LRC / LIBRARY
MORAINE VALLEY COMMUNITY COLLEGE
WITHDRAWN
PALOS HILLS, ILLINOIS 60465

D0203378

BF 721 .H242 1983 v.3

HANDBOOK OF CHILD PSYCHOLOGY

DEMCO

HANDBOOK OF CHILD PSYCHOLOGY

HANDBOOK OF CHILD PSYCHOLOGY

Formerly CARMICHAEL'S MANUAL
OF CHILD PSYCHOLOGY

PAUL H. MUSSEN EDITOR

FOURTH EDITION

Volume III
COGNITIVE DEVELOPMENT

John H. Flavell/Ellen M. Markman
VOLUME EDITORS

JOHN WILEY & SONS
NEW YORK CHICHESTER BRISBANE TORONTO SINGAPORE

Copyright 1946 © 1954, 1970, 1983 by John Wiley & Sons, Inc.

All rights reserved. Published simultaneously in Canada.

Reproduction or translation of any part of
this work beyond that permitted by Sections
107 and 108 of the 1976 United States Copyright
Act without the permission of the copyright
owner is unlawful. Requests for permission
or further information should be addressed to
the Permissions Department, John Wiley & Sons.

Library of Congress Cataloging in Publication Data
Main entry under title:

Cognitive development.

   (Handbook of child psychology; v. 3)
   Includes index.
   1. Cognition in children.   I. Flavell, John H.
II. Markman, Ellen M.   III. Series. [DNLM: 1. Child
psychology. WS 105 H2354]
BF721.H242   1983 vol. 3   155.4s   [155.4'13]   83-3468
[BF723.C5]
ISBN 0-471-09064-6

Printed in the United States of America

10 9 8 7 6 5 4 3

PREFACE TO THE FOURTH EDITION

The *Handbook of Child Psychology* is a direct descendant of three editions of the *Manual of Child Psychology*. The first and second editions, edited by Leonard Carmichael, were published in 1946 and 1954, the third, called *Carmichael's Manual of Child Psychology*, which I edited, was published in 1970. Each of these editions attempted to provide a definitive account of the state of knowledge of child psychology at the time of its publication.

In the 13 years since the publication of the third edition of *Carmichael's Manual*, child psychology has been an extraordinarily lively and productive discipline, expanding in many directions and at a rapid rate. Only a few of the most important of the countless changes will be reviewed here. The volume of the research activity and the annual output of research articles and books have accelerated enormously. As more information accumulates, new questions are generated, new research approaches are invented and older ones are applied in new versions, established theories are challenged and revised, novel theories are proposed, concepts are redefined, and specialized fields of interest and investigation evolve. These changes are closely intertwined and consequently have an impact on one another. Investigation of a new issue (or a revised version of an older one) often requires novel research techniques and approaches. New research findings may evoke questions about the conclusions derived from earlier studies and about underlying theories, and these questions, in turn, lead to further research. These cycles of events are repeated, progress in the field is continuous, and the amount of accumulated data snowballs. Consequently, even an authoritative 1970 publication cannot give an adequate picture of the field in the 1980s. A brand new source book is needed and the present volumes are intended to satisfy this need.

This *Handbook* attempts to reflect the changes in child psychology that have occurred since 1970 and to present as comprehensive, balanced, and accurate a survey of the contemporary field as possible. It is twice the size of the earlier two-volume work and differs from it in many ways. The coverage is broader and more topics are included, discussed in greater depth, and organized according to different principles. Discussions of topics of enduring interest that were presented in chapters in the last edition of *Carmichael's Manual*—for example, Piaget's theory, learning, language, thinking, aggression, sex-typing, socialization in the family and peer group—are reconceptualized and brought up to date in chapters in this *Handbook*.

The reader may get a clearer understanding of the structure and contents of the *Handbook* by noting some of the most significant contrasts between it and the last edition of *Carmichael's Manual*. The *Handbook* includes more chapters on theories and fundamental approaches to research in child psychology (Volume I). The chapter by Piaget on his own theory has been retained. In addition, there are chapters on information processing and systems theories—previously applied to issues in perception, learning, cognition, and social organization—which have proven useful in integrating a substantial body of the data of developmental psychology and in stimulating research. Cross-cultural and field studies have become very fruitful in the last 20 years and these too are discussed in separate chapters, as are the latest advances in general research methodology and assessment. And, as the discipline has matured, there is heightened (or renewed) interest in its philosophical and historical antecedents, so two chapters of Volume I are centered on these issues.

Developmental psychologists have always been interested in the *origins* of behavior, and the factors involved in very early development have become more prominent foci of research attention in the last 10 or 15 years. The psychological study of infants has burgeoned, while advances in research methodology in physiology, ethology, genetics, and neurology have made possible more refined and penetrating explorations of the biological bases of behavior. These research emphases are examined in Volume II of this *Handbook*.

The content area of greatest activity since 1970 has been cognitive development and the results of this activity are apparent in Volume III. For example, the third edition of *Carmichael's Manual* contained one chapter on language development and it dealt almost exclusively with the acquisition of grammar. In contrast, the *Handbook* has separate chapters on grammar, meaning, and communication. Much of the recent research in cognitive development confirms and extends Piaget's conclusions, but the results of other studies challenge aspects of Piagetian theory. Both kinds of findings are included in chapters in Volume III.

Several research areas that were new in 1970 have become well established, vigorous, and fruitful. Among these are social cognitive development, moral reasoning, and prosocial behavior; each of these is the topic of a chapter in this *Handbook*. In addition a number of traditional issues that had been somewhat neglected until recently have become more prominent in the literature of developmental psychology. For example, this *Handbook* contains chapters on representation, on logical thinking, play, the self, and on the school as an agent of socialization. None of these topics was discussed in the 1970 edition of *Carmichael's Manual*.

In response to social needs, developmental psychologists in increasing numbers conduct research on practical problems and attempt to apply their research findings to the solution of urgent problems, spelling out the implications of basic data for such areas as educational practice and social policy (see particularly the chapters on intervention and on risk factors in development in Volume II, on learning, memory, and comprehension in Volume III, and on treatment of children with emotional problems in Volume IV). The results of these activities are highly salutary for advancing the field of child psychology, for they extend the definitions of concepts investigated, test the findings of laboratory research in real-life settings, and illuminate the limitations of available data and theory.

The volume editors (William Kessen of Yale University, Marshall Haith and Joseph Campos of the University of Denver, John Flavell and Ellen Markman of Stanford, and E. Mavis Hetherington of the University of Virginia) and I met to plan and organize this *Handbook* over five years ago. Our objective was clear and straightforward: to prepare a source book that would present as complete, accurate, balanced, and up-to-date a view of the field as possible.

Although there is no entirely satisfactory way of subdividing and organizing all of the vast body of theory, methods, and data in a field as large, varied, and ever-changing as developmental psychology, we constructed a table of contents that in our opinion included all the key topics—that is, all the topics that are currently receiving substantial amounts of research and theoretical attention. It soon became obvious that four volumes would be required, and we decided to arrange the material in accordance with the four predominent divisions of the field—theory and methods, biological bases of behavior and infancy, cognitive development, and social and personality development.

Comprehensive coverage was not our only aim; integrative summaries were to be accompanied by new perspectives and insights, critical analyses, and explications of deficiencies in existing data and theoretical orientations. We hoped to produce more than an encyclopedic review of accumulated knowledge; our goal was a source book that would encourage sophisticated thinking about fundamental issues, formulation of questions and hypotheses, and, ultimately, more good research.

We selected and invited a group of distinguished authorities in developmental psychology and related fields who were highly qualified to contribute chapters that would accomplish these goals. Almost all of our invitations were accepted and the assignments were carried out with extraordinary diligence, care, and thoughtfulness. Each working outline, preliminary draft, and final manuscript was reviewed by the volume editor, the general editor, and another authority on the subject, and suggestions for revision were communicated to the author. Although three of the chapters included in the original plan are missing, all the key chapters are included. We are therefore convinced that the *Handbook* provides the most comprehensive picture of contemporary child psychology that exists in one place.

If the objectives of the *Handbook* have been achieved, it is due primarily to the painstaking work, dedication, and creativity of the contributors and the volume editors. The lion's share of the basic work—preparation of scholarly, integrative, and critical chapters—was done by the authors. The contribution of the volume editors was indispensable; in their difficult roles of critic, advisor, and guardian of high standards, they were infinitely wise, patient, and persistent. My debts to all these individuals are incalculable.

PAUL H. MUSSEN

PREFACE TO VOLUME III

This volume contains rich and insightful pictures of the current state of knowledge and belief in most contemporary areas of cognitive development and the artists who painted these pictures include some of the best scientists and scholars in the field. We asked them to write the only kind of review chapter that we thought busy and talented people would consider writing. Please write a chapter that presents a fair and adequate review of the literature, we asked, but also one that is selective, thoughtful, and interesting. We want a responsible, thorough survey, of course, but feel free to refer the reader to good secondary sources for any subareas you do not feel warrant detailed coverage. Long review chapters can be rather dull, we said. Try to make yours lively and compelling by conspicuously putting your own stamp on it. Make its organization, coverage, ideas, and conclusions reflect your hard-won wisdom and expertise in the area. That wisdom and expertise deserve to be shared with the reader, not hidden in a thicket of study summaries and literature citations. Besides, the opportunity to speak your mind on matters of great interest and importance to you is one of the few recompenses you will have for all your drudgery and suffering.

We hoped that almost everyone invited to write would agree to do so, but of course we never thought it would really happen. But it did happen: To our delight and gratitude, almost everyone we asked said yes. Unfortunately, the drudgery and suffering were also unavoidable, and were even worse than anticipated. Some things just have to be experienced to be imagined and writing a review chapter of this length, scope, and depth is one. It entails innumerable hours of very hard work. Worse, it involves repeated frustrations at the organization or integration scheme that won't come, battered self-esteem for the vision and creativity one is supposed to have but seemingly doesn't, and other torments known only to authors of such reviews. "Mussen chapters," as we all came to call them, are plain hell on

wheels to write. They may have some delights, but they certainly have many devils.

However, the months did pass and the chapters did get planned, replanned, drafted, critiqued, revised, copy edited, proofread, and—now, at long last—published. We couldn't be more pleased with the final results. These chapters provide masterly, insightful reviews that, in our opinion, will prove to be truly significant and lasting contributions to the field. We think they are treasure troves of information and ideas about what the field presently is, and also about where it may or should be heading. A person who absorbs what is in these chapters will understand the contemporary scene in the field of cognitive development with a breadth and depth previously unavailable to anyone, however expert and knowledgeable. We are sure that working through them had that profound an effect on our own understanding, and for this we feel deeply indebted to the authors. We can only hope the chapters will have the same deep and abiding effect on your command of this fascinating field.

The field of cognitive development has greatly changed since the publication of the 1970 *Carmichael's Manual of Child Psychology,* and, in our opinion, it has greatly improved. In reading these chapters, we were continually struck by the experimental ingenuity of investigators, by the many surprising new empirical discoveries, and by the theoretical advances that have been made. In the last decade, every subfield in the area has gained a more explicit appreciation of the subtlety and complexity of cognitive development.

One of the more striking changes is the movement away from orthodox Piagetian theory. It is a tribute to Jean Piaget's greatness that almost everything people think and do in this field has some connection with questions that Piaget raised. This was true during most of the 1960s and all of the 1970s, is true today, and probably will continue to be true for a long time. Although investigators continue to address these fundamental Piagetian questions of cognitive development, the nature of the answers has changed greatly. Piaget's theory and research findings, while never uncontroversial, are more and more being challenged from all quarters. There is growing criticism, and burgeoning efforts at reinterpretation, revision, and extension. This is not surprising, given all Piaget did and wrote, and given the extraordinary amount of thought and research the field has addressed to the problems that he raised. This change, we feel, is also a sign of progress.

Another noticeable change is that researchers across many different areas have become skeptical of stage-theoretic accounts of development. Piaget's logical-algebraic models of concrete- and formal-operational thought seem to have all types of problems. Cognitive development may not be as stagelike as he thought, or, if it is, its stages or *coupures naturelles* may be somewhat different from those he postulated.

In the past, we may have been too wedded to particular Piagetian methodologies to measure many cognitive abilities adequately. This situation has been remedied in part by the more sensitive assessment procedures that have been developed to uncover early cognitive competence. Preschool children have been shown to have more cognitive potential than Piaget believed, and infants more than he or anyone else would have dreamed a few years ago. The field of infant cognition is clearly in its Golden Age. Researchers are discovering many important and often surprising things about babies' sensory, perceptual, conceptual, learning, and memory capabilities. Highly interesting research is also being done on a wide range of early-childhood cognitive phenomena, some of it representing fruitful extensions or revisions of Piagetian work but much of it involving essentially new directions. Examples include research on young children's knowledge of number and classification, logical reasoning, and social cognition. One other important new focus is the concern with characterizing developing knowledge structures (e.g., schemas, scripts, etc.). There are now many elegant studies suggesting that very young children may have the capacity to represent knowledge in a format quite like that of the adult. Methodological and conceptual advances have paved the way for these revised assessments of capacity.

At the other end of ontogeny, adolescents and adults do not appear to be as consistently formal-operational or otherwise rational as Piaget's theory suggested. It no longer seems feasible to expect total uniformity of cognitive level in the way any individual approaches cognitive problems. Instead, it is now clear that the formal structure of any given problem is only one factor affecting its solution. A solution derived from a formal logical analysis may conflict with one based on a more practically oriented reasoning. A child's familiarity with the material, experience in solving similar problems, and many other factors will affect performance. This conclusion is emphasized by cross-cultural, individual-differences, and life-span-developmental psychologists.

To oversimplify, one way of summing up these changes is to point to the recent movement toward information-processing approaches to cognitive development. Here we refer to information-processing approaches in the most general sense, rather than to any specific model. This approach emphasizes careful analysis of the processing requirements implicit in any task and the recognition that failure on a given problem could result from a breakdown in any one of the processes. Another important assumption of these models is that humans have limited capacity to process information. This approach underlies much of the recent research directed at revising and refining Piagetian theory as well as the more radical departures from Piaget. It can be seen in such areas as the development of logical reasoning and related intellectual abilities, of communication skills, and of social cognition, to name only a few. In each case, developmental differences in performance could result from any number of factors that consume resources more rapidly for children than for adults, without assuming fundamental differences in the nature of representation or of cognitive competence.

One factor that is gaining increasing attention is the amount of information and knowledge that children have on any given topic compared to adults. Children's lack of expertise in an area could result in striking developmental differences even if there were only minor age changes in the basic processes themselves.

Another consequence of this shift is the emphasis on different strategies that children use to solve problems. This in turn is one reason that metacognition (i.e., knowledge and cognition concerning cognition) and such related processes as executive functioning and cognitive monitoring have become popular research topics in recent years. Work in this area initially addressed children's developing knowledge and cognition concerning language (metalanguage) and memory (metamemory) but now includes knowledge and cognition about perception, attention, comprehension, learning, communication, and problem solving.

Also, partially as a result of this new emphasis, the relationship of cognitive competence to behavior has become a near-ubiquitous issue. To what extent do we use and express in everyday behavior that which we know and know how to do? To what extent and under what circumstances are our metacognitive knowledge and know-how translated into effective cognitive strategies? How, and to what extent, is our social-cognitive knowledge about self and others actually used, "on line," in everyday social interactions? What about the relationship between our ability to reason morally and our moral behavior? And somewhat differently, how much concordance between linguistic competence and linguistic performance should we expect to see?

In addition to information processing, there have been many new theoretical approaches guiding developmental research. Examples include attribution theory and other theories from social psychology; linguistic and psycholinguistic theories concerning phonology, morphology, syntax, semantics, and pragmatics; and many cognitive theories dealing with perception, attention, memory, comprehension, knowledge, problem solving, logical reasoning, judgments and decisions, and other processes. This expansion of new approaches has led to a greater diversity in the kinds of questions that have been formulated about development and in the kinds of empirical studies conducted. The compatibility of developmental and nondevelopmental accounts of cognition can lead to a more unified approach to studying cognitive processes from childhood through adulthood. This can have the advantage of clarifying and emphasizing the importance of studying development, in seeing how successive changes result in the adult performance. Thus we expect to see a growing integration of research in developmental and adult cognition, with theories of adult performance influencing developmental accounts and with what is known about development constraining theories of adult cognition.

The authors and we are very grateful to Thomas J. Berndt, Jill deVilliers, Rachel J. Falmagne, Nancy S. Johnson, Paul H. Mussen, and Tom Trabasso for their help in critically evaluating chapter drafts, and to Sophia Cohen and Peter Coles for their assistance in translating the Bullinger and Chatillon chapter from French into English. We also want to thank Paul Mussen for his help and wise counsel throughout the book's genesis.

JOHN H. FLAVELL
ELLEN M. MARKMAN

CONTENTS

HANDBOOK OF CHILD PSYCHOLOGY

THE DEVELOPMENT OF PERCEPTION | 1

ELEANOR J. GIBSON, *Cornell University*
ELIZABETH S. SPELKE, *University of Pennsylvania*

CHAPTER CONTENTS

INTRODUCTION

What Is Perception?

Perception is the process by which animals gain knowledge about their environment and about themselves in relation to the environment. It is the beginning of knowing, and so is an essential part of cognition. More specifically, to perceive is to obtain information about the world through stimulation. The perceptual systems of animals have evolved to detect patterns of light, of sound, and of pressure on the skin that carry information about the events, things, and places in the world. This information is in the world, but it is not the events and places themselves. It is to be found in the structure of stimulation, and it specifies the world that an animal perceives. To understand perception, we must first understand what aspects of the world an animal perceives and what information specifies the things it perceives.

Perceiving is an active process; it depends on perceptual systems that pick up stimulus information. Stimulation does not simply fall passively upon a receptor surface like rain upon the ground, for the perceptual systems are more than receptor surfaces. We do not just see, for example, we look, and in the course of looking, our pupils adjust to the level of illumination, our eyes converge or diverge, we move our heads or change our position to get a better view of something, and sometimes we even put on spectacles.

If the perceptual systems are active and are adjusted constantly to optimize the information being picked up, it is obvious that perception is selective. A continuous flow of information is available in the flux of stimulation; what is actually extracted by the animal's perceptual systems is only a part of it. It is this aspect of perception that can be referred to as attention, but attending is not really separable from perceiving itself.

What Is Perceived?

A description of perception starts with the events and things in the world and proceeds to the information in stimulation that is actually picked up by the perceptual systems. Do we, then, perceive this information? Such an answer can be immediately rejected. We do not perceive stimuli or even any momentary representation of them on a receptor surface, such as a retinal image. We perceive the events and things in the world. To perceive any event or thing, the information in stimulation must correspond to it, in the sense of *specifying* it. Events and things are specified in many ways for us, for example, in light, in sound, and in pressure patterns on the surfaces of the body. These sources of energy provide information to the visual system, the auditory system, and the haptic system. But through the activity of the perceptual systems, we perceive a unitary world, not separate collections of visual, auditory, and tactile impressions. This review is organized in terms of what is in the world for humans to perceive: events, objects, places, and artifacts that represent them.

Events

What goes on in the world goes on in a continuous stream with no full stops and starts and with few displays that remain perfectly still while one contemplates them. Nor does the perceiver herself stand still. Heads containing eyes and ears and noses and vestibular organs are almost continually moving. This chapter does not focus, then, on perception of static displays but on perception of continuous happenings in the world, specified by continuously changing arrays of stimulation. These happenings are events, and they seem to have a beginning and an end, even though the information for them is continuous over time. When a perceiver observes an event, she perceives changes that occur over time as well as a persisting, underlying layout of objects and places.

Objects

The world is furnished with objects, closed surfaces that are substantial and that retain their integrity over time. Many objects, such as people, stones, and books, are detached; they are capable of moving around or being moved. Some objects are attached to immoveable surfaces, such as a tree that is fixed to the terrain. Although attached objects are not moveable, they can be walked around. Each object is perceived as a unit, a separate whole, and it has properties that are perceived as well. The unity and most of the properties of an object are specified by information in a flow of stimulation that occurs as the object participates in events.

Places

Places are segregated parts of the layout of the world at which surfaces meet one another, often forming an enclosure. Places may have vistas and paths that can be seen or walked through, walls that constitute obstacles and conceal things, a ground that can be walked on, and dropoffs that must be avoided. An animal always lives and acts in some place. After a certain age, it can move around in that place and even move out of it, but the place persists. At any given moment, the animal occupies one point of observation, but that point changes continuously as the animal moves, and it can be exchanged with the vantage point of another animal. As the animal changes its location in a layout, objects come in and out of view; they are occluded and disoccluded. Over these changes, there is information to specify the persisting layout of the environment.

Pictures

Many of the furnishings of the world are artifacts, and some of these represent the events, objects, and places of the world. Pictures are representations par excellence, and they afford a means of obtaining knowledge about the world secondhand. They are very interesting for the study of perception because of their dual character as objects and as serviceable, although imperfect, representations of real scenes and events.

The Point of View

We approach the problems and the literature of perception by beginning with the ecology of an animal, its way of life as a species, and the biological structures with which it has been endowed by nature. Every species has evolved in a habitat, and in the long course of evolution, its niche and its biological structures have developed in reciprocity with one another. The perceptual systems developed in the context of this mutual relationship. They have adapted to enable the perceiver to extract the information that he needs for survival in the kind of world he lives in, especially to extract information about the affordances of things.

Affordances are a way of talking about meaning, but a special way. The term was introduced by J. J. Gibson (1979):

The *affordances* of the environment are what it *offers* the animal, what it *provides* or *furnishes,* either for good or ill. . . . I mean by it something that refers to both the environment and the animal in a way that no existing term does. It implies the complementarity of the animal and the environment. (p. 127)

Places, objects, and events all have affordances for human animals. A floor affords support, and it can be walked on. A wall is an obstacle that affords collision, but a doorway in the wall affords walking through. A cave affords shelter from the rain, which affords getting wet. Water affords drinking, but not

walking on. A screen affords hiding. A fire affords warming oneself and reading by its light. Affordance is a functional term that emphasizes the utility of some aspect of the environment for an animal (E. J. Gibson, 1982).

The properties of events, objects, and places are specified by constant, higher order relationships in the flow of stimulation, relationships that we, after J. J. Gibson (1966, 1979), call invariants. Invariants are abstract and relational. Many are also available to more than one modality, that is, the same higher order relationship may be constant over changing stimulation to the eye, the ear, and the skin. Perhaps the most familiar case of an invariant is the optical structure that persists over movements of the eyes, head, or body. As a person moves over the ground, or moves a rigid object in his hands, there is a continuous transformation of the stimulation projected to his eyes. Nevertheless, the projective properties of the optic array, such as the cross-ratio of the distances between any four collinear points, remain constant. Despite the optical flow, these projective properties are invariant and provide information about the layout of surfaces and the objects resting upon them. In this case, as in others to be described throughout this chapter, "the flow of the array does not destroy the structure beneath the flow" (J. J. Gibson, 1979, p. 310).

An animal perceives events, objects, places, and their affordances by seeking out and detecting invariants. Some mechanisms for detecting invariants are present at birth, but sensitivity to invariants increases as new perceptual and exploratory abilities mature or become modified by experience. Furthermore, the child's developing perceptual systems provide information that is increasingly accessible for new purposes. For the very young infant, perception of an affordance might guide only a limited repertoire of adaptive actions. For the older child, perception of an affordance will come to guide actions of many kinds and can even become an object of thought.

The point of view espoused in this chapter is not constructivist. We do not conceive of perception as the building of a representation of the world from a collection of elementary sensations through processes of association, inference, or assimilation to a schema. We stress, instead, that perception depends on a search for invariance in stimulation that is continually changing. An important function of perception is to search for the persisting structures and the invariants that provide information about the environment and its affordances. Perception develops not through the construction of new descriptions of the world, but through the discovery of new information about it.

EXPLORING AND ATTENDING

Over the course of development, animals gain knowledge about the events, objects, and layout of the world and of what they afford for behavior. By what means is a human infant prepared to proceed with this massive program? Human infants are far from being precocial; nature has given them little in the way of ready-to-go knowledge about the situations they will encounter in the world. But they are richly endowed with the means of finding out about the environment. Active exploration begins at birth, and exploratory skills increase with maturation and with practice. An infant's looking and listening and to some extent her feeling, smelling, and tasting are inherently coordinated for obtaining information. Furthermore, coordinated multimodal exploration, such as auditory-visual coordination, is functional very early and does not appear to depend on learning. These precoordinated systems provide a way of learning about the world at an early age, and we have seen in recent years that infants are motivated to use them actively in seeking information. From infancy to childhood, exploration appears to become more specific in its direction, more economical, and more systematic, but it has a purposeful look from the start.

The Beginnings of Information Pickup

Visual Exploration

Visual exploration provides the major means of information gathering for very young infants. Fixating high-contrast patterns, tracking moving ones, and moving the head and upper trunk to assist in localizing and following objects are all preadapted coordinated systems, imperfect but functional at birth. These exploratory activities improve rapidly during the first few months with maturation of the visual system.

Infants of 1 month reliably turn in the direction of a target by saccadic movements of the eyes when the target is introduced as far as 30° from the line of sight along horizontal and diagonal axes and as far as 10° along the vertical axis (Aslin & Salapatek, 1975). The first saccade is not very accurate: It is usually short of the target and is followed by one or more saccades of equal amplitude. Infants shift their gaze further when the target is farther away, however, showing adaptation to the target's distance. Evidence from directionally appropriate first saccades

and multiple saccades following them led Aslin and Salapatek to conclude that the infants were motivated to look at the targets.

Even newborn infants shift their gaze toward the side of the field in which a peripheral target is introduced (Harris & MacFarlane, 1974). Localization of a peripheral target is swifter and occurs for a target at a greater distance if there is no central stimulus present. The probability of locating a distant peripheral target is enhanced if the central target is stationary and the peripheral one is in motion (Tronick, 1972). The effective visual field was thought to expand with age by earlier investigators (see Tronick, 1972), but no expansion was found between 1 and 7 weeks when a competing central stimulus was introduced with a peripheral one (MacFarlane, Harris, & Barnes, 1976), suggesting that selective attention to a centrally located target occurs at both ages.

Infants under 2 months do not track a moving stimulus with smooth-pursuit movements that match the velocity and direction of the stimulus; instead, following occurs in the form of a jerky series of saccadic refixations (see Salapatek & Banks, 1978). Kreminitzer, Vaughan, Kurtzberg, and Dowling (1979) observed that smooth pursuit occurred only about 15% of the time in newborn infants. Its velocity increased with target velocity up to 19°/sec. and deteriorated at faster speeds. Tracking occurs at 8 weeks when an object is displaced relative to a background, but not when the object and background move together (Harris, Cassel, & Bamborough, 1974). When an object moves against a stationary background it successively occludes texture in the background field. Occlusion and disocclusion of a stationary field provide information for differentiating objects from background surfaces.

Movements of the head in relation to a peripheral stationary target or a target moving across the field have been studied less, probably because infants have usually been observed in a supine position making head control difficult. Bullinger (1977) observed neonates seated in a chair before a white background. A flock of red wool was dangled at the infant's eye level, 70-cm distant. The object was presented at the left, right, or center for 1 min. Infants oriented head and eyes toward the object. When the object was swung in front of the infant, both head and eyes turned slowly to follow it, but the movements were jerky rather than smooth and were not well calibrated to the object's rate of motion.

Auditory-Visual Exploration

Visual exploration of sounding objects is a precoordinated system of particular interest because it provides a basis for perceiving a unified world. Does the very young infant turn head and eyes to look at a sound source and explore it visually? Evidence for innate coordination was reported by Wertheimer (1961); a newborn infant turned her eyes in the direction of a sound (a click). Other experimenters have reported different results. Butterworth and Castillo (1976) observed that newborn infants moved their eyes away from a loud click. Sound intensity may affect the direction of looking (Hammer & Turkewitz, 1975). McGurk, Turnure, and Creighton (1977) also failed to find ipsilateral eye movements to clicks in neonates. Several more recent experiments with persisting, structured sounds nevertheless have obtained results that confirm Wertheimer's (1961) earlier observation.

Mendelson and Haith (1976) used a 40-sec. presentation of human speech. It was presented laterally, and there was a stationary bar on either the same or the contralateral side of the infant's visual field. Visual scanning of the field was influenced by the speech; infants turned at first toward the sound, then away from it. The authors interpreted this as an extended search for a change in the visual field. A signal detection analysis of eye turning to the sound of a human voice saying ''baby'' was performed by Crassini and Broerse (1980). The infants turned toward the sound at significantly greater than chance level. The frequency of these turns was not high, but it was greater than the frequency of turns in the absence of a laterally presented sound. Alegria and Noirot (1978) reported that infants turned their heads in the direction of a human voice as well, opening their eyes as they did so.

Identification of the conditions that promote visual exploration to sounds has been extended in further experiments. Muir and Field (1978) investigated head turning toward sound (a rattle produced by shaking a plastic bottle containing popcorn) in neonates held in such a way that they could turn their heads spontaneously. All babies turned correctly on the majority of trials, appearing to investigate the locus of the shaking rattle: ''They hunched their shoulders, actively pulled their heads up, turned to the side of the stimulus, and then seemed to inspect the sound source visually'' (p. 432). The importance of a more continuous sound and a free-to-move head are apparent. In a further experiment, Field, DiFranco, Dodwell, and Muir (1979) presented 2½-month-old infants with a recording of a woman's voice reading poetry. Infants turned both head and eyes toward the voice. Sustained, complex, auditory stimulation again seemed to favor visual orientation. Field, Muir, Pilon, Sinclair, and Dodwell (1980)

compared infants aged 1, 2, and 3 months for head and eye turning to a sound produced by shaking a popcorn-filled bottle. Infants turned reliably at 1 and 3 months, but less reliably at 2 months.

Several experiments indicate that introduction of auditory stimulation enhances visual exploration in early infancy. Haith, Bergman, and Moore (1977) studied visual scanning of an adult's face by infants who were 3 to 11 weeks old. A dramatic increase in fixation of the face occurred between 5 and 7 weeks, and the introduction of a voice intensified scanning, particularly in the eye area (see also Hainline, 1978). Horowitz (1974) and her colleagues conducted a series of studies of habituation to visual displays with and without auditory accompaniment. Infants of 5 to 14 weeks habituated to a visual pattern accompanied by a continuous sound, such as a voice reading poetry, and subsequently dishabituated when the sound was changed. The change in sound led to further looking without a change in the visual display, as if the infant were searching for a change in the visual scene as well (see also Walker, 1982).

Exploration of the visible source of an ongoing sound has been observed with a preference method (Spelke, 1976). Motion picture films of two events were presented side by side on a small screen before the baby. During the filming for each event, a sound track was made. One of the two sound tracks was played from a central location as the baby viewed the films. An observer stationed behind the screen monitored the baby's looking so that the total looking time to each film could be assessed. Infants looked longer at the film specified by the sound track. A search test given after presentation of the films and both sound tracks provided further evidence for coordination (Spelke, 1979, 1981). The films were again presented side by side. On each of a series of trials, the baby's gaze was centered by means of a flashing light, a short burst of one sound track was given, and the baby's orientation to one film or the other was noted. Infants looked to the event specified by each sound. A number of experiments using this method have now been performed with 4-month-old infants (e.g., Bahrick, 1980; Bahrick, Walker, & Neisser, 1981; Spelke, 1976, 1979; Walker, 1982). These experiments have displayed a variety of events, including peekaboo, pat-acake, hands playing musical instruments, and bouncing puppets (see *Obtaining Information About Events*). Visual-auditory exploration of a temporally extended event is highly functional by 4 months.

Finally, there is some evidence that sound influences visual tracking of an object that moves laterally and is temporarily occluded (Bull, 1978, 1979).

A sound moving with the occluded object facilitated looking to the object's point of reappearance from behind the occluding screen at 4 months of age.

Haptic Exploration

Haptic exploration occurs earliest in the form of mouthing, whereas active manual exploration of objects appears considerably later. There is reason to think that mouthing activity of neonates is spatially oriented toward external events, as is activity of the visual system. Alegria and Noirot (1978, 1982) observed asymmetrical mouthing as a function of absence versus presence of a human voice and as a function of the voice's location. Asymmetrical mouthing came to be directed toward the voice within the first three feedings. Breast-fed babies (held either on the right or left arm for feeding) oriented toward the voice, whereas bottle-fed babies showed mouthing in the direction of the arm that characteristically held them. Asymmetrical mouthing was negligible in the control condition when the baby was held but not spoken to.

An experiment by Meltzoff and Borton (1979) provides evidence that mouthing is exploratory, that it furnishes information about the surface properties of objects, and that it is coordinated with looking at objects. Infants 4 weeks of age were allowed to explore by mouth one of two objects—a smooth sphere or a sphere with nubs. The objects (actually, larger versions of them) were then presented as a pair for visual inspection. The infants were reported to look preferentially at the object similar to the one familiarized by mouthing. Infants 4 months old, in a similar experiment, looked longer at the novel object (Meltzoff, 1981). The infants apparently learned something about the object from haptic exploration that was also detectable visually. However, a recent experiment with infants 1, 3, and 5 months old failed to replicate these effects (Baker, Brown, & Gottfried, 1982).

Oral exploration was used by Gibson and Walker (1982) in an experiment on intermodal perception of substance by 4-week-old infants. A cylinder-shaped object made of either lucite or spongy rubber was inserted in the baby's mouth and left until the baby had mouthed it for 60 sec. A test of preferential looking followed. Identical cylindrical objects were displayed simultaneously side by side before the infant, one object rotating in a pattern characteristic of a rigid substance and the other object deforming in a pattern characteristic of a spongy substance. The infants looked preferentially toward the object moving in the pattern of the *novel* substance. This experiment also provides evidence for detection of an intermodal correspondance.

Oral exploratory behavior was investigated directly by Allen (1982), who recorded pressure changes during oral exploration of objects. Infants of 3 months showed a decreased rate of sucking during familiarization with one object. They subsequently differentiated between the familiar object and a novel object of a different shape, sucking more vigorously on the novel object.

Infants learn very readily to suck at high amplitudes to obtain some contingent, seemingly arbitrarily related display, such as a human voice uttering "ba" or "ga" (e.g., Eimas, Siqueland, Jusczyk, & Vigorito, 1971). This learning may be facilitated by the exploratory function of mouthing, which is especially adapted for the pickup of information about affordances at an early age when other means of exploration are limited. An experiment by Kalnins and Bruner (1973) supports this interpretation. Infants 5 to 12 weeks old quickly learned to suck at high amplitudes when sucking brought a motion picture display into focus. But in the symmetrical condition, in which a picture came into focus only when the infant inhibited sucking, no learning occurred. Instrumental learning in infancy appears to build on the infant's inherent propensity to explore.

Mouthing continues as a means of exploration all through the first year of life. It is still used in preference to manual exploration between 8 and 9 months. Kopp (1974) studied visual-manipulative behavior of infants between 32 and 36 weeks of age when presented with a rigid object. Types of behavior included examining by turning an object in the hands and looking at it, mouthing, and actions like banging or sliding the object on the tabletop. Mouthing was the predominant behavior, followed by examining. Some infants still only explored the object visually.

Active touching and manipulation of an object with differentiated finger movements is late in developing. The precedence of the mouth over the hands for haptic exploration recalls Gesell's anatomical rule of head-downward and proximodistal development. But by 1 year children do explore the affordances of objects manually to some extent, differentiating elastic and rigid substances with such behaviors as squeezing versus banging (Gibson & Walker, 1982). Ruff (in preparation) reported an increase in exploratory fingering of objects between 6 and 12 months, particularly when the objects varied in surface texture.

Visual-Haptic Exploration

What is especially interesting about the haptic system is its tie-in with the visual system, which generally instigates haptic exploration. The hand-to-mouth coordination (look at an object, pick it up, and then mouth it) does not occur until about 6 months, but there are intimations of coordinated looking and reaching much earlier.

Research by Bower suggested that even a new-born infant will reach for a visible object under suitable conditions (see Bower, 1974, 1979, for reviews). Newborn infants were reported to extend an arm more toward a solid object than to a flat, extended surface depicting that object (Bower, 1972; Bower, Dunkeld, & Wishart, 1979), and more to an object within reaching distance than to one too far away (Bower, 1972). The newborn's arm extensions were reported to be adapted to the object's visible direction (Bower, 1974) and even its shape (Bower, 1972; Bower, Broughton, & Moore, 1970a). However, other investigators have failed to replicate these observations in studies with neonates (Ashmead, Lockman, & Bushnell, 1980; Dodwell, Muir, & DiFranco, 1976; Rader & Stern, 1981; Ruff & Halton, 1978). DiFranco, Muir, and Dodwell (1978) found many of the components of mature reaching in very young infants, but little evidence of the control characteristic of mature reaching. The arm extensions of neonates may be visually triggered without being as yet visually guided.

Two recent studies have more carefully examined the orientation of arm movements to visually presented targets in very young infants. McDonnell (1979) performed a signal detection analysis on the distribution of arm movements as a target changed position from center to the left or right side with infants from 3 to 8 weeks old. Results supported the view that infant limb movements are oriented to visual targets and that there is improvement in the accuracy of these movements from 3 to 8 weeks. Von Hofsten (1982) studied arm and hand movements in newborns presented with a slowly moving object. The relative frequency of forward extensions increased when the infant fixated the object. These extensions were analyzed by a technique that took into consideration the three-dimensional properties of arm-hand movements. The movements performed while the infant fixated the object were aimed closer than other extensor movements. They clustered round the object and the hand also slowed down, in the best aimed movements, as it neared the object. There does, thus, seem to be a primitive eye-arm coordination in the newborn that is adapted to the three-dimensional layout of objects well before grasping and active manipulation occur. This embryonic form of eye-hand coordination appears to have an orienting function. From the beginning, the infant focuses on events in the world.

Further experiments provide evidence of behavior precursory to reaching by 2 months of age. Bruner and Koslowski (1972) observed infants between 8 and 22 weeks and concluded that they were "able to make use of visual information in the regulation of early pre-reaching—information prior to that provided by feedback from early attempts at visually directed reaching" (p. 13). Infants who were not yet capable of a successful visually directed reach were, nevertheless, able to stretch their hands to midline in the presence of a small graspable object and did so more than in the presence of a larger, nongraspable object. A swiping motion, more akin to palpating than to grasping, was likely to be evoked by the larger object. Provine and Westerman (1979) observed infants' extension of one arm when the other arm was restrained. At 9 weeks, all infants tested reached for and touched an object presented in front of the shoulder of the freely moving arm, although they could not as yet cross the midline to touch an object in front of the opposite shoulder. At 18 to 20 weeks, all infants crossed the midline, opened the hand, and extended the fingers toward the object. Many infants succeeded in grasping it as well as touching it.

The development of reaching skill has been studied in detail in the past (see Gesell & Amatruda, 1964) and will not be examined here. But recent studies of reaching at an early age in relation to properties of an object or surface are of interest. The distance of the object from the infant, for example, may affect early prehensile behavior. J. Field (1976a) observed both the reaching and looking of 2- and 5-month-old infants in the presence of objects placed at several distances within and beyond possible reaching contact. Only the 5-month-old infants adjusted their reaching to the object's distance, but visual attention was affected by object distance in the younger group (see also McKenzie & Day, 1972). The 2-month-olds also showed differentiation in one category of arm adduction that appeared to reflect a distinction between reachable objects and objects far beyond reach.

In another study (J. Field, 1976b), infants from 13 to 25 weeks old were shown solid objects and pictures of objects placed at three distances. Pictures cut from paper were pasted upon the same board that was placed behind the objects. Both reaching and visual attention were observed. There was a significant effect of distance on the frequency of reaching toward the objects at every age level. From reaching alone, there was no evidence that infants discriminated between objects and their pictures until 24 weeks. There was little active manipulation before 24 weeks when most infants grasped the object and touched the wall or the picture. Even the youngest age group differentiated the object from its picture, however, as indicated by longer periods of looking at the object. Both a surface within reach (wall with pictures) and an object within reach apparently trigger visually elicited reaching and touching at these ages. Young infants do not fail to distinguish a flat surface from an object but show primitive tendencies to explore both.

Reaching for a moving object has been studied by von Hofsten (1979, 1980) and von Hofsten and Lindhagen (1979). Catching a moving object would appear to be far more difficult than grasping a stationary one, because extending the arm and opening the hand must be coordinated with the velocity and the trajectory of the approaching object. It is truly fascinating to discover, from these expert longitudinal studies, that infants reach successfully for moving objects as soon as they master reaching for stationary ones. The infants anticipate an object's future location after a time lapse, reaching and grasping to its anticipated position. Von Hofsten and Lindhagen (1979) seated the infants within reaching distance of a point in the trajectory of an attractive object mounted on a sort of boom that traveled at a velocity of 30 cm/sec. in a horizontal circular path. Infants 18 weeks old caught the object as it moved. Reaching skill improved during the period studied; the number of movement elements decreased with age and the first visually elicited step increased in speed and amplitude (von Hofsten, 1979). But reaching was predictive in the lowest age group; the hand was aimed at the point where it would meet the object rather than the point where the object was seen when the reach was initiated (von Hofsten, 1980). These results do not suggest a gradual integration or mapping of manual and visual schemata, with glances from hand to object, but rather a preadapted coordination.

Attention to tactually given information (manual, at least) is far from being as strong as attention to visually given information in the early months (Bower et al., 1970a; Gratch, 1972). Active, exploratory touching (squeezing, fingering, poking, and rotating) becomes skillful only as the infant becomes able to coordinate the use of both hands. The question here is, How early do visual and haptic exploration occur together, permitting discovery of intermodal invariants?

Hutt (1967) made an extensive study of a 7-month-old infant's manipulatory and visual exploration of novel objects. Manipulation began with a clutching pattern, often followed by half-turns of the wrist that resulted in different aspects of the object being viewed. Later in the month, the object began to be turned over and over while held in both hands. All these movements were accompanied by visual inspection and an intent facial expression.

Harris (1971) found that 8-month-old infants searched more for an object that they had examined both visually and manually than for one examined only visually, so touch would seem to be playing some role at that age. In another study Harris (1972) asked whether infants of 6 to 14½ months touched and looked at the same time; he concluded that visual and tactual inspection were synchronized. Older infants sought to touch an object that they had only inspected visually before, as if they wished to confirm its properties. Later studies are in some disagreement as to whether infants touch and look concordantly as early as 6 months (see Rubenstein 1974; Ruff, 1976; Schaffer, 1975; Schaffer, Greenwood, & Parry, 1972; and Schaffer & Parry, 1970).

Visually directed reaching, although well established, may not necessarily be followed by continued synchronous visual-tactual exploration when the haptic system is still rather poorly controlled, particularly when the object reached for lacks interesting or novel tactual-haptic properties. Steele and Pederson (1977) compared the effect of changes in shape, texture, and color of the objects to be inspected visually and manually by infants of 6 months. Looking and manipulation increased upon introduction of a novel object when shape or texture were changed, but only looking increased when color alone was changed. Concordance of visual-manual exploration was apparent only when new information common to both modalities was introduced. Exploration is, thus, appropriately selective even at this early age.

Other properties of objects that might induce visual inspection and also manipulation are not necessarily apparent until some manipulation has occurred, for example, substance and sound-making properties. An object's substance (e.g., hardness vs. plasticity) is observable visually when it is handled (via rigid vs. deforming motions), but not necessarily when it is stationary. An object's characteristic sounds (e.g., rattle noises) are often revealed only when it is manipulated. Properties such as plasticity and sound potential were found to be attractive ones for inducing manipulatory play and concordant visual regard by 8½ months, whereas sheer configural complexity was not found to be very effective (McCall, 1974).

In a study of the development of play between 7 and 20 months, Fenson, Kagan, Kearsley, and Zelazo (1976) recorded episodes of "simultaneous visual and tactual contact with a toy." Such episodes lasted an average of 8 min, even at 7 months of age. The nature of the play changed with age from mouthing and banging to activities involving several objects and a variety of actions. Even banging, however, provides information about an object's substance, weight, and sound potential.

Auditory-Haptic Exploration

We may conclude that a seen object elicits arm extension and primitive forms of exploration very early; so perhaps does an object that is specified by sound alone, although it loses this power later in infancy. Wishart, Bower, and Dunkeld (1978) studied auditory-manual coordination in sighted babies tested with a noise-making toy in the dark. They reported that the tendency to extend the arm toward a noise-making object was present in early months, peaked at about 5 months, and then declined. Bower (1979) felt that this decline indicated the beginning of "dissociation of the senses," which he assumed to be undifferentiated at birth. Actually, discontinuous sounds are poor sources of information for a layout with continuous surfaces that persist and support objects. Blind babies are notoriously late in reaching for noise-making objects (Adelson & Fraiberg, 1974), as are sighted babies tested under analogous conditions at around 9 to 10 months.

Search for an unseen sound-producing object was less successful than searching for a soundless object that was seen being hidden (Freedman, Fox-Kolenda, Margileth, & Miller, 1969). Bigelow (1980) found that search for a sounding object was not pursued once it was no longer seen until children had reached or passed Piaget's Stage 4 of development of object permanence. These findings were confirmed and extended by Uzgiris and Benson (1980) in several experiments on the use of sound in the search for objects by infants between 9½ and 11½ months. Sound was more effective in directing search in younger infants if the sounding

object had been seen, manipulated, and made to sound before being hidden. Search was less successful when a previously unseen, untouched, and unheard toy was sounded in a hiding place, although the infants frequently oriented toward the sound.

In these experiments, children do not explore an object for knowledge of its properties but hunt for an object in the environment by using sound as a guide. It is hardly surprising that a young infant's skill in this enterprise is limited, since sound is the least rich source of information about objects and places for humans, and it is a poor guide to search at any age. Sounds do not direct exploration of objects at all in many cases, but when they do (crumpling paper, shaking things that rattle, banging things together), they are attended to with interest and provide information about the object's properties, especially about what the object affords.

The Development of Selectivity

Although the exploratory activities of infants are far from random, they appear to become increasingly specific and systematic with age. Exploratory skills develp along with the development of knowledge of what has utility for a task and of differentiation of relevant from irrelevant information (Gibson & Rader, 1979). This development is particularly evident when children attempt to perform tasks set for them by others, such as to compare two objects or scenes, to follow one event and ignore another, or to find an object in a cluttered scene.

Zinchenko, van Chzhi-Tsin, and Tarakanov (1977) presented preschool children with an irregularly shaped object for visual inspection. Visual fixations were recorded and a subsequent shape-matching task was administered. Children 6 years old tended to fixate all around the boundaries of the object and performed well on the matching task. Younger children were more apt to fixate the center of the object, where the lens of the eye-movement camera was located. Not surprisingly, the children who attended to the camera lens performed less well on the shape-matching task. These findings may reflect only age differences in comprehension of the task demands or in motivation to fulfill them. But, alternatively, they may reflect developmental changes in the ability to engage in systematic visual exploration for the purpose of some task.

As children grow, their haptic exploration of objects also develops. Zinchenko (cited in Zaporozhets, 1969) presented preschool children with the same irregularly shaped object to explore manually, and he followed this exploration with a haptic-matching task. By 6 to 7 years, children systematically traced the contours of the object with their fingers. Younger children tended to clutch the object in one place, with little exploration of its boundaries. The children who explored systematically performed better on the matching task. Haptic exploration, driven by the demands of a task, evidently improves over the preschool years.

In the above studies, children must explore an object as fully as possible to recognize an identical object on the matching task. Other studies have required children to discriminate between two objects. A discrimination task requires that the child explore the objects in search of the critical information that distinguishes them. Over the course of childhood, this search becomes increasingly economical.

Nodine and his colleagues (Nodine & Evans, 1969; Nodine & Lang, 1971; Nodine & Simmons, 1974; Nodine & Stuerle, 1973) investigated the eye movements of children in the early school years while they made same/different judgments of pairs of letters and letters presented in strings. Scanning became much more efficient with age. Scanning between critical target comparison areas increased, unnecessary scanning within letters or within a letter string declined, and the number of fixations decreased markedly. The oldest children (third graders) appeared to know what letter in a string and what aspects of that letter contained the critical information for discrimination, and they looked for that information directly.

The development of increasingly efficient, task-directed information pickup is evident in many experiments. An experiment by Lehman (1972) will serve as an illustration. She used a haptic comparison task to investigate school children's (K through sixth grade) information-gathering strategies. When the children were instructed to match two objects of the same shape or texture, with both dimensions varying, even kindergarten children restricted their manual exploration of the objects to the relevant property. But when the children were not told what feature was relevant and the two features were redundant so that only one needed to be explored for a correct choice, the older children learned to explore only one feature early in the task, whereas the younger children took longer either to discover the redundancy or to perceive its utility. When the redundancy was pointed out, selective exploration was enhanced at all ages.

Pick, Christy, and Frankel (1972) used a visual comparison task to study development of selectivity in second and sixth graders by means of wooden animals that varied in shape, color, and size. In one task, the children were told which aspect to compare before viewing a pair of the wooden animals. In another task, they were informed only after stimulus presentation. Reaction times were facilitated by prior instruction, especially for the older children. In another study, Pick and Frankel (1974) used the same sort of task, but the relevant feature for comparison was either predesignated for blocks of trials or else randomly designated from trial to trial. Random presentation was more disturbing to the younger children, leading the authors to conclude that older children are more flexible in their strategies of selective attention (see also Pick & Frankel, 1973; Pick, Frankel & Hess, 1975).

The degree to which one can generalize from any one experiment to another situation is always a problem. Flexibility of selection may develop rather specifically, depending on the task. An experiment by Condry, McMahon-Rideout, and Levy (1979) is in many ways comparable to the Pick et al. (1973, 1975) experiments, but the materials and the judgments were different. Second- and fifth-grade children as well as adults made similarity judgments on sets of three words projected on a screen before them with respect to graphic, phonetic, or semantic information. The words were arranged in a triangular display, with the upper word as standard and the two lower ones for comparison. The subject might be given a set of words, with one pair close in meaning, and asked to choose the word that looked, sounded, or meant most nearly the same as the standard. For half the subjects, the judgments were arranged in blocks, with all the trials in a block requiring a match on just one of the three properties. The other subjects were presented with sequences in a random arrangement, and the required comparison was designated just before the trial began. All the subjects were facilitated by the blocked arrangement; there was no interaction of blocking with age, as Pick and Frankel (1973) had found. Overall improvement in performance increased with age (reaction times decreased) and irrelevant information had a less detrimental effect, but flexibility in shifting attention without blocking did not increase.

An aspect of selectivity that has often been shown to develop with age is a trend toward more efficient use of specific features of information presented. Perception in tasks that are repeated becomes progressively more economical through detection of only those features of available information that have greatest utility for performing the behavior required. Detection of the affordance of the minimal criterial information has been demonstrated repeatedly (see E. J. Gibson, 1969, pp. 462 ff.; Gibson & Levin, 1975, pp. 43 ff.). When critical features for guidance of performance are defined redundantly, the most economical information tends to be selected. Pick and Unze (1979) had preschool and older children select a set of three designated letters from a box containing a collection of letters. As redundancy was introduced (e.g., coloring the designated letters differently from the rest of the assortment), children of all ages profited, especially the older ones. The youngest group profited even more when the redundancy was pointed out. Seeing the affordances and making economical use of them begins early and increases developmentally.

In the above tasks, children were presented with either a single object or a pair of objects for exploration and comparison. In other tasks, children have been presented with an displays of objects to explore. With age, exploration of such arrays becomes increasingly systematic and efficient as well.

A number of developmental studies of exploring and comparing two displays were performed by Vurpillot (for summaries, see Vurpillot, 1972/1976, chap. 9; Vurpillot & Ball, 1979). The task was to judge whether pairs of line drawings of houses were the same or not. Each house in a pair contained six windows that were arranged in two vertical columns of three. Within each window were pictures varying details (plants, curtains, laundry on a line, etc.). A pair of houses could be identical with all the sets of six windows matching or they might vary in one or a number of details in one or more pairs of windows.

Children's scan paths (eye movements of comparison) became increasingly economical between 4 and 9 years. The proportion of comparison movements between houses increased, as did the proportion of these movements that were horizontal (most informative). The most efficient strategy was homologous comparison: an eye movement that went directly from window *a* in one house to window *a*, its homologue, in the other. The number of subjects making such comparisons were 0 out of 18 in the youngest group and 18 out of 20 in the oldest group. Above age 6, nearly all the children made some homologous comparisons. Vurpillot & Ball (1979) consistently found that the preschool children based their judgments on only a limited amount of the available information, whereas older

children used any potential difference between the stimuli in making their judgments.

Vurpillot and Ball (1979) suggested that the development of search reflected a change in how children understood the comparison task. Young children may have thought that two houses should be judged the same if they were equivalent in their overall structure; older children may have thought that the two houses should be judged identical only if they were identical in all their contents and in the arrangements of those contents. It seems possible, however, that children also developed new and more systematic strategies of search.

Experiments on search behavior by Russian psychologists support the latter interpretation (see Venger, 1977). Children of 3 to 7 years were observed while searching for a designated target (a strip of given magnitude or a color chip) in a series of strips varying in magnitude or in a color array classified according to hue, brightness, and saturation. In some cases, the items of the array were arranged systematically; in some they were randomized. In searching for a strip of designated length, the youngest children seldom referred back to the model and failed to examine many elements of the array, even when the array was arranged systematically. Search time increased in a middle group, with more looks at the model and more elements examined. In the oldest group, search time decreased and proceeded systematically. The youngest children scanned a random series in much the same way as an ordered one. The older children took account of the series properties and scanned a "bracketed" area in an economical fashion in the ordered arrays. Some of them appeared to use the series properties even when the series was randomized.

When colors were presented in an ordered array, age differences were especially apparent. The youngest children searched nearly as chaotically as with a random array. The older children divided the process of searching into two stages, as disclosed by their eye movements. The first stage consisted of vertical and diagonal sweeps, followed by horizontal movements increasing regularly in fixation time until the match was selected. They were using the properties of the color system, searching first for the required hue and then scanning horizontally within a graduated series of shades lying within the chosen hue. Search strategies based on affordances and order in the array are developing during the early school years, yielding even more economical search behavior.

Finally, a few studies have investigated children's exploration of a three-dimensional layout in search of an object. These studies, too, reveal that search becomes more efficient and systematic.

Drozdal and Flavell (1975) presented children of 5 to 10 years with a model house consisting of 14 connecting rooms and two dolls representing a boy (Charlie Brown) and a frog. As these objects were placed in the first room, a story was told in which Charlie and the frog were said to move through the house. The children could not see the movements of the dolls because the walls of the house were opaque, but the story was illustrated with cartoon drawings. As Charlie entered the fifth room, the frog was said to be present; by the seventh room, it was discovered to be lost. Charlie Brown continued through the house alone. Children were asked, at the end of the story, where they should look for the frog. They were probed to determine whether they realized that the frog had to be within a critical search area, in rooms 5, 6, or 7. Children 10 years old uniformly appreciated this fact; children 5 years old did not. Drozdal and Flavell concluded that this aspect of logical search behavior develops in middle childhood.

Because Drozdal and Flavell's (1975) study involved a model environment that the child never encountered directly, developmental changes in logical search may partly reflect the older child's greater ability to imagine unseen paths through an unseen environment. Studies by Wellman, Somerville, and Haake (1979) provide evidence for logical search at younger ages in a study in which an object was lost in a playground. The logic of the study was similar to that of Drozdal and Flavell (1975). A child of 3 to 5 was taken by an experimenter through a playground divided into eight areas. In the third area, the experimenter took the child's picture. In the seventh area, the camera was discovered to be missing. The child completed the path through the eighth area and then was asked to search for the camera. Children of all ages tended to search first in the third area, where the picture had been taken. Most of the 3-year-olds did not search at a second location; those who did tended to search outside the critical area, in the first or second locations. Older children were more likely to confine their second searches to the critical area. These findings indicate that the tendency to search comprehensively within a critical area develops over the preschool and early school years.

The study by Wellman et al. (1979) indicated that preschool children have some capacity to search logically for an object if it is lost in a natural setting that the child has walked through. But even

this study may underestimate young children's abilities because the children were led through the playground by the experimenter. A child may locate objects in a large setting even more effectively if she has been allowed to explore that setting actively. Feldman and Acredolo (1979) introduced 3- to 4-year-olds and 9- to 10-year-olds to a network of corridors within which they found a cup. Half the children searched for the cup on their own, the experimenter following behind. The others looked for the cup as they were led through the corridor by the experimenter. All children were subsequently asked to find the place where the cup had been. The older children were more accurate in their estimates of the cup's location, but at both ages, the children were more accurate if they had explored the corridor actively. By exploring, children evidently pick up more information about an environmental layout.

Following an event is always selective because, at any given time, multiple changes are taking place in the flux of stimulation. Selective exploration of events becomes especially remarkable when the attended event is accompanied by other, potentially confusable happenings that could distract the child. Do children become better able to resist such distraction as they grow and to follow one event exclusively?

This question has been addressed through studies of selective listening. In such studies, the child is instructed to attend to and report about one of two tape-recorded verbal messages. The earliest research with children was performed by Maccoby and her colleagues (1967). Each of two very short messages was presented to different ears or in voices of different sex. Children as young as 5 years could attend to one voice selectively, although the number of intrusions from the unattended message declined with age. Related experiments by Anooshian and McCulloch (1979), Anooshian and Prilop (1980), Clifton and Bogartz (1968), and Doyle (1973) have generally found some developmental improvement, but the measure has typically been retention rather than detection of appropriate information.

Experiments by Geffen and Sexton (1978) and Sexton and Geffen (1979) used detection tasks more pertinent to perceptual selectivity. The subjects (children from 7 to 11 years and adults) were to listen to pairs of words presented simultaneously and press a key if the target word was heard. The words were played to different ears or spoken by different voices. When 7-year-olds were instructed simply to attend to one ear exclusively, their hit rate was as good as in a control condition with no competing voice. Hit rate increased with age in general and number of intrusions decreased. Age effects were most notable as instructions became more difficult to follow (e.g., "attend to one ear, but press the key if you hear the target word in the other"). The ability to divide attention (listen to both ears equally) did not change with age. Thus, older children appear better able to follow complicated instructions in a flexible manner.

It is interesting that even the youngest children can attend to one message selectively in simple detection tasks. Can infants attend to a voice selectively as well? Benson (1978) investigated this ability in infants of 12 and 25 weeks, both with and without spatial separation of background noise and signal. The background noise consisted of a babble of voices (four men's and four women's voices reading aloud). It was played continually from a loudspeaker directly in front of the infant. At specified intervals, a new voice was added from a loudspeaker either in front of the infant or 90° to the side. This signal was either the mother's voice greeting the infant or a control signal consisting of a segment of the babble. Heart rate was monitored continuously. There was a significant deceleration of heart rate when the mother's voice was added, but not when babble was played. Detection was facilitated when the mother's voice was separated from the babble, but there was a small, reliable deceleration even without any spatial separation. The older infants showed a larger deceleration, but there was significant detection of the mother's voice at 12 weeks. More infants smiled, also, after hearing the mother's voice than after exposure to the added babble. Figure and ground, under these conditions at least, are separated. Even young infants do not hear simply a "blooming, buzzing confusion" and can attend to a meaningful event despite competing contextual information.

The mother's voice is an event of special significance to the child, and it might be attended selectively for that reason. But a final study (Bahrick et al., 1981) indicates that 4-month-old infants can attend selectively to other events as well. This experiment used a visual analogue of a selective listening task, in which two visible events are presented so that they overlap each other on a screen and the subject is asked to follow one of them (Neisser & Becklen, 1975). In the present case, filmed events of four hands playing a clapping game and of two hands operating a slinky toy were superimposed. Infants could not, of course, be asked to follow one of them, so a variant of Spelke's (1976) auditory-visual preference method was used. The two movies were projected one on top of the other and the sound track to one movie was played. The infants were apparently able to segregate the events and to follow the event accompanied by sound. After familiarization with this display, projection of the two films silently and without superposition indicated that the infants had habituated to the one accompanied by sound and now looked at the other one. It appears, therefore, that perception is selective from the start, at least when the infant is given the opportunity to follow an event.

Overview

Exploring the environment is the key to detecting information about it, and the human neonate is well provided with coordinated systems for exploring. These systems, moreover, are coordinated with each other to foster perception of a unitary world by looking, listening, and touching. Nevertheless, some perceptual systems are more mature at birth than others (the visual vs. haptic systems for example), and each system will undergo enormous changes with development. Children will come to explore objects, events, and places more efficiently and flexibly.

As children progress to the performance of instructed tasks, they must learn to explore and search for relevant information economically. They become better able to do this as they come to understand a task better, as perception becomes more differentiated, and as their exploration becomes more flexible. But exploration is active, selective, and systematic from the start, as infants investigate objects and events spontaneously for the purpose of discovering their affordances.

OBTAINING INFORMATION ABOUT EVENTS

The active perceptual systems of the young infant provide stimulation that is continuously changing. In this flux of stimulation, there is information both about changes in the surface layout and about the stable characteristics of the layout. Through changing arrays of stimulation, perceivers obtain information about events. These events, in turn, provide information about objects, surfaces, and their persisting properties, since invariant relationships are preserved over change. This section focuses on the perception of events and their properties. In later sections, we will discuss the role of events in specifying constant properties of objects and places.

Two Views of Event Perception

Our focus on events is hardly traditional. In the early history of experimental psychology, research on perception was confined largely to static phenomena, for example, color, illusions, and depth observed under purely static conditions. The reasons for this choice may have had to do with limitations of equipment and probably, too, with the then current theoretical background of British empiricism. Most early psychologists believed that perception depended on elementary sensations joined together by association. Perception of movement was thought to be derived from the integration of static impressions.[1] This view penetrated to developmental psychology: It led to research on "the problem of temporal integration" and to the hypothesis that integration was improved or speeded up developmentally (e.g., see Schnall, 1968). Research on this problem has customarily presented subjects with separate piecemeal glimpses of a display presented sequentially, thus, forcing integration (Girgus, 1973; Girgus & Hochberg, 1970). It is interesting that, even under these impoverished conditions, young children can sometimes perceive objects and events. A succession of static displays, if presented with appropriate rapidity, leads to perception of an event with change over space and time. Perceiving such an event, for example, stroboscopic motion, does not depend on associative learning, because it is perceived by neonates (Tauber & Koffler, 1966).

We will be concerned here with the perception of events in which information is flowing naturally over time rather than with a succession of frozen displays, for we conceive of perception as primarily and primitively the pickup of information within a continuous spatiotemporal flow (J. J. Gibson, 1950, 1966, 1979). By this view, events are the principal aspects of the world that require and receive the attention of an animal. They supply structured information for the perceptual systems; and they are perceived as unitary, bounded, meaningful happenings. The development of event perception occurs through a process of differentiation rather than integration, and this differentiation begins early in life. Event perception is not a late achievement that results from an integration of static pictures but a fundamental ability that underlies the perception of the constant properties of the world.

What Is an Event?

Events have been variously defined. To J. J. Gibson, events are of three kinds: "Change in the layout of surfaces, change in the color and texture of surfaces, or change in the existence of surfaces" (1979, p. 94). To Johansson, an event is "a generic concept denoting various kinds of relational change over time in a structure" (1978, p. 677). Both definitions imply that an event involves both transformation and invariance—both a changing and an unchanging structure. These changes and invariances can be considered distally (as physical changes in a stable layout), proximally (as patterns of change and invariance in the information available to pickup systems), and perceptually (as the registration of change and constancy by an organism). However defined, an event involves a change over time and an invariant property that persists. Invariants of events are abstract and usually amodal, for example, a rhythm. Rhythmic patterns can be presented acoustically, optically, or on the skin and still keep their identity as a pattern. Invariants confer unity on events—an event has a beginning and an end and many events have points of articulation or centers of underlying structure. Invariants also specify the properties of events and their affordances.

Johansson's studies of motion perception provide one particularly interesting example of how the unity of an event is specified by abstract invariant information. Johansson filmed motion patterns representing the activity of locomotion in man without any concomitant pictorial information. This was achieved by means of a moving-dot technique (see Johansson, 1978). Ten small luminous points were attached to the main limb joints of an actor who was filmed in near darkness while walking, running, or dancing. Nothing was recorded on the film but a group of 10 bright dots, each moving in its own path. What is perceived is not a swarm of dots, but a moving person. Schoolchildren shown the films for as little as 200 msec reported seeing a walking man. They perceived the man as persisting over changes in his posture and location. The information for this invariance is entirely relational, abstract, and changing, and it specifies an event with coherence, structure, and meaning. Johansson describes this information in terms of vector addition—although the dots move in different directions, they share a common component direction. Detection of this common component leads to perception of the unity and persistence of the person, whereas detection of the remaining components of motion leads to perception of changes in the person's posture.

In Johansson's studies, the movements of dots must be perceived relative to each other for any coherent whole to be defined. Must an infant learn to perceive relative motion rather than unrelated absolute motions? Existing evidence indicates not. Lasky and Gogel (1978) in an experiment with patterns of three moving dots showed that infants of 5 months perceived their motions relative to each other. As we will see later, such relative motions provide information about the unity of an object for infants as well as for adults.

Another important characteristic of events is their hierarchical structure: Small events are embedded within larger events and may be differentiated into even smaller events. This hierarchical structure is particularly obvious in acoustic events such as speech and music. Segmentation of speech and music involves differentiation and analysis at many levels. In listening to speech, we segment the acoustic stream into sentences, phrases, words, and syllables. In listening to music, segmentation occurs at many levels also. Preschool children, before learning to read, may have difficulty breaking the speech stream into event units that are not determined by meaning (see Gibson & Levin, 1975, pp. 119 ff.). In the case of music, untutored listeners are less able to relate smaller events to superordinate themes (Frances, 1958). Perception of a high degree of embeddedness thus may come late in development. But some degree of embeddedness is perceived quite early, especially when the larger event contains repetitive subunits, like a game of peekaboo. Greenfield (1972) found that a 4-month-old infant quickly learned the structure of the game and anticipated the key feature of the subevent (reappearance after disappearance) even after specific vocal cuing was dropped.

Events have affordances. Speech affords communication with another, games afford socializing. These affordances are perceived with such immediacy that it is difficult to describe an event otherwise. Speech in one's native language cannot ordinarily be perceived as a jumble of meaningless sounds, try as one might. And even inanimate events with distinctive sounds like branches of a tree crackling in the wind, and man-made ones, like uncorking a bottle of champagne, are identified as meaningful readily and accurately by adults and even quite well by preschool children (VanDerveer, 1979).

Finally, events are not only given by the world around us. They are also created by the observer. Information about many things in the world, including the self, is only available by active participation in an event. A good example is touch. Touch must be active to get information about substance, texture, shape, and weight of objects. Touching is usually combined with active fingering, pressing, squeezing, poking, rubbing, and other activities. Even when some information is available without activity, an observer is likely to enhance his opportunities by adjustments that optimize exploration. As discussed earlier, some of these exploratory activities are present at the beginning of life.

Following Events by Young Infants

Events provide information about the world from the start of life. We have already noted, in the discussion on preadapted coordination, that neonates can follow an object moving in translation across the field of view. The fact that very young infants attend to and follow events is strong evidence against an integration view of event perception. Babies do not seem to perceive a series of frozen images, for they attend to moving objects consistently. For example, infants of 2 months look longer to moving objects than to stationary objects (Ames & Silfen, 1965; Carpenter, 1974; Cohen, 1969; McKenzie & Day, 1976; Wilcox & Clayton, 1968). Infants of 1- to 3-months also look to objects in the periphery more quickly if they are moving than if they are stationary (Milewski & Genovese, 1980). Finally, when an object is presented away from the infant's fixation point, the infant will turn to look at it over a greater range of distances, both laterally (Tronick, 1972) and in depth (McKenzie & Day, 1976), if it is moving.

What happens when infants are presented with motions more complicated than simple translation, where there is a change in the path of motion or an object's trajectory? Mundy-Castle and Anglin (1969) presented infants with a two-window display in which a decorative ball moved up in one window and then down in the other after a brief interval of occlusion. Infants under 1 month tended to fixate one window or the other, with few cross-looks. But by 30 days, there was an increase in the number of anticipatory cross-looks toward the opposite window after the disappearance of a fixated ball. Around 14 weeks, many infants followed an assumed trajectory over the top of the box containing the windows, during the ball's occlusion. So by 1 month, looking behavior began to be coordinated with the pattern of events. This experiment was repeated by Mundy-Castle (reported in Dasen, Inhelder, Lavallée, & Retschitzki, 1978) with Nigerian infants with similar results. Beginning at 25 to 70 days, they anticipated the appearance of the ball in the second window.

In real-life events, as in Mundy-Castle's experiments (1969, 1978), objects are frequently occluded either by other objects that pass in front of them or by objects that they pass behind. As adults, we do not perceive the occluded object as vanishing into thin air. We perceive, instead, an event in which one thing goes behind something else. There is no reason to suppose this perception is the result of an integration of frozen snapshots with the mind supplying an inference about the object, because there is information at the occluding edge for something going behind. The progressive deletion of structure of a target object as it is occluded (Gibson, Kaplan, Reynolds, & Wheeler, 1969; G. A. Kaplan, 1969) provides information for the continued presence of the object despite change. In an experiment by Yonas (1982), translation of a surface between a viewer and a second surface was specified by accretion and deletion of texture elements. For adults, these displays specify the interposition of one surface moving in front of another. Infants 7 months old reached more frequently to the virtually closer surface, whereas they did not with static presentation of the dot patterns.

There have been a number of experiments studying the effects of temporary occlusion of an object upon infants' perception of the object's continued presence and their apparent expectation that the object will reappear. The experiments have been motivated, for the most part, by an interest in the development of object permanence, knowledge of the identity and continued existence of an object when it is out of sight. In that light, results of the experiments are as yet ambiguous; it is not clear whether young infants conceive of an object as permanent (see Harris , vol. II, chap. 9). Nevertheless, these experiments are of interest for event perception.

The first of these experiments was performed by Bower (1967a). Two contrasting events involving disappearance were compared: one involved temporary occlusion of an object by a moving screen via a progressive deletion and then accretion of structure at the edges of the screen; the other event provided information for going out of existence by a sudden implosion. Infants between 49 and 55 days of age were observed with an operant procedure. The infants treated progressive occlusion as they would a nondisappearance, but reacted quite differently to the implosive disappearance. When spontaneous sucking was used as a response indicator, suppression of sucking provided evidence that a progressively occluded object was perceived as persisting.

Most subsequent experiments have focused on perception of the temporary occlusion of an object as it passed behind a screen, by observing the infants' anticipatory eye movements at the time appropriate for the object's emergence. If infants perceived the trajectory of a moving object as a unitary event, they would presumably follow the trajectory as if they were tracking a visible object. There is evidence that infants as young as 8 weeks do this, turning their eyes to the exit side of the screen and reaching it before or as the moving object emerges (Bower, Broughton & Moore, 1971a). In another experiment, Nelson (1971) reported that anticipatory looking did not occur the first time the object disappeared and that it occurred with only gradually increasing frequency on successive trials. However, Nelson's occluder (a tunnel through which a toy train engine passed) was 27-in. long (more than five times as long as that in Bower et al., 1971). Furthermore, the duration of occlusion changed randomly from one revolution to the next; only one of the durations was commensurate with the velocity of the engine. Infants may have failed to anticipate the emergence of the train because the duration of disappearance was too great or because the occlusion time was not commensurate with the observed velocity.

There are many parameters of these experiments that can be varied; for example, the duration of occlusion, the width of the occluder, the speed of the object's travel, the path of the trajectory, the attractiveness of the target object, and the response selected for observation. Unfortunately, all of these factors may affect the results, making apparent contradictions almost inevitable. However, some of the variations are of interest developmentally and theoretically. In one of the experiments of Bower et al. (1971a), conditions of the movement that specified the original trajectory were disrupted (inappropriate speed at emergence or too long a period of occlusion before reemergence). If an infant were really extracting an invariant trajectory specified by the beginning of the event, these conflicting conditions should produce disruptions of behavior. In fact, an "impossible" final trajectory (accelerated movement at emergence) resulted in no systematic anticipations, although a possible one regularly did. Nelson's (1971) experiment as well as an experiment by Moore, Borton, and Darby (1978) are consistent with this finding. The evidence, thus, confirms that quite young infants perceive invariant information for an event, specification of a trajectory over a transformation involving temporary occlusion. This result is by no means trivial because the information during occlusion is amodal and abstract (see, in particular, the discussion of the "rabbit-hole phenomenon" in Michotte, Thinès, & Crabbé, 1964). The result also complements nicely von Hofsten's (1980) finding that infants predict the trajectory of a moving object.

Picking up information for an event does not, however, guarantee that the event is fully differentiated. Does an infant also perceive featural details of an object that is being moved? In one experiment, Bower et al. (1971a) substituted one moving object for another during occlusion so that an object of a different color and shape emerged, moving along the correct trajectory. Up to 20 weeks, infants did not react to the change, but after that time they suppressed tracking and glanced back. There is conflicting information for the event in this case, which is resolved by young infants in favor of the invariant trajectory information rather than the object's static properties. This experiment was repeated by Goldberg (1976), who recorded heart rate as well as tracking. If infants were surprised by a change in features of the object, their heart rate was expected to decelerate. No evidence of such change was found in infants 20 to 24 weeks old. Neither was there change in visual fixation with a change in the object during occlusion, as Bower et al. (1971a) had found. Various conditions of the experiment (e.g., longer occlusion time) differed from the Bower et al. experiments, however.

A developmental comparison of perception of an object's motion trajectory, differentiation of its features, and permanence was conducted by Moore et al. (1978) with 5- and 9-month-old infants. The experiment presented three conditions designed to violate an infant's presumed expectations if she had knowledge of each of the three types. To violate expectations about an object's trajectory, an object reappeared from behind a screen faster than its original trajectory would have specified. To violate expectations about an object's features, the object disappeared behind a screen and a featurally different object appeared from the other side on the initial trajectory. To violate expectations about an object's continuous displacement, an object disappeared behind the first of two separated screens, but failed to

appear in the space between them before emerging on the correct trajectory. The behavior observed was any indication of disrupted tracking (looking back, looking away, monitoring screen edges). Each condition had an appropriate control. Infants 5 months old quite consistently showed disrupted tracking behavior when the trajectory and the feature conditions were violated. The 9-month-old infants displayed evidence of disrupted tracking in all three conditions, including the continuity condition. The younger infants evidently expected the object to move smoothly without changing its color or shape, and the older infants also expected it to move continuously over space and through time.

Two further experiments have investigated the effect of changing the moving object while it is occluded. Muller and Aslin (1978) observed tracking of infants at 2, 4, and 6 months, with the shape or the color of a moving target changed during occlusion. Infants at all three ages showed smooth tracking as the object passed behind the screen and emerged, with no disruption because of changes in the object. Infants were capable of disrupting their tracking, however, and they did so if the object stopped short of going behind the occluder. When occlusion duration was varied, a longer occlusion led to some disruption of tracking, but there was no interaction with change in the object, even at 6 months. Muller and Aslin concluded that disruption of tracking was a poor measure for investigating the object concept or object identity because of spontaneous or chance disruptions of tracking.

Von Hofsten and Lindhagen (in press) performed the change-of-object experiment with 19-week-old infants using a measure of cardiac deceleration, as Goldberg (1976) had done, but with a much briefer duration of occlusion (less than 1 sec. as compared with 4 sec.). A habituation procedure, followed by a test for dishabituation, was used. When the object was changed behind the screen, deceleration occurred, but not when it was only occluded. Tracking data did not show disruption when the object was changed behind the occluding screen. Looking at these results as a whole, it does not seem possible to conclude anything about object permanence, except that numerous variables may affect the results; but the evidence does seem conclusive and plentiful that quite young infants perceive invariant information specifying the trajectory of an object over occlusion.

What do infants perceive when an event involves motion toward or away from the observer? Motion away from the observer is akin to information for disappearance, if the recession continues long enough. It indicates that something is moving out of the immediate surroundings. Progressive minification of the image of the object projected to the eye specifies the event. This is exactly what happens in nature when imprinting is observed in precocial animals. The mother moves away on a vanishing course; the precocial duckling or chick begins to run. It is interesting that artificial production of information for vanishing by means of a contracting pattern with a shadow caster is effective for inducing imprinting in chicks in the absence of featural information about a target object (Tronick, 1967). Safe following (without losing a target or colliding with it) follows the rule, stabilize the expansion pattern at the eye (J. J. Gibson, 1979). Adult drivers do this on highways, as do precocial animals in following the herd. Motion toward the observer provides information for imminent collision, and it is specified by a symmetrical, accelerated expansion pattern. The event is typically referred to as looming. Responses to looming with both simulated (shadow-caster) events and events involving real objects have been studied in infants. (For a detailed discussion, see *Perceiving Affordances of the Layout*.)

Events are specified acoustically as well as visually, and there is evidence that some of these are followed at an early age. It was noted earlier that neonates respond to certain kinds of acoustic stimulation, especially continuous sounds, by turning the eyes and head toward the sound source. They may also follow the event and differentiate its properties. For example, 2-month-old infants have been shown to discriminate simple repetitive rhythmic sequences (Demany, McKenzie, & Vurpillot, 1977). Perception of temporal grouping in auditory patterns has been studied with 5-month-old infants by Chang and Trehub (1977b). Following habituation of a cardiac response to a six-tone sequence with 2, 4 grouping, infants were given the same tonal sequence with 4, 2 grouping, with ensuing dishabituation. A sequence of eight notes arranged in ascending order was presented 4, 8, or 12 times for familiarization to 5½-month-old infants by McCall and Melson (1970). The same notes were then presented in a rearranged sequence. Cardiac deceleration to the rearranged sequence occurred, increasing as the number of familiarization trials increased (replicated by Melson & McCall, 1970).

Although infants in these experiments must have obtained some event information of a relational sort, it is not clear that the sequence of eight tones was heard as a whole. An experiment by Chang and Trehub (1977a) presented infants 4½ to 6 months old with a six-tone pattern of notes over 15 habituation trials. The response indicator was cardiac deceleration. Transpositions of the habituated pattern (three higher and three lower) as well as a pattern of the same notes in scrambled order were presented for dishabituation. Response recovery was not evident when the shift was to a transposed pattern, but it was evident when the shift was to a scrambled pattern. In the absence of a no-change control group, a conclusion is dubious, but the infants may have detected relational information in the tonal patterns—a property of the melody that was invariant over changes in its absolute frequency.

The events so far considered were specified by either optical or acoustical information alone. Events in the real world, however, are normally multimodally specified. We watch them, hear them, and often get kinesthetic and vestibular information about them. As adults, we perceive these events as units—unique happenings with one meaning. It may be that the best information for unity of an event is given in invariant information that is specified in many modes, for example, both optically and acoustically or both optically and haptically. Dynamic event properties, like tempo and rhythm, would provide event structure specifiable as the same in many modes. Adults are aware of such properties, for example, in watching and listening to a ballet or when dancing themselves. Preadapted coordinated systems for pickup of information are ideally suited to extract information for these abstract, amodal invariants. Is multimodally specified invariant information detected by infants?

Earlier research on so-called intersensory patterning with subjects from the early grades (Abravanel, 1968; Birch & Lefford, 1967) sometimes gave the impression that perceptual systems become increasingly integrated with age. The tasks that were used required matching of patterns across visual, auditory, or tactile presentations. But research with suitable intrasensory comparisons (Milner & Bryant, 1970) has made the integration interpretation dubious, and an experiment on intermodal perception of temporal sequences in infancy (Allen, Walker, Symonds, & Marcell, 1977) has stripped it of plausibility. Allen et al. presented infants of about 6 months with audible and visible sequences of three elements in two temporal patterns. An habituation procedure with one pattern was followed by a test for recovery with a new pattern or the same pattern as a control. There were four groups, varying in mode of presentation of the two tests: auditory-auditory, visual-visual, auditory-visual, and visual-auditory. Heart rate and skin potential were the response indicators. Infants generalized habituation to the same pattern presented in a new mode, and all the infants dishabituated to a new pattern. Infants in the intersensory presentation conditions showed greater recovery to new patterns than did infants in the intrasensory conditions.

The events studied in these experiments were extremely simple and of short duration. As noted earlier, there is now evidence that infants follow more complex natural events specified optically and acoustically and attend to the bimodally specified information. Four-month-old infants look and listen preferentially to events such as a woman playing peekaboo and a hand beating a rhythm on simple percussion instruments (Spelke, 1976). Infants of 4½ months also look preferentially to sound-specified events that are less familiar: slinky toy and a hand-clap game (Bahrick et al., 1981). There was no common spatial information in these studies; the infants responded to internal temporal structure invariant over the two modalities.

Further experiments have investigated the information for unity in such bimodally specified events (see Spelke, in press, for a review). In one series of studies (Spelke, 1979), films were prepared using unfamiliar objects (toy stuffed animals) and sounds (thumps and gongs presented in sequences of locomotion and bouncing produced via puppet strings) accompanied by a sound track bearing some aspect of temporal invariance with the depicted locomotion in any given film. Each object made a different percussion sound. A pair of films with different objects and temporal sequences was displayed while one sound track located in a central position was played. The quality of the sound, being artificially produced, bore no intrinsic relation to either object. Infants could respond to the auditory-visual relationship only by detecting a temporal invariant. Three experiments tested whether infants could perceive a unitary event by detecting the synchrony or the common tempo of sounds and impacts. In Experiment 1, a sound occurred whenever the appropriate object landed on the ground, and the sound and impacts occurred at a distinctive tempo. In Experiment 2, each sound occurred in the same tempo as one of the objects, but it was not simultaneous with the impacts of either object. In Experiment 3, sounds were simultaneous with the impacts of one object, but their tempo was common to both the events portrayed so that only synchrony of burst

and impact provided temporal invariance for uniting one film with the sound track. Infants detected the temporal relationships in all three experiments. Infants at 4 months of age do appear to be able to perceive unitary audible and visible events either by detecting the synchrony or the common tempo of sounds and impacts. Further studies indicated that infants can perceive a unitary event by detecting temporal relationships between sounds and other visible movements of an object—movements not culminating in an impact (Spelke, Born, & Chu, in press).

Other aspects of event structure could also provide information for bimodal unity. Microstructure within the event specifying properties of a substance (e.g., hard vs. spongy) may carry optical and acoustic information for unity (see Bahrick, 1980, which will be described in *Obtaining Information About Objects*). It is possible, also, that simultaneous information about the affordance or meaning of an event may be picked up visually and aurally to unite the event sequence. The affordance of an event, such as scissors converging on a piece of paper and cutting it in two, is easily perceived visually, and it is also perceived and identified correctly by an adult when only the sound, played over a tape recorder, is available (VanDerveer, 1979). When bimodal information is available, both the temporal structure and the affordance of the event might specify its unity to an infant. Could the affordance alone?

The question was explored by Walker (1982) in experiments on perception of expressive behavior in infants. Expressive behavior of adults, as revealed in changes in facial structure and accompanying vocalizations, provides information about the kind of interaction that can be expected, for example, pleasant, comforting, playful versus harsh, inattentive, somber. Walker prepared films of a woman displaying expressive behaviors judged as happy, neutral, or sad. She projected two films side by side and played the sound track for only one of them in a central location. Infants of both 7 and 5 months consistently looked longer to a filmed event when its appropriate sound track was played. Synchrony of temporal patterns could well have been responsible for perception of unity by the infants. But when the sound track was played out of phase with the event, so as to destroy synchrony, the infants were at first upset and looked back and forth at length, then settled down after 60 sec. or so to watching the film appropriate to the sound track. It seems plausible that they detected the common affordance of vocal and facial expressions and thus perceived a unitary event.

Differentiating the Properties of Events

Reversibility

One useful way of classifying events is on the basis of reversibility or nonreversibility. A reversible event is one for which there exists a transformation that can be applied to the final state to produce the initial state. Changes of location of an object in the surface layout are generally of this kind. As a man walks into the distance toward his mailbox, stimulation projected to the eye changes continuously, rendering the image smaller and smaller. But he peers in his mailbox and retraces his route, returning to his original position. Motion toward and away from an observer provides information for a persisting property of a movable object—its size. Such an event is very frequent in the world, even in the world of an infant, who sees his caretaker moving toward him and then away again or who moves his own hand toward his eyes and away in a cyclic pattern. These events provide information for the constant size of an object. Like many of the events that follow, they are reversible in a special sense, because the transformation that restores the initial state is similar to the original transformation.

Another type of reversible event gives information for so-called shape constancy. An object that turns or rotates provides optical information via a series of continuous perspective transformations for a persisting shape of the object itself. The continuity of the transformation and its reversibility can be duplicated by an observer's walking around an object or turning it in his hand. Such information is picked up by infants quite early.

Information for substance, another persisting property of objects, is also revealed in reversible transformations of different kinds. Rigid objects, when moved, retain constant cross-ratios for points in linear relation on their surfaces, no matter what the angle of rotation. Nonrigid objects may deform when moved, especially when squeezed or subjected to pressure. Cyclic deformation is information for elasticity of substance (rubbery or fluid transformations) and is also picked up early. (For experiments on the development of size and shape constancy and detection of substance, see *Obtaining Information About Objects*.)

Reversible paths in a layout that can be walked through provide a continuous series of reversible vistas that give information for an objective, permanent environment in which objects and oneself can move around (see *Obtaining Information About Places*). As one moves, surfaces are occluded and disoccluded—a most important reversible event that provides information for persisting properties of both objects and the layout. Looking at a landscape through a window, one perceives a continuous lawn or expanse of terrain. Much of this expanse is occluded by trees, buildings, and so on, but we perceive that the full expanse is there. We can procure direct information for it by moving our viewing position so that what was concealed is revealed.

An irreversible event is one for which there exists no transformation, in the ordinary world, that will restore the event's initial state. Irreversible transformations hold information for nonconstancy or change of state. They occur in events like evaporating, breaking, and being consumed. Infants do not experience many such events until the beginning of the second year when they not only witness but also create events such as spilling milk, breaking toys and dishes, and consuming cookies.

There has been rather little research on the child's differentiation of reversible and irreversible events and perception of their affordances. Bower's experiment (1967a) comparing a perspectival with an implosive disappearance is one. Another method has been developed to study the perception of reversibility and irreversibility in more complex natural events. Gibson and Kaushall (1973) filmed events that were reversible and irreversible and presented them in pairs, one projected correctly and one with the film reversed. Adults perceive the irreversible event (e.g., spilling ink on a blotter) as absurd when the film is run backward. The method was adapted for children by Megaw-Nyce (1979). Films were prepared of events that were thought to be natural for young children (e.g., bouncing a ball, breaking an egg, spilling milk) and were shown to 4 year olds, first correctly projected and then reversed. Half the filmed events were deemed (by adults) reversible-event sequences and half irreversible. When the reversed films were shown, the children were asked whether the event was one they had been shown before (the same as one they had seen) and then whether the event was possible or was magic. The children were aware of the distinction between reversible and irreversible events; they noticed no change in the reversible ones but made it clear that a change in the order of the irreversible ones altered the meaning as a real and possible occurrence. It seems likely that information about persistent properties of things is picked up in continuous cycles of reversible events long before 4 years (e.g., information for constancy of size and shape).

Experimental paradigms for the study of perception of persisting properties of objects, places, and events over reversible transformations are variously referred to as investigations of constancy, object permanence, identity, or conservation. Two of these, object permanence and conservation, imply more than perceiving a persistent property because the terms are generally used to imply conceptual knowledge. They are discussed in other chapters (see *Gelman & Baillargeon, vol. III, chap. 3; Mandler, vol. III, chap. 7; Harris, vol. II, chap. 9*). It is worth pointing out, however, that even conceptual knowledge about persistence is rooted in observations of reversible events.

Reciprocity

Social events are especially rich sources for studying event structure, especially in early social interchanges. The many studies of mother-infant interaction in recent years have emphasized again and again the reciprocity of interaction within these events, cycles of turn-taking (Brazelton, Koslowski, & Main, 1974). This interaction foreshadows the development of event perception more generally, for example, in game structures.

Peekaboo is perhaps the earliest game in which infants typically take part, and a reciprocal rule structure as well as articulated substructure (disappearance and reappearance) is found in almost anybody's version of the game (see Bruner & Sherwood, 1979). The reciprocal relations and the articulated points of subevents are perceived as early as 4 months (Greenfield, 1972). Infants do not usually control the game until later, but the structural relations are picked up. It is interesting to note that the actions in this game are both reciprocal and reversible and that discovery of this structure is enjoyable. The degree of embedding of substructures is kept to a minimum in this nursery game (as in others, like patacake), demonstrating the commonsense knowledge of parents and caretakers that simple, repetitive event structure is appreciated early and that deeper embedding (like story structures) is appreciated only later in development.

Nonreciprocal events may also provide information about social encounters—encounters in which different participants assume different roles. This information can even be portrayed without any pictorial information about the participants' features. Movies made by animation techniques that depict abstract figures, like circles and squares, moving about can lead to perceiving actions of one person or another, such as pushing, running, following, fighting (Bassili, 1976). Such movies can also depict people with distinct personalities, moods, and social roles (Heider & Simmel, 1944).

Causal Structure

Perception of causal relations in events has long been a topic for dispute among philosophers and psychologists, the disagreement taking place along typical lines: Is a causal relation inferred only as the result of interpretation based on past experience or is it perceived directly? The first view is historically attributed to the philosopher Hume, although a different version of this view has been suggested by Piaget. Piaget did not believe that causality was immediately perceptible but thought that it developed with age and was based on the development of action (see Piaget, 1969, pp. 234ff., for his interpretation of Michotte's [1946/1963] experiments; see E. J. Gibson, 1969, for a discussion of Piaget's views on causality and experiments performed by his collaborators).

The second view was developed by Michotte (1946/1963), who spent much of his life as a psychologist studying the perception of causality. Michotte was interested in causal events of a mechanical nature, like one billiard ball hitting another and sending it off on a path with a velocity that is specified by conditions attending the collision. Michotte studied several such events (e.g., launching, triggering, and entraining), simulating them with ingenious displays on rotating cardboard discs that were not, however, very lifelike (see Runeson, 1977). Adult viewers described the event relations in these displays as causal and so, on the whole, did young children (Olum, 1956, 1958), although children segregated parts less within the event. Perceived causality, Michotte (1946/1963) pointed out, was amodal, in that no specific sensory experience attended it. Piaget took a third view of the perception of causality.

Research with very young children on perception of causal relations of a mechanical type is rare. Keil (1979) studied the development of anticipation of the outcomes of causal events in children 1½ and 2½ years old. The events involved removal of crucial supports from a block structure. Anticipation was measured by degree of surprise when a causal relation was violated. When an object lost its support but remained suspended in midair, children of both ages showed surprise. The event itself was meaningful for the younger group if viewed as a whole, but not if presented as two static before and after displays when some kind of inference was presumably necessary.

Younger infants (9 to 12 weeks) were tested by Ball (1973) in an investigation of perception of a simulated causal relation somewhat like Michotte's (1946/1963) demonstrations. A red Styrofoam object disappeared behind a screen and then a white object emerged from the other side, with a delay and velocity appropriate for a concealed collision to have taken place. Infants were habituated to this condition. Then half the subjects witnessed 10 trials in which a red object collided with a white one, whereas the other half witnessed motion of the two objects (red toward white followed by motion of white) without any contact (no continuity of motion). There was no concealment in these cases. Infants in the noncollision, no-contact condition tracked the display longer during the test trials. Ball interpreted his results as supporting those of Michotte, in that perceived continuity of motion (despite occlusion) was presumed to be an essential condition for perception of a mechanical causal relation. An experiment by Borton (1979) investigated whether 3-month-old infants could distinguish between a causal and a noncausal event. There were three events: (1) a single object moving across a horizontal track; (2) one object moving toward a second stationary one, colliding, and launching it; and (3) the first object approaching the second but stopping short of collision as the second moved off. Disrupted tracking was more apparent in the noncontact than the contact condition. There were no differences between the contact and the single object conditions. Spatiotemporal continuity of movement seems again to be a distinguishing feature for the infants. But it is not clear in either of these studies whether the mover object was perceived as a separate object from the one moved. To perceive that one object causes a change in another, the two objects must be distinguished from one another.

Mechanical events are only one type of causal relation. Self-controlled events, often characterized as intentional, are another type, and, indeed, have often been considered as providing the most primitive experience of causality from which other types (use of tools, perceiving others as agents, mechanical causality) are eventually differentiated. Such, in essence, is Piaget's (1953) view. An infant begins with primitive causality, a feeling of efficacy linked with his own activity. There is a progression from egocentric causality to spatialization of causality, which means perceiving external objects in causal relations of the kinds we have just described.

Self-controlled events are of great interest to infants, whether or not they are perceived as intentional, and these events may enter into development of the perception of causal relations in ways different from that envisaged by Piaget. Piaget's secondary circular reactions (see *Harris, vol. II, chap. 9*) testify to infants' interest in self-produced events and their affordances. Even more dramatic testimony is provided by experiments performed over the last decade on infants' perception of contingency and the apparent reinforcing effect of self-initiated contingencies. Examples are so plentiful in the infant literature that it is hard to choose one. Papoušek may have been the first to show that infants would suck contingently, long after hunger was appeased, apparently for the pure motive of controlling a predictable event contingent upon their own behavior (see Papoušek, 1979, for a recent discussion; also see *Exploring and Attending*).

Other examples show how perceived contingency enters into discoveries about control of one's own actions and their consequences. Watson (1966, 1972) observed head and limb movements of infants in response to a stimulus display that changed contingently with their actions. Infants of 2 to 3 months discovered the contingency and increased their own movements to produce a change in what they saw. Moreover, increasing awareness of a clear contingency produced vigorous smiling and cooing, leading Watson (1972) to refer to such a sequence as "the game." The critical condition here seems to be the interplay of perceived control and a changing event sequence. The contingent change, whatever it may be, is related to the infant's activity, as is the change when an adult guides the path of a car by turning a steering wheel. The wheel, when turned, brings into view a changing path with new affordances. Infants, like adults, are motivated to explore events that they can control—to monitor the outcome of their own actions and look for their utility. The continuous interplay of acting and perceiving can bring to light the affordances of events.

A third (but basically similar) kind of causal relation is the use of tools to effect some desired consequence. Selection and use of a tool depends on perceiving the affordance of the tool (J. J. Gibson, 1979). The affordance is perceived, in the first place at least, within an event structure. Classic examples of perceiving the affordance of tools are found in Köhler's *The Mentality of Apes* (1925). Apes, like people, may discover that sticks can be used as levers, as jumping poles, and as extensions to one's arm to obtain a desired out-of-reach object.

Premack has also emphasized the ape's knowledge of causality (Premack, 1976; Premack & Woodruff, 1978) with tasks showing that a causal relation is perceived between a tool and some antecedent and end state (a knife and a cut apple for example). Chimpanzees presented with a whole apple and then with a cut apple were able to choose the correct tool (a knife) from a collection containing a pen, a nail, an eraser, etc. There was evidence that a transformation was perceived and that the tool for effecting it was recognized—a cause-effect relation. Similar experiments with positive results have been performed with 3- and 4-year-old children (Gelman, Bullock, & Meck, 1980).

Human youngsters may begin to perceive the affordance of tools as soon as they manipulate a mobile toy and perceive a contingency between their own actions and the ensuing event, but exploration and experiment with toys and utensils leads to more explicit knowledge (see *Affordances: Perceiving for Some Purpose*). Children will use a rake to reach a desired toy around 14 to 16 months. They will rotate a moveable surface to obtain an object resting on it between the ages of 16 and 18 months, the ages being quite similar across several cultures (see Dasen et al., 1978).

Speech as an Event: An Example

Spoken language occurs in a stream over time and presents us with all the essential features of an event. The change is mainly over time rather than spatiotemporal, but the changes are relational and invariant properties are retained. Speech events occur in units, and they are structured and bounded. The units are segmented so that small ones are embedded in larger ones in relations of greater or less depth. Speech events have affordances for behavior, the most general one being communication, but they may be of many degrees of specificity. Finally, linguistic events, including speech, are not merely passively perceived, but they are created by the observer in an active fashion. Active perception may not be so obvious in listening to speech, although some prominent theories of speech perception are active ones (Walthen-Dunn, 1967), but activity is obvious in reading written language, where the perceiver moves his eyes over the page to create the sequencing of the event. We cannot go into development of the perception of language, but we will illustrate how speech fulfills our definition of an event and is perceived as one.

Speech is the first form of language perceived by the infant, and it appears to be an event with meaningful affordances from the beginning, although these change toward greater specificity rapidly. Speech is attended to strongly and preferentially, it would seem, from birth. Alegria and Noirot (1978), in an experiment similar to some described earlier (see *Exploring and Attending*), investigated neonates' responses to speech sounds, monitoring head movements, opening of the eyes, mouthing, and crying. As in other studies, they found significantly more head turning in the direction of speech sounds than in the absence of them. They also noted that the eyes opened when the head turn was elicited by speech. The voice also enhanced mouthing and crying, as if the infant expected to be able to suck. Onset of crying took place most frequently when the infants were facing the source of sound and when preceding head movement had led to an approach. When natural nonspeech sounds are presented (e.g., a faucet turning on or a door slamming), infants also turn their heads, but they are less apt to open their eyes or suck (Alegria & Noirot, 1982).

Newborn infants will suck for contingent auditory stimulation, provided by tapes of folk songs (Butterfield & Siperstein, 1972), whereas contingent white noise is ineffective. And in a recent study that allowed neonates to suck in either of two different ways to produce the voice of the mother or a stranger, it was reported that infants modify their sucking specifically to hear the mother (DeCasper & Fifer, 1980). This study indicates that infants begin to recognize the mother's voice soon after birth and that human speech, especially the mother's speech, is an effective motivator for them.

What aspects of human speech might be differentiated by the human infant at such an early age? The more global structural features of auditory events would seem to be likely candidates, such as rhythm (Condon & Sander, 1974), frequency variation (Butterfield & Siperstein, 1972; Eisenberg, 1970), and intonation. Intonation is particularly interesting because intonation and stress carry so much information for sophisticated linguistic structure, both semantic and syntactic. E. L. Kaplan presented 4- and 8-month-old infants with repetitions of a three-word sentence in either rising or falling intonation (E. L. Kaplan, 1969; see also Kaplan & Kaplan, 1971). An habituation procedure was used, with cardiac and behavioral measures. At 4 months, the intonations were not differentiated by this method, but at 8 months they were.[2] An experiment by Morse (1972), however, found positive evidence for discrimination of a rising from a falling intonation in infants from 40 to 54 days of age, using a nonnutritive conjugate sucking procedure. The speech sample presented was a single syllable.

An experiment by Mehler, Bertoncini, Barriere, and Jassik-Gerschenfeld (1978) found evidence of differentiation of intonation in connected speech at 1 month. The infants were reinforced, contingent upon nonnutritive sucking, with either their own mother's voice or that of a stranger. In each case, there was one condition in which the speech was aimed at communicating with the infant and one in which the speech lacked prosodic and intonational qualities of natural speech (the speaker read from a text, backward). Infants sucked more for the mother's voice than the stranger's, but only when the speech contained natural intonation. The stranger's voice also elicited more sucking when naturally intoned.

Intonation over a continuous speech event thus appears to be perceived early, demonstrating pickup of structural relations over a temporal stream. One can ask, then, about the other side of the coin: To what extent is the speech event segmented? There is now ample evidence that very young infants discriminate many phonemic contrasts categorically, in the so-called speech mode (Jusczyk, 1979). But that is not the same thing as segmenting a continuous speech event into meaningful subunits. Such differentiation occurs progressively and extends well into the language-learning process. But articulatory substructure may perhaps be differentiated to some extent before meaningful constituent units are abstracted from the total event. A recent experiment suggests that infants 2 months old segment a stream of speech into syllables (Bertoncini & Mehler, 1981). But not until much later are words segmented from the continuous acoustic stream as the semantic information in speech is abstracted. Segmenting sentences into words actually occurs rather late, as does the ability to segment words into phonemic constituents (see Gibson & Levin, 1975, pp. 119 ff.).

Finally, we can illustrate the pickup of invariant relations in ongoing speech events. Phonemes must carry invariant information over multiple tokens for speech to convey the same information over different speakers or even the same voice in different contexts. Perception of invariant relations in phonemic contrasts over varying contexts is sometimes referred to as perceptual constancy and demonstrations of it have been provided by Kuhl (1980). Infants were trained to make a head turn when a background vowel was changed in a speech sample. When infants had learned to respond to the contrast, variations were introduced into the tokens

for each category by introducing changes in pitch contour and by presenting tokens produced by different speakers. The subjects continued to respond to the contrast as invariant over these changes, a situation somewhat analogous to responding to melodies as invariant over transpositions. Syntactic and semantic aspects of surface structure of a spoken message can also be transformed radically while maintaining invariant information for a sophisticated listener. These are essential invariants of a speech event, but they are beyond our assignment here.

Reading written language requires as much attention to an event as does listening to speech, and the same syntactic and semantic information (except for the prosodic features of speech) is there to be extracted. Other structured information is also present—graphic and orthographic structure. As in listening, the beginning reader must differentiate contrastive relations in abstract invariants over changing contents. For example, distinctive features permit identification of alphabetic characters and invariant relations permit their recognition over varying typefaces and handwriting. Orthography provides constraints and rules that structure higher order units in sequences of letters that are distributed spatially but that must be processed as an event as well. These constraints are abstracted during the early stages of learning to read, yielding more economical units of processing (see Barron, 1980).

One more form of language, sign language for the deaf, exemplifies a linguistic event, a spatiotemporal event in this case. It has syntactic and semantic invariants as do other modes of linguistic communication, but it has invariant relations in its own mode as well. Information is conveyed by hand shaping and especially by movement. Motion trajectories vary in many ways, but they are structured and abstract. Variations in speaker style, hand preference, and size of the signing space moved through can all change while the essential relations remain invariant.

The structured use of space and movement in space is particularly important in conveying morphological transformations in sign language (Klima & Bellugi, 1979, chap. 12). Elaborate variations of motion trajectory occur when a base morpheme, such as "give," is embedded in an array of morphological transformations, such as "give me," "I give you," "I am giving you." The abstract, invariant character of these transformations is apparent in that signers, given the base morpheme, can differentiate the transformations when they are performed in the dark with only light spots on the shoulder, elbow, and wrist joints of the speaker to carry the information about the motion (Poizner, Bellugi, & Lutes-Driscoll, 1981).

Little is known as yet about how the human infant exposed to signing as his first language develops the ability to differentiate the invariant information in these complex transformations, but such observations as exist suggest that it occurs naturally by pickup of structural relations in the signed gestures, much as a hearing infant exposed to speech abstracts invariants and differentiates distinctive relations in the speech stream, and that progress occurs at about the same rate, with the same timetable (Holmes & Holmes, 1980; Newport, 1980).

OBTAINING INFORMATION ABOUT OBJECTS

Perceiving the Unity and Boundaries of an Object

The world is furnished with objects: unitary, bounded, persisting things—each of a particular substance, shape, texture, and coloring and perhaps a characteristic odor, taste, and sound. At any given time, each object in an array is only partly in view, that is, its back is hidden and even parts of its forward surfaces may be occluded. It may be next to or resting upon other objects, and all these objects rest on a substratum. Adults perceive each object as unitary, bounded, and complete. When and how does a child perceive where one object ends and another object or surface begins?

Three Views

One general account of the adult's perception of unitary objects centers on the concepts of sensation and association. As an object is encountered in different settings, the various sensations evoked by its visible parts will occur at the same time and become associated. An adult perceives the separateness of an object from its background or from an adjacent object because the sensations evoked by one object are highly associated to each other but less associated with sensations evoked by its surroundings. According to this view, young infants should not perceive the unity of an object and should come to do so only as the object is repeatedly encountered in different places.

A second view, offered by the gestalt psychologists, proposes that animals perceive the boundaries of objects in an array in accordance with certain principles of organization (Koffka, 1935; Wertheimer, 1923/1958). Perceivers group together parts of an array that are close together, that are similar, and that move together in accordance with the principles of proximity, similarity, and common fate. They also group together regions that lie within the same closed area, regions whose contours are aligned, or regions that form simple figures in accordance with the principles of closure, good continuation, and good form. These principles allow a perceiver to see an object as separate from the background, as separate from an adjacent object, and as continuing behind an occluder (Koffka, 1935; Michotte et al., 1964). The principles are believed to reflect the structure of the brain and so are thought to be independent of learning.

We shall argue for a third view (Spelke, 1982). A child perceives an object whenever she detects a topologically connected arrangement of surfaces that retains its connectedness as it moves. The arrangement and the movements of surfaces in a scene are richly specified. For example, the separateness of an object from the background is specified, as the object or the observer moves, by the accretion and deletion of background texture at the edges of the object. The unity of a moving object is further specified by the relationship between the movements of its parts. If the object moves rigidly, its projection at the eye undergoes a continuous series of perspective transformations, with all the invariant properties of projective geometry (Gibson & Gibson, 1957). If the object is jointed, such as a person, motions of its parts share a common directional component (Johansson, 1978). Perception of objects depends on the detection of such invariants. Infants and children should perceive the unity of an object as soon as they can perceive the appropriate arrangement and movements of its surfaces.

Objects as Separate from the Background

Studies of reaching provide the best evidence that infants perceive a single object, suspended in front of a uniform background, as a separate whole. Infants begin systematically to reach for objects at about 4½ months (see *Exploring and Attending*). At that time, their reaching is adapted, to some degree, to an object's visually given distance, direction, movement, and size. The size of an object, in particular, could not be registered if the object were not perceived as a separate thing.

Infants of 6 months indicate that they perceive the unity of a visible object in an additional way. They appear to expect that a suspended object can move independently of its background and that the object must move as a whole. Spelke and Born (1982) presented infants with a three-dimensional object in front of a flat surface that began to move toward them in two ways. In one condition, the object alone moved, as a whole; in the other condition, part of the object moved in tandem with part of the background. Infants were judged by a naive observer to be surprised or puzzled when they witnessed the breakup of the object, but not when they witnessed the unitary movement of that object. An infant's surprise may reflect her expectation that an object will move as a whole. Such an expectation implies that she perceives the object as unitary and separate from its surroundings.

It is difficult to investigate the perception of unitary, bounded objects by infants who are not yet able to reach. The studies that have attempted this, however, suggest that the capacity to perceive suspended objects develops very early. It has been shown, for example, that 3-month-old infants will swipe at objects even though they do not reach for them. And like later reaching, their swiping is affected by an object's size, direction, and distance. Furthermore, 3-month-olds, like 6-month-olds, show signs of surprise at movements of an array that break up the boundaries of an object (Spelke & Born, 1982).

Young infants evidently perceive the boundaries of a visible object by detecting the spatial separation between the object and its background, for they do not appear to perceive objects when no such separation is present. Infants show no surprise when a pictured object breaks apart (Spelke & Born, 1982). Infants may perceive the spatial separation of object and background by detecting discontinuities in the velocities of texture elements from the object and background, contingent on head and eye movements. Alternatively, they may detect the accretion and deletion of background texture at the occluding edges of the object, a pattern that is also produced by head movements. In either case, motion would seem to bring information about the boundaries of an object.

Adjacent Objects

Two adjacent surfaces sometimes belong to the same object and sometimes do not. As adults, we perceive adjacent surfaces as connected or separate in accordance with the gestalt principles of organization. Studies of infants suggest that the ability to perceive these connections and separations does not emerge as early as the capacities discussed above.

Piaget (1954) observed the development of one infant's reaching for objects under a variety of conditions. He reported that this infant would not reach for an object on a small support—a box, a book, or the palm of a hand—until 8 to 10 months. The same infant did reach successfully for a dangling object or an object on an extended support. Although recent research suggests that younger infants do attempt to touch supported objects, they reach more directly for an object perched on someone's fingertips than for an object lying on another object (Bresson, Maury, Pieraut-le-Bonniec, & de Schonen, 1977; Bresson & de Shonen, 1976–1977). The young infant's difficulties may stem from problems in motor control. But a more interesting possibility, originally suggested by Piaget (1954), is that the child fails to perceive that a supported object is a unit separate from its support. It is noteworthy that Piaget's infant did reach for a supported object if it moved relative to its support. This motion may have specified the object's unity and boundaries for the infant.

A recent experiment provides evidence that young infants perceive two adjacent objects as one unit. Prather and Spelke (1982) presented one group of 3-month-old infants with a succession of displays each containing one rectangular solid object. A variety of objects, differing in color, shape, and size, were presented in a variety of locations. A second group of infants was presented with a succession of displays each containing two objects of different dimensions but the same color, presented so that they were spatially separated in the frontal plane. The colors, shapes, sizes, and locations of the objects again varied from one display to the next. It had previously been shown that infants can be habituated to the number of objects in an array (Starkey, Spelke, & Gelman, 1980; Strauss & Curtis, 1981). It was hoped, therefore, that infants in this experiment would habituate either to one-object or to two-object displays.

After habituation, infants in both groups were presented with two objects that had not been shown previously; they were of the same color but different shapes. These objects were presented in a one-object and a two-object display to determine if infants would dishabituate to a change in number. In addition, the objects were presented in two new configurations. In one display, they were adjacent, side by side. In the other display, they were separated in depth—one object stood directly in front of the other and partly occluded it so that their projections at the eye overlapped. Many infants did not show the predicted dishabituation to a change in number. Among those who did respond to number, most of the infants who had been habituated to one-object arrays showed greater dishabituation to the objects separated in depth, and most of the infants habituated to two-object arrays showed greater dishabituation to the adjacent objects. It appeared that the infants perceived two adjacent objects as one unit and perceived two objects separated in depth as two units. This experiment suggests that the ability to see two adjacent objects as separate develops after 3 months. Young infants may not perceive object boundaries in accordance with the principles of good form and good continuation.

Partly Occluded Objects

When—and how—do infants perceive the complete shapes of partly hidden objects? Research by Michotte et al. (1964) suggested that adults perceive partly hidden objects in accordance with the principles of good continuation and good form. An experiment by Bower (1967b) suggested that some of these principles are effective for infants as well. Infants 6 weeks old were conditioned to suck in the presence of a wire triangle with a long, vertical cylinder suspended in front of it and partly occluding it. Sucking generalized to a complete triangle more than to a variety of other displays. Infants appeared to perceive the unity of the triangle. This ability was not evident, however, in a further experiment by Bower (1967b) in which infants viewed a two-dimensional representation of the occluded triangle.

Infants' perception of occluded objects was investigated further in a series of experiments (Kellman & Spelke, 1979, 1981). In one experiment, 4-month-old infants were habituated to a straight rod whose center was occluded by a block, and then they were tested with alternating presentations of a complete, nonoccluded rod and a rod with a gap where the occluder had been. The infants looked equally to the two test displays. Their equal looking did not reflect a failure to discriminate the test rods; infants in two control experiments, presented with the same test displays after habituation to a nonoccluded complete or broken rod, looked longer to the test rod they had not seen. Moreover, infants habituated to a partly occluded rod looked longer to a new rod display with a gap larger than the area where the occluder had been. It appears that infants in the original experiment perceived the two visible ends of the original, partly occluded rod neither as definitely connected nor as definitely separate. In a further experiment, infants were presented with a partly occluded triangle very similar to that used by Bower (1967b). Habituation to this display also generalized equally to complete and broken triangle displays. Thus, the gestalt principles of good continuation, good form, and similarity did not jointly lead infants to perceive a unitary object.

In the next experiment, infants viewed the partly occluded rod and block display, but now the rod moved. In one condition, the visible parts of the rod moved in tandem to the left and to the right. In other conditions, the rod and block moved together as a unit or the block moved while the rod remained stationary. The center of the rod never came into view during these movements. After habituation, infants who had viewed the rod moving against a stationary block looked more to the broken test rod. The other infants looked equally to the two test displays. It was concluded that infants do perceive the unity of similar, aligned ends of a partly hidden object if the ends move together independently of the other surfaces in the scene. Subsequent studies revealed that any translatory movement through a scene—movement in depth as well as lateral movement—provided information to infants that the ends of the rod were connected behind the occluder (Kellman & Spelke, 1981).

A final experiment investigated whether infants would perceive the unity of two parts of an object that moved together if the parts were not similar in color, texture, or shape and were not aligned. Two different nonaligned objects protruded from behind the same occluding block and moved together. After habituation, infants viewed these objects without the block, connected or separated. A separate experiment indicated that the two test displays were equally attractive to infants. But infants who had habituated to the objects moving together looked longer to the display of separated objects. Infants, thus, seem to perceive a unitary, partly occluded object when its visible parts move as a whole, even when the principles of similarity and good continuation work against that impression for an adult.

In sum, the unity and bounds of an object might be specified for a young infant only by its spatial separation from other things and its movement relative to those things (Spelke, 1982). Infants may not perceive the separateness of two stationary, adjacent objects because the boundary between them is specified only by their dissimilarity and nonalignment. Infants may fail to track an object moving in tandem with its background (Harris et al., 1974) because an object and background are perceived as a single unit when they move together. Finally, Piaget's (1954) infant might not have been able to reach for a supported object unless it moved relative to its support because the independent motion of object and support specified that they were separate. Neither association theory nor gestalt theory can easily account for these findings. The boundaries of objects are first given in events.

Perceiving the Properties of an Object

Objects have many affordances for a perceiver. The potential affordances of an object depend on such properties as its substance, texture, and shape. Many of the properties of an object are specified to more than one perceptual system. We focus here on some of the more important amodal properties of objects.

Substance

Objects can be rigid or flexible. If rigid, they can be brittle or strong, solid or hollow, and made of such substances as stone, wood, bone, or metal. If flexible, they can be fuzzy or elastic, stretchable or deformable, and made of such materials as rubber or fur. Objects can also vary in density and, thus, in weight. When do children begin to perceive these properties and their affordances?

Infants have been found to differentiate between rigid and flexible objects visually, aurally, and haptically in a coordinated fashion. A series of studies has investigated visual perception of rigid and flexible objects. In the first (Gibson, Owsley, & Johnston, 1978), infants of 5 months were presented with a sponge-rubber object undergoing three different rigid motions. These presentations continued until visual attention had habituated, then new events were presented for several test trials. On some trials, the object was seen to undergo a fourth rigid motion. On others, it was seen to undergo a deforming motion. The subjects dishabituated to the deforming motion, whereas presentation of a fourth rigid motion yielded results similar to a no-change control condition. In subsequent studies, infants of 3½ months were shown to respond to invariant information for rigidity over a class of rigid motions even as the objects undergoing these motions changed in shape (Gibson, Walker, Owsley, & Megaw-Nyce, 1979). They were also shown to habituate to a class of deforming motions and to dishabituate to a new rigid motion (Walker, Owsley, Megaw-Nyce, Gibson, & Bahrick, 1980). These studies indicate an early sensitivity to optic information for the rigidity or flexibility of an object.

The substance of an object can be specified haptically and aurally as well as visually. Infants are sensitive to some of these sources of information as well, and they detect correspondences between visual and aural information for the substance of an object. Bahrick (1980) investigated auditory-visual perception of substance in 4½-month-old infants. Infants were presented with films of two events. In one, two wooden blocks repeatedly struck each other, producing a clacking sound. In the other, two wet sponges struck each other, producing a squishing sound. Infants viewed the films side by side, accompanied by one synchronized sound track played through a central speaker. In one condition, each sound was synchronized with the movements of the appropriate object. In a second condition, each sound was synchronized with the inappropriate object, that is, squishes accompanied the impacts of blocks and clacks accompanied the impacts of sponges. Infants looked preferentially to the aurally synchronized object only if the motion of that object provided information for the same substance as was specified by the sound. This study and others (see Bahrick, 1980) suggest that infants detect information for rigidity and flexibility both by looking and by listening.

Haptically, infants of 12 months differentiate objects of rigid and elastic substance by handling them differently. Rigid, hard objects are banged on available surfaces (a tabletop or another object). Elastic, spongy objects are squeezed, pressed, and wiped on surfaces rather than banged. Following handling an object of a hard or an elastic substance, infants looked preferentially at a film of an object of the familiarized substance moving in an appropriate pattern (Gibson & Walker, 1982). As noted earlier (see *Exploring and Attending*), even 1-month-old infants appeared to differentiate rigid from flexible substances during oral exploration: they detected a correspondence between a rigid or flexible object in the mouth and an object moved rigidly or flexibly in a visual presentation (Gibson & Walker, 1982).

These studies suggest that infants can perceive one aspect of the substance of an object and that they do so as the object participates in events. It is not known whether infants can perceive other aspects of the substance of an object. Although they differentiate rigid from nonrigid objects, they may not be sensitive to differences among classes of rigid or nonrigid objects, differentiating wood from glass or metal or rock, differentiating a person's skin from cloth or rubber, and so on. But they do appear to perceive one other aspect of an object's substance very early, its weight.

When an infant in the second half-year picks up an object, he adjusts the tension in his arm to the object's perceived weight (Halverson, 1931). Furthermore, such an infant can use vision to provide information about an object's weight. An infant of 9 months or more who is handed the same object repeatedly will come to anticipate the muscle tension needed to hold it (Mounoud & Bower, 1974). If a larger object is then presented, an infant of 15 months will increase the arm tension, as if expecting the larger object to weigh more. Such an infant can be fooled by changes in the visual appearance of an object. If a spherical ball of clay, repeatedly held by the infant, is flattened into a pancake, the infant seems to anticipate that it will weigh more; he increases the tension in his arm as it is handed to him and his arm flies abruptly into the air. By 18 months, the infant no longer makes this error: he comes to appreciate that the weight of an object is invariant over changes in its shape (Mounoud & Bower, 1974). Five or six years pass before the child comes to use this information when he makes explicit judgments about the weights of objects (Piaget & Inhelder, 1941). Perhaps the perceptual invariance that is detected at 18 months only later becomes accessible to thought.

Texture

The surfaces of objects can be rough or smooth, hard or soft, finely or coarsely grained. These distinctions can be perceived visually and haptically by adults. Some properties of texture are also detectable by infants. As noted in our earlier discussions, 6-month-old infants discriminate haptically between objects of different textures (Steele & Pederson, 1977). Infants of this age can also perceive the constant texture of an object over changes in its color (Ruff, 1980). After habituation to a series of differently colored objects, all with the same texture (depressions or protrusions in its surface), infants dishabituated to a new object of a different texture but not to one of the same texture. Finally, it is possible that very young infants perceive texture intermodally by mouthing and looking (see *Exploring and Attending*).

Infants evidently can perceive aspects of an object's texture both by vision and by touch, and they can coordinate visual and haptic information about a texture. It is not clear, however, how sensitive infants are to texture differences. Adults are very sensitive to small changes in the roughness of tex-

ture, both visually and haptically (Bjorkman, 1967). The development of this sensitivity has not, to our knowledge, been studied.

Shape

Very young infants discriminate visually between flat and solid objects (Cook, Field, & Griffiths, 1978; Fantz, 1961; J. Field, 1977) and between many pairs of objects that differ only in shape (see Ruff, 1980, for a review). But perceiving the characteristic shape of an object requires more than these accomplishments reveal. One must perceive the shape as constant over changes in its orientation, and over the resulting projective transformations at the eye. This, in turn, would seem to require that the infant perceive the orientation of an object in a three-dimensional layout, detecting stimulus relationships that remain constant as the orientation of an object changes. Research now indicates that young infants can perceive the constant shape of an object.

The first evidence for shape constancy in early infancy was provided by Bower (1966). Infants of 2 months were conditioned to turn their heads in the presence of a rectangular surface presented at 45°; generalization was tested with several rectangular and trapezoidal surfaces at several orientations. Infants responded more to the real shape, even when it was presented in a new orientation. Positive evidence for shape constancy in the first 4 months has also been reported by Day and McKenzie (1973) and by Caron, Caron, and Carlson (1979).

Studies of infants do not indicate how precise the perception of shape is. Experiments with children, using judgment methods, have investigated developmental changes in the precision of shape constancy. Such research suffers from certain methodological problems (for discussions, see E. J. Gibson, 1969; Piaget, 1969; and Wohlwill, 1963)—when age differences are found, it is rarely clear whether they are caused by developmental changes in the constancy mechanisms themselves or in other judgmental processes. Nevertheless, there appear to be few age changes in the precision of shape constancy. For example, Meneghini and Leibowitz (1967) and Kaess, Haynes, Craig, Pearson, and Greenwell (1974) presented children and adults with textured, flat objects of different dimensions at different orientations. Children were told to pick the frontal comparison object that matched the shape of the standard. There was no improvement with age on shape judgments when the standard and comparison objects were presented at the same distance. In the Kaess et al. (1974) study, shape constancy was equally high from age 4 to age 19, whereas in Meneghini and Leibowitz's study (1967), shape constancy was most accurate at the youngest age. Govorova (cited in Venger, 1977) reported similar findings using a different procedure. Shape-constancy judgments did improve with age when the standard object was presented at five times the distance of the comparison object. This age difference may reflect a tendency for younger children to be less attentive to objects at farther distances or less able to compare two objects presented at different distances.

As children grow, they come to differentiate shapes of ever greater complexity. Developmental changes in haptic shape perception are especially marked. By 10 months of age, infants have been found to discriminate and recognize certain simple shapes that they have explored manually. Soroka, Corter, and Abramovitch (1979) presented infants with one solid object in the dark for 2 min. Then, the infants were given the same or a differently shaped object. Infants manipulated the novel object for a longer time; they evidently could recognize the familiar one. In addition, infants of 8 to 12 months have been found to recognize visually an object they have felt (Bryant, Jones, Claxton, & Perkins, 1972; Gottfried, Rose, & Bridger, 1977), but this ability has not always been found with 6-month-old infants or with 1-year-old infants of low socioeconomic status (Rose, Gottfried, & Bridger, 1978). Although these failures may reflect only the insensitivity of current tests of tactile recognition, it seems likely that the ability to perceive shape manually develops slowly over the course of infancy along with the development of haptic exploration (see *Exploring and Attending*).

Young infants may have difficulty perceiving the shapes of objects if the shapes are complex and if other properties vary. Ruff (1978) presented 6- and 9-month-old infants with two objects, each of which was a unique combination of cubes, blocks, spheres, and cylinders. One shape was presented at a variety of orientations, positions, and colors; in some conditions, an object was seen to move, whereas in others it was not. After a series of familiarization trials, discrimination was tested with familiar/novel shaped objects. Infants of 6 months did not appear to recognize the familiar shapes as the same when presented with an object of a new color, size, and orientation. Infants of 9 months did recognize the familiar shape under some conditions but not under others.

Visual shape perception continues to develop throughout childhood (see *Exploring and Attending*). Preschool children do not explore the contours of objects as consistently as older children, and they perform less well on visual- and haptic-matching tasks (Zaporozhets, 1969; Zinchenko et al., 1977). Young children also have difficulty with certain tasks involving simple shapes.

Zaporozhets (1969) presented children of 6 months to 3 years with a form-fitting problem. A child was shown a board with two apertures of the same shape standing in front of two objects of different shapes. Both apertures were the same shape as one of the objects. The child could obtain that object by reaching through the aperture and pulling the object through the opening. The other object could not be obtained in this way. Children attempted to obtain these objects on a series of trials. Initially, they all approached this task by trial and error, reaching for both objects. Children of 2 years eventually learned to take account of the shape of the object, reaching only for an object of one particular shape, but they continued to reach for that object after the aperture shape was changed. These children never learned to take account of the relationship between the shape of the object and the aperture. Older children do take account of this relationship.

It seems that the younger children could not perceive the relationship between the shape of an object and the shape of the corresponding aperture. Possibly this task was difficult because the young child cannot abstract one aspect of an object's shape, its two-dimensional silhouette. The young child may be able to perceive the shapes of blocks but may have difficulty deciding whether an object's outline shape at its greatest extension corresponds to the outline shape of the aperture.

In summary, young infants have certain limited abilities to perceive shape. They can discriminate and recognize simple shapes but not complex, embedded ones. They have a capacity for visual-shape constancy, although it is not clear how accurate their shape constancy is. They are not adept at perceiving shape haptically, especially through active manipulation. Finally, their capacity to perceive shape may be functional for some purposes, such as discriminative responding, but not for other purposes, such as object-aperture matching of one contour. As children grow, they explore more effectively shapes of greater complexity and embedding, and they may perceive more subtle relationships among the shapes of solid objects.

Size

As noted in our earlier discussion, *Exploring and Attending,* infants of 3 months differentiate between an object of graspable size and an object too large to grasp (Bruner & Koslowski, 1972). Infants, thus, respond to some degree to the size of an object, perhaps in relation to the size of the hand. To perceive the sizes of objects flexibly and adaptively, however, one must perceive their sizes as invariant over changes in distance. Bower (1966) investigated this capacity for size constancy in early infancy. He conditioned 6- to 12-week-old infants to turn their heads in the presence of a 12-in. cube 3 ft. away. The cube was placed on a table in a room whose walls remained visible. Thus, a perceiver could, in principle, assess the object's size by taking account of its distance, or she could perceive its size relative to the width of the table. Generalization testing was given with cubes of several sizes and distances. Generalization was greatest to a cube with the same true size at a new distance, even though that object now subtended a much smaller angle at the eye. Bower concluded that infants innately perceive size as constant over changes in distance.

Although a number of subsequent experiments failed to provide evidence for size constancy (Day & McKenzie, 1977), such evidence has recently been obtained. Day and McKenzie (1981) presented 4-month-old infants with an object that moved continuously through a limited range of distances from four different starting points. After habituation, infants were presented with the same object as well as with an object twice or half its size that moved through the same range of distances. Habituation generalized to the moving object of the same true size, despite the change in the angle it subtended at the eye.

These studies indicate that some capacity for perceiving size over changes in distance appears very early in life, but they do not indicate how precise the infant's size constancy is. Studies of children have addressed this question.

The literature on the development of size constancy in children is long and complex (for reviews, see E. J. Gibson, 1969; Piaget, 1969; Wohlwill, 1960). Depending on the stimulus and task conditions, many different patterns of developmental change have been obtained. Four conclusions, nevertheless, appear to be established. First, at the youngest ages tested, judgments of real size are far more accurate than judgments of projected size, insofar as the latter can be tested (Brunswik, 1956;

Piaget, 1969). Second, evidence for size constancy is obtained at very young ages under conditions that do not require verbal judgments (see E. J. Gibson, 1969; Tanaka, 1967). Third, judgments of size over changing distance improve, at all ages, when objects are presented on a richly textured ground. The benefits of a textured ground suggest that children detect information for a continuous spatial layout and use this information in perceiving object size. Finally, there is, in some situations, a tendency toward increasing over-constancy with age. Over-constancy may reflect a bias in the child's judgments rather than her perceptions (Wohlwill, 1963). On the other hand, it may result from a change in the information used in a size-constancy task (Sedgwick, 1980).

Animacy

Animate objects differ in many ways from inanimate objects, and there is some reason to think that they are differentiated very early in life (see Gelman & Spelke, 1981, for a preliminary analysis of these differences and the child's appreciation of them). Brazelton et al. (1974) compared infants' responsive behavior to an inanimate object (a toy monkey suspended on a wire) and to a person. At 6 weeks, the infants stared fixedly at the toy and followed it with the gaze when it was moved to one side or the other. Fingers and toes appeared to point jerkedly at the object. Attention was intense and rapt. But when the person (the child's mother) was the object, attention occurred in cycles of alternating interest and withdrawal as if the infant expected a response from the object. Trevarthen (1977) reported similar differences between the infant's response to a person and a toy. In particular, he noted that expressive behavior and gesturing were much more frequent in the presence of the person.

A young infant not only seems to expect other people to respond to him, he may become upset if this expectation is not fulfilled. Such reactions have been reported many times (see Bloom, 1977; Brazelton et al., 1974; T. M. Field, 1979; Fogel, Diamond, Langhorst, & Demos, 1979; Trevarthen, 1977). For example, Tronick, Adamson, Wise, Als, & Brazelton (1975) observed infants of 6 to 16 weeks in interaction with the mother. On cue, the mother was instructed to become unresponsive. Infants of all ages were distressed by this manipulation. These findings suggest an early differentiation of animate from inanimate objects and an early appreciation that animate objects respond to one's acts.

Responsiveness is certainly one of the essential affordances of an animate object, and many authors have written of the importance of a responsive environment for· normal development. Infant monkeys deprived of social rearing with members of their own species may be at a disadvantage in later dealings with their environment, but any responsive environment, even the company of a dog, appears to be better than a nonresponsive one, however comfortable otherwise (Mason, 1978). Responsiveness is a characteristic of objects that is revealed only in events, especially those contingent on the infant's own actions.

Animate objects are not only responsive, they move differently from most inanimate objects. Inanimate objects for the most part move rigidly; animate objects do not. Some animate objects, like worms, move only in cycles of deformation; some, like vertebrates, have a rigid skeleton and can move the limbs rigidly like levers, but they are jointed and so the total skeletal movement is deforming, as is the movement of the musculature (particularly noticeable in faces). These differences may be detectable to infants. Several recent studies suggest that infants early in the first year discriminate changes in structure in dynamic light patterns representing biological motion that are not discriminated in successive static displays. Bower (1982) reported that infants discriminated gender in moving point-light displays; Bertenthal and Proffitt (1982) and Fox and McDaniel (1982) reported that infants discriminated moving-light displays of walkers from other displays of nonbiological motion.

Perhaps above all, the source of motion of an animate and an inanimate object is different. Animate objects can move from within, in the absence of any external force. Inanimate objects move only when some force is applied. Thus, animate objects provide a different type of information for perception of causal events than inanimate objects, and this difference could serve as a further basis for distinguishing these kinds of objects. We have already noted that infants may be sensitive to some information for a causal relationship (see *Obtaining Information About Events*). Moreover, preschool children have been observed to refer to the causes of an object's movement when they are asked whether a toy with certain animate features (a doll or a puppet) is capable of walking, talking, thinking, and so on. Most children judge that dolls cannot walk, for example, "unless someone moves it" (Gelman, Spelke, & Meck, 1982).

Overview

There are modality-specific properties of objects, such as color, temperature, and scent as well as the properties described above. Infants and young children are known to be sensitive to some of these (see *vol. II, chaps. 1 and 2*): But the above examples should serve to illustrate a few general principles. First, very young infants have rudimentary abilities to perceive the properties of objects. They are sensitive to stimulus information that specifies the substances, textures, shapes, sizes, and perhaps the animacy of objects. Second, perception of objects becomes increasingly differentiated as children develop strategies of exploration and manipulation. Third, objects are first perceived, and best perceived, when they participate in events. And, in events, their most important affordances are revealed.

Reactions to Conflicting Visual and Haptic Information

We have reviewed evidence suggesting that young infants perceive the unity of an object they see and hear or see and feel. They can coordinate auditory and visual information about the location, movement, and substance of an object as well as visual and haptic information about its shape. We have also reviewed evidence suggesting that the earliest actions, such as reaching, are guided by an object's visually given distance, direction, motion, size, and shape. These early coordinations suggest that perception of the unity of a multiple specified object depends not on associative learning or on the integration of action schemes but on the perception of object properties and affordances.

Yet one source of evidence seems to contradict this conclusion. A number of experiments have been conducted in which visual and haptic or visual and auditory information have been made to conflict. The reactions of infants to these conflicts have been observed. If different modalities are coordinated with each other and if perception is truly coordinated with action, then infants might be surprised or distressed when intermodal and perceptual-motor relationships are altered. In most cases, young infants do not respond noticeably to such rearrangements.

In a series of ingenious studies, Bower (Bower, 1974; Bower et al., 1970a, 1970b) presented infants with the visible image of an intangible object. Using a stereoscopic shadow caster he was able to create what for adults is the visual impression of an object suspended within reach. When the infant extended her arm, however, she encountered empty space. Bower et al. (1970b) reported that 1-week-old infants became distressed when their reach did not lead to contact with an object. Older infants (5 and 6 months) explored the source of the discrepancy, for example, they systematically tested their hands for numbness (Bower et al., 1970b).

These results have been difficult to obtain in other laboratories. J. Field (1977) used a mirror device to present an intangible visible object to 3-, 5-, and 7-month-old infants. The infants were attentive to the visible object and inclined to reach for it, but they showed no surprise or distress when their hands encountered empty space. Yonas and his colleagues (see Yonas, 1979) investigated developmental changes in reactions to an intangible visible object, again using a stereoscopic shadow-casting device. They found no evidence for surprise and no discernible tendency to test the hands for numbness in infants as old as 9½ months. Thus, young infants may show no discernible reaction to this discrepancy, whereas older infants may systematically explore the object with their hands but show no surprise or distress.

In further studies of visual-haptic perception, objects were presented through a mirror device so that one object could be felt at the location at which a second object was seen. Two kinds of visual-haptic conflict are introduced with this device. First, as the infant reaches for an object at its visible location, his hand does not come into view. Second, the object that the infant contacts manually can be made to differ in size, shape, texture, or substance from the object that he sees. Lasky (1977) investigated 2½- to 6½-month-old infants' reactions to reaching for an object with or without sight of the hand. Failure to see the hand reduced the reaching of 5½-month-olds, but not of younger infants. The frequency of reaching at younger ages was very low in both conditions, however. E. W. Bushnell (1979, 1980) investigated infants' reactions to touching an object with different properties from the object they saw. When infants reached for a visible object, they encountered an object of a different shape and texture. In a control condition, infants encountered an object with the same properties as the visible object. Infants were videotaped and their facial and manual reactions were observed. Infants of 8 months reacted equally in the two conditions. Infants of 9½ and 11 months, however, were more inclined to explore visually and manually in the discrepant condition.

These findings present a puzzle. Because young infants are sensitive to relationships between the visible and tactual substance of an object felt in the mouth (Gibson & Walker, 1982) and because they reach for visible objects that are nearby and graspable (Bruner & Koslowski, 1972), why are they not surprised when a visible object turns out to be intangible? There would seem to be four possible explanations. First, haptic exploration has its own developmental course (see *Exploring and Attending*). Infants may not be sensitive to all of the properties of an object held in the hand until manual exploratory skills increase. Exploration by the mouth, in contrast, appears to mature very early. Second, young infants may not respond emotionally to events in ways that adults can interpret. Expressions of surprise, fear, or distress may themselves develop (Sroufe & Waters, 1976). Third, infants may be subject to capture effects, as are adults (Welch & Warren, 1980). Visual information for an object of one shape may modify the infant's haptic perception of that shape so as to eliminate any perceived discrepancy. Fourth, young infants may be able to use their perceptual capacities only in limited ways. In Rozin's (1976) terms, young infants may have only limited access to the information that their perceptual systems provide. For example, an infant may be able to register the relationship between visual and haptic information for the shape of an object, and this capacity may guide reaching for a visible object or looking at an object that has been felt. But when there is a discrepancy between the information detected by the eye and hand, the discrepancy that is registered may not serve to guide a search for the source of the discrepancy and may not elicit emotional communications. The accessibility hypothesis proposes that developmental acquisitions are rooted in innate structures that have evolved for quite specific purposes. But developmental changes of considerable importance will occur as these mechanisms come to function in new ways.

Perceiving Another Person: An Example

We close this section on object perception by focusing on the development of the perception of people. Within the first six months, infants become sensitive enough to the properties of the face to discriminate one face from another in pictures, in three-dimensional representations, and in live presentations. For example, Fagan (1972) familiarized infants with a photograph of one face and then paired that photograph with one of a different face for a preference test. Infants of 5½ months exhibited a preference for the face they had not seen, whereas 4-month-olds exhibited no reliable preference. The negative results with 4-month-olds may, however, be attributable to the techniques Fagan used—infants as young as 3 months have been found to discriminate between photographs of two different faces in studies using a habituation technique (Barrera & Maurer, 1981; Maurer & Heroux, 1980). There appears to be no reliable evidence that infants can discriminate between photographs of two different faces below 3 months, even if one photograph portrays the infant's own mother (G. Olson, 1981).

These studies show that infants are sensitive to some property or relationship that distinguishes a photograph of one face from a photograph of another face, but they do not indicate what relationships infants perceive. To address the latter question, investigators have studied infants' reactions to schematic faces. With these displays, specific features and feature combinations can be varied systematically, and infants' responses to these variations can be assessed. This literature has been reviewed in detail by Sherrod (1981). We mention only a few findings. Two-month-old infants have been shown to discriminate normally arranged faces from a variety of bizarre arrangements when tested with a visual-preference procedure (Fantz, 1966) or a habituation procedure (Maurer & Barrera, 1981). This discrimination has also been reported with newborn infants, in a study using a visual tracking procedure (Goren, Sarty, & Wu, 1975). Older infants have been shown to respond to changes in particular features of schematic faces. For example, Caron, Caron, Caldwell, and Weiss (1973) presented infants of 4 and 5 months with one schematic face for habituation, followed by a second test face. The test stimulus was always a regular schematic face; the habituation stimulus was the same face with one or several features missing or misplaced. The youngest infants were most sensitive to changes in large external features of the face, such as the hair. Changes in the eyes were noticed next, and changes in the nose and mouth were noticed last, at 5 months.

These studies and many others (see E. J. Gibson, 1969) suggest a rapid development of face perception in infancy. But even these studies may underestimate the young infant's perceptual competence, because they all presented infants with static representations. Natural faces are active and constantly changing in expression. The face undergoes deformations in which different surfaces move relative to each other and some surfaces are stretched or wrinkled.

One experiment presented 4- and 5½-month-old infants with films of the head and shoulders of an unfamiliar woman (Spelke, 1975). During a habituation phase, the person was seen to engage in six different repetitive actions, with different expressions, for 20 sec. each. The actions included smiling, nodding, yawning, and the like. In the test that followed, the same person or a different person—same age, sex, and coloring—engaged in two new actions, with new expressions. Infants of both ages looked longer to the new person during the test; habituation to presentation of a person performing several actions generalized to presentations of new actions by that person. Infants can perceive some continuity in events in which one person does different things. They may perceive that person to persist over changes in what she does.

Infants may be less able to perceive the identity of a person over different poses if that person is presented only in still photographs, but they eventually become able to do so. Fagan (1976) presented 7-month-old infants with a photograph of a single face presented in a frontal orientation. After familiarization, infants received a preference test with the same and a very different face, both presented at a different orientation, that is, a profile or a three-quarter view. Infants exhibited a novelty preference for the photograph of the person they had not previously seen. Thus, 7-month-old infants appear to recognize a face in two different photographs.

Fagan's (1976) experiment indicates that infants perceive some similarity between two different photographs of the same person. It suggests that they may recognize the person in the two views. But children continue to have some difficulty recognizing people in photographs and in very short filmed episodes until adolescence. They have trouble recognizing a person over changing facial expressions, hairstyles, and even accessories, provided that the comparison person is similar in appearance.

Carey and Diamond (1977) asked children of 6 to 10 years which of two photographs depicted the same person as an original inspection photograph. The two test pictures portrayed women of the same hair color. The correct person's hairstyle, clothing, and expression sometimes changed from the inspection to the test photograph. There was a gradual increase in accuracy with age, and a gradual decline in attention to accessories and other features extraneous to the face. Young children appeared especially apt to match faces by considering individual features such as the mouth; older children appeared to attend to the total configuration of facial features. The developing ability to perceive the distinctive configuration of a face appears to be tied, in part, to maturational changes occurring at the time of puberty (Carey, 1978). Marked improvements with age in face perception were also reported by Dirks (1976) who showed preschool and school-aged children short videotapes of unfamiliar people performing different actions. It is interesting that children perform better at this task if they are allowed to see more than one view of a person. The identity of a person appears to be perceived better if the person performs varied or extended actions.

Infants not only perceive the identity of a person over changes in his actions and expressions; they also appear to discriminate some actions and expressions. The most dramatic evidence for perception of another person's actions comes from studies of imitation. Newborn infants have been reported to imitate some of the actions of an adult (Church, 1970; Dunkeld, 1978; Maratos, 1973; Meltzoff & Moore, 1977, 1979; Trevarthen, 1977). They seem particularly apt to imitate gestures of the mouth, such as tongue protrusion (Church, 1970; Meltzoff & Moore, 1977, 1979). Early imitation has not been found by all investigators (Hamm, Russell, & Koepke, 1979; Hayes & Watson, 1979), and some of the studies reporting imitation have been criticized (see Meltzoff & Moore [1977] for a critique of earlier studies; also see Anisfeld [1979], Masters [1979], and Meltzoff & Moore [1979]). If young infants do imitate actions of the face, they must have considerable ability to perceive faces and their actions. Note, however, that the young infant's ability to imitate an expression appears, even by the most generous estimate, to be quite limited. The ability to imitate actions outside of the child's normal repertoire, and to do so in a deliberate manner, develops slowly over the course of infancy and childhood (Aronfreed, 1968; Parton, 1976; Piaget, 1951).

The development of sensitivity to the expressive behavior of others has become a topic of considerable interest. This development seems to begin in infancy, although it continues through childhood. It is difficult to determine whether an infant responds to an emotional expression as such (Oster, 1981).

Nevertheless, infants appear to discriminate among certain expressions of emotions, particularly if one expressed emotion is joy and the other is anger, sorrow, or surprise (Barrera, 1981; Kreutzer & Charlesworth, 1973; LaBarbera, Izard, Vietze, & Parisi, 1976; Walker, 1982; Young-Brown, Rosenfeld, & Horowitz, 1977).

Research by Walker (1982) suggests that infants perceive and react to the affordances of an expressive face in at least a rudimentary way. Infants were videotaped as they watched a film of a happy or sad face. Experimentally blind but experienced observers using a forced-choice procedure judged better than chance what film a baby watched by looking at her facial expression alone. Walker's observers were unable to describe explicitly the basis of their judgments.

There are developmental changes in the child's sensitivity to the emotional expression of a face, particularly when he views the face only in a photograph. The development of sensitivity to facial expressions has been studied in diverse ways. For example, children have been asked to label the emotion expressed in a picture or to choose the pictured face whose expression is most appropriate in some given context. Findings vary across tasks, but, in general, there appears to be a steady increase in sensitivity to expression over the childhood years (Oster & Ekman, 1978). As in the infant studies, children seem most sensitive to expressions of joy. They are least able to identify fear in pictures. Other emotions show no consistent ordering of difficulty (Oster & Ekman, 1978).

In nature, faces do not come alone. A child encounters people with characteristic voices, movements, actions, and odors. Recent studies have focused on the infant's sensitivity to one of these relationships, that between the voice and the visible movements of a speaking person.

When a person speaks, his face moves in synchrony with his speech. Adults are sensitive to the synchrony and are disturbed when it is disrupted, as in poorly dubbed movies. As we have already noted, infants 12 to 16 weeks old are sensitive to this synchrony as well (Dodd, 1979; Spelke & Cortelyou, 1981). By 8 months, infants also respond to relationships between auditory and visual information about the sex of a person. Presented with photographs of a man and a woman's face while one man or woman's voice is played between them, infants tend to look preferentially to the face of the person whose sex matches the voice (Miller & Horowitz, 1980). Finally, Walker (1982) showed that infants of 5 and 7 months can coordinate auditory and visual information about the emotional expression of a person (see *Obtaining Information About Events*). Young infants perceive innately, or learn rapidly, about many of the properties of a face both optically and acoustically specified.

The preceding studies suggest that infants perceive people as meaningful objects. They do not discriminate and recognize people, their expressions, and their actions as meaningless patterns. Infants perceive and respond to the affordances of a person as an object that can move, gesture, and engage the infant in reciprocal interactions. Perceptual development seems to involve not the imposition of a constructed meaning on a meaningless pattern, but the discovery of new affordances of objects that are already perceived as meaningful.

OBTAINING INFORMATION ABOUT PLACES

The environmental layout consists of surfaces—surfaces that meet, surfaces that are nested within other interlocking surfaces, and surfaces that extend indefinitely into the distance. Where surfaces end or turn abruptly, there are edges; where they break, there are apertures; where they meet, there are corners; and beyond the edges of any surface are vistas through which a layout of more distant surfaces can be seen. This layout of surfaces has affordances for behavior. Most flat, rigid, extended surfaces afford support and locomotion. Apertures and tunnels afford passage to a locomoting animal, whereas upright surfaces placed in his path are obstacles that prevent locomotion or afford collision. To an adult, the surface layout is perceived to extend beyond the immediate field of view, and the properties and affordances of the layout are perceived as constant over changes in the point of observation. Thus, the environmental layout can serve as a reference system within which a perceiver can locate himself in relation to other objects and objects in relation to each other.

The development of perception and knowledge of the spatial layout has occasioned debate on many topics. Philosophers and psychologists have pondered the origins of space perception and the role experience plays in its development, the nature of the child's knowledge of spatial relationships and the proper mathematical description of spatial knowledge. We will examine these and other issues in the course of this discussion. Our focus is not, however, on perception of space as such, but on perception of the environment.

Two Views

According to one class of theories, perceptual knowledge of space is a construction, a system of inferences based on the child's action. Theorists as different as Berkeley and Piaget have proposed that the child comes gradually to appreciate the spatial properties of things as she acts on the world and as activities of the hand and body endow her visual sensations with three-dimensionality. According to Piaget (1954), knowledge of space begins to develop over the infancy period. Near space is constructed before far space, because the child's range of effective actions broadens only gradually. Moreover, the child constructs space in relation to herself before she constructs an objective spatial layout. As the child gains the capacity for symbolic thought, her knowledge of space gradually becomes objective and comes to bear the formal properties of progressively higher geometries.

In contrast to these views is the theory that the environmental layout is specified by invariants in the optic array and that perceivers detect the layout as they move about. Space need not be inferred from action. Instead, properties of the spatial layout can be detected by mechanisms that are attuned to the appropriate stimulus invariants (J. J. Gibson, 1966, 1979). J. J. Gibson spent much of his life attempting to describe the invariants underlying perception of that layout, and his work has led to a number of discoveries and suggestions.

A developmental theory based on J. J. Gibson's analysis (see E. J. Gibson, 1969, 1982) has proposed that mechanisms for detecting invariants specifying properties of the spatial layout develop very early. The child uses perceived properties of the layout as relational information for the positions, orientations, and movements of objects, including the self. This analysis emphasizes the role of events, often brought about by the observer himself, in specifying surfaces. Extended surfaces are best found out about by looking or moving around. Walking toward a wall provides evidence at once—by the optical expansion pattern produced—of its orientation relative to the observer. And exploring the larger spatial layout—the layout of one's house or school or town—can only be accomplished through locomotion. Perception and locomotion are reciprocal, for walking around is itself guided by visual information about the layout of surfaces.

Visual Proprioception

Adults rely heavily on visual information about their own movements and posture when they stand

and locomote. If all the elements of the optic array begin to flow outward from a single point, we perceive ourselves to be moving in the direction of the focus of expansion (J. J. Gibson, 1966; Warren, 1976). If the array begins to rotate to the right, we soon feel ourselves spinning to the left, even in some cases to the point of nausea. If the array is tilted to an oblique angle, we feel ourselves tilting the opposite way (Witkin, Lewis, Hertzman, Machover, Meissner, & Wapner, 1954). If surfaces in the environment suddenly swing from their normal orientation to a forward tilted orientation, we feel ourselves falling forward and may falsely compensate for this movement so far that we lose our balance (Lishman & Lee, 1975). All these phenomena reflect the adult's perception of the layout as permanent and immoveable, and of himself as a moveable object within it. Moreover, these phenomena testify to the adult's perception of the invariant relation between his own upright posture and the orientation of the walls and the ground.

A constructivist theory of development should predict that the effect of vision on proprioception will grow with age, but in fact, the effect diminishes. Subjects aged 8 years to adult have been placed in a tiltable chair in a tilted room and asked to adjust the chair until it was upright. Subjects of all ages were influenced by the orientation of the room, and this influence was greatest at the youngest ages (Witkin et al., 1954).

In other studies, even infants have been shown to use visual information as a guide for posture control. Lee and Aronson (1974) placed 11-month-old infants who had recently learned to stand in a room whose walls could be made to swing toward and away from them. The infant stood on the ground in front of the mother; both the mother and the floor remained stationary as the walls moved. The effects were even more dramatic than with adults. When the room was swung toward them, infants evidently perceived themselves to be falling toward the wall, for they leaned sharply backward and lost their balance. The opposite pattern was obtained when the room was swung away from them. Despite the presence of the mother, the stationary ground, and vestibular information that the child was upright and unmoving, infants evidently felt themselves to move and the walls to stand still in response to the discordant visual flow pattern. Infants evidently use visual information about the extended surfaces in the environment to guide locomotion. The absence of this posture-control system in blind infants may partly explain their considerable delay in onset of locomotion.

Lee and Aronson's infants were beginning to walk. It is conceivable that they learned about the correlation of optical motions and posture changes during a fall. Such learning is less likely to explain the results of studies by Butterworth (Butterworth & Cicchetti, 1978; Butterworth & Hicks, 1977; for a review, see Butterworth, 1981). Butterworth and Hicks (1977) observed the reactions of infants of 10 and 16 months who were seated in a swinging room. The older infants were capable of standing; the younger infants were not. Infants of both ages reacted to the visually specified information for movement. In fact, further research suggested that younger infants in a seated position are more responsive to this information than older infants (Butterworth & Cicchetti, 1978). Finally, infants of only 2 months made appropriate postural adjustments of the head to compensate for a swinging room (Pope, cited in Butterworth, 1981). Because these infants had never stood or walked on their own, it is unlikely that they had learned to correlate visual information with posture control. Infants may have unlearned visuomotor programs that use optical motions to guide postural adjustments.

Perceiving Affordances of the Layout

Obstacles

When a perceiver faces a wall or an obstacle and walks directly toward it, a projection of the obstacle expands symmetrically in the field of view, its contours moving at a geometrically increasing rate. As the moment of impact approaches, the obstacle comes rapidly to fill the field of view. This explosive pattern of expansion is called looming, and it specifies imminent collision. Adults detect this flow pattern and use it to guide locomotion and avoid running into things. Once infants can walk, they too avoid walking into walls and other surfaces. Do toddlers learn to avoid obstacles by trial and error, or are they innately sensitive to information for impending collision? These questions are addressed by studies in which an obstacle is brought toward an infant who is much too young to locomote, and the infant's reactions are observed.

Schiff (1965) originally observed responses to looming optical displays in a variety of newborn animals. Animals were presented with a screen projection of an object that was produced by a shadow-casting device. The projection was made to expand in a looming pattern. Monkeys, kittens, and crabs all backed away from the looming display, but not from a display in which an object appeared to recede. The same response was observed with a variety of objects. Schiff concluded that these animals perceived an impending collision with the object and acted to avoid it.

Observations of human infants initially supported the same conclusion. Bower, Broughton, and Moore (1971b) presented 2-week-old infants with a real object that approached them or receded. Infants were reported to widen their eyes, withdraw their heads, and interpose their hands between their faces and the object as the object reached the near point of approach. When the object was replaced by a shadow pattern presenting the same expansion pattern without other information for depth, the response was still observed, although it was reduced. When air displacement from an approaching object was presented with no accompanying visual information, no defensive response was obtained. Bower et al. (1971b) concluded that the infants were sensitive to visual information for the approach of an object. Optical expansion patterns seemed to provide part of this information, although other optical information might contribute as well, such as information for distance.

Ball and Tronick (1971) compared infants' responses to approaching objects and expanding shadow patterns when the optical expansion was symmetrical (specifying that the object was moving toward a collision with the infant) or asymmetrical (specifying that the object would pass by the infant with no collision). Infants reacted differently to these events. When the object pattern expanded asymmetrically (on a miss course) infants followed the expanding pattern with interest, exhibiting no avoidant behavior. It was concluded that infants perceive the approach of an object and its affordance for collision.

This conclusion has been questioned, because infants under 8 months exhibit no discernible fear of a looming object as they withdraw from it (Cicchetti & Sroufe, 1978). Perhaps, then, the defensive reaction has been misinterpreted. Yonas, Bechtold, Frankel, Gordon, McRoberts, Norcia, & Sternfels (1977) proposed that behavior labeled defensive is really exploratory, that is, infants may attempt to maintain visual fixation on the rising contour of a shadow pattern, retracting the head in order to do so. Yonas et al. (1977) discovered that patterns that do not specify collision will also elicit head withdrawal under certain conditions, provided that the upper contour rises.

Despite these considerations, it now seems clear that very young infants do show avoidant behavior when given visual information for the approach of an object (see Ball & Vurpillot, 1976; Pettersen,

Yonas, & Fisch, 1980; Yonas, Pettersen, & Lockman, 1979; Yonas, Pettersen, Lockman, & Eisenberg, 1980). Bower reported that infants will show appropriate reactions to an impending collision with an object whose contour does not rise (Bower, 1979; Dunkeld & Bower, 1980). Infants of 2 to 4 weeks were presented with the shadow of a rectangle undergoing continuous perspective transformations, specifying rotation about a horizontal axis. As the upper contour neared its lowest position, the object appeared about to fall on the infants. At that point, the infants backed away.

Finally, Carroll & Gibson (1981) investigated 3-month-old infants' reactions to two patterns of symmetrical expansion with very different affordances. One display consisted of a patterned panel against a patterned background. The panel approached the infant on a hit path. In the other condition, the display that approached the infant was an identically shaped aperture in a larger panel through which a stationary rear surface with the same pattern could be seen. Infants responded to the approach of the obstacle in the characteristic way, withdrawing their heads and extending their arms toward the object. The response to the aperture was very different. Infants initially tracked the rising contour, but then they turned to one side to track an edge of the surface as it moved close. Measures of changing head pressure differentiated the two events. This study indicates that avoidant behaviors are not elicited by an expanding contour as such. Instead, an approaching surface has affordances for the infant, and the affordances depend on whether it is an obstacle or an aperture. Patterns of occlusion and disocclusion serve to distinguish these affordances. If an obstacle approaches, more and more of the background surface becomes occluded. If an aperture approaches, more and more of the background surface becomes disoccluded. Young infants may perceive rigid surfaces, openings, and their affordances by detecting this information.

Surfaces of Support

When do infants first perceive that a solid, flat, rigid surface will support them and their locomotion? Studies of responses to a visual cliff indicate that this perceptual ability is innate in some animals. Gibson and Walk placed animals such as rats, chicks, and kids on a board from which they could descend onto either of two transparent surfaces (Gibson & Walk, 1960; Walk & Gibson, 1961). On the shallow side, there was a patterned surface directly beneath the glass; on the deep side, the patterned surface was several feet below. Newborn kids and chicks immediately descended to the shallow side, but all avoided the deep side, as did dark-reared rats. Human newborns could not be tested because they do not locomote independently, but infants were tested when they could crawl. The majority of them avoided the deep side of the cliff. It appeared that a flat, opaque rigid surface is perceived as affording support as soon as locomotion is possible. The development of perception of these affordances seemed not to depend on trial-and-error learning.

Other observations seem to challenge this conclusion. First, infants of many species show little fear of the deep side of the cliff. Although baby goats avoid the deep side of the cliff from birth, they do so with no signs of fear. Young human infants who are placed directly on the deep side of the cliff do not seem to be afraid either; their faces remain calm, they do not cry, and their heart rate does not accelerate (Campos, Langer, & Krowitz, 1970; Scarr & Salapatek, 1970). Second, not all human infants avoid the deep side of the cliff in any experiment. Third, young prelocomotor infants who have learned to locomote with the aid of a walker show no avoidance of the deep side of the cliff, they will cross in the walker to either side with equal readiness (Rader, Bausano, & Richards, 1980; see also Scarr & Salapatek, 1970). Older infants who refuse to crawl onto the deep side will also cross to that side if placed in a walker (Rader et al., 1980).

These findings have prompted reinterpretations of the development of avoidance of the deep side of the visual cliff. Campos, Hiatt, Ramsay, Henderson, & Svejda (1978) proposed that, for humans, experience plays a role in the development of perception of a dropoff and its consequences. Children learn—perhaps by trial and error—that visually specified dropoffs do not afford support and should be avoided. Rader and her colleagues (Rader, et al., 1980; Richards & Rader, 1981) presented evidence against this interpretation. In several studies, they examined the development of cliff avoidance in babies that varied in age, amount of crawling experience, and age of onset of crawling. If infants learn to avoid the deep side, then those who are older or more experienced crawlers should show greater avoidance. This did not occur. The only reliable predictor of cliff avoidance was age of onset of crawling. Babies who began to crawl at an early age (before 6½ months) showed little avoidance of the cliff, regardless of when they were tested. Babies who began to crawl at a later age showed a strong tendency to avoid the deep side.

Rader et al. (1980) proposed that cliff avoidance depends on a visuomotor program that matures at about the time that crawling begins. The visuomotor program leads infants to shift their weight forward—the first step in crawling—only when they detect visual information for a supporting surface. Rader et al. proposed that this program depends on no specific experience for its development. For infants who are late crawlers, the program will have matured by the time crawling begins, and thus late crawlers will avoid the deep side of the cliff. But infants who begin crawling before the program matures must use nonvisual information for a supporting surface—probably tactile information—to guide their locomotion. For these infants, crawling may continue to be guided by tactual information. Because the deep side of the cliff feels safe, early crawlers will not avoid it.

In summary, infants seem able to perceive, without specific experience, that obstacles afford collision and that rigid, flat opaque surfaces afford support. Nevertheless, these abilities are very restricted in expression. Young infants withdraw from an object on a collision course, but they are not distressed by an impending collision. Most infants avoid crawling onto a cliff as soon as they are able to crawl, but they show no fear of the cliff until months later and may cross over the cliff if placed in a walker. For a young infant, information about an impending collision or a dropoff may not be accessible to systems for communicating a state of personal danger to others (such as expressions of fear) or to actions that are not species-specific adaptive responses to an impending collision or a dropoff (such as maneuvering a walker). As we grow, the affordances we perceive may come to guide a greater and greater repertoire of behavior.

Paths for Locomotion

There is more to perceiving the layout than perceiving obstacles, openings, and supporting surfaces. Most environmental layouts consist of an arrangement of surfaces that form potential supports, obstacles, passages, and vistas. A perceiver must plot a course through this layout, getting from where he is to where he wants to go without hitting obstacles or running into blind alleys. Furthermore, there are usually many potential paths through a layout, and it is desirable to choose the most efficient one.

The development in children of the ability to navigate through a cluttered environment has received very little study. Lockman (1980) conducted a longitudinal study with infants aged 8 to 12 months. Infants were presented with a desirable toy that was then moved behind an opaque or transparent barrier. In some conditions, the infants had to crawl around the barrier. In other conditions, they could obtain the toy by reaching around the barrier. In addition, infants were given an object-permanence task in which they had to retrieve an object that had been placed under a cloth. All the infants succeeded at this object-permanence task before succeeding at the barrier task. The ability to navigate around barriers evidently requires more than a capacity to search for things that are out of view. Among the detour conditions, the reaching tasks were solved at a younger age than the crawling tasks and the tasks with opaque barriers were solved earlier than the tasks with transparent barriers. Confronted with a transparent barrier, many of the younger infants attempted to reach through the barrier and abandoned all attempts to obtain the object when that procedure failed.

Knowledge of Larger Layouts

As children begin to locomote, they come to navigate over a larger and larger terrain. A young child must not only plot a course across a room, avoiding obstacles, but also get from the kitchen to the dining room, from the living room to the bedroom, from the front door to the backyard. These courses involve routes and goals that are not visible to the child as she begins her journey. She must use knowledge of the layout to direct her locomotion. What do children know about the layout of familiar environments like their homes, their schools, and their neighborhoods?

Children's knowledge of a familiar environment—a classroom or a school library—has been studied by H. L. Pick, Jr., and his colleagues with preschoolers (H. L. Pick, Jr., 1972) and with children in the first and fifth grades (Hardwick, McIntyre, & Pick, 1976). In these studies, children were asked to indicate where objects were without looking at them. They stood behind screens in different corners of the room and aimed a sighting tube at the objects. Preschoolers were as consistent as adults when they pointed to the same object from different places, but the adults were more accurate. Accuracy increased from first grade to fifth grade, although not from fifth grade to adulthood. But the accuracy of young children was impressive. For example, the average error for sighting was 9.58° for first graders compared to 6.53° for adults. Children know a good deal about the spatial layout of their schools.

Young children also have rudimentary knowledge of the layout of their homes. In one experiment (Pick & Lockman, 1979), children living in two-story apartments were asked to aim a sighting tube at targets in other rooms of the apartment. Aiming accuracy improved with age, but it was high at all ages. For example, the average aiming error was 11.5° for adults and 27.1° for children aged 4 to 6. Accuracy was higher within a floor than across floors for all the children, particularly the youngest, although not for the adults. In a further study, 4- and 5-year-olds were able to identify rooms of their homes while standing outside, and they were able to construct a rudimentary map of the furniture in individual rooms in the house (Pick, Acredolo, & Gronseth, 1973).

Finally, Cohen, Baldwin, and Sherman (1978) investigated children's knowledge of a familiar, larger scale environment. Children of 9 and 10 years were asked to estimate distances between places at their summer camp. Children's estimates of distance were systematically related to the true, euclidean distances between points. However, both children and adults overestimated distances that were difficult to travel between relative to distances that were easily traveled. Kosslyn, Pick, & Fariello (1974; see also Anooshian & Wilson, 1977) familiarized preschool children and adults with an artificial environment containing objects and barriers. Barriers could be opaque or transparent. The subjects were then asked to estimate distances between pairs of objects. The adults overestimated the distance between two objects only if an opaque barrier separated them. Children overestimated that distance if either an opaque or a transparent barrier separated them. Nevertheless, children's and adults' estimates were related to euclidean distances.

Most of these studies suggest that children's knowledge of space is somehow affected by their locomotion. Thus, Pick & Lockman (1979) found that children know more about spatial relationships between rooms on the same floor, which they can walk between with ease, than they do about rooms on different floors, which are separated by stairways. And Cohen et al. (1978) and Kosslyn et al. (1974) found that children overestimate distances between two points if the route one must travel between them is longer. It is not surprising that locomotion should play a role in the child's spatial knowledge for it is only by locomoting that one can obtain the sequence of vistas that provides information about the larger environmental layout. But what is most striking about these experiments is how limited the effects of locomotion are. Children and adults overestimate distances between points separated by a barrier, but their distance estimate is not nearly as great as is the length of the path that would be needed to circumvent the obstacle. Children are more accurate at judging the direction of an object in a different room if that room is more easily walked to, but their estimates reflect the true direction of the object, not the direction in which they would need to walk to get to the object. Thus, children are able to gain spatial knowledge that goes beyond the paths they have taken.

In light of these findings, one might expect that children, who are introduced to a new environment and are taken through that environment along some set of paths, would gain knowledge of the spatial layout of that environment and so generate new paths they have never taken. That rats can sometimes do this is well known (Maier, 1929; Olton, 1977; Tolman, 1948). Nevertheless, some research suggests that young children have trouble charting new routes through familiar environments (Hazen, Lochman & Pick, 1978; Maier, 1936). Hazen et al. (1978) introduced children aged 3 to 6 years to a novel environment consisting of three rooms, each with four doors and each containing a toy animal. The children were taken along one route through the rooms repeatedly until they were able, on entering a room, to choose the correct door leading out to the next room and to report the animal they would encounter there. After training, the children were able to travel the familiar route in reverse with high accuracy. They were also able to anticipate the animals they would encounter as they traveled the route in reverse, although 3-year-olds made more errors than the older children on this task. Performance was poor, however, especially at the younger ages, when children were asked what animals lay behind doors they had *not* traveled through. Young children apparently did not perceive the layout of the rooms as a single unified place.

In experiments with simpler environments, however, very young children have been shown to be capable of finding new routes through a layout. Hazen (1979) taught children one route through three rooms. Then, a door normally traveled along the route was blocked, and the children were asked to choose another door. The 3-year-olds usually chose a door that led efficiently to the goal. Moreover, even a congenitally blind 2½-year-old child, and sighted, blindfolded children of that age, have been observed to find new, direct paths between objects (Landau, Gleitman, & Spelke, 1981). The children were placed in an unfamiliar room and

taken from one object (*A*) to each of two others (*B* and *C*). When they were then asked to travel between *B* and *C*, they did so directly without returning to *A*. During their travels along the two training paths, the children evidently came to know the spatial relationships among all three objects.

As children grow, they come to use maps to find their way in a new place. We do not describe studies of map-reading and map-drawing here (see, e.g., Bluestein & Acredolo, 1979; Herman, Allen, & Kirasic, 1979; Siegel, Herman, Allen, & Kirasic, 1979; Siegel & White, 1975; Tonkonogaya, 1961; see also Mandler, Vol. III, Chap. 7). Suffice it to say that the development of map-reading seems to build on a prior ability, the gaining and using of knowledge of spatial layouts that children explore directly by locomotion.

Locating Moveable Objects

The environmental layout provides information about the spatial locations of objects. With development, children become increasingly adept at using this information to locate objects, especially objects that are out of sight.

There is a voluminous literature on the early development of search for hidden objects, research that springs from Piaget's theory of the development of the object concept (Piaget, 1954). That theory is only tangentially relevant to our present concerns and is reviewed elsewhere in these volumes (see *Mandler, vol. III, chap. 7; Harris, vol. II, chap. 9*). Infants below 8 months will rarely, if ever, search for an object that is fully out of view. Once infants begin to search for hidden objects, they do not always confine their search to the last place in which they saw an object disappear. If the object is displaced while it is out of view—for example, if it is hidden in someone's hand and then dropped into a box—children under 18 months may be completely baffled.

By the end of the second year, children can not only find an object that has just been hidden but can also find an object after a delay. DeLoache (1979) observed mothers playing an object-hiding game with children from 18 to 30 months of age. As the child watched, the mother hid a small toy somewhere in the home, for example, in a drawer or under a pillow. The child had to wait for 1, 3, or 5 min. and then find the object. Children found the object directly—with no errors—on the great majority of the trials. There was some developmental improvement, but even the youngest children found the object without error on 67% of the trials. In a second study, three objects were hidden on each trial. After a delay of 3 or 5 min., the children were asked to find one specific object, and they did so with high accuracy. Young children are surprisingly good at noting and remembering the locations of hidden objects.

In DeLoache's studies (1979), children had observed the objects as they were hidden. Many of the times that we search for things, however, we do not know where they are. We may forget where we left something or we may have dropped it inadvertently. In such situations, adults are usually able to search for the missing object systematically, narrowing down its possible locations and checking these one by one. As described earlier in our discussion of *Exploring and Attending,* search for objects becomes increasingly systematic over the course of early childhood (Drozdal & Flavell, 1975; Wellman et al., 1979). Children come increasingly to confine their search to a critical area—the only area in which the object could possibly be—and to search that area exhaustively.

To retrieve a hidden object, the child must mark its location in some way. Children have been thought to locate objects in terms of three frames of reference. First, they may locate an object relative to themselves, noting that a toy is hidden ''on my right'' or ''above my head.'' This self-oriented, or ''egocentric,'' reference system will serve the child well as long as she herself does not change position. Second, children may locate an object relative to some other object or objects, noting that a toy is hidden ''under the sofa'' or ''behind the door.'' This landmark-oriented reference system will serve to locate the object as long as the landmark is unique (there must not be two identical sofas under which the object might be hidden) and does not move. Finally, the child may note the location of a hidden object relative to the larger, permanent spatial layout—the sky, the horizon, the walls of a room, or the perimeters of a piece of land. Because the layout as a whole never changes, the object's location can be retained indefinitely in a layout-oriented reference system, no matter how the child or other objects happen to move.

There have been many recent studies of the development of the use of these reference systems (for a review, see Pick, Yonas, & Rieser, 1978). Acredolo (1976) investigated children's use of the three frames of reference to locate a place in a room. In one study, 3- and 4-year-old children were introduced into an unfamiliar room with one door and one window, containing only a table to the right of the entry point. The child was taken to the table, was blindfolded, and was walked around the room until he lost his bearings. During this time, the table was discreetly moved. Then the child was led to a new place in the room, the blindfold was removed, and he was asked to find his initial starting point. A self-oriented reference system would dictate that the child move to the right, a landmark-oriented system would dictate that he move to the table, and a layout-oriented system would dictate that he move to the wall to the right of the door. There were two experimental conditions, one in which self-oriented and landmark-oriented systems were pitted against the layout-oriented system, and one in which self-oriented and layout-oriented systems were pitted against the landmark-oriented system. Children of both ages moved in a specific direction relative to the self.

In a follow-up experiment, these conditions were replicated in a smaller room with walls of different colors. In addition, a third condition was run in which the self-oriented system was pitted against the landmark- and layout-oriented systems. Each child was run in all these conditions. The 3-, 4-, and 10-year-old children showed no tendency to move in a particular direction relative to the self. At all ages, most children moved in a direction specified by the room itself. Those younger children who did not locate the object relative to the room tended to use the table rather than themselves as a reference point. Children may be less apt to locate objects relative to the self if they are in a room that is small, that has distinctive markings of its own (walls of different colors) or that is familiar.

In a further experiment, Acredolo (1977) trained 3-, 4-, and 5-year-old children to find a trinket under one of two cups on repeated trials. Then the children were taken to the opposite side of the room and asked to look for the trinket. If they located the trinket relative to their initial position, they should now move to the cup that had previously been empty. If they kept track of their own movements and located the cup relative to the layout, they should move in a new direction, to the old cup. Children were observed either in a room devoid of landmarks or in a room with tables or patterns on the wall that could serve as landmarks. Few of the children at any age used the self-oriented system. Use of this system declined with age and was lower, at all ages, when landmarks were present. Taken together, these studies suggest that even 3-year-old children are capable of locating an object relative to other objects and surfaces. They seem not to be bound to an egocentric reference system.

The use of a layout-oriented reference system at

age 3 raises questions about its antecedents. Studies of infants and toddlers now suggest that even the youngest children can respond to the spatial position of an object relative to other objects and surfaces, although they only do so under restricted conditions. The tendency to locate objects relative to the self may be more prevalent in infancy than later in life.

Bremner and Bryant (1977) presented 9-month-old infants with a task resembling Piaget's (1954) object-search task. The infant faced two containers, one to his left and one to his right. After an object was hidden and retrieved five times in one container, the infant was moved to the other side of the table for five more search trials in which the object was placed under the same or a different container. Infants of this age sometimes tend to persist searching in the direction in which an object was formerly hidden, even if it is now hidden elsewhere. If infants do not take account of their own change of position, they should make more errors if the object is hidden under the original container (in a new egocentric direction) than if it is hidden under the other container (same egocentric direction). These errors occurred frequently, even when the color of the table could serve to mark the constant location of each box. However, in a follow-up study in which Bremner (1978b) used covers of distinctive colors, the number of egocentric errors declined. Infants showed some tendency to search under the cover with the color under which they had searched previously. Bremner concluded that 9-month-old infants can respond to the objective spatial position of an object; they are not inevitably egocentric. However, infants can only respond to an objective location in space if there are distinctive landmarks by which they can identify that location.

Similar findings have been obtained from research by Acredolo (1978), Acredolo and Evans (1980), and by Rieser (1979). Infants were trained to look to the left or right in anticipation of seeing a person, and then they were rotated to a new position. Infants tested in a room without landmarks tended to anticipate seeing the person in a particular direction relative to the self; those tested with distinctive landmarks tended to anticipate seeing the person in a particular direction relative to the landmarks. For example, Rieser's 6-month-old infants responded to the landmarks on 70% of the trials after a 90° rotation. Landmark-oriented search was particularly prevalent when infants were tested in their own homes (Acredolo, 1979).

By 18 months of age (and perhaps by 14 months), children can take account of changes in their own position and can perceive the constant location of an object even without landmarks. This ability has been demonstrated in ingenious studies by Heiman and Rieser (1980). Toddlers were trained to approach and touch one of eight identical windows arrayed in a circle. During training, the child always faced in the same direction—the target window was always straight ahead or to one side. After training, the child was rotated to face in a new direction, and then further testing began. Rather than turning in the trained egocentric direction, the toddlers spontaneously rotated themselves toward the true target. Most remarkably, they chose the shorter direction of rotation to get to the target. These children perceived a constant layout over changes in their motion without landmarks to guide them.

These studies suggest that children can localize objects relative to the self and to other things from a very early age. As children grow, they seem increasingly to rely on landmarks and distant surfaces as reference points. Nevertheless, we end this discussion with a caution. It is very difficult for any experimental study to provide conclusive evidence for or against the use of any reference system, because most spatial tasks can be performed in several different ways. Virtually all of the tasks in which a response is reinforced or a landmark is provided could be performed with no spatial reference at all.

For a child to use a self-oriented frame of reference, he must perceive or conceive of an object in space with a definite location relative to himself. An egocentric responder in the above studies need not do this. He may simply repeat a response that was successful in obtaining an object in the past. For example, consider an infant who has repeatedly seen a person through a window to his left and is rotated about the room so that a new window is to his left, opposite the original window. The infant may turn to the left in search of the person because he perceives that window to be the *place* where the person was seen before—this perception would reflect use of a self-oriented system. But alternatively, the child may turn to the left because he has been taught that leftward turning produces the person. The latter case involves no spatial reference at all.

A similar interpretation for landmark responding may be offered. To use a landmark-oriented spatial reference system is to perceive or conceive of an object in its spatial relationship to a second object. But children who respond to landmarks in the above studies need not do this. They might, alternatively, learn a nonspatial rule, such as "to see the woman, turn to the striped wall, wherever that is'' or ''to retrieve the object, lift the black cloth.'' The developmental progression from a preference for self-oriented searching to a preference for object-oriented searching may reflect not a developmental change in spatial reference systems but a change in a preferred response rule. Younger children may tend to persist in a given set of motor movements, whereas older children may tend to persist in responding to a particular object.

Because many tasks can be solved nonspatially, studies of spatial localization may underestimate the infant's spatial capacities. For example, training studies may actually encourage infants to rely on nonspatial task solutions, bypassing their knowledge of a spatial layout. Many studies have trained infants to act in a certain way to achieve a particular effect. The first time the infant responds, his action may be directed to a location in the layout. As the action is repeated, however, the infant may discover a contingency between his action and the event that it produces. We noted earlier that young infants actively search for such contingencies. Thus, an infant may adopt a simple response rule in these learning studies rather than relying on knowledge of the spatial layout. Such response learning has been reported to occur systematically in studies of spatial localization by children as old as 7 years (Lasky, Romano, & Wenters, 1980). But the fact that infants can discover contingencies between their actions and other events does not mean that they lack perceptual knowledge of spatial layouts.

Despite these problems, the studies by Acredolo (1977) and Heiman and Rieser (1980) indicated that preschool children can sometimes perceive the constant spatial positions of objects and surfaces as they themselves move. Further evidence for this conclusion comes from studies involving no training. Shantz and Watson (1970, 1971) allowed 3-, 4-, and 5-year-old children to walk through a room. As they did so, the room was rotated so that the direction of the walls relative to the child remained constant. Children of all ages were markedly surprised by this. They evidently expect changes in their own positions to be accompanied by changes in their spatial relationship to other objects and surfaces. Rieser, Doxsey, McCarrell, & Brooks (1980) gave toddlers an aerial view of a simple two-choice maze with the mother at its end and then allowed the children to crawl or walk to the mother when she called. Infants 25 months old tended to crawl in the correct (nonbarricaded) direction. Without any training, the 2-year-olds evidently coordinated information picked up in the aerial view

(even a side view) with information available on the ground. A similar conclusion emerges from the studies, discussed above, of spatial localization in blind and blind-folded, sighted children (Landau et al, 1981).

Finally, Bremner (1978a) allowed infants to observe an object hidden repeatedly in one of two distinctively colored containers. Then the infants observed the hiding from the opposite side of the table so that the cup appeared in a new egocentric direction. Some of the children had searched for and retrieved the object during the initial familiarization, others had only watched the hiding and uncovering. Infants who had searched for the object previously tended to search perseveratively in the wrong location. Those who had only watched the hiding did not. Infants are, thus, capable of perceiving and responding to an object's new spatial location, and they are apt to use this ability when their task does not encourage them to rely on a well-rehearsed action.

Coordination of Perspectives

Children—even very young ones—seem able to perceive the properties of objects and places rather than the properties of their own perspective views. Yet, there are times when one must perceive properties of an array that are tied to one perspective. Most artists do this when they draw. And all perceivers need to take account of their own perspectives—and the perspectives of others—when they consider what they and others can and cannot see.

The ability to take account of the perspectives of other people appears to develop quite gradually over the course of early childhood. Young children have difficulty determining what a layout would look like from another's point of view, that is, what objects would be to the left, what to the right, what in front, and what behind. Three explanations for this difficulty have been offered. First, Piaget (Piaget & Inhelder, 1956) proposed that young children are egocentric: They cannot mentally adopt the perspectives of others. Thus, they are unable to appreciate that an array could look different to another person than it does to themselves. Second, it has been proposed that young children have difficulty transforming any mental representation of a scene. They cannot rotate a scene so as to imagine it from another point of view (e.g., Huttenlocher & Presson, 1973, 1979). Third, it has been proposed that young children have difficulty with perspective-taking tasks because they cannot easily abstract *any* perspective view of an array, including their own (E. J. Gibson, 1977; a similar hypothesis has been advanced by Flavell, 1977). Young children's perception is focused on objects and events—on what things are—rather than on any one perspective view of those events. In perceiving objects and events, the child extracts information from a flow of stimulation over time as he moves his head and body and as objects and surfaces move. If events provide the normal information for perception, it may be difficult for a child to abstract the single frozen array that is captured by any one perspective view. With development, children become increasingly sensitive to these individual perspectives and their vicissitudes.

Piaget's position and the information processing alternatives are discussed elsewhere (see *Gelman & Baillargeon, vol. III, chap. 3; Mandler, vol. III, chap. 7*), so we will focus on the third theory. There is considerable evidence that children are not very sensitive to a single, frozen perspective on an array. As we have noted, children can judge the real size of objects with considerable accuracy, but they appear to be poor at estimating the projected size of an object. Even infants are more sensitive to real changes in an object than to changes in their own perspective view of the object (Bower, 1966; Day & McKenzie, 1973). Children also appear insensitive to the limits of what they can see in a single glance. Asked to draw an object, they typically draw more than can be seen from any single perspective (Freeman & Janikoun, 1972; Hagen & Jones, 1978; Sazont'yev, 1961). When asked to describe a scene, they describe what they know to be there, not what they actually "see" (Piaget & Inhelder, 1969). Finally, children of 3 to 7 years do not always seem to appreciate that two people occupying the same location will have the same view of a scene and that two people with different locations will see the array from a different perspective (Flavell, Omanson, & Latham, 1978), perhaps with a different degree of clarity (Flavell, Flavell, Green, & Wilcox, 1980).

If the young child perceives an object better than a particular perspective view, he might find it easier to determine if another person can see an object at all rather than to determine what the other person's perspective view of the object is. Recent evidence suggests that young children are quite good at determining what object and surfaces another person can see. (For a fuller discussion, see Flavell, 1977, and *Gelman & Baillargeon, vol. III, chap. 3*.) For example, if an adult asks a young child to show her

a picture, the child will usually orient the picture so that the adult can see it (Lempers, Flavell, & Flavell, 1977). Even a blind child of 3½ has learned how to hold things so that an adult has an unobstructed view of them, taking account of the adult's line of sight and of any obstacles (Landau, 1981).

Most dramatically, infants are often able to detect which of several objects an adult is looking at. Infants as young as 4 months change their direction of gaze in response to the shifts of gaze of an adult with whom they are interacting (Scaife & Bruner, 1975). Butterworth & Cochran (1980) observed 12-month-old infants in face-to-face interaction with the mother. On signal, the mother broke off the interaction and looked to one of several visible objects. The infant's looking patterns were then observed. In the first experiment, four objects were present: some were in the infant's immediate field of view and some were not. When the mother turned to fixate a target, the infants watched her momentarily and then looked to an object as well, often pointing and looking back to the mother. Infants nearly always chose a target in the same lateral direction as the mother's glance, but they did not always choose the same target as the mother. When the mother fixated a target behind the baby, the infant usually chose a target within his own immediate visual field; he looked behind himself at the correct object only 25% of the time. When the mother fixated a target within the baby's visual field, however, the infant's accuracy rose to 85%. In a second experiment, 6-, 12-, and 18-month-old infants were presented with only one object at a time, either within or outside the immediate visual field. When the mother looked at the object, infants were likely to look at it as well, as long as both the object and the mother remained in the visual field. Infants would not follow the mother's gaze to an object if the object and mother could not be seen at the same time. Infants can determine what object another person is looking at, as long as they can view the person and the object at once.

Perceiving Geometric Relationships

This discussion of the child's perception of objects and surfaces in a spatial layout has so far bypassed a question of central interest: What are the spatial relationships among objects and surfaces that children perceive and know? This question has been raised most directly by Piaget (Piaget & Inhelder, 1956), who focused on the child's knowledge of topological, projective, and euclidean spatial properties. We follow Piaget's lead, discussing each of these sets of properties in turn.

Geometrical properties can be defined by the transformations that leave them invariant. Euclidean properties are those properties that are preserved over any rigid motions—rotations, reflections, and translations of points, lines, planes, or higher spaces. Most notably, distance and angle are invariant over any rigid motion, and so are all the geometric properties that can be derived from distance and angle. Projective properties are those properties of geometric objects that are invariant over any transformations that map one set of points into another set by projection from another point in space (of finite or infinite distance). These transformations usually change the distances between points and the angles formed by intersecting lines, but they preserve collinearity, the cross-ratio of four collinear points, and other properties that can be derived from these properties. Topological properties are those properties that are invariant over all continuous transformations that result in a one-to-one mapping of one set of points onto another set. Topological transformations generally do not preserve collinearity or the cross-ratio. They do preserve the connectivity of curves or surfaces, inside-outside relationships defined by a closed curve or surface, and incidence relationships such as the point of intersection of two curves. Topological, projective, and euclidean properties form a hierarchy: every geometric property that is invariant over all topological transformations will also be invariant over all projective transformations, and every property that is invariant over all projective transformations will also be invariant over all euclidean transformations. The converse statements are not true.[3]

What might it mean, then, for a child to have topological, projective, or euclidean knowledge of space? If a child had projective knowledge, he should be sensitive to all the properties of objects that are invariant under projection. This statement, in turn, implies two capacities. First, the child should be able to discriminate between any two objects that differ with respect to some projective property, such as a triangle and a square. Second, the child should perceive an equivalence between any two objects that are projectively equivalent, for example, any two triangles should be seen as somehow alike, since all triangles are identical under projection.

With this framework, we may consider which geometry or geometries best capture the child's spatial knowledge. Piaget and Inhelder (1956) and Laurendau and Pinard (1970) proposed that children progress from perceiving topological, to projective, to euclidean properties of space. This proposal has received little support. Cousins and Abravanel (1971) obtained similarity judgments of pairs within triads of cutout forms from 3½- to 5-year-old children. They found that the majority of judgments at all ages were based on euclidean features such as rectilinearity. Laurendau and Pinard (1970) obtained confusion errors from children, (2½, 3, 4, and 5 years of age) on an intermodal shape-matching task. They concluded from the pattern of errors that Piaget and Inhelder's (1956) theory was substantially correct. However, they reported that the youngest children tested could discriminate certain topologically identical objects as well as topologically distinct objects. Moreover, when their data were reanalyzed with a nonmetric multidimensional scaling procedure by Rieser and Edwards (1979), the solutions did not provide support for Piaget's theory. Younger children's confusions were based on relatively global properties, like angularity and curvilinearity; the older children's confusions were based on these plus more specific properties, like rectilinearity and jaggedness. All these properties, however, are euclidean. Moreover, Rieser and Edwards presented new data on the judgments of similarity of a parallelogram to 12 geometrical transformations of it. The judgments of 5-year-old children appeared to be based on projective and euclidean relations to an even greater degree than were the judgments of adults. Developmentally, there was evidence of differentiation of features, with similarity of euclidean properties easiest to detect. Recall that children's knowledge of the layout of an experimental space divided into quadrants and separated by transparent and opaque barriers was studied by Kosslyn et al. (1974). The subjects (preschool children and adults) judged distances between all pairs of objects located within the layout. Multidimensional scaling techniques applied to the data found that a euclidean solution described well the judgments of both children and adults, the children being remarkably accurate.

Recent evidence suggests that even infants are sensitive to euclidean spatial relationships. In a series of experiments, Schwartz and Day (1979) investigated discrimination by 8- to 17-week-old infants of simple two-dimensional figures. Infants viewed squares, rectangles, diamonds, or simple crosses. They were habituated to one figure and then presented with one of several other figures for discrimination testing. The test figures could differ from the original figure in orientation, angular relationship within the figure, or both. Results were strikingly consistent across figures. Infants generalized habituated to the same figure at a novel orientation, but not to a figure composed of the same lines meeting at different angles from the original. Angle is a euclidean property unchanged by any rigid motion; orientation is changed by rigid motions. The fact that infants 2 and 3 months old discriminated changes in angle and generalized over changes in orientation suggests that they detected the euclidean properties. A recent study suggests that infants 6 weeks old, however, respond more to changes in orientation than to changes in angle (Younger & Cohen, 1982).

A child who is sensitive to euclidean spatial relationships, such as distance and angle, should be able to develop knowledge of a unified layout of objects at definite distances from each other and to use that knowledge to direct locomotion along new paths through that layout. We have already referred to evidence that young children have this ability (e.g., Hazen, 1979; Landau et al., 1981).

Overview

Infants and young children perceive surfaces as potential supports and obstacles, and they use visual information about these surfaces as a guide to the earliest locomotion. The information used by infants seems to be abstract and relational, obtained as the infant moves about. Infants use the perceived layout of surfaces as information about their own position and the positions and movements of other objects. They also have rudimentary abilities to take account of another perceiver's perspective. In all these cases, children seem to perceive the euclidean properties of the layout: the distances and angular relationships among points, edges, and surfaces in a scene.

Given these early abilities, it is not surprising that children gain spatial knowledge rapidly as they begin to walk. As children locomote, they encounter new vistas in which new aspects of the layout can be seen. Over this succession of views they gain knowledge of the layout as a whole. Their knowledge goes beyond the paths they have taken, for children perceive, from these paths, a unified layout of objects and surfaces.

There are developmental changes in the child's perception of the environmental layout. Older children live in a larger environment, of course, and they are more sensitive to its potential landmarks. They also know more about the particular tableau that a spatial array projects to an eye—their own or someone else's. And their perception of the layout and its affordances seems to become more and more accessible to action and thought. But there is no doubt that the spatial layout of the infant is a coherent, unified, three-dimensional place with affordances for action. The spatial layout does not seem to be constructed by the child through her action. It is perceived at a time when the child can act in only very limited ways, and perception guides action from the start. Moreover, the information for the layout used at an early age resides primarily in events that are produced as the infant moves about.

OBTAINING INFORMATION THROUGH PICTURES

Pictures and the Layout of the World

A picture consists of texture, shading, color, and form on a static, two-dimensional surface. It may represent an array of objects and surfaces, even events, but it is very different from any natural scene that it depicts. The amount of detail and the range of brightness in a real scene far exceed that in a picture. Moreover, a real scene contains objects and surfaces arranged in depth and objects that move; a picture never does. Perhaps above all, projections to the eye from a real scene change in regular ways as the observer moves. Near surfaces progressively occlude and disocclude far surfaces, and the visible points on all surfaces are displaced in directions and velocities determined by the three-dimensional distances and orientations of these surfaces. When an observer moves while looking at a picture, no occlusion and disocclusion is produced, and the motions of points on its surface specify the uniform, flat surface of the picture itself.

How, then, does a picture represent a natural layout of objects and surfaces? As J. J. Gibson (1950) has emphasized, there is information for the layout in a single frozen image, information produced by the gradients of texture of any surface in that scene. An observer may perceive depth in a picture by detecting those texture gradients. Appropriate texture gradient information will be available whenever a picture conforms to the laws of perspective. These laws are principles for projecting any real scene onto the plane of a picture from a single point of observation. They produce not only texture gradient information for depth but also linear perspective (convergence of objectively parallel lines with increasing depth) and size perspective (diminution of objectively equal-sized objects with increasing depth).

For an adult perceiver, then, a pictorial representation can be experienced in two ways. It can be seen as a plane surface, whose two-dimensionality is specified by motion perspective and other primary information for depth such as binocular disparity. And it can be seen as the scene that it represents, a scene whose three-dimensionality is specified by texture gradients and by linear and size perspective. Adults typically see a picture in both ways at once, that is, as a two-dimensional depiction of a three-dimensional layout.

How do children perceive the layout in pictures? According to one view of perceptual development, the static image is primary and should be the easiest configuration to perceive. According to the view guiding this chapter, invariance over change is primary and static perception is a special case. Young perceivers are attuned to invariant stimulus relationships that are produced as they move about. Perception of static forms in pictures should develop later than perception of objects and events. It remains possible, however, that infants are also sensitive to invariant information within a single glimpse, such as texture gradient information. If that were true, then infants might perceive a three-dimensional array in a picture if the two-dimensionality of the picture itself were deemphasized.

We begin our review by discussing the sensitivity of infants and children to information in static, two-dimensional, patterned surfaces. Then we discuss their perception of three-dimensional objects and scenes represented in pictures.

Perceiving Abstract Patterns

Volumes have been written on children's developing perception of structure and meaning in two-dimensional forms (see Salapatek, 1975; Vurpillot, 1976; also see *Salapatek & Banks, vol. II, chap. 1*). We will not review this literature but will discuss representative findings in a few substantive areas. In general, it seems that infants and young children are sensitive to certain patterns and structure in pictures but that they are much more sensitive to structure in the natural world.

Unity

The ability to perceive stable units in a picture— to perceive what goes with what—was described by the gestalt psychologists whose principles we have already encountered. Briefly, adults perceive relationships among elements in a picture united by the principles of proximity, similarity, good continuation, closure, and good form. (Common fate, a most important gestalt principle, depends on movement and so plays no role in pictorial perception.) We noted that infants show little sensitivity to these gestalt properties when they perceive objects (Spelke, 1982). We might expect, then, that infants will show little tendency to group parts of pictures together according to the gestalt principles. Research on infants largely supports this expectation.

Bower (1965, 1967) investigated the development of perceptual unity with infants in their first 2 months. He presented infants with patterns of dots or overlapping simple forms and then he moved the patterns in various ways. Adults organize these stationary patterns into groups in accordance with various gestalt principles. Bower sought to determine whether infants perceived the same organization by comparing their reactions to movements that preserved that organization with their reactions to movements that destroyed it. If infants grouped the patterns as adults do, they were expected to show surprise or increased attention to movements that broke up the units that adults perceive. Infants showed no surprise at the breakup of configurations whose unity followed from the gestalt principles of proximity, good continuation, and good form. Infants were surprised at the breakup of a pattern whose unity followed from the principle of common fate (Bower, 1965). Most likely, young infants are insensitive to the gestalt relationships that unite elements in a static picture.

A similar conclusion can be drawn from research by Salapatek (1975). Salapatek investigated 2-month-old infants' visual scanning of a matrix of identical forms containing a small region of different forms. For an adult, the gestalt principles of similarity, and possibly good continuation, immediately segregate this smaller region from the rest of the matrix. Adults and even 2-year-old children tended spontaneously to shift their direction of gaze toward that region. The infants did not. They did look at a region of distinct elements if it was brighter than the rest of the display, but not if it only differed in form. It seemed that the gestalt grouping principles did not define for infants a discontinuity in the matrix.

The results of these studies support those reviewed in our earlier discussion *Perceiving the Unity and Boundaries of an Object*. Infants are sensitive to the spatial arrangements and to the movements of surfaces, but they do not appear to perceive either objects or forms by detecting their static gestalt properties.

Forms

Although infants do not organize patterns into groups as do adults, they may, nevertheless, discriminate one pattern from another. Twenty years of research on pattern perception in infancy suggests that they do. This research is reviewed elsewhere (see *Salapatek & Banks, vol. II, chap. 1*). In brief, even newborn infants can discriminate between certain patterns, such as a bull's-eye and a checkerboard, under optimal conditions (Fantz, 1961). The basis of many of their discriminations seems to be the density of contour in a pattern (Karmel, 1969) or the curvature of individual contours (Fantz, Fagan, & Miranda, 1975).

Infants also perceive relational information in two-dimensional drawings. As noted in the section on the layout, Schwartz and Day (1979) studied the ability of 8- to 17-week-old infants to perceive very simple outline forms, such as angles, forked figures, and squares in various orientations. Angular relationships in such figures appeared to be perceived as invariant over rotation in the picture plane. Bornstein and his coworkers (Bornstein, Gross, & Wolf, 1978; Bornstein, Ferdinandsen, & Gross, 1981) investigated infants' perception of vertical symmetry in random patterns. Infants habituated more rapidly to symmetrical than to asymmetrical patterns, provided that the two halves of the pattern were suitably close together. Infants evidently detected the redundancy in vertically symmetrical patterns and perceived their structure more economically. By kindergarten age, and perhaps before, children are sensitive to horizontal symmetry (Boswell, 1976). Use of other kinds of redundancy in a pattern appears to emerge later in childhood (Chipman, 1977; Chipman & Mendelson, 1975).

One study suggests that young infants perceive a triangle as a coherent form. Milewski (1979) presented 3-month-old infants with a series of visual displays, each containing three dots in the shape of a triangle. In different displays, the sizes and positions of the dots (and, hence, the size of the triangle) varied, yet a triangle could always be seen by adults, with the three dots as vertices. Infants were presented with these displays, contingent on a suck of high amplitude. The presentations continued until their high-amplitude sucking habituated to a criterion level. Then infants were shown new displays of three dots forming a straight line. They dishabituated to this change in configuration.

Adults perceive contours in a two-dimensional array where no physical contour is given if other contours of the array follow certain constraints specifying an occluding surface. This tendency has traditionally been considered a demonstration of perceiving higher order relations (Kanizsa, 1976; see also Michotte et al., 1964, on amodal completion). Bertenthal, Campos, and Haith (1980), using the habituation method, found evidence of sensitivity to such contours in two-dimensional displays with 7-month-old but not 5-month-old infants.

Another difference between young and older infants has been found when the infant is presented with simple embedded patterns. Salapatek observed the scanning patterns of infants who viewed simple figures containing one embedded element (see Salapatek, 1975, for a general discussion). Infants under 2 months tended to scan only the external boundary of these figures; infants over 2 months scanned the internal boundary as well. Salapatek speculated that the younger infants were insensitive to the embedded form. Evidence consistent with this claim was provided by Milewski (1976), using a high-amplitude sucking procedure. Infants of 1 and 4 months sucked to bring to view one of Salapatek's (1975) embedded displays. After sucking had habituated, either the external or the internal figure in the display was changed in form, for example, a square embedded in a circle might change to a square embedded in a triangle or a triangle embedded in a circle. Infants of 4 months dishabituated to either change. Infants of 1 month dishabituated only to a change in the external figure. Sensitivity to embedded forms in a pictorial display appears to develop some time after 1 month.

Although young infants do not appear sensitive to an internal figure in a static display, they might be sensitive to internal regions of an object if those regions moved independently of the surrounding contour. I. W. R. Bushnell (1979) tested and confirmed this suggestion. He presented 1- and 3-month-old infants with an embedded form, such as those used by Milewski (1976) and Salapatek (1975), in a habituation-of-looking time procedure. In the first study, the display was stationary. As expected, 3-month-olds dishabituated to a change in the internal form, but 1-month-olds did not. In a second study, the internal form moved back and forth inside the stationary external form during both habituation and test. This movement had a marked effect on the younger infants' perception; they now dishabituated to a change in the internal element. A further experiment indicated that the movement of the internal element relative to the boundary was critical, not just the presence of movement per se. I. W. R. Bushnell (1979) concluded that young infants can perceive embedded forms in a display, but only if their movement segregates them from the rest of the display. Similar conclusions were reached by Girton (1979), who presented 5-week-old infants with eyes moving in a schematic face.

Perceiving Representations

Objects in Pictures

The ability to recognize an object in a picture appears to develop quite early. This has been demonstrated in studies of discrimination learning in which children are trained to respond differently to each of two objects or pictures and then are transferred to the opposite mode. For example, Steinberg (1974) trained children from 2 to 3 years old to discriminate among toy farm animals and then observed their transfer to pictures of the animals. Successful transfer was observed at 28 months, although not at 24 months. However, using a somewhat different procedure, Daehler, Perlmutter, and Myers (1976) obtained nearly perfect transfer from objects to pictures, and the reverse, at 2 years.

Most 2-year-olds have had considerable experience with pictures, playing games in which pictured objects are named. Yet, one study indicates that such experience is not necessary for the development of the ability to identify objects in pictures (Hochberg & Brooks, 1962), and more recent studies indicate that the ability to perceive certain objects in pictures is present at birth. Many of these studies involve pictures of faces, and have already been reviewed. For example, we have noted that newborn infants follow visually a picture of a regular face more than a scrambled face (Goren et al., 1975) and infants recognize the mother in a photograph by 3 months of age (Barrera & Maurer, 1981). Finally, infants of 5 months show some recognition of an unfamiliar person in a photograph. Dirks and Gibson (1977) presented infants of 5 months with a live, unfamiliar face for habituation. After looking time had declined, infants were shown photographs of the same face, one of different sex, skin color, and hairstyle, or one of the same sex, coloring, and hairstyle. Habituation generalized to the photograph of the same face and the similar one, but not to the one with very different features. These studies indicate that young infants can perceive some similarity between a face and a photograph of a face. As we already noted in the review of face perception, however, infants seem to be less sensitive to a face in a still photograph than to a face that is three-dimensional and animate.

Transfer from three-dimensional patterned arrays to photographs of them was demonstrated by Rose (1977) in 6-month-old infants. The patterns were simple designs, like a sunburst or an arrangement of four diamonds. Infants could visually differentiate a three-dimensional pattern from its representation and could also transfer responding from pictures to objects. DeLoache, Strauss, and Maynard (1979) investigated recognition of pictures of objects of varying degrees of fidelity to the object in infants of 5 months. Infants were familiarized with a real doll and given preference tests with the same doll and a new one or with photographs of the two dolls in color or in black and white. Infants showed a reliable preference for looking at the novel doll in all three conditions. In a second experiment, color photographs of two faces of women served as familiarization stimuli; black-and-white photographs and line drawings of the two faces as well as color photographs served as test stimuli. Infants tended to look longer at pictures of the novel person in all cases.

The Spatial Layout in Pictures

Can infants perceive a layout of objects in depth when given a static pictorial representation? It now appears that they can, as early as 6½ months of age, under certain restricted conditions. But infants and young children are less apt to perceive depth relationships in pictures than are older children and adults.

Yonas, Cleaves, and Petterson (1978) obtained evidence for pictorial depth perception through a study of reaching to a flat object whose spatial orientation was specified by perspective information. Infants were presented with a frontal trapezoid that was patterned so that it appeared (to adults) to be a slanted rectangular window (Ames, 1951). In one condition, infants viewed the window binocularly; thus, the frontal orientation of one window was specified by binocular disparity, whereas pictorial information suggested an oblique orientation. In the other condition, infants viewed the window monocularly; thus, less information for the true orientation was available to conflict with the pictorial information for a slanted surface. If the infants perceived the stimulus as a rectangular surface slanting in depth, they would be expected to reach for the pictorially "near" side. The 6-month-old infants reached more often to that side in the monocular condition, but not in the binocular condition. Infants of 5 months and younger reached equally to both sides under both conditions. Yonas, Cleaves, & Petterson (1978) concluded that 6-month-olds are sensitive to pictorial information for a three-dimensional layout, whereas 5-month-olds are not clearly so. They further concluded that when pictorial and stereoscopic depth information are placed in conflict, the latter wins.

These findings are consistent with the now large literature on pictorial depth perception in childhood. In brief, it has been found that children are sensitive to pictorial depth information, but they use this information less accurately than adults. Moreover, children's depth perception is facilitated by conditions that reduce information for two-dimensionality of the picture surface. For example, 3-year-olds appear to use linear perspective as information about the relative sizes of two objects in a picture if the objects pictured are three-dimensional and firmly planted on the surface (Benson & Yonas, 1973; Yonas & Hagen, 1973), but not if the objects are two-dimensional forms (Wilcox & Teghtsoonian, 1971), perhaps because such forms can appear to "float" above the perspective drawing (Benson & Yonas, 1973). Older children and adults use pictorial information for relative size in both cases. As another example, first graders, like adults, can use a texture gradient as information about the slant of a surface, but the accuracy of their judgments of slant increases with age (Degelman & Rosinski, 1976; Rosinski & Levine, 1976).

The above studies suggest that there are quantitative improvements with age in sensitivity to pictorial information for depth, particularly texture gradients and linear perspective. There may be qualitative changes as well, as the child becomes sensitive to new kinds of pictorial information for the relative distances of two objects. Children as young as 2 years have been shown to be sensitive to interposition in a distance-judgment task—an object was reported to be nearer than a second object when the first object occluded part of the second object in the picture (R. K. Olson, 1975; Olson & Boswell, 1976). Using reaching as a measure, Yonas & Granrud (1981) obtained evidence for sensitivity to interposition in 7-month-old infants as well. Young children are also sensitive to relative height in the picture plane as information for depth (Benson & Yonas, 1973; R. K. Olson, 1975; Olson & Boswell, 1976). But very young children do not consistently perceive the smaller of two objects as being farther away if all other information for depth

is removed from the picture (R. K. Olson, 1975; Olson & Boswell, 1976; but see also Yonas & Granrud, 1981).

A second kind of change concerns the child's use of shading as information for the shape and depth of an object. Children as young as 3 years are sensitive to shading information when the pictured objects are lit from above and they are viewed in their normal orientation (Benson & Yonas, 1973; Yonas, Goldsmith, & Hallstrom, 1978). But young children can be misled by shading information if the direction of lighting is not the usual one and particularly if the direction of lighting in the picture differs from the direction of lighting in the testing room (Hagen, 1976; Yonas, Kuskowski, & Sternfels, 1979). In this respect, children may have difficulty perceiving a picture as independent of the surroundings in which it is viewed.

A third kind of change concerns the child's perception of suggested movement in pictures. Movement of an object in a picture may be conveyed in a variety of ways, but most fall into two categories. First, an object is perceived to be moving if it is depicted in an unstable position, for example, a person in a running posture with legs off the ground. Second, an object may be perceived to be moving if its motion is represented by cartoon conventions, such as lines or clouds of dust to represent vibrations or swift motion forward. Friedman and Stevenson (1975) presented children aged 4, 6, and 12 as well as adults with cartoon figures of a person whose movement was depicted posturally or conventionally. All the subjects were sensitive to the postural information for movement. Only the sixth graders and adults, however, were sensitive to the conventional information for movement.

A final developmental change is perhaps the most interesting. When adults view a picture at an oblique angle, the perspective information they receive is distorted. Yet, adults appear to perceive the pictured spatial array more or less as the artist intended it to be, not according to the oblique projection received from their less-than-optimal station point. Studies of the development of this ability have uncovered a complex pattern of change (Hagen, 1976; Hagen & Elliott, 1976; Hagen & Jones, 1978). In general, adults are better able to perceive the spatial properties of objects from an oblique view than are children, provided that the surface qualities of the picture are made obvious. Adults are better able to perceive from an oblique view if they can detect what the angular orientation of the picture plane is. For 4-year-old children, perception of the spatial properties of a pictured object is less accurate from an oblique view than from the "correct" station point. Hagen (1976) speculates that a mechanism compensating for an oblique view develops over the course of childhood.

Hagen's (1976) work underscores what she calls the special character of pictorial perception. On one hand, pictures incorporate information that also specifies the three-dimensionality of the normal spatial layout—the gradients of texture that are produced when one textured plane is projected from one point onto another plane. On the other hand, a picture presents a special kind of optic array that captures the properties of the layout only in a frozen moment of time, from a single point of observation and on a two-dimensional surface. To perceive the layout in a picture, one must attend to the scene that is depicted rather than to the picture as an object. To perceive movement in pictures, one must detect the instability of an object's position or follow certain artistic conventions. To perceive spatial relationships from an oblique station point, one must detect the invariant relation between one's own perspective and the artist's perspective. Even young infants can perceive objects in pictures and are sensitive to certain pictorial information for the layout. But perception seems to progress toward recognizing the special character of pictures, perceiving both their three-dimensionality and their two-dimensionality, both movement and stasis, and both the layout and a projection of the layout.

AFFORDANCES: PERCEIVING FOR SOME PURPOSE

Three Views

In our view, perception is intrinsically active, purposeful, and meaningful. Perception is active and purposive because it results from a search for invariance, be this the scanning of a newborn infant who follows a moving object or the systematic exploration of a biologist examining tissue under a microscope. Perception is inherently meaningful because we perceive the affordances of the world—the possibilities for action that are offered by the objects, events, and places that surround us. The gropings of a newborn are as actively oriented toward the discovery of possibilities for action as are the investigations of an adult.

The perception of affordances undoubtedly develops. As the child acquires new knowledge about the world and develops new capacities to act in it, her exploration becomes more diversified and her goals become more specific and explicit. As adults, we are often aware that we are perceiving for some purpose—to avoid the oncoming traffic, to locate our spectacles, to make out the handwriting of a student's midterm essay, to learn how to operate a new tool that someone is demonstrating. Yet, the perception of a 15-month-old trying to steer a spoon to her mouth seems equally purposeful, however incapable the child is of describing her purposes.

Many perceptual theories have denied that perception is inherently purposeful and oriented to action. To those who adopt the perspective of traditional learning theory, for example, perception is not guided by any intrinsic purpose at all. The goals of perception are provided by the environment through positive and negative reinforcement. Thus, perception is itself a passive process, one devoid of intrinsic meaning and incapable, in itself, of bringing knowledge. From this view, we do not perceive affordances but merely learn to respond in certain ways to certain patterns of stimulation. What appears to be the perception of meaning is really the association of responses to meaningless patterns of sensation.

For those who view perception from the perspective of information-processing theory as well, perception is passive and devoid of meaning. An information-processing theorist would contend that the goals of perception are not intrinsic to perception but are provided by cognitive representations and the relations that those representations express. From this view, affordances are not perceived; knowledge of affordances results from the interpretation, or categorization, of sensory information through operations on mental representations. These representations and operations are also sometimes conceived to be associative in nature.

These three perspectives differ in their accounts of how new affordances are learned. A traditional learning theorist would contend that this development depends on the acquisition of new forms of behavior through reinforcement; an information processing theorist would contend that this development depends on the construction of new mental representations, or categories, again perhaps by association. We suggest that this development depends on the search for, and detection of, new invariants and transformations in arrays of stimulation.

Affordances and Action

Exploration aimed at the discovery of new affordances would seem to begin in earliest infancy (see

Exploring and Attending). From the beginning of life, infants tend to look and listen to objects with the most important affordances. For example, the voice of the mother is selectively attended to in a field of noise (Benson, 1978), and infants will act to make it available if possible (DeCasper & Fifer, 1980). As children grow, however, they make greater and greater efforts to discover new affordances through active exploration.

This exploration becomes very pronounced in the second year of life, as was described vividly by Piaget (1952). Piaget noted that his children, beginning at about 12 months of age, began to act on the world systematically in new ways to observe the consequences of those actions. For example, he describes how Jacqueline, in her bath:

> engages in many experiments with celluloid toys floating on the water. At 1,1 (20) and the days following, not only does she drop her toys from a height to see the water splash or displace them with her hand in order to make them swim, but she pushes them half way down in order to see them rise to the surface. (Piaget, 1952, p. 273)

It seems very likely that children discover many of the basic affordances of the world through such experimentation.

Active experimentation also brings the child information about tools. Piaget (1952, pp. 279 ff.) has described how a child learns to use a string that is attached to an object as a means to bring the desired object within reach. At first, the child reaches for the object directly, ignoring the string. At other times, he may pull the string but without noticing the systematic effect of this action on the location of the object. Finally, the child grasps the relation between the position of the string and the position of the object. In the future, the string will serve as an instrument that can be used to retrieve that object (see also H. M. Richardson, 1932). In these cases, the child does not appear to learn through random trial and error. He actively searches for information about the invariant relationships between objects and the affordances for action that they provide.

If the instrument in question is more specialized, the process of discovering its affordances is more involved. Koslowski and Bruner (1972) examined in detail the strategies employed by children learning to use a rotating lazy Susan lever to bring a toy into reach (see also Piaget, 1952, p. 284; H. M. Richardson, 1934). The children were between 12 and 24 months of age. A bar rested on a rotatable circular platform, the whole mounted on a table beside which the child was placed. A toy was secured to one end of the bar, directly opposite the child, but out of reach. At first the children maneuvered directly along the line of sight of the toy, reaching for it, then pushing or pulling on the lever. The next step was discovery of rotation: the bar was simply oscillated back and forth, an interesting affordance of its own. If the child was somehow distracted from operation of the lever and caught sight of the goal, he reached for it if it was nearby. It was necessary to focus on rotating the lever, to the momentary exclusion of the goal, and then to detect the goal's position. Finally the child discovered the lever/goal relation. Discovery of this affordance depended on perception of a relationship between two events, the rotation of the lever and the movement of the object. Moreover, each event had to be perceived in relation to the child's actions of turning the lever and of reaching for the goal object. Once this relationship was detected, it was highly generalizable— an affordance had been discovered for a kind of tool.

As children grow, they perceive the affordances of more and more tools as they discover the relationship between a tool and the consequences that it can produce. A child of 5 knows, for example, that the slicing of an apple can be accomplished with a knife and the cutting of paper accomplished with scissors (Gelman et al., 1980). These discoveries appear to come about as the child acts on objects with other objects, perceiving both the transformations that his actions bring and the properties of objects that they leave invariant.

In all of the above examples, children discover the affordances of objects as they act on them directly. But children also discover affordances by observing objects being transformed by others. As studies of observational learning reveal, children are often attentive to the actions of other people on objects, and they are apt to repeat those actions (see Stevenson, 1970, for a review). We think that they do so because the actions of others provide information about the affordances of the world. An experiment by Bandura and Menlove (1968) illustrates change in the perceived affordance of a class of objects through observation. A group of children who were markedly fearful of dogs was shown a series of films in which models interacted nonanxiously with dogs of varying size and fearsomeness. Significant reductions in the children's avoidance behavior resulted.

In summary, the perceived affordances of objects change with experience. As the child observes objects participating in events and as he acts on those objects himself, he discovers more and more of their possibilities for action. We believe that this learning brings a change in the child's perception of those objects, not merely a change in the child's responses to certain stimuli as a traditional learning theorist might contend. A theory of response learning by association fails to account for the active nature of exploration in the cases we have described. It also overlooks the information in stimulation, the invariant relationships that can specify an affordance and lead to perceiving the object in a new relation to other things and to the perceiver. Information about these relations specifies the object's affordance and is abstracted from all other information about it. The extraction of new information specifying an affordance usually has two interrelated consequences: (1) differentiation of the object from otherwise similar objects lacking the affordance and (2) perception of correspondences between different objects with the same affordance. We now consider these two kinds of change.

Affordances and Differentiation

When a child or an adult explores the distinctive affordances of a set of very similar objects, he learns to differentiate among those objects. The fledgling bird watcher learns to differentiate between a nuthatch and a chickadee; the novice little leaguer learns to distinguish a fast ball from a slider; the apprentice carpenter learns to discriminate walnut veneer from mahogany. Studies of differentiation are now legion, and have been discussed in detail (E. J. Gibson, 1969). Unfortunately, these studies were rarely carried out with real objects and events—the kinds of things that we most often learn to differentiate in the natural world. It may be that it is difficult to specify what the basis for differentiation could be in an interesting and internally confusable set of natural objects: What is the information by which we identify a chickadee? A human face? Nevertheless, real objects and events appear to be the first things that children differentiate.

Other people are objects with particularly varied and important affordances for infants, and infants begin to differentiate them at birth. Research on the development of perception of human faces was described earlier. It is notable that the earliest distinction made seems to be between faces and nonfaces. The usual misleads presented have been bizarre arrangements of facial structure. As we pointed out,

this research does not reveal how one face is distinguished from another, nor do we know exactly how adults recognize faces. It seems likely, however, that we recognize particular faces by detecting certain invariant relationships in the face, in particular its unique configuration of features (Carey, 1978). Sensitivity to these invariants may develop rather slowly. The research to date suggests that whereas children do recognize particular people at an early age, they do so by relying more than adults do on superficial characteristics (e.g., a hairstyle), at least when they are given only momentary static information, such as a photograph. But it remains possible that infants would abstract invariant properties of a face if they observed a person in action.

One recent study has been taken to suggest that infants do not analyze component features of faces at all. Fagan and Singer (1979) presented infants 5 to 6 months old with photographs of babies or adults of either sex who were similar or dissimilar in some gross features, such as hair (bald vs. full heads of hair), face shape (round or oval), eyebrows (prominent or not), and so on. The photographs were selected so that pairs of faces disparate in age or sex were judged as having fewer feature differences than pairs of same sex or age. The method was familiarization followed by a preference test. Faces judged as similar in many features but different in age or sex were easily discriminated by the infants, but pairs of like-sex, like-age faces with features rated very dissimilar were not distinguished. This finding seems to rule out feature analysis as the basis of the infants' discrimination of faces, but only on the assumption that the experimenter manipulated the right set of features. A possible difficulty may be that features were judged as absolute, whereas the information that distinguishes one face from another is relational. For example, features like eyebrows are embedded in a larger facial structure. Because the larger structure appears to be differentiated first, it seems likely that the embedded structures would be segregated, whenever they are, in relation to the larger structure rather than as isolated components. Indeed, if infants were not sensitive to some relational structure, it is hard to see how they could differentiate between faces of differing ages and sex.

A wealth of research on discrimination of alphanumeric characters and forms suggests that children of school age become increasingly sensitive to contrastive relations in this domain (see Gibson & Levin, 1975, for a review). How does such skill improve? An experiment by A. D. Pick (1965) sought to compare two hypotheses. According to the schema hypothesis, sensory input about objects is matched to a representation of the object that has been built through repeated experience and is stored in memory. Improvement in discriminating or identifying objects would occur as new schemes are constructed. According to the differentiation hypothesis, subjects learn the contrastive relations that serve to distinguish among the items. Improvement consists of discovering the transformations by which the members of the set are distinguished from one another. A. D. Pick's experiment utilized letterlike forms to be discriminated by kindergarten children. A training session with a set of standard forms and three transformations of each of them was followed by one of three transfer conditions. In one (a base condition) a new set of standards and three new transformations of them were presented for discrimination. In a second, the original standards were presented along with new transformations of each of them. In a third, there were new standards, but the same transformations for each of them were presented. Both conditions two and three yielded positive transfer compared to the base condition, but group three (retaining the transformations already learned about) showed most facilitation. A. D. Pick carried out further experiments with comparable forms and transformations adapted for tactual discrimination. When the subject felt the forms to be discriminated successively, conditions two and three were both superior to the base condition but did not differ from one another. In another experiment, tactual discrimination was carried out simultaneously, one form being explored by each hand. In this case, only condition three (same transformations retained) was facilitated. Differentiation depended in large part on the discovery of the transformations defining critical contrastive relations within the set of forms.

A large number of experiments on learning to discriminate letterlike forms and real letters have been performed since A. D. Pick's experiment, many of them providing training in the discovery of contrastive relationships (e.g., Samuels, 1973). Comparisons of such training with other methods of learning to discriminate and identify forms have often been made. Silver and Rollins (1973), for example, compared acquisition and transfer of letterlike forms following both visual and verbal emphasis on contrastive relations, visual or verbal emphasis alone, or observation of the forms without such emphasis. Visual emphasis of the distinctions among forms was most effective. Zelniker and Oppenheimer (1973, 1976) compared several methods of training impulsive children to discriminate letterlike forms. Training in differentiating transformations was more effective than training in matching identical forms.

Because the objects presented in these tasks were created by the experimenter and depended necessarily on the transformations that were built into the material, the results may not capture the course of perceptual differentiation of natural objects. It does seem appropriate to conclude, however, that in tasks where distinctions must be made, children come increasingly to attend to the relevant contrastive relationships among objects. As they attend to more and more of these relationships, perception becomes increasingly differentiated. Moreover, it seems to us that this differentiation is brought about through the child's efforts to distinguish objects with different affordances. The affordances of the material used in these tasks are far removed from the affordances of a human face, a hammer, or a baseball pitch. Nevertheless, perception becomes differentiated in all these cases because each object has distinctive affordances within the context of the task. A child of school age knows that alphabetic characters have affordances—they mark the crucial distinctions between one word and another in written language. The child becomes able to act on the affordances as he differentiates between letters by detecting the invariant relationships that distinguish them.

Affordances and Categorization

Discriminably different objects may have the same affordances. A cup, a glass, and a jar all afford containment of water and drinking—emptying their contents into the mouth. The characters t, T, and *t* all afford distinguishing the word *table* from *cable* or *fable*. When a child is engaged in a task and is oriented toward the discovery of the relevant affordances for that task, she will focus on those invariant properties of all containers or all Ts that specify their common affordance. It could be said that she treats all those different objects equivalently and that all of them form a category for her.

One of the clearest cases of perceptual equivalence arises in the domain of speech perception. Phonemic distinctions are made categorically along many of the acoustic dimensions on which speech gestures differ, such as voice-onset-time and place of articulation. Stimulus samples ranging along a physical continuum, such as voice-onset-time, are identified over a considerable range as corresponding to a single articulatory gesture. Moreover, discrimination among them seems to be poor, at least in certain tasks. The end of this range appears to constitute a sharp boundary, partitioning off another distinct category when it is crossed; discrimination at this boundary is high. Categorical perception of speech was first noted with adult subjects (Liberman, Harris, Kinney, & Lane, 1961; Lisker & Abramson, 1970) and led to the notion that there was a special, learned mode for perceiving speech.

About 10 years after the original discovery, the role of learning came to be questioned. Experiments by Eimas et al. (1971) indicated that categorical perception of speech gestures differing in voice-onset-time was present in very young human infants. Experiments on infants' categorical perception of phonemic distinctions now abound (see Aslin & Pisoni, 1980; Eimas, 1975; Jusczyk, 1979; Strange & Jenkins, 1978, for recent summaries). There is evidence, however, that infants born into one language group perceive certain phonemic distinctions categorically even though their parents do not, that is, despite the lack of a categorical distinction in the language they are hearing. Nature seems to have provided for sensitivity to all the contrasts that different languages embody, but learning is presumably responsible for the increasing correspondence between phonemic perception and the phonological structure of a given language.

Many species of animals, insects as well as vertebrates, have evolved auditory systems that are selectively attuned to those classes of acoustic information that have utility for them, particularly information specifying gestures of other conspecifics (Marler, 1970). A nice example of this selectivity is the sensitivity to predator alarm calls in vervet monkeys. Adult monkeys give alarm calls for predators that are specific to different classes of predators and elicit appropriate defensive behavior (e.g., snake alarms elicit looking to the ground, whereas eagle alarms elicit looking up and running into dense bush). Infants respond to these alarm calls, but their responses are generalized to nonpredators and are not sharply differentiated. Even for infants, however, alarm calls are differentiated according to relatively general predator classes in relation to appropriate behavior. Further differentiation of affordances of species within a class develops with experience (Seyfarth, Cheney, & Marler, 1980).

Human infants and adults are said to perceive speech categorically. What does this mean? Cognitive theorists have provided two different accounts of categorization. Some have proposed that the child detects certain discrete attributes of an item (in this case, an utterance) and categorizes the item in accordance with a rule specifying those attributes all items in a particular category have in common. Others have proposed that the child has a representation of an ideal example, or prototype, corresponding to each category and that he categorizes incoming items in terms of their similarity to each of the prototypes. But neither of these accounts seems very plausible when applied to speech perception in infancy. A third view proposes that the child performs no special act of categorization but rather detects certain dynamic invariant relations in the acoustic waveform—relations that correspond to phonemic distinctions based on articulatory gestures of a speaker (Bailey & Summerfield, 1980). These invariants are abstract and potentially intermodal (MacDonald & McGurk, 1978).

Each of these views provides a different general account of the categorization of natural objects. The view that all categorization depends on a rule defined over a set of attributes has been predominant in psychology and has played a major role in philosophy and linguistics as well. To study the development of categorization, psychologists have generally made use of highly artificial material, such as combinations of forms and colors or schematic line drawings of faces with fixed numbers of attributes combined by a rule arbitrarily imposed by the experimenter. The subject is forced to abstract a rule to describe a class of items, each of which is obliged to possess the defining attributes. But we doubt that the natural concepts of infants or children are abstractions from a few dimensions. By 28 or 30 weeks, infants can categorize photographs of real faces as those of a man or woman (Cohen & Strauss, 1979; Cornell, 1974; Fagan, 1976) and real voices as those of a man or woman (Miller, Younger, & Morse, 1980). In these cases, it seems unlikely that the infants are constructing a class on the basis of a few discrete attributes shared by every token. The experimenters themselves could define no such combination over the variety of exemplars they provided.

As has been noted many times, it is hard to define any natural concept completely in terms of a set of physical attributes. In light of this difficulty, it has been argued that natural categories do not have sharply defined boundaries nor a logical definition that presupposes a small set of discrete attributes or components shared by all members. Instead, categories in nature are organized around a prototype or best example to which other members of the category are related to a greater or lesser degree (Rosch, 1973a, 1973b; Rosch & Mervis, 1975; Wittgenstein, 1953).

Rosch's work began with categorization of colors and forms, but she subsequently focused on categories of natural objects that share clear affordances, for example, furniture, tools, and vehicles. Unfortunately, it is difficult to describe such categories in terms of a prototype and members that are globally similar to it. A car may be a prototypical vehicle, but a toy car—which is not a vehicle at all and lacks its principal affordance—is featurally more similar to the prototype than is another genuine vehicle, such as a sailboat. In view of such problems, Rosch and Mervis (1975) described the prototypes of these categories not in terms of global similarity, but in terms of features—mostly physical attributes—and they rooted the process of categorization in the analysis of features and the applications of rules, much as do the psychologists whose view of concepts Rosch opposes. Thus, many of the problems of the older approach remain.

A different view of concepts and categories emerges if one acknowledges that perception is always abstract and meaningful and that normal perception always depends on the detection of invariance over change. From this view, the acquisition of a concept depends on the extraction of invariance over transforming events. For example, consider a particular kind of affordance, that of rigidity of substance. A rigid object in motion is differentiated, whatever its trajectory, from an object changing its form (Johansson, von Hofsten, & Jansson, 1980). As we have noted, invariant information for rigidity of substance is differentiated from elasticity of substance in infants as early as 3 months (see *Obtaining Information About Objects*). The objects used in these experiments (E. J. Gibson et al., 1978; E. J. Gibson et al., 1979) were identical in all their static properties; no static presentation of the object ever occurred. Therefore, the information for rigidity versus elasticity had to be the invariant provided by the contrasting types of motion. Whether one calls the perception of rigidity over perspective transformations a concept depends on what one thinks a concept is. If one believes (as we do not) that perception is concrete and conception is abstract and that to have a concept is to apply an abstract rule to a set of concrete exemplars, then these experiments say nothing about the concept of rigidity. The infants in these experiments cannot be storing a set of discrete, frozen images of an object, applying some rule to each image, and abstracting a category. They are detecting invariance and change

in a continuous stimulus flow. The end product of their activity is not, we think, the construction of a category representation in the mind, but the perception of an affordance of the world.

As a second example, consider a very different set of concepts, concepts of number. The number of objects or events in a collection contributes greatly to the affordances of that collection—affordances for action often depend on the number of pennies in one's hand or the number of times one has been caught speeding on the highway. It is now clear that young infants are sensitive to the number of objects in a display or the number of events in a sequence, provided that the total number is small. For example, Starkey et al. (1980) presented 6- to 8-month-old infants with a series of photographic slides of arrays of natural objects (see also Strauss & Curtis, 1981). For infants in one group, every slide in the series contained two objects; for the infants in the other group, every slide contained three objects. The particular objects within each slide were heterogeneous—they varied in color, shape, and size. Moreover, the objects changed from one slide to the next, and their configuration changed as well (in slides of three objects, the objects could form any of a large set of differently shaped triangles or differently oriented lines). The infants in both groups were habituated to the slides in these series. After habituation, they looked hardly at all at slides of new objects in new configurations if the number of objects remained the same. When a display containing a different number of objects was presented, infants looked with renewed attention. It seems, therefore, that infants can detect a very abstract invariant property—the number of objects in a display—over changes in the particular objects and their configurations. Subsequent studies (Starkey, Spelke, & Gelman, 1982) revealed that infants 6 to 8 months old can detect a numerical invariance over even greater changes—they detect a correspondence between the number of visible objects in a spatial layout and the number of audible beats in a temporal sequence.

There is, of course, more to the human conception of number than these experiments reveal. For an adult, numbers form an ordered series; it is not clear if this is so for infants. Moreover, adults appreciate that different numbers are related by transformations of addition and subtraction. Preschool children appear to know this as well (Gelman, 1972), but it is not certain whether infants do. It seems likely, as Gelman speculates, that the operations of addition and subtraction come to be understood by children as they witness the application of those transformations to actual collections, observing the reversible nature of the transformations and discovering their effects on the number of objects in the collections. Conceptions of number also appear to develop as the child acts on collections of objects to produce a very important reversible event, counting (Gelman & Gallistel, 1978).

Whether or not one considers the abstraction of number as a perceptual or a conceptual achievement depends, once again, on what one means by these terms. Yet, number concepts illustrate the continuity of perception and cognition. Like concepts of substance, number cannot easily be viewed as the application of a rule to concrete physical attributes: What are the attributes of *three*? Neither is number easily viewed as organized around a prototype (see Armstrong, Gleitman, & Gleitman, in press). Instead, it seems that number is an abstract property of a set of objects or events that is invariant over a particular set of transformations. Number is abstracted over changes in the color, size, or spatial configuration of objects. Specific numbers are distinguished from each other by other transformations—addition and subtraction. Children appear to come to understand number as they observe these transformations and discover both the changes they bring and the properties they leave unchanged.

From our view, there is no firm line to be drawn between perception and cognition as the child gains knowledge of the affordances of the world—affordances that eventually are given conceptual descriptions, such as rigid, square, animal, or three. Knowledge of all these properties depends on the detection of invariance over change. As the child grows, he will discover things about substance, form, animacy, and number that he cannot perceive, discoveries that are formalized in science and mathematics. These discoveries may depend on innate and developing structures that are not related in a direct way to the child's perceptual systems. But the underlying continuity between perception and conception remains. Both perception and conception are abstract and meaningful. Both depend on the detection of invariance and are directed to the discovery of affordances. Both perceptual and conceptual knowledge are always less specific than the infinitely dense and variable world that is there to be known. Meaningful groupings of objects and events in the world inevitably result from the very nature of perception itself. No special act of categorization need be postulated to explain them.

It would be a mistake to think that information in the world is so random, unordered, piecemeal, and unrelated that economy of perception could only be achieved by forming categories on the basis of arbitrary and accidental combinations of recurring elements. Order and invariance exist in nature. Perception shows a trend toward economy by abstracting from changing temporal contexts the order that exists.

Overview

We have suggested that perception is inherently purposeful. It results from an active search for invariants in stimulation, and it is oriented toward the discovery of the affordances of the world. This search leads to the differentiation of perception through the discovery of new contrastive relations between objects, a way of learning about the world (E. J. Gibson, 1969). It also leads to the discovery of affordances that different objects share, properties like rigidity and animacy.

Our view contrasts sharply with the approach of traditional learning theories to purpose and meaning in perception. Perception and action are interleaved, and the relation between them cannot easily be explained in terms of association and extrinsic reinforcement. Actions, both exploratory and performatory, reveal new affordances, and perception of new affordances makes possible new actions.

Our view also contrasts with the approach of information processing theories. Perception and cognition are interrelated, but perception does not depend on cognitive processes by which representations of meaningless sensory impressions are categorized and given meaning. Perception depends on the detection of invariance and change. The development of many concepts may depend, in turn, on detecting these invariant relationships.

Perception is an autonomous, developing domain of competence. It depends, for its development, on its own intrinsic processes of exploring, detecting invariance, and perceiving affordances.

THE COURSE OF PERCEPTUAL DEVELOPMENT: A SUMMING UP

To perceive is to monitor the environment and what happens in it in the service of guiding one's behavior. Perception depends on obtaining information about the environment from an array of potential stimulation. We have stressed three concepts in describing this process—exploration, discovery, and differentiation, and we have stressed the reciprocity between the animal and the environment through the concept of affordance.

Obtaining knowledge of the environment begins with exploring it. Different species of animals are endowed with different means of doing so. Some precocial animals seem to be extraordinarily ready to act on the perceived affordances of events such as the retreat of the mother; of places such as a surface that is safe for locomotion; and of things such as a grain that is edible. Humans are not a precocial species, but the means for exploring the events, objects, and layout of the world are adequate at birth to begin the long process of gaining knowledge about the surrounding environment and themselves in it. Means of exploring develop and become more skillful for many years—extending even into an adult's professional life when exploration with tools like telescopes and stethoscopes may be required—but the competence of the perceptual systems is impressive even in neonates.

Exploration results in the discovery of persisting aspects of the layout like ground, sky, and walls; of events like things approaching and things going away; and of properties of objects like their shape and substance. All of these have affordances for behavior, some of them probably perceived immediately as the infant actively explores by sucking and looking.

The third concept, differentiation, refers particularly to development (E. J. Gibson, 1969). Perceptual learning seems most appropriately thought of as a process of differentiation, of perceiving progressively more deeply embedded structure and more encompassing superordinate invariant relations. Progressive differentiation of structure is particularly obvious as children learn language or music. But it is also apparent in perceiving other events such as games, and in developing recognition of faces and objects such as toys and tools, although the latter have been little studied. The literature on developing perception of places seems especially well interpreted as a process of differentiation. Features of places, such as doorways, barriers, and dropoffs, are differentiated early (Carroll & Gibson, 1981; Walk & Gibson, 1961), but paths through a large space and places where things get lost are differentiated later as more far-ranging behavior needs guidance.

Perception of affordances develops along with differentiation of objects, places, and events; it is their affordances that are perceived. A toy may at first afford only grasping, later chewing, later rolling along the floor, still later taking apart, and finally fitting into a large construction of blocks, like a parking lot or a garage. A pair of pliers for a 12-month-old infant usually has the affordance of an object for banging and noise making. For the average adult, it has the affordance of a useful tool. Its affordance as a tool for a new purpose, such as weighting a pendulum, is not always apparent even to the adult, but it can be made to be if the adult looks at the pliers with a new requirement.

What kind of changes and continuities stand out in the course of development? We have found no indication of stages in perceptual development; continuity seems to be far more apparent than abrupt change. Five kinds of change are worthy of comment. First, there are changes in the selective, purposeful aspect of perception. Traditional theories have usually implied that perception is initially inflexible, unguided, and nonselective, but here is a case where continuity, as we look at the research of recent years, is remarkable. Exploration of the world appears to be directed and selective, to some extent at least, from the start. Selecting one event to follow, when more than one is going on, is a particularly striking case (Bahrick et al., 1981; Spelke, 1976). Nevertheless, perception comes to serve a greater range of purposes with development. Exploration becomes more systematic and makes more use of order in events and in the available information. Tasks become more specific as goals diversify and as other people's requirements constrain patterns of exploration (Gibson & Rader, 1979).

Second, awareness of affordances increases as children grow. We do not endorse the traditional view that perceptual development proceeds from the meaningless to the meaningful, from sensation to knowledge. Nevertheless, it is clear that children come to perceive new affordances of the world as they explore it. Again, development is continuous: the child discovers new affordances of a world that already has affordances for action.

Third, as differentiation occurs, perception increases in specificity (E. J. Gibson, 1969). Diversity and detail, fine structure, invariant relations and affordances of a greater subtlety are detected. At the same time, higher order structure is differentiated. But along with this increase in sensitivity to information about the world goes a fourth trend toward increasing economy. Perceiving becomes more efficient as exploratory skills increase and as the critical, minimal information for guiding action is detected. This change has often been noted in the past (E. J. Gibson, 1969) and research in recent years confirms it. There is continuity even here, for the youngest infant appears to search for invariants—the information for persisting structure over the maelstrom of change. As this search becomes successful, what is picked up is more and more what is sufficient for the task in hand. Guidance of skillful performance of motor tasks, like catching a moving object, is a nice case. At 4½ months, an infant aims predictively (von Hofsten, 1979, 1980), but guided movements later become fewer and more ballistic. An outfielder in a baseball game is so efficient at picking up the information for where the ball will be that it appears magical to the unskilled. Eye movements of comparison become more efficient in children as contrastive relations are detected. These cases show the interplay between perceiving and exploring.

The fifth change is the increasing generalizability of perceived affordances of things and places to new situations and to newly developing action systems. In early perceptual development, perceiving an affordance of an object for action may be effective only as a guide to limited actions in certain narrow contexts. Properties of things that have been detected through actions or through observations of events may be perceived, but often a child is slow to detect their utility when a different kind of action is required or a quite new task arises. Increasing ability to relate perceived affordances of things to new task demands and to different actions may be a key factor in perceptual development.

Metacognition has become a popular concept in developmental psychology (see Brown, Bransford, Ferrara & Campione, Vol. III, Chap. 2; Flavell, 1978). Do children become more aware of what they perceive and of the invariants that specify things in the world? This is an interesting question, and it is possible that developing awareness can hasten perceptual differentiation. But it is clear that a perceiver need not reflect on the properties of the world to perceive them. To perceive the world is not to describe it to oneself. It is to extract information about its affordances, information that keeps an active animal in touch with the world around it.

NOTES

1. This position was developed most clearly by Helmholtz, Wundt, and Titchener. An early opponent was Mach. See Johansson, 1978, and Johansson, von Hofsten, and Jansson, 1980, for a discussion of these opposing positions.

2. One should be wary of concluding that discrimination was impossible for the 4-month-old infants because negative evidence does not guarantee lack of competence, especially in the absence of a no-change control group. This danger has often been remarked by researchers who work with animals and preverbal children (Gibson & Olum, 1960; Kagan, Linn, Mount, & Reznick, 1979).

3. There are other, noneuclidean metric geometries that also preserve distance, angle, and all projective and topological properties. We do not discuss them here.

REFERENCES

Abravanel, E. The development of intersensory patterning with regard to selected spatial dimensions. *Monographs of the Society for Research in Child Development,* 1968, *38* (Serial No. 118).

Acredolo, L. P. Frames of reference used by children for orientation in unfamiliar spaces. In G. Moore & R. Golledge (Eds.), *Environmental knowing.* Stroudsburg, Pa.: Dowden, Hutchinson & Ross, 1976.

Acredolo, L. P. Developmental changes in the ability to coordinate perspectives of a large-scale space. *Developmental Psychology,* 1977, *13,* 1–8.

Acredolo, L. P. Development of spatial orientation in infancy. *Developmental Psychology,* 1978, *14,* 224–234.

Acredolo, L. P. Laboratory vs. home: The effect of environment on the 9-month-old infant's choice of spatial reference system. *Developmental Psychology,* 1979, *15,* 666–667.

Acredolo, L. P., & Evans, D. Developmental changes in the effects of landmarks on infant spatial behavior. *Developmental Psychology,* 1980, *16,* 312–318.

Adelson, E., & Fraiberg, S. Gross motor development in infants blind from birth. *Child Development,* 1974, *45,* 114–126.

Alegria, J., & Noirot, E. Neonate orientation behaviour toward human voice. *International Journal of Behavioral Development,* 1978, *1,* 291–312.

Alegria, J., & Noirot, E. On early development of oriented mouthing in neonates. In J. Mehler, M. Garrett, & E. Walker (Eds.), *Perspectives on mental representation*. Hillsdale, N.J.: Erlbaum, 1982.

Allen, G. L., Kirasic, K. C., Siegel, A. W., & Herman, J. F. Developmental issues in cognitive mapping: The selection and utilization of environmental landmarks. *Child Development*, 1979, *50*, 1062–1070.

Allen, T. W. Oral-oral and oral-visual object discrimination. Paper presented at the meeting of the International Conference on Infant Studies, Austin, Tex., March 1982.

Allen, T. W., Walker, L., Symonds, L., & Marcell, M. Intrasensory and intersensory perception of temporal sequences during infancy. *Developmental Psychology*, 1977, *13*, 225–229.

Ames, A. Visual perception and the rotating trapezoidal window. *Psychological Monographs*, 1951, *67*(7, Whole No. 324).

Ames, E., & Silfen, C. Methodological issues in the study of age differences in infants' attention to stimuli varying in movement and complexity. Paper presented at the meeting of the Society for Research in Child Development, Minneapolis, March 1965.

Anisfeld, M. Interpreting ''imitative'' responses in early infancy. *Science*, 1979, *205*, 214–215.

Anooshian, L. J., & McCulloch, R. A. Developmental changes in dichotic listening with categorized word lists. *Developmental Psychology*, 1979, *15*, 280–287.

Anooshian, L. J., & Prilop, L. Developmental trends for auditory selective attention: Dependence on central-incidental word relations. *Child Development*, 1980, *51*, 45–54.

Anooshian, L. J., & Wilson, K. L. Distance distortions in memory for spatial locations. *Child Development*, 1977, *48*, 1704–1707.

Armstrong, S., Gleitman, L. R., & Gleitman, H. On what some concepts might not be. *Cognition*, in press.

Aronfreed, J. The problem of imitation. In L. P. Lipsitt & H. W. Reese (Eds.), *Advances in child development and behavior* (Vol. 4). New York: Academic Press, 1968.

Ashmead, D. H., Lockman, J. J., & Bushnell, E. W. The development of anticipatory hand orientation during reaching. Paper presented at the meeting of the International Conference on Infant Studies, New Haven, Conn., April 1980.

Aslin, R. N., & Pisoni, D. B. Some developmental processes in speech perception. In G. Yeni-Komshian, J. F. Kavanaugh, & C. A. Ferguson (Eds.), *Child phonology: Perception and production*. New York: Academic Press, 1980.

Aslin, R. N., & Salapatek, P. Saccadic localization of visual targets by the very young human infant. *Perception and Psychophysics*, 1975, *17*, 293–302.

Bahrick, L. E. *Infants' perception of properties of objects as specified by amodal information in auditory-visual events*. Unpublished doctoral dissertation, Cornell University, 1980.

Bahrick, L. E., Walker, A. S., & Neisser, U. Selective looking by infants. *Cognitive Psychology*, 1981, *13*, 377–390.

Bailey, P. J., & Summerfield, Q. Information in speech: Observations on the perception of [s]-stop clusters. *Journal of Experimental Psychology: Perception and Performance*, 1980, *6*, 536–563.

Baker, R. A., Brown, K. W., & Gottfried, A. W. Ontogeny of tactile-visual cross-modal transfer. Paper presented at the meeting of the International Conference on Infant Studies, Austin, Tex., March 1982.

Ball, W. A. The perception of causality in the infant. Paper presented at the meeting of the Society for Research in Child Development, Philadelphia, March 1973.

Ball, W. A., & Tronick, E. Infant responses to impending collision: Optical and real. *Science*, 1971, *171*, 818–820.

Ball, W. A., & Vurpillot, E. Perception of movement in depth in infancy. *L'Année Psychologique*, 1976, *76*, 383–399.

Bandura, A., & Menlove, F. L. Factors determining vicarious extinction of avoidance behavior through symbolic modeling. *Journal of Personality and Social Psychology*, 1968, *8*, 99–108.

Barrera, M. E. The perception of facial expressions by the three-month-old. *Child Development*, 1981, *52*, 203–206.

Barrera, M. E., & Maurer, D. Recognition of mother's photographed face by the three-month-old infant. *Child Development*, 1981, *52*, 714–716.

Barron, R. W. Development of visual word recognition: A review. In T. G. Waller & G. E. Mackinnon (Eds.), *Reading research: Advances in theory and practice* (Vol. 2). New York: Academic Press, 1980.

Bassili, J. N. Temporal and spatial contingencies in the perception of social events. *Journal of Personality and Social Psychology*, 1976, *33*, 680–685.

Benson, K. A. The development of auditory figure-ground segregation in young infants. Paper presented at the meeting of the International Conference on Infant Studies, Providence, R.I., March 1978.

Benson, K. A., & Yonas, A. Development of sensitivity to static pictorial depth information. *Perception and Psychophysics, 1973, 13,* 361–366.

Bertenthal, B. I., Campos, J. J., & Haith, M. M. Development of visual organization: The perception of subjective contours. *Child Development, 1980, 51,* 1072–1080.

Bertenthal, B. I., & Profitt, D. R. Development of infant sensitivity to biomechanical motion. Paper presented at the International Conference on Infant Studies, Austin, Tex., March 1982.

Bertoncini, J., & Mehler, J. Syllables as units in infant speech perception. *Infant Behavior and Development, 1981, 4,* 247–260.

Bigelow, A. Object permanence for sound-producing objects: Parallels between blind and sighted infants. Paper presented at the meeting of the International Conference on Infant Studies, New Haven, Conn., April 1980.

Birch, H. G., & Lefford, A. Visual differentiation, intersensory integration, and voluntary motor control. *Monographs of the Society for Research in Child Development, 1967, 32,* 2(Serial No. 110).

Bjorkman, M. Relations between intra-modal and cross-modal matching. *Scandanavian Journal of Psychology, 1967, 8,* 65–76.

Bloom, K. Patterning of infant vocal behavior. *Journal of Experimental Child Psychology, 1977, 23,* 367–377.

Bluestein, N., & Acredolo, L. P. Developmental changes in map-reading skills. *Child Development, 1979, 50,* 691–697.

Bornstein, M., Ferdinandsen, K., & Gross, C. G. Perception of symmetry in infancy. *Developmental Psychology, 1981, 17,* 82–86.

Bornstein, M. H., Gross, C., & Wolf, J. Z. Perceptual similarity of mirror images in infancy. *Cognition, 1978, 6,* 89–116.

Borton, R. W. The perception of causality in infants. Paper presented at the meeting of the Society for Research in Child Development, San Francisco, March 1979.

Boswell, S. L. Young children's processing of symmetrical and asymmetrical patterns. *Journal of Experimental Child Psychology, 1976, 22,* 309–318.

Bower, T. G. R. The determinants of perceptual unity in infancy. *Psychonomic Science, 1965,*

3, 323–324.

Bower, T. G. R. The visual world of infants. *Scientific American, 1966, 215,* 80–92.

Bower, T. G. R. The development of object-permanence: Some studies of existence constancy. *Perception and Psychophysics, 1967, 2,* 411–418. (a)

Bower, T. G. R. Phenomenal identity and form perception in an infant. *Perception and Psychophysics, 1967, 2,* 74–76. (b)

Bower, T. G. R. Object perception in infants. *Perception, 1972, 1,* 15–30.

Bower, T. G. R. *Development in infancy.* San Francisco: W. H. Freeman, 1974.

Bower, T. G. R. *Human development.* San Francisco: W. H. Freeman, 1979.

Bower, T. G. R. *Development in infancy* (2nd ed). San Francisco: W. H. Freeman, 1982.

Bower, T. G. R., Broughton, J. M., & Moore, M. K. The coordination of visual and tactual input in infants. *Perception and Psychophysics, 1970, 8,* 51–53. (a)

Bower, T. G. R., Broughton, J. M., & Moore, M. K. Demonstration of intention in the reaching behavior of neonate humans. *Nature, 1970, 228,* 679–680. (b)

Bower, T. G. R., Broughton, J. M., & Moore, M. K. Development of the object concept as manifested in tracking behavior of infants between 7 and 20 weeks of age. *Journal of Experimental Child Psychology, 1971, 11,* 182–193. (a)

Bower, T. G. R., Broughton, J. M., & Moore, M. K. Infant responses to approaching objects: An indication of response to distal variables. *Perception and Psychophysics, 1971, 9,* 193–196. (b)

Bower, T. G. R., Dunkeld, J., & Wishart, J. G. Infant perception of visually presented objects (technical comment). *Science, 1979, 203,* 1137–1138.

Brazelton, T. B., Koslowski, B., & Main, M. The origins of reciprocity: The early mother-infant interaction. In M. Lewis & L. Rosenblum (Eds.). *The effect of the infant on its care-giver.* New York: Wiley, 1974.

Bremner, J. G. Egocentric vs. allocentric spatial coding in nine-month-old infants: Factors influencing the choice of code. *Developmental Psychology, 1978, 14,* 346–355. (a)

Bremner, J. G. Spatial errors made by infants: Inadequate spatial cues or evidence of egocentrism? *British Journal of Psychology, 1978, 69,* 77–84. (b)

Bremner, J. G., & Bryant, P. E. Place vs. response

as the basis of spatial errors made by young infants. *Journal of Experimental Child Psychology*, 1977, *23*, 162–171.

Bresson, F., Maury, L., Pieraut-le-Bonniec, G., & de Schonen, S. Organization and lateralization of reaching in infants: An instance of asymmetric function in hand collaboration. *Neuropsychologia*, 1977, *15*, 311–320.

Bresson, F., & de Schonen, S. À propos de la construction de l'espace et de l'objet: La prise d'un objet sur un support. *Bulletin de Psychologie*, 1976–1977, *30*, 3–9.

Bruner, J. S., & Koslowski, B. Visually preadapted constituents of manipulatory action. *Perception*, 1972, *1*, 3–14.

Bruner, J. S., & Sherwood, V. Early rule structure: The case of peekaboo. In J. S. Bruner, A. Jolly, & K. Sylva (Eds.), *Play: Its role in evolution and development*. London: Penguin, 1979.

Brunswik, E. *Perception and the representative design of psychological experiments*. Berkeley: University of California Press, 1956.

Bryant, P. E., Jones, P., Claxton, V., & Perkins, G. H. Recognition of shapes across modalities by infants. *Nature*, 1972, *240*, 303–304.

Bull, D. Auditory-visual coordination in infancy: The perception of moving sights and sounds. Paper presented at the meeting of the International Conference on Infant Studies, Providence, R.I., March 1978.

Bull, D. Infants' tracking of auditory-visual events. Paper presented at the meeting of the Society for Research in Child Development, San Francisco, March 1979.

Bullinger, A. Orientation de la tête du nouveau-né en présence d'un stimulus visuel. *L'Année Psychologique*, 1977, 357–364.

Bushnell, E. W. Infants' reactions to cross-modal discrepancies. Paper presented at the meeting of the Midwestern Psychological Association, Chicago, May 1979.

Bushnell, E. W. The ontogeny of intermodal relations. In H. L. Pick, Jr., & R. D. Walk (Eds.), *Intersensory perception and sensory integration*. New York: Plenum, 1980.

Bushnell, I. W. R. Modification of the externality effect in young infants. *Journal of Experimental Child Psychology*, 1979, *28*, 211–229.

Butterfield, E., & Siperstein, G. N. Influence of contingent auditory stimulation upon non-nutritional suckle. In J. Bosma (Ed.), *Third Symposium on Oral Sensation and Perception: The Mouth of the Infant*. Charles C. Thomas: Springfield, Ill.: 1972.

Butterworth, G. Structure of the mind in human infancy. Paper presented at the meeting of the International Society for the Study of Behavioral Development, Toronto, August 1981.

Butterworth, G., & Castillo, M. Coordination of auditory and visual space in newborn human infants. *Perception*, 1976, *5*, 155–160.

Butterworth, G., & Cicchetti, D. Visual calibration of posture in normal and motor retarded Down's syndrome infants. *Perception*, 1978, *7*, 513–525.

Butterworth, G., & Cochran, E. What minds have in common in space: A perceptual mechanism for joint reference in infancy. *International Journal of Behavior Development*, 1980, *3*, 253–272.

Butterworth, G., & Hicks, L. Visual proprioception and postural stability in infancy. A developmental study. *Perception*, 1977, *6*, 255–262.

Campos, J. J., Hiatt, S., Ramsay, D., Henderson, C., & Svejda, M. The emergence of fear on the visual cliff. In M. Lewis & L. Rosenblum (Eds.), *The development of affect*. New York: Plenum, 1978.

Campos, J. J., Langer, A., & Krowitz, A. Cardiac responses on the visual cliff in prelocomotor human infants. *Science*, 1970, *170*, 196–197.

Carey, S. A case study: Face recognition. In E. Walker (Ed.), *Explorations in the biology of language*. Montgomery, Vt.: Bradford Books, 1978.

Carey, S., & Diamond, R. From piecemeal to configurational representation in faces. *Science*, 1977, *195*, 312–315.

Caron, A. J., Caron, R. F., Caldwell, R. C., & Weiss, S. T. Infant perception of the structural properties of the face. *Developmental Psychology*, 1973, *9*, 385–399.

Caron, A. J., Caron, R. F., & Carlson, V. R. Infant perception of the invariant shape of an object varying in slant. *Child Development*, 1979, *50*, 716–721.

Carpenter, G. C. Visual regard of moving and stationary faces in early infancy. *Merrill-Palmer Quarterly*, 1974, *20*, 181–194.

Carroll, J. J., & Gibson, E. J. Differentiation of an aperture from an obstacle under conditions of motion by three-month-old infants. Paper presented at the meeting of the Society for Research in Child Development, Boston, April 1981.

Chang, H-W., & Trehub, S. E. Auditory processing of relational information by young infants. *Journal of Experimental Child Psychology,* 1977, *24,* 324–331. (a)

Chang, H-W., & Trehub, S. E. Infant's perception of temporal grouping in auditory patterns. *Child Development,* 1977, *48,* 1666–1670. (b)

Chipman, S. F. Complexity and structure in visual patterns. *Journal of Experimental Psychology: General,* 1977, *106,* 269–301.

Chipman, S. F., & Mendelson, M. J. The development of sensitivity to visual structure. *Journal of Experimental Child Psychology,* 1975, *20,* 411–429.

Church, J. Techniques for the differential study of cognition in early childhood. In J. Hellmuth (Ed.), *Cognitive Studies* I. New York: Brunner/Mazel, 1970.

Cicchetti, D., & Sroufe, L. A. Emotional expression in infancy II: Early deviations in Down's syndrome. In M. Lewis & L. Rosenblum (Eds.), *The development of affect.* New York: Plenum, 1978.

Clifton, C., & Bogartz, R. Selective attention during dichotic listening by preschool children. *Journal of Experimental Child Psychology,* 1968, *6,* 483–491.

Cohen, L. B. Observing responses, visual preferences, and habituation to visual stimuli in infants. *Journal of Experimental Child Psychology,* 1969, *7,* 419–433.

Cohen, L. B. Commentary on M. Schwartz and R. H. Day, "Visual shape preception in early infancy." *Monographs of the Society for Research in Child Development,* 1979, *44*(No. 182).

Cohen, L. B., & Strauss, M. S. Concept acquisition in the human infant. *Child Development,* 1979, *50,* 419–424.

Cohen, R., Baldwin, L. M., & Sherman, R. C. Cognitive maps in a naturalistic setting. *Child Development,* 1978, *49,* 1216–1218.

Condon, W. S., & Sander, L. W. Neonate movement is synchronized with adult speech: Interactional participation and language acquisition. *Science,* 1974, *183,* 99–101.

Condry, S., McMahon-Rideout, M., & Levy, A. A. A developmental investigation of selective attention to graphic, phonetic, and semantic information in words. *Perception and Psychophysics,* 1979, *25,* 88–94.

Cook, M., Field, J., & Griffiths, K. The perception of solid form in early infancy. *Child Development,* 1978, *49,* 866–869.

Cornell, E. Infants' discrimination of photographs of faces following redundant presentations. *Journal of Experimental Child Psychology,* 1974, *18,* 98–106.

Cousins, D., & Abravanel, E. Some findings relevant to the hypothesis that topological spatial features are differentiated prior to Euclidean features during growth. *British Journal of Psychology,* 1971, *62,* 475–479.

Crassini, B., & Broerse, J. Auditory-visual integration in neonates: A signal detection analysis. *Journal of Experimental Child Psychology,* 1980, *29,* 144–155.

Daehler, M. W., Perlmutter, M., & Myers, N. Equivalence of pictures and objects for very young children. *Child Development,* 1976, *47,* 96–102.

Dasen, P. R., Inhelder, B., Lavallée, M., & Retschitzki, J. *Naissance de l'intelligence chez l'enfant baoulé de Côte d'Ivoire.* Berne: Hans Huber, 1978.

Day, R. H., & McKenzie, B. E. Perceptual shape constancy in early infancy. *Perception,* 1973, *2,* 315–320.

Day, R. H., & McKenzie, B. E. Constancies in the perceptual world of the infant. In W. Epstein (Ed.), *Stability and constancy in visual perception: Mechanisms and processes.* New York: Wiley, 1977.

Day, R. H., & McKenzie, B. E. Infant perception of the invariant size of approaching and receding objects. *Developmental Psychology,* 1981, *17,* 670–677.

DeCasper, A. J., & Fifer, W. P. Of human bonding: Newborns prefer their mothers' voices. *Science,* 1980, *208,* 1174–1176.

Degelman, D., & Rosinski, R. R. Texture gradient registration and the development of slant perception. *Journal of Experimental Child Psychology,* 1976, *21,* 339–348.

DeLoache, J. S. A naturalistic study of memory for object location in very young children. Paper presented at the meeting of the Society for Research in Child Development, San Francisco, March 1979.

DeLoache, J. S., Strauss, M. K., & Maynard, J. Picture perception in infancy. *Infant Behavior and Development,* 1979, *2,* 77–89.

Demany, R., McKenzie, B. E., & Vurpillot, E. La perception du rhythme chez le nourrisson. *Nature,* 1977, *266,* 718–719.

DiFranco, D., Muir, D., & Dodwell, P. C. Reaching in very young infants. *Perception*, 1978, *7*, 385–392.

Dirks, J. A. *Children's recognition of moving people*. Unpublished doctoral dissertation, Cornell University, 1976.

Dirks, J. A., & Gibson, E. Infants' perception of similarity between live people and their photographs. *Child Development*, 1977, *48*, 124–130.

Dodd, B. Lip reading in infants: Attention to speech presented in- and out-of-synchrony. *Cognitive Psychology*, 1979, *11*, 478–484.

Dodwell, P. C., Muir, D., & DiFranco, D. Responses of infants to visually presented objects. *Science*, 1976, *194*, 209–211.

Doyle, A. B. Listening to distraction: A developmental study of selective attention. *Journal of Experimental Child Psychology*, 1973, *15*, 100–115.

Drozdal, J. G., & Flavell, J. H. A developmental study of logical search behavior. *Child Development*, 1975, *46*, 389–393.

Dunkeld, J. *The function of imitation in infancy*. Unpublished doctoral dissertation, University of Edinburgh, 1978.

Dunkeld, J., & Bower, T. G. R. Infant response to optical collision. *Perception*, 1980, *9*, 549–554.

Eimas, P. D. Speech perception in early infancy. In L. B. Cohen & P. Salapatek (Eds.), *Infant perception: From sensation to cognition* (Vol. 2). New York: Academic Press, 1975.

Eimas, P. D., Siqueland, E., Jusczyk, P. W., & Vigorito, J. Speech perception in infants. *Science*, 1971, *171*, 303–306.

Eisenberg, R. B. *Auditory competence in early life*. Baltimore: University Park Press, 1976.

Fagan, J. F., III. Infants' recognition memory for faces. *Journal of Experimental Child Psychology*, 1972, *14*, 453–476.

Fagan, J. F., III. Infants' recognition of invariant features of faces. *Child Development*, 1976, *47*, 627–638.

Fagan, J. F., III, & Singer, L. T. The role of simple feature differences in infants' recognition of faces. *Infant Behavior and Development*, 1979, *2*, 39–45.

Fantz, R. L. The origins of form perception. *Scientific American*, 1961, *204*, 66–72.

Fantz, R. L. Pattern discrimination and selective attention as determinants of perceptual development from birth. In A. H. Kidd & J. L. Rivoire (Eds.), *Perceptual development in children*. New York: International Universities Press, 1966.

Fantz, R. L., Fagan, J. F., III, & Miranda, S. B. Early visual selectivity as a function of pattern variables, previous exposure, age from birth and conception, and expected cognitive deficit. In L. B. Cohen & P. Salapatek (Eds.), *Infant perception: From sensation to cognition* (Vol. 1). New York: Academic Press, 1975.

Feldman, A., & Acredolo, L. The effect of active vs. passive exploration on memory for spatial location in children. *Child Development*, 1979, *50*, 698–704.

Fenson, L., Kagan, J., Kearsley, R. B., & Zelazo, P. R. The developmental progression of manipulative play in the first two years. *Child Development*, 1976, *47*, 232–236.

Field, J. The adjustment of reaching behavior to object distance in early infancy. *Child Development*, 1976, *47*, 304–308. (a)

Field, J. Relation of young infant's reaching to stimulus distance and solidity. *Developmental Psychology*, 1976, *12*, 444–448. (b)

Field, J. Coordination of vision and prehension in young infants. *Child Development*, 1977, *48*, 97–103.

Field, J., DiFranco, D., Dodwell, P. C., & Muir, D. Auditory-visual coordination in 2½-month-old infants. *Journal of Infant Behavior*, 1979, *2*, 113–122.

Field, J., Muir, D., Pilon, R., Sinclair, M., & Dodwell, P. C. Infants' orientation to lateral sounds from birth to three months. *Child Development*, 1980, *51*, 295–298.

Field, T. M. Visual and cardiac responses to animate and inanimate faces by young term and preterm infants (3 months old). *Child Development*, 1979, *50*, 188–194.

Flavell, J. H. The development of knowledge about visual perception. In C. B. Keasey (Ed.), *Nebraska Symposium on Motivation* (Vol. 25). University of Nebraska Press, 1977.

Flavell, J. H. Metacognitive development. In J. M. Scandura & C. J. Brainerd (Eds.), *Structural-process theories of complex human behavior*. Alphen aan den Rijn, the Netherlands: Sijthoff and Noordhoff, 1978.

Flavell, J. H., Flavell, E. R., Green, F. L., & Wilcox, S. A. Young children's knowledge about visual perception: Effect of observer's distance from target on perceptual clarity of target. *Developmental Psychology*, 1980, *16*, 10–12.

Flavell, J. H., Omanson, R. C., & Latham, C. Solving spatial perspective-taking problems by rule vs. computation: A developmental study. *Developmental Psychology*, 1978, *14*, 462–473.

Fodor, J. D. *Semantics: Theories of meaning in generative grammar*. New York: Crowell, 1978.

Fogel, A., Diamond, G. R., Langhorst, B. H., & Demos, V. Alteration of infant behavior as a result of "still-face" perturbation of maternal behavior. Paper presented at the meeting of the Society for Research in Child Development, San Francisco, March 1979.

Fox, R., & McDaniel, C. Perception of biomechanical motion in human infants. Paper presented at the International Conference on Infant Studies, Austin, Tex., March 1982.

Frances, R. *La perception de la musique*. Paris: Librairie T. Urin, 1958.

Freedman, D., Fox-Kolenda, B., Margileth, D., & Miller, D. The development of the use of sound as a guide to affective and cognitive behavior—a two-phase process. *Child Development*, 1969, *40*, 1099–1105.

Freeman, N. H., & Janikoun, R. Intellectual realism in children's drawings of a familiar object with distinctive features. *Child Development*, 1972, *43*, 1116–1121.

Friedman, S. L., & Stevenson, M. B. Developmental changes in the understanding of implied motion in two-dimensional pictures. *Child Development*, 1975, *46*, 773–778.

Geffen, G., & Sexton, M. A. The development of auditory strategies of attention. *Developmental Psychology*, 1978, *14*, 11–17.

Gelman, R. The nature and development of early number concepts. In H. W. Reese (Ed.), *Advances in child development and behavior* (Vol. 7). New York: Academic Press, 1972.

Gelman, R., Bullock, M., & Meck, E. Preschoolers' understanding of simple object transformations. *Child Development*, 1980, *51*, 691–699.

Gelman, R., & Gallistel, C. R. *The child's understanding of number*. Cambridge: Harvard University Press, 1978.

Gelman, R., & Spelke, E. S. The development of thoughts about animate and inanimate objects: Implications for research on social cognition. In J. H. Flavell & L. Ross (Eds.), *Social cognitive development: Frontiers and possible futures*. London: Cambridge University Press, 1981.

Gelman, R., Spelke, E. S., & Meck, E. Preschoolers' use of criteria for distinguishing animate from inanimate objects. Paper presented at the NATO Conference on the Acquisition of Symbolic Skills, Keele, England, July 1982.

Gesell, A. L., & Amatruda, C. S. *Developmental diagnosis* (2nd ed.). New York: Hoeber, 1964.

Gibson, E. J. *Principles of perceptual learning and development*. New York: Appleton-Century-Crofts, 1969.

Gibson, E. J. Presentation at the Eric H. Lenneberg Memorial Symposium, Cornell University, 1977.

Gibson, E. J. The concept of affordances in development: The renascence of functionalism. In W. A. Collins (Ed.), *Minnesota Symposia on Child Psychology* (Vol. 15). *The concept of development*. Hillsdale, N.J.: Erlbaum, 1982.

Gibson, E. J., & Levin, H. *The psychology of reading*. Cambridge: MIT Press, 1975.

Gibson, E. J., & Olum, V. Experimental methods of studying perception in children. In P. H. Mussen (Ed.), *Handbook of research methods in child development*. New York: Wiley, 1960.

Gibson, E. J., Owsley, C. J., & Johnston, J. Perception of invariants by five-month-old infants: Differentiation of two types of motion. *Developmental Psychology*, 1978, *14*, 407–415.

Gibson, E. J., Owsley, C. J., Walker, A. S., & Megaw-Nyce, J. S. Development of the perception of invariants: Substance and shape. *Perception*, 1979, *8*, 609–619.

Gibson, E. J., & Rader, N. Attention: The perceiver as performer. In G. A. Hale & M. Lewis (Eds.), *Attention and cognitive development*. New York: Plenum, 1979.

Gibson, E. J., & Walk, R. D. The "visual cliff." *Scientific American*, 1960, *202*, 64–71.

Gibson, E. J., & Walker, A. Intermodal perception of substance. Paper presented at the meeting of the International Conference on Infant Studies, Austin, Tex., March 1982.

Gibson, J. J. *The perception of the visual world*. Boston: Houghton-Mifflin, 1950.

Gibson, J. J. *The senses considered as perceptual systems*. Boston: Houghton-Mifflin, 1966.

Gibson, J. J. *The ecological approach to visual perception*. Boston: Houghton-Mifflin, 1979.

Gibson, J. J., & Gibson, E. J. Continuous perspective transformations and the perception of rigid motion. *Journal of Experimental Psychology*, 1957, *54*, 129–138.

Gibson, J. J., Kaplan, G. A., Reynolds, H. N., & Wheeler, K. The change from visible to invisible: A study of optical transitions. *Perception and Psychophysics*, 1969, *5*, 113–116.

Gibson, J. J., & Kaushall, P. (Producers). *Reversible and irreversible events*. State College, Pa.: Psychological Cinema Register, 1973. (Film)

Girgus, J. S. A developmental approach to the study of shape processing. *Journal of Experimental Child Psychology*, 1973, *16*, 363–374.

Girgus, J. S., & Hochberg, J. E. Age differences in sequential form recognition. *Psychonomic Science*, 1970, *21*, 211–212.

Girton, M. R. Infants' attention to intrastimulus motion. *Journal of Experimental Child Psychology*, 1979, *28*, 416–423.

Goldberg, S. Visual tracking and existence constancy in 5-month-old infants. *Journal of Experimental Child Psychology*, 1976, *22*, 478–491.

Goren, C. G., Sarty, M., & Wu, P. Y. K. Visual following and pattern discrimination of face-like stimuli by new-born infants. *Pediatrics*, 1975, *56*, 544–549.

Gottfried, A. W., Rose, S. A., & Bridger, W. H. Crossmodal transfer in human infants. *Child Development*, 1977, *48*, 118–123.

Gratch, G. A study of the relative dominance of vision and touch in six-month-old infants. *Child Development*, 1972, *43*, 615–623.

Greenfield, P. M. Playing peekaboo with a four-month-old: A study of the role of speech and non-speech sounds in the formation of a visual schema. *Journal of Psychology*, 1972, *82*, 287–298.

Hagen, M. A. Influence of picture surface and station point on the ability to compensate for oblique view in pictorial perception. *Developmental Psychology*, 1976, *12*, 57–63.

Hagen, M. A., & Elliott, H. B. An investigation of the relationship between viewing conditions and preferences for true and modified linear perspective with adults. *Journal of Experimental Psychology: Human Perception and Performance*, 1976, *2*, 479–490.

Hagen, M. A., & Jones, R. K. Differential patterns of preference for modified linear perspective in children and adults. *Journal of Experimental Child Psychology*, 1978, *26*, 205–215.

Hainline, L. Developmental changes in visual scanning of face and non-face patterns by infants. *Journal of Experimental Child Psychology*, 1978, *25*, 90–115.

Haith, M. M., Bergman, T., & Moore, M. J. Eye contact and face scanning in early infancy. *Science*, 1977, *198*, 853–855.

Halverson, H. M. An experimental study of prehension in infants by means of systematic cinema records. *Genetic Psychology Monographs*, 1931, *10*, 107–286.

Hamm, M., Russell, M., & Koepke, T. Neonatal imitation? Paper presented at the meeting of the Society for Research in Child Development, San Francisco, March 1979.

Hammer, M., & Turkewitz, G. Relationship between effective intensity of auditory stimulation and directional eye-turns in the human newborn. *Animal Behaviour*, 1975, *23*, 287–290.

Hardwick, D. A., McIntyre, C. W., & Pick, H. L., Jr. The content and manipulation of cognitive maps in children and adults. *Monographs of the Society for Research in Child Development*, 1976, *41* (3, Serial No. 166).

Harris, P. L. Examination and search in infants. *British Journal of Psychology*, 1971, *62*, 469–473.

Harris, P. L. Infants' visual and tactual inspection of objects. *Perception*, 1972, *1*, 141–146.

Harris, P. L., Cassel, T. Z., & Bamborough, P. Tracking by young infants. *British Journal of Psychology*, 1974, *65*, 345–349.

Harris, P. L., & MacFarlane, A. The growth of the effective visual field from birth to seven weeks. *Journal of Experimental Child Psychology*, 1974, *18*, 340–348.

Hayes, L. A., & Watson, J. S. Neonatal imitation: Fact or artifact? Paper presented at the meeting of the Society for Research in Child Development, San Francisco, March 1979.

Hazen, N. L. Young children's knowledge and exploration of large-scale environments. Unpublished doctoral dissertation, University of Minnesota, 1979.

Hazen, N. L., Lockman, J. J., & Pick, H. L., Jr. The development of children's representations of large-scale environments. *Child Development*, 1978, *49*, 623–636.

Heider, F., & Simmel, M. An experimental study of apparent behavior. *American Journal of Psychology*, 1944, *57*, 243–259.

Heiman, M. L., & Rieser, J. Spatial orientation at 18 months of age: Search mediated by self-movement. Paper presented at the meeting of the International Conference on Infant Studies,

New Haven, Conn., April 1980.

Hochberg, J. E., & Brooks, V. Pictorial recognition as an unlearned ability: A study of one child's performance. *American Journal of Psychology,* 1962, *75,* 624–628.

Hofsten, C., von. Development of visually directed reaching. The approach phase. *Journal of Human Movement Studies,* 1979, *5,* 160–178.

Hofsten, C., von. Predictive reaching for moving objects by human infants. *Journal of Experimental Child Psychology,* 1980, *30,* 369–382.

Hofsten, C., von. Eye-hand coordination in newborns. *Developmental Psychology,* 1982, *18,* 450–461.

Hofsten, C., von, & Lindhagen, K. Observations on the development of reaching for moving objects. *Journal of Experimental Child Psychology,* 1979, *28,* 158–173.

Hofsten, C., von, & Lindhagen, K. Perception of visual occlusion in 4½-month-old infants. *Infant Behavior and Development,* in press.

Holmes, K. M., & Holmes, D. W. Signed and spoken language development in a hearing child of hearing parents. Paper presented at the meeting of the International Conference on Infant Studies, New Haven, Conn., April 1980.

Horowitz, F. D. (Ed.). Visual attention, auditory stimulation, and language discrimination in young infants. *Monographs of the Society for Research in Child Development,* 1974, *39*(Serial No. 158).

Hutt, C. Effects of stimulus novelty on manipulatory exploration in an infant. *Journal of Child Psychology and Psychiatry,* 1967, *8,* 241–247.

Huttenlocher, J., & Presson, C. C. Mental rotation and the perspective problem. *Cognitive Psychology,* 1973, *4,* 277–299.

Huttenlocher, J., & Presson, C. C. The coding and transformation of spatial information. *Cognitive Psychology,* 1979, *11,* 375–394.

Johansson, G. Visual event perception. In R. Held, H. W. Leibowitz, & H-L. Teuber (Eds.), *Handbook of sensory physiology: Perception.* Berlin: Springer-Verlag, 1978.

Johansson, G., Hofsten, C., von, & Jansson, G. Event perception. *Annual Review of Psychology,* 1980, *31,* 27–63.

Jusczyk, P. W. Infant speech perception: A critical appraisal. In P. D. Eimas & J. L. Miller (Eds.), *Perspectives on the study of speech.* Hillsdale, N.J.: Erlbaum, 1979.

Kaess, D. W., Haynes, S. D., Craig, M. J., Pearson, S. C., & Greenwell, J. Effect of distance and size of standard object on the development of shape constancy. *Journal of Experimental Psychology,* 1974, *102,* 17–21.

Kagan, J., Linn, S., Mount, R., & Reznick, J. S. Asymmetry of inference in the dishabituation paradigm. *Canadian Journal of Psychology,* 1979, *33,* 288–305.

Kalnins, I. V., & Bruner, J. S. The coordination of visual observation and instrumental behavior in early infancy. *Perception,* 1973, *2,* 307–314.

Kanizsa, G. Subjective contours. *Scientific American,* 1976, *234,* 48–52.

Kaplan, E. L. *The role of intonation in the acquisition of language.* Unpublished doctoral dissertation, Cornell University, 1969.

Kaplan, E. L., & Kaplan, G. A. The prelinguistic child. In J. Eliot (Ed.), *Human development and cognitive processes.* New York: Holt, Rinehart & Winston, 1971.

Kaplan, G. A. Kinetic disruption of optical texture: The perception of depth at an edge. *Perception and Psychophysics,* 1969, *6,* 193–198.

Karmel, B. Z. The effect of age, complexity, and amount of contour on pattern preferences in human infants. *Journal of Experimental Child Psychology,* 1969, *7,* 339–354.

Keil, F. The development of the young child's ability to anticipate the outcomes of simple causal events. *Child Development,* 1979, *50,* 455–462.

Kellman, P. J., & Spelke, E. S. Perception of partly occluded objects in infancy. Paper presented at the meeting of the Society for Research in Child Development, San Francisco, March 1979.

Kellman, P. J., & Spelke, E. S. Infant perception of partly occluded objects: Sensitivity to movement and configuration. Paper presented at the meeting of the Society for Research in Child Development, Boston, April 1981.

Klima, E. S., & Bellugi, U. *The signs of language.* Cambridge: Harvard University Press, 1979.

Koffka, K. *Principles of gestalt psychology.* New York: Harcourt, Brace & World, 1935.

Köhler, W. *The mentality of apes.* New York: Harcourt, Brace, 1925.

Kopp, C. B. Fine motor abilities of infants. *Developmental Medicine and Child Neurology,* 1974, *16,* 629–636.

Koslowski, B., & Bruner, J. S. Learning to use a lever. *Child Development,* 1972, *43,* 790–799.

Kosslyn, S. M., Pick, H. L., Jr., & Fariello, G. R. Cognitive maps in children and men. *Child Development*, 1974, *45*, 707–716.

Kremenitizer, J. K., Vaughan, H. G., Jr., Kurtzberg, D., & Dowling, K. Smooth-pursuit eye movements in the newborn infant. *Child Development*, 1979, *50*, 442–448.

Kreutzer, M. A., & Charlesworth, W. R. Infants' reactions to different expressions of emotions. Paper presented at the meeting of the Society for Research in Child Development, Philadelphia, March 1973.

Kuhl, P. K. Perceptual constancy for speech-sound categories. In G. H. Yeni-Komshian, J. F. Kavanagh, & C. A. Ferguson (Eds.), *Child phonology*, vol. 2, *Perception*. New York: Academic Press, 1980.

LaBarbera, J. D., Izard, C. E., Vietze, P., & Parisi, S. A. Four-and-six-month-old infants' visual responses to joy, anger, and neutral expressions. *Child Development*, 1976, *47*, 535–538.

Landau, B., Gleitman, H., & Spelke, E. S. Spatial knowledge and geometric representation in a child blind from birth. *Science*, 1981, *213*, 1275–1278.

Lasky, R. E. The effect of visual feedback of the hand on the reaching and retrieval behavior of young infants. *Child Development*, 1977, *48*, 112–117.

Lasky, R. E., & Gogel, W. C. The perception of relative motion by young infants. *Perception*, 1978, *7*, 617–623.

Lasky, R. E., Romano, N., & Wenters, J. Spatial localization in children after changes in position. *Journal of Experimental Child Psychology*, 1980, *29*, 225–245.

Laurendau, M., & Pinard, A. *The development of the concept of space in the child*. New York: International Universities Press, 1970.

Lee, D. N., & Aronson, E. Visual proprioceptive control of standing in human infants. *Perception and Psychophysics*, 1974, *15*, 529–532.

Lehman, E. B. Selective strategies in children's attention to task-relevant information. *Child Development*, 1972, *43*, 197–209.

Lempers, J. D., Flavell, E. R., & Flavell, J. H. The development in very young children of tacit knowledge concerning visual perception. *Genetic Psychology Monographs*, 1977, *95*, 3–53.

Liberman, A., Harris, K., Kinney, J., & Lane, H. The discrimination of relative onset time of the components of certain speech and nonspeech patterns. *Journal of Experimental Psychology*, 1961, *61*, 379–388.

Lishman, T. R., & Lee, D. N. The autonomy of visual kinesthesis. *Perception*, 1975, *2*, 287–294.

Lisker, L., & Abramson, A. The voicing dimension: Some experiments in comparative phonetics. *Proceedings of the Sixth International Congress of Phonetic Sciences, Prague, 1967*. Prague: Academia, 1970.

Lockman, J. J. The development of detour knowledge during infancy. Paper presented at the meeting of the International Conference on Infant Studies, New Haven, Conn., April 1980.

Maccoby, E. E. Selective auditory attention in children. In L. P. Lipsitt & C. C. Spiker (Eds.), *Advances in child development and behavior* (Vol. 3). New York: Academic Press, 1967.

MacDonald, J., & McGurk, H. Visual influences on speech perception processes. *Perception and Psychophysics*, 1978, *24*, 253–257.

MacFarlane, A., Harris, P. L., & Barnes, I. Central and peripheral vision in early infancy. *Journal of Experimental Child Psychology*, 1976, *21*, 532–538.

Maier, N. R. F. Reasoning in white rats. *Comparative Psychology Monographs*, 1929, *6*(Serial No. 3).

Maier, N. R. F. Reasoning in children. *Journal of Comparative Psychology*, 1936, *21*, 357–366.

Maratos, O. *The origin and development of imitation in the first six months of life*. Unpublished doctoral dissertation, University of Geneva, 1973.

Marler, P. A. A comparative approach to vocal learning: Song development in white crowned sparrows. *Journal of Comparative and Physiological Psychology Monograph*, 1970, *71*(2, Pt. 2).

Mason, W. A. Social experience and primate cognitive development. In G. Burghardt & M. Berkoff (Eds.), *The development of behavior: Comparative and evolutionary aspects*. New York: Garland, 1978.

Masters, J. C. Interpreting "imitative" responses in early infancy. *Science*, 1979, *205*, 215.

Maurer, D., & Barrera, M. Infants' perception of natural and distorted arrangements of a schematic face. *Child Development*, 1981, *52*, 196–202.

Maurer, D., & Heroux, L. The perception of faces by three-month-old infants. Paper presented at the meeting of the International Conference on Infant Studies, New Haven, Conn., April 1980.

McCall, R. B. Exploratory manipulation and play in the human infant. *Monographs of the Society for Research in Child Development*, 1974, *39*(2, Serial No. 155).

McCall, R. B., & Melson, W. H. Amount of short-term familiarization and the response to auditory discrepancies. *Child Development*, 1970, *41*, 861–869.

McDonnell, P. M. The development of visually guided reaching. *Perception and Psychophysics*, 1975, *19*, 181–185.

McDonnell, P. M. Patterns of eye-hand coordination in the first year of life. *Canadian Journal of Psychology*, 1979, *33*, 253–267.

McGurk, H., Turnure, C., & Creighton, S. J. Auditory-visual coordination in neonates. *Child Development*, 1977, *48*, 138–143.

McKenzie, B. E., & Day, R. H. Object distance as a determinant of visual fixation in early infancy. *Science*, 1972, *178*, 1108–1110.

McKenzie, B. E., & Day, R. H. Infants' attention to stationary and moving objects at different distances. *Australian Journal of Psychology*, 1976, *28*, 45–51.

Megaw-Nyce, J. S. Perception of reversible and irreversible events by pre-schoolers. Paper presented at the meeting of the Society for Research in Child Development, San Francisco, March 1979.

Mehler, J., Bertoncini, J., Barriere, M., & Jassik-Gerschenfeld, D. Infant recognition of mother's voice. *Perception*, 1978, *7*, 491–497.

Melson, W. H., & McCall, R. B. Attentional responses of 5-month-old girls to discrepant auditory stimuli. *Child Development*, 1970, *41*, 1159–1171.

Meltzoff, A. N. Intermodal matching in early infancy. Paper presented at the meeting of the Society for Research in Child Development, Boston, April 1981.

Meltzoff, A. N., & Borton, R. W. Intermodal matching by human neonates. *Nature*, 1979, *282*, 403–404.

Meltzoff, A. N., & Moore, M. K. Imitation of facial and manual gestures by human neonates. *Science*, 1977, *198*, 75–78.

Meltzoff, A. N., & Moore, M. K. Interpreting "imitative" responses in early infancy. *Science*, 1979, *205*, 217–219.

Mendelson, M. J., & Haith, M. M. The relation between audition and vision in the human newborn. *Monographs of the Society for Research in Child Development*, 1976, *41*(4, Serial No. 167).

Meneghini, K. A., & Leibowitz, H. W. The effect of stimulus distance and age on shape constancy. *Journal of Experimental Psychology*, 1967, *74*, 241–248.

Michotte, A. *The perception of causality* (T. R. Miles & E. Miles trans.). London: Methuen, 1963. (Originally published, 1946.)

Michotte, A., Thinès, G., & Crabbé, G. *Les compléments amodaux des structures perceptives*. Louvain, Belg.: Publications Universitaires de Louvain, 1964.

Milewski, A. E. Infants' discrimination of internal and external pattern elements. *Journal of Experimental Child Psychology*, 1976, *22*, 229–246.

Milewski, A. E. Visual discrimination and detection of configurational invariance in 3-month infants. *Developmental Psychology*, 1979, *15*, 357–363.

Milewski, A. E., & Genovese, C. M. The effects of stimulus movement on visual attentional processes in one- and three-month infants. Paper presented at the International Conference on Infant Studies, New Haven, Conn., April 1980.

Miller, C. L., & Horowitz, F. D. Integration of auditory and visual cues in speaker classification by infants. Paper presented at the meeting of the International Conference on Infant Studies, New Haven, Conn., April 1980.

Miller, C. L., Younger, B. A., & Morse, P. A. Categorization of male and female voices in infancy. Paper presented at the meeting of the International Conference on Infant Studies, New Haven, Conn., April 1980.

Milner, A. D., & Bryant, P. E. Crossmodal matching by young children. *Journal of Comparative and Physiological Psychology*, 1970, *71*, 453–485.

Moore, M. K., Borton, R. W., & Darby, B. L. Visual tracking in young infants: Evidence for object identity or object permanence? *Journal of Experimental Child Psychology*, 1978, *25*, 183–198.

Morse, P. I. The discrimination of speech and non-speech stimuli in early infancy. *Journal of Experimental Child Psychology*, 1972, *14*, 477–492.

Mounoud, P., & Bower, T. G. R. Conservation of weight in infants. *Cognition*, 1974, *3*, 29–40.

Muir, D., & Field, J. Newborn infants orient to

sounds. *Child Development*, 1978, *50*, 431–436.

Muller, A. A., & Aslin, R. N. Visual tracking as an index of the object concept. *Infant Behavior and Development*, 1978, *1*, 309–319.

Mundy-Castle, A. C., & Anglin, J. The development of looking in infancy. Paper presented at the meeting of the Society for Research in Child Development, Santa Monica, Calif., March 1969.

Neisser, U., & Becklen, R. Selective looking: Attending to visually specified events. *Cognitive Psychology*, 1975, *7*, 480–494.

Nelson, K. E. Accommodation of visual tracking patterns in human infants to object movement patterns. *Journal of Experimental Child Psychology*, 1971, *12*, 182–196.

Newport, E. L. Constraints on structure: Evidence from American sign language and language learning. In W. A. Collins (Ed.), *Minnesota Symposia on Child Psychology* (Vol. 14). Hillsdale, N.J.: Erlbaum, 1980.

Nodine, C. F., & Evans, J. D. Eye movements of prereaders to pseudowords containing letters of high and low confusability. *Perception and Psychophysics*, 1969, *6*, 39–41.

Nodine, C. F., & Lang, M. J. The development of visual scanning strategies for differentiating words. *Developmental Psychology*, 1971, *5*, 221–222.

Nodine, C. F., & Simmons, F. Processing distinctive features in the differentiation of letter-like symbols. *Journal of Experimental Psychology*, 1974, *103*, 21–28.

Nodine, C. F., & Stuerle, N. L. Development of perceptual and cognitive strategies for differentiating graphemes. *Journal of Experimental Psychology*, 1973, *97*, 158–166.

Olson, G. The recognition of specific persons. In M. E. Lamb & L. R. Sherrod (Eds.), *Infant social cognition*. Hillsdale, N.J.: Erlbaum, 1981.

Olson, R. K. Children's sensitivity to pictorial depth information. *Perception and Psychophysics*, 1975, *17*, 59–64.

Olson, R. K., & Boswell, S. L. Pictorial depth sensitivity in two-year-old children. *Child Development*, 1976, *47*, 1175–1178.

Olton, D. S. Spatial memory. *Scientific American*, 1977, *236*, 82–98.

Olum, V. Developmental differences in the perception of causality. *American Journal of Psychology*, 1956, *69*, 417–423.

Olum, V. Developmental differences in the perception of causality under conditions of specific instructions. *Vita Humana*, 1958, *1*, 191–203.

Oster, H. "Recognition" of emotional expression in infancy? In M. E. Lamb & L. R. Sherrod (Eds.), *Infant social cognition*. Hillsdale, N.J.: Erlbaum, 1981.

Oster, H., & Ekman, P. Facial behavior in child development. In W. A. Collins (Ed.), *Minnesota Symposia on Child Psychology* (Vol. 11). Hillsdale, N.J.: Erlbaum, 1978.

Papoušek, H. From adaptive responses to social cognition: The learning view of development. In M. H. Bornstein & W. Kessen (Eds.), *Psychological development from infancy: Image to intention*. Hillsdale, N. J.: Erlbaum, 1979.

Parton, D. A. Learning to imitate in infancy. *Child Development*, 1976, *47*, 14–31.

Petterson, L., Yonas, A., & Fisch, R. O. The development of blinking in response to impending collision in preterm, full-term, and post-term infants. *Infant Behavior and Development*, 1980, *3*, 155–165.

Piaget, J. *Play, dreams, and imitation in childhood*. New York: W. W. Norton, 1951.

Piaget, J. *The origins of intelligence in children*. New York: International Universities Press, 1952.

Piaget, J. *The construction of reality in the child*. New York: Basic Books, 1954.

Piaget, J. *The mechanisms of perception*. London: Routledge, 1969.

Piaget, J., & Inhelder, B. *Le développement des quantités chez l'enfant*. Neuchâtel, Switz.: Delachaux et Niestlé, 1941.

Piaget, J., & Inhelder, B. *The child's conception of space*. New York: W. W. Norton, 1956.

Piaget, J., & Inhelder, B. *The psychology of the child*. London: Routledge, 1969.

Pick, A. D. Improvement of visual and tactual form discrimination. *Journal of Experimental Psychology*, 1965, *69*, 331–339.

Pick, A. D., Christy, M. D., & Frankel, G. W. A developmental study of visual selective attention. *Journal of Experimental Child Psychology*, 1972, *14*, 165–175.

Pick, A. D., & Frankel, G. W. A study of strategies of visual attention in children. *Developmental Psychology*, 1973, *9*, 348–357.

Pick, A. D., & Frankel, G. W. A developmental study of strategies of visual selectivity. *Child Development*, 1974, *45*, 1162–1165.

Pick, A. D., Frankel, D. G., & Hess, V. L. Children's attention: The development of selectivity. In E. M. Hetherington (Ed.), *Review of child development research* (Vol. 5). Chicago: University of Chicago Press, 1975.

Pick, A. D., & Unze, M. G. The development of visual-motor search and the use of redundant information. *Bulletin of the Psychonomic Society,* 1979, *14,* 267–270.

Pick, H. L., Jr. Mapping children . . . mapping space. Paper presented at the meeting of the American Psychological Association, Honolulu, September 1972.

Pick, H. L., Jr., Acredolo, L. P., & Gronseth, M. Children's knowledge of the spatial layout of their homes. Paper presented at the meeting of the Society for Research in Child Development, Philadelphia, March 1973.

Pick, H. L., Jr., & Lockman, J. J. The development of spatial cognition in children. Paper presented at the meeting of the Mind, Child, and Architecture Conference, Newark, N.J., October 1979.

Pick, H. L., Jr., Yonas, A., & Rieser, J. Spatial reference systems in perceptual development. In M. H. Bornstein & W. Kessen (Eds.), *Psychological development from infancy*. Hillsdale, N.J.: Erlbaum, 1978.

Poizner, H., Bellugi, U., & Lutes-Driscoll, V. Perception of American sign language in dynamic point-light displays. *Journal of Experimental Psychology,* 1981, *7,* 430–440.

Prather, P., & Spelke, E. S. Three-month-olds' perception of adjacent and partly occluded objects. Paper presented at the meeting of the International Conference on Infant Studies, Austin, Tex., March 1982.

Premack, D. *Intelligence in ape and man.* New York: Wiley, 1976.

Premack, D., & Woodruff, G. Does the chimpanzee have a theory of mind? *Behavioral and Brain Sciences,* 1978, *4,* 515–526.

Provine, R. B., & Westerman, J. A. Crossing the midline: Limits of early eye-hand behavior. *Child Development,* 1979, *50,* 437–441.

Rader, N., Bausano, M., & Richards, J. E. On the nature of the visual-cliff avoidance response in human infants. *Child Development,* 1980, *51,* 61–68.

Rader, N., & Stern, J. D. The neonatal reaching response to objects. Paper presented at the meeting of the International Society for the Study of Behavioral Development, Toronto, August 1981.

Richards, J. E., & Rader, N. Crawling-onset age predicts visual cliff avoidance in infants. *Journal of Experimental Psychology: Human Perception and Performance,* 1981, *7,* 382–387.

Richardson, H. M. The growth of adaptive behavior in infants: An experimental study of seven age levels. *Genetic Psychology Monographs,* 1932, *12,* 195–359.

Richardson, H. M. The adaptive behavior of infants in the utilization of the lever as a tool: A developmental and experimental study. *Journal of Genetic Psychology,* 1934, *44,* 352–377.

Rieser, J. Spatial orientation of six-month-old infants. *Child Development,* 1979, *50,* 1078–1087.

Rieser, J., Doxsey, P., McCarrell, N., Brooks, P. Emergence of cognitive mapping: Toddler's use of information from an aerial view of a maze. Paper presented at the meeting of the International Conference on Infant Studies, New Haven, Conn., April 1980.

Rieser, J., & Edwards, K. Children's perception and the geometries: A multidimensional scaling analysis. Paper presented at the meeting of the American Psychological Association, New York, September 1979.

Rosch, E. H. Natural categories. *Cognitive Psychology,* 1973, *4,* 328–350. (a)

Rosch, E. H. On the internal structure of perceptual and semantic categories. In T. E. Moore (Ed.), *Cognitive development and the acquisition of language.* New York: Academic Press, 1973. (b)

Rosch, E. H., & Mervis, C. B. Family resemblances: Studies in the internal structure of categories. *Cognitive Psychology,* 1975, *7,* 573–605.

Rose, S. A. Infants' transfer of response between two-dimensional and three-dimensional stimuli. *Child Development,* 1977, *48,* 1086–1091.

Rose, S. A., Gottfried, A. W., & Bridger, W. H. Crossmodal transfer in infants: Relationships to prematurity and socio-economic background. *Developmental Psychology,* 1978, *14,* 643–652.

Rosinski, R. R., & Levine, N. P. Texture gradient effectiveness in the perception of surface slant. *Journal of Experimental Child Psychology,* 1976, *22,* 261–271.

Rozin, P. The evolution of intelligence and access to the cognitive unconscious. *Progress in Psychobiology and Physiological Psychology,* 1976, *6,* 245–279.

Rubenstein, J. Concordance of visual and manipulative responsiveness to novel and familiar stimuli in six-month-old infants. *Child Development*, 1974, *45*, 194–195.

Ruff, H. A. The coordination of manipulation and visual fixation: A response to Schaffer (1975). *Child Development*, 1976, *47*, 868–871.

Ruff, H. A. Infant recognition of the invariant form of objects. *Child Development*, 1978, *49*, 293–306.

Ruff, H. A. The development of perception and recognition of objects. *Child Development*, 1980, *51*, 981–992.

Ruff, H. A. Infants' manipulative exploration of objects. Paper in preparation, 1982.

Ruff, H. A., & Halton, A. Is there directed reaching in the human neonate? *Developmental Psychology*, 1978, *14*, 425–426.

Runeson, S. *On visual perception of dynamic events*. University of Uppsala (Sweden), 1977. (Doctoral dissertation)

Salapatek, P. Pattern perception in early infancy. In L. B. Cohen & P. Salapatek (Eds.), *Infant perception: From sensation to cognition* (Vol. 1). New York: Academic Press, 1975.

Salapatek, P., & Banks, M. S. Infant sensory assessment: Vision. In F. D. Minifie & L. L. Lloyd (Eds.), *Communicative and cognitive abilities—early behavioral assessment*. Baltimore: University Park Press, 1978.

Samuels, S. J. Effect of distinctive feature training on paired-associate learning. *Journal of Educational Psychology*, 1973, *64*, 164–170.

Sazont'yev, B. A. The development of spatial perception and spatial concepts in preschool children. In B. G. Anan'yev & B. F. Lomov (Eds.), *Problems of spatial perception and spatial concepts*. Moscow: 1961. (Available from NASA through the Office of Technical Services, Department of Commerce, Washington, D.C.)

Scaife, M., & Bruner, J. S. The capacity for joint visual attention in the infant. *Nature*, 1975, *253*, 265–266.

Scarr, S., & Salapatek, P. Patterns of fear development during infancy. *Merrill-Palmer Quarterly*, 1970, *16*, 53–90.

Schaffer, H. R. Concordance of visual and manipulative responses to novel and familiar stimuli: A reply to Rubenstein (1974). *Child Development*, 1975, *46*, 290–291.

Schaffer, H. R., Greenwood, A., & Parry, M. H. The onset of wariness. *Child Development*, 1972, *43*, 165–176.

Schaffer, H. R., & Parry, M. H. The effects of short-term familiarization on infants' perceptual-motor coordination in a simultaneous discrimination task. *British Journal of Psychology*, 1970, *61*, 559–569.

Schiff, W. The perception of impending collision: A study of visually directed avoidant behavior. *Psychological Monographs*, 1965, *79*(Whole No. 604).

Schnall, M. Age differences in the integration of progressively changing visual patterns. *Human Development*, 1968, *11*, 287–295.

Schwartz, M., & Day, R. H. Visual shape perception in early infancy. *Monographs for Research in Child Development*, 1979, *44*(7, Whole No. 182).

Sedgwick, H. A. Perceiving spatial layout: The ecological approach. Paper presented at the meeting of the American Psychological Association, Montreal, September 1980.

Sexton, M. A., & Geffen, G. Development of three strategies of attention in dichotic monitoring. *Developmental Psychology*, 1979, *15*, 299–310.

Seyforth, R. M., Cheney, D. L., & Marler, P. A. Monkey responses to three different alarm calls: Evidence of predator classification and semantic communication. *Science*, 1980, *210*, 801–803.

Shantz, C. U., & Watson, J. S. Assessment of spatial egocentrism through expectancy violation. *Psychonomic Science*, 1970, *18*, 93–94.

Shantz, C. U., & Watson, J. S. Spatial abilities and spatial egocentrism in the young child. *Child Development*, 1971, *42*, 171–182.

Sherrod, L. R. Issues in cognitive-perceptual development: The special case of social stimuli. In M. E. Lamb & L. A. Sherrod (Eds.), *Infant social cognition*. Hillsdale, N.J.: Erlbaum, 1981.

Siegel, A. W., Herman, J. F., Allen, G. L., & Kirasic, K. C. The development of cognitive maps of large- and small-scale spaces. *Child Development*, 1979, *50*, 582–585.

Siegel, A. W., & White, S. H. The development of spatial representations of large scale environments. *Advances in Child Development and Behavior* (Vol. 10). N.Y.: Academic Press, 1975.

Silver, J. R., & Rollins, H. A. The effects of visual and verbal feature-emphasis on form discrimination in preschool children. *Journal of Experimental Child Psychology*, 1973, *16*, 205–216.

Soroka, S. M., Corter, C. M., & Abramovitch, R. Infants' tactual discrimination of novel and familiar tactual stimuli. *Child Development*, 1979, *50*, 1251–1253.

Spelke, E. S. Recognition of facial identity over varying activities in infancy. Paper presented at the meeting of the American Psychological Association, Chicago, August 1975.

Spelke, E. S. Infants' intermodal perception of events. *Cognitive Psychology,* 1976, *8,* 533–560.

Spelke, E. S. Perceiving bimodally specified events in infancy. *Developmental Psychology,* 1979, *15,* 626–636.

Spelke, E. S. The infant's acquisition of knowledge of bimodally specified events. *Journal of Experimental Child Psychology,* 1981, *31,* 279–299.

Spelke, E. S. The development of intermodal perception. In L. B. Cohen & P. Salapatek (Eds.), *Handbook of infant perception.* New York: Academic Press, in press.

Spelke, E. S. Perceptual knowledge of objects in infancy. In J. Mehler, M. Garrett, & E. Walker (Eds.), *Perspectives on mental representation.* Hillsdale, N.J.: Erlbaum, 1982.

Spelke, E. S., & Born, W. S. Perception of visible objects by 3-month-old infants. Unpublished manuscript, 1982.

Spelke, E. S., Born, W. S., & Chu, F. Perception of moving, sounding objects in infancy. *Perception,* in press.

Spelke, E. S., & Cortelyou, A. Perceptual aspects of social knowing: Looking and listening in infancy. In M. E. Lamb & L. R. Sherrod (Eds.), *Infant social cognition.* Hillsdale, N.J.: Erlbaum, 1981.

Sroufe, L. A., & Waters, E. The ontogenesis of smiling and laughter: A perspective on the organization of development in infancy. *Psychological Review,* 1976, *83,* 173–189.

Starkey, P., Spelke, E. S., & Gelman, R. *Number competence in infants: Sensitivity to numeric invariance and numeric change.* Paper presented at the meeting of the International Conference on Infant Studies, New Haven, Conn., April 1980.

Starkey, P., Spelke, E. S., & Gelman, R. *Detection of intermodal numerical correspondence by human infants.* Paper presented at the meeting of the International Conference on Infant Studies, Austin, Tex., March 1982.

Steele, D., & Pederson, D. R. Stimulus variables which affect the concordance of visual and manipulative exploration in six-month-old infants. *Child Development,* 1977, *48,* 104–111.

Steinberg, B. M. Information processing in the third year: Coding, memory, transfer. *Child Development,* 1974, *45,* 503–507.

Stevenson, H. W. Learning in children. In P. H. Mussen (Ed.), *Carmichael's manual of child psychology* (Vol. 1). New York: Wiley, 1970.

Strange, W., & Jenkins, J. J. Role of linguistic experience in the perception of speech. In R. D. Walk & H. L. Pick (Eds.), *Perception and experience.* New York: Plenum, 1978.

Strauss, M. S., & Curtis, L. E. Infant perception of numerosity. *Child Development,* 1981, *52,* 1146–1152.

Tanaka, K. Developmental studies of size constancy. In Y. Akishige (Ed.), Experimental researches on the structure of the perceptual space. *Kyushu Psychological Studies,* 1967, *4,* 98–128.

Tauber, E. S., & Koffler, S. Optomotor response in human infants to apparent motion: Evidence of innateness. *Science,* 1966, *152,* 382–383.

Tolman, E. C. Cognitive maps in rats and men. *Psychological Review,* 1948, *55,* 189–208.

Tonkonogaya, Y. P. Relationship between spatial and quantitative concepts in students in the fourth to sixth grades. In B. G. Anan'yev & B. F. Lomov (Eds.), *Problems of spatial perception and spatial concepts.* Moscow: 1961. (Available from NASA through the Office of Technical Services, Department of Commerce, Washington, D.C.)

Trevarthen, C. Descriptive analyses of infant communicative behavior. In H. R. Schaffer (Ed.), *Studies in mother-infant interaction.* London: Academic Press, 1977.

Tronick, E. Approach of domestic chicks to an optical display. *Journal of Comparative and Physiological Psychology,* 1967, *64,* 529–531.

Tronick, E. Stimulus control and the growth of the infant's effective visual field. *Perception and Psychophysics,* 1972, *11,* 373–376.

Tronick, E., Adamson, L., Wise, S., Als, H., & Brazelton, T. B. The infant's response to entrapment between contradictory messages in face to face interaction. Paper presented at the meeting of the Society for Research in Child Development, Denver, March 1975.

Uzgiris, I. C., & Benson, J. Infant's use of sound in search for objects. Paper presented at the International Conference on Infant Studies, New Haven, Conn., April 1980.

VanDerveer, M. J. *Ecological acoustics: Human perception of environmental sounds*. Unpublished doctoral dissertation, Cornell University, 1979.

Venger, L. A. The emergence of perceptual acts. In M. Cole (Ed.), *Soviet developmental psychology*. White Plains, N.Y.: M. E. Sharpe, 1977.

Vurpillot, E. *The visual world of the child* (W. E. C. Gillham, trans.). New York: International Universities Press, 1976. (Originally published, 1972.)

Vurpillot, E., & Ball, W. A. The concept of identity and children's selective attention. In G. A. Hale & M. Lewis (Eds.), *Attention and cognitive development*. New York: Plenum, 1979.

Walk, R. D., & Gibson, E. J. A comparative and analytical study of visual depth perception. *Psychological Monographs*, 1961, *75*(15, Whole No. 519).

Walker, A. S. Intermodal perception of expressive behaviors by human infants. Journal of Experimental Child Psychology, 1982, *33*, 514–535.

Walker, A. S., Owsley, C. J., Megaw-Nyce, J. S., Gibson, E. J., & Bahrick, L. E. Detection of elasticity as an invariant property of objects by young infants. *Perception*, 1980, *9*, 713–718.

Walthen-Dunn, W. (Ed.). *Models for the perception of speech and form*. Cambridge: MIT Press, 1967.

Warren, R. The perception of ego motion. *Journal of Experimental Psychology: Human Perception and Performance*, 1976, *2*, 448–456.

Watson, J. S. The development and generalization of "contingency awareness" in early infancy: Some hypotheses. *Merrill-Palmer Quarterly*, 1966, *12*, 123–135.

Watson, J. S. Smiling, cooing, and "the game." *Merrill-Palmer Quarterly*, 1972, *18*, 323–340.

Welch, R. B., & Warren, D. H. Immediate perceptual response to intersensory discrepancy. *Psychological Bulletin*, 1980, *88*, 638–667.

Wellman, H. M., Somerville, S. C., Haake, R. C. Development of search procedures in real-life spatial environments. *Developmental Psychology*, 1979, *15*, 530–542.

Wertheimer, M. Principles of perceptual organization. (M. Wertheimer, trans.). In D. C. Beardslee & M. Wertheimer (Eds.), *Readings in perception*. Princeton, N.J.: Van Nostrand, 1958. (Originally published in German, 1923.)

Wertheimer, M. Psychomotor coordination of auditory and visual space at birth. *Science*, 1961, *134*, 1692.

Wilcox, B. L., Teghtsoonian, M. The control of relative size by pictorial depth cues in children and adults. *Journal of Experimental Child Psychology*, 1971, *11*, 413–429.

Wilcox, B. M., & Clayton, F. L. Infant visual fixation on motion pictures of the human face. *Journal of Experimental Child Psychology*, 1968, *6*, 22–32.

Wishart, J. G., Bower, T. G. R., & Dunkeld, J. Reaching in the dark. *Perception*, 1978, *7*, 507–512.

Witkin, H. A., Lewis, H. B., Hertzman, M., Machover, K., Meissner, P. B., & Wapner, S. *Personality through perception*. New York: Harper, 1954.

Wittgenstein, L. *Philosophical investigations*. New York: Macmillan, 1953.

Wohlwill, T. R. Developmental studies of perception. *Psychological Bulletin*, 1960, *57*, 249–288.

Wohlwill, T. R. The development of "over constancy" in space perception. *Advances in Child Development and Behavior*, 1963, *1*, 265–312.

Yonas, A. Studies of spatial perception in infancy. In A. D. Pick (Ed.), *Perception and its development: A tribute to Eleanor J. Gibson*. Hillsdale, N.J.: Erlbaum, 1979.

Yonas, A. Motion carried information for spatial layout and shape. Paper presented at the meeting of the International Conference on Infant Studies, Austin, Tex., March 1982.

Yonas, A., Bechtold, A. G., Frankel, D. G., Gordon, F. R., McRoberts, G., Norcia, A., & Sternfels, S. Development of sensitivity to information for impending collision. *Perception and Psychophysics*, 1977, *21*, 97–104.

Yonas, A., Cleaves, W. T., & Petterson, L. Development of sensitivity to pictorial depth. *Science*, 1978, *200*, 77–79.

Yonas, A., Goldsmith, L. T., & Hallstrom, J. L. Development of sensitivity to information provided by cast shadows in pictures. *Perception*, 1978, *7*, 333–341.

Yonas, A., & Granrud, C. E., Development of depth sensitivity in infants. Paper presented at the Harry Frank Guggenheim Conference on Infant and Neonate Cognition, New York, November 1981.

Yonas, A., & Hagen, M. A. Effects of static and motion parallax depth information on perception of size in children and adults. *Journal of Experimental Child Psychology*, 1973, *15*, 254–265.

Yonas, A., Kuskowski, M., & Sternfels, S. Role of frames of reference in the development of responsiveness to shading information. *Child Development,* 1979, *50,* 495–500.

Yonas, A., Petterson, L., & Lockman, J. J. Sensitivity in 3- to 4-week-old infants to optical information for collision. *Canadian Journal of Psychology,* 1979, *33,* 268–276.

Yonas, A., Petterson, L., Lockman, J. J., & Eisenberg, P. The perception of impending collision in three-month-old infants. Paper presented at the meeting of the International Conference on Infant Studies, New Haven, Conn., April 1980.

Young-Browne, G., Rosenfeld, H. M., & Horowitz, F. D. Infant discrimination of facial expressions. *Child Development,* 1977, *48,* 555–562.

Younger, B. A., & Cohen, L. B. Infant perception of angular relations. Paper presented at the International Conference on Infant Studies, Austin, Tex., March 1982.

Zaporozhets, A. V. Some of the psychological problems of sensory training in early childhood and the preschool period. In M. Cole & I. Maltzman (Eds.), *A handbook of contemporary Soviet psychology.* New York: Basic Books, 1969.

Zelniker, T., & Oppenheimer, L. Modification of information processing of impulsive children. *Child Development,* 1973, *44,* 445–450.

Zelniker, T., & Oppenheimer, L. Effect of different training methods on perceptual learning in impulsive children. *Child Development,* 1976, *47,* 492–497.

Zinchenko, V. P., Chzhi-Tsin, V., & Tarakanov, V. V. The formation and development of perceptual activity. In M. Cole (Ed.), *Soviet developmental psychology.* White Plains, N.Y.: M. E. Sharpe, 1977.

LEARNING, REMEMBERING, AND UNDERSTANDING*

2

ANN L. BROWN, *University of Illinois*
JOHN D. BRANSFORD, *Vanderbilt University*
ROBERTA A. FERRARA, *University of Illinois*
JOSEPH C. CAMPIONE, *University of Illinois*

CHAPTER CONTENTS

INTRODUCTION

Scope of Chapter

It seems somewhat perverse to begin a chapter, particularly one of this length, with details of what will not be included. But the title of learning, remembering, and understanding affords such an open-ended task that we felt it necessary to limit quite stringently the boundaries of the domain we would cover. Given the length of the chapter, some might question whether we were stringent enough!

In the section of the previous Handbook devoted to cognitive development (Mussen, 1970), there were two chapters on learning, one on reasoning and thinking, and one on concept development—but

*Preparation of this work was supported in part by USPHS grants HD-05951, HD-06864, and Research Career Development Award HD-00111 from the National Institute of Child Health and Human Development.

none on memory. In contrast, despite the somewhat catholic title of this chapter, the main data base we will review can broadly be termed memory research, although by memory we include understanding as well as rote recall. We will also be concerned with acquisition mechanisms in a variety of domains that would not traditionally be included in a chapter on memory. This emphasis reflects the gradual change in the late 1960s and in the 1970s away from a concentration on learning mechanisms in a traditional "learning theory" sense toward a consideration of remembering, learning, and understanding within a more eclectic framework. At the end of the 1960s, a great deal of work was conducted on children's learning; during the 1970s, the main emphasis shifted to memory research. We will argue that, at the end of the 1970s and into the 1980s, the focus will again be on learning mechanisms, but this time guided by a cognitive theory of learning that draws its theoretical insights and empirical support from much wider domains than was previously the case.

For a variety of reasons, not least of them being space restrictions, we chose to concentrate on what might be called academic cognition, which differs from everyday cognition along three main axes—effortful-effortless, individual-social, and cold-hot. Everyday cognition is relatively effortless, social, and hot. Bleak though it may sound, academic cognition is relatively effortful, isolated, and cold.

Academic cognition is effortful because the primary focus is on deliberate and often painful attempts to learn. It is demanding of cognitive efficiency; it takes time and effort. Academic cognition is also relatively isolated because it is concerned with how individuals come to be capable of learning on their own. Although a great deal of learning is social, schools measure success largely in terms of independent competence. Finally, academic cognition is cold, in that the principal concern is with the knowledge and strategies necessary for efficiency, with little emphasis placed on emotional factors that might promote or impede that efficiency. Although all these barriers are weakening, a great deal of work in cognitive development can be subsumed under the effortful, isolated, and cold categories, and we will confine ourselves primarily to a review of this work. We were, however, somewhat uneasy with the decision to follow these traditional separations for it does force us to neglect some areas where fascinating new research is being conducted. But as we interpreted our task in this chapter, it was (1) to provide an overview and interpretation of the work already completed on children's learning, remembering, and understanding, and the vast majority of that

work has been on academic learning, and (2) to complement other chapters in the Handbook.

Excellent treatments of effortless, social, and hot cognition do appear elsewhere in these volumes. The importance of environmental factors, particularly other people, on the forms and functions of human learning is discussed at length in the Laboratory of Comparative Human Cognition chapter in this Handbook (*vol. I, chap. 7*). Similarly, Dweck (*vol. IV, chap. 8*) gives an in-depth treatment of emotional factors involved in learning effectiveness. And Mandler (see *vol. III, chap. 7*) deals with scripted learning that guides a great deal of our day-to-day concourse with the world. The early emergence of powerful scripted knowledge permits much everyday cognition to be relatively effortless and undemanding of cognitive resources, in contrast to the labor-intensive state often required in academic learning situations. Although we do deal with social and emotional factors in the latter part of this chapter, we look at these primarily in terms of how they promote effective academic learning, which is in keeping with our declared focus.

Even within our restricted focus, this chapter will not represent a review of the literature. First, this would be impossible because the majority of experimental work in cognitive development in the 1970s was concerned with memory or learning in the broad sense, and there is just too much to cover. Second, this would be unnecessary as previous reviews of the topic are legion; predating this chapter are more than 60 chapters and an excellent book (Kail & Hagen, 1977). Instead, we have chosen to select for consideration areas of research that illustrate some key theoretical questions and the two basic themes of the chapter, the interactive nature of learning and the dynamic nature of learning.

Plan of Chapter

The chapter is divided into four main sections. The first is a brief overview of the principal trends of the 1970s and a statement of the quite dramatic advances in our understanding of children's learning that were made during that period. The second is a selected review of the literature that highlights the interactive nature of learning. The literature is organized within a framework that we refer to as the tetrahedral model through which we consider the activities and characteristics of learners in response to variations in criterial tasks and stimulus materials. In the third section, we deal with some of the controversies surrounding metacognition and other concepts with which it shares a family resemblance. In the fourth section, we concentrate on the implication of work in this area for instruction as well as on the importance of considering instructional effects when formulating basic developmental theory. As this chapter is so long, we have attempted to write each section in such a way that, although there is repeated cross-reference across sections, it is possible for the reader to understand each section in isolation from the others.

MAJOR TRENDS IN RESEARCH AND THEORY BETWEEN 1970 AND 1980

As a chapter on children's learning, this discussion is the historical descendant of those of Stevenson (1970), White (1970), and to a lesser extent Berlyne (1970) in the preceding Handbook (Mussen, 1970); the reader is referred to these excellent pieces for continuity. In this section, we will argue that several fundamental changes, already heralded in the Stevenson, White, and Berlyne discussions, occurred in the study of children's learning in the past decade. Under the influence of American learning theory, the dominant metaphor that was extended to children during the 1960s was that of a passive organism responding to environmental influences. Gradually, the metaphor became that of an active organism, with the child seen as acting upon the environment and through this action defining it—a metaphor of the ''genetic'' approach that White (1970) contrasted with ''learning theory'' approaches to children's learning. Throughout the 1970s the emphasis shifted to the learner's side of the learner—environment equation and a heavy concentration on learners' activities and strategies was a prime characteristic of the decade.

A second major change in the decade was in the nature of the materials that children were set to learn; this change resulted in a reconsideration of knowledge factors. Compatibility between prior knowledge and new learning together with issues of access to, and use of, knowledge became prominent concerns. Another change that followed from the liberation of the concept learning from its traditional boundaries was that essential developmental questions of qualitative growth and change became a main focus of discussion. And, finally, epistemological boundaries that separated ''learning theory'' approaches from, for example, the ''genetic'' approach (White, 1970) were considerably weakened; psychologists from quite disparate backgrounds became concerned with essentially similar issues. These changes in emphasis had a dramatic

effect on the kind of children's learning considered, the methods by which it was examined, and the developmental theories it generated.

Munn (1954) in an earlier version of the Handbook summarized the state of the art in children's learning somewhat depressingly:

So far as discovering anything fundamentally new concerning the learning process, the investigations on learning theory in children have failed. One possible reason for this is that such investigations have from the first been patterned too much after the lines of earlier research with animals and adults in the laboratory. A more likely reason, however, is that the phenomenon of learning is fundamentally the same whether studied in the animal, child, or adult. (p. 449)

The dominating learning theories at the time were those of Hull (1943), Skinner (1938), and Tolman (1932) and, indeed, Munn was in accord with their existing belief in the species independence of the main principles of learning. Although the critical differences between these theories were sufficiently compelling to occupy empirical psychology for 30 years, they also share common features that make them less than ideal models for developmental psychology. All derived their primary data base from rats and pigeons learning arbitrary things in arbitrary situations. All three hoped that their systems would have almost limitless applicability. True to a creed of panassociationism, they shared a belief that laws of learning of considerable generality and precision could be found and that there were certain basic principles of learning that could be applied uniformly and universally across all kinds of learning and all kinds of species. These principles were thought of as species indifferent, activity indifferent, and context indifferent (Brown, 1982a; Turvey & Shaw, 1979).

The theories had very little to say about species variation. Attempts were made to place animal species (also humans differing in age) on a ladder of increasing intellectual capacity. For example, fish were designated less intelligent than rats because they display less of a certain type of learning (Bitterman, 1965). The skills selected as measures of intelligence were quite arbitrary (species independent), as indeed were the situations selected in which to test the presence/absence of the skills (e.g., impoverished environments where the skills to be learned had no adaptive value for the species in question). In summary of this type of enterprise, it has been said (Schwartz, quoted in Rozin, 1976) that, by studying the behavior of pigeons in arbitrary situations, we learned nothing about the behavior of pigeons in nature, but a great deal about the behavior of people in arbitrary situations.

Of more importance to this chapter, the theories had very little to say about developmental issues. The growth of the knowledge base was simply incremental. Although later there were some attempts to deal with reorganization of small basic units into larger complex forms, it was by no means dominant in these theories and by no means an unqualified success. Children learned by the same rules as adults (or pigeons for that matter) and the result of experience was seen as an accumulation of associations varying in strength, with strength determined by the amount and recency of reinforcement/contiguity relations. In short, the theories did not confer special status to age or species differences and, thus, provided a somewhat unlikely metaphor for those whose primary goal is to understand human growth and learning (Brown, 1982a; Rozin, 1976; White, 1970).

Munn's theme was repeated in both the Stevenson and the White chapters on learning that appeared in the previous Handbook (Mussen, 1970). Both were in agreement: ''Research on children's learning is for the most part a derivation of psychological studies of learning in animals and human adults'' (Stevenson, 1970, p. 849); ''No learning theory has even been constructed from studies of children or been specifically directed toward them. Strictly speaking, there is no learning theory in child psychology'' (White, 1970, p. 667). Note that in so stating, White contrasts the ''genetic approach''of Piagetian, Wernerian, and Soviet origin with ''learning theory,'' a commonly accepted division before this decade.

Children's learning became included in the bailiwick of learning theories because its proponents adopted the specialized methods common to investigations of learning in animals.

In most of the specialized procedures, the subject's time to observe or act is partialed out in trials. The time and place of learning is fixed and the environment is isolated, uninterrupted, and asocial. Discrete cues are made prominent. Criteria, set up by observer or instrument, are enforced so that countable, timeable, scorable responses are fished from the stream of behavior. These typical research procedures for the study of learning have regularized it, made the learning situation more repeatable across individuals and laboratories. The (dominant) theories of learning were based upon the possibilities of controlled variation and experimentation possible when learning had been so regularized. (White, 1970, p. 667)

And a great deal of progress was made in systematizing the study of children by subjecting them to learning tasks developed originally for the investigation of animal learning. Many of the main headings in Stevenson's (1970) review reflect this influence: conditioning, drive level, delay of reward, stimulus familiarization, stimulus generalization, satiation and deprivation, extinction, secondary reinforcement, discrimination learning, learning sets, oddity learning, transposition, and reversal-nonreversal shifts were all studied originally with animals. Stevenson and White provide extensive reviews of the great deal of information that was gathered from a consideration of children learning in such settings. This was a prolific period of research and we gained a great deal of information of lasting value, especially concerning selective attention (Zeaman & House, 1963), symbolization (Berlyne, 1970; Kendler & Kendler, 1962; Reese, 1962), hypothesis testing (Levine, 1969), curiosity and exploration (Berlyne, 1970), learning sets (Harlow, 1959; Reese, 1968), stimulus differentiation (Tighe, 1965), social learning (Bandura & Walters, 1963), and behavioral engineering (Bijou & Baer, 1967; Lumsdaine & Glaser, 1960; Skinner, 1971).

Whereas Munn in 1954 seemed quite content with the age and species independence of learning principles, Stevenson (1970) and White (1970) reflected the concern during the 1960s with species differences and particularly with age differences in learning, which they reviewed extensively. Furthermore, in both of their earlier chapters in Mussen (1970), one senses the beginning of a dissatisfaction with the types of learning investigated and their potential contribution to a developmental theory of learning. For example, Stevenson questions whether the principles of learning gained in the confines of the traditional laboratory task will hold up in a variety of settings, particularly those of a social or everyday nature. White queries whether ''these experimental situations and their variations offer too narrow a window through which to explore the underlying developmental process'' (White, 1970, p. 671). Further, White calls for a consideration of mechanisms of age change rather than just descriptions of ''before and after the learning process,'' all themes that are current today.

White contrasted the learning theory approach to that of the genetic tradition, always attractive to developmental psychologists but supplanted for a while because of the sheer elegance of the models and methods of learning theory at a time when ''the transcription of the genetic point of view into a rigorous and tough-minded program for maintaining and continuing research'' had not taken place (White, 1970, p. 663). These approaches were seen as essentially incompatible and a merger impossible unless basic tenets were abandoned or softened to permit an accommodation. We will argue that the seeds of such a merger were planted and did come to fruition in the 1970s. Next, we will consider some of the shifts in emphasis that could at least enable a merger, even if not actually bring it about.

One legacy of the learning theory approach was that of an essentially passive organism (see Reese, 1973, 1976, for a discussion of this metaphor). To improve learning from this perspective, one would not try to change the learner; instead, one would change the stimulus environment to which the learner is responsive. For example, one might improve learning by increasing the number, immediacy, and quality of the reinforcement or one might vary the type or saliency of the stimulus dimensions, and so on. There is nothing wrong with this approach; apart from anything else, it works—learning improves. But the focus is heavily directed to one side of the learner—context interaction. During the late 1960s and early 1970s, this focus shifted, with the learner's activities receiving the lion's share of attention. Influenced by European (Flavell, 1963; Hunt, 1961) and Soviet (Cole & Maltzman, 1969) genetic traditions and by the landmark work of Bruner (Bruner, Goodnow, & Austin, 1956; Bruner, Olver, & Greenfield, 1966) and Flavell (1970b), attention turned to the child's strategies for learning.

One reflection of this shift is that by the middle 1970s, developmental journals were dominated by studies of children's knowledge and use of strategies, particularly those devised in the service of deliberate remembering. As many reviews predate our chapter (e.g., Belmont & Butterfield, 1977; Brown, 1975, 1978; Flavell, 1970b; Hagen, Jongeward, & Kail, 1975; Kail & Hagen, 1977; Meacham, 1972; Ornstein, 1978), we will not review this work in detail. Suffice it to say that a major contribution of the 1970s was the impressive body of knowledge generated on the subject of the development of active acquisition strategies of learning, such as rehearsal (Atkinson, Hansen, & Bernbach, 1964; Belmont & Butterfield, 1971; Bray, 1973; Brown, Campione, Bray, & Wilcox, 1973; Flavell, Beach, & Chinsky, 1966; Hagen, Hargrave, & Ross, 1973; Hagen, Meacham, & Mesibov, 1970;

Hagen & Stanovich, 1977; Keeney, Cannizzo, & Flavell, 1967; Kingsley & Hagen, 1969; Ornstein & Naus, 1978), categorization (see *Mandler, vol. III, chap. 7*, for a review; see also Moely, 1977; Puff, 1979), elaboration (Borkowski, in press; Borkowski & Wanschura, 1974; Jensen & Rohwer, 1970; Rohwer, 1973; Turnure & Thurlow, 1973), and retrieval mechanisms (Buschke, 1974; Keniston & Flavell, 1979; Kobasigawa, 1974, 1977; Ritter, Kaprove, Fitch, & Flavell, 1973), together with the child's developing knowledge and control of her repertoire of strategic action, that is, metacognition (Borkowski & Cavanaugh, 1979; Brown, 1975, 1978, in press-a; Butterfield & Belmont, 1977; Butterfield, Siladi, & Belmont, 1980; Campione, in press-b; Campione & Brown, 1977, 1978; Flavell, 1971a, 1976; Flavell & Wellman, 1977; Wellman, in press).

A second major change that was consolidated during the 1970s was in the type of materials children were required to learn. Prior emphasis on color/form stimuli, nonsense syllables, and words and pictures in isolation was supplanted by a focus on organized or potentially organizable material (see *Mandler, vol. III, chap. 7*, for a review). Children in the 1970s were asked to learn picture sequences (Brown, 1975, 1976; Brown & Murphy, 1975; Day, Stein, Trabasso, & Shirey, 1979; Horowitz, Lampel, & Takanishi, 1969), sentences (Paris & Lindauer, 1977), stories (Brown & Smiley, 1977; Brown, Smiley, Day, Townsend, & Lawton, 1977; Mandler & Johnson, 1977; Stein & Glenn, 1979; Stein & Trabasso, in press; Trabasso, Stein, & Johnson, in press; also see *Mandler, vol. III, chap. 7*, for a review), and expository texts (Brown & Day, in press; Brown, Palincsar, & Armbruster, in press; Markman, 1979).

Perhaps an even more dramatic change was in the subject matter to be learned, for toward the end of the decade children as well as adults were examined as they attempted to learn in semantically rich domains, such as chess (Chi, 1978), physics (Larkin, Heller, & Greeno, 1980), mathematics (Resnick, 1976), and history and social sciences (Voss, in press). With these shifts in emphasis, questions about the knowledge base also changed from a consideration of the accumulation of facts and their reinforcement histories to a consideration of the organization and coherence of information along with the compatibility of new information to prior experience (Brown, 1975; Paris & Lindauer, 1977). Providing an inspiration for this trend in the developmental literature was the work of Bransford (see Bransford, 1979) with adults and the work on contextual sensitivity of learning generated by cross-cultural psychologists (for recent reviews see the Laboratory of Comparative Human Cognition, in press-a, in press-b; Rogoff, 1981).

The third major change that occurred during the 1970s is that, to some extent, the boundaries that were clear in the chapters of Mussen (1970) were weakened in the movement toward a cognitive theory of learning. To illustrate, we will give a brief and oversimplified description of the major trends in the 1970s as reflected in reports in the developmental journals.

The beginning of the 1970s saw the formation of a somewhat uneasy alliance between developmental psychologists trained in the tradition of neo-behavioral learning theories and their descendants, information processing models, and psychologists influenced by the traditional developmental schools, such as those of Piaget and Werner. This alliance was forged through a common interest in learning strategies.

Information processing psychologists, deeply influenced by the prototypic memory model of Atkinson and Shiffrin (1968), began to emphasize the importance of control processes, that is, strategies and routines for making more efficient use of a limited capacity information processing system. Such common control processes as rehearsal received considerable attention. Typical of this approach in developmental psychology was the work of Belmont and Butterfield (1971, 1977), Brown and Campione (Brown, 1974; Brown et al., 1973; Campione & Brown, 1977), Hagen (Hagen & Stanovich, 1977), and Ornstein and Naus (1978).

Contemporaneous with this work, influenced primarily by John Flavell's pioneering efforts, cognitive developmental psychologists became interested in memory strategies, defined as deliberate planful activities introduced in the service of remembering. Following the landmark paper of Flavell et al. (1966), rehearsal mechanisms again received the lion's share of attention, followed closely by organization and elaboration. Together, developmental psychologists from both backgrounds provided a rich description of the development of mnemonics for learning common laboratory (and often school) material. Thus, developmental psychologists originally influenced by the dominant adult approaches as well as those initially influenced by Piaget became interested in the activities of the learner and in the acquisition of principled rules and strategies (Gelman & Gallistel, 1978; Siegler, 1976).

The result of these shared interests was a common concern with production deficiencies, a term originally introduced in the context of learning theories (Kendler, 1964; Reese, 1962) and adopted by Flavell et al. (1966). Flavell (1970b) extended the concept "beyond the simple cue-producing responses to which it had been limited in Hull-Spence theory and applied it to mnemonic strategies and other complex cognitive operations—making it much more consistent with Vygotsky's usage" (Reese, 1979; for a recent discussion, see Paris, 1978). In short, from a variety of backgrounds, developmental psychologists became interested in the use of strategies, whether naturally evolved or deliberately trained. This led the information processing group to embark on a series of training studies to examine whether children's memory deficits were largely the result of inefficient use of control processes or the result of structural limitations in the system—a problematic theoretical distinction (see Belmont & Butterfield, 1977; Brown, 1974). Meanwhile, Flavell (1970b) and his coworkers were concerned with a very similar issue: Do children fail to use strategies (1) because they do not think to, or (2) because strategies will not help, or (3) because children cannot use them? Neo-Piagetians were also concerned with training studies as a method of revealing competencies often obscured by performance factors (see Flavell, 1970a; also see *Gelman & Baillargeon, vol. III, chap. 3,* for a history of this debate).

Thus, one reason for a merger was methodological; training studies were employed by psychologists from diverse backgrounds to address questions about the nature of developmental change. Regardless of the theoretical impetus, the results of this spate of studies are clear. Briefly, immature learners tend not to introduce strategies to aid their learning. They can, however, be trained to do so, and their performance dramatically improves when they receive such instruction. Unfortunately, it also became clear that in the absence of specific instructions, the immature learner rarely uses such strategic activities intelligently, even following relatively explicit and extensive training (Belmont & Butterfield, 1977; Brown, 1974, 1978; Brown & Campione, 1978; Butterfield et al., 1980; see also *Intervention Research*). Similarly, competencies of young children uncovered by workers in the genetic tradition (see Gelman, 1978) were also shown to be extremely fragile (Flavell, 1982).

The dramatic failure of training studies to effect major changes in the intelligent use of strategies was a main feature of research in the middle 1970s and provided a prime impetus to the growth of the concept of metacognition. Impressed by the pervasive nature of production deficiencies, Flavell and his colleagues became interested in children's awareness of their own memory processes and the subject, task, and strategy variables that influence learning (Flavell & Wellman, 1977). It is this form of self-knowledge that Flavell dubbed metamemory (Flavell, 1971a). The information processing group also began to concentrate on issues of executive control, long a cause of theoretical controversy within their models. The executive is imbued with a wide range of overseeing functions, including predicting, monitoring, reality testing, and the coordination and control of deliberate strategies for learning (Brown, 1978); and it was in performing these executive routines that young children experienced difficulty. The work of Belmont and Butterfield (1977), Borkowski (in press), and Brown and Campione (Brown, 1975, 1978; Brown & Campione, 1981) are good examples of this approach. Failures to plan, monitor, and oversee were thought to be in large part responsible for transfer failures in the young, as was the lack of relevant declarative knowledge concerning the domain memory. These somewhat separable forms of metacognition—executive control and declarative knowledge—were examined extensively in the later part of the decade. Similarly, Piaget and his colleagues (Inhelder, Sinclair, & Bovet, 1974; Karmiloff-Smith, 1979a, 1979b; Karmiloff-Smith & Inhelder, 1974/1975; Piaget, 1976, 1978) also became increasingly concerned with the twin forms of metacognition, self-regulation during learning and conscious control of the learning process. Despite some thorny theoretical confusion, there is considerable agreement concerning the young child's peculiar difficulties in this domain (see *Metacognition, Executive Control* . . . and *Intervention Research*).

Toward the later part of the 1970s, points of common interest so far outnumbered original differences that the old barriers between learning theorists and cognitive development theories were no longer viable. The common interest in strategies and their control, never a major concern in the adult literature, weaned a great many developmental psychologists from their dependence on adult models and paved the way for a merger between those from the genetic tradition and those whose training had been primarily influenced by dominant adult models. From all directions came a concern for developing a cognitive theory of learning that would give a central place to the developmental issues of growth and change (Brown, 1979, 1982a).

Janus-faced at the onset of the 1980s, developmental psychologists seem to be in remarkable agreement concerning the major advances in the 1970s and the key questions facing the construction of a cognitive learning theory in the 1980s. First, it is increasingly clear that the model will be essentially interactive. To illustrate this point, we have chosen to organize our review of the literature around a tetrahedral interactive learning model introduced by Jenkins (1979). To understand learning, it is necessary to consider both subject (activity, prior knowledge, capacity, etc.) and environmental factors (task demands, materials, contexts, etc.) as well as the state of mutual compatibility between them.

A second major issue that has an honorable history is that of stages versus continuous age changes in acquisition (see *Brain and Behavioral Sciences,* 1978; for recent reviews of this question, see also Brown, 1982b; Case, 1981; Feldman, 1980; Fischer, 1980; Flavell, 1971b, 1982; Gelman, 1978). One current instantiation of this traditional topic is the question of accessibility of knowledge (Brown, 1982a; Brown & Campione, 1981; Gelman & Gallistel, 1978; Rozin, 1976). The prime question concerns the fragility of early competence versus the robust transitional nature of mature forms of the same skill. In an influential paper on the topic of access, Rozin (1976) made two main points. First is the notion of welding (Brown, 1974; Fodor, 1972; Shif, 1969)—intelligence components can be strictly welded to constrained domains, that is, skills available in one situation are not readily used in others, even though they are appropriate. Quite powerful computational processes may be available to the very young child but only for the performance of quite specific forms of computations (Fodor, 1972). Rozin argues that young children's programs are "not yet usable in all situations, available to consciousness or statable." Development is "the process of gradually extending and connecting together isolated skills with a possible ultimate extension into consciousness" (Rozin, 1976, p. 262). The second part of both of these quotes refers to Rozin's second main point, that of conscious access. Even if skills are widely applicable rather than tightly welded, they need not necessarily be conscious and statable. Conscious access to the routines available to the system is the highest form of mature human intelligence.

Pylyshyn (1978) made a similar distinction between multiple and reflective access. Multiple access refers to the ability to use knowledge flexibly. Knowledge is informationally plastic, in that it can be systematically varied to fit a wide range of conditions. Reflective access refers to the ability to mention as well as use the components of the system. Similarly, Gardner (1978) cites as hallmarks of human intelligence (1) generative, inventive, and experimental use of knowledge rather than pre-programmed activities (multiple access) and (2) the ability to reflect upon one's own activity (reflective access). The twin concepts of flexibility and reflection are important issues with wide implications for theories of learning and development, and they will be a main theme of this chapter (see *Metacognition, Executive Control . . .* and *Intervention Research*).

Finally, a main theme of the chapter, which we believe will be the principal question of the 1980s, is that of mechanisms of growth and change. A basic problem in understanding learning is to explain how the learner progresses from knowledge gained in specific learned experiences to the stage when she can use knowledge flexibly. This is the question behind access theories: How do isolated skills become connected together, extended, and generalized? (Brown & Campione, 1981; Rozin, 1976). Development is the process of going from the specific-context bound to the general context free, although truly general, context-free, statable laws may be a chimera—an idealized end point. Knowledge in some sense must always be context bound, but contextual binding permits of degrees. It is the range of applicability of any particular process by any particular learner that forms the diagnosis of expertise or cognitive maturity. The less mature, less experienced, less intelligent suffer from a greater degree of contextual binding, but even the expert is bound by contextual constraint to some degree (Brown, 1982a). Thus, a key developmental question is how children go from strict contextual binding to more powerful general laws. One commonly suggested mechanism is conflict—conflict induces change, a notion basic to learning theories (Berlyne, 1970), dialectic theories (Wozniak, 1975), as well as Piagetian models (Inhelder et al., 1974). A serviceable hypothesis is maintained until a counterexample, an invidious generalization, or an incompatible outcome ensues. Conflict generated by such inconsistencies induces the formulation of a more powerful rule to account for a greater range of specific experiences (see *Metacognition, Executive Control . . .*).

Brown (1982a) described three methods that developmental psychologists are beginning to use widely to attack the problem of development head-on. The first method is to provide as rich and detailed a description as possible of the qualitative differences in both factual and strategic knowledge between young (novice) and older (expert) learners (Chi, 1978, 1981; Siegler, 1981). Based on this in-

formation, it is possible to address the transition process directly by observing learning actually taking place within a subject over time. This is essentially the microgenetic approach advocated by Vygotsky (1978) and Werner (1961). The majority of developmental data to date has been cross-sectional. The performance of groups of children, varying in age or level of expertise, is compared and contrasted. Even a great deal of longitudinal research has a surprisingly cross-sectional flavor, in that we tend to see frozen shots of behavior taken at quite long intervals. Both approaches provide a picture of cognition in stasis rather than evolving, as it were, right before one's eyes. The revived interest in microgenetic analysis of both adult (Anzai & Simon, 1979) and children's (Karmiloff-Smith, 1979a, 1979b) learning enables psychologists to concentrate not only on qualitative descriptions of stages of expertise but also to consider transition phenomena that underly the progression from beginning to expert states. As we come to understand more about qualitative descriptions of the stages of expertise and about the mechanisms that seem to induce change, a third approach is made possible, that is, to attempt to understand change better by engineering it (see *Intervention Research*). Each approach serves a complementary function in contributing to our knowledge about learning processes. As a result of such an attack, we should become better able: (1) to describe the stages of development, that is, model developmental progressions and trajectories within a domain; (2) to model self-modification processes in individual learners acquiring expertise; and (3) to engineer transition by the provision of appropriate experience. If so, we must come to understand better the essential elements of learning. Armed with such understanding we would be in a better position to help the less mature acquire the appropriate self-awareness to enable them to learn how to learn (see *Metacognition, Executive Control . . .* and *Intervention Research*).

Central themes of this chapter are, then, acquisition of information, access and use of knowledge, and transition mechanisms that are involved in change. We argue that the learning model that will be necessary to incorporate these themes will be an interactive model. Redressing earlier unbalanced treatments that were either heavily learner centered or heavily task centered, the interactive models of the 1980s will be primarily concerned with learner/task compatibility. We would like to emphasize, however, that it is only because of the exponential increases in our knowledge concerning activities, knowledge, materials, and task variations in relative isolation that we are in the current position of preparedness to attack the complexity of interactive models, the subject of our next section.

A TETRAHEDRAL FRAMEWORK FOR EXPLORING PROBLEMS OF LEARNING

The majority of developmental memory research conducted in the late 1960s and throughout the 1970s led to the establishment of a fairly detailed picture of how the child becomes a school expert, that is, how the young learner acquires academic skills and comes to know how to learn deliberately. To illustrate the current state of our knowledge, we would like to introduce the diagram in Figure 1. At first glance this seems like a simple model, particularly in comparison with the elaborate flow diagrams favored by modern cognitive psychologists, who were imprinted on the computer in their formative years. Unfortunately, as is often the case in psychology, the simple model becomes more complex on closer examination. It does, however, provide a useful aid to help us remember the major factors that should be taken into account when considering any aspect of learning. We would like to stress that not only should we, the psychologists, consider the tetrahedral nature of the learning process but also that this is exactly what expert learners come to consider when they design their own plans for learning (Flavell & Wellman, 1977; also see *Metacognition, Executive Control . . .*).

There are a minimum of four factors that comprise the learner-in-context, and these factors interact in nontrivial ways. The four factors are: (1) the learner's activity, (2) the characteristics of the learner, (3) the nature of the materials to be learned, and (4) the criterial task. Because of the sheer weight of empirical evidence, we will give only a few illustrations of the types of factors that have been considered under each of these rubrics and then provide selected examples of the essentially interactive nature of the model.

Learning Activities

The activities that the learner engages in are a prime determinant of efficiency. Some systematic activities that learners use are referred to as strategies, although what is strategic and what is not has not been made particularly clear in the literature. We will concentrate primarily on deliberate plans and routines called into service for remembering, learning, or problem solving, although we recognize that

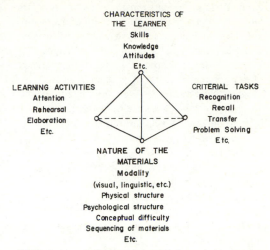

Figure 1. An organizational framework for exploring questions about learning. (Adapted from Jenkins, 1979, and Bransford, 1979.)

a great deal of cognition is not as effortful as this (Brown, 1975; Hasher & Zacks, 1979; Naus & Halasz, 1979).

Strategies are part of the knowledge base and, therefore, could be classified as a characteristic of the learner within the model. But the learner's activities are not necessarily synonymous with the strategies available in the knowledge base. Learners can access strategies or any other form of knowledge to help learning, but they need not. Having knowledge, of any kind, does not necessitate using it effectively. In this section, we will concentrate on the systematic application of a plan, routine, or activity designed to enhance learning.

One of the most established facts is the active strategic nature of a great deal of learning in older children. During the 1960s and 1970s, developmental psychologists provided a rich picture of the development of strategies for learning and remembering as well as quite convincing evidence that efficient performance in a wide variety of tasks is in large part dependent on the appropriate activities the subject engages in, either on his own volition when trained to do so or even when tricked into doing so by means of a cunning incidental orienting task. As children mature, they gradually acquire a basic repertoire of strategies, first as isolated task-dependent actions, but gradually these may evolve into flexible, and to some extent generalizable, skills. With extensive use, strategic intervention may become so dominant that it takes on many of the characteristics of automatic and unconscious processing (Shiffrin &

Schneider, 1977). Under instructions to remember, the mature learner employs a variety of acquisition and retrieval strategies that are not readily available to the developmentally less mature individual.

As we stressed earlier, this is an influential area of developmental psychology where a great deal of progress has been made. We would like to emphasize just how robust the strategy-performance link is by pointing out (1) the *reliability* of the finding that increased strategy use leads to increased memory performance and (2) the *magnitude* of the effect that is due to strategic intervention. For example, there is ample evidence that the extent, consistency, and type of rehearsal use is intimately related to recall efficiency (Belmont & Butterfield, 1977; Ornstein & Naus, 1978). Mature use of a rehearsal strategy following training can increase the performance of retarded children to the level set by untrained adults (Butterfield & Belmont, 1977). Similarly, mature application of an organizational strategy increases recall of college students by a large order of magnitude (Bower, Clark, Lesgold, & Winzenz, 1969). The reliability and magnitude of the effect that is to strategic intervention should not be overlooked.

Although this is one area where psychologists have been successful at providing a rich description of development, there are still some notable holes in the picture. Until recently, there has been a marked paucity of information concerning the early emergence of plans and strategies for learning. Although Flavell and his colleagues have always been interested in memory in preschool children (Flavell, 1970b; Wellman, 1977) and although there is currently increasing research activity in this area (Perlmutter, 1980), it is still true that our knowledge about early cognition is somewhat limited and rather negative, consisting of many more descriptions of what young children cannot do than of what they can do (Brown & DeLoache, 1978; Gelman, 1978).

The problem of defining early competence has been especially acute in the area of memory research. Until recently, the prime concern was with the competencies that define the school-aged child, specifically the shift to more adequate understanding that seems to occur between ages 5 and 7 (White, 1965). The bulk of studies during the early 1970s concerned rote learning of lists and the emergence of rehearsal, categorization, or elaboration as tools to enhance performance (Kail & Hagen, 1977). These strategies tend to emerge in a recognizable form between 5 and 8 years of age. One by-product of this focus is that, indeed, we do know a great deal concerning the development of classic strategies (rehearsal, elaboration, etc.) during the grade-school

years, but we know less about the precursors of these strategies. If young children are not, for example, rehearsing on a deliberate memory task, we have no way of knowing what it is that they *are* doing.

The second gap in our knowledge about strategic development is again due to paucity of data, this time concerning the development of memory and learning strategies *after* the middle grade-school years. There are several excellent programs of research that detail the refinement and elaboration of list-learning strategies during the high school years, notably those of Belmont and Butterfield (1971, 1977), Neimark (1976), Ornstein and Naus (1978), and Rohwer (1973); but, until recently, there was little attention paid to strategies other than rehearsal, categorization, and elaboration. This question is beginning to be addressed in interesting and exciting ways, and we will review some of the recent work on strategic development in adolescents in this section.

A third change in our attack on the strategy-development issue has been greater emphasis on the interplay of knowledge factors and strategic action. Although no one denied the importance of knowledge (Brown, 1975; Flavell, 1970b), it has only recently been the subject of extensive empirical investigation (Chi, 1981; Ornstein & Corsale, 1979; Ornstein & Naus, 1978), at least intraculturally. Elegant intercultural demonstrations of the importance of knowledge factors in memory performance (Laboratory of Comparative Human Cognition, in press-a, in press-b; Rogoff, 1981) still provide the most extensive empirical support for the position.

As it would clearly be impossible to give a detailed review of the development of strategic learning, and there are many prior sources for perusal by the devotee, we will illustrate this topic with a brief description of one classic example, the development of rehearsal. The remainder of this section will be devoted to the relatively neglected areas of (1) the early emergence of precursors of strategic intervention and (2) the development of strategies in the adolescent period. Knowledge-based issues will be reserved until later (*Characteristics of the Learner*).

A Prototypical Memory Strategy: Rehearsal

Developmental psychologists are not alone in their dependence on rehearsal strategies for theory building. A strong dependence on rehearsal can be found in the proliferation of memory models in the adult literature of the early 1970s; this is true of both the ''modal model'' (Atkinson & Shiffrin, 1968; Murdock, 1967; Waugh & Norman, 1965) and the ''levels-of-processing'' varieties (Craik & Lockhart, 1972). We have chosen rehearsal as our illustration of traditional strategies research, not because we accord undue status to this activity but simply because the description of developmental processes is particularly rich in this domain.

A typical study of the late 1960s and early 1970s was one where the relationship of strategy use to memory performance was investigated. Prototypical experiments of this genre consisted of an assessment phase and a training phase (Flavell et al., 1966). It was readily shown that young or slow children tended not to produce mnemonic strategies in the assessment phase but could readily be trained to do so; and, in so doing, they greatly improved their memory performance. We would like to stress that this prototypical finding has been replicated many times and is one of the most robust findings in the developmental literature (Belmont & Butterfield, 1977; Brown, 1975, 1978; Flavell, 1970a; Hagen et al., 1975; Kail & Hagen, 1977; Ornstein & Naus, 1978; etc.).

A neat twist on this procedure is that if older students are prevented from using a strategy, for example, rehearsal they produce levels and patterns of performance that are very similar to younger or slower learners (Belmont & Butterfield, 1977; Brown, Campione, Bray, & Wilcox, 1973). These findings were taken as strong evidence in favor of the utility of strategic intervention. Young children trained to rehearse perform like older spontaneous users of the strategy; spontaneous users prevented from so indulging perform like the young children (for limitations on the effects of training, see *Intervention Research*).

Considerable evidence exists to support a basic presence/absence position; when rehearsal is present the result is good performance, when rehearsal is absent the result is bad performance. However, the presence/absence argument was always bedevilled by confusion as to what rehearsal was and what activities could be counted as rehearsallike. Thus, in studies where observation (Flavell et al., 1966) or electromyographic recordings (Locke & Fehr, 1970) of lip activity have been used to denote rehearsal, children as young as 4 or 5 are credited with strategy use. Evidence of systematic coordination of acquisition and retrieval demands for complex rehearsal plans is not readily apparent until well into the high school years (Belmont & Butterfield, 1977; Neimark, 1976; Ornstein & Naus, 1978).

A thumbnail sketch of the development of spontaneous rehearsal strategies follows a path that could be traced through studies concerned with other acquisition and retrieval strategies (e.g., Keniston & Flavell, 1979; Kobasigawa, 1977; Reese, 1977; Rohwer, 1973; see also *Mandler, vol. III, chap. 7*).

Primitive precursors of rehearsal are preschoolers' sporadic attempts to maintain material via naming, pointing, or eye fixation (Wellman, Ritter, & Flavell, 1975). By 5 years of age, children attempt to name (label) some of the items some of the time. Labeling becomes well established during the early grade-school years and is a prime example of what has been called maintenance rehearsal (Craik & Watkins, 1973; Cuvo, 1975; Ornstein & Naus, 1978). The prototypical pattern of rehearsal from third graders would be a rote repetition of single items. With increasing sophistication, children begin to employ more items in their rehearsal sets and, hence, are said to engage in cumulative rehearsal (Belmont & Butterfield, 1971). Development during the later grade-school and early high school years consists of the continual refinement of a cumulative rehearsal strategy that includes planning of both the acquisition and retrieval components (Butterfield, Wambold, & Belmont, 1973) and increasing attention to the size and composition of the rehearsal set (Ornstein & Naus, 1978). Finally, children begin to produce elaborated rehearsal (the contrast to maintenance rehearsal). They become increasingly sensitive to the presence of conceptual organization in the to-be-remembered list and capitalize on this inherent structure whenever possible (Ornstein & Naus, 1978). Thus, the rehearsal plans of high school children and adults are active, systematic, elaborative procedures, whereas those of younger children are rote-maintenance procedures. The systematic refinement of the rehearsal strategy is gradual; the evolution is not fully completed until adulthood, if then. In general, however, college students devise spontaneous rehearsal plans that are readily tailored to meet the specific, and even the changing, demands of the particular task at hand (Butterfield & Belmont, 1977). Finally, even with this supposedly most content free of all strategies, rehearsal use is intimately related to knowledge and capacity factors (Ornstein & Naus, 1978).

Early Emergence of Strategies

In the mid to late 1960s, developmental psychologists were interested in a phenomenon known as the 5-to-7 shift (White, 1965), that is, did a qualitative change in cognitive functioning occur at the point where children were making the passage to formal schooling? (Rogoff, Sellers, Pirrotta, Fox, & White, 1975). Interest in this question was shown by developmental psychologists with quite diverse backgrounds. Learning theorists disputed whether a qualitative shift occurred between nonmediated learning in the preschooler to mediated learning in the older child (Kendler & Kendler, 1962; Zeaman & House, 1963). Similarly, a shift from absolute to relational learning was contested (Brown & Scott, 1972; Kuenne, 1946; Reese, 1968). At the same time, Piagetians were interested in the qualitative changes that accompany the transition from pre-operational to concrete operational thought, also believed to occur between 5 and 7 years of age (see *Gelman & Baillargeon, vol. III, chap. 3*).

It was in this context that the early work on the development of memory strategies was often interpreted as yet another exemplar of the ubiquitous 5-to-7 shift. Although Flavell and his colleagues did consider earlier production of strategies (Flavell et al., 1966), there was some question concerning the leniency of the criteria that attributed strategic thinking to the preschool child (Wellman, 1977). For the most part, investigators concentrated on the emergence of the three common strategies: rehearsal, categorization, and mnemonic elaboration. The age trend they found tended to confirm the impression of another 5-to-7 shift. Prior to 5 years of age, children were deemed passive, nonstrategic, and nonplanful in memory tasks, just as they were judged to be preoperational, precausal, and egocentric in classical Piagetian tasks and nonmediated responders in learning tasks.

Recent evidence suggests that in many domains preschool children have more competence than was initially supposed (Gelman, 1978). A successful method for uncovering early competence is to situate the experiment in a manner ideally suitable for the preschoolers' interests and abilities. The idea is to look for evidence of competence not only in the traditional laboratory tasks but also in situations where that competence could most readily be shown. To considerably oversimplify the comparative literature, the two major techniques that have been used to expose early competency have been (1) to *strip away* all but the most essential elements of the task to reveal its cognitive demands in the simplest possible form and (2) *to situate the experiment in the familiar*. A combination of these two techniques marks the better cross-cultural experimental work (see *Laboratory of Comparative Human Cognition, vol. I, chap. 7*) and also reveals early competence in preschool children. For example, Shatz (1978) argued cogently that earlier (or later) competence in communicative situations can readily be accounted for by the excess baggage of the task. In unfamiliar situations with arbitrary stimuli, where the children must expend considerable cognitive effort identifying the items and comprehending the nature of the game, they appear unable to communicate adequately with a peer. In situations where the game is familiar, the information to be conveyed is meaningful, and, therefore, cognitive capacity is freed for the communicative aspect of the task, the younger children look far more reasonable; they communicate well. Flavell and his colleagues (Salatas & Flavell, 1976) have also shown that complexity and familiarity are important factors leading to a diagnosis of egocentrism in children. Similarly, Gelman and her colleagues (Gelman, 1978; Gelman & Gallistel, 1978; see also *Gelman & Baillargeon, vol. III, chap. 3*) have made this point quite graphically for several concrete operational tasks (for early discussions of these points see Flavell, 1970a, and Flavell & Wohlwill, 1969).

A consideration of the memory development research in the 1970s also suggests that a gradual progression to competency is more representative than the idealized 5-to-7 shift from nonstrategic to strategic status. Although full-blown forms of rehearsal, categorization, and elaboration are not apparent before 5 and relatively stable by 7 to 8 (at least in a recognizable form), it is an illegitimate inference to conclude that, therefore, the propensity to be planful is absent prior to the emergence of these activities. Recent concentration on preschool learners and memorizers has revealed a very early propensity to be strategic in situations where the goal of the activity is clear to the child, the setting familiar, and the index of strategic use more lenient (Meacham, 1972; Wellman, 1977). We will consider some of this evidence next.

There have been two major approaches to the study of preschool memory. That of Perlmutter and Myers (1979) and their associates is to assume that strategies are largely absent before 5 years of age and then to find an alternative explanation of why memory on both recall and recognition improves from 2 to 4 years. They assume that the improvement is due to increased knowledge, and, of course, they are right. Increases in knowledge are very likely to result in changes in memory performance on tasks that tap that knowledge. Perlmutter and Myers have successfully documented this point. Their evidence concerning the absence of strategies is largely inferential however; indeed, it is very difficult to distinguish between changes that are due to strategies and changes that are due to knowledge on a free-recall task, a point to which we will return.

The second main approach is to assume that although full-blown versions of rehearsal, categorization, and so on, are not likely to be present before 7, early indices of strategic intervention can be found, and they are related to efficiency. Istomina (1975) in research conducted in 1943, provided a rich picture of the gradual emergence of strategies in preschool children. Istomina set children the task of remembering a list of items either to be bought at a play store or as a lesson. Recall was superior in the game situation. Istomina argued that the improved memory in the shopping condition followed because the goal of the activity made sense to the child. Although the youngest children knew what it meant to remember, this was not enough: "They must not only know what remembering is by itself, but also be able to see it as an end result, an objective to which activity must be directed, i.e., to grasp it as a goal" (Istomina, 1975, p. 59). Istomina's study produced a delightful set of protocols detailing individual children's emergent procedures for remembering. The strategies adopted and the way in which they were used became increasingly complex and sophisticated over the age period of 4 to 6.

Two contemporary research programs aimed at the early emergence of planful memory have shown competence at even younger ages than Istomina. Wellman and his colleagues (1977) were concerned with engineering situations in which evidence could be found for the emergence of primitive precursors of strategic action. For these reasons, Wellman abandoned the traditional free-recall task in favor of such problems as memory for future activities, preparation for future retrieval demands, and search strategies (Wellman, 1977; Wellman & Somerville, in press).

A nice example of this approach is a study by Wellman et al. (1975). Children of 2 and 3 were shown a toy dog that was subsequently hidden under one of a set of containers. The experimenter left the room and asked the child either to wait with the dog or to remember where the dog was hidden. Their behavior in the experimenter's absence was observed via a one-way mirror. It proved difficult to obtain data from the 2-year-olds, who preferred not to wait around in the experimenter's absence! The 3-year-olds in the memory condition, however, displayed a variety of delightful strategies, such as looking fixedly at the hiding place, retrieval practice (such as looking at the target container and nodding yes, looking at the nontarget containers and nodding no), and baiting the correct container (by resting their hand on it, by moving it to a salient position, etc.). Children who demonstrated some activity in anticipation of future recall did remember better.

Wellman and his colleagues have also studied logical search strategies in young children. An object might be lost in a particular location in their playground and the children's attempts to retrace their steps in a logical fashion measured. For example, in a study by Wellman, Somerville, and Haake (1979), a search was conducted for a camera lost in one of eight locations on a playground. The child's picture was taken by the to-be-lost camera at locations 1, 2, and 3. Evidence of logical search would be the child's initial search directed to location 3 as the site of the last place the camera had been used. From age 3 1/2 upwards, the evidence for such logical search is quite compelling.

Some recent work by DeLoache and Brown (1979; 1981a; 1981b) combines the location search method of Wellman et al. (1975) and the large-scale environmental method of the Wellman et al. (1979) study. Using an overlearned hide-and-seek game, they found evidence of planful preparation for memory tests in children as young as 18 months of age. In a series of six studies, the children were required to find a toy hidden in a location in a large-scale environment (e.g., behind a chair, under a pillow, etc.). The main difficulty in these tasks was finding conditions that produced less than ceiling performance! We will discuss only one of these studies here because of the somewhat unusual pattern of results. Children between 18 and 23 months of age were divided into two groups; one group played the hide-and-seek game in the laboratory, the other in the home. During the delay interval the child's activities were videotaped. Evidence of planning for future retrieval included (1) verbalizing about the toy or its hiding place, (2) looking toward the hiding place, (3) pointing at the hiding location, (4) approaching the hiding location (the child walked toward and hovered around the correct location), (5) peeking at the hidden toy, and (6) attempting to retrieve the toy (reaching for it, an attempt that was foiled by the experimenter).

The proportion of overt indices of planning was twice as high in the laboratory than in the home. This might at first seem surprising (it was replicated twice) as it is generally assumed that familiar settings afford a suitable environment for the display of any strategic propensities that young children might be harboring. But consider one factor, accuracy. In both conditions, the children's performance was extremely high (85% or above correct). We argue that it is only in the unfamiliar setting that planning is necessary. Faced with the more demanding task of locating a hidden object in an unusual location, even children under 2 will show some overt signs that they plan for their anticipated retrieval attempts (DeLoache & Brown, 1981a).

The early emergence of learning strategies is an area wide open for future research. For example, we need to understand more about the conditions under which primitive precursors of memory strategies occur, the stability with which they are used by the same child across different settings, the similarities and differences between earlier and later forms of the activity, and so on. Similarly, we know little about the influence of knowledge-based factors, and the terms ''familiar setting,'' ''ecological validity,'' and so on, need a great deal of ''unpacking.'' But, the initial work on these topics is both exciting and illuminating.

Late Development of Strategies

The majority of work concerned with the development of strategies has focused on activities that enhance rote recall of words or pictures, but these are not the only form of learning. Indeed, in the high school years, although list learning is still a common activity, the emphasis shifts to strategies for coping with much richer semantic domains. And learning shifts to texts; students must not only perfect their reading, but they must learn how to learn from reading (Brown, 1981, 1982b). A great deal of the adolescent's school life is devoted to learning content from text and developing skills of scientific reasoning. The student must develop strategies for dealing with materials that are principled, organized, and coherent.

In this section, we will consider examples of the strategies students develop to enable them to handle such situations. We would like to point out, however, that although the strategies have changed, the developmental methodology and theory that guided the investigation of ''simple'' rote-recall activities has also been influential in guiding the investigations of more complex activities. In many senses, the qualitative developmental pattern found between grades 6 and 12 on reading and writing tasks is very similar to that found between grades 1 to 6 on simple rote-recall tasks. First, there is the early sporadic emergence of an appropriate activity, followed by increasing stability and transituational application with repeated use. These activities gradually become systematized and consolidated into a robust, reliable pattern of attacking reading and writing tasks. Production deficiencies and inefficiencies (Flavell, 1970b) occur along the way and these are related to performance decrements exactly as they are in young children undertaking simpler list-learning tasks. Precocious maturity with the strategies leads to adultlike patterns and levels of performance. Mature learning is in large part the result of strategic application of rules and principles and the systematic suppression of serviceable, but less mature, habits.

And, even more striking in this domain, strategic activities cannot be understood in isolation from the other factors in the tetrahedron.

Literacy is the primary aim of schooling. Learning to read and write demands strategies that are appropriate to the ''literacy domain,'' just as learning to remember demands strategies appropriate to the ''remembering domain.'' In this section, we will examine some aspects of studying from texts, expository writing, and scientific reasoning, the three prime tasks of academic literacy.

Studying. There is a long history of interest in the types of knowledge and strategies students bring to the task of learning from texts—notetaking, underlining, adjunct aids, question asking, outlining, and so on (Anderson & Armbruster, in press; Brown, 1981, 1982b, in press-a). In the past, however, the work has been limited in several ways: first, the majority of prior work has concentrated almost exclusively on the study activity of adults, usually college students. Second, the majority of studies have been correlational rather than manipulative. And third, the most important limitation is that the majority of studies have shared a concentration on product rather than on process. That is, the main focus has been on some outcome measure, such as the test scores of students who do or do not use a certain strategy. Little or no consideration has been given to the activity of the studier, what she is *actually doing* while studying. An example of this is the large number of experiments that have considered the product (how well studiers do on tests), for example, of notetakers, but have ignored the processes that the notetaker employs; even the notes themselves are not examined for evidence of the process that the taker of notes might be using (Brown & Smiley, 1978).

In a series of studies with high school students, Brown and her colleagues have been investigating these common study strategies, using theories and methodologies adapted from developmental psychology. Of particular interest has been the relation between the activity spontaneously generated as an aid to learning and the performance levels achieved on a variety of retention and comprehension measures. A main focus has been on the influence of various forms of knowledge on the development and maintenance of a variety of selective attention (Brown, 1981, 1982b) and effort-allocation (Wellman, in press) strategies.

As a preliminary to this program of research, Brown and Smiley (1977) estimated the ability of students from 3rd to 12th grade to rate the units of complex texts for importance to the theme. The 12th graders could reliably distinguish the four levels of importance that had been rated previously by college students. The 7th graders did not differentiate the two intermediate levels of importance, but they did assign their lowest scores to the least important and highest scores to the most important elements. The 3rd graders made no reliable distinction between levels of importance in their ratings and even 5th graders could only distinguish the highest level of importance from all other levels.

These initial findings have important implications for studying. To go beyond retention of just a few main points, that is, to achieve a more complete fleshed-out memory of the text, one must engage in active strategies to ensure increased attention to important material that will not be retained automatically. If young children have difficulty distinguishing what is important, they will also have difficulty studying. Quite simply, one cannot selectively attend to important material in the absence of a fine sensitivity to what *is* important (Brown, in press-a).

As children mature, they become better able to identify what are the essential organizing features and crucial elements of texts (Brown & Smiley, 1977). Thanks to this foreknowledge, they make better use of extended study time (Brown & Smiley, 1978). For example, when given an extra period for study, the majority of younger students (grades 5 to 7) appear to favor the strategy of passive, even desperate, rereading. But a certain proportion of students at all ages take notes or underline during study; the proportion increases with age. An analysis of the notes taken reveals a clear concentration on text segments previously rated as important.

The subsequent recall of the strategy users was superior to that of the nonstrategy users, and there was a clear relation of strategy use to increased efficiency after extra study time. Even 5th and 7th graders who spontaneously underlined or took notes showed an adultlike pattern and used extra study differentially to improve their recall of important elements. We would like to emphasize that efficiency of recall after extra study was not a function of age per se but of efficient strategy use. The 7th graders who took effective notes recalled as well as college students. The 11th graders who did not take suitable notes recalled like 7th graders. Similarly, in a summary-writing task, 5th and 7th graders who make adequate rough drafts before attempting a final version perform like college students (Brown, Day, & Jones, in press).

This sensitive relation between knowledge of textual importance, knowledge of suitable strategies, and estimation of one's current state of mastery has been found in a series of schoollike tasks, such as notetaking, outlining, summary writing, and retrieval-cue selection (Brown, 1980, 1981; Brown & Day, in press; Brown & Smiley, 1978; Brown, Smiley, & Lawton, 1978). Here we will describe only one project in detail because it illustrates a pervasive problem we wish to emphasize, that is, students are often impeded in their development toward more mature study habits by the existence of a serviceable, well-used, inferior strategy that results in partial success.

Within the series of studies conducted by Brown and her colleagues, qualitative differences were repeatedly found in the type of notes, summaries, and outlines produced by spontaneous users of a selective attention strategy. For example, the principal condensation rules used to summarize were found to be: (1) deletion of trivia, (2) deletion of redundancy, (3) substitution of either a superordinate term for a list of exemplars or substitution of a superordinate event for a list of subordinate episodes, and (4) selection of topic sentence if one were thoughtfully provided by the writer or invention of a topic sentence if one were needed. To map the developmental progression associated with the use of the basic condensation rules, Brown and Day (in press) examined the ability of students from grades 5, 7, and 10 as well as various college students to use the rules while summarizing. Even the youngest children were able to use the two deletion rules with above 90% accuracy; but, on the more complex rules, developmental differences were apparent. Students became increasingly adept at using the topic-sentence-selection rules, with college students performing extremely well. However, the most difficult rule, invention, was rarely used by 5th graders, used on only a third of appropriate occasions by 10th graders, and on only half the occasions when it was appropriate, even by college students. Of interest is the fact that junior college students, a population suspected of having difficulty with critical reading and studying, performed like 5th graders on the summarization task (Brown & Day, in press). Experts (rhetoric teachers), however, used the selection and invention rules almost perfectly.

One explanation for the differential difficulty of the basic condensation rules is that they demand differing degrees of cognitive manipulation and depart to a greater or lesser extent from the already existing strategy favored by the younger participants, the copy-delete strategy. Grade 5 students tend to treat the task of summarizing as one of deciding whether to include or delete elements that actually occur in the surface structure of the original text. The strategy is as follows: (1) read text elements sequentially, (2) decide for each element whether to include or to delete, (3) if inclusion is the verdict, copy the unit more or less verbatim from the text (Brown, Day, & Jones, in press). The same general strategy is employed by grade 5 and grade 7 notetakers (Brown & Smiley, 1978), and it is also applied to the task of outlining. Interviews conducted with students in grades 7 to 8 concerning their study and research habits again suggest that this is a common method (Brown, 1981).

The simple copy-delete strategy is then used consistently in a variety of text-processing tasks by 11- to 14-year-old students, and it works relatively well, in that it gets the job done—it results in a product that is recognizably a summary, an outline, or a set of notes. It is because the simple copy-delete strategy is so generally applicable and meets with partial success that it is difficult to get students to attempt to use more complex rules. The fact that a student must replace a primitive strategy that works adequately with a more sophisticated approach is often a difficult impediment to progress.

Experts' strategies are a radical departure from the copy-delete strategy. They systematically depart from both the surface wording and the temporal sequence of the text, combining across paragraphs, rearranging by topic cluster, and stating the gist in their own words. They rely heavily on the invention rule that demands a synopsis in their own words of the implicit meaning of the paragraph. The invention rule requires that the students add information rather than just delete, select, or manipulate sentences. It is these processes that are the essence of good summarization, that are used with facility by experts, and that are most difficult for novice learners (Brown & Day, in press; Brown, Day, & Jones, in press).

In summarizing the results of an extensive series of experiments on study skills, Brown (1981) emphasized four main points. The first three were: (1) the gradual emergence of strategic planning; (2) the relationship between effective plans and efficiency, age per se is not the crucial variable; and (3) the close interdependence of strategic action and the remaining points in the tetrahedron. During junior high and high school years, students develop and increasingly fine tune a battery of serviceable skills for learning from texts. These include underlining and taking notes on main ideas (Brown & Smiley, 1978); developing macrorules for comprehension, retention, and synopsis writing (Brown & Day, in press); outlining and mapping (Armbruster, 1979); self-questioning (André & Anderson, 1978; Brown, Palincsar, & Armbruster, in press; Palincsar & Brown, 1981);

concentrating on previously missed or difficult segments of text (Brown, Campione, & Barclay, 1979; Brown, Smiley, & Lawton, 1978); and the general propensity of treating studying as a purposive attention-directing and self-questioning act.

A fourth, more speculative point is that partially adequate strategies are often developed and that these impede progress toward the more efficient strategy. Once students have developed the inefficient strategy, they tend to apply it consistently in a variety of situations and maintain it for quite long periods of time. It is only with a great deal of practice that they abandon it in favor of the more mature strategy, indeed, many high school (and college) students never do. We will examine other examples of this phenomenon in the work of Scardamalia and Bereiter (1980) on writing and Kuhn and Phelps (in press) on scientific reasoning.

Writing.   Expository writing is the second major school activity that has recently received considerable attention from cognitive and instructional psychologists. As we do not have space to detail the natural history of the development of writing and revising skills, the reader is referred to excellent recent papers by Bereiter and Scardamalia (1980, in press), Collins and Gentner (1980), Nold (1980) and Scardamalia and Bereiter (1980, in press). Here we will concentrate primarily on the development of the partially adequate knowledge-telling strategy (Bereiter & Scardamalia, 1980).

Bereiter and Scardamalia describe the executive decisions demanded of children who are faced with a typical school writing problem. Thinking of what to write is a very difficult problem for the young student, both at the beginning of the task and throughout. For example, Keeney (1975) found that children who ceased writing after producing less than 100 words invariably reported that their problem was simply that they could not think of anything more to say. With a little prompting, however, it could readily be shown that such children had a great deal of potentially usable knowledge. Nondirective prompts, such as "another reason is" or "on the other hand," were sometimes all it took to get the writing process going again (Bereiter & Scardamalia, 1980). Planning problems in writing are apparent even when the child is writing about a domain of which she has considerable knowledge.

A typical composition of primary grade children will consist of the form, I think X because of Y. The child might then give another reason for X or (rarely) explicate the link between X and Y. Usually at this junction the child will indicate that there is nothing left to say. The second common tactic that young children employ to extend their texts is to introduce a new theme based on *Y*. For example, when writing an essay on winter, the child might begin with, "I think winter is the best time of year because you can make snowmen." The child will then proceed for many more sentences telling all she knows about snowmen. Having exhausted that topic, the child will declare that the composition is ended, seemingly having forgotten the original purpose of the essay (Bereiter & Scardamalia, 1980). This general ploy is referred to as the knowledge-telling strategy (Bereiter & Scardamalia, in press).

A prototypical example of the knowledge-telling strategy is that adopted by many college students. In an essay examination, there is a question that cannot be answered. Instead of leaving the question blank, the student writes down everything he knows about that topic, even though the product in no way constitutes an adequate answer to the specific question. College students resort to knowledge telling in times of desperation. However, knowledge telling is the dominant mode of the young writer who, using key words to set the process in motion, tells all he knows about a domain without tailoring or fine tuning the output in response to the actual question. Flower (1979) has referred to this approach, charitably, as writer-based prose, that is, prose dominated by the writer's memory of the domain rather than the reader's needs.

Flower and Hayes (1980), considering talk-aloud protocols during writing, have noted the absence of advanced planning strategies in knowledge-telling subjects. Elaboration, restatement, and revision of the goals and subgoals of the assignment are repeatedly stated by experts. Knowledge-telling, writer-based novices do not often indulge in these refinements.

Reader-based, expert writers have reasonable criteria for terminating their writing task. The job is done, the goal is reached, the question is answered. How then do knowledge-telling writers exit the arena? Termination rules for them include more mundane criteria, such as "the end of the page," "I have three paragraphs and an essay must have three paragraphs," and so on.

The knowledge-telling strategy is distinguished by (1) a lack of goal-related planning; (2) a lack of internal constraints in the text, one sentence being as deletable as any other; (3) a lack of interconnectedness in the written output; (4) reliance on purely forward-acting serial production rather than recursive forward-backward revision processes; and finally (5) a remarkable lack of anything other than merely cosmetic revision (Nold, 1980).

The knowledge-telling strategy gives way to reader-based, responsive, mature writing only with great difficulty. It is an inefficient strategy that is retained because it meets with at least partial success. Like most production inefficiencies (Flavell, 1970b), it lies halfway between the younger child's failure to find any content for writing, and the mature strategy of tailoring the output to the goal via executive strategies of goal-directed actions. It shares with the copy-delete strategy (Brown, 1981) its resistence to change because it results in a product that in many cases is acceptable; it shares with copy-delete the problem that it impedes the development of high-level activities. Fortunately, it also shares with copy-delete the fact that training can be introduced to overcome this obstacle to effective performance (Brown, Campione, & Day, 1981; Day, 1980). For example, Scardamalia and Bereiter (in press) describe a variety of training devices for helping children develop (1) search and selection strategies prior to writing and (2) on-line processes needed to revise, evaluate, and correct written output. The primary aim of these procedures is to get children to concentrate on the higher level nodes in their discourse structure and prevent them from "downsliding" (Collins & Gentner, 1980) to details or lists of possible entries under a node. They aim to keep the child focused on the task, for example, of writing about winter and discourage downsliding to all the information in the node snowman. The child learns to forego knowledge telling terminated by arbitrary exit rules and to develop reader-based, topic-responsive, mature expository writing.

Scientific Reasoning. High schools demand of their successful clients not only increased sophistication in literacy skills but also the development of formal operational skills of mathematic and scientific reasoning. Space limitations are such that we cannot deal with this topic in any reasonable detail (see *Siegler, vol. I, chap. 4*). Instead, we will describe one program that again illustrates the difficulty learners have in abandoning an existing strategy that results in partial success.

Kuhn and Phelps (in press) examined the development of scientific reasoning in the combination-of-elements task introduced by Inhelder and Piaget (1958). Their approach was to select fourth- and fifth-grade students who are (or should be) at a transition point for the skill in question and to examine their increasing sophistication with the task over a period of 3 months. By adopting a microgenetic approach (Werner, 1961), they hoped to study the process of development directly. Typical of Piagetian learning situations, the only feedback the students received was that generated by their own actions on the physical material (Inhelder et al., 1974; Karmiloff-Smith & Inhelder, 1974/1975; Piaget, 1976; see also *Self-regulation* in our discussion, *Roots of Metacognition*).

The problem requires that the students determine which chemical of three present in a demonstration mixture is responsible for producing a chemical reaction (simplest problem); students must systematically isolate elements in such a way that they are able to determine unambiguously which of the potential elements is causally related to the outcome of chemical change. The mature strategy is to test, in isolation, each element in the outcome-producing combination to assess its individual effect. Subjects were judged to have solved the initial problem if they specified the single effective element and excluded all other elements; they then moved on to more complex problems where two elements, and then three, were combined to produce the effect.

We will give only the flavor of the results. The most striking feature was the variability in the strategies a subject applied to the problem both within and across sessions. Far from a smooth gradual progression in expertise, the students, at least in the initial sessions, were very patchy in their strategy use. Students' insight into the problem shown in early sessions did not necessarily carry over to later sessions. Although many of the advanced strategies appeared in the initial sessions, stabilization and consolidation of this early competence was not achieved until quite late. Performance mastery was attributable to both this consolidation and systematization of advanced strategies (Karmiloff-Smith, 1979a) *and* a gradual, reluctant discarding of previously used, but less adequate, strategies. Kuhn and Phelps (in press) argue that it is the second of these processes, that is, the freeing from the clutches of inadequate but attractive strategies, that was the most formidable impediment to learning.

The most attractive lure in the combination-of-elements task was the tendency to seek evidence that confirms rather than refutes a current hypothesis (Bartlett, 1958; Tschirgi, 1980; Wason & Johnson-Laird, 1972). The second inadequate but preferred strategy was that of false-inclusion, that is, the tendency to infer that whatever occurs in conjunction with the outcome is causally related to that outcome. These two false strategies were difficult for subjects to relinquish on the easy problems, thereby impeding initial success; and they tended to recur among subjects who went on to the more advanced problems. We would like to argue that the confirmation-seeking and false-inclusion strategies share common features with the copy-delete and knowledge-telling strategies just reviewed. All are maintained because they do result in partial success and are recognizable attempts to get the job done. They are resistant to change because they are typical of everyday reasoning (Bartlett, 1958; Cole, Hood, & McDermott, 1978), where demands for the most efficient strategy are rarely stringent. The process of development is not just one of acquiring increasingly more refined and sophisticated strategies; development involves the systematic consolidation and growing conviction of the appropriateness of the mature strategies combined with the rejection of plausible but less efficient habits.

Strategy Development Revisited

In summary, we are beginning to map out the development of strategies for learning over a greatly increased age range and over a greater diversity of tasks than was the case in the late 1960s and early 1970s. Strategic activities can be observed at very young ages if the observer knows for what to look. In contrast, faced with the academic task of writing, studying texts, or scientific-reasoning problems, much older learners are surprisingly sporadic in their strategic intervention. But, we would argue that the development of complex strategies demanded by advanced academic tasks traces a route that is similar in kind to that followed during the acquisition of list-learning routines. Rather than being a question of presence or absence, development involves the systematic organization and refinement of effective routines at the expense of ineffective activities. Major impediments to progress are attractive intermediate strategies that meet with partial success and are consistent with the type of reasoning that dominates everyday cognition (Bartlett, 1958).

We argued that for any strategic activity one must distinguish between the early fragile state and its later robust quality (Flavell & Wohlwill, 1969). Although it is possible to find primitive precursors at a very young age, the activity is fragile and can easily disappear. The activity is also tightly welded, or restricted, to limited domains of activity (Brown, 1974, 1982a; Fischer, 1980; Fodor, 1972; Rozin, 1976). The fact that the child thinks to prepare for retrieval in a toy-hiding game does not necessarily mean that he will select a suitable cue to bait the correct container in a very similar retrieval-cue-selection task. The appearance of strategies is patchy, the propensity to be strategic has not become so ingrained that the child will routinely search for ways to be strategic.

Although we have ample evidence from the early

memory literature that stripping away unessential demands and situating the experiment in the familiar are procedures that result in surprising competence in preschool children, we would not like to give the impression that it is only the nature of laboratory tasks that has led us to underestimate the cognitive maturity of the preschooler (Flavell, 1982). It is just as important to note that 2-year-olds show fleeting glimpses of their capabilities only under circumstances where considerable ingenuity has been expended in selecting a suitable setting. And, even then, young children's learning and problem-solving strategies are unreliable. Sometimes they do show signs of knowing a great deal more than was previously supposed. But more often they do not. In the current trend to prove the early emergence of almost any cognitive capacity, we should not overlook the obvious fact that 6- and 7-year-olds are able to show their understanding in a wider range of situations, including the much-maligned laboratory task. The cognitive competence of the grade-school child is far more robust; it is manifested on many criterial tasks. This compares sharply with the fragile nature of the preschooler's fleeting moments of insight. We would like to argue (Karmiloff-Smith, 1979a; Piaget & Inhelder, 1973; Thornton, in press; see also *Gelman & Baillargeon, vol. I, chap. 3*, and *Metacognition, Executive Control* . . .) that early competence tends to be rather tenuous, consisting of a set of juxtaposed procedures that have not been organized into a systemic, coherent body of knowledge.

It is the coherence, sturdiness, and resistance to counter suggestions that sets the older child apart from the very young learner. The propensity to be strategic on a variety of learning tasks is much greater, and a considerable degree of ingenuity is often needed on the part of the experimenter to prevent the older child from being strategic. The mature form of the strategy differs from the earlier forms not only in terms of its stability but also in terms of its relatively transituational quality. For example, the young child's use of a primitive rehearsal strategy is unreliable; he fails to refine it to conform with changing task demands, and he often fails to use it in a variety of situations where it would be applicable. Strategy use in mature users is characterized by its robust nature, its internal coherence, and its transituational applicability. There are, of course, limits to this transituational flexibility. Everyone's knowledge is context-bound to a certain degree (Brown, 1982a) and this is true of strategy utilization. We will return to this point later (when we discuss *Intervention Research*).

Our final point on strategies is that we cannot emphasize enough the importance of other factors in the tetrahedron for determining the form and function of strategic intervention. Strategies and knowledge factors are intimately related. Even the prototypic knowledge-free strategy of rehearsal (one can perfectly well rehearse meaningless material) is influenced by the nature of the material to be rehearsed and the knowledge that the subject has concerning the potential organization of that material (Ornstein & Naus, 1978). The nature of the criterial task is again a crucial factor in determining whether a strategy will be used. Adults do not rehearse when the list is either too long or too short or when another strategy can be applied with less effort. And young children are only spontaneously strategic in circumstances where the criterial task represents a goal that they understand (e.g., finding a toy); remembering for remembering's sake is not a situation that will reveal young children's propensity to make active attempts to learn. Strategic action must be evaluated as one part of the tetrahedron, influenced by the subjects' knowledge and capacities, the nature of the materials to be learned, and the end point of learning, the criterial task.

Characteristics of the Learner

We turn now to the general question of what it is that the learner brings to the learning situation. This is no small topic! The characteristics of the learner include, of course, the previously described repertoire of strategic skills that the learner may or may not access when planning her learning activities. Some of the many other factors that can be considered under this heading are those general catch-all categories of knowledge, variously referred to as knowledge-of-the-world, the knowledge base, memory in the broad sense, schematic knowledge, and so on (Brown, 1975). Further, there is the popular topic of metacognition (Flavell & Wellman, 1977); one characteristic of the learner is, indeed, the declarative knowledge that she has concerning her own knowledge, be it factual or strategic. And finally, a major characteristic of the learner that continues to be controversial is her capacity.

In this section we will consider only (1) some recent work reaffirming the importance of subjects' factual knowledge in determining their learning activities and efficiencies and (2) the topic of capacity limitations affecting efficiency of learning. Both topics will be treated primarily as illustrative of the necessity to consider the learners' characteristics when viewing the interactions of the tetrahedron.

We will defer to a separate section our discussion of metacognition.

Factual Knowledge

The obvious fact that what a person currently knows must influence what he can learn has received considerable attention in recent years. Developmental psychologists must be concerned with issues of differential knowledge because age and knowledge are usually highly correlated. There has been, however, a tendency to act as if the prime consideration was to control or equate for knowledge factors. Developmental variations in knowledge are often regarded as a source of extraneous variability. For example, in standard memory tasks an attempt is made to insure that even the youngest subjects are familiar with the stimuli, at least to the level that they can name them. If a name is not readily given by a young participant, the experimenter generously provides one and then operates as if stimulus familiarity were equated across ages. That familiarity may involve more than access (or even speed of access) to the name code was rarely considered in early studies of memory development. Variations in performance across ages were attributed to factors other than variations in knowledge, for example, capacity limitations or strategy deficits (Chi, 1976).

Perhaps a more enlightened way that developmental psychologists have expressed concern with differential knowledge has been in their treatment of instruction. If one wishes to instruct a child to perform in a way he previously could not, the most intelligent way to proceed is to uncover his starting level of competence. It is a widespread assumption of developmental psychologists of quite divergent theoretical viewpoints that the distance between the child's existing knowledge and the new information he must acquire is a critical determinant of how successful training will be (Inhelder et al., 1974; Piaget, 1971; Siegler, 1981). Thus, it is a critical concern for those involved in instruction to detail the stages through which the learner must pass. The map between the child's current understanding and the instructional routine selected is a critical determinant of the success of that instruction.

Then there is the question of task difficulty. A task is easy or hard and material is comprehensible or not to the extent that it maps onto the preexisting knowledge and preferences of the learners. Young thinkers who lack some basic knowledge should be hindered in their comprehension and retention of any information that presupposes the existence of that prior knowledge. A good example would be studies that show a clear link between children's ability to free-recall material and the compatibility of that material with their own knowledge (Denney & Ziobrowski, 1972; Naron, 1978; Perlmutter & Ricks, 1979; Stolz & Tiffany, 1972). This area of research is plagued with methodological difficulties (Murphy, Puff, & Campione, 1977), but there does seem to be support for the influence of stimulus familiarity on children's recall performance. For example, Richman, Nida, and Pittman (1976) used familiar words known to all their subjects, but the children's judgment of their meaningfulness varied as a function of age. When common lists were used, the older children outperformed the younger ones, but when the lists were tailored to the child by equating them for meaningfulness in an age-appropriate manner, no age differences were reported. Similarly, Lindberg (1980) used standard taxonomic lists versus lists made up of categories relevant to the children's lives (i.e., names of school teachers, television shows, books in their reading curriculum, etc.). Again, the age difference disappeared on the familiar materials, thus, providing strong positive evidence of the effects of knowledge on recall performance.

Another successful ploy is to show that experimentally induced preexisting knowledge determines what is understood and retained from passages. This has been successfully demonstrated with both children (Brown, Smiley, Day, Townsend, & Lawton, 1977) and adults (Anderson & Pichert, 1978; Bransford, 1979; Chiesi, Spilich, & Voss, 1979); even young children disambiguated vague or misleading sections of text in a manner congruent with their preexisting expectations (Stein & Trabasso, in press). Indeed, it is not necessary in a standard prose-recall situation to manipulate age as well as preexisting knowledge. Inducing adults to take different perspectives before reading a passage is an ideal way of demonstrating that comprehension is an interaction of expectations and actual textual materials (Anderson & Pichert, 1978; Bower, Black, & Turnure, 1979; Bransford, 1979).

Recent work by Chi has shown an intriguing inverse finding that is just as pertinent to our argument. Chi has been investigating the memory and metamemory performance of skilled chess players, an honorable psychological pursuit dating back at least to Binet (1894). Chi's twist is that in her sample of players knowledge is negatively correlated with age; the children are the experts, whereas the adults are the novices. It is the experts who outperform the novices both in terms of actual memory performance and in predicting in advance how well they will perform.

Let us consider another of Chi's studies in detail, the dinosaur expert (Chi & Koeske, in press). Chi's subject was a 4 1/2-year-old boy who knew more than anyone need know about dinosaurs. The child was asked to generate the names of all the dinosaurs he knew. In seven sessions the child generated 46 dinosaurs of which 20 were selected to be the better known and 20 the lesser known set. Assignment to a set was based on frequency of generation (4.5 vs. 1) and the frequency with which the dinosaurs occurred in the texts from which the child had been read.

Chi established both the properties the child could recognize and generate in a clue game in which the experimenter and the child took turns generating properties that the other had to identify. Using the properties and frequency data, a network representation was mapped with directional links between nodes representing generation or recognition. The number of links between nodes indicated the frequency of mention. The links fell into seven main types: habitat, locomotion, appearance, size, diet, defense mechanism (e.g., spines), and nickname. On the basis of these mappings, Chi could identify what knowing more means; knowing more is identified with the number of property nodes associated with each concept node, the number of interrelations among the nodes, and the frequency with which each dinosaur node shows a particular property node. The better known set differed from the lesser known set quite dramatically in terms of the complexity, density, and interrelatedness of the representation. Although it may not be possible to equate for knowledge in psychological experiments, Chi's elegant study does point to ways of mapping a child's representation and of quantifying what it means to know more.

Having mapped the knowledge base concerning well-known and not-so-well-known dinosaurs, Chi looked at the child's free recall of the two sets. The lists were read to the child and he was required to recall them three times. The number of items recalled across trials for the better known dinosaurs was 10, 9, and 9, and for the lesser known dinosaurs it was 6, 5, and 4. The child's recall for the better known set was twice as high as for the lesser known set.

What is not clear in the dinosaur study is the significance of the findings vis-à-vis the strategies and knowledge interrelationship. The free-recall task is a difficult vehicle for studying the interaction of strategies and knowledge. Improved recall over trials and even clustering occur in adults and children exposed to taxonomic lists that they are not set to learn deliberately, that is, under incidental learning situations (Murphy & Brown, 1975; Ritchey, 1980). Chi would like to argue, as does Lange (1978), that improvement in both the quality and quantity of recall across ages is not solely the result of strategic intervention, as has often been claimed, but is more the result of the corresponding growth in knowledge as a function of age. Hence, she concludes that "the elaborateness and richness of the representation of the concepts in memory *determines* the quantity and quality of recall" (Chi & Koeske, in press).

We would argue that although Chi has positive evidence for the importance of knowledge factors, she has only indirect evidence concerning strategic factors. And further, we would argue that the critical experiment, although technically difficult, is feasible and has not yet been undertaken.

Consider the recall trials data. Chi's dinosaur aficionado recalled 10 of the 20 well-known animals and 5 of the less well-known. Performance, if anything, dropped over the three trials. If the learner were using an organizational strategy to guide recall, one would expect him to improve over trials; indeed, in developmental work it is essential to give multiple trials for evidence of strategy use to show up (Murphy et al., 1977). Chi's learner did not show this prototypical improvement over trials, thus providing some indirect evidence that strategies for learning were not employed. But Chi's expert was 4 years old.

Consider a fictitious 8-year-old dinosaur expert who has at her command not only an organized knowledge base but also a serviceable repertoire of memory strategies. We presume that this learner would show a superiority based on knowledge factors, that is, she would recall more from her familiar than from her unfamiliar set. But, in addition, she would be able to employ deliberate strategies to help her improve over trials on both sets. If the task were modified somewhat so that the dinosaurs were presented on cards (pictures), one might gain additional evidence of strategic activity, such as sorting into categories (habitat, locomotion, etc.), *in the service of* memorizing. Sorting should be easier and more stable for the familiar than less familiar sets; if so, one might predict greater improvement over trials for the better known set. Relationships between input and output organization might also provide additional evidence of the interrelation of strategies and knowledge.

Persistent controversy in the memory development literature has surrounded this issue of inferring something about the nature of the *representation* of knowledge (semantic memory) on the basis of *per-*

formance in memory tasks. One controversial instantiation of this problem was the concern with putative improvements over time in memory for logical organizations (Liben, 1977; Piaget & Inhelder, 1973). A less esoteric version of the problem is the routine attribution of knowledge structures only to those who use them in the common free-recall task. Furthermore, there is no reason to suppose that the presence of organized recall *necessarily* implicates the use of deliberate strategies. Lange (1978) has pointed out that clustering may very well be the more-or-less automatic result of strong interitem associations in the knowledge base. Lange's argument is one of semantic capture, that is, the compatibility between the organization of the material and the organization in the head is such that, willy-nilly, output is organized. Unfortunately, it is difficult to distinguish between effects that are due to automatic semantic capture and the use of deliberate organization strategies in free-recall tasks (*Mandler, vol. III, chap. 7*).

Tasks other than free recall that tap the child's organizational structure provide a different picture of the child's knowledge base. For example, in a semantic priming task (Sperber, McCauley, Ragin, & Weil, 1979), the speed of identifying the second word of a pair is greater if the two words are drawn from the same, as opposed to different, categories. The latency to identify the word cat is faster if the previous word was horse than if it were house. On such tasks, very young and quite severely impaired learners appear to be sensitive to the taxonomic structure of the lists. Comparable data can be gleaned from developmental studies of release from proactive inhibition (Kail & Siegel, 1977).

We would like to argue that the nature of the criterion task is in large part responsible for the attribution of a certain kind of knowledge to a certain kind of knower. At least this is true in the current literature. We should also be wary about leaping to conclusions about knowledge factors without systematically examining the nature of both the materials and the criterion task. Consider the following study by Smiley and Brown (1979). Children from kindergarten, first and fifth grade, college students and elderly adults were given a picture-matching task and asked to indicate which two items of three were alike. The items could be paired taxonomically or thematically, that is, a horse could be paired either with a saddle (thematic grouping) or a cow (taxonomic grouping); a needle with a pin (taxonomic) or a thread (thematic). Younger (kindergarten and first-grade) and older (chronological age [CA] = 80) subjects reliably chose the thematic grouping,

whereas the schooled samples (fifth graders and college students) chose the taxonomic grouping. But consider a slight change in the criterial task. After the students had made and justified their original choice, they were asked if there were any way that the alternate pairing could be justified; the subjects were perfectly happy to give the alternative explanation. Choice of thematic or taxonomic organization reflected preference rather than a fundamental change in underlying organization. This preference affected both learning rate (Smiley & Brown, 1979) and memory performance (Overcast, Murphy, Smiley, & Brown, 1975).

Whereas there is little evidence as yet to suggest that there are fundamental qualitative differences in the nature of representation as a function of age (see *Mandler, vol. III, chap. 7,* for a detailed discussion), there are differences in preference for various organizational formulas and differences in the facility with which experts and novices can gain access to the organization that they have. For example, the young child's taxonomic knowledge may be revealed in passive situations, like the semantic priming task, but this does not mean that she can access that organization to form the basis of a systematic sort or—even more demanding—harness that organization to design a strategy in the service of deliberate remembering. If we use only the most demanding task, we will have a pessimistic picture of what the child knows. The nature of the criterial task must be scrupulously examined before we make inferences concerning the organization of knowledge or the child's propensity to be strategic.

Dynamic Versus Static Conceptions of Knowledge

It is not uncommon for theorists to attempt to explain performance differences between young and old, good and poor, or expert learners and novice learners in terms of the adequacy of their factual knowledge base. The group that performs well does so because it has already acquired the background knowledge necessary to perform the task, whereas the less successful group lacks this knowledge. These claims are undoubtedly true, but perhaps of greater interest to a developmental psychologist is how these differences in knowledge came about and how these differences affect strategy utilization, and so on.

Issues concerning the importance of content knowledge can be approached from two different perspectives that are complementary rather than mutually exclusive. From a *static perspective,* the major question is, ''How does the current state of one's knowledge affect performance?'' The major question from the alternate perspective, the *dynamic perspective*, is, ''How did one's knowledge base get to be the way it is, and how does it change?''

Many of the traditional theories borrowed from the adult, cognitive literature reflect the static perspective—theories of frames, scripts, and schemata represent a case in point. From the perspective of these theories, it seems clear that lack of relevant knowledge contributes strongly to many problems, such as the inability to learn or remember new sets of information. The dynamic perspective suggests a different approach to this issue, that is, lack of relevant content knowledge can be viewed as a *symptom*, as well as a cause. Thus, a theorist can assume that the knowledge base is one major determinant of current performance (a static perspective), yet still believe that something else accounts for, or at least contributes to, differences in the development of the knowledge base (a dynamic perspective). We argue here that the something else is access—people differ in the degree to which they spontaneously utilize potentially available information in order to understand and learn.

Imagine a prototypical developmental study. One group of children (the older, more experienced, etc.) performs better than the other. But, for the sake of argument, make the additional assumption that both groups possess the content knowledge necessary for successful performance. In such cases, the key factor is the degree to which people spontaneously access or utilize potentially available resources to understand and learn new information. For example, in a recent study by Bransford, Stein, Shelton, and Owings (1981), academically successful and less successful fifth graders were asked to learn a passage about two kinds of robots. The first paragraph of the passage included a brief introduction and a description of the function of each robot. The extendible robot could extend itself to the height of a two-story house and was used to wash outside windows in two-story houses. The nonextendible robot was designed to wash outside windows in tall high-rise apartment buildings. The remaining paragraphs described particular properties of each robot, properties that were potentially meaningful given the tasks that each robot had to perform. For example, the robot for high-rise buildings had suction-cup feet to help it climb; it was light and had a parachute in case it should fall. The robot for two-story buildings was made of heavy steel for stability and had spiked feet to stick into the ground, and so on. The relevance of the various properties was not explicitly explained.

Academically successful students spontaneously used information about the function of each robot to understand the relevance of various properties. Their memory for the properties was excellent, and the students were generally able to explain why each robot possessed its various properties. Another group of academically successful students received an explicit version of the robot passage in which the relevance of each property was explained in the text. The ability of these students to remember the properties and explain their significance was no better than that of students in the implicit group.

The academically less successful students exhibited a different pattern of performance. Those who received the implicit version had a difficult time recalling properties and explaining their significance. Performance for those receiving the explicit version was considerably better. It became clear that the less successful students who received the implicit version had the potential to understand the significance of the properties (or the vast majority of the properties at least), but they failed to ask themselves how previously available information about the functions of each robot might make each fact more relevant or significant. The less successful students did not spontaneously activate knowledge that could clarify the significance or relevance of the properties. They had the potential to do so but did not do this spontaneously; they had to be explicitly prompted to ask themselves relevant questions about the information they were trying to learn. These additional prompts were not required by the successful students, who could provide them for themselves.

The tendency of some children to miss significant details that would alter their interpretation can have pervasive effects on their abilities to learn from experience. For example, Bransford et al. (1981) asked their fifth graders to read a passage about camels; part of the passage emphasized problems, such as surviving desert sandstorms, other parts discussed facts, for example, ''Camels can close their nasal passages and have special eyelids to protect their eyes.'' Many of the academically less successful students failed to utilize information about the sandstorm to interpret the significance of facts about the camels' nasal passages and eyelids. However, successful students who did understand how various properties of camels help them survive desert sandstorms had a basis for understanding a new passage that described the clothing worn by desert people (e.g., these students could understand the significance of wearing veils or other forms of face protection). Hannigan, Shelton, Franks, and Bransford (1980) have devised analogues of situations where particular events are or are not interpreted as instances of more general principles and have assessed the effects on students' abilities to deal with novel-but-related materials. Students who were prompted to interpret each acquisition event as an instance of more general principles exhibited a much greater ability to transfer to novel-but-related events (see *Intervention Research*).

Bransford et al. (1981) have discussed several studies designed to explore how children approach the problem of learning new information. The children in these studies had the background knowledge necessary to learn the information, but some of them consistently failed to access this knowledge; they failed to ask themselves how potentially available information could clarify the significance or relevance of new factual content. The failure to perform these activities could affect the development of an adequate knowledge base and, hence, jeopardize the chance to learn subsequent related information. Repeated superficial processing of this type would lead to a cumulative deficit or a knowledge base impoverished over a wide range of factual topics. Inadequacies in the development of the knowledge base are not only causes of various problems but may be symptoms as well.

Of course, the performance of less successful learners can be improved by explicitly prompting them to use appropriate strategies or to activate relevant knowledge. This prompting may take the form of leading questions, or it may involve direct instruction. One problem with this approach to directed learning or teaching is that a teacher or writer cannot always anticipate what each learner needs to know to understand a message. An even greater problem is that this approach may, indeed, help people better understand and remember particular sets of materials, but it does not necessarily help them know how to structure their own learning activities. The development of the ability to learn on one's own is the learning-to-learn problem (Bransford et al., 1981; Brown, 1982b). To function efficiently as an independent learner, the child must be able to access his available knowledge and apply it appropriately. Students vary not only in what they know but also in what they do with what they know. Knowledge is necessary but not sufficient for performance, for it is the efficiency with which a learner uses whatever is available that defines intelligence (Brown & Campione, in press; Campione & Brown, in press; see also *Intervention Research*).

Capacity

A continuing controversy in the literature surrounds our second characteristic of the learner, that is, her working memory or attentional capacity. This is, indeed, an important feature of the learner. Few would doubt that novices and young children are hampered in their efforts to learn by a limit on what they can hold concurrently in memory. And convincing arguments have been put forward that overloading a child's working capacity is an important factor that leads to immature behavior on a variety of tasks. For our purposes here, we will concentrate on the central idea that one cannot talk about capacity differences without considering all four factors of the tetrahedron.

It has been amply demonstrated that the *functional* capacity of the human information processing system increases developmentally (e.g., Dempster, 1978; Huttenlocher & Burke, 1976). However, whether this reflects changes in capacity per se, or in the efficient use of that capacity is a debatable issue. The resolution of this controversy has been hampered by the complexity of an essentially interactive system. The answer is not going to be a simple "it's all knowledge," "it's all strategies," "it's amount of space," "it's durability," and so on. Concomitant to the observed increase in capacity with age, other characteristics of the child, for example, the complexity of her knowledge base and her repertoire of learning activities, are also developing and the rate at which these factors are changing varies widely both within and between individuals. Moreover, the interdependencies existing between these factors have not been completely specified. This greatly complicates the task of constructing a pure measure of capacity that can be applied to people of different ages. We will elaborate on this problem in the following discussion of the developmental data. Research suggesting that changes in (1) mental space, (2) basic processing operations, (3) the knowledge base, and (4) strategy use underlie observed changes in functional capacity will now be considered.

Mental Space and Capacity. Pascual-Leone (1970) hypothesized that the Piagetian stages of cognitive development are determined primarily by the growth in capacity of a central computing space, a construct that he terms M-space. M-space is equivalent to the number of schemes or discrete units of information that can be operated upon simultaneously. This quantitative construct is assumed to develop as a linear function of age (i.e., from 1 unit at age 3 to 7 units at age 15). To test this hypothesis, Pascual-Leone (1970) constructed the compound-stimuli visual-information task. His subjects (ages 5, 7, 9, and 11) first learned a different response (e.g., clap hands, open mouth) to each of a number of positive instances of a variety of visual-stimulus dimensions (e.g., red color, large size). The children were then presented with compound visual stimuli that were to be decoded by responding appropriately to each of the cues present in the stimuli. According to Pascual-Leone, the number of correct responses a child emitted in this task corresponded to the maximum number of schemes that she could integrate without exceeding her available information processing capacity. In support of the model, Pascual-Leone found that performance increased as a function of age; he concluded that these developmental increments were primarily due to increased M space. Corroborating evidence has been obtained within other domains by Case (e.g., 1972, 1974).

Pascual-Leone's (1970) model and his tests of that model have been criticized on a number of grounds, including procedural, statistical, and metatheoretical ones; by far the most damaging criticisms concern the confounding of M-demands with demands on certain basic processes, on strategies, and on executive control (Rohwer & Dempster, 1977; Trabasso, 1978; Trabasso & Foellinger, 1978; for a reply to these criticisms, see Pascual-Leone, 1978; Pascual-Leone & Sparkman, 1980). Case asserts that "according to Pascual-Leone's neo-Piagetian theory of development, a subject's performance on any given cognitive task is a function of three parameters: the mental strategy with which she approaches the task, the demand which the strategy puts on her mental capacity (its M-demand), and the mental capacity which she has available (her M-space)" (1974, p. 382). Thus, to infer a difference in M-space between two children of different ages, it is necessary at minimum to insure that they are using the same strategy that places an equivalent drain on mental capacity in each case. The tasks used by Pascual-Leone (1970) and Case (1972, 1974) are obviously facilitated by certain skills and strategies (e.g., analysis of complex stimuli and ordering skills) that undergo development during the age range of interest.

Basic Processing Operations and Capacity. More recently, Case and his colleagues (Case, Kurland, & Goldberg, 1982) have suggested that a person's total processing space is composed of space available for *storing* information and space available for *executing* cognitive operations. Although total processing space is assumed to remain constant as one develops, its two components are believed to fluctuate with a tradeoff existing between them. Thus, Case et al. (1982) propose that the improved functional capacity that accompanies development reflects increases in storage space, which accompany the decreasing amounts of operating space necessary for performance. The decrements in necessary operating space occur as a result of the growing

speed, efficiency, and automaticity of basic processes (e.g., encoding and retrieval).

Case et al. (1982) reported a series of studies supporting their model. In the first study, they demonstrated that between the ages of 3 and 6, word span (i.e., roughly the maximum number of words that a person could repeat in any order) was linearly related to the speed of repeating individual words. In a second study, word familiarity was manipulated (i.e., adults were given nonsense words) to equate adults and 6-year-olds on their speed of word repetition. This manipulation resulted in the disappearance of age-related differences in word span. The amount of space the adults required for basic operations increased in the case of nonsense words, with a concomitant decrease in the amount of available storage space in short-term memory.

Similar results were reported in a third study in which a counting span task was administered to children from kindergarten through sixth grade. This test required the children to count each of a number of arrays and, subsequently, to recall the number of dots in each of those arrays. A linear relationship was found between developmental increments in counting span and developmental increments in counting speed. Furthermore, in a fourth study, by requiring adults to count in an artificial language, both the speed of counting and the counting span of adults were reduced to a first-grade level. Case et al. (1982) concluded that there is no developmental increase in total processing space but rather that reductions in the necessary operating space are responsible for the developmental increments in span. They acknowledge, however, that this conclusion rests upon the validity of their operational definitions of the amount of required operating space. The source (or sources) of any increases in operational efficiency (e.g., maturation, experience) and the mechanisms by which such changes might increase memory span (e.g., less attentional interference, more time for rehearsal, or other strategies) are also issues that remain to be addressed.

Huttenlocher and Burke (1976) arrived at a similar conclusion. They obtained measures of digit span from 4-, 7-, 9-, and 11-year-olds. Their experimental manipulation was to vary the sound pattern (melody, prosody, or monotone) and the temporal groupings. The effects of sound pattern were quite small and not clearly related to age. Temporal grouping, however, improved the spans of all age groups to roughly the same extent, suggesting that differences in subject-imposed organization cannot be responsible for developmental differences in memory span. They conclude that the growth of memory span is probably not due to the development of active strategies and that, therefore, it probably results from improvements in basic processes, such as the identification of individual items and the encoding of order information. In a comprehensive review of the literature, Dempster (1981) came to a similar conclusion.

Knowledge Base and Capacity. It is possible that knowledge-base restrictions may underlie the child's relatively poor memory span and perhaps his processing inefficiencies as well. Chi (1976) suggests that a young child can be restricted by his knowledge base in three different ways. First, the chunks of information that constitute his knowledge base may be smaller (Simon, 1972, 1974). Materials that are less familiar to a child than to an adult may correspond to more chunks of smaller size for the child. Second, the chunks in the child's knowledge base may be less accessible in the sense of fewer associations between chunks in the network. Third, the child may simply lack chunks in his knowledge base for totally unfamiliar stimuli. Chi (1976) reviewed research demonstrating that materials that supposedly vary in familiarity (i.e., digits, letters, concrete words, and geometric figures) resulted in varying memory spans for adults, but not for children. She concluded that this is because there are greater variations in the structure of the knowledge base for different types of material in adults than in children.

Strategies and Capacity. It has been suggested throughout the cognitive literature that grouping and rehearsal are the two major strategies that provide advantages in tasks, such as memory span, but there is not a great deal of evidence to support this position. Experimenter-imposed grouping does not eliminate age differences in span performance (Huttenlocher & Burke, 1976). On the contrary, such manipulations have sometimes accentuated age differences. For example, McCarver (1972) found that 10-year-olds and college students displayed greater probed short-term memory for pictures when spatial and temporal cues as well as grouping instructions were provided, but that 6- and 7-year-olds did not improve under these conditions. Generally, however, grouping improves the performance of young and old alike (Baumeister, 1974; Harris & Burke, 1972; Huttenlocher & Burke, 1976).

We know of no positive research demonstrating active recoding of stimulus items in short-term memory tasks by young children; in general, little investigation has been done in this area. Failure to recode might be due to at least a couple of different problems (Chi, 1976). First, a child may not know when or how to go about recoding. Secondly, recognizable chunks appropriate for recoding might not yet exist in the knowledge base for many types of stimuli. In general, then, there is little evidence to suggest that developmental increases in memory span are due to the acquisition of grouping strategies, although the *paucity of data* should be noted. The same might be said for rehearsal strategies (see Frank & Rabinovitch, 1974; Huttenlocher & Burke, 1976 for a discussion of this issue).

We regard the capacity-development issue as moot given current evidence. But we tentatively conclude that there is little evidence to suggest that total processing capacity per se changes at least after 4 years of age (there are no data on younger children). Instead, developmental increases in span are due to an interaction of three general factors that undergo changes during childhood. These factors are the structure of the knowledge base, the use of strategies, and the efficiency of basic processes. Which of these variables will be most responsible for differential performance across ages may depend upon such things as the constraints of the task, the type of materials, and the ages of the subjects.

We would also like to argue that many of the changes that underlie age-related increases in functional capacity may be similar to those that occur with the development of expertise in general. Furthermore, it remains to be seen to what extent the allocation of short-term memory capacity is automatic and to what extent it is a volitional process, requiring fairly sophisticated executive monitoring skills (Shiffrin & Schneider, 1977). Equally speculative at this stage is Chi's (1977) implication that the development of metacognitive skills may play a role in the increasing efficiency of capacity allocation with age.

Despite the flurry of recent activity in this area, we have little evidence to refute or substantiate Olson's (1973) characterization of capacity increments:

> The changes we find are associated with the child's ability to recode or encode, to plan and monitor, to integrate and unitize. Broad limits on information processing capacity, which may be biological in origin, are relatively constant, but how the child operates within these limits undergoes systematic and profound development. (p. 153)

The Nature of the Materials

The third point of the tetrahedron concerns the nature of the materials. We will use only one example here of the importance of considering the materials to be learned, that is, the controversy surrounding developmental trends in recognition memory. However, an important theme throughout the chapter is the influence varying forms of materials have on the learning process (see *Mandler, vol. III, chap. 7,* for a full treatment of this question).

Recognition Memory

One issue that concerned developmental psychologists during the early 1970s was the existence of developmental effects in recognition memory. The original question that motivated the research was whether there existed some class of memory task that would place little demands on capacity limitations, strategies, or knowledge factors and, therefore, would result in excellent performance in young subjects notorious for their poor memory performance. The argument was that it is uninteresting to point out that retarded children, for example, have poor memories. More informative would be studies showing areas of relative strength as well as areas of weakness (Brown, 1974; see also Wellman, 1977, for an extension of this argument to young children). The initial studies in recognition memory did, to some extent, provide the needed data. Young children and retarded learners showed excellent recognition memory for particular kinds of stimulus materials—such children could readily identify previously seen distinct familiar pictures from a set of such items (Brown & Scott, 1971). Children could even tolerate some quite similar distractor items, such as the same character in a different pose (Brown & Campione, 1972) or two quite similar instances of the same conceptual category (Siegel, Kirasic, & Kilburg, 1973).

The original work with recognition memory was interpreted as an attempt to show that the process of recognition itself was developmentally insensitive, as if "recognition" were somehow identifiable in isolation. We would like to argue that this question is not well motivated because it is impossible to consider the development of recognition memory without asking, "Recognition of what?" A particular recognition memory task will be easy or hard depending on (1) the nature of the materials, for example, the similarity of the distractors along physical and conceptual dimensions; (2) the compatibility of the materials with the analyzing structures of the learner (knowledge-base factors); and (3) the extent to which deliberate strategies can be used to enhance learning (learning activities). If the subsequent spate of recognition memory studies are analyzed in this light, the picture to emerge becomes quite cohesive.

Perlmutter and Myers (1979) reviewed the research on recognition memory in the years prior to 5 and found that age-related increases in performance, if they occur at all, can be attributed to (1) acquisition factors, such as more efficient scanning, encoding, and information pickup; (2) knowledge factors—if the items are differentially familiar to the older and younger children, a developmental trend accrues; (3) comparison factors, such as matching; and (4) response factors, such as response bias changes with age. In general, Perlmutter and Myers's (1979) early recognition memory studies suggest excellent performance if the materials are familiar and the items distinct. There are no age differences under such circumstances. Age differences become apparent when the stimuli are complex or differentially familiar and when sustained systematic scanning and comparison processes are required.

A similar pattern emerges when older children serve as subjects. Dirks and Neisser (1977) asked adults and children from grades 1, 3, and 6 to view complex scenes and then tested them on recognition items with elements of the scene deleted or rearranged. There was a sizable improvement in performance as a function of age. On the basis of these data, Dirks and Neisser rejected the notion that picture recognition is an automatic process that undergoes no development. Recognition performance improved with age, and the cause of its improvement depended on the particular kind of information being tested (i.e., the nature of the materials).

Not only did the nature of the materials affect the developmental trend but also the differential use of strategies. Dirks and Neisser found that their older subjects had at their disposal various strategies useful for picking up and storing the kinds of information the test required. Older children were more likely to scan the array systematically, to notice that neighboring items can form meaningful groups, to pay attention to nuances of spatial arrangement, or to formulate verbal descriptions of minor details. Dirks and Neisser concluded that recognition was not a function of automatically encoded visual traces but depends crucially on specific and gradually developing cognitive skills.

The work of Jean Mandler and her colleagues confirms the picture. Mandler has been interested in recognition memory for complex visual arrays that are organized or disorganized (Mandler & Johnson, 1977; Mandler & Ritchey, 1977; Mandler & Robinson, 1978) and for orientation and spatial information in complex pictorial arrays (Mandler & Day, 1975: Mandler & Parker, 1976; Mandler & Stein, 1974; Stein & Mandler, 1974; for a review of their work, see *Mandler, vol. III, chap. 7*). For our purposes, it is sufficient to state that the improvement with age found in these complex recognition memory tasks is a function of changes in the nature to the materials (stimulus complexity), scanning strategies, and knowledge.

The accumulated literature suggests that recognition memory is clearly not impervious to developmental differences. A prime determinant of levels of performance is the nature of the stimulus materials and the relationship among target and distractor items. By cleverly manipulating the compatibility of the stimulus materials with the child's existing knowledge, it should be possible to generate any pattern of age effects in recognition. For example, one might adopt Chi's (1978) procedure and manipulate stimulus familiarly in such a way that younger children are the experts and, hence, can recognize what to the older novice look like very similar stimuli. Or one could vary the similarity of the distractor and target items along some scale of semantic similarity not yet salient to the young but distracting to the old. The less mature child would not be snared by the related distractor and should outperform the confused older participant.

In summary, the recognition memory literature provides an excellent illustration of the interactive nature of the tetrahedral framework. To predict performance on any recognition task, one would need to know something about the nature of the actual task (number of distractors, response demands, etc.), the nature of the materials (the relationships between target and distractor items), the compatibility of the organization in the material with the child's extant knowledge, and the demands placed on active strategies, such as scanning and systematic comparison processes (Brown & DeLoache, 1978).

The Criterial Task

We turn now to the last entry in our tetrahedral framework, the criterial task. Learning is not undertaken in a vacuum; there is always an end product in mind, and effective learners are often cognizant of this end product and tailor their learning activities accordingly (Bransford, 1979; Brown, 1979, 1982; Meacham, 1972). For example, to be effective in a memory task, learners need to know whether the demand is for gist rather than for verbatim recall, for recognition rather than reconstruction. They need to know if memory for the material is required as the end product or whether they will be called upon to apply the acquired information to novel instances (Bransford, 1979; Nitsch, 1977). In

short, learners' activities are purposive and goal directed, and the nature of the criterial task will play an important role in determining the effective activity that must be undertaken.

It follows, then, that an appropriate learning activity must be one that is compatible with the desired end state. One cannot, therefore, discuss appropriate learning activities unless one considers the question, Appropriate for what end?, or the compatibility between the learning activity and the goal of that activity. Effective learners tailor their strategies in tune with changes in task demands. And there is a great deal of evidence in the educational research literature that the more the student knows concerning the criterial task to which her knowledge must be put, the better the outcome of reading and studying (Anderson & Armbruster, in press; Baker & Brown, in press-a).

Consider the following example from Bransford et al. (1981), concerning where and when a certain strategy is appropriate. Imagine that students are given a passage about blood circulation and that they must learn to differentiate between arteries and veins—arteries are thick, elastic, and carry blood from the heart that is rich in oxygen; veins are thinner, less elastic, and carry blood rich in carbon dioxide back to the heart. To the biological novice, even this relatively simple set of facts can seem arbitrary and confusing. Was it veins or arteries that are thin? Was the thin one or the thick one elastic? Which one carries carbon dioxide from the heart (or was it to the heart)?

There are several ways to deal with the problem of learning factual content that initially seems unfamiliar and arbitrary. One is simply to rote rehearse the facts until they are mastered, the brute force approach. Sometimes, a more efficient approach is to use various mnemonic elaboration strategies (Rohwer, 1973). For example, the fact that arteries are thick could be remembered by forming an image of a thick, hollow tube that flashes the word artery. An alternate technique is to use verbal elaboration, for example, ''*Art*(ery) was *thick* around the middle so he wore pants with an *elastic* waistband. . . .'' There is a considerable amount of literature documenting the fact that the formation of images and linking sentences can facilitate retention (Reese, 1977), and researchers have also explored the possibility of explicitly teaching various mnemonic techniques to improve people's abilities to learn (Rohwer, 1970; Weinstein, 1978).

Mnemonic techniques are useful for *remembering facts* about veins and arteries, but one may have to take a very different approach to learning to develop an *understanding* of the functions of veins and arteries; an understanding that would be necessary if the criterial task were not remembering facts but, for example, designing an artificial artery. If students used only mnemonics, however clever, intended to produce rote recall of facts, they would not necessarily be prepared for a criterial task demanding understanding of principles.

To understand, learners must seek information about the significance or relevance of facts. For example, the passage about veins and arteries stated that arteries are elastic. What's the significance of elasticity? Because arteries carry blood *from* the heart, there is a problem of directionality. Why does not the blood flow back into the heart? This will not be perceived as a problem if one assumes that arterial blood always flows downhill, but let us assume that our passage mentions that there are arteries in the neck and shoulder regions. Arterial blood must, therefore, flow uphill as well. This information might provide an additional clue about the significance of elasticity. If arteries expand from a spurt of blood and then contract, this might help the blood move in a particular direction. The elasticity of arteries might, therefore, serve the function of a one-way valve that enables blood to flow forward but not backward. If one were to design an artificial artery it might, therefore, be possible to equip it with valves and hence make it nonelastic. However, this solution might work only if the spurts of blood did not cause too much pressure on the artificial artery. Suppose that our imaginary passage does not provide enough information about pressure requirements; if so, the learner would have to look elsewhere for this information. Note, however, that an efficient learner would realize the need to obtain additional information. The learner's activities are not unlike those employed by good detectives or researchers when they confront a new problem. Although their initial assumptions about the significance of various facts may ultimately be found to be incorrect, the act of seeking clarification is fundamental to the development of new expertise. In contrast, the person who simply concentrates on techniques for memorizing facts does not know whether there is something more to be understood (Bransford et al., 1981).

This somewhat detailed example illustrates that the nature of the criterion task determines the appropriate processing strategy. If the desired outcome is rote recall, perhaps the most appropriate strategy is mnemonic elaboration; if, however, the desired outcome is comprehension of the significance of information contained in the material or the application of the information to a novel prob-

lem, then the appropriate activity would change. Consider an experimental example from Nitsch (1977). Students heard definitions of six new concepts (such as, to minge: to gang up on a person or thing) and then received a series of study-test trials that required them to identify examples of each concept. Students in one group learned the concepts in the *same contexts,* each of the examples for a particular concept was drawn from a common context (all examples of "minge" involved restaurants, examples of "crinch" involved cowboys, etc.). Students in the second group also learned the concept definitions, but they were presented in *varied contexts* (examples for "minge" might, therefore, range over several contexts, cowboy contexts, restaurant contexts, etc.). After students had learned the concepts, they were asked to rate their degree of mastery. There were no differences between the groups, and students in both groups were relatively confident that they knew the concepts, which they did by some criteria. They were then given a new test requiring them to identify examples of concepts that occurred in novel contexts, contexts never experienced during acquisition. Students who had received the varied-context training performed much better on the new test. Varied-context experience was a better preparation for the actual criterial task of using the concept, whereas same context experience produced faster rote learning of the particular exemplar in the original task.

An important aspect of Nitsch's (1977) study is that students who received training on same-context examples had an inaccurate and overinflated sense of mastery. However, one does not want to argue that students in Nitsch's same-context condition had fewer metacognitive skills than students who received the varied-context training. A much more plausible interpretation is that students who received same-context training had set up inappropriate expectations concerning the actual criterial task, that is, they were expecting a test that was similar to their acquisition training but not anticipating the type of transfer task actually administered. Their assessment of mastery was accurate *given* their assumptions about the type of criterial task to be performed.

Nitsch (1977) asked the students to rate their feelings of mastery a second time; this time *after* they had taken the transfer test. Under these conditions the sense of mastery ratings for the same-context students were lower than those of the varied-context students. Thus, an important question concerns the degree to which students learn something when confronted with a criterial task that they are not prepared to handle adequately. For example, imagine that students in Nitsch's same-context condition had taken the transfer test and were then asked to learn six additional concepts. Assume further that they could structure their own acquisition activities, ask questions, and so forth. Would these students inquire about the nature of the test? Would they learn in a way that would enable them to identify novel examples? In other words, would they modify their learning strategy in light of their new-found knowledge concerning the actual nature of the criterion task?

A recent study by Bransford and his colleagues (Bransford et al., 1981) is relevant to the present discussion. They presented academically successful and less successful fifth graders with pairs of sentences. One member of each pair was completed with a precise (or meaningful) elaboration (e.g., The hungry man got into the car to go to the restaurant), the other with an imprecise (or random) elaboration (e.g., The hungry man got into the car to go for a drive). Children were shown that each pair of sentences was about a different type of man (hungry, short, etc.) and were informed that their task was to choose the member of each pair that would make it easier to remember which man did what (see also Tenney, 1975).

The majority of academically successful fifth graders performed like college students and chose the sentences that were precisely elaborated. In contrast to the successful students, all but one less successful student chose sentences on the basis of something other than precision. Most chose the sentence that was shorter because they felt that shorter items would be easier to remember. This is a reasonable hypothesis of course.

On a subsequent memory test, the children were much better at remembering precise sentences; they, therefore, had an opportunity to use their memory performance to evaluate their original hypotheses about the variables that influenced sentence memory. The few successful students who initially had not entertained hypotheses about precision changed their hypothesis on the second set of sentence pairs; they chose the precise sentences and adequately explained why. One less successful student changed his hypothesis after the first test and focused on precision; the rest of the less successful children made no change at all. These data are consistent with other reports that immature learners often fail to revise hypotheses in the face of conflicting information or fail to change their strategies after doing poorly on a test (Belmont & Butterfield, 1977; Brown, Smiley, & Lawton, 1978). The ability to modify one's activities in light of

changes in the criterial task is an essential factor in efficient learning.

Summary

We have argued that for psychologists to fully understand learning, it is necessary to design experiments that are sensitive to the four points of the tetrahedral model. We would like to argue that just as psychologists need to understand how the four points interact (Jenkins, 1979) so, too, do learners. On her road to becoming an expert in the domain of intentional learning, the child will be greatly helped if she can develop the same insights into the demands of the tetrahedral model that the psychologist needs. To be an effective learner, she will need to know something about her own characteristics, her available learning activities, the demand characteristics of various learning tasks, and the inherent structure of materials (Flavell & Wellman, 1977). She must tailor her activities finely to the competing demands of all these forces to be a flexible and effective learner. In other words, she must *learn how to learn*.

The use of terms, such as ''know,'' ''be aware of,'' and so on, brings us face to face with the controversial topic of metacognition in its various manifestations. As this is a popular area of research, we will turn now to a relatively in-depth treatment of some of the issues.

METACOGNITION, EXECUTIVE CONTROL, SELF-REGULATION, AND OTHER EVEN MORE MYSTERIOUS MECHANISMS[1]

What Is Metacognition?

In this section, we will describe some of the historical roots and discuss the current status of the fashionable but complex concept of metacognition and other topics with which it shares a family resemblance. Various forms of metacognition have appeared in the literature and some of these instantiations are puzzling and mysterious. For example, Marshall and Morton (1978) refer to the mechanism that permits the detection and correction of errors in speech production as an EMMA—even more mysterious apparatus; it is a mechanism that could be an optional extra. We will argue that far from being an optional extra, the processes that have recently earned the title metacognitive are central to learning.

Metacognition refers to one's knowledge and control of the domain cognition. Two primary problems with the term are that (1) it is often difficult to distinguish between what is meta and what is cognitive and (2) there are many different historical roots from which this area of inquiry arose.

Consider first the interchangeability of cognitive and metacognitive functions. Recent reviews of the literature on, for example, metacognition and reading have been justly criticized on the grounds that they have encouraged the practice of dubbing as metacognitive any strategic action. For example, metacognitive skills of reading include the following activities previously dignified with the title of mere strategies: establishing the purpose for reading; modifying reading rate because of variations in purpose; identifying important ideas; activating prior knowledge; evaluating the text for clarity, completeness, and consistency; compensating for failures to understand; and assessing one's level of comprehension (Baker & Brown, in press-b). Just which of these activities should be deemed metacognitive or, more subtly, which components of these complex activities are meta is not clear.

A second source of confusion concerning the widespread use of the term metacognition is that, within the modern psychological literature, it has been used to refer to two distinct areas of research, namely *knowledge about cognition* and *regulation of cognition*. The two forms of metacognition are indeed closely related, each feeding on the other recursively; attempts to separate them lead to over-simplification. However, they are readily distinguishable, and they do have quite different historical roots.

Knowledge about cognition refers to the relatively stable, statable, often fallible, and late-developing information that human thinkers have about their own cognitive processes and those of others (Flavell & Wellman, 1977). This form of knowledge is relatively *stable*. One would expect that knowledge of pertinent facts about a domain, for example, memory (that it is fallible, that it is severely limited for short-term verbatim retention, etc.), would be a permanent part of one's naive theory on the topic. This form of knowledge is often *statable*, in that one can reflect on the cognitive processes involved and discuss them with others. Of course, this form of knowledge is often *fallible*, in that the child (or adult for that matter) can perfectly well know certain facts about cognition that are not true. Naive psychology is not always empirically supportable. Finally, this type of knowledge is usually assumed to be *late developing*, in that it requires that learners step back and consider their own cognitive processes as objects of thought and reflection (Flavell & Wellman, 1977).

The second cluster of activities dubbed meta-

cognitive in the developmental literature consists of those used to regulate and oversee learning. These processes include *planning* activities prior to undertaking a problem (predicting outcomes, scheduling strategies, various forms of vicarious trial and error, etc.), *monitoring* activities during learning (testing, revising, rescheduling one's strategies for learning), and *checking* outcomes (evaluating the outcome of any strategic actions against criteria of efficiency and effectiveness). It has been assumed that these activities are not necessarily statable, somewhat unstable, and relatively age independent, that is, task and situation dependent (Brown, 1978, 1980, in press-a).

Although knowledge and regulation of cognition are incestuously related, the two forms of activity have quite different roots and quite different attendant problems. The tension generated by the use of the same term, metacognition, for the two types of behavior is well illustrated by the fact that even the leading proponents in the field tend to answer questions about the nature of metacognition with, ''It depends.'' Is metacognition late developing? It depends on the type of knowledge or process to which one refers. Is metacognition conscious? It depends. . . . In the next section, we will consider four separate stands of inquiry where the current issues of metacognition were introduced and originally discussed.

Roots of Metacognition

We will discuss four historically separate, but obviously interlinked, problems in psychology that pertain to issues of metacognition. First, there are the enduring questions concerning the status of verbal reports as data (Ericsson & Simon, 1980). Can people have conscious access to their own cognitive processes? Can they report on these processes with verisimilitude? And how does the act of reporting influence the processes in question? Second, there is the issue of executive mechanisms within an information processing model of human and machine intelligence. What is responsible for regulation of cognition? With what knowledge or form of knowledge must an executive be imbued? How do such models deal with the infinite regression of homunculi within homunculi? How do such models deal with the problems of consciousness, intention, and purpose? Third, we will deal with the issues of self-regulation and conceptual reorganization during learning and development that have always been featured in Genevan developmental psychology and have played a major role in Piaget's modern writings (1976, 1978) and those of his coworkers, notably Karmiloff-Smith (1979a, 1979b; Karmiloff-Smith & Inhelder, 1974/1975) and Inhelder (Inhelder et al., 1974). And, finally, we will discuss the transference from other-regulation to self-regulation central to Vygotsky's (1978) theory of development.

Verbal Reports as Data

Several theorists from quite disparate schools agree that the most stringent criteria of understanding involve the availability of knowledge to consciousness and reflection, thus permitting verbal reports (for reviews, see Brown, 1982a; Brown & Campione, 1981; Rozin, 1976). Early investigations into children's knowledge about cognition focused on metamemory; many studies relied on the direct approach of simply asking children to report what they knew. Kreutzer, Leonard, and Flavell (1975) interviewed children in kindergarten and grades 1, 3, and 5 about the effects of a number of variables on remembering. They found that even the youngest subjects knew that information in short-term memory can decay rapidly, that the relearning of forgotten information tends to be faster and easier than the original learning, that study time affects subsequent retrieval attempts, and that the number of items and their familiarity also affect retention. Children at all ages tended to rely on external mnemonic resources (e.g., other persons, notes) rather than internal ones. Third and fifth graders seemed to be more planful and self-aware; they suggested a greater variety of mnemonic strategies and showed better understanding of the potential interactions among variables in their effects upon memory. Wellman's (in press) findings that 10-year-olds were far better than 5-year-olds in judging the interaction of two memory relevant variables, although not in judging the effect of a single variable, are consistent with the results of Kreutzer et al. (1975).

Even preschoolers have some information concerning what makes a memory task easy or hard (Wellman, 1977). They come to understand the memory relevance of certain variables according to the following developmental sequence: (1) number of items; (2) distraction; (3) age of rememberer, assistance from others, study time; and (4) associative cues. Wellman (1977) also found that the knowledge that certain factors (e.g., body-build, type of clothing, etc.) are irrelevant to memory increased from ages 3 to 5 years. He suggested that children will tend more easily to recognize the role of a relevant variable if it occurs frequently in their own experience, if it concerns their own behavior, and if its various manifestations are easily discriminable to the young child.

Since the original questionnaire studies, a great deal of evidence has accumulated that demonstrates older children's greater knowledge about memory (Flavell & Wellman, 1977), attention (Miller & Bigi, 1979), communication (Yussen & Bird, 1979), reading (Baker & Brown, in press-a; Markman, 1979; Myers & Paris, 1978), studying (Baker & Brown, in press-a; Paris & Myers, 1981), problem solving (Piaget, 1976), and so on. As Kreutzer et al. (1975) point out, questionnaire studies provide an interesting insight into the child's understanding of a particular domain; however, these data should be followed with careful empirical examination of the phenomena in question.

As part of a body of converging evidence, verbal reports of cognitive processes are extremely valuable. But there are nontrivial problems associated with reliance on self-reports in the absence of corroboration. An obvious problem is the difficulty associated with asking children to inform on the content of their own conscious processes. As Piaget (1976) and others have pointed out, children are as likely to distort and modify their observations of their thought processes as they are their observations of the world around them. Eyewitness testimony is fallible, no less for the objects and events of the internal world than for the external.

Another problem concerns reliability. Will children be consistent in their opinions and beliefs about cognitive processes? Few investigators have considered the problems of reliability or of validity, an equally thorny problem. What is the relationship between what an informant says and what he does? Studies with children have yielded only a moderate relation, for example, between performance on a restricted class of memory tasks and children's statable knowledge of sometimes a different class of memory phenomena (Cavanaugh & Borkowski, 1979; Justice & Bray, 1979; Kelly, Scholnick, Travers, & Johnson, 1976; Kendall, Borkowski, & Cavanaugh, 1980; Salatas & Flavell, 1976), although there have been some recent studies where a clearer relationship was found (Perlmutter, 1978; Waters, in press). In many of these studies, the rationale for why one would expect a link between the particular form of metamemory probed and actual performance is weak (Wellman, in press). Similarly, as Flavell and Wellman (1977) point out, there are many reasons why there should *not* be a close link between metamemorial knowledge and memory performance in any one particular task.

Many forms of knowledge about things cognitive can be assumed to be stable, others transient and elicited only in certain situations. Stable forms are the kinds of declarative knowledge learners may possess about themselves (and others) in the learning context, the tetrahedral model if you will. People know about the demands of certain classes of problems and the necessity of tailoring their learning activities finely in tune with specific criterial tasks. These are the types of knowledge that Flavell and his colleagues (Flavell, 1980, 1981; Flavell & Wellman, 1977) have classified as person, task, and strategy variables. Learners possess naive theories of what it takes to learn certain classes of materials and to meet certain criterial task demands as well as naive theories of their repertoire of available strategies to accomplish certain ends, and so on. That young children are less informed about stable characteristics of learning is amply documented (for reviews see Baker & Brown, in press-a, in press-b; Brown, 1978, 1980; Cavanaugh & Perlmutter, 1982; Flavell & Wellman, 1977; Kluwe, in press; Kreutzer et al., 1975; Myers & Paris, 1978; Weinert, in press; Wellman, in press).

Transient forms of knowledge include insights that are elicited while actually performing a particular task; with adult subjects this is often the form of information obtained from on-line talk-aloud protocols. Protocol analyses of performers actually solving problems have been restricted to adult subjects or adolescents, supposedly because young children are judged to be incapable of the split mental focus that is required for simultaneously solving problems and commenting on the process. Instead, developmental psychologists have typically asked children to predict what they will do in imaginary situations. For example, preschool and early grade-school children have difficulty predicting their span for lists of pictures (Flavell, Friedrichs, & Hoyt, 1970; Markman, 1973; Worden & Sladewski-Awig, 1979; Yussen & Levy, 1975), and they are likely to predict that categorized lists are as easy to recall as random ones (Moynahan, 1973; Yussen, Levin, Berman, & Palm, 1979). Predicting in advance of an actual trial is difficult for the young, although they do seem better able to report retrospectively on their own actually experienced performance (Brown & Lawton, 1977; Moynahan, 1973), and they do take this information (and false norms about other learners) into account when predicting again (Brown, Campione, & Murphy, 1977; Markman, 1973; Yussen & Levy, 1975).

But it is a common and problematic procedure in the developmental literature to ask children to describe how they would behave in certain hypothetical situations. Asking adult informants to imagine possible worlds and how they might act in them is one of the practices highlighted by Nisbett and Wilson (1977) in their attack on the status of verbal reports as data; this was also heavily criticized by Ericsson and Simon (1980). But the questionnaire studies of children's knowledge consist primarily of situations in which the child must imagine scenarios and how she might act in them. Of the 14 main items contained in the Kreutzer et al. (1975) questionnaire, 10 are completely imaginary, for example, the child is asked to imagine how other children might perform in a task. It might help to clarify matters if a distinction were made between (1) predictive verbalizations about possible performance before the event, (2) concurrent verbalizations as one is actually performing, and (3) retrospective verbalization after the event has transpired.

Another important distinction is whether information is being sought concerning specific or very general knowledge. Questions of the form "How do you perform these tasks?" implicitly request very general information and leave open to the informant the creative task of constructing a general rule by drawing on a variety of specific experiences, including general knowledge of what one ought to do in such tasks. As Ericsson and Simon (1980) point out, in areas of applied psychology where verbal questioning has a long history, subjects are rarely asked for their general theories or impressions. Instead, Flanagan (1954) and others used what is referred to as the critical incident technique whereby informants are asked to report only about very specific incidents. For example, combat pilots would be asked to describe a particular, actually experienced incident and then to answer questions on how they thought or felt within that specific event. In general, however, questionnaire and experimental studies of children's metacognition demand reflection on quite general cognitive processes. Asking children to describe general processes that they might use in imaginary situations is the least favorable circumstance for producing verbal reports that are closely linked with the cognitive processes under discussion.

Finally, an adequate theory of the relation of verbal reports to actual performance should include some a priori predictions of when verbal reports will be related to, or will influence, performance and when they will not. Ericsson and Simon (1980) believe that verbal reports will have a positive, negative, or neutral effect on performance depending on the function of the reports in the ongoing learning process. The effect will be neutral under circumstances where the subject is asked to describe information that is already available (i.e., in short-term memory). If the subject is asked to report on information that is available, but not in verbal or propositional form, the translation process may slow down performance but will not otherwise interfere. Ericsson and Simon quote a great deal of experimental evidence to support these claims.

Of greater interest are situations where the relation between thinking aloud and problem solving can be beneficial. This occurs most commonly when the type of verbalization that is required is a statement of a rule or a reason for an action. Good problem solvers (adults) spend more time than poor learners identifying and evaluating what they did or are doing, stating rules and evaluating their efficiency (Dörner, 1978; Goldin & Hayes-Roth, 1980; Thorndyke & Stasz, 1980). And, on standard laboratory puzzles, such as the Tower of Hanoi, instructions to state a rule significantly accelerate the learning process and facilitate transfer across isomorphic and homomorphic versions of the same physical puzzle (Gagné & Smith, 1962) or story problem (Gick & Holyoak, 1980). Although there is little data, the same effect seems to work for children. On mathematic problems requiring invention (Resnick & Glaser, 1976), Pellegrino and Schadler (1974) required children to look ahead by verbalizing a sequence of goals, a procedure that produced a dramatic increase in the number of successful inventions by grade-school children. And, in an ongoing study, Crisafi and Brown (in preparation) found greater transfer across problem isomorphs of an inferential reasoning task when 3- and 4-year-old learners were required to describe the solution after each problem to Kermit the frog so that Kermit could also do the task.

Verbal reports can often have a negative effect on the learning process. Prime examples of such situations are where the requirement for overt verbalization competes for central processing capacity with the processes that must be reported. In on-line protocols it is characteristic that verbalization stops when the going gets difficult and starts up again when the cognitive load is lessened. Similarly, requiring verbal reports of information that is not generally available to consciousness is a disruptive procedure. For example, one reason why Piaget (1976, 1978) experienced so much difficulty getting children to describe their actions may be because the subject of those descriptions was just that, actions. Perceptual motor activities are notoriously difficult to describe, and it is, indeed, true that we can do a great deal that we cannot describe (Broadbent, 1977). And, as many current information processing models claim, many of the intermediate steps of both thought and action become auto-matized with repeated practice and, thereby, even less available to conscious introspection (Norman & Schallice, 1980; Schneider & Shiffrin, 1977; Shiffrin & Schneider, 1977). Asking subjects to report on internal events that are not readily available to such inspection can significantly impair the processes upon which they must report.

In summary, desperately needed in the developmental literature are systematic evaluations of children's verbal reports on their own cognitive processes when stringent attention is paid to (1) the temporal relation between these reports and the cognition in question, (2) the nature of the cognitions under evaluation, and (3) the influence of reflection on the operations of thought. It is simplistic to ask whether or not a certain group of children have reflective access to their own cognitions without specifying exactly the conditions under which these observations are made. Ideally, one would like to see programmatic research aimed at uncovering a certain child's range of understanding within a task domain. Under what conditions is it reasonable to ask for verbal reports? Can the child make predictive, concurrent, or retrospective statements about actual or potential cognitive activity within a problem space? Do the specific restrictions on adults' verbalizations under varying circumstances apply to children or do young learners experience particular difficulties with, for example, imagining possible actions in situations as yet unexperienced? Do children have particular problems talking about general rules rather than specific activities? In short, we need to progress from the current piecemeal study of certain isolated metacognitions concerning intuitively appealing but somewhat haphazardly chosen cognitive tasks to a systematic evaluation of the function of verbal reports in specific learning situations. Such data would provide an invaluable source of evidence concerning what a child knows, when he knows it, and how knowing influences performance.

Executive Control

The second historical root of things metacognitive is the notion of executive control taken from information processing models of cognition. The majority of information processing models attribute powerful operations to a central processor, interpreter, supervisor, or executive system that is capable of performing intelligent evaluation of its own operations:

The basic requirements of such an executive, demonstrate the complexity of the issue. It must include the ability to (a) predict the system's capacity limitations, (b) be aware of its repertoire of heuristic routines and their appropriate domain of utility, (c) identify and characterize the problem at hand, (d) plan and schedule appropriate problem-solving strategies, (e) monitor and supervise the effectiveness of those routines it calls into service, and (f) dynamically evaluate these operations in the face of success or failure so that termination of activities can be strategically timed (Brown, 1978, p. 152).

Thus, very complex operations are attributed to something within the system, a problem of attribution that is, to say the least, theoretically problematic (Boden, 1978; Dennett, 1978).

Information processing theories emerged in the mid-1960s, along with the growing interest in computer competence and machine simulation of thought. The concurrent development of psychological models was greatly influenced by the theories and jargon of synthetic intelligence, and the computer metaphor has dominated theories of human cognition during the past 15 years. By adopting the notion of a central processor or executive system imbued with very fancy powers, developmental psychologists gained a powerful analogy through which to consider the development of efficient learning. (For a detailed review of information processing models and developmental psychology, see Klahr & Wallace, 1976; Siegler, 1981; see also *Siegler, vol. I, chap. 4*).

Central within the prototypical information processing model are the concepts of executive control, whether implicitly or explicitly stated, and automated and controlled processes; these notions are interlinked. We will describe the automated-controlled distinction and then the executive systems.

Automatic and Controlled Processes. A two-process approach to thinking predates information processing models. A notably lucid description of the distinction between automatic and controlled process was provided by James (1890) who stressed the freedom from attention and effort that automatization provides: "The more details of our daily life we can hand over to the effortless custody of automatism, the more our higher powers of mind will be set free for their own proper work" (p. 122).

Automatic processing is a fast, parallel process that is not limited by short-term memory, that requires little subject effort, and that demands little direct subject control. Controlled processing is a comparatively slow, serial process that is limited by short-term memory constraints, that requires subject effort, and that provides a large degree of subject control (Schneider & Shiffrin, 1977).

The distinction between automatic and controlled processing is now a common feature of both the adult and developmental literatures, although it masquerades under different titles. For example, in the adult literature are Posner and Snyder's (1974) "conscious strategies" and "automatic activation," Shiffrin's (1975) "controlled vs. systemic processing," Norman and Bobrow's (1975) "resource limited" and "data limited processing," and LaBerge's (1975) "automatic focusing." The year 1975 was obviously a good one for this theoretical concept. More recent theories come from Shiffrin and Schneider (1977) and Logan (1978, 1979). Developmentalists also discuss "deliberate and involuntary" (Brown, 1975), "effortful and automatic" (Hasher & Zacks, 1979) and "strategic versus automatic" (Naus & Halasz, 1979) processing.

There are many interesting questions for developmental psychologists concerning automatization. A major notion is that a great deal of the development that occurs with increasing expertise (age) is the result of processes that were originally controlled, effortful, and laborious becoming automated (Brown, 1975; Hasher & Zacks, 1979; Naus & Halasz, 1979; Shiffrin & Dumais, 1981). A second well-aired notion is that processes that do not demand a great deal of strategic control are efficient even in the young and are less sensitive to developmental changes (Brown, 1975; Hasher & Zacks, 1979). But of particular interest in this section is the notion of who or what does the controlling and who or what deciphers the output of the automatized system.

Heterarchies, Hierarchies, and Demons All the Way Down. Within the information processing system, executive power in large or small degrees must be attributed, and it is with this attribution that the models run into epistemological problems of long standing, problems that have proven particularly recalcitrant and uncomfortably metaphysical for a psychology never truly weaned from a strict radical behaviorist tradition. The major problem is the traditional one of consciousness and who has it. The problem is nicely stated by Norman (1981b) in his inaugural address to the Cognitive Science Society:

Consciousness is a peculiar stepchild of our discipline, agreed to be important, but little explored in research and theory. There are legitimate reasons for this relative neglect. This is a most difficult topic, one for which it is very difficult to get the hard, sensible evidence that experimental disciplines require. . . . We cannot understand (thinking) until we come to a better appreciation of the workings of the mind, of the several simultaneous trains of thought that can occur, of the differences between conscious and subconscious processing, of what it means to focus upon one train of thought to the exclusion of others. What-who-does the focusing? — And what does it mean to have *conscious* attention? Can there be attention that is not conscious? What — who — experiences the results of conscious attentional processes? (p. 280)

Norman's self-conscious use of who or what immediately conjures up a spectre traditionally feared and derided by psychologists, the ghost in the machine, the homunculus. Skinner refers to this entity as the "inner man" whose function is "to provide an explanation which will not be explained in turn" (Skinner, 1971, p. 14). Such theories are, indeed, easy to deride, but hard to replace with an alternative. As Dennett (1978) points out (see also Boden, 1972, 1978), Skinnerian outrage at such "mentalisms" can be reduced to the axiom, "don't use intentional idioms in psychology." It is one of the liberations of current theories of cognitive science that we admit that human beings are intentional and that an adequate explanation of human behavior necessitates reference to the intention or the meaning of the behavior to the individual who performs it, that is, the individual's understanding of what she is doing (Boden, 1977; Brown, 1982a; Dennett, 1978; Flores & Winograd, 1978; Norman, 1981b; Shaw & Bransford, 1977).

How do information processing models deal with the inner man? Most of the original models were hierarchical, unidirectional systems with a central processor initiating and interpreting lower level actions. More recent models tend to be heterarchical so that control can be distributed throughout the system (Hayes-Roth, 1977; Hayes-Roth & Hayes-Roth, 1979; Turvey & Shaw, 1979). Heterarchical control is clearly evident in animal physiological systems (Gallistel, 1980; Green, 1971; Turvey, 1977), skilled performance and action (Gallistel, 1980; Norman, 1981a; Norman & Schallice, 1980; Turvey, 1977), and human speech perception (Turvey, 1977). Several recent theorists have claimed that heterarchies are the simplest class of system that could perform processing tasks of the complexity typical of human behavior (Gallistel, 1980; Green, 1971; Koestler, 1979; Turvey, 1977; Turvey, Shaw, & Mace, 1978).

Such systems do not rid themselves of inner men making decisions; the demons do not go away, they get distributed—a democratic solution that is much favored in current information processing models (Hayes-Roth & Hayes-Roth, 1979; Norman & Schallice, 1980) that trace their historical roots to Selfridge's (1959) original Pandemonium model. But, even within the democratic confederacies or heterarchies there are supervisory processors (Lindsay & Norman, 1977) or decision demons (Selfridge, 1959) who listen to the pandemonium produced by the lower level demons and select the most obtrusive. Conflicts for attentional resources must occur when several subordinate processors compete for the same resources. Some conflict resolution procedure must be provided in such systems (McDermott & Forgy, 1978; Norman & Schallice, 1980); it is these conflict resolution devices that sound very like metacognitive demons to the untrained ear.

Planning. Most central to the issues of metacognition are computer planning models that attempt to model problem-solving behavior. The concept of planning was introduced to artificial intelligence by the programmers of the General Problem Solver (GPS) (Newell & Simon, 1972). The main planning strategy of GPS was means-end analysis, a hierarchical planning strategy that works backward from a clear idea of the goal to be achieved. The GPS works quite well for closed-problem systems that have well-defined goals that can be reached by fixed means. But, GPS is a simple state-by-state planning strategy that does not produce an overall strategic plan of the problem before the solution is started. Such a decision maker has limited flexibility in revising and evaluating plans. Sacerdoti (1974) argues that although it is not sensible to formulate an epistemologically adequate plan before attempting problem solution, a broad outline of the plan should be scheduled first so that the system can see what adjustments need to be made during execution. Machine programs can no more foresee all possible contingencies than can humans and, therefore, some form of contingency planning is needed.

Sacerdoti's Network of Organized Action Hierarchies (NOAH) constructs a preplan that can be altered on a contingency basis during execution; NOAH works by means of a successive refinement approach to planning. But NOAH is essentially a top/down processor, with the planner making high-level abstract plans that guide and restrict the subsequent development of low-level details. Similarly, the model assumes that the initial plan is relatively complete and subject only to refinement at lower levels. Therefore, NOAH is essentially a hierarchical planning model.

Recently, Hayes-Roth and Hayes-Roth (1979)

have developed an Opportunistic Planning Model (OPM) that departs from the top/down, hierarchical, complete preplan assumptions of prior planning models. The OPM permits planning at many different levels, allows several tentative, incomplete plans to coexist and is, therefore, essentially a heterarchical system. The OPM has great flexibility, in that it can shift among several planning levels opportunistically. At any one point in the planning process, the planner's current decisions and observations afford new opportunities for plan development, and these are followed up by the model. Sometimes these opportunistic decisions result in orderly top/down routes, but often less coherent sequences are engaged in, just as in human thinking.

The OPM achieves this flexibility by assuming that the planning process consists of the independent actions of many distinct cognitive specialists (demons), each able to make tentative decisions for potential incorporation within a plan. As in the classic Pandemonium model (Selfridge, 1959), the specialists record these decisions in a common data structure known as the blackboard, thus enabling them to interact with each other, to influence and be influenced by each other's decisions.

The blackboard is divided into five conceptual planes that correspond to different categories of decision. These include: (1) *metaplan* decisions that deal with the general approach to the problem; (2) *plan-abstraction* decisions that describe ideal plans, that may or may not be feasible, that is, what kinds of actions are desirable; (3) *plan* decisions that cover what specific actions to take; (4) *world-knowledge* decisions that take note of specific problem environments; and (5) *executive* decisions that are involved with the on-line organization of the planning process itself. Each plane on the blackboard is also potentially served at several levels of abstraction. For example, the levels of the metaplan involve problem definition, selection of an appropriate problem-solving model, policy setting, and establishment of appropriate evaluation criteria. The executive plan involves decisions of priority, scheduling, and general allocation of cognitive resources.

In a recent series of studies, Goldin and Hayes-Roth (1980) tested the OPM model by examining the planning strategies of adults. The task was to schedule a series of errands in a fictional town. The subjects read a scenario that described a series of desired errands, a starting time and location, an ending time and location, and sometimes some additional constraints. The allotted time was invariably insufficient to perform all of the errands and,

therefore, the planners were obliged to set priorities concerning which errands to perform as well as to organize their schedule in the most economical manner. The primary data consisted of the protocols of the subject's on-line descriptions of their planning processes.

Good planners made many more metaplan and executive decisions and exercised more deliberate control over their planning processes. Good planners also made more use of world-knowledge information. They showed greater flexibility than poor planners, in that they frequently shifted the focus of their attention among the different plans of decisions (within the OPM framework) and among the different loci within the route. More of the decisions of good planners were at a high level of abstraction; good planners recognized the importance of global planning, in contrast to the heavy reliance on local control or bottom/up plans shown by the poor planners. Poor planners tended to switch back and forth between objectives in an idiosyncratic (and often chaotic) fashion. In contrast, effective planners developed a prototypical procedure for accomplishing the errands, which they maintained over several instantiations of the task.

The details of GPS, NOAH, and OPM are not important for our purposes here; the lesson is that with increasing sophistication, information processing and artificial intelligence models have gained more power by paying increasing attention to the metacognitive aspects of thinking. Crudely, all such models distinguish between preplanning and planning-in-action (Rogoff & Gardner, in press), planning and control (Hayes-Roth & Hayes-Roth, 1979), preaction and troubleshooting (Norman & Schallice, 1980), and planning and monitoring (Brown, 1978). Preplanning involves the formulation of general methods of procedure prior to the actual onset of action. During the ongoing attempt to solve the problem, there is continual planning-in-action, troubleshooting, or control processing that involves monitoring, evaluating, and revising. Intelligent systems, be they machine or human, are highly dependent on executive orchestration, resource allocation, and monitoring functions. Nonintelligent systems, be they inadequate programs or humans, are assumed to be deficient in these planning functions.

Poor problem solvers lack spontaneity and flexibility in both preplanning and monitoring. Extreme examples of planning deficits in adults come from the clinical literature on patients with frontal-lobe syndrome. Such patients typically omit the initial preaction component (Luria, 1966); they also experience extraordinary difficulty with error correction

(Milner, 1964). Such patients have been described as simultaneously perseverative and distractible, a failure in intelligent focusing attributed to damage to the supervisory attentional mechanism or executive system (Norman & Schallice, 1980). Although pathological cases are extreme, many descriptions of young and retarded children's planning are very similar.

Developmental Studies of Monitoring. Currently, there is considerable interest in planning and monitoring processes, and developmental data to support the theoretical models are accumulating in a variety of domains, notably studies of social planning (Bruce & Newman, 1978; Newman, 1981), problem solving (Klahr, 1978; Klahr & Robinson, 1981; Klahr & Siegler, 1978), planning and monitoring during reading and studying (Bransford et al., 1981; Brown, 1980, 1981; Flavell, 1981; Markman, 1981), and training research designed to improve the ability to plan and monitor in the developmentally young (Brown, 1978; Brown & Campione, 1981; also see *Intervention Research*). We will illustrate with two related examples of on-line monitoring from the area of learning from texts: (1) comprehension monitoring while listening and reading and (2) effort allocation while studying.

Comprehension Monitoring. Comprehension monitoring is a topic that has received considerable attention and been subjected to a great deal of theoretical speculation (Baker & Brown, in press-a, in press-b; Bransford et al., 1981; Brown, 1980; Collins & Smith, 1981; Flavell, 1980, 1981; Garner, in press; Markman, 1981, in press; Stein & Trabasso, in press), although the data base to support these speculations is somewhat sparse. Studies by Markman reaffirmed a traditional claim (Thorndike, 1917) that children are surprisingly tolerant of ambiguities, inconsistencies, and just plain untruths in passages they must listen to (Markman, 1977, 1979, 1981, in press) or read (Garner, in press). For example, Markman (1979) had children in third, fifth and sixth grades listen to short essays containing inconsistent information; they were then probed for their awareness of the inconsistencies. Some of the inconsistencies could only be noticed if the child made an inference, whereas others were quite explicit. Children in all grades were poor at reporting the inconsistencies, although they were somewhat more successful with the blatant problems. Markman also found that when children were specifically warned in advance that a problem might be present in the text, both third and sixth graders were more likely to report the inconsisten-

cy. Nevertheless, many children still failed to report the inconsistencies.

In a recent series of experiments, Garner and her colleagues (Garner, in press; Garner & Kraus, 1980; Garner & Taylor, 1980) have shown that junior high students, particularly those identified as poor readers, are also poor at evaluating texts for internal consistency. The students were asked to rate brief passages for ease of understanding and to justify whatever low ratings they gave. Poor readers were less likely to rate inconsistent text as difficult to understand, although good readers were by no means proficient at this task. The poor readers were better at identifying comprehension problems that were due to difficult vocabulary items than to inconsistencies (Garner, in press).

Garner and Taylor (1980) also found differences in the amount of assistance required to notice inconsistencies. After reading a brief passage, fourth, sixth, and eighth graders were provided with increasingly more specific hints as to the source of difficulty. Even after the experimenter underlined the two sentences that conflicted with one another and told the child they did not make sense, fourth graders and older poor readers were rarely able to report the exact nature of the problem. However, the intervention did increase the likelihood that better readers would notice the inconsistency.

Listeners and readers are more likely to notice inconsistencies if they are in a single sentence (Garner & Kraus, 1980) or in adjacent sentences (Markman, 1979) than if they are separated by a more substantial body of text, suggesting that one common shortcoming in children's comprehension monitoring is a failure to consider relationships across noncontiguous sentences in a text. Although they may be capable of evaluating their understanding of single sentences, they still need to develop the skills to integrate and evaluate information across larger segments of text. Even college students may have difficulty with the more demanding task (Baker, 1979).

One possible problem with these studies is that children were required to report the inconsistencies, and their putative lack of sensitivity could be due to a reluctance to criticize or to the general problems with verbal reports discussed earlier. This interpretation is a little far fetched, however, because the insensitivity is reported in studies that used button pressing (Markman & Gorin, in press), rating comprehensibility (Garner, in press), and replaying a recorded message (Flavell, Speer, Green, & August, 1981) as the index of comprehension failure.

One method to avoid the problem of verbal reporting is to take on-line evidence of comprehension monitoring. For example, adults return to previously read information and make regressive eye movements when they encounter pronouns whose referents are unclear (Baker, 1979; Carpenter & Just, 1978; Garrod & Sanford, 1977), and they require more time to read paragraphs that violate conventional organizational structure (Greeno & Noreen, 1974; Kieras, 1978). When such on-line measures are used, children are credited with more sensitivity to textual anomalies. We will give two examples, one with quite young children listening to confusing tape-recorded messages, the other with older children reading confusing text. The similarity in pattern of results across disparate tasks and ages is striking.

Flavell et al. (1981) instructed kindergarten and second-grade children to construct block buildings identical to those described on tape by a confederate child. Some of the instructions contained ambiguities, unfamiliar words, insufficient information, or unattainable goals. Children were encouraged to replay the tape as often as necessary to help them construct the buildings. The children were videotaped as they attempted to carry out the instructions, and the videotapes were analyzed for nonverbal signs of problem detection, that is, looking puzzled or replaying the tape. The children later were asked if they had succeeded in making a building exactly like the confederate's and if they thought the other child did a good job in conveying the instructions.

As expected, the older children were more likely to notice the inadequacies in the messages than were the younger. Even though both kindergartners and second graders showed nonverbal signs of puzzlement at appropriate points during the task, the kindergartners were less likely to report later that some of the messages were inadequate. Several other investigators have also reported on-line evidence of problem detection in listening tasks despite failures to report the inadequacies verbally (Bearison & Levey, 1977; Lloyd & Pavlidis, 1978; Patterson, Cosgrove, & O'Brien, 1980).

Turning to comprehension monitoring while reading, Harris, Kruithof, Terwogt, and Visser (1981) reported an analogous finding; 8- and 11-year-olds were asked to read passages that contained sentences that were or were not anomalous depending on the title. For example, the sentence "He sat in the chair and watched his hair get shorter" would be acceptable if the title were "A Visit to the Barber," but anomalous if the title were "A Visit to the Dentist." Children at both ages read the anomalous sentence more slowly, but the proportion of subjects reporting that they had detected a text problem was much greater in the 11-year-old sample. This finding has also been reported by Capelli and Markman (1980); of interest in their study was that sixth graders decreased their reading time more dramatically than third graders in response to text anomaly. Capelli and Markman, Flavell et al. (1982), and Harris et al. (1981) all suggest that younger students have difficulty interpreting their own feelings of discomfort in the face of hitches in smooth comprehension.

One problem, then, with estimating children's comprehension-monitoring ability is the measure that is used for assessing sensitivity; on-line measures, such as time expended, facial signs of confusion, and so on, reveal earlier sensitivity than the more stringent demands for verbal reporting. A second problem is that familiarity of materials or knowledge-base factors are extremely influential in both listening and reading (Patterson, O'Brien, Kister, Carter, & Kotsonis, in press; Stein & Trabasso, in press). If children are familiar with the domain in question, they are more likely to note inconsistencies and to devise plausible hypotheses on how to resolve them. Furthermore, the development of the ability to monitor one's comprehension is not due to the development of a unitary "metacognitive faculty" or "demon" that automatically sounds an alarm at every possible misinterpretation or lack of mastery. One of the difficulties of constructing such a comprehension-monitoring demon to assess the adequacies of one's current state of understanding and mastery is that different information is necessary for different purposes. For example, nearly all adults know the concept of gold (as in gold watch or gold bar), and most adults would also confidently proclaim they knew the concept (Miller, 1978); indeed, they *do* know it sufficiently well for many purposes. If forced to differentiate real gold from fool's gold, however, most would quickly realize the need for more information. Technical concepts of gold are necessary for some purposes, but most adults experience no difficulties with their nontechnical knowledge of gold. If a comprehension-monitoring demon sounded an alarm at anything less than nontechnical knowledge, it would be an extreme pain in the head (or elsewhere depending on one's theory of localization).

In summary, the ability to monitor one's comprehension of texts is not just a function of age. The blatancy of the anomaly, its centrality to the reading task at hand, relevant background information, and the ability to interpret correctly the discomfort generated by various degrees of misunderstanding are all important factors determining efficiency. An important point here is that obtaining nonverbal measures of comprehension monitoring is an important addition because such nonverbal measures are often more sensitive to on-line monitoring than retrospective reporting.

Effort and Attention Allocation. Another nonverbal method of measuring on-line monitoring is to observe how learners deploy their attention and effort. The ability to attend selectively to relevant aspects of a task is a traditional index of learners' understanding of that task, be it discrimination learning (Crane & Ross, 1967; Hagen & Hale, 1973; Zeaman & House, 1963), rote memorizing (Hagen & Hale, 1973; Hale & Alderman, 1978), or learning from texts (Brown, 1981). Shifting attention as a response to increments in learning is a nonverbal reflection of on-line monitoring that can be examined developmentally. For example, consider such a shift in a rote-memory task. Belmont and Butterfield (1977) observed students who were trained to use (or who spontaneously devised) a cumulative rehearsal strategy for remembering lists of digits. Without warning, a particular list was presented repeatedly, a departure from the usual procedure of presenting a novel list on each trial. Clear developmental differences were found in the speed and efficiency with which the students (1) abandoned the strategy when it was no longer needed (i.e., the list was learned) and (2) modified the strategy when it was appropriate (when lists composed of old and new segments were used). The link between effective monitoring and effort allocation was quite clear.

There is considerable evidence in the educational literature that good learners adjust their degree of effort commensurate with the difficulty of the test they face. For example, Smith (1967) reported that students of high school age who were good readers adjusted their reading efforts depending on whether they were reading for details or general impressions, whereas those who were poor readers used the same behaviors for both purposes. Similarly, Forrest and Waller (1981) asked good and poor readers, third through sixth grade, to read stories for four different purposes: (1) for fun, (2) to make up a title, (3) to find one specific piece of information as quickly as possible, and (4) to study. The older and better readers were more likely to expend additional effort on the more demanding tasks and to distribute effort to relevant parts of the text (skim appropriately). Interestingly, in light of the preceding discussion concerning the relation of

nonverbal to verbal indices of monitoring, the majority of children know by fourth grade how to skim for specific facts, although they cannot describe how they do this until much later (Kobasigawa, Ransom, & Holland, in press). As they become more experienced text learners, children become better able to adjust their effort allocation in an economical manner.

An excellent method of studying effort allocation is the study-time apportionment task introduced by Masur, McIntyre, and Flavell (1973). Grade-school children were given lists of pictures to learn in a multitrial free-recall study. On each trial but the first, they were permitted to select half of the items for further study. By third grade, students selectively chose items they had missed on previous recall attempts for extra study. Even retarded children can be trained to use this strategy (Brown & Campione, 1977).

However, this strategy is not so simple if one wants to apply it to the task of learning from texts. The learner must still select for extra study material she has failed to recall, but judging one's mastery of the gist of texts is more difficult than judging verbatim recall of a list of items (Brown, Campione, & Barclay, 1979). While attempting to learn a text to mastery, it is necessary to shift attention finely in tune with one's subjective impression that certain points are known well enough to risk a test and that others need extra study. In addition, one must estimate which segments of the material are important enough to warrant attention and which are trivial and can, therefore, be ignored. For example, the ideal strategy is to concentrate first on the most important elements of text and, then, as these become well known, shift to lesser and lesser elements until a full representation of the text is built up—as one's degree of learning improves, one must shift attention from a concentration on main points to an attempt to fill in the details.

Brown and her colleagues examined effort and attention allocation as an index of memory monitoring while studying texts (Brown & Campione, 1978; Brown, Smiley, & Lawton, 1978). Students from 5th through 12th grade together with college students were asked to study prose passages until they could recall all the details in their own words. They were allowed repeated study trials. The passages were divided into constituent idea units rated in terms of their importance to the theme; there were four levels of rated importance. On each trial, the students were allowed to select a subset of the idea units (15%) to keep with them while they attempted recall.

On the first trial, the majority of students at all

ages selected the most important units to help them recall. Children below high school age continued to do this, even though they became perfectly able to recall the most important information without aid, but they persistently failed to recall additional details. College students, however, modified their selection as a function of their degree of learning: on the first trial, they selected predominantly important (Level 4) units for retrieval aids. On the second trial, they shifted to a preference for Level 3 units, whereas on the third trial, they preferred Level 2 units. As they learned more and more of the material, college students shifted their attention allocation to reflect their estimated state of knowledge.

Older high school students showed the same basic pattern as the college students, but they were one trial behind; they did not begin to shift to less important units until the third trial. This lag could be due to slower learning, that is, both groups shifted when they reached the same criterion of learning, but the younger students took an extra trial to reach that criterion. It could also be due to a slower shift in attention allocation, that is, both groups learned as much on each trial, but it took high school students longer to realize that they should adjust their attention. The latter appears to be the correct interpretation for, even when students were matched on the basis of degree of learning on each trial, the younger students still took longer to change their effort-allocation pattern in the face of their level of mastery.

The ability to fine tune one's allocation of attention to reflect mastery level is a late-developing skill, perhaps because it requires the coordination of various forms of knowledge. To allocate his attention in a manner responsive to his state of existing knowledge, the learner must have (1) information concerning the current state of knowledge, that is, what he knows and what he does not yet know; (2) knowledge of the task demands of gist recall; (3) knowledge of the fine gradiation of importance of various elements of texts, that is, what is important to know and what can be disregarded; and (4) the strategic knowledge to adjust his allocation of effort in response to this information.

In short, the ability to monitor one's state of learning depends on the sensitivity one has to the factors in the tetrahedral model; strategy, knowledge, material, and task demands all influence the degree to which a child will be able to coordinate his plans and engage in active monitoring. Nonverbal indices of monitoring seem to be more reliable than verbal reports, although the exact relationship between the two deserves attention. Effort allocation as measured by reading speed (Baker, 1979; Capelli & Markman, 1980; Greeno & Noreen, 1974; Harris et al., 1981; Kieras, 1978) or attention deployment (Belmont & Butterfield, 1977; Bisanz, Vesonder, & Voss, 1978; Brown & Campione, 1977, 1978; Brown & Smiley, 1978; Brown, Smiley, & Lawton, 1978; Masur, McIntyre, & Flavell, 1973; Posnansky, 1978; Wellman, in press) seems to be a sensitive index of memory, learning, and comprehension monitoring that deserves further attention.

Self-regulation

Any active learning process involves continuous adjustments and fine tuning of action by means of self-regulating processes and "other even more mysterious" mechanisms (Marshall & Morton, 1978). Psychologists interested in mechanisms of growth and change have traditionally been concerned with such self-regulating processes. Of course, substantial contributions are made by external agents, which we will discuss later in the chapter. But even without external pressure, human thinkers "play" with thinking (Gardner, 1978), that is, subject their own thought processes to examination and treat their own thinking as an object of thought. Similarly, learners regulate and refine their own actions, sometimes in response to feedback concerning errors, but often in the absence of such feedback. Indeed, even if the system with which one is experimenting is adequate, active learners will improve upon their original production (Karmiloff-Smith, 1979a, 1979b).

Recently, the term metacognition has been extended to encompass such regulatory functions as error detection and correction (Brown & DeLoache, 1978; Clark, in press), but the historical roots of such concepts can be found in most of the major developmental theories. For example, Binet was fascinated by individual differences in his daughters' cognitive styles of self-regulation (Binet, 1890, 1903) and, following intensive study with both normal and retarded children, he selected *autocriticism* (Binet, 1909) as a central component of intelligence.

Given space limitations, we will concentrate here primarily on relatively recent Genevan research on self-regulatory mechanisms in children's thinking and on the growing emphases in developmental psycholinguistics on error correction, systematization, and metalinguistic awareness.

Piaget's Theory of Regulation. In the latter part of his career, the transformational period (Riegel, 1975), Piaget became more and more interested in mechanisms of learning and the influence of both conscious and unconscious regulatory functions in promoting conceptual change. Again, owing to space restrictions, we cannot begin to describe the complex theory of Piaget's latter years and the reader is referred to the excellent treatment by Gelman and Baillargeon (*vol. III, chap. 3*). Briefly (and probably too simplistically), Piaget distinguished between three primary types of self-regulation: autonomous, active, and conscious.

Autonomous regulation is an inherent part of any knowing act; learners continually regulate their performance, fine tuning and modulating actions, however small the learner and however simple the action (Bruner, 1973; Koslowski & Bruner, 1972). *Active regulation* is more akin to trial and error, where the learner is engaged in constructing and testing theories-in-action (Karmiloff-Smith & Inhelder, 1974/1975). Under the guidance of a powerful theory-in-action, the learner tests a current theory via concrete actions that produce tangible results. Not until a much later stage can the learner mentally construct and reflect upon the hypothetical situations that would confirm or refute a current theory without the need for active regulation. *Conscious regulation* involves the mental formulation of hypotheses capable of being tested via imaginary counterexamples or confirmatory evidence.

Consciousness first emerges as the child becomes capable of reflecting upon her own actions in the presence of the actual event. At this initial stage, consciousness is tied to concrete action but does not direct it. The child's "reactions remain elementary, the subject is likely to distort conceptualizations of what he observes, instead of recording it without modification." Such distortion can be quite dramatic. For example, having witnessed an event that is contrary to a tenaciously held belief, the "subject contests the unexpected evidence of his own eyes and thinks that he sees what he predicted would happen" (Piaget, 1976, p. 340).

At the most mature level, which Piaget would prefer to restrict to the stage of formal operations, the entire thinking process can be carried out on the mental plane. The learner can consciously invent, test, modify, and generalize theories and discuss these operations with others:

> Finally, at the third level (from eleven to twelve years) which is that of reflected abstraction (conscious products of reflexive abstraction) the situation is modified in that cognizance [consciousness] begins to be extended in a reflexion of the thought itself—This means that the subject has become capable of theorizing and no longer only of "concrete," although logically

structured, reasoning. The reason for this is the child's new power of elaborating operations on operations.—he thereby becomes capable of varying the factors in his experiments, of envisaging the various models that might explain a phenomenon, and of checking the latter through actual experimentation. (Piaget, 1976, pp. 352–353)

In brief, the developmental progression is from unconscious autonomous regulation to active regulation but in the absence of anything more than a "fleeting consciousness." The beginning of conscious reflection occurs when the child is capable of considering her actions and describing them to others, albeit sometimes erroneously. The mature level of reflected abstraction, however, is characterized by conscious processes that can be carried out exclusively on the mental plane. Mature learners can create imaginary worlds and theories to explain actions and reactions within them. Such theories can be confirmed or refuted by means of the further construction of mental tests, conflict trials, or thought experiments that extend the limits of generality of the theory. This is the essence of scientific reasoning and the end state for a Piagetian development progression of "child as scientist."

The progress to conscious regulation of problem solving via thought experiments, hypothesis testing, and reflected abstraction is well illustrated in Anzai and Simon's (1979) microgenetic analysis of an adult who is systematically refining her procedures for solving a five-disc Tower of Hanoi problem. Within a single session, the subject progressed through three stages. First, she was totally concerned with the goal of completing the task by whatever means possible. In the intermediate stage, she became theory driven, seeking to understand the principles behind the task, guiding herself explicitly by mentioning intermediate goals, and pausing after each goal had been reached to plan for the next goal. Theories-in-action (Karmiloff-Smith & Inhelder, 1974/1975) were being created and tested in this phase. In the third phase, the subject shows Piaget's "transcendance of action by conceptualization," that is, "reflection-directing action." *Before* undertaking to solve the puzzle again, the subject tested her understanding by reviewing the moves of the component one-, two-, three-, and four-disc problems. In so doing, she explicitly stated the main principle of recursivity and the essential notion of the transfer of pyramids of discs (Anzai & Simon, 1979).

The microgenetic learning route followed by this adult subject is recapitulated macrogenetically.

Piaget collected protocols on children solving The Hanoi Tower (Piaget, 1976). In the early stage of solution, children complete a three-disc problem by trial and error without being conscious of the principles. None of the younger subjects (5 years old) made a plan, or were able to predict how they were going to move the tower (see, however, Klahr, 1978, for earlier evidence of planning on this task). After the fact, their justifications and explanations were noninformative. In an intermediate stage, correct solutions became stable for three-disc problems but were not readily transferred to more difficult problems. There was some evidence of planning ahead and the beginning of the ability to describe the procedures used during a successful attempt. The final stage (at approximately 11 years of age) was characterized by rapid and stable success on three-disc problems and increasingly inferential anticipation of the rules for solving five-disc problems. Having completed a four-disc problem, one child asked to predict how to solve a five-disc problem responded:

> There's one more, you have to make more moves, otherwise it's the same system—you always take away the smaller one, then the middle one, then you put the small one on the middle one and you can get at the bigger one; that makes a small pyramid there, and then the way is clear to do it all again. I can start all over again; it's the same story afterward." (Piaget, 1976, p. 298)

By Piaget's Stage 3, the child's understanding of the principles of recursivity and the pyramid-subgoal strategy (Anzai & Simon, 1979) is not only fully articulated, but it directs the subsequent problem-solving attempt. The entire procedure can be corrected, examined, and revised in thought before it is attempted in action. This is the essence of conscious control of action, the hallmark of formal operations.

Metaprocedural Reorganization and Systematization. Piaget's colleagues, Inhelder and Karmiloff-Smith, have introduced another concept relevant to this discussion of self-regulation, that of *metaprocedural reorganization* (Karmiloff-Smith, 1979a; Karmiloff-Smith & Inhelder, 1974/1975). The basic idea is that learning within a domain follows a predictable sequence that is characterized by internal pressure to systematize, consolidate, and generalize knowledge. The prototypical microgenetic sequence is that the child first works on developing an adequate partial theory for a salient aspect of the problem space; the partial theory is practiced and perfected until it is fully operational. Only

when the partial theory is consolidated and functioning efficiently can the child step back and consider the system as a whole. Typically, the child will develop several juxtaposed theories adequate for various parts of the problem space, each theory operating in isolation from the other. Once the procedures are functioning well, the next stage of development is possible and the child "steps up" and reconsiders the problem-space metaprocedurally. Once children become aware of the discrepancies or contradictions resulting from the simultaneous existence of several different partial theories, they begin attempts to reconcile the differences and obviate contradictions resulting from the juxtaposition (Inhelder et al., 1974).

A concrete example might help to clarify this complicated theoretical notion. Karmiloff-Smith and Inhelder (1974/1975) asked 4- to 9-year-old children to balance rectangular wooden blocks on a narrow metal rod fixed to a larger piece of wood. Length blocks had their weight evenly distributed, and the correct solution was to balance the blocks at the geometric center. With weight blocks, the weight of each "side" varied either conspicuously (by gluing a large square block to one end of the base rectangular block) or inconspicuously (by inserting a hidden weight into a cavity on one end of the rectangular block).

At first, the children made the blocks balance by brute trial and error, using proprioceptive information to guide action. Behavior was purely directed at the goal of balancing. This ploy was obviously successful; the children balanced each block in turn. There was no attempt to examine the properties of the objects that led to balance and no attempt to subject each block to a test of a unified theory.

This early errorless, but unanalyzed, phase was supplanted by the emergence of strong theories-in-action. These theories were directed at uncovering the rules governing balance in the miniature world of these particular blocks. Unfortunately, they were incomplete rules that produced errors. A common early theory developed by the children was to concentrate exclusively on the geometric center and attempt to balance all blocks in this fashion. This works for unweighted blocks. When the theory did not result in balance, the blocks involved were discarded as exceptions ("impossible to balance").

After this theory was well established and working well for length blocks, the children became discomforted by the number of, and regularity of, the errors. A new juxtaposed theory was then developed for the conspicuous weight blocks. For these, the children compensated for the weight that was obviously added to one end and adjusted the point of balance accordingly. For a time, however, length and weight were considered independently. Length blocks were solved by the geometric center rule and conspicuous weight blocks were solved by the rule of estimate weight first and then compensate. Inconspicuous weight problems still generated errors; they looked identical to the unweighted blocks and were, therefore, subjected to the dominant geometric center rule. When they did not conform to the theory they were discarded as anomalies that were "impossible to balance." The children's verbal responses reflected these juxtaposed solutions, with exclusively length justifications given for unweighted blocks and weight justifications given for conspicuously weighted blocks.

Gradually and reluctantly, the children entered the period of metaprocedural reorganization, which was only possible when both their juxtaposed procedures were working smoothly. Now, the young theorists were made uncomfortable by the remaining exceptions to their own rules and began to seek a rule for them. In so doing, a metaprocedural reorganization was induced that resulted in a single rule for all blocks. The children abandoned the simple theories and reorganized the problem space so that a single unifying theory predominated. Now, the children paused before balancing any block and roughly assessed the point of balance. Verbal responses reflected their consideration of both length and weight, for example, "You have to be careful, sometimes it's just as heavy on each side and so the middle is right, and sometimes it's heavier on one side." *After* inferring the probable point of balance, and only then, did the child place the block on the bar.

There are three main points to note about this example: first, there is the finding of a developmental lull or even a seemingly retrogressive stage when errors predominate. Initially, the children made no errors; all blocks were balanced. But, during the quest for a comprehensive theory of balance, the children generated partially adequate procedures that resulted in errors. Only when the unifying theory was discovered did the children revert to perfect performance. If errors alone formed the data base, a U-shaped developmental growth curve would be apparent (Strauss & Stavey, in press). Actually, what was happening was that the children were analyzing the problem space to generate a theory that would incorporate all the blocks. In so doing, they made what looked like errors but what were often tests of the existing partial theory.

A second main point is that metaprocedural reorganization leading to a "stepping up" in theory complexity is only possible when the partially ade-quate, juxtaposed systems are well established (see also Siegler, 1981). It is essential that the child gain control of simple theories in her quest for a more complex and more adequate theory. Karmiloff-Smith and Inhelder refer to this as creative simplification:

> The construction of false theories or the overgeneralization of limited ones are in effect productive processes. Overgeneralization, a sometimes derogatory term, can be looked upon as the *creative simplification* of a problem by ignoring some of the complicating factors (such as weight in our study). This is implicit in the young child's behavior but could be intentional in the scientist's. Overgeneralization is not just a means to simplify but also to unify; it is then not surprising that the child and the scientist often refuse counterexamples since they complicate the unification process. However, to be capable of unifying positive examples implies that one is equally capable of attempting to find a unifying principle to cover counterexamples . . . [there is] a general tendency to construct a powerful, yet often inappropriate hypothesis which [learners] try to verify rather than refute. This temporarily blinds the [learner] to counterexamples which should actually suffice to have them reject their hypothesis immediately. (Karmiloff-Smith & Inhelder, 1974/1975, p. 209)

Progress comes only when the inadequate partial theory is well established and the learner is free to attempt to extend the theory to other phenomena. In this way, the theorists, be they children or scientists, are able to discover new properties that, in turn, make it possible for new theories to be constructed.

The third main point is that metaprocedural reorganization is not solely a response to external pressure or failure but rather occurs spontaneously when the child has developed well-functioning procedures that are incomplete but adequate for the task at hand. It is not failure that directs the change but success, success that the child wishes to extend throughout the system.

A similar U-shaped developmental pattern has been observed in children's language acquisition (Bowerman, in press; Karmiloff-Smith, 1979a). The phenomena under consideration are errors in children's spontaneous speech. The particular errors of interest are those that are preceded by a period of correct usage; these are, hence, referred to as late errors (Bowerman, in press). For example, consider the child's use of plural (-s) and past tense (-ed) morphemes. The typical developmental progression is that children produce correct instances of plural and past tense forms of both the regular (dog*s*, cat*s*, tree*s;* walk*ed,* jump*ed,* climb*ed*) and irregular (mice, feet; went, broke) kinds (Bowerman, in press). Next, the irregular pattern is replaced by an incorrect, overgeneralization of the regular form (foots, mouses; goed, breaked). Eventually the correct forms reappear.

The explanation for this U-shaped development is that the original correct usage was due to the child having learned the irregular (as well as regular) forms as individual cases. With repeated experience with the regular pattern, the child recognizes the systematicity involved, abstracts the general rule, and applies it too broadly to all plurals (hence, mouses) or all past tense forms (hence, goed and breaked). Errors occur where they had not previously. When the system is fully established, the child is ready to admit exceptions to the dominant rule and the irregular forms reappear; this time they are part of an integrated theory however and are regarded as exceptions to the rule, not just isolated forms (For many other examples, see Bowerman, in press; Karmiloff-Smith, 1979a).

Levels of Self-regulation. In this brief and oversimplified synopsis of latter-day Genevan psychology and language-acquisition data, a central place in theoretical speculation is afforded to the concept of self-regulation; there is basic agreement that self-regulatory functions are integral to learning and are central mechanisms of growth and change. Similarly, in the emergent field of metacognition, the notion of self-regulatory mechanisms has a central place (Brown & DeLoache, 1978).

All agree that there are many degrees of self-regulation and that self-regulation is essential for any knowing act. It is important to note, however, that a sharp distinction is made in both theories of language acquisition and in Genevan psychology, a sharp distinction that has not been made as clearly in the metacognitive literature. The distinction is between conscious awareness and direction of thought versus self-correction and regulation that can proceed below this level.

Piaget (1976, 1978) distinguishes sharply between active regulation as part of any knowing act and conscious regulation and direction of thought, the keystone of formal operations. The first process is age independent, even the young learner succeeds in action by regulating, correcting, and refining his current theories. Some form of error correction must be part of any active learning attempt, even very young children are capable of regulating

their activities by means of a systematic procedure of error detection and correction. For example, in a recent study, DeLoache, Sugarman, and Brown (1981) observed young children (24 to 42 months) as they attempted to assemble a set of nesting cups. Children in this age range did not differ in the likelihood of their attempting to correct a set of nonseriated cups. They did, however, differ in their strategies for correction.

The most primitive strategy, used frequently by children below 30 months, was brute force. When a large cup was placed on a smaller one, the children would press down hard on the nonfitting cup. Variants of brute pressure were twisting and banging, but the same principle held—the selected cup will fit if only one can press hard enough. Older children also used the brute-force approach, but only after an unsuccessful series of maneuvers; for them, it appeared to be a last resort.

A second strategy initiated by some of the younger subjects was that of trying an alternative. After placing two nonfitting cups together, the child removed the top cup and did one of two things. He either looked for an alternative base for the nonfitting cup or he tried an alternative top for the original base. Both ploys involve minimal restructuring and necessitate considering the relation between only two cups at any one time. The third characteristic ploy of children below 30 months was to respond to a cup that would not fit into a partially completed set of cups by dismantling the entire set and starting again.

Older children (30 to 42 months) faced with a nonfitting cup engaged in strategies that involved consideration of the entire set of relations in the stack. For example, one sophisticated strategy was insertion; the children took apart the stack at a point that enabled them to insert the new cup in its correct position. A second strategy, reversal, was also shown by older children. After placing two nonfitting cups together, the child would *immediately* reverse the relation between them (5/4 immediately switched to 4/5).

The rapidly executed reversal strategy was not shown by the younger group. Some young children would repeatedly assemble, for example, cups 4 to 1, starting with 4 as a base and then inserting 3, 2, and 1. Then, they encountered the largest cup, that is, 5 and attempted to insert it on top of the completed partial stack, pressing and twisting repeatedly. When brute force failed, they would dismantle the whole stack and start again. Similarly, having assembled 1, 2, 4, and 5 and then encountering 3, the younger children's only recourse was to begin again.

The DeLoache et al. (1981) study of self-correction in young children is used as one example (see also Koslowski & Bruner, 1972) of the obvious fact that even very young children correct their errors while solving a problem. Of more interest is the demonstration that the child's error-correction strategies provide us with a window through which to view the child's theories-in-action. The very processes used to correct errors reflect the level of understanding the child has of the problem space. Similarly, developmental psycholinguists have argued that production errors are most informative, "the tongue slips into patterns" (Nooteboom, 1969). Such errors reveal a great deal about the organization of the semantic knowledge of the speaker (Bowerman, in press; Clark, in press).

Important though these early regulatory actions may be, the distinction between theories-in-action and reflection should not be overlooked. Error correction during language production is integral to the processes of using language and is present no less in young children (Bowerman, in press; Clark, in press) than in adults (Fromkin, 1973; Nooteboom, 1969). Metalinguistic awareness, in contrast, is assumed to be a product of adolescent rather than childhood thinking. The ability to step back and consider one's own thought (or language) as itself an object of thought and, to go further, use the subsequent conceptualization to direct and redirect one's cognitive theories is currently believed to be late developing.

Confused in the metacognitive literature, even lost in some versions of the concept, is this essential distinction between self-regulation during learning and knowledge of, or even mental experimentation with, one's own thoughts. Whatever distinctions must be made to render metacognition a more malleable concept, this one is a fine candidate for inclusion in the list.

Other-Regulation

The last strand of metacognitive inquiry to be addressed is the notion of a transference from other-regulation to self-regulation. Important as the processes of self-regulation may be, a great deal of learning occurs in the presence of, and is fostered by, the activity of others. Supportive others, such as parents, teachers, peers, and so on, guide a novice to mastery, and there seems to be a systematic regularity in how this guidance works.

A great deal of the work conducted on other-regulation has taken place within the framework of Vygotsky's (1978) theory of internalization. Vygotsky argues that all psychological processes are initially social, shared between people, particularly between child and adult, and that the basic interpersonal nature of thought is transformed through experience to an intrapersonal process. Thus, for Vygotsky, the fundamental process of development is the gradual internalization and personalization of what was originally a social activity.

Social settings where the child interacts with experts in a problem-solving domain are settings where a great deal of learning occurs. Indeed, some would argue that the majority of learning is shaped by social processes (*Laboratory of Comparative Human Cognition, vol. 1, chap. 7*). A great deal of this learning involves the transfer of executive control from an expert to the child. Children first experience active problem-solving procedures in the presence of others, then gradually come to perform these functions for themselves. This process of internalization is gradual; first, the adult (parent, teacher, etc.) controls and guides the child's activity, but gradually the adult and the child come to share the problem-solving functions, with the child taking initiative and the adult correcting and guiding when she falters. Finally, the adult cedes control to the child and functions primarily as a supportive and sympathetic audience (Brown & French, 1979; Brown & Ferrara, in press; Laboratory of Comparative Human Cognition, in press-b; Wertsch, 1978). Again, we have selected illustrations that span a wide age and task range to demonstrate the generality of this pattern; the first involves mother-child dyads and the second teacher-pupil interactions.

At least in middle-class homes, one stable locus of mother-child interaction is picture book "reading." Ninio and Bruner (1978) observed one mother-infant dyad longitudinally, starting when the child was only 8 months old and terminating (unfortunately) when he was 18 months old. From the very beginning, their mother-child interaction could best be described as a *dialogue*, with the timing of the mother's and child's behaviors following an almost complete alternation pattern, strikingly similar to the turn-taking conventions observed in dialogue. In this dyad, the mother initially was very much in command and any participation from the child was encouraged. Indeed, Ninio and Bruner (1978) point out that the mother accepted an astonishing variety of responses as acceptable turn-taking behavior, interpreting anything as having a "specific, intelligible content." The "imputation of intent and content" to the child's activities constitutes "an important mechanism by which the child is advanced to more adult-like communicative behavior" (p. 8).

A dramatic shift in responsibility, however, came when the child began to use labels by himself. The mother began to act as if she believed the child had uttered words rather than babble. The mother's "theory of the child" changed and so did her actions. At first, she appeared to be content with any vocalization but, as soon as actual words can be produced, the mother "stepped up" her demands and asked for a label with the query, "What's that?" The mother seemed to increase her level of expectation, first "coaxing the child to substitute a vocalization for a nonvocal sign and later a well-formed word for a babbled vocalization" (Ninio & Bruner, 1978, p. 12). Initially the mother did all the labeling because she assumed that the child could not, but later the mother started

a cycle with a label *ONLY* if she thinks that the child will not label the picture himself, either because he does not yet know the correct word, or because he is not attentive enough to make the effort at labelling. If circumstances seem more favorable for labelling to occur, she will usually start the cycle with a *"What's that?"* question. (p. 14)

Responsibility for labeling is transferred from the mother to the child in response to his increasing store of knowledge, finely monitored by the mother. During the course of the study, the mother constantly updated her inventory of the words the child had previously understood and repeatedly attempted to make contact with his growing knowledge base. For example:

1. "You haven't seen one of those; that's a goose."
2. "You don't really know what those are, do you? They are mittens; wrong time of year for those."
3. "It's a dog; I know you know that one."
4. "We'll find you something you know very well."
5. "Come on, you've learned ''bricks'."

DeLoache (in preparation) repeated many of these observations in a cross-sectional study of mothers reading to their children. In this study, the children range from 17 to 38 months. The mothers of the youngest children pointed to the objects and labeled them, sometimes providing some additional information. In the middle age group, the children were much more active. Their mothers asked them

to point to and label objects and to provide other information about the picture. These children often spontaneously provided labels ("There's a horsie") or asked the mothers for labels ("What's this?"). In the oldest group studied, more complex stories were introduced and the mothers again assumed control, but they did much more than simply point to and label objects. They talked about the relation among the objects in the picture, related them to the child's experience, and questioned the child about their outside experience (e.g., "That's right, that's a beehive. Do you know what bees make? They make honey. They get nectar from flowers and use it to make honey, and then they put the honey in the beehive."). When the child was quite advanced with respect to naming the objects and knowing something about them, the mother then used the situation and the material to provide the child with a great deal of background information only loosely related to the actual pictures. It is not simply that the amount of help changes as the child becomes more competent, but the quality of help is finely geared to the child's current level.

In both the Ninio and Bruner (1978) and DeLoache (in preparation) dyads, the mother is repeatedly seen functioning in the child's "region of sensitivity to instruction" (Wood & Middleton, 1975) or "zone of proximal development" (Vygotsky, 1978). As the child advances so does the level of collaboration demanded by the mother. The mother systematically shapes their joint experiences in such a way that the child will be drawn into taking more and more responsibility for the dyad's work. In so doing, she not only provides an optimal learning environment but also models appropriate comprehension-fostering activities; these crucial regulatory activities are thereby made overt and explicit.

Ideally, teachers function as just such mediators in the learning process, acting as promotors of self-regulation by nurturing the emergence of personal planning as they gradually cede their own direction. In schools, effective teachers are those who engage in continual prompts to get children to plan and monitor their own activities (Schallert & Kleiman, 1979) and model many forms of critical thinking for their students (Collins & Stevens, 1981), processes that the students must internalize as part of their own problem-solving activities if they are to develop effective skills of self-regulation (Brown et al., in press).

In a recent study, Palincsar and Brown (1981) developed a training procedure based on this theory of the internalization of comprehension-fostering skills first experienced in social contexts. The basic situation was an interactive tutoring dyad, where seventh graders were receiving instruction aimed at improving their reading-comprehension skills. The children were referred by their teachers because, although they were able to decode at grade level, they had severe comprehension problems. Over many sessions, the tutor and the child engaged in an interactive learning game that involved taking turns in leading a dialogue concerning each segment of text. Both the tutor and the child would read a text segment and then the dialogue leader would paraphrase the main idea, question any ambiguities, predict the possible questions that might be asked about that segment, and hypothesize about the content of the remaining passage segments. The dialogue leader would then ask the other a question on the segment. In the next segment, the roles were reversed.

Initially, the tutor modeled these activities, and the child had great difficulty assuming the role of dialogue leader when his turn came. The tutor was forced to resort to constructing paraphrases and questions for the tutee to mimic. In this initial phase, the tutor was modeling effective comprehension-fostering strategies, but the child was a relatively passive observer.

In the intermediate phase, the tutee became much more capable of playing his role as dialogue leader and by the end of 10 sessions was providing paraphrases and questions of some sophistication. For example, in the initial sessions, 55% of questions produced by the tutees were judged to be nonquestions or questions needing clarification but, by the end of the sessions, only 4% of responses were so judged. At the beginning of the sessions, only 11% of the questions were aimed at main ideas. But, by the end of the sessions, 64% of all questions probed comprehension of salient gist. Similar progress was made in producing paraphrases of the main ideas of the text segment. At the beginning of the sessions, only 11% of summary statements captured main ideas, whereas, at the end, 60% of summary statements were so classified. The comprehension-monitoring activities of the tutees certainly improved, becoming more and more like those modeled by the tutor. With repeated interactive experiences, with the tutor and child mutually constructing a cohesive representation of the text, the tutees became able to employ these monitoring functions for themselves.

This improvement was revealed not just in the interactive sessions but also on privately read passages where the students were required to answer comprehension questions on their own. In the laboratory, such tests of comprehension were given throughout the experiment. On these independent tests, performance improved from 10% to 85% correct. And in the classroom, the students moved from the 7th to the 40th to 70th percentile when compared with all other seventh graders in the school. Not only did the students learn to perform comprehension-fostering activities in interaction with their tutor, they were also able to internalize these procedures as part of their own cognitive processes for reading. Through the intervention of a supportive, knowledgeable other, the child is led to the limits of his own understanding. The teacher does *not*, however, tell the child what to do; the teacher enters into an interaction where the child and the teacher are mutually responsible for getting the task done. As the child adopts more of the essential skills initially undertaken by the adult, the adult relinquishes control. Transference of power is gradually and mutually agreed on.

Although the supportive other in the laboratory is usually an experimenter, these interactive learning experiences are intended to mimic real-life learning. Mothers (Wertsch, 1978, 1979), teachers (Schallert & Kleiman, 1979), and mastercraftsmen (Childs & Greenfield, 1980) all function as the supportive other, the agent of change responsible for structuring the child's environment in such a way that he will experience a judicious mix of compatible and conflicting experiences. The interrogative, regulatory role becomes internalized during the process, and the child becomes able to fulfill some of these functions for himself via self-regulation and self-interrogation.

Mature thinkers are those who provide conflict trials for themselves, practice thought experiments, question their own basic assumptions, provide counterexamples to their own rules, and so on. Although a great deal of thinking and learning may remain a social activity (Laboratory of Comparative Human Cognition, in press-a), mature reasoners become capable of providing the supportive-other role for themselves through the process of internalization. Under these systems of tutelage, the child learns not only how to get a particular task done independently but also learns how to set about learning new problems. In other words, the child learns how to learn (Bransford et al., 1981; Brown, 1982a, 1982b; see also *Intervention Research*).

Status of Metacognition as a Concept

In the preceding review, it is clear that metacognition is not only a monster of obscure parentage but also a many-headed monster at that. In this final section, we will make an attempt to estimate the current status of the offspring and list some of the problems we see with the current use of the term.

We would like to emphasize our belief that in many ways this status report is premature. Scientific theorizing, like any other, must pass through stages. Consider, as an example, the novice block balancers (Karmiloff-Smith & Inhelder, 1974/1975) described earlier. Initially, they are merely goal oriented; they concentrate on getting the new theory to work. The next stage is to develop and refine juxtaposed subsystems so that they work fluently. Only when these subsystems are functioning efficiently can the theorist step back and consider the entire problem space and systematize or reorganize it into a cohesive whole.

The recent history of theory development in the realm of metacognition can be viewed in this light. In the early seventies, attracted by the lure of a new-sounding concept, developmental psychologists engaged in demonstration studies to see how the new idea would work. These early studies were often ingenious and the wave of enthusiasm they provoked was justified.

The initial stage is now over and we believe that the current stage is, and should be, devoted to the task of developing workable theories and procedures for separate parts of the problem space. It is for this reason that we chose to look separately at the strands of inquiry that gave rise to the stepchild, metacognition. Currently a great deal of systematic work is being undertaken that we hope will lead to fluently functioning subsystems that are juxtaposed, existing, and developing side by side. But this is an essential stage of theory building. Later, perhaps, when the main subsystems are better understood, metaprocedural reorganization (Karmiloff-Smith, 1979a) may be possible and a full understanding of the domain of metacognition will be attained.

Doubt remains, however, concerning whether the domains covered by metacognition will be tractable enough for such a total systematization. If one takes the wide view, metacognition as currently used refers to understanding in a very broad sense. What we have on our hands is no simple problem space!

In a recent review, Wellman (in press) referred to metacognition as a fuzzy concept, as others have done before. Wellman, however, went on to discuss four features of the fuzzy concept:

First, the concept encompasses an essential, central distinction. However, this distinction serves to anchor the concept not intentionally define it. Second, prototypic central instances of the concept are easily recognized. However,

third, at the periphery agreement as to whether an activity is legitimately metacognitive breaks down; the definitional boundaries are truly fuzzy. Related to this, and fourth, different processes all of which partake of the original distinction may be related only loosely one to another. Thus the term metacognition or metamemory serves primarily to designate a complex of associated phenomena. (pp. 3–4)

This is nicely put and well illustrates the loose confederation of topics included under the blanket term, metacognition. Of some concern, however, is whether the associated phenomena are closely linked enough to warrant the use of a single family name, that is, Are we talking about family resemblances within an ill-defined, natural, or fuzzy category, or about many categories? Would we not be better off at this stage to abandon the global term and work at the level of subordinate concepts, which are themselves somewhat fuzzy?

One suggestion is that the use of the term could be limited to one of its original usages, knowledge about cognition, where that knowledge is stable and statable (Gleitman, in press). Process terms, such as planning ahead, monitoring, resource allocation, self-questioning, self-directing, and so on, would then be used alone without the addendum, metacognition. Thus, for clarity and communicative efficiency, a case could be made that the term metacognition should be pensioned off or at least severely restricted in its extensional reference. Let us hasten to add that this is not because the phenomena subsumed under the term are trivial but rather because issues of fundamental importance may be obscured by the current arguments surrounding things metacognitive; arguments that are obscured because the participants do not always make it clear which head of the beast they are attacking or defending.

This brings us back to the problems mentioned at the beginning of this section. At present it is difficult to answer critical questions about metacognition—such as, "Is it late developing?" "Is it general or domain specific?" "Is it conscious?"—without pausing to ascertain which type of knowledge or process is in question. Although metacognition may turn out to be a fuzzy concept with indistinct boundaries, this degree of imprecision provides an insecure basis for scientific inquiry. By referring to the process/knowledge under discussion by its subordinate name, that is, planning ahead, error correction, hypothesis testing, and so on, many of the current controversies, but by no means all, would evaporate. At least, we would know where we have real problems and which problems are those of communication failures.

We end by emphasizing one of the real advances spurred by the interest in metacognition, that is, the revived concern for mechanisms of change. This has always been the hidden agenda of developmental psychologists but, until recently, there have been surprisingly few attempts to study change directly. Many of the studies reviewed here depart from the typical cross-sectional age-comparison approach, and this is because many of the studies that have been inspired by the metacognitive boom have involved microgenetic analyses of children learning by doing on their own or learning to develop self-regulatory skills through the intervention of supportive others. We turn now to a more detailed consideration of training studies, another area that has been considerably influenced by the interest in metacognition.

INTERVENTION RESEARCH

In this section, we will concentrate on research that has involved some attempt to elevate the performance of groups of learners; the major issue concerns the ways in which cognitive developmental research and theory can inform these attempts. A more traditional title for this section might be educational implications. Although that title would not be inappropriate, we believe it suggests a unidirectional flow of information—"basic" research leads to advances in understanding, which, in turn, enables an increasingly sophisticated and powerful treatment of more "applied" problems. As we learn more about cognitive development, we are in a position to outline more effective instructional packages. This will, in fact, be the major emphasis here. However, we would argue strongly that the flow of information is bidirectional.

Intervention research itself represents one important way of attempting to build and evaluate cognitive theory. If we understand the cognitive processes and learning mechanism involved in some domain and something about developmental differences, we should be in a strong position to teach someone to perform more effectively. The outcome of such training attempts allows us to evaluate the quality of our underlying theories of the domain, learning, and individual differences. Further, consideration of the ways in which intervention fails and must be supplemented or modified to effect improvement in performance provides not only information about shortcomings in the original guiding theories but also positive suggestions about

the way in which those theories need to be altered. In this view, intervention research serves both as a way of providing converging evidence for a variety of theoretical formulations and as a tool for developing and refining those theories.

As we have described thus far, we have come quite a long way in our understanding of the factors and their interactions that comprise adequate performance in a variety of learning and comprehension situations. Compared with a decade or so ago, we have a better representation of expertise within a variety of domains, more detailed descriptions of the developmental path toward expertise, and a considerably more elaborated analysis of the ways in which the "typical" developmental trajectory can break down. Armed with this information, we are better able to specify some of the skills that need to be taught, as well as some of the ways in which they might be taught.

The majority of the studies we will describe fits into the broad category of intervention research. Within this category, it is possible to distinguish a number of different emphases, those aimed at changing the learner, those concerned with altering the learning materials, and those in which the essential approach is to modify the learning situation in general. As with many subdivisions, these approaches are not mutually exclusive; nonetheless, different studies and educational practices do rest primarily on one or other of these emphases. As a simple example of the difference, consider a group of students who are having difficulty in learning some material from a reading assignment. To circumvent the problem, we might attempt to teach them strategies for studying and comprehending texts (modify the learner). An alternative would be to design more readable, better formed narratives that would minimize the need for more powerful comprehension activities (modify the materials). Or the teacher might do both. An additional choice she has is to inform, or not to inform, the students of her purposes.

In our review, we will be concerned with three classes of questions: (1) *what* to teach, (2) *how* to teach it, and (3) how to adapt what and how to individual differences, that is, *who* is being taught. Note that (1) requires a theory of the components of academic performance, both within and across academic disciplines; that (2) requires a theory of learning; and that (3) requires theories of developmental and comparative differences: How do students of varying ages differ? Within age, how do good and poor performers differ? Although a complete theory does not as yet exist, we argue that the data available constrain those theories sufficiently so that it is possible to derive some important conclusions.

To begin with, we will center our discussion on the issue of *what* should be taught and return to the *how* and *who* later. One way of providing a context for this topic is to assume, as Rohwer did in the 1970 Handbook, that on the most general level, the aims of education are: (1) teaching the content knowledge, both declarative and procedural, sufficient for expertise within some academic domain and (2) teaching learning to learn, that is, enabling students to proceed more efficiently and independently.

Although these aims might be regarded as complementary, it may be more accurate to say that they are somewhat antagonistic in practice. Teachers frequently regard the amount of time they have to teach a particular course as insufficient for that purpose. If a large amount of time is devoted to teaching learning skills, that of necessity reduces the amount of time available for transmitting course content. And it is course content on which the students (and teachers) are generally evaluated.

A fairly clear example of the conflict can be seen in debates regarding various types of teaching formats. For example, the use of Socratic dialogue as a teaching approach embodies the modeling of many important learning activities, such as self-questioning, seeking relations, probing for further examples and counterexamples, and so on (Collins & Stevens, 1981). In this way, it would seem to represent a promising vehicle for teaching students how to learn. Its less than universal acceptance, however, can be attributed in part to the fact that the rate at which specific content is transmitted is relatively low (Collins & Stevens, 1981). Although students *may* be learning to learn, they are not necessarily learning much geography or history or math or. . . . This learning process-learning product tension has been expressed succinctly by one well-known educator in discussing the "revolution in mathematics teaching known as the 'new math'." He noted that the emphasis of the "new math" was on knowing and understanding what you were doing "rather than getting the right answer" (Lehrer, 1965).

From our perspective, the emphases of educational practice and cognitive developmental research have been somewhat different—and for good reasons. The main target of school programs has been the goal of teaching content knowledge; the preferred criterion measures have been performance on knowledge-based examinations. Students do well in school to the extent that they perform well on achievement tests in various subject areas.

Given this criterion measure, it should not be surprising that the main goal is to somehow instill a powerful, well-organized knowledge base. But achievement tests provide only indirect measures of learning ability. If students were tested for the efficiency of their learning, there would be a greater likelihood that learning processes would be a part of the school curriculum; that is, there is a tendency for teachers to teach to the test or, more positively stated, they take the criterion task into account in designing their instruction. If learning skills were to be evaluated, they would be more likely to be taught. We do not wish to leave the impression that it would be an easy task to evaluate learning skills. Those who would undertake the task of developing a theory-based assessment instrument of learning would have to confront most of the thorniest problems in cognitive development. A central subset of the issues would include: Do learning skills as such exist? If so, what are they? How might they be assessed in such a way as to minimize the influence of specific knowledge? These are in fact some of the questions that have recently been attracting the attention of investigators interested in instructional research (Chipman, Segal, & Glaser, in press).

In contrast to the knowledge emphasis in schools, the major target in the developmental research literature has been on procedures for learning or, more recently, on learning to learn. As an example of the difference between the two areas, we might say that a target of a geography curriculum would be to have the students know what the 50 states and their capitals are. More typical research questions would concern the specific strategies different children would use to set about the task of learning the information. There would also be concern with a specification of the factors underlying any developmental differences in the approaches adopted. More recently, the research on the role of specific strategies has been supplemented by a renewed interest in identifying more general content-free activities, such as the metacognitive skills just discussed.

This emphasis on learning activities in the research literature represents both a strength and a weakness. On the positive side, the work has documented the centrality of such activities to learning and has shown that their inclusion in training programs can have important consequences. One weakness of this emphasis on learning activities, both specific and general, is that we know less about the development of extensive knowledge bases and the overall effects of increases in domain-specific knowledge. This relative lack is also not surprising; the acquisition of a well-articulated knowledge base in a semantically rich domain takes a considerable amount of time (Simon, 1979). Ideally, what we would like to be able to do is to track the development of a knowledge base in some domain in a sample of students differing in age and ability. We would then be in a position to ask what the specific and general effects of incrementing knowledge are in students who differ in their experience with, and success in, school-learning tasks. This would involve extensive longitudinal analysis of relatively few subjects, that is, a case study methodology (Campione, Brown, & Ferrara, in press). As we argued earlier, the use of microgenetic investigation is already contributing substantially to our understanding of learning mechanisms.

We have characterized educational practice as emphasizing knowledge rather than learning factors. First, note that we believe the difference is one of emphasis. We do not wish to argue that educators are not concerned with teaching students to learn. Instead, our point is that general learning activities, or cognitive skills (cf. Chipman et al., in press), tend not to be taught directly. By directly, we mean an *explicit* attempt on the part of teachers to transmit the skills. This, in turn, could be because the lack of such instruction is defensible or appropriate; and this view does have its proponents. Reasons for not teaching general cognitive skills include: (1) they do not exist; (2) if they do, they are a consequence of a well-developed knowledge base; or (3) if they do exist, they are acquired incidentally as a result of the modeling that is an integral part of instruction and, hence, do not need to be taught explicitly.

The first point is straightforward. Schools may not teach general thinking skills because such skills do not exist. The second is also popular; all skills are heavily context dependent and, thus, are an inherent part of the knowledge base of any semantically rich domain. This specificity/generality issue is one of the oldest debates going and has been a central issue at a number of recent conferences on thinking and problem-solving skills (e.g., Chipman et al., in press; Reif & Tuma, 1979). For example, in his role as the concluding speaker at the Carnegie-Mellon Conference on Problem Solving and Education, Newell noted that "if there is one dichotomy that permeated this conference, it concerned the basic nature of problem solving. Specifically the poles are

> Domain-independence of
> Problem-Solving
> vs.
> Domain-specificity of
> Problem-Solving

The dichotomy is an old one" (Newell, 1979, p. 184).

Thus, one important set of research questions deals with the existence and identification of any general learning skills. For example, on the one hand, Goldstein (1979) asserts that "the fundamental problem of understanding intelligence is not the identification of a few powerful techniques, but rather the question of how to represent large amounts of knowledge in a fashion that permits their effective use" (p. 127). On the other hand, Simon (1979) argues that "bare facts, however they are stored in memory, do not solve problems" (p. 85). The weight of the current evidence is that some fairly general skills have been identified and that their acquisition is essential for efficient learning. For example, Simon argues that:

> The evidence from close examination of AI [artificial intelligence] programs that perform professional-level tasks, and the psychological evidence from human transfer experiments, indicate both that powerful general methods do exist and that they can be taught in such a way that they are relevant. (Simon, 1979, p. 86)

Similarly Brown, Collins, and Harris (1978) argue that:

> We have begun to see some surprising similarities in the kind of strategies and knowledge used in these different domains (story comprehension, solutions to mathematical problems and electronic circuits). This suggests that there may be general learning strategies that will enhance a student's comprehension over a wide range of content areas. Rigney (1976) has claimed that "The approach to teaching students cognitive strategies has been through content-based instruction and maybe this is wrong and should be reversed; that is content-independent instruction." (p. 108)

In summary, we have argued that schools have emphasized the acquisition of domain-specific knowledge bases, whereas cognitive developmental researchers have centered their more recent efforts on the development of learning skills, both "specific" (e.g., rehearsal strategies) and "general" (e.g., performance monitoring). This emphasis on knowledge development could be justified in several ways: (1) if there were no general learning skills or (2) if learning skills, general or specific, emerge without being explicitly taught. Relevant research questions, then, concern the existence of general skills, the extent to which they result automatically from a developing knowledge base, and the extent to which they are acquired incidentally through modeling in specific content areas. Although the evidence is far from overwhelming, we argue that there are general but weak (Newell, 1979) skills and that in many cases they do need to be taught explicitly. This view is coming to be adopted more frequently by educators (cf. Chipman et al., in press), particularly by, although by no means only by, those concerned with poorer learners.

Schools have emphasized the knowledge aspect of the tetrahedral model, researchers the activities component. Over the last decade, the two groups have come to the realization that both knowledge factors and learning activities along with their interaction need to be considered. In the following discussion, we will argue that developmental research has much to say about ways in which educational programs might be modified and that some of the implications we can draw are, in fact, being implemented.

Intervention Studies in Developmental Research: Early Trends

A notable feature of the last decade has been an increase in the number of studies aimed at the instruction of simple learning or remembering activities. An intervention methodology has become increasingly prominent, and investigators have asked a wide variety of questions about the ways in which performance in a number of domains can be improved. The vast majority of studies in the 1960s and 1970s were entirely theoretically motivated. In fact, the training study has historically been one of the favorite tools in the repertoire of the developmental psychologist because it lends itself well to the analysis of a number of central issues. It represents a vehicle for investigating key factors involved in learning and development. For example, one way of studying change is to attempt to engineer it (Brown, 1982a). Hence, interest in theories of change can lead fairly naturally to the use of intervention research.

Although the use of training studies is popular, their interpretation is not a simple matter. A great deal has been written about both the importance of training studies in comparative and developmental research and their underlying rationale. Although we will touch on some of those issues later, we do not have the space available to go into any detail. In-depth discussions of the various strengths and weaknesses of this approach to theory construction can be found in Belmont and Butterfield (1977), Brown and Campione (1978, 1981), Butterfield et al. (1980), and Campione et al. (in press).

Over the course of the decade, the type of instructional study has changed as researchers have begun to pay more attention to educational issues. These changes have stemmed from two, not independent, causes. One is that a number of psychologists have become more interested in questions of potential educational significance and have expended more of their efforts on understanding the components of performance in more typical academic pursuits, such as mathematics and reading. At the same time, this decade has seen a steady increase in our knowledge about cognitive development and individual differences. As the emergent data and theories provided more detailed insights into a number of pertinent issues, developmental psychologists were better able to address educational issues. We would argue that it was these advances in our understanding that encouraged many to undertake instructional research.

Here we will trace some of the changes that have occurred in the learning-strategies training literature (see Flavell, 1970b; see also Gelman & Baillargéon, this volume, for a review of the Piagetian training studies). Brown, Campione, and Day (1981) have classified training studies into three broad categories: blind, informed, and self-control. They differ in terms of when they were conducted historically, the nature of the interaction between the subject and the experimenter, the reasons for undertaking the research, and the criterion against which the outcomes were evaluated.

Blind Training Studies

Blind training studies are historically the first in the sequence we will describe. These studies are termed blind because they tended to leave the subjects in the dark about the importance of the activities they were being induced to use. The studies were by no means blind from the perspective of the experimenter. The choice of the activities to be trained was based on a well-articulated and insightful analysis of the demands of a number of memory or problem-solving situations, and the studies' main purpose was to evaluate hypotheses regarding both the processes involved in efficient performance on some tasks as well as the sources of developmental or comparative differences on those tasks. In this regard, they were extremely successful; one impressive feature of a number of these studies was the finding that large improvements in performance could be engineered. It was this fact that encouraged those interested in educational issues to expend more effort on instructional research aimed at improving subjects' use of learning activities. In summary, these studies were designed for theoretical reasons and were not addressed to educational issues, in contrast to some of the later studies we will describe. They were, however, directly responsible for the ensuing research.

A prototypical study might begin with the hypotheses that: (1) efficient performance requires the use of some task-appropriate strategy or learning activity, and (2) differences between individuals, or groups of individuals, reflect variations in the spontaneous use of such activities. If those hypotheses were correct, the question of why the less efficient were less likely to exploit such activities was addressed. Were the differences because of a failure to engage a usable activity, such as rehearsal (production deficiency), or an inability to profit from the activity (mediation deficiency)? To address these questions, a training study might be conducted to induce the younger subjects to rehearse. If performance improved significantly and approached the level of older subjects, support for three propositions would be inferred: (1) rehearsal is an important component of task performance, otherwise, training its use should not help; (2) developmental differences are in part due to differential rehearsal because inducing the younger children to use it did reduce the performance difference; and (3) the deficiency operating prior to training was one of production, not mediation. Very simple training studies provide data relevant to a number of important developmental issues, although their interpretation is not unequivocal (Campione, in press-a).

The typical procedure in blind training studies is that children are instructed or induced to perform particular processing routines but are not helped to understand the significance of such activities. They are told what to do or are led to do it, but they are not informed why they should act this way or that it helps performance or that it is an activity appropriate to a particular class of situations, materials, goals, and so on. Although, for some children, this is sufficient in that they can infer the significance of the activity for themselves, for many this is not so.

As one illustration, consider tasks involving free recall of categorizable materials. Children can be induced to categorize through the use of clever incidental orienting instructions (Murphy & Brown, 1975), the material can be blocked into categories (Gerjuoy & Spitz, 1966), or recall can be cued by category names (Green, 1974). None of these procedures guarantee that the child understands why, or even if, recall is improved. But, all these methods are extremely successful in improving children's performance on a particular set of materials.

Similarly, in the area of paired-associates learn-

ing, subjects can be instructed to generate either verbal or imaginal elaborations involving the to-be-associated items (e.g., Rohwer, 1973) or the experimenter can engage the subjects in an activity that results in such elaborations (e.g., Turnure, Buium, & Thurlow, 1976). Alternatively, the pairs of items can be introduced in an already elaborated form, either verbal or visual. They can be presented in a sentence frame or in a scene involving some interaction between them (e.g., Reese, 1977). Any of these methods can speed learning.

The sheer frequency and, on occasion, magnitude of intervention effects caught the attention of those interested in remediation. Although there are numerous examples, we will mention only two here. One involves elaboration and the other rehearsal. In an experiment by Turnure et al. (1976), educable retarded children (IQs around 70) and normal children matched for CA (about 7 years) were given a 21-item paired-associates list to learn. There was one study trial followed by a single test trial. In the labeling condition, subjects simply repeated the names of the items (e.g., soap/jacket) after the tester. In three other conditions, the subjects were required to answer what or why questions about the pair, for example, "What is the soap doing under the jacket?", "Why is the soap hiding in the jacket?". The aim of these procedures was to lead the subjects to think about the meaning of the individual items and to force them to generate elaborations involving possible relations between the members of each pair.

The differences among the conditions were dramatic. The children in the labeling condition averaged 2.0 items correct, whereas those in the what and why groups were correct on an average of 14.4 items, an increase in recall of over 600%. This finding was true of both the retarded and nonretarded children; normal children of this age have not yet begun to use these kinds of elaborative strategies spontaneously (see Reese, 1977; Rohwer, 1973); as a result, they performed poorly unless given the questioning procedures during study, in which case they also improved dramatically.

The rehearsal study we will describe represents a much more intensive attempt to improve the short-term memory performance of retarded children; the goal was to bring them to the level of untrained college students. It is an important study both for the magnitude of the effects it produced and because the study addressed a number of additional theoretical points. Butterfield et al. (1973) employed a standard probed short-term memory paradigm in which subjects were shown a series of six items and then asked to indicate the position in which a randomly selected one had appeared. They used a subject-paced procedure in which the participants pressed a button to view each successive item; thus, the subject was allowed to pause as long as she wished at any point in the series. College students deal with tasks of this type through the use of rehearsal strategies. A typical strategy (Belmont & Butterfield, 1971) would involve studying the first three items as a set (i.e., pausing for an extended period following exposure of the third item) and then inspecting the last three items quickly (a 3–3 active/passive strategy). Retarded adolescents, like normal children below 10 years of age, showed no evidence of the use of rehearsal strategies and performed poorly—they were correct on approximately 35% of the trials.

They were then programmed to use the 3–3 strategy adopted by adults. The subjects were told to view the first three items and then to pause and repeat them as a set a number of times. After this, they were to expose and view the last three items quickly. This strategy raised the level of performance for the first three letters in the sequence, but recall of the last items was surprisingly poor. Butterfield et al. (1973) hypothesized that although the subjects were using the *rehearsal* strategy, they were not using an appropriate *retrieval* strategy. The most effective retrieval strategy would have two parts. First, when the probe item was presented the last three items would be searched, taking advantage of the fact that these items would not yet have faded from memory. Second, if the letter were not among the last three, the rehearsed items would then be searched. An alternative approach, that of searching the initial rehearsed set first, would result in the subjects converting the task to one of serial recall, a task for which the 3–3 study strategy would be inappropriate. The fact that after initial training, retarded adolescents performed relatively well on the initial set of three items, together with some subsequent analyses of latency data, indicated that this conversion did take place, thus impairing performance. This result emphasizes the interactive nature of the various components of performance in a given task. The study strategy is effective only if coupled with a compatible retrieval plan. In this case, the instructional design problem was complicated by the fact that the students were setting themselves a criterion task that was different from the one assumed by the experimenter.

These considerations led to a revised training procedure aimed at both the acquisition and retrieval component. The subjects were initially taught the acquisition strategy. They were then informed about, and led through, the correct retrieval plan. Finally, they were given *explicit* instruction in the coordination of the two. In the most detailed condition, the subjects achieved an accuracy level of around 85%, some 140% above their initial level and comparable to that of nonretarded adolescents given some, but not so detailed, training. It is important to note that the provision of the components of the overall plan was not sufficient to result in their effective use. Butterfield et al. (1973) also had to include explicit instruction in their sequencing and coordination. This is one of the earliest training studies in which the importance of executive functioning was emphasized. Butterfield et al. (1973) conclude from the series of studies that:

> We can now elaborate two deficiencies in addition to the lack of rehearsal that hold retarded subjects so far below their capacity. They do not properly sequence rehearsal and non-rehearsal learning techniques, and they neither intercoordinate multiple retrieval strategies nor coordinate these retrieval strategies with strategies of acquisition. (p. 667)

and

> If this failure of executive control is transitutional, and we assume that it is, then the appropriate level of analysis for future research is the level of selecting, sequencing, and coordinating processes that are in the cognitive repertoire. Trying to train executive function instead of the particular skills for whose success it must ultimately be responsible may save much effort and yield more general theory in the bargain. (p. 668)

Inducing subjects to employ task-appropriate activities can result in dramatic improvements in their performance. This can be done by teaching them the routines necessary (Butterfield et al., 1973), augmenting the original learning situation (Turnure et al., 1976), or by modifying the learning materials (Reese, 1977; Spitz, 1966). (As we will see, the same findings obtain when the goals are comprehension of text.) Although direct comparisons are impossible, it also appears that altering the learning activities of the learner has a larger effect than restructuring the materials (Butterfield & Belmont, 1977). What particularly caught the attention of those interested in education was the impressive magnitude of the effects achievable through direct instruction of learning activities.

The implications of this work are clear. If the goal is to enhance the learning and retention of specific (although presumably limited) sets of information, there are ways of engineering that learning. We have come to know a great deal about some of the activities that result in rapid learning and durable memory, and intervention studies have shown that getting young or poor learners to carry out some of those activities does result in greatly enhanced performance. It does not matter much whether the learner knows why or even what is being done. This is not trivial, as in many cases the learning of specific packets of information is either a goal in itself or necessary for further learning.

There are, of course, also limitations to these conclusions. The first problem is that there are clear limits on the extent to which restructured learning environments can be expected to lead to positive effects. What can be learned depends on the initial knowledge or capabilities of the performer. The learner's entering knowledge can determine if a particular intervention will be successful. An extremely simple case of instruction is to provide for learners examples from which a rule can be inferred. An example of this approach and of a knowledge × instruction interaction can be found in a number of experiments involving the balance-beam problem reported by Siegler (1976, 1978). Subjects are shown a series of weight arrangements and asked to predict whether the beam will balance or whether one side or the other will fall if support is withdrawn. Siegler (1976) has analyzed the problem in terms of a number of increasingly complex rules that represent progressive changes toward a full understanding of the principles involved. Rule I in Siegler's taxonomy is based on a consideration of weight factors only. If the amount of weight on either side of the fulcrum is the same, the scale will balance, otherwise, the side with more weight will drop.

Siegler (1978) worked with groups of 3- and 4-year-olds who had not yet acquired this rule. Their predictions were essentially random. Interested in how his subjects might acquire Rule I, Siegler administered a series of feedback trials. The subjects would predict what would happen to the beam when supports holding it in place were removed, then the supports were withdrawn and the subjects were allowed to observe what actually happened. It could be said that the process of formulating hypotheses, obtaining data, and then reevaluating those hypotheses was being simulated. The main result was that the 4-year-olds tended to learn, or more specifically to acquire Rule I, whereas the 3-year-olds did not. Subsequent experiments showed that 4-year-olds, although random responders on prediction trials prior to any feedback, did encode or attend to (Zeaman & House, 1963) the relevant

weight dimension, whereas 3-year-olds did not. In some sense, the 4-year-olds may be said to know more about the balance problems (i.e., that weight is a relevant dimension) than the 3-year-olds and that this knowledge is necessary for the intervention to produce learning. In fact, 3-year-olds taught to encode weight and then given the feedback trial showed an increased tendency to acquire Rule I.

In this situation, we would like to emphasize the developmental pattern obtained. The performance of the 3- and 4-year-olds did not differ significantly prior to the presentation of the feedback series (they were both random). However, after the treatment, the groups did differ significantly. This divergent effect, in which intervention results in increasing the difference between younger and older children, is a far from uncommon finding; in fact, as we will emphasize later, it is quite typical in some classes of instructional studies. This effect stems from the fact that the instruction afforded requires some underlying competency for it to be effective. Older children tend to exploit that competency and profit from instruction, whereas younger children do not, thus, the instruction is less effective.

A second problem is that blind training techniques can, and often do, help people learn a *particular* set of materials, but existing data suggest that they do not necessarily help people change their general approach to the problem of learning new sets of materials. In short, these procedures fail to result in maintenance (durability) and generalization (transfer) of the learning strategies (Brown & Campione, 1978; Campione & Brown, 1977). Children neither perform these activities subsequently on their own volition nor transfer them to new but similar learning situations. Something other than blind training, therefore, seems to be necessary to help many children learn on their own.

In summary, blind training studies demonstrated powerful effects following training or the inducing of appropriate activities during the acquisition and retrieval of to-be-learned material. One immediate implication of these studies is that it is possible to design instructional interventions to facilitate the mastery of specific bits of information. These implications are limited by a number of other considerations. One is that simply simulating the desired activities does not result in facilitation for all learners in all situations (i.e., the activities × subject characteristics or activities × knowledge interactions inherent in the tetrahedral model). Another is that although such interventions may lead to mastery of specific materials, they may not lead to transfer (the activities × criterial-task interaction).

The transfer issue, or the learning versus learning-to-learn distinction, can be seen in many school situations. For example, consider the case of a teacher providing the acronym HOMES to students in an attempt to help them learn the names of the Great Lakes. This is a very reasonable thing to do, and it does work. If the goal is learning the lake names, nothing else is of much import. If, however, the teacher also wants the students to come to use this mnemonic/retrieval activity to help them learn other sets of arbitrary material, the problem would be an entirely different one, and the subjects' ability to generate those activities appropriately on new occasions would be the target of instruction.

This distinction maps nicely onto the state of affairs in the early 1970s. Brief instruction could result in impressive improvements in task-specific performance, but transfer following that intervention was exceedingly limited. The strongest statement that could be made was that extending the amount of training seemed sufficient to produce greater maintenance (e.g., Borkowski & Wanschura, 1974), but generalized effects of instruction were more difficult to bring about (Brown, 1974; Campione & Brown, 1977). But it was necessary to first identify appropriate learning activities and show that teaching them to young or poor learners would result in enhanced performance before it would make any sense to consider transfer issues. Transfer of nonhelpful activities would not be of much interest. It was the successes obtained in the early training studies that led to more intensive research on factors involved in transfer.

As investigators shifted their criterial task, seeking transfer rather than only task-specific improvement, they also searched for suggestions about how to go about modifying instruction. Providing the requisite learning activities to immature learners did not seem sufficient to lead to flexible access to those routines. To redesign instruction, it would be necessary to know what other skills or activities would have to be taught to improve access. It was around this time that some of Flavell's early work on metamemory began to appear (e.g., Flavell, 1971a; Flavell et al., 1970; Masur, McIntyre, & Flavell, 1973). In an insightful series of studies, Flavell and his colleagues demonstrated that younger children tended not to know as much about their memory system as older children and did not appear as capable as older children of regulating and monitoring that system. Similarly, mildly retarded children also appeared to demonstrate particular problems in areas (Brown, 1974, 1978). One global statement of the overall pattern of results is that young children and poor learners, those who were the targets of the blind training studies, did

not seem to know much about the memory system that the trainers were attempting to modify, nor were they particularly capable of overseeing the resources that instructors provided for them.

It is interesting to note that Flavell's early interest in metacognitive factors arose in the context of production deficiencies. Brief training was sufficient to induce the use of a number of memory-enhancing activities, and one question that was raised by this finding was why the subjects failed to employ those activities spontaneously. Even more provocative were those cases (e.g., Brown, Campione, & Barclay, 1979; Keeney et al., 1967) where subjects, for example, rehearsed when told to do so and performed significantly better; when prompting to rehearse was withdrawn, rehearsal was abandoned and performance returned to base-line levels. These data could be explained if the subjects did not know why rehearsal was helpful or even that it was helpful, that is, if the subjects did not understand the significance of the activities. And the metamemory data seemed to support these notions.

In this context, the failure to find transfer of instructed routines could be assumed to result from an incomplete treatment of the initial problems responsible for the strategy deficits. At this point, research aimed at assessing the effects of inducing metacognitive supplements to strategy training was undertaken. As a rough distinction, we can consider two types of experiments, those involving *informed* training and those involving *self-control* training (Brown et al., 1981). Generally subjects in informed training studies are given some additional information about the strategy they have been instructed to use; those in self-control studies are also given explicit instruction about overseeing, monitoring, or regulating the strategies (Campione, in press-a, in press-b).

Informed Training

Brown et al. (1981) refer to intermediate levels of instruction as informed training. Here, children are not only prompted to perform particular activities, but they are also provided with information about the significance of these activities. As one example, Kennedy and Miller (1976) were able to show that an instructed rehearsal strategy was more likely to be maintained in the absence of experimenter prompts if it had been made clear to the subject that the use of the strategy did result in improved recall. This effect can be obtained with a variety of strategies and subject populations. For example, a similar result with retarded children was obtained by Kendall et al. (1980) in work centering on the use of elaborative strategies to hasten paired-associates learning. Somewhat more elaborate instructional packages have been investigated by other authors, including Burger, Blackman, Holmes, and Zetlin (1978) with retarded children and Ringel and Springer (1980) with children in regular classes. The hallmark of these studies was the inclusion, during and following training, of much more detailed information about the need for, and effects of, the instructed routines. Again, the result of these extended instructions was to lead to enhanced transfer. For example, in the Burger et al. study, the subjects who were taught to use a categorization plan to facilitate free recall continued 3 weeks after training to show significant superiority over an untrained control group with regard to both clustering and amount recalled.

One can also inform subjects indirectly of some aspects of strategy use. To demonstrate the transitutional nature of a strategy, one can train the use of a particular routine in multiple contexts (Brown, 1978). For example, Belmont, Butterfield, and Borkowski (1978) compared groups of subjects who had received rehearsal training in one versus two contexts. The two contexts differed slightly in their response requirements, thereby demanding that the rehearsal strategy be varied accordingly to take this into account. The two-context group was more likely to show transfer to a third context. This is, of course, not a new finding; precedents can be found in the discrimination learning literature (e.g., Johnson & Zara, 1960; Sherman & Strunk, 1964). In that literature can also be found evidence that, on some occasions, multiple training is effective only if appropriate exemplars are found (e.g., Beaty & Weir, 1966).

Another relevant finding is that the tendency to maintain a strategy seems to be a function of the efficiency and precision with which the strategy was carried out during training (Borkowski, Cavanaugh, & Reichart, 1978; Butterfield & Belmont, 1977). Students who execute a strategy well at the time of training are more likely to maintain that strategy subsequently. For example, Paris, Newman, and McVey (in press) looked at the process of strategy acquisition in a study that included a number of the features of informed training. After 2 days of baseline performance on free recall of categorized lists, Paris et al. divided their 7- and 8-year-old subjects into two training groups. In one, the nonelaboration (blind in our terminology) group, the subjects were told how to carry out some mnemonic activities: grouping, labeling, cumulative rehearsal, and recalling by groups. The second, or elaboration (informed) group, was in addition given a brief rationale for each of the different be-

haviors; they were also provided feedback about their performance after recall. The elaboration group outperformed the nonelaboration group on both the training session and on subsequent maintenance probes. In this study, information was provided prior to training, and the effect was to augment the immediate effects of training. Furthermore, as in the other informed studies, there was a longer term effect, that is, increased maintenance.

Elaborated training resulted in better acquisition performance. Subjects so trained carried out the strategies more frequently and effectively and were also the ones who showed greater maintenance. We might generalize a bit and propose that any procedure that leads to efficient strategy execution during training will result in maintenance. One suggestion from these data is that to facilitate transfer, subjects need to be run to some criterion of mastery during acquisition.

Paris et al. (in press) prefer another explanation and offer some data in support. They argue that provision of information about the rationale underlying each component activity leads subjects to understand the significance of those activities, that is, they become aware of the strategies' benefits, and that this awareness is, in part, responsible for continued unprompted use. To evaluate this possibility, they obtained metacognitive judgments throughout the course of the experiment. In fact, the subjects in the elaborated training condition did show increased awareness of the role of sorting activities compared with those in the nonelaborated condition. Also, awareness scores were significantly correlated with both strategy use and recall performance.

We conclude this discussion with a general comment. Many of the studies included here could be said to be multiple-confounded, in the sense that the training packages include many components, for example, extended practice, information about significance, information about effectiveness, general praise and attention, and so on. As such, it is difficult, if not impossible, to ascribe benefits unambiguously to one factor or set of factors. Although this is, of course, a problem, it also represents one reasonable research strategy. Given that transfer is difficult to obtain, it makes sense to assemble a powerful package designed to elicit it. If the intervention is successful, follow-up studies can be designed to track down the more specific components responsible. Such tracking down is theoretically necessary. Regarding the implications for education, confounded treatments that work are extremely interesting in themselves. Clarification of the specific factors responsible for positive effects may allow refinements of the package (Campione & Armbruster, in press), but an intervention that works (for any of a number of reasons) is a desirable outcome in its own right.

Self-control Training Studies

The final category involves self-control studies, the main feature of which is the inclusion of explicit training of general executive skills, such as planning, checking, and monitoring. In the informed training approach, instruction of the target activities is supplemented with the provision of information about the activity and its effects. In self-control studies, the instructions include help with overseeing the activity.

Direct instruction of self-control skills should be particularly important in the context of transfer. For subjects participating in blind training, the experimenter does the executive work, telling the learner what to do and frequently for how long to do it (e.g., Belmont & Butterfield, 1971; Brown et al., 1973). Self-control training can be regarded as an attempt to emulate more closely the activity of the spontaneous producer—the trained subject is taught to produce *and regulate* the activity. Telling subjects to monitor and regulate their activities should produce the effects aimed at in informed training attempts, that is, if a subject does monitor her performance, she can see for herself that performance is improving and she provides her own information about strategy effectiveness. To the extent that this occurs, training self-regulation might be expected to lead to more widespread effects than would the provision of information about specific strategies because a consistent tendency to monitor performance would enable subjects to ascertain the effectiveness of a number of routines (see Campione, in press-b).

Although there are fewer self-control training studies available than those from other categories, the initial results are encouraging. For example, in a series of experiments with mildly retarded children, Brown and her colleagues (Brown & Barclay, 1976; Brown et al., 1979) adapted the recall readiness paradigm employed by Flavell et al. (1970). The subjects were required to study a supraspan set of items for as long as they wanted until they were sure they could recall all the items. Base-line performance was poor and instruction was undertaken. In one condition, subjects were taught a rehearsal strategy to learn the list; in another, they were asked to anticipate list items before exposing them. In both conditions, the subjects were also induced to engage in self-checking activities to see that

learning was occurring. The effects of this strategy plus regulation training for an older group of subjects (MA = 8 years)—but not for a younger group (MA = 6 years)—were (1) immediate beneficial effects of training, (2) maintenance of the strategy over a one-year period, and (3) evidence for generalization to a quite different task, that is, studying and recalling prose passages. The younger group showed only immediate effects of training; on maintenance probes, they reverted to base-line levels of performance, although mild prompts were sufficient to elicit the trained activities even one year later.

We would like to emphasize two points from this study. The first is that teaching-strategy use in a fashion that also instilled self-checking or monitoring activities did lead to more impressive transfer performance than previously had been the case. Inclusion of executive-control components in training is important. The second point is that these transfer effects were obtained only for the older group. To appreciate the developmental pattern a bit more, note that if we adjust performance for entering memory span differences, the older and younger groups did not differ prior to instruction. If we consider performance on unprompted maintenance tests later, there were large and significant differences between the groups. Thus, as in the Siegler (1976, 1978) experiments, the effect of providing training was to increase the difference between the older and younger subjects.

Summary

The series of blind, informed, and self-control studies leads to a number of conclusions. It is clear that the learning activities engaged in are an important determinant of performance and that we can specify in some detail a number of those activities. We also see that the evidence indicates the existence of both specific sets of activities, which are powerful but limited to a highly constrained set of circumstances, as well as more general ones, which are weaker but both broadly applicable and possibly necessary for the effective use of, or access to, the more specific routines. As we have begun to know more about essential processing components, we have become better able to program the student to execute them. Finally, for those effects to be obtained, it is not necessary that the learner be aware of what is being done to bring about learning.

That represents the good news, but there are also clear limitations. First, the beginning competence of the learner needs to be considered. Knowledge differences can limit the benefits that might result from inducing the subjects to carry out reasonable learning activities (e.g., Siegler, 1976, 1978). As Case (1978) has emphasized, it is also important to identify the particular strategies or approaches that students bring with them to the training situation. Examples of the importance of identification of entering states have been provided earlier (*A Tetrahedral Framework* . . .) in the context of composing (Bereiter & Scardamalia, in press; Scardamalia & Bereiter, in press), summarizing prose passages (Brown & Day, in press), and scientific reasoning (Kuhn & Phelps, in press). Differences in functional memory capacity can also result in training programs that are successful with some students, but less so for others (Case, 1978).

Even in the best cases, where the learner can be led to use the activities to speed learning, the impact is lessened by transfer limitations. In this arena, recent research has resulted in some worthwhile results. One is that it is not difficult to get learners to maintain activities on new occurrences of familiar problem types. Also, there appear to be considerable savings. Mild prompts to use a previously taught strategy can result in its effective use (e.g., Brown et al., 1979). Finally, as investigators have become more interested in programming transfer rather than simply expecting it (Stokes & Baer, 1977), the evidence for transfer has begun to increase. In these efforts, the major factor has been an increasing attempt to foster the understanding of the specific skills being taught, both by providing knowledge about those skills (informed training) or by explicitly including general self-regulatory, or executive, functions in the tutorial interaction (self-control training). How effective these training attempts to orchestrate transfer will be in the long run remains to be seen, but the early results are encouraging.

Intervention Research: More Recent Questions and Emphases

In classifying the studies contributing to our conclusions thus far, the reader will note that they have involved almost exclusively young or poor learners in situations requiring deliberate memorizing or problem solving. This feature of our review reflects the bias in the literature; the majority of the instructional work stimulated by cognitive developmental theory has featured this combination of learners and domains. Although we will speculate why this might be the case later, the obvious questions concern the extent to which the findings and conclusions can be generalized to situations involving older or more capable learners performing in other areas. We will deal first with the comparative/

developmental issue and then summarize some recent work on comprehension-fostering interventions. These discussions will be somewhat brief, in part a result of the relative paucity of data. We argue that the overall patterns do generalize quite broadly, and that the results obtained to date do indicate some areas where more work is needed.

A third issue is that of transfer, or more accurately, the difficulty of inducing learners to transfer the fruits of their learning experiences. In this context, we have discussed the role of more general learning skills in fostering learning to learn. We will return to a consideration of the general-specific tradeoff after discussing the developmental/comparative issues and work in the area of comprehension.

Developmental/Comparative Considerations

When young or poor learners are the targets of instructions to remember, it is clear that they need to be taught both specific powerful procedures and their overseeing and control. In the majority of training studies, only young or poor learners are involved. Although we cannot prove it, we believe this feature of the literature reflects the assumption that older or more capable learners already have or soon will have both the specific skills and the means for overseeing them. There are, of course, data consonant with this assumption. Although the memorization skills studied in the laboratory are not taught explicitly in schools, they are, in fact, acquired incidentally; one outcome of schooling does appear to be the emergence and use of such learning activities (Rogoff, 1981; Scribner & Cole, 1973). Given this view, it is not necessary to teach such skills to developmentally more capable students.

There is, however, another possibility. More advanced students may not be as capable as this view would have us believe, with the result that they would also profit from instruction. Even if they do show evidence of using memorization strategies, their use may be far short of optimal. That even highly selected learners are far from expert is clear if we contrast the performance of college students with that of expert mnemonists. More generally, there are increasing numbers of educators and educational researchers questioning the competence of college students' study skills (Chipman et al., in press). There is little doubt that there is still room for improvement.

Such speculation aside, the matter is an empirical one—the necessary experiment involves instructing groups of learners differing in level of cognitive maturity, young versus old or less successful versus more successful, that is, an instruction × levels factorial design. To illustrate the need for such designs and their potential complexity, consider the typical training study as it appears in the developmental literature. A young group of subjects, who initially perform less well than an older group, are given training on some process, the more effective use of which is presumed responsible for the developmental difference. Following such training, the performance of the young group improves, let us say to the level of the older group. One conclusion might be that the training was necessary for one group but not the other, the assumption is that training would have little or no effect on the efficient as they are already carrying out the trained process well. An excellent example of this approach is that of the study of Butterfield et al. (1973) in which training of cumulative rehearsal resulted in bringing the performance of retarded adolescents up to the level of untrained adults and to the level of less stringently trained nonretarded adolescents. Note that the best learners in this example were not trained; we simply assume their ceiling performance.

An evaluation of that assumption requires that the older or more capable groups be given the *same* instruction. There are, then, a number of possible outcomes to the hypothetical expanded experiment. These different outcomes are of both theoretical and educational significance because they indicate where remediation is or is not necessary and allow us to sharpen our account of developmental differences. We emphasize, again, that the interpretation of training studies, even the elaborated ones called for here, is not simple (Brown & Campione, 1978; Campione, in press-a). To illustrate the various outcomes and indicate the types of information they can provide, we will describe five different patterns. Three involve relative convergence, in which developmental differences are reduced after training. A fourth is parallel improvement. And the final outcome is divergence, where instruction results in an increase in the magnitude of developmental differences.

Consider first a pattern of results that would allow the strongest conclusion about developmental differences and the assumed competence of older learners. In our hypothetical factorial design, age and presence/absence of instruction interact in the following way: instruction improves the performance of the younger but not older students, and following instruction, there are no developmental differences. A clear example of such a pattern was

obtained by Brown in a judgment-of-relative-recency task (Brown, 1973; Brown, Campione, & Gilliard, 1974). There were no developmental differences between young and old on the task if there were no background cues to anchor the temporal series. If background cues were provided, however, the old capitalized on this information and outperformed the young. It seemed that the old, but not the young, exploited the background cues and that this alone was responsible for the difference. Instructing students how to use the background cues did not change the excellent (but not ceiling) performance of the old, but it did succeed in bringing the young up to their level. This outcome is the strongest possible evidence that differential use of the trained component was the major, if not sole, determinant of developmental differences and that training was, in fact, unnecessary for the older.

A number of other outcomes involving relative convergence after instruction would also be informative. For example, instruction might affect only the young subjects but their performance could still be poorer than the older students—the implication here might be that the old are proficient with regard to the trained process *and* that there are additional sources of developmental differences involved in task performance. Alternatively, both the young and old groups might improve, but the younger might improve more so. The simplest conclusions in this case would be that the older subjects were not completely proficient in the use of the target process (else training would not help), that differential use did contribute to the original developmental differences (equating use did reduce those differences), and that there remain further sources of performance variations.

It is also possible, however, that training would have the *same* effect on both ages, that is, in our age × instruction design, there would be two main effects but no interaction. Although there are a number of ways in which such interactions could arise, a simple interpretation would be that the process trained was important for performance on the target task but that it did not contribute to developmental differences. As one example, Huttenlocher and Burke (1976) set out to evaluate the hypothesis that developmental differences in digit span were due to the fact that older children grouped the input into richer chunks. In a standard condition, they found the usual developmental differences. In a grouped condition, in which the input string was grouped by the experimenter to simulate the chunking presumably done by older subjects, both the young and old subjects improved to about the same degree. Thus, the intervention that might have been expected to reduce the developmental difference by being more effective or necessary for the younger group was equally effective for all subjects. Similar effects have been obtained by Lyon (1977) using college students who differ in terms of memory span. Interventions designed to reduce individual differences by providing "expert help" to the lower scores improved everyone's performance and had no effect on the magnitude of individual differences.

A final possibility is that age (or ability) and instruction will interact, but that group differences will get larger rather than smaller. For example, young children may do more poorly than an older group before training, but after both groups have been trained, the difference may have increased. This divergent effect has already been noted in the Siegler (1978) and Brown et al. (1979) studies reviewed earlier and is a far from infrequent finding (Cronbach, 1967; Snow & Yalow, in press). In fact, when performance in some open-ended domain is being investigated, it may be the modal outcome. The implication of this pattern would be that the trained routine was not exploited efficiently (if at all) by the more advanced students prior to training and that its use requires some additional skills or knowledge before it can be utilized to maximal effect. More capable learners are better able to profit from incomplete instruction as they are more likely to possess those necessary resources.

Some examples of this divergence have already been noted in the discussion of the Siegler (1978) and Brown et al. (1979) studies reviewed earlier. It is also important to emphasize that the particular pattern obtained in any study—convergence, parallel improvement, or divergence—can depend upon the criterion against which the training is evaluated. To illustrate this point, consider the Brown et al. recall-readiness training study (Brown et al., 1979). Which of the three patterns best typifies the results? Remember that if we adjust for memory span differences, the MA 6 and MA 8 groups did not differ significantly prior to training. Immediately after training, the subjects were given a prompted posttest (on which they were told to continue executing the trained activity); both groups improved significantly, and there was still no reliable difference between them. Given these data, parallel improvement could be said to be the result. When unprompted tests were given a day later, however, the younger group abandoned the trained routines, and their performance reverted to baseline levels. The older subjects, in contrast, continued to perform well, and for the first time, there was a signifi-

cant difference between the groups. If degree of independent (unprompted) learning is the criterial task, a divergent pattern is obtained. If we add to that the fact that the older children demonstrated transfer to a recall task, the divergent pattern becomes even more pronounced. Thus, even studies that produce convergence when initial response to instruction is the metric might turn out to produce a divergent effect if maintenance and transfer probes are included (Campione & Brown, in press). To the extent that this is true, the frequency of these effects would be underestimated in the literature as the majority of studies have centered on the immediate effects of training.

As Snow and Yalow (in press) have suggested, a divergent effect is a frequent finding. Our interpretation is that it indicates that advanced students can profit from some of the same, or at least similar, programs administered to less capable students. The kinds of instructional variables and interventions investigated with young and poor learners, far from being unnecessary or inappropriate with average to above-average learners, may actually produce more pronounced benefits when applied to them. We will elaborate on this conclusion after considering some work in the area of comprehension.

Comprehension Research

Although there has been considerably less relevant instructional research in the area of comprehension, we would argue that the patterns that are beginning to emerge are very similar to those in the memory area. We might first note that there is a good reason why there has been a relative lack of intervention research in this area, that is, we do not understand understanding as well as we understand deliberate memorizing. Whereas we can specify in some detail the activities and variables that can be expected to lead to durable memory of some sets of information and can, thus, be quite explicit in terms of instruction, this is not true to the same extent for comprehension. Although it may be true that a *learner* need not be aware of a set of processes being employed in the service of memory or comprehension for those processes to produce the desired effect, it is much more difficult to see how a teacher could transmit such skills explicitly if *she* is not aware of them. As more empirical and theoretical attention has been expended on comprehension processes (Spiro, Bruce, & Brewer, 1980), we have become better able to devise methods of improving students' ability to comprehend texts—and the number of instructional studies is increasing rapidly.

Before addressing the instructional research, we can note some high-level similarities between the comprehension and memory areas. The tetrahedral model offered by Jenkins (1979) as a way of organizing the memory literature works equally well and with only minor modifications when applied to comprehension (Brown et al., 1981). To illustrate some parallels, comprehension and recall of texts are influenced by the reader's activities, the reader's schematic and specific knowledge, and the interactions among these variables.

In this sphere of activities, Brown and Smiley (1978) reported that over a wide age range, subjects' ability to profit from a study period depended upon the study behaviors they displayed. Subjects, regardless of age, who demonstrated some appropriate study activity, either underlining or notetaking, recalled more on their second attempt; again age independent, those who did not show evidence of such activities failed to improve from their first to second recall.

Regarding schematic knowledge, research inspired by the story-grammar approach (e.g., Mandler & Johnson, 1977; Rumelhart, 1975; Stein & Glenn, 1979; Stein & Trabasso, in press) has succeeded in formalizing some of the structural properties of well-formed stories, properties that are appreciated by even quite young children. Texts that correspond closely to this structure tend to be more readily comprehended and recalled (Baker & Stein, 1981; Mandler, 1979; see also *Mandler, vol. III, chap. 7*). Furthermore, as pointed out earlier, the availability of specific background knowledge influences both the form and amount of what is comprehended and recalled from a narrative, be the learner a college student (e.g., Sulin & Dooling, 1974) or a child (Brown, Smiley, Day, Townsend, & Lawton, 1977).

An example of a learning activities × knowledge interaction can also be found in the Brown and Smiley (1978) series of experiments. The ability of their subjects to profit from reasonable learning activities depended upon those subjects' ability to make use of specific knowledge about the domain being studied. Subjects who underlined or took notes during study did not benefit from those activities unless they were able to identify the main points of the story. That is, subjects at any of the different ages studied could profit from an additional study period only if they knew what the main points of the narrative were *and* engaged in an appropriate learning activity.

We can now turn to some of the parallels in the intervention research. Again, there are two major avenues open to those who would try to enhance

performance—modify the materials or modify the learner. Regarding materials, the data generated by the story-grammar approach represent one relevant example. Stories written to conform to a canonical form are better understood than those that are not.

A second example of the modify-materials approach, and an extremely popular one among researchers, is to provide adjunct questions to go along with the text (see Anderson & Biddle, 1975, for a review of much of this work). These questions can be inserted in various portions of the text, for example, before or after students read a particular text segment. We can also distinguish different functions those questions might play. They might be expected to have either attention-directing or comprehension-inducing properties. Attention-directing questions would be aimed at specific points students are to master; they could, for example, be expected to help the students identify main points. Comprehension-inducing questions, in contrast, would represent attempts to increase overall comprehension scores, for example, by leading the students to engage in some "deeper processing" of the material being read. An attention-getting (adjunct) question would be successful if students were more likely to answer a subsequent (test) question on specific material than if it had not been highlighted during reading. A successful comprehension-inducing question would result in an increase in test accuracy on both items that had and had not been specifically questioned. As Anderson and Biddle (1975) report, the specific effects are much more impressive than the general ones.

One implication of these results is that such adjunct aids can be used to increase the likelihood that students know what the main points of the lesson are, an accomplishment that is far from trivial. The immediate benefit is that students are more likely to learn the important points given a single reading of the text than might otherwise be the case. An additional, and more subtle, outcome is that students should be in a better position to benefit from additional study than they would be without the questions. Recall that in the Brown and Smiley (1978) experiments, only students who were able to demonstrate that they could identify the main points of a passage demonstrated further gains in recall as a result of extra study time; simply rereading the passages produced no improvement. In these ways, attention-directing questions can be extremely helpful.

Note that the interventions aimed at the materials follow the general format of blind training studies. Stories are restructured or additional questioning is provided, but the students are not taught to facilitate their own learning in situations where the narrative is not well formed or where helpful questions are not provided. In our view, these studies are aimed at facilitating learning of a particular text, but not learning to learn from texts in general (Bransford et al., 1981; Brown, 1982b).

There are also a number of studies in which the main aim has been to modify the activities of the learners by teaching them some comprehension-related skills. One prerequisite of training studies of this type is the specification of the critical skills or activities in sufficient detail to enable an instructor to outline them to the student. As an example, we will use training basic rules of summarization. Brown and Day (in press) described in detail the developmental progression associated with the use of five rules that were (in order of difficulty): (1) deletion of trivia, (2) deletion of redundancy, (3) superordination of exemplars of a concept, (4) selection of topic sentences, and (5) invention of topic sentences (see *A Tetrahedral Framework* . . . for a discussion). Day (1980) taught these rules to junior college students. The students differed in ability and in the type of instruction afforded them. The "control" treatment was similar to traditional summary-writing instructions; the students were told to be economical with words, include all the main ideas, and so on, but no further details were provided to help students follow these instructions. Another condition involved a listing and demonstration of the set of rules developed in the prior research (similar to informed training); and yet another included both the rules and explicit instructions regarding the management and overseeing of those rules (self-control training).

Consider first only the highest ability group, students with no diagnosed reading or writing problems. Prior to training, their summaries were generally poor; they used the simplest deletion rules quite well but showed little evidence of use of the more complex rules. They did, however, respond to training and began to produce better summaries. Also of significance, the students continued to manifest this improvement in class assignments administered several weeks later by their teachers.

As with less mature learners in the earlier memory studies, it appears that these older students have not acquired some specific skills that are needed to facilitate performance in summarization tasks. Instruction based on an in-depth analysis of the underlying cognitive processes (Brown & Day, in press) does lead to substantial improvement. Consider also a comparison of the informed and self-control treatments. Differences as a function of instructional conditions were found but only in the case of the most complex rule taught. For simple and intermediate-difficulty rules (deletion, superordination, and selection), informed training was sufficient to lead to maximal performance levels; however, for the most difficult rule, invention, use was better in the self-control than in the informed condition. When complex (for the particular learner) routines are being taught, inclusion of a self-control component appears necessary for optimal use of those routines.

Day (1980) also worked with students varying in ability. She included groups of junior college students who were average (in regular classes) or poor (in remedial classes) writers. For the simplest rules, nothing dramatic occurred; all students used those rules well prior to and following training. We will consider here only the more difficult rules—superordination, selection, and invention. The ability groups did not differ significantly in their use of any of these rules prior to training. For the superordination rule, both groups improved to approximately the same extent; a pattern of parallel improvement was obtained. With the most difficult rules, a divergent ability × instruction interaction was found; although both groups improved significantly following training, average writers improved significantly more than poor writers. Thus, within this experiment, the form of the ability × instruction interaction varied as a function of rule difficulty. The more difficult the rule being taught, the greater the tendency toward a divergent effect. Day (1980) also included a group of students who were taking both remedial reading and writing courses. These more severely learning-impaired students did not differ from the other groups prior to training, but the divergent effect was even more pronounced on, for example, the selection rule when their data were included. With the most difficult invention rule, these students with severe reading and writing problems did not improve at all, even after the most explicit (self-control) instruction. Overall, the tendency toward divergence increased as rule difficulty increased, and the magnitude of that divergence increased as the ability difference increased.

In summary, if we consider a number of instructional experiments that have included groups of students differing in age or ability and that have involved manipulations of the complexity of the skills being taught, a general pattern begins to emerge. The most basic point is that poor performance often results from a failure of the learner to bring to bear specific routines or skills important for optimal performance. In this case, she needs to be taught explicitly what those rules are. This, in turn, requires a detailed theoretical analysis of the domain in question; otherwise, we cannot specify the skills in sufficient detail to enable instruction. A second recurrent theme is that this requirement is more pronounced the poorer the learner because the need for complete instruction increases with the severity of the learning problem.

Given that specific skills need to be taught, is it necessary for their teaching to be supplemented by the inclusion of more general self-control routines? One generalization that emerges is that the answer to this question depends upon the complexity of the routines being taught. We emphasize, however, that complexity is determined not only by the specific skills to be trained but also by learner characteristics, such as prior knowledge, interest, overall ability, and so on. Complexity does not reside solely in the skills but is an interactive function of the factors involved in the tetrahedral model. More mature learners already have some practice with executive/regulatory skills in other domains and, hence, are better able to supplement blind training regimes for themselves; but even in their case, as complexity increases, metacognitive supplements to instruction may be needed before optimal effects of instruction can be found.

General and/or Specific Skills?

Throughout the discussion of training studies, we have made reference to specific and general skills, although we appreciate that the terms are problematic. Nonetheless, there are a number of important questions that arise in this context concerning the kinds of activities we should target for instruction. Should we teach specific skills or general skills, or both? To reduce the ambiguity, we can refer to a helpful discussion of the general-specific issue provided by Newell (1979). He made use of an inverted cone metaphor, the base of which contains many (hundreds?) of specific routines; these specific routines are also powerful ones. They are specific in that they are serviceable in only a highly limited number of cases; they are powerful in that once they are accessed, problem solution should follow (assuming only that they are executed properly). An example would be a task-specific rehearsal strategy. It is important to note that as we move up the cone, there is a tradeoff between generality and power. At the tip of the cone, there are a few highly general but weak routines—general in that they are applicable to almost any problem-solving situation, but weak in that they alone will not lead to problem solution. Examples here include exhortations to stay on task or to monitor progress. These are weak in that, for example, merely noticing that progress is not being made or that learning is not occurring cannot rectify the situation unless the student brings to bear more powerful routines that can result in better learning.

In this view, one answer to the question of teaching general or specific skills is clear. Both types are necessary. If there are students who do possess most of the specific procedures needed for mastery within some domain, instruction aimed primarily at general self-regulatory skills would be indicated. It is in situations of this type that Meichenbaum has produced very impressive results (Meichenbaum, 1977; Meichenbaum & Asarnow, 1978). In contrast, there may be students who have internalized many of the self-regulatory routines and are highly likely to employ them whenever learning. What they may lack in a new problem are the powerful and specific procedures unique to that domain. As we have already discussed, the relative emphasis on general and specific skills in a particular case will vary as a function of both the ability of the learner and the complexity of the procedures being taught.

Within this view, we can characterize the research we have described thus far as involving very specific and very general skills. This general-specific dimension is also related to ease of transfer. Specific skills are powerful enough to enable problem solution *if* they are accessed; but the problem of access or transfer remains a major one. The executive, self-regulatory skills that are weak evade the transfer problem as they are appropriate in almost any situation; no subtle evaluation of task demands is necessary. The result of including both types of skills in training programs is clear; use of the instructed activity is more effective on the original training task (Paris et al., in press), and there is evidence for increased transfer (Brown et al., 1979). Note, however, that the experimental work has involved single strategies and their use, not larger sets of specific skills, and it is the latter case that is more typical of educational settings. For example, some reading programs involve upwards of 200 separate skills (Campione & Armbruster, in press). Even presuming that the list could be dramatically reduced, the task of accessing, coordinating, and sequencing those skills remains a formidable one.

Rather than teaching a large number of specific routines and some extremely general supervisory ones, an alternative approach would be to identify and teach intermediate-level skills or packages of skills. These would be more general than the extremely specific routines investigated in much of the literature and taught in many school settings, but, at the same time, more powerful than the self-regulatory skills that have attracted so much recent interest. We will describe one example of a successful attempt of this type and, at the same time, indicate some of the interplay between theory development and instructional research.

The experiment we will use, reported by Palincsar and Brown (1981; see also *Metacognition, Executive Control . . .*), can be related to the adjunct-question literature. One major difference is that whereas in prior research, the questions were provided for the student in an attempt to facilitate learning, Palincsar and Brown attempted to teach students to provide their own questions. In this way, they hoped to foster both learning and learning to learn. A second major difference is in the nature of the questions involved. In the adjunct-question literature, the effects were extremely limited; students' learning of specifically questioned items improved, but the more general comprehension-inducing consequences were limited at best. This is not surprising in retrospect as there was no compelling theoretical rationale underlying the construction and choice of questions. In fact, many investigators did not even believe it necessary to provide examples (Anderson & Biddle, 1975).

It is in the context of question generation that recent theoretical ideas become important. The notion that readers should engage in periodic self-interrogation while reading is not new, although it has become an even more common suggestion of late (Baker & Brown, in press-a; Brown, 1980; Collins & Smith, 1981; Flavell, 1981; Markman, 1981). Of more direct interest are specific suggestions about the kinds of questions students should be taught to ask. Although the list is a long one, there is considerable agreement that the questions should both allow comprehension monitoring and facilitate comprehension.

To cite a few examples, Collins and Smith (1981) emphasize the continuous process of hypothesis generation, evaluation, and revision while reading. They distinguish between two main types—interpretations and predictions. Interpretations are hypotheses about what is happening now; predictions are hypotheses about what will happen next. It is clear that good readers engage in these activities while reading, just as they make and test inferences of many kinds (Trabasso, Stein, & Johnson, in press). They also engage in critical evaluation of ambiguous and contradictory segments of texts (Markman, 1981; Stein & Trabasso, in press). Poor readers are much less likely to generate these activities. Novice readers also experience difficulties with lower level functions, such as checking that they remain on task (Bommarito and Meichenbaum cited in Meichenbaum & Asarnow, 1978) and simply paraphrasing sections to see if they understand and remember the gist of sections they have read (Brown & Day, in press).

As described earlier (*Metacognition, Executive Control . . .*), the training program devised by Palincsar and Brown (1981) was based on these analyses; they set out to teach students to paraphrase and summarize sections of the texts they were reading, anticipate questions that might be asked, and predict what the author might go on to say next. As the results have already been described, we will simply mention that large improvements in comprehension and recall (500% to 600% increases on laboratory measures) were obtained and that those improvements were found on passages that the students read *independently*, in both laboratory and classroom settings. Compared with the skills typically investigated in instructional research, teaching this routine was not easy. The instructor worked individually with students for many sessions, modeling the kinds of questions she wished students to produce and initially helping them formulate some of their attempts. Students were continually reminded of why these activities were useful, given feedback concerning their effectiveness, and told that they should engage in such self-questioning any time they studied. Improvement took time, but eventually the students were able to generate appropriate questions without help. The return on the investment appears well worth the extra time and effort. The self-questioning approach is quite general, being applicable to a wide variety of texts. In this way, the transfer problem is in some sense finessed, as the occasions for use of the instructed activities are quite clear.

The Problem of Transfer

We have spent considerable time talking about transfer and its importance to both developmental theory and educational practice. Throughout, we argued that major differences between young and old learners reside in their ability to access and flexibly use competencies they are known to possess (see also Brown, 1982a; Brown & Campione, 1981; Flavell, 1982). Development consists in part of going from the context-dependent state where resources are welded to the original learning situation to a *relatively* context-independent state where the learner extends the ways in which initially highly constrained knowledge and procedures are used.

Transfer tests also play a central role in the evaluation of educational programs. For example, we are reluctant to say that someone has learned elementary physics or mathematics if they can solve only the problems they have practiced in class. Similarly, the ability to read one and only one text is not viewed as evidence of reading (except perhaps by some proponents of machine intelligence).

No one would want to claim that a student had learned how to remember if the only data involved the student's ability to recite one set of materials that had been practiced frequently. Thus, the entire discussion of learning to learn is really a discussion of the importance of transfer. In this section, we would like to elaborate upon our earlier discussions and deal with the transfer issue in more depth.

Relationships Between Learning and Transfer

Our first point concerns the interdependence of learning and transfer. Consider some prototypical situations where transfer tasks are used for purposes of assessment. When evaluating training studies or school curricula, we frequently say that one method produced greater transfer than the other; similarly, we sometimes speak of individuals who "learned the training materials but failed to transfer." Such statements as these can often be misinterpreted in that transfer is seen as some process that occurs after learning has taken place.

Imagine a situation where students practice until they are able to solve all the problems in a text (a statistics text for example) and then receive new, but similar, problems on an examination. If they fail the examination, does it make sense to say that they learned but failed to transfer? It seems equally if not more appropriate to say that, in a very important sense, they failed to learn. Similarly, imagine that groups of children receive instruction on calculating the area of squares and triangles; some learn by memorizing formulas and others learn by "insight" (Resnick & Glaser, 1976). Imagine that the two groups now receive a new problem that requires them to calculate the area of a parallelogram and that the insight group does better. Has this second group transferred farther or has it learned different things?

It seems clear that the concepts of learning and transfer are closely interrelated (Brown, 1982a; Brown & Campione, 1981; Campione et al., in press; Ferguson, 1954; Hebb, 1949). Furthermore, it could be misleading to assume that transfer is solely due to some process that happens *after* learning occurs. A major problem with the latter assumption is that it presupposes a unitary and clear-cut definition of learning, yet there are many ways to define learning. For example, Bransford (1979) describes the study activities of a student preparing for an examination in statistics. The student could solve all the problems on the study sheets and, hence, felt prepared for the examination. A friend cut out the problems from each sheet, shuffled them, and asked the student to try again. This time

the student failed miserably; he thought he had learned to solve the problems, but he was inadvertently relying on chapter cues to choose the formulas and principles that were applicable to each problem. The student had learned something, of course, but he had not learned in a way that would allow him to function without the explicit use of chapter cues. (Note that the experiment conducted by the friend could have been done by the student himself. We will argue that such self-testing is the kind of activity that characterizes successful academic performers.)

It may be possible operationally to specify an acquisition point (where some skill or bit of knowledge is originally acquired) and a later transfer or retrieval point (where that information is to be used) nonetheless, it is a mistake to think of the processes involved as unrelated. What is learned and the related issue of how it is learned influence subsequent use. Indeed, one traditional use of transfer tests is to assess what it is that people have learned. And the act of learning something new is itself a type of transfer task; people must activate potential skills and knowledge to understand and master new content and principles. But this is not to say that learning automatically leads to transfer. When the new learning situation is introduced, it is frequently necessary for the student to search actively for the resources she has which are relevant to the solution of that problem (see *Dynamic Versus Static Conceptions of Knowledge* in our discussion on *Characteristics of the Learner*); both the tendency to search for, and the ability to find, appropriate resources are intimately involved in successful performance. To advance our theories of development and refine our educational programs, we need to identify the kinds of search and problem-solving strategies, both strong and weak, used by successful learners.

The Recognition of Problem Isomorphs

Many of the difficulties of transfer seem to involve the process of recognizing problem isomorphs (Brown, 1982a; Brown & Campione, 1981; Gick & Holyoak, 1980; Newell, 1979; Rumelhart & Norman, 1981; Simon, 1979), that is, recognizing that the new situation is similar to one encountered previously. For example, Gick and Holyoak (1980) presented college students with a task such as Duncker's (1945) radiation story. The problem is that a certain ray can destroy a malignant tumor. If the rays reach the tumor with sufficient intensity, the tumor will be destroyed. Unfortunately, at this intensity, healthy tissue will also be destroyed. The solution is to send the rays from different angles so that they meet simultaneously at the point of the tumor and hence summate to produce the required intensity. Healthy tissue is not destroyed because the single rays are not strong enough to do damage.

Students who had successfully solved this problem were given the structurally isomorphic problem of the attack-dispersion scenario. A fortress is located in the center of a country. Many roads radiate from the fortress, but they are guarded so that any large body of men attempting to infiltrate the fortress would be apprehended. A general who wishes to attack the fortress must adopt the solution of dispersing his troops and sending them in small groups to meet at the attack point, the fortress. The dispersion and summate rule is nearly identical to the rule required for the radiation/tumor problem.

In the absence of hints to use the preceding story to help them solve the new problem, students' transfer was less than impressive. Similar studies examining transfer between homomorphic or isomorphic versions of well-defined laboratory puzzle problems, such as missionaries and cannibals (Reed, Ernst, & Banerji, 1974) and Towers of Hanoi (Hayes & Simon, 1977), have also failed to find a great deal of spontaneous transfer. It should not be surprising, therefore, that young children also need hints that formally identical problems with different surface structures are indeed occasions for transfer (Crisafi & Brown, in preparation).

What is at issue in the recent research on problem isomorphs is a revival of the traditional Thorndike and Woodworth (1901) transfer theory of identical elements; they argued that transfer will occur across tasks only to the extent that the tasks share identical elements. Some version of identical-elements theories has persisted (Ellis, 1965; Gagné, 1967; Osgood, 1949). Thorndike and Woodworth (1901) defined identical elements primarily in terms of physical features of the tasks. But as an earlier identical-elements theorist (Höffding, 1892) pointed out, the real problem with transfer lies not in the physical dimensions of the task environment but in the perceived similarity of task domains as constructed by the learner. Höffding's position is very similar to contemporary theories of transfer of training. In addition to noting that degree of physical similarities among task contexts can determine transfer, Höffding was concerned with perceived similarity between situations—how new situations elicit old responses and how a new situation comes to be connected with the stored trace of previous learning, that is, the famous Höffding-step (1892) that is still in its many guises a central problem for psychology.

Common elements may be the key to transfer, but they are difficult to define. If people use the wrong elements for classifying the current situation, one would expect many errors. Studies of expert versus novice problem solvers suggest that the elements used to recognize problem types can have important effects on performance. For example, novices tend to use key words in the problem format when they are asked to sort problems into types; in contrast, experts generally sort on the basis of underlying conceptual identities (Chi, Feltovich, & Glaser, 1981; Larkin et al., 1980; Simon, 1979). An important outcome of increasing expertise within a domain and an important determinant of transfer may, therefore, involve the ability to recognize the appropriate types of commonalities; otherwise, a problem may be misclassified and, hence, approached in an inappropriate way.

Assumptions about the importance of recognizing that a new situation is similar to old ones seem to underlie many methods of training. When we explicitly train for transfer, we often try to help people learn to identify appropriate elements. For example, training in multiple contexts is a principle that is endorsed by many theorists because it decreases the likelihood that a particular piece of information will be welded to a particular context, and, hence, it increases the probability of performing well on transfer tasks (Belmont et al., 1979; Brown, 1974, 1978; Brown et al., 1981). Similarly, the practice of encouraging learners to state a general rule is effective in inducing transfer because it highlights that general rule and makes it explicit (Gagné & Smith, 1962; Thorndike & Stasz, 1980). Training in multiple contexts with explicit statements made concerning the general rule increases the probability of effective transfer.

Related examples of training for transfer involve what Feuerstein and colleagues (1980) call bridging. Students may learn a general principle and then be helped to see how it applies to particular situations, such as social-problem solving, learning mathematics, and so forth. That is, explicit instruction is given in the range of applicability of the concept (Brown, 1978; Brown & Campione, 1981). The assumption underlying bridging is that the children need to see how particular principles apply to new situations, otherwise, they may fail to utilize the principles in these situations.

To summarize, the preceding examples suggest that problem recognition plays an important role in transfer. If people are unable to see how a new situation is related to ones previously encountered, it is difficult to imagine how transfer could occur. When we train for transfer, we are implicitly acknowledging the importance of problem recognition; people who are simply asked to memorize principles, formulas, or concept definitions or who learn a strategy only in one context may not recognize that these are applicable in other situations. By illustrating a variety of situations or contexts in which learners may profitably use their knowledge and strategies, we are increasing the probability that transfer will occur.

Static Versus Dynamic Approaches to Transfer

In many of the examples we have discussed, the aim is to modify instruction to lead to transferable learning products. Training in multiple contexts, for example, is designed to teach not only a rule (strategy, bit of knowledge, etc.) but also to provide information that the rule is of somewhat general use. Further, an attempt is made to illustrate something about the range of applicability of the rule in question. Seeing the rule applied in several contexts allows the learner to understand its significance and to infer some of the properties of situations in which it is applicable. The rule thus learned has become in some sense a transferable item in the learner's knowledge base. We see this as a static aspect of transfer. The learner has acquired a resource that can be brought to bear in a number of situations; when those situations appear, she is likely to access the specific rule and, thus, perform well.

There is, however, another aspect of transfer we would like to emphasize. We can consider situations in which specific resources necessary for problem solution are not in the learner's repertoire and ask what, if any, transfer might be expected in that case. To be more concrete, the present authors would be unable to solve numerous physics problems because we lack the content knowledge necessary to do so; in this situation, whatever general skills and strategies we possess would do us little good. Should one, therefore, conclude that there is no transfer from the present author's area of psychology to many areas of physics? Our answer is that it depends upon the approach to transfer that one takes.

The transfer task just described (asking psychologists to solve physics problems) represents a static approach to transfer; the basic question being addressed is, What do these psychologists know at this particular point in time? This is very different from the question, Can these psychologists *learn* to solve physics problems? From the perspective of this dynamic approach, there *can* be transfer from psychology to the physics domain.

Recently, one of the present authors (Bransford) decided to learn about a new area of physics and to keep a log of the experience. A physicist picked a particular topic and supplied relevant material to be read. The psychologist found the task difficult but it seemed clear that there were many general skills and strategies that facilitated learning. These included:

1. A general sense of what it meant to understand something rather than merely memorize it.
2. The ability to recognize that some texts were more advanced than others and that the advanced texts were not the place to begin.
3. The ability to recognize when certain technical terms were crucial and needed to be understood more adequately.
4. Knowledge of the need to search for relevant examples of certain concepts and principles that were defined abstractly in a particular passage.
5. Knowledge of the importance of removing examples and example problems from the text context, randomizing them, and seeing if one really understood them.
6. The ability and willingness to formulate questions to ask a physicist when the texts would not suffice.
7. The ability to determine whether the physicist's answers to those questions made sense (to the learner, that is).

Perhaps the most important information available to the experienced learner was that the texts were objectively difficult; fault did not rest with his learning potential but with inadequacies in his background knowledge. The learner was, therefore, willing to ask questions of the expert rather than give up the endeavor for fear of seeming stupid. In general, the learner knew something about how to learn and, hence, was aware of the difficulties to be expected as well as some of the mistakes to avoid (merely memorizing rather than trying to understand, looking up each and every unknown word, placing equal weight on all concepts for example).

Note that the psychologist's knowledge of how to approach the problem of learning new information could not be tapped by a static measure that simply assessed the ability to solve physics problems. The psychologist lacked information necessary to solve these problems; if this information is not available in the testing environment, it is impossible to assess the degree to which someone is able to use it to learn. Questions about learning and transfer require a dynamic approach (Brown & Ferrara, in press).

Both the static and dynamic approaches to transfer are important and valid; we sometimes want to assess what someone knows (static approach) and at other times to assess what they can learn (the dynamic approach). For example, most current measures of achievement are static measures that assess the current state of people's knowledge and skills. This information can be important and useful; we often need to know whether a learner has the necessary skills and knowledge for handling a particular course or job. It would be unwise for a physics department who needed an expert in astrophysics to hire our psychologist who knows no physics because the psychologist knows how to learn. Even efficient learners would require too much time to develop the necessary expertise; expertise takes time to acquire (Simon, 1979).

There are other situations where the static approach becomes much more questionable, where we use static measures to make claims that actually require the dynamic approach. Measures of intelligence are a prime case in point. Like achievement tests, most intelligence tests are also static measures of an individual's current level of skills and knowledge. However, when interpreting intelligence tests we tend to translate a static score into a ranking number (e.g., IQ = 92) that is assumed to hold for all time.

We argued earlier that a static test makes it difficult for us to measure people's abilities to learn to perform more adequately. Imagine that we give a physics test to our psychologist who knows no physics (but knows how to learn) and compare his performance with a student who has muddled through one course in physics but does not know how to learn efficiently. The physics test may reveal that student X is much "better" than the psychologist, but this tells us nothing about the latter's abilities to *learn* physics; indeed, the learning skills of our hypothetical psychologist may be far superior to student X. If we used the initial test to measure the intelligence of the two individuals, we would be using a static test to make a claim that actually requires a dynamic test.

Of course, creators of general intelligence tests do not use items such as those found on physics tests because they know that people differ greatly in terms of their experience with physics concepts. Intelligence tests are, therefore, putatively composed of familiar items that everyone should have had an equal opportunity to learn or that are relatively unfamiliar to everyone. Needless to say, there are many debates about whether these conditions can ever be met, thus, we may always face some version of the psychologist/person X problem when using static measures. However, imagine that we *could* ensure that everyone had had equal exposure to information required for answering questions on an intelligence test. We could then assess the degree to which people were adept at learning from their experience; however, the fact that person A learned less from his experience than person B does not mean that person A cannot learn how to learn. If one is interested in learning potential, the problem requires a dynamic rather than static approach (Brown & Ferrara, in press; Feuerstein, 1980).

This brings us back to one of the questions we raised at the outset of our discussion of *Intervention Research*. Are there general learning skills? Can and should they be taught? We believe that the answer to each question is yes. Efficient learners bring to bear on typical learning situations a number of resources that facilitate learning in new domains; they have learned to learn. They tend to profit more—learn more rapidly and transfer more broadly—than poorer learners from objectively identical learning situations because they know more about learning and *supplement for themselves* the information afforded. They apportion effort appropriately, continually monitor progress, know when and how to seek advice, and so on.

Efficient learners also prepare for transfer and engage in sophisticated reasoning aimed at accessing and using current knowledge. They prepare for transfer, for example, by regarding new problems, not as isolated problems, but as instances of a general class (e.g., Scribner & Cole, 1973); they expect that what they learn may be relevant elsewhere and entertain hypotheses about where and when. Simply knowing that transfer is desirable from prior situations to the current one or from the current one to future ones is itself part of the battle. Good learners perform thought experiments, seek appropriate analogies, and understand some of the principles involved in learning and reasoning from incomplete knowledge (e.g., Collins, Warnock, Aiello, & Miller, 1975). To repeat, good learners supplement incoming information in a number of clever ways to facilitate their own learning. Instruction may well be incomplete, but they have the skills to complete it for themselves.

We conclude this section by noting that these skills tend not to be taught explicitly and that there is growing evidence that even many college students do not acquire them incidentally (Chipman et al., in press). Given this growing awareness, fostered in large part by basic research efforts, it is not surprising that this situation is changing and that the amount of attention devoted to teaching cognitive skills is increasing.

Beyond Cold Cognition

In this section, we would like to emphasize that there is more to effective learning to learn than the issue of how instructors should impart "pearls of cognitive wisdom." Important factors involved in learning to learn are emotional as well as strictly cognitive. Poor performance can be due to objective facts, such as deficient materials, inappropriate learning activities, or unexpected criterial tasks. But many children may add to their difficulties by attributing their poor performance to themselves (to their lack of intelligence for example) rather than to other factors in the tetrahedral framework (Diener & Dweck, 1978; see also *Dweck, vol. IV, chap. 5*). Variations in opinions about oneself as a learner seem to be extremely important for understanding normal and atypical development and for designing programs that might help students learn to learn more effectively.

Virtually everything we have discussed so far involves what many would call the "cold cognitive" aspect of learning (Zajonc, 1980). But there are other dimensions to learning that are extremely important; for example, people have feelings about particular learning tasks and about themselves as learners that can have pervasive effects on their performance (Bransford, 1979; Brown, 1978; Henker, Whalen, & Hinshaw, 1980; Holt, 1964). Some individuals may be convinced of their inability to learn mathematics for example (Tobias, 1978) or of their incapacity to solve certain types of problems. Some children actively resist learning because their peers think it inappropriate or demeaning (McDermott, 1974) or because of their own diagnosis of personal incompetency. A particularly sweeping self-diagnosis was given by Daniel, a learning disabled 10-year-old, who worked with the first author. Upon encountering his first laboratory task, Daniel volunteered this telling comment: "Is this a memory thing?" (it wasn't)—"Didn't they tell you I can't do this stuff?"—"Didn't they tell you I don't have a memory?" Given this devastating estimate of his own ability, it is not surprising that Daniel would be diagnosed as passive, even resistant in situations that he classified as tests of his nonexistent faculty. It would take many sessions of systematically mapping out the specific nature of his memory problem and providing feedback about just where the problem was acute but also where there were no problems at all before Daniel could derive a more realistic evaluation of his learning problem and, as a consequence, would be willing to attempt active learning strategies to overcome a recognized problem.

It is by no means difficult, therefore, to imagine ways that negative feelings about a task or about oneself can affect learning. Nor is it surprising that people tend to avoid situations that tap their areas of weakness, thus conspiring to provide themselves with less practice in areas where it is most needed. Teachers inadvertently conspire to help students do this by, for example, addressing questions to students capable of answering and passing by those that need help to save everyone embarrassment. For example, recent observations of reading groups (Au, 1980; McDermott, 1978) have shown that good and poor readers are not treated equally. Good readers are questioned about the meaning behind what they are reading, asked to evaluate and criticize material, and so on. By contrast, poor readers receive primarily drill in pronunciation and decoding. Rarely are they given practice in qualifying and evaluating their comprehension (Au, 1980). There is considerable evidence that teachers give less experience in this learning mode to those who, because of their lack of prior experience, need it most (Gumperz & Hernandez-Chavez, 1972).

A plausible emotional block to effective learning involves an inefficient use of limited attention because a significant amount of cognitive effort is being directed to self-defeating, anxiety-producing self-evaluation. If learners focus on thoughts, such as "I can't do this" or "I'm going to fail again," they will not be able to attend to the details of the actual problem. Such negative ideation (Meichenbaum, 1977) can have a paralyzing effect on learning (*Dweck, vol. IV, chap. 8*).

Another related block to learning includes a lack in the confidence necessary to debug one's own errors. Some learners may not be sufficiently secure to enable them to tolerate mistakes; hence, they may ignore any errors they make or forget about them as quickly as possible (Bransford, 1979; Holt, 1964). Others may refuse to take the risk of responding incorrectly and, hence, be deprived of valuable feedback. It seems clear that the cold cognitive aspects of learning are only part of a much larger system that influences development; indeed, the purely cognitive aspects may be less primary than we like to think they are.

Beyond Isolated Cognition

In this last section, we would like to stress that learning is not only a less purely cognitive activity than we often suppose but it is also a less individual activity than might be readily apparent from a consideration of learning studies. We do not have space to deal in depth with this issue, but an excellent treatment is given in a companion volume to this one (*vol. I, chap. 7*). Here we will discuss only one issue to illustrate the importance of social mediation in learning. We will concentrate on tutors as agents of change in cognitive development (see also *Roots of Metacognition* in our discussion of *Metacognition, Executive Control . . .*).

In our previous discussion of training studies, we portrayed parents, teachers, and researchers as dispensers of pearls of cognitive wisdom. Effective mediators do much more than focus on particular concepts and strategies that may improve task performance, they respond to *individuals* who may feel confident, anxious, enthused, threatened, defiant, and so forth. Cognitively oriented developmental researchers who derive most of their developmental information from laboratory tasks often deal almost exclusively with relatively enthused individuals (Bransford, 1981). Good experimenters go to considerable lengths to design experiments that are interesting and nonthreatening; they attempt to structure the situation in ways that will minimize potential problems of hot cognition. This strategy is both practical and humane, of course, but it can also lead researchers to overlook emotional resistance to learning because they rarely confront it in their experimental work (Bransford, 1981). In addition, many of the experimental procedures for insuring cooperation, enthusiasm, and so forth, are relegated to the domain of lab lore rather than viewed as an integral part of a theory of development. As researchers, we routinely use our intuitions to structure optimal learning environments, yet give little thought to the fact that the learner and experimenter are interacting within the confines of that environment. If the situation were changed, if we were unable to convince people to cooperate in a training study for example, any pearls of cognitive wisdom we wished to offer would have very little effect.

The literature on parent/child interactions provides illuminating examples of the social basis of teaching and learning. The basic unit of learning and teaching is one of dialogue (both verbal and nonverbal) rather than a monologue (Schaffer, 1977, 1979; Vygotsky, 1978); children and their mediators influence one another and make mutual adjustments. For example, effective mediators use feedback from the learner to determine whether to repeat an instruction, put the instruction into simpler words, and so forth. Effective mediators estimate the child's "region of sensitivity to instruction" and work from there (Wood & Middleton, 1975); even teachers who seem to be lecturing in a monologue attempt to anticipate the needs of their audience and make use of student feedback.

Many of the activities employed by effective mediators are specifically focused on cold cognitive aspects of instruction, on particular concepts, factual knowledge, or strategies for example. But effective mediators do much more than impart cognitive lore. They encourage children, try to help them stay on task, express joy at the child's accomplishments, and so forth. Learning proceeds smoothly when child and mediator are in synchrony (Schaffer, 1977, 1979). But it is often very difficult to establish and maintain this synchrony; many of the moves made by effective mediators are designed to do just this.

To give one example, a side benefit of the zone-of-proximal-development testing procedures being developed (Brown & Ferrara, in press; Campione et al., in press) is that of increasing the child's feelings of competence. The procedure is such that if children fail to solve a problem unaided, they are given a set of increasingly explicit hints toward solution. The interactive and collaborative value of the adult/child relationship is such that the children believe that they are collaborating in the problem-solving process. Even when the adult provides such explicit clues that the answer is virtually given to the children, the prior collaboration leads the children to maintain faith in their own vital part in the learning solution. They seem to feel they have worked toward a solution that they eventually discover for themselves (Brown & Ferrara, in press). This interpretation was not generally made by a group of elderly women who took part in a similar zone-of-proximal-development study (French, 1979). Threatened by the testlike problems and deeply unsure of their own cognitive competence, the women interpreted the hints as an indication of their failure. Help often had to be terminated after two or three hints as the situation became intolerable. These data point out the importance of the learner's attitude in training studies and testing situations. Having in general a healthy self-image, academically successful children are able to capitalize on hints, even when given inadvertently in standard testing situations (see Mehan, 1973). Children who have already experienced more than their fair share of academic failure often fail to benefit from such aid because they are too busy covering up their supposed incompetence.

Mediators vary in how effectively they can establish the necessary empathy so that learning can occur. The present authors have had the opportunity to observe videotapes of Feuerstein (1980) working with academically less successful adolescents. Feuerstein is a gifted clinician, a cognitive therapist, if you will. He does a great deal of prompting to help children improve their approaches to various academic problems, but this is only part of his function; many of the moves that he makes are designed to alter the child's general reactions to the situation and the task. For example, one child faced with her first figural analogy problem said, in an extremely agitated and whiney voice: "I can't do that! I'm not used to that kind of problem." Feuerstein's response was: "Of course you can't do it—*yet*. Nobody can do things well until they have learned them. You can *learn* to do these problems, and I'm going to help you learn to do them." The girl did indeed learn to solve the problems (much to her amazement as well as that of her parents); furthermore, the session ended with the girl demanding to be given more problems when Feuerstein decided that it was time to stop.

Note that the moves Feuerstein made were designed to alter the student's reactions to the situation; to move her from a whiney resistive state dominated by negative ideation (Meichenbaum, 1977) to a more positive self-appraisal. Feuerstein did much more than simply dispense pearls of cognitive wisdom. The literature in clinical psychology contains some valuable information that is relevant in this context; for example, Strupp and his colleagues (Strupp, 1980a, 1980b, 1980c; Strupp & Hadley, 1977) discuss the importance of developing a working alliance and Horowitz (1979) analyzes the importance of helping clients move from resistive states to working states.

Feuerstein's success has been criticized on the grounds that, "it's all Feuerstein." A similar argument is that children learn simply "because of good teachers" or that clinical therapy works "because of gifted therapists." The assumption behind such criticisms seems to be that some mediators are "gifted" or "magic" and that is all there is to it. Much of cognitive development is an inherently social phenomenon that depends on effective mediation; it is not, then, sufficient simply to assume that some mediators are "magic" or "gifted" and that some are not. In their fascinating book, *The Structure of Magic,* Bandler and Grinder (1975) analyze the procedures used by successful therapists to make their procedures more explicit and, hence, learnable by novices. Similar analyses of the methods of effective agents of change, be they teachers, tutors, mastercraftsmen, priests, politicians, or clinicians, represent important activities for cognitive psychologists. The recent attempt by Collins and Stevens .(1981) to seek regularities in the activities of a variety of outstanding Socratic teachers is an important contribution to the literature.

There is an ever-present conflict faced by mediators, a conflict between their humanitarian side and their cold cognitive side. Mediators hesitate to push too hard for fear of making learners anxious and unhappy (sometimes rebellious perhaps). But the failure to push at all may protect the child from learning something new. Effective learning environments are those where the humanitarian and cold cognitive side of mediators are not in direct conflict. Many of the moves made by successful mediators can be viewed as attempts to create and maintain a balance between these two dimensions. If the balance is not developed and maintained, effective mediation does not occur.

There are many things that mediators do intuitively that eventually need to become part of a comprehensive theory of learning. When working with less successful students who are anxious about being tested, an effective mediator may adapt the role of helper or benefactor rather than tester. There are other common ploys that enhance learning. For example, rather than emphasizing the student's ability (or inability) to remember information one can focus on the degree to which the material is easy or difficult. Students, then, focus on evaluating the material rather than themselves and are open to suggestions concerning methods of making difficult materials easier to learn. Similarly, the ability to detect errors in one's own work and then make revisions can be viewed as a positive achievement rather than a sign of failure.

One of the most important aspects of effective mediation may involve procedures that enable children to experience a sense of mastery, that let them see that they have some control over learning situations, and that systematic analysis can lead to successful performance. An important outcome of such mediation may be a more positive attitude toward the general task of learning and problem solving and toward one's self as a learner. These outcomes may be as important as number of problems solved successfully, although one would hope that they would be positively correlated. Successful mediation involves much more than the act of dispensing pearls of cognitive wisdom. Successful researchers in cognitive development implicitly know this, of course, and use the information to design effective experiments and training studies; but it is important to move this knowledge from the domain of lab lore to the domain of theory. If we do not, we may be ignoring some of the most important influences on development that exist. The emotional cannot be divorced from the cognitive nor the individual from the social.

NOTE

1. A considerably expanded version of this section can be found in Brown (in press-a).

REFERENCES

Anderson, R. C., & Biddle, W. B. On asking people questions about what they are reading. In G. H. Bower (Ed.), *Psychology of learning and motivation* (Vol. 9). New York: Academic Press, 1975.

Anderson, R. C., & Pichert, J. W. Recall of previously unrecallable information following a shift in perspective. *Journal of Verbal Learning and Verbal Behavior*, 1978, *17*, 1–12.

Anderson, T. H., & Armbruster, B. B. Studying. In P. D. Pearson (Ed.), *Handbook of reading research*. New York: Longman, in press.

André, M. D. A., & Anderson, T. H. The development and evaluation of a self-questioning study technique. *Reading Research Quarterly*, 1978/1979, *14*, 605–623.

Anzai, Y., & Simon, H. A. The theory of learning by doing. *Psychological Review*, 1979, *86*, 124–140.

Armbruster, B. B. *An investigation of the effectiveness of ''mapping'' text as a studying strategy for middle school students*. Unpublished doctoral dissertation, University of Illinois, 1979.

Atkinson, R. C., Hansen, D. N., & Bernbach, H. A. Short-term memory with young children. *Psychonomic Science*, 1964, *1*, 255–256.

Atkinson, R. C., & Shiffrin, R. M. Human memory: A proposed system and its control processes. In K. W. Spence & J. T. Spence (Eds.), *Advances in the psychology of learning and motivation research and theory* (Vol. 2). New York: Academic Press, 1968.

Au, K. *A test of the social organizational hypothesis: Relationships between participation structures and learning to read*. Unpublished doctoral dissertation, University of Illinois, 1980.

Baker, L. Comprehension monitoring: Identifying and coping with text confusions. *Journal of Reading Behavior*, 1979, *11*, 363–374.

Baker, L., & Brown, A. L. Cognitive monitoring in reading. In J. Flood (Ed.), *Understanding reading comprehension*. Newark, Del.: International Reading Association, in press. (a)

Baker, L., & Brown, A. L. Metacognition and the reading process. In P. D. Pearson (Ed.), *Handbook of reading research*. New York: Longman, in press. (b)

Baker, L., & Stein, N. L. The development of prose comprehension skills. In C. Santa & B. Hayes (Eds.), *Children's prose comprehension: Research and practice*. Newark, Del.: International Reading Association, 1981.

Bandler, R., & Grinder, J. *The structure of magic*. Palo Alto, Calif.: Science and Behavior Books, 1975.

Bandura, A., & Walters, R. H. *Social learning and personality development*. New York: Holt, Rinehart & Winston, 1963.

Bartlett, F. C. *Thinking: An experimental and social study*. New York: Basic Books, 1958.

Baumeister, A. A. Serial memory span thresholds of normal and mentally retarded children. *Journal of Educational Psychology*, 1974, *66*, 889–894.

Bearison, D. J., & Levey, L. M. Children's comprehension of referential communication: Decoding ambiguous messages. *Child Development*, 1977, *48*, 716–720.

Beaty, W. E., & Weir, M. W. Children's performance on the intermediate-size transposition problem as a function of two different pretraining procedures. *Journal of Experimental Child Psychology*, 1966, *4*, 332–340.

Belmont, J. M., & Butterfield, E. C. Learning strategies as determinants of memory deficiencies. *Cognitive Psychology*, 1971, *2*, 411–420.

Belmont, J. M., & Butterfield, E. C. The instructional approach to developmental cognitive research. In R. V. Kail, Jr., & J. W. Hagen (Eds.), *Perspectives on the development of memory and cognition*. Hillsdale, N.J.: Erlbaum, 1977.

Belmont, J. M., Butterfield, E. C., & Borkowski, J. G. Training retarded people to generalize memorization methods across memory tasks. In M. M. Gruneberg, P. E. Morris, & R. N. Sykes (Eds.), *Practical aspects of memory*. London: Academic Press, 1978.

Bereiter, C., & Scardamalia, M. From conversation to composition: The role of instruction in a developmental process. In R. Glaser (Ed.), *Advances in instructional psychology* (Vol. 2). Hillsdale, N.J.: Erlbaum, 1980.

Bereiter, C., & Scardamalia, M. Does learning to write have to be so difficult? In J. Pringle, J. Yalden, & A. Friedman (Eds.), *Writing skills*. New York: Longman, in press.

Berlyne, D. E. Children's reasoning and thinking. In P. H. Mussen (Ed.), *Carmichael's manual of child psychology* (Vol. 1). New York: Wiley, 1970.

Bijou, S. W., & Baer, D. M. *Child development: A systematic and empirical theory*. New York: Appleton-Century-Crofts, 1967.

Binet, A. Perceptions d'enfants. *Revue Philosophique*, 1890, *30*, 582–611.

Binet, A. *Psychologie des grands calculateurs et joueurs d'échecs*. Paris: Hachette, 1894.

Binet, A. *L'étude expérimentale de l'intelligence*. Paris: Schleicher Frères, 1903.

Binet, A. *Les idées modernes sur les infants*. Paris: Ernest Flammarion, 1909.

Bisanz, G. L., Vesonder, G. T., & Voss, J. F. Knowledge of one's own responding and the relation of such knowledge to learning. *Journal of Experimental Child Psychology*, 1978, *25*, 116–128.

Bitterman, M. E. The evolution of intelligence. *Scientific American*, 1965, *212*, 92–100.

Boden, M. A. *Purposive explanation in psychology*. Boston: Harvard University Press, 1972.

Boden, M. A. *Artificial intelligence and natural man*. Hassocks, Eng.: Harvester Press, 1978.

Borkowski, J. G. Signs of intelligence: Strategy generalization and metacognition. In S. R. Yussen (Ed.), *Development of reflection in children*. New York: Academic Press, in press.

Borkowski, J. G., & Cavanaugh, J. C. Maintenance and generalization of skills and strategies by the retarded. In N. R. Ellis (Ed.), *Handbook of mental deficiency: Psychological theory and research*. Hillsdale, N.J.: Erlbaum, 1979.

Borkowski, J. G., Cavanaugh, J. C., & Reichart, G. J. Maintenance of children's rehearsal strategies: Effects of amount of training and strategy form. *Journal of Experimental Child Psychology*, 1978, *26*, 288–298.

Borkowski, J. G., & Wanschura, P. B. Mediational processes in the retarded. In N. R. Ellis (Ed.), *International review of research in mental retardation* (Vol. 7). New York: Academic Press, 1974.

Bower, G. H., Black, J. B., & Turnure, T. J. Scripts in memory for text. *Cognitive Psychology*, 1979, *11*, 177–220.

Bower, G. H., Clark, M. C., Lesgold, A. M., & Winzenz, D. Hierarchical retrieval schemes in recall of categorized word lists. *Journal of Verbal Learning and Verbal Behavior*, 1969, *8*, 323–343.

Bowerman, M. Starting to talk worse: Clues to language acquisition from children's late speech errors. In S. Strauss (Ed.), *U-shaped behavioral growth*. New York: Academic Press, in press.

Brain and Behavioral Sciences, 1978, *1*. (whole issue.)

Bransford, J. D. *Human cognition: Learning, understanding, and remembering*. Belmont, Calif.: Wadsworth, 1979.

Bransford, J. D. Social-cultural prerequisites for cognitive research. In J. Harvey (Ed.), *Cognition, social behavior, and the environment*. Hillsdale, N.J.: Erlbaum, 1981.

Bransford, J. D., Stein, B. S., Shelton, T. S., & Owings, R. A. Cognition and adaptation: The importance of learning to learn. In J. Harvey (Ed.), *Cognition, social behavior, and the environment*. Hillsdale, N.J.: Erlbaum, 1981.

Bray, N. W. Controlled forgetting in the retarded. *Cognitive Psychology*, 1973, *5*, 288–309.

Broadbent, D. E. Levels, hierarchies and the locus of control. *Quarterly Journal of Experimental Psychology*, 1977, *29*, 181–201.

Brown, A. L. Mnemonic elaboration and recency judgments in children. *Cognitive Psychology*, 1973, *5*, 233–248.

Brown, A. L. The role of strategic behavior in retardate memory. In N. R. Ellis (Ed.), *International review of research in mental retardation* (Vol. 7). New York: Academic Press, 1974.

Brown, A. L. The development of memory: Knowing, knowing about knowing, and knowing how to know. In H. W. Reese (Ed.), *Advances in child development and behavior* (Vol. 10). New York: Academic Press, 1975.

Brown, A. L. The construction of temporal succession by preoperational children. In A. D. Pick (Ed.), *Minnesota symposia on child psychology* (Vol. 10). Minneapolis: University of Minnesota, 1976.

Brown, A. L. Knowing when, where, and how to remember: A problem of metacognition. In R. Glaser (Ed.), *Advances in instructional psychology* (Vol. 1). Hillsdale, N.J.: Erlbaum, 1978.

Brown, A. L. Theories of memory and the problem of development: Activity, growth, and knowledge. In L. S. Cermak & F. I. M. Craik (Eds.), *Levels of processing in human memory*. Hillsdale, N.J.: Erlbaum, 1979.

Brown, A. L. Metacognitive development and reading. In R. J. Spiro, B. Bruce, & W. Brewer (Eds.), *Theoretical issues in reading comprehension*. Hillsdale, N.J.: Erlbaum, 1980.

Brown, A. L. Metacognition and reading and writing: The development and facilitation of selective attention strategies for learning from texts. In M. L. Kamil (Ed.), *Directions in reading: Research and instruction.* Washington, D.C.: National Reading Conference, 1981.

Brown, A. L. Learning and development: The problem of compatibility, access, and induction. *Human Development*, 1982, *25*, 89–115. (a)

Brown, A. L. Learning to learn how to read. In J. Langer & T. Smith-Burke (Eds.), *Reader meets author, bridging the gap: A psycholinguistic and social linguistic perspective.* Newark, N.J.: Dell, 1982 (b).

Brown, A. L. Metacognition, executive control, self-regulation, and other even more mysterious mechanisms. In F. E. Weinert & R. H. Kluwe (Eds.), *Learning by thinking.* West Germany: Kuhlhammer, in press. (a)

Brown, A. L., & Barclay, C. R. The effects of training specific mnemonics on the metamnemonic efficiency of retarded children. *Child Development*, 1976, *47*, 71–80.

Brown, A. L., & Campione, J. C. Recognition memory for perceptually similar pictures in preschool children. *Journal of Experimental Psychology*, 1972, *95*, 55–62.

Brown, A. L., & Campione, J. C. Training strategic study time apportionment in educable retarded children. *Intelligence*, 1977, *1*, 94–107.

Brown, A. L., & Campione, J. C. Permissable inferences from cognitive training studies in developmental research. In W. S. Hall & M. Cole (Eds.), *Quarterly Newsletter of the Institute for Comparative Human Behavior*, 1978, *2*, 46–53.

Brown, A. L., & Campione, J. C. Inducing flexible thinking: A problem of access. In M. Friedman, J. P. Das, & N. O'Connor (Eds.), *Intelligence and learning.* New York: Plenum, 1981.

Brown, A. L., & Campione, J. C. Modifying intelligence or modifying cognitive skills: More than a semantic quibble? In D. K. Detterman & R. J. Sternberg (Eds.), *How and how much can intelligence be increased.* Norwood, N.J.: Ablex, in press.

Brown, A. L., Campione, J. C., & Barclay, C. R. Training self-checking routines for estimating test readiness: Generalization from list learning to prose recall. *Child Development*, 1979, *50*, 501–512.

Brown, A. L., Campione, J. C., Bray, N. W., & Wilcox, B. L. Keeping track of changing variables: Effects of rehearsal training and rehearsal

prevention in normal and retarded adolescents. *Journal of Experimental Psychology*, 1973, *101*, 123–131.

Brown, A. L., Campione, J. C., & Day, J. D. Learning to learn: On training students to learn from texts. *Educational Researcher*, 1981, *10*, 14–21.

Brown, A. L., Campione, J. C., & Gilliard, D. M. Recency judgments in children: A production deficiency in the use of redundant background cues. *Developmental Psychology*, 1974, *10*, 303.

Brown, A. L., Campione, J. C., & Murphy, M. D. Maintenance and generalization of trained metamnemonic awareness by educable retarded children: Span estimation. *Journal of Experimental Child Psychology*, 1977, *24*, 191–211.

Brown, A. L., & Day, J. D. Macrorules for summarizing texts: The development of expertise. *Journal of Verbal Learning and Verbal Behavior*, in press.

Brown, A. L., Day, J. D., & Jones, R. S. The development of plans for summarizing texts. *Child Development*, in press.

Brown, A. L., & DeLoache, J. S. Skills, plans and self-regulation. In R. S. Siegler (Ed.), *Children's thinking: What develops?* Hillsdale, N.J.: Erlbaum, 1978.

Brown, A. L., & Ferrara, R. A. Diagnosing zones of proximal development. In J. Wertsch (Ed.), *Culture, communication, and cognition: Vygotskian perspectives.* New York: Cambridge University Press, in press.

Brown, A. L., & French, L. A. The zone of potential development: Implications for intelligence testing in the year 2000. *Intelligence*, 1979, *3*, 255–277.

Brown, A. L., & Lawton, S. C. The feeling of knowing experience in educable retarded children. *Developmental Psychology*, 1977, *13*, 364–370.

Brown, A. L., & Murphy, M. D. Reconstruction of arbitrary versus logical sequences by preschool children. *Journal of Experimental Child Psychology*, 1975, *20*, 307–326.

Brown, A. L., Palincsar, A. S., & Armbruster, B. B. Inducing comprehension-fostering activities in interactive learning situations. In H. Mandl, N. L. Stein, & T. Trabasso (Eds.), *Learning from texts.* Hillsdale, N.J.: Erlbaum, in press.

Brown, A. L., & Scott, M. S. Recognition memory for pictures in preschool children. *Journal of Experimental Child Psychology*, 1971, *11*, 401–412.

Brown, A. L., & Scott, M. S. Transfer between the oddity and relative size concepts: Reversal and extradimensional shifts. *Journal of Experimental Child Psychology*, 1972, *13*, 350–367.

Brown, A. L., & Smiley, S. S. Rating the importance of structural units of prose passages: A problem of metacognitive development. *Child Development*, 1977, *48*, 1–8.

Brown, A. L., & Smiley, S. S. The development of strategies for studying texts. *Child Development*, 1978, *49*, 1076–1088.

Brown, A. L., Smiley, S. S., Day, J. D., Townsend, M., & Lawton, S. Q. C. Intrusion of a thematic idea in children's recall of prose. *Child Development*, 1977, *48*, 1454–1466.

Brown, A. L., Smiley, S. S., & Lawton, S. Q. C. The effects of experience on the selection of suitable retrieval cues for studying texts. *Child Development*, 1978, *49*, 829–835.

Brown, J. S., Collins, A., & Harris, G. Artificial intelligence and learning strategies. In H. F. O'Neil (Ed.), *Learning strategies*. New York: Academic Press, 1978.

Bruce, B. C., & Newman, D. Interacting plans. *Cognitive Science*, 1978, *2*, 195–233.

Bruner, J. S. Organization of early skilled action. *Child Development*, 1973, *44*, 1–11.

Bruner, J. S., Goodnow, J. J., & Austin, G. A. *A study of thinking*. New York: Wiley, 1956.

Bruner, J. S., Olver, R. R., & Greenfield, P. M. *Studies in cognitive growth*. New York: Wiley, 1966.

Burger, A. L., Blackman, L. S., Holmes, M., & Zetlin, A. Use of active sorting and retrieval strategies as a facilitator of recall, clustering, and sorting by EMR and nonretarded children. *American Journal of Mental Deficiency*, 1978, *83*, 253–261.

Buschke, H. Components of verbal learning in children: Analysis by selective reminding. *Journal of Experimental Child Psychology*, 1974, *18*, 488–496.

Butterfield, E. C., & Belmont, J. M. Assessing and improving the executive cognitive functions of mentally retarded people. In I. Bialer & M. Sternlicht (Eds.), *Psychological issues in mentally retarded people*. Chicago: Aldine, 1977.

Butterfield, E. C., Siladi, D., & Belmont, J. M. Validating process theories of intelligence. In H. W. Reese & L. P. Lipsitt (Eds.), *Advances in child development and behavior* (Vol. 15). New York: Academic Press, 1980.

Butterfield, E. C., Wambold, C., & Belmont, J. M. On the theory and practice of improving short-term memory. *American Journal of Mental Deficiency*, 1973, *77*, 654–669.

Campione, J. C. The logic of training studies: Application to reading comprehension interventions. In H. Mandl, N. L. Stein, & T. Trabasso (Eds.), *Learning from texts*. Hillsdale, N.J.: Erlbaum, in press. (a)

Campione, J. C. Metacognitive components of instructional research with problem learners. In F. E. Weinert & R. H. Kluwe (Eds.), *Learning by thinking*. West Germany: Kuhlhammer, in press. (b)

Campione, J. C., & Armbruster, B. B. Acquiring information from texts: An analysis of four approaches. In S. Chipman, J. Segal, & R. Glaser (Eds.), *Cognitive skills and instruction*. Hillsdale, N.J.: Erlbaum, in press.

Campione, J. C., & Brown, A. L. Memory and metamemory development in educable retarded children. In R. V. Kail, Jr., & J. W. Hagen (Eds.), *Perspectives on the development of memory and cognition*. Hillsdale, N.J.: Erlbaum, 1977.

Campione, J. C., & Brown, A. L. Toward a theory of intelligence: Contributions from research with retarded children. *Intelligence*, 1978, *2*, 279–304.

Campione, J. C., & Brown, A. L. Learning ability and transfer propensity as sources of individual differences in intelligence. In P. H. Brooks, C. McCauley, & R. D. Sperber (Eds.), *Learning and cognition in the mentally retarded*. Baltimore: University Park Press, in press.

Campione, J. C., Brown, A. L., & Ferrara, R. A. Mental retardation and intelligence. In R. J. Sternberg (Ed.), *Handbook of human intelligence*. New York: Cambridge University Press, in press.

Capelli, C. A., & Markman, E. M. *Children's sensitivity to incomprehensible material in written texts*. Unpublished manuscript, Stanford University, 1980.

Carpenter, P. A., & Just, M. A. Reading comprehension as eyes see it. In M. A. Just & P. A. Carpenter (Eds.), *Cognitive processes in comprehension*. Hillsdale, N.J.: Erlbaum, 1977.

Case, R. Validation of a neo-Piagetian mental capacity construct. *Journal of Experimental Child Psychology*, 1972, *14*, 287–302.

Case, R. Structures and strictures: Some functional limitations on the course of cognitive growth. *Cognitive Psychology*, 1974, *6*, 544–573.

Case, R. A developmentally based theory and technology of instruction. *Review of Educational*

Research, Summer 1978, *48*, 439–463.

Case, R. *The search for horizontal structure in children's development*. Paper presented at the meeting of the Society for Research in Child Development, Boston, April 1981.

Case, R., Kurland, D. M., & Goldberg, J. Operational efficiency and the growth of short-term memory span. *Journal of Experimental Child Psychology*, 1982, *33* (3), 386–404.

Cavanaugh, J. C., & Borkowski, J. G. The metamemory-memory "connection": Effects of strategy training and transfer. *Journal of General Psychology*, 1979, *101*, 161–174.

Cavanaugh, J. C., & Perlmutter, M. Metamemory: A critical examination. *Child Development*, 1982, *53*, 11–28.

Chi, M. T. H. Short-term memory limitations in children: Capacity or processing deficits? *Memory and Cognition*, 1976, *4*, 559–572.

Chi, M. T. H. Age differences in memory span. *Journal of Experimental Child Psychology*, 1977, *23*, 266–281.

Chi, M. T. H. Knowledge structures and memory development. In R. S. Siegler (Ed.), *Children's thinking: What develops?* Hillsdale, N.J.: Erlbaum, 1978.

Chi, M. T. H. Knowledge development and memory performance. In M. Friedman, J. P. Das, & N. O'Connor (Eds.), *Intelligence and learning*. New York: Plenum, 1981.

Chi, M. T. H., Feltovich, P., & Glaser, R. Categorization and representation of physics problems by experts and novices. *Cognitive Science*, 1981, *5*, 121–152.

Chi, M. T. H., & Koeske, R. D. Network representations of knowledge base: Exploring a child's knowledge and memory performance of dinosaurs. *Developmental Psychology*, in press.

Chiesi, H. L., Spilich, G. J., & Voss, J. F. Acquisition of domain-related information in relation to high and low domain knowledge. *Journal of Verbal Learning and Verbal Behavior*, 1979, *18*, 257–273.

Childs, C. P., & Greenfield, P. M. Informal modes of learning and teaching: The case of Zinacanteco weaving. In N. Warren (Ed.), *Studies in cross-cultural psychology* (Vol. 2). London: Academic Press, 1980.

Chipman, S., Segal, J., & Glaser, R. *Cognitive skills and instruction*. Hillsdale, N.J.: Erlbaum, in press.

Clark, E. V. Language change during language acquisition. In M. E. Lamb & A. L. Brown (Eds.), *Advances in developmental psychology* (Vol. 2). Hillsdale, N.J.: Erlbaum, in press.

Cole, M., Hood, L., & McDermott, R. P. *Ecological niche-picking: Ecological invalidity as an axiom of experimental cognitive psychology* (Working Paper 14). New York: Rockefeller University, Laboratory of Comparative Human Cognition and the Institute of Comparative Human Development, 1978.

Cole, M., & Maltzman, I. (Eds.), *A handbook of contemporary Soviet psychology*. New York: Basic Books, 1969.

Collins, A., & Gentner, D. A framework for a cognitive theory of writing. In I. L. Gregg & E. Steinberg (Eds.), *Processes in writing*. Hillsdale, N.J.: Erlbaum, 1980.

Collins, A., & Smith, E. E. Teaching the process of reading comprehension. In D. K. Detterman & R. J. Sternberg (Eds.), *How and how much can intelligence be increased*. Norwood, N.J.: Ablex, in press.

Collins, A., & Stevens, A. Goals and strategies of inquiry teachers. In R. Glaser (Ed.), *Advances in instructional psychology* (Vol. 2). Hillsdale, N.J.: Erlbaum, in press.

Collins, A., Warnock, E., Aiello, N., & Miller, M. Reasoning from incomplete knowledge. In D. G. Bobrow & A. Collins (Eds.), *Representation and understanding: Studies in cognitive science*. New York: Academic Press, 1975.

Craik, F. I. M., & Lockhart, R. S. Levels of processing: A framework for memory research. *Journal of Verbal Learning and Verbal Behavior*, 1972, *11*, 671–684.

Craik, F. I. M., & Watkins, M. J. The role of rehearsal in short-term memory. *Journal of Verbal Learning and Verbal Behavior*, 1973, *12*, 599–607.

Crane, N. L., & Ross, L. E. A developmental study of attention to cue redundancy following discrimination learning. *Journal of Experimental Child Psychology*, 1967, *5*, 1–15.

Crisafi, M. A., & Brown, A. L. *Very young children's transfer of an inferential reasoning rule across familiar and unfamiliar instantiations of the problem*. University of Illinois, in preparation.

Cronbach, L. J. How can instruction be adapted to individual differences? In R. M. Gagné (Ed.), *Learning and individual differences*. Columbus, Ohio: Charles E. Merrill, 1967.

Cuvo, A. Developmental differences in rehearsal and free recall. *Journal of Experimental Child Psychology*, 1975, *19*, 265–278.

Day, J. D. *Training summarization skills: A comparison of teaching methods*. Unpublished doctoral dissertation, University of Illinois, 1980.

Day, J. D., Stein, N. L., Trabasso, T. A., & Shirey, L. *A study of inferential comprehension: The use of a story scheme to remember picture sequences.* Paper presented at the meeting of the Society for Research in Child Development, San Francisco, March 1979.

DeLoache, J. S. *Mother-child reading dyads.* University of Illinois, in preparation.

DeLoache, J. S., & Brown, A. L. Looking for Big Bird: Studies of memory in very young children. *Quarterly Newsletter of the Laboratory of Comparative Human Cognition,* 1979, *1,* 53–57.

DeLoache, J. S., & Brown, A. L. *Precursors of mnemonic strategies in very young children's memory for the location of hidden objects.* Unpublished manuscript, University of Illinois, 1981. (a)

DeLoache, J. S., & Brown, A. L. *Young children's memory for the location of objects hidden in large- and small-scale spaces.* Unpublished manuscript, University of Illinois, 1981. (b)

DeLoache, J. S., Sugarman, S., & Brown, A. L. *Self-correction strategies in early cognitive development.* Paper presented at the meeting of the Society for Research in Child Development, Boston, April 1981.

Dempster, F. N. Memory span and short-term memory capacity: A developmental study. *Journal of Experimental Child Psychology,* 1978, *26,* 419–431.

Dempster, F. N. Memory span: Sources of individual and developmental differences. *Psychological Bulletin,* 1981, *89,* 63–100.

Dennett, D. C. *Brainstorms: Philosophical essays on mind and psychology.* Montgomery, Vt.: Bradford Books, 1978.

Denney, N. W., & Ziobrowski, M. Developmental changes in clustering criteria. *Journal of Experimental Child Psychology,* 1972, *13,* 275–282.

Diener, C. I., & Dweck, C. S. An analysis of learned helplessness: Continuous changes in performance, strategy, and achievement cognitions following failure. *Journal of Personality and Social Psychology,* 1978, *36,* 451–462.

Dirks, J., & Neisser, U. Memory for objects in real scenes: The development of recognition and recall. *Journal of Experimental Child Psychology,* 1977, *23,* 315–328.

Dörner, D. Theoretical advances of cognitive psychology relevant for instruction. In A. Lesgold, J. Pellegrino, S. Fokkena, & R. Glaser (Eds.), *Cognitive psychology and instruction.* New York: Plenum, 1978.

Duncker, K. On problem solving. *Psychological Monographs,* 1945, (*58,* Whole No. 270).

Ellis, H. C. *The transfer of learning.* New York: Macmillan, 1965.

Ericsson, K. A., & Simon, H. A. Verbal reports as data. *Psychological Review,* 1980, *87,* 215–251.

Feldman, D. H. *Beyond universals in cognitive development.* Norwood, N.J.: Ablex, 1980.

Ferguson, G. A. On learning and human ability. *Canadian Journal of Psychology,* 1954, *8,* 95–112.

Feuerstein, R. *Instrumental enrichment: An intervention program for cognitive modifiability.* Baltimore: University Park Press, 1980.

Feuerstein, R., Rand, Y., Hoffman, M., Hoffman, M. & Miller, R. Cognitive modifiability in retarded adolescents: Effects of instrumental enrichment. *American Journal of Mental Deficiency,* 1979, *83,* 539–550.

Fischer, K. W. A theory of cognitive development: Control and construction of hierarchies of skills. *Psychological Review,* 1980, *87,* 477–531.

Flanagan, J. C. The critical incident technique. *Psychological Bulletin,* 1954, *51,* 327–358.

Flavell, J. H. *The developmental psychology of Jean Piaget.* Princeton, N.J.: Van Nostrand, 1963.

Flavell, J. H. Concept development. In P. H. Mussen (Ed.), *Carmichael's manual of child psychology* (Vol. 1). New York: Wiley, 1970. (a)

Flavell, J. H. Developmental studies of mediated memory. In H. W. Reese & L. P. Lipsitt (Eds.), *Advances in child development and behavior* (Vol. 5). New York: Academic Press, 1970. (b)

Flavell, J. H. First discussant's comments: What is memory development the development of? *Human Development,* 1971, *14,* 272–278. (a)

Flavell, J. H. Stage-related properties of cognitive development. *Cognitive Psychology,* 1971, *2,* 421–453. (b)

Flavell, J. H. Metacognitive aspects of problem solving. In L. B. Resnick (Ed.), *The nature of intelligence.* Hillsdale, N.J.: Erlbaum, 1976.

Flavell, J. H. Cognitive monitoring. In W. P. Dickson (Ed.), *Children's oral communication skills.* New York: Academic Press, 1981.

Flavell, J. H. On cognitive development. *Child Development,* 1982, *53,* 1–10.

Flavell, J. H., Beach, D. H., & Chinsky, J. M. Spontaneous verbal rehearsal in memory tasks as a function of age. *Child Development,* 1966, *37,* 283–299.

Flavell, J. H., Friedrichs, A. G., & Hoyt, J. D. Developmental changes in memorization processes. *Cognitive Psychology*, 1970, *1*, 324–340.

Flavell, J. H., Speer, J. R., Green, F. L., & August, D. L. The development of comprehension monitoring and knowledge about communication. *Monographs of the Society for Research in Child Development*, 1981 (*46*, Whole No. 192).

Flavell, J. H., & Wellman, H. M. Metamemory. In R. V. Kail, Jr., & J. W. Hagen (Eds.), *Perspectives on the development of memory and cognition*. Hillsdale, N.J.: Erlbaum, 1977.

Flavell, J. H., & Wohlwill, J. F. Formal and functional aspects of cognitive development. In D. Elkind & J. H. Flavell (Eds.), *Studies in cognitive development: Essays in honor of Jean Piaget*. New York: Oxford University Press, 1969.

Flores, C. F., & Winograd, T. *Understanding cognition as understanding*. Unpublished manuscript, Stanford University, 1978.

Flower, L. Writer-based prose: A cognitive basis for problems in writing. *College English*, 1979, *41*, 19–37.

Flower, L., & Hayes, J. Plans that guide the composing process. In C. Frederiksen, M. Whiteman, & J. Dominic (Eds.), *Writing: The nature, development, and teaching of written communication*. Hillsdale, N.J.: Erlbaum, 1980.

Fodor, J. A. Some reflections on L. S. Vygotsky's *Thought and language*. *Cognition*, 1972, *1*, 83–95.

Forrest, D. L., & Waller, T. G. *Meta-memory and meta-cognitive aspects of decoding in reading*. Paper presented at the meeting of the American Educational Research Association, Los Angeles, April 1981.

Frank, H. S., & Rabinovitch, M. S. Auditory short-term memory: Developmental changes in rehearsal. *Child Development*, 1974, *45*, 397–407.

French, L. A. *Cognitive consequences of education: Transfer of training in the elderly*. Unpublished doctoral dissertation, University of Illinois, 1979.

Fromkin, V. A. (Ed.), *Speech errors as linguistic evidence*. The Hague: Mouton, 1973.

Gagné, R. M. (Ed.), *Learning and individual differences*. Columbus, Ohio: Charles E. Merrill, 1967.

Gagné, R. M., & Smith, E. C. A study of the effects of verbalization on problem solving. *Journal of Experimental Psychology*, 1962, *63*, 12–18.

Gallistel, C. R. *The organization of action: A new

synthesis*. Hillsdale, N.J.: Erlbaum, 1980.

Gardner, H. Commentary on animal awareness papers. *Behavioral and Brain Sciences*, 1978, *4*, 572.

Garner, R. Monitoring of passage inconsistency among poor comprehenders: A preliminary test of the "piecemeal processing" explanation. *Journal of Educational Research*, in press.

Garner, R., & Taylor, N. *Monitoring of understanding: An investigation of the effects of attentional assistance*. Unpublished manuscript, University of Maryland, College Park, 1980.

Garner, T., & Kraus, C. *Monitoring of understanding among seventh graders: An investigation of good comprehender-poor comprehender differences in knowing and regulating reading behaviors*. Unpublished manuscript, University of Maryland, College Park, 1980.

Garrod, S., & Sanford, A. Interpreting anaphoric relations: The integration of semantic information while reading. *Journal of Verbal Learning and Verbal Behavior*, 1977, *16*, 77–90.

Gelman, R. Cognitive development. *Annual Review of Psychology*, 1978, *29*, 297–332.

Gelman, R., & Gallistel, C. R. *The child's understanding of number*. Cambridge: Harvard University Press, 1978.

Gerjuoy, I. R., & Spitz, H. H. Associative clustering in free recall: Intellectual and developmental variables. *American Journal of Mental Deficiency*, 1966, *70*, 918–927.

Gick, M. L., & Holyoak, K. J. Analogical problem solving. *Cognitive Psychology*, 1980, *12*, 306–355.

Gleitman, H. Some trends in the study of cognition. In S. Koch & D. E. Leary (Eds.), *A century of psychology as science: Retrospectives and assessments*. New York: McGraw-Hill, in press.

Goldin, S. E., & Hayes-Roth, B. *Individual differences in planning processes* (Tech. Rep. No. N–1488–ONR). Santa Monica, Calif.: Rand Corporation, 1980.

Goldstein, I. Developing a computational representation for problem-solving skills. In D. T. Tuma & F. Reif (Eds.), *Problem solving and education: Issues in teaching and research*. Hillsdale, N.J.: Erlbaum, 1979.

Green, J. M. Category cues in free recall: Retarded adults of two vocabulary age levels. *American Journal of Mental Deficiency*, 1974, *78*, 419–425.

Green, P. H. Introduction. In I. M. Gelford, U. S. Garjinkel, S. V. Fourer, & M. L. Tsetlin

(Eds.), *Model of the structural functional organization of certain biological systems.* Cambridge: MIT Press, 1971.

Greeno, J. G., & Noreen, D. L. Time to read semantically related sentences. *Memory and Cognition,* 1974, *2,* 117–120.

Gumperz, J. J., & Hernandez-Chavez, E. Bilingualism, dialectalism, and classroom interaction. In C. B. Cazden, V. P. John, & D. Hymes (Eds.), *Functions of language in the classroom.* New York: Teachers College Press, 1972.

Hagen, J., & Hale, G. The development of attention in children. In A. D. Pick (Ed.), *Minnesota symposia on child psychology* (Vol. 7). Minneapolis: University of Minnesota Press, 1973.

Hagen, J. W., Hargrave, S., & Ross, W. Prompting and rehearsal in short-term memory. *Child Development,* 1973, *44,* 201–204.

Hagen, J. W., Jongeward, R. H., & Kail, R. V., Jr. Cognitive perspectives on the development of memory. In H. W. Reese (Ed.), *Advances in child development and behavior* (Vol. 10). New York: Academic Press, 1975.

Hagen, J. W., Meacham, J. A., & Mesibov, G. Verbal labeling, rehearsal, and short-term memory. *Cognitive Psychology,* 1970, *1,* 47–58.

Hagen, J. W., & Stanovich, K. G. Memory: Strategies of acquisition. In R. V. Kail, Jr., & J. W. Hagen (Eds.), *Perspectives on the development of memory and cognition.* Hillsdale, N.J.: Erlbaum, 1977.

Hale, G. A., & Alderman, L. B. Children's selective attention with variation in amount of stimulus exposure. *Journal of Experimental Child Psychology,* 1978, *26,* 320–327.

Hannigan, J. L., Shelton, T. S., Franks, J. J., & Bransford, J. D. The role of episodic and semantic effects in the identification of sentences masked by white noise. *Memory and Cognition,* 1980, *8,* 278–284.

Harlow, H. F. Learning set and error factor theory. In S. Koch (Ed.), *Psychology: A study of science, Study I. Conceptual and systematic* (Vol. 2). New York: McGraw-Hill, 1959.

Harris, G. J., & Burke, D. The effects of grouping on short-term serial recall of digits by children: Developmental trends. *Child Development,* 1972, *43,* 710–716.

Harris, P. L., Kruithof, A., Terwogt, M. M., & Visser, P. Children's detection and awareness of textual anomaly. *Journal of Experimental Child Psychology,* 1981, *31,* 212–230.

Hasher, L., & Zacks, R. T. Automatic and effortful processes in memory. *Journal of Experimental Psychology: General,* 1979, *108,* 356–388.

Hayes, J. R., & Simon, H. A. Psychological differences among problem isomorphs. In N. J. Castellan, Jr., D. P. Pisoni, & G. R. Potts (Eds.), *Cognitive theory* (Vol. 2). Hillsdale, N.J.: Erlbaum, 1977.

Hayes-Roth, B. Evolution of cognitive structure and process. *Psychological Review,* 1977, *84,* 260–278.

Hayes-Roth, B., & Hayes-Roth, F. A cognitive model of planning. *Cognitive Science,* 1979, *3,* 275–310.

Hebb, D. O. *The organization of behavior.* New York: Wiley, 1949.

Henker, B., Whalen, C. K., & Hinshaw, S. P. The attributional contexts of cognitive intervention strategies. *Exceptional Education Quarterly,* 1980, *1,* 17–30.

Höffding, H. *Outlines of psychology* (M. E. Lowndes, trans.). London: Macmillan, 1892.

Holt, J. H. *How children fail.* New York: Dell, 1964.

Horowitz, L. M., Lampel, A. K., & Takanishi, R. N. The child's memory for unitized scenes. *Journal of Experimental Child Psychology,* 1969, *8,* 375–388.

Horowitz, M. J. *States of mind: Analysis of change in psychotherapy.* New York: Plenum, 1979.

Hull, C. L. *Principles of behavior: An introduction to behavior theory.* New York: Appleton-Century-Crofts, 1943.

Hunt, J. McV. *Intelligence and experience.* New York: Ronald Press, 1961.

Huttenlocher, J., & Burke, D. Why does memory span increase with age? *Cognitive Psychology,* 1976, *8,* 1–31.

Inhelder, B., & Piaget, J. *The growth of logical thinking from childhood to adolescence.* New York: Basic Books, 1958.

Inhelder, B., Sinclair, H., & Bovet, M. *Learning and the development of cognition.* Cambridge: Harvard University Press, 1974.

Istomina, Z. M. The development of voluntary memory in preschool-age children. *Soviet Psychology,* 1975, *13,* 5–64.

James, W. *Principles of psychology* (Vol. 1). New York: Holt, 1890.

Jenkins, J. J. Four points to remember: A tetrahedral model and memory experiments. In L. S. Cermak & F. I. M. Craik (Eds.), *Levels of processing in human memory.* Hillsdale, N.J.: Erlbaum, 1979.

Jensen, A. R., & Rohwer, W. D., Jr. The effects of verbal mediation on the learning and retention of paired associates by retarded adults. *American Journal of Mental Deficiency*, 1963, *68*, 80–84.

Johnson, R. C., & Zara, R. C. Relational learning in young children. *Journal of Comparative and Physiological Psychology*, 1960, *53*, 594–597.

Justice, E. M., & Bray, N. W. *The effects of context and feedback on metamemory in young children*. Paper presented at the meeting of the Society for Research in Child Development, San Francisco, March 1979.

Kail, R. V., Jr., & Hagen, J. W. (Eds.), *Perspectives on the development of memory and cognition*. Hillsdale, N.J.: Erlbaum, 1977.

Kail, R. V., Jr., & Siegel, A. W. Development of mnemonic encoding in children: From perception to abstraction. In R. V. Kail, Jr., & J. W. Hagen (Eds.), *Perspectives on the development of memory and cognition*. Hillsdale, N.J.: Erlbaum, 1977.

Karmiloff-Smith, A. Micro- and macro-developmental changes in language acquisition and other representational systems. *Cognitive Science*, 1979, *3*, 91–118. (a)

Karmiloff-Smith, A. Problem solving construction and representations of closed railway circuits. *Archives of Psychology*, 1979, *47*, 37–59. (b)

Karmiloff-Smith, A., & Inhelder, B. If you want to get ahead, get a theory. *Cognition*, 1974/1975, *3*, 195–212.

Keeney, M. L. *An investigation of what intermediate-grade children say about the writing of stories*. Unpublished doctoral dissertation, Lehigh University, Bethlehem, Pa., 1975.

Keeney, T. J., Cannizzo, S. R., & Flavell, J. H. Spontaneous and induced verbal rehearsal in a recall task. *Child Development*, 1967, *38*, 953–966.

Kelly, M., Scholnick, E. K., Travers, S. H., & Johnson, J. W. Relations among memory, memory appraisal, and memory strategies. *Child Development*, 1976, *47*, 648–659.

Kendall, C. R., Borkowski, J. G., & Cavanaugh, J. C. Metamemory and the transfer of an interrogative strategy by EMR children. *Intelligence*, 1980, *4*, 255–270.

Kendler, H. H., & Kendler, T. S. Vertical and horizontal processes in problem solving. *Psychological Review*, 1962, *69*, 1–16.

Kendler, T. S. Verbalization and optional reversal shifts among kindergarten children. *Journal of Verbal Learning and Verbal Behavior*, 1964, *3*, 428–436.

Keniston, A. H., & Flavell, J. H. A developmental

study of intelligent retrieval. *Child Development*, 1979, *50*, 1144–1152.

Kennedy, B. A., & Miller, D. J. Persistent use of verbal rehearsal as a function of information about its value. *Child Development*, 1976, *47*, 566–569.

Kieras, D. E. Good and bad structure in simple paragraphs: Effects on apparent theme, reading time, and recall. *Journal of Verbal Learning and Verbal Behavior*, 1978, *17*, 13–28.

Kingsley, P. R., & Hagen, J. W. Induced versus spontaneous rehearsal in short-term memory in nursery school children. *Developmental Psychology*, 1969, *1*, 40–46.

Klahr, D. Goal formation, planning, and learning by preschool problem solvers. In R. S. Siegler (Ed.), *Children's thinking: What develops?* Hillsdale, N.J.: Erlbaum, 1978.

Klahr, D., & Robinson, M. Formal assessment of problem-solving and planning processes in preschool children. *Cognitive Psychology*, 1981, *13*, 113–148.

Klahr, D., & Siegler, R. S. The representation of children's knowledge. In H. W. Reese & L. P. Lipsitt (Eds.), *Advances in child development and behavior* (Vol. 12). New York: Academic Press, 1978.

Klahr, D., & Wallace, J. G. *Cognitive development: An information processing view*. Hillsdale, N.J.: Erlbaum, 1976.

Kluwe, R. H. The development of metacognitive processes and performances. In F. E. Weinert & R. H. Kluwe (Eds.), *Learning by thinking*. West Germany: Kuhlhammer, in press.

Kobasigawa, A. K. Utilization of retrieval cues by children in recall. *Child Development*, 1974, *45*, 127–134.

Kobasigawa, A. K. Retrieval strategies in the development of memory. In R. V. Kail, Jr., & J. W. Hagen (Eds.), *Perspectives on the development of memory and cognition*. Hillsdale, N.J.: Erlbaum, 1977.

Kobasigawa, A. K., Ransom, C. C., & Holland, C. J. Children's knowledge about skimming. *Canadian Journal of Psychology*, in press.

Koestler, A. *Janus: A summing up*. New York: Random House, 1979.

Koslowski, B., & Bruner, J. S. Learning to use a lever. *Child Development*, 1972, *43*, 790–799.

Kreutzer, M. A., Leonard, S. C., & Flavell, J. H. An interview study of children's knowledge about memory. *Monographs of the Society for Research in Child Development*, 1975, *40*(1, Serial No. 159).

Kuenne, M. R. Experimental investigation of the

relation of language to transposition behavior in young children. *Journal of Experimental Psychology,* 1946, *36,* 471–490.

Kuhn, D., & Phelps, K. Microgenetic studies of scientific reasoning. In H. W. Reese & L. P. Lipsitt (Eds.), *Advances in child development and behavior.* New York: Academic Press, in press.

LaBerge, D. Acquisition of automatic processing in perceptual and associative learning. In P. M. A. Rabbitt & I. Dornic (Eds.), *Attention and performance V.* New York: Academic Press, 1975.

Laboratory of Comparative Human Cognition. Intelligence as cultural practice. In R. J. Sternberg (Ed.), *Handbook of human intelligence.* New York: Cambridge University Press, in press. (a)

Laboratory of Comparative Human Cognition. The zone of proximal development: Where culture and cognition create one author. In J. V. Wertsch (Ed.), *Culture, communication and cognition: Vygotskian perspectives.* New York: Cambridge University Press, in press. (b)

Lange, G. Organization-related processes in children's recall. In P. A. Ornstein (Ed.), *Memory development in children.* Hillsdale, N.J.: Erlbaum, 1978.

Larkin, J. H., Heller, J. I., & Greeno, J. G. Instructional implications of research on problem solving. In W. J. McKeachie (Ed.), *Cognition, college teaching, and student learning.* San Francisco: Jossey-Bass, 1980.

Lehrer, T. *That was the year that was.* San Francisco: Reprise Records, 1965.

Levine, M. Neo-noncontinuity theory. In G. H. Bower & J. T. Spence (Eds.), *The psychology of learning and motivation: Advances in research and theory* (Vol. 3). New York: Academic Press, 1969.

Liben, L. S. Memory in the context of cognitive development: The Piagetian approach. In R. V. Kail, Jr., & J. W. Hagen (Eds.), *Perspectives on the development of memory and cognition.* Hillsdale, N.J.: Erlbaum, 1977.

Lindberg, M. The role of knowledge structures in the ontogeny of learning. *Journal of Experimental Child Psychology,* 1980, *30,* 401–410.

Lindsay, P. H., & Norman, D. A. *Human information processing* (2nd ed.). New York: Academic Press, 1977.

Lloyd, P., & Pavlidis, G. T. *Child language and eye movements: The relative effects of sentence and situation on comprehension.* Unpublished manuscript, University of Manchester, Eng., 1978.

Locke, J. L., & Fehr, S. Young children's use of the speech code in a recall task. *Journal of Experimental Child Psychology,* 1970, *10,* 367–373.

Logan, G. D. Attention in character classification tasks: Evidence for automaticity of component stages. *Journal of Experimental Psychology: General,* 1978, *107,* 32–63.

Logan, G. D. On the use of a concurrent memory load to measure attention and automaticity. *Journal of Experimental Psychology: Human Perception and Performance,* 1979, *2,* 189–207.

Lumsdaine, A. A., & Glaser, R. *Teaching machines and program learning.* Washington, D.C.: National Education Association, 1960.

Luria, A. R. *Higher cortical function in man.* London: Tavistock Press, 1966.

Lyon, D. R. Individual differences in immediate serial recall: A matter of mnemonics? *Cognitive Psychology,* 1977, *9,* 403–411.

Mandler, J. M. Categorical and schematic organization in memory. In C. R. Puff (Ed.), *Memory organization and structure.* New York: Academic Press, 1979.

Mandler, J. M., & Day, J. D. Memory for orientation of forms as a function of their meaningfulness and complexity. *Journal of Experimental Child Psychology,* 1975, *20,* 430–443.

Mandler, J. M., & Johnson, N. S. Remembrance of things parsed: Story structure and recall. *Cognitive Psychology,* 1977, *9,* 111–151.

Mandler, J. M., & Parker, R. E. Memory for descriptive and spatial information in complex pictures. *Journal of Experimental Psychology: Human Learning and Memory,* 1976, *2,* 38–48.

Mandler, J. M., & Ritchey, G. H. Long-term memory for pictures. *Journal of Experimental Psychology: Human Learning and Memory,* 1977, *3,* 386–396.

Mandler, J. M., & Robinson, C. A. Developmental changes in picture recognition. *Journal of Experimental Child Psychology,* 1978, *26,* 122–136.

Mandler, J. M., & Stein, N. L. Recall and recognition of pictures by children as a function of organization and distractor similarity. *Journal of Experimental Psychology,* 1974, *102,* 657–669.

Markman, E. M. *Factors affecting the young child's ability to monitor his memory.* Unpublished doctoral dissertation, University of Pennsylvania, 1973.

Markman, E. M. Realizing that you don't understand: A preliminary investigation. *Child Development,* 1977, *46,* 986–992.

Markman, E. M. Realizing that you don't understand: Elementary school children's awareness of inconsistencies. *Child Development*, 1979, *50*, 643–655.

Markman, E. M. Comprehension monitoring. In W. P. Dickson (Ed.), *Children's oral communication skills*. New York: Academic Press, 1981.

Markman, E. M. Comprehension monitoring: Developmental and educational issues. In S. Chipman, J. Segal, & R. Glaser (Eds.), *Cognitive skills and instruction*. Hillsdale, N.J.: Erlbaum, in press.

Markman, E. M., & Gorin, L. Children's ability to adjust their standards for evaluating comprehension. *Journal of Educational Psychology*, in press.

Marshall, J. C., & Morton, J. On the mechanics of EMMA. In A. Sinclair, R. J. Jarvella, & W. J. M. Levelt (Eds.), *The child's conception of language*. Berlin: Springer-Verlag, 1978.

Masur, E. F., McIntyre, C. W., & Flavell, J. H. Developmental changes in apportionment of study time among items in a multitrial free-recall task. *Journal of Experimental Child Psychology*, 1973, *15*, 237–246.

McCarver, R. B. A developmental study of the effect of organizational cues on short-term memory. *Child Development*, 1972, *43*, 1317–1325.

McDermott, J., & Forgy, C. Production system conflict resolution strategies. In D. A. Waterman & F. Hayes-Roth (Eds.), *Pattern-directed influence systems*. New York: Academic Press, 1978.

McDermott, R. P. Achieving school failure: An anthropological approach to illiteracy and social stratification. In G. Spindler (Ed.), *Education and cultural process: Toward an anthropology of education*. New York: Holt, Rinehart & Winston, 1974.

McDermott, R. P. Some reasons for focusing on classrooms in reading research. In P. D. Pearson & J. Hansen (Eds.), *Reading: Disciplined inquiry in process and practice*. Clemson, S.C.: National Reading Conference, 1978.

Meacham, J. A. The development of memory abilities in the individual and in society. *Human Development*, 1972, *15*, 205–228.

Mehan, H. Assessing children's language-using abilities: Methodological and cross cultural implications. In M. Armer & A. D. Grimshaw (Eds.), *Comparative social research: Methodological problems and strategies*. New York: Wiley, 1973.

Meichenbaum, D. *Cognitive behavior modification: An integrative approach*. New York: Plenum, 1977.

Meichenbaum, D., & Asarnow, J. Cognitive behavior modification and metacognitive development: Implications for the classroom. In P. Kendall & S. Hollon (Eds.), *Cognitive behavioral interventions: Theory, research and procedure*. New York: Academic Press, 1978.

Miller, G. A. Lexical meaning. In J. F. Kavanagh & W. Strange (Eds.), *Speech and language in the laboratory, school, and clinic*. Cambridge: MIT Press, 1978.

Miller, P., & Bigi, L. The development of children's understanding of attention. *Merrill-Palmer Quarterly of Human Behavior and Development*, 1979, *25*, 235–250.

Milner, B. Some effects of frontal lobectomy in man. In J. M. Warren & K. Avert (Eds.), *The frontal granular cortex and behavior*. New York: McGraw-Hill, 1964.

Moely, B. E. Organizational factors in the development of memory. In R. V. Kail, Jr., & J. W. Hagen (Eds.), *Perspectives on the development of memory and cognition*. Hillsdale, N.J.: Erlbaum, 1977.

Moynahan, E. D. The development of knowledge concerning the effect of categorization upon free recall. *Child Development*, 1973, *44*, 238–246.

Munn, N. L. Learning in children. In L. Carmichael (Ed.), *Manual of child psychology* (2nd ed.). New York: Wiley, 1954.

Murdock, B. B., Jr. Recent developments in short-term memory. *British Journal of Psychology*, 1967, *58*, 421–433.

Murphy, M. D., & Brown, A. L. Incidental learning in preschool children as a function of level of cognitive analysis. *Journal of Experimental Child Psychology*, 1975, *19*, 509–523.

Murphy, M. D., Puff, C. R., & Campione, J. C. *Clustering measures and organization*. Paper presented at the meeting of the Society for Research in Child Development, New Orleans, March 1977.

Mussen, P. H. (Ed.), *Carmichael's manual of child psychology* (Vol. 1). New York: Wiley, 1970.

Myers, M., & Paris, S. G. Children's metacognitive knowledge about reading. *Journal of Educational Psychology*, 1978, *70*, 680–690.

Naron, N. K. Developmental changes in word attribute utilization for organization and retrieval in free recall. *Journal of Experimental Child Psychology*, 1978, *25*, 279–297.

Naus, M. J., & Halasz, F. G. Developmental perspectives on cognitive processing. In L. S. Cermak & F. I. M. Craik (Eds.), *Levels of processing in human memory*. Hillsdale, N.J.: Erlbaum, 1979.

Neimark, E. D. The natural history of spontaneous mnemonic activities under conditions of minimal experimental constraint. In A. D. Pick (Ed.), *Minnesota symposia on child psychology* (Vol. 10). Minneapolis: University of Minnesota Press, 1976.

Newell, A. One final word. In D. T. Tuma & F. Reif (Eds.), *Problem solving and education: Issues in teaching and research*. Hillsdale, N.J.: Erlbaum, 1979.

Newell, A., & Simon, H. A. *Human problem solving*. Englewood Cliffs, N.J.: Prentice-Hall, 1972.

Newman, D. *Children's understanding of strategic interaction*. Unpublished doctoral dissertation, City University of New York, 1981.

Ninio, A., & Bruner, J. S. The achievement and antecedents of labeling. *Journal of Child Language*, 1978, *5*, 1–15.

Nisbett, R. E., & Wilson, D. Telling more than we know: Verbal reports on mental processes. *Psychological Review*, 1977, *84*, 231–279.

Nitsch, K. E. *Structuring decontextualized forms of knowledge*. Unpublished doctoral dissertation, Vanderbilt University, 1977.

Nold, E. Revising. In C. Frederiksen, M. Whiteman, & J. Dominic (Eds.), *Writing: The nature, development, and teaching of written communication*. Hillsdale, N.J.: Erlbaum, 1980.

Nooteboom, S. C. The tongue slips into patterns. In A. G. Sciarone, A. J. Van Essen, & A. A. Van Raad (Eds.), *Nomen: Leyden studies in linguistics and pragmatics*. The Hague: Mouton, 1969.

Norman, D. A. Cognitive engineering and education. In D. T. Tuma & F. Reif (Eds.), *Problem solving and education: Issues in teaching and research*. Hillsdale, N.J.: Erlbaum, 1979.

Norman, D. A. Twelve issues for cognitive science. In D. A. Norman (Ed.), *Perspectives on Cognitive Science*. Norwood, N.J.: Orblex, 1981. (b)

Norman, D. A. Categorization of action slips. *Psychological Review*, 1981, *88*, 1–15. (a)

Norman, D. A., & Bobrow, G. A. On data-limited and resource-limited processes. *Cognitive Psychology*, 1975, *7*, 44–64.

Norman, D. A., & Schallice, T. *Attention to action: Willed and automatic control of behavior* (CHIP Tech. Rep. 99). LaJolla: University of California, December 1980.

Olson, D. What is worth knowing and what can be taught. *School Review*, 1973, 24–43.

Ornstein, P. A. *Memory development in children*. Hillsdale, N.J.: Erlbaum, 1978.

Ornstein, P. A., & Corsale, K. Organizational factors in children's memory. In C. R. Puff (Ed.), *Memory organization and structure*. New York: Academic Press, 1979.

Ornstein, P. A., & Naus, M. J. Rehearsal processes in children's memory. In P. A. Ornstein (Ed.), *Memory development in children*. Hillsdale, N.J.: Erlbaum, 1978.

Osgood, C. E. The similarity paradox in human learning: A resolution. *Psychological Review*, 1949, *56*, 132–143.

Overcast, T. D., Murphy, M. D., Smiley, S. S., & Brown, A. L. The effects of instruction on recall and recognition of categorized lists in the elderly. *Bulletin of the Psychonomic Society*, 1975, *5*, 339–341.

Palincsar, A. S., & Brown, A. L. *Training comprehension-monitoring skills in an interactive learning game*. Unpublished manuscript, University of Illinois, 1981.

Paris, S. G. *Metacognitive development: Children's regulation of problem solving skills*. Paper presented at the meeting of the Midwestern Psychological Association, Chicago, 1978.

Paris, S. G., & Lindauer, B. K. Constructive aspects of children's comprehension and memory. In R. V. Kail, Jr., & J. W. Hagen (Eds.), *Perspectives on the development of memory and cognition*. Hillsdale, N.J.: Erlbaum, 1977.

Paris, S. G., & Myers, M. Comprehension monitoring memory and study strategies of good and poor readers. *Journal of Reading Behavior*, 1981, *13*, 5–22.

Paris, S. G., Newman, R. S., & McVey, K. A. From tricks to strategies: Learning the functional significance of mnemonic actions. *Journal of Experimental Child Psychology*, in press.

Pascual-Leone, J. A mathematical model for the transition rule in Piaget's development stages. *Acta Psychologica*, 1970, *63*, 301–345.

Pascual-Leone, J. Compounds, confounds and models in developmental information processing: A reply to Trabasso and Foellinger. *Journal of Experimental Child Psychology*, 1978, *26*, 18–40.

Pascual-Leone, J., & Sparkman, E. The dialectics of empiricism and rationalism: A last methodological reply to Trabasso. *Journal of Experimental Child Psychology*, 1980, *29*, 88–101.

Patterson, C. J., Cosgrove, J. M., & O'Brien, R.

G. Nonverbal indicants of comprehension and noncomprehension in children. *Developmental Psychology,* 1980, *16,* 38–48.

Patterson, C. J., O'Brien, C., Kister, M. C., Carter, D. B., & Kotsonis, M. E. Development of comprehension monitoring as a function of context. *Developmental Psychology,* in press.

Pellegrino, J. W., & Schadler, M. *Maximizing performance in a problem-solving task.* Unpublished manuscript, University of Pittsburgh, 1974.

Perlmutter, M. What is memory aging the aging of? *Developmental Psychology,* 1978, *14,* 330–345.

Perlmutter, M. A developmental study of semantic elaboration and interpretation in recognition memory. *Journal of Experimental Child Psychology,* 1980, *29,* 413–427.

Perlmutter, M., & Myers, N. A. Development of recall in 2- to 4-year-old children. *Developmental Psychology,* 1979, *15,* 73–83.

Perlmutter, M., & Ricks, M. Recall in preschool children. *Journal of Experimental Child Psychology,* 1979, *27,* 423–436.

Piaget, J. *Psychology and epistemology.* New York: Viking, 1971.

Piaget, J. *The grasp of consciousness: Action and concept in the young child.* Cambridge: Harvard University Press, 1976.

Piaget, J. *Success and understanding.* Cambridge: Harvard University Press, 1978.

Piaget, J., & Inhelder, B. *Memory and intelligence.* New York: Basic Books, 1973.

Posnansky, C. J. Age and task related differences in the use of category size information for retrieval of categorized items. *Journal of Experimental Child Psychology,* 1978, *26,* 373–382.

Posner, M. I., & Snyder, C. R. R. Attention and cognitive control. In R. L. Solso (Ed.), *Information processing and cognition: The Loyola symposium.* Potomac, Md.: Erlbaum, 1974.

Puff, C. R. (Ed.), *Memory organization and structure.* New York: Academic Press, 1979.

Pylyshyn, Z. W. When is attribution of beliefs justified? *Behavioral and Brain Sciences,* 1978, *1,* 592–593.

Reed, S. K., Ernst, G. W., & Banerji, R. The role of analogy in transfer between similar problem states. *Cognitive Psychology,* 1974, *6,* 436–450.

Reese, H. W. Verbal mediation as a function of age level. *Psychological Bulletin,* 1962, *59,* 502–509.

Reese, H. W. *The perception of stimulus relations: Discrimination learning and transposition.* New York: Academic Press, 1968.

Reese, H. W. Models of memory and models of development. *Human Development,* 1973, *16,* 397–416.

Reese, H. W. Models of memory development. *Human Development,* 1976, *19,* 291–303.

Reese, H. W. Imagery and associative memory. In R. V. Kail, Jr., & J. W. Hagen (Eds.), *Perspectives on the development of memory and cognition.* Hillsdale, N.J.: Erlbaum, 1977.

Reese, H. W. *Verbal self-regulation in historical perspective.* Paper presented at the meeting of the Society for Research in Child Development, San Francisco, March 1979.

Resnick, L. B. Task analysis in instructional design: Some cases from mathematics. In D. Klahr (Ed.), *Cognition and instruction.* Hillsdale, N.J.: Erlbaum, 1976.

Resnick, L. B., & Glaser, R. Problem solving and intelligence. In L. B. Resnick (Ed.), *The nature of intelligence.* Hillsdale, N.J.: Erlbaum, 1976.

Richman, C. L., Nida, S., & Pittman, L. Effects of meaningfulness on child free-recall learning. *Developmental Psychology,* 1976, *12,* 460–465.

Riegel, K. F. Structure and transformation in modern intellectual history. In K. F. Riegel & G. C. Rosenwald (Eds.), *Structure and transformation: Developmental and historical aspects.* New York: Wiley, 1975.

Rigney, J. *On cognitive strategies for facilitating acquisition, retention, and retrieval in training and education* (Tech. Rep. No. 78). Los Angeles: University of Southern California, 1976.

Ringel, B. A., & Springer, C. On knowing how well one is remembering: The persistence of strategy use during transfer. *Journal of Experimental Child Psychology,* 1980, *29,* 322–333.

Ritchey, G. H. Picture superiority in free recall: The effects of organization and elaboration. *Journal of Experimental Child Psychology,* 1980, *29,* 460–474.

Ritter, K., Kaprove, B. H., Fitch, J. P., & Flavell, J. H. The development of retrieval strategies in young children. *Cognitive Psychology,* 1973, *5,* 310–321.

Rogoff, B. Schooling and the development of cognitive skills. In H. C. Triandis & A. Heron (Eds.), *Handbook of cross-cultural psychology* (Vol. 4). Boston: Allyn & Bacon, 1981.

Rogoff, B., & Gardner, W. P. Developing cognitive skills in social action. In B. Rogoff & J. Lave (Eds.), *Everyday cognition: Its develop-*

ment in social context. Cambridge: Harvard University Press, in press.

Rogoff, B., Sellers, M. J., Pirrotta, S., Fox, N., & White, S. H. Age of assignment of roles and responsibilities to children. *Human Development,* 1975, *18,* 353–369.

Rohwer, W. D., Jr. Implications of cognitive development in education. In P. H. Mussen (Ed.), *Carmichael's manual of child psychology.* New York: Wiley, 1970.

Rohwer, W. D., Jr. Elaboration and learning in childhood and adolescence. In H. W. Reese (Ed.), *Advances in child development and behavior* (Vol. 8). New York: Academic Press, 1973.

Rohwer, W. D., Jr., & Dempster, F. N. Memory development and educational processes. In R. V. Kail, Jr., & J. W. Hagen (Eds.), *Perspectives on the development of memory and cognition.* Hillsdale, N.J.: Erlbaum, 1977.

Rozin, P. The evolution of intelligence and access to the cognitive unconscious. *Progress in Psychobiology and Physiological Psychology,* 1976, *6,* 245–280.

Rumelhart, D. E. Notes on a schema for stories. In D. G. Bobrow & A. Collins (Eds.), *Representation and understanding: Studies in cognitive science.* New York: Academic Press, 1975.

Rumelhart, D. E., & Norman, D. A. Analogical processes in learning. In J. R. Anderson (Ed.), *Cognitive skills and their acquisition.* Hillsdale, N.J.: Erlbaum, 1981.

Sacerdoti, E. D. A structure for plans and behavior. In D. Michie (Ed.), *On machine intelligence.* New York: Wiley, 1974.

Salatas, H., & Flavell, J. H. Behavioral and metamnemonic indicators of strategic behaviors under remember instructions in first grade. *Child Development,* 1976, *47,* 81–89.

Scardamalia, M., & Bereiter, C. *Audience-adaptedness in knowledge-telling and problem-solving strategy.* Paper presented at a Conference on Models and Processes of Children's Writing, Albany, N.Y., March 1980.

Scardamalia, M., & Bereiter, C. The development of evaluative, diagnostic, and remedial capabilities in children's composing. In M. Martlew (Ed.), *The psychology of written language: A developmental approach.* London: Wiley, in press.

Schaffer, H. R. Early interactive development. In H. R. Schaffer (Ed.), *Studies in mother-infant interaction.* London: Academic Press, 1977.

Schaffer, H. R. Acquiring the concept of the dialogue. In M. H. Bornstein & W. Kessen (Eds.), *Psychological development from infancy: Image to intention.* Hillsdale, N.J.: Erlbaum, 1979.

Schallert, D. L., & Kleiman, G. M. *Some reasons why the teacher is easier to understand than the text book* (Reading Education Report No. 9). Urbana: University of Illinois, Center for the Study of Reading, 1979. (ERIC Document Reproduction Service No. ED 172 189)

Schmidt, C. R., & Paris, S. G. Operativity and reversability in children's understanding of pictorial sequences. *Child Development,* 1978, *49,* 1219–1222.

Schneider, W., & Shiffrin, R. M. Controlled and automatic human information processing: I. Direction, search, and attention. *Psychological Review,* 1977, *84,* 1–66.

Scribner, S., & Cole, M. Cognitive consequences of formal and informal education. *Science,* 1973, *182,* 553–559.

Selfridge, O. Pandemonium: A paradigm for learning. In *The symposium on the mechanization of thought.* London: H.M. Stationery Office, 1959.

Shatz, M. On the development of communicative understandings: An early strategy for interpreting and responding to messages. *Cognitive Psychology,* 1978, *10,* 271–301.

Shaw, R., & Bransford, J. D. Approaches to the problem of knowledge. In R. Shaw & J. D. Bransford (Eds.), *Perceiving, acting, and knowing: Toward an ecological psychology.* Hillsdale, N.J.: Erlbaum, 1977.

Sherman, M., & Strunk, J. Transposition as a function of single versus double discrimination training. *Journal of Comparative and Physiological Psychology,* 1964, *58,* 449–450.

Shif, Z. I. Development of children in schools for mentally retarded. In M. Cole & I. Maltzman (Eds.), *A handbook of contemporary Soviet psychology.* New York: Basic Books, 1969.

Shiffrin, R. M. The locus and role of attention in memory systems. In P. M. A. Rabbitt & S. Dornic (Eds.), *Attention and performance V.* New York: Academic Press, 1975.

Shiffrin, R. M., & Dumais, S. T. The development of automatism. In J. R. Anderson (Ed.), *Cognitive skills and their acquisition.* Hillsdale, N.J.: Erlbaum, 1981.

Shiffrin, R. M., & Schneider, W. Controlled and automatic human information processing: II. Perceptual learning, automatic attending, and a general theory. *Psychological Review,* 1977, *84,* 127–190.

Siegel, A. W., Kirasic, K. C., & Kilburg, R. R. Recognition memory in reflective and impulsive preschool children. *Child Development,* 1973, *44,* 651–656.

Siegler, R. S. Three aspects of cognitive development. *Cognitive Psychology,* 1976, *8,* 481–520.

Siegler, R. S. The origins of scientific reasoning. In R. S. Siegler (Ed.), *Children's thinking: What develops?* Hillsdale, N.J.: Erlbaum, 1978.

Siegler, R. S. Developmental sequences within and between concepts. *Monographs of the Society for Research in Child Development,* 1981, *46* (Whole No. 189).

Simon, H. A. On the development of the processor. In S. Farnham-Diggory (Ed.), *Information processing in children.* New York: Academic Press, 1972.

Simon, H. A. How big is a chunk? *Science,* 1974, *183,* 482–488.

Simon, H. A. Problem solving and education. In D. T. Tuma & F. Reif (Eds.), *Problem solving and education: Issues in teaching and research.* Hillsdale, N.J.: Erlbaum, 1979.

Skinner, B. F. *The behavior of organisms: An experimental analysis.* New York: Appleton-Century-Crofts, 1938.

Skinner, B. F. Behaviorism at fifty. In T. W. Wann (Ed.), *Behaviorism and phenomenology.* Chicago: University of Chicago Press, 1964.

Skinner, B. F. *Beyond freedom and dignity.* New York: Knopf, 1971.

Smiley, S. S., & Brown, A. L. Conceptual preference for thematic and taxonomic relations: A nonmonotonic age trend from preschool to old age. *Journal of Experimental Child Psychology,* 1979, *28,* 249–257.

Smith, H. K. The responses of good and poor readers when asked to read for different purposes. *Reading Research Quarterly,* 1967, *3,* 53–84.

Snow, R. E., & Yalow, E. Education and intelligence. In R. J. Sternberg (Ed.), *Handbook of human intelligence.* Boston: Cambridge University Press, in press.

Sperber, R. D., McCauley, C., Ragin, R., & Weil, C. Semantic priming effects on picture and word processing. *Memory and Cognition,* 1979, *7,* 339–345.

Spiro, R. J., Bruce, B. C., & Brewer, W. F. (Eds.), *Theoretical issues in reading comprehension.* Hillsdale, N.J.: Erlbaum, 1980.

Spitz, H. H. The role of input organization in the learning and memory of mental retardates. In N. R. Ellis (Ed.), *International review of research in mental retardation* (Vol. 2). New York: Academic Press, 1966.

Stein, N. L., & Glenn, C. G. An analysis of story comprehension in elementary school children. In R. O. Freedle (Ed.), *Discourse processing: Advances in research and theory* (Vol. 2). Norwood, N.J.: Ablex, 1979.

Stein, N. L., & Mandler, J. M. Children's recognition of geometric figures. *Child Development,* 1974, *45,* 604–615.

Stein, N. L., & Trabasso, T. What's in a story: Critical issues in comprehension and instruction. In R. Glaser (Ed.), *Advances in instructional psychology* (Vol. 2). Hillsdale, N.J.: Erlbaum, in press.

Stevenson, H. W. Learning in children. In P. H. Mussen (Ed.), *Carmichael's manual of child psychology* (Vol. 1). New York: Wiley, 1970.

Stokes, T. F., & Baer, D. M. An implicit technology of generalization. *Journal of Applied Behavior Analysis,* 1977, *10,* 349–367.

Stolz, W. S., & Tiffany, J. The production of "child-like" word associations by adults to unfamiliar adjectives. *Journal of Verbal Learning and Verbal Behavior,* 1972, *11,* 38–46.

Strauss, S., & Stavey, R. U-shaped behavioral growth: Implications for theories of development. In W. W. Hartup (Ed.), *Review of child development research* (Vol. 6). Chicago: University of Chicago Press, in press.

Strupp, H. H. Success and failure in time-limited psychotherapy: A systematic comparison of two cases: Comparison 1. *Archives of General Psychiatry,* 1980, *37,* 595–603. (a)

Strupp, H. H. Success and failure in time-limited psychotherapy: A systematic comparison of two cases: Comparison 2. *Archives of General Psychiatry,* 1980, *37,* 708–716. (b)

Strupp, H. H. Success and failure in time-limited psychotherapy: Further evidence: Comparison 4. *Archives of General Psychiatry,* 1980, *37,* 947–954. (c)

Strupp, H. H., & Hadley, S. W. A tripartite model of mental health and therapeutic outcomes. With special reference to negative effects in psychotherapy. *American Psychologist,* 1977, *32,* 187–196.

Sulin, R. A., & Dooling, D. J. Intrusion of a thematic idea in retention of prose. *Journal of Experimental Psychology,* 1974, *103,* 255–262.

Tenney, Y. J. The child's conception of organization and recall. *Journal of Experimental Child Psychology,* 1975, *19,* 100–114.

Thorndike, E. L. Reading as reasoning: A study of

mistakes in paragraph reading. *Journal of Educational Psychology*, 1917, *8*, 323–332.

Thorndike, E. L., & Woodworth, R. S. The influence of improvement in one mental function upon the efficiency of other functions. *Psychological Review*, 1901, *8*, 247–261, 384–395, 553–564.

Thorndyke, P., & Stasz, C. Individual differences in procedures for knowledge acquisition from maps. *Cognitive Psychology*, 1980, *12*, 137–175.

Thornton, S. Challenging "early competence": A process-oriented analysis of children's classification. *Cognitive Science*, in press.

Tighe, L. S. Effect of perceptual training on reversal and non-reversal shifts. *Journal of Experimental Psychology*, 1965, *70*, 397–385.

Tobias, S. *Overcoming math anxiety*. New York: W. W. Norton, 1978.

Tolman, E. C. *Purposive behavior in animals and men*. New York: Appleton-Century, 1932.

Trabasso, T. On the estimation of parameters and the evaluation of a mathematical model. A reply to Pascual-Leone. *Journal of Experimental Child Psychology*, 1978, *26*, 41–45.

Trabasso, T., & Foellinger, D. B. Information processing capacity in children: A test of Pascual-Leon's model. *Journal of Experimental Child Psychology*, 1978, *26*, 1–17.

Trabasso, T., Stein, N. L., & Johnson, L. R. Children's knowledge of events: A causal analysis of story structure. In G. Bower (Ed.), *The psychology of learning and motivation: Advances in research and theory* (Vol. 15). New York: Academic Press, in press.

Tshirgi, J. E. Sensible reasoning: A hypothesis about hypotheses. *Child Development*, 1980, *51*, 1–10.

Tuma, D. T., & Reif, F. *Problem solving and education: Issues in teaching and research*. Hillsdale, N.J.: Erlbaum, 1979.

Turnure, J. E., Buium, N., & Thurlow, M. L. The effectiveness of interrogatives for prompting verbal elaboration productivity in young children. *Child Development*, 1976, *47*, 851–855.

Turnure, J. E., & Thurlow, M. L. Verbal elaboration and the promotion of transfer of training in educable mentally retarded children. *Journal of Experimental Child Psychology*, 1973, *15*, 137–148.

Turvey, M. T. Preliminaries to a theory of action with reference to vision. In R. Shaw & J. D. Bransford (Eds.), *Perceiving, acting, and knowing: Toward an ecological psychology*.

Hillsdale, N.J.: Erlbaum, 1977.

Turvey, M. T., & Shaw, R. E. The primacy of perceiving: An ecological reformulation of perception for understanding memory. In L. G. Nilsson (Ed.), *Perspective on memory research: Essays in honor of Uppsala University's 500 Anniversary*. Hillsdale, N.J.: Erlbaum, 1979.

Turvey, M. T., Shaw, R. E., & Mace, W. Issues in the theory of action: Degrees of freedom, coordinative structures and coalitions. In J. Requin (Ed.), *Attention and performance VII*. Hillsdale, N.J.: Erlbaum, 1978.

Voss, J. F. Knowledge factors in learning in text. In H. Mandl, N. L. Stein, & T. Trabasso (Eds.), *Learning from texts*. Hillsdale, N.J.: Erlbaum, in press.

Vygotsky, L. S. *Mind in society: The development of higher psychological processes* (M. Cole, V. John-Steiner, S. Scribner, & E. Souberman, eds. and trans.). Cambridge: Harvard University Press, 1978.

Wason, P. C., & Johnson-Laird, P. N. *Psychology of reasoning: Structure and content*. Cambridge: Harvard University Press, 1972.

Waters, H. S. Memory development in adolescence: Relationships between metamemory, strategy use and performance. *Journal of Experimental Psychology*, in press.

Waugh, N. C., & Norman, D. A. Primary memory. *Psychological Review*, 1965, *72*, 89–104.

Weinert, F. E. Theoretical relationships between the development of metacognition, attribution style, and self-directed learning. In F. E. Weinert & R. H. Kluwe (Eds.), *Learning by thinking*. West Germany: Kuhlhammer, in press.

Weinstein, C. Elaboration skills as a learning strategy. In H. F. O'Neil (Ed.), *Learning strategies*. New York: Academic Press, 1978.

Wellman, H. M. The early development of intentional memory behavior. *Human Development*, 1977, *20*, 86–101.

Wellman, H. M. Knowledge of the interaction of memory variables: A developmental study of metamemory. *Developmental Psychology*, 1978, *14*, 24–29.

Wellman, H. M. Metamemory revisited. In M. T. H. Chi (Ed.), *What is memory development the development of? A look after a decade. Human Development*, in press.

Wellman, H. M., Collins, J., & Gleiberman, G. Understanding the combination of memory variables: Developing conceptions of memory limitations. *Child Development*, in press.

Wellman, H. M., Ritter, K., & Flavell, J. H. Deliberate memory behavior in the delayed reactions of very young children. *Developmental Psychology*, 1975, *11*, 780–787.

Wellman, H. M., & Somerville, S. C. The development of human search ability. In M. E. Lamb & A. L. Brown (Eds.), *Advances in developmental psychology* (Vol. 2). Hillsdale, N.J.: Erlbaum, in press.

Wellman, H. M., Somerville, S. C., & Haake, R. J. Development of search procedures in real-life spatial environments. *Developmental Psychology*, 1979, *15*, 530–542.

Werner, H. *Comparative psychology of mental development*. New York: Wiley, 1961.

Wertsch, J. V. Adult-child interaction and the roots of metacognition. *Quarterly Newsletter of the Institute for Comparative Human Development*, 1978, *1*, 15–18.

Wertsch, J. V. *The social interactional origins of metacognition*. Paper presented at the meeting of the Society for Research in Child Development, San Francisco, March 1979.

White, S. H. Evidence for a hierarchical arrangement of learning processes. In L. P. Lipsitt & C. C. Spiker (Eds.), *Advances in child development and behavior* (Vol. 2). New York: Academic Press, 1965.

White, S. H. The learning theory tradition for child psychology. In P. H. Mussen (Ed.), *Carmichael's manual of child psychology* (Vol. 1). New York: Wiley, 1970.

Wood, D., & Middleton, D. A study of assisted problem-solving. *British Journal of Psychology*, 1975, *66*, 181–191.

Worden, P., & Sladewski-Awig, L. *Children's mnemonic judgments and meta-memory*. Paper presented at the meeting of the Society for Research and Child Development, San Francisco, March 1979.

Wozniak, R. H. Psychology and education of the learning disabled child in the Soviet Union. In W. M. Cruickshank & D. P. Hallahan (Eds.), *Perceptual and learning disabilities in children*. Syracuse, N.Y.: Syracuse University Press, 1975.

Yussen, S. R., & Bird, J. E. The development of metacognitive awareness in memory, communication, and attention. *Journal of Experimental Child Psychology*, 1979, *28*, 300–313.

Yussen, S. R., Levin, J. R., Berman, L., & Palm, J. Developmental changes in the awareness of memory benefits associated with different types of picture organization. *Developmental Psychology*, 1979, *15*, 447–449.

Yussen, S. R., & Levy, V. M., Jr. Developmental changes in predicting one's own span of short-term memory. *Journal of Experimental Child Psychology*, 1975, *19*, 502–508.

Zajonc, R. B. Feeling and thinking: Preferences need no inferences. *American Psychologist*, 1980, *35*, 151–175.

Zeaman, D., & House, B. J. The role of attention in retardate discrimination learning. In N. R. Ellis (Ed.), *Handbook of mental deficiency*. New York: McGraw-Hill, 1963.

A REVIEW OF SOME PIAGETIAN CONCEPTS*

ROCHEL GELMAN, *University of Pennsylvania*
RENÉE BAILLARGEON, *University of Pennsylvania*

CHAPTER CONTENTS

OVERVIEW

Our task was to examine Piagetian concepts in light of recent research and theory on cognitive development. This breathtaking assignment was made somewhat easier by the fact that elsewhere in the *Handbook* there are discussions of the first (sensorimotor intelligence) and last (formal operations) of Piaget's proposed stages of development. This allowed us to focus on Piaget's two intermediary stages of development, those of preoperational and concrete-operational thought. But we still had to make choices. In the end, we tried to put together a review that would reflect the impact of Piagetian theory as well as our own views on the current status of the theory. The result is a review that is critical, yet in agreement with some of the fundamental tenets of the theory. Thus, we accept the position that there is much to be learned about cognitive development by studying the acquisition of such concepts as number, space, time, and causality. We also have no quarrel with the idea that cognition involves structures that assimilate and accommodate to the environment; indeed, we do not see how it could be otherwise. However, we do question the notion of there being broad stages of development, each characterized by qualitatively distinct structures. As we will see, the experimental evidence available today no longer supports the hypothesis of a major qualitative shift from preoperational to concrete-operational thought. Instead, we argue for domain-specific descriptions of the nature as well as the development of cognitive abilities.

Our review of Piagetian concepts starts with matters of *structure* and ends with matters of *function*, or development proper. That is, we take up first the

*Supported in part by NSF grants to Rochel Gelman and fellowships to Renée Baillargeon from the NSERC of Canada and The Quebec Department of Education. We thank our editors and K. Cheng, C. R. Gallistel, R. Golinkoff, J. Mandler, and F. Murray for their careful readings of an earlier draft of this chapter and E. Meck for keeping us on task. All new translations of the French are due to Renée Baillargeon.

what and then the *how* of cognitive development. We begin by examining some of Piaget's ideas about the nature of preoperational and concrete-operational thought. We then review in some detail the research that has been conducted in several cognitive domains, including numerical and quantitative reasoning and classification. In the final section, we examine Piaget's ideas about the sources of cognitive structures and the processes—assimilation, accommodation, equilibration, and so on—that account for their development.

ASSESSMENT OF THE CHARACTERIZATION OF CONCRETE OPERATIONS

When tested on the standard Piagetian tasks in the standard way, preschool children typically err in their responses. Thus, when asked whether a bouquet composed of six roses and four tulips contains more roses or more flowers, they quite invariably answer more roses. Similarly, when presented with two even rows of chips and asked, after watching the experimenter spread one row, whether the two rows still contain the same number of chips, preschoolers typically respond that the longer row has more.

No one seriously questions the reliability of these (and other similar) observations, which have all been widely replicated. What is very much at issue, however, is how preschoolers' failure on the standard Piagetian tasks should be interpreted. The fact that children less than 6 years of age typically fail these tasks and that children 6 years of age and older typically succeed on these tasks suggests that there are important differences in their cognitive capacities. The question is, How should these differences be characterized?

Piaget's account of the differences involved granting the older child reversible structures, or operations, while limiting the younger child to irreversible structures: hence the use of the terms operational and preoperational to describe the cognitive capacities of the older and the younger child respectively. Piaget believed that children's (at first concrete and later formal) operations are organized into well-integrated sets, or structured wholes, and he and his colleagues developed logicomathematical models to characterize these wholes. (The reader who is not familiar with these models is referred to Flavell, 1963; Gruber and Vonèche, 1977; and Piaget, 1942, 1957).

Evaluation of the theory of concrete operations has proceeded along several lines. One has been to assess whether success on different Piagetian tasks (e.g., conservation, classification, seriation, per-

spective taking) is indeed related. Another has been to explore the preschool child's alleged intellectual incompetence relative to the older child. Still another line of evaluation, closely related to the third, has been to devise training studies that might bring to the fore unsuspected competencies. In the next sections, we review some of the work that has been done along each of these lines.

Are There Structures d'Ensemble?

Do Multiple Correlations Obtain?

Many studies have been conducted to compare children's ability to classify, seriate, conserve, measure, give predictions and explanations, assume another's visual or social perspective, and so on. Most such studies have failed to show high intercorrelations between the various abilities tested (e.g., Berzonsky, 1971; Dimitrovsky & Almy, 1975; Jamison, 1977; Tomlinson-Keasey, Eisert, Kahle, Hardy-Brown, & Keasey, 1979; Tuddenham, 1971). Such findings are not really inconsistent with Piagetian theory. Piaget never really claimed (1) that all concrete-operational abilities are based on, or are derived from, a single underlying structure; or (2) that all concrete-operational abilities emerge in a strictly parallel, perfectly synchronous fashion (Vyuk, 1981). To the contrary, Piaget's writings are filled with theoretical claims concerning the order of emergence within each developmental stage of distinct cognitive abilities, with the earlier abilities viewed as precursors of, or as prerequisites for, the later abilities. For example, Piaget (1952a) argued that numerical reasoning is the product of the joint development of the child's classification and seriation abilities. In addition, Piaget often noted in his empirical writings that cognitive abilities, once acquired, are not always applied uniformly in all contexts. Instead, cognitive abilities are frequently applied in one context at a time, with considerable décalages between successive applications. Thus, Piaget (1962) reported that children do not conserve number before the age of 6 or 7; mass, before the age of 8; weight, before the age of 10; and so on.

All of these theoretical and empirical claims obviously mitigate against the possibility of anyone finding high correlations between children's performance on many or all of the concrete-operational tasks. Contrary to what is sometimes held to be the case, investigators' repeated failure to find high correlations across tasks does *not* constitute definite evidence against the notion of a concrete-operational mentality in the (relatively diffuse) sense intended by the theory. Still, such consistently negative results do raise difficulties when it comes to the interpretation of certain studies. Psychologists and educators often attempt to relate children's performance on a given task to their level of cognitive development (e.g., preoperational, concrete-operational) as assessed by any of the standard Piagetian tasks. Were it the case that performance on all standard Piagetian tasks was highly correlated, then, obviously, any task would be as good as any other as a test of children's mastery of concrete-operational thought. But as we just saw, that is far from the case. For this reason, studies that report relationships between, say, children's ability to use metamemorial strategies and children's ability to conserve (taken to demonstrate their entry into the concrete-operational stage) are difficult, if not impossible, to interpret vis-à-vis Piagetian theory.

Are Sequences as Predicted?

The studies we discussed in the previous section tested for the synchronous emergence of different abilities during the concrete-operational period. Other studies have tested whether the order in which abilities develop within that period is as predicted by Piagetian theory. Several investigators have focused on the development of numerical reasoning in the child. As mentioned earlier, Piaget (1952a) maintained that the concept of number develops from the coordination of classification and seriation structures. According to Piaget (1952a), the construction of number

consists in the equating of differences, i.e., in writing in a single operation the class and the symmetrical relationship. The elements in question are then both equivalent to one another, thus participating of the class, and different from one another by their position in the enumeration, thus participating of the asymmetrical relationship. (p. 95)

Piagetian theory generally assumes that success on standard number-conservation tasks indexes a true understanding of number and that success on standard class-inclusion tasks indexes a true understanding of classification. If Piaget's (1952a) account of the development of the concept of number was correct, one should not find children who pass standard number-conservation tasks well before they pass standard class-inclusion tasks. As Brainerd (1978a) recently pointed out, however, exactly the oppostie sequence obtains. The vast majority of children conserve number by age 6 or 7; but it is not until age 9 or 10 that they truly understand the princi-

ple of class inclusion (see also Markman, 1978; Winer, 1980). Such facts clearly call into question the claim that numerical reasoning is the product of the joint development of classification and seriation abilities. Additional evidence against this claim comes from a study by Hamel (1974).

Hamel (1974) analyzed Piaget's (1952a) account of number and concluded that it predicts a strong relationship between: (1) number conservation; (2) provoked correspondence; (3) spontaneous, that is, unprovoked correspondence; (4) seriation; (5) cardination-ordination; and (6) class inclusion. The correlations between the various number tests were significant and quite high (.50 to .80). Likewise, correlations between the multiple-classification tasks and the various number subtasks were also significant, ranging from .45 to .66. However, there were no significant relationships between the class-inclusion task and *any of the other tasks*. Dodwell (1962) reported similar results.

There are other studies that fail to observe some of the between-task predictions derived from the theory (e.g., Brainerd, 1978a; Kofsky, 1966; Little, 1972). There are even studies that fail to observe the same sequence of development across children—whether or not the sequence is predicted by the theory. For example, in a longitudinal study, Tomlinson-Keasey, et al. (1979) found that 13 of 38 subjects passed a class-inclusion task before they conserved amount, 12 passed it after, and 13 passed it at the same time.

What should we make of investigators' failure to confirm the between-tasks sequences predicted by the theory? Should we take it to suggest that Piaget was wrong in claiming that the concrete-operational stage is characterized by the coordinated emergence of superficially disparate but structurally related cognitive abilities? Not necessarily. It could be argued that to do so would be to confuse the issue of whether or not specific abilities develop in the order predicted by Piagetian theory with the more general issue of whether or not abilities from different cognitive domains develop in a well-integrated, coordinated fashion. Piagetian theory could be right in supporting the general issue and still be wrong in any of its specific predictions. Piaget's (1952a) account of the development of the child's understanding of number could be wrong—and as we will see, Piaget (1975a, 1977) himself later abandoned his earlier account—but the general hypothesis that development in other domains contributes to the emergence of the child's concept of number could still be right.

There obviously is no rebuttal to this argument. As the saying goes, the proof is in the pudding. What

Piagetian theory must provide is a satisfactory account of numerical (or causal, or spatial, or logical, etc.) development that posits real, nontrivial interactions between domains. To the extent that such an account can be provided, then to the same extent will the notion of a stage of concrete operations be reinforced. (As we will see below, however, the trend in recent years has been to move away from stage-like, across-the-cognitive-board accounts of development. More and more, investigators appear to focus on the possibility of parallel, domain-specific lines of development.)

Test of the Logicomathematical Model

It is sometimes argued that the reason why investigators have failed to find high correlations between various concrete-operational abilities or have failed to confirm the order in which their abilities develop has to do with the way in which abilities are measured (see Flavell, 1972; Jamison & Dansky, 1979; Tuddenham, 1971). Different investigators use different tasks. Further, it is not always clear whether the tasks used provide a good test of the abilities under study. In addition, there are statistical nightmares. How does one estimate measurement error? Is it constant across tasks? And what if one finds only one child whose performance contradicts the expected pattern—should the theory be rejected?

One way to get around some of these difficulties is to work directly from the logicomathematical model of concrete operations Piaget and his collaborators proposed. Osherson (1974), for instance, used Grize's (1963) axiomatization of these operations. The choice of this axiomatization was based in large part on Piaget's (1967) endorsement of it. Further, Grize's axioms are easily interpreted into statements about classes and relations.

To start, Osherson (1974) derived a set of theorems that followed from Grize's (1963) axioms. He then translated a subset of the theorems into a set of length-inclusion and class-inclusion tasks designed to embody the derived theorems and, thus, provide a test of children's ability to use them. Finally, he made predictions about the patterns of successes and failures that should obtain. That is, he specified which tasks children should pass or fail, given that they had passed or failed certain other tasks. The predictions were based on the analysis of which and how many axioms a particular theorem was derived from. To illustrate, assume Theorems 1 and 2 were derived from Axioms 1 and 2, respectively and Theorem 7 was derived from Axioms 1 and 2. The child who passed the task designed to test for Theorem 7 should likewise have passed the tasks designed to test Theorems 1 and 2 by themselves.

Osherson (1974) found that despite an overall comparable success rate on the length-inclusion and class-inclusion tasks, the patterns of errors made in the two sets of tasks were *not* comparable. These findings suggest that the logicomathematical structures proposed by Piaget and his collaborators are not appropriate for modeling performance in these two task domains. Indeed, one might take these results to call into question the idea that the *same* structures underlie children's ability to solve length-inclusion and class-inclusion problems.

At this point, however, one might point out that Osherson's findings need no longer be taken into account as there have been changes in the formal theory of concrete-operational thought, as well as further developments in the efforts to axiomatize the theory (Piaget, 1977; Wermus, 1971). In addition, one could argue (as before) that even if Piagetian theory, in spite of its recent revisions, still fails to provide an adequate formal description for the logicomathematical structures underlying concrete operations, one need not conclude that no such structures exist: perhaps one has not yet succeeded in finding their proper characterization.

Whether or not the revised Piagetian model serves as a better model has yet to be determined. But as Sheppard (1978) pointed out, it is not clear that the more recent axiomatizations are all that different from the original ones.

Are Within-Domain Relations as Predicted?

Investigators' repeated failure to verify the developmental sequences described by Piagetian theory has led many authors to doubt the claim that cognitive abilities emerge in a coordinated, orderly fashion across domains. Perhaps for this reason, some authors have sought to test the developmental sequences predicted by the theory *within* domains rather than *across* domains. If one interprets Piagetian theory to mean that performance within each domain is based on operations that are organized into a well-integrated, reversible structure, then one might expect to find relatively high correlations between tasks testing abilities assumed to be derived from that same structure. However, attempts to verify this particular hypothesis have not faired well.

Consider, for instance, the work of Hooper, Sipple, Goldman, and Swinton (1979) and Kofsky (1966), who tested Inhelder and Piaget's (1964) description of the development of classification abilities. Kofsky (1966) found that although she could discern a rank order of difficulty for her different classification tasks, only 27% of her subjects fit this pattern. Hooper and his colleagues (1979) later replicated Kofsky's overall developmental sequence.

Some of their findings also led them to doubt that this sequence represented the development of only one common classificatory structure. For instance, Hooper et al. found that the ability to multiply classes as assessed in a cross-class matrix task does *not* predict the ability to solve class-inclusion problems. Indeed, they, like many others (e.g., Brainerd, 1978a; Dimitrovsky & Almy, 1975; Dodwell, 1962; Hamel, 1974; Kofsky, 1966; Tuddenham, 1971; Winer, 1980) found that class-inclusion tasks are much more difficult—and are accordingly solved much later—than are other concrete-operational tasks. They concluded that some four separate factors contribute to the development of classificatory abilities.

Studies that examined the development of ordering abilities have yielded comparable results (Dimitrovsky & Almy, 1975; Tuddenham, 1971). Tuddenham reported a .28 (nonsignificant) correlation between the ability to seriate and solve a transitive inference task. Dimitrovsky and Almy compared children's ability to seriate and reorder, that is, place back in order stimuli that are mixed up before them. Of the 408 children tested, 134 passed the seriation task; in contrast, only 41 passed the reordering task.

Attempts to confirm Piaget's (1952a, 1975a, 1977) prediction that the ability to compensate precedes or co-occurs with the ability to conserve have also been unsuccessful. According to Piaget, the child who truly understands that the amount of liquid in a glass is conserved when it is poured into a container of different dimensions also understands the principle of compensation: "conservation . . . involves quantities that are not perceptive, but have to be constructed by compensation between two different dimensions" (Piaget, 1967a, p. 533). In his first presentation of this position Piaget (1952a) predicted that all children who conserved liquid would reveal an understanding of compensation. This meant that a child could pass a compensation task and fail a conservation task but not the reverse. In a subsequent presentation of the argument, Piaget considered the kinds of predictions children at different stages in the development of conservation should make before the transformation phase of both the conservation and compensation tasks (e.g., Inhelder, Bovet, Sinclair, & Smock, 1966; Piaget & Inhelder, 1974). At an initial stage, the nonconserver should predict that there will be conservation after the transformation and that the water level in the new beaker will *not* change. At the second stage, the nonconserver should predict that there will not be conservation and the water level *will* change. Finally, the true conserver should predict that the water level will change *and* that conservation will obtain in

the face of this perceptual change. In either version of the conservation account, one should not observe a child who passes the conservation task and, nevertheless, fails the compensation task. Piaget and Inhelder (1963) reported that all but 5% of children who conserved were able to anticipate the level of water that would be reached if the contents of a standard beaker were poured into a beaker of different dimensions. Although details of the data are not presented, Piaget (1952a) noted that almost all children who conserved passed a compensation test that required children to pour as much water into an empty beaker as there was in a standard beaker of different dimensions. Piaget and Inhelder (1971) also reported a study of the ability to pass conservation and compensation tasks in support of their account of conservation. However, there are now many studies that do not support their account.

Acker (1968) found children who conserved but failed the anticipation task used by Piaget and Inhelder (1963). Lee (1971) found that when children were required to pass both tests of conservation and compensation in order to be judged true conservers, the proportion of conservers fell from 11 of 15 to 6 of 15. Gelman and Weinberg (1972) reported that 17% of their subjects who conserved failed to compensate, that is, failed to match the water level of the standard when pouring the "same amount" into a beaker of different dimensions.

More recently, Acredelo and Acredelo (1979) tested the extended version of Piaget's account of the relationship between the abilities to conserve, compensate, and anticipate conservation or compensation. They reported that 37.5% of their sample revealed success and failure patterns *not* predicted by Piagetian theory. These disconfirming patterns were expected with their alternative identity theory of conservation however. This alternative theory allows children to conserve even if they fail to compensate. Such children are viewed as being in an early stage of conservation; they focus on the absence of an addition/subtraction operation or the irrelevance of displacement transformations and pay little attention to the perceptual conflict that obtains after the transformation. Children then go on to learn that compensation is a consequence of conservation. This fits with Gelman and Weinberg's (1972) observation that the understanding of the compensation principle, as manifested in verbal statements, continues to develop well after the age at which the child's ability to conserve liquid may be taken for granted. Further, it removes the puzzle of how a child could understand compensation without presupposing an equivalence relation—as Piaget would have them do.

In sum, even when we assess the Piagetian account within a single domain (e.g., classification, seriation, conservation), the results do not lend support to the theory. The idea that concrete-operational thought is not dependent on one or even several structures d'ensemble is probably related to the turn away from Piaget's stage theory (e.g., Brainerd, 1978a, 1978b; Feldman, 1980; Fischer, 1980; Flavell, 1982; Siegler, 1981; but see also Davison, King, Kitchener, & Parker, 1980). Evidence that preoperational thought may not be preoperational makes it even harder to maintain the stage account.

Is Preoperational Thought Really Preoperational?

To say of a child that he is preoperational is to say more than that he has no concrete operations. Preoperational thought is not defined (or explained) solely in terms of what it lacks; it is also said to possess several dominant characteristics. According to Piagetian theory, the preoperational child is egocentric or (to use the more recent label) centered. His reasoning processes are perception bound: he is easily distracted by the perceptual or spatial properties of objects and, for this reason, often fails to detect more abstract, invariant relations among objects. In addition, the preoperational child is usually unable to coordinate information about states and transformations.

Are preschoolers truly preoperational? A host of recent investigations have raised questions about the validity of this characterization. In general, these studies show that under certain conditions, even young preschoolers behave in a nonegocentric manner, ignore misleading perceptual cues, integrate information about states and transformations, and so on.

Consider the claim that preschoolers are egocentric. In the perspective-taking task designed by Piaget and Inhelder (1956), children are shown a model of three mountains. A doll is placed at various positions around the model and children are asked to indicate how the mountains look to the doll from each of the positions. Children less than 6 years of age tend to choose a picture or small replica that depicts their own view rather than the doll's view. According to Piaget and Inhelder (1956), the young child is "rooted to his own viewpoint in the narrowest and most restricted fashion, so that he cannot imagine any perspective but his own" (p. 242). Similarly, when asked to describe the workings of a water tap or to repeat to another child a story he has been told, the young child does terribly. This is be-

cause "he feels no desire to influence his listener nor to tell him anything; not unlike a certain type of drawing room conversation where everyone talks about himself and no one listens" (Piaget, 1959, p. 32).

Do young children really believe that an observer standing in a different location than theirs sees the same thing they see? Recent work by Masangkay, McCluskey, McIntyre, Sims-Knight, Vaughn, and Flavell (1974) and by Lempers, Flavell, and Flavell (1977) indicates that the answer to this question is negative. In the study by Masangkay et al., a card with different pictures on each side was held vertically in front of children who were asked: "What do *you* see?" and "What do *I* see?" All of the 3-year-olds and half of the 2-year-olds tested responded correctly. In the study by Lempers et al., children 1 to 3 years of age were given hollow cubes with a photograph of a familiar object glued to the bottom of the inside. Children's task was to show the photograph inside the cube to an observer sitting across from them. Lempers et al. found that virtually all children 2 years and older turned the cube opening *away from themselves* to face the observer. These results indicate that the young child is not so egocentric as to believe others see whatever *he* sees. What then could be the source of the young child's difficulty on Piaget and Inhelder's (1956) mountain task?

Flavell (1974) distinguished between the child's identification of *what* object another sees and the more complex concept of *how* the object is seen. The findings of Masangkay et al. (1974), Lempers et al. (1977), and others (e.g., Coie, Constanzo, & Farnill, 1973) indicate that the rudimentary ability to determine what another person sees is present by age 2. The ability to recognize how an object or a scene appears to another person develops much more slowly. Borke (1975) showed that the age at which children demonstrate nonegocentric perspective-taking ability is heavily influenced by such task variables as the nature of the test displays and the type of response required. Borke's (1975) procedure was the same as that of Piaget and Inhelder (1956), with two important exceptions. First, two of the three displays Borke used were scenes containing familiar toy objects. Display 1 consisted of a small lake with a toy sailboat, a model of a house, and a miniature horse and cow. Display 2 contained different groupings of miniature people and animals in natural settings (e.g., a dog and doghouse). Display 3 was a replica of Piaget and Inhelder's (1956) three mountains. Second, Borke asked her subjects to indicate the doll's perspective by rotating duplicates of the displays. On Displays 1 and 2, Borke found that 3- and 4-year-old children correctly assessed the doll's perspective for all three positions tested between 79% and 93% of the time. In contrast, on Piaget and Inhelder's display, 3-year-olds gave 42% and 4-year-olds 67% correct responses for the three positions. Borke concluded that her results "raise considerable doubt about the validity of Piaget's conclusion that young children are primarily egocentric and incapable of taking the viewpoint of another person. When presented with tasks that are age appropriate, even very young subjects demonstrate perceptual perspective-taking ability" (p. 243). Additional support for Borke's conclusion comes from a recent study by Flavell, Flavell, Green, and Wilcox (1981). Flavell and his colleagues found that preschoolers understand that objects with different sides (e.g., a house) look different from different perspectives, whereas objects with identical sides (e.g., a ball) look the same from all perspectives.

Taken together, the results of Borke (1975) and Flavell et al. (1981) clearly indicate that children as young as 3 years of age (1) are aware that an individual looking at a display (e.g., a house) from a position other than their own will have a different view of the display; and (2) are able to compute how the display looks to this individual under certain optimal conditions. With time, children become more and more proficient at identifying how a display appears to another individual. It should be noted that this ability continues to develop well into the school years. Huttenlocher and Presson (1973, 1978), for example, found that school-aged children do better on perspective-taking tasks if they are allowed to walk around the covered display before giving their response.

Similar nonegocentric results have been obtained in other types of perspective tasks. Markman (1973a) found that preschoolers correctly predicted that 2-year-olds would fail on a memory task but would achieve some degree of success on a motoric task. Shatz and Gelman (1973) reported that 4-year-olds used shorter and simpler utterances when talking to a 2-year-old than when talking to peers or adults. Speech to the 2-year-olds typically involved remarks aimed at obtaining and maintaining the child's attention as well as show-and-tell talk. In marked contrast, adult-directed speech usually involved comments about the child's own thoughts and requests for information, classification, or support. Speech to the adults also included hedges, which are commonly assumed to mark the speaker's recognition that the listener is better informed, older, and so on (Gelman & Shatz, 1978). Maratsos

(1973) reported that 3- and 4-year-olds pointed to indicate the positions of toys to a sighted adult. When the same adult covered her eyes, however, children tried—as best as they could—to describe the toys' respective positions. Likewise, Marvin, Greenberg, and Mossler (1976) reported that children as young as 4 recognized that a person who did not see an event did not know this event: Knowledge of the event could be shared only by those who had witnessed it. These are hardly the sorts of things one would expect fundamentally egocentric thinkers to be able to do (for further evidence see Donaldson, 1978; Shatz, 1978; *Shatz, vol. III, chap. 13*).

In all fairness to Piaget, we should point out that our criticism of the characterization of the young child as egocentric is addressed more to interpreters and followers of Piaget than to Piaget himself. In our survey of the Genevan literature since 1965, we never encountered the term egocentric. As Vyuk (1981) noted, Piaget switched to the term *centered* in his later writings to avoid the surplus meaning of the term egocentric.

What evidence is there that the preoperational child is *centered,* in the sense Piaget intended? One version of the centration hypothesis holds that the preoperational child's failure to conserve number or quantity is due, in part, to a proclivity to center on one dimension (e.g., length in the case of number conservation, height in the case of liquid conservation) and ignore the other dimension (e.g., density in the case of number conservation, width in the case of liquid conservation). However, Anderson and Cuneo (1978) provide compelling evidence against this version of the centration hypothesis. In one study, children 5 years of age and older were shown rectangular cookies that varied systematically in width and in height. Their task was to rate how happy a child would be to be given the different cookies to eat. During pretesting, children were taught how to use the rating scale. This scale consisted of a long rod with a happy face at one end and a sad face at the other. The children's task during the test was to point to the place on the rod that reflected their judgment of how happy or sad a child would be if he ate a cookie of a given size. Analyses of the ratings yielded significant effects of both width and height—even for preschool subjects. In a subsequent study, Cuneo (1980) obtained similar results with 3- and 4-year-old children. Analyses of the children's ratings indicated that they were using a height + width rule to evaluate the area of the test cookies. As before, there was no evidence of centering on one dimension.

What of the characterization of the preoperational child as perception bound? An early conservation training study by Bruner et al. (1966) appeared to lend support to this characterization. Children were shown two identical beakers filled with water and were asked whether or not they contained the same amount. Next, children were shown a third, empty beaker of different dimensions. This new beaker was placed behind a screen, and the contents of one of the original beakers was poured into it. Children were then asked whether the screened and the unscreened beakers contained the same amount of water. It was found that children were less likely to give up their initial judgment of equivalence with the screen present.

A conservation study by Markman (1979) makes it difficult to accept the Bruner et al. position that children's failure to conserve reflects the perception bound quality of their thought processes. Markman asked 4- and 5-year-olds to participate in one of two versions of the number conservation task. The only difference between the two versions was the terms used to label the displays. In one version—the standard Piagetian version—*class* terms (e.g., trees, soldiers, birds) were used. In the other version, *collection* terms (e.g., forest, army, flock) were used. Children in the class condition did poorly. In contrast, children in the collection condition averaged 3.2 correct judgments out of 4 *and* were able to provide explanations for their judgments. Because both versions of the task involved the exact same displays, one cannot explain the class subjects' failure to conserve on the ground that preschoolers are perception bound. Subjects in both experimental conditions obviously had equal opportunity to become distracted by the perceptual appearance of the posttransformation displays. The fact that the collection children did not raises doubt about the validity of the characterization of the preoperational child as fundamentally perception bound.

Additional evidence that preschoolers are not always perception bound comes from studies that examined their ability to distinguish between appearance and reality. Fein (1979), for instance, found that by age 3 children have no difficulty distinguishing the pretend activities involved in play from other activities. Flavell, Flavell, and Green (in press) reported that even 3-year-olds have some ability to distinguish between real and apparent object properties. In one experiment, children were shown a white paper that looked pink when placed behind a piece of pink plastic. More than half of the 3-year-olds tested correctly differentiated between the appearance (pink) and the reality (white) of the paper. In a similar vein, Gelman, Spelke & Meck (in press)

found that 3-year-olds recognize that a doll and a person are more alike perceptually than are a doll and a rock. But they also understand—as evidenced by spontaneous comments to this effect—that a doll can only "pertend" walk, sit, eat, and so on.

Work by Gelman, Bullock, and Meck (1980) raises questions about yet another characterization of preschool thought, which is that preschoolers have serious difficulty relating states (in Piaget's terms, figurative knowledge) and transformations (operative knowledge). The experiment was based on Premack's (1976) finding that chimpanzees are able to select the appropriate instrument (e.g., a scissors) to relate two different states of an object (e.g., a whole apple and a cut apple). In the Gelman et al. study, 3- and 4-year-olds were asked to select one of three choice-cards to fill in the missing element in three-item picture sequences. Test sequences had either the first, second, or third position empty. Each completed sequence consisted of an object (e.g., a cup), an instrument (e.g., a hammer), and the same object transformed by the application of the instrument (e.g., a broken cup). Half the sequences depicted familiar events (e.g., cutting a piece of fruit), half depicted unusual events (e.g., sewing the two halves of a banana together or drawing on a piece of fruit). Performance in both age groups was nearly perfect, indicating that the children could reason about the relationship between object states before and after the application of various instruments.

In a second experiment, Gelman et al. (1980) showed 3- and 4-year-olds picture sequences in which the deleted item was always the instrument. The children's task was to relate the two object states first from one direction (e.g., whole apple, cut apple) and then from the opposite direction (e.g., cut apple, whole apple). As in the first experiment, performance in both age groups was very good, indicating that children could represent reciprocal transformations. Gelman and her colleagues concluded that although preschoolers may not *always* be able to represent the same object states with reference to reciprocal transformations (e.g., pretransformation and posttransformation displays in a clay-conservation task), there are clearly cases where they can do so.

In this section, we have reviewed a number of studies that indicate preschool children are not fundamentally egocentric, centered, or perception bound. The general implication of these studies is that the mentality of the preschool child is qualitatively more similar to that of the older child than Piagetian theory leads one to suspect. This is not to deny, obviously, the cognitive limitations of the young child. After all, preschool children do fail standard conservation, classification, and seriation tasks. As we will see in the next section, however, it is no longer clear what such failures signify because more and more investigators discover that startlingly modest amounts of training are sufficient to make conservers out of nonconservers, seriators out of nonseriators, and so on.

Inducing Success on Concrete-Operational Tasks

According to Piagetian theory, learning involves the assimilation of novel information to a previously existing structure, with concomitant changes in the structure as it accommodates to the incoming information. Hence, if there is no cognitive structure relevant to an input, there can be no assimilation and likewise no accommodation—in other words, no learning. One implication of this view is that children who possess part of a structural capacity (e.g., transitional conservers) are more likely to benefit from training than are children who possess none (e.g., nonconservers) (Inhelder, Sinclair, & Bovet, 1974).

We would like to turn the Piagetian argument on its head. That is, we would like to argue the following: to the extent that preschoolers can be shown to benefit from training on some concrete-operational task, then to the same extent they can be assumed to possess (at least part of the) structural capacities relevant to this task. If it is true that the mental structures of preschoolers are more like those of older children than was traditionally assumed (as we concluded at the end of the previous section), it should be possible to design simple training conditions that induce success on concrete-operational tasks—and thus reveal hitherto concealed competencies. As we will see later, that is indeed possible.

It used to be commonplace to claim that training had no effect on concrete-operational abilities (see Flavell, 1963, for a review of the early training literature). In recent review sources, however, just the opposite conclusion is reached (e.g., Beilin, 1971, 1977; Brainerd & Allen, 1971; Modgil & Modgil, 1976; Murray, 1978). Since these review sources are available, we focus on a select number of studies.

Gelman (1969) worked with 5-year-olds who failed on pretests to conserve number, length, liquid amount, and clay amount. Children in the experimental group received a learning-set training on length and number tasks that was designed to focus attention on quantity-relevant relations and away from quantity-irrelevant relations. In all, the experi-

mental children received 32 problem sets with 6 trials in each set; half the problems involved length, half number. On each trial the children were asked which two of three rows of chips (or sticks) had the same (different) number (or length); feedback was then provided. On Trial 1 of each set, the arrays were arranged to elicit a correct answer, even if the child was attending to irrelevant properties of the display. This was done by arranging the displays so that the relevant and irrelevant cues were redundant. Thus, for example, two rows containing the same number of equally spaced chips were aligned one above the other. A third row containing a different number of chips was placed so that its ends were not aligned with the ends of the other rows. On Trials 2 to 5 of the problem set, the children watched as the experimenter transformed one or two displays so that the number-relevant (length-relevant) cues were now in conflict with the number-irrelevant (length-irrelevant) cues. Then, if children responded on the basis of number-irrelevant cues, they made an error. On Trial 6, irrelevant cues were not present at all, allowing Gelman to determine whether the children could accurately respond to length and number.

Because Gelman created a conflict between perceptual and quantitative cues within each problem set, she thought she was providing children with attention training (Harlow, 1959; Trabasso & Bower, 1968). As we will see, there are other interpretations. But whatever the interpretation, the training worked. During learning-set training, nonconserving children quickly reached plateau; when asked to choose two arrays that contained the same (different) number (length), they responded on the basis of quantity. Further, they transferred what they learned on posttest conservation tasks. Performance on length- and number-conservation tasks were near ceiling and children were able to justify their choices. The majority of liquid- and clay-conservation trials also yielded correct choices and explanations. Finally, the effects of training were maintained over a period of 2 to 3 weeks.

The Gelman (1969) training experiment is typically classified as one in the learning theory tradition (e.g., Beilin, 1971, 1977; Modgil & Modgil, 1976). It is no longer obvious to Gelman (Gelman & Gallistel, 1978) that this characterization holds. Recall that within each problem set, Gelman created a conflict between perceptual and quantitative cues. Feedback probably guaranteed that the child noticed the conflict. Perhaps the study accomplished what Piagetian theory requires for training to be effective—that the child encounter a conflict between schemes. Beilin (1977) makes a similar suggestion about the learning-set procedure. But note that for this interpretation to hold, it is necessary to assume that the subject had begun to develop some quantity schemes. Otherwise, there could have been no conflict for the subject.

Piagetian training studies focus on highlighting contradictions or conflicts. And the evidence is good that this training can be effective, especially with children who show some initial evidence of having moved from preoperational to operational thought (Inhelder, Sinclair, & Bovet, 1974). However, it is not clear that such training is either sufficient or necessary. In a thorough review of the vast array of conflict-training procedures, Beilin (1977) pointed out that some conflict-training procedures work (e.g., Lafèbvre & Pinard, 1974; Smedslund, 1961a, 1961b; Winer, 1968) and others do not (e.g., Beilin, 1965; I. D. Smith, 1968; Wohlwill & Lowe, 1962). Further, a variety of training procedures that do not induce conflicts also work. Reversibility-training studies are a clear case in point.

The Wallach and Sprott (1964) study was probably the first successful reversibility-training study. It involved a series of problems, each using two displays, one of N dolls and one of N beds. The number of items per array varied from problem to problem. Within each problem, children were first shown that each doll fit in a bed; then the dolls were removed from the bed and either the row of beds or the row of dolls was spaced further apart or closer together. Children who said there were no longer as many beds as dolls were shown that each doll did have a bed. The idea was that the children would learn reversibility and, thus, be able to predict that the dolls would always fit back in beds. Roll (1970) followed up on the Wallach and Sprott (1964) study and included transfer tasks to see if the learning was resistant to the Smedslund (1961b) extinction method. There still was considerable transfer.

A variety of investigators have studied the effect of having a nonconserver watch models who do conserve (e.g., Murray, 1972, 1981; Silverman & Geiringer, 1973; Silverman & Stone, 1972). In general, the opportunity to interact with, or simply watch, conservers and nonconservers was found to help induce conservation. Botvin and Murray (1975) assigned black first-graders who failed to conserve mass, weight, amount, and number to one of two kinds of modeling conditions. In one condition, two nonconservers and three conservers participated in a discussion. The discussion began with the experimenter's request that each child participate in the mass-conservation and weight-conservation tasks. The children were then left on their own to discuss

their different answers and reach an agreement. A second group of nonconservers watched while the experimenter tested another group of children. These children did not participate in a subsequent discussion. Both groups showed a dramatic amount of specific transfer (to weight and mass tasks) as well as general transfer (to number and length tasks). Comparison of the explanations given by the original conservers and the trained conservers ruled out the possibility that the trained conservers were simply mimicking what they had heard. The original conservers were more inclined to give compensation and reversibility accounts in justifying their judgments; the trained conservers were more inclined to point out that nothing had been added or subtracted or that the transformations were irrelevant. The latter kinds of explanations were also prevalent in Markman's (1979) collection condition, and her subjects were even younger.

Are results like Botvin and Murray's (1975) consistent with the Piagetian hypothesis that conflict conditions caused development? Those children who participated in the discussion condition probably did enter a state of conflict and because they eventually reached agreement with the conservers, they could be said to have also resolved the conflict. However, we find it more difficult to maintain this position for the children who simply watched the testing of conservers and nonconservers. Even if we allow that some "inner" conflict occurred and was resolved, a problem remains. How could the opportunity simply to watch a conserver be effective so quickly unless the child already had some understanding of quantitative invariance?

Like us, Gold (1978) maintains that it is appropriate to conclude that a child has an understanding of quantity if very little pretest experience leads her to focus on quantity: "If this occurs, it seems likely that the successful 'training' was due simply to the reinterpretation by the subject of the experimenter's question, and not to the acquisition of a conservation concept as such" (p. 407). A similar argument is made by Donaldson (1978) and McGarrigle and Donaldson (1974) who show that 4- to 6-year-olds are much more likely to conserve if the transformations are made accidentally by a "naughty" teddy bear.

A simple training study by Gold (1978) yielded results consistent with his position. Subjects (around 5½ years of age)[2] were given eight pretest trials. The pretest displays resembled posttransformation displays in the standard equivalence and nonequivalence conservation tasks, that is, the two rows were different or the same length respectively. During the pretests, the child was told to count the items in each row and then was asked whether the two rows had the same cardinal values or not (where the numbers in each row were different). A control group of children was shown the same pretest displays and was simply asked whether the rows had the same number or not. That is, they were not asked to determine the specific values in each display before being asked the standard posttransformation conservation questions. The transfer tests yielded remarkable results. Of the 29 children in the experimental group, 22 and 20 respectively, conserved on the two standard number-conservation tasks. What is more, when retested 6 weeks later, 22, 20, and 19 children conserved on the number, beads, and liquid tasks respectively. And 14 weeks later, conservation scores were slightly better on all three tasks! In contrast, none of the control group ($N = 29$) conserved on any task at any time.

Gelman (1982) gave 3- and 4-year-olds a brief pretest experience much like the one Gold (1978) used. Children were asked to count one of two displays; indicate its cardinal value; count the other display; indicate its cardinal value; and then decide whether the number in each row was the same. In the pretest phases, children worked with set sizes of 3 and 4. The standard conservation tasks involved set sizes of 5 (and 4 on conservation of difference trials) and 10 (or 8). To Gelman's surprise, the pretest experience transferred to *both* the small and the large set trials. In addition, children gave the same sort of explanations observed by Markman (1979).

The vast majority of training studies have focused on the conservations. But there have also been successful training studies of children's ability to draw transitive (or related) inferences.

Bryant and Trabasso (1971) suggested that young children's difficulty with transitive inferences was more a problem of memory than logical inference. Accordingly, they gave their subjects memory training. They showed their subjects pairs of sticks from a set of five sticks (A, B, C, D, E) that differed in length and color. Using a discrimination learning procedure, they taught children which of a pair of sticks was the longer (or shorter) stick. To start, children were taught the AB pair, then the BC, CD, and DE pairs. Subsequently, they were shown a random selection of pairs of sticks (other than the BD pair) and were again required to learn which of the two was the longer (or shorter) stick. Children were never shown the actual lengths of the sticks during training; the bottoms of each pair of sticks were hidden in a box and their tops protruded to the same height. Thus, they had to learn to code the

relative heights that corresponded to the different colors. Following training, children were tested without feedback on all 10 possible pairs of sticks. As before, only the tops of the sticks were visible so that children had to rely on the color of the sticks to decide which was longer or shorter. The crucial test involved the BD pair and the adjacent BC and DC pairs. Recall that children were not trained on the BD comparison. Furthermore, during training, the B, C, and D sticks were as often the longer as the shorter stick in an array. The correct responses on the BD comparison ranged from 78% to 92% (well above chance). As predicted, success on the critical test pair was highly correlated with a child's ability to remember the relative values of the elements in the BD and CD pairs.

De Boysson-Bardies and O'Regan (1973) tried to account for the Bryant and Trabasso (1971) results without granting the children transitive inference abilities. We think their alternative interpretation presumes that young children go out of their way to make their task difficult for themselves. Consider the three assumptions made by de Boysson-Bardies and O'Regan. First, they assume the children only learn the pairs of stimuli AB, BC, CD, and DE. They also associate *long* with A, *short* with B; *long* with B, *short* with C; and so on. Second, children treat sticks that are labeled both *long* and *short* as nonentities. The effect of this step is to eliminate labels for all sticks but A, which remains *long,* and E, which remains *short*. Finally, children learn to associate *long* with the stick that is paired with A and *short* with the stick that is paired with E. Thus, they assign B (of the AB pair) a *long* label and D (of the DE pair) a *short* label. Having done all this, they can pass the critical transfer trials on the basis of a paired-associate learning strategy as opposed to a transitive-inference one. Harris and Bassett (1975) found no evidence to support this alternative account.

The de Boysson-Bardies and O'Regan (1973) account was motivated by the claim that the Bryant and Trabasso (1971) subjects did not use the operation of transitivity. Without accepting their paired-associate hypothesis, it is possible to make this point in another way, as Trabasso (1975) showed. Trabasso tested the hypothesis that children construct ordered linear images of stimuli and then "read" their answers off these images. This, indeed, seems to be what children do; but then adults do likewise. Both children and adults have been found to construct ordered linear representations when confronted with a wide variety of materials that represent differences in height, weight, happiness, and even niceness

(Riley, 1976). Even if one does not want to claim that Bryant and Trabasso's (1971) subjects used the operation of transitivity, there is no getting around the fact that they were able to construct an ordered set of mental objects. On the Piagetian assumption that performance reflects available structures, it must be that children had available at least an ordering relation (see Gelman, 1978, for further evidence).

Some may object that the Bryant and Trabasso (1971) study provided extensive training and feedback. With so many feedback trials, perhaps the concept of transitivity was trained in and not simply uncovered. Findings from a study by Timmons and Smothergill (1975) argue against such a possibility. These authors worked with kindergarten children who did poorly on tasks requiring them to seriate six values of brightness or length. The children were given same/different judgment trials on either or both dimensions without feedback. This training was sufficient to facilitate seriation performance. Because Timmons and Smothergill did not run a transitive-inference task during posttesting, one might still object that the seriation performance was not based on an operatory scheme. We submit this is unlikely given Brainerd's (1978a) and Bryant and Kopytynska's (1976) demonstrations of the early use of transitive inference (see Brainerd, 1978a for a review). Hooper, Toniolo, and Sipple (1978) also reported kindergarten children receiving scores of 3.65 and 4.46 out of 5 on length and weight transitivity tasks.

As for conservation and transitivity, it is now clear that preschoolers benefit from training designed to alter their typical classification solutions. Nash and Gelman (cited in Gelman & Gallistel, 1978) gave 3- to 5-year-old children experience at sorting a set of eight wooden blocks that varied in size, shape, and color. To start, the children were told to "put the blocks together that go together." If necessary the experimenter showed the child a way of doing the task or even asked the child to copy her sort. Sorting experience continued until the child had successfully sorted the blocks in two ways. On a subsequent day, the child was asked to place 25 toys into one of five clear plastic boxes. The toys represented five categories (fruits, vehicles, kitchen furniture, flowers, and animals) and were withdrawn one at a time from a bag. The block-sorting experience helped children sort consistently by taxonomic category, as did the opportunity for children to sort the toys until they achieved a stable sort on two successive trials. Of the 3-, 4-, and 5-year-olds who

had block-sorting and toy-sorting experience, 66%, 83%, and 89% respectively, used taxonomic categories.

As in the case of conservation and transitivity training, classification training need not be extensive consistently. Smiley and Brown (1979) showed that preschoolers prefer to sort materials according to thematic as opposed to taxonomic relations. Nevertheless, they can and do use both kinds of relations. Further, they can be trained to use taxonomic relations consistently. Smiley and Brown's training involved showing children triads that represented both a taxonomic and a thematic relation. In each triad, an experimenter demonstrated and explained the taxonomic response (or thematic response in the control group). The opportunity to observe the experimenter use taxonomic criteria influenced the children's choices—these were then predominantly taxonomic. Markman, Cox, and Machida (1981) reported a shift from graphic sorts to consistent taxonomic sorts in 3- and 4-year-olds when asked to sort objects in plastic bags rather than on a table. Apparently, the latter condition encourages the use of spatial and configurational relations.

Odom, Astor, and Cunningham (1975) gave 4- to 6-year-old children repeated trials on a matrix classification task and found a significant decrease in errors over trials: "This strongly suggests that repeated presentations may be required to obtain a valid assessment of a young child's cognitive ability to classify multiplicatively" (p. 762). It likewise raises the possibility that the ability to classify taxonomically is underestimated in standard procedures where children are assessed on the basis of one or two sorting trials. As Worden (1976) points out, most classification studies with adults have them classify repeatedly until a stable sort is achieved. The failure to do the same with children may elicit immature preferences but these need not preclude the ability to assign correctly the extension of a given class.

The training literature on class inclusion yields results that are in line with what by this point is a consistent theme; it is possible to "train" a child on many concepts with limited training experience. Siegel, McCabe, Brand, and Matthews (1977) provided 3- and 4-year-olds with but six trials, with feedback to their answers to such questions as "How many red buttons are there?" "How many white buttons?" "How many buttons?" "Are the red ones buttons?" Both age groups benefited from training, although the 4-year-olds' gains were greater on a posttest. Judd and Mervis (1979) drew 5-

year-olds' attention to the fact that the results of counting the members of the superordinate and subordinate classes conflicted with their erroneous answer to the class-inclusion question. The experimental group received such training on but three problems. Yet 23 of the 30 children in this group were perfect on posttests.

Overall, the training literature supports the view that preschoolers are more competent than their failure on standard concrete operational tasks implies. Some authors go further and take these results to suggest that the differences in the cognitive structures of preschoolers and older children are minimal—if there are any at all. We believe that such a conclusion is premature. Preschoolers do fail the standard Piagetian tasks; they do in many cases need tailored pretest experience or training to reveal some competency and, even then, they often show limited transfer. Before we accept an hypothesis of no qualitative differences, it is necessary to take a close look at the abilities as well as the inabilities preschoolers show. Although we admittedly must grant more capacity to the preschooler, his or her capacities could still be limited compared to those of the older child. In the following sections, we focus on the development of quantity and classification concepts. We chose these Piagetian concepts because enough research has been done to permit a careful analysis of how cognitive development in these domains might proceed. In addition, the research is far enough along for us to start to address some of the general issues raised by Piaget about the nature of cognitive development.

A CLOSER LOOK AT THE DEVELOPMENT OF SOME CONCRETE-OPERATIONAL CONCEPTS

Conservations During Middle Childhood

Of all the Piagetian tasks, the conservation ones are those that have received the most attention. Hundreds and hundreds of studies have considered whether a nonconserver can be trained to conserve and, if so, under what conditions. A countless number of studies have investigated the effects of socioeconomic status (e.g., Gaudia, 1972; Hanley & Hooper, 1973); schooling (e.g., Price-Williams, Gordon, & Ramirez, 1969); IQ (e.g., Field, 1977; Inhelder, 1968; linguistic prowess (e.g., Siegel, 1977); and variations in the conservation tasks (Bryant, 1974; Mehler & Bever, 1967) on the emergence of conservation. Despite the abundance of research activity, there is one issue that has received very little attention outside of Geneva: that is,

the relationship between the conservation of discrete and continuous quantities. This is a central question in much of the recent Genevan work on conservation (e.g., Inhelder et al., 1974; Inhelder, Blanchet, Sinclair, & Piaget, 1975):

> Some subjects had great difficulty in applying a reasoning which had proved adequate for problems dealing with discrete elements to other situations where quasi-continuous materials were used. This would suggest that the developmental link between the conservation of discrete and continuous quantities is neither simple nor direct. (Inhelder et al., 1974, p. 80)

We agree, although, as will become clear at the end of this section, for somewhat different reasons.

We question whether the understandings of discrete and continuous quantities are all that similar. In the case of discrete quantities, there is a way to obtain a specific representation of the quantities represented—that is, to count. It is also possible to use a rule of one-to-one correspondence to determine whether an equivalent number of items is present in two displays. No such quantification processes are available for continuous quantities. Siegler (1981) provides evidence that these differences at least matter to adults. He showed adults the posttransformation displays of the number-, liquid-, and mass-conservation problems he planned to use with children and asked them to judge whether the displays were equal or not (half were and half were not). The adults were always correct on the number problems, and they often counted. In contrast, they were correct on only 60% and 61% of the mass and liquid problems—presumably because they had no verification procedures.

Further, as noted by Schwartz (1976), the conditions of application of arithmetic operations differ, depending on whether discrete or continuous quantities are involved. Consider: "Two peaches and two peaches make four peaches" versus "A cup of water at $10°$ C added to a cup of water at $10°$ C make a glass of water at $20°$ C." The former is correct; the latter is not. Or consider: "Two peaches and three pears make five pieces of fruit" versus "100 cc of alcohol and 90 cc of water make 190 cc of liquid." At a more basic level, the natural numbers can be used by themselves as adjectives with count nouns (e.g., one boy, six apples), but not with mass nouns (e.g., one water). The use of count words with continuous quantities depends on the selection of some attribute over which to quantify (e.g., volume or density) and the correct choice of unit. Thus, it is acceptable to talk of one gallon or one glass of water, but not one water. These are but a few of the issues raised by Schwartz when comparing knowledge about discrete and continuous quantities. All such considerations lead to the view that the development of the understanding of discrete and continuous quantities could differ. Siegler's (1981) reexamination of the conservations of liquid, mass, and number points in this direction.

Siegler (1981) tested children ranging in age from 3 to 9 years on 24 number, liquid, and mass-conservation problems. Within each set of 24 problems, the trials were designed to obtain meaningful patterns of yes/no answers to the question of whether the posttransformation displays were equivalent or not. They were not always equivalent because Siegler used addition and subtraction transformations as well as the standard displacement ones. On the basis of his own previous work as well as that of others—especially Piaget's (1952a)—Siegler predicted that the children's judgments would be consistent with one of four different rules, with development involving a move from Rule I → Rule II → Rule III → Rule IV. The assignment of a rule to a given child was to be done on the basis of the pattern of his responses to the posttest transformations. Children who consistently judged on the basis of one dominant dimension (e.g., length on number problems and height on liquid problems) were to be classified as Rule I users. Children who also considered the subordinate dimension (e.g., density on number problems and width on liquid problems) when the values of the dominant dimension were equal were to be classified as Rule II users. Rule III children would be those who always considered both dimensions but could not resolve conflicts and, therefore, performed at chance on such trials. Children who responded to all trials on the basis of transformation type were to be assigned Rule IV.

As it turned out, judgments on the conservation of liquid and mass tasks could be characterized with but two rules, I and IV. That is, there was no evidence of transition rules; the tendency to use Rule I declined with age and the tendency to use Rule IV increased with age. In both cases, the trend to use Rule IV was not complete by 9 years of age.

The developmental sequence on the number-conservation tasks was decidedly different from that observed for the two continuous-quantity tasks. If children were observed using Rule I, they were the younger children. But even the 4- to 6-year-olds were more likely to use one of two advanced rules,

either the expected Rule IV or a combination of Rules I and IV, which Siegler identifies as Rule IIIa. According to Siegler, Rule IIIa reflects a tendency to sometimes use Rule I and sometimes Rule IV. If anything was added to a row, it was judged to have more regardless of whether the rows became equal because of the addition or whether the rows differed in length. A similar strategy was invoked when subtraction occurred. When there was neither addition nor subtraction, children used Rule I.

Almost all 7-, 8-, and 9-year-olds used Rule IV on number trials. Parenthetically, the failure to identify any Rule II children suggests that the relative density of items in the displays had little salience (Baron, Lawson, & Siegel, 1974; Gelman, 1972b; Smither, Smiley, & Rees, 1974). Returning to the Siegler (1981) results for number conservation, the transitional children, that is, those who used a combination of Rule I and Rule IV, were better able to deal correctly with addition and subtraction than other transformations. No differential effect of transformation type occurred with the two continuous-quantity conservations.

As one might expect, number-conservation ability was advanced compared to the other conservation abilities. Children's performance in the two continuous tasks were remarkably alike, which gives more evidence for the hypothesis of a common structure for the liquid and mass tasks (Tuddenham, 1971).

Siegler (1981) provides a plausible account for the differences in strategies used across conservation tasks. On number-conservation tasks, a child can use up to three strategies correctly, that is, one based on counting, another based on one-to-one correspondence, and another based on the analysis of the transformations performed. In the liquid and mass tasks, only the latter is available. Thus, Siegler concludes that liquid and mass tasks may be harder than number conservation. Our objection to this account is simply that it does not go far enough. Presumably, the use of a given strategy reflects some underlying concept. Otherwise, why that particular strategy as opposed to some other strategy? What does the young child know about number that leads him or her to shift from one strategy to another as the need arises? Moreover, there is more to the understanding of continuous quantity than an appreciation of the roles of relevant and irrelevant transformations (Schwartz, 1976). In an effort to achieve some insight on the matter, we will go over what is known about the development of notions of discrete quantity. We will then return to considering concepts of continuous quantity.

Number Concepts

Abstraction Versus Reasoning

Gelman (1972a) distinguished between two kinds of numerical abilities: (1) the abilities we use to abstract the specific or relative numerosity of one or more displays—Gelman and Gallistel (1978) call these our *number-abstraction abilities;* and (2) the abilities we use to reason about number—Gelman and Gallistel call these our *number-reasoning abilities*. These abilities, which derive from arithmetic *reasoning principles,* allow us to reach inferences about the effects of transformations, the relations that hold between sets, and the effects of a combination of operations. Thus, we know not only that addition increases and decreases set size but also that the effect of addition can be canceled by subtraction. One reason for making this distinction is to highlight the possibility that number-abstraction and number-reasoning abilities could interact—especially in young children. In particular, Gelman and Gallistel thought that a preschooler might be able to reason only about those set sizes for which he can achieve a specific numerical representation. When the task requires reasoning about nonspecified values, as is the case in many conservation tasks, the child might fail to reveal reasoning abilities. Such considerations led Gelman and her collaborators to investigate the processes by which preschoolers represent the number of items in a display and the effects set size has on their numerical reasoning abilities.

Counting in Preschoolers?

There are two primary candidate processes by which a preschooler could represent number. These are counting and perceptual apprehension. In the latter case, the argument is that young children might be able to recognize twoness and threeness by virtue of a pattern-detection process. If so, one could argue, as Piaget (1952a) has, that the young child has little, if any, understanding of number. First, the recognition of patterns could be directly associated with labels, just as is the recognition of a three-dimensional object. The child need not know that a display of 3 items contains more than a display of 2 items and less than a display of 4 items. Second, on the assumption that the range of set sizes that could be apprehended is related to the span of apprehension, the ability to represent ''number'' should be limited to small set sizes. Since this is, indeed, the case (see Gelman & Gallistel, 1978, for a review), the argument could be made that the young child has little, if any, numerical ability.

The idea that the preschooler perceives differences in numerosity without some concomitant understanding of number is discredited by a converging set of research findings however. First, although it is true that the young child's ability to judge accurately how many items there are in a display drops off rapidly around set sizes of 4 or 5, she still knows that a set size of 7 items contains more items than does a set size of 5 items; likewise, that a set size of 11 items is greater in numerosity than one with 7 items. As Gelman and Gallistel (1978) report, 3-year-olds in the Gelman and Tucker (1975) experiment tended to represent larger and larger set sizes with number words that come later in the counting sequence, even though they encountered the variations in set size in a random order. Thus, the 3-year-olds tended to use the number words two, three, four, five, six, ten, and eleven to represent set sizes of 2, 3, 4, 5, 7, 11, and 19 respectively. Older children were more accurate, although they too made errors in assigning numerical values. Such results hardly fit with the characterization of numerical ability that follows from an apprehension-only hypothesis. To the contrary, they suggest that young children know something about counting. How else can one account for the tendency to use number words of higher ordinal values for the larger set sizes? But to grant preschoolers some understanding of counting is to go against a common notion—that early counting is but rote counting, but the simple reeling off of words in a list without any appreciation of the fact that these words have numerical meaning. When researchers began to consider the possibility that very young children's counting involves something more than reeling off number words (e.g., Fuson & Richards, 1979; Gelman & Gallistel, 1978; Schaeffer, Eggelston, & Scott, 1974; Shotwell, 1979), they soon found that this was the case. Young children do have an implicit understanding of counting and its use in quantification.

What is involved in the understanding and use of counting? According to Gelman and Gallistel (1978), successful counting reflects the coordinated application of five principles: (1) the one-to-one correspondence principle—all items in an array must be tagged with unique tags; (2) the stable-order principle—the tags used to correspond to items in an array must be arranged and chosen in a stable order; (3) the cardinal principle—the final tag used in tagging the items in an array represents the cardinal value of the array; (4) the abstraction principle—the first three principles (i.e., the how-to-count principles) can be applied to any collection of discrete items; it matters not what the items are, whether they are homogeneous or heterogeneous, real or imagined, actual objects or only spaces between objects, and so on; and (5) the order-irrelevance principle—the order in which items are enumerated is irrelevant; it matters not whether a given object is tagged as one (1), two (2), three (3), and so on, as long as the how-to-count principles are honored.

There are three reasons for maintaining that preschoolers have some understanding of the counting principles. The first is that counting behaviors in young children are systematic. Perhaps the most compelling evidence for the claim of systematicity is the use of what Fuson and Richards (1979) call nonstandard lists and what Gelman and Gallistel (1978) call idiosyncratic lists. These appear in very young children (i.e., 2½-year-olds), when they count even small set sizes, and in somewhat older children when they count larger set sizes. Although the lists are nonstandard, they are nevertheless used systematically. Thus, for example, a 2½-year-old child might say "2, 6" when counting a 2-item array and "2, 6, 10" when counting a 3-item array (the one-one principle). The same child will use her own list over and over again (the stable-order principle) and, when asked how many items are present, will repeat the last tag in her list (the cardinal principle). The fact that young children settle on their own lists suggests that the counting principles are guiding the search for appropriate tags. Such errors in counting are like the errors made by young language learners (e.g., I runned). In the latter case, such errors are taken as evidence that the child's use of language is rule governed and that these rules come from the child herself. We rarely hear adult speakers of English (outside of psycholinguistic classes) say runned, footses, mouses, unthirsty, and so on. Gelman and Gallistel (1978) use a similar logic to account for the presence of idiosyncratic lists.

A second reason for believing that some basic principles of understanding serve to guide the young child's acquisition of skill at counting is that young children spontaneously self-correct their count errors and often are inclined to count without any request to do so. Indeed, they will apply the counting procedure to a variety of item types, be they toys, steps, pieces of candy, or what have you. Presumably, these self-generated practice trials make it possible for the child to develop skill at applying the principles. A third reason for crediting preschoolers with counting knowledge is that they can invent counting algorithms.

Groen and Resnick (1977) taught 4½-year-olds to use a counting algorithm to solve simple addition problems. The algorithm consisted of first counting two separate groups of objects, then combining the

groups of objects into one collection, and then counting the number of objects in that group. Across sessions, half of the children spontaneously began to employ a more efficient algorithm than they had been taught. This was to count on from the cardinal value of the greater of the to-be-added numbers. Gelman (1977) also reports that 3- and 4-year-olds count spontaneously when confronted with unexpected changes in the set size of a given array. It is hard to maintain that the counting behavior of young children reflects nothing but rote learning. How, then to explain its spontaneous use to solve simple arithmetic problems? In this regard, it is of interest that Ginsburg and his colleagues (e.g., Ginsburg, 1982) report a similar use of counting algorithms in unschooled cultures.

An Interaction Between Number Abstractors and Reasoning Principles

The strong version of the interaction hypothesis is that young children will not be able to reason arithmetically unless they reason about numerosities they can represent accurately. Working from this assumption, Gelman (1972b) focused on whether preschool children could apply a number-invariance scheme when asked to consider small set sizes (2 to 5 at most) but not larger sets. The paradigm used in these studies was developed to control for many of the possible confounding variables in the standard conservation paradigm, for example, the child's failure to understand the use of "more," and "less," the child's tendency to be distracted by changes in irrelevant variables, and so on (see Gelman, 1972a). The paradigm involved children in a two-phase procedure. During Phase I, children learned to identify one of two rows of items as the winner, and the other as the loser. Identification could be based on either a difference in the number of items or a redundant perceptual cue, that is, length or density. The identification phase involved covering and shuffling the two displays and then asking the child to guess which of the two covered displays (which were side by side) was the winner. Children's answers to probe questions revealed that they established an expectancy for two displays of specific numerical values during this phase. Phase II began unbeknownst to the children. Depending on the experiment and condition children were in, the experimenter made a surreptitious change in either one or both of the displays. Changes could be number irrelevant (e.g., lengthening or shortening the display, changing the color of an item, substituting a new object for a familiar one). They could also be number relevant (e.g., adding or subtracting one or more items).

Gelman (1977) found that when set sizes were small and when addition/subtraction involved but one item, even 2½- and 3-year-olds responded correctly when they encountered the unexpected changes in the array. Changes that were produced by number-irrelevant transformations were recognized as such. Changes that were produced by number-relevant transformations were likewise recognized as such. The children often intimated, in their own way, that there had to have been surreptitious addition or subtraction to produce the observed number change. One child claimed "one flew out." Another said "Jesus took it." When asked, they also said that the effects of addition (or subtraction) could be undone by subtraction (or addition). In the conditions where children encountered unexpected changes in the length of a display, color of items, or type of items, the children would say these were irrelevant because the numbers were the same as expected.

On the basis of these findings with the magic paradigm, Gelman and Gallistel (1978) maintain that preschool children do know that addition and subtraction are number relevant *and* that displacement and substitution are number irrelevant. This knowledge is, in turn, related to the ability to decide whether two arrays represent equivalent or nonequivalent numerical values and, if not, which is the greater (see Gelman & Gallistel, 1978, chap. 10, for details). Note that this statement applies for the magic paradigm where displays are placed side by side and where children achieve specific representations of number. Children's reactions during Phase II tell us that they know the conditions under which a specific numerosity is preserved and the conditions under which it is not. Such results do *not* tell us whether children know when an equivalence or nonequivalence relation between two sets is conserved.

It was the latter consideration that led Gelman and Gallistel (1978) to accept Piaget's (1952a) view that the number-conservation task requires the use of a principle of one-to-one correspondence. They further maintained that preschoolers could not use this principle because they could not reason about nonspecified numerical values: hence, their failure on the traditional conservation task. Our review of the training literature (see *Is Preoperational Thought Really Preoperational?*) makes clear that this hypothesis regarding number-abstraction abilities and the use of arithmetic-reasoning principles make too strong a claim.

The Gelman (1982) conservation-training experiment was designed as a test of the Gelman and Gallistel (1978) hypothesis. The idea was to encourage young children to recognize that the specific

cardinal value of the two displays placed one above the other was either the same or different. It was hypothesized that children would then be able to conserve on small set sizes (4, 5) but not larger set sizes (8, 10). As it turned out, 3- and 4-year-olds conserved on all set sizes *and* gave explanations for their judgments. Because most children this age cannot count accurately set sizes greater than 4 or 5, the only way they could have conserved equivalence judgments for larger arrays was on the basis of one-to-one correspondence. And such explanations were offered, particularly by the 3-year-olds.

Gelman and Gallistel's account of conservation resembles somewhat Piaget's (1975a, 1977) more recent treatment of number. Piaget's (1952a) early treatment focused on the role of transformations. In his later writings, Piaget turned his attention to the conditions that a child must recognize before he or she can deal with transformations. He maintained the child first discovers the correspondences between two states to make comparisons. At this early stage, the child can determine correspondences but is unable to apply the rules of transformations. Next in development he can use transformations but only after he establishes correspondences. Finally, the child understands the system of transformations as it generally applies to quantity. We suggest that Gelman and Gallistel's distinction between number abstraction and reasoning principles parallels Piaget's distinction between correspondence and transformation.

By Piaget's (1975a) account, it should be possible to observe "precocious conservation" if a child can be brought to recognize that one-to-one correspondence indicates a corresponding number of items. Indeed, Inhelder et al. (1975) succeeded in producing precocious number conservation. Their experiments involved showing 4- and 5-year-olds displays in one-to-one correspondence and then a series of item-removal and replacement transformations. For example, one item in an array was removed and the child was asked if the number of items in both rows was the same; then that item was put back into the array but at a different position and again the child was asked about equivalence. The idea in these experiments was to highlight the "commutability" of items in a discrete set, that is, that the act of adding an item at one point (in space) is undone by taking out an item from another point in space. Note that tasks like these involve permuting the positions of items within the set. In contrast, the standard conservation task involves displacing items. According to Inhelder et al. (1975), "when one simply displaces the objects, the child only attends to their point of arrival and does not concern himself with the fact that they have been removed from an initial position to be added elsewhere'' (p. 26).

Piaget (1977) takes the fact that experience with the ''commutability'' of items transferred to the standard task as evidence for the view that it is the understanding of commutability that underlies true conservation. We are not sure. First, Gelman (1982) did show children length changes. Second, no such training was required in Markman's (1979) study, indeed, no training at all was required. In addition, a closer consideration of the Inhelder et al. (1975) experiments makes clear that their children were also counting and representing cardinal values. Gelman (1982) argues that these three sets of results together show that there are some special conditions that make accessible the principle of one-to-one correspondence. The younger the child, the more likely the tendency to restrict arithmetic reasoning to conditions where the child can achieve specific representations of number. Nevertheless, there is some ability to work with nonspecified values—an ability that will eventually dominate the initial tendency to restrict arithmetic reasoning to conditions where the child can achieve specific representations of number. We suspect this is related to the fact that the young child's skill at counting and knowledge about counting go through a considerable amount of development.

Some Implicit Knowledge Does Not Imply Full or Explicit Knowledge

Counting. Although Gelman and Gallistel (1978) claim that even 2½-year-olds can obey the how-to-count principles, they do not mean that children this age have explicit knowledge of the principles. Nor do they mean that little or no development occurs past this age—indeed, quite the contrary. Gelman and Gallistel point out that first there are limits on how many items a child can count, how long a tag list she can remember, how well she coordinates the many component processes involved in the counting procedure, and even how well she tags unorderly arrays (Potter & Levy, 1968; Schaeffer et al., 1974; Shannon, 1978). But with practice come skill and speed and greater efficiency (cf. Case & Serlin, 1979). The period over which this skill accrues is protracted at least into kindergarten (Fuson & Richards, 1979).

Gelman and Gallistel (1978) found that the number of items in a set interacts with the tendency to apply the cardinal principle. As set size increases, the tendency to use the last tag to index the cardinal value of the set drops off. Some have suggested that

this means the child does not yet have the cardinal principle as part of her counting scheme. Gelman and Gallistel maintain they do, but once again its application is at first variable. What evidence is there that the cardinal principle is available, even if it is applied sporadically? If Gelman and Gallistel are correct that the variable use of the cardinal principle in a young child derives from the performance demands of applying the counting principles, there should be conditions that elicit its consistent use. And when attention is drawn to the role of counting in quantification, the likelihood of its use should increase.

If 3- and 4-year-olds did not have the cardinal principle available, Markman (1979) should not have been able to show an increase in its use under a change in question conditions. Yet, she did. To expand, Markman reasoned that cardinal number tasks require children to think of a display as an aggregate to which a particular number applies. As we mentioned earlier, Markman contends that class terms, for example, children, trees, soldiers, emphasize the individuality of the members in an aggregate, whereas collection terms, for example, class, forest, army, lead one to think of a display as an aggregate to which a particular cardinal number applies. Accordingly, Markman (1979) predicted that children would find it easier to apply the cardinal number principle when collection terms, as opposed to class terms, were used to describe the display.

Children in Markman's collection-terms condition were instructed as follows: ''Here is a nursery school class (forest, etc.). Count them. How many children (trees, etc.) in the class?'' Children in the class-terms condition were told: ''Here are some nursery-school children (trees, etc.). Count them. How many children (trees, etc.) in the class?'' Set sizes were 4, 5, or 6. Collection-terms children gave the last number in their count list on 86% of the trials. In contrast, class-terms children were as likely to recount the array as to repeat the last number. The tendency of young children to recount a display when asked how-many questions has been cited as evidence that they do not yet have the cardinal principle (Fuson & Richards, 1979; Schaeffer et al., 1974). If so, Markman's (1979) results are inexplicable.

Recently, Gelman and Meck (1982) conducted a direct test of the idea that performance demands limit the young child's tendency to apply the cardinal principle. In their study, 3- and 4-year-old children watched a puppet count displays of 5, 7, 12, and 20 objects. Children were told the puppet often made mistakes when counting and their job was to tell the puppet whether it was right or wrong. They were also encouraged to correct the puppet's errors. Note that the children did not have to generate the counting performance themselves; they only had to monitor it for conformance to the counting principles. Children did very well. For example, the 4-year-olds attempted to correct 90% of the puppet's errors and did so correctly 93% of the time. The comparable figures for the 3-year-olds were 70% and 94% respectively. The failure for Gelman and Meck to find an effect of set size means that the children did as well on set size 7 as they did on set size 20. Obviously, the children had implicit knowledge of the cardinal principle.

When all facts are considered, it seems reasonable to say that young children do honor the cardinal principle but that their tendency to do so is restricted and first revealed in only certain conditions. Further, they need to practice the application of the counting procedure, presumably so as to automatize it and thereby limit the amount of attention required in its use (cf. Case & Serlin, 1979; Schaeffer et al., 1974). The effect of this is to make it easier to focus on the cardinal value—and, we suspect, acquire explicit knowledge of the cardinal principle.

In considering the foregoing, it is essential to recognize the distinction between implicit and explicit understanding of principles. This distinction is well known in psycholinguistics. Young children are granted implicit knowledge of linguistic structures well before they are granted explicit knowledge of any of these (cf. deVilliers & deVilliers, 1972; Gleitman, Gleitman, & Shipley, 1972). The explicit knowledge is often characterized as metalinguistic knowledge, a knowledge that continues to develop into adulthood and is a function of general education level, training in linguistics, and so on (Gleitman & Gleitman, 1979). A similar distinction regarding knowledge of the counting principles helps sort out some seemingly contradictory conclusions about counting principles (Greeno, Riley, & Gelman, 1981). When children as young as 3 years of age are asked to count repeatedly a set of given value, they are indifferent to the order of the items as it changes across trials. Such behavior is what one would expect if the child had an implicit understanding of the order-irrelevance principle. It does not index explicit understanding of this principle. Indeed explicit understanding is at best weak in the 3-year-old child. However, the development of explicit understanding of this principle is well advanced by 5 years of age. This is illustrated in the 5-year-olds' performance on a modified counting task (see Gelman & Gallistel, 1978, chap. 9).

The modified count task requires that a child first count a linear array of x heterogeneous items (e.g.,

5). Almost all children do this by starting at one end or another of the array, thereby setting the stage for the modified count trials. These start with the experimenter pointing to some item in the middle of the array and saying, "count all these but make this be the 1." On subsequent trials, the child is asked to make the designated item the 2, 3, 4, . . . and $x + 1$, that is, 1 more than the cardinal value of the set. The 5-year-olds are nearly perfect on the modified count trials. Further, they try to say something about how movement of the items per se does not affect the tagging process. Perhaps most important in this context, they say they cannot designate any item $x + 1$ (6 in the case of a 5-item array) because "there are only 5, I need another 1." Clearly, these children have achieved an explicit understanding of cardinality vis-à-vis the counting procedure. Put differently, they know a count is conserved no matter how the items are arranged. Perhaps this is a stepping stone to the use of one-to-one correspondence in the typical number-conservation task.

Just as there is development from an implicit to an explicit understanding of the cardinal-count principle so there is, of course, for the other counting principles. Apparently, 3-year-olds can indicate which count sequences have double count, omit, errors, and so on, but only older children can say why (Fuson & Richards, 1979). Mierkiewicz and Siegler (1981) find that 3-year-olds are able to recognize some counting errors, especially the skipping of an item. They also find 4- and 5-year-olds can recognize a diverse set of counting errors (omitting or adding an extra tag, skipping an item, or doubly counting an item). What is more, they also recognize that it is all right to count alternate items and then back up to count the remaining in-between items or to start counting in the middle of a row. But it is not until children are school aged that they are able to say why an error-free count sequence that involves the alphabet as tags is a better count trial than one that uses the conventional count words but includes errors (Saxe, Sicilian, & Schonfield, 1981). Thus, we see the development of an understanding of the one-one and stable-order counting principles becoming more explicit. Saxe and Sicilian (in press) also found that, despite a young child's tendency to self-correct, the ability to say whether they were accurate develops after 5 years of age.

It is not only the explicit understanding of the counting procedure that develops but also the appreciation of the fact that counting is an iterative process that is unbounded. Evans (1982) reports that kindergarten children typically resist the idea that each addition of one (1) item will increase number. Interestingly, their resistance is highly correlated with their ideas of what constitutes a big number. These are usually under 100 or made-up combinations like "forty-thirty-a hundred." Apparently, children need some experience with largish numbers before they can move on to the recognition that counting is iterative. At the next level of development, children talk about a million and other large numbers when asked what is a very large number. But even this advancement does not guarantee that they will accept the consequence of continued iteration, that is, that there is no upper bound on the natural numbers. Instead, they maintain that despite the possibility of another, and another, and another yet-larger number being created with each addition of one (1), there is, nevertheless, a largest number. Finally, by 8 or 9 years of age, children recognize and accept the possibility of nonending iteration. There seems to be a progressive boot-strapping of one level of understanding to the next with intermediate plateaus where children assimilate enough examples to achieve (in Piagetian terms) a *reflective abstraction*, of their earlier levels of knowledge to a new level of understanding.

Just as the understanding of counting develops through steps, so apparently does the understanding of arithmetic principles, equivalence procedures, and conservation.

Arithmetic Principles. Fundamentally, the principles of addition and subtraction require that one understands that addition increases and subtraction decreases the numerical values of sets. Several studies support the view that preschool children have some understanding of these principles. Smedslund (1966) had 5- and 6-year-olds indicate whether two arrays of equal value ($N = 16$) were equal; then the arrays were screened. When one of the arrays was transformed by adding one object to it or subtracting one object from it, the children were able to indicate which array contained more objects. The same finding was obtained in 4- and 5-year-olds by Brush (1972) and in 3-, 4-, and 5-year-olds by Cooper, Starkey, Blevins, Goth, and Leitner (1978). Also, Gelman (1972a, 1972b; 1977) and Cooper et al. (1978) found that 3-, 4-, and 5-year-olds can infer the occurrence of a screened addition or subtraction by comparing the pretransformation and post-transformation values of arrays. Thus, preschoolers understand the directional effects on numerosity of addition and subtraction and can, under some conditions, infer their unobserved occurrence.

The value of the augend and minuend affect the preschool child's ability to solve simple tasks in mental arithmetic. Starkey and Gelman (1982) have tested 3-, 4-, and 5-year-olds on a variety of addition

and subtraction tasks. Each task began by having the child establish the number of pennies held in the experimenter's open hand. The child was asked, "How many pennies does this bunch have?" The experimenter then closed her hand and thereby screened the augend (or minuend) array of pennies and placed the added array in the hand holding the augend while saying: (1) "Now I'm putting x pennies in my hand; how many pennies does this bunch have?" or (2) "Now I'm taking x pennies out. . . ." The two values to be added or subtracted were never simultaneously visible. Problems involving zero were not used. The majority of the 5-year-olds could solve problems that involved starting with 1 to 6 items and then adding or subtracting 1 to 4 items. The 4-year-olds did well on problems involving the addition or subtraction of 1 or 2 items to (from) set sizes of 1 to 4 items. At least 50% of 3-year-olds could manage $1 + 1, 1 + 2, 2 + 1, 3 - 1$, $3 - 2$, and $4 - 2$. Thus, there was an interaction between set size and age. As expected, many children used a counting algorithm, even though the items were screened.

Preschoolers have at least some implicit understanding of the inverse relationship between addition and subtraction. Starkey and Gelman (1982) included some $x + 1 - 1, x - 1 + 1, x + 2 - 2, x - 2 + 2$ tasks in their experiment. The vast majority of 4- and 5-year-olds solved these problems where $x = 1$ through 4. And even the majority of 3-year-olds could arrive at the correct answer for values of $x = 1, 2$, and 3 and for problems involving a $+ 1, - 1$ sequence. The studies by Brush (1972) and Cooper et al. (1978) make it clear that inversion tasks are more difficult for preschoolers if the children have to represent two arrays (generated by an iterative, temporal one-to-one correspondence procedure) to start and then make judgments of relative numerosity after transformations are performed on one of the arrays, for example, x and $x + 1 - 1$. And when arrays of equivalent Ns are placed one above the other, thereby introducing a conflicting spatial cue, the tasks become even harder—although not impossible. A similar trend holds for compensation tasks, that is, where the two arrays are equal to start ($x = y$) and then the act of adding (or subtracting) of 1 (or more) items to array x is compensated by the act of adding or subtracting some number of items to array y. Indeed, Starkey (1978) reports that compensation tasks wherein spatial cues conflict are harder than the standard conservation task.

So once again we see more arithmetic competence in preschoolers than expected; however, the development of understanding occurs over a protracted span of years—in some cases past the time the child conserves number (see Siegler & Robinson, 1982, for a similar point for older children). Regarding this latter observation, it is noteworthy that many of Evans's (1982) subjects could conserve number and still not accept the idea of continued iteration. We expect that research designed to follow the shift from an implicit to explicit understanding of inversion and compensation will reveal a similar pattern to that observed regarding the counting principles and iteration. That is, we expect that children need to have some experience with local rules before they can move on to recognize the generality of that rule. As in the case of the counting principles, they have the benefit of some implicit understanding of the principles of addition and subtraction as well as their own counting algorithms with which to steer the course of acquisition.

Equivalence. The developmental story regarding the understanding of equivalence involves a by now familiar account. At early ages, there is at least an implicit understanding of the equivalence relation; to start, this understanding has an on-again, off-again characteristic, and its development is protracted.

In their account of the preschooler's arithmetic-reasoning principles, Gelman and Gallistel (1978) maintain that the young child recognizes an equivalence relation. For evidence they point to the way young children behaved in those magic experiments when the surreptitious change involved transformations that were irrelevant to number, for example, lengthening, item-type substitution. In nearly all cases, the children regarded the altered array as still equivalent to the original array. When the children who noticed the changes were probed about the reason for their equivalence judgment, they characteristically indicated that the number of items was the same, even though other features of the display were not. In Gelman and Tucker's (1975) experiment, there was an opportunity for children to construct two equivalent displays to give themselves two winners. Half the children did just this. It is difficult to explain such findings without allowing that the young child's arithmetic-reasoning principles include an equality relation.

A similar line of evidence and argument led Gelman and Gallistel (1978) to maintain that preschool children recognize that a difference between numerosities does not satisfy an equivalence relation. Further, in the case where $x \neq y$, the child believes that either x is more than y or that y is more than x. In short, the child recognizes that an ordering relation holds between x and y. Siegel (1974) showed that

preschoolers could consistently respond to a numerical-ordering relation between two sets. Bullock and Gelman (1977) showed that even 2½-year-olds can compare the set size pair of 1, 2 with 3, 4 and, therefore, select 3 (or 4) as the winner after first learning that 1 (or 2) was the winner. Interestingly, it will be a good while before the very young child will use correctly the terms "more" and "less" (e.g., Clark & Clark, 1977).

We have already discussed the two-candidates procedure by which preschoolers achieve a representation of numerical equivalence—counting and one-to-one correspondence. In Gelman's (e.g., 1972a, 1972b) magic experiments, there was no obvious way to use a rule of one-to-one correspondence; the arrays were placed side by side. Under these conditions, counting served as the algorithm by which children made judgments of equivalence or nonequivalence. Because the preschooler's ability to count accurately is limited, it is no surprise that his ability to use a counting algorithm to determine equivalence is too. Thus, Saxe (1979) finds that young preschool children can use the counting procedure to establish equivalence between a standard small set and another set. It is not until 5 or 6 years of age that children do the same with much larger sets.

Studies by Brush (1972), Bryant (1974), Cooper et al. (1978), and Starkey (1978) show that there are conditions under which preschool children can reach a decision about numerical equivalence or nonequivalence on the basis of one-to-one correspondence. Such conditions involve controlling for the potential conflict with spatial extent. Piaget (1952a) describes the various stages children pass through before they can use a principle of one-to-one correspondence in the face of conflicting cues.

Work by Russac (1978) and Saxe (1979) provides evidence that the ability to use a counting algorithm to determine equivalence develops ahead of the ability to use one-to-one correspondence. Russac's research is especially informative on this matter because he used a test of one-to-one correspondence that did not require the child to ignore competing spatial extent cues. The counting task involved showing 5-, 6-, and 7-year-olds cards with 7, 8, 9, or 10 dots. The children were then instructed to count the number of dots and put the same number in a box. In the correspondence task, the child was asked, without counting, to put as many items on a card as were already there; the instruction was to place the blue items beside the red items, thereby alleviating the possibility of confusion with spatial extent. The proportion of correct trials was .96, 1.00, and .95 respectively for the 5-, 6-, and 7-year-old groups. In contrast, the respective figures for the correspondence task were .125, .313, and .688.

An earlier study by Stock and Flora (1975) makes it clear that there is development in the ability to apply the one-to-one correspondence procedure. Whereas Russac (1978) had children produce equivalence, Stock and Flora did not. They showed children displays containing alternating red and blue dots where there were 3, 5, 6, or 8 pairs of dots. Control tasks had one extra red (or blue) dot. The subjects were in preschool (x̄ age, 55.8 months), kindergarten (x̄ age, 70.2 months) and first grade (x̄ age, 81.5 months); their task was to indicate, without counting, whether the number of red and blue dots was the same or not. The proportions correct of equivalence judgments on this single-row correspondence task were .33, .66, and 1.00 for the preschool, kindergarten, and first-grade groups respectively. In contrast, the proportions correct for the double-row task used by Brainerd (1973) were .00, .07, and .18. Parenthetically, we should note that this Stock-Flora correspondence task was easier for the children than a length-ordination task. This reverses Brainerd's (1973) findings regarding the acquisition of ordinal and cardinal concepts and highlights the critical role of task complexity in assessments of developmental sequences (Brainerd, 1977).

Flora and Stock (1975) note that their single-row task elicited explicit explanations, for example, "there's 2, and 2, and 2, . . ." for a judgment of equivalence; "there's 2 and 2 . . . and 1 left over" for nonequivalence judgments. Clearly, the children were using a principle of one-to-one correspondence. Still, they did poorly on the double-row task, indicating that their ability to apply the correspondence principle was not yet completely general. We suspect it is a very, very long time before they will be able to follow Cantor's proofs regarding transfinite numbers. Again, there is some competence at an early age but this competence is restricted; it is not applied generally and is probably not explicitly understood.

Conservation. Markman (1979) suggests that the kinds of explanations offered by young conservers differ from those of older natural conservers. Her subjects justified their equivalence judgments either with reference to the irrelevance of the transformation (e.g., "you just spread them"), or the fact that nothing was added or subtracted, or a specific reference to number. She fails to report any reference to reversibility. Gelman (1982) found that her young subjects used the same kinds of explanations as did Markman's (1979). These two studies

lend support to Piaget's (1975a, 1977) hypothesis that a child's understanding of number conservation goes through levels. The suggestion from the above studies is that explanations involving reversibility, and therefore an explicit understanding of reversibility, develop later—an account that is consistent with Piaget's. A similar conclusion was reached by Botvin and Murray (1975) regarding the conservation of continuous quantity. Their trained conservers referred to the absence of addition and subtraction as well as the irrelevance of a displacement operation; unlike their controls, natural conservers, they did not refer to reversibility and compensation arguments. Whether it is the case that reversibility explanations become prevalent at a later age is not known. Thus, as reasonable as the hypothesis may be, it needs further support.

The kinds of explanations offered by Gelman's (1982) preschoolers go against Gelman and Gallistel's (1978) account of what might distinguish precocious conservations from those obtained later. Recall that they hypothesized that preschoolers would not be able to use a principle of one-to-one correspondence when applying their reasoning principle regarding equivalence. Gelman (1982) finds that they did; indeed, if anything, the younger the child the greater the tendency. Of the 3-year-olds' explanations, 21% were of this type as opposed to only 9% of the 4-year-olds' explanations. Thus, the Gelman and Gallistel hypothesis has to be modified to acknowledge that there are some conditions where children as young as 3 can access one-to-one correspondence. It may be that Gelman and Gallistel are correct about the tendency of preschoolers to yoke their application of operational knowledge of number to quantification procedures that can determine whether, in fact, an equivalence relation holds. That is, they may be more dependent on having an empirical confirmation of a judgment of conservation than older children. In Piagetian terms, this would involve a dependence on using correspondence procedures when applying operatory knowledge. Older children can think solely in terms of operations. Perhaps this happens at the time when children likewise articulate one or more versions of a reversibility hypothesis as regards number conservation.

Summary. We have reviewed evidence on the young child's understanding of counting, addition and subtraction, equivalence and nonequivalence, and conservation. In all cases, it can be seen that the preschooler knows more about number than was assumed as little as 5 or 6 years ago. However, despite this early competence, there is considerable development that will occur. Indeed, it begins to look as if the development will be more protracted than one might have expected. Thus, there seems to be a paradoxical result, that is, more competence in the pre-operational period but less in the concrete-operational period. We will return to what we make of this paradox in the final section of the chapter.

Continuous-Quantity Concepts

Conservation

We have seen that preschoolers know that the operations of addition and subtraction change number, whereas those involving displacement or change in item type or color do not. Further, preschoolers can in some cases use this knowledge in explanations of their number-conservation judgment. Because in adult, scientific thought, quite similar reasoning principles are applied to a wide range of continuous quantities, for example, length, mass, heat, electric charge, one might think the generalization to continuous quantity would be a small step for the child. One might expect it to be easy to apply the same explanations with continuous quantities. In some cases, this seems to have happened. Gelman (1969) reported transfer from training on length and number items to length and number conservation as well as liquid and mass. The explanations regarding mass and liquid involved appeal to the irrelevance of the transformations of displacement, pouring, and the like. But if the only thing involved in the development of the understanding of conservation of continuous quantity were the recognition of the common status of such operations vis-à-vis length, liquid, and malleable clay, then surely the natural development of these would follow quickly after the stable understanding of number conservation. Training studies designed to build the development of an understanding of continuous quantity on that available for number conservation should be successful. Yet, judging from a series of Genevan training studies (Inhelder et al., 1974; Inhelder et al., 1975), this does not seem to be true. Before we look at these studies on the relationship between number and continuous quantities, a brief digression is in order.

The concept of length, which is probably the easiest of the continuous quantities to understand, can be understood at two levels (at least). A great deal of reasoning about length can go on without the notion of a unit—as Euclid long ago demonstrated. Lengths may be ordered, equivalent lengths recognized, and so on, without ever considering the question of how many units long a length is. To question how long a length is, is to consider length at the second level. The question of how long a length is requires the arithmetization of the concept of magnitude and the arbitrary choice of a unit. Euclid and the other Greek mathematicians, having discovered the problem of incommensurables—which rears its head when one tries to let numbers represent lengths—kept their geometry and arithmetic strictly separate (see Kline, 1972, for an excellent treatment of this topic).

At the second level we identify, the understanding of length entails an understanding of scaling, the processes by which numbers may be made to represent various continuous quantities. Historically, the development of processes for scaling continuous quantities has gone hand in hand with the development of a scientific understanding of those quantities. Although it is perhaps obvious to adults what length is and, therefore, how it must be defined for purposes of scaling and how in principle to scale it, once defined, the same cannot be said for heat or electric charge. Even liquid quantity, on extended consideration, behaves in a way that presents the would-be applier of numbers with perplexing problems. Recall that the abstraction principle of counting asserts that the identity of the unit is irrelevant. However, this is not true for liquid quantity. Three cups of water plus three cups of alcohol do not yield six cups of liquid. This is because liquid mass, but not liquid volume, is conserved when mutually soluble (i.e., missible) liquids are combined. Scaling (i.e., measuring) heat, electric charge, liquid volume, and so on, cannot be done satisfactorily in the absence of some scientific understanding of these quantities.

The point of these remarks is that the application of arithmetic reasoning to continuous quantity is not as straightforward as it may seem at first. Even in the case of length, the child must have the idea of magnitudes that can be counted, that is, measured. As we will see, the problem of the unit is not trivial, even in the case of length or sweetness (Strauss & Stavy, 1981). Now back to the Genevan studies that have focused on trying to lead the child from his ability to make ordinal comparisons to ones involving an understanding of the fact that a given continuous quantity can be considered in terms of units.

The findings of Inhelder et al. (1974) highlight the difficulty a child who conserves number can have with length tasks. They also show that it is not enough to be able to count and conserve number to be able to conserve length. In one experiment, children were shown two roads made up of the same number of matchsticks, laid end to end to yield two continuous roads. A small wooden house was glued

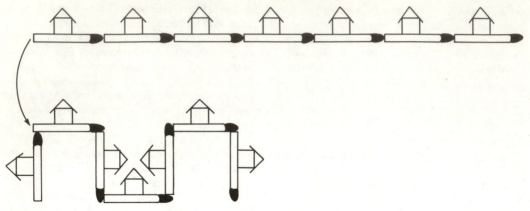

Figure 1. Illustration of the effect of transforming one row of matches and houses. (After Inhelder, Sinclair, and Bovet, 1974, p. 138.)

to the middle of each matchstick. Thus, the same number of houses appeared on two roads of equal length. The experimenter then rearranged the sticks in one row into the pattern shown in Figure 1. There were children who maintained that after the rearrangement, the number of houses in the two displays remained the same but that the length of the roads did not; the resulting road in Figure 1 was said to be shorter. Some children said that both were the same because there were the same number of matches—as if to take the length task and treat it as a number task. This may seem a perfectly good answer if we assume that the child realized that there were an equal number of equal units in each. However, a further task showed that the children who responded this way were indifferent to the issue of equality of the units. Consider a condition where the length of the individual sticks (i.e., of the units) in each row varied themselves in length. Thus, a row with 5 matchsticks stretched end to end was as long as one with 7 shorter pieces of wood also laid end to end. Believe it or not, some children said that the latter would be a longer road to traverse because it had 7 pieces. These children failed to realize that the units in both rows were of different sizes themselves. Therefore, the comparison was not valid, a fact that the children seemed not to know.

Findings such as the above led Inhelder et al. (1974) to conclude that the relationship between conservation of number and length was quite complex. In a subsequent set of experiments, Inhelder et al. studied the relationship between number and the continuous quantity in a malleable clay ball. This work takes off from Piaget's (1975a) more recent account of number conservation, that is, the need for

the child to realize that items within a display are commutable. The issue was whether the argument could be developed to explain the understanding of continuous quantity. The experiments that were designed to inform the issue involved different small colored pieces of clay. These pieces could be left as such for tests of number conservation or put together for the continuous tests. It turned out that "in going from the discontinuous to the continuous, subjects regress and substitute for the 'operatory envelop' (a collection whose quantity equals the sums of the parts, and which is conserved during form or shape transformations) a 'preoperatory envelop' where the total quantity is, in general, more" (Inhelder et al., 1974, p. 46). To get beyond this, the child has to understand that the small pieces which were rolled into a clay ball are "commutable" under displacement. To do this requires knowing that it does not matter to where the pieces are moved nor does it matter what shape the pieces or the whole object are as they are moved.

We confess that we have a less than full understanding of the recent Piagetian theory of what takes the child from nonconservation to conservation of continuous quantity and how this, in turn, relates to the understanding of discontinuous quantity. For us, the recent experiments highlight the difficulty children have with the notion of a unit of a quantity, a fact that is not dealt with in this new account of conservation. The child who says that 7 short matchsticks cover more ground than 5 long matchsticks is making a fundamental error by comparing units of different extents. This, we submit, occurs because he does not yet think of length in our second sense, where relative lengths are considered with reference to a countable unit of a fixed magnitude. If the child lacks this idea of length, then he cannot begin to understand that he is mixing apples and oranges let alone comprehend the conditions under which he might be able to compare numbers that count comparable units (Schwartz, 1976). Similarly, when asked to compare two clay balls that are each made up of three smaller pieces, we doubt that the child recognizes that the ability to decompose the continuous quantities into pieces in this situation is an example of a general principle, that is, that continuous quantities can be represented in units which thereby renders them measurable. Indeed we doubt that the child who quantifies discrete sets realizes that he has both encountered a unit problem and solved it.

Given that the counting principles are applied indifferently to different types, shapes, colors, and so on, of objects, a child need not know that counts involve the iterative production of yet another one (1). The problem of the unit in counting (and, therefore, discrete quantification) is solved for the child by virtue of the abstraction principle. Yet, this could be, and probably is, an implicit understanding of the principle at first. Recall that it is a while before children come to realize that the successive natural numbers are generated by an iterative process. It would seem hard to understand that continuous quantities can be represented in terms of concatenated units without the latter being implicitly understood; but even this is not enough. The child has to know what dimension to quantify and, as shown by the examples of heat, electrical charge, and even liquid volume, this is far from obvious.

We seem to be in disagreement with the Genevans on two matters. First, although they do point out the quite different status of the notion of unit vis-à-vis discrete as opposed to continuous quantities, they maintain "the fact that the unit is given in discrete quantities, and must be constructed in continuous quantities is important, mostly with respect to measurement which comes in long after conservation" (Inhelder et al., 1974, p. 54). As indicated, we see a closer relationship between the development of an understanding of continuous quantities and the development of measurement concepts. Strauss & Stavy, (1981) provide a lovely example of this relationship in their work on the child's concept of sweetness. As children develop the ability to use more powerful scales, for example, ordinal versus interval scales, so they come to understand the variables that do and do not affect the sweetness of a liquid. Second, the Genevans seem to suggest that the understanding of a given continuous concept is

an all-or-none matter. Work by Shultz, Dover, and Amsel (1979) highlights the danger of such an assumption. They point out that changes in shape can and do alter quantity under certain conditions, and likewise, that some properties of a container can profoundly affect whether the liquid in it is conserved over time.

If the same amount of water is poured from a tall, narrow container into a very wide but shallow dish, as opposed to a yet taller and narrower glass, there will be a difference in the amounts in each container when both are measured 24 hr. later. For the greater the exposed surface of the water, the greater the rate of evaporation. Shultz et al. (1979) report that 10-year-old children who passed the standard liquid conservation did poorly in predicting the 24-hr. difference that would obtain as a function of differences in degree of exposed surfaces. Lest one think that such tricks can be performed only under conditions of the passage of time, it should be sobering to know that some shape transformations that involve continuous quantity alter the amount immediately. Shultz et al. go over the fact that the shape changes of two-dimensional closed figures can alter the area or perimeter of that figure. Because most of us either did not learn or have forgotten the relevant geometric proofs, we are likely to do as the McGill University undergraduates did—maintain a judgment of conservation when we should not. Shultz et al. (1979) were able to teach their subjects about the effects of shape transformations on closed two-dimensional figures, and they did so "on the premise that the effects of shape transformations could best be grasped if the quantities were readily identified in standard unit measures" (p. 113).[3]

We have come a long way from the Siegler (1981) paper on conservation. We were dissatisfied with his account of the difference between conservation of number and the two continuous quantities of liquid and clay amount. It was not because we thought what he said was wrong. Rather, it was because we thought it was just the beginning of a longer account of how children think about the processes of quantification—an account that will have to allow for the continued development of some conservation beliefs as a function of knowledge about a given domain and how to define units in that domain.

Other Concepts of Continuous Quantity
Given the possibility that children will go through two levels at least in their understanding of continuous quantity, is there any evidence for the understanding of the first level at an early age? Work by Brainerd (1973) and Trabasso (1975) show pre-

schoolers able to order the relative lengths of sticks when they cannot know their exact lengths. Indeed, the evidence of an early ability to make transitive inferences about length and weight fit well in this context. And the work on functions of Piaget et al. (1977) is motivated by the need to explain the primacy of order judgments (i.e., relative extents) over judgments based on quantification during the preschool years. Piaget wants to argue that concepts of number and extent are not yet differentiated. In a sense we agree.

If we are right that concepts of continuous quantity are at first not recognized as quantifiable in terms of some unit, we should begin to see results reporting findings of such early concepts of other continuous quantities. Levin's research on the development of time concepts can be interpreted in this context (Levin, 1977, 1979; Levin, Israeli, & Darom, 1978). Levin (1977) presented 5- to 6½-year-olds and 8½-year-olds with three different tasks. These were the still-time, rotational-time, and linear-time tasks. Each successive task was designed to be more complex than the previous one. We focus on the still-time task, which asked children to decide whether two dolls slept as long as each other and if not which slept longer. The children were asked to answer these questions after witnessing four conditions: (1) the dolls went to sleep and woke up at the same time, (2) the dolls went to sleep but one woke up first, (3) one doll went to sleep first but both woke up together, and (4) one doll went to sleep first and woke up before the other, however both slept as long. Even the 5-year-olds did well on the first three problems. Moreover, their explanations made it clear they were taking succession into account and rationalizing their duration judgments in terms of the relative starting and ending times. As task complexity increased—in item 4 of the still-time task as well as in other tasks that put time and other factors, like speed and extent, into conflict—the younger children's performance scores decreased. Levin and her colleagues argue that much of the decrease is due to the young child's tendency to be distracted by irrelevant variables. We also suspect that the development of time-measurement skills is involved for much the same reasons outlined above regarding other continuous quantities.

Further evidence for an early ability to perform relative comparisons of continuous quantities comes from experiments that require children to match a standard with another display. Gelman (1969) found that her 5-year-old subjects could select the two of three sticks of the same length if none of the sticks overlapped. Anderson and his colleagues (e.g., An-

derson & Cuneo, 1978; Cuneo, 1980; Wilkening, 1981) repeatedly report children of this age able to indicate how much area, time, distance, and so on, is represented in a given display or event; children as young as 3 are able to point reliably to different relative positions on a scale. Thus, for example, Cuneo (1977) had young children indicate how happy (or sad) they would be eating a particular cookie where over trials the area of the cookie varied systematically.

Wilkening's (1981) work raises the possibility that 5-year-old children make *implicit* use of arbitrary units. As such, it could be that later development of this ability is better thought of as the development of an *explicit* understanding of the role of measurement vis-à-vis decisions of relative amounts. Wilkening points out that all research on the child's understanding of the relationship between time, speed, and distance involves a choice paradigm wherein the child is required to choose that animal, that train, or what have you, that went further or faster or took longer, and so on. He suggests that these paradigms may have failed to reveal an early ability to integrate information from two of the dimensions in order to reach an inference about the third because they are not appropriate tests of this ability. Instead, he argues that they are tests of the child's ability to ignore one or more dimensions (cf. Levin, 1979). The proof of the argument lies in Wilkening's (1981) results. Subjects in each of three age groups (5, 10, and adults) were tested on three tasks that required subjects to integrate velocity, distance and time. We consider the first.

The velocity-time integration task involved a display of a dog sitting close to the exit of its den. The dog and its den were on the left side of a 3-m by 1-m screen. A bridge led out of the den across a lake. A metal strip, fixed to the bridge, served as a scale to which subjects were to attach an animal—a turtle, guinea pig, or cat. Subjects were told that these animals were afraid of the dog whenever it barked, and that, whenever the dog barked, the animals started running across the bridge and stopped when the barking stopped. Note that the three animals have differential natural speeds. In a pretest, even the 5-year-olds could arrange the animals in the correct order. Not only does this mean they can represent relative velocities, it means Wilkening could do his experiment. Children (and adults, of course) listened to the dog bark for either 2, 5, or 8 sec. and then placed a given animal at the spot on the bridge he could have reached during these barking intervals. Because a centimeter scale was attached to the back of the metal strip, the distance in centimeters served as the true dependent variable. All age groups implicitly integrated time and velocity values with a multiplicative rule. This is revealed by significant interaction effects in an analysis of variance between time and velocity. How did such young children do this? Wilkening's eye-movement data show that the children (as well as the older subjects) followed the imaginary movement of an animal along the bridge. When the dog stopped barking, they pointed to the position their eyes had reached. Because they adjusted the rate of their eye movements as a function of animal, the fact that the time × velocity interactions were significant is explained.

Wilkening points out that the ability to integrate distance and velocity to judge time requires the use of a division rule, likewise the ability to judge velocity as a function of distance and time. Furthermore, the definition of the unit is more complex, as are the information processing demands of tasks that require these integrations. The youngest group did not succeed on distance, that is, the velocity task, where success is defined in terms of the use of a division rule. Whether these velocity tasks require an explicit understanding of the relevant units of measurement remains a question for further research. What is clear now is that even young children can, under some conditions, make correct judgments of relative amounts of continuous quantities. Still, there is much room for development.

Classification

In an earlier section (*Assessment of the Characterization of Concrete Operations*), we discussed the role classification structures play in Piaget's (1952a) theory of the development of numerical reasoning. In this section, we focus on Inhelder and Piaget's (1964) theory of the development of classification skills, and on the implications this theory has for concept acquisition.[4]

Concepts have traditionally been characterized in terms of classes and class-inclusion hierarchies. Like classes, concepts are said to have both an intensional and an extensional component. The *intension*, or definition, of a concept specifies the criterion elements must satisfy to be regarded as members of the concept. The *extension* of a concept consists of all the elements that are appropriately described as members of that concept. (The reader is referred to Schwartz, 1977, for a review of a philosophical work that proposes an alternative approach to concepts, and to Smith & Medin, 1981, for a review of psychological research conducted within this approach.)

To Vygotsky (1962), Inhelder and Piaget (1964), and Olver and Hornsby (1966)—all of whom shared the traditional view of concepts as classes—the study of children's classifications was of special interest for two reasons. First, it was thought that analyses of the structure of children's classifications would shed light on the structure of their concepts and, more generally, would show how this structure successively approximates the logical class structure of adults' concepts. Second, it was hoped that an examination of the basis of children's classifications would reveal something of the content—whether concrete or abstract—of their concepts. Because the young child was viewed as locked in a concrete, immediate reality (e.g., Piaget, 1970; Bruner et al., 1966), it was predicted (e.g., Olver and Hornsby, 1966) that young children would establish equivalences on the basis of perceptual similarities, whereas older children would make use of more abstract criteria.

Background

Structural Properties of Children's Groupings. According to Inhelder and Piaget (1964), classification begins when the child groups together two objects that look alike in some way. The child's ability to discover similarities between objects is *not* regarded as sufficient, however to warrant the conclusion that the child can classify. True classification is said to involve the active construction of classificatory systems.

Inhelder and Piaget (1964) began their investigation of classification skills with a detailed examination of children's productions in free-sorting tasks. They found three main phases in the development of free classification. In the first phase (2 to 5½ years), graphic collections, three types of grouping were obtained: alignments, collective objects, and complexes. All three types are based on configurational variables rather than similarity. The child becomes distracted by the spatial arrangement of the objects, or by the descriptive properties of the whole, and builds without regard for similarity. The geometric design objects form or the representative, situational content they evoke (e.g., a train, a cake, a castle) sway the child's attention away from the perceived likeness and differences of the objects themselves. In the second phase (5½ to 7 years), nongraphic collections, the child is no longer misled by considerations of patterns: objects are assigned to groups on the basis of similarity alone. Inhelder and Piaget list four types of nongraphic collections. At the least advanced level, a number of small groups are formed, each based on a different criterion. Further, only some of the objects that constitute the array are assigned to groups. The second type of nongraphic collections again involves various small groups based on a multiplicity of criteria. At this level, however, there is no unclassified remainder: all of the objects in the array are classified. At the next level, fluctuations of criterion are eliminated. Objects are now assigned to groups on the basis of a single, stable criterion without any remainder and without overlap. At the fourth and most advanced level, groups formed on the basis of one criterion are subdivided according to a second, stable criterion.

Children are, thus, able, by the end of the nongraphic collections phase, to form stable, nonoverlapping collections and to divide these into subcollections. Can children, at this point, be said to be able to classify? Inhelder and Piaget argue that, although these children's classifications may be so differentiated and hierarchized as to closely resemble class-inclusion hierarchies, they are *still* preoperational. According to Inhelder and Piaget, "the true criteria by which we can distinguish such preoperations from true classification are the ability of the subject to appreciate the relations 'all' and 'some,' and his power to reason correctly that A < B [i.e., that the subclass is smaller than the class in which it is included]" (Inhelder & Piaget, 1964, p. 54). That is, the preoperational child is still unable to grasp fully the logical relation of inclusion. When shown 12 roses and 6 tulips, for example, and asked, "Are there more flowers or more roses?," the preoperational child typically answers, "more roses." He is capable of adding subclasses to form a larger class (flowers = roses + tulips), but he is unable to simultaneously perform the inverse transformation (roses = flowers − tulips). As a result, he is unable to make a quantitative comparison of the class and its larger subclass. For such a comparison requires that the child separate the class into its subclasses to isolate the larger subclass, while at the same time maintaining the integrity or identity of the class, the other term in the comparison. In other words, the child must be able to attend at once to the part and to the whole, and that is precisely what the preoperational child cannot do. As soon as the subclasses are isolated, the child loses sight of the whole. As a result, he compares the two subclasses rather than the class and the larger subclass. It is only when both operations (addition and division of classes) are present and fully coordinated that the child becomes capable of contemplating at once the class and the subclass and of comparing the two. At this point (the third and last phase of development of classificatory abilities),

the child's groups are no longer simply juxtaposed but constitute well-articulated, logical, class-inclusion hierarchies.

Using somewhat different procedures, Vygotsky (1962) and Bruner et al. (1966) have also studied the development of classification abilities. Although there are many differences in the types of classificatory responses reported across the three programs of research, there are also striking similarities. In particular, all three studies suggest that young children go through an initial stage in which they are caught by relationships among the elements themselves—whether spatial arrangements, thematic relations, or idiosyncratic resemblances. Further, all three studies indicate that children go through an intermediary stage in which groups are formed on the basis of similarity alone, but the criterion for grouping fluctuates. During the last stages, children progressively learn to group objects into stable, exhaustive classes and to organize the classes thus formed into logical hierarchies.

Basis of Children's Groupings. Olver and Hornsby (1966) maintained that children's classifications exhibit semantic as well as syntactic properties and that both sets of properties undergo developmental change. The syntax of classification is defined as the formal structure of the class or grouping formed. The semantics of classification are the features of objects or events children use to establish equivalences.

Working with the theory of cognitive development of Bruner et al. (1966), Olver and Hornsby proposed that in the early stage, when the child's mode of representation of the world is essentially ikonic, children would group objects solely on the basis of perceptual properties. Older children, whose mode of representation is symbolic, were expected to use more abstract criteria. In particular, it was assumed that what uses objects have and what functions they serve constitute a more abstract notion and require more "going beyond the information given" than what objects look like. Accordingly, it was predicted that younger children would form concepts based on perceptual attributes whereas older children would form concepts based on functional attributes.

Olver and Hornsby (1966) report the results of two experiments, one by each author. In Olver's study (see also Bruner & Olver, 1963) children aged 6 to 19 were presented with a series of concrete nouns and were asked how each new item was similar to, and different from, the items previously introduced. For example, the words banana and peach would be presented, and, then, the word potato would be added to the list. At this point, the child would be asked, "How is potato different from banana and peach?" and "How are banana and peach and potato all alike?" This procedure was continued until a list of nine items had been presented (e.g., banana, peach, potato, meat, milk, water, air, germs, and stones). Hornsby's procedure was closer to that of Inhelder and Piaget (1964). Children of 6 to 11 years were shown an array of 42 drawings representing familiar objects (e.g., doll, garage, bee, pumpkin, sailboat, etc.). The children's task was simply to select a group of pictures. Their grouping completed, children were asked how the pictures they had chosen were alike. The pictures were then returned to their original position in the array, and children were asked to form another group. The entire procedure was repeated 10 times.

In both Olver's and Hornsby's tasks it was found that 6-year-olds based more of their groupings on perceptual attributes (color, size, shape, position in space) than did older children. In Olver's verbal task, the use of functional attributes increased steadily from 49% at age 6 to 73% at age 19. Conversely, the use of perceptual attributes decreased steadily from roughly 25% to 10%. In Hornsby's picture task, there was again a steady decline in perceptually based equivalence from 47% at age 6 to 20% at age 11. In contrast, the use of functional and nominal attributes increased from 30% and 6% respectively to 48% and 32% respectively. Comparing these two sets of findings, Olver and Hornsby noted that the same pattern of development obtained whether words or pictures were presented and whether items were presented in random or predetermined order. They described this pattern in the following terms:

> Equivalence for the six-year-old reflects a basis in imagery, both in what he uses as a basis for grouping and in how he forms his groups. . . . With the development of symbolic representation, the child is freed from dependence upon moment-to-moment variation in perceptual vividness and is able to keep the basis of equivalence invariant. (1966, p. 84)

We are not convinced that Olver and Hornsby's data support the notion of a stage-by-stage progression from a perceptually based to a functionally based equivalence. At no age were children's groupings based solely on perceptual properties. To the contrary, even Olver and Hornsby's younger children produced a sizable percentage of functional re-

sponses. (Indeed, the largest category of responses produced by the 6-year-olds in Olver's study was functional [49%], *not* perceptual [25%].) What these results suggest to us is that if there does exist a difference between younger and older children with respect to the basis they select for classifying objects, it is one of degree and not of kind. Younger children may use perceptual criteria somewhat more frequently than do older children; but they clearly do not use perceptual criteria to the exclusion of all others. What specific criterion is selected as basis for equivalence in any given situation appears to reflect less a particular mode of representing reality than the interplay of a large number of factors. These include the mode of presentation (verbal versus visual) of the stimuli; the readiness with which the stimuli presented can be subsumed under a single, conventional label (both factors seem to have influenced subjects' performance in Olver and Hornsby's studies); the child's style of conceptualization (e.g., Kagan, Moss, & Sigel, 1963) or organizational preference (Smiley & Brown, 1979); and so on. Support for this interpretation comes from a study by Miller (1973).

Miller (1973) gave 6-year-olds and college students eight oddity problems. Each problem involved a set of four objects (e.g., an orange, a plum, a banana, and a ball), and subjects were asked to remove "the thing that doesn't belong." The same question was repeated twice, and subjects were encouraged to take out a different object each time. The sets of four objects were constructed in such a way that removal of one object left a perceptual subset (e.g., an orange, a plum, and a ball) and removal of a different object left an abstract subset (e.g., an orange, a banana, and a plum). In general, the 6-year-olds had little difficulty forming both types of subsets. Indeed, in two of three problems where reliable differences were obtained between the 6-year-olds and college students, the significant result was due to the children's inability to generate a perceptual subset. Both children and adults tended to form abstract subsets on their first correct trial. Taken together, these results suggest that: (1) 6-year-olds *can* form categories on the basis of both concrete and abstract criteria and (2) 6-year-olds do not necessarily differ from college students with respect to the kind of criterion they *prefer* to use.

A variable that may have contributed to the 6-year-olds' superior performance, in Miller's (1973) task, is the use of modeling. Miller took children through two training problems prior to testing and showed them how two different solutions (one perceptual, one more abstract) could be provided for each. There is little doubt that such careful coaching must have left children in no uncertainty as to the nature of the task or the types of responses that were expected from them (Nash & Gelman, cited in Gelman & Gallistel, 1978; Smiley & Brown, 1979).

Classification and Basic Categories

The work of Inhelder and Piaget (1964) gave rise to much experimental interest in the development of the structure of children's free classifications. By and large, the evidence collected supported Inhelder and Piaget's claim that young children are unable to sort objects into classes (see Flavell, 1970, for a review of the free-classification research published prior to 1969). However, recent work by Rosch, Mervis, Gay, Boyes-Braem, and Johnson (1976) and Sugarman (1979) indicates that even very young children can, and do, sort objects taxonomically when presented with appropriate sets of stimuli.

Rosch and her colleagues (1976) noted that the stimuli used in classification experiments were typically stimuli (e.g., a table, a dresser, a bed) that could be grouped taxonomically only at the superordinate level (e.g., furniture). They pointed out that taxonomies of concrete objects include a level of categorization (e.g., chairs, apples, shirts) that is less abstract than the superordinate level; categories formed at this level are referred to as *basic* categories. In a number of experiments, Rosch and her colleagues found basic categories to be the most inclusive categories whose members (1) possess significant numbers of attributes in common, (2) are used by means of similar motor movements, and (3) possess similar shapes.

Rosch and her colleagues (1976) predicted that basic-level categories would be the first to develop. Rosch et al. reasoned that if young children encode the world by means of sensorimotor schemes (e.g., Piaget, 1970) or images (e.g., Bruner et al., 1966), then basic objects should be learned easily. In one experiment, kindergartners and first-, third-, and fifth-graders were assigned to one of two sorting conditions (basic or superordinate). Stimulus materials were color photographs of clothing (shoes, socks, shirts, pants), furniture (tables, chairs, beds, dressers), vehicles (cars, trains, motorcycles, airplanes), and people's faces (men, women, young girls, infants). Subjects in the superordinate condition were given one picture each of the four different objects in each of the four superordinate categories. Subjects in the basic condition received four different pictures of a basic object in each of the four superordinate categories. The results were straightforward. As in previous studies, only half the kindergarten and first-grade subjects could sort objects at the superordinate level. In contrast, there were no developmental differences in the ability to sort basic-level objects—basic-level sorts were virtually perfect at all age levels. In a second experiment, 3- and 4-year-olds as well as kindergartners and first-, third-, and fifth-graders were given oddity problems with either basic-level or superordinate relations. Again, basic sorts were virtually perfect at all age levels. For the 3-year-olds, the percentage correct was 99%; for all older age groups, it was 100%. As expected, the 3-year-olds performed poorly (55% correct) on triads that could only be sorted at the superordinate level. It is interesting to note, however, that the 4-year-olds' performance was almost perfect, with 96% correct.

Recent findings indicate that even 1½- to 3-year-old children may be capable of consistent sorting at the basic level (e.g., Nelson, 1973; Ricciuti, 1965; Ross, 1980; Stott, 1961; Sugarman, 1979). In Sugarman's (1979) study, children between 12 and 36 months of age were given six grouping tasks. Materials in each task were eight small objects evenly divided into two classes, for example, four dolls and four rings. Each task involved (1) a phase of spontaneous manipulation and (2) a phase during which children were given several grouping-elicitation probes. Two types of classificatory activity were examined: (1) the order in which objects were manipulated (sequential classification) and (2) the arrangement of objects in space (spatial classification). Spontaneous and elicited performance usually coincided. In general, the results suggested a shift in children's classifications from a sequential, stimulus-bound organization of single classes to an anticipatory representation and coordination of the two classes in the array. The 12-month-olds showed a reliable tendency to manipulate identical objects successively: they repeatedly selected items from one of the two classes, generally that with greater tactile-kinesthetic salience. Their arrangement of objects in space, however, was haphazard. Complete spatial groupings of single classes (e.g., all the dolls *or* all the rings) did not appear until 18 months of age. By 24 months, sequential selection of similar objects extended to both classes and objects within a basic category were spatially grouped. Finally, whereas all but one of the younger children who grouped two classes at any point in the experiment arranged the objects one class at a time, more than half the 30- and 36-month-olds shifted between classes as they sorted. These children clearly could attend to both classes at once. Whether they constructed one-to-one correspondences between dissimilar objects (e.g., a doll in each ring) or sorted identical objects into spatially distinct groups, their actions were always swift and deliberate. Indeed, it often appeared to Sugarman as if the older children had mentally constructed some classification in which both classes were represented and, seizing objects more or less at random, were arranging them according to the scheme they had formed.

Inhelder and Piaget (1964) themselves reported having observed, along with the graphic-collections characteristic of the first phase of development of free classification, other, less frequent productions that are quite similar to those reported by Sugarman (1979). Specifically, Inhelder and Piaget (1964) found that young children would at times successively select similar objects and then toss them into a pile or hold them in their hands without attempting to build them into a configurational structure. Inhelder and Piaget minimized the significance of these productions, which they viewed as a very primitive type of nongraphic collection. They argued that the similar objects were manipulated sequentially on the basis of "successive assimilations" and were not formed into a classification (collection) proper.

Should the classifications produced by Sugarman's (1979) infants also be construed as resulting from successive assimilations? After all, each of the arrays Sugarman used in her grouping tasks contained two classes of identical objects, and Inhelder and Piaget (1964) have never denied the fact that children, even very young children, can discern physical similarities between objects. One could argue that where such similarity is high, as was obviously the case in Sugarman's (1979) experiment, the young child successively explores similar objects precisely because the perceived resemblance is particularly salient and catches and holds her attention. Conversely, where the similarity between objects is low, as was the case in Inhelder and Piaget's (1964) own experiments (recall that the stimuli used could only be sorted at the superordinate level), the child becomes distracted by the configurational properties of the objects and as a result builds without regard for similarity.

We do not believe that the productions Sugarman (1979) obtained resulted solely from sequential, stimulus-bound assimilations, which mimic classifications based on similarity. One might doubt that successive manipulations of identical objects unambiguously reveal classificatory behavior. But add to this the ability to place the groups in two separate locations, thereby using space to keep the two categories separate, and it becomes hard to deny a true classificatory competence with basic-level objects. Sugarman's data demonstrate that sequential classifications, with no spatial arrangement of the objects, occur only at the earliest ages. By 18 months of age, infants successively selected *and* grouped together spatially all of the objects that belonged to one of the two classes in the array. For us, such findings support the notion that significant classificatory competencies are present from the earliest ages (which is not to say, obviously, that no development remains to take place). This conclusion is supported by the recent reports of Cohen and Younger (1981) and Ross (1980). Both studies used habituation and recovery-from-habituation responses to show that infants do categorize some sets of objects.

The work of Rosch et al. (1976) and that of Sugarman (1979) demonstrate that children as young as 3 years of age can sort objects according to a consistent criterion and without remainder or overlap. Indeed, there is evidence that still younger children can do the same. These demonstrations clearly challenge Inhelder and Piaget's (1964) description of the development of free classification. At the very least, they force us to abandon the notion that a stage of graphic collections invariably precedes that of nongraphic collections. In addition, they provide clues about some of the processes that contribute to the young child's acquisition of knowledge—in both factual and linguistic domains.

Primacy of Basic Categorization

According to Rosch and her colleagues (1976) basic categories are the primary cuts we make on our environment. We can and do establish equivalences at higher and lower levels of abstraction, but the basic level is the *primary* level at which we form equivalences—the primary level at which we chunk objects in our environment. There is some support for the notion that our most spontaneous or immediate categorization of the world is in terms of basic categories. Experiments with adult subjects have shown that concrete objects are typically first recognized as members of their basic-level category and are normally referred to by their basic-level name (Rosch et al., 1976; Shipley, Kuhn & Madden, 1981). Is there evidence that infants and young children carve their world into basic categories? We think so. First, there is the infant's often spontaneous (Sugarman, 1979) sorting of arrays into basic categories; second, there is the infant's differential and appropriate reactions to different objects; and third, there is the young child's use of basic-level terms for basic objects.

We have already discussed the infant's sorting

behavior. Young children also reveal their classificatory competence through their actions—other than sorting—upon objects. We might say that sorting is an object-independent action in the sense that all classes of objects—roses, books, cups, and so on—can be sorted in the same way. By contrast, actions, such as drinking, rolling, and so on, are object dependent or object specific. When we talk here about the infant's actions on objects, we have in mind these object-specific responses. When given a new instance of a familiar category, for example, a shoe, or a cup, 1-year-old children may try to put it on their feet, or bring it to their lips respectively. In other words, they behave differentially and appropriately when presented with new examples of presumably known basic categories (Nelson, 1977). Of course, there is the question of what this capacity means. Inhelder and Piaget (1964) maintained that the infant's assimilatory activity is only analogous to classification. We believe that the infant's assimilation of novel objects to existing sensorimotor schemas is in fact a *primitive form* of classification.

Rosch et al. (1976) reasoned that if by the time the child begins to acquire words, he or she has available mostly basic-level concepts, then basic-object names should be the first nouns acquired. Rosch and her colleagues (1976) carefully analyzed Brown's (1973) protocols of the spontaneous speech of his subject, Sarah, during her initial period of language acquisition. Two judges read Sarah's protocols, and utterances of an item in any of the taxonomies Rosch et al. (1976) had studied were recorded. The results were straightforward. Basic-level names were essentially the only names used by Sarah at that stage. Similarly, vocabulary studies reviewed by Clark (1978) suggested that of the first 50 or so object words that children learn, many of them are basic-level terms. Additional support for the primacy of basic-level names in children's acquisition of concrete nouns is provided by the study of Rosch et al. (1976) of the names 3-year-olds give to pictures of objects. Of the 270 names collected, all but one was a basic-level name. True, not all of the names provided by the children were correct, but errors were typically basic-level names for objects other than those pictured (e.g., blueberries instead of grapes).

On a comprehension test, Anglin (1977) found that young children responded accurately when asked about a dog as opposed to collie or animal. In seeming contrast, more were accurate when asked about an apple as opposed to fruit or food. Anglin concluded that young children tend to use terms at that level of generality which maximally discriminates among objects in their everyday environment. Rosch et al. (1976) also noted that what objects are treated as basic level does not necessarily coincide with the biological definition of superordinates and subordinates. As an example, individuals who think trees are those objects one sits under to avoid the penetrating heat of the sun probably do not know whether the trees they sit under are maples, oaks, and so on. For these individuals, the seeming superordinate is psychologically a basic-level concept (i.e., a tree is a tree is a tree).

Young children's overgeneralizations of nouns are sometimes held as evidence against the view that early noun usage reflects the availability of basic concepts. Recent evidence points to a different interpretation of children's generalizations however. Briefly, it appears that these reflect the child's attempt at using as meaningful a label as he can when he does not yet know the appropriate label. Instead of selecting a label at random, he selects one from within the same hierarchy. Two lines of evidence support this hypothesis. First, 2- and 3-year-old children who produce overextensions, nevertheless, accurately comprehend adult terms (Gruendel, 1977; Huttenlocher, 1974; Thomson & Chapman, 1977). Second, several investigators (Bloom, 1973; Gruendel, 1977; Rescorla, 1980, 1981) have observed that a period of relatively accurate use of category name is often followed by overextensions to exemplars of a common superordinate. For example, the initial accurate use of the term car is followed by its use for many diverse objects within the broader category of vehicle. This overextension could signify either the formation of, or an already-present, superordinate category. Recall that Rosch et al. (1976) found that children's labeling errors typically involved using inaccurate basic-level names, such as blueberries instead of grapes. Both names reflect basic level categories from the same superordinate category. These results suggest that some early concepts may be more richly organized than the basic-level analysis suggests. Children of a very young age may be capable of using hierarchical-classification schemes to at least represent and organize their knowledge about objects. Put differently, what young children's overextensions may reveal is their implicit use of an organization scheme long before that organization can be explicitly accessed and used in sorting tasks.

We have reviewed evidence that indicates that even very young children are capable of forming categories according to stable, consistent criteria. We submit that this finding is surprising only in the context of an expectation to the contrary. It is hard to see how the child could master her environment as quickly and as efficiently as she does if she were incapable of forming stable categories. For the most economical means of mastery must necessarily involve the generalization to all novel, unfamiliar instances of what is known or what has been discovered to be true about a small set of familiar instances. Clearly the formation of categories that are at least consistent is indispensable if such generalization is to bear fruit. We want the child to be able to generalize from old cup to new cup that which is true about cups and from old shoe to new shoe that which is true about shoes. In each case, the recognition that the old and the new objects belong to the same category creates a basis for generalization. In other words, the fact that the child can categorize upon the basis of similarity—however that similarity may be recognized—means that she does have a capacity for projecting or generalizing information to appropriate instances. A child who always categorized objects on the basis of their spatial configurations would make one erroneous generalization after the other.

We have also considered evidence that suggests that the first categories the child learns are basic categories. Rosch et al. (1976) describe characteristics of the basic categorization process that help elucidate why it is that basic categories are primary, why it is that so many of our perceptions and conceptions involve basic categories, and why—we add—it is especially adaptive for the young child to form basic categories as opposed to categories at other levels of abstraction.

Rosch and her colleagues (1976) argue that, far from being unstructured, the world we live in is highly determined: real-world attributes do *not* occur independently from each other. Creatures with feathers are more likely to have wings than creatures with fur; and objects that look like chairs are more likely to have the property of sit-on-ableness than objects that look like birds. Given that combinations of attributes do not occur uniformly, it is to the individual's advantage to form classifications that mirror (at some level of abstraction) the correlational structure of real-world objects. For such classifications would enable the individual to predict from knowing any one property an object possesses many of the other properties that may be present.

The level of abstraction at which categories are formed that best delineates the correlational structure of the environment is *not* the basic level but the *sub*ordinate level. Objects that belong to the category of rocking chair share a larger set of attributes than do objects belonging to the basic category of chair.

However, the gain in correlational value between the features of members of a category, as one goes from a basic to a subordinate category, is accompanied by a severe loss in generality or inclusiveness. It makes intuitive good sense that one should wish one's categories to be, on the whole, as inclusive as possible. Clearly, the broader the category, the larger the number of items for which a summary description is simultaneously provided. Superordinate categories obviously are more inclusive than basic categories. However, their members share fewer attributes in common. Thus, Rosch et al. (1976) argue for the priority of basic categories. They are at the most inclusive level that still delineates the correlational structure of the environment.

Put somewhat differently, the argument is that basic categories dominate as a consequence of two opposite principles. On the one hand, categorization must help reduce the near-infinite variety of the environmental array to behaviorally and cognitively usable proportions. Attempts at fulfilling this goal lead to the formation of a few very large categories, with the greatest possible number of discriminably different objects being assigned to the same category. On the other hand, it is obvious that the more differentiated an individual's categories, the greater his ability to predict and, generally, control occurrences in his environment. Fulfillment of *this* particular goal calls for the formation of a larger number of small, distinct categories that correspond to detailed discriminations among stimuli. The basic level of categorization is the level that maximizes the conflicting demands of information richness and cognitive economy.

Thus, following Rosch et al. (1976), formation of categories at the basic level, as opposed to higher or lower levels of abstraction, presents significant adaptive advantages for the young child. At birth, all the objects, places, and events that the child experiences are novel. The first years of life must be largely devoted to resolving these novel experiences into familiar, recognizable forms and predictable events. A child who is inclined to form basic categories is effectively breaking down or parsing his environment into the most functional units, units that allow him to generalize the largest amount of information to the largest number of objects.

Classification and Hierarchies of Classes

Inhelder and Piaget (1964) recognized that were one "to find a mixture of graphic and non-graphic collections from the beginning . . . one could argue that classificatory behavior owes its origin to nongraphic collections alone" (1964, p. 31). The previous sections indicate that a mixture of graphic and nongraphic collections *is* found from the beginning. Whether young children group objects on the basis of similarity alone (nongraphic collections) or on the basis of some other criterion, such as the objects' joint contributions to pleasing spatial configurations (graphic collections), depends heavily upon the nature of the arrays they get. Objects that can be sorted at the basic level of categorization are typically, and often spontaneously, sorted into consistent, exhaustive categories; objects that can only be sorted at the superordinate level are not. Why?

As Inhelder and Piaget (1964) claimed, it could be that the child's grasp of classificatory is not fully adequate. However, many extralogical factors appear to contribute to the ease or difficulty with which the child builds hierarchical classifications. In the next sections, we discuss some of these factors.

Competing Behavioral Tendencies. One possibility as to why young children do poorly on hierarchical sorting tasks is suggested by the work of Ricciuti. Ricciuti (1965) tested infants between 12 and 20 months of age with a procedure very similar to that used by Sugarman (1979) and obtained essentially the same results. He subsequently retested some of his 20-month-old subjects when they were 40 months old (Ricciuti & Johnson, 1965). Not surprisingly, complete spatial groupings of both object classes were by then far more frequent. What was surprising, however, was that children also produced groupings that were distinctly illogical from a classificatory point of view. They would, for instance, form two separate groupings, each containing two objects from each class. Moreover, the objects within each grouping would be arranged in such a way as to form, as Flavell (1970) put it, "what looked suspiciously like a 3-year-old's version of an interesting design or pattern" (p. 993).

Ricciuti and Johnson's (1965) findings suggest that young children develop, around the ages of 3 or 4, a taste for interesting, novel configurations. Instead of simply grouping the identical objects in an array in different locations, the child combines them in creative, fanciful ways. Her grouping activity, in other words, is no longer governed by a classificatory scheme alone; other dispositions or tendencies compete with, and at times prevent (as Ricciuti and Johnson have shown), the formation of logical classifications.

Assume for a moment that 3-year-olds do prefer building creative designs or patterns to forming symmetrical logical classifications. It seems reasonable to suppose that the more heterogeneous the array of objects, the greater the likelihood of a child forming some illogical configuration or other. Both Sugarman (1979) and Ricciuti and Johnson (1965) used arrays that contained two different classes of identical objects. Such arrays, it would seem, offer only limited possibilities in the way of figural masterpieces. Were one to increase the perceptual *dissimilarity* between the objects in the array, one might expect to find fewer and fewer logical classifications. To put the matter differently, whether 3-year-olds group objects together on the basis of common attributes *or* on the basis of their joint contribution to the creation of pleasing spatial configurations might depend on the nature of the objects used. Arrays that are composed of highly similar subsets might elicit classificatory responses; arrays composed of dissimilar objects, might elicit varying building responses.

Recall that Rosch et al.(1976) demonstrated that objects belonging to the same superordinate category tend to possess few perceptual attributes in common to have highly dissimilar shapes. Hence, a superordinate sorting task confronts the young child with perceptually dissimilar objects—the kind we propose as likely to elicit building as opposed to classificatory responses. If this account has merit, it is reasonable to conclude that the young child's well-documented failure to sort objects taxonomically at the superordinate level is due *not* to an inadequate grasp of classificatory logic but rather, in part, to the emergence (and continued intervention), of competing behavioral dispositions (Bever, 1970).

One implication of the preceding argument is that a reduction in the salience of the perceptual contrast between objects would facilitate the production of taxonomic sorts. Some support for this is provided by a study by Markman, et al. (1981). They asked 3- and 4-year-olds to sort the same set of objects twice, once on pieces of paper placed on a table, and once in transparent plastic bags. The objects to be sorted fell into four superordinate classes: furniture (kitchen chair, easy chair, table, couch), vehicles (motorcycle, car, plane, truck), people (boy, woman, man, fireman), and trees (evergreen, rust-colored trees, a deciduous tree, and a tree with needlelike leaves). Markman et al. reasoned that having the children sort the objects into transparent bags that did not readily allow for spatial arrangement would tend to reduce the impact of perceptual and configurational variables. The result would be to facilitate the formation of logical classifications. As predicted, there was a marked improvement in both 3- and 4-year-olds' sorting when they sorted into plastic bags. The authors concluded that young children fail to sort objects taxonomically in part because they become distracted by spatial variables and not because they have different principles of classification.

Competing Hierarchical Organizations. Until now, we have been concerned only with classifications based on relations of similarity, assuming (after Inhelder and Piaget, 1964) that classifications based on other relations were primitive productions whose existence was due to the child's inadequate grasp of classificatory logic. Recently, however, a number of authors (e.g. Nelson, 1978; Mandler, 1979, see also Mandler, vol. III, chap. 7.) have challenged the claim that the only, or even the most important, way in which our knowledge is organized is in terms of classes and hierarchies of classes. According to these authors, children and adults possess an alternative mode of conceptual organization— one which is based on *spatiotemporal* relations. The fundamental units in this type of organization are not categories but schemas. The tendency to use schemas might very well interfere with an ability to impose a classification structure on the environment.

Modern cognitive psychology's use of the construct *schema* is both like and unlike Piaget's use of scheme. (See Mandler, 1981; Mandler, vol. III, chap. 7 for a detailed discussion of the differences.) Both are taken to be mental structures that organize memory, perception, and action. However, for Piaget, the emphasis is more on the logico-mathematical structures that underly and constrain schemes. For schema theorists (e.g., Rumelhart, 1980, Rumelhart & Ortony, 1977, Schank & Abelson, 1977) the emphasis is more on the representations of everyday knowledge that are embodied in the schemas—be they face schemas, restaurant scripts or grammars for folktales. Some evidence for young children's sensitivity to spatiotemporal information . . . studies of causal reasoning in young children. Bullock and Gelman (1979) found that children as young as 3 select as cause the event that precedes rather than the event that follows the effect to be explained. Gelman, et al. (1980) also found that young children, when presented with pictures of an object and an instrument, have no difficulty selecting a third picture depicting the outcome of applying the instrument to the object. These and other similar findings (see Bullock, Gelman, & Baillargeon, 1982, for a review) suggest that children develop causal schemas that faithfully portray the sequencing of events in causal sequences and that specify what transformations can be applied to objects and with what effects.

A second source of evidence that children can detect and make use of temporal/spatial structure comes from studies that examine children's descriptions of event sequences. For example, Nelson (1978) analyzed preschoolers' descriptions of such event sequences as eating dinner at home, having lunch at a daycare center, and eating at MacDonald's restaurant. She found that the children generally agreed on where the sequence started and stopped and on the order in which events took place. To do this, children must have been able to keep track of event order. This conclusion would seem to go against Piaget's (1959) work on children's recall of stories. Piaget (1959) reported that his young subjects were very poor at maintaining the correct sequence of events when retelling stories. As Mandler (1981) pointed out, however, Piaget's subjects may have had difficulty keeping track of sequence because the stories used were poorly motivated and poorly structured. When 5- and 6-year-olds hear stories that contain clear and temporal and causal connections, they have no trouble retelling them correctly (e.g., Mandler & Johnson, 1977; Stein & Glenn, 1979).

The existence of an alternative mode of conceptual organization, one that emphasizes spatial and temporal relations, may well serve as another reason why young children fail to produce taxonomic classifications. Recall, for example, the representative constructions Inhelder and Piaget (1964) obtained (e.g., a train station); such productions can be attributed to the child's use of an alternative mode of organization rather than to a fundamental inability to grasp hierarchical relations between objects. Some support for this interpretation comes from Smiley and Brown (1979), who found that preferences for sorting materials into thematic or taxonomic groupings showed a curvilinear relationship across age. Younger children and older adults preferred thematic categories. It seems reasonable to suppose that what is changing is not the ability to classify objects logically but rather the choice of a basis to use in a task that allows for more than one possible organization. In other words, young children's tendency to produce thematic groupings may be due to in part to their greater preference for organizations that rely on spatial or temporal relations (Markman, 1981).

In a way, the two previous alternative accounts regarding the failure of a young child to classify reduce to one, that is, that the child's figural and thematic constructions both reflect a preference for a part-whole organization as opposed to a class organization (Markman & Siebert, 1976). When the young child is presented with meaningless objects, such as building blocks and geometric shapes, he uses them to build creative designs or configurations (e.g., Denney, 1972a; Inhelder and Piaget, 1964;

Ricciuti & Johnson, 1965); when presented with more meaningful stimuli, such as real objects or toy-size reproductions, he constructed scenes and situations with which he is familiar (e.g., Inhelder & Piaget, 1964; Markman et al., 1981); and when presented with verbal items and asked about similarities and differences among them, the young child relates the items in terms of a story that may be inspired or guided by the schemas he has formed (e.g., Bruner & Olver, 1963). In all cases, the organization that is imposed is not one of class relations but one in which parts are joined together to create some whole—whether a spatial configuration or a simple sequence of events, depending on the nature of the items with which the child is presented (Flavell, 1970). The relation between element and totality is one of part to whole rather than class member to class or subclass to class.

It is interesting, in this context, to consider Markman's (e.g., 1973a, 1980) work on collections. Recall that collections are the referents of collective nouns, such as forest, pile, family, and army. According to Markman, collections and classes differ in several ways. First, collections are organized into part-whole relations and classes are organized, obviously, into class-inclusion relations. Thus, we can say that petunias are part of a bouquet or that together they constitute a bouquet. We can also say that petunias are a type of flower or that they are instances of flowers; but we cannot say that petunias are kinds of bouquets or that they are instances of bouquets. This is because in a class-inclusion hierarchy, an element possesses (by definition) all of the properties that specify elements higher up in the hierarchy. That is, if element X is a member of category Y, the defining properties of X will include those of Y. In a part-whole hierarchy, however, the defining properties of the whole are distinct from the defining properties of the parts. We cannot say that petunias are a bouquet or are bouquets because the defining features of bouquets are not included in those of petunias and the "is a" relation cannot hold. Second, to form a collection, elements must be related to each other. For petunias to form a bouquet, for trees to form a forest, they must be in close spatial proximity; for children and adults to form a family, they must be related by some biological/parenting bond. To determine membership in a collection, then, one must consider the properties individual elements possess as well as the particular relationships that obtain between them. To determine membership in a class, one need only consider what properties individual elements possess—their relation to other elements does not enter into the deci-

sion. Finally, because of these differences in their internal structure, collections might be expected to have greater psychological stability, or coherence, than classes. That is, it should be simpler to conceptualize collections as organized totalities than to do so for classes. After all, classes are wholes only in an abstract sense. In contrast, collections are empirical, finite sets of elements that are characterized by specifiable relationships to one another.

According to Inhelder and Piaget (1964), children are unable to pass the class-inclusion test until 8 or 9 years of age because they lack the requisite concrete operations. Instead of comparing the superordinate class to its larger subclass (flowers and petunias), young children typically compare the two subclasses (petunias and daisies). Markman and Siebert (1976) suggested that this is because the superordinate class lacks psychological coherence once it is divided into its subclasses. If collections have greater psychological coherence than classes, then children should be better able to keep the whole in mind while attending to its subparts and, thus, should perform better on tasks that require comparing the whole to its subparts. Accordingly, Markman and Siebert gave kindergarten and first-grade children two different versions of the Piagetian class-inclusion task. Only children who failed a pretest consisting of two standard class-inclusion questions were included in the study. All children received four questions that involved part-whole comparisons (collection questions) and four questions that involved subclass comparisons (class questions). The same four sets of stimuli (e.g., a set of 10 blue and 5 red building blocks) were used for both types of questions. As an illustration, the collection question was, "Who would have more toys to play with, someone who owned the blue blocks or someone who owned the pile?" The class question modeled after the standard Piagetian question was, "Who would have more toys to play with, someone who owned the blue blocks or someone who owned the blocks?" Performance on the collection questions was reliably superior to that on the standard class questions. Markman and her collaborators have now completed several studies that show children able to solve problems with collections that they are unable to solve with classes. In all of these studies, children who heard class descriptions and children who heard collection descriptions viewed identical displays. Substituting collection terms for class terms markedly improved children's ability to answer correctly.

These results show that the part-whole structure of collections is easier for children to operate upon or reason with than the class-inclusion structure of classes. Recently, Markman et al. (1980) have suggested that part-whole structures might be easier for children to form as well. If part-whole relations do reflect a psychologically simpler principle of hierarchical organization, then one might expect that children left relatively free to impose their own structure on a novel hierarchy would construct a collection rather than a class hierarchy.

To test this hypothesis, Markman et al. (1980) taught subjects (aged 6 to 17 years) novel class-inclusion hierarchies. Four categories (each composed of two subcategories) were constructed. Nonsense syllables were used to refer to the four categories and eight subcategories. Children in each of the four age groups were assigned to one of two training conditions, ostension and inclusion. For children in the ostension condition, the experimenter simply pointed to and labeled the entire category and each of the two subcategories (members of each subcategory were grouped together, and the two subcategories were placed a few inches apart). Training continued until subjects were able to provide all three correct labels. Children in the inclusion condition went through the same pointing and labeling procedure as did children in the ostension condition. The only difference was that they were given additional information about category membership. That is, they were told: "A's are a kind of C''; "B's are a kind of C''; and "A's and B's are two kinds of C's" (where, obviously, A and B are the labels of the two subordinate categories that comprise the category C). This information was given immediately after the labeling and pointing.

Children in both conditions were tested with the exact same procedure. Each child was asked questions about an entire category (C) and its subcategories (A and B). For the entire category, the questions were: "Show me a C''; "Put a C in the envelope''; "Is this a C?'' (pointing to an A); and "Is this a C?'' (pointing to a B). For the subcategories the questions were: "Show me an A''; "Put an A in the envelope''; "Is this a B?'' (pointing to an A); and "Is this a B?'' (pointing to a B). It was expected that children in the inclusion condition, who were given class-inclusion information, would achieve class-inclusion interpretations of the material. In contrast, it was predicted that children in the ostension condition, who received minimal information about the hierarchical relation, might (erroneously) impose a part-whole collection organization upon it. The results confirmed the predictions. Subjects in the inclusion condition correctly interpreted the relation as one of class inclusion. Subjects in the ostension con-

dition mistakenly imposed a collection structure on the inclusion hierarchies. Children as old as 14 years of age denied that any single element (A or B) was a C and picked up several elements when asked for a C or when asked to put a C in an envelope.

These results are especially surprising when one considers that plural labels were used during training, for example, "These are A's." "These are B's." "These are C's." And singular labels were used during testing, for example, "Show me a C." (this is analogous to saying, e.g., "These are petunias." "These are daisies." "These are flowers.") To impose a part-whole organization on the hierarchy, the subject had to systematically ignore the cues provided by the syntax.

The fact that the 14-year-olds in the Markman et al. (1980) study spontaneously and erroneously imposed a part-whole organization on the novel hierarchies they were taught certainly refutes any suggestion that the young child's classifications reflect a qualitatively distinct, more primitive conceptual organization that is based on part-whole relations and is replaced in time by an adult-type conceptual organization. Instead, it appears that both the collection and class modes of hierarchical organization are available from a very early age. Because the part-whole mode of organization is psychologically simpler, it is the preferred mode of organization—one that children and adolescents alike will impose when the situation does not unambiguously call for a class-inclusion hierarchy. Thus, the young child's tendency to group elements into wholes—stories, patterns, or scenes—rather than class-inclusion hierarchies, might be interpreted as indicative of a systematic and enduring preference for part-whole organizations. This preference might be rooted in the psychological characteristics of this type of organization, that is, the fact that it appears to be easier to operate on, to conceptualize, to establish, and so on.

We are not suggesting that very young children are just as good as teenagers at solving problems that involve part-whole or class-inclusion hierarchies. Clearly, the older children will be superior on most tasks. What we are suggesting, though, is that both types of organization are available to younger and older children and that all children may find it easier to, and may prefer to, impose part-whole as opposed to class-inclusion structures on hierarchies. Thus, whatever development there is in terms of establishing, maintaining, and operating on each type of organization, would take place over a considerable amount of time, and possibly would represent improvements in degree rather than kind.

Finding a Basis for Classification. Why do

young children adhere to a criterion when sorting objects at the basic but not at the superordinate level? One explanation offered above is that there is greater perceptual dissimilarity among members of superordinate categories than among members of basic categories (Rosch et al., 1976). As the child takes in the different properties of the objects before him, his attention sways away from the property initially selected as basis for classification and is captured first by one property, then by another property, and so on. In short, the child keeps switching criteria. In addition, young children might fail to group objects according to a consistent criterion at the superordinate level, *not* because they are incapable of adhering to the same criterion throughout their classification, but because they are incapable of *uncovering* a criterion that could serve as basis for classification. By this account, the young child's failure to group objects consistently at the superordinate level is due to the child's having difficulty in coming up with a satisfactory criterion—not to his being unable to systematically apply the criterion selected. This explanation presupposes that once children have selected or hit upon a criterion by which to classify objects, they always know to apply it consistently. Given this assumption, inconsistent or haphazard groupings are naturally interpreted as reflecting the child's inability to discover in the array before him a basis for classification.

It is easy to see why the young child would have little difficulty coming up with a satisfactory criterion when presented with objects that must be sorted at the basic, as opposed to the superordinate, level. Children can group objects into basic categories according to any or all of a number of criteria: shape, function, motor programs involved in their use, and so on. A basis for classification is easily found as several are available and because the overall physical similarity of members of the same basic category is usually very salient. The child who is presented with an array containing objects that belong to (two or three) different basic categories is, thus, faced with highly contrasting subsets of objects that have perceptually clear-cut boundaries. It is not difficult for the child to identify the instances of each basic category represented in the array. These tend to be similar to one another along a number of separate dimensions as well as different from the instances of the other categories. On all these counts, it appears that it would be easy for the child to select a basis for classification and to carry out the grouping of basic-level objects consistently and exhaustively.

The superordinate categories with which we have

been mainly concerned have all been categories of real-world, concrete objects. But the same argument regarding the criterion selected could be extended to categories of blocks that vary along a number of dimensions. For instance, one might say that the greater the number of dimensions that must be ignored, the less obvious or salient the basis for classification and the more difficult the task. Partial support for this hypothesis comes from traditional concept-learning experiments that have shown that adding irrelevant stimulus dimensions increases the difficulty of learning for adults (Haygood & Stevenson, 1967; Walker & Bourne, 1961) and for nursery-school and elementary-school children (Osler & Kofsky, 1965).

Additional support for the above hypothesis comes from Fischer and Roberts (1980) who assessed children between 15 and 75 months of age on a developmental sequence of classificatory skills. The sequence was predicted from Fischer's (1980) skill theory. A total of 12 distinct steps were differentiated and over 95% of the children tested fit the sequence perfectly. Because the first 4 steps of the sequence are the most relevant to our argument, we will be concerned exclusively with these. It was predicted that by 15 months of age children would be able to handle single categories (Step 1). When presented with blocks that varied along a single dimension (e.g., shape), children would group together all the blocks that belonged to the same category. For example, they would pick circles from triangles when the blocks were all the same color and size (recall Sugarman's [1979] finding that 18-month-olds will produce complete spatial groupings of one of the two classes in an array). At about 2 years of age, children were expected to be able to handle several categories simultaneously (Step 2). For example, with blocks like those in Step 1, children would sort blocks into three categories—circles, triangles, and squares (again, recall Sugarman's [1979] findings that by 24 months of age both classes in the array were spatially grouped). At 2½ years, children were expected to sort blocks into three categories, even if there were variations within each of the categories. For example, different types of triangles, circles, and squares might make up the three categories (Step 3). Finally, by 3 or 3½ years of age, the child was expected to handle not only simple categories but also categories where there were variations on an interfering dimension. That is, when the blocks varied in both color and shape simultaneously (but presented no within-category variations as in Step 3), the child was still expected to be able to sort them into three shape categories and then subdivide each category into three color categories (Step 4).

Fischer and Roberts' (1980) subjects were 70 children between the ages of 15 and 75 months. Each of the four tasks required the child to sort blocks into (one or more) boxes. Boxes were used to minimize the need for verbal instructions and to make the nature of the task as obvious and as simple as possible. A separate box was used for each category. For tasks that involved two or three categories, identical boxes were arranged in a line before the child.

The experimenter first demonstrated how the blocks were to be sorted and described how he had sorted them. Then, he put them in a scrambled pile before the child and said, "Put the blocks in the boxes so they go together like the way I put them in." If the child erred in sorting the blocks, the experimenter re-sorted them correctly and then urged the child to try a second time (cf. Nash & Gelman cited in Gelman & Gallistel, 1978). After the second trial, the experimenter went on to the next task. For every step, the child had to sort *all* blocks correctly to pass the step.

The performance profiles of all 70 children fit the hypothesized sequence perfectly. The results from this and a second experiment (which assessed later steps in the sequence predicted from skill theory) indicate that children acquire classificatory skills in a gradual sequence that starts by 15 months of age (if not before). These results clearly contradict Inhelder and Piaget's (1964) analysis of the development of classification. Other attempts at testing the sequence Inhelder and Piaget proposed (e.g., Hooper et al., 1979; Kofsky, 1966) have also failed to support it. However, the latter studies did report the same general trend from poor, inconsistent classification to skilled, consistent classification that Inhelder and Piaget found. Fischer and Roberts' (1980) results are particularly interesting in that they indicate that young preschool children possess far more classificatory ability than the results of previous studies (whether or not they found the developmental pattern predicted by Inhelder & Piaget, 1964) led one to expect. Fischer and Roberts, (1980) also show—and this is the point we wished to make—that this ability is somewhat dependent on the particular array of objects with which the child is presented. At first, the child can only sort arrays that are composed of single categories that represent variations along only one dimension, that is, the blocks are identical except for variations in one dimension, such as shape. Later on, the child can sort arrays into single categories and ignore irrelevant variations within each category, for example, different types of circles, triangles, or squares. Later still, the child becomes able (1) to tackle arrays that are composed of objects that vary along two dimensions and (2) to divide them first according to one dimension and then to subdivide them according to the other dimension.

It is hard to believe that the child learns anew at each step of the sequence how to sort objects into consistent, exhaustive classes. On grounds of parsimony alone, one would want to reject such an assumption. Instead, one might suggest that the child understands quite well that one should sort according to a stable, consistent criterion and does so from the earliest ages. What would change over time, then, is not the ability to adhere to a criterion throughout a classification, but the ability to parse more and more complex arrays—to uncover amidst the complexity a criterion or a set of criteria that would permit the child to sort the array without remainder and without overlap.

In other words, one might say that the ability to construct consistent, exhaustive classes is there very early on and that what improves in time is the ability to apply this competence to more and more complex arrays. Arrays that contain objects that vary simultaneously along a number of dimensions (some relevant, some irrelevant) require more complex processing than do arrays that are composed of two types of very distinct objects (such as those Sugarman, 1979, and Ricciuti, 1965, used). The nature of the psychological processes involved in the abstraction of a basis for classification in simpler and more complex arrays still remains to be specified. Once we have some idea of the nature of these processes and how they develop over time, we may have a much better idea of the nature of the young child's difficulty with superordinate sorting tasks.

At this point, one might make the following claim. If it is correct to assume that a child *always* applies a criterion consistently once she has succeeded in uncovering it, then were we to show or tell the child what the criterion is, she should have no difficulty in picking out the instances of the category and doing so consistently. However, this strong prediction of the hypothesis is not borne out by the facts. First, modeling a classification is not sufficient to get a child to classify objects correctly. In Fischer and Roberts' (1980) experiment, the experimenter first sorted the objects and then had the child do the same. The children could not always sort the blocks as the experimenter had; they followed a clear-cut developmental sequence in terms of the classifications they could imitate. Thus, more is involved than just the ability to use a criterion consistently.

Horton and Markman (1980) provide additional evidence that telling the child what the criterion is, is not necessarily helpful to the child. Horton and Markman investigated 4-, 5-, and 6-year-olds' acquisition of artificial animal categories. They found that (1) basic-level categories were acquired more easily than superordinate categories from exposure to exemplars alone; (2) the specification of the criterial features was beneficial for the acquisition of only the superordinate categories, that is, basic-level categories were not learned better when criteria were specified; and (3) only the older children benefited from the specification of the criteria, and then only when learning superordinate categories (this is the result that is relevant to the present discussion). The 4-year-old children did not benefit from the specification of criteria at the superordinate level. In contrast, both the 5- and the 6-year-old children were better able to learn superordinate categories when the criteria were specified.

Given that criterial information can be helpful in the acquisition of superordinate categories—as the older children's performance demonstrates—why the failure of younger children to use it? Horton and Markman (1980) rule out a failure in understanding. Children could understand the descriptions and could sort objects based on each individual criterion when so instructed. Horton and Markman argue that the information processing demands of the task were too great. In addition, it could have been a question of poor strategic skills. There are many instances in the literature where young children fail to make use of information or skills that are at their disposal. The rehearsal literature is a particularly good case in point (e.g., Flavell & Wellman, 1977). There is some evidence that the same might be going on here. For instance, Anglin (1977) asked preschoolers to define common nouns and later to classify objects into categories denoted by the terms they had been asked to define. Anglin reports that when classifying, the children often failed to use their own definitions for the categorization of the objects.

Factual Knowledge and Classification Abilities. Above we argued that the child may have difficulty forming superordinate categories because the basis for classification is abstract and not immediately accessible to the young child. However, in some cases it may be the features that characterize a higher order category are inaccessible, not because they are abstract and difficult to discern but because the child has not yet acquired the necessary or relevant knowledge to appreciate their significance.

Chi's (1980) study of preschoolers who are interested in dinosaurs makes this point. The more a child knows about dinosaurs, the more complex a classification scheme reflected in his recall of the names of dinosaurs. Carey's (1978) work on childrens' concept of "animal" helps illustrate how there could be an interaction between knowledge and the use of a classification structure.

Carey has done a series of studies on the development (from 4 to 7 years) of the understanding of the concept of animal (Carey, 1978; in preparation). In these studies, children were presented with a number of animate and inanimate objects, some familiar and some unfamiliar. For example, children were shown pictures of a person, a dog, an aardvark, a dodo, a hammerhead, a fly, a worm, an orchid, a baobab, the sun, clouds, a bus, a harvesting machine, a garlic press, a hammer, and a rolltop desk. They were asked several questions about each picture. Some questions involved properties of the particular object ("Is the sun hot?"); others involved properties of an immediate superordinate of an object ("Does a hammerhead live in water?"), or properties of animals ("Does a worm eat?"), or properties of living things ("Does a dodo grow?"). The animal properties probed were, eats, breathes, has a heart, has bones, sleeps, thinks, and has babies. The properties of living things were, is alive, grows, and dies.

Animals that adults take as more peripheral exemplars of the class were systematically assigned fewer animal characteristics by the children. In addition, there was a marked absence of a clear differentiation among animal properties. Thus, Carey found a stable ordering of the animals in terms of how often they were attributed animal properties. Roughly, this ordering was: people, mammals, birds, insects, fish, and worms. Even though the most peripheral animals were credited with a particular animal property only 20% to 40% of the time, each child credited every animal with at least one animal property. That is, the ordering of the animals does not seem to reflect some children's failure to appreciate that the peripheral animals were animals. Although the animals were ordered, the properties were not. Subjects were no more likely to credit animals with eating than with having bones or thinking. Adults, on the contrary, attribute eating, breathing, and having babies to all animals, sleeping and having hearts to fewer, having bones to fewer still, and thinking to fewest of all. Thus, 4- to 7-year-olds were likely to attribute only one or two animal properties to the peripheral animals, but those properties were just as likely to be having bones and thinking as eating and having babies. The animal properties clearly were not differentiated from each other in the subjects' patterns of responses.

Carey takes her result to suggest that the child's concept of animal is embedded in a very impoverished biological theory. This follows from both the tendencies to underattribute animal properties to peripheral cases of animals and not to differentiate animal properties from each other. We agree with Carey's interpretation. But more important in this context, her findings have considerable implications for the way young children will behave on classification tasks.

If peripheral animals are not known to have a heart, they presumably will not be classified together with animals who are known to have a heart. Similarly, if children do not know that not all animals have bones, they may end up classifying items together that they should not. Children's erroneous classifications might be taken as evidence of an inability to apply criteria (e.g., "has-a-heart," "has-bones") consistently. But, in fact, this would reflect children's ignorance of biological facts rather than an inability to maintain a hierarchical classification scheme.

We have explored a number of reasons why the young child has difficulty sorting arrays that are composed of objects that can only be sorted at the superordinate level. We have argued that despite his poor performance in superordinate sorting tasks, the young child does possess (at least some of) the relevant logical abilities. Actually, we believe there is enough evidence in the young child of a capacity for hierarchical organization to suggest that what needs explaining is the fact that this ability is not *always* displayed—rather than the fact that it is not displayed at all. This argument was used to interpret results from a variety of free-classification studies with preschoolers (e.g., Denney, 1972a, 1972b; Fischer & Roberts, 1980; Nash & Gelman cited in Gelman & Gallistel, 1978). It is buttressed by studies that used simplified classification tasks as well as memory studies.

Oddity tasks and matching tasks are simpler than free-classification tasks in that they do not require the child to group objects together into consistent, exhaustive categories. All that is required is that the child be able to perceive that two of a small number of elements belong to the same category.

We have already presented oddity data that support the notion that young children are sensitive to, and can pair items on the basis of, superordinate relations. Recall the study of Rosch et al. (1976) in which children 3 years of age and older were given oddity problems. Performance on the basic-level

problems was virtually perfect at all ages tested. Performance on the superordinate level problems was significantly worse, especially in the youngest age group. Still, the 3-year-olds' mean correct percentage was 55% and the 4-year-olds' was 96%. These data suggest that children find it easier to sort items that belong in the same basic, as opposed to superordinate, category—not that they are fundamentally unable to perform the latter kind of task.

Daehler, Lonardo, and Bukatko (1979) examined the difficulty very young children have in matching stimuli at several levels of perceptual and conceptual similarity. Four different types of relationships between stimuli were tested: (1) identical stimuli, (2) stimuli belonging to the same basic category, (3) stimuli belonging to the same superordinate category, and finally (4) stimuli bearing a complementary relation to one another (e.g., crayon-coloring book, hammer-nail). Subjects were 16 children at each of 3 age levels 21 to 22, 27 to 28, and 31 to 33 months. Stimuli consisted of real objects or toy objects. The exemplars for each basic-level category differed in size and color and, where possible, detail and shape as well. Stimuli were never labeled during test trials; the experimenter simply held out the standard to the child and instructed her to "find the one (of four choices) that goes with this one." Any child who failed to respond to the experimenter's instructions was led to the table as the instructions were repeated. A response was recorded whenever the subject placed the standard beside one of the four alternatives or touched or picked one of the alternatives. Correct responses were verbally reinforced. If the child made an error, she was asked to respond again. If she were still not correct, the correct response was modeled. At the completion of each trial, the correct response alternative was removed, a new item was added, and all four stimuli in the array were rearranged. Thus, all stimuli in the array were eventually relevant. Because children were invariably attracted to each new item, they were allowed to play with it briefly as prior testing indicated that the opportunity to become familiar with each new item before a trial helped reduce a substantial response bias for selecting it on the subsequent trial. There were 6 distinct trials for each type of relationship examined (24 altogether).

The results were straightforward. Performance improved with age in every condition. Moreover, the order of difficulty of conditions for each age group was consistent—identity matches were easiest, followed by basic-level, superordinate level, and complementary matches. Finally, children in all age groups responded above chance level in all four conditions, with the exception of the youngest age group matching complementary stimuli. The fact that performance on stimuli belonging to superordinate taxonomic categories was well above chance at all ages again suggests that from a very early age (in this case less than 2 years) children are able to detect and make use of superordinate relations. However, the equivalences selected by Daehler and his colleagues (1979) do lend themselves to alternative interpretations. Their superordinate pairs were camel-cow, fork-spoon, boat-truck, apple-banana, and pants-shirt. The underlined pairs appear especially ambiguous as they represent items that the child, no doubt, must have had ample opportunities to see together and so the basis of his matching, or equivalence judgment, is unclear.

Adults are better at remembering words from lists that contain subsets from the same taxonomic categories than words from randomly generated lists (e.g., Cofer, Bruce, & Reicher, 1966). In addition, if the words that are taxonomically related are separated in the list, adults tend to cluster them by meaning in output (e.g., Bousfield, 1953). It has been reported that young children do not remember words from lists with taxonomically related subsets better than words from unrelated lists (e.g., Hasher & Clifton, 1974; Nelson, 1969). In addition, the degree of clustering has been found to increase with age, from grade school through college (e.g., Bousfield, Esterson, & Whitmarsh, 1958; Neimark, Slotnick, & Ulrich, 1971). The preschooler's alleged inability to detect and benefit from the hierarchical organization of to-be-remembered lists has been thought to reveal a fundamental inability to appreciate or impose hierarchical relations on stimuli. Such conclusions, however, are beginning to look unwarranted (Huttenlocher & Lui, 1979).

There is now evidence that young children are better at remembering items that are all from the same taxonomic category than items that are unrelated (e.g., Cole, Frankel, & Sharp, 1971; Kobasigawa & Orr, 1973). In the study of Kobasigawa and Orr (1973), for example, kindergarten subjects were presented with 16 pictures in four category sets (e.g., animals: zebra, lion, camel, and elephant; vegetables: corn, onion, carrot, and pumpkin); or in a random order with one item from each category composing the four presentation sets. The categorically grouped presentation facilitated free-recall performance, both in terms of number of items recalled and the speed with which items were recalled; it also increased the amount of clustering in recall.

Even 2-year-olds have been found to recall pairs of objects better when they are from the same, rather than from different, categories. Goldberg, Perlmutter, and Myers (1974) tested children aged 29 to 35 months on a task requiring free recall of two-item lists. Each of the three trials consisted of the randomly ordered presentation of six boxes, each containing a pair of objects selected from three categories (food, animals, and utensils). For three of these pairs, the objects belonged to the same taxonomic category (e.g., cookie-lollipop; elephant-giraffe; fork-spoon). The three remaining pairs were formed of unrelated items from the same categories (e.g., M&M's-lion; apple-cup; dog-plate). (Pilot work showed that labels were readily produced for all pictures and that although fork and spoon were associated responses for a few children, none of the other items were given in response to each other.) The mean number of correct responses was higher for related items than for unrelated items.

Additional evidence that young children impose hierarchical organization on objects is Keil's (1977, 1979) finding that a hierarchical structure constrains the development of ontological knowledge. Keil had children make acceptability judgments of what predicates could be true about certain objects and events. Over and over again he found children's judgments reflected an underlying hierarchical structure. Thus, for example, they failed to assign animate predicates to inanimate objects and vice versa. Such results indicate that young children can make *implicit* use of a hierarchical classification scheme. They do not demonstrate *explicit* use of the same structure—a point to which we will return below.

Class Inclusion Revisited

For Inhelder and Piaget (1964), complete mastery of hierarchical classification is indexed by the mastery of the inclusion relation, and it is not attained until the stage of concrete operations. The preoperational child is incapable of class inclusion because she lacks the two reversible operations of class addition (e.g., flowers = petunias + begonias) and class subtraction (petunias = flowers − begonias). Until she acquires these two operations, the child is unable to attend simultaneously to the class and its subclasses and is, thus, incapable of making quantitative class-subclass comparisons (e.g., "Are there more flowers or more petunias?").

We do not believe that class-inclusion tests should be taken as criterial measures of the ability to classify objects hierarchically. Mastery of the class-inclusion relation, with all its implications, is a relatively late development (Winer, 1980); hierarchical classification, by contrast, emerges in the first few years of life. We have seen evidence of hierarchical organization in the 2-year-old's grouping of objects—in his correct usage of superordinate terms, in his free recall performance, and so on. As more ingenious methods of investigating the prelinguistic child's cognition and knowledge are developed, one may find that even younger children are capable of constructing simple, well-formed hierarchies.

Winer (1980) in an extensive review of the literature on class inclusion notes that "the studies showing late development far outnumber those showing early development," and concludes that "the results clearly refute the claim of Piaget and others that class-inclusion is developed by age 7 or 8" (p. 310). There is also evidence that children less than 11 years of age who do pass the class-inclusion test may still have only an incomplete grasp of the logic of inclusion. Markman (1978) tested whether children who render correct class-inclusion judgments do so on the basis of logical or empirical considerations. Because her earlier work (Osherson & Markman 1974–1975) showed that children often treat tautological statements as though they were empirical statements, Markman thought that children might also treat the greater numerosity of a class over its subclass as an empirical fact rather than as a logical consequence of inclusion.

Markman (1978) reasoned that children who do appreciate the logical necessity of the class being larger than its subclass (1) should be willing to make the class-subclass comparison, even when they have no empirical means of judging the relative numerosity of the two, (2) should understand that no addition of elements could ever result in the subclass containing more elements than the class, and finally (3) should be willing to compare a class to its subclass even when given only minimal information about the subclass. A study was designed to test each of these hypotheses. Results indicated that children take the greater numerosity of the class to be an empirical fact until about 11 years.

Although performance on the standard class inclusion task points to a relatively late development, there is evidence that even 4-year-olds are able to represent and implicitly evaluate inclusion relations. C. L. Smith (1979) tested 4- to 7-year-olds on three different tasks. The first task involved quantified inclusion questions of the form, "Are all Xs Ys?" and "Are some Xs Ys?," where X could be a subset of Y. No pictures were used; children answered on the basis of their knowledge of the terms and the objects they denoted.

The other two tasks were inference tasks. One was a class inference task. Children were given problems of the form, "A _____ is a kind of X. Does a _____ have to be a Y?" (where _____ was a real word children did not know). There were three types of problems, depending on whether the inference was valid (e.g., "A pug is a kind of dog. Does a pug have to be an animal?"); indeterminate (e.g., "A pug is an animal. Does a duplex have to be a fence?"); or invalid (e.g., "A pug is an animal. Does a pug have to be a cat?"). The other inference task was a property inference task. Problems were of the form: "All Xs have _____. Do all Ys have to have _____" (where _____ was filled with a new word for a property). Again, there were three types of problems—where the inference was valid (e.g., "All milk has lactose. Does all chocolate milk have to have lactose?"); where the inference was invalid (e.g., "All milk has lactose. Do all sneakers have to have lactose?"); and, finally, where the inference was indeterminate (e.g., "All milk has lactose. Do all drinks have to have lactose?").

Smith reports group as well as individual data for each of the three tasks. However, the results that are most relevant to the present discussion are those that concern the children's patterns of responding *across* the three tasks. Overall, 90% of the 4-year-olds and all of the older children succeeded on at least one of the tasks. As Smith points out, such results definitely argue against characterizing young children as being unable to represent and reason about inclusion relations. For, if such a characterization were correct, children would have failed all three inclusion tasks. The fact that almost all children met criterion on at least one task and many children on more than one task suggests that children are able to represent inclusion relations. It also suggests that under favorable conditions children can solve problems that require them to evaluate such relations.

A subsequent experiment was designed to explore further 4-year-olds' ability to draw inferences on the basis of inclusion relations. In this experiment, 10 children, aged 48 to 56 months, were given four valid and four invalid inference problems. These problems were slightly different from those used in the first experiment; they gave the children additional information that, presumably, made the inference easier, for example, "A yam is a kind of food, but not meat. Is a yam a hamburger?" and "A pawpaw is a kind of fruit, but not a banana. Is a pawpaw food?" The results were quite striking; children were correct 91% of the time, and 8 of the 10 children made only one or fewer errors.

These results indicate that success on the standard Piagetian class-inclusion test should not be held up as the sine qua non condition of the ability to embed classes within one another. It is best to think of inclusion not as a unitary, all-or-none ability, but to think of it as one does classification, numerical reasoning, and so forth. One can devise tasks that will result in a very broad range of performance success—inclusion tasks that 4-year-olds solve without any difficulty (e.g., C. L. Smith, 1979) and inclusion tasks that children less than 11 years of age systematically fail. Recall also the Markman et al. (1980) unexpected result that even 14-year-olds will mistake a class-inclusion hierarchy for a collection hierarchy when the situation provides minimal information to guide or constrain their interpretation. There is reason to suppose that some inclusion ability is available at an early age but that this ability is at first relatively limited and is only displayed under limited, favorable conditions (see Trabasso, Isen, Dolecki, McLanahan, Riley, & Tucker, 1978, for a careful consideration of limiting conditions). As the child develops, he becomes capable of carrying out more and more complex computations on the inclusion relation between classes. The standard Piagetian test is only one of the many tests that require the child to evaluate and operate on inclusion relations.

We do not mean to suggest that the ability to classify objects hierarchically is fully present from the start. The bulk of the experimental evidence we have reviewed indicates that there is considerable improvement with age. However, the evidence also suggests that the improvement is one of degree, not of kind. As the child's information-processing capacities develop, as his knowledge of the world increases, and as his perceptual and cognitive strategies become more efficient, we find that his ability to detect, and make use of, hierarchical structure also develops.

It seems reasonable to suppose that as mastery of hierarchical classification is progressively achieved, the child becomes better able to represent for himself the relations that exist between classes at the same and different levels within hierarchies. Further, as the child's ability to represent interactions among classes develops, so does his ability to reason about such interactions. It is in this light (it seems to us) that one can best make sense of the empirical work on class inclusion. Quantitative comparisons of superordinate classes and their subclasses are not successfully performed until quite late—by contrast, inclusion tasks that involve simpler, less demanding comparisons are solved at an early age.

More on the Same Themes

Our review of some core concrete-operational concepts highlighted several themes. First, preschool children have more knowledge about quantity and classification than any of us anticipated—say 10 years ago. Second, despite the new-found brilliance of the young child, there is still much to develop within the various domains of cognition. The development will be protracted, in some cases taking until 13 to 14 years of age. Third, the younger the child, the fewer the task settings with which he can cope. That is, their abilities are uncovered within a rather limited set of situations. Fourth, what is known early is often implicit. That is, the child's behavior is systematically governed by underlying structures (e.g., the counting principles) that are not known to the child. Thus, at least in some cases, a part of development is making explicit what was initially implicit (for a similar argument see Flavell & Wellman, 1977, on the development of metamemory). Finally, the evidence on the relationships among abilities across domains is too weak to support a theory of overarching structures. This leaves open the possibility that there are domain-specific structures rather than domain-independent structures (cf. Chomsky, 1965; Keil, 1981).

We believe that many of the same conclusions will emerge as we gain further knowledge about various domains of cognition. Indeed, there is already sufficient evidence regarding the abilities to seriate and reason about physical cause-effect relations.

We have already noted the strong tendency of very young children to impose an order relation on objects (e.g., Bryant, 1974; Bryant & Trabasso, 1971). Additional evidence on the ability of young children to seriate comes from Cooper, Leitner, and Moore (1981), Greenfield, Nelson, and Saltzman (1972), Koslowski (1980). Greenfield et al. reported that even 3-year-old children could construct a series out of stacking cups and could correctly insert a new cup into the stack.

As Koslowski (1980) notes, early demonstrations of operational competence may not meet Piaget's definition. In the case of seriation, Inhelder and Piaget (1964) require that a child be able to perform a systematic seriation in a constant direction, insert additional items into an already-established series, and correct an erroneous insertion by someone else. Koslowski (1980) tested 3- and 4-year-olds on her own abbreviated tasks as well as the traditional tasks used by Inhelder and Piaget (1964). The difference between the two sets of tasks was simply in the number of sticks used. The traditional tasks require a child to work with a 10-stick series to start; Koslowski (1980) had them work with a 4-stick series to start. Otherwise, the two sets of tasks were identical and met the above crucial criteria. On the basis of their performance on the 10-stick tasks, Koslowski (1980) assigned children to the standard three Piagetian stages of seriation ability. Of the many children who were classified as Stage 1 (no ability to seriate), 75% could construct a systematic series of 4 sticks, 81% could insert 2 new sticks in a 4-stick series, and 100% could correct incorrect insertions. What we see here is a powerful effect of set size—one that yields contradictory classifications of the same children. It is hard to deny these young children a seriation scheme, even if it is applied in a restricted range.

Work by Cooper et al. (1981) leads us to conclude that despite the young child's competence vis-à-vis seriation, it is nevertheless fragile. These researchers find 3-year-olds able to discriminate between a seriated and nonseriated set of rods under some conditions. Yet, they have difficulty discriminating between series on the basis of the direction increase.

The theme that "the young know more and that the old know less" applies to seriation as does it to other domains. Recent work by Piaget (1980) supports this conclusion as well as the idea of development proceeding from the implicit to the explicit.

With Bullinger, Piaget (1980) studied the way children between 5 and 12 years solved a conflict over what they saw. Children were shown a display containing seven discs in a zigzag row. The thicknesses of all the discs were the same; the diameters increased progressively by steps of 0.2 mm—a nondiscriminable difference. Because the discs were arranged in a zigzag, the child could compare only adjacent pairs of discs and, therefore, would conclude that each pair of discs shared the same diameter. However, because the last disc could be removed and compared with the first in the display, the child could see that these two did differ in diameter. Children younger than 11 years had difficulty resolving the conflict between their initial *conclusion* that the first and last discs were equal in diameter and their *perception* that they were not. To resolve the conflict, one has to maintain that the discs *had* to get progressively bigger, even if one could not physically see this. That is, one had to impose a presumed ordering on the stimuli. It is hard to imagine how one could do this without an explicit understanding of seriation and the principle of transitivity. Piaget (1980) reports that only the older children (at least 11 years old) could resolve the conflict successfully. This leads us to suggest that an explicit understanding of the principle of transitivity is rather late in developing, a conclusion that is also supported by Moore's (1979) work.

Recent work on the understanding of physical causality reinforces the conclusion that order relations are quite salient for the young child. Bullock and Gelman (1979) had children watch the exact same event—a ball rolling down a runway and disappearing into a box—before *and* after Jack jumped up from the box. When asked to chose the ball that made Jack jump, 3- to 5-year-old children systematically chose the ball that was dropped first. They did this even when the order information conflicted with a cue of spatial contiguity, that is, when the *before*-event was in a runway that was separated from the jack-in-the-box but the *after*-event was not. Bullock and Gelman took these findings as evidence in favor of the view that preschoolers honor a principle of priority when reasoning about physical cause-and-effect relations. That is, young children implicitly apply the rule that causes cannot follow their effects but can only precede or coincide with their effects. Other lines of converging evidence are reviewed in Sedlak and Kurtz (1981) and Weiner and Kun (1976).[5]

Bullock, Gelman, and Baillargeon (1982) go beyond granting preschoolers the implicit principle of priority. Bullock et al. maintain that preschoolers also apply the principle that cause-effect relations are mediated by mechanisms. Those familiar with Piaget's early (1930) and recent work (e.g., 1974) on physical causality will recognize that this latter conclusion is at odds with his ideas about the development of the understanding of physical causality.

Piaget was probably the first psychologist to investigate systematically the development of the young child's conception of physical causality. He and his collaborators asked children to explain a variety of natural (e.g., the cycle of the moon, the floating of boats) and mechanical (e.g., the operation of bicycles and steam engines) phenomena. Analyses of the explanations collected led Piaget to characterize the young child's thought as fundamentally precausal.

According to Piaget, "immediacy of relations and absence of intermediaries . . . are the two outstanding features of causality around the age of 4 to 5 (1930, p. 268). Thus, the pedals of a bicycle are said to make the wheels turn without being in any way attached to them. A fire lit alongside an engine is said to make the wheels of the engine turn, even if it is 2 ft. away; the sun is said to follow us as we walk down the street. "Not a thought is given to the question of distance or of how long the action would take in travelling from cause to effect" (Piaget, 1930, p. 268).

In his early work on child causality, Piaget

(1930) claimed the young child had no assumption of contact between cause and effect. The idea was that the young lacked an assumption of mechanism. With development, the young child came to learn about chains of intermediary events. In Piaget's more recent treatment of causality (e.g., Piaget, 1974), the account of development is different. However, the young child is still characterized as lacking a principle of mechanism. By his most recent account, children have to come to attribute to objects the operations they have mastered. According to Piaget, "There is a remarkable convergence between the stages of formation of operations and those of causal explanation; the subject understands the phenomena only by attributing the objects . . . operations more or less isomorphic to his" (Piaget, 1974, p. 4). In one experiment used to make this point, children were asked to explain why the last of a row of still marbles rolled away after the first was hit by a moving marble. Children in the initial stage (4 to 5 years) explained this as if they believed the moving marble acted at a distance. Children in the subsequent stage (6 years) assumed each marble in the row pushed the one next to it. According to Piaget (1974), it was not until they reached the next stage (i.e., until the advent of operational transitivity, 7 to 8 years) that children began to form a notion of mediate transmission.

The idea that an assumption of mechanism is lacking in the preschooler is contradicted by several lines of research. Bullock (1979) adapted her runway and jack-in-the-box apparatus to give children a choice between two events as possible causes. In one experiment, children saw a ball and a light source move down parallel runways and disappear at the same time into the jack box (the perception of light movement was due to an induced phi-phenomenon). In the experiment, 3-, 4- and 5-year-olds consistently chose the ball running down the runway as cause, presumably on the assumption that steel balls are more likely to hit something and release the jack-in-the-box. Support for the conclusion that 4- and 5-year-olds made such inferences follows from what happened in Bullock's next experiment.

In the second Bullock experiment, the runway portion of the apparatus was separated from the jack-in-the-box portion. Otherwise the experiment was exactly the same. (The jack-in-the-box was operated by remote control.) In this experiment, 4- and 5-year-olds did *not* choose the rolling ball. Instead, they attributed causality to the moving light. Put differently, children chose that event as cause that was most plausible. Balls do not produce impact at a distance; however, electrical devices often cause ef-

fects at a distance. Given their ability to take into account changes of conditions when making causal attributions, it is difficult to deny 4- and 5-year-olds an implicit concern for mechanism. A similar conclusion follows for even younger children, given work by Baillargeon, Gelman, and Meck (1981) and Shultz (1982).

In two separate experiments, Baillargeon et al. (1981) showed children the working of a three-part apparatus. The initial piece consisted of a long rod that could be pushed through a hole in a post; the intermediate piece was a set of five upright blocks; the end part was made up of a lever and a toy rabbit (Fred) sitting on a box next to a toy bed. Children in the experiment were first given a demonstration of the working apparatus: when the rod was pushed through the hole it hit the first block. The first block fell and created a domino effect. The last block landed on the lever that made Fred-the-rabbit fall into his bed. After the demonstration, the children were asked to predict whether Fred would fall into his bed given variations in the first, intermediate, and final parts of the apparatus. Modifications were of two types: *relevant* ones, those that disrupted the sequence, and *irrelevant* ones, those that did not disrupt it. For example, a short stick was used and, hence, could not reach the first block (a relevant change). In contrast, a long glass tube could reach the first block, and, thus, when used, constituted an irrelevant change. Similarly, the removal of one intermediate block versus the laying down of blocks was relevant as opposed to irrelevant. In the first experiment, prediction trials were run on a fully visible apparatus. In the second experiment, the block and lever portion of the apparatus was screened.

Baillargeon et al. (1981) reasoned as follows. If young children wrongly believe that the very occurrence of the first event in a causal sequence is sufficient to bring about the final event, they should treat all modifications of the first event as potentially disruptive and all modifications of the intermediary events as nondisruptive. On the other hand, if children do understand that the intermediary events in a causal sequence effectively connect the first and last events in the sequence, they should regard all and only the *relevant* modifications—whether of the initial or intermediary events—as likely to disrupt the sequence. In the first experiment all 20 children in the experiment were correct on at least 75% of their 23 predictions. Indeed, the average correct responses for the 3-year-olds was 85%; that for the 4-year-olds was 90.5%. In the second experiment, where the screen hid the intermediate mechanism, the children did almost as well: 19 met the 75%

correct criterion. Differential predictions at this level of accuracy could only have occurred if the children were using the intermediary events as such.

Shultz (1982) has concluded that even 2-year-olds assume that a cause produces its effects via a transmission of force, be it either direct (as in one ball hitting another) or through an intermediary. In Shultz's first experiment, after a brief initial demonstration of a cause-effect sequence, children were asked to assign causal attributions to one of two energy sources. As an example, children were shown that turning on a blower had the effect of putting out a candle. They were then shown two blowers (one white, the other green), each of which was surrounded on three sides by a Plexiglass shield. The critical difference between the two blowers was whether the open side was facing a lit candle—and, therefore, one could blow out the candle. If considerations of mechanism do not influence young children, they should choose randomly between blowers as cause. They did not; they systematically chose the blower whose opening faced the candle. Similar effects held for the transmission of a sound source from a tuning fork and the transmission of light from a battery. The consistent result was that children took note of barriers that would stop the transmission of light and sound when they made causal attributions. Interestingly, a similar result held in Shultz's (1982) study of Mali children in West Africa—whether or not they were in school environments.

If we acknowledge that young children's search for explanations of their world is governed by the implicit principles of priority and mechanism, we can account for the kinds of results reviewed here. But to grant these causal principles is not to say young children know they are using them. In the case of causal reasoning, we doubt whether most adults know they are using it. As before, we allow for the implicit use of principles, just as psycholinguists allow for the implicit use of rules that guide the use and comprehension of speech.

Again, to say the young child has some competence is not to say she has a complete, correct understanding of physical causality. As Baillargeon (1981) shows, the development of the ability to explain why a prediction is correct evolves very slowly. And as McCloskey, Caramazza, and Green (1980) show, even undergraduates at Johns Hopkins University make erroneous assumptions about the world. The kinds of predictions made are more consistent with Aristotle's writings on physics than anything Newton ever wrote! Wrong theories have abounded in the history of science. But, whatever the theory, assumptions must have been made about

priority, mechanism, and weak determinism (Bullock et al., 1982), otherwise there could hardly be a history of science.

Like Carey (1980) we ascribe to the view that Piaget's (1974) recent experiments on causal reasoning should be viewed as experiments on the acquisition and change of explanation systems. Looking back to the Piaget (1974) experiment on the child's understanding of the transmission of force, we suspect many of our readers wanted to know what was wrong with the 6-year-olds' explanation of why the final marble moved. It certainly included an assumption of possible mechanism, albeit a naive one.

Our preceding point goes beyond a standard anti-Piagetian argument, that is, young children are bad explainers. We do not mean that causal understanding is simply a matter of being able to provide explanations per se. There is the separate issue of whether one understands the *correct* explanation. When viewed from this perspective, it is possible to allow that there are qualitatively different theories of physical reality as a function of development or even schooling—just as Aristotelean and Newtonian theory are. It is not, however, necessary to deny the young or uneducated a causal attitude that is governed by principles of causal reasoning.

There are further cases of earlier cognitive competence than once expected—either within a Piagetian framework or not. Many of these appear in other chapters (e.g., see *Brown, Bransford, Ferrara, & Campione, vol. III, chap. 2; Mandler, vol. III, chap. 7;* or *Shatz, vol. III, chap. 13*). We trust our main point is clear by now. Earlier competence? *Yes*. Full competence? *Certainly not*.

SUMMING UP

Structures of Thought?

When we began our review we simply announced our support of the Piagetian view that what we think, perceive, and remember is mediated by structures of thought. We did so without even justifying this position. That we did not is a sign of how heavily Piaget *has* influenced all of us. Piaget's ideas that cognitive structures set the limits of problem-solving abilities as well as influence both how we perceive the world "out there" and influence the contents of memory, were either ignored altogether or dismissed as unnecessary. As Flavell (1982) noted, the idea that structures determine our memories, perceptions, and problem-solving abilities is so pervasive in modern cognitive psychology that it is almost a puzzle as to what the fuss was once about. "Piaget, Newell and Simon, Chomsky and others have now convinced just about everyone that adult and child minds alike are inhabited by exceedingly rich structures of knowledge and cognitive processes" (Flavell, 1982, p. 4). This volume is full of evidence in support of this view. However, given the subject of this review, we must point out that it is not true that everyone accepts Piaget's views.

First, there are still advocates of the learning theory view (e.g., Kendler, 1979). Second, we believe that Piaget still would hold that some of the current work in the information processing tradition tends to lose sight of the role of structure in cognitive development (see *Siegler, vol. I, chap. 4,* for a review of the work in this tradition). When we are told that a child fails task *x, y,* or *z* because of a memory problem or a limit in short-term memory or a failure to encode a crucial stimulus, the issue is, What exactly is being said? There could be the implicit assumption that the child has the requisite structures but we are not sure. The question is not confronted directly, and so we hesitate to put words in an author's mouth. In some cases it seems a legitimate inference (as in Trabasso's, 1975, work); in other cases the issue is more complex.

Consider Siegler's (1981) hypothesis that what changes in development is what is encoded. But why does what is encoded change? Piaget's answer is that the cognitive structures change. And because the structures determine what is assimilable, it follows that what is encoded will change. Siegler (1981) might very well accept this interpretation. But if he did, then we would ask for a description of the structure. Sure, we are asking for a lot, perhaps more than yet can be accomplished. (But see the recent publication by Siegler & Robinson, 1982.)

Our point simply is that we cannot be satisfied with a zeitgeist that accepts the notion of structure. What is needed are descriptions of these structures—all the more now that the evidence goes against Piaget's particular descriptions. Further, we need to determine the interaction between structural and information processing constraints as they influence cognitive development. Such thoughts are more than in the air. A variety of investigators and theoreticians are trying to accomplish this (e.g., Case, 1978; Fischer, 1980; Halford & Wilson, 1980; Pascual-Leone, 1970). The Halford and Wilson paper is interesting because it offers an a priori definition of a unit of information processing. To do this they work with category theory.[6] We reserve judgment on the descriptive adequacy of this theory. As Halford and Wilson (1980) point out, it needs further empirical support. Still, we see here an effort to use a known mathematical structure to define a unit and then to make predictions about information processing demands. Newport (1980) makes a similar attempt in the domain of language acquisition by using linguistic theory to define structural units. We suspect this is just the beginning of such theorizing.

In any case, we trust that Flavell (1982) is right and that the notion of structure is here to stay. Piaget's influence on this outcome in cognitive developmental circles has been, and will continue to be, enormous. We obviously believe that the ultimate characterizations of these structures will be different than those offered by Piaget. In particular, we anticipate that the structures underlying arithmetic thought will not be the same ones underlying the tendency to form cause-and-effect explanations. No matter what, the fact remains that there is a need for a structural account—be it logic or a set of reasoning principles—about those domains of knowledge to which Piaget turned our attention.

Stages of Cognitive Development?

In our opinion there is little evidence to support the idea of major stages in cognitive development of the type described by Piaget. Over and over again, the evidence is that the preoperational child has more competence than expected. Further, the evidence is that the concrete-operational child works out concepts in separate domains without using the kind of integrative structures that would be required by a general stage theory. In addition, there is evidence in some cases that the structure underlying the way a preschooler reasons about a problem is much like that used by older children and even adults, for example, the principles of causal reasoning. In other cases, the evidence is that there is structural change reflected in the development of a concept. The case of number concepts is one clear example of the latter.

None of the foregoing points eliminates the possibility of there being within-domain stages of development. It could even turn out that there are some cognitive developmental domains wherein there is evidence of stages and others wherein there is no evidence. Flavell's (in press) recent work on visual perspective-taking abilities is perhaps one such candidate. And the domain of number concepts may be yet another, although Gelman and Gallistel's (1978) version of the stages needs modification.

Recall Gelman and Gallistel's hypothesis. The preschooler could only reason about specific numerical values. In contrast, the elementary school-aged child could reason about nonspecified numbers. The proposed stages were that Stage 1, reflected arithmetic competence with countables; Stage 2 reflected an advance to algebraic reasoning about numbers. Unfortunately, the data contradict the hypothesis. Under certain conditions, preschoolers can and do use a principle of one-to-one correspondence to reason about number. And they do this with set sizes they cannot count accurately. Evans (1982) further finds no correlation between the development of the concepts of zero, infinity, and negative numbers in elementary school-aged children. Indeed the seemingly related concepts of forever and infinity fail to show a within-subject correlation. So even in the case of number concepts, the evidence for a transtask stage development is weak at best.

There is one possible way to retrieve the stage argument for within-cognitive-domain developments. This involves representing a given level of competence in terms of hierarchies of related concepts and then characterizing each stage in terms of the dominant tendencies at a given time. A similar strategy has been used by Kohlberg (1969). We hesitate to guess whether this or other efforts to characterize cognitive development in terms of stages (e.g., Case, 1978; Feldman & Toulmin, 1975; Halford & Wilson, 1980; Pascual-Leone, 1970) will prove more successful.

One of Piaget's better known positions is that the course of cognitive development must be paced, that is, there is little that can be done to engineer a truly accelerated rate of development (Piaget, 1966). Although the many successful training studies serve as evidence against this position, notions of readiness still abound—and we suspect they always will. Siegler (1978) reports that a 5-year-old who uses the same rule as does an older child does not benefit as much from the same training as does the older child. This is in part due to a weaker tendency on the part of the younger child to encode the relevant information; the latter fact raises the question of whether time itself must pass before the training is effective or whether differences involving encoding strategies, processing space, knowledge, and so on, need to be modified during this time. More generally, the question is what happens during a given time period to enable learning to go forward (see Siegler & Klahr, 1981, for an extended discussion).

How Does Development Happen?

Up to this point we have focused almost exclusively on matters of structure. We now turn to matters of function. How do an individual's cognitive structures operate (i.e., How do they respond to inputs from the environment?)? The central notions in Piaget's (e.g., 1970) account are assimilation, accommodation, and equilibration. And which functional mechanisms are responsible for the emergence of each stage of development? The crucial notions here are those of abstraction réfléchissante and équilibration majorante (Piaget, 1975b).

For Piaget, all cognitive functioning involves the two fundamental, complementary processes of assimilation and accommodation. Piaget defines assimilation as the incorporation of external elements (objects or events) into sensorimotor or conceptual schemes. Thus, for example, thumb sucking in the infant is described as the assimilation of a novel element, the infant's thumb, into the existing sucking scheme. Similarly, the concrete-operational child who orders a set of rods is said to have assimilated the rods into a seriation scheme.

In his book, *L'équilibration des structures cognitives,* Piaget (1975b) postulates that every scheme tends to feed itself, that is, to incorporate into itself external elements that are compatible with its nature. The child's schemes are, thus, seen as constituting the motivational source, or the motor of development. Schemes do not merely constrain the nature and range of exchanges the child has with her environment, but they actively bring about such exchanges in their effort to feed or actualize themselves. The child's activity is, thus, necessary, in that it alone provides inputs to the child's assimilation schemes.

Many consider the foregoing notions vague. Yet, as indicated in our opening remarks, we said we accepted the idea that development proceeds as a function of assimilation and accommodation. To show why, we apply these notions to some of our work.

An example of the way in which schemes guide as well as motivate behavior comes from Gelman and Gallistel (1978). These authors found that even very young children obey the how-to-count principles that underlie counting behavior in older children and adults. Consider, for instance, the case of a 2½-year-old child who said, "2, 6, 10, 16" when engaging in what appeared to be counting. When shown one object and asked how many there were, the child answered "2." When shown two objects and asked how many there were, the child said, "2, 6, *6*" (emphasis on the last digit). Finally, when shown three objects and asked to count them, the child counted "2, 6, 10," and when asked how many there were, simply replied "10." This child can be said to have applied all of the how-to-count principles because he assigned one unique tag to each object, he used the same list over trials, and he repeated the last tag in a count when asked the cardinal-number question.

According to Gelman and Gallistel, the child's adherence to the how-to-count principles reveals the availability of a counting scheme, which embodies these (and possibly other) counting principles. The counting scheme guides and motivates the child's behavior. It must be clear from the foregoing how the counting scheme structures the child's counting performance. Evidence that the counting scheme serves a motivating role as well comes from at least two separate sources. The first is the existence of nonconventional or idiosyncratic count lists, such as the one cited above (children have also been found to count with letters as well as numbers). The children who use such lists do not do so because they have been taught them or heard them. They must have created them themselves using elements from the two lists they have had most occasion to hear, that is, the alphabet and the counting numbers. Gelman and Gallistel argue that the creation of these nonconventional lists points to the presence of a scheme that requires the count list to be stably ordered, but leaves unspecified the nature of the items that will constitute the list. What we have, then, is a scheme in search of a list. The scheme assimilates items that can then be stably ordered to create an acceptable count list, that is, a list that is compatible with the scheme itself.

The second source of evidence that counting schemes serve a motivating function is the frequency with which spontaneous counting is observed in the young child. Young children appear to have a compulsion to count, be it cows they pass while in a car, toys, candies, leaves on a tree, and so on. How else to explain this, Gelman and Gallistel argue, if not in terms of a scheme that presses children to search for items that can be readily assimilated? Because young children are not instructed to practice counting, a theory that required extrinsic (as opposed to intrinsic) motivation would be on difficult grounds. In their theory, the motivation would come from the schemes themselves, that is, the schemes would continually have to assimilate external elements to subsist and develop, and, hence, would press children to engage in activities whose results will be compatible with the schemes themselves.

In an assimilation, external elements are structured by, or adjusted to, the individual's schemes. In an accommodation, by contrast, the individual's schemes must adjust themselves to the demands of the environment. A scheme must always accommodate itself to the particular characteristics of the element (object or event) it is trying to assimilate. Thus, for example, the infant's grasping scheme will be applied differently when dealing with small as applied to large objects. In the very act of assimilating, or grasping the object, the infant must accommodate

her action to the specific contour, weight, size, and so on, of the object she is attempting to grasp. The young child who uses an idiosyncratic count list eventually will accommodate to the conventional one. Otherwise communications involving counting and numbers will be exceedingly difficult.

Another example of schemes accommodating themselves comes from Saxe's (1980) work with the Papuans in Papua New Guinea. The Papuans use a 53-item count list that has no base rules embodied in it. With recent exposure of some men to money has come the shift to a base-20 system—presumably to make it possible to deal with large numbers.

To summarize, for Piaget, the child's schemes are the motivational source of development because they actively assimilate and accommodate. But the process of assimilation does more than constrain the nature and range of exchanges that a child will have with his environment. The process of assimilation also involves the seeking out of stimuli that are assimilable to a given scheme. As such, the scheme obtains the necessary inputs that feed the scheme. Because accommodation is always part of the assimilation process, it guides the eventual change in structures. We have illustrated how the processes of assimilation and accommodation might work in the development of counting skill and knowledge. By postulating that the counting principles form a scheme that assimilates and accommodates, we can account for the appearance of unusual count lists, the child's seeming compulsion to practice counting without a request, the tendency to self-correct and the further development of counting. We know of no other way to do so and, hence, accept Piaget's view that assimilation and accommodation are fundamental developmental processes. Indeed, because the characteristics of young children's counting behaviors are ubiquitous in other domains of development (e.g., language aquisition), it seems plausible that assimilation and accommodation are likewise ubiquitous during the course of development and later knowledge acquisition.

If every cognitive act involves schemes that assimilate and accommodate, how can there ever be stability of cognitive structures, or at least enough stability for one to recognize a stage? Piaget dealt with this issue by distinguishing between different kinds of assimilation-accommodation functions and the consequent different kinds of equilibration (Piaget, 1975b). In cases were accommodation is readily effected either by repetition of a previous accommodation or by relatively insignificant alterations of the individual's schemes, Piaget talks of simple, limited equilibrations that do no more than preserve or restore the existing state of equilibrium. In cases where accommodation is unsuccessful, however, and assimilation of a given element proves impossible without significant modifications of the individual's schemes or cognitive systems, Piaget talks of equilibrations majorantes or major improvements that generate qualitatively distinct, superior states of cognitive equilibrium.

Obviously the latter situations—those unsuccessful accommodations that call for an improved (majorante) equilibration—are the most important ones from a developmental point of view. Exactly how does the major equilibration happen? It is hard to find a clear account in Piaget's writings. One thing is clear, this is that Piaget thought that qualitatively new concepts could emerge from the process of reflective abstraction.[7]

We admit to having been less than successful in our efforts to understand fully the notion of reflective abstraction. Again, we resort to an example from Evans' (1982) work on the acquisition of the concept of infinity. Evans suggests that some children acquire, on their own, the notion that there is no largest number on the basis of their self-initiated counting trials. The idea is that some children set themselves the task of counting up to the largest number and eventually come to recognize that they will never get there because there is no largest number. Piaget would say the child who reaches this conclusion does so via the process of a reflective abstraction from the set of count trials that were self-generated. Parenthetically, the self-generated count trials are examples of what Piaget means by logical as opposed to physical abstraction (Piaget, 1975b).

We suspect that part of the resistance to accepting the idea that schemes assimilate and accommodate is due to the absence of detailed accounts of how the assimilation and accommodation processes yield development. Piaget (1975b) tried to do this in his more recent treatments of the processes of equilibration and reflective abstraction. We see this work as part of Piaget's continuing efforts to detail the nature of assimilation and accommodation. However, we confess that we still are far from a full understanding of the various processes postulated in Piaget's treatment of reflective abstraction and equilibration. Yet, we do not think it necessary to throw up our hands in despair. Perhaps work by Rumelhart and Norman (1978) on schema development or Siegler and Klahr (1981) on developmental transition processes will serve this end. And Rozin's (1976) notion of accessing has much in common with Piaget's (1975b) notion of reflective abstraction. Further, to repeat, there can be no denying something like assimilation

and accommodation as being involved in learning and development. Those familiar with the theoretical work of Rumelhart and his colleagues (e.g., Rumelhart and Norman, 1978; Rumelhart & Ortony, 1977) will recognize the use of similarly active processes in their account of how schemata are formed and developed. Whether Piaget's particular version of how schemes develop will stand the test of time, we do not know. But we are sure that notions akin to assimilation and accommodation will. And by now, they are no more mysterious to us than are the processes of association and selective attention.

Whence Come Structures?

The issue of whence concepts was taken up in the Piaget-Chomsky debate held in France in 1975 and published in English with Piatelli-Palmarini (1980) serving as editor and commentator. Not only were Piaget and Chomsky present, so were Bateson, Fodor, Inhelder, Jacob, Mehler, Monod, Papert, and Premack—to list but some of the distinguished participants. The debate was supposed to focus on the Piagetian and Chomskian accounts of language acquisition but was, in fact, a broader debate about Piaget's constructivism versus Chomsky's and Fodor's innatism. Piaget defended his view that structures are constructed and not inherited. He maintained that cognitive functions, but not cognitive structures, were innate. Fodor and Chomsky were on the side of innate ideas.

The nub of the disagreement between Chomsky and Piaget concerns the origin of mental structure. Chomsky and Fodor maintain that structure begets structure and that this is logically necessary. Fodor's argument is that learning involves hypothesis testing; hypotheses are either rejected or accepted. For one to induce the correct hypotheses, one must be able to formulate those hypotheses. Therefore, the hypotheses must already be available to the organism.

> To let such a device [a learning device] do what it is supposed to do, you have to presuppose the field of hypotheses, the field of concepts on which the inductive logic operates. In other words, to let this theory do what it is supposed to do you have to be in effect a nativist. You have to be a nativist about the conceptual resources of the organism because the inductive theory of learning simply doesn't tell you anything about that. (Fodor in Piatelli-Palmarini, 1980, pp. 146–147)

As noted by the biologists at the debate, the nativist position (outlined here) does not, of course, mean that the adult's mental structures are present from the outset any more than it means—to translate the argument to a purely biological example—that adult sexual organs are present in the newly fertilized ovum. Work in ethology provides ample evidence that constructivist and nativist positions need not be contradictory. The acquisition of bird song provides a lovely example. The adult white-crowned sparrow has a characteristic song. By varying the kind of environment available to the young white-crowned sparrow, Marler (1970) has been able to show that experience plays a central role in the development of the song that is characteristic of the region in which the bird lives. For, if a baby sparrow is raised in isolation, it will sing a distinctly odd song as an adult. Experts agree that this odd song is the basic form of the adult song. It is odd because it is never heard in nature and lacks those characteristics that give it the status of one dialect or another. If the young bird is exposed to the adult song during its first 10 to 50 days of life, but never again, the bird will sing the adult characteristic song. This is true, even if the young bird is deafened after the exposure. What matters is not the opportunity to sing the song—the young cannot—but the opportunity to hear the song of the region. There is a critical period during which the bird must hear the adult model. If the isolated bird hears the song for the first time at 100 days, the experience will have no effect. Likewise, if the acoustic input is provided during the first days of life, it does not take. Subsequent deafening does inhibit acquisition. Marler argues from such findings that the white-crowned sparrow is born with template for the basic song. Experience serves to tune that template to allow the young bird to learn its particular dialect. The bird brings to the interaction with the environment a structural advantage that helps it focus attention on, that is, assimilate one set of songs as opposed to another. In interacting with the environment, the bird develops the particular song of its locale, that is, the basic template is accommodated. The idea is *not* that development involves a bit of innate structure and a bit of learning but *that development is a function of the organism's interaction with its environment*. The potential for structural change is not reached unless there is development, that is, an interaction between structure and environment. Nevertheless, the potential is innately given.

For Chomsky and Fodor, the complexity and power of the final structure is preordained by the complexity of the initial structure. This is precisely where Piaget disagrees. Piaget insists that each successive structure in the stagelike course of development is not only different from, but more complex and powerful than, the preceding structure. Piaget fosters a notion of developmental process as divorced from structure. He grants that the processes or developmental functions are innate, but he does not grant that complex processes presuppose a complex structure for their realization. Piaget argues that cognitive functions foster the emergence of structures more complex than prior ones. Carrying this argument back to the very beginning of development, he maintains there is only process or function and no structure: "I have my doubts . . . [that the point of departure is innate], because I am satisfied with just a functioning that is innate" (Piaget in Piatelli-Palmarini, 1980, p. 157). The tendency of the subject to assimilate and accommodate is enough to bring him into interaction with his environment and this interaction yields cognitive structures.

Piaget's distinctly Lamarkian hypothesis was criticized by the biologists at the debate. For example, Jacob pointed out:

> In the case of the small animals from the bottom of Lake Geneva, the observed variations are always those allowed by their genotype. One always remains within the working margin authorized by the genes. . . . *There is regulation only on structures and with structures that exist and that are there to regulate*. . . . They adjust, of course, the allowed working margin, but it is, once more, the genotype that prescribes the limits. (Jacob in Piatelli-Palmarini, p. 62)

Despite persistent efforts by the biologists, Piaget stood by his view that structures are not determined innately. Rather than granting Fodor's view that successive structures must be represented in prior structures, he maintained that a prior structure can contain the subsequent structure *only as possibilities*, possibilities that do not get formed until they are constructed or created in the course of an interaction with the environment. The interaction itself alters the prior structures and, thus, more complex structures develop.

We agree with Chomsky and Fodor regarding the ultimate origin of the structures mediating the kinds of concept Piaget describes as being present during the early school years. First, we cannot make sense of the notion of a functioning divorced from a structure. If structures do not guide functioning, then we fail to see how the developmental process gets started on the *same* developmental course for *all* normal children. But, if we allow innate structural constraints on the course of development, then we can begin to make sense of the fact that children all over the world seem to develop the same concepts in about the same sequence up to around the beginning of the concrete-operational period. Further, the evidence points to innate structural dispositions in infants (e.g., Haith, 1980; Spelke, 1980). Likewise, much of the recent evidence regarding the cognitive capacities of preschoolers points to the early availability of rich and complex reasoning structures. As more evidence like this comes in, it becomes harder and harder to escape the argument that there are innate structural constraints on the course and nature of cognitive development. Osherson (1978) and Keil (1981) have made some progress in characterizing these constraints.

To say that young children's reasoning structures are rich is not to say that they are the same as the adult structures. Indeed, we noted the many conceptual domains where (despite the presence of early capacities) young children's reasoning structures are nowhere near those of older children, which, in turn, seem impoverished compared to adult's capacities. As far as we are concerned, to say there are rich cognitive structures to start is just the beginning. There remain the questions of what those structures are and how they determine the emergence of advanced structures, given an appropriate range of experience. And, of course, the account of what the appropriate range of experiences are has to be related to the nature of the structures that set the range. Finally, the obvious fact that humans have considerable conceptual plasticity, has to be reconciled with the idea that there are innate structural constraints on the course of cognitive development. For an example of how this might be accomplished we turn to Rozin's Accessing theory of intellectual development.

Rozin (1976) has attempted to deal with the facts that (1) highly "intelligent" behavioral mechanisms are available to species low down on the phylogenetic scale and (2) even though more "intelligent" organisms have genetically specified behavior programs, they are less constrained by these programs or are more open to environmental variations.

Rozin begins by calling attention to the highly "intelligent" nature of many special-purpose behavioral mechanisms in animals. Foraging bees, for example, record the location of food sources in polar coordinates, with the home nest as the origin of the coordinate system and the sun as the point of angular reference. It is now known that almost all of such "intelligent" behavior is founded on genetically

specified computational machinery that prepares the bees to learn the location of a food source. The learning here does not reflect some general-purpose faculty of association. Instead, the learning ability appears within genetically constrained behavioral circumstances and the bees' "knowledge" of celestial mechanics, which is implicit in the bees' behavior and is unavailable for use in other aspects of the bees' behavior.

According to Rozin, the genetically determined behavioral machinery in lowly creatures is unaccessible for use in contexts other than the specific context that shape the evolution of the requisite neural machinery in the first place. Rozin's thesis is that the evolution of general-purpose intelligence in higher mammals has involved the evolution of more general access to computational processes that originally served specialized behavioral purposes. Still, he stresses the fact that even in humans, there are many computational routines whose outputs are not generally accessible. For example, our visual system makes extensive computations that draw on a great deal of implicit knowledge of trigonometry and optics. The end result, our perception of the world around us, is generally accessible. But the intermediate computations are not. Likewise, humans appear to possess genetically specified neural machinery for computing phonetic representations of the speech they hear (Eimas, 1974). This phonetic representation is an intermediate stage in the computation of a semantic representation of what humans hear. The evidence indicates that the phonetic representation is not *consciously* available to preschool-aged children (Gleitman & Rozin, 1977; Liberman, Shankweiler, Liberman, Fowler, & Fischer, 1977; Rozin & Gleitman, 1977).

Rozin and Gleitman (1977) hypothesize that the ability to read rests heavily on the ability of humans eventually to gain conscious access to the phonetic representation of what they hear. Spelling rules relate written English to a phonetic representation of spoken English. Every fluent reader can give decidedly nonarbitrary pronunciations of words she has never seen (Baron, 1977). Thus, it seems hard to deny that an important aspect of learning to read is learning to compute a phonetic representation of written material by using the lawful relations between spelling and pronunciation. Learning to compute such phonetic representations of visual inputs must be very difficult if one does not have conscious access to the phonetic representation of what one hears. But it is known (see above) that the young child has limited access to the phonetic representation. Hence, the Rozin and Gleitman (1977) argument that reading ability requires the development of conscious access to the phonetic representation.

Note that Rozin does not contend that the ability to read per se is coded in the genes but that related abilities as well as a general accessing ability (reflective abstraction?) are. The notion of accessing by itself does not constitute a solution to the developmental problem, that is, how to account for new concepts within a nativist frame of reference. Instead, it points to the form such a solution might take. If the notion is to be taken seriously, one must raise *and* answer the following questions: What is it about the early representation of a given set of experiences that prevents their being worked on by a given piece of computational machinery? How must this representation be altered for the machinery to operate on it? What are the processes that produce such alterations and what experiences bring these processes into play?

We introduce Rozin's theory because it has the form of the theory that is needed to deal with the facts about the concepts that Piaget has studied. Their development is more domain specific than not. Very young children have considerable cognitive abilities. Still, some, if not most, are exceedingly hard to demonstrate, and the range of application of these abilities is oftentimes remarkably restricted compared to that in older children. Hence, their ubiquitous tendency to fail may related tasks. Eventually, what are rigid, undergeneralized capacities become fluid, generalized capacities.

A Concluding Remark

There are at least three important ways in which Piaget's work has influenced the field of child cognitive psychology. First, Piaget was among the first modern psychologists to insist on the active role the child plays as a learner. Traditional learning theory tended to characterize development in terms of the passive registering and gradual accumulation of environmental contiguities. In marked contrast, Piaget portrayed the young child as one who continually engages in the selection and interpretation, as well as the storage, of information. Second, Piaget was also among the first modern psychologists to underscore the role cognitive structures play in young children's reasoning. Again and again Piaget demonstrated that young children's cognitive structures determine their perception and understanding of the world and delimit the nature and range of knowledge they acquire at each point in their development. Third, Piaget is undoubtedly the psychologist who has most contributed to our knowledge of the facts of cogni-

tive development. His work covers the development of a remarkably wide and varied set of concepts: object permanence, number conservation, class-inclusion, length, distance, and so on. As we repeatedly pointed out in the chapter, investigators may not always agree with Piaget's interpretation of the developmental phenomena he reported—but they do not deny their reliability or interest.

On the debit side, we would argue that Piaget's work presents two major drawbacks. Throughout his career, Piaget maintained that all cognition develops through four successive stages, with each stage characterized by the emergence of qualitatively distinct structures. It seems to us that Piaget's strong commitment to this view, though praiseworthy in some respects, also had some unfortunate consequences. In particular, it appears to have led him to disregard—and even at times summarily dismiss—alternative accounts of his findings that were at least as plausible as those he proposed himself. The second drawback is analogous to the first. Having commited himself to the view that cognitive structures are actively constructed by the child, Piaget seems never to have seriously considered alternative views of the development of these structures. True, Piaget's treatment of developmental issues almost invariably includes a discussion of the rationalist and empiricist standpoints. However, his presentations of these views are usually so simplistic as to border on the charicatural. One lesson of modern research in child psychology is that accounts of how development proceeds can no longer ignore the possibility that at least some of the structures that underlie our systems of knowledge are innate. Another lesson is that in order to do justice to the richness and complexity of the learning processes involved in the acquisition of cognitive structures, far more sophisticated investigative and descriptive tools than were hitherto available must be developed. Piaget's account of the manner in which cognitive structures emerge appears extremely limited. But then, it is always easy to examine the past in terms of the present. What is more difficult is to create the future. It will be hard, very hard, to do as well as Piaget.

NOTES

1. Osherson (1974) provides a proof that the groupings themselves are either inconsistent or tautological.

2. Gold provided the information about subjects' ages upon request from the authors. These are not in his text.

3. Shultz et al. (1979) make as good a case as

anyone for treating separately issues of a belief in logical necessity and the understanding of many conservations.

4. For a complete list of the properties of classificatory systems see Inhelder & Piaget, 1964, p. 48.

5. Our comments about causal reasoning are restricted to the domain of physical causality. See Gelman & Spelke (1981) for a discussion of possible differences in reasoning about physical causality and social causality.

6. An example of the difficulty in defining a unit of M-space is taken up in Trabasso and Foellinger (1978). Pascual-Leone (1978) considers the critique unjustified on many counts. However, there still remains the question of how to define a unit on a priori grounds.

7. This is but one of Piaget's uses of the concept of reflective abstraction. See Vyuk (1981) for an excellent coverage of this and related concepts.

REFERENCES

Acker, N. *Conservation and coordination of relations*. Unpublished doctoral dissertation, Institute of Child Development, University of Minnesota, 1968.

Acredolo, C., & Acredolo, L. P. Identity, compensation, and conservation. *Child Development*, 1979, *50*, 524–535.

Anderson, N. H., & Cuneo, D. O. The height + width rule in children's judgments of quantity. *Journal of Experimental Psychology: General*, 1978, *107*, 335–378.

Anglin, J. M. *Word, object and concept development*. New York: W. W. Norton, 1977.

Baillargeon, R. *Young children's understanding of causal mechanisms*. Unpublished doctoral dissertation, University of Pennsylvania, 1981.

Baillargeon, R., Gelman, R., & Meck, E. Are preschoolers truly indifferent to causal mechanisms? Paper presented at the meeting of the Society for Research in Child Development, Boston, Mass., April 1981.

Baron, J. What we might know about orthographic rules. In S. Dornic & P. M. A. Rabbitt (Eds.), *Attention and performance* (Vol. 6). Hillsdale, N.J.: Erlbaum, 1977.

Baron, J., Lawson, G., Siegel, L. S. Effects of training and set size on children's judgments of number and length. *Developmental Psychology*, 1974, *11*, 583–588.

Beilin, H. Learning and operational convergence in logical thought development. *Journal of Experimental Child Psychology*, 1965, *2*, 317–339.

Beilin, H. The training and acquisition of logical operations. In M. F. Rosskopf, L. P. Steffe, & S. Taback (Eds.), *Piagetian cognitive development research and mathematical education*. Washington, D.C.: National Council of Teachers of Mathematics, 1971.

Beilin, H. Inducing conservation through training. In G. Striner (Ed.), *Psychology of the 20th century*, vol. 7, *Piaget and beyond*. Zurich: Kinder, 1977.

Berzonsky, M. Interdependence of Inhelder and Piaget's model of logical thinking. *Developmental Psychology*, 1971, *4*, 469–476.

Bever, T. G. The cognitive basis for linguistic structures. In J. R. Hayes (Ed.), *Cognition and the development of language*. New York: Wiley, 1970.

Bloom, L. *One word at a time*. The Hague: Mouton, 1973.

Borke, H. Piaget's mountains revisited: Changes in the egocentric landscape. *Developmental Psychology*, 1975, *11*, 240–243.

Botvin, G. J., & Murray, F. B. The efficacy of peer modeling and social conflict in the acquisition of conservation. *Child Development*, 1975, *46*, 796–797.

Bousfield, W. A. The occurence of clustering in the recall of randomly arranged associates. *Journal of General Psychology*, 1953, *49*, 229–240.

Bousfield, W. A., Esterson, J., & Whitmarsh, G. A. A study of developmental changes in conceptual and perceptual associative clustering. *Journal of Genetic Psychology*, 1958, *92*, 95–102.

Brainerd, C. J. Mathematical and behavioral foundations of number. *Journal of Genetic Psychology*, 1973, *88*, 221–281.

Brainerd, C. J. Response criteria in concept development research. *Child Development*, 1977, *48*, 360–366.

Brainerd, C. J. *Piaget's theory of intelligence*. Englewood Cliffs, N.J.: Prentice-Hall, 1978. (a)

Brainerd, C. J. The stage question in cognitive developmental theory. *Behavioral and Brain Sciences*, 1978, *1*, 173–182. (b)

Brainerd, C. J., & Allen, T. W. Experimental inductions of the conservation of "first-order" quantitative invariants. *Psychological Bulletin*, 1971, *75*, 128–144.

Brown, R. *A first language: The early stages*. Cambridge, Mass.: Harvard University Press, 1973.

Bruner, J. S., & Olver, R. R. Development of equivalence transformations in children. In J. C. Wright & J. Kagan (Eds.), Basic cognitive processes in children. *Monographs of the Society for Research in Child Development, 1963, 28 (2, Serial No. 86).*

Bruner, J. S., Olver, R. R., Greenfield, P. M., Hornsby, J. R., Kenney, H. J., Maccoby, M., Modiano, N., Mosher, F. A., Olson, D. R., Potter, M. C., Reich, L. C., & McKinnon-Sonstroem, A. *Studies in cognitive growth.* New York: Wiley, 1966.

Brush, L. R. *Children's conceptions of addition and subtraction: The relation of formal and informal notions.* Unpublished doctoral dissertation, Cornell University, 1972.

Bryant, P. E. *Perception and understanding in young children: An experimental approach.* New York: Basic Books, 1974.

Bryant, P. E., & Kopytynska, H. Spontaneous measurement by young children. *Nature, 1976, 260,* 773.

Bryant, P. E., & Trabasso, T. R. Transitive inferences and memory in young children. *Nature,* 1971, *232,* 456–458.

Bullock, M. *Aspects of the young child's theory of causation.* Unpublished doctoral dissertation, University of Pennsylvania, 1979.

Bullock, M., & Gelman, R. Numerical reasoning in young children: The ordering principle. *Child Development,* 1977, *48,* 427–434.

Bullock, M., & Gelman, R. Preschool children's assumptions about cause and effect: Temporal ordering. *Child Development,* 1979, *50,* 89–96.

Bullock, M., Gelman, R., & Baillargeon, R. The development of causal reasoning. In W. F. Friedman (Ed.), *The developmental psychology of time.* New York: Academic Press, 1982.

Carey, S. The child's concept of animal. Paper presented at the meeting of the Psychonomic Society, San Antonio, Texas, November 1978.

Carey, S. *Are children fundamentally different kinds of thinkers and learners than adults?* Paper presented at the NIE-LRDC Conference on Thinking and Learning, University of Pittsburgh, October 1980.

Carey, S. The concept of life: On the acquisition of natural kind terms. Unpublished manuscript, Massachusetts, Institute of Technology, 1982.

Case, R. Intellectual development from birth to adulthood: A neo-Piagetian interpretation. In R. S. Siegler (Ed.), *Children's thinking: What develops?* Hillsdale, N.J.; Erlbaum, 1978.

Case, R., & Serlin, R. A new process model for predicting performance on Pascual-Leone's test of *M*-space. *Cognitive Psychology,* 1979, *11,* 308–326.

Chi, M. T. H. *Interactive roles of knowledge and strategies in development.* Paper presented at the NIE-LRDC Conference on Thinking and Learning, University of Pittsburgh, October 1980.

Chomsky, N. *Aspects of the theory of syntax.* Cambridge, Mass.: MIT Press, 1965.

Clark, E. V. Building a vocabulary: Words for objects, actions and relations. In P. Fletcher & M. A. Garman (Eds.), *Studies in language acquisition.* Cambridge, Mass.: Cambridge University Press, 1978.

Clark, H. H., & Clark, E. V. *Psychology and language: An introduction to psycholinguistics.* New York: Harcourt Brace Jovanovich, 1977.

Cofer, C. N., Bruce, D. R., & Reicher, G. M. Clustering in free recall as a function of certain methodological variations. *Journal of Experimental Psychology,* 1966, *71,* 858–866.

Cohen, L. B., & Younger, B. A. Perceptual categorization in the infant. Paper presented at the Symposium of the Jean Piaget Society, Philadelphia, May 1981.

Coie, J. D., Costanzo, P. R., & Farnill, D. Specific transitions in the development of spatial perspective-taking ability. *Developmental Psychology,* 1973, *9,* 167–177.

Cole, M., Frankel, F., & Sharp, D. Development of free-recall learning in children. *Developmental Psychology,* 1971, *4,* 109–123.

Cooper, R. G., Leitner, E. F., & Moore, N. J. The development of seriation: The skills underlying the perception and construction of series. Unpublished manuscript, University of Texas, Austin, 1981.

Cooper, R. G., Starkey, P., Blevins, B., Goth, P., & Leitner, E. Number development: Addition and subtraction. Paper presented at the Symposium of the Jean Piaget Society, Philadelphia, June 1978.

Cuneo, D. O. Judgments of numerosity: Developmental changes in the integration of length and density. Paper presented at the meeting of the Psychonomic Society, Washington, D.C., November 1977.

Cuneo, D. O. A general strategy for quantity judgments: The height and width rule. *Child Development,* 1980, *51,* 299–301.

Daehler, M. W., Lonardo, R., & Bukato, D. Matching and equivalence judgments in very young children. *Child Development,* 1979, *50,* 170–179.

Davison, M. L., King, P. M., Kitchener, K. S., & Parker, C. A. The stage sequence concept in cognitive and social development. *Developmental*

Psychology, 1980, *16*, 121–131.

de Boysson-Bardies, B., & O'Regan, K. What children do in spite of adults' hypotheses. *Nature*, 1973, *246*, 531–534.

Denney, N. W. A developmental study of free classification in children. *Child Development*, 1972, *43*, 221–232. (a)

Denney, N. W. Free classification in preschool children. *Child Development*, 1972, *43*, 1161–1170. (b)

deVilliers, J. G., & deVilliers, P. A. A cross-sectional study of the development of semantic and syntactic acceptability by children. *Journal of Psycholinguistic Research*, 1972, *1*, 299–310.

deVilliers, J. G., & deVilliers, P. A. *Language acquisition*. Cambridge, Mass.: Harvard University Press, 1978.

Dimitrovsky, L., & Almy, M. Linkages among concrete operations. *Genetic Psychology Monographs*, 1975, *92*, 213–229.

Dodwell, P. C. Relations between the understanding of the logic of classes and of cardinal number in children. *Canadian Journal of Psychology*, 1962, *16*, 152–160.

Donaldson, M. *Children's minds*. New York: W. W. Norton, 1978.

Eimas, P. D. Linguistic processing of speech by young infants. In R. L. Shiefelbusch & L. L. Lloyd (Eds.), *Language perspectives: Acquisition, retardation, and intervention*. Baltimore: University Park Press, 1974.

Evans, D. *Understanding infinity and zero in the early school years*. Unpublished doctoral dissertation, University of Pennsylvania, 1982.

Fein, G. G. Play and the acquisition of symbols. In L. Katz (Ed.), *Current topics in early childhood education*. Norwood, N.J.: Ablex, 1979.

Feldman, C. F., & Toulmin, S. Logic and the theory of mind. In J. K. Cole & W. J. Arnold (Eds.), *Nebraska Symposium on Motivation* (Vol. 23). Lincoln: University of Nebraska Press, 1975.

Feldman, D. H. *Beyond universals in cognitive development*. Norwood, N.J.: Ablex, 1980.

Field, D. The importance of the verbal content in the training of Piagetian conservation skills. *Child Development*, 1977, *48*, 1583–1592.

Fischer, K. W. A theory of cognitive development. *Psychological Review*, 1980, *87*, 477–525.

Fischer, K. W., Roberts, R. J. A developmental sequence of classification skills in preschool children. Unpublished manuscript, University of Denver, 1980.

Flavell, J. H. *The developmental psychology of Jean Piaget*. Princeton, N.J.: Van Nostrand, 1963.

Flavell, J. H. Concept development. In P. H. Mussen (Ed.), *Carmichael's manual of child psychology* (Vol. 1). New York: Wiley, 1970.

Flavell, J. H. An analysis of cognitive-developmental sequences. *Genetic Psychology Monographs*, 1972, *86*, 279–350.

Flavell, J. H. The development of inferences about others. In T. Mischel (Ed.), *Understanding other persons*. Oxford, Eng.: Blackwell, Basil, and Mott, 1974.

Flavell, J. H. Structures, stages, and sequences in cognitive development. In W. A. Collins (Ed.), *The concept of development*. Minnesota Symposiam on Child Psychology (Vol. 15). Hillsdale, N.J.: Erlbaum, 1982.

Flavell, J. H. *Cognitive development* (2nd ed.). Englewood Cliffs, N.J.: Prentice-Hall, in press.

Flavell, J. H., Flavell, E. R., & Green, F. L. Development of the appearance-reality distinction. *Cognition*, in press.

Flavell, J. H., Flavell, E. R., Green, F. L., & Wilcox, S. A. The development of three spatial perspective-taking rules. *Child Development*, 1981, *52*, 356–358.

Flavell, J. H., & Wellman, H. M. Metamemory. In R. V. Kail, Jr., & J. W. Hagen (Eds.), *Perspectives on the development of memory and cognition*. Hillsdale, N.J.: Erlbaum, 1977.

Fuson, K. C., & Richards, J. Children's construction of the counting numbers from a spew to a bidirectional chain. Unpublished manuscript, Northwestern University, 1979.

Gaudia, G. Race, social class, and age of achievement of conservation on Piaget's tasks. *Developmental Psychology*, 1972, *6*, 158–165.

Gelman, R. Conservation acquisition: A problem of learning to attend to relevant attributes. *Journal of Experimental Child Psychology*, 1969, *7*, 167–187.

Gelman, R. The nature and development of early number concepts. In H. W. Reese (Ed.), *Advances in child development and behavior* (Vol. 7). New York: Academic Press, 1972. (a)

Gelman, R. Logical capacity of very young children: Number invariance rules. *Child Development*, 1972, *43*, 371–383. (b)

Gelman, R. How young children reason about small numbers. In N. J. Castellan, D. B. Pisoni, G. R. Potts (Eds.), *Cognitive theory* (Vol. 2), Hillsdale, N.J.: Erlbaum, 1977.

Gelman, R. Cognitive development. *Annual Review of Psychology*, 1978, *29*, 297–332.

Gelman, R. Accessing one-to-one correspondence: Still another paper on conservation. *British Jour-*

nal of Psychology, 1982, *73,* 209–220.

Gelman, R., Bullock, M., & Meck, E. Preschoolers' understanding of simple object transformations. *Child Development,* 1980, *51,* 691–699.

Gelman, R., & Gallistel, C. R. *The child's understanding of number.* Cambridge, Mass.: Harvard University Press, 1978.

Gelman, R., & Meck, E. Preschoolers' counting: Principles before skill or skill before principles? Unpublished manuscript, University of Pennsylvania, 1982.

Gelman, R., Spelke, E. & Meck, E. What preschoolers know about animate and inanimate objects. In J. Sloboda, D. Rogers, P. Bryant & R. Cramer (Eds.), Acquisition of symbolic skills. London: Plenum, in press.

Gelman, R., & Shatz, M. Appropriate speech adjustments: The operation of conversational constraints on talk to two-year-olds. In M. Lewis & L. A. Rosenblum (Eds.), *Interaction, conversation, and the development of language.* New York: Wiley, 1978.

Gelman, R., & Spelke, E. S. The development of thoughts about animates and inanimates: Some implications for research on the nature and development of social cognition. In J. H. Flavell & L. Ross (Eds.), *Social cognitive development: Frontiers and possible futures.* Cambridge: At the University Press, 1981.

Gelman, R., & Tucker, M. F. Further investigations of the young child's conception of number. *Child Development,* 1975, *46,* 167–175.

Gelman, R., & Weinberg, D. H. The relationship between liquid conservation and compensation. *Child Development,* 1972, *43,* 371–383.

Ginsburg, H. P. The development of addition in the contexts of culture, social class and race. In T. P. Carpenter, J. M. Moser, & T. A. Romberg (Eds.), *Addition and subtraction: A developmental perspective.* Hillsdale, N.J.: Erlbaum, 1982.

Gleitman, L. R., & Gleitman, H. Language use and language judgment. In C. F. Fillmore, D. Kempler, & W. S.-Y. Wang (Eds.), *Individual differences in language ability and language behavior.* New York: Academic Press, 1979.

Gleitman, L. R., Gleitman, H., & Shipley, E. F. The emergence of the child as grammarian. *Cognition,* 1972, *1,* 137–164.

Gleitman, L. R., & Rozin, P. The structure and acquisition of reading: I. Relations between orthographies and the structure of language. In A. S. Reber & D. L. Scarborough (Eds.), *Toward a psychology of reading: The proceedings of the CUNY conferences.* Hillsdale, N.J.: Erlbaum, 1977.

Gold, R. On the meaning of nonconservation. In A. M. Lesgold, J. W. Pellegrino, S. D. Fokkema, & R. Glaser (Eds.), *Cognitive psychology and instruction.* New York and London: Plenum, 1978.

Goldberg, S., Perlmutter, M., & Myers, N. Recall of related and unrelated lists by 2-year-olds. *Journal of Experimental Child Psychology,* 1974, *18,* 1–8.

Greenfield, P. M., Nelson, K., & Saltzman, E. The development of rulebound strategies for manipulating seriated cups: A parallel between action and grammar. *Cognitive Psychology,* 1972, *3,* 291–310.

Greeno, J. G., Riley, M. S., & Gelman, R. Young children's counting and understanding of principles. Unpublished manuscript, University of Pittsburgh and University of Pennsylvania, 1981.

Grize, J. B. Des groupements à l'algebre de Boole: Essai de filiation des structures logiques. In L. Apostel, J. B. Grize, S. Papert, & J. Piaget, *La filiation des structures.* Paris: Presses Universitaires de France, 1963.

Groen, G., & Resnick, L. B. Can preschool children invent addition algorithms? *Journal of Educational Psychology,* 1977, *69,* 645–652.

Gruber, H. E., & Vonèche, J. J. (Eds.). *The essential Piaget:* An interpretative reference and guide. London: Routledge & Kegan Paul, 1977.

Gruendel, J. M. Referential extension in early language development. *Child Development,* 1977, *48,* 1567–1576.

Haith, M. *Rules that babies look by.* Hillsdale, N.J.: Erlbaum, 1980.

Halford, G. S., & Wilson, W. H. A category theory approach to cognitive development. *Cognitive Psychology,* 1980, *12,* 356–411.

Hamel, B. R. *Children from 5 to 7: Some aspects of the number concept.* Rotterdam: Rotterdam University Press, 1974.

Hanley, J. G., & Hooper, F. H. A developmental comparison of social class and verbal ability influences on Piagetian tasks. *Journal of Genetic Psychology,* 1973, *122,* 235–245.

Harlow, H. F. Learning set and error factor theory. In S. Koch (Ed.), *Psychology: A study of science,* vol. 2, *General systematic formulations, learning, and special processes.* New York: McGraw-Hill, 1959.

Harris, P. L., & Bassett, E. Transitive inferences by 4-year-old children? *Developmental Psychol-*

ogy, 1975, *11*, 875–876.

Hasher, L., & Clifton, D. A developmental study of attribute encoding in free recall. *Journal of Experimental Child Psychology*, 1974, *17*, 332–346.

Haygood, R. C., & Stevenson, M. Effects of number of irrelevant dimensions in nonconjunctive concept learning. *Journal of Experimental Psychology*, 1967, *74*, 302–304.

Hooper, F. H., Sipple, T. S., Goldman, J. A., & Swinton, S. S. A cross-sectional investigation of children's classification abilities. *Genetic Psychology Monographs*, 1979, *99*, 41–89.

Hooper, F. H., Toniolo, T. A., & Sipple, T. S. A longitudinal analysis of logical reasoning relationships: Conservation and transitive inference. *Developmental Psychology*, 1978, *14*, 674–682.

Horton, M. S., & Markman, E. M. Developmental differences in the acquisition of basic and superordinate categories. *Child Development*, 1980, *51*, 708–719.

Huttenlocher, J. The origin of language comprehension. In R. L. Solso (Ed.), *Theories in cognitive psychology*. Hillsdale, N.J.: Erlbaum, 1974.

Huttenlocher, J., & Lui, P. The semantic organization of simple nouns and verbs. *Journal of Verbal Learning and Verbal Behavior*, 1979, *18*, 141–162.

Huttenlocher, J., & Presson, C. C. Mental rotation and the perspective problem. *Cognitive Psychology*, 1973, *4*, 277–299.

Huttenlocher, J., & Presson, C. C. The coding and transformation of spatial information. *Cognitive Psychology*, 1979, *11*, 375–394.

Inhelder, B. *The diagnosis of reasoning in the mentally retarded*. New York: Chandler, 1968.

Inhelder, B., Blanchet, A., Sinclair, A., & Piaget, J. Relations entre les conservations d'ensembles d'éléments discrets et celles de quantités continues. *Année Psychologique*, 1975, *75*, 23–60.

Inhelder, B., Bovet, M., Sinclair, H., & Smock, C. D. On cognitive development. *American Psychologist*, 1966, *21*, 160–164.

Inhelder, B., & Piaget, J. *The early growth of logic in the child*. New York: W. W. Norton, 1964.

Inhelder, B., Sinclair, H., & Bovet, M. *Learning and the development of cognition*. Cambridge, Mass.: Harvard University Press, 1974.

Jamison, W. Developmental inter-relationships among concrete operational tasks: An investigation of Piaget's stage concept. *Journal of Experimental Child Psychology*, 1977, *24*, 235–253.

Jamison, W., & Dansky, J. L. Identifying developmental prerequisites of cognitive acquisition. *Child Development*, 1979, *50*, 449–454.

Judd, S. A., & Mervis, C. B. Learning to solve class-inclusion problems: The roles of quantification and recognition of contradiction. *Child Development*, 1979, *50*, 163–169.

Kagan, J., Moss, H. A., & Sigel, I. E. Psychological significance of styles of conceptualization. In J. C. Wright & J. Kagan (Eds.), Basic cognitive processes in children. *Monographs of the Society for Research in Child Development*, 1963, *28* (2, Serial No. 86).

Keil, F. C. *Semantic and conceptual development*. Cambridge, Mass.: Harvard University Press, 1979.

Keil, F. C. Constraints on knowledge and cognitive development. *Psychological Review*, 1981, *88*, 197–227.

Kendler, T. S. The development of discrimination learning: A levels-of-functioning explanation. In H. W. Reese & L. P. Lipsitt (Eds.), *Advances in child development and behavior*. (Vol. 13), New York: Academic Press, 1979.

Kline, M. *Mathematical thought from ancient to modern times*. New York: Oxford University Press, 1972.

Kobasigawa, A., & Orr, R. R. Free recall and retrieval speed of categorized items by kindergarten children. *Journal of Experimental Child Psychology*, 1973, *15*, 187–192.

Kofsky, E. A scalogram study of classificatory development. *Child Development*, 1966, *37*, 191–204.

Kohlberg, L. Stage and sequence: The cognitive-developmental approach to socialization. In D. A. Goslin (Ed.), *Handbook of socialization theory and research*. Chicago: Rand McNally, 1969.

Koslowski, B. Quantitative and qualitative changes in the development of seriation. *Merrill-Palmer Quarterly*, 1980, *26*, 391–405.

Lee, L. C. The concomitant development of cognitive and moral modes of thought: A test of selected deductions from Piaget's theory. *Genetic Psychology Monographs*, 1971, *83*, 93–146.

Lefèbvre, M., & Pinard, A. Influence du niveau initial de sensibilité au conflict sur l'apprentissage de la conservation des quantités par une méthode de conflic cognitif. *Revue Canadienne des Sciences du Comportement*, 1974, *6*, 398–413.

Lempers, J. D., Flavell, E. R., & Flavell, J. H. The development in very young children of tacit knowledge concerning visual perception. *Genetic Psychology Monographs*, 1977, *95*, 3–53.

Levin, I. The development of time concepts in

young children: Reasoning about duration. *Child Development*, 1977, *48*, 435–444.

Levin, I. Interference of time-related and unrelated cues with duration comparisons of young children: Analysis of Piaget's formulation of the relation of time and speed. *Child Development*, 1979, *50*, 469–477.

Levin, I., Israeli, E., & Darom, E. The development of time concepts in young children: The relations between duration and succession. *Child Development*, 1978, *49*, 755–764.

Liberman, I. Y., Shankweiler, D., Liberman, A. M., Fowler, C., & Fischer, F. W. Phonetic segmentation and recoding in the beginning reader. In A. S. Reber & D. L. Scarborough (Eds.), *Toward a psychology of reading: The proceedings of the CUNY conferences*. Hillsdale, N.J.: Erlbaum, 1977.

Little, A. A longitudinal study of cognitive development in young children. *Child Development*, 1972, *43*, 1024–1034.

Mandler, J. M. Categorical and schematic organization in memory. In C. R. Puff (Ed.), *Memory organization and structure*. New York: Academic Press, 1979.

Mandler, J. M. Structural invariants in development. In L. S. Liben (Ed.), *Piaget and the foundations of knowledge*. Hillsdale, N.J.: Erlbaum, 1981.

Mandler, J. M., & Johnson, N. S. Remembrance of things parsed: Story structure and recall. *Cognitive Psychology*, 1977, *9*, 111–151.

Maratsos, M. P. Nonegocentric communication abilities in preschool children. *Child Development*, 1973, *44*, 697–700.

Markman, E. M. *Factors affecting the young child's ability to monitor his memory*. Doctoral dissertation, University of Pennsylvania, 1973. (a)

Markman, E. M. Facilitation of part-whole comparisons by use of the collective noun "family." *Child Development*, 1973, *44*, 837–840. (b)

Markman, E. M. Empirical versus logical solutions to part-whole comparison problems concerning classes and collections. *Child Development*, 1978, *49*, 168–177.

Markman, E. M. Classes and collections: Conceptual organization and numerical abilities. *Cognitive Psychology*, 1979, *11*, 395–411.

Markman, E. M. Two different principles of conceptual organization. In M. E. Lamb & A. L. Brown (Eds.), *Advances in developmental psychology* (Vol. 1). Hillsdale, N.J.: Erlbaum, 1981.

Markman, E. M., Cox, B., & Machida, S. The stan-

dard object-sorting task as a measure of conceptual organization. *Developmental Psychology*, 1981, *17*, 115–117.

Markman, E. M., Horton, M. S., & McLanahan, A. G. Classes and collections: principles of organization in the learning of hierarchical relations. *Cognition*, 1980, *8*, 227–241.

Markman, E. M., & Siebert, J. Classes and collections: Internal organization and resulting holistic properties. *Cognitive Psychology*, 1976, *8*, 561–577.

Marler, P. A comparative approach to vocal learning: Some development in white-crowned sparrows. *Journal of Comparative and Physiological Psychology*, 1970, *6*, 1–25.

Marvin, R. S., Greenberg, M. T., & Mossler, D. G. The early development of conceptual perspective taking: Distinguishing among multiple perspectives. *Child Development*, 1976, *47*, 511–514.

Masangkay, Z. S., McCluskey, K. A., McIntyre, C. W., Sims-Knight, J., Vaughn, B. E., & Flavell, J. H. The early development of inferences about the visual percepts of others. *Child Development*, 1974, *45*, 357–366.

McCloskey, M., Caramazza, A., & Green, B. Curvilinear motion in the absence of external forces: Naive beliefs about the motion of objects. *Science*, 1980, *210*, 1139–1141.

McGarrigle, J., & Donaldson, M. Conservation accidents. *Cognition*, 1974–1975, *3*, 341–350.

Mehler, J., & Bever, T. G. Cognitive capacity of very young children. *Science*, 1967, *158*, 141–142.

Mierkiewicz, D. B., & Siegler, R. S. Preschoolers' ability to recognize counting errors. Paper presented at the meeting of the Society for Research on Child Development, Boston, April 1981.

Miller, R. The use of concrete and abstract concepts by children and adults. *Cognition*, 1973, *2*, 49–58.

Modgil, S., & Modgil, C. *Piagetian research: Compilation and commentary*. Atlantic Highlands, N.J.: Humanities Press, 1976.

Moore, G. W. Transitive inferences with seriation problems assessed by explanations, judgments and strategies, *Child Development*, 1979, *50*, 1164–1172.

Murray, F. B. The acquisition of conservation through social interaction. *Developmental Psychology*, 1972, *6*, 1–6.

Murray, F. B. Teaching strategies and conservation training. In A. M. Lesgold, J. W. Pellegrino, S. D. Fekkema, & R. Glaser (Eds.), *Cognitive psychology and instruction* (Vol. 1). New York and

London: Plenum, 1978.

Murray, F. B. The conservation paradigm. In D. Brodzinsky, I. Sigel, & R. Golinkoff (Eds.), *New directions in Piagetian research and theory.* Hillsdale, N.J.: Erlbaum, 1981.

Neimark, E., Slotnick, N. S., & Ulrich, T. Development of memorization strategies. *Developmental Psychology,* 1971, *5,* 427–432.

Nelson, K. The organization of free recall by young children. *Journal of Experimental Child Psychology,* 1969, *8,* 284–295.

Nelson, K. Some evidence for the cognitive primacy of categorization and its functional basis. *Merrill-Palmer Quarterly,* 1973, *19,* 21–39.

Nelson, K. Variations in children's concepts by age and category. *Child Development,* 1974, *45,* 577–584.

Nelson, K. Cognitive development and the acquisition of concepts. In R. C. Anderson, R. J. Spiro, & W. E. Montague (Eds.), *Schooling and the acquisition of knowledge.* Hillsdale, N.J.: Erlbaum, 1977.

Nelson, K. How children represent knowledge of their world in and out of language: A preliminary report. In R. S. Siegler (Ed.), *Children's thinking: What develops?* Hillsdale, N.J.: Erlbaum, 1978.

Newport, E. L. Constraints on structure: Evidence from American sign language and language learning. In W. A. Collins (Ed.), Minnesota Symposia on Child Psychology (Vol. 14). Hillsdale, N.J.: Erlbaum, 1980.

Odom, R. D., Astor, E. C., Cunningham, J. G. Effects of perceptual salience on the matrix task performance of four- and six-year-old children. *Child Development,* 1975, *46,* 758–762.

Olver, R. R., & Hornsby, J. R. On equivalence. In J. S. Bruner, R. R. Olver, & P. M. Greenfield et al. (Eds.), *Studies in cognitive growth.* New York: Wiley, 1966.

Osherson, D. N. *Logical abilities in children,* vol. 1, *Organization of length and class concepts: Empirical consequences of a Piagetian formalism.* Hillsdale, N.J.: Erlbaum, 1974.

Osherson, D. N. Three conditions on conceptual naturalness. *Cognition,* 1978, *6,* 263–289.

Osherson, D. N., & Markman, E. Language and the ability to evaluate contradictions and tautologies. *Cognition,* 1974–1975, *3,* 213–226.

Osler, S. F., & Kofsky, E. Stimulus uncertainty as a variable in the development of conceptual ability. *Journal of Experimental Child Psychology,* 1965, *2,* 264–279.

Pascual-Leone, J. A mathematical model for the transition rule in Piaget's developmental stages. *Acta Psychologica,* 1970, *32,* 301–345.

Pascual-Leone, J. Compounds, confounds, and models in developmental information processing: A reply to Trabasso and Foellinger. *Journal of Experimental Child Psychology,* 1978, *26,* 18–40.

Piaget, J. *The child's conception of physical causality.* London: Routledge & Kegan Paul, 1930.

Piaget, J. *Classes, relations et nombres: Essai sur les groupements de la logistique et sur la réversibilité de la pensée.* Paris: Vrin, 1942.

Piaget, J. *The child's conception of number.* London: Routledge & Kegan Paul, 1952. (a)

Piaget, J. *The origins of intelligence in children.* New York: International Universities Press, 1952. (b)

Piaget, J. *Logic and psychology.* New York: Basic Books, 1957.

Piaget, J. *The language and thought of the child* (3rd ed.). London: Routledge & Kegan Paul, 1959.

Piaget, J. Le temps et le développement intellectuel de l'enfant. *La vie et le temps.* Rencontres internationales de Genève. Neuchâtel: La Baconnière, 1962.

Piaget, J. Nécessité et signification des recherches comparatives en psychologie génétique. *Journal International de Psychologie,* 1966, *1,* 1–13.

Piaget, J. Les méthodes de l'épistémologie. In J. Piaget (Ed.), *Logique et connaissance scientifique. Encyclopédie de la Pléiade* (Queneau ed.) Paris: Gallimard, 1967. (a)

Piaget, J. Cognitions and conservations: Two views. *Contemporary Psychology,* 1967, *12,* 530–533. (b)

Piaget, J. *Piaget's theory.* In P. H. Mussen (Ed.), *Carmichael's manual of child psychology* (Vol. 1). New York: Wiley, 1970.

Piaget, J. *Biology and knowledge.* Chicago: University of Chicago Press, 1971.

Piaget, J. *Understanding causality.* New York: W. W. Norton, 1974.

Piaget, J. On correspondences and morphisms. Paper presented at the symposium of the Jean Piaget Society, Philadelphia, 1975. (a)

Piaget, J. *L'équilibration des structures cognitives: Problème central du développement.* Études d'épistémologie génétique, Vol. 33. Paris: Presses Universitaires de France, 1975. (b)

Piaget, J. Some recent research and its link with a new theory of groupings and conservations based on commutability. *Annals of the New York Academy of Sciences,* 1977, *291,* 350–358.

Piaget, J. *Success and understanding,* London and Henley-on-Thames: Routledge & Kegan Paul, 1978.

Piaget, J. *Experiments in contradiction.* Chicago and London: University of Chicago Press, 1980.

Piaget, J. et al. *Epistemology and psychology of functions.* Dordrecht, the Netherlands: D. Reidel, 1977.

Piaget, J., & Inhelder, B. *The child's conception of space.* London: Routledge & Kegan Paul, 1956.

Piaget, J., & Inhelder, B. L'image et la pensée: Le rôle de l'image dans la préparation ou dans le fonctionnement des opérations. In P. Fraisse & J. Piaget (Eds.), *Traité de psychologie expérimentale,* (vol. 7), *L'intelligence.* Paris: Presses Universitaires de France, 1963.

Piaget, J., & Inhelder, B. *Mental imagery in the child.* London: Routledge & Kegan Paul, 1971.

Piaget, J., & Inhelder, B. *The child's construction of quantities.* London: Routledge & Kegan Paul, 1974.

Piatelli-Palmarini, M. (Ed.). *Language and learning: The debate between Jean Piaget and Noam Chomsky.* Cambridge, Mass.: Harvard University Press, 1980.

Potter, M. C., & Levy, E. I. Spatial enumeration without counting. *Child Development,* 1968, *39,* 265–272.

Premack, D. *Intelligence in ape and man.* Hillsdale, N.J.: Erlbaum, 1976.

Price-Williams, D. R., Gordon, W., & Ramirez, M. Skill and conservation: A study of pottery-making children. *Developmental Psychology,* 1969, *1,* 769.

Rescorla, L. A. Overextension in early language development. *Journal of Child Language,* 1980, *7,* 321–336.

Rescorla, L. A. Category development in early language. *Journal of Child Language,* 1981, *8,* 225–238.

Ricciuti, H. N. Object grouping and selective ordering behavior in infants 12 to 24 months old. *Merrill-Palmer Quarterly,* 1965, *11,* 129–148.

Ricciuti, H. N., & Johnson, L. J. Developmental changes in categorizing behavior from infancy to the early pre-school years. Paper presented at the meeting of the Society for Research in Child Development, Minneapolis, March 1965.

Riley, C. A. The representation of comparative relations and the transitive inference task. *Journal of Experimental Child Psychology,* 1976, *22,* 1–22.

Roll, S. Reversibility training and stimulus desirability as factors in conservation of number. *Child Development,* 1970, *41,* 501–507.

Rosch, E., Mervis, C. B., Gay, W. D., Boyes-Braem, P., & Johnson, D. N. Basic objects in natural categories. *Cognitive Psychology,* 1976, *8,* 382–439.

Ross, G. S. Categorization in 1- to 2-year-olds. *Developmental Psychology,* 1980, *16,* 391–396.

Rozin, P. The evolution of intelligence and access to the cognitive unconscious. In J. M. Sprague & A. D. Epstein (Eds.), *Progress in psychobiology and physiological psychology* (Vol. 6). New York: Academic Press, 1976.

Rozin, P., & Gleitman, L. R. The structure and acquisition of reading: II. The reading process and the acquisition of the alphabetic principle. In A. S. Reber & D. L. Scarborough (Eds.), *Toward a psychology of reading: The proceedings of the CUNY conferences.* Hillsdale, N.J.: Erlbaum, 1977.

Rumelhart, D. E. Schemata: The building blocks of cognition. In R. J. Spiro, B. Bruce, & W. Brewer (Eds.), *Theoretical issues in reading comprehension.* Hillsdale, N.J.: Erlbaum, 1980.

Rumelhart, D. E., & Norman, D. A. Accretion, tuning and restructuring: Three modes of learning. In J. W. Cotton & R. Klatzky (Eds.), *Semantic factors in cognition.* Hillsdale, N.J.: Erlbaum, 1978.

Rumelhart, D. E., & Ortony, A. The representation of knowledge in memory. In R. C. Anderson, R. J. Spiro, & W. E. Montague (Eds.), *Schooling and the acquisition of knowledge.* Hillsdale, N.J.: Erlbaum, 1977.

Russac, R. J. The relation between two strategies of cardinal number: Correspondence and counting. *Child Development,* 1978, *49,* 728–735.

Saxe, G. B. Cognition about counting and its relation to number conservation. Paper presented at the Symposium of the Jean Piaget Society, Philadelphia, June 1979.

Saxe, G. B. Developing forms of arithmetic operations among the Oksapmin of Papua, New Guinea. Unpublished manuscript, City University of New York, 1980.

Saxe, G. B., & Sicilian, S. Children's interpretation of their counting accuracy: A developmental analysis. *Child Development,* in press.

Saxe, G. B., Sicilian, S., & Schonfield, I. Developmental differences in children's understanding of conventional properties of counting. Unpublished manuscript, Graduate Center of the City University of New York, 1981.

Schaeffer, B., Eggleston, V. H., & Scott, J. L. Number development in young children. *Cognitive Psychology,* 1974, *6,* 357–379.

Schank, R. A., & Abelson, B. *Scripts, plans, goals and understanding*. Hillsdale, N.J.: Erlbaum, 1977.

Schwartz, J. L. The semantic aspects of quantity. Unpublished manuscript, Massachusetts Institute of Technology, 1976.

Schwartz, S. P. *Naming, necessity and natural kinds*. Ithaca, N.Y.: Cornell University Press, 1977.

Sedlak, A. J., & Kurtz, S. T. A review of children's use of causal inference principles. *Child Development*, 1981, *52*, 759–784.

Shannon, L. Spatial strategies in the counting of young children. *Child Development*, 1978, *49*, 1212–1215.

Shatz, M. The relationship between cognitive processes and the development of communication skills. In C. B. Keasey (Ed.), *Nebraska Symposium on Motivation* (Vol. 25). Lincoln: University of Nebraska Press, 1978.

Shatz, M., & Gelman, R. The development of communication skills: Modifications in the speech of young children as a function of listener. *Monographs of the Society for Research in Child Development*, 1973, *38*(5, Serial No. 152).

Sheppard, J. L. A structural analysis of concrete operations. In J. A. Keats, K. F. Collis, & G. S. Halford (Eds.), *Cognitive development: Research based on a neo-Piagetian approach*. Chichester, Eng.: Wiley, 1978.

Shipley, E. F., Kuhn, I. F., & Madden, E. C. Mother's use of superordinate category terms. Unpublished manuscript, University of Pennsylvania, 1981.

Shotwell, J. Counting steps. *New Directions for Child Development*, 1979, *3*, 85–96.

Shultz, T. R. Rules of causal attribution. *Monographs of the Society for Research in Child Development*, 1982, *47*(1, Serial No. 194).

Shultz, T. R., Dover, A., & Amsel, E. The logical and empirical bases of conservation judgments. *Cognition*, 1979, *7*, 99–123.

Siegel, L. S. Development of number concepts: Ordering and correspondence operations and the role of length cues. *Developmental Psychology*, 1974, *10*, 907–912.

Siegel, L. S. The cognitive basis of the comprehension and production of relational terminology. *Journal of Experimental Child Psychology*, 1977, *24*, 40–52.

Siegel, L. S., McCabe, A. E., Brand, J., & Matthews, J. Evidence for the understanding of class-inclusion in preschool children: Linguistic factors and training effects. Unpublished manuscript, McMaster University, 1977.

Siegler, R. S. The origin of scientific thinking in R. S. Siegler (Ed.), *Children's thinking: What develops?* Hillsdale, N.J.: Erlbaum, 1978.

Siegler, R. S. Developmental sequences between and within concepts. *Monographs of the Society for Research in Child Development*, 1981, *46*(2, Serial No. 189).

Siegler, R. S. & Klahr, D. What do children learn? The relation between existing knowledge and the acquisition of new knowledge. In R. Glaser (Ed.), *Advances in instructional psychology* (Vol. 2). Hillsdale, N.J.: Erlbaum, 1981.

Siegler, R. S., & Robinson, M. The development of numerical understandings. In H. W. Reese & L. P. Lipsitt (Eds.), *Advances in child development and behavior* (Vol. 14). New York: Academic Press, 1982.

Silverman, I. W., & Geiringer, E. Dyadic interaction and conservation induction: A test of Piaget's equilibration model. *Child Development*, 1973, *44*, 815–820.

Silverman, I. W., & Stone, J. Modifying cognitive functioning through participation in a problem-solving group. *Journal of Educational Psychology*, 1972, *63*, 603–608.

Smedslund, J. The acquisition of conservation of substance and weight in children: III. Extinction of conservation of weight acquired "normally" by means of empirical controls on a balance. *Scandinavian Journal of Psychology*, 1961, *2*, 85–87 (a).

Smedslund, J. The acquisition and conservation of substance and weight in children: V. Practice in conflict situations without external reinforcement. *Scandinavian Journal of Psychology*, 1961, *2*, 156–160 (b).

Smedslund, J. Microanalysis of concrete reasoning: I. The difficulty of some combinations of addition and subtraction of one unit. *Scandinavian Journal of Psychology*, 1966, *1*, 145–156.

Smiley, S. S., & Brown, A. L. Conceptual preference for thematic or taxonomic relations: A nonmonotonic trend from preschool to old age. *Journal of Experimental Child Psychology*, 1979, *28*, 249–257.

Smith, C. L. Children's understanding of natural language hierarchies. *Journal of Experimental Child Psychology*, 1979, *27*, 437–458.

Smith, E. E., & Medin, D. L. *Categories and concepts*. Cambridge, Mass.: Harvard University Press, 1981.

Smith, I. D. The effects of training procedures upon the acquisition of conservation of weight. *Child Development*, 1968, *39*, 515–526.

Smither, S. J., Smiley, S. S., & Rees, R. The use of perceptual cues for number judgment by young children. *Child Development,* 1974, *45,* 693–699.

Spelke, E. S. Perceptual knowledge of objects in infancy. Unpublished manuscript, University of Pennsylvania, 1980.

Starkey, P. *Number development in young children: Conservation, addition and subtraction.* Unpublished doctoral dissertation, University of Texas at Austin, 1978.

Starkey, P., & Gelman, R. The development of addition and subtraction abilities prior to formal schooling. In T. P. Carpenter, J. M. Moser, & T. A. Romberg (Eds.), *Addition and subtraction: A developmental perspective.* Hillsdale, N.J.: Erlbaum, 1982.

Stein, N. L., & Glenn, C. G. An analysis of story comprehension in elementary school children. In R. Freedle (Ed.), *New directions in discourse processing* (Vol. 2). Norwood, N.J.: Ablex, 1979.

Stock, W. & Flora, J. Cardination and ordination learning in young children. Unpublished manuscript, Arizona State University, 1975.

Stott, D. H. An empirical approach to motivation based on the behavior of a young child. *Journal of Child Psychology and Psychiatry,* 1961, *2,* 97–117.

Strauss, S., & Stavy, R. U-shaped behavioral growth: Implications for theories of development. In W. W. Hartup (Ed.), *Review of child development research* (Vol. 6). Chicago: University of Chicago Press, 1981.

Sugarman, S. *Scheme, order & outcome: The development of classification in children's early block play.* Unpublished doctoral dissertation, University of California at Berkeley, 1979.

Thomson, J. R., & Chapman, R. S. Who is 'Daddy' revisited: The status of two-year-olds' over-extended words in use and comprehension. *Journal of Child Language,* 1977, *4,* 359–375.

Timmons, S. A., & Smothergill, D. W. Perceptual training of height and brightness seriation in kindergarten children. *Child Development,* 1975, *46,* 1030–1034.

Tomlinson-Keasey, C., Eisert, D. C., Kahle, L. R., Hardy-Brown, K., & Keasey, B. The structure of concrete operational thought. *Child Development,* 1979, *50,* 1153–1163.

Trabasso, T. R. Representation, memory and reasoning: How do we make transitive inferences? In A. D. Pick (Ed.), *Minnesota Symposia on Child Psychology* (Vol. 9). Minneapolis: University of Minnesota Press, 1975.

Trabasso, T. R., & Bower, G. *Attention in learning: Theory and research.* New York: Wiley, 1968.

Trabasso, T. R., & Foellinger, D. B. Information processing capacity in children: A test of Pascual-Leone's model. *Journal of Experimental Child Psychology,* 1978, *26,* 1–17.

Trabasso, T. R., Isen, A. M., Dolecki, P., McLanahan, A. G., Riley, C. A., & Tucker, T. How do children solve class inclusion problems? In R. S. Siegler (Ed.), *Children's thinking: What develops?* Hillsdale, N.J.: Erlbaum, 1978.

Tuddenham, R. D. Theoretical regularities and individual idiosyncracies. In D. R. Green, M. P. Ford, & G. B. Flamer (Eds.), *Measurement and Piaget.* New York: McGraw-Hill, 1971.

Vygotsky, L. S. *Thought and language.* Cambridge, Mass.: MIT Press, 1962.

Vyuk, R. *Overview and critique of Piaget's genetic epistemology, 1965–1980,* (2 vols.). London: Academic Press, 1981.

Walker, C. M., & Bourne, L. E., Jr. The identification of concepts as a function of amounts of relevant and irrelevant information. *American Journal of Psychology,* 1961, *74,* 410–417.

Wallach, L., & Sprott, R. L. Inducing number conservation in children. *Child Development,* 1964, *35,* 1057–1071.

Weiner, B., & Kun, A. The development of causal attributions and the growth of achievement and social motivation. In S. Feldman & P. Bush (Eds.), *Cognitive development and social development.* Hillsdale, N.J.: Erlbaum, 1976.

Wermus, H. Formalisation de quelques structures initiales de la psychogenèse. *Archives de Psychologie,* 1971, *41,* 271–288.

Wilkening, F. Integrating velocity, time, and distance information: A developmental study. *Cognitive Psychology,* 1981, *13,* 231–247.

Winer, G. A. Induced set and acquisition of number conservation. *Child Development,* 1968, *39,* 195–205.

Winer, G. A. Class-inclusion reasoning in children: A review of the empirical literature. *Child Development,* 1980, *51,* 309–328.

Wohlwill, J., & Lowe, R. C. Experimental analysis of the development of the conservation of number. *Child Development,* 1962, *33,* 153–167.

Worden, P. E. The effects of classification structure on organized free recall in children. *Journal of Experimental Child Psychology,* 1976, *22,* 519–529.

RECENT THEORY AND RESEARCH OF THE GENEVAN SCHOOL* | 4

ANDRÉ BULLINGER, *University of Geneva*
JEAN-F. CHATILLON, *University of Aix-Marseille II*

CHAPTER CONTENTS

INTRODUCTION

The title of this chapter is borrowed from Piaget (1976b), who, in the postscript to a work in his honor, wrote the following lines:

In reading the results of all these fine studies, I had the comforting impression that together, their authors and myself, we form a ''school'' (even called the Genevan School). . . . It is the nature of a school . . . that a common orientation, even if it is born of the master's theories, in no way excludes discussion on any point where opinions might diverge. Nor does a school hinder progress, of any kind, in areas where gaps become apparent and where new questions should be raised. (p. 223)

The research to which Piaget referred covers a wide variety of areas: clinical psychology, social psychology, psycholinguistics, infant development, educational psychology, cross-cultural psychology,

ethology, problem solving, and others. Researchers trained in Geneva have made contributions in all of these areas.

If these studies have extended Piaget's work, they are, nonetheless, distinguishable from it on a number of important points. Here, we will concentrate on these divergences. To understand fully the direction in which current research is evolving (and will doubtless continue to evolve), it should be borne in mind that the central concern of the researchers has changed.

All of Piaget's endeavors aimed at an understanding of the formation of knowledge *in general*. This was, therefore, an epistemological question and to answer it he made use of psychology and, in particular, the psychology of intelligence. The studies carried out in this area, thus, have the status of a tool—a means to study the general problem of the genesis of knowledge. In fact, Piaget thought that by observing the intellectual development of the young child he would be able to identify the mechanisms through which new knowledge is formed. The study of intellectual development was not the only means used by Piaget to deal with this epistemological question; his research into the history of science was also aimed at the same goal.

All the current research is centered on psychological issues. Research on intellectual development is directed toward an identification of the steps and mechanisms of development itself and the variables that may modify its progress (its rate or even its

*This work was carried out with partial support of the Swiss National Science Foundation, Grant No.: 1–828.0–78. The authors wish to express their special thanks to the translators, Peter Coles and Sophia Cohen, for this difficult task, which required not only a knowledge of the two languages but also of theoretical nuances of the Genevan school. Our discussion on *Developmental Psycholinguistic Studies* was written in close collaboration with the psycholinguistic research team in Geneva. Thanks are also due to M. Hoegen, J. Aouizerate, and M. Bauget for typing the manuscript.

content). The observation of behaviors produced by subjects while solving problems aims both (1) to separate out the mechanisms whereby subjects elaborate their solution strategy and the role of the operatory (opératoire) structures available to them and (2) to isolate those variables that have an influence on the solution itself.

With certain exceptions, the contributions from researchers of the Genevan School are increasingly centered on the study of the complex relationships between action and representation at different points in development. A number of developmental studies attempt to identify the mechanisms governing the transition from a given structure to the next. Others look at mechanisms underlying the formation of the whole ensemble of representational instruments (various kinds of operation and representation) based on subjects' actions. The main problem is the role of action in overall cognitive development (and not just in the crucial period of sensorimotor intelligence). The study of strategies for solving problems attempts to specify the manner in which subjects do or do not make use of the mental means available to them to produce an action within a defined task. These studies are, thus, concerned with the relationships existing between representation and action. These relationships are different from those taken into account in developmental studies.

These contributions have opened up a new field of research and have led to some important theoretical distinctions. One such distinction, concerning the epistemic and the psychological subject, was briefly sketched by Inhelder (1978):

> You will perhaps be surprised that we are moving away from the epistemic subject, which for decades was our central concern, in order to further our interests in the psychological subject: the child in his progressive discoveries of the means destined to resolve problems that are indissociable from concrete and specific contexts.
> By *epistemic subject* we mean that which is in common in the knowledge structures of subjects at the same level and by *psychological subject,* that which is common to individual subjects, for example, their need for their own organization in order to remedy the incoherence of initially isolated means and ends. (pp. 99–100)

The study of problem-solving procedures has not only led Genevan researchers to make new theoretical distinctions. They have also emphasized the importance of the phase of representational coding for the solution of the problem. In this decisive phase in the elaboration of solutions, two aspects have to be taken into account: (1) the subject's current possibilities and (2) the difficulties the subject may encounter in representing in a useful manner the situation upon which he has to act. Reality is, thus, more or less able to resist the subject's assimilatory activity. This resistance of reality underlies the existence of what Piaget (1941, 1955) called horizontal décalages.

We will briefly describe the principal research areas, without pretending to be comprehensive, and will summarize some of the results obtained. We will then move on to a discussion of the complex relationships between the subject's actions and the cognitive means available to him at various periods in his development. These relationships between different psychological realities comprise an entire object for study and, thus, have to be analyzed, both at a theoretical and a methodological level.

At a theoretical level, the nature of the relations between thought and action will be discussed by investigating the manner in which actions of a given kind form, organize, and finally transform themselves. The status of these relations may vary not only according to the subject's level of cognitive development but also according to the moment at which one considers the selected action. That is, the links between a subject's reasoning abilities at a given level of development are not the same when he or she is in the process of developing this action as when he or she is repeating an already stabilized action.

At a methodological level, these complex interactions will finally lead us to discuss the choice of behavioral indices retained for analyses. These indices reflect psychological realities that are not directly accessible and, therefore, assume a kind of mediation role. This mediation is always partial, distorting and changing throughout development and over time. The problem of how various indices relate to underlying psychological realities is raised by many studies and yet has been very little studied in its own right.

KNOWLEDGE STRUCTURES AND PROBLEM SOLVING

Researchers trained in Geneva are becoming more and more interested in the *functioning of thought.* Studies so far carried out are attempting to specify the role of the cognitive structures available to a given subject when she is faced with a concrete problem to solve. Focusing on the study of solution procedures and the strategies developed by individuals, these studies are looking at the relationships between subjects' means for mental assimilation and the actions they perform with the experimental materials.

From the point of view of intellectual development, we know that individuals first construct the means for a practical assimilation of the world, in the form of sensorimotor schemes, and only later the means to effect a mental assimilation, namely, the representational schemes of intelligence. To study the functioning of thought is to specify under which conditions and according to which modalities mental assimilation may or may not be used for practical assimilation. Thus formulated, the problem is especially raised for the developmental periods in which the individual has representational means for assimilation because, in the sensorimotor period, thought and action are indissociable.

By asking themselves about the manner in which individuals do or do not use what they know in what they are doing, researchers have come to be interested only in a certain class of relationships between thought and action. Thus, for example, the question of knowing how and by what process representational thought derives from the subject's actions is *not* a dominant area of concern for researchers working in the area of the study of the functioning of thought.

Having carried out a structural study of the child's thought at different moments in her development, Piaget attempted to tease out the mechanisms through which knowledge structures are formed via the subject's actions, but he was never particularly concerned with studies of functioning. Nevertheless, despite the absolute priority in Geneva given to the analysis of structures, Inhelder has long been interested in the use subjects could make of these structures to deal with the problems they had to solve. Her investigations provided material for a paper (1954) and also led to the writing of a book that was never published; Gréco (1956) refers to this work in a discussion of the relationships between induction, deduction, and learning. Using the experimental protocols from the structural analysis of adolescent thought (Inhelder & Piaget, 1955), Inhelder carried out a functional analysis whose importance and timeliness she stressed: "In fact we knew the main lines of the child's conception of the world and yet we are fully aware of the fact that this picture shows two considerable gaps that concern, on the one hand, the *functional aspect* of thought and, on the other hand, reasoning in the adolescent" (Inhelder, 1954, p. 272, emphasis added). This study of the functioning of thought raises specific questions.

It is not sufficient that the child has acquired a certain instrument of knowledge or reasoning mechanism for her to know how to use them. We also need to ask about the manner in which she chooses or actualizes a given structure rather than another to assimilate the situation facing her. In this generally complex assimilation process, it is also appropriate to analyze what role each particular form of reasoning plays in the set of solution processes.

The new questions raised above may only be asked if we know enough about the adaptive instruments (cognitive structures) available to individuals at different stages in their development. As Inhelder (1954) quite rightly points out, "the labor of operatory analysis thus calls for an effort at functional synthesis" (p. 272). If we accept that the main objective of psychologists is to understand subjects' behaviors (including especially those that are complex), we must realize that knowledge of the different adaptive means at their disposal is not sufficient. Knowing the repertoire of an individual's instruments for cognitive adaptation, we are not able to use this directly to deduce what she will do in a given situation or when faced with a given task. This is particularly true when we are dealing with adults who have very different and varied means for adaptation, ranging from sensorimotor or mental skills to capacities for sophisticated anticipatory reasoning made possible by formal operations. Finally, we might consider the research on the functioning of thought as responding to a series of questions generated by studies of its structural characteristics. That is, the studies carried out on the problem of structures raise the question of the study of functioning, or procedures.

The first studies of functioning (Inhelder, 1954) aimed to show how subjects organized the reality presented to them and to find out which aspects of it were taken into account. The analysis, thus, rested on the kind of investigation that subjects applied to the different experimental situations presented to them, for example, the scientific-reasoning tasks involving billiards, the pendulum, the mixture of liquids, and so on.

The protocols obtained from a large number of children (1,600 interviews) permitted the study of the functioning of inductive reasoning. This study analyzed the different acts that make up the children's scientific research process. The different forms that this process takes define the techniques used by subjects to organize their experiment to extract laws and to test the degree of generalizability of these laws. At different periods in their development, subjects with different modes of reasoning naturally develop different research techniques. A classification of techniques was carried out to look at the different research directions adopted by the child (his motives), the set of steps he used to organize the experiment (his tactics), his interpretation of reality (his reading), and the kind of connections he makes between his predictions and what he reads (his verification). An analysis of the protocols showed the following developmental progression:

Imaginative techniques are most frequently used by young children. At this level the child acts for the sake of acting. This global action on reality, although it gives the child great pleasure, does not constitute a means of investigating the apparatus and its properties. The child may notice the successes and failures in what he does, but these are not used to organize an interrogation of reality. Two examples will enable us to illustrate the behaviors encountered with young children.

In the experiment combining liquids, young subjects create mixtures with several liquids solely to discover the result. This result, once noticed, is not used to organize the experiment. Successive actions *and* the results obtained make up totalities that are sufficient in themselves. In the billiards situation, similarly, young children often hit the billiard balls harder and harder without changing the orientation of the cue, being convinced that they will end up hitting the target ball. Their activity often has nothing to do with the problem given to them.

Concrete techniques are developed by slightly older children. At this point, the child acts to succeed, that is, to achieve the assigned goal in a practical way. His action is, thus, a means to the attainment of the goal set by the experimenter, and this means has to be effective. The child looks for new relationships between causes (his actions) and effects (what happens to the apparatus) and tries to make generalizations by degrees. In the billiards experiment, he is able to notice that different trajectories of the billiard ball correspond to different angles of the cue. Using the correspondence between these positions and trajectories, he will be able to determine how to change the angle of the cue if the position of the target changes, but he will not be able to calculate the exact position to guarantee hitting the target. He still has to "try and see" (as children often say) in order to regulate his action by the results obtained. At this point in development, it is obvious that action is as much a means to reach the goal as a means to the child's understanding of the phenomenon in question.

Scientific techniques are at the base of adoles-

cents' and preadolescents' performances. The specific actions carried out are particularly aimed at verifying if what they think is true or false. Less preoccupied with obtaining practical results, the subjects use action upon the materials as a means either to verify their calculations or to prove the correctness of their calculations to an external observer. This change of status for action characterizes the performance of adolescents, who do not rush into action but think before they act (Inhelder, 1954). Subjects will *first* translate the situation into a series of mental substitutes (images, propositions, or other representations) upon which they will make mental calculations to solve the problem and only *then* act to verify. Observation of behavior shows that actions carried out are preceded by phases of reasoning by the subject. In the combination-of-liquids experiment, for example, observation of adolescents shows that what they do is planned; some subjects are even able to list the possible combinations of two liquids, then three, and so on. Having carried out the mixing of two liquids and noted the results, they are able to proceed to the mixing of three liquids, using the completed mixing of two liquids as their new point of departure. Thus, carrying out the mixing of two liquids is simultaneously a means to discover the results of this combination as well as a step in carrying out combinations of three liquids. The relevance for functioning is clearly indicated in these early studies, but the analysis of the structures of thought is equally present.

The functional perspective developed in the mid-fifties should be stated more precisely. Inhelder (1954) was studying the functioning of inductive reasoning on a *general* level. Her objective ignored individual subjects in favor of a hypothetical subject, a model of the development of inductive reasoning (i.e., the epistemic subject). The situations retained from previous research had to invoke active research on laws and their governing causes rather than on research in problem solving. On this level, these experimental situations are far removed from daily life, which requires of the subject less a systematic understanding of these laws or causes than the giving of a response or the attaining of a goal. Learning to drive a car or driving it, once one has learned to do so, is not a matter of understanding how a combustion engine works or how the commands are transmitted to the different parts concerned but of being able to use the car to get from one space to another without accident and without getting into trouble with the police (by respecting certain driving rules). If knowledge of how an automobile functions is one subject for research (it is able to tell us about the possibilities for analysis of the epistemic subject), the use of the automobile constitutes another subject that should be distinguished from the first (it will lead us to ask questions about the cognitive aspects of the behavior of psychological subjects).

Put briefly, the 1954 studies of the functioning of a particular mode of reasoning must be distinguished from studies of the functioning of thinking of individuals who have to solve practical problems. In the latter case, individuals may or may not be able to use the set of cognitive resources available to them. Despite their special nature, these early studies show up the clear change with age in the status of action within the subject's performance, a change that is confirmed by later research (Bullinger, 1973). Initially existing for itself (isolated), the action later becomes an employable means to attain a practical goal and finally becomes a means to verify and prove. This change of status for action is accompanied by a temporal structuring peculiar to the activity. If young children literally throw themselves into action, adolescents defer their access to the experimental apparatus to reflect before acting.

Owing to the accumulation of findings regarding the structural aspects of development and the dynamics of the mechanisms for passing from one stage to another, the conditions under which current research is being carried out within this functional perspective are radically different from those of the 1950s. The aim of this current research is quite different from that of the earlier studies. It is no longer a matter of observing the functioning of a particular mode of reasoning or the generalization of a given analysis to a set of modes of reasoning possessed by subjects. Instead, it concentrates on the functioning of the psychological subject to discover its mechanisms. Within this perspective, the emphasis is placed on the study of the procedures for solving problems:

Now the time has come to turn our interests to the subject's processes of invention or discovery in his/her search for solutions to very different problems. . . . Invention with regard to a particular problem always consists of a set of individual procedures that may vary from subject to subject, or from situation to situation. . . . We hope that the several methods and facts reported will permit an understanding of the general laws of functioning, a new and considerable task. (Inhelder, Ackermann-Valladao, Blanchet, Kar-

miloff-Smith, Kilcher-Hagedorn, Montangero, & Robert, 1976, p. 59)

At several points Inhelder insists on the continuity between previous work (aimed at the mechanisms of understanding the world and thereby constructing general structures) and her present interests:

I think that a procedural study of problem solving only has real meaning when inserted in the framework of a constructivist epistemology, when it is based upon the previous structuralist analysis, and when it is supported by the functional laws of the growth of knowledge. (1978, p. 100)

Current research centers on the study of the strategies developed by subjects when asked to solve problems. Beyond the strategies developed, it is the mechanisms of their elaboration that are targeted: "The object of our current studies is the search for the functional mechanisms in use in each individual subject's strategies at different levels in his/her development" (Inhelder, 1978, p. 102). To carry out this project successfully, a number of distinctions have to be made and several new concepts defined.

The actions produced by subjects in the different experimental situations allow for the analysis of *action procedures* considered as "responses oriented toward the solution of a problem that the subject sets for himself (or that someone else may set for him)" (Saada-Robert, 1979, pp. 179–180). The term *strategy* is used to designate "any system and sequence of procedures that are strictly determined by an end or goal ('finalized'), that are repeatable and transferable, and that constitute for the subject the means for attaining his/her goal" (Inhelder, 1978, p. 102). The systemic nature of strategies is underlined. The emphasis is put on the organization that characterizes the strategy as well as on its properties.

These are the properties that Piaget usually attributed to action schemes or operatory schemes, which he defined as being the structure or outline of an action or operation; it was that which was repeatable in identical situations or generalizable in analogous situations. This quasi-identity in the definitions of the notion of strategy and the notion of scheme led Piaget (1976a) to propose new theoretical distinctions to remove this ambiguity. Thus, he defined three kinds of schemes and their properties.

1. *Presentative schemes* (schèmes présentatifs) are "those which relate to the permanent and simultaneous characteristics of comparable objects"

(Piaget, 1976a, p. 286). For the subject, they constitute one of the means available to her to translate the stable aspects of reality. This category simultaneously brings together representational schemes, concepts (e.g., the red ones, the triangles, dogs), and sensorimotor schemes enabling the child to recognize certain characteristics of the objects with which she has already dealt. For example, suspended objects may be recognized because they can be made to swing; distant objects may be recognized because they are impossible to get hold of or to handle. Through the action of recognitory assimilation, practical classes are constituted—objects to be swung, distant objects, and so on. Thus, heterogeneous schemes (representational and sensorimotor) are grouped together under the heading of presentative schemes. The function of these schemes is to present reality and to translate it by reducing it to one or another of its invariant qualities. These schemes also may easily be generalized or abstracted out of their context. They remain, even if they are subclasses of larger sets. (The concept of cat does not disappear because the class of cats is included in that of animals for example.)

2. *Procedural schemes* (schèmes procéduraux) are "action sequences serving as means to attain a goal" (Piaget, 1976a, p. 286). These (procedural) schemes are "finalized" and are consequently difficult to generalize and to abstract from the precise context in which they have been constructed and used. They are preserved only for a limited duration because once the goal has been reached, "they no longer have a use" (Piaget, 1976a, p. 286).

3. *Operatory schemes* (schèmes opératoires) "are in one sense procedural, but make use of regulated and general means (operations)" (Piaget, 1976a, p. 287). They are coordinated and form structures, which may be described by their properties (e.g., the additive grouping of classes, or more generally, classifications). These structures are presentative, in that they enable the relations between objects to be translated (resemblances for classifications or differences for seriation). Piaget considers operatory schemes to be a synthesis of the other two kinds of schemes (presentative and procedural).

These theoretical distinctions make it possible to differentiate two large systems within the set of cognitive mechanisms. Although complementary, these two systems have different finalities. One serves to *understand* the world, that is, the set of physical realities, logicomathematical relations, or the laws or causality of phenomena. This system provides the bases for mental assimilation. It is shaped by the ensemble of presentative and operatory schemes. The other serves to *succeed* in the world in the various situations confronting subjects. This system provides the bases for practical assimilation in its broad sense. It is made up of the set of procedural schemes. It may also include operatory schemes if they are considered as the means to attain a goal, for example, arranging sticks in serial order is certainly to construct an ordered relation whose properties may be listed (operatory aspect), but it could also be used to construct a staircase for the doll to get to the first floor of the house (procedural aspect).

By studying the processes by which the means adjust themselves and make it possible to arrive at the goal, functional studies aim to specify how understanding may be employed for success. Three kinds of problems have interested researchers:

The first has to do with the relationships between action procedures and the interpretive systems that support the sets of actions produced by the subject. These interpretive systems, sometimes called implicit theories or theories in action (Karmiloff-Smith & Inhelder, 1975), refer to the means available to the child for understanding the world.

The second problem concerns the mechanisms for the elaboration of solution procedures. Behavior observation has led to the distinction of two kinds of procedure on the basis of the manner in which they are formed. If the action sequence enabling the goal to be reached is built up by degrees, using the general property of actions to produce a result, we speak of the productive order. In this case, the order in which actions are determined and are carried out are in exact correspondence. If, on the other hand, the combination of actions is carried out on the basis of characteristics of the goal (determining what should be done and in what order), we speak of the precursive or teleonomic order. Here the elements making up the sequence are determined in exactly the inverse of the order in which they are carried out.

The third problem deals with the systems of meanings attributed, first to the means and to the goal and second to the subject's interventions with the experimental situation to instantiate the problem the subject has been set. Studies in this area focus on the mechanisms used by the child to determine which solution means is pertinent for the problem posed.

The experimental situations used by the group of researchers were such that to attain a particular goal, the subject had to produce a connected set of actions.

The observation of these action chains, therefore, would allow inferences to be made regarding the underlying cognitive processes. The experimenter intervened as little as possible so as not to disrupt the unfolding of the child's behaviors. Modifications to the materials were used to vary the constraints placed on activity. The resistance of the situation to the child's actions was *directly* manipulated on the materials and not (as was the case in earlier Genevan research) by giving the child verbal suggestions or countersuggestions. The child was thereby able to discover and interpret the effects of his or her actions directly, via the results of the effects in the situation.

The experiments conducted used the developmental method, that is, the strategies in most of the research are studied in the course of their evolution. The data used are observations of the subject's actions. Certain properties of the actions allow inferences to be made about the underlying cognitive processes and make it possible to specify the role of these processes. The detailed study of what a subject does in the various situations allows us to infer the interpretive systems that underlie the actions produced.

The results of one experiment in which subjects were required to balance blocks on a support (Karmiloff-Smith & Inhelder, 1975) are especially illustrative of the relations between what subjects do (their actions) and what they think about the situation (the kind of interpretation they have).

Some of the blocks used in this study would balance at their geometric center; others would not because, for example, they contained hidden weights concentrated at one end. Observation of the behavior of very young children shows that they do not distinguish between that which pertains to the action they produce and that which results from the properties of the object itself. Certain actions definitely have special powers. For example, after a failure to balance a block, young subjects put the block on the support again and pushed hard with their finger. The protocols collected show that these children frequently explore the blocks by acting on them—they place them on the support according to their various dimensions. These phases of systematic exploration of the characteristics of an object often take place after subjects have already succeeded in balancing a block. These facts led Inhelder (1978) to wonder whether children do not draw from the reservoir of their presentative schemes to find those that might serve as procedural schemes. Ineffective procedures are often replaced by effective ones in the course of the experiment. Discovering, for example, that it is not sufficient to push hard on the block for it to

remain balanced, children modify their behavior, for example, supporting the block with one finger at each end, they move it until it does balance. This sensorimotor kind of effective sequence can be applied to all the different situations of the materials and in this way constitutes a problem-solving procedure that is both *effective* and *general*. This is a method that may be generally characterized as being proprioceptive and allows the child to achieve a state of balance by successive adjustments. This solution method then disappears but may reappear in older children when they are asked to balance a block with their eyes closed.

With an older age group, the protocols show that the children develop completely different attempts at solution. They systematically place the block at its geometric center. In all cases where this positioning does not lead to balancing (e.g., because of the hidden weights), they can, at most, execute several small displacements that barely move the block from its initial, geometric-center positioning. Most important, these children seem to ignore the proprioceptive information that the youngest children used perfectly to succeed. If they close their eyes, the use of differences in pressure is again possible, but once they open their eyes, they modify the position of the block by bringing its geometric center back in line with the vertical axis of the support.

In these cases, previous solution procedures disappear as the subject attributes a priviledged and exclusive role to the geometric center of the solid. This generates failures—children using this procedure are less successful than are the younger children. These responses are evidence of the role the child attributes to the geometric center in balancing an object. Above all, the responses show that action systems are no longer elaborated, bit by bit, by integrating visual and proprioceptive information. Instead, the responses are organized by taking into account what the child thinks is the role played by a certain property of the object. This geometric-center theory persists despite the negative responses of the material to the subject's action.

This interpretive system will change slowly with development, and it is only quite gradually that the oldest children will begin to use the center of gravity of objects. This change has several causes. First, the property of mass of objects is progressively constructed. Its role in balance becomes clearer. Second, this elaboration makes children increasingly sensitive to negative responses from the milieu and makes them extract and interpret the regularity of failures. Finally, there is a coordination of the properties of the geometric center and those of the center of gravity within a single interpretive system. This allows not only the regularity of successes but also the regularity of failures to be taken into account—the children can then provide a complete explanation of the events that might occur in the situation.

This evolution is manifested in the children's behavior by various modifications to their activity. First, the falling of blocks is used positively, bringing with it changes in the position of the block on the support that go in the right direction for the solution. Second, the temporal unfolding of the activity changes. Subjects can defer their actions; they do not rush immediately away to the materials. At this level, the children are able simultaneously to consider ends and means and, consequently, to plan action. Very gradually the mental means of assimilation available to the children will change places with and replace the practical means of assimilation used by the youngest children to solve the problem.

It should be pointed out that Karmiloff-Smith and Inhelder (1975) speak of sensorimotor understanding to interpret this behavior of the youngest children. This interpretation must be discussed on the basis of the facts it takes into account and also on the basis of the theoretical distinctions that this kind of experiment has made necessary.

As far as the facts are concerned, the protocols show that the very young children do succeed in balancing the various blocks offered to them on the support. This balancing relies on a very particular procedure. After the first attempt to position the block, the very young children carry out a series of displacements of the point of contact, checking after each modification to see if the goal has been attained. Without knowing why, they end up by placing the center of gravity on the support and so the block is balanced.

The theoretical problem consists in knowing if the behavior of these young children is evidence of the use of an interpretive system responsible for the organization of the procedure developed or whether this procedure is simply made up of the repetition of actions of the same kind. In both cases, these actions displace the block's point of contact with the support. No matter at which moment in the process, what the subject does is to correct the state produced by what she has previously done, taking into account the various perceptual clues. The sequence of actions making up the procedure is not only determined but also organized by a general functioning "closing the gap." The organization of the procedure developed by the subject appears to be only a by-product (it is a result for which she was not looking) of the very general process of regulating activity through its result. Thus, there is nothing in the re-

ported facts that is evidence of the intervention of the cognitive system that enables the subject to understand the world, only mechanisms are called upon that enable her to succeed in the world.

Of course something quite different is happening when the older subjects use first the geometric center and then the center of gravity to effect a balance. This systematic use of the geometric or gravitational center is evidence of presentative schemes and of the intervention of the system of understanding in the regulation of action.

This discussion of the role attributed to interpretive systems raises the question of the mechanisms by which individuals develop strategies to solve a problem. Different but congruent approaches to this problem have been undertaken in Geneva (Cellerier, 1979a, 1979b; Inhelder et al., 1976; Leiser, Cellerier, & Ducret, 1976) and elsewhere (Chatillon, 1980; Chatillon & Baldy, 1975; Pailhous, 1971; Pailhous, in press).

The distinction between the two previously defined procedural orders allows Inhelder and her collaborators to propose three possibilities for the direction of the assembly or organization of strategies: (1) the assembly is governed solely by a productive order, (2) the assembly is governed solely by a precursive or teleonomic order, or (3) the assembly is governed by a particular coordination of the two orders.

At certain points in development, one can note that children's actions follow one another, using the effects of each of the previous actions. The organization of the strategy then rests on the use of causal relations in the broadest sense of the term. The assembly of strategies is accomplished by successive adjustments relative to the effect (or effects) of the previous action. The strategy is constructed by reducing the gap between the productions currently realized and the goal that is to be attained. Its means of regulation is retroactive.

An experiment by Ackermann-Valladao (1977) confirms this predominance of solution procedures based on successive adjustments. The task requires the building of towers of equivalent heights from the table by fitting blocks of different heights into hollow boxes. To achieve the assigned goal, one has to compensate for the differences in the heights of the blocks by placing a shelf at different heights in the hollow containers. The height of the shelf serving as a base could be regulated by sliding it into the containers through one of four slots on their front surfaces. The total height of each tower is determined by the height of the block itself and the height of the empty space separating the shelf from the base of the tower. The shelf pieces and blocks of various heights are provided jumbled up and all together; the child subject can handle them as he wishes. The child himself decides the levels for the summits of the various towers.

The results of this experiment show that the youngest children preferentially use solution procedures based on the use of productive relations. They initially place the base pieces (shelves) in a position that does not take account of the heights of the blocks that have to be fitted into the containers. Placing of the blocks is carried out after this first phase and leads to unequal heights from the table for the towers. This inequality causes some subjects to stop what they are doing; they consider the task impossible. Others transform the situation by constructing distinct groups of towers (two for example) that have equivalent heights, but they do not modify the positions of the shelves. Other young children finally (and these are the most interesting behaviors) manage progressively to adjust the position of the base pieces by using their observation of the inequalities in heights. These readjustments of positions generally come after a whole series of attempts to equalize the heights by changing the blocks. The behavior described shows that there is no use of a goal-determined procedure to find the position of the shelf.

It is the reverse for the older subjects. They proceed in their construction from top to bottom. They fix themselves a reference in the goal to be attained that immediately intervenes to organize their actions in the inverse order to that usually used in contruction (from the bottom upwards). In this case, activity is really organized mentally as a function of this goal, and its achievement rests upon a sequence of anticipations that constitute a system of precursory planning of the action. This activity is constantly directed by the goal and its unfolding is continuous, each step necessarily preparing the way for the next. Thus, each action has a determined place within an overall executive process.

If, in order to be solved, the situations require the coordination of the two orders of procedure, as in the situations used by Blanchet (1977) or Boder (1978), the child encounters specific difficulties. For example, if they have to load different colored blocks onto a truck that then unloads them at different points on a circular route, the children have enormous difficulty in coordinating the loading order with that for unloading. For the blocks to be unloaded at their respective destinations, the last to be unloaded must be the first to be loaded.

The existence of two principal modes of control of thought and their coordination is studied from a position clearly influenced by cybernetic and information processing models. This research tries to get at "the cyclical process of interaction between the level of reflection and the level of execution . . . [that] . . . in the course of solution elaborates the means as such and differentiates the goal while specifying it" (Boder, 1978, p. 87). The tasks used permit the study of the directing idea that assures "the transition from the initial representation of the goal to the first action to be executed" (Boder, 1978, p. 87). Translation of the directing idea into procedures defines a top-down mode of controlling activity; successive changes to this directing idea based on the results obtained defines a bottom-up mode of controlling activity. Solving the problem has as a necessary condition the coordination of these two modes of control, that is, top-down (precursive) and bottom-up (productive).

This perspective, in which cybernetic models play an important role, has been developed at the theoretical level by several Genevan researchers. The idea of a system, and especially of the representational function, has also been defined. Leiser et al. (1976) stress the role and the importance of representation for apprehending the initial state of the problem. They also emphasize the role of the elaboration of representations useful in the solution. In this representational system, they distinguish between a static aspect, referring to the current state of the subject's knowledge of the problem, and a dynamic aspect, the functional nucleus comprising operators responsible for transformations of state. There is also a control system that determines which operator to use. This control system has an organizational function with regard to an individual's activity in a given situation, in that it both selects and combines the operators.

This emphasis placed on the assembly of operators underlines the importance of the concept of scheme, a central concept in the study of the application of instruments of knowledge to particular situations (Cellerier, 1979a, 1979b). The problem posed is that of the pragmatic transformation of knowledge into action, described by Miller, Galanter, and Pribram (1960). The question is how to coordinate the analysis built from the classic structuralist positions with that developed by the cognitivists whose central interests are with the doable and with action. This coordination is Cellerier's (1979a, 1979b) goal when, starting with the notion of scheme, he tries to analyze the mechanisms and the conditions of their assembly through the study of different types of control and its means.

The study of adult cognitive functioning has given rise to other research projects. Task performance was studied and analyzed in terms of *specific schemes* for analyzing the situation (Chatillon, 1980; Chatillon & Baldy, 1975). Subjects' initial representations were closely tied to the type of procedure developed for attaining the goal (a procedure that gradually approaches a solution or one that is highly structured toward the goal). The initial representations strongly influenced the subject's performance—the best results were from those individuals who were able most precisely to imagine the different steps of the transformation of the object (a top-down control of activity seems particularly important). In the domain of adult spatial problem solving, Pailhous (1971, in press) approaches the problem of the combination of schemes by defining the concept of *executive principle*. This concept takes into account the fact that an individual confronted with a problematic situation will organize his instruments of knowledge more or less powerfully to generate a system for processing and for specific representation that allows this problem to be solved. These executive principles are to be found in the child as well as in the adult. Their power is determined by two parameters: (1) the size of the class of images and rules that might be generated and (2) their efficiency, that is, whether they lead to the goal.

If the problem is posed in these terms, it then becomes necessary to identify the rules governing the application of the cognitive instruments to new situations. From this perspective, several authors think a single rule can account for subjects' behavior when they are placed in new situations. Speaking in terms of microgenesis, transitory disequilibrium, or registers or levels of functioning Vermersch (1976, 1979), for example, is of the opinion that in new situations individuals use their instruments of knowledge in the ontogenetic order in which they were acquired. The passage from behavior of a given type to another would be guaranteed by processes of reequilibration. The idea according to which there would exist registers of functioning (whose characteristics are closely related to those of child behavior at a given developmental level) takes into account the coexistence in the adult of several possible modes of cognitive functioning. The use of a class of instruments defines the register of the subject's functioning. For example, the involvement of isolated sensorimotor instruments in a given situation defines the subject's use of a sensorimotor register.

These hypotheses have been applied in a series of studies on adults learning to use an oscilloscope. In interpreting individuals' behavior, Vermersch (1979) suggests that the first time the subject encounters an oscilloscope the sensorimotor register alone is used. The subject proceeds without anticipating. It is by the use of perturbations (introduction of a signal) and restoring control after periods of confusion following the introduction of perturbations that the subject learns how to control the oscilloscope, in other words the subject constructs a knowledge of the object.

This notion is no doubt appealing in its simplicity. In this way, it is related to the varieties of recapitulation theories that periodically manifest themselves in psychology. However, if we allow that inside each adult sleep several children, it is clear that when they awaken, it is the adult who carries them, who acts, and who is responsible for managing their actions. An adult faced with a problematic situation could behave in such a way that the *external* signs were the same as behavior produced at the sensorimotor level. We must ask ourselves, however, about the meaning and the function that these behaviors have. This questioning will no doubt lead to the conclusion that the sensorimotor behavior observed in the adult has nothing to do with sensorimotor behavior produced by a child less than 2 years of age.

The mechanism by which the subject chooses the elements necessary for the solution of a problem is based on the meaning she attributes to the elements during the solution process. These meaning systems (or meaningful representations) link comprehension with the procedures themselves. They require particularly sensitive analysis because they do not lend themselves well to direct observation. It is especially clear that the actions produced by a subject working with task materials only partially reflect these systems of meaning. The transformation of a given action sequence is, however, a more direct reflection of the meaningful representations implied. If modification to the course of activity can be taken as an index of change of functional significance, it is clear that some observable manifestations of meaning (Blanchet, 1977) must be sought beyond these. A certain number of behaviors that accompany performance are meaningful. "Facial expressions, incipient gestures or verbalizations, gaze path, hesitations, modification of the work rhythm, etc. . . . allow us to reconstruct each action as a function of the meaning that the subject gives it" (Blanchet, 1977, p. 50). The inference made from observation of these indices allows us to grasp "the system of planning actions invented by the child as a function of a concrete goal" (Inhelder, Blanchet, Boder, De Caprona, Saada-Robert, & Ackermann-Valladao, 1980, p. 646), or to reconstruct the representational model constructed by the individual (Blanchet, 1980). In a way, to be interested in the problem of meaning is to ask why a particular meaningful unit seems relevant to the subject and will thereby orient her activity. In this way, these interests are close to those of researchers concerned with the problem of action formation within other theoretical frameworks (Galpérine, 1966).

Several studies are beginning to yield data on the study of problem solving (Ackermann-Valladao, 1980; Blanchet, Ackermann-Valladao, Kilcher, & Saada-Robert, 1978; Boder, 1978; Saada-Robert, 1979, 1980). These studies show that the strategy developed can only be interpreted in the functional context in which it was generated.

Finally, the relationships between structures and procedures have not proved to be simple to analyze (Inhelder & Piaget, 1979). The available data show that there are different types of interaction between material actions and the conceptual representation that the individual has at his disposal (Montangero, 1977). The procedures developed by a subject while solving a problem do not appear to depend directly on fixed structural levels—several procedures of different types can be produced by the same individual at different points in the execution of the solution (Kilcher & Robert, 1977).

We are witnessing a veritable explosion of research on the functioning of thought. The number of studies makes it difficult to present a synthesis and, a fortiori, an exhaustive account of the state of the problem.

DEVELOPMENTAL PSYCHOLINGUISTIC STUDIES

Genevan psycholinguistic research underwent both methodological and theoretical changes during the 1970s. Briefly, the main changes can be characterized as follows:

1. Experimental methods became more varied, in the sense that different levels of language competence were taken into account. Some interviewing techniques are apt to show children's capacities for reflecting *on* language; others, particularly those that insert target patterns into natural discourse, come closer to a study of competence in everyday language use.

2. Theoretically speaking, the main object of study became the changes in the ways children approach language problems rather than the structural levels in their mastery of a particular sentence pattern. Consequently, the search for parallels between

the acquisition of certain syntactic structures and the basic cognitive structures brought to light by Piaget was given up in favor of a search for processes and strategies that might be common to the treatment children give to various sentence patterns and the procedures they develop in other problem-solving situations.

In the early 1970s, results of research on the acquisition of syntax (considered as an autonomous part of language knowledge) carried out with comprehension, production, and repetition techniques in several languages raised a number of problems:

1. How should one account for the fact that identical sentence patterns are more or less difficult for children to understand according to the content words used? What are the extralinguistic factors that influence the interpretation of sentences? What is, in acquisition, the importance of the interaction between syntax, pragmatics, and semantics?

2. How do children elaborate the various functions fulfilled by sets of morphosyntactic markers, such as verb-determiners and noun-determiners (conjugation forms and articles, etc.)?

3. How can one encourage children to produce certain sentence patterns? Do certain patterns carry particular functional meanings? How do children understand such instructions as "I would like you to begin your sentence with the word *X*"? Do such instructions presuppose some reflection on language? If so, how does such metalinguistic or epilinguistic awareness develop?

Several series of experiments were designed to deal with these questions.

Syntax, Pragmatics, and Semantics

The intricate relationships between semantics and syntax are particularly clear in Barblan's (1977) continuation (in French) of C. Chomsky's research (1969) on such sentences as "The doll is easy to see." This sentence was one of several chosen because of the particular relation between deep structure and surface structure in such constructions. Many 5- and 6-year-olds (both English- and French-speaking) think that this sentence means something like, "The doll sees easily." (Compare this to the sentence, "Paul is ready to help." The interpretation of this sentence is, indeed, something like, "Paul helps readily.") Several linguistic studies have proposed different transformational derivations for such sentences. The best solution has appeared to be a transformation that introduces a displacement of an element of the deep structure in such a way that a fronting of the object is obtained; this transformation is called tough movement.

Barblan (1977) presented children with several sentences, such as: "Le chien est prêt à manger." ["The dog is ready to eat."] / "Le garçon est difficile à entendre." ["The boy is difficult to understand."] / Le paquet est lourd à porter." ["The parcel is heavy to carry."] / "Le lapin est doux à toucher." ["The rabbit is soft to touch."] The results showed that "easy to see" is by far the most difficult example of that particular construction. Although the rabbit sentence could give rise to the same type of error noted with the doll sentence (the rabbit touches softly), this interpretation is almost never given by children, not even by 4-year-olds. Barblan concluded from lengthy interviews with his subjects that the main factor of the difficulty of the doll sentence is to be sought in the fact that—in contrast to the rabbit sentence, which describes an intrinsic property of all rabbits—the doll sentence concerns a momentary property ("easy to see" for whom? From where?). Moreover, the expression "to see easily" has rather particular connotations for young children, who think, for example, that one cannot say that Peter sees Paul easily unless Paul can also see Peter easily. The results of the experiment, thus, indicated clearly that semantics as well as pragmatics and syntax have to be invoked to account for the different approaches children use to interpret sentences of this type.

Another example of relationships between syntax and semantics is to be found in the area of pronouns. Definitions of pronouns stress two aspects that interplay during comprehension. The first is the search for an antecedent (noun or noun phrase) and the second is the understanding of a case function (for the attribution of agent, patient, beneficiary roles). Examples of pronouns carrying these functions are: "He [agent] bought a book." / "The boy kissed her [patient]." / "The boy gave her [beneficiary] a book." Pronouns may also carry semantic information: distinction between sexes, animate/inanimate, possession, quantity, and so on. The mastery of this complex system has been the object of a series of developmental studies that have concentrated on comprehension rather than production.

Chipman (1974, 1980) investigated the child's comprehension of sentences that contained third-person personal (e.g., he, she) and possessive pronouns (e.g., his, hers) as well as relative (e.g., that) pronouns in English. The pronouns were inserted in sentences representing two actions that the child was able to perform easily; thus, difficulties because of extralinguistic problems were eliminated to focus comprehension on the syntactic aspect.

The findings for the three types of pronouns brought to light three levels of acquisition. At the first level, subjects (aged 3 to 5 approximately) use primitive word-order strategies (similar to those noted by Sinclair and Bronckart, 1972) that lead to an intrapropositional treatment. At this level, the child treats two simple SV0 (subject-verb-object) clauses linked by a pronoun as two more or less independent units. For example, "The boy pushes the girl and then she washes the other boy." This is understood as meaning that a first boy pushes the girl and that a second girl washes a second boy. If possible, the children also use real-world knowledge in their interpretations, as in the possessive pronoun experiment for example. In this case, ideas about games and pets are reflected in the understanding of such a sentence (where the boy and the girl each have a dog) as "The boy pushes his and then the girl pets his." This is acted out as boy and girl each playing with their own dog, which is frequently the case in real-life situations. At the second level, from 5 to 7, children extensively apply a role-conserving coordination strategy, that is, the semantic function of the antecedent as an agent or a patient is transferred to the pronoun and both clauses are acted out keeping either the same agent or the same patient. The use of these strategies is so overriding that any semantic marking of pronouns (e.g., he, she) is ignored. This means that in the above example with personal pronouns, the first boy is used as agent for both actions. In relative-clause sentences, the following sentence is easily and correctly understood: "The dog that pushes the cat licks the squirrel." It is understood precisely because the dog is the agent of both actions. The third level begins around age 7 when the child correctly treats whatever information is available from the pronoun's morphological marker. The child considers the surface structure of sentences in his search for the referent; at this point, center-embedded clauses become difficult for the child. The above example of a relative-clause sentence is now less easily understood, not only because of the insertion of the relative clause within the main clause (thus upsetting the canonical SVO order) but also because the child begins to wonder what the pronoun "that" actually means.

Ferreiro, Othenin-Girard, Chipman, and Sinclair (1976) compared English results to those obtained in French and Spanish for similar sentences. Generally, results are similar, in particular as far as the role-conserving strategies are concerned. However, there were differences in the percentages of success obtained with different types of relative clauses. Right-branching subject-relative clauses appeared easier in French than in English or Spanish; center-embedded relative-subject clauses appeared easier in Spanish than in English or French. These differences may be due to the morphological marking of the French pronouns (qui/que) and of the Spanish article (el/al), which are case marked for nominative or accusative functions. Moreover, the results of a production experiment and of a study on children's grammatical judgments of sentences with relative clauses allowed for some further interpretation of children's construction of the pronominal system. In all languages, it is easier to add a relative clause to an agent than to a patient; in French and in Spanish children seem to oscillate between two values of *que* (as an anaphoric pronoun and as a subordinating link between two propositions); even when these two values have become coordinated, the minimal distance rules constraining the position of relative pronouns have not yet been mastered.

Functional Aspects of Sets of Markers

Bronckart (1976) studied how children (2 1/2 to 9) use French verbal forms. For adult French speakers, the main function of tenses (perfect, imperfect, pluperfect, present, and future) is to express the relation (simultaneity, posteriority, or anteriority) of the event described to the moment of speaking. An experimenter showed the children some simple events acted out with toys. The children were asked to go to another experimenter and to tell him what they had seen. Before age 6, children seem to attach more importance to the distinction between perfective and imperfective events than to the temporal relation between event and moment of speaking. Imperfective actions (with no clear result, such as swimming or running) were almost never expressed by past tenses. For perfective actions, the use of the present was the more frequent the greater the probability of the children taking into account the unaccomplished part of the action. This probability is partly determined by the duration of the action. The predominant aspectual feature in the use of verb forms is the distinction between the result of an action and its process. Focusing on the result implies attributing a "past" character; focusing on the process projects the action into a kind of perpetual "present." Thus, when the event shown was, for example, a horse galloping in a field, the children would report, "The horse is galloping." When the horse was shown to

jump a hurdle, the children would say, "The horse jumped over the barrier." Thus, they used a "present" and a "passé composé" respectively.

Within this new direction of research on the construction of multifunctional sets of morphosyntactic markers, Karmiloff-Smith (1979) explored the gradual mastery of noun determiners. The special role of the conjunction "and" in the child's comprehension of conjoined utterances was studied by Rappe du Cher (1977). Among the many functions of "and" is that of allowing deletion of certain elements in phrasal or sentential coordinations, for example, "John pushed the dog and petted the cat." "John petted the dog and Mary the cat." In such languages as English only word order determines the agent and patient roles; in other languages, the words "dog" and "cat" may be case marked as accusatives or special particles may be introduced that make the different relationships clear. For example, take the sentence, "John petted the dog and Mary the cat." This sentence often raised problems for English- and French-speaking subjects, who wondered whether there was somewhere a cat called Mary and what this cat was doing. Similar sentences in case marking Turkish never led to any mistakes for even the youngest (3-year-olds) Turkish-speaking subjects. This research was carried out in five languages belonging to three language families (Indo-European: French, English, German; Altaic: Turkish; Hametic-Semitic: Hebrew). The results show beyond doubt that flexion and special surface markers that govern sentence construction in Turkish, German, and Hebrew determine the ease or difficulty with which children deal with agent-patient relationships.

Functional Aspects of Syntactic Patterns

The functional perspective emphasized another problem, that is, the status of what in generative terminology are called transformations. Is their only function stylistic? Are they determined by linguistic context or by the desire of the speaker to underline certain elements and to distinguish old from new information? For example, "I know the driver of that green car: she's a pretty girl who drives rather recklessly." / "That green car belongs to a pretty girl I know; she drives rather recklessly." / "That pretty girl has a green car she drives rather recklessly; I know her." All the above sentences describe the same objective state of affairs but, according to subtle shades of meaning and context, speakers will choose one of them rather than another. Is it possible to render the reasons for this choice explicit and thereby ascribe particular functions to the different patterns? In the examples given, what are the functions of the relative-subject and relative-object clauses? Such clauses can almost always be replaced by simple coordinations or juxtapositions. Why use complex subordination? Our lack of knowledge on this point creates a methodological problem (as well as a theoretical one). If we want to study the production of certain sentence patterns with young subjects, we will have to know something about the contexts in which adult native speakers use them; otherwise, we are reduced to impose metalinguistic or epilinguistic instructions, such as "I want you to use the word *that* . . ." or to give models that the subjects are asked to imitate.

However, there are some complex sentence patterns for which it is possible to find a context. One such context, for the elicitation of conditional utterances, has been used by Berthoud and Sinclair (1978). After an introductory period during which experimenter and child construct bridges under which trucks can run, the experimenters presented the children with a new set of construction blocks inside an opaque bag and, before opening the bag, asked whether the children thought they could construct a bridge with the new material. Children between 4 and 9 produced a large number of conditional utterances, many of them "if/then" sentences, others incorporating expressions, such as "maybe," "it's possible," and morphological markers of conditionality. These various utterances appear to fulfill different functions and to be closely related to the way the child approaches the problem, that is, his conception of the possibilities of constructing the bridge and his attitude toward uncertainty (the ability to form hypotheses).

For example, "if/then" utterances produced by 5-year-olds appear to express the causal rather than the conditional link and, moreover, seem mainly to be used to express a negative value, for example, "I can make the bridge because the blocks are big. If they're small, the bridge falls down." Around 6 or 7 years of age, children can take uncertainty as a starting point for reasoning. Their "if/then" utterances express an opposition between condition *p*, which implies a certain consequence, and condition non-*p*, which gives the opposite result. These children produce what can be called symmetric utterances: "If the blocks are big, I can make a bridge; if they are small, I can't." For older children, the use of "if/then" appears to acquire a genuine hypothetical function, and they will produce several successive conditional utterances, indicating several possibilities and their consequences: "If there are small blocks, one could make a bridge, but the truck could not go underneath." / "If there are a lot, but they are small. . . ."

Apart from methodological issues, the question of the function of certain sentence patterns is a theoretical linguistic problem that needs clarification. From a psycholinguistic point of view, it appears that for the study of the subject's competence to produce and understand certain sentence types, the *how* of the mechanisms of production and comprehension cannot be separated from the *why*.

Currently other research in this field is being carried out in even more spontaneous settings. Discussions on how to prepare a certain dish or on how to play a particular game appear to elicit temporal and (to a lesser degree) conditional clauses; discussing a physical phenomenon surprising to the subjects appears to elicit subordinate clauses with "because" (without the experimenter asking "Why?").

Othenin-Girard (1978) analyzed narratives and dialogues obtained in a free-discourse situation with 4- to 7-year-old children acquiring French as a second language. In particular, she studied certain subordinate constructions, that is, temporal and relative clauses. The results show that subordinate clauses introduced by "quand" [when] express various relations between events, some not specifically temporal. The relative clauses produced in this spontaneous context do not show evidence of the role-conservation strategies found in comprehension. Presumably, this is due to the fact that when children spontaneously produce relative clauses there is something in the total context of communication that incites them to do so. Such contextual elicitation is absent in the experimental situation and sentences presented for comprehension may, therefore, seem unnatural to the child. In his search for a reason for the use of a particular pattern, she may mentally transform it. Most utterances produced spontaneously were right-branching ones, and the relative pronouns functioned as grammatical subjects. This particular type of construction appears to be due to the speaker's desire to express new information in the predicate rather than in the subject of a sentence.

Children's Linguistic Awareness

Berthoud-Papandropoulou (1978) studied 4- to 12-year-old children's metalinguistic awareness in a series of experiments on their understanding of the term "word" (see also Papandropoulou, 1976). It appears that, for 4-year-olds, words exist on the same plane as the things or events to which they refer (e.g., Strawberry is a word "because it grows in the garden." / Train is a long word "because there are lots of railroad cars.''). At 5 to 6 years of age, children identify words with the activity of speaking (e.g., ''A word is when you talk.''); when asked to tell the experimenter a ''long word,'' children produce complete utterances (e.g., ''I go inside the house and take off my shoes.''). Around 6 or 7 years of age, words are differentiated from the reality to which they refer and are thought of as existing independently, either as graphic or as phonic entities. Similarly, words become differentiated from speaking; at around the age of 7, words are thought of as constituent elements of the speaking activity (e.g., ''A word is a bit of a story, it's a part of a sentence.''). Finally, from the age of 10 onward, words are explicitly defined as elements that have a meaning (e.g., ''A word means something.''). That is, words have a specific link with extralinguistic reality and are organized into a system that has its own rules and its own categories (at this age, children talk about verbs, about agreement between noun and verb, etc.).

Starting from a hypothesis that for a naive subject the concept of a speech sound comprises characteristics of both acoustic and articulatory natures, Zei (1979) carried out an experiment to investigate awareness of phonetic activity. Children from 4 to 9 were asked to pronounce successively 14 different syllables and to describe how they produced them or what they felt ''happening inside themselves.'' They expressed an awareness of six different organs that take part in sound production, that is, the mouth, the lips, the tongue, the teeth, the throat, and the abdominal muscles. They also mentioned breathing, blowing, vibrations, and the acoustic properties of sounds (mostly by comparing them with various noises). At all ages, the mouth was by far the most frequently mentioned, next came the tongue, then the lips followed by mention of throat and acoustic features. Furthermore, the results show that mention of mouth and abdomen decreases in number with age, whereas mention of the tongue, lips, throat, and breathing increases with children from 5 to 8 years of age; mention of teeth remains fairly constant; reference to acoustic features increases with age. On the whole, children's descriptions of speech sounds are remarkably accurate and throw some light on the articulatory parameters that appear as being of psychological importance to speech production.

Brami-Mouling (1977) studied how children adapt their way of talking to the age of the child to whom they are speaking. Her subjects first told a story to a child of their own age and then they told the same story to a younger child. Children 6 years old are already clearly aware of the fact that their younger partner does not share their own knowledge of the world or of language. To make themselves understood, they choose what they consider to be simple words, they use attention-getting and attention-keeping devices, and they check that they have been understood. In contrast with the findings of other authors, Brami-Mouling noted the production of long and often complex sentences, that is, lexical terms are defined (e.g., ''The closet, you know, the place where you put your clothes.'') and events are explained (e.g., ''The birds fly away, they are afraid; cats are nasty to birds.''). These explanations, which do not occur when the subject is talking to a child of her own age, bear witness to the child's awareness of the need to compensate for the listener's presumed lack of knowledge. This awareness, however, long remains tacit; an interview after the storytelling shows that various means of clarification and simplification are only made explicit years after the subjects have regularly used them.

In Berthoud's (1978) research on children's ideas about words, there were indications that written language plays a role in their reflections on language, for example, certain children maintain that pronouns or articles ''are not words, they don't have enough letters.'' Written language is present in many forms in urban environments (words on toys and cans; street signs and posters; books and newspapers, etc.). At a very early age, children start thinking about these peculiar squiggles. Ferreiro (1978, 1979) devised a series of studies to explore children's conceptualization of our writing system. How do children come to believe that the squiggles they encounter in many different situations have a meaning? Once this first link is established, how do they come to understand that in alphabetic systems this meaning is linked to a representation of a series of sounds? How do they separate the properties of the spoken utterance that are represented in the written text (linear order, approximate phonological correspondance) from those that are not (prosody, intensity, etc.) and from the properties that are specific to graphic representation (left-right, up-down, spaces between words, etc.)? Written texts often accompany pictures, which are another way of symbolizing reality. One of the first problems young children face is to differentiate between these two modes of representation. A subtle difference is introduced by many prereaders: children are asked such questions as ''What is drawn here?'' / ''What is this a picture of?'' In response, they answer, for example, ''A duck.'' They are then asked, ''And what do you think is written underneath?'' The children say, ''duck'' (even if there are several words). When the experimenter reads out a written sentence, following the writing with her finger, and then asks the children what they think is written (indicating different words in different places in the sentence), it appears that 4- to 5-year-olds believe that only nouns are written. They interpret the graphic entities for which they cannot account (articles, verbs, etc.) in their own way (e.g., take the sentence, "The girl bought a candy bar." The children indicate that girl and candy bar are written somewhere, and they interpret the words that are left over as, "shop," "money," "mummy," etc.). From a wealth of such data, Ferreiro concludes that, by means of many compromise solutions and contradictions (some internal, some derived from information given by parents or siblings), the children gradually modify hypotheses to come to an understanding of the internal rationality of the system while accepting the arbitrariness of the representation itself. Only then do what may be called problems of orthography appear. This gradual reconstruction appears at many points to interact with children's awareness of their own verbal activity.

Bronckart (1977) set up a research program to explore theoretical notions and experimental data from Genevan psycholinguistic studies in an educational setting. The basic metalinguistic notions used and taught in elementary school (word classes: noun, verb, adjective; the sentence; grammatical functions: subject and object) were the topic of collective and individual interviews. Verb determiners (tense, aspect, and modality) were studied with cloze techniques applied to oral and written discourse and narratives. The identification of word classes and the concept "sentence" were surprisingly difficult for all elementary school children. School instruction bases word classes on morphosyntactic criteria, and these were mentioned by children; but, in reality, their identification procedures were semantically founded. The analysis of grammatical functions remains difficult even for older children; often they do not seem to understand that in many cases (e.g., passives) agent and patient roles do not correspond to grammatical subject and object functions. The main difficulty seems to lie in the children's syntactic strategies, although the different methods by which grammar is taught in school also seem to play a part (Bronckart, 1979).

As for verb determiners, Besson and Jeanrenaud's results (1974) showed that mastery of narrative verb forms depended on aspectual features of the actions described.

To make a start in tackling the vast number of problems, linguistic and psycholinguistic, raised by the comprehension and production of texts in high school, Bronckart (1979) elaborated a framework for a typology of texts. Texts can be classed on two distinct axes, one for discourse and one for narratives. Discourse (e.g., dialogue) is produced in close connection with the general context of enunciation and is organized according to this context. Narratives (e.g., historical writings and novels) entertain a mediate relation with their production context and are structured in a more autonomous way, depending partly on the chronology of the event described. The discourse axis shows two poles: (1) situational texts, which are maximally dependent on the production context (speaker and listener or writer and reader; moment and place of enunciation) and (2) theoretical texts, which are produced with the intention of maximal freedom from the enunciation context. Surface markers characteristic of situational texts are use of second-person pronouns, use of enunciation modalities (e.g., interrogatives and imperatives), absence of passé simple, absence of elements that introduce narrative and that organize texts, and low syntagmatic density (i.e., the ratio between the occurrence of nouns and that of lexical qualifiers). Theoretical texts, by contrast, show few pronouns but many enunciation modalities and passives. The narrative axis also shows two poles, that of autobiographical narrative and that of historical narrative. Its surface markers are the absence of second-person pronouns, the use of passé simple and imparfait, and the use of narrative introductions and of story modulation. Autobiographical narratives combine some of these markers with those of situational discourse. It would seem that once a detailed topology has been established students could be led to an awareness of appropriate markers; such awareness might assist both their comprehension and their production of written texts.

Underlying all Genevan research in developmental psycholinguistics is the question of the interaction of language knowledge with other types of knowledge. Initially, it was thought that this interaction could be studied in comparing particular structures, for example, the different developmental levels in the structure of the concept of time as studied by Piaget and the different levels of the temporal structures in language as they appear in the child's comprehension and production of utterances with conjunctions, such as "when," "before," and so on. Subsequently, the main emphasis was put on the interaction of construction processes in the various types of knowledge, their differences and similarities, and their (possible) specificity. Comparing children's behavior in a particular language task and in a related (mainly nonverbal) problem-solving task was now felt to be too atomistic an approach— Piaget's principle of interactionist constructivism does *not* mean that development consists of separate processes that interact from time to time. From an epistemological point of view, it is often possible to isolate certain cognitive structures, but the interaction between the various procedures and strategies subjects use in different problem-solving tasks are in constant interaction.

Although the changes in theory and methodology of developmental psycholinguistic research in Geneva are (in a sense) endogenous, that is, generated by the results of the various experiments and the problems they raised, they do show a very close parallel with recent trends in cognitive research in Geneva and elsewhere. However, in psycholinguistics, the structural approach and the search for models borrowed from logic or mathematics never yielded results comparable to those obtained by Piaget and his collaborators in his studies of the epistemologically important concepts. No crucial experiments, such as conservation tasks, were invented. Is psycholinguistics still waiting for its Piaget? Or is language mastery, because of its very nature, not a scientific object that can be analyzed in terms of general developmental levels? It seems unlikely that this fundamental question will be decided in the near future. In the meantime, the search for processes and functions is beginning to yield some interesting results and appears to be a promising trend in psycholinguistic research.

CROSS-CULTURAL STUDIES

Indirectly, the research domain of cross-cultural studies has a long history in the Genevan School. Numerous authors have replicated Piagetian tasks in very different human environments, eventually constructing materials valid for such studies. Until around the 1960s, these replications were mainly carried out on Western cultures. Later, research on other cultures was undertaken (Piaget, 1966). Epistemologically, the fundamental interest of this research has been to test the stability of the sequence of developmental stages and the generality of the instruments of knowledge. The effects of parameters of the physical and social environment on the speed of acquisition as well as the synchrony among fields of knowledge have been studied over the last 10 years in Geneva.

A study carried out in Africa on Piaget's developmental stages in infancy (Dasen, Inhelder, Lavallée, & Retschitzki, 1978) shows that: (1) the structures of

sensorimotor intelligence are almost certainly universal, (2) the rate of development is influenced by environmental factors, (3) with the emergence of the semiotic function, the contents of the child's imitations are culturally relative.

In this study, the African infants reached the various substages of sensorimotor intelligence somewhat earlier (on the average) than French babies, but this precocity was not homogeneous over different experimental situations, and the rate of development was found to be somewhat slower in those infants who suffered from moderate malnutrition. Differences were also found in the style of the behavior, for example, movements were often observed to be slow but harmonious in these African children or, before finding their own solution to a problem (e.g., to attain an object placed out of reach), they first attempted to have their mother solve it for them.

The same stages as those described for European children were found in the development of the semiotic function, but the Africans, of course, imitated models from their own culture, for example, carrying a doll on the back, whereas a French child would be more likely to sit the doll on the pram.

Formal schooling seems to be a necessary, although insufficient, condition for the development of the stage of formal operations (Laurendeau-Bendavid, 1977), but not enough cross-cultural research has been carried out on this topic. In some cases, even the last substage of the concrete operatory stage is not attained by all individuals for all the concepts, a fact that represents an important limitation on the universality of developmental sequences (Dasen & Heron, 1981).

An investigation of this problem with samples from three cultures shows substantial temporal décalages in the developmental curves for classical Piagetian tasks (Dasen, 1977). Dasen relates these to ecocultural demands, that is, those concepts that are needed for subsistence activities are culturally valued and are developed early in all subjects. This is the case, for example, of spatial concepts in nomadic, hunting populations or of precise quantification (i.e., conservation of liquids) in sedentary, agricultural populations. On the other hand, concepts that are less needed are less valued and their development tends to be slower and sometimes incomplete. These décalages can be diminished or overcome through training techniques (Dasen, Ngini, & Lavallée, 1978).

Such a global cross-cultural approach, focusing on populations, neglects individual differences within a single group. As Lautrey (1980a) shows, educational practices and the structure of family environments are dimensions relevant to cognitive development. Dasen (1979–1980) joins this perspective with observations on an African milieu showing that different educational practices have repercussions for cognition.

This line of research, which takes into account the ecocultural dimensions of human environments, shows some limitations of Piaget's theory and, at the same time, enriches and enlarges it by taking cultural factors into account. It shows the extent to which the structural invariants described at the epistemological level are valid. The cultural differences underline the importance of the interactions between the child and those properties of an environment relevant to the construction of knowledge.

The importance of the observed décalages suggests that individuals elaborate instruments of knowledge in domains that traditional experimental situations and analyses have not been able to tap. As Greenfield (1976) has pointed out, the ideal developmental end point in other cultures is not necessarily Western scientific thinking. Following Piaget's own example, one should ascertain what the ideal end state in a particular culture is and then find out the developmental steps by which an infant grows up to this culturally defined end state.

ETHOLOGICAL STUDIES

Several Genevan experiments in the field of ethology are aimed at a comparative study of object permanence in animals. In this section, the term object permanence is to be taken in its broadest sense: to what extent does an organism (1) take into account the identity and continuous existence of objects (or living beings) and (2) integrate these objects into a coherent organization of space and time. However complex the concept of object permanence may be from a conceptual and epistemological point of view, at a behavioral level it can be studied through relatively simple experimental situations, which involve the disappearance of an object in standardized conditions. The reactions in this context represent an adequate and rich criterion for the assessment of organization at the sensorimotor level. For Etienne (1972), this criterion can be applied to the human infant in the preverbal period of development as well as to animal species at various zoological levels.

At the invertebrate level, the aquatic, carnivorous dragonfly larva, *Aeschna cyanea M.*, reacts to the disappearance of a prey with stereotyped behavior based on physiological aftereffects following the presentation of the prey: (a) after a brief presentation of a lure, the larva remains orientated in the direction where the prey disappeared and thus increases the probability of a further encounter with the same prey (Etienne, 1972); (b) if however, the larva has been pursuing an escaping prey in vain for some time, it reacts to the prey's disappearance with a series of backing and turning movements "that decrease the likelihood that the same prey may be rediscovered, and at the same time favor the discovery of new prey objects" (Etienne, 1976, 1977a, 1977b). Behavior (a) depends on the intensity of the prey stimulus, which determines aftereffects of a certain duration within the insect's optical system; behavior (b), on the other hand, is controlled by the larva's energy expenditure during the pursuit of the previously presented prey (Etienne, 1978). Both behaviors, which imply (a) a very limited principle of object permanence as well as (b) a principle of counterpermanence, are of adaptive value with respect to the economy of the larva's predatory behavior.

Among birds, very young domestic chicks can learn to find a prey object that has disappeared within a standardized test situation. Search behavior in the chick is, however, not generalized to other situations, and it does not vary with the animal's age and general preliminary experience (Etienne, 1973b, 1974). Thus, chicks of various ages develop stereotyped search strategies that are restricted to a given spatial and temporal context; these strategies are not generalized to new situations and remain, therefore, quite limited.

Search behavior that is immediately adapted to various new situations is found in certain birds as well as in various mammalian orders. Search of this type suggests an elaboration of principles of invariance that integrates objects or events into systems with general laws and properties. Species that show an organization of their environment according to these principles share a prolonged ontogeny during which the fundamental programming of behavior undergoes repeated changes (Etienne, 1973a). Ontogenetic development of this nature always follows the same basic steps, independently of the species's taxonomic status, but it may reach different levels of final differentiation in different species (Etienne, 1976–1977).

STUDIES OF SENSORIMOTOR DEVELOPMENT

Piaget's work on the first years of life is contained in his now-famous writings that date from the 1930s. They are as much concerned with the theory as with the facts that support it. It was in the 1960s that, in laboratories throughout the world, the production of experimental and theoretical articles on the young infant began to grow. This increase was facilitated by new methodologies and data-acquisition techniques that resulted from technical progress. The Genevan School is not unaware of this trend, and research in this area has been oriented in a fairly specific manner by the extant epistemological and psychological framework.

Inhelder, Lezine, Sinclair, and Stambak (1972) put forward sensorimotor behaviors as the means to attain a knowledge about actions and objects prefiguring later semiotic productions. The approach adopted by Mounoud for the study of sensorimotor intelligence in the infant originates from research on the practical intelligence of 4- to 8-year-old children (the construction of simple instruments). In his first studies, Mounoud (1968, 1970/1976) showed how the conception that the child finally develops of an instrument or tool is elaborated from the knowledge the child has of the characteristics of his or her own prehension (tracking, reaching, grasping, hooking, etc.). This led Mounoud to study the prehension of objects during the sensorimotor period, which, in turn, led him to change certain Piagetian theses radically and to reject others. In particular, Mounoud thought that it must be possible to show practical conservations at the sensorimotor stage corresponding to those studied by Piaget and Szeminska (1941) at the concrete-operatory stage. In situations requiring babies to grasp and to lift objects, Mounoud sought to indicate the ways that infants' actions take into account the physical properties of the object. The results showed that the knowledge elaborated by infants of 16 to 18 months leads them to grasp the same object with equal force regardless of variations in its form (this has been called conservation of weight in the infant). Similarly, the infants showed an ability to seriate forces that they developed for grasping objects of increasing size and weight (seriation of weight) (Mounoud, 1973, 1974; Mounoud & Bower, 1974).

The theoretical premises of these first studies were formulated in a paper that made explicit several differences of opinion with Piaget's position, specifically, on the problem of the initial state of intersensorimotor coordination of the baby's behavior and on the problem of the existence of representational systems as early as the sensorimotor period (Mounoud, 1971). These first studies gave rise to a general model of development conceived in terms of revolution (Mounoud, 1976). So-called early conservations or invariants raise the problem of the relationships between identity and conservation in Piaget's psychological theory. The internal contradictions in Piagetian theory brought to light by these

studies will help us to specify the originality of Mounoud's approach. When early conservations were demonstrated in the 2- to 3-year-old child (by Bruner, Bower, Mehler, Bryant, etc.), Piaget vigorously refused to accept them as operatory conservations (Piaget, Sinclair, Vinh Bang, 1968). Piaget defined them as the first form of the qualitative identities of the object and contrasted them with operatory conservation. According to Piaget, the origin of identities lies in a process of dissociation of the properties of objects (so-called constitutive properties versus nonconstitutive properties). These identities or identifications are not at the origin of conservations, even if they constitute a preliminary condition. Conservations are the result of quantitative compositions of transformations. It is this point of view that led Piaget to redefine object permanence as a first, global form of the qualitative identity of the object. The object is not elaborated in respect of its transformations but uniquely in terms of its positions and movement. It is a question of the existence or the assimilation of a simple object and not the conservation of a quantifiable quality of the object or the conservation of a collection of objects.

According to Mounoud (1974), however, objects are elaborated at the sensorimotor stage as much in terms of the relationships between objects as of the relationships between the parts of the object. For this reason, it seemed to Mounoud erroneous to consider the permanent object as a preliminary form of individual identity. Mounoud has shown that during the first 18 months the infant elaborates conservations in the strict sense (i.e., resulting from a composition of transformations) by means of her actions. These conservations are elaborated by means of a perceptual coding of reality, which Mounoud clearly distinguishes from later conceptual codings upon which the conservations of the concrete-operatory stage depend. It is on the basis of the construction of perceptual cues, which Mounoud currently prefers to speak of as perceptual representations, that the infant becomes capable of performing the inferences leading her to conservations. Developing this point of view, Mounoud and Hauert (Hauert, 1980; Mounoud & Hauert, 1975, 1976; Mounoud, Mayer, & Hauert, 1979) believed that the knowledge elaborated by the child, at the sensorimotor stage as well as at later stages, has as a principal goal the organization and the control of actions. For these authors, the physical characteristics of actions (displacement, speed, acceleration) are sources of information about their degree of programming or of control. These depend on the subject's knowledge of *object properties* and of *the characteristics of the child's actions*. This is a new methodological orientation to the study of the development of knowledge. It is in this regard that the study of the characteristics of action, not only in the infant, but equally in the child and the adult, have been analyzed. A presentation that pulls together this research and makes clearer its ties with cognitive development can be found in two recent papers (Mounoud & Hauert, 1982a, 1982b).

A more extreme criticism of Piagetian theory has developed in the past few years (Mounoud, 1977, 1979; Mounoud & Vinter, 1981). The child does not construct structures in the Piagetian sense of the word, rather he constructs representations in the sense of internal models or internal memories. From this point of view, the structures as information processing capacity are thought to be preformed as are coding abilities. However, the representations constructed by the child by means of his different coding systems depend directly on the situations the subject has happened to experience. It is, thus, that Mounoud (1973) was led to reinterpret the invariants or conservations demonstrated by Piaget (1962). Mounoud no longer considers them as the sign of the achievement of new (formal) structures of thought (operatory instruments) but as the result of the structuring or organization (by means of preformed logical capacities) of certain object dimensions translated through various coding systems. In conclusion, it is possible to say that although wishing to arrive at structures (the formal instruments of our thought and actions), Piaget did study the elaborations of certain contents—but the least specific contents possible or those common to a very large number of objects. He studied how certain object dimensions isolated by the experimenter are mastered by the child without taking into account the pathway or the steps necessary for their isolation, extraction, or identification. In the same way (again according to Mounoud, 1979), Piaget did not study the genesis of the general instruments used for figuration or encoding. Instead, he studied the genesis of the representations of various contents or dimensions of objects by means of coding capacities which could be considered to be preformed.

These criticisms may be colored by recent developments in Piagetian theory, but they appear, nonetheless, justified with respect to classical aspects of that theory. Studies by Maratos (1973) on imitative behavior during the first 6 months of life are the source for follow-up research undertaken by Meltzoff and Moore (1977) among others. In the same age range, Widmer-Robert-Tissot's (1980) research on discrimination among people in the infant rests on the same theoretical base as does the work of Piaget and Mounoud.

Bullinger's (1981) work using currently available techniques to analyze the infant's oculomotor and postural activities aims to specify the stages leading to the coordination between vision and prehension described by Piaget (1952). For Piaget (and this point of view is often forgotten), it is activity itself that is the object of the assimilation and accommodation of schemes in the levels preceding the coordination of vision and prehension. This activity constitutes the "aliments for action schemes." At this level, there is no polarization of self-contained subject and object; it is the coordination of these schemes that allows the constitution of a subject and an object. Nevertheless, Piaget, describing the stages of development prior to object permanence, speaks in terms of the coordination of schemes (subject pole); after this conquest, he speaks of the permanence of properties attributed to object (object pole).

For Bullinger (1981) cognitive elaborations are always and simultaneously applied to the organism, objects, and space. Through its functionings in interaction with other objects in the milieu, the organism is an object to be known. Here Bullinger makes a clear distinction between functioning, which refers to the organism (and alone is observable), and activity, which refers to the unobservable cognitive processes. The behavioral cues measured are always related to functionings. Thus, cognitive structures are always accessed indirectly. To use these indices to infer the activity of a subject, it is necessary to observe an evolution or modification of functioning over time. Such changes would be ascribable to a change in the cognitive direction of behavior. If this procedure is not used, there is always the risk that one will observe a functioning that is stable and that primarily reflects biological adaptations rather than cognitive structures.

The position adopted leads to a consideration of sensorimotor development as bearing upon a functioning determined by the organism's biological properties, on the one hand, and upon the physical and social properties of the environment, on the other hand. To illustrate this point of view, let us briefly analyze so-called early-reaching behaviors. We know that in his interaction with the environment, the newborn is characterized by a global engagement in a task. These behaviors are often described as preprogrammed or precoordinated. It is possible to analyze early reaching in terms of this global involvement (more than just the arm may be seen to move). Precoordination, thus, derives from the total participation of the organism in the action without the elements being coordinated in their own right. The preprogrammed and rigid aspects of behavior rest upon biological determinants that are not specific to the body segments concerned. With repetition, this biologically determinated functioning leads a dynamic configuration of physiological signals to be reproduced in forms that are similar to one another. Cognitive activity acts upon these signals and extracts from them invariants that may be used to control behavior in a new way. One could speak of a progressive making sense of these repeated signals or of a coordination, in psychological terms this time, that create a subject, an object, and a space for the properties that have been coordinated (Bullinger, in press). From this level onward, one may speak of representations that relate essentially to the body parts involved in the action. The hand takes on the status of a tool in an activity that is now organized to carry out the task and is recognized as such.

Using visual indices, this point of view has been applied in the analysis of the newborn's activities for the pursuit of a mobile object (Bullinger, 1977, 1979; Kaufmann & Bullinger, 1980). Results show a progressive releasing from biologically determined structures (involving the entire organism) and the correlated instrumentation of the head, which becomes a tool taking into account the properties of space and of the object. At a later stage, this elaboration enables the coordination of vision and prehension and allows objects to be seized.

The analysis of oculomotor functioning (Mayer, Bullinger, & Kaufmann, 1979) in spatial tasks, such as the test for conservation of length described by Piaget (1948), has allowed the relevance of these indices to be specified for cognitive-spatial tasks involving school-aged children. The results demonstrate the remarkable stability of oculomotor functioning, evidence of a relatively advanced state of automatization. Given that any automatized activity primarily demonstrates the interaction of the sensorimotor system with objects in the milieu, such activity is often of little relevance if we are trying to grasp the potentially underlying cognitive activity (Pailhous & Bullinger, 1978). For example, in a spatial field where discrete objects are placed 10° apart, the distribution of saccade amplitudes is quite likely to show an anomaly at 10° compared to a distribution of amplitudes if the objects are placed randomly. This anomaly shows up the properties of the interaction between the visual system and the stimulus and says very little about any underlying cognitive activity. If, however, we observe a distortion with respect to the stabilized functioning, we may hypothesize that this is indicative of a cognitive activity. An example of such a distortion may be seen when the child is in a transitional phase of beginning elaboration of the conservation of length.

It is also possible to disrupt automatized functioning by introducing a device between a subject's sensory system and the spatial field to be explored. Pailhous and Bullinger (1978) and Bullinger and Pailhous (1980) asked children and adults to explore a model village by means of a television camera equipped with a narrow angle of view. To establish spatial relations between objects in the model, it was necessary to coordinate the spatial effects of displacements of the camera with the displacements themselves. Such coordinations were only seen in older children and adults, who could be said to have explored the field. For these subjects, unlike the younger children who were preoccupied with the camera and its movements, exploration was possible because the interposed device had become transparent (i.e., it was used to see with). It had become instrumented in the same way, for example, as a hammer used to drive in a nail.

On a theoretical level, these results converge with those obtained in the infant, who in some ways has to make her sensory systems her own. Mechanisms for cognitive elaborations are similar, whether they are applied to the infant's phylogenetically determined sensory systems or to protheses offered to children or adults. In each case, the minimal criteria for a subject to be able to make a sensory system her own, be it biologically determined or an artificial device, are the following:

1. These sensory systems must engender regularities in interactions created with the milieu, that is, the same movement must produce similar sensations. These sensations provide a basis for processes for extracting invariances.

2. The subject must have access to algorithms generating these regularities (access to the algorithms emphasizes the fact that movements must be produced by the subject herself).

New research within this perspective is being planned to look at sensorimotor protheses for the handicapped infant.

APPLIED STUDIES

The results obtained from the study of development led very quickly to research aimed at defining practical tools (Inhelder, 1943). The volume of these studies increased because it was thought that by providing a theoretical framework, they might revive certain aspects of differential approaches. There are three different strands in this line of research. They differ from one another in their goals, methodologies, and the aspects of the theory they draw upon.

The first includes research aimed at evaluation, that is, at diagnosing the level of operational reasoning. This research draws principally from the notion of stages of intellectual development and its properties. Some studies also take into account the current work on the functioning of thought.

The second strand includes research aimed at educational psychology. These studies make use of what is known about the evolution of intellectual possibilities in children as well as other aspects of the theory, for example, the status and the role of action in the formation of instruments of knowledge.

The goal of the third set of studies is to study the activity of individuals (usually adults) in work situations or in physical activities and sports.

The diagnostic studies are an active line of research. Started by Inhelder's (1943) study of reasoning in the mentally retarded and pursued in connection with neuropsychiatric teams, this research has made it possible to specify the cognitive disturbances that accompany certain mental illnesses. The problem was posed in terms of operatory deficit relative to the epistemic subject, which was considered to be the model of normal development. Moreover, this idea underlies the training in operatory diagnosis, which is an integral part of Genevan instruction in clinical psychology.

The same kinds of procedures have been developed elsewhere. One can cite the work of Dodwell (1963), Elliot, Murray, and Pearson (1977), Furth (1970), Goldschmid and Bentler (1968), Hatwell (1966), Longeot (1967, 1969, 1974, 1978), Lowell, Healy, and Rowland (1962), and Oléron (1957). We will examine the work done in France by Longeot because it is among the most systematic.

Longeot's goal is clear. He would like to define the conditions of a differential developmental psychology and to derive from it instruments for evaluating the operatory level. These instruments are for the use of practitioners interested in scholastic and professional guidance. To this end, he makes use principally of the concept of stages and their properties. Based on Nassefat's (1963) results from quantitative studies, Longeot proposed two types of evaluation instruments for developmental levels, ranging from concrete to formal. The first is an individually administered scale of logical thought. The second is a series of paper-and-pencil tests for group administration, that is, tests for formal operations. Both tests are meant to be interpreted in terms of the developmental stage attained by the individual test-

ed. A series of methodological precautions were taken during the construction of these tasks. In addition, strict controls for content validity were carried out from a number of viewpoints.

By considering operatory schemes as possible sources of variation in subject performance, Longeot has established that the tests make it possible to evaluate the level of construction of characteristic schemes of the period of formal operations. Factorial analyses show that certain subtests are strongly saturated by one factor called the combinatory, others by a factor called the INRC (INRC refers to the mathematical group of transformations— where I = identical transformation, N = inverse transformation, R = reciprocal transformation, and C = correlative transformation—observable in the child who has reached the stage of formal operations). A third set of subtests involves the interaction of these two sources of variation. By using hierarchical analysis, Longeot (1969) set out to test whether there was a hierarchy in the difficulty of the situations presented and whether this hierarchy conformed to the system of developmental stages. This kind of control is essential due to the proposed method of interpreting the results.

The use of hierarchical analysis is a delicate enterprise and calls for a few comments. It is not, in fact, sufficient to extract a hierarchy of difficulty in the situations used to conclude that these situations call upon different modes of reasoning. Hierarchical analysis can judge whether the tests presented to subjects differ in difficulty, but it gives absolutely no information about the nature of this difference nor about its origin. The choice of situations comprising the tests is critical—only situations whose solution requires a certain mode of reasoning should be used. For example, one might set out to research situations that might be mastered by the use of instruments characteristic either of concrete thinking (the logic of classes or relations) or of formal thinking (combinatory, propositional logic and INRC group structure). If this condition is fulfilled, any hierarchy extracted from the results may be attributed to a hierarchy of modes of reasoning because situations whose solution requires concrete thought are always resolved before those requiring formal thought. Then, the order of difficulties encountered by subjects in the solution of the tasks given them reflects the order of developmental stages. The origin of the difficulties is that responsible for vertical décalages (Piaget, 1941, 1955). Under these conditions, hierarchical analysis makes it possible to verify the tests in two ways. The results make it possible, first of all, to verify that the situations in which the solution reveals a different mode of reasoning do, in fact, represent different degrees of difficulty (they form a hierarchy that is stable). Second, the results must show that situations requiring the same mode of reasoning for their solution are of the same degree of difficulty (they do not form a hierarchy).

In broad terms, the analysis carried out confirms these hypotheses. There is, it appears, a hierarchy related to different modes of reasoning (i.e., to the stages). Nevertheless, the results also show that situations that require the use of a given mode of reasoning are of different degrees of difficulty. This latter point shows how hard it is, in the construction of tests of this kind, to eliminate variations in difficulty owing to variations in content.

These investigations have confirmed the existence of an intermediary level between the concrete and the formal first noted by Nassefat (1963). If the existence of this intermediate level (or intermediate stage, or even preformal stage) can be demonstrated statistically, its status in the general model of development is ambiguous. This particular level is often defined by saying that subjects are able to apply concrete operations to formal contents or formal operations to certain concrete contents. (Nassefat had noted that the same items could give rise to both kinds of solution.)

Some new attempts at verification are currently being carried out by Lautrey (1979, 1980b). The results show that (1) hierarchical analyses are most sensitive to the experimental populations, (2) the contents play an important role owing to their different degrees of difficulty, and (3) the results confirm those of several studies showing great intraindividual variability in operatory level when the individual is given a set of different situations. Concerning the greater or lesser role played by the content in solving the problems posed, Lautrey wonders if the attempts to apply the developmental model to the description of psychological subjects has not been too hasty. Focusing essentially on the steps in the development of reasoning, the model furnished by the epistemic subject leaves little room to study the contents and their role.

Current Genevan studies in this domain are taking greater account of the functioning of thought (Schmid-Kitsikis, 1976). Interests are moving away from analysis in terms of the level of development toward those taking into account deficient mental functioning (Schmid-Kitsikis, 1979).

We will not here attempt to review the whole field of educational psychological research as the number of studies is extremely large. They make use of various aspects of the operatory theory. Some of these studies concentrate on our knowledge of the successive steps in cognitive development with the aim of revising teaching programs to make them compatible with pupils' cognitive capacities. Pierrehumbert's research (1980) makes much more use of the central role played by the subject's activity in the formation of knowledge. Within this general set of educational psychological research, it is possible to separate two main categories:

1. Those who aim to understand and, thus, improve what happens in teaching situations; here, authors often use the term didactics, usually in a specific sense, for example, mathematical didactics.

2. Those who aim to understand and, thus, improve certain practices developed by educational and career guidance professionals. These practices come within the framework of educational psychological research because they set out to unify the necessary conditions for the elaboration of knowledge.

We will first look at the didactic research, in particular that dealing with mathematical didactics. To work within didactics, one has to identify and judge the role of variables involved in the acquisition of a series of concepts. Here we are concerned with the cognitive aspects of the acquisition of well-defined concepts. We will be looking at the form of constructive interaction between an individual or individuals and these concepts as well as at the task or subject variables helping or hindering elaboration in the form of knowledge.

We will briefly analyze the difficulties manifested by children in the solution of problems dealing with proportions. The choice of this problem is interesting for two reasons. First, the notion of proportion has been the subject of research by Piaget and his collaborators, and their results led them to consider "the scheme of proportionality" as one of the important acquisitions of formal thinking (Inhelder & Piaget, 1955; Piaget, Orsini, Meylan-Backs, & Sinclair, 1968). Second, proportion is a subject taught at school, beginning at age 9 to 10 and continuing for 3 to 4 years, and it is likely that this will provide children with numerous opportunities favoring the construction of this scheme. In fact, the results are clear: at least between the age of 13 and 14 years, large numbers of children fail when they are given problems dealing with proportions to solve.

Several research groups have looked into this

problem and results show that many variables are at work. In an experiment on the teaching of mechanics to 13-year-olds, Halbwachs and Lakermance (1978) have shown that some of the children's failures are related to an incomplete understanding of the notion of proportion and not, as one would think, of notions in mechanics. The apparatus used in the experiment consisted of a length of cord passed over a pulley with variable weights attached to the two ends. The aim of the experiment was to study the influence of differences in suspended weights on the acceleration of motion. The children had to compare different situations in which an equal difference in weight between the two sides of the pulley pull different masses. The results obtained show that if 13-year-olds are able to understand a situation with a simple variation in one magnitude (double, triple), the great majority, nevertheless, fail when the variations in magnitude are in terms of fractions.

In another project that concerns proportions, Vergnaud, Marthe, Ricco, Metregiste, and Boucher (1978) are developing an analysis of the procedures used by students to deal with certain classes of problems characterized by their relational structure. The authors make a distinction between classes of relational problems, those based on "the isomorphism of measure" and those where there is a "product of measurement." The first kinds of situation are more easily solved by 11-year-olds. The type of relational structure of the problem is another variable that affects difficulty of problem solution in school children.

Vinh Bang and Lavallée (1978) use problems that involve fractions to look at the roles played by quantification and the use of number in 9- to 10-year-olds. The situations are such that two magnitudes directly covary. There is a functional relationship between two variables. In some situations the variables, such as surfaces and lengths, are continuous; in others, such as numeric quantities, they are discrete. The results obtained show that the fact of working with continuous or discontinuous variables does not alter the degree of problem difficulty. When numbers may be used, the results show that the children no longer reflect on the actual situation but only on the numbers available. They often regard the problem as a simple numerical progression. The possibility of using numbers seems to cause the meaning of the situation (i.e., proportionality) to disappear. The child no longer sees the necessity of using a system of multiplication. One could speak of a number-screen effect, which may go so far as to make the problem disappear.

According to another set of studies (Chatillon, Fialon, & Massabo, 1978), the way the situation is presented seems to be a variable in the difficulty of finding a solution. There were three strictly isomorphic groups of situations. Subjects were 12 years of age and had received 3 years of teaching about proportions. The results show that situations expressed using actual apparatus (a) are more easily solved than if the problem is presented as a table of numbers (b) or as a series of propositional statements (c). The effects of transfer were used as a means of studying the relationships between the different situations (their cognitive kinship). The results show that whereas positive transfer effects may be seen between (a) and (c), there is no transfer between (b) and (c). It is interesting to consider these findings with respect to the status of number tables in teaching proportions—they do not seem to be the instruments for solving this kind of problem and may even have a screen effect of the kind described by Vinh Bang and Lavallée (1978) for number, in as much as they present an obstacle to arriving at a solution. This research shows how difficult it is to make applications within the domain of educational psychology and also shows the complexity of the effort to improve teaching theory.

A certain number of problems raised by work in the areas of professional and educational guidance and advice may be included with applications in educational psychology. Advice is provided to extend schoolchildrens' knowledge about future life situations or jobs. Within this advisory area, a number of studies have been carried out (Chatillon & Paterne, 1975; Chatillon, Rayssac, & Taillard, 1976; Huteau, 1975, 1979; Huteau & Lautrey, 1978). Moreover, they are laying the foundations for a study of the cognitive aspects of individuals' choice of profession and are beginning to define a teaching methodology for professional advice.

A great deal of research in industrial psychology is employing the Piagetian approach concerning either structures or procedures. These conceptual developments are being used to study the tasks individuals have to carry out in real-life work situations as well as the activity carried out. The research of Leplat and Bisseret (1965) on the activity of aerial navigators, Pailhous (1971) on taxi drivers' itineraries, or Savoyant (1971) on the activity of human operators in the chemical industry are all good examples.

This research trend has emphasized the importance of analysis of the task in terms of the necessary conditions to carry it out. The use of Piagetian operatory theory makes it possible to define and identify the necessary cognitive conditions for task execution. The taking into account of the structural characteristics of the situation is critical for the analysis of the individual's activity. The study of operators' behavior at a work station (especially its cognitive dimension) may have a number of goals; these studies in industrial psychology have provoked a number of theoretical questions that extend well beyond the field of the analysis of work. Being confronted with the problems of studying behavior in work situations, researchers have been led to ask questions about the mechanism involved in the genesis (in the broad sense of the word) of behaviors. This study of behavior through the steps of its formation may be transferred to the child at school and could change certain aspects of educational psychological research.

THEORETICAL AND METHODOLOGICAL PROBLEMS RAISED BY CURRENT RESEARCH

Research on learning the structures of knowledge (Inhelder, Sinclair, & Bovet, 1974) has led the way for research on problem solving. The study of the mechanisms underlying the transition from one stage to another has attracted attention to the role played by strategies in the generalization of newly acquired forms of reasoning. The increasing importance accorded to this study of strategies has raised new theoretical and methodological problems. An approach dealing with procedures requires a specially adapted theoretical framework. Concepts such as "problem," "goal," and "task" have to be defined and spelled out. So far the only changes have been rearrangements of the classical theory, for example, concerning the concept of scheme (Piaget, 1976). In this section, we would like, first of all, to analyze some of the theoretical aspects of this problem and later to discuss some of the methodological issues.

When subjects have a *problem* to solve they are in a *situation* that may be described as *problematic*. If we qualify a situation as being problematic, we are dealing with an analysis of the relationships between the state of the subject and the state of the environment. We may speak of a problematic situation for a given subject at a given time if the state of the environment does not correspond to the state of his needs or expectations. Thus, the term "problem" indicates that there is discordance *for the subject* between his state and that of the environment (Vergnaud, 1968). In natural situations subjects are very often confronted with problematic situations, for example, a child or adult who is trying to achieve a goal out of his reach has a problem to be solved. Usually

in experimental situations, the discordance is defined by the experimenter, that is, externally. The subject's behavior has to satisfy a certain number of conditions. These include the conditions of the job or experiment, the objectives of the results to be attained and the conditions for execution (instructions, instruments, or tools the subject can use). The set of these conditions to be satisfied by the behavior constitutes the subject's *task*. The notion of task is distinguishable from that of problem on the following points:

1. A task exists outside of, and independently of, the subject. A problem is always a discordance for a given subject between the state in which he finds himself and the state of the environment. The autonomy of the task in relation to the subject makes it possible for it to be analyzed independently of any subject. The analysis of the task may make it easier to analyze the subject's behavior, as Leplat and Pailhous (1977) have shown.
2. Not every task poses a problem for the subject. A task becomes a problem only if the subject takes account of the discordance defined by the experimenter. A great many experiments show that very young subjects do not behave like this; they act for the sake of acting and not to attain a goal set by the task. In certain work situations where the tasks are repetitive, the problematic aspect has disappeared.
3. The notion of task carries with it the idea that there are conditions that the subject's behavior must satisfy. This is the normative aspect of the task and is not necessarily present in the problem.

In summary, whereas a given task may pose a problem for a given subject, not every task necessarily poses a problem for every subject. Conversely, some, but not all, problematic situations may be tasks. In natural situations, it is not always possible to talk about tasks because the subject often has the choice of means solution.

Situations used in the study of procedures are characterized by the existence of a *goal*. This goal has to be attained by the subject, who first of all has to subordinate her means (the activity she develops) to this end. We agree with Inhelder (1978) who considers that it is not the goal as such that acts in a causal manner on the means but the current representation of the goal joined with the awareness of the needs to be satisfied.

If, like Vergnaud (1968), we consider that to reach a goal is to exit from a problematic situation—

to eliminate the discordance between the current state of the subject and that of the environment—it is clear that we are speaking of the subject's goal (the goal of her activity). Thus, it is important to distinguish the goal set by the experimenter and that which the subject sets herself. That the goals of experimenter and subject may not coincide is attested to by observations of young childrens' behavior. For young children, action is a means of obtaining a result that (in the majority of cases) has nothing to do with that for which the experimenter is looking. The subject aims for her own goals. We can more easily analyze the subject's representation of the goal when this goal coincides with that assigned by the experimenter. In this case, the subject's representation of the goal may guide the formation and coordination of the means to reach it. There are two ways in which this guidance by the goal may operate:

1. The assigned goal may be used by the individual as a reference, making it possible for the subject to judge the success or failure of her activity and sometimes the gap separating the obtained result from that to be attained. Proceeding in this way, the individual may reach the goal, but the goal functions only to help her estimate the gap (in this case, we could say error) separating the current result from the final result. The organization of the action depends upon the use of the results it produces for a comparison with those to be obtained. In fact, the activity of the subject leads her to optimize her action systems when faced with an explicit goal. In the block-balancing experiment (Karmiloff-Smith & Inhelder, 1975), the behavior of certain young children provides examples of the use of the goal as reference (see *Knowledge Structures and Problem Solving*).

2. The goal assigned to the subject's activity also constitutes the product of a determined sequence of transformations applied to the initial state. The subject's knowledge (or representation) of the goal as being the product of a set of transformations makes it possible for her to choose and mentally to assemble the means (i.e., the transformations) that will enable her to reach this goal. When a subject plans her action, she coordinates the means and ends. She *mentally* organizes the solution and this allows her to eliminate the discordance between her current state and that of the environment. This possibility radically transforms the kind of subordination of the subject's activity to reaching the goal because the subject is able to make use of the properties of the solution. The error is not simply a gap

separating the result obtained and result to be achieved, it also reveals an inadequacy in the representation of the imagined means with respect to those required by the situation (Leplat, 1976). The subject can detect the faults in her imagined solution and can mentally proceed to the necessary modifications.

The experimental work of Boder (1978) shows that there is a progressive elaboration of the goal in such a way that the means are coordinated with the ends within the framework of the process of problem solving. This elaboration is essentially a coordination of the different functions of the goal. Ackermann-Valladao (1980) has shown that young children first of all explore productive relations, whereas precursive behavior comes later. These results could also be interpreted as a change in function of the goal.

On a methodological level, these studies raise the problem of the indices one chooses to use to infer the cognitive activity underlying the observed behavior. The meaning of these indices may vary with time (during the process and during development). The choice of indices and their link with the activity should be discussed. The analysis of strategies is based upon the use of indices recorded during the execution phase. This raises two questions.

The first concerns the relationship between the observable aspects of behavior and cognitive activity. Inhelder et al. (1976) consider that the relationship between the observed actions (execution) and the subject's cognitive activity (planning) is a direct one as long as the situations have been suitably chosen. If this condition is fulfilled, observation of the subject's actions makes it possible to have direct access to the unfolding of his thought. Other authors (e.g., Leplat, 1976) take a very wise position on this point. For Leplat, the mechanisms of the subject's activity cannot be deduced simply from observable actions. Chatillon, Combes, and Faynet (1981) have shown that the nature of the link between the observable part of the behavior and the cognitive activity varies with subject characteristics, the conditions his behavior has to satisfy, and the status of the action. The organization of the action enabling the goal to be reached may reflect a cognitive activity of the subject if the latter is in the process of developing a new action. On the other hand, if the action has been regularly repeated and is automatized, its organization no longer reflects a current cognitive activity of the subject. The action maintains the trace of a preceding cognitive activity that has been sedimented. In this case, one could join Rey (1935) by saying that active intelligence has been removed from the subject's behavior. A number of studies have shown that automatized behaviors are efficient and involve a very light mental load.

The second question asks which behavioral indices should be used to infer the subject's cognitive activity under the best conditions. There is great variety in the practices of researchers on this point. Saada-Robert (1980) uses the modifications in the course of the activity of execution to analyze subjects' cognitive activity. Blanchet (1977) suggests the use of convergent configurations of indices. Some of these indices are outside of the solution procedure in the subject's accompanying behaviors, such as facial expression, eye movements, and so on. Often the indices collected from the observable part of the behavior can be supplemented by others whose link with the subject's representational activity is well known. For example, drawings made before the action is executed makes it possible to see how the subject imagines the solution to the problem.

Chatillon and his colleagues (Chatillon, 1980; Chatillon et al., 1981) analyze the temporal structure of the subject's behavior to see if he plans his action or if he uses a skill available in his repertoire. If the subject deals with situations at a representational level, this will require time during which he will not act on the situation. On the other hand, if the subject employs an available skill, he will act on the situation without delay, even if this skill is not directly applicable and has to be accommodated. Studies of latencies and their durations and suspension of actions (their number and duration) make it possible to distinguish different kinds of behavior. In a spatial task, it has been shown that either the subject passes through a preliminary phase of mental assimilation or he becomes directly involved in a practical assimilation of the situation. Chatillon (1980) try to gain access to the subject's mechanisms for elaborating his strategy by requiring him to externalize his plan of action. In a spatial task, the subject has verbally to guide the experimenter to place constituent elements in a spatial configuration. The results clearly show up the distortions affecting the representation of the third dimension.

Examination of the research emphasizes the methodological difficulties encountered by researchers when they have to choose indices from which to infer subjects' cognitive activity. For example, in the case of very young subjects, developmental research draws behavioral indices from the organism's functionings and interprets them in terms of the relation of the infant with its milieu. This uncomfortable position has often been opted for by reducing the infant to biological dimensions alone and minimizing the role of intrinsic properties of the human milieu. This tendency leads to a biologizing view of the development of human young. In contrast, theories focused on the social or affective aspects reduce the infant to his social or affective dimensions alone and neglect the biological bases of behavior. This rift reappears in educational practice, psychology teaching, and . . . manuals. Clearly, the development of research underway assumes a whole line of theoretical and methodological progress that remains to be achieved.

CONCLUSION

A presentation of recent Genevan work is difficult because the rich theoretical foundation has allowed research to develop in diverse fields. These studies go beyond the strict Piagetian framework and increasingly bear the stamp of psychological analysis. This reequilibration of the issues, in which the psychological is no longer just a necessary means for epistemological analysis, is making itself felt in all the domains. The more clearly psychological interests of current research makes possible the fruitful confrontation of different issues through a common analysis of experimental problems. Researchers are not only basing their work on classical Genevan findings but also on Anglo-American information processing models or the model of action formation developed by one of the Soviet schools (Galpérine, 1966). The facts will eventually show in what respects these different approaches are in genuine opposition and in what respects they complement each other.

The interests of researchers of the Genevan School are in establishing new relations with trends in applied research. At the same time, the applied studies in different areas are leading to the definition of specific conceptual frameworks for the study of behavior. Developmental psychology can profit from this research in the functional studies it is currently pursuing. Such constructive interactions involve an interpenetration of so-called fundamental research and applied studies to the benefit of both. These kinds of interactions are equally present in infancy research and enlarge the field by breaking down partitions between areas. This density of all kinds of exchange (conceptual and methodological) is enriching Genevan psychology and providing it with an approach to behavior that is closer to the complexities of human reality.

REFERENCES

Ackermann-Valladao, E. Analyse des procédures de résolution d'un probleme de composition de hauteurs. *Archives de Psychologie,* 1977, *45,* 101–125.

Ackermann-Valladao, E. Etude des relations entre procédures et attribution des significations dans une tâche de construction de chemin. *Archives de Psychologie,* 1980, *48,* 59–93.

Barblan, L. [*Developmental problems concerning sentences with "easy to see."*] Paper presented at the Salzburger Jahrestagung für Linguistik. Salzburg, Aus., August 1977.

Berthoud, I., & Sinclair, H. L'expression d'éventualités et de conditions chez l'enfant. *Archives de Psychologie,* 1978, *46,* 205–233.

Berthoud-Papandropoulou, I. An experimental study of children's ideas about language. In A. Sinclair, R. J. Jarvella, & W. J. M. Levelt (Eds.), *The child's conception of language* (Vol. 2). Heidelberg, W. Ger., Springer, 1978.

Besson, M. J., & Jeanrenaud, D. L'emploi de l'imparfait et du passé simple dans la langue écrite des enfants de 7 à 12 ans. *Travaux de Pédolinguistique* (Vol. 13). Geneva: University of Geneva, 1974.

Blanchet, A. La construction et l'équilibre du mobile. Problèmes méthodologiques. *Archives de Psychologie,* 1977, *45,* 29–52.

Blanchet, A. *Etude génétique des significations et des modèles utilisés par l'enfant lors de résolutions de problèmes.* Unpublished doctoral dissertation, University of Geneva, 1980.

Blanchet, A., Ackermann-Valladao, E., Kilcher, H., & Saada-Robert, M. Une hypothèse sur les connaissances utilisées en situation de résolution de problème. *Cahiers de Psychologie,* 1978, *21,* 111–117.

Boder, A. Etude de la composition d'un ordre inverse: Hypothèse sur la coordination de deux sources de contrôle du raisonnement. *Archives de Psychologie,* 1978, *46,* 87–113.

Brami-Mouling, M. A. Notes sur l'adaptation de l'expression verbale de l'enfant en fonction de l'âge de son interlocuteur. *Archives de Psychologie,* 1977, *45,* 225–234.

Bronckart, J.-P. *Genèse et organisation des formes verbales chez l'enfant.* Brussels: Dessart & Mardaga, 1976.

Bronckart, J.-P. *Théories du langage. Une introduction critique.* Brussels: Dessart & Mardaga, 1977.

Bronckart, J.-P. L'élaboration des opérations langagières. Un exemple à propos des structures ca-

suelles. *Cahiers de l'Institut de Linguistique de Louvain,* 1979, *5,* 139–157.

Bullinger, A. Comparaison, mesure et transitivité. *Archives de Psychologie,* Monographie N°1, August 1973.

Bullinger, A. Orientation de la tête du nouveau-né en présence d'un stimulus visuel. *L'Année Psychologique,* 1977, *2,* 357–364.

Bullinger, A. La réponse cardiaque comme indice de la sensibilité du nouveau-né à un spectacle visuel. *Cahiers de Psychologie,* 1979, *22,* 195–208.

Bullinger, A. Cognitive elaboration of sensorimotor behaviour. In G. Butterworth (Ed.), *Infancy and epistemology.* Hassocks, Eng.: Harvester Press, 1981.

Bullinger, A. Space, the organism and objects: Their cognitive elaboration in the infant. In A. Hein & M. Jeannerod (Eds.). *Spatially oriented behavior.* New York: Springer-Verlag, in press.

Bullinger, A., & Pailhous, J. The influence of two sensorimotor modalities on the construction of spatial relations. *Communication and Cognition,* 1980, *13,* 25–36.

Cellerier, G. Structures cognitives et schèmes d'action I. *Archives de Psychologie,* 1979, *47,* 87–104. (a)

Cellerier, G. Structures cognitives et schèmes d'action II. *Archives de Psychologie,* 1979, *47,* 107–122. (b)

Chatillon, J.-F. Etude des aspects cognitifs nécessaires à la réalisation d'une tâche d'habileté manuelle. *Laboratoire de Psychologie de l'Apprentissage. Publications de l'Université d'Aix-Marseille II, N°5,* 1980.

Chatillon, J.-F., Antonetti, J., Hernandez, G. L'élaboration et la coordination des points de vue. Les implications psychopédagogiques. *Publications de l'Université d'Aix-Marseille II, N°11,* 1980.

Chatillon, J.-F., Baldy, R. Evaluation des apports initiaux des stagiaires entrant au Centre de Préformation de Marseille. *Publications de l'Université d'Aix-Marseille II, N°3,* 1975.

Chatillon, J.-F., Beziaud, A., Fundoni, J.-C., Grellet, P., & Thomas, A. A propos de l'intelligence pratique: Une analyse: le passalong. *Publications de l'Université d'Aix-Marseille II, N°10,* 1980.

Chatillon, J.-F., Combes, L., & Faynet, M. Problèmes d'intelligence pratique et mécanismes sous-jacents à l'élaboration des stratégies. *Publications de l'Université d'Aix-Marseille II, N°12,* 1981.

Chatillon, J.-F., Fialon, J., & Massabo, Y. Les difficultés de l'enseignement de la proportionnalité. Contribution à l'étude du problème. *Publications de l'Université d'Aix-Marseille II, N°8,* 1978.

Chatillon, J.-F., Paterne, J.-C. Le choix et la représentation de la profession. *Publications de l'Université d'Aix-Marseille II, N°2,* 1975.

Chatillon, J.-F., Rayssac, M., Taillard, C. Les représentations professionnelles. Notion de référentiel des professions: Extension et niveaux d'organisation. *Publications de l'Université d'Aix-Marseille II, N°6,* 1976.

Chipman, H. *Children's construction of the English pronominal system.* Berne: Hans Huber, 1980.

Chipman, H., & de Dardel, C. A developmental study of the comprehension and the production of the pronoun "it." *Journal of Psycholinguistic Research,* 1974, *3,* 91–99.

Chomsky, C. *The acquisition of syntax in children from 5 to 10.* Cambridge, Mass.: MIT Press, 1969.

Dasen, P. Are cognitive processes universal? A contribution to cross-cultural Piagetian psychology. In N. Warren (Ed.), *Studies in cross-cultural psychology* (Vol. 1). London: Academic Press, 1977.

Dasen, P. Différences individuelles et différences culturelles. *Bulletin de Psychologie,* 1979–1980, *33,* 675–683.

Dasen, P., & Heron, A. Cross-cultural tests of Piaget's theory. In H. C. Triandis & A. Heron (Eds.), *Handbook of cross-cultural psychology,* vol. 4, *Developmental psychology.* Boston: Allyn and Bacon 1981.

Dasen, P., Inhelder, B., Lavallée, M., & Retschitzki, J. *Naissance de l'intelligence chez l'enfant Baoulé de Côte d'Ivoire.* Berne: Hans Huber, 1978.

Dasen, P., Ngini, L., & Lavallée, M. Cross-cultural training studies of concrete operations. In L. Eckensberger, W. Lonner, & Y. Poortinga (Eds.), *Cross-cultural contributions to psychology.* Lisse, the Netherlands: Swets & Zeitlinger, 1978.

Dodwell, P. C. Children's understanding of spatial concepts. *Canadian Journal of Psychology,* 1963, *17,* 141–161.

Elliot, C. D., Murray, D., & Pearson, L. *The British ability scales.* Windsor, Eng.: National Foundation for Education Research, 1977.

Etienne, A. S. The behaviour of the dragonfly larva. *Aeschna cyanea M.* after a short presentation of a prey. *Animal Behaviour,* 1972, *20,* 724–731.

Etienne, A. S. Developmental stages and cognitive structures as determinants on what is learned. In R. A. Hinde & J. S. Hinde (Eds.), *Constraints on learning limitations and predispositions.* New York and London: Academic Press, 1973. (a)

Etienne, A. S. Searching behaviour towards a disappearing prey in the domestic chick as affected by preliminary experience. *Animal Behaviour,* 1973, *21,* 749–761. (b)

Etienne, A. S. Age variability shown by domestic chicks in selected spatial tasks. *Behaviour,* 1974, *50,* 52–76.

Etienne, A. S. Stereotyped pattern of locomotion controlled by duration of previous tracking by a predatory insect. *Nature,* 1976, *260,* 426–428.

Etienne, A. S. L'étude comparative de la permanence de l'objet chez l'animal. *Bulletin de Psychologie,* 1976–1977, *30,* 187–197.

Etienne, A. S. The control of two antagonistic locomotor activities in a predatory insect. *Behaviour,* 1977, *60,* 122–177. (a)

Etienne, A. S. A descriptive and functional analysis of a stereotyped pattern of locomotion after target tracking in a predatory insect. *Animal Behaviour,* 1977, *25,* 429–446. (b)

Etienne, A. S. Energy- versus time-dependent parameters in the determination of behavioural sequence in the *Aeschna cyanea M.* larva. *Journal of Comparative Psychology,* 1978, *127,* 89–96.

Ferreiro, E. What is written in a written sentence? A developmental answer. *Journal of Education,* 1978, *160,* 25–39.

Ferreiro, E., Othenin-Girard, C., Chipman, H., & Sinclair, H. How do children handle relative clauses? *Archives de Psychologie,* 1976, *45,* 229–266.

Ferreiro, E., & Teberosky, A. *Los sistemos de escritura en el desarrollo del nino.* Mexico City and Madrid: Siglo XXI, 1979.

Furth, H. *An inventory of Piaget's developmental tasks.* Washington, D.C.: Catholic University Center for Research in Thinking and Language, 1970.

Galpérine, P. Essai sur la formation par étapes des actions et des concepts. In *Recherches psychologiques en U.R.S.S.* Moscow: Editions du Progrès, 1966.

Goldschmid, M. L., & Bentler, P. M. *Concept assessment kit—conservation.* San Diego, Calif.: Educational and Industrial Testing Service, 1968.

Gréco, P. Induction, déduction et apprentissage. In *Etudes d'épistémologie génétiques* (Vol. 10). Paris: Presses Universitaires de France, 1956.

Greenfield, P. M. Cross-cultural research and

Piagetian theory: Paradox and progress. In K. Riegel & J. Meacham (Eds.), *The developing individual in a changing world* (Vol. 1). The Hague: Mouton, 1976.

Halbwachs, F., & Lakermance, C. *Etude sur le maniement des proportions chez les élèves de 4e*. Action Thématique Programmée: Travail de l'Elève. Paris: Publications du Centre National de la Recherche Scientifique, 1978.

Hatwell, Y. *Privation sensorielle et intelligence. Effets de la cécité précoce sur la genèse des structures logiques de l'intelligence*. Paris: Presses Universitaires de France, 1966.

Hauert, C.-A. Propriétés des objets et propriétés des actions chez l'enfant de 2 à 5 ans. *Archives de Psychologie*, 1980, *48*, 95–168.

Huteau, M. La représentation du monde professionel chez l'adolescent. *Bulletin de l'Association des Conseillers d'Orientation de France*, 1975, *252*, 4–15.

Huteau, M. L'évolution des critères de catégorisation des métiers. *L'Orientation Scolaire et Professionnelle*, 1979, *8*, 325–346.

Huteau, M., & Lautrey, J. L'utilisation des tests d'intelligence et de la psychologie cognitive dans l'éducation et l'orientation. *L'Orientation Scolaire et Professionnelle*, 1978, *7*, 99–174.

Inhelder, B. *Le diagnostic du raisonnement chez les débiles mentaux*. Neuchâtel, Switz., and Paris: Delachaux & Niestlé, 1943.

Inhelder, B. Les attitudes expérimentales de l'enfant et de l'adolescent. *Bulletin de Psychologie*, 1954, *7*, 272–282.

Inhelder, B. De l'approche structurale à l'approche procédurale, introduction à l'étude des stratégies. In *Actes du XXIe congrès international de psychologie*, Paris: Presses Universitaires de France, 1978.

Inhelder, B., Ackermann-Valladao, E., Blanchet, A., Karmiloff-Smith, A., Kilcher-Hagedorn, H., Montangero, J., & Robert, M. Des structures cognitives aux procédures de découverte. Esquisse de recherches en cours. *Archives de Psychologie*, 1976, *44*, 57–72.

Inhelder, B., Blanchet, A., Boder, A., De Caprona, D., Saada-Robert, M., & Ackermann-Valladao, E. Procédures et significations dans la résolution d'un problème concret. *Bulletin de Psychologie*, 1980, *33*, 645–648.

Inhelder, B., Lezine, I., Sinclair, H., Stambak, M. Les débuts de la fonction symbolique. *Archives de Psychologie*, 1972, *40*, 187–243.

Inhelder, B., & Piaget, J. *De la logique de l'enfant à la logique de l'adolescent. Essai sur la construc-tion des structures opératoires formelles*, Paris: Presses Universitaires de France, 1955.

Inhelder, B., & Piaget, J. Procédures et structures. *Archives de Psychologie*, 1979, *47*, 165–176.

Inhelder, B., Sinclair, H., & Bovet, M. *Apprentissage et structures de la connaissance*. Paris: Presses Universitaires de France, 1974.

Karmiloff-Smith, A., Inhelder, B. "If you want to get ahead, get a theory." *Cognition*, 1975, *3*, 195–212.

Karmiloff-Smith, A. *A functional approach to child language. A study of determiners and reference*. Cambridge: At the University Press, 1979.

Kaufmann, J.-L., & Bullinger, A. Exploration oculaire en situation de règle dépendante (quelques faits de sondage sur des aspects cognitifs dans le contrôle du système oculomoteur). *Cahiers de Psychologie*, 1980, *23*, 3–22.

Kilcher, H., & Robert, M. Procédures d'action lors de constructions de ponts et d'escaliers. *Archives de Psychologie*, 1977, *45*, 53–83.

Laurendeau-Bendavid, M. Culture, schooling and cognitive development. A comparative study of children in French Canada and Rwanda. In P. R. Dasen (Ed.), *Piagetian psychology: Cross-cultural contributions*. New York: Wiley, 1977. (Gardner Press)

Lautrey, J. Théorie opératoire et tests opératoires. *Revue de Psychologie Appliquée*, 1979, *29*, 161–177.

Lautrey, J. *Classe sociale, milieu familial, intelligence*. Paris: Presses Universitaires de France, 1980. (a)

Lautrey, J. *La variabilité intra-individuelle du niveau de développement opératoire et ses implications théoriques*. Manuscript submitted for publication, 1980. (b)

Leiser, D., Cellerier, G., Ducret, J.-J. Une étude de la fonction représentative. *Archives de Psychologie*, 1976, *44*, 83–96.

Leplat, J. Analyse du travail et genèse des conduites. Quelques perspectives théoriques en psychologie appliquée. *International Review of Applied Psychology*, 1976, *25*, 3–14.

Leplat, J., & Bisseret, A. Analyse des processus de traitement de l'information chez le contrôleur de la navigation aérienne. *Bulletin du Centre d'Etude et de Recherches Psychotechniques*, 1965, *14*, 51–67.

Leplat, J., & Pailhous, J. La description de la tâche: Statut et rôle dans la résolution de problèmes. *Bulletin de Psychologie*, 1977, *31*, 149–156.

Longeot, F. Aspects différentiels de la psychologie génétique. *Bulletin de l'Institut National d'Ori-*

entation Professionelle, 1967. (Numéro spécial)

Longeot, F. *Psychologie différentielle et théorie opératoire de l'intelligence*. Paris: Dunod, 1969.

Longeot, F. *L'échelle de développement de la pensée logique. Manuel d'instructions*. Issy-les-Moulineaux, France: Editions Scientifiques et Psychologiques, 1974.

Longeot, F. *Les stades opératoires de Piaget et les facteurs de l'intelligence*. Grenoble, France: Presse Universitaires de Grenoble, 1978.

Lowell, K., Healy, D., Rowland, A. D. Growth of some geometrical concepts. *Child Development*, 1962, *33*, 751–767.

Maratos, O. *The origin and development of imitation in the first six months of life*. Unpublished doctoral dissertation, University of Geneva, 1973.

Mayer, E., Bullinger, A., Kaufmann, J.-L. Motricité oculaire et cognition dans une tâche spatiale. *Archives de Psychologie*, 1979, *47*, 309–320.

Meltzoff, A. N., & Moore, M. K. Imitation of facial and manual gestures by human neonates. *Science*, 1977, *198*, 75–78.

Miller, G. A., Galanter, E., & Pribram, K. H. *Plans and the structure of behavior*. New York: Holt, Rinehart & Winston, 1960.

Montangero, J. Expérimentation, réussite et compréhension chez l'enfant, dans trois tâches d'élévation d'un niveau par immersion d'objets. *Archives de Psychologie*, 1977, *45*, 174.

Mounoud, P. Construction et utilisation d'instruments chez l'enfant de 4 à 8 ans. *Revue Suisse de Psychologie*, 1968, *27*, 200–208.

Mounoud, P. *Structuration de l'instrument chez l'enfant. Intériorisation et régulation de l'action*. Neuchâtel, Switz., and Paris: Delachaux & Niestlé, 1970. (Translated in *Piaget's Reader*. New York: Springer-Verlag, 1976.)

Mounoud, P. Développement des systèmes de représentation et de traitement chez l'enfant. *Bulletin de Psychologie*, 1971, *25*, 5–7, 261–272.

Mounoud, P. Les conservations physique chez le bébé. *Bulletin de Psychologie*, 1973, *312*, 13–14, 722–728.

Mounoud, P. La construction de l'objet par le bébé. *Bulletin d'Audiophonologie*, 1974, *4*(6 suppl.), 419–438.

Mounoud, P. Les révolutions psychologiques de l'enfant. *Archives de Psychologie*, 1976, *44*, 103–114.

Mounoud, P. Relations entre les régulations biologiques et les processus cognitifs. Développement sensorimoteur et développement conceptuel.

Vers l'Education Nouvelle, 1977, 173–180. (Special issue)

Mounoud, P. Développement cognitif: Construction de structures nouvelles ou construction d'organisations internes, *Bulletin de Psychologie*, 1979, *33*, 107–118.

Mounoud, P., Bower, T. G. R. Conservation of weight in infants. *Cognition*, 1974, *3*, 29–40.

Mounoud, P., & Hauert, C.-A. L'organisation de la préhension par rapport aux différentes propriétés des objets. *Revue Suisse de Psychologie*, 1975, *34*, 264–265.

Mounoud, P., & Hauert, C.-A. Préparation et contrôle des actions de soulèvement d'objets. *Cahiers de Psychologie*, 1976, *19*, 226.

Mounoud, P., & Hauert, C.-A. The development of sensori-motor organization in the child: Grasping and lifting objects. In G. Forman (Ed.), *Action and thought: From sensorimotor schemes to symbolic operations*. New York: Academic Press, 1982. (a)

Mounoud, P., & Hauert, C.-A. Sensori-motor and postural behavior: Its relation to cognitive development. In W. W. Hartup (Ed.), *Review of child development research* (Vol. 6). Chicago: University of Chicago Press, 1982. (b)

Mounoud, P., Mayer, E., & Hauert, C.-A. Preparation of actions to lift objects of varying weight and texture in the adult. *Journal of Human Movement Studies*, 1979, *5*, 209–215.

Mounoud, P., Vinter, A. Representation and sensorimotor development. In G. Butterworth (Ed.), *Infancy and epistemology*. Hassocks, Eng.: Harvester Press, 1981.

Nassefat, M. *Etude quantitative sur l'évolution des opérations intellectuelles*. Neuchâtel, Switz., and Paris: Delachaux & Niestlé, 1963.

Oléron, P. *Recherches sur le développement mental des sourds-muets*. Paris: Editions du Centre National de la Recherche Scientifique, 1957.

Othenin-Girard, C. Unpublished doctoral dissertation, University of Geneva, 1978.

Pailhous, J. Elaboration d'images spatiales et de règles de déplacement: Une étude sur l'espace urbain. *Le Travail Humain*, 1971, *34*, 299–324.

Pailhous, J. Les fonctions d'organisation des conduites et des données (conduite de l'adulte). In J. Piaget, J. P. Bronckart, & P. Mounoud (Eds.), *Psychologie*. Paris: La Pleiade, in press.

Pailhous, J., & Bullinger, A. The role of interiorization of material properties of information-acquiring devices in exploratory activities. *Communication and Cognition*, 1978, *11*, 209–234.

Papandropoulou, I. La réflexion métalinguistique

chez l'enfant. Unpublished doctoral dissertation. University of Geneva, 1976.

Piaget, J. Le mécanisme du développement mental. *Archives de Psychologie*, 1941, *28*, 218–271.

Piaget, J. The origins of intelligence. New York: International Universities Press, 1952.

Piaget, J. Les stades du développement intellectuel de l'enfant et de l'adolescent. In *Le problème des stades en psychologie de l'enfant, symposium de l'Association de Psychologie Scientifique de Langue Française*. Paris: Presses Universitaires de France, 1955.

Piaget, J. Nécessité et signification des études comparatives en psychologie génétique. *Journal International de Psychologie*, 1966, *1*, 3–13.

Piaget, J. Le possible, l'impossible et le nécessaire. *Archives de Psychologie*, 1976, *44*, 281–499. (a)

Piaget, J. Post-face. *Archives de Psychologie*, 1976, *44*, 223–228. (b)

Piaget, J., Inhelder, B., & Szeminska, A. *La géometrie spontanée de l'enfant*. Paris: Presses Universitaires de France, 1948.

Piaget, J., Orsini, F., Meylan-Backs, M., & Sinclair, H. De la regularité à la proportionalité. *Etudes d'épistémologie génétiques* (Vol. 23). Paris: Presses Universitaires de France, 1968.

Piaget, J., Sinclair, H., & Vinh Bang. Epistémologie et psychologie de l'identité. *Etudes d'épistémologie génétiques* (Vol. 24). Paris: Presses Universitaires de France, 1968.

Piaget, J., Szeminska, A. *La genèse du nombre chez l'enfant*. Neuchâtel, Switz., and Paris: Delachaux & Niestlé, 1941.

Pierrehumbert, B. La question des représentations et de leur utilisation lors de la résolution de problème. *Cahiers de Psychologie*, 1980, *23*, 107–134.

Rappe du Cher, E. A comparative study of children's comprehension of derived sentences. *Salzburger Beiträge zur Linguistik*, 1977, *4*, 103–116.

Rey, A. *L'intelligence pratique chez l'enfant (observations et expériences)*. Paris: F. Alcan, 1935.

Saada-Robert, M. Procédures d'action et significations fonctionnelles chez des enfants de 2 à 5 ans. *Archives de Psychologie*, 1979, *47*, 177–235.

Saada-Robert, M. *Les modifications du déroulement de l'activité observable comme indices d'un changement de significations fonctionnelles*. Unpublished doctoral dissertation, University of Geneva, 1980.

Savoyant, A. Diagnostic dans une étude de poste de l'industrie chimique. *Le Travail Humain*, 1971, *34*, 177–183.

Schmid-Kitsikis, E. The cognitive mechanisms underlying problem-solving in psychotic and mentally retarded children. In *Piaget and his school*. New York: Springer-Verlag, 1976.

Schmid-Kitsikis, E. Modes de fonctionnement mental et modèles du développement psychologique. *Cahiers de Psychologie*, 1979, *22*, 43–48.

Sinclair, H., & Bronckart, J.-P. A linguistic universal? A study in developmental psycholinguistics. *Journal of Child Experimental Psychology*, 1972, *14*, 329–348.

Vergnaud, G. *La réponse instrumentale comme solution de problème: Contribution*. Unpublished doctoral dissertation, University of Paris, 1968.

Vergnaud, G., Marthe, R., Ricco, G., Metregiste, R., & Boucher, A. *Acquisition des structures multiplicatives*. Action Thématique Programmée: Travail de l'Elève. Paris: Publications du Centre National de la Recherche Scientifique, 1978.

Vermersch, P. *Une approche de la régulation de l'action chez l'adulte. Registres de fonctionnement, déséquilibre transitoire et microgenèse. Un exemple: l'analyse expérimentale de l'apprentissage du réglage de l'oscilloscope cathodique*. Unpublished doctoral dissertation, University of Paris, 1976.

Vermersch, P. Peut-on utiliser les données de la psychologie génétique pour analyser le fonctionnement cognitif des adultes? Théorie opératoire de l'intelligence et registre de fonctionnement. *Cahiers de Psychologie*, 1979, *22*, 59–74.

Vinh Bang, & Lavallée, M. *Rapport de recherche sur les fractions chez l'enfant*. Geneva: Faculté de Psychologie et de Sciences de l'Education, University of Geneva, 1978.

Widmer-Robert-Tissot, C. *Les modes de communication du bébé. Postures, mouvements et vocalises*. Neuchâtel, Switz., and Paris: Delachaux & Niestlé, 1980.

Zei, B. The psychological reality of phonemes. *Journal of Child Language*, 1979, *6*, 375–381.

LOGICAL REASONING* | 5

MARTIN D. S. BRAINE AND BARBARA RUMAIN, *New York University*

CHAPTER CONTENTS

*This review was aided by a research grant (MH30162, Martin D. S. Braine, principal investigator) and a predoctoral fellowship awarded to Barbara Rumain (MH08302). We are very grateful to Rachel Falmagne for her careful reading and comments on an earlier draft.

Traditionally, logic has to do with forms of argument that are valid across content areas. Thus, individual disciplines and content areas (e.g., physics, chemistry, law, and especially the various branches of mathematics) have ways of arguing that are specific to their respective subject matters; In addition, however, there are certain general forms of argument that all areas of knowledge share—and usually take for granted—that do not depend on the specific content discussed. These are the province of logic, and our topic.

In practice, logic has to do with arguments that seem to depend on the meanings of certain kinds of linguistic structures, for instance, words like *and, or, if,* and *unless;* whether a statement is negated or not and how it is negated; words like *all, every, each, any, some,* the articles *a* and *the, other, only, except, whatever,* and *whenever;* whether a noun is singular or plural; certain auxiliary verbs, especially *can, could, may, might, must, have to, should,* and *ought to;* and certain adjectives and adverbs, for example, *possible, necessary,* and *perhaps.* To say that reasoning often depends on the meanings of such expressions is to say that they have logical functions. The enumeration of English expressions that have logical functions is very hard to complete. For one thing, there are very many words that combine logical with nonlogical functions, for example, conjunctions like *but* and *although* seem to have the same logical function as *and,* but they convey something over and above that (e.g., information about what the speaker expects that the listener believes). For another thing, ''logic'' itself is a concept that is fuzzy at its boundaries.

Formal logic—the subject studied and developed by logicians—arose as an attempt to formulate and standardize the kinds of argument that are valid (i.e., that always lead from true premises to true conclusions). In due course, logicians developed their own vocabulary and notational systems independent of natural language, in large part to avoid the ambiguities and vagueness of ordinary language expressions. Logic developed its own subdivisions, and it is convenient to use these subdivisions to organize this review. So, let us enumerate the main ones.

There is, first of all, propositional logic. Its content consists of statements, usually represented by letters, conventionally p, q, and r. The logical vocabulary comprises the connectives that join statements to each other. The English words that most nearly correspond to the connectives are *and, or, if,* and *not.* (There are numerous points of noncorrespondence that we will consider later.) Propositional logic is concerned with arguments about the truth or falsity of statements that depend only on the meanings of the connectives.

Second, there is a group of systems that overlap in their domains—the Aristotelian categorical syllogism (the logic of *all* and *some*), the Boolean class algebra, and (first-order) predicate logic. In general, these three systems represent information about what classes objects belong to, what properties they have, and how they are related to other objects. The inferences that can be made lead from this kind of information to other statements of the same sort. In natural-language reasoning that corresponds to the domain of predicate logic, the inferences depend not only on the meanings of such words as *all, each, every, any,* and *some,* but also on rather subtle aspects of linguistic form, for example, the nature of the article that accompanies a noun, whether a phrase is singular or plural, aspects of word order, what the antecedent of a pronoun is, and the like. Predicate logic is the most inclusive of the three systems: Anything that can be represented within the categorical syllogism or within the class algebra can be represented within predicate logic, but predicate logic is more powerful in that many things can be represented in it that cannot be represented in the other two systems.[1] A major reason for the breadth of predicate logic is that it can represent relations, whereas the class algebra and the syllogism are only concerned with class and property statements. In addition, the categorical syllogism only represents very simple property statements, those of the forms *All* (or *some*) *A are* (or *are not*) *B;* more complex statements, for example, *All A that are not B are either C or D,* are not covered. Although it has been much used in psychological studies, the syllogism is mainly of historical interest for logicians.

Table 1 provides some sample problems to illustrate the difference between propositional reasoning and reasoning of the broader predicate-logic domain.

Predicate logic includes propositional logic and is the most solidly systematized province of logic. There are a variety of systems that include and extend predicate logic in various ways. There is set theory, which can equally be regarded as a branch of mathematics, but which in any case is not relevant for this review. More notably, there are modal, deontic, and various intensional logics. Modal logic incorporates sentence modifiers that aim to capture certain uses of the adverbs *necessarily* and *possibly* (and corresponding auxiliary verbs, such as *must, can,* etc.). As usual, the correspondences between the English and logical expressions are complex. There are a variety of similar systems of modal log-

Table 1. **Some Problems to Illustrate the Difference Between Propositional Reasoning and Reasoning of a Predicate-Logic Type That Is Not Propositional**

Propositional Problems	Predicate-Logic Problems
1. If there is either a "B" or an "R," then there is a "Z" There is a "B" ? There is a "B" and a "Z" ?	1. None of the pictures was painted by anyone I know I know Hank's sister ? Did she paint one of the pictures ?
2. If there is an "R," then there is not an "X" It is false that there is not an "R" ? There is an "X" ?	2. All the raincoats in the closet are yellow Some children in this room do not have yellow raincoats ? Are there some children in this room who do not own any of the raincoats in the closet ?
3. There is a "B" or a "Z" There is not a "Z" It is not true that there is both a "B" and an "R" ? There is not an "R" ?	3. All the boys in this room play baseball Some girls do not like any boys who play baseball ? Are there some girls who do not like any of the boys in this room ?
4. If there is an "F," then there is an "L" If there is not an "F," then there is a "V" ? There is an "L" or a "V" ?	4. Either each block is oak, or each block is square and each block is red ? For each block: If it is not oak then it is square?
5. If there is an "A," then there is a "D" If there is not an "A," then there may or may not be a "D"; you cannot tell There is not a "D" ? There is an "A" ?	5. Everything on my desk is a masterpiece Anyone who wrote a masterpiece is a genius Someone obscure wrote a novel on my desk ? Is some obscure person a genius ?

The propositional problems are from Braine, Reiser, and Rumain (1981). Three of the predicate-logic problems are from Hill (1961), one from Copi (1967) and one from Osherson (1976). Some problems are worded to have the answer "true" and some to have the answer "false."

ic. Deontic logic is concerned with sentence modifiers that correspond (more or less) to expressions like *ought to* and *may* (in the sense of 'allowed').

A great deal of work in logic is concerned with analyzing established systems and proving things about them (as opposed to proving things *in* them). The language of the examination is separate from the language of the system examined. In this metalogical work, the relevant logical concepts are notions like "prove" or "provable," "entails" (see *entailment* in the logical glossary), and most important, "true" and "false."

For much of the last half century, logicians and philosophers have put a good deal of effort into the analysis of the properties of some English expressions that are not logically well behaved, that is, they resist translation into predicate logic because ordinary inference principles do not hold for them. These include, for instance, certain "mental" verbs (the prototypes are *believe* and *want*). In recent years, this type of work has become a rich research frontier where logic and linguistics are indistinguishable (e.g., Montague, 1973, 1974). Most of the phenomena discussed are not relevant to this review because, unfortunately, there is no relevant psychological work. One such phenomenon on which some work in psychology is beginning to be done is the distinction between two kinds of logical relations: presupposition and entailment. Unlike an entailment, a presupposition is an inference that would normally be drawn from a statement regardless of whether it is affirmative or negative. Thus, *George has stopped smoking* and *George has not stopped smoking* are different assertions; however, unless one was deliberately being pedantic, one would infer *George smoked* from both of them; hence, we say they presuppose *George smoked*.

We will construe "logical reasoning" to include all kinds of reasoning that correspond to the domains and topics just summarized. We are, of course, concerned with ordinary reasoning, that is, reasoning performed in ordinary language by ordinary subjects untutored in logic. Because such reasoning depends on subjects' understanding of linguistic forms and expressions, we will also be concerned with all available information on the development of understanding of these forms and expressions, much of which comes from studies that are not studies of reasoning. In general, we will be concerned with work of whatever nature that might throw light on the basis of subjects' behavior on logical-reasoning tasks.

The first major section of the review considers, in a general way, what a model of logical reasoning might be expected to look like. A model must account for both correct responses and errors, and we consider mechanisms that have been proposed for each of these as well as their developmental implications. In particular, the search for an explanation of error takes us into a long discussion of the nature of comprehension processes on logical-reasoning tasks.

The second section takes up a necessary preliminary to discussion of developmental data on reasoning error—the development of the response of "undecidable."

The next major section is devoted to propositional reasoning, including work concerned with the development of comprehension of the relevant English conjunctions and the development of truth judgments, as well as command of inference principles of propositional reasoning and characteristic sources of reasoning error.

The fourth major section is concerned with reasoning of a predicate-logic type, that is, reasoning about classes, properties, and relations. We review relevant work on comprehension, similarities and differences between natural styles of reasoning and those of standard predicate logic, sources of error in reasoning, and work on the categorical syllogism.

The fifth section discusses Piaget's logic and issues relating to the stage of formal operations. The section that follows reviews other kinds of logical reasoning, primarily studies relating to perceptions of possibility and necessity, and work on young children's knowledge of presuppositions.

As noted earlier, "logic" is a notion that has no well-defined boundaries. There are kinds of deductive reasoning that we shall not review that would be considered "logical" under some construals of that term. We shall not discuss so-called "lexical" reasoning, that is, inferences that are specific to particular words (unless the words are relevant to reasoning of the kinds summarized or the work has to do with the notion of presupposition). For example, given *Jack killed John on Wednesday*, one can infer *John died on Wednesday*. Specific entailments like this seem more relevant to the development of lexical memory (here, the meaning of *kill*) than reasoning. Along with this omission, we shall not review work on "transitivity," for example, deductions from such premises as *A is larger than B, B is larger than C*, to *A is larger than C*. Such inferences are viewed as "logical" by Aristotle and Piaget, although not

by such modern logicians as Quine (1953b) because they depend on empirical fact, that is, the fact that the relation *larger than* is indeed transitive. They are reviewed by Gelman and Baillargeon in their discussion, *A Review of Some Piagetian Concepts* (see *vol. III, chap. 3*).

WHAT SHOULD A THEORY OF LOGICAL REASONING BE LIKE?

Here we discuss the relation between logic and ordinary reasoning. We consider sources of error in reasoning, the nature of the logical component of a model of reasoning, and what other components such a model would need.

The Controversy Over the Relation Between Logic and Reasoning

There is a longstanding issue about whether or not ordinary reasoning is based on logical principles. From the time of Aristotle until late in the nineteenth century, it was largely taken for granted that there was a close relation between logic and reasoning. Psychology was not an independent discipline; almost all serious thinking about cognitive processes was done by philosophers. For them, logic was the science of reasoning. In a brief historical survey, Henle (1962) notes that Kant (1885) held that logic was a "science of the necessary laws of thought" (p. 3) and that Mill (1874) viewed it as "the science of reasoning." Similarly, Boole (1854) entitled his book *An Investigation of the Laws of Thought* and regarded the laws of the symbols of logic as "deducible from a consideration of the operations of the mind in reasoning" (p. 46).

Toward the end of the nineteenth century, psychology and philosophy became separate disciplines. However, the new psychology brought no fresh insights into the psychology of reasoning that would clarify the relation between logic and thinking. On the philosophical side, there were important new developments in logic and the philosophy of logic, especially in the work of Frege (Frege, 1879, 1884/1950; Geach & Black, 1952); predicate logic became systematized in pretty much its present form, with its own notation that depended little on the meaning of natural-language expressions. It became clear, as Russell (1904) noted, that the study of logic does not presuppose mental processes. Most philosophers came to view the relation of logic to thinking as purely normative, that is, logic provides criteria by which the validity of reasoning can be evaluated, but logical principles do not describe the reasoning process. The fact that ordinary reasoning is often fallacious appeared to provide strong support for this view. Because psychology and philosophy were separate disciplines now, philosophers did not, of course, have to confront the problem of trying to account for correct reasoning without assuming that the subjects were following logical principles. The view that the relation of logic to reasoning is purely normative is probably held by most philosophers today. This was the dominant view in modern psychology until midcentury when it began to be questioned by some psychologists, first by Piaget (1953) and then for different reasons by others, notably Henle (1962, 1971). During this half century or so, only a little work was done on logical reasoning in psychology; no comprehensive theoretical framework for explaining reasoning was developed under the aegis of the doctrine that logic has only a normative relation to thinking.

The pendulum swung back with Henle's (1962) influential article. She discussed reasoning errors in some detail, and she provided suggestive evidence that they were rarely due to illogicality but rather to subjects' interpreting problems in a way not intended by the problem setter. Thus, a common source of error (Henle, 1962; Henle & Michael, 1956; Richter, 1957) occurs when a subject does not distinguish between a conclusion that is logically valid (i.e., that follows from the premises) and one that the subject believes to be factually correct. Other kinds of errors of interpretation are also common, for example, subjects sometimes omit a premiss, or they may give a statement a meaning that was not intended, or they may slip in an additional premiss, especially one that comes from their general knowledge of the subject matter. In such cases, the reasoning is correct for the problem as it is construed, so that the "error" is an error of construal, not a logical error. It is interesting that this is exactly the explanation of error in reasoning that was assumed more than a century ago by Mill and Kant. According to this view, the reasoning itself typically follows logical principles correctly.

This issue of the relation of logic and reasoning leads, then, to a classical dilemma. We may assume that there is no logical component in reasoning. In that case, we have a ready explanation for error—if the reasoner has no command of logical principles we should expect little else but error—but we then have to confront the problem of how to explain correct reasoning when it occurs. Alternatively, we can assume that reasoning is based on logical principles. In that case, we have a ready explanation for correct reasoning (although we will need to specify the logical principles), but we have to confront the problem of explaining error.

Which promises to be easier—to account for correct reasoning without logic, or to assume a logic and account for error? We think that the second horn contains the viable route out of the dilemma and that Henle's (1962) discussion of error points the way. For propositional reasoning, there is a fair consensus in favor of the second horn—there are specific proposals about the "natural logic" used in ordinary reasoning and no competing nonlogical proposals. For reasoning about classes and properties, however, the matter is not settled: Here, the logical route is poorly worked out, and on the other side, there are some examples of nonlogical approaches focused on a narrow range of subject matter—categorical syllogisms, for example, the imagistic theory of Erickson (1974) and the analogical theory of Johnson-Laird and Steedman (1978). Very recently, the analogical theory has been developed into the only deliberate attempt we know of to take the first horn of the dilemma seriously (Johnson-Laird, 1981). We discuss these nonlogical approaches when we discuss categorical syllogisms. In the meantime, we follow the second horn and now consider sources of error in more detail.

Comprehension Processes as Sources of Error

Let us start with Henle's view that characteristics of comprehension are a major source of error, and let us consider the general nature of comprehension processes and how they could be expected to affect behavior on reasoning tasks. Donaldson (1976) suggests that one should distinguish two kinds of language comprehension. The first kind is ordinary comprehension. Its goal is to arrive at the meaning that a speaker or writer intends by a statement. The comprehension process uses all the information available—what the comprehender knows about the speaker and the speaker's motives, specific knowledge of the subject matter, general knowledge of the world, general conventions about speaking and writing (e.g., Grice, 1975, 1978), as well as the words used and their grammatical organization within the sentence being decoded. This kind of comprehension is typical of conversation and reading for pleasure. It is ordinarily a fast process since it takes place at conversation and reading speeds. We can take it for granted that all normal human beings have a lot of practice at ordinary comprehension and develop a fair degree of skill at it.

The other kind of comprehension is very different. Its purpose is to discover the meaning of a sentence—not what the speaker means by the sentence, but what the sentence itself means. We will call it "analytic" comprehension. This kind of comprehension is involved in a number of sophisticated verbal tasks. For instance, it is common in a variety of kinds of legal work that a close analysis of the *language* of the law is required, for example, whatever the spirit of the law, few people willingly pay a tax if they can see that the language of the law does not clearly require them to pay. A good example of analytic comprehension occurs in a jury summons received from New York State. It states that "By law you may claim exemption from jury service if you are: . . . (2) A licensed physician, dentist, pharmacist, optometrist; psychologist, podiatrist, registered nurse, practical nurse, embalmer or a Christian Science nurse exempt from licensing regularly engaged in the practice of his profession." Deciding whether that says that an unlicensed nonclinical professor of psychology can claim exemption illustrates analytic comprehension. (Note that the issue is what New York State says, not what New York State intends.) A well-known further example is the discussion of the dog-walking ordinance by a certain borough council as reported by Graves & Hodge (1943) or Nagel (1956). Analytic comprehension is also involved in editing and in the self-editing that goes on in good writing; the major objective of both endeavors is to contrive sentences that mean just what the writer intends them to mean. As most writers know, this is by no means a simple task. Analytic comprehension, then, is a comprehension process that deliberately ignores normal aids to understanding, such as the speaker's intent or whether the presumptive meaning is plausible or not, in order to focus on the commitments of the sentences themselves.

Ordinary comprehension has been well studied, for example, psycholinguistic studies of sentence comprehension (e.g., Bever, 1970; Gough, 1965) are studies of ordinary comprehension.[2] Analytic comprehension has been discussed in the context of writing (e.g., Olson & Hillyard, in press), and there are occasional studies that may well demand analytic comprehension without identifying it as such (e.g., the paraphrasing of noun compounds demanded by Gleitman & Gleitman, 1970). Otherwise, it has been hardly studied at all by psychologists. It is obvious, however, that analytic comprehension is ordinarily a much slower and more careful process than ordinary comprehension, and common observation suggests that it is a relatively high-level verbal skill in which there are large individual differences among adults.

The distinction between ordinary and analytic comprehension is relevant here because formal reasoning from premises demands analytic comprehension of the premises. For one reason or another, however, a subject may use ordinary comprehension processes. This may happen because he or she fails to preceive that analytic comprehension is demanded or because they lack analytic comprehension skills. Children, in particular, have very little experience with any but ordinary comprehension. "Error" in reasoning is likely to occur whenever ordinary comprehension yields an appreciation of the premises that differs from that yielded by analytic comprehension; such errors can be expected to be the norm in young children.

It is worth noting in this context that by comparison with ordinary social communication events, logical-reasoning tasks can be decidedly peculiar. Imagine a young child taken into a little room by a stranger. The stranger explains that the child is going to do some puzzles in which he or she will be told some things and then asked a question. In one of the puzzles, they are told: *If this is Room 12, it's a fifth-grade classroom. This is a fifth-grade classroom. Is it Room 12?*

Let us consider what our young subject might make of this event. Common sense suggests that the first response is likely to be a certain amount of mystification. What is the point of saying *If this is Room 12, it's a fifth-grade classroom* if you already know it is a fifth-grade classroom? It is an implicit rule of ordinary interaction not to be vague without reason. Not being definite when you could be implies lack of knowledge, so a speaker who says *If this is Room 12, it's a fifth-grade classroom* is implying that they do not know whether or not it is Room 12 or whether or not it is a fifth-grade classroom. (They just know that Room 12 is a fifth-grade classroom.) The second premiss contradicts this conversational implicature however. So the child's ordinary comprehension, aimed at determining the speaker's intent, may have difficulty arriving at a result. If the child is confused, the consequence for the investigator is that a random element is thrown into the data, one that will mask whatever reasoning abilities the child has.

But let us suppose that the child retains his or her wits and tries to consider the problem on its merits. For example, the child—particularly an older child—may be acquainted with examination-type situations, and that may provide a familiar framework for assimilating the event. However, the child is still faced with some things that are strange when measured by the standards of ordinary interactions, even including tests. Consecutive statements on the same subject matter are usually additive in meaning, that is, each statement adds information that can be integrated with the previous information. So, given that it is a fifth-grade classroom, what could a speaker who says *If this is Room 12, it's a fifth-grade classroom* mean to communicate relevant to whether or not it is Room 12? Obviously, they probably mean that if it is a fifth-grade classroom, it will be Room 12. This assumption accords with another conversational rule—not to be misleading if you can avoid it. It is one of the normal courtesies of conversational interaction (also of good test making) that one adds caveats that cancel aspects of statements that are likely to mislead. Thus, an adult who did not wish to be misunderstood might well alert the listener by adding some caveat, like *but if it isn't Room 12, then I don't know if it's a fifth-grade classroom or not.* Given a tacit convention not to mislead, the absence of a caveat itself helps guide the listener to the speaker's intent. So, sensitivity to discourse norms should encourage the child to assume that the speaker meant that if it was not Room 12, it would not be a fifth-grade classroom. Thus, ordinary comprehension dictates a yes response to the question, *Is it Room 12?* The child will then be classified as having fallen into one of the traditional fallacies.

In such cases, one can expect the responses of young children to contain fallacies of this sort combined with some admixture of random responding. One can hope to diminish the amount of random responding by careful preparation of how the task is presented to the child. However, to eliminate the traditional fallacies, the subject must not only be aware that analytic comprehension is demanded but also have a moderate degree of this verbal skill.

The conventions that speakers and listeners observe in conversation have been extensively discussed by Grice (1975, 1978). Speakers and listeners try to adhere to what Grice calls the "cooperative principle." That is, speakers try to be as informative, truthful, relevant, and clear as they can, and listeners assume that speakers are trying to be so when interpreting what they say. These cooperative conventions allow much to be left inexplicit in conversation and much to be inferred that is not said. An important part of ordinary comprehension must consist in knowing and using these conventions. They are important for understanding behavior on logical-reasoning tasks because the traditional ways of writing logical-reasoning problems typically flout the cooperative principle, sometimes to an extraordinary degree.

These conversational habits are relevant to the interpretation of the logical vocabulary of natural language. Geis and Zwicky (1971) note that some natural-logical forms have characteristic "invited inferences." Thus, a statement of the form *If p then q* invites the inference *If not p then not q.* We can add that a statement of the form *Some F are G* invites the inference *Some F are not G.* Note that these invited inferences are not part of the essential meaning of the logical expressions *if* and *some* because they can be countermanded without contradiction. For example, it is not contradictory—in fact, perfectly comprehensible—to say *Some, perhaps all of the F are G;* similarly, one can cancel the inference invited by the form *If p then q* by adding, for example, *but if not p, then q may be true or it may be false.*[3] (The essential meaning cannot, of course, be countermanded, that is, one cannot say *Some, perhaps none of the F are G* or *If p then q, but if p, then q may be true or it may be false!*) It also seems that the form *p or q* invites the inference *but not both*—which can be countermanded by adding *or both.* Invited inferences are probably made more or less automatically in ordinary comprehension unless they are countermanded either explicitly by the speaker or implicitly by something in the subject matter talked about that makes them implausible. Successful analytic comprehension sets them aside.

It is not clear exactly how these invited inferences enter into the native speaker's competence. One possibility is that the lexical entries for particles like *if, or,* and *some* contain the essential meanings, and that the invited inferences are produced whenever relevant by ordinary comprehension processes that use the Gricean discourse conventions mentioned earlier. The other possibility is that the invited inferences are actually part of the lexical entries for the logical particles. In that case, these entries would have to have two parts: One part would specify the essential meaning (whose nature we discuss later), marked as essential; the other part would be the invited inference, marked as likely but not necessary. In the latter case, it might be a tenable hypothesis that at early stages of development children's lexical entries do not distinguish the essential and invited components of meaning, that is, mark both parts as equally essential. This hypothesis is implicit in some suggestions in the literature that at some ages *if* is the biconditional of standard logic (e.g., Peel, 1967; Sternberg, 1979).

Of course, there are other possible developmental hypotheses, for example, that the essential meanings develop first and that the invited inferences accrue later, possibly as a result of increasing mastery of conversational conventions. To anticipate the data, this hypothesis has little support. At least for *if,* the most studied particle, the data seem to indicate that children make the invited inferences as early as they make coherent responses at all.

It is clear from what has been said that such expressions as "the meaning of *if*," "the meaning of *or*," and so on, are ambiguous: They could refer to how a listener understands *if* or *or* on some occasion of utterance, or they could refer to the meaning encoded in semantic memory, the lexical entry. This is a pernicious ambiguity; to avoid it, we shall use the terms "construal" and "lexical entry," respectively. It is axiomatic that in ordinary comprehension construal of an expression usually depends on many factors beyond the content of the lexical entry, such as the subject matter of the discourse and conversational implicatures.

The Difference Between Formal and Practical Logical Reasoning

Formal logical reasoning uses explicit premises and is concerned with what statements follow from the premises. However, there is a purely practical kind of logical reasoning that occurs in everyday-life situations. Thus, you know from general knowledge that if a certain thing is the case some other thing will be too. You then discover that the second thing is not so; so you expect the first not to be also. Or, you have reason to believe that one or another of a pair of alternatives holds; at some later point in time, you discover that one of them does not hold; so you conclude that the other does. For instance, you have a friend in Boston who is coming to visit you. He says he has not decided whether he'll come by plane or train; if he comes by plane he'll telephone at 6:00 P.M. just before the plane leaves, so you can meet him at the airport. If he comes by train he doesn't need to be met. At 6:30 P.M. he hasn't telephoned. So, you infer by a completely logical train of thought that he's not coming by plane and so the other alternative must be correct, that he's coming by train. This is the sort of everyday logical reasoning that Aristotle called the "practical syllogism."

There are obvious differences between formal and practical reasoning. In formal reasoning, the starting information is set out in the premises. In practical reasoning, the starting information may come from general knowledge, from specific facts that have been discovered, or from verbal communications that have been understood through ordinary comprehension processes. Typically it comes from some mixture of these sources. Also, the pieces of starting information ordinarily come from different sources, often at different times; the reasoning is a kind of integration of the pieces.

These differences amount to two important functional differences. First, formal reasoning demands analytic comprehension, whereas practical reasoning does not: Insofar as the starting information comes from verbal communciation (rather than from observation or by retrieval from memory) only ordinary comprehension is typically involved. Second, formal reasoning demands a compartmentalization of information: The reasoner must separate the information gained from the premises from whatever other information he or she may have about the subject and use only the information in the premises. Practical reasoning makes no such demands. Although formal and practical reasoning differ in how the starting information is established, they probably have much in common in the inference-making process itself. Practical reasoning includes inferences based on plausibility, but some part of it is logical—all of it, in the example of our visitor from Boston. For this part, there is every reason to assume that the principles that govern the movement from one step to another in a chain of reasoning are the same as those in formal reasoning. These principles are presumably where the logical component of ordinary reasoning is to be found. Thus, we may conclude that formal and practical reasoning differ in how the starting information is arrived at and in the inclusion of merely plausible inferences in practical reasoning, but, otherwise, formal and practical reasoning share a common logic.

Formal reasoning from premises is something that emerged as a relatively specialized scholarly exercise rather late in human cultural evolution—in the last 2,500 years and only in environments of highly literate culture. Practical logical reasoning is undoubtedly much older, probably as old as organized language itself. The logical particles of natural language presumably developed to serve the purposes of everyday practical reasoning. Practical reasoning is clearly a much more basic and universal human cognitive activity than formal reasoning.

These considerations suggest that the inferential process itself—the principles and processes that determine the movement from one step to another in reasoning, separate from analytic comprehension ability—may be manifest most straightforwardly in information-integration tasks that mimic practical reasoning, that is, tasks in which the pieces of starting information come from different sources and in which verbally communicated information is presented in a way that conforms to the Gricean cooperative principle as far as possible.

The Logical Component of a Model of Reasoning

We now have to face the question of the nature of the logical principles in reasoning. Standard logic offers two kinds of approaches. One is through truth tables; the other is through inference schemas. We consider each in turn.

Truth Tables

The usual truth-table approach assumes that the natural connectives (*and, or, if*) are defined by the conditions under which the compound propositions containing them (i.e., of the form *p and q, p or q, if p then q*) are true or false. These conditions are customarily summarized in truth tables. *And* would have the truth table of standard logic &; *or* would be ambiguous between two tables, that for v ("inclusive or") and w ("exclusive or"); *if* would have the truth table for ⊃. Under a variant of the approach, *if* would be ambiguous between the tables for ⊃ and for the biconditional (≡). (See the *Logical Glossary* for definition of the truth tables.) In the development of logical competence, the truth-table theory would hold that part of what is acquired are the truth tables.

There are overwhelming arguments against all forms of the truth-table theory. The differences between the behavior of the natural connectives and that predictable from the corresponding truth tables are well known. See Strawson (1952) for a philosophical perspective and Lakoff (1971) for a linguistic one; Fillenbaum (1977) summarizes much data on all three connectives from a psychological standpoint and Braine (1978) provides a recent discussion of *if*. In studies that we review later, there is evidence that children are able to make basic inferences based on the meaning of *or* before they are able to make sensible judgments of the truth of propositions containing *or* (Braine & Rumain, 1981). Similarly, some ability to reason from statements containing *if* develops quite early, but even adults do not judge the truth of such statements in accordance with any truth table (e.g., Johnson-Laird & Tagart, 1969). There is also general agreement that ordinary propositional reasoning does not use truth tables (e.g., Osherson, 1975b; Wason & Johnson-Laird, 1972). In general, then, if one is seeking within logic for a model relevant to reasoning, truth tables are not it.

Inference Schemas

We have concluded that it is the movement from one step to another in a chain of inferences that is governed by logical principles. Does logic offer a model for a deductive step?

One common way of presenting modern logic is as a set of axioms together with a small number of inference schemas. Axioms are sentence forms, all instances of which are true. They do not have the form of an inference, moving from given information to something inferred, and so have not seemed an appropriate form for a model of reasoning (Braine, 1978; Gentzen, 1935/1964; Johnson-Laird, 1975; Osherson, 1975b; Wason & Johnson-Laird, 1972). However, it is possible, as the logician Gentzen (1935/1964) showed, to present logic entirely in the form of inference schemas.

An inference schema specifies a kind of inference by specifying the form of the conclusion that can be drawn when given starting information of a certain form. In the usual notation, there is a horizontal line, the inference line; above the line, the form of the starting information is specified; below the line, the form of the conclusion is given. Letters of the alphabet are used as variables, for example, p, q, and r (for propositions), as in the following inference schemas:

$$\textbf{(1)} \qquad \frac{\text{IF } p \text{ THEN } q; \ p}{q}$$

$$\textbf{(2)} \qquad \frac{p \text{ OR } q; \ \text{IF } p \text{ THEN } r; \ \text{IF } q \text{ THEN } r}{r}$$

An inference is formed by substituting actual propositions for p, q, and r; any inference so formed is a valid step in a chain of reasoning. For instance, the following inference is formed by substitution in Schema 2:

$$\textbf{(3)} \qquad \frac{\begin{array}{l}\text{Either Carter wins or Reagan wins.}\\ \text{If Carter wins, we will have a deficit.}\\ \text{If Reagan wins, we will have a deficit.}\end{array}}{\text{We will have a deficit.}}$$

Inference schemas provide a model capable of defining deductive steps. Gentzen (1935/1964) proposed a set of such schemas for predicate logic. Each schema defined a kind of inference, and the set defined the repertory of allowed kinds of inferences, that is, the repertory of elementary deductive steps. Thus, every argument in predicate logic consisted of a chain of such inferences. Gentzen's motives were in part psychological: He wished "to set up a formal system that came as close as possible to actual reasoning" (p. 288). This goal is reflected in the name, "Natural deduction," that he gave to the system. Systems of predicate logic consisting of inference schemas are now presented in most elementary logic textbooks.

Before considering psychological theories that posit inference schemas, it may be well to consider a possible objection to them in principle. Given a set of inference schemas involving a connective, it is often possible to deduce a truth table for that connective. (It is always possible in standard logic.) Consequently, it might be thought that the objections to the truth-table theory that we have just noted would also count as objections to inference schemas. This is not in fact the case. Consider, for example, a basic inference schema involving *or:*

(4)
$$\frac{\text{p OR q; NOT p}}{\text{q}}$$

The schema states that if one of a pair of alternatives is false, the other must be correct. It is hard to see how an ordinary *or*-statement could be comprehensible to someone who did not have this schema, and someone with this schema need not have worked out a truth table to understand many sentences with *or.* The schema can explain many responses much more directly than a truth table could, for example, the fact that subjects paraphrase such statements as *Get out of my way or I'll hit you* as *If you don't get out of my way I'll hit you* (Fillenbaum, 1974b).

Or consider Modus Ponens (i.e., Schema 1, above). It is hard to see how any *if-then* statement could be comprehensible to someone who did not have this schema. In fact, much of the meaning of *if* seems to be contained in it. As reviewed later, when subjects are given a Modus Ponens reasoning problem (i.e., a problem with two premises of the form *If p then q* and *p*, and a conclusion *q* to be evaluated), they are almost unanimous in responding that *q* is true from about age 6 onward. When adults are asked to explain why they think *q* must be true, the most common explanation is to point to the premiss *If p then q* and say, "It says so" (Braine, 1978). Thus, Schemas 1 and 4 seem to capture more of the meaning of *if* and *or* than any truth table.

Counterfactual conditionals provide an excellent case in which ordinary evaluations of statements are in direct conflict with a truth-table approach but are completely rational if it is assumed that the meanings of the connectives are given by inference schemas. Consider the following two sentences:

(5) If Hitler had had the atomic bomb in 1940, he would have won the war.

(6) If Hitler had had one more airplane in 1940, he would have won the war.

Most people would consider Sentence 5 probably correct and 6 incorrect. However, according to the truth table for the conditional ($\supset$), both sentences are true merely because their first clauses are false. Let us now consider the following inference schema, which is a version of what logicians often call the "rule of conditional proof":[4]

(7)
$$\frac{(\text{p and } \Sigma) \text{ entails q; } \Sigma}{\text{If p then q}}$$

The schema says, given that *q* follows from *p* together with some conditions or assumptions (Σ), and given also that the assumptions are true, then one can conclude *If p then q.* Schema 7 provides a method of evaluating a conditional: One looks for some set of assumptions or conditions (Σ) that are true and that taken together with *p* permit one to establish *q.* If one is successful, one can conclude *If p then q.* This seems to be just the way one evaluates sentences like 5 and 6. To evaluate 5, one would consider various facts about the nature of the bomb and the state of Europe in 1940. One would take these together with the supposition that Hitler had the bomb and see whether these led one to conclude that he would have won the war. One would perform the same procedure with 6, using the supposition that Hitler had one more plane than he had. No doubt, one would conclude for 5 that he would have won the war and for 6 that it would not have made any difference (i.e., for 6, one would convince oneself of the opposite conditional—*If Hitler had had one more airplane he would not have won the war*). Hence, one would evaluate 5 positively and 6 as invalid. Thus, the approach using inference schemas can straightforwardly explain behavior that is not explicable on a truth-table approach.[5]

Inference schemas will not explain all uses of *and, or,* and *if* in discourse. We still need to assume knowledge of discourse conventions, including the Gricean cooperative principles. But the way the connectives are used in discourse would itself be inexplicable if people did not know certain inference schemas. On the other hand, the discussion obviously does not endorse all schemas that anyone might propose. Schemas offer a potentially useful model for the inferential steps in reasoning, but they need to be evaluated on a case by case basis.

In recent years, several sets of inference schemas have been proposed as models of competence in various forms of logical reasoning. Ennis (1976) presents such a set, together with a set of "invalid" schemas that define common fallacies. These are offered as a framework for conceptualizing logical competence. The development of competence would consist in understanding that the valid schemas are valid and that the invalid ones are fallacious, also in resisting the effects of suggestive content on reasoning, and in acquiring skill in handling various kinds of complexities in chains of reasoning. Ennis suggests that the schemas differ in difficulty and in age of initial mastery.

In the other proposals (Braine, 1978; Braine, Reiser, & Rumain, 1981; Johnson-Laird, 1975; Osherson, 1974, 1975a, 1976), each schema purports to define a kind of deductive step possible in a chain of reasoning. A step would consist of applying a schema either to the starting information or to the output of previous reasoning steps. The models of Johnson-Laird and Braine are proposed as complete repertories of the kinds of deductive steps in natural propositional reasoning. Osherson (1974, 1975a, 1976) proposes limited sets of schemas for a number of logical domains and seeks to show that subjects use these schemas in reasoning. Details are reviewed later.

The Overall Form of a Model of Logical Reasoning

A complete model will contain much more than a repertory of deductive steps. There obviously must be components that determine what the starting information is, and that select from the repertory the steps to be used. Braine (1978) proposed that a complete model would have a performance component in addition to the repertory of inference schemas of the logical component. The performance component would contain two main kinds of processes. One is a set of comprehension processes that decode the information given into the representations used in the schemas. The other consists of reasoning programs—routines and strategies that draw on the repertory of deductive steps and put together a line of reasoning that leads from the starting information to a conclusion. Johnson-Laird's (1975) model for propositional reasoning also has reasoning programs in addition to the repertory of schemas.

There are, undoubtedly, occasions in which subjects' reasoning programs have difficulty finding a line of reasoning using the schemas in the repertory. An additional part of the performance component—possibly a very important part—would consist of any nonlogical strategies people use to try to reach a conclusion under these circumstances. Some errors in reasoning may be due to such strategies.

Developmental Questions

Some developmental questions follow from the model outlined. An important one concerns the origin of schemas. For Ennis (1975) and Falmagne (1980) schemas are learned as valid steps in reasoning. Ennis argues that different schemas are learned at different ages, and some perhaps not universally learned at any age. On the other hand, Johnson-Laird (1975) and Braine (1978) regard their schemas as a universal repertory. It seems likely to us that the lexical entries for the connectives are in large part given by inference schemas, an idea that is consistent with the "procedural" approach to semantics in which meaning is given by procedures for operating on information (e.g., Johnson-Laird, 1977; Winograd, 1972, 1975). In that case, many schemas would be acquired as part of learning the language, and simple inferences based on them should be available early to children and be among the early pieces of evidence for understanding the words.

A second developmental task is to describe changes with age in comprehension processes that affect how information given is understood, and in associated error tendencies in reasoning.

A third issue concerns the development of reasoning strategies. A potentially important distinction here is between "direct" and "indirect" lines of reasoning. In direct reasoning, the reasoner starts from the premises and makes an inference from them, and then makes further inferences from the premises together with the just inferred proposition(s), until the desired conclusion is reached or contradicted. (When the conclusion to be reached is an *if*-statement, one can also consider a line of reasoning to be direct if it starts from the premises together with the antecedent of the *if*-statement, and then works toward the consequent by direct reasoning.) An indirect line of reasoning has a point of departure outside the premises. For instance, in Table 1, direct lines of reasoning solve the first three propositional problems, whereas Problems 4 and 5 require indirect reasoning (in 4, the starting point is the proposition *There is an "F" or there is not an "F"*, which is not one of the premises; Problem 5 involves seeing that the supposition that there is an "A" would lead to a contradiction). In general, more strategic skill may be required to discover an indirect line of reasoning than a direct one of the same length, and so direct and indirect reasoning abilities could well have different developmental histories.

Some additional issues arise out of existing developmental theories, notably the Piagetian framework. For instance, are schema models related to the Piagetian logical models of the Concrete and Formal Operations? Are there cognitive changes in the bases or organization of responses on deductive-reasoning tasks that are consonant with the Piagetian stages?

The first of these requires a discussion of Piaget's logic (reserved for a later section). We discuss the second issue as relevant occasions arise.

DEVELOPMENT OF THE RESPONSE OF "UNDECIDABLE"

"Undecidable" is a cognitively complex response category. It encodes distinctions—like that between knowing that one knows and knowing that one does not know—that are closely related to the modal concepts of necessity and possibility and that are quite likely to be subtle for a young child. However, the broader questions concerning the development of modal concepts are left until later.

The simplest experimental task we have found that involves a notion akin to "undecidable" occurs in a study of the distinction between knowing and guessing by Miscione, Marvin, O'Brien, and Greenberg (1978). Subjects were 3 to 7 years old. An object was hidden in one of three boxes. Sometimes the child saw the object hidden (and could, therefore, know where it was) and sometimes did not see; children had to pick the box where they thought the object was, and say whether they "knew" where it was or whether they were "guessing." The "know/guess" judgment was sometimes made before knowing whether the location chosen was correct and sometimes after. The youngest children made no distinction at all. There was an intermediate pattern of saying "know" when they had seen and when they guessed correctly and of saying "guess" when they guessed incorrectly. Most of the 6-year-olds, half the 5-year-olds, but hardly any younger children properly distinguished knowing from guessing.

Somerville, Hadkinson, and Greenberg (1979) presented simple inference problems to 5- and 6-year-olds in three experiments. In the main type of problem, the child was shown a boy doll and told that this boy's house had a particular object in the front yard (e.g., a blue table). Then the subject was shown a pair of identical houses, one of which was the boy's house; both houses had objects in their front yards. The objects might or might not permit an inference to be made, for example, a blue table and a yellow dog outside one house and a yellow table and a white dog outside the other would permit an inference to be made, whereas when each had a blue table outside, no inference was possible. Both types of trials were used. The child had to respond to the question "Do you think you can choose which is the boy's house or would you have to ask somebody because you can't tell?" Test trials were preceded by four training trials in which responses were cor-

rected and the correct answers explained. All subjects responded that they could choose on decidable trials, and they correctly made the inference called for. However, the "can't tell/ask somebody" response was underused: Only a few 5-year-olds used it, although most of the 6-year-olds did so, appropriately.

Several of Pieraut-Le Bonniec's (1974, 1980) experiments on modal reasoning have to do with judgments of undecidability. One study with mostly 6-year-olds presented two boxes containing plastic sticklike objects that could be fitted together to make shapes. One box (A) contained both straight and curved pieces; the other box (B) contained only straight pieces. Objects made with the pieces were presented and subjects had to say from which box the pieces came and justify their choice. Curved objects came only from A, but straight objects could come from either A or B (i.e., one could not tell). Although almost all subjects were correct in the decidable case, very few indicated that the choice was indeterminate for the straight objects.

Another study used a box with two holes of different size on top. Sticks and marbles went into the box; the marbles could fit only through the large hole; the sticks could fit through either hole. The objects fell into drawers beneath the holes which could be inspected. A subject was first carefully shown which objects could go through which holes. Then he or she was asked questions to find out if they could tell when it was necessary to look in the drawer, in order to tell which object had been inserted (given information about the hole it was inserted through) or which hole had been used (given information about which object had been inserted). Subjects were 4 to 10 years old. Setting aside some of the younger children who were merely confused, subjects were correct on questions with decidable answers; however, when the answer was not decidable, only the 10-year-olds and some 9-year-olds showed any substantial use of the undecidable response category (i.e., "One must look in the drawer"); the others guessed, although the guesses of the older subjects were often qualified ("I think," "I'm not sure"). In a further experiment, half the 8-year-olds used the undecidable response category appropriately. Pieraut-Le Bonniec concludes that at around the age of 8, one half or more of children command the three-way distinction: "I know that p," "I know that not-p," "I don't know whether p or not." But it is only at 10 years that most children distinguish "I don't know whether p or not" from "One can't know whether p or not."

It should be noted that unless there is unusually

elaborate explanation, the common response-category-label "can't tell" is ambiguous between "I do not know" and "one cannot know."

The work summarized indicates that one cannot expect an undecidable response category to be understood before age 6, but one can expect it at around age 9 or 10. For intermediate ages, the status of the response is uncertain: It is not clear why Somerville et al. found more comprehension at a younger age than Pieraut-Le Bonniec. A possible reason is that Somerville et al. incorporated more training trials into their procedure than Pieraut-Le Bonniec did. Thus, 6 years may be the age at which children can be readily trained.

Falmagne (1975a) also succeeded in eliciting "undecidable" responses in 6-year-olds. Stimulus materials consisting of colored geometric forms were shown to subjects and then some were placed in an envelope (the subject did not see which ones). One instruction was, for instance, *In this envelope there are only circles.* The subject then judged a series of statements with three possible responses: "True" (e.g., *There is a circle*), "You are lying" (e.g., *There is a green square*), or "Nobody could tell" (e.g., *There is a blue circle*). The response categories were carefully explained and the explanation repeated if necessary. In three experiments, the 6-year-olds tended to use the undecidable category appropriately. Exact figures are not given for two experiments, but in the third about 70% of the undecidable statements elicited the response "Nobody could tell." The purpose of the experiments was not to demonstrate that 6-year-olds could make judgments of "undecidable" (which Falmagne apparently took for granted), but to find out whether the judgments were based on imaging the possible contents of the envelope. Sometimes the stimulus materials contained just two colors, sometimes six or eight. If subjects were mentally envisaging the possible kinds of circles there might be in the envelope, they should take longer to respond when there were six or eight colors than when there were just two. Response latencies were measured. Undecidable statements involving colors (e.g., *There is a blue circle*) did indeed take longer to evaluate for sets with more colors; for undecidable statements not involving color (e.g., *There is a big circle*), there were no differences between the sets nor were there differences for true or false statements. Thus, the evidence is that for the undecidable statements, the subjects ran through the possible kinds of circles relevant to the statement in their minds. They apparently did not do this for the decidable statements, which could be answered by direct deduction: Given

There are only circles, one can answer "false" to *There is a blue square* without envisaging anything in the envelope, but for *There is a blue circle* one has to remember what colors of circles there were in the original set.

Although the studies of Falmagne (1975a) and Somerville et al. (1979) do not require the distinction between the labels "don't know" and "can't know," they do indicate that a useful kind of "can't tell" response can be elicited from 6-year-olds. However, the entire group of studies indicates that there is a response bias against "can't tell" responses that extends well past this age: Errors consist in responses of "true" and "false" to undecidable stimuli, not the reverse.

Some data on the amount of training needed to overcome the bias is provided by Rumain, Connell, and Braine (in press). The subjects (second and fifth graders and adults) reasoned about the contents of some boxes. A variety of simple practice problems were designed to elicit "can't tell" responses. For example, the experimenter read a rule, *If there's a cat in this box there's an apple;* then he looked inside and announced "There's a cat," and then asked, "Is there an orange?" Initially, half the adults and 70% of the child groups answered "No." It required five reinforced problems with this degree of transparency before all the adults were reliably responding "can't tell"; somewhat more reinforced problems were required for the children. However, except for 20% of the 7-year-olds, all subjects did learn. The data indicate that even when they transparently cannot know from the information available, most subjects of all ages start off assuming the experimenter wants a decision of "true" or "false," and they may require several negative reinforcements before they abandon this assumption. In adults, a strong bias against undecidable responses has also been noted for categorical syllogisms (e.g., Dickstein, 1976; Revlis, 1975a).

It is doubtful that a single factor is responsible for the bias; instead, there appear to be a number of influences whose importance probably varies with the task and the age group, for example:

1. In the experience of most subjects, questions asked on tests and by academic authority figures no doubt usually turn out to have been decidable, and "can't tell" responses to be a confession of improper ignorance.

2. Questions asked may have subtle implicatures. For instance, in the example *If there's a cat in this box there's an apple; There's a cat; Is there an orange?*, the responses that were not "can't tell"

were always "no," suggesting that subjects read the first premiss as implicating 'There's just an apple.'

3. Subjects' reasoning strategies are probably geared toward making rather than shelving decisions, and other things being equal, they prefer poorly based decisions to no decision.

4. In syllogisms, subjects may expect more problems to be decidable than actually are. Revlis (1975a) reported that when subjects were informed how often "no valid conclusion" was the correct response, the proportion of error on undecidable problems dropped from almost 80% to below 45% without affecting correctness on decidable syllogisms. However, Dickstein (1976) found that even when this factor was removed, there was still a bias against the response of "no valid conclusion."

5. Subjects probably lack strategies for proving undecidability, so that an undecidable judgment will often be the result of a failed search for a valid conclusion and not the result of directly establishing undecidability. Thus, any error or hastiness will lower the frequency of responses of "undecidable."

Factors (4) and (5) are probably major influences for categorical syllogisms.

PROPOSITIONAL REASONING

We begin with theories of the repertory of kinds of inferences available to educated adults untutored in logic. We then review how the natural connectives are used and understood early in life, the development of competence with various kinds of inference in simple problem situations, the basis of fallacies, how truth judgments are made, and how complexity in propositional reasoning is handled. Finally, we consider the bearing of the evidence on some old philosophical issues.

Schema Models of Natural Propositional Reasoning

Sets of schemas intended to model inferences made in ordinary propositional reasoning have been presented by Osherson (1975a), Johnson-Laird (1975), and Braine (1978). The latter system attempted to improve on the earlier systems—it has much in common with Johnson-Laird's—and is revised in Braine et al. (1981) on the basis of reasoning data. The revised set is shown in Table 2, and it is the basis of discussion here. Before reviewing the empirical work, we discuss some assumptions about the relations between linguistic and logical structure implicit in this kind of model.

Surface Structure, Semantic Representation, and Standard Logical Form

The inference schemas of Table 2 employ a vocabulary of semantic elements: AND, OR, NEG-, F, and IF-THEN. These cannot be equated with the corresponding English words, but they are included in the meanings of most English conjunctions that are not temporal. However, the relations between these elements and surface structure are complex, as a brief survey shows.

Although *and* is no doubt the commonest realization of AND in English, *but* and *although* can be viewed as pragmatically motivated realizations of AND. One says *p but q* instead of *p and q* to countermand an assumed expectation of the hearer that not-*q* or to mark a semantic contrast between parallel expressions in the two clauses (G. Lakoff, 1971; R. Lakoff, 1971; Osgood & Richards, 1973). Braine (1978) suggests that *p* AND *q* is realized as *q although p* when the hearer is thought to expect that *q* would likely not be true when *p* was. Thus, the function of *but* and *although* is to counter presumed hearer expectancies that might hinder comprehension of *and*.

Similarly, most uses of *because* and *so* as well as nontemporal uses of *since* appear to express IF plus special additional entailments (Braine, 1978; von Kutschera, 1974). Thus, the main difference between *John was happy because (since) he got a cookie* and *If John got a cookie he was happy* appears to be that the latter makes no claim about John's actually getting a cookie and becoming happy, whereas the *because*-sentence entails that the event occurred. There is also a sentence form that expresses the same cause-effect relation but assumes that the event did not occur, for example, *If John had gotten a cookie he would have been happy*.

Although AND is often realized as *and,* there are uses of *and* and *or* that do not join propositions and thus cannot be realizations of AND and OR. In surface structure, *and* and *or* can join phrases as well as sentences. Some of these phrases can be regarded as transformationally derived by conjunction reduction from conjoined sentences—for example, *Jane and Jill felt sad* from *Jane felt sad and Jill felt sad* (e.g., Chomsky, 1957; Gleitman, 1965)—*and* can then be taken as realizing AND. However, some phrases clearly cannot be so derived. From *Jane and John are a married couple,* one cannot infer, by Schema N2 of Table 2, that Jane is a married couple because the sentence does not come from *Jane is a married couple and John is a married couple* (Strawson, 1952). See, for instance, Lust and Mervis (1980) for some developmental work on phrasal and sentential conjunction. Nonpropositional usage of *or* occurs in *or*-questions, for example, *Do you want sugar or no sugar in your coffee? Or* here is in principle ambiguous. Interpreted analytically, it could be propositional ('Is it true that you either want sugar or do not want sugar?'), in which case the proper answer is "necessarily yes." Taken in context, however, such questions are always nonpropositional, a request to make a choice, and they do not realize OR. It is as if the semantic representation were like that of a *what*-question (*What do you want in your coffee?*) coupled with an enumeration of the answer set (sugar, no sugar) from which the choice is to be made. We will refer to this as the "choose-one" sense of *or*.

An important difference between AND and *and* has to do with clause order. In logic, *p* & *q* is the same as *q* & *p*. But in English, the order of clauses joined by *and* is often not free, for example, *They got married and had a child ≠ They had a child and got married* (Strawson, 1952). Sometimes *and* is understood temporally, as 'and then,' as noted by Johnson-Laird (1969a) and Staal (1968), and as extensively documented by Fillenbaum (1971, 1974c, 1977), all of whom note that *and* may also be construed causally, as in Morgan's (1975) example *Spiro told a joke and infuriated Paul.*

However, Braine (1978), Grice (1975), Kempson (1975), and Wilson (1975) argue that it is not necessary to postulate a multiplicity of meanings for *and* (i.e., temporal, causal, logical). Grice (who is not without critics, e.g., Cohen, 1971) argues that only one meaning (logical conjunction) is needed for nonphrasal uses, together with the application of some conversational principles, such as "Be relevant" and "Be orderly," so that the narration of events reflects their sequence. The temporal and causal meanings are conversational implicatures. Braine (1978) argues that the ordering constraint comes in the realization of AND in surface structure, that is, when the clauses represent events, their order must correspond to the time order of the events, with causes before effects. *And* is constrained, but not AND.

And and *or* are sometimes pragmatically equivalent to conditionals, notably in pseudoimperative threats and promises (Fillenbaum, 1974b, 1977; Springston & Clark, 1973), for example, *Sit down and I'll scream* is paraphrasable as *If you sit down I'll scream* and *Get out of my way or I'll hit you* as *If you don't get out of my way I'll hit you*. (Of course, ordinary *p or q* has the immediate entailment *If not p then q*.) These uses of *and* and *or* are inherently ordered, and the clause order presumably comes from the implied *if*-statement (i.e., reversing the

order would correspond to an anomalous *if*-statement). On the basis of reaction-time data in adults, Springston and Clark argue that pseudoimperative *p and q* is represented as $p \equiv q$, and *p or q* as $Not\,(p \equiv q)$. The reaction-time data show that the implicated *if*-statement (*If you get out of my way I won't hit you*) is computed just as fast as the more directly intended one (*If you don't get out of my way I'll hit you*). Some languages often use a conjunction compounded of *if* and *not* (e.g., Italian *senno*, French *sinon*) to translate this and similar uses of ordered *or* in English. For instance, Clancy, Jacobsen, and Silva (1976) cite a 2-year-old Italian child saying "No, no via . . . senno lo ovino," which they gloss as 'No, no off . . . or I'll ruin it.' (The child is talking about her new dress, which she wants to take off.)

Because of the differences between surface structure and the semantic representations used in the schemas, it follows that before schemas can be used in reasoning there must be a decoding step in which verbal information is understood in terms of the representations provided in the numerators of the schemas.

AND, OR, NEG- versus &, v, ~. Although AND, OR, etc., in Table 2 are quite similar to the standard logical connectives, there are some formal differences that prevent their identification.

In standard logic, & and v are binary, that is, join only two propositions: *p* & *q* & *r* is either *(p* & *q) & r* or *p* & *(q* & *r)*, likewise *p* v *q* v *r* is either *(p* v *q) v r* or *p* v *(q* v *r)*. AND and OR are taken here as coordinate (i.e., capable of connecting n coordinate propositions) because there is no evidence for binary constituents in the deep structure or semantic representations underlying strings of English propositions joined by *and* or *or* (Gleitman, 1965; McCawley, 1981).

Also, in logic, ~ can be iterated (~*p*, ~~*p*, ~~~*p*, etc.) and used to negate compound propositions (e.g., ~*(p* & *q)*). However, in English, only simple sentences can be negated by adding *not;* compound and already negated propositions are denied by asserting their falsity, that is, by prefixing *It is false (not the case) that*, not by grammatically negating them (Braine, 1978). For this reason, Table 2 uses F (. . .) 'it is false that' to deny negations and compound propositions.

Empirical Work on the Repertory of Propositional Inferences

There are two series of studies. Osherson (1975a) conducted several studies with adolescents to examine the psychological reality of some inference sche-

Table 2.   Inference Schemas of "Natural" Propositional Reasoning (Braine et al., 1981) with Example Inferences

N1.
$$\frac{p_1;\ p_2;\ \ldots\ p_n}{p_1 \text{ AND } p_2 \text{ AND } \ldots \text{ AND } p_n}$$
E.g., There is a "G"; There is an "S" /∴ There is a "G" and an "S"

N2.
$$\frac{p_1 \text{ AND } \ldots \text{ AND } p_i \text{ AND } \ldots \text{ AND } p_n}{p_i}$$
E.g., There is an "O" and a "Z" /∴ There is an "O"

N3.
$$\frac{p;\ \ \ \ \text{NEG-}p}{\text{INCOMPATIBLE}}$$
E.g., There is an "M"; There is not an "M" / INCOMPATIBLE

N4.
$$\frac{p_1 \text{ OR } \ldots \text{ OR } p_n;\ \text{NEG-}p_1 \text{ AND } \ldots \text{ AND NEG-}p_n}{\text{INCOMPATIBLE}}$$
E.g., There is an "R" or a "W"; There is not an "R" and there is not a "W" / INCOMPATIBLE

N5.
$$\frac{\text{F(NEG-}p)}{p}$$
E.g., It is false that there is not a "W" /∴ There is a "W"

N6.
$$\frac{p \text{ AND } (q_1 \text{ OR } \ldots \text{ OR } q_n)}{(p \text{ AND } q_1) \text{ OR } \ldots \text{ OR } (p \text{ AND } q_n)}$$
E.g., There is a "B," and there is an "L" or an "R" /∴ There is a "B" and an "L," or there is a "B" and an "R"

N7.
$$\frac{\text{IF } p_1 \text{ OR } \ldots \text{ OR } p_n \text{ THEN } q;\ p_i}{q}$$
E.g., If there is either a "C" or an "H," then there is a "P"; There is a "C" /∴ There is a "P"

N8.
$$\frac{p_1 \text{ OR } \ldots \text{ OR } p_n;\ \text{NEG-}p_i}{p_1 \text{ OR } \ldots \text{ OR } p_{i-1} \text{ OR } p_{i+1} \text{ OR } \ldots \text{ OR } p_n}$$
E.g., There is a "D" or a "T"; There is not a "D" /∴ There is a "T"

N9.
$$\frac{\text{F}(p_1 \text{ AND } \ldots \text{ AND } p_n);\ p_i}{\text{F}(p_1 \text{ AND } \ldots \text{ AND } p_{i-1} \text{ AND } p_{i+1} \text{ AND } \ldots \text{ AND } p_n)}$$
E.g., It is false that there is both a "G" and an "I"; There is a "G" /∴ There is not an "I"

N10.
$$\frac{p_1 \text{ OR } \ldots \text{ OR } p_n;\ \text{IF } p_1 \text{ THEN } q;\ \ldots;\ \text{IF } p_n \text{ THEN } q}{q}$$
E.g., There is an "F" or an "R"; If there is an "F" then there is an "L"; If there is an "R," then there is an "L" /∴ There is an "L"

N11.
$$\frac{p_1 \text{ OR } \ldots \text{ OR } p_n;\ \text{IF } p_1 \text{ THEN } q_1;\ \ldots;\ \text{IF } p_n \text{ THEN } q_n}{q_1 \text{ OR } \ldots \text{ OR } q_n}$$
E.g., There is an "I" or a "B"; If there is an "I," then there is an "N"; If there is a "B," then there is a "T" /∴ There is an "N" or a "T"

mas he proposed. The set does not include many types of inference modeled in Table 2. He presented reasoning problems consisting of one or more premisses and a conclusion. Subjects judged whether or not the conclusion followed from the premisses and rated the difficulty of the inference. Some of the problems could be solved in one step, by applying one of his schemas; other problems were multistep, requiring the successive application of two or more schemas for their solution. The mean rated difficulties of the multistep problems were correlated with their predicted difficulties, where the predicted difficulty of a problem was the sum of the difficulties of its component steps (obtained from the ratings of the one-step problems). In nine experiments, correlations between the obtained and the predicted mean difficulties ranged from .54 to .90. Although these correlations are fairly high, the work has problematic aspects. First, high correlations mean only that whatever inferences were used to solve the one-step problems are included in those used to solve the multistep problems—not that these inferences are the ones in Osherson's set. Second, for several of Osherson's schemas, when they are embodied in problems involving no reasoning step other than the schema itself, an unusually large number of subjects (sometimes more than half the sample) did not believe that the conclusion follows from the information given. Although Osherson did not seem perturbed by this fact, it suggests to us that these schemas are not basic inference principles for subjects.

The other set of studies is by Braine et al. (1981) and examined the schemas of Table 2. Osherson's

Table 2. (Continued)

N12.
$$\frac{\text{IF p THEN q; p}}{q}$$

E.g., If there is a "T," then there is an "L"; There is a "T" /∴ There is an "L"

N13.   Given a chain of reasoning of the form

$$\Sigma; \{p\}$$

- - - -

- - - -

q

One can conclude: IF p THEN q

N14.
$$\frac{*}{\text{p OR NEG-p}}$$

N15.
$$\frac{*}{\{p\}}$$

N16.   Given a chain of reasoning of the form

$$\{p\}$$

- - -

- - -

INCOMPATIBLE

One can conclude: NEG-p

N17.
$$\frac{\text{IF p THEN q; IF q THEN r}}{\text{IF p THEN r}}$$

E.g., If there is a "J," then there is a "Q"; If there is a "Q," then there is a "D" /∴ If there is a "J," then there is a "D"

Where there are subscripts, *i* indicates any one of the subscripted propositions. In N5 and N9, F(. . .) indicates that . . . is false. (NEG-p and Fp are semantically equivalent, but NEG- is restricted to simple propositions—see Braine, 1978, for fuller elucidation.) In N13, Σ is starting information (e.g., premises); in N13, N15, and N16, the braces mark *p* as a supposition. Thus, N13 says that if *q* can be proved from the supposition *p* and the premises Σ, one can conclude *If p then q;* N16 says that a supposition leading to an incompatibility is false. In N14 and N15, the asterisk indicates that the denominator can be introduced at any point in an argument. Thus, N15 allows a supposition to be made at any time. (Anything proved with a supposition is itself a supposition, except as provided for in N13 and N16.) The order of conjuncts and disjuncts and of the propositions in numerators is immaterial. The example inferences are mainly from Braine et al. (1981)—subjects reason about letters on an imaginary blackboard. We do not give examples of N13 to N16 because they can occur only in combination with other schemas. The use of N14 is exemplified in the first step of the solution of Problem 4 in Table 1 to postulate *There is an "F" or there is not an "F."*

(1975a, 1976) general methodology was used to test Schemas N1 through N13. Problems with direct solutions were given to adult subjects. For each problem, the subjects indicated whether the conclusion was true or false, given the premises, and they rated the difficulty of the problem. The schemas were tested by seeing how well the rated difficulty of a problem could be predicted from the sum of the difficulty weights of the component mental steps needed to solve it plus some independently measured difficulty contributed only by problem length. One set of data was used to estimate difficulty weights for each schema. Using these weights, the predicted difficulties were found to correlate well ($r = .91$) with the subjective difficulties as rated by the subjects. Cross-validation with new subjects and a partially new set of problems yielded an equally high correla-

tion with no new estimation of parameters. Other measures of problem difficulty (errors, and a latency measure) were also well predicted. Moreover, subjects almost never rejected conclusions that followed in one step from the premises according to the schemas of Table 2. Osherson's (1975a) data were shown to be consistent with Table 2; in the few places where Johnson-Laird's (1975) system differs materially from Table 2, the data supported Table 2.

In the work of Braine et al. (1981) the main data analyses focused on Schemas N1 through N13 because N14 through N16 are only used in indirect reasoning. However, N14 was found to be used by all the subjects. The data for N16 were less clear, and we return to them when we discuss the reductio ad absurdum reasoning strategy. In general, these schemas undoubtedly constitute the best current hypothesis about the repertory of elementary propositional inferences available to adult subjects untutored in logic.

The Use and Comprehension of Connectives

Negation, and *and, but, or, because* and *if* (and their translation equivalents in other languages studied) are usually present by about 3 years of age. See, for instance, Bellugi (1967), Bloom (1970), Klima and Bellugi (1966), McNeill and McNeill (1973), Pea (1980a, 1980b), and Wode (1977) on the development of negation; and Bates (1974, 1976), Bloom, Lahey, Hood, Lifter, and Fiess (1980), Clancy et al. (1976), E. V. Clark (1970, 1973), Ferreiro and Sinclair (1971), Hood and Bloom (1979), Hood, Lahey, Lifter, and Bloom (1978), Kuczaj and Daly (1979), Lust and Mervis (1980), and Werner and Kaplan (1963) for the conjunctions. *And* appears first and is the most frequent conjunction used by children; *or* is later and rarer. In E. V. Clark's (1970) preschoolers *because* and *when* were next in frequency after the "and" connectives (*and, and so, and then*); *because* is used more often than *if*.

Propositional and nonpropositional uses both appear early. Bloom (1970) notes that negation occurs in rejections (*no bed* 'I do not want to go to bed') as well as denials (e.g., *No David fun play* 'David is not fun to play with'). Alongside propositional uses, *and* may be used to enumerate objects and *or* used in the choose-one sense (Johansson & Sjolin, 1975).

In their longitudinal study, Hood et al. (1978) called the first use of *and* "concomitance"; no meaning is conveyed by the clause order, for example, *I'm sitting here and you can sit there* or *Now you drive and I be waiting over here*. Somewhat later, the combination of the two clauses conveyed causality (e.g., *She put a band-aid on her shoe and it maked it feel better*) or antithesis (e.g., *That train broke down and dis train did not broke down*). Clancy et al. (1976) found a similar sequence in four languages. E. V. Clark (1970, 1973) and Ferreiro and Sinclair (1971) noted that *and* is used in the first descriptions of temporal sequence.

Clancy et al. (1976) and other work cited below call a relation "conditional" if it could have been sensibly expressed using *if* and call it "causal" if it could have been sensibly expressed with *because* or *so* (or their equivalents in other languages). Used this way, "causal" includes both physical cause-effect relations and cases in which one clause states a motive or reason for the other, for example, *Qua fatta bua/duto pe terra* 'here made hurt, fell on

ground,' *I can't do it/I not big enough* (Clancy et al., 1976), *Get another one/it dirty, It's gonna cut you/let's get away from it* (Hood & Bloom, 1979).

Clancy et al. found that both causality and conditionality appeared at roughly 2 or 3 years of age in children learning to speak English, Italian, German, and Turkish, with causality appearing somewhat earlier than conditionality. Many early child utterances that "express causality" contain no connective, as in the examples just cited. Sometimes *and* is used, in which case the order of clauses is always cause before effect, for example, *I gonna step in the puddle with sandals and get it all wet* (Hood et al., 1978). Like adults, children also often use *when* to express conditionality. Hood and Bloom (1979) found that whether 2- and 3-year-olds acquired *because* or *so* first depended on the particular clause order a child used before the acquisition. Children whose causal statements had the clause containing the cause or reason before the effect used *so* first and *because* later; those with the cause or reason second acquired *because* before *so;* those with no clause order predominating used *because* and *so* at about the same time.

The most frequent semantic relation that *because* expresses for young children is psychological motivation, the *because*-clause giving a motive or reason, for example, *I want this doll because she's big* (Limber, 1973) or *I'm blowing on this cause it's hot* (Hood et al., 1978), (see Hood & Bloom, 1979, for further content analysis). The use of *because* to express entailment (e.g., *It's a boat because it hasn't any wheels*, Piaget, 1928) comes later (Corrigan, 1975; Piaget, 1928).

Comprehension of *and* and *or* has been tested by asking children to obey commands of the form *Do A and do B* and *Do A or do B* (Beilin & Lust, 1975; Johansson & Sjolin, 1975). Subjects have also been asked to indicate which items of a set satisfy a description like *birds or black* (e.g., Hatano & Suga, 1977; Johansson, 1977; Neimark, 1970; Neimark & Slotnick, 1970; Nitta & Nagano, 1966; Suppes & Feldman, 1971). Some comprehension of *and* was shown by 2-year-olds, and most 4-year-olds knew to obey *or*-commands by doing one of the things requested. On the other hand, *or* as set union (e.g., *all figures that are blue or square* construed to mean 'all the blue figures and all the squares') is much more difficult and is rare before late childhood.

The development of understanding of the contrasts marked by *but* has been studied by Hutson and Shub (1975). Subjects first-grade through adult completed sentences with *but* or *and* for three types of sentences: (1) identical (e.g., *Mr. Green is rich *[and/but] his son is rich/poor*), (2) related (e.g., *Mr. Green is rich [and/but] he has a shiny new car/rusty old car*), and (3) unrelated (e.g., *Mr. Green is rich [and/but] he is tall/short*). What emerged was a developmental trend from a period in which *and* was selected in all sentence types to a stage where similarity of clauses was indicated by *and* and contrast was indicated by *but;* in a final stage, *but* was not used for the contrasts of the unrelated sentences. Katz and Brent (1968) found a similar developmental trend: Comprehension was poor in the first grade, fair in the sixth grade, and perfect only in adults. They also studied *although* and obtained an identical developmental pattern.

An interesting series of comprehension studies has explored conditionals. Amidon (1976) asked 5-, 7-, and 9-year-olds to control a car according to instructions that included *You move the car if the light comes on* (or . . . *does not come on*). All age groups could follow this instruction. However, the task does not demand understanding of the difference between *The light comes on if you move the car* and *You move the car if the light comes on.* Consequently, it only indicates appreciation that *if* expresses a contingency, not a grasp of its directionality.

Amidon also investigated *unless* with the same procedure and obtained worse-than-chance performance in all age groups. The children missed the negative component of *unless* and systematically misinterpreted it as *if.*

Emerson (1980) investigated children's comprehension of *if* by asking them to judge the acceptability of *if*-sentences. *If* was sometimes attached to the wrong clause, for example, *If it starts to rain, I put up my umbrella, I put up my umbrella if it starts to rain* versus *If I put up my umbrella, it starts to rain, It starts to rain if I put up my umbrella;* the latter two sentences were referred to as "silly." The children were asked to correct the silly sentences to make them sensible and to change the sensible sentences to make them silly. Differentiating between the sensible and anomalous sentences would mark that *if* had become directional, the *if*-clause indicating the cause or condition and the other clause the consequence. Emerson concludes that the differentiation appears at about 7 or 8 years of age. However, her criterion appears overly severe—the 5-year-olds made correct judgments (though not changes) of silly and sensible sentences about 75% of the time, with better performance for the order *if p, q* than *q if p.* By 6 years of age, the children made both correct judgments and changes of both types of sentences over 60% of the time.

The "sensible/silly" method has also been used to investigate children's comprehension of *because* (Corrigan, 1975; Emerson, 1979, Expt. 2; Johnson & Chapman, 1980). Emerson (1979) concluded that full comprehension of *because* does not develop before 8 years of age and Johnson and Chapman (1980) place it as late as 11 to 12 years of age. However, the criterion of mastery is again problematic. The reason these investigators place the development late appears to be that they used a high criterion: In all the studies, the 6- or 7-year-olds made correct judgments of both the correct-order and reversed-order sentences 60% or more of the time. Kuhn and Phelps (1976) obtained somewhat earlier success with their method: They showed children a picture and asked them to choose the sentence that best described the picture, *A because B* versus *B because A.* They found that 82% of the choices made by the 6- and 7-year-olds were correct.[6] Similarly, Katz and Brent (1968) found a large majority of first graders preferred a sensible *because*-sentence to no connective, and they rejected a silly one in favor of the corresponding sentence with *and.* The reason the last two studies obtained earlier evidence of mastery is probably that judging which of two alternative sentences is the more sensible is easier than judging a single sentence as sensible or silly.

Emerson (1979) and Emerson and Gekoski (1980) used four other tasks to investigate children's comprehension of the directionality of *because* and *if.* In all of these, comprehension was found to occur later than in the work reviewed so far. In one task, called the Picture Sequence Task, children were given *if* and *because* sentences that were reversible (i.e., *if* and *because* could attach to either clause without anomaly). For each sentence, the child was shown two three-frame cartoon strips, one picture sequence corresponding to the direction of causation of the presented sentence and the other to that of the reversed sentence. Children did not select the correct one reliably until 8 years of age.

In another task, children had to put two pictured events in order, to match a sentence with *because.* The children tended to ignore the directionality of *because* and used an order-of-mention strategy, that is, they put the picture representing the first-mentioned clause first.

Emerson's third task presented sentences of the form *X because Y* and *X if Y.* For each *X because Y* sentence, children judged whether it meant the same as the corresponding sentences *X then Y* (same order of mention, meaning different) and *Because Y, X* (structure different, meaning the same). Similarly, for each *X if Y* sentence presented, children judged its equivalence to sentences *X so Y* (same order of mention, meaning different) and *If Y, X* (structure different, meaning the same). For both the *because/ then* and *if/so* sets, most children at all ages judged sentences that were structurally different but had the same meaning as "same"; however, sentences that were structurally similar but different in meaning were correctly judged as "different" more than half the time only by 9- to 10-year-olds. One might conclude from this task that the young children had a "same" response bias and that it is only by 9 to 10 years of age that children appreciate the meanings of *because* and *if*. However, the task makes noteworthy memory demands: The child must, in succession, extract the gist from two complex and potentially confusable sentences and then make a similarity judgment.

In the fourth task, children first chose picture sequences to represent each of two sentences (as in the picture-sequence task described above), and then they judged whether the sentences were equivalent in meaning, as in the third task. The two sentences had the same connective and meaning but a different structure (e.g., *X if Y/If Y, X; X because Y/Because Y, X*) or parallel structure but different connectives and meaning (e.g., *X because Y/X then Y; X if Y/X so Y*). Responding was random for 6- and 7-year-olds. For 8-year-olds, a majority of judgments were correct; for the older children, performance was somewhat better, although there were still many errors, especially for *if*. There was a tendency across age to judge sentences as equivalent.

It is apparent that the tasks that have been used to test comprehension of *because* and *if* vary widely in difficulty, and it seems to us that many of them make cognitive demands over and above comprehension of the connectives (e.g., memory demands, conventions for representing order of events in cartoon strips). These demands could be the cause of many of the difficulties. Nevertheless, the work as a whole suggests that comprehension of the directionality of *because* and *if* develops relatively late and may extend into the school years.

The results present a striking contrast to the work previously summarized on spontaneous speech. Bloom et al. (1980), Clancy et al. (1976), Hood and Bloom (1979), and Hood et al. (1978) found that even 3-year-olds overwhelmingly put the connectives in the right place in their spontaneous speech. Directionality errors are characteristic of comprehension tests not of speech. The discrepancy is puzzling.

Hood and Bloom (1979) explained the discrepancy by noting that the comprehension studies in-volved physical causality, whereas the children's spontaneous talk was about intentions and motivational reasons. However, Corrigan (1975) found that even for such psychological content, it was not until 6 years of age that a majority of children were able to correctly judge reversed *because*-sentences as wrong.

Kuhn and Phelps (1976) remarked that a child might produce correct sentences with *because* as a result of hearing these often from adults, yet might not be sensitive to the directionality of *because* and do poorly on comprehension. Emerson (1980) makes the same proposal for *if*. This explanation also seems quite implausible, that is, unless the spontaneous *because* and *if* utterances are rote imitations, the children must have a linguistic rule that locates *because* and *if* in the right clause. In principle, any such rule could provide a basis for anomaly judgments like those of the comprehension tasks. It is extremely unlikely that all the *because* and *if* utterances observed by Hood, Bloom, Clancy, and their co-workers were rote learned.

There would seem to be three directions to look for an explanation. First, there are other examples in which children appear to fail to use ordering rules in comprehension that they use in production (Chapman & Miller, 1975)—presumably because the plausibility strategy used in comprehension preempts other possible strategies that use sentence structure. Second, there could be some not-yet-understood basis (other than rote copying) for the correct early productions that would not be useful in comprehension. Third, the comprehension tasks that test the directionality of *if* and *because* use metalinguistic judgments (and some make other cognitive demands as well), and the difficulty could lie in the metalinguistic attitude demanded.

Development of Simple Inferences and Fallacies

Conditional Syllogisms

We consider first the development of performance on the classical problems involving *if:* Modus Ponens, Denying the Antecedent, Asserting the Consequent, and Modus Tollens (see Table 3). Modus Ponens is N12 in Table 2. Problems involving it have been found to be the easiest of those of Table 2 and can be solved by 6-year-olds; Denying-the-Antecedent and Asserting-the-Consequent problems are the most difficult, and children have almost always fallen into these fallacies (Ennis, 1971; Ennis & Paulus, 1965; Hill, 1961; Kodroff & Roberge, 1975; Miller, 1969; O'Brien, 1972; O'Brien & Shapiro, 1968; Roberge 1970, 1972; Ru-

Table 3. The Standard Conditional Reasoning Problems

Problem Name	Major Premiss	Minor Premiss	Question	Response Alternatives
Modus Ponens	If p then q	p	q?	True, false, undecidable
Denying the Antecedent	If p then q	not-p	q?	True, false, undecidable
Asserting the Consequent	If p then q	q	p?	True, false, undecidable
Modus Tollens	If p then q	not-q	p?	True, false, undecidable

main et al., in press; Shapiro & O'Brien, 1970; Staudenmayer & Bourne, 1977; Taplin, 1971; Taplin, Staudenmayer & Taddonio, 1974). Adult performance has varied considerably among studies, for example, Shapiro (cited in Wason & Johnson-Laird, 1972) found 20% to 25% of her subjects falling into the fallacies, whereas Taplin and Staudenmayer (1973) reported 80% to 85%. It is not clear how far the variation is due to differences in problem content (as Falmagne, 1980, would expect), in manner of presentation of problems, or in subject populations.

Legrenzi (1970) provided evidence for the influence of one kind of content—situations in which the clauses of the conditional each refer to one of only two possible states of affairs, for example, *If the switch is up the light is on.* Then, the invited inference *If the switch is down the light is off* seems particularly compelling. Rips and Marcus (1977) varied the structure of this type of situation and found that the construal of *if* is controlled by the subjects' beliefs about the nature of the correlation between the states of affairs referred to.

The usual explanation offered for children's falling into the fallacies is that they interpret the connective in the major premiss as the biconditional—*if* would mean 'if and only if' to children (e.g., Matalon, 1962; Peel, 1968; Sternberg, 1979; Taplin et al., 1974; Wildman & Fletcher, 1977). Knifong's (1974) suggestion that children use "transductive logic" in conditional reasoning seems basically similar to the biconditional explanation. The concept of transduction appears to mean that the events or states of affairs represented by the two clauses are viewed simply as going together—both present or both absent. This explanation implies that children's lexical entry for *if* does not distinguish necessary from invited inferences. An alternative explanation is that children do distinguish necessary and invited inferences but accept the invited inferences on the classic problems because they lack analytic comprehension skills. To decide between these explanations, Rumain et al. (in press) used the fact that necessary

inferences cannot be countermanded without contradiction, whereas invited inferences can be. In one experiment, 10-year-olds and adults reasoned about cards with a letter on their top half and a number on their bottom half. The classic problems were presented in two forms. In one form, the major premiss was a simple *if-then* sentence (e.g., *If the bottom has 3, then the top has R*). In the other form, the invited inferences were countermanded by adding *But if the bottom doesn't have 3, then the top may have R or it may have some other letter; and if the top has R, then the bottom may have 3 or it may have some other number.* The expanded major premiss raised the number of "can't tell" responses on the fallacies very significantly for both children and adults, indicating that the invited inferences can be countermanded. On the biconditional explanation, children should find the expanded premisses contradictory and be confused—but they were not.

The countermanding of the invited inferences was merely implicit in a second experiment in which 7- and 10-year-olds and adults reasoned about the content of some boxes. In half the problems, the major premiss was presented as a set of three rules, e.g., *If there's a cat in the box, then there's an orange in the box; if there's a dog in the box, then there's an orange in the box; if there's an elephant in the box, then there's a banana in the box.* The inference invited by the first conditional (*If there isn't a cat there isn't an orange*) is countermanded by the second conditional. Consequently, subjects able to do so should reject the invited inference. The findings were that performance improved markedly with the presence of the three-rule major premiss and was barely distinguishable from adult performance, indicating that most 7-year-olds could distinguish necessary from invited inferences. Thus, in both experiments the evidence was that children's lexical entry for *if* is not the biconditional. In sum, Modus Ponens is available at an early age and developmental differences on the fallacies have to do with whether the invited inferences are accepted or not.

Let us now turn to Modus Tollens, a fourth type

of problem in Table 3. It, like Modus Ponens, is a valid inference, but performance on Tollens is usually poorer than that on Ponens (e.g., Ennis, 1976; Kodroff & Roberge, 1975; O'Brien, 1972, 1973; Rumain et al., in press; Taplin et al., 1974). The common adult error is to respond "undecidable," for example, Shapiro (cited in Wason & Johnson-Laird, 1972) found that half of her adult subjects erroneously responded "can't tell." Children generally make more correct responses on Tollens than adults (e.g., O'Brien & Overton, in press; O'Brien & Shapiro, 1968; Rumain et al., in press; Shapiro & O'Brien, 1970; Wildman & Fletcher, 1977). Falmagne (1980) has reported that children's responses on Tollens can be improved by training, and especially, their generalization across different kinds of content increased.

In the absence of training, there are three levels of sophistication in responses to Tollens. First, children's correct "false" responses to Tollens problems usually result from assuming that the states of affairs represented by p and q are either both present or both absent. The same process, of course, is involved in the fallacies, and anyone (child or adult) who accepts the invited inferences would be expected to respond "false" on Tollens. The intermediate level is represented by subjects who reject the invited inference but who do not find a line of reasoning that determines a response; they respond "can't tell." Typically, subjects justify the response by explaining that the major premiss does not say what p will be if q is false—it only says what q will be if p is true. This increase in sophistication results in an increase in the number of "can't tell" responses and, therefore, in an increase in the number of errors. At the most sophisticated level, subjects find a line of reasoning, a reductio ad absurdum argument (Wason & Johnson-Laird, 1972), and correctly respond with "false." As typically verbalized, the line of reasoning has the form "If p were true q would be; but it isn't, so p is false," that is, the assumption that p is true leads to a contradiction with the minor premiss, therefore, the assumption must be wrong.

In the experiments of Rumain et al. summarized above, the countermanding of the invited inference caused an increase in "can't tell" responses on Modus Tollens. This change can be interpreted as due to a movement of responses from the lowest to the intermediate level of sophistication—one would expect that blocking the invited inferences should cause such a shift. Thus, children's responses to Tollens are ordinarily at the lowest level of sophistication, and adults' responses represent a mixture of all three levels.

The difficulty of Modus Tollens is related to the directionality of if. Modus Tollens becomes much easier relative to Modus Ponens when the major premiss has the form p $only$ if q instead of If p $then$ q. Although these two forms are analyzed by logicians as having the same truth conditions and as leading to the same inferences, they do not have the same meaning because they differ in directionality: If p $then$ q carries the hearer from information about p to information about q, whereas p $only$ if q can be paraphrased as If not q, $then$ not p, and this tends to reverse the directionality, moving from information about q to information about p (Braine, 1978; McCawley, 1974, 1981). The directionality of if and the change of directionality caused by $only$ allow one to predict that when a major premiss has the form If p $then$ q, Modus Tollens should be more difficult (e.g., more errors and longer latencies) than Modus Ponens; on the other hand, for the form p $only$ if q, Tollens should become relatively easier than Ponens. Evans (1977) found that adults made more correct responses on Tollens problems when the major premiss had the form p $only$ if q than If p $then$ q, and more correct responses on Ponens with the latter form than with the former. Braine (1978) also summarizes two studies using error and latency measures that confirmed these predictions.

Other Kinds of Propositional Inferences

We now survey the development of other inference forms, focusing on those of Table 2. In each case, we primarily consider studies where correct responses depend only on command of the inference form. Complexity in reasoning is considered later.

Schemas N1 and N2 are so manifestly simple that both are likely to be available very early. Schema N1 dictates that the form p and q should be considered true when both p and q are true. That the truth of p and q is incompatible with either or both p and q being false follows from Schema N2 taken with N3. In fact, as we review later, none of these truth judgments pose any difficulty to children.

It is convenient to discuss N3 jointly with N14. Schema N3 says that a proposition and its negation cannot both be true, and N14 says that one of them has to be true. In a study of Osherson and Markman (1975), the experimenter concealed a chip and said sentences like The $chip$ in my $hand$ is $white$ and it is not $white$ or $Either$ the $chip$ in my $hand$ is $yellow$ or it is not $yellow$. Subjects were to evaluate each statement by saying "true," "false," or "can't tell." Second graders and even most of some sixth graders did not treat the statements as contradictions and tautologies, respectively. The dominant response was "can't tell." However, this response could mean that the subjects thought they were being asked to decide whether or not the chip was the color mentioned. Because the chip was concealed, it would be natural for the subjects to say they could not tell. They may have assimilated the statements to *or*-questions, which are usually requests to make a choice. We (1981) changed the procedure by having two puppets. One said of a closed box "There's a dog in the box" and the other "There's no dog in the box." The subjects were asked, first, whether both puppets could be right, then, whether one of them had to be right. Three quarters of the 5- and 6-year-olds and essentially all the older subjects said that both puppets could not be right, suggesting that Schema N3 is available to kindergartners.

Responses were more equivocal to the question whether one of the puppets had to be right. There was no automatic short-latency "yes" response. Although a clear majority of subjects 7 years of age and older either responded "yes" or argued themselves into a "yes" response in an inquiry following the task, some subjects thought that both puppets could be wrong because "there might be 'other things' in the box." (!) The main use of N14 is in a certain type of indirect reasoning that, as we review later, is rare among young children; N14 is probably not part of early reasoning competence.

Schema N4 states that an *or*-statement is incompatible with the falsity of all its clauses—in effect, that an *or*-statement is false if all its clauses are false. When discussing truth judgments later, we note that this is the one truth condition for *or*-statements that all subjects, down to 5- and 6-year-olds, are clear about (Braine & Rumain, 1981; Paris, 1973).

There are two lines of evidence on Schema N5 (canceling a negative). First, as discussed later, models of sentence verification (e.g., Carpenter & Just, 1975) assume that canceling a negative is involved in evaluating true negative sentences; this is a task that a majority of 6-year-olds can do (Slobin, 1966). Schema N5 was also investigated in unpublished work of Rumain in which a puppet said of a closed box that there was no apple in it; the experimenter then peeped inside and said that the puppet was wrong. A fifth of the kindergartners and 90% of the 10-year-olds gave responses indicating that they understood that there had to be an apple. The result suggests that canceling a negative develops in the early school years.

No data are available on young children for Schema N6, but inferences patterned on it are easy for junior high schoolers (Osherson, 1975a), and Braine et al. (1981) found it to be one of the easiest schemas for adults.

We (1981) tested competence on Schemas N7, N8, and N10, using reasoning problems in which the subject had to make an inference about the contents of a closed box. The premises were provided by the experimenter giving the subject some information about what was contained in the box; this was followed by an assistant looking inside the box and giving a hint about what was there, this hint providing the last premiss. Various control problems were presented to control for noninferential responses. It was found that all age groups tested, including children of 5 and 6 years, could make the inferences defined by each of these schemas. Hill (1961) also found that inferences patterned on Schema N8 were made by 6-year-olds.

There are no data relevant to Schemas N9 and N11 for children. Schema N12 is Modus Ponens: The data reviewed earlier indicated that it is available to 6-year-olds. Schema N13 is the Rule of Conditional Proof; so far as we know, problems involving it have not been presented to children. This is an unfortunate gap in the literature, because an important aspect of competence with *if* lies in understanding what sort of reasoning is needed to support a conditional. Braine et al. (1981) included many problems involving N13 in work with adults, for whom it proved to be very easy indeed. It may well be available quite early to children.

Schemas N14 through N16 can only occur in combination with other schemas, in what we have called indirect reasoning. We have already discussed N14. N15 is involved in suppositional reasoning and N16 in reductio ad absurdum arguments. These are reviewed later, and it is concluded that there is no evidence for N16 early in childhood and that suppositional reasoning is not part of early reasoning competence.

Transitivity problems (Schema N17) typically provide two premises of the form *If p then q* and *If q then r*, and a conclusion *If p then r*. A quite similar kind of problem provides three premises of the form *If p then q*, *If q then r*, and *p;* the conclusion *r* has to be evaluated. There has been a strange lack of consistency in results. Hill (1961) included nine problems of the second type, some with correct answer "yes" and some with correct answer "no" (e.g., of the form *If p then q, If q then ~r, p/r?*). These were solved by three quarters of Hill's 6-year-olds and larger majorities of her 7- and 8-year-olds. On the other hand, Ennis and Paulus (1965) did not find mastery until subjects were 17 years of age, and Mason, Bramble, and Must (1975) found errors in graduate students. Intermediate results were found by Ennis, Finkelstein, Smith, and Wilson (1969) and Roberge (1970). The late errors are hard to understand. Ennis and Paulus (1965) and Roberge

(1970) used group-administered paper-and-pencil tests, which are liable to be misunderstood because they flout Grice's (1975) cooperative principle discussed earlier; also, they included some items with counterfactual quantified conditionals (e.g., *If an animal is a turtle, then it can fly*) which could be confusing. Perhaps such factors account for the poor performance.

One schema of standard logic that is not included in Table 2 is:

$$\frac{p}{p \text{ or } q}$$

The schema dictates that *or* be taken inclusively. Strawson (1952) comments that once one has established the truth of *p*, it is not natural to infer the weaker statement *p or q*. Subjects also do not find the inference natural: Inferences of this form were rejected as invalid about half the time in Braine et al. (1981); Osherson's (1975a) adolescents also often rejected them even though they had been coached to take *or* inclusively. The schema has not been tested for young children, but the data suggest it is not a schema of natural logic.

In summary, the schemas of Table 2 about which there is developmental evidence appear to divide into two classes: those that develop by or during the first school years and those for which there is little clear evidence until considerably later. The "early" schemas include N1 through N5, N7, N8, N10, and N12. The "late" schemas comprise N14 through N16, which are involved in indirect reasoning. About the others (N6, N9, N11, N13, and N17), there is no information or, in one case, conflicting information; however, these schemas are not tied to complex reasoning strategies, and the first four, at least, pose no difficulty for adults; they could all well turn out to belong to the early group of schemas.

Truth Judgments

Awareness of the truth or falsity of simple affirmative statements comes early. Pea (1980b) found that 30-month-olds—and to a lesser extent even 18- and 24-month-olds—dissented from false affirmatives but not from true ones.

The evaluation of negative statements faces a potential ambiguity. Consider a negative question, for example, *Isn't that a pear?*, or *That isn't a pear?* with rising intonation. If the object is not a pear, the usual English response is *No, that isn't a pear*. The response of *no* is an evaluation of the underlying affirmative, *That is a pear*, as false, not an evaluation of the negative, *That is not a pear*, as true. This

is not the only possible linguistic convention, for example, in Japanese, one would say, *Yes, that is not a pear*, evaluating the negation as true. Similarly, according to the English system, the denial is *Yes, that is a pear*, but according to the Japanese system, it is *No, that is a pear* (Akiyama, 1979; McNeill & McNeill, 1973). Akiyama studied 4-year-old English and Japanese monolingual and bilingual children and found that the English system is easier to acquire and that the bilingual children use the English system to answer Japanese negative questions.

One would expect this dual answering system to create difficulties in making truth judgments of negative sentences. Suppose one is asked to evaluate *This is not a ball*. If the object is a ball, should one say "Yes, it is" or "No, it is"? Pea (1980b) reports this conflict. His 30- and 36-month-olds significantly disagreed with false negative sentences, but their responses to true negatives could not be interpreted.

In a standard paradigm for eliciting truth judgments, a sentence and a picture are presented and the subject has to say whether the sentence is true or false of the picture. In effect, the paradigm demands the Japanese answering system. A common finding is that true negatives are more difficult (in terms of error or latency data) than false negatives (e.g., Chase & Clark, 1972; H. H. Clark, 1974; Clark & Chase, 1972, 1974; Gough, 1966; Just & Carpenter, 1971; Slobin, 1966). Slobin found several 6-year-olds who did not accept any negative sentences as true, but otherwise all his age groups (6 to 20 years of age) were able to make the judgments.

Wason (1965) noted that true negatives are pragmatically most appropriate when the negative is about something unusual or exceptional, that is, a "plausible denial." Using a sentence-completion task, he found that adults responded with a shorter latency when the denials were plausible. De Villiers and Tager-Flusberg (1975) have replicated this effect in preschoolers, after a failure to replicate by Donaldson (1970).

Starting from an idea of Gough (1966), models of how a sentence is judged against a picture have posited that a subject first judges the truth of the underlying affirmative statement against the picture coded propositionally; then, the subject takes account of the negation in the statement (Carpenter & Just, 1975). When the underlying affirmative is true (e.g., *The dots are not red*, when they are), the incompatibility leads to a response of "false"; when the underlying affirmative is false, the falsity is registered and then canceled because of the negation in the proposition to be evaluated. For example, in judging *The dots are not red* against black dots, the underlying *The dots are red* is coded "false," and then "not false" is recoded as "true." Thus, the reason that true negatives are harder is that they involve cancelation of a negative. Thus, if this model is interpreted in terms of the schemas of Table 2, evaluating a false negative involves Schema N3, whereas evaluating a true one involves N5.

Truth judgments for other connectives have been investigated by Paris (1973, 1975) who reports data for *and, both-and, but, or, either-or, if,* and *if and only if.* He presented sentences like *The boy is riding a bicycle and* (*or, if,* etc.) *the bird is in its nest.* A pair of slides accompanied each sentence, for example, one slide showing a boy either riding or not riding a bicycle and the other showing a bird in or not in its nest. Judgments were obtained for each of the four truth conditions (i.e., with slides such that both clauses were true, just one true, and neither true), from subjects second grade through adult. We have used a formally similar procedure to obtain judgments for *or* (Braine & Rumain, 1981), that is, a puppet made statements of the form *Either there's a* (name of an animal) *or there's a* (name of another animal) *in the box,* referring to a box containing toy animals. The subject looked in the box and judged whether or not the puppet was right. The youngest subjects were 5 and 6 years old. Johnson-Laird and Tagart (1969) have investigated adult judgments of *if*-sentences: Sentences like *If there is an A on the left, then there is a 7 on the right* were presented along with cards with various symbols on the left and right of each card. A novel feature of the procedure was that subjects were allowed the response category of "irrelevant" in addition to "true" and "false."

Paris (1973) found that performance with *and, both-and,* and *but* was nearly perfect at all ages. For *or* and *either-or,* all age groups in both relevant studies considered the *or*-statement false when both clauses were false. When one clause was true and the other false, the older children and adults usually considered the statement true. Our younger subjects often said the puppet was partly right and sometimes counted that as wrong; Paris found a similar response tendency in his younger subjects. When both clauses were true, most children considered the *or*-statement true, whereas the adults split—some considered it true and some false, with a slight plurality for false.

It seems that the youngest subjects merely assess the truth of each clause separately; they do not use the meaning of the connective to integrate the two clauses. Thus, an *or*-statement is partly right if one clause is true and wholly right if both are true. Older children (e.g., 9 to 13) usually interpret the connective and give the response pattern for inclusive *or.* The pattern for exclusive *or* appears later, in some of the oldest subjects. However, both studies found that a quarter or more of the adults gave neither the response pattern for inclusive *or* nor for exclusive *or,* but something less intelligible. Thus, it appears that sensible truth judgments for *or* are made later than elementary inferences involving *or* (e.g., N4, N7 through N9), and are not consistently made by all adults.

Paris's (1973) subjects' judgments did not differentiate *if* and *if and only if* at any age. When both antecedent and consequent clauses were true, they considered both conditionals and biconditionals to be true. When the antecedent was false and the consequent true, they usually responded "false." When both antecedent and consequent were false, the younger children responded "false," and the older subjects' responses were split. On the other hand, Johnson-Laird and Tagart (1969) found that adults usually judged conditionals with false antecedents as irrelevant rather than true or false. Paris's subjects did not have this response option.

In general, no subjects treated *if*-statements as having the truth conditions of the truth-functional conditional (see ⊃ in the *Logical Glossary*). Adults apparently prefer not to assign a truth value at all (i.e., regard the statement as irrelevant) when the antecedent is false, and children may well have the same opinion. When subjects are constrained to respond true or false, the younger subjects overwhelmingly assign to both *if* and *if and only if* the truth conditions of conjunction (&); the older subjects split, some assigning the truth conditions of conjunction, some those of the biconditional. It is apparent that the meaning of *if* for subjects is not given by truth conditions.

If the lexical entries for the connectives are given by inference schemas, one would expect that truth judgments that follow immediately from the schemas should appear early and be made consistently. The truth judgments that are given directly by the schemas of Table 2 comprise both judgments of negative sentences (by N3 and N5, as discussed earlier), the truth conditions for conjunction (by N1, and N2 + N3), the fact that an *or*-statement is false when both clauses are false (by N4), and the fact that an *if*-statement is false when the antecedent is true and the consequent is false (by N12 + N3). All these judgments are made by children by age 7 or earlier; older subjects are essentially unanimous about them.

The judgments that appear late or not at all (i.e., the judgments for *or* when one or both clauses are true and for *if* for false antecedents) are those that would require relatively complex and indirect lines of reasoning to reach using the schemas of Table 2.

Braine (1978) argues that native speakers are largely unaware of what can be proved from their inference schemas. Schemas are procedures and are not themselves accessible to introspection. It is the products of reasoning that are accessible—the propositions that are the output of one reasoning step and the input to the next. There is no way that a native speaker can retrieve from long-term memory a neat list of schemas as in Table 2 and then work out the things that a logician could work out given Table 2. Playing metalogician to one's own logic is blocked as a possible psychological activity. In particular, although a truth table for *if* can be proved from the system, the native speaker is completely unaware of it (except only that an *if*-statement must be wrong if the antecedent is true and the consequent false). Judgments and intuitions are, therefore, not conditioned by knowledge of truth conditions for *if*.

Sternberg (1979) reports a fairly elaborate study that demands more than truth judgments, but analyzes the data in terms of coding categories that depend on the truth-table conception of the connectives. He used two kinds of tasks, which he called "encoding" and "combinations." Subjects (second grade through adult) were given statements with *and, or, if, only if, if and only if,* and *not* as the major premiss of problems (e.g., *There is a circle in the box and there is a square in the box, If there is a circle in the box, then there is a square,* etc.). In the encoding task, the subject was then given a statement to evaluate as "true," "false," or "maybe true and maybe false," given the premiss; the statement was always a conjunction of two clauses, of one of the four forms, $p \& q$, $p \& \sim q$, $\sim p \& q$, and $\sim p \& \sim q$, where p states that there is a circle in the box and q that there is a square in the box. The two clauses of these conjunctions were separated in the combinations task: One became the minor premiss (i.e., *There is a circle* or *There is not a circle*) and the other became the conclusion to be evaluated.

Sternberg argues that the encoding task is a comprehension task and that the combinations task involves both the comprehension demanded in the encoding task and reasoning as well. However, it is not clear that one task must involve relatively more comprehension and less reasoning than the other, still less that the mental operations of the encoding task must be included in those of the combinations. For instance, a combinations item presents both the premisses *If there is a circle then there is a square* and *There is a circle,* and it asks the subject to evaluate *There is a square.* The parallel encoding item presents *If there is a circle then there is a square* and asks the subject to evaluate *There is a circle and there is a square.* Here the combinations item is manifestly the more straightforward, that is, it demands only a Modus Ponens inference, whereas the encoding item requires a moderately elaborate chain of reasoning (e.g., "There is a circle or there isn't; If there is, there is a square, and so there are both; If there is not, there cannot be both, so the conclusion could be true or could be false. So the response is 'maybe' ").

Sternberg analyzed the data by seeking to establish the truth function that most closely approximated the way each major premiss connective was interpreted. Each of the possible truth tables predicts a pattern of responses across the set of encoding and combinations problems (assuming all other processing of the problems is done optimally) with which the obtained pattern was compared. *And* was found to have a good fit with & and *or* showed a change from inclusive to exclusive disjunction with age. None of the truth functions fitted *if* well for the second graders; in older children, there was a preference for the biconditional, and the conditional was preferred to the biconditional at the college level. *If and only if* was quite variably interpreted at all ages. Overall, these results resemble those from Paris's truth-judgment task. However, many response patterns appear to have fitted none of the truth functions well, and the wholistic method of analyzing the data conceals some possible bases for responses, for example, bias against the "maybe" response category, imperfect processing of negations, and the like.

Complexity in Propositional Reasoning

Complexity in Direct Reasoning

As we have seen, there are a number of reasoning schemas that are available by around 6 or 7 years of age. At this age, there must exist an elementary reasoning procedure that consists in seeking a schema that can be applied to the available starting information, and then applying it. Complexity in direct reasoning lies in iterating this procedure so that inferences are chained. Osherson's (1975a) youngest subjects were of junior high school age, and they were clearly able to construct chains of a few steps; some such capacity is probably present much earlier.

Difficulty Caused by Negation. Negations are a kind of complexity that has been much studied, although mostly in adults. Negations often cause confusion, but not inevitably; nor is the amount of difficulty proportional to the number of negations present. For instance, in conditional reasoning, a negation in the consequent of the major premiss (*if p then not q*) does not increase difficulty over the unnegated form; a negation in the antecedent does (*if not p then q*), but negations in both clauses are not worse than a negation in just the antecedent (Evans, 1972b, 1977; Roberge, 1971, 1974; Wildman & Fletcher, 1977). In reasoning about alternatives, making inferences from premises like *John is intelligent or he is rich; he is not rich* is slightly easier than making inferences from *John is intelligent or he is rich; he is poor* (which contains no negation), and much easier than making inferences from *John is intelligent or he is not rich; he is rich* (Johnson-Laird & Tridgell, 1972). For reasoning that involves either of Schemas N8 or N9 of Table 2, a negation in just one of the clauses of the major premiss causes more difficulty than a negation in both of them (Roberge, 1976a, 1976b).

It has been suggested that the difficulty arises when a negative has to be denied (Evans, 1972b; Wason & Johnson-Laird, 1972). This could explain difficult cases of Modus Tollens (i.e., *If not p then q, not q, ∴ p* and *If not p then not q, q, ∴ p*) in which a negative assumption, *not p*, has to be denied to reach the conclusion. However, it would not explain the fact that reasoning about alternatives is less confusing when both alternatives are negated than when one is (e.g., *Not p or not q, p, ∴ not q* is less difficult than *Not p or q, p, ∴ q*), since these cases are equal in terms of denial of negations. Wason and Johnson-Laird (1972) also suggest that the confusion has to do with losing track of information; that may well be correct, although lacking in detail.

The Development of Indirect Reasoning Strategies

Indirect reasoning has a point of departure outside the given starting information. There are data concerning two common strategies of indirect reasoning.

One strategy involves positing alternatives a priori: One supposes each alternative in turn and works out its consequences; then Schema N10 or N11 is applied. Commonly, the initial alternatives have the form *p or not p*, obtained via Schema N14. The simplest possible reasoning problem that requires this strategy has two premises of the form *If p then q* and *If not p then q;* the conclusion to be evaluated is *q*. In Braine and Rumain (1981), subjects reasoned about a box and had premises like *If there's a dog in the box there's an orange, If there isn't a dog in the*

box there's an orange; Is there an orange? About half the 10-year-olds and a large majority of adults solved the problems and gave explanations like ''either way there's an orange''; those who failed gave answers of ''can't tell.'' The problems involved just two reasoning steps, Schema N14 followed by N10. We also found that problems involving N10 alone (e.g., *If there's a cat in the box there's some string, If there's a dog in the box there's some string, There's either a cat or a dog*) were solved by most 6-year-olds. Thus, the greater difficulty of the indirect-reasoning problem probably lies in the fact that it has to occur to the child that either there is a dog or there is not a dog.

A question requiring the same kind of reasoning was included in a study of Pieraut-Le Bonniec (1980, Expt 5). There were three objects, one red, one blue, and one wrapped in foil but which could only be red or blue. The child was asked (in effect) whether there had to be two objects of the same color. It has to occur to the child to posit the alternatives, that is, that the unknown is either red or blue. Some of the 9- and two-thirds of the 10-year-olds could do so. Thus, the data from both studies suggest that (given an average Western-world school and class environment) this kind of indirect reasoning strategy probably becomes available to children at around 10 years of age.

The other kind of indirect reasoning involves Schema N16 and leads to a supposition being deemed false because it leads to an incompatibility, that is, a reductio ad absurdum. Braine et al. (1981) included a problem with two premises of the form *If p then q* and *If p then not q:* subjects (adult) had to evaluate *p*. Because the assumption of *p* leads to a contradiction, *p* must be false. One third of the subjects reached this conclusion; most of the others responded ''undecidable.'' Evans (1972a), discussed by Wason (1977) and Wason and Johnson-Laird (1972), attempted to present a structurally similar problem more naturalistically: Little Jeremy asks each of his parents if he may go to the movies tonight with one of his friends, and also asks if he may go for a walk tomorrow with another friend. His father replies *You must either go to the pictures tonight or not go for a walk tomorrow, but not both*. His mother replies *If you go to the pictures tonight, then you must not go for a walk tomorrow*. The subject's problem is to determine what Jeremy must do to obey both his parents. (If Jeremy goes to the movies, he will face incompatible demands from his parents on the morrow. So, his only way of obeying both parents is not to go to the movies tonight.) Only 10 of 24 adult subjects found the reductio ad absurdum solution to the problem; only 2 found it for a parallel problem in which the supposition that led to the incompatibility was negative (so that the difficulty of denying a negative was added to the difficulty of the reductio ad absurdum argument).

Other discussions of reductio ad absurdum have concerned the solution of Modus Tollens problems. Recall that there are three developmentally ordered responses. The least sophisticated is a response of "false" by a subject who accepts the invited inferences and assumes that the events represented by p and q are either both present or both absent. The most advanced is a response of "false" based on a reductio ad absurdum argument ("If p were true, q would have to be also, but it isn't, so p can't be true"). The intermediate response is to reject the invited inference, fail to find the reductio ad absurdum, and respond "undecidable." Over a variety of studies in the literature, the proportion of "false" as a response among adults has varied from 50% to almost 100%, with 75% as a very rough average. However, some of these "false" responses are undoubtedly of the unsophisticated type. Braine et al. (1981) and Rumain et al. (in press) contained problems in which the major premiss countermanded the invited inferences, sometimes implicitly and sometimes explicitly (e.g., using the form *If p then q; but if not p, then q may be true and it may be false*). With the unsophisticated response thus impeded, adults responded "false" 50% to 65% of the time; fifth graders averaged about 50%; however, some of their responses probably had the unsophisticated basis because some children made the Asserting-the-Consequent fallacy despite the countermanding of the invited inferences. A fair summary would appear to be that in maximally propitious circumstances, a half to two thirds of adults and a minority of 10- and 11-year-olds find the reductio ad absurdum solution to Modus Tollens.

As discussed by logicians, the reductio ad absurdum strategy "consists in assuming the contradictory of what has to be proved and looking for trouble" (Quine, 1959, p. 173). We doubt that the subjects in the work reviewed deliberately selected a supposition with the goal of proving it false. Their reductio ad absurdum solutions probably consisted of assuming the antecedent of a conditional in the premises and following out the consequences of that assumption, interpreting the antecedent as false if an incompatibility was discovered. Even so, this way of reasoning appears to be a relatively late development which is not universally available to adults.

Empirical Status of Three Old Philosophical Issues

How Many Truth Values?

The schemas of Table 2 assume that natural logic has just two truth values. A competing view is that there are three. The third value, "neither true nor false," would hold when a presupposition is violated (e.g., Keenan, 1971, 1972; Lakoff, 1970). Thus, statements like the following would have this value:

(8) The present king of France is bald.
(9) Smith is pleased that New York City is in Colorado.

Within such a three-valued logic, some of the inference schemas of Table 2 would have to be modified or given up (e.g., N14 could scarcely be valid). However, there may be more than one way to develop the logic, and that enterprise is fraught with subtle obscurities (cf. Rescher, 1969; McCawley, 1981). It is not clear exactly what modifications to Table 2 would be required. Thus, at present, one cannot resolve the issue of number of truth values empirically by comparing Table 2 with a set of schemas for a logic with a neither-true-nor-false value, to investigate which set best describes the inferences subjects make. Even given such a set of three-value schemas, the test would face problems. For instance, it seems likely that reasoners normally assume that presuppositions are not violated, that is, that the truth value of "neither true nor false" will not apply. In that case, the effective logic would be two-valued. We return to the subject of presupposition later.

The response of "undecidable" does not, of course, constitute a third truth value. It does not deny that a proposition evaluated is either true or false; instead, it assumes that the proposition has one of these values and records the judgment that one cannot know which value.

The Meaning of *Or*

It has been debated since antiquity whether *or* is inclusive ('either . . . or . . . or both') or exclusive ('. . . and not both'). Four points of view are to be found in the literature. The first, expressed by the *Oxford English Dictionary* and by R. Lakoff (1971), is that the meaning of *or* is exclusive. Pragmatically, there is good evidence that *or*-statements taken in context are most often construed as being exclusive by listeners. This is demonstrated, for instance, by the paraphrases listeners give (Fillenbaum, 1974a, 1974b, 1977). However, *or* is not always taken exclusively. It is easy to find *or*-statements that are clearly inclusive, for example, *Either Zorn's lemma or the Axiom of Choice will allow me to prove Exercise 12* (Pelletier, 1977). Also, inferences of the form of N7, or *If p or q then r,∴ If p then r*, are made regularly by subjects (Braine & Rumain, 1981; Braine et al., 1981; Osherson, 1975a) but are not valid for exclusive *or*.

Second, a popular view (especially in textbooks of elementary logic) is that *or* is ambiguous between inclusive and exclusive senses (see Pelletier, 1977, for a list of 24 references). However, if *or* is ambiguous, people should hesitate about making inferences like N7 or about inferring *If p then r* from *If p or q then r*, just as they hesitate about inferring *p or q* from *p*. Yet, the former inferences are regularly made, and the latter inference is often rejected.

The third view, developed by Pelletier (1977), is that the meaning of *or* is always inclusive. When *or* appears to have an exclusive meaning, it is because the possibility of both clauses being true is ruled out or rendered highly improbable by factors other than the meaning of *or*, that is, something in the content or context makes it unlikely, or there is some applicable discourse convention that makes it expected that only one clause holds. In effect, in most circumstances, the presumption, 'not both' is a conversational implicature of an *or*-statement, but it can be readily countermanded. However, this view, like the preceding one, does not provide a satisfactory account of people's lexical entry for *or*. Since Pelletier equates *or* with standard logic v. presumably the entry would either be the truth table or include the schema *p, ∴ p or q*, which is the schema of standard logic that dictates inclusive *or*. Neither of these options is satisfactory because (as reviewed) coherent judgments of the truth of *or*-statements emerge relatively late and are not universal in adults, and *p, ∴ p or q* is not a kind of inference that is regularly made.

A fourth view, proposed by Braine (1978) and adopted here, is that the lexical entry for *or* is not given by a truth table but by the inference schemas involving OR. These do not include *p, ∴ p OR q*. This view agrees with Strawson (1952, p. 91) that this inference is not a "logically proper step." It also agrees with Pelletier (1977) that the common exclusive construal of *or* is the product of context and conversational implicature. It correctly predicts the data reviewed—that inferences involving *or* will emerge earlier than sensible truth judgments for *or*-

statements, and that subjects of all ages will make correct inferences on simple problems more consistently and regularly than they make the truth judgments.

The Meaning of *If*

Argument about the meaning of *if* is as ancient as that about *or*, and more complicated. There are three current approaches. The first is by means of truth tables, the second provides a semantic interpretation in terms of "possible worlds," and the third is a procedural approach which identifies the lexical entry with the inferences that *if* permits.

The Truth-Table Approach. In its usual form in the psychological literature, the truth-table approach regards *if* as ambiguous. *If* may represent the conditional (⊃) of standard logic; alternatively—particularly in children (as we have noted)—it would represent the biconditional (≡) (see the *Logical Glossary* for definition of the truth tables). A third possibility, proposed by Wason and Johnson-Laird (1972), is that *if* can have a defective truth table, that is, *If p then q* is true if both *p* and *q* are true and it is false if *p* is true and *q* false, but it has no truth value when *p* is false.

This approach is criticized in detail by Braine (1978) on the principal grounds that (1) it is ad hoc, in that there is no theory of when one meaning should be applicable and when another; (2) no interpretation is assigned to counterfactual conditionals; and (3) it does not account for the directionality of *if*, that is, that *If p then q* moves from information about *p* to information about *q*. (Thus, inter alia, the approach cannot account for the greater difficulty noted of Modus Tollens over Modus Ponens.)

The "Possible-Worlds" Theory. Philosophical work on modal logic has yielded a very different approach to conditionals. C. I. Lewis (1918; Lewis & Langford, 1932) defined a connective, "strict implication" ($p \dashv q$ p strictly implies q'), in which the consequent is deducible from the antecedent, that is, it is logically impossible for *p* to be true and *q* false. *p* $\dashv$ *q* holds only when the truth of *p* $\dashv$ *q* is a logical necessity, as is the case when *q* can be deduced from *p*. Strict implication has been proposed as a theory of *if* (e.g., Grandy, 1979). However, it cannot provide a satisfactory theory because, as pointed out by Braine (1979a), in most ordinary *if-then* sentences the consequent is not deducible from the antecedent. The relationship can even be arbitrary, as in many psychology experiments (e.g., *If the bottom has 27,* *then the top has Q, If there is a nupittle, then there is a coolt*).

Recently, it has become common to define a semantics for modal logic in terms of "possible worlds" (e.g., Hintikka, 1969; Kripke, 1963). A number of quite similar interpretations of *if* have been proposed within this framework (Kutschera, 1974; D. Lewis, 1973; Stalnaker, 1968). For example, for Stalnaker, *If p then q* is true if and only if *q* is true in the world most similar to this one in which *p* is true; for Kutschera, *If p then q* is true if and only if the worlds that are consistent with *p* being true are included in the worlds that are consistent with the truth of *q*. It is not explicitly claimed that such truth conditions are the native speaker's lexical entry for *if*, but this claim is necessary for such theories to explain the usages and intuitions that they aim to explain. It seems to us that there is room for concern about the strength of the assumptions about the psychological reality of the set of possible worlds that may be required for the logical apparatus to yield its results. Johnson-Laird (1978) remarks that the set of possible worlds is not recursively enumerable so it would not be reasonable to assume that a subject could construct and mentally scan it.

The main goal and achievement of this line of work is to provide a conception of *if* that does not encounter the difficulties with counterfactual conditionals that are suffered by the truth-table approach. However, the *if* that is defined lacks a number of commonly accepted logical properties. Notably, it is not transitive and the schema of conditional proof (N13) is not valid for it. Transitivity has been assumed by investigators (e.g., Ennis, 1976; Johnson-Laird, 1975). The counterexamples to it of D. Lewis (1973) and Stalnaker (1968) do not seem valid (Braine, 1979b), and they offer no direct counterexamples to the schema of conditional proof. There is certainly a good intuitive basis for this schema (Braine, 1979a) and evidence that it is part of adult reasoning competence (Braine et al., 1981).

The trial of the possible-worlds approach in the psychological literature has barely begun, and our comments may be prematurely prosecutorial. So far as we know, Rips and Marcus (1977) is the only psychological work that has tried to make significant use of it.

The Inference-Rule Theory. Braine (1978) proposed that the logical function of *if* is to state inference rules, that is, it is the same as that of the inference line in schemas. For instance, if a parent tells a child *If it rains tomorrow we'll go to the movies*, the parent is warranting the rule:

$$(10) \quad \frac{\text{It rains tomorrow}}{\text{We go to the movies tomorrow}}$$

Thus, *if-then* is "a convenient device that permits inference rules to be supplied ad hoc for the duration of their relevance (usually transient) to any matter at hand" (Braine, 1978, p. 8).

As defined, *if* is manifestly directional, for example, carrying from *It rains tomorrow* to *We go to the movies tomorrow* in Rule 10. The theory also accords with the kind of data that led to the concept of the defective truth table: A rule like *If there is an A on the left then there is a 7 on the right* (Johnson-Laird & Tagart, 1969) would not apply to a card without an A on the left, thus, it is predictable that subjects would classify the rule as irrelevant to such a card.

Of course, it follows immediately from this conception that Modus Ponens is valid for *if*. It is also postulated that the Conditional Proof schema (N13) is valid. In fact, the conception seems operationally equivalent to the claim that the native speaker's lexical entry for *if* is given by these schemas. In particular, Modus Ponens is a procedure for using an *if*-statement and Conditional Proof a procedure for attempting to reach one. Evaluations of counterfactual conditionals are accounted for by assuming that the evaluator tries to use the Conditional Proof schema (see the earlier discussion on *Inference Schemas*).

Comment. It is important to understand that in any logic that has a conditional connective for which both Modus Ponens and Conditional Proof are valid, it will be provable that the connective has the truth conditions of the standard conditional ($\supset$). That is a constraint that logic imposes on any seeker after a theory of *if*.

All three approaches reviewed can be seen as attempts to cope with the counterintuitiveness of the standard truth table. The first does so by multiplying truth tables, and it is manifestly wrong. The second gets rid of the truth table by rejecting the schema of Conditional Proof. This improves predictions of truth judgments, but, not surprisingly, leads to poorer coverage of phenomena that motivated the Conditional Proof schema in the first place. The third approach keeps both schemas but argues that people are not explicitly aware of their schemas as such and cannot, therefore, play metalogician to their own logic; they never work out the truth table, so their judgments are not influenced by it.

Developmental Summary

There is a good deal of evidence that a fairly broad repertory of inferences is (or becomes) available around school-entering age. The early types of inferences comprise many, but not all, of those in Table 2. Although children's ability to chain inferences in direct reasoning has not been studied systematically, some such ability may well arise quite early too. In general, children's logical competence is related to inference schemas, not to truth conditions. The knowledge of truth conditions that children acquire tends to follow, not precede, the acquisition of schemas, and to be confirmed to rather immediate inferences from the schemas.

Certain schemas seem to be tied to indirect reasoning strategies, and the evidence indicates that these and the associated strategies are a later-developing aspect of reasoning skill. Some strategies, like the reductio ad absurdum, seem not to be spontaneously available to all adults.

Not much thought has yet been given to the origin of schemas. We have suggested that the early-developing inferences are probably acquired as part of learning the language. But that merely situates the question; it does not answer it. One who has thought about the matter is Falmagne (1980). She proposes that schemas arise, at least in part, ''from a concept-learning process whereby the child encounters instances of a given pattern of inference . . . , is given feedback either by other speakers or reality . . . and abstracts the logical structure common to those instances'' (p. 182). Falmagne reports some evidence that Modus Tollens (*If p then q, not q, ∴ not p*) can be acquired this way in second- to fifth-grade children. However, Modus Tollens is not one of the early-developing inferences. It would be interesting to know whether this concept-learning explanation can be generalized to the inferences that seem most basic to the meanings of *and, or,* and *if.*

Several aspects of comprehension are worthy of note. Children are sensitive to some discourse properties of *or* and *if* quite early. The inferences invited by *if* seem to be made as early as Modus Ponens. Nevertheless, the classic fallacies can be countermanded in children as young as 7 years old, indicating that their lexical entry for *if* marks only Modus Ponens as necessary. Young children also often confuse the orders *p if q* and *q if p*. This error is found in comprehension only, not in spontaneous speech. It is reminiscent of the conversion errors in categorical syllogisms that we discuss later, and its source has not been established.[7]

Discourse properties of connectives are not always understood early, for example, for *but*, knowledge of the truth conditions precedes comprehension of the discourse properties by several years.

REASONING ABOUT HOW OBJECTS ARE RELATED AND THE PROPERTIES THEY HAVE

No concrete proposals for a natural predicate logic exist yet and so the only logic available as a reference framework for this section is standard predicate logic itself.[8] We begin by reviewing major relevant differences between predicate logic and natural language in linguistic structure and habitual modes of reasoning, and we take a small step in the direction of a natural predicate logic. Next, we review data on the development of comprehension of aspects of linguistic structure that have logical functions. The remaining subsections focus on reasoning—the development of simple kinds of inference of a predicate-logic sort, then on categorical syllogisms and other reasoning studies, ending with work in which hypotheses in the form of quantified sentences are assessed against evidence.

Predicate-Logic and Natural-Language Reasoning Compared

Linguistic Structure and Notation

It is well known that natural languages can express ideas that are not expressible in predicate logic. Briefly, predicate logic is limited to expressing relations among objects that do not depend on how they are conceived by sentient organisms (e.g., many sentences containing *want* or *believe* have no translation). We will not dwell on the differences because we are concerned with reasoning about that large segment of English that is translatable. However, even within the common field of operation, English and logic work in some notably different ways.

Standard predicate logic analyzes propositions into four kinds of elements (apart from parentheses): connectives, quantifiers, predicates, and arguments. The connectives are those of propositional logic and need no further comment. There are two quantifiers: the universal quantifier, $\forall x(. . .)$, 'for every x, . . .', and the existential quantifier, $\exists x(. . .)$, 'for some x, . . .' or 'there is an x such that . . .'.

Predicates may have one argument (monadic predicates or properties) or more than one argument (relations). Very roughly, monadic predicates correspond to English nouns, adjectives, and intransitive verbs, and relations to transitive verbs and prepositions. In discussions of form, it is common to use capital letters (F, G, etc.) as predicates. Arguments are the objects that have the properties or are related by the relations; they correspond to the Noun Phrases (NPs) that are subjects, objects, indirect objects, and so on, of the predicates. The simplest kind of formula consists of a predicate and its arguments. In complex propositions, formulas may be joined by connectives or preceded by quantifiers, or both.

There are three ways of identifying arguments. First, there are names. Second, there are descriptions, which correspond to definite singular NPs that contain enough information to identify an object uniquely, for example, *the author of ''Waverly''* (but not *the man, the book,* etc., which do not uniquely identify out of context). Third, there are variables. Names and descriptions identify an argument directly, by naming or describing it. Variables identify arguments only indirectly. They have a cross-referencing function, that is, a variable occurs in more than one place in a proposition and indicates that the same object is referred to in all occurrences of the variable. For example, in $\forall x\ (Fx \supset \exists yGxy)$ 'For every x, if it is an F, then there is a y such that x bears the relation G to that y' (or, more colloquially, 'The Fs all gee something or other'), the x identifies the first argument of G with the argument of F, and associates it with the quantifier, $\forall$. Although English does not have variables, it has elements (pronouns and definite NPs) that play some of the roles of variables (cf. Quine, 1953a, on pronouns as variables). Thus, parallel to a predicate-logic sequence like $\exists x(Fx \& \ldots x \ldots)$, English typically uses an indefinite NP, *an F,* to correspond to the first occurrence of the variable, and a definite NP or pronoun, *the F* or *he/she/it,* to correspond to subsequent occurrences. The relation of definite NPs and pronouns to their antecedents performs the cross-reference function of variables.

Quantifiers and Scope Cues. As opposed to the two logical quantifiers, there are many quantifying phrases in English, including some that have no counterpart in logic, for example, *only* (Keenan, 1971), and *many, several, few,* and so on. However, these have not been the subject of reasoning studies.

Quite a rich variety of English forms can correspond to the universal quantifier, for example, *all, every, any, each,* and unmodified plural NPs; see Vendler, (1967) for some discussion of differences among these; there are a large number of linguistic articles that include some relevant discussion (e.g., Carden, 1976). There are also many different English forms corresponding to the existential quantifier, for example, the indefinite article and *some.* The English phrases that correspond to a given quantifier often depend in a complex manner on aspects of sentence structure outside the quantifier phrase itself. (Some examples are cited later in discussing cues to the scopes of quantifiers.)

Apart from these matters of vocabulary, there are great differences in form between English and logical notation. In English surface structure, words like *all, every, some,* and so on, are noun modifiers and thus part of the NP in which they occur, that is, in terms of logical structure they are part of the argument phrase. In logic, the quantifier is not part of an argument, it is a separate element outside the predicate and arguments of a proposition. The question arises whether English deep structures and semantic representations retain this formal feature of the surface structure, or whether they are more like the logical representations. The motivation for treating the quantifier as an outside element is that it permits logic to neatly handle differences in the relative scopes of quantifiers and connectives. Consider the following ambiguous English sentence:

(11) The components all pass inspection or the factory discards them.

This could mean 'Each component passes inspection or the factory discards it,' that is, '$\forall x$ (x is a component $\supset$ [x passes inspection v the factory discards x])' or it could mean 'The components all pass inspection or the factory discards them all,' that is, '$\forall x$ (x is a component $\supset$ x passes inspection) v $\forall x$ (x is a component $\supset$ the factory discards x)'.

Some linguists (e.g., Carden, 1976) have thought that English deep structures are like the logical representations in having the quantifier outside the proposition. However, this assumption requires unusual kinds of transformation to yield English surface structure (e.g., Jackendoff, 1968, 1972). Moreover, it is hard to see why a natural language would have surface structures so gratuitously different from its deep structures and semantic representations. On the other hand, there is no accepted way of writing pairs of semantic representations that distinguish the two senses of sentences like 11 while retaining the property that the quantifier is part of the argument phrase in both representations. A natural predicate logic would have to resolve the issue of how the two senses of 11 are to be represented.

Cues to the relative scopes of quantifiers with each other and with negation are often complex and subtle. Moreover, they are often ambiguous, the scopes understood by a reader or listener being determined by plausibility as dictated by context or content. The scope signals are not well understood, except that what follows a logical element in the surface structure is usually within its scope (e.g., Jackendoff, 1968, 1969; Johnson-Laird, 1969a, 1969b). However, there are many factors that can override the order-of-occurrence cue. For instance, suppose a group of boys and girls are playing at camp, and consider:

(12a) The boys (*or* All the boys) hid behind a cabin, corresponding to '$\exists y_{cabin} \forall x_{boy}$ (x hid behind y).'

This contrasts with:

(12b) The boys (*or*, All the boys) hid behind cabins, corresponding to '$\forall x_{boy} \exists y_{cabin}$ (x hid behind y).'

Here, English uses the singular/plural distinction to convey what logic conveys by the position of the quantifier. Or consider the following contrasting pairs.

(13a) Mary doesn't like the boys in her class.
(13b) Mary doesn't like all the boys in her class.
(14a) Mary isn't driving a car.
(14b) Mary isn't driving the car.

In 13a and 13b, if Tom is one of the boys, we can infer *Mary does not like Tom* from 13a but not from 13b. In 14a, Mary could be walking or riding a bike, whereas in 14b, a car is in the action—either Mary is doing something else to it or someone else is driving it. In both cases, the simple, unadorned definite NP, singular or plural, is outside the scope of the negation. This is probably because definite NPs indicate identity with antecedents that are themselves outside the scope of the negation.

Reasoning in Predicate Logic and in English

When predicate logic is formulated with inference schemas, the set of schemas comprises the schemas of propositional logic together with four additional schemas particular to predicate logic. These four are commonly called "universal instantiation," "existential instantiation," "universal generalization," and "existential generalization." Their exact form varies slightly from one textbook of logic to another, but essentially they are as follows. We use the notation $S(x)$ to refer to any condition on an argument variable, x (i.e., to any formula containing one or more occurrences of x)

(15) $\dfrac{\forall x S(x)}{S(a)}$ (universal instantiation)

The schema states that, given that every object satisfies the condition, S, then any object a satisfies the condition, where a names some object, which may be arbitrarily chosen.

(16) $\dfrac{\exists x S(x)}{S(a)}$ (existential instantiation)

Schema 16 states that, given that there is an object that satisfies a condition, S, then one can give that object a name, a, and thus conclude $S(a)$. It is as if one said, "There is such an object, let us call it a." The name chosen must be one that has not previously occurred in the discourse. In a proposition of the form $S(a)$ derived by existential instantiation, a cannot refer to an arbitrarily chosen object, whereas in the case of universal instantiation it may.

The instantiation schemas eliminate quantifiers. For example, from $\forall x \exists y S(x, y)$ one obtains first $\exists y S(a, y)$ by Schema 15 and then $S(a, b)$ by Schema 16; $S(a, b)$ provides a quantifier-free proposition in which a may name an arbitrarily chosen object, but b does not.

(17) $\dfrac{S(a)}{\forall x S(x)}$ (universal generalization)

The schema has the restriction that a must designate an arbitrarily chosen object, that is, it cannot have been introduced by Schema 16. The schema states that, given that an arbitrarily chosen object satisfies a condition, then every object does.

(18) $\dfrac{S(a)}{\exists x S(x)}$ (existential generalization)

The schema states that if a specified object satisfies a condition, then there is an object that satisfies it.

A chain of reasoning in predicate logic has a standard form with three stages: One begins with instantiating, a process that results in propositions that contain no quantifiers; then one reasons, using schemas of propositional logic; finally, one generalizes and regains the quantifiers.

Ordinary reasoning rarely seems to present these three stages. To see what replaces them, let us take an example problem and make an intuitive comparison of predicate-logic and natural reasoning. For some sets, F, G, and H, suppose we are given the premise *All H are either F or G* and asked if it follows that all H that are not F are G.

In predicate logic the reasoning exemplifies the three-stage form:

$\forall x (Hx \supset Fx \lor Gx)$ (premiss)

Let a name an arbitrary object, then

$Ha \supset Fa \lor Ga$ (universal instantiation)

Suppose Ha, then

Fa v Ga   (Modus Ponens: Schema
                  N12 of Table 2)

Also, suppose ~Fa, then

Ga   (Schema N8 of Table 2)

∴Ha & ~ Fa ⊃ Ga (Conditional Proof: Schema
                  N13 of Table 2)

∴ ∀x(Hx & ~Fx ⊃ Gx) (universal generalization)

However, in ordinary reasoning the answer "yes" to the problem seems immediate. Adults we have asked say that the conclusion follows directly. This behavior suggests that they have an inference schema that takes them from premiss to conclusion in a single step. To see what kind of schema this is, we have to consider the schemas of Table 2 in a novel way. Let us take as examples Schema N1 and a modified form of N8 (p OR q / IF NOT p THEN q), that we will call N8′. Let *p* be *Fa* and *q* be *Ga*, where *a* names some object. Then N1 and N8′ become respectively:

$$\frac{Fa; \quad Ga}{Fa \text{ AND } Ga} \quad \text{and} \quad \frac{Fa \text{ OR } Ga}{\text{IF NOT } Fa \text{ THEN } Ga}$$

Now suppose that *a* names an object arbitrarily chosen from a set, α. That is, *Fa* comes by instantiation from a statement that α's are either F or G. Because *a* is arbitrarily chosen, we can generalize the conclusion to all objects of α. If we leave out the intermediate steps, that is, just consider the premiss before the instantiation and the conclusion after the generalization, we arrive at schemas that we can represent informally as follows:

N1 (modified) $\dfrac{\alpha\text{'s are F; } \alpha\text{'s are G}}{\alpha\text{'s are both F and G}}$

N8′ (modified) $\dfrac{\alpha\text{'s are either F or G}}{\alpha\text{'s that are not F are G}}$

These schemas collapse the three steps into one. N8′ (modified) solves the problem cited above in one step, with α = H. Such schemas explain why the instantiation and generalization steps are not apparent in subjects' reasoning.

If *F* and *G* above name properties or classes, the schemas could be expressed as Boolean class schemas, for example, N1 (modified) could be expressed as:

N1 (twice modified) $\dfrac{\alpha \subset F; \alpha \subset G}{\alpha \subset F \cap G}$

In fact, however, these kinds of inference are not confined to class and property statements. For in-

stance, from *Either the cars have stickers or the guards have them towed away,* one can infer *The guards have the cars that don't have stickers towed away.* The inference has the form of N8′ (modified), although the predicates corresponding to *F* and *G* are relations ('have stickers,' 'cause to be towed away'), and one of the relations has an embedded equivalent of an existential quantifier (*the cars have stickers* means 'for each car there is a sticker').

Inference forms that can be derived from propositional schemas N1 through N12 in the manner described above are shown as PL1 through PL12 in Table 4,[9] using a somewhat ad hoc notation (see table footnote). It may be noted that PL12, the analogue of Modus Ponens, is a version of Universal Instantiation. The last two schemas of Table 4, PL13 and PL14, are not derived from the propositional schemas but are relevant to some of the work reviewed later. PL13 is a version of Existential Generalization. PL14 describes inferences from negative phrases like *none, not . . . any,* and *no* + NP.[10] We will call it "negative instantiation."

It seems a plausible hypothesis that the kinds of inferences summarized in Table 4 constitute an important part of natural predicate logic.

Comprehension of Logical Structure

Articles, Pronouns, and Reference Making

There is evidence that by the end of the second year, many children distinguish names of individuals from class terms and use the presence or absence of articles as a cue to the distinction. Thus, for a doll introduced by the locution *That's a gav,* followed by subsequent references to *the gav, gav* was usually taken as indicating a type of doll, whereas if it was introduced by *That's gav* followed subsequently by *gav,* the term was more often taken as a name of the individual doll (Katz, Baker, & Mac-Namara, 1974).

The two most common uses of the indefinite article are to mark predicate nouns (as in *That's a . . .*), and to indicate indefinite reference to one of a kind. There is much evidence that the use to mark predicate nouns is mastered first and mastered very early (e.g., Bresson, 1974; Brown, 1973; Karmiloff-Smith, 1979). For indefinite reference, children tend to overuse the definite article, at least until around the age of six or seven (Bresson, 1974; Karmiloff-Smith, 1979; Warden, 1976). One reason for this overuse appears to be a preference for a specific description, for example, instead of saying just *a car,* a preschooler may say *the red car with a little scratch on the side* (Karmiloff-Smith, 1979).

The definite article is used to refer to a specific object that has been previously identified lin-

Table 4. **Some Possible Inference Schemas of Natural-Predicate Logic**

PL1.	$\dfrac{S_1[\alpha];\ S_2[\alpha]}{(S_1\ \text{AND}\ S_2)[\alpha]}$	E.g., The blocks are new; Grandpa brought the blocks /∴ The blocks are new and Grandpa brought them.
PL2.	$\dfrac{(S_1\ \text{AND}\ S_2)[\alpha]}{S_1[\alpha]}$	E.g., The blocks are new and Grandpa brought them /∴ Grandpa brought the blocks.
PL3.	$\dfrac{S[\alpha];\ \text{NEG-}S[\alpha]}{\text{INCOMPATIBLE}}$	E.g., The blocks are red; The blocks are not red / INCOMPATIBLE.
PL4.	$\dfrac{(S_1\ \text{OR}\ S_2)[\alpha];\ (\text{NEG-}S_1\ \text{AND}\ \text{NEG-}S_2)[\alpha]}{\text{INCOMPATIBLE}}$	E.g., The cars had stickers or the guards towed them away; the cars didn't have stickers and the guards did not tow them away / INCOMPATIBLE
PL5.	$\dfrac{(F(\text{NEG-}S))[\alpha]}{S[\alpha]}$	E.g., It is false that the boys did not help Mary /∴ The boys helped Mary.
PL6.	$\dfrac{(S_1\ \text{AND}\ (S_2\ \text{OR}\ S_3))[\alpha]}{((S_1\ \text{AND}\ S_2)\ \text{OR}\ (S_1\ \text{AND}\ S_3))[\alpha]}$	E.g., Everyone takes Math and either French or German /∴ Everyone takes Math and French or Math and German.
PL7.	$\dfrac{S_1(\alpha\colon S_2) + (\alpha\colon S_3);\ S_2[\beta][\beta]{\subset}[\alpha]^a}{S_1[\beta]}$	E.g., The square blocks and the round blocks are red; The blocks Jane used are square /∴ The blocks Jane used are red.
PL8.	$\dfrac{(S_1\ \text{OR}\ S_2)[\alpha]}{S_2[\alpha\colon\text{NEG-}S_1]}$	E.g., All the cars had stickers or the guards towed them away /∴ The cars that the guards did not tow away had stickers.
PL9.	$\dfrac{\text{NEG-}(S_1\ \text{AND}\ S_2)[\alpha]}{\text{NEG-}S_2[\alpha\colon S_1]}$	E.g., The men did not wear both suits and sneakers /∴ The men who wore sneakers did not wear suits.
PL10.	$\dfrac{(S_1\ \text{OR}\ S_2)[\alpha];\ S_3[\alpha\colon S_1];\ S_3[\alpha\colon S_2]}{S_3\ [\alpha]}$	E.g., All the cars in the lot have stickers or the guards tow them away; The cars that have stickers are Toyotas; The cars that the guards tow away are Toyotas /∴ All the cars are Toyotas.
PL11.	$\dfrac{(S_1\ \text{OR}\ S_2)[\alpha];\ S_3[\alpha\colon S_1];\ S_4[\alpha\colon S_2]}{(S_3\ \text{OR}\ S_4)[\alpha]}$	E.g., The blocks are all round or square; The round blocks are red; The square blocks are blue /∴ The blocks are all red or blue.
PL12.	$\dfrac{S[\alpha];\ [\beta]{\subset}[\alpha]^a}{S[\beta]}$	E.g., β Singular: All men are mortal; Socrates is a man /∴ Socrates is mortal. β Plural: All B are C; All A are B /∴ All A are C.
PL13.	$\dfrac{S[\beta];\ [\beta]{\subset}[\alpha]^a}{S[\text{some}\ \alpha]}$	E.g., β Singular: F16 is heavy; F16 is a block /∴ At least one block is heavy. β Plural: The green blocks are square /∴ Some of the blocks are square.
PL14.	$\dfrac{S[\text{no}\ \alpha];\ [\beta]{\subset}[\alpha]^a}{\text{NEG-}S\ [\beta]}$	E.g., β Singular: None of Joe's sisters is here today; Molly is one of Joe's sisters /∴ Molly is not here today. β Plural: No B are C; All A are B /∴ All A are not-C (i.e., No A are C).

$S[\alpha]$ means that the alpha (or all the alphas when there are more than one) satisfy the condition S. Similarly, NEG-$S[\alpha]$ means the alpha(s) (all) lack the condition S; $(S_1\ \text{OR}\ S_2)[\alpha]$, each alpha satisfies either S_1 or S_2. $[\alpha\colon S]$ = the alphas that satisfy S. [some α] indicates some unspecified member(s) of alpha. + indicates set union.

Alongside several schemas there is a parallel schema that interchanges the roles of S_1 and S_2 (or S_2 and S_3), for example, alongside PL2, the parallel schema has the conclusion $S_2[\alpha]$. The parallel schemas are obvious and are omitted for the sake of compactness. The example inferences sometimes exemplify the parallel schemas.

^{a}Read $[\beta]{\subset}[\alpha]$ as $[\beta]$ *is an* $[\alpha]$ if β is singular.

guistically or whose identity is clear from context. Maratsos (1974, 1976) reports two experiments in which children as young as 3 years old used or understood the indefinite article to indicate nonspecific reference and the definite article specific reference—to indicate the same object as one mentioned previously. However, Maratsos's conclusions differ from those of Warden (1976), and Karmiloff-Smith (1979) did not obtain Maratsos's results in those of her experiments that were similar to his. Warden and Karmiloff-Smith found that it is not until well into the school years that children develop the sequence in which the indefinite article is used to introduce a new referent, followed by a subsequent use of the definite article or pronoun to refer to it. Karmiloff-Smith (1979) concludes that, until around the age of 6, children typically use pronouns and definite articles to refer to something in the local environment (often accompanied by pointing) or to an exemplar of some concept in their heads. After that, pronouns often refer to the thematic topic of the discourse (Karmiloff-Smith, 1981). It is not until age 12 or so that pronouns and definite NPs are used with genuine anaphoric reference (i.e., reference back to a purely linguistic antecedent).

Articles and Scope of a Negation.   To find out how a negative sentence was understood, de Boysson-Bardies (1977) asked children to draw what was happening. For *Le lapin ne mange pas une carotte* 'The rabbit is not eating a carrot,' the children often left the carrot out of the drawing, but they rarely did so for *Le lapin ne mange pas la carotte* 'The rabbit isn't eating the carrot.' Thus, the negation negated just the verb for the definite NP, but the whole verb phrase (VP) (i.e., *eating a carrot*) for the indefinite NP. Rumain (1982) asked subjects to select a picture or describe a scene. All age groups (7 and 10 years as well as adult) tended to exclude subject NPs and definite NPs from the scope of the negation. For instance, the picture or scene was quite likely to contain a man for both *The man isn't driving a car* and *A man isn't driving the car*, but more likely to do so for the former. Subjects became more sensitive to the articles with age.

Understanding Quantified Phrases

It has been vigorously argued by Piaget and his collaborators that young children do not develop an adult notion of class until the stage of "concrete operations," at around age 7 (Inhelder & Piaget, 1964; Piaget & Szeminska, 1941/1952). One consequence is that preoperational children cannot understand the relation of class inclusion and cannot properly interpret expressions containing *all*. Children

who lack a notion of class should interpret general terms and plural NPs in unexpected ways, and an understanding of class inclusion is a conceptual prerequisite to much logical reasoning.

According to Inhelder and Piaget (1964), the preoperational child groups elements into collections rather than classes. The most primitive form of collection (Stage 1, 3 to 4 years old) is a grouping of objects by situational belongingness. Thus, in sorting objects, the items grouped together will not all share a common property; they may form a spatial arrangement that seems appropriate, for example, a square under a triangle that serves as a roof; or they may be thematically related, for example, a mother, a baby, and a baby carriage because they "go together." Part-whole relations take the place of inclusion. At Stage 2, typically around 5 to 7 years of age, collections become more like classes, in that they have members that share a common property. However, theme and spatial arrangement are still important and the protoclass loses its psychological coherence when the elements are separated; the child still has no real notion of inclusion that is separate from part-whole relations. Thus, given, for example, a grouping of four blue circles, four red squares, and two blue squares, the child cannot correctly understand questions like *Are all the circles blue?* because, according to Piaget, he or she cannot simultaneously form, hold in mind, and compare the two classes "the blue ones" and "the circles." Similarly, given, for example, a drawing of 20 poppies and 3 bluebells, the child cannot understand the question *Are there more poppies or more flowers?* because the lack of an inclusion concept means that the two classes (poppies and flowers) cannot be simultaneously available as psychological objects for comparison.

Markman (1973, 1978, 1979a) and Markman and Seibert (1976) have pointed out that a collection is not just a stage of development of the notion of class, but is a type of natural concept in its own right, denoted by singular collective nouns like *family, team, bunch, army, forest,* and so on. Membership in collections is determined by one form or another of spatial proximity, not just by intrinsic properties. In many ways, a collection is like an object with parts, being coherent in a sense that a class is not; also like objects, one cannot have a null collection, although there are lots of null classes.

Although collections are like complex objects in many ways, the parts of an object are typically not similar to each other (e.g., a shoulder is not like a leg), whereas the parts of a collection are elements of the same type. It is a property of the part-whole relation that a part of a part is part of the whole. Thus, a part of a leg, for example, the knee, is part of the body. But when we say that the Smith family's daughters are part of the Smith family, the notion "part" does not have this property, for example, the youngest daughter's left knee (say) is not part of the Smith family in the same sense that the daughter herself is. In this formal respect, the relation between an element and a collection is a genuine membership relation, not just a part-whole one. Markman and Seibert suggest that there is a continuum of increasing coherence from class to collection to object.

To show that collections are more concrete psychological units than classes, Markman (1973) and Markman and Seibert (1976) reformulated Piaget's class-inclusion question using a collective noun, for example, *Who would have a bigger birthday party, someone who invited the boys, or someone who invited the (kindergarten) class?* Children correctly answered this question more readily and at a younger age than the same question with *children* in place of *class*. Markman (1979a) shows a similar facilitation of number conservation.

Markman does not claim that her inclusion data threaten the Piagetian theory. She finds plenty of younger children who do not respond correctly to the reworded question. A Piagetian might argue that the use of the collective noun renders the question accessible to the kinds of mental structures (i.e., collections) available to Stage 2 children. However, Dean, Chabaud, and Bridges (1981) claim that the results are due to collective nouns being suggestive—they may tend to suggest "a lot" of members—and children are responding to this suggestiveness without really comparing the collection with part of itself. This argument remains to be resolved.

Many investigators (e.g., Donaldson, 1976; Hayes, 1972; Kalil, Youssef, & Lerner, 1974) have thought that the poor performance of young children might have more to do with their language comprehension processes than with the nature of their class concepts. It is known that children's errors come from comparing one subset with another, for example, asked *Are there more flowers or more buttercups?* (given 15 buttercups and 2 bluebells), the response "more buttercups" is because "there are only two bluebells" (Piaget, 1952, p. 167). The referent of *flowers* is taken as just the bluebells. The comprehension-process theory holds that the child does not pay attention to the experimenter's choice of words, but uses plausibility to arrive at the speaker's intent. The child searches for a referent for

flowers in the question and finds the bluebells to be the only plausible one. A similar tendency can be elicited in adults, for example, in the question *In the APA, are there more psychologists or more clinicians?* the term *psychologists* would likely be taken as meaning 'nonclinicians', and the question construed as a snide attack on clinicians (Klahr & Wallace, 1972). A request to compare two sets quantitatively seems to invite the assumption that the sets are disjoint. Shipley (1979) has shown that comprehension is aided when linguistic markers are added to guide the intended interpretation (e.g., *Which is more, only the lemons or all the fruit?*).

The comprehension-process theory is consistent with much evidence for variability in the average age of correct responding to inclusion questions as a function of experimental conditions, for example, the nature of the array and the way the question is posed. The age may be as early as age 4 (McGarrigle, Grieve, & Hughes, 1978) and as late as age 10—see the review of Winer (1980) and Klahr and Wallace's (1972) discussion of the results of Ahr and Youniss (1970), Kofsky (1966), Smedslund (1964), and Wohlwill (1968).

Strong support for the comprehension-process theory is provided by evidence that the same kind of error occurs in problems that are not class-inclusion problems. The best evidence consists of studies in which there are two sets, A and B (say), each composed of large and small subsets (A_1 and A_2, and B_1 and B_2). Children make about as many errors when asked to compare A_1 with B as A_1 with A, despite the fact that the A_1/B comparison is not an inclusion. Piaget himself presented data of this sort (Piaget, 1952, pp. 169–170; cf. the discussion of Hayes, 1972, p. 180). More systematic data are presented by Trabasso, Isen, Dolecki, McLanaham, Riley, and Tucker (1978), McGarrigle et al. (1978), and Grieve and Garton (1981). For example, in one of the studies of McGarrigle et al., four horses (three black and one white) faced four cows (two black and two white) across a wall; the children were asked questions like *Are there more black horses or more cows?* Only 14% of 5-year-olds responded correctly. The poor performance together with the nature of the explanations indicates that the children use a comprehension strategy in which one of the subsets indicated in the question is compared with another disjoint subset, whose selection is influenced by guessing from the possibilities available in the stimulus array, for example, they compare the black horses with the black cows or with the white horses.

This comprehension strategy masks whatever

understanding of inclusion young children have. It has not proved easy to countermand the strategy, but there appear to be some circumstances in which it can be done. Using a task that involves figural collections rather than classes, McGarrigle et al. (1978, Expts. 4 and 5) found that most 4-year-olds were successful. They presented an array consisting of six small disks with a teddy at one end, a chair alongside the fourth disk, and a table after the sixth. The question *Are there more steps [for the teddy] to go to the chair, or more steps to go to the table?* was answered correctly by a majority of the subjects. It is also the case that performance on standard class-inclusion questions can readily be improved with training (e.g., Ahr & Youniss, 1970; Judd & Mervis, 1979; Siegel, McCabe, Brand, & Matthews, 1978). In what is probably the most thorough of the training studies, Kohnstamm (1963, 1967) showed that in a half hour of didactic training almost all 5-year-olds reach a state in which they solve new types of class-inclusion problems with appropriate explanations, and they retain what they have learned for at least 3 weeks. The training is easily interpretable as training to understand which sets the question really refers to. These results indicate that children can show at least some grasp of class inclusion well before the age at which they usually answer Piagetian questions correctly.

Other questions and instructions, involving the word *all*, also lead to errors in young children. Working mainly with 3- and 4-year-olds, Donaldson and Lloyd (1974) and Donaldson and McGarrigle (1974) obtained results consistent with a comprehension process that does not distinguish the forms *All the F are G* and *All the G are F*. In some important studies with slightly older children, Inhelder and Piaget (1964, Ch. 3) used displays, such as one consisting of red squares, blue squares, and blue circles. Four questions were asked. For two questions, *Are all the red ones squares?* and *Are all the circles blue?*, the subject set is included in the predicate set so that the correct answer is "yes." For the two other questions, *Are all the squares red?* and *Are all the blue ones circles?*, there is no inclusion and the correct answer is "no."

Inhelder and Piaget found that young children make many errors in answering these questions. They discuss two main types of error. Some of the youngest children (Stage 1) refer the question to the entire set, for example, *Are all the circles blue?* is construed as if it meant 'Are they all blue circles?' A somewhat later error is to construe it as 'Are all the circles all of the blue things?' with *all* applying to both the subject and the predicate set—an error In-

helder and Piaget call "false quantification of the predicate." At Stage 3 (7 to 8 years) the questions are interpreted and responded to correctly.

It should be noted that the second characteristic error is the same as an error that many investigators have noted on categorical syllogisms. They have called it a "conversion" error: It consists in interpreting *All F are G* to mean 'All F are G and All G are F'—obviously the same as 'All the F are all the G.'

Inhelder and Piaget report numerical data that appear not to be fully in accord with their discussion. It may be recalled that in two of the four questions there was an inclusion relation, and that in two there was not. Both the interpretive errors predict incorrect responses to the questions where there is an inclusion, and correct responses (for the wrong reasons) where there is no inclusion. For example, given the display of red squares, blue squares, and blue circles, if the question *Are all the circles blue?* is interpreted either as 'Are they all blue circles?' or as 'Are all the circles all the blue things?' one would expect an erroneous response of "no." On the other hand, the question *Are all the squares red?* should yield a correct response (of "no") however it is interpreted. Thus, Inhelder and Piaget's account predicts that almost all errors should consist of saying "no" to questions where there is an inclusion. Table 5 summarizes data for the two kinds of questions from their three studies and from a study by Bucci (1978) that uses quite similar material.

It can be seen in Table 5 that in Inhelder and Piaget's data (in contrast to their discussion) errors occur nearly equally on questions with and without the inclusion. On the other hand, Bucci's data do reveal a preponderance of error on inclusion questions. It is hard to know what to make of the inconsistency. The safest conclusion is that there are indeed more errors on inclusion questions, but that there are also many errors on questions where there is no inclusion, whose basis is not accounted for. Both data sets show an overall improvement with age and that even the youngest subjects are not merely guessing.

Bucci offers a theory that is not the same as Piaget's. She proposes that children tend to use a sentence-comprehension process that pays little attention to syntactic structure. A sentence of the form *All F are G* is often given a syntactic decoding that she calls "structure neutral"; it has the form 'All; F; G,' with the three terms independent, that is, syntactic subordination in the verbal stimulus is ignored. The semantic interpretation that is arrived at is a joint product of guessing strategy, the possibilities sug-

Table 5. **Percentages of Correct Responses at Various Ages to Questions of the Form "Are All the F G?" for Sets F and G**

Age	Inhelder and Piaget[a]			Inhelder and Piaget[b]			Bucci (1978)		
	N	F $\subset$ G	F $\not\subset$ G[c]	N	F $\subset$ G	F $\not\subset$ G[c]	N	F $\subset$ G	F $\not\subset$ G[c]
5	35	43	46	20	35	20			
6	41	38	54	20	37	53 ⎫			
7	24	54	63	25	47	44 ⎪	37	38	84
8	20	75	85	20	66	56 ⎭			
9	18	78	89	16	89	62			
11–12							38	58	83
Adult							28	88	82

[a]Compiled from Tables 1 and 1a of Inhelder and Piaget (1964, pp. 63–64).
[b]Compiled from Table 3 of Inhelder and Piaget (1964, p. 88).
[c]When F $\subset$ G the correct response is "yes"; when F $\not\subset$ G the correct response is "no." Inhelder and Piaget asked two questions of each type, and so chance is 25%; because Bucci asked three questions, chance is 12.5% for her data.

gested by the array and by the dictates of the task, and any factual knowledge that is relevant. (Factual knowledge is not relevant to the task under discussion. It would be relevant to a sentence like *All oaks have acorns*, which, according to Bucci, would be syntactically decoded as 'all; oaks; have acorns,' and then the elements would be recombined using factual knowledge to yield a construal like 'All oaks have acorns and all acorn-bearing trees are oaks.') This comprehension process strikingly resembles the one previously discussed for the inclusion task.

Bucci goes on to propose that the usual outcome of a structure-neutral decoding is an interpretation of the form 'All the objects are F and G' (e.g., 'Are they all blue circles?'). This predicts the bias in her results, as does Piaget's account, although neither account predicts the errors on questions without an inclusion. However, it is not clear why Bucci's conception requires that the favored interpretation be 'All the objects are F and G.' In principle, there would seem to be four possible interpretational outcomes of a structure-neutral decoding. 'All; F; G' could be interpreted as:

1. All the objects are F and G
2. All the F are G
3. All the G are F
4. All the F are G and all the G are F

If the question involves an inclusion (F $\subset$ G), then interpretations (1), (3), and (4) will lead to an erroneous response of "no." If there is no inclusion of F in G, then interpretations (1), (2), and (4) will yield correct responses of "no," and (3) will yield an incorrect response of "yes." The obtained

"yes" responses to the questions where F $\not\subset$ G must come from interpretation (3) (unless they come from pure guessing with no interpretive process at all). Thus, a slightly revised Bucci model that assumed random selection from these four interpretations, except for increasing selection of the correct interpretation with age, would account for all the trends and biases in the data rather better than either Inhelder and Piaget's or Bucci's original account. To settle what the probability hierarchy is among the four interpretations (and the frequency of guessing without any interpretation) would require further work that varied the set relationships present in the array.

Another part of Bucci's experiment—actually the main part—presented subjects with many wooden blocks varying in shape, color, and size; the subjects were given a series of instructions like *Make a building in which all the yellow blocks are square*. In follow-up probe questions, a type of block not used by the subject was indicated (e.g., a red rectangle), and the subject was asked *Could you use any of these in a building in which* [for example] *all the yellow blocks are square?* The predominant response was to use only blocks with the combination of attributes named (e.g., only yellow squares), and the probe questions were answered accordingly, for example, "No, you said it had to be yellow and it had to be square," "Why do you keep telling me to make these stupid little buildings?" For almost all the 6- to 8-year-olds and most of the sixth graders, all the buildings made were of this type, with probe questions answered consistently. Only in the adult group did subjects properly understand which blocks were allowed and disallowed. In general, this study demonstrates interpretational errors that appear to be of

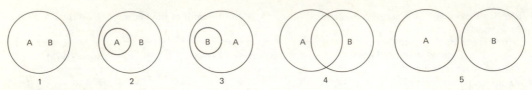

Figure 1. Euler circles illustrating the possible relations between two sets, A and B.

the same kind as those found in the tasks previously described, but these errors are appearing now in older children. Bucci argues that the instruction induces a set to scan the embedded clause for a specification of the kind of blocks to be used; the clause is given a structure-neutral syntactic decoding ('all; yellow; square'), and then the elements are recombined semantically under the influence of the interpretive set, that is, the blocks used are to be all yellow squares.

C. L. Smith (1979, 1980) posed *all*-questions and *some*-questions about familiar content (e.g., *Are all boys people?*, *Are all people boys?*) to children aged 4 to 7 years of age. The questions were given in blocks. Children of all ages who received a block of *all*-questions first did well on that block. *All*-questions not in this first-given block were responded to less well, giving rise to the same kinds of errors that Bucci (1978) and Inhelder and Piaget (1964) observed. Nevertheless, a majority of kindergartners and first graders responded accurately overall. No groups had any difficulty with *some*-questions.

Children's difficulties with *all* clearly do not have to do with the word, per se. As Inhelder and Piaget note, from Stage 2 onwards, "*all* is the set of elements of a collection, without exception" (1964, p. 94). Instead, children often have difficulty translating sentence structures containing *all* into appropriate logical representations. The difficulty is a function of content as well as sentence structure. When questions are about inclusion relations stored in long-term memory, as in C. L. Smith's (1979, 1980) tasks, even 4-year-olds show some initial understanding and a majority of 6-year-olds meet a success criterion. In the Piagetian task, the difficulty is overcome a year or two later, but even 11- and 12-year-olds are subject to it when the *all*-sentence is embedded, as in Bucci's (1978) block-building task. As we will see later, similar difficulties reappear in adults in syllogistic reasoning problems.

Errors for *some* have not been noted, except that at Stage 1 it may have an absolute connotation—a small number—so that when a collection has only two or three objects its meaning merges with *all* (Inhelder & Piaget, 1964).

Neimark and Chapman (1975) have studied the understanding of *some* and *all* among older subjects, age 12 through adult. They aimed to clarify how subjects interpret the sentence forms used in categorical syllogisms when the forms are presented in isolation. The statements *All A are B, No A are B, Some A are B*, and *Some A are not B* were each presented twice; other statements presented all possible combinations of the forms (*All A are B and all B are A, All A are B and no B are A*, etc.). There were six response alternatives: Five were the Euler circles of Figure 1, and the sixth was the word "incompatible" (i.e., the relation is impossible, as in *All A are B and no B are A*). Subjects had to indicate all the alternatives described by each statement.

A majority of responses to *All A are B* and *No A are B* were correct in all age groups. *No A are B* had least errors. For *All A are B*, responses increased from 60% to 65% to about 95% correct with age. The only error of the older subjects was to choose only one of Alternatives 1 and 2 (Fig. 1); younger subjects also sometimes elected the inclusion relation for the reversed proposition (Alternative 3), either in addition to or instead of the correct inclusion.

Some was understood with the usual conversational implicatures. Thus, *Some A are B* was taken to mean 'Some A are B and some are not'; it was not taken to comprehend *All A are B*, nor was *Some A are not B* taken to include *No A are B*. Only a quarter of the adults and almost none of the 12-year-olds interpreted these statements in the analytically correct manner. The most common response of the younger subjects was to select Alternative 4 for both *Some A are B* and *Some A are not B*. The next favorite response, and the most common in the older subjects was to select the proper inclusion (Alternative 3) as well.

In general, the response to the compound propositions was consistent with what one would predict from the way the simple forms were interpreted.

Simple Quantificational Inferences and Fallacies

Probably the simplest kind of quantificational inference is the instantiation of a class, as in PL12 of

Table 4 when β is singular, for example,

(19) All the people in Tundor [an imaginary city] are happy
Jean lives in Tundor
Is Jean happy? (Kuhn, 1977)

As noted earlier, this kind of instantiation is analogous to Modus Ponens. Quantificational analogues also exist for Modus Tollens and for the fallacies of Denying the Antecedent and Asserting the Consequent. The four problem types are shown in Table 6.

Several studies have compared the types. The usual result has been that performance is best on the simple instantiation analogous to Modus Ponens, that performance on the two valid inferences is better than on the fallacies, and that the Denying-the-Antecedent fallacy is easier to avoid than the Asserting-the-Consequent one. Kuhn (1977) used content like that of the example above (19) with first- through fourth-grade children. All grades generally responded according to logical canon on the valid forms; most children responded with "maybe" on the Denying-the-Antecedent fallacy from the second grade on; from one third to one half did so on the Asserting-the-Consequent fallacy. However, no one else has obtained quite such sophisticated results on the fallacies, age for age, as Kuhn did.

Bucci (1978, Experiment 2) used three age groups—6 to 8 years of age, 11 and 12 years of age, and adults. She compared three kinds of content, which she called "broad predicate," "narrow predicate," and "abstract." These were likely to affect the fallacies differently. Thus, in a broad predicate item like *All football players are strong; The man I'm thinking of is strong; Is he a football player?*, a subject is likely to know of strong people that are not football players, whereas in a narrow predicate item like *All oak trees have acorns; The thing I'm thinking of is an acorn; Does it come from an oak tree?*, the possibility of acorns that do not come from oak trees is unlikely to suggest itself. Consequently, responses of "not sure" are more likely for the for-

mer. The abstract items were about blocks in a closed bag, for example, *All the pink blocks are rectangles; The block in my hand is pink; Is it a rectangle?* Responses on the analogues of Modus Ponens and Tollens were usually correct for all kinds of content and age groups. The fallacies were resisted best for the broad predicate content: The adults were almost always correct, the 11- and 12-year-olds somewhat less than half the time, and the youngest subjects much less often. The children gave only a few responses of "not sure" to the narrow predicate and abstract contents, and adults gave such responses only 50% to 75% of the time. In another study, Roberge (1972) and Roberge and Paulus (1971) used group-administered written test materials with 4th, 6th, 8th, and 10th graders and found a very high incidence of the fallacies; performance was best with naturalistic and worst with symbolic content, just as in Wilkin's (1928) original study of the effect of content on logical reasoning.

It should be noted that the incidence of the fallacies has usually been greater than would be expected from Neimark and Chapman's (1975) direct data on comprehension. As reviewed earlier, they found that 60% to 65% of 12-year-olds and 95% of the adults correctly represented the form *All A are B* as set inclusion, not as set identity. The fallacies imply an understanding of the major premise as set identity. Thus, subjects' construal of the form *All A are B* is less sophisticated in the inference task than it is in a direct test of comprehension. We discuss why later, when the same question comes up again with categorical syllogisms.

In work by P. Harris (1975) and C. L. Smith (1979), one premiss came from general knowledge. Harris first established that the children (4½ to 5½ years of age) knew that men and birds eat food and that airplanes and houses do not, and that birds and airplanes have wings and men and horses do not. The second premiss used a nonsense word and was given verbally, for example, *A mib is a man.* The child was then asked questions like *Does a mib eat*

Table 6. Quantificational Analogues of the Standard Conditional Reasoning Problems

Analogous Conditional Problem	Major Premiss	Minor Premiss	Question	Response Alternatives
Modus Ponens	All F are G[a]	x is F	Is x G?	True, or False, or Undecidable
Denying the Antecedent	All F are G[a]	x is not F	Is x G?	
Asserting the Consequent	All F are G[a]	x is G	Is x F?	
Modus Tollens	All F are G[a]	x is not G	Is x F?	

[a]Or any paraphrase, e.g., *Every F is G, If a thing is an F, then it as a G,* and so on.

food?, Does a mib have wings? The inference has the form of PL12 (Table 4). The huge majority of responses were correct. In two further experiments, 5- and 6-year-olds were told, for instance, *A mib is a bird*. They were asked whether a mib had wings (PL12 [Table 4], as before), and were then asked *Is a mib a robin?* Note that a "yes" response to this question would be analogous to the Asserting-the-Consequent fallacy (or, equally, the fallacy *All A are B, All C are B, ∴ All A are C*). The responses on the valid inference were almost always correct and greatly superior to the responses on the fallacy, which were about chance level. Because there was no "can't tell" response category (which children of this age would not readily use), the responses on the fallacy could well represent guessing.

C. L. Smith's (1979) inference tasks were similar to P. Harris's (1975), but evaded the problem of the "can't tell" response category by using the modal verb *have to* in the question (e.g., *A pug is a kind of dog, Does a pug have to be an animal?* / *All milk has lactose, Does all chocolate milk have to have lactose?* vs. *A tody is a kind of bird, Does a tody have to be a robin?* / *All milk has lactose, Do all drinks have to have lactose?*—the words *pug, tody, lactose,* etc., were effectively nonsense words for the children). Even the 4-year-olds got better than chance scores, and half the kindergartners and most first graders got virtually all answers correct. Errors in the younger children indicated failure to understand *have to*. In a further study, most 4-year-olds made correct responses of "no" as well as "yes" on the valid inference problems (e.g., *A bongo is a kind of animal but not a dog, Is a bongo a poodle?*).

The work reviewed indicates that inferences of the form of PL12 (Table 4) are available at the time children enter school, and even earlier when the major premiss is implicit in general knowledge. In the latter case, the problem of decoding *All F are G* is eliminated (because the proposition is not spoken and the child knows already that $F \subset G$ and $F \neq G$); it is an interesting feature of C. L. Smith's data that fallacies of the Asserting-the-Consequent type then essentially vanish, even in 6-year-olds. We may note, too, for later reference, that the work places the development of comprehension of *have to* as logical necessity during the period of 4 to 7 years of age.

The simplest kind of existential inference is from a statement of the form *a is F*, where *a* names some object, to *There is something that is F* (Schema PL13 [Table 4] with β singular). Such inferences were among the easiest explored by Osherson (1976) with fifth-grade children, and their intuitive simplicity suggests that they are probably available to much younger children.

Premisses containing *none, no* + NP, or *not . . . any* have been used primarily in categorical syllogisms, and only rarely in work with children. A few problems involving inferences of the form of Schema PL14 were included in Hill (1961; see an example in Table 4). The children made somewhat more errors than they did on simple instantiations, but such problems were solved by a large majority of at least 8-year-olds.

Only is a natural language quantifier with no direct correspondence in predicate logic (although sentences with *only* can usually be translated into logical notation). A typical inference involving *only* has the form:

S (only F) (i.e., only Fs satisfies the condition S)
x is not an F
∴ not-S(x)

Hill's study included a few inferences of this general type. They were not among her earliest types but were solved by her 6- to 8-year-olds far more often than not.

Since analogous class and conditional problems can be constructed, they can be compared. Roberge (1972) and Roberge and Paulus (1971) compared problems using the categorical forms with analogous problems employing simple conditionals, that is, the problems of Table 6 with those of Table 3. They also included problems involving transitivity (i.e., *All A are B, All B are C, ∴ All A are C* vs. *If p then q, If q then r, ∴ If p then r*) and contraposition (*All A are B, ∴ All non-B are non-A* vs. *If p then q, ∴ If not-q then not-p*). Across these six types of problems and three kinds of content, they found that the categorical problems were slightly but significantly easier than the propositional, with some interactions that fell into no coherent pattern. They suggested that children may be suspicious of the word *all*, and thus more likely to respond with "maybe" on categorical problems, thereby giving more correct answers on the fallacies. An alternative explanation might be that the invited inferences are more seductive for a conditional, for example, perhaps *If p then q* invites *If not p then not q* more readily than *All F are G* invites *All non-F are not G*. In any case, the overall comparison does not seem very meaningful because of the variety of psychological processes involved: Correct responses on simple instantiation and Modus Ponens, as well as on the transitivity problems probably reflect basic inference patterns; correct responses on the fallacies depend on comprehension processes that resist invited inferences and conversion; and, as seen in the discussion of propositional reasoning, responses on Modus Tollens and contraposition are complexly determined—

the least and the most sophisticated subjects are likely to be correct for different reasons and the subjects of intermediate sophistication to give incorrect responses of ''can't tell.''

Universal statements can be expressed in a variety of ways, for example, *All F's are G*, *An F is a G*, *If a thing is an F, then it is a G*. There is nothing in standard logic that corresponds to these differences; they are all ways of rendering $\forall x(Fx \supset Gx)$ into English.[11] The question arises whether the verbal form affects reasoning. The two most different forms are the categorical, *All F's are G*, and the quantified conditional, *If a thing is an F, then it is G*. Note that there is a difference between a quantified conditional and the simple (unquantified) conditional of propositional reasoning. The following two problems illustrate the difference:

(20) If a person lives in Tundor, then they are happy.
       Jean lives in Tundor.
       Is Jean happy? (Kuhn, 1977)

(21) If Jean lives in Tundor, then she is happy.
       Jean lives in Tundor.
       Is Jean happy?

Problem 21, with the simple conditional, involves only a Modus Ponens inference, whereas Problem 20 involves an instantiation in addition, that is, the instantiation of *a person* as *Jean*. One might reasonably expect that the additional instantiation step for the quantified conditional should cause some increment in difficulty, but the data reviewed suggest that if there is a difference it is small.

Kuhn (1977) found no difference between the categorical and quantified conditional forms (cf. Problem 19 with Problem 20) for the four problem types of Table 6. Similarly, adult subjects evaluate quantified conditional and categorical propositions against evidence in much the same way (Johnson-Laird & Wason, 1970a; Moshman, 1979); Moshman's study (described in more detail later) also found no difference between the negative forms *No F are G* and *If a thing is F it is not G*.

Osherson (1974) compared a similar pair of verbal forms over a variety of inferences in 10- to 13-year-olds. Logically parallel problems were presented in either a ''quantifier'' or ''sentential'' idiom, and concerned one or the other of two kinds of content—figurines (called ''toks'') that varied in color and other properties, or a toy playground composed of tiles of various colors and sizes. The problems all presented a premiss in the form of a hint, followed by a question. For example, in the quantifier idiom, one problem gave the hint *All the red toks have spots*, followed by the question *All the red toks*

which are not tall—is every one of these a spotted tok which is not tall? An isomorphic problem in the sentential idiom gave the hint *If I'm thinking of a blue tok, then I'm thinking of a starred tok*, followed by *If I'm thinking of a blue tok that is not short, am I thinking of a starred tok that is not short?* The difficulties of isomorphic problems correlated about .7 across idioms and .9 across contents. Thus, keeping the same idiom and varying content changed problem difficulty hardly at all; keeping the same content and altering the idiom of presentation changed difficulty only a little. Inspection of the few problems where there were discrepancies suggests that they are due to subtly different conversational implicatures associated with each idiom. However, problem structure, not idiom or content, was the major determinant of difficulty.

The main purpose of Osherson's study was not to compare the two idioms, but to see whether subjects use certain inference schemas (see Table 7).[12] Each schema was associated with certain problem conditions that call for its application. The schemas, with their conditions of application, predict a unique series of mental steps that solves each problem by starting with the premiss and applying a sequence of schemas.

Difficulty weights were assigned to each schema, and the difficulty of a problem was predicted to be the sum of the difficulty weights of the schemas used in solving it. The predicted difficulties were correlated with the actual difficulties (the number of subjects solving each problem). Over the several sets of data the correlations ranged around .8. The correlations are high, but they are hard to evaluate because, although the weights are plausibly assign-

Table 7. The Schemas of Osherson (1974) in Class Form

01. $\dfrac{F \cup G}{-(-F \cap -G)}$	02. $\dfrac{F \cap G}{-(-F \cup -G)}$
03. $\dfrac{(F \cup G) \subset H}{F \subset H}$	04. $\dfrac{F \subset (G \cap H)}{F \subset G}$
05. $\dfrac{F \subset G}{-G \subset -F}$	
06. $\dfrac{F \subset G}{(F \cup H) \subset (G \cup H)}$	07. $\dfrac{F \subset G}{(F \cap H) \subset (G \cap H)}$
08. $\dfrac{F \subset G}{F \subset (G \cup H)}$	09. $\dfrac{F \subset G}{(F \cap H) \subset G}$

Alongside some of these schemas, there is a commutational variant that interchanges the roles of F and G, or G and H. For instance, alongside 03, there is $(F \cup G) \subset H/G \subset H$. These variants are obvious and have been omitted for simplicity.

ed, the number of problems is small for the number of schemas.

We have another reservation about the model, that is best illustrated with an example problem:

Premiss: all the blue toks and all the short toks have stars. (B ∪ Sh ⊂ St)

Conclusion: all the blue toks which are not short—is every one of these a starred tok? (B ∩ ~Sh ⊂ St?)

Osherson's model predicts the following solution:

B ∪ Sh ⊂ St	(premiss)
∴ B ⊂ St	(by 03 of Table 7)
∴ B ∩ ~Sh ⊂ St	(by 08 of Table 7)

That is, since all the blue toks and all the short toks have stars, all the blue toks have stars, therefore, all the blue toks that are not short have stars.

Subjects on whom we have tried this problem report a line of reasoning that goes: All the blue toks that are not short are blue and, therefore, starred. Unlike Osherson's model, they do not start with the premiss and successively transform it; they start from the first term of the conclusion (*All the blue toks which are not short*) and use the premiss to show that the predicate of the conclusion applies to this set. Thus, the model conflicts with verbal reports. The report of the example is consistent with PL7 of Table 4.

Osherson (1976) investigated a different set of schemas. They included the propositional ones of Osherson (1975a—discussed earlier), and 14 schemas involving quantifiers. Two were universal instantiation and existential generalization; six involved distribution of quantifiers over conjunction and disjunction (e.g., *Each F is G and each F is H/ ∴ Each F is both G and H*); and six involved relations between quantifiers (e.g., *Each F is not G/ ∴ It is not true that at least one F is G*). Only one quantifier could appear in a proposition.

Subjects were 10 and 16 to 17 years old. As in Osherson (1975a), the difficulties of multistep problems (rated by subjects) were correlated with their predicted difficulties (the sum of the difficulty ratings for the individual steps, obtained from one-step problems). Correlations were moderately high, and the same in both age groups. The results suggest that the reasoning used in the multi-step problems usually incorporated that used to solve the one-step problems. However, that does not show that the elementary inferences were those specified in the schemas. It is also problematic that for some of the sche-

mas, many subjects did not think the conclusion followed from the premiss in the simplest exemplifying problems.

Both sets of studies (Osherson, 1974, 1976) indicate that by 10 years of age children can chain inferences together in short chains of direct reasoning.

Categorical Syllogisms

Categorical syllogisms have two premisses and a conclusion. All propositions have one of the four forms (A) *All A are B*, (E) *No A are B*, (I) *Some A are B*, and (O) *Some A are not B*. The labels "A," "E," "I," and "O" are traditional. The order of terms in a proposition can vary, and the possible order combinations are called the "figures" of the syllogism. These are defined in Table 8, with a sample problem for each.

Traditionally, problems are identified by the types of premisses and the figure. Thus, AI–1 means a syllogism with a major premiss of the form *All B are C*, a minor premiss of the form *Some A are B*, and a conclusion with *A* as first term and *B* as the second term. Since each premiss is of one of the four types, there are 16 possible pairs of premisses in each figure, and thus 64 possible problems in the four figures. Of these, 19 have a valid conclusion.

Syllogism problems have primarily used two formats. One format is open-ended: Subjects are given pairs of premisses, and are asked to deduce a conclusion, or to conclude that there is no conclusion that follows. The other, and commonest, format is the multiple-choice one illustrated in Table 8. These two formats have complementary costs and benefits. Open-ended problems allow subjects to choose the order of terms in the conclusion (e.g., *Some A are B* vs. *Some B are A*), whereas in the multiple-choice format, the direction of the conclusion is specified in the response alternatives. On the other hand, certain inferences (e.g., those of Figure 4—see Table 8) can only be studied in the multiple-choice format because subjects do not spontaneously make inferences in the required direction.

There are two main theories of how subjects solve syllogisms—the set-analysis theory and the analogical theory.[13] There is also a line of analytic studies aimed at discovering the bases of erroneous responses on particular classes of problems. We start with that.

Response Preferences and Error Tendencies
The Figure Effect. There are strong directional preferences in responses to syllogisms (Johnson-Laird & Steedman, 1978). For instance,

Table 8. The Figures of the Categorical Syllogism with an Example Problem Type in the Multiple-Choice Format for Each Figure

Figure 1	Figure 2	Figure 3	Figure 4
M — P	P — M	M — P	P — M
S — M	S — M	M — S	M — S
S — P	S — P	S — P	S — P
E.g.,	E.g.,	E.g.,	E.g.,
All M are P	All P are M	All M are P	All P are M
Some S are M	Some S are M	Some M are S	Some M are S

Response choices:
(A) All S are P
(E) No S are P
(I) Some S are P
(O) Some S are not P
(−) None of the above.
"S" labels the term destined to be the subject of the conclusion, "P" the term destined to be the predicate, and "M" the other (middle) term.

consider the following two premiss pairs, from Figures 1 and 4 (see Table 8), respectively:

(22) Some A are B
  All B are C
(23) All B are A
  Some C are B

Subjects greatly prefer the response *Some A are C* to Problem 22, and the response *Some C are A* to Problem 23. Both conclusions are valid for both problems, but for Problem 23 the conclusion specified in Figure 4 in Table 8 is the nonpreferred *Some A are C*. Such premises can be combined as a forward chain, from S to M to P, and this favors Figure 1 over Figure 4 (Frase, 1968). Order preferences are negligible for Figures 2 and 3.

Conversion. Conversion consists in construing the form *All A are B* as 'All A are B and all B are A' (i.e., 'A = B') and the form *Some A are not B* as 'Some A are not B and some B are not A.' (Conversion of E and I propositions may also occur, but cannot cause errors because these do entail their converses.) Much empirical work has been concerned with conversion since Chapman and Chapman (1959) first proposed it (e.g., Begg & Denny, 1969; Ceraso & Provitera, 1971; Mazzocco, Legrenzi, & Roncato, 1974; Revlin & Leirer, 1978; Revlis, 1975a, 1975b).

A number of facts indicate that conversion is a real source of error. Subjects make significantly more errors on problems where conversion would cause error than on those where it would maintain the correct response (Revlin & Leirer, 1978; Revlis 1975a, 1975b). In addition, responses predicted by conversion occur more frequently when the convert-ed proposition is one that subjects believe than when it is not (Revlin & Leirer, 1978; Revlis, 1975a, 1975b). Moreover, giving premises in a form that explicitly blocks conversion reduces errors (Ceraso & Provitera, 1971).

There are limitations to what conversion can explain. It would not cause errors on a majority of problems, and in fact it accounts well only for errors on problems where the premises include an A proposition. In addition, because conversion creates a symmetrical proposition, it cannot account for the figure effect (Johnson-Laird & Steedman, 1978). The evidence for the reality of conversion also creates a new question. In Neimark and Chapman's (1975) data on comprehension, older subjects did not construe the form *All A are B* as 'A = B.' Why then is it that conversion of universal propositions happens mainly when subjects are asked to reason, not just to understand?

Other Error Tendencies. Dickstein (1978b) reports evidence for two sources of error pertinent on problems where conversion cannot explain errors. One tendency occurs on problems that combine two I premises or that combine I with O. Given, say, *Some M are P* and *Some M are S*, the subject assumes that the Ms that are S are the ones that are P, and concludes *Some S are P*. The other tendency occurs when both premises are negative: In effect, one premiss denies a relation between S and M and the other between M and P. The subject fails to see that S and P might be related other than through M, and concludes that some or all S are not P. The two types of error were statistically independent.

The three error tendencies discussed (i.e., conversion, and Dickstein's two) may be the source of most adult errors on syllogisms. They are undoubtedly exacerbated by the bias against responses of "undecidable" discussed earlier (see *Development of the Response of Undecidable*).

"Atmosphere." Woodworth and Sells (1935), Sells (1936), and Woodworth (1938) proposed that responses are based on the "atmosphere" of the premises. Universal premises contribute a universal atmosphere, particular premises (I and O) a particularistic atmosphere, and negative premises a negative atmosphere. People like to choose a conclusion with the same atmosphere as the premises. As formulated by Begg and Denny (1969), when there is a particular premiss, subjects prefer a particular conclusion; when there is a negative premiss, subjects prefer a negative conclusion; otherwise, the preference is for universal and positive conclusions.

The theory predicts the type of conclusion only, not the order of the terms in it; thus, it cannot explain directionality effects in responses. Also, it predicts the same errors as the other error tendencies where they apply. However, there is positive evidence for the other sources of error, but no hard evidence for an effect of atmosphere. In recent work, atmosphere has served only as a biasing factor in theories mainly relying on other processes (Erickson, 1974; Revlis, 1975a).

We now turn to theories that aim to explain correct responses as well as error.

The Set-Analysis Theory

In the set-analysis theory (Erickson, 1974, 1978), the subject construes the set relations in each premiss in terms of mental diagrams, using Euler circles or the like. These are combined mentally, and the subject selects a response compatible with the combined diagram. However, many additional assumptions are required because more than one diagram can capture a premiss (e.g., four pairs of Euler circles in Fig. 1 are consistent with I premisses); also, there is more than one way of combining two diagrams in one, and more than one proposition could describe any final diagram. Dickstein (1978b) notes that the best model makes 18 probability assumptions, and much of its accuracy comes from positing that universal premises are usually converted. Also, because many diagrams are symmetric, the theory does not account for the figure effect. Johnson-Laird and Steedman (1978) also point out the serious limitation that relational premises with more than one quantifier (e.g., *All the boys kissed some of the girls*) cannot be represented by Euler circles; consequently, the set analysis theory could not be extended to other reasoning of a predicate-logic sort.

The Analogical Theory

Johnson-Laird (1975, 1981) and Johnson-Laird and Steedman (1978) propose a different type of mental model. The subject represents each premiss by imagining members of the subject class and mentally tagging some or all of them as belonging to the predicate class (see Fig. 2 for the representation they propose). In the second stage, the models of the two premises are joined by linking end items through middle items, and the subject reads a tentative conclusion off the combined representation. Finally, the subject tries to test this conclusion by altering the representation while remaining faithful to the meanings of the premises. Figure 2 shows how the second-stage model of *All A are B, Some B are C* suggests *Some A are C,* and how the final stage could refute this.

The analogical theory explains most errors by positing that subjects are poor at testing conclusions (although the possibility of "converted" representations is left open). The errors are the tentative conclusions of the second stage.

The theory has the virtue that the links in the representations are inherently directional, thus, it can predict the order of items in subjects' conclusions. The method for combining premises builds in Dickstein's (1978b) two sources of error. Moreover, the same kind of mental model could be used for relational premises with multiple quantifiers, so the theory is not limited to syllogisms. However, evidence for the model is all quite indirect.

Figure 2. The analogical theory (Johnson-Laird & Steedman, 1978): (1) The representations suggested for the proposition types; (2) an example of the combination of the representations at two stages of processing a problem. Lower-case letters represent imagined class members, the vertical arrow represents belonging, and the blocked line represents 'is not.'

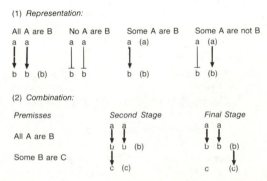

Discussion

The set-analysis and analogical theories posit that subjects' responses depend on manipulating mental models. They are thus apparently in opposition to the "inference-schema" account of logical reasoning. Indeed, Johnson-Laird (1981) suggests that inference schemas (at least those concerned with classes and relations) are psychologically secondary, being a learned consequence of mental manipulation of models.

If subjects are representing premises with either kind of mental model, there should be traces of that fact in introspective reports on how they solved problems. The only introspective reports we know of (Störring, 1908, 1925, 1926) suggest that subjects' reasoning is often purely verbal; these reports provide no support for the idea that most subjects solve most syllogisms by means of the mental models proposed.

Could an inference schema approach account for the directionality in responses and for the main error tendencies? We think it could—rather easily. Consider PL12 and PL14 of Table 4. They apply immediately to the valid syllogisms of Figure 1 (see Table 8 for the figures); they do not apply immediately to those of Figures 2 and 3; and they apply to some of the premiss combinations of Figure 4, but they would lead to a response in the opposite direction to that required by the figure, that is, the direction preferred by subjects. Thus, they would explain the directional preferences and also the well-known fact that the valid syllogisms of Figure 1 are the easiest (Aristotle, cited in Kneale & Kneale, 1962; Dickstein, 1978a; Johnson-Laird & Steedman, 1978).

We propose that subjects start by trying to apply these schemas. That solves some easy problems. However, the schemas do not apply directly to most problems and many subjects lack the indirect reasoning strategies needed to solve them. So they switch to one or the other of two nonlogical heuristics. One is a recast strategy, that is, the subject seeks to reconstrue one or both premises so as to put a problem in a form to which the schemas do apply directly. This causes conversion errors, for example, PL12 (Table 4) will not apply to *All M are P, All M are S*, but if the latter is recast as *All S are M*, it will apply to yield *All S are P*. Note that if conversion occurs primarily as part of this recast strategy and not automatically, then we have an explanation for the puzzle that conversion of universal propositions occurs so much more often in reasoning than in the simple comprehension tasks of Neimark and Chapman (1975).

The other nonlogical heuristic is to construct a mental model and reason from that, as Erickson and Johnson-Laird propose—inference schemas by no means exclude the use of mental models.

What are the indirect reasoning strategies that subjects often lack? The main one that would be useful on valid syllogisms is to decide to consider the Ss (usually a subset of all the Ss) that are or are not M, according to the second premiss, and then to try to use the first premiss to prove that these Ss are or are not P. For instance, given *All M are P, All M are S*, one decides to consider the subset of Ss that are M—whose existence the second premiss guarantees—and one concludes that this subset is P by PL12 (Table 4) and the first premiss, whence some S are P by PL13. The fact that adults usually get this problem wrong (Dickstein, 1978b; Johnson-Laird & Steedman, 1978) suggests that their logical reasoning programs are not very good. Subjects also certainly lack good strategies for establishing a response of "no valid conclusion." They are thus left, on most problems, with no recourse but the nonlogical strategies.

We have now described the adult stage of development. The only study we know with children that included some syllogisms is Hill (1961): The premisses and a conclusion were given, and the children had to say whether or not the conclusion was correct. (A control group was given the same problems lacking one of the premisses, and over all the problems they obtained chance scores.) Hill included two examples each of AA–1, AI–1, and EA–2 as well as one each of AE–2 and OA–3. These are among the easiest of the valid syllogisms for adults. Most of the 8-year-olds also solved each problem. Thus, the available data suggest that young children have some capability with syllogisms—but probably little more than that supplied by the basic inference schemas.

Inferences Involving Relations and Multiple Quantification

There is very little work indeed on logical reasoning from information that includes relational predicates and more than one quantifier. Hill's (1961) study with 6- to 8-year-olds contained a grab bag of items of this sort. Predicate-logic Problems 2 and 3 of Table 1 are examples. The children were mostly successful with the items, especially the oldest children.

Johnson-Laird (1969c) used sentences like *Some medicine cures every disease, Every disease is cured by some medicine* and *Every child likes some toy,*

Some toy is liked by every child. The sentences were used both as premises and as putative conclusions to be judged as valid or invalid by adult subjects. In general, the order of mention of the quantifiers was crucial, that is, *Every disease is cured by some medicine* was usually taken as entailed by *Some medicine cures every disease,* but not vice versa; and *Every child likes some toy* was usually taken as following from *Some toy is liked by every child,* but not vice versa. The results suggested that the sentences were decoded into a logical representation in which the quantifier occurring first in the surface structure has outside scope—as some linguists (e.g., Jackendoff, 1968, 1969) have theorized and as Johnson-Laird (1969b) found in a separate study on comprehension of such sentences.

It is a great pity that so little work has been done on reasoning that involves relations and more than one quantifier. It means that nothing like the full range of natural reasoning of a predicate-logic type has been sampled by psychologists. The neglect encourages undue attention to miniature theories (e.g., the atmosphere and set-analysis theories of syllogistic reasoning) that focus on a narrow range of phenomena and have little potential for general applicability.

Judging Universally Quantified Sentences Against Data

The work on propositional reasoning showed that simple inferences are often made earlier and more consistently than truth judgments. There are analogous results for quantified sentences. Most work concerns quantified conditionals and indicates inadequacies in evaluating such conditionals at surprisingly advanced ages.

Kuhn (1977, Experiment 3) presented second, fourth, sixth, and eighth graders with a scenario about a Mr. Jones who had just three kinds of bugs in his garden: big striped bugs, small striped bugs, and small black bugs, each kind represented in a picture. The subjects were shown eight sentences of the form *If a bug is _____ it is _____,* with *big* or *small,* and *striped* or *black* in the blanks. They had to indicate which sentences were true things that Mr. Jones could say about the bugs in his garden. The eighth graders correctly identified just *If a bug is big it is striped* and *If a bug is black it is small* as true. However, most second and fourth graders treated the sentences as if they meant 'There are bugs that are _____ and _____.' The sixth grade was intermediate. The correct response pattern showed a moderate correlation with a Piagetian "formal-oper-

ations" task involving isolation of variables. Kuhn proposed that assessing quantified conditionals against data belongs to the formal-operations stage, whereas making inferences from them only requires concrete operations.

Moshman (1979) presented subjects (7th, 10th grades and college) with "theories" in the form of statements of the four following types: *If a thing is F it is G, All F are G, If a thing is F it is not G, No F are G* (e.g., *If a person uses fluoridated toothpaste, he will have healthy teeth* exemplifies the first form). Instances were presented of each possible combination of the presence and absence of the mentioned attributes, for example, *Albert uses fluoridated toothpaste and has healthy teeth* for F and G present. For each instance, subjects had to indicate whether it proved the theory true, whether it proved it false, or whether it provided no proof. Each set of responses for a subject was classified according to the interpretation it implied of the theory statement—as a conditional, a biconditional, or as having no consistent interpretation. There was a strong age trend: almost half of the 7th-grade responses were inconsistent and less than 20% reflected an interpretation as a conditional; conditional interpretations underlay a majority—but not a large majority—of the college students' responses. The most common conditional pattern was to regard the forms *If F then G* and *All F are G* as proved true by an object that was F and G, as proved false by one that was F and not G, and to regard other objects as "no proof." This is essentially the same pattern that Johnson-Laird & Tagart (1969) found for simple conditionals. Only a few subjects appreciated that an object with both attributes should not be regarded as proving a conditional true.

These data appear to indicate a rather poor understanding of quantified conditionals in surprisingly mature subjects. However, it seems to us that part of the inconsistency and apparent lack of sophistication could be due to subjects having difficulty in fitting their own categories to those of the experimenter. For example, a subject might regard a quantified conditional as a rule for predicting. The person who uses fluoridated toothpaste and has cavities still falsifies the prediction *If a person uses fluoridated toothpaste, he will have healthy teeth.* But Albert, who uses fluoridated toothpaste and has healthy teeth would be a case of the prediction confirmed.[14] The person who doesn't use fluoridated toothpaste but who has cavities might also be regarded as a confirming case, but weaker than Albert. On the other hand, the person who doesn't use fluoridated toothpaste but has healthy teeth counts on the negative side—as indicating that using fluoridated tooth-paste is not necessary for having healthy teeth, ruling out a strong interpretation of the connection. Such categories would provide a ranking of evidence from supportive to falsifying. Subjects could have them but not map them accurately and consistently onto those provided by Moshman, especially if they were casual in attending to Moshman's definitions.

Moshman also asked questions to see if subjects were inclined to use a falsification strategy in testing hypotheses. He found that barely half the college students did and hardly any seventh graders. Most subjects sought to evaluate the theories by attempting to verify rather than falsify them.

This finding is in line with a great deal of work with adults—much of it using versions of Wason's (1968a) "four-card" problem—indicating that many people evaluate an hypothesis by attempting to verify rather than falsify it (Bracewell & Hidi, 1974; Evans & Lynch, 1973; Gilhooly & Falconer, 1974; Goodwin & Wason, 1972; Johnson-Laird, Legrenzi, & Legrenzi, 1972; Johnson-Laird & Wason, 1970b; Lunzer, Harrison, & Davey, 1972; Van Duyne, 1973, 1974; Wason, 1960, 1966, 1968b, 1969; Wason & Golding, 1974; Wason & Johnson-Laird, 1970, 1972; Wason & Shapiro, 1971). In the original version of the four-card task, a subject is given four cards, each with a number on one side and a letter on the other side, and a sentence. The sentence is a rule like *If there is a D on one side then there is a 3 on the other* or *All cards that have a D on one side have a 3 on the other;* the cards might show, respectively, D, K, 3, and 7 on their face-up sides. The task is to specify the smallest number of cards that need to be turned over in order to find out whether the rule is true or false for the four cards. The answer is two cards, the D and the 7, but very few subjects say that the 7 has to be turned over. Insight into the need to try to falsify comes more readily, although not universally, when familiar content is used (Bracewell & Hidi, 1974; Gilhooly & Falconer, 1974; Johnson-Laird et al., 1972; Wason & Johnson-Laird, 1972; Wason & Shapiro, 1971), for example, rules like *Every time I go to Manchester I travel by car*.

Wason and Johnson-Laird (1969) found that an analogous four-card problem using quantified disjunctions was much easier (e.g., *Every card has a number which is even on one side, or a letter which is a vowel on the other*). Even when one of the propositions was negative, performance was still much better than for conditional rules, despite the truth-table identity of $\sim p \vee q$ and $p \supset q$. Moshman (1977) found it was easier to select examples consistent with a disjunction than with a conditional.

Working with third and seventh graders and college students, O'Brien and Overton (1980) explored the effects of evidence contradicting an expectation on the interpretation of a quantified conditional. Their starting point was a task of Wason's (1964). A conditional like *If a worker is _____ years of age, or older, then that person will receive at least $350 each week* is presented, accompanied by instances, for example, someone 25 earning $200, someone 60 earning $400; the subject has to say whether the instance provides information about the age of the rule, and what information. Wason found that although adults correctly inferred that the age in the rule must be 25 or over given a 25-year-old earning $200, they usually incorrectly inferred that the age must be under 60 given a 60-year-old earning $400. The erroneous inference usually disappeared if subjects were presented with an instance contradicting it (e.g., a 60-year-old earning $200). O'Brien and Overton (1980) gave such contradictory evidence to half their subjects, but not to the other half. The contradictory evidence caused a significant shift only in the adults' responses. Thus, Wason's (1964) result is easily obtainable only in the college-age group with which he worked. (Of course, a series of contradictory instances might affect the younger groups.) O'Brien and Overton (1980) also explored transfer to two versions of the Wason four-card task. They found transfer only in the college subjects, but even in this group, there were many logically unsophisticated responses on all the tasks.

We are puzzled by the work on the assessment of universally quantified conditionals against evidence. It is apparent that even college students—and, a fortiori, younger subjects—have a strong bias to evaluate by trying to verify rather than falsify, and they fail to appreciate that confirming a prediction does not prove something true. What is not clear is why. As we suggested in discussing Moshman's (1979) experiment, subjects may have evaluative categories that are logically defensible for some ordinary evaluative goals, even though they are not appropriate to the task defined by the experimenter. For instance, subjects may tend to construe the task as a request to try to determine the nature of the contingency relation between the attributes of the antecedent and consequent clauses, and for this purpose it is not only the falsifying case that is relevant.

In any case, the poor quality of the performance on these tasks confirms that subjects' logical understanding is reflected more directly in simple deductions than in evaluations and truth judgments. Competence given only by inference schemas would not easily be brought to bear on these tasks.

Developmental Summary

The themes of the work on propositional reasoning find echoes in this section. First, there is evidence for the emergence of some basic inferences by school-entering age, notably the kinds of instantiation captured by PL12 and PL14 of Table 4. Other kinds of inferences represented in Table 4 may well also be available early, but relevant studies are lacking.

There is a second parallel in the development of reasoning strategies. Children are capable of short chains of direct reasoning about classes and relations by fourth grade (Osherson, 1974), but more complex strategies are a much more sophisticated acquisition. The work on syllogisms indicates that even adults have few logical reasoning skills that go beyond a direct-reasoning chain, and they have quick recourse to nonlogical strategies.

The earlier finding of the relative difficulty of truth judgments (over simple deductions) finds an analogy here in the difficulties that adolescents and even many adults have in evaluating universally quantified statements against evidence. Evaluating quantified statements against evidence is a hallmark of the Piagetian "formal operations" (which we discuss next) and would be predicted on those grounds to be a developmentally advanced skill.

We again meet evidence that certain fallacies are closely related to language-comprehension processes. The culprit here is the tendency to convert universal propositions. The tendency depends complexly on content, task, and age. Thus, questions of the form *Are all the F G?* are distinguished from *Are all the G F?* by kindergartners if they are about familiar content (C. L. Smith, 1979), but they are not distinguished until about 8 years of age if they are about objects in a display (Inhelder & Piaget, 1964). The set relations that are consistent with the form *All F are G* are correctly checked by most 12-year-olds and by almost all adults (Neimark & Chapman, 1975). However, when the form is embedded (*Make a building in which all the yellow blocks are square*), it is understood by adults but by few sixth graders (Bucci, 1978). The form is especially difficult when it serves as the major premiss of reasoning problems; then conversion is common even in adults, giving rise to the Asserting-the-Consequent fallacy and many errors of syllogistic reasoning. Apparently, the location of *all* in the sentence becomes increasingly important as a determinant of the scope of *all* with age, but is readily overridden by contextual factors at all ages. A particularly powerful factor is the convenience of finding a construal that facilitates direct reasoning.

PIAGET'S LOGIC AND THE STAGE OF FORMAL OPERATIONS

There are serious problems in interpreting Piaget's logic, so we consider first the structure of the logic and then the interpretive problems. We then discuss the function of the logic, that is, the psychological content or processes it is intended to model. Elements other than the logic that constitute the formal operations stage are then briefly reviewed, and finally the kind of evidence available is considered.

Piaget's Logic

The Logic as an Uninterpreted System

The internal organization of the system is clear so we present that first, and leave the difficult questions of interpretation until afterwards. The system consists of 16 formulas. Two kinds of symbols are used in the formulas: (1) content symbols: p and q, and (2) connective symbols: ., v, and $-$, for conjunction, disjunction, and negation respectively. Determining just what kinds of entities p, q, and the formulas as wholes are intended to represent is the problem of interpreting the system.

The 16 formulas consist of all possible combinations of the four conjuncts ($p \cdot q$, $\bar{p} \cdot q$, $p \cdot \bar{q}$, and $\bar{p} \cdot \bar{q}$) taken one, two, three, or all four at a time, with the conjuncts joined by v, plus a null formula. They are set out in the second column of Table 9, under the heading "Piaget's Form." In the first column, each formula is given a number, a name, and Piaget's symbolic shorthand. The 16 formulas are called "operations" by Piaget, but because it is not clear to us what this term is intended to convey, we will stick to the more neutral term "formula."

Piaget describes four kinds of relations, which he calls "transformations," that formulas can have to each other. One formula can be the "inverse" (N) of another: 1 and 2, 3 and 4, 5 and 6, 7 and 8, 9 and 10, 11 and 12, 13 and 14, 15 and 16 of Table 9 are inverse pairs. Each formula also has a reciprocal formula (R) and a correlated formula (C). For instance, for any formula, s, the reciprocal, $R(s)$, is the same formula with the signs of p and q changed (e.g., Formulas 3 and 6 are reciprocals, and Formula 11 is its own reciprocal); the correlate is the negation (inverse) of the reciprocal. Taken with the identity transformation (I), these transformations are related so that the set of 16 formulas has the abstract algebraic structure of a "four-group," for example, for any formula, the correlate of its reciprocal is its inverse, that is, $C(R[s]) = N(s)$. For more on the system, see Piaget (1949, 1953) and Inhelder and Piaget (1958).

Problems in Interpreting Piaget's Logic

Although Piaget refers to the logic as a propositional logic, it turns out that p and q in the formulas are not to be taken as propositions. Both in his illustrations of the formulas (Piaget, 1949, ch. 6) and in his use of them (Inhelder & Piaget, 1958), p and q stand for attributes or propositional functions (e.g., thinness or flexibility of a rod). Propositional functions are sentence frames like *x is thin* or *x is a mammal*. They have no truth value and do not assert anything until x is identified or a quantifier is prefixed, for example, *For every x* . . . or *There is an x such that* . . . . Whichever quantifier is chosen, the mere fact that p and q are propositional functions rather than propositions means that the logic is not a propositional logic, as Piaget usually refers to it, but some sort of predicate logic, or property logic (because the propositional functions are always monadic).

Ennis (1975) finds several passages in the Genevan writings that suggest that the existential quantifier is intended. This quantifier forms the basis of Ennis's interpretation, which follows Parsons (1960) and is consistent with Flavell (1963), Papert (1963), and Ginsburg and Opper (1969). If we take p as Fx and q as Gx, $p \cdot q$ becomes $\exists x Fx \cdot Gx$. As shown in Table 9, complete affirmation is then represented $\exists x Fx \cdot Gx$ & $\exists x \bar{F}x \cdot Gx$ & $\exists x F\bar{x} \cdot Gx$ & $\exists x \bar{F}x \cdot \bar{G}x$,[15] that is, there are objects with all combinations of values on the attributes F and G, hence, whether or not an object has the one attribute is independent of whether or not it has the other. For other formulas, this interpretation assumes that they contain unexpressed negative statements indicating the attribute combinations that do not occur. For instance, corresponding to implication (Formula 7 in Table 9), we have not only $\exists x Fx \cdot Gx$ & $\exists x \bar{F}x \cdot Gx$ & $\exists x \bar{F}x \cdot \bar{G}x$ but also need to add & $\sim \exists x Fx \cdot \bar{G}x$, which has nothing that corresponds to it in Piaget's disjunct form. The Parsons-Ennis interpretations of all the formulas are given in Table 9. Essentially, according to this interpretation, to establish any formula one establishes that there are cases of certain attribute combinations and no cases of others, and this is what a formula asserts. Note that Piaget's v's all become &'s in the Parsons-Ennis interpretation.

If this interpretation is accepted, the logic is anomalous in at least four ways (Ennis, 1975, 1978; Parsons, 1960). First, in the case of the four triplex formulas (4, 5, 7, and 9 in Table 9), it does not correspond to English (or French) usage to require that there be cases of each attribute combination mentioned in order to assert the corresponding natural-language expression. For example, to assert *If a rod is thin it is flexible*, it is not necessary to establish that there are thick flexible rods; indeed, all that really seems to be necessary is to establish that there are no thin rigid ones (the negative part of Formula 7 that is not mentioned in Piaget's disjunct form). Similarly, to examine a disjunction of the form *The things* [in some domain] *are either F or G* (Formula 5), one might proceed by seeing what combinations existed; but to justify the statement, it suffices that there be no objects that are neither F nor G.

Second, under the Ennis-Parsons interpretation, implication and converse implication (i.e., $p \supset q$ and $q \supset p$) turn out to be incompatible and neither is compatible with equivalence. Implication requires $\exists x \bar{F}x \cdot Gx$, and if that holds, converse implication cannot hold and neither can equivalence. Piaget clearly believes that the three formulas are compatible in his logic and that (in his logic as in standard propositional logic) $p \equiv q$ is the same as $p \supset q$ & $q \supset p$. It follows that either Piaget has made a mistake or that this interpretation is not what he intended; yet he has failed to take numerous opportunities to clear the matter up (e.g., Piaget, 1967).

Third, under this interpretation, the affirmation of p (Formula 13) is incompatible with the affirmation of q (Formula 15): To affirm p requires $\sim \exists x \bar{F}x \cdot Gx$, whereas to affirm q requires $\exists x \bar{F}x \cdot Gx$. In Ennis's example, suppose the domain is men and p is *x is mortal* and q is *x is a vertebrate*. To affirm p requires that there be no immortal vertebrates—but there must be some to affirm q.

These three troubles arise from the fact that under this interpretation the logic requires the existence of certain cases that ordinary intuition does not require. The fourth trouble has a different source, the requirements that certain cases not exist. Here, again, these requirements are too strong. For instance, to deny implication it suffices to establish $\exists x Fx \cdot \bar{G}x$; it is not necessary also to establish $\sim \exists x Fx \cdot Gx$, $\sim \exists x \bar{F}x \cdot Gx$, and $\sim \exists x \bar{F}x \cdot \bar{G}x$.

This point can be generalized. In Piaget's logic the formulas come in mutually contradictory pairs, that is, if one formula is taken as an hypothesis about how attributes are related in some domain, then the inverse formula is intended to define the evidence that will serve as the counterexample that would disprove the hypothesis. But, in the Parsons-Ennis interpretation, the inverse pairs never have this relation. Thus, the evidence needed to disprove conjunction is not defined by the Parsons-Ennis formula for incompatibility but rather is evidence that $\exists x Fx \cdot \bar{G}x$ v $\exists x \bar{F}x \cdot Gx$ v $\exists x \bar{F}x \cdot \bar{G}x$; similarly, counterexamples to incompatibility are not given by the formula for conjunction, but rather by $\exists x Fx \cdot Gx$— and so on for each pair.

Under the Parsons-Ennis interpretation, Piaget's

Table 9. The Formulas of Piaget's Logic and Their Various Possible Interpretations

Operation	Piaget's Form	Parsons-Ennis Interpretation	Revised Leiser Interpretation[a]	
			As Hypothesis	As Counterexample
1. Complete Affirmation: p * q	p·q v p·q̄ v p̄·q v p̄·q̄	∃xFx·Gx & ∃xFx·Ḡx & ∃xF̄x·Gx & ∃xF̄x·Ḡx	∀x(Fx·Gx v Fx·Ḡx v F̄x·Gx v F̄x·Ḡx)	∃xF̄x·Gx v ∃xFx·Ḡx v ∃xF̄x·Gx v ∃xF̄x·Ḡx
2. Complete Negation: "0"	—	—	—	—
3. Conjunction: p·q	p·q	∃xFx·Gx & ~∃xFx·Ḡx & ~∃xF̄x·Gx & ~∃xF̄x·Ḡx	∀xFx·Gx	∃xFx·Ḡx
4. Incompatibility: p/q	p·q̄ v p̄·q v p̄·q̄	∃xFx·Ḡx & ∃xF̄x·Gx & ∃xF̄x·Ḡx & ~∃xFx·Gx	∀x(Fx·Ḡx v F̄x·Gx v F̄x·Ḡx)	∃xFx·Ḡx v ∃xFx·Gx
5. Disjunction: p v q	p·q v p·q̄ v p̄·q	∃xFx·Gx & ∃xFx·Ḡx & ∃xF̄x·Gx & ~∃xF̄x·Ḡx	∀x(Fx·Gx v Fx·Ḡx v F̄x·Gx)	∃xFx·Gx v ∃xF̄x·Ḡx
6. Conjunctive Negation: p̄·q̄	p̄·q̄	∃xF̄x·Ḡx & ~∃xFx·Gx & ~∃xFx·Ḡx & ~∃xF̄x·Gx	∀xF̄x·Ḡx	∃xF̄x·Ḡx
7. Implication: p ⊃ q	p·q v p̄·q v p̄·q̄	∃xFx·Gx & ∃xF̄x·Gx & ∃xF̄x·Ḡx & ~∃xFx·Ḡx	∀x(Fx·Gx v F̄x·Gx v F̄x·Ḡx)	∃xFx·Gx v ∃xF̄x·Gx
8. Nonimplication: p·q̄	p·q̄	∃xFx·Ḡx & ~∃xFx·Gx & ~∃xF̄x·Gx & ~∃xF̄x·Ḡx	∀xFx·Ḡx	∃xFx·Gx
9. Converse implication: q ⊃ p	p·q v p·q̄ v p̄·q̄	∃xFx·Gx & ∃xFx·Ḡx & ∃xF̄x·Ḡx & ~∃xF̄x·Gx	∀x (Fx·Gx v Fx·Ḡx v F̄x·Ḡx)	∃xFx·Gx v ∃xF̄x·Gx
10. Converse Nonimplication: q·p̄	p̄·q	∃xF̄x·Gx & ~∃xFx·Gx & ~∃xFx·Ḡx & ~∃xF̄x·Ḡx	∀xF̄x·Gx	∃xF̄x·Gx
11. Equivalence: p ≡ q	p·q v p̄·q̄	∃xFx·Gx & ∃xF̄x·Ḡx & ~∃xFx·Ḡx & ~∃xF̄x·Gx	∀x(Fx·Gx v F̄x·Ḡx)	∃xFx·Gx v ∃xF̄x·Gx
12. Reciprocal Inclusion: p w q	p̄·q v p·q̄	∃xF̄x·Gx & ∃xFx·Ḡx & ~∃xFx·Gx & ~∃xF̄x·Ḡx	∀x(F̄x·Gx v Fx·Ḡx)	∃xFx·Gx v ∃xF̄x·Gx
13. Affirmation of p: p[q]	p·q v p·q̄	∃xFx·Gx & ∃xFx·Ḡx & ~∃xF̄x·Gx & ~∃xF̄x·Ḡx	∀x(Fx·Gx v Fx·Ḡx)	∃xFx·Gx v ∃xF̄x·Gx
14. Negation of p: p̄[q]	p̄·q v p̄·q̄	∃xF̄x·Gx & ∃xF̄x·Ḡx & ~∃xFx·Gx & ~∃xFx·Ḡx	∀x(F̄x·Gx v F̄x·Ḡx)	∃xFx·Gx v ∃xF̄x·Gx
15. Affirmation of q: q[p]	p·q v p̄·q	∃xFx·Gx & ∃xF̄x·Gx & ~∃xFx·Ḡx & ~∃xF̄x·Ḡx	∀x(Fx·Gx v F̄x·Gx)	∃xFx·Gx v ∃xF̄x·Gx
16. Negation of q: q̄[p]	p·q̄ v p̄·q̄	∃xFx·Ḡx & ∃xF̄x·Ḡx & ~∃xFx·Gx & ~∃xF̄x·Gx	∀x(Fx·Ḡx v F̄x·Ḡx)	∃xFx·Gx v ∃xF̄x·Gx

[a]Leiser's (1982) interpretation is equivalent to the formula under the heading *As Hypothesis*.

logic is so paradoxical that it does not merit the attention of psychologists; it is not a system that could conceivably develop in children around adolescence. Although much that Piaget says suggests that he had in mind this interpretation without awareness of its problems (see Ennis, 1975, for textual discussion), Piaget is far from completely clear about what he intended. So let us ask: Are there other, more reasonable, interpretations of Piaget's logic? There are suggestions in Inhelder and Piaget (1958) that rather than actual existence of attribute combinations, Piaget may have meant possible existence. Let P (. . .) represent *It is possible that* . . . . Under this interpretation, the implication formula would presumably be interpreted as '$P(\exists xFxGx)$ & $P(\exists x\bar{F}x \cdot Gx)$ & $P(\exists x\bar{F}x \cdot \bar{G}x)$ & $\sim \exists xFx \cdot \bar{G}x$' (or something of the sort), and the other formulas interpreted analogously. Ennis (1975) mentions this interpretation, but no one has developed it with any precision, perhaps because it does not look as if it could cure the troubles of the Parsons-Ennis interpretation. For instance, in English the proposition *If a pendulum is long it is slow* does not need the possibility of existence of short and slow pendulums to be true. Similarly, the inverse pairs of formulas are not related as hypothesis and counterexample on the ''possible-existence'' interpretation any more than on the Parsons-Ennis interpretation.

Leiser (1982) has recently proposed what he calls an ''epistemic'' interpretation. This is an interpretation in terms of what is possible from the standpoint of a subject's current knowledge (''epistemic'' possibility). Like the Parsons-Ennis interpretation, Leiser's interpretation also concords well with certain passages in Inhelder and Piaget (1958). To take implication as the example again, $p \supset q$ can be regarded as an ''addition'' of seven possibilities:

1. $p.q \lor \bar{p}.q \lor \bar{p}.\bar{q}$
2. $p.q \lor \bar{p}.q$
3. $p.q \lor \quad\quad \bar{p}.\bar{q}$
4. $\quad\quad \bar{p}.q \lor \bar{p}.\bar{q}$
5. $p.q$
6. $\quad\quad \bar{p}.q$
7. $\quad\quad\quad\quad \bar{p}.\bar{q}$

Leiser accepts the interpretation of the conjuncts as existence statements, so, under this interpretation, Piaget's implication becomes interpreted as:

(24) $((\exists xFx \cdot Gx$ & $\exists x\bar{F}x \cdot Gx$ & $\exists x\bar{F}x \cdot \bar{G}x) \lor (\exists xFx \cdot Gx$ & $\exists x\bar{F}x \cdot Gx) \lor (\exists xFx \cdot Gx$ & $\exists x\bar{F}x \cdot \bar{G}x) \lor (\exists x\bar{F}x \cdot Gx$ & $\exists x\bar{F}x \cdot \bar{G}x) \lor \exists xFx \cdot Gx \lor \exists x\bar{F}x \cdot Gx \lor \exists x\bar{F}x \cdot \bar{G}x)$ & $\sim \exists xFx \cdot \bar{G}x$

And the other Piagetian formulas are interpreted analogously. Because existence of each mentioned attribute combination is no longer required, the first trouble of the Parsons-Ennis interpretation disappears. Leiser notes that under his interpretation, implication and converse implication are compatible and that when they both hold, the formula for equivalence is met. So the second problem of the Parsons-Ennis interpretation also disappears. And so does the third problem: The affirmations of p and q are now compatible.

Surprisingly, Leiser does not propose that the Parsons-Ennis interpretation be abandoned in favor of his interpretation. He considers that there are passages in various works that indicate that Piaget intended both interpretations. He proposes that the two interpretations correspond to different stages of the subject's knowledge. Thus, the formulas represent hypotheses, or the subject's current knowledge state about which attribute combinations occur in reality and which do not (e.g., which attributes of a pendulum can co-occur with rapid oscillation, and which with slow). Early in the subject's experimentation with the apparatus, Leiser proposes, his interpretation is appropriate: The subject does not yet know exactly which combinations are possible and a formulation like *If a pendulum is long it is slow* is to be interpreted as in Expression 24, as indicating a set of possibilities. When a subject's knowledge is complete, the subject knows which possibilities are actual; then, Leiser thinks, the Parsons-Ennis interpretation is appropriate.

We find this proposal very strange indeed. It would mean, for instance, that a quantified *if-then* statement (e.g., *If a pendulum is long it is slow*) and its converse (*If a pendulum is slow it is long*) are not contradictory while the subject is experimenting with pendulums, but they become so when the experimentation is complete!

Can Leiser's interpretation be simply substituted for Parsons-Ennis'? Let us look at Leiser's proposal in more detail. First, it is possible to simplify the formulation enormously, by noting that Expression 24 above is equivalent to:

(25) $\forall x(Fx \cdot Gx \lor \bar{F}x \cdot Gx \lor \bar{F}x \cdot \bar{G}x)$

We adopt this form forthwith. The interpretation of each formula using $\forall$ is shown in Table 9, in the ''As Hypothesis'' column under ''Revised Leiser Interpretation.''

Although Leiser does not note the fact, it can be seen that the fourth trouble of the Parsons-Ennis interpretation remains. The formulas that are supposed to be inverses are not each the negation of the other.

For instance, conjunction, $\forall xFx \cdot Gx$, is not the negation of incompatibility, $\forall x(Fx \cdot \bar{G}x$ v $\bar{F}x \cdot Gx$ v $\bar{F}x \cdot \bar{G}x)$; nor is it the negation of p (14, Table 9) the negation of the affirmation of p (13, Table 9). The difficulty is not curable within the confines of a mere interpretation of Piaget's system. In the final column, under the head "As Counterexample," we show what each formula would have to be to negate its Piagetian inverse in the As Hypothesis column. (Thus, the counterexample formulas in Rows 1, 3, 5, 7, 9, 11, 13, and 15 contradict the Hypothesis formulas in Rows 2, 4, 6, 8, 10, 12, 14, and 16, respectively.) It is as if every Piaget formula is systematically ambiguous; it has one interpretation that uses the universal quantifier and is a possible hypothesis or generalization about some domain, and it has another interpretation that uses the existential quantifier and defines what would count as a counterexample disproving the "inverse" hypothesis.

Is there any evidence that Piaget intended some such double interpretation of his formulas? We have found no explicit recognition of the two interpretations. But in practice, when Inhelder and Piaget discuss evidence that serves as counterexample to a hypothesis or generalization, it is evidence that supports the As Counterexample form (e.g., when nonimplication is used to disprove implication, the observation shows that $\exists xFx \cdot \bar{G}x$ not that $\forall xFx \cdot \bar{G}x$; similarly, a case of reciprocal inclusion that disproves equivalence shows that $\exists x\bar{F}x \cdot Gx$ v $\exists xFx \cdot \bar{G}x$). On the other hand, evidence that supports a generalization or hypothesis is evidence for either the form with the universal quantifier, or (usually) evidence for the Parsons-Ennis formula (see Ennis, 1975, and Leiser, in press, for discussion of relevant passages from Inhelder and Piaget, 1958, and Piaget, 1949). Of course, every Parsons-Ennis formula in Table 9 entails the revised-Leiser As Hypothesis formula to its immediate right (although the converse entailment does not hold). So a subject could establish the revised Leiser formula by establishing the Parsons-Ennis one by observation of cases. The passages that appear to support the Parsons-Ennis interpretation may be describing this strategy.

It seems very doubtful that Piaget ever worked through the interpretation of his system. He could hardly have failed to discover the paradoxes of the Parsons-Ennis interpretation or to recognize the ambiguity of the Piagetian formulas revealed in the revised Leiser interpretation. We strongly doubt that there are other interpretations Piaget might have had in mind.

The revised Leiser interpretation could be regarded as a system in its own right, consisting of 32 formulas grouped in hypothesis and counterexample pairs. As such, it is formally very similar to Piaget's system—if the quantifiers are erased, the system collapses into Piaget's. It is hard to imagine that Piaget's system could have any useful logical or psychological property that would not be inherited by the revised Leiser system.[16] And the revised Leiser system has the huge additional virtue of clarity.

In sum, Piaget's logic is badly paradoxical under one interpretation, its formulas are systematically ambiguous under another, and no more satisfactory interpretation is likely to appear. However, there is a system formally quite similar to Piaget's that does not suffer the same problems. Piagetians might consider substituting it for Piaget's system in their theoretical system; neither the merits nor the defects of the theory would be much changed. Without such substitution, claims about the formal operations stage are left without any theoretical foundation. For Piaget's logic clearly cannot develop at adolescence, or at any time—it is too problematic to stand as a psychological model of anything.

The Intended Function of the Logic

Let us now consider what the logic was intended to do. Our reading of Inhelder and Piaget (1958)—and in this we were helped by Leiser (1982)—is that the formulas represent possible hypotheses, conjectures, generalizations, or states of knowledge about the relationships among attributes in a domain being investigated. Despite Piaget's term "operation," the formulas are not mental operations at all: They are a way of coding data, not of manipulating it. A formula represents an hypothesis before it has been proven, and represents a state of knowledge afterward. Essentially, then, the function of the logic is to provide a framework that imposes an hypothesis space on a domain. With two attributes, a space of 16 hypotheses is defined. Of course, many problem domains contain more than two attributes. The system can be expanded to three, four, or more attributes, although with many attributes, the hypothesis space becomes enormous. With three attributes (see Piaget, 1952) there are 256 formulas (512 in the corresponding revised Leiser system). The claim that the logic develops at adolescence is, then, a claim that the typical adolescent has a general framework or scheme that can generate an hypothesis space containing all the ways the attributes in a problem domain might be related to each other, at least for the kinds of problem domains cited by Inhelder and Piaget (1958). Inhelder and Piaget's description of the adolescent as reasoning by hypothesis and supposition is to be understood in terms of this scheme. The adolescent's reasoning is hypothetical in the sense of having a scheme that generates all possible hypotheses and of allowing reasoning within this space. If we understand correctly, the claim is not that the younger child is incapable of making a possibly counterfactual hypothesis, but rather that the younger child lacks a scheme that defines the possible hypotheses.

Assuming our reading of Piaget is correct, the purpose of his logic is not the same as that of the inference schemas considered in previous sections. These defined steps in a chain of reasoning; they do not code knowledge gained in a problem domain, or specify hypotheses, as Piaget's logic is intended to do. Thus, although the same term "logic" has been used, the theoretical functions are quite different and the ideas not competitive.

One might ask, what does define the mental steps that test the hypotheses of a Piagetian hypothesis space, in order to select the correct generalization? One must note that the kinds of problems used by Inhelder and Piaget (1958) are not deductive reasoning problems like those reviewed in previous sections. As Falmagne (1975a, 1980) has elaborated, they explore a scientific type of reasoning; they involve obtaining and interpreting evidence, and study the child as scientist rather than the child as logician. For instance, in the pendulum problem (Inhelder & Piaget, 1958), the child is given apparatus in which pendulums can vary in length, weight, height of release, and force of push, and the child has to discover which factor determines the frequency of oscillation. Thus, the mental steps of the subject's reasoning are those involved in selecting a test to be run (e.g., in the pendulum study, which pendulums to compare) and in interpreting the results. These mental steps are not described as such in Piagetian theory (as we understand it), although they may be largely determined by a general plan—to vary one variable at a time while holding others constant—which it is claimed develops alongside the formal operations.

Newell and Simon (1972) have argued that there is no essential psychological difference between inductive and deductive reasoning—the discovery of a proof involves a search through a problem space just as much as the solution to a scientific problem. It is also true that once a finite hypothesis space has been defined for a scientific domain, computing which hypotheses are eliminated and which are still viable as each datum come in is purely a deductive matter. Then, wherein lies the difference between the tasks used by Inhelder and Piaget and the logical deduction of the preceding sections?

In the problem-solving literature, solving a problem is regarded as a search for a path from some initial situation to a goal. Some strategies are described, for example, hillclimbing, means-end analysis, and planning a solution path by analogy either to problems for which a path is known or to an abstracted problem (e.g., Hayes, 1978). Such general strategies do not seem to differentiate deductive and scientific-type problems. But there are specific strategies relevant to finding a deductive argument that seem to have small relevance for Inhelder and Piaget's (1958) problems, for example, the strategy of supposing the negation of a desired conclusion and trying to prove a reductio ad absurdum. As Falmagne (1980) notes, there are also specific strategies that are useful on scientific problems and that have no relevance to proof finding. These are strategies of data gathering: For example, varying one variable at one time while holding others constant is one; the method of successive fractionation of an hypothesis space (as in the 20-questions game) is another. Of course, logic, in the sense of the inference schemas discussed earlier, plays a role in interpreting scientific data, but it does not shape the choice of the data to be gathered.

The Operational Schemas

In addition to the logic, the stage of formal operations is characterized by the development of the "operational schemata" and the investigative strategy of varying one factor while holding others constant. The operational schemata are a set of useful concepts or strategies that are separate from the logic but that are claimed to be related to it, in that their development presupposes the logic. Eight such are described by Inhelder and Piaget (1958). They include several that have to do with the coordination or mutual compensation of variables, for example, a notion of proportion and a concept of mechanical equilibrium. The schemata also include a systematic method for enumerating all combinations or permutations of a set of elements, as well as qualitative statistical notions of probability and correlation.

The theoretical ties between the schemata and the logic do not seem to be spelled out clearly, and we find the discussion of the relationship (Inhelder & Piaget, 1958, pp. 307–329) hard to summarize. Some of the reasoning seems analogical. According to Piaget, the notion of mutual compensation of variables (e.g., in a balance, increase in weight compensated by decrease in distance from the fulcrum) is dependent on the Reciprocity transformation of the INRC group. However, as Flavell (1963) points out, following Parsons (1960), in physical systems like a balance scale or a hydraulic press, the realization of the four group is physical rather than logical. For example, in a balance scale, one can increase the weight in the pan (p, say) or move the pan further from the fulcrum (q, say). One can undo each of these changes—note that undoing an action is not the same as negating a proposition—by decreasing weight (p^*, say) or distance (q^*, say). Similarly, one can compensate for increasing weight by decreasing distance, and one can compensate for increasing distance by decreasing weight (i.e., p and q^*, and p^* and q, are reciprocals in Piaget's terminology). There is an implicit assumption that all realizations of a four group, whether physical or logical, are psychologically equivalent (Flavell, 1963). A parallel assumption is made in discussing the emerging ability to enumerate all combinations of a set of elements—that enumerating all combinations of a set of tokens is not psychologically different from forming all combinations of a set of conjunctions of a pair of propositional functions.

In places, Inhelder & Piaget (1958) seem to suggest that it is not the logic that is fundamental to the formal operations stage. Instead, it is some content-free notion of an INRC group, together with the ability to construct all combinations of a set. All subject matters are then equivalent, and the logic is merely one manifestation (albeit an important one) where these two join to organize a domain. Such a conception would tie the logic and many of the operational schemata together theoretically. But it is a very abstract notion that is at many removes from data. And it is suggested as a possibility, not adopted as part of the theory.

Evidence

The concept of the formal operations stage can be formulated as the claim that the following elements of thinking are rare prior to the age of 11 to 12 years, but they become typical in late adolescence:

1. The ability to form an hypothesis space that specifies all possible dependency relations among the attributes present in a problem domain (i.e., the logic).
2. The strategy of varying one factor at a time, holding the others constant.
3. The operational schemata.

Because the logic itself is paradoxical, one should obviously not expect much in the way of supporting evidence for it. However, the notion of the develop-

ment of an ability to construct an hypothesis space impresses us as interesting and important, and because there is a system very similar to Piaget's that is not paradoxical, Element (1) should not, we think, be rejected merely because of the defects of Piaget's logic.

In Inhelder and Piaget (1958), the first set of chapters are directed toward elements (1) and (2), and the rest to element (3). We will not attempt a detailed review and will largely ignore work on many of the schemata, several of which seem remote from our topic. In general, we find the evidence of Inhelder and Piaget and that from subsequent work with similar tasks (see later) to be indirect and suggestive. The evidence convinces us that children with age become increasingly systematic in their exploration of scientific-type problems, with the adolescents both more systematic than the preadolescents and often using the strategy of varying one factor at a time. Systematicity in hypothesis testing implies a conception of the possible hypotheses, but it says nothing precise about the nature of the schema that generates the hypothesis space. Inhelder and Piaget's observations are consistent with the possibility that the adolescent's conception of some of the dependencies between variables resembles some of those posited by Piaget, but the observations leave a great deal to be desired in the way of detail (Bynum, Thomas, & Weitz, 1972).

A great deal of research has simply treated the formal operations stage as operationally defined by one or more of Inhelder and Piaget's tasks, and administered the tasks to various groups with an explicit scoring procedure and a tabulation and statistical treatment of results, sometimes exploring correlational relationships among tasks. This kind of work has usually replicated the general lines of Inhelder and Piaget's findings, with perhaps some small revision upwards of the usual age of development. Good performance usually develops during adolescence, although there are differences among tasks, not much correlation among tasks, and often a minority (even a sizable minority) of college students do not perform well (e.g., Burt, 1971; Danner & Day, 1977; Keating, 1975, 1979; Kuhn & Brannock, 1977; Kuhn & Ho, 1977; Lawson, 1977; Martorano, 1977; Roberge & Flexer, 1979). However, the poor performance of college students is probably often due to temporary processing difficulties and older preadolescent children show some ability to learn (e.g., Kuhn & Angelev, 1976; Kuhn, Ho, & Adams, 1979; Siegler & Liebert, 1975; Siegler, Liebert, & Liebert, 1973; Stone & Day, 1978). Two aspects of the stage have been the subject of more work than others—the development of a systematic method for finding all combinations (or all permutations) of a set of elements (one of the operational schemata), and the strategy of varying only one variable at a time. Both show the usual developmental course, the latter having been shown to be teachable to older preadolescents (e.g., Conan, 1978; Siegler & Liebert, 1975), although not always spontaneously adopted by college students (e.g., Bruner, Goodnow, & Austin, 1956; Danner & Day, 1977). Kuhn and Brannock (1977) found that the preadolescents' difficulty is not just one of executing the strategy: They usually have difficulty interpreting the kind of data yielded by the strategy. There also has been work on closely related strategies—that of seeking to falsify rather than verify, and the successive fractionation strategy of the 20-questions game (e.g., Denney, 1974; Denney & Conners, 1974; Moshman, 1979).

The hypotheses that Piaget's logic is intended to generate are universally quantified statements. At the end of the preceding section we reviewed work indicating that difficulties are often present into adulthood in evaluating such statements against evidence, especially quantified conditionals.

The use of strategies for isolating variables implies an organized hypothesis space of some sort, but there has been almost no work investigating the development of children's schemes for imposing an hypothesis space on a problem and defining the kinds of dependencies among variables envisaged as possible in the space. That seems to be the central challenge imposed by Piaget's claims about the formal operations stage, and although difficult to investigate, it is clearly an interesting and important aspect of intellectual development for study, quite independently of Piagetian theory.

MODALITY, PRESUPPOSITION, AND RELATED MATTERS

In this section we discuss a variety of things related to logical reasoning that fall outside the previous sections. We begin with modality, that is, notions having to do with necessity and possibility.

Modal and Metalogical Concepts and Reasoning

Logical and Linguistic Considerations

Modality is a tricky subject that the psychologist should approach warily. There is a tradition of subtle distinctions about necessity and possibility that comes down from the scholastic philosophers (Bochenski, 1961; Kneale & Kneale, 1962). Mod-

ern modal logic is not in a settled state. Several systems were proposed early this century (C. I. Lewis, 1918), and although the subject is controversial (e.g., Quine, 1953c, 1961), it is an active research area in which there have been recent advances. However, the correspondences between the natural-language concepts and those of the logics are far from straightforward. In current modal logics, *necessarily true* is interpreted in terms of some version of the Leibnizian "true in all possible worlds" (e.g., Hintikka, 1969; Kripke, 1963). The psychological reality of this sort of interpretation can be questioned (e.g., Johnson-Laird, 1978). It seems to us that possible worlds are not the psychological basis of people's possibility concepts and suppositional processes, but rather a philosophical reification created from them.

One characteristic of the logical systems that is shared by natural language is that necessity and possibility are interdefinable with the aid of negation. Let N and P be sentence prefixes meaning 'of necessity' and 'possibly,' respectively, and let p be any proposition. Then, $Np = \sim P(\sim p)$; alternatively, $Pp = \sim N(\sim p)$.

From the point of view of logical reasoning, an important kind of necessity lies in the notion of logical consequence, of one statement following logically from another. The technical term for this is "entailment." Although this is a metalogical rather than modal notion, its import can readily be expressed in modal logic: *"p" entails "q"* can be rendered by $N(p \supset q)$.[17]

Now let us consider English modal expressions. It is well known that the modal auxiliaries can have several different kinds of meaning. First of all, one can separate off one sense of *can*, 'be able to' (as in *George can ride a unicycle*), as not being genuinely modal and thus not of concern here.[18] Next, one can distinguish a deontic (moral, ethical) system from more "logical" ones. In the deontic system, N means 'obligatory' rather than 'necessary,' and P is "permissible" rather than 'possible.' We contrast the two systems in Table 10. There is overlap in the auxiliaries used in the two systems but there are also several nonconcordances, for example, *may not* aligns with $N(\sim p)$ in the deontic system (i.e., 'obligatorily not') but it aligns with $P(\sim p)$ on the logical side.

"Epistemic" Versus "Alethic." Within just the Logical Systems part of Table 10, it is possible to distinguish more than one kind of possibility and necessity. It turns out that most uses of modal terms in English have a sense, called "epistemic" by philosophers, that is different from the sense rendered

Table 10.   The English Modal Auxiliary Systems: Logical Correspondences

Logic	English (Logical Systems)			English (Deontic System)		
Np	$(2^{1.76})$	must be / has to be	(3.56).	(John)	must / should / ought to	(eat pork).
Pp	$(2^{1.76})$	may be / could be	(3.56).	(John)	may / can	(eat pork).
$\sim Pp = N(\sim p)$	$(2^{1.76})$	cannot be / could not be	(3.56).	(John)	must not / should not / may not	(eat pork).
$\sim Np = P(\sim p)$	$(2^{1.76})$	may not be	(3.56).	(John)	need not	(eat pork).

N = 'necessary', P = 'possible' in the logical systems; N = 'obligatory', P = 'permissible' in the deontic system.

by the common modal logic systems. In an instructive paper, Karttunen (1972) points out three differences. First, in modal logics *Np* is a stronger statement than just *p* because *Np* means that *p* is not merely true but necessarily true. However, in English the reverse is usually the case, for example, *John must have left* is usually weaker than *John has left*. In the former, the *must* indicates that John's leaving is only inferred, not directly known.

Second, on modal logics $\sim p$ and *Pp* are consistent. However, in English there is obviously some kind of incompatibility between the two clauses of:

(26) It isn't raining in Chicago, but it may be raining there.

Third, in modal logics the form $N(p \supset q)$ makes a quite different statement from $p \supset Nq$. Yet there is often little or no difference in corresponding English forms, for example, *It must be that if Bill has a diamond ring, he stole it from someone* means much the same as *If Bill has a diamond ring, he must have stolen it from someone*.

Karttunen concludes that in English *must* and *possible* usually indicate inference from knowledge (hence "epistemic"). Thus, *It must be that p* means 'from what I know it follows that p.' This is quite different from any true-in-all-possible-worlds version of necessity. Similarly, *It may be that p* means 'there is nothing in what I know from which it follows that not-p.' (The incompatibility in Sentence 26 is then explained by the fact that its first clause is equivalent to *I know it isn't raining in Chicago,* and the second clause denies this knowledge.) It is possible to write a logic for epistemic necessity and possibility (Hintikka, 1962), but it is part of a logic of knowledge and belief, not a version of ordinary modal logic.

We can contrast further the difference between epistemic and modal-logic notions of necessity by considering the following schema:

(27) $$\frac{\Sigma; \, \Sigma \text{ entails } p,}{Np}$$

where Σ is available factual information. The schema expresses the fact that one can show that a propo-

sition, *p*, "must" (epistemically) be true, by showing that it follows from available information, Σ, known to be true. In standard modal logics, the same conclusion would hold only if Σ were itself not merely true but also necessarily true.

The entailment in Schema 27 need not, of course, be purely logical; it could be any sort of cause-effect chain. Thus, suppose Σ represents some state of affairs, Σ^*, and *p* some event, p*. Then we can write 27 as:

(27′) $$\frac{\Sigma; \, \Sigma^* \text{ results in } p^*}{Np}$$

That is, if Σ is true and p* is an inevitable result of Σ^*, then p* must occur, that is, *p* is necessarily true. If Σ^* is a necessary but not a sufficient condition of p* and there is no other information that would rule out p*, then the conclusion is *Pp:* As Johnson-Laird (1978) points out, to evaluate a claim that something is possible, one often determines a referent situation (i.e., Σ^*) and then attempts mentally to construct a sequel to it that leads to the event whose possibility is being evaluated (i.e., p*).

A kind of undecidability can be expressed in terms of epistemic possibility and necessity: *p is undecidable* $= Pp \, \& \, P(\sim p)$, that is, 'from what I know, *p* is possible and $\sim p$ is also possible.' Equally, *p is decidable* $= Np$ or $N(\sim p)$. Thus, entailment, epistemic necessity and possibility, and decidability are a semantically closely interrelated group of concepts.

It is possible in English to express notions of necessity and possibility that can be construed in terms of modal logic's possible worlds. These are often called "alethic" in contrast to "epistemic." For instance, although Sentence 26 is anomalous, one can say *It isn't raining in Chicago, but it could be* (e.g., if the clouds hadn't dispersed); *could* there expresses a notion of possibility that is not epistemic (Karttunen, 1972).

The deontic-epistemic-alethic distinction can affect the choice of auxiliary verb and must, therefore, be recognized in some form in adults' lexical entries for the modal auxiliaries. Thus, some such distinctions must be acquired as part of learning linguistic structure. There seems to be no need to assume that the same holds for the distinctions that can be made within the alethic and epistemic categories (i.e., between logical, physical, psychological, or other kinds of possibility and necessity).[19]

Psychological Data

We begin with children's appreciation of incompatibility and entailment. First, we may recall from a study summarized earlier (Braine & Rumain, 1981) that 5- and 6-year-olds recognized a logical incompatibility (one puppet saying about a closed box "There's a dog in the box" and another saying "There's no dog in the box," followed by the question "Can they both be right?"), and they associated this incompatibility with impossibility ("That can't be," "That's impossible"). However, recognizing an incompatibility in these ideally simple circumstances is a far cry from identifying one under other conditions. In some interesting studies, Markman (1977, 1979b) presented children with descriptions that contained either explicit or implicit contradictions. For example, part of a passage containing an implicit contradiction read:

> there is absolutely no light at the bottom of the ocean. Some fish that live at the bottom of the ocean know their food by its color. (1979b, p. 646)

In the explicit condition, the passage read:

> there is absolutely no light at the bottom of the ocean. It is pitch black down there. When it is that dark the fish cannot see anything. They cannot even see colors. Some fish that live at the bottom of the ocean can see the color of their food. (p. 646)

When the children (third, fifth, and sixth graders) were asked merely to judge the comprehensibility of the stories (with some probe questions), almost none noticed the contradiction in the implicit condition and only about half noticed it in the explicit condition (with no age differences). Yet there was good recall of the information, and adults noticed the contradiction in the implicit condition. With instructions to "try and spot the problem," and "tell me what it was that did not make any sense," most of the 12-year-olds were successful, but only half the 8-year-olds were, even for the explicit passage. We may note, too, that 8 is the age at which items requiring identification of "verbal absurdities" enter the Stanford-Binet Test (Terman & Merrill, 1937).

Some early work of Piaget's on the development of *because* concerned entailment. Piaget (1928) de-

scribed three uses of *because* developing around age 7 or 8. One reflected physical causation, another psychological motivation, and the third logical entailment. Corrigan (1975) took up the same subject more systematically. She examined the three types (labeled "affective," "physical," and "logical") in both usage and comprehension. Her usage test required subjects to complete a *because*-clause (e.g., for "affective": *Jon laughed at Sue. She hit Jon because* . . . [he laughed at her]). Her comprehension tests required a "right" or "wrong" judgment. A descriptive statement was presented followed by two clauses joined by *because:* in half the items the two clauses were ordered appropriately and in the other half they were reversed. For instance, a logical example is *All the blocks were white* followed by either *Jon had a white block because there were only white ones* or *There were only white ones because Jon had a white block* (reversal). The basis of responses was clarified by follow-up questions. Subjects were age 2½ to 7½ years old. In each task, the affective reasons were easiest and the logical ones hardest. All kinds of affective items were solved by a majority of subjects at about age 6, the physical and logical items at age 7. Thus, this study agrees with Piaget (1928) on the age at which *because* can express entailment.

The experiments of Pieraut-Le Bonniec (1980) are the only programmatic series of studies on modality. They divide into two groups, one set with preschool children and the second set with older children. The work on the preschoolers is presented as exploring a "pragmatic" modality concerned with the "makability" of objects given certain kinds of materials. Most of the experiments used plastic elements that could be fitted together to make objects. Elements were of three types: curved (for making bracelets), straight (for sticks), and semidisks called "moons"—two moons could make a wheel; these elements were of various colors. In an initial experiment, in which a girl doll had access to only curved elements and a boy doll to only straight elements, 60% of the 4-year-olds and all the 5-year-olds correctly answered the question *Can the boy/ girl doll make a bracelet/stick?*

In the next experiment, the girl doll had blue, yellow, and green curved elements, and the boy doll had curved, straight, and moon elements, all yellow. A series of questions were asked. The easiest questions, answered by most of the 4-year-olds, asked about the kinds of objects a doll could make (*Can she make a bracelet/stick/yellow object/green object?*). The next easiest, answered by some of the 4-year-olds and most of the 5-year-olds, asked about objects negatively defined (*Can she make something that is not a bracelet/a bracelet that is not yellow?*). The hardest, answered only by a third of the 5-year-olds, concerned kinds of objects the dolls were obliged to make, or need not make (*She doesn't want to make anything yellow; Must she?/Must she make bracelets?/When she makes bracelets, is she obliged to make a green one?*). Thus, in this situation, questions about possibility and impossibility are understood before questions about necessity. Confusions in the latter type are illustrated by a child who said "She must make a yellow bracelet, but she can also make a green one."

The next experiment included the temporal quantifying terms *always, sometimes,* and *never.* There were six dolls, each with a box of elements; one had only curved elements, one only moons, three had two types of elements, and one had all three types. The easiest questions, solved by both 4- and 5-year-olds, were of the form *Show me the dolls that can/cannot make bracelets/wheels.* The hardest, solved by only 30% of the 5-year-olds, had to do with necessity (*Show me the dolls that are/are not obliged to make bracelets/wheels*). These results are like the previous ones. The questions using time quantifiers were of intermediate difficulty (*Show me the dolls that always make bracelets/wheels; or that sometimes but not always make bracelets/wheels*).

Another experiment explored the development of the time quantifiers further. The material consisted of three cars (various colors) and three trucks. A candy was hidden in one—if it was a big candy it was in one of the trucks, and if a small candy in one of the cars, and this fact was learned. Certain time-quantifier questions were easy and solved by most of the 4-year-olds (e.g., *Are the big candies always or not always in the trucks/sometimes or never in the cars?*). In these, the correct responses can be regarded as just adding emphasis to the unquantified declarative (e.g., in *The big candies are always in the trucks, always* could be deleted without disturbing truth value). Other time-quantifier questions were solved by only half the 5-year-olds (*Are the small candies always or not always/always or sometimes/in this red car?*); only in these questions is there a contrast between *sometimes* and *always,* and *sometimes* and *never;* some of the children spontaneously say *not never* for *sometimes.* Pieraut-Le Bonniec suggests that success on this set reflects the ability to construct a class: When the child has to select just three vehicles to look for the hidden candy in, knowing the candy's size, only about half the 5-year-olds consistently selected the appropriate set (all the cars or all the trucks).

Kuczaj (1975) also finds that the meanings of *always, never,* and *sometimes* become understood during the preschool period. His data are consistent with *always* and *never* being understood first, but they suggest considerable variability in what is understood by the terms in the very early stages. He suggests a final organization by degree of frequency—*never < seldom < sometimes < usually < always*—with *usually* and *seldom* developing after the other terms, *usually* developing well before *seldom.* However, his procedure is not such as would elicit the logical oppositions among *always, sometimes,* and *never.*

Pieraut-Le Bonniec concludes that in what concerns "makability," notions of possibility and impossibility are constructed before those of necessity, and that the time quantifiers develop during the same age period. The children begin with the opposition *possible-impossible* (i.e., makable-unmakable), then add the third element *possible . . . not;* next, the dichotomy *obligatory-prohibited* (i.e., forced to make-prevented from making) is formed and the third element (*need not*) added. Then, at around age 7, the systems are integrated: prohibited = impossible and possible-not-to-make = need not make.

The first of Pieraut-Le Bonniec's (1980) experiments with older children presented two boxes: Box A contained both straight and curved pieces and Box B only straight pieces. A collection of finished objects was presented, and for each object the 6-year-old subjects had to say which box contained the pieces used to make it. They had no difficulty answering in the decidable cases, but only 20% of the subjects gave a response of undecidable when asked about straight objects, although some others showed doubt.

The next study found 11- and 12-year-olds able to make some judgments of "possibly true" for undecidable statements. Two other experiments explored the development between 6 and 11 years of age. We summarized the first of these (Pieraut-Le Bonniec, 1980, Experiment 4) earlier (see *Development of the Response of Undecidable*). The experiment did not find a substantial majority of undecidable responses until 10 years of age, although subjects often qualified their responses with expressions of doubt from about 6 years of age on. The other experiment (Pieraut-Le Bonniec, 1980, Experiment 5) used two situations. In one, the subject had two moons; one was of known color (red, say), and one of unknown color (red or blue). The subject was asked questions like (1) *Can you be sure you can make an all-red wheel?* (2) *Are you sure you can make a monocolored wheel?* and (3) *Given that the wheel is monocolored, can you tell which color?* Note that some of these questions involved reasoning by supposition, that is, considering both possibilities, red and blue, for the unknown moon, and pursuing the consequences of each supposition. Four levels are distinguished in the responses. The youngest children showed no understanding. The next level showed some doubt on the undecidable questions, for example, "Yes I'm sure [I can make an all-red wheel], because *maybe* that one [unknown] is red." Many 6-, most 7-, and half the 8-year-olds fell into this category. At the third level, undecidability was understood: On undecidable questions, subjects would enumerate both possibilities and say one could not be sure. Half the 8-year-olds and almost all the 9- and 10-year-olds reached at least this level, and some of the 9- and two thirds of the 10-year-olds reached the final level at which decidable questions that required reasoning by supposition were answered correctly. The kind of reasoning by supposition required here was discussed earlier (see *The Development of Indirect Reasoning Strategies*).

As we have seen, Pieraut-Le Bonniec interprets her experiments on younger children as having to do with a "pragmatic" modality of doing (makability). She views the period of doubt (without undecidable responses) as reflecting some grasp of the epistemic distinction between *I know that p* and *I do not know that p*, whence *I do not know whether p or not*. After that, she proposes, alethic possibility and necessity become understood, leading to a grasp of undecidability (both eventualities are possible and neither is necessary). This construction culminates in an ability to reason by supposition—to suppose each of the open possibilities in turn.

Let us consider whether or not there are possible alternative interpretations for this pioneering set of experiments. First, it does not seem to us that the possibility and necessity of the second set of experiments summarized is alethic. In Experiment 5, when a child says, for instance, "forcément elle sera rouge," the necessity felt is clearly not of the true-in-all-possible-worlds type; instead, the child means that it is logically "forced" [*forcément*] by the information given. That puts it in the epistemic category, according to the distinctions made earlier (i.e., it is a necessity sanctioned by Schema 27).

Second, although the first set of experiments can be construed narrowly (as concerned with makability), it seems to us that a broader interpretation is also open. The kind of possibility and necessity considered there does seem to be of the true-in-all-possible-worlds type, for example, in no possible world could one make straight sticks out of curved elements. Thus, it could be that the results of these experiments reflect the development of general (alethic) concepts of possibility and necessity. Such a conclusion would fit with the evidence cited that around age 5 or 6, simple cases of logical incompatibility (when noticed) are recognized as indicating an impossible state of affairs. Thus, it may be that at age 6 or so, children have developed a general concept of possibility and necessity.

Epistemic possibility and necessity is a kind of possibility and necessity that is conditional on knowledge, that is, it is allowed or entailed by a known specific state of affairs. As such, it must be dependent on a grasp of entailment, which the data cited from Corrigan (1975) and Piaget (1928) suggest becomes available at around age 7. Thus, at this age, if our speculative construction is correct, the three intellectual components for constructing epistemic possibility and necessity would be available—some grasp of entailment and general concepts of possibility and necessity. Because undecidability is definable in terms of epistemic possibility (as $P(p)$ & $P(\sim p)$), one would expect it to be grasped as part of developing an understanding of epistemic possibility and necessity—a result with which the data are consistent.

This reinterpretation of the data is, of course, extremely speculative, and much more work on the development of these conceptually slippery concepts is needed. Moreover, there is a further caution to be heeded. As we noted earlier (see *Development of the Response of "Undecidable"*), there is a strong response bias against "can't tell" responses, and it may be that the age at which children are able to respond "undecidable" is heavily a function of the pains the experimenter took to counter this bias. As was noted, "can't tell" responses have been elicited in 6-year-olds (Falmagne, 1975a; Somerville et al., 1979). Although the status of these responses is not proven—they may mean 'do not know' or they may mean 'cannot know'—it may be that most children who make guesses accompanied by doubt are actually capable of responses of "undecidable," and could be led to make them with suitable pretest preparation.

There is one further group of studies to be considered. The later chapters of Osherson (1976) ask whether subjects use certain schemas for the domains of time, alethic possibility and necessity, and obligation and permissibility. The methodology used is that of Osherson's other work (1975a, 1976) that was reviewed earlier. Reasoning problems were given; some could be solved in one step, using one of the schemas, and others required chaining two or more schemas together to reach the conclusion. The psychological reality of a set of schemas was assessed by correlating the mean rated difficulties of the multistep problems with their predicted difficulties (the sum of the difficulties of the individual steps in the one-step problems). Subjects ranged from fifth graders to high school seniors. The correlations ranged from .29 to .90 with a median of .73—moderately high but not compellingly so—with little suggestion of a difference among the domains or between the younger and the older subjects.

In what concerns modality, the most interesting schemas were those that convert between possibility and necessity, that is, *P (not p) = not Np; not P(p) = N(not p)*, and so on. Although it is not credible that the high school seniors did not understand the correspondences, some of these were often rejected in the simplest exemplifying problems; one would have liked some information about how the subjects understood the wording used. The uneven acceptance of the supposedly basic inferential steps diminishes somewhat the interest of the work.

Presuppositions and Mental Verbs

Verbs like *realize, believe, know,* and *remember* are "mental" in that understanding them involves understanding a mental state or activity. Typically, they represent a relation between a person (subject of the verb) and a proposition expressed in a sentential complement.

Mental verbs are of interest here for two reasons. First, the development of modal notions, especially epistemic ones, could well be associated with a developing codification of mental activity itself, for example, epistemic possibility and necessity are a function of knowledge, and (as noted earlier) there is an obvious connection possible between the response of "can't tell" and understanding whether or not one "knows." Secondly, statements containing mental verbs frequently have presuppositions.

We review the topics of presuppositions and mental verbs together because, although many other lexical items also carry presuppositions, it is primarily presuppositions associated with mental verbs that have been studied developmentally.

The Definition of "Presupposition"

A presupposition of a proposition is something taken for granted by both speaker and hearer. It is often defined (e.g., Keenan, 1971b; Strawson, 1952) as something entailed by both the proposition and its negation.

(28) *p* presupposes *q* $=_{\text{def}}$ *p* entails *q*. & *not-p* entails *q*.

For instance,

(29) George knew that Jack came

is said to presuppose

(30) Jack came

because, it is said, Proposition 30 is entailed not only by Proposition 29 but also by:

(31) George did not know that Jack came.

However, Definition 28 is highly controversial (e.g., Kempson, 1975; Wilson, 1975), for two reasons. First, the definition is incompatible with a two-valued logic,[20] requiring a third truth value "neither true nor false," which holds whenever a presupposition is violated. The issue of two versus three truth values is hard to resolve (see *How Many Truth Values?*); nevertheless, it should be resolved on its merits, not surreptitiously, through a definition of presupposition.

The second objection to Definition 28 is that by no means everybody shares the intuition that negations like Proposition 31 logically entail their corresponding presuppositions like Proposition 30. It seems that Proposition 31 could hardly logically entail Proposition 30, given that:

(32) If Jack did not come, then George cannot have known that he came

appears to be necessarily true (whereas if Proposition 31 entailed that Jack came, then, if Jack did not come, one would expect Proposition 31 to be false [or perhaps, neither true nor false]; but according to Proposition 32, Proposition 31 has to be true if Jack did not come).

In normal usage Proposition 31 conversationally implicates Proposition 30. So a less tendentious definition of presupposition might read:

(33) *p* presupposes *q* $=_{\text{def}}$ *p* entails *q* & *not-p* implicates *q*.

This definition is compatible with a two-valued logic and would have no practical effect on linguists' classifications of what is or is not a presupposition.

Developmental Data

Some understanding of mental verbs appears to begin at around age 4. Johnson and Maratsos (1977) told 3- and 4-year-olds stories of the form "X hid Y's toy under this box (A), but X told Y it was under this box (B) and Y believed it"; they then asked questions about what the hider and the seeker "thought" and "knew" about where the toy was. The 3-year-olds were merely confused, but the 4-year-olds showed some understanding that what one "thinks" may be false, but what one "knows" is true. Macnamara, Baker, and Olson (1976) examined 4-year-olds' understanding of *pretend, forget,* and *know,* also by telling a story and asking questions. In general, *forget* was understood better than *pretend,* and both were understood better than *know* (for which little understanding was shown). Macnamara et al. concluded "some four year olds are able to grasp unstated presuppositions and entailments" (1976, p. 68), for example, that a sentence like *She forgot to bring the ball* presupposes *She was supposed to bring the ball* and entails *She did not bring the ball.* Wellman and Johnson (1979) also found some beginning understanding of *remember* and *forget* at 4 years of age (*remember* means correctness, *forget* incorrectness), with an increasing understanding of the reference to internal mental states between 4 and 7 years of age. It will be recalled that Miscione et al. (1978) found that most 6-year-olds properly distinguished "knowing" from "guessing," although no distinction was made at all by most children under age 4. M. C. Smith (1978) found most 6-year-olds drew an adultlike distinction between intentional and unintentional acts, although his 4-year-olds did not.

Children's knowledge of the presuppositions and entailments of various factive, counterfactive, and nonfactive verbs have been examined in more detail in work of Ackerman (1978), R. J. Harris (1975), and Hopmann and Maratsos (1978). All the studies involved presenting sentences (in a story context in the case of Ackerman, 1978), followed by questions to see whether the subject understood the presupposition or entailment. Half the time, the verb at issue was negated, for example, *It is/is not surprising that . . . ,* or *A knows/does not know that . . . .* Some of the verbs presupposed the truth of the complement sentence (e.g., *know, be surprising, be sad* [*that*]), some presupposed the falsity of the complement (e.g., *pretend*), and some had no presuppositions (e.g., *be true* [*that*], *be possible* [*that*], *say, think*). In general, at least by 7 or 8 years of age, and often younger, the children gave anticipated responses to both the positive and negative forms of the factive and counterfactive verbs. There were differences among verbs, for example, Hopmann and Maratsos (1978) found that the presuppositions of affective factive verbs (e.g., *be happy/sad that . . .*) were less well understood than of the neutral verbs (*know, be surprised*), which were understood by their 5-year-olds. There was more variability with the nonfactive verbs, the children often responding on a pragmatic rather than logical basis (e.g., they usually denied the complements for *did not say that* and *does not desire that*). Ackerman (1978) and R. J. Harris (1975) both found developments after 8 years of age, but these seem tangential to understanding of presuppositions of lexical items. For ex-

ample, Ackerman presented some sentences in a context indicating irony or sarcasm, and this was not well diagnosed by his 8-year-olds; and Harris found development into the adult years on a task involving judgments of anomaly.

There is also work on adults' understanding of presupposition (e.g., R. J. Harris, 1974; Hornby, 1974; Just & Clark, 1973; Offir, 1973) that we do not summarize. In general, the evidence indicates that the age range of 4 to 7 is the important period for developing a grasp of mental verbs and their presuppositions, although (not surprisingly) there is variation from one verb to another.

CONCLUSIONS

There are three themes that recur repeatedly in this review. The first is that some basic logical competence is available to children early, at least by around school-entering age. This competence comprises a repertory of inferences. In propositional reasoning, it includes Modus Ponens, several schemas for reasoning about alternatives, and indeed, all of Schemas N1 through N13 of Table 2 that have been tested. It also includes the principle that the properties of a class are inherited by its subclasses, and probably several other schemas of Table 4. It includes some notion of possibility and necessity and some understanding of the entailments and presuppositions of several mental verbs.

We have suggested that this early logical competence is acquired as part of learning the language. This suggestion is not based on empirical data that connect inferences to language learning; instead, it comes from the consideration that the inferences that comprise the early competence appear to be closely tied to the meanings of words like *if, or, all, may, know,* and the like. It is hard to see how one could be said to understand the words without knowing the inferences.

The second theme is that certain aspects of logical reasoning are *not* present early. A collection of rather disparate skills typically begins to appear in late childhood, many of which are by no means universally present in college students. We can broadly divide these skills into two categories: those that have to do with strategies of deductive reasoning and those that involve assessing statements against evidence.

Let us first consider deductive-reasoning strategies. The only reasoning procedure that is implicit in the early logical competence consists in direct reasoning from starting information to conclusion, that is, the procedure seeks an inference schema that can be applied to reach a conclusion, and applies it.

One can surmise that this procedure early becomes iterable, and then allows at least short chains of direct reasoning, for example, inferences from starting information to an intermediate statement and from thence to a conclusion. But there is no evidence in young children for reasoning strategies richer than a direct-reasoning chain. Some strategies of indirect reasoning begin to emerge in late childhood. The strategy of setting up alternatives a priori (to see if they all lead to the same conclusion) is available to essentially all adults and to some 9- and 10-year-olds, but apparently not to younger children. The reductio ad absurdum is readily available to some adults, but by no means all. Nevertheless, although some strategies of indirect reasoning are acquired, the evidence indicates that the strategies available to many adults are only a little richer than the direct-reasoning-chain procedure. The literature on categorical syllogisms documents the poverty of the logical-reasoning heuristics available even to adults. The syllogisms that are regularly solved are those for which a direct-reasoning procedure yields a solution. When this procedure fails, as it does for most syllogisms, many adults apparently do not have other logical-reasoning heuristics that can be brought to bear, but instead have recourse to nonlogical or quasi-logical strategies, for example, reconstruing a premiss so that the direct-reasoning procedure can apply (leading to the so-called conversion errors), or constructing some mental model that can be manipulated. It is very likely that the quality of the logical-reasoning strategies available to adults is influenced by cultural and educational experience. Of course, late childhood is an age at which a wide variety of strategies for accomplishing various problem-solving goals are acquired.

The other aspect of logical reasoning that emerges late has to do with assessing statements, especially quantified statements, against evidence. Particularly noteworthy are the impressive gaps in insight into quantified conditionals of older children and many adults. It is clear that evaluating a quantified statement is a very different and much more cognitively demanding task than drawing an inference from one.

This division into early- and late-appearing logical abilities is reminiscent of the Piagetian distinction between the concrete and the formal operations; Kuhn (1977) draws the parallel explicitly. However, the concrete operations manifestly provide a very poor theoretical account indeed of the early appearing competence. On the other hand, many of the late-appearing abilities do have much in common with abilities involved in tasks used to study the formal operations. However, the late-appearing skills are quite heterogeneous in nature and vary widely in difficulty, from 10-year-old to bright-adult levels. It is hard to find any unity among them that would justify the term ''stage,'' and certainly, Piaget's logic does not provide a satisfactory unifying concept.

The third theme is the recurring evidence for extensive inadequacies of comprehension at all ages. Young school-age children may not notice that adjacent sentences of a text contradict each other. They often fail to attend to which clause the word *if* or *because* is attached to, and do not use this as a cue to which event is cause and which effect. Similarly, they fail to register which noun the word *all* modifies, so that *All F are G* may not be distinguished from *All G are F*. A similar inattention to wording causes malcomprehension of questions of the form *Are there more F or more G?* Moreover, these comprehension errors easily recur in older subjects when the context of comprehension is complicated somewhat. These errors reflect a habit of comprehension in which guessing guided by plausibility plays a much larger role than the detailed character of the input sentences. This kind of comprehension program undoubtedly derives from the social context of most discourse. Such a program probably optimizes speed and effectiveness of comprehension in a world in which most communication is commonplace and speakers put little care into how they put their thoughts into words.

Such a comprehension program is the opposite of what we earlier called ''analytic'' comprehension (in which meaning is obtained from analysis of the statement itself in abstraction from situational cues). Although it is not surprising to find children unable to set aside plausibility in context, we were surprised at the lack of evidence for programs in which sentence structure contributes substantially to meaning, in addition to plausibility. The fact that many young school-age children use the primitive plausibility-plus-guessing program even in test situations suggests that they do not have ready access to a program that provides for nonsuperficial processing of linguistic structure.

These conclusions suggest to us that certain lines of applied research could usefully be undertaken. In the elementary grades, we think there is a need for research on how to increase the role played by the detailed character of the input sentences in children's comprehension programs. At the high school level, we suspect that both analytic comprehension and reasoning strategies would turn out to be readily teachable and to have broad beneficial effects in improving argumentation and reasoning as well as in helping students write so that ideas are put into words from which the ideas can be recovered. Research could determine teachability and whether the benefits warrant the investment of teaching time.

LOGICAL GLOSSARY

Logical Notation

The following symbols are used for the connectives and quantifiers of standard logic and for set relations. We give the symbol, any technical names for it, and an approximate gloss (translation) into English for formulas containing the symbol.

Connectives

In the glosses given, *p* and *q* represent any propositions. Also, each connective is associated with truth conditions, see *Truth Tables*.

Symbol	Technical Name	Formula	Approximate Gloss
~	Negation	~p	not p
&	Conjunction	p & q	p and q
v	Disjunction (inclusive), Inclusive *or*	p v q	p or q, or both
w	Disjunction (exclusive), Exclusive *or*	p w q	p or q, but not both
⊃	Conditional	p ⊃ q	if p then q
≡	Biconditional	p ≡ q	p if and only if q

Quantifiers

In the glosses given, *F* and *G* represent properties or relations, and *x* and *y* represent objects that bear the properties or are related by relations.

Symbol	Technical Name	Formula	Approximate Gloss
∃	Existential quantifier	∃xFx	There is an object, x, that has the property F
∀	Universal quantifier	∀xFx	For every object, x, x has the property F *or* Every object (in the universe of discourse) has the property F

Set Relations

In the glosses given, *F* and *G* represent classes. (The terms set and class are used interchangeably here.)

Symbol	Technical Name	Formula	Approximate Gloss
⊂	Class inclusion	F ⊂ G	F is included in G
∩	Intersection	F ∩ G	The class composed of all objects that are members of both F and G
∪, +	Union	F ∪ G or F + G	The class composed of the objects of F plus objects of G

Truth Tables

Truth conditions for compound propositions, containing connectives, are given by the following tables for each connective.

Negation

p	$\sim p$	
T	F	E.g., The first row says that when p is true (T), $\sim p$ is false (F)
F	T	

Other Connectives

p	q	$p \,\&\, q$	$p \lor q$	$p \lor w \, q$	$p \supset q$	$p \equiv q$
T	T	T	T	F	T	T
T	F	F	T	T	F	F
F	T	F	T	T	T	F
F	F	F	F	F	T	T

E.g., the third row says that when p is false and q is true, then $p \,\&\, q$ is false, $p \lor q$ is true, $p \lor w \, q$ is true, $p \supset q$ is true, and $p \equiv q$ is false.

Entailment

Entailment is a relation between propositions: *"p" entails "q"* means that q is deducible from p, using only logically necessary truths in the deduction (i.e., no factual truths other than p and q).

Entailment Versus the Conditional. *"p" entails "q"* differs from $p \supset q$ semantically, in that empirical facts (e.g., factual premises of problems) can be used to support $p \supset q$, but not *"p" entails "q"*; or said in another way, when p entails q, $p \supset q$ is necessarily true, that is, its truth does not depend on the accuracy of any factual statements.

NOTES

1. A qualification to this statement is that Aristotelian logic has certain existence presuppositions that do not correspond to entailments of predicate logic, so that certain syllogisms are not valid in predicate logic. See the discussion and defense of the syllogism by Strawson (1952) who points out that the existence assumptions of Aristotle seem to concord better with the natural language than do those of predicate logic.

2. Psycholinguistic studies of sentence comprehension often try to make competing interpretations equally plausible (e.g., by using so-called "reversible" sentences). This permits study of the contribution that linguistic structure makes in ordinary comprehension, but it does not turn such studies into studies of analytic comprehension. In analytic comprehension there is an effort by the comprehender to confine interpretation to that required by lexical entries and sentence structure.

3. The form *Even if p then q* blocks the invited inferences more neatly, but it is suitable only if there are other *if*-statements with the same consequent that can be taken as true with greater certainty (e.g., a confident fan might say *Even if our third-best pitcher pitches, the team will win*).

4. Another (equivalent) version occurs as Schema N13 of Table 2.

5. The "possible worlds" approach, which we describe later, provides a method of evaluation that is operationally hard to distinguish from the one described here (Rips & Marcus, 1977; Stalnaker, 1968).

6. In these studies, Corrigan (1975) and Kuhn and Phelps (1976) used nonreversible sentences, and Emerson (1979) and Emerson and Gekoski (1980) criticize them on the ground that children may use a

pragmatic plausibility strategy for such sentences. Thus, they suggest that children may rely on extra-linguistic knowledge that a shining sun may cause snow to melt to understand the nonreversible sentence *The snowman started to melt because the sun started to shine*. Such a strategy could not be used for a reversible sentence like *Betty was angry because Archie took Veronica for a ride in his car* because reversing the clauses (*Archie took Veronica for a ride in his car because Betty was angry*) also yields a sensible sentence. Although children undoubtedly use pragmatic plausibility in comprehension, it is hard to see that the strategy could help them make a judgment of anomaly: To judge *The sun started to shine because the snowman started to melt* as ''silly,'' the child must appreciate that the clause or reason follows *because*.

7. It is possible that the two fallacies have somewhat different bases. It may be that the Denying-the-Antecedent fallacy is due only to the invited inference *If not p then not q,* whereas both invited inference and a tendency to ''convert'' and then apply Modus Ponens to the converted proposition contribute to the Asserting-the-Consequent fallacy.

8. McCawley (1981) develops a logic that has structural features that are intuitively more ''natural'' than standard logic, but it is not clear to us what theoretical status he intends to claim for the system. In any case, his study and that of Reichenbach (1947) are basic (and complementary) references on logic/language relationships.

9. Purely for simplicity, to maximize readability, we have treated AND and OR as binary in Table 4, that is, not as joining *n* coordinates as in Table 2.

10. The notation, $S[No\ \alpha]$, in PL14 is particularly badly ad hoc. However, there is no consensus about the proper semantic representation of *not . . . any* and *no* + NP, and this is not the place for us to argue the question. There are two reasonable candidate analyses: one is equivalent to '$\forall x_\alpha \sim S(x)$', and the other to '$\sim \exists x_\alpha S(x)$'. (Read x_α as 'x that is an α.')

11. It is likely that when we have a natural predicate logic we will understand the source of these differences, for example, each surface structure probably corresponds to a different type of underlying formula of natural predicate logic.

12. Osherson (1974) presents the schemas in propositional form, but he notes that they could equally well be presented in terms of class operations. The table uses that form because it seems to us more appropriate to the problem content.

13. There is now a third theory—Guyote and Sternberg (1981)—which appeared too late for discussion here.

14. How supportive a case of both attributes is depends on base rates of the attributes in the population. If each is common, finding a case of both tells nothing: But if the attributes are rare, a case of both could encourage the idea of their being a contingency relation of some sort.

15. Between clauses, we use & rather than · and $\sim$ rather than $-$ to save parentheses.

16. For whatever interest the observation has, we note that the 32 formulas of the modified Leiser system have a kind of structure analogous to the four group of the 16 formulas of Piaget's logic. To get the group structure, one replaces the identity transformation of the INRC system by a Q-transformation that relates the hypothesis and counterexample formulas to each other by exchanging quantifiers and adjusting their scopes. Then, with R and C defined as in Piaget's system, the INRC group becomes QNRC in the revised Leiser system, with analogous relations holding, for example, for any formula, s, $N(Q[s]) = R(C[s])$.

17. There are logically important differences between ''p'' entails ''q'' and $N(p \supset q)$, but they are of little relevance here because they primarily concern quantification (Quine, 1953c): *Entails* is always outside the scope of any quantifier inside the propositions it relates, whereas N is not so restricted.

18. Note, for instance, that there is no corresponding ''necessity'' concept, for example, there is no *N(George rides a unicycle)* with the meaning 'It is not the case that George is able not to ride a unicycle.'

19. The distinction between physical and logical impossibility is not always transparent. For instance, it follows from the definition of the words that *curved* entails *not straight*. Thus, a straight curve is a logically impossible object (as well as physically impossible). But now consider a construction set that contains straight and curved pieces that can be fitted together (as in one of Pieraut-Le Bonniec's, 1980, studies). Is the impossibility of making a straight stick out of curved elements a logical or merely physical impossibility?

20. Suppose a standard two-valued logic, and suppose that Definition 28 is not vacuous, that is, there are propositions (*a* and *b*, say) that satisfy it, for example, *a* presupposes *b*. Suppose now that *b* is false. Because *a* entails *b*, it follows that *not-a*, and because *not-a* entails *b*, it follows that *not-not-a*, that is, *a*—thus, *a* & *not-a*, which is absurd.

REFERENCES

Ackerman, B. P. Children's comprehension of presupposed information: Logical and pragmatic inferences to speaker belief. *Journal of Experimental Child Psychology*, 1978, *26*, 92–114.

Ahr, P. R., & Youniss, J. Reasons for failure on the class-inclusion problem. *Child Development*, 1970, *41*, 131–143.

Akiyama, M. M. Yes-no answering systems in young children. *Cognitive Psychology*, 1979, *11*, 485–504.

Amidon, A. Children's understanding of sentences with contingent relations. *Journal of Experimental Child Psychology*, 1976, *22*, 423–437.

Bates, E. The acquisition of conditionals by Italian children. *Proceedings of the 10th Regional Meeting of the Chicago Linguistic Society*. Chicago: Chicago Linguistic Society, 1974.

Bates, E. *Language and context: The acquisition of pragmatics*. New York: Academic Press, 1976.

Begg, I., & Denny, J. P. Empirical reconciliation of atmosphere and conversion interpretations of syllogistic reasoning errors. *Journal of Experimental Psychology*, 1969, *81*, 351–354.

Beilin, H., & Lust, B. A study of the development of logical and linguistic connectives. In H. Beilin (Ed.), *Studies in the cognitive basis of language development*. New York: Academic Press, 1975.

Bellugi, U. The acquisition of negation. Unpublished doctoral dissertation, Harvard University, 1967.

Bever, T. G. The cognitive basis for linguistic structures. In J. R. Hayes (Ed.), *Cognition and the development of language*. New York: Wiley, 1970.

Bloom, L. *Language development: Form and function in emerging grammars*. Cambridge: MIT Press, 1970.

Bloom, L., Lahey, M., Hood, L., Lifter, K., & Feiss, K. Complex sentences: Acquisition of syntactic connectives and the semantic relations they encode. *Journal of Child Language*, 1980, *7*, 235–261.

Bochenski, I. M. A history of formal logic (I. Thomas trans.). South Bend, Ind.: Notre Dame University Press, 1961.

Boole, G. *An investigation of the laws of thought*. London: Walton & Maberly, 1854.

Bracewell, R. J., & Hidi, S. E. The solution of an inferential problem as a function of stimulus materials. *Quarterly Journal of Experimental Psychology*, 1974, *26*, 480–488.

Braine, M. D. S. On the relation between the natural logic of reasoning and standard logic. *Psychological Review*, 1978, *85*, 1–21.

Braine, M. D. S. If-then and strict implication. A response to Grandy's note. *Psychological Review*, 1979, *86*, 154–156. (a)

Braine, M. D. S. On some claims about *if-then*. *Linguistics and Philosophy*, 1979, *3*, 35–47. (b)

Braine, M. D. S., Reiser, B. J., & Rumain, B. *Some empirical justification for a theory of natural propositional logic*. Unpublished manuscript, 1981.

Braine, M. D. S., & Rumain, B. Development of comprehension of "or": Evidence for a sequence of competencies. *Journal of Experimental Child Psychology*, 1981, *31*, 46–70.

Bresson, F. Remarks on genetic psycholinguistics: The acquisition of the article system in French. In F. Bresson (Ed.), *Problèmes actuels en psycholinguistique*. Paris: Centre National de la Recherche Scientifique, 1974.

Brown, R. W. *A first language: The early stages*. Cambridge: Harvard University Press, 1973.

Bruner, J. S., Goodnow, J. J., & Austin, G. A. *A study of thinking*. New York: Wiley, 1956.

Bucci, W. The interpretation of universal affirmative propositions: A developmental study. *Cognition*, 1978, *6*, 55–77.

Burt, W. M. The factor structure of formal operational thought. *British Journal of Educational Psychology*, 1971, *41*, 70–77.

Bynum, T. W., Thomas, J. A., & Weitz, L. J. Truth-functional logic in formal operational thinking: Inhelder and Piaget's evidence. *Developmental Psychology*, 1972, *7*, 129–132.

Carden, G. *English quantifiers: Logical structure and linguistic variation*. New York: Academic Press, 1976.

Carpenter, P. A., & Just, M. A. Sentence comprehension: A psycholinguistic processing model of verification. *Psychological Review*, 1975, *82*, 45–73.

Ceraso, J., & Provitera, A. Sources of error in syllogistic reasoning. *Cognitive Psychology*, 1971, *2*, 400–410.

Chapman, L. J., & Chapman, J. P. Atmosphere effect reexamined. *Journal of Experimental Psychology*, 1959, *58*, 220–226.

Chapman, R., & Miller, J. Word order in early two and three word sentences. *Journal of Speech and Hearing Research*, 1975, *18*, 355–371.

Chase, W. G., & Clark, H. H. Mental operations in the comparison of sentences and pictures. In L.

Gregg (Ed.), *Cognition in learning and memory*. New York: Wiley, 1972.

Chomsky, N. *Syntactic structures*. The Hague: Mouton, 1957.

Clancy, P., Jacobsen, T., & Silva, M. The acquisition of conjunction. *Papers and Reports on Child Language Development*, 1976, *12*, 71–80.

Clark, E. V. How young children describe events in time. In G. B. Flores d'Arcais & W. J. M. Levelt (Eds.), *Advances in psycholinguistics*. Amsterdam: North Holland, 1970.

Clark, E. V. How children describe time and order. In C. A. Ferguson & D. I. Slobin (Eds.), *Studies of child language development*. New York: Holt, Rinehart & Winston, 1973.

Clark, H. H. Semantics and comprehension. In T. A. Sebeok (Ed.), *Current trends in linguistics, vol. 12, Linguistics and adjacent arts and sciences*. The Hague: Mouton, 1974.

Clark, H. H., & Chase, W. G. On the process of comparing sentences against pictures. *Cognitive Psychology*, 1972, *3*, 472–517.

Clark, H. H., & Chase, W. G. Perceptual coding strategies in the formation and verification of descriptions. *Memory & Cognition*, 1974, *2*, 101–111.

Cohen, L. J. Some remarks on Grice's views about the logical particles of natural language. In Y. Bar-Hillel (Ed.), *Pragmatics of natural language*. Dordrecht, the Netherlands: D. Reidel, 1971.

Conan. M. H. Mastery of a formal operations problem-solving strategy: A developmental study. Unpublished doctoral dissertation, New York University, 1978.

Copi, I. M. *Symbolic logic*. New York: Macmillan, 1967.

Corrigan, R. A scalogram analysis of the development of the use and comprehension of *because* in children. *Child Development*, 1975, *46*, 195–201.

Danner, F. W., & Day, M. C. Eliciting formal operations. *Child Development*, 1977, *48*, 1600–1606.

De Boysson-Bardies, B. On children's interpretation of negation. *Journal of Experimental Child Psychology*, 1977, *23*, 117–127.

de Villiers, J. G., & Tager-Flusberg, H. B. Some facts one simply cannot deny. *Journal of Child Language*, 1975, *2*, 279–286.

Dean, A. L., Chabaud, S., & Bridges, E. Classes, collections and distinctive features: Alternative strategies for solving inclusion problems. *Cogni-*

tive Psychology, 1981, *13*, 84–112.

Denney, D. R. Recognition, formulation, and integration in the development of interrogative strategies among normal and retarded children. *Child Development*, 1974, *45*, 1068–1076.

Denney, N. W., & Connors, G. J. Altering the questioning strategies of preschool children. *Child Development*, 1974, *45*, 1108–1112.

Dickstein, L. S. Differential difficulty of categorical syllogisms. *Bulletin of the Psychonomic Society*, 1976, *8*, 330–332.

Dickstein, L. S. The effect of figure on syllogistic reasoning. *Memory & Cognition*, 1978, *6*, 76–83. (a)

Dickstein, L. S. Error processes in syllogistic reasoning. *Memory & Cognition*, 1978, *6*, 537–543. (b)

Donaldson, M. Developmental aspects of performance with negatives. In G. B. Flores d'Arcais & W. J. M. Levelt (Eds.), *Advances in psycholinguistics*. Amsterdam: North-Holland, 1970.

Donaldson, M. Development of conceptualization. In V. Hamilton & M. D. Vernon (Eds.), *The development of cognitive processes*. New York: Academic Press, 1976.

Donaldson, M., & Lloyd, P. Sentences and situations: Children's judgments of match and mismatch. In F. Bresson (Ed.), *Problèmes actuels en psycholinguistique*. Paris: Centre National de la Recherche Scientifique, 1974.

Donaldson, M., & McGarrigle, J. Some clues to the nature of semantic development. *Journal of Child Language*, 1974, *1*, 185–194.

Emerson, H. F. Children's comprehension of "because" in reversible and non-reversible sentences. *Journal of Child Language*, 1979, *6*, 279–300.

Emerson, H. F. Children's judgments of correct and reversed sentences with "if." *Journal of Child Language*, 1980, *7*, 137–155.

Emerson, H. F., & Gekoski, W. L. Development of comprehension of sentences with "because" or "if." *Journal of Experimental Child Psychology*, 1980, *29*, 202–224.

Ennis, R. H. Conditional logic and primary children. *Interchange*, 1971, *2*, 127–132.

Ennis, R. H. Children's ability to handle Piaget's propositional logic. *Review of Educational Research*, 1975, *45*, 1–41.

Ennis, R. H. An alternative to Piaget's conceptualization of logical competence. *Child Development*, 1976, *47*, 903–919.

Ennis, R. H. Conceptualization of children's logical

competence: Piaget's propositional logic and an alternative proposal. In L. S. Siegel & C. J. Brainerd (Eds.), *Alternatives to Piaget: Critical essays on the theory*. New York: Academic Press, 1978.

Ennis, R. H., Finkelstein, M. R., Smith, E. L., & Wilson, N. H. *Conditional logic and children* (Final Report, New York State Education Department). Ithaca, N.Y.: Cornell University, 1969. (ERIC Document Reproduction Service No. ED 040 437)

Ennis, R. H., & Paulus, D. H. *Critical thinking readiness in Grades 1–12* (Phase 1: *Deductive reasoning in adolescence*) (Final Report, U.S. Office of Education Cooperative Research Project No. 1680). Ithaca, N.Y.: Cornell University, 1965. (ERIC Document Reproduction Service No. ED 003 818)

Erickson, J. R. A set analysis theory of behavior in formal syllogistic reasoning tasks. In R. L. Solso (Ed.), *Theories in cognitive psychology: The Loyola symposium*. New York: Academic Press, 1974.

Erickson, J. R. Research on syllogistic reasoning. In R. Revlin & R. E. Mayer (Eds.), *Human reasoning*. Washington, D.C.: V. H. Winston, 1978.

Evans, J. St. B. T. Deductive reasoning and linguistic usage (with special reference to negation). Unpublished doctoral thesis, University of London, 1972. (a)

Evans, J. St. B. T. Reasoning with negatives. *British Journal of Psychology*, 1972, *63*, 213–219. (b)

Evans, J. St. B. T. Linguistic factors in reasoning. *Quarterly Journal of Experimental Psychology*, 1977, *29*, 297–306.

Evans, J. St. B. T., & Lynch, J. S. Matching bias in the selection task. *British Journal of Psychology*, 1973, *64*, 392–397.

Falmagne, R. J. Deductive processes in children. In R. J. Falmagne (Ed.), *Reasoning: Representation and process in children and adults*. Hillsdale, N.J.: Erlbaum, 1975. (a)

Falmagne, R. J. Introduction. Overview. Reasoning, representation, process, and related issues. In R. J. Falmagne (Ed.), *Reasoning: Representation and process in children and adults*. Hillsdale, N.J.: Erlbaum, 1975. (b)

Falmagne, R. J. The development of logical competence: A psycholinguistic perspective. In R. Kluwe & H. Spada (Eds.), *Developmental models of thinking*. New York: Academic Press, 1980.

Ferreiro, E., & Sinclair, H. Temporal relationships in language. *International Journal of Psychol-*

ogy, 1971, *6*, 39–47.

Fillenbaum, S. On coping with ordered and unordered conjunctive sentences. *Journal of Experimental Psychology*, 1971, *87*, 93–98.

Fillenbaum, S. Information amplified: Memory for counterfactual conditionals. *Journal of Experimental Psychology*, 1974, *102*, 44–49. (a)

Fillenbaum, S. OR: Some uses. *Journal of Experimental Psychology*, 1974, *103*, 913–921. (b)

Fillenbaum, S. Pragmatic normalization: Further results for some conjunctive and disjunctive sentences. *Journal of Experimental Psychology*, 1974, *102*, 574–578. (c)

Fillenbaum, S. Mind your *p*'s and *q*'s: The role of content and context in some uses of *and, or,* and *if*. In G. Bower (Ed.), *The psychology of learning and motivation* (Vol. 11). New York: Academic Press, 1977.

Flavell, J. H. *The developmental psychology of Jean Piaget*. New York: Van Nostrand, 1963.

Frase, L. T. Associative factors in syllogistic reasoning. *Journal of Experimental Psychology*, 1968, *76*, 407–412.

Frege, G. *Begriffsschrift*. Halle, Ger.: Louis Nebert, 1879.

Frege, G. *The foundations of arithmetic*. New York: Philosophical Library, 1950. (Originally published, 1884.)

Geach, P. T., & Black, M. (Eds.). *Frege's philosophical writings*. Oxford: Basil Blackwell, 1952.

Geis, M., & Zwicky, A. M. On invited inferences. *Linguistic Inquiry*, 1971, *2*, 561–566.

Gentzen, G. II. Investigations into logical deduction. *American Philosophical Quarterly*, 1964, *1*, 288–306. (Originally published, 1935.)

Gilhooly, K. J., & Falconer, W. A. Concrete and abstract terms and relations in testing a rule. *Quarterly Journal of Experimental Psychology*, 1974, *26*, 355–359.

Ginsburg, H., & Opper, S. *Piaget's theory of intellectual development*. Englewood Cliffs, N.J.: Prentice-Hall, 1969.

Gleitman, L. R. Coordinating conjunctions in English. *Language*, 1965, *51*, 260–293.

Gleitman, L. R., & Gleitman, H. *Phrase and paraphrase*. New York: W. W. Norton, 1970.

Goodwin, R. Q., & Wason, P. C. Degrees of insight. *British Journal of Psychology*, 1972, *63*, 205–212.

Gough, P. B. Grammatical transformations and speed of understanding. *Journal of Verbal Learning and Verbal Behavior*, 1965, *4*, 107–111.

Gough, P. B. The verification of sentences: The

effects of delay of evidence and sentence length. *Journal of Verbal Learning and Verbal Behavior*, 1966, *5*, 492–496.

Grandy, R. E. Inference and if-then. *Psychological Review*, 1979, *86*, 152–153.

Graves, R., & Hodge, A. *The reader over your shoulder*. New York: Macmillan, 1943.

Grice, H. P. Logic and conversation. In P. Cole & J. L. Morgan (Eds.), *Syntax and semantics, vol. 3, Speech acts*. New York: Academic Press, 1975.

Grice, H. P. Further notes on logic and conversation. In P. Cole (Ed.), *Syntax and semantics, vol. 9, Pragmatics*. New York: Academic Press, 1978.

Grieve, R., & Garton, A. On the young child's comparison of sets. *Journal of Experimental Psychology*, 1981, *32*, 443–458.

Guyote, M. J., & Sternberg, R. J. A transitive-chain theory of syllogistic reasoning. *Cognitive Psychology*, 1981, *13*, 461–525.

Harris, P. Inferences and semantic development. *Journal of Child Language*, 1975, *2*, 143–152.

Harris, R. J. Memory and comprehension of implications and inferences of complex sentences. *Journal of Verbal Learning and Verbal Behavior*, 1974, *13*, 626–637.

Harris, R. J. Children's comprehension of complex sentences. *Journal of Experimental Child Psychology*, 1975, *19*, 420–433.

Hatano, G., & Suga, Y. Understanding the use of disjunction in children. *Journal of Experimental Child Psychology*, 1977, *24*, 395–405.

Hayes, J. R. The child's conception of the experimenter. In S. Farnham-Diggory (Ed.), *Information processing in children*. New York: Academic Press, 1972.

Hayes, J. R. *Cognitive psychology: Thinking and creating*. Homewood, Ill.: Dorsey Press, 1978.

Henle, M. On the relation between logic and thinking. *Psychological Review*, 1962, *69*, 366–378.

Henle, M. Of the scholler of nature. *Social Research*, 1971, *38*, 93–107.

Henle, M., & Michael, M. The influence of attitudes on syllogistic reasoning. *Journal of Social Psychology*, 1956, *44*, 115–127.

Hill, S. A. A study of logical abilities in children. Unpublished doctoral dissertation, Stanford University, 1961.

Hintikka, K. J. J. *Knowledge and belief: An introduction to the logic of the two notions*. Ithaca, N.Y.: Cornell University Press, 1962.

Hintikka, K. J. J. *Models for modalities: Selected essays*. Dordrecht, the Netherlands: D. Reidel, 1969.

Hood, L., & Bloom, L. What, when and how about why: A longitudinal study of early expressions of causality. *Monographs of the Society for Research in Child Development*, 1979, *44*(6, Serial No. 181).

Hood, L., Lahey, M., Lifter, K., & Bloom, L. Observation and descriptive methodology in studying child language: Preliminary results in the development of complex sentences. In G. Sackett (Ed.), *Observing behavior* (Vol. 1). Baltimore: University Park Press, 1978.

Hopmann, M. R., & Maratsos, M. D. A developmental study of factivity and negation in complex syntax. *Journal of Child Language*, 1978, *5*, 295–309.

Hornby, P. Surface structure and presupposition. *Journal of Verbal Learning and Verbal Behavior*, 1974, *13*, 530–538.

Hutson, B. A., & Shub, J. Developmental study of factors involved in choice of conjunctions. *Child Development*, 1975, *46*, 46–52.

Inhelder, B., & Piaget, J. *The growth of logical thinking from childhood to adolescence*. New York: Basic Books, 1958.

Inhelder, B., & Piaget, J. *The early growth of logic in the child*. London: Routledge & Kegan Paul, 1964.

Jackendoff, R. S. Quantifiers in English. *Foundations of Language*, 1968, *4*, 422–442.

Jackendoff, R. S. An interpretive theory of negation. *Foundations of Language*, 1969, *5*, 218–241.

Jackendoff, R. S. *Semantic interpretation in generative grammar*. Cambridge: MIT Press, 1972.

Johansson, B. S. Levels of mastery of the coordinates *and* and *or* and logical test performance. *British Journal of Psychology*, 1977, *68*, 311–320.

Johansson, B. S., & Sjolin, B. Preschool children's understanding of the coordinates "and" and "or". *Journal of Experimental Child Psychology*, 1975, *19*, 233–240.

Johnson, C. N., & Maratsos, M. D. Early comprehension of mental verbs: *Think* and *know*. *Child Development*, 1977, *48*, 1743–1747.

Johnson, H. L., & Chapman, R. S. Children's judgment and recall of causal connectives: A developmental study of "because," "so," and "and." *Journal of Psycholinguistic Research*, 1980, *9*, 243–259.

Johnson-Laird, P. N. '&.' *Journal of Linguistics*, 1969, *6*, 111–114. (a)

Johnson-Laird, P. N. On understanding logically complex sentences. *Quarterly Journal of Experimental Psychology*, 1969, *21*, 1–13. (b)

Johnson-Laird, P. N. Reasoning with ambiguous

sentences. *British Journal of Psychology*, 1969, *60*, 17–23. (c)

Johnson-Laird, P. N. Models of deduction. In R. Falmagne (Ed.), *Reasoning: Representation and process in children and adults*. Hillsdale, N.J.: Erlbaum, 1975.

Johnson-Laird, P. N. Procedural semantics. *Cognition*, 1977, *5*, 189–214.

Johnson-Laird, P. N. The meaning of modality. *Cognitive Science*, 1978, *2*, 17–26.

Johnson-Laird, P. N. Mental models in cognitive science. In D. A. Norman (Ed.), *Perspectives on cognitive science*. Norwood, N.J.: Ablex, 1981.

Johnson-Laird, P. N., Legrenzi, P., & Legrenzi, M. S. Reasoning and a sense of reality. *British Journal of Psychology*, 1972, *63*, 395–400.

Johnson-Laird, P. N., & Steedman, M. The psychology of syllogisms. *Cognitive Psychology*, 1978, *10*, 64–99.

Johnson-Laird, P. N., & Tagart, J. How implication is understood. *American Journal of Psychology*, 1969, *82*, 367–373.

Johnson-Laird, P. N., & Tridgell, J. When negation is easier than affirmation. *Quarterly Journal of Experimental Psychology*, 1972, *24*, 87–91.

Johnson-Laird, P. N., & Wason, P. C. Insight into a logical relation. *Quarterly Journal of Experimental Psychology*, 1970, *22*, 49–61. (a)

Johnson-Laird, P. N., & Wason, P. C. A theoretical analysis of insight into a reasoning task. *Cognitive Psychology*, 1970, *1*, 134–148. (b)

Johnson-Laird, P. N., & Wason, P. C. *Thinking: Readings in cognitive science*. Cambridge: Cambridge University Press, 1977.

Judd, S. A., & Mervis, C. B. Learning to solve class-inclusion problems: The roles of quantification and recognition of contradiction. *Child Development*, 1979, *50*, 163–169.

Just, M. A., & Carpenter, P. A. Comprehension of negation with quantification. *Journal of Verbal Learning and Verbal Behavior*, 1971, *10*, 244–253.

Just, M. A., & Clark, H. H. Drawing inferences from the presuppositions and implications of affirmative and negative sentences. *Journal of Verbal Learning and Verbal Behavior*, 1973, *12*, 27–31.

Kalil, K., Youssef, Z., & Lerner, R. M. Class-inclusion failure: Cognitive deficit or misleading reference? *Child Development*, 1974, *45*, 1122–1125.

Kant, I. *Introduction to logic and essay on the mistaken subtilty of the four figures*. London: Longman's Green, 1885.

Karmiloff-Smith, A. *Functional approach to child language*. Cambridge, Eng.: At the University Press, 1979.

Karmiloff-Smith, A. The grammatical marking of thematic structure in the development of language production. In W. Deutsch (Ed.), *The child's construction of language*. London: Academic Press, 1981.

Karttunen, L. Possible and must. In J. P. Kimbal (Ed.), *Syntax and semantics*, vol. I. New York: Seminar Press, 1972.

Katz, E., & Brent, S. Understanding connectives. *Journal of Verbal Learning and Verbal Behavior*, 1968, *7*, 501–509.

Katz, N., Baker, E., & MacNamara, J. What's in a name? A study of how children learn common and proper names. *Child Development*, 1974, *45*, 469–473.

Keating, D. P. Precocious cognitive development at the level of formal operations. *Child Development*, 1975, *46*, 276–280.

Keating, D. P. Adolescent thinking. In J. P. Adelson (Ed.), *Handbook of adolescence*. New York: Wiley, 1979.

Keenan, E. L. Quantifier structures in English. *Foundations of Language*, 1971, *7*, 255–284. (a)

Keenan, E. L. Two kinds of presupposition in natural language. In C. J. Fillmore & D. T. Langendoen (Eds.), *Studies in linguistic semantics*. New York: Holt, Rinehart & Winston, 1971. (b)

Keenan, E. L. On semantically based grammar. *Linguistic Inquiry*, 1972, *3*, 413–461.

Kempson, R. M. *Presupposition and the delimitation of semantics*. Cambridge, Eng.: At the University Press, 1975.

Klahr, D., & Wallace, J. G. Class-inclusion processes. In S. Farnham-Diggory (Ed.), *Information processing in children*. New York: Academic Press, 1972.

Klima, E. S., & Bellugi, U. Syntactic regularities in the speech of children. In J. L. Lyons & R. J. Wales (Eds.), *Psycholinguistics Papers*. Edinburgh: University of Edinburgh Press, 1966.

Kneale, W., & Kneale, M. *The development of logic*. Oxford, Eng.: Oxford University Press, 1962. (Clarendon Press)

Knifong, J. D. Logical abilities of young children—Two styles of approach. *Child Development*, 1974, *45*, 78–83.

Kodroff, J. K., & Roberge, J. J. Developmental analysis of the conditional reasoning abilities of primary-grade children. *Developmental Psychology*, 1975, *11*, 21–28.

Kofsky, E. A scalogram study of classificatory development. *Child Development*, 1966, *37*, 191–204.

Kohnstamm, G. A. An evaluation of part of Piaget's theory. *Acta Psychologica*, 1963, *21*, 313–356.

Kohnstamm, G. A. *Teaching children to solve a Piagetian problem of class inclusion*. The Hague: Mouton, 1967.

Kripke, S. A. Semantical considerations on modal logic (*Proceedings of a colloquium on modal and many-valued logics*). *Acta Philosophica Fennica*, 1963, *16*, 83–94.

Kuczaj, S. A. On the acquisition of a semantic system. *Journal of Verbal Learning and Verbal Behavior*, 1975, *14*, 340–358.

Kuczaj, S. A., & Daly, M. J. The development of hypothetical reference in the speech of young children. *Journal of Child Language*, 1979, *6*, 563–579.

Kuhn, D. Conditional reasoning in children. *Developmental Psychology*, 1977, *13*, 342–353.

Kuhn, D., & Angelev, J. An experimental study of the development of formal operational thought. *Child Development*, 1976, *47*, 697–706.

Kuhn, D., & Brannock, J. Development of the isolation of variables scheme in experimental and "natural experimental" contexts. *Developmental Psychology*, 1977, *13*, 9–14.

Kuhn, D., & Ho, V. The development of schemes for recognizing additive and alternative effects in a "natural experiment" context. *Developmental Psychology*, 1977, *13*, 515–516.

Kuhn, D., Ho, V., & Adams, C. Formal reasoning among pre- and late adolescents. *Child Development*, 1979, *50*, 1128–1135.

Kuhn, D., & Phelps, H. The development of children's comprehension of causal direction. *Child Development*, 1976, *47*, 248–251.

Kutschera, F. von. Indicative conditionals. *Theoretical Linguistics*, 1974, *1*, 257–269.

Lakoff, G. Linguistics and natural logic. *Synthese*, 1970, *22*, 151–271.

Lakoff, G. The role of deduction in grammar. In C. J. Fillmore & D. T. Langendoen (Eds.), *Studies in linguistic semantics*. New York: Holt, Rinehart & Winston, 1971.

Lakoff, R. If's, and's and but's about conjunction. In C. J. Fillmore & D. T. Langendoen (Eds.), *Studies in linguistic semantics*. New York: Holt, Rinehart & Winston, 1971.

Lawson, A. E. Relationships among performances on three formal operational tasks. *Journal of Psychology*, 1977, *96*, 235–241.

Legrenzi, P. Relations between language and reasoning about deductive rules. In G. B. Flores d'Arcais & W. J. M. Levelt (Eds.), *Advances in psycholinguistics*. Amsterdam: North-Holland, 1970.

Leiser, D. Piaget's logical formalism for formal operations: An interpretation in context. *Developmental Review*, 1982, *2*, 87–99.

Lewis, C. I. *A survey of symbolic logic*. Berkeley: University of California Press, 1918.

Lewis, C. I., & Langford, C. H. *Symbolic logic*. New York: Century, 1932.

Lewis, D. *Counterfactuals*. Cambridge: Harvard University Press, 1973.

Limber, J. The genesis of complex sentences. In T. E. Moore (Ed.), *Cognitive development and the acquisition of language*. New York: Academic Press, 1973.

Lunzer, E. A., Harrison, C., & Davey, M. The four-card problem and the generality of formal reasoning. *Quarterly Journal of Experimental Psychology*, 1972, *24*, 326–339.

Lust, B., & Mervis, C. A. Development of coordination in the natural speech of young children. *Journal of Child Language*, 1980, *7*, 279–304.

Macnamara, J., Baker, E., & Olson, C. L. Four-year-olds' understanding of *pretend, forget*, and *know:* Evidence for propositional operations. *Child Development*, 1976, *47*, 62–70.

Maratsos, M. P. Preschool children's use of definite and indefinite articles. *Child Development*, 1974, *45*, 446–455.

Maratsos, M. P. *The use of definite and indefinite reference in young children*. Cambridge, Eng.: At the University Press, 1976.

Markman, E. M. The facilitation of part-whole comparisons by use of the collective noun "family." *Child Development*, 1973, *44*, 837–840.

Markman, E. M. Realizing that you don't understand: A preliminary investigation. *Child Development*, 1977, *48*, 986–992.

Markman, E. M. Empirical vs. logical solutions to part-whole comparisons concerning classes and collections. *Child Development*, 1978, *49*, 168–177.

Markman, E. M. Classes and collections: Conceptual organization and numerical abilities. *Cognitive Psychology*, 1979, *11*, 395–411. (a)

Markman, E. M. Realizing that you don't understand: Elementary school children's awareness of inconsistencies. *Child Development*, 1979, *50*, 643–655. (b)

Markman, E. M., & Siebert, J. Classes and collections: Internal organization and resulting holistic properties. *Cognitive Psychology*, 1976, *8*,

561–577.

Martorano, S. C. A developmental analysis of performance on Piaget's formal operational tasks. *Developmental Psychology*, 1977, *13*, 666–672.

Mason, E. J., Bramble, W. J., & Mast, T. A. Familiarity with content and conditional reasoning. *Journal of Educational Psychology*, 1975, *67*, 238–242.

Matalon, B. Etude génétique de l'implication. *Etudes d'epistémologie génétique, vol. 16, Implication, formalisation et logique naturelle*, 1962.

Mazzocco, A., Legrenzi, P., & Roncato, S. Syllogistic inference: The failure of the atmosphere effect and the conversion hypothesis. *Italian Journal of Psychology*, 1974, *1*, 157–172.

McCawley, J. D. *If* and *only if. Linguistic Inquiry*, 1974, *5*, 632–635.

McCawley, J. D. *Everything that linguists have always wanted to know about logic but were ashamed to ask*. Chicago: University of Chicago Press, 1981.

McGarrigle, J., Grieve, R., & Hughes, M. Interpreting inclusion: A contribution to the study of the child's cognitive and linguistic development. *Journal of Experimental Child Psychology*, 1978, *26*, 528–556.

McNeill, D., & McNeill, N. B. What does a child mean when he says "no"? In C. A. Ferguson & D. I. Slobin (Eds.), *Studies of child language development*. New York: Holt, Rinehart & Winston, 1973.

Mill, J. S. *A system of logic* (8th ed.). New York: Harper, 1874.

Miller, W. A. A unit in sentential logic for junior high school students: Involving both valid and invalid inference patterns. *School Science and Mathematics*, 1969, *69*, 548–552.

Miscione, J. L., Marvin, R. S., O'Brien, R. G., & Greenberg, M. T. A developmental study of preschool children's understanding of the words "know" and "guess." *Child Development*, 1978, *49*, 1107–1113.

Montague, R. The proper treatment of quantification in ordinary English. In K. J. J. Hintikka, J. M. E. Moravcsik, & P. Suppes (Eds.), *Approaches to natural language*. Dordrecht, the Netherlands: D. Reidel, 1973.

Montague, R. *Formal philosophy: Selected papers of Richard Montague* (R. Thomason, Ed.). New Haven, Conn.: Yale University Press, 1974.

Morgan, J. L. Some interactions of syntax and pragmatics. In P. Cole & J. L. Morgan (Eds.), *Syntax and semantics*, vol. 3, *Speech acts*. New York: Academic Press, 1975.

Moshman, D. Consolidation and stage formation in the emergence of formal operations. *Developmental Psychology*, 1977, *13*, 95–100.

Moshman, D. Development of formal hypothesis-testing ability. *Developmental Psychology*, 1979, *15*, 104–112.

Nagel, E. Symbolic notation, haddocks' eyes and the dog-walking ordinance. In J. R. Newman (Ed.), *The world of mathematics* (Vol. 3). New York: Simon & Schuster, 1956.

Neimark, E. D. Development of comprehension of logical connectives: Understanding of "or." *Psychonomic Science*, 1970, *21*, 217–219.

Neimark, E. D., & Chapman, R. H. Development of the comprehension of logical quantifiers. In R. J. Falmagne (Ed.), *Reasoning: Representation and process in children and adults*. Hillsdale, N.J.: Erlbaum, 1975.

Neimark, E. D., & Slotnick, N. S. Development of the understanding of logical connectives. *Journal of Experimental Psychology*, 1970, *61*, 451–460.

Newell, A., & Simon, H. A. *Human problem solving*. Englewood Cliffs, N.J.: Prentice-Hall, 1972.

Nitta, N., & Nagano, S. Basic logical operations and their verbal expressions. *Research Bulletin of the National Institute for Educational Research* (Japan), 1966, No. 7.

O'Brien, D., & Overton, W. F. Conditional reasoning following contradictory evidence: A developmental analysis. *Journal of Experimental Child Psychology*, 1980, *30*, 44–61.

O'Brien, D., & Overton, W. F. Conditional reasoning and the competence-performance issue. *Journal of Experimental Child Psychology*, in press.

O'Brien, T. C. Logical thinking in adolescents. *Educational Studies in Mathematics*, 1972, *4*, 401–428.

O'Brien, T. C. Logical thinking in college students. *Educational Studies in Mathematics*, 1973, *5*, 71–79.

O'Brien, T. C., & Shapiro, B. J. The development of logical thinking in children. *American Educational Research Journal*, 1968, *5*, 531–543.

Offir, C. Recognition memory for presuppositions of relative clauses. *Journal of Verbal Learning and Verbal Behavior*, 1973, *12*, 636–643.

Olson, D. R., & Hillyard, A. Writing and literal meaning. In M. Martlew (Ed.), *Psychology of writing*, in press.

Osgood, C. E., & Richards, M. M. From yang and yin to *and* and *but. Language*, 1973, *49*, 380–412.

Osherson, D. N. *Logical abilities in children*, vol. 2, *Logical inference: Underlying operations*. Hillsdale, N.J.: Erlbaum, 1974.

Osherson, D. N. *Logical abilities in children*, vol. 3, *Reasoning in adolescence: Deductive inference*. Hillsdale, N.J.: Erlbaum, 1975. (a)

Osherson, D. N. Models of logical thinking. In R. J. Falmagne (Ed.), *Reasoning: Representation and process in children and adults*. Hillsdale, N.J.: Erlbaum, 1975. (b)

Osherson, D. N. *Logical abilities in children*, vol. 4, *Reasoning and concepts*. Hillsdale, N.J.: Erlbaum, 1976.

Osherson, D. N., & Markman, E. M. Language and the ability to evaluate contradictions and tautologies. *Cognition*, 1975, *3*, 213–226.

Papert, S. Sur la logique Piagetienne. In L. Apostel, J. B. Grize, S. Papert, and J. Piaget (Eds.), *Etudes d'epistémologie génétique*, vol. 15, *La filiation des structures*. Paris: Presses Universitaires de France, 1963.

Paris, S. G. Comprehension of language connectives and propositional logical relationships. *Journal of Experimental Child Psychology*, 1973, *16*, 278–291.

Paris, S. G. *Propositional logical thinking and comprehension of language connectives: A developmental analysis*. The Hague: Mouton, 1975.

Parsons, C. Inhelder and Piaget's "The growth of logical thinking." II. A logician's viewpoint. *British Journal of Psychology*, 1960, *51*, 75–84.

Pea, R. D. Development of negation in early child language. In D. R. Olson (Ed.), *The social foundation of language and thought: Essays in honor of Jerome Bruner*. New York: W. W. Norton, 1980. (a)

Pea, R. D. Logic in early child language. In V. Teller & S. J. White (Eds.), *Studies in child language and multilingualism. Annals of the New York Academy of Sciences*, 1980, *345*, 27–43. (b)

Peel, E. A. A method for investigating children's understanding of certain logical connectives used in binary propositional thinking. *British Journal of Mathematical and Statistical Psychology*, 1967, *20*, 81–92.

Pelletier, F. J. Or. *Theoretical Linguistics*, 1977, *4*, 61–74.

Piaget, J. *Judgment and reasoning in the child*. New York: Harcourt Brace, 1928.

Piaget, J. *Traité de logique*. Paris: Colin, 1949.

Piaget, J. *Essai sur les transformations des opérations logiques: Les 256 opérations ternaires de la logique bivalente des propositions*. Paris: Presses Universitaires de France, 1952.

Piaget, J. *Logic and psychology*. Manchester, Eng.: Manchester University Press, 1953.

Piaget, J. Logique formelle et psychologie génétique [including discussion]. In *Les modèles et la formalization du comportement*. Proceedings of the International Colloquium of the National Center for Scientific Research, Paris, July 1965. Paris: Centre Nationale de la Recherche Scientifique, 1967.

Piaget, J., & Szeminska, A. *The child's conception of number*. New York: Humanities Press, 1952. (Originally published, 1941.)

Pieraut-Le Bonniec, G. *Le raisonnement modal, étude génétique*. The Hague: Mouton, 1974.

Pieraut-Le Bonniec, G. *The development of modal reasoning: Genesis of necessity and possibility notions*. New York: Academic Press, 1980.

Quine, W. V. O. *From a logical point of view*. Cambridge, Mass.: Harvard University Press, 1953. (a)

Quine, W. V. O. Mr. Strawson on logical theory. *Mind*, 1953, *62*, 433–451. (b) (Reprinted in W. V. O. Quine, *The ways of paradox*. New York: Random House, 1966.)

Quine, W. V. O. Three grades of modal involvement. *Proceedings of the XI International Congress of Philosophy*, 1953, *14*, 65–81. (c) (Reprinted in W. V. O. Quine, *The ways of paradox*. New York: Random House, 1966.)

Quine, W. V. O. *Methods of logic*. New York: Holt, Rinehart & Winston, 1959.

Quine, W. V. O. Reply to Professor Marcus. *Synthese*, 1961, *13*, 323–330. (Reprinted in W. V. O. Quine, *The ways of paradox*. New York: Random House, 1966.)

Reichenbach, H. *Elements of symbolic logic*. New York: Macmillan, 1947.

Rescher, N. *Many-valued logic*. New York: McGraw-Hill, 1969.

Revlin, R., & Leirer, V. O. The effect of personal biases on syllogistic reasoning: Rational decisions from personalized representations. In R. Revlin & R. E. Mayer (Eds.), *Human reasoning*. Washington, D.C.: V. H. Winston, 1978.

Revlis, R. Syllogistic reasoning: Logical decisions from a complex data base. In R. J. Falmagne (Ed.), *Reasoning: Representation and process in children and adults*. Hillsdale, N.J.: Erlbaum, 1975. (a)

Revlis, R. Two models of syllogistic reasoning: Feature selection and conversion. *Journal of Verbal Learning and Verbal Behavior*, 1975, *14*, 180–195. (b)

Richter, M. N. The theoretical interpretation of errors in syllogistic reasoning. *Journal of Psychol-

ogy, 1957, *43*, 341–344.

Rips, L. J., & Marcus, S. L. Suppositions and the analysis of conditional sentences. In M. A. Just & P. A. Carpenter (Eds.), *Cognitive processes in comprehension*. Hillsdale, N.J.: Erlbaum, 1977.

Roberge, J. J. A study of children's abilities to reason with basic principles of deductive reasoning. *American Educational Research Journal*, 1970, *7*, 538–595.

Roberge, J. J. Some effects of negation on adults' conditional reasoning abilities. *Psychological Reports*, 1971, *29*, 839–844.

Roberge, J. J. Recent research on the development of children's comprehension of deductive reasoning schemes. *School Science and Mathematics*, 1972, *70*, 197–200.

Roberge, J. J. Effects of negation on adults' comprehension of fallacious conditional and disjunctive arguments. *Journal of General Psychology*, 1974, *91*, 287–293.

Roberge, J. J. Effects of negation on adults' disjunctive reasoning abilities. *Journal of General Psychology*, 1976, *94*, 23–28. (a)

Roberge, J. J. Reasoning with exclusive disjunctive arguments. *Quarterly Journal of Experimental Psychology*, 1976, *28*, 419–427. (b)

Roberge, J. J., & Flexer, B. K. Further examination of formal operational reasoning abilities. *Child Development*, 1979, *50*, 478–484.

Roberge, J. J., & Paulus, D. M. Developmental patterns for children's class and conditional reasoning abilities. *Developmental Psychology*, 1971, *4*, 191–200.

Rumain, B. Pragmatics of interpretation of negation: A developmental study. Unpublished doctoral dissertation, New York University, 1982.

Rumain, B., Connell, J., & Braine, M. D. S. Conversational comprehension processes are responsible for reasoning fallacies in children as well as adults: *If* is not the biconditional. *Developmental Psychology*, in press.

Russell, B. The axiom of infinity. *Hibbert Journal*, 1904, *2*, 809–812.

Sells, S. B. The atmosphere effect: An experimental study of reasoning. *Archives of Psychology*, 1936, *29*, 3–72.

Shapiro, B. J., & O'Brien, T. C. Logical thinking in children aged six through thirteen. *Child Development*, 1970, *41*, 823–829.

Shipley, E. F. The class-inclusion task: Question form and distributive comparisons. *Journal of Psycholinguistic Research*, 1979, *8*, 301–331.

Siegel, L. S., McCabe, A. E., Brand, J., & Matthews, J. Evidence for the understanding of class-inclusion in preschool children: Linguistic factors and training effects. *Child Development*, 1978, *49*, 689–693.

Siegler, R. S., Liebert, D. E., & Liebert, R. M. Inhelder and Piaget's pendulum problem: Teaching preadolescents to act as scientists. *Developmental Psychology*, 1973, *9*, 97–101.

Siegler, R. S., & Liebert, R. M. Acquisition of formal scientific reasoning by ten and thirteen year olds. *Developmental Psychology*, 1975, *11*, 401–402.

Slobin, D. I. Grammatical transformations in childhood and adulthood. *Journal of Verbal Learning and Verbal Behavior*, 1966, *5*, 219–227.

Smedslund, J. Concrete reasoning: A study of intellectual development. *Monographs of the Society for Research in Child Development*, 1964, *29*(2, Serial No. 93).

Smith, C. L. Children's understanding of natural language hierarchies. *Journal of Experimental Child Psychology*, 1979, *27*, 437–458.

Smith, C. L. Quantifiers and question answering in young children. *Journal of Experimental Child Psychology*, 1980, *30*, 191–205.

Smith, M. C. Cognizing the behavior stream: The recognition of intentional action. *Child Development*, 1978, *49*, 736–743.

Somerville, S. C., Hadkinson, B. A., & Greenberg, C. Two levels of inferential behavior in young children. *Child Development*, 1979, *50*, 119–131.

Springston, F. J., & Clark, H. H. *And* and *or*, or the comprehension of pseudoimperatives. *Journal of Verbal Learning and Verbal Behavior*, 1973, *12*, 258–272.

Staal, J. F. "And." *Journal of Linguistics*, 1968, *4*, 79–81.

Stalnaker, R. C. A theory of conditionals. In N. Rescher (Ed.), *Studies in Logical Theory*. *American Philosophical Quarterly*, Monograph No. 2, 1968.

Staudenmayer, H., & Bourne, L. Learning to interpret conditional sentences: A developmental study. *Developmental Psychology*, 1977, *13*, 616–623.

Sternberg, R. J. Developmental patterns in the encoding and combination of logical connectives. *Journal of Experimental Child Psychology*, 1979, *28*, 469–498.

Stone, C. A., & Day, M. C. Levels of availability of a formal operational strategy. *Child Development*, 1978, *49*, 1054–1065.

Störring, G. Experimentelle Untersuchungen über einfache Schlussprozesse. *Archiv für die gesamte Psychologie,* 1908, *11,* 1–127.

Störring, G. Allgemeine Bestimmungen über Denk-prozesse und kausale Behandlung einfacher experimentell gewonnener Schlussprozesse. *Archiv für die gesamte Psychologie,* 1925, *52,* 1–60.

Störring, G. Psychologie die zweiten und dritten Schlussfigur und allgemeine Gesetzmässigkeiten der Schlussprozesse. *Archiv für die gesamte Psychologie,* 1926, *54,* 23–84.

Strawson, P. F. *Introduction to logical theory.* London: Methuen, 1952.

Suppes, P., & Feldman, S. Young children's comprehension of logical connectives. *Journal of Experimental Child Psychology,* 1971, *12,* 304–317.

Taplin, J. E. Reasoning with conditional sentences. *Journal of Verbal Learning and Verbal Behavior,* 1971, *10,* 218–225.

Taplin, J. E., & Staudenmayer, H. Interpretation of abstract conditional sentences in deductive reasoning. *Journal of Verbal Learning and Verbal Behavior,* 1973, *12,* 530–542.

Taplin, J. E., Staudenmayer, H., & Taddonio, J. L. Developmental changes in conditional reasoning: Linguistic or logical? *Journal of Experimental Child Psychology,* 1974, *17,* 360–373.

Terman, L. M., & Merrill, M. A. *Measuring Intelligence.* Boston: Houghton Mifflin, 1937.

Trabasso, T., Isen, A. M., Dolecki, P., McLanaham, A. G., Riley, C. A., & Tucker, T. How do children solve class-inclusion problems? In R. S. Siegler (Ed.), *Children's thinking: What develops?* Hillsdale, N.J.: Erlbaum, 1978.

Van Duyne, P. C. A short note on Evans' criticism of reasoning experiments and his matching bias hypothesis. *Cognition,* 1973, *2,* 239–242.

Van Duyne, P. C. Realism and linguistic complexity in reasoning. *British Journal of Psychology,* 1974, *65,* 59–67.

Vendler, Z. *Linguistics in philosophy.* Ithaca, N.Y.: Cornell University Press, 1967.

Warden, D. A. The influence of context on children's use of identifying expressions. *British Journal of Psychology,* 1976, *67,* 101–112.

Wason, P. C. On the failure to eliminate hypotheses in a conceptual task. *Quarterly Journal of Experimental Psychology,* 1960, *12,* 129–140.

Wason, P. C. The effect of self-contradiction on fallacious reasoning. *Quarterly Journal of Experimental Psychology,* 1964, *16,* 30–34.

Wason, P. C. The contexts of plausible denial. *Journal of Verbal Learning and Verbal Behavior,* 1965, *4,* 7–11.

Wason, P. C. Reasoning. In B. M. Foss (Ed.), *New horizons in psychology, 1.* Harmondsworth, Eng.: Penguin, 1966.

Wason, P. C. Reasoning about a rule. *Quarterly Journal of Experimental Psychology,* 1968, *20,* 273–281. (a)

Wason, P. C. On the failure to eliminate hypotheses—a second look. In P. C. Wason & P. N. Johnson-Laird (Eds.), *Thinking and reasoning.* Harmondsworth, Eng.: Penguin, 1968. (b)

Wason, P. C. Regression in reasoning? *British Journal of Psychology,* 1969, *60,* 471–480.

Wason, P. C. Self-contradictions. In P. C. Wason & P. N. Johnson-Laird (Eds.), *Thinking: Readings in cognitive science.* Cambridge, Eng.: At the University Press, 1977.

Wason, P. C., & Golding, E. The language of inconsistency. *British Journal of Psychology,* 1974, *65,* 537–546.

Wason, P. C., & Johnson-Laird, P. N. Proving a disjunctive rule. *Quarterly Journal of Experimental Psychology,* 1969, *21,* 14–20.

Wason, P. C., & Johnson-Laird, P. N. A conflict between selecting and evaluating information in an inferential task. *British Journal of Psychology,* 1970, *61,* 509–515.

Wason, P. C., & Johnson-Laird, P. N. *Psychology of reasoning: Structure and content.* Cambridge: Harvard University Press, 1972.

Wason, P. C., & Shapiro, D. Natural and contrived experience in a reasoning problem. *Quarterly Journal of Experimental Psychology,* 1971, *23,* 63–71.

Wellman, H. M., & Johnson, C. N. Understanding of mental process: A developmental study of "remember" and "forget." *Child Development,* 1979, *50,* 79–88.

Werner, H., & Kaplan, B. *Symbol formation.* New York: Wiley, 1963.

Wildman, T. M., & Fletcher, H. J. Developmental increases and decreases in solutions of conditional syllogism problems. *Developmental Psychology,* 1977, *13,* 630–636.

Wilkins, M. C. The effect of changed material on the ability to do formal syllogistic reasoning. *Archives of Psychology,* 1928, *16,* No. 102.

Wilson, D. *Presuppositions and non-truth-conditional semantics.* New York: Academic Press, 1975.

Winer, G. A. Class-inclusion reasoning in children: A review of the empirical literature. *Child Development,* 1980, *51,* 309–328.

Winograd, T. *Understanding natural language.* New York: Academic Press, 1972.

Winograd, T. Frame representations and the declarative/procedural controversy. In D. G. Bobrow & A. Collins (Eds.), *Representation and understanding: Studies in cognitive science*. New York: Academic Press, 1975.

Wode, H. Four early stages in the development of L1 negation. *Journal of Child Language*, 1977, *4*, 87–102.

Wohlwill, J. F. Responses to class-inclusion questions for verbally and pictorally presented items. *Child Development*, 1968, *39*, 449–465.

Woodworth, R. S. *Experimental psychology*. New York: Holt, 1938.

Woodworth, R. S., & Sells, S. B. An atmosphere effect in formal syllogistic reasoning. *Journal of Experimental Psychology*, 1935, *18*, 451–460.

THE DEVELOPMENT OF INTELLIGENCE* | 6

ROBERT J. STERNBERG, *Yale University*
JANET S. POWELL, *Yale University*

Everyone agrees that intelligence develops; few people agree as to what intelligence is (Miles, 1957). The problem is confounded in that there is also little consensus as to just what develops or whether the intelligence that develops is the same thing at different ages. Thus, not only does intelligence develop in some fashion but also what it is that develops may develop as well!

We attempt in this chapter to make some sense of the perplexities surrounding the development of intelligence. The major thesis underlying our attempt is that sufficient information is now available about the nature of intelligence and its development to render possible the formulation of a reasonably unified and coherent view of intellectual development that crosscuts and, we hope, transcends specific para-

digms for the study of the development of intelligence. First, we consider implicit theories of intelligence and its development, that is, intuitive theories people have in their minds regarding what intelligence is and how it develops. Next, we consider explicit theories of intelligence, that is, the theories that have been proposed by researchers on intelligence to account for intelligent behavior and its development. We consider four kinds of explicit theories: behavioristic, psychometric, Piagetian, and information processing ones—with emphasis on psychometric and information processing theories. For the most part, these alternative conceptions highlight different aspects of the nature of intelligence and its development; they differ most in what aspects of intelligence they emphasize rather than in what they aver intelligence to be. We conclude our case in the third and final part of the chapter, where we propose what we believe to be a set of transparadigmatic principles of intellectual development. These principles crosscut the theorizing of many of the alternative conceptions described in the earlier

*This chapter was written while Janet S. Powell was a National Science Foundation predoctoral fellow in the Psychology Department at Yale University. We wish to thank Elizabeth Charles, Barbara Conway, and Jeff Powell for their valuable comments on this chapter.

parts of the chapter and seem reasonably central to many, if not most, notions of intellectual development. We suggest that the principles of intellectual development that are worth pursuing are, in general, those that are not specific to any one paradigm, that is, those that cut across such paradigms as the psychometric, information processing, Piagetian, and so on. This notion stems not from a belief in majority rule in science but from a belief that basic truths about intellectual development will tend to reveal themselves through research conducted within the framework of multiple psychological paradigms.

We begin by a consideration of several alternative conceptions of the nature of intelligence and its development. We describe what we believe to be the five major conceptions: the prototypical, stimulus-response (S-R), psychometric, Piagetian, and information processing conceptions. In addition, we will discuss some conceptions that combine elements of these five major conceptions. The five views are not given equal weight in the discussion because of the different impacts they are currently having on the field of intelligence as well as to minimize overlap with other chapters. Further, the more intuitive, prototypical view differs in kind from the others and is considered separately.

IMPLICIT CONCEPTIONS OF INTELLIGENCE: INTELLIGENCE AS A PROTOTYPE

An implicit conception of intelligence is one that resides in the minds of the individuals to whom the theory applies: the objects of the theory are by definition the creators of the theory. In this case, people's commonsense notions of what intelligence is are viewed as defining intelligence. Data from human subjects are used as the basis for constructing the prototypical theory rather than merely as the basis for testing and perhaps later revising the theory. The data of interest are people's descriptions of intelligence or intelligent behavior rather than their manifestations of it (through tasks that require reasoning, problem solving, learning, or whatever). Studies of implicit conceptions of intelligence are studies of people's notions of what intelligence is.

One question that needs to be answered is that of whose notions are to serve as the data base for a theory. Traditionally, the subjects in this approach have been experts in the field of intelligence. On this view, then, intelligence is what one or more experts define as intelligence. The most well-known implementation of this approach to defining the nature of intelligence was a symposium that appeared more than 60 years ago in the *Journal of Educational Psy-*chology (see "Intelligence and Its Measurement," 1921). In this symposium, 14 experts gave their views on the nature of intelligence, with definitions involving such activities as the ability to carry on abstract thinking, learning or having the ability to learn to adjust oneself to the environment, the ability to adapt oneself adequately to relatively new situations in life, the capacity for knowledge and knowledge possessed, and the capacity to learn or to profit by experience.

Viewed narrowly, there seem to have been as many definitions of intelligence as there were experts asked to define intelligence. Viewed broadly, however, two themes seem to run through at least several of these definitions: the capacity to learn from experience and adaptation to one's environment. Indeed, a view of intelligence accepted by many of these experts is one of intelligence as general adaptability to new problems and situations in life.

A contemporary version of the same kind of study was conducted by Sternberg, Conway, Ketron, and Bernstein (1981). These investigators compiled a list of behaviors that were described as intelligent, academically intelligent, or everyday intelligent by laypeople filling out a brief open-ended questionnaire either at a train station, at a supermarket, or in a college library. The complete list of behaviors was sent to experts in the field of intelligence (faculty members in psychology departments of major universities whose research interests are in the area of intelligence, broadly defined). These experts were asked to rate either how characteristic each behavior was of an ideally intelligent, academically intelligent, and everyday intelligent person or how important each behavior was in defining the experts' conceptions of an ideally intelligent, academically intelligent, and everyday intelligent person. Ratings of the 65 experts who responded to the characteristicness questionnaire were factor analyzed; only items that were classified as high in importance by the experts (a mean rating of 6.3 or above on a 1-to-9 scale) were retained in the factor analysis. Three major factors were obtained for the ratings of intelligence. The first, labeled "verbal intelligence," showed high loadings for such behaviors as "displays a good vocabulary," "reads with high comprehension," "is verbally fluent," and "converses easily on a variety of subjects." The second factor, labeled "problem solving," showed high loadings for such behaviors as "able to apply knowledge to problems at hand," "makes good decisions," "poses problems in an optimal way," and "plans ahead." The third factor, labeled "practical intelligence," showed high loadings for such behaviors as "sizes up situations well," "determines how to achieve goals," "displays awareness to world around him or her," and "displays interest in the world at large." Factors for academic and everyday intelligence were somewhat similar to those for intelligence, although slanted (as one might expect) toward the academic and everyday sides of intelligence respectively.

Some psychologists have argued that laypersons should form at least one population to be studied in research on people's conceptions of intelligence. On this view, intelligence was originally and still is largely a concept created by the person in the street for the person in the street. A leading proponent of this point of view is Neisser (1979), who is largely responsible for reawakening modern interest in people's conceptions of intelligence.

According to Neisser (1979):

> "*Intelligent person*" is a prototype-organized Roschian concept. Our confidence that a person deserves to be called "intelligent" depends on that person's overall similarity to an imagined prototype, just as our confidence that some object is to be called "chair" depends on its similarity to prototypical chairs. There are no definitive criteria of intelligence, just as there are none for chairness; it is a fuzzy-edged concept to which many features are relevant. Two people may both be quite intelligent and yet have very few traits in common—they resemble the prototype along different dimensions. Thus, there is no such quality as *intelligence*, any more than there is such a thing as *chairness*—resemblance is an external fact and not an internal essence. There can be no process-based definition of intelligence, because it is not a unitary quality. It is a resemblance between two individuals, one real and the other prototypical. (p. 185)

Neisser notes that he is not the first to express such a view, which he traces back at least to E. L. Thorndike (1924):

> For a first approximation, let intellect be defined as that quality of mind (or brain or behavior if one prefers) in respect to which Aristotle, Plato, Thucydides, and the like, differed most from Athenian idiots of their day, or in respect to which the lawyers, physicians, scientists, scholars, and editors of reputed greatest ability at constant age, say a dozen of each, differ most from idiots of that age in asylums. (p. 241)

Wittgenstein (1953) has also proposed similar views. Neisser (1979) suggests that such tests as the Stanford–Binet have been reasonably successful because they consist of large numbers of items that assess resemblance to different aspects of the prototype. Individual items function, like individual dimensions of a chair, in the construction of a prototype.

Neisser collected informal data from Cornell undergraduates regarding their conceptions of what intelligence is; more formal studies were conducted by Bruner, Shapiro, and Tagiuri (1958); Cantor and Mischel (1979); and Sternberg, Conway, Ketron, and Bernstein (1981) in the United States and by Wober (1974) among the Kiganda. The data of Sternberg and his colleagues suggest that laypersons' conceptions of intelligence are remarkably similar to experts'. Characteristicness ratings of experts and laypersons were correlated .96; importance ratings were correlated .85. Thus, the two groups of individuals seem largely to agree as to what behaviors are characteristic of, and important in, defining the ideally intelligent person. Differences in views among populations can be found however. People in a college library described as intelligent behaviors those that were similar to the ones they described as academically intelligent; people at a train station (largely business commuters) and in a supermarket (largely housewives) described as intelligent behaviors those that were similar to the ones they described as everyday intelligent. Similar patterns were displayed in self-ratings, where the students showed higher correlations between their self-ratings of intelligence and academic intelligence than between their self-ratings of intelligence and everyday intelligence. The commuters showed the reverse pattern (Sternberg, Conway, Ketron, & Bernstein, 1981).

Although there is little evidence of any transition in views regarding the nature of intelligence between nonexpert and expert levels of technical sophistication and knowledge, there is evidence of a transition in views regarding the nature of intelligence with increasing age. Yussen and Kane (in press) studied conceptions of intelligence as reflected in the interview responses of first, third, and sixth graders. Children were asked questions concerning such issues as visible signs of intelligence, qualities associated with intelligence, the constancy or malleability of intelligence, and the definition of intelligence. The authors found that older children's conceptions were more differentiated than those of younger children, that with increasing age children increasingly characterize intelligence as an internalized quality, that older children are less likely than younger ones to think that overt signs signal intelligence, and that older children are less global in the qualities they associate with intelligence than are younger children. There was also a tendency for younger children to think of intelligence largely in terms of social skills, but for older children to think of it largely in terms of academic skills.

Siegler and Richards (in press) conducted a study that in some respects might be viewed as complementary to that of Yussen and Kane (in press). Rather than asking individuals of different ages what they thought intelligence was, Siegler and Richards asked people of a given age (college students) what they thought intelligence was at different ages. In particular, subjects were asked to describe the nature of intelligence in 6-month-olds, 2-year-olds, 10-year-olds, and adults. The authors reported (in the order of the frequency with which they were mentioned) the five traits must often mentioned as characterizing intelligence at different ages. At 6 months old, these traits were recognition of people and objects, motor coordination, alertness, awareness of environment, and verbalization. At 2 years old, they were verbal ability, learning ability, awareness of people and environment, motor coordination, and curiosity. At 10 years old, they were verbal ability, followed by learning ability, problem-solving ability, reasoning ability—all tied for second place in frequency of mention—and creativity. At the adult level, the traits were reasoning ability, verbal ability, problem-solving ability, learning ability, and creativity. Clearly, there is a trend toward conceiving of intelligence as less perceptual motor and as more cognitive with increasing age.

We believe that research on implicit theories of intelligence has been and will continue to be important in the psychology of intelligence and its development: first, because the importance of intelligence in our society makes it worthwhile to know what people mean by intelligence; second, because implicit theories serve as the basis of informal, everyday assessment (as in college or job interviews) and training (as in parent/child interactions) of intelligence; and third, because implicit theories may suggest aspects of intelligent behavior that need to be understood but are overlooked in available explicit theories of intelligence. We now turn our attention to explicit theories.

EXPLICIT CONCEPTIONS OF INTELLIGENCE

An explicit theory of intelligence is one that attempts to ferret out what intelligence is by investi-gating its manifestations in the behavior of human subjects. The investigator's assumptions about, or implicit theory of, intelligence guide his or her choice of tasks and direct his or her vision toward certain characteristics, but the data of interest are people's performances on specific tasks chosen by the experimenter to require intelligent behavior. Data from human subjects are the basis for testing and perhaps revising the investigator's theory of intelligence and its development. The subject's own beliefs about intelligent behavior are irrelevant to an explicit theory of intelligence, except insofar as they color people's performance on reasoning, problem-solving, and learning tasks.

We have chosen for inclusion in this chapter those explicit theories we believe have made, and are continuing to make, a significant impact on students of intelligence and of intellectual development. The explicit theories included here are behaviorism or learning theory, psychometric theory, Piagetian theory, and information processing theories of intelligence. Although these approaches often begin with very different views of intelligence and although they use very different methodologies to test their theories, we will argue that the approaches actually have much in common, and we conclude with some suggested *transparadigmatic* principles of intellectual development that we see emerging from these different explicit theories.

The Learning Theory Conception of Intelligence

Whereas in the last, two-volume edition of *Carmichael's Manual of Child Psychology*, edited by Mussen, the learning theory approach to development was quite prominent (see Stevenson, 1970; White, 1970), it is interesting to note that in the current four-volume edition, this is not the case at all. Whereas some S-R theorists still are active in research, they have not been prominent in the past decade in the formulation of theories of children's cognitive development. But there is still an effect of associative theorizing on the formulation of current theories. Therefore, the purpose of this section is to summarize briefly and evaluate the contribution of learning theory to conceptions of intelligence and intellectual development as well as to outline likely areas for further input.

The S-R or learning theory view of intelligence is perhaps best stated by Thorndike, Bregman, Cobb, & Woodyard (1926):

The hypothesis which we present and shall defend—asserts that in their deeper nature the higher forms of intellectual operation are identical with mere association or connection forming, depending upon the same sort of physiological connections but requiring *many more of them*. By the same argument the person whose intellect is greater or higher or better than that of another person differs from him in the last analysis in having, not a new sort of physiological process, but simply a large number of connections of the ordinary sort. (p. 415)

In the associative learning theorist's view, then, all behavior—no matter how complex or "intelligent"—is seen as of a single type, and one's "intelligence" is seen as simply a function of the number and strength of the S-R connections one has formed and, perhaps, the rate at which new ones can be formed.

The learning theorist's emphasis is always on the observed behavior of the organism; traditional learning theorists tend to shun any hint of mentalistic operations or of any internal processes that must be inferred rather than directly observed. All behavior, be it physical or intellectual, is seen as of a single type, established by the formation of S-R connections; all organisms, be they pigeons or humans, are seen as following the same associative laws of learning (see Rachlin, 1976). However, because researchers consistently find qualitative differences in behavior between lower animals and adult humans or even between children of different ages (see White, 1970), some S-R researchers have questioned the strict learning theorist's assumptions that all behavior is of a single type and that simple behaviors capture the essence of complex behaviors. Neobehaviorists, such as the Kendlers (Kendler & Kendler, 1975; T. Kendler, 1970, 1979a) and White (1965), have departed from radical learning theory by assuming that associationist theory is fine for some types of behavior and for some periods of human development but that modifications must be made to traditional S-R theory to account for higher, more conceptual behaviors, such as many of those characterizing the mature human.

In the discussions that follow, we will briefly present and evaluate some relatively recent learning theories exemplifying two approaches to the relationship between simple and complex learning. (See Sternberg & Powell, 1980, for a more detailed description of these theories.) The first approach is one in which all behavior is seen as following the associative laws of learning, but which specifies a hierarchy of learning types (Gagné, 1965, 1968). The second approach is one in which the applicability of

associative learning principles is seen as limited to simple behaviors or to the behavior of young children; qualitatively different cognitive processes are hypothesized to develop with maturation and gradually to take over behavioral control from the more primitive associative processes (Kendler & Kendler, 1975; T. Kendler, 1970, 1979a; White, 1965). Finally, we suggest ways in which learning theory might make a greater contribution in the future to understanding the nature of cognitive development.

Gagné's Hierarchy of Learning

Gagné's theory (1965, 1968) is in line with more traditional S-R theories, in that it views cognitive development as the accumulation of past learning (which is described as always of an associative nature); but it departs from traditional theory in its delineation of eight types of associative learning, each requiring different conditions for its establishment and arranged so that types higher in the hierarchy describe more conceptual learning. The eight types of learning, in order of ascending complexity, are signal learning, S-R learning, chaining, verbal association, multiple discrimination, concept learning, principle learning, and problem solving. Each level of the hierarchy has been seen by Gagné as providing a basis for the higher, more complex forms of learning in the hierarchy.

Gagné has proposed that his theory can explicitly account for the developmental progression of the child from a limited capacity to perform simple learning tasks to the ability to master complex types of learning. He has written:

> Learning contributes to the intellectual development of the human being because it is *cumulative* in its effects. The child progresses from one point to the next in his development, not because he acquires one or a dozen new associations, but because he learns an ordered set of capabilities which build upon each other in progressive fashion through the processes of differentiation, recall, and transfer of learning. (Gagné, 1968, p. 181)

Gagné, thus, has described qualitative changes in learning as the child matures, and he has noted that maturation imposes limits on behavioral development (1968); but his emphasis has been on describing the role of experience in development and on determining the prerequisite conditions for learning to occur rather than on the role of maturation per se.

Gagné's cumulative learning theory is the best S-R account of thinking and problem solving available, and as an approach to task analysis and to training higher order processes, it is very valuable. But Gagné's approach is more task centered than person centered, and so it tells us less than one might hope about how a person actually forms associations of the various types, that is, what cognitive processes are involved. What is the nature of the qualitative change involved as one progresses to higher types of learning? To be of maximal use in illuminating the nature of complex cognitive behavior, it is not enough to say that complex learning builds upon simpler forms of learning; one must specify the nature of the added element. Gagné's hierarchy suggests that this added something is a higher level organization, consisting of more general, higher order associations. But, one might well ask, What guides the formation of these higher order associations? And why did Gagné think they developed with age? It seems that some higher order processes are perhaps implied that guide the ability to see more general associations, to perceive similarities, to discriminate differences, and to guide the transfer of learning from one familiar situation to another novel one. Thus, we must question the reductionist claim that all learning, all thought, is really of a single type; by increasing conceptual complexity, as when one progresses up in Gagné's hierarchy, one may well be introducing some sort of higher order processing. Gagné's task analysis has had considerable influence on textbook writers and curriculum designers (e.g., Mager, 1972, 1975), but as a method for understanding intellectual performance, the theory has been possibly less useful. It does show promise, however, as a way of exploring the validity of the reductionist argument that complex behavior can be broken into simpler units and that the whole will still be equal to the sum of the parts. (See Sternberg and Powell, 1982, for a further discussion of reductionism.)

Mediation Theory and Qualitative Shifts in the Nature of Intellectual Performance

A second major attempt to extend traditional S-R theories to account for both simple and complex behaviors was pioneered by Kuenne (1946) and by the Kendlers and their associates (Kendler & Kendler, 1964, 1975; T. Kendler, 1970). Underlying these theories is the assumption that simple and complex behavior can both be explained by the traditional associative laws of learning *if* one proposes that the S-R connections comprising behavior may also include covert links or mediating responses that intervene between an overt stimulus and an overt response. A mediation view of learning holds that the S-R description of behavior may actually be short-

hand for a chain of stimuli and responses, some of which may be internal. Language is a commonly proposed mediator of behavior—although not the only type of mediator possible—and the work of the Kendlers and their associates as well as that of Kuenne, Luria, and others, has focused on the development of verbal mediation. A more complete description of the work on mediation theory is presented in Sternberg and Powell (1980). In the interest of brevity, we will just note here that many of these studies by associative learning theorists—using a discrimination learning task—noted a strategy change that occurs sometime between the age of 3 and the child's entry into school (Kendler & Kendler, 1964; T. Kendler, 1970; T. Kendler, Kendler, & Wells, 1960; T. Kendler & Ward, 1972). The Kendlers proposed that the development of mediated responses, linked to, but not synonymous with, the development of language, well describes the behavioral changes that occur as higher order concepts are first acquired and, then, later come to serve as mediators (guides) of behavior. These findings coincide with Luria's (1961) view of the development with age of the child's speech as a regulator of his or her behavior and with Piaget and Inhelder's (1969) description of the development of representational thought that occurs during preschool years.

It is interesting to note how learning theorists account for the qualitative shift in children's cognitive functioning that occurs as mediational processes are gradually acquired. Kendler (1979a) has proposed a levels-of-functioning theory, and White (1965) suggests a temporal stacking theory to account for these phenomena; both theories suggest that, whereas associative learning processes may account for the behavior of younger children, older children gradually develop more conceptual, or mediational, processes that lead to behavior of a qualitatively different sort.

Kendler's Levels-of-Functioning Theory. Kendler (1979a) has proposed a levels-of-functioning theory, based on the maturation of the nervous system, that postulates a dual-component central processing system that develops gradually and that increasingly comes to mediate behavior. This dual-component central processor consists of an encoding component that "analyzes, integrates, and stores the stimulus input" and a behavior-regulation component that "initiates, monitors, and evaluates the behavioral output" (p. 111). In a tentative, first formulation of the levels-of-functioning theory, Kendler proposed that each component consists of at least two hierarchically arranged modes of functioning that mature at different rates; other levels, Kendler noted, may be specified at a later date. The encoding component consists of an early-to-develop nonselective mode, which registers all of the input stimuli that the organism can process, and a later-to-develop selective mode, which abstracts and records only those cues relevant to the task at hand. The behavior-regulation component consists of (1) a basic incremental-learning mode that regulates reinforcement-determined associative learning and (2) a slower developing hypothesis-testing mode that uses the information provided by the reinforcement contingencies to test hypotheses, rules, and strategies. Thus, Kendler's levels-of-functioning theory poses two qualitatively distinct, competitive levels of functioning: an earlier developing associative level and a later developing, more selective cognitive level. Kendler proposed a gradual development of the higher order cognitive capabilities, with the selective encoding system being the first of the higher processes to emerge and allowing, but not guaranteeing, the emergence of hypothesis-testing behavior. Such a gradual model of cognitive development provides for an in-between developmental stage (as described above) in which the child possesses mediating concepts but in which these concepts have no influence over behavior.

Some learning theorists have objected to Kendler's departure from a strict associationistic account of learning and have countered with their own theories of the development and functioning of mediating processes. (See Gholson & Schuepfer, 1979; T. Kendler, 1979a, 1979b; and Spiker & Cantor, 1979, for a sample of the ongoing debate.) Other researchers deny the existence of central mediational processes at all and account for these changes in discrimination-task performance by proposing age changes in attentional processes (Zeaman & House, 1967) or by developmental changes in stimulus differentiation (Tighe, 1965; Tighe & Tighe, 1967; Youniss & Furth, 1965).

White's Temporal Stacking Theory of Cognitive Functioning.   After an extensive review of the literature, covering not only the development of the mediating processes but also a vast assortment of changes appearing in the child's cognitive functioning as she or he matures, White (1965) proposed the existence of a great divide that is crossed by the child—again, as in other theories, around the age of 5 to 7. On the younger side of this cognitive divide, according to White, most of the child's learning is based on the associative processes described by traditional learning theories. But around 5 to 7 years of age, White claimed that the child begins a transition that can best be described as moving from animal-like to humanlike learning. Whereas associative learning processes still exist and still are operative

for the child after this transition is completed, the older child begins to construct cognitive or conceptual processes as well, that is, she or he develops those processes characterizing what we usually consider to be thinking. White described the coexistence of these two types of processes in the more mature child or adult as parallel associative and cognitive layers, stacked in a competitive hierarchy. As the child matures, she or he becomes better able to inhibit the manifestation of the more basic associative processes so that the slower conceptual processes can occur and regulate behavior. Thus, in White's view, cognitive development involves a qualitative transition from behavior that can be completely characterized by the associative links of learning theory to thought. This cannot be explained solely by the formation of S-R connections but rather represents a new level and a new type of functioning. White noted that the qualitative transition appears related to the increased influence of language upon development, but he did not specify the causal nature of the development of the hierarchical arrangement of the learning processes or of the temporal inhibition of the lower, less conceptual types of processes.

Note that whereas both Kendler's and White's theories described how simple and complex thought processes can coexist in the same individual and how the latter are gradually acquired by the time the child enters school, neither theory proposed any further qualitative development within the individual or any specific source of differences across individuals. The basic distinction these researchers saw is between associative and conceptual processes. Presumably (it is never explicitly stated), both theorists would account for individual differences in cognitive functioning by saying that they are due to the degree to which the individual utilizes the higher order conceptual processes that are, potentially, equally available to all individuals.

In conclusion, we believe that learning theory has not made as much of a contribution to the development of theories of cognitive development in the past decade as it could have, primarily for two reasons. First, by stressing so much the general laws of learning—laws that apply across species and across individuals—learning theorists have tended to ignore differences in individuals with similar experience. Learning theorists traditionally stress the leveling (or, as we will see below, the uplifting) effect of experience, as in the famous quote from J. B. Watson, the father of behaviorism:

Give me a dozen healthy infants, well-formed, and my own specified world to bring them up in and I'll guarantee to take any one at random and train him to become any type of specialist I might select—doctor, lawyer, artist, merchant-chief and, yes, even beggar-man and thief, regardless of his talents, penchants, tendencies, abilities, vocations, and race of his ancestors. (1930, p. 104)

Such a theoretical approach, whether we agree or disagree with its basic premises, could contribute much to research on cognitive development in the next decade by focusing more on why differences in individuals exist in spite of, or because of, what experiences and what learning situations can be set up to overcome weaknesses and build up strengths in the individual's cognitive performance. Information processing psychologists have begun to look at aptitude-strategy interactions, that is, at how people of different abilities use different strategies to solve a given task, but little has been done on the interaction of aptitudes and situations, and this is an area where the interests of the learning theorists and the needs of researchers in cognitive development may well intermesh.

A second reason why learning theory has not affected the mainstream of research on intelligence as much as it could have is the learning theorists' unconcern with the actual processes involved in a given task—other than to say that they are always, or always up to a point, associative in nature. Cognitive research has been, and is likely to continue to be, vitally concerned with cognitive processes, both those involved in simple tasks, such as choice reaction-time tasks, and in complex problem solving. Learning theory, with its stress on the continuity between tasks, has a great potential for contributing to an investigation into the relation between simple and complex tasks. There is a definite need in the cognitive-development literature for a theory of tasks describing both the continuity between tasks of different levels of complexity and the continuity between performances exhibited by individuals of different ages. By concentrating more on task analysis—in terms of human processes required as well as in terms of task complexity—learning theory has a greater potential to contribute to further discussions of the development of intelligence than a quick look at the past decade might lead one to expect. We, as students of cognitive development, hope to see learning theorists continue to move more in these directions.

Psychometric Conceptions

Psychometric conceptions of intelligence and its development have in common their reliance upon individual-differences data as a means of testing theories, and, in some cases, as a heuristic aiding the formulation of the theories. Psychometric researchers use techniques of data analysis, such as factor analysis, to discover common patterns of individual differences across tests. These patterns are then hypothesized to emanate from latent sources of individual differences, namely, mental abilities.

Psychometric theory and research seem to have evolved along three interrelated but, nevertheless, distinguishable lines. These traditions have conveyed rather different impressions of what intelligence is and of what it is that develops. The three traditions can be traced back to Sir Francis Galton, Alfred Binet, and Charles Spearman. We will consider each of these traditions in turn and, then, consider separately the meaning of intelligence in infancy.

The Tradition of Sir Francis Galton

The publication of Darwin's (1859) *The Origin of Species* had a profound impact upon many lines of scientific endeavor. One of these lines of endeavor was the investigation of human intelligence and its development. Darwin's book suggested that the capabilities of humans were in some sense continuous with those of lower animals and, hence, could be understood through scientific investigations of the kind that had been conducted upon animals. There was also the intriguing possibility that in intelligence, as in physical properties, ontogeny might recapitulate phylogeny, that is, that the development of intelligence in humans over age might in some way resemble the development of intelligence across successively higher species.

Darwin's cousin, Sir Francis Galton, was probably the first to explore the implications of Darwin's book for the study of intelligence. For seven years (1884–1890), Galton maintained an anthropometric laboratory at the South Kensington Museum in London where, for a small fee, visitors could have themselves measured on a variety of psychophysical tests, such as weight discrimination and pitch sensitivity. In his theory of the human faculty and its development, Galton (1883) proposed two general qualities that distinguished the more from the less gifted. The first was energy or the capacity for labor. The second was sensitivity to physical stimuli:

The discriminative facility of idiots is curiously low; they hardly distinguish between heat and cold, and their sense of pain is so obtuse that some of the more idiotic seem hardly to know what it is. In their dull lives, such pain as can be excited in them may literally be accepted with a welcome surprise. (p. 28)

James McKean Cattell brought many of Galton's ideas from England to the United States. As head of the psychology laboratory at Columbia University, he was in a good position to publicize the psychophysical approach to the theory and measurement of intelligence. J. McK. Cattell (1890) proposed a series of 50 psychophysical tests, such as dynamometer pressure (greatest possible squeeze of one's hand), rate of arm movement over a distance of 50 cm, the distance on the skin by which two points need to be separated for them to be felt separately, and letter span in memory. Underlying all of these tests was the assumption that physical tests measure mental ability. For example, "the greatest squeeze of the hand may be thought by many to be a purely physiological quantity. It is, however, impossible to separate bodily from mental energy" (J. McK. Cattell, 1890, p. 374).

The coup de grace for the Galtonian tradition—at least in its early form (we will argue later that the tradition has resurfaced recently in a different guise)—was administered by one of Cattell's own students, Clark L. Wissler. Wissler (1901) investigated 21 psychophysical tests. His line of approach was correlational. The idea was to show that the various tests are fairly highly intercorrelated and, thus, define some common entity (intelligence) that underlies all of them. Wissler's results were disappointing however. He found the tests generally to be unrelated, and he concluded that his results "lead us to doubt the existence of such a thing as general ability" (p. 55). However, psychologists did not give up hope of finding a construct of general intelligence because an alternative approach to its discovery was leading to greater success.

The Tradition of Alfred Binet

In 1904, the Minister of Public Instruction in Paris named a commission charged with studying or creating tests that would insure that mentally defective children received an adequate education. The commission decided that no child suspected of retardation should be placed in a special class for the retarded without first being given an examination "from which it could be certified that because of the state of his intelligence, he was unable to profit, in an average measure, from the instruction given in the ordinary schools" (Binet & Simon, 1916a, p. 9). Binet and Simon devised tests to meet this placement need. Thus, whereas theory and research in the tradition of Galton grew out of pure scientific concerns, theory and research in the tradition of Binet grew out of practical educational concerns.

At the time, definitions for various degrees of subnormal intelligence lacked both precision and standardization. Personality and intellectual deficits were seen as being of the same ilk. Binet and Simon noted a case of one institutionalized child who seemed to be a victim of the state of confusion that existed: "One child, called imbecile in the first certificate, is marked idiot in the second, feebleminded (*débile*) in the third, and degenerate in the fourth" (Binet & Simon, 1916a, p. 11).

Binet and Simon's conception of intelligence and of how to measure it differed substantially from that of Galton and Cattell, whose tests they referred to as "wasted time." To Binet and Simon, the core of intelligence is:

Judgment, otherwise called good sense, practical sense, initiative, the faculty of adapting one's self to circumstances. To judge well, to comprehend well, to reason well, these are the essential activities of intelligence. A person may be a moron or an imbecile if he is lacking in judgment; but with good judgment he can never be either. Indeed the rest of the intellectual faculties seem of little importance in comparison with judgment. (1916a, pp. 42–43)

Binet cited the example of Helen Keller as someone of known extraordinary intelligence whose scores on psychophysical tests would be notably inferior and, yet, who could be expected to perform at a very high level on tests of judgment.

Binet and Simon's (1916a) theory of intelligent thinking in many ways foreshadowed the research being done today on the development of metacognition (see, e.g., Brown & DeLoache, 1978; Flavell & Wellman, 1977). According to Binet and Simon (1916b), intelligent thought is composed of three distinct elements: direction, adaptation, and criticism.

Direction consists in knowing what has to be done and how it is to be accomplished. When we are required to add two numbers, for example, we give ourselves a series of instructions on how to proceed, and these instructions form the direction of thought. These instructions need not always be conscious:

In the beginning, when we commence an art not yet learned, we have the full consciousness of the directions we are to follow; but little by little, the influence of the directing state becomes weaker on the movement of the thought and of the hand. One no longer needs to make an express appeal to the verbal formula of the instructions; it falls into the vague state of an intellectual feeling, or even completely disappears. (Binet & Simon, 1916b, p. 137)

In many respects, these ideas about the development of direction over time foreshadow current theorizing regarding automaticity of information processing (see, e.g., Schneider & Shiffrin, 1977; Shiffrin and Schneider, 1977). According to Binet and Simon (1916b), retarded individuals show an absence or weakness of direction that manifests itself in two different forms: "either the direction, once commenced, does not continue, or it has not even been commenced because it has not been understood" (p. 138).

Adaptation refers to one's selection and monitoring of one's strategy during the course of task performance:

> There is not only a direction in the movement of thought, there is also a progress; this progress manifests itself in the nature of the successive states through which one passes; they are not equivalent, the first is not of the same value as the last. One arrives at the last state only because he has already passed the first state. (Binet & Simon, 1916b, pp. 139–140)

Thought consists of a series of selections:

> It consists in constantly choosing between many states, many ideas, many means, which present themselves before it like routes which diverge from a crossroad. . . . To think is constantly to choose in view of the end to be pursued. (Binet & Simon, 1916b, p. 140)

Retarded children, according to Binet and Simon (1916b), show a lack of adaptive ability, which manifests itself in part in terms of what these authors call *n'importequisme* ("no-matter-whatism"). No-matter-whatism derives from a lack of critical sense, a lack of differentiation in thinking, and an absence of persistence of intellectual effort. Suppose, for example, an individual is presented with a puzzle in which a whole pattern can be reconstructed by joining pieces of the cards to reconstruct the whole, as in a jigsaw puzzle. The normal person tries many different solutions. When one combination does not succeed, the person tries other combinations and either maintains successful parts of previous constructions or abandons previous ideas and visualizes new schemes. On the other hand, "not only does the imbecile content himself with something nearly true, owing to the absence of critical sense, but moreover the number of attempts which he makes is extremely small, two or three for example, where a normal would make ten" (Binet & Simon, 1916b, p. 145).

Criticism or control is the ability to criticize one's own thoughts and actions. Binet and Simon (1916b) believed much of this ability to be exercised beneath the conscious level. Defectives show a lack of control. Their actions are frequently inappropriate to the task at hand. For example, a retarded individual "told to copy an 'a' scribbles a formless mass at which he smiles in a satisfied manner" (1916b, p. 149).

In a later paper, Binet and Simon (1916b) distinguished between two types of intelligence, ideational intelligence and instinctive intelligence. Ideational intelligence operates by means of words and ideas. It uses logical analysis and verbal reasoning. Instinctive intelligence operates by means of feeling. It refers not to the instinct attributed to animals and to simple forms of human behavior, but to the "lack of a logical perception, of a verbal reasoning, which would permit of explaining and of demonstrating a succession of truths" (Binet & Simon, 1969b, p. 316). It seems to be very similar to what we might refer to as an intuitive sense. Retardates are seen as deficient in both, to greater or lesser extents.

The above formulation should make clear that contrary to the contemporary conventional wisdom, Binet was not atheoretical in his approach to intelligence and its development. To the contrary, he and Simon conceived of intelligence in ways that were theoretically sophisticated—more so than most of the work that followed theirs—and that resembled in content much of the most recent thinking regarding metacognitive information processing. Whatever may be the distinction between the thinking of Binet and that of Galton, it was not (as some would have it) that Galton was theoretically motivated and Binet atheoretically motivated (see, e.g., Hunt, Frost, & Lunneborg, 1973). If anything, Binet had a more well-developed theory of the nature of intelligence. Instead, it was in the way these scientists selected items for the tests that they proposed to measure intelligence. Galton's test items had construct validity in terms of his theory that intelligence is closely related to physical abilities, but Galton did not empirically validate his test items. Binet's test items had construct validity in terms of his theory of intelligence, in that these test items measured the kinds of judgmental abilities that Binet theorized constituted intelligence, but they were also chosen so that they would differentiate between the performance of children of different ages or mental capacities as well as be intercorrelated with each other at a reasonable level. What were the kinds of items Binet and his successors (e.g., Terman & Merrill, 1973) used to measure intelligence at various age levels?

The Stanford–Binet scale in its contemporary form (Terman & Merrill, 1973) starts with tests for children of age 2. Examples of tests at this level are a three-hole form board, which requires children to put circular, square, and triangular pieces into holes on a board of appropriate shape; identification of parts of the body, which requires children to identify body parts on a paper doll; block building, which requires children to build a four-block tower; and picture vocabulary, which requires children to identify pictures of common objects.

Six years later, by age 8, the character of the tests changes considerably, although the tests are still measuring the kinds of higher cognitive processes that the tests for age 2 attempt to tap. At age 8, the tests include vocabulary, which requires children to define words; verbal absurdities, which requires recognition of why each of a set of statements is foolish; similarities and differences, which requires children to say how each of two objects is the same as, and different from, the other; comprehension, which requires children to solve practical problems of the sort encountered in everyday life; and naming the days of the week.

Six more years later, when subjects are 14, there is some overlap in tests, although on the average the tests are still more difficult. They include vocabulary; induction, in which the experimenter makes a notch in an edge of some folded paper and asks subjects how many holes the paper will have when it is unfolded (the test seems to be more spatial than inductive in character); reasoning, which requires solution of an arithmetic word problem; ingenuity, which requires individuals to indicate the series of steps that could be used to pour a given amount of water from one container to another; orientation, requiring reasoning about spatial directions; and reconciliation of opposites, which requires individuals to say in what ways two opposites are alike.

The most difficult level, "Superior Adult III," includes measures of vocabulary; interpretation of proverbs; orientation; reasoning; repetition of the main ideas in a story; and solution of analogies.

The early Binet tests, like the early Galton tests (as modified and expanded by J. McK. Cattell), were subjected to empirical test rather early on. Sharp (1899) undertook a large-scale experiment to discover the usefulness of the Binet–Simon tests in applied settings. Sharp "provisionally accepted [the notion] that the complex mental processes, rather than the elementary processes, are those the variations of which give most important information in regard to the mental characteristics whereby individuals are commonly classed" (p. 348). Sharp used a curious sample of tests however. They included

five memory tests, a mental imagery test, a test of imagination, a test of attention, a test of discrimination, and a test of taste and tendencies. The heavy emphasis upon memory tests was peculiar, especially in view of Binet and Simon's (1916a) belief that memory is not an important aspect of intelligence:

> At first glance, memory being a psychological phenomenon of capital importance, one would be tempted to give it a very conspicuous part in an examination of intelligence. But memory is distinct from and independent of judgment. One may have good sense and lack memory. The reverse is also common. (p. 43)

Unfortunately, Binet and Simon's point was lost not only on Sharp but on many of her successors. A review of the fairly extensive post-Binet literature on the relationship between memory and intelligence reveals the truth of what Binet recognized many years ago—that memory is not a particularly integral part of intelligence (see Estes, in press). It should come as no surprise that Sharp's (1899) results were only slightly more encouraging than Wissler's (1901). But the fact that Sharp's data had much less impact than did Wissler's is probably due not to the questionable aspects of her selection of materials but to the fact that Binet, like Galton, had a popularizer in this country—one who was much more successful than Cattell in marketing new ideas about how to measure intelligence.

Lewis M. Terman, a professor of psychology at Stanford University, constructed the earliest versions of what have come to be called the Stanford–Binet Intelligence Scales (Terman & Merrill, 1937, 1973). The tests already described are from Terman's versions of the Binet scales. Terman is well known for his applied rather than his theoretical work. One example of such work, of course, is the set of Stanford–Binet scales. A second example of equal renown is the longitudinal study of the gifted conducted by Terman and his successors (e.g., Terman, 1925; Terman & Oden, 1959). In his sample of the gifted, Terman included California children under age 11 with IQs over 140 as well as children in the 11- to 14-age-bracket with slightly lower IQs (to allow for the lower ceiling at this age in test scores). The mean IQ of the 643 subjects selected was 151; only 22 of these subjects had IQs of under 140. The accomplishments in later life of the selected group were extraordinary by any criterion. By 1959, there were 70 listings among the group in *American Men of Science* and 3 memberships in the highly prestigious National Academy of Science. In addition,

31 men were listed in *Who's Who in America* and 10 appeared in the *Directory of American Scholars*. There were numerous highly successful business-men as well as individuals who were succeeding unusually well in all of the professions. The sex bias in these references is obvious. Because most of the women became housewives, it is impossible to make any meaningful comparison between the men on the one hand (none of whom were reported to be house-husbands) and the women on the other hand.

Terman's other major accomplishment, the Stan-ford–Binet Intelligence Scale, is still (in its present 1973 version) probably the most widely used indi-vidual test of intelligence. In earlier versions of the scale and in much of the literature on the develop-ment of intelligence, three interrelated concepts have played a critical role. The first concept, chron-ological age, refers simply to a person's physical age from time of birth. The second concept, mental age, refers to a person's level of intelligence in compari-son to the "average" person of a given age. If, for example, a person performs at a level comparable to that of an average 12-year-old, the person's mental age will be 12 regardless of the person's chronologi-cal age. The third concept, intelligence quotient (IQ), traditionally refers to the ratio between mental age and chronological age multiplied by 100. A score of 100 signifies that mental age is equivalent to chronological age. Scores above 100 indicate above-average intelligence; scores below 100 indicate be-low-average intelligence.

For a variety of reasons, the concept of mental age has proven to be something of a weak link in the psychometric analysis of intelligence. First, in-creases in mental age seem to slow at about the age of 16. The interpretation of the mental-age concept above this age, thus, becomes equivocal. Second, increases in mental age vary nonlinearly with chron-ological age, even up to the age of 16. The in-terpretation of mental ages and of IQs computed from them may, therefore, vary for different chrono-logical ages. Third, the unidimensionality of the mental-age scale seems to imply a certain sameness over age levels in the concept of intelligence—a sameness that the contents of the tests do not bear out. For these and other reasons, IQs have tended in recent years to be computed on the basis of relative performance within a given age group (see, e.g., Terman & Merrill, 1973)—one's performance is evaluated relative only to the performance of others of the same age. Commonly, scores have been stan-dardized to have a mean of 100 and a standard devia-tion of 15 or 16. These deviation IQs (as they are called) have been used in much the same way as the original ratio IQs, although in spirit they are quite different. In fact, the deviation IQs are not quotients at all!

Deviation IQs are used in the second major indi-vidual intelligence scale applied in contemporary as-sessment. This scale is the Wechsler Adult Intel-ligence Scale (Wechsler, 1958) and its companion scale for children, the Wechsler Intelligence Scale for Children (Wechsler, 1974). These two scales are known as the WAIS and the WISC, respectively.

These scales are based on Wechsler's (1974) no-tion of intelligence as "the overall capacity of an individual to understand and cope with the world around him" (p. 5). It is conceived of as a global entity in which no one particular ability is of crucial or overwhelming importance:

> Ultimately, intelligence is not a kind of ability at all, certainly not in the same sense that reason-ing, memory, verbal fluency, etc., are so re-garded. Rather it's something that is inferred from the way these abilities are manifested under different conditions and circumstances. . . . General intelligence, however viewed, is a mul-tifaceted construct. Most definitions differ not so much by what they include as by what they omit. They cover only a modest range of the many abilities and aptitudes that may enter into or de-termine intelligent behavior, and these pertain primarily to cognitive skills or processes (e.g., ability to reason, ability to learn, ability to solve problems, etc.). Intelligent behavior, however, may also call for one or more of a host of apti-tudes (factors) which are more in the nature of conative and personality traits than cognitive ca-pabilities. These involve not so much skills and know-how as drives and attitudes, and often what may be described as sensitivity to social, moral, or aesthetic values. They include such traits as persistence, zest, impulse control, and goal awareness—traits which, for the most part, are independent of any particular intellectual ability. For this reason, they are best designated as *non-intellective* factors of intelligence. (pp. 5–6)

The Wechsler intelligence scales, like the Stan-ford–Binet scales, are wide ranging in their content. However, these scales do not do full justice to the breadth of their originator's conception of the nature of intelligence. Indeed, it is unlikely, even today, that any scale could be constructed that would do full justice to the broad conceptions of Binet and Wechsler.

The most recent version of the WISC, the WISC-R

(Wechsler, 1974), is appropriate for children in the age range from 6 to 16. The test contains 12 subtests, 10 of which are considered mandatory and 2 of which are considered optional. The content of the test is almost identical to that of the adult scale, except that items are easier, as befits their lower targeted age range. The tests are equally divided into two parts, verbal tests and performance tests. Each part yields a separate deviation IQ, and it is possible as well to obtain a deviation IQ for the full scale. Like the Stanford–Binet, the test must be individually administered. In both tests, one administers only items appropriate to the age and ability of the subject. Subjects begin with items easier than appropriate for their age and end with items difficult enough to result in repeated failure of solution on the part of the child.

The verbal part of the test includes as subtests: information, which requires the demonstration of knowledge about the world; similarities, which requires an indication of a way in which two different objects are alike; arithmetic, which requires the solution of arithmetic word problems; vocabulary, which requires definition of common English words; comprehension, which requires understanding of societal customs; and, optionally, digit span, which requires recall of strings of digits presented forward in one section of the subtest and backward in another. The performance part of the test includes as subtests: picture completion, which requires recognition of a missing part in a picture of an object; picture arrangement, which requires rearrangement of a scrambled set of pictures into an order that tells a coherent story from beginning to end; block design, which requires children to reproduce a picture of a design, constructed from a set of red, white, and half-red/half-white blocks, by actually building the design with physical blocks; object assembly, which requires children to manipulate jigsaw-puzzle pieces to form a picture of a common object in the real world; coding (the analogue of digit-symbol at the adult level), which requires rapid copying of symbols that are paired with pictures of objects according to a prespecified key that links the pictures with the objects; and, optionally, mazes, which requires tracing of a route through each of a set of mazes from beginning to end.

Several studies have been conducted of just what it is that the Stanford–Binet and Wechsler tests measure at different age levels. Most of these studies have been conducted by using a methodology that grew not out of the tradition of Alfred Binet, but out of the tradition of another key psychologist in the history of research on intelligence, Charles Spear-

man. To understand these results, it is necessary first to understand something about this methodology, so we defer a presentation of these results until we describe the methodology Charles Spearman invented—factor analysis.

The Tradition of Charles Spearman

Substance and method have rarely been as closely intertwined as in the investigation of intelligence in the tradition of Spearman. Indeed, use of the most widely accepted method of data analysis in differential psychology, factor analysis, has become almost synonymous with use of the psychometric (or differential) approach to intelligence.

Factor analysis takes as its input a matrix of correlations (or less commonly, covariances) between all possible pairs of a set of tasks or tests. The method seeks to reduce the rank of the matrix by finding a relatively small number of latent variables that are then proposed in some sense to account for measured variation on the individual tests. For example, there might be two factors, a verbal one and a spatial one, underlying a battery of tests that includes vocabulary, mental rotation of geometric forms, reading comprehension, mental paper folding, spelling, and comparison of the sameness or difference of pictures of cubes, presented in different orientations, for which some of the faces are missing. Although the methodology will extract the factors and indicate the degree of relationship between each of the factors and tests, it is the investigator's responsibility to assign names to the factors that plausibly describe what each of the factors represents.

What, exactly, is a factor? Users of factor analysis have never reached a complete consensus on this matter (see Coan, 1964; Royce, 1963; R. J. Sternberg, 1977b; Thurstone, 1947). Thurstone (1947) noted that "factors may be called by different names, such as 'causes,' 'faculties,' 'parameters,' 'functional unities,' 'abilities,' or 'independent measurements' " (p. 56). Royce (1963) added to this list "dimensions, determinants, . . . and taxonomic categories" (p. 522). Moreover, R. B. Cattell (1971) referred to factors as "sources traits," and Guilford (1967) described a factor as "an underlying, latent variable along which individuals differ" (p. 41). Guilford (1967) also said, "It is an intervening variable, conceived by the investigator, and has a status like that of *drive* and *habit,* which are also inferred from observed data" (p. 37). Our own view is similar to Guilford's with the added stipulation that factors be viewed as conveniently descriptive—as "categories for classifying mental or behavioral performances" (Vernon, 1971, p.

8)—rather than as causal. Factors provide one of a number of alternative descriptive systems for understanding the structure of mental abilities (R. J. Sternberg, 1980c, 1980f). They give us a useful way of identifying constellations of individual differences that in some sense go together, whether because of communalities in process, structure, content, or whatever.

Factor theorists have included in their theories abilities of the kind studied both by Galton (e.g., Burt, 1940) and by Binet (e.g., Thurstone, 1938). What has unified these theorists of intelligence, on the one hand, and distinguished them from Galton and Binet, on the other hand, is their heavy, indeed, almost exclusive reliance upon factor-analytic methodology both in the conceptualization of their theories (in terms of factors) and in the testing of their theories. This almost exclusive reliance upon a single theoretical and data-analytic system has perhaps resulted in a narrowing of view regarding the nature of intelligence. With the exception of a very few theorists (e.g., Royce, 1973), factor theorists have separated theorizing about intelligence from theorizing about motivation and affect. Although most factor theorists have been more heavily influenced by Binet than by Galton in their choice of test content, their theoretical notions about the nature of intelligence have lacked the inclusiveness that characterized the theorizing, if not the tests, of Binet and Wechsler.

Spearman—originator of the factorial tradition—was not narrow in his conceptualization of intelligence. But his breadth of conceptualization was not transmitted to his successors for a very curious reason indeed, one that might be regarded very loosely as a kind of intellectual schizophrenia on Spearman's part. Spearman's theorizing about intelligence developed and was presented in two clearly identifiable parts. The first part was heavily psychometric and even antiexperimental in character, in that Spearman (1904) believed that experimental psychology

> does not immediately handle the things which really interest us, but other things which are believed to accurately enough betoken the former; to be identical with those of the more complex terms. . . . The results of all good experimental work will live, but as yet most of them are like hieroglyphics awaiting their deciphering Rosetta stone. (pp. 203–204)

The second part was cognitive in its prescient characterization of information processing. Indeed, some of Spearman's theorizing could be viewed as a precursor to the information processing theories that were to come later. But Spearman's information processing theorizing had almost no effect upon subsequent psychometric theorists, and even Spearman never really integrated his information processing theorizing with his psychometric theorizing.

Spearman's mislabeled psychometric theory of intelligence—the two-factor theory—proposes two kinds of factors of human intelligence (not just two factors). According to this theory, there is (1) a general factor, which pervades all intellectual performances and (2) a set of specific factors, each of which is relevant to one particular task. In Spearman's (1904) words: "All branches of intellectual activity have in common one fundamental function (or group of functions), whereas the remaining or specific elements of the activity seem in every case to be wholly different from that in all the others" (p. 284). Spearman's belief that a single factor of intellect was responsible for whatever was common in intellectual performance across tasks constituted what he believed to be a law of the Universal Unity of the Intellective Functions (Spearman, 1904).

What was the actual psychological mechanism that gave rise to such a unity of intellective functions—to what Spearman referred to as the g factor? Spearman (1927) considered a number of possible explanations, such as attention, will, plasticity of the nervous system, and the state of the blood, but he finally settled upon an explanation in terms of mental energy. According to Spearman, the concept of mental energy originated with Aristotle. But the concept had a somewhat different meaning for Aristotle than it had for Spearman. For Aristotle, energy signified any actual manifestation of change, whereas for Spearman, the energy "was but the latent potentiality for this" (1927, pp. 117–118). For Spearman, unlike Aristotle, energy could be an entirely mental construct.

Brown and Thomson (1921) pointed out that Spearman's theory of mental energy was not the only theory consistent with Spearman's factor-analytic results that showed a general factor running across tasks or tests. They argued that the obtained general factor could be indicative of a mathematical rather than a psychological unity. The important point was thereby established for future times that multiple psychological theories could map onto single mathematical (in this case, factorial) ones. Thomson (1939) proposed a theory of bonds in which the mind is conceived of as possessing an enormous number of bonds, including reflexes, habits, learned associations, and the like. Performance on any one task would activate a large number of these bonds. Related tasks, such as those used in mental tests, would sample overlapping subsets of bonds. A factor analysis of a set of tests might, therefore, give the appearance of a general factor, when in fact what was common to the tests was the elicitation of a multitude of overlapping bonds.

Holzinger (1938) proposed what he called a bifactor theory, which retained the general and specific factors of Spearman, but also permitted group factors common to some tests but not others. The theory, thus, expanded upon (rather than contradicted) the foundation of Spearman's two-factor theory, and Holzinger and Spearman actually collaborated at some points in the development of the bifactor theory.

Thurstone (1938), unlike Spearman, Thomson, and Holzinger, eschewed the notion of a general factor. He proposed a theory that tentatively included seven primary mental abilities, which were identified through his method of multiple factor analysis. The abilities were verbal comprehension, number, memory, perceptual speed, space, verbal fluency, and inductive reasoning. These primary mental abilities were used as the basis for the later formulation of the Primary Mental Abilities Tests (Thurstone & Thurstone, 1962). These tests, suitable for children of kindergarten level and above as well as for adults, measure the primary mental abilities in a pencil-and-paper, group-testing format. The contents of the tests vary considerably in difficulty over the age range covered by the tests, but they vary only slightly in the abilities measured. Perceptual speed, for example, is measured only at the lower grade levels. As it happens, scores on factors representing the primary mental abilities are almost always correlated. If the factor scores are factor analyzed (in much the same way that task or test scores would be), a second-order general factor emerges from the analysis. Before his death, Thurstone was obliged to concede the existence of a general factor, which he, nevertheless, believed to be of little importance and of second-order status only. Complementarily, Spearman was eventually forced to concede the existence of group factors, which, unsurprisingly, he believed to be of little importance.

Guilford proposed an extension of Thurstone's theory that incorporates Thurstone's factors (Guilford, 1967; Guilford & Hoepfner, 1971). It splits the primary mental abilities, however, and adds new abilities so that the number of factors is increased from 7 to 120. According to Guilford, every mental task requires three elements: an operation, a content, and a product. Guilford pictured the relation among these three elements as that of a cube, with each of the elements—operations, contents, and products—representing a dimension of the cube. There are five kinds of operations: cognition, memory, divergent production, convergent production, and evaluation. There are six kinds of product: units, classes, relations, systems, transformations, and implications. And there are four kinds of content: figural, symbolic, semantic, and behavioral. Because the subcategories are independently defined, they are multiplicative, yielding $5 \times 6 \times 4 = 120$ different mental abilities. Each of these 120 abilities is represented by Guilford as a small cube embedded in the larger cube. Guilford and his associates have devised tests measuring many of the 120 mental abilities. Cognition of figural relations, for example, is measured by such tests as figural analogies or matrices. Memory for semantic relations is measured by presenting subjects with series of relationships, such as ''Gold is more valuable than iron,'' and then testing their retention of these relationships using a multiple-choice test. The theory of 120 independent factors might seem implausible to some; indeed, the methodology Guilford (1967) has used to confirm his theory—Procrustean rotation of principal-factor solutions—has been shown to be problematical in many respects when used in the way that Guilford used it (see Horn, 1967; Horn & Knapp, 1973).

Burt (1949) proposed a five-level hierarchical model of human intelligence. At the top of the hierarchy is the human mind. At the second level, the relations level, are g (the general factor) and a practical factor. At the third level are associations; at the fourth level, perception; and at the fifth level, sensation. The hierarchical model proposed by Vernon (1971) is probably more sophisticated. At the top of the hierarchy is g. At the second level are two major group factors, verbal-educational ability and practical-mechanical ability; at the third level are minor group factors; and at the fourth level are specific factors.

How could one methodology—factor analysis—support such a wide variety of theories of intelligence? There are a number of ways in which differences in factor-analytic outcomes can arise: method of factor analysis, statistical model underlying the factor analysis, criteria for deciding when to stop extracting further factors, selection of tests, selection of subjects, and alternative substantive interpretations of identical solutions. But we believe that the primary reason for the differences in factorial theories resides in different criteria for rotating factorial solutions (see R. J. Sternberg, 1977b). Most methods of factor analysis yield a multidimensional factor space in which the locations of points (usually tests) in the space are fixed, but the orientation of axes (factors) is not. The axes can be rotated in any of an infinite number of ways that retain the integrity of the factorial space, that is, are consistent with a fixed location for the set of points. Different rotations of axes can result in radically different depictions of the structure of mental abilities. A given solution to a factor analysis might support Spearman's theory if left unrotated, Thurstone's theory if rotated to what Thurstone (1947) called simple structure, and at least aspects of Guilford's theory if rotated in a particular Procrustean manner. Mathematically, all of these solutions are "correct." And no one has found any widely accepted psychological criterion for accepting one kind of rotation and rejecting others. In fact, British theorists have tended to prefer unrotated solutions (certainly not because Spearman was British!), and American theorists have tended to prefer solutions rotated to simple structure (certainly not because Thurstone was American!). We will argue later that the choice of a criterion for rotation is purely one of theoretical or practical convenience. No one rotation is "correct," and in fact, all theories that can be factorially supported are special cases of a single psychometric theory that can be understood equally well in information processing terms.

Psychometric Conceptions and Intellectual Development

Substantial literatures exist regarding the nature of intelligence and the development of intelligence as perceived from a psychometric point of view. Yet, the two literatures are surprisingly autonomous: on the one hand, few of the major factor theorists of intelligence have given serious and detailed consideration to the place of intellectual development in their theories. On the other hand, few of the major developmental students of intelligence have given serious and detailed consideration to the place of theories of the nature of intelligence in their research. Despite notable exceptions (e.g., Horn, 1970; Stott & Ball, 1965), the literature on the development of intelligence has been very largely empirical in its orientation (see, e.g., Bayley's, 1970, review of the literature on the development of mental abilities), and some of the work has been almost entirely atheoretical (see, e.g., Broman, Nichols, & Kennedy, 1975). We do not wish to overstate the separation between theory and data in the developmental literature, but merely to point out that the integration between them has often not been as nearly complete as one might have hoped. We attempt here to provide a framework for interrelating more closely work on the nature of intelligence with work on the development of intelligence. The basis for

this integration is an enumeration of some of the possible loci of intellectual development in the factorial theories. The various loci are not mutually exclusive; to the contrary, it seems highly likely that multiple loci exist.

Changes in Number of Factors with Age. One possible locus of intellectual development is in the number of abilities and, hence, of factors that constitute measured intelligence at different ages. Arguments in favor of change in number of factors as a locus of intellectual development usually take the form of differentiation theories. Although it is conceivable that intelligence could become either more or less differentiated with advancing age, the former position has been by far the more popular, and certainly more plausible, one. Perhaps the most noted proponent of this point of view has been Henry E. Garrett (1938, 1946). Garrett (1946) defined intelligence as comprising the abilities demanded in the solution of problems that require the comprehension and use of symbols. According to his developmental theory of intelligence, "abstract or symbol intelligence changes in its organization as age increases from a fairly unified and general ability to a loosely organized group of abilities or factors" (Garrett, 1946, p. 373). This theory has obvious implications for how various psychometric theories of intelligence might be interrelated:

> It seems to effect a rapprochement between the Spearman General Factor and the Group Factor theories [e.g., that of Thurstone, 1938]. Over the elementary school years we find a functional generality among tests at the symbol level. Later on this general factor of "*g*" breaks down into the quasi-independent factors reported by many investigators. (Garrett, 1946, p. 376)

Several sources of evidence provide at least tentative support for the differentiation theory. Garrett, Bryan, and Perl (1935), for example, administered 10 tests of memory, verbal ability, and number ability to children of ages 9, 12, and 15. With one exception, intercorrelations among the three kinds of tests showed a monotone decrease between the ages of 9 and 12 and 12 and 15, suggesting increasing independence of the abilities with age. A factor analysis of the correlations showed a decrease in the proportion of variance accounted for by a general factor with increasing age. Similar results were found by Asch (1936), who found a decrease in the correlation between verbal and numerical tests from ages 9 to 12. M. P. Clark (1944) administered an early version of the Primary Mental Abilities Test to boys of ages 11, 13, and 15 and found that scores on tests of verbal, number, spatial, memory, and reasoning abilities showed decreasing correlations with increasing age. Other studies considered together (e.g., Schiller, 1934, for third and fourth graders; Schneck, 1929, for college students) also tend to support the hypothesis of a decrease in correlations with age. Reviewing the literature on changes in the organization of mental abilities with age, Bayley (1955) concluded that there was fairly substantial support for the differentiation notion.

In summary, then, one possible reconciliation among the various theories of the nature of intelligence is in terms of increasing differentiation of abilities with age. (See also, Werner's, 1948, views of increasing differentiation of thought as cultures and individuals develop.) Theories postulating small numbers of interesting factors, such as Spearman's, may be relevant for younger children; theories postulating large numbers of interesting factors, such as Thurstone's or conceivably Guilford's, may be relevant for older children and adults.

Changes in the Relevance or Weights of Factors with Age. A second possible locus of intellectual development is in the relevance or weights of factors as contributors to individual-differences variance in intelligence at different age levels. For example, a perceptual-motor factor may decrease in weight, whereas a verbal factor may increase in weight with age. Thus, it is not total number of factors, but importance of individual factors that changes with age. In this view, what makes one person more intelligent than another can be quite different across ages because the abilities that constitute intelligence can shift dramatically in their importance. Variants of this viewpoint have been very popular in the literature on the development of intelligence (e.g., Hofstaetter, 1954). Despite their differences, these variants have virtually all been consistent with the notion that abilities of the kind proposed by Galton and successors in his tradition to constitute intelligence seem most relevant for infants and very young children; abilities of the kind proposed by Binet and successors in his tradition seem most relevant for older children and adults. These views, then, like the differentiation views, seem to point the way toward a developmental reconciliation of theoretical positions. An interesting ramification of these views is that developmental theorizing becomes essential rather than adjunct to understanding theories of intelligence originally proposed for adults.

One of the most well-known data sets supporting the notion that factors change in relevance with age is that of Hofstaetter (1954). Hofstaetter factor analyzed data from Bayley's (1933, 1943, 1949, 1951) Berkeley Growth Study, which assessed intellectual performance from infancy through adulthood. Hofstaetter found that up to 20 months of age, a first factor, which he named sensorimotor alertness, accounted for most of the individual-differences variance in children's performance on intelligence tests. From the age of 40 months onward, this factor accounted for practically none of the variance in mental-age scores. Between 20 and 40 months, the dominant source of individual-differences variance was in a second factor that Hofstaetter tentatively labeled persistence. From 48 months onward, almost all of the individual-differences variance could be accounted for by a third factor that seemed appropriately labeled manipulation of symbols or simply abstract behavior. Hofstaetter suggested that this factor corresponds to Spearman's (1927) *g*, but he further noted that it was only because of limitations in the data that the factor appeared to be unitary in nature. Hofstaetter concluded from his data that:

> The term "an intelligent child" seems to refer to a lively (alert) infant at first and to a rather stubborn child at an age of three before it acquires the connotations which predominate all through the school-age. In talking about the development of "intelligence" we actually refer to the switches from one connotational pattern to another rather than to unidirectional growth. To the extent that test batteries truly reflect the meaning of the term "intelligence" as applied to infants and children, the changing composition of such batteries indicates also the connotational changes which the term itself undergoes when used with regard to children of differing age-levels. (p. 163)

Semantic use of the term intelligence, thus, reflects the factors that show the highest weights at a given age level. In his concern with the changing nature of intelligence as a reflection of changes in the use of the term intelligence, Hofstaetter foreshadows Siegler (1976) in his later concern with changes in people's conceptions of intelligence as applied to children of differing ages.

Bayley's (1955) own view of her data is very similar to that of Hofstaetter (1954). Like Piaget (1976), however, Bayley has emphasized how the abilities of greater importance in later life build upon the abilities of greater importance in earlier life:

> Intelligence appears to me . . . to be a dynamic succession of developing functions, with the

more advanced and complex functions in the hierarchy depending on the prior maturing of earlier simpler ones (given, of course, normal conditions of care). (1955, p. 807)

For example, verbal tasks require perceptual processing for their completion.

Bayley (1933) identified six factors in the correlational data from her First-Year Scale and six factors in the data from her Preschool Scale. Like Hofstaetter (1954), she found that the factors that contributed substantially to individual differences in measured intelligence varied with age (see, especially, Bayley, 1970, Fig. 4.) Up to 10 months, the factors with the highest weights were visual following, social responsivity, perceptual interest, and manual dexterity; vocal communications came to be of some importance at the very end of this time period. In the range from 10 to 30 months, factors with highest weights were perceptual interest (a carryover from the earlier period), vocal communications, meaningful object relations, and perceptual discrimination. Factors of object relations (dexterity), memory for forms, and verbal knowledge were beginning to be of some importance, especially at the end of the time period. In the range from 30 to 50 months, the most important factors were object relations (a carryover), memory for forms, and verbal knowledge. In the period of time from 50 to 70 months, memory for forms and verbal knowledge (carryovers) were important, as were complex spatial relations and vocabulary. By the last period assessed in this particular analysis, 70 to 90 months, the important factors were verbal knowledge, complex spatial relations, and vocabulary. The factor of memory for forms, important in the immediately preceding period, had dropped out. Thus, we see a general tendency for the more complex factors to become of greater importance to individual differences in intelligence with increasing age.

Stott and Ball (1965) factor analyzed data from intelligence tests administered to children in the age range from 3 to 60 months. They used Guilford's (1956, 1957) structure-of-intellect model as the theoretical framework within which to interpret their results. Although they found significant loadings for 31 of Guilford's factors at one age or another and although many factors appeared at multiple age levels, results for the younger age levels (especially below 1 year) included important other factors, such as gross psychomotor skills, locomotor skill, and hand dexterity, that did not fit into the Guilford model and that did not apply at the upper age levels. Thus, the Guilford factors appeared not to be relevant at all ages.

Changes in the Content (Names) of Factors Within a Given Factor Structure. Whereas the point of view discussed above suggests that the structure of mental abilities (or at least the factor structure important for generating individual differences) changes with age, the point of view considered here suggests that, for a given theory, structure stays essentially the same across age groups but that the content that fills in this structure changes. For example, g, or general ability, might be conceived as perceptual motor in nature at the infant level but as cognitive in nature later on. In each case, the factorial structure could be the same, that is, there is a single general factor, but the content of that factor differs across ages. The difference between structure and content is not always a clear-cut one, and we doubt that theorists propounding each of these two positions actually intended to be placed in separate camps. Nevertheless, the empirical claims of the two positions differ: support for the preceding position requires a different factor structure at each age level; support for the present position requires a different content filling in the structure at each level. Historically, proponents of this present position have tended to be most interested in the changing composition of Spearman's g over ages. They extract a general factor at each level but find that what is general changes with age.

McCall, Hogarty, and Hurlburt (1972) factor analyzed data from the Gesell Developmental Schedule administered to children participating in the Fels Longitudinal Study. Children were studied at 6, 12, 18, and 24 months of age. The authors were interested primarily in the first principal component (general factor) at each age level. At 6 months, they found that items loading on this factor tended to measure visually guided exploration of perceptual contingencies. At 12 months, the factor reflected a mixture of sensorimotor and social imitation as well as rudimentary vocal-verbal behavior. The joint presence of sensorimotor and social imitation was interpreted as consistent with Piaget's (1976) notion that imitation mediates the transition between egocentric sensorimotor behaviors, on the one hand, and more decentered verbal and social behaviors, on the other hand. At 18 months, items loading on the first principal component reflected verbal and motor imitation, verbal production, and verbal comprehension. By 24 months, highly loading items measured verbal labeling, comprehension, fluency, and grammatical maturity. Again, we see transition between the types of behaviors studied by Galton (1883) at the lower levels and the types of behaviors studied by Binet and Simon (1916a, 1916b) at the upper levels. It is important to note that the items loading on the first principal component are factorially but not behaviorally unitary: multiple behaviors are general across the tests that McCall et al. (1972) studied at each age level. Thus, they load on a single general factor. The authors interpreted their data as supporting what they and Kagan (1971) before them had called a heterotypic model of mental development. In such a model, there is a discontinuity in the overt developmental function (i.e., the behaviors responsible for individual differences in intelligence), but there is stability in patterns of individual differences across these behaviors (i.e., in people's rank orders at different ages, despite the differences in the behaviors of consequence). This model was contrasted with five other models that were not as well supported. One such model, for example, was a homotypic model in which individual differences are purported to remain stable, as are the behaviors that generate the individual differences.

McCall, Eichorn, and Hogarty (1977) studied "transitions in early mental development" in much the same ways as had McCall and his colleagues in an earlier study (1972). In this study, however, the investigators used the developmental data from the Berkeley Growth Study, as had Hofstaetter before them. Whereas Hofstaetter factor analyzed data across age levels, McCall et al. factor analyzed data within age levels. The investigators interpreted their data (for infants) as supporting a five-stage model of intellectual development. During Stage 1 (0 to 2 months), the infant is responsive primarily to selected stimulus dimensions that in some sense match the structural predispositions of the infant's sensory-perceptual systems. Stage 2 (3 to 7 months) is characterized by more active exploration of the environment, although the infant's view of the world is alleged still to be completely subjective. At Stage 3 (8 to 13 months), means for doing things begin to be differentiated from ends. The separation is complete by Stage 4 (14 to 18 months), by which time the child is able to associate two objects in the environment without acting on either of them. Symbolic relationships emerge during Stage 5 (21+ months).

The emphasis on change in the composition of the first principal component or factor that characterizes the work described above does not emerge in all factor-analytic studies, although the difference in emphasis may reflect primarily differences in ages studied. McNemar (1942) reported factor analyses of the Stanford–Binet for children of ages 2 to 18 years. (Thus, infants were excluded.) He found that a general factor did pervade the subtests at each of the age levels and that, at most age levels, the single factor was sufficient to account for the intercorrelations between subtests. At the age levels where a

single factor was insufficient (2, 2½, 6, and 18 years), there was evidence of additional specific factors (in line with the Spearman, 1927, model), but the study was not sufficiently powerful (by McNemar's, 1942, own admission) to identify group factors if they occurred. Finally, the content of the tests loading most highly on the first factor were approximately the same across age levels. McNemar concluded (perhaps a bit too strongly):

> There is just one common factor at each level and also that the various levels are identical or nearly so, [so] that the I.Q.'s for individuals of differing mental-maturity levels or for the same individual at different stages of development are comparable quantitatively and qualitatively. (1942, p. 123)

Although McNemar did not find evidence of group factors in the Stanford–Binet, there is at least some evidence that such factors can indeed appear (Jones, 1954).

Changes in Factor Scores of Fixed Factors with Age. The views expressed in the above discussions are all ones of qualitative changes in the nature of intelligence with age. However, most of the voluminous literature reflecting the psychometric approach to the development of intelligence has dealt with quantitative changes and how to account for them. The preponderance of studies has been atheoretical, although our emphasis here will be upon the more theoretically motivated research.

Two basic findings in the literature that have needed to be accounted for are, first, that absolute level of intelligence (as measured, say, by mental age or a comparable construct) increases with age and, second, that correlations between measurements of intelligence decrease with increasing intervals of time between measurements (see, e.g., Bayley, 1933, 1970; Dearborn & Rothney, 1941; Honzik, 1938; Sontag, Baker, & Nelson, 1958). An elegant attempt to account for these findings was made by J. E. Anderson (1940), who proposed that correlations of IQ at various ages with terminal IQ (say, at about the age of 16) increase because "the prediction of final status is based upon a larger proportion of that which is included in the total; that is, scores at 10 years include more of that which is present at 16 years than do scores at 3 years" (p. 388). Anderson suggested that the increase in overlap between final scores and successively later scores would be predicted by a model in which increments to intelligence are additive over the age span and uncorrelated (or only modestly correlated) with each other and with the current level of intelligence.

Anderson tested this simple model by reanalyzing data from the Harvard Growth Study (Dearborn, Rothney, & Shuttleworth, 1938) and the Honzik (1938) study. He compared mental growth curves from these data to Monte Carlo curves generated by cumulating the first to the sixteenth random number (where each number represented a "year" of mental growth) in a table of random numbers of 300 artificial subjects. In the random-number table, of course, successive increments in the accumulated sum will be uncorrelated both with each other and with the current value of the sum. According to Anderson's model, the closer in time two measurements are, the less time there has been for intervening changes to take place and, hence, the more highly related those two measurements will be. Fits of the data to the model were quite good, providing at least tentative support for the model.

Most of the research that has been done on quantitative development of intelligence has assumed, as did Anderson, that intelligence increases in absolute amount over age and that one's goal should be to plot the form of this function and to account in some way for why the function takes this form. Bayley (1966, 1968), for example, plotted mental growth curves from infancy to 36 years on the basis of her data from the Berkeley Growth Study. Her findings were typical of this literature: absolute level of intelligence increased fairly rapidly until early adolescence, showed some decrease in the rate of increase from early to mid adolescence, and then pretty much leveled off in mid to late adolescence. However, the assumption of a monotonic growth curve throughout the life span has been challenged as representing a composite of two different component functions, each of which is purported to show a different pattern of growth throughout the life span. The two component functions, in this view, represent what R. B. Cattell (1963, 1971) and Horn (1968) have referred to as fluid and crystalized intelligence.

Fluid and crystalized intelligence are proposed by R. B. Cattell (1963, 1971) and Horn (1968) to be subfactors of general intelligence (g). Fluid ability is best measured by tests that require mental manipulation of abstract symbols, for example, figural analogies, series completions, and classification problems. Crystalized ability is best measured by tests that require knowledge of the cultural milieu in which one lives, for example, vocabulary, general information, and reading comprehension. Horn and Cattell (1966) reported that although the mean level of fluid intelligence was systematically higher for younger adults than for older adults, the mean level of crystalized intelligence was systematically higher

for older adults than for younger adults. In general, crystalized ability seemed to increase throughout the life span, whereas fluid intelligence seemed to increase up until the 20s and slowly to decrease thereafter.

Schaie (1974) questioned what he called the myth of intellectual decline, namely, that some or all intellectual functions decline after some point in adulthood. Schaie noted that the evidence on the question of decline had been mixed. Cross-sectional studies have tended to support the notion of a decline (e.g., Jones & Conrad, 1933; Wechsler, 1939), whereas longitudinal studies have not (e.g., Bayley & Oden, 1955; Owens, 1953). Studies of both kinds have been subject to reasonable criticism. Cross-sectional studies are susceptible to cohort (age-group) differences: differences in scores may reflect differences in measured intelligence across different subjects of different cohorts rather than differences in measured intelligence across the same individuals within a given cohort. Longitudinal studies are susceptible to sampling bias as a result of differential dropout: those who remain in a study over a large number of years are unlikely to be a representative sample of the total group that started the study. Schaie (1965, 1973) suggested what he believed to be a way out of this apparent dilemma, and he has summarized the results that are obtained when this way out is followed:

> Two approaches are needed: The first requires the replication of cross-sectional studies over several points in time. The second involves the carrying of several cohorts over the age ranges of interest. In our own work we have now done both and the results are indeed revealing. They show with great clarity that a much larger proportion of the variance associated with age can be attributed to generation differences than to ontogenetic change and that both peak levels and slopes of change in ability are changing in a positive direction. (Schaie, 1974, p. 804)

Schaie further suggested that the actual declines in test scores within a given individual that did occur in some cases might be attributable to increased cautiousness or reduced risk taking on the part of older subjects (Birkhill & Schaie, 1975; Botwinick, 1967; Wallach & Kogan, 1961) or to the fact that test items might be biased in their construction toward younger adults.

Horn and Donaldson (1976) attempted to refute the view advanced by Schaie (1974) and also the view that what has appeared to be a gradual intellectual decline in adulthood is in fact a decline appearing only just before death (Jarvik, Eisdorfer, & Blum, 1973; Riegel & Riegel, 1972). They argued, in the first place, that none of the sampling designs, including the ones advocated by Schaie (1974), were free of sampling bias, but that even the data obtained through these biased designs tend to support the notion of a decline in later life. The thrust of their argument was that the major evidence arguing against intellectual decline in many (if not all) individuals was based upon sampling bias and wishful thinking in the interpretation of research.

A final reply (for our purposes) by Baltes and Schaie (1976) seems to us to defuse the debate and to call into question whether there was much substantive basis for the debate in the first place. These authors argued that Horn and Donaldson (1976) had misrepresented the earlier positions taken by Schaie and Baltes (Baltes & Schaie, 1976; Schaie, 1974):

> Schaie and Baltes do not reject the notion of intellectual decline *in toto*. Within the framework of a dialectical interpretation of intelligence in adulthood and old age, Schaie and Baltes emphasize plasticity as evidence in large interindividual differences, multidimensionality, multidirectionality, modifiability, and the joint import of age- and cohort-related determinants. (Baltes & Schaie, 1976, p. 720)

We doubt there are any substantive points in the above statement with which Horn and Donaldson would disagree. Both sets of authors seem to agree that, at the level of individual cases, later decline may or may not occur. There may be some disagreement as to trends in group means. But when group means camouflage multiple systematic patterns in data rather than reflect a single systematic pattern, their interpretability is doubtful in the first place. All parties seem to agree that *some* decline *sometimes* occurs. The substantive question that no one has yet resolved is: What circumstances lead to declines and why do they do so? If a debate is to continue, it will have to take a new form.

Not all of the debate regarding growth functions in intelligence has concerned the issue of whether intelligence or a part of it declines in the later years after an initial incline in the early years. Jensen (1970) has suggested that intelligence shows a monotonic increase with age but that each of two different kinds of intelligence increases at a different rate. Jensen has further proposed that this rate is mediated by socioeconomic status. Jensen has distinguished between two kinds of intelligence, which he refers to as Level I and Level II abilities. Level I ability is measured by standard episodic memory tests, such as digit span, whereas Level II ability is measured by tests of comprehension and inferential ability:

> Level I ability is essentially the capacity to receive or register stimuli, to store them, and to later recognize or recall the material with a high degree of fidelity. . . . It is characterized especially by the lack of any need of elaboration, transformation or manipulation of the input in order to arrive at the output. The input need not be referred to other past learning in order to issue effective output. A tape recorder exemplifies Level I ability. . . . Level II ability, on the other hand, is characterized by transformation and manipulation of the stimulus prior to making the response. . . . Semantic generalization and concept formation depend upon Level II ability; encoding and decoding of stimuli in terms of past experience, relating new learning to old learning, transfer in terms of concepts and principles, are all examples of Level II. Spearman's characterization of *g* as the "eduction of relations and correlates" corresponds to Level II. (Jensen, 1970, pp. 156–157)

Jensen has suggested that Level I ability shows a rather steep increase in the early years up to about the age of 4 and that the rate of increase decreases with increasing age. Thus, the function is approximately exponential in shape. Growth curves for populations of middle and low socioeconomic status are almost the same, with a slight advantage shown by the middle-class individuals. The amount of advantage increases with age but remains small throughout the age range about which Jensen has theorized (0 to 14 years). Jensen has suggested that Level II ability increases according to an S-shaped function, with the sharpest increase occurring in the age range roughly from 4 to 8 years. Jensen again suggests that the difference in ability levels between middle-socioeconomic-class and low-socioeconomic-class individuals increases with age, but in this case, the mean difference becomes fairly substantial as time progresses.

Jensen's distinction between Level I and Level II abilities seems useful insofar as tests of basic learning ability (Level I) are at best moderately correlated with tests of higher order reasoning ability (Level II) of the kind that predominate in the measurement of IQ (see, e.g., Denny, 1963; House & Zeaman, 1960; Hunt et al., 1973; Hunt, Lunneborg, & Lewis, 1975; Lipman, 1963; Woodrow, 1946). But whereas tests of higher order reasoning abilities tend to be fairly highly intercorrelated among themselves, tests of basic-learning abilities tend to show only low to moderate intercorrelations (Hunt et al., 1975). We are, therefore, not yet convinced that Level I ability coheres as a unitary construct in the same way that Level II ability does.

Jensen's claim of a social-class difference in measured *g* (or Level II ability) is by now fairly well documented (see Scarr & Carter-Saltzman, in press). We believe little is to be gained from denying the preponderance of evidence in favor of such a difference (although it should be noted that we view the evidence supporting racial differences in *g* as exceedingly weak and at the present time nonsupportive of such a hypothesis; see Scarr & Carter-Saltzman, in press). We believe as well, however, that little is to be gained by attributing the difference to social class per se because social class is uninformative with regard to the functional psychological variables that, in our opinion, are likely to be responsible for the observed difference. In our view, then, the present need is to study psychological (and we believe largely motivational) differences that lead to observed differences in IQ-test performance across social class. Little is to be gained now from more studies simply documenting the existence of such differences.

Heritability of Intelligence

Research on the inheritance of intelligence, like that on the nature of intelligence, can in large part be traced back to Sir Francis Galton. Galton's (1869) research on hereditary genius in particular and on the inheritance of intelligence not only motivated much of the substance of later research but also, unfortunately, the spirit in which the research was carried out. Galton left no doubt as to where his own predispositions lay:

> I have no patience with the hypothesis occasionally expressed, and often implied, especially in tales written to teach children to be good, that babies are born pretty much alike, and that the sole agencies in creating differences between boy and boy, and man and man, are steady application and moral effort. It is in the most unqualified manner that I object to pretensions of natural equality. (p. 56)

Many of the researchers who succeeded Galton also left no doubt as to where their own predispositions

lay, and in almost every case, their views regarding the heritability of intelligence have closely matched their predispositions.

The issues surrounding the heritability of intelligence are extraordinarily complex, and we could not attempt to do justice to these complexities here. Our own reading of the literature is the conventional one—that heredity, environment, and the interactions between them all play large roles in determining the intellectual performance of children and adults. Even though intelligence is almost certainly inherited in part, environment will largely determine whether an individual lives up to his or her inherited potential. Because we do not yet have the basic knowledge or technology to inform us of what the limits of intellectual performance are, any attempts to explain away reduced levels of intellectual performance in terms of hereditary limitations are premature. We believe that the study of the effects of heredity, environment, and their interaction on intellectual performance constitutes a legitimate area of scientific inquiry; attempts to suppress such inquiry are often antiscientific in spirit. But we also believe that psychologists doing research in this area should suppress their understandable desire to apply the knowledge they have gained to educational and societal problems. Our present level of knowledge in this area is rudimentary at best, and premature attempts to apply tentative understandings to real-world problems can cause, and probably already have caused, as much harm as good.

For balanced reviews of the literature on heredity, environment, and intelligence, we recommend Scarr and Kidd's chapter on behavior genetics (*vol. 2, chap. 6*) in this Handbook; Loehlin, Lindzey, and Spuhler (1975); and Scarr and Carter-Saltzman (in press). An extremely interesting critique and history of research on the heritability of intelligence is provided by Kamin (1974), although Kamin's strong environmentalist leanings should be kept in mind as one reads through his book.

Conclusions

Looked at from a psychometric point of view, there are probably multiple sources of intellectual development. We find the evidence at least fairly persuasive that abilities differentiate over time, that the importance of various aspects of intelligence changes over the life span, and that eventual deterioration of intelligence almost certainly occurs in some people late in life. There is no persuasive evidence that deterioration occurs in everyone, and, indeed, it is not clear to us that anyone now claims that such universal deterioration occurs. If deterioration of fluid kinds of abilities occurs in some people but not in others, there may be an average decreasing trend that represents not a group pattern but the pattern of one or more particular subgroups. There is certainly a need to know more about what physiological or psychological characteristics lead to decline in some people but not others.

If one uses perceptual-motor tests to measure intelligence in infancy, there seems to be a discontinuity in intellectual development between infancy and the remainder of the life span. (See the chapters in Lewis, 1976, for differing views on the nature of this discontinuity.) In infancy (certainly during the first year of life and probably during most of the second year), rudimentary perceptual-motor abilities form an ''intelligence'' of a kind different from that measured later. Correlations of infant perceptual-motor tests with performance in later childhood and adulthood are close to zero (see Bayley, 1970). In fact, it is not until about the age of 4 years that one begins to obtain reasonably high-level prediction of IQ-test performance in mid adolescence and adulthood.

We believe that there is at least one aspect of intelligence that is stable over the life span. This is the part of intelligence that involves the seeking, finding, learning, and solving of novel problems and aspects of problems. This view dovetails nicely with findings of Lewis and Brooks-Gunn (1981) and of Fagan and McGrath (1981) on novelty preference in infancy and with findings of R. J. Sternberg (1981a) on the handling of novelty by adults. Fagan and McGrath (1981) found that infants' visual preferences for novel targets in recognition memory at 7 months predicted later performance on vocabulary tests of intelligence at 3 years. Lewis and Brooks-Gunn (1981) found that habituating to redundant stimuli and recovering to novel stimuli at 3 months of age predicted later intellectual functioning at 24 months better than did 3-month perceptual-motor or object-permanence scores. In terms of information processing skills, recovery to novel stimuli predicts later intelligence-test scores better than did habituation. The total package of results is consistent with the notion that attitude toward, and performance on, novel tasks or aspects of tasks is an important part of intelligence from infancy onward. Obviously, the way in which measurement operations are conducted for assessing behavior will differ greatly across age levels. Both our own results and those of other authors suggest that converging operations for measurement of the behaviors of interest are both

possible and feasible. We are, therefore, prepared to suggest that attitude toward, and performance on, novel tasks or aspects of tasks form the basis for at least one developmental continuity in intelligence.

How can this view be reconciled with the massive evidence suggesting that scores on infant intelligence tests do not correlate with scores on tests of intelligence administered later? Reconciliation is possible in terms of the particular aspects of intelligence one chooses to measure. Sensorimotor intelligence is, no doubt, a major part of infantile development, but it is also, without doubt, only a minor part of postinfantile development. There is not now and never has been any reason to expect high correlations between tests of sensorimotor abilities, on the one hand, and of more cognitive abilities, on the other hand. Indeed, the two kinds of tests do not even correlate highly *within* age level, as Galton (1883) found out years ago and as others have found out again and again. The problem has been to find some aspect or aspects of intelligence that are present in both infants and older people *and* that can be measured in both. The greatest stumbling block has been in finding measurable aspects of infant behavior that would continue to be important sources of individual differences in intelligence later on. The present studies increase our confidence that attitude toward, and performance on, novel (nonentrenched) tasks or parts of tasks is a key aspect of intelligence from infancy onward.

To conclude, developmental theories are of particular interest because they provide one kind of reconciliation between alternative psychometric theories of intelligence. For example, some abilities theorized to be important in intelligence by Galton do indeed appear to be important in infancy and perhaps for a few years thereafter. As infancy draws to a close, however, these abilities seem to become less important, and the abilities theorized to be of consequence in intelligence by Binet and Simon (1916a) seem to acquire greater importance. By adulthood, the latter kinds of abilities seem to be of much greater importance in measured intelligence, and probably in general adaptation to most adult environments, than do the former kinds of abilities. A reconciliation of sorts among some of the factor theories is also possible on the differentiation view, according to which the number and fineness of factors increases with age. Although we believe that some differentiation probably occurs, we believe that whatever it is that constitutes the general factor probably remains of primary importance throughout most or all of one's later lifetime. The constituents of group factors are important as well, but at a secondary level.

The Piagetian Conception of Intelligence

Jean Piaget first entered the field of cognitive development when, working in Binet's laboratory, he became intrigued with children's *wrong* answers to Binet's intelligence-test items. To understand intelligence, Piaget reasoned, one's investigation must be twofold. First, and as was done by Binet, one must look at the way a person acts upon the environment—at a person's performance. But also, and here is where Piaget began to part company with Binet, one must consider *why* the person performs as she or he does, taking account of the cognitive structures underlying the individual's actions. Through his repeated observation of children's performance and particularly their errors in reasoning, Piaget concluded that there are coherent logical structures underlying children's thought but that these structures are different from those underlying adult thought. In the six decades that followed, Piaget focused his research on delineating what these cognitive structures might be at different stages of development and how they might evolve from one stage to the next.

What Is Intelligence?

Piaget thought that there were two interrelated aspects of intelligence: its function and its structure. Piaget, a biologist by training, saw the function of intelligence to be no different than the function of other biological activities, that is, adaptation, which includes assimilating the environment to one's own structures (be they physiological or cognitive) and accommodating one's structures (again, either physical or mental) to encompass new aspects of the environment. "A certain continuity exists . . . between intelligence and the purely biological process of morphogenesis and adaptation to the environment" (Piaget, 1952b, p. 1). In Piaget's theory, the function of intelligence—adaptation— provided this continuity with lower biological acts.

Intelligence is thus only a generic term to indicate the superior forms of organization or equilibrium of cognitive structuring. . . . Intelligence . . . is essentially a system of living and acting operations. (Piaget, 1976, p. 7)

He rejected the sharp delineation proposed by the gestaltists and others between intelligent acts, which were proposed to require insight or thought, and nonintelligent acts, or habits and reflexes. Instead, he preferred to speak of a continuum in which "behavior becomes more intelligent as the pathways between the subject and the objects on which it acts cease to be simple and become progressively more complex" (Piaget, 1976, p. 10).

Piaget further proposed, however, that the internal organizational structures of intelligence and how intelligence will be manifested differ with age. It is obvious that an adult does not deal with the world in the same way as does a neonate. For example, the infant typically acts on his or her environment via sensorimotor structures and, thus, is limited to the apparent, physical world; the adult, on the other hand, is capable of abstract thought and, thus, is free to explore the world of possibility. Much of Piaget's research was a logical and philosophical exploration of how knowledge structures might develop from primitive to sophisticated forms. Guided by his interest in epistemology and his observations of children's behavior, Piaget divided the intellectual development of the individual into discrete, qualitative stages. "Each stage is characterized by an overall structure in terms of which the main behavior patterns can be explained" (Piaget & Inhelder, 1969, p. 153). As the child progresses from one stage to the next, the cognitive structures of the preceding stage are reorganized and extended, through the child's own adaptive actions, to form the underlying structures of the equilibrium characterizing the next stage. Piaget wrote:

At each new stage, the mechanisms provided by the factors already in existence make for an equilibrium which is still incomplete, and the balancing process itself leads to the next level. (Piaget, 1976, p. 49)

This equilibrium process is repeated as "intelligence tries to embrace the universe" (p. 49).

Piaget's theory described the stages of the development of intelligence from birth to adolescence. Piaget was in agreement with many psychometricians in seeing infant intelligence as set apart from adult intelligence. But Piaget not only saw the infant's intellectual structures as different from those of the adult but he also hypothesized still other intellectual structures for childhood. In fact, Piaget (1976) proposed three distinct periods, or stages, of development: the sensorimotor period (which lasts from birth to approximately age 2), the period of preparation for and organization of concrete operations (which is often subdivided into a preoperational and a concrete operational stage, lasting approximately from age 2 to age 12), and the formal operational period (which is begun at approximately age 12 and which continues through adulthood). Because of space limitations, we will not describe Piaget's stages of intellectual development in this chapter. Instead, we refer the reader to the summaries by Flavell (1963), Ginsburg and Opper (1979), Sternberg and Powell (1980), and, of course, the myriad works of Piaget and his colleagues, especially the summaries contained in Piaget (1970, 1976) and in Piaget and Inhelder (1969). (See also *Gelman & Baillargeon, vol. III, chap. 3.*)

Underlying Piaget's description of the child's intellectual development are three core assumptions about the nature of this developmental process. First, in Piaget's view, there are four factors that interact to bring about the development of the child. Three of these factors are the ones usually proposed: maturation, experience of the physical environment, and the influence of the social environment. To these three factors, however, Piaget added a fourth, which coordinates and guides the other three: equilibration, that is, the child's own self-regulatory processes (Piaget, 1970). Thus, Piaget's theory centers on the assertion that the child is a very active participant in the construction of his or her own intelligence. Second, Piaget asserted that this intellectual development results in the appearance of developmental stages and that these stages follow an invariant sequential order, with each succeeding stage incorporating and extending the accomplishments of the preceding stage. Third, although the rate of development may vary across children, the stages themselves and their sequence were considered by Piaget to be universal. In sum, Piaget's theory asserted that there is a single route of intellectual development that *all* humans follow, regardless of individual differences, although their progression along this route may be at different rates and they may stop off somewhere along the way rather than follow the route to completion.

Aside from the equilibration model, proposed to handle structural change at the broadest level of development as well as at the level of performance on a specific task (Piaget, 1977), Piaget spoke very little about actual thought processes or how these processes develop. The primary purpose of his research was to understand and describe the structures underlying the child's thought, and not primarily to investigate how the child actually performs on a given task or set of tasks, or how the components of the child's performance change with age. Thus, except for the fact that Piaget insisted that structure and process are interdependent and evolve together, Piaget's model is vague concerning the "how" of cognitive development, and many researchers, especially information-processing theorists (see below), would argue that Piaget is equally vague on the "what."

In general, cross-cultural and other studies support the universal sequence of the appearances of Piaget's major stages, but these same studies contest the invariant sequence of the individual psychological operations within a stage (Dasen, 1977). Training studies, even some done by members of the Genevan camp (e.g., Inhelder, Sinclair, & Bovet, 1974), suggest that there may be more than one developmental route to the acquisition of some constructs. Again, the reader is referred to other sources for a detailed presentation of criticisms of Piaget's theory (e.g., Brown & Desforges, 1979; Siegel & Brainerd, 1978; see also, *Gelman & Baillargeon, vol. III, chap. 3*) but the next section deals with some of the major challenges to Piaget's theory.

Methodological and Theoretical Challenges to Piaget's Theory of Intellectual Development: A Brief Overview

Piaget's theory adds a great richness to our conception of intellectual development; not the least of his contributions are the Piagetian tasks and a vast data base describing the child's performance on these tasks. Spada and Kluwe (1980) describe his impact as follows:

> Almost no investigation of cognitive development is made without referring to or basing the work on the theory of Piaget and his Genevan collaborators. The empirical studies by these authors are unsurpassed in richness of detail and findings, and their theory is the only one that claims to explain cognitive development so completely. (p. 2)

However, his theory has also come under fierce attack on both theoretical and methodological grounds. Brown and Desforges (1979) have written an excellent psychological critique of Piaget's theory, and Siegel and Brainerd (1978) provide an edited collection of papers proposing alternatives to Piagetian theory. The following four challenges to Piaget's theory draw extensively upon these sources.

1. *Replicability.* Much attention has been focused by researchers attempting to replicate Piaget's results on the tasks that he uses. Interexperimenter variance owing to the flexibility of Piaget's clinical method is a major problem in such replica-

tion attempts. At least one researcher, Tuddenham (1971), has attempted to construct a standardized battery of Piaget's tasks to help alleviate this problem. (See Green, Ford, & Flamer, 1971, for an example of the dialogue going on between psychometricians and Piagetians.) But, as Brown and Desforges (1979) note, most of Piaget's critics are not questioning the replicability of his observations per se; instead, their criticisms rest on the validity of the Piagetian methodology and on the interpretation of Piaget's observations of the child's performance.

2. *Interpretation: are apparent failures really failures and successes really successes?* At the heart of this controversy is the issue of identifying the ages at which different Piagetian constructs appear. Challenges to Piaget's theory falling in this camp come from two major directions: defining successful performance on a given Piagetian task and ensuring the age- and culture-appropriateness of a given task.

Much controversy has been created over the criteria used by the investigator to define successful completion of a task. In general, the Genevans (preferring to err in favor of fewer false successes) argue for more stringent criteria with resulting later acquisition ages for the various constructs; other researchers (preferring to err in favor of fewer false negatives) argue for less stringent criteria so that the tasks identify the absolute earliest age at which a psychological construct appears.

Bower (1967, 1974) and Cornell (1978), for example, have argued that the object-permanence concept appears earlier than proposed by Piaget but that Piaget's performance criteria are too high to recognize the presence of the construct. A similar criterion problem exists in a typical Piagetian conservation task in which the child is asked to judge whether or not two quantities are equal with respect to some empirical factor. In such a task, after affirming the initial equality of the quantities, the child witnesses some transformation of one or both of the quantities and then is again questioned as to whether the quantities are equivalent. In addition, the child is required to justify or explain his or her response and, sometimes (especially in situations where the effects of training are being assessed) the child is expected also to resist the examiner's attempt to dissuade the child from his or her convictions by surreptitiously making additions to or deletions from the quantity under consideration.

In the conservation tasks, much of the debate centers around whether a correct response is sufficient evidence for conservation (judgment-only criterion) or whether the child should also be expected to justify his or her response (judgment-plus-explanation criterion)—the former is, of course, a much less stringent requirement than the latter and, thus, would provide for earlier acquisition ages than the latter. Brainerd (1977) has attempted to resolve the debate by claiming that whether one's criteria err in the direction of including actual nonconservers or excluding actual conservers is irrelevant; instead, one's criteria should be the ones resulting in the lowest error rate, which, he argues, means that judgment alone, without explanation, is the preferred, that is, most accurate, response.

Other critics have further argued not only that the experimenter's criteria are sometimes too high but also that the criteria often result in the experimenter's leading the child to give a wrong answer. Hall and Kaye (1978) have objected to the experimenter's requirement, especially the Genevans' requirement in training studies, that the child, in addition to responding correctly and justifying his or her response, must resist the investigator's attempts to shake the child's conviction. Hall and Kaye suggest that requiring the child to appeal to logical necessity ("but it has to be the same!") in the face of conflicting evidence surreptitiously set up by the experimenter is asking the child to exhibit within the special context of the experiment a behavior that is normally maladaptive for learning and development in general. If one sticks consistently to one's belief regardless of the apparent facts, then, indeed, how can learning or development come to pass at all? Therefore, Hall and Kaye argue that such a logical-necessity criterion should not be employed in the assessment of conservation.

Rose and Blank (1974) have gone even further by arguing that the very way in which the conservation tasks are usually structured (i.e., the use of pre- and posttransformation questions as to equality) requires a response that is unnatural in comparison to what is expected in nonexperimental contexts. These investigators suggest that the fact that the examiner is asking the same question twice implies to the child that the intervening transformation must have involved change on the relevant dimension. Indeed, Rose and Blank found that children do perform better, earlier, on one-question (after-only) tasks and that this improvement carries over to standard, two-question forms of the tasks.

The issue of the age- and culture-appropriateness of a given task has yielded even more debate between the Genevans and critics. Many of the cross-cultural attempts at validation of Piaget's theory (see, e.g., Dasen, 1977) have found that the Piagetian tasks are often failed by non-Western children if presented in their traditional forms; but when the tasks are translated into content more familiar to the children, then non-Western children's performance more nearly resembles that of Western children. (See also Greenfield, 1969; Price-Williams, Gordon, & Ramirez, 1969). Familiarity with the materials makes a difference in cross-cultural studies of children's abilities. Therefore, the issue arises: How much should one make allowances for a child's background in designing, administering, and interpreting performance on Piagetian tasks and how much does making such allowances leave out phenomena of interest?

Researchers investigating the earliest ages at which Piaget's constructs appear—especially those researchers attempting to train young children in developmentally more mature tasks—are concerned with the problem of how one makes a Piagetian task age appropriate. The extensive reliance on language in Piagetian tasks, especially on the child's own verbalizations, is particularly at issue when investigators attempt to use the traditional Piagetian tasks with younger children (Siegel, 1978). Some researchers (e.g., Braine, 1968) have attempted to generate nonverbal tasks for use with preschool-age children. In general, these nonverbal tasks support Piaget's theory of the sequence of development, but they consistently produce evidence for the appearance of Piaget's constructs, especially concrete operations, at earlier ages than do the traditional Piagetian tasks. Piagetians rebut these claims by arguing that the nature of the criterion task has been changed in these nonverbal tasks. S. A. Miller (1976) also warns that in such attempts to modify the traditional Piagetian tasks, great care must be taken to be sure that the alternative versions of the tasks still measure the same constructs as did the original tasks (see also Sigel & Hooper, 1968). But this is a difficult criticism to get around because the tasks are designed to define the operations. In addition there have been relatively few information processing analyses of the tasks to see what processes children actually have to use to solve each kind of task—this leads us to the next of the challenges to Piaget's theory to be discussed.

3. *Interpretation: what does "failure" or "success" on a given task mean in terms of evaluating a child's intelligence?* Two issues arise under this heading of drawing conclusions about a child's intelligence. First is the issue of construct validity: Does the task measure what it is proposed to measure and nothing else? Second, given that an individual operation is found to be or not to be used by a child, can one then go on to conclude that the child is in a given stage of development, possessing the attendant broad cognitive structures proposed by Piaget?

In regard to the first issue, some researchers have questioned whether even the original Piagetian tasks necessarily measure the hypothesized psychological constructs that Piaget intended them to measure. Because of his primary interest in epistemology rather than in psychological processes per se, Piaget did not systematically investigate the strategies and processes children actually use to solve various tasks. Instead, he made process assumptions on the basis of his logicomathematical model of intelligence and concentrated his empirical energies on finding evidence to support his hypothetical constructs. Riley and Trabasso (1974) have noted a problem with this lack of attention to the actual information processing demands of Piaget's tasks. These researchers reported successfully training preoperational children to solve a transitive inference task involving a series of sticks of different lengths; this outcome contradicts Piaget's theory, according to which children cannot use transitive inference (i.e., cannot coordinate the members of two premises via a middle term) until the concrete operational period of development. Upon further investigation, however, Riley and Trabasso concluded that these preoperational children were not using transitive inference, as it is usually defined, to solve the problem. Instead, the children were creating a mental spatial array and then answering inferential questions by scanning this internal array. Riley and Trabasso's results serve as a reminder that one cannot assume that there is only one strategy possible for task solution; some sort of task analysis from the viewpoint of the task's information processing requirements definitely appears to be needed. As Brown and Desforges assert: "If we wish to establish the absence or presence of a particular operation we need tasks which require the use of that and only that operation and which can be done in no other way" (1979, p. 50). In this regard, information processing theorists working with Piaget's theory are making some headway (e.g., Case, 1978; Pascual-Leone, 1970, 1980).

Stages, according to Piaget's theory, are characterized by specific underlying cognitive structures that organize the child's thought and other activities. Piaget assumed that, through his tasks, an investigator could tap these cognitive structures and thereby ascertain the child's current stage of development. But is there consistency in performance across tasks proposed to reflect a given cognitive structure? Existing empirical evidence on consistency of performance is not encouraging for stage theory. As Brown and Desforges (1979) observe, cognitive structures should be content-free; yet, the content of a task seems to make a great deal of difference for the individual's performance (see Martorano, 1977; Uzgiris, 1968). A number of studies (e.g., Brown & Desforges, 1979; Pascual-Leone, 1970; Sigel & Hooper, 1968) have referred to low correlations between alternative measures of a particular operation. The lack of a strong relationship between tasks using different content to measure the same construct or between tasks measuring multiple constructs theoretically proposed to emerge in the same stage of development (because they share a common structure), pose problems for evaluating Piaget's stage theory of intellectual development. In explaining such data, Piagetians point to the existence of transitional stages and of horizontal décalage, in which a cognitive structure is exhibited first in content areas most familiar to the child and later in more abstract and unfamiliar tasks (Lovell, 1971; Piaget, 1972). Flavell (1971) notes that it is not necessary in a stage theory to postulate abrupt all-or-nothing stages of development. (See Beilin, 1980, for a revisionist's view of apparent inconsistencies within a stage.) Yet, one wonders whether because so much fuzziness is attached to Piaget's stage theory, it would not be better to abandon, at least for the time being, notions of a coherent underlying structures d'ensemble and to focus instead on the development of individual processes and strategies. And, as Siegel and Brainerd's (1978) book illustrates, alternative explanations of Piaget's observations (i.e., explanations not requiring the postulation of general stages of development) are rampant. Piagetians have done little empirical work designed to eliminate such alternative interpretations, whereas these alternatives are often testable and, when tested, fit Piaget's data quite well. For these reasons, the theory is not faring extremely well today as a psychological theory of intellectual development, despite its many extremely admirable features.

4. *Usefulness of the theory.* Unfortunately, Piaget's theory has often been used only to attach yet another label to children while telling us little about the child's specific abilities in his or her daily functioning (see, e.g., Green et al., 1971). But apart from how the theory *has* been used is the question of how it could be used. Piaget (1976) noted that his model is a competence model and not a model of the individual's specific performance on a specific task; performance does not necessarily equal competence, and contextual and content factors often influence how an individual will perform at a given time. Piagetians basically try only to determine whether or not a construct is there, not whether it is ordinarily

used or even under what conditions it will be used. Information processing theorists argue that a much more constructive approach to evaluating a child's intellectual capabilities would be to look first at the child's usual performance—at the cognitive processes and strategies that the child utilizes—and at the nature of the interaction between external and internal determinants of performance.

Piaget's theory is further limited, in that, except for the admission that rate of intellectual development may vary across individuals, it pays insufficient attention to individual differences in children's ability. The theory assumes that the reason individuals differ in their cognitive functioning is that some are further advanced along the route of cognitive development than are others. Level of cognitive development is equated with intelligence, and no mention is made of possible differences between children within a common stage of development or of inherent differences in ability. These criticisms are not necessarily damning of Piaget's theory, in the sense that the existence of individual differences disproves the theory, but rather they point to the limited usefulness of the theory in explaining and predicting many aspects of performance.

In conclusion, it appears that although Piaget's formal theory of development is indeed elegant, the elegance is due to the fact that the theory tends to be derived from epistemological considerations and only later verified by the observation and testing of children. Some aspects of the theory are untestable; other aspects, when tested, prove inadequate as descriptions of, and explanations for, children's development (see Brown & Desforges, 1979; Siegel & Brainerd, 1978). Yet, in spite of these criticisms, it is certainly true that, whether we agree with the theory or not, Piaget has changed the way we think about children's thinking. And, as Beilin (1980), a researcher offering a revisionist view of Piaget's theory, wrote: "Piaget's theory has been with developmental psychology for some 60 years despite almost continuous criticism, but [it] appears in no immediate danger of being superseded" (p. 245).

Information Processing Conceptions

Information processing conceptions of intelligence and its development have in common their primary reliance upon stimulus (rather than subject) variation as their primary means for testing theories of intelligent functioning. Underlying all of these conceptions is a view of intelligence as deriving from the ways in which people mentally represent and process information. Information processing researchers use techniques of data analysis, such as computer simulation and mathematical modeling, to discover patterns of stimulus variation that suggest strategies of information processing in tasks requiring the exercise of one's intelligence.

Information processing research has used the computer program as a metaphor and a heuristic for understanding how humans process information. The major distinguishing feature of the approach, however, is not its reliance upon cybernetic notions but rather its concern with how information is processed during the performance of various kinds of tasks. A history of the information processing approach could cite any number of seminal books and articles; we will necessarily be selective in our brief summary.

Certainly, one of the earliest and most important articles propounding the information processing approach was that of Donders (1868). Donders proposed that the time between a stimulus and a response can be decomposed into a sequence of successive processes, with each process beginning as soon as the previous one ends. The durations of these processes can be ascertained through the use of a subtraction method, that is, subjects solve each of two tasks proposed by the experimenter to differ only in that the more difficult task requires one more component process for its solution than does the simpler task. The duration of this process can then be computed by subtracting the time taken to solve the easier task from the time taken to solve the harder task. The subtraction method was popular for several decades (Jastrow, 1892) but then came into disfavor (Külpe, 1895) because of the method's assumption of strict additivity: One had to assume that one could insert into, or delete from, a task a given process without somehow affecting the execution of other processes. This assumption seemed so unreasonable at the time (and still does to many people) that the method went into hibernation for about a century, until it was reawakened in modified form.

Although the subtraction method lay dormant, psychologists were still interested in information processing and the isolation of component processes. One such psychologist was Charles Spearman. Spearman, one of the most influential figures in the psychometric tradition for studying intelligence, might also have been one of the most influential figures in a revival of the information processing tradition had the times been right. The times apparently were not right however. Whereas Spearman's (1904, 1927) psychometric theory and methodology were eagerly adopted by workers in the laboratory and in the field, Spearman's (1923)

information processing theory was not, perhaps because there was no methodology yet available to provide adequate testing of the theory. Spearman proposed three qualitative principles of cognition that might as easily have been proposed as three fundamental processes of cognition. The principles are best illustrated in the context of analogy solution (which is how, in fact, Spearman illustrated the principles). The first principle, apprehension of experience, states that "any lived experience tends to evoke immediately a knowing of its characters and experiencer" (Spearman, 1923, p. 48). In an analogy, such as lawyer is to client as doctor is to _____, apprehension of experience would correspond to the encoding of each analogy term whereby the problem solver perceives each word and understands its meaning. The second principle, eduction of relations, states that "the mentally presenting of any two or more characters (simple or complex) tends to evoke immediately a knowing of relation between them" (Spearman, 1923, p. 63). In the sample analogy, eduction of relations would correspond to inferring the relation between lawyer and client (e.g., that a lawyer provides professional services to a client). The third principle, eduction of correlates, states that "the presenting of any character together with any relation tends to evoke immediately a knowing of the correlative character" (Spearman, 1923, p. 91). In the sample analogy, eduction of correlates would correspond to the application of the rule previously inferred to generate an acceptable completion to the analogy, such as patient. Spearman also proposed five quantitative principles of cognition—mental energy, retentivity, fatigue, conative control, and primordial potency—that he believed controlled the amount (as opposed to kind) of cognition that occurred within a given individual. Our mere listing of Spearman's principles does not do justice to the scope of his theory, although perhaps it conveys a sense of the form the theory took.

Almost 40 years later, two works (Newell, Shaw, & Simon, 1960; Miller, Galanter, & Pribram, 1960) appeared in a single year that revived the information processing approach. The goal of both programs of research was, as Miller et al. put it, "to discover whether the cybernetic [computer-based] ideas have any relevance for psychology" (p. 3). Both groups of investigators concluded that they did have relevance, and, moreover, that the computer could be a highly useful tool in psychological theorizing. Miller et al. sought to understand human behavior in terms of Plans, where a Plan was defined as "any hierarchical process in the organism that can control the order in which a sequence of operations is to be performed'' (p. 16). Critical for the information processing approach was the authors' view that ''a Plan is, for an organism, essentially the same as a program for a computer'' (p. 16). The authors did not wish to confuse matters, however, by failing to distinguish altogether between computer and human information processing:

> We are reasonably confident that ''program'' could be substituted everywhere for ''Plan'' in the following pages. However, the reduction of Plans to nothing but programs is still a scientific hypothesis and is still in need of further validation. For the present, therefore, it should be less confusing if we regard a computer program that simulates certain features of an organism's behavior as a theory about the organismic Plan that generated the behavior. (p. 16)

The Miller et al. (1960) and Newell et al. (1960) works proposed both theories of information processing and a methodology for implementing and testing information processing theories, that is, computer simulation. Newell et al. (1960) proposed a General Problem Solver (GPS) that could actually solve complex problems of the sort that give people considerable difficulty. Subsequent versions of the program (e.g., Ernst & Newell, 1969) could solve large numbers of problems (e.g., Missionaries and Cannibals, Tower of Hanoi, Water Jugs) by using just a small set of routines that were applicable across the entire range of problems.

The computer simulation method allowed experimental psychologists to test theories of human information processing by comparing predictions generated by computer simulation to actual data collected from human subjects. Some investigators have preferred to test their theories by using quantitative models with parameters estimated directly from the human data. Saul Sternberg (1969a) proposed an additive-factor method that can do just that. The additive-factor method is a substantial modification of the subtraction method that avoids the restrictive assumptions of the subtraction method. In particular, it does not require one to assume that the experimenter can insert and delete stages of information processing into a task at will. The method uses patterns of additivity and interaction in a multifactor experimental design to infer the stages of processing used in performing a task (see Pachella, 1974, for a particularly lucid description of the method). S. Sternberg (1969a, 1969b) also reinstituted use of the subtraction method in some of his data analyses, and

R. J. Sternberg (1977b) later proposed that several tests could be performed to determine whether the strict assumptions of additivity made by the subtraction method were indeed being met. Subsequent to S. Sternberg's (1969a, 1969b) papers, quantitative modeling based on reaction-time data joined computer simulation as a popular method for testing information processing theories of human behavior because both approaches emphasized internal mental operations.

The Unit of Behavior

Whereas many psychometric theorists of intelligence have agreed upon the factor as the fundamental unit in terms of which intellectual behavior should be analyzed, many information processing theorists have agreed upon the elementary information process as the fundamental unit of behavior (Newell & Simon, 1972). It is assumed that all behavior of a human information processing system is the result of combinations of these elementary processes. The processes are elementary in the sense that they are not further broken down into simpler processes by the theory under consideration. The level of analysis that is considered to be ''elementary'' will depend upon the type of behavior under consideration and the level at which the theory attempts to account for the behavior. The processes must be well defined, and the collection of them must be sufficiently general and powerful to compose all macroscopic performances of the human information processing system (Newell & Simon, 1972).

The notion of an elementary information process is obviously a general one. Some investigators have sought to specify further the notion and the ways multiple elementary information processes might combine to form macroscopic performances. We consider now some of these further specifications.

The TOTE.   Miller et al. (1960) proposed as the fundamental unit of intelligent behavior the TOTE (Test-Operate-Test-Exit). Each unit of behavior begins with a test of the present outcome against the desired outcome. If the result of the test is congruent with the desired outcome (called an Image), an exit is made. If not, another operation is performed to make the result of the next test conform as closely as possible to the Image. If the result of the next test is congruent with the Image, an exit is made. Otherwise, still another operation is performed and so on down the line until a test result corresponds to the Image (which may have been modified along the way to make it conform more closely to the demands of reality). An individual

TOTE, a hierarchy of TOTEs, or a sequence of TOTEs (which may include hierarchies) executed to realize an Image is what we earlier referred to as a Plan. The concept of a TOTE leads quite naturally to the flow chart as a representation for sequences of TOTEs. Such a chart represents the flow of control from one subsequence of behavior to another and represents the state of one's progress in problem solving from the beginning of solution to the end.

Although the notion of the TOTE has had considerable influence upon theorizing in information processing psychology, the TOTE itself has not seen much subsequent use since its presentation by Miller et al. (1960). Probably the most important contribution of the TOTE is an historical one. The TOTE was introduced as a more powerful alternative to the unit of behavior that at the time was still in fashion in much of American experimental psychology. This unit was the reflex arc.

> The present authors feel that the TOTE unit, which incorporates the important notion of feedback, is an explanation of behavior in general, and of reflex action in particular, fundamentally different from the explanation provided by the reflex arc. . . . Stimulus and response must be seen as phases of the organized, coordinated act . . . the stimulus processes must be thought of not as preceding the response but rather as guiding it to a successful elimination of the incongruity. That is to say, stimulus and response must be considered as aspects of a feedback loop. (Miller et al., 1960, pp. 29–30)

The Component. R. J. Sternberg (1979b, 1980c, 1980f) has expanded the notion of the elementary information process by proposing that elementary information processes, or what he calls components, can be subdivided in two mutually orthogonal ways: by function and by level of generality.

Components can be distinguished on the basis of function into five different kinds: metacomponents, performance components, acquisition components, retention components, and transfer components. Metacomponents are higher order control processes that are used for executive planning and decision making in problem solving. Metacomponents (1) decide just what the problem is that needs to be solved; (2) select lower order components to effect solution of the problem; (3) select a strategy for combining lower order components, (4) select one or more representations or organizations of information upon which the lower order components and strategies can act; (5) decide upon a rate of problem solving that will permit the desired level of accuracy or solution quality; and (6) monitor progress toward a solution. Performance components may be viewed as executing the plans and implementing the decisions laid down by the metacomponents. Performance components in a variety of tasks tend to organize themselves into four stages of strategy execution (R. J. Sternberg, 1981c). One or more of these components are usually needed to (1) encode the elements of a problem; (2) combine these elements in the execution of a working strategy; (3) compare the solution obtained to available answer options; and (4) respond. Acquisition components are processes involved in learning new information, retention components are processes involved in retrieving information that has been previously acquired, and transfer components are processes involved in carrying over retained information from one situational context to another. Although we have not yet isolated components of these last three types, we are investigating the hypothesis that the variables that affect acquisition, retention, and transfer include (1) amount of experience with a given type of problem or information, (2) variability of the contexts in which the problem or information has been encountered, (3) importance of the problem or information to the task context in which it occurs, (4) recency of occurrence of a given type of problem or piece of information, (5) helpfulness of context to understanding the problem or information, and (6) helpfulness of stored information to understanding the problem or new piece of information (Powell & Sternberg, 1981; Sternberg, Ketron, & Powell, 1982).

The various kinds of components are theorized to be interrelated in four basic ways. First, one kind of component can directly activate another. Second, one kind of component can indirectly activate another. Third, one kind of component can provide direct feedback to another kind of component. Fourth, one kind of component can provide indirect feedback to another kind of component. Direct activation (feedback) refers to the immediate passage of control or information from one kind of component to another kind. Indirect activation (feedback) refers to the mediate passage of control or information from one kind of component to another via a third kind of component.

In the proposed system of interrelations, only metacomponents can directly activate and receive feedback from each other kind of component. Thus, all control to the system passes directly from the metacomponents, and all information from the system passes directly to the metacomponents. The other kinds of components can activate each other only indirectly, and they receive information from each other only indirectly; in each case, mediation must be supplied by the metacomponents. For example, acquisition of information affects retention of information and various kinds of transformations (performances) upon that information but only via the link of the three kinds of components to the metacomponents. Feedback from the acquisition components can be passed to any other kind of component but only through the filter of the metacomponents.

The metacomponents are able to process only a limited amount of information at a given time. In a difficult task, the amount of information being fed to the metacomponents may exceed the capacity of the metacomponents to act upon this information. In this case, the metacomponents may become overloaded, and valuable information that cannot be processed will simply be lost. The total information-handling capacity of the metacomponents will, thus, be an important limiting aspect of the system.

R. J. Sternberg (1980f) has proposed that the system of interrelations described above can account for several ways in which children might become smarter as they grow older. The system of interrelations contains several dynamic mechanisms by which cognitive growth can occur.

First, the components of acquisition, retention, and transfer provide the mechanisms for a steadily developing knowledge base. Increments in the knowledge base, in turn, allow for more sophisticated forms of acquisition, retention, and transfer and possibly for greater ease in execution of performance components. For example, some transfer components may act by relating new knowledge to old knowledge. As the base of old knowledge becomes deeper and broader, the possibilities for relating new knowledge to old knowledge, and, thus, for incorporating that new knowledge into the existing knowledge base, increase. There is, thus, the possibility of an unending feedback loop, that is, the components lead to an increased knowledge base, which leads to more effective use of the components, which leads to further increases in the knowledge base, and so on.

Second, the self-monitoring metacomponents can, in effect, learn from their own mistakes. Early on, allocation of metacomponential resources to varying tasks or kinds of components may be less than optimal, with resulting loss of valuable feedback information. Self-monitoring should eventually result in improved allocation of metacomponential resources, in particular, to the self-monitoring of

the metacomponents. Thus, self-monitoring by the metacomponents results in improved allocation of metacomponential resources to the self-monitoring of the metacomponents, which, in turn, leads to improved self-monitoring, and so on. Here, too, there exists the possibility of an unending feedback loop, one that is internal to the metacomponents themselves.

Finally, indirect feedback from kinds of components other than metacomponents to each other and direct feedback to the metacomponents should result in improved effectiveness of performance. Acquisition components, for example, can provide valuable information to performance components (via the metacomponents) concerning how to perform a task, and the performance components, in turn, can provide feedback to the acquisition components (via the metacomponents) concerning what else needs to be learned to perform the task optimally. Thus, other kinds of components, too, can generate unending feedback loops in which performance improves as a result of interactions between the kinds of components or between multiple components of the same kind.

Components also can be distinguished on the basis of level of generality into three different kinds: general components, class components, and specific components. General components are processes used in the accomplishment of all tasks within a given universe. If, for example, tasks on IQ tests constitute a task universe of interest, a metacomponent, such as that enabling selection of performance components, and performance components, such as encoding and response, would probably constitute general components, in that they would be needed for the solution of virtually any test problems. Class components are processes used in the accomplishment of a proper subset of tasks (including at least two tasks) within a given task universe. In the universe of IQ-test problems, for example, inference (used in finding the relation between the first two terms of an analogy or series-completion problem) would constitute an example of a class (performance) component, in that this component is used in analogy and other inductive reasoning problems but not in, say, spatial visualization problems. Specific components are processes used in the accomplishment of single tasks within a given task universe. Such components are of little interest to a theory of intelligence because of their specificity of application.

R. J. Sternberg (1980c, 1980f) has used the taxonomy of components proposed above to reinterpret the apparent conflict among various psychometric theories of intelligence. The proposal is made that various factorial theories of intelligence are all special cases of a single higher order theory. The individual factorial theories differ from each other primarily as a result of the way a given factorial solution is rotated. The choice of a rotation is mathematically arbitrary, although different rotations of a given solution highlight different psychological elements. Consider some examples.

According to Spearman's (1927) two-factor theory, intelligence is to be understood in terms of two kinds of factors: one general factor and a number of specific factors. Evidence supporting this theory tends to be obtained in unrotated factorial solution. According to one proposed componential theory (R. J. Sternberg, 1980f), individual differences in the general factor are attributable to individual differences in the effectiveness with which general components are executed. In other words, the general factor comprises a set of general components that is common to a wide variety of intellectual tasks; specific factors comprise specific components. As it happens, the metacomponents have a much higher proportion of general components among them than do any of the other kinds of components, presumably because the executive routines needed to plan, monitor, and possibly replan performance are highly overlapping across tasks of a widely differing nature. Metacomponents are not solely responsible for the appearance of a general factor however. Most behavior, and probably all of the behavior exhibited on intelligence tests, is learned. Thus, there are certain to be acquisition components as well as retention and transfer components whose past influence will have a present effect upon individual differences in general ability. Finally, certain performance components, such as encoding and response, may be general to a wide variety of tasks and, thus, also have an effect upon individual differences in general factor.

According to Thurstone's (1938) theory of primary mental abilities, intelligence can be viewed as comprising a small set of multiple factors, or primary mental abilities: verbal comprehension, number, spatial visualization, word fluency, perceptual speed, reasoning, and memory. A multiple-factor solution such as this one tends to appear when factorial solutions are rotated to simple structure. Simple-structure solutions, like unrotated solutions, seem to have a special appeal to psychometricians, and we believe there is a psychological basis for this appeal. Whereas the unrotated solution seems to provide the best overall measure of individual differences in general components, a simple-structure solution seems to provide the best overall measure of individual differences in class components, that is, there seems to be minimal overlap in class components across factors when factors are rotated in this way. Although overlap among class components is minimized, one would nevertheless expect some correlation between pairs of primary mental abilities because of their overlap in general components. Indeed, when simple-structure solutions are factored, they tend to yield a second-order general factor, which we believe captures the shared variation across primary mental abilities owing to general components.

In Cattell and Horn's theory of fluid and crystalized ability (e.g., R. B. Cattell, 1971; Horn, 1968), g is subdivided into the kinds of things measured by figural analogies, series completions, and classifications, on the one hand, and the kinds of things measured by vocabulary, general information, and reading comprehension, on the other hand. Factors such as these seem to result from hierarchical forms of factor analysis. On the componential view, crystalized-ability tests seem best to separate out the products of acquisition, retention, and transfer components, whereas fluid-ability tests seem best to separate out the execution of performance components. Whereas the measurement of crystalized ability involves accumulated products of past executions of components of acquisition, retention, and transfer, measurement of fluid ability involves current execution of components of performance.

The difference in the way the two sets of components are measured may explain why, at least for some people, crystalized ability tends to increase indefinitely with increasing age (short of senility), whereas fluid ability starts to decline in early to middle adulthood. Products of performance are already established and unlikely to show deterioration, except through the effects of senility. Current execution of performance components or any other kind of component may well deteriorate with age however.

To conclude, the componential theory can provide at least a tentative sketch of how different forms of rotation might support seemingly different factorial theories of intelligence. Each factorial theory is viewed as a special case of a single theory, with each special case highlighting different constellations of individual differences. Which constellation of individual differences is important will depend upon the purpose a given theory or test is supposed to serve. This reconciliation of theories, it should be noted, complements the developmental one described earlier; that is, the differentiation-of-abilities hypothesis proposes a reconciliation across age levels, whereas the componential hypothesis proposes a reconciliation within age levels. From a componential point of view, availability and accessibility of components increase with age. From a factorial point of view, levels of factorially based abilities increase with age. On the above analysis, these may both amount to the same thing.

We have emphasized R. J. Sternberg's (1980f) view of information processing components because it is the one we (not disinterestedly!) favor. Two alternative views that have also been elaborated in considerable detail are those of Carroll (1980, 1981) and of Hunt (1978). Carroll does not distinguish among different kinds of components, but has identified 10 components of information processing that he believes are common to large numbers of information processing tasks. These include components such as a Monitor process, an Attention process, an Apprehension process, and so on. Hunt divides what he refers to as mechanistic processes into two kinds: automated and controlled (see also Schneider & Shiffrin, 1977; Shiffrin & Schneider, 1977). Controlled processes require the allocation of attention for their execution; automatic processes do not. This distinction has proven to be a useful one in understanding performance in a variety of information processing tasks. At the present time, the various typologies of components seem more useful heuristically than predictively; we do not have adequate ways of testing their validity.

The Production. A production is a condition-action sequence. If a certain condition is met, then a certain action is performed. Sequences of ordered productions are called production systems.

The executive for a production system is hypothesized to make its way down the ordered list of productions until one of the conditions is met. The action corresponding to that condition is executed and control is returned to the top of the list. The executive then makes its way down the list again, trying to satisfy a condition. When it does so, an action is executed, control returns to the top, and so on. Hunt and Poltrock (1974) have suggested that the productions may be probabilistically ordered so that the exact order in which the list is scanned may differ across subsequent scannings of the list.

An example of a simple production system for crossing the street is the following (Newell & Simon, 1972):

> traffic-light red—stop;
> traffic-light green—move;
> move and left-foot-on-pavement—step-with-right-foot;

move and right-foot-on-pavement—step-with-left-foot.

In this production system, one first tests to see whether the light is red. If it is red, one stops, and again tests to see whether the light is red. This sequence will be repeated until the light turns green, at which point one will start moving. If one is moving and one's left foot is on the pavement, one will step with the right foot; if one is moving and one's right foot is on the pavement, one will step with the left foot. This particular production system is obviously an oversimplification; for example, if the light were to turn red while one were in the middle of the street, according to this production system, one would stop dead in one's tracks, a probably nonadaptive strategy if stopped cars in the perpendicular direction start racing toward one!

The TOTE and the production are related. The test of the former is analogous to the condition of the latter, and the operation of the former is analogous to the action of the latter. The major difference seems to be in the control structure that puts together sequences of TOTEs or productions: the Plan (usually represented as a flow chart) versus the production system. Although these two control structures are different in nature, Carpenter and Just (1975), Hunt and Poltrock (1974), and Newell (1973) have shown that execution of complex tasks can often be conceptualized in either way. It is not clear at present whether the two control structures are even distinguishable experimentally.

Cognitive development is assumed to occur through the operation of self-modifying production systems (see Klahr, 1979, for a review of the literature on such production systems). The basic idea is that the action in a condition-action sequence is to build a new production. Anderson, Kline, and Beasley (1979) have proposed four transition mechanisms by which modification could occur. A designation production is one that simply has as its action the instructions to build a new production of a certain kind. A strengthening mechanism increases the probability that a production will be activated. A generalization mechanism weakens the specific conditions that activate a production so that the production is more likely to be executed under a broader variety of circumstances. And a discrimination mechanism strengthens the specifications for activation of a production so that the production will be activated only when more specific conditions are met than was originally the case. Notice that a critical assumption underlying these last three mechanisms is that productions have differential strengths that affect the likelihood of being executed if they are reached. A rough analogy would be to eliciting conditions necessary to fire a neuron in the nervous system. Intellectual development, thus, is a continuing matter throughout one's lifetime and is largely a matter of learning, which can alter the productions constituting a production system and, thus, the person's way of going about problem solving of various kinds.

Schemes. The notion of a scheme as proposed by Juan Pascual-Leone (1970) and elaborated by Robbie Case (1974a, 1974b, 1978) is viewed by Pascual-Leone and Case as neo-Piagetian, drawing as it does on the basic Piagetian notion of the scheme. What these investigators have done, however, is to specify the notion of a scheme more precisely than has Piaget. They have described the notion in terms amenable to information processing analysis. Thus, one could look at this notion as a translation (with fairly substantial modification) of Piaget's scheme notion and other notions associated with it into information processing terms. The following account is based upon Case (1974b).

In the neo-Piagetian system proposed by Pascual-Leone (1970) and Case, schemes are defined as the units of thought, much as TOTEs and components are in the systems described earlier. There are three basic kinds of schemes: figurative, operative, and executive. Figurative schemes are "internal representations of items of information with which a subject is familiar, or of perceptual configurations which he can recognize" (Case, 1974b, p. 545). These schemes are roughly equivalent to what G. A. Miller (1956) has called chunks. If, for example, a subject described a photograph as depicting a picture of his or her house, one could say that the subject assimilated the sensory input to a figurative house scheme. Operative schemes are "internal representations of functions (rules), which can be applied to one set of figurative schemes, in order to generate a new set" (Case, 1974b, p. 545). Schemes of this kind correspond to what Inhelder and Piaget (1958) have referred to as transformations or to what Newell and Simon (1972) have referred to as elementary information processes. If, for example, a subject looked at two different photographs of a house and judged them to be depicting the same house, one would describe the subject as applying an operative scheme representing a sameness function to the figurative schemes representing the features of each of the two photographs. Executive schemes are "internal representations of procedures which can be applied in the face of particular problem situations, in an attempt to reach particular objectives" (Case,

1974b, p. 546). These schemes correspond to what Miller et al. (1960) referred to as Plans or to what Newell and Simon (1972) have labeled executive programs. These schemes are to a large extent responsible for determining what figurative and operative schemes a subject activates in a particular problem situation. The figurative and operative schemes suggested above for the comparison of two photographs, for example, would presumably be activated only if they were part of some larger executive scheme that required the particular comparison.

Although the three kinds of schemes perform somewhat different functions, they share three basic characteristics. First, they are all active, that is, they act on input and transform it. Second, they are all functional units, albeit ones that can vary in content and structural complexity. Third, they all consist of two components, an initial set of conditions under which they can apply (what might be called a releasing component) and a subsequent set of conditions that they can generate (which might be called an effecting component). In these respects, they bear a certain similarity to the condition-action sequence of a production.

The complete set of schemes activated at any given moment is asserted to constitute the content of an individual's thought. Certain postulates are asserted to characterize the processes of this thought. First, in attempting to solve a problem, a subject's initial step is to activate some general executive scheme (or set of metacomponents, to use R. J. Sternberg's, 1980f, language). The choice of a particular executive scheme will depend upon the nature of the constraints posed by the problem, the nature of the perceptual field, the nature of the subjects's past problem-solving experience, and the nature of the subject's emotional reaction to the situation. Second, a particular executive scheme having been activated, that scheme directs the activation of a sequence of figurative and operative schemes (or strategies for combining performance, acquisition, retention, and transfer components, to use R. J. Sternberg's, 1980f, language). Third, the sequence of figurative and operative schemes is assumed to be constituted of discrete mental steps (or sequentially executed components in R. J. Sternberg's, 1980f, language). Fourth, figurative schemes that are the product of past operations are carried forward or practiced so that they can be utilized in future operations. (Transfer of strategies is thereby made possible.) Fifth, unless its releasing component is activated directly by the immediate perceptual input, the activation of any scheme requires the application of mental effort (to use Kahneman's, 1973, term) or mental energy (to use Spearman's, 1927, term). Because the amount of mental effort that can be applied at any one moment is limited, the number of schemes that can be activated at any one moment is limited as well. Sixth, when a scheme (or set of schemes) that corresponds to the subject's original objective is finally generated, the executive scheme directs an appropriate terminal response (exit, to use Miller et al.'s, 1960, term) or response component (to use R. J. Sternberg's, 1980f, term). Finally, if, at any time, two schemes are activated whose content is incompatible (e.g., one scheme states that object x is larger than object y, whereas another states that object x is smaller than object y), cognitive conflict ensues. Conflict is resolved by activating any schemes that might be relevant to resolution of the conflict and by deciding to use the scheme that is compatible with the largest number of other schemes.

Whether or not a subject actually solves a particular problem is assumed to depend upon four basic factors. The first is the repertoire of schemes that a subject brings to the problem. The second is the maximum number of schemes that the subject's psychological system is capable of activating at any one time. The maximum mental effort a subject can apply to a problem is referred to as M-power and is assumed to vary both within and between age groups. M-power is viewed as at least one source of individual differences within and between age levels in overall general ability, or g. M-power is assumed to increase linearly with age. The third factor is a subject's tendency to utilize the full M-power the subject has available; some subjects are assumed to be more willing than others to apply full M-power; in general, subjects differ in the proportion of their M-power they typically exploit. Finally, a fourth factor is the relative weights assigned to cues from the perceptual field, on the one hand, and to cues from all other sources (e.g., task instructions), on the other hand.

Given the above characterization of the nature of schemes, how does intellectual development occur? Case (1974b) describes several ways in which new schemes can be acquired. First, they can be acquired by modification of old schemes. Second, new schemes can be acquired by the combination or consolidation of multiple old schemes. Each of these two ways of acquiring new schemes can be further subdivided, resulting in multiple means by which intellectual growth can occur. The important point is that "in the course of everyday interaction with the world, . . . subjects are assumed to be constantly applying, and constantly modifying, their basic repertoire of schemes" (Case, 1974b, p. 547). Intellec-

tual development, then, continues throughout the life span.

Rules (or principles). "The basic assumption underlying the rule-assessment approach is that cognitive development can be characterized in large part as the acquisition of increasingly powerful rules for solving problems" (Siegler, 1981, p. 3). Rules or principles, like schemes, emphasize knowledge rather than process as the basic unit of development. Obviously, there must be development in both knowledge and process, so the two emphases are compatible.

Rules can be considered to be mini-Plans or mini-strategies for solving problems of various kinds. As the child grows older, the complexity of his or her rules increases, generally because earlier rules fail to take into account all of the relevant information in a given problem. Siegler has used rules most often to translate Piaget's stages of performance on various tasks into information processing terms (Siegler, 1976, 1977, 1978, 1981; Siegler & Vago, 1978). He has carried this form of analysis further, however, in devising Piagetian types of tasks that are also susceptible to analysis by the rule-assessment approach. Consider, as Siegler (1981) does, Piaget's (1952a) description of the developmental sequence of the conservation of liquid quantity. The rules used at different age levels in this task are quite representative of the kinds of rules Siegler has proposed, and they also appear to be generalizable, with slight modifications, to a variety of tasks. In this task, typically, subjects are shown water being poured from a tall, thin jar (or beaker) into a short, thick jar (or beaker), or vice versa, and they are asked which jar (or beaker) is holding more water. Conservers will state that both jars are holding the same amount of water; nonconservers will state that the tall, thin jar is holding more water. The rule-assessment approach seeks to explain the differences in the ways information is processed by conservers and nonconservers as well as to explain intermediate stages of processing.

In Piaget's Stage 1, a child is said to be "unable to reckon simultaneously with the height and cross section of the liquids . . . he takes into account only the heights" (Piaget, 1952a, p. 12). Siegler's Rule I, corresponding to Piaget's Stage 1, begins with the child asking him or herself whether the values of the dominant dimension (usually the height of a column of water in each of two jars) are equal. If the heights (or values on some other dominant dimension) are judged to be equal, the child responds that the alternatives are equal (even though the widths of the jars may be grossly unequal). If the heights (or other dominant values) are judged to be unequal, the child responds that the jar or beaker with the water at greater height (or other dominant dimension) has more water in it. Thus, Piaget's concept of nonconservation has been translated into information processing terms as a rule (or Plan) actualized through self-interrogation.

In Piaget's Stage 2, "a second relation, that of the width, is explicitly brought into the picture . . . [but] when he is concerned with the unequal levels he forgets the width, and when he notices the difference in width he forgets what he has just said about the relation between the levels" (Piaget, 1952a, p. 16). In Siegler's Rule II, the child asks himself or herself whether the values of the dominant dimension are equal. If they are, the child asks whether the values of the subordinate dimension are equal. If so, the child responds that the alternatives are equal; if not, the child responds that the jar or beaker with the greater value on the subordinate dimension has more water in it. Suppose, though, that the values of the dominant dimension are perceived as unequal. In this case, the subject responds that the jar or beaker with the greater value on the dominant dimension has more water in it. Note that using this rule, the child will respond correctly if the values of the dominant dimension are equal (say, two beakers of equal height). In this case, the child attends to both the dominant and subordinate dimensions (usually height and width). The child will respond incorrectly, however, if the values on the dominant dimension are unequal, unless the values on the subordinate dimension are equal. When the values on the dominant dimension are unequal, the child ignores the subordinate dimension and gets the problem correct only if it so happens that for the particular problem, the value of the subordinate dimension does not affect the answer to the problem (as when the widths of the two jars are equal). Siegler has also proposed a Rule III that corresponds to a slightly more advanced substage of Piaget's Stage 2, but which we will not consider here.

In Piaget's Stage 3, "children state immediately, or almost immediately that the quantities of liquid are conserved, and this irrespective of the number and nature of the changes made" (Piaget, 1952a, p. 17). In Siegler's Rule IV, corresponding to Piaget's Stage 3, all information about both dimensions is taken into account. The child first asks whether the values of the dominant dimension are equal. If they are, the child asks whether the values of the subordinate dimension are equal. If so, the alternatives are judged to be equal; if not, the jar with the greater value of the subordinate dimension is said to hold more water. Suppose the values of the dominant dimension are unequal. The child still asks whether the values of the subordinate dimension are equal (unlike in Rule II, where this question was not asked in this case). If the answer is yes, the jar with the greater value of the dominant dimension is judged to hold more water; if the answer is no, the values of the dominant and subordinate dimensions are appropriately combined.

Gelman and Gallistel (1978), like Siegler, have used rules, or, as they have called them, principles, as a unit of cognitive development. They have proposed five principles that they believe govern and define the act of counting. Three of these principles deal with how to count, one with what to count, and a final one with a combination of both. The counting principles will be described later in the discussion on *Number Ability*. The important point to be made here is that early number ability as manifested in counting is believed to develop through increasing knowledge of the counting principles. These principles seem roughly analogous in the domain of number to Siegler's rules in the domain of problem solving. There are two important differences however. First, in Siegler's (1981) formulation, more sophisticated rules are believed to replace simpler rules; in Gelman and Gallistel's (1978) formulation, later principles are added onto (rather than replacing) earlier ones. Second, Gelman and Gallistel's rules are more content based than are Siegler's, dwelling as they do on counting in particular rather than cognitive processing in general.

To summarize this section on units of behavior, several different units have been proposed under the information processing rubric. We believe the units are all compatible with each other. A TOTE may be viewed as a three-component sequence (test, operate, exit). TOTEs combine into Plans, which are essentially equivalent to the strategies into which components combine. The component is itself an elaboration of the concept of an elementary information process, in that there can be components of different kinds. The production is a particular instantiation of an elementary information process with a specific kind of control mechanism, the production system. Schemes and rules may be viewed as knowledge structures that are both created by and operated on by elementary information processes of various sorts. As the various kinds of units are further specified, incompatibilities among them may start to emerge, although we do not believe these incompatibilities have yet been shown to exist.

These information processing notions are compatible with psychometric notions as well as with each other. It has been shown how factor theories of intelligence can be explained in componential terms, or, symmetrically, how components can be explained in terms of factors. At this time, we have no firm basis for saying which kind of unit is more basic, nor is it entirely clear what more basic would mean in this instance. At best, we can hope that different kinds of analysis will converge upon the same basic truths, increasing our confidence that we are gaining a valid understanding of the human mind and how it develops.

Instantiations of Units of Behavior in Tasks Requiring Intelligent Performance

The information processing literature that could be construed as dealing with the development of intelligence is immense. We will of necessity be highly selective in the literature we review, guiding ourselves loosely by Thurstone's (1938) theory of primary mental abilities in the selection and organization of topics we will cover. We recommend highly Siegler and Richards's (in press) review of this same literature for an alternative (but compatible) perspective on the same topic. The topics we will cover here (in greater or, usually, lesser detail) include inductive reasoning, deductive reasoning, problem solving, verbal comprehension, number, spatial visualization, and memory. The item types that have been studied are similar or identical to those that appear on many IQ tests.

Inductive Reasoning. Because most of the research that has been done on inductive reasoning has been concerned with reasoning by analogy, we will concentrate on that topic. Our contention will be that a wide variety of studies employing a number of alternative paradigms seem to converge upon a few basic conclusions about analogical reasoning and its development.

The first conclusion is that there are roughly three stages in the development of analogical reasoning. The first, extending roughly through the ages of 7 to 10 years, seems to be marked by an inability of subjects to discern second-order relations in analogies (i.e., the relation between the first-order *A–B* and *C–D* relations). The second stage, approximately between 9 and 12 years, is marked by a preliminary or tentative level of ability to discern these second-order relations. The third stage, beginning to show in children of 11 or so, is characterized by full ability to understand second-order relations.

Piaget with Montangero and Billeter (1977) has suggested three stages in the development of reasoning by analogy. The three stages, resembling those described above, were inferred from experimental data. The investigators presented 29 children between the ages of 5 and 13 with sets of pictures. They asked the children to arrange the pictures into pairs. The children were then asked to put together those pairs that went well together, placing groups of four pictures into 2×2 matrices that represented relations of analogy among the four pictures. Children who had difficulty at any step of the procedure were given prompts along the way. Children who finally succeeded were presented with a countersuggestion to their proposed solution, by which the investigators hoped to test the strength of the children's commitment to their proposed response. At all steps along the way, children were asked to explain their reasons for grouping things as they did. In the first proposed stage of Piaget's model, characterizing the performance of children of ages 5 and 6, children can arrange pictures into pairs, but the children ignore the higher order relations between pairs. Thus, although these children can link *A* to *B* or *C* to *D*, they cannot link *A–B* to *C–D* in the analogy, "*A* is to *B* as *C* is to *D*." In the second stage, characterizing the performance of children from about 8 to 11 years of age, children can form analogies, but when challenged with countersuggestions, they readily rescind their proposed analogies. Piaget interprets this finding as evidence of only a weak or tentative level of analogical reasoning ability. In the third stage, characterizing the performance of children from age 11 and up, children form analogies, are able to state explicitly the conceptual bases of these analogies, and resist countersuggestions from the experimenter.

Lunzer (1965) presented children of ages 9 through 17+ with verbal analogies taking several different forms. Some had just one term missing (which could be *A*, *B*, *C*, or *D*); others had two terms missing (which could be either *C* and *D*, *A* and *B*, *B* and *C*, or *A* and *D*). As would be expected, analogies with a single term missing were easier to solve than analogies with two terms missing. Those with *C* and *D* missing or with *A* and *B* missing were found to be less difficult than those with *B* and *C* missing or with *A* and *D* missing. Presumably, this was because for the latter two kinds of problems, there was no single relation linking the missing pair; each of the two missing terms was involved in a different relation within the analogy. Lunzer further found that children had great difficulty with even the simplest analogies until about 9 years of age, and they did not show highly successful performance until the age of 11. Lunzer concluded that even the simplest analogies require recognition of higher order relations (i.e., relations between the first and second halves of an analogy) that are not discernible to children who are not yet formal operational. The suggestion of three stages in Lunzer's work (before age 9, between ages 9 and 11, and after age 11) seems correspondent to the suggestion of Piaget (1977) regarding three stages of reasoning by analogy.

Gallagher and Wright (1977, 1979) have done research comparing the relative abilities of children in grades 4 to 6 to provide what these investigators have called symmetrical or asymmetrical explanations of analogy solutions. Symmetrical explanations showed awareness of the higher order relation linking $A-B$ to $C-D$. Asymmetrical explanations ignored this relation, dealing either only with the $C-D$ relation or with both the $A-B$ and $C-D$ relations, but in isolation from each other. Percentages of symmetrical responses increased with age and were associated with higher levels of performance on the analogies.

Levinson and Carpenter (1974) presented verbal analogies (e.g., bird is to air as fish is to ?) and quasi analogies (e.g., A bird uses air; a fish uses ?) to children of ages 9, 12, and 15 years of age. The standard analogies required recognition of the higher order analogical relationship; the quasi analogies essentially supplied this relationship by suggesting what is common (in the example, use of a medium in which to breathe) to the two halves of the analogy. The investigators found that whereas 9-year-olds could answer significantly more quasi analogies than analogies correctly, 12- and 15-year-olds answered approximately equal numbers of each kind of item correctly. Moreover, whereas performance on the standard analogies increased monotonically across age levels, performance on the quasi analogies did not increase, presumably because it is the mapping of the higher order relationship given in the quasi analogies that challenges the younger children. We interpret these results as providing still further evidence for the ability of third-stage children, but not first-stage children, to discover second-order relations in the solution of verbal analogies.

A second conclusion or generalization is that children become more nearly exhaustive in their information processing in solving analogies with advancing age. This generalization seems to extend beyond analogical reasoning to a variety of other tasks as well (Brown & DeLoache, 1978) and is considered again later as a possible general principle of development. The trend appears regardless of whether the information being processed is a set of attributes of a single analogy term or the set of terms that constitute the analogy as a whole.

Sternberg and Rifkin (1979) investigated the role of exhaustive information processing in the development of analogical reasoning processes. Two kinds of schematic-picture analogies were used. One kind was the People Piece analogy used by R. J. Sternberg (1977a, 1977b); the other kind was also a schematic figure of a person. But, whereas the People Piece analogies were composed of perceptually integral attributes, the schematic-figure analogies were composed of perceptually separable attributes (see Garner, 1974). In the perceptually integral attributes, the levels of one attribute depend upon levels of other attributes for their existence. For example, in the People Pieces, which varied on four binary attributes—sex (male, female), height (tall, short), clothing shading (black, white), and weight (fat, thin)—a level of height cannot be represented without representing some level of weight and vice versa. In the perceptually separable attributes, which also varied on four binary attributes—hat shading (white, black), vest pattern (striped, polka dots), handgear (suitcase, umbrella), and footwear (shoes, boots)—the color of a hat can be represented without also representing the type of footwear a figure has. Multiple-regression modeling was used to predict the data. For the analogies with perceptually integral attributes, it was found that second graders used a maximally self-terminating strategy, encoding and comparing the minimum possible numbers of attributes needed to solve the problems; fourth graders encoded terms exhaustively (i.e., they perceived all attributes of each term) but compared attributes in a self-terminating fashion. Sixth graders and adults encoded terms exhaustively and performed inference of the $A-B$ relation exhaustively, but they performed mapping of the higher order relation between $A-B$ and $C-D$ and application of the $C-D$ relation in a self-terminating fashion. Moreover, it was found that although fourth graders, sixth graders, and adults solved the analogies by mapping the higher order relation between the two halves of the analogies, second graders did not. Once again, then, we have support for a late-developing ability to recognize and utilize higher order relations. For the analogies with perceptually separable attributes, subjects at all ages used the same strategy, namely, the same one that second graders used for the perceptually integral attributes. All operations, including encoding of analogy terms, were executed with self-termination. Mapping of the higher order relation between the first and second half of the analogy was not used or was used for a constant amount of time across items types. (The two outcomes were experimentally indistinguishable.) Thus, it appears that for analogies with integral attributes, strategy changes with age, whereas for analogies with separable attributes, it does not. Perhaps this is because in analogies with separable attributes, subjects are unable to integrate attributes, and hence the memory load for all models, except the most self-terminating one (which requires the lowest load) exceeds working-memory capacity.

Sternberg and Nigro (1980) presented analogies to third, sixth, and ninth graders as well as to adults that took each of the following three forms:

1. NARROW : WIDE :: QUESTION : (TRI-AL, STATEMENT, ANSWER, ASK);
2. WIN: LOSE :: (DISLIKE : HATE), (EAR : HEAR), (ENJOY : LIKE), (ABOVE : BELOW);
3. WEAK : (SICK :: CIRCLE : SHAPE), (STRONG :: POOR : RICH), (SMALL :: GAR-DEN : GROW), (HEALTH :: SOLID : FIRM).

Numbers of answer options ranged from two to four. These authors, using mathematical modeling of latency data, found that whereas the third and sixth graders were self-terminating in their search among the answer options (i.e., they stopped option search as soon as they found a plausible response option), ninth graders and adults were exhaustive, always looking at all of the options before responding. We see once again, then, the tendency to become more nearly exhaustive in processing with increasing age.

A third conclusion is that use of word association in solving verbal analogies is common among younger children, but it decreases with age. Sternberg and Nigro (1980), for example, found that third and sixth graders used word association to guide their search among the answer options, with higher association responses being examined before lower association ones. This heavy use of word association may represent an extreme example of the use of a self-terminating strategy, in that these children select the first response that comes to mind—the response most highly associated with another term in the analogy regardless of the relationships conveyed by the analogy. The ninth graders and adults, on the other hand, did not use word association in any discernible way.

The pioneering studies on the role of word association in analogy solution were conducted by Achenbach (1970a, 1970b, 1971), who found that children in the intermediate and even early secondary school grades differ widely in the extent to which they use word association as a means of choosing one from among several response options. In using word association, subjects choose the response option that is most highly semantically related to the third term of the analogy stem rather than choosing

the option that is related to the third analogy term in the same way that the second analogy term is related to the first. Moreover, the extent to which children use word association serves as a moderator variable in predicting classroom performance—correlations between performance on IQ tests and school achievement were substantially lower for children who relied primarily on word association than for children who relied primarily on reasoning processes. Gentile, Tedesco-Stratton, Davis, Lund, and Agunanne (1977) further investigated children's associative responding by using Achenbach's Children's Associative Responding Test (CART). They found that associative priming can have a marked effect on test scores, leading children either toward or away from correct solutions.

At least some of the transitions that have been observed in analogy solution seem to be ones that characterize other forms of intellectual behavior as well (e.g., increased ability to discern second-order relations or increased use of exhaustive information processing). This observation lends support to the notion of many investigators (e.g., Mulholland, Pellegrino, & Glaser, 1980; Spearman, 1923; R. J. Sternberg, 1977a, 1977b; Whitely, 1977) that analogies tap a central part of whatever it is we mean by general intelligence, or *g,* and may also play a central role in more specialized kinds of thinking as well, for example, legal reasoning (Levi, 1949) and scientific reasoning (Oppenheimer, 1956).

To summarize, the research on the development of inductive reasoning seems to converge on three conclusions: first, there appear to be three stages in the development of analogical reasoning (a pre-analogical stage, a transitional stage, and an analogical stage in which full analogical reasoning is possible); second, children become more nearly exhaustive in their processing of induction problems with increasing age; third, the use of word association in solving analogies is common in young children, but it decreases with age. There is also fairly good agreement as to what processes are needed to solve analogies. What seems most to be needed is research that tests the degree to which these or other processes are used in a variety of induction tasks.

Deductive Reasoning. Deductive reasoning covers a wide domain of research, including the encoding and combination of statements using logical connectives, transitive inference, propositional reasoning, and the like. We will briefly consider here some of the major issues in each of these three subareas as well as some of the pertinent research that has been done in each.

1. *Encoding and combination of statements using logical connectives.* Understanding of logical con-

nectives is essential to intelligent comprehension of, and reasoning about, ideas presented in everyday speech and reading because these connectives tie together what otherwise would be disconnected and unintelligible strings of ideas. Probably the most fundamental theoretical as well as practical question concerning development in the understanding of logical connectives is the relative roles of logical and linguistic processes in this understanding. The connectives needing to be understood include, among others, *and, or, if-then, only if, if and only if,* and *not* (which, strictly speaking, is a unary operator rather than a connective).

One viewpoint is that understanding of development is to be sought through an analysis of logical operations. The theoretical framework of Piaget asserts that the kinds of complex rules required in the encoding and combination of logical connectives require competence in the use of propositional calculus and that this calculus is not available until the formal operational period associated with early adolescence and beyond (Inhelder & Piaget, 1958). In this view, systematic and logical interpretations of logical connectives could not be expected to emerge until quite late in development. This prediction, however, is falsified by any number of data sets showing logical thinking in preadolescent, concrete-operational children (e.g., Paris, 1973; R. J. Sternberg, 1979a; Taplin, Staudenmayer, & Taddonio, 1974). The falsification of this key prediction does not require abandonment of the position asserting the primacy of logical operations though. Several authors have argued that Piaget is simply wrong in his view that propositional calculus does not become available to children until they become formal operational (e.g., Brainerd, 1976; Ennis, 1975, 1976). Their research suggests that it is available much earlier; moreover, Brainerd asserts that it is actually required for later developing operations to emerge. Thus, the logical position may be tenable, even if Piaget's particular version of it is not.

A second and increasingly widely accepted viewpoint is that understanding of simple relations, such as conjunctions, and more complex relations, such as conditionals, can be understood in terms of their relative frequencies of occurrence in children's experience and in terms of their semantic complexity. Support for a linguistic interpretation of development has come from the seminal work of Taplin et al. (1974) with conditionals; they found that children of varying ages were approximately equally likely to use some (logical) truth table in their processing of conditionals. What changed over age was the particular truth table that tended to be used.

The third viewpoint, advanced by Staudenmayer and Bourne (1977), is that the first two viewpoints cannot really be disentangled, that it is undesirable to maintain that "the interpretation of the premises is separable from the inferences involved in evaluating the conclusions of syllogistic arguments in the conditional reasoning task" (p. 617). In their view, which focuses upon the information processing strategies children might employ in dealing with logical connectives, development can be understood in terms of perceptual, associative, and abstract logical properties of elements.

What we believe to be the best evidence on this issue (R. J. Sternberg, 1979a; Taplin et al., 1974) supports the view that both linguistic and logical factors matter but that linguistic factors are of greater importance than logical ones. When one compares children's difficulty in linguistically encoding the meaning of each connective to their difficulty in combining these meanings, one finds that encoding accounts for most of the difficulty in performance. (A review of this literature can be found in R. J. Sternberg, 1979a; see also *Braine & Rumain, vol. III, chap. 5.*)

2. *Transitive inference.*   A typical transitive inference problem is, "John is taller than Mary; Mary is taller than Susan; who is tallest?" The thinking required to solve this problem is referred to as transitive because it involves a chain of reasoning in which the relation between two objects in an array that are not explicitly linked is inferred from the relations between two pairs of objects that are explicitly linked. The importance of the child's ability to make transitive inferences appears first to have been recognized by Burt (1919), who used such transitive inference problems as the one above on a subtest of intelligence.

The developmental literature on transitive inference has focused upon two key questions. The first is that of the age at which the ability to make transitive inferences first appears. The second is that of how children of different ages actually make transitive inferences. A recent review of both literatures is provided by Thayer and Collyer (1978).

Consider first the question of the age at which transitive inference first becomes possible. The conclusion that will be drawn from our brief literature review is that even preoperational children as young as 4 years of age appear able to make successful transitive inferences. Originally, however, Piaget (see, e.g., Piaget, 1928, 1955; Piaget, Inhelder, & Szeminska, 1960) proposed that children are unable to make transitive inferences until they reach the stage of concrete operations at about the age of 7 or 8. In fact, transitivity tasks have often been used by Piagetian psychologists as a test to determine whether a child has become capable of concrete operational thinking. In this view, the young child whose thinking is preoperational is unable to reorganize perceptual input to perform the reasoning needed for a transitive inference. Perceptual domination and the inability of the preoperational child to understand the reversibility of ordered relations prevent such a child from making the needed inference (Bryant, 1973).

Bryant and Trabasso (1971) proposed instead that memory rather than reasoning limitations were responsible for the failure of preoperational children to solve the transitive-inference task. They suggested that the child could not answer the question if he or she was unable to remember the premises. These authors designed an elegant experiment to test their hypothesis. Training of each child began by showing the child a pair of red and blue colored sticks that appeared to be of equal height because part of each stick was hidden, but that were in fact of unequal length. The child was asked which stick was longer (or shorter), the red or the blue, and was then given either visual or verbal feedback regarding the correctness of the choice. Visual feedback consisted of actually showing the child the difference between the lengths of the pair of sticks; this was done by making each stick fully visible. Verbal feedback consisted of such a statement as either ''Yes, the red stick is longer'' or ''No, the blue stick is shorter.''

Training was done in two phases, each involving feedback of the kinds described above. In the first phase, four comparisons—A–B, B–C, C–D, and D–E—were trained separately and in order from either the tallest stick to the shortest one or vice versa. Each pair was learned to a criterion of 8 out of 10 successful learning trials. In the second phase, which immediately followed the first, all four pairs were presented in a random order on consecutive trials. Presentation of the pairs in various orders continued until a given child responded correctly to 6 successive presentations of each pair.

Testing followed immediately after completion of the second training phase. The testing procedure was the same as the second phase of training (with mixed presentation of pairs), except that no feedback was given. Each child was tested four times on every one of the 10 possible pairs of colored sticks, including the 4 initially trained direct comparisons and 6 new, indirect (i.e., transitive) comparisons. The critical transitive comparison was the B, D one because B was shorter than one item (A) and taller than three others (C, D, E,), whereas D was shorter than three items (A, B, C) and taller than one (E). In all other transitive comparisons (A–C, A–D, A–E,

B–E, C–E), at least one item was either taller or shorter than every other item so that correct responding might have been due to use of linguistic surface structure in the item rather than to a genuine transitive inference.

Performance on all of the six transitive-inferential comparisons was well above the chance level of .50 for children of 4, 5, and 6 years of age. On the critical (B, D) comparison, proportions of correct responses were .78, .88, and .92 for 4-, 5-, and 6-year-olds respectively. These proportions were sufficiently high to reject the null hypothesis of chance performance at the .01 level of statistical significance. Thus, preoperational children as young as 4 years of age were able to succeed quite well in performing transitive inferences. Moreover, the authors argued that what failures there were could be attributed to retrieval failure for the premises rather than to reasoning failure. A simple mathematical model based on retrieval failure predicted the three critical proportions noted above quite well; furthermore, performance on the nontransitive pairs was highly correlated across subjects with performance on the transitive pair, suggesting that the same factors that led to failure on the adjacent pairs may well have led to failure on the transitive pair. The factors could not be ones of transitive inference because the adjacent pairs did not require such an inference; because the modeling data were consistent with a retrieval-failure interpretation, this one seemed plausible.

In an unpublished study by Trabasso (cited in Trabasso, 1975), 17 of the original 20 children in the Bryant and Trabasso (1971) study were retrained so as to improve their memories for the trained pairs. Retraining resulted in significant improvements in performance on the transitive relations. In fact, performance of the retrained 4-year-olds reached the level of the 6-year-olds who had been trained just once. Again, retrieval of relations was highly correlated ($r = .8$) with level of success on the transitive-inference problems, suggesting that memory factors were likely to be responsible for many of the children's failures to perform transitive inferences correctly.

Consider next research on how children actually solve the transitive-inference problems. The conclusion to be drawn is that children almost certainly use a mixture of linguistic and spatial processes and representations. Again, Trabasso and his colleagues have probably been the key investigators addressing this question. Riley and Trabasso (1974) were particularly interested in how information about pairs of terms is encoded. They trained 4-year-old children either on the traditional transitive-inference problem, in which only one comparative term is used (e.g., longer), or on the problem as presented by Bryant and Trabasso (1971), where both comparatives were used (e.g., longer and shorter). Training was most effective when both comparatives were used. They found that when children were trained with only one comparative term, they tended to encode the relations nominally rather than contrastively, that is, they tended, in their verbal reports, to reduce statements, such as "red is longer than blue," to "red is long" and "blue is not long." But this nominal encoding leads to contradictions between successive pairs because a given stick can be longer than one other stick but shorter than another stick (e.g., B is longer than C but shorter than A). In the double-comparative condition, on the other hand, children seemed to encode the terms contrastively.

Although the Riley and Trabasso (1974) study deals with encoding of single relations, it does not directly deal with the question of how a linear ordering is constructed from paired-ordering information. This question was directly addressed by Trabasso, Riley, and Wilson (1975). These authors set out to explain marked serial-position effects that occur during the second phase of training of the kind used by Trabasso and his colleagues (where the pairs learned during the first phase in fixed order, from longest to shortest or vice versa, are then learned in variable orders). Two basic hypotheses were considered. One was that children first learn each pair as an ordered set: $A,B; B,C; C,D; D,E$. Relations between other pairs are then computed at the time of retrieval as needed. Because pairs A,B and D,E each contain a member that has only one comparative associated with it, learning of these pairs should be facilitated. Pairs B,C and C,D should cause problems because all of these have members with double functions. Factors such as response competition would produce higher error rates and the serial-position effect for the middle pairs. This explanation fails, however, on six-term problems, where it predicts that pair C,D will be equal in difficulty to pairs B,C and D,E because each term in each pair is longer than some terms but shorter than others. In fact, the middle pair C,D is the hardest one to learn. This verbal-learning type of model was contrasted with an ends-inward spatial model, which could account for the six-term problem results. In this model, children are assumed first to isolate end-anchor members of the array (sticks A and E). This isolation is assumed to be done by finding the stick that is taller than all of the other sticks (and, thus, shorter than none) and, then, the

stick that is shorter than all other sticks (and, thus, taller than none). Once the end points are identified, children are proposed to construct a spatial linear ordering, working from the ends inward.

Trabasso et al. (1975) also investigated speed of retrieval for pairs of terms. They found that subjects were faster in retrieving more distant pairs than closer ones, even though subjects had been trained on the closer (but not more distant) pairs! This "symbolic distance effect" (Moyer, 1973) is consistent with retrieval from a spatial linear ordering, but not with storage merely of individual pairs of terms. More detailed descriptions of this and other work by Trabasso and his colleagues can be found in Trabasso (1975) and in Trabasso and Riley (1975). (See also Riley, 1976, for further evidence supporting the linear-ordering hypothesis for children of varying ages.)

Other investigators have concentrated their attention on a different form of transitive-inference problem, the verbal three-term series problem of the kind presented at the beginning of this section. The developmental literature on the three-term series problem can be traced back at least to Hunter (1957), who proposed a model of linear syllogistic reasoning that he tested on 11- and 16-year-olds. The model, which asserts that people solve linear syllogisms by rearranging premises into a canonical form whereby the second term of the first premise matches the first term of the second premise (as in "John is taller than *Mary, Mary* is taller than Pete"), has not held up under subsequent investigation and is no longer considered to be viable (see H. H. Clark, 1969a, 1969b; Huttenlocher, 1968; Johnson-Laird, 1972).

There are currently four major models of linear syllogistic reasoning. First, DeSoto, London, and Handel (1965) proposed a spatial model, according to which people represent the terms of a linear syllogism in the form of a spatial array. The model has been refined and expanded by Huttenlocher (1968) and by Huttenlocher and Higgins (1971). Trabasso et al. (1975) drew heavily on this model in their construction of a model for performance of the transitive-inference task using colored sticks. Second, H. H. Clark (1969a, 1969b) has proposed an alternative linguistic model according to which linear syllogisms are solved via inferences on functional relations represented by linguistic deep structures. Third, Quinton and Fellows (1975) have suggested an algorithmic model for the solution of linear syllogisms that seems almost to bypass the need for reasoning altogether. Using this model, people can solve determinate linear syllogisms (those in which the complete ordering of the three terms can be inferred) by supplying a series of simple, essentially mechanical steps. Finally, R. J. Sternberg (1980d, 1980e) has proposed a mixed model of linear syllogistic reasoning that combines selected features of the spatial and linguistic models and that contains new features of its own. Several individuals have also proposed strategy-change variants of the spatial and linguistic models. For example, Wood, Shotter, and Godden (1974) proposed that early on during practice, subjects use a spatial model, later switching to a linguistic model. Shaver, Pierson, and Lang (1974) have proposed the reverse hypothesis, arguing that subjects switch from a linguistic to a spatial strategy.

Keating and Caramazza (1975) collected error data from children in the fifth and seventh grades who solved linear syllogisms under a 10-sec.-deadline procedure. In this procedure, a response was counted as an error if it was either incorrect or was not given before the end of 10 sec. Keating and Caramazza's data were supportive of the linguistic model, although the authors did not directly pit this model against any others. R. J. Sternberg (1980b) pitted the four models described above against each other for children in grades 3, 5, 7, 9, and 11. Solution latencies for three-term series problems were mathematically modeled, using quantitative implementations of each of the four models described briefly above. The data supported the mixed model over the other models at every grade level except 9, where the linguistic model was preferred. However, the superiority of the linguistic model was limited to the first session of practice; in the second session, the mixed model was better. This was the only grade level at which there was any evidence of a possible strategy change. At all other levels, the mixed model was preferred in each session. Component latencies for the mixed model decreased with age. These data were generally supportive of results for adults (R. J. Sternberg, 1980d, 1980e; Sternberg & Weil, 1980). The mixed model was found to be superior to the alternative models across adjectives as well as sessions. Not all subjects used this model however; a minority of subjects in each experiment used one of the other three models.

To summarize, children of all ages appear to use a mixture of linguistic and spatial representations and processes in the solution of transitive-inference problems of various kinds. The exact nature of the mixture probably depends upon the format of the problem (e.g., colored sticks versus verbal statements) and the context in which it is presented. There is no strong evidence for strategy change over age (Riley, 1976; R. J. Sternberg, 1980b), although available evidence suggests that preoperational children are limited by their working memory capacities (in Case's, 1974b, terminology, M-power) in the effectiveness with which they can implement a working strategy.

3. *Propositional reasoning.* By propositional reasoning, we refer to reasoning of the kind used in formal logical proofs. Perhaps the most elegant work on propositional reasoning in children has been done by Osherson (1974, 1975, 1976). We will briefly describe here a small portion of Osherson's theory.

Osherson (1974) proposed that a subset of logical thinking in children could be understood in terms of their use of 15 logical operations:

> These operations operate on formulas of sentential logic, changing them into other formulas, not necessarily distinct from the original. The operations are arranged in a specified order, $O_1, \ldots O_n$ so that the output of operation O_j is the input to operation O_{j+1}. The operations are *context sensitive* in the sense that whether or not they effect their change on a given formula depends not only on the structure of that formula but also on properties of the larger formula within which the given formula is embedded. (p. 53)

Examples of the kinds of operations that appear in Osherson's theory appear below. Each operation can be interpreted as an instruction to rewrite the formula above the line as the formula below the line, provided that certain conditions (to be described) are met. The child reads or hears statements (e.g., "The grass is brown or it is green"), converts the statements to their logical equivalents, operates upon these abstract logical equivalents, and then reconverts the computed solution to the language of the original statements:

Demorgan's Law (&):
$$\frac{p \lor q}{-(-p \;\&\; -q)}$$

Deletion (V):
$$\frac{p \lor q \rightarrow r}{p \rightarrow r}$$

Contraposition:
$$\frac{p \rightarrow q}{-q \rightarrow -p}$$

Addition (&):
$$\frac{p \rightarrow q}{p \;\&\; r \rightarrow q}$$

The operations can be viewed as applying to the antecedent conditional of a logical formula, that is, to the $p \rightarrow q$ section of $(p \rightarrow q) \rightarrow (r \rightarrow s)$. The output of the ordered set of operations (including all 15 of the formulas in Osherson's theory) is another conditional not necessarily different from the original antecedent conditional that served as the input to the set of formulas.

To convey the nature of the conditions that must be met for the formulas to be applied, three definitions are necessary. The *current antecedent* conditional of a formula is the antecedent conditional of that formula. The *upper formula* is the formula above the line in a given operation. The *lower formula* is the formula below the line. In general, an operation applies when three conditions are met: first, the current antecedent conditional does not already match the consequent conditional; second, the current antecedent conditional has the logical structure shown in the upper formula; and third, the operation helps to make the current antecedent conditional match the consequent conditional. (Osherson specifies in some detail what he means by an operation helping to make the current antecedent conditional match the consequent conditional, but we will not present the rather detailed specification here.)

Osherson (1974) tested his theory using two different sets of 14 formulas from sentential logic. These were formulas such as $(A \lor B \rightarrow C) \rightarrow (A \& -B \rightarrow C)$, $(A \lor A \rightarrow C) \rightarrow (-C \rightarrow -B)$, and $(A \rightarrow B) \rightarrow (B \& -C \rightarrow A)$. Obviously, no children would understand formulas presented in this form. In fact, the formulas were presented to the subjects (fourth, fifth, and sixth graders in Osherson's Experiment 1) in concrete rather than abstract forms. There were two concrete forms, one making use of figurines called toks and one making use of objects in an imaginary playground. These two kinds of concrete content were crossed with two idioms of presentation: quantified and sentential. For example, the first formula mentioned above, $(A \lor B \rightarrow C) \rightarrow (A \& -B \rightarrow C)$, expressed in quantified form via toks would be, "All the blue toks which are not short—is everyone of those toks a starred tok?" The same formula, expressed in sentential form via objects in the playground on which small pictures of children could be placed would be, "If I'm thinking of a yellow square which is not small, am I thinking of a boys' square?" To solve these problems, subjects needed what Osherson called a hint. In the first instance, the hint was that "all the blue toks and all the short toks have stars." In the second instance, it was that "If I'm thinking of either a yellow square or a small square, then I am thinking of a boys' square."

Osherson's (1974) competence model—that subjects solve logical reasoning problems using the 15 ordered formulas in his theory—does not make predictions about the kinds or numbers of errors people make in solving logical reasoning problems. In fact, it predicts errorless performance! It was, therefore, necessary for Osherson to supplement his competence model with a performance model that makes predictions about errors. In fact, Osherson tested several alternative performance models; he did not find one that was best but rather identified a class of models that worked quite well. We will describe only a single example. In this performance model, which well accounted for the data, the probability of passing a task with x operations is asserted to equal $p^x q$ (p to the x power times q), where p is the probability of successfully executing a given operation (for simplicity, p is assumed in some analyses to be the same for all formulas—this assumption is later relaxed), q is the probability of unsuccessfully executing a given operation (where again, for simplicity, q is assumed initially to be the same for each operation), and x is the number of operations. To make the model viable, it was necessary to weight operations according to their difficulty of execution. When this was done, Osherson was able to obtain quite respectable correlations between the predicted and observed difficulties of logical problems that he presented to his subjects. These correlations were generally in the low .80s.

This very brief description cannot do justice to the power and elegance of Osherson's models, which include theories of response time as well as of response difficulties. We hope, however, the description conveys a sense of what Osherson is trying to accomplish. In terms of our earlier descriptions of units of analysis, Osherson's operations would seem most similar to subrules of Siegler's (1981) rules. One strings together the operations in Osherson's models as one strings together the component decisions in Siegler's rules, to arrive at a final conclusion. The operations in Osherson's models, like the rules in Siegler's, are knowledge based. Errors are made either through lack of knowledge regarding the content of particular operations (e.g., not yet knowing DeMorgan's Law) or through performance limitations, that is, one lacks the mental capacity (*M*-power, to use Case's, 1974b, terminology) to perform the sequence of operations necessary to solve a given problem. Successful deductive reasoning thus requires both the knowledge and *M*-power to complete a problem successfully.

Problem Solving. A great deal of work has been done on problem solving in children (e.g.,

Beilin, 1969; Brainerd, 1973, 1974; Klahr & Wallace, 1973, 1976; Siegler, 1976) and we cannot, of course, review anything resembling the whole body of literature here. Hence, we will not even try. Instead, we will describe briefly two well-conceived, if not necessarily representative, approaches to problem solving, those of Siegler and Klahr.

Siegler's elegant rule-based approach to understanding the development of problem-solving abilities is epitomized by his work on the balance-scale problem (Siegler, 1976). Our summary is based on the account of this work presented in Siegler (1978). In Siegler's approach, it will be recalled, it is assumed (1) that children's problem-solving strategies are rule governed, with the rules progressing in level of sophistication with increasing cognitive development and (2) that it is possible to infer the rules children of different ages use in solving problems by constructing problems on which patterns of correct and erroneous responses suggest the rules children are using.

In the balance-scale task, children are presented with a balance scale, such as that used by Inhelder and Piaget (1958), that has four equally spaced pegs on each side. The arm of the balance scale can fall down to the left or right or it can remain in balance, depending upon the distribution of metal weights that are placed on the pegs. The child's task is to predict which (if either) side of the balance scale will descend if a lever that holds the scale motionless is released.

Siegler (1976) combined Inhelder and Piaget's (1958) analysis of the problem with his own to formulate four rules that he believed governed solution of balance-scale problems. The idea is that children pass from simpler to more complex rules as they grow older; more complex rules are defined as those that take into account more information that is present in the problem situation. The simplest rule, Rule I, takes into account only the numbers of weights on each side of the fulcrum. If these numbers (and, hence, total weight) are the same, the scale is predicted to balance; if they are different, the scale is predicted to fall in the direction of the arm with more weights on it. The next rule, Rule II, takes into account distance as well as number of weights, but only if the number of weights on the two sides is equal. If the number of weights is equal, the scale is predicted to balance only if the distance from the fulcrum is equal; otherwise, it is predicted to fall in the direction of the weight further from the fulcrum. If, however, the number of weights is unequal, the scale is simply predicted to fall in the direction of the greater number of weights. The subsequent rule,

Rule III, takes into account distance as well as number of weights in all cases. If both distance and weight (numbers of disks on the scale) on both sides of the fulcrum are equal, the child predicts that the scale will balance. If either distance or weight, but not both, are equal, the other determines the outcome, for example, if distance but not weight is equal, then the scale will fall in the direction of the greater number of weights. If both distance and weight are unequal on the two sides of the fulcrum and if one side of the scale has the greater value on both distance and weight, that side is predicted to fall; if, however, one side has greater value on weight and the other on distance, the rule does not permit resolution of the conflict and the child is assumed to muddle through. The most complex rule, Rule IV, involves computation of the torques on each side of the fulcrum by multiplying the number of weights on each peg on each side of the fulcrum by the distance of that peg from the fulcrum and, then, summing the products. For example, if there were five weights on the third peg to the left of the fulcrum and four weights on the fourth peg to the right, the child would compare $5 \times 3 = 15$ to $4 \times 4 = 16$, decide that 15 is less than 16, and predict that the right side of the balance scale would descend.

Siegler (1976) employed six kinds of balance-scale problems to infer from subjects' responses which rules they were using:

1. Balance problems, with the same configuration of weights on pegs on each side of the fulcrum.

2. Weight problems, with unequal amounts of weight equidistant from the fulcrum.

3. Distance problems, with equal amounts of weight different distances from the fulcrum.

4. Conflict-weight problems, with more weight on one side and more "distance" (i.e., occupied pegs farther from the fulcrum) on the other, and the configuration arranged so that the side with more weight goes down.

5. Conflict-distance problems, similar to conflict-weight except that the side with greater distance goes down.

6. Conflict-balance problems, like other conflict problems, except that the scale remains balanced.

Use of each rule predicts a certain level of responding on each of these kinds of problems. The critical fact for inferring subjects' rules is that the predicted pattern of responses for the six kinds of problems is different for each rule. Consider each rule and the

Problem Type	Rule				Comment
	I	II	III	IV	
Balance	100%	100%	100%	100%	
Weight	100	100	100	100	
Distance	0	100	100	100	Rule I predicts balance.
Conflict weight	100	100	33	100	Rule III performance at chance.
Conflict distance	0	0	33	100	Rules I and II fail to take into account greater effect of distance than weight; Rule III performance at chance.
Conflict balance	0	0	33	100	Same comments as conflict distance.

predicted level of performance on each kind of problem as shown in the table.

Using the paradigm described, Siegler (1976) found that the rule models successfully characterized the performance of 89% of the 120 children he studied—5-, 9-, 13-, and 17-year-olds in a girls' private school in Pittsburgh. Children's verbal descriptions of how they solved the problems accorded well with the proposed rules. Data analyses revealed that of those classifiable as using one of the rules, all of the 5-year-olds used Rule I; 9-year-olds were split among Rules I, II, and III (with 2, 3, and 4 cases using each respective rule); 13-year-olds were also split among these rules, but with more subjects using more advanced rules (1 using Rule I, 2 using Rule II, and 7 using Rule III); and 17-year-olds were split among Rules II, III, and IV (with 2, 6, and 2 cases of each rule respectively). Siegler's rule-based assessment procedure, thus, revealed a sensible pattern of cognitive development in solution of the balance-scale problem. Almost identical rules have been applied to, and tested for, other problem-solving tasks, with similar results, which suggests that the rules and the procedures for assessing them are generalizable across tasks and subjects (see Siegler, 1978, 1981).

Klahr's approach to problem solving emphasizes a production-system formalism rather than a rule-based formalism, although the two formalisms are highly related and, indeed, Siegler and Klahr have collaborated in some of their analyses of problem solving in children (see Klahr & Siegler, 1978). As an example of Klahr's research, we will discuss Klahr's (1978) analysis of the Tower of Hanoi problem.

The standard version of the Tower of Hanoi problem consists of a series of three pegs and a set of n disks of decreasing size. The disks are initially placed on one of the three pegs. The subject's goal is to move the entire n-disk configuration from that peg to another one. There are two constraints to this movement however: (1) that only one disk can be moved at a time and (2) that at no time can a larger disk be placed atop a smaller one. In the initial configuration, in fact, disks are placed in order of increasing size from top to bottom.

Klahr presented this problem with $n = 3$ to children ranging in age from 3 to 6 years, with three minor modifications that made the problem suitable for the youngsters. First, Klahr used cans instead of pegs. The cans had to be stacked with larger ones in inverted form atop smaller ones. The larger cans fit snugly into the smaller ones so that part of each smaller can showed. If the child inverted the order, placing a smaller can atop a larger one, the smaller can simply fell off and, so, the child was cued in to the fact that he or she had made a mistake. Second, there were two sets of three cans, one for the experimenter and one for the child. The child's cans showed the final configuration and the experimenter's cans showed the initial one. The child had to show the experimenter, who was described as a copycat, how to attain the final configuration represented by the child's cans. Third, the problem was presented with a cover story in which the cans were monkeys who wanted to jump from tree to tree.

Klahr (1978) describes an idealized model for solution of this task, taken from Simon (1975). The model, which Simon called a "sophisticated perceptual strategy," consists of seven steps (Klahr, 1978, p. 187):

1. Compare the current state to the goal state and note all items that are not in their final location.
2. Find the most constrained item (in our

case, the smallest can; in the standard form of the problem, the largest disk) that is not yet on its goal peg.

3. Establish the goal of moving that item to its goal peg.

4. Determine the smallest can (if any) that is preventing you from making the desired move.

5. If there is no such can (no culprit), then make the desired move and start all over again (go to step 1).

6. If you can't make the move, then *replace* the current goal with a goal of moving the culprit from its current location to a peg other than the two involved in your current goal.

7. Then return to step 4.

Klahr did not represent this particular routine as a production system in his research report because he felt the simplicity of the task did not merit the complexity of a production system for the level of analysis he intended. He did represent the routine as a computer program however. To give a feel for the kind of notation Klahr uses in his research, the steps in this program are reproduced here (Klahr, 1978, p. 188):

SOLVE (C,G)   C = Current state;
                               G = goal state

S1:   Find differences between C and G. If none, then done.
S2:   n ⟨-(Select smallest can).
S3:   New goal ⟨-(Move can n from X to Y) ⟨X = current peg of n, Y = goal peg of n⟩.
S4:   culprit ⟨-TEST (new.goal)
S5:   If culprit = nil, then MOVE (nXY); go to S1.
S6:   else new.goal (Move culprit from X′ to Y′); go to S4.
      ⟨X′ = current peg of culprit,
      Y′ = other of (X,Y)⟩

TEST (nXY)
T1:   f.list ⟨-See.from (X) ⟨all cans above n on X⟩
T2:   t.list ⟨-See.to (Y) ⟨all cans on Y larger than n⟩
T3:   if f.list = nil & t.list = nil, then culprit ⟨-nil
T4:   else culprit ⟨-min (f.list,t.list); exit

We will not draw further on this computer-program description however.

This model, which Klahr refers to as the SOLVE model, is a very powerful one, in that it will generate the solution having the minimum number of moves

for any *n*-disk problem. There are also alternative strategies of equal power, but Klahr believes them much less likely to be used in human performance. Klahr's greatest interest as a developmental psychologist is in the partial strategies subjects of different ages may use that approach the SOLVE model in terms of the power with which they can be used in finding a solution. Klahr presents three partial strategies in computer-program form: SOLVE.2, SOLVE.4, and SOLVE.5. We will summarize their main features here in verbal terms.

SOLVE.2, the most elementary of the partial strategies Klahr considers, will solve all problems correctly so long as they do not require more than two moves. It will fail on most problems of greater complexity. In its second step, this strategy determines which of the differences involves the smallest can. It then establishes as a goal the movement of that can directly to its goal peg. Having set that goal, the strategy calls for the making of that move without any further perceptual testing or comparison. The difficulty with this strategy is that it calls for an immediate attempt to move to the goal peg the smallest can that is not yet on that peg. But in most problems, such an attempt is illegal, because the smallest can is not at the top of the initial stack. Thus, the SOLVE. 2 strategy differs from the SOLVE strategy in that (1) it does not test the feasibility (i.e., legality) of the move it wants to make; (2) the only goal it sets always includes the ultimate goal peg rather than any temporary, internally generated subgoal peg; and (3) it never determines the smaller of two obstructors (Klahr, 1978).

SOLVE.4, a strategy of intermediate complexity, will solve all problems up to five-move problems correctly. It is similar to SOLVE, with two important exceptions. First, when a culprit is detected, this strategy does not call for the establishment of a new goal and then a return to what is labeled step 4 in the seven-step strategy described earlier. Instead, it calls for immediate movement of the culprit. Second, the strategy does not have the concept of other (see step 6 in the seven-step strategy). The target peg for the culprit is simply an empty peg. There are also minor differences between this strategy and SOLVE that we will not go into here.

SOLVE.5, a strategy of greater but still intermediate complexity, will also solve all problems up to five-move problems correctly and then will begin to make moves that are not on the shortest solution path. Unlike SOLVE.4, SOLVE.5 has the concept of other when determining where to move the culprit, but like SOLVE.4, it makes the move directly rather than generating a new goal.

Klahr (1978) tested 10 children, each of ages 3, 4, and 5, in their ability to solve the monkey version of the Tower of Hanoi problem. The experiment had several goals, but of major interest to us is the extent to which the models described above characterized children's performance. The children did seem to show signs of the developmental sequence suggested by the pattern of strategies described above, although Klahr, unlike Siegler, did not provide formal tests of the extent to which performance of children of each age was characterized by each of the alternative models.

To summarize, research on the development of problem solving has taken two primary courses, one based on an analysis of the rules children use in solving problems, the other based on an analysis of problem solving in production-system terminology. As we find so often to be the case, the two approaches are compatible, in that rules can easily be expressed in the production-system formalism. What is unclear is whether to do so genuinely increases the psychological validity of the problem-solving model. At present, the various formalisms seem more distinguishable on the basis of their heuristic value than on the basis of their psychological validity. Indeed, we know of no tests that distinguish among alternative formalisms. Hence, we are reluctant to argue strongly in favor of one formalism or another. Instead, we are inclined to evaluate formalisms in terms of their heuristic value in expressing and providing a basis for testing particular theories. As described above, both these formalisms do seem to describe changes with age in children's problem-solving strategies.

Verbal Comprehension. Verbal comprehension refers to a person's ability to comprehend verbal materials, such as words, sentences, and paragraphs. At present, there are many different streams of research that can be loosely classified as dealing with verbal comprehension. In particular, the literature on children's reading is enormous. We could not begin to cover it here, nor will we try to do so in the course of the chapter. Instead, in the present review, we will limit ourselves to just two approaches to the question of what it is that leads some children—and later some adults—to have richer vocabularies than others. The two streams of research we will discuss are those of Keating and his colleagues (Keating & Bobbitt, 1978; Keating, Keniston, Manis, & Bobbitt, 1980), which derives from the approach of Hunt and his coworkers (Hunt, 1978; Hunt et al., 1975); and our own approach (Powell & Sternberg, 1981; Sternberg, Powell, &

Kaye, in press), which derives from the approach of Werner and Kaplan (1952). These two approaches view the antecedents of verbal comprehension ability in quite different ways, although they are potentially complementary, since the two may be viewed as dealing with different aspects of verbal-comprehension ability.

According to Hunt (1978), two types of processes underlie verbal ability—knowledge-based processes, which are the kind we emphasize in our analyses of verbal ability, and mechanistic, or information-free processes, which are the kind Hunt and Keating emphasize. In particular, Hunt et al. (1975) studied three aspects of what they called current information processing that they believed to be key determinants in individual differences in developed verbal ability. These were:

(a) the sensitivity of overlearned codes to arousal by incoming stimulus information, (b) the accuracy with which temporal tags can be assigned, and hence order information can be processed, and (c) the speed with which the internal representations in STM and intermediate term memory (ITM, memory for events occurring over minutes) can be created, integrated, and altered. (Hunt et al., 1975, p. 197)

The basic hypothesis motivating their work is that intelligence tests indirectly measure these information processing skills by directly measuring the products of these skills. For example, higher vocabulary as measured by a vocabulary test can be interpreted as deriving from increased information processing skills that earlier in life enabled acquisition of this vocabulary; reduced vocabulary reflects lesser information processing skills that earlier in life enabled acquisition of only a more limited vocabulary.

Keating and Bobbitt (1978) took tasks studied by Hunt et al. (1973) and Hunt et al. (1975) and studied them in the context of a developmental paradigm. Their self-stated major goal was to "discover whether reliable individual differences in cognitive processing exist in children and, if so, whether these differences are systematically related to age and ability" (Keating & Bobbitt, 1978, p. 157). Like Hunt and his colleagues, their primary interest was in individual differences in the component processes of information processing activities rather than in global response times or error rates reflecting a conglomeration of processes.

The subjects in Keating and Bobbitt's experiments were 20 subjects in each of grades 3 (average

age, 9), 7 (average age, 13), and 11 (average age, 17). Half of the subjects at each age level were characterized as being of high mental ability (scores in roughly the 90th to 95th percentile of the Raven Progressive Matrices), and half were characterized as being of average mental ability (scores in roughly the 40th to 45th percentile of the Raven Progressive Matrices).

The authors were interested in children's performance on three basic sets of information processing tasks. The first set included simple reaction-time and choice reaction-time tasks. In the simple reaction-time task, subjects were instructed to press a button as soon as a red light appeared; in the choice reaction-time task, subjects were instructed to press a green button whenever a green light appeared or a red button whenever a red light appeared. Subjects did not know, of course, which color of light would appear on a given trial. The second set of tasks involved retrieval and comparison of information in memory. This set included two letter-matching tasks, a physical-match task, and a name-match task, based upon the tasks adopted by Hunt et al. (1975) from Posner, Boies, Eichelman, and Taylor (1969). In the physical-match task, subjects were asked to sort cards that had pairs of letters printed on them that either were or were not physical matches. Examples of the former would be "AA" and "bb"; examples of the latter would be "Aa" and "Ba." In the name-match task, subjects were presented with cards to sort that had pairs of letters printed on them that either were or were not name matches. Examples of the former would be "Aa," "BB," and "bB"; examples of the latter would be "Ab," "ba," and "bA." In the first task, the subject had to sort the cards by the physical appearance of the stimuli; in the second task, the subject had to sort by the names of the stimuli. The third set of tasks involved scanning sets of either one, three, or five digits held in working memory. In this task, which Hunt et al. (1973) adopted from the varied-set procedure of S. Sternberg (1969b), subjects are asked to store the short list of items in memory. This list, thus, becomes a memory set. Subjects are then presented with a target item and are asked to indicate as quickly as possible whether the target is one of the items in the memory set. For example, if the memory set were "3, 9, 6," an affirmative response would be required for "9," but a negative response would be required for "2."

The results of the experiments on the three sets of tasks generally confirmed Keating and Bobbitt's (1978) hypothesis of developmental differences. In the simple reaction-time and choice reaction-time

tasks, the investigators found significant main effects of age, ability level, and task (simple or choice reaction time). In each case, means were in the expected direction, with older and brighter children performing the tasks more rapidly and with simple reaction time faster than choice reaction time. Of somewhat greater interest was a significant age-by-task interaction whereby the difference between choice reaction time and simple reaction time was greater for younger children than for older children. The ability level by task interaction was nonsignificant, but in the expected direction, with lesser ability children showing a greater increment in choice relative to simple reaction time than was shown by higher ability children. Thus, increased task complexity affected the response times of less able (at least as measured by age and possibly as measured by Raven score) children more than it affected the response times of more able children.

In the letter-retrieval and comparison task, there were significant main effects of age, ability, and task (physical or name match). Again, the results were as expected: older and brighter children were faster in card sorting, and the name-match condition took longer than the physical-match condition. Again, there were significant age-by-task and ability-by-task interactions, with older and brighter children less differentially affected by the added demands of the name-match task than were younger and duller children.

In the memory-scanning task, significant main effects were found for age, ability level, and set size, with all effects in the expected directions. There was also a significant interaction between set size and ability, with lesser ability children showing a greater effect of set size than was shown by higher ability children. To understand better this interaction and the main effects as well, subjects' performance on this task was decomposed into two parameters, a slope and an intercept. The former parameter estimated the duration of the comparison process hypothesized to be performed between the target item and each member of the memory set; the latter parameter estimated the duration of all processes that were constant in duration across set sizes, such as target encoding time and time to respond. The linear model used to estimate these parameters accounted for over 98% of the variance in the latency data and, hence, could be expected to yield meaningful parameter estimates. The authors found in the analysis of slopes that only the main effect of ability was significant, although the age by ability interaction approached significance. In contrast, the intercept was only marginally related to ability level, but strongly related to age. The reason for this particular pattern of findings was not clear.

In an effort to put together the results of the various experiments, correlations were computed between component processes from different tasks. These processes were hypothesized either to be highly related psychologically (e.g., intercept from the memory-scanning task and choice reaction time) or to be only poorly related (e.g., intercept from the memory-scanning task and difference between name and physical match times). In general, the parameters hypothesized to be highly related showed higher intercorrelations (median = .72) than did the parameters hypothesized to be only poorly related (median = .28). An attempt was also made to predict Raven Progressive Matrix scores from three hypothesized components of information processing—choice reaction time minus simple reaction time, name minus physical match time, and memory-scanning slope. These three parameters accounted for 62% of the variance in the Raven Progressive Matrix scores across all ages combined. Age alone accounted for 47% of the variance, however, leaving 15% explained by the central-processing variables.

Keating et al. (1980) followed up on this work by isolating slope and intercept parameters from both a memory- and a visual-scanning task. The visual-scanning task is like the memory-scanning task described earlier, except with the presentation order of the target item and the set of items reversed, that is, in this task, the single item is presented first and the subject must then visually scan a set of items to determine whether the target is in that set. This research attempted to do for children what Chiang and Atkinson (1976) had previously done for adults—they had found the corresponding parameters across tasks to be highly correlated (slopes with slopes, intercepts with intercepts), but the noncorresponding parameters to be only modestly correlated (slopes with intercepts). Keating et al. found that the intercepts were highly correlated across tasks but that the correlations between slopes were no higher than the correlations between slopes and intercepts. The evidence, thus, does not support the notion that the comparison process in children is the same for visual as for memory scanning. Further delineation of the developmental changes that occur in these comparison processes needs yet to be done.

As forebears of the second stream of research to be discussed, Werner and Kaplan (1952) proposed:

The child acquires the meaning of words principally in two ways. One is by explicit reference either verbal or objective; he learns to understand verbal symbols through the adult's direct naming of objects or through verbal definition. The second way is through implicit or contextual reference; the meaning of a word is grasped in the course of conversation, i.e., it is inferred from the cues of the verbal context. (p. 3)

Werner and Kaplan were interested especially in the second method of word-meaning acquisition, acquisition from context. They devised a task in which subjects were presented with an imaginary word followed by six sentences using that word. The subjects' task was to guess the meaning of the word on the basis of the contextual cues they were given. One example (from the 12 such imaginary words they used) is "contavish," which they intended to mean "hole." They did not, of course, tell the children in their study the meaning of the word but rather presented them with these six sentences (Werner & Kaplan, 1952, p. 4):

1. You can't fill anything with a contavish.
2. The more you take out of a contavish the larger it gets.
3. Before the house is finished the walls must have contavishes.
4. You can't feel or touch a contavish.
5. A bottle has only one contavish.
6. John fell into a contavish in the road.

Children ranging in age from 8 to 13 years were tested in their ability to acquire new words presented in this way. Developmental patterns were analyzed by a number of different means. Werner and Kaplan found that (1) performance improves gradually with age, although the various processes that underlie performance do not necessarily change gradually—some change gradually, but others change abruptly; (2) there is an early and abrupt decline in signs of immaturity that relate to inadequate orientation toward the task itself; (3) the processes of signification for words undergo a rather decisive shift between approximately 10 and 11 years of age; and (4) language behavior shows different organizations at different ages.

Van Daalen-Kapteijns and Elshout-Mohr (1981) have recently revived the work of Werner and Kaplan (1952). By using a task very similar to theirs but collecting thinking-aloud protocols as well, they have obtained congruent findings to the Werner and Kaplan studies. These researchers found differences in the way high- and low-verbal subjects use a known word's meaning as a model for an unknown word and in the way subjects transform the sentence contexts to apply the contexts to the word. As compared to low-verbal subjects, high-verbals tended to be more analytic in their processing—more able to pick and choose between elements of familiar concepts used as approximate models for the unknown word and more able to combine these selected elements into a coherent whole. Low-verbal subjects, on the other hand, were more holistic in their processing—less able to separate out only specific elements from the familiar concepts and less likely to combine these disparate elements into a new whole.

Our own approach (Powell & Sternberg, 1981; see also Sternberg, Powell, & Kaye, 1981) to the acquisition of word meanings is loosely based on that of Werner and Kaplan (1952) and uses a task similar to one used by Heim (1970) for psychometric assessment of intellectual performance. To understand the theory underlying the research, it helps first to know something about our task.

All subjects in our study (high school students) received a set of 33 brief reading passages such as might be found in newspapers, magazines, novels, or textbooks. Embedded within these passages were from one to four very low-frequency words, which could be repeated from zero to three times either within or between passages, but not both. An example of such a passage is:

> Two ill-dressed people—the one a tired woman of middle years and the other a tense young man—sat around a fire where the common meal was almost ready. The mother, Tanith, peered at her son through the <u>oam</u> of the bubbling stew. It had been a long time since his last <u>ceilidh</u> and Tobar had changed greatly; where once he had seemed all legs and clumsy joints, he now was well-formed and in control of his hard, young body. As they ate, Tobar told of his past year, re-creating for Tanith how he had wandered long and far in his quest to gain the skills he would need to be permitted to rejoin the company. Then all too soon, their brief <u>ceilidh</u> over, Tobar walk-ed over to touch his mother's arm and quickly left.

Subjects were divided into two experimental and two control groups. In the first experimental group, subjects were asked to provide ratings regarding the low-frequency words and their surrounding contexts. These ratings (described below) concerned various aspects of the passage that were hypothesized to affect the subjects' ability to learn the meanings of the new words. When a given word

occurred more than once in a given passage, subjects were asked also to provide separate ratings for each token occurrence. In the second experimental group, subjects were asked to state the main idea of the passage and to define as best they could each of the underlined (low-frequency) words. When a single word appeared twice in a passage, subjects only needed to define the word once, but if a given word appeared again in a later passage, subjects had to redefine the word later on. Subjects were allowed to view the passage they had just read at the time they defined the word, but they were not allowed to look back at previous passages. Subjects in the first control group were asked to read each of the passages and to choose the best title from four possible titles given for each. Thus, subjects in this group were exposed to the same passages as the experimental subjects, but their attention was directed to more global comprehension of the passages and not to the low-frequency words per se. Finally, subjects in the second control group never saw the passages at all. All subjects received a pretest and a retest that contained passages very much like those in the main part of the study.

We proposed two types of variables, a set of contextual cues and a set of mediating variables, that interact to account for the acquisition, retention, and transfer of the meanings of unfamiliar vocabulary presented in context. The set of contextual cues specifies the particular kinds of context cues that individuals can use to figure out the meanings of new words from their surrounding contexts. The mediating variables specify those constraints imposed by the relationship between the previously unknown word and the context in which the word occurs that affect, for better or worse, how well a given set of clues will be utilized in a particular task and situation.

For our contextual cues, we identified eight categories of context clues that represented the various types of information that possibly could be gleaned about a word from a passage. (Alternative and related classification schemes have been proposed in the past by, among others, Ames, 1966; McCullough, 1958; and Miller & Johnson-Laird, 1976.) Briefly, the eight contextual cue categories used for our modeling were: temporal clues, spatial clues, value clues, clues describing static properties, functional descriptive clues, causal/enablement clues, class-membership clues, and equivalence clues.

The mediating variables, proposed to affect the application of the contextual cues, were derived from the ratings provided by our first group of experimental subjects and included number of occurrences of the unknown word, variability of contexts in which the multiple occurrences of the unknown word appears, importance of the unknown word to understanding the context in which it is embedded, the helpfulness of the surrounding context to understanding the meaning of the unknown word, the location of the helpful context part, density of unknown words, concreteness of the unknown word and of its surrounding context, and, finally, usefulness of previously known information in cue utilization.

The idea in this research is to model quality of definitions of words presented in context on the basis of our proposed contextual cues and mediating variables. Obviously, these do not constitute a complete list of variables that affect learning, but they seem to serve as a beginning. Acquisition components are based on modeling of quality of definitions of words presented for the first time. Transfer components are based on modeling of improvement in quality of definitions of words from earlier presentations of the words to later presentations. Retention components are based upon modeling of performance in a final definitions test presented outside the context of reading passages. In each case, the independent variables (as listed above) are the same; only the context of the modeling changes. Although we have not yet completed analyses for the retention and transfer components, by using our combined contextual cues and mediating variables, we were able to predict acquisition of word meaning from context. The correlation between predicted and observed definition goodness ratings were .92 for literary passages, .74 for newspaper passages, .85 for science passages, and .77 for history passages—all statistically significant. Also, our task does appear to measure antecedents of verbal comprehension ability—correlations of scores on our learning-from-context task with scores on standardized tests of verbal ability were generally in the .50s and .60s.

To summarize, there have been two major approaches to the investigation of the development of verbal comprehension. The first looks at development in mechanistic processes, such as speed of lexical access, and particularly investigates changes in process latency with increasing age. The second approach looks at the development of children's abilities to learn meanings of words presented in natural contexts. The two approaches seem to address different aspects of verbal comprehension and, hence, are not directly comparable. Correlations of scores obtained from the latter approach with psychometrically measured verbal ability tend to be considerably higher than correlations obtained from the former approach, suggesting the possibility that the learning-from-context approach may tap abilities closer to what we usually mean by verbal comprehension than do the very simple name-comparison and similar tasks used by Hunt, Keating, and others. However, the mechanistic-process approach is useful in terms of specifying some low-level information processing abilities involved in individual differences in verbal ability.

Number Ability. Number ability can mean a number of different things: rapidity and accuracy of arithmetical calculations, ability to solve word problems, and understanding of numerical or mathematical concepts, among other things. We will discuss here two approaches to number ability. One, primarily associated with Rochel Gelman, involves development of counting principles in very young children. The other, associated with a number of investigators, including Herbert Ginsburg, Guy J. Groen, and Lauren B. Resnick, concerns the processes whereby children solve simple arithmetic problems.

Gelman and Gallistel (1978) have proposed five principles that they believe underlie children's ability to count, particularly children's understanding of how to count and of what to count. Their first three principles deal with the *how* of counting; the fourth principle deals with the *what* of counting; the last principle involves a composite of features of the other four principles.

1. *The one-one principle.* A distinct tag must be assigned to each object in an array and only one tag may be assigned to each object. The authors emphasize that these tags need not be conventional numerals. They take as evidence of mastery of the principle in particular, and of counting in general, the assignment by young children of letters of the alphabet to successive objects. Satisfaction of the principle does not even require that the letters or numbers be assigned in conventional order as long as the assignment of tags to objects is unique. Implementation of this principle requires coordination of two processes: partitioning and tagging. Partitioning is the process whereby two categories of items are maintained—those that have been counted and those that have yet to be counted; items must be transferred one at a time from the first partition to the second. Tagging is the process whereby a distinct tag is retrieved from memory and assigned to each item.

2. *The stable-order principle.* The tags must be arranged in a stable (repeatable) order and the number of tags must be as large as the number of objects in the array.

3. *The cardinality principle*. The tag applied to the final object in an array must represent the number of objects in that array. This principle involves recognition of a special property of the last tag used, namely, that this tag represents the cardinality of the array of objects.

4. *The abstraction principle*. The preceding principles can be applied to any array or collection of entities, whether physical or nonphysical. The importance of this principle lies in the inability of very young children to recognize that nonphysical entities, such as the number of minds in a room, can be counted in the same way that physical entities can be counted. As the authors point out, very young children often do not recognize the possibility of counting together members of ludicrous sets, such as the set of all minds and all chairs in a room.

5. *The order-irrelevance principle*. The order in which objects in an array are tagged is irrelevant to the number of objects in that array.

These principles are not proposed as unitary processes or components of performance. Instead, acquisition and utilization of each principle is alleged to consist of several component processes, for example, partitioning of items into already-counted and to-be-counted sets and tagging of the items in accordance with the one-one principle. Moreover, application of principles can be partial. For example, children's ability to apply the first three, how-to-count principles, is a function of set size. The authors conclude that many 2- and 3-year-olds cannot count reliably beyond 3 or 4, but nevertheless, the children show some differentiation among higher quantities in making absolute judgments about them. Finally, abilities to apply the various principles are not fully independent. Application of the cardinality principle, for example, presupposes successful application of the one-one and stable-order principles.

The general stance of Gelman and Gallistel (1978) is that the cognitive capacities in general, and the numerical capacities in particular, of very young children have been underestimated. They set out to show what these young children can do, rather than what they cannot do. Indeed, the authors show convincingly that 3-year-olds and even some 2-year-olds have rudimentary counting abilities that they can use in simple counting tasks. The reader is referred to Gelman and Gallistel's (1978) book for lucid descriptions of the studies that have led to these findings.

In the second approach to number ability that we will consider, subjects have generally been older—at least of elementary-school age and in some of the early studies, adults. This approach emphasizes people's construction of inventive strategies for solving arithmetic problems:

> People acquire most new mathematical knowledge by constructing for themselves new organizations of concepts and new procedures for performing mathematical operations. I call this process *invention* because something new is constructed from the material already available. People also, of course, acquire from outside certain new facts and information about mathematics operation or conventions of representation. However, I assume that these externally-given pieces of information take on significance—indeed are retained—only to the degree that they are incorporated by the learner into organized and interconnected systems of knowledge. (Resnick, 1980, pp. 2–3)

Note that Resnick's perspective on arithmetic differs greatly from the conventional wisdom, according to which the algorithm by which people solve simple arithmetic problems, such as $2 + 3 = ?$, is simply a matter of retrieving from memory a fact memorized during one's school days.

Consider as an example, then, how children perform simple additions, such as $2 + 3 = ?$. Three information processing models of addition have been proposed (Groen & Parkman, 1972; Suppes & Groen, 1967; see also Resnick, 1980), representing alternative "intelligent" strategies for doing arithmetic. The models have in common the stipulation of a mental counter that is initialized at some value and then incremented as needed. The counter is initially set at some value, a. The individual then enters an incrementing loop. Before each increment (i.e., addition of one unit), a test is made to determine whether the needed number of increments has been made. If it has been, the incremental process stops; if it has not been, the number of increments already made (say, x) is increased by yet one more.

In the first model we will consider (using as an example the simple addition problem, $2 + 3 = ?$), the counter is initialized at 0, then incremented two times (corresponding to the value of the first addend), and then incremented three more times (corresponding to the value of the second addend). The final value of the counter is thus 5. This reasonable way of solving addition problems is fairly similar to what children are taught in school (Resnick, 1980).

In the second model, which would seem on its face to be more efficient than the first, the counter is initially set at the value of the first number in the equation, in our case, 2. The counter is then incremented the number of times required by the second addend, in our case, 3. Again, the obtained sum is 5.

In the third model, which would seem to be the most efficient of the three models, the counter is initialized at the value of the greater of the two addends. It is then incremented a number of times equal to the lesser of the two addends. Hence, in our example, the counter is initialized at 3 and incremented by 2. Again, a sum of 5 is reached. This model minimizes the number of increments needed to solve the problem.

Note that these three models make different predictions regarding patterns of response latencies for various arithmetic problems. In the first model, the slope of the latency function for solving addition problems is a function of the sum of the two numbers; in the second model, the slope is a function of the second of the two numbers; and in the third model, the slope is a function of the smaller of the two numbers. Hence, it is possible to distinguish the predictions of the models empirically and to test what children actually do when confronted with simple additions.

Groen and Parkman (1972) found that the data of virtually all of the first grade children they studied conformed to the predictions of the third and most efficient model they proposed. Thus, even very young children were solving addition problems in a highly efficient way, with differences in their rate of solution for different problems a function only of the smaller of the two addends. There was one notable set of exceptions to this rule, namely, problems in which both addends were equal, for example, 3 + 3 = ?. These problems were all solved very quickly, perhaps because the answers to these problems are stored in a highly accessible form in long-term memory and can, thus, be read off directly.

Similar research has been performed for subtraction by Woods, Resnick, and Groen (1975), who compared second and fourth graders. These investigators studied three alternative models of how subjects might perform simple subtractions, such as 7 − 2 = ?. In the first model, a counter is set initially to the larger of the two numbers, and a decremental counter counts down the number of units indicated by the subtrahend (in this case, 2). In the second model, a counter is set initially to the lower of the two numbers and an incremental counter counts up to the value of the higher number (in this case, 7). Which model would be more efficient would depend upon the relative sizes of the two terms in the subtraction. This fact suggests a third possible model in which subjects use whichever of the first two models is most efficient in a given situation. For example, 8 − 3 = ? would be solved using the decrementing (first) model, whereas 8 − 5 = ? would be solved using the incrementing (second) model. The first model comes closest to what we are presumably taught in school, but it does not come closest to what most children in fact do. The investigators found that one fifth of the second graders used the first model and the remainder used the third. All of the fourth graders used the third model. Thus, again, children seem to have invented highly efficient strategies for dealing with simple arithmetic problems, strategies they almost certainly were not taught in school.

To summarize, two main approaches to the development of number ability (but by no means the only approaches) have looked at the development of rules for counting and the development of algorithms for arithmetical computation. It appears that it is possible to model computation processes in much the same way cognitive psychologists have modeled reasoning and problem-solving processes, despite the subjective feeling that arithmetic facts are simply recalled from memory. One thing that seems to be missing is a link between the development of counting abilities, on the one hand, and the later development of computational abilities, on the other hand. Given the prominence of counting in the computational models, it would seem that there must be some link between the two streams of research, but at the present, it is not at all clear what form this link would take.

Spatial Visualization. Spatial visualization can refer to imagery ability, ability to orient oneself in one's spatial surround, or ability to manipulate in one's head mental representations of objects of various kinds. It is the third ability that is measured by many standard tests of intelligence; therefore, we will limit our discussion here to that particular aspect of spatial ability.

Although a fairly large number of studies have been performed of adults' abilities to rotate mental representations of objects (e.g., Cooper, 1973; Cooper & Shepard, 1973; Shepard & Metzler, 1971), the number of studies with children has been limited. In fact, we were able to locate only a handful (Huttenlocher & Presson, 1973; Kail, Pellegrino, & Carter, 1980; Marmor, 1975, 1977) that took an information processing approach to the problem. We will summarize here the Kail et al. (1980) study, which is the one closest in its conceptualization to the studies that have been done with adults in studying performance on intelligence-test types of problems.

In the Kail et al. (1980) study, subjects in grades 3, 4, 6, and college judged whether pairs of stimuli were identical to each other or mirror-image reversals of each other. One stimulus in each pair was presented in an upright position; the other was rotated either 0°, 30°, 60°, 90°, 120°, or 150° from the standard. The pairs comprising each stimulus item were either alphanumeric symbols (4, 5, *F, G, J, L, P, R*) or unfamiliar, letterlike characters of the sort found on the Science Research Associates' (SRA's) Primary Mental Abilities spatial visualization test. The authors were interested in response latencies as a function of stimulus type, degree of angular rotation, and age of subjects. The main results were that (1) speed of mental rotation increased with age, (2) unfamiliar characters were rotated more slowly than were the familiar alphanumeric characters, and (3) unfamiliar characters were encoded and compared more slowly than were alphanumeric symbols by an amount that decreased with development.

These findings raised several interesting psychological questions about mental rotation in children and adults. A first question is that of why rate of mental rotation increases with increasing age. The authors suggested two possible and related explanations. The first was that younger children may rotate the entire stimulus, whereas older children rotate only part of it. The second explanation was that older children may rotate stimuli in a more analytic way so that each component is rotated separately. The data were insufficient to distinguish between these two explanations or between these two explanations and a third, which is simply that the older children do the same thing as the younger ones, except more speedily. A second question is that of why the unusual (primary mental abilities) characters were encoded and rotated more slowly than the more familiar alphanumeric ones. The authors suggested that the difference might be due to the activation by the familiar characters of an already existing, easily accessible pattern in memory, in contrast to the need for the subjects to form a new pattern corresponding to each of the unfamiliar stimuli. This study, although obviously forming only the beginning of an investigation of spatial ability in children, seems to suggest a useful direction in which future studies might proceed.

Memory.   The literature on memory and its relationships to intellectual functioning is without question the largest of the seven information processing literatures we have considered. Because it is also the topic of a chapter in this work (*Brown, Bransford, Ferrara, & Campione, vol. III, chap. 2*) and of several books (Kail, 1979; Perlmutter, 1980),

we will limit ourselves to referring readers to these sources, to two recent volumes that contain excellent reviews of recent research on memory (Kail & Hagen, 1977; Siegler, 1978), and to discussing briefly one line of research that we see as particularly promising for the investigation of the interface between memory and intelligence.

This line of research is that which deals with cognitive or comprehension monitoring. The line of research has evolved from research on metamemory and metacognition, although it might as easily have evolved from research on verbal comprehension. In large measure, it represents a cross-fertilization between these two areas. Investigators pursuing this line of research include Ann L. Brown, John H. Flavell, Ellen M. Markman, and Scott G. Paris. A recent review that deals with this literature and the general metamemory literature as well has been written by Cavanaugh and Perlmutter (1982). Our own assessment of the literature is more favorable than that of Cavanaugh and Perlmutter, particularly with regard to the work on monitoring.

A. L. Brown (1978; see also Brown & De-Loache, 1978) has characterized cognitive monitoring as consisting of several related skills. One is ''the realization that there is a problem of knowing what you know and what you do not know'' (Brown, 1978, p. 82; see also Brown, 1975). Brown quotes from John Holt's (1964) *How Children Fail,* and we repeat that quotation here because it so well describes the issues involved:

> Part of being a good student is learning to be aware of one's own mind and the degree of one's own understanding. The good student may be one who often says that he does not understand, simply because he keeps a constant check on his understanding. The poor student who does not, so to speak, watch himself trying to understand, does not know most of the time whether he understands or not. Thus the problem is not to get students to ask us what they don't know; the problem is to make them aware of the difference between what they know and what they don't. (Holt, 1964, pp. 28–29)

A second skill is prediction, which, in the meta-memory literature, refers to the ability to predict one's accuracy prior to an attempt to remember something. A third skill is planning, including one's own knowledge about the efficiency of the attempt to plan. Thus, there are some aspects of one's life for which one can reasonably plan (a 17-year-old deciding whether to apply to colleges), whereas there are other aspects of one's life one cannot reasonably plan for (an 8-year-old deciding whether or not to get married in later life). The fourth skill is checking and monitoring one's behavior, for example, determining whether a problem-solving strategy is leading toward a successful solution. These kinds of cognitive-monitoring skills are identical in character to what we have referred to as metacomponents, and, indeed, the notion of metacomponents draws heavily on the metacognitive notions of A. L. Brown, J. H. Flavell, and others.

In his earlier work on metacognition, Flavell (Flavell, 1976; Flavell & Wellman, 1977; see also Flavell, 1981) perceived metamemory as being of two basic types. One type, sensitivity, refers to a child's sense of when a particular situation calls for voluntary and intentional efforts at remembering. Thus, a more sophisticated individual will know when to call upon strategies for storage and retrieval of information, whereas a less sophisticated person might well not. The second type, variables, refers to knowledge of what variables in a given problem situation act and in what ways they act to affect one's memory performance. Flavell characterized the variables as being of three kinds. Person variables include all of the things one could learn about oneself and others as mnemonic beings. Flavell has given as examples your possible belief that you are better at remembering faces than names, that your spouse has a better memory for most things than you do, and that everybody's memory is fallible. Task variables include knowledge of what aspects of a task affect the difficulty level of a memory problem. For example, one might know that it is harder to remember larger bodies of information than smaller ones and that it is harder to remember material from poorly organized text than from well-organized text. Finally, strategy variables include knowledge of the various things one can do to improve one's recall. These include mnemonics, such as imagery, relating new knowledge to old knowledge, and looking for distinctive cues in what one has to memorize.

In more recent work, Flavell (1981) has proposed a model of cognitive monitoring that includes four basic components: cognitive goals, cognitive actions, metacognitive knowledge, and metacognitive experiences. Each of these components influences each of the others. Cognitive goals are the explicit or implicit objectives that instigate and maintain a cognitive enterprise. These goals vary from one enterprise to another and may actually change during the course of a single enterprise. Cognitive actions are actions undertaken to achieve the goals of an enterprise, for example, trying to understand the intended

meaning of what someone says. Metacognitive knowledge consists of long-term memory representations of knowledge about one's own cognitions. Finally, metacognitive experiences are conscious experiences (ideas, thoughts, feelings, etc.) related to any aspect of a given enterprise, for example, the feeling of knowing or of not understanding.

Markman (1981) has suggested some signals people can use to detect failure to comprehend verbal materials. These signals constitute part of what might be construed as means of effective comprehension monitoring. One signal is perceived absence of structure. If one finds it difficult or impossible to impose a structure on verbal materials, then this failure should serve as a signal that the information is not well understood. A second signal is multiple perceived structures. In the sentences "John and Bill went to the store. He bought some bread," at least two possible structures can be imposed, signaling the difficulty one has in understanding the message the writer intended to communicate. A third signal is the discovery of inconsistencies, which has been the topic of some of Markman's recent research (e.g., Markman, 1977, 1979). Inconsistencies may indicate misstructuring of information comprehended earlier so that the imposed structure does not work for information that is comprehended later. A fourth signal is inability to use structure to formulate expectations. Except in the case of highly novel material, if one cannot formulate plausible expectations about what is to come next on the basis of what has come already, this failure may indicate lack of comprehension of the text.

Markman (1981) has further proposed that there are two essential characteristics of understanding, the systematization of knowledge and the use of inferential or constructive processing. Systematization of knowledge, in particular, improves one's comprehension-monitoring abilities in three ways. First, it enables one to integrate separate items into higher order structures. Second, it permits the generation of detailed, tightly organized knowledge structures that generate plausible expectations. Finally, it enables one to gain explicit knowledge about the cognitive structures one has formed and about the principles that organize this knowledge.

Paris (1978) has proposed a system for organizing metamemorial information that differs in at least some respects from those considered above. He has hypothesized that there are three major components of metacogniton. The first, content variables, are similar in their conceptualization to Flavell's (1981) content variables. Included in this component are person, task, strategy, and context variables that influence one's ability to recall information. The second, evaluation procedures, or executive processes, are similar in their conceptualization to Brown's (1978) metacognitive activities. These include predicting task difficulty, generating and inventing memory strategies, planning when to use strategies, selecting the most appropriate strategies, monitoring and checking ongoing activity, testing and evaluating strategies, changing strategies if necessary, and sequencing strategies. The third component, modulating factors, include sensitivity to, and coordination of, information and cultural milieu.

To conclude, these four systems for organizing aspects of metacognitive knowledge and action seem a promising step toward integrating what have previously been rather separate research domains, memory and problem solving (see Brown & DeLoache, 1978). Although we agree with critics of metamemory research (such as Cavanaugh and Perlmutter, 1982) that there has been a great deal of vagueness and failure to relate metacognitive variables to interesting cognitive ones, we believe that these systems are at least on the right track and are likely to yield productive research in the future.

Conclusions

Looked at from an information processing point of view, there are a number of different loci of intellectual development. We list here what we believe to be some of the most important ones.

1. *Knowledge base.* Obviously, the knowledge base upon which one operates increases in extent with age. The knowledge base includes knowledge about the external world as well as knowledge about one's internal cognitions. Metacognitive theorists, in particular, have claimed that the latter kind of knowledge plays a major role in one's ability to acquire the former kind of knowledge. Although the evidence in support of this claim is still weak, we view metacognitive knowledge as of interest in its own right, without regard to whether or not it interacts strongly with knowledge of the world.

To understand how the knowledge base increases in extent, one has to understand the processes that operate on it. But the highly process-oriented approach to research during the early and mid-1970s sometimes failed to take into account the bidirectionality of spheres of influence. Processes need a knowledge base on which to operate, and the extent of the knowledge base in large part determines what processes can operate when, as well as how effectively they can operate. Sometimes the distinction between knowledge and process is not a clear one. In part, this is due to unfortunate semantic confusions. In the literature on metacognition, for example, the term metacognition has sometimes been used to refer to a kind of knowledge (knowledge about cognition) and other times to a kind of process (control processes, i.e., processes that control other processes). The understandable tendency to blame metacognitive theorists for this and other semantic confusions has sometimes obscured the more important issue, namely, the presumably close but poorly understood relation between knowledge and processes. This lack of understanding has often led to a tendency to attempt to study knowledge in isolation from process or vice versa. This tendency has been unfortunate because the close relationship between the two means that one cannot be fully understood without a full understanding of the other (see J. R. Anderson, 1976). Although we are quite a way off from full understanding, we believe it important to continue what we see as a present trend to study processes in knowledge-rich domains.

2. *Processes.* An important source of intellectual development resides in the new availability and increased accessibility of processes with increasing age. We saw, for example, in the domain of analogical reasoning that concrete-operational children seem to be at best poorly able to map second-order relations, and we saw in the domain of metacognition that young children seem to lack at least some of the metacomponents necessary for monitoring their comprehension. Further research is needed on the processes that are available at different ages.

The early and mid-1970s saw a perhaps necessary initial tendency to undertake task analyses that isolated processes involved in particular tasks but that did not attempt to relate these processes either to each other (within and across tasks) or to external referents. Now that we do have some knowledge of how to decompose performance on a fairly large class of tasks as well as of what the outcomes of these task analyses look like, we believe it important to begin to seek an understanding of interrelations of processes and relations of processes to other variables. In this way, we would hope it would become possible in our developmental research to start with cognitive theories that specify processes used in the solution of fairly large numbers of tasks rather than to start with tasks, specify the processes used in their solution, and then trace the development of what may in many cases be task-specific processes. We see a tendency in that direction, and our own research has definitely been moving that way (e.g., R. J. Sternberg, 1980a, 1981c). We hope this direction for research will continue.

3. *Memory.* Despite the enormous amount of research that has been done on memory development (see, e.g., Kail & Hagen, 1977), our understanding

of what exactly it is that develops in memory is still surprisingly meager. People still do not even agree as to whether memory capacity (expressed in terms of some kind of slot notion) increases with age. We believe memory capacity, or processing space (Osherson, 1974), does increase (see also Case, 1974a, 1974b, 1978), as does one's effective use of mnemonics to increase one's learning and memorial efficiency. The importance of studying memory development can be seen dramatically in the research we reviewed of Trabasso and his colleagues (e.g., Bryant & Trabasso, 1971), where what had seemed to be a process limitation of sorts in the ability of preoperational children to perform transitive inferences now appears more likely to be a memory limitation, which can in fact be overcome with appropriate training.

4. *Strategies.* Many of the tasks we have reviewed, for example, analogies and balance-scale problems, show changes in the strategies applied to them with increased intellectual development. Moreover, these strategy changes reflect increasingly intelligent ways of solving problems. Indeed, it is not the strategy change per se that is of interest, but what it tells us about the developing mind. For example, in both analogy and balance-scale problems, there is an increased tendency to use more of the information given in the problem in a more integrative way as children grow older. We believe it of particular importance in the study of strategies as in the study of processes, that investigators not become bogged down in task-specific aspects of strategy development, but rather focus upon what it is about strategy development that reflects generally increasing cognitive competence. We further believe it of importance to continue what we see as a present tendency to study strategy formation and implementation in real-world as well as in laboratory tasks.

5. *Representations of information.* Processes and strategies act on a knowledge base, and this knowledge base must be represented in some form. One thing that may develop with age is the ability to represent information in a way that renders the information easily accessible and highly relatable to other pieces or kinds of information. In pictorial analogies, for example, a tendency was observed to move from more separable to more integral representations of attribute information, and Kail et al. (1980) suggested the possibility that in spatial tasks also, older subjects may represent forms to be rotated mentally in a more holistic way. On the other hand, we know that in some cases the developmental trend is to move from more integral to more separable representations of information (see van Daalen-Kapteijns & Elshout-Mohr, 1981; Shepp, 1978; Smith & Kemler, 1978; Werner & Kaplan, 1952). Thus, we need to learn a lot more about the circumstances under which children of different ages represent information in different ways. It appears that changes in representation can be understood only in terms of the sense they make in the context of particular task environments or, at least, classes of task environments.

6. *Process latencies, difficulties, and probabilities.* Many recent studies we reviewed, such as those of analogical and linear syllogistic reasoning as well as of spatial visualization, have sought to isolate component processes and to assign values of some kind (e.g., duration) to these processes. We see this as a necessary ingredient in information processing research, although it is important to retain a sense of why this is so. In general, process values (such as latencies or difficulties) are not so much of interest in their own right as they are of interest in comparison to other process values. Thus, it is important to know what it is, say, that makes one analogy more difficult than another, one kind of balance-scale problem more difficult than another, or one addition problem more difficult than another. Moreover, it is essential to be able to isolate these values at the level of individual as well as group data because sources of difficulty in intelligent performance may differ widely across different individuals. In order eventually to attempt remediation, we need to know what it is that needs remediation in each individual rather than what it is that needs remediation on the average.

7. *Executive control.* Finally, we stress the importance of executive control in intellectual development. Although this item could be incorporated as a kind of process, we separate it here from processes to distinguish it from the kinds of processes that are used merely in the execution of one kind of problem or another. During the past several years, there has been an increasing tendency to study the executive in human functioning (e.g., Brown & DeLoache, 1978; R. J. Sternberg, 1980f; Sternberg & Ketron, 1982), and we believe that this trend should continue. Unfortunately, there has been a tendency on some people's parts to lump together more interesting research of this kind with more pedestrian research that does not go much beyond demonstrating, for example, that people know more about their memories as they grow older (without any demonstration of why what they know matters). The core of intelligence, it seems to us, is in the allocation and adaptation of one's mental resources to a given task environment, and we believe that future research on intellectual development should

give these aspects of functioning high priority.

In sum, we believe the information processing approach to intellectual development has been highly successful in isolating important loci of development and in elucidating just what it is that develops at many of these loci. We hasten to add that these loci are not independent but rather are highly interactive, as, for example, when processes embedded in a strategy act upon knowledge stored in some form of representation. We believe that information processing research has been highly complementary with psychometric research (see R. J. Sternberg, 1980a, 1981c), and we described in the discussion on the component as a unit of analysis how it is possible to intermap psychometric and information processing constructs. We hope that present attempts to interrelate the two literatures will continue because we believe they represent important sources of converging operations for identifying those aspects of intellectual development that appear, without regard to the paradigm under which they are discovered.

TRANSPARADIGMATIC PRINCIPLES OF INTELLECTUAL DEVELOPMENT

In our review of some of the alternative approaches that have been used to study intellectual development, certain prospective loci of intellectual development seem to have emerged and reemerged in one approach after another. These loci of development are of particular interest to us because they suggest the possibility that it may be possible to pose a fairly small set of transparadigmatic principles of development, ones that emerge from research almost without regard to the kind of research it is. We will attempt to integrate the findings of the various approaches by suggesting some possible principles that we view as having emerged. Obviously, our suggestions are only a first pass at such principles; we make no claim that every approach would be consistent with these proposals or that other interpretations of the identical data could not lead to a somewhat different set of principles. Nevertheless, we believe that an attempt to pose tentative principles of development is probably a reasonable direction in which developmental psychology might proceed at this point in its history.

More Sophisticated Control Strategies (Metacomponents) Develop with Age

Control strategies, executive functioning, or whatever one chooses to call the homunculus that directs everything else, are an essential element of almost everyone's definition (implicit theory) of in-

telligence. In the Sternberg, Conway, Ketron, and Bernstein (1981) factor analyses of experts' and laypersons' views of intelligence, for example, such behaviors as "makes good decisions" and "plans ahead" were critical to the problem-solving factor. Even the earliest theorists recognized the importance of executive functioning. As noted earlier, Binet and Simon (1909a) believed that intelligent thought consists of three distinct elements: the tendency to take and maintain a definite direction; the capacity to make adaptations for the purpose of attaining a desired end; and the power of self-criticism. All of these elements are metacomponential in nature. Spearman (1927) referred to "intellectual judgment" as a "great stage in the development of the Intellect" (p. 277); Thurstone (1924) believed that the capacity to inhibit merely instinctive adjustments was an essential aspect of human intelligence.

The idea of metacomponents and control of one's own learning is foreign to an S-R view of an organism on which learning is imposed from without; yet, upon closer inspection, metacomponents seem to creep in through the back door of neobehavioristic theory, even as traditional learning theorists judiciously guard the front. Thurstone's "capacity to inhibit merely instinctive adjustments" is exactly the concept involved in White's (1965) theory of the development of the ability to inhibit lower level associative responses so that the higher order conceptual processes will have time to take effect. In a similar vein, Kendler's (1979a) notion of a central processing system with coexisting modes of functioning suggests that some metacomponential functions must be involved in the triggering of the alternative modes. Other indirect evidence for the existence and development of metacomponents can be found in the learning theory literature. For example, Stevenson and his colleagues (Stevenson, Iscoe, & McConnell, 1955; Weir & Stevenson, 1959) found a curvilinear relationship between age and rate of learning in a simple discrimination task. They explained this phenomenon by suggesting that the older subjects appeared unable to accept that the problems could really be as simple as they appeared. Instead, Stevenson et al. suggested, older subjects would develop complex hypotheses about task solution that, in fact, overcomplicated the task and hindered performance. Such an explanation assumes planning and strategy selection on the part of the older subjects. Whenever learning theorists admit the possibility of multiple types of functioning—as in mediated versus unmediated learning (Kendler & Kendler, 1975; T. Kendler, 1970, 1979a; Spiker & Cantor, 1979)—or the possibility of more cognitive processes—such as hypothesis testing (Eimas, 1970; Gholson, Levine, & Phillips, 1972), rule or principle formation (Gagné, 1965), or inferential problem solving (Gagné, 1965; Kendler & Kendler, 1967)—a metacomponential interpretation of some sort that allows the organism internal control of its behavior is at least possible.

Psychometric analyses of intelligence and its development have tended not to emphasize executive processes. We believe the reason for this deemphasis is largely historical—most factor-analytic investigations of intelligence were done at a time when concern with executive processes had not yet arisen. Some of the more recent factor-analytic work does in fact reflect the more recent emphases in psychological theorizing on executive functions. Das, Kirby, and Jarman (1975), for example, have sought to confirm and extend factor analytically Luria's (1966a, 1966b, 1973) theory of cognitive information processing. In this theory, information may be processed as some kind of unitary or holistic composite that is primarily spatial in character, or it may be processed in a way that is primarily sequential in nature, following a set temporal order. Das et al. refer to the two kinds of processing as simultaneous and successive syntheses. Each kind of synthesis may be viewed as representing a different mode of executive decision making as well as action upon the information about which decisions have been made (see Jarman & Das, 1977). Carroll (1980) has conducted the largest scale set of factor analyses on information processing tasks ever to be undertaken. He has used this set of factor analyses to provide guidance in proposing a set of basic processes used in information processing tasks. One of the processes Carroll has identified is what he calls the Monitor process, whereby subjects utilize instructions, rules, and guidelines for task performance. "Usually, the process has a hierarchical structure in the sense that it has one or a very small number of major goals, each of these having one or a small number of minor goals or 'subgoals'" (Carroll, 1980, p. 34), and so on, down to the finest possible level of analysis. Development of the Monitor process occurs as the quantity and quality of instructions, rules, and guidelines increase.

Piaget described the increased systematization of thought involved in the child's development from sensorimotor modes of interacting with the world to formal operational reasoning (Inhelder & Piaget, 1958; Piaget, 1976; Piaget & Inhelder, 1969). Not only does the child develop more efficient and more sophisticated schemes as she or he matures—a process that itself suggests the guidance of some sort of metacomponents—but the child also develops a more inclusive and more integrated underlying logical structure that allows for the construction and coordination of these schemes. Thus, Piaget's view of intellectual development can be seen as emphasizing the development of metacomponential processes as much as, if not more than, it emphasizes the development of specific information processing capabilities. Piaget (1976) defined intellectual development as the movement toward greater flexibility and increased intentionality of thought, and his research program detailed the child's transition from reflex behavior, controlled by heredity and the environment (Piaget, 1952b), to the development of formal operations in which the child has such control over his or her own mental processes that he or she has little need to deal with the concrete world at all, but, instead, can use mental representations of reality and possibility (Inhelder & Piaget, 1958). Using a variety of tasks, such as the colored-liquids problem that requires the child to discover what combinations of four liquids produces a specific chemical reaction, Piaget found that, with increasing age, the child is better able to plan beforehand how she or he will attack a problem, carry out this planned investigation systematically, and monitor the results and evaluate various hypotheses until she or he arrives at the best explanation for the phenomena observed (Inhelder & Piaget, 1958; Lovell, 1961). So, Piaget and his colleagues have also demonstrated that the child develops more sophisticated planning, regulatory, and evaluative processes, that is, more sophisticated metacomponents, with increasing age.

We have devoted considerable space to information processing accounts of the development of control strategies; therefore, we will only summarize some of the points we have made. All of the information processing units we have considered—TOTEs, components, productions, schemes, and rules—make allowances for executive processing in development and for the development of executive processing. Executive processing is handled by higher order TOTEs, metacomponents, productions that drive productions, executive schemes, or high-level rules. R. J. Sternberg's (1980f) analysis of the development of intellect, primarily in reasoning, has led to the postulation of six metacomponential loci of intellectual development. Brown's (1978) analysis of memory and metamemory development has led her to postulate four metacognitive operations driving cognitive processing; Flavell (1981) has proposed a model of cognitive monitoring that includes four basic components; and Markman (1981) has also proposed four signals that people use in monitoring their comprehension. Butterfield and Belmont (1977) have shown that a key aspect of developmentally advanced functioning is the ability to select and apply optimal mnemonic strategies in learning. Almost no matter where one looks in the information processing literature we have reviewed, executive processes (called by whatever name) are seen as critical to intellectual development. R. J. Sternberg's (1980f) list of metacomponents—(1) deciding just what the problem is that needs to be solved, (2) selecting lower order components to effect solution of the problem, (3) selecting a strategy for combining lower order components, (4) selecting one or more representations or organizations of information upon which the lower order components and strategies can act, (5) deciding upon a rate of problem solving that will permit the desired level of accuracy or solution quality, and (6) monitoring progress toward a solution—is fairly typical of the kinds of executive processes information processing researchers have identified as developing with age.

Information Processing Becomes More Nearly Exhaustive with Increasing Age

The importance of thoroughness in information processing has been recognized by experts and laypersons alike in their notions about intelligence. In Peterson's (1921) definition of intelligence, for example, intelligence was believed to reflect the ability "by which the effects of a complexity of stimuli are brought together and given a somewhat unified effect in behavior" (p. 198). Part of intelligence, then, is the thorough encoding of the complexity of stimuli that needs to be brought together. In numerous conceptions of intelligence citing intelligence, in part, as the ability to profit from experience (e.g., Dearborn, 1921), a major idea is that some people fail to encode in their experiences the relevant information that will be helpful to them later (see also Schank, 1980). In the Sternberg, Conway, Ketron & Bernstein (1981) study of people's conceptions of intelligence, a thread running through all of the factors was the ability to glean the most possible information from a given situation. More intelligent people were believed to use all of the information at hand (rather than only part of it) and to use it to maximum advantage.

Because the primary focus in learning theory research as been on locating and manipulating environmental variables that affect learning and not on modeling how the organism processes stimuli, there is little, if any, direct evidence in the S-R literature on whether or not information processing becomes

more nearly exhaustive with age. Performance on learning tasks is generally found to improve with age (Stevenson, 1970), but the nature of this improvement is usually not specified in terms of the child's increased information processing skills.

The psychometric tradition has generally not emphasized process modeling so that there are not many places to look for discussions of how information is encoded. Guilford's (1967) factor-analytically based theory is probably the most exhaustive collection of abilities that has been compiled, and it is also the one that probably takes greatest account of information processing abilities. Tests used to measure Guilford's cognition ability—"immediate discovery, awareness, rediscovery, or recognition of information in its various forms; comprehension or understanding" (Guilford & Hoepfner, 1971, p. 20)—measure, in part, thoroughness with which information is encoded and processed, as do some of the tests measuring Guilford's evaluation ability—"comparison of items of information in terms of variables and making judgments concerning criterion satisfaction (correctness, identity, consistency, etc.)" (Guilford and Hoepfner, 1971, p. 20). In one of Guilford's cognition tests (measuring cognition of symbolic units), for example, subjects must identify words with their vowels replaced by blanks, for example, m_g_c. Obviously, one skill that will improve performance on this task is the ability and willingness to try out large numbers of vowel combinations. In solving syllogisms (an evaluation test), performance will be improved to the extent that subjects can generate all possible set relations that derive from the encoding and combination of the two syllogistic premises. Some of the Binet and Wechsler tests that measure recognition of absurdities and incongruities in pictures also test in part a child's ability to encode the pictures fully enough to detect what is wrong with them. Performance on a number of Carroll's (1980) factor-analytically derived components can also be improved by more thorough processing—apprehension, perceptual integration, encoding, and comparison.

There is a great deal of evidence within Piaget's research to support the claim that information processing becomes more nearly exhaustive with age. Much of this evidence lies in Piaget's descriptions of the development of the conservations. In numerous studies, Piaget and his colleagues demonstrated that as the child matures, his or her thought becomes increasingly decentered, that is, as the child develops, she or he learns to use all of the information at hand rather than allow his or her judgments to be inappropriately dominated by only a portion of this input (Elkind, 1961; Piaget, 1952a; Piaget & Inhelder, 1962). This increasing liberation from appearances resulting from more exhaustive processing enables the child to construct the conservations of the object's permanence, mass, weight, volume, and so on, through transformations of appearance. Piaget also demonstrated that with age, the child becomes more able to generate all possible combinations of variables and to carry out these combinations systematically and to compare their results. An older child is less likely to be satisfied with the first explanation of a phenomenon or solution to a problem that she or he happens upon. Instead, he or she is more likely to test thoroughly the solution or explanation for correctness; an older child is also more likely to look for alternative solutions or multiple causes of a phenomenon (Inhelder & Piaget, 1958; Lovell, 1961). The older the child, the more likely he or she is to go beyond the immediately presented situation and to extend his or her solution—classification, seriation, hypothesis, and so on—to account for future events and possibilities, not just present circumstances (Inhelder & Piaget, 1958, 1964; Piaget, 1952a). Thus, the research of Piaget and his colleagues definitely supports the conclusion that with increasing age the child becomes more capable of exhaustively exploring reality and possibility.

Brown and DeLoache (1978) reviewed the information processing literatures on extracting the main idea of a passage, visual scanning, and retrieval processes, and they concluded that in all of these kinds of tasks, a characteristic of intellectual development was the increase in the number of exhaustive attempts at information processing that were made. In visual scanning, for example, Vurpillot (1968) found that young children (e.g., age 4) almost never exhaustively scanned pictures of two houses to determine whether they were identical, whereas older children (e.g., age 9) frequently did. In retrieval, Kobasigawa (1974) found that in recalling categories of words, first graders who spontaneously used an available category cue recalled fewer items than did third graders—the younger children failed to scan exhaustively and, hence, to recall the items listed under each category in their memories. Istomina (1948/1975) also noted the tendency of younger children not to scan their memories exhaustively—when trying to recall a list of words from memory, 4- and 5-year-olds rarely tried to retrieve words not immediately recalled. Siegler (1978) found that a major cause of failure of younger children to solve balance-scale problems was in their failure to encode information relevant to all of the dimensions that affected the way in which the scale

balanced. Kogan, Connor, Gross, and Fava (1980) found that younger children's failure to pair pictures metaphorically was due in part to their failure to make all possible comparisons between pictures. Both Siegler (1978) and Kogan et al. (1980) found that training of children to use exhaustive information processing could improve their performance on the tasks investigated. Sternberg and Nigro (1980) and Sternberg and Rifkin (1979) found that in analogical reasoning, there was a tendency for information processing to become more nearly exhaustive with age, both in encoding of stimuli and in comparisons made on the stimuli that have been encoded. In sum, the information processing of children does seem to become more nearly complete with increasing age.

The Ability to Comprehend Relations of Successively Higher Orders Develops with Age

We have essentially no idea of when the ability to comprehend first-order relations between given terms of a problem first develops. To our knowledge, there is no evidence of any kind that children of any given age cannot understand first-order relations (simple comparisons) of any kind. Evidence described in this chapter and presented here suggests (1) that the ability to comprehend second-order relations, at least of the kind used in analogical reasoning (as in the connections between two halves of an analogy), develops around the age of 12 and (2) that the ability to comprehend third-order relations (as in analogies between analogies) develops during adolescence. The ability to use these kinds of relations may develop before the ability to discover them.

We have not found any implicit theories of intelligence that explicitly propose ability to comprehend relations of different orders as a source of developmental or individual differences in intelligence. Such a notion seems implicit in some of Terman's (1921) ideas about intelligence as the ability to carry on abstract thinking, where increasingly higher levels of abstraction would be associated with higher levels of intelligence. The ability to think abstractly also emerged as a behavior associated with intelligent performance in the Sternberg, Conway, Ketron, and Bernstein (1981) study of people's conceptions of intelligence, and it seems that in everyday thinking about intelligence, people associate ''deeper thoughts'' with higher levels of intelligence. One way in which thoughts can be deeper, we propose, is in terms of the level of abstraction they entail. People like Einstein or Newton are considered to have been extremely intelligent, in large part because of their ability to think at very high levels of complexity that, presumably, most of us cannot reach. A shallow person is presumably one who cannot reach high levels of abstraction, or possibly, any levels at all—less intelligent people are generally thought to be highly concrete in their thinking.

Within the learning theory literature, Gagné's (1968) hierarchy of learning processes assumes that the ability to form and use higher order relations, such as concepts and principles, develops with the age and experience of the child. Concept-learning studies also support the claim that the ability to comprehend relations of successively higher orders develops with age. For example, Odom (1966) and Osler and Kofsky (1966), using subjects ranging in age from 5 to 14, have found that younger subjects tend to form concepts by rote learning of individual S-R relations for the various instances of a concept, whereas older subjects tend to employ higher order categories as a basis for their responding. For instance, when Osler and Kofsky systematically varied the number of dimensions represented in a concept-learning task and the total number of values possible on each dimension, they found that younger subjects were more sensitive to the absolute size of the stimulus set, whereas older subjects were more sensitive to the number of independent dimensions or categories represented in the stimulus set.

One of the most explicit statements of the role of higher order relations in intelligent performance has been made by Raymond B. Cattell, the noted psychometrician. Cattell, like Terman, has viewed intelligence as comprising in part the ability to think abstractly (R. B. Cattell, 1971; Cattell & Cattell, 1963). In particular, R. B. Cattell sees abstract thinking as critical to "fluid intelligence," which he and others have identified in numerous factor-analytic investigations of intelligence. Because for Cattell (1971), "abstraction . . . is intrinsically a building up of relations among relations" (pp. 185–186), he would presumably be sympathetic to our notion that part of what develops in intelligence is the ability to perceive relations of a successively higher order. Indeed, in his and others' intelligence tests, difficulty of abstract-reasoning items is largely a function of the order of relations one needs to perceive. In the most difficult items in the Cattell Culture Fair Scale (Level 3) and in the Raven Progressive Matrices, it is necessary to see higher order relations to solve the problems. For example, in a series problem, one may not only have a change in the angular rotation of a series of figures but also a change in the rate at which the degree of angular rotation changes.

Spearman's (1927) theory of general intelligence posited eduction of relations as one of three qualitative principles that constituted intelligent cognition. Eduction of relations is that which we have referred to as inference of the relation between two terms, such as the first two terms of the analogy, $A : B :: C : D$. Spearman (1927) showed how the difficulty of transitive-inference problems could be understood in terms of the order of relations one needed to comprehend. Consider, for example, the problem, A is larger than B, B is larger than C, and C is larger than D. On Spearman's (1927) analysis (which is probably not wholly correct), one can educe the relation between A and D by comprehending first the first-order relations between $A–B$, $B–C$, and $C–D$; then the second-order relation (not given explicitly in the problem) between $A–B$ and $B–C$; and so on. Thus, the fact that A is larger than D is recognized by the hierarchical solution of the problem.

Piaget has also demonstrated how, as the child matures, she or he becomes better able to comprehend higher order relations. By the middle-to-end of the concrete operational period of development, the child has mastered the first-order relations involved in understanding classifications, seriations, causation, and so on (Inhelder & Piaget, 1958, 1964; Piaget, 1952a, 1952b, 1954, 1970, 1976). According to Piaget's theory, however, the child is not capable of performing second-order operations on the results of these first-order, concrete operations until she or he attains formal operational thought. Thus, the attainment of formal operational thought marks the attainment of the ability to perceive and construct relations between relations (Inhelder & Piaget, 1958; Piaget, 1976). As the child grows older, she or he is more likely to be able to perceive and to propose more abstract, higher order connections between phenomena. Older children are also more likely to look for higher order relations; Inhelder and Piaget (1958) found that older children are less likely to be content with a situation-specific task solution and are more likely to seek generalizable, abstract rules or principles when presented problems to solve. Thus, Piaget found that an increasing ability to handle higher order relations and more abstract forms of reasoning characterizes the child's development.

In the information processing domain, Case (1978) has proposed that "the search for 'development beyond formal operations' should . . . concentrate on clarifying the nature of second-order intellectual operations and on searching for third-order operations" (p. 63). We have pursued this interesting suggestion in the context of analogical reasoning

(Sternberg & Downing, 1982). A number of information processing investigations of analogical reasoning have discovered that the ability to map second-order relations appears around the transition between childhood and adolescence (e.g., Gallagher & Wright, 1979; Levinson & Carpenter, 1974; Lunzer, 1965; Piaget with Montangero & Billeter, 1977; Sternberg & Rifkin, 1979). None of these investigations have found further strategy development during adolescence, however, perhaps because by this time the most conceptually difficult aspect of analogical reasoning, mapping of second-order relations, is already expeditiously accomplished. Sternberg and Downing (1982) tested students of junior high school, high school, and college levels in their ability to perceive analogies between analogies—subjects would be presented with two analogies of the form $A : B :: C : D$ and asked how analogous they were. We were particularly interested in the degree to which higher order mapping between the domain (first analogy) and range (second analogy) of this higher order analogy problem would affect judgments of higher order analogy. Analogies were rated by other subjects not involved in the primary task for a number of attributes, including goodness of the higher order mapping. We discovered that there was a monotone increase in the use of higher order mapping with increasing age. Thus, older children seemed better able than younger children to comprehend relations of a third order, a finding consistent with the principle of intellectual development we tentatively propose here.

Flexibility in Use of Strategy or Information Develops with Age

Flexibility in strategy or information utilization means that an individual knows when to change strategy or transfer information and when not to do so. One often associates intellectual immaturity with inflexibility in strategy change and information transfer. But changing strategy when it is unnecessary or harmful or transferring information when the information is inappropriate to the use to which one puts it can be just as dangerous as failing to change or transfer. The locus of development, then, is not so much the ability to change as the ability to know when to change.

Flexible thinking emerges from the Sternberg, Conway, Ketron, and Bernstein (1981) conceptions-of-intelligence study as an aspect of intelligent behavior, as does the ability to engage in situation-appropriate behaviors. Many people have defined intelligence in terms of adaptation or adjustment to the environment in which one finds oneself (e.g., Colvin, 1921; Pintner, 1921; R. J. Sternberg, 1981a, 1981b), and we view flexibility as an integral part of adaptation to the continual changes one finds in one's environment. To be a bit more dramatic, the ability of a species to survive depends in large part on its flexibility in meeting changes in the environment for which it might not have been genetically (or environmentally) prepared. Ferguson's (1954) view of intelligence as the ability to transfer information is consistent with the present point of view, as is Cole's (1980) analysis of intelligent functioning in everyday "niche-picking."

A number of studies exist in the learning theory literature that demonstrate the greater inflexibility of younger children's thought relative to that of older children. Odom and Coon (1966) found that, when presented a three-choice problem in which a left/middle/right position sequence of responses was reinforced for 90 trials and followed by 20 trials in which no responses were reinforced, 6-year-old subjects continued in the previously reinforced pattern, whereas 11- and 19-year-old subjects demonstrated extinction of this response pattern. Kessen and Kessen (1961) presented 3- and 4-year-old children a two-choice discrimination problem in which the response probabilities were changed halfway through the experiment. Again, younger subjects showed a greater inflexibility in rule application, whereas older subjects were more likely to modify their behavior to reflect the changed reinforcement conditions. Other findings supporting greater appropriateness in strategy utilization with increased age come from the hypothesis-theory literature (Gholson & Beilin, 1979; Gholson, Levine, & Phillips, 1972). Younger subjects are more likely to make stereotyped responses based on stimulus preference, position preference, or a preference for position alteration rather than on feedback from past responses. Older children and adults, however, tend to use more and more sophisticated prediction hypotheses, which they then modify to conform to feedback until they reach problem solution. Even when younger children employ systematic prediction hypotheses, they do not appropriately revise their hypotheses to reflect feedback. Several investigators, using subjects ranging in age from 3 to 16, have found an increase with age in win-stay behavior, that is, older subjects are more likely to stay with a winning hypothesis than are younger subjects (Eimas, 1969; Gholson et al., 1972; Kendler, 1979a; Tighe & Tighe, 1972). Cantor and Spiker (1978) demonstrated that the performance of kindergarten and first-grade children on a discrimination-learning task improved when they were trained in a "win-stay, lose-shift" strategy, that is, to stay with a winning hypothesis and to shift to a previously untested hypothesis following negative feedback. Cantor and Spiker also found that younger children tended not to use systematic strategies spontaneously, and that when younger children used systematic strategies, they often focused on irrelevant stimulus information to form these strategies. Thus, much support exists in the learning theory literature for the claim that greater flexibility and more appropriate strategy or information utilization develop with age.

Flexible thinking is measured in a number of different ways by a number of different psychometric tests of intellectual ability. In the Guilford (1967) tests of divergent thinking and in similar creativity tests, flexible thinking is measured by items such as those requiring subjects to think of unusual uses for ordinary objects, like coathangers or fishing rods. In some forms of the Miller Analogies Test, flexibility is measured by set-breaker items that require the test-taker to perceive nonsemantic analogical relations, for example, ones based on the sounds rather than on the meanings of the words constituting the analogy item. Even in less exotic types of test items, flexibility may be measured by one's ability to perceive relations that are out of the ordinary or to solve what seem to be difficult problems in simple ways. On the mathematical aptitude section of the Scholastic Aptitude Test, for example, so-called insight problems are ones that can be solved laboriously by a time-consuming algorithm that is usually immediately obvious or that can be solved simply and quickly by a shortcut procedure whose applicability will generally not be immediately obvious. One of the more interesting, if indirect, measurements of flexibility is provided by tests such as the in-basket (Frederiksen, Saunders, & Ward, 1957), which requires an individual to simulate important functions of the job of a person in some occupation, usually a business executive. The individual is presented with more tasks to accomplish than can possibly be accomplished in the time allotted, and the individual must allocate his or her time flexibly to fulfill as well as possible the most important tasks. The importance of flexibility in psychometric thinking about intelligence can be seen in theoretical as well as in practical work. R. B. Cattell's (1935a, 1935b) research led him to believe that flexibility is an important aspect of g, where flexibility is defined as a switch-over from some old, accustomed, overlearned activity to a new way of effecting the same end. R. B. Cattell contrasted this view of flexibility with Spearman's (1927) notion of it as the degree of

impedance from interference in switching from one mental process to another. Thurstone (1944) also believed flexibility to be an important aspect of the perceptual aspects of intelligence. To summarize, flexibility in various forms seems to enter into a large number of psychometric conceptions of intellectual functioning and its development.

A major element of Piaget's (1976) definition of intellectual development is the progression toward greater mobility or flexibility of thought. Sensorimotor thought begins with rigid sensorimotor reflexes and gradually is extended through the development of the semiotic function to handle representational thought. As the child matures and constructs concrete operations, thought becomes reversible and the child becomes capable of integrating these concrete operations into higher order systems providing still greater flexibility of thought. For example, Inhelder and Piaget (1964) found that the child first learns to construct rigid series and classes by trial and error and is unable to extend them to incorporate additional elements until later in development. As the child moves toward the development of formal operational thought, she or he becomes more capable of handling possibility as well as reality. Piaget proposes the development of two complex logical structures, the combinatorial system and the four-group of transformations, to explain this ultimate flexibility of thought (Piaget, 1976; Piaget & Inhelder, 1969). Thus, as the child develops, his or her cognitive structures become more flexible and better able to assimilate reality. In task after task, Piaget reports that younger children tend to approach problems with preformed convictions about their solution, and they remain convinced about these stereotyped notions, even in the face of contradictory evidence. Older children are more likely to respond to findings that contradict, or that are not accounted for by, their explanation. Not only are older children more likely to be able to solve a larger variety of Piaget's tasks but they are also more willing to look for alternative ways of reaching the same result (Inhelder & Piaget, 1958, 1964; Piaget, 1976; Piaget & Inhelder, 1962, 1969).

Flexible thinking of various kinds has played an important role in information processing investigations of intelligence and their antecedents. The importance of flexibility as a psychological construct in such investigations can be traced back at least to Luchins's (1942) famous water-jug problems. In these problems, subjects solved a number of items requiring them to state an algorithm by which water could be poured from one jug to another via a third jug. A number of problems were presented that could be solved by one formula; then, problems were presented that could be solved by this formula or a much simpler one. Strong effects of "set" were found whereby subjects failed to recognize that they could change their strategy to a much simpler one. Recently, Atwood and Polson (1976) have proposed an information processing model of performance on this task. In the literature on loci of deficiency in the retarded, the ability to transfer information flexibly has been identified by a number of investigators as a major source of difference in performance between normals and retarded (see, e.g., Butterfield & Belmont, 1977; Campione & Brown, 1974; Feuerstein, 1979, 1980). Recently, Brown and Campione (1982) have proposed that inducing flexible thinking is one of the major needs of any program for training intelligent performance, whether in retarded or normal individuals. It was stated earlier that flexible thinking includes knowing when not to change strategy or transfer information as well as knowing when to do so—a consistent characteristic of more intelligent people both within and between age levels is their ability to settle upon a strategy that is generalizable across a large class of problems rather than to settle upon very specific strategies that need to be changed as a result of slight variations in problem type (Bloom & Broder, 1950; Jensen, 1982; Sternberg & Nigro, 1980; Sternberg & Rifkin, 1979). To summarize, flexibility in a variety of forms seems to be an essential ingredient of intelligent behavior.

CONCLUSION

In this chapter, we have described not only the implicit conceptions of intelligence and its development underlying people's interactions with each other and with their world but also the explicit conceptions underlying the work of S-R, psychometric, Piagetian, and information processing psychologists. We have produced evidence for the existence of some agreement among these different world views, and we end our chapter with several suggested principles of cognitive development. We must confess our pleasure at finding that not only can one speak of general principles of intellectual development but also that one finds these same principles emerging in the work of psychologists with very different approaches. Just as converging operations yielding similar results reassure the investigator that she or he is on the right track, so does the fact that one can find transparadigmatic agreement on certain higher order principles proposed to describe the development of human intelligence.

REFERENCES

Achenbach, T. M. The children's associative responding test: A possible alternative to group IQ tests. *Journal of Educational Psychology*, 1970, *61*, 340–348. (a)

Achenbach, T. M. Standardization of a research instrument for identifying associative responding in children. *Developmental Psychology*, 1970, *2*, 283–291. (b)

Achenbach, T. M. The children's associative responding test: A two-year followup. *Developmental Psychology*, 1971, *5*, 477–483.

Ames, W. S. The development of a classification scheme of contextual aids. *Reading Research Quarterly*, 1966, *2*, 57–82.

Anderson, J. E. The prediction of terminal intelligence from infant and preschool tests. In G. M. Whipple (Ed.), *Intelligence: Its nature and nurture* (Thirty-Ninth Yearbook, National Society for the Study of Education). Bloomington, Ill: Public School Publishing Co., 1940.

Anderson, J. R. *Language, memory, and thought*. Hillsdale, N.J.: Erlbaum, 1976.

Anderson, J. R., Kline, P. J., & Beasley, C. M., Jr. A general learning theory and its application to schema abstraction. In G. Bower (Ed.), *The psychology of learning and motivation* (Vol. 13). New York: Academic Press, 1979.

Asch, S. A study of change in mental organization. *Archives of Psychology*, 1936, Whole No. 195.

Atwood, M. E., & Polson, P. G. A process model for water jug problems. *Cognitive Psychology*, 1976, *8*, 191–216.

Baltes, P. B., & Schaie, K. W. On the plasticity of intelligence in adulthood and old age: Where Horn and Donaldson fail. *American Psychologist*, 1976, *31*, 720–725.

Bayley, N. Mental growth during the first three years: A developmental study of 61 children by repeated tests. *Genetic Psychology Monographs*, 1933, *14*, 1–92.

Bayley, N. Mental growth during the first three years. In R. G. Barker, J. S. Kounin, & H. F. Wright (Eds.), *Child behaviour and development*. New York: McGraw-Hill, 1943.

Bayley, N. Consistency and variability in the growth of intelligence from birth to eighteen years. *Journal of Genetic Psychology*, 1949, *75*, 165–196.

Bayley, N. Development and maturation. In H. Helson (Ed.), *Theoretical foundations of psychology*. New York: Van Nostrand, 1951.

Bayley, N. On the growth of intelligence. *American Psychologist*, 1955, *10*, 805–818.

Bayley, N. Learning in adulthood: The role of intelligence. In H. J. Klausmeier & C. W. Harris, (Eds.), *Analysis of concept learning*. New York: Academic Press, 1966.

Bayley, N. Behavioral correlates of mental growth: Birth to thirty-six years. *American Psychologist*, 1968, *23*, 1–17.

Bayley, N. Development of mental abilities. In P. H. Mussen (Ed.), *Carmichael's manual of child psychology* (3rd ed., Vol. 1). New York: Wiley, 1970.

Bayley, N., & Oden, M. H. The maintenance of intellectual ability in gifted adults. *Journal of Gerontology*, 1955, *10*, 91–107.

Beilin, H. Stimulus and cognitive transformation in conservation. In D. Elkind & J. H. Flavell (Eds.), *Studies in cognitive development: Essays in honor of Jean Piaget*. London: Oxford University Press, 1969.

Beilin, H. Piaget's theory: Refinement, revisionism, or rejection? In R. H. Kluwe & H. Spada (Eds.), *Developmental models of thinking*. New York: Academic Press, 1980.

Binet, A., & Simon, T. *The development of intelligence in children*. Trans. by E. S. Kite. Baltimore: Williams & Wilkins, 1916. (a)

Binet, A., & Simon, T. *The intelligence of the feeble-minded*. Trans. by E. S. Kite. Baltimore: Williams & Wilkins, 1916. (b)

Birkhill, W. R., & Schaie, K. W. The effect of differential reinforcement of cautiousness in intellectual performance among the elderly. *Journal of Gerontology*, 1975, *30*, 578–582.

Bloom, B. S., & Broder, L. *Problem-solving processes of college students*. Chicago: University of Chicago Press, 1950.

Botwinick, J. *Cognitive processes in maturity and old age*. New York: Springer Publishing, 1967.

Bower, T. G. R. The development of object-permanence: Some studies of existence constancy. *Perception and Psychophysics*, 1967, *2*, 411–418.

Bower, T. G. R. *Development in infancy*. San Francisco: W. H. Freeman, 1974.

Braine, M. D. S. The ontogeny of certain logical operations: Piaget's formulation examined by nonverbal methods. In I. E. Sigel & F. H. Hooper (Eds.), *Logical thinking in children: Research based on Piaget's theory*. New York: Holt, Rinehart & Winston, 1968.

Brainerd, C. J. Order of acquisition of transitivity, conservation, and class inclusion of length and weight. *Developmental Psychology*, 1973, *8*, 105–116.

Brainerd, C. J. Neo-Piagetian training experiments revisited: Is there any support for the cognitive-developmental stage hypothesis? *Cognition*, 1974, *2*, 349–370.

Brainerd, C. J. "Stage," "structure," and developmental theory. In G. Steiner (Ed.), *The psychology of the twentieth century*. Munich: Kindler, 1976.

Brainerd, C. J. Response criteria in concept development research. *Child Development*, 1977, *48*, 360–366.

Broman, S. H., Nichols, P. L., & Kennedy, W. A. *Preschool IQ: Prenatal and early developmental correlates*. Hillsdale, N.J.: Erlbaum, 1975.

Brown, A. L. The development of memory: Knowing, knowing about knowing, and knowing how to know. In H. W. Reese (Ed.), *Advances in child development and behavior* (Vol. 10). New York: Academic Press, 1975.

Brown, A. L. Knowing when, where, and how to remember: A problem of metacognition. In R. Glaser (Ed.), *Advances in instructional psychology* (Vol. 1). Hillsdale, N.J.: Erlbaum, 1978.

Brown, A. L., & Campione, J. C. Discussion: How, and how much, can intelligence be modified? In D. K. Detterman & R. J. Sternberg (Eds.), *How and how much can intelligence be increased?* Norwood, N.J.: Ablex, 1982.

Brown, A. L., & DeLoache, J. S. Skills, plans and self-regulation. In R. S. Siegler (Ed.), *Children's thinking: What develops?* Hillsdale, N.J.: Erlbaum, 1978.

Brown, G., & Desforges, C. *Piaget's theory: A psychological critique*. Boston: Routledge & Kegan Paul, 1979.

Brown, W., & Thomson, G. H. *The essentials of mental measurement*. Cambridge: Cambridge University Press, 1921.

Bruner, J. S., Shapiro, D., & Tagiuri, R. The meaning of traits in isolation and in combination. In R. Tagiuri and L. Petrullo (Eds.), *Person perception and interpersonal behavior*. Stanford, Calif.: Stanford University Press, 1958.

Bryant, P. E. What the young child has to learn about logic. In R. Hinde & J. Hinde (Eds.), *Constraints on learning*. New York: Academic Press, 1973.

Bryant, P. E., & Trabasso, T. Transitive inferences and memory in young children. *Nature*, 1971, *232*, 456–458.

Burt, C. The development of reasoning in school children. *Journal of Experimental Pedagogy*, 1919, *5*, 68–77.

Burt, C. *The factors of the mind*. London: University of London Press, 1940.

Burt, C. Alternative methods of factor analysis and their relations to Pearson's method of "principal axes." *British Journal of Psychology, Statistical Section*, 1949, *2*, 98–121.

Butterfield, E. C., & Belmont, J. M. Assessing and improving the executive cognitive functions of mentally retarded people. In I. Bialer & M. Sternlicht (Eds.), *Psychological issues in mental retardation*. New York: Psychological Dimensions, 1977.

Campione, J. C., & Brown, A. L. The effects of contextual changes and degree of component mastery on transfer of training. In H. W. Reese (Ed.), *Advances in child development and behavior* (Vol. 9). New York: Academic Press, 1974.

Cantor, J. H. & Spiker, C. C. The problem-solving strategies of kindergarten and first-grade children during discrimination learning. *Journal of Experimental Child Psychology*, 1978, *26*, 341–358.

Cantor, N., & Mischel, W. Prototypes in person perception. In L. Berkowitz (Ed.), *Advances in experimental social psychology*. New York: Academic Press, 1979.

Carpenter, P. A., & Just, M. A. Sentence comprehension: A psycholinguistic processing model of verification. *Psychological Review*, 1975, *82*, 45–73.

Carroll, J. B. *Individual difference relations in psychometric and experimental cognitive tasks* (NR 150–406 ONR Final Report). Chapel Hill, N.C.: L. L. Thurstone Psychometric Laboratory, 1980.

Carroll, J. B. Ability and task difficulty in cognitive psychology. *Educational Researcher*, 1981, *10*, 11–21.

Case, R. Mental strategies, mental capacity, and instruction: A neo-Piagetian investigation. *Journal of Experimental Child Psychology*, 1974, *18*, 372–397. (a)

Case, R. Structures and strictures: Some functional limitations on the course of cognitive growth. *Cognitive Psychology*, 1974, *6*, 544–573. (b)

Case, R. Intellectual development from birth to adolescence: A neo-Piagetian interpretation. In R. Siegler (Ed.), *Children's thinking: What develops?* Hillsdale, N.J.: Erlbaum, 1978.

Cattell, J. McK. Mental tests and measurements. *Mind*, 1890, *15*, 373.

Cattell, R. B. On the measurement of "perseveration." *British Journal of Educational Psychology*, 1935, *5*, 76–92. (a)

Cattell, R. B. Perseveration and personality: Some experiments and a hypothesis. *Journal of Mental Science*, 1935, *61*, 151–167. (b)

Cattell, R. B. Theory of fluid and crystallized intelligence: An initial experiment. *Journal of Educational Psychology*, 1963, *54*, 105–111.

Cattell, R. B. *Abilities: Their structure, growth, and action*. Boston: Houghton-Mifflin, 1971.

Cattell, R. B., & Cattell, A. K. S. *Test of g: Culture Fair, Scale 3*. Champaign, Ill.: Institute for Personality and Ability Testing, 1963.

Cavanaugh, J. C., & Perlmutter, M. Metamemory: A critical examination. *Child Development*, 1982, *53*, 11–28.

Chiang, A., & Atkinson, R. C. Individual differences and interrelationships among a select set of cognitive skills. *Memory and Cognition*, 1976, *4*, 661–672.

Clark, H. H. The influence of language in solving three-term series problems. *Journal of Experimental Psychology*, 1969, *82*, 205–215. (a)

Clark, H. H. Linguistic processes in deductive reasoning. *Psychological Review*, 1969, *76*, 387–404. (b)

Clark, M. P. Changes in primary mental abilities with age. *Archives of Psychology*, 1944, *291*, 30.

Coan, R. W. Facts, factors and artifacts: The quest for psychological meaning. *Psychological Review*, 1964, *71*, 123–140.

Cole, M. *Niche-picking*. Unpublished manuscript, 1980.

Colvin, S. S. Contribution to "Intelligence and its measurement: A symposium." *Journal of Educational Psychology*, 1921, *12*, 136–139.

Cooper, L. A. *Internal representation and transformation of random shapes: A chronometric analysis*. Unpublished doctoral dissertation, Stanford University, 1973.

Cooper, L. A., & Shepard, R. N. Chronometric studies of the rotation of mental images. In W. G. Chase (Ed.), *Visual information processing*. New York: Academic Press, 1973.

Cornell, E. H. Learning to find things: A reinterpretation of object permanence studies. In L. S. Siegel & C. J. Brainerd (Eds.), *Alternatives to Piaget: Critical essays on the theory*. New York: Academic Press, 1978.

Daalen-Kapteijns, M. M., van, & Elshout-Mohr, M. The acquisition of word meanings as a cognitive learning process. *Journal of Verbal Learning and Verbal Behavior*, 1981, *20*, 386–399.

Darwin, C. *The origin of species*. London: John Murray, 1859.

Das, J. P., Kirby, J., & Jarman, R. F. Simultaneous and successive syntheses: An alternative model for cognitive abilities. *Psychological Bulletin*,

1975, *82*, 87–103.

Dasen, P. R. *Piagetian psychology: Cross-cultural contributions*. New York: Gardner Press, 1977.

Dearborn, W. F. Contribution to "Intelligence and its measurement: A symposium." *Journal of Educational Psychology*, 1921, *12*, 210–212.

Dearborn, W. F., & Rothney, J. W. M. *Predicting the child's development*. Cambridge, Mass.: Science-Art Publishing, 1941.

Dearborn, W. F., Rothney, J. W. M., & Shuttleworth, F. K. Data on the growth of public-school children (from the materials of the Harvard Growth Study). *Monographs of the Society for Research in Child Development*, 1938, *3*, 1(Serial No. 14).

Denny, M. R. Learning. In R. Hever and H. Stevens (Eds.), *Review of research in mental retardation*. Chicago: University of Chicago Press, 1963.

DeSoto, C. B., London, M., & Handel, S. Social reasoning and spatial paralogic. *Journal of Personality and Social Psychology*, 1965, *2*, 513–521.

Donders, F. C. Over de snelheid van psychoische processen. Onderzoekingen gedaan in het Physiologisch Laboratorium der Utrechtsche Hoogeschool, 1868–1869. *Tweede reeks, II*, 92–120.

Eimas, P. D. A developmental study of hypothesis behavior and focusing. *Journal of Experimental Child Psychology*, 1969, *8*, 160–172.

Eimas, P. D. Effects of memory aids on hypothesis behavior and focusing in young children and adults. *Journal of Experimental Child Psychology*, 1970, *10*, 319–336.

Elkind, D. Children's discovery of the conservation of mass, weight, and volume: Piaget replication study II. *Journal of Genetic Psychology*, 1961, *98*, 219–227.

Ennis, R. H. Children's ability to handle Piaget's propositional logic: A conceptual critique. *Review of Educational Research*, 1975, *45*, 1–41.

Ennis, R. H. An alternative to Piaget's conceptualization of logical competence. *Child Development*, 1976, *47*, 903–919.

Ernst, G. W., & Newell, A. *GPS: A case study in generality and problem-solving*. New York: Academic Press, 1969.

Estes, W. K. Learning, memory, and intelligence. In R. J. Sternberg (Ed.), *Handbook of human intelligence*. New York: Cambridge University Press, in press.

Fagan, J. F., III, & McGrath, S. K. Infant recognition memory and later intelligence. *Intelligence*, 1981, *5*, 121–130.

Ferguson, G. A. On learning and human ability. *Canadian Journal of Psychology*, 1954, *8*, 95–112.

Feuerstein, R. *The dynamic assessment of retarded performers: The learning potential assessment device, theory, instruments, and techniques*. Baltimore: University Park Press, 1979.

Feuerstein, R. *Instrumental enrichment: An intervention program for cognitive modifiability*. Baltimore: University Park Press, 1980.

Flavell, J. H. *The developmental psychology of Jean Piaget*. New York: D. Van Nostrand, 1963.

Flavell, J. H. Stage related properties of cognitive development. *Cognitive Psychology*, 1971, *2*, 421–453.

Flavell, J. H. Metacognitive aspects of problem solving. In L. B. Resnick (Ed.), *The nature of intelligence*. Hillsdale, N.J.: Erlbaum, 1976.

Flavell, J. H. Cognitive monitoring. In W. P. Dickson (Ed.), *Children's oral communication skills*. New York: Academic Press, 1981.

Flavell, J. H., & Wellman, H. M. Metamemory. In R. V. Kail, Jr., & J. W. Hagen (Eds.), *Perspectives on the development of memory and cognition*. Hillsdale, N.J.: Erlbaum, 1977.

Frederiksen, J. R., Saunders, D. R., & Ward, B. The in-basket test. *Psychological Monographs*, 1957, *71* (9, Whole No. 438).

Gagné, R. M. *The conditions of learning*. New York: Holt, Rinehart & Winston, 1965.

Gagné, R. M. Contributions of learning to human development. *Psychological Review*, 1968, *75*, 177–191.

Gallagher, J. M., & Wright, R. J. *Children's solution of verbal analogies: Extension of Piaget's concept of reflexive abstraction*. Paper presented at the meeting of the Society for Research in Child Development, New Orleans, March 1977.

Gallagher, J. M., & Wright, R. J. Piaget and the study of analogy: Structural analysis of items. In J. Magary (Ed.), *Piaget and the helping professions* (Vol. 8). Los Angeles: University of Southern California, 1979.

Galton, F. *Hereditary genius*. London: Macmillan, 1869.

Galton, F. *Inquiries into human faculty*. London: Macmillan, 1883.

Garner, W. R. *The processing of information and structures*. Hillsdale, N.J.: Erlbaum, 1974.

Garrett, H. E. Differentiable mental traits. *Psychological Record*, 1938, *2*, 259–298.

Garrett, H. E. A developmental theory of intelligence. *American Psychologist*, 1946, *1*, 372–378.

Garrett, H. E., Bryan, A. I., & Perl, R. The age factor in mental organization. *Archives of Psychology*, 1935, *176*, 1–31.

Gelman, R., & Gallistel, C. R. *The child's understanding of number*. Cambridge, Mass.: Harvard University Press, 1978.

Gentile, J. R., Tedesco-Stratton, L., Davis, E., Lund, N. J., & Agunanne, B. A. Associative responding versus analogical reasoning by children. *Intelligence*, 1977, *1*, 369–380.

Gholson, B., & Beilin, H. A developmental model of human learning. In H. W. Reese & L. P. Lipsitt (Eds.), *Advances in child development and behavior* (Vol. 13). New York: Academic Press, 1979.

Gholson, B., Levine, M., & Phillips, S. Hypotheses, strategies, and stereotypes in discrimination learning. *Journal of Experimental Child Psychology*, 1972, *13*, 423–446.

Gholson, B., & Schuepfer, T. Commentary on Kendler's paper: An alternative perspective. In H. W. Reese & L. P. Lipsitt (Eds.), *Advances in child development and behavior* (Vol. 13). New York: Academic Press, 1979.

Ginsburg, H., & Opper, S. *Piaget's theory of intellectual development: An introduction* (2nd ed.). Englewood Cliffs, N.J.: Prentice-Hall, 1979.

Green, D. R., Ford, M. P., & Flamer, G. B. *Measurement and Piaget*. New York: McGraw-Hill, 1971.

Greenfield, P. M. On culture and conservation. In D. R. Price-Williams (Ed.), *Cross-cultural studies*. Harmondsworth, Eng.: Penguin, 1969.

Groen, G. J., & Parkman, J. M. A chronometric analysis of simple addition. *Psychological Review*, 1972, *79*, 329–343.

Guilford, J. P. The structure of intellect. *Psychological Bulletin*, 1956, *53*, 267–293.

Guilford, J. P. A revised structure of intellect (Reprint No. 19). Los Angeles: University of Southern California, Psychological Laboratory, 1957.

Guilford, J. P. *The nature of human intelligence*. New York: McGraw-Hill, 1967.

Guilford, J. P., & Hoepfner, R. *The analysis of intelligence*. New York: McGraw-Hill, 1971.

Hall, V. C., & Kaye, D. B. The necessity of logical necessity in Piaget's theory. In L. S. Siegel & C. J. Brainerd (Eds.), *Alternatives to Piaget: Critical essays on the theory*. New York: Academic Press, 1978.

Heim, A. *Intelligence and personality: Their assessment and relationship*. Harmondsworth, Eng.: Penguin, 1970.

Hofstaetter, P. R. The changing composition of intelligence: A study of the *t*-technique. *Journal of Genetic Psychology*, 1954, *85*, 159–164.

Holt, J. *How children fail*. New York: Pitman, 1964.

Holzinger, K. J. Relationships between three multiple orthogonal factors and four bifactors. *Journal of Educational Psychology*, 1938, *29*, 513–519.

Honzik, M. P. The constancy of mental test performance during the preschool period. *Journal of Genetic Psychology*, 1938, *52*, 285–302.

Horn, J. L. On subjectivity in factor analysis. *Educational and Psychological Measurement*, 1967, *27*, 811–820.

Horn, J. L. Organization of abilities and the development of intelligence. *Psychological Review*, 1968, *75*, 242–259.

Horn, J. L. Organization of data on life-span development of human abilities. In L. R. Goulet & P. B. Baltes (Eds.), *Life-span developmental psychology: Research and theory*. New York: Academic Press, 1970.

Horn, J. L., & Cattell, R. B. Refinement and test of the theory of fluid and crystallized general intelligences. *Journal of Educational Psychology*, 1966, *51*, 253–270.

Horn, J. L., & Donaldson, G. On the myth of intellectual decline in adulthood. *American Psychologist*, 1976, *31*, 701–719.

Horn, J. L., & Knapp, J. R. On the subjective character of the empirical base of Guilford's structure-of-intellect model. *Psychological Bulletin*, 1973, *80*, 33–43.

House, B. J., & Zeaman, D. Visual discrimination learning and intelligence in defectives of low mental age. *American Journal of Mental Deficiency*, 1960, *65*, 51–58.

Hunt, E. B. Mechanics of verbal ability. *Psychological Review*, 1978, *85*, 109–130.

Hunt, E. B., Frost, N., & Lunneborg, C. Individual differences in cognition. In G. Bower (Ed.), *The psychology of learning and motivation* (Vol. 7). New York: Academic Press, 1973.

Hunt, E. B., Lunneborg, C., & Lewis, J. What does it mean to be high verbal? *Cognitive Psychology*, 1975, *7*, 194–227.

Hunt, E. B., & Poltrock, S. Mechanics of thought. In B. Kantowitz (Ed.), *Human information processing: Tutorials in performance and cognition*. Hillsdale, N.J.: Erlbaum, 1974.

Hunter, I. M. L. The solving of three term series problems. *British Journal of Psychology*, 1957, *48*, 286–298.

Huttenlocher, J. Constructing spatial images: A strategy in reasoning. *Psychological Review*,

1968, *75*, 550–560.

Huttenlocher, J., & Higgins, E. T. Adjectives, comparatives, and syllogisms. *Psychological Review*, 1971, *78*, 487–504.

Huttenlocher, J., & Presson, C. C. Mental rotation and the perspective problem. *Cognitive Psychology*, 1973, *4*, 277–299.

Inhelder, B., & Piaget, J. *The growth of logical thinking from childhood to adolescence*. New York: Basic Books, 1958.

Inhelder, B., & Piaget, J. *The early growth of logic in the child: Classification and seriation*. New York: W. W. Norton, 1964.

Inhelder, B., Sinclair, H., & Bovet, M. *Learning and the development of cognition*. Cambridge, Mass.: Harvard University Press, 1974.

"Intelligence and its measurement: A symposium." *Journal of Educational Psychology*, 1921, *12*, 123–147, 195–216, 271–275.

Istomina, Z. M. The development of voluntary memory in preschool-age children. *Soviet Psychology*, 1975, *13*, 5–64. (Originally published, 1948.)

Jarman, R. F., & Das, J. P. Simultaneous and successive syntheses and intelligence. *Intelligence*, 1977, *1*, 151–169.

Jarvik, L. F., Eisdorfer, C., & Blum, J. E. *Intellectual functioning in adults*. New York: Springer Publishing, 1973.

Jastrow, J. Some anthropological and psychological tests on college students—a preliminary survey. *American Journal of Psychology*, 1892, *4*, 420.

Jensen, A. R. Hierarchical theories of mental ability. In W. B. Dockrell (Ed.), *On intelligence*. Toronto: Ontario Institute for Studies in Education, 1970.

Jensen, A. R. The chronometry of intelligence. In R. J. Sternberg (Ed.), *Advances in the psychology of human intelligence* (Vol. 1). Hillsdale, N.J.: Erlbaum, 1982.

Johnson-Laird, P. N. The three-term series problem. *Cognition*, 1972, *1*, 57–82.

Jones, H. E. The environment and mental development. In L. Carmichael (Ed.), *Manual of child psychology* (2nd ed.). New York: Wiley, 1954.

Jones, H. E., & Conrad, H. S. The growth and decline of intelligence: A study of a homogeneous group between the ages of ten and sixty. *Genetic Psychology Monographs*, 1933, *13*, 223–298.

Kagan, J. *Change and continuity in infancy*. New York: Wiley, 1971.

Kahneman, D. *Attention and effort*. Englewood Cliffs, N.J.: Prentice Hall, 1973.

Kail, R. V. *The development of memory in children*. San Francisco: W. H. Freeman, 1979.

Kail, R. V., & Hagen, J. W. (Eds.), *Perspectives on the development of memory and cognition*. Hillsdale, N.J.: Erlbaum, 1977.

Kail, R. V., Pellegrino, J., & Carter, P. Developmental changes in mental rotation. *Journal of Experimental Child Psychology*, 1980, *29*, 102–116.

Kamin, L. J. *The science and politics of I.Q.* Hillsdale, N.J.: Erlbaum, 1974.

Keating, D. P., & Bobbitt, B. L. Individual and developmental differences in cognitive-processing components of mental ability. *Child Development*, 1978, *49*, 155–167.

Keating, D. P., & Caramazza, A. Effects of age and ability on syllogistic reasoning in early adolescence. *Developmental Psychology*, 1975, *11*, 837–842.

Keating, D. P., Keniston, A. H., Manis, F. R., & Bobbitt, B. L. Development of the search-processing parameter. *Child Development*, 1980, *51*, 39–44.

Kendler, H. H., & Kendler, T. S. Vertical and horizontal processes in problem-solving. In R. J. C. Harper, C. C. Anderson, C. M. Christensen, & S. M. Hunka (Eds.), *The cognitive processes: Readings*. Englewood Cliffs, N.J.: Prentice-Hall, 1964.

Kendler, H. H., & Kendler, T. S. From discrimination learning to cognitive development. A neobehavioristic odyssey. In W. K. Estes (Ed.), *Handbook of learning and cognitive processes* (Vol. 1). Hillsdale, N.J.: Erlbaum, 1975.

Kendler, T. S. Development of mediating responses in children. In P. H. Mussen, J. J. Conger, & J. Kagan (Eds.), *Readings in child development and personality* (2nd ed.). New York: Harper & Row, 1970.

Kendler, T. S. The development of discrimination learning: A levels-of-functioning explanation. In H. W. Reese & L. P. Lipsitt (Eds.), *Advances in child development and behavior* (Vol. 13). New York: Academic Press, 1979. (a)

Kendler, T. S. Reply to commentaries. In H. W. Reese and L. P. Lipsitt (Eds.), *Advances in child development and behavior* (Vol. 13). New York: Academic Press, 1979. (b)

Kendler, T. S., & Kendler, H. H. Experimental analysis of inferential behavior in children. In L. P. Lipsitt & C. C. Spiker (Eds.), *Advances in child development and behavior* (Vol. 3). New York: Academic Press, 1967.

Kendler, T. S., Kendler, H. H., & Wells, D. Reversal and nonreversal shifts in nursery school children. *Journal of Comparative and Physiological Psychology*, 1960, *53*, 83–88.

Kendler, T. S., & Ward, J. W. Optional reversal probability is a linear function of the log of age. *Developmental Psychology*, 1972, *7*, 337–348.

Kessen, W., & Kessen, M. L. Behavior of young children in a two-choice guessing problem. *Child Development*, 1961, *32*, 779–788.

Klahr, D. Goal formation, planning, and learning by pre-school problem solvers or: "My socks are in the dryer." In R. S. Siegler (Ed.), *Children's thinking: What develops?* Hillsdale, N.J.: Erlbaum, 1978.

Klahr, D. *Problem solving and planning by pre-school children*. Paper presented at the meeting of the Society for Research in Child Development, San Francisco, March 1979.

Klahr, D., & Siegler, R. S. The representation of children's knowledge. In H. Reese & L. P. Lipsitt (Eds.), *Advances in child development and behavior* (Vol. 12). New York: Academic Press, 1978.

Klahr, D., & Wallace, J. G. The role of quantification operators in the development of conservation of quantity. *Cognitive Psychology*, 1973, *4*, 301–327.

Klahr, D., & Wallace, J. G. *Cognitive development: An information processing view*. Hillsdale, N.J.: Erlbaum, 1976.

Kobasigawa, A. Utilization of retrieval cues by children in recall. *Child Development*, 1974, *45*, 127–134.

Kogan, N., Connor, K., Gross, A., & Fava, D. Understanding visual metaphor: Developmental and individual differences. *Monographs of the Society for Research in Child Development*, 1980, *45*(1, Whole No. 183).

Kuenne, M. R. Experimental investigation of the relation of language to transposition behavior in young children. *Journal of Experimental Psychology*, 1946, *36*, 471–490.

Külpe, O. *Outlines of psychology*. New York: Macmillan, 1895.

Levi, E. H. *An introduction to legal reasoning*. Chicago: University of Chicago Press, 1949.

Levinson, P. J., & Carpenter, R. L. An analysis of analogical reasoning in children. *Child Development*, 1974, *45*, 857–861.

Lewis, M. *Origins of intelligence*. New York: Plenum, 1976.

Lewis, M., & Brooks-Gunn, J. Visual attention at three months as a predictor of cognitive functioning at two years of age. *Intelligence*, 1981, *5*,

131–140.

Lipman, R. S. Learning: verbal, perceptual-motor and classical conditioning. In N. R. Ellis (Ed.), *Handbook of mental deficiency*. New York: McGraw-Hill, 1963.

Loehlin, J. C., Lindzey, G., & Spuhler, J. N. *Race and intelligence*. San Francisco: W. H. Freeman, 1975.

Lovell, K. A follow-up study of Inhelder and Piaget's *The growth of logical thinking*. *British Journal of Psychology*, 1961, *52*, 143–153.

Lovell, K. Some problems associated with formal thought and its assessment. In D. R. Green, M. P. Ford, & G. B. Flamer (Eds.), *Measurement and Piaget*. New York: McGraw-Hill, 1971.

Luchins, A. S. Mechanization in problem solving. *Psychological Monographs*, 1942, *54*(6, Whole No. 248).

Lunzer, E. A. Problems of formal reasoning in test situations. In P. H. Mussen (Ed.), European research in cognitive development. *Monographs of the Society for Research in Child Development*, 1965, *30*(2, Serial No. 100).

Luria, A. R. *The role of speech in the regulation of normal and abnormal behavior*. New York: Liveright, 1961.

Luria, A. R. *Higher cortical functions in man*. New York: Basic Books, 1966. (a)

Luria, A. R. *Human brain and psychological processes*. New York: Harper & Row, 1966. (b)

Luria, A. R. *The working brain*. London: Penguin, 1973.

Mager, R. F. *Goal analysis*. Belmont, Calif.: Lear Siegler/Fearon, 1972.

Mager, R. F. *Preparing instructional objectives* (2nd ed.). Belmont, Calif.: Fearon, 1975.

Markman, E. M. Realizing that you don't understand: A preliminary investigation. *Child Development*, 1977, *48*, 986–992.

Markman, E. M. Realizing that you don't understand: Elementary school children's awareness of inconsistencies. *Child Development*, 1979, *50*, 643–655.

Markman, E. M. Comprehension monitoring. In W. P. Dickson (Ed.), *Children's oral communication skills*. New York: Academic Press, 1981.

Marmor, G. S. Development of kinetic images: When does the child first represent movement in mental images? *Cognitive Psychology*, 1975, *7*, 548–559.

Marmor, G. S. Mental rotation and number conservation: Are they related? *Developmental Psychology*, 1977, *13*, 320–325.

Martorano, S. C. A developmental analysis of performance on Piaget's formal operations tasks. *Developmental Psychology*, 1977, *13*, 666–672.

McCall, R. B., Eichorn, D. J., & Hogarty, P. S. Transitions in early mental development. *Monographs of the Society for Research in Child Development*, 1977 (Whole No. 171).

McCall, R. B., Hogarty, P. S., & Hurlburt, N. Transitions in infant sensorimotor development and the prediction of childhood IQ. *American Psychologist*, 1972, *27*, 728–748.

McCullough, C. M. Context aids in reading. *Reading Teacher*, 1958, *11*, 225–229.

McNemar, Q. *The revision of the Stanford–Binet scale: An analysis of the standardization data*. Boston: Houghton-Mifflin, 1942.

Miles, T. R. On defining intelligence. *British Journal of Educational Psychology*, 1957, *27*, 153–165.

Miller, G. A. The magical number seven plus or minus two: Some limits on our capacity for processing information. *Psychological Review*, 1956, *63*, 81–97.

Miller, G. A., Galanter, E., & Pribram, K. H. *Plans and the structure of behavior*. New York: Holt, Rinehart & Winston, 1960.

Miller, G. A., & Johnson-Laird, P. N. *Language and perception*. Cambridge, Mass.: Harvard University Press, 1976.

Miller, S. A. Nonverbal assessment of Piagetian concepts. *Psychological Bulletin*, 1976, *83*, 405–430.

Moyer, R. S. Comparing objects in memory: Evidence suggesting an internal psychophysics. *Perception and Psychophysics*, 1973, *13*, 180–184.

Mulholland, T. M., Pellegrino, J. W., & Glaser, R. Components of geometric analogy solution. *Cognitive Psychology*, 1980, *12*, 252–284.

Mussen, P. H. (Ed.), *Carmichael's manual of child psychology* (3rd ed.). New York: Wiley, 1970.

Neisser, V. The concept of intelligence. In R. J. Sternberg & D. K. Detterman (Eds.), *Human intelligence: Perspectives on its theory and measurement*. Norwood, N.J.: Ablex, 1979.

Newell, A. Production systems: Models of control structures. In W. G. Chase (Ed.), *Visual information processing*. New York: Academic Press, 1973.

Newell, A., Shaw, J., & Simon, H. A. Report on a general problem-solving program. In *Proceedings of the international conference on information processing*. Paris: UNESCO, 1960.

Newell, A., & Simon, H. A. *Human problem solving*. Englewood Cliffs, N.J.: Prentice-Hall,

1972.

Odom, R. D. Concept identification and utilization among children of different ages. *Journal of Experimental Child Psychology*, 1966, *4*, 309–316.

Odom, R. D., & Coon, R. C. The development of hypothesis testing. *Journal of Experimental Child Psychology*, 1966, *4*, 285–291.

Oppenheimer, J. R. Analogy in science. *American Psychologist*, 1956, *11*, 127–135.

Osherson. D. N. *Logical abilities in children*, vol. 2, *Logical inference: Underlying operations*. Hillsdale, N.J.: Erlbaum, 1974.

Osherson, D. N. *Logical abilities in children*, vol. 3, *Reasoning in adolescence: Deductive inference*. Hillsdale, N.J.: Erlbaum, 1975.

Osherson, D. N. *Logical abilities in children*, vol. 4, *Reasoning and concepts*. Hillsdale, N.J.: Erlbaum, 1976.

Osler, S. F., & Kofsky, E. Structure and strategy in concept learning. *Journal of Experimental Child Psychology*, 1966, *4*, 198–209.

Owens, W. A., Jr. Age and mental abilities: A longitudinal study. *Genetic Psychology Monographs*, 1953, *48*, 3–54.

Pachella, R. G. The interpretation of reaction time in information processing research. In B. Kantowitz (Ed.), *Human information processing: Tutorials in performance and cognition*. Hillsdale, N.J.: Erlbaum, 1974.

Paris, S. G. Comprehension of language connectives and propositional logical relationships. *Journal of Experimental Child Psychology*, 1973, *16*, 278–291.

Paris, S. G. *Metacognitive development: Children's regulation of problem-solving skills*. Paper presented at the meeting of the Midwestern Psychological Association, Chicago, May 1978.

Pascual-Leone, J. A mathematical model for the transition rule in Piaget's developmental stages. *Acta Psychologica*, 1970, *63*, 301–345.

Pascual-Leone, J. Constructive problems for constructive theories: The current relevance of Piaget's work and a critique of information-processing simulation psychology. In R. H. Kluwe & H. Spada (Eds.), *Developmental models of thinking*. New York: Academic Press, 1980.

Perlmutter, M. (Ed.), *Children's memory: New directions for child development*. San Francisco: Jossey-Bass, 1980.

Peterson, J. Contribution to "Intelligence and its measurement: A symposium." *Journal of Educational Psychology*, 1921, *12*, 198–201.

Piaget, J. *Judgment and reasoning in the child*. London: Routledge & Kegan Paul, 1928.

Piaget, J. *The child's conception of number*. New York: W. W. Norton, 1952. (a)

Piaget, J. *The origins of intelligence in children*. New York: International Universities Press, 1952. (b)

Piaget, J. *The construction of reality in the child*. New York: Basic Books, 1954.

Piaget, J. *The language and thought of the child*. New York: New American Library, 1955.

Piaget, J. Piaget's theory. In P. H. Mussen (Ed.), *Carmichael's manual of child psychology* (3rd ed., Vol. 1). New York: Wiley, 1970.

Piaget, J. Intellectual evolution from adolescence to adulthood. *Human Development*, 1972, *15*, 1–12.

Piaget, J. *The psychology of intelligence*. Totowa, N.J.: Littlefield, Adams, 1976.

Piaget, J. *The development of thought: Equilibration of cognitive structures* (trans. Arnold Rosin). New York: Viking, 1977.

Piaget, J., & Inhelder, B. *Le développement des quantités physiques chez l'enfant: Conservation et atomisme* (2nd ed.). Neuchâtel, Switz.: Delachaux et Niestlé, 1962.

Piaget, J., & Inhelder, B. *The psychology of the child*. New York: Basic Books, 1969.

Piaget, J., Inhelder, B., Szeminska, A. *The child's conception of geometry*. New York: Basic Books, 1960.

Piaget, J. (with Montangero, J., & Billeter, J.). Les correlâts. *L'Abstraction réfléchissante*. Paris: Presses Universitaires de France, 1977.

Pintner, R. Contribution to "Intelligence and its measurement: A symposium." *Journal of Educational Psychology*, 1921, *12*, 139–143.

Posner, M., Boies, S., Eichelman, W., & Taylor, R. Retention of visual and name codes of single letters. *Journal of Experimental Psychology Monograph*, 1969, *79*(1, Pt. 2).

Powell, J. S., & Sternberg, R. J. *Acquisition of vocabulary from context*. Paper presented at the meeting of the American Psychological Association, Los Angeles, August 1981.

Price-Williams, D. R., Gordon, W., & Ramirez, W. G. Skill and conservation: A study of pottery-making children. *Developmental Psychology*, 1969, *1*, 769.

Quinton, G., & Fellows, B. "Perceptual" strategies in the solving of three-term series problems. *British Journal of Psychology*, 1975, *66*, 69–78.

Rachlin, H. *Introduction to modern behaviorism* (2nd ed.). San Francisco: W. H. Freeman, 1976.

Resnick, L. B. *The role of invention in the develop-ment of mathematical competence*. Unpublished manuscript, 1980.

Riegel, K. F., & Riegel, R. M. Development, drop, and death. *Developmental Psychology*, 1972, *6*, 306–319.

Riley, C. A. The representation of comparative relations and the transitive inference task. *Journal of Experimental Child Psychology*, 1976, *22*, 1–22.

Riley, C. A., & Trabasso, T. Comparatives, logical structures, and encoding in a transitive inference task. *Journal of Experimental Child Psychology*, 1974, *17*, 187–203.

Rose, S. A., & Blank, M. The potency of context in children's cognition: An illustration through conservation. *Child Development*, 1974, *45*, 499–502.

Royce, J. R. Factors as theoretical constructs. *American Psychologist*, 1963, *18*, 522–527.

Royce, J. R. The conceptual framework for a multi-factor theory of individuality. In J. R. Royce (Ed.), *Multivariate analysis and psychological theory*. London: Academic Press, 1973.

Scarr, S., & Carter-Saltzman, L. Behavior genetics and intelligence. In R. J. Sternberg (Ed.), *Handbook of human intelligence*. New York: Cambridge University Press, in press.

Schaie, K. W. A general model for the study of developmental problems. *Psychological Bulletin*, 1965, *64*, 92–107.

Schaie, K. W. Developmental processes and aging. In C. Eisdorfer & M. P. Lawton (Eds.), *The psychology of adult development and aging*. Washington, D.C.: American Psychological Association, 1973.

Schaie, K. W. Translations in gerontology—from lab to life. *American Psychologist*, 1974, *29*, 802–807.

Schank, R. How much intelligence is there in artificial intelligence? *Intelligence*, 1980, *4*, 1–14.

Schiller, B. Verbal, numerical and spatial abilities of young children. *Archives of Psychology*, 1934, *161*, 1–69.

Schneck, M. R. The measurement of verbal and numerical abilities. *Archives of Psychology*, 1929, *107*, 1–49.

Schneider, W., & Shiffrin, R. M. Controlled and automatic human information processing: I. Detection, search, and attention. *Psychological Review*, 1977, *84*, 1–66.

Sharp, S. E. Individual psychology: A study in psychological method. *American Journal of Psychology*, 1899, *10*, 329–391.

Shaver, P., Pierson, L., & Lang, S. Converging

evidence for the functional significance of imagery in problem solving. *Cognition, 1974, 3,* 359–375.

Shepard, R. N., & Metzler, J. Mental rotation of three-dimensional objects. *Science, 1971, 171,* 701–703.

Shepp, B. From perceived similarity to dimensional structure: A new hypothesis about perspective development. In E. Rosch & B. B. Lloyd (Eds.), *Cognition and categorization.* Hillsdale, N.J.: Erlbaum, 1978.

Shiffrin, R. M., & Schneider, W. Controlled and automatic human information processing: II. Perceptual learning, automatic attending, and a general theory. *Psychological Review, 1977, 84,* 127–190.

Siegel, L. S. The relationship of language and thought in the preoperational child: A reconsideration of nonverbal alternatives to Piagetian tasks. In L. S. Siegel & C. J. Brainerd (Eds.), *Alternatives to Piaget: Critical essays on the theory.* New York: Academic Press, 1978.

Siegel, L. S., & Brainerd, C. J. (Eds.), *Alternatives to Piaget: Critical essays on the theory.* New York: Academic Press, 1978.

Siegler, R. S. Three aspects of cognitive development. *Cognitive Psychology, 1976, 4,* 481–520.

Siegler, R. S. The 20-question game as a form of problem-solving. *Child Development, 1977, 4,* 481–520.

Siegler, R. S. The origins of scientific reasoning. In R. S. Siegler (Ed.), *Children's thinking: What develops?* Hillsdale, N.J.: Erlbaum, 1978.

Siegler, R. S. Developmental sequences within and between concepts. *Monographs of the Society for Research in Child Development, 1981, 46*(2, Whole No. 189).

Siegler, R. S., & Richards, D. D. The development of intelligence. In R. J. Sternberg (Ed.), *Handbook of human intelligence.* New York: Cambridge University Press, in press.

Siegler, R. S., & Vago, S. The development of a proportionality concept: Judging relative fullness. *Journal of Experimental Child Psychology, 1978, 25,* 371–395.

Sigel, I. E., & Hooper, F. H. *Logical thinking in children: Research based on Piaget's theory.* New York: Holt, Rinehart, & Winston, 1968.

Simon, H. A. The functional equivalence of problem-solving skills. *Cognitive Psychology, 1975, 7,* 268–288.

Smith, L. B., & Kemler, D. G. Levels of experienced dimensionality in children and adults. *Cognitive Psychology, 1978, 10,* 502–537.

Sontag, L. W., Baker, C. T., & Nelson, V. L. Mental growth and personality development: A longitudinal study. *Monographs of the Society for Research in Child Development, 1958, 23*(2, Whole No. 68).

Spada, H., & Kluwe, R. H. Two models of intellectual development and their reference to the theory of Piaget. In R. H. Kluwe & H. Spada (Eds.), *Developmental models of thinking.* New York: Academic Press, 1980.

Spearman, C. "General intelligence," objectively determined and measured. *American Journal of Psychology, 1904, 15,* 201–293.

Spearman, C. *The nature of "intelligence" and the principles of cognition.* London: Macmillan, 1923.

Spearman, C. *The abilities of man.* New York: Macmillan, 1927.

Spiker, C. C., & Cantor, J. H. The Kendler levels-of-functioning theory: Comments and an alternative schema. In H. W. Reese & L. P. Lipsitt (Eds.), *Advances in child development and behavior* (Vol. 13). New York: Academic Press, 1979.

Staudenmayer, H., & Bourne, L. E., Jr. Learning to interpret conditional sentences: A developmental study. *Developmental Psychology, 1977, 13,* 616–623.

Sternberg, R. J. Component processes in analogical reasoning. *Psychological Review, 1977, 84,* 353–378. (a)

Sternberg, R. J. *Intelligence, information processing, and analogical reasoning: The componential analysis of human abilities.* Hillsdale, N.J.: Erlbaum, 1977. (b)

Sternberg, R. J. Developmental patterns in the encoding and combination of logical connectives. *Journal of Experimental Child Psychology, 1979, 28,* 469–498. (a)

Sternberg, R. J. The nature of mental abilities. *American Psychologist, 1979, 34,* 214–230. (b)

Sternberg, R. J. Componentman as vice-president: A reply to Pellegrino and Lyon's analysis of "The components of a componential analysis." *Intelligence, 1980, 4,* 83–95. (a)

Sternberg, R. J. The development of linear syllogistic reasoning. *Journal of Experimental Child Psychology, 1980, 29,* 340–356. (b)

Sternberg, R. J. Factor theories of intelligence are all right almost. *Educational Researcher, 1980, 9,* 6–13, 18. (c)

Sternberg, R. J. A proposed resolution of curious conflicts in the literature on linear syllogisms. In R. Nickerson (Ed.), *Attention and performance*

(Vol. 8). Hillsdale, N.J.: Erlbaum, 1980. (d)

Sternberg, R. J. Representation and process in linear syllogistic reasoning. *Journal of Experimental Psychology: General*, 1980, *109*, 119–159. (e)

Sternberg, R. J. Sketch of a componential subtheory of human intelligence. *Behavioral and Brain Sciences*, 1980, *3*, 573–584. (f)

Sternberg, R. J. Intelligence and nonentrenchment. *Journal of Educational Psychology*, 1981, *73*, 1–16. (a)

Sternberg, R. J. Novelty-seeking, novelty-finding, and the developmental continuity of intelligence. *Intelligence*, 1981, *5*, 149–155. (b)

Sternberg, R. J. Toward a unified componential theory of human intelligence: I. Fluid abilities. In M. Friedman, J. P. Das, & N. O'Connor (Eds.), *Intelligence and learning*. New York: Plenum, 1981. (c)

Sternberg, R. J., Conway, B. E., Ketron, J. L., & Bernstein, M. People's conceptions of intelligence. *Journal of Personality and Social Psychology: Attitudes and Social Cognition*, 1981, *41*, 37–55.

Sternberg, R. J., & Downing, C. The development of higher-order reasoning in adolescence. *Child Development*, 1982, *53*, 209–221.

Sternberg, R. J., & Ketron, J. L. Selection and implementation of strategies in reasoning by analogy. *Journal of Educational Psychology*, 1982, *74*, 399–413.

Sternberg, R. J., Ketron, J. L., & Powell, J. S. Componential approaches to the training of intelligence. In D. K. Detterman & R. J. Sternberg (Eds.), *How and how much can intelligence be increased?* Norwood, N.J.: Ablex, 1982.

Sternberg, R. J., & Nigro, G. Developmental patterns in the solution of verbal analogies. *Child Development*, 1980, *51*, 27–38.

Sternberg, R. J., & Powell, J. S. *The development of intelligence* (Tech. Rep. No. 10, Cognitive Development Series). New Haven, Conn.: Yale University, 1980.

Sternberg, R. J., & Powell, J. S. Theories of intelligence. In R. J. Sternberg (Ed.), *Handbook of human intelligence*. New York: Cambridge University Press, 1982.

Sternberg, R. J., Powell, J. S., & Kaye, D. B. *The nature of verbal comprehension. Poetics*, in press.

Sternberg, R. J., & Rifkin, B. The development of analogical reasoning processes. *Journal of Experimental Child Psychology*, 1979, *27*, 195–232.

Sternberg, R. J., & Weil, E. M. An aptitude-strat-egy interaction in linear syllogistic reasoning. *Journal of Educational Psychology*, 1980, *72*, 226–234.

Sternberg, S. The discovery of processing stages: Extensions of Donder's method. *Acta Psychologica*, 1969, *30*, 276–315. (a)

Sternberg, S. Memory-scanning: Mental processes revealed by reaction-time experiments. *American Scientist*, 1969, *4*, 421–457. (b)

Stevenson, H. W. Learning in children. In P. H. Mussen (Ed.), *Carmichael's manual of child psychology* (3rd ed., Vol. 1). New York: Wiley, 1970.

Stevenson, H. W., Iscoe, I., & McConnell, C. A developmental study of transposition. *Journal of Experimental Psychology*, 1955, *49*, 278–280.

Stott, L. H., & Ball, R. S. Infant and preschool mental tests. *Monographs of the Society for Research in Child Development*, 1965, *30*(3, Whole No. 101).

Suppes, P., & Groen, G. J. Some counting models for first-grade performance data on simple addition facts. In J. M. Scandura (Ed.), *Research in mathematics education*. Washington, D.C.: National Council of Teachers of Mathematics, 1967.

Taplin, J. E., Staudenmayer, H., & Taddonio, J. L. Developmental changes in conditional reasoning: Linguistic or logical? *Journal of Experimental Child Psychology*, 1974, *17*, 360–373.

Terman, L. M. Contribution to "Intelligence and its measurement: A symposium." *Journal of Educational Psychology*, 1921, *12*, 127–133.

Terman, L. M. *Genetic studies of genius*, vol. 1, *Mental and physical traits of a thousand gifted children*. Stanford, Calif.: Stanford University Press, 1925.

Terman, L. M., & Merrill, M. A. *Measuring intelligence*. Boston: Houghton-Mifflin, 1937.

Terman, L. M., & Merrill, M. A. *Stanford–Binet intelligence scale: Manual for the third revision, Form L-M*. Boston: Houghton-Mifflin, 1973.

Terman, L. M., & Oden, M. H. *Genetic studies of genius*, vol. 4, *The gifted group at midlife*. Stanford, Calif.: Stanford University Press, 1959.

Thayer, E. S., & Collyer, C. E. The development of transitive inference: A review of recent approaches. *Psychological Bulletin*, 1978, *85*, 1327–1344.

Thomson, G. H. *The factorial analysis of human ability*. London: University of London Press, 1939.

Thorndike, E. L. The measurement of intelligence: Present status. *Psychological Review*, 1924, *31*,

219–252.

Thorndike, E. L., Bregman, E. O., Cobb, M. V., & Woodyard, E. I. *The measurement of intelligence.* New York: Columbia University, Teachers College, 1926.

Thurstone, L. L. *The nature of intelligence.* New York: Harcourt, Brace, 1924.

Thurstone, L. L. *Primary mental abilities.* Chicago: University of Chicago Press, 1938.

Thurstone, L. L. *A factorial study of perception.* Chicago: University of Chicago Press, 1944.

Thurstone, L. L. *Multiple factor analysis.* Chicago: University of Chicago Press, 1947.

Thurstone, L. L., & Thurstone, T. G. *SRA Primary Mental Abilities.* Chicago: Science Research Associates, 1962.

Tighe, L. S. Effect of perceptual pretraining on reversal and nonreversal shifts. *Journal of Experimental Psychology,* 1965, *70,* 379–385.

Tighe, T. J., & Tighe, L. S. Discrimination shift performance as function of age and shift procedure. *Journal of Experimental Psychology,* 1967, *4,* 466–470.

Tighe, T. J., & Tighe, L. S. Reversals prior to solution of concept identification in children. *Journal of Experimental Child Psychology,* 1972, *13,* 488–501.

Trabasso, T. Representation, memory, and reasoning: How do we make transitive inferences? In A. D. Pick (Ed.), *Minnesota symposia on child psychology* (Vol. 9). Minneapolis: University of Minnesota Press, 1975.

Trabasso, T., & Riley, C. A. On the construction and use of representations involving linear order. In R. L. Solso (Ed.), *Information processing and cognition: The Loyola symposium.* Hillsdale, N.J.: Erlbaum, 1975.

Trabasso, T., Riley, C. A., & Wilson, E. G. The representation of linear order and spatial strategies in reasoning: A developmental study. In R. Falmagne (Ed.), *Reasoning: Representation and process.* Hillsdale, N.J.: Erlbaum, 1975.

Tuddenham, R. D. Theoretical regularities and individual idiosyncracies. In D. R. Green, M. P. Ford, & G. B. Flamer (Eds.), *Measurement and Piaget.* New York: McGraw-Hill, 1971.

Uzgiris, I. C. Situational generality of conservation. In I. E. Sigel & F. H. Hooper (Eds.), *Logical thinking in children: Research based on Piaget's theory.* New York: Holt, Rinehart, & Winston, 1968.

Vernon, P. E. *The structure of human abilities.* London: Methuen, 1971.

Vurpillot, E. The development of scanning strategies and their relation to visual differentiation. *Journal of Experimental Child Psychology,* 1968, *6,* 632–650.

Wallach, M. A., & Kogan, N. Aspects of judgment and decision-making: Interrelationships and changes with age. *Behavioral Science,* 1961, *6,* 23–36.

Watson, J. B. *Behaviorism* (Rev. ed.). Chicago: University of Chicago Press, 1930.

Wechsler, D. *The measurement of adult intelligence.* Baltimore: Williams & Wilkins, 1939.

Wechsler, D. *The measurement and appraisal of adult intelligence.* Baltimore: Williams & Wilkins, 1958.

Wechsler, D. *Manual for the Wechsler Intelligence Scale for Children—Revised.* New York: Psychological Corp., 1974.

Weir, M. W., & Stevenson, H. W. The effect of verbalization in children's learning as a function of chronological age. *Child Development,* 1959, *30,* 143–149.

Werner, H. *Comparative psychology of mental development* (Rev. ed.). New York: International Universities Press, 1948.

Werner, H., & Kaplan, E. The acquisition of word meanings: A developmental study. *Monographs of the Society for Research in Child Development,* 1952, *15*(1, Serial No. 51).

White, S. H. Evidence for a hierarchical arrangement of learning processes. In L. P. Lipsitt and C. C. Spiker (Eds.), *Advances in child development and behavior* (Vol. 2). New York: Academic Press, 1965.

White, S. H. The learning theory tradition and child psychology. In P. H. Mussen (Ed.), *Carmichael's manual of child psychology* (3rd ed., Vol. 1). New York: Wiley, 1970.

Whitely, S. Information-processing on intelligence test items: Some response components. *Applied Psychological Measurement,* 1977, *1,* 465–476.

Wissler, C. L. The correlation of mental and physical tests. *Psychology Review Monograph Supplement,* 1901, *3*(6).

Wittgenstein, L. *Philosophical investigations.* Oxford: Basil Blackwell, 1953.

Wober, M. Toward an understanding of the Kiganda concept of intelligence. In J. W. Berry and P. R. Dasen (Eds.), *Culture and cognition: Readings in cross-cultural psychology.* London: Methuen, 1974.

Wood, D., Shotter, J., & Godden, D. An investigation of the relationships between problem solving strategies, representation and memory. *Quarterly Journal of Experimental Psychology,* 1974,

26, 252–257.

Woodrow, H. The ability to learn. *Psychological Review*, 1946, *53*, 147–158.

Woods, S. S., Resnick, L. B., & Groen, G. J. An experimental test of five process models for subtraction. *Journal of Educational Psychology*, 1975, *67*, 17–21.

Youniss, J., & Furth, H. G. Discrimination shifts as a function of degree of training in children. *Journal of Experimental Psychology*, 1965, *70*, 424–427.

Yussen, S. R., & Kane, P. Children's concept of intelligence. In S. R. Yussen (Ed.), *The growth of insight in the child*. New York: Academic Press, in press.

Zeaman, D., & House, B. J. The relation of IQ and learning. In R. M. Gagné (Ed.), *Learning and individual differences*. Columbus, Ohio: Charles E. Merrill, 1967.

REPRESENTATION* | 7

JEAN M. MANDLER, *University of California, San Diego*

CHAPTER CONTENTS

INTRODUCTION

The Two Senses of Representation

There are two principal senses in which the term representation has been used. The first of these, and the sense that will be the focus of this chapter, refers to knowledge and the way in which it is organized. This is a complex conception, since it refers both to what is known and how that knowledge is structured. Thus, we can ask *whether* some piece of information is represented, and we can also ask *how* it is

represented. To illustrate, in their chapter, "The Representation of Children's Knowledge," Klahr and Siegler (1978) discuss the kinds of information children have about the workings of a balance scale. They then discuss several theories about the form that representation might take, for example, a decision tree or a production system. Each of these is a theory about representation in our first sense of the term.

The second usage is the more traditional and familiar one, namely, representation as the use of symbols. Representation in this sense refers to words, artifacts, or other symbolic productions that people use to represent (to stand for, to refer to) some aspect of the world or some aspect of their knowledge of the world. In this usage, representation involves a relationship between a symbol and its referent, as in the relationship between a road map and a terrain or a

*Preparation of this chapter was supported in part by National Institute of Mental Health Grant MH–24492. For their many helpful comments, I am grateful to the editors of this volume, the members of my laboratory, and Rochel Gelman, William Kessen, Stephen Kosslyn, and George Mandler. I am particularly indebted to Nancy Johnson for her detailed and insightful comments.

portrait and the object of the portraiture. Thus, x represents y is taken to mean that x stands for or portrays y. Because symbols are involved, representation in this sense has a communicative function, telling someone (or sometimes oneself) that when x is used it is meant to stand for a piece of shared knowledge.

Within the framework of developmental psychology, the distinction between the two senses of the term has been captured nicely by Deregowski (1977):

> Representation . . . has to a[n] empirical psychologist . . . at least two distinctive meanings. One of these refers to the artifacts created by the child which are intended to represent the external world, the other to the internal schema or frames of reference which the child uses in his interaction with the external world. Unlike the former, the latter are not directly accessible and have to be elicited by a variety of techniques, including analysis of children's artifacts. (p. 219)

Both uses of the term are respectable and useful, but they are often not clearly distinguished. Thus, in the book of essays on the child's representation of the world from which the Deregowski quote was taken (Butterworth, 1977a), one finds first one usage, then another. Most of the essays concentrate on children's pictorial representations (representations as symbols). However, some of the chapters, especially those having to do with spatial representation, examine children's abstract knowledge of space (representation as knowledge). What one knows about space must be carefully separated from the use of a square on a piece of paper to stand for a house or a curving line to stand for the route to a school.

The use of representation as knowledge is not concerned with the issue of how one should characterize the relationship between a representation and the world, an issue that has traditionally been thought to be the heart of the matter. Such questions as ''What must the relation be between a symbol and its referent?'' or ''Must a symbol resemble that which it represents?'' have an ancient philosophical and aesthetic history.[1] However, as just discussed, the use of representation as knowledge does not imply a symbolic, referential, or communicative function. From our point of view as individuals, knowledge of dogs or houses or how to get to school or what happens in a restaurant does not *stand for* or *communicate about* those objects or events. Instead, such knowledge constitutes our model of the world.

Given that this model, our knowledge base, is the *only* information we have about the world, it can only be said to stand for the world in a loose and somewhat circular sense; that is, in the equation x represents y, we only know about x (and the correspondence between our x and someone else's).[2] (See Huttenlocher & Higgins, 1978, for a similar point of view.)

The use of representation to refer to knowledge and how it is organized is a relatively recent shift in emphasis from the more traditional use of the term. Although the concept of representation as knowledge is itself not new, this focus has become more common as psychological theorizing has changed over the last decade or so (see Pylyshyn, 1973). In part, the shift stems from the move away from behaviorism, with its denigration of mental events, to cognitive theories that directly focus on those events (sometimes to the exclusion of other kinds of behavior). The shift was reinforced by developments in computer science. The practical and demanding business of constructing a computer program to simulate some psychological domain necessarily leads to a focus on the kinds of knowledge the program must have and how that knowledge is to be organized and expressed. The representation itself cannot be vague; choices must be made and a knowledge base written into the program. The arguments that have ensued over practical and impractical ways of doing this have focused psychologists' thinking on the organization of knowledge more acutely than ever before. (See Boden, 1977, for a highly readable account of the early history of this field.)

A variety of models of the way in which information is stored in the human mind have developed over the past 10 years, all of them influenced in one degree or another by computer science (e.g., Anderson, 1976; Anderson & Bower, 1973; Collins & Quillian, 1969; Kintsch, 1974; Miller & Johnson-Laird, 1976; Norman, Rumelhart, & LNR Research Group, 1975; Quillian, 1968; Schank, 1972, 1975; Schank & Abelson, 1977). These models vary as to the domain of knowledge they cover. Quillian (1968), for example, was interested in how to represent what has come to be called semantic memory, that is, our knowledge about concepts and their interrelationships. Others were more concerned with how we understand sentences (e.g., Anderson & Bower, 1973), and still others were more interested in how we understand discourse (Kintsch, 1974) or events (Schank, 1972, 1975). In all of these theoretical models, however, a concern with what knowledge is to be represented and how it is to be expressed is central, and this concern has come to dominate much current psychological theory and experimentation.

We are on the threshold of this enterprise and at present there is little consensus as to the form such theories should take. Worse, there is much confusion attendant on our explorations. Palmer points out that psychologists have been lost in a sea of notational systems and theories to represent knowledge and have ascribed to different notational systems significances that they may lack:

> We, as cognitive psychologists, do not really understand our concepts of representation. We propose them, talk about them, argue about them, and try to obtain evidence in support of them, but we do not understand them in any fundamental sense. Anyone who has attempted to read the literature related to cognitive representation quickly becomes confused—and with good reason. The field is obtuse, poorly defined, and embarrassingly disorganized. Among the most popular terms, one finds the following: visual codes, verbal codes, spatial codes, physical codes, name codes, image codes, analog representations, digital representations, first-order isomorphisms, second-order isomorphisms, multidimensional spaces, templates, features, structural descriptions, relational networks, multicomponent vectors, and even holograms. (Palmer, 1978, p. 259)

Discouragingly, this characterization is quite true. However, lest the reader stop at this point, I hasten to add that this chapter will not discuss the merits or demerits of this list. In a sense, we are hardly far enough along in our characterization of children's knowledge to worry about such details. We are still at the stage where we are disputing what kinds of knowledge children have; for the most part, we have not advanced to the point where we can argue whether one set of terms is better than another or whether two theories end by making exactly the same predictions. Although I will touch on these issues when discussing different ways in which knowledge might be organized, the chapter, for the most part, will proceed at a fairly general level and will not be concerned with differences in notational systems.

The notion of representation as symbols standing for referents will also arise in several places, and I will have occasion to discuss children's acquisition and use of symbols, but it will be only a minor focus. (For detailed discussions of the development of symbol systems, see Gardner, 1979; Huttenlocher & Higgins, 1978; Smith & Franklin, 1979; Wolf &

Gardner, 1981.) The issue of symbols arises in part because psychologists often use children's symbolic representations to study their representation of knowledge, as in the use of children's drawings to inform us of what they know. The issue of symbolic development also arises because of the crucial role it plays in the theories of Piaget (and others) of a qualitative shift in the nature of representation at the end of the sensorimotor period.

The plan of the chapter is to cover several aspects of children's representation of the world and to raise questions about developmental changes in knowledge and its organization. Following some further introductory comments, representation in infancy will be discussed. Then the chapter will consider imagery, space, events, and categorical knowledge. The chapter is necessarily highly selective because people have knowledge about concepts, events, language, space, memories, how to walk and speak—a veritable ''Whole-Earth Catalogue.'' Such knowledge does not have to be conscious of course. Many aspects of our world view that profoundly affect our behavior are not conscious and many may not, in principle, be available to consciousness (see Pylyshyn, 1973; Rozin, 1976). For example, our normal use of language demonstrates our knowledge of grammar. We do not know what that grammar is, however, and those who think they do have not kept up with the controversies in linguistics. We clearly have representations of grammatical rules, but only certain parts of them can be consciously accessed. Many other examples could be given, such as our knowing how to walk without easily bringing that knowledge to awareness (Piaget, 1976). The kinds of knowledge that are most difficult to access are those called procedures (or ways of doing things), which will be examined in the discussion on *Procedural Versus Declarative Representation*. In addition, the problem of conscious access to different aspects of our knowledge base will occur throughout the chapter.

Piaget's View of Representation

Because developmental psychology's interest in representation has been so strongly influenced by Piaget's theory, we must clarify his uses of the term. Piaget uses the term in both our senses. His use of representation as knowledge, or ''representation in the broad sense,'' is defined as ''identical with thought, *i.e.,* with all intelligence which is based on a system of concepts or mental schemas and not merely on perceptions and actions'' (Piaget, 1951, p. 67). He sometimes refers to this kind of representation as ''conceptual representation.'' His other use of the term, usually qualified as "representation in the narrow sense," refers to representation as symbols, that is, "the capacity to evoke by a sign or a symbolic image an absent object or an action not yet carried out" (Piaget, 1952, p. 243). Piaget considers the presence of symbols to be necessary for recall and probably for all thought. That is, thinking is assumed to make use of symbols to refer to the underlying concepts that form the knowledge we have about the world. To think, in this view, one must be able to call forth a symbol into active or working memory so that it can be put into relation to another symbol or otherwise manipulated for purposes of recall, problem solving, making inferences, and so forth.

This conception of the role of symbols in cognition is in accord with common sense and intuitions about our own thought processes but, nevertheless, is fraught with ambiguity. A good deal of thinking probably takes place without symbol manipulation. For example, in models of semantic memory that are based on the notion of activation spreading through a network of nodes (Collins & Loftus, 1975), much of the work of thinking is accomplished not by symbol use but by paths being activated among the nodes themselves. In his discussion of symbol use, Piaget may be referring to conscious thought. To the extent that thought is conscious, it must involve symbols or other representations that are necessarily not the same as the underlying concepts to which they refer. However, much of our "thinking" takes place beyond the reach of consciousness and may not involve symbol manipulation at all.

According to Piaget, both types of representation develop more or less simultaneously in Stage 6 of sensorimotor development, that is, in the second half of the second year of life. Before this time, children are said to lack both concepts and symbols. Hence, this position ascribes no representational system to the minds of children younger than 1½. Because Piaget concedes that sensorimotor children know a great deal, we can see that his use of the term representation is more restrictive than that adopted in this chapter. He is unwilling to accord them a representational capacity because he believes they do not have conceptual knowledge. What kind of knowledge is it then that sensorimotor children have? To address this question, we need to mention the distinction between declarative and procedural knowledge.

Procedural Versus Declarative Representation

Both in common parlance and in philosophical and psychological writings, two kinds of knowledge are often distinguished: knowing how and knowing that. We know how to tie our shoes or hit a golf ball, usually without being able to specify the actions that we take in so doing. This kind of knowing seems quite different from knowing facts, such as the name of the President of the United States or the product of 3×4. In current terminology, these two kinds of knowing are often called procedural and declarative respectively. (See Rumelhart, 1979, and Winograd, 1975, for detailed discussions of this distinction.)

The distinction between procedural and declarative knowledge became important with the arrival of modern computer programs designed to model psychological processing. How much of a program's knowledge should be in the form of a data base of facts and how much in the form of information about how to carry out actions or find a factual answer? Various solutions have been attempted. Some programs consist largely of a set of facts with very general procedures, or rules of inference, that operate on them; the procedures themselves are not tied to any particular content. Others consist primarily of procedures, or sets of actions designed to arrive at particular answers. For example, a program may not know that $3 \times 4 = 12$, but it knows how to go about finding the result and does it so easily and rapidly that it does not need to store the answer in its data base. The difference might be characterized as having stored the multiplication tables versus not having any of the answers stored but knowing how to multiply.

Each of these kinds of representation has advantages (Winograd, 1975). A primarily declarative system is more flexible and economical, in the sense that a given piece of knowledge only has to be stored in one place where it can be reached when needed from any other part of the system. It is also easy to add new information to a declarative data base; you merely add another line to a list or a new node to a network. A primarily procedural system, on the other hand, often seems more natural for representing much of our knowledge, especially knowledge of actions. It is difficult to understand how many of our familiar action routines could be described as a data base of facts plus some very general rules for operating on them. The corresponding disadvantage of a purely procedural system is that specific facts can be accessed only by running through the particular routine in which they are embedded and, in many instances, are not generally accessible.

An example of buried knowledge can be taken from the area of perceptual recognition. Perceptual processing seems to be largely procedural in nature; we usually do not use "facts" to recognize something, and much of the information we do use in pattern matching is not available to other parts of the system. For example, we have all seen hundreds of thousands of faces, but without artistic training few of us "know" the proportions of the human face. We use this information over and over again during the course of recognizing, but do not have a stored list telling us that the eyes, ears, nose, and mouth are all in the lower two thirds of the face or that the eyes and ears both appear at approximately the same height. Without attention being drawn to them, these "facts" are not only not accessible to consciousness but may also not be available to other procedures within the system. This knowledge is context bound and seems to be used only within a single recognition procedure.

It is also possible to turn one kind of knowledge into the other; after following a procedure to find an answer to a question, the answer may be separately stored so that it is not necessary in the future to carry out the procedure to access it. Running through a routine to locate or generate a piece of information may result in that information forming part of a declarative knowledge system. To take an old example, suppose you are asked how many windows there are in your house. You probably do not "know" the answer but can generate the information by mentally walking around your house "looking" at the windows and counting them. However, once having carried out this procedure you *can* add the result of the process to your knowledge base as an independently accessible fact associated with your house. The next time someone asks you how many windows there are in your house you can answer immediately without having to repeat the procedural analysis. A new node to which you have direct access has been added to a network of concepts associated with your house.

The question of accessibility is considered in more detail in the discussion on *Representation in Infancy*. Here it is sufficient to note that accessibility is implicated in the distinction between procedural and declarative knowledge. To the extent that a bit of information is embedded within a given procedure, it may not be easily found and used when relevant to another situation. The question of accessibility looms large for developmental psychology because children gradually become able to access knowledge beyond the demands of the immediate (procedural) context. The simplest form of this increased accessibility is the ability to recall absent things, that is, to locate an item in memory without any current perceptual support. Other more sophisticated forms of accessibility appear during the course of develop-

ment—how and when is a problematical issue that will be raised at several points in this chapter.

As mentioned above, many of these issues became important with the advent of computer science and its work on machine understanding. Most computer programs consist of a mixture of these two kinds of knowledge, having some kind of propositional data base as well as sets of procedures; the mix that is used depends to some extent on the domain being modeled. Questions of the organization and accessibility of knowledge are equally relevant to understanding representation in the human mind, but the problems are vastly more complex. This point becomes obvious when we consider Piaget's theory of the development of representation. A summary of his characterization is that the infant's representational system is procedural in nature and gradually shifts over the course of the preoperational period to one that includes major declarative components. The infant can only access knowledge by executing familiar motor programs that are tied to particular domains. Either concrete or formal operations, on the other hand, can be described as a system with a declarative data base (i.e., a system of concepts) and a very general set of content-free procedures that operate on it. The formation of such a system in the concrete operational period is said to develop only after a long, slow process of interiorization of motor actions.

REPRESENTATION IN INFANCY

According to Piaget, the sensorimotor child before Stage 6 (18 to 24 months) does not have a capacity for representation in the true sense, but only sensorimotor intelligence. Knowledge about the world consists only of perceptions and actions; objects are only understood through the child's own actions and perceptual schemata. It is a most un-Proustian life, not thought, only lived. Sensorimotor schemata (or, in our sense, representation as knowledge) enable a child to walk a straight line but not to think about a line in its absence, to recognize his or her mother but not to think about her when she is gone. It is a world very difficult for us to conceive, accustomed as we are to spend much of our time ruminating about the past and anticipating the future. Nevertheless, this is the state that Piaget posits for the child before 1½, that is, an ability to recognize objects and events but an inability to recall them in their absence. Because of this inability, this lack of concepts of things and symbols to represent them, Piaget does not consider the sensorimotor child's knowledge to be "mental" representation; to be mental means to be thought and the sensorimotor child cannot think. Note that lack of thought in this view does not merely mean that the child is still missing the ability to reason or make deductive inferences; it means that the child cannot even remember what he or she did a few minutes ago, what his room looks like or what she had for lunch, except accidentally in the course of carrying out actions relevant to these past perceptions and activities. What is missing, according to Piaget, is both a system of concepts and a mobile, flexible symbol system capable of pointing to, or referring to, those concepts.

A point of view similar to Piaget's has been offered by Bruner (Bruner, Olver, & Greenfield, 1966). Bruner calls the action-saturated knowledge of the sensorimotor child "enactive representation" but, in contrast to Piaget, he recognizes that this kind of knowledge is a form of representation like any other. The child does not merely act but has knowledge about how to act, in the sense that there are mental structures (schemata) guiding and controlling action. The sensorimotor schemata are considered to be both mental and a form of representation. This difference between Bruner and Piaget is probably more terminological than substantive (with Bruner's usage more in accord with current cognitive theory). Both posit sensorimotor schemata as the earliest type of knowledge. Bruner stresses, as does Piaget, that these schemata are generative; they do not consist of fixed action patterns nor of behavior solely under the control of the environment. Rather, they are goal-directed plans for action that guide ongoing behavior with a good deal of flexibility, a characteristic that becomes more prominent over the first few months of life. (See Piaget, 1952, for a detailed presentation of the growth and development of sensorimotor schemata during the first 18 months; see Head, 1926, and Lashley, 1951, for early discussions of the general character of motor or action schemata; see Gallistel, 1980, and Saltzman, 1979, for current accounts of their complex details.)

Using the terminology of the previous discussion, the infant is a purely procedural organism in this view. Furthermore, the procedures are limited to those governing motor behavior and perception. Both are sharply distinguished from conceptual, or declarative, knowledge. A related characteristic is the lack of symbols that would enable the system to query its memory or to solve problems without recourse to action—in short, to think. The emergence of a conceptual knowledge base and a symbol system to refer to it is said to be a slow development over the course of the first 2 years of life.

Piaget's conception of the sensorimotor, nonconceptual character of early knowledge seems to have been widely, if perhaps uncritically, accepted. In particular, although he distinguishes between two senses of representation (conceptual and symbolic), he appears unwilling to admit that one can be present without the other. Development in infancy will not be considered to be conceptual unless, and until, it is accompanied by symbol use and has become freed from the infant's action schemata. Because Piaget links symbols and concepts so closely in his discussion of development in infancy, I will begin with his view of the gradual emergence of symbolic representation. The interest in symbols here is not to chart the course of symbolic development per se but because symbol use gives evidence of a knowledge system that is not entirely action based. To the extent that infants manipulate symbols, one can assume an underlying conceptual structure at least partially independent of the sensorimotor routines in which they usually engage.

Next I will consider the rather slim evidential base for symbol use in infancy. Positive findings of symbolization would indicate earlier development of conceptual knowledge than Piaget posits; negative findings, however, would not tell us that conceptual knowledge is absent. Then, because Piaget uses recall as one of his main criteria for the presence of symbols, I will evaluate this kind of data as another means of assessing the ability to access concepts independently of sensorimotor procedures. Then, the discussion continues with more general evidence for conceptual activity during the sensorimotor period.

Throughout this discussion, the theme is that a declarative knowledge base is being laid down during the first 2 years. To some extent, this must be seen as a simplifying assumption. It is not clear that conceptual knowledge must be considered to be declarative in nature. Most schemata governing our understanding of various concepts seem to be a mixture of procedural and declarative knowledge (Rumelhart, 1980b; Winograd, 1975). Procedures, of course, do not involve only the control of motor actions; they can consist of rules telling us what to do next in a situation or how to go about finding out something. A more conservative view, in that it makes fewer assumptions about the format of the representational system, is that concepts gradually become less context bound, first less tied to actual physical activities and then less tied to the contexts in which they were developed. Later, I will discuss the notion of a transition from context-bound to more context-free knowledge and consider the question of the accessibility of knowledge.

Piaget's Theory of the Emergence of Symbolic Thought

Piaget uses a strict criterion for the onset of the symbolic function. He takes pains to chart its growth in detail but is conservative in his ascription of symbolic thought to the child. This approach follows the rule of parsimony; an ascription of symbolic representation will be eschewed until it can no longer be avoided. Piaget believes that attribution of "true" representation is unnecessary until Stage 6 (18 to 24 months). Earlier behavior, which might appear symbolic or closely related to symbolic behavior, is considered to lack one or more characteristics that are defining of symbol use for Piaget—the symbol must be completely internalized; the symbol must be a mentally evoked image (or an intentionally chosen object used to stand for a class of objects or events); the symbol must be able to be used retrospectively for purposes of recall and prospectively for purposes of anticipating the future.

According to Piaget, the earliest precursors of true symbols show none of these characteristics. The infant very early learns connections between "signals" and events to follow. Piaget's view of these connections is similar to the notion of a discriminative stimulus in conditioning theory. The signal is an early form of an "indicator," the latter being defined as a perception that "announces the presence of an object or the imminence of an event (the door which opens and announces a person)" (Piaget, 1952, p. 192). Although this sequence allows some predictability about the future, Piaget found no indication of interiorization, that is, the ability to access the indicator and its implications independently of present perception or its use to recall the past; a stimulus from the environment has merely become capable of triggering a fairly complex motor or perceptual schema. (Actually, "becoming freed from the context in which the indicator was learned" would be a more accurate expression than "interiorization" because the perception of the indicator is already an interior event.)

In Stage 3 (4 to 8 months), Piaget observed a phenomenon he called motor recognition. He observed his children occasionally performing abbreviated versions of motions in which they typically engaged when interacting with a particular object:

At 0;6 (12) Lucienne perceives from a distance two celluloid parrots attached to a chandelier and which she had sometimes had in her bassinet. As soon as she sees them, she definitely but briefly shakes her legs without trying to act upon them from a distance. This can only be a matter of motor recognition. So too, at 0;6 (19) it suffices that she catches sight of her dolls from a distance for her to outline the movement of swinging them with her hand. (Piaget, 1952, p. 186)

Piaget calls these gestures acts of recognitory assimilation, in which the child merely notes an event and both recognizes and classifies it without attempting to act upon it directly. This interesting observation, which to my knowledge has not been reported by others, suggests the beginning of an interiorization of a symbol used to represent an object. To be sure, the gestures are still external, but the motor schemata from which they derive are being used for a new purpose and not just to control direct action. The process by which such interiorization might occur is reminiscent of Osgood, Suci, and Tannenbaum's (1957) theory in which meaning is said to reside in internalized abbreviated responses derived from originally external action (see Flavell, 1963).

In Stage 4 (8 to 12 months), the child becomes capable of "prevision," that is, the use of one sight as a *sign* that another will follow. Piaget ascribes to the indicators that allow prevision a greater degree of flexibility and some detachment from familiar action patterns of the child. For example, a movement of a person in the child's vicinity is a sign to the child that the person is about to leave and is accompanied by signs of distress. Piaget hastens to add, however, that for such signs to occur with prevision does not imply that the child can *picture* the signed object or event. "It is enough that the sign set in motion a certain attitude of expectation and a certain schema of recognition" (Piaget, 1951, p. 252).

In Stage 5 (12 to 18 months), prevision becomes more elaborate and still further freed from the child's own activities, giving rise to practical anticipations based upon generalization from earlier experience with objects. This development is not differentiated in kind from that of Stage 4. The notion of a practical anticipation is similar to Werner and Kaplan's (1963) concept of anticipatory behavior. Werner and Kaplan had some difficulty distinguishing between anticipatory motor activities and similar activities used in the service of representing or depicting some action. They cite the case of a 13-month-old child approaching a staircase and lifting his legs in a climbing motion before he got there, and they contrast this anticipatory action with the same child at 15 months looking for a sand spoon and making shoveling movements with his arm, holding his hand in a scooping position. They considered the latter case to be an instance of a representative (symbolic) activity (see *Declarative Representation in Infancy*).

Finally, in Stage 6, a whole host of complex behaviors occur that seem to require some sort of symbolic representation. Piaget observed his children engaging in symbolic play in which objects in the environment were used to represent other objects. They began to engage in problem solving in which new means were invented mentally rather than merely being tried out in a groping way in the environment. They imitated complex behaviors previously seen but no longer present. They could follow a series of hidden displacements of objects (e.g., an object being dumped out of a container under a blanket) and figure out where the object must be, thus reaching the culmination of the notion of object permanence. They showed signs of detailed anticipation of the consequences of some of their actions. Most convincingly of all, his children began to engage in verbal recall during this period. In addition to labeling objects in their presence, they began to use words to refer to absent objects and previous events. Because the ability to evoke absent objects is Piaget's hallmark for the presence of a representational ability, verbal recall is convincing evidence.

Declarative Representation in Infancy

The Use of Symbols

Some of the evidence that symbolic activity appears earlier than indicated by Piaget comes from his own observations (1951). Particularly in describing the sequences in Stage 4 in which infants learn to imitate actions that they cannot see themselves perform, such as blinking the eyes and sticking out the tongue, Piaget documented a kind of analogical response. When, for example, Piaget blinked his eyes, one child opened and closed her hand, then opened and closed her mouth. Somewhat later she covered and uncovered her face with a pillow. Piaget calls such mistakes "intelligent confusion: the model is assimilated to an analogous schema susceptible of translating the visual into the kinesthetic"(Piaget, 1951, p. 44).

Although Piaget does not interpret them so, these kinds of responses could plausibly be related to the use of a symbol to express an abstract relationship. The child appears to be using an unrelated motor schema as a means of expressing analogically the

notion of opening and closing or, in the case of using the pillow, seeing and not seeing. This does not indicate recall nor anticipation of the future but rather use of a motorically expressed representation in the service of problem solving. The example appears qualitatively similar to the Stage 6 behavior of one of Piaget's children opening and closing her mouth to represent the widening of a slit in a matchbox. About the latter behavior, Piaget states that "the attempt at representation which she thus furnishes is expressed plastically, that is to say, due to inability to think out the situation in words or clear visual images she uses a simple motor indication as 'signifier' or 'symbol'" (Piaget, 1952, p. 338).

In the matchbox example, it is easier to assume that mouth-opening expressed a symbolic function because it did not occur in the context of attempting to match another person's behavior. Nevertheless, it is possible to attribute symbolic activity to the earlier behavior instead of assuming that it was merely a series of mistaken generalizations. In any case, the systematic trial-and-error attempts to imitate complex actions that Piaget observed during Stage 4 suggest conceptual activity in which problem solving on the basis of analogical comparison is taking place.

Similar observations can be made about the development of symbolic play. Piaget does not report true symbolic play until Stage 6. However, earlier instances of play in Stage 4 appear similar in form and meaning. Piaget noted very similar ritual behavior in two of his children, one of whom was in Stage 4, the other in Stage 6. In both cases, the children went through a series of actions typically accompanying going to sleep at night, but only in the case of the Stage 6 child was the ritual accompanied by smiling (suggesting awareness of pretense). Piaget states that the Stage 4 child's ritual was the evocation of a schema by familiar circumstances; she was in bed at the time. Therefore, he termed it only ritualization preparing for true symbolic play in which the child actually pretends to sleep, that is, is aware of make-believe. The difference between completing a schema evoked by a situation and actual pretense seems clear, although pretense in the Stage 4 example is difficult to rule out.

As in the case of the practical anticipations discussed earlier, the context in which activities are carried out tends to be given heavy weight in their interpretation. The child raising his legs before climbing the stairs was acting in sight of the stairs and in the context of a familiar activity. When he made the scooping motion with his hand, the sand spoon for which he was searching was absent. In all of these cases, when the activity occurs out of its usual context, one feels more confident in ascribing symbolic representation to the child; nevertheless, there is some danger of missing the occurrence of genuine symbolic behavior by maintaining such a strict criterion.

Other investigators have reported symbolic play earlier than would be predicted by Piaget's theory. For example, Bates, Camaioni, and Volterra (1975) and Bates, Benigni, Bretherton, Camaioni, and Volterra (1977, 1979) report symbolic play occurring around 12 months and generally ahead of several other measures of Stage 6 behavior. In general, much recent research aimed at assessing sensorimotor development indicates a faster progression than suggested by Piaget. Thus, symbolic play occurring at 12 months does not necessarily mean symbolic play occurring in Stage 4; it could equally well be interpreted as a child reaching the earliest of Stage 6 behaviors at a precocious age. If this interpretation is reasonable, then we are merely haggling over age norms, not establishing a particular kind of representational capacity throughout the period in which Piaget claims it is absent. Let us examine other kinds of evidence.

Recall

Before the onset of language production most of the evidence for recall of absent objects is indirect. Nevertheless, there are several findings that suggest that sensorimotor children can remember things in their absence. Some evidence comes from studies that report comprehension of words referring to absent objects that is accompanied by search for them. Huttenlocher (1974) describes the following sequence, beginning about 1 year of age or slightly younger and developing over the next 2 or 3 months. First, children can locate named objects when they are present in the room, even though not necessarily in sight. In the initial stages, success may result from contentless searching, followed by recognition of the object. Next, children can locate named objects in other rooms if the objects are in their accustomed places. Finally, they can locate absent objects that are in temporary locations, for example, going to the dining table in the next room when asked, "Where are the cookies?" (Werner & Kaplan, 1963, cite similar examples from earlier literature). Comprehension of these words precedes production, and Huttenlocher (1974) suggests that it is easier for the child to recognize a word and recall its referent (word comprehension) than to recognize an object or event and recall its label (word production). In any case, data such as these indicate that the child understands that the utterance refers to an absent object,

can recall the referent and its location, and can hold both in mind long enough to find it.

Incidental observations in studies on the development of object permanence have also been used to indicate recall of absent objects, especially several studies of the A$\bar{\text{B}}$ error in Stage 4. This term refers to the finding that when an object has been hidden at location A and then, while the child watches, is moved to and hidden at location B, the child attempts to recover it at location A (Piaget, 1954). The question of interest is whether or not the child has a concept or representation of the absent object independent of the action patterns involved in reaching for it or trying to find it. Piaget believes that the notion of an object's location in this stage (not necessarily the object itself) is still bound to the child's activities. During earlier stages, objects gradually come to have properties independent of action, but the most difficult property to disassociate from motor activity is that of location. Thus, in Stage 4, infants who see an object moved from one location to a new one will attempt to find the object by reaching to the place where they have reached for it before.

Although the existence of the A$\bar{\text{B}}$ error amply illustrates confusion about the location of hidden objects, it is difficult to determine exactly what the child does recall, in part because more than one trial is routinely given and because, even on a single trial, the child often reaches to more than one location. For purposes of demonstrating recall independent of the child's actions, it may be more relevant to ask whether or not the child recalls the particulars of the hidden object, that is, whether or not the child maintains a representation of the object itself in its absence. This is a difficult question to address in preverbal children because many responses that might indicate recall are also indicative of recognition; the latter capacity is present in neonates. For example, a decrease in looking time (habituation) is assumed to indicate recognition, whereas an increase in looking time (dishabituation) is assumed to indicate a response to novelty; neigher necessarily indicates recall. What other responses could be used?

LeCompte and Gratch (1972) report gradually increasing surprise in infants from 9 to 18 months when a new object is discovered in the place where a former object was hidden. Surprise is a difficult response to quantify, however, and difficult to distinguish from a response to novelty per se, which (as just mentioned) does not necessarily involve recall. Inspection of the nominal scale that these authors used to measure surprise indicates, indeed, that the reactions of the 9-month-old children (the mean response being "a long, careful, and decided stare at the [new] toy" [p. 390]) are consistent with a dishabituation response and not necessarily an indication that the child recalled the former object. Similar conclusions can be drawn from the measurement of instrumental searching when a new object was discovered. The 9-month-olds typically showed "a recognition of the new toy by actively exploring it" (p. 390) rather than a pattern of persistent search indicating recall of the former object.

Piaget suggests that persistent search for a missing object is an adequate criterion for recall because it requires a representation above and beyond any familiar actions. Ramsay and Campos (1975, 1978) found different patterns of search in 8-month-olds and smiling in 10- to 11-month-old children following discovery of an old or a new toy in a hiding task. They interpreted their results to indicate that the children had maintained a representation of the original object. Even persistent search, however, may be an ambiguous criterion. It is possible for search to be initiated by a failure of recognition without maintaining a clear representation of the object for which one is searching. That is, these data may be similar to the early examples of word comprehension discussed above.

Ashmead and Perlmutter (1980) have recently attempted to get more direct evidence of recall in children under 1 year. Parents of children aged 7, 9, and 11 months were asked to keep diaries of any incidents that indicated memory for past events on the part of their children. Ashmead and Perlmutter report that all of the children showed some spontaneous (uncued) memory episodes that suggested recall. The most direct evidence was found in the infants demonstrating knowledge of the locations of absent objects. The younger infants were more likely to remember permanent locations of objects; by 9 months, temporary locations were remembered as well. A typical example, cited in an earlier paper (Ashmead & Perlmutter, 1979), was the following: A 9-month-old girl opened a drawer where ribbons were usually kept. The ribbons had been moved to another drawer. She searched all the drawers until she found the ribbons. The next day she crawled to the chest and went directly to the new ribbon drawer.

It is difficult to disentangle recall from recognition in the preverbal child and also difficult to separate recall from the carrying out of habitual actions. Nevertheless, data such as these as well as some of the findings from the object-permanence studies suggest that an ability to maintain a representation of an absent object develops well before the end of the first year of life. Kessen and Nelson (1978) suggest

that this ability develops in the second half of the first year and that the formation of organized routines creates a context for developing notions of objects that can eventually be uncoupled from them. They hypothesize:

> At some point the information about familiar figures against familiar grounds has become so well organized that the child notices when a context or setting that should imply a familiar person, object, or event fails to do so; the structure of the familiar context leads the child to note the *absence* of a familiar person or object. . . . For example, when the suppertime and bedtime context usually contains his father's homecoming, then his father's approaching footsteps or his father's arriving car imply to the child the appearance of his father at this time. But if his father does not appear as usual, the child's contextual structure may lead him to notice the absence of the expected familiar person in the familiar context and to indicate this by looking out the window, fussing, or even saying "Dada." (Kessen & Nelson, 1978, p. 25)

The implication of this hypothetical example is not only that the child recognizes that something is missing but also, within the confines of a given context, is gradually able to access a concept from memory. Such an event would be a step beyond simple recognition. The expectations that have been created through repetition of the routine seem to allow access to the thought of an absent object.

Piaget cites many instances in which infants use expectations to anticipate future events (e.g., 1952). The phenomenon of prevision (described in *Piaget's Theory of the Emergence of Symbolic Thought*) seems to be of this nature. Because prevision occurs before the onset of word use, there is no possibility for infants to name the sight they expect to see; yet, it is not clear that Piaget would accept any other evidence in this situation for the presence of "true" conceptual representation.

Conceptual Development in Infancy

As we have seen, Piaget makes a sharp distinction between sensorimotor and conceptual intelligence. He ascribes a good deal of knowledge about objects and events even to quite young infants, but because this knowledge has to do with perception and the infant's own actions, it seems to be accorded a second-class, or merely practical, status. More seriously, because of his binding of the notion of conceptual representation to the use of symbols (which do indicate a degree of flexibility in use that mere anticipations do not), Piaget tends to underplay the extent to which conceptual knowledge is developing in the presymbolic child. From his own examples, it is difficult to find a qualitative difference in the nature of the expectations of sights to follow an indicator in Stage 4 and the expectations of sights to follow that the child labels in Stage 5 or 6. The qualitative difference seems to come more in the ability to *refer* to these expectations than in the nature of the underlying representation itself.

Perception, for Piaget, is a sensorimotor or procedural affair, and it does not involve concepts. The question arises, however, whether it is possible to have a perceptually sophisticated organism without a related conceptual system integrated with its perceptual functioning. The conceptual system may be procedural in the first instance, but if so, it is purely mental with little connection to action or motor schemata as these are commonly conceived. Conceptual knowledge is involved in all classificatory activity. The classification systems that eventually grow out of this activity should probably be considered declarative or at least context free in nature.

Classificatory activity begins at birth. At its simplest, it involves the recognition of similarity and dissimilarity. Even primitive similarity judgments based on purely physical dimensions tend to result in distinct categories. Categorical perception has been demonstrated in infants for hue (Bornstein, Kessen, & Weiskopf, 1976), speech sounds (Bertoncini & Mehler, 1981; Eimas, Siqueland, Jusczyk, & Vigorito, 1971), and musical sounds (Jusczyk, Rosner, Cutting, Foard, & Smith, 1977). (See Bornstein, 1979, for a review of these areas of research.) In addition, recent work indicates that from an early age highly sophisticated processes are involved in forming more complex categories, leading to categorization that is not based on physical information alone. For example, work by Fagan and Shepherd (1979) and Watson (1966) suggests that faces are conceptualized in a canonical orientation (upright), in spite of the fact that they are frequently seen in many other orientations (perhaps especially so by infants in arms). That a 4- to 5-month-old can recognize a face more easily when it is upright than when it is upside down indicates that perception is being facilitated by a concept of faceness, or a face schema. This does not mean, of course, that the infant's face schema is the same as that of adults (see Carey, Diamond, & Woods, 1980). Even 5- to 6-month-olds treat infant faces as a category different from adult faces, and women's faces as different from men's faces. These category differences occur even when the man's and woman's (or infant's and

adult's) faces are judged by adults to be physically more similar than two within-category faces (Fagan & Singer, 1979).

Although the study of categorization in infants is still relatively new, it has already been shown that 10-month-olds average feature values from facelike stimuli to form a prototypical representation of the category in a fashion quite similar to the processes that have been identified in adults (Strauss, 1979). They learn so-called natural categories, taking into account several sources of information to do so (Husaim & Cohen, 1980). Ross (1980) has suggested that by 12 months, infants respond differentially to superordinate categories. She found that infants of this age, after having seen several exemplars of a category (such as animals, food, or furniture), preferred to look at a new instance of a new category rather than at a new instance of an old one. There is still a great deal of work to be done in this area, including the difficult task of controlling visual similarity along all the relevant dimensions. Nevertheless, the evidence at this time strongly suggests that at least basic-level categories (Rosch, Mervis, Gray, Johnson, & Boyes-Braem, 1976) are formed during the first year of life. We return to this issue in the discussion of *Categorical Representation*.

It would require a rather strained interpretation in most instances to account for these concepts as internalization of motor activity. Piaget quite correctly emphasized that perception is a constructive process and not merely a passive registration of stimulation. In his work on the development of spatial concepts in preoperational children, he implicated constructive activity by reference to motor activity, for example, tactual exploration or eye movements (Piaget & Inhelder, 1956). The implication of this work is that the youngest preoperational children are relatively passive in their perception, which leads to incomplete spatial concepts. Although there are many aspects of this interpretation that are appealing, on the whole it seems to place too great an emphasis on physical action. Constructive activity, in the sense of abstracting and categorizing information, is woven into the very fabric of perception itself and must be considered operative from birth. Perceptual analysis undoubtedly increases in sophistication with development, but even for the youngest infants, it is not possible to consider perceptual schemata without at the same time considering conceptual schemata.

The concepts that arise from perceiving form the basis of a conceptual system that is quickly elaborated and full of rich interconnections. Many of these early concepts may be procedural in nature, in the sense of consisting of rules about functional relations among things and actions, but this does not imply that these concepts are only accessible by means of action related to them. Children well under the age of 1 year "know" that cups contain things, whether they are interacting with them or not; that shoes go on feet and not on hands; and so forth. Many parental games with infants rely on such knowledge by violating these expectations to produce laughter. Piaget (1952) also recorded many examples of this kind of knowledge.

There are various ways to explore this kind of conceptual knowledge in the laboratory. A recent example is work by Freeman, Lloyd, and Sinha (1980) who used the search and transposition paradigms developed in studies of object permanence to demonstrate that children have a concept of containment at least by the age of 9 months. They found that infants were more likely to succeed in locating an object when it was hidden by an upright cup than by an inverted one. They argue that the infant already knows that cups have canonical orientations and that inverted cups are not reliable cues for finding things. These authors suggest that the performance they observed indexes "conceptual behaviour, for the infant is accessing an entry in memory which contains a knowledge of the predictable characteristics of an object in its canonical and non-canonical orientation" (Freeman et al., p. 259).

There may be alternate explanations for these particular findings. However, continuation of such studies as this—designed to unravel early conceptual knowledge about relationships, such as in, on, and under—should be fruitful for our further understanding of the conceptual development taking place before the onset of language. The infant may not be able to refer to these developing concepts, but lack of reference does not mean that they do not exist. Further, there is little reason at present to assume that these concepts are solely procedurally based, insofar as early procedures are considered to involve action, except, perhaps, in the earliest stages of their formation.

Transitions from Procedural to Declarative Representation

Although I have suggested that there is evidence for symbolization, recall, and concepts independent of familiar procedures, nevertheless, Piaget's many observations bear testimony to the extent to which representation in sensorimotor children is procedurally bound. For example, his careful analyses of his children's imitation suggests the extent to which parts of motor procedures are not accessible as independent units. In Stage 3, his children found

it difficult to imitate opening and closing their hands, even though the movements were familiar to them and well practiced in the context of grasping or waving bye-bye (Piaget, 1951). This kind of restriction, as discussed earlier, is often true of procedural representation. As Piaget describes it:

> It seems that the child at this stage is capable of imitating all movements of the hands that he can make spontaneously, but is unable to imitate those movements which are part of a more complex whole and which must first be differentiated as independent schemas. (Piaget, 1951, p. 25)

At present we have little information about the course of freeing parts of procedures into generally accessible pieces of knowledge. In some cases (as in knowledge about faces discussed in *Procedural Versus Declarative Representation*), information may remain embedded within particular routines throughout life. In other cases, decontextualization seems to happen rapidly. The acquisition of language is one of these. Language, of course, may be a special case because it is a symbol system used to refer to other knowledge. In addition, procedures learned through verbal instruction seem to be more readily accessible than many others.

Procedurally bound representation of early language has been suggested by data on both comprehension and production of the earliest words. Nelson (1977) cites a 1½-year-old child who could identify her nose, hair, eyes, and other parts of her face upon demand, but who did not understand the word face. However, when asked to wash her face, she would go through the motions of rubbing her hands against her face. Nelson suggests that the word face was embedded in a single procedure and could not be responded to independently. Huttenlocher (1974) offers a number of examples of the limited contexts in which the first words are produced. For example, one of the children she studied initially used the word "hi" only in her crib when someone entered the room; not until later did she use it productively for people appearing in other contexts. Each of the four words in production at the time she was studied showed similar limitations. For example, "Mommy" was used in the context of wanting to be picked up from the highchair or playpen. An interesting observation comes from her acquisition of the term "sit down," which she said only during the brief period of time when she had learned to stand up but not yet to sit herself down again. Her mother would help her to sit, saying "sit down" while she did so. The child began to produce this term when in desperate straits to be seated, but as soon as she learned to do so by herself, the term dropped out of her vocabulary.

Greenfield and Smith (1976) make similar observations. Both of the children they studied began first to use language in a performative manner. For example, one of the earliest words of one child was a nonreferential "dada," which accompanied many actions at about 9 months of age. Similarly, "bye-bye" was first used only as an accompaniment to waving; the word was not freed from this context for some (unspecified) period of time. Greenfield and Smith comment:

> The earliest Performatives are on the borderline of language proper. These examples lack complete separation of words and referent and are part of the child's own nonverbal action. With development, more language-like forms appear. These forms are more decentered and less tied to the child's own action: The word substitutes for an action rather than merely accompanying it. For example, the greeting *hi* is first part of the act of waving; later, it functions as a greeting without a wave. (pp. 81–83)

Bates, Bretherton, Shore, and McNew (in press) describe the early history of their subject Carlotta's use of the term "Bam." It was used first in a game of knocking blocks over, apparently always occurring at a regular point in the routine. Several weeks after this routine had become well established, Carlotta, sitting among but not playing with her toys, said "Bam" and then began to pound on her toy piano. They suggest that the sound had become decontextualized from the routine within which it had originally been embedded. A number of Piaget's (e.g., 1951) observations of his children's earliest word use illustrate similar limitations to single contexts or routines, and this kind of interpretation can also be given to many examples of underextension of word meanings as well. Huttenlocher (1974) suggests that the earliest words might act as stimuli that are directly wired to a particular motor plan.

These data suggest that the earliest language occurs in a limited set of contexts and is not freely accessible over many situations. Nonetheless, it seems proper to call it language. As Kessen and Nelson (1978) put it:

> The nameable does not have to be context-independent or context-indifferent; rather it need only be defined over several different contexts. . . . The baby can make sense of and, perhaps, even aggregate presentations that appear in only a few contexts; thus, it is not necessary for a potential nameable to be disconnected from all its backgrounds. (p. 21)

It should be noted that most accounts of early word use analyze selected samples rather than following the day-to-day course of the acquisition of individual words. In addition, data typically are aggregated across a considerable time span, making determination of the extent to which the earliest words are procedure bound uncertain. Whether or not it is an adequate characterization of the earliest words to say that they are embedded within particular procedures, the most salient aspect of language acquisition is how quickly words become productive and context free (e.g., Bloom, 1973; Greenfield & Smith, 1976).

Accessibility

The contexts within which the earliest recall and language use take place must be conceived more widely than the child's own action procedures. Recognition of objects and the development of concepts about them take place not only within the framework of the child's own actions but also within the larger framework of the observation of the event sequences that surround them. Piaget stressed that the insertion of objects into more than one schema (e.g., looking and grasping) is a prerequisite for their objectification. We must attend to their insertion into larger frameworks as well; it may be necessary for objects to occur in a variety of event sequences (many of which are only partially controlled by the child) to be thought of out of context.

The schematic organization of scenes and event sequences that form the larger context for the child will be discussed in detail later. Here I will only note that the schemata that organize our knowledge of familiar scenes and event sequences are also a form of procedural knowledge. Much of our knowledge of the world, even as adults, is organized around expectations of what we will see next or what will happen next. A major difference between the sensorimotor child and the adult, however, appears to be the extent to which knowledge is confined to certain procedures or is accessible under a variety of conditions.

I have made the simplifying assumption that knowledge that is generally accessible has been stored in a declarative format. It may or may not enter the representational system in the first place as part of a procedure. Under what conditions might procedural knowledge become generally accessible? I suggested earlier (in the example of counting the windows of your house and storing the answer) one way in which information could be extracted from procedures. The suggestion implies that you now have a fact as part of a list or network of facts associated with the concept of your house.

The notion of deriving independently accessible facts from procedural knowledge may be a way to conceptualize Bartlett's puzzling notion of "turning around on one's own schemata" (Bartlett, 1932). Bartlett wrestled with the problem of how people can find an item of knowledge embedded within temporally organized, familiar sequences. For example, the alphabet is organized in a fairly rigid unidirectional manner, and both children and adults find it difficult to access the names of letters preceding given ones (Klahr & Chase, 1978; Nissen, 1979). Nevertheless, if given a reason to do so, adults can enter the sequence at several different places, run through it in a forward direction, stop at a particular point, and note the name of the preceding letter; children have more difficulty with this task. Given enough practice and conscious analysis of the sequence, presumably people could learn to disembed some or all of the relationships among the letters from the unidirectional procedure in which they have been learned and used.

Relatively little is known about the kinds of analysis that are required to produce such flexibility or whether such analyses need to be conscious. (See Norman & Shallice, 1980, for a discussion of this issue; see also Jones, 1974, J. G. Martin, 1972, and Restle, 1970, 1976, for suggestive work in the auditory sphere.) In any case, it is clear that adults can access many items of knowledge embedded within various types of procedures. It is less clear whether young children can access items embedded within a procedure or easily extract them, and this problem may not be confined to the sensorimotor period (see *Representation of Events*).

Whenever and however it occurs, the ability to access concepts in a flexible fashion is an important development and one that seems to form a qualitative shift in a representational system. The onset of the ability need not be abrupt or even general across the entire system. Indeed, many of Piaget's observations in the sensorimotor period suggest a gradual acquisition of this ability. Especially from Stage 4 onward (i.e., beginning around 8 months), Piaget documented increasing flexibility of behavior. The sensorimotor schemata begin to be used in an in-

creasingly mobile fashion, being combined and recombined in novel ways. Behavior seems markedly less stereotyped than in the earlier stages and means-end analyses appropriate to novel situations begin to appear. This increasing flexibility is apparent whether or not it is accompanied by an ability to represent concepts in symbolic form.

Whenever an increase in flexibility occurs, it provides an advance in intellectual functioning (see Brown & Campione, 1980). Rozin (1976) ascribes the ability to use a representation in other than the context in which it was originally learned (or in the case of lower organisms, the context for which it was designed) as an evolutionary advance. Bees, for example, do not have this flexibility of access; humans do. The youngest humans may be limited in this regard, but at least in some domains, they quickly gain a capacity for multiple access (Pylyshyn, 1978). This term refers to the ability to call forth a concept from many different contexts or activities. Language is a case in point because words are rapidly freed from the contexts in which they were originally acquired. Other representations may remain tied to particular contexts throughout life or be freed from them only by specific training.

Pylyshyn (1978) contrasts multiple access with the notion of reflective access, which refers to the ability to mention concepts as well as use them. This concept is similar to the notion of consciousness, at least that aspect of consciousness that allows awareness of some of our representations. To be conscious does not mean that we are aware of our processing, only that we have access to the products of some of that processing and can represent these products for ourselves and others (see G. Mandler, 1975, in press; Shallice, 1972). Increase in the ability to engage in this kind of access occurs throughout development, but the likelihood of its emergence is dependent on the nature of the representations themselves; some kinds of knowledge are more accessible to consciousness than others. Gleitman and Rozin (1977) and Rozin and Gleitman (1977) suggest, for example, that phonemic representations are unusually difficult to bring to awareness (see Hirsh-Pasek, Gleitman, & Gleitman, 1978, for other examples). Keil (1981a) speculates that the more inborn constraints there are on the structuring of knowledge in a given domain, the more difficult access will be.

In general, the literature on metacognitive development (e.g., Flavell, 1978, 1979), which is about reflective access, suggests a gradual development of this kind of accessibility. On the other hand, reflective access, or thinking about one's own thinking, may not be as important to functioning as multiple access; that is, the ability to move around freely in a representational system may be more important than being able to represent the system to oneself. The latter may be what Marshall and Morton (1978) call an optional extra. Some kind of internal device to detect and correct errors may not be a necessary component to functioning but it is clearly a desirable one. In the case of language acquisition, some monitoring ability develops quite early (Clark, 1978; Slobin, 1978). As yet we know little about how error detectors work, nor the extent to which all of them imply conscious awareness. Nevertheless, some kind of "even more mysterious apparatus," or EMMA for short, can be seen at work in the 2-year-old's self-corrections and in slightly older children's comments about the linguistic mistakes of others (Marshall & Morton, 1978). The very name these authors chose to label the monitoring function indicates how little we know about this aspect of development.

IMAGERY AS A FORM OF REPRESENTATION

Piaget posits a fundamental change in the nature of representation at the end of the sensorimotor period. The child's habitual action patterns gradually become internalized over the course of many months and become reformulated as concepts (to be precise, as preconcepts, because for Piaget true concepts require a stable classification system). The first preconcepts are abstract schemata (representation in the broad sense), but they are represented in the narrow sense by symbols, or images.[3] Piaget has relatively little to say about why he chose to equate the first symbols with images. He merely states:

The concept is an abstract schema and the image a concrete symbol, and in spite of the fact that we no longer consider thought to be merely a system of images, it is possible that all thought is accompanied by images, for if thinking consists in relating meanings, the image would be a 'signifier' and the concept a 'signified.' (Piaget, 1951, p. 67)

It may be that Piaget equates symbols with images because symbols are said to be related to the signified by some form of resemblance, as opposed to words, which are arbitrary signs. He also recognizes the presence of symbolic activity in apes, who are (or were, in Piaget's prime, and perhaps once again have become) languageless.

Possibly Piaget was influenced by the long history of the belief that thinking is accomplished by means of imagery. Although the Würzburg school had demonstrated imageless thought (see Mandler & Mandler, 1964, for a historical account)—and Piaget agrees that thought is not composed of images—the assumption of some relationship between imagery and thought has been a remarkably enduring notion. Unless one posits a more abstract level of representation than either images or words (such as the abstract propositional representations espoused by many current cognitive psychologists), it is probably necessary to supplement a theory of language-based thought with some other symbolic form. In Piaget and Inhelder's more recent book on imagery (1971), thinking is said to require a broad semiotic function, including nonverbal symbols as well as words. Language is found to be insufficient to account for many types of thought, especially those that involve current or past perceptions:

If one wishes to evoke in thought some past perception, it is necessary to supplement the verbal sign system with a system of imaginal symbols. Without some semiotic means it would be impossible to think at all. The image, then, is a symbol in that it constitutes the semiotic instrument necessary in order to evoke and think what has been perceived. (Piaget & Inhelder, 1971, p. 381)

In addition, Piaget wishes to combat the old associationist view of the image as a copy of perception, replacing this ancient idea with the more modern view that images reflect what we know rather than what we see (or hear, or feel). To the extent that images are more than copies or extensions of perception and, hence, have a constructed, "non-primitive" character, they tend "to acquire the status of a symbol" (Piaget & Inhelder, 1971).

In any case, the shift from sensorimotor to preoperational representation is characterized by the acquisition of symbols, and it is assumed that the first purely mental symbols (as opposed to gestures) are images. So far as I know, no evidence is adduced for this assumption other than the fact that symbol use can occur without the use of language. It may be that if Piaget's theory of early representational development were to be systematized, this assumption would become an axiom. The second assumption is that the formation of symbols is based on imitation. Piaget states that child psychology "has defined the conditions of the formation of the symbolic function as based on imitation, which consequently might also be the source of the images" (Piaget & Inhelder, 1971, p. xv). Although imitation as the source of images is thus considered to be more speculative than imitation as the source of symbolization, in fact Piaget's various discussions of the end products of imitation all revolve around the development of images.

The Origins of Imagery

As we have seen, Piaget does not find it necessary to posit the presence of symbols until Stage 6 of the sensorimotor period. Therefore, he does not admit the presence of imagery before this time. The problem to be explained, then, is, What causes the appearance of imagery at this stage? Where do images come from? Piaget's solution to the problem, namely, that imitation produces imagery, immediately raises another problem. He needs imagery (or other symbolic processes) to account for the phenomenon of deferred imitation, which he first observed in Stage 6. The most widely cited example is Jacqueline's delayed imitation of a little boy's temper tantrum, a phenomenon that she had recently seen for the first time (Piaget, 1951). To account for her ability to reproduce this strange event after a delay of more than 12 hr. requires some symbolic representation (recall) of the incident. Clearly, there is danger of circularity here. On the one hand, deferred imitation is to be accounted for by representation; on the other hand, representation is to be accounted for by imitation and possibly by deferred imitation. Although Piaget recognizes the problem, he does not directly address it. The closest approach to a description of the sequence involved is the following:

> There is a sensori-motor imitation consisting of an actual representation and action acquired in the first instance in the presence of the object. At a later stage it is able to assume a "deferred" form (in other words a new imitative act is carried out without the object); it then becomes an evocation proper, though still in terms of action. If it is then internalized . . . it is prolonged as an image. (Piaget & Inhelder, 1971, p. xvi)

If Piaget were to admit the development of imagery through perception or action alone, the problem of circularity would not arise. That is, repeated perceptions or actions could give rise to images of those perceptions and actions, which could then be used for purposes of evocation or recall to enable deferred imitation. However, because of his insistence that imagery is more than a passive recapitulation of per-

ception, he sought another mechanism for its development. Hypothesizing that mechanism to be imitation was an inspired notion because it places the development of imagery squarely in the arena of the active analysis of things perceived. For Piaget, imitation involves active attempts to copy some aspect of the environment. His account of the development of imitation in infancy is devoted to the increasingly important role played by analytic activity—not just looking and doing but looking and attempting to dissect what is seen and done to understand it well enough to make a copy of it. Looking alone will not produce an image according to this view, only looking accompanied by analysis. When such analysis has been carried out, the resulting image may be precise enough to become a "draft of potential imitation" (Piaget, 1951, p. 70) and, thus, to mediate future reproduction.

There are remarkably few data available to evaluate the claim that imagery develops from imitation, nor is it entirely clear just what the claim implies. On the one hand, there is the question of how the capacity to imagine develops in the first place and, on the other hand, there is the question of what is required to form an image at any age. Piaget and Inhelder (1971) answer both questions with the same solution: imagery always requires an active internalized imitation. The notion suffers from a good deal of vagueness. It is difficult to know what to look for in the way of evidence because it is not clear either what exactly is supposed to be imitated or what kinds of activity are required to carry out the active analysis that imitation implies.

Piaget and Inhelder interpret the notion of activity rather broadly and include eye movements as well as more overt activity. They suggest that the demonstration of similarity of eye movements and visual images would not only support the notion of the imitative character of imagery but also would counteract the notion of an image as no more than a residual perception. The evidence on eye movements is mixed and its interpretation is complex. Some imagery studies find that eye movements are correlated with vividness, amount of imagery, or the size of the image (e.g., Tikhomirov, 1971; Weber & Malmstrom, 1979), but others have not found such relationships (e.g., Marks, 1973; Weiner & Erlichman, 1976; Zikmund, 1972). It has even been suggested that eye movements must be suppressed for vivid imagery to occur (Singer, Greenberg, & Antrobus, 1971).

In any case, it is not clear that the presence of eye movements during visual imagery, even if correlated with aspects of the stimulus, would support

Piaget's notion that imagery is *imitative*. Evidence showing that eye movements are associated with constructing or scanning a visual image has been used to support the notion of the image as a reinstatement of a perceptual process (e.g., Hebb, 1949, 1968; Neisser, 1967). Such a position might be hard to distinguish from the "recreation or prolongation of past perception" that Piaget wishes to deny. Furthermore, scanning by the mind's eye, a notion supported by some (e.g., Kosslyn, 1978a; Paivio, 1975), would not require eye movements, yet might be considered active imitation.

Piaget and Inhelder also suggest that children are better at using imagery to reconstruct a display following their own construction of it than when they merely look at the display or watch an experimenter construct it (Piaget & Inhelder, 1971, chap. 7). They conclude that imagery is facilitated if it is the result of the child's own action and that the image is more accurate if the action is overt rather than merely consisting of perceptual activity. In general, the comparison of recognition of displays that have been constructed with those that have merely been observed is not a viable technique for assessing imagery. Accounting for mistakes in the initial construction and difficulty in disentangling recognition from recall during reconstruction are just two of the problems endemic to this method.

Unfortunately, most of the available work of other investigators has used an even more indirect method of assessing the role that active manipulation plays in forming an image. Levin and his associates (e.g., Levin, McCabe, & Bender, 1975; Wolff & Levin, 1972) have carried out a number of studies on this question using success at paired-associate learning as their measure of imagery. The use of such a measure to study imagery stems from the traditional belief that imaginal elaboration leads to more effective learning (see Pressley, 1977, and Reese, 1977, for reviews). A typical finding is that motor manipulation of the objects to be learned improves young children's performance. However, because no direct measure of imagery is employed, the results are ambiguous. There could be many reasons why manipulation of objects facilitates paired-associate learning, such as greater attention to, or interest in, the task, and so forth.

Somewhat more direct information on the development of imagery through motor activity comes from a set of serendipitous observations accompanying a study of the overlearning of new motor patterns (Mandler & Kuhlman, 1961). Adult subjects were required to learn to pull in correct sequence a series of 8 randomly assigned switches on a 64-switch

board. Practice on this task was continued either until errorless performance was attained or for 50 trials past criterion. A postexperimental interview was conducted during which subjects described their behavior and method of accomplishing the task. Overtrained subjects were significantly more likely to report visual imagery than were subjects trained to mastery only; the latter subjects more often referred to tactile or motor imagery. These data suggest the possibility of a gradual development of visual imagery during extended practice. To my knowledge, however, this phenomenon has not been directly investigated as a subject of study in its own right. Even if such a sequence should prove reliable, by itself it would not separate the effects of repeated activity (or perception) from active attempts at analysis of either the visual display or the pattern of movements. The question does seem amenable to experimental test, however, and might inspire a productive line of research on the question of the origin of various sorts of imagery.

The Theory of Imagery as the Major Form of Representation in Early Childhood

We have seen that Piaget posits a new form of representation (imaginal) at the end of the sensorimotor period, one that heralds the onset of the preoperational period. Bruner formulates a similar hypothesis (Bruner et al., 1966). The preoperational child is said to be perception bound, captured by the surface appearance of things, unable to dig beneath the surface to represent deeper meanings. Deeper meanings, for Piaget, consist of an understanding of changes of states rather than the states themselves as well as an understanding of the complex interrelationships among concepts, such as the addition and multiplication of classes and relations. Until the child becomes concrete operational, thinking will depend heavily on images, which at all ages are better at representing states than transformations. That is, imagery by its very nature, according to Piaget, remains more static than kinetic, but it gradually becomes subordinate to, and influenced by, operational thought as the child enters the concrete operational period.

Generally speaking, preoperational thought may be thought of as a system of notions within which figurative treatment of states takes precedence over comprehension of transformations. Consequently, at this level images govern thought, while the situation is reversed at the operational level. (Piaget & Inhelder, 1971, p. 197)

Piaget's account takes little notice of the verbal system in the preoperational child, although it is clearly well developed long before the onset of concrete operational thought. To the extent that language is discussed in Piaget's various writings about the preoperational period, it is usually to point out that many verbally expressed concepts have shifting and uncertain meanings. Some oft-cited examples are terms denoting extension, such as "some" and "all"; kinship and other relational terms; and difficulties in relating subordinate to superordinate terms. Difficulties with these expressions might indicate conceptual differences between children and adults (see *Categorical Representation*) but by themselves do not indicate a lack of a semantic representational system nor implicate an imaginal format for such a system. Nevertheless, Piaget suggests that preoperational concepts (or preconcepts) are represented by images of prototypical exemplars.

The preconcepts of this level can be considered to be still half-way between the symbol and the concept proper . . . the preconcept involves the image and is partially determined by it, whereas the concept, precisely because of its generality, breaks away from the image and uses it only as an illustration. . . . Since in the case of the preconcept . . . there is assimilation to a selected object without generalized accommodation to all [members of the same class], accommodation to this specific object is necessarily continued as image when the child's thought is projected on to the others. The image intervenes as essential aid to assimilation, and therefore as privileged signifier, and to some extent as substitute. (Piaget, 1951, p. 229)

It should be noted that a statement that a category is organized in terms of prototypes or degrees of prototypicality says nothing about the format in which a prototype is represented. Although the work of Rosch and her associates (Rosch, 1975; Rosch & Mervis, 1975; Rosch et al., 1976) has sometimes been taken as evidence for a perceptual (imaginal) basis for prototypes (e.g., Paivio, 1978), Rosch (1978) herself disclaims such a notion, pointing out that a prototype can be represented by either a propositional or an imaginal system.

The position that imagery is the primary form of representation in the preoperational period has come under attack from two sources (Fodor, 1972, 1975; Kosslyn, 1978c). Fodor and Kosslyn complain about the vagueness of Bruner's (1966) and Piaget's (1951) formulation; in particular, the exact nature of imagery is left unspecified as well as its consequences for thought. Both authors justly point out that what people of various ages are interested in, or attend to, does not tell us how that information is represented. It may be true that young children are more concerned with the physical appearances of things than with concepts that lie behind those appearances.

Such considerations may argue for a special salience of perceptibles in the child's psychological economy. If so, they tell us something interesting about what children think *about*. But it doesn't follow that they also tell us something about what children think *with*. . . . One cannot, in general, infer from *what* is represented to the nature of the *vehicle* of representation. Information about enactive or perceptual properties of the environment *could*, after all, be stored as descriptions (i.e., "symbolically" in Bruner's sense of the term). For this reason, to demonstrate an ontogenetic shift in the features of the environment that the child attends to is not more than the first step in demonstrating the very radical thesis that the medium of internal representation changes with development. (Fodor, 1975, p. 177)

Kosslyn (1978c) has several suggestions about how to clarify and test the notion of a shift in *usage* of imaginal representation. He suggests that children may not encode information exclusively in the form of images, but they might rely on imagery more for querying their memory and for certain kinds of inferential thinking. He uses an example similar to the one cited earlier about accessing the number of windows in your house. His example is to ask, "What is the shape of a Doberman pinscher's ears?" Many people say that to answer this question they image a Doberman and inspect its ears. He suggests that ear shape may not be explicitly represented in memory but only implicitly embedded within an image.

The more frequently a given fact about a concrete (imageable) object is accessed, the more likely it is to be represented in an explicit way as well as in an image. Because children have presumably accessed the bulk of their knowledge less frequently than have adults, they presumably have had fewer opportunities for recoding imaginal representations. Hence, it makes sense to conjecture that a greater proportion of the child's memories, relative to the adult's, are encoded solely in an imaginal format. In the course of development, however, an increasing proportion of the representations in memory would be [in] an explicit, language-like format. (Kosslyn, 1978c, pp. 162–163)

Kosslyn expands this notion to account for possible differences in thinking between a child using an imaginal format and an adult who, owing to frequent access, has added explicit information to his or her knowledge base. For example, an adult who is asked whether a Doberman has four legs should not need to consult an image in the same way as to answer the question about the shape of its ears. Long experience with four-leggedness has resulted in a node being appended to the superordinate "dog"; therefore, the question can be answered immediately. The child may have made fewer image inspections and so not have extracted that piece of information and stored it directly with the concept. Consequently, the child may need to imagine a Doberman to find out how many legs it has.

This formulation of a representational-shift hypothesis is attractive because it is clearer as to what is being hypothesized and because it is potentially subject to experimental test. The hypothesis is an imaginal variant of the suggestion made earlier that an important aspect of development is the gradual formation of a declarative knowledge system from the continued applications of procedures. Using a procedure to query knowledge implicit in an image and then adding the answer to a propositional network would be one way for a declarative knowledge base to grow. The main difference between the two positions is that Kosslyn's formulation does seem to imply that this kind of information is stored in imagelike form in the first place. I took a more neutral position about the nature of the original storage. The point common to both views is that in whatever format the knowledge was encoded, it is not accessible in the form in which it was originally stored. It can be made accessible either by using the stored information to generate an image that can then be inspected or perhaps by extracting a piece of information embedded in a more abstractly conceived procedure.

One indirect finding that is consistent with these points of view about developmental differences in accessing information is that task familiarity affects the use of imagery. Weber and Malmstrom (1979) report that adults visualize familiar words as smaller images than they do for unfamiliar letter strings. These authors also comment on Tikhomirov's (1971) finding that when imagining chess moves, chess masters make fewer and smaller sized eye movements than do novices. They speculate that this

difference might be due to differences in familiarity with chess positions; in the case of chess masters, knowledge may have been transformed from an imaginal to a propositional format. This proposal echoes Kosslyn's (1978c) developmental hypothesis. Some suggestively similar results were reported by Kail, Pellegrino, and Carter (1980). They found that images of unfamiliar shapes were rotated more slowly than images of familiar alphanumeric characters. They did not find developmental differences in this regard, but they did not include children younger than the third grade.

The most relevant developmental evidence comes from Kosslyn (1976b). First and fourth graders and adults were presented with the name of an animal, followed by the name of a possible part. The animal parts were varied so that the smaller parts (e.g., claws for a cat) were more highly associated with the particular animal than were the larger parts (e.g., head). The rationale for the design was the notion that if people use a propositional store to do the task, they should be faster in accessing more highly associated parts, which presumably would be stored closer in a list or a network to the animal concept itself. If, on the other hand, people use imagery to do the task, they should be faster in accessing larger parts because previous work (Kosslyn, 1976a) had shown that larger parts of images are located more quickly than are smaller parts. In the present experiment, no mention of imagery was made in the first block of trials, but in the second block subjects were asked to decide whether or not the animal had the part by visualizing it and seeing if the part looked right. Consistent with previous results, when imagery instructions were given, it took longer to verify small than large parts. When no imagery instructions were given, fourth graders and adults verified the smaller (more highly associated) parts more rapidly than the larger ones. First graders, on the other hand, tended to respond more rapidly to the larger parts. However, there were considerable individual differences among the first graders. The nine children who reported using visual imagery in the no-imagery condition were faster in verifying large parts, whereas the five children who did not report using imagery behaved more like the fourth graders and adults; that is, they were slightly faster in verifying small parts. Most of the older children and adults reported they did not use visual imagery when no imagery instructions were given.

In contrast with this line of research, which investigates image use directly, most traditional work on imagery has not been germane to the question of how children encode and represent information from various types of tasks. Kosslyn (1978c) provides an extensive critique of a number of experiments that have been used to suggest that young children rely more on imagery than on verbal mechanisms. The brunt of his argument is similar to that discussed above in relation to paired-associate learning: the data are simply too indirect to address the issue of how the material is encoded. For example, studies on verbal mediation in which children were shown not to label pictures spontaneously (e.g., Flavell, 1970; Hagen, 1972) cannot be used to support an imaginal representation hypothesis. Aside from the fact that even very young children often *do* spontaneously label pictures they are asked to remember (Perlmutter & Myers, 1976), lack of spontaneous verbalization simply does not tell us what has been encoded or how it is stored. The notion seems to have been that if something is not encoded in words then it must be encoded as an image. Such reasoning by exclusion, as Kosslyn (1978c) points out, rests on an unduly simple notion of the possible encoding mechanisms at the child's disposal. Similar problems of inappropriate methods are found in studies claiming that imagery becomes less static and more dynamic in later childhood.

Changes in Imagery During Childhood

Both Bruner (1966) and Piaget and Inhelder (1971) claim that the preoperational child's imagery is static. For Bruner, the change that occurs around ages 6 to 8 is that the child's representational system becomes more symbolically and linguistically based. Having gradually mastered the linguistic rules involving categorization and hierarchical structure, the child learns to apply them to conceptual organization as well. For Piaget, the change that occurs is due to the onset of concrete operations. Piaget emphasizes more than Bruner that even the young child's imagery is at least partly symbolic in nature, but because children cannot accurately perceive or understand transformations, a fortiori their images cannot represent such information. Young children may be able to represent movements relating to their own actions (such as body movements), but they are unable to imagine the kinds of transformations of objects that are relevant to concrete operational thought (such as the transformations involved in conservation tests).

Recent work has begun to show that preschool children are more knowledgeable about transformations than Piaget's work has suggested (see Gelman & Gallistel, 1978, on number transformations; Bullock & Gelman, 1979, and Gelman, Bullock, &

Meck, 1980, on causal transformations). Nevertheless, it may still be the case that they have more difficulty representing such transformations in their imagery. Much of Piaget and Inhelder's imagery book (1971) suggests that they do. Piaget and Inhelder make a distinction between kinetic imagery, which involves movement of objects (change in position), and transformational imagery, which involves change in form of objects. It might be thought that the latter kind of imagery would give the preoperational child the most trouble because transformations, not movements, are involved in the concrete operations and because movement is a highly salient aspect of perception from infancy onward. Nevertheless, Piaget and Inhelder's work indicates that both movement and transformations of objects are difficult for children to image before the concrete operational period.

According to this view, preoperational imagery is so static that it cannot even represent the end state of a simple movement that the child must have seen a great many times. For example, Piaget and Inhelder showed children two squares sitting on top of each other. Then, the child was asked to imagine that the top square was moved slightly to the right and asked to draw the result (or occasionally to choose from among several drawings). The interpretation of the results is complex because most of the 4-year-olds and many of the 5-year-olds could not even correctly draw the final result when it was shown to them. However, Piaget and Inhelder's point is that the representation of the *imagined* end state lagged behind. Of the 5½- to 6-year-olds, 79% could draw the end state when it was shown to them, but not until the age of 7 could 78% of the children draw the end state from imagination alone.

A number of other investigators have reported findings that appear to support the static, nonanticipatory character of preoperational children's imagery (Beilin, Kagan, & Rabinowitz, 1966; De Lisi, Locker, & Youniss, 1976; Lipton & Overton, 1971). However, others have not found the predicted relationship between operational level and kinetic imagery (Anooshian & Carlson, 1973; Jackson, 1974; Marmor, 1975, 1977). Marmor (1977) and Kosslyn (1978c) both argue that many studies merely *assume* that static imagery is the cause of failure in certain tasks. That is, it is posited that anticipatory kinetic imagery is required for success. Their argument can be illustrated using the De Lisi et al. (1976) paper. These investigators found a relationship between failure on spatial perspective problems and the horizontal water-level task. It was assumed that the solution to these problems requires anticipatory kinetic imagery, that is, the ability to imagine unseen movements through space. The possibility that people can solve these problems by using specific rules rather than by using imagery was not considered. In fact, it is not necessary to imagine an object moving through space to solve the water-level problem. One can simply know that water is always horizontal and find an appropriate frame of reference (e.g., the table top) to express that knowledge. Similar arguments can be made for the perspective-taking task. Rules—such as, "If it is on my right, it must be on your left" or "If it is close to me, it must be far from you"—are sufficient to accomplish these tasks. This is not to say that such rules *are* used, only that to *assume* that performance on spatial tasks tells us about the nature of imagery is unwarranted. Hunt, for example, has shown that there are two distinct algorithms that can be used to solve matrix and certain perceptual problems, one spatio-perceptual, the other analytic (Hunt, 1974; Hunt, Frost, & Lunneborg, 1973). There are likely to be multiple solutions to many other problems.

Related difficulties arise from using children's drawings to analyze the nature of their imagery, which was one of Piaget and Inhelder's (1971) most frequent methods of assessment. It has been pointed out by many investigators that although drawings are influenced by what one knows, drawing requires complex rules of its own (Freeman, 1980; Goodnow, 1977; Goodnow & Levine, 1973; Maccoby, 1968). According to Freeman:

> There are different kinds of mental imagery theory but their kernel is that you can read off the child's mental imagery from the drawn product. For example, if you get a tadpole man drawn, such a theory would entail that the child had a mental image that corresponds to the drawing. My own view is that all drawings involve the labour of production. There is no privileged way of reading off from the drawing what the mental image is. (Freeman, 1977, p. 45)

Freeman concludes that children have more knowledge available than they can access unless they are given proper retrieval cues. They also have production problems in handling such things as serial order and coordination of various frames of reference, in addition to operating under a "perpendicular bias" (Bassett, 1977; Freeman, 1980). Kosslyn, Heldmeyer, & Locklear (1977) also make a cogent argument for the difficulty of separating children's knowledge of pictorial conventions from the content of their internal representations. They

suggest that it is unlikely that we can gain information about the format of representations from the format of children's drawings (see also Hayes, 1978).

Once again we see the need for a more direct method of studying imagery. Marmor's work falls into this class (1975, 1977; see also Childs & Polich, 1979). She investigated the use of kinetic imagery in 5- and 8-year-olds using the Shepard and Cooper technique of studying rotational movement (Shepard & Metzler, 1971; Cooper & Shepard, 1973, 1978). This technique has become one of the most convincing demonstrations of the use of imaginal processing. In one version of their tasks, subjects are shown pairs of pictures at the same or different orientations and are asked whether the pairs are identical or mirror images of each other. When the pairs are displayed at the same orientation, a simple match or mismatch can be made. When one of the pictures is rotated in the picture plane, however, subjects claim that they imagine the first picture rotating in space until it is superimposed on the other, at which time a match or mismatch judgment is made. The findings have been surprisingly robust, showing a linear increase in reaction time to make the judgments as a function of degree of rotation of one of the pictures.

When Marmor (1975) carried out this kind of experiment on children, she found the same linear relationship between amount of rotation and reaction time as found for adults. The slopes of the functions were steeper, suggesting a slower rate of rotating the image, but the linear relationship between reaction time and angular separation between the stimuli was as impressive as for the adults. If such results are considered to be evidence for kinetic imagery in adults, then one must conclude that it exists in 5-year-old children as well.

Marmor noted that her results may have differed from those of Piaget and Inhelder because children in her experiment were specifically told to use mental rotation as a method of accomplishing the task, whereas Piaget and Inhelder did not tell children how to approach the problems they set them. In a later experiment, Marmor (1977) tested this variable. Working with 4- and 5-year-old children and adults, she gave half of them training designed to induce the use of rotational imagery and gave no instructions to the others. Exactly the same results were found as in the previous experiment, with no effect of instructions. Again, slopes decreased with age, suggesting that rate of rotation of an image increases as a function of age, but the same linear relationship was found even with the 4-year-olds. In addition, no relationship was found between mental rotation and number conservation. These results strongly suggest that kinetic imagery is spontaneously used by preoperational children.

In summary, when more direct measures of imagery are used than have typically been used in the past, little evidence is found for qualitatively different *kinds* of imagery in children and adults. The only evidence of differences in *usage* of imagery are the Kosslyn (1976b) data suggesting that children may rely more on imagery for certain kinds of inferential thinking than adults. These data are still preliminary, although they do suggest that children *may* have more of their knowledge stored in imaginal form. These conclusions do not imply that the *content* of children's imagery is the same as adults' imagery. To the extent that images are influenced by rules that we know or perceptual details that we have noticed, we should expect differences in sophistication of content across ages. Thus, if a child does not know that water remains horizontal and does not notice its horizontality when observing a glass of water, his or her image is unlikely to contain this information (see Liben & Golbeck, 1980).

This consideration raises the issue of what it means to store information in the form of an image. If an image were a replica or copy of perception, then the information about water level would seem to be there, available for inspection. As we will see in the following discussion, the nature of imagery is hotly disputed. Almost the only thing that is agreed upon is that an image is not a "raw" picture in the head.

Theories of Imagery

I have discussed the development of imagery and its possible use as a form of representation without specifying exactly what is meant by the term. I have relied on our intuitions about imagery, and all of us have them, although some more positively than others. Yet, specifying the nature of an image in any detail has turned out to be an extremely difficult task, and there still remains no satisfactory account. Instead, how to account for imagelike or perceptionlike representations and the processes that operate on them has become one of modern psychology's most acrimonious battlegrounds. The two sides of the fray (which is sometimes called the analog-propositional dispute) can be roughly characterized as follows. Side 1 claims that imagery is a form of representation that has a continuous (analog) character fundamentally different from a discrete propositional representation. In the case of visual imagery, the representation occurs in a spatial medium that

may be the same as that used in visual perceptual processing (Kosslyn, 1981). At this end of the field, the major combatants (and representative recent publications) have been Cooper and Shepard (1978), Kosslyn (1980), Kosslyn & Pomerantz (1977), and Paivio (1977, 1978). Side 2, at the other end of the field, claims that there is a single form of representation and this is propositional. The combatants here are principally Fodor (1975), Palmer (1975b), and Pylyshyn (1973, 1979a). After several years of struggle, Anderson (1978) attempted to act as a (slightly biased) arbitrator and was roundly denounced by both sides for his efforts (Hayes-Roth, 1979; Pylyshyn, 1979b). Most recently a new round of salvos has been presented by Pylyshyn (1981) and Kosslyn (1981). There the matter currently stands— either a cold war or a tired truce, depending on how you look at it.

Although the arguments may soon exhaust their usefulness to the discipline, as often happens in both hot and cold wars, many of the participants engaged in normal activity in the interstices of the fighting and the result has been a greatly expanded data base and a number of findings about imagery that future theories must take into account. On the whole, it seems to this bystander (with her own biases) that Side 1 has grown in stature during the course of the arguments and has ended in a stronger position than the one from which it began.

In its earlier form (see Paivio's original dual-code theory, 1971), which influenced many of the developmental studies we have discussed, Side 1's argument for images appeared somewhat simplistic. Words were encoded as words and percepts as images. Pylyshyn (1973) argued cogently against such a notion and it is no longer held today (Kosslyn & Pomerantz, 1977). It is generally accepted that words are encoded in a more abstract underlying format (e.g., Clark & Clark, 1977; Kintsch, 1977a; Norman et al., 1975). In addition, perception has been shown to be a highly interpreted process (Garner, 1962; Neisser, 1967; Palmer, 1975c). We do not see raw sense data but only data interpreted by our conceptual system. If the relevant concepts and schemata are represented in propositional networks or the like, then perception necessarily involves propositional knowledge. Because images are based on perceptual processes, one might expect them to involve propositional knowledge as well. Nevertheless, current holders of the imagery position all espouse some version of a dual-code theory, albeit more sophisticated versions than earlier formulations.

Propositional theorists emphasize the vagueness

of imagery theorists' claims and particularly decry the notion that introspective accounts should be taken as evidence for the primitives of the representational system. As Anderson (1978) puts it, "there is no reason to suppose that the best representation to account for verbal reports of picturelike properties of an image is a picture" (p. 259). It has also been argued that some sort of abstract underlying knowledge is necessary to account for the ease with which we describe pictures in words and create pictures from verbal descriptions. We often confuse the source of information and after a while cannot remember whether we saw or heard or read it. These considerations suggest that all incoming information is encoded into a common format or interlingua (Pylyshyn, 1973) that is neither verbal or visual but more abstract than both (Anderson & Bower, 1973; Chase & Clark, 1972; Potter, Valian, & Faulconer, 1977).

Another argument is that because perception must also be given a propositional interpretation, it is more parsimonious or economical to couch all representations in the single format that has been shown to be necessary for many cognitive activities. The argument for parsimony is a two-edged sword, however, particularly because no one has yet implemented a full-scale model of human cognition. Although it is fairly generally agreed that any kind of knowledge *can* be represented in propositional format, the issue is whether such representations would constitute an unrealistic form for a theory of imaginal representation. In one sense, a single-format model is parsimonious; if it means a cumbersome, unduly time-consuming type of processing, however, the system is no longer economical. It is fair to say that although claims have been made that the complexities of imagery can be represented purely propositionally, no one has tried to do so in any detail (although see Baylor, 1971, for a propositional account of a simple image system; see also Gips, 1974).

There are also compelling arguments for different modes of representation that are tailored for different kinds of processing. Imagery theorists assume that an image is a spatial representation similar in nature to, and derived from, perceptual processing (Shepard, 1978). This assumption does not entail any conclusions as to whether or not perceptual processes result in propositionally interpreted information. Furthermore, a great deal of evidence has accumulated over the past few years about the characteristics of imagery and the processes that operate on it so that the claim of vagueness is largely outdated (see Shepard & Podgorny, 1978, for an account of some types of research that can be used to assess the properties of images). Images can be rotated, as discussed earlier. Images can be scanned, and it takes longer to arrive at parts that are farther away from the starting point (Kosslyn, Ball, & Reiser, 1978). It is easier to find parts on large images than on small ones (Kosslyn, 1975). One can zoom in on an image and enlarge it to the point of overflow, that is, until it becomes fuzzy around the edges and disappears (Kosslyn, 1978b).

With varying degrees of strain, each of these phenomena can potentially be explained by a propositional account, but in the long run, the outcome will be determined by the practical success of the theorizing. Currently, the most promising imagery theory is that of Kosslyn and Shwartz (Kosslyn, 1980; Kosslyn & Shwartz, 1977, 1978). They have developed a computer program to simulate imagery and its processing. The model uses an underlying representation, consisting of both propositional and semantically uninterpreted perceptual information, which can generate images and process them in ways that conform to the data Kosslyn has collected over the years. In addition, the theory has begun to specify the characteristics of the spatial medium in which images occur (Finke & Kosslyn, 1980; Kosslyn, 1980). This work is providing us with much more detailed information about imaginal processing than many of us would have thought possible a few years ago.

It may seem that we have strayed afield from the central issue of how to characterize children's imagery. But so much weight has been placed on imagery in explanations of development that it is crucial to understand the import of what is being claimed. Considering that the concept of the image has been central to psychological theory since its inception, it may seem surprising how little we still understand about it. Great strides have been made in the past decade, and the new techniques devised by Shepard, Cooper, and Kosslyn promise to enhance our understanding of imagery considerably. The application of these techniques to children's imagery is still in its infancy, or perhaps preoperational period, and we still have much to learn. It is clear that developmental work on imagery must incorporate the current sophisticated theory and experimental techniques and leave behind the simpler measures with which we are more familiar if the development of imagery is to be understood.

Developmental studies of imagery may also help us resolve some major theoretical issues. For example, the most recent skirmish in the imagery war concerns the role of experimenter demands and tacit knowledge of perception as an explanation for imagery findings (Pylyshyn, 1981; Richman, Mitchell, & Reznick, 1979). Kosslyn (1981) rebuts these arguments forcefully, pointing out that many imagery phenomena are indeed related to perceptual processes but also include processes of which subjects are not aware. Developmental studies, such as those of Marmor, (1975, 1977) which find similar imagery phenomena in very young children, decrease the likelihood that the use of tacit knowledge can explain imagery phenomena because these children are too young to be aware in a sophisticated way of their perceptual processing. This may be an arena in which developmental work can settle a general psychological issue—an all too rare phenomenon.

REPRESENTATION OF SPACE

Many of the issues examined in the discussion on imagery are pertinent to the question of how children represent space. This is so in part because images themselves are thought to be spatial representations and because it has commonly been assumed that children use imagery to solve a variety of spatial problems. Because the issue of the format of spatial representations has already been discussed at length, the present exposition will concentrate on the types of spatial knowledge that children are capable of representing at various stages of development.

The temptation is strong to assume that both our perception and representation of space directly reflect a euclidean reality. We look at the world and see straight lines, curves, angles, circles, cubes, and spheres—all contained in a great three-dimensional expanse. If we close our eyes, we can imagine (represent) all sorts of lines and angles without difficulty. The representation seems to follow directly from the perception. One of Piaget's most important contributions was to demonstrate that this folk psychology does not accurately convey the complex relations between perception and the conception of space.

Piaget emphasizes that the representation of space is a construction, not a simple reflection of perception. He notes that children's knowledge of space does not necessarily match what they see. The young child may see a straight line, but not be able to imagine one; discriminate squares from circles, but not be able to reproduce the difference from memory. Furthermore, children's conceptions direct their perception; if they are not attuned to subtleties in the perceptual scene, it is unlikely that those fine details will be included in any representation they carry away with them. Needless to say, this interplay between knowledge and perception is not confined to childhood (Bobrow & Norman, 1975; Friedman, 1979; Palmer, 1975c; Rumelhart & Ortony, 1977). One of the reasons why most of us are such poor artists is our lack of analysis of perceptual relationships. As mentioned at the beginning of the chapter, we have all observed literally hundreds of thousands of faces; yet, most of us cannot specify the proportions of the human face or the proper relationships among eyes, ears, and forehead.

Piaget may not have carried the implications of his constructive characterization of space far enough. Our folk psychology leads us all to overestimate the euclidean accuracy of our spatial knowledge. Piaget's major thesis is that the adult conception of space is primarily a euclidean one that is gradually constructed out of more primitive topological beginnings. The implications of this view are two: first, that there is a radical restructuring of spatial conceptions during the course of development; second, that the mature concept of space eventually achieves a veridical euclidean character. This discussion will suggest that each of these views may be exaggerated.

The discussion opens by examining the extent to which infants encode space in terms of relationships to their own bodies as opposed to a more objective framework. Next, preoperational children's conception of space and the issue of topological versus euclidean representations are considered in some detail. Then, the issues of how cognitive maps of small-scale and large-scale environments are formed and what characteristics these maps have at various ages are examined. Finally, the topic of scene representation and the types of information about familiar scenes that children encode and retain are covered.

Spatial Representation in Infancy

Piaget's (1954) discussion of the development of spatial concepts in infancy parallels his work on the development of the object concept (see *Piaget's Theory of the Emergence of Symbolic Thought*). He suggests that in the early stages of the sensorimotor period, the conception of space is primitive indeed; to the extent that children at this stage can represent space at all (as opposed to perceive it), it is in terms of their own actions. In this view, the early conception of space has a strongly procedural base: the child knows how to locate objects in space or remembers where to find them in terms of his or her accustomed acts of reaching for and manipulating them. "True" representation of space, in Piaget's view, will only be achieved when these actions become coordinated and internalized.

In the earliest stages, Piaget suggests that there is not a single unitary space but rather a series of unrelated spaces associated with different activities and sensory modalities. This view of a lack of intersensory coordination, with its implications of James's (1890) conception of a blooming, buzzing confusion, has come under attack recently (see *Gibson & Spelke, vol. III, chap. 1,* in which infant perception is discussed in detail). Regardless of intersensory coordination, Piaget claims that infants do not have knowledge of an objective framework in which objects can be located independent of their actions on them. Even when various sensory modalities become coordinated, the child still conceives near or graspable space differently from far or nongraspable space (Piaget, 1954).

The shift in representation from a subjective, procedurally based conception to a more objective view of space as a motionless container in which both subjects and objects are independently placed, which Piaget terms the child's "Copernican revolution," has been characterized as a shift from an egocentric to an allocentric code (Bremner, 1978a, 1978b; Butterworth, 1977b; Harris, 1977). In an egocentric code, positions of objects in space are coded in relation to oneself; for example, objects can be coded as being to one's right or left, in front or behind, and so forth. In an allocentric code, some external frame of reference is used to locate objects' positions. Such a framework need not be a euclidean one; a simple framework in which proximity to landmarks is used would be sufficient, although it might lead to local mistakes owing to lack of information about an object's distance from a landmark. The egocentric and allocentric codes might also be combined; an object might be encoded as being near a landmark while, at the same time, the relation to the landmark (left or right) might be encoded egocentrically. Harris (1977) has suggested that the typical patterns of errors found in various sensorimotor spatial tasks indicate that this is indeed what the infant is learning: to coordinate egocentric and allocentric codes, a task, by the way, that is not fully completed even in the adult.

Several studies have charted a gradual shift during the sensorimotor period from an egocentric representation of object locations to an allocentric one (Acredolo, 1978, 1979; Bremner, 1978a, 1978b; Bremner & Bryant, 1977; Cornell & Heth, 1979). The rationale of these experiments is based on old experiments with rats on place (allocentric) versus response (egocentric) learning (Tolman, Ritchie, & Kalish, 1946). Adult rats are place learners, but apparently human infants are not. Acredolo (1978)

taught 6-month-old infants to make a left (or right) turning response to find an attractive object. When the infants were then moved 180° so that they now faced the display from the opposite direction, they continued to make the same response as before and, thus, looked in the wrong direction. This egocentric response was unaffected by the presence of salient landmarks. The pattern gradually changed to an allocentric response by 16 months. The exact time course is still to be determined because Bremner (1978a, 1978b) found that salient landmark cues encourage allocentric responding by 9 months of age, and a more recent study by (Rieser, 1979) suggests that even by 6 months of age, infants can engage in some allocentric encoding in the presence of a landmark. Although the tendency toward egocentric encoding increases when the child is allowed to reach for the object, it occurs even without such training (Acredolo, 1979); therefore, the egocentric code appears to be related to the use of one's body to encode spatial location rather than being a purely procedural response based on one's actions vis-à-vis the object.

Both Bremner (1978a) and Acredolo (1978) suggest that the shift from egocentric to allocentric representation of space is dependent on the child's increasing mobility, starting with crawling and accelerating when walking begins. Although the infant appears to derive some information from being carried, active, self-generated movement seems to be more effective (cf. Hein, 1972). As one begins to move around one's environment, an egocentric code not only becomes increasingly unworkable but one also acquires more and more information about the independence of objects from one's own position, what they look like from different points of view, and so forth.

In case the notion of an egocentric code seems an unusually primitive way of representing space, Hutchins (in press) has noted that adults use an egocentric code vis-à-vis the solar system. We do not move (or at least most of us have not) through outer space. We are hopelessly earthbound to our notion that the sun comes up in the morning rather than that we are moving around the sun. The real Copernican revolution did not seem to affect these views very much. Indeed, given that we have no traffic with the other bodies in the solar system, our egocentric encoding of the sun in relation to the earth is a quite efficient conception. Hutchins has documented a similar adult system of egocentric encoding for the Caroline Island navigators. These intrepid sailors cover vast distances in the South Pacific without benefit of compass or other navigational device; during most of their journeys, they are out of sight of any landmark. Their navigational system is highly successful and its principle is egocentric. The sailer conceives of his boat as standing still while the invisible landmarks (charted by the horizon positions of star settings) flow by him. It seems that use of an egocentric or allocentric code per se is not a question of a primitive or sophisticated notion of space but rather one that is influenced by one's opportunities for seeing a region from many points of view.

A final observation may be made about these two spatial codes. Acredolo (1979) found that 9-month-old infants were much more likely to demonstrate allocentric knowledge about space when tested in their homes than when tested in an unfamiliar environment. This finding is clearly relevant to the notion that an "objective" knowledge of space develops as one explores it from many points of view. Unless we are very clever when taking a walk through an unfamiliar town and turn around often to acquire knowledge about how things look from the other direction, we may have little information to guide our way back again except in terms of an egocentric record of our various turns. Most of our knowledge of new spaces consists of route knowledge and, as we will see in the discussion on *Large-Scale Spaces,* even adults do not behave very differently than young children in unfamiliar surroundings.

Euclidean Versus Topological Representation of Space

Neither an egocentric nor allocentric code speaks to the issue of the characteristics of the spatial framework that is being used. In both codes, distance can be represented by either euclidean or topological relations. Topological characterizations of space do not include the metric aspects of euclidean geometry. Instead, space is characterized by relations of proximity or neighborhoods, continuity of lines, order of succession of points, and enclosure or surrounding. This branch of mathematics is aptly dubbed "rubber geometry" because the relations it defines remain invariant when the surface on which lines and shapes are drawn is stretched like rubber. Thus, a straight line can be stretched to be made longer or twisted so that it is curved, yet its continuity and the order of its points remain unchanged. These relationships can only be changed by poking a hole through the surface or otherwise tearing it. Many of the most basic aspects of space can be quite adequately represented by topological relations alone, without calling upon the metric properties of projective or euclidean geometry. (See the transla-

tor's introduction to Piaget and Inhelder, 1956, for a brief description of topological relations.)

Metric properties of space add restrictions to the topological conceptions. These properties begin to appear when considering projective space, in which objects are described in relation to each other through lines of regard or points of view. In projective space, linear order becomes rectilinear order, and the distinction between straight and curved lines is thus made; in addition, rectilinearity remains invariant when the point of view changes. Euclidean concepts introduce the notion of coordinate axes and include many of our most familiar notions about space, such as right angles and the metric concepts of distance.

Piaget and Inhelder (1956) posit that the earliest representations of space are topological and do not contain information stemming from either projective or euclidean geometry. Although they imply that the topological relations they discuss can be given a strict mathematical interpretation, in fact their definitions of topological terms are not the same as those of mathematicians (Kapadia, 1974; J. L. Martin, 1976). Because their usage of various terms, such as continuity, proximity, and separation, differs from strictly mathematical terminology, the set of distinctions that they call topological might better be specified as a list of primitive, or global, properties of spatial representations. For example, "above" and "below" may be represented as early as "inside" and "outside," yet with some exceptions involving tangents, the latter relations are distinguished in topology, whereas the former are not. To my knowledge, no typology of spatial relations that does not depend upon euclidean conceptions has been worked out other than the one offered by Piaget and Inhelder (1956). In the remainder of this discussion, I will continue to use their terminology, only reminding the reader that topological relations, from a psychological point of view, have not yet been well specified.

Piaget and Inhelder (1956) assume that the earliest perception in infancy also has a topological basis and that perception of euclidean space is one of the main achievements of the sensorimotor period. For example, they state that not until Stage 3 or 4 of the sensorimotor period is the infant able to perceive a straight line. These notions about early perception, developed as they were before the recent spurt of sophisticated studies of infant perception (see *Gibson & Spelke, vol. III, chap. 1*), have since been shown to be incorrect. As a single example, Fantz and Miranda (1975) have demonstrated that even neonates are capable of distinguishing between straight and curved lines. However, it is not necessary for Piaget and Inhelder's (1956) theory of spatial representation that it be preceded by similar perceptual phenomena because, as we have seen, they emphasize that representational space is a construction and not a simple reflection of perception. In any case, following the sensorimotor period, during which the child is not considered to have attained representational concepts of space (only practical, procedural methods of dealing with space), there is thought to be a gradual construction of spatial understanding that proceeds from a topological to a projective and euclidean nature. Hence, the preoperational child is thought not to make euclidean distinctions when imagining spatial concepts.

A series of experiments representative of those Piaget and Inhelder used to document their theory required children to explore two-dimensional shapes with their hands and then either to draw what they had felt or to choose the same shapes from a series of pictures. The rationale for these studies is that to draw or recognize visually a shape that has been encoded only by tactile-kinesthetic means requires some spatial representation; because no direct visual information has been given, the child's response must be derived from a conceptual analysis of the tactile task. Piaget and Inhelder's (1956) studies documented preoperational children's seeming inability to make distinctions between rectilinear and curvilinear shapes, let alone the more sophisticated distinctions between squares and rectangles or circles and ellipses. At the same time, preoperational children were found to be able to represent differences between shapes that differed on various topological properties, such as inside and outside or open and closed.

Piaget and Inhelder did observe a number of examples of crude preoperational attempts to portray euclidean distinctions. A square might be drawn as a circle with hatch marks on it to represent angles. This kind of drawing suggests that euclidean information is represented and can even be expressed symbolically but that the child is having trouble translating the information onto the page. As discussed in the section on imagery, the complex relationships between spatial knowledge and the expression of that knowledge in drawing have been extensively documented (e.g., Freeman, 1980). Piaget and Inhelder, however, maintained a strict criterion for asserting that euclidean representations are present; unless a drawing more or less accurately portrayed angle and distance information, the child was said to lack euclidean concepts.

Piaget and Inhelder's view of the primacy of to-

pological representations seems to have been widely accepted in spite of several challenges that have been offered. In two of the early replications, Lovell (1959) and Page (1959) found that children could represent the difference between curvilinear and rectilinear shapes from an early age. This finding was confirmed by Laurendeau and Pinard (1970). Nevertheless, after elaborate analyses, the latter authors argued strongly for a predominantly topological representation in the preoperational period, and this view seems to have prevailed.

By itself, an ability to represent differences between rectilinear and curvilinear shapes would not be fatal to a psychologically defined topological hypothesis. Although a triangle and a circle are both closed continuous figures and, thus, topologically indistinguishable in the mathematical sense, the sharp angles of a triangle may be discontinuous in a psychological sense. As suggested earlier, the hypothesis of topological primacy could be bolstered by abandoning a mathematical interpretation and substituting a psychological notion of continuity instead (perhaps in terms of shifts in eye or finger movements). However, Laurendeau and Pinard (1970) also found that children were able to represent the difference between a circle and an ellipse and between a square and a rectangle as early as the difference between straight and curved shapes.

There are many problems with all of these experiments on shape representation, some of which were recognized by Laurendeau and Pinard. The choice of shapes seems to have been somewhat haphazard rather than based on a careful analysis of the concepts that were to be investigated. The stimulus sets did not represent the various concepts in equal numbers, thus making analysis of choices extremely complex. A great many stimuli were usually offered in the recognition tests, in many cases undoubtedly exceeding young children's attentional capacity. The most important problem perhaps was ignoring the extent to which children actually explored the various shapes. Piaget and Inhelder's assumption had been that tactile exploration would mimic visual exploration, but this assumption remains to be proven; in addition, even visual exploration tends not to be thorough at young ages (Mackworth & Bruner, 1970; Vurpillot, 1968). Both groups of investigators noticed that the youngest children tended to be quite passive in their exploration so that many features of the objects were not encoded and, therefore, could not be represented. This observation has been replicated and quantified by Kleinman (1979).

Hence, there seems to be merit to the alternate position offered by Lovell (1959) that children may have euclidean representations from the start and that the documented changes in accuracy of recognition of various kinds of shapes can equally well be described in euclidean as in topological terms. Lovell's claim is that the genetic primacy of topological spatial representation is unproven. Some recent work on spatial representation in young blind children is relevant to this claim. Landau, Gleitman, and Spelke (1981) found that a blind child less than 3 years old could make what appear to be euclidean spatial inferences. Upon being led from the door of a strange room to an object by one wall and back, then to an object by another wall and back, and finally to an object by the third wall and back, the child could subsequently find her way with a remarkable degree of precision among the three objects, even though she had never traversed those routes before. She made some mistakes on the way, only sometimes self-corrected, but in general one must attribute to the child a spatial representation that included both angle and distance information, concepts most easily described in terms of euclidean geometry.

Another task used by Piaget and Inhelder (1956) and studied frequently since (Laurendeau & Pinard, 1970; Lovell, 1959; Mandler & Stein, 1977; Olson, 1970) concerns the child's ability to construct a straight line. If the topological theory of spatial representation in preoperational children is correct, they should not have a concept of a straight line and, consequently, should not be able to construct one. Piaget and Inhelder (1956) report that up to about 4 years, children are unable to reproduce a straight line from a set of posts under any circumstances. From roughly ages 4 to 7, children can construct a straight line only when it lies parallel and close to a perceptually given reference line, such as the edge of a table. Only after about age 7 is the child said to have the projective concept of a straight line.

As in the case of shape recognition discussed above, the replication studies have varied a good deal, both in how the task is presented and in the criterion for correct performance. Laurendeau and Pinard (1970) found roughly the same sequence and age norms in this task as reported by Piaget and Inhelder, but they also used quite a strict criterion. A single post out of place or a straight line that did not connect the relevant end points were counted as errors, in spite of the fact that the child had mostly or entirely constructed a straight line. An indication of the strictness of their criterion is that a number of the 8- and 9-year-old children in their study were still making errors, especially when constructing diagonal lines. Lovell (1959), on the other hand, found more than half of his 4½- to 5-year-old subjects

could construct a straight or nearly straight line; he reports aiming and straightening behavior as well, behavior that Piaget and Inhelder found only in older children. Lovell (1959) also reports that almost all the 3½- to 4-year-olds could construct a straight line when the posts were to be placed near a table edge.

Many of the well-documented difficulties young children have with this kind of task stem from the particular requirement to construct a diagonal line (Olson, 1970). Bryant (1974) suggests that children have unusual difficulty with the diagonal because, lacking any internal representation of orientation, they attempt to match a line's orientation against some external frame of reference; typically such frames provide primarily horizontal and vertical axes, such as the table on which the stimuli rest and the room itself. However, even 3- to 4-year-old children can learn to discriminate between diagonal lines if external frames of reference are removed (Fisher, 1979; but see Williamson & McKenzie, 1979, for a failure with 5-year-olds). The problem seems not to be one of a lack of internal representation of diagonality or directionality per se, but a conflict that is induced when what may be a rather fragile representation is confronted with a powerful and opposing perceptual field.[4] This problem may be partly responsible for the age lag in accurately drawing a diamond after successful mastery of drawing a square. As Freeman (1980) points out, these drawing tasks are carried out using convenient pieces of rectangularly shaped paper. Children's ability to represent the diagonal may be underrated by asking them to draw a square within a context that supports it and a diamond within a context that works against it (Naeli & Harris, 1976).

We know that 4-year-olds can correctly reproduce a diagonal on a circular field and are better if the task requires setting a rod rather than drawing (Berman, Cunningham, & Harkulich, 1974; Berman & Golab, 1975). Similarly, Mandler and Stein (1977) found that 5-year-olds were more accurate at reproducing a diagonal, even on a rectilinear background if they merely had to place a bar on the field rather than take a recognition test. When confronted with the presence of more than one alternative, their memory for the original seemed to be disrupted. They had even more difficulty in a reconstruction test of the sort used by Piaget and Inhelder. Children tended to start their construction correctly, but the difficulty of reconstructing a whole from its parts was sufficient to overcome the initial representation, and they began to follow the horizontal and vertical axes in the middle of their construction. The more pieces there were, the more difficulty they had.

It appears that construction of a figure from arbitrary parts, such as checkers or matchsticks, has some of the difficulties associated with drawing. Freeman (1980) has shown that children are responsive to diagonal information when asked to complete a human figure whose head has already been drawn on the page, but their behavior is influenced by a number of cues. The relationships between the orientation of their own bodies to the page, the framework of the page itself, and the angle of the predrawn head all interact to control details of performance, such as where the pencil hits the page and how lines are continued. Thus, accurate responding in both reconstruction and drawing requires planning and careful perceptual analysis as well as continual monitoring of the various frames of reference within which the figure is situated.

Children's representation of space is clearly less detailed and exact than that of adults. Nevertheless, it does not seem to have been demonstrated that the earliest form of spatial representation is purely topological in nature or that euclidean properties only gradually appear during the preoperational period. A more conservative hypothesis is that the less familiar something is (the fewer opportunities to observe it) or the less perceptual analysis that has taken place (even when the display is familiar), the less detailed and exact the representation will be. This hypothesis applies to adults as well as children. As an exercise, try to reconstruct the details of the last new room you encountered. You will probably find that it is your real-world knowledge of likely placement of furniture, windows in walls, and so on, that accounts for most of the details of your representation, rather than your actual observation of them (see *Representation of Scenes*). Your representation is also unlikely to be very exact. As another example, Mandler and Day (1975) found that memory for the orientation of familiar figures was better than for nonmeaningful figures at all ages from kindergarten to adulthood. There was little change in accuracy of recognition of orientation of the meaningful figures from the second grade onward, but pronounced developmental trends occurred in recognition of orientation of the nonmeaningful figures.

Throughout our life span, most of the spatial encoding we engage in is strongly "topologically" determined. This does not mean that our representations do not have euclidean properties, only that such properties tend to be crudely encoded, which may seem to give them a topological character. It is not just the young child who encodes liquid as being "in" a container without noticing its horizontal levels, even some adults have been shown to ignore this property (Rebelsky, 1964; Thomas & Jamison, 1975). Similarly, few of us have noted that eyes and ears tend to occur at the same level on a face, although we have noted such euclidean properties as that eyes are ellipses and noses extend at a right angle from the line of the eyes. In the main, global "topological" properties are the most essential and basic aspects of spatial knowledge. Things are inside or outside of others, nearby landmarks, and ordered serially. We have to look hard to notice more exact details and because they are often not necessary for our traffic with the environment we often do not bother. The blind child discussed earlier probably *had* to bother to negotiate comfortably in unseen space.

Part of the sketchiness of our spatial representations, whether the properties be topological or euclidean, stems from the role played by our knowledge and expectations in perceptual activity. One of the great advantages of knowing how the world typically looks is that we do not have to pay much attention to it (Bobrow & Norman, 1975). Much of this knowledge is probably represented in topological terms. We tend to know about neighborhoods and proximate positions rather than exact distances, about serial order rather than linear order. We do tend to know about rectilinearity and curvilinearity, but that knowledge appears in children's spatial representations as well. We also remember things as more symmetrical and regular than they in fact are (Stevens & Coupe, 1978; Tversky, 1981). This property also appears to be characteristic of young children's representations (Laurendeau & Pinard, 1970). Our spatial representations are also strongly influenced by our nonspatial knowledge about the world. These influences will be discussed under the next heading, where the development of representation of small-scale and large-scale spaces is considered.

Representation of Small-, Medium-, and Large-Scale Spaces

I have divided this topic into three parts to separate work that has been done on spaces of three different scales. Studies have been carried out on the representation of small-scale spaces, such as arrays on table tops or small models of larger spaces (e.g., Piaget & Inhelder, 1956; Laurendeau & Pinard, 1970). People usually acquire information about such arrays from a single perspective, and they stand outside the space, not in it (Ittleson, 1973; Kuipers, 1977). Other studies have investigated representation of medium-sized spaces, such as rooms, in which one moves about and takes in information from a number of perspectives (e.g., Acredolo, 1977; Hardwick, McIntyre, & Pick, 1976). Finally, studies have been conducted on the representation of large-scale spaces, such as houses, towns, and countries, in which most spatial relationships cannot be directly observed, but must be constructed from the routes one takes through the space (e.g., Downs & Stea, 1973; Siegel, Kirasic, & Kail, 1978; Siegel & White, 1975). Typically a distinction has been drawn only between small spaces seen from the outside and large spaces that surround and enclose the observer. Our knowledge of rooms, however, seems to fall between these two scales. It is possible to stand in a doorway and take in a room as a whole, although more typically we move around in the space. In addition, there are probably some differences between houses and immediate neighborhoods and very large-scale spaces, such as states and countries; in the latter cases, it may not be appropriate to speak of a space surrounding and enclosing one because much of our knowledge comes from studying maps, perhaps supplemented by occasional aerial glimpses.

Small-Scale Spaces

In many of the studies of spatial representation, two topics have been considered: (1) the contents and form of this type of representation and (2) the manipulation of such representations for purposes of spatial problem solving. The latter topic has dominated the study of the representation of small-scale spaces and has been the focus of a vast literature on the development of perspective taking and the ability to imagine a rotated array from another point of view (e.g., Borke, 1975; Fishbein, Lewis, & Keiffer, 1972; Flavell, Omanson, & Latham, 1978; Freeman, 1980; Harris & Bassett, 1976; Huttenlocher & Presson, 1973, 1979; Piaget & Inhelder, 1956; Pufall & Shaw, 1973; Salatas & Flavell, 1976; Shantz, 1975). This fascinating developmental problem primarily concerns the processes that operate on representations rather than the nature of the representations themselves and would take us too far afield from the main topic of this chapter. It may be noted, however, that a rudimentary appreciation of different viewpoints appears as early as 2 to 3 years of age (Flavell, Everett, Croft, & Flavell, 1981; Masangkay, McCluskey, McIntyre, Sims-Knight, Vaughn, & Flavell, 1974) and that the level and sophistication of this understanding develops considerably during the preschool period (Flavell, Flavell, Green, & Wilcox, 1981).

Because much of the work on small-scale spaces has concerned rotation problems, there is relatively little information about the types of spatial knowledge children encode and retain merely from inspecting spatial displays. (Other types of information derived from viewing scenes will be examined in the discussion on *Representation of Scenes*.) Laurendeau and Pinard (1970) found that the majority of 3-year-olds could reproduce correctly the positions of many objects in a nonrotated display. They found that most of the children's placements followed topological principles, in that objects near salient landmarks were most apt to be placed correctly, and errors of placement tended to respect topological categories, such as inside and outside. As noted above, it is difficult in most of these tasks to determine whether a representation is topologically "accurate" or euclidean and inexact. The finding that both children and adults respect neighborhood boundaries but that adults are quantitatively more exact does not necessarily imply that children have not encoded any metric information at all. In most studies, age-related improvement is found on both types of measure.

Mandler, Seegmiller, and Day (1977) found that subjects from age 5 to adult performed in a qualitatively similar fashion in recalling both objects and their locations from a small-scale display under both incidental and intentional memory conditions. There was a steady progression across grades in number of objects recalled and an apparent leveling off in recall of locations by the sixth grade; however, none of the age-related interactions were significant, suggesting similarity of functioning at all ages. This experiment did not address the issue of euclidean accuracy because the locations of objects were specified and subjects only had to identify which objects went with which locations. Similar findings have been reported by Day (1977) for recall of objects and their locations in a small display representing a house. In this study, absolute accuracy of placement could be measured in addition to such topological measures as enclosure (locating the objects in the correct room of the house). Accuracy of placement on both measures increased from kindergarten to fifth grade in both incidental and intentional conditions; again there were no age-related interactions. Laurendeau and Pinard (1970) report similar improvement on both types of measure for their various tasks.

Medium-Scale Spaces

Because of the different methods of obtaining information in small- and large-scale spaces, representations of the two might be expected to differ.

Indeed, Acredolo (1977) found that 3- to 4-year-old children were less accurate in their representations of a room than were 5-year-olds, but they showed comparable performance to 5-year-olds on a small-scale space. To test this hypothesis further, Siegel, Herman, Allen, and Kirasic (1979) studied children from kindergarten to the fifth grade in their ability to reconstruct a medium-scale model town (laid out in an area of 4.5 × 6 m) when working with the same-scale space or with a small-scale model representing that space. In addition, they showed the children a small-scale model of the same layout (80 × 100 cm) and tested their ability to reconstruct it on the same scale or on the larger scale. Accuracy of reconstruction was equivalent for the two types of spaces but suffered when children viewed the small space and had to reconstruct it in the medium-sized space. Performance improved with age, but the deleterious effects of change in scale during reconstruction remained the same for all ages. It is not known whether or not adults would suffer the same translation problems.

Although in general the data suggested fewer differences in generalizing from a medium-scale space to a small-scale space than might have been predicted, they do speak to the issue of problems that arise in various methods of assessing internal representations. Drawing ability may be a confounding factor, as we have seen, and ability to change scale may be another. It may be noted, however, that even 3-year-olds show some mapping ability and an understanding that a small-scale model can represent a larger space (Blaut & Stea, 1974; Bluestein & Acredolo, 1979). Bluestein and Acredolo found that the majority of the 3-year-olds they tested could use a map of a room with an object marked on it to find that object in the actual room. By 5 years, all children were successful at this task. In addition, most of the children were able to interpret a vertically held map correctly; that is, they translated up and down to mean far and near in the horizontal plane.

Two methods of assessing spatial representations have recently been used that may be less subject to contamination than are verbal or construction methods. One of these is the triangulation technique used by Hardwick et al. (1976). In several studies, children from the first and fifth grades as well as college students were asked to use a sighting tube to point to various objects around a school library room from a series of station points at each of the four walls. Some subjects carried out this task with the objects in view, others with their view obstructed by a screen. These data were used to construct cognitive maps of the area. Although there was improvement

with age, even the first graders possessed quite accurate and coherent cognitive maps. The data suggested that the distortions in locational accuracy that did occur tended to be random for the first graders, but for the fifth graders and adults, errors stemmed from the tendency to treat the layout as more symmetrical than it actually was. Hardwick et al. suggest that an organizing principle is gradually learned that sacrifices a certain amount of absolute accuracy in spatial representation for the sake of cognitive economy.

Another technique that has been used to study medium-sized spaces is multidimensional scaling derived from ordinal judgments of proximity. Kosslyn, Pick, and Fariello (1974) showed both 4- to 5-year-old children and adults a room divided into four quadrants either by opaque or transparent barriers. There were 10 toys scattered in the space. Subjects practiced placing the toys on their marked locations until the space was well memorized. Subjects then left the room and were asked to make judgments from memory of the relative distances among the toys. The first toy was designated and the subject had to choose the toy that had been closest to it, then the toy next closest to it, and so forth. When these judgmental data were submitted to multidimensional scaling, a map of the remembered locations was produced that could be compared to a map of the actual locations. For both children and adults, a euclidean metric described their mental maps better than did a city-block metric (which might have been thought to be more important in a space that had barriers requiring one to walk in indirect routes to reach various objects). Once again, there was improvement in accuracy with age, although even the preschool children's data yielded fairly good spatial representations.

This study provides a better basis for speculations about children's reliance on topological concepts in their cognitive maps than many others. First, it is possible to interpret the children's maps as indicating placement of objects merely within the four quadrants rather than reflecting the actual distances among them. Kosslyn et al. (1974) suggest that objects in the children's representations were repelled by both opaque and transparent barriers and were clustered in the middle of the quadrants. The adults' data showed a similar phenomenon but only in the case of the opaque barriers. The children also appeared to represent the distance between two objects with no barrier as less than the same distance separated by a transparent barrier. Similar results were found for adults but again only for opaque barriers. Thus, visible distance played a larger role in determining the spatial representation of adults than did functional distance. Further, the children seemed to have more difficulty integrating the four subspaces into an overall map.

Functional distance does influence the spatial representations of older children and adults, however. Cohen, Baldwin, and Sherman (1978) had 9- and 10-year-olds and adults estimate distances in a camp with which they were familiar. The presence of hills or barriers, such as buildings and trees, led to overestimation of distances for all three groups. These authors suggest that cognitive maps are influenced by ease of travel among the various points. Cohen and Weatherford (1980) found similar results with second and sixth graders and adults in a medium-scale space.

A final comment about the presence of topological and euclidean frames of reference in young children's representations may be made, one that is also relevant to the following section on large-scale spaces. Familiarity and experience with the environment to be mapped play a major role in the accuracy of children's representations. This is hardly a surprising observation in itself, and it is equally true for adults (e.g., Appleyard, 1970; Lynch, 1960). Its importance stems from the tendency to study children's representations of new spaces in which there is little control over the extent to which attention has been paid to various aspects of the space. Herman (1980) reports, for example, that the kindergarten children he studied frequently did not even look at all the parts of the small model town they were asked to remember. He finds, as have Siegel and Schadler (1977) and Herman and Siegel (1978), that kindergarten children become much more accurate in their reconstructions as a function of the number of times the environment is explored.

That relatively limited increases in experience should markedly increase the accuracy of a reconstruction suggests that young children do not suffer as much from a lack of euclidean representation or an inability to use external frames of reference as from lesser experience with, and lesser attention to, their environment. Lack of attention will naturally produce a less detailed representation but does not imply that children's spatial representations are fundamentally different in kind from those of older children and adults. In any case, it is clear that many factors other than the underlying nature of spatial representation itself are influencing performance. Familiarity with the items is one of the most important of these. The relative importance of the other factors that have been considered here, such as the extent and systematicity of visual exploration, the

deliberate deployment of attention to spatial relations, and the degree of integration among units in the representation of space, is still little understood. It seems likely, however, that all three factors will develop with age and experience.

Large-Scale Spaces

In a recent review of this literature, Siegel et al. (1978) stress three different kinds of knowledge about large-scale environments: landmarks, routes, and configurational knowledge. Landmarks are fixed salient points around which route knowledge is organized. Use of landmarks, as we have seen, is often considered to be topologically based knowledge, although it involves projective knowledge as well if left/right and front/behind relations are coded with respect to the landmark. Routes involve a series of decisions about changes in bearing and are sequentially organized one-dimensional paths through a space with at least two dimensions. Siegel et al. suggest that these paths may be formed through serial learning, but that they more likely consist of a series of paired associates (e.g., ''go left at the market''). They speculate that routes may be relatively empty of content between landmarks, although for adults, the paths between landmarks eventually are characterized by ordinal or even interval scales. The development of route maps is prior to the construction of overall configurational or survey maps (Shemyakin, 1962) that join landmarks and routes into an integrated whole.

Hazen, Lockman, and Pick (1978) found that 3- to 5-year-old children could construct route maps through a new environment and follow them in the reverse direction as well. However, the 3-year-olds had difficulty in remembering the sequence of landmarks in the reverse direction. As mentioned earlier, adults may have some difficulty in this regard as well but presumably less than young children do. There has been little systematic work on this question, but a study by Siegel, Allen, and Kirasic (1979) found that accuracy in judging distances between landmarks on a pictorialized walk through a city increased from second grade to adulthood. Second graders did not differ in accuracy of their judgments for the two directions, but fifth graders were more accurate in judging distances in the forward than in the reverse direction. Adults approached ceiling performance for both directions. In a similar study, Allen, Kirasic, Siegel, and Herman (1979) found that children were less capable than adults of selecting potential landmarks as cues and that the ability to *use* a landmark developed before the ability to pick out informative ones. For example, the children tended to choose colorful awnings and window displays as reference points, even though the route contained many of these and, thus, they were not as informative as a proper landmark should be. This finding again suggests that some of the developmental improvement in accuracy of representation is a function of planful, strategic deployment of attention in addition to increasing knowledge about what will be helpful for route finding and following. It might also be noted that the method of teaching people about a route or a region by means of a series of slides is somewhat artificial; it may require more strategic knowledge than do tasks carried out in natural environments (e.g., Cohen & Scheupfer, 1980).

Concerning configurational knowledge, Piaget, Inhelder, and Szeminska (1960) and Shemyakin (1962) studied children's understanding of the areas around their schools. They found a developmental progression in representation: from uncoordinated landmarks in the preoperational period, to series of uncoordinated route maps in the early school years, to overall coordinated survey maps by 11 or 12 years of age. Although these results clearly suggest a developmental sequence from accurate understanding of local parts to appreciation of a whole terrain, the extent of the age change was undoubtedly affected by experience in the areas. To the extent that children have not followed a particular route to school, for example, they will find it difficult to integrate it into an overall configuration. In a recent experiment Anooshian and Young (1981) studied cognitive maps of a recently built neighborhood in which children from the first to the eighth grades had all lived for about the same amount of time. Using a technique similar to that of Hardwick et al. (1976), they found that even the youngest children showed good configurational knowledge, although there were increases in accuracy up to the fourth and fifth grades. Very similar results were reported by Curtis, Siegel, and Furlong (1981) for children's knowledge of the spatial layout of their school.

Throughout this discussion of children's spatial representation, two main points have been emphasized. First, the differences between children's and adults' spatial knowledge are partly due to differences in experience and familiarity with the various spaces tested. The longer one lives in an environment or the more one has interacted with a particular spatial configuration the more likely one is to pick up detailed information about it. This point has been elegantly demonstrated by Chi (1978) in the context of playing chess. Children who had extensive experience with and knowledge about chess were better able to remember chess positions than

were adults who were chess novices. Although the point that development is confounded with age seems obvious, we frequently tend to ignore it and assume that some developmental process is occurring that stops or is much attenuated in adulthood. It is true that as we get older we are apt to meet less frequently with totally new experiences (and often are clever at arranging our lives so that we do not). Nevertheless, developmental theory can benefit from studies of the acquisition of new knowledge by adults. Because the question of spatial representation has been studied extensively by geographers as well as psychologists, we are fortunate to have many such comparisons. In general, the course of acquisition of knowledge about new environments appears to be similar for adults and children. Appleyard (1969, 1970), for example, found that as their length of residence in an area increases, people tend to produce more configurational maps than route maps.

In many cases, however, we do not know either for the adult or the child which kinds of spatial knowledge will increase with experience and which will not. I referred earlier to adults' lack of detailed knowledge about many aspects of faces; at some point, further experience does not seem to lead to further detail. This observation leads to the second focus of this discussion, namely, that it is difficult to separate topological from euclidean aspects of spatial representations. The difficulty is partly conceptual because it is often not clear exactly which kinds of spatial encoding should be classified as topological or as euclidean. The difficulty is compounded by the persistent finding that improvement on both topological and euclidean measures occurs throughout childhood. This finding suggests that rather than emphasizing the distinction between topological and euclidean aspects of space, we should be concerned with the overall framework in which spatial knowledge is organized. Much of the superstructure of spatial knowledge at all ages is apt to be topological in character, organized around landmarks, linear orderings, and relations of enclosure and relative proximity. Such a focus might lead us to value topological encoding rather than devalue it and suggests the importance of investigating how such general frameworks encourage or discourage detailed metric encoding.

A good example of such an approach is a study by Stevens and Coupe (1978; see also Tversky, 1981). They found that adults systematically distort the locations of cities owing to a schematic representation of the superordinate regions to which the cities belong. Thus, even residents of San Diego tend to think that their city is west of Reno because it is in a region (California) that for the most part is west of the region that contains Reno (Nevada). Stevens and Coupe suggest that superordinate structure systematically distorts the representation of spatial relationships. They further suggest that spatial information is stored hierarchically, with regions centered around key landmarks or features. Metric information may be stored directly for certain places within a region or between regions themselves. When asked to make a distance comparison between a subunit of one region and a subunit of another, a computation must be performed and an estimate made because the information has not been directly encoded. In such a system, higher level units in the hierarchy probably weigh more heavily in the computations. Because most subjects have not had occasion to encode the geographical relationships between the two cities in question, they use their knowledge of the higher level units to compute the answer—wrongly in this case.

A recent experiment by Allen (1981) studied the development of this kind of schematic organization of large-scale space and the kinds of processes that operate on it. Children from the second and fifth grades as well as adults agreed almost unanimously on the boundaries of subdivisions in a pictorialized walk. When required to judge which of two sites was closer to a given reference point, all subjects were strongly influenced by the boundaries. A site that crossed a subdivision boundary was judged incorrectly to be farther away from the reference point than a more distant site that was within the same subdivision as the reference point. (Compare with the Kosslyn et al., 1974, and Cohen et al., 1978, studies described earlier). There were no significant developmental trends in this regard. However, there was significant improvement in the ability to judge the relative distances of two sites both of which were within the same subdivision as the reference point. Allen suggests that subdivisional organization is a primary source of information for judgments of distance for both children and adults but that metric accuracy of within-unit judgments increases with age.

Comparisons such as these of the development of different aspects of spatial representations are potentially informative. For example, Pick (1972) found that young children were poor at identifying the rooms on the other side of the walls in their homes. A similar phenomenon has been found in adults (Norman, 1973). At present we do not know whether the adults would be more accurate at judging metric distances within rooms while remaining as inaccurate at

judging distance between rooms, although much of the data presented in this section suggests that this might be the case. For both children and adults, however, spatial inferences about relationships that have not been directly observed or that involve successive views of large-scale spaces seem to be schematically organized in a very general framework. This notion is developed further in the next section.

Representation of Scenes

Perception of even the simplest stimuli is saturated with knowledge. Nor is it the case that we see first and interpret afterwards; the entire perceptual process from its earliest stages is interactive and influenced by our knowledge and expectations (Biederman, 1981; Palmer, 1975c; Rumelhart & Ortony, 1977). A fortiori, our representations are influenced by the semantics of what we see. This meaning base in spatial perception is particularly evident when we consider the representation of scenes, that is, the rooms and buildings, the streets, and other familiar places we encounter in our daily activities. Our knowledge about scenes affects how rapidly and accurately we perceive them (Biederman, 1972, 1981; Biederman, Glass, & Stacy, 1973; Biederman, Rabinowitz, Glass, & Stacy, 1974) as well as the kinds of information we encode and retain from them (Brewer & Treyens, 1981; Friedman, 1979; Mandler & Johnson, 1976; Mandler & Parker, 1976; Mandler & Stein, 1974).

The organization of our knowledge about how places look has been called a scene schema (Biederman, 1981; J. M. Mandler, 1979). There are several different kinds of knowledge that become integrated into this kind of cognitive structure. First, there is knowledge about physical relations such as support (most objects typically do not float in the air), the likely size, and the solidity and opaqueness of objects. Second, there is knowledge about the kinds of objects one is apt to see in particular places (stoves in kitchens, buildings on a street) as well as their likely relationships to each other (chairs facing tables, pictures on walls rather than on the floor, and so forth). Both of these kinds of knowledge are integrated into a cognitive representation, or a scene schema, that governs what we expect to see upon looking at or entering a particular scene. The variables in this mental structure consist of categories of objects and their relationships to each other.

Scene schemata vary in their generality, in the sense that we have knowledge relevant to all places (e.g., support relations); knowledge relevant to certain classes of places, such as rooms (e.g., they have walls); and proceeding down to highly specific places, such as living rooms or one's own living room. The structure of such schemata seems to be hierarchical, in that specific parts, which are governed by schemata of their own, are embedded in larger schemata. Rumelhart and Ortony (1977) use the example of a face schema to illustrate this point. A face schema has constituent parts, such as eyes and mouths, that may be considered as basic-level units. However, our knowledge of eyes and mouths are schemata in their own right, and their constituent parts, such as pupils, eyelids, and eyelashes, serve the same function for our recognizing an isolated eye as the eye does for a face. This embedding property explains many of the effects of context on the amount of stimulus information required for recognition to take place. With no context, an eye needs quite a bit of detail to be recognized but, within the context of a face, an appropriately placed ellipse will do (Palmer, 1975c). Similarly, a window in isolation may take quite a bit of information to be recognized but, within the context of a room, a simple rectangle will suffice.

Scene schemata provide a great deal of economy in our processing of the surround. We do not need to notice many details to recognize a window when we enter a room; a brief glimpse is sufficient to allow this information to be encoded. However, the economy of this sort of top-down, or conceptually driven, processing (Bobrow & Norman, 1975) means that much of what we think we have actually seen, we have only inferred. Scene schemata have typical, or default, values associated with their variables. These values are derived from past experience and tell us what is the most likely thing to have been seen. When we do not actually process some part of the environment, the schema automatically fills in the default value. One of the results of this process is that our representations of past events are often more canonical and regular than reality warrants.

Many studies have shown the operation of the processes just described in scene perception and memory. We encode objects faster when they are presented in the context of a normal scene than when the scene is jumbled, disorganized, or inappropriate (Biederman, 1972; Biederman et al., 1974; Palmer, 1975a). We are more accurate in remembering organized scenes and remember them longer (Mandler & Johnson, 1976; Mandler & Ritchey, 1977). We distort our memories of disorganized scenes toward forms more canonical than they actually were (Mandler & Parker, 1976). We recognize anomalous objects and violations of physical relationships within the first eye fixation (Biederman, 1981; Parker,

1977), indicating that our knowledge about scenes affects their processing from the earliest stages of perception (Palmer, 1975a; Potter, 1975, 1976). It has also been shown that the likelihood of an object's occurring in a scene markedly affects the amount of processing that is expended on it and what is remembered from it afterwards (Loftus & Mackworth, 1978). The more probable the object is, the less processing it receives (Friedman, 1979). It takes longer to identify a low-probability object (Biederman, 1981), but once we have identified it, more time and attention is devoted to its details.

Because the phenomena just described depend upon our knowledge of the world, the question arises as to when children acquire enough of this kind of information to have the same kind of scene representations and to use them in the same way in their processing and memory. Presumably, the most general kinds of information would be the first to be acquired, such as the physical relationships of support, size, interposition, and so on. More content-oriented aspects of scene schemata, such as knowledge about particular types of rooms, might be later acquisitions. Some specific kinds of information are acquired extremely early, such as the development of a face schema in infancy (see *Gibson & Spelke, vol. III, chap. 1*). With development, however, changes in detail, elaboration, and even cohesiveness might be expected to occur in many domains, leading to quantitative improvements in encoding and memory.

One recent experiment indicates that scene schemata for familiar rooms in the home may be well established as early as 2 years of age. Ratner and Myers (1981) found that even 2-year-olds were quite accurate in identifying typical items found in the kitchen and the bathroom and only slightly less accurate in rejecting inappropriate items. There was some increase in accuracy of identification between ages 2 and 3 and a large increase between ages 2 and 4 in the number of items the children could produce verbally upon request. At all three ages, however, core items that define the function of these rooms constituted the highest percentage of the productions and typically used items were the next highest; inappropriate items were rarely mentioned.

This is one of the few experiments to explore very young children's representations of familiar scenes. More work has been carried out on children age 6 or older. In general, most of these studies have found that the principles applicable to adult representations apply to children's representations as well. G. S. Goodman (1980) found that 7- and 9-year-old children as well as adults were all less likely to recognize high-probability than low-probability items in pictures of previously viewed scenes, thus replicating Friedman's (1979) effect with children. Hock, Romanski, Galie, & Williams (1978) found that concrete operational children and adults were better able to recognize previously viewed scenes of physically possible but low-probability arrangements of objects than scenes of high-probability arrangements or completely unorganized (impossible) scenes. However, 6-year-old children who failed a standard conservation test did not show this effect, leading the authors to suggest that preoperational children were less able to use a scene schema to mediate recognition.

At present, little theoretical work has been done to relate the concept of a scene schema (or the event schemata to be discussed in the next section) to the Piagetian concepts of concrete operations (see J. M. Mandler, in press-b). Even within the Piagetian framework, schemata are the building blocks of cognition from birth, and there is little reason to suppose that the perceptual and knowledge schemata we are discussing here are linked to the developments of the concrete operational period. This is not to say that such a linkage may not be found, only that there are few theoretical bridges and precious little data at the present time. It seems clear, however, that the current use of the term schema by cognitive psychologists does not make as sharp a distinction between figurative and operative knowledge as does Piaget's usage. If anything, a scene or an event schema is closer in conception to a sensorimotor schema than to a concrete operative one. Concrete-operational schemata, such as conservation or seriation, involve the grouping properties of identity and reversibility; these are structural characteristics far removed from the theoretical description of the schemata being discussed here.

In the various studies by J. M. Mandler and her associates, different types of distractors have been used in recognition tests to assess the kinds of information encoded either from pictures conforming to a scene schema or from disorganized collections of the same objects. Four types of information have been studied: inventory information, or the objects that a scene contains; descriptive information, or the figurative details of objects; spatial relation information, such as relative positions, size, and orientation of objects; and spatial composition information, or areas of blank and filled space. In a series of studies, inventory and spatial relation information were found to be the two kinds of information most affected when a picture is schematically organized into a coherent scene. Descriptive information seems to

be relatively neutral vis-à-vis a scene schema, and spatial composition is sometimes even better encoded from a disorganized picture.

Very similar patterns of responding to these types of information have been found in recognition tests of organized and disorganized scenes by first-, third-, and fifth-grade children and adults (Mandler & Robinson, 1978). The effects of organization were least evident in first graders however, a finding consistent with the Hock et al. (1978) data. Newcombe, Rogoff, and Kagan (1977), on the other hand, found no interaction between type of information and age in a study testing 6- and 9-year-olds as well as adults. Dirks and Neisser (1977), using miniature three-dimensional scenes as well as photographs of them, also found that performance was similar for first, third, and sixth graders and for adults. Pezdek and Hancock (1978) reported that when the context in which an object had been viewed was retained in a recognition test, recognition of the object was improved for 7- and 10-year-olds in the same fashion as for adults. Parker (1977) found that 8-year-old children as well as adults showed similar eye-movement patterns and responses in a recognition test of complex scenes. Both groups were sensitive to the "semantic distance" of the changed items used in the distractors; the less well the object fit into the overall scene, the faster the distractor was rejected.

A recent finding by Kirasic, Siegel, and Allen (1980) suggests that kindergarten children are also influenced by scene schemata. These authors found better recognition of objects in context than out of context for kindergarten children as well as for fourth graders and adults. In contrast to the older subjects, the kindergartners were slower to recognize objects in than out of context, leading the authors to suggest that they have less well-developed scene schemata; nevertheless, the effects of a schema were clearly shown in the accuracy data. Variability in the data of the youngest children that have been studied may be due to the complexities of the procedures used. I expect that future work, perhaps along the line of the Ratner and Myers (1981) study, will show the effects of scene schemata at increasingly younger ages.

In all of these experiments *quantitative* improvement occurred with development. Adults are faster and more accurate in recognizing the many different types of changes that have been used as distractors in the recognition tests. Adults also retain information from scenes for longer periods of time than do children (G. S. Goodman, 1980), even though rate of forgetting appears to be independent of age

(Fajnsztejn-Pollack, 1973). As for *qualitative* differences, very few have been found. Quantitative differences in speed and accuracy need to be explained of course. The explanation for this kind of change, however, seems less likely to be found in the nature of the representations than in various processing variables.

Although principles of perceptual organization have been explored for more than a century (see Hochberg, 1974, for a review of Gestalt principles), the organization of our representations of real-world scenes is a relatively new field of study. We have much to learn about the organization of this kind of knowledge and how it develops. As we will see in the next section, our understanding of the representation of events is also still in a primitive stage.

REPRESENTATION OF EVENTS

Here we are concerned with the representation of common event sequences, that is, sequences of action and changes of states that occur frequently enough for us to develop expectations about the way in which they are structured. The focus of the discussion will be on the overall structure of events and how that structure might be represented rather than on comprehension of individual acts, states, or occurrences within a given sequence.[5] Our knowledge of familiar event sequences can be characterized as having a schematic organization similar to that discussed for scenes. The main difference is that event schemata are temporally rather than spatially organized.

An event schema, then, can be defined as a temporally organized representation of a sequence of events or as a set of expectations about what will occur and when it will occur in a given situation. Just as for scene schemata, event schemata are hierarchically organized; each variable in an event schema has embedded within it descriptions at a greater level of detail. Again, as for scenes, event schemata vary in their generality. Some concrete schemata have been called scripts (Schank & Abelson, 1977). An example is a restaurant script that describes the typical sequence of events that occur when one goes to a restaurant to eat. A script has a series of temporally ordered variables, such as entering the restaurant, ordering food, eating it, and leaving. These variables (sometimes called scenes), in turn, have more detailed subparts, for example, ordering consists of getting a menu, reading it, making a decision about what you want to eat, telling the waiter, and so forth. This kind of schema can be made even more concrete by specifying the type of restaurant: fast-

food restaurant, French gourmet restaurant, and so forth. As the schema is specified in more detail, the acceptable range of values for the variables becomes narrower and the events more predictable. If you have a favorite restaurant where you have eaten for years, a great many variables will have relatively fixed values, perhaps including the items on the menu and the jokes of the waiters. Even here, however, precise content is not necessarily specified. You may have a slot for "chatting with the waiter before ordering" without any particular specification of what will be talked about.

Many sequences of events are not as predictable as those encountered in a restaurant, the local supermarket, or getting to work in the morning, although a little reflection suggests that a remarkable number of our daily experiences as adults are routinized. Within these routines, new events do take place, of course, and are comprehended without interrupting our expectations about the larger sequence within which they occur. Such new events may be encoded as irrelevant to the ongoing sequence and paid little attention or encoded as script deviations in which something out of the ordinary has taken place (Graesser, 1981). In either case, new events must be comprehended through more bottom-up, or data-driven, processing (Bobrow & Norman, 1975).

When we observe activities that do not fit known sequences of events, the bottom-up search for explanation often involves activating schemata that are more general than scripts. Schank and Abelson (1977) call these more general schemata plans. Plans are sets of expectations about activities that are organized around our knowledge of goals and motivations and various ways of achieving particular goals. To the extent that such plans are highly general formulations, the range of their variables is much broader. We may not be in a position to follow a restaurant or cooking script when we are hungry, but whatever we do to satisfy our hunger can be subsumed under a general, all-purpose plan of finding food, getting to it (or it to us), and eating it. Our interpretation of the actions of other people also often requires searching for general plans to account for their behavior, and, of course, we use such plans to guide our own actions in nonroutine situations as well.

An example of a highly general schema, one that has been much studied of late, is our knowledge about the structure of events in traditional stories, such as folktales, fables, and myths. This kind of schema specifies the general type and sequence of events in a story, but the variables are quite open as to content. When hearing "Once upon a time, ..."

an adult listener can generate a surprising number of predictions without any particular expectations as to whether the content will be about dragons and princesses or hares and tortoises. The study of story understanding has turned out to be an excellent method of investigating some of the more abstract aspects of event schemata, in part because a long history of linguistic and literary analysis has aided psychologists in analyzing the materials upon which story schemata are based.

Event schemata of all sorts are obviously learned through experience. The most general psychological questions concern how this type of knowledge affects comprehension and memory. The most interesting developmental questions concern when such structures are formed and whether young children use them in representing and interpreting the world in the same fashion as adults. Schank and Abelson (1977) made some informal observations of one or two very young children that suggest the presence of this kind of organization of knowledge from 1 year or so of age, or even younger; indeed, the distress a change in daily routines often causes young infants testifies to the early onset of this kind of knowledge. Moreover, Schank and Abelson suggest that the earliest form of organized knowledge revolves round the scriptlike daily episodes that occur in the infant's life. Nelson (1977) seconds this suggestion and adds that the earliest concepts, which are formulated within the context of ongoing events, are probably contextually bound for some period of time:

> Both elemental concepts and the sequences or scripts within which they fit are important organizing structures for the young child. Concepts are defined in relation to larger event sequences in space and time. The selection principle for concept formation, what is novel and interesting, must therefore depend not only on the characteristics of the object or event in itself, but also upon the characteristics of the episodic *structure* within which it occurs (p. 226).

This suggestion echoes our earlier discussion of the procedural basis of early knowledge organization; it fits with the observations of Piaget (1951) and others that many early concepts seem to be tied to the contexts in which they were first formed, leading to such phenomena as underextension of word-meanings (see *E. V. Clark, vol. III, chap. 12*). Hence, the early organization of knowledge around scriptlike activities may play a profound role in the child's developing conceptual life. Nelson and Gruendel (1981) suggest that early generalized event representations are in fact the basic building blocks of cognitive development.

To my knowledge, no research has been carried out on the development of scripts in infancy. However, a small amount of work has been done on preschool and older children's acquisition of script representations. This work, along with an equally meager amount of adult work, is discussed first, followed by a discussion of the somewhat larger body of work that has been carried out on the acquisition and use of story schemata.

Before turning to the empirical studies, a comment should be made about the theoretical framework within which the work on the representation of event sequences from daily life has been conducted. This area of research is quite new and the theoretical specification of this type of representation is still in its infancy. Even workers using the script concept have expressed doubt about the ultimate utility of the notion as it is currently formulated (e.g., Bower, 1978b; Schank, 1980). Bower points out that the level of abstraction at which scripts should be described is unclear. Should we describe a visit-doctor script or a more specific script, such as visit pediatrician or perhaps a more general script, such as visit professional? Although these versions are related in a superordinate-subordinate hierarchy, it is not clear from which script or at which level slots are instantiated during a given experience. Schank (1980) has concluded that scripts may be too large and too rigid structures to account for processing. He suggests that smaller units of knowledge, which could be either more or less general than the scenes in scripts, would allow a more economical and flexible representational system. He calls these smaller units memory organization packets or MOPs for short. What are described as scripts in this section could then be considered not as permanent memory structures but as temporary structures built up out of MOPS as they become relevant. Thus, one might have a waiting-room MOP, which could be called upon during visits to a wide variety of professional offices.

There is much theoretical ferment in this field and it seems likely that scripts as presently conceived will have disappeared before the next Handbook is out. Nevertheless, many of the principles of representation and the use of representation in processing examined in this and the previous discussion of scenes seem valid and important to our understanding of the mind and its development. For this reason and because the script formulation is the only even moderately well-developed theory at present, I will discuss empirical work within its framework.

Scripts and the Representation of Common-Event Sequences

The first substantive piece of research on scripts was done by Bower, Black, and Turner (1979). They conducted a number of experiments investigating adults' representations of such routine activities as eating in a restaurant, going to the doctor, making coffee, and so forth. The series began with the collection of norms. Not surprisingly, there was a good deal of agreement on the events involved and on the sequences in which they occur. Of more interest was the finding that people agree on what constitutes an individual event in a sequence of activities and describe it at approximately the same level of generality. For example, when they describe getting up in the morning, people say such things as "Make the bed," not "Smooth the bottom sheet, then pull up the top sheet, . . ." let alone "Take the upper right corner of the top sheet by your right hand. . . ." The level of description that subjects use is reminiscent of Rosch's concept of basic-level categories of objects (Rosch et al., 1976). That is, there appears to be a potentially specifiable level of generality at which basic categories of events are conceptualized. At present, however, we have only subject-generated protocols, such as those of Bower et al. (1979); with the exception of philosophical and linguistic analysis (e.g., van Dijk, 1976), essentially no theoretical work exists on the principles that account for why people segregate events at one level of generality rather than another.

In their next experiment, Bower et al. (1979) wrote little stories that closely followed the collected script norms. When asked to divide the stories into parts, subjects agreed fairly well on the segmentation of the scripts into scenes, that is, where one set of events ended and the next began; such data indicate a hierarchical structure to the knowledge representation. It seems likely that these higher order units of scripts are centered around the goals and subgoals and changes in location involved in the activity the script represents (see also Lichtenstein & Brewer, 1980). Again, however, little theoretical work, such as has been accomplished for traditional stories (see *Representation of Stories*), has been carried out on what accounts for the division of event sequences into subparts. The task may not be easy; we have found that the division of scripts into scenes is influenced by the surface format (sentences or phrases) and length of the materials that subjects are asked to judge (Mandler & Murphy, 1982).

Bower et al. (1979) demonstrated a number of ways in which scripts influence processing. When presented with stories describing common event sequences, subjects tended to confuse actions that had been mentioned with those that also belong to the script but were not actually stated. They also showed a strong tendency to recall scrambled stories in their canonical script order. The underlying schema was also shown to influence reading times; the second of two adjacent sentences was read faster if it represented the next event to occur in the script rather than one that was further away. Finally, goal-relevant deviations from a script were remembered better than the usual, or expected, script events. Similar results have also been reported by Graesser, Gordon, and Sawyer (1979) and Graesser, Woll, Kowalski, and Smith (1980). It may be noted that many of these findings are similar to those reported in the earlier discussion on memory for scenes (such as remembering low-probability objects better than high-probability objects) and, as we will see under the next heading, the data are also similar to those collected for memory for stories. In fact, one of the interesting aspects of schematic organizations is the commonality of functioning associated with them across many different domains.

Turning to the development of script representation, Nelson and her colleagues have begun to explore young children's acquisition of script representations. Nelson (1978a) studied 4- to 5-year-old children's descriptions of the events that occur when eating at home, in their daycare center, or at a McDonald's restaurant. The protocols show remarkable similarities to those collected from adults by Bower et al. (1979). From the protocols Nelson (1978a) derived a set of common elements, or basic events. These consisted of events that were mentioned by several children and that were not broken down into subparts; thus, they correspond to the basic-level events discussed above. Because a common structure of these event sequences was found, Nelson was able to identify the beginning and ending (anchor) events in the sequences as well as those events that were central and those that were optional. There was also uniformity in sequencing, the only exception being some uncertainty in the McDonald's script about the temporal location of paying (an activity with which presumably the children had relatively little experience).

In a second study, Nelson tested children's knowledge of eating at the daycare center shortly after they began school for the first time and 3 months later. More basic events were added to the script descriptions as the children became more familiar with the situation. Documenting the development of other scripts, Gruendel (1980) found that the number of conditional paths in scripts increased from ages 4 to 8. That is, the older children produced more alternate paths when describing activities, such as making a campfire, indicating growth in the structural complexity of scripts and increasing flexibility in describing the possible paths to be followed.

In another study, Nelson and Gruendel (1979) found that when 4-year-olds were playing in the context of a shared, mutually understood script, the dialogue that ensued showed less of the egocentrism often observed in young children's playtime conversations (Kohlberg, Yeager, & Hjertholm, 1968; Piaget, 1926; Vygotsky, 1962). Nelson and Gruendel (1979) suggest that it is under circumstances in which children do not have a shared knowledge base that egocentric speech is most apt to occur.

More recent work in this series (Nelson & Gruendel, 1981) indicates that preschool children make use of a canonically ordered event representation to sequence their recall. The children were presented either with a correctly arranged scriptlike story or one that had one event out of its correct temporal position. When recalling the misarranged stories, the children tended either to omit the misordered event altogether or to put it back in its canonical position.

Further, French and Nelson (1981) found that when retelling familiar event sequences, 3- and 4-year-old children sometimes would spontaneously repair their own errors; if they recalled an event after the point in the sequence where it belonged, the children would say ''before'' or ''but first.'' As French and Nelson point out, such temporal repairs indicate an ability to move bidirectionally within the representation of an event sequence, suggesting a degree of reversibility typically thought to be beyond the capabilities of the preschool child.

Wimmer (1979) found that the majority of 4-year-olds and all 6-year-olds studied could recognize deviations from a script about buying groceries. The script was presented in the form of a story accompanied by pictures in which the shopper lost her wallet on the way to the store. When asked to complete the story from the point at which the shopper reaches the cashier, most children were able to say that she could not pay. Those 4-year-olds who did not seem to recognize the deviation were shown in another experiment to have not realized that the shopper no longer had the wallet. Thus, the failures were apparently caused by a wrong representation of a condition of the script, not an inability to recognize

a deviation per se. Wimmer notes that in the context of a standard script, young children show greater recognition of anomalies than has been found when they listen to descriptions (Markman, 1979).

Overall, these data on young children's representation of event sequences show a more mature understanding of sequential order than was found in the classic studies of Piaget (1926, 1969). Piaget attributes the child's failure to reconstruct a given temporal sequence to the lack of reversibility of preoperational thought. Yet, as Brown (1976a) notes, Piaget does ascribe to the preoperational child the ability to seriate familiar events. This discrepancy is not resolved in Piaget's writings; on the one hand, reversibility of thought is required for true seriation and, on the other hand, at least some seriation ability precedes logical reversibility. As far as the data are concerned, part of the difference between Piaget's results and the more recent work just described is due to differences in the type of materials used. For example, Piaget reports that children up to 7 years of age mixed up the order of events when retelling fairy tales. However, Stein and Trabasso (1982b) note that inversions of events in the sample protocols that Piaget reported were not as frequent as he implied, and Mandler and Johnson (1977) pointed out that the stories in which inversions did occur were ill structured and did not have a clear causal-temporal sequence of events. It has since been shown that when stories follow a canonical sequence of events, even very young children do not mix up the order in their recall (Johnson & Gandel, in preparation; Mandler & Johnson, 1977; Stein & Glenn, 1979; Wimmer, 1980).

There are two separate issues to be considered here. One concerns the child's familiarity with the material to be ordered; in general, the more familiar the material, the less likely there are to be inversions in sequencing. The work on scripts carried out by Nelson and others involves sequences with which the child is, by definition, quite familiar. The other issue concerns the degree to which a sequence to be ordered has an invariant temporal structure, a causal structure, or an enabling structure in which each event is a precondition for the next. Although many scripts rest on causal or enabling ordering, not all do. The sequence of washing hands, eating, and taking a nap may appear to have enabling, or at least nonarbitrary, connections to an adult, but it is not obvious that the basis of the sequence is apparent to the young child learning this sequence at nursery school. Even if arbitrary, however, with experience, an invariant sequence becomes represented in a canonical form from which deviations are recognized as such.

When a sequence has causal or enabling connections, less experience with it is required for children to order it correctly. Nelson and Gruendel (1981) report that preschool children were quite accurate in sequencing all the scripts that were studied, but the youngest children were more likely to put events together if they stood in a causal or enabling relation than if they were merely linked by custom. Brown (1975, 1976a) and Brown and Murphy (1975) found that preschool children were responsive to event sequences based on enabling relations, even when new and unusual material was presented, and they did better on them than on arbitrarily ordered material. Even when the events themselves did not form a sensible sequence but were made meaningful by being included in a connected narrative, preschool children tended not to make ordering mistakes.

Preschool children also show false recognition of consistent but not actually presented items in a series of pictures depicting an event sequence (Brown, 1976b). Interestingly enough, the younger children were more likely to make false recognitions than the older ones. Because accuracy improved for all types of items (presented items, consistent and inconsistent foils), this finding may merely indicate a lesser degree of attention in the younger children. However, Rabinowitz, Valentine, and Mandler (1981) also found that fifth graders made more false recognitions of consistent foils than did adults in a recognition task involving a lunch-time script. There were no differences between the two age groups in recognizing either inconsistent foils or actually presented items, so an explanation in terms of differential attention seems unlikely. There are wide age differences between these two studies, but the data suggest the possibility that children may be more dependent on the representation of familiar sequences to guide their encoding and memory than are adults.

Representation of Stories

Brown (1976a) heads a section of her chapter with a quote from Lewis Carroll that is most apt for story recall:

"Where shall I begin?" asked the White Rabbit. "Begin at the beginning," the King said gravely, "and go on till you come to the end, then stop." (Carroll, 1865)

The notion that any story, no matter what its content, has a clear-cut beginning and end may seem unduly obvious, yet it reflects a structural appreciation of some psychological significance. Traditional stories, such as fairy tales, folktales, and fables, as well as children's self-generated stories that derive from them not only have beginnings and endings but also a whole series of quite specific parts in between. A great deal of work has been done in the past few years on the structure of this kind of story and the ways in which the representation of that structure affects processing.

There has been an upsurge of interest in text and discourse processing of all kinds in recent years, but the interest in stories arises from the limited number of forms they display. Traditional stories originated in nonliterate societies and the limitations in their structures may reflect limitations on human memory. Mandler and Johnson (1977) speculated that for a story to survive in an oral tradition, it must either be highly memorable in the first place or become so through repeated retellings. To the extent that such stories have common formats, repeated experience with them allows generalizations about their structure to be formed. These structural representations (often signaled by stock phrases, such as "Once upon a time . . .") enable listeners to engage in a good deal of top-down processing in which their comprehension is guided by, and partially controlled by, their expectations of what is to come.

Much of the current interest in stories, therefore, has less to do with their content than with their structure just because they do have normal or canonical forms. It is for this reason that most characterizations of story structure have specifically limited their domain to stories of a particular type (such as stories stemming from the oral tradition); they are not meant to tell us how people process modern short stories or detective stories, let alone newspaper articles and the like. For most kinds of discourse, we must rely much more on bottom-up processing to build an overall representation of the meaning of what is being said.

Current interest in models of the constituent structure of stories and their implications for story schemata stems primarily from two sources. One is the work of Kintsch and van Dijk (Kintsch, 1977b; Kintsch & van Dijk, 1975, 1978), which is based on linguistic work in text analysis and on Kintsch's propositional analyses of prose. The other source is Rumelhart (1975), whose work is related to earlier analyses by Propp (1928/1968) and Colby (1973). Using Rumelhart's (1975) model as a base, several variations and elaborations have been offered (Mandler & Johnson, 1977; Stein & Glenn, 1979; Thorndyke, 1977). Most recently, Johnson and Mandler

(1980) have extended their analyses to longer, multi-episode stories and have described transformational rules relating underlying and surface structures. Rumelhart's (1975) and the more recent models have been called story grammars, a perhaps unfortunate label, because of the tendency to impute too many linguistic overtones to what is basically a psychological enterprise.[6]

The availability of the story grammars as a means of analyzing texts and as a heuristic in the study of comprehension and memory accounts in part for the increasing volume of work on stories, much of it developmental in character. Until a method of analyzing stories into meaningful units was devised, it was difficult to study story processing in a developmentally informative way. As long as stories were analyzed only according to phrase or clause divisions or according to units determined by pauses during reading or speaking (R. E. Johnson, 1970), developmental analyses tended to be limited to purely quantitative statements or else retained an ad hoc character. The story grammars offered a principled way of analyzing stories into meaningful parts so that results could be compared across different stories and different populations.

The general notion of the story grammars is that traditional stories have an underlying structure consisting of a setting component in which the protagonist and background information are introduced, followed by one or more episodes that form the skeletal plot structure of the story. Each episode has some kind of beinning, or initiating, event, to which a protagonist reacts. Typically, the protagonist formulates a goal in response to the beginning event, although the goal is frequently obvious enough that it is omitted from the surface structure of the story. Nevertheless, it is assumed to be present in the underlying structure because the protagonist and his or her goal form the core around which an episode is built. There follows next an attempt to attain the goal and the outcome of that attempt (success or failure). The episode comes to a close with an ending, which may consist of a statement of the long-range consequences of the episode, responses of the protagonist or other character to the events that have taken place, or an emphatic statement, such as ''They lived happily ever after.'' As can be seen from this brief description, the constituent units or categories (often called nodes) of an episode are both temporally and causally connected to each other; each constituent is the cause of the next, which follows it in correct temporal sequence.

Episodes can be either causally or temporally connected. Causal connections between episodes

occur through the embedding property of several of the constituent units. Most frequently, embedding occurs at the outcome or ending node of an episode; that is, these units may be rewritten into entire new episodes. This embedding property is similar to that found in sentences, in which relative clauses, which are sentences in their own right, can be embedded within longer sentences. Temporal connections between episodes produce structures that are looser and less coherent than causally connected ones. Not only are causal connections missing, but each episode in such a sequence is complete in its own right, that is, no embedding occurs and, at each such connection, the story could in principle stop. It is rare to find stories in the oral tradition that consist *only* of temporally connected episodes, but such sequences do occur, especially within long stories or stories of the picaresque type.

Although the embedding property of stories allows many episodes to be conjoined and a number of sequences to occur, nevertheless, if this characterization of story structure is correct, there are still relatively few formats to follow, and in each case the listener should have little trouble keeping track of the story line. In addition, there is another feature of traditional stories that facilitates comprehension: there seem to be relatively few deletions or movements of units in the surface structure (Johnson & Mandler, 1980). The most common deletion is to omit the statement of the goal in an episode because most goals can be easily inferred by listeners familiar with the culture from which the story derives. Because there are relatively few deletions or movements in the surface structure of the story (the story as actually told), the underlying structure is usually relatively transparent to the listener. This structure can be used to form an organized representation of the particular content of the story and presumably is one of the bases of its cohesion (Halliday & Hassan, 1976).

It can be seen that traditional stories share many of the properties of scripts; they consist of familiar action sequences arranged in a specified manner, with beginning and ending points. The main difference is that a story schema, even though its units are content based, is more abstract than a script; it specifies the overall structure or skeleton of a plot in a story without any *particular* content. The commonalities, however, are many. Both stories and scripts provide ready-made schemata that guide comprehension and retrieval, and the characteristics of processing for both kinds of schematic structures are similar in kind.

People use story structure to provide inferences

about information not actually stated in the text; consequently false recognition of expected, but not presented, material tends to be high. Disruptions in comprehension occur when events are described in other than their expected order or when parts are deleted. As for recall, because what is retained is the underlying gist of the story, many details of the surface structure are lost. Recall is, thus, schematic rather than exact. Further, people use the ideal schema to infer appropriate material if they forget the details of content of some unit, leading to intrusions in recall. Events are recalled in their correct order when stories are told in canonical form and when they are told in scrambled or mixed-up form, recall tends to approximate the ideal order as well. Finally, people use the underlying structure to summarize the gist of a story. A number of studies have documented these claims.

Studies of Comprehension

The most detailed studies of the effects of story structure on comprehension have used reading time as a measure and so have tended to use adults as subjects. Examples of recent work are the finding that reading times of individual sentences can be predicted in part on the basis of story structure (Cirilo & Foss, 1980; Olson, Duffy, & Mack, in press) and that reading time increases at the boundaries of episodes (Haberlandt, 1980; Haberlandt, Berian, & Sandson, 1980). Haberlandt ascribes this increase to a kind of episode-processing strategy; when the schema indicates that an episode is finished, readers must prepare for a new topic, repackaging the previous episode into more abstract form. Mandler and Goodman (1982) also observed an increase in reading time at episode boundaries and, in addition, found increased reading times at the boundaries of each constituent within an episode. They also found that reading times increased when a story constituent was moved out of its correct place, even when the movement was given a temporal marker so that the intended real-time sequence of events could be unambiguously determined. Data such as these have been taken to demonstrate the psychological validity of the analyses of the constituent structure of stories as well as the notion that stories have canonical sequences.

Whether following scripts or stories, both children and adults make a great many context-driven inferences (Barclay & Reid, 1974; Bower, 1978a; Bransford & Johnson, 1972; Kail, Chi, Ingram, & Danner, 1977; Omanson, Warren, & Trabasso, 1978; Paris & Upton, 1976). For example, Brown, Smiley, Day, Townsend, & Lawton (1977) found

that children from the second to the seventh grades behaved like adults in making content-related intrusions in their recall of stories and in having difficulty in distinguishing their own embellishments from content actually presented. Relatively little work has been done on the effects of story structure per se (as opposed to general context effects) on inferences, although some suggestive evidence is reported by Hildyard and Olson (1978). These investigators report that fifth graders made inferences central to the structure of a story more frequently than inferences about incidental material. It is of some interest that subjects listening to stories, rather than reading them, were somewhat more dependent on the structure of the story—a finding that fits well with the speculation that memory limitations may have loomed large in forming the characteristic structure of traditional stories.

Inferences based on contextual and real-world knowledge play such a large role in understanding stories (or for that matter any discourse) that the notion of an inference chain has even been offered as an alternative to a structural analysis of stories (Warren, Nicholas, & Trabasso, 1979). However, the two types of analysis should not be considered to be in opposition. One of the functions of story structure should be to make certain inferences more prepotent than others. The use of story structure in making inferences can be seen in the tendency of both children and adults to invent structurally appropriate material when they cannot recall a particular component (Mandler & Johnson, 1977). Similarly, when a unit of a story is omitted in the telling, children are able to add information that is appropriate to the form of the missing component (Whaley, 1981). It must be stressed that there is no reason to pit structural and content analyses against each other, as has occasionally been done (Black & Wilensky, 1979; Omanson, in press; see also J. M. Mandler, in press-a; Mandler & Johnson, 1980; and Rumelhart, 1980a, for replies). It would be a mistake to assume that either a purely structural approach or a purely content-oriented approach to stories would be sufficient in itself to account for the many aspects of story understanding; too many sources of knowledge are used during comprehension for any one source to be considered preeminent.

Recall of Stories

As noted in the discussion of scripts, Piaget (1926; see also Fraisse, 1963) suggested that children find it difficult to maintain the temporal sequence of stories in their recall. However, it has since been shown that when well-formed stories are used even 4-year-old children make relatively few inversions in recall (Johnson & Gandel, in preparation; Wimmer, 1980). In addition, several studies have shown that when stories are told in other than their canonical form, both children and adults reorder their recall to follow the canonical sequence. J. M. Mandler (1978) wrote two-episode stories in which the episodes were interleaved rather than presented separately and sequentially. From second grade to adult, subjects tended to separate the two episodes in their recall, thus following canonical story form rather than the form in which the stories had been told. A similar result was reported by Glenn (1978). Mandler and DeForest (1979) found that even when instructed to maintain the presented order, subjects had great difficulty in doing so. This difficulty was even greater for the children than for the adults, again suggesting the hypothesis that children are more dependent in their retrieval upon the use of familiar schemata. As a rule, adults seem to have more flexibility in their methods of retrieval, although in this situation even they have difficulty using an alternate retrieval scheme.

Stein and Nezworski (1978) also found that adults tended to recall slightly disordered stories in canonical form; however, when the stories were presented completely randomly, they could no longer uncover the underlying structure and consequently their recall no longer mimicked the ideal order (nor matched the input order very well either). McClure, Mason, and Barnitz (1979) report similar findings for third, sixth, and ninth graders, although ability to arrange misordered stories improved with age. On the other hand, when simple narratives that do not have the form of traditional stories are used and there is no story schema to guide recall, input order plays an increasingly important role (Baker, 1978). Baker interprets her results as failing to support a "strict schema-based approach to comprehension"; however, if the materials are not such as to activate a particular schema, it is not surprising that it is not used.[7]

Amount recalled from various story constituents has also been shown to produce stable patterns across many populations. Although any particular story category can be made unusually salient and, therefore, recalled unusually well by adding stress or unusual or crucial material (Stein & Trabasso, 1982a), nevertheless, highly similar patterns of recall of various story categories have been found in many studies using different stories (Glenn, 1978; J. M. Mandler, 1978; Mandler & Johnson, 1977; Stein & Glenn, 1979; Yussen, Mathews, Buss, & Kane, 1980). The same patterning is also found in dyslexic children (Weaver & Dickinson, in press), language-impaired children (Graybeal, 1981), learning-disabled adults (Worden, Malmgren, & Gabourie, 1982), and deaf children (Gaines, Mandler, & Bryant, 1981). Mandler, Scribner, Cole, and DeForest (1980) found virtually identical patterns of recall in American schoolchildren and adults; Liberian children; and schooled and nonschooled, literate and nonliterate Liberian adults. In all of these studies, amount recalled increases with age, but the patterning of recall is qualitatively similar at all ages studied.[8]

Because of the cross-cultural stability in patterns of recall, Mandler et al. (1980) suggested that at least one kind of story schema may be universal. They noted that this kind of schematic organization produces much more similar cross-cultural and developmental data than has typically been found when lists of categorized words are studied. This point is discussed again later; here, it is only noted that if the same schemata are found cross-culturally and if they are used in a top-down fashion to structure comprehension and to order retrieval automatically, it is not surprising that commonality across many groups is found. Kintsch and Greene (1978) have suggested that story schemata may be culturally specific because they found that American college students had more trouble recalling an Apache folktale than a Grimm brothers' fairy tale. However, the Apache tale consisted of temporally connected episodes and the Western tale of causally connected ones. The former kind of story is typically less well recalled, but both kinds of stories are found in many cultures (Johnson & Mandler, 1980). There are probably some kinds of story schemata that do differ cross-culturally, but it is important to disentangle structural differences from cultural ones when attempting to study this question.

The only exception to the uniformity in patterns of recall across development occurs in the case of motivational states and goals. These story units are the least likely to be recalled by adults, but children are even more apt to omit them. It is not clear why this should be so because children know and use this kind of information. Stein and Glenn (1979) used probe questions following recall and found that first graders were typically able to answer questions about goals and motivational states, even when they had been omitted in recall. Even 4-year-olds are able to infer the intentions and internal states of characters in simple stories (Stein & Trabasso, 1982b).

There is, of course, development in knowledge about motivations, goals, and plans that should affect story understanding (Goldman, in press; Sedlak, 1979). The likelihood of understanding complex motivations may also interact with the complexities of plot structure. Newman (1980) found that young children were less likely than older children and adults to interpret story characters' actions in terms of deception. For example, young children typically did not understand the deceptive intricacies found in some of the Bert and Ernie sketches on the television show ''Sesame Street.'' Newman points out that the presence of deception requires the understander to represent more embedding in the ''belief spaces'' of the characters (Bruce & Newman, 1980) as well as to comprehend asymmetry among different characters' beliefs. Bisanz (in press) suggests that young elementary school children simplify protagonist-antagonist stories by reinterpreting them as simpler single-protagonist stories; perhaps this is due to their lack of recognition of the trickery that often characterizes such stories.

Part of the reason for the omission of motivational statements in children's recall, then, may sometimes be due to lack of appropriate knowledge about why the characters act as they do. This explanation, however, does not account for the omission of the simple goals that are often found in traditional stories. Mandler et al. (1980) also found that nonliterate Liberian adults were somewhat more likely than American adults to omit such story statements in recall. Such factors as a tendency to omit redundant information or to concentrate exclusively on events when retelling a story may be at work (Kareev, 1981), but this issue has not been systematically explored.

Generating Stories

One way to address the question of how early a story schema is formed is to examine the structure of children's own stories. Earlier analyses of children's stories tended to concentrate on the content, with special reference to children's affective life (e.g., Pitcher & Prelinger, 1963). Other more recent research has examined children's knowledge of narrative conventions, their ability to maintain a narrative line, and so forth (Menig-Peterson & McCabe, 1978; Rubin & Gardner, 1980; Rubin & Wolf, 1979). For example, Rubin and Gardner report that 3-year-olds have learned some fairy tale conventions, such as ''Once upon a time. . . .'' Of particular interest for understanding how story knowledge is organized, however, are analyses of structural changes in children's productions. Inspection of the corpus of stories Pitcher and Prelinger (1963) col-

lected from children aged 2 to 5 suggests the gradual growth of a story schema during this period. Applebee (1978), Botvin and Sutton-Smith (1977), and Stein and Glenn (1982) report an increase in complexity of stories and their conformity to an ideal story schema during the elementary school years. Botvin and Sutton-Smith found embedded episodes appearing only toward the older ages. However, Stein and Glenn found complete episodes and embedding in a number of stories produced by kindergarten children. Many of the stories of the young children did consist of scriptlike sequences. It may be easier to produce a script of one's daily activities than to create upon demand a problem or a goal to reach. Trabasso, Stein, and Johnson (1981) also report that when young children's story productions do have episodic form, the sequence of story categories closely matches a story-grammar format, including the deletion rules proposed by Johnson and Mandler (1980).

Analysis of children's productions is informative, but it may underestimate the age at which the schematic components of story understanding appear; the technique suffers from some of the problems found in the analysis of children's drawings. The labor of production almost certainly results in simpler or less sophisticated stories than children can understand. Many of the stories generated by preschool children are quite primitive in structure; yet Poulsen, Kintsch, Kintsch, and Premack (1979) found that 4-year-old children used a story schema to interpret a series of pictures that composed a reasonably complex story, and Johnson and Gandel (in preparation) found that 4-year-olds could recall both temporally and causally connected episodes quite well. Such results suggest that a story schema may be used in encoding and retrieving stories earlier than it can be used to create a new story.

Summarization and Judgments of Importance

Kintsch and van Dijk (1975, 1978) and Rumelhart (1977) have provided sets of rules, based on the notion of a story schema, that adults use when summarizing stories. It has traditionally been thought that summarizing requires an awareness of story structure and an analysis of the important elements in a story beyond the skill of young children. However, N. S. Johnson (in press) found that even first graders could summarize stories if they were familiar with them or if the stories had clear simple structure. Of the two major summarization techniques, deletion and condensation, first graders relied more on deletion, and their summaries were less sophisticated than those of older children and adults; nevertheless, an ability to formulate the gist of a story is present at least in a rudimentary form by the first grade.

Apparently, summarizing a story is an easier task for young children than is judging the importance of various story constituents. Yussen et al. (1980) found that there was marked improvement in ability to pick out the most important structural units in episodes between the second and fourth grades. Using a different measure of structural importance and considerably more complex stories, Brown and Smiley (1977) found that both third and fifth graders were poor at judging the importance of story parts. Similarly, Brown, Smiley, and Lawton (1978) found increasing improvement from the fifth grade to adulthood in the ability not only to judge the importance of story parts but also to judge which parts would make good retrieval cues.

Although little is still known about summarizing, it may be an easier task than judging the importance of various units because it is possible to summarize on the basis of activating a schema. N. S. Johnson (in press) suggests that to the extent that a deletion strategy is being used, the child could use the story schema in its accustomed way, successively retrieve each constituent unit, and make a decision at each point whether to delete or not. Condensation of several units into one is a more complex strategy, requiring some scanning back and forth in memory and comparison among units. Presumably, judging the importance of story units requires this kind of flexibility as well and, in addition, requires a kind of metacognitive awareness about discourse in much the same way that knowledge of what makes a good retrieval cue requires awareness of the capacity and workings of one's memory.

Another task requiring the ability to bring a story schema to awareness is making judgments about the constituent structure of stories. Work by Pollard-Gott, McCloskey, and Todres (1979) and Mandler (1982) has shown that many adults can divide stories into their constituent units (and the results largely agree with the story-grammar analyses), but even college students often have difficulty in the separation of lexical, semantic, and structural factors required by this kind of task. A good deal of sophistication is needed to reflect on the structure of language (Gleitman & Gleitman, 1970; Levelt, 1974). Given the difficulty children have in making judgments about the importance of story units, it would be surprising if they could accomplish a pure structural judgment task, although even second graders can make overall judgments about what is and what is not a story that match their teachers' judgments quite well (Stein, in press).

Related findings have been reported about children's monitoring of their comprehension. Markman (1979) found that children throughout the elementary school years were poor at monitoring their comprehension of textual materials. Even obvious inconsistencies appeared to slip by their notice. Such a finding does not imply, however, that the children do not engage in constructive, integrative processing during the course of reading. Harris, Kruithof, Terwogt, & Visser (1981) found that both 8- and 11-year-old children slowed down in their reading when they reached a sentence inconsistent with the previous text, even though they did not report the inconsistency. Detection and awareness of inconsistencies are two different matters, the latter apparently being a more slowly developing process than the former.

In contrast to tasks requiring either the strategic application of knowledge or metacognitive awareness, the typical use of schematic organizations—whether in the form of a script, a story, or knowledge of what a face looks like—operates automatically and normally out of the reach of awareness. Indeed, one of the advantages of schematic organizations for comprehension and retrieval is that they do not require conscious application. As we will see later, children's use of categorical organizations does not always operate so automatically.

Before turning to the topic of categorization, let me sum up some of the characteristic aspects of the knowledge of scenes and events that have been discussed in this and the previous section. I have suggested that scene and event knowledge is organized in the form of schemata. Some schemata are quite abstract (as we have seen in the case of stories) specifying structure more than content; others are quite concrete (as in the case of our knowledge of what our home looks like or what happens in the local restaurant). These kinds of knowledge become organized on the basis of personal experience through daily contact with spatial and temporal co-occurrences in the environment. We have an innate tendency to organize our experiences, and if we encounter sets of co-occurrences often enough, we come to know them well, to conceive of them as units, having parts and sections, each with its own meaning and connections to the whole.

There are, of course, constraints on this process. I have not considered here the mechanisms that control the nature of the units that can become chunked together. Recent work suggests that even very young infants integrate auditory and visual stimuli that show common temporal patterns (Spelke, 1976, 1979, 1981). There is also some indication that spatial congruency (auditory and visual information coming from the same location) is necessary for such integration to take place (Lawson, 1980). (This issue is treated at length in *Gibson & Spelke, vol. III, chap. 1*.) The primary concern of the present chapter has been to describe larger organizations of collections of objects and sequences of events, and I have proceeded as if we already knew how infants come to conceive objects and events in the first place.

Whatever the mechanisms involved in forming object and event schemata, our lives quickly become filled with regularities. We can use these packages of knowledge to guide the encoding and storing of new information with predictable effects of such guidance—gist encoding, and construction of details in memory by means of default processing, and so on. As discussed earlier (*Representation in Infancy*), these schemata not only represent information but they also act as procedures. Comprehension involves the search for, and activation of, appropriate schemata to account for incoming data (Rumelhart, 1980b). A schema also provides a highly effective retrieval mechanism: it is automatically activated by a familiar situation and it provides a starting point, a rule for ordering output, and a stop rule. It seems to be a mechanism by which ''natural'' or incidental remembering can occur, in which retrieval does not require deliberate or planful search strategies (J. M. Mandler, 1979).

The data discussed here strongly suggest that these procedural forms of knowledge develop early and remain qualitatively similar throughout life. There are several ways, however, in which developmental change in this kind of knowledge takes place, most of which are still imperfectly understood. First, it seems likely that increasing experience with a variety of situations similar in structure, content, or both, allows more abstract and general scene and event schemata to emerge. At the same time, there may well be limits on the abstractness of the similarities between situations that people will notice in the course of their daily lives unless special attention is drawn to them (J. M. Mandler, in press-b). Second, flexibility in the application of schemata seems to develop. The data that I have reported here only hint at such change; both experimental and theoretical work will be needed to understand this type of growth.

Finally, the ability to reflect on knowledge in a conscious way (metacognition) is clearly one of the major accomplishments of development (see Flavell, 1978). We still know little about these processes in the area of schematically organized knowledge. We do not know the extent to which conscious attention to the structure of a story, say, can be used strategically for deliberate remembering, story creation, and so forth. We do not know the extent to which this kind of knowledge, when called to attention, becomes reorganized into a more easily accessible declarative format. To date, we know more about the development of access to, and the use of, categorical forms of knowledge, which is the final topic of this chapter.

CATEGORICAL REPRESENTATION

We will now consider the development of knowledge about the interrelationships among classes, or categories, of things. The discussion will not be concerned with concept formation per se, but with how sets of things that are considered equivalent are related to each other to form taxonomic classification systems. The world of things (and events) can be categorized in a great many ways by varying the dimensions on which the classification is based. The most common bases are functional and perceptual similarity, and these two bases often overlap; that is, things that have common function also often look alike or have sets of features in common. In addition, idiosyncratic classifying principles of all sorts can be used, from ''things that I like'' to the vagaries of the ancient Chinese Celestial Emporium of Benevolent Knowledge that Rosch (1978) describes.

This discussion will focus on objects rather than on events and particularly on the cognitive structures that govern our understanding of superordinate, subordinate, and coordinate classes. These relationships are hierarchical in nature, although whether or not they are mentally represented in the form of hierarchies is a disputed point. In addition to knowledge about what items belong in given categories, categorical knowledge includes the more abstract knowledge of class-inclusion relations that are used in both inductive and deductive thinking (Inhelder & Piaget, 1964).

Categorizing itself is a basic ability, one that almost certainly must be posited as a primitive of psychological functioning. It is a natural by-product of the processes of assimilation and accommodation, and in its basic sense cannot be distinguished from schema formation. The infant quickly learns to categorize objects at the basic level (Rosch et al., 1976), presumably on the basis of their perceptual characteristics and their functional relations to the child's and others' activities (Nelson, 1979). However, here we are concerned with the relationships *among* categories and how children learn, for example, that dogs and cats are both animals. This kind of information is not experienced directly in the same way that individual objects and events are encoded. Recognizing an object or event at the basic level depends upon spatiotemporal organization. The formation of superordinate classes is a generalization based on more complex similarities of function and to a lesser extent on appearance; presumably, it is influenced by caretakers' labeling as well. It is more abstract than basic-level categorizing, just as a higher order schema, such as going shopping, is a more abstract formulation than a script about going to the corner supermarket.

It seems reasonable to assume that the earliest categorization of things as belonging to the same superordinate class takes place within the daily repetitive episodes that lead to the formation of scripts and other schemata (J. M. Mandler, 1979). Dogs and cats not only look somewhat alike but also are treated similarly as pets. Knives, forks, and spoons also look rather alike; they also occur together or as substitutes for each other in the daily activities revolving around eating. Hence, at the same time that infants are learning to organize the world spatially (leading to perceptual categorization) and temporally (leading to categories of events), they must be forming the foundation for the eventual understanding of the hierarchical relationships involved in the formation of superordinate categories of animals, eating utensils, furniture, types of food, and so forth. It is for this reason that Nelson and Gruendel (1981) suggest that generalized event representations are the building blocks of cognition; the formation of superordinate classes may be due in large part to a generalization across the things that go into particular slots in scripts and other schemata. If so, we should expect the functional characteristics of superordinate classes to play a heavier role in their definition than perceptual ones, a characteristic that may or may not be true for basic-level categories (Gentner, 1978; Nelson, 1982; Tomikawa & Dodd, 1980; see also *Clark, vol. III, chap. 12*).

The established wisdom on the formation of superordinate classes is that such understanding takes a great many years to be accomplished. Inhelder and Piaget (1964) and countless replications of their work have shown that until at least 7 or 8 years of age, children tend to be somewhat confused about categorical relations. In particular, the whole body of work on class-inclusion concepts suggests that

children are unclear as to the extension of individual classes and their relations to each other (see Markman, 1981; Trabasso, Isen, Dolecki, McLanahan, Riley, & Tucker, 1978; and Winer, 1980, for reviews of this work. See also *Gelman & Baillargeon, vol. III, chap. 3*). Several related areas of research lead to the same conclusion. At the same age at which Nelson (1978a) found that young children could verbalize their knowledge of scripts, others have found that children have great difficulty verbalizing hierarchical classificatory relations (Anglin, 1977; Mcnamara, 1972). Some studies have suggested that young children can sort items into basic-level categories but have difficulty sorting them into superordinate ones (Inhelder & Piaget, 1964; Olver & Hornsby, 1966; Rosch et al., 1976). Finally, a large body of research indicates that children are not as responsive to the hierarchical structure of categorized lists of words as adults and their recall does not show the same degree of clustering of items into categories (see Ornstein & Corsale, 1979, for a review of this literature).

On the other hand, another body of research indicates responsiveness to categorical relations from an early age. Many of these studies have used priming, recognition, and habituation techniques to measure the extent to which a superordinate category is automatically activated by the presentation of an exemplar. The tension between these two bodies of research may be resolvable in terms of the degree of conscious awareness of categorical relations the tasks require. Many of the verbal, sorting, and recall tasks require active thinking about categories, whereas priming and recognition studies do not. I will discuss the latter group of studies first, followed by a small amount of work that has explored the question of the depth of hierarchicalization in the conceptual system, that is, the extent to which levels more abstract than basic-level objects and their immediate superordinate classes are present. Then I will take up the question of conscious awareness versus automatic activation of categorical representations in more detail.

Hierarchical Representation of Categories

Analyses of early language production indicate the formation of superordinate categories at least by the second year of life. Rescorla (1980) collected samples of 1- to 1½-year-old children's speech production and examined them for use of overextensions. She found that more than half of the overextensions consisted of using a basic-level word to refer to a superordinate class. The mislabeling itself is not surprising, given the limited vocabulary that children of this age have to express such relationships. Nelson, Rescorla, Gruendel, and Benedict (1978) also noted that children of this age often understand the correct referents of object words, but in production they use a prototypical member of the class to refer to the class as a whole. Similarly, Mervis (1981) observed that when 1- to 2-year-old children begin to bring a basic-level category into closer agreement with adult conceptions, the old category label seems to continue to function as a superordinate label. Somewhat older children have no difficulty in producing exemplars of superordinate categories upon request. Nelson (1974) found that 5-year-olds produced fewer instances of categories than older children and adults, but the organization of the classes was similar at all ages.

If we are to understand the extent to which categorical knowledge is present in young children or if we wish to explore the boundaries of their categories, we must be wary of relying on verbal data alone. Obviously, the technique is useless for studying preverbal children, and a vast literature testifies to newly verbal children's slow progress in bringing their language into congruence with that of the adult community (see *Clark, vol. III, chap. 12*). For reasons that are not entirely clear (although limited vocabulary may be one of them), the expression of hierarchical relationships among concepts appears later than their demonstrable presence in the child's representational system (see Nelson, 1978b). For example, Anglin (1977) notes that there is a fundamental distinction between the child's verbal expressions and the underlying conceptual system that supports them and that the child may know more than he or she can express in language. At the same time, Anglin states that there is an absence of a hierarchical system in the conceptual structures underlying the child's terms of reference, a conclusion that too strongly equates verbal production with conceptual understanding. Nonverbal measures can often tell us more about children's classificatory systems than verbal ones.

One recent study (Ross, 1980) used looking time in a habituation/dishabituation paradigm to explore 1-, 1½-, and 2-year-old children's knowledge of superordinate categories. She presented the children with instances of what might be considered basic-level categories (wooden models of *M*'s, *O*'s and toy men) or of superordinate categories (models of animals, food, and furniture). All three groups of children decreased their looking times to successive exemplars in the basic categories, but not to the superordinate ones, suggesting greater perceptual dissimilarity among the members of the superordinate classes (cf. Rosch et al., 1976). For all catego-

ries, however, following exposure to instances of one class, looking time increased when an instance of a new class was presented. The implication is that the increase in looking was due to a change in category, although without careful specification of the degree of perceptual similarity within and across classes, it is difficult to be certain that the result was not due to the greater perceptual dissimilarity of the test items. Additional experimental work, such as that carried out by Fagan and Singer (1979), discussed earlier (*Representation in Infancy*), should decide the issue.

Related studies have shown that at least by 2 years of age children habituate to new members of an old taxonomic category when looking at pictures (Faulkender, Wright, & Waldron, 1974) and that by 3 years of age children show release from proactive inhibition when a new category is introduced in a memory task (Esrov, Hall, & LaFaver, 1974; Hoemann, DeRosa, & Andrews, 1974; Huttenlocher & Lui, 1979). Children 2 years old can choose a categorically related item from an array at above-chance levels (Daehler, Lonardo, & Bukatko, 1979). Also, 2- to 3-year-old children recall more from categorically related lists than from unrelated lists, and they usually show above-chance clustering in their recall (Goldberg, Perlmutter, & Myers, 1974; Perlmutter & Myers, 1979; Rossi & Rossi, 1965). Similarly, Huttenlocher and Newcombe (1976) found that blocking items into categories increased memory spans for 4-year-old children in the same fashion that it did for adults.

Other techniques, such as false recognition and latency to respond to related words, have also been used to study the activation of categorical information, although typically with somewhat older children. Mansfield (1977) studied errors and latencies in recognition of target words that had previously been presented in sentences. Subjects ranged from kindergarten age to adult. In the most relevant experiment, the distractors were either subordinates or superordinates of the target words, stood in a part or whole relationship to the targets, or were unrelated. All subjects showed more errors and longer latencies to reject superordinate and subordinate distractors than part-whole distractors or unrelated words. Mansfield concluded that young children show the same hierarchical organization of categories as do adults.

A similar conclusion was reached by Hall and Halperin (1972) and Steinberg and Anderson (1975). Hall and Halperin (1972) found greater false recognition for verbal associates and categorical superordinates than for unrelated items by 3- and 4-year-olds. Steinberg and Anderson (1975) found that superordinate terms, whether close or remote (i.e., one or two steps up a taxonomic hierarchy), served as better retrieval cues for first graders recalling previously seen pictures than did coordinate terms, which could also be either close or remote associates. This experiment is unusual because it assessed more than one level of hierarchical structure.

In general, in spite of a few negative findings (Heidenheimer, 1978; McCauley, Weil, & Sperber, 1976), most of the work in recent years supports the notion that even young children have representations of superordinate as well as basic-level categories. This is not to say that developmental changes do not occur in the extensiveness of the knowledge base and the strength of the connections in the semantic networks by which such relationships are represented (see Saltz, Soller, Sigel, 1972). As an example, Kareev (1980) measured the degree of semantic activation between superordinate classes and their exemplars, using the Stroop interference technique. Children in the second, fourth, and sixth grades were presented with words representing concepts and their superordinate and subordinate classes (such as, dog, animal, and collie). First, one of these words was presented as a prime; then another of the words was presented, written in color. Subjects had to name as quickly as possible the color in which the word was written. The more that the word written in color has been activated by the prime word, the slower the response to name the color should be. Using this interference measure, Kareev found an increase in the strength of the association between concepts and their superordinate classes over the age range studied and a decrease in the strength of association between concepts and their subordinate exemplars.

It should also be noted that the existence of a hierarchically organized categorical system does not by itself speak to the formal understanding of class inclusion that Piaget was most interested in, although it is hard to imagine a hierarchically arranged system that did not imply *some* understanding of class inclusion. Indeed, C. L. Smith (1979) found that under favorable conditions 4- to 6-year-old children answered class-inclusion questions above chance. She used three different kinds of multitrial problems and found that 90% of the younger children and 100% of the older children could answer the questions in at least one of the tasks in an "adult" fashion (one error or less). She points out that her data lead to the conclusion that children must have a representational system that contains class-inclusion information; otherwise, they would not be able to answer *any* class-inclusion problems above

chance levels. The most likely hypothesis is that young children have a hierarchical representation of categories but have difficulty in using that knowledge to draw certain kinds of conclusions. They are most apt to be able to use such knowledge if the classification is concrete rather than abstract (Inhelder & Piaget, 1964) or if the superordinate class is bound to its exemplars by spatial or part-whole relations (Markman, 1981; Markman & Seibert, 1976).

For the most part, the studies just described only address the issues of whether or not young children have any superordinate information and whether or not such information is activated when basic-level instances are processed. Relatively little work has been carried out on the question of whether children have higher level representations of relationships among superordinate classes themselves. Much of this work has revolved around the animate/inanimate distinction; that is, Do children understand that animals and plants can both be represented by a single "animate" class, one that is contrasted with an inanimate class of objects? Piaget (1929) and Laurendeau and Pinard (1962) thought that this higher level understanding was a fairly late acquisition.

In a fascinating treatise on the development of ontological knowledge, Keil (1979) has shown not only that preschool children's categorical representation is hierarchical in nature but also that it typically includes animate and inanimate branches (see also Keil, 1981b). In a series of studies using people's judgments about anomalies in the application of various predicates to classes of terms, Keil found suggestive evidence that there may be a rigid hierarchical structure to our categories of "things" in the world.[9] Certain predicates can be applied only to humans (honest, sorry); other predicates apply not only to humans but also to all animals (asleep, hungry). Similarly, another set of predicates can be applied to all living things (dead, sick), and still broader predicates to solid objects of any sort (tall, skinny). Continuing up the ontological tree, we find predicates that apply to all physical objects regardless of their category and others (such as spatial location) that apply both to objects and to events. At the top of the tree are predicates that can refer to any class of terms (interesting, thought about), whether they be objects, events, or abstract ideas. In the data Keil presents, adults were almost invariant in their judgments about which predicates were applicable to the various terms, and these judgments respected the hierarchical nature of the tree. That is, all predicates higher in the tree were considered to be appropriate (not necessarily true) for all terms on branches under them (e.g., it is all right to say that a pig is interesting); predicates at lower levels were considered to be anomalous when applied to any term above them (e.g., it is not all right to say that a box is sleepy).

Keil's (1979) experiments indicate some very general constraints on human categorization and its development; not only is there the tendency to impose hierarchical structure on concepts from an early age but also the type of hierarchy seems to be the same at all ages, even though the younger children's have many fewer branches. The experiments do not tell us all that can be said about language with respect to underlying conceptual structure, however, because not all predicates are as neatly hierarchically applied as those Keil used (Gerard & Mandler, in press). In particular, predicates that apply to events seem not to fall into as clean a hierarchy as those that apply to objects.

Overall, Keil's data do not support Piaget's (1929) conclusion that children frequently tend to attribute animate properties to inanimate objects. Children do tend to misattribute some animal properties to plants, but only occasionally make an animacy error. When they do, they are apparently consistent in their attributions to the misassigned term (Keil, 1981b). Keil relates a charming example of a 5-year-old who thought that rocks were alive; when probed, it was discovered that he believed they could have babies (pebbles), grow (perhaps into boulders?), and die, as evidenced by their just lying around and being still!

Other recent work also indicates less confusion between animate and inanimate classes than suggested by Piaget. Flavell, Shipstead, and Croft (1979) report that young children agree with the statement that people can know their names but dolls cannot. Similarly, Johnson and Wellman (1979) found that 4-year-olds know that a doll does not have a brain, although 3-year-olds are more likely to think that a doll does. Carey (1978) taught 4-year-olds the name of a new predicate (such as omentum) without giving them any information other than that a specific animal had the part in question. Then she asked them whether other things had the part as well. The tendency to ascribe the part to other animals was a function of their similarity to the animal for which the part had originally been designated and rarely was it ascribed to inanimates (see also Harris, 1975).

Although Carey (in preparation) believes that a full understanding of the concept of animacy depends on extensive biological knowledge and, thus, is a late acquisition, many investigators have found a more adequate and consistent understanding of the distinction between animate and inanimate classes in the preschool year than the Piagetian work implied. Gelman and Spelke (1981) point out that Piaget tended to ask questions about objects that young children know little about, such as the moon and the wind, and that the questions he asked were ones that must have been very difficult for young children to know how to answer. Keil adds that to ask whether the sun knows where it is moving is in fact an anomalous question because the correct answer is neither yes or no!

Another method of assessing the hierarchical character of categorical knowledge and one that has the advantage of relying less on the use of language, is to scale similarity judgments. In a recent study in my laboratory, we asked kindergartners, third grade children, and adults to make triad judgments of similarity among various animals and plants, in each case choosing the two things that were most alike. The resulting similarity matrices were submitted to hierarchical clustering analyses; these analyses, in turn, were used to generate tree structures depicting the similarity relations among the various categories. Although the kindergarten data were more variable than those of the older children's and the adults', a great deal of commonality in the hierarchical relationships was found at all three ages. The main distinction between the children's and the adults' judgments was the children's separation of people from other animals; college students grouped people as part of a primate class. Here is a case of a shift in conception that seems to result from biological training in school. One interesting finding was that most of the young children tended to consider insects to be more similar to other animals than to plants. Children of this age will rarely agree that insects are animals (Anglin, 1977), yet their knowledge of the relationship between the two classes can be demonstrated. It seems fairly obvious that an uncertain linguistic mapping of terms onto an underlying conceptual structure accounts for such discrepancies in results.

Conscious Awareness Versus Automatic Activation of Categorical Organizations

One of the most robust findings in the developmental literature is the lesser tendency of children to organize their free recall around taxonomic categories, even when the presented material has a categorical structure. The findings cannot be due to the absence of categorical representation because, as we have seen, even 2-year-olds show some clustering in their recall of categorized lists. Although such results might be accounted for on the basis of associative relatedness rather than categorical activation (see Lange, 1978), 6-year-olds, who usually do not spontaneously use the categorical organization of a list to order their recall, will, nevertheless, when asked to sort the items into groups, do so on a taxonomic basis (Worden, 1974).

Nash and Gelman (reported in Gelman & Gallistel, 1978) found that 3- to 5-year-olds showed moderate amounts of clustering in recall of a categorized group of toys after they had played with them for about 15 min. Children who were given the same amount of time in a training procedure, in which they practiced consistent sorting, showed considerably higher clustering in their recall of the toys (and higher recall as well). Gelman and Gallistel conclude that the classificatory ability must have already been present in these young children because its effects were noticeable after such a brief training procedure. Note also that at least half of the children in all groups spontaneously sorted the toys into taxonomic categories.

What can we conclude from such results? A likely hypothesis is that conscious attention has to be paid to categorical information for it to be used to organize a set of disparate items into an overall structure. This suggestion can be contrasted with various theories of semantic memory (see E. E. Smith, 1978) and the results reported earlier (*Hierarchical Representation of Categories*) that superordinate information is automatically activated when an object is encoded. But this does not mean that categorical information must always be activated sufficiently to bring it to awareness or for it to serve as the basis of organization for retrieval.

Both children and adults can encode lists of items and not be aware of their overall categorical structure, although adults are more likely to notice such information. Whether or not the information is noticed depends in large part on the nature of the task. Both children and adults, if engaged in a categorizing task (such as sorting), *will* encode the categorical information and use it as the basis of retrieval (G. Mandler, 1967; Murphy & Brown, 1975; Worden, Mandler, & Chang, 1978). Sorting requires the active maintenance of a criterion for grouping; if the criterion is a taxonomic one, then the taxonomic structure of the materials is necessarily brought to one's attention. However, when not given such a task, adults do not always discover and use the categorical structure of a list, even in deliberate memory situations (Puff, Murphy, & Ferrara, 1977). In incidental tasks, recall and clustering fall to lower levels, again depending on the nature of the task. For example, we have found in my laboratory that if an incidental task requires a judgment of prototypicality of the items (i.e., a categorical judgment), recall and clustering improve for both children and adults. If the incidental task involves making judgments about the quality of individual items and, thus, does not require categorical information, recall and clustering decline.

These data suggest that there is an important difference between processing a list of categorized items and processing material that is schematically organized. It is typical for young children not to discover the categorical structure of a list of words; it is rarer, but it still occurs in adults. In cross-cultural studies, it is even the rule for nonschooled adults to miss the categorical structure of lists of words (Cole & Scribner, 1977). As we have seen earlier, however, it is almost impossible for either children or adults to miss the schematic structure of a script or story or not to call upon this kind of organization in retrieval.

One of the reasons for the optional character of attention to the similarity relations involved in taxonomic classification may be their abstractness. The similarity between two exemplars of a basic-level category is more likely to be noticed than that between two exemplars of a superordinate category. The similarity among exemplars of still higher classes is still more unlikely to be noticed; indeed, it is often very difficult to bring to awareness. For example, the animate/inanimate basis of similarity is quite abstract and not salient even to many adults, who presumably have full command of the distinction; witness the fact that animacy is the basis for solution of the final item on the Similarities subtest of the Weschler Adult Intelligence Scale (see also Schaeffer, Lewis, & Van Decar, 1971).

Another reason for optional attention to categorical relations is the multiple bases on which categorization can be carried out. Many kinds of similarity relations are available and may be noticed during the processing of a list of words; each will provide a different kind of retrieval cue. No overall single categorical structure is automatically activated, allowing greater variation in what will be attended to than in a situation in which a spatial or causal-temporally organized structure is automatically activated and guides the entire process of encoding. When similarity relations constitute the only available structure, which of many will be noticed depends on the materials themselves, the nature of the task, and also on the subjects' preferences.

Many studies have shown that preference for attending to different aspects of stimuli varies as a function of age (Denney & Moulton, 1976; Kemler, in press; Melkman & Deutsch, 1977; Smiley & Brown, 1979; Smith & Kemler, 1977). That people prefer to attend to different kinds of similarity relations does not speak to the underlying organization of their knowledge however, unless these tendencies are so strong as to exclude encoding of certain kinds of information. For example, Melkman, Tversky, and Baratz (1981) report that preschool children showed a preference for color as a basis of grouping and older children preferred taxonomic grouping, but categorical cues were more effective as retrieval cues for both groups. Sophian and Hagen (1978) and Ceci, Lea, and Howe (1980) report similar findings.

Children's knowledge about conceptual relationships must be separated from their ability to use stored information in specific tasks (Kemler, in press; Scarborough, 1977; L. B. Smith, 1979). Even sorting tasks, which have routinely been used to assess conceptual preferences, have their pitfalls. Markman, Cox, and Machida (1981) found that the sorting performance of 3- and 4-year-olds varied as a function of the specifics of the task. When children were asked to sort objects into transparent bags rather than on a table in front of them, the salience of spatial configurations was reduced and their classifications became more like standard taxonomic sorting, as did their justifications for their sorts.

One of the reasons for conflicting data from preference tests is that some methods make it more likely that the child will note the categorical relations in the first place or make it easier for the child to keep that structure in mind. One of the classic studies suggesting that young children are unable to sort taxonomically (Olver & Hornsby, 1966) used large numbers of pictures belonging to many categories, a situation likely to cause difficulty in maintaining a consistent basis for the groupings. Another "negative" finding (Rosch et al., 1976) was based on a very strict criterion of success—children were said to sort taxonomically only when *no* errors were made. Because young children have both smaller and somewhat more idiosyncratic classes than adults, such a criterion may be unrealistic.

In short, we must be cautious when generalizing about the organization of knowledge from preferences for various kinds of similarity relations. Preferences are strongly influenced by the task and materials, by culture, and by training in school (Sharp, Cole, & Lave, 1979). Smiley and Brown (1979), for example, found that older people, like very young children, tend to prefer thematic organizations to taxonomic ones in a grouping task. Taxonomic preferences were more common in school-aged children as well as in adults. It seems unlikely that the underlying organization of knowledge changes in such a curvilinear fashion. Even college students, with their well-known proclivity for taxonomic organization, will often use an event-based organizing activity in preference to a categorical one. Rabinowitz

and Mandler (in press) presented short phrases that could be organized either taxonomically or as simple schematic sequences. More subjects sorted the items into schematically organized groups than into taxonomic ones. When the phrases were replaced by the nouns that occurred in each phrase, subjects tended to revert to a taxonomic organization. Nevertheless, for both nouns and phrases, subjects recalled more from lists blocked according to the schematic organizations than from lists blocked according to the taxonomic categories.

Suggestive as such data are of a tendency to organize information around event schemata, they do not address the question of the underlying bases of knowledge as a whole. We are far from answering that question because, in the absence of a theory of the relationships among various kinds of knowledge, our experiments have tended to address quite limited aspects of comprehension and memory. Nevertheless, I will close this section with some speculation about the organization of knowledge that might be considered a framework for thinking about the development of a general representational system.

The many studies showing a shift in dimensional preferences during the early years have often been assumed to indicate a shift in the way knowledge is represented. Nelson (1977) in particular, following work by Schank (1975) and Schank and Abelson (1977), has suggested that knowledge is originally organized around episodes and only gradually are context-free, hierarchically organized taxonomic structures added onto episodic structures.[10] This suggestion was supported by Brown (1977) and J. M. Mandler (1979). Although I still find this view appealing, I would emphasize today a slightly different aspect of some of the changes that appear to be taking place. It seems an eminently sensible and plausible view that knowledge is originally organized around the daily episodes that control infants' earliest experiences. The repetitive regularity of certain event sequences (and constant aspects of the immediate physical environment) must provide the framework within which to notice similarities and to categorize the variety of changing objects with which the infant interacts. That is, as suggested before, many of the earliest divisions of the world into classes of similar things are made in the context of familiar routines and are undoubtedly strongly influenced by them. This may be one of the reasons for the functional character of many of our classification systems. However, we have also seen the influence of categorical organization on a variety of types of processing by very young children, suggesting that it is not added on but an integral part of the processing of scenes and events from an early age.

On the one hand, decontextualization of categorical organizations from the contexts in which they were learned clearly takes place; it gradually becomes possible to contemplate collections of things in terms of their similarity relations alone. On the other hand, it is not at all clear that categorical organization becomes a separate system in its own right, operating independently of the episodic system. Schematic organization of various spatial and temporal sequences, or episodes, may remain the predominant form of organization throughout life and play a much more important role in our processing than has usually been credited to it. If so, the kind of developmental tasks we have chosen to study may have overemphasized the importance of taxonomic classification systems. We may also have exaggerated the notion of a shift in representation from an event-bound knowledge system in the young child to a categorically organized system in the older child and adult.

CONCLUSIONS

One of the most widely accepted characteristics of cognitive development is that qualitative shifts in representation and thinking occur at various ages. Three shifts that match the major Piagetian stages have been widely noted, whether or not the theorist is of the Piagetian persuasion. These are a shift in functioning (1) from infancy to early childhood, (2) from early childhood to the school years (the 5-to-7 shift), and (3) from late childhood to adolescence. The topics I have covered in this chapter have not been directed toward changes that may occur at the onset of adolescence, but I will briefly touch on this issue after reviewing the two earlier periods in which major shifts have been claimed to occur.

Observations of a shift in functioning in the period from 5 to 7 have been so widespread that it is hard to believe that something fundamental is not occurring (even though claims of an important shift have also been made for the period from 3 to 5). Nevertheless, insofar as representation is concerned, we have seen essentially no evidence for a qualitative shift in the way that knowledge is structured from early childhood throughout the elementary school years. Although information about the preoperational period is still sketchy (see Gelman, 1978), what we have gleaned about representation during this age range suggests that imagery, the representation of space, scenes, and events, as well as the hierarchical organization of conceptual knowledge are not different in

kind from those found in later years. This is not to say that various kinds of functioning do not change during this period; given the onset of formal schooling, it would be surprising if changes in thinking and other behavior did not occur. However, the changes wrought by formal schooling may have misled us into thinking that the fundamental structuring of knowledge changes as well. In contrast, the contention of this chapter has been that this is not the case. I see no evidence that young children encode the world only in images or that their imagery is greatly different from that of older children and adults. There is little evidence that euclidean representation is lacking in early childhood. Events also seem to be represented in the same way as in later years. And in a sense most impressively, given the long-standing belief to the contrary, young children *do* seem to have a hierarchically organized conceptual system.

Turning to the shift from infancy to early childhood, there is one undeniable change that takes place: children learn to talk. One might expect the onset of language to have profound implications for the organization of knowledge and, indeed, that may be the case. To date, however, specific effects of learning to code the world through language seem remarkably hard to document. It is clear that it will be a difficult task to uncouple growing conceptual development from growing facility with language. It is not obvious that in many cases the addition of language per se produces a qualitative change in the representation of concepts already acquired. Language undoubtedly provides the conceptual system with additional and better specified information, but that does not mean that the concepts themselves are necessarily changing in nature.

The onset of language, however, does mean that another, if more subtle (and certainly less observable) change has already taken place. The roots of language lie in the ability to symbolize, to let one thing refer to another. The ontogenesis of symbolic thought is still little understood, but at the least its development occurs more rapidly than Piaget suggested. This statement is not meant as a quibble over age norms but to suggest that the boundary between the sensorimotor and preoperational periods is so fluid as to make the idea not notably useful.

The notion that the infant is a purely sensorimotor (or procedural) organism who at some point shifts to being a conceptual one is undoubtedly an exaggeration. The position that infants know the world only through their own actions is difficult to maintain. The formation of basic-level categories of objects and events, as packages of knowledge in large part independent of the infant's actions, seems to begin very early. There is some evidence that their aggregation into larger groups forms at least a minimal hierarchical knowledge system by the end of the first year. This development may occur even earlier, but the relevant data have not yet been collected.

This kind of representation may be called declarative to the extent that it can be accessed independently of the infant's sensorimotor procedures; the ability to do so seems to emerge much earlier than we once thought, most likely in the second half of the first year. If, as Piaget suggested, symbols are required for recall, then they must appear quite early. On the other hand, perhaps the capacity to symbolize should be divorced from the ability to access representations of objects in their absence. In this case, the growth of symbolization, while important for language and complex thought, may not be particularly related to the development of a declarative form of conceptual representation.

The other side of this coin is whether the procedural organization of knowledge, which seems to be predominant in infancy, is left far behind during the course of development. Manifestly, this is not the case. Much of our knowledge in adulthood remains procedurally organized. Adults do, however, have easier access to aspects of various procedures as well as to bodies of facts. In general, they are not as context bound and show greater flexibility in their thinking.

A major source of a declaratively based knowledge system, of course, is being told "facts," a source of knowledge that begins as soon as the child starts to understand language. Such information is added directly to the system in a declarative format and may, in general, be more easily accessible than information induced from observation of objects and events and from carrying out daily routines. But, in addition to gaining knowledge by word of mouth or book, we also learn to extract information from familiar procedures and regroup it into independently accessible form. I have suggested that we can query procedures for this purpose, and Kosslyn (1978c) has suggested that we query imagery as well. Such queries, whether of imagery or not, would be one way for shifts in representational format to take place. How or when such queries begin is unknown, although the absence of an object or event from its expected routine may be one of the early sources. To the extent that children have not engaged in as much of this kind of activity, they may be more dependent than adults on imagery or procedural knowledge. This does not mean that they think in images however, only that to the extent that their knowledge is less

immediately accessible, they may use imagery as an adjunct to answer questions more than do adults.

As discussed throughout this chapter, a major developmental change is the gradually increasing accessibility of knowledge. Karmiloff-Smith (1979) suggests that this is a continuous process; each time a procedure becomes practiced and can operate at an automatic level, the child becomes able to move to a metaprocedural level and to consider the procedure as a unit in its own right. The result of this process presumably is an increasingly integrated representational system. Whether or not such changes require awareness is unknown. In any case, the ability to reflect on one's conscious processing is another major change that occurs with development. Its roots also begin in early childhood (Wellman, in press), possibly even in infancy, but it seems to play an increasingly important role in governing thought and behavior as the child grows. Many of the developmental changes in thinking that Piaget and others have so clearly documented can be accounted for, at least in part, by the increasing tendency to think consciously about complex relationships among classes, to search for new connections among concepts already represented, to seek verification and proof, and so forth. Consciousness is itself a representational system (Thatcher & John, 1977), but one that has resisted our explorations; we understand even less about its role in our mental life than we do about many other facets of representation and thinking. The relationships between error detection and correction, flexible access to information, and cognitive monitoring of a type that requires conscious attention (Brown, 1978; Flavell, 1981) are topics that will become increasingly important in our theorizing in the next decade.

The view that much of our knowledge is organized procedurally leads to an emphasis on familiarity and experience with a given domain as a crucial factor in the ability to access and manipulate information in a flexible fashion. To the extent that acquisition of knowledge is domain specific rather than consisting of sets of broad principles applied to many areas of thought and behavior, major implications for development follow. This view allows shifts in representation to occur but neither confines them to particular periods of life nor assumes that they are concentrated in particular periods. Instead, it stresses *continual shifts* in the accessibility of knowledge as a function of experience in a domain. Hence, one would expect décalages in performance in different areas within the organism at any one period of time (see Chi, in press).

Although the concept of horizontal décalage has been with us for many years, most accounts of discrepancies in performance on structurally similar tasks have consisted of attempts to apply a production-deficiency proviso to the notion of a broader underlying competence (e.g., Piaget, 1972). If a child reasons well about conservation of quantity in one stimulus domain and not in another, it has been assumed that the discrepancy is due to such factors as the information processing load in a given task and not to a lack of generalizable competence (see Case, 1978; Pascual-Leone, 1970). Indeed, the concept of horizontal décalage has been the safety valve of a stage-theoretic concept of development; however, as has been widely noted, the concept is a descriptive, not an explanatory one. It may well be that in many areas of thinking there is no generalized competence, only hard won principles wrested anew from each domain as it is explored.

Stage-theoretic views of development have been fueled by the belief that in adulthood we find broadly applicable principles of reasoning that do not exist at earlier ages. This view, however, has been called into question in recent years in many different areas of functioning (see Keating, 1979, for a review). More and more evidence has accumulated that many décalages persist into adulthood. Thus, the notion of a final shift to a period of formal operations, as a fundamentally different form of representation, may be called into question as well.

Adults who understood problem-solving principles in one task often show total lack of transfer to formally identical problems with different content. As one example, adults who learn the principles necessary to solve the Towers of Hanoi problem show great difficulty transferring to the same problem couched in the form of a tea ceremony or a "monster" problem (Hayes & Simon, 1977; Simon & Hayes, 1976). As another, adults who appear to demonstrate good command of conditional reasoning principles in a domain with which they are familiar show such poor performance on identical problems in a relatively unfamiliar domain that mastery of the general principles may be considered to be illusory. For example, college students can solve conditional reasoning problems fairly well when they are expressed in the form of working in a department store and checking charge slips for the presence of a supervisor's signature. The problem is solved in part on the basis of knowledge about the factors that are apt to be important in this situation in the real world (a $1,000 charge may be financially risky). But when the structurally identical problem is couched in the form of working in a label factory and checking slips of paper for the presence of arbitrary letters or numbers, performance drops dramatically (Johnson-Laird & Wason, 1977; J. M. Mandler, in press-b; Wason, 1968). Only abstract knowledge of conditional reasoning will carry the day in this unfamiliar situation, and relatively few college students manage the task successfully.

To the extent that décalages are many and extend over wide age ranges, the safety valve of a stage theory appears to be more of an open tap. Stage theory has particular trouble in this regard with the notion of an exclusive stage of adult thought. Many developmental studies find competence at formal operational tasks at an early age and less than formal competence in adults. Conditional reasoning begins to appear in the elementary school years or earlier (Falmagne, 1980; Greenberg, Marvin, & Mossler, 1977; Kuhn, 1977) but remains incomplete and imperfectly used even in adulthood. Elementary school children look much like adults in isolating variables, and both depend primarily on pragmatic strategies geared to their daily problem-solving activities (Capon & Kuhn, 1979; Tschirgi, 1980). Truly abstract thought is a rarity and, if it appears in the adult at all, it seems to be dependent on specialized training (Pitt, 1976; Scribner, 1979). Typically people think and solve problems in the context of familiar routines and on the basis of the knowledge they have accumulated in those domains.

These considerations have led a number of investigators to reject the notion of general stage shifts across development and to substitute domain-specific models of knowledge acquisition instead (Feldman, 1980; Fischer, 1980). This change in emphasis from classic stage-theoretic views of development does not mean that universal shifts will never be found. As Brown (1982) has pointed out, there may be characteristics of the child as a universal novice that differ from the adult who is a novice in a particular area. These characteristics have only recently come under study (Bransford, Nitsch, & Franks, 1977; Brown & DeLoache, 1978; Chi & Brown, 1981). Although schooled adults may approach some problems more abstractly, the commonalities between children's and adults' learning of new skills may be greater than has often been assumed. In any case, this view does focus our attention on developmental changes that are linked to specific domains and training rather than to age and, thus, broadens the scope of our field considerably (Feldman, 1980). Most important for purposes of this chapter, focusing on domain-specific knowledge shifts the emphasis in development from broad stage-like changes in underlying modes of representation to questions of how transitions are made within the representation of a given domain, that is, how specific learning takes place (see *Brown, Bransford, Ferrara, & Campione, vol. III, chap. 2*).

One of Piaget's main contributions to our understanding of development was his insistence that the way in which knowledge is acquired remains functionally invariant throughout life. The principles of assimilation and accommodation together with the universal tendency to organize incoming information can be seen in all aspects of learning and development regardless of the age at which it is taking place. Piaget, however, uncoupled these notions from the structures that result from them and suggested that the functional invariants result in qualitatively different knowledge structures at different stages. When we examine particular domains in detail and consider structure at a microlevel, this view is undoubtedly correct. As an example, the knowledge that children have of the workings of a balance scale can be characterized as having different structural characteristics at different ages (Siegler, 1978). Qualitative changes can be discerned in the development of the understanding of number (see *Gelman & Baillargeon, vol. III, chap. 3*), and even the increasingly dendrated trees that Keil (1979) finds in the development of ontological knowledge can be described in terms of structural additions.

Nevertheless, examination of some of the more fundamental aspects of knowledge discussed in this chapter suggests that basic forms of representation are structurally similar throughout development. The schematic organization of our knowledge of objects, scenes, and events seems to be one such basic form and the organization of concepts into hierarchical systems of categories another. The primary changes that take place in these forms of knowledge seem to be differentiation and elaboration rather than fundamental changes in format, a point made by Werner long ago (e.g., Werner, 1957). One must suspect that integration of disparate realms of knowledge increases as well, but the chasms that appear between one domain and another in adult thinking must make us a little wary of just how much integration we can expect to find.

The similarities in representation and basic modes of processing information that have been documented in this chapter suggest that there are strong constraints on development, constraints that guide our representational system into a common mold. We can view such constraints in either of two ways. We can follow the nativist arguments and consider universal structures to be genetic givens (see the debate between Piaget and Chomsky cited in Piattelli-Palmarini, 1980). On this view we are innately prepared to form certain kinds of perceptual units rather than others, to hold only certain kinds of hypotheses about language, to form rigid ontological categories, and so on. Or we can emphasize, as did Piaget, that we are only biologically constrained by certain modes of intellectual functioning. The latter view opens the way, of course, to a theory of major structural change over the course of development—the route that Piaget followed.

However, even a theory that rests primarily on functional rather than structural constraints can be made to produce universal structures. Such a theory might result if we expand Piaget's conception of functional invariants in processing to include the tendency to impose particular *kinds* of spatial, causal, and temporal organization on objects and events. Indeed, it is hard to imagine how assimilation and accommodation could operate to form schemata without the tendency to impose at least ordinal divisions on space and sequence from birth, in addition to the tendency to classify on the basis of similarity. There must also be innate mechanisms that determine the size and kind of chunks into which the world can be divided. The rest may follow naturally. If we combine these rather general constraints on processing with the broader notion of the functional invariants and consider both in relation to a highly structured environment, some structural invariants in representation may become inevitable.

NOTES

1. It is often assumed that the symbol x represents y to the extent that x is similar to y and that the more similar, the more faithful or true the representation. This assumption has been successfully demolished by N. Goodman (1968). Related arguments from a psychologist's point of view can be found in Palmer (1978). It should also be noted that the distinction made here between the two senses of representation is not always accepted. Newell (1980) and Palmer (1978) consider the mind to be a symbol system that stands for the world.

2. Representation as knowledge does not imply anything about veridicality. I may well "know" that an acquaintance is a tyrant without that being the case at all. Nevertheless, it is my knowledge, my representation of that acquaintance. Whether a person's representation of the world is more or less veridical is clearly a matter of great interest, perhaps especially to developmental psychologists. This issue, however, is a knotty philosophical problem that

is beyond the scope of this chapter, and I will not attempt to distinguish between knowledge and belief.

3. Piaget's term schema has been translated variously as scheme and schema. Whichever of the two terms is chosen as the name of the cognitive, operational structures, the other is used to refer to simplified images. In this chapter, we are concerned with the more general, cognitive type of structure, and I use the term schema to designate it to emphasize the similarities between Piaget's conception and that of many cognitive psychologists. Both Piaget's and the current conceptions derive from Kant's notion, but although similar in the main, they do not map perfectly onto each other; the current cognitive usage includes many of the figurative characteristics that Piaget assigned to perception and images. Some of the differences between the two conceptions are examined in the discussion on *Representation of Scenes*.

4. Piaget and Inhelder (1956) make this point as well. Again we can see how different conclusions are reached depending on the stringency of one's criteria for asserting that a child has represented some kind of information. When remembered information conflicts with current perceptual input, should we say that the information has not been represented, not stably represented, or that the child has difficulty in using the representation to maintain active control over behavior?

5. For discussions of the early acquisition of knowledge about the structure of simple movements and actions see *Gibson and Spelke, vol. III, chap. 1*; see also Huttenlocher and Smythe-Burke, in press.

6. A good deal of confusion has arisen from the failure to distinguish between a story grammar and a story schema. A story grammar is a formal description of the structure of a kind of text. A story schema is a representation of story structure, which may or may not be accessible to consciousness. It is formed on the basis of reading or hearing stories with common underlying structures. Which of the regularities found in texts are incorporated into a story schema is an empirical question to which a number of the current story studies are addressed. Confusion has also arisen from the mistaken assumption that the rewrite rules in which story grammars are couched are meant to express psychological processing rules; they are not. It may also be noted that the general principles mentioned in this discussion depend primarily on the concept of a story schema and not on the details of the story grammars that have been proposed.

7. The study of the processing of stories and other narratives is still relatively new, and it would be unwise to assume that they are all processed in the same way. Processing should be characteristically different, depending upon the amount of structural information available to the processor. This is true not only for narratives but also for other kinds of text as well; the more one knows about the subject matter being read, the more one is apt to use previously acquired knowledge in a top-down fashion to interpret new information.

8. It has frequently been suggested that recall should be predictable on the basis of the hierarchical importance of each of the units (e.g., Black & Bower, 1980). In itself, this suggestion is quite reasonable, but it is important not to equate the tree structure that results from the application of rewrite rules with the notion of a hierarchy of importance. This point becomes obvious by considering sentences. The underlying structure of sentences can also be characterized by a tree structure, but that does not predict whether a noun phrase or verb phrase or which of two relative clauses will be considered more important or be better recalled. In the case of stories, the units most likely to be recalled are the beginning (initiating event) and the outcome; the least likely to be recalled are internal states and goals, in spite of the fact that goals are the pivotal notion around which episodes revolve.

9. Rigid does not mean that we cannot categorize in many ways, only that we apply predicates to object terms in a strictly hierarchical way.

10. This use of the term episode should not be confused with the term episodic memory coined by Tulving (1972). I have suggested elsewhere (J. M. Mandler, 1979) that episodic memory in Tulving's sense should be called autobiographical memory to distinguish it from the use of the term to refer to episodes or event sequences in Schank and Abelson's (1977) sense. As Nelson and Brown (1978) have pointed out, lack of specification of the use of these terms has led to rampant confusion in the developmental literature.

REFERENCES

Acredolo, L. P. Developmental changes in the ability to coordinate perspectives of a large-scale space. *Developmental Psychology*, 1977, *13*, 1–8.

Acredolo, L. P. Development of spatial orientation in infancy. *Developmental Psychology*, 1978, *14*, 224–234.

Acredolo, L. P. Laboratory versus home: The effect of environment on the 9-month-old infant's choice of spatial reference system. *Developmental Psychology*, 1979, *15*, 666–667.

Allen, G. L. A developmental perspective on the effects of "subdividing" macrospatial experience. *Journal of Experimental Psychology: Human Learning and Memory*, 1981, *7*, 120–132.

Allen, G. L., Kirasic, K. C., Siegel, A. W., & Herman, J. F. Developmental issues in cognitive mapping: The selection and utilization of environmental landmarks. *Child Development*, 1979, *50*, 1062–1070.

Anderson, J. R. *Language, memory, and thought*. Hillsdale, N.J.: Erlbaum, 1976.

Anderson, J. R. Arguments concerning representations for mental imagery. *Psychological Review*, 1978, *85*, 249–277.

Anderson, J. R., & Bower, G. H. *Human associative memory*. Washington, D.C.: V. H. Winston, 1973.

Anglin, J. M. *Word, object, and conceptual development*. New York: W. W. Norton, 1977.

Anooshian, L., & Carlson, J. A study of mental imagery and conservation within the Piagetian framework. *Human Development*, 1973, *16*, 382–394.

Anooshian, L. J., & Young, D. Developmental changes in cognitive maps of a familiar environment. *Child Development*, 1981, *52*, 341–348.

Applebee, A. N. *The child's concept of story: Ages two to seventeen*. Chicago: University of Chicago Press, 1978.

Appleyard, D. Why buildings are known. *Environment and Behavior*, 1969, *1*, 131–156.

Appleyard, D. Styles and methods of structuring a city. *Environment and Behavior*, 1970, *2*, 100–118.

Ashmead, D. H., & Perlmutter, M. Infant memory in everyday life. Paper presented at the meeting of the American Psychological Association, New York, September 1979.

Ashmead, D. H., & Perlmutter, M. Infant memory in everyday life. In M. Perlmutter (Ed.), *New directions for child development: Children's memory* (Vol. 10). San Francisco: Jossey-Bass, 1980.

Baker, L. Processing temporal relationships in simple stories: Effects of input sequence. *Journal of Verbal Learning and Verbal Behavior*, 1978, *17*, 559–572.

Barclay, J. R., & Reid, M. Semantic integration in children's recall of discourse. *Developmental Psychology*, 1974, *10*, 277–281.

Bartlett, F. C. *Remembering: A study in experimental and social psychology*. Cambridge: At the University Press, 1932.

Bassett, E. M. Production strategies in the child's drawing of the human figure: Toward an argument for a model of syncretic perception. In G. Butterworth (Ed.), *The child's representation of the world*. New York: Plenum, 1977.

Bates, E., Benigni, L., Bretherton, I., Camaioni, L., & Volterra, V. From gesture to the first word: On cognitive and social prerequisites. In M. Lewis & L. Rosenblum (Eds.), *Interaction, conversation and the development of language*. New York: Wiley, 1977.

Bates, E., Benigni, L., Bretherton, I., Camaioni, L., & Volterra, V. Cognition and communication from nine to thirteen months: Correlational findings. In E. Bates (Ed.), *The emergence of symbols: Cognition and communication in infancy*. New York: Academic Press, 1979.

Bates, E., Bretherton, I., Shore, C., & McNew, S. Names, gestures and objects. In K. E. Nelson (Ed.), *Children's language* (Vol. 4). Hillsdale, N.J.: Erlbaum, in press.

Bates, E., Camaioni, L., & Volterra, V. The acquisition of performatives prior to speech. *Merrill-Palmer Quarterly*, 1975, *21*, 205–226.

Baylor, G. W. A treatise on the mind's eye. Unpublished doctoral dissertation, Carnegie-Mellon University, 1971.

Beilin, H., Kagan, J., & Rabinowitz, R. Effects of verbal and perceptual training on water level representation. *Child Development*, 1966, *37*, 317–329.

Berman, P. W., Cunningham, J. G., & Harkulich, J. Construction of the horizontal, vertical, and oblique by young children: Failure to find the "oblique effect." *Child Development*, 1974, *45*, 474–478.

Berman, P. W., & Golab, P. Children's reconstructions of the horizontal, vertical and oblique in the absence of a rectangular frame. *Developmental Psychology*, 1975, *11*, 117.

Bertoncini, J., & Mehler, J. Syllables as units in infant speech perception. *Infant Behavior & Development*, 1981, *4*, 247–260.

Biederman, I. Perceiving real world scenes. *Science*, 1972, *177*, 77–80.

Biederman, I. On the semantics of a glance at a scene. In M. Kubovy & J. R. Pomerantz (Eds.), *Perceptual organization*. Hillsdale, N.J.: Erlbaum, 1981.

Biederman, I., Glass, A. L., & Stacy, E. W., Jr. On the information extracted from a glance at a scene. *Journal of Experimental Psychology*, 1973, *97*, 22–27.

Biederman, I., Rabinowitz, J. C., Glass, A. L., & Stacy, E. W., Jr. Scanning for objects in real world scenes. *Journal of Experimental Psychol-*

ogy, 1974, *103,* 597–600.

Bisanz, G. L. Knowledge of persuasion and story comprehension: Developmental changes in expectations. *Discourse Processes,* in press.

Black, J. B., & Bower, G. H. Story understanding as problem-solving. *Poetics,* 1980, *9,* 223–250.

Black, J. B., & Wilensky, R. An evaluation of story grammars. *Cognitive Science,* 1979, *3,* 213–230.

Blaut, J. M., & Stea, D. Mapping at the age of three. *Journal of Geography,* 1974, *73,* 5–9.

Bloom, L. *One word at a time: The use of single word utterances before syntax.* The Hague: Mouton, 1973.

Bluestein, N., & Acredolo, L. Developmental changes in map-reading skills. *Child Development,* 1979, *50,* 691–697.

Bobrow, D. G., & Norman, D. A. Some principles of memory schemata. In D. G. Bobrow & A. Collins (Eds.), *Representation and understanding: Studies in cognitive science.* New York: Academic Press, 1975.

Boden, M. A. *Artificial intelligence and natural man.* New York: Basic Books, 1977.

Borke, H. Piaget's mountains revisited: Changes in the egocentric landscape. *Developmental Psychology,* 1975, *11,* 240–243.

Bornstein, M. C. Perceptual development: Stability and change in feature perception. In M. H. Bornstein & W. Kessen (Eds.), *Psychological development from infancy: Image to intention.* Hillsdale, N.J.: Erlbaum, 1979.

Bornstein, M. H., Kessen, W., & Weiskopf, S. Color vision and hue categorization in young human infants. *Journal of Experimental Psychology: Human Performance and Perception,* 1976, *2,* 115–129.

Botvin, G. J., & Sutton-Smith, B. The development of complexity in children's fantasy narratives. *Developmental Psychology,* 1977, *13,* 377–388.

Bower, G. H. Experiments on story comprehension and recall. *Discourse Processes,* 1978, *1,* 211–232. (a)

Bower, G. H. Representing knowledge development. In R. S. Siegler (Ed.), *Children's thinking: What develops?* Hillsdale, N.J.: Erlbaum, 1978. (b)

Bower, G. H., Black, J. B., & Turner, T. J. Scripts in memory for text. *Cognitive Psychology,* 1979, *11,* 177–220.

Bransford, J. D., & Johnson, M. K. Contextual prerequisites for understanding: Some investigations of comprehension and recall. *Journal of Verbal Learning and Verbal Behavior,* 1972, *11,* 717–726.

Bransford, J. D., Nitsch, K. E., & Franks, J. J. Schooling and the facilitation of knowing. In R. C. Anderson, R. J. Spiro, & W. E. Montague (Eds.), *Schooling and the acquisition of knowledge.* Hillsdale, N.J.: Erlbaum, 1977.

Bremner, J. G. Egocentric versus allocentric spatial coding in nine-month-old infants: Factors influencing the choice of code. *Developmental Psychology,* 1978, *14,* 346–355. (a)

Bremner, J. G. Spatial errors made by infants: Inadequate spatial cues or evidence of egocentrism? *British Journal of Psychology,* 1978, *69,* 77–84. (b)

Bremner, J. G., & Bryant, P. E. Place versus response as the basis of spatial errors made by young infants. *Journal of Experimental Child Psychology,* 1977, *23,* 162–177.

Brewer, W. F., & Treyens, J. C. Role of schemata in memory for places. *Cognitive Psychology,* 1981, *13,* 207–230.

Brown, A. L. Recognition, reconstruction, and recall of narrative sequences by preoperational children. *Child Development,* 1975, *46,* 156–166.

Brown, A. L. The construction of temporal succession by preoperational children. In A. D. Pick (Ed.), *Minnesota Symposia on Child Psychology* (Vol. 10). Minneapolis: University of Minnesota Press, 1976. (a)

Brown, A. L. Semantic integration in children's reconstruction of narrative sequences. *Cognitive Psychology,* 1976, *8,* 247–262. (b)

Brown, A. L. Development, schooling and the acquisition of knowledge about knowledge. In R. C. Anderson, R. J. Spiro, & W. E. Montague (Eds.), *Schooling and the acquisition of knowledge.* Hillsdale, N.J.: Erlbaum, 1977.

Brown, A. L. Knowing when, where, and how to remember: A problem of metacognition. In R. Glaser (Ed.), *Advances in instructional psychology.* New York: Halsted Press, 1978.

Brown, A. L. Learning and development: The problems of compatibility, access, and induction. *Human Development,* 1982, *25,* 89–115.

Brown, A. L., & Campione, J. Inducing flexible thinking: The problem of access. In M. Friedman, J. D. Das, & N. O'Connor (Eds.), *Intelligence and learning.* New York: Plenum, 1980.

Brown, A. L., & DeLoache, J. S. Skills, plans, and self-regulation. In R. S. Siegler (Ed.), *Children's thinking: What develops?* Hillsdale, N.J.: Erlbaum, 1978.

Brown, A. L., & Murphy, M. D. Reconstruction of arbitrary versus logical sequences by preschool children. *Journal of Experimental Child Psy-*

chology, 1975, *20*, 307–326.

Brown, A. L., & Smiley, S. S. Rating the importance of structural units of prose passages: A problem of metacognitive development. *Child Development*, 1977, *48*, 1–8.

Brown, A. L., Smiley, S. S., Day, J. D., Townsend, M. A. R., & Lawton, S. C. Intrusion of a thematic idea in children's comprehension and retention of stories. *Child Development*, 1977, *48*, 1454–1466.

Brown, A. L., Smiley, S. S., & Lawton, S. Q. C. The effects of experience on the selection of suitable retrieval cues for studying texts. *Child Development*, 1978, *49*, 829–835.

Bruce, B., & Newman, D. Interacting plans. *Cognitive Science*, 1978, *2*, 195–233.

Bruner, J. S., Olver, R. R., & Greenfield, P. M. *Studies in cognitive growth*. New York: Wiley, 1966.

Bryant, P. E. *Perception and understanding in young children*. London: Methuen, 1974.

Bullock, M., & Gelman, R. Preschool children's assumptions about cause and effect: Temporal ordering. *Child Development*, 1979, *50*, 89–96.

Butterworth, G. *The child's representation of the world*. New York: Plenum, 1977 (a).

Butterworth, G. Object disappearance and error in Piaget's stage IV task. *Journal of Experimental Child Psychology*, 1977, *23*, 391–401 (b).

Capon, N., & Kuhn, D. Logical reasoning in the supermarket: Adult females' use of a proportional reasoning strategy in an everyday context. *Developmental Psychology*, 1979, *15*, 450–452.

Carey, S. The child's concept of animal. Paper presented at the meeting of the Psychonomic Society, San Antonio, Texas, November 1978.

Carey, S. The child's concepts of animals and living things. Book in preparation, 1982.

Carey, S., Diamond, R., & Woods, B. Development of face recognition—A maturational component? *Developmental Psychology*, 1980, *16*, 257–269.

Carroll, L. *Alice's adventures in wonderland*. London: Macmillan, 1865.

Case, R. Intellectual development from birth to adulthood: A neo-Piagetian interpretation. In R. S. Siegler (Ed.), *Children's thinking: What develops?* Hillsdale, N.J.: Erlbaum, 1978.

Ceci, S. J., Lea, S. E. G., & Howe, M. J. A. Structural analysis of memory traces in children from 4 to 10 years of age. *Developmental Psychology*, 1980, *16*, 203–212.

Chase, W. G., & Clark, H. H. Mental operations in the comparison of sentences and pictures. In L. W. Gregg (Ed.), *Cognition in learning and memory*. New York: Wiley, 1972.

Chi, M. T. H. Knowledge structures and memory development. In R. S. Siegler (Ed.), *Children's thinking: What develops?* Hillsdale, N.J.: Erlbaum, 1978.

Chi, M. T. H. Interactive roles of knowledge and strategies in development. In S. Chipman, J. Segal, & R. Glaser (Eds.), *Thinking and learning skills: Current research and open questions*. Hillsdale, N.J.: Erlbaum, in press.

Chi, M. T. H., & Brown, A. L. The development of knowledge and expertise. Paper presented at the meeting of the Society for Research in Child Development, Boston, April 1981.

Childs, M. K., & Polich, J. M. Developmental differences in mental rotation. *Journal of Experimental Child Psychology*, 1979, *27*, 339–351.

Cirilo, R. K., & Foss, D. J. Text structure and reading time for sentences. *Journal of Verbal Learning and Verbal Behavior*, 1980, *19*, 96–109.

Clark, E. V. Awareness of language: Some evidence from what children say and do. In A. Sinclair, R. J. Jarvella, & W. J. M. Levelt (Eds.), *The child's conception of language*. New York: Springer-Verlag, 1978.

Clark, H. H., & Clark, E. V. *Psychology and language: An introduction to psycholinguistics*. New York: Harcourt Brace Jovanovich, 1977.

Cohen, R., Baldwin, L. M., & Sherman, R. C. Cognitive maps of a naturalistic setting. *Child Development*, 1978, *49*, 1216–1218.

Cohen, R., & Schuepfer, T. The representation of landmarks and routes. *Child Development*, 1980, *51*, 1065–1071.

Cohen, R., & Weatherford, D. L. Effects of route traveled on the distance estimates of children and adults. *Journal of Experimental Child Psychology*, 1980, *29*, 403–412.

Colby, B. N. A partial grammar of Eskimo folktales. *American Anthropologist*, 1973, *75*, 645–662.

Cole, M., & Scribner, S. Cross-cultural studies of memory and cognition. In R. V. Kail, Jr., & J. W. Hagen (Eds.), *Perspectives on the development of memory and cognition*. Hillsdale, N.J.: Erlbaum, 1977.

Collins, A. M., & Loftus, E. F. A spreading-activation theory of semantic processing. *Psychological Review*, 1975, *82*, 407–428.

Collins, A. M., & Quillian, M. R. Retrieval time from semantic memory. *Journal of Verbal*

Learning and Verbal Behavior, 1969, *8,* 240–247.

Cooper, L. A., & Shepard, R. N. Chronometric studies of the rotation of mental images. In W. G. Chase (Ed.), *Visual information processing.* New York: Academic Press, 1973.

Cooper, L. A., & Shepard, R. N. Transformations on representations of objects in space. In E. C. Carterette & M. P. Friedman (Eds.), *Handbook of perception,* vol. 8, *Perceptual coding.* New York: Academic Press, 1978.

Cornell, E. H., & Heth, C. D. Response versus place learning by human infants. *Journal of Experimental Psychology: Human Learning and Memory,* 1979, *5,* 188–196.

Curtis, L. E., Siegel, A. W., & Furlong, N. E. Developmental differences in cognitive mapping: Configurational knowledge of familiar large-scale environments. *Journal of Experimental Child Psychology,* 1981, *31,* 456–469.

Daehler, M. W., Lonardo, R., & Bukatko, D. Matching and equivalence judgments in very young children. *Child Development,* 1979, *50,* 170–179.

Day, J. D. Veridical and inferential memory for the spatial layout of a small house. Unpublished master's thesis, University of Illinois, 1977.

De Lisi, R., Locker, R., & Youniss, J. Anticipatory imagery and spatial operations. *Developmental Psychology,* 1976, *12,* 298–310.

Denney, D. R., & Moulton, P. A. Conceptual preferences among preschool children. *Developmental Psychology,* 1976, *12,* 509–513.

Deregowski, J. B. Pictures, symbols and frames of reference. In G. Butterworth (Ed.), *The child's representation of the world.* New York: Plenum, 1977.

van Dijk, T. A. Philosophy of action and theory of narrative. *Poetics,* 1976, *5,* 287–338.

Dirks, J., & Neisser, U. Memory for objects in real scenes: The development of recognition and recall. *Journal of Experimental Child Psychology,* 1977, *23,* 315–328.

Downs, R. M., & Stea, D. (Eds.), *Image and environment: Cognitive mapping and spatial behavior.* Chicago: Aldine, 1973.

Eimas, P. D., Siqueland, E. R., Jusczyk, P., & Vigorito, J. Speech perception in infants. *Science,* 1971, *171,* 303–306.

Esrov, L. V., Hall, J. W., & LaFaver, D. K. Preschoolers' conceptual and acoustic encodings as evidenced by release from PI. *Bulletin of the Psychonomic Society,* 1974, *4,* 89–90.

Fagan, J. F., III, & Shepherd, P. A. Infants' perception of face orientation. *Infant Behavior & Development,* 1979, *2,* 227–234.

Fagan, J. F., III, & Singer, L. T. The role of simple feature differences in infants' recognition of faces. *Infant Behavior & Development,* 1979, *2,* 39–45.

Fajnsztejn-Pollack, G. A developmental study of decay rate in long-term memory. *Journal of Experimental Child Psychology,* 1973, *16,* 225–235.

Falmagne, R. J. The development of logical competence: A psycholinguistic perspective. In R. H. Kluwe & H. Spada (Eds.), *Developmental models of thinking.* New York: Academic Press, 1980.

Fantz, R. L., & Miranda, S. B. Newborn infant attention to form of contour. *Child Development,* 1975, *46,* 224–228.

Faulkender, P. J., Wright, J. C., & Waldron, A. Generalized habituation of concept stimuli in toddlers. *Child Development,* 1974, *45,* 1002–1010.

Feldman, D. H. *Beyond universals in cognitive development.* Norwood, N.J.: Ablex, 1980.

Finke, R. A., & Kosslyn, S. M. Mental imagery acuity in the peripheral visual field. *Journal of Experimental Psychology: Human Perception and Performance,* 1980, *6,* 1126–1139.

Fischer, K. W. A theory of cognitive development: Control and construction of hierarchies of skills. *Psychological Review,* 1980, *87,* 477–531.

Fishbein, H. D., Lewis, S., & Keiffer, K. Children's understanding of spatial relations. *Developmental Psychology,* 1972, *7,* 21–33.

Fisher, C. B. Children's memory for orientation in the absence of external cues. *Child Development,* 1979, *50,* 1088–1092.

Flavell, J. H. *The developmental psychology of Jean Piaget.* Princeton, N.J.: Van Nostrand, 1963.

Flavell, J. H. Developmental studies in mediated memory. In H. W. Reese & L. P. Lipsitt (Eds.), *Advances in child development and behavior* (Vol. 5). New York: Academic Press, 1970.

Flavell, J. H. Metacognitive development. In J. M. Scandura & C. J. Brainerd (Eds.), *Structural-process theories of complex human behavior.* Leyden, the Netherlands: Sijthoff, 1978.

Flavell, J. H. Metacognition and cognitive monitoring: A new area of cognitive-developmental inquiry. *American Psychologist,* 1979, *34,* 906–911.

Flavell, J. H. Cognitive monitoring. In W. P. Dickson (Ed.), *Children's oral communication skills*. New York: Academic Press, 1981.

Flavell, J. H., Everett, B. A., Croft, K., & Flavell, E. R. Young children's knowledge about visual perception: Further evidence for the Level 1–Level 2 distinction. *Developmental Psychology*, 1981, *17*, 99–103.

Flavell, J. H., Flavell, E. R., Green, F. L., & Wilcox, S. A. The development of three spatial perspective-taking rules. *Child Development*, 1981, *52*, 356–358.

Flavell, J. H., Omanson, R. C., & Latham, C. Solving spatial perspective-taking problems by rule versus computation: A developmental study. *Developmental Psychology*, 1978, *14*, 462–473.

Flavell, J. H., Shipstead, S. G., & Croft, K. What young children think you see when your eyes are closed. Unpublished manuscript, Stanford University, 1979.

Fodor, J. A. Some reflections on L. S. Vygotsky's *Thought and Language*. *Cognition*, 1972, *1*, 83–95.

Fodor, J. A. *The language of thought*. New York: Crowell, 1975.

Fraisse, P. *The psychology of time*. New York: Harper & Row, 1963.

Freeman, N. Discussion of the papers by Norman Freeman and Lorna Self. In G. Butterworth (Ed.), *The child's representation of the world*. New York: Plenum, 1977.

Freeman, N. H. *Strategies of representation in young children: Analysis of spatial skills and drawing processes*. London: Academic Press, 1980.

Freeman, N. H., Lloyd, S., & Sinha, C. G. Infant search tasks reveal early concepts of containment and canonical usage of objects. *Cognition*, 1980, *8*, 243–262.

French, L., & Nelson, K. Taking away the supportive context: How preschoolers talk about the "then-and-there." Paper presented at the Sixth Annual Boston University Conference on Language Development, Boston, 1981.

Friedman, A. Framing pictures: The role of knowledge in automatized encoding and memory for gist. *Journal of Experimental Psychology: General*, 1979, *108*, 316–355.

Gaines, R., Mandler, J. M., & Bryant, P. Immediate and delayed story recall by hearing and deaf children. *Journal of Speech and Hearing Research*, 1981, *24*, 463–469.

Gallistel, C. R. *The organization of action: A new synthesis*. Hillsdale, N.J.: Erlbaum, 1980.

Gardner, H. Developmental psychology after Piaget: An approach in terms of symbolization. *Human Development*, 1979, *22*, 73–88.

Garner, W. R. *Uncertainty and structure as psychological concepts*. New York: Wiley, 1962.

Gelman, R. Cognitive development. *Annual Review of Psychology*, 1978, *29*, 297–332.

Gelman, R., Bullock, M., & Meck, E. Preschoolers' understanding of simple object transformations. *Child Development*, 1980, *51*, 691–699.

Gelman, R., & Gallistel, C. R. *The child's understanding of number*. Cambridge, Mass.: Harvard University Press, 1978.

Gelman, R., & Spelke, E. S. The development of thoughts about animates and inanimates: Implications for research on social cognition. In J. H. Flavell & L. Ross (Eds.), *Social cognitive development: Frontiers and possible futures*. New York: Cambridge University Press, 1981.

Gentner, D. What looks like a jiggy but acts like a zimbo? *Papers and Reports on Child Language Development*, 1978, *15*, 1–6.

Gerard, A. B., & Mandler, J. M. Sentence anomaly and ontological knowledge. *Journal of Verbal Learning and Verbal Behavior*, in press.

Gips, J. A syntax-directed program that performs a three-dimensional perceptual task. *Pattern Recognition*, 1974, *6*, 189–199.

Gleitman, L. R., & Gleitman, H. *Phrase and paraphrase: Some innovative uses of language*. New York: W. W. Norton, 1970.

Gleitman, L. R., & Rozin, P. The structure and acquisition of reading I: Relations between orthographies and the structure of language. In A. S. Reber & D. L. Scarborough (Eds.), *Toward a psychology of reading*. Hillsdale, N.J.: Erlbaum, 1977.

Glenn, C. G. The role of episodic structure and of story length in children's recall of simple stories. *Journal of Veral Learning and Verbal Behavior*, 1978, *17*, 229–247.

Goldberg, S., Perlmutter, M., & Myers, N. Recall of related and unrelated lists by 2-year-olds. *Journal of Experimental Child Psychology*, 1974, *18*, 1–8.

Goldman, S. R. Knowledge systems for realistic goals. *Discourse Processes*, in press.

Goodman, G. S. Picture memory: How the action schema affects retention. *Cognitive Psychology*, 1980, *12*, 473–495.

Goodman, N. *Languages of art*. Indianapolis: Bobbs-Merrill, 1968.

Goodnow, J. *Children's drawing*. Cambridge, Mass.: Harvard University Press, 1977.

Goodnow, J. J., & Levine, R. A. "The grammar of action": Sequence and syntax in children's copying. *Cognitive Psychology*, 1973, *4*, 82–98.

Graesser, A. C. *Prose comprehension beyond the word*. New York: Springer-Verlag, 1981.

Graesser, A. C., Gordon, S. E., & Sawyer, J. D. Recognition memory for typical and atypical actions in scripted activities: Tests of a script pointer + tag hypothesis. *Journal of Verbal Learning and Verbal Behavior*, 1979, *18*, 319–332.

Graesser, A. C., Woll, S. B., Kowalski, D. J., & Smith, D. A. Memory for typical and atypical actions in scripted activities. *Journal of Experimental Psychology: Human Learning and Memory*, 1980, *6*, 503–515.

Graybeal, C. M. Memory for stories in language-impaired children. *Applied Psycholinguistics*, 1981, *2*, 269–283.

Greenberg, M. T., Marvin, R. S., & Mossler, D. G. The development of conditional reasoning skills. *Developmental Psychology*, 1977, *13*, 527–528.

Greenfield, P. M., & Smith, J. H. *The structure of communication in early language development*. New York: Academic Press, 1976.

Gruendel, J. Scripts and stories: A study of children's event narratives. Unpublished doctoral dissertation, Yale University, 1980.

Haberlandt, K. Story grammar and reading time of story constituents. *Poetics*, 1980, *9*, 99–118.

Haberlandt, K., Berian, C., & Sandson, J. The episode schema in story processing. *Journal of Verbal Learning and Verbal Behavior*, 1980, *19*, 635–650.

Hagen, J. W. Attention and mediation in children's memory. In W. W. Hartup (Ed.), *The young child: Reviews of research* (Vol. 2). Washington, D.C.: National Association for Education of Young Children, 1972.

Hall, J. W., & Halperin, M. C. The development of memory-encoding processes in young children. *Developmental Psychology*, 1972, *6*, 181.

Halliday, M. A. K., & Hassan, R. *Cohesion in English*. London: Longman, 1976.

Hardwick, D. A., McIntyre, C. W., & Pick, H. L., Jr. The content and manipulation of cognitive maps in children and adults. *Monographs of the Society for Research in Child Development*, 1976, *41*(Serial No. 166).

Harris, P. L. Inferences and semantic development. *Journal of Child Language*, 1975, *2*, 143–152.

Harris, P. L. Subject, object and framework: A theory of spatial development. Unpublished manuscript, University of Lancaster, England, 1977.

Harris, P. L., & Bassett, E. Reconstruction from the mental image. *Journal of Experimental Child Psychology*, 1976, *21*, 514–523.

Harris, P. L., Kruithof, A., Terwogt, M. M., & Visser, T. Children's detection and awareness of textual anomaly. *Journal of Experimental Child Psychology*, 1981, *31*, 212–230.

Hayes, J. Children's visual descriptions. *Cognitive Science*, 1978, *2*, 1–15.

Hayes, J. R., & Simon, H. A. Psychological differences among problem isomorphs. In N. J. Castellan, Jr., D. B. Pisoni, & G. R. Potts (Eds.), *Cognitive theory* (Vol. 2). Hillsdale, N.J.: Erlbaum, 1977.

Hayes-Roth, F. Distinguishing theories of representation: A critique of Anderson's "Arguments concerning mental imagery." *Psychological Review*, 1979, *86*, 376–382.

Hazen, N. L., Lockman, J. J., & Pick, H. L., Jr. The development of children's representations of large-scale environments. *Child Development*, 1978, *49*, 623–636.

Head, H. *Aphasia and kindred disorders of speech*. Cambridge: At the University Press, 1926.

Hebb, D. O. *Organization of behavior*. New York: Wiley, 1949.

Hebb, D. O. Concerning imagery. *Psychological Review*, 1968, *75*, 466–477.

Heidenheimer, P. A comparison of the roles of exemplar, action, coordinate, and superordinate relations in the semantic processing of 4- and 5-year-old children. *Journal of Experimental Child Psychology*, 1978, *25*, 143–159.

Hein, A. Acquiring components of visually guided behavior. In A. D. Pick (Ed.), *Minnesota Symposia on Child Psychology* (Vol. 6). Minneapolis: University of Minnesota Press, 1972.

Herman, J. F. Cognitive maps of large-scale spaces: Effects of exploration, direction, and repeated experience. *Journal of Experimental Child Psychology*, 1980, *29*, 126–143.

Herman, J. F., & Siegel, A. W. The development of cognitive mapping of the large-scale environment. *Journal of Experimental Child Psychology*, 1978, *26*, 398–406.

Hildyard, A., & Olson, D. R. Memory and inference in the comprehension of oral and written discourse. *Discourse Processes*, 1978, *1*, 91–118.

Hirsh-Pasek, K., Gleitman, L. R., & Gleitman, H. What did the brain say to the mind? A study of the detection and report of ambiguity by young children. In A. Sinclair, R. J. Jarvella, & W. J. M. Levelt (Eds.), *The child's conception of language*. New York: Springer-Verlag, 1978.

Hochberg, J. Organization and the Gestalt tradition. In E. C. Carterette & M. P. Friedman (Eds.), *Handbook of Perception*, vol. 1, *Historical and philosophical roots of perception*. New York: Academic Press, 1974.

Hock, H. S., Romanski, L., Galie, A., & Williams, G. S. Real-world schemata and scene recognition in adults and children. *Memory & Cognition*, 1978, *6*, 423–431.

Hoemann, H. W., DeRosa, D. V., & Andrews, C. E. Categorical encoding in short-term memory by 4- to 11-year-old children. *Bulletin of the Psychonomic Society*, 1974, *3*, 63–65.

Hunt, E. A. Quote the Raven? Nevermore! In L. W. Gregg (Ed.), *Knowledge and cognition*. Potomac, Md.: Erlbaum, 1974.

Hunt, E. A., Frost, N., & Lunneborg, C. Individual approaches to cognition: A new approach to intelligence. In G. H. Bower (Ed.), *The psychology of learning and motivation* (Vol. 7). New York: Academic Press, 1973.

Husaim, J. S., & Cohen, L. B. Infant learning of ill-defined categories. Paper presented at the International Conference on Infant Studies, New Haven, Conn., April 1980.

Hutchins, E. Understanding Micronesian navigation. In D. Gentner & A. Stevens (Eds.), *Mental models*. Hillsdale, N.J.: Erlbaum, in press.

Huttenlocher, J. The origins of language comprehension. In R. L. Solso (Ed.), *Theories in cognitive psychology: The Loyola symposium*. Hillsdale, N.J.: Erlbaum, 1974.

Huttenlocher, J., & Higgins, E. T. Issues in the study of symbolic development. In W. A. Collins (Ed.), *Minnesota Symposia on Child Psychology* (Vol. 11). Hillsdale, N.J.: Erlbaum, 1978.

Huttenlocher, J., & Lui, F. The semantic organization of some simple nouns and verbs. *Journal of Verbal Learning and Verbal Behavior*, 1979, *18*, 141–162.

Huttenlocher, J., & Newcombe, N. Semantic effects on ordered recall. *Journal of Verbal Learning and Verbal Behavior*, 1976, *15*, 387–399.

Huttenlocher, J., & Presson, C. C. Mental rotation and the perspective problem. *Cognitive Psychology*, 1973, *4*, 277–299.

Huttenlocher, J., & Presson, C. C. The coding and transformation of spatial information. *Cognitive Psychology*, 1979, *11*, 375–394.

Huttenlocher, J., & Smythe-Burke, T. Event encoding in infancy. In P. Salapatek & L. Cohen (Eds.), *Handbook of infant perception*. New York: Academic Press, in press.

Inhelder, B., & Piaget, J. *The early growth of logic in the child*. London: Routledge & Kegan Paul, 1964.

Ittelson, W. H. Environment perception and contemporary perceptual theory. In W. H. Ittelson (Ed.), *Environment and cognition*, New York: Academic Press, 1973. (Seminar Press)

Jackson, J. P. The relationship between the development of gestural imagery and the development of graphic imagery. *Child Development*, 1974, *45*, 432–438.

James, W. *The principles of psychology*. New York: Holt, 1890.

Johnson, C. N., & Wellman, H. M. Children's conception of the brain: A developmental study of knowledge about cognitive processes. Unpublished manuscript, Michigan University, 1979.

Johnson, N. S. What do you do if you can't tell the whole story? The development of summarization skills. In K. E. Nelson (Ed.), *Children's language* (Vol. 4). Hillsdale, N.J.: Erlbaum, in press.

Johnson, N. S., & Gandel, R. G. Effects of story organization on preschool children's recall. Article in preparation, 1982.

Johnson, N. S., & Mandler, J. M. A tale of two structures: Underlying and surface forms in stories. *Poetics*, 1980, *9*, 51–86.

Johnson, R. E. Recall of prose as a function of the structural importance of the linguistic units. *Journal of Verbal Learning and Verbal Behavior*, 1970, *9*, 12–20.

Johnson-Laird, P. N., & Wason, P. C. A theoretical analysis of insight into a reasoning task. In P. N. Johnson-Laird & P. C. Wason (Eds.), *Thinking: Readings in cognitive science*. Cambridge: At the University Press, 1977.

Jones, M. R. Cognitive representations of serial patterns. In B. H. Kantowitz (Ed.), *Human information processing: Tutorials in performance and cognition*. Hillsdale, N.J.: Erlbaum, 1974.

Jusczyk, P. W., Rosner, B. S., Cutting, J. E., Foard, C. F., & Smith, L. B. Categorical perception of nonspeech sounds by 2-month-old infants. *Perception & Psychophysics*, 1977, *21*, 50–54.

Kail, R. V., Jr., Chi, M. T. H., Ingram, A. L., & Danner, F. W. Constructive aspects of children's reading comprehension. *Child Development*,

1977, *48*, 684–688.

Kail, R., Pellegrino, J., & Carter, P. Developmental changes in mental rotation. *Journal of Experimental Child Psychology*, 1980, *29*, 102–116.

Kapadia, R. A critical examination of Piaget-Inhelder's view on topology. *Educational Studies in Mathematics*, 1974, *5*, 419–424.

Kareev, Y. A priming study of developmental changes in the associative strength of class relations. Unpublished manuscript, Hebrew University of Jerusalem, 1980.

Kareev, Y. Developmental differences in memory for temporally neutral and temporally tagged information. *Journal of Experimental Child Psychology*, 1981, *31*, 310–320.

Karmiloff-Smith, A. Micro- and macro-developmental changes in language acquisition and other representational systems. *Cognitive Science*, 1979, *3*, 91–118.

Keating, D. P. Thinking processes in adolescence. In J. Adelson (Ed.), *Handbook of adolescent psychology*. New York: Wiley, 1979.

Keil, F. C. *Semantic and conceptual development: An ontological perspective*. Cambridge, Mass.: Harvard University Press, 1979.

Keil, F. C. Constraints on knowledge and cognitive development. *Psychological Review*, 1981, *88*, 197–227. (a)

Keil, F. C. On the emergence of semantic and conceptual distinctions. Unpublished manuscript, Cornell University, 1981. (b)

Kemler, D. G. Wholistic and analytic modes in perceptual and cognitive development. In T. Tighe & B. E. Shepp (Eds.), *Interactions: Perception, cognition, and development*. Hillsdale, N.J.: Erlbaum, in press.

Kessen, W., & Nelson, K. What the child brings to language. In B. Z. Presseisen, D. Goldstein, & M. H. Appel (Eds.), *Topics in cognitive development*, vol. 2, *Language and operational thought*. New York: Plenum, 1978.

Kintsch, W. *The representation of meaning in memory*. Hillsdale, N.J.: Erlbaum, 1974.

Kintsch, W. *Memory and cognition*. New York: Wiley, 1977. (a)

Kintsch, W. On comprehending stories. In M. A. Just & P. A. Carpenter (Eds.), *Cognitive processes in comprehension*. Hillsdale, N.J.: Erlbaum, 1977. (b).

Kintsch, W., & van Dijk, T. A. Comment on se rapelle et on résume des histoires. *Langages*, 1975, *40*, 98–116.

Kintsch, W., & van Dijk, T. A. Toward a model of text comprehension and production. *Psychological Review*, 1978, *85*, 363–394.

Kintsch, W., & Greene, E. The role of culture-specific schemata in the comprehension and recall of stories. *Discourse Processes*, 1978, *1*, 1–13.

Kirasic, K. C., Siegel, A. W., & Allen, G. L. Developmental changes in recognition-in-context memory. *Child Development*, 1980, *51*, 302–305.

Klahr, D., & Chase, W. G. Developmental changes in latency patterns for access to the alphabet. Paper presented at the meeting of the Psychonomic Society, San Antonio, Texas, November 1978.

Klahr, D., & Siegler, R. S. The representation of children's knowledge. In H. W. Reese & L. P. Lipsitt (Eds.), *Advances in child development and behavior*. New York: Academic Press, 1978.

Kleinman, J. M. Developmental changes in haptic exploration and matching accuracy. *Developmental Psychology*, 1979, *15*, 480–481.

Kohlberg, L., Yeager, J., & Hjertholm, E. Private speech: Four studies and a review of theories. *Child Development*, 1968, *39*, 691–736.

Kosslyn, S. M. Information representation in visual images. *Cognitive Psychology*, 1975, *7*, 341–370.

Kosslyn, S. M. Can imagery be distinguished from other forms of internal representation? Evidence from studies of information retrieval times. *Memory & Cognition*, 1976, *3*, 291–297. (a)

Kosslyn, S. M. Using imagery to retrieve semantic information: A developmental study. *Child Development*, 1976, *47*, 434–445. (b)

Kosslyn, S. M. Imagery and internal representation. In E. Rosch & B. B. Lloyd (Eds.), *Cognition and categorization*. Hillsdale, N.J.: Erlbaum, 1978. (a)

Kosslyn, S. M. Measuring the visual angle of the mind's eye. *Cognitive Psychology*, 1978, *10*, 356–389. (b)

Kosslyn, S. M. The representational-development hypothesis. In P. A. Ornstein (Ed.), *Memory development in children*. Hillsdale, N.J.: Erlbaum, 1978. (c)

Kosslyn, S. M. *Image and mind*. Cambridge, Mass.: Harvard University Press, 1980.

Kosslyn, S. M. The medium and the message in mental imagery. *Psychological Review*, 1981, *88*, 46–66.

Kosslyn, S. M., Ball, T. M., & Reiser, B. J. Visual images preserve metric spatial information: Evidence from studies of information retrieval time. *Journal of Experimental Psychology: Human*

Perception and Performance, 1978, *4*, 47–60.

Kosslyn, S. M., Heldmeyer, K. H., & Locklear, E. P. Children's drawings as data about internal representations. *Journal of Experimental Child Psychology*, 1977, *23*, 191–211.

Kosslyn, S. M., Pick, H. L., Jr., & Fariello, G. R. Cognitive maps in children and men. *Child Development*, 1974, *45*, 707–716.

Kosslyn, S. M., & Pomerantz, J. R. Imagery, propositions, and the form of internal representations. *Cognitive Psychology*, 1977, *9*, 52–76.

Kosslyn, S. M., & Shwartz, S. P. A simulation of visual imagery. *Cognitive Science*, 1977, *1*, 265–295.

Kosslyn, S. M., & Shwartz, S. P. Visual images as spatial representations in active memory. In E. M. Riseman & A. R. Hanson (Eds.), *Computer vision systems*. New York: Academic Press, 1978.

Kuhn, D. Conditional reasoning in children. *Developmental Psychology*, 1977, *13*, 342–353.

Kuipers, B. J. Representing knowledge of large-scale space (Memo 359). Cambridge, Mass.: MIT Artificial Intelligence Laboratory, 1977.

Landau, B., Gleitman, H., & Spelke, E. Geometric representation in a child blind from birth. *Science*, 1981, *213*, 1275–1278.

Lange, G. Organization-related processes in children's recall. In P. A. Ornstein (Ed.), *Memory development in children*. Hillsdale, N.J.: Erlbaum, 1978.

Lashley, K. S. The problem of serial order in behavior. In L. A. Jeffress (Ed.), *Cerebral mechanisms in behavior*. New York: Wiley, 1951.

Laurendeau, M., & Pinard, A. *Causal thinking in the child: A genetic and experimental approach*. New York: International Universities Press, 1962.

Laurendeau, M., & Pinard, A. *The development of the concept of space in the child*. New York: International Universities Press, 1970.

Lawson, K. R. Spatial and temporal congruity and auditory-visual integration in infants. *Developmental Psychology*, 1980, *16*, 185–192.

LeCompte, G. K., & Gratch, G. Violation of a rule as a method of diagnosing infants' levels of object concept. *Child Development*, 1972, *43*, 385–396.

Levelt, W. J. M. *Formal grammars in linguistics and psycholinguistics*, vol. 3, *Psycholinguistic applications*. The Hague: Mouton, 1974.

Levin, J. R., McCabe, A. E., & Bender, B. G. A note on imagery-inducing motor activity in young children. *Child Development*, 1975, *46*, 263–266.

Liben, L. S., & Golbeck, S. L. Sex differences in performance on Piagetian spatial tasks: Differences in competence or performance? *Child Development*, 1980, *51*, 594–597.

Lichtenstein, E. H., & Brewer, W. F. Memory for goal-directed events. *Cognitive Psychology*, 1980, *12*, 412–445.

Lipton, C., & Overton, W. F. Anticipatory imagery and modified anagram solutions: A developmental study. *Child Development*, 1971, *42*, 615–623.

Loftus, G. E., & Mackworth, N. H. Cognitive determinants of fixation location during picture viewing. *Journal of Experimental Psychology: Human Performance and Perception*, 1978, *4*, 565–572.

Lovell, K. A follow-up study of some aspects of the work of Piaget and Inhelder on the child's conception of space. *British Journal of Educational Psychology*, 1959, *29*, 104–117.

Lynch, K. *The image of the city*. Cambridge, Mass.: MIT Press, 1960.

Maccoby, E. E. What copying requires. *Ontario Journal of Educational Research*, 1968, *10*, 163–170.

Mackworth, N. H., & Bruner, J. S. How adults and children search and recognize pictures. *Human Development*, 1970, *13*, 149–177.

Macnamara, J. Cognitive basis of language learning in infants. *Psychological Review*, 1972, *79*, 1–13.

Mandler, G. Organization and memory. In K. W. Spence & J. T. Spence (Eds.), *The psychology of learning and motivation* (Vol. 1). New York: Academic Press, 1967.

Mandler, G. *Mind and emotion*. New York: Wiley, 1975.

Mandler, G. The construction and limitation of consciousness. In V. Sarris & A. Parducci (Eds.), *Perspectives in psychological experimentation: Toward the year 2000*. Hillsdale, N.J.: Erlbaum, in press.

Mandler, G., & Kuhlman, C. K. Proactive and retroactive effects of overlearning. *Journal of Experimental Psychology*, 1961, *61*, 76–81.

Mandler, J. M. A code in the node: The use of a story schema in retrieval. *Discourse Processes*, 1978, *1*, 14–35.

Mandler, J. M. Categorical and schematic organization in memory. In C. R. Puff (Ed.), *Memory organization and structure*. New York: Academic Press, 1979.

Mandler, J. M. An analysis of story grammars. In F. Klix, J. Hoffman, & E. van der Meer (Eds.), *Cognitive research in psychology*. Amsterdam, the Netherlands: North-Holland, 1982.

Mandler, J. M. Some uses and abuses of a story grammar. *Discourse Processes,* in press. (a)

Mandler, J. M. Structural invariants in development. In L. Liben (Ed.), *Piaget and the foundations of knowledge.* Hillsdale, N.J.: Erlbaum, in press. (b)

Mandler, J. M., & Day, J. Memory for orientation of forms as a function of their meaningfulness and complexity. *Journal of Experimental Child Psychology,* 1975, *20,* 430–443.

Mandler, J. M., & DeForest, M. Is there more than one way to recall a story? *Child Development,* 1979, *50,* 886–889.

Mandler, J. M., & Goodman, M. S. On the psychological validity of story structure. *Journal of Verbal Learning and Verbal Behavior,* 1982, *21,* in press.

Mandler, J. M., & Johnson, N. S. Some of the thousand words a picture is worth. *Journal of Experimental Psychology: Human Learning and Memory,* 1976, *2,* 529–540.

Mandler, J. M., & Johnson, N. S. Remembrance of things parsed: Story structure and recall. *Cognitive Psychology,* 1977, *9,* 111–151.

Mandler, J. M., & Johnson, N. S. On throwing out the baby with the bathwater: A reply to Black and Wilensky's evaluation of story grammars. *Cognitive Science,* 1980, *4,* 305–312.

Mandler, J. M., & Mandler, G. *Thinking: From association to Gestalt.* New York: Wiley, 1964.

Mandler, J. M., & Murphy, C. M. Subjective judgments of script structure. Article submitted for publication, 1982.

Mandler, J. M., & Parker, R. E. Memory for descriptive and spatial information in complex pictures. *Journal of Experimental Psychology: Human Learning and Memory,* 1976, *2,* 38–48.

Mandler, J. M., & Ritchey, G. H. Long-term memory for pictures. *Journal of Experimental Psychology: Human Learning and Memory,* 1977, *3,* 386–396.

Mandler, J. M., & Robinson, C. A. Developmental changes in picture recognition. *Journal of Experimental Child Psychology,* 1978, *26,* 122–136.

Mandler, J. M., Scribner, S., Cole, M., & DeForest, M. Cross-cultural invariance in story recall. *Child Development,* 1980, *51,* 19–26.

Mandler, J. M., Seegmiller, D., & Day, J. On the coding of spatial information. *Memory & Cognition,* 1977, *5,* 10–16.

Mandler, J. M., & Stein, N. L. Recall and recognition of pictures by children as a function of organization and distractor similarity. *Journal of Experimental Psychology,* 1974, *102,* 657–669.

Mandler, J. M., & Stein, N. L. Encoding and retrieval of orientation: A new slant on an old problem. *Bulletin of the Psychonomic Society,* 1977, *10,* 9–12.

Mansfield, A. F. Semantic organization in the young child: Evidence for the development of semantic feature systems. *Journal of Experimental Child Psychology,* 1977, *23,* 57–77.

Markman, E. M. Realizing that you don't understand: Elementary school children's awareness of inconsistencies. *Child Development,* 1979, *50,* 643–655.

Markman, E. M. Two different principles of conceptual organization. In M. E. Lamb & A. L. Brown (Eds.), *Advances in developmental psychology* (Vol. 1). Hillsdale, N.J.: Erlbaum, 1981.

Markman, E. M., Cox, B., & Machida, S. The standard object-sorting task as a measure of conceptual organization. *Developmental Psychology,* 1981, *17,* 115–117.

Markman, E. M., & Seibert, J. Classes and collections: Internal organization and resulting holistic properties. *Cognitive Psychology,* 1976, *8,* 561–577.

Marks, D. F. Visual imagery differences and eye movements in the recall of pictures. *Perception and Psychophysics,* 1973, *14,* 407–412.

Marmor, G. S. Development of kinetic images: When does the child first represent movement in mental images? *Cognitive Psychology,* 1975, *7,* 548–559.

Marmor, G. S. Mental rotation and number conservation: Are they related? *Developmental Psychology,* 1977, *13,* 320–325.

Marshall, J. C., & Morton, J. On the mechanics of Emma. In A. Sinclair, R. J. Jarvella, & W. J. M. Levelt (Eds.), *The child's conception of language.* New York: Springer-Verlag, 1978.

Martin, J. G. Rhythmic (hierarchical) versus serial structure in speech and other behavior. *Psychological Review,* 1972, *79,* 487–509.

Martin, J. L. An analysis of some of Piaget's topological tasks from a mathematical point of view. *Journal for Research in Mathematics Education,* 1976, *7,* 8–24.

Masangkay, Z. S., McCluskey, K. A., McIntyre, C. W., Sims-Knight, J., Vaughn, B. E., & Flavell, J. H. The early development of inferences about the visual percepts of others. *Child Development,* 1974, *45,* 357–366.

McCauley, C., Weil, C. M., & Sperber, R. D. The development of memory structure as reflected by semantic-priming effects. *Journal of Experimen-*

tal Child Psychology, 1976, *22*, 511–518.

McClure, E., Mason, J., & Barnitz, J. An exploratory study of story structure and age effects on children's ability to sequence stories. *Discourse Processes*, 1979, *2*, 213–249.

Melkman, R., & Deutsch, C. Memory functioning as related to developmental changes in bases of organization. *Journal of Experimental Child Psychology*, 1977, *23*, 84–97.

Melkman, R., Tversky, B., & Baratz, D. Developmental trends in the use of perceptual and conceptual attributes in grouping, clustering and retrieval. *Journal of Experimental Child Psychology*, 1981, *31*, 470–486.

Menig-Peterson, C. L., & McCabe, A. Children's orientation of a listener to the context of their narratives. *Developmental Psychology*, 1978, *14*, 582–592.

Mervis, C. B. Tigers and leopards are kitty-cats: Mother-child interaction and children's early categories. Paper presented at the Interdisciplinary Conference, Park City, Utah, January 1981.

Miller, G. A., & Johnson-Laird, P. N. *Language and perception*. Cambridge, Mass.: Harvard University Press, 1976.

Murphy, M. D., & Brown, A. L. Incidental learning in preschool children as a function of level of cognitive analysis. *Journal of Experimental Child Psychology*, 1975, *19*, 509–523.

Naeli, H., & Harris, P. L. Orientation of the diamond and the square. *Perception*, 1976, *5*, 73–77.

Neisser, U. *Cognitive psychology*. New York: Appleton-Century-Crofts, 1967.

Nelson, K. Variations in children's concepts by age and category. *Child Development*, 1974, *45*, 577–584.

Nelson, K. Cognitive development and the acquisition of concepts. In R. C. Anderson, R. J. Spiro, & W. E. Montague (Eds.), *Schooling and the acquisition of knowledge*. Hillsdale, N.J.: Erlbaum, 1977.

Nelson, K. How children represent knowledge of their world in and out of language: A preliminary report. In R. S. Siegler (Ed.), *Children's thinking: What develops?* Hillsdale, N.J.: Erlbaum, 1978. (a)

Nelson, K. Semantic development and the development of semantic memory. In K. E. Nelson (Ed.), *Children's language* (Vol. 1). New York: Gardner Press, 1978. (b)

Nelson, K. Explorations in the development of a functional semantic system. In W. A. Collins (Ed.), *Minnesota symposia on child psychology*

(Vol. 12). Hillsdale, N.J.: Erlbaum, 1979.

Nelson, K. The syntagmatics and paradigmatics of conceptual development. In S. A. Kuczaj II. (Ed.), *Language development:* Vol. 2. *Language, thought and culture*. Hillsdale, N.J.: Erlbaum, 1982.

Nelson, K., & Brown, A. L. The semantic-episodic distinction in memory development. In P. A. Ornstein (Ed.), *Memory development in children*. Hillsdale, N.J.: Erlbaum, 1978.

Nelson, K. & Gruendel, J. M. At morning it's lunchtime: A scriptal view of children's dialogues. *Discourse Processes*, 1979, *2*, 73–94.

Nelson, K., & Gruendel, J. M. Generalized event representations: Basic building blocks of cognitive development. In M. E. Lamb & A. L. Brown (Eds.), *Advances in developmental psychology* (Vol. 1). Hillsdale, N.J.: Erlbaum, 1981.

Nelson, K., Rescorla, L., Gruendel, J., & Benedict, H. Early lexicons: What do they mean? *Child Development*, 1978, *49*, 960–968.

Newcombe, N., Rogoff, B., & Kagan, J. Developmental changes in recognition memory for pictures of objects and scenes. *Developmental Psychology*, 1977, *13*, 337–341.

Newell, A. Physical symbol systems. *Cognitive Science*, 1980, *4*, 117–133.

Newman, D. Children's understanding of strategic interaction. Unpublished doctoral dissertation, City University of New York, 1980.

Nissen, M. J. Interactions among levels of processing. *Memory & Cognition*, 1979, *7*, 124–132.

Norman, D. A. Memory, knowledge and the answering of questions. In R. L. Solso (Ed.), *Contemporary issues in cognitive psychology: The Loyola symposium*. Washington, D.C.: V. H. Winston, 1973.

Norman, D. A., Rumelhart, D. E., & LNR Research Group. *Explorations in cognition*. San Francisco: W. H. Freeman, 1975.

Norman, D. A., & Shallice, T. Attention to action: Willed and automatic control of behavior (Center for Human Information Processing Technical Report No. 99). La Jolla: University of California, San Diego, 1980.

Olson, D. R. *Cognitive development: The child's acquisition of diagonality*. New York: Academic Press, 1970.

Olson, G. M., Duffy, S. A., & Mack, R. L. Knowledge of writing conventions in prose comprehension. In W. J. McKeachie & K. Eble (Eds.), *New directions in learning and teaching*. San Francisco: Jossey-Bass, in press.

Olver, R. R., & Hornsby, J. R. On equivalence. In

J. S. Bruner, R. R. Olver, & P. M. Greenfield, *Studies in cognitive growth*. New York: Wiley, 1966.

Omanson, R. C. An analysis of narratives: Identifying central, supportive, and distracting content. *Discourse Processes,* in press.

Omanson, R. C., Warren, W. H., & Trabasso, T. Goals, inferential comprehension, and recall of stories by children. *Discourse Processes,* 1978, *1,* 323–336.

Ornstein, P. A., & Corsale, K. Organizational factors in children's memory. In C. R. Puff (Ed.), *Memory organization and structure.* New York: Academic Press, 1979.

Osgood, C. E., Suci, G. J., & Tannenbaum, P. H. *The measurement of meaning.* Urbana: University of Illinois Press, 1957.

Page, E. I. Haptic perception: A consideration of one of the investigations of Piaget and Inhelder. *Education Review,* 1959, *11,* 115–124.

Paivio, A. *Imagery and verbal processes.* New York: Holt, 1971.

Paivio, A. Perceptual comparisons through the mind's eye. *Memory & Cognition,* 1975, *3,* 635–647.

Paivio, A. Images, propositions, and knowledge. In J. M. Nicholas (Ed.), *Images, perception and knowledge: The Western Ontario series in philosophy of science.* Dordrecht, the Netherlands: D. Reidel, 1977.

Paivio, A. The relationship between verbal and perceptual codes. In E. C. Carterette & M. P. Friedman (Eds.), *Handbook of perception,* vol. 8, *Perceptual coding.* New York: Academic Press, 1978.

Palmer, S. E. The effect of contextual scenes on the identification of objects. *Memory & Cognition,* 1975, *3,* 519–526. (a)

Palmer, S. E. The nature of perceptual representation: An examination of the analog/propositional debate. In R. C. Schank & B. L. Nash-Webber (Eds.), *Theoretical issues in natural language processing.* Arlington, Va.: Tinlap Press, 1975. (b)

Palmer, S. E. Visual perception and world knowledge: Notes on a model of sensory-cognitive interaction. In D. A. Norman, D. E. Rumelhart, & LNR Research Group (Eds.), *Explorations in cognition.* San Francisco: W. H. Freeman, 1975 (c).

Palmer, S. E. Fundamental aspects of cognitive representation. In E. Rosch & B. B. Lloyd (Eds.), *Cognition and categorization.* Hillsdale, N.J.: Erlbaum, 1978.

Paris, S. G. & Upton, L. R. Children's memory for inferential relationships in prose. *Child Development,* 1976, *47,* 660–668.

Parker, R. E. The encoding of information in complex pictures. Unpublished doctoral dissertation, University of California, San Diego, 1977.

Pascual-Leone, J. A mathematical model for the transition rule in Piaget's developmental stages. *Acta Psychologica,* 1970, *32,* 301–345.

Perlmutter, M., & Myers, N. A. Recognition memory in preschool children. *Developmental Psychology,* 1976, *12,* 271–272.

Perlmutter, M., & Myers, N. A. Development of recall in 2- to 4-year-old children. *Developmental Psychology,* 1979, *15,* 73–83.

Pezdek, K., & Hancock, N. Context characteristics and the context effect. Paper presented at the meeting of the Psychonomic Society, San Antonio, Texas, November 1978.

Piaget, J. *The language and thought of the child.* New York: Harcourt, Brace, 1926.

Piaget, J. *The child's conception of the world.* New York: Harcourt, Brace, 1929.

Piaget, J. *Play, dreams and imitation in childhood.* New York: W. W. Norton, 1951.

Piaget, J. *The origins of intelligence in children.* New York: International Universities Press, 1952.

Piaget, J. *The construction of reality in the child.* New York: Basic Books, 1954.

Piaget, J. *The child's conception of time.* London: Routledge & Kegan Paul, 1969.

Piaget, J. Intellectual evolution from adolescence to adulthood. *Human Development,* 1972, *15,* 1–12.

Piaget, J. *The grasp of consciousness: Action and concept in the young child.* Cambridge, Mass.: Harvard University Press, 1976.

Piaget, J., & Inhelder, B. *The child's conception of space.* London: Routledge & Kegan Paul, 1956.

Piaget, J., & Inhelder, B. *Mental imagery in the child: A study of the development of imaginal representation.* London: Routledge & Kegan Paul, 1971.

Piaget, J., Inhelder, B., & Szeminska, A. *The child's conception of geometry.* New York: Basic Books, 1960.

Piattelli-Palmarini, M. (Ed.), *Language and meaning: The debate between Jean Piaget and Noam Chomsky.* Cambridge, Mass.: Harvard University Press, 1980.

Pick, H. L., Jr. Mapping children—mapping space. Paper presented at the meeting of the American Psychological Association, Honolulu, September 1972.

Pitcher, E. G., & Prelinger, E. *Children tell stories: An analysis of fantasy*. New York: International Universities Press, 1963.

Pitt, R. B. Toward a comprehensive model of problem solving: Applications to solutions of chemistry problems by high school and college students. Unpublished doctoral dissertation, University of California, San Diego, 1976.

Pollard-Gott, L., McCloskey, M., & Todres, A. K. Subjective story structure. *Discourse Processes*, 1979, *2*, 251–282.

Potter, M. C. Meaning in visual search. *Science*, 1975, *187*, 965–966.

Potter, M. C. Short-term conceptual memory for pictures. *Journal of Experimental Psychology: Human Learning and Memory*, 1976, *2*, 509–522.

Potter, M. C., Valian, V. V., & Faulconer, B. A. Representation of a sentence and its pragmatic implications: Verbal, imagistic, or abstract? *Journal of Verbal Learning and Verbal Behavior*, 1977, *16*, 1–12.

Poulsen, D., Kintsch, E., Kintsch, W., & Premack, D. Children's comprehension and memory for stories. *Journal of Experimental Child Psychology*, 1979, *28*, 379–403.

Pressley, M. Imagery and children's learning: Putting the picture in developmental perspective. *Review of Educational Research*, 1977, *47*, 585–622.

Propp, V. *Morphology of the folktale* (2nd ed.). Austin: University of Texas Press, 1968. (Originally published, 1928.)

Pufall, P. B., & Shaw, R. E. Analysis of the development of children's spatial reference systems. *Cognitive Psychology*, 1973, *5*, 151–175.

Puff, C. R., Murphy, M. D., & Ferrara, R. A. Further evidence about the role of clustering in free recall. *Journal of Experimental Psychology: Human Learning and Memory*, 1977, *3*, 742–753.

Pylyshyn, Z. W. What the mind's eye tells the mind's brain: A critique of mental imagery. *Psychological Bulletin*, 1973, *80*, 1–24.

Pylyshyn, Z. W. When is attribution of beliefs justified? *Behavioral and Brain Sciences*, 1978, *1*, 592–593.

Pylyshyn, Z. W. The rate of "mental rotation" of images: A test of a holistic analogue hypothesis. *Memory & Cognition*, 1979, *7*, 19–28. (a)

Pylyshyn, Z. W. Validating computational models: A critique of Anderson's indeterminacy of representation claim. *Psychological Review*, 1979, *86*, 383–394. (b)

Pylyshyn, Z. W. The imagery debate: Analogue media versus tacit knowledge. *Psychological Review*, 1981, *88*, 16–45.

Quillian, M. R. Semantic memory. In M. Minsky (Ed.), *Semantic information processing*. Cambridge, Mass.: MIT Press, 1968.

Rabinowitz, M., & Mandler, J. M. Organization and information retrieval. *Journal of Experimental Psychology: Learning, Memory, and Cognition*, in press.

Rabinowitz, M., Valentine, K. M., & Mandler, J. M. A developmental comparison of inferential processing: When adults don't always know best. Paper presented at the meeting of the American Psychological Association, Los Angeles, September 1981.

Ramsay, D. S., & Campos, J. J. Memory by the infant in an object notion task. *Developmental Psychology*, 1975, *11*, 411–412.

Ramsay, D. S., & Campos, J. J. The onset of representation and entry into Stage 6 of object permanence development. *Developmental Psychology*, 1978, *14*, 79–86.

Ratner, H. H., & Myers, N. A. Long-term memory and retrieval at ages 2, 3, 4. *Journal of Experimental Child Psychology*, 1981, *31*, 365–386.

Rebelsky, F. Adult perception of the horizontal. *Perceptual and Motor Skills*, 1964, *19*, 371–374.

Reese, H. W. Imagery and associative memory. In R. V. Kail, Jr., J. W. Hagen (Eds.), *Perspectives on the development of memory and cognition*. Hillsdale, N.J.: Erlbaum, 1977.

Rescorla, L. A. Overextension in early language development. *Journal of Child Language*, 1980, *7*, 321–335.

Restle, F. Theory of serial pattern learning: Structural trees. *Psychological Review*, 1970, *77*, 481–495.

Restle, F. Structural ambiguity in serial pattern learning. *Cognitive Psychology*, 1976, *8*, 357–381.

Richman, C. L., Mitchell, D. B., & Reznick, J. S. Mental travel: Some reservations. *Journal of Experimental Psychology: Human Perception and Performance*, 1979, *5*, 13–18.

Rieser, J. J. Spatial orientation of six-month-old infants. *Child Development*, 1979, *50*, 1078–1087.

Rosch, E. Cognitive representation of semantic categories. *Journal of Experimental Psychology:*

General, 1975, *104*, 192–233.

Rosch, E. Principles of categorization. In E. Rosch & B. B. Lloyd (Eds.), *Cognition and categorization*. Hillsdale, N.J.: Erlbaum, 1978.

Rosch, E., & Mervis, C. B. Family resemblances: Studies in the internal structure of categories. *Cognitive Psychology*, 1975, *7*, 573–605.

Rosch, E., Mervis, C. B., Gray, W. D., Johnson, D. M., & Boyes-Braem, P. Basic objects in natural categories. *Cognitive Psychology*, 1976, *8*, 382–439.

Ross, G. S. Categorization in 1- to 2-year-olds. *Developmental Psychology*, 1980, *16*, 391–396.

Rossi, E. L., & Rossi, S. I. Conceptualization, serial order and recall in nursery-school children. *Child Development*, 1965, *36*, 771–778.

Rozin, P. The evolution of intelligence and access to the cognitive unconscious. In J. M. Sprague & A. A. Epstein (Eds.), *Progress in psychobiology and physiological psychology* (Vol. 6). New York: Academic Press, 1976.

Rozin, P., & Gleitman, L. R. The structure and acquisition of reading II: The reading process and the acquisition of the alphabetic principle. In A. S. Reber & D. L. Scarborough (Eds.), *Toward a psychology of reading*. Hillsdale, N.J.: Erlbaum, 1977.

Rubin, S., & Gardner, H. Once upon a time: The development of sensitivity to story structure. Unpublished manuscript, Harvard University, 1980.

Rubin, S., & Wolf, D. The development of maybe: The evolution of social roles into narrative roles. *New Directions for Child Development*, 1979, *6*, 15–28. ("Fact, fiction, and fantasy in childhood" issue, E. Winner & H. Gardner [Eds.].)

Rumelhart, D. E. Notes on a schema for stories. In D. G. Bobrow & A. Collins (Eds.), *Representation and understanding: Studies in cognitive science*. New York: Academic Press, 1975.

Rumelhart, D. E. Understanding and summarizing brief stories. In D. LaBerge & S. J. Samuels (Eds.), *Basic processes in reading: Perception and comprehension*. Hillsdale, N.J.: Erlbaum, 1977.

Rumelhart, D. E. Analogical processes and procedural representation (Center for Human Information Processing Technical Report No. 81). La Jolla: University of California, San Diego, 1979.

Rumelhart, D. E. A reply to Black and Wilensky. *Cognitive Science*, 1980, *4*, 313–316. (a)

Rumelhart, D. E. Schemata: The building blocks of cognition. In R. Spiro, B. Bruce, & W. F. Brewer (Eds.), *Theoretical issues in reading comprehension*. Hillsdale, N.J.: Erlbaum, 1980. (b)

Rumelhart, D. E., & Ortony, A. The representation of knowledge in memory. In R. C. Anderson, R. J. Spiro, & W. E. Montague (Eds.), *Schooling and the acquisition of knowledge*. Hillsdale, N.J.: Erlbaum, 1977.

Salatas, H., & Flavell, J. H. Perspective-taking: The development of two components of knowledge. *Child Development*, 1976, *47*, 103–109.

Saltz, E., Soller, E., Sigel, I. E. The development of natural language concepts. *Child Development*, 1972, *43*, 1191–1202.

Saltzman, E. Levels of sensorimotor representation. *Journal of Mathematical Psychology*, 1979, *20*, 91–163.

Scarborough, H. S. Development of visual, name, and conceptual memory codes for pictures. *Journal of Experimental Child Psychology*, 1977, *24*, 260–278.

Schaeffer, B., Lewis, J. A., & Van Decar, A. The growth of children's semantic memory: Semantic elements. *Journal of Experimental Child Psychology*, 1971, *11*, 296–309.

Schank, R. C. Conceptual dependency: A theory of natural language understanding. *Cognitive Psychology*, 1972, *3*, 552–631.

Schank, R. C. *Conceptual information processing*. New York: Elsevier, 1975.

Schank, R. C. Language and memory. *Cognitive Science*, 1980, *4*, 243–284.

Schank, R. C., & Abelson, R. *Scripts, plans, goals and understanding*. Hillsdale, N.J.: Erlbaum, 1977.

Scribner, S. Modes of thinking and ways of speaking: Culture and logic reconsidered. In R. O. Freedle (Ed.), *New directions in discourse processing* (Vol. 2). Norwood, N.J.: Ablex, 1979.

Sedlak, A. J. Developmental differences in understanding plans and evaluating actors. *Child Development*, 1979, *50*, 536–560.

Shallice, T. Dual functions of consciousness. *Psychological Review*, 1972, *79*, 383–393.

Shantz, C. U. The development of social cognition. In E. M. Hetherington (Ed.), *Review of child development research* (Vol. 5). Chicago: University of Chicago Press, 1975.

Sharp, D., Cole, M., & Lave, J. Education and cognitive development: The evidence from experimental research. *Monographs of the Society for Research in Child Development*, 1979, *44* (Serial No. 178).

Shemyakin, F. N. Orientation in space. In B. G. Anayev, et al. (Eds.), *Psychological science in the U.S.S.R.* (Vol. 1). Washington, D.C.: Office of Technical Services, 1962.

Shepard, R. N. The mental image. *American Psychologist*, 1978, *33*, 125–137.

Shepard, R. N., & Metzler, J. Mentation rotation of three-dimensional objects. *Science*, 1971, *171*, 701–703.

Shepard, R. N., & Podgorny, P. Cognitive processes that resemble perceptual processes. In W. K. Estes (Ed.), *Handbook of learning and cognitive processes* (Vol. 5). Hillsdale, N.J.: Erlbaum, 1978.

Siegel, A. W., Allen, G. L., & Kirasic, K. C. Children's ability to make bidirectional distance comparisons: The advantage of thinking ahead. *Developmental Psychology*, 1979, *15*, 656–657.

Siegel, A. W., Herman, J. F., Allen, G. L., & Kirasic, K. C. The development of cognitive maps of large- and small-scale spaces. *Child Development*, 1979, *50*, 582–585.

Siegel, A. W., Kirasic, K. C., & Kail, R. V., Jr. Stalking the elusive cognitive map: The development of children's representations of geographic space. In J. F. Wohlwill & I. Altman (Eds.), *Human behavior and environment* (Vol. 3). New York: Plenum, 1978.

Siegel, A. W., & Schadler, M. Young children's cognitive maps of their classroom. *Child Development*, 1977, *48*, 388–394.

Siegel, A. W., & White, S. H. The development of spatial representations. In H. W. Reese (Ed.), *Advances in child development and behavior* (Vol. 10). New York: Academic Press, 1975.

Siegler, R. S. The origins of scientific reasoning. In R. S. Siegler (Ed.), *Children's thinking: What develops?* Hillsdale, N.J.: Erlbaum, 1978.

Simon, H. A., & Hayes, J. R. Understanding complex task instructions. In D. Klahr (Ed.), *Cognition and instruction*. Hillsdale, N.J.: Erlbaum, 1976.

Singer, J. L., Greenberg, S., & Antrobus, J. S. Looking with the mind's eye: Experimental studies of ocular motility during daydreaming and mental arithmetic. *Transactions of the New York Academy of Sciences*, 1971, *33*, 694–709.

Slobin, D. I. A case study of early langage awareness. In A. Sinclair, R. J. Jarvella, & W. J. M. Levelt (Eds.), *The child's conception of language*. New York: Springer-Verlag, 1978.

Smiley, S. S., & Brown, A. L. Conceptual preference for thematic or taxonomic relations: A nonmonotonic trend from preschool to old age. *Journal of Experimental Child Psychology*, 1979, *28*, 249–257.

Smith, C. L. Children's understanding of natural language hierarchies. *Journal of Experimental Child Psychology*, 1979, *27*, 437–458.

Smith, E. E. Theories of semantic memory. In W. K. Estes (Ed.), *Handbook of learning and cognitive processes* (Vol. 5). Hillsdale, N.J.: Erlbaum, 1978.

Smith, L. B. Perceptual development and category generalization. *Child Development*, 1979, *50*, 705–715.

Smith, L. B., & Kemler, D. G. Developmental trends in free classification: Evidence for a new conceptualization of perceptual development. *Journal of Experimental Child Psychology*, 1977, *24*, 279–298.

Smith, N. R., & Franklin, M. B. *Symbolic functioning in childhood*. Hillsdale, N.J.: Erlbaum, 1979.

Sophian, C., & Hagen, J. W. Involuntary memory and the development of retrieval skills. *Journal of Experimental Child Psychology*, 1978, *26*, 458–471.

Spelke, E. S. Infants' intermodal perception of events. *Cognitive Psychology*, 1976, *8*, 553–560.

Spelke, E. S. Perceiving bimodally specified events in infancy. *Developmental Psychology*, 1979, *15*, 626–636.

Spelke, E. S. The infant's acquisition of knowledge of bimodally specified events. *Journal of Experimental Child Psychology*, 1981, *31*, 279–299.

Stein, N. L. The concept of a story. In H. Mandl, N. L. Stein, & T. Trabasso (Eds.), *Learning from text*. Hillsdale, N.J.: Erlbaum, in press.

Stein, N. L., & Glenn, C. G. An analysis of story comprehension in elementary school children. In R. O. Freedle (Ed.), *New directions in discourse processing* (Vol. 2). Norwood, N.J.: Ablex, 1979.

Stein, N. L., & Glenn, C. G. Children's concept of time: The development of a story schema. In W. J. Friedman (Ed.), *The developmental psychology of time*. New York: Academic Press, 1982.

Stein, N. L., & Nezworksi, T. The effects of organization and instructional set on story memory. *Discourse Processes*, 1978, *1*, 177–194.

Stein, N. L., & Trabasso, T. Children's understanding of stories: A basis for moral judgment and dilemma resolution. In C. J. Brainerd & M. Pressley (Eds.), *Verbal processes in children: Progress in cognitive development research*. New York: Springer-Verlag, 1982. (a)

Stein, N. L., & Trabasso, T. What's in a story? An approach to comprehension and instruction. In R. Glaser (Ed.), *Advances in the psychology of instruction* (Vol. 2). Hillsdale, N.J.: Erlbaum, 1982. (b)

Steinberg, E. R., & Anderson, R. C. Hierarchical semantic organizaton in 6-year-olds. *Journal of Experimental Child Psychology*, 1975, *19*, 544–553.

Stevens, A., & Coupe, P. Distortions in judged spatial relations. *Cognitive Psychology*, 1978, *10*, 422–437.

Strauss, M. S. Abstraction of prototypical information by adults and 10-month-old infants. *Journal of Experimental Psychology: Human Learning and Memory*, 1979, 5, 618–632.

Thatcher, R. W., & John, E. R. *Foundations of cognitive processes*. Hillsdale, N.J.: Erlbaum, 1977.

Thomas, H., & Jamison, W. On the acquisition of understanding that still water is horizontal. *Merrill-Palmer Quarterly*, 1975, *21*, 31–44.

Thorndyke, P. W. Cognitive structures in comprehension and memory of narrative discourse. *Cognitive Psychology*, 1977, *9*, 77–110.

Tikhomirov, O. K. [*The structure of human activity*], Arlington, Va.: Joint Publications Research Service, 1971. (JPRS 53982 and JPRS 52119)

Tolman, E. C., Ritchie, B. F., & Kalish, D. Studies in spatial learning: II. Place learning versus response learning. *Journal of Experimental Psychology*, 1946, *36*, 221–229.

Tomikawa, S. A., & Dodd, D. H. Early word meanings: Perceptually or functionally based? *Child Development*, 1980, *51*, 1103–1109.

Trabasso, T., Isen, A. M., Dolecki, P., McLanahan, A. G., Riley, C. A., & Tucker, T. How do children solve class-inclusion problems? In R. S. Siegler (Ed.), *Children's thinking: What develops?* Hillsdale, N.J.: Erlbaum, 1978.

Trabasso, T., Stein, N. L., & Johnson, L. R. Children's knowledge of events: A causal analysis of story structure. In G. H. Bower & A. R. Lang (Eds.), *The psychology of learning and motivation* (Vol. 15). New York: Academic Press, 1981.

Tschirgi, J. E. Sensible reasoning: A hypothesis about hypotheses. *Child Development*, 1980, *51*, 1–11.

Tulving, E. Episodic and semantic memory. In E. Tulving & W. Donaldson (Eds.), *Organization and memory*. New York: Academic Press, 1972.

Tversky, B. Distortion in memory for maps. *Cognitive Psychology*, 1981, *13*, 407–433.

Vurpillot, R. Judging visual similarity: The development of scanning strategies and their relation to differentiation. *Journal of Experimental Child Psychology*, 1968, *6*, 632–650.

Vygotsky, L. S. *Thought and language*. Cambridge, Mass.: MIT Press, 1962.

Warren, W. H., Nicholas, D. W., & Trabasso, T. Event chains and inferences in understanding narratives. In R. O. Freedle (Ed.), *New directions in discourse processing* (Vol. 2). Norwood, N.J.: Ablex, 1979.

Wason, P. C. Reasoning about a rule. *Quarterly Journal of Experimental Psychology*, 1968, *20*, 273–281.

Watson, J. S. Perception of object orientation in infants. *Merrill-Palmer Quarterly*, 1966, *12*, 73–94.

Weaver, P. A., & Dickinson, D. K. Scratching below the surface structure: Exploring the usefulness of story grammars. *Discourse Processes*, in press.

Weber, R. J., & Malmstrom, F. V. Measuring the size of mental images. *Journal of Experimental Psychology: Human Perception and Performance*, 1979, *5*, 1–12.

Weiner, S. L., & Ehrlichman, H. Ocular motility and cognitive process. *Cognition*, 1976, *4*, 31–43.

Wellman, H. M. A child's theory of mind: The development of conceptions of cognition. In S. R. Yussen (Ed.), *The growth of insight in the child*. New York: Academic Press, in press.

Werner, H. The concept of development from a comparative and organismic point of view. In D. Harris (Ed.), *The concept of development*. Minneapolis: University of Minnesota Press, 1957.

Werner, H., & Kaplan, B. *Symbol formation: An organismic-developmental approach to language and the expression of thought*. New York: Wiley, 1963.

Whaley, J. F. Readers' expectations for story structures. *Reading Research Quarterly*, 1981, *17*, 90–114.

Williamson, A. N., & McKenzie, B. E. Children's discrimination of oblique lines. *Journal of Experimental Child Psychology*, 1979, *27*, 533–543.

Wimmer, H. Processing of script deviations by young children. *Discourse Processes*, 1979, *2*, 301–310.

Wimmer, H. Children's understanding of stories: Assimilation by a general schema for actions or coordination of temporal relations? In F. Wilkening, J. Becker, & T. Trabasso (Eds.), *Information integration by children*. Hillsdale, N.J.: Erlbaum, 1980.

Winer, G. A. Class-inclusion reasoning in children: A review of the empirical literature. *Child Development*, 1980, *51*, 309–328.

Winograd, T. Frame representations and the declarative-procedural controversy. In D. G. Bobrow & A. Collins (Eds.), *Representation and understanding: Studies in cognitive science*. New York: Academic Press, 1975.

Wolf, D., & Gardner, H. On the structure of early symbolization. In R. Shiefelbusch & D. Bricker (Eds.), *Early language: Acquisition and intervention*. Baltimore: University Park Press, 1981.

Wolff, P., & Levin, J. R. the role of ovrt activity in children's imagery production. *Child Development*, 1972, *43*, 537–547.

Worden, P. E. The development of the category-recall function under three retrieval conditions. *Child Development*, 1974, *45*, 1054–1059.

Worden, P. E., Malmgren, I., & Gabourie, P. Memory for stories in learning disabled adults. *Journal of Learning Disabilities*, 1982, *15*, 145–152.

Worden, P. E., Mandler, J. M., & Chang, F. R. Children's free recall: An explanation of sorts. *Child Development*, 1978, *49*, 836–844.

Yussen, S. R., Mathews, S. R., II, Buss, R. R., & Kane, P. T. Developmental change in judging important and critical elements of stories. *Developmental Psychology*, 1980, *16*, 213–219.

Zikmund, V. Physiological correlates of visual imagery. In P. W. Sheehan (Ed.), *The function and nature of imagery*. New York: Academic Press, 1972.

SOCIAL COGNITION* | 8

CAROLYN UHLINGER SHANTZ, *Wayne State University*

CHAPTER CONTENTS

How do children conceptualize and reason about their social world—the people they observe, the relations between people, and the groups in which they participate? What are the developmental changes in such concepts and reasoning? And how is social-cognitive functioning related to social behavior? These are the central questions addressed in the area of social-cognitive development. The major theories that provide conceptual frameworks for these questions and the research studies that provide some of the answers to them will be examined in this chapter.

The development of social knowledge and reasoning has been both very recent and an intense focus of study, only emerging during the past 15 years or so. The reason for this may well lie in the history of the field itself. Social development and cognitive development historically were studied largely in isolation from one another. Despite the need at times to divide up complex behavior to study

it, the division was an uncomfortable breach for many who wished to understand unified, adaptive behavior as it changes in ontogenesis. The importance of the field of social-cognitive development, then, is that it is focused specifically on understanding the relation between social behavior and cognitive development. One basic assumption is that the way in which one conceptualizes and reasons about others has a major effect on how one interacts with them. For example, a child who thinks a peer purposely destroyed his puzzle is likely to retaliate aggressively, whereas the inference that the destruction was accidental will not as likely lead to aggression (Dodge, 1980). The corollary assumption is that social interaction and experiences have a major influence on the child's social conceptions (e.g., Damon & Killen, 1982). A second, important effect of this field of study is that it affords an extension of the study of cognitive development from the traditional nonsocial problems and processes to social ones.

Social cognition as an area of inquiry can be seen, then, as arising in response to some historical dichotomies made in psychology: between thinking and behaving, and between social and nonsocial knowing. Such dichotomies are not without their

*I wish to acknowledge and thank the many colleagues who have contributed to my thinking about this topic through their enlightening conversations and lively debates. John H. Flavell and Ellen M. Markham's encouragement and thoughtful critique of the first draft of this review are especially appreciated. This chapter is dedicated to the memory of Dr. Susan Jane Uhlinger.

critics. For example, some see the social/nonsocial distinction as a false dichotomy, but they then hold opposing positions: (1) that all knowledge is basically social, in that people largely construct their worlds mentally, and that the basic categories and relations of knowledge are embedded within the social-symbol system of language, and so on, or (2) that all knowledge is basically nonsocial, in that social "objects" are much like physical objects in the ways they are perceived and represented. These differences have philosophical roots that deserve discussion far beyond the limits of this chapter (see, e.g., Broughton, 1978; Chandler, 1976; Damon, 1981; Glick & Clarke-Stewart, 1978; Sigel & Vandenberg, 1975).

For those who see the social/nonsocial dichotomy as useful, important, or "true," the primary differences that have been suggested are: actions on physical objects have much more predictable and stable effects than actions on or with people; the range of possible actions of objects is much less than that of people; the causal locus of action is within a social being, but it is external for inanimate objects; affective relations are more critical or intense between people than between objects and people; and person-person relations, but not object-person relations, are marked by mutual, coordinated intentions. The point is not that the validity of these distinctions need to be adjudicated by the field at large in the future but that views held on this issue have influenced and will continue to influence what is selected for study in social-cognitive functioning and how it is studied, as will be evident at later points in the discussion.

We will consider first a brief historical overview of the field as a confluence of theories of cognitive development and adult social psychology to understand the kinds of assumptions, questions, and methods brought to the field. The major stream of work on children and adolescent's social knowledge and reasoning has come directly or indirectly from Piagetian theory of cognitive development. By and large, Piaget's theory and research traced the ontogenetic odyssey of "the child as a symbolic logician" and "the child as a physicist" of the world, to put it, perhaps, too succinctly. From research on such basic concepts as space, number, causality, logical classification and relations, Piaget constructed a broad stage theory of mental development. A small portion of his work dealt with more social concepts and reasoning, such as how children communicate with one another and how they understand the rules of games. Although Piaget found less clear evidence for stages of social-concept develop-

ment than in the nonsocial areas, this work led to his positing the construct of egocentrism, which has been a focal point of a good deal of research. Most simply put, egocentrism refers to the lack of differentiation between the self and other, which is indexed by the proclivity of selves to attribute their own thoughts, viewpoints, attitudes, and the like, to other people. Likewise, Werner's comparative organismic theory (1948) posits a shift from egocentrism to perspectivism between and (interestingly) within stages of development and systems of action (i.e., sensorimotor, perceptual, and contemplative). In keeping with these stage theories of mental development of Piaget and Werner, there are several stage theories of social-conceptual development—such as stages of perspective coordination (Selman, 1980), of authority and friendship relations (Damon, 1977; Selman, 1980), and of social-rule concepts (Damon, 1977; Turiel, 1975)—to be described later (see *Conceptions of Relations Between Individuals*).

Adults' social reasoning and social judgments, as studied by social psychologists, have been another contributing stream of research. This stream has a much longer history than developmental social cognition, yet it is some of the more recent social psychological theories, known collectively as attribution theories, that have had a great impact on developmental research. Most derive from Heider's theory (1958) concerning the way in which the average adult understands the behavior of others, specifically the causes of behavior. Heider proposed that adults categorize causes as either external (environmental) or internal (person), the latter subdivided into ability and two components of intention and effort. That is, we make causal attributions by considering the circumstances the person is in and by inferring what the person "can" do and is "trying" to do. Several derivations and elaborations of this basic model have been made, for example, Kelley's process model (1973) of causal attribution and Jones and Davis's attribution theory (1965). To understand the development of causal attribution, most research has employed Kelley's (1973) model, examining both the covariation principle and the causal schemata. The covariation principle, for example, states that a person attributes an action or effect to a cause with which it covaries. A behavior that occurs in a particular situation in most people most of the time will be seen as caused by that situation, whereas a behavior of an individual that occurs in most situations most of the time will be seen as caused by some aspect of the person. Developmental work based on Kelley's model and a related model, concerned specifically with attributions about success and failure in achievement situations (Weiner, 1974), will be described later (see *Inferences About the Causes of Behavior*).

Another stream of research has appeared recently, one that is not identified with any single theory or model. It takes the position that the way to reveal explicit and tacit social knowledge and reasoning is to observe social interaction, that is, the child not as a knower *about* the social world but as an actor *in* it. One such perspective is that of symbolic interactionism in which the focus is on the child's own negotiations with the social world (e.g., Cooley, 1902; Mead, 1934), the meanings of social actions, and the implicit rules of conduct between individuals (e.g., Goffman, 1974; Harré, 1974). Using interactions of individuals to reveal their structuring of social situations, relational knowledge, and rule following has been a strategy from such diverse traditions as cognitive anthropology and linguistics. Some specific examples include children's conversational abilities (e.g., Garvey & Hogan, 1973), the explicit and implicit social skills revealed in children's play (e.g., Forbes, Lubin, & Anderegg, 1980; Goldman & Ross, 1978), and children's distinctions in natural settings between social-conventional rules and moral ones (e.g., Nucci & Turiel, 1978). The emergence of this relatively new approach to social cognition among developmentalists in part reflects the premise shared by some that all knowledge is basically social in nature, that the proper focus of study is on the knowledge and processes of social *relations* as made manifest in actual social interactions of the child with others, and that many experimental paradigms used heretofore do not allow for, or are poor analogues of, actual social interactions and meaningful social contexts (Bearison, in press; Damon, 1979). In summary, by far the major wellsprings of social-cognitive development are the cognitive-developmental theories of Piaget and Werner, to a lesser extent the adult attribution theories, and to a still lesser extent the positions focused on social knowledge-in-action-in-context.

In this chapter, three major topics of the child's conception of others are considered: the other person as an individual, the social relations between people (dyadic level), and the social relations among people (group level). Within each topic, the cognitive changes that occur in ontogenesis are described and, in some cases, the relation of these changes to social behavior. Specifically, the first topic is the way in which the child represents and explains the *behavior* of others as well as the way others are conceptualized as *persons*. Such social inferences and knowledge are then related to some characteristics of children and characteristics of social-cognitive tasks. Finally, social-cognitive abilities in relation to aggression and prosocial behavior are considered. The second major topic of dyadic social-relation conceptions deals with concepts of authority, friendship, and conflict. The third topic, the group level, includes: conceptions of social structure as revealed in power and liking relations within groups, concepts of deviant behavior, and social role. The final section is a summary of some of the themes of social-cognitive development, recommendations concerning future theory and research, and areas of applications to the lives of children.

Having stated what is covered in this chapter, it is equally important to note which of the usual topics of social cognition are not covered. Some "gerrymandering of conceptual boundaries" (to use Chandler's, 1976, phrase) is required to delimit a reasonable corpus of theory and research. The perimeter was partially determined by the goal of selecting topics and emphases that represent the diversity of theoretical, methodological, and substantive approaches to social-cognitive development. Earlier reviews (e.g., Chandler, 1976; Kurdek, 1978a; Shantz, 1975a) dealt primarily with the voluminous literature on person perception and perspective-taking abilities. These two topics still are a substantial portion of recent research and, thus, the inclusion of such studies is more highly selective, given the goal of the chapter and the sheer constraint of space. On the other hand, conceptions of social institutions have been so rarely studied (one example of neglect) that no important additions can be made to Flavell's review (1970). In general, research has been favored that is readily available in published sources.

Some of the gerrymandering of topics is a function of the field itself, in the sense that there is such an extensive literature on some topics that they deserve separate chapter presentations. Self-conception, moral reasoning, and communication development are not included here for that reason, although they are usually considered social-cognitive topics. Likewise, the extensive coverage of infant development in the Handbook (vol. II) includes social-cognitive development. Other chapters in the Handbook that can be considered "companion pieces" to the dual foci of this chapter on cognition and social behavior are those on concepts and representation (see *Clark, vol. III, chap. 12; Mandler, vol. III, chap. 7*) and the peer system (*Hartup, vol. IV, chap. 2*).

Before proceeding to the substantive topics, it is worth noting that much of the early work in social-cognitive development was decidely cognitive in emphasis, that is, exploring children's representations of others, their causal reasoning, and developing tests of social-reasoning abilities and examining their interrelationships. There seemed to be little interest in determining whether differences in social-cognitive abilities made a difference in the ways children relate to one another (Shantz, 1975a). But that situation has changed. A noticeable increase has occurred in posing such questions as to whether children who are advanced in various perspective-taking skills behave more positively (helpfully, cooperatively) and less antisocially with their peers than those less advanced. This change seems not only to reflect cognitive psychologists' interests in knowing the kinds of relations between thinking and behaving but also social psychologists' increasing interest in cognitive aspects of social behavior. Traditionally, those who studied social behavior of children used either a psychoanalytic or social learning theory, neither of which had any explicit account of the child as a thinking social being. But social learning theory, in particular, has been substantially modified in the last decade to emphasize cognitive factors in behavioral acquisitions. For example, Bandura noted that imitation is strongly influenced by the cognitive capacities of the child:

> Social learning theory . . . assumes that *modeling influences operate principally through their informative function,* and that observers acquire mainly symbolic representations of modeled events rather than specific stimulus-response associations. (1971, p. 16)

Mischel (1973) has offered an even more explicit cognitive social learning view in which various information processing strategies, expectations, and cognitive capabilities of the individual are proposed as important determinants of behavior in various circumstances.

CONCEPTIONS OF THE INDIVIDUAL

Two fundamental aspects of conceptualizing others are understanding the meaning of the behavior of others and understanding others as persons. That is, the child as a student of the social world presumably focuses attention on, and reasons about, both the behavior of people and people as behavers, just as science does. For example, a child observes or participates in fights in the playground. He can focus on fighting behavior, such as what is fought about, or on what strategies lead to winning or losing fights. Or, the focus can be on individual children as fight-

ers: Is *X* someone who hits or just calls names, someone I can probably beat or not? Although it is sometimes implied that behavior perception is more fundamental than person perception, it is probably more appropriate to view them as different foci that afford different types of knowledge about the social world.

It is assumed here that one of the long-term goals of social-cognitive theory and research is to understand the child's conceptualization and reasoning about others as the child both participates with them and observes them. Ideally, this discussion would begin with studies of children as participants in actual social situations, but such studies are sufficiently rare and diverse in topic that they do not yet form a solid and coherent body of work. Thus, those methods that most closely replicate the experiential social world are considered first, specifically filmed social behavior. The basis of replication is the dynamic, event-based nature of filmed behavior as opposed to the much more frequently used static "summarized" social events presented in stories and pictures. The separate consideration of filmed behavior is based on my conjecture that event perception and event representation may provide in the future a substantially different view of human cognition than that based on static stimuli (e.g., Johansson, von Hofsten, & Jansson, 1980; Mandler, 1979). Following this discussion on filmed behavior, we will consider children's descriptions, inferences, and causal attributions about people as individuals.

The Other's Behavior

Descriptions and Explanations of Filmed Social Behavior

Movement is a fundamental attribute of behavior. It is a particularly salient aspect of the environment that elicits and maintains attention from infancy onward, and it influences the types of causal attributions made (e.g., Heider & Simmel, 1944; Michotte, 1946/1963). In describing events as they occur and in recalling events, the child chunks the ongoing behavioral stream into units or episodes as parts of the larger whole or theme of behavior. However, there appears to be no systematic research on this elementary level of behavior perception. Instead, the focus has been on the content (descriptions and explanations) of observed behavior. In most of the research described here, fairly complicated social behavior is represented in a story framework, and the children are asked after viewing the film to describe what happened and are questioned about various aspects of the film. The responses rest on children's attention, interpretation, memory, and skills of verbal expression.

An illustrative study of behavior perception and cognition using dramatized events is a study by Flapan (1968) conducted with 60 girls, drawn equally from ages 6, 9, and 12. Two excerpts, about 20 min. in duration, from the commercial movie, *Our Vines Have Tender Grapes,* were shown to each girl; after each of five subsections, she was asked to give an account of what she had seen. One episode involved a strained relationship between a girl and her father; the other was about a girl's guilt for accidently killing a squirrel. The verbatim spontaneous accounts were coded into three large categories: (1) describing/reporting observable events and situations (which included obvious feelings, such as crying and stated intentions); (2) explaining events as due to the situation, psychological factors, or interpersonal perceptions; and (3) interpreting/inferring the feelings, thoughts, intentions, motives, and perceptions of the actors.

The results were: (1) 6-year-olds' accounts were largely restricted to the reporting/describing level, with practically all children noting obvious feelings and half of them using some explanations of events. However, virtually all such explanations cited situational factors as causal. The greatest differences in descriptions occurred between the 6- and 9-year-old groups. The 9-year-olds supplemented descriptions of events with more explanations and some interpretation of the actors' feelings, thoughts, and intentions. The oldest group showed a similar pattern, except that a great number inferred feelings and thoughts, and so on; (2) in all three age groups, behavior was most often explained by situational factors, but over half of the older two groups used psychological explanations; (3) when making social inferences, most often there was a trend toward inferring the thoughts of others, then inferring intentions/motives, followed less often by inferences about feelings.

Wood (1978) basically confirmed Flapan's (1968) findings in her study of 6- to 14-year-old British children's understanding of four short silent films depicting jealousy, rejection, desire to impress others, and malicious pleasure. Children were asked specifically for explanations of behavior and inferences about the actors' thoughts and feelings. Descriptions of observable behavior and perceptible causes decreased significantly with increasing age, simple causal inferences occurred equally at all ages, and dispositional causes increased significantly with increasing age. Like Flapan, Wood found all three levels of causal inference present at all age levels, but the degree to which they occurred (Wood, 1978) and the number of children who used them (Flapan, 1968) showed the same trends with age. Further, Wood's study (1978) revealed no significant differences in descriptions and inferences for girls versus boys nor for working-class versus middle-class children. Rappoport and Fritzler (1969) used a quasi-movie technique of presenting four slides in rather quick succession. Geometric shapes represented people. For example, a large circle approached a small circle, and at the end of the demonstration, they are apart again with the large circle larger and the small one smaller—interpreted as taking and giving by adults. In children's descriptions, 6½-year-olds restricted themselves almost entirely to movement, whereas the 9½- and 12-year-olds most frequently inferred intentions/motives (here giving to, sharing) on slide cartoons that were "easy." On more difficult ones, however, older children used largely movement and quantity changes in their descriptions.

In summary, these studies of free descriptions of filmed behavior indicate that children about 6 years of age tend largely (although not exclusively) to describe obvious movement, observable events, and expressive behavior of people. With increasing age, there is a greater frequency of making simple-to-complex inferences about intentions, feelings, and the causes of behavior. Causes are usually attributed to situational factors at first; later in development, psychological factors and interpersonal perception are cited more often. However, Livesley and Bromley (1973) reported a pilot study using excerpts of a 12-min. silent film of Dr. Livesley's morning, which showed him arising, having breakfast, doing routine tasks, and driving off to work. This film was not dramatized, activities were presented in real time with minimal editing. Children gave a running commentary rather than recalling what they had seen. Without benefit of statistical data, some of the same developmental trends were noted here as those summarized previously, but the authors found that the youngest children, ages 4 to 5, as well as the older children, evidenced awareness of the inner states of the actor, such as needs and intentions (e.g., "He wants to know." "He's trying to. . . ." "He needs. . . ."). In short, these findings show that preschoolers do infer intentions of actors more often than other reviewed research suggests. The appearance of such competencies may relate to aspects of the film (highly familiar events and slow pace), or to the responses (running descriptions rather than recall), or to both. There is supportive evidence of preschoolers' inferences about intentions, which is discussed later (see *Attributions of Intentional Behavior*).

To this point, we have considered what children attend to, infer, remember, and relate about filmed behavior. But how *accurate* are children in perceiving social behavior and what factors influence their accuracy? These questions cannot be answered in any general way for two reasons: (1) there has been no systematic sampling of filmed behavior and (2) accuracy is sometimes confounded with the importance or centrality of information. In the first case, any general statement about developmental changes in accuracy would be based on a fairly representative or systematically varied sample of films as to complexity, text structure of the story, length, subtlety of themes, and so on. Data that are sometimes interpreted as normative data on children's accuracy are, in fact, captive to one particular film in each study.

The second problem is that children can be quite accurate about behavior that is irrelevant to the plot and fail to describe aspects central to it. Consider, for example, the descriptions of one episode in Flapan's study (1968) by a 12-year-old:

And then as he (the father) was passing, they (boy and girl) both got on the fence. And then as he was coming back, she asked if red squirrels were bad, and the father said he didn't know. She was trying to get him to say they were. . . . (p. 31)

And the same episode described by a 6-year-old:

The father said, "Come on." So they went with the father. The boy went on the fence first. Then after the boy went on the fence, the girl went on. The girl didn't get on the same way the boy did. So the father lifted the girl down. . . . (p. 31)

The description of fence climbing by the 6-year-old was accurate but had little to do with the equally accurate central theme of the episode of assuaging guilt. Thus, accuracy about what aspects of the film are described is a major issue. Usually, researchers have handled this problem by having adults judge how central or peripheral the information is to the plot. The general findings are: (1) children's spontaneous or elicited recognition or recall of information central to the plot (necessary) increases in a linear manner with increasing age (from second to ninth grades) (Collins, 1970; Collins, Wellman, Keniston, & Westby, 1978); (2) second- and third-graders' average correct recall for central informa-

tion is 66% and at eighth and ninth grades about 80% to 90% (e.g., Collins et al., 1978); (3) the recall of information peripheral to the plot also tends to increase with age, sometimes in a curvilinear pattern (Collins, 1970) and sometimes in a linear manner (Collins et al., 1978); somewhat less peripheral information (50% to 70%) is recalled than central information (75% to 80%) in grades two to eight; (4) the ability to infer information correctly (e.g., the reasons someone behaved as they did) also improves with increasing age (Collins et al., 1978; Collins, Berndt, & Hess, 1974; Flapan, 1968); (5) observable behavior and its observable effects (e.g., shooting someone and being arrested, Collins et al., 1974) are accurately recalled by a high proportion of all children from kindergarten to eighth grade, but the motives are less often inferred, recalled, or reported (Collins et al., 1974); (6) children recall more central information in a complex film shown in an ordered sequence than when the film is jumbled (randomly ordered scenes) (Collins et al., 1978).

It is worth reiterating that the degree to which these results are reliable as trends and, particularly, their timing in ontogenesis await further research on a wide variety of films. For example, some of the data summarized above is based on a single unspecified situation-comedy or on a film about a Vietnam war veteran turned police officer who is angered by city officials compromising with antiwar demonstrators, and so on. In the latter case, kindergarten and second-grade children have no political/historical framework for easily understanding the emotions and intentions portrayed, and they would be likely to focus on observable acts and consequences in such a difficult film (Rappoport & Fritzler, 1969). If behavior perception is quite sensitive to certain parameters of films, then the use of a single film is unlikely to reveal reliable normative data or reliable evidence of discontinuities in perceptual development, if discontinuities exist. The robustness of the broad developmental trends evident to date should be assessed by the systematic variation of film parameters or by a broad sampling of films in cross-sectional and longitudinal designs. Stimulus factors (such as the pace, length, and informational content of films) constitute only one source of variation in behavior perception. Another set that deserves exploration includes factors that tap the *relation* of the perceiver to the perceived (such as the familiarity of the themes of films to the perceivers, the similarities of the characters and their circumstances to the perceivers).

The work on children's understanding of filmed social behavior has proceeded for the most part without benefit of theoretical guidance. But in the highly related area of children's comprehension of stories (as read by, or to, them) there are a number of models that have been developed recently to describe and explain how children encode, comprehend, and remember narratives. Much of the work (e.g., Mandler & Johnson, 1977; Rumelhart, 1975; Stein & Glenn, 1979) is based on Bartlett's schema theory (1932). The proposed internal organization of story knowledge has been approached in the form of rewrite rules that contain generic structural knowledge of stories or as goal-directed episodes to account for the comprehension and retrieval of stories. Story grammars assist in elucidating the structure of the text and in relating such structure to the representations given by the reader or listener. A good deal of the research (see reviews, e.g., by Baker & Stein, 1981; Stein & Trabasso, in press) concerns children's understanding of causal relationships in one-episode or multiepisode stories, what categories of information are more memorable (e.g., the setting, protagonist, initiating events, major goals, and consequences), and what categories are more forgettable (e.g., the thoughts and emotional reactions of characters). As such, the models offer some ways to analyze story structure and its representation. These models go beyond, for example, measures of how much central and peripheral information (as defined by adults) is recalled. At the same time, work in social-cognitive development of causal reasoning, attributions, and inferences may aid in specifying some aspects of the schemata children of different ages are likely to bring to the task of understanding stories of social events.

Attributions of Intentional Behavior

Making others' behavior meaningful and predictable depends to a large degree on the "naive" perceiver distinguishing between acts that are intended and those that are accidental (Barker & Wright, 1955; Heider, 1958; Jones & Davis, 1965). Judgments of morality and responsibility rest in part on the extent to which a person is perceived as producing an act as well as effects that are intended or not, thus, whether he should be blamed, credited, or excused. As such, the concept of intentionality is not the same as the concept of motive. Motive *assumes* intended acts, what one is trying to do, one's purposes and goals. In this discussion, we deal with only one of the many previously discussed aspects of behavior—inferences of intention and accident.

Following Smith (1978), intended acts are those that involve voluntary movement that results in one or more intended effects, that is, the actor foresees the effect at the time he acts. Some acts are only (or largely) done intentionally, such as singing and grasping, and some are done both intentionally and unintentionally, such as kicking and dropping. Do children as they observe behavior distinguish between accidental acts and intentional ones? Three studies (Berndt & Berndt, 1975; King, 1971; Smith, 1978) provide some answers. King (1971) used four short films showing two boys running. One boy accidently falls or falls from being pushed, combined with either neutral or negative consequences. Answers to standard questions ("What happened?" "Why did it happen?") were ranked from explicit statements of accident to explicit intention statements. Most 4-year-olds did not distinguish between intended and accidental acts. Significantly greater differentiation occurred for 5½-year-olds, and there was further differentiation for 9-year-olds. There was, apparently, no association between the accident/intention distinction and the type of outcome.

These results were, in the main, replicated by Berndt and Berndt (1975), based on four two-min. videotapes portraying instrumental aggression, accidental damage, altruism, and displaced aggression between two boys. Preschoolers (nearly 5 years old) and 8- and 11-year-olds were asked, among other things, whether the actor injured the victim on purpose (yes/no). With films (as opposed to stories of the same episodes), the two younger groups were correct much less often than the oldest group. Half the preschoolers were correct on both the intended (instrumental) aggression and accidental injury films (but not stories). Unfortunately for our purposes, the percentage of correct judgments was based on both film and story data combined; however, the data are interesting, in that correct judgments were much higher for intended acts than for accidental ones. Indeed, correct judgments of the accident film and story were at a chance level, 48% (cf. Keasey's reanalysis, 1978, of Berndt and Berndt's data). Thus, young children recognize intended acts as intended (perhaps reflecting a bias of *assuming* that all acts are intended), but it appears that they lag in their ability to recognize or infer accidental acts.

A study by Smith (1978) clarified and extended these findings. Three types of human movement were shown in short films: voluntary (walk; chew) versus involuntary (sneeze; yawn) versus objectlike movements (being pushed by an object; arm moved by an umbrella hook). These movement types were combined with desirable or undesirable effects and whether the actress was looking at what she was doing or not. Children were asked three things: what happened in the film; what the actress was trying to do, for example, "Did she try to trip?"; and what she wanted to do, for example, "Did she want to sneeze?". Smith (1978) found, like King (1971), that 4-year-olds tended not to differentiate between intentional and unintentional acts. What they *did* do was important: 4-year-olds regarded all acts/movements as well as their effects as intended by the actor. *Assumed* intentionality of young children is consistent with Piaget's view (1929) that they tend indiscriminately to attribute purpose to others' behavior as well as to nonsocial events. Piaget speculated that this tendency is based on two factors: first, the lack of differentiation between the self and other (knowledge of one's own intentions for acts gives rise to assuming others also intend their acts) and second, young children have little conception of chance and probability.

Smith (1978) found that 5-year-olds, on the other hand, clearly tended to discriminate between intentional acts and both objectlike and involuntary acts; they were also beginning to discriminate intended versus unintended *effects* of acts. In this age group, however, desirable effects were often seen as intended and undesirable effects as unintended. The 6-year-olds were similar to adults, largely in distinguishing voluntary from involuntary and objectlike movements. There were differences within each of these two age groups as to whether an act and its effects were intended when the effects were undesirable and the actress was not looking as she acted. Finally, it seems rather unlikely that the age differences in recognizing intentional actions are due solely to children's imperfect understanding of "try." Almost identical results were found in response to the "want" questions, suggesting that "try" and "want" have the same or a highly similar conceptual referent.

In summary, most preschoolers appear to *assume* that others' behavior is intended, and that assumption (bias) leads them not to recognize or infer accidental acts as accidental. Preschoolers' running descriptions of filmed behavior (Livesley & Bromley, 1973) and recall of short films (Berndt & Berndt, 1975; King, 1971; Smith, 1978) support this. Why, then, do some studies (e.g., Collins et al., 1974; Flapan, 1968) indicate that even 5- and 6-year-olds seldom recognize or infer intentions and motives? It may be that if intention is assumed, then actors' intentions are not worth mentioning from the child's viewpoint when describing what was seen; or, given complex films with a good deal of action, it may be that obvious acts and outcomes swamp the importance of inferring and recalling actors' intentions. In short, young children's scarce mention of intentions in their free descriptions or answers to probes cannot

be viewed as a direct indication of an inability to make such inferences. On the other hand, it is important not to assume an all-or-none ability to infer any-and-all accidents and intentions. That is, it may well be that under some circumstances intentions and accidents are quite easy to discriminate or infer, but not under others; and very likely, that some types of intentions and accidents are more readily inferred than others. The familiarity to the child of the circumstances and events portrayed and the complexity of the story are two noticeable differences among research films that might influence performance on distinguishing intention from accident.

To continue the summary, most children show rapid improvement during the ages of 5 and 6 in distinguishing acts of accident and intent; at the same time, they show an emerging distinction between accidental *effects* and intentional effects. There is some tendency to assume good outcomes are intended and bad ones unintended, but this bias begins to wane during the early elementary school years. Most studies show continued development of intention inferences throughout the following years.

A closely related body of research that deals with inferences of intent versus accident combined with positive or negative outcomes is that of moral-reasoning development. Because researchers of this topic usually require children to judge the "naughtiness" of the actor (rather than directly assessing intention inferences) and use stories rather than filmed behavior, that extensive literature is not reviewed here (see Karniol, 1978; Keasey, 1978; see also *Rest, vol. III, chap. 9*).

Conceptions of Behavior-in-Context

Such theories as Heider's (1958) emphasize that the context in which behavior occurs greatly influences the meaning attributed to it. That is, the situation (defined physically, socially, etc.) provides both opportunities and limits on behavior. As such, it influences the interpretation of behavior by defining what a person can and cannot do and induces expectancies for certain types of behavior. Despite the theoretical importance of situational influences, there has been no direct research (apparently) on the child's understanding of the ways in which social and physical contexts influence others' behavior. Various studies reviewed in this chapter, however, give testimony to the fact that young children are aware of situational influences, and, in fact, appear to have some bias toward attributing causes to situation factors more than person factors.

There is some recent research relevant to this area in which children's knowledge of events in particular settings or occasions are explored (e.g., Nelson, 1981). Here we depart from research based on films of events to data based on the child's own real experience. The term, social script, is used to describe the child's representation of, and memory for, ordered events that occur when, for example, one makes cookies or goes shopping. As the term implies, the script is an event structure involving (typically) a small set of actors in various roles (Schank & Abelson, 1977). The importance of scriptal knowledge on the cognitive side rests on the notion that representation of actions in space and time may be quite different from category, word-based representations (e.g., Goffman, 1974; Mandler, 1979). On the social side, scriptal knowledge provides a clue as to the way the dynamic stream of behavior between individuals is structured and, to the degree there are shared scripts, the coordination of behavior is facilitated.

The developmental questions addressed thus far concern the occurrence of scripts at various ages, events that are central at all ages, and the major changes in scripts in ontogenesis. For example, Nelson and Gruendel (1979) asked 60 children, ages 3 to 8, "what happens" when you have a birthday party, plant a garden, and so on. The youngest children's construction and memory for sequenced activities are general and skeletal (to illustrate, an entire birthday party script for a 3-year-old: "You cook a cake and eat it."). The major changes in development in scripts is an increase in the social aspect (e.g., 6½-year-olds often include birthday guests arriving and playing games; 8½-year-olds add the inviting of guests); an increase in the length of act sequences; a decrease in simple sequences, with an increase in complex sequential and hierarchical structuring. There are certain aspects of different scripts mentioned at all ages, that is, certain events are central. Even children as young as 3 evidence over 90% agreement and accuracy in sequencing their "day at school" when interviews and enaction are used. Scriptal knowledge, then, is one index of shared social customs in particular settings as the young understand them, and it has potential for elucidating the structuring (segmenting and ordering) of routine social activities in which the child participates or observes.

The general developmental findings of children's understanding of filmed social behavior are: (1) a relative shift from attention to, and representation of, obvious and external aspects of behavior to less obvious behavior and internal states of people; (2) a shift from merely describing behavior and events to both describing and explaining behavior; (3) a shift from the apparent assumption by young children that all behavior of others is intended to a distinction between intended and accidental behavior and effects; and (4) accurate recall of central events of episodes or stories increases in a linear manner with increasing age. Because there are many other data relevant to these trends that will be discussed in later parts of this review, a discussion of the possible reasons for these trends will be deferred. Although the ontogenetic trends just noted may hold in future research using a more representative sample of films and behaviors, the ages at which any discontinuities occur in the types of inferences, distinctions, and so on, are likely to vary somewhat with the features of films in relation to the child's experiences and cognitive abilities. For example, if children are shown a complex film about unfamiliar events, it is likely that even older children will tend to focus on more obvious aspects (actions, observable consequences, etc.) of the filmed behavior (Rappoport & Fritzler, 1969).

It is important not only to sample stimuli more adequately to determine the validity of these trends and developmental timing but also to sample responses more broadly. A good deal of the work thus far has relied on free descriptions or very general open-ended questions. As such, it is prone to errors of the child knowing more than he says and saying more than he actually knows. Other methods might provide clarifying information. For example, the extent to which children infer intentions, motivations, and personality traits to actors may be more sensitively tested by having children predict the future behavior of the actors because inferences of intentions and goals should lead to predictions of relevant behaviors and trait attributions should elicit trait-consistent behavioral predictions to the actors (e.g., Rotenberg, 1980).

Describing developmental trends is not the only important goal in this area of behavior perception; it is equally important to determine how children use information to attribute meaning and causes to filmed behavior. For example, the control and systematic variation of different types of person and situation information would clarify how children of different ages combine information, make it meaningful, attribute causes, and so on.

In general, very little research has been directed at children's conceptions and reasoning about behavior they observe, which is both surprising and lamentable, given the utility of such information in a number of applied areas. For example, to what extent are most children at various ages capable of providing fairly accurate eyewitness testimony in court proceedings? Virtually no systematic data are available to guide such legal decisions. (According to the *American Law Reports* of 1962, children under 5 are rarely judged competent to testify; those 6 and older often are; and in 34 states, children age 10 and older are presumed competent.) Such research could determine the selective attention, inferential accuracies and biases, and causal reasoning to which children of different ages are prone to help guide methods of judging children's competencies to testify. Likewise, little is known with certainty about what children learn from that which they see and hear on television. Most research on television has been directed at documenting certain aspects of programs (rates of violence, degree of sex stereotyping, etc.) and its effects on children's behavior (Stein & Friedrich, 1975). Little work has been directed at children's understanding of such aspects and images (see *Descriptions and Explanations of Filmed Social Behavior*). Do young children understand the motives behind commercial advertisements on television? What do they make of a hero detective who engages in a long series of illegal acts and violence for a (subtle and long-delayed) prosocial goal? Clearly, such questions bear on business practices and social policy; as yet, there is little systematic work to inform such concerns.

The Other as a Person

We turn from the conception of behavior to the conception of the person. The child and adolescent's understanding of the other as an individual constitutes the largest area of social-cognitive theory and research. Specifically, it includes person description; inferential processes, such as perspective taking; and causal attributions. Given the extensive work in this area, the review will present some of the major developmental findings and factors related to it while noting many review articles that supplement this one: Chandler, 1976; Flavell, 1978; Guttentag and Longfellow, 1978; Hill and Palmquist, 1978; Livesley and Bromley, 1973; Sedlak and Kurtz, 1981; and Shantz, 1975a.

There are two discernably different views of the child as a social cognizer vis-à-vis the social world, that is, the knower-known relationship. Some research is focused on the child's discriminating cues—discovering characteristics of the other, learning about social rules, and so on—which are suggestive of an underlying view of the developing child as increasingly sensitive to, and knowledgeable about, other persons and their inner attributes.

This view, in its most extreme form, conceptualizes the child as passive and as one who largely *discovers* social reality, an external given. The other view emphasizes the child's own mental activities in structuring the social world, giving it stability and meaning. The child is viewed as an active cognizer, largely *constructing* or creating social reality. Or, put differently, social reality is in an important sense in the eye and mind of the beholder.

Although these positions are not often as sharply drawn in research as this description suggests, it is important to note such underlying assumptions in this area of study. Indeed, these may represent another false dichotomy, in the sense that most contemporary psychology recognizes the joint contributions of the knower and the known. An example of some research relevant to this issue is a study by Dornbusch, Hastorf, Richardson, Muzzy, and Vreeland (1965). Children, ages 11 to 13, at summer camp were asked to describe some of their tentmates. The descriptions were classified for the types of categories (a total of 69) used when (1) two children described the same child, (2) when one child described two different children, and (3) when two children each described two different children. The question concerned the degree of overlap in the *types* of categories used in the descriptions, that is, how often the same categories, such as friendliness, neatness, and so on, were mentioned (but not agreement on the degree within a category, such as how friendly or how neat). If the person being described largely determines the categories used to describe him, then two describers of the person should have high overlap in the categories they use. If, on the other hand, the describer's available or preferred categories largely determine descriptions, then there should be high overlap in descriptions of two different people. These represent the two views of the child presented earlier: the child as perceiver of an external social reality versus the child as constructor of a social reality.

The results were these. When two children described one other person, there was a 45% overlap in the categories they used, but when one child described two different people, the overlap was 57%. The higher overlap of 57%, versus 45%, is a demonstration of the important role of the perceiver. At the same time, the magnitude of the percentages makes the opposite point—children are not autistic creators of their social world but share (45%; and not, say, 10%) their characterizations of the other. And, furthermore, when two children each described two different children, the mean overlap of categories was 38%. This degree of overlap may reflect the fact that children of the same age group in a common setting and from a common culture have some similarity in the way they represent other children. The point is simply that what one perceives in the social world is best conceived as a joint function of the characteristics (attention and representations) of the perceiver and the characteristics of the perceived.

Descriptions of Others

We move from this demonstration study of the descriptions of others to the developmental changes found in research. Usually, these studies are referred to as studies in ''person perception,'' the close counterparts in adult social psychological research being ''impression formation'' (Asch, 1946), ''implicit personality theory'' (Cronbach, 1955), or again, ''person perception'' (Bruner & Taguiri, 1954). The question is how children and adolescents conceptualize people they know in their everyday lives. Of all the things they *could* say about known others, what do they say? Are there systematic changes in development in the content and organization of descriptions? Two points are useful here. First, just as with the descriptions of filmed social behavior, descriptions are presumed to reflect a mixture of what children attend to, the meaning they attribute, memory, and their linguistic abilities to express their concepts. Second, accuracy of descriptions is not at issue but rather the form they take.

The most frequent method is merely to ask children to describe (orally or in writing) individuals whom they know (e.g., ''Tell me about ————.'' or ''What sort of person is ————?''). The free description method, although making substantial demands on expressive verbal skills, is a less constrained and biased method compared to requiring children to use the experimenter's preselected adjectives to attribute or rank an individual. The adjectives and traits children freely select index their spontaneous personal construct system (Kelly, 1955), and traits have been found to represent only a small part (20%) of most children's descriptions (Livesley & Bromley, 1973).

An illustration of the kind of descriptions children give in this area of research is useful to understand person perception. The following protocols were obtained by Livesley and Bromley (1973) in their extensive study of person perception of 320 English children, ages 7 to 16. The children here are describing different children they know.

Max sits next to me, his eyes are hazel and he is tall. He hasn't got a very big head, he's got a big pointed nose. (p. 213 [age 7½])

He smells very much and is very nasty. He has no sense of humour and is very dull. He is always fighting and he is cruel. He does silly things and is very stupid. He has brown hair and cruel eyes. He is sulky and 11 years old and has lots of sisters. I think he is the most horrible boy in the class. He has a croaky voice and always chews his pencil and picks his teeth and I think he is disgusting. (p. 217 [age 9 years, 11 months])

Andy is very modest. He is even shyer than I am when near strangers and yet is very talkative with people he knows and likes. He always seems good tempered and I have never seen him in a bad temper. He tends to degrade other people's achievements, and yet never praises his own. He does not seem to voice his opinions to anyone. He easily gets nervous. (p. 221 [age 15 years, 8 months])

She is curious about people but naive, and this leads her to ask too many questions so that people become irritated with her and withhold information, although she is not sensitive enough to notice it. (p. 225 [young adult])

Such descriptions in most research are broken into single-idea units and categorized. For example, Livesley and Bromley used two large categories: (1) peripheral or external aspects, such as appearance, name, age, sex, routine habits, possessions, social roles, and so on, and (2) central or psychological aspects that were more abstract and inferential, such as personality traits, general habits, motives, values, attitudes, and so on. In addition, the specific content within these two categories were studied as were the use of qualifying and organizing terms (e.g., explanations, how situations influence behavior, etc.).

It was found that the number and proportion of central statements increased significantly with increasing age, a finding well documented now (e.g., Barenboim, 1978; Gollin, 1958; Peevers & Secord, 1973; Scarlett, Press, & Crockett, 1971). Children age 7 and younger usually focus mainly on observable, concrete aspects of persons and on their behavior, possessions, family, home, and so on, the latter list suggesting that the person is conceived largely in terms of his environmental circumstances, that is, the person ''is'' what he owns and where he lives. Often global evaluative terms are used by younger children (e.g., good, bad, mean, nice). Around 8 years of age, there is usually a shift that occurs toward relatively more abstract and inferential concepts, such as the regularities in behavior of a person, traits, abilities, and so on. In fact, Livesley and

Bromley found that the only significant increase in psychological statements occurred between 7½- and 8½-year-olds; this coupled with substantial changes in three other indices (number of categories used, the use of traits, and use of qualifying and organizing terms) led them to view the 8th year as a critical point in the development of person perception (1973, p. 174). In short, there is a major shift from a highly concrete level and global evaluative orientation to a more inferential level in which more covert aspects, such as values, beliefs, and so on, are described. Such a change suggests that the child becomes less bound to the surface aspects of people and increasingly abstracts regularities across time and situations and infers motives for behavior.

Some research shows no significant changes in person descriptions after age 8 for the number of categories used (Livesley & Bromley, 1973; Yarrow & Campbell, 1963). However, there appears to be a substantial change between 12 and 14 years of age in person perception, as measured by significant increases in the use of qualifying terms (sometimes, quite) and organizing terms (implicit and explicit explanations of behavior and specifications of how traits are manifested or in what situations) (Barenboim, 1977; Leahy, 1976; Livesley & Bromley, 1973). This is an important change, in that it reflects the adolescent's emerging sensitivity to, and understanding of, causal networks in which neither very general trait attributions nor total situational factors are adequate; instead, it reflects a situation and person interaction (as reflected in Mischel's position, 1973). These changes were more evident when adolescents were describing liked rather than disliked peers (Barenboim, 1977; Leahy, 1976). There is one indication (Barenboim, 1977) of another substantial increase in the qualifying/organizing measure between 14 and 16 years of age for most subjects.

If one were to view the child as a psychologist who subscribes to certain positions or theories, the developmental changes, broadly put, suggest the following: prior to 7 or 8 years of age, the child conceives of persons largely as one who is both a demographer and a behaviorist would, defining the person in terms of her environmental circumstances and observable behavior; during middle childhood, persons are conceived more as a trait-personality theorist would, ascribing unqualified constancies to persons; and by the onset of adolescence, a more interactionist position emerges in which people and their behavior are often seen as a joint function of personal characteristics and situational factors.[1]

Having drawn this very general developmental picture, it is important to note that it is influenced by characteristics of the person being described, by characteristics of the describer other than age, and by characteristics of both the describer and the target. For example, more psychological statements are used by children, in general, when describing children than when describing adults (Livesley & Bromley, 1973). Further, in a study on children's implicit personality theory, Olshan (1970) found the child versus adult dimension was salient in descriptions for third graders but was not for either sixth or ninth graders. Children may have a more differentiated view of children than adults because they have more diverse interactions with children on which to base inferences, and children are more similar to one another and can more easily infer similar attitudes, motives, and the like. Also, Livesley and Bromley (1973) found more psychological statements were used by children in describing males than females, but there were few sex differences found for describers, that is, boys and girls tended not to differ in the ways they described others at each age but whether children were describing males or females did influence descriptions. Finally, children of higher intelligence used more central statements than those of lower intelligence, particularly at older ages, but whether one liked or disliked the target had less systematic effect. This latter factor, the liking or disliking relation, has been found to have an effect on various aspects of descriptions in some studies (e.g., Honess, 1980; Peevers & Secord, 1973; Scarlett et al., 1971).

There are other ways the developmental changes in descriptions have been conceptualized: as a shift from egocentric to other-oriented descriptions and from concrete to abstract. Such conceptualizations are usually drawn from Werner's (1948) model of cognitive development, which shares some major aspects of Piaget's (1970) model. The egocentrism dimension is variously defined but in general shows a shift in orientation—from personally oriented descriptions to third-party-observer descriptions with increasing age (e.g., Livesley & Bromley, 1973; Peevers & Secord, 1973; Scarlett et al., 1971). The shift from concrete to abstract descriptions is well documented, as previously discussed. Although valuable as a dimension in its own right for describing developmental changes, the dimension, nonetheless, presents some difficulties. Indexing descriptions only as concrete or abstract fails to reveal some important developmental changes (e.g., in content and organizing features), and more important, concrete descriptions cannot be assumed to reflect immaturity per se. Children and adolescents (not to mention novelists, biographers, and playwrights) sometimes use concrete episodes as vignettes to capture a particularly central aspect of a person. What is important is not just whether descriptions are concrete but how such descriptions function. That is, concrete descriptions may directly reflect the *only* way the child conceives of the person or they may be used as a vivid means to express a particularly telling quality of the person.

Children's conceptions of people they know change developmentally in some of the same ways their conceptions of behavior of unknown others in films change (not surprisingly): a relative shift from external, overt aspects of the person to internal psychological aspects (beliefs, motives, etc.) and a shift from descriptive statements to spontaneous attempts to explain behavior. In person descriptions, there are also indications of a change from specific behaviors of the person to more abstract statements (e.g., trait attributions) that seem to reflect an ability to find invariances or regularities over time and situations. Finally, there appear changes between middle childhood and adolescence from using unqualified trait attributions to qualified ones (qualified temporally and by situational influences) and from egocentric descriptions (involving specific relations between the self and target) to other-oriented descriptions (as a third-party observer of the other's social relations with other people).

The major changes in person concepts are perhaps best captured by the notion of differentiation. The young child, in contrast to the older child (1) seems not to differentiate clearly a person as a *psychological* being separate from his physical surround (i.e., a person *is,* in an important sense, what he owns, where he lives); (2) tends not to differentiate outward, observable aspects of a person from inward, covert aspects (i.e., a person *is* how he looks and behaves); (3) tends not to differentiate clearly his conceptions of a person from other possible conceptions of that same person (i.e., the person *is* as the child conceives him to be); and, finally, (4) tends not to differentiate within the person both good and bad qualities, contradictory tendencies, and the like (i.e., a person *is* good or *is* bad). As such, these show substantial similarities to some general characteristics of young children's thinking about their nonsocial world (e.g., in their attempts to understand physical phenomena, to solve conservation problems, to classify objects, and the like). As abstracted by Piaget and Werner, younger children tend to be "stimulus bound," to not differentiate appearance and reality, to assume their conception *of* reality *is* reality, and so on. During middle childhood particularly, the differentiations begin to occur

and stabilize: the near fusion of the psychological person and his circumstances is supplanted by a differentiation of person and surround; the outward and observable aspects are supplemented with inferences about the other's attitudes, beliefs, abilities, motives; the contradictory tendencies within individuals and the way their traits manifest themselves in different situations become differentiated from global evaluative and global personality attributions; and, finally, the qualifying and organizing statements in the descriptions of children and adolescents indicate their awareness that they are interpreters of the others' behavior and that other interpretations are possible.

This account of developmental changes along one dimension of differentiation could doubtless be supplemented with other types of dimensions. It is notable that there does not seem to be clear evidence, at least at this time, for stages of person conceptions. This may be due in part to the kind of data available and how it has been analyzed up to this time. For example, children are asked merely to describe others and the responses are not systematically probed for how they arrived at such conceptions. How children reason about people is more likely to show coherent patterns than the bare descriptions of others.

The similarity of findings among several studies of person conception may be due in part to the use of a single method, free description. As noted earlier, this method has several important advantages in the early, exploratory phase of research in an area, but it has some well-known problems as well (Barenboim, 1977; Berndt & Heller, 1979; Shantz, 1975a). Two shortcomings deserve mention. The first is that children are seldom asked to elaborate on what they intend by what they say about a person (e.g., two children attribute the word "mean" to a person; in one case the import is "she's always hurting kids' feelings" but in another case the import is "she got mad when I took her candy bar"). Just as one cannot assume that children use words with highly similar referents or that these referents are similar to most adults, one cannot assume (unfortunately) that researchers' definitions are similar—the second problem. For some, the word "mean," for example, is categorized as a trait, for others, as a global evaluative statement. At the least, criteria for each category require presentation.

To determine the validity of the developmental trends found in free descriptions, to explore the relative weighting of factors in children's impression formation, and to begin study of children's implicit personality theories, it would seem advisable to use some different methods, such as more standard question formats with probing, rating scales, and predictions of a person's behavior (Berndt & Heller, 1979; Rotenberg, 1980).

Inferences About Psychological States and Processes

The relation between understanding the self and the other person is a peculiarly complex topic, and it is one of the major issues addressed in several cognitive, social, and personality theories (e.g., James Mark Baldwin, 1906; Fritz Heider, 1958; Jean Piaget, 1932; Harry S. Sullivan, 1953; Heinz Werner, 1948). Both of the major developmental theorists, Piaget and Werner, have characterized ontogenetic changes in the self/other relation as a movement from egocentrism to perspectivism. Because the concept of egocentrism has had such an important role in the research and models to be described shortly, a brief synopsis of Piaget's views of the self/other relation is in order.

Egocentrism is a descriptive concept of a state of fusion or undifferentiation between the self and nonself. Piaget characterized infancy as a period of "profound" egocentrism in which there is no separateness between self and nonself. Only toward the end of the first year does the infant begin to recognize that objects have existence apart from the self's experiencing them (seeing them, touching them, etc.). That is, the hallmark of the separateness of self and other (objects and people) is the recognition that objects are neither created nor maintain their existence by the self's acts but exist apart from self's actions. Thus begins, according to Piaget, a sensorimotor objectification of "reality" in which the self is organized in space and time in relation to other objects.

The toddler/preschool period of mental development is characterized by Piaget as evidencing less profound egocentrism than in infancy but still showing considerable tendencies to fuse self and nonself. For example, there is a lack of differentiation of the physical world and social world as revealed in the child's attribution of psychological characteristics to physical objects and events (animism); its opposite, the attribution of physical characteristics to psychological events (realism); and the attribution of psychological purposes to physical effects (artificialism). Likewise, there is a lack of differentiation between the self's psychological states (thoughts, wishes, feelings) and those of other people, the fusion being reflected in the young child's *assumption* of similarity of others to his own wishes, thoughts, and so on. The young child also fails to distinguish

between what he knows and the thing known. That is, the self is not reflective about his knowing: reality is as he understands it to be. The picture that Piaget painted of the preoperational child as one who massively construes (assimilates) in terms of the self is, as we will see later, a focus of current controversy.

Piaget found in a variety of studies with different groups of children a significant decline in egocentrism in most children around 6 or 7 years of age. Specifically, the child clearly recognizes that other people may have different thoughts, perspectives, wishes than the self and becomes increasingly accurate in inferring exactly what those thoughts are in others. For example, children take into consideration the listener's characteristics much more often when communicating, and they begin to infer the appearance of objects to another who is at a different spatial location than the self. Piaget posited that the decline in egocentrism is facilitated by conflicts with others, particularly with peers. For example, the child increasingly confronts a social world of peers who also want the largest piece of pizza, want to watch the television show they prefer, and so on. This has the effect of forcing the child to reflect upon himself as a (correct) position holder in opposition to other position holders to persuade, trick, or somehow win the conflict.

At adolescence, egocentrism further declines in general but takes a new form from previous periods as a result of the "use and abuse" of new mental abilities, formal operations. The adolescent can engage in lengthy recursive thinking ("I thought about myself the other day, and then I began to think about thinking about myself, and then I began wondering why I was thinking of myself thinking about myself . . ."). Elkind (1967) has extrapolated Piaget's notions of egocentrism during adolescence to describe two types of imbalance between self and others: (1) the "imaginary audience," constructed by adolescents in the belief that others' concerns are the same as theirs, namely themselves, with a high degree of self-consciousness ensuing; and (2) the "personal fable," in which one construes others' feelings and experiences as totally different from the self's own. The underdifferentiation and overdifferentiation these constructions represent are partially corrected for most adolescents, Elkind suggests, by their confronting the lack of match between their notions and those of their intimate friends.

This is a very brief summary of Piaget's views (with some extrapolation) of the broad developmental changes in the self/other relations. It has engendered a great deal of theoretical work and research on children's social understanding, and it has engendered some controversy. Critics of Piaget's views have focused on several aspects. First, despite Piaget's theoretical stance that mental development is an interaction of the current level of mental functioning and the environmental aspects upon which the mind operates, his research is largely focused only on one side of the interaction: the mind. The other side, the environment, has been largely neglected. For example, the impact of the ways in which others interpret events to the child or the impact of formal schooling appear irrelevant to mental development. In short, the child is viewed as too captive to her own mental processes, with little appreciation of the influence of the social environment and the essential social nature of mental processes. Second, the theory overestimates, critics charge, the intellectual ineptness of the child vis-à-vis the social world. For example, Piaget's work emphasizes the inabilities and interpretive biases of the preschooler (particularly in comparison to the concrete-operational stage), which are at odds with the considerable social knowledge and skills of young children. Finally, there is no specific delineation in the theory of the important role of affect in the child's mental development. Some of these issues will be addressed at various points in the presentation of studies.

To have sufficient background to evaluate the methods and results of research in this area, some further discussion is required on the construct of egocentrism (Shantz, 1981). First, the prior presentation of Piaget's ideas should make it clear that egocentrism does not refer to the fact that children tend to make more errors of social judgment or more extreme errors than do adults; it refers only to their tendency to make a particular kind of error: attributing to others their own knowledge, viewpoint, feelings, and so on.

Second, the attribution of self's characteristics to another is not necessarily an egocentric attribution. If the self recognizes potential differences between self and other, analyzes and *infers* similarity between self and other, the attribution is not egocentric because there is an initial recognition of possible differences. If, on the other hand, self automatically *assumes* similarity, the attribution would be considered egocentric. The assumption of similarity is an index of the fusion of self and other.

Third, not all correct social judgments indicate nonegocentric functioning. One may be judging another who is very similar to the self, and by merely attributing one's own characteristics under the assumption of similarity, one could often be correct. Likewise, one may use information true of the self or people in general to arrive at a correct judgment of another person. For example, one may know another is sad when crying because the self is sad when the self cries; most people are sad when they cry; or losing something one likes makes others and self sad. In short, there are many social concepts and processes and much social information that can be brought to bear to arrive at correct social inferences other than "taking the role of the other."

Fourth, not all incorrect social judgments indicate egocentric functioning. One may know that the self and other differ in knowledge for example, but be unable to determine what it is specifically the other knows. To illustrate, one may know that objects appear differently to a person at a different spatial location than the self, but because the self's spatial relational knowledge or spatial rotational skills are wanting, one may make errors on the task.

Finally, apart from the correctness of social inferences, the relation between egocentrism and role taking requires comment. There has been a confusion in the literature because egocentrism is often viewed as the opposite of role taking, and, conversely, nonegocentrism is equated with role taking. It is not a relation of identity or equality but rather an asymmetric relation: nonegocentric functioning is necessary for role taking, but role taking is not necessary for nonegocentric functioning. In the first case, once one has recognized that the other thinks about things differently than the self in a particular context, then role taking, as an inferential process, can be used as one means for generating social information about another to specify what the differences between self and other's perspectives may be. Further, in the second case, that is, role taking is not necessary for nonegocentric functioning, one may recognize that there *is* a difference and use any number of other methods for specifying the differences (as previously discussed); or one may have insufficient inferential abilities or knowledge about people to take their role (as previously discussed). In short, the failure to role take does not mean ipso facto that the person is egocentric. In this sense, then, nonegocentrism is not the same as role taking nor is egocentrism the opposite of role taking. Role taking assumes nonegocentrism, but the converse does not hold.

Yet another error in the literature is to view sociocentrism as the opposite of egocentrism. Piaget (1970) saw sociocentrism as highly similar to egocentrism, in that there is still a fusion of the self and other. In this case, though, the self's thoughts and wishes are accommodated to others' thoughts and wishes (e.g., when the child assumes parental wishes are her own wishes—see Damon's [1977] first stage of authority reasoning in children). In the discussion here, we will use the term nonegocentrism as the opposite of egocentrism. Also, perspective taking has been adopted recently by many as preferable to the term role taking, possibly owing to the confusion of the term role as used by social psychologists to refer to a set of behaviors or functions, as in social roles of mother, teacher, firefighter, and so on.

In summary, then, the construct of egocentrism refers to the *assumption* of similarity between self and other; it is not the opposite of role taking or sociocentrism; and nonegocentric functioning is neither necessary nor sufficient for many correct social judgments of others (see Flavell, Botkin, Fry, Wright, & Jarvis, 1968; Shantz, 1981).

Models of Perspective Taking and Methods. There are two major models of the ability to infer and adopt the perspective of another. The first is John H. Flavell's model (Flavell et al., 1968), in which perspective taking is conceptualized more as a verb, so to speak, than a noun. That is, it is an information processing model that details a sequence of cognitive acts involved in learning to take the role of another. Four classes of mental acts are said to occur in the following order: (1) The social cognizer assesses the possibility that the other has a point of view (knowledge, attitude, etc.) different from the self's, that is, the recognition that different points of view *can* exist. This is labeled the *Existence* phase; it is the phase that involves egocentric or nonegocentric functioning, (previously discussed), and "it is not defined as including any cognitive mechanisms for discovering what the other's perspective actually consists of" (Flavell et al., 1968, p. 209). (2) Next there is a recognition of the *Need* to make inferences about the other's viewpoint, usually in the service of some interpersonal goals, such as persuading the other, winning a game, and so on. That is, the child may recognize the existence of possible differences and have considerable skills of inference, in fact, but if there is no perceived need to engage in such acts, no effective perspective taking occurs. (3) The third phase, *Inference,* includes all those mental actions that go beyond the social data at hand. The purpose of such mental actions is to infer "what the pertinent role attributes (of the other) are in a given situation" (Flavell et al., 1968, p. 209). (4) The last phase, *Application,* occurs when one uses such inferential information about others by applying it to self's forthcoming behavior (what one says to the other, how one says it, etc.).

Flavell's sequential model can be interpreted as both an ontogenetic and microgenetic process model. First, in the development of the individual, the Existence phase would be the first fundamental recognition that one's point of view is not the *only* point of view possible, that is, that other viewpoints *can* exist. Likewise, children presumably change in their ability to recognize times when social inferences of these types would be useful (Need) and change in how they go about making such inferences, and so on. The microgenetic use of the model is the notion that in every full-fledged act of perspective taking by the child or adult, the sequential steps occur over milliseconds of time. For example, for the Existence step, the child recognizes that in a particular situation that self and other *do* differ in viewpoints, not just that they *can* differ, and recognizes the need to infer, make inferences, and so on. The microgenetic process has not been directly examined to my knowledge, but the ontogenetic model, especially the Existence phase, has been studied extensively by Flavell and his colleagues in spatial perspective taking (e.g., Flavell, 1978).

Robert L. Selman (1980) has developed a more structural than process model that describes the different types of perspective coordination that occur in ontogenetic development. The self is taken as always in some relation to others, and the focus is describing self's conceptualization of that relation. Selman proposes an orderly ontogenetic series of perspective-taking relations that have developmental-stage properties. Further, perspective coordination is assumed to be a basic structure underlying social conceptions in four interpersonal domains: concepts of individuals, friendship, peer/group relations, and parent/child relations. Each perspective-coordination level is logically necessary but not sufficient for any manifestation of "a structurally parallel social conception."

The five levels of perspective coordination are briefly summarized here, but the reader has other sources for a full description of this broad model of perspective taking (e.g., Selman, 1971, 1980; Selman & Byrne, 1974). Level 0, usually occurring in children between ages 3 and 7, is labeled "egocentric or undifferentiated perspectives" in which the child is said to be capable of recognizing the reality of subjective states of the self and other, but frequently they are not distinguished. Some sublevels (A and B) apparently part of Level 0, have been described as follows (Selman, 1971). Level A is the simple attribution of the self's own viewpoint to the other, that is, egocentric judgments. Level B is characterized by the child's unwillingness to make any attribution to the other ("I can't read his mind!''). This suggests that in the wake of the early awareness that another *might* think differently than the self, the child assumes that the other *does* think differently, and so differently that the child conceives of no communality (Brandt, 1978). Levels C and D appear to be part of the larger Level 1 of perspective coordination, labeled ''subjective or differentiated perspective,'' as evidenced in children from ages 4 to 9. Level C includes responses where the child again attributes his own perspective to the other, but apparently because the other is in the same *situation* the self is or has been in. Here the rule ''same situation = same viewpoint'' is used with the naive assumption that the other will respond just as the child would. Level D includes various attributions to the other but with clear indication that it is not possible to know for certain the other's preferences, viewpoints, and so on.

At Level 1, the child understands that even in similarly perceived social circumstances, the self and other's perspective may be either the same or different and shows concern for the unique psychological life of people. Level 2, ''self-reflective or reciprocal perspectives,'' is marked by the child's ability to reflect on his own thoughts and feelings from another's perspective, that is, ''to put [himself] in the other's shoes and to see the self as a subject to other'' (Selman & Jacquette, 1978, p. 274). This level usually occurs somewhere between ages 6 and 12. The awareness of the relation of perspectives of the self and other is a ''second-person perspective'' that allows for reciprocity of thought. Level 3, ''third-person or mutual perspectives,'' is shown by awareness of the recursive nature of reciprocal perspectives (e.g., ''She thinks that I think that she wants . . .'') and by the ability to abstractly move to a third-party position to understand the mutuality of human perspectives. This level occurs usually between 9 and 15. Finally, the fourth level is labeled ''society or in-depth perspective,'' and in normal development usually begins after 12 years of age to adulthood. Here perspectives among individuals are seen as forming a network or system, and generalized concepts of society's viewpoints are held (legal, moral, etc.). There is, in addition, an understanding that the mutuality of persons exists not only at superficial levels of shared expectations but at deeper levels of unverbalized feelings and values. The primary data source for this model of perspective coordination has been children and adolescents' reasoning about moral and social dilemmas, using a ''clinical method'' of semistructured interviewing to probe the network of social concepts held.

Finally, a structural model of recursive thought (''thinking about thinking . . .'') has been described by Flavell and his colleagues (Flavell et al., 1968; Miller, Kessel, & Flavell, 1970). It will be described in the next section.

The paradigms used to assess perspective taking differ in at least three important ways: (1) the *content* of the problem—the assessment of another's thoughts or knowledge, spatial perspective, or feelings. These are often referred to, in order, as cognitive (conceptual) perspective taking, spatial (or visual) perspective taking, and affective perspective taking or empathy. For convenience, the research will be covered by different content, with no implication that content is important in task performance; (2) the *function* of perspective taking—sometimes it is an end in itself; in some research it is a means to an interpersonal goal, such as winning a game, persuading someone, and so on; (3) the *structure* of the task. Structure varies in many ways among tasks, but perhaps the most important is that in some tasks the child is a ''participant'' with one or two others or is in the role of observer of others. In participant situations, the child either has information the other does not have (as in hiding games or ''priviledged-information'' tasks) or the child's information is different from the other's information (as in the spatial task). An example of the priviledged-information format is the dog-and-apple-tree task of Flavell et al. (1968): seven cartoonlike drawings are presented in sequence that depict a boy walking, a dog starting to chase him, the boy climbing an apple tree for safety, and then the boy eating an apple as the dog in the distance wanders off. Three cards that show the dog chasing the boy are removed, another (hypothetical or real) person sees only the four remaining cards then, and the child is asked to pretend he is this person and tell the story the person would tell. If the child attributes to the other information in the missing three cards, he is deemed egocentric. Other levels of performance index the degree to which a child can inhibit attribution of his own information and supply a different motive than fear for the boy climbing the tree. Finally, in some tasks, the child is in the role of observer of others who are in some dilemma, and the measure is the degree to which the child can understand the dilemma from each story character's viewpoint.

Thoughts and Intentions. Piaget's original research on egocentrism (e.g., spatial and communicative) indicated that most children prior to 6 years of age did not differentiate between their knowledge and that of others. More recent research has revealed less egocentrism in preschoolers however. Studies have found that when a simple, concrete priviledged-information task is presented, one third to two thirds of 4-year-olds perform nonegocentrically and that 85% and 100% respectively of 5- and 6-year-olds performed nonegocentrically; however, all 2-year-olds and most 3-year-olds readily attribute information known only to themselves to another (Marvin, Greenberg, & Mossler, 1976; Mossler, Marvin, & Greenberg, 1976). In one study (Mossler et al., 1976), for example, children ages 2½ to 6½ were individually shown short television shows while their mothers were out of the room; upon her return, both mother and child saw but could not hear information carried on the audio track. The children were questioned, "Does mommy know . . . (the auditory information)? Yes/No?"[2] Because children had a 50% chance of responding correctly in this and other studies, these data are indicative of some 4-year-olds showing nonegocentric responding in simple situations (when given a yes/no question) and rapid improvement in nonegocentric performance between 4 and 6 years of age (Brandt, 1978; Marvin et al., 1976; Mossler et al., 1976). Largely corroborative data were obtained by DeVries (1970) in a hide-the-penny game. The 3-year-olds showed no recognition of the need for secrecy, sometimes offering the penny to the opponent rather than hiding it. It was not until 5 years of age that most children seemed to recognize the opposing goals of the player (chagrin at defeat and glee at winning) and tried to deceive their opponent by hiding the penny in different hands (although regularly shifting) at each trial.

A wide variety of conceptual perspective-taking tasks has been administered to children between 4 and 12 years of age. They differ in structure and function (previously described). But there is an additional important feature, most of these tasks measure more than egocentric functioning (differentiation of self's and other's viewpoint). They are scored in such a way as to measure the degree to which the child accurately infers the other's information (the Need, Inference, Application steps in the Flavell et al., 1968, process model). In short, it is a misnomer to refer to most of these tasks as "egocentrism tasks"; instead, they are perspective-taking tasks that include both measures of egocentrism and the ability to infer another's viewpoint. Most of the frequently used tasks have shown satisfactory, although not always robust, degrees of interscorer and test-retest reliabilities (Ford, 1979; Kurdek, 1978a).

First, perspective-taking ability as variously measured has been significantly and consistently related to increasing chronological age, as indicated by significant linear grade effects (Kurdek, 1977; Kurdek & Rodgon, 1975; Rubin, 1978) and signifi-

cant correlations with increasing age (e.g., Brandt, 1978; Flavell et al., 1968; Kurdek, 1977; Rubin, 1973). It is not possible to determine whether or when in the late preschool through elementary school years that marked improvements occur because across studies different tasks and scoring are used and different data are presented (e.g., mean performance or percentage of subjects passing). The most direct data are provided by Kurdek (1977) in which four widely used conceptual perspective tasks were scored in the same way: passing was defined as the ability to infer the cognitions of another person (Kurdek, 1977, p. 1507). The tasks included two observer-role tasks, Selman's dilemmas (Selman & Byrne, 1974) and Feffer's role-taking task (Feffer & Gourevitch, 1960), which assess the degree to which the child takes the role of the story characters and coordinates their perspectives. There were also two participant-role tasks, Chandler's cartoon task (1973), which is similar in most respects to the dog-and-apple-tree task described earlier, and the Flavell et al. (1968) nickel-and-dime task. The latter involves the child reasoning about how to fool an opponent to pick one of two cups from which money has been removed. The four tasks differed considerably in difficulty level: dilemmas were easiest, followed (in order) by Feffer's task, the cartoon task, and the nickel-and-dime hiding task, which was the most difficult. This order of difficulty was true for the total sample, grades 1 through 4, as well as at each grade level. The dilemmas and Feffer task, which a factor analysis revealed loaded on the same factor, elicited substantial improvement between grades 2 and 4, whereas performance on the cartoon task and nickel-and-dime task improved between grades 3 and 4. The absolute level of performance is reflected at grade 3, with 50% passing the dilemmas, 33% Feffer's task, 8% the cartoon task, and 4% the nickel-and-dime task. If these tasks reflect the ability to determine the knowledge and thoughts of another person, why are there such differences in performance? Kurdek suggests that the dilemmas task and Feffer's role-taking measure are easier because they are not designed to create a clear difference between the child (self) and others: "The child could merely be attributing his own social cognitions about the social interaction to the other person and . . . need not separate his view of the social interaction from that of the other person" (1977, p. 1509). Such a difference is built into the cartoon and nickel-and-dime tasks. In these, the child has to inhibit attributions of her own information to the other, infer the other's thoughts, and coordinate her own and other's knowledge. The clear difference between self's and other's knowledge engineered in the latter two tasks has some merit in explaining the data. However, it apparently is not the only important difference because other tasks that do this too, elicit higher performance at much earlier ages (e.g., DeVries' penny-hiding game vs. Flavell's nickel-and-dime hiding game; Marvin's priviledged information ''secret'' game vs. Chandler's cartoon task of priviledged information). Those tasks that are passed at earlier ages involve making inferences about perspective taking from the child's behavior (DeVries' task) versus a verbalized strategy (nickel-and-dime game) and measuring egocentrism only (Marvin's ''secret'' task) versus egocentrism and perspective taking (cartoon task).

In summary, there is yet no available evidence to determine whether there are any periods of substantial improvement of conceptual perspective-taking abilities with increasing age. The most direct data (Kurdek, 1977) are correlational, based on four tasks that differ in many ways and, therefore, cannot be considered definitive. An analysis of the differences among these tasks has the heuristic value, at least, of suggesting some factors that might influence performance and thereby clarify age trends. First, for example: Is the task constructed so that the child is a participant or an observer? To my knowledge, no conceptual perspective-taking tasks have been systematically varied by providing information only to the self-as-participant versus providing the same information about others (self-as-observer) to determine the impact on performance. Data from other sources, such as children's awareness of intentionality in judging others' naughtiness and self's naughtiness (Keasey, 1978) indicate that intentionality attributions are made correctly more often for self than for others' behavior for kindergartners, but not first graders. Although indirect, these data give a modicum of credence to the importance of analyzing perspective-taking tasks for ''the role of the child'' so that incorrect generalizations are avoided. Second: Does the task measure only egocentrism or does it, in addition, measure other social inferential skills? Such an analysis will clarify when in ontogenesis egocentric functioning is unlikely in certain circumstances and when it is the inferential skills (abstraction and use of category information, role taking, etc.) that are weak. Third, on the response side: Is perspective taking inferred from the child's behavior or verbalizations? Each has its strengths and weaknesses. Behavior-based data presumably reflect such skills-in-action without contaminating ability to reflect on what one knows; but they also require considerable confidence both in the correctness of the researcher's inferences and that the behavior has one primary basis, perspective taking. On the other hand, verbal data often can be taken at face value with more confidence than the researcher's inferences as to what the subject consciously knows and does not know; but they also are dependent on linguistic and communicative abilities and may underestimate what the child tacitly knows but can not reflect on.

One type of conceptual perspective thinking is the understanding of the recursive nature of thought. It defines, in part, different levels of perspective-coordination in Selman's model (1980); a structural model of recursive thinking has been offered by Flavell and his colleagues (Flavell et al., 1968; Miller et al., 1970). The model distinguishes between four levels of thinking: the subject conceptualizes thinking about contiguous people (''the boy is thinking of the girl,'' ''. . . is thinking of himself''); conceptualizes thinking about action between people (''the boy is thinking that the girl is talking to her father''); one-loop recursive thought in which the subject conceptualizes thinking about thinking (''the boy is thinking that the girl is thinking of father,'' . . . of herself,'' . . . of himself''); and two-loop recursive thought—thinking about thinking about thinking (e.g., ''the boy is thinking that the girl is thinking of the father thinking of the mother'') (Miller et al., 1970).

Rubin (1973) found that the ability to understand recursive thinking at various levels improves significantly with increasing age during the elementary school years. The ability to understand one-loop recursion, Miller et al. (1970) found, improves substantially between grades 2 and 3 (20% to 40% responses correct), but it remains at or under 50% correct through sixth grade. Two items in one-loop recursion were significantly harder: when ''the boy is thinking that he is thinking of himself'' or ''. . . that the girl is thinking of herself''—testimony to the difficulty of others' self-reflective thoughts versus thoughts about others. Two-loop recursion abilities were rare, even in children as old as 12 (Miller et al., 1970). But do children spontaneously use one-loop recursive thinking? Barenboim (1978) analyzed free descriptions of peers and found very few 10- and 12-year-olds mentioned peers' thinking about thinking, but 65% of 16-year-olds did. Likewise, Flavell et al. (1968) found that recursive thinking, measured by verbalized strategies to fool an opponent in a hiding game, developed during adolescence; even at 16 years of age, fewer than half used or verbalized recursive strategies.

Up to this point, studies have been reviewed that assess preexisting conceptual perspective-taking skills. Training studies offer the possibility of identifying what kinds of experiences in the training (presumed analogues of natural acquisition experiences) do and do not facilitate perspective taking. Is there any indication such abilities can be elicited or improved by certain experiences? Yes, several studies have found significant improvement after training in the conceptual perspective taking of children of preschool and elementary school age (e.g., Burns & Brainerd, 1979; Chandler, 1973; Chandler, Greenspan, & Barenboim, 1974; Iannotti, 1978; Saltz & Johnson, 1974). These results were found in several studies controlling for pretest scores; trained groups performed significantly better than control groups who had no training. Two of the five studies involved special populations: preadolescent delinquents (Chandler, 1973) and emotionally disturbed children (Chandler et al., 1974).

One type of training most consistently elicited improved perspective taking—role enactment. That is, children or adolescents were given a dramatic theme, situation, or made up their own skits and then enacted different roles, sometimes switching roles in the same play or between plays. Often training sessions were about one-half hour once or twice a week spread over 2 to 10 weeks. Prior to examining possible reasons for such effects of role enactment, these additional findings should be noted: (1) small-group cooperative activity training also can significantly improve perspective taking (Burns & Brainerd, 1979); (2) role enactment of fantasy-type roles as well as more real-world roles seem effective (although the latter were not successful in one study, Saltz & Johnson, 1974); (3) role-enactment training has most consistently improved conceptual perspective-training performance as measured by such tasks as Chandler's cartoon task and Selman's dilemmas, and it has less consistently improved affective perspective taking.

It is difficult to determine, given the multiple experiences involved in such role-enactment sessions, what factors are critical and can account for the gains children show. What is rather remarkable about the training is that it is quite "distant" from perspective taking as measured by the tasks, that is, the training does not employ any of the standardized tasks nor variants of them but rather is interactive play that apparently generalizes well to tasks. At the same time, there are some similarities that might be important in linking role enactment to perspective taking. For example, it may be that the ability to infer another's perspective is enhanced by as if experiences, that is, *behaving* as if one were Red Riding-hood, a firefighter, or a mother facilitates *symbolic* acts of reference. Or it may be that role reversals and role switching help to make children aware of differences in viewpoints and provide opportunities to coordinate such differences as they interact with others. These are only two possibilities of many and may or may not apply to cooperative play sessions that also elicited improved perspective taking (Burns & Brainerd, 1979).

Finally, the question is raised: Are the effects of role-enactment training specific to perspective taking or are they evident in other cognitive tasks as well? There are few data to answer this because most studies have assessed only perspective taking or social knowledge. The exceptions (e.g., Saltz, Dixon, Johnson, 1977; Saltz & Johnson, 1974) indicate some effects on causal reasoning, story-sequence memory, and conceptual tempo. Such results could suggest low discriminant validity of the training; however, such skills as these may be related themselves to the ability to take the perspective of another. The discriminant validity of role-enactment training remains, then, an open question.

Visual Experience of the Other. This area of research is concerned with the child's ability to determine *what* another person sees and *how* it is seen (perspective) when the other is in a different spatial location than the self. This, then, is the most literal form of the "ability to put oneself in another person's place," and of all the social-inference tasks, it is, in a sense, the least social. That is, the only thing a child needs to consider in most situations is the location of the other in relation to the objects viewed and not such subtleties as the psychological situation of the other, characteristics peculiar to an individual, and so on—as is true in many other social-inference tasks. Because this research has been reviewed in a number of places (e.g., Flavell, 1974, 1978; Shantz, 1975a), only the major developmental changes and recent research are presented.

The proclivity of young children to attribute their own experience to others was most dramatically illustrated, perhaps, by Piaget and Inhelder's classic three-mountain problem (1956). Children, from ages 4 to 6 (approximately), when asked to select a picture that showed *how* the three-mountain replica appeared to a person at a different location than the child, produced predominately one error: they attributed their own spatial perspective to another, the definition of egocentric responding. In addition, it was not until 9 or 10 years of age that most children accurately inferred the other's perspective from most locations (Laurendeau & Pinard, 1970; Piaget

& Inhelder, 1956).

These findings, although replicated by many and valid for the method used to obtain them, proved to be a hazardous basis for generalizing downward in development, that is, that prior to 6 years of age children are egocentric and devoid of spatial-perspective abilities. Largely owing to the work of Flavell and his colleagues (1974, 1978) toddlers and preschoolers have been shown to have some understanding of the spatial experiences of another person. There are two levels of inferences that have been examined: Level 1 is the ability of the child to correctly infer *what* another person sees or does not see; Level 2 is the inference of *how* the object appears to another (the other's perspective).

Level 1 understanding emerges in late infancy and is well established in most children by 3 years of age (e.g., Flavell, Everett, Croft, & Flavell, 1981; Flavell, Shipstead, & Croft, 1978; Lempers, Flavell, & Flavell, 1977; Masangkay, McCluskey, McIntyre, Sims-Knight, Vaughn, & Flavell, 1974). Using simple objects and motor responses, many children by 18 months of age indicated awareness that another does not see what the self sees and "produces percepts" in the other by pointing to objects and showing, thereby sharing the self's experience with another. And by 2 years of age, most children can produce percepts in the other while at the same time depriving themselves of the percept, as in holding a hollow cup in such a way that another can see the picture glued to its bottom (Lempers et al., 1977). Further, virtually all 2½-year-olds could move an object to hide it from another person by moving the object behind a screen; by a year later, most could deprive another of seeing the object by moving the screen between the object and the other person (Flavell, Shipstead, & Croft, 1978). In general, then, percept-production ability seems to develop prior to percept-deprivation ability.

How an object or an array of objects appears to another (Level 2) is an inference ability that seems to have a much longer developmental course. The first indications of such understanding emerge around 3 or 4 years of age, using simple tasks and simple responses (motor responses, yes/no answers), and undergoes rapid improvement and greater consistency in performance with more complex visual arrays through middle childhood and into early adolescence. The preschool data on the emergence of the ability to diagnose another's visual perspective are not entirely consistent, appearing to fluctuate some with various task features. For example, most 3-year-olds failed a one-object task to determine whether a turtle appeared right-side up or upside down to the experimenter (Flavell et al., 1981), and most children this age also failed to understand how distance from an object determines how clearly a person can see it (Flavell, Flavell, Green, & Wilcox, 1980). However, Borke (1975) and Fishbein, Lewis, and Keiffer (1972) found that most 3-year-olds could indicate another's visual experience by turning an array of objects to produce for themselves what the other was seeing. It may be that these discordant findings reflect the impact of certain task and response features: children's difficulty in understanding terms like upside down might underestimate abilities, whereas turning an array to reproduce another's experience may overestimate the child's abilities if the child is using a kind of topological rule to put the object nearest to the other also nearest to the self (and, thus, perhaps fortuitously, produce the other's experience).

There is substantial improvement on multiple-object arrays throughout the elementary school years (e.g., Coie, Costanzo, & Farnill, 1973; Cox, 1978; Flavell et al., 1968; Huttenlocher & Presson, 1973; Laurendeau & Pinard, 1970; Liben, 1978; Rubin, 1973; Shantz & Watson, 1971), often measured by having the child select a picture of the array as he thinks it appears to another at various sites around the array. And depending on the complexity of the array and other features, perfect or near-perfect spatial inferences develop through adolescence (e.g., Cox, 1978; Flavell et al., 1968; Laurendeau & Pinard, 1970). It should be clear, however, that such tasks measure both the self/other differentiation (i.e., the other's perspective is different than the self's) and the child's spatial coordinate concepts (i.e., exactly what the other's perspective is, given other's location). If it is true (as the preschool studies indicate) that children are rapidly learning that another does see something different than the self at different sites, then one would not expect to find egocentric errors very often in children of elementary school age. And, indeed, of all the errors made on such tasks, the specific egocentric error of attributing one's own viewpoint is only a small percentage, usually 8% to 25% (e.g., Coie et al., 1973; Cox, 1978; Eliot & Dayton, 1976). The bulk of errors are nonegocentric errors of inferring exactly how objects appear to another, for example, when the other is opposite to the self, the inference is made that objects near for self are far away for the other, or that those on self's right are on the other's left, and so on (Coie et al., 1973; Cox, 1978). Such errors indicate that egocentrism is not the problem during middle childhood, but the inferences based on spatial concepts the child has in relation to the other and to the self do provide problems and are only slowly developed.

These developmental trends are abstracted from a variety of studies that indicate that performance is related to other factors beside the age of the subject. For example, some of the task and response features that influence performance are: the number of objects in an array and the symmetry of their placement in relation to one another (Liben, 1978; Piaget, Inhelder, & Szeminska, 1960; Pufall, 1975); the complexity of the objects themselves (Brodzinsky & Jackson, 1973; Flavell et al., 1968); the type of response required (e.g., turning an array, reconstructing the scene, selecting a picture) (Piaget & Inhelder, 1956); the location of the other in relation to the self (e.g., opposite, 90° to self's left or right) (Cox, 1978; Nigl & Fishbein, 1974; Shantz & Watson, 1970, 1971). It may be that the impact of these factors has more to do with the child's spatial representation than social inference skills per se, as previously suggested (Ford, 1979; Shantz, 1975a). Yet, if there is some consistency across social inference tasks as to features that have direct substantial effects on performance or that consistently interact with age, then they may serve to illuminate underlying processes in the development of perspective-taking ability (Wohlwill, 1973).

There are two psychological factors that have been recently suggested as explanations of children's proclivity to select the egocentric view in spatial perspective-taking tasks: (1) intellectual realism (Liben & Belknap, 1981), and naive realism in relation to the spatial field (Presson, 1980). In the first case, Liben and Belknap (1981) examined 3- to 5-year-olds' ability to indicate correctly their *own* perspective of an array when the array was constructed in front of them versus when the array was presented in completed form to them and when all objects in the array were visible versus some objects were hidden by other objects in the array. Overall, children had difficulty separating what they *knew* to be in the arrays from what they actually *saw* in the arrays, a form of intellectual realism (also evident in children's drawings, e.g., when two eyes are drawn on a profile). The point is simply that some of the child's errors in computing what another person sees in much research may be based on the more fundamental problem of computing what *oneself* actually sees; (2) Presson (1980) reasoned that selection of the egocentric picture might be due largely to the fact that it is the only one in most picture choices to maintain the fixed relation between the array and the room in which the child is tested. If such spatial-field dependency or naive realism is operative, then providing the child with a change in the field that accompanies a change in viewer site (90°, 180°, 270° from the child's position) might decrease egocentric functioning. A miniature model of the room was provided that was turned to represent the position of the other at different sites. Egocentric responding was substantially lower at 90° and 270° compared to the same children's response in a standard perspective-taking task, although even with the model, egocentric responding occurred at well above chance level at all grades (first, third, and fifth). The lack of effect of the model at 180° is not clear. Although intellectual realism and naive spatial realism are offered as explanations of egocentrism, they themselves are not explained. Indeed, Piaget (1926, 1929) seemed to vacillate as to whether realism, animism, and the like, were explanations of egocentrism or whether egocentrism was an explanation of realism, and so on. It may be neither but instead that egocentrism, realism, syncretism, and such descriptive concepts are indices of either some more fundamental process as-yet-to-be formulated or the process of centration that Piaget (1970) seemed to favor.

The ways in which children solve spatial perspective-taking problems are not nearly as clear as the developmental trends and the types of problems they encounter in solving the task. Two primary types of processes have been suggested and studied: the development and use of spatial rules and mental rotation strategies. First, the problem of understanding self/other differences in spatial perspectives can be conceptualized as learning two rules: "same position = same view" (of self and other) and "different positions = different view." Salatas and Flavell (1976) and Flavell, Omanson, and Latham (1978) found that most children by kindergarten age evidence knowledge and use of the "same position = same view" rule, and half to two-thirds of the children in the first and third grades knew and used the difference rule. Mental rotation strategies have not been directly assessed. Indirect data (e.g., Huttenlocher & Presson, 1973; Shantz, Asarnow, & Berkowitz, 1974) suggest that imaginally "putting oneself in another's position" is quite difficult for children. It may be, if rotational strategies are used at all, that instead children tend to rotate the array and other to self's position and "read off" the resulting imaged display, a strategy frequently reported by adults (Huttenlocher & Presson, 1973).

Can spatial perspective-taking be taught? If so, by what means? One obvious method is to take children to the other's position to see how, in fact, objects look from there. This training procedure with preschoolers resulted in only mild effects in one study (Flavell et al., 1981) and no effects in another (Cox, 1977). On the other hand, confronting the child with the difference between his perspective and the other's while the child remains in his position has been shown to be quite successful with kindergartners immediately after training and again 15 weeks after training (Cox, 1977). This is, of course, the basic mechanism Piaget (1932, 1967) suggested as causing significant decreases in egocentrism, that is, confronting the self with the differences in self's and other's viewpoints (figuratively or literally). Interestingly, there is some evidence in referential communication-training studies that confronting the speaker with the inadequacies of a message for the listener also results in greater improved performance than role-reversals of the speaker becoming the listener and vice versa (Shantz, 1981). But definitive answers to the relative efficacy of different training procedures await further research.

Feelings. The child's understanding of another's feelings has been given a critical role in some major social and personality theories (e.g., Mead, 1934; Sullivan, 1953) for the development of social understanding in general and in the development of positive social behavior. It has been studied under such titles as empathy, affective perspective-taking, and, the more general term, social sensitivity. The discussion here will be on the developmental changes and issues because there are many available recent reviews (e.g., Deutsch & Madle, 1975; Feshbach, 1978; M. L. Hoffman, 1978; Shantz, 1975a).

There are two definitions of empathy, one cognitive and the other affective. The cognitive definition is the child's *understanding* of another's emotions as provided by the discrimination and recognition of cues of affect and inferences about the internal emotional states of others, particularly inferences based on taking the perspective of another. The affective definition of empathy is the *emotional* response of the self to, or with, the other's affect. Specifically, empathy is thought of as having the same emotion as the other (upon seeing another fearful, the self feels fear, too, e.g., Feshbach, 1978) or of having the same or different emotion (upon seeing another fearful, the self feels sadness or fear, e.g., M. L. Hoffman, 1978). Although it is possible to divide a response of the self to another's feelings into a cognitive component and an affective component, it is not assumed here (nor by most others) that they occur independently or in a particular order. The two major models of empathy, Feshbach's (1978) and M. L. Hoffman's (1978), include both cognitive and affective components. This review is based on some research that includes both understanding and emotional response to another's feelings because the methods used in many studies combine the two components.

Preschoolers' ability to identify emotions of others in posed photographs of adults' faces has shown that pleasant versus unpleasant emotions are reliably distinguished, and often, particular emotions can be identified when the verbal label is given and the child merely selects a picture to go with it (Gitter, Mostofsky, & Quincy, 1971; Izard, 1971). Children are less often correct, however, if required to supply the name of the emotion to the photograph. Most children by 4 or 5 years of age know the typical emotions another person would experience in simple, familiar situations (Borke, 1971, 1973). For example, in Borke's Interpersonal Perception Test (1971), short stories about losing a toy, having a favorite snack, and so on, are read and each is accompanied by a picture illustrating the situation but not the face of the main character. The child is asked what the story character feels and answers by selecting one of four stylized drawings of faces showing fear, anger, happiness, or sadness. On the whole, happy and sad situations were identified more reliably than anger and fear situations among preschoolers and first graders (Borke, 1971; Feshbach & Roe, 1968).

The meaning of these findings has been the subject of some debate. Whereas to some these abilities of preschoolers indicated empathic abilities that, in turn, were thought to be based on nonegocentric functioning, others (e.g., Chandler & Greenspan, 1972) have suggested that correct responses could be the result of many different processes, only one of which might be "affective perspective-taking." For example, when only situational information is given, the child may correctly identify the emotion of another by knowing how most people feel in that situation (normative social information), how they themselves have felt in that situation, or a simple association of situation with emotion (e.g., birthday parties = happy times). Gove and Keating (1979) and Hughes, Tingle, and Sawin (1981) found support for this last possibility. With facial cues available, it is also possible to arrive at a correct answer in a variety of ways. In short, the child's understanding of how another feels can be based on any one of a number of possible processes. Regardless of the process, the important fact remains that significant increases in understanding others' emotions and situations that elicit emotions occur between the ages of 3 and 6.

It has been suggested that "when situations are

familiar and/or the person being judged is similar to the judger, accuracy (in identifying the other's emotion) may be the result of a simple attribution of one's own response or characteristics'' (Shantz, 1975a, p. 280). There is evidence that higher empathy scores (identifying the other's emotion or feeling the same emotion) occur when the judge and judgee are the same sex (Deutsch, 1975; Feshbach & Roe, 1968) or the same race (Klein, 1971), and scores on comprehension are lower when the judge and judgee differ in age (i.e., children judging adults vs. other children) (e.g., Flapan, 1968; Rothenberg, 1970). Likewise, children's judgments about individuals' emotions often seem to be based on the familiar situation the other is in rather than cues of affect from the person. For example, when a pictured child in a familiar setting (birthday party) shows an emotion (sadness) different from what most people or the self would probably feel, children often err toward the situation (judge happy) (Burns & Cavey, 1957; Deutsch, 1974).

During the elementary school years, comprehension of others' emotions improves, at least when measured by tasks in which "appropriate" emotions are expressed in particular situations (e.g., Kurdek & Rodgon, 1975; Rothenberg, 1970). However, when "inappropriate" emotions are shown (i.e., the incongruous task described in the preceding paragraph), some studies show significantly poorer performance with increasing age (e.g., Iannotti, 1978; Kurdek & Rodgon, 1975). The reasons for this trend are not at all clear. On the one hand, a simple methodological factor may account for the finding, Kurdek and Rodgon (1975) suggest, in that older children may be more attentive to the verbal narration that describes the situation (but not the emotions). Or it could be that the simple and highly familiar situations are more apt to elicit from older children well-learned normative emotions for situations, or projections. Indeed, Kurdek and Rodgon found increasing projection with increasing age from kindergarten through sixth grade. If the trend is not a method artifact, the findings speak to heavy reliance on situation cues in attributing emotions throughout middle childhood when the situation and expressed emotions are in conflict.

Rothenberg (1970) used a different method than the incongruous-emotions tasks to maximize the dissimilarity of the self and other. She had children judge adults' emotions in situations the child had not experienced herself (e.g., having to prepare dinner quickly for unexpected guests). Under these conditions, 8½-year-olds had difficulty correctly identifying emotions (happiness, sadness, anger, and anx-

iety), changes of emotions, and their causes. The 10½-year-olds were significantly more accurate. These findings parallel quite well Flapan's data (1968), described earlier, of children in this age range increasingly spontaneously identifying or inferring others' emotions in filmed stories as well as their increasing attempts to explain others' emotions.

The study of children's understanding of emotions has a very short history; it has been focused in the main on only four basic emotions (happy, sad, fear, anger) to the exclusion of more complex blends of emotions (e.g., chagrin, jealousy, pride) or on conflicting emotions and, for the most part, emotions as they occur in simple situations. Very little research has been addressed to children's understanding of the causes of emotion, the influence of emotion on behavior, or how emotional expressions of others' may be misleading as to their internal state.

Inferences About the Causes of Behavior

"Why did he do that?" is a ubiquitous question. Inferring *why* a person behaved as she did (aggressed, helped, failed or passed a test) is a fundamental way in which others' behavior is made meaningful and predictable (Heider, 1958). Social causal inference theories, known collectively as attribution theories, and the bulk of research on causal thinking are not developmental. The major theories (Heider, 1958; Jones & Davis, 1965; Kelley, 1967, 1973) deal with the ways in which the average adult makes causal inferences, given certain information about the other's behavior, situation, and so on. Only during the last decade have these theories been used to study the development of causal reasoning.

First, let us recall the propensity children have for making and stating causal inferences at all prior to examining how they go about making such inferences. The most relevant data, although sparse, indicate a steady increase from middle childhood through early adolescence in spontaneous attempts to explain behavior observed in films (Collins et al., 1974; Flapan, 1968) and in people known to children (e.g., Livesley & Bromley, 1973). Flapan (1968), for example, found that half the 6-year-old girls tested never explained any behavior they saw in two films, contenting themselves merely with description, whereas virtually all the 9- and 12-year-olds spontaneously attempted at least some explanations. Livesley and Bromley (1973) also found that spontaneous explanations of central statements increased significantly with increasing age, particularly around 13 years of age. These data indicate what children *do* when asked to describe behavior or persons, and not what they *can* do in making causal inferences, and thereby may underestimate the use of causal schemes.

All major social-attribution theories distinguish two loci of causes: internal causes (characteristics of the person, such as their abilities, effort, attitudes, etc.) or external causes (outside-the-individual factors, such as the situation or thing toward which behavior is directed). For example, in Kelley's theory (1967), various types of information are hypothesized as influencing whether causes of behavior are attributed to something about the person or about the situation. The types of information are: (1) *consistency,* that is, whether the actor usually behaves the way he just did (high consistency) or whether he rarely, if ever, behaves that way (low consistency); (2) *distinctiveness,* that is, whether the actor responds the same way to similar entities (people or objects), labeled low distinctiveness, or whether he behaves differently toward similar entities (high distinctiveness); (3) *consensus,* which concerns how other people than the actor usually behave in relation to the entity, high consensus meaning that the actor behaves like most other people and low consensus meaning that he does not. For example, if one wanted to explain why John gave Bob a piece of candy, it is likely we would attribute it to something about the person, that is, the actor, John, if (1) hardly anyone else gives Bob candy (low consensus); or (2) John also gives candy to many other people (low distinctiveness); or (3) in the past, John has often given candy to Bob (high consistency) (adapted from DiVitto & McArthur, 1978). If, on the other hand, the opposite information, that is, reversals of highs and lows on consensus and distinctiveness were present, we would likely attribute the giving of candy to something about the entity, Bob. Kelley's principle of covariation (1967) is basic to drawing inferences. He proposes that observers consider whether an effect (candy giving here) covaries with the particular actor, entity, or circumstance. In the example, each single covariant implicates John and the configuration (low consensus, low distinctiveness, and high consistency) strongly implicates John, not Bob, as the locus of the cause.

Do children use the covariation principle in the predicted way? There are not extensive data, but it appears that most children by age 5 or 6 use the covariation principle to attribute causes to social behavior, particularly in the case of consistency information and distinctiveness information (e.g., DiVitto & McArthur, 1978; Leahy, 1979). The use of consensus information, and particularly the developmental onset of its use, is not as clear (DiVitto & McArthur, 1978; Ruble, Feldman, Higgins, & Karlovac, 1979; Sedlak & Kurtz, 1981; Shaklee, 1976). Even for adults, consensus information has been found to have so little effect on inferences that the effect, as some authors put it, appears "to violate not only common sense of attribution theory, but any kind of common sense at all" (Nisbett, Borgida, Crandall, & Reed, 1976, p. 115). It is worth drawing attention to the fact that many adults do not evidence unbiased inference making: they tend to ignore important and logically compelling data in everyday induction, they often prefer concrete and vivid events to abstract data (Nisbett et al., 1976), and they often overestimate the role of person factors (dispositions) and underestimate the impact of situation factors (e.g., Ross, 1977).

There are more complexities to social-attribution theories and research than suggested up to this point. Because there are extensive reviews of this literature available (Guttentag & Longfellow, 1978; Ruble & Rholes, 1981; Sedlak & Kurtz, 1981) only a few causal schemes will be presented here, particularly those on social-causal (not physical) reasoning involving a sufficient number of developmental studies where some consistent findings have emerged.

Sometimes covariation information is incomplete for the observer, Kelley (1973) notes. In such cases, the observer relies on causal schemata, according to the theory, such as those of multiple *sufficient* causes (MSC) and multiple *necessary* causes (MNC). Causes may be, of course, either facilitative (increasing the probability of an effect occurring) or inhibitory (decreasing the probability). An example of MSC schema use with facilitative causes is provided by the studies of Smith (1975) and Karniol and Ross (1976). The task for the children was to decide which of two story characters really wanted to play with a toy, the one whose mother either rewarded toy playing or commanded toy playing versus the one who had no such external factors but just played on her own (the internal factor of intrinsic interest). Using the MSC schema, the effect (toy playing) can be attributed to one or more sufficient causes. If a sufficient cause is present, then the observer cannot be certain a second sufficient cause is also operative. The observer may apply the discounting principle: "The role of a given cause in producing a given effect is discounted if other plausible causes are also present" (Kelley, 1971, p. 8). If a child has the discounting principle available, presumably she would recognize that the mother's rewards or commands are sufficient to cause toy playing and would discount intrinsic interest. Kindergartners did not use discounting, and although second graders did so more often, it was not until fourth grade that adultlike use was evident. Costanzo, Grumet, and Brehm (1974) used a similar task and found that sixth graders used discounting, but not first graders. What kindergarten and first graders apparently tended to do in these studies, instead, was to use an additive principle: the child who was commanded or rewarded *also wanted* to play with the toy, the children thought. This reasoning has been called a halo schema (Heider, 1958) or augmentation error (Sedlak & Kurtz, 1981) in which a sufficient cause augments or is added to another cause rather than being discounted. This error on this task is reminiscent of Damon's findings (1977) that the young child tends not to differentiate between an authority's wishes and the child's own wishes. (It bears noting that there is some controversy in the attribution literature about the correctness of the assumption that MSC schema imply discounting, given *independent* sufficient causes, or whether discounting is only implied in the more complex graded-effects schema of *interdependent* causes. A full discussion is offered by Kun, Murray, Sredl, 1980, and Sedlak & Kurtz, 1981.)

In summary, the discounting principle appears to emerge usually between 7 and 9 years of age and to be evident in most children's causal inferences between 9 and 11. Younger children seem to err by adding one sufficient cause to another (augmentation error) rather than discounting one. But there is some disagreement as to the ontogenetic patterns because responses differ, depending on the use of stories versus film (Shultz & Butowsky, 1977), whether sufficient causes are internal only, external only, or pitted against one another (e.g., Costanzo et al., 1974; Karniol & Ross, 1979), and further, whether children's attributions might better be described by different schemata other than the multiple sufficient causal schema (Kun et al., 1980).

One particular attribution area, achievement, has received a good deal of study and is based primarily on the theoretical model proposed by Weiner (1974). In this model, causes for success or failure at a task are classified along two dimensions: internal versus external and stable versus unstable. In combination, the internal/stable cause is ability; the internal/unstable cause is effort; the external/stable cause is task difficulty; and the external/unstable cause is luck. Children's expectancies and attributions for their own and others' successes and failures have important implications, of course, for their future schoolwork and their self-esteem (see Dweck, 1978). In addition, it is one of the few areas of so-cial-cognitive development that has shown consistent sex differences, with the general tendency for girls to attribute failure to lack of ability but for boys to attribute it to lack of effort (Dweck, 1978).

There are two aspects of much of the achievement-attribution work that bear mentioning at the outset. First, in most studies children are given outcome information (success, failure, or gradations between them) and are asked to select among the four major causes of ability, effort, luck, and task difficulty, that is, restricted choices. When they *are* free to supply their own causes, they seldom use luck, often mention effort, ability, and task difficulty, and, in addition, use intrinsic motivation (wanting to do well) and an ability-and-task relation ("the task was too hard for him") (Frieze & Snyder, 1980). Second, most research has been done with real or hypothetical *academic* achievement problems. Thus, it may, as a body of research, represent achievement attributions in general or it may be specific to academic-task situations. For example, in a more playful achievement task of catching frogs, the reasons for success were quite different from those used for academic outcomes Frieze and Snyder (1980) found. Ability and intrinsic motivation were seldom invoked for frog catching, but task difficulty and effort were.

It would be expected that most children and adults viewing a person succeeding over several trials at a task (consistency information) would infer high ability, and viewing a person failing over several trials, would infer low ability; also, if several others are seen to succeed at a task (consensus information), the task would be judged easy but if they all failed, judged difficult. Shaklee (1976) gave children information about one child having all success, all failure, and mixed outcomes while playing a game (to elicit ability inferences) and about four children playing one game (to elicit task-difficulty inferences). She found that preschool children only made a clear distinction between total success and total failure in attributing task ease or difficulty, whereas kindergartners and second graders made more discriminations based on mixed outcome patterns. Ability inferences for both preschoolers and kindergartners showed gross differentiation of ability, but second graders were significantly better in ability inferences. It was not clear whether younger children have difficulty summarizing data over trials or in using such summaries in making inferences. A later study (Shaklee & Tucker, 1979) suggested that summarizing is not the problem, but that using summaries to make correct inferences about another is.

Most achievement-attribution studies give children summarized outcome information. Nicholls (1978) used a unique format (for this area of research), however, by offering open-ended questions after children had seen short films of a diligent child and a lazy child doing mathematics problems. They were asked to explain why both children succeeded, both did poorly, and why the hard worker did poorly and the lazy one did well. Consistent with Shaklee's findings (1976), kindergarten and first-grade children did not make correct effort and ability attributions, instead they seemed not to have effort, outcome, and ability well differentiated. A kind of halo scheme was evident: ''people who try harder are smarter—even if they [fail]'' (p. 812). Children ages 7 to 9 (approximately) showed a higher level of reasoning in which clear cause-and-effect relationships were used between effort and outcome, but ability inferences were not well established (and ability inferences needed to be made to explain how equal performance can result from unequal effort). It was only at Level 4, usually beginning about 10 years of age and evident in most 12- and 13-year-olds, that outcomes were seen as jointly determined by effort and ability. It appears, then, that when children do begin to differentiate possible causes, effort is assumed to be the primary cause of success (or the lack of it for failure), and only later is ability used (Karabenick & Heller, 1976; Kun, 1977). A less direct method was used by Weiner and Peter (1973), and they obtained similar results. They presented stories, such as, ''Carolyn is not good at working puzzles. She is trying to do this puzzle. She gets it put together,'' and asked the child whether (and how much) to reward or punish the story character. With stories varying ability, effort, and outcome, they found rewards were more determined by effort and outcome for children age 4 and older and ability had little impact in rewarding until 13 years of age. By 16 to 18 years of age, lack of ability associated with success is rewarded more than success with ability, quite possibly owing to the inference that the less able tried harder.

In sum, children differentiate effort before ability in development, tend to account for success in terms of effort rather than ability, and reward effort more than ability. Why this primacy of effort over ability? The maxim of ''try hard and you will succeed'' has been suggested (Guttentag & Longfellow, 1978) as a frequently taught rule and one that might function to preserve self-esteem because one has more control over effort than ability. As such, success is attributed to effort and effort is rewarded. Why the internal-person characteristic of effort is conceptualized in development prior to the internal charac-

teristic of ability is not clear. It is possible that the notion of trying (in terms of intention as well as exertion) has a privileged status from early childhood onward in development. From the earlier studies reviewed on intention, there is evidence that young children assume all behavior of others is intended (goal directed) and, presumably, one exerts some effort to reach one's goals. Likewise, it may be that children find it difficult to differentiate ability from task difficulty. That is, the perceptible task is given the attributes hard or easy with no recognition that those are not absolute characteristics of the task but are relative to the (less perceptible) abilities of the person (and vice versa). In a sense, then, children may be physicalizing ability by equating it with task difficulty. This same equating of internal states with external referents was found in young children in the case of understanding emotions of others (Gove & Keating, 1979).

Up to this point, we have considered children's causal attributions for straightforward, obvious human behavior (e.g., failing a task, giving a cookie, or aggressing against someone). What about less obvious behavior and causal links? Whiteman (1967) and Chandler, Paget, and Koch (1978) examined children's ability to understand typical defense mechanisms, for example, why a boy whose baby brother just ruined his model airplane would bang his own head on a tree. Chandler et al. (1978) examined the logical operations involved in various defense mechanisms, classifying them as follows: simple inversions (repression and denial); simple reciprocals (rationalization, reaction formation, displacement, turning against the self); and negations of propositional statements (projection and introjection). Children were tested on conservation and combinatorial tasks to assign them to the Piagetian stages of preoperations, concrete operations, and formal operations. In general, preoperational children did not understand any defense mechanism. Concrete-operational children understood defenses involving inverse and reciprocal operations. Those in the formal stage understood, on the whole, all types—inverse, reciprocal, and combined inverse and reciprocal (negations of propositions). Chandler et al. suggest that some of the difficulties of young children relate not only to deficient logical abilities but also to their tendency to use situational-proximal causes rather than distal causes to explain behavior (see Berndt & Berndt, 1975). This suggestion relates to children's use of the principle of spatial contiguity to infer a relation between cause and effect. This principle as well as temporal order and formal similarity between cause and effect, as principles for inferring cause-effect relations, have been studied in children (e.g., Shultz & Ravinsky, 1977; Siegler & Liebert, 1974). Because a good deal of this research deals with causal reasoning about *physical* events rather than *social* events (e.g., Shultz & Ravinsky, 1977), it will not be reviewed here (see Sedlak & Kurtz, 1981).

Finally, it should be pointed out that some perspective-taking tasks in part assess children's abilities to make causal inferences. For example, the dog-and-apple-tree task of Flavell et al. (1968) is scored both for the ability to inhibit the attribution of self's knowledge to an uninformed bystander and the ability to think of some other cause than fear-of-dog for climbing the tree (e.g., to get an apple, to have a view). Indeed, methods used to assess children's understanding of others' thoughts, feelings, and causes for their behavior overlap a good deal, more than may be implied by the organizational scheme of this chapter.

Factors Related to Social Inference and Knowledge

The broad developmental picture of social knowledge and inference abilities sums over many factors, and in this section we will address briefly a few of the characteristics of the child and of the task that are related to performance.

Characteristics of Children

Cognitive Abilities. Is performance on various perspective-taking tasks related to general intelligence? What specific cognitive abilities are related to performance? These two questions are the major ones addressed in the literature. In the first case, standardized psychometric tests of intelligence (e.g., Peabody Picture Vocabulary Test, California Test of Mental Maturity) have been administered, and the relationship between IQ and various perspective-taking tasks has been found most often to range between .20 and .40, seldom higher and sometimes no relation is found (e.g., Coie & Dorval, 1973; DeVries, 1970; Flavell et al., 1968; Hudson, 1978; Irwin & Ambron, 1973; Rothenberg, 1970; Rubin, 1978). The magnitude of the relations vary somewhat with the type of intelligence test used (e.g., Coie & Dorval, 1973; Rothenberg, 1970) and with age. Rubin (1978) found, for example, that the average correlation between IQ and six perspective-taking tasks to be highest at the preschool level (.39) and lowest at the fifth-grade level (.10). In general, the low to moderate relation of performance on social-cognitive tasks such as these and IQ gives little

support to the notion that such social-cognitive abilities are nothing more than a reflection of general intelligence. The intelligence quotient, an individual difference variable, is not as high a correlate as mental age, a developmental variable. The only study to my knowledge in which MA has been reported (Rubin, 1973) found correlations of .43 to .77 between MA and six perspective-taking tasks for children between the ages of 5½ and 11½. Further, the other developmental marker, CA, which correlates with MA at .85, also correlated with perspective-taking performance to the same degree as MA (.47 to .78). These meager data, then, provide psychometric support for the notion that social-cognitive development is significantly related to mental development and to chronological age, but is less related to individual differences in IQ.

As previously noted (Shantz, 1975a), such relationships between psychometric measures and social-cognitive skills are not very useful to determine what specific processes or cognitive abilities may be involved because intelligence tests themselves often tap many abilities and combine them, or they tap only one skill, such as receptive verbal ability (e.g., the Peabody Picture Vocabulary Test). It is somewhat paradoxical (given the placement of this topic in the Handbook volume on cognitive development) that little research has been devoted to identifying cognitive skills and processes of social inference. One presumed index of concrete-operational abilities, conservation, has been found to be positively and significantly related to various perspective-taking task performances (e.g., Feffer & Gourevitch, 1960; Rubin, 1973; but not always (Hollos, 1975). Although conservation may be useful as one index of levels of cognitive functioning, it does not help solve the riddle of underlying processes involved because conservation itself can be solved by many means (e.g., addition/subtraction schema, reversibility, multiplication of relations of height and width). Kurdek (1977) used two tasks that presumably tap the ability to relate simultaneously separate elements (cross-modal coding and the Raven Progressive Matrices Test) and found they were significantly related to four conceptual perspective-taking tasks, particularly loading with Chandler's cartoon task and Flavell's nickel-and-dime game. These relations, Kurdek suggested, are consistent with the notion that these two tasks require the simultaneous coordination of perspectives (in comparison to other perspective-taking tasks that do not).

There has been speculation as to the types of cognitive processes that underlie various causal attributions, often based on the age at which children exhibit certain abilities and then are presumed to be within the stages of mental development outlined by Piaget. Actual assessment of such cognitive abilities apparently has not been done. Some of the causal attribution work as well as some in the related areas of moral reasoning (Surber, 1977) and equity (Anderson & Butzin, 1978) has examined the ways in which children integrate different types of information (e.g., additively or multiplicatively).

Sex Differences. There is a frequent assumption that there are substantial sex differences in social-cognitive abilities, usually that females are more socially sensitive and more adept at social inferences than males. The developmental literature, in general, does not provide support for this assumption. This needs some specification however. On most perspective-taking tasks, girls and boys do not show significant differences in performance (Cutrona & Feshbach, 1979; Hudson, 1978; Kurdek, 1977, 1979; Rothenberg, 1970; Rubin, 1978). A few studies have found differences and these indicate higher spatial perspective-taking in boys than girls (Coie & Dorval, 1973; Kurdek & Rodgon, 1975) but not consistently so (Cutrona & Feshbach, 1979). Some studies using composite measures of social perspective-taking and social knowledge have not found sex differences (e.g., Jennings, 1975), whereas others have (e.g., Gilbert, 1969; Zahn-Waxler, Radke-Yarrow, & Brady-Smith, 1977). However, empathy research gives somewhat more evidence of sex differences. Feshbach (1978) reviewed empathy findings and concluded that *understanding* how another feels usually does not differ by gender, but *affective matching* does—girls showing more affect matching. Even this is somewhat suspect however. Feshbach suggests this may reflect girls' lower inhibition in stating feelings, particularly because the largest sex differences occur in response to stating one feels fear (vs. feeling happy or sad).

Characteristics of Tasks

The social problems presented to children to assess their abilities to infer another's perspective and to assess their social knowledge differ in so many ways as to defy any simple or even systematic analysis. That these differences are important is evident by substantial differences in performance on tasks designed to measure "the same thing," in terms of difficulty level, types of errors made, and correlations in performance between tasks. Only a very few of the many differences in the tasks, on the one hand, and responses measured, on the other hand, can be addressed here.

Task Format. Two aspects of tasks, their structure and content, are considered first. Differences in structure were addressed briefly earlier (see *Thoughts and Intentions*), and will only be summarized here. Perspective-taking and empathy tasks differ in the degree to which they are so structured as to present a clear difference between the self and the other person. This aspect is important if one wishes to measure the child's recognition (inference) of a difference when it exists, that is, to measure egocentric functioning. If there is no clear difference between the child and other, then a "correct" answer can be obtained by any number of means, including egocentric attribution of the self's knowledge, and so on. As Cronbach (1955) noted in research on adults' accuracy in judging others, actual similarity between the judge and the person being judged can be the basis for high social-inference scores by assumed similarity, projection, and so on. In short, social-inferential ability is confounded with actual similarity.

Priviledged-information tasks, game-playing tasks, and spatial perspective-taking tasks clearly engineer differences between the self's knowledge and experience and that of the other person being judged. However, most of these are scored in ways that combine self/other differentiation (egocentrism) and the accuracy in inferring the other's knowledge, spatial perspective, and so on. (And some scores also reflect the *consistency* of differentiation + inference by using the number of items scored at certain levels or the number passed.) Those tasks most often used with toddlers and preschoolers are the ones that present both a clear self/other difference and score only the child's ability to infer that the difference exists (e.g., Brandt, 1978; Flavell, 1978; Mossler et al., 1976). As discussed earlier, those tasks used with school-age children are usually scored for correct inferences about others, assuming a correct inference rests on distinguishing a difference between self and other but sometimes erroneously assuming that an incorrect answer is an index of egocentrism. This is, of course, not necessarily the case. The child may know full well a difference exists between her knowledge and another's, but not have the inferential ability or social concepts to specify what the other knows, feels, or sees (see *Inferences About Psychological States and Processes*). In short, not all tasks of perspective taking are clearly and only measures of egocentrism. It is inappropriate, then, to dismiss the construct of egocentrism as having any validity when it is found that perspective-taking tasks intercorrelate at only low to moderate levels (see reviews by Ford, 1979;

Kurdek, 1978a; Shantz, 1975a) if, as proposed here, many of these tasks assess many abilities in addition to egocentric functioning.

Some tasks do not create as specific and clear differences between the child and the other but rather present social-problem situations that others are in and assess the level of reasoning and solutions (e.g., Selman's dilemmas, Feffer's role-taking task). For example, in Selman's story where a little girl, Holly, has promised her father not to climb trees and then is asked by her friend to rescue the friend's kitten in a tree, the child's ability to infer the differences in perspectives and coordinate them is assessed. Here, the self is not pitted as directly against the other as in priviledged-information tasks, spatial tasks, and game tasks, and the child may or may not identify with one of the story characters. This description should not be interpreted as indicating these dilemma tasks are somehow flawed or invalid. They present merely a different problem to be solved in relation to self, a problem, in fact, that the child often experiences. That is, the child observes differences in opinions, knowledge, and wishes between two other people and tries to understand and coordinate them. Unfortunately, there is little evidence one way or the other that such structural differences in tasks do influence children's performance. The most direct (but by no means sufficient) information is provided by Kurdek's study (1977), described previously, in which, when all tasks were scored for the same level of reasoning, social-dilemma story tasks were significantly easier than priviledged-information tasks. This suggests, then, that the degree to which the self is engaged in the problem (i.e., observer vs. participant with others) influences the ease of the problem, but more direct examination of the task feature is required.

Does the *content* of the inference make a difference in performance—whether one is inferring another's thoughts versus feelings for example? In terms of difficulty level, the available evidence suggests that understanding *if* another sees or does not see an object (Flavell, 1978) is an easier task under a variety of conditions than understanding *if* another knows or does not know a fact (Flavell et al., 1981; Marvin et al., 1976). But beyond this point, it is not possible to discern whether spatial perspective inferences develop ontogenetically before those inferences dealing with thoughts and feelings because tasks vary on so many dimensions other than content.

In general, if content is an important determiner of performance then one would expect moderate cor-

relations among measures *within* one content area (e.g., several measures of affective perspective taking) and certainly higher correlations *within* than *between* different content areas. The relevant data are not very consistent, but they do suggest that content does not have a clear determining role in performance. Rubin (1978) found no relation within affective tasks (Borke's empathy measure, 1971, and Rothenberg's social-sensitivity task, 1970) and only low-order correlations within cognitive perspective-taking tasks. Kurdek (1977), however, did find substantial correlations in the latter case. More to the point, Rubin (1978) found correlations *between* different content areas (affective and cognitive) to be in many cases as high as those within one area (cognitive). A further comparison between different content areas is afforded by correlations between spatial perspective-taking and other perspective-taking tasks that have indicated a greater number of positive correlations (than no relations) and sometimes significant moderate correlations: with Flavell's dog-and-apple-tree task (Hollos, 1975; Zahn-Waxler et al., 1977), with Miller and his colleague's recursive-thinking task (Rubin, 1973), with communication tasks (Moir, 1974; Rubin, 1973), and with variations of nonspatial perspective-taking tasks (e.g., Burns & Brainerd, 1979). In sum, the content of perspective-taking tasks has not yet been shown to have a major impact on performance as reflected in difficulty level or intercorrelations among tasks.

Task Responses. Two aspects of the task on the response side are now considered. Are differences in performance largely due to verbal versus nonverbal response measures? Although sometimes suggested to be so, it seems unlikely this gross difference is critical. For example, the data just reviewed on the rather frequent moderate correlations between performance on the *nonverbal* spatial task (selecting a picture, turning a model, etc.) and tasks requiring considerable *verbal* production (retelling a story, citing reasons, etc.) would not support the idea that the verbal/nonverbal factor is critical.

However, what is being asked and how the child can respond do have an impact on performance. Brandt (1978), for example, gave two simple privileged-information tasks (Chandler's droodles and Ambron and Irwin's story task) and asked children: "What will (the other) think?" "Will the other think X or Y?" (X = what the self knows; Y = nonegocentric knowledge.) "Does the other know X?" The third question, requiring only a yes/no answer, not surprisingly, elicited the best performance at all ages (preschool and grades 1 and 3); of course, children had a 50% chance of being correct. But the second question, which also offered an alternative, was much more difficult than the third question. The reason it was is not at all clear. Suffice it to say, there are considerable complexities suggested by question/response relations, even when all questions have to do with the basic recognition that the other does not know what the self knows.

A second feature is the *level* of perspective taking that can be represented in how responses are scored or built into the task itself. Stage or level models of perspective taking posit qualitatively different types of relations between self and other (DeVries, 1970; Feffer, 1970; Flavell et al., 1968; Miller et al., 1970; Selman, 1980). Many of these models relate to the recursive nature of thinking, that is, the subject's ability to infer what another is thinking, that another is thinking of thinking, etc. The point is that in a stage model, one would expect higher correlations among tasks that tap the same level of recursive thinking than tasks that tap different levels. It is possible, for example, that some of the relatively modest or low intercorrelations among perspective-taking tasks that have been reported occur in part because various tasks measure different levels of perspective taking. There is some recent evidence (Kurdek, 1977; Landry & Lyons-Ruth, 1980) that tasks scored or designed for a particular level of recursive thought evidence higher correlations than those found in most intercorrelational studies.

In contrast to perspective-taking studies, little systematic research has been done on task and response factors that influence children's performance on causal-attribution tasks, although there has been speculation concerning memory demands, order of information given, and the type of response (e.g., forced choice vs. free response) (see Guttentag & Longfellow, 1978; Sedlak & Kurtz, 1981).

We have considered here two characteristics of task format (the structure of self/other relations; content) and two task response measures (verbal/nonverbal; level of reasoning), some of which seem to influence performance and some of which do not apparently. The impact of task factors is often interpreted as masking underlying competencies (in the competence/performance distinction). This view of task factors has encouraged two errors of interpretation of children's performance: (1) the age at which children succeed on task X (e.g., Piaget's classic three-mountain problem) is taken as evidence that they now possess competency Y (spatial perspective-taking) and younger children who fail task X have no competency Y; (2) simplifications of the task (usually intuitively derived by the researcher) then yield evidence that young children do indeed have some perspective-taking skills and, by inference, that the only reason older children fail some other spatial tasks is due to a variety of performance factors (number of items, memory demands, verbal requirements, etc.). Such interpretations are based on viewing competencies as very abstract concepts or rules that cannot be instantiated (applied, used) in particular tasks because of the inhibiting features of the task, that is, the task stimuli or responses mask the "true" abilities. Rather than such an absolute view of either having a competency or not having it, an interactionist position would suggest that competencies be considered in relation to the task at hand, that is, a competency-by-task unit. Instead of seeing the task as producing error, it is taken seriously as a partial determinant of performance that may itself change with age. Such a conceptualization offers a more systematic approach to task properties.

Further, it is possible to see some task characteristics as analogues of the way social situations themselves vary. Consider some of the features of tasks noted in the review thus far. Social situations that require some inferences typically vary (like the research tasks themselves) as to the role of the child, that is, whether the child is a participant or an observer. Social situations also vary as to whether one largely shares the same information as others or not; whether one is given (told, shown) information or must infer it; whether others' emotional responses are normative or not; whether the others are similar to the child or not; and so on. By reconceptualizing task factors in this way, the kinds of social information—structure and content—that may influence and interact with the child's social reasoning at different ages may be clarified and, possibly, may be more evident in social situations that vary on these same properties. Clearly, researchers have been rather successful at simplifying and complicating tasks, but often such task properties result in a plethora of things that *can* influence performance without any indication as to their relative importance as determiners or their meaning in relation to social-adaptation problems. As a result, we have little theory of the task (situation) or theory of the task × competency.

Relations of Social Inferences to Social Behavior

Most major developmental theories of social behavior, such as those of Freud, Erikson, Mead, and Sullivan, are based in part on the assumption of a close relation between the changing interpersonal behavior of the child and adolescent and the changing cognitive abilities in ontogenesis. The current work on social-cognitive/social-behavior relations, however, does not seem to be based on any one of the theories. Instead, some provide a general framework, for example, Mead's emphasis (1934) of the impact on social behavior of "taking the role of the other," Sullivan's notions concerning the importance of peers in the development of interpersonal relations, and ego-psychologists' focus on adaptive, coping skills for personality development. And the great bulk of research on children's social behavior, whether studied in an experimental or natural setting, whether from a social-learning perspective or an ethological perspective, has stayed largely at a behavioral level. There has been little, if any, examination of how children conceptualize or reason about the social situation in which they participate or which they observe.

In short, there is not specific and detailed theory guiding the research on social-cognitive/social-behavior relations. Perhaps the most frequently investigated position is that advanced social-cognitive abilities (of various kinds) are positively related to the frequency of prosocial behavior and negatively related to the frequency of antisocial behavior. It is unclear (except, perhaps, in theories of empathy) why this position is so widely held because social information and understanding, however derived (from normative knowledge, perspective taking, or self-knowledge), can be used for social good or ill.

Aggressive Behavior

Two questions have largely dominated inquiries into the relation between aggression and social-cognitive abilities: Is empathy related to aggression? What is the role of the child's ability to infer intentions of the other in the child's aggressive behavior?

Feshbach (1978) has proposed the following relation of empathy to aggressive behavior: the cognitive component of empathy allows the child "to examine a conflict situation from the perspective of another person [which] should result in greater understanding, accompanied by a lessening of conflict and aggression" (p. 29); the affective component of empathy provides for the observer of a victim's pain and distress to experience a vicarious distress, the affective empathy functioning then as an inhibitor of the child's own aggressive tendencies. In short, Feshbach posits, "children high in empathy should manifest less aggression than those low in empathy" (1978, p. 30), including both instrumental and anger-mediated aggression.

In developmental studies using the Feshbach and Roe Affective Situation Test for Empathy (FASTE), some limited support for the inverse relation has been provided in studies by Fay (1970), Huckabay (1971), and Feshbach and Feshbach (1969) using teacher-rated aggression measures. However, in the Feshbach and Feshbach (1969) study, no relation was found between empathy and aggression for girls (ages 4 to 7); and young boys (ages 4 to 5) showed a positive relation, that is, the more empathic were more aggressive. Feshbach (1978) has interpreted the latter finding, similarly to Murphy (1937), as a reflection of high social activity rather than hostility. In sum, the inverse relation between empathy and aggression is most often found for boys over 5 years of age and is not found for girls.

Rothenberg (1970) assessed third- and fifth-graders' abilities to identify emotions in adults and the reasons for changes in emotions in short vignettes. This ability, called social sensitivity, was related to peer- and teacher-nominations of children's behavior on a cruel-to-kind dimension. The relations were mixed: the predicted inverse relations between social sensitivity and cruelty were found at a modest level for peer-nominated third graders ($-.33$) and teacher-nominated fifth graders ($-.28$) but not for peer-nominated fifth graders or teacher-nominated third graders.

What of the relation between perspective taking and aggression? It, too, seems inconsistent. For delinquent boys (ages 11 to 13) who had lengthy police and court records Chandler (1973) found that their ability to take the perspective of another (Chandler's cartoon task) was quite deficient, about the level of normal children half their age. Burka and Glenwick (1975) also found that fourth-grade boys who were low in perspective taking were rated by their teachers as aggressive, acting-out, unpopular with peers, and so on. On the other hand, Kurdek (1978b), using four standard perspective-taking tasks, found in first through fourth grades that *high* perspective-taking abilities were associated with being disruptive in the classroom, fighting and quarreling, and general behavior problems, especially for boys. This latter study along with Feshbach and Feshbach's similar (1969) finding for preschool boys, indicates that there may be no simple relationship between aggression and perspective taking/empathy. The issues are abundant however. For example, what teachers perceive as aggression may be in part a teasing and baiting of peers (a kind of exercising of social skills); although certainly disruptive of a classroom, it may not have much of a hurtful intent as the term aggression usually implies. Whether such findings indicate problems in defining aggression, an artifact of high social activity, or a demonstration of the many purposes to which perspective-taking skills can be put will await further research.

The degree to which children can and do infer whether a peer's behavior is intended or accidental can have important consequences for the ensuing interaction. If, for example, a child thinks that another bumped into him or destroyed his puzzle accidently rather than intentionally, the child would be less likely to respond aggressively. This premise was examined by Dodge (1980). He compared the reaction of boys who were known as aggressive or nonaggressive (as rated both by teachers and peers) in a situation where their half-completed puzzle was dropped by another child either (1) with stated hostile intent, (2) stated accident, or (3) with an ambiguous statement. First, both aggressive and nonaggressive boys were more aggressive in the hostile-intent condition. Further, only in the ambiguous condition was there a difference between aggressive and nonaggressive boys: the aggressive ones responded *as if* the peer had acted with hostile intent (the responses being to hit objects in the room, take apart the provoker's puzzle, etc.). Interviews by other experimenters on other days confirmed the inference from the puzzle-destruction experiment: aggressive boys attributed hostile intent to a peer in hypothetical stories under ambiguous-intent conditions 50% more often than did nonaggressive boys.

There has been only one study, apparently, that has specifically involved training of perspective-taking skills to determine their efficacy in lessening antisocial behavior. In the Chandler study (1973) referred to earlier, it was found that 10 weeks of role-enactment training with delinquent preadolescents resulted in significant increases in perspective-taking ability, and, at 18 months after training, significant decreases in known delinquent acts. (Other training studies concerning aggressive behavior in relation to social skills and social problem-solving will be reviewed later.)

Prosocial Behavior

The ability to take another's perspective or empathize with another is postulated as central in the development of a variety of prosocial behaviors—cooperation, friendliness, kindness, generosity, altruism (e.g., Aronfreed, 1968; Feshbach, 1978; M. L. Hoffman, 1978; Kohlberg, 1969; Murphy, 1937; Piaget, 1967). This centrality should not be construed as suggesting that perspective taking and empathy are the only determining factors in prosocial behavior. Clearly, there are many other factors, both situational and personal, that influence its occurrence. The developmental literature specifically on prosocial behavior is extensive, as is that on the relation of prosocial behavior to social-cognitive development (see reviews by Bryan, 1975; Deutsch & Madle, 1975; Feshbach, 1978; M. L. Hoffman, 1978; Kurdek, 1978a). It bears noting, however, that prosocial behaviors, such as altruism, are not defined the same way by various investigators, and different behaviors, such as helping and generosity, are often not consistently or highly related to one another (Bryan, 1975). Indeed, terms, such as prosocial and antisocial, are problematic. They usually refer to behavior that has immediate positive or negative outcomes for the other person and, as such, tend to ignore the function of the behavior. That is, antisocial behavior can serve prosocial ends (as when a girl hits a bully to defend her brother) and apparent prosocial behavior can serve antisocial goals.

In contrast to the aggression literature, most of the published studies do not measure behavior by peer or teacher nominations but rather observe altruistic behavior with peers in natural settings or with adults in experimental settings. First, there are several studies that show no relation between perspective taking/empathy and altruism. For example, Zahn-Waxler et al. (1977) used 10 role-taking tasks (spatial and conceptual), and for 4- to 6-year-olds, the summed performance bore no relation to children's sharing, helping, or comforting an adult, although significant modest correlations occurred for 3-year-olds. Two studies found no relationship between empathy (measured by FASTE) and sharing and helping for 6- to 8-year-olds (Feshbach, 1978) or for preschoolers (Eisenberg-Berg & Lennon, 1980). In the latter study, when a summed spontaneous-altruism score was used, it was negatively related to empathy.

Some studies show mixed results. Iannotti (1978) found significant relations between perspective taking and altruism for 9-year-old boys, but not for 6-year-old boys, and Eisenberg-Berg and Mussen (1978) found significant relations between helping and empathy for adolescent boys, but not for adolescent girls. And some studies have shown quite consistent positive results. Buckley, Siegel, and Ness (1979), studying children from 3½ to 9 years of age, found that those children who helped or shared with a peer in an experimental situation, compared to those who did not, were significantly higher in perspective-taking and empathy (Borke, 1971) scores. Likewise, Hudson, Peyton, and Brion-Maisels (1976) reported 7-year-olds who were advanced on a variety of perspective-taking tasks were more helpful, friendly, and evidenced more social problem solving while tutoring kindergartners than were poor perspective takers. In sum, then, studies have shown the complete range from negative to positive relations. There are so many differences among them as to defy a systematic comparison (e.g., the ages studied, prosocial behaviors measured, social-cognitive skills measured). Yet, there is one aspect of the pattern of these results that may, in part, account for the differences. Those studies showing negative or mixed relations between prosocial behavior and social-cognitive abilities, with one exception (Eisenberg-Berg & Lennon, 1980), used as a recipient of donating, helping, sharing, and so on, either a hypothetical peer or an actual adult (who was a stranger). In both studies that showed positive relations, the recipients were actual peers of the child. The importance of the recipient has been recently demonstrated by Payne (1980) who found that prosocial behaviors clustered together according to whether the recipient was a hypothetical unknown peer (donating and helping) or an actual classmate (cooperating and sharing). Thus, the *relationship* of the child to the recipient may be important in the degree to which and the consistency with which the child behaves positively. That relationship seems to implicate such factors as similarity and familiarity, specifically, whether a peer or adult, a real individual or a hypothetical one, an acquaintance or a stranger, and whether the act is private or public (Payne, 1980).

A less dispositional approach to the behavior-cognition relation was taken by Barnett, King, and Howard (1979). They directly manipulated children's focusing on the other child's needs by having them recount sad events that occurred to another child, recount their own sad experiences, or recount the others' happy experiences. Those who recounted sad events of others subsequently donated more than children in the other two conditions. This suggests that focusing on other's sad experiences induces sad feelings for, or with, another, and it heightens awareness of past need states that are sufficient to influence donation behavior.

What do children, themselves, think are the causes of their own prosocial behavior? Eisenberg-Berg and Neal (1979) studied this by on-the-spot interviewing of preschoolers immediately after they had shared, comforted, or helped another during a 12-week period in nursery school. Of 11 categories of reasons, two were cited most frequently: the psychological or physical needs of the other child (25%) and pragmatic considerations (25%). An additional 40% of the reasons fell in three categories: mutual gain, friendship, and just wanting to help, share, or comfort. There was an almost total absence of such reasons as the stereotyped, "it's nice to help," concern about authorities' potential punishment for not helping, expectation for selfish gain, or to obtain social approval. Although preschoolers' reasoning about the causes of their own behavior may not be an unsullied report of actual causes, their perceptions of the causes of their behavior are noteworthy in their own right. Another study (Eisenberg-Berg & Hand, 1979) of preschoolers' reasoning about stories in which prosocial behavior was pitted against self-gain also implicated the importance of the recognition of the needs of others. In this case, needs-oriented reasoning was significantly related to spontaneous sharing with peers. These three studies (Barnett et al., 1979; Eisenberg-Berg & Hand, 1979; Eisenberg-Berg & Neal, 1979) suggest that a critical factor in empathy is the inference or recognition of the needs of others and such sensitivity is related to appropriate prosocial behavior. These data are consistent with M. L. Hoffman's view (1978) that empathy may serve as a prosocial motive rather than a self-serving motive.

In conclusion, the expected relation of perspective taking and empathy with various kinds of antisocial and prosocial behavior have been found in many studies, but not in all. And, in fact, a few show the opposite relation to that expected. It is difficult to assume that this body of data is definitive, given several considerations. For example, (1) perspective-taking abilities are, at best, only moderately correlated with one another so that any one of them can hardly be taken as an index of a general social-cognitive ability or to be related to other social-cognitive abilities; (2) various types of prosocial behaviors are not highly correlated often (e.g., Bryan, 1975; Staub, 1971); (3) although observation of behaviors in actual social situations has clear advantages to ratings, and so on, often *opportunities* to behave prosocially vary for children so widely that their prosocial act frequencies may be less a reflection of their dispositions to help or cooperate than a reflection of the opportunities that came their way; (4) we have virtually no information about the circumstances under which children use the social-cognitive abilities they may possess (the "need" component in Flavell's processing model). The expectation of a *direct* relationship between social-cognitive abilities and behavior may well be too simple a formulation. A variety of factors may influence the kind of relation found between the two domains—for example, the ambiguity of the other's intentions (Dodge, 1980), the assertiveness of the child in interpersonal relations (Barrett & Yarrow, 1977), the similarity of the self to the recipient of prosocial behavior (e.g., Payne, 1980; Staub, 1971), to cite a few.

There are certain parallels of this cognition-behavior relation that have been confronted in social psychology, as in the relations between attitudes and social behavior—relations that were often found to be less consistent and weaker than initially expected. In attempting to understand interpersonal behavior, there is a legacy of the field at large to approach the problem by emphasizing the determining role of "person" factors (attitudes, personality traits, cognitive abilities) *or* the determining role of situational factors. It may be that children differ in the degree to which their social behavior is determined by situational or person aspects, as has been suggested for adults by social psychologists (e.g., Bem & Allen, 1974; Snyder & Monson, 1975). Cutrona and Feshbach (1979) did find differences among children in their memory for, and use of, dispositional (person) versus situational information. Specifically, they assessed these differences by presenting stories in which both types of information were given, and children predicted the story characters' actions and justified the predictions. Children who remembered and used dispositional information were rated by their teachers as less aggressive and more prosocial than children who remembered and used only external, situation information. The dispositionally oriented also showed advanced perspective-taking skills. These data suggest that a child who does not attend to the psychological characteristics of those with whom she interacts will have difficulty interpreting the meaning of others' behavior. It is for the future to determine whether such an individual-differences reformulation of the classic trait versus situation controversy in psychology will prove fruitful.

CONCEPTIONS OF RELATIONS BETWEEN INDIVIDUALS

Up to this point, we have examined social-inference development as it applies to inferences about another individual. Now, we turn to the relations between individuals, specifically the relations of authority, friendship, and conflict. Some have suggested that to understand the development of social behavior and social cognition, a reconceptualization is required, one in which social events are viewed as part of larger social-relational systems (e.g., Bell, 1968; Damon, 1977; Hartup, 1976; Youniss, 1975).

Such a formulation is illustrated in the recent extensive work in attachment in the infant-mother dyad. In this discussion, we will examine this rather new focus in social-cognitive development on dyadic relations—primarily how children conceptualize them and reason about them.

Authority Relations

Hartup (1980) has suggested that there are "two social worlds of childhood," the adult/child world and the world of peers. The first is marked by the fundamental relation of authority of the adult to the child, authority in the sense of greater power physically, socially, mentally, and financially. This is in contrast to the peer world in which equal power relations exist. The difference in the two worlds is not absolute, of course, because authority relations exist among children, as in the roles of team captain, gang leader, and so on, just as equalitarian relations can exist between adults and children. Research on children's conceptions of authority relations has involved interviewing children, and, in most cases, conceptualizing their responses in terms of stages or levels of social-cognitive development.

Damon (1977) interviewed children between 4 and 9 years of age in cross-sectional and longitudinal studies. In the first study, social dilemmas were presented: in one, a boy had to choose between obeying his mother's dictum to clean up his room or disobeying to go with peers on a picnic (adult/child problem); the second involved a boy who is told by a peer captain of a team that he cannot play the position on the team he wants (child/child problem). Damon found two key issues that showed substantial developmental change: the legitimacy of authority and the rationales for obedience to authority. (Two other issues showed no developmental change: the boundaries of authority and the "rightness" of obedience to authority.) In both the cross-sectional and longitudinal studies, authority conceptions appear to undergo sequential qualitative change in ontogenesis. At Level 0, children tend not to differentiate what they want and what an authority expects of them; this then evolves (in the second substage of Level 0) into a differentiation of the two, but with a focus on the pragmatic effects of obedience ("It is right because it gets you what you want"). At Level 1, there is a shift to a more moral orientation in which the child basically endorses the concept of "might makes right" and authority is legitimized by the power to enforce. Bad consequences are viewed by the child as a just outcome for disobedience. Later in this level, usually beginning about 6 or 7 years of age, authority is legitimized by having special talents or abilities and obedience is justified as fair payback (reciprocal exchange) for the assistance of the authority. At this same time, children begin to see authority figures as less than omniscient, a concept that Elkind (1967) elaborated (to be described later). At Level 2, usually beginning about 9 years of age, children start to separate pragmatic and constrained obedience to an authority from obedience that is voluntary and cooperative. Authority is vested in those who have special experiences and are better leaders, children think. These concepts evolve later in this level to authority being vested in those who have abilities to best address the specific situational problems. At this point, children see authority as a consensual relation among people that is adopted temporarily by one person for the welfare of the many. The general superiority of an authority is no longer assumed by most children.

There was no evidence that children had more advanced concepts about adult/child versus child/child authority relations because 92% scored at the same or adjacent level on both stories. There were no sex differences in authority reasoning, but there was a fairly strong relationship to chronological age (.58 to .60).

Does reasoning about hypothetical authority issues bear any relation to reasoning about the same issues in relevant real-life situations? Yes, according to Damon's second study (1977), in which 64 children between 4 and 10 years of age were interviewed before and after selecting team captains and playing basketball games. Levels of reasoning about legitimacy of authority and obedience about this specific actual situation corresponded quite highly to levels of reasoning about hypothetical peer authority (.75 to .80; partialled for age, .41 to .53). There was no systematic lag for hypothetical compared to real-life reasoning.

Selman and his colleagues (Cooney & Selman, 1978; Selman & Jacquette, 1978) have examined one type of children's peer-authority concepts, specifically, leadership conceptions. From children's responses to interviews, Selman, like Damon (1977), posits sequential stages of reasoning. These bear some major similarities to Damon's levels. At Stage 0, Selman and Jacquette (1978) found, leadership is conceptualized as physical power over others and telling people what to do. During early middle childhood, leadership is based on leader-knows-best deference, and authority is legitimized by superior knowledge or skills. This unilateral authoritarian relationship of leader to followers is supplanted in the next stage by a bilateral conception. Now, a good

leader is seen as an arbitrator, not a dictator, with reciprocity underlying the role. At Stage 3, adolescents conceptualize the group as a social system in which the leader reflects group concerns rather than imposing her own concerns, and the leader serves as a catalyst for structuring the group.

The changing conceptions of authority figures that occurs in middle childhood has been discussed by Elkind (1967). When children discover that adults are not infallible or omniscient, many of them generalize this into an assumptive reality that adults are rather stupid. As they begin to note the many things they know that adults do not, they view themselves often as quite clever in contrast to adults, a belief called cognitive conceit. Elkind bases these descriptions on clinical and everyday observations, such as the kinds of humor children enjoy at this age period (e.g., rhymes and jokes about things adults take seriously and that make adults look inept) and the themes of books they prefer (e.g., the children in Peter Pan outwitting the adult Captain Hook or Nancy Drew solving mysteries that baffle her lawyer father). There is no evidence to date of the generality of these characterizations, either across American subcultures or across other cultures.

Finally, it should be pointed out that authority conceptions, although important in their own right, are of additional importance because of their role in moral-development theories. In its simplest form, the origins of morality for such theorists as Piaget (1932) and Kohlberg (1969) lie in the obedience of children to authorities from a general orientation of deference and to avoid punishment. Damon (1977) has disagreed with this authority-based view of moral origins, suggesting instead that moral development derives more directly from the child's own experiences with peers that relate to justice (i.e., fair treatment, sharing, kindness, etc.). These issues are discussed in greater detail by Rest (*vol. III, chap. 9*).

Friendship

Friendship among children undoubtedly plays an important role in social development, particularly with its emergence during the early preschool years as the first attachments outside the family group. But it has only been recently that the study of friendship has moved from a focus on how children behave with friends to how they conceptualize friendship itself. Several aspects require comment. First, like authority, it deals with a relation between individuals. As defined by most adults, the friendship relation is not a unilateral attachment, liking, or attraction of one individual for another but a reciprocated relation between two individuals. Second, liking another is assumed as part of friendship but not as sufficient to define the relation, that is, one may like another without being a friend to the other.

How do children understand this social relation and how do conceptualizations change with increasing age? To answer these questions, most investigators employ a modified interview asking children to name their best friend, asking why the named child is the best friend, or asking more hypothetical questions of what the children expect of a best friend. Youniss has investigated the operations of friendship (Youniss, 1975; Youniss & Volpe, 1978), that is, the transformations to and from a friendship state (how one becomes a friend and how friendships end).

In accord with much of the research in other areas of social cognition, the friendship conceptions undergo a good deal of change in development, the major changes appearing to be: (1) from defining friendship as a concrete, behavioral, surface relationship of playing together and giving goods to more abstract, internal dispositional relationships in adolescence of caring for one another, sharing one's thoughts and feelings, and comforting each other; (2) from a self-centered orientation of the friend as satisfying one's wants and needs to a mutually satisfying relation; (3) from momentary or transient good acts between individuals to relations that endure over time and occasional conflicts (e.g., Berndt, 1981; Bigelow, 1977; Damon, 1977; Selman, 1981; Youniss & Volpe, 1978).

These developmental changes have been viewed, almost without exception, as stages-of-friendship conceptions. The types of stages abstracted and the ages at which they typically occur has varied a good deal however. The first to be considered is that of Damon (1977) who interviewed children about their knowledge of friendship. The interview included questions about their best friend, the reasons for the friendship, how they know the best friend likes them, how they make friends and enemies, and then a series of questions to probe the limits of friendship, such as whether a sibling or parent can be a friend. Damon drew out three stages of friendship conceptions. At Level 1, typical of 5- to 7-year-olds usually, friends are playmates who share material goods, act nice, and are fun to be with. The relation is seen as momentary and transient, with little individuality associated with a friend, that is, "all friends are the same." Level 2 conceptions, usually occurring from middle to late childhood, are focused on friends as people who help one another either spontaneously or in response to an expression of need. The two most central features of this level are the notion of trusting one another and liking certain dispositions or traits in the friend.

Finally, about age 11 or so Damon found, friends are defined as persons who understand one another, share their innermost thoughts and feelings (including secrets), help each other with psychological problems, and avoid causing each other problems. Compatibility of interests and personality are the bases for selecting one as a friend, and the termination of friendship is viewed likely if one shows bad faith to a friend. Adolescents' reasoning at this level also emphasizes communication as critical to friendship, both as an end in itself and as a means to share and assist one another.

Youniss has focused his work on the knowledge of friendship relations, defined as "a system of procedures pertaining to interpersonal interactions" (Youniss & Volpe, 1978, p. 19). Further, despite the oft-cited distinction between knowing about something versus knowing how to do something (Ryle, 1949), Youniss and Volpe (1978) take the position that "psychological understanding of one's relation to another person is not abstractly separated from one's knowing how to interact with the other person" (p. 19). As such, the focus is on the social operations, or interpersonal actions, that serve to establish or dissolve a friendship relation. In the studies conducted, children are interviewed and write stories about "showing you are friends," or telling how one friend did something that another friend did not like and how to undo the breach. Children age 6 and 7 know friendly procedures (sharing material goods, playing together) and have a rulelike orientation toward such procedures. Older children, ages 9 to 10, integrate such rules into a conception of a relation based on equality and reciprocity. Now, the bases of friendship are psychological and emphasis is on mutuality (sharing one another's burdens, having responsibility, etc.). When friendship is violated, the older children require some *acknowledgement* of violation before the relation can be repaired, whereas younger children merely require the behavioral indices, that is, the resuming of friendly actions.

Another stage approach to friendship conceptions is Selman's (1981), which shares some features with that of Damon (1977) and of Youniss and Volpe (1978). In this case, Selman presented a dilemma for children and adolescents to reason about: Should a child go with a new acquaintance to a special event that is scheduled at the same time as a previous engagement with a long-time best friend? The new acquaintance and the best friend do not like each other. (A modified version was used for older subjects.) In an interview, the child's reasoning about the dilemma was explored, specifically the six issues identified as critical to friendship relations: formation, intimacy, trust and reciprocity, jealousy, conflict resolution, and termination. The matrix of conceptions on these issues defines stages in the reflective understanding of friendship as follows. Stage 0, usually occurring in children younger than 7, is labeled momentary physicalistic playmate to denote the friendship relation as based on proximity (a friend is someone who lives nearby) and with whom one plays at the moment. Friendship is playmateship. Intrusion of someone into the play is conceptualized as specific fights over specific toys rather than conflicts involving personal feelings or affection.

In Selman's Stage 1, one-way assistance, the focus is on the specific acts performed by the friend that meet the self's wishes. The child assumes a standard or rule and is vigilant that friends act in accord with that standard. A close friend at this stage (usually occurring between ages 4 and 9) is one known better than others, and known better means having more accurate knowledge of the other's likes and dislikes. Stage 2, usually occurring somewhere between 6 and 12 years of age, is labeled fairweather cooperation. Now that reciprocal perspectives are recognized, the manifestation of that recognition in friendship concepts is a change from matching one person's standard and expectations to the notion of coordinating and adjusting both the self's and other's likes and dislikes. The coordination of such attitudes at the moment defines the relation, that is, fairweather friends, in which arguments sever the relation. (Selman's Stages 1 and 2 are described, in part, by only one level in Damon's, 1977, scheme.) Stage 3, intimate and mutually shared relationships, occurs roughly between 9 and 15 years of age. Evidence of the concept of continuity of the relation and affectional bonds is given. Friendship is a means of developing mutual intimacy and support, not just escaping boredom and loneliness. The limitation is the possessiveness felt for a friend, which appears to arise out of the adolescent's realization of the difficulty in forming and maintaining friendship.

Several studies (e.g., Bigelow, 1977; Bigelow & LaGaipa, 1975; Reisman & Shorr, 1978) have focused on the *expected* behavior of friends. For example, Bigelow (1977) and Bigelow and LaGaipa (1975) examined essays on friendship written by Canadian and Scottish children from ages 6 to 14 (approximately), coded the content into 21 categories, and rated the degree of emphasis the categories were given in the essays (from major theme to omission). The results of the cross-cultural validation (Bigelow, 1977) indicated that general play decreased in frequency of mention with increasing age and, surprisingly, four categories occurred in less than 5% of the essays: mutual activities, similarity of person characteristics, physical attractiveness, and ritualistic social exchange. Most of the major developmental changes were reflected in categories similar to those found in the work by Damon, Youniss, and Selman, such as common activities, acceptance, loyalty, commitment, intimacy, common interests, and similarity in attitudes.

In two studies of preschoolers, Hayes also found corroborating data (Hayes, 1978; Hayes, Gershman, & Bolin, 1980) in that the reasons children cited for liking their best friends were: propinquity, physical possessions, general play, common activities, and evaluation. However, the first two bases (propinquity and physical possessions) were found in the Hayes et al. study (1980) to be the bases for unilateral relationships, that is, where one child cites another as a best friend but the best friend does not cite that child. The two bases of common activities and evaluation were evident in reciprocal friendships, and play was frequently cited as a reason in both unilateral and reciprocal relations of liking. Note that the relation and its bases seem to be treated at the same level for some preschoolers: friends are those who play together and those who play together are friends. In both of the Hayes studies, the reasons cited for disliking another child were aggressive behavior, rule violations, and aberrant behavior (see also Youniss & Volpe, 1978). Friendship conceptions continue to change in late adolescence and adulthood (Antonucci, 1976; Reisman & Shorr, 1978; Selman, 1981).

The semistructured-interview method with probing, the primary method used in friendship studies, is useful to bring out the broad developmental sweep of concept differences and to have some confidence that meanings and concepts are being categorized rather than mere words. What is not clear, however, is the extent to which these stage models are describing some of the conceptions of some of the children some of the time. That is, it is important to move beyond demonstrating that these conceptions can and do occur to examine in detail (1) how exhaustive these attributes and themes are of friendship conceptions, (2) how reliably they co-occur to form patterns at any one age period, (3) what proportion of children at any one age period show all, some, or few of the patterns of reasoning, and (4) how reliable the conceptions are across short time periods and across types of friendship, for example, unilateral versus mutual friendships. Note, for example, the degree of heterogeneity in preschoolers' reasoning and behavior (Hayes, Gershman, & Bolin, 1980), which appears to span Selman's Stage 0 to 2, where Stages 1 and 2 are supposed to be typical of middle childhood reasoning. Such analyses in future research may discriminate between individual differences and developmental differences in the way friendship relations are conceptualized.

The study of the relation between conceptions of friends and behavior of friends has been too rare to draw conclusions. There is some evidence that behavior toward friends differs in some respects from behavior toward nonfriends and that behavior changes occur between friends in ontogenesis (see *Hartup, vol. IV, chap. 2*).

Conflict Relations

Coming into conflict with others is an everyday part of social life, such as a child telling a friend's secret to others or a child refusing to go to bed when the parent wishes it. In this section we will focus not on children's conceptions of conflict but on their knowledge of, and reasoning about, ways to solve interpersonal conflict. As such, the topic touches on a large area of theory and research related to social competence and social adjustment of children as well as various educational and therapeutic programs to teach children ways to solve social problems (often referred to as social-skill training). Much of the literature will not be reviewed here because it only deals in small measure with interpersonal conflict per se, and children's changing conception and reasoning about interpersonal behavior ception and reasoning about interpersonal behavior are not directly studied.

One extensive program of research that has examined children's reasoning about conflicts and the relation of reasoning to behavioral adjustment is that of Spivack and Shure (Shure & Spivack, 1978; Spivack & Shure, 1974). They posit that social adjustment of children and adolescents is largely determined by the capacity to think through social problems, specifically the ability: (1) to think of alternative ways of solving problems, (2) to know the likely response of another to certain solutions, and (3) to use means-end problem solving. A few major aspects of this extensive body of research is presented here because recent reviews of it are available (e.g., Krasnor & Rubin, 1981; Shure, in press). For example, the number and kinds of strategies to solve conflict is assessed by the Preschool Interper-

sonal Problem-Solving (PIPS) Test in which two short story dilemmas are presented: How can a child get a toy another has? How can a child avoid a mother's anger after damaging property? The *number* of alternative strategies preschoolers can think of (e.g., trading toys, finagling, grabbing, getting an adult to intercede, etc.) or the number of alternative actions to reach a specific goal and obstacles anticipated (means-end problem solving) are two cognitive abilities that have been found to be related to children's adjustment (e.g., Elias, Larcen, Zlotlow, & Chinsky, 1978; Hopper & Kirschenbaum, 1979; Johnson, Yu, & Roopnarine, 1979; Shure & Spivack, 1979; Spivack & Shure, 1974). Not all studies have documented the relationship however (e.g., Butler, 1978; Enright & Sutterfield, 1980; Krasnor & Rubin, 1981; Sharp, 1978). It may be that the different ways in which adjustment has been assessed in these studies accounts in part for the mixed findings (e.g., teacher- or observer-rated behaviors in natural settings, sociometric status, etc.) or the differential relationship of problem solving and behavior at various ages.

Although social problem-solving skills appear in most studies not to be significantly related to IQ, there is little known about the relation of problem solving to other social-cognitive abilities. Perspective taking has shown very modest (if any) correlations with social problem solving (e.g., Marsh, Serafica, & Barenboim, 1980; Shure, in press), except in one case where substantial relations were found (Johnson et al., 1979). Selman (1981) has analyzed children's conflict-resolution conceptions in relation to perspective-coordination but specific to conflicts between friends.

A program of training children how to think about social problems has been developed by Spivack and Shure (Shure & Spivack, 1978; Spivack, Platt, & Shure, 1976; Spivack & Shure, 1974); it has been shown in several cases, but not all, to increase significantly problem-solving strategy alternatives and to improve social adjustment (e.g., Elardo & Caldwell, 1979; Gesten, de Apodaca, Rains, Weissberg, & Cowen, 1978; McClure, Chinsky, & Larcen, 1978; Shure, in press; Shure & Spivack, 1978; Spivack & Shure, 1974).

Most of the studies noted to this point have used the *number* of alternative strategies as the main dependent variable, presumably reflecting the repertoire and flexibility with which children can approach conflict situations. The *kinds* of solutions generated have not been subject to much study yet, particularly in relation to increasing age (e.g., Krasnor & Rubin, 1981). Maternal child-rearing style (variously defined) has been found to relate to daughters' problem-solving skills, but not to those of sons (Shure, in press), and to the kinds of strategies children use (Jones, Rickel, & Smith, 1980). In the latter study, for example, restrictive child-rearing practices were associated with evasive strategies in children and negatively related to negotiation strategies and personal appeal, whereas maternal nurturance was associated with children's use of authorities in solving hypothetical problem situations. It would seem reasonable (1) that child-rearing strategies that focus on conflict as a problem to be solved, encourage children's thinking about solutions, and (2) that point out the relation between different solutions and others' covert responses (e.g., inductive techniques of discipline, M. L. Hoffman, 1970) might foster the problem-solving abilities of children in interpersonal conflicts (e.g., Bearison & Cassel, 1975). But whether or not parents use such inductively oriented strategies appears to depend in part on characteristics of the children (e.g., Keller & Bell, 1979) and the type of conflict (e.g., Grusec & Kuczynski, 1980). Direct observation of parent/child dyads and child/child dyads as they confront a conflict of goals would be a useful addition to understanding the process of social problem solving.

In conclusion, children's reasoning and knowledge about interpersonal relations, a recent focus of inquiry, shows some striking similarities to their reasoning about individuals, but equally important, there are some unique aspects of relational reasoning. In the first case, there is again evidence of the problem of self/other differentiation of young children, as when the authority's wishes and the child's own are assumed by the child to be the same. Likewise, the developmental change from a physicalistic basis to a psychological one is evident, as in reasons for selecting a person as a friend or leader or reasons for obeying an authority.

There are some other developmental trends that are more specific to relational concepts: the shift from a unilateral to bilateral to social-system conceptualization; from a view of relations as constrained by power to relations that are voluntary for individuals and consensually agreed to; from relations largely dominated by self-interest to those focused on mutual gain and responsibility; from a concrete, behavioral definition (e.g., acting friendly) to a definition based on interpersonal principles, such as trust; from a fusion of a role with the individual to a differentiation of the role from the person occupying it. Although these appear from this early research to be some of the dimensions of develop-

mental change, such dimensionalization of development is inadequate by itself to reflect other important aspects of ontogenetic change. First and foremost, there are different patterns of reasoning evident at different age levels that reflect the *kinds* of organized reasoning that dimensions alone do not reveal. The richness and subtlety of these patterns can not be summarized here in a few sentences; the reader must be referred back to the primary sources for descriptions of various levels of reasoning as outlined by Damon, Selman, Youniss, and others. Second, dimensions such as those suggested here minimize the content of the relation, that is, authority, friendship, leadership, and so on. Given the different function of such interpersonal relations, it is likely that concepts and reasoning about them will differ somewhat. To obtain a complete and differentiated understanding in future research and theoretical work, both a dimensional and levels approach will probably be fruitful if they are sensitive to the communalities and differences of various types of social relations.

CONCEPTS OF RELATIONS AMONG INDIVIDUALS

We turn now to children's social conceptions at the next larger level of organization, the social group. The term is used here loosely, to apply to children's perceptions and knowledge about small-group structure, such as in preschool play groups and classrooms, to broader societal concepts, such as social roles, normative information, and social rules. The focus, most succinctly put, is on the child as a social psychologist.

Concepts of Social Structure

Among the many ways to characterize social groups, a central aspect is their structure. Organizational patterns in a group reflect relations among members that transcend the characteristics of individuals who make up the group or specific dyads within the group. What is of interest here is the degree to which children perceive (or conceptualize) group structure in those groups in which they participate. Presumably, shared perception of status on various dimensions among individuals in a group serves predictability of interactions among members of the group and the functioning of the group as a whole. Three dimensions in particular have been studied (Glidewell, Kantor, Smith, & Stringer, 1966) in children and adolescents: social power ("Who can get you to do what they want you to do?"); affiliation ("Who likes whom?"), and competence ("Who is good at doing the things you do here [in school, at camp]?"). The first two dimensions will be discussed here.

Power Structure

Power has often been studied as it is manifested in a dominance hierarchy in a group. Dominance linearity, although defined and measured in different ways, is colloquially a pecking order usually occurring in the context of interpersonal conflict and indexed variously by who initiates conflicts, who wins and who loses, and sometimes by who is perceived as toughest in the group. Glidewell et al. (1966) summarized a good deal of the available studies done between the 1930s and 1960s. Virtually all of this research uses the concept of social power, defined as the ability to influence others, making no distinction between dominance and leadership. Interestingly enough, children themselves distinguish social power from coercive power in the classroom (Gold, 1958).

Preschool children when asked who is tougher (by which most children mean being aggressive or physically strong according to Omark, 1980) show a low level of agreement among themselves about each other—as studied in America (Edelman & Omark, 1973; Omark & Edelman, 1975), in England (Sluckin & Smith, 1977), and in Switzerland (Omark, Omark, & Edelman, 1975). The usual low level of agreement among young children could mean, of course, that they are less accurate perceivers of a dominance hierarchy or that there is less hierarchy to perceive. The latter seems unlikely if we assume adults are more accurate perceivers than preschoolers. Adult observers usually do perceive a dominance hierarchy in preschool groups that have been formed for several months (e.g., McGrew, 1972; Strayer & Strayer, 1976). The correlations between the adult-perceived hierarchy and the child-perceived hierarchy are usually below chance levels of agreement (Edelman & Omark, 1973; Omark & Edelman, 1975; Sluckin & Smith, 1977). However, in two preschools, the last-named authors found that about a fourth of the children, most of whom were 4 years old, gave reliable rankings. They also found a general tendency for preschoolers to overestimate how tough they were relative to others. (The kinds of behaviors and facial expressions that appear to be related to perceived rank and winning conflicts are described by Camras, 1980; Ginsburg, Pollman, & Wauson, 1977; Zivin, 1977.)

Children of elementary school age show a good deal more agreement among themselves than do preschoolers on the rank ordering within their group, well above chance level and including an "accurate" perception of where they rank in the group on power. For example, Lippitt, Polansky, Redl, and Rosen (1960) found a .90 correlation among boys at a summer camp. There was 62% to 73% agreement on who was toughest in grades one through four in studies by Edelman and Omark (1973) and Omark and Edelman (1975). In general, there are usually moderate-to-high correlations between children's and teachers' perceptions of power hierarchies in classrooms, perceptions that remain quite stable within and between years of school (Glidewell et al., 1966). For example, Weisfeld, Omark, and Cronin (1980) found first- and third-grade children largely maintained their relative dominance ranks eight years later in high school ($r = .69$ to .74).

So, too, lines of power are perceived within adolescent groups among members of gangs or at summer camp (e.g., Savin-Williams, 1976, 1979; Sherif, Harvey, White, Hood, & Sherif, 1961; Sherif & Sherif, 1964; Suttles, 1968). To illustrate: Savin-Williams (1976, 1979) found significant agreement among cabinmates at a summer camp in rankings of dominance within the first week of camp and again at the end of camp for all the boys' cabins (1976, 1979), but only for some of the girls' cabins (1979). There was high correspondence between adolescents' dominance perceptions and those of camp counselors (.90 or higher) for boys, but less, again, for girls.

In sum, then, preschoolers seem to have less agreement among themselves than older children and adolescents on the question, "Who can make who do what they want them to do?" But it is not clear whether increasing agreement in development means increasingly accurate perceptions of hierarchies or increasingly clear hierarchies to be perceived. There is, actually, yet another possibility that relates to the measurement of preschooler-perceived dominance rank. In most studies, children only make paired comparisons among group members as to whom is tougher, but they do not actually rank order the entire group (the researcher compiles the hierarchy from judgments of dyads). This is, perhaps, tacit recognition of preschoolers' difficulty in ordering a series of differences (even with physical objects, such as length of sticks). Indeed, it may be that preschoolers are more sensitive to dyad relations than to entire-group relations, and mostly to extreme dyads (very tough vs. very not tough) in the group. The causal relation between perception and behavior is, of course, a highly debated topic, that is, the extent to which perceptions influence behavior and behavior influences perceptions. Suffice it to say that the substantial agreement among children and adolescents on dominance hierarchies, the stability of agreement over time, and the moderate-to-high agreement of children and adult observers' hierarchy rankings suggest that social power is a highly relevant phenomenon of social-group perception. It does not appear to be merely a social-halo phenomenon, in that several studies indicate that when the dimensions of power, acceptance, and competence rankings are intercorrelated and each pair partialed on the third dimension, the correlations are as follows: power/competence = .30; power/acceptance = .60; and competence/acceptance = .40 (Glidewell et al., 1966). This discussion, it should be noted, has summed across a host of factors that are associated with ranked-power perception, for example, the size of the group, the length of time it has been formed, the position of the perceiver in the rank, and so on, and has ignored some of the conceptual controversies about dominance as a measure of animal- and human-group organization.

Liking Structure

The liking structures and related friendship structures that occur in groups are thought to fulfill the same function as dominance structures, that is, to make interactions more predictable and the group cohesive. Because the liking or acceptance structure of a group is elicited often by having children name their three best friends, the concepts of friendship and liking are merged in most of this literature. The research on liking is more briefly reviewed than dominance research because friendship conceptions have been discussed, there appears to be less research on the perception of friendship networks, and some of the findings concerning dominance hold here too, that is, the awareness of liking patterns in the group, stability over time, and agreement with adult observers' perceptions. For example, Hayes et al. (1980) found that among preschoolers who named each other as best friends (mean age 4 years), all but one pair of 24 children played together 78% of the time or more during free play and 100% of their parents when asked to name their child's best friend, named the reciprocated best friend. There seems to be a fair degree of stable agreement among preschoolers of who likes whom in the group (perhaps, for this age group, this means their perceptions about "who plays with whom") (Asher, Singleton, Tinsley, & Hymel, 1979; Marshall & McCandless, 1957). Among children of elementary school age and older, friendship relations within the group are widespread with approximately 85% to 90% of the children being named by someone as a friend (e.g.,

Bonney, 1943; Hymel & Asher, 1977). Jones (1980) found in same-sex afterschool activity groups of 6- and 7-year-olds that mutual best friends (from sociometric nominations) among boys were observed to play together more but that there was no relation between liking and play frequency for girls. It is worth noting that preferred friend/playmates tend not to be the same as preferred workmates (e.g., Oden & Asher, 1977). Perhaps this is related to the relative independence of competence and acceptance previously reported and recently demonstrated (Rubenstein, Fisher, & Iker, 1975). And, like dominance perceptions, there is considerable agreement among children as to their degree of acceptance (e.g., Goslin, 1962; Potashin, 1946). The reader is referred to Hartup (*vol. IV, chap. 2*) on behavioral correlates of perceived friendship structure.

Socially Deviant Behavior Conceptions

Are children aware of behavior that adults consider atypical or deviant? To what do they attribute such behavior? Perhaps we should first consider, "Deviant from what?" There are at least three common ways of thinking of norms: (1) the empirical typicality of some behavior for most people, usually in terms of its frequency or intensity, which is called in attribution research consensus information or base-line rates of behavior; (2) some widely shared standard of behavior; and (3) the norm for a particular individual, which in attributional work falls within the category consistency information. Most research has implicitly or explicitly studied children's conceptions of deviancy in the first two senses, from a social norm or social standard, specifically, behavior that is antisocial, withdrawn, paranoidlike, school phobic, or borderline psychotic.

Children's conceptions of such behavior has not been studied at the preschool level, although anecdotal observation suggests some awareness in this age group of deviancy, as when children refer to other children's behavior as different, queer, or silly. Such references could mean merely that the behavior is novel to them or that it is different from what they themselves do, or (less likely) it could imply deviation from an abstract social norm.

Clear empirical developmental data begin with 7-year-olds. Coie and Pennington (1976) interviewed children ages 7, 10, 13, and 17, first asking them to identify known peers (not by name) who "act differently . . . from most other kids" and to describe what they do. Then, short stories were told of a character who evidenced either antisocial loss of control or paranoid-type distorted perceptions of thoughts and feelings. What did the children consider deviant? Children 7-years-old cited—(1) verbal or physical aggression and often (2) self-referent attributions in which the describer noted differences in interests of peers with whom she had a personal grievance. Such self-reference dropped out in the older age groups of 10- and 13-year-olds, but these groups continued to emphasize aggression as deviant and included social-norm violations (being silly, engaging in age-inappropriate behavior, showing off or snobbishness, etc.). Only at age 17 was social withdrawal recognized as an important deviant behavior; aggression was much less often mentioned than in the younger age groups.

Most studies employ short vignettes of deviant behavior and through ratings of the behavior and interviews assess children's conceptions and causal schemes about deviancy. The findings suggest (1) peers who exhibit deviant behavior are seen as less attractive and less similar to the self than "normal" peers (Novak, 1974); (2) with increasing age, children are more likely to see adult-defined deviant behavior as deviant (Coie & Pennington, 1976; Marsden & Kalter, 1976); and (3) recognition increases with greater severity of the disorder (e.g., school phobia vs. borderline psychosis or antisocial vs. paranoidlike perceptions) (Coie & Pennington, 1976; Marsden & Kalter, 1976). Recognition in the Coie & Pennington study, however, included both the accurate recounting of the disordered behavior after hearing the story twice and some reasonable cause for such behavior. Virtually no 7-year-olds recognized, in this sense, the antisocial or paranoidlike behavior as deviant per se but instead reconstructed the story to give plausible causes. This, in effect, normalized the deviancy (e.g., the antisocial child was provoked or the paranoid child was fearful because other children *were* talking about him and *were* mean to him). It was not until 17 years of age that more than half the subjects recognized, as defined earlier, deviant behavior as such.

The types of causes suggested by children for deviant behavior also change with age (Maas, Merecek, & Travers, 1978). The physical state of the story character is cited as the primary cause by a majority of 7-year-olds, a third of the 9-year-olds, and only 15% of the 11½-year-olds. Physical state means such reasons as "he was born that way," "he fell on his head," or "he smoked too much dope." Experiential causes were cited with increasing frequency at older ages (i.e., the way the person was treated by family, friends, and teachers or the experiences the person had had). Physical causes were attributed to withdrawal more than to self-punitive or antisocial behavior. About a quarter of the children at each grade level thought the story character "wants to act" that way, particularly the antisocial character. That character was thought to enjoy the "rewards" of being antisocial; persistent antisocial behavior, children thought, was due to lack of effort in trying to change.

The developmental changes, then, seem to indicate that in the early elementary school years, children use differences-from-self as sufficient to label behavior as deviant, and so they use aggression too. This use (of aggression) as deviant is true of children up to 17 years of age. Violations of social norms are a primary basis for labeling behavior as deviant in children 10 and older. (Of course, given a "normal" sample of public school children, behaviors that are deviations from general norms are also deviations from self's behavior in most cases.) There is a suggestion, secondly, of a bias to normalize deviant behavior in young children, that is, to assume deviancy has reasonable causes and, not unexpectedly, reasonable often refers to the physical situation or physical state of the deviant person. Older children cite experiential factors more often than situational ones to explain deviant behavior. As such, the ontogenetic changes in causes of deviancy seem to parallel historical changes of Western societal conceptions.

The concept of deviancy implies a process of comparison (to self, to standard, or to norms). But social-comparison processes, interestingly enough, have not been studied much despite the fact that they would seem to have important implications for learning of standards and rules as well as for self-concept and self-esteem. Although very young children certainly can and do compare themselves to others on a concrete level (e.g., how much they have of something vs. others; Masters, 1971), social-comparison research has been largely limited to achievement behavior. Ruble (in press) in a series of studies (e.g., Ruble, Feldman, & Boggiano, 1976; Ruble, Parsons, & Ross, 1976; Ruble, Boggiano, Feldman, & Loebl, 1980) has done some pioneer work on achievement and gathered evidence that led

to the surprising conclusion that social comparison information has little impact on children's self-evaluations, or on behaviors based on self-evaluations until at least 7 to 8 years of age. Furthermore, this is true even though most of the prerequisite cognitive skills, motivations, and strategies are evident during the preschool years. (Ruble, in press)

These findings are also consonant with the weak effect consensus information (what most people do) has on causal attributions (described earlier). It may be that children at first use themselves as the referent or standard and only later use abstract social-normative information as the referent upon which to base a judgment of deviancy as suggested by the findings of Coie and Pennington (1976). And, it is likely that comparison behavior occurs earlier for concrete behavior, characteristics (''Who's strongest?'' ''Who's tallest?''), and possessions than comparison of internal attributes, such as abilities, motives, and so on (see Barenboim, 1981). The area deserves more inquiry to determine whether these speculations have any validity.

Social-Role Conceptions

An important part of children's societal conceptions is their understanding of social roles. Roles are defined as a set of ''functions a person performs when occupying a particular characterization (position) within a particular social context'' (Shaw & Costanzo, 1970, p. 326). As such, role refers to societally shared expectations for certain ''appropriate'' behaviors; as a concept, it is related to the previously discussed relational concepts, social norms, and social deviancy. Role theorists who have most directly addressed the self/other relations relative to development include Cooley (1902), Mead (1934), and, in the case of role socialization within the family, Parsons and Bales (1955). However, those theories have had little discernible impact on role research, the major work emerging instead from Piaget's theory.

There are many different social-role conceptions and stereotypes that have been studied, but the most frequent of these is children's sex-role conceptions. That extensive literature is not reviewed here because it is in other sources (e.g., Maccoby & Jacklin, 1974; see also *Harter, vol. IV, chap. 4*). A related topic is children's perceptions of parental roles. Dubin and Dubin (1965) reviewed 16 studies prior to 1965 that indicate that at least by 5 years of age, children ascribe different functional roles to each parent along the usual male/female stereotype. Parent roles are, however, a function of both age-role and sex-role prescriptions so that most parent-role conceptions are combinations of these two roles. For example, Emmerich (1959, 1961) found that age roles in the family were perceived more in terms of power differences than functional differences, high power ascribed to parents and low power to children, whereas sex roles in the family were perceived in terms of both power and function. High-power and interference statements were attributed to fathers and low power and facilitation were attributed to mothers. The difficulty in interpreting such findings is that it is unclear whether children's perceptions of parental roles have changed in any fundamental ways in 20 years, that is, the possible presence of cohort effects, given the marked increase in working mothers and indications of less traditional roles in the family in some segments of society. Apart from studies of perceptions of the working mother (e.g., L. W. Hoffman, 1974), there appear to be few developmental studies conducted recently of parent-role and age-role perceptions (e.g., Appel, 1977; Heilbrun & Landauer, 1977). Relevant to this topic, however, is children's conceptions of the authority of adults (reviewed earlier).

Sibling-role concepts were examined by Bigner (1974); he found that older siblings were consistently assigned more power than younger siblings (consistent with Emmerich's, 1959 and 1961, findings of power differentiation by age) and that sibling roles were differentiated by function, with facilitation being attributed to older siblings rather than interference. These ascriptions were made by second-born children 7 years of age and older but not as clearly so among 5-year-olds. Sibling sex roles were also discriminated by power and function. It bears noting, however, that power and function were the only attributes offered to children in the Emmerich (1959, 1961) and Bigner (1974) studies, and although children can and do discriminate roles on these two bases, it is not clear whether they are the most prominent attributes were children freely to describe parent and sibling roles.

Watson and Fischer (1980) have provided evidence for the development of toddler and preschoolers' role concepts of mother, father, boy, girl, teacher, student. In a semimodeling-assessment task of acting out a story with dolls and in solitary free play with dolls, a developmental sequence in social-role development was found for children ages 1½ to 7½. By 2 years of age, most children could make a doll act as an independent agent (have the doll drink or walk for example); most of the 3-year-olds could make the doll carry out several behaviors that fit the role of doctor; and by ages 4 to 5, most children were able to show social-role behavior in the more usual sense of complementary roles by having a doctor doll, for example, interact appropriately with a patient doll. And around 6 years of age children began to show some understanding of one person being able to occupy two social roles, as a father who is a doctor also interacting with his daughter who is also his patient. In free play, young preschoolers frequently showed the highest level of social-role conception that they had evidenced in the assessment phase, but older preschoolers less often did so.

The stability of role concepts has been examined by Sigel, Saltz, and Roskind (1967). For example, a child is presented the following: "This father gets up early in the morning and goes to work where he joins this group of doctors. He is a doctor, too. Is he still a father?" Not to most 6-year-olds; they deny such multiple-role membership as possible or fail to conserve social roles, depending on one's interpretation. These data appear basically consistent with Watson and Fischer's (1980) findings. But 8-year-olds knew that a father could be a doctor too; however, when a father was transformed via a story into a negative role (a drunkard), 8-year-olds no longer considered him a father (Saltz & Hamilton, 1968). In a later study by Saltz & Medow (1971), role transformations were made from good to good, good to bad, and bad to good (e.g., mother to saleslady; good baseball player to liar; thief to saleslady). Both the attributes of the role and the role label were measured for conservation. As might be expected, good-to-good transformations resulted in conservation of roles and attributes by a higher percentage of children than the good-to-bad or bad-to-good transformations at both ages 5 and 8. Under the latter two transformations, attributes as well as labels were often changed, for example, for many children, a ballplayer who becomes a liar loses his ability to play baseball.

A related conservation paradigm was used by Jordan (1980) on kinship roles, the transformations being *time* (e.g., Is John still a son when he is 27 years old?), multiple inclusive *kinship roles* (a mother who is also a sister) versus exclusive roles (a brother can not also be a sister), and sex-stereotyped *occupational roles* (father as doctor vs. father as nurse). By 5 years of age, most children recognize that opposite-sex kinship pairs cannot exist simultaneously, but even 7-year-olds did not accept the inclusive kinship roles (e.g., mother and sister) as other research has suggested. Likewise, the time transformation had a significant impact: a son is no longer a son when he is an adult, although recognition of the constancy of *self's* role as son or daughter into adulthood is often recognized.

In sum, then, whereas even young children ascribe different behaviors, functions, and powers to various familiar roles, such as father, mother, and sibling, the stability of role concepts undergoes a rather long developmental course. First, most children up to the age of 7 or so have difficulty understanding that a person can occupy two or more roles at the same time, which, as a finding, accords well with the onset of multiple-class membership concepts in nonsocial material (e.g., Kofsky, 1966). However, it is not entirely clear, given children's tendency to understand roles as behaviors, that denials of multiple-role membership by young children merely mean one cannot behave motherly while behaving sisterly for example. Second, some changes and aspects of people influence children's ability to conserve social roles (whether a child who grows up to be an adult is still a daughter to her parents) and attributes of people in roles (e.g., a baseball player who becomes a liar loses his ability to play ball well). Two points: it is well documented that children have difficulty conserving several kinds of quantitative dimensions as well as class membership prior to 7 years of age (Kofsky, 1966; Piaget, 1970), and their difficulty conserving social roles is in keeping with those data. Second, role membership can be viewed as a class-membership instance ("She is a mother." "I am a brother.") or as a relation between people ("I have two brothers." "She is my mother.") (Elkind, 1962; Piaget, 1928). Young children often treat a relational term, such as brother, as an absolute characteristic (e.g., "Brother is a boy.") and tend to construe relational concepts (social or spatial) to classes or absolutes. Future research will determine the extent to which social-role concepts show some of these same features. There is a hint in one case (Jordan, 1980) that social-role conservation for self's own roles may develop prior to conservation of others' roles.

Finally, social rules are another broad topic of relations among individuals, whether those rules are moral or social-conventional. The interested reader is referred to Rest's chapter on moral development (*vol. III, chap.* 9) and the work of Damon (1977), Nucci & Turiel (1978), Shantz (in press), and Turiel (1975).

CONCLUDING REMARKS

Although the stated topic of this review was children's conceptions of others and not themselves, the chapter is a testimony to their essential indivisible nature. The self/other *relation* is a primary issue of development, it appears. Not only is that true in the relative lack of differentiation of self and other in many judgments of the other (as Piaget, 1967, captured in the construct of egocentrism) but also the footprints of the self are all over other developmental phenomena—the substantial impact exerted on inferences by the similarity between self and other, the tendency to use self as a standard for judging deviant behavior, the long developmental course of understanding the relations between self's and other's perspectives, the assumption of others' intentional behavior, to name a few. Given the centrality of the self/other relation in social cognition, it is not surprising that a great deal of research and theory has focused on perspective taking, considered both as a process by which one generates information about the other and as a structure of self/other relations of different types or levels. Although this focus has produced substantial insight into the child's social reasoning (and is likely to continue to do so), there have been certain distinctions about perspective taking, particularly as a process, that have seldom been made. Some of these distinctions have been discussed in this review: the difference between assumed similarity versus inferred similarity and the relations among egocentrism, sociocentrism, and perspective taking (see also Shantz, 1981, and Higgins's elaborations, 1981).

Although the research to date has begun to reveal the richness and subtlety of the child's odyssey in understanding others and the self/other relations, there are some areas of relative neglect that deserve comment. Three are focused on here: the processes by which social judgments are made, the analysis of the social environment, and various methods and designs used in research.

One surprising topic of neglect is what a child (or adult) actually does mentally when she makes a social judgment about another person, that is, the mental acts that occur. One particular process, role taking, has been the primary postulated process since the time of Mead's theoretical (1934) work, and, more contemporaneously, the pioneering research of John Flavell et al. (1968) on role taking and communication. Role taking has been defined metaphorically as putting oneself in another's position or seeing the world through another's eyes. Apparently, the metaphor has been too satisfying or the task too difficult to interest many to go beyond the metaphor to specify the means by which one mentally infers or constructs another's understanding of a situation or another's viewpoint. Flavell et al., in fact, noted years ago the difficulty in specifying social analysis and inference:

> Assuming the child knows all the foregoing [that perspectives can exist and the situation calls for analysis of the other], he still faces the considerable problem of actually carrying out the intended analysis of the other person's role attributes. There is obviously a great deal we don't

know about how this is done. Our working conception has been that role-taking activity usually takes the form of an inferential process of some sort, a process of making guesses about what the pertinent role attributes are in a given situation on the basis of our general knowledge of human behavior, together with whatever specific information we can extract from the immediate situation. (1968, p. 209)

Let us examine some possible ways in which information about another can be generated, that is, general social-judgmental processes, with no assumption about their relation to role taking as one judgmental process. First, as hinted in Flavell et al. (1968), a child can infer certain information about another by knowing what *most* people do, feel, or think—in general or in this particular situation. This has been called previously (Shantz, 1975b) *normative* information and is clearly related to Kelley's (1967) notion of consensus information (as used in causal reasoning) and to a more specific form called *social-category* information (Higgins, 1981), that is, the use of specific classes of people to infer normative attributes. For example, one might predict a child's food aversion, not by taking his role but merely by classifying the child as a member of the class children, who are known (believed) in general to dislike stew, as compared to the class adults, who are known (believed) in general to like (or tolerate) stew. In short, one does not need necessarily to take the role of the other to discern likely attributes (preferences, feelings, thoughts, attitudes), one can derive them sometimes by classification. Second, one can make inferences about another based on that person's past behavior, preferences, attitudes, thoughts, and feelings (i.e., *consistency* information in Kelley's model) in general or in particular situations. Presumably, the child's developing abilities to abstract regularities in a person's behavior and to construct an implicit personality theory of relating traits to one another would form part of the bases for judging another's psychological response and future behavior. Third, *generalizations from the self* could generate substantial information about the other (Shantz, 1975b). This rests on the notion that, as humans, we often think, feel, and behave similarly in certain situations and that use of the self as a model of others' likely reactions (internal and behavioral) leads very often to accurate and adaptive judgments. The critical point, as outlined earlier, is whether this similarity is assumed (egocentric functioning) or inferred (nonegocentric functioning). If the latter, one can presumably make inferences by symbolically putting oneself in another's situation ("What would I do, feel, think if I were in that situation?") or symbolically becoming another ("What would I do, feel, or think if I were that person?"), labeled respectively situational role taking and individual role taking (Higgins, 1981). Of course, labeling a process as generalizations from the self, whether situational or individual, still largely begs the difficult question of process, that is, what is generalized and how and when it is done.

This excursion into three possible means of generating social information is done in part to delimit the definition of role taking as a process that is likely operative under certain conditions rather than, as is sometimes the case, being used as a catchall term or assumed process underlying *any* social information. In concert with this delimitation is Higgins's suggestion: "Judgments involve role taking when there is an inference about a target's viewpoint (or response) under circumstances where the judge's own viewpoint is salient and different from the target's" (1981, p. 133).

As important as the explication of role taking (or perspective taking) as a process is, it is equally critical to examine the implications of perspective taking as structure, that is, the levels of inference and coordination among viewpoints. There is certainly a psychological revolution that occurs phenomenologically when, for example, one suddenly becomes aware that one is not only the observer/inferrer about another but also that oneself is the subject of another's inferences; or, when, as one is involved in a dyadic exchange, one steps outside the dyad to understand the exchange from a symbolic third-person perspective. The developmental description of such restructurings of the social field is almost entirely due to the extensive work of Selman (1980) and Flavell et al. (1968, pp. 44–55). The importance of perspective-coordination development, in Selman's view, is that it is a fundamental restructuring in the way an individual views social relations and, as such, is predictive of the conceptual level of reasoning about friends, authorities, peers, and the self. It holds promise for relating diverse domains of social reasoning and deserves extensive study. Here, as in perspective-taking-as-process, we know very little about the kinds of cognitive abilities required for such restructuring at various levels. It is unlikely that it is adequately described by the mere ability to take into account more elements (Higgins, 1981). Also, little is known about the kinds of social experiences that foster such restructuring. Here one can only speculate that some diverse and potent social experiences may restructure the field for the

child, which, in turn, foster the child's own reorganizations (e.g., being fooled by a peer because, the peer gloats, he knew what the self had in mind; or having a parent interpret the self's classroom behavior from the teacher's perspective).

The importance of perspective coordination, implying as it does "qualitative differences in the way social reality is organized" (Selman, 1980, p. 76), lies not only in its usefulness in understanding ontogenetic changes but also in its usefulness in understanding individual differences among adults and the conditions under which various structurings occur. The data to this point suggest adult functioning almost uniformly at the highest levels of perspective coordination (Selman, 1980) from interview data. However, it is likely adults differ substantially in their ability or willingness to consistently function at the highest levels. Besides the variations that occur in the "average" adults' day-to-day, situation-by-situation constructions, it is equally likely, although less obvious, that such difficulties are also true of "average" adult scientists' structuring of the reality they study. For example, Sameroff (1982) has noted the problem scientists have in understanding their "location" in scientific systems of inquiry and thereby structuring their relationship to their "fields." He notes, by way of illustration, that the two great revolutions in physics provided by Copernicus and Einstein were related to perspective-coordination: the fact that mankind is not the center of the universe and that the organization of physical reality is known only in relation to the observer's position in time and space. The subarea of perspective coordination, then, may have substantial utility for lifespan developmental psychology in explicating the organization of social and physical reality as constructed by most adults and adult scientists as well as children (e.g., the child as a natural philosopher, Broughton, 1978; Wellman, 1982).

The second major area of neglect in social-cognitive research is the examination of the social world of the child. That is, most research has been focused on the child's thinking and reasoning about his or her social world and not much attention has been given to the social world reasoned about. The emphasis may be a legacy from the guiding influence of Piaget and Werner, each of whom detailed the organism's mental processes and largely assumed an "average expectable environment" for the developing organism. Piaget, of course, in his theoretical writings emphasized an interactionist view of the organism and environment, but his research focused almost entirely on the organism side. This slighting of the environment in both Piaget's and social-cognitive research has given an impression sometimes of children bootstrapping their way to social knowledge and adaptive social reasoning. The examination of the social world—its informational properties, its structure, and particularly the changing social environment in ontogenesis—would be a worthwhile endeavor to understand the interaction and reciprocal influences between organism and environment (e.g., Higgins & Parsons, in press; Shantz, in press).

The third area of neglect is highlighted by the fact that the vast majority of studies reviewed here are based on cross-sectional designs and are nomothetic, using *group* data to infer *individuals'* mental structuring and reasoning. In the first case, age *differences* in performance (in causal reasoning, perspective taking, person perception, etc.) are used to infer age *changes* rather than examining changes directly by the longitudinal method. As such, this area is no different than the field of developmental psychology in general. It would be most useful to have some of the major findings shown in cross-sectional work confirmed or disconfirmed by longitudinal study. Second, there has been very little work devoted to the intensive study of a few individuals' social-cognitive knowledge profiles to detail intrapsychic patterns (e.g., conceptions of friends, authorities, and persons in general; perspective coordination and causal reasoning). Because different groups of children are often studied for different concepts or processes, we have little guidance except by way of age-related performance to the possible relationships of these concepts and processes *within* children. More use can be made of idiographic approaches because they deal directly with one of the primary aims of social-cognitive research: to describe the individual's pattern of social reasoning and knowledge about the social world and how that pattern changes in development.

Some additional aspects of methods of research deserve comment. One method often used is the semistructured (clinical) interview of children and adolescents; most researchers using this method have found evidence of qualitatively different reasoning (stages or levels) to occur sequentially in development. Although some of the limitations of this method are well recognized, it has a strength particularly important during the early phases of research: the minimal constraining of the child's responses and the probing of what children mean by what they say. This latter aspect is best contrasted with the experimental dictum of presenting the same stimulus to each subject to examine systematically differences in responses. It would be assumed, for example, that asking each child "Who is your best

friend?" is asking the same question of all. But, as has been detailed, perceivers of questions may give very different meanings to the same question, for example, the one question is equivalent to asking one child "Who do you play with most?", whereas for another it is "Who is it you trust and share secrets with?" As such, perceivers can do some violence to scientists' experimental canons. And just as stimuli have different meanings, so do responses. By not knowing what a child means when he says someone is liked because the person is loyal, the researcher may well err toward sorting words rather than sorting meanings and concepts.

Both interviewing and more test-oriented approaches (as in perspective-taking tasks of many kinds) have been frequent means to reveal social-cognitive abilities, reasoning, and representations. Another method that has not been as frequently adopted is the examination of social-knowledge-in-action. Typically, in this method, children are studied in natural settings or close analogues thereof as they interact with one another. Their social behavior and statements are used to infer their tacit social knowledge and structuring of social relations. Tacit knowledge refers to the procedures and rules, for example, that children may know and use, but they do not know they know them in the sense of being able to represent them (in analogy with the slavish following of syntactical and adjective-ordering rules, for example, by users of a language who, nonetheless, do not represent them as rules). Examples of such descriptive work is children's structuring of social situations around interpersonal issues of ownership (e.g., Newman, 1978), breaches of interpersonal rules (e.g., Much & Shweder, 1978), and third-party entry into an ongoing dyad (e.g., Forbes, Lubin, & Anderegg, 1980).

Social-knowledge-in-action, as a research approach, can provide not only important new descriptive data but also can be used to study more directly the processes of social-cognitive change as children debate and discuss various social issues or social tasks. Recently, there have been several studies, mostly restricted to moral-reasoning development, that examine the dynamics of peer interactions to determine their influence on reasoning changes (e.g., Bearison, in press; Berkowitz, Gibbs, & Broughton, 1980; Damon & Killen, 1982). The importance of this approach is its potential for explicating the mechanisms by which peers influence each other's social reasoning (e.g., through conflict, imitation, co-construction, etc.).

Of the many latent and manifest issues in this field of inquiry, two will be addressed here. The first concerns the relation between hypothetical and real-world reasoning. Does real-world reasoning overestimate or does it underestimate the child's social knowledge? Or, the issue is sometimes posed: Does level *X* reasoning systematically occur in real-world context before (in development) it occurs in hypothetical contexts, or the reverse? The issue is important in many respects, not the least of which is the fact that so much of the data base of social-cognitive development rests on hypothetical stories and packaged causal information. Damon (1977) has discussed this issue and presented evidence that whether one precedes or lags in development may depend on the degree to which self-interest is an issue in a particular domain of reasoning. For example, in distributive-justice situations, about half the children reasoned at the same level in both real and hypothetical contexts, but when there was a difference, it was clear that higher levels occurred in hypothetical situations (Damon, p. 107). However, when children reasoned about authority issues, essentially no differences between contexts occurred (Damon, 1977). Bearison and Gass (1979) found children used significantly higher levels of appeals in persuading another in a real situation (being paid for good persuasion) versus a hypothetical situation. (The major difference was the simple begging did not occur in the real condition but accounted for 41% of the appeals in the hypothetical situation.) Damon (1977) posited that when self-gain conflicts with equity principles, the practical situation is likely to elicit lower levels of reasoning because self-gain is at stake. Self-gain does not conflict with principles of persuasion, and, thus, it is understandable that persuasive levels were higher in the real than hypothetical setting. Likewise, in authority problems, such as choosing and obeying a team captain, the child's self-interest does not conflict with others' interest: everyone's self-interest is at stake. In short, the role self-interest plays in different situations is likely to be at least one critical factor in determining whether reasoning is higher or lower in different contexts or precedes or lags in development.

The second issue concerns the degree of rationality of the child. The literature on the cognitive processes possibly involved in social reasoning runs the risk of painting a picture of a very rational social child, one prone to be lost in social thought in the midst of the peer group, so to speak. Unfortunately, there are no data to speak to the veracity of this picture, but several considerations make one question it. For example, an environmental press is caused by the fact that social events occur rapidly in real time, and there are limits to the attentional sys-

tem and mental capacity of the child. It may well be that children, as has been speculated for adults (e.g., Langer, 1978; Taylor & Fiske, 1978), engage in a good deal of simple perceptions and global impressions as well as simple habits in their everyday interactions. Simple means here those nonanalytic ways of coding or giving meaning to another's behavior, for example, affective coding, global intuitions or images. Most likely, social inferences would occur primarily in those situations in which the social environment in some way resists simple and habitual processes and acts. For example, simple expectations are not predictive, the situation is novel and old perceptions and routines cannot be applied, or known scripts fail to run off. What is being suggested here is that the law of least mental effort applies until the environment provides circumstances where it fails, that is, it resists application.

It is clear that social-cognitive development, as an area of theory and active research that has evolved primarily during the last 15 years, not only is addressed to some important academic issues but also has substantial usefulness in applied fields. In education, for example, children's attributions as to why they and others succeed or fail at tasks is of concern to the children themselves as well as to teachers and parents, and these attributions have demonstrated relations to expectancies for achievement (e.g., Dweck, 1978). Likewise, there are a number of programs of social problem solving (e.g., Shure & Spivack, 1978) and social-skill training (e.g., Asher & Renshaw, 1981) that have been employed in homes, preschools, and classrooms for children with interpersonal problems. Some of the findings on perspective taking have been applied also to children and adolescents with more severe problems (e.g., Chandler, 1976; Selman, 1980). In a new area of investigation, Kurdek, Blisk, and Siesky (1981) have found that children's adjustment to their parents' divorce is related to the children's level of interpersonal reasoning. Much of the applied research, which is only briefly sampled here, is a direct response to children's social problems. It is equally important that the research reviewed in this chapter, most of which was motivated by more academic issues, be used wherever possible to address the various social problems of children by those intimately involved in their lives as well as those at the broader societal level of social policy, the legal system, television broadcasting, and education.

This new field of psychological inquiry has only begun to afford glimpses of the complexities and subtleties of the development of social knowledge and reasoning. The complexity and subtlety appear to have encouraged, not discouraged, a tolerance of different theoretical and methodological approaches and investigations into a wide variety of different phenomena. Perhaps this strength is to be expected in a hybrid area that brings together developmentalists and nondevelopmentalists, cognitive psychologists and social psychologists, academic interests and applied interests. It is hoped that this review will help to maintain such diversity and, at the same time, provide indications of common pursuits and findings to reveal some of the coherence underlying the diversity. If the pace of studying children's understanding of their social world continues to accelerate, as it appears to be doing, we can anticipate with confidence more contributions in the interests of children and the enrichment of related areas of developmental psychology.

NOTES

1. A study by Josephson as reported by Ross (1981) partially confirms this broad picture. Subjects ages 5, 8, 11, 15, and 20 heard stories that gave dispositional information or situational information and then predicted what the actor would do. All age groups made person and situation inferences, but the youngest children gave the greatest weight to the situation and the least to the person; the 8-, 11-, and 15-year-olds were more inclined to give heavy weight to person factors and *relatively* light weight to the situation (it is unclear if data were scored to reveal person × situation interaction); but (interestingly) the 20-year-olds were most like the 5-year-olds. Ross hypothesized that the college students may have "reverted" to situationalism from their exposure in the college setting to ideologies stressing relativism and situationalism.

2. This particular methodology may have underestimated nonegocentric functioning because there is some evidence (Hayes & Birnbaum, 1980) that preschoolers remember more visual than auditory information of televised events.

REFERENCES

Anderson, N. H., & Butzin, C. A. Integration theory applied to children's judgments of equity. *Developmental Psychology*, 1978, *14*, 593–606.

Antonucci, T. Attachment: A life-span concept. *Human Development*, 1976, *19*, 135–142.

Appel, Y. H. Developmental differences in children's perception of maternal socialization behavior. *Child Development*, 1977, *48*, 1689–1693.

Aronfreed, J. *Conduct and conscience: The socialization of internalized control over behavior.* New York: Academic Press, 1968.

Asch, S. E. Forming impressions of personality. *Journal of Abnormal and Social Psychology*, 1946, *41*, 258–290.

Asher, S. R., & Renshaw, P. D. Children without friends: Social knowledge and social skill training. In S. R. Asher & J. M. Gottman (Eds.), *The development of children's friendships.* New York: Cambridge University Press, 1981.

Asher, S. R., Singleton, L. C., Tinsley, B. R., & Hymel, S. A reliable sociometric measure for preschool children. *Developmental Psychology*, 1979, *15*, 443–444.

Baker, L., & Stein, N. L. The development of prose comprehension skills. In C. Santz & B. Hayes (Eds.), *Children's prose comprehension: Research and practice.* Newark, Del.: International Reading Association, 1981.

Baldwin, J. M. *Social and ethical interpretations of mental development.* New York: Macmillan, 1906.

Bandura, A. *Psychological modeling: Conflicting theories.* Chicago: Aldine-Atherton, 1971.

Barenboim, C. Developmental changes in the interpersonal cognitive system from middle childhood to adolescence. *Child Development*, 1977, *48*, 1467–1474.

Barenboim, C. Development of recursive and non-recursive thinking about persons. *Developmental Psychology*, 1978, *14*, 419–420.

Barenboim, C. The development of person perception in childhood and adolescence: From behavioral comparisons to psychological constructs to psychological comparisons. *Child Development*, 1981, *52*, 129–144.

Barker, R. G., & Wright, H. F. *Midwest and its children.* New York: Harper & Row, 1955.

Barnett, M. A., King, L. M., & Howard, J. A. Inducing affect about self or other: Effects on generosity in children. *Developmental Psychology*, 1979, *15*, 164–167.

Barrett, D. E., & Yarrow, M. R. Prosocial behavior, social inferential ability, and assertiveness in children. *Child Development*, 1977, *48*, 475–481.

Bartlett, F. C. *Remembering: A study in experimental and social psychology.* Cambridge: Cambridge University Press, 1932.

Bearison, D. J. New directions in studies of social interaction and cognitive growth. In F. Serafica

(Ed.), *Social cognitive development in context.* New York: Guilford Press, 1982.

Bearison, D. J., & Cassel, T. Z. Cognitive decentration and social codes: Communicative effectiveness in young children from differing family contexts. *Developmental Psychology,* 1975, *11,* 29–36.

Bearison, D. J., & Gass, S. T. Hypothetical and practical reasoning: Children's persuasive appeals in different social contexts. *Child Development,* 1979, *50,* 901–903.

Bell, R. Q. A reinterpretation of the direction of effect in studies of socialization. *Psychological Review,* 1968, *75,* 81–95.

Bem, D. J., & Allen, A. On predicting some of the people some of the time: The search for cross-situational consistencies in behavior. *Psychological Review,* 1974, *81,* 506–520.

Berkowitz, M. W., Gibbs, J. C., & Broughton, J. M. The relation of moral judgment stage disparity to developmental effects of peer dialogues. *Merrill-Palmer Quarterly,* 1980, *26,* 341–357.

Berndt, T. J. Effects of friendship on prosocial intentions and behavior. *Child Development,* 1981, *52,* 636–643.

Berndt, T. J., & Berndt, E. G. Children's use of motives and intentionality in person perception and moral judgment. *Child Development,* 1975, *46,* 904–912.

Berndt, T. J., & Heller, K. Predictions of future behavior, trait ratings, and responses to open-ended questions as measures of children's personality attributions. Paper presented at the Growth of Social Insight During Childhood Conference, University of Wisconsin, Madison, October 1979.

Bigelow, B. J. Children's friendship expectations: A cognitive-developmental study. *Child Development,* 1977, *48,* 246–253.

Bigelow, B. J., & LaGaipa, J. J. Children's written descriptions of friendship: A multidimensional analysis. *Developmental Psychology,* 1975, *11,* 857–858.

Bigner, J. J. A Wernerian developmental analysis of children's descriptions of siblings. *Child Development,* 1974, *45,* 317–323.

Bonney, M. E. The relative stability of social, intellectual, and academic status in grades II to IV, and the interrelationships between these various forms of growth. *Journal of Educational Psychology,* 1943, *34,* 88–102.

Borke, H. Interpersonal perception of young children: Egocentrism or empathy? *Developmental Psychology,* 1971, *5,* 263–269.

Borke, H. The development of empathy in Chinese and American children between three and six years of age: A cross-cultural study. *Developmental Psychology,* 1973, *9,* 102–108.

Borke, H. Piaget's mountains revisited: Changes in the egocentric landscape. *Developmental Psychology,* 1975, *11,* 240–243.

Brandt, M. M. Relations between cognitive role-taking performance and age, task presentation, and response requirements. *Developmental Psychology,* 1978, *14,* 206–213.

Brodzinsky, D. M., & Jackson, J. P. Effects of stimulus complexity and perceptual shielding in the development of spatial perspectives. Paper presented at the meeting of the Society for Research in Child Development, Philadelphia, March 1973.

Broughton, J. M. Development of concepts of self, mind, reality, and knowledge. In W. Damon (Ed.), *New directions for child development: Social cognition.* San Francisco: Jossey-Bass, 1978.

Bruner, J., & Tagiuri, R. The perception of people. In G. Lindzey (Ed.), *Handbook of social psychology.* Cambridge, Mass.: Addison-Wesley, 1954.

Bryan, J. H. Children's cooperation and helping behaviors. In E. M. Hetherington (Ed.), *Review of child development research* (Vol. 5). Chicago: University of Chicago Press, 1975.

Buckley, N., Siegel, L. S., & Ness, S. Egocentrism, empathy, and altruistic behavior in young children. *Developmental Psychology,* 1979, *15,* 329–330.

Burka, A. A., & Glenwick, D. S. Egocentrism and classroom adjustment. Paper presented at the meeting of the Jean Piaget Society, Philadelphia, May 1975.

Burns, N., & Cavey, L. Age differences in empathic ability among children. *Canadian Journal of Psychology,* 1957, *11,* 227–230.

Burns, S. M., & Brainerd, C. J. Effects of constructive and dramatic play on perspective taking in very young children. *Developmental Psychology,* 1979, *15,* 512–521.

Butler, L. J. The relationship between interpersonal problem-solving skills and peer relations and behavior. Paper presented at the meeting of the Canadian Psychological Association, Ottawa, June 1978.

Camras, L. A. Children's understanding of facial expressions used during conflict encounters. *Child Development,* 1980, *51,* 879–885.

Chandler, M. J. Egocentrism and antisocial behavior: The assessment and training of social perspective-taking skills. *Developmental Psychology,* 1973, *9,* 326–332.

Chandler, M. J. Social cognition: A selective review of current research. In W. F. Overton & J. M. Gallagher (Eds.), *Knowledge and development* (Vol. 1). New York: Plenum, 1976.

Chandler, M. J., & Greenspan, S. Ersatz egocentrism: A reply to H. Borke. *Developmental Psychology,* 1972, *7,* 104–106.

Chandler, M. J., Greenspan, S., & Barenboim, C. Assessment and training of role-taking and referential communication skills in institutionalized emotionally disturbed children. *Developmental Psychology,* 1974, *10,* 546–553.

Chandler, M. J., Paget, K. F., & Koch, D. A. The child's demystification of psychological defense mechanisms: A structural and developmental analysis. *Developmental Psychology,* 1978, *14,* 197–205.

Coie, J. D., Costanzo, P. R., & Farnill, D. Specific transitions in the development of spatial perspective-taking ability. *Developmental Psychology,* 1973, *9,* 167–177.

Coie, J. D., & Dorval, B. Sex differences in the intellectual structure of social interaction skills. *Developmental Psychology,* 1973, *8,* 261–267.

Coie, J. D., & Pennington, B. Children's perceptions of deviance and disorder. *Child Development,* 1976, *47,* 407–413.

Collins, W. A. Learning of media content: A developmental study. *Child Development,* 1970, *41,* 1133–1142.

Collins, W. A., Berndt, T. J., & Hess, V. L. Observational learning of motives and consequences for television aggression: A developmental study. *Child Development,* 1974, *45,* 799–802.

Collins, W. A., Wellman, H. M., Keniston, A. H., & Westby, S. D. Age-related aspects of comprehension and inference from a televised dramatic narrative. *Child Development,* 1978, *49,* 389–399.

Cooley, C. H. *Human nature and the social order.* New York: Scribner's, 1902.

Cooney, E. W., & Selman, R. L. Children's use of social conceptions: Toward a dynamic model of social cognition. In W. Damon (Ed.), *New directions for child development: Social cognition.* San Francisco: Jossey-Bass, 1978.

Costanzo, P. R., Grumet, J. F., & Brehm, S. S. The effects of choice and source of constraint on children's attributions of preference. *Journal of Experimental Social Psychology,* 1974, *10,* 352–364.

Cox, M. V. Perspective ability: The conditions of change. *Child Development,* 1977, *48,* 1724–1727.

Cox, M. V. Order of the acquisition of perspective-taking skills. *Developmental Psychology,* 1978, *14,* 421–422.

Cronbach, L. J. Processes affecting scores on "understanding others" and "assumed similarity." *Psychological Bulletin,* 1955, *52,* 177–193.

Cutrona, C. E., & Feshbach, S. Cognitive and behavioral correlates of children's differential use of social information. *Child Development,* 1979, *50,* 1036–1042.

Damon, W. *The social world of the child.* San Francisco: Jossey-Bass, 1977.

Damon, W. Why study social-cognitive development? *Human Development,* 1979, *22,* 206–211.

Damon, W. Exploring children's social cognition on two fronts. In J. H. Flavell & L. Ross (Eds.), *Social cognitive development: Frontiers and possible futures.* New York: Cambridge University Press, 1981.

Damon, W., & Killen, M. Peer interaction and the process of change in children's moral reasoning. *Merrill-Palmer Quarterly,* 1982, *28,* 347–367.

Deutsch, F. Female preschoolers' perceptions of affective responses and interpersonal behavior in videotaped episodes. *Developmental Psychology,* 1974, *10,* 733–740.

Deutsch, F. The effects of sex of subject and story character on preschoolers' perceptions of affective responses and interpersonal behavior in story sequences: A question of similarity of person. *Developmental Psychology,* 1975, *11,* 112–113.

Deutsch, F., & Madle, R. Empathy: Historic and current conceptualizations, measurement, and a cognitive theoretical perspective. *Human Development,* 1975, *18,* 267–287.

DeVries, R. The development of role-taking as reflected by the behavior of bright, average, and retarded children in a social guessing game. *Child Development,* 1970, *41,* 759–770.

DiVitto, B., & McArthur, L. Z. Developmental differences in the use of distinctiveness, consensus, and consistency information for making causal attributions. *Developmental Psychology,* 1978, *14,* 474–482.

Dodge, K. A. Social cognition and children's aggressive behavior. *Child Development,* 1980, *51,* 162–170.

Dornbusch, S. M., Hastorf, A. H., Richardson, S. A., Muzzy, R. E., & Vreeland, R. S. The perceiver and perceived: Their relative influence on categories of interpersonal perception. *Journal of Personality and Social Psychology*, 1965, *1*, 434–440.

Dubin, R., & Dubin, E. R. Children's social perceptions: A review of research. *Child Development*, 1965, *36*, 809–838.

Dweck, C. S. Achievement. In M. E. Lamb (Ed.), *Social and personality development*. New York: Holt, Rinehart & Winston, 1978.

Edelman, M. S., & Omark, D. R. Dominance hierarchies in young children. *Social Sciences Information*, 1973, *12*, 103–110.

Eisenberg-Berg, N., & Hand, M. The relationship of preschoolers' reasoning about prosocial moral conflicts to prosocial behavior. *Child Development*, 1979, *50*, 356–363.

Eisenberg-Berg, N., & Lennon, R. Altruism and the assessment of empathy in the preschool years. *Child Development*, 1980, *51*, 552–557.

Eisenberg-Berg, N., & Mussen, P. Empathy and moral development in adolescents. *Developmental Psychology*, 1978, *14*, 185–186.

Eisenberg-Berg, N., & Neal, C. Children's moral reasoning about their own spontaneous prosocial behavior. *Developmental Psychology*, 1979, *15*, 228–229.

Elardo, P. T., & Caldwell, B. M. The effects of an experimental social development program on children in the middle childhood period. *Psychology in the Schools*, 1979, *16*, 93–100.

Elias, M., Larcen, S., Zlotlow, S., & Chinsky, J. An innovative measure of children's cognitions in problematic interpersonal situations. Paper presented at the meeting of the American Psychological Association, Toronto, August 1978.

Eliot, J., & Dayton, C. M. Egocentric error and the construct of egocentrism. *Journal of Genetic Psychology*, 1976, *128*, 275–289.

Elkind, D. Children's conceptions of brother and sister: Piaget replication study V. *Journal of Genetic Psychology*, 1962, *100*, 129–136.

Elkind, D. Egocentrism in adolescence. *Child Development*, 1967, *38*, 1025–1034.

Emmerich, W. Young children's discriminations of parent and child roles. *Child Development*, 1959, *30*, 403–419.

Emmerich, W. Family role concepts of children ages six to ten. *Child Development*, 1961, *32*, 609–624.

Enright, R. D., & Sutterfield, S. J. An ecological validation of social cognitive development. *Child Development*, 1980, *51*, 156–161.

Fay, B. The relationships of cognitive moral judgment, generosity, and empathic behavior in six and eight year old children. Unpublished doctoral dissertation, University of California, Los Angeles, 1970.

Feffer, M. H. Developmental analysis of interpersonal behavior. *Psychological Review*, 1970, *77*, 197–214.

Feffer, M. H., & Gourevitch, V. Cognitive aspects of role-taking in children. *Journal of Personality*, 1960, *28*, 383–396.

Feshbach, N. D. Studies of empathic behavior in children. In B. A. Maher (Ed.), *Progress in experimental personality research* (Vol. 8). New York: Academic Press, 1978.

Feshbach, N. D., & Feshbach, S. The relationship between empathy and aggression in two age groups. *Developmental Psychology*, 1969, *1*, 102–107.

Feshbach, N. D., & Roe, K. Empathy in six- and seven-year-olds. *Child Development*, 1968, *39*, 133–145.

Fishbein, H. D., Lewis, S., & Keiffer, K. Children's understanding of spatial relations: Coordination of perspectives. *Developmental Psychology*, 1972, *7*, 21–33.

Flapan, D. *Children's understanding of social interaction*. New York: Teachers College Press, 1968.

Flavell, J. H. Concept development. In P. H. Mussen (Ed.), *Carmichaels' manual of child psychology* (Vol. 1) (3rd ed.). New York: Wiley, 1970.

Flavell, J. H. The development of inferences about others. In T. Mischel (Ed.), *Understanding other persons*. Totowa, N.J.: Rowman & Littlefield, 1974.

Flavell, J. H. The development of knowledge about visual perception. In C. B. Keasey (Ed.), *Nebraska Symposium on Motivation* (Vol. 25). Lincoln: University of Nebraska Press, 1978.

Flavell, J. H., Botkin, P. T., Fry, C. L., Jr., Wright, J. W., & Jarvis, P. E. *The development of role-taking and communication skills in children*. New York: Wiley, 1968.

Flavell, J. H., Everett, B. A., Croft, K., & Flavell, E. R. Young children's knowledge about visual perception: Further evidence for the Level 1-Level 2 distinction. *Developmental Psychology*, 1981, *17*, 99–103.

Flavell, J. H., Flavell, E. R., Green, F. L., & Wilcox, S. A. Young children's knowledge about visual perception: Effect of observer's distance from target on perceptual clarity of target. *Developmental Psychology*, 1980, *16*, 10–12.

Flavell, J. H., Omanson, R. C., & Latham, C. Solving spatial perspective-taking problems by rule versus computation: A developmental study. *Developmental Psychology*, 1978, *14*, 462–473.

Flavell, J. H., Shipstead, S. G., & Croft, K. Young children's knowledge about visual perception: Hiding objects from others. *Child Development*, 1978, *49*, 1208–1211.

Forbes, D. L., Lubin, D. A., & Anderegg, D. The development of children's third-party entry strategies. Unpublished manuscript, Harvard University, 1980.

Ford, M. E. The construct validity of egocentrism. *Psychological Bulletin*, 1979, *86*, 1169–1188.

Frieze, I. H., & Snyder, H. N. Children's beliefs about the causes of success and failure in school settings. *Journal of Educational Psychology*, 1980, *72*, 186–196.

Garvey, C., & Hogan, R. Social speech and social interaction: Egocentrism revisited. *Child Development*, 1973, *44*, 562–568.

Gesten, E. L., de Apodaca, F. R., Rains, M. H., Weissberg, R. P., & Cowen, E. L. Promoting peer related social competence in young children. In M. W. Kent & J. E. Rolf (Eds.), *Primary prevention of psychopathology* (Vol. 3). Hanover, N.H.: University Press of New England, 1978.

Gilbert, D. The young child's awareness of affect. *Child Development*, 1969, *39*, 619–636.

Ginsburg, H. J., Pollman, V. A., & Wauson, M. W. An ethological analysis of nonverbal inhibitors of aggressive behavior in male elementary school children. *Developmental Psychology*, 1977, *13*, 417–418.

Gitter, A. G., Mostofsky, D. I., & Quincy, A. J. Race and sex differences in the child's perception of emotion. *Child Development*, 1971, *42*, 2071–2075.

Glick, J., & Clarke-Stewart, K. A. (Eds.), *The development of social understanding*. New York: Gardner Press, 1978.

Glidewell, J. C., Kantor, M. B., Smith, L. M., & Stringer, L. A. Socialization and social structure in the classroom. In L. W. Hoffman & M. L. Hoffman (Eds.), *Review of child development research* (Vol. 2). New York: Russell Sage Foundation, 1966.

Goffman, E. *Frame analysis*. New York: Harper & Row, 1974.

Gold, M. Power in the classroom. *Sociometry*, 1958, *25*, 50–60.

Goldman, B. D., & Ross, H. S. Social skills in action: An analysis of early peer games. In J. Glick & K. A. Clarke-Stewart (Eds.), *The devel-*

opment of social understanding. New York: Gardner Press, 1978.

Gollin, E. S. Organizational characteristics of social judgment: A developmental investigation. *Journal of Personality*, 1958, *26*, 139–154.

Goslin, D. A. Accuracy of self-perception and social acceptance. *Sociometry*, 1962, *25*, 283–296.

Gove, F. L., & Keating, D. P. Empathic role-taking precursors. *Developmental Psychology*, 1979, *15*, 594–600.

Grusec, J. E., & Kuczynski, L. Direction of effect in socialization: A comparison of the parent's versus the child's behavior as determinants of disciplinary techniques. *Developmental Psychology*, 1980, *16*, 1–9.

Guttentag, M., & Longfellow, C. Children's social attributions: Development and change. In C. B. Keasey (Ed.), *Nebraska Symposium on Motivation* (Vol. 25). Lincoln: University of Nebraska Press, 1978.

Harré, R. The conditions for a social psychology of childhood. In M. P. M. Richards (Ed.), *The integration of a child into a social world*. London: Cambridge University Press, 1974.

Hartup, W. W. Peer interaction and the behavioral development of the individual child. In E. Schopler & R. J. Reichler (Eds.), *Psychopathology and child development*. New York: Plenum, 1976.

Hartup, W. W. Two social worlds: Family relations and peer relations. In M. Rutter (Ed.), *Scientific foundations of developmental psychiatry*. London: Heinemann, 1980.

Hayes, D. S. Cognitive bases for liking and disliking among preschool children. *Child Development*, 1978, *49*, 906–910.

Hayes, D. S., & Birnbaum, D. W. Preschoolers' retention of televised events: Is a picture worth a thousand words? *Developmental Psychology*, 1980, *16*, 410–416.

Hayes, D. S., Gershman, E., & Bolin, L. J. Friends and enemies: Cognitive bases for preschool children's unilateral and reciprocal relationships. *Child Development*, 1980, *51*, 1276–1279.

Heider, F. *The psychology of interpersonal relations*. New York: Wiley, 1958.

Heider, F., & Simmel, M. An experimental study of apparent behavior. *American Journal of Psychology*, 1944, *57*, 243–259.

Heilbrun, A. B., & Landauer, S. P. Stereotypic and specific attributions of parental characteristics by late-adolescent siblings. *Child Development*, 1977, *48*, 1748–1751.

Higgins, E. T. Role-taking and social judgment: Alternative developmental perspectives and processes. In J. H. Flavell & L. Ross (Eds.), *Social cognitive development: Frontiers and possible futures*. New York: Cambridge University Press, 1981.

Higgins, E. T., & Parsons, J. E. Stages as subcultures: Social-cognitive development and the social life of the child. In E. T. Higgins, W. W. Hartup, & D. N. Ruble (Eds.), *Social cognition and social development: A sociocultural perspective*. New York: Cambridge University Press, in press.

Hill, J. P., & Palmquist, W. J. Social cognition and social relations in early adolescence. *International Journal of Behavioral Development*, 1978, *1*, 1–36.

Hoffman, L. W. Effects of maternal employment on the child: A review of the research. *Developmental Psychology*, 1974, *10*, 204–228.

Hoffman, M. L. Moral development. In P. H. Mussen (Ed.), *Carmichael's manual of child psychology* (Vol. 2) (3rd ed.). New York: Wiley, 1970.

Hoffman, M. L. Empathy, its development and prosocial implications. In C. B. Keasey (Ed.), *Nebraska Symposium on Motivation* (Vol. 25). Lincoln: University of Nebraska Press, 1978.

Hollos, M. Logical operations and role-taking abilities in two cultures: Norway and Hungary. *Child Development*, 1975, *46*, 638–649.

Honess, T. Self-reference in children's descriptions of peers: Egocentricity or collaboration? *Child Development*, 1980, *51*, 476–480.

Hopper, R. B., & Kirschenbaum, D. S. Social problem-solving skills and social competence in preadolescent children. Paper presented at the meeting of the American Psychological Association, New York, September 1979.

Huckabay, L. M. A developmental study of the relationship of negative moral-social behaviors to empathy, to positive social behaviors and to cognitive moral judgment. Unpublished doctoral dissertation, University of California, Los Angeles, 1971.

Hudson, L. M. On the coherence of role-taking abilities: An alternative to correlational analysis. *Child Development*, 1978, *49*, 223–227.

Hudson, L. M., Peyton, E. F., & Brion-Maisels, S. Social reasoning and relating: An analysis of videotaped social interactions. Paper presented at the meeting of the American Psychological Association, Washington, D.C., September 1976.

Hughes, R., Jr., Tingle, B. A., & Sawin, D. B.

Development of empathic understanding in children. *Child Development*, 1981, *52*, 122–128.

Huttenlocher, J., & Presson, C. C. Mental rotation and the perspective problem. *Cognitive Psychology*, 1973, *4*, 277–299.

Hymel, S., & Asher, S. R. Assessment and training of isolated children's social skills. Paper presented at the meeting of the Society for Research in Child Development, New Orleans, March 1977.

Iannotti, R. J. Effect of role-taking experiences on role-taking, empathy, altruism, and aggression. *Developmental Psychology*, 1978, *14*, 119–124.

Irwin, D. M., & Ambron, S. R. Moral judgment and role-taking in children ages three to seven. Paper presented at the meeting of the Society for Research in Child Development, Philadelphia, March 1973.

Izard, C. E. *The face of emotion*. New York: Appleton-Century-Crofts, 1971.

Jennings, K. D. People versus object orientation, social behavior, and intellectual abilities in preschool children. *Developmental Psychology*, 1975, *11*, 511–519.

Johansson, G., von Hofsten, C., & Jansson, G. Event perception. *Annual Review of Psychology*, 1980, *31*, 27–64.

Johnson, J. E., Yu, S., & Roopnarine, J. Social cognitive ability, interpersonal behaviors, and peer status within a mixed age group. Paper presented at the meeting of the Southwestern Society for Research in Human Development, Lawrence, Kans., April 1979.

Jones, D. C. The social structure of children's activity groups. Unpublished doctoral dissertation, Wayne State University, 1980.

Jones, D. C., Rickel, A. U., & Smith, R. L. Maternal childrearing practices and social problem-solving strategies among preschoolers. *Developmental Psychology*, 1980, *16*, 241–242.

Jones, E. E., & Davis, K. E. From acts to dispositions: The attribution process in person perception. In L. Berkowitz (Ed.), *Advances in experimental social psychology* (Vol. 2). New York: Academic Press, 1965.

Jordan, V. B. Conserving kinship concepts: A developmental study in social cognition. *Child Development*, 1980, *51*, 146–155.

Karabenick, J. D., & Heller, K. A. A developmental study of effort and ability attributions. *Developmental Psychology*, 1976, *12*, 559–560.

Karniol, R. Children's use of intention cues in evaluating behavior. *Psychological Bulletin*, 1978, *85*, 76–85.

Karniol, R., & Ross, M. The development of causal

attributions in social perception. *Journal of Personality and Social Psychology*, 1976, *34*, 455–464.

Karniol, R., & Ross, M. Children's use of a causal attribution schema and the inference of manipulative intentions. *Child Development*, 1979, *50*, 463–468.

Keasey, C. B. Children's developing awareness and usage of intentionality and motives. In C. B. Keasey (Ed.), *Nebraska Symposium on Motivation* (Vol. 25). Lincoln: University of Nebraska Press, 1978.

Keller, B. B., & Bell, R. Q. Child effects on adult's method of eliciting altruistic behavior. *Child Development*, 1979, *50*, 1004–1009.

Kelley, H. H. Attribution theory in social psychology. In D. Levine (Ed.), *Nebraska Symposium on Motivation* (Vol. 15). Lincoln: University of Nebraska Press, 1967.

Kelley, H. H. *Attribution in social interaction*. New York: General Learning Press, 1971.

Kelley, H. H. The processes of causal attribution. *American Psychologist*, 1973, *28*, 107–128.

Kelly, G. A. *A theory of personality: The psychology of personal constructs*. New York: W. W. Norton, 1955.

King, M. The development of some intention concepts in young children. *Child Development*, 1971, *42*, 1145–1152.

Klein, R. Some factors influencing empathy in six and seven year olds varying in ethnic background. Unpublished doctoral dissertation, University of California, Los Angeles, 1971.

Kofsky, E. Developmental scalogram analysis of classificatory behavior. *Child Development*, 1966, *37*, 191–205.

Kohlberg, L. Stage and sequence: The cognitive-developmental approach to socialization. In D. A. Goslin (Ed.), *Handbook of socialization theory and research*. Chicago: Rand McNally, 1969.

Krasnor, L. R., & Rubin, K. H. The assessment of social problem-solving skills in young children. In T. Merluzzi, C. Glass, & M. Genest (Eds.), *Cognitive assessment*. New York: Guilford Press, 1981.

Kun, A. Development of the magnitude-covariation and compensation schemata in ability and effort attributions of performance. *Child Development*, 1977, *48*, 862–873.

Kun, A., Murray, J., & Sredl, K. Misuses of the multiple sufficient causal scheme as a model of naive attributions: A case of mistaken identity. *Developmental Psychology*, 1980, *16*, 13–22.

Kurdek, L. A. Structural components and intellec-

tual correlates of cognitive perspective taking in first- through fourth-grade children. *Child Development*, 1977, *48*, 1503–1511.

Kurdek, L. A. Perspective taking as the cognitive basis of children's moral development: A review of the literature. *Merrill-Palmer Quarterly*, 1978, *24*, 3–28. (a)

Kurdek, L. A. Relationship between cognitive perspective-taking and teachers' ratings of children's classroom behavior in grades one through four. *Journal of Genetic Psychology*, 1978, *132*, 21–27. (b)

Kurdek, L. A. Generality of decentering in first through fourth grade children. *Journal of Genetic Psychology*, 1979, *134*, 89–97.

Kurdek, L. A., Blisk, D., & Siesky, A. E., Jr. Correlates of children's long-term adjustment to their parents' divorce. *Developmental Psychology*, 1981, *17*, 565–579.

Kurdek, L. A., & Rodgon, M. Perceptual, cognitive, and affective perspective-taking in kindergarten through sixth-grade children. *Developmental Psychology*, 1975, *11*, 643–650.

Landry, M. O., & Lyons-Ruth, K. Recursive structure in cognitive perspective-taking. *Child Development*, 1980, *51*, 386–394.

Langer, E. J. Rethinking the role of thought in social interaction. In J. H. Harvey, W. J. Ickes, & R. F. Kidd (Eds.), *New directions in attribution research* (Vol. 2). Hillsdale, N.J.: Erlbaum, 1978.

Laurendeau, M., & Pinard, A. *Development of the concept of space in the child*. New York: International Universities Press, 1970.

Leahy, R. L. Developmental trends in qualified inferences and descriptions of self and others. *Developmental Psychology*, 1976, *12*, 546–547.

Leahy, R. L. Development of conceptions of prosocial behavior: Information affecting rewards given for altruism and kindness. *Developmental Psychology*, 1979, *15*, 34–37.

Lempers, J. D., Flavell, E. R., & Flavell, J. H. The development in very young children of tacit knowledge concerning visual perception. *Genetic Psychology Monographs*, 1977, *95*, 3–53.

Liben, L. S. Perspective-taking skills in young children: Seeing the world through rose-colored glasses. *Developmental Psychology*, 1978, *14*, 87–92.

Liben, L. S., & Belknap, B. Intellectual realism: Implications for investigations of perspective taking in young children. *Child Development*, 1981, *52*, 921–924.

Lippitt, R., Polansky, N., Redl, F., & Rosen, S. The dynamics of power. In D. Cartwright & A.

Zander (Eds.), *Group dynamics*. Evanston, Ill.: Row & Peterson, 1960.

Livesley, W. J., & Bromley, D. B. *Person perception in childhood and adolescence*. London: Wiley, 1973.

Maas, E., Marecek, J., & Travers, J. R. Children's conceptions of disordered behavior. *Child Development*, 1978, *49*, 146–154.

Maccoby, E., & Jacklin, C. *The psychology of sex differences*. Stanford, Calif.: University of Stanford Press, 1974.

Mandler, J. M. Schematic and categorical organization in memory. Paper presented at the meeting of the Society for Research in Child Development, San Francisco, March 1979.

Mandler, J. M., & Johnson, N. S. Remembrance of things parsed: Story structure and recall. *Cognitive Psychology*, 1977, *9*, 111–151.

Marsden, G., & Kalter, N. Children's understanding of their emotionally disturbed peers. *Psychiatry*, 1976, *36*, 227–238.

Marsh, D. T., Serafica, F. C., & Barenboim, C. Effect of perspective-taking training on interpersonal problem solving. *Child Development*, 1980, *51*, 140–145.

Marshall, H. R., & McCandless, B. R. A study in prediction of social behavior of preschool children. *Child Development*, 1957, *28*, 149–159.

Marvin, R. S., Greenberg, M. T., & Mossler, D. G. The early development of conceptual perspective taking: Distinguishing among multiple perspectives. *Child Development*, 1976, *47*, 511–514.

Masangkay, Z. S., McCluskey, K. A., McIntyre, C. W., Sims-Knight, J., Vaughn, B. E., & Flavell, J. H. The early development of inferences about the visual percepts of others. *Child Development*, 1974, *45*, 357–366.

Masters, J. E. Social comparison by young children. *Young Children*, 1971, *27*, 37–60.

McClure, L. F., Chinsky, J. M., & Larcen, S. W. Enhancing social problem-solving performance in elementary school settings. *Journal of Educational Psychology*, 1978, *70*, 504–513.

McGrew, W. *An ethological study of children's behavior*. New York: Academic Press, 1972.

Mead, G. H. *Mind, self, and society*. Chicago: University of Chicago Press, 1934.

Michotte, A. *The perception of causality*. New York: Basic Books, 1963. (Originally published, 1946.)

Miller, P. H., Kessel, F. S., & Flavell, J. H. Thinking about people thinking about people thinking about . . . : A study of social cognitive development. *Child Development*, 1970, *41*, 613–623.

Mischel, W. Toward a cognitive social learning reconceptualization of personality. *Psychological Review*, 1973, *80*, 252–283.

Moir, D. J. Egocentrism and the emergence of conventional morality in preadolescent girls. *Child Development*, 1974, *45*, 299–304.

Mossler, D. G., Marvin, R. S., & Greenberg, M. T. Conceptual perspective-taking in 2- to 6-year-old children. *Developmental Psychology*, 1976, *12*, 85–86.

Much, N. C., & Shweder, R. A. Speaking of rules: The analysis of culture in breach. In W. Damon (Ed.), *New directions for child development: Social cognition*. San Francisco: Jossey-Bass, 1978.

Murphy, L. B. *Social behavior and child personality: An exploratory study of some roots of sympathy*. New York: Columbia University Press, 1937.

Nelson, K. Social cognition in a script framework. In J. H. Flavell & L. Ross (Eds.), *Social cognitive development: Frontiers and possible futures*. New York: Cambridge University Press, 1981.

Nelson, K., & Gruendel, J. M. From personal episode to social script: Two dimensions in the development of event knowledge. Paper presented at the meeting of the Society for Research in Child Development, San Francisco, March 1979.

Newman, D. Ownership and permission among nursery school children. In J. Glick & K. A. Clarke-Stewart (Eds.), *The development of social understanding*. New York: Gardner Press, 1978.

Nicholls, J. G. The development of the concepts of effort and ability, perception of academic attainment, and the understanding that difficult tasks require more ability. *Child Development*, 1978, *49*, 800–814.

Nigl, A. J., & Fishbein, H. D. Perception and conception in coordination of perspectives. *Developmental Psychology*, 1974, *10*, 858–867.

Nisbett, R. E., Borgida, E., Crandall, R., & Reed, H. Popular induction: Information is not necessarily informative. In J. S. Carroll & J. W. Payne, *Cognition and social behavior*. Hillsdale, N.J.: Erlbaum, 1976.

Novak, D. Children's reactions to emotional disturbance in imaginary peers. *Journal of Consulting and Clinical Psychology*, 1974, *42*, 462.

Nucci, L. P., & Turiel, E. Social interactions and the development of social concepts in preschool children. *Child Development*, 1978, *49*, 400–407.

Oden, S., & Asher, S. R. Coaching children in social skills for friendship making. *Child Development*, 1977, *48*, 495–506.

Olshan, K. The multidimensional structure of person perception in children. Unpublished doctoral dissertation, Rutgers University, 1970.

Omark, D. R. The Umwelt and cognitive development. In D. R. Omark, F. F. Strayer, & D. G. Freedman (Eds.), *Dominance relations: An ethological view of human conflict and social interaction*. New York: Garland, 1980.

Omark, D. R., & Edelman, M. S. A comparison of status hierarchies in young children: An ethological approach. *Social Sciences Information*, 1975, *14*, 87–107.

Omark, D. R., Omark, M., & Edelman, M. S. Formation of dominance hierarchies in young children: Action and perception. In T. Williams (Ed.), *Psychological Anthropology*. The Hague: Mouton, 1975.

Parsons, T., & Bales, R. F. (Eds.). *Family, socialization, and interaction process*. New York: Free Press, 1955.

Payne, F. D. Children's prosocial conduct in structured situations and as viewed by others: Consistency, convergence, and relationships with person variables. *Child Development*, 1980, *51*, 1252–1259.

Peevers, B. H., & Secord, P. F. Developmental changes in attribution of descriptive concepts to persons. *Journal of Personality and Social Psychology*, 1973, *27*, 120–128.

Piaget, J. *The language and thought of the child*. New York: Harcourt, Brace, 1926.

Piaget, J. *Judgment and reasoning in the child*. New York: Harcourt, Brace, 1928.

Piaget, J. *The child's conception of the world*. New York: Harcourt, Brace, 1929.

Piaget, J. *The moral judgment of the child*. London: Kegan Paul, 1932.

Piaget, J. *Six psychological studies*. New York: Random House, 1967.

Piaget, J. Piaget's theory. In P. H. Mussen (Ed.), *Carmichael's manual of child psychology* (Vol. 1) (3rd ed.). New York: Wiley, 1970.

Piaget, J., & Inhelder, B. *The child's conception of space*. London: Routledge & Kegan Paul, 1956.

Piaget, J., Inhelder, B., & Szeminska, A. *The child's conception of geometry*. New York: Basic Books, 1960.

Potashin, R. A sociometric study of children's friendships. *Sociometry*, 1946, *9*, 48–70.

Presson, C. C. Spatial egocentrism and the effect of an alternate frame of reference. *Journal of Experimental Child Psychology*, 1980, *29*, 391–402.

Pufall, P. B. Egocentrism in spatial thinking: It depends on your point of view. *Developmental Psychology*, 1975, *11*, 297–303.

Rappoport, L., & Fritzler, D. Developmental responses to quantity changes in artificial social objects. *Child Development*, 1969, *40*, 1145–1154.

Reisman, J. M., & Shorr, S. I. Friendship claims and expectations among children and adults. *Child Development*, 1978, *49*, 913–916.

Ross, L. The intuitive psychologist and his shortcomings: Distortions in the attribution process. In L. Berkowitz (Ed.), *Advances in experimental social psychology* (Vol. 10). New York: Academic Press, 1977.

Ross, L. The "intuitive scientist" formulation and its developmental implications. In J. H. Flavell & L. Ross (Eds.), *Social cognitive development: Frontiers and possible futures*. New York: Cambridge University Press, 1981.

Rotenberg, K. J. Children's use of intentionality in judgments of character and disposition. *Child Development*, 1980, *51*, 282–284.

Rothenberg, B. B. Children's social sensitivity and the relationship to interpersonal competence, intrapersonal comfort, and intellectual level. *Developmental Psychology*, 1970, *2*, 335–350.

Rubenstein, G., Fisher, L., & Iker, H. Peer observation of student behavior in elementary school classrooms. *Developmental Psychology*, 1975, *11*, 867–868.

Rubin, K. H. Egocentrism in childhood: A unitary construct? *Child Development*, 1973, *44*, 102–110.

Rubin, K. H. Role taking in childhood: Some methodological considerations. *Child Development*, 1978, *49*, 428–433.

Ruble, D. N. The development of comparison processes and their role in achievement-related self-socialization. In E. T. Higgins, W. W. Hartup, & D. N. Ruble (Eds.), *Social cognition and social development: A sociocultural perspective*. New York: Cambridge University Press, in press.

Ruble, D. N., Boggiano, A. K., Feldman, N. S., & Loebl, J. H. Developmental analysis of the role of social comparison in self-evaluation. *Developmental Psychology*, 1980, *16*, 105–115.

Ruble, D. N., Feldman, N. S., & Boggiano, A. K. Social comparison between young children in achievement situations. *Developmental Psychology*, 1976, *12*, 192–197.

Ruble, D. N., Feldman, N. S., Higgins, E. T., &

Karlovac, M. Locus of causality and the use of information in the development of causal attributions. *Journal of Personality*, 1979, *47*, 595–614.

Ruble, D. N., Parsons, J. E., & Ross, J. Self-evaluative responses of children in an achievement setting. *Child Development*, 1976, *47*, 990–997.

Ruble, D. N., & Rholes, W. S. The development of children's perceptions and attributions about their social world. In J. H. Harvey, W. Ickes, & R. F. Kidd (Eds.), *New directions in attribution research* (Vol. 3). Hillsdale, N.J.: Erlbaum, 1981.

Rumelhart, D. E. Notes on a schema for stories. In D. G. Bobrow & W. A. Collins (Eds.), *Representation and understanding*. New York: Academic Press, 1975.

Ryle, G. *The concept of mind*. New York: Barnes & Noble, 1949.

Salatas, H., & Flavell, J. H. Perspective taking: The development of two components of knowledge. *Child Development*, 1976, *47*, 103–109.

Saltz, E., Dixon, D., & Johnson, J. E. Training disadvantaged preschoolers on various fantasy activities: Effects on cognitive functioning and impulse control. *Child Development*, 1977, *48*, 367–380.

Saltz, E., & Hamilton, H. Concept conservation under positively and negatively evaluated transformations. *Journal of Experimental Child Psychology*, 1968, *6*, 44–51.

Saltz, E., & Johnson, J. E. Training for thematic-fantasy play in culturally disadvantaged children: Preliminary results. *Journal of Educational Psychology*, 1974, *66*, 623–630.

Saltz, E., & Medow, M. L. Concept conservation in children: The dependence of belief systems on semantic representation. *Child Development*, 1971, *42*, 1533–1542.

Sameroff, A. J. Development and the dialectic: The need for a systems approach. In W. A. Collins (Ed.), *The concept of development: Minnesota Symposia on Child Psychology* (Vol. 15). Hillsdale, N.J.: Erlbaum, 1982.

Savin-Williams, R. C. An ethological study of dominance formation and maintenance in a group of human adolescents. *Child Development*, 1976, *47*, 972–979.

Savin-Williams, R. C. Dominance hierarchies in groups of early adolescents. *Child Development*, 1979, *50*, 923–935.

Scarlett, H. H., Press, A. N., & Crockett, W. H. Children's descriptions of peers: A Wernerian developmental analysis. *Child Development*,

1971, *42*, 439–453.

Schank, R. C., & Abelson, R. *Scripts, plans, goals and understanding*. Hillsdale, N.J.: Erlbaum, 1977.

Sedlak, A. J., & Kurtz, S. T. A review of children's use of causal inference principles. *Child Development*, 1981, *52*, 759–784.

Selman, R. L. Taking another's perspective: Role-taking development in early childhood. *Child Development*, 1971, *42*, 1721–1734.

Selman, R. L. *The growth of interpersonal understanding*. New York: Academic Press, 1980.

Selman, R. L. The child as a friendship philosopher. In S. R. Asher & J. M. Gottman (Eds.), *The development of friendships*. New York: Cambridge University Press, 1981.

Selman, R. L., & Byrne, D. F. A structural-developmental analysis of levels of role taking in middle childhood. *Child Development*, 1974, *45*, 803–806.

Selman, R. L., & Jacquette, D. The development of interpersonal awareness: A working draft manual. Unpublished scoring manual, Harvard-Judge Baker Social Reasoning Project, Cambridge, Mass., 1978.

Selman, R. L., & Jacquette, D. Stability and oscillation in interpersonal awareness: A clinical-developmental analysis. In C. B. Keasey (Ed.), *Nebraska Symposium on Motivation* (Vol. 25). Lincoln: University of Nebraska Press, 1978.

Shaklee, H. Development in inferences of ability and task difficulty. *Child Development*, 1976, *47*, 1051–1057.

Shaklee, H., & Tucker, D. Cognitive bases of development in inferences of ability. *Child Development*, 1979, *50*, 904–907.

Shantz, C. U. The development of social cognition. In E. M. Hetherington (Ed.), *Review of child development research* (Vol. 5). Chicago: University of Chicago Press, 1975. (a)

Shantz, C. U. Empathy and social-cognitive development. *Counseling Psychologist*, 1975, *5*, 18–21. (b)

Shantz, C. U. The role of role-taking in children's referential communication. In P. Dickson (Ed.), *Children's oral communication development*. New York: Academic Press, 1981.

Shantz, C. U. Children's understanding of social rules and the social context. In F. C. Serafica (Ed.), *Social–cognitive development in context*. New York: Guilford Press, 1982.

Shantz, C. U., Asarnow, J., & Berkowitz, M. W. Situational and intellectual factors influencing perspective-taking performance in children. Paper presented at the meeting of the Southeastern Society for Research in Child Development, Chapel Hill, N.C., April 1974.

Shantz, C. U., & Watson, J. S. Assessment of spatial egocentrism through expectancy violation. *Psychonomic Science*, 1970, *18*, 93–94.

Shantz, C. U., & Watson, J. S. Spatial abilities and spatial egocentrism in the young child. *Child Development*, 1971, *42*, 171–181.

Sharp, K. C. Interpersonal problem-solving capacity and behavioral adjustment in preschool children. Paper presented at the meeting of the American Psychological Association, Toronto, August 1978.

Shaw, M. E., & Costanzo, P. R. *Theories of social psychology*. New York: McGraw-Hill, 1970.

Sherif, M., Harvey, O. J., White, B. J., Hood, W. R., & Sherif, C. W. *Intergroup conflict and cooperation: The robbers cave experiment*. Norman: University of Oklahoma Press, 1961.

Sherif, M., & Sherif, C. W. *Reference groups*. New York: Harper & Row, 1964.

Shultz, T. R., & Butkowsky, I. Young children's use of the scheme for multiple sufficient causes in the attribution of real and hypothetical behavior. *Child Development*, 1977, *48*, 464–469.

Shultz, T. R., & Ravinsky, F. B. Similarity as a principle of causal inference. *Child Development*, 1977, *48*, 1552–1558.

Shure, M. B. Interpersonal problem solving: A cog in the wheel of social cognition. In F. C. Serafica (Ed.), *Social–cognitive development in context*. New York: Guilford Press, 1982.

Shure, M. B., & Spivack, G. *Problem-solving techniques in childrearing*. San Francisco: Jossey-Bass, 1978.

Shure, M. B., & Spivack, G. Interpersonal cognitive problem solving and primary prevention: Programming for preschool and kindergarten children. *Journal of Clinical Child Psychology*, 1979, *3*, 89–94.

Siegler, R. S., & Liebert, R. M. Effects of contiguity, regularity, and age on children's causal inferences. *Developmental Psychology*, 1974, *10*, 574–579.

Sigel, I. E., Saltz, E., & Roskind, W. Variables determining concept conservation in children. *Journal of Experimental Psychology*, 1967, *74*, 471–475.

Sigel, I. E., & Vandenberg, B. The development of person schema. Paper presented at the meeting of the Society for Research in Child Development, Denver, March 1975.

Sluckin, A. M., & Smith, P. K. Two approaches to the concept of dominance in preschool children. *Child Development*, 1977, *48*, 917–923.

Smith, M. C. Children's use of the multiple sufficient cause schema in social perception. *Journal of Personality and Social Psychology*, 1975, *32*, 737–747.

Smith, M. C. Cognizing the behavior stream: The recognition of intentional action. *Child Development*, 1978, *49*, 736–743.

Snyder, M., & Monson, T. C. Persons, situations, and the control of social behavior. *Journal of Personality and Social Psychology*, 1975, *32*, 637–644.

Spivack, G., Platt, J. J., & Shure, M. B. *The problem-solving approach to adjustment: A guide to research and intervention*. San Francisco: Jossey-Bass, 1976.

Spivack, G., & Shure, M. B. *Social adjustment of young children: A cognitive approach to solving real-life problems*. San Francisco: Jossey-Bass, 1974.

Staub, E. The use of role playing and induction in children's learning of helping and sharing behavior. *Child Development*, 1971, *42*, 805–816.

Stein, A. H., & Friedrich, L. K. Impact of television on children and youth. In E. M. Hetherington (Ed.), *Review of child development research* (Vol. 5). Chicago: University of Chicago Press, 1975.

Stein, N. L., & Glenn, C. G. An analysis of story comprehension in elementary school children. In R. O. Freedle (Ed.), *Advances in discourse processing: New directions in discourse processing* (Vol. 2). Norwood, N.J.: Ablex, 1979.

Stein, N. L., & Trabasso, T. What's in a story: Critical issues in comprehension and instruction. In R. Glaser (Ed.), *Advances in the psychology of instruction* (Vol. 2). Hillsdale, N.J.: Erlbaum, in press.

Strayer, F. F., & Strayer, J. An ethological analysis of social agonism and dominance relations among preschoolers. *Child Development*, 1976, *47*, 980–989.

Sullivan, H. S. *The interpersonal theory of psychiatry*. New York: W. W. Norton, 1953.

Surber, C. F. Developmental processes in social inference: Averaging of intentions and consequences in moral judgment. *Developmental Psychology*, 1977, *13*, 654–665.

Suttles, G. D. *The social order of the slum*. Chicago: University of Chicago Press, 1968.

Taylor, S. E., & Fiske, S. T. Salience, attention,

and attribution: Top of the head phenomena. In L. Berkowitz (Ed.), *Advances in experimental social psychology* (Vol. 11). New York: Academic Press, 1978.

Turiel, E. The development of social concepts: Mores, customs, and conventions. In D. J. De-Palma & J. M. Foley (Eds.), *Moral development: Current theory and research*. Hillsdale, N.J.: Erlbaum, 1975.

Watson, M. W., & Fischer, K. W. Development of social roles in elicited and spontaneous behavior during the preschool years. *Developmental Psychology*, 1980, *16*, 483–494.

Weiner, B. *Achievement motivation and attribution theory*. Morristown, N.J.: General Learning Press, 1974.

Weiner, B., & Peter, N. A cognitive-developmental analysis of achievement and moral judgments. *Developmental Psychology*, 1973, *9*, 290–309.

Weisfeld, G. E., Omark, D. R., & Cronin, C. L. A longitudinal and cross-sectional study of dominance in boys. In D. R. Omark, F. F. Strayer, & D. G. Freedman (Eds.), *Dominance relations: An ethological view of human conflict and social interaction*. New York: Garland, 1980.

Wellman, H. M. The child's theory of mind: The development of conceptions of cognition. In S. R. Yussen (Ed.), *The growth of insight in the child*. New York: Academic Press, 1982.

Werner, H. *Comparative psychology of mental development*. New York: International Universities Press, 1948.

Whiteman, M. Children's conception of psychological causality. *Child Development*, 1967, *38*, 143–155.

Wohlwill, J. F. *The study of behavioral development*. New York: Academic Press, 1973.

Wood, M. E. Children's developing understanding of other people's motives for behavior. *Developmental Psychology*, 1978, *14*, 561–562.

Yarrow, M. R., & Campbell, J. D. Person perception in children. *Merrill-Palmer Quarterly*, 1963, *9*, 57–72.

Youniss, J. Another perspective on social cognition. In A. Pick (Ed.), *Minnesota Symposia on Child Psychology* (Vol. 9). Minneapolis: University of Minnesota Press, 1975.

Youniss, J., & Volpe, J. A relational analysis of children's friendships. In W. Damon (Ed.), *New directions for child development: Social cognition*. San Francisco: Jossey-Bass, 1978.

Zahn-Waxler, C., Radke-Yarrow, M., & Brady-Smith, J. Perspective-taking and prosocial behavior. *Developmental Psychology*, 1977, *13*, 87–88.

Zivin, G. On becoming subtle: Age and social rank changes in the use of a facial gesture. *Child Development*, 1977, *48*, 1314–1321.

MORALITY* | 9

JAMES R. REST, *University of Minnesota*

CHAPTER CONTENTS

DEFINITIONS OF MORALITY AND THE DOMAIN OF MORAL PSYCHOLOGY

Psychologists have used a variety of criteria as indicators of a person's morality: (1) behavior that helps another human being, (2) behavior in conformity with societal norms, (3) the internalization of social norms, (4) the arousal of empathy or guilt or both, (5) reasoning about justice, and (6) putting another's interests ahead of one's own. Each of these

*I wish to thank the College of Education, University of Minnesota for support of this chapter, to thank the researchers who sent preprints of their work, to thank editors J. H. Flavell, E. M. Markman, and P. H. Mussen for their extraordinary help. Also, I benefited greatly from the criticisms and suggestions of the following colleagues (although some of them may wish I had benefited a bit more from their comments): N. H. Anderson, M. W. Berkowitz, T. J. Berndt, H. Black, R. Burton, J. L. Carroll, W. Damon, J. Darley, C. P. Edwards, N. Eisenberg-Berg, R. D. Enright, J. Gallatin, J. Gibbs, M. L. Hoffman, B. Hoffmaster, R. Karniol, L. Kohlberg, L. Kuhmerker, L. A. Kurdek, C. Levine, G. Lind, L. Nucci, F. Oser, M. Radke-Yarrow, J. P. Rushton, T. Trabasso, E. Turiel, L. J. Walker, H. Weinreich-Haste, and from many students at the University of Minnesota. This review was originally completed in June, 1980, and revised in August, 1981.

notions captures something important about morality, but as a complete definition of morality, each has limitations.

Behavior that helps other human beings is certainly part of morality. Indeed, whenever a person's behavior affects the welfare of another person, a question of morality is involved. But morality cannot be defined as *any* activity that helps people. Otherwise we would have to regard intestinal bacteria that aid digestion as behaving morally or the ozone layer in the upper atmosphere that filters out harmful rays of the sun as behaving morally. If we define morality in terms of helpful consequences, we would have to regard as moral the actions of a wife who tries to poison her husband by putting harsh chemicals in his food, but instead of killing him, cures his gout. Moral behavior implies activity regulated by certain internal processes, not any and every activity that helps human beings.

Behaving in conformity with social norms also touches on an important aspect of morality. Morality is a societal enterprise involving the establishment of cooperative social structures (promises, institutions, laws, roles, and contracts) that individuals must support to accomplish shared goals (e.g., mutual protection, economic coordination, and education of the young). Individuals who violate group norms are refusing to accept their part in making that system work, and might be showing contempt for the shared goals of the group as well.

Sometimes, however, particular norms of a society are actually inconsistent with cherished social goals; and sometimes certain social arrangements may place a disproportionate burden on some members of the society. There can be various types of nonconformists: those who are purely self-serving and want to avoid social cooperation and those who protest norms that are unjust or inconsistent with ideal social goals and who are willing to incur punishment to dramatize their cause. Such nonconformists as Socrates, Sir Thomas More, Gandhi, and Martin Luther King obviously differ from such nonconformists as Al Capone, Lee Harvey Oswald, and Jack the Ripper. Conformity to group norms, therefore, is an inadequate criterion of morality. Furthermore, many matters of conformity are not primarily moral matters, such as eating etiquette, dress styles, and many customs of business, politics, and social intercourse. In addition, the smooth functioning of a society need not imply a high level of morality: the societies of bees and ants are well coordinated, but we do not regard their behavior as moral because such coordination is not governed by individual choice and a desire to cooperate for shared goals, but by instinct. Likewise, a society tyrannized by a few people enslaving the masses may have a high degree of conformity to social norms, but that coordination of activity is based on coercion, not morality.

Some writers have described moral development as an internalization process whereby behavior comes to be governed by internal standards in the absence of external reinforcement. This notion is consistent with the comment above, namely, that behavior produced by coercion cannot be regarded as morality. The internalization notion is appealing, in that it emphasizes that morality involves an internal governance system. Indeed, one aspect of moral development is a person's becoming increasingly independent of the pressures and temptations of the immediate situation and more governed by long-term plans and more encompassing goals. Internalized behavior usually is described as a pattern of behavior originally established by external pressure that later persists in the absence of external pressure. Yet the notion of internalization by itself does not capture the active *social* constructive side of morality that involves the balancing of one's own interests with other's interests and the coordination of long-term plans and goals with other persons in unified schemes of cooperation. But such behavior would include phobias and mindless habits, and this misses the social-constructive character of morality. Becoming increasingly internalized per se (free of external constraints) could mark the onset of autism or schizophrenia.

The arousal of empathy is an important motivator of moral action. Acting in accord with empathy is not necessarily moral however, for instance, the new medical intern who cannot administer an injection into the arm of a crying child because he empathizes too much; the teacher who gives certain children advantages because she empathizes with some children more than others; the mother who overprotects her child because she is too emotionally identified with the child for the child's own good. Similarly, the arousal of guilt indicates the presence of inner standards and that emotion also is an important motivator. However, the capacity for guilt cannot be the defining characteristic of morality for then guilt-ridden neurotics would have to be regarded as the height of moral perfection. Theories that define morality in terms of behavior driven by the emotion of empathy and guilt are deficient in at least two respects: first, these emotions are not always dependable guides; second, the emotions of empathy and guilt are generally considered "good" emotions in contrast to the "bad" emotions of envy and sadism. The value placed on the emotions of empathy and guilt is grounded on some more fundamental criteria of goodness; it is not just that any behavior that follows from a strong human emotion is good. Otherwise we would promote envy and sadism as much as empathy and guilt.

Reasoning about justice must surely be part of the moral process because so many moral problems involve finding some balance between competing claims and interests. Yet, moral reasoning per se is not all there is to morality; good reasoning does not necessarily translate into good deeds. Furthermore, sophisticated reasoning can sometimes mask or defend self-serving behavior.

Putting another's interests ahead of one's own is the operational definition of much recent research on prosocial behavior. In the typical study of prosocial behavior, the subject is given the choice of acting to help another at cost to oneself or to help oneself at cost to another. If the prosocial act costs something to the decision maker, we have more assurance that helping another is not really selfishly motivated. But considering only situations in which self-interest is opposed to another's interests eliminates cooperative situations (in which the self both gains and gives). Consequently, cooperation is not included as prosocial. In cooperative arrangements, one does not martyr self-interest (the self's interests are as important as anyone else's, although not more so). Some prosocial writers seem to suggest that self-interest is intrinsically less important than someone else's interest (by labeling the *prosocial* alternative as the one in which the self loses and the other gains). But in many situations, self-sacrifice is not morally justified (e.g., the demonstrator who sets fire to himself to publicize a grievance when other means could have been effective or the wife who sacrifices her integrity and individual development to cater to the whims and conveniences of her husband).

Psychologists who have used one or another of these characteristics of morality have not claimed to be offering a comprehensive definition of morality, but they have proposed operational definitions to be able to identify subjects as more or less moral for the purposes of their studies. Much of this research has contributed to our understanding. Nevertheless, the limitations of these conceptions need to be noted because each by itself leads to an underestimation of what is involved in morality. In some cases the phenomenon of morality has been trivialized beyond recognition. We need to attempt a fuller, more complicated, more integrated picture of morality and to envision how the part processes are organized.

The domain of morality envisioned in this chapter borrows from some moral philosophers (e.g., Frankena, 1970), although it must be admitted that moral philosophers are not in agreement on the matter. Alston (1971, p. 276) states: "It is notorious that moral philosophers agree no more about what is distinctive of the moral than about anything else." (See also Wallace & Walker, 1970.) Nevertheless, Frankena (1970) and others regard morality (considered abstractly as a domain of human functioning) as standards or guidelines that govern human cooperation—in particular, how rights, duties, and benefits are to be allocated. Given that people live together and that their activities affect each other, morality provides guidelines and rationales for how each person's activities should affect the other's welfare. The guidelines are not fashioned to serve any one person's interests but are constructed with consideration for each person's interests and each individual's intrinsic value. The implications of this conception of morality will be elaborated in the course of the chapter, but at the onset, it may be useful to note (1) that not all human values or ideals are regarded as *moral* values (e.g., morality is distinguishable from aesthetic and religious values and from ideals of personal perfection)[1]; and (2) that

morality, at least in principle, deals with sharable values because moralities are proposals for a system of mutual coordination of activities and cooperation among people.

A sketch of the major psychological processes involved in the production of moral behavior is presented later. This may help flesh out the conceptions of morality presupposed in this chapter. Also, the presentation of this overview may help place the special focus of this chapter in perspective. Because this volume of the Handbook focuses on cognitive development, this chapter focuses on cognitive development in morality. Therefore, not all aspects of morality are given equal consideration here—the chapter will concentrate on what shall be called Component II. Research pertaining to the other components, however, is discussed at length in other chapters in the Handbook. Before beginning the detailed discussion of cognitive development in morality, I want to emphasize its interrelatedness with other aspects and to make it clear that I am not proposing a *cognitive* theory of morality in contrast to noncognitive theories but am attempting to identify the various cognitive elements along with affective elements in an ensemble of processes involved in the production of moral behavior. The various linkages of cognition with affect and behavior will be sketched before the intensive review of cognitive development.

Major Components of Morality

Reviews of morality commonly subdivide the area into thoughts, behavior, and emotions: cognitive developmentalists are said to study moral thought, behaviorists study behavior, and psychoanalytic psychologists study emotions. This kind of presentation suggests that three basic psychological elements exist, each governed by different processes (e.g., equilibrating cognitive structures, conditioning and modeling, and identification and the operations of the superego). Such reviews usually end by lamenting the uncertain relationships among the three elements and calling on future research to elucidate how cognition and affect are connected, how thought relates to action, and so on.

Dividing morality into these three subareas is inadequate in several respects. First, the three subareas of morality do not represent empirical clusters; various moral behaviors (e.g., resistance to temptation, sharing or helping behavior) are no more highly correlated among themselves than are the correlations between thought and behavior (see Blasi, 1980; Burton, 1976; Rushton, 1976, 1980). Second, dividing reality into thoughts, behavior, and emotions does not provide theoretically clear units of analysis: What is an emotion disembodied from cognitive referents? What is a behavior without intention or thoughts without any feeling component? Third, cognitive developmentalists are not the only psychologists interested in cognition. Social learning theorists (e.g., A. Bandura and W. Mischel) and many social psychologists (e.g., attribution theorists) also study cognition, although not in the Piagetian tradition. There are many kinds of cognition now and, therefore, cognition is no longer the private property of cognitive developmentalists. Fourth, a considerable amount of research undertaken in the past 10 years indicates many kinds of cognitive-affective interactions, and there is not just *one* interface between cognition and affect, cognition and behavior.

To represent the diverse kinds of cognitive processes involved in morality and in an attempt to present a more integrated picture of morality, I propose a four-part framework. Let us imagine that the production of moral behavior in a particular situation involves (1) interpreting the situation in terms of how people's welfare is affected by possible actions of the subject, (2) figuring out what the ideally moral course of action would be, (3) selecting among valued outcomes to intend to do the moral course of action, and (4) executing and implementing what one intends to do.[2]

Component I

Component I, interpreting the situation, involves the identification of possible courses of action in a situation that affect the welfare of someone else. Many factors complicate such interpretation and people often have difficulty in imagining what they might do and in realizing how their actions affect others. Sometimes, the other people who are affected are distant, not personally identifiable, and are affected indirectly through a complicated chain of events (e.g., I may be unaware that my use of a certain brand of coffee supports the exploitation of peasant workers in South America). Sometimes, another's welfare is affected indirectly by violating a general practice or undermining a commonly held standard. Political decisions almost always involve uncertainty in how one's action will affect various people because the effects are mediated through complex social structures and involve unpredictable chains of events (e.g., who knows with certainty what abolishing the military draft will accomplish or what tighter credit will do). The prediction of the effects of one's action entails knowledge about how

the world works, and often our knowledge is not very good (e.g., the surgeon who is not sure whether to perform an operation, the diplomat who wonders how certain policies will work out). Sometimes, we are not very accurate in knowing what other people really want or what their real needs are.

Three findings regarding Component I stand out from psychological research: (1) many people have difficulty in interpreting even relatively simple situations, (2) striking individual differences exist among people in their sensitivity to the needs and welfare of others, and (3) the capacity to make these inferences generally develops with age. Consider first some striking findings from the research on bystander reactions to emergencies. In a much publicized event in New York City, Kitty Genovese was repeatedly attacked and stabbed by an assailant while 38 of her fellow apartment dwellers looked on. Why did not the bystanders do anything to stop the attacks? Interviews with the apartment dwellers indicated that they were uncertain about what was happening to Genovese. Some thought the commotion might be a lover's quarrel and did not want to interfere. Pursuing this lead, systematic studies have found that the ambiguity of situations (hence, the ability to carry out Component I processes) is significantly related to bystander helping behavior in emergency situations (Staub, 1978). Interpreting such situations often entails identifying the pattern and meaning of behavior of several people in interaction with each other, inferring what their respective wants and needs are, imagining what one might do to help in the situation and how the participants would likely react to such an act. To the degree that the subject has difficulty in interpreting the situation in any of these regards, moral behavior is less likely to occur.

Second, research by Schwartz (1977) indicates individual differences in ''the spontaneous tendency to attend to possible consequences of one's behavior for the welfare of others'' (p. 243). Some people seem to recognize how their actions affect others only when the most blatant signs of human suffering are present, whereas other people are supersensitive, seeming to see momentous moral implications in every utterance, gesture, and sneeze and a moral problem under every bush. Moral sensitivity has been linked to moral behavior (Schwartz, 1977).

Third, social cognition research (see *Shantz, vol. III, chap. 8*) documents the developmental character of the ability to make inferences about the thoughts, feelings, and perceptions of others. Insofar as a person was unable to make these inferences, the ability to understand how one's actions would affect others would be limited. The development of these abilities is generally seen as a process of becoming less egocentric (although recent research indicates that egocentrism may not be a unitary process and that many factors affect role-taking abilities). A considerable amount of research has investigated the linkage between social-cognitive development and moral behavior (Kurdek, 1978; Rushton, 1980; Staub, 1978, 1979; see also *Shantz, vol. III, chap*. 8). Many studies show a significant relationship, although results are mixed. A variety of methodological issues and differences in assessment procedures may explain the inconsistent results. It should be noted, in addition, that social cognition measures generally are designed to measure more elementary parts of Component I, that is, measures of social cognition often assess whether a subject can make a specific kind of inference about one other person in one situation. Social cognition is rarely assessed of several people interacting in complex ways, with multiple motives, presented in a flood of information in which relevant cues are embedded and scattered. As one exception, research by Collins and his associates has attended to social inference making in such complex situations (Collins, 1973; Collins, Berndt, & Hess, 1974; Collins, Wellman, Keniston, & Westby, 1978), using television programs to portray the situations. They found that young subjects had trouble understanding the motives of the characters and misunderstood their patterns of interaction in television dramas; young children missed relevant cues, failed to integrate information from various parts of the presentation, and consequently drew false inferences, made erroneous moral evaluations, and advocated inappropriate behavior. Studies of more complex forms of social cognition like that in Collins's research are more likely to show linkages between social cognition and moral development because these assessments of social cognition embody more of what is involved in Component I processes.

So far, the discussion of Component I has emphasized the cognitive aspects of perceiving and interpreting a situation. Also involved is the arousal of affect. Affective arousal does not seem to wait for an unambiguous interpretation of events and even misperceptions of situations can trigger strong emotional arousal (e.g., "I'm extremely agitated because I thought for a moment you were hurting him, even though I knew it couldn't be true"). Even when we do not fully understand social situations, we experience alarm, empathy, anger, envy, exhilaration, and so on. Zajonc (1980), for instance, contends that affective reactions precede complex cognitive operations and can be elicited independently of extensive cognitive encoding. Our own affective arousal, then, is part of what needs to be interpreted when faced with a problem situation. Sometimes the affective arousal serves to highlight salient cues and motivate our "better" selves, for instance when we strongly empathize with a victim and go to his aid. But sometimes the affects aroused in a situation can hamper our better judgment, for instance when we dislike the way someone looks and want to deny the person his full rights.

Hoffman (1975, 1976, 1978, 1981, in press) has emphasized the role of empathy in morality and, like Zajonc (1980), views the arousal of empathy as a primary response that need not be mediated by complex cognitive operations. The rudiments of empathy (distress triggered by distress in another) can be aroused in very young infants and requires very little cognitive development for its activation (Hoffman, 1976), for instance, when newborns cry upon hearing other babies cry. Hoffman's account is particularly interesting in suggesting how this primary affective response comes to interact with cognitive development to produce more complex forms of empathy:

1. During the first year, the child may be discomforted and become alarmed upon seeing distress cues from others. At this point, however, the child does not clearly distinguish herself from others and is unclear about what is happening to whom.

2. Then, gradually, the child comes to realize a clear distinction between the self and others, thus, when another person is hurt, the child knows it is not the self, but still feels sympathy for the other. Nevertheless, the child may respond to the other person in ways that would comfort oneself but are not appropriate for the other (e.g., to offer one's own doll to the other).

3. At 2 or 3 years, the child is aware that other people's feelings and needs can differ from her own and begins to use information about the world and others to infer what is required in the situation to give effective help to the other.

4. By late childhood, the child has developed a conception of other people as each having her own particular life history and identity. The child's empathy at this point may be aroused by the awareness of some deprivation in the other person's general life situation rather than by specific signs of distress. For instance, one may feel sad for a retarded child even while observing the retarded child playing joyfully in a playground.

Hoffman's account, therefore, depicts how affective responses (the arousal of empathic distress) interact with the development of conceptions of the other.

Many writers have proposed that empathy provides the motive for altruism, that is, our sensitivity to the needs and wishes of others is what motivates us to act to help others. At first, it may seem that the constructs of empathy and altruism provide all that is necessary for an explanation of morality or prosocial behavior: the perception of certain social stimuli arouses empathy, which, in turn, creates the motive to act to help others. Despite the current surge of research interest in empathy and altruism, however, the limitations of these constructs need to be noted for they cannot serve as a general model for morality (or prosocial behavior), important as they may be. There are at least three major limitations:

1. Research on empathy and altruism focuses on a very limited range of moral situations and ignores other situations. The typical situation in empathy-altruism research is one in which a subject must decide whether or not to help a stranger in an emergency or whether or not to do something that harms another person. Typically, being selfish and callous is opposed to doing something on behalf of another (i.e., being empathic, caring, altruistic). But there are other types of moral situations. Consider the legend of wise King Solomon. Two women claimed the same baby as their own and Solomon had to decide to whom to give the baby. It was not adequate for Solomon to express his sympathy for the baby and the two women. If all that Solomon could do with that situation was to show sympathy for all the parties involved (or even for all the women of the world wanting babies), he would not have addressed the crucial aspect of this situation (the conflict of interests and the necessity of prioritizing the claims), and it is doubtful that he would have become known as *wise* King Solomon. So also, many of our most vexing moral problems today are situations in which the crux of the matter is a conflict of interest: taxation, abortion, affirmative action, and so on. The crux of these problems is not whether to help another person or not, but whom to help to what degree.

2. Another limitation of the empathy-altruism model of morality is that acting in accord with empathy is sometimes immoral: for instance, the teacher who empathizes more with some children than others and who plays favorites; the mother who smothers her child by overreacting to the child's fears and overprotects the child; the judge who feels greater empathy with one side than the other and takes sides. Because people make moral judgments that can override empathy in some situations (that is, acting in accord with empathy is sometimes morally wrong), a psychological model of morality must postulate another level of cognitive processing that arbitrates when following empathy is right and when it is wrong. Going directly from empathy to altruism to action is not sufficiently complex to depict this additional level of cognitive processing (which is Component II in the present model).

3. The single-person-in-need situation, as a general paradigm for moral psychology, is inadequate, too, in its isolation from a societal or historical context. Although some moral problems may involve two strangers in isolation, many moral problems must be considered with reference to social institutions designed to meet human needs. For instance, we attempt to meet the needs of poor orphans systematically through charitable organizations and tax-supported government agencies rather than just giving a handout to begging children we happen to meet on the streets. Any paradigm of morality that neglects the societal-historical context of human interaction is likely to underestimate institutional and programmatic ways of meeting human needs and one's duties and rights within a set of ongoing social arrangements. Sometimes a person charged with the responsibility for a social organization must act in opposition to his empathy for specific people. For instance, the director of an orphanage might have to fire an employee whom he likes but whose work is jeopardizing the organization. Therefore, an adequate model of morality must consider social-historical contexts because people are related to each other through social structures and history, not only in isolated face-to-face encounters. The arousal of empathy is an important component of morality, but there are other major components.

Component II

Given that a person is aware of alternate courses of action in a situation and is aware of how these actions affect others, Component II involves integrating the various considerations (e.g., person A's needs, person B's needs, my needs, expectations founded on previous promises or roles or instituted practices) insofar as they count for or against the alternative courses of action. Component II involves determining what course of action would best fulfill a moral ideal, what *ought* to be done in the situation. A subject may simultaneously (or as a substitute) be figuring out what course of action optimizes other nonmoral ideals as well (e.g., religious ideals). Later, in discussion of Component III, we will consider how a person decides between conflicting ideals or goals (e.g., to decide for the moral ideal as opposed to an aesthetic ideal), but in discussion of Component II, we consider how a subject determines what the moral ideal is.

To appreciate what is involved in Component II, consider Kohlberg's (1969) well-known moral dilemma about Heinz:

> In Europe, a woman was near death from a special kind of cancer. There was one drug that the doctors thought might save her. It was a form of radium that a druggist in the same town had recently discovered. The drug was expensive to make, but the druggist was charging ten times what the drug cost him to make. He paid $200 for radium and charged $2,000 for a small dose of the drug. The sick woman's husband, Heinz, went to everyone he knew to borrow the money, but he could only get together about $1,000 which is half of what it cost. He told the druggist that his wife was dying, and asked him to sell it cheaper or let him pay later. But the druggist said, "No, I discovered the drug and I'm going to make money from it." So Heinz got desperate and broke into the man's store to steal the drug for his wife. (p. 379)

Note that in such verbally presented dilemmas, much of the processing of Component I is already verbally encoded: the needs and motives of the chief actors are identified, as are the ways that the actions of the participants affect each other; the situation is already represented as a moral dilemma (Heinz's action to help his wife is also clearly hurting—stealing from—the druggist); therefore, the consequences to others by an action are already identified. Given these considerations, the subject is asked to make a judgment about the proper course of action and to explain the rationale. This is the business of Component II.

Two major research traditions offer descriptions of mechanisms involved in Component II: One from social psychology postulates that *social norms* govern how a moral course of action is to be defined. Social norms are of the form, "In a situation with X circumstances, a person ought to do Y." A variety of social norms have been postulated: social responsibility (Berkowitz & Daniels, 1963), equity (e.g., Adams, 1963; Walster, Berscheid, & Walster, 1973), reciprocity (e.g., Gouldner, 1960), the norm of giving (e.g., Leeds, 1963). For instance, the norm of social responsibility prescribes that if you perceive a need in another person and the other person is dependent on you, then you should help the other person. This norm might be applied to the Heinz dilemma as follows: Heinz should steal the drug because his wife needs the drug and cannot get it herself.

Norms are rules or widely held expectations taught by socializing agents and reinforced by one's culture either subtly, by sensing what people expect, or not so subtly, through concrete reward and punishment. Social norms prescribe forms of behavior that are useful and necessary for the regulation, coordination, and prosperity of the social group. According to the social-norm explanation, when a person is confronted with a moral problem, she interprets the situation, and in doing so, notices a particular configuration of circumstances relevant to a particular social norm (e.g., in the above example, the circumstance that someone dependent on Heinz is in need).

> Exposure to the need of others often leads to the activation of social expectations (norms) which define the appropriate responses in a given situation. Activation means a directing of attention to expectations sufficient to bring them into the stream of information processing. Activation does *not* necessarily bring the expectation into focal attention where the individual becomes self-consciously aware that he is considering them. (Schwartz, 1977, p. 225)

Activation, then, is a sort of pattern recognition that classifies the situation as falling under a certain norm; in turn, the norm prescribes the moral course of action. I will return later to a discussion of research on various social norms and developmental studies of social norms.

The second major research tradition dealing with the process of formulating a moral course of action is cognitive-developmental research, notably that influenced by Piaget and Kohlberg. In contrast to the social norm that focuses on the acquisition of a number of norms, the cognitive-developmental approach focuses on the progressive understanding of the purpose, function, and nature of social arrangements. The focus is on the rationale for establishing cooperative arrangements, particularly on how the participants in cooperation are mutually benefiting. In cooperative arrangements, the participants each benefit and incur obligations; justice deals with reciprocating the benefits and obligations in some balanced way. Development consists in the subject's conception of what kinds of cooperative arrangements are possible (concepts of social organization) and in the ways to balance the benefits and obligations (concepts of justice). Children are first aware of fairly simple schemes of cooperation that involve only a few people who know each other through face-to-face encounters and who reciprocate in concrete, short-term exchanges. Gradually, they become aware of more complicated schemes of cooperation that involve long-term societywide networks, institutionalized role systems, divisions of labor, and law-making and law-enforcement systems. The various schemes of cooperation (or justice structures) are called various stages of moral reasoning, each characterized in terms of its distinctive notion of the possibilities and requirements for arranging cooperation among wider circles of participants. Each successive stage is said to build upon and elaborate the previous stage, introducing more complexity for the sake of achieving a more balanced reciprocity of benefits and obligations. The more advanced stages presuppose greater understanding about society and social structures. Each stage is viewed as an underlying general framework of assumptions about how people ought to act toward each other. Each stage provides a "grammar" or "deep structure" for organizing one's construal of social situations. Consequently, each stage provides a framework for prioritizing and integrating considerations to formulate what one's duties and rights are in a specific situation. In the cognitive-developmental view, a person defines what ought to be done in a situation by assimilating the elements of the situation according to one or another general scheme of cooperation and defines the duties of a specific actor by invoking the requirements of maintaining the cooperative arrangements of that general scheme.

For illustration, consider the Heinz dilemma again and how Kohlberg's Stage 4 (1971) might formulate a moral course of action. Stage 4, Law-and-Order Orientation, views all human interaction as taking place within an organized social system, governed by formal law with rights and duties assigned to each role position. The people who occupy those role positions have rights and duties to each other as prescribed by the laws and institutions of the social system. Thus, the social system provides societywide coordination of human activity, stabilizes expectations about what people can expect from one another, provides protection from irresponsible individuals within and from the enemy without. Each person should do his job and stay within the law expecting that other people will do the same. Thus, Heinz might believe that the druggist is a scoundrel and feel desperation about helping his wife; however, Heinz's moral duty is to stay within the law. What is involved is more than a personal transaction between Heinz and the druggist; maintenance of law and order of the entire social network is at stake. Far more human suffering and waste would occur if the system of law were undermined and people began taking the law into their own hands. If a legal way can be found to force the druggist to give up the drug, Heinz is certainly justified in using that recourse, but it can never be right to violate another person's legal rights (out of respect for the social system, not respect for the particular druggist).

Note that in such a formulation, the specific moral dilemma is assimilated into a general way of looking at social cooperation. The derivation of a moral course of action in a specific situation follows from a generalized structure that defines obligations and rights. Therefore, a moral judgment stage differs from a social norm, in that the former is a view about moral relationships in general, whereas the latter applies to a particular type of situation. A social norm does not necessarily involve a generalized view about society or human relationships, nor does it give a *rationale* for allocating moral rights and responsibilities. Social norms entail a recognition of a pattern and a prescription. By the social-norm account, it is difficult to distinguish moral prescriptions from the prescriptions of etiquette, aesthetics, or other social conventions.

The application of Stage 4 concepts to the Heinz dilemma is actually less tidy than portrayed above. Stage 4 concepts could be applied in a different way to the Heinz dilemma. Some subjects focus on Heinz's duties as a husband (who presumably took a formal oath at the time of the marriage vows) and argue that Heinz has a duty as a husband in protecting his wife, possibly even to the point of stealing the drug. Thus, the features of the Heinz dilemma can be organized in several ways in accordance with a Stage 4 perspective; thus, the general perspective of a stage does not always generate a unique solution to a dilemma. The subject must construct the linkages between a stage perspective and the features of a dilemma. This is not to say that a person's stage orientation should in principle have nothing to do with how he solves moral dilemmas, as some writers have contended. Instead, stage structure provides the rationale for formulating a moral course of action and in some multifaceted dilemmas, some stage structures can be used to formulate more than one rationale.

Although some writers regard Piaget's or Kohlberg's stage theories as furnishing a total theory of moral development (and some writers even seem to regard them as theories of general personality development), the framework of this chapter represents their theories mainly as contributions to Component II processes. Reasoning about justice is no more the whole of morality than is empathy.

Component III

Component III involves deciding what one actually intends to do. In Component II, the morally ideal course of action is defined, but it remains for the person to choose what to do. Typically, a person is aware of a number of possible outcomes of different courses of action, each presenting different values and activating different motives. For instance, a student taking an examination might be asked by a classmate to allow a look at her paper. This situation might evoke a motive to resist temptation and not allow cheating; it might evoke a motive of affiliation, expecting that helping the classmate in this situation would solidify their friendship; it might evoke a motive of need achievement if the student wanted to show her superiority over the classmate and others; it might evoke the motive of self-protection if the classmate was menacing. Therefore, parallel to formulating a *moral* course of action, a person may be formulating courses of action oriented toward other values. Oftentimes, other values are so important to a person that they preempt or compromise moral values. For instance, John Dean writes in his book *Blind Ambition* that his activities as special counsel to President Nixon were motivated by his ambitions to succeed in the Nixon administration and that questions of morality and justice were preempted by more pressing concerns. Research by Damon (1977) is another case in point. Damon asked young children how 10 candy bars ought to be distributed as rewards for making bracelets. In interviews, the children described various schemes for a fair distribution of rewards, explaining why they thought a particular distribution ought to be followed. However, when these same children actually were given the 10 candy bars to distribute, they deviated from their espoused fairness schemes and instead gave themselves a disproportionate number of candy bars. The children's espoused moral ideals were thus compromised by self-interest. Recent research by Sobesky (in press) also suggests the distinction between Component II and Component III. When subjects were asked, what *should* Heinz do, they gave different responses than when asked, what *would* most people do in Heinz's situation.

Two kinds of questions are relevant in Component III: (1) How can we represent the decision-making process? That is, what are the elements that enter into the decision-making process, how are they organized, how do they interact, and what factors influence the process? (2) What motivates moral behavior? Why is morality prized more than other values by some people but not by others? Where do moral values come from?

Models of Decision Making. Behavioral decision theory (see reviews by Rappoport & Wallsten, 1972; Slovic, Fischhoff, & Lichtenstein, 1977) offers some possible candidates for models. For instance, Pomazal and Jaccard (1976) applied Fishbein's subjective expected utility model (1967) to moral decision making. In this model, the human decision maker is depicted as maximizing the sum of the products of utility and probability, that is, the decision maker identifies the various consequences of each course of action, calculates the value to the self of each consequence, calculates the subjective probability of each consequence occurring, and calculates how significant other people would favor each action alternative; all these calculations are algebraically combined to yield an overall value for each course of action, and then the actor picks the course of action that maximizes utility and probability. Such models of decision making have the advantage of including many variables that seem to influence decisions (variables, such as the person's subjective estimates of the probability of events, the cost to oneself of doing various acts, etc.). In some studies (e.g., Pomazal & Jaccard, 1976), this model has accounted for a sizable amount of the variance. However, there are numerous difficulties in regarding such a model as generally representative of moral decision making.

1. When the consequences are many and when there is difficulty in estimating the probabilities of occurrence, it is doubtful that many people actually carry out such complex calculations and algebraically combine them according to some systematic algorithm—most human heads are boggled by too much calculation (Slovic et al., 1977).

2. Another complication in applying behavioral decision theory to moral decision making is that some subjects, in some situations, may not calculate the gains and losses of different courses of action but may respond to the call of duty without calculation. That is, in some circumstances, some people may decide to fulfill a moral obligation without weighing the costs and benefits—they do it "just because it is right." Therefore, moral decision making may sometimes have a different dynamic than other forms of decision making that assume a maximum-gain orientation. Indeed, one of the interesting aspects of *moral* decision making may be to determine whether or when moral obligation overrides cost/benefit calculations.

3. Another complication in modeling moral decision making is that sometimes subjects engage in defensive evaluations to deny or neutralize feelings of moral obligation. As the costs of moral action are recognized, a person may neutralize the feelings of obligation by denying the need to act, by denying

personal responsibility to act, by reappraising the situation to make other alternatives more appropriate, or by devaluating persons in need (e.g., Bandura, Underwood, & Fromson, 1975; Lerner, 1971; Schwartz, 1977; Staub, 1978; Walster & Walster, 1975). In this case, preliminary processing of Component III leads to reappraisal of Component I processes.

4. Another complication in modeling moral decision making is that transitory fluctuations in mood seem to affect it. For instance, Isen (1970) found that subjects who were induced to feel happy by being provided a success experience (being told they did extremely well on a perceptual-motor task) tended to donate more money for charity than subjects with a failure experience (being told they did extremely poorly) or than controls. Similar results have been found in studies of children donating more to charity after success in a bowling game, of college students volunteering to participate in a study after being given a cookie, of people who helped pick up spilled papers after finding a dime in a pay phone, and of children giving more to charity who had reminisced about happy experiences (see review in Staub, 1978). The general finding is that people who are in a good mood (from remembering pleasant memories, from a recent success experience, from being given something) usually are more positive, generous, and willing to cooperate. These researchers talk about "the warm glow of success" and the "positive effects of looking on the bright side." Isen, Shalker, Clark, and Karp (1978) speculate on the cognitive-affective processes that may produce this relationship between good mood and decision making:

> When a person is confronted with a situation in which he or she can help, presumably, cognitions concerning both the advantages and disadvantages of helping are available in memory from past experience in similar situations. These advantages and disadvantages, however, may not all be equally accessible or retrievable to the person at the moment, and thus, they may not all come to mind. What we are suggesting is that mood plays a role in what comes to mind. (p. 2)

In summary, at present we have some notions about what elements and factors have to be considered in models of moral decision making (in the sense described as Component III), but is has been studied very little and its developmental character is virtually unknown. We must also entertain the possibility that no single *general* model adequately covers all cases.

Moral Motivation. Given that a person is aware of various possible courses of action in a situation, each leading to a different kind of outcome or goal, why then would a person ever choose the moral alternative, especially if it involves sacrificing some personal interest or enduring some hardship? What motivates moral behavior? A number of classical, centuries' old answers to this question have been proposed, and there are a number of recent versions and new hybrids as well.

1. One classical answer is that morality is rooted in basic human nature—people behave morally because that is the way they are made. This notion is exemplified by optimistic views of humans as transcendent beings made in the image of God and created apart from the beasts. A more modern version of this view is advanced by sociobiologists who postulate biologically based altruistic instincts. Wilson (1975), for instance, cites cases of animals helping fellow members of the species at cost to the self and argues by analogy that human evolution must have made similar genetic provisions for biologically based altruism in human beings, given that they cannot have survived without altruism.

2. Another classical answer is that people are moral because "conscience makes cowards of us all." That is, we cannot bring ourselves to violate certain moral standards because of the guilt, shame, or anxiety that accompanies transgression. For some people, the fear of God may insure compliance with moral standards. Freud's notion of the punishing, tyrannical superego is another version of this general view of conscience (however linked to Freud's own peculiar speculations about childhood sexuality and early childhood relationships with parents). A more recent version in the social-learning tradition is given by Aronfreed (1968), who attempted to analyze conscience in terms of the conditioning of anxiety to socially disfavored acts. In laboratory settings, Aronfreed demonstrated that children would obey adult prescriptions, even when tempted to deviate and even when the children thought no one was watching. Eysenck (1976) also depicts the motivational force underlying morality in terms of avoidance conditioning, essentially like the acquisition of a phobia—however, conscience consists of socially approved phobias.

3. A related view is that special motivation to be moral is an illusion. People do not really behave counter to reinforcement or social exigencies, it only appears so to external observers who are not aware of the subtle reinforcement that may be operating in a situation or not aware of the particular reinforcement histories of individuals. Goldiamond (1968) is

one proponent of the view that morality is not a scientifically useful construct for the analysis of behavior. He emphasizes complex reinforcement schedules and extinction curves to explain away the illusion of *special* moral motives. Bandura (1977) is another theorist who sees nothing special about moral learning to distinguish it from any other kind of social learning, but he emphasizes modeling effects and self-reward mechanisms as underlying all social behavior.

4. Another classical answer is the cognitivist view, that is, social understanding leads to moral motivation:

> Ultimate moral motives and forces are nothing more or less than social intelligence—the power of observing and comprehending social situations—and social power—trained capacities of control—at work in the service of social interests and aims. (Dewey, 1959, p. 42)

> Once the powers of understanding mature and persons come to realize their place in society and are able to take up the standpoint of others, they appreciate the mutual benefits of establishing fair terms of social cooperation. We have a natural sympathy with other persons and an innate susceptibility to the pleasures of fellow feeling and self-mastery, and these provide the affective basis for the moral sentiments once we have a clear grasp of our relations to our associates from an appropriately general perspective. Thus this tradition regards the moral feelings as a natural outgrowth of a full appreciation of our social nature. (Rawls, 1971, pp. 459–460)

The ideological tradition of liberal enlightenment has assumed that social understanding leads to moral motivation: education can cure prejudice and provincialism, one of the outcomes of schooling is broadening one's perspectives, exposure to great thinkers fosters social responsibility, and public education must be provided for the electorate in a democracy to ensure enlightened participation in the democratic process. Piaget is a modern proponent of the cognitivist view. Although his book on moral judgment (1932/1965) is usually regarded as only concerned with cognition, it also presents a view of moral motivation. As children come to understand the purpose, function, and nature of cooperative arrangements, children come to have mutual respect for their coparticipants and develop a sense of solidarity with them. In other words, with development, the child comes to appreciate his stake in supporting certain social arrangements; his "ego boundaries"

are extended to include others in a social system of mutual respect whereby each individual values the other, each realizing that by cooperating they can do much together in creating a social world of great value. At the beginning of development, the child is not cognizant of the possibilities of social organization that later become the major motivators of morality. Therefore, according to this view, as cognition develops, moral motivation is not just rechanneled or retargeted but is fundamentally transformed, in that the goals and objects of motives change. Kohlberg's discussion of cognitive-affective parallelism essentially takes the same view (1969). The cognitivist view assumes that development in logical forms of thinking, in turn, makes possible new structures of meaning that have both logical and effective aspects.

5. Another classical view of moral motivation is that it derives from a sense of awe and self-subjugation to something greater than the self, such as identification with some cause or crusade, dedication to one's country or collective, or respect for the sacred. The motivation to be moral comes from dedication and identification with some supraindividual entity that gives purpose and dignity to one's life. Erikson (1958, 1968) describes a tendency to some adolescents to resolve their identity crisis by committing themselves to an ideology or cause with great moralist fervor. Durkheim (1925/1961) proposed that moral education ought to begin early to instill in the child a feeling of respect for the larger social group, acceptance of discipline, and a willingness to sacrifice oneself for the greater good. Moral education in traditionalist societies as well as in some of the modern Communist states seems to be oriented to this view (Bronfenbrenner, 1962; Garbarino & Bronfenbrenner, 1976).

6. Another view involving the self-concept is that moral motivation derives from a person's self-identity as a moral being. That is, one's sense of moral responsibility and integrity, and a view of oneself as a fair, honorable, and self-respecting person is what provides the motivation to choose moral values over other values (Blasi, in press; Schwartz, 1977).

7. Hoffman's theory of moral internalization is a hybrid theory that has attracted much recent attention (e.g., Hoffman, 1976, 1978, in press). "Moral internalization" is an explanation of "how children come to subordinate their egoistic desires in favor of moral considerations" and why "most people do not go through life viewing society's moral norms . . . [as] external, coercively imposed pressures to which they must submit" (in press). Al-

though Hoffman allows that internalization may take place according to the classical cognitivist and socialization mechanisms, his distinct formulation of an additional internalization process has four basic postulates. First (discussed above), humans are constitutionally predisposed to be discomforted by perceiving distress in others. The assumption of a constitutional predisposition is somewhat similar to the sociobiologists, although Hoffman does not argue for altruistic genes. Nevertheless, Hoffman believes that the rudiments of empathic distress are as basic and inevitable as egoistic, self-serving motives: "We are built in such a way that distress will often be contingent not on our own, but on someone else's painful experience" (1976, p. 132). It is human nature to want to relieve empathic distress.

Second, the basic motive to relieve empathic distress is modified and transformed by developing conceptions of the other person. With greater understanding of how the other is different from the self and with greater appreciation of the total life circumstances of the other person, the child becomes increasingly accurate in perceiving distress in the other and able to do so on the basis of more subtle and complex cues. Cognitive development also enables the self to relieve the other's distress with greater accuracy. Hoffman's (1978) characterization of the developing conceptions of the other is a kind of cognitive developmental sequence. It differs, however, from the cognitive developmentalist's notion of moral development, in that the latter is focused on how perspectives can be coordinated so that cooperative arrangements can be established in which benefits and duties are reciprocally balanced. Nevertheless, both assume that shifts in meaning (the development of social understanding) lead to transformations in the direction and purpose of behavior.

Third, Hoffman (1978, in press) postulates that the development of empathy and the expression of altruism is facilitated by socialization pressure from parents. Note that the postulation of empathic distress only implies that you are discomforted by perceiving distress in another; two equally viable ways of relieving that discomforture are either to help the other person to relieve her distress or to get far enough away from the other person so that her distress will not bother you (especially when helping the other person would cost something). If a person converts empathy to sympathy, he then opts for the first alternative, relieving the discomforture by helping the other. Hoffman believes that parents are influential in fostering the developmental transformation of empathy to sympathy, especially by using inductive disciplining techniques. That is, when the child misbehaves, the parent disciplines the child by highlighting how the child's misbehavior is causing harm to another. Unlike the classical cognitivist view that assumes that children develop by reflecting on their own experience, Hoffman postulates a more active socialization role of parents, one in which the consequences of the child's actions for others are called to attention rather than just letting the child discover these on his own. Hoffman's socialization role of parents is different, however, from the classical socialization approach in focusing on the inner cognitive and emotional states of the child rather than on the manipulation of external rewards.

Fourth, Hoffman postulates that the child comes to experience his altruistic motives as coming autonomously from within (not as compliance with parental pressure) by the special operation of episodic and semantic memory. According to research by Tulving (1972), semantic memory is memory for material that is cognitively processed, encoded, and stored in basic systems of meaning, whereas episodic memory is memory for situational details, like who said what, what particular words were used, and details of the physical setting in which events occurred. Basic meanings in semantic memory are much better recalled than details in episodic memory. Hoffman (in press) conjectures that children retain the basic meaning of parental inductions (i.e., they remember the basic strictures about not hurting others) but that children forget the episodic details of the discipline encounter (e.g., exactly where and when they heard the parents' inductions, what the specific circumstances were, what exactly the dialogue was like). Indeed, Hoffman supposes that children even forget that it was the parents who gave the directives in the first place. Consequently, "having no external agent to whom to attribute the ideas and the guilt feelings associated with them, the child may experience them as originating within himself" (Hoffman, in press). Therefore, according to Hoffman, the sense of autonomy in internalized morality is due to deficient episodic memory and the misattribution of ideas to oneself that really originate elsewhere.

It is not clear how far Hoffman would go with this explanation of moral internalization. If humans had better episodic memory, then, would autonomous morality be much rarer? Is the strength of a moral conviction related to the degree of episodic forgetting? Did the saints and martyrs who were persecuted for their moral convictions have poorer episodic memory than usual? If someone had reminded Socrates about the details of his discipline encounters with his parents, would he have been less eager to drink the hemlock?

Although Hoffman's account of internalization is cognitivist, it differs from a Piagetian, cognitive-developmental view. With regard to the semantic-episodic distinction of memory systems, according to cognitive developmentalists, the sense of inner conviction and self-acceptance of moral standards comes from their meaningfulness in semantic memory, not from forgetfulness in episodic memory. That is, moral standards are internalized as a self-reflexive judgment that the standards make sense in terms of one's understanding of the social world. A person develops strength of conviction in moral standards as he sees how they lead to mutual welfare, to a balancing of the benefits and burdens of cooperation, and to a sense of solidarity and mutual respect for fellow participants. What matters is what happens in the organization of semantic memory, not deficiencies in episodic memory—according to a cognitive-developmental view.

8. One last hybrid view about moral motivation will be mentioned. The philosopher John Rawls (1971)—often cited by cognitive developmentalists—interestingly enough, contends that cognitive understanding is not enough by itself to ensure the motivation to be moral. In addition to understanding the logic of how cooperating systems work, moral motivation develops as the child experiences the love and fidelity and largess of living in just and caring communities. Rawls speculates that moral motivation begins as the child experiences the love of her parents and recognizes their caring for her good; in turn, the child loves them, trusts their directives, and wants to carry out their wishes. Second, as the child experiences the larger community and recognizes that others take their duties seriously and try to live up to the ideals of their station, the child, in turn, develops trust, respect, and a sense of fellow feeling toward others in the association. Third, as the child realizes how social arrangements that are governed by principles of justice have promoted her good and the good of those for whom she cares, the child comes to appreciate the abstract ideals of just human cooperation. Significantly, Rawls puts first the experience of living and benefiting in just communities and afterwards the cognitive understanding and sense of commitment (in contrast to the classical cognitivist view that social understanding by itself brings moral commitment along with it). Good community experiences and good relationships come first and having "developed a taste" for this way of living, then the person is motivated to understand and perpetuate it.[3]

In connection with this view, the recent experience of Kohlberg and his colleagues (1974) in attempting moral education among prisoners and problem adolescents is instructive. Quite early in their attempts, Kohlberg and his associates sensed that asking prisoners to sharpen their reasoning ability by discussing Heinz-and-the-drug-type dilemmas was a weak impetus for moral development and personality transformation. Prisoners commonly come from disrupted families and predatory neighborhoods, and the communal life in prison itself is less than benign. Therefore, the social experience of prisoners is likely to disconfirm any high-level conception of cooperation that is imagined in hypothetical moral discussions. Whereas moral discussion among youth from privileged and benign social backgrounds is likely to reflect positively upon their social experience, the social experience of prisoners is likely to work against higher level conceptualization. And even if discussing moral dilemmas did foster development in Component II processes, that is not the whole of moral development or personality reconstruction. In a change of tactics, Kohlberg and his colleagues then expanded their intervention program beyond moral discussion groups to attempt to establish just communities within the prison itself (Kohlberg, Kauffman, Scharf, & Hickey, 1974). Part of the rationale for establishing just communities is that people who are cynical, self-protective and brutalized need to have more than just the cognitive awareness of the possibility of harmonious living; they need concrete experience in a just community in actual operation, they need to experience that their contributions to the community are reciprocated and that support from others is really there; they need confirmation and reconfirmation that cooperation is a workable—and even preferable—way to live. Although Kohlberg and his colleagues have conceptualized the just-community approach variously as a return to Durkheim, as neo-Platonic, as Deweyian participatory democracy, and as other things (e.g., Kohlberg, 1980), nevertheless it is significant that Kohlberg, one of the foremost proponents of the purely cognitivist view, changed his views about the singular efficacy of pure cognitive advancement after becoming involved with people lacking in positive social experiences.

In summary, the eight theories about moral motivation indicate the diversity of views on the issue. None of these views is supported by very strong, complete, or compelling research evidence.[4] Because this chapter emphasizes cognitive development, I will not review here the bits and pieces of evidence used to support each view but will only note that even in the question of moral motivation, cognition plays a role—in some theories a major role, in others a minor role. Along with modeling the decision-making process, an enormous amount of work needs to be done on this aspect of Component III.

Component IV

Components I, II, and III have accomplished the interpretation of a social situation, the formulation of a moral plan of action, and the decision to carry out that plan rather than other alternatives. And yet, as popular wisdom advises, good intentions are a long way from good deeds. Component IV, executing and implementing a plan of action, involves figuring out the sequence of concrete actions, working around impediments and unexpected difficulties, overcoming fatigue and frustration, resisting distractions and other allurements, and not losing sight of the eventual goal. Perseverance, resolutions, competence, and character are virtues of Component IV. Psychologists sometimes refer to these processes as involving ego strength or self-regulation skills. Somewhat earlier, Paul the Apostle noticed that intentions to perform a course of action sometimes falls short: "The good that I would, I do not; but the evil which I would not, that I do" (Romans 7:19). Weakness of the flesh is Biblical terminology for failures in Component IV processes. However, firm resolve, perseverence, iron will, strong character, ego strength, and so on, are qualities that can be used for ill or good. One needs ego strength to rob a bank, prepare for a marathon, rehearse for a piano concert, or carry out genocide.

Mischel and Mischel (1976) discuss research on ego strength and delay of gratification:

> Correlational studies indicate that the person who chooses larger delayed rewards or goals for which he must either wait or work . . . is more likely to be oriented toward the future . . . and to plan carefully for distant goals, . . . have high scores on ego-control measures, high achievement motivation; to be more trusting and socially responsible; and to show less uncontrolled impulsivity and delinquency. (p. 98)

Grim, Kohlberg, and White (1968) reported significant correlations between measures of attention (resistance to distraction on monotonous tests—an ego-strength index) and resistance to temptation on a cheating task. In another study, R. L. Krebs (1967) reported that Stage 4 Law-and-Order subjects on Kohlberg's measure who were high on a measure of ego strength showed less cheating than Stage 4 subjects who were low on ego strength—presumably, those subjects with high ego strength had the strength of their convictions, whereas the Stage 4 subjects with low ego strength had such convictions but did not act on them.

Various other lines of research also suggest that a certain inner strength, an ability to mobilize oneself to action, is a factor in the production of moral behavior. Barrett and Yarrow (1977) found that social assertiveness was an important component in children's prosocial behavior. London (1970) interviewed people who were involved in saving persecuted Jews in Nazi Germany and remarked on their adventurousness. Hornstein (1976) describes a motivational force that maintains goal-directed behavior and increases in intensity as the desired goal is approached—a Zeigarnick effect in moral behavior. Mischel (1974) and Masters and Santrock (1976) describe techniques for enhancing persistence in effortful tasks.

The Four-Component Model and the Definition of Morality

The conception of morality in this chapter implies that failure to behave morally (i.e., behavior that is morally commendable) can result from deficiencies in any component. If a person is insensitive to the needs of others or if a situation is too ambiguous to interpret, the person may fail to act morally (deficient in Component I). Or a person may be deficient in formulating a moral course of action or may have simplistic and inadequate moral reasoning (Component II). Or moral values can be compromised or preempted by other values (Component III). Or it may be that a person has decided upon a moral course of action but loses sight of the goal, is distracted, or just wears out (Component IV). Moral development entails gaining proficiency in all these component processes. Moral education should be concerned with all these processes.

Furthermore, the conception of morality in this chapter implies that behavior can be called moral only on the basis of knowing both the observable behavior and the processes giving rise to the behavior.[5] If only the externally observable behavior is known (or its consequences), we may refer to the behavior as helpful, or socially conforming, or lawful, and so on, but we may not apply the term moral to it. To some researchers, the cumbersomeness of using the term moral in this way would prompt them simply to give up using the term and to reinterpret the goal of their research as the study of helping behavior, prosocial behavior, and so on. This strategy is appealing in simplifying the job of initial assessment; however, one can not assume that the class of helping behavior is a uniform and homogeneous phenomenon. As mentioned before, a wife trying to poison her husband, the ozone layer, and intestinal bacteria may all be helpful to some people, but the processes and circumstances whereby they help people are very different and generalization from the occurrence of one instance of helpful behavior to another is very problematic. Of course, in the context of specific studies, it may not be necessary to assess all four inner components plus the external behavior of subjects to say something about their morality—it may be reasonable to infer certain inner processes from other processes or from the pattern of behavior. But it should be understood that the underlying conception of morality involves inferences about a full set of inner processes, even if not all of these are actually measured.[6]

The four-component model is not presented as a linear decision-making model. That is, we do *not* suppose that subjects go through each component one at a time in a certain order. Although the four components suggest a logical sequence, each component influences the other components through feedback and feedforward loops. A number of studies suggest the interactive nature of the components. For instance, Dienstbier and his associates (Dienstbier, Hillman, Lehnhoff, Hillman, & Valkenaar, 1975; Dienstbier & Munter, 1971) manipulated the interpretation of the emotion aroused in a situation (Component I) and found differences in behavior related to the manipulation (probably owing to influences in decision making, Component III). Dienstbier et al. (1975) further suggest that the particular ways that a person thinks of moral ideals (Component II) influences the interpretation of aroused affect (Component I). As another instance, Darley and Batson (1973) manipulated the ease with which a task could be carried out (time pressure in preparing and delivering a talk) and found that subjects under great time pressure were less likely to notice someone in need. In other words, subjects who were so engrossed in faithfully completing one task (highly invested in Component IV) were less attentive to detecting the needs of another person in another situation (Component I). Overload in attending to one component decreased efficiency in another component. Also, mention was made earlier of how subjects sometimes defensively reappraise the situation as the personal costs of moral action become clear (Component III influencing Component I).

It should also be obvious from this account that there are many kinds of cognitive and affective processes involved in the production of moral behavior and that there are many interfaces between cognition and affect. Various researchers have studied different cognition-affect connections. Dienstbier and his associates (1975) were concerned with cognitive labeling given to aroused emotions. Hoffman (1976) emphasized the role of cognition in discriminating subtle cues that trigger empathic affect and in guiding and targeting the expression of altruism. Isen et al. (1978) referred to selective memory processes that operate on decision making as a function of a pervasive mood state. Kohlberg (1969) described the feelings that accompany cognitive structure because both are aspects of meaning. Masters and Santrock (1976) focused on how cognitively induced affective states can aid in task perseverance. Indeed, cognitive-affective interactions abound; when one focuses on some particular process, the cognitive aspects are difficult to separate from the affective aspects.

An all-inclusive review of morality research would discuss all four components, both the affective and cognitive aspects, both developmental and nondevelopmental aspects, both individual and group processes. However, in keeping with the special focus of this volume, this chapter will emphasize individual cognitive development. Furthermore, it will focus on Component II processes because the other processes are discussed elsewhere in the Handbook. Components I and IV deal with processes that are essential parts in the production of moral behavior but involve processes that are not distinctively or uniquely moral. Very little research exists on moral decision making in the sense of Component III. Component II has a long and rich history of research (bibliographic references total in the thousands),[7] and deals with cognitive processes that are distinctively and uniquely moral.

THE DEVELOPMENT OF MORAL KNOWLEDGE AND JUDGMENT

Piaget's Approach

As with so many areas of cognitive development, the place to start is with Jean Piaget. Piaget (1932/1965) published his book, *The Moral Judgment of the Child,* almost 50 years ago and it still remains one of the most influential and seminal works. Its importance lies in its general, programmatic direction rather than in the details of particular research methodology or specific research findings. Piaget did not propose to provide a detailed description of moral judgment but rather intended to outline an alternative to Durkheim's impressive and important view. Durkheim (1925) had emphasized the influence of society in shaping the behavior of individuals to conform to social norms and viewed moral development as essentially instilling respect for the social group in each individual so that each member of the group would accept its discipline and abide by its rules. It is useful to regard Piaget's book as a counterargument to Durkheim: Piaget cites Durkheim on the first page, makes more references to Durkheim than to any other person, and repeatedly comes back to make further arguments against him. Piaget does not dispute that morality *begins* in the child as learning social norms, and he agrees with Durkheim with regard to the young child. Society in general and socialization agents in particular command the child to act in certain ways; morality at this stage is essentially conformity to social prescriptions and proscriptions. Piaget's main thrust, however, is to depict the limitations of this kind of morality and to contend that as the child develops, a general understanding of the social world develops (in particular, an understanding of the possibilities and conditions of cooperation) and the fundamental nature of morality changes. There is not one morality, but two. There is the morality of constraint and, later, as cognitive development proceeds, the morality of cooperation. The dynamics and organizing principles of these two moralities are different. For the purpose of arguing with Durkheim, it was not necessary for Piaget to give a detailed description of the course of development nor to define tightly unified stages; it was only necessary that he build a case that all morality is not "imposed by the group upon the individual and by the adult upon the child" (1932/1965, p. 341).

There are two levels on which Piaget characterizes the different moralities: the more abstract level, which represents the deep structures or general knowledge about the social world; and the more concrete level, at which about a dozen particular features are described and related to specific responses of actual subjects. Piaget describes the deep structure (or organizing principles) of the morality of constraint:

The morality of constraint is that of duty pure and simple and of heteronomy. The child accepts from the adult a certain number of commands to which it must submit whatever the circumstances may be. Right is what conforms with these commands; wrong is what fails to do so; the intention plays a very small part in this conception, and the responsibility is entirely objective. (1932/1965, p. 335)

Unilateral respect of the child for the adult provides the motivation for morality at this stage. The child regards the adult as wiser, more powerful, greater, and superior to himself—a mixture of fear, affection, and admiration—and, therefore, the child learns and respects the social prescriptions of adults and is socialized.

The child, however, is interacting constantly with peers. With others who are similar in status and power, a certain amount of give and take is required to negotiate and coordinate plans, settle disagreements, make and enforce rules and promises. In this social experience, the child gradually comes to realize that social rules can be used as instruments for coordinating social activity, that cooperative social arrangements can lead to mutually valued goals, that promises and contracts are obligatory because each partner wants the benefits of cooperation. Thus, the child gradually discovers the possibilities and conditions of cooperation that are not motivated by unilateral respect, but by the mutual respect of collaborators for each other and by their solidarity in coordinating their activity for mutual benefit.

In contrast to Durkheim's emphasis on adults as socializers, Piaget emphasizes peer interaction as crucial for development. Piaget regards adults as typically so overbearing in manner and so opaque to children about their intentions and reasoning that adult moral teaching is perceived by children as commands for blind obedience. Although the content of adult prescriptions and proscriptions are understood (children know they are supposed to do this or that), the rationale is not understood, nor is there the sense of working out some arrangement for mutual benefit. Hence, interaction with adults informs the child what ought to be done but short-circuits the process of building a deeper understanding of cooperative arrangements. In contrast, when children interact with other children, they all have equal status and must communicate their intentions and win over their peers with reasons.

Piaget describes the morality of cooperation as more equilibrated than the morality of constraint. The equilibration theme runs throughout all his works, in which the individual establishes equilibrium with his environment through evolving cognitive structures. In the morality work, Piaget depicts morality as the equilibrium of individuals in society, as individuals each reciprocating with each other individuals according to rules that balance the benefits and burdens of cooperation. A social system can be said to be equilibrated if its rules balance the benefits and burdens among participants in a way that is viewed as fair, adjudicate conflicts between individuals without destroying the social system, and attract support from its participants because they appreciate the fairness of the system. Piaget's analysis of morality centers on the concept of justice, which prescribes how reciprocity among individuals is to be balanced. (For Piaget, morality is not primarily a generalized love of humanity or a sense of the sacred, the good, or pure duty.)

Although Piaget referred to his two moralities as stages, he, nevertheless, disclaimed that they were tightly organized or clearly separated from each other (e.g., 1932/1965). In light of subsequent research, Piaget's two moralities probably are best regarded as characterizations of the poles of development, that is, the two moralities are rough descriptions of the beginning and end points of the course of development rather than the successive transformations in cognitive systems over the course of development. Later theorists have offered more detailed descriptions of successive cognitive structures in development (e.g., Kohlberg's, 1969, six stages). Piaget's use of the stage concept in his 1932 morality research is looser and weaker than in his later discussions of logicomathematical stages (e.g., 1960). However, a moral stage for Piaget seems to imply at least two notions: (1) a stage is a logically coherent system of ideas about morality that is said to underlie specific moral judgments. It is the deep structure or framework of assumptions that provides a general point of view from which specific situations are analyzed. Actual people when making moral judgments may mix perspectives and jumble the ideas inconsistently, thus, a particular person may manifest a mixture of stages (or a mixture of perspectives). It is the definition of a stage that is a consistent, logical system of ideas; people may be inconsistent. Further, for Piaget, subjects need not be able to describe their own stage—in fact, they may not even be consciously aware of their tacit assumptions and intuitive understanding. Stage structures work "behind the scenes" in organizing the subject's moral judgments. (2) Piaget also implies by stage that the different structures of moral thinking are developmentally sequenced. Over time, people shift away from Stage 1 to Stage 2, and Stage 2 is conceptually more adequate—it takes more things into account, it provides more adequate directives for making decisions.

Piagetian Research

Having discussed the deep structure of the stages, let us consider Piaget's descriptions of the two stages at the more concrete level. The more concrete level ties the deep structures to empirical data. Piaget's strategy was to interview children on a number of topics and to demonstrate that the younger children (presumably less developed) show "childish" and inadequate judgments, whereas the older children (presumably more developed) show adultlike, more adequate judgments. Even though the younger children have learned many social norms, their answers to Piaget's questions display striking misunderstanding of the nature and function of social rules. Thus a socialization view of morality (learning social norms) is insufficient to account for the general framework of understanding in which specific social norms are imbedded and that adults regard as mere common sense.

Piaget investigated about a dozen different dimensions of children's moral thinking, predominantly by presenting hypothetical moral stories and interviewing children about them. Reviews of Piaget's research and subsequent follow-up research are given by Hoffman (1970), Karniol (1978), Keasey (1978), and especially Lickona (1976). Several of the dimensions closely follow from Piaget's view that the young child is presented with moral rules by an adult and the child does not know their rationale, derivation, or function. Moral rules seem to the child to be permanent fixtures in reality, like gravity and other physical laws. When Piaget interviewed children about the possibility of changing moral rules, some of the younger children seemed to regard rules as sacred and unchangeable, rooted in parental and divine authority. Younger children also seemed to assume that the adult view is the morally right view and that every other view is simply wrong. This exaggeration of the absolutism of social rules is possible only if the child lacks general understanding about the nature and origin of social rules. Related to this characteristic is the child's belief in immanent justice, that is, the belief that wrongdoing inevitably leads to punishment. To the young child, physical accidents and misfortunes are punishments willed by God or produced by inexorable immanent justice, and they are confused with social sanctions. Furthermore, if an act is punished, then the younger child assumes that the act must have been wrong. Lacking a general framework of understanding about social rules, the child applies rules to specific situations in a literal, wooden way, attending most to the obvious aspects of objective conformity and attending less to subtle, subjective, ameliorating circumstances. Piaget refers to the younger child's sense of *objective* responsibility (focus on the obvious, concrete aspects of rule conformity), in contrast to the older child's sense of *subjective* responsibility (understanding enough about the nature and functions of rules that ameliorating circumstances can be taken into account, including the actor's intentions). Piaget's book presents a counterargument to Durkheim's (1925/1965) view by showing that younger children know social prescriptions but do not understand their origin, function, or nature; thus, there is not just one kind of inner organization to morality and, therefore, moral development involves more than learning social rules.

From Piaget's characterization of heteronomy, one might expect young children to be perfectly obedient. Yet Piaget notes that young children are notoriously perfidious. So how can the children who have such a reverential—almost mystical—view of rules also be the ones who flagrantly disregard them? Piaget attempts to explain this paradox by contending that the reverential view and the flagrant disregard of rules are both aspects of egocentrism (1932/1965). According to Piaget, both are elements of the same basic structure, and in fact, the inconsistency itself is said to be a sign of childhood egocentrism. It seems to me, however, that a less tortured explanation could be advanced by distinguishing between Component II and Component III processes. The child's conception of social rules and her understanding of the dynamics of social cooperation are aspects of Component II—essentially involving how one defines the moral ideal, as one sees it. If young children are asked questions about social rules and they depict rules as sacred, eternal fixtures, then that shows their limitations in understanding what cooperation is about and in formulating moral ideals. However, when it comes to Component III and the valuing of moral ideals in competition with other desirable goals, we can understand how young children do not feel they have much of a stake in upholding moral ideals because social rules are just handed down to them secondhand. Adult constraint may not only sustain primitive social understanding but may also provide little motivation to abide by social rules. In any case, Piaget (as have many cognitive developmentalists since) assumes that moral development is a unitary process and that the subject's view about social rules as well as conformity to rules are both elements of the same basic cognitive structure.

Piaget presents his evidence in terms of listing case after case of interview material, with extensive comment and discussion. Occasionally, a tabulation is presented of the percent of younger children at various stages of thinking contrasted with the percent of older children at various stages; the results show more younger children using lower stage thinking and more older children using higher stage

thinking. By today's journal standards, the presentation of such cross-sectional data (comparisons of younger and older subjects) would be considered rather sparse evidence for claiming a developmental sequence without supporting evidence from longitudinal studies, discriminant validity (e.g., partialing out IQ), interjudge reliability, test-retest stability, and so on. Yet, all these methodological shortcomings are secondary to the general direction of Piaget's approach: to draw attention to the complex inner processes that underlie adult common sense and to propose that morality is rooted in a person's basic understanding of the social world. Subsequent research in the cognitive-developmental tradition has improved on Piaget's methodology, but only elaborated Piaget's general vision.

Subsequent research following Piaget's methods has frequently (but not invariably) replicated the stage differences between younger and older subjects on many dimensions: absolutism, rules as unchangeable, immanent justice, objective responsibility, focus on punishment, expiatory punishment, and obedience to authority over allegiance to equality (see Lickona, 1976, for review and references). In addition, a number of studies have found Piaget's dimensions to correlate positively and significantly with IQ and socioeconomic status (SES) (see Hoffman, 1970), which, along with the age trends, are consistent with the view that these dimensions are developmental (presuming that advantage enhances development). And yet the intercorrelations among the dimensions (e.g., immanent justice with objective responsibility) are quite low, test-retest stability is poor, and subjects are inconsistent, even on the same dimension, when a variety of test stimuli are used (see review by Lickona, 1976). Furthermore, recent research (see *Post-Piagetian Research*) has demonstrated a plethora of deficiencies in Piaget's materials and methods and has challenged his interpretation of his findings. Therefore, although Piaget's morality research suggested developmental differences in the fundamental organization of people's thinking, there is considerable doubt that Piaget's particular characterizations and research methodology provide incisive ways of studying the phenomena, particularly in light of more powerful research findings from alternative schemes.

Kohlberg's Extension of Piaget

For many years Piaget's morality work was virtually ignored along with his other work. In the mid-1950s Kohlberg began his doctoral dissertation, which initially was to be a replication of Piaget's work on an American sample using somewhat different assessment techniques. Kohlberg's dissertation (1958) in effect launched a new brand of morality research that has generated more studies, commentary, and controversy than any other. A comparison of Piaget's work with Kohlberg's can be summarized as follows:

1. Like Piaget, Kohlberg's emphasis is on basic cognitive structures that are said to underlie and organize moral reasoning, not upon learning specific moral rules. Like Piaget, Kohlberg has two levels of description: the deep-structure level that portrays a stage of reasoning as a unified global perspective about morality and a more concrete level that describes specific features or dimensions by which actual utterances of subjects can be scored. Unlike Piaget, Kohlberg's specific scoring features are not as well known as the deep-structure stage descriptions—in part, this is due to ongoing revisions of the scoring system since 1968. Unlike Piaget, Kohlberg collapses information from each scoring feature into an overall stage score rather than reporting each feature separately.

2. Like Piaget, Kohlberg describes stages of development that represent successive transformations in the way thinking is organized. Whereas Piaget's two stages give a rough characterization of the overall course of moral judgment development, Kohlberg describes six stages that are intended to portray more closely the successive patterns of thinking in development. Whereas Piaget's major point was that children's development involves fundamental transformations in the organization of thought, Kohlberg's purpose was to describe the many specific transformations that occur from childhood through adulthood, including even development among moral philosophers. One never gets the impression that Piaget was trying to describe the organizing principles of moral philosophers but rather was interested in showing that younger children do not have the understanding about social rules that adults regard as common sense. Kohlberg (1971) is much bolder and even goes so far in his most advanced stages (Stage 5 and Stage 6) to propose that some moral philosophers are more advanced than others.

3. Not only does Kohlberg describe more stages, but he uses the stage concept itself in a different way than Piaget did in his morality work. Whereas Piaget was tentative and indefinite about his moral judgment stages, Kohlberg makes strong statements about the properties and implications of his stages. Kohlberg uses Piaget's later descriptions of logicomathematical stages (Piaget, 1960) as characteristics of his own (Kohlberg's) moral-judgment stages.

4. The central concept in Kohlberg's system, like Piaget's, is justice (rather than love of humanity, or the intuitive sense of sacred duty, or survival of the human race). Both view moral development as establishing greater social equilibrium among individuals interacting with each other. For both, the central problem of morality is to determine the legitimate claims of people in a situation and to prioritize and balance those claims according to principles that impartial, rational people could accept as governing principles for cooperative interaction. In this sense, morality is discussed as the "logic of action" (Kohlberg, 1973; Piaget, 1932/1965). Kohlberg, however, uses the notion of equilibrium in different ways than Piaget, focusing more on attaining an equilibrated perspective from which to view a moral dilemma.

5. Like Piaget, Kohlberg believes that the clinical interview is the preferred technique for assessing moral judgment. Presumably, a skilled clinician can pose questions in ways tailored to the individual's own system of meaning, and the clinician knows how to probe and unearth the important features of a person's thinking without leading the subject. Like Piaget, Kohlberg presents hypothetical stories to subjects and interrogates them about their judgments in those cases. Whereas Piaget's stories are focused on one dimension (e.g., immanent justice) and the discussion is fairly limited to gaining information about that one feature, Kohlberg's stories are open ended and the discussion can range over a large number of features and topics. The freedom of Kohlberg's stories has led to the identification of many new forms and features of thinking previously unnoticed. However, the complexity and diversity of responses to Kohlberg's dilemmas have raised vexing problems in scoring that kind of data. The recent scoring system developed at Harvard by Kohlberg and his colleagues (Colby, Gibbs, Kohlberg, Speicher-Dubin, Power, & Candee, 1980) is impressive in devising ways to deal with such complex free-flow interview material (see *Measurement Operations and the Scoring System*). But one of the effects of the new scoring system is that an idea in a subject's protocol must be explicitly stated to credit the subject with that concept. Ideas not clearly articulated are assumed not to exist in the subject's head. This scoring policy is necessary for obtaining good interjudge agreement in a system as complex as Kohlberg's (otherwise, variance among scorers arises as a function of the scorer's intuition). However, this departs from the notion of deep structure as behind the scenes organizing principles.

6. Like Piaget, Kohlberg uses age-trend data as the primary empirical support for his stages. However, Kohlberg has collected longitudinal data (testing

about 50 boys about every 3 or 4 years over a 20-year period) rather than relying only on cross-sectional data. In addition to age-trend studies, Kohlberg and his associates have developed support for the six-stage model in studies of experimental manipulations, correlations, cross-cultural comparisons, internal structure, and so on. Thus, many new research strategies and research paradigms have emerged.

7. Like Piaget, Kohlberg does not regard didactic instruction from adults as especially important in the child's moral development. What is important is that children attend to the reasons for social arrangements and to their functions and purposes. Peer interaction and negotiation is an important experience. However, Kohlberg conceptualizes the critical aspect of social experience more broadly than Piaget's peer interaction—for Kohlberg, the crucial social experiences for moral development are "role-taking opportunities." By this Kohlberg does not mean empathizing with lots of people in distress (nor did Piaget), but rather discussing with others their respective points of view, participating in the decision-making process of groups, and participating in the secondary institutions of law, government, and business. Role-taking opportunities provide information out of which the child constructs concepts of interpersonal and institutional cooperative schemes. Interaction with peers can supply role-taking opportunities, but parents and the community at large also provide these experiences. Moreover, Kohlberg has gone beyond Piaget not only in speculating about the experiences that foster development but also in developing moral education programs to put these ideas into practice.

8. Like Piaget, Kohlberg's style of scholarship is more in the European grand speculative tradition than in the American modest-but-rigorous tradition. Kohlberg has been foremost the visionary and proposer rather than the documentor or instrumentor. His theorizing goes beyond rigorously established facts, that some people appreciate for suggesting new and exciting areas of research and other people depreciate for being speculation, or contrary to their own speculations, or unclear and inconsistent.

Kohlberg's Characterizations of Development

Over the years, a number of different scoring systems and stage descriptions have evolved. (Although for convenience, the system will be called Kohlberg's, he readily acknowledges the enormous contributions of his associates, in particular Anne Colby and John Gibbs.) The changes in the scoring system have not been trivial: One report cites a correlation of only .39 between moral judgment scores

of subjects scored by the 1958 system and the 1978 system.[8] As another indication of the changes, Kohlberg's 1958 dissertation study showed 16-year-old boys scoring an average of about 40% at Stages 5 and 6, whereas in later scoring systems, Stage 5 is a rarity even among adults and Stage 6 is not listed at all as a scoring possibility in the latest scoring systems. Thus, there is not just one set of stage descriptions and scoring systems but a family of them.

The general outlines of Kohlberg's stage definitions are well known. Table 1 presents one of the more recent versions. A one-table summary may give some impression of the kinds of characteristics that distinguish each stage, but it must be realized that Kohlberg and his associates at Harvard have developed an 800-page scoring guide containing hundreds of scoring features (in contrast to Piaget's dozen or so), and a full understanding of the system can best be gained by studying the scoring manual.

The rationale for claiming that one stage is more advanced and more adequate than its predecessor is crucial to any developmental theory. That is, in what sense is a higher stage any better than a lower stage? Kohlberg in various places has proposed at least three different kinds of arguments: (1) each stage in the sequence is progressively more differentiated and integrated; (2) with development, each new stage employs cognitive operations that are more reversible and equilibrated; (3) with development, each stage has a more encompassing perspective on society. It is not clear whether these three lines of argument translate completely into each other, but each has been used to characterize the stages and argue that they comprise a developmental order.

The first notion, that each stage is more differentiated and integrated, draws upon Heinz Werner's concept of development (1957): development is essentially change from global, diffuse, and confused thinking to systematic, articulate, and hierarchical thinking. For instance, Kohlberg (1971) quotes one young subject who thinks that it is more important to save many people from death than just one person because of the furniture they own: "One man just has the one house, maybe a lot of furniture, but a whole bunch of people have an awful lot of furniture . . ." (p. 168). This is cited as the confusion in Stage 1 between moral values and physical properties or characteristics. At Stage 2, this particular confusion is no longer present, but the moral value of life is still confused with the instrumental and hedonistic value to the subject, for example, "If a pet dies you can get along without it—it isn't something you really need. Well, you can get a new wife, but it's not really the same" (Kohlberg, 1971, p. 168). Likewise, on through the stages, progressive development is portrayed as peeling away the layers

Table 1. Kohlberg's Moral Judgment Stages

Level and Stage	Content of Stage		Social Perspective of Stage
	What Is Right	Reasons for Doing Right	
LEVEL I—PRECON-VENTIONAL Stage 1—Heteronomous Morality	To avoid breaking rules backed by punishment, obedience for its own sake, and avoiding physical damage to persons and property.	Avoidance of punishment, and the superior power of authorities.	*Egocentric point of view.* Doesn't consider the interests of others or recognize that they differ from the actor's; doesn't relate two points of view. Actions are considered physically rather than in terms of psychological interests of others. Confusion of authority's perspective with one's own.
Stage 2—Individualism, Instrumental Purpose, and Exchange	Following rules only when it is to someone's immediate interest; acting to meet one's own interests and needs and letting others do the same. Right is also what's fair, what's an equal exchange, a deal, an agreement.	To serve one's own needs or interests in a world where you have to recognize that other people have their interests too.	*Concrete individualistic perspective.* Aware that everybody has his own interest to pursue and these conflict so that right is relative (in the concrete individualistic sense).
LEVEL II—CONVEN-TIONAL Stage 3—Mutual Interpersonal Expectations, Relationships, and Interpersonal Conformity	Living up to what is expected by people close to you or what people generally expect of people in your role as son, brother, friend, etc. "Being good" is important and means having good motives, showing concern about others. It also means keeping mutual relationships, such as trust, loyalty, respect, and gratitude.	The need to be a good person in your own eyes and those of others. Your caring for others. Belief in the Golden Rule. Desire to maintain rules and authority which support stereotypical good behavior.	*Perspective of the individual in relationships with other individuals.* Aware of shared feelings, agreements, and expectations which take primacy over individual interests. Relates points of view through the concrete Golden Rule, putting yourself in the other guy's shoes. Does not yet consider generalized system perspective.
Stage 4—Social System and Conscience	Fulfilling the actual duties to which you have agreed. Laws are to be upheld except in extreme cases where they conflict with other fixed social duties. Right is also contributing to society, the group, or institution.	To keep the institution going as a whole, to avoid the breakdown in the system "if everyone did it," or the imperative of conscience to meet one's defined obligations (easily confused with Stage 3 belief in rules and authority).	*Differentiates societal point of view from interpersonal agreement or motives.* Takes the point of view of the system that defines roles and rules. Considers individual relations in terms of place in the system.

(*continued*)

Table 1.—Continued

Level and Stage	Content of Stage		Social Perspective of Stage
	What Is Right	Reasons for Doing Right	
LEVEL III—POSTCONVENTIONAL or PRINCIPLED Stage 5—Social Contract or Utility and Individual Rights	Being aware that people hold a variety of values and opinions, that most values and rules are relative to your group. These relative rules should usually be upheld, however, in the interest of impartiality and because they are the social contract. Some nonrelative values and rights like *life* and *liberty*, however, must be upheld in any society and regardless of majority opinion.	A sense of obligation to law because of one's social contract to make and abide by laws for the welfare of all and for the protection of all people's rights. A feeling of contractual commitment, freely entered upon, to family, friendship, trust, and work obligations. Concern that laws and duties be based on rational calculation of overall utility, "the greatest good for the greatest number."	*Prior-to-society perspective.* Perspective of a rational individual aware of values and rights prior to social attachments and contracts. Integrates perspectives by formal mechanisms of agreement, contract, objective impartiality, and due process. Considers moral and legal points of view; recognizes that they sometimes conflict and finds it difficult to integrate them.
Stage 6—Universal Ethical Principles	Following self-chosen ethical principles. Particular laws or social agreements are usually valid because they rest on such principles. When laws violate these principles, one acts in accordance with the principle. Principles are universal principles of justice: the equality of human rights and respect for the dignity of human beings as individuals.	The belief as a rational person in the validity of universal moral principles and a sense of personal commitment to them.	*Perspective of a moral point of view from which social arrangements derive.* Perspective is that of any rational individual recognizing the nature of morality or the fact that persons are ends in themselves and must be treated as such.

(Kohlberg, 1976, pp. 34–35)

of confusion until at Stage 6 the subject has disentangled nonrelevant considerations in valuing human life.

The second line of argument, that each successive stage employs new cognitive operations that are more reversible and equilibrated, draws upon Piaget's line of argument for a developmental order in his logical stages (i.e., concrete operations, formal operations). Kohlberg moves from Piaget's discussions of development as progressive equilibrium to a similar claim for moral stages: each new stage involves a new logical operation, this new operation creates a new and more integrative or equilibrated form of justice, and this new form of justice is the

core of a social-moral order (1971). In Kohlberg's most extensive discussion of developmental progress through the stages (1971), it is not always clear just what the new logical operation is at each stage, nor what it is that is being equilibrated (e.g., Is it the conflicting claims of people in a situation or different points of view about the proper course of action?), nor how the variety of characteristics used to score each stage logically cohere and relate to the new operation. Furthermore, the most recent scoring systems, 1978 and later, have redefined the six stages in some major ways and, therefore, pre-1978 discussions of the stages may not be current.

The clearest statement regarding new logical operations and equilibrium is in Kohlberg's article (1973a) addressed to a philosophical audience that focuses on Stage 6. Kohlberg invokes the notion of reversibility in Piaget's scheme:

> According to Piaget and others, the keystone of logic is reversibility. A logical train of thought is one in which one can move back and forth between premises and conclusions without distortion. (1973a, p. 641)

Then a parallel is claimed in moral thinking:

> Reversibility of moral judgment is what is ultimately meant by the criterion of the fairness of a moral decision. Procedurally, fairness as impartiality means reversibility in the sense of a decision on which all interested parties could agree insofar as they can consider their own claims impartially, as the just decider would. (1973a, p. 641)

As an illustration, Kohlberg discusses Stage 6 reversibility applied to the Heinz dilemma:

> In the Heinz dilemma, Heinz must imagine whether the druggist could put himself in the wife's position and still maintain his claim and whether the wife could put herself in the druggist's position and still maintain her claim. Intuitively we feel the wife could, the druggist could not. As a result, it is fair for the husband to act on the basis of the wife's claim. We call the process by which a reversible moral decision is reached "ideal role-taking." . . . A decision reached by playing "moral musical chairs" corresponds to a decision as to what is ultimately "just" or "fair." Ideal role-taking is the decision procedure ultimately required by the attitudes of respect for persons and of justice as equity recognized at higher stages. (1973a, pp. 643, 645)

Thus, the new operation at Stage 6 is "ideal role-taking," or complete reversibility, or "moral musical chairs." An equilibrated decision is one that all parties would support if they considered all the claims from all the perspectives, choosing that action that they could endorse regardless of which participant they were (e.g., even the druggist would have to admit that if it were his life at stake, he would favor preserving life over property rights).

Kohlberg's third line of argument that the six stages comprise a developmental order is focused on social perspective. Here, Kohlberg acknowledges similarities to Selman's theory of social perspective taking (1976). The characterization of social perspective taking at each moral stage is given in the right-hand column in Table 1. Kohlberg illustrates a preconventional social perspective with an interview from a 10-year-old subject:

> (*Interviewer:* Why shouldn't you steal from a store?)
>
> *Subject:*   It's not good to steal from the store. It's against the law. Someone could see you and call the police. (Kohlberg, 1976, p. 36)

Kohlberg says that this response views law as something enforced by the police and the reason for obeying the law is to avoid punishment. It is the perspective of an individual considering his own interests or those of other isolated individuals.

In contrast, here is the response by the same subject at 17 years of age:

> (*Interviewer:* Why shouldn't you steal from a store?)
>
> *Subject:*   It's a matter of law. It's one of our rules that we're trying to help protect everyone, protect property, not just to protect a store. It's something that's needed in our society. If we didn't have these laws, people would steal, they wouldn't have to work for a living and our whole society would get out of kilter. (Kohlberg, 1976, p. 36)

Kohlberg says this response reflects a Level II (i.e., conventional level) sociomoral perspective. The subject is concerned about keeping the law for the good of society as a whole. The subject views himself not as an isolated individual but as a member of society who is attending to the needs of the group and their shared relationship.

The same subject was reinterviewed at 24 years of age:

> (I: Why shouldn't someone steal from a store?)
>
> S: It's violating another person's rights, in this case to property.
>
> (I: Does the law enter in?)

S: Well, the law in most cases is based on what is morally right so it's not a separate subject, it's a consideration.

(I: What does "morality" or "morally right" mean to you?)

S: Recognizing the rights of other individuals, first to life and then to do as he pleases as long as it doesn't interfere with somebody else's rights. (Kohlberg, 1976, pp. 36–37)

Kohlberg says this response reflects a Level III (i.e., postconventional) sociomoral perspective. Although the subject is aware of the member-of-society perspective, a person's commitment to society's laws and values are derived from the moral value that they embody and operationalize. Society's laws and values must be ones that any impartial, reasonable person could accept (in the sense of "ideal role-taking" or "moral musical chairs"), that is, ones based on principle. According to this view, the wrongness of stealing is that it violates the moral rights of individuals, which are prior to laws and society.

Kohlberg has been a master at interpreting moral judgment interview material. He brings in philosophical concepts to characterize development in ways more detailed and incisive than Piaget's rather vague and loose stages. Kohlberg's stages seem to capture better the underlying organization and assumptive base of people's moral judgments. His scoring system depicts development according to the three lines of argument just described (development as progressive differentiation, as new logical operations of reversibility and greater equilibrium, as more encompassing and sociomoral perspective taking). From time to time, other criteria have been mentioned for claiming that one stage is more cognitively advanced than another—for instance, Kohlberg's flirtation with the correlativity of rights and duties, influenced by the philosopher Raphael (1955) (see Kohlberg, 1973a)—but these other types of analysis have not had much impact on the scoring system or the analysis of actual interview material.

The Stage Concept

Having discussed Kohlberg's approach to the analysis of developmental progressions, now let us consider Kohlberg's notions about the stage concept itself. Kohlberg has made extremely bold claims about a subject's consistency in moral judgment stage usage across situations; he believes that his six stages comprise a universal, invariant, irreversible, step-by-step sequence; that stages are structural wholes; and that trained scorers can reliably identify stages in all sorts of material. (Quotes from Kohlberg are cited in J. R. Rest, 1979a, to document advocacy of these views.) Kohlberg finds it comfortable to talk about a person being "in" a particular stage, and he characterizes movement as going through each stage one step at a time in the prescribed order. Furthermore, in the development of the scoring system, scoring criteria and scoring rules have been selected (or discarded) on the basis of how well the data generated conform to strict stage expectations (no reversals in longitudinal data, minimal stage mix, no stage skipping).

I believe that Kohlberg's strong stand on the stage concept is based on four considerations. First, his analysis of underlying structures in people's responses to open-ended dilemmas (e.g., the Heinz dilemma) is far more powerful and incisive than that provided by Piaget's two stages. As an illustration, go back to the interview material presented earlier and classify the responses as morality of constraint or morality of cooperation. Piaget's stages are difficult to apply in this way, and even if they could be reliably applied, much of the underlying assumptive framework of these people's thinking would have been missed. Kohlberg's analysis is much more finely tuned to the subjects' organizations of thinking. Kohlberg can justifiably claim that his depictions of cognitive structures are "truer" stages (better depictions of the underlying organization of thinking) than Piaget's (at least in this interview material). Second, the results of the recent longitudinal analysis (Colby, Kohlberg, Gibbs, & Lieberman, in press) can be construed as giving support to a strong stage model. Kohlberg and his associates argue that all other studies and other measures have confused content with structure and that because this study is the only one that does not, only its findings can be seriously considered. Other studies presupposing inadequate conceptions of stage structure and using inadequate measures simply do not count. Third, Kohlberg stresses the distinction between qualitative and quantitative analysis. Whereas trait psychology and most psychometric approaches view the person as an aggregate of quantitative dimensions (where each person has more or less of the various trait or dimension), the cognitive-developmental approach uses ideal-typological constructs that emphasize the patterning of behavior rather than its quantitative descriptors (frequency, amplitude, intensity, latency, etc.). In this connection, the story is often told of Piaget working in Binet's laboratory: Binet was concerned with the number of correct answers to a bat-tery of test items, but Piaget was concerned with the qualitative organizations of thinking that led to wrong answers. The qualitative/quantitative distinc-tion in moral judgment research calls attention to the cognitive developmentalists' interest in identifying underlying patterns of thought—the various organi-zations of thinking that are called different stages. But Kohlberg goes further and assumes that the char-acterization of one specimen of material from a sub-ject implies that the subject can be generally charac-terized as being at that stage—for instance, if a subject is scored Stage 4 on the Heinz dilemma, then the subject is "at" Stage 4 generally. This assumes that only one organization of thinking is present at one time in a subject, discounting the possibility of multiple patterns or of different patterns manifested in response to different situations. Although Kohlberg's view is logically consistent with the qualitative/quantitative distinction, it is not required by the distinction and is an overextension of the initial interest in studying patterns of thinking. Fourth, back in the 1950s and 1960s, structuralists were arguing with associationists that a subject's behavior (or judgment) does not consist of aggre-gates of isolated S-R bonds but rather that behavior is generated from general underlying cognitive structures that the subject calls forth from long-term memory in actively construing the situation and in organizing activity in accord with the situation. One line of argument that structuralists advanced in be-half of the existence of underlying structures (and the notion of an active human cognizer who makes meaning by assimilating experience to general struc-tures) was to contend that a close examination of the myriad of responses of a person would reveal per-sistent patterns of organization. Presumably, the greater the consistency of pattern across more and more situations, the better the argument for the exis-tence of underlying structures. Ironically, today the structuralists' basic position is widely accepted, that is, that humans actively construe situations accord-ing to general systems of meaning (Flavell, in press), however, what remains controversial are the specific proposals for characterizing these structures and the contention that subjects use the same organi-zations of thinking regardless of the situation. To-day, the structuralists' conclusion has greater accep-tance than the empirical premises designed to argue for that conclusion.

When Kohlberg began his work on moral judg-ment, Piaget's type of analysis of inner thought pro-cesses (assuming deep structures characterized in terms of stages) was virtually the only show in town.

Since then, other cognitive psychologists have pro-posed other types of cognitive organization scripts, schema, frames, grammars, prototypes, and so on (Abelson, 1981; Bartlett, 1932; Bobrow & Norman, 1975; Hastie, in press; Mandler & Johnson, 1977; Minsky, 1975; Rumelhart, 1977; Schank & Abel-son, 1977). These types of structures differ from Piagetian stages in at least two important ways: (1) Unlike Piagetian stages, they are not defined in terms of abstract logical operations (like INRC groups) but are closer to phenomenal experience (like schema, for organizing the basic elements of a story or folktale; a frame, for recognizing spatial relations in a room; or a script, for behaving in a restaurant). In other words, like Piagetian stages, these structures guide attention to certain features of experience, provide a heuristic for anticipating events and relationships, and establish a framework for organizing experience in perception and in mem-ory; however, unlike Piagetian stages, these struc-tures are depicted at a more concrete level of abstrac-tion. (2) Unlike stages in Piagetian theory, these structures are more sensitive to particular eliciting conditions and stimuli. Many factors affect their evocation and use. They are also not so deep, that is, they are not presumed to underlie all thinking at one time period. The main reason for postulating such structures is not that subjects display them with such consistency and tenacity but rather that structures have to be postulated when we see how subjects selectively attend to, and remember, certain fea-tures; how subjects draw inferences beyond what is given directly; how they "correct" material so that it corresponds better to "good form"; and how they "chunk" and organize experience. In short, one can postulate underlying cognitive structures without fashioning them in terms of Piagetian stages.

Measurement Operations and the Scoring System

The Kohlberg group's major research effort over the last decade has been to revise the scoring system. Why did this take so long and why did it seem so important? One set of reasons has to do with han-dling interview material. Kohlberg's procedure in gathering data is much more open ended than Piaget's, and this had led to a much richer and fuller description of the organizing structures in moral judgment development. Nevertheless, free response data to open-ended dilemmas pose vexing problems in setting up a reliable scoring system. First, there is the problem of establishing a unit of analysis. In Kohlberg's 1958 work, two scoring systems were devised: one using the sentence or completed thought as the basic unit of analysis, the other (global rating) using all the subject's utterances to a dilemma as the unit of analysis. Both of these solutions had serious shortcomings. When using the sentence as the basic unit, stage scoring was too much influenced by concrete-word usage. Furthermore, a repeated idea was scored as many times as it was repeated. When the global-rating system was used, invariably the subject said some things that seemed at one stage, but other things that seemed at another stage. Therefore, because subjects did not give responses that completely fit the stage typology, there was the problem of knowing how to classify conflicting themes. A second problem with free-response data is that different subjects bring up different topics and touch on different aspects of the dilemma. For instance, in the Heinz dilemma, some subjects start out speaking of the druggist's property rights, other subjects pay attention to Heinz's marriage vows. Therefore, information from different subjects is not comparable, and we do not know whether to attribute this phenomenon to fleeting quirks of attention or to fundamental organizing structures. A third problem is in specifying how explicitly the subject must state an idea to be credited with ''having'' it, or how ''clinically'' it can be inferred. A fourth problem is in deciding what is ''content'' (i.e., inconsequential features that are discarded in the analysis) and what is ''structure'' (i.e., features at the level of abstraction that is the particular concern of the analysis). In other words, how formalistic, deep, or abstract should the analysis be? A fifth problem is in knowing how to combine conflicting cues from various parts of an interview over several dilemmas into a single summary score that describes the subject in general.

The Kohlberg group over the last decade has identified these problems, devised strategies for dealing with them, and tested and revised strategies in light of their workability. Their new scoring system is impressive, particularly for its methods of dealing with the problems inherent in scoring free-interview material. Indeed, researchers concerned with interview material who have no interest in morality per se would be well advised to look at the new scoring system to see how it handles these methodological problems. Furthermore, the derivation of the scoring system is noteworthy for using longitudinal, not just cross-sectional, data. The Kohlberg group has construed their task as using longitudinal data to devise a scoring scheme that will produce scores that are consistent for a subject across dilemmas at one point in time and that over time *each* subject shows step-by-step movement through the stages without reversals and without skipping any stages. Using longitudinal data instead of cross-sectional data sets more constraints because the patterns must hold true for each individual, not just for the averages of groups. Presumably this greater stringency gives greater assurance that such a scoring system is tapping true ontogenetic change rather than cohort or sample differences.

The old 1958 scoring system actually showed more than passable interjudge agreement (Kohlberg, 1976) and produced data trends that are satisfactory by current journal standards (see Kohlberg's review of studies in 1969). Yet, from a theoretical point of view, the system was loose, inelegant, ad hoc, and lacked a clean conceptual architecture. The original impetus for revising the system was not to develop a standardized test or to provide an easier method of scoring (more to be said about quick and easy assessment later); instead, the goal was to develop a method of logical analysis of people's moral thinking that captured its grammar, analogous to Chomsky's (1957) grammar of language. The hope was that the fundamental categories and logical operations of people's moral thinking could be described and that these descriptors would be valid for all dilemmas and for all kinds of spoken or written material, not just for responses to the Heinz story and company. Other dilemmas might involve minor adjustments in scoring, some stage definitions might need realignment, other data gathering methods might require some recalibration—nevertheless, the aim was to make the major breakthrough in setting the categories and descriptors of analysis.

As a source of ideas about basic categories and descriptors, Kohlberg turned to academic moral philosophy. Philosophers distinguish different kinds of moral questions (e.g., Who has a responsibility to act in a given situation? Assuming responsibility, exactly what is a person obligated to do? If a person falls short of her obligation, how should she be treated?) Furthermore, philosophers differentiate principles of justification (justice, utility, prudence, perfection, etc.). And philosophers differentiate contexts in which a problem is set (law, affectional relations, property, or punishment). In the early 1970s, Kohlberg attempted to create a cross-classification system on all the major sets of philosophical distinctions in which any possible moral judgment could be located and related to all other possible moral judgments. In these scoring systems, ease of scoring and practicality were not major concerns, as evidenced by the fact that one system had over 2 million possible scoring categories. As might be imagined, the complications in this work are bewildering; in more recent years, the emphasis has shifted from philosophical analysis to a more workable scoring system.

Another impetus to revise the scoring system was the occurrence of some disconfirming data. Using the 1958 system, Kohlberg and Kramer (1969) found some reversals in the developmental sequence of some subjects between the testing in high school and the testing in college. In high school, some students had been scored at Stages 4 and 5, but as sophomores in college, they were scored at Stage 2. In other data, some anomalies were found in subjects moving from Stage 4 back to Stage 3 or skipping from Stage 3 to Stage 5 (Kohlberg, 1976). These irregularities were a major challenge to Kohlberg's strong stage model, which requires that there be no anomalies ("A stage sequence disregarded by a single child is no sequence," Kohlberg, 1973b, p. 182). Given the clash between his hard-line stage model and the disconfirming data, rather than soften his stage model, Kohlberg's response was to revise the scoring system, assuming that the fault must be in confusing content with structure. Consequently, the trend in scoring system revisions has been to purge more and more content from structure, that is, to key stage distinctions on progressively more abstract and formalistic descriptors. As Colby (1978, p. 91) puts it, "We can view this history as a progressive differentiation of content from structure. Each major scoring change has involved an important redefinition of the content-structure distinction." For instance, a subject might respond to the Heinz dilemma by saying, "Heinz shouldn't steal because it'd be against the law." We would want to know how the subject regards "the law"—as simple fear of legal punishment, as concern for the social system, or as what. One must go beyond content concerns (life, law, affiliation) to get to the underlying structure.

The recent scoring systems purge content from stage differentiations by holding content constant (Kohlberg, Colby, Gibbs, Speicher-Dubin, 1978). It does this by a four-tier classification system: the interview material for each dilemma is first separated into issues (2 for each dilemma), then into norms (12 possible for each issue), then into elements (17 possible for each norm), and only then is scored by stage. For instance, one subject said, "Heinz shouldn't steal. If everyone went around breaking the law, things would be wild; stealing, murder. You couldn't live." Because this response favors not stealing, it is classified under the law *issue*. It invokes a concern for the law as a reason for obeying the law, therefore, the *norm* is law. The specific type of concern about the law has to do with

group consequences, so it is classified as *element* II.9. Only after these classifications are made do we finally get to decide what stage it is. At this point, the scoring manual presents us with these choices:

Stage 3 scoring criteria: "One should obey the law because if everybody breaks the law there would be chaos, things would be wild, or everything would be topsy-turvy; *OR* because without laws immoral people would cause chaos." (The response above is scored as an example of Stage 3 structure.) (Kohlberg et al., 1978, Pt. 3, p. 96)

Stage 3/4 scoring criteria: "People should obey the law because otherwise laws will no longer be a guide to people; *OR* because otherwise a bad example or precedent will be set; *OR* because otherwise people will steal even if they don't really have to, will steal without thinking, or will think stealing is okay." [*Example of a subject's response scored under this criteria:* "Yes, I mean in general this type of precedent would be established for any kind of a want that somebody wants to satisfy. Just go ahead and rob or something like that, the results would be." (Scored Stage 3/4—Law II.9.)] (Kohlberg et al., 1978, Pt. 3, p. 97)

Stage 4 scoring criteria: "People should obey the law because the law is essential if society or civilization is to survive; *OR* because the law is necessary for social organization, general social order, or smooth social functioning; *OR* because giving way to individual beliefs or values and decisions will cause disorganization." [*Example:* "If it's just, if it's necessary to preserve order. (Why do we need laws?) Well, I think without laws there would be chaos, there wouldn't be any order so to speak. I am talking about just laws now." (Scored Stage 4—Law II.9.)] (Kohlberg et al., 1978, Pt. 3, p. 107)

Stage 5 scoring criteria: "One should obey the law because if individuals are to live together in society, there must be some common agreement; *OR* because laws represent a necessary structure of social agreement." [*Example:* "Because it is so hard for people to live together unless there are some laws governing their actions. Not everybody is good certainly and we have to go by some code, so to speak, that we have to follow to make sure that everybody has their own individual rights." (Scored Stage 5—Law II.17.)] (Kohlberg et al., 1978, Pt. 3, p 117)

Notice that by the time we are able to score a response by stage, the distinctions have become exceedingly fine. The new scoring system purges content with a vengeance. In effect, the Kohlberg group contends that there is no developmental significance in whether a subject appeals to a husband's affection or to maintaining social order; what is important is the particular subvariety of social order the subject envisions (e.g., the subclassifications above) or what concept of affection the subject has (many subvarieties of this are also distinguished by stage). By the new system, a stage score would not reflect the difference between a response that appealed to a Stage 3 affectional concern from a response that appealed to a Stage 3 social-order concern. Variance in stage scores reflects the kind of distinctions embodied in the four examples above. One might ask, has something important been lost on the road to purging content? (See J. R. Rest, 1979a, for further discussion.)

Because the new scoring system is so new, only the initial research on its reliability and validity by the Kohlberg group has been reported. But these results are spectacular (Colby et al., in press). Test-retest correlations were .96, .99, and .97 (using different data and different raters). Interrater correlations were .98, .96, and .92 for forms A, B, and C, respectively. Correlations between Form A and Form B was .95. On the longitudinal data of subjects tested at 3- to 4-year intervals over 20 years, 56 of 58 subjects showed upward change with *no* subjects skipping any stages; only 6% of the 195 comparisons showed backward shifts between two particular testings. The internal consistency of scores is also impressive: between 67% and 72% of the scores were at one stage and only 1% to 3% of the scores were spread further than two adjacent stages; Cronbach's alpha was .92, .96, and .94 for Forms A, B, and C respectively.

Results like these—if cross-validated on other samples—[9]would seem to vindicate Kohlberg's hard-line stage model as well as the ferocious purging of content. But some qualifications need to be made. First, with respect to the upward movement, even though the trends are remarkably unambiguous, nevertheless, the amount of change over 20 years was not great: most subjects moved up less than two full stages; one full stage shift (e.g., Stage 2 to Stage 3 or Stage 3 to Stage 4) takes on the average 13.9 years. Most subjects start out around Stage 2 and end up around Stage 4. Stage 5 even in minor traces is a rarity; Stage 6 is not scored in this material at all. Second, with respect to stage consistency, it must be pointed out that the consistency of scores in Kohlberg's data is not a strong test of stage consistency in a person's moral thinking. Various scoring rules have been devised to weed out stage mixture, thus, the procedure is biased toward stage

consistency (see J. R. Rest, 1979a). For instance, the upper stage inclusion rule requires that whenever a subject gives material that matches the scoring criteria at a lower stage, it is not recorded on the scoring sheet if elsewhere in the discussion of that dilemma, the subject gives more elaborated material that matches a higher stage. For example, suppose that a subject started out discussing the Heinz dilemma with the response scored Stage 3 (above example), then later in the discussion the subject gave the response scored Stage 4; the lower stage response would not be recorded at all and would not contribute to stage mixture. The theoretical justification for such a procedure is that higher stage statements hierarchically include the lower stage idea. Such scoring rules give the Kohlberg measure good internal reliability and make sense as methods for inducing good interrater reliability. Nevertheless, this procedure does not allow disconfirmation of the hard-stage model.

Hundreds of studies have been conducted with one or another version of Kohlberg's scoring systems. These have generated a wealth of ideas and findings and will be reviewed along with related research later. Critics and revisionists of the system have also been plentiful. Gibbs (1979):

Kohlberg's stage theory of moral judgment development, we learn from many of his critics, is ethnocentric (Simpson, 1974), ideological (Sullivan, 1977), elitist (Frankel, 1978), restrictively abstract (Aron, 1977a, [1977]b; Gilligan, 1977), and perniciously individualistic (Hogan, 1975; Reid and Yanarella, 1977). My own critical opinion (Gibbs, 1977), which is among the more sympathetic (e.g., Bereiter, 1978; Broughton, 1978), is that although Kohlberg's theory is in fact ailing from these excesses, it will be fine once its proportions return to those of its proper constitutional frame. (p. 90)

For Gibbs (1979), the "proper constitutional frame" is a more rigorous application of the Piagetian stage model. Rather than considering the merits of each of these critics in the abstract, let us turn to some revisions and alternate proposals that have initiated a program of research.

Defining Issues Test Research

The Defining Issues Test (DIT) began as an attempt to develop an easier method of assessment based on Kohlberg's approach. Rather than the Kohlberg group's search for an analytic scheme for all moral thinking, DIT research began with the more modest goal of using some of the then-recognized developmental features of people's thinking (identified by Kohlberg's research) and devising an assessment procedure based on subjects' ratings and rankings of stage-prototypical statements instead of interviewing subjects. The hope was to provide an easily administerable, objectively scorable assessment tool on which a much needed data base could be built. Since 1974, several hundred studies have been completed (see J. R. Rest, 1979a, 1982) that provide the largest data base yet accumulated on a single measure of moral judgment (counting Kohlberg's different scoring systems as different measures). Many researchers have played central roles in DIT research, collecting data from thousands of subjects in many regions and countries and using techniques from several branches of psychology. As findings have accumulated and, with the benefit of hindsight, several important reformulations of theory have been proposed, including the stage concept itself, definitions of moral judgment stages and the major dimensions of development, the relation of moral judgment to behavior, the meaning of validation for moral judgment measures, the role of formal education in fostering moral judgment development, and many issues of research strategy and design. Before discussing these theoretical reformulations, however, a brief description of the DIT as an assessment procedure follows.

The DIT Measurement Operations

The DIT assumes that people at different developmental stages construe moral dilemmas differently—particularly in what they define as the crux of a moral problem and in what considerations they regard as the most important ones. Presumably, if people are presented with different statements about the issues of a moral dilemma, people at different developmental stages will choose different statements as representing the most important issue.

The DIT uses 6 moral dilemmas—3 of which were taken from Kohlberg's Interview (1958) and 3 from Lockwood's dissertation (1970)—chosen after extensive interviewing had shown what kinds of things people spontaneously say in response to these dilemmas and because short, distinct DIT items could be written for these dilemmas. The DIT dilemmas include the familiar story about Heinz and the drug. After a subject reads a dilemma, 12 issue-statements are listed. The subject is asked to read each one and indicate on a 5-point rating scale how important each issue-statement is in making a decision about what ought to be done in the dilemma. For instance, regarding the Heinz dilemma, the subject

first reads the issue: "Whether a community's laws are going to be upheld." If the subject thinks that this issue is the crux of the dilemma and of great importance in deciding what Heinz ought to do, then the subject is instructed to rate that item high. If the item has some relevance but seems not to be decisive in and of itself, then the subject is instructed to give the item a medium rating. If the item is ridiculous, irrelevant, or does not make sense, then the item is to be rated low. Other items for the Heinz dilemma include: "Isn't it only natural for a loving husband to care so much for his wife that he'd steal?" / "Is Heinz willing to risk getting shot as a burglar or going to jail for the chance that stealing the drug might help?" / "What values are going to be the basis for governing how people act toward each other?" These four items were designed to represent the way that the crucial issue might be conceived from a Stage 4, Stage 3, Stage 2, and Stage 6 point of view respectively. There are 12 items in all that are presented to subjects for each of the 6 dilemmas, producing ratings on 72 items. After *rating* the items for each dilemma, subjects are asked to *rank* the 4 most important items from the set of 12.

A variety of scores can be derived from these ratings and rankings. One of the most useful scores has been the P index: the relative importance that a subject gives to Stage 5 and 6 items (Principled considerations). Operationally, the P index is the percentage of top rankings given to Stage 5 and 6 items. In addition, Davison and his colleagues (Davison, 1977; Davison & Robbins, 1978; Davison, Robbins, & Swanson, 1978) have recently developed a scaling technique (based on the metric unfolding model) that yields an overall composite index of development, the D index, based on weighted rating data. Scores for Stages 2, 3, and 4 can also be derived from subjects' questionnaires, although the reliability of these scales is not as high as the P and D indices. (See J. R. Rest, 1979c, for scoring details and technical data on various scales.) A detailed discussion of the rationale of DIT construction and design features is contained in J. R. Rest, 1979a and 1980. There, a number of technical issues are discussed: the number of items written for each stage, item order, item length, continuous indexing versus stage-typing indices, relation of decision data to item evaluation, and so on.

As with every method of assessment, there are advantages and disadvantages to the DIT's method. The three most serious threats to the internal and external validity of a test like the DIT are that: (1) subjects may randomly check off responses without even reading the items, dilemmas, and instructions;

(2) subjects may pick out items that seem complex and sophisticated, even when they do not understand their meaning; and (3) subjects may try to fake high on a recognition task because they do not have to discuss or justify their answers. Special features were built into the DIT to deal with these problems. For random checking, a Consistency Check between the rating and ranking is used to identify subjects who are putting check marks down in a meaningless pattern. If subjects are too discrepant between their ratings and rankings, the questionnaire is discarded from further analysis. Similarly, to identify subjects who are picking items on the basis of their apparent complexity or verbal sophistication rather than on their meaning, the DIT contains a number of M items, that is, items written to sound impressive and sophisticated but which do not mean anything (e.g., "Whether the essence of living is more encompassing than the termination of dying, socially and individually"). If a subject selects too many of these M items, the questionnaire is also discarded. Third, several studies have been conducted to determine if subjects can fake high without invalidating their questionnaire on the M score. It seems subjects cannot fake high without raising their M score too high, although they can fake low (see J. R. Rest, 1979a). In a report of reliability studies, Davison and Robbins (1978) cite test-retest correlations in the .70s and .80s and internal reliabilities (Cronbach's alpha) in the same range.

The DIT procedure raises some basic theoretical-methodological issues. For one, it might be argued that a standardized objective test that prestructures the response alternatives in prototypical statements prevents the discovery of the structuring activity of the subject—the multiple-choice format by its very nature defeats the purpose of cognitive-developmental assessment by preventing subjects from explaining their thinking in their own terms. Furthermore, devotees of the interview method (e.g., Damon, 1977) claim that the flexible clinical interview is the only means for adjusting for a subject's idiosyncratic understanding of the task and materials; a skilled clinical interviewer accommodates to each person's peculiarities to insure comparable understanding of the questions being asked them. Arguments for and against the interview method versus standardized objective tests have been forthcoming for 50 years at least and have been particularly pointed and intense regarding Piaget's *methode clinique* (Braine, 1959, 1962; Inhelder & Sinclair, 1969; Smedslund, 1963, 1969). For instance, against the interview method, there is no evidence that skilled interviewers can accommodate to individual peculiarities without

confounding the assessment with more error variance owing to task and stimuli changes. Further, Brainerd (1973, 1978) argues that interview methods are so confounded by differences in subjects' verbal ability that interviewing produces less valid results than standardized objective methods. At this point, it seems that all methods of assessment (interview and standardized objective tests) have many possible sources of error and have their particular confounds; the question is not one of finding an error-free test but rather of minimizing the kinds and amounts of error. Comparing the DIT with Kohlberg's interview method, the DIT credits subjects with more advanced thinking than does Kohlberg's test, and the two are only moderately correlated (as high as the .70s in heterogeneous samples, but lower in homogeneous samples) (see J. R. Rest, 1979a). Nevertheless, the two tests thus far seem to produce similar longitudinal trends (with about the same amount of regression), similar correlates with other cognitive and attitudinal variables, and similar changes in response to educational and experimental interventions. Therefore, the superiority (in terms of greater validity) of one technique over the other is not established. The two techniques probably are vulnerable to different sources of error, but the total amount of error variance is not demonstrably different.

Another basic issue that the DIT procedure raises is that developmental assessment is expressed in terms of a continuous variable (e.g., the P or D indices) rather than in terms of locating a subject in a stage. If cognitive developmentalists analyze people's thinking in terms of qualitative organizations (stages), should not a test score tell us in what stage a subject is? There are two subissues involved in this question: one deals with the concept of stage and will be discussed later; the other concerns the matter of indexing, that is, what rules should be used to compute a subject's score, given the data from some information-collection procedure? In the case of the DIT, how should the various ratings and rankings be used to compute a developmental score for each subject? In general, how are scores to be derived from the various pieces of information that come from interviewing, or responses to items, and so on?

Many ways of indexing have been proposed by researchers: a subject's score is that stage that is used most (Kohlberg, 1958); a subject's score is the highest stage that is used (Damon, 1977); a subject's score is based on the extent to which the lower stages are rejected (Rest, 1981); a subject's score is a continuous variable representing the weighted average of the extent of use of the various stages (Kohlberg's moral maturity quotient, 1958); and the DIT's P and D scores are also variants. Actually, in DIT research, several dozen indices have been examined (see J. R. Rest, 1979a). The recommendation of the P and D indices comes from systematically comparing dozens of indices on several criteria: test-retest stability, power-of-age trends, most distinct pattern of convergent-divergent correlations, and so on. In this kind of systematic comparison, the P and D indices consistently produced the best data trends theoretically expected of a measure of moral judgment. Therefore, the use of those particular indices for the DIT is based on empirical grounds. To my knowledge, no other research program in moral judgment has published a systematic empirical justification of the particular index employed in the measure. Typically, researchers treat their method of indexing as if it were the only one possible; sometimes researchers inconsistently use one index in some studies and another index in different studies (e.g., Damon in 1977 uses a highest stage index, but in 1980a he uses a modal-stage index).

Several shortcomings of the DIT should be noted. For one, the procedure cannot be used with young subjects (subjects having less than a 12-year-old reading level), thus preventing assessment in subjects whose development is perhaps the most dramatic. Second, as with all multiple-choice procedures, the items limit the possible ways of thinking that are taken into account. If a subject is thinking about some issue not presented in the provided item set, there is no way that a score can take this into account. Third, there is evidence that at least some items (particularly items having bad psychometric properties) are interpreted in various ways (see Lawrence, 1978); thus, ratings and rankings of such items have different meanings to different subjects and confound interpretation (and validity) of test scores, at least to some extent.

The Stage Concept

Any approach to studying the underlying structures of moral thinking hinges on its concept of these structures. Piaget's work on the developing structures of logical thought has been so brilliant that moral judgment researchers have been captivated by the prospect of finding analogous structures in moral thinking, at times seeming to seek the moral equivalent of the INRC structure and to define moral stages in terms of reversibility operations or the lack thereof. To Piagetians, the structure d'ensemble of stages is such a dominating rule system that being in a stage is like being in a country: when you are within its borders, you must obey the laws that govern it; leaving the borders of that country for another might get you another set of laws but then you are subject to that system. Many discussions by cognitive developmentalists seem to imply that if one disputes Piagetian stages, then one will be thrown into the clutches of Skinnerian philistines who categorically forbid exploring the inner world of the mind.

Many discussions of Piaget's stage concept have appeared in recent years (e.g., Flavell, 1970, 1971, 1977, in press; Flavell & Wohlwill, 1969; Wohlwill, 1973), pointing to problems in the concept and its fit with empirical evidence. A detailed discussion of the stage concept in moral judgment research appears in J. R. Rest, 1979a. A stage model of moral judgment development did not lead us to anticipate certain findings:

1. The acquisition of cognitive structures is gradual rather than abrupt; acquisition is not an all-or-nothing matter but rather is better depicted as a gradual increase in the probability of occurrence. Although stages (or cognitive structures) are qualitatively distinguished, their occurrence in a person's thinking needs to be quantitatively described (in terms of more or less). In DIT research, the amount of stage usage is calculated in terms of percentages for every stage. In Kohlberg's research, relative amounts of stage usage are represented in terms of major stage usage and minor stage usage, in only about one third of the cases are subjects scored as pure types (Colby et al., in press). Therefore, both quantitative and qualitative assessments of thought organizations are necessary.

2. Subjects fluctuate in their use of a stage structure even on the same tasks. Short time test-retest correlations on the DIT and on most versions of Kohlberg's test are typical for measures of this sort (.70s and .80s). Even with Kohlberg's latest scoring system, which has test-retest correlations in the high .90s, about 30% of the subjects show fluctuations of one third of a stage over a 2-week period, for example, dominant on Stage 2 and minor on Stage 3 to dominant on Stage 3 and minor on Stage 2, which is more than negligible considering that on the average, one third of a stage is the equivalent of 4-years' natural movement in Kohlberg's longitudinal study. In short, subjects are not simply "in" one stage or another but fluctuate within a developmental range.

3. Varying the specific type of testing material, instructions, procedures, scoring criteria, and stringency produces considerable variance in stage scores. Indeed, a major interest in post-Piagetian research in moral judgment has been to document

just that. Similar manipulation of the Kohlbergian stories has also produced fluctuations in stage scores (e.g., Leming, 1978; Levine, 1976; McGeorge, 1974; Sobesky, in press). Although Piagetians have invoked the notion of décalagé (unevenness in development), the amount of it and the variety of factors that produce it were not anticipated.

4. The organization of thinking imposed on a problem is partially determined by the type of task and the type of response that are used in assessment. For instance, Kohlberg's test asks subjects to discuss and justify a course of action; the DIT asks subjects to rate and rank stage-prototypical statements—subjects are scored lower on Kohlberg's spontaneous production task than on the DIT's recognition and preference task. That different tasks and response modes made a difference in stage scores is another empirical disconfirmation of a simple stage model (see also Gibbs & Widaman, 1982; Levine, 1976, 1979).

Given these empirical findings, development needs to be portrayed in more complex terms than the picture of a subject as being in one stage and moving step by step through a series of stages. All assessment is relative to the particular tasks, test materials, conditions, and procedures used. A given subject uses a variety of stage structures to a greater or lesser extent, depending on many factors. The basic question of assessment should not be, "What stage is a subject in?" but rather, "To what extent and under what circumstances does a subject display various organizations of thinking?" Development is the gradual shifting from the use of lower stages to higher stages. (For a defense of a stronger model, however, see Colby et al., in press.)

The DIT research has assumed that it is useful to postulate general organizations of thinking that underlie moral judgments and that these organizations of thinking have a developmental order. However, the notion of stage in DIT research is modified from Kohlberg's use of the term. Stage mixture, stage fluctuation, and sensitivity to contextural and stimulus variation are assumed to be facts of life. Other researchers using other paradigms have challenged and rejected all use of the stage concept; we will consider their research and arguments later, after reviewing the research generated by the six-stage model (using both the DIT and various varieties of Kohlberg's scoring systems). But first, let us consider the reformulation of moral judgment development proposed in DIT research.

Characterization of Development

Instead of assuming with Kohlberg that moral judgment development should conform to a strict stage model and that, therefore, people's thinking must be purged of all "content" and characterized in terms of highly abstract operations (reversibility, "moral musical chairs"), DIT research assumes that the basic organizations of moral thinking are different schemes of cooperation, that is, generalized views of how people cooperate in social relationships (e.g., as mentioned earlier when discussing Component II, one such is the Law and Order scheme of Stage 4). Different stages are postulated as a formalistic but shorthand way of describing: the pattern of considerations that a subject highlights and considers crucial, how a subject balances and prioritizes the various claims of subjects, and the subject's rationale for advocating one or another course of action. A subject may not be completely aware of these organizing tendencies in making moral judgments, nevertheless, subjects experience an intuitive sense of fairness about a particular solution.

Development is portrayed in terms of the progressive understanding of the various possibilities of cooperative relationships, how rights and duties are balanced, and the conditions that sustain the cooperative schemes. Theoretically, progressive understanding is characterized in terms of six distinct schemes of cooperation. The new recognitions or new accomplishments of each new stage over its predecessor is describable in terms of two dimensions. The first is the conceptualization of how *shared* expectations can be coordinated among people, that is, how it is possible for one person to know what to expect from other individuals and to coordinate plans and goals with others. This is a kind of metacognition in Flavell's sense (1979), and has parallels to Selman's interpersonal perspective taking (1980) up through his Stage 4. The first column in Table 2 describes for each stage the distinctive notion about how expectations can be coordinated and shared, beginning at Stages 1 and 2 with direct commands (you know what the other wants from you if given commands) and concrete agreements (you and the other person explicitly bargain for what favor you will do, what favor he will do), moving through formal law at Stage 4 (you know what to expect from others, even those you have never met before, by knowing the law), to anticipating at Stages 5 and 6 the coordination of expectations by figuring out what rational and impartial people should accept. (An extended discussion is contained in J. R. Rest, 1979a, including specific criteria for scoring subjects' responses and quotes from sub-

Table 2. Stages of Moral Judgment

Stage	Coordination of Expectations About Actions (How Rules Are Known and Shared)	Schemes of Balancing Interests (How Equilibrium Is Achieved)	Central Concept for Determining Moral Rights and Responsibilities
Stage 1	The caretaker makes known certain demands on the child's behavior.	The child does not share in making rules but understands that obedience will bring freedom from punishment.	The morality of obedience: "Do what you're told."
Stage 2	Although each person is understood to have his own interests, an exchange of favors might be mutually decided.	If each party sees something to gain in an exchange, then both want to reciprocate.	The morality of instrumental egoism and simple exchange: "Let's make a deal."
Stage 3	Through reciprocal role taking, individuals attain a mutual understanding about each other and the ongoing pattern of their interactions.	Friendship relationships establish a stabilized and enduring scheme of cooperation. Each party anticipates the feelings, needs, and wants of the other and acts in the other's welfare.	The morality of interpersonal concordance: "Be considerate, nice, and kind, and you'll get along with people."
Stage 4	All members of society know what is expected of them through public institutionalized law.	Unless a societywide system of cooperation is established and stabilized, no individual can really make plans. Each person should follow the law and do his particular job, anticipating that other people will also fulfill their responsibilities.	The morality of law and duty to the social order: "Everyone in society is obligated and protected by the law."
Stage 5	Formal procedures are institutionalized for making laws, which one anticipates rational people would accept.	Law-making procedures are devised so that they reflect the general will of the people, at the same time insuring certain basic rights to all. With each person having a say in the decision process, each will see that his interests are maximized while at the same time having a basis for making claims on other people.	The morality of societal consensus: "You are obligated by whatever arrangements are agreed to by due process procedures."
Stage 6	The logical requirements of nonarbitrary cooperation among rational, equal, and impartial people are taken as ideal criteria for social organization which one anticipates rational people would accept.	A scheme of cooperation that negates or neutralizes all arbitrary distribution of rights and responsibilities is the most equilibrated, for such system is maximizing the simultaneous benefit to each member so that any deviation from these rules would advantage some members at the expense of others.	The morality of nonarbitrary social cooperation: "How rational and impartial people would organize cooperation is moral."

jects.) And so, for instance, if a person does not yet realize that law can be an instrument for coordinating the expectations of people about how to behave toward each other (even among strangers), then the scheme of cooperation at Stage 4 will not make sense.

The second dimension of developmental advance from stage to stage concerns the kind of social organization that the subject realizes is possible, particularly in the ways that cooperation can be structured. With each form of social organization, a notion of justice defines how reciprocity among participants is balanced—in effect, achieving a social equilibrium. The second column in Table 2 sketches the progression, beginning with rather lopsided reciprocity at Stage 1 to highly idealized reciprocity at Stage 6. The third column in Table 2 indicates how the ascription of rights and responsibilities follow from each scheme of cooperation and the particular rationale for making moral judgments. Each stage portrays a distinctive way of defining what is most important and for directing action in specific moral dilemmas.

At every stage, there is an intuitive sense of what is right and fair. This moral sense changes as more complexities of social life are taken into account and the subject envisions new possibilities for arranging cooperation. Stage 1 provides a normative structure (the superior's demands) for the regulation of human interaction; however, in this system of cooperation great inequality exists between parties and there is hardly any reciprocity. The system is largely determined by accidents of birth, that is, who was born first, who is bigger and more powerful, and so on. Stage 2 makes significant progress toward establishing a more balanced reciprocity among participants through recognizing each person's special point of view and through the device of simple exchange. Stage 2, however, provides only a temporary and fragmentary system of social cooperation and is arbitrarily bound by the contingency that parties can get together and have favors that each one wants at that time. Stage 3 provides for a more enduring system of cooperation through relationships of mutual caring and affection, each party being generally committed to the other's welfare; however, the scheme of Stage 3 is arbitrarily limited to whatever friendships have been established at a given time. Stage 4 establishes a societywide system of cooperation through the concept of formal social systems governed by law and in which all parties reciprocate with each other by carrying out their own roles. Stage 4, however, can allow gross inequalities and arbitrary distribution of the benefits and burdens of cooperation because the social order itself may be set up legally to give advantage to some at the expense of others (e.g., a slave society). Stage 5 attempts to eliminate arbitrary rules by providing procedures for making rules that reflect the will of the people, giving each person an equal say in determining the arrangements of society. Stage 5, therefore, has gone a long way in neutralizing inequities and lopsided reciprocity owing to accidents of birth, historical accidents, and other arbitrary circumstances, and at the same time, it has provided for enduring social structures that can win the support of the participants. Stage 5, however, has not completely insured that

the *outcomes* of duly enacted laws produce a nonarbitrary balancing of people's interests; the collective judgment of the people at one time may be unfair as viewed by the people at a later time (e.g., the acceptance of slavery in early America). In Rawls's (1971) terminology, Stage 5 guarantees procedural justice but not substantive justice. Stage 6 maintains, therefore, that although a majority of people may want a law (or social policy), that still does not necessarily make it moral because the ultimate test of morality goes beyond due process and social consensus. The defining feature of Stage 6 is its appeal to ideal principles of justice (e.g., Brandt's extended rule utilitarianism, 1959; Kant's categorical imperative; Rawls's two principles of justice, 1971, etc.), which are presented so that rational, equal, and impartial people could choose them as the governing terms of their cooperative interaction. According to this characterization of Stage 6, most modern moral philosophers would be scored at Stage 6 insofar as their conceptions of fairness are principles of social organization that balance competing claims of individuals, which attempt to optimize everyone's stake in that social order and eliminate or neutralize arbitrary factors.

The definition of stages here in terms of schemes of cooperation is less based on abstract logical operations and more on various conceptions of social relationships and structures (e.g., two-person bargains, enduring positive relationships, formal societal order, ideal schemes of reciprocity and balance). One consequence is that, according to these definitions, it is possible to find more Stage 5 and 6 thinking than with Kohlberg's method (in which a subject must deliver a philosophical lecture in response to the Heinz and the drug story to be credited with higher stage thinking). Nevertheless, the similarities of the DIT stage definitions with the various Kohlberg scoring systems is much more striking than the dissimilarities; therefore a review of research on the six-stage model will combine studies using the DIT and the various versions of Kohlberg's test.

Research on the Six-Stage Model

Studies using various versions of Kohlberg's test and studies using the DIT total well over 1,000, undoubtedly the largest body of research in the area of moral knowledge and judgment. Fortunately, several intensive critical reviews of subareas of this literature have appeared recently and the reader will be referred to them for more complete documentation and references. The research will be discussed under four headings: (1) research relating to developmental sequence; (2) research bearing on the claim that moral judgment stages are governed primarily by cognitive processes and that higher stages are cognitively more advanced; (3) research on conditions, manipulations, and factors affecting change in moral judgment; and (4) research linking moral judgment test scores to real-life behavior.

Developmental Sequence

One of the central implications of any developmental theory is, of course, that people change over time. One of the first studies that researchers do is to look for cross-sectional age trends, that is, following Piaget, younger children are compared with older children to see if older children use more advanced types of thinking. Kohlberg's dissertation (1958) compared boys at ages 10, 13, and 16, and many cross-sectional studies have extended these age groups in both directions (see Kohlberg, 1969, for partial review). Likewise, many DIT studies have looked for and found age trends when comparing junior high school subjects with senior high school subjects, college students, and graduate students. The largest cross-sectional study involving over 4,500 students in these four groupings found that age/education accounted for 38% of the variance (Rest, Davison, & Robbins, 1978). Other studies have attributed almost 50% of the variance to age/education (J. R. Rest, 1979a). In DIT studies, students in doctoral programs in moral philosophy and political science have the highest scores as a group, although some individuals without that specialized training also have scores as high. Correlations of moral judgment scores with age are in the .60s and .70s in several reports (Colby et al., in press; J. R. Rest, 1979a).

Among nonstudent adults, moral judgment is associated more with level of education than chronological age. After adults finish formal schooling, they seem to plateau in moral judgment development. Schooling seems to be a formative period after which adults become settled in their ways. However, training studies (reviewed later) indicate that moral judgment development is not simple learning of verbal terminology or formulas. Colby et al. (in press) report that in adult subjects, the correlation of moral judgment with educational level was between .53 and .69, whereas the correlation with age was nonsignificant. Some further evidence using the DIT comes from comparing current medical students with practicing physicians, current college students with adults having a college education, current high school students with adults having only a high school education, and so on. In each case, the older

group have scores similar to those of the young group with comparable educational level (J. R. Rest, 1979a).

Some special limitations of these studies should be noted in addition to the usual limitations of cross-sectional data, such as possible generational or cohort effects. For one, the DIT cannot be used with subjects below a 12-year-old reading level and, thus, provide no evidence for developmental sequence at the lower stages. On the other hand, Kohlberg's test in its various versions has generated data of unknown comparability from study to study (although within the specific studies age trends are shown). Furthermore, the use of Stages 5 and 6 in Kohlberg's scheme is very sparse, therefore, providing little evidence for developmental sequence at the highest stages. Both tests taken together provide evidence for developmental shifts from Stage 1 to Stage 6—movement from Stage 1 to 4 on Kohlberg's test, movement from Stage 4 to 6 on the DIT. However, because the tests are not equivalent, the significance of this is not completely clear.

Age trends in cross-sectional studies also have been found using other tests of moral judgment based on the six-stage model besides the Kohlberg or DIT (Bode & Page, 1980; Carroll, 1980; Gibbs & Widaman, 1982; Maitland & Goldman, 1975).

Longitudinal studies testing the same subjects repeatedly at 1- to 4-year intervals provide stronger data for developmental sequence. About a dozen longitudinal studies are reviewed in Rest et al., 1978 (see Holstein, 1976; Kohlberg & Kramer, 1969; Kuhn, 1976; Turiel, Edwards, & Kohlberg, 1978; White, Bushnell, & Regnemer, 1978). To these should be added the Colby et al. (in press) study and five recent longitudinal studies of the DIT.[10] In general, subjects show significant change in the direction postulated by the six-stage theory. However, there are these qualifications: many subjects show no change between two testings; adult subjects who are not in school tend to stay the same; a small portion of student subjects (about 7%) actually move downward; developmental change is more dramatic over longer intervals of time (4 years and more); change appears to be slow; and no clear longitudinal evidence exists that Stage 6 follows Stage 5 (because Kohlberg's test does not score for Stage 6 and the DIT collapses Stages 5 and 6 together in its indices). Nevertheless, more than 10 times as many subjects move upward than move downward over a 3- to 4-year interval.

As in the cross-sectional studies, the DIT longitudinal studies show shifts to the higher stages; in the studies using Kohlberg's test, the shifts are mostly within the first four stages. Kohlberg's recently completed 20-year longitudinal study on 58 subjects, starting at age 10 (Colby et al., in press), is especially interesting: 56 of the 58 subjects showed upward movement, 2 vacillated slightly over 20 years; only 6% of the cases showed a downward shift between any two testings; no subject skipped over any stages; none of the subjects solidly reached Stage 5, although 8 subjects showed some Stage 5 thinking; few subjects gained more than two full stages over 20 years, most showing a little over one whole-stage shift; changes over a 3- to 4-year interval were usually less than a whole stage; and Stage 4 is the most typical end point. Time-sequential and cohort-sequential analyses (as suggested by Baltes, 1968, and Schaie, 1965) on DIT data over a 6-year span indicate that the age trends in DIT data are not attributable to cohort or generation effects (J. R. Rest, 1979a). Also sample bias and retesting effects do not seem to explain the age trends obtained.

A different line of evidence for the sequential order of the stages comes from Davison's work on the internal structure of the DIT. Using techniques derived from multidimensional scaling, Davison found that the average scale values of the stages are empirically ordered in the way theory predicts (the lowest stages have the lowest scale scores; the scale scores increase along with the theoretical ordering of the stages). The findings on a sample of 160 subjects were cross-validated on a sample of 1,080 subjects (Davison, 1977; Davison et al., 1978).

Further corroboration of the developmental nature of the six stages comes from its correlations with other developmental measures. Also, in educational and intervention studies designed to stimulate more rigorous and more defensible moral thinking, whenever a significant change occurred, it was always upward (described later). Therefore, the evidence is fairly compelling that moral judgment does generally change over time in the pattern roughly indicated by the six-stage model (in its various versions).

The Cognitive Nature of Moral Judgment

A number of subquestions involved in this issue require different sorts of answers:

1. In what sense is each higher stage more conceptually adequate than the preceding stage? This theoretical-philosophical question has been discussed in connection with the description of stages. Kohlberg spoke in terms of progressive differentiation, new role-taking operations, and more encompassing perspectives on society. I dealt with the

question in terms of increasingly more adequate concepts of coordinating social expectations and balancing individual interests in cooperative social systems.

2. Another questions is: Is not morality more a matter of the heart than of the head? Or restated, Is not morality governed more by affective processes than cognitive ones? This question presupposes a separation of affect and cognition that was criticized earlier in this chapter. Moreover, I suspect that people who raise this question probably are thinking of morality primarily in terms of empathic arousal (Component I), or the relative importance of moral values over other values (Component III), or the ego strength to follow through on one's beliefs (Component IV). These other aspects of morality all are part processes (Components I, III, and IV), just as moral judgment is a part process (Component II)—and all have both affective and cognitive sides. However, if the intent of the question is to suggest that moral judgment (as defined and operationalized here) can be accounted for by some personality trait (such as Rokeach's Value Survey, 1973) or attitude (such as Hogan's Survey of Ethical Attitudes, 1975), the evidence available is decidedly against this view. A review of 200 correlations of moral judgment with personality and attitude variables shows low or inconsistent correlations (J. R. Rest, 1979a; see also Sullivan & Quarter, 1972; Wonderly & Kupfersmid, 1979), whereas the correlations of moral judgment with cognitive variables (IQ, Piagetian measures, achievement tests, etc.) are consistently significant, generally in the .20s to .50s range (Colby & Kohlberg, 1975; Kohlberg, 1969; J. R. Rest, 1979a). This should not be too surprising if we recall that moral judgment (as a Component II process) involves the identification of legitimate claims of people in a situation and the prioritization or balancing of these claims by integrative concepts.

3. Another set of questions is, What evidence is there that the six moral stages comprise an order of increasing psychological complexity and difficulty for subjects? Even if the theoretical description depicts increasing complexity, perhaps the *subjects* themselves do not find it any more difficult to use the concepts of the higher stages than lower stages. Furthermore, what is the evidence that people's use of the higher stages is limited by their cognitive capability to think in those terms? What is the evidence that subjects are using the concepts at the upper limits of their capacity?

One line of research has addressed this issue by devising a test of the ability to understand arguments at each stage (for review see J. R. Rest, 1979a; see also Lawrence, 1978). A test of moral comprehension differs from a test of moral judgment in that a test of comprehension does not ask subjects which concepts they use in making a moral decision but rather inventories which concepts a subject understands. One type of comprehension test asks a subject to paraphrase and discuss statements exemplifying the various stages (to show that the subject understands the main idea of the statement). Another type asks a subject to match one statement with the best equivalent among a list of alternatives (where presumably a correct match indicates comprehension of the stage-distinctive idea). The major conclusions of the comprehension studies are:

Comprehension of the stages is cumulative, that is, Stage 1 concepts are easiest to understand, then Stage 2, then Stage 3, and so on. A person who shows high comprehension of Stage 4, for instance, also shows high comprehension of Stages 1, 2, and 3.

Subjects who comprehend high-stage concepts tend to use those concepts in their judgments about what ought to be done. Subjects who show low comprehension tend to have low moral judgment scores. In two studies using Kohlberg's test and in eight studies using the DIT, comprehension scores were related significantly to moral judgment scores—in five studies the correlations were in the .50s and .60s. Only in one study using a shortened version of the comprehension test was the relation nonsignificant (see J. R. Rest, 1979a).

Longitudinal studies indicate that as subjects increase in comprehending high-stage concepts, they also increase in moral judgment scores. Of the subjects who showed upward patterns of movement on the DIT over 4-years, 81% also showed upward movement in comprehension (J. R. Rest, 1979a). Although there are problems in the reliability of the comprehension measures, these data generally support the idea that *cognitive* advancement is a major concomitant in moral-judgment advancement.

Experimental studies support the conclusions of the comprehension studies (see especially McGeorge, 1975, and the review in J. R. Rest, 1979a). To manipulating test instructions, subjects were given the special incentive to raise their scores by being asked to fake high in one condition, to fake low in another condition, and to take the DIT under the usual instructions in a third condition. The fake-high instructions were as follows:

Please assist us by trying to fill in the questionnaire so that it records the highest, most mature level of social and ethical judgment possible. Fill in the questionnaire as someone concerned only with the very highest principles of justice would fill it in. (McGeorge, 1975, p. 108)

Subjects had been forewarned about meaningless items and told that if an item did not make sense to them, it should be rated low. Under the fake-high condition, subjects did not increase their scores nor was the M score (endorsement of meaningless items) increased. It seems that as long as subjects are choosing only items that are meaningful, they cannot increase their scores. Under the fake-low condition, subjects dramatically lowered their scores. Presumably, subjects understood well the lower stage items and found it easy to choose lower items. This suggests that generally under normal conditions, subjects are using the highest concepts that they understand, rejecting those at lower stages because of their inadequacy and not choosing the higher items because they do not make sense. Lawrence (1978) corroborated these findings by intensively interviewing subjects about reasons for their ratings of DIT items.

It should not be concluded, however, that having a higher stage concept *inevitably* leads to using that concept in making a moral judgment. Although the previous studies indicate that this is *usually* the case, Lawrence's study (1978) indicates that under special circumstances people may set aside their own best notions of fairness in a situation and use an externally defined code for selecting and justifying an action. Among other subject groups, Lawrence studied a group of ultraconservative seminarians. These seminarians considered their radical religious dogmatism to be a sign of faith and a condition of salvation. Lawrence noticed that the DIT scores of this group were much lower than what would be expected from their comprehension scores and education. In fact, these subjects' endorsement of Stage 4 on the DIT was higher than ever seen before. Lawrence intensively interviewed the subjects about how they went about making their moral judgments. She found that the seminarians deliberately set aside their own notions of fairness in the situation and instead reacted to the DIT items according to the item's congruence with religious doctrine. Some stated that value judgments should not be based on earthbound, human rationality but on divine revelation. Therefore, any DIT item that seemed to agree with their religious ideology was given a high rating, and items not in conformity with their religious ideology were downrated regardless of whether it made sense personally to them or not. Lawrence's study indicates that ideology and commitment to dogma can preempt judging on the basis of a rational analysis of a social situation and one's own notions of fairness. Perhaps in other cultures (especially non-Western cultures that are not so rationalistic-individualistic) such preempting by ideology is not so rare as in the American populations involved in our studies.

4. Another set of questions is: What are the basic cognitive building blocks of moral judgment? Are certain stages of Piagetian logical operations prerequisite to certain moral-judgment stages? Are certain stages of role taking prerequisite?

The correlation of moral judgment with measures of cognitive ability has already been discussed. In the case of Piagetian measures of formal operations and measures of role taking, some studies report correlations with moral judgment as high as the .60s and .70s (Colby & Kohlberg, 1975). But the question here is not whether measures developed in the cognitive developmental tradition (Piagetian logical operations or role-taking measures) correlate with moral judgment nor whether they correlate more highly than psychometric cognitive measures developed in the individual-differences tradition (IQ, achievement, and aptitude tests). Instead, the question is whether elementary components of moral judgment can be identified in terms of Piagetian logical operations and social perspective taking. Indeed, this has been a major emphasis throughout the 1970s of what might be called the Harvard Structuralist School (Broughton, 1978; Byrne, 1974; Colby, 1973; Damon, 1975; Fritz, 1974; Keasey, 1975; Kuhn, Langer, Kohlberg, & Haan, 1977; Selman, 1971, 1976; Walker, 1980; Walker & Richards, 1979). The cornerstone of this approach is that new constellations of ideas (new perspectives, new stages) are made possible by new logical operations. Piaget, of course, is the originator of this view in describing, for instance, the acquisition of concrete operations in terms of the logical operations of reversibility, coordination of classes, and so on, and the acquisition of formal operations in terms of the INRC operations. The Harvard structuralists attempt to carry this program into the social and moral domain by postulating a succession of new logical operations that, in turn, make possible new transformations of thinking about morality and the social world. This work cannot be described in detail here, but an example will illustrate the general approach. Inhelder and Piaget (1955/1958) discuss the coordination of inversion and reciprocity as a logical operation that makes possible a new organization of thinking that begins formal operations. Byrne

(1974) and Selman (1976) postulate that this new logical operation makes possible "mutual perspective taking" (Selman's Stage 3 of social perspective taking), and Colby and Kohlberg (1975) postulate that these new operations make possible Stage 3 of moral judgment, the morality of interpersonal concordance. Colby and Kohlberg state (1975):

> At Stage 3 [of moral judgment,] role-taking becomes mutual in the sense that each individual can consider each other's point of view both simultaneously and mutually, while at the same time taking a third party "impartial" perspective and orienting to the relationship between the individuals. The complexity of this role-taking can be illustrated by an analysis of the Golden Rule, which is first understood at moral judgment Stage 3. The role-taking involved in understanding the Golden Rule, a role-taking level which is presupposed by moral judgment Stage 3, involves the coordination of inversion and reciprocity. "Do unto others as they do unto you." A correct understanding of the Golden Rule necessitates both the taking of at least two perspectives, either in some sequence or simultaneously, and the comprehension of the reciprocal nature of functioning among these alternative viewpoints. The mutual role-taking involved in a correct use of the Golden Rule involves the negation of an action (e.g., hitting the other) on the basis of a reciprocal operation, the taking of another's perspective as recipient of this action. (pp. 39–40)

Other correspondence between Piaget's logical stages with Selman's perspective-taking stages and Kohlberg's moral judgment stages also are postulated. In each case, the logical operation is seen as a prerequisite to the parallel social role-taking stage, and each role-taking stage is prerequisite to the corresponding moral judgment stage; the new operation makes possible the new organization of thinking at each stage in each domain (logical, social perspective, moral).

Several research paradigms have been used to study prerequisite relationships. One paradigm (that might be called contemporaneous contingent association) tests subjects on two variables (e.g., Piagetian formal-operations tasks and moral judgment) and examines the pattern of association between the two variables. For instance, if beginning formal operations is a prerequisite for Stage 3 moral judgment, then we can expect to find some subjects who lack both, some subjects who have both, and some subjects who have the prerequisite beginning formal operations but not Stage 3 moral judgment. We expect to find no subjects who lack beginning formal operations but do have Stage 3 moral judgment (if Piagetian logical operations are necessary but not sufficient for the corresponding stage of moral judgment). In other words, the crucial test of this paradigm is to find no subjects in one cell of a 2 × 2 contingency table. Colby and Kohlberg's review (1975) reports that pooled data from five studies show that only 1% of the subjects who lacked beginning formal operations were at Stage 3 moral judgment.

In Kurdek's review (1978) of the relation of role taking to moral judgment, "only about half of the reported associations are significant" (p. 8). Kurdek, however, cautions against using these inconsistent findings to conclude that role taking is not related to moral judgment, citing methodological shortcomings of the studies reviewed and the variety of measures of both constructs. The Harvard structuralists have not claimed that *all* measures of role taking are related to *all* measures of moral judgment—in fact, when Selman's measure of social perspective taking is related to Kohlberg's more recent measure of moral judgment, consistent relationships are reported (Colby & Kohlberg, 1975; Selman, 1976; Walker, 1980). Furthermore, researchers have not always been clear or in agreement about the theoretical relationship of role taking to moral judgment. A variety of linkages are conceivable between role taking and moral judgment:

1. Selman and the Harvard structuralists claim that Selman's stages of social perspective taking and Kohlberg's moral judgment stages share fundamental cognitive operations so that social perspective taking is a prerequisite to the corresponding moral judgment stage. This relation is most appropriately demonstrated not by product-moment correlations but by showing that the moral judgment stages are never higher than the corresponding social perspective stage.

2. Alternatively, other researchers seem to view the relation of role taking to moral judgment as asserting that acuity in interpreting social situations is related to sophistication in formulating moral ideals, that is, Component I is related to Component II. The two presumably are related because one has to see a problem before reasoning about it.

3. Some researchers seem to postulate a connection as stemming from a general prosocial orientation—thinking of others is related to wanting to help others and valuing others and more lofty moral ide-

als. It is all part of being a warm and nice person.

4. Another view of the connection is that role taking involves decentering from one's own exclusive point of view and coordinating the perspectives of others (anticipating what each person wants and values, how each person is aware of the internal states of others, and how each person is aware of mutual understandings and agreements); so also schemes of cooperation involve balancing each participant's interests and establishing a shared basis of mutually beneficial interaction.

Thus, various interpretations about the relation of role taking to moral judgment come from studies using different measures, different types of association (e.g., correlations rather than the missing cell in contingency tables), and different theoretical expectations about the nature of the connection—but such studies do not invalidate the prerequisite notion of the Harvard structuralists.

A second paradigm (that might be called longitudinal prerequisite movement) examines the patterns of change on two variables over successive testings and stipulates that over time the prerequisite variable can shoot ahead of the dependent variable, but not vice versa. For instance, Selman (1973) examined longitudinal cases on both moral judgment and social perspective taking and found no instance where moral judgment was at a higher stage than the corresponding social perspective stage, although moral judgment sometimes lagged behind social perspective taking.

The third paradigm (intervention readiness) pretests and posttests subjects before and after an intervention; it stipulates that subjects who already have the prerequisite operation will respond more to the intervention than subjects who do not have the prerequisite. The most impressive studies of this kind are by Walker (Walker, 1980; Walker & Richards, 1979). For instance, in one part of these studies, Walker identified subjects at Stage 2 moral judgment, some of whom had the logical and perspective-taking prerequisites for moral Stage 3, some of whom did not. As an intervention, Walker exposed subjects to conflicting advice, using Stage 3 reasoning. A sizable proportion of Stage 2 subjects with the prerequisites showed movement to Stage 3, whereas *none* of the subjects without the prerequisites moved to Stage 3. Walker's studies are exemplary in the use of control groups and follow-up posttesting, and for producing strong data trends.[11]

In general, a number of studies using a number of approaches support the hypothesis that certain

Piagetian logical operations and certain Selman stages of perspective taking are prerequisite components of certain Kohlbergian moral judgment stages. Even so, several fundamental problems remain. For one, the accounts do not agree about which logical operations are crucial for each moral judgment stage. Kuhn et al. (1977) and Keasey (1976) cite different moral operations and relationships with Piagetian cognitive operations than Colby and Kohlberg (1975). Furthermore, a systematic and comprehensive account has not yet been written that logically relates all the scoring features used to define a moral judgment stage with the supposed operations that give rise to the stage structure. Second, the research paradigms presuppose a hard-stage model of development. Subjects are said to "have" or "not have" certain operations and to be "in" one stage or another; stage-by-stage comparisons are made between constructs (i.e., this stage of Piagetian stages is paralleled by that stage of moral judgment). As mentioned before, the difficulty with such notions is that all developmental assessment is both method and situation specific. Different scoring systems, different dilemmas, different conventions for indexing, or different stringency in scoring standards would shift around the subjects' stage scores in any study and give a different set of correspondences between moral judgment stage and Piagetian stages than those postulated here. A mischievous researcher could probably devise tasks and scoring rules for each construct so that the results would support the opposite prerequisite relationships than those proposed here (e.g., that moral judgment was a prerequisite to Piagetian formal operations rather than vice versa). Furthermore, the prerequisite operation is typically assessed in a different domain (e.g., formal operations in a chemistry task) than the moral domain, and there is no reason to suspect that showing certain operations in one domain indicates the presence of those operations in the other domain. The stage-by-stage correspondences that the research to date supports must be understood as applying to specific sets of assessment techniques; generalization beyond these specific sets of situations, test instruments, response modes, or scoring conventions is unknown. Third, as research into cognitive processes continues, many researchers have increasing reservations about Piaget's specific descriptions of cognitive operations as completely adequate accounts of cognitive organization (see Flavell, 1978; see other chapters in this volume). A theoretical approach to social cognition and moral judgment that is so closely tied to Piaget's specific characterizations is vulnerable to the same criticisms.

5. Another set of questions is: Can moral judgment be reduced to more general cognitive development or to verbal facility? Is moral judgment development distinct from other kinds of cognitive development? What information do moral judgment scores give beyond IQ or verbal facility or Piagetian scores?

Some writers state that it is not parsimonious to regard moral judgment as distinct from general cognitive ability and that moral-judgment scores represent little more than verbal fluency or nonspecific reasoning skills. The available evidence goes against this view.

a. There are some subjects who have very high scores on general aptitude measure and very low scores on moral judgment. The film maker, Stanley Kubrick, gave us a memorable character a few years ago, Dr. Strangelove. The doctor was portrayed as a genius in technical matters but rather obtuse about questions of fairness. He was intelligent, articulate, fond of fine-sounding phrases, like "duty to humanity" and "moral obligation," but the structure of his thinking never rose above self-serving Stage 2. The existence of Dr. Strangelove types speaks against the parsimony view.

b. Correlational studies show that measures of moral thinking cluster among themselves more highly than they intercorrelate with nonmoral cognitive measures (J. R. Rest, 1979a).

c. A number of studies show that moral judgment scores have unique and significant predictability to behavior and other criteria even when the shared variance with general aptitude is statistically partialed out or is controlled by design and subject selection (J. R. Rest, 1979a). Moral-judgment scores convey useful information not conveyed in general ability measures.

d. Experimental evidence for the distinctiveness of moral judgment comes from a study of the differential effects of ethics classes and logic classes. College students were pretested and posttested on the DIT and a test of logical thinking: students taking the ethics course gained on the DIT but not on the logic test; students taking the logic course gained on the logic test but not on the DIT. The interaction of the type of course with the type of gain was significant, indicating the distinctiveness of moral reasoning from reasoning in general (J. R. Rest, 1979a).

In summary, moral judgment is significantly related to other cognitive variables, but cannot be reduced to general aptitude or verbal ability.

Determinants, Conditions, and Mechanisms of Change

From Piaget come two suggestions for what promotes structural change in moral judgment: cognitive disequilibrium and peer interaction. The first follows from Piaget's general discussions of assimilation and accommodation and his view that all cognitive structures are forms of organizing experience and action, hence, are forms of equilibration. When new experience cannot be assimilated into existing cognitive structures, then the person is in a state of disequilibrium and searches for new cognitive structures to reestablish cognitive equilibrium. Piaget's other suggestion for what produces structural change in moral judgment is more concrete: social interaction of peers who negotiate and bargain with each other for arranging mutually beneficial agreements. This give and take among peers fosters a recognition of the *reciprocity of cooperation,* of the *equality among peers* (each is free to enter into cooperative agreements and each must be satisfied with the arrangement for it to work); and it also fosters *role-taking opportunities,* that is, trying to figure out what the situation must look like from the other person's point of view. Experiences in coordinating, reconciling, and balancing various points of view are said to be crucial determinants in moral development.

Short-term Intervention Studies. Turiel (1966, 1972) has elaborated the notion of cognitive disequilibrium as the mechanism of change in moral judgment. He introduced an ingenious experimental paradigm for studying change and has influenced a major feature of Kohlbergian moral educational programs (discussion of controversial moral problems and +1 modeling). In a short-term experimental intervention, Turiel exposed one group of subjects to arguments one stage above their own stage (the +1 condition), another group to two stages above their own (+2), and a third group to arguments one stage below their own (−1). Turiel predicted that the group exposed to arguments one stage above their own would show the greatest change on a posttest because, in such a condition, subjects could grasp the significance of the argument and would experience disequilibrium (hence supplying the crucial condition for the transformation of cognitive structures). In the −1 condition, subjects would be unimpressed with arguments less adequate than their own. In the +2 condition, the arguments would be too far advanced for the subjects to understand. A number of short-term experimental studies have used the basic paradigm of inducing change through exposure to different stage reasoning than the subject's own predominant stage (Arbuthnot, 1975;

Berkowitz, Gibbs, Broughton, 1980; Keasey, 1973, 1974; Matefy & Acksen, 1976; Tracy & Cross, 1973; Walker & Richards, 1976; see also Walker, 1979, for a review of published studies). Unfortunately, these studies have not produced consistent or powerful findings. Furthermore, journal publishing is biased toward selecting studies that have found some sort of significant trend, rejecting those that have found no significant trends. It is my impression that more studies of the latter sort have been done than are published, among them being a large-scale, exquisitely designed study that Turiel (1973) planned as a replication and extension of his 1966 study. As is the case for short-term disequilibration studies in general, the results of Turiel's 1973 study present a jumble of contradictions and no convincing trends. For instance, no significant differences were found between experimental and control groups on the full pretests and posttests; no significant differences were found on the basis of stage exposure, method of presentation, or time of posttest; only some paradoxical differences were found on the stories used in the treatment condition (e.g., the +2 condition produced more change than the +1 condition).

More has been learned from the disequilibration studies about general research strategy than about moral development in particular. Several writers (e.g., Flavell, 1977; Kuhn, 1974; McCall, 1977; J. R. Rest, 1979a; and Wohlwill, 1973) have pointed out difficulties in the training study as a paradigm for discovering the determinants of development. The problems include:

1. The development of cognitive structures may come about by many routes, helped by various combinations of experiences. Therefore, a strategy (the experimental method) designed to isolate *the* necessary and sufficient condition for developmental change falsely assumes that a single antecedent regularly precedes an event. The most powerful experimental manipulation in developmental research may be the deprivation study rather than the enhancement study.

2. Short-term treatments (sometimes only 20 min.) may be too brief to simulate a slowly moving process like moral-judgment development (in Kohlberg's recent longitudinal data (in Colby, et al., in press) it takes 13.9 years on the average to move one full stage). Measures of moral judgment were designed to chart the major epochs in lifespan development and, therefore, are too gross for such short-term studies. Furthermore, if a 20-min. intervention is effective in shifting development stage, then one must question if basic cognitive organization is real-

ly being changed or whether the shifts reflect changes in the evocation and utilization of the basic structures.

3. The disequilibration studies assume that the exposure to different stage reasoning is disequilibrating—they assume that an external manipulation can initiate an internal state. No evidence supports this assumption (see Flavell, 1977, for further discussion of disequilibration), and furthermore, attempts to detect the occurrence of the state of disequilibrium (e.g., confusion, contradiction, and inconsistency) have been unsuccessful (Berkowitz, 1981).

4. It is not clear that current methods of assessment are sensitive enough for short-term training studies. Not only are the measures coarse grained but also the experimental treatments themselves may violate the assumptions implicit in testing naive subjects. Also the test-retest reliabilities may not be sufficiently high for the microscopic shifts expected from the treatments.

5. Most short-term experimental studies have assumed a hard-line view of the stage concept, that is, if a subject produces explanations scored at Stage 3 on the Heinz-and-the-drug dilemma, then that subject is "in" Stage 3, will be "in" Stage 3 going into the intervention, and that moral arguments advanced by others not at Stage 3 on new dilemmas will be foreign to the subject's thinking on the new dilemma (+1, or +2, or −1, etc.). But because subjects have several stage schemes available to them and because different contexts and tasks evoke different organizing schemes, these inferences from the standard interview may not be valid.

One promising outgrowth of the disequilibration intervention studies is the work of Berkowitz and colleagues on the fine-grained analysis of ongoing dialogue between individuals (Berkowitz, 1980; Berkowitz & Gibbs, 1981). Concentrating on how individuals reason with each other when discussing moral dilemmas, Berkowitz describes the transactions with such terms as "competitive paraphrase," "justification request," "counterconsideration," "common ground, integration," "competitive juxtaposition," and so on. A scoring manual to analyze transcriptions of two-person dialogue now provides a way of describing in detail what goes on in moral discussions; consequently, these experiences can be related to development in moral reasoning.

Educational Programs. Longer term interventions have been undertaken as educational programs. The primary purpose of these studies has been practical (Can educational programs be devised to foster moral judgment development?) rather than

to gather purely scientific evidence on the nature of moral judgment. As is common in educational research, the researchers usually cannot exercise tight control over the schools or students, and shortcomings exist in the design and execution of many studies. The rationale for most of the programs is that structural change is facilitated by disequilibration and peer interaction. Accordingly, peer discussion of controversial moral problems has been a major feature of Kohlbergian moral education (see Hersh, Paolitto, & Reimer, 1979, for discussion of studies and newer educational developments). Presumably, practice in solving moral dilemmas, mutual probing of each other's solutions, and accommodating and negotiating with others are the key ingredients. The study by Blatt and Kohlberg (1975) was the first and remains one of the most impressive in terms of design and strength of trends. The major finding was that peer discussion of controversial moral dilemmas seems to foster moral judgment development. Many studies on variations of the theme have ensued (see reviews of several dozen studies in Lawrence, 1980; Lockwood, 1978; J. R. Rest, 1979a), and perhaps half of the interventions have produced significantly greater gains for the experimental group over the control groups. I have the following impressions from the intervention studies:

1. It is difficult to raise the average moral-judgment scores of any group by an intervention. Many studies show no change; when change occurs, it tends to be slight (typically one tenth to one twentieth of the effective range of the Kohlberg test or the DIT); and the final scores of the "treated" groups are still far from the scores of moral philosophy/political science doctoral students. In a way, this recalcitrance to change suggests that moral judgment scores reflect something basic in a person's thinking and not the learning of superficial verbal phrases or tricks of argumentation.

2. When students have been encouraged to discuss moral dilemmas among themselves and to scrutinize each other's reasoning, whenever change occurred from pretest to posttest, it was upward (according to the theory).

3. The interventions that have an explicit and heavy emphasis on moral reasoning (rather than broad cultural exposure, an artistic emphasis, general philosophy, or social studies) are more likely to produce change.

4. Interventions shorter than three months are unlikely to produce significant change.

5. There is no evidence that +1 modeling is the effective condition for growth (see Berkowitz, 1981).

6. Teaching Kohlberg's six-stage theory in the intervention is likely to complicate interpretation of change scores. On the posttest, if a subject starts enunciating arguments and characteristics that she has read or heard are Stage 6 in Kohlberg's theory, it is often difficult to determine how well the subject understands these arguments.

7. It is as yet unclear what specific pedagogical practices or curriculum material are most effective (or what works with whom and under what conditions).

Correlates of Development.   In addition to intervention studies that seek to manipulate the experience of subjects, many correlational studies address the question of which experiences foster moral-judgment development. Of course, with correlational findings, one can never be sure that the crucial variable has been identified nor can one be sure of unidirectional causality, but many of the correlational studies have the virtue of drawing information from naturalistic settings and of studying conditions that have been operative for years (not just 20 min. or even several months). Correlational studies have investigated the influences of the three sources of role-taking opportunities discussed by Kohlberg (1969): peers, parents, and participation in the institutions of the wider culture.

Consistent with both Kohlberg and Piaget, moral judgment development is correlated with indices of peer interaction: several studies report that moral judgment development is correlated with participation in clubs and special activity groups, popularity among peers, and service in leadership roles (Harris, Mussen, & Rutherford, 1976; Keasey, 1971; Kohlberg, 1958). Moreover, studies by Edwards (1978) and Maqsud (1977) of students in Kenya and Nigeria found that college and secondary students attending culturally diverse schools (presumably providing more challenging exchange of different points of view than culturally homogeneous schools) were more advanced in moral judgment development; that students in residential or semiresidential schools (presumably intensifying the peer interaction) were more advanced than students living at home (a finding also reported for American college students in J. R. Rest, 1979b); and that students attribute the greatest changes in their personal values to encountering ethnic and racial heterogeneity at school and to going away from home to live (Edwards, 1980).

Although Piaget deemphasized the positive influence by parents on moral-judgment development, Kohlberg has characterized a positive but *not unique* influence of parents. Several studies have indicated

a positive influence of democratic family-discussion styles (Dickinson, 1979; Holstein, 1972; Parikh, 1980; Schoffeitt, 1971), and of the induction style of discipline (Hoffman, 1970; Saltzstein, 1976). Edwards (1980) characterizes the kind of parent that facilitates growth in children in contrast to Piaget's view of parents as constraining:

> The most successful parents are expected to be those verbal and overtly rational people who encourage warm and close relations with children and who promote a ''democratic'' style of family life. That is, they foster discussions oriented toward reasoned understanding of moral issues and toward a fair consideration of everyone's viewpoint. (p. 31)

Both peer influence and parent influence on development are consistent with Kohlberg's concept of role-taking opportunities. Moreover, the concept extends to the influence of cultural and class differences. Although Kohlberg claims that his moral judgment stages describe development cross-culturally—as Piaget claims for his stages of logical-physical development, Kohlberg also postulates that differences in role-taking opportunities among cultures and socioeconomic class can speed up or slow down development through the stages. Lower socioeconomic classes in several countries seem to go through the stages slower than high SES groups (Kohlberg, 1969):

> The lower class cannot and does not feel as much sense of power in, and responsibility for, the institutions of government and economy as does the middle class. This, in turn, tends to generate less of a disposition to view these institutions from a generalized, flexible and organized perspective based on various rules as vantage points. (pp. 401–402)

Similarly, Kohlberg states that people in underprivileged, non-Western countries have a slower development rate in moral judgment than affluent, Western countries: ''The Mexican, Turkish, and Taiwanese villager grows up with a sense of participation in the village, but little in the more remote political, economic, and legal system'' (p. 402). Therefore, the lack of participation in secondary institutions (the national legal system and government, bureaucracies of industry) makes it less likely that those people will evolve the conceptual schemes of Stages 4, 5, and 6 that deal especially with moral problems at this more abstract level.

Edwards (1980) reviews studies using Kohlberg's test in Mexico, Taiwan, Kenya, the Bahamas, Honduras, India, Nigeria, Israel, Thailand, Turkey, Great Britain, Canada, New Zealand, and the Yucatan. Two studies (one in Turkey, the other in the Bahamas) report longitudinal age trends (Turiel et al., 1978; White et al., 1978), the other studies report cross-sectional age trends and various correlates of moral judgment. The major findings to come from these studies are that:

1. Kohlberg's interview technique and scoring guides can be modified for use in other cultures, producing scorable material and satisfactory inter-judge agreement.
2. Age trends in other countries also show younger subjects using the lower stages and older, more educated subjects using the higher stages.
3. Stages 4 and above do not appear in the protocols of semiliterate people coming from peasant or tribal communities.

Simpson (1974) contends that the absence of Kohlberg's so-called higher stages in foreign cultures is evidence against the universality of the six-stage scheme. Simpson argues that Kohlberg's whole approach is a flagrant case of cultural bias: Kohlberg portrays his particular interpretation of the Western philosophical tradition as the standard by which all people's morality is to be judged; he makes invidious comparisons with people who use different strategies to explore and explain the world, who do not use the language of graduate philosophy students or who do not orient their values to the particular institutions of the Western, industrialized democracies.

Admittedly, finding that protocols from foreign cultures can be coded and that they display age trends according to theory does not ensure either that the testing procedure has been sensitive to their capacity or that the categories of the scoring system adequately capture the particular patterns of thinking developed in a particular culture. It could be that forcing the responses of non-Western people into Kohlberg's scheme is a distortion of the underlying organization of their thinking. But in favor of the Kohlberg position, the research done so far has succeeded in using the Kohlberg scheme as a classification tool (sometimes by researchers native to the culture) and has replicated the sequentiality of at least the lower stages. Furthermore, that some people in one culture score higher than people in another culture is not proof of bias in the measuring procedure—otherwise, we would have to say that the

foot-ruler was ethnocentric because the average American is taller than the average Japanese. The crux of the controversy is whether other organizational structures develop in people in foreign cultures than those depicted in the six-stage model. Note that we are not concerned here with people's overall morality (in the sense of all four components); the issue of Kohlbergian stages is concerned with the organizational schemes a person uses to prioritize and balance the competing claims of the parties in a moral dilemma. If structures develop in different cultures other than those depicted in the six-stage model, they must still provide guidelines (as do the six stages) for dealing with certain perennial human problems, such as, What special duties go along with friendship and kinship? What role does personal interest play in deciding what one ought to do? Is it ever right to violate established social expectations? On what basis can I press a claim on other people—that they ought to do something for me? Under what conditions should I follow the commands of someone else? Should social rules ever be changed, if so, how? The schemes of the six-stage model address these questions and others, and it remains to be seen if other organizational structures can be identified that supply answers. Furthermore, as suggested earlier in discussion of the Lawrence (1978) study, it may be that in some cultures people typically handle moral problems by invoking religious or other ideological rules rather than attempting to solve them through their own developing sense of what is fair or right.

Recently a number of writers (Gilligan, 1977; Holstein, 1976) have claimed that the six-stage scheme is sexist because (allegedly) women usually are credited with no development beyond Stage 3 (good-boy/good-girl orientation) and men typically are scored higher. Because of revisions in the Kohlberg scoring system that may affect this point, it is problematic to summarize general trends across studies. It is clear that the six-stage model has produced a mix of trends, some studies finding males ahead of females, some the opposite, but most with no difference. A review of the DIT studies (J. R. Rest, 1979a) shows that over 90% of them show no sex difference and Walker (1982) shows a similar trend for studies using Kohlberg's test. The evidence at hand hardly supports the view that the six-stage model is biased against women. When sex differences occur, they are likely owing to differences in educational opportunity, suggesting a bias in the social system, not in the definitions of the stages. The claim that women are more sensitive and more caring than men may or may not be true, but it has relevance to Component I or III processes and is of questionable relevance to Component II.

In addition to Kohlberg's notion of role-taking opportunities (involving the influence of peers, parents, and the cultural milieu), another influence must be recognized: formal education. Indeed, formal schooling has been the most powerful correlate of DIT scores, even more so than chronological age when adult subjects are included. Education is also a powerful correlate among adults in the Kohlberg data. As mentioned previously, cross-sectional data suggest that moral judgment development reaches a plateau whenever people stop their formal education. A small longitudinal study (J. R. Rest, 1979b) confirms the cross-sectional data: one subgroup of subjects went from high school to college, another subgroup of subjects did not. In high school, the subgroups were not significantly different on the DIT or moral comprehension test, but as the years passed, the college group increasingly diverged from the noncollege group on the DIT and on the moral comprehension test. Another corroboration of the importance of formal education comes from cross-cultural studies: Within a given country, the more highly educated have higher moral judgment scores.

Developmentalists in the Piagetian tradition have deemphasized the influence of formal education because they contend that basic cognitive structures are not directly learned but are self-constructed general schemes. Cognitive developmentalists insist that basic schemes of meaning involve self-discovery and active integration of experience, not the passive incorporation of direct teachings. Often, the impact of formal schooling is viewed as learning superficial verbalisms, not the forging of the fundamental structures of meaning. And yet, the influence of formal education is too striking to deny its structural effect. The mechanisms of the effects of formal education need not be mindless indoctrination nor the memorization of empty verbalisms. Evidence already has been cited that moral judgment development involves development in moral comprehension and that moral judgment cannot be reduced to verbal skills. It is at least plausible that formal education directs the mind to attend to certain problems and proposes certain solutions that, when understood, become conceptual tools in one's own thinking (even if not spontaneously discovered de novo). Even so, formal education (and particularly formal courses in moral philosophy) does not seem to be absolutely necessary for higher stages of moral judgment development. Some subjects without high levels of formal education experiences attain high scores. Furthermore, students without any moral philosophy show the influence of formal education. In fact, the available evidence suggests that the impact of formal education comes from many aspects of the experience (milieu and extracurricular activities as well as purely academic activities) and that different people are affected by different aspects (J. R. Rest, 1979b; Volker, 1980).

Moral Judgment and Behavior

Why should moral judgment be related to behavior? Enough research has shown that morality is not a strong unitary trait in which all measures of thinking, feeling, prosocial and antisocial behavior tightly cohere. Moral judgment is part of Component II processes, involving how the various considerations and claims of participants in a moral dilemma are given priorities or balanced. The six-stage model postulates that people have basic, generic schemes about cooperation—how people balance their interests, help each other, and coordinate their activity for shared goals—and that the six stages represent these ideas. Furthermore, when a person is faced with the conflicting claims of a situation, he invokes one (or more) of these basic schemes as a basic pattern for organizing his thinking about that situation. Subjects differ among themselves in the degree to which the higher stage schemes are generally available and can be used (this difference is reflected in the subject's developmental score). But subjects also may differ in how they apply the scheme to a particular situation (e.g., recall the example earlier of two ways of applying Stage 4 to the Heinz dilemma); they may differ in the degree to which religious or other ideological doctrines preempt or influence their sense of fairness in judging the situation; they may differ in all the other processes of Components I, III, and IV (note that none of these differences are reflected in the moral judgment score). Therefore, moral judgment is one player in a large cast of players, and even if it is a star, it is not the whole show.

The relation of moral judgment to behavior, therefore, is complicated and mediated by many other factors. Researchers who correlate moral judgment measures with behavior measures usually have not attended to other factors, nor have they typically undertaken a logical analysis to describe how one stage scheme may predispose action within a particular situation, whereas another stage scheme may predispose other action. For some of the behaviors studied (e.g., smoking marijuana, being a virgin) it is difficult to work out a clear directive from the six stages, much less predict a developmental trend in behavior that logically parallels the development in moral judgment.

A further complication should be mentioned.

The current methods of assessing moral judgment (in the Kohlberg tradition) involve verbal reports of subjects about hypothetical dilemmas. Information of this sort has been invaluable for discovering organizational structures in people's moral thinking. However, we have no direct assurance that the schemes that a person verbalizes in a hypothetical situation are those operative in actual decision making in real situations. Usually researchers have assumed that the schemes invoked by a subject in response to the Heinz dilemma are also the schemes operative in some other actual behavioral situation. In one of the few studies on this point, Haan (1975) compared moral reasoning in a student protest situation with the standard hypothetical dilemmas and found little correspondence. Damon (1977), on the other hand, using different notions of moral judgment development, compared reasoning on hypothetical dilemmas with reasoning in actual dilemmas and found close correspondence, although neither reasoning measure correlated highly with actual patterns of behavior. The problem needs much more research.

Despite these complications, however, many studies have found that moral judgment does significantly predict important social phenomena. First, let us consider research relating moral judgment to the value stances that people take on controversial public policy issues. Six studies found significant relationships of the DIT with people's stands on the right to free speech, due process protections of people accused of crimes, and civil rights demonstrations (see review in R. J. Rest, 1979a). In addition, G. J. Rest (1978) found significant relationships with people's views of the Democratic and Republican platform planks in the 1976 presidential election and also with how they voted. Candee (1976) found a correlation of .57 between moral judgment and attitudes toward the Watergate and Lt. Calley situations, scoring answers as either favoring human rights or favoring maintenance of conventions and institutions (e.g., Should American officers be convicted for war crimes ordered by their superiors?). Fishkin, Keniston, and Mackinnon (1973) found that Stage 4 was correlated (.68) with endorsement of conservative slogans (e.g., "America: love it or leave it," "I fight poverty—I work"), whereas the preconventional stages correlated (.34) with violent radical slogans ("Kill the pigs," "Revolution for the hell of it"). Fontana and Noel (1973) found that Stage 4 correlated (.35) with right-wing ideology (e.g., "Protestors in our society do more harm than good because of the aid they give to the Communist cause") and that Stages 5 and 6 were nonsignificantly correlated. Kohlberg and Elfenbein (1975)

found a biserial correlation of .76 between moral judgment and opposition to capital punishment. These studies indicate that variance in the use of stage schemes (as indicated by moral judgment scores) is related to the way people construe certain value controversies. Although moral judgment is distinct from the construct of liberal/conservative attitudes (as discussed earlier, the correlations of moral judgment with general measures of liberalism/conservatism are inconsistent or low), nevertheless, when different schemes of cooperation logically lead to distinct interpretations of specific public policy issues, then the linkages can be strong. Note also that whenever subjective opinions about public policy issues are publicly expressed (as for instance, in voting, in Gallup polls, or in communications to law makers), then these opinions can have impact on the flow of events in the real world.

Blasi (1980) reviewed 75 studies relating moral judgment to behavior in the more usual sense and found that 76% of the studies (57 out of 75) report some significant relationship of behavior with moral judgment. For instance, Campagna and Harter (1975); Fodor (1972, 1973); and McColgan (1975) found moral judgment correlated significantly with delinquency and sociopathic behavior. Haan, Smith, and Block (1968) found relationships with student protest behavior. Harris, Mussen, and Rutherford (1976); R. L. Krebs (1967); Leming (1978); Malinowski (1978); and Schwartz, Feldman, Brown, and Heingartner (1969) found relationships with cheating behavior. Anchor and Cross (1974) and Jacobs (1977) found relationships with behavior in the prisoner's dilemma game. Andreason (1976) and Staub (1974) found relationships with prosocial behavior (aiding someone in distress). Gunzburger, Wagner, and Anooshian (1977) found relationships with patterns of distributive justice. Andreason (1976), Fodor (1971), Froming and Cooper (1976), Rothman (1976), and Saltzstein, Diamond, and Belenky (1972) found relationships with resistance to conformity behavior.

Of course, not all the studies have found significant relationships, and even when found, the relationships are not very strong. Nevertheless, enough studies are affirmative for Blasi's conclusion: "The body of research reviewed here seems to offer considerable support for the hypothesis that moral reasoning and moral action are statistically related" (1980, p. 37). The prospects for increased power in predicting behavior would seem to lie in multivariate studies that take all four components into account. Figuring out how to do this poses a challenge. The problem is not unique to morality but has parallels in social psychology relating attitudes to behavior or in cognitive psychology when relating Piaget's formal operations or IQ tests to real-life adaptive intelligence, and so forth. Studies that simply pick a behavior out of a hat and correlate it with some measure of moral judgment do not add much to our present knowledge.

Other Cognitive-Developmental Approaches

In addition to Piaget and Kohlberg and their direct descendants, other researchers have developed different approaches to studying moral judgment, still, however, drawing on many assumptions and research strategies of the cognitive developmental tradition. These other approaches propose different types of stories and dilemmas, different scoring systems and developmental descriptors, different content areas, and different views of underlying structure. Representatives of these approaches are discussed later, concentrating on those who have established a program of research rather than just a few studies. Each is considered in greater brevity than the foregoing approaches because many fewer studies are involved in each case, in contrast to the hundreds of studies of the previous approaches. This does not necessarily represent a judgment about their future promise but simply reflects differences in data bases.

The Moral Judgment of Young Children

Research on the six-stage model typically involves subjects aged 10 and older, thus missing the development that occurs in young children. Furthermore, the Kohlbergian dilemmas raise issues that are far from the typical involvements of young children (e.g., stealing a drug to save one's dying wife). Damon (1977), for one, has argued that the most appropriate context for studying young children's thinking is the immediate milieu of the child, the situations with which children are most familiar and come into most frequent contact (although it would be interesting to see if a child's thinking is noticeably deficient about dilemmas in a Star Trek setting or in the Saturday morning TV cartoons, all of which are even further removed from the real life of children than the situations in Kohlberg dilemmas). Damon presents children 4 to 12 years old with the following kind of situation:

Here are four little children just about your age. Well, actually, George here is a couple of years younger than the other three. Let's pretend that they were at school one day when their teacher, Miss Townsend, asked them to go outside with a

couple of men. The men told the four kids that they really liked bracelets made by little children, and they asked the kids if they would make some bracelets for them. The kids spent about fifteen or twenty minutes making lots of bracelets for the men. Michelle, here, made a whole lot of bracelets, more than anyone else, and hers were the prettiest ones, too. John and Ellen made some nice bracelets, too; and, as you can see, John is the biggest boy there. George, the younger kid, didn't do so well. He only made half of a bracelet, and it was not very pretty.

Well, one of the men thanked them all for making bracelets, and put before them ten candy bars, which he said was their reward for making the bracelets. But he said that the kids would have to decide what the best way was to split up the candy bars between themselves. Let's pretend that these are the ten candy bars [represent (*sic*) with poker chips]. How do you think the kids should split them up between themselves? (pp. 64–65)

Solidly in the cognitive-developmental tradition, Damon is interested in analyzing subjects' responses to such dilemmas in terms of a taxonomy of underlying principles. Damon classifies response to this dilemma into six response types or levels (1977): At Level 0–A, the child confuses a person's desire with notions of positive justice. At Level 0–A there is no awareness of a need to justify a justice choice with sharable or objective reasons ("I should get more because I like candy bars"). At Level 0–B, the child cites an objective attribute as the basis of distribution—a rudimentary sense of deserving, but one which lacks the more advanced notion of reward for good deeds or special work. The child seems to recognize the necessity of justifying his choice on more general grounds than personal wishes, but appeals to arbitrary characteristics ("We should get more because we're girls"). At Level 1–A, the subject recognizes that each participant in the situation has an interest in the rewards and thinks that the way to resolve conflicts of interest is through administration of strictly equal rewards. Equality is derived from the subject's belief in the similarity of each person's wants and claims. Equal treatment is the only way to deal with conflicts; no mitigating circumstances are allowed ("Give everybody the same"). At Level 1–B, positive justice is the payback of being good or doing well. At Level 1–B, the child recognizes that all participants may have an equal interest or desire for rewards but that some people may have a more deserving claim on rewards, deserving being based on achievement or investment of talent or effort

("Michelle worked hardest and deserves more"). At Level 2–A, the child recognizes a plurality of disparate claims to justice (e.g., merit, need). The special perspective of each party is respected equally while at the same time weighing each claim and adjusting his or her rewards accordingly. A participant with special need or deprivation is given a little extra consideration to affirm the equal respect for all parties. Level 2–A, thus, involves recognizing all claims and working out some sort of compromise that reflects all these diverse claims ("Michelle should get a little more because she made more, but George shouldn't suffer on account of his age"). At Level 2–B, the child recognizes all the diverse claims but goes on further to exclude some claims that are seen as irrelevant to the particular situation. The child at Level 2–B construes the justice solution to a particular situation as serving some larger social good (such as establishing a reward system to encourage overall production or as an opportunity to affirm group cohesion and mutual caring, etc.). Thus, while all participants' claims are considered (because all participants are inherently equal), nevertheless, only those claims are given special weight that create a social structure that furthers certain goals. At Level 2–B, claims are integrated in a variety of ways depending on the contexts ("I'd give more to the kids who produced more because that way they'll all do better next time. But John shouldn't get any more just because he's bigger—giving him more wouldn't help the class next time"). (This discussion only briefly sketches Damon's taxonomy. To appreciate the detail and richness of Damon's analysis, one must read the case material in his 1977 book or the scoring manuals.)

In the tradition of Heinz Werner, Damon suggests, "the best way to conceptualize these levels is as a sequence of unfolding confusions in the mind of the child. Each mental confusion is less sophisticated than the following one" (1977, pp. 74–75). At Level 0–A, fairness is confused with individual desire; at Level 0–B, fairness is confused with some quasi-objective criterion; at Level 1–A, fairness is confused with strict equality; at Level 1–B, comes a confusion with deserving; at Level 2–A, comes a confusion with compromise; at Level 2–B, fairness is confused with "a situational kind of ethic." Damon, however, does not present a clear account for ordering this set of six confusions from least sophisticated to most sophisticated (e.g., Why is the deserving confusion less sophisticated than the compromise confusion?) nor is it clear how resolving the particular confusion at one level inevitably leads to

the particular confusion at the next level (e.g., How does resolving the confusion of strict equality inevitably leave us with the confusion of deserving?). Nevertheless, when one gets beyond this "official" explanation for the ordering of the levels or examines Damon's analysis of cases, one can see a logical progression in the young child's social-moral understanding: the youngest children seem to have little idea about what a sharable plan of action would be that could win support from the other participants; gradually, they get this notion but at first settle on the most obvious solution that could win group support ("everybody gets the same"); eventually, they begin to notice and take account of special circumstances that warrant deviation from simple equality (taking into account harder work, greater talent, special need); and lastly, subjects begin to fit the whole situation into some larger social context. Damon's intriguing analyses of both the distributive justice situation and the authority problem are original and involve a more thorough probing of underlying assumptions and cognitive processes than is found in the social psychology literature that deals with the same type of problem (discussed later).

Damon's approach differs from Kohlberg's in several important ways. Mention has already been made of the focus on a younger age group and on Damon's concern with using child-oriented situations. An important consequence of this is to depict the young child as a much more active social negotiator and more attuned to the purposes and functions of social arrangements than Piaget's heteronomous stage or Kohlberg's Stage 1 would suggest for children in this age range. Another difference lies in the content-structure distinction. All research using the six-stage model has separated subjects' advocacy of one or another action choice (e.g., Heinz should steal or he should not steal) from their reasoning for justifying that choice (which is used to derive stage scores). In contrast, in Damon's research, the particular action choice that a subject advocates (e.g., "give Michelle more," "give all the children the same") is a large determinant of the levels. It is unclear how much scorers using Damon's system rely on the subject's action choice and to what degree the scores reflect different levels of processing and integrating the diverse claims (or whether action choice is distinguishable from reasoning). Furthermore, Damon differs from the Piaget and Kohlberg tradition in not invoking stages. It is somewhat ironic that the title of Damon's book, *The Social World of the Child* (1977), is reminiscent of Piaget's book, *The Child's Conception of the World* (1929/1963), and yet unlike Piaget, Damon does not attempt to represent the general-knowledge structures of the child about the world as they inform and guide the child's construal of concrete social experience. Damon does not characterize how general social knowledge is represented in long-term memory and only postulates in the subject's head the existence of particular concepts that apply to specific kinds of moral problems. Just what kind of cognitive structures a concept is, is not described in any meta-theoretical way. Subjects seem to have one kind of concept when solving the positive-justice tasks (distributing rewards) and another kind of concept when solving authority tasks (1977), and Damon does not postulate any necessary connection between the two. One advantage of Damon's agnostic position regarding stages is that it allows research to progress without being tied to a commitment on the characterization of general knowledge structures. And it may well be that young children's thinking—and perhaps that of many adults(?)—is not all that coherent and systematic and that the attempt to cast young children as miniature philosophers, each with a moral system, is ill conceived. Nevertheless, the thinking of some people is definitely systematic, not an aggregate of disconnected concepts—each concept is bounded and clarified by its connectedness within a system. Therefore, at some point, more encompassing systems of thinking and knowledge have to be posited. Furthermore, if one kind of concepts apply to only one type of moral situation, then we need to study many additional moral problems (and their accompanying concepts or levels) to have a complete picture of the young child. If Damon's levels indicate nothing more general and fundamental than solutions to the specific problems of positive justice and authority, then we do not have any information about children's moral thinking regarding lying, promise keeping, fighting and self-defense, punishment, cheating on games or school tests, being disruptive and unruly, special responsibilities to friends and kin, performing assigned chores, and all the other situations in a child's life that involve moral issues.

Damon has suggested that other researchers in moral judgment need to reexamine the postulation of global stages and that a finer grained analysis at the level of his concepts or of Kohlberg's issues (punishment, life, authority, contract, etc.) may be more profitable:

My own view is that all of Kohlberg's moral issues are potentially distinct. I see no reason to assume a priori that these separate concerns are subparts of a coherent, unified "moral" system; and Kohlberg has never adequately demonstrated empirical relations between them. (Damon, 1980b, p. 52)

Yet, the recent work of the Kohlberg group could not be more supportive of the global-stage position and against Damon's separate-issue position. Colby et al., (in press) show that the correlations of each issue across stories and across forms is no higher (typically in the .60s) than the correlation between different issues (also typically in the .60s); furthermore, factor analysis of issue scores reveals only one large factor on which all issues are loaded (factor loadings all in the .7 to .8 range). Some unpublished cluster analyses of DIT items also indicate the same thing: separating issues as the unit of developmental analysis is not warranted by the data. Perhaps, in the future, a more fine-grained unit of analysis will be identified, but presently, the global stages portray the empirical clusterings better than any finer unit in data from older children and adults.

Enright and his colleagues (Enright, Enright, Manheim, & Harris, 1980; Enright, Franklin, & Manheim, 1980; Enright, Manheim, Lapsley, & Enright, 1981) have recently developed a standardized and objective method for assessing positive-justice levels in young children, presenting paired comparisons of pictures that depict the various solutions to distributing rewards. Despite Damon's strong advocacy of the clinical interview method for children (1977), no systematic comparison has yet been made to demonstrate the superiority of either method, although that of Enright and his colleagues is clearly less time consuming and less costly. In addition, Kurdek and his colleagues (Kurdek, 1980; Larsen & Kurdek, 1979) have also modified Damon's scoring method for the positive-justice task to make it more workable for their data.

Research on moral judgment in early childhood by Damon, Enright, and Kurdek and their associates has generally involved the same kinds of research strategies and designs as research based on the six-stage model:

1. *Reliability.* Interjudge agreement, internal consistency, and alternative-form correlations have all been good for the Damon measures. For Enright's objective measure, interjudge reliability is, of course, no problem and internal consistency is typically in the .60s. For Kurdek's measure, only interjudge agreement is reported and that is high.

2. *Age trends.* Age trends in cross-sectional

studies of subjects 4 to 10 years old have been reported for both the Damon and Kurdek measures (Damon, 1977; Enright, Franklin, & Manheim, 1980; Kurdek, 1980; Larsen & Kurdek, 1979) and for longitudinal age trends (Damon, 1977, 1980a; Kurdek, 1980). It remains to be seen if other investigators testing other samples also find longitudinal trends on either measure. Enright and associates (1981) have carried out the most extensive exploration of age trends, including two time sequential studies (two sets of cross-sectional samples from the same populations tested at different times) and two cross-sequential studies (two sets of longitudinal samples retested at a 1-year interval). Although the cross-sectional studies generally showed age trends, the longitudinal findings failed to do so, perhaps because of the instability of response in younger subjects and the short time intervals (1 year).

3. *Correlations.* Damon (1977) reported sizable correlations between positive-justice, authority, and developmental measures of friendship and social convention (ranging from .52 to .78) as well as extremely high correlations between moral judgment and Piagetian logical tasks (ranging from .76 to .88). However, Kurdek, using a modified version of the positive-justice task, found much lower correlations among the moral-judgment measures and other social-cognitive measures (Kurdek, 1980; Larson & Krudek, 1979). Curiously, in a cross-lagged correlational analysis, Kurdek (1980) found evidence suggesting that moral judgment caused development in cognitive perspective taking rather than perspective taking making possible moral judgment as usually hypothesized (Kohlberg, 1976; Selman, 1976). In relating moral judgment to behavior, Damon (1977) found little predictability between children's justice solutions in a hypothetical task and their actual behavior in settings carefully matched to those in the hypothetical task. He attributed the discrepancy to the influence of self-interest (a Component III process that nullified the impact of Component II). However, Enright and Sutterfield (1980) found a low but significant correlation between positive justice and observed socially constructive behavior in a naturalistic setting (school classroom). They also found significant correlations between their measure of positive justice and sociometric ratings of popularity, being fair, and socioeconomic status. Also, Kurdek (1980) found some significant correlations of his measure of positive justice with some parent ratings of social skills, achievement, and adjustment.

4. *Discriminant validity.* In many studies, IQ-type measures were statistically partialed from the correlations and uniformly demonstrated that the trends could not be accounted for by IQ. In no study was sex of subject an important variable.

Research on the moral-judgment development of young children looks promising, but it is too early yet for replicated and convergent studies to have completely clarified the status of the developmental levels. The most vexing question concerning positive justice is how this developmental research articulates with about two dozen studies on equity theory conducted from a social psychology approach (discussed in more detail later; social psychology studies are listed in Hook & Cook, 1979). Both the cognitive developmental and social psychology studies are concerned with similar problems: how to distribute rewards. Both approaches have basic similarities in classifying response types: distribution of rewards according to self-interest, according to strict equality, according to merit, or according to need. Yet, researchers in the social psychology tradition do not always find age differences in children in response types (e.g., Lerner, 1974); furthermore, some studies have adults using various response types, when according to the developmental research we would expect only the highest level in subjects well beyond 10 years old (e.g., see Gunzburger et al., 1977). Damon (1977) states:

> The ordering of these early levels bears no implication about the relative worth of meritarian, egalitarian, or benevolent philosophies of distribution as employed by adults. . . . A distribution-of-rewards problem in adulthood is usually considered in the context of major political traditions and prevailing economic realities. In such a case, positive justice reasoning takes on an entirely different form, with different sorts of organizing principles at work. (p. 77)

But what are these different organizing principles and why should a distribution-of-rewards problem for children "bear no implication" for the same sort of problem for adults? In many cases, the tasks presented to the adults seem almost identical to those presented to children and contain no political or economic references (e.g., Gunzburger et al., 1977). If methodological differences, stimulus differences, or differences in scoring responses account for the inconsistencies between the cognitive-developmental and social psychological studies, then what are these differences, why are they so important, and what does this imply about the generality and robustness of the phenomena of positive justice? A thorough probing and comparison of these two literatures is needed.

Prosocial Moral Reasoning

Many writers have noted that the Kohlberg dilemmas do not sample the full diversity of moral problems. In recent years, researchers have studied moral dilemmas about the environment (Iozzi, 1980), politics (Lockwood, 1970), sex (Gilligan, Kohlberg, Lerner, & Belenky, 1971), and so on. Eisenberg-Berg (1976) has identified another dimension, prosocial moral dilemmas. Prosocial dilemmas are ones "in which the individual must choose between satisfying his own wants, needs, and/or values and those of others, particularly in contexts in which laws, punishment, and formal obligations are irrelevant or de-emphasized" (p. 552). Examples of prosocial dilemmas are: citizens of a town must choose between sharing or not sharing food with another town after a flood when sharing would result in the benefactors going hungry themselves; a young woman is asked to go into the hospital to donate blood over a period of weeks, when doing so would make her weak, make her lose her job, and disrupt her college studies; a man must choose between helping a woman who is being mugged and protecting himself. In these dilemmas, helping another person is in direct opposition to self-interest, the cost in helping is extremely great to the actor, and the burden of helping the victim cannot be spread among a large number of other people. Prosocial in these situations essentially means self-sacrifice. Philosophers refer to this behavior as "acts of supererogation"—that is, good deeds over and above one's duty as derived from maintaining ongoing relationships, past contracts and promises, considerations of fairness, general social practice, or special roles of responsibility. It is in this sense that the prosocial dilemmas involve "contexts in which laws, punishment, and formal obligations are irrelevant" (Eisenberg-Berg, 1976, p. 552) and in which "there are few available criteria . . . to dictate the proper course of action" (Eisenberg-Berg, 1979a, p. 129).

Eisenberg-Berg differentiates prosocial dilemmas from Kohlberg dilemmas in the following way:

Most of this research [Kohlberg's] has dealt with only one domain of moral judgment, that of prohibition-oriented reasoning. In nearly all of Kohlberg's dilemmas, laws, rules, authorities, and formal obligations are salient concerns and frequently dominate the individual's reasoning about the conflicts. (Eisenberg-Berg, 1979a, p. 128)

A differentiation should be made between prosocial and constraint-oriented moral reasoning analogous to the differentiation between helping behaviors and prohibition behaviors (e.g., not stealing or breaking the law). (1976, p. 552)

Although it is clear that prosocial dilemmas are different from Kohlberg's, the characterization of Kohlberg dilemmas as "prohibition-oriented reasoning" is not apt. Prohibition usually refers to the forbidding by an external authority of an act that a person is otherwise inclined to perform. But Eisenberg-Berg does not differentiate obligation derived from the demands of an external power (Stage 1) from all the other bases of obligation derived from commitment to various schemes of cooperation. For Eisenberg-Berg, a prohibition includes commitments to maintaining an ongoing love relationship, commitments based on past promises and agreements, duties arising from a sense of justice, expectations based on past cooperation, and duties arising from a cooperative division of labor and role responsibilities. It is misleading to characterize all these different sources of moral obligation as prohibition morality or as negative morality.

A second way that Eisenberg-Berg's approach differs from the Kohlberg tradition illustrates some further options in researching moral judgment. Eisenberg-Berg constructed her taxonomy for scoring responses differently than the classical cognitive-developmental approach. Cognitive developmentalists usually construct the categories or features of their taxonomies in a way that both describes a type of response and also anticipates how one category is developmentally more or less advanced than another category. A developmental-structural analysis attempts to describe the inner constructive process of the subject in generating a response and to portray, in an ordered sequence of organizational types, how the more advanced types evolve from the less advanced types (e.g., by taking more bits of information into account than the less advanced types; by discriminating superficial, surface features from deeper, more subtle features; by utilizing new cognitive operations or integrating principles, etc.). In other words, cognitive developmentalists construct their basic descriptive systems (their taxonomy of response-types) not only to capture some differentiable features of the responses but also to furnish a description of the inner constructive process by which the responses are generated[12] and to indicate how the successive organizations lead up to the most advanced type of response. In contrast, Eisenberg-Berg (1979a) constructed her categories more simply by picking out some differentiable features in the response to her dilemmas. There was no attempt to describe the inner constructive process that generates the responses nor was there an attempt to construct the categories logically so as to order the processes from simple to those more advanced. Eisenberg-Berg states:

> Subjects' moral judgments were coded into a variety of categories (henceforth called *moral consideration categories*), each representing a moral concern expressed by the subjects (e.g., concern with potential gain for the self, concern with improving interpersonal relationships as the result of one's actions, and concern with living up to one's own internalized values). These categories were devised empirically. (1979a, p. 130)

Thus, in the initial characterization of the phenomena, "the categories are not ordered developmentally, that is, no one category is considered more advanced than any other cateogry" (1979a, p. 130). Later on, Eisenberg-Berg notices that some of the response categories empirically clustered and that some clusters were used more by older subjects and other clusters were used more by younger subjects. On this empirical basis, Eisenberg-Berg refers to four stages of prosocial reasoning "somewhat similar to Kohlberg's stages" (1979b, p. 88):

> (1) hedonistic reasoning (e.g., "I wouldn't help because I might be hungry."); (2) stereotypic, approval-oriented reasoning (e.g., "It's only natural to help." "His parents would be proud of him if he helped."); (3) empathic reasoning (e.g., "They'd be happy if they had food."); (4) reasoning based on internalized values and responsibilities (e.g., "I'd feel good knowing that I had lived up to my principles." "If everyone helps, society would be a lot better."). (Eisenberg-Berg, 1979a, pp. 130–131)

Notwithstanding the similarities to Kohlberg's stages, it is important to call attention to the differences in rationale and research strategy. Eisenberg-Berg's scoring categories are differentiations logically closer to Kohlberg's norm/element/mode classification (Kohlberg's content) than to the differentiation he uses as stages (structure). Kohlberg's stages are said to be developmentally ordered primarily on the basis of a logical analysis of the constructive processes of each type of organization that generates the responses; Kohlberg collects age-trend data to confirm empirically the theoretical order. In contrast, Eisenberg-Berg's stages are based on empirical age trends. The various features of Kohlberg's stages are said to cohere on the basis of their supposed derivation from a single underlying organization of thinking; Eisenberg-Berg's stages represent empirically derived clusters from one sample.

Despite the differences in deriving the stages, Eisenberg-Berg and her associates have conducted similar kinds of studies to those using the six-stage model:

1. *Reliability*. Interjudge reliability in classifying responses into the major categories in Eisenberg-Berg's scheme is good. However, internal consistency (correlations of scores across several dilemmas) is usually not reported, and in the one study in which it was reported (Eisenberg-Berg & Hand, 1979), the correlations were unacceptably low. Often nonsignificant, the highest correlation was .35. Test-retest consistencies are not reported. Thus, there is some question about the reliability and representativeness of prosocial reasoning scores even if scorers can usually agree on the classification of responses.

2. *Age trends*. In Eisenberg-Berg's thesis (1979a), cross-sectional age trends in subjects ranging from grade 2 to grade 12 were found in 14 out of 37 of the original moral-consideration categories. Because the claim of developmental stages in prosocial reasoning is based on empirical grounds, not theoretical grounds, it is important to replicate these age trends in other samples. Cross-sectional age trends were also found in another sample of adolescents in grades 7 to 12, using a different version of the prosocial reasoning test (Eisenberg-Berg, 1976). Two other studies, Eisenberg-Berg (1979b) and Eisenberg-Berg and Mussen (1978), using the same instrument as reported in Eisenberg-Berg (1979a), apparently used some of the same subjects (reporting on different facets of the dissertation study). Therefore, these studies cannot be regarded as replications. Still another version of the prosocial reasoning test was developed for preschool subjects and a longitudinal study over an 18-month period (Eisenberg-Berg & Roth, 1980) found decreases in hedonistic reasoning and increases in needs-oriented and approval-oriented reasoning. Within the samples of preschoolers, however, cross-sectional age trends were not found (probably because of the narrow age range of 66 to 81 months).

3. *Correlations*. In an adolescent sample, the

correlation with empathy was in the .30s and .40s in one study (Eisenberg-Berg & Mussen, 1978), but in a sample of preschoolers, the correlation with role taking was nonsignificant (Eisenberg-Berg & Roth, 1980). In one sample of adolescents (Eisenberg-Berg, 1976), the correlations of prosocial moral reasoning with two measures of liberal/humanitarian political attitudes was .34 and .21; with another adolescent sample (Eisenberg-Berg, 1979b), the correlations of women with political attitudes was .35 (partialed for age) and .09 for men (partialed for age). In one study of preschoolers (Eisenberg-Berg & Hand, 1979), prosocial reasoning was correlated with some indices of prosocial behavior as high as the .30s and .40s; however, in a study of adolescents, the correlation of prosocial moral reasoning with prosocial behavior was nonsignificant (Eisenberg-Berg, 1979b).

4. *Discriminant validity.* About the highest correlation (.54) reported for measures of prosocial reasoning was with religious participation (Eisenberg-Berg & Roth, 1980). The authors state: "It is not clear whether the effects of religious participation reflect training for selflessness, rote memorization of desirable responses, or some other process or motivation" (p. 376). Sex and IQ do not seem to account for the variance of prosocial reasoning. The hope that prosocial moral reasoning might more powerfully predict to prosicial behavior or prosocial attitudes than "prohibition-oriented" (Kohlbergian) moral reasoning has not been demonstrated. Thus far, studies using Kohlbergian measures have produced more powerful trends in prosocial behavior than those using prosocial reasoning (Blasi, 1980; J. R. Rest, 1979a). In one study that directly compared prosocial reasoning with prohibition reasoning (Eisenberg-Berg, 1976), the prosocial measure produced correlations with political attitudes of .34 and .21, whereas the prohibition measure produced correlations of .28 and .16; not only are these differences in correlations undramatic but also the lower correlations of prohibition reasoning can be accounted for by the fact that the prohibition measure in this study had been shortened to one third its recommended length and also changed in other ways. In summary, the special usefulness of prosocial moral reasoning has not been demonstrated by dramatically strong and consistent correlations with prosocial behavior in comparison with prohibition reasoning.

One clear contrast between reasoning to prosocial and prohibition dilemmas, however, has been that in dilemmas designed to eliminate the relevance of prohibitions by authorities (the prosocial dilemmas), even young subjects seldomly invoke prohibitions by authorities as reasons for action—thus, subjects in the age range usually scored at Kohlberg's Stage 1 do not invariably give Stage 1 type reasonings when the dilemma makes it inappropriate. Again, as in Damon's work, there is evidence that Kohlberg's Stage 1 is not a complete picture of the young child's capacities and that young children show surprising sophistication when the strictures of adults do not dominate the situation. In general, an intriguing aspect of this prosocial line of research is that many significant relationships are discovered even when two central characteristics of the cognitive-developmental tradition are abandoned: a deemphasis on concepts of cooperation and reciprocal social systems and a deemphasis on structural analysis and underlying cognitive operations.

Additional Cognitive-Developmental Studies

Other studies in the cognitive-developmental tradition illustrate yet different options in conceiving of, and in conducting research on, moral judgment. Because extended programs of research have not yet emerged, it is difficult to appraise the reliability of the phenomena described by these studies; space only allows a listing: Bar-Tal, Raviv, and Leiser (1980); Bloom (1977); Boyce and Jensen (1978); Bronfenbrenner (1970); Bull (1969); Gilligan and Murphy (1978); Haan (1978); Hogan (1970); D. L. Krebs (1978); and Saltzstein (1976). See also Eckensberger's (in press) review of moral development research in Germany.

Morality is distinguishable but related to other social phenomena: politics, law, and economics (Furth, 1980; Gallatin, 1980; Merelman, 1972; Renshon, 1977; Tapp and Levine, 1977); religion (Fowler, 1976; Oser, Gmuender, & Fritzsche, 1979); interpersonal relationships (Selman, 1980); and social convention (Nucci, 1981; Turiel, 1978a, 1978b). Turiel has been particularly outspoken on the relation of morality to social convention and initiated a research program focused on this relationship. Turiel (1978a, 1978b) proposes that social convention and morality constitute two distinct conceptual domains and that they develop independently. Social conventions include, for instance, table manners, modes of dress, forms of address, modes of greeting. Turiel contends that researchers in the tradition of Piaget and Kohlberg have confused social convention with morality, construing conventionality as an inferior form of morality (Turiel, 1978b). In fact, Turiel contends, people conceptualize rules that apply to the moral domain differently from rules that apply to social convention and that development in understanding social convention comprises a different sequence of stages than the moral stages. As empirical support for distinguishing morality from convention, for example, children and youth were asked how wrong it would be, on the one hand, to commit certain acts like hitting another, lying, or stealing (examples of violating moral rules) or, on the other hand, acts like addressing a teacher by a first name, a boy entering a girl's bathroom, or eating lunch with one's fingers (examples of violating rules of social convention) (Nucci, 1981). Children and youth (from the second grade to college) consistently viewed the moral violations as more wrong than violations of social convention. The moral violations are viewed as more wrong because they result in harm to another, violate rights, and "never should be committed"; whereas violations of social conventions are viewed as merely impolite or disruptive and "making a mess." Thus, judgments of moral events are "based on the intrinsic consequences of actions upon others," whereas judgments of social convention are based on the "perception of the acts as affecting the social order established by rules emanating from authority or social consensus" (Nucci, 1981, p. 115). Rules of social convention are instituted to coordinate activity in a community but are arbitrary and relative—both in the sense that other rules could be devised to accomplish the same thing and that other communities may adopt different rules. The arbitrariness and relativity of rules was studied in the following way: children were asked if it would be right for another country to have no rule prohibiting stealing and if it would be right for a person to go ahead and steal in a country that had no rule against stealing. Most children at every age from 6 to 17 replied that it would still be wrong to steal. By comparison, children were asked if it would be right for people in another country to play a game by different rules if the people agreed to play it by different rules, virtually all children responded that the rules of a game could be changed. Because young children as well as older youths distinguish moral violations from social-convention violations (in terms of degree of wrongness, relativity to the culture, and in terms of arbitrary/intrinsic consequences), Turiel and his colleagues contend, therefore, that morality and social convention comprise distinct domains with separate courses of development.

What is the basic difference, then, between morality and social convention? Turiel states: "Morality is defined not by coordination of interactions within social organizations but by principles of justice prescriptive of behavior. . . . We . . . have distinguished between (1) convention, which is part of social systems and is structured by underlying concepts of social organization and (2) morality, which is structured by underlying concepts of justice (Turiel, 1978a, p. 60). In this passage, Turiel seems to be separating concepts of justice (on the morality side) from concepts of social organization (on the social-convention side). But this distinction is not adequate because concepts of social organization are logically implicated in both morality and social convention—concepts of justice provide standards by which to judge social organization. How could there be justice or morality *without* social organization? As the philosopher John Rawls states:

> Justice is the first virtue of social institutions, as truth is of systems of thought. . . . The primary subject of justice is the basic structure of society, or more exactly, the way in which the major social institutions distribute fundamental rights and duties and determine the division of advantages from social cooperation. (1971, p. 7)

Furthermore, Piaget's concept of justice as an equilibrated social system, Kohlberg's discussion of his stages in terms of perspectives on society, and the discussion of the six stages in this chapter all link justice to concepts of social organization. This is not to say that all forms of social organization are just or that existing social organizations define justice. However, as people become aware of new forms of social organization (e.g., long-term enduring friendships, societywide networks of role positions, communities organized and governed to further certain ideals), they also face the moral question of how to balance the benefits and burdens of participants, of how to set up fair reciprocity. Development of concepts of justice presupposes development of concepts of social organization.

Is any developmental scheme that postulates a conventional level of morality guilty of confusing conventionality with morality? Not necessarily—stages of moral judgment should be understood as basic rationales for defining what is fair. Stage 3 and Stage 4 thinking is not conventional in the sense of being unreflective or conforming to the commonplace or simply reflecting prevailing social pressures. Schemes of cooperation serve as active integrative structures for organizing one's thinking about fairness and providing directives for allocating rights and duties. The Stage 3 scheme is interpersonal harmony among caring and sensitive individuals and the Stage 4 scheme of cooperation is an orchestrated social system with each person doing her particular job. Stages 3 and 4 are conventional in that their concepts of fairness direct one to do one's part in maintaining existing social arrangements: for Stage 3, it is to maintain the other's expectations; at Stage 4, it is to uphold the existing social system (the familiar theme of the Law-and-Order orientation). But such a view of Stages 3 and 4 does not commit one to the view that all thinking about social conventions is nothing but inferior morality.

Turiel's analysis of the conventional-moral distinction is inadequate for several reasons. He construes the morality of acts only in terms of their direct and intrinsic effects upon the welfare of another person (hitting the person, stealing from him, etc.). But a person's welfare is also affected indirectly by general social structures and social arrangements. For instance, a judge who makes judicial decisions on the basis of helping a friend rather than on the basis of law is a case of one person helping another but at the cost of undermining a social arrangement designed for the general welfare of that society. Many social institutions and social arrangements are devices for furthering human welfare (even though such arrangements usually contain an element of arbitrariness and are relative to the particular history and circumstances of that society). For instance, driving on the right hand of the street, paying income tax on April 15, having presidential elections every 4-years in November—these instances are all somewhat arbitrary and certainly relative. They are not intrinsically helpful or harmful to people, but they are institutionalized practices (conventions) designed to further human welfare at least indirectly; therefore, we cannot relegate these social practices to a domain separate and independent of morality. Indeed, an interesting topic of research would be to study the development of children's understanding of the moral rationale (or lack of it) of certain institutional practices and conventions. Young children may well regard many social practices (e.g., having presidential elections, filling out income tax forms) as "just a bunch of silly rules" having no more purpose than dress styles or eating etiquette. It is when one cannot discern any moral rationale or social utility of an institutionalized practice that one refers to the practice as "merely a social convention." Moral-judgment stages presuppose social organization and social convention. Stages 5 and 6 provide abstract criteria or standards for judging the fairness of conventional arrangements. As early as Stage 3, human relationships are seen as mediated by social structures and conventions. For instance, at Stage 3, being nice and considerate to

another is often seen in terms of conventional-role stereotypes. Therefore, morality deals not only with acts that have direct and intrinsic effects on other people but also with the indirect effects of acts, social practices, and social conventions—an aspect of morality that Turiel's analysis overlooks. Furthermore, violation of a social convention that has no intrinsic harmful effect can, nevertheless, cause human suffering by hurting another's feelings or showing contempt for the other's dignity. For instance, wearing a bikini bathing suit to the funeral of one's father would be a breach of our social conventions, but I think would be something more as well. And lastly, some acts that directly and intrinsically inflict pain or harm upon a person are not necessarily immoral when understood in the context of particular social conventions. For instance, the ritualistic circumcision rites in some societies are surely intrinsically painful but have to be understood within the context of the social conventions of those societies. Moral violations cannot simply be defined as acts that are intrinsically harmful. In summary, morality and social convention have many complex relationships and are not simply separate and independent domains. A more penetrating theoretical analysis of the distinctions and interrelationships is needed for morality and other social phenomena.

The data produced by Turiel and Nucci and their colleagues are interesting in suggesting that even young children strive to understand the purpose and rationale of social rules. Children do not mindlessly learn social rules of all kinds but rather attend to their functions and strive to see the sense of social rules. Social development is not simply a matter of adding one more regulation of behavior to an unorganized list of rules but rather involves the construction of conceptions about how the social world is organized and how it ought to function. This research (as does that of Damon and Eisenberg-Berg) indicates that even young children are well along in building this knowledge.

Social Psychological Approaches: Social and Personal Norms

Some social psychologists postulate social norms as internalized regulators of moral behavior. Three norms (and their variants) have received most attention: the norm of social responsibility (e.g., Berkowitz, 1972), the norm of reciprocity (e.g., Gouldner, 1960), and the norm of equity (e.g., Adams, 1963; see also Staub, 1978, for a general review of social norms). The norm of social responsibility prescribes that people should help another person who is dependent upon them. The norm of equity prescribes that when individuals are in a cooperative relationship, the ratio of rewards to investments should be the same for each person. Particular social norms apply to particular situations; one norm does not regulate all social-moral behavior. Social norms are not general understandings about human relationships (comparable to deep structures in the cognitive developmental approach) nor are they intended to be representations of general knowledge about the sociomoral world. (In this regard, social norms seem somewhat akin to Damon's concepts.) As a person becomes aware of the applicability of a particular norm to a particular situation, the norm guides and motivates the person to act in the prescribed way in that particular situation. Certain situational variations may increase or diminish the feeling of obligation to comply with the norm, and certain personality variables may also affect compliance with the norm (see Schwartz, 1977). Generally, social norms are considered to be prevailing rules or shared expectations of one's social group, learned from and reinforced by one's group, that is, social rules that owe their existence to their role in enhancing the integrity and welfare of the group as a whole.

The social-norm approach is especially interesting in using *behavioral* data to infer the existence of social norms, not solely *verbal* data. For instance, with regard to the norm of social responsibility, Berkowitz and Daniels (1963) asked college students to follow the directions of an alleged supervisor in training. Students in one condition were informed that the supervisor was greatly dependent upon high work levels from the student subjects, whereas another group of students was told that the supervisor was not dependent upon the students' work level. Students worked harder when the alleged supervisor was highly dependent. The authors attribute the difference in work levels between the student groups to the norm of social responsibility, activated in the first set of circumstances but not in the second.

Significantly, the evidential basis for postulating social norms inside the human cognizer depends on behavioral differences in the averages of groups exposed to different situational conditions. This contrasts with the cognitive-developmental approach to morality that relies on subjects' verbal explanations and their rationales. The social-norm approach is somewhat piecemeal (no one knows how many social norms exist, what they are, or what their boundaries are) and somewhat post hoc (the cognitive processes in applying a social norm to a particular

situation are discovered by finding out whatever situational manipulations affect the behavior—invent a new situational manipulation that produces behavioral differences and you have discovered an additional consideration to which subjects allegedly attend in applying a norm to a situation). Also, there is difficulty in specifying precisely what norm (or cognitive process) is operative in determining a specific behavioral pattern. In many situations, several different norms can be invoked to explain the same behavior. The basic problem is that it is just as difficult to specify unique internal processes from overt behavior as it is to predict specific behavior from verbal representations of internal processes. Although the current formulations of internal processes from the social-norm approach are still preliminary, it seems worthwhile to continue this avenue of research, particularly if verbal data (subjects' descriptions of their reasoning, explanations of their rationales) can be integrated with behavioral data. Working both sides of the street may produce more robust descriptions of the operative internal processes governing actual behavior.

Although a large number of studies have used the social-norm approach, they will not be reviewed here because they do not focus on cognitive processes nor do they have a developmental focus. A notable exception is some recent research by Hook (Hook, 1978; Hook & Cook, 1979) who investigated the basic cognitive components requisite to the application of the social norm of equity. Equity research deals with problems of distributive justice (similar to Damon's positive justice). For instance, if one person produces three times as much as another person, then how should the rewards be divided? Subjects' responses to this problem are usually classified as self-interest, equality, or equity. Hook, however, distinguishes ordinal equity and proportional equity. If one person does three times the work of another and they are to divide 20¢, then according to strict proportional equity, the first subject should get 75% of the 20 pennies (or 15¢) as reward and the second should get 25% (or 5¢). In ordinal-equity solutions, the subject who contributes more should get something more, but not in strict proportion to the inputs. For instance, an ordinal-equity solution to the case above would be to give the first subject 12¢ and the second subject 8¢ (the first subject is rewarded with a little more for his extra work, but not in proportion to the relative amount of work). Hook's major point is that to allocate rewards according to strict proportional equity (as the formulators of the norm of equity—Adams, 1963; Walster, Berschied, & Walster, 1973—postulate), the subject must be able to compute and compare proportions. However, according to Piagetian research, this logicomathematical capacity to compute proportions does not ordinarily appear until about 12 years old. Therefore, strict proportional-equity solutions should not appear until this age. In a review of over two dozen studies on the norm of equity, Hook and Cook (1979) found that indeed, subjects under 13 years did not show proportional-equity solutions but only ordinal-equity solutions, whereas subjects over 13 did show proportional equity. Further, in a cross-sectional study of 5-, 9-, and 13-year-olds, Hook (1978) found Piagetian logicomathematical reasoning to be related to solutions to distributive-justice problems. Therefore, Hook introduces a line of research similar to the Harvard structuralists (see section titled *The Cognitive Nature of Moral Judgment*) into social-norm research, a line of research that focuses on clarifying the cognitive components of processes regulating moral behavior (not just moral judgment).

Post-Piagetian Research

Since 1970, over 100 studies have used and modified Piaget's basic paradigms introduced in 1932 (Piaget, 1932/1965), not with the intent of replicating his work but to modify it and in many cases to challenge Piaget's interpretations. The research is post-Piagetian in the sense of recognizing Piaget's work and studying the phenomena he identified, but it departs from Piaget either on methodological or theoretical points. By far the greatest attention has been given to Piaget's paradigm studying the use of intentionality and consequence information in making moral judgments. Piaget's method was to present two brief stories to a subject, for instance, one boy breaking 15 cups while helping his mother, and another boy breaking 1 cup while trying to get some jam. Piaget asked the subject to judge which boy was naughtier and which boy should be punished more. Piaget reported that under 10 years of age, children often based judgments on consequences information (e.g., how many cups were broken), but after age 10, children based judgments on intentions only (e.g., trying to help his mother or trying to sneak some jam).

First, it should be recognized that making judgments of naughtiness and punishability are a special type of moral judgment. The kind of moral judgment emphasized in most morality research deals with the question of deciding what an actor ought to do in a given social situation. It deals with deciding and justifying a course of action, of defining rights and obligations, and prioritizing and balancing competing claims. Philosophers refer to this type of moral judgment as "judgments of moral obligation" (Frankena, 1963, p. 9). In contrast, Piaget's intentionality-consequence stories raise the question of judging naughtiness (blameworthiness and praiseworthiness) and punishability—issues that philosophers call "judgments of moral value" (Frankena, 1963, p. 9). The kinds of considerations and the underlying logic for making these two kinds of moral judgments are different (see Brandt, 1959). Piaget's stories do not ask what a person ought to do in a given situation (what should Henry do if he wants some jam when his mother is away and the jam is out of reach in a cupboard?); instead, they ask how bad a person is who acts in a certain way in a given situation when certain events have occurred. Figuring out how bad a person is despite excuses and extenuating circumstances is a large part of judgments of moral value. On the other hand, figuring out what to do despite conflicting claims and loyalties is a large part of judgments of obligation. For convenience, let us refer to judgments of moral value as moral evaluation and to judgments of moral obligation as moral judgment.

The complexity of moral evaluation can be glimpsed by the following example. Suppose one person has shot to death another person. How blameworthy is the killer and what punishment, if any, is justified? Even practical institutions, such as the criminal justice system, make many distinctions and take many sorts of information into account. The consequences (death of a person) are, of course, relevant, as is the intent of the actor (Did the actor try to shoot the victim or did the gun misfire while cleaning it?). In addition, one must determine the circumstances in which the shooting took place (e.g., a hunting accident, during a holdup), the societal role of the actor (e.g., a soldier firing at the enemy, a police officer in a gun battle with terrorists), the mental state of the actor (e.g., being drunk, hypnotized, or insane), the provocation by the victim (e.g., Was the victim burglarizing the actor's home or was the victim in a lover's quarrel?), the prior planning of the act (e.g., premeditated murder vs. an act in a fit of passion), and so on. These considerations are all involved in establishing the guilt of the actor. Determining a punishment involves further considerations and integrative principles (e.g., Is any punishment justified at all? The death sentence? Imprisonment with possibility of parole?). (See Pennington & Hastie, 1981, for discussion of juror decision-making models and the complexities of making moral evaluations.)

Piaget's paradigm does not go very far in explicating moral evaluation. The intention/consequence distinction furnishes only a crude and partial representation of what is involved; furthermore, Piaget's stories confound several elements, and the two-story format presents several special problems as well. Post-Piagetian research has proceeded in three major directions. One direction has been to sort out the various components involved in moral evaluation, systematically studying the parameters of the various factors and devising task formats that avoid some of the problems of Piaget's tasks. Most of this research is atheoretical, manipulating stimulus characteristics, using experimental designs, and ANOVA techniques. Instead of having only Piaget's two factors (intentions and consequences), studies have shown the influence of a multitude of factors: whether the consequences are negative or positive and their extent or degree; whether the object of the consequence is an inanimate object, animal, or person—and if a person, whether the effects of the action were physical or psychological; whether the consequences were intended or happened accidentally or through carelessness or recklessness; if intended, whether the person was provoked, forced, or pressured or whether the consequences were willful and premeditated; whether the specific activity was part of an overall plan to be helpful, malicious, or selfish or part of no plan at all; whether the person doing the evaluating is the offender, the offended, or a third-party bystander; the age, sex, and relation of the actor to the recipient of action; whether social sanctions followed the act, negative or positive, mild or severe, physical or verbal, and so on (see Rostollan, 1979). In addition, characteristics of the stimulus material have been shown to influence moral evaluation: whether the stimulus material is presented via videotape or verbally; whether the format is to pick one of the two characters who is naughtier or to rate a single story character on a Likert scale; in what order the stimuli are presented; whether the story setting is a familiar one or not; whether the actor's intentions are explicitly mentioned or have to be inferred. Furthermore, the mode of response affects moral evaluation: whether subjects are asked to make ratings on a Likert scale, to explain their evaluations, or are assessed in terms of reaction time in choosing.

What are the general implications of finding that so many factors influence moral evaluations? One would be that assessment with Piagetian-type stories must be understood to give only a partial picture of the processes of moral evaluation at best. Another implication is to challenge a hard-line stage concept in yet another domain (which Piaget himself disclaimed for his morality research). However, a major problem in this body of research is its lack of theoretical coherence. We now have a long list of factors that influence moral evaluations and that probably interact with each other in complex ways (at least sometimes in some subject groups); the list gets longer as psychologists invent new stimulus manipulations. The programmatic implications of this research are unclear: Is it to carry out Piaget's original program with greater methodological rigor and descriptive detail? Is it to replace Piaget's concepts with an alternative set of explanations of the phenomena to which Piaget alerted us? Is it to deny that morality is a distinct domain of psychological functioning and to assert that moral phenomena are best understood in terms of more general processes of memory, attention, and stimuli control of responses, and so on? Is it to assert that with experiences in the social world, people do not develop an understanding of cooperative arrangements and the function of social rules but only develop an ability to distinguish certain stimulus characteristics of situations?

Recent reviews of the intentionality-consequence literature (Karniol, 1978; Keasey, 1978) emphasize the development and use of social-cognitive processes in making moral evaluation, that is, the emphasis is on Component I processes as prerequisites to moral evaluation, similar to the work on social-cognitive prerequisites to Kohlbergian moral judgments. Keasey points out the importance of distinguishing the concept of intentionality (deliberately trying to bring about some consequence in contrast to accidentally bringing it about) from the concept of motive (trying to do something good or bad) and that "the two concepts seem to follow different developmental sequences, with the concept of motive emerging earlier" (p. 26). Similarly, Karniol (1978) suggests that children use social-cognitive cues about ill-intentioned acts in their moral evaluations before using cues about well-intentioned acts; he also proposes different developmental courses for the two kinds of acts on the basis of this distinction. The details of the intentionality-consequence research will not be reviewed here because the emphasis is more on social-cognitive processes (Component I) than on moral reasoning per se (Component II). Indeed, Wellman, Larkey, and Somerville (1979) recently pointed out the lack of attention to moral criteria (Component II in the present scheme) in addition to the social-cognitive prerequisites of moral evaluation. However, good examples of research attending to moral criteria are studies by

Darley, Klossen, and Zanna (1978) and by Rule, Nesdale, and McAra (1974). Nevertheless, the interest of most researchers doing post-Piagetian moral evaluation studies is not primarily in morality, as is evident in the last sentence of Keasey's review: "It might be better to study children's developing understanding of the concepts of intentionality and motive outside the sphere of morality" (1978, p. 256). Therefore, although a large number of studies have used moral evaluation as a major variable (and have "moral judgment" in their titles), the main interest has been elsewhere. Researchers have easily adapted the intentionality-consequence paradigm to ask subjects to make attributions other than moral evaluations: Baldwin and Baldwin (1970) modified the paradigm to study kindness attributions, Farnill (1974) studied attributions of a person's potential helpfulness, Morrison and Keasey (1977) studied attributions of niceness and potential friendship, Weiner and Peter (1973) studied attributions of achievement.

A second major new direction in post-Piagetian research has been the melding of a social psychological approach with the cognitive-developmental approach. Accordingly, moral reasoning is described in terms of the acceptance of social norms and the moral evaluation is recast as an attribution process (as described by Heider, 1958; Jones & Davis, 1965; or Kelley, 1972). Heider (Heider, 1958; see also Keasey's review, 1978) describes five ways by which a subject might attribute moral responsibility (i.e., blameworthiness) to another person:

1. The subject might attribute blame to a person for any effect that is in any way associated with the person.
2. The subject might blame a person for anything caused by the person (similar to Piaget's objective responsibility).
3. The subject might blame a person for any event that a person could have foreseen.
4. The subject might blame a person for only those effects that were intended (similar to Piaget's subjective responsibility).
5. The subject might blame a person for only those effects that were intended and not under severe environmental pressure.

Heider's five types of attributing responsibility (or blame) are:

successive stages in which attribution to the person decreases and attribution to the environment increases . . . personal responsibility then var-

ies with the relative contribution of environmental factors to the action outcome. (1958, p. 113)

Although Heider's five types represent more differentiations than those in Piaget's work, only a few studies have used Heider's classification scheme and age trends have not been dramatic.

Another example of research drawing both from social psychological and cognitive-developmental approaches is work by Berndt regarding "the reciprocity norm." Berndt (1977) studied how moral evaluations are affected by reciprocity information (e.g., If person A has previously been provoked by person B, is person A's aggression seen as less bad than if person A aggresses against person B without provocation?). Berndt found that actors who are reciprocating harm for previous harm are evaluated by 6-year-old subjects and adults as less bad than actors who aggress without provocation. Likewise, reciprocating favor for previous favor was evaluated as less good than giving favors without receiving previous favors. In another study, Berndt (1979) found that young preschool children do not yet accept reciprocity norms, that is, their moral evaluations of an actor are not affected by information about previous actions by a recipient person. (For other examples, see Peterson, Hartmann, & Gelfand, 1977; Smith, Gelfand, Hartmann, & Partlow, 1979).

A third major direction in post-Piagetian research is the merging of American cognitive psychology with the cognitive-developmental approach. One example of this is the use of Anderson's information integration theory to explain moral evaluation and moral judgment (Anderson, 1980; Anderson & Butzin, 1978; Lane & Anderson, 1976; Leon, 1980; Surber, 1977). The central idea is that moral evaluations and moral judgments involve the integration of various pieces of information, that is, these judgments are multiply caused and various considerations must simultaneously be taken into account. Anderson (1980) proposes several algebraic models to represent how people may integrate information, and he provides procedures for testing the fit of these mathematical models to judgment data. The developmental difference between young subjects and older subjects may be due to deficiencies in younger subjects' ability to handle simultaneously all the pieces of information (similar to Piaget's notion of centration) or, alternatively, people at different developmental levels may weigh the variables differently. Studies have applied this approach to the intentionality-consequence paradigm and to equity judgments. An important advantage of the approach—in contrast to Piaget's forced-choice, two-story format—is that it allows the experimenter to determine whether the subject is attending to only one set of cues or integrating information from more than one set of cues. Moreover, the approach offers procedures for determining whether the integration is according to an additive rule, an averaging rule, some other algebraic rule, or according to no simple algebraic rule at all. The level of analysis is not limited to group data but allows analysis of the integrative patterns of individual subjects. As yet, however, studies have not been conducted to show how information integration analyses are useful in illuminating predicting behavior in real-life settings (e.g., If a subject uses an additive integration rule on one set of stories, does she generally use an additive rule in other situations? How does this help predict behavior in some socially important situations?). Pennington and Hastie (1981) review and critique the information integration approach and other mathematical models in depicting decision making by jurors.

Another example of this third direction is the application of theories of story comprehension to explain the extraction of information from moral-judgment stories (Grueneich & Trabasso, in press; Nezworski, Stein, & Trabasso, n.d.). The authors describe the detailed processes in which the motives and intentions of an actor in a story are inferred. They demonstrate that inferences about a story actor's intentions can come from a variety of information sources—not only from explicit statements about the actors's intentions but also from descriptions of the actor's activity or even from descriptions of consequences that follow an action. Therefore, the distinction between intention and consequence cues is not hard and fast because inferences about the actor's subjective states can be drawn from many sources. Furthermore, the authors point out that the extraction of intentionality information from complex or ambiguous stories is an ability that develops; therefore, some of the age differences in the use of intentionality in moral-judgment studies may reflect the ability to extract information from story material rather than differences in moral criteria in making moral evaluations. In addition, the authors point out order effects in the presentation of story information—younger subjects tend to evaluate actors by whatever information cues are presented last in the stories. Although the authors do not make a case that *all* of the age differences in the intentionality-consequence literature are due to ambiguous story information or order effects (especially because many recent studies have contained explicit intentionality

information and have been controlled and analyzed for order effects), nevertheless, the authors explicate important confounds in this research and provide guidelines for constructing improved story materials.

Additional examples of the integration of American cognitive psychology with cognitive-developmental approaches are in Carroll and Payne (1977), Gottlieb, Taylor, and Ruderman (1977), Karniol (1980), and Lawrence (1979).

Post-Piagetian approaches attend especially to the influence of stimuli, context, and task demands upon a person's judgment, and they provide a more fine-grained analysis of the steps that people go through in making moral evaluations and judgments. They point to the processes of disembeding cues from masses of information, of the limits of memory in holding relevant material in mind, of the integration of information, of the many distinctions and complexities in making inferences about the wishes, intentions, and needs of others. Post-Piagetian research adds much in areas that cognitive developmentalists have neglected; however, post-Piagetian research tends to neglect the issue in which cognitive developmentalists have traditionally been most interested, namely, What do we have to suppose about subjects' understanding and representation of the sociomoral world to account for their judgments and their rationales for their judgments? Cognitive developmentalists postulate stages or general schemes to characterize people's understanding of the purpose and function of cooperative social structures. Cognitive developmentalists, then, invoke this understanding about the sociomoral world to explain why subjects regard some solutions to moral problems as more adequate than other solutions. In contrast, information processing accounts specify how younger, less advanced subjects are deficient in extracting information, or deficient in combining information, or deficient in decentering from superficial cues and, thus, missing the more subtle cues. These deficiencies explain why younger subjects cannot do what older subjects do, but the information processing analysis does not explain why older subjects, who have the option to act like the younger subjects or older subjects, choose to do the more complex processing. Given that younger children may be deficient in extracting information from complex story material, why is it that they or the older children want certain kinds of information in the first place? Given that younger children may be deficient in information integration, why would anybody want to trouble with complex integrations at all? Given that younger children are swamped over with obvious, superficial cues so that they miss the more subtle, beneath-the-surface cues, why are not older children satisfied with obvious cues? Given that younger children do not accept certain social norms, why do older children think it is good to do so? Information processing accounts help explain why younger children are unable to do certain things but they do not explain why more competent subjects think it is better to use more complex forms of reasoning.

CONCLUSIONS

Morality arises because people live in groups and their actions affect each other. Morality concerns how people determine rights and responsibilities in their social interactions, how people arrange the terms of cooperation and the promotion of their mutual welfare. The more behavior of an individual in a particular situation involves an ensemble of psychological processes. The major components are:

1. Interpreting the situation to identify how one's actions will affect the welfare of others.
2. Figuring out what the ideally moral course of action would be.
3. Selecting from among multiple values what one actually intends to do.
4. Executing and implementing the moral plan of action.

Each component involves both affective and cognitive processes. Although each component is crucial to the production of moral behavior, the focus of this chapter is on the cognitive development of the second component because that component is distinctive in the moral domain and has been extensively researched.

The major thrust of cognitive developmentalists—beginning with Piaget over 50 years ago—has been to argue that moral judgments about particular situations are influenced by a person's general understanding of the social world. Children do not just learn lists of prescriptions and prohibitions, they also come to understand the nature and function of social arrangements (e.g., promises, bargains, role-defined divisions of labor, institutions, and principles and procedures for organizing societywide systems of cooperation). This general knowledge can be represented in terms of schemes of cooperation— different ways of understanding the possibilities and conditions of cooperation. Traditionally, the different schemes of cooperation are referred to as stages insofar as: (1) they provide a general structure for construing concrete social situations—providing a way of comprehending the situations, highlighting the salient features, and integrating the considerations in such a way as to define one line of action or another as more morally justifiable, and (2) the stages are ordered logically so that the higher stages are elaborations of the lower stages, taking more into account, requiring more difficult cognitive operations, and also providing a more satisfactory rationale for balancing the various claims of people and promoting general welfare. The theoretical function of stages or deep structures, then, is: (1) to represent general knowledge about the social world (especially that pertaining to cooperative and reciprocating arrangements) that affects people's judgments about rights and responsibilities in specific situations, (2) to characterize (in part) the cognitive operations involved in identifying cues and considerations and in the integration of considerations into advocacy of one line of action or another, and (3) to explain people's intuitive sense of fairness and rightness about their solutions to moral problems (an intuitive sense of rightness that has a counterpart in people's sense of logical necessity derived from the application of basic logical schemes to phenomena). Hence, for researchers in this tradition, development in Component II is not just stamping in more rules by the ministrations of socializing agents or even learning subtleties in how to apply the rules or in learning more complex rules (although progress in these regards might go along with development) but rather development is the progressive understanding of why people have rights and responsibilities—understanding what kinds of social arrangements are possible and what it takes to create and sustain them.

A considerable amount of research has been generated in the cognitive-developmental tradition over the years. Controversies exist over ways to define developmental features, over methods of assessing moral thinking, over the stage concept itself, and over many issues of research strategy—this chapter describes these controversies. Nevertheless, fairly strong evidence supports the general claim that over time people generally change in the direction of making moral judgments on the basis of a better understanding of social relationships and social arrangements. Also, fairly strong evidence supports the claim that these shifts in moral judgment reflect new cognitive capacities—yet, moral thinking cannot be reduced to general cognitive and linguistic development. Concepts about bargaining, sustaining loyalty in relationships, doing one's share of the duties in social organizations, participating in consensus government, taking account of ameliorating circumstances in judgments of blameworthiness—such ideas involve more than just formal logic, propositional thinking, or the learning of special jargon. The evidence is less strong regarding the conditions and determinants of change: moral discussion with peers and parents seems to facilitate development, as does formal education, social interaction, and involvement in complex social organizations. Although the Kohlberg system has been successfully used in the analysis of moral thinking in other cultures, it is not clear whether some other characterization of developmental features would better capture progress in those different life circumstances. Although many studies have shown significant links of moral judgment to behavior, the relationships are not strong and the precise role of moral judgment in interaction with other variables and processes has yet to be clarified (this chapter proposes one possibility). Current research activity is devoted to studying moral thinking about a greater variety of situations, to proposing various representations of social-moral knowledge that underlie the construal of concrete social situations, to exploring varieties of assessment techniques, to studying the cognitive prerequisites of moral thinking, to determining the coherence and cross-situational stability of general systems of moral thinking, to determining what life experiences foster moral development, and to determining the role of moral judgment in behavior.

Research on moral thinking that draws on other traditions (social psychology approaches, information processing approaches) has attended to the way that variations in stimuli, task requirements, and context affect the way people make moral judgments. This research has suggested the importance of processes that do not draw on distinctively *moral* concepts, such as the extraction of information from story material, drawing inferences about the motives and intentions of others, holding various bits of information in mind and combining them, and selectively attending to one or another set of cues. Generally, the differences between younger children and older people are explained in terms of deficiencies in not attending to all the information, in not holding and integrating information, and in being too much swayed by obvious cues at the expense of noticing more subtle ones. This research has not addressed the question of whether general knowledge about the social world (how people cooperate, how social arrangements are made) affects moral judgments in specific situations, nor has it explained why older, more sophisticated subjects prefer to use more complex forms of reasoning (it only explains why younger, less sophisticated subjects have difficulty in carrying out the complex forms of reasoning). One future direction for this approach would be to represent general social knowledge about the world in terms of scripts, frames, schemas, plans, and so on. In other words, to characterize structures of social knowledge differently than Piaget-type stages—not so deep and all pervasive, not defined in terms of logicomathematical operations, not invariant and universal step-by-step sequences, but very sensitive to situational and task conditions—and to investigate how this knowledge is related to a person's determination of what is morally right or wrong in concrete situations. Interesting research might emerge, for instance, by explaining selective memory effects or false representations of social situations in terms of the operation of such structures. And, as with virtually all research on cognitive development in all domains, the relevance of this research to naturalistic real-life behavior needs to be clarified and demonstrated.

NOTES

1. Some writers (e.g., Wallace & Walker, 1970) define morality as encompassing all questions of value, including duties to oneself that involve no one else. I have chosen a narrower definition, one focusing on *social* morality (questions of duty to others, justice, the conditions of social cooperation), not because these wider questions of value are unimportant or unworthy of research but because little developmental research has been done and because there is no evidence that the core notions and psychological processes related to social morality are the same as those relating to other values. It is true that conceptions of duty and fairness are closely tied to conceptions of the "good" (an argument for not separating social morality from other questions of value); however, it is also true that conceptions of duty and fairness are closely tied to conceptions of human life (Is a 2-month fetus a human life?), self (Is one person's self bounded by his skin or does it include his children, work, interests?), rationality, society, and so on. Rather than taking up the whole network of interconnected thought, social morality will be delineated as a special domain, which is the focus of this chapter.

By defining the domain of morality as separable from other domains of value, I do imply that all individuals always distinguish moral questions (how to determine rights and responsibilities) from other value questions (e.g., those of aesthetics, religion, convention). Indeed, there is evidence that some individuals sometimes answer moral questions with aesthetic or other nonmoral value considerations (e.g., ''He doesn't deserve to get the job because he looks funny and has long hair''). Nevertheless, we can delimit the scope of what to include in our study of morality by considering how subjects deal with situations in which their actions have welfare consequences for others.

2. This four-part framework assumes that the major question of moral psychology relevant to this volume is to explain individual moral behavior—that is, the processes, organization, and determinants of the individual acting in a publically observable way that impacts the flow of events in the real world. Thus, we do not deal with the processes and dynamics of group decision making or the morality of social organizations and cultures as units of investigation. Also, we deemphasize those inner, subjective feelings and thoughts that are never publically manifested (such as hidden guilt, judgments that are never uttered or acted upon); however, we do consider inner feelings and thoughts as important determinants in the production of behavior.

3. Rawls does not address the problem of explaining the motivation of moral leaders who are ahead of their contemporaries and whose vision brings new just communities into existence.

4. Social learning proponents may object to my saying that no theories have produced very strong or compelling evidence for their view. It is true that many demonstrations exist that social reinforcement and modeling opportunities influence social behavior (e.g., Rushton, 1980; Staub, 1978, 1979), including behavior that is often called moral behavior. However, evidence that some condition influences behavior is not sufficient grounds for concluding that one has explained the motivational basis for the behavior. Consider the following analogy: it can be demonstrated that wind affects the speed of a car (if the wind is blowing against the car it slows it down); however, it would be false to conclude that the basic motive power of cars is wind power. Cars are fundamentally different than sailboats. So also, in showing that certain modeling experiences increase or decrease the amount of sharing behavior, one cannot conclude that the basic motivation to share is due to modeling experiences.

5. The term morality is used in common speech for a variety of purposes (see Wallace & Walker, 1970), and in this chapter we do so also. In one sense, morality is used to distinguish one domain from another, for example, a moral consideration as opposed to a nonmoral consideration. The moral domain as an area of psychological study is the response of subjects to problems involving the deter-

mination of rights and duties. Also, moral is sometimes used as shorthand for morally commendable (as opposed to immoral), for example, in talking about the deficiencies in any component leading to moral failure, whatever subjects do in response to a problem of rights and duties is a moral response in the first sense (relevant to the psychological study of morality) but may not be moral in the second sense (morally commendable). A third use of the term moral is in reference to the particular inner processes that cause a behavior (in this chapter, defined in terms of the four components). The point being made here is that if the inner processes are not known or involve fundamentally different processes, then the behavior cannot be classified as governed by moral processes. In the third sense, moral implies a particular psychological analysis of the processes causing the behavior.

6. A similar case could be made for calling behavior intelligent. The term refers not only to some outwardly observable behavior but also to the inner processes that gave rise to the behavior.

7. The number of bibliographic entries in the area of moral development is now probably around the 5,000 mark. Useful listings have been compiled by Hill, Klafter, and Wallace (1976) for works up through 1975; since 1975, a listing of references for each year is provided in the spring issue of Kuhmerker's *Moral Education Forum*.

8. The 1978 system was described in a proposal, ''Assessment of Moral Judgment in Childhood and Youth,'' that L. Kohlberg, A. Colby, and W. Damon presented to the National Institutes of Health when requesting a grant.

9. Because the Kohlberg group has studied these cases so intensively for so many years, there is the lingering concern about generalizability to other samples (even though the latest system was worked out on a few construction cases and then the rest of the sample was scored blind). Partial replication comes from a recent series of studies by Gibbs and Widaman (1982). Using a modified form of the Harvard test (which correlates .85 with the original), Gibbs and Widaman studied five different samples (totaling over 700 subjects) and found interrater reliabilities (among trained raters) generally in the .80s, a test-retest correlation of .87, parallel form correlation of .90, and internal consistencies (Cronbach's alpha) in the .80s and .90s. Also powerful cross-sectional age trends were found ($r = .65$ and .71), the test discriminated delinquents from nondelinquents and showed significant gains owing to an educational intervention. Thus, even though the test by Gibbs and Widaman is not exactly equivalent to

the new Harvard test and even though they do not report longitudinal data, nevertheless, they both embody the same reconceptualization of stage features and produce results on different samples that bolster confidence in the new scoring system.

10. Additional, more recent longitudinal studies reporting significant movement on the DIT are by Broadhurst, 1980; Kaseman, 1980; Mentkowski, in preparation; Sheehan, Husted, & Candee, 1981; Whiteley, 1982.

11. Kurdek (1980) has introduced a fourth paradigm for the study of prerequisite relationships; however, the measure of moral judgment was not the six-stage model. The design uses cross-lagged panel correlations. If perspective taking is a prerequisite to moral judgment, then the expectation is that perspective taking at Time 1 should correlate with moral judgment at Time 2, higher than moral judgment at Time 1 should correlate with perspective taking at Time 2. Unexpectedly, "the present results indicate that the preponderance of causation was in the direction of children's early moral judgment abilities operating as a cause of their latter cognitive perspective-taking ability" (Kurdek, 1980, p. 116).

12. For example, Kohlberg (1976) talks about his Stage 3 involving the coordination of inversion and reciprocity—taking various perspectives and comprehension of the reciprocality among these viewpoints. Damon (1977) describes his positive justice levels in terms of the type of justice conflict that the child recognizes, the means by which the child resolves the conflict, the identification of relevant participants, and the nature of the justification.

REFERENCES

Abelson, R. P. Psychological status of the script concept. *American Psychologist*, 1981, *36*, 715–729.

Adams, J. S. Toward an understanding of inequity. *Journal of Abnormal and Social Psychology*, 1963, *67*, 422–436.

Alston, W. P. Comments on Kohlberg's "From is to ought." In T. Mischel (Ed.), *Cognitive development and epistemology*. New York: Academic Press, 1971.

Anchor, K. N., & Cross, H. G. Maladaptive aggression, moral perspective, and the socialization process. *Journal of Personality and Social Psychology*, 1974, *30*, 163–168.

Anderson, N. H. Information integration theory in developmental psychology. In F. Wilkening, J. Becker, & T. Trabasso (Eds.), *Information integration by children*. Hillsdale, N.J.: Erlbaum, 1980.

Anderson, N. H., & Butzin, C. A. Integration theory applied to children's judgments of equity. *Developmental Psychology*, 1978, *14*, 593–606.

Andreason, A. W. The effects of social responsibility, moral judgment, and conformity on helping behavior (doctoral dissertation, Brigham Young University, 1975). *Dissertation Abstracts International*, 1976, *36*, 585A–613A. (University Microfilms No. 76–9,829)

Arbuthnot, J. Modification of moral judgment through role playing. *Developmental Psychology*, 1975, *11*, 319–324.

Aron, I. E. Moral philosophy and moral education. A critique of Kohlberg's theory. *School Review*, 1977, *85*, 197–217. (a)

Aron, I. E. Moral philosophy and moral education-II. The formalist tradition and the Deweyan alternative. *School Review*, 1977, *85*, 513–534. (b)

Aronfreed, J. *Conduct and conscience*. New York: Academic Press, 1968.

Baldwin, C. P., & Baldwin, A. L. Children's judgment of kindness. *Child Development*, 1970, *41*, 30–47.

Baltes, P. B. Longitudinal and cross-sectional sequences in the study of age and generation effects. *Human Development*, 1968, *11*, 145–171.

Bandura, A. *Social learning theory*. Englewood Cliffs, N.J.: Prentice-Hall, 1977.

Bandura, A., Underwood, B., & Fromson, M. E. Disinhibition of aggression through diffusion of responsibility and dehumanization of victims. *Journal of Research in Personality*, 1975, *9*, 253–269.

Barrett, D. E., & Yarrow, M. R. Prosocial behavior, social inferential ability, and assertiveness in children. *Child Development*, 1977, *48*, 475–481.

Bar-Tal, D., Raviv, A., & Leiser, T. The development of altruistic behavior: Empirical evidence. *Developmental Psychology*, 1980, *16*, 516–524.

Bartlett, F. C. *Remembering*. Cambridge: At the University Press, 1932.

Bereiter, C. The morality of moral education. *Hastings Center Report*, 1978, *7*, 20–25.

Berkowitz, L. Social norms, feelings, and other factors affecting helping and altruism. In L. Berkowitz (Ed.) *Advances in experimental social psychology* (Vol. 6). New York: Academic Press, 1972.

Berkowitz, L., & Daniels, L. R. Responsibility and dependency. *Journal of Abnormal and Social Psychology*, 1963, *66*, 429–436.

Berkowitz, M. W. The role of transactive discussion in moral development: The history of six-year program of research—Part II. *Moral Education Forum*, 1980, *5*, 15–27.

Berkowitz, M. W. A critical appraisal of the educational and psychological perspectives on moral discussion. *Journal of Educational Thought*, 1981, *15*, 20–33.

Berkowitz, M. W., & Gibbs, J. C. Transactive communication as a condition for moral development. Paper presented at the meeting of the Society for Research in Child Development, Boston, Mass., April 1981.

Berkowitz, M. W., Gibbs, J. C., Broughton, J. M. The relation of moral judgment stage disparity to developmental effects of peer dialogues. *Merrill-Palmer Quarterly*, 1980, *26*, 341–357.

Berndt, T. J. The effect of reciprocity norms on moral judgment and causal attribution. *Child Development*, 1977, *48*, 1322–1330.

Berndt, T. J. Lack of acceptance of reciprocity norms in preschool children. *Developmental Psychology*, 1979, *15*, 662–663.

Blasi, A. Bridging moral cognition and moral action: A critical review of the literature. *Psychological Bulletin*, 1980, *88*, 593–637.

Blasi, A. Moral identity: Its development and role in moral functioning. In W. M. Kurtines & J. L. Gewirtz (Eds.), *Morality, moral development, and moral behavior: Basic issues in theory and research*. In preparation.

Blatt, M., & Kohlberg, L. The effects of classroom moral discussion upon children's level of moral judgment. *Journal of Moral Education*, 1975, *4*, 129–161.

Bloom, A. H. Two dimensions of moral reasoning: Social principledness and social humanism in cross-cultural perspective. *Journal of Social Psychology*, 1977, *101*, 29–44.

Bobrow, D. G., & Norman, D. A. Some principles of memory schemata. In D. Bobrow & W. A. Collins (Eds.), *Representation and understanding*. New York: Academic Press, 1975.

Bode, J., & Page, R. The ethical reasoning inventory. In L. Kuhmerker, M. Mentkowski, & V. L. Erikson (Eds.) *Evaluating moral development and evaluating educational programs with a value dimension*. Schenectady, N.Y.: Character Research Press, 1980.

Boyce, W. D., & Jensen, L. C. *Moral reasoning: A psychological-philosophical integration*. Lincoln: University of Nebraska Press, 1978.

Braine, M. D. S. The ontogeny of certain logical operations: Piaget's formulation examined by non-verbal methods. *Psychological Monographs*, 1959, *73*(5, Whole No. 475).

Brainerd, C. J. Judgments and explanations as criteria for the presence of cognitive structure. *Psychological Bulletin*, 1973, *79*, 172–179.

Brainerd, C. J. *Piaget's theory of intelligence*. Englewood Cliffs, N.J.: Prentice-Hall, 1978.

Brandt, R. R. *Ethical theory*. Englewood Cliffs, N.J.: Prentice-Hall, 1959.

Broadhurst, B. P. Report: Defining Issues Test. Unpublished manuscript, Colorado State University, 1980.

Bronfenbrenner, U. Soviet methods of character education—some implications for research. *American Psychologist*, 1962, *17*, 550–565.

Bronfenbrenner, U. Reaction to social pressure from adults versus peers among Soviet day-school and boarding-school pupils in the perspective of an American sample. *Journal of Personality and Social Psychology*, 1970, *15*, 179–189.

Broughton, J. M. The cognitive-developmental approach to morality: A reply to Kurtines and Greif. *Journal of Moral Education*, 1978, *7*, 81–96.

Bull, N. J. *Moral judgment from childhood to adolescence*. Beverly Hills, Calif.: Sage Publications, 1969.

Burton, R. Honesty and dishonesty. In T. Lickona (Ed.), *Moral development and behavior: Theory, research and social issues*. New York: Holt, Rinehart & Winston, 1976.

Byrne, D. F. The development of role-taking in adolescence (Doctoral dissertation, Harvard University, 1973). *Dissertation Abstracts International*, 1974, *34*, 5647B. (University Microfilms No. 74–11,314).

Campagna, A. F., & Harter, S. Moral judgment in sociopathic and normal children. *Journal of Personality and Social Psychology*, 1975, *31*, 199–205.

Candee, D. Structure and choice in moral reasoning. *Journal of Personality and Social Psychology*, 1976, *34*, 1293–1301.

Carroll, J. L. & Rest, J. R. Development in moral judgment as indicated by rejection of lower-stage statements. *Journal of Research in Personality*, 1981, *15*, 538–544.

Carroll, J. S., & Payne, J. W. Judgments about crime and the criminal: A model and a method for investigating parole decisions. In B. D. Sales (Ed.), *Perspectives in law and psychology: The criminal justice system* (Vol. 1). New York: Plenum, 1977.

Chomsky, N. *Syntactic structures*. The Hague:

Mouton, 1957.

Colby, A. Logical operational limitations on the development of moral judgment (doctoral dissertation, Columbia University, 1973). *Dissertation Abstracts International*, 1973, *34*, 2331B. (University Microfilms No. 73–28,193)

Colby, A. Evolution of a moral-developmental theory. In W. Damon (Ed.), *New directions for child development*. San Francisco: Jossey-Bass, 1978.

Colby, A., Gibbs, J., Kohlberg, L., Speicher-Dubin, B., Power, C., & Candee, D. *Standard form scoring manual*. Cambridge, Mass.: Harvard Graduate School of Education, Center for Moral Education, 1980.

Colby, A., & Kohlberg, L. The relation between logical and moral development. Unpublished manuscript, Harvard University, 1975.

Colby, A., Kohlberg, L., Gibbs, J., & Lieberman, M. A longitudinal study of moral judgment. *Monographs of the Society for Research in Child Development*, in press.

Collins, W. A. Effect of temporal seperation between motivation, aggression, and consequences: A developmental study. *Developmental Psychology*, 1973, *8*, 215–221.

Collins, W. A., Berndt, T. J., & Hess, V. L. Observational learning of motives and consequences for television aggression: A developmental study. *Child Development*, 1974, *45*, 799–802.

Collins, W. A., Wellman, H. M., Keniston, A., & Westby, S. D. Age-related aspects of comprehension and inference from a televised dramatic narrative. *Child Development*, 1978, *49*, 389–399.

Damon, W. Early conceptions of positive justice as related to the development of logical operations. *Child Development*, 1975, *46*, 301–312.

Damon, W. *The social world of the child*. San Francisco: Jossey-Bass, 1977.

Damon, W. Patterns of change in children's social reasoning: A two-year longitudinal study. *Child Development*, 1980, *51*, 1010–1017. (a)

Damon, W. Structural-developmental theory and the study of moral development. In M. Windmiller, N. Lambert, & E. Turiel (Eds.), *Moral development and socialization*. Boston: Allyn & Bacon, 1980. (b)

Darley, J., & Batson, C. D. From Jerusalem to Jericho: A study of situational and dispositional variables in helping behavior. *Journal of Personality and Social Psychology*, 1973, *27*, 100–108.

Darley, J. M., Klossen, E. C., and Zanna, M. P. Intentions and their contexts in the moral judgments of children and adults. *Child Development*, 1978, *49*, 66–74.

Davison, M. L. On a unidimensional, metric unfolding model for attitudinal and developmental data. *Psychometrika*, 1977, *42*, 523–548.

Davison, M. L., & Robbins, S. The reliability and validity of objective indices of moral development. *Applied Psychological Measurement*, 1978, *2*, 391–403.

Davison, M. L., Robbins, S., & Swanson, D. Stage structure in objective moral judgments. *Developmental Psychology*, 1978, *14*, 137–146.

Dewey, J. *Moral principles in education*. New York: Philosophical Library, 1959.

Dickinson, V. M. The relation of principled moral thinking to commonly measured sample characteristics and to family correlates in samples of Australian Senior High School adolescents and family triads. Unpublished doctoral dissertation, Macquarie University, Austral., 1979.

Dienstbier, R. A., Hillman, D., Lehnhoff, J., Hillman, J., & Valkenaar, M. C. An emotion-attribution approach to moral behavior: Interfacing cognitive and avoidance theories of moral development. *Psychological Review*, 1975, *82*, 299–315.

Dienstbier, R. A., & Munter, P. O. Cheating as a function of the labeling of natural arousal. *Journal of Personality and Social Psychology*, 1971, *17*, 208–213.

Durkheim, E. *Moral education*. New York: Free Press, 1961. (Originally published, 1925.)

Eckensberger, L. H. Research on moral development in Germany. *German Journal of Psychology*, in press.

Edwards, C. P. Social experiences and moral judgment in Kenyan young adults. *Journal of Genetic Psychology*, 1978, *133*, 19–30.

Edwards, C. P. The comparative study of the development of moral judgment and reasoning. In R. L. Munroe, R. Munroe, & B. B. Whiting (Eds.), *Handbook of cross-cultural human development*. New York: Garland, 1980.

Eisenberg-Berg, N. The relation of political attitudes to constraint-oriented and prosocial moral reasoning. *Developmental Psychology*, 1976, *12*, 552–553.

Eisenberg-Berg, N. Development of children's prosocial moral judgment. *Developmental Psychology*, 1979, *15*, 128–137. (a)

Eisenberg-Berg, N. Relationship of prosocial moral reasoning to altruism, political liberalism, and intelligence. *Developmental Psychology*, 1979, *15*, 87–89. (b)

Eisenberg-Berg, N., & Hand, M. The relationship

of preschoolers' reasoning about prosocial moral conflicts to prosocial behavior. *Child Development*, 1979, *50*, 356–363.

Eisenberg-Berg, N., & Mussen, P. H. Empathy and moral development in adolescence. *Developmental Psychology*, 1978, *14*, 185–186.

Eisenberg-Berg, N., & Roth, K. The development of young children's prosocial moral judgment: A longitudinal follow-up. *Developmental Psychology*, 1980, *16*, 375–376.

Enright, R. D., Enright, W. F., Manheim, L. A., & Harris, B. E. Distributive justice development and social class. *Developmental Psychology*, 1980, *16*, 555–563.

Enright, R. D., Franklin, C. C., & Manheim, L. A. Children's distributive justice reasoning: A standardized and objective scale. *Developmental Psychology*, 1980, *16*, 193–202.

Enright, R. D., Manheim, L. A., Lapsley, D. K., & Enright, W. F. An alternative to *Method Clinique:* A standardized scale of children's distributive justice reasoning. Paper presented at the meeting of the International Interdisciplinary Conference on Piagetian Theory and the Helping Professions, January 1981.

Enright, R. D., & Sutterfield, S. J. An ecological validation of social cognitive development. *Child Development*, 1980, *51*, 156–161.

Erikson, E. *Young man Luther*. New York: W. W. Norton, 1958.

Erikson, E. *Identity: Youth and crisis*. New York: W. W. Norton, 1968.

Eysenck, H. J. The biology of morality. In T. Lickona (Ed.), *Moral development and behavior: Theory, research, and social issues*. New York: Holt, Rinehart & Winston, 1976.

Farnill, D. The effects of social-judgment set on children's use of intent information. *Journal of Personality*, 1974, *42*, 276–289.

Fishbein, M. Attitude and prediction of behavior. In M. Fishbein (Ed.), *Readings in attitude theory and measurement*. New York: Wiley, 1967.

Fishkin, J., Keniston, K., & MacKinnon, C. Moral development and political ideology. *Journal of Personality and Social Psychology*, 1973, *27*, 109–119.

Flavell, J. H. Concept development. In P. H. Mussen (Ed.), *Carmichael's manual of child psychology* (Vol. 1, 3rd ed.). New York: Wiley, 1970.

Flavell, J. H. Stage-related properties of cognitive development. *Cognitive Psychology*, 1971, *2*, 421–453.

Flavell, J. H. *Cognitive development*. Englewood Cliffs, N.J.: Prentice-Hall, 1977.

Flavell, J. H. Metacognition and cognitive monitoring: A new area of cognitive-developmental inquiry. *American Psychologist*, 1979, *34*, 906–911.

Flavell, J. H. Structures, stages, and sequences in cognitive development. In W. A. Collins (Ed.), *Minnesota Symposium on Child Psychology*, in press.

Flavell, J. H., & Wohlwill, J. F. Formal and functional aspects of cognitive development. In D. Elkind & J. H. Flavell (Eds.), *Studies in cognitive development: Essays in honor of Jean Piaget*. New York: Oxford University Press, 1969.

Fodor, E. M. Delinquency and susceptibility to social influences among adolescents as a function of level of moral development. *Journal of Social Psychology*, 1972, *86*, 257–260.

Fodor, E. M. Moral development and parent behavior antecedents in adolescent psychopaths. *Journal of Genetic Psychology*, 1973, *122*, 37–43.

Fontana, A., & Noel, B. Moral reasoning at the university. *Journal of Personality and Social Psychology*, 1973, *3*, 419–429.

Fowler, J. W. Stages in faith: The structural developmental approach. In T. Hennessey (Ed.), *Values and moral development*. New York: Paulist Press, 1976.

Frankel, J. R. The Kohlbergian paradigm: Some reservations. In P. Scharf (Ed.), *Readings in moral education*. Minneapolis: Winston Press, 1978.

Frankena, W. K. *Ethics*. Englewood Cliffs, N.J.: Prentice-Hall, 1963.

Frankena, W. K. The concept of morality. In G. Wallace & A. D. M. Walker (Eds.), *The definition of morality*. London: Methuen, 1970.

Fritz, B. R. The cognitive requisites for conventional moral judgment (doctoral dissertation, Yeshiva University, 1974). *Dissertation Abstracts International*, 1974, *35*, 1887B. (University Microfilms No. 74–23,547)

Froming, W., & Cooper, R. G. Predicting compliance behavior from moral judgment scales. Unpublished manuscript, University of Texas, 1976.

Furth, H. G. *The world of grown-ups: Children's conceptions of society*. New York: Elsevier, 1980.

Gallatin, J. Political thinking in adolescence. In J. Adelson (Ed.), *Handbook of adolescent psychology*. New York: Wiley, 1980.

Garbarino, J., & Bronfenbrenner, U. The socialization of moral judgment and behavior in cross-cultural perspective. In T. Lickona (Ed.), *Moral development and behavior: Theory, research, and social issues*. New York: Holt, Rinehart & Winston, 1976.

Gibbs, J. C. Kohlberg's stages of moral judgment: A constructive critique. *Harvard Educational Review*, 1977, *47*, 43–61.

Gibbs, J. C. Kohlberg's moral stage theory: A Piagetian revision. *Human Development*, 1979, *22*, 89–112.

Gibbs, J. C., & Widaman, K. F. *Social intelligence: Measuring the development of sociomoral reflection*. Englewood Cliffs, N.J.: Prentice-Hall, 1982.

Gilligan, C. F. In a different voice: Women's conceptions of self and morality. *Harvard Educational Review*, 1977, *47*, 481–517.

Gilligan, C. F., Kohlberg, L., Lerner, T., & Belenky, M. Moral reasoning about sexual dilemmas: The development of an interview and scoring system. In *Technical report of the commission on obscenity and pornography* (Vol. 1) (No. 5256–0010). Washington, D.C.: U.S. Government Printing Office, 1971.

Gilligan, C., & Murphy, J. M. The philosopher and the ''dilemma of the fact.'' Unpublished manuscript, Harvard University, 1978.

Goldiamond, I. Moral development: A functional analysis. *Psychology Today*, 1968, *2*, 31–34, 70.

Gottlieb, D. E., Taylor, S. E., & Ruderman, A. Cognitive bases of children's moral judgments. *Developmental Psychology*, 1977, *13*, 547–556.

Gouldner, A. W. The norm of reciprocity. *American Sociological Review*, 1960, *25*, 165–167.

Grim, P. F., Kohlberg, L., & White, S. H. Some relationships between conscience and attentional processes. *Journal of Personality and Social Psychology*, 1968, *8*, 239–252.

Grueneich, R., & Trabasso, T. The story as a social environment: Children's comprehension and evaluation of intentions and consequences. In J. Harvey (Ed.), *Cognition, social behavior and the environment*. Hillsdale, N.J.: Erlbaum, in press.

Gunzburger, D. W., Wagner, D. M., & Anooshian, L. Moral judgment and distributive justice. *Human Development*, 1977, *20*, 160–170.

Haan, N. Hypothetical and actual moral reasoning in a situation of civil disobedience. *Journal of Personality and Social Psychology*, 1975, *32*, 225–270.

Haan, N. Two moralities in action contexts: Relationships to thought, ego regulation, and development. *Journal of Personality and Social Psychology*, 1978, *30*, 286–305.

Haan, N., Smith, M. B., & Block, J. H. The moral reasoning of young adults: Political-social behavior, family background, and personality correlates. *Journal of Personality and Social Psychology*, 1968, *10*, 183–201.

Harris, S., Mussen, P. H., & Rutherford, E. Some cognitive, behavioral, and personality correlates of maturity of moral judgment. *Journal of Genetic Psychology*, 1976, *128*, 123–135.

Hastie, R. Schematic principles in human memory. In E. T. Higgins, C. Sherman, & M. Zanna (Eds.), *The Ontario symposium on personality and social psychology: Social cognition*. Hillsdale, N.J.: Erlbaum, in press.

Heider, F. *The psychology of interpersonal relations*. New York: Wiley, 1958.

Hersch, R., Paolitto, D., & Reimer, J. *Promoting moral growth from Piaget to Kohlberg*. New York: Longman, 1979.

Hill, R. A., Klafter, M. B., & Wallace, J. D. *A bibliography on moral/values education*. Philadelphia: Research for Better Schools, Inc., 1976.

Hoffman, M. L. Moral development. In P. H. Mussen (Ed.), *Carmichael's manual of child psychology* (Vol. 2, 3rd ed.). New York: Wiley, 1970.

Hoffman, M. L. Developmental synthesis of affect and cognition and its implications for altruistic motivation. *Developmental Psychology*, 1975, *11*, 607–622.

Hoffman, M. L. Empathy, role-taking, guilt, and development of altruistic motives. In T. Lickona (Ed.), *Moral development and behavior: Theory, research and social issues*. New York: Holt, Rinehart & Winston, 1976.

Hoffman, M. L. Empathy, its development and prosocial implications. In C. B. Keasey (Ed.), *Nebraska Symposium on Motivation* (Vol. 25). Lincoln: University of Nebraska Press, 1978.

Hoffman, M. L. Is altruism part of human nature? *Journal of Personality and Social Psychology*, 1981, *40*, 121–137.

Hoffman, M. L. Affective and cognitive processes in moral internalization. In E. T. Higgins, D. Ruble, & W. Hartup (Eds.), *Social cognition and social behavior*. New York: Cambridge University Press, in press.

Hogan, R. A dimension of moral judgment. *Journal of Consulting and Clinical Psychology*, 1970, *35*, 205–212.

Hogan, R. Theoretical egocentrism and the problem of compliance. *American Psychologist*, 1975,

30, 533–540.

Holstein, C. B. The relation of children's moral judgment level to that of their parents and to communication patterns in the family. In R. Smart & M. Smart (Eds.), *Readings in child development.* New York: Macmillan, 1972.

Holstein, C. B. Irreversible, stepwise sequence in the development of moral judgment: A longitudinal study of males and females. *Child Development,* 1976, *47,* 51–61.

Hook, J. G. The development of equity and logicomathematical thinking. *Child Development,* 1978, *49,* 1035–1044.

Hook, J. G., & Cook, T. D. Equity theory and the cognitive ability of children. *Psychological Bulletin,* 1979, *86,* 429–445.

Hornstein, H. A. *Cruelty and kindness. A new look at aggression and altruism.* Englewood Cliffs, N.J.: Prentice-Hall, 1976.

Inhelder, B., & Piaget, J. *The growth of logical thinking from childhood to adolescence* (A. Parsons & S. Milgram, trans.). New York: Basic Books, 1958. (Originally published, 1955).

Inhelder, B., & Sinclair, H. Learning cognitive structures. In P. H. Mussen, J. Langer, & M. Covington (Eds.), *Trends and issues in developmental psychology.* New York: Holt, Rinehart & Winston, 1969.

Iozzi, L. The environmental issues test. In L. Kuhmerker, M. Mentkowski, & V. L. Erikson (Eds.), *Evaluating moral development and evaluating educational programs with a value dimension.* Schenectady, N.Y.: Character Research Press, 1980.

Isen, A. M. Success, failure, attention and reaction to others: The warm glow of success. *Journal of Personality and Social Psychology,* 1970, *15,* 294–301.

Isen, A. M., Shalker, T. E., Clark, M., & Karp, L. Affect, accessibility of material in memory and behavior: A cognitive loop? *Journal of Personality and Social Psychology,* 1978, *36,* 1–13.

Jacobs, M. K. Women's moral reasoning and behavior in a contractual form of prisoners' dilemma. In J. R. Rest (Ed.), *Development in judging moral issues—a summary of research using the Defining Issues Test* (Minnesota Moral Research Projects, Tech. Rep. No. 3), 1977. (ERIC Document Reproduction Service No. ED 144 980)

Jones, E. E., & Davis, K. E. From acts to disposition: The attribution process in person perception. In L. Berkowitz (Ed.), *Advances in experimental social psychology* (Vol. 2). New York: Academic Press, 1965.

Karniol, R. Children's use of intention cues in evaluating behavior. *Psychological Bulletin,* 1978, *85,* 76–86.

Karniol, R. A conceptual analysis of immanent justice responses in children. *Child Development,* 1980, *51,* 118–130.

Kaseman, T. C. A longitudinal study of moral development of the West Point class of 1981. West Point, N.Y.: U.S. Military Academy, Department of Behavioral Sciences and Leadership, 1980.

Keasey, C. B. Social participation as a factor in the moral development of preadolescents. *Developmental Psychology,* 1971, *5,* 216–220.

Keasey, C. B. Experimentally induced changes in moral opinions and reasoning. *Journal of Personality and Social Psychology,* 1973, *26,* 30–38.

Keasey, C. B. The influence of opinion agreement and the quality of supportive reasoning in the evaluation of moral judgments. *Journal of Personality and Social Psychology,* 1974, *30,* 477–482.

Keasey, C. B. Implicators of cognitive development for moral reasoning. In D. J. De Palma & J. M. Foley (Eds.), *Moral development: Current theory and research.* Hillsdale, N.J.: Erlbaum, 1975.

Keasey, C. B. A longitudinal study of the relationship between cognitive and social development. Paper presented at the meeting of the American Educational Research Association, San Francisco, April 1976. (ERIC Document Reproduction Service No. ED 122 966)

Keasey, C. B. Children's developing awareness and usage of intentionality and motives. In C. B. Keasey (Ed.), *Nebraska Symposium on Motivation,* (Vol. 25). Lincoln: University of Nebraska Press, 1978.

Kelley, H. H. Moral evaluation. *American Psychologist,* 1971, *26,* 293–300.

Kohlberg, L. The development of modes of moral thinking and choice in the years 10 to 16. Unpublished doctoral dissertation, University of Chicago, 1958.

Kohlberg, L. State and sequence: The cognitive-developmental approach to socialization. In D. Goslin (Ed.), *Handbook of socialization theory and research.* Chicago: Rand McNally, 1969.

Kohlberg, L. From is to ought: How to commit the naturalistic fallacy and get away with it in the study of moral development. In T. Mischel (Ed.), *Cognitive development and epistemology.* New York: Academic Press, 1971.

Kohlberg, L. The claim to moral adequacy of a highest stage of moral judgment. *Journal of Philosophy*, 1973, *40*, 630–646. (a)

Kohlberg, L. Continuities in childhood and adult moral development revisited. In P. B. Baltes & K. W. Schaie (Eds.), *Life-span developmental psychology: personality and socialization*. New York: Academic Press, 1973. (b)

Kohlberg, L. Moral stages and moralization: The cognitive-developmental. In T. Lickona (Ed.), *Moral development and behavior: Theory, research, and social issues*. New York: Holt, Rinehart & Winston, 1976.

Kohlberg, L. High school democracy and educating for a just society. In R. Mosher (Ed.), *Moral education: A first generation of research and development*. New York: Praeger, 1980.

Kohlberg, L., Colby, A., Gibbs, J., & Speicher-Dubin, B. *Standard form scoring manual*. Cambridge, Mass.: Harvard Graduate School of Education, Center for Moral Education, 1978.

Kohlberg, L., & Elfenbein, D. The development of moral judgments concerning capital punishments. *American Journal of Orthopsychiatry*, 1975, *45*, 614–640.

Kohlberg, L., Kauffman, K., Scharf, P., & Hickey, J. *The just community approach to corrections*. Cambridge, Mass.: Moral Education Research Foundation, 1974.

Kohlberg, L., & Kramer, R. Continuities and discontinuities in childhood moral development. *Human Development*, 1969, *12*, 93–120.

Krebs, D. L. A cognitive-developmental approach to altruism. In D. L. Krebs (Ed.), *Altruism, sympathy and helping*. New York: Academic Press, 1978.

Krebs, R. L. Some relations between moral judgment, attention, and resistance to temptation. Unpublished doctoral dissertation, University of Chicago, 1967.

Kuhmerker, L. (Ed.). *Moral Education Forum*. 1975–1982. (Spring issues)

Kuhn, D. Inducing development experimentally: Comments on a research paradigm. *Developmental Psychology*, 1974, *10*, 590–600.

Kuhn, D. Short term longitudinal evidence for the sequentiality of Kohlberg's early stages of moral judgment. *Developmental Psychology*, 1976, *12*, 162–166.

Kuhn, D., Langer, J., Kohlberg, L., & Haan, N. The development of formal operations in logical and moral judgment. *Genetic Psychology Monographs*, 1977, *95*, 97–188.

Kurdek, L. A. Perspective taking as the cognitive basis of children's moral development: A review of the literature. *Merrill-Palmer Quarterly*, 1978, *24*, 3–28.

Kurdek, L. A. Developmental relations among children's perspective taking, moral judgment, and parent-rated behavior. *Merrill-Palmer Quarterly*, 1980, *26*, 103–121.

Lane, J., & Anderson, N. H. Integration of intention and outcome in moral judgments. *Memory & Cognition*, 1976, *4*, 1–5.

Larson, S., & Kurdek, L. A. Intratask and intertask consistency of moral judgment indices in first-, third-, and fifth-grade children. *Developmental Psychology*, 1979, *15*, 462–463.

Lawrence, J. A. The component procedures of moral judgment-making. Unpublished doctoral dissertation, University of Minnesota, 1978. *Dissertation Abstracts International*, 1979, *40*, 896-B. (University Microfilms No. 7918360)

Lawrence, J. A. Components of moral judgment-making about social issues. *Australian Psychologist*, 1979, *14*, 214ff.

Lawrence, J. A. Moral judgment intervention studies using the Defining Issues Test. *Journal of Moral Education*, 1980, *9*, 178–191.

Leeds, R. Altruism and the norm of giving. *Merrill-Palmer Quarterly*, 1963, *9*, 229–240.

Leming, J. S. Cheating behavior, situational influence, and moral development. *Journal of Educational Research*, 1978, *71*, 214–217.

Leon, M. Integration of intent and consequence information in children's moral judgments. In F. Wilkening, J. Becker, & T. Trabasso (Eds.), *Information integration by children*. Hillsdale, N.J.: Erlbaum, 1980.

Lerner, M. J. Observer's evaluation of a victim: Justice, guilt and veridical perception. *Journal of Personality and Social Psychology*, 1971, *20*, 127–135.

Lerner, M. J. The justice motive: "Equity" and "parity" among children. *Journal of Personality and Social Psychology*, 1974, *29*, 539–550.

Levine, C. Role-taking standpoint adolescent usage of Kohlberg's conventional stage of moral reasoning. *Journal of Personality and Social Psychology*, 1976, *34*, 41.

Levine, C. Stage acquisition and stage use. An appraisal of stage displacement explanations of variation in moral reasoning. *Human Development*, 1979, *22*, 145–164.

Lickona, T. Research on Piaget's theory of moral development. In T. Lickona (Ed.), *Moral development and behavior: Theory, research, and social issues*. New York: Holt, Rinehart & Winston, 1976.

Lockwood, A. L. Relations of political and moral thought. Unpublished doctoral dissertation, Harvard University, 1970.

Lockwood, A. L. The effects of values clarification and moral development curriculum on school-age subjects: A critical review of recent research. *Review of Educational Research*, 1978, *48*, 325–364.

London, P. The rescuers: Motivational hypotheses about Christians who saved Jews from the Nazis. In J. Macaulay & L. Berkowitz (Eds.), *Altruism and helping behavior*. New York: Academic Press, 1970.

Maitland, K. A., & Goldman, J. R. Moral judgment as a function of peer group interaction. *Journal of Personality and Social Psychology*, 1974, *30*, 699–704.

Malinowski, C. Moral judgment and resistance to the temptation to cheat. Paper presented at the meeting of the American Psychological Association, Toronto, Canada, September 1978.

Mandler, J. M., & Johnson, N. S. Remembrance of things passed: Story structure and recall. *Cognitive Psychology*, 1977, *9*, 111–151.

Maqsud, M. The influence of social heterogeneity and sentimental credibility on moral judgments of Nigerian Muslim adolescents. *Journal of Cross-Cultural Psychology*, 1977, *8*, 113–122.

Masters, J. C., & Santrock, J. W. Studies in the self-regulation of behavior: Effects of contingent cognitive and affective events. *Developmental Psychology*, 1976, *12*, 334–348.

Matefy, R. E., & Acksen, B. A. The effect of role-playing discrepant positions on change in moral judgments and attitudes. *Journal of Genetic Psychology*, 1976, *128*, 189–200.

McCall, R. B. Challenges to a science of developmental psychology. *Child Development*, 1977, *48*, 333–344.

McColgan, E. Social cognition in delinquents, pre-delinquents, and non-delinquents. (Doctoral dissertation, University of Minnesota, 1975.) *Dissertation Abstracts International*, 1975, *37*, 199A. (University Microfilms No. 76–14,931)

McGeorge, C. M. Situational variation in level of moral judgment. *British Journal of Educational Psychology*, 1974, *44*, 116–122.

McGeorge, C. M. The susceptibility to faking of the Defining Issues Test of moral development. *Developmental Psychology*, 1975, *11*, 108.

Mentkowski, M. Evaluation of the Alverno College values education project. In preparation.

Merelman, R. M. The adolescence of political so-cialization. *Sociology of Education*, 1972, *45*, 134–166.

Minsky, M. A framework for representing knowledge. In P. Winston (Ed.), *The psychology of computer vision*. New York: McGraw-Hill, 1975.

Mischel, W. Processes in delay of gratification. In L. Berkowitz (Ed.), *Advances in experimental social psychology* (Vol. 7). New York: Academic Press, 1974.

Mischel, W., & Mischel, H. N. A cognitive social learning approach to morality and self-regulation. In T. Lickona (Ed.), *Moral development behavior*. New York: Holt, Rinehart & Winston, 1976.

Morrison, L., & Keasey, C. B. Children's use of intentionality and consequences under different instructional sets. Unpublished manuscript, University of Nebraska-Lincoln, 1977.

Nezworski, T., Stein, N. L., & Trabasso, T. Story structure versus content effects on children's recall and evaluative inferences. Unpublished manuscript, University of Minnesota, n.d.

Nucci, L. Conceptions of personal issues: A domain distinct from moral or social concepts. *Child Development*, 1981, *52*, 114–121.

Oser, F., Gmuender, P., & Fritzsche, U. Stages of religious judgment. Unpublished manuscript, University of Fribourg, Switz., 1979.

Parikh, B. Development of moral judgment and its relation to family environmental factors in Indian and American families. *Child Development*, 1980, *51*, 1030–1039.

Pennington, N., & Hastie, R. Juror decision-making models: The generalization gap. *Psychological Bulletin*, 1981, *89*, 246–287.

Peterson, L., Hartmann, D. P., & Gelfand, D. M. Developmental changes in the effects of dependency and reciprocity cues on children's moral judgments and donation rates. *Child Development*, 1977, *48*, 1331–1339.

Piaget, J. The general problem of the psycho-biological development of the child. In J. M. Tanner & B. Inhelder (Eds.), *Discussions on child development* (Vol. 4). New York: International Universities Press, 1960.

Piaget, J. *The child's conception of the world*. Paterson, N.J.: Littlefield, Adams, 1963. (Originally published, 1929.)

Piaget, J. *The moral judgment of the child* (M. Gabain, trans.). New York: Free Press, 1965. (Originally published, 1932).

Pomazal, R. J., & Jaccard, J. J. An informational

approach to altruistic behavior. *Journal of Personality and Social Psychology*, 1976, *33*, 317–327.

Raphael, D. *Moral judgment*. London: Allen & Unwin, 1955.

Rappoport, A., & Wallsten, T. S. Individual decision behavior. *Annual Review of Psychology*, 1972, *23*, 131–175.

Rawls, J. *A theory of justice*. Cambridge, Mass.: Harvard University Press, 1971.

Reid, H., & Yanarella, E. J. Critical political theory and moral development. On Kohlberg, Hampden-Turner, and Habermas. *Theory Soc.*, 1977, *4*, 479–500.

Renshon, S. A. *Handbook of political socialization: Theory and research*. New York: Free Press, 1977.

Rest, G. J. Voting preference in the 1976 presidential electional and the influences of moral reasoning. Unpublished manuscript, University of Michigan, 1978.

Rest, J. R. *Development in judging moral issues*. Minneapolis: University of Minnesota Press, 1979. (a)

Rest, J. R. *The impact of higher education on moral judgment development* (Tech. Rep. No. 5). Minneapolis: Minnesota Moral Research Projects, 1979. (b)

Rest, J. R. *Revised manual for the Defining Issues Test*. Minneapolis: Minnesota Moral Research Projects, 1979. (c)

Rest, J. R. Development in moral judgment research. *Developmental Psychology*, 1980, *16*, 251–256.

Rest, J. R. Bibliography of DIT research. Unpublished manuscript, University of Minnesota, 1982.

Rest, J. R., Davison, M. L., & Robbins, S. Age trends in judging moral issues: A review of cross-sectional, longitudinal, and sequential studies of the Defining Issues Test. *Child Development*, 1978, *49*, 263–279.

Rokeach, M. *The nature of human values*. New York: Free Press, 1973.

Rostollan, D. The effect of situational factors on post-behavior moral judgments of third and sixth grade children. Unpublished master's thesis, Illinois Institute of Technology, 1979.

Rule, B. G., Nesdale, A. R., & McAra, M. J. Children's reactions to information about the intentions underlying an aggressive act. *Child Development*, 1974, *45*, 794–798.

Rumelhart, D. E. Understanding and summarizing brief stories. In D. LaBerge & S. J. Samuels (Eds.), *Basic processes in reading: Perception and comprehension*. Hillsdale, N.J.: Erlbaum, 1977.

Rushton, J. P. Socialization and the altruistic behavior of children. *Psychological Bulletin*, 1976, *83*, 898–913.

Rushton, J. P. *Altruism, socialization and society*. Englewood Cliffs, N.J.: Prentice-Hall, 1980.

Saltzstein, H. D. Social influence and moral development: A perspective on the role of parents and peers. In T. Lickona (Ed.), *Moral development and behavior: Theory, research and social issues*. New York: Holt, Rinehart & Winston, 1976.

Saltzstein, H. D., Diamond, R. M., & Belenky, M. Moral judgment level and conformity behavior. *Developmental Psychology*, 1972, *7*, 327–336.

Schaie, K. W. A general mode for the study of developmental problems. *Psychological Bulletin*, 1965, *64*, 92–107.

Schank, R. C., & Abelson, R. P. *Scripts, plans, goals, and understanding*. Hillsdale, N.J.: Erlbaum, 1977.

Schoffeitt, P. G. The moral development of children as a function of parental moral judgments and childrearing. Unpublished doctoral dissertation, George Peabody College for Teachers, 1971.

Schwartz, S. H. Normative influences on altruism. In L. Berkowitz (Ed.), *Advances in experimental social psychology* (Vol. 10). New York: Academic Press, 1977.

Schwartz, S. H., Feldman, K. A., Brown, M. E., & Heingartner, A. Some personality correlates of conduct in two situations of moral conflict. *Journal of Personality*, 1969, *37*, 41–57.

Selman, R. The relation of role-taking ability to the development of moral judgment in children. *Child Development*, 1971, *42*, 79–91.

Selman, R. The relation of role-taking levels to stage of moral judgment: A theoretical analysis of empirical studies. Unpublished manuscript, Harvard University, 1973.

Selman, R. L. Toward a structural analysis of developing interpersonal relationship concepts: Research with normal and disturbed preadolescent boys. In A. Pick (Ed.), *Tenth Annual Minnesota Symposia on Child Psychology*. Minneapolis: University of Minnesota Press, 1976.

Selman, R. L. *The growth of interpersonal understanding*. New York: Academic Press, 1980.

Sheehan, T. J., Husted, S. D., & Candee, D. The development of moral judgment over three years in a group of medical students. Paper presented at the meeting of the American Educational Research Association, Los Angeles, April 1981.

Simpson, E. L. Moral development research: A case of scientific cultural bias. *Human Development,* 1974, *17,* 81–106.

Slovic, P., Fischhoff, B., & Lichtenstein, S. Behavioral decision theory. *Annual Review of Psychology,* 1977, *28,* 1–39.

Smedslund, J. Development of concrete transitivity of length in children. *Child Development,* 1963, *34,* 389–405.

Smedslund, J. Psychological diagnostics. *Psychological Bulletin,* 1969, *71,* 237–248.

Smith, C. L., Gelfand, D. M., Hartmann, D. P., & Partlow, M. Children's causal attributions regarding help giving. *Child Development,* 1979, *50,* 203–210.

Sobesky, W. E. The effects of situational factors on moral judgments. *Child Development,* in press.

Staub, E. Helping a distressed person: Social, personality, and stimulus determinants. In L. Berkowitz (Ed.), *Advances in experimental and social psychology* (Vol. 7). New York: Academic Press, 1974.

Staub, E. *Positive social behavior and morality: vol. 1, Social and personal influences.* New York: Academic Press, 1978.

Staub, E. *Positive social behavior and morality: vol. 2, Socialization and development.* New York: Academic Press, 1979.

Sullivan, E. V. A study of Kohlberg's structural theory of moral development. A critique of liberal social science ideology. *Human Development,* 1977, *20,* 325–376.

Sullivan, E. V., & Quarter, J. Psychological correlates of certain postconventional moral types: A perspective on hybrid types. *Journal of Personality,* 1972, *40,* 149–161.

Surber, C. F. Developmental processes in social inference: A verging of intentions and consequences in moral judgment. *Developmental Psychology,* 1977, *13,* 654–665.

Tapp, J. L., & Levine, F. J. (Eds.). *Law, justice, and the individual in society.* New York: Holt, Rinehart & Winston, 1977.

Tracy, J. J., & Cross, H. J. Antecedents of shift in moral judgment. *Journal of Personality and Social Psychology,* 1973, *26,* 238–244.

Tulving, E. Episodic and semantic memory. In E. Tulving & W. Donaldson (Ed.), Organization of memory. New York: Academic Press, 1972.

Turiel, E. An experimental test of the sequentiality of developmental stages in the child's moral judgments. *Journal of Personality and Social Psychology,* 1966, *3,* 611–618.

Turiel, E. Stage transition in moral development. In R. M. Travers (Ed.), *Second handbook of research on teaching.* Chicago: Rand McNally, 1972.

Turiel, E. The effects of cognitive conflicts on moral judgment development. Unpublished manuscript, Harvard University, 1973.

Turiel, E. Distinct conceptual and developmental domains: Social-convention and morality. In C. B. Keasey (Ed.), *Nebraska Symposium on Motivation* (Vol. 25). Lincoln: University of Nebraska Press, 1978. (a)

Turiel, E. Social regulations and domains of social concept. *New directions for child development,* 1978, *1,* 45–74. (b)

Turiel, E., Edwards, C. P., & Kohlberg, L. Moral development in Turkish children, adolescents, and young adults. *Journal of Cross-Cultural Psychology,* 1978, *9,* 75–86.

Volker, J. Moral reasoning and college experience. Unpublished master's thesis, University of Minnesota, 1980.

Walker, L. J. Cognitive and perspective-taking prerequisites for the development of moral reasoning. (Doctoral dissertation, University of Toronto, 1978). *Dissertation Abstracts International,* 1979, *40,* 901B. (National Library of Canada, Ottawa, No. 38,867)

Walker, L. J. Cognitive and perspective-taking prerequisites for moral development. *Child Development,* 1980, *51,* 131–139.

Walker, L. J. Sex differences in the development of moral reasoning: A critical review of the literature. University of British Columbia, 1982, manuscript submitted for publication.

Walker, L. J., & Richards, B. S. The effects of a narrative model on children's moral judgments. *Canadian Journal of Behavioral Science,* 1976, *8,* 169–177.

Walker, L. J., & Richards, B. S. Stimulating transitions in moral reasoning as a function of stage of cognitive development. *Developmental Psychology,* 1979, *15,* 95–103.

Wallace, G., & Walker, A. D. M. (Eds.), *The definition of morality.* London: Methuen, 1970.

Walster, E., Berscheid, E., & Walster, G. W. New directions in equity research. *Journal of Personality and Social Psychology,* 1973, *25,* 151–176.

Walster, E., & Walster, G. W. Equity and social justice. *Journal of Social Issues,* 1975, *31,* 21–43.

Weiner, B., & Peter, N. A cognitive-developmental

analysis of achievement and moral judgments. *Developmental Psychology,* 1973, *9,* 290–309.

Wellman, H. M., Larkey, C., Somerville, S. C. The early development of moral criteria. *Child Development,* 1979, *50,* 869–873.

Werner, H. The concept of development from a comparative and organismic point of view. In D. B. Harris (Ed.), *The concept of development.* Minneapolis: University of Minnesota Press, 1957.

White, C., Bushnell, N., & Regnemer, J. Moral development in Bahamian school children: A three-year examination of Kohlberg's stages of moral development. *Developmental Psychology,* 1978, *14,* 58–65.

Whiteley, J. *Character development in college students* (vol. 1). Schenectady, N.Y.: Character Research Press, 1982.

Wilson, E. O. *Sociobiology: The new synthesis.* Cambridge, Mass.: Harvard University Press, 1975. (Belknap)

Wohlwill, J. F. *The study of behavioral development.* New York: Academic Press, 1973.

Wonderly, D. M., & Kupfersmid, J. H. The relationship between moral judgment and selected characteristics of mental health. *Character Potential,* 1979, *9,* 111–116.

Zajonc, R. B. Feeling and thinking: Preferences need no inferences. *American Psychologist,* 1980, *35,* 151–175.

STYLISTIC VARIATION IN CHILDHOOD AND ADOLESCENCE: CREATIVITY, METAPHOR, AND COGNITIVE STYLES*

NATHAN KOGAN, *New School for Social Research*

CHAPTER CONTENTS

*Preparation of this chapter was facilitated by discussions with Neil J. Salkind. I am grateful for his interest and for providing me with drafts of unpublished material. Much of the bibliographic burden was borne by Mindy Chadrow and Montie Mills, and I am most thankful for their efforts. Despite the pressure of other work, Claire Martin assumed responsibility for typing a substantial portion of the manuscript, and I am most grateful for her support. Finally, I owe a special debt to the editors of this volume for their useful comments and criticisms of an earlier draft of this chapter. Any shortcomings that remain are clearly the responsibility of the author.

INTRODUCTION

The third edition of *Carmichael's Manual of Child Psychology* (Mussen, 1970) contained several chapters concerned in whole or in part with individual differences in the cognitive functioning of children. Two of those chapters can be considered as intellectual ancestors of the present one—the chapter by Kagan and Kogan (1970) on ''Individual Variation in Cognitive Processes'' and the chapter by Wallach (1970) on ''Creativity.'' The Kagan and Kogan essay dealt largely with the cognitive styles and strategies of children; Wallach's contribution emphasized the distinction between divergent-thinking performance and the traditional domain of intelligence, and it spelled out the construct-validational evidence for divergent thinking as an index of the broader notion of breadth-of-attention deployment. Both chapters focused on cognitive variables that were stylistic in character, but both recognized that *styles* of cognition in children necessarily overlapped with the study of children's problem solving and general intellectual functioning.

Although the foregoing two chapters offer an excellent point of departure for the present contribution, it is important to observe that there is no direct continuity from the work of more than a decade ago to that of the present. Issues that were at the forefront of theoretical and empirical activity in the mid-to-late 1960s had in some cases virtually faded from view by 1980. The Kagan and Kogan (1970) chapter, for example, devoted considerable space to the ego-psychoanalytic construct of cognitive controls and its relevance for individual differences in children's cognitive processes. Since the appearance of the Gardner and Moriarty (1968) volume, however, there has been a veritable dearth of relevant research. A recent book by Santostefano (1978) has sought to revive this earlier tradition, but that work as a whole appears to be directed more toward the interests of clinical child psychologists than to those of basic researchers in developmental psychology. Even more space in the Kagan and Kogan (1970) chapter was given over to Wernerian and Lewinian approaches to the issues of differentiation and hierarchic integration as a background for the developmental study of cognitive complexity (Bieri, 1966; Harvey, 1966). Despite the lively interest in that latter topic in the 1960s, there is little trace of it evident now.

Other topics treated in the Kagan and Kogan chapter have continued to flourish, and these, of course, will receive extended coverage here. Included in this category are reflection-impulsivity (R-I) and field dependence-independence (FDI). For each of these, the 1970s represented a decade of active exploration; hence, their current status warrants evaluation. It should be noted that the author (Kogan, 1976a) reviewed the foregoing styles for children of preschool age and younger; hence duplication of this material will be avoided. At the same time, that review is now more than six years old, and I will endeavor to update it wherever feasible.

In respect to the Wallach (1970) chapter on creativity, it would seem fair to say that the climate has changed considerably over the course of a decade. The enormous enthusiasm that accompanied children's creativity research in the 1960s has waned, and only a few of the issues paramount a decade ago continue to generate new research. Possibly, the major preoccupation of creativity researchers through the early 1970s concerned the discriminant-validational issue of the statistical independence of divergent- and convergent-thinking measures (see Wallach, 1971). That issue appears to have been resolved in favor of relative independence—that is, when significant correlations are observed, they are so small as to be of virtually no practical significance.

Both construct and extrinsic validation of divergent-thinking measures in children have continued to appear on a limited scale, and I will discuss this work in the present chapter. It is far from the case that interest in children's creativity has disappeared. Rather, the focus of research concern has expanded beyond divergent thinking to include such issues as children's symbolic play, metaphoric production and comprehension, and aesthetic development. Only a small portion of this more recent body of work, however, has inquired into individual differences among children.

In a chapter devoted to stylistic variation in children and adolescents, one might well ask whether the four topics selected for review—creativity, metaphor, and the cognitive styles of FDI and R-I—provide a reasonably exhaustive account of the current state of the field. How does one justify the absence of styles of categorization and conceptualization, especially in the light of the separate chapters devoted to each in the author's previously published book (Kogan, 1976a)? The omission can be readily explained. Much of the material in the two chapters at issue was devoted to developmental change in linguistic and conceptual overextension and underextension (breadth vs. narrowness) and in the bases for concept acquisition (e.g., complementarity vs. similarity, perceptual, functional, nominal). Such matters, of course, lie at the very heart of the cognitive-developmental enterprise and are amply treated elsewhere in the present volume.

Although the topic of individual differences in language and conceptual development has become more prominent (Nelson, 1981), only a minute portion of that work is relevant to stylistic variation. The chapter on categorization styles in Kogan (1976a) discussed the research of Nelson and Bonvillian (1973) on early concept acquisition because of its relevance to breadth of categorization in early childhood. The latter work has been extended (Nelson & Bonvillian, 1978) in a longitudinal study across the age interval of 2½ to 4½. Concept overgeneralization (breadth) at the former and latter ages correlated significantly ($r = .58$) over the two-year period in a small sample of middle-class children. In addition, conceptual breadth indices obtained at both ages were examined in relation to divergent thinking and Stanford-Binet IQ assessed at age 4½. Correlations with divergent thinking were significant, but breadth and IQ were not significantly associated. These findings are consistent with those reported by Wallach and Kogan (1965) on a sample of fourth-grade children who were given the children's version of the Pettigrew (1958) category-width test. The striking aspect of the Nelson and Bonvillian (1978) outcomes, however, is the predictive power of concept overgeneralization at age 2½ vis-à-vis divergent thinking two years later. Such results are quite exciting because they point to the possibility of tapping into creativity-relevant processes quite early in childhood.

In sum, although some of the data on stylistic aspects of early concept and word acquisition are quite provocative, there is simply not enough of it at present to warrant a separate section in the present chapter. Note should also be taken of other work cited in the Kogan (1976a) chapter on categorization styles. Considerable space was devoted to unpublished research by Jack and Jeanne Block on personality correlates in early childhood of performance on a set of breadth-of-categorization tasks. This research has since been published (Block, Buss, Block, & Gjerde, 1981) and extended to 7-year-olds in their longitudinal study. The overall pattern of the findings, however, is quite close to that reported by Kogan (1976a); hence, further discussion here does not appear to be warranted.

The chapter devoted to styles of conceptualization in Kogan (1976a) placed much emphasis on the conceptual-styles test (Kagan, Moss, & Sigel, 1963) and revised versions of that test for younger children (Sigel, 1967, 1972). In this author's view, the strictly developmental aspects of the research by the foregoing authors has been absorbed into the mainstream of research on conceptual development (e.g., Den-

ney, 1975; Denney & Moulton, 1976). The examination of conceptual styles from an individual-differences perspective, on the other hand, has generated little new work of interest. There have been limited applications to the field of educational psychology (e.g., Gray, 1974), and the longitudinal research of the Blocks has generated personality correlates of conceptual styles (reported in preliminary form in Kogan, 1976a). Conceivably, the eventual publication of these latter data may help to revitalize this area of inquiry.

In the case of each of the domains treated in this chapter, there is no intention of presenting an exhaustive review of all of the relevant published and to-be-published material. Given the availability of the Wallach (1970) and Kagan and Kogan (1970) chapters, I will focus on work that appeared subsequent to their publication. Readers approaching the present topics for the first time might find it helpful to consult the two chapters cited above before attempting to assimilate the present one. In the course of the discussion of the creativity, metaphor, and cognitive-style areas, I will make periodic reference to recent published reviews. Readers seeking a complete bibliography should find such sources helpful. In the present chapter, references to empirical research reports will be in the service of illustrating and discussing key issues in the field. Complete citation of all research pertinent to these issues is not feasible. Space limitations and readability dictate selectivity; omission of a reference should not be interpreted automatically as an indicator of lesser importance.

A Classification of Styles

As a prelude to the discussion of specific stylistic dimensions in childhood and adolescence, it would appear worthwhile to ask about the forces that led to the emergence of the constructs considered in this chapter. A return to the time before divergent thinking and cognitive styles appeared on the psychological scene would reveal an almost exclusive focus on cognitive individual-differences research in the domain of convergent abilities. Accuracy of performance, of course, is the primary criterion in such ability assessments. In due course, there came the realization that accuracy or efficiency did not exhaust the cognitive domain and concern shifted to studies of styles and strategies where form and manner rather than sheer skill in cognitive performance became a major topic of inquiry. An even more fundamental difference between traditional intelligence researchers and the new wave of cognitive-style and creativity investigators was the concern with motivational and personality factors as contributors to individual differences in cognitive functioning.

As research on stylistic dimensions proliferated, it became evident that the domain included constructs quite different from one another. Styles emerged from different theoretical traditions. Some were largely adult based, others derived from research on children. Some were quite close to the ability domain or virtually indistinguishable from it; others assumed the character of cognitive strategies or preferences and appeared quite distinct from abilities in the conventional sense. This closeness versus remoteness of a style from the ability domain provided the basis for a threefold style classification (Kogan, 1973).

Styles of the *first* type employ operational indices that reflect level of accuracy of performance. In the case of FDI, for example, location of a simple figure embedded in a complex geometrical pattern is a primary index of the style in question. Performance on such a task is clearly related to, or possibly even a form of, spatial ability. That FDI is characterized as a style rather than as an ability rests on the theoretical conceptualization of the construct, not on the means employed to assess it.

Accuracy is not a relevant issue for the *second* type of cognitive style, although performance is characterized in explicitly or implicitly evaluative terms. In respect to styles of conceptualization in children, for example, an analytic (common-dimension) grouping of stimulus objects is evaluated more positively than a relational (i.e., complementary) grouping. This value judgment may be made on either theoretical or empirical grounds. Certain stylistic modes may be considered developmentally more advanced than other modes. Alternatively, a particular style may be deemed to have higher value by virtue of positive correlations with ability indices. Although creativity in the divergent-thinking sense has not traditionally been treated as a cognitive style, the ideational-fluency component of divergent thinking (the number of associates generated in response to a stimulus) can readily be conceived as a style of the second type. Production of a larger number of ideas is considered superior to the generation of a smaller number of ideas.

There is, finally, a *third* type of style for which neither accuracy of performance nor other forms of value judgment are of relevance. Early research on styles of categorization, for example, was essentially neutral in respect to the advantage of breadth or narrowness in the categorization of diverse stimuli.

It must be noted that the designation of a particular style in the foregoing typology is not immutable. A style of the third type is transformed into a style of the second type if it should prove to be related to increasing developmental maturity or to dimensions of ability. Similarly, a style of the first type, such as the error component of R-I (degree of success in perceptual matching under conditions of response uncertainty), becomes a style of the third type in the hands of those investigators (Zelniker & Jeffrey, 1976) who assert that reflectives are better at detail processing, whereas impulsives are better at global processing. The evaluative component of RI is reduced in the foregoing case, but not entirely eliminated. Because the reflective style (i.e., detail processing) appears to be advantageous in a variety of school-related tasks, matters of value continue to pervade the RI domain.

Individual Differences and Cognitive Development

A number of years ago, Cronbach (1957) proposed the existence of "two disciplines of academic psychology"—the experimental and the differential, each with its distinctive research designs and associated statistical methods. It is of interest that Cronbach included developmental psychology within the differential camp by virtue of its concern with the issue of age *differences*. For Cronbach, age was but another variable associated with a range of human differences and, hence, well suited to correlational methodology. As Wohlwill (1973) has more recently pointed out, however, the dominant tradition within the field of cognitive development—that of Jean Piaget and his associates and disciples—has been marked by disinterest in within-age or within-stage variation among children and adolescents. Further, such disinterest continues to characterize much cognitive-developmental work, quite apart from the theoretical base from which it derives. The neglect of such individual variation is in many respects analogous to its relegation to sampling error in the research designs favored by traditional experimental psychologists.

Cognitive styles, creativity, and metaphor—the constructs under review in this chapter—represent domains where cognitive-developmental and individual-difference issues have come together. It has been an uneasy meeting ground, however, for as Wohlwill (1973, p. 334) has so astutely observed in his critique of the Kagan and Kogan (1970) chapter, the "unifying theme around which the developmental and differential aspects of cognitive functioning might be welded together . . . remains largely unrealized." Wohlwill (1973) has placed great confidence in the methodological proposals advanced by a new breed of lifespan developmentalists (e.g., Baltes & Nesselroade, 1973). This latter group as well as others (e.g., Nesselroade & Baltes, 1979) have made major methodological advances in integrating correlational and factor-analytic methodology with issues of developmental change, but these advances have not yet had much of an impact in the substantive areas under review in this chapter.

In respect to the meaning of individual differences in development, Wohlwill (1973) has posed the issues quite elegantly. Hence, I will offer a compressed version of his position. Cognitive-style dimensions can have a dual significance. On the one hand, they may simply reflect individual differences in childhood or adolescence that have little diagnostic relevance for current developmental status or subsequent developmental change; on the other hand, a child's score on a cognitive-style index may be quite informative in respect to his or her rate of development and, hence, of his or her eventual terminal level on the dimension of interest. In the case of the former, the focus is often on the interindividual stability of a dimension. Is there, in other words, a significant correspondence in the rank ordering of children for a particular cognitive style at ages 5 and 8 for example? Age changes across this longitudinal span are of secondary concern, although many investigators do report and comment upon the significance of mean differences across the age span under investigation.

The alternative view of cognitive styles as an indicator of developmental growth rate has received relatively less attention. Witkin, Dyk, Faterson, Goodenough, and Karp (1962) have maintained that psychological differentiation (in the Wernerian sense) proceeds at faster or slower rates in different individuals and that cognitive-style indices of differentiation reflect this rate of growth. It has been noted by Wohlwill (1973), however, that differential growth rates necessarily imply increasing interindividual variability with increasing age—a type of fanning-out process. Yet an examination of relevant data from Witkin, Lewis, Hertzman, Machover, Meissner, and Wapner (1954) failed to demonstrate progressively increasing variances between the ages of 8 and 17 on relevant cognitive-style indicators. Hence, the application of cognitive-style measures to the prediction of the course of developmental change was not effectively established. Nor can one point to more recent work in the areas of concern here that has generated more successful outcomes.

One can point to a third perspective on the linkage between stylistic individual-difference measures and the matter of developmental change. When multivariate designs are employed, it is possible to inquire into the onset of particular stylistic dimensions. Is there, for example, a coherent dimension of FDI emergent at age 5, although not in evidence at age 4? Do boys and girls vary in the age at which a particular stylistic dimension becomes manifest? Questions such as these are thoroughly elucidated in the Kogan (1976a) volume and, hence, will receive only cursory attention here.

A fourth perspective on individual differences and cognitive development inquires into the causal status of cognitive-style variables in relation to various developmental milestones (e.g., the achievement of conservation, the waning of egocentrism, the onset of formal operations). With the advent of such techniques as cross-lagged correlational analysis (e.g., Kenny, 1979), the opportunity for drawing causal inferences from longitudinal data becomes feasible (if particular psychometric assumptions have been met). If cognitive-style variables can be shown to operate as causal antecedents vis-à-vis the emergence of operational thought, one would necessarily have to conclude that stylistic individual differences are of major importance in the cognitive-developmental enterprise. A study (Brodzinsky, 1982) along the lines described above is discussed later in the chapter.

Much of the discussion thus far is based on the premise of longitudinal age comparisons. Although longitudinal designs have been employed in the cognitive-style and creativity domains, it must be noted that such designs characterize a small portion of the relevant published work. A large part of the research discussed in this chapter is based on a single age group of children or adolescents and represents a functionally based approach to the study of individual differences. Investigators in the areas of creativity, metaphor, and cognitive styles have generally operated on the premise that their favored constructs are relevant to the minds and behaviors of children and adolescents. From such a premise, it naturally follows that one should wish to examine the antecedents and correlates of the constructs at issue as well as to attempt to discover whether these constructs are experimentally modifiable. Accordingly, in the pages to follow, studies are described that focus on such matters as possible child-rearing antecedents, correlates in the realm of interpersonal behavior, and comparisons of socioeconomic groups. Further, both laboratory and more naturalistic classroom experiments are discussed with emphasis on the specific environmental conditions responsible for facilitating (or hindering) performance in the creativity, metaphor, and cognitive-style domains. It is important to note in this regard that the stylistic constructs treated in this chapter have been cast in the role of both independent and dependent variables. When dealing with individual variation in cognitive structures and processes, one can in a sense move backward in a search for antecedents or move forward to seek behavioral consequents. Both approaches are represented throughout the chapter.

CREATIVITY

General Background

The term creativity has been chosen as a heading less for its aptness than for the sake of maintaining continuity with past usage in the literature. Unlike the labels attached to most of the other cognitive styles discussed in the present chapter, the creativity label suffers severely from surplus meaning. It evokes associations having to do with civilization's greatest creative geniuses and the particular creative products that they forged. When the term creative is applied to children's thinking by developmental psychologists, however, the referent is considerably more constricted and mundane. Children's creativity essentially refers to performance on tests of the divergent-thinking type (Guilford, 1967). Within this general rubric, it is the component of ideational fluency that has been the primary focus of research attention for the past 15 years. Ideational fluency refers to the sheer number of ideas elicited by a stimulus in a divergent-thinking task (e.g., "Tell me all the ways that a cork can be used."). Other referents for the creativity term in children have sometimes been advanced—for example, fantasy, artistic expression, playfulness—but these have never constituted the core of the construct. Instead, they are often treated as correlates of divergent thinking in construct-validational research.

In a controversial paper, Wallach (1971) spelled out many of the issues confronting the ideational-fluency approach to creativity. Some of these issues were deliberately put forth as fallacies, no doubt with the intent of discouraging further research along such lines. As we will presently discover, many psychologists have not been convinced by these arguments because work has continued unabated along allegedly fallacious tracks. Wallach's arguments assumed the following form:

1. Ideational fluency is an imperfect predictor of real-world creativity, therefore, it is unreasonable to treat them as equivalent.

2. Flowing from this is the view that the search for correlates of ideational fluency is of little value where the aim is to delineate linkages with genuine creativity.

3. Similarly, all experimental efforts to enhance ideational fluency are misguided because such enhancement in no sense implies that the individual's real level of creativity has been increased.

It is important to note that Wallach's (1971) position is largely adult based because, as one descends the age continuum, the meaning of genuine or real-world criteria becomes progressively less clear. Where preschool children are the subjects of one's research, for example, it is dubious whether any criterion (e.g., art products, teacher ratings, story construction) represents a "truer" index of creativity than the divergent-thinking test performance itself. Beginning with the primary-school years, the predictor-criterion framework becomes more viable, whether applied to concurrent relationships or longitudinal data extending from childhood through adolescence and beyond. Nevertheless, such school-age criteria are intermediate, and their validity with respect to the ultimate creativity criteria of adulthood remains an open question (Kogan, 1973).

Regardless of subject age, however, ideational fluency and other divergent-thinking indices represent modes of thought and, hence, can legitimately be studied as such within a developmental and construct-validational framework. Certainly, given the present state of knowledge, the exclusion of either approach on scientific grounds cannot be justified. The special nature of the creativity construct assures that both basic and applied orientations will prevail, and one can only hope that the area is more likely to prosper from the active articulation of the two than from the single-minded pursuit of either one alone.

The Creativity-Intelligence or the Convergent-Thinking/Divergent-Thinking Distinction

Possibly, the most robust finding in the creativity domain is the statistical separation of divergent- and convergent-thinking measures across a wide span of age groups extending from nursery school children to university students (Kogan, 1971a, 1973). These results are based on the Wallach and Kogan (1965) tasks. There is somewhat greater doubt about the extent of the divergent-convergent separation with other test batteries (see Wallach, 1970).

Although the issue of whether creativity and intelligence tests tap relatively independent modes of thought appears to have been definitively settled, the matter of the context necessary to achieve the separation has continued to engender considerable controversy (see Hattie, 1977). In the initial Wallach and Kogan (1965) work, a relaxed and untimed gamelike context was employed for the assessment of creativity. As further research accumulated, however, considerable ambiguity developed over the necessity of a gamelike context for achieving a sharp divergent-convergent distinction. Indeed, Wallach (1971) publicly asserted that he found it necessary to change his mind on the issue. His final statement represents a strong claim for the irrelevance of testing context—creativity and intelligence are claimed to be distinct modes of thought quite apart from the gamelike or testlike context in which each is assessed. Hattie (1977) has extended this assertion in a prescriptive direction, maintaining that "there is little evidence against using timed test-like conditions as the norm for administering creativity tests" (p. 1249). If there is no invidious distinction between contexts on strictly scientific grounds, pragmatic considerations would clearly favor testlike conditions that offer greater ease, economy, and standardization of administration.

The battle has been fought largely along psychometric lines. If the divergent-thinking measures correlate among themselves, but do not correlate with convergent-thinking measures, then the necessary convergent and discriminant validation has been achieved. Despite the Wallach (1971) and Hattie (1977) assertions that there is little to choose between testlike and gamelike conditions in respect to psychometric criteria, data sets continue to appear that fail to support such a claim. Even in Hattie's (1980) own data, the few significant divergent-convergent correlations emerged in the testlike context; there were none under gamelike conditions. In one of the better designed studies in the field, Nicholls (1971) obtained strikingly clear outcomes pointing to the presence of discriminant validation for convergent- and divergent-thinking tasks under gamelike conditions and the absence of such validation in the testlike condition. More recently, Milgram and Milgram (1976) obtained results similar to those reported by Nicholls (1971) in the case of fourth-grade to eighth-grade children of average intelligence.

Regrettable as it may sound, it would seem somewhat premature to close the book completely on the impact of testing context on the creativity-intelligence distinction. Yet, one cannot help wondering whether further effort directed toward this issue is warranted. Should choice of context rest entirely on intrinsic psychometric criteria or should one inquire into the differential extrinsic predictability of divergent-thinking scores generated under testlike and gamelike conditions? There is a dearth of research focused on this issue. Possibly, the only relevant study in child or adolescent samples has been carried out by Vernon (1971). That author selected diverse external criteria of creativity in junior high school students (e.g., rated creativity of an autobiography, creativity on a draw-a-man procedure, and artistic leisure-time interests) and endeavored to find out whether these criteria could be more accurately predicted from creativity test scores obtained under gamelike or testlike conditions. The general correlational pattern clearly supported the greater concurrent validity of divergent-thinking indices obtained in a gamelike context.

Components of Divergent Thinking

In his structure-of-intellect model, Guilford (1967) spelled out a diversity of presumably independent divergent-thinking factors. An exhaustive review of the relevant literature by Wallach (1970) pointed strongly to the ideational-fluency factor as the one most distinct from convergent-thinking and problem-solving processes in general. Further confirmation of this conclusion is contained in a recent article by Houtz and Speedie (1978). Those authors administered a wide variety of problem-solving tasks to a sample of fifth-grade children (including divergent-thinking tasks). Factor analysis yielded a distinct factor with loadings derived exclusively from tasks with a divergent open-ended structure. Comparable results have been reported by Hargreaves and Bolton (1972) in a study of 10- to 11-year-old British children.

Of further interest is the evidence that a spontaneous-flexibility index (number of different categories of response) also loaded on the divergent-thinking factor in both of the foregoing studies. This raises the important issue of how divergent-thinking tasks should be scored, because it is clearly possible and often desirable to go beyond a simple frequency count of the number of responses generated to a task item (ideational fluency). In the Wallach and Kogan (1965) research, a uniqueness index was obtained to reflect the number of responses produced by a child that no other child in the sample produced. One can also apply a quality criterion to the child's responses by employing judges to rate them on a quality scale. The major question at issue is the degree to which these different indices are tapping a common process.

On measurement grounds alone, one would anticipate some relation between the foregoing indices of fluency, spontaneous flexibility, uniqueness, and quality. As sheer response output increases, the likelihood of a larger number of categories spanned also increases (Hargreaves & Bolton, 1972; Houtz & Speedie, 1978). Further confirmation is provided by Yando, Seitz, and Zigler (1979) who obtained a highly significant fluency-flexibility correlation of .48 in their sample of second graders and third graders. The link between ideational fluency and uniqueness derives from the creativity model proposed by Mednick (1962) and has been thoroughly elaborated by Wallach (1970). Unique responses come later in a series of emitted responses; hence, a larger output increases the likelihood that at least one of them will be unique (e.g., Milgram & Rabkin, 1980). Even in the case where unique responses are fairly evenly distributed across a series, as in data from young children reported by Ward (1969b), the more fluent child again has a greater probability of generating a unique response. Because the fluent child continues to generate responses after the less fluent child has ceased, a correlation between fluency and uniqueness is assured.

Can the foregoing reasoning for uniqueness be extended to the quality of the responses generated by the child? It is important to note that uniqueness is but one component of quality. The highly unusual response may be discounted on quality grounds if it does not offer an elegant fit to the stimulus requirements posed by the item in question. Quality, of necessity, reflects a blend of originality (uniqueness) and appropriateness. On these grounds, one would expect the fluency-quality link to be attenuated in comparison to the fluency-uniqueness relationship.

Ward, Kogan, and Pankove (1972) reported the use of a 7-point scale for judging idea quality in a sample of low socioeconomic status (SES) fifth graders. A mean quality score for each subject was obtained by averaging the ratings across all of his or her responses to the items of the Wallach and Kogan (1965) tasks. Interrater reliability proved to be quite adequate, but intertask consistency for quality was quite low. Ward et al. (1972) raised the possibility that the quality score might exhibit greater generality in more advantaged samples of children, possibly because of greater variance in the quality scores for such samples. In this regard, note should be taken of the modest convergent validity of quality scores in college students reported by Hocevar (1979).

The quantity/quality issue has been pursued more recently by Milgram, Milgram, Rosenbloom, and Rabkin (1978) in an Israeli sample of sixth graders and high school seniors who responded to the Wallach and Kogan (1965) tasks. The major inference drawn from the research by its authors concerns the scientific value of quality scoring of divergent-thinking responses. With overall ideational-fluency and quality scores correlating at the level of .65 and .84 for younger and older subjects respectively, a strong case can obviously be made for exclusive reliance on the more easily scorable ideational-fluency index. Further support is provided by Yando et al. (1979) who also found that fluency and judged originality were highly correlated ($r = .82$) in their sample of second graders and third graders.

The overall implication that flows from the preceding review is that the correlations among the different ways of scoring responses from divergent-thinking tasks may be sufficiently high to warrant selection of the most reliable and economical index—the sheer number of different responses generated, that is, ideational fluency. Scoring for spontaneous flexibility, uniqueness, and quality is cumbersome, time consuming, and less reliable than a frequency count. There is little point in undertaking such scoring unless it can be shown that valuable information would be lost by discarding the more complex measure. Of course, one can retain a set of separate indices despite high intercorrelations, as Torrance (1966) prefers to do for his fluency, flexibility, originality, and elaboration measures. It is dubious, however, whether this latter choice would withstand a benefit-cost analysis in the absence of other compelling reasons for the retention of separate components.

Further evidence in favor of dropping all indices but ideational fluency is reported by Hocevar (1979). When that index was statistically controlled, uniqueness and quality scores in college students became quite unreliable and lacked convergent validity. Hocevar interpreted these findings as a reflection of the serious contamination of uniqueness and quality by the fluency component. Although such an interpretation may have a certain psychometric appeal, it loses force in the face of creativity theory (e.g., Mednick, 1962) that considers fluency of response to represent the route through which uniqueness and quality are attained. In a later section, we will return to the issue of the separate components and suggest that they may in fact be tapping distinctive processes. We will also explore the possibilities that testing context may have a differential impact on the various components of divergent thinking.

Processes of Divergent Thinking

In two major publications, Wallach (1970, 1971) outlined the bright and the dark side of creativity research. In the earlier publication, an impressive case was developed for breadth-of-attention deployment as the major explanatory construct responsible for superior performance on divergent-thinking tasks. This construct refers to extensive and adaptive scanning of the external environment and memory storage. Such scanning is presumed to take place in an associational rather than strictly logical manner and may be purposeful (i.e., in the service of problem solving) or less purposeful in character. In this latter connection, Wallach (1970) described the links between ideational fluency on the one hand and both elicited and spontaneous fantasy on the other hand. Superior performers in the divergent-thinking domain tend to produce novel stories to Thematic Apperception Test (TAT) cards (e.g., Maddi, 1965) and there are strong suggestions in Singer's (1973) research that divergent thinking may also be associated with daydreaming activity. Possibly the most striking evidence for the adaptive value of breadth-of-attention deployment is Ward's (1969a) observation that ideationally fluent children are much more likely than their less fluent peers to seek out cues in the external environment as an aid to responding on divergent-thinking tasks. All of the foregoing findings are rendered more impressive by the indication that individual differences in intelligence have no impact on them.

In marked contrast to an attention-deployment interpretation of creative thinking, Wallach (1971) subsequently introduced a much less flattering interpretation of high productivity in the divergent-thinking domain. We now learn that performing well in that domain may be symptomatic of such tendencies as obsessiveness, suggestibility, and susceptibility to experimenter-demand characteristics. Thus, ideationally fluent children are presumed to be unable to let go of an item, preferring to go on in a nitpicking fashion if necessary rather than stop and proceed to the next item. Further, such children are now seen as particularly eager to please an examiner, hence generating a large number of responses to make a good impression.

Factor analysis has taught us that the variance of a particular test can be spread across two or more orthogonal or oblique factors and that may, in fact, best account for the apparent paradox in Wallach's two interpretations. One can argue, of course, that the foregoing assertion is more a matter of description than of explanation. It is quite rare in the psychological literature to have two such contrasting views of the same phenomenon, and one would naturally like to find the key to a resolution of the dilemma.

A promising avenue toward such resolution is suggested by Caudle's (1976) dissertation research. Working with seventh graders who were administered selected items from the Wallach and Kogan

(1965) tasks as a base-line index, Caudle then divided her subjects into three groups for a second administration of different Wallach and Kogan items. The three groups represented random assignment to neutral-control, authoritarian-demand, and role-playing (a creative person) conditions. Results indicated that an experimenter demanding that subjects produce more creative responses proved effective in eliciting higher levels of ideational fluency from subjects. On the other hand, such a condition either had no effect on, or actually depressed, the number of high-quality responses generated. In striking contrast, an experimenter lightheartedly encouraging subjects to role play a creative person produced a significant enhancement in quality level. The outcomes of the Caudle investigation as a whole clearly demonstrated that both of Wallach's interpretations are viable if one allows for distinctive divergent-thinking criteria—fluency and quality in the present case. Contrary to claims made earlier, then, these two components may not necessarily represent alternate means of measuring the same thing. Obsessively sticking with an item or attempting to make a good impression on an examiner can apparently enhance the sheer fluency of ideas, but a price may be paid in the form of a diminished level of quality.

Further evidence for the importance of a quality/quantity distinction is offered by Harrington, Block, and Block (1983). Teacher ratings of the Q-set item—"creative in perception, thought, work or play" (a sixth-grade creativity criterion)—were significantly predicted by the Ward (1968) adaptation of the Wallach and Kogan instances and alternate-uses tasks administered at ages 4 and 5. In contrast, intelligence test data obtained at those early ages had little predictive value for teacher-rated creativity. Of particular significance in the present context is the evidence that the divergent-thinking effects were observed in the case of quality rather than fluency scores. In other words, quality appears to be superior to quantity in predicting an external creativity criterion. As noted previously, fluency and quality scores are often significantly correlated and fluency may represent the route through which quality is achieved; nevertheless, there is now good reason to believe that, at least in early childhood, fluency and quality reflect distinctively different aspects of the divergent-thinking domain.

Research by Kogan and Morgan (1969) offers further evidence on differential task-context effects in elementary school children (fifth graders). In the case of the verbal alternate-uses task, testlike relative to gamelike conditions generated higher levels of fluency and uniqueness. Yet, spontaneous flexibility (the number of response categories) did not share in this relationship. How can one explain this puzzling outcome? Kogan and Morgan suggested that the testlike condition encourages a category-exhaustion strategy where, to speed the associative flow, children will seize upon some pivotal category (e.g., cutting in the case of a knife) and proceed to exhaust the exemplars that flow from it (e.g., cutting bread, butter, fruit, etc.). Under such circumstances, the child may think of something to cut that is unique to the sample. The reason why spontaneous flexibility remains unaffected should now be clear. A strategy of category exhaustion necessarily implies the building up of specific categories as opposed to frequent switching across categories.

Examination of comparable data for the figural pattern-meanings task failed to reveal the foregoing pattern. No test-game main effects were found. This very likely reflects the fact that the category-exhaustion strategy previously described cannot work with such a figural task as pattern meanings, where each response is likely to be a category in its own right. In sum, it appears that verbal and figural divergent-thinking tasks may elicit distinctive cognitive strategies in children, with the salience of the strategy dependent upon task context. Lending further weight to the importance of the verbal-figural contrast is recent evidence (McKinney & Forman, 1977) indicating that the verbal and figural Wallach and Kogan (1970) tasks load on separate factors.

The strategies discussed in the Kogan and Morgan (1969) research represent inferences from the data; they were not observed directly. More recently, La Greca (1980) attempted to study strategies of divergent thinking in a more direct manner through interviews of third graders and sixth graders exposed to both verbal (instances and alternate uses) and figural (Rorschach cards) tasks. Thus, children reported the use of a strategy akin to category exhaustion. In addition, children described such strategies as placing the object in a familiar context and scanning the immediate environment for ideas. Of interest is the evidence that the high divergent-thinking performers were able to verbalize their strategies, whereas the low performers were poor at such verbalization and seemed to adopt a passive approach of simply waiting for ideas to emerge. Regrettably, La Greca did not examine her verbal and figural tasks separately in search of possibly distinctive strategies, hence ruling out any direct comparison with the Kogan and Morgan (1969) research.

There was also some indication in La Greca's data that the more creative children were more effective than their low-creative counterparts in making effective use of externally provided [...] dence is consistent with the outcom[...] (1969a) study cited earlier in which [...] children seemed better able than the [...] peers to take advantage of an enriched [...] This kind of advantage is prototy[...] in the creativity literature and represents the outcome one would expect from a theoretical perspective stressing breadth-of-attention deployment.

In sum, two distinct approaches can be discerned in the study of divergent-thinking processes. One has focused directly on the role of task variables in influencing the level of performance on the various dimensions of divergent thinking. The other has employed a prior classification of children on a divergent-thinking dimension and then has proceeded to examine how those high and low on that dimension vary in their response to relevant tasks and testing conditions. The overall evidence suggests that children respond differently to variation in the content of divergent-thinking tasks and in the context within which they are administered. This does not imply that the situational aspects of divergent-thinking testing can exclusively account for performance variation. Instead, there are salient individual differences in strategy selection and use in the divergent-thinking domain, and these appear to interact with differences in task content (e.g., verbal vs. visual) and task setting (e.g., cue-rich vs. cue-poor environments).

Relation to Play

If there is any sort of new look to recent process-oriented research on children's creativity, it is the repeated demonstration of linkages between play behaviors and dispositions on the one hand and divergent-thinking performance on the other hand. The relevant literature contains both correlational and experimental studies. Before we describe this research, however, it may be helpful to consider the theoretical and empirical precursors of a creativity-play relationship. As we noted earlier, Wallach (1970) devoted considerable attention to the connection between ideational fluency and various indices of fantasy. Despite the obvious link between fantasy and play, explicit evidence linking divergent thinking to play variables was quite meager at the time Wallach (1970) prepared his chapter.

On the conceptual side, a strong relationship between divergent thinking and play can be readily envisioned, and one can only express surprise that so little empirical research on this topic was carried out prior to the 1970s. In its higher forms, both divergent thinking and play entail cognition and behavior that extend or transform the central functional purpose of stimulus objects. Thus, in the prototypical alternate-uses task, the child to do well must forsake the category of obvious uses and search out less obvious, although appropriate, uses. Where play is concerned, single-minded concentration on an object's dominant quality or function will eventually lead to stereotyped behavior. To remain constructive, the play must engage the child's imagination in a search for alternative modes of relating to the object. From these descriptions, it should be apparent that we are talking about children's free-play behaviors, not about play involving rule-bound games or puzzles. The former type of play has often been referred to as make-believe and symbolic play.

The formal similarities between the divergent-thinking and play processes outlined here are quite striking and basically suggest three types of research, each of which is represented by at least one study in the published literature. In the direct correlational approach, children's play behaviors are rated and the resultant ratings are examined in relation to divergent-thinking performance measured concurrently or after a considerable lapse of time. In the experimental approach, children are assigned to play and to various control treatments, and they are subsequently assessed on one or more divergent-thinking tests. In the mixed approach, children are classified as high or low on play behavior prior to assignment to play and control conditions. It should be noted that each approach has generated findings supportive of a play-creativity association.

Let us begin with the individual-differences research. In the 1960s, a number of articles were published on "playfulness," and the outcomes of this work have been incorporated in a book by Lieberman (1977). In one of the studies reported in that book, teachers' playfulness ratings were significantly correlated with the divergent-thinking measures of ideational fluency, spontaneous flexibility, and originality derived from performance on the Torrance (1966) tests. At the same time, however, both the "playfulness" ratings and the Torrance indices were significantly correlated with the mental-age score derived from the Peabody Picture Vocabulary Test (PPVT). Unfortunately, no partial correlations were computed to determine whether the playfulness/divergent-thinking correlations remained significant with MA controlled.

The teacher-ratings approach to playfulness was also employed by Singer and Rummo (1973) in a study of kindergarten-age children. There were 15 rating scales developed, subsequently reduced to three factors via factor analysis. One of these was labeled "playfulness and openness to experience," with substantial loadings on scales of openness, communicativeness, curiosity and novelty seeking, humorous and playful attitude, and emotional expressiveness. The Wallach and Kogan (1965) tasks provided measures of divergent thinking. For males, all of the foregoing scales were significantly related to ideational fluency. For females, on the other hand, creativity/IQ-interaction effects were found. No clear explanation is provided for these sex-moderated effects. We are, thus, forced to conclude that the assessment of playfulness via the teacher-rating route yields a clear play-creativity association only in the case of kindergarten boys. For kindergarten girls, the relationship is more complex and not yet fully understood.

Teacher ratings, of course, represent a rather indirect method for the assessment of a child's play behavior. An obvious alternative is the direct observation of play, the approach taken in research carried out by J. E. Johnson (1976). Low SES preschool children were systematically observed during free play at their nursery school. Play units were scored for social- and nonsocial-fantasy play. The former involved make-believe activities in which two or more children interacted; the latter involved individual make-believe activity. The PPVT and the picture-completion subtest of the Wechsler Preschool and Primary Scales of Intelligence (WPPSI) were employed as convergent-thinking (intelligence) indices, and alternate-uses and story-completion tasks were used to assess divergent thinking. Neither the convergent- nor the divergent-thinking measures were related to nonsocial-fantasy play. In contrast, partial correlational analysis supported the dominant influence of divergent over convergent thinking in respect to incidence of social-fantasy play. Somewhat stronger effects were found for girls than for boys.

Why are the foregoing effects confined to social-fantasy play? J. E. Johnson (1976) argues that such play requires a higher level of cognitive maturity than does nonsocial-fantasy play. In the former case, the child must obviously translate private symbolism into a communicative form if the play episode is to proceed in a constructive fashion. Of interest in this regard is the indication that children below the median on both convergent-thinking measures exhibited little social-fantasy play. Hence, such play would appear to require better than average intelligence as a necessary, if not a sufficient, condition.

The J. E. Johnson (1976) investigation is based on concurrent assessments of abilities and play. Evidence for the long-term predictive power of data on nursery school play in respect to divergent-thinking performance—the Wallach and Kogan tasks—at primary school (a four-and-one-half-year interval) is offered in a brief report by Hutt and Bhavnani (1972). Prior research by Hutt (1966) demonstrated that 3- to 5-year-olds could be placed into one of three categories on the basis of responses to a new toy: (1) nonexplorers who merely approached and looked at the toy, (2) explorers who actively inspected the toy but did little with it, and (3) inventive explorers who, following investigation of the toy, found imaginative ways to play with it. For both sexes, the highest uniqueness scores were obtained by those children who had been categorized as inventive explorers four to five years earlier, although the effects were stronger for boys than for girls.

We turn next to play-creativity research of an experimental character. In one of the first such studies, Feitelson and Ross (1973), working with kindergarten children, examined the effects of play training on divergent-thinking indices derived from the Torrance (1966) nonverbal Thinking Creatively with Pictures test. Of the four experimental conditions employed, the major focus was on play tutoring intended "to raise the level and amount of combinatory play and to decrease dependence on ready-made toys. Fancifulness and inventiveness were encouraged" (p. 212). Consistent with expectations, play sophistication and originality on the Torrance tests increased significantly only in the case of the foregoing condition. However, because play training rather than spontaneous play as such was responsible for the observed effects, the findings might reflect the sheer presence of a participating adult rather than the content of the activity between adult and child. The principal contribution of the present investigation is the demonstration that engagement in combinatory play is not a spontaneous occurrence in kindergarten children. An adult modeling such play can apparently induce children to increase the combinatory quality of their play behavior. Thus, what has often been viewed as a universal attribute of young preschool and kindergarten children may well represent a dimension of individual differences in its own right.

The major flaw of the Feitelson and Ross (1973) study—the questionable nature of the play manipulation—is overcome in the work of Dansky and Silverman (1973). Nursery school children were randomly assigned to a free-play, imitation, or control condition. A variety of stimulus material was made available in the play condition (paper towels, screwdrivers, paper clips, match boxes), and chil-

dren were given 10 min. to play with these materials. As a dependent measure, the experimenter selected one of the objects listed above and asked the child to think of all of the possible things one might do with it. These were scored as standard and nonstandard uses. No treatment differences were observed for standard uses. In contrast, for nonstandard (unusual) uses, children assigned to the play condition generated a significantly larger number of responses for each of the four objects employed than did the children in the imitation and control conditions (who did not differ from each other). Further, the nonstandard responses were generally faithful to the properties of the objects. Bizarre responses were rare.

Unclear from the preceding experiment is whether the additional uses generated by children in the play condition derive from specific behavioral components of the play activity itself. Such a process has much more limited theoretical implications than one in which play is viewed as a general facilitator of divergent thinking. To settle this issue, Dansky and Silverman (1975) conducted a second experiment (with the same age group of children) that explicitly separated the objects made available for play purposes from those to which the children subsequently responded in a divergent-thinking context. Results were highly comparable to those obtained in the initial 1973 study, thus clearly pointing to play as a general facilitator of thought processes compatible with the requirements of divergent-thinking tasks.

In a more recent study by Dansky (1980a), an effort is made to elucidate the mediating variables responsible for the linkage between play and divergent thinking. To achieve a fuller understanding of this issue, Dansky proposes an examination of individual differences among children in their spontaneous make-believe play behaviors. The presence of such differences is suggested by the Feitelson and Ross (1973) observation reported earlier. Thus, when children are encouraged to play for a duration of time with a specified set of toy materials, there is no reason to expect that all the children exposed to this condition would necessarily engage in make-believe play. If it could be shown that children who naturally engage in make-believe play are more strongly influenced by a congruent play treatment (in the sense of enhanced divergent-thinking scores) than are children who show no natural inclination toward make-believe play, a strong case could then be made for the disposition toward make believe as the mediator of the play/divergent-thinking association.

The Dansky (1980a) investigation employed preschool children who were observed in a free-play setting over four 5-min. periods. Children who engaged in make believe more than 25% of the time were designated players; those manifesting make believe less than 5% of the time were labeled nonplayers. The children within each category were then randomly assigned to experimental treatments, that is, free-play, imitation, and convergent problem-solving treatments. Note further that the toy objects employed for the divergent-thinking assessment were different from those used in the experimental treatments. In respect to results, main effects were obtained for both treatments and subjects (players vs. nonplayers). Greater alternate-uses fluency was found in the free play relative to the other conditions and among players in comparison with nonplayers. Of primary interest, however, was the evidence of a significant interaction in which children in the free-play/player cell generated significantly more uses than subjects in any of the other cells comprising the study design. Further, observations of the children in that cell indicated that more than 85% of them actually engaged in make-believe play. In sum, the outcomes of the Dansky (1980a) research strongly reinforce the view that the make-believe elements in symbolic play have much in common with the cognitive processes characterizing skill in divergent thinking.

Most of the research exploring the facilitative effects of free play on divergent thinking has been based on middle-class children. Dansky (1980a) has demonstrated that children vary in the degree to which they spontaneously engage in free play, and in further work (Dansky, 1980b), he has argued that economically disadvantaged children would profit least from free-play opportunities. Consistent with earlier work by Smilansky (1968), Dansky (1980b) exposed disadvantaged preschoolers to sociodramatic play training in which an adult (using a variety of props) guided the children's behavior around particular themes (e.g., a grocery store situation). The study also included a free-play control in which children were given the same props, but no adult guidance. In a third condition, children were exposed to exploration training emphasizing the physical properties of the available props. Spontaneous free-play behaviors were observed both prior to and one week after the interventions.

The results showed that sociodramatic play training substantially increased the extent and the imaginativeness of make-believe play relative to the effects observed for free-play and exploration training. Further, on the Wallach and Kogan (1965) alternate-uses task, ideational-fluency levels were significantly higher for children in sociodramatic play than for children assigned to the other play conditions. In brief, whether the make-believe play is spontaneous (more likely for middle-class children) or induced by an adult trainer (more likely to be required for economically disadvantaged children), the ultimate effect is one of enhanced performance in the divergent thinking domain.

In summary, the research directed toward the issue of the play-creativity linkage may well represent the most promising set of findings in the children's creativity literature over the past decade. Of course, there are a number of loose ends that remain to be tied together, but this does not detract from the strength of the evidence. Let us, however, consider some of these unresolved issues. As we have noted, the individual-differences approach is plagued by variation in the patterning of sex differences, a recurrent finding in the creativity literature (see Kogan, 1974). On the whole, it would appear that social-fantasy play yields stronger effects for girls, whereas object play generates stronger effects for boys. On the matter of play tutoring (and its enhancement of divergent thinking and other cognitive accomplishments), Smith and Syddall (1978) have shown that a comparable duration of contact with an adult in a skill-learning context as opposed to play context produced a similar level of cognitive enhancement. Regrettably, however, those authors failed to include a divergent-thinking task among their cognitive assessments; hence, the Feitelson and Ross (1973) demonstration of the efficacy of play tutoring for divergent-thinking originality has not been directly challenged. Further, Dansky and Silverman (1973, 1975) have rather clearly shown that the mere opportunity to play with various toy materials in the absence of any adult instruction is sufficient to bring about an increase in the number of unusual uses attributed to common objects. These represent immediate postexperimental effects however. We presently do not know how play affects divergent thinking on a longer term basis.

In a recent paper, Smith and Dutton (1979) have taken issue with the use of divergent-thinking indices as a criterion for the evaluation of play effects. They argue that such responses in young children, although innovative, frequently are not functionally useful. One cannot deny this assertion, and it raises the possibility of refining or expanding the scoring of divergent-thinking procedures to include indices of appropriateness or usefulness as well as novelty. Smith and Dutton (1979) as well as others (Saltz, Dixon, & Johnson, 1977; Saltz & Johnson, 1974) have shown that play can also enhance problem-solving skill (convergent thinking). This is of particular interest in the light of the statistical independence of divergent- and convergent-thinking measures in preschool children (Williams & Fleming, 1969).

Although play may well enhance both divergent and convergent thinking, the question of the nature of the play that facilitates these distinctive thinking modes has not yet been answered. There is little doubt that the play materials offered to the child can be convergent or divergent in character. It would be of considerable interest, of course, to know how such contrasting play materials affect subsequent performance on convergent and divergent problem-solving tasks.

In a recent experiment, Pepler and Ross (1981) addressed themselves to the above issue. Children 3 and 4 years old were provided either with an assorted set of colored pieces, each of which fit into a formboard (convergent play), or with the pieces alone, which consisted of free-standing animals, vehicles, regular shapes, random shapes, and squares (divergent play). Observation of the children indicated that the provided materials fostered the kinds of play intended. All of the participating children were then given convergent tasks (e.g., puzzles involving color or form matching with irrelevant cues) and divergent tasks (e.g., alternate uses).

The Pepler and Ross (1981) study generated an array of provocative findings. First, consistent with research described earlier, divergent play enhanced the uniqueness of responses offered on divergent-thinking tasks, even though such tasks bore little formal similarity to the play materials. No such effects on divergent tasks were found for children in the convergent-play or no-play control groups. Further, the relatively broad transfer effects observed within the divergent-task domain in the divergent-play group also extended to the convergent domain. Children engaging in divergent play "appeared to be more flexible in abandoning ineffective strategies as they sought problem solutions" (Pepler & Ross, 1981, p. 1210). Comparable effects have also been reported by Dansky (1980b), by Sylva, Bruner, and Genova (1976) and by Smith and Dutton (1979). Convergent play, by contrast, seemed to enhance performance exclusively on convergent-thinking tasks similar to those employed during the play period. In sum, the Pepler and Ross (1981) work is of particular significance in its demonstration that the beneficial effects of divergent play are not confined to divergent-thinking tasks but rather are suggestive of a heightened flexibility in problem-solving performance conceived more generally. The importance of such outcomes must be acknowledged, although one must also note that, consistent with prior research, the longer term effect of the play experience on diverse cognitive performances remains unknown.

Little attention has been directed thus far to possible motivational elements in play and its aftermath. Bruner (1972) has argued that the play of young children may be a prime example of intrinsic motivation. Nonplay control conditions conceivably lack such motivation. Thus, the intrinsic motivation and positive affect aroused by the play experience might well be maintained in the subsequent criterial phase, thereby enhancing both convergent- and divergent-thinking performance. Such a position is also consistent with Vandenberg's (1980) recent statement. That author argues that the link between play and divergent thinking does not depend on specific behavioral subassemblies that the two have in common. Rather, to quote Vandenberg (1980, p. 64), "play seems to develop a more generalized attitude and/or schema which predisposes the individual to creating and using novelty." Separating out these motivational processes from more strictly cognitive attention-deployment and combinatorial processes cannot be easily achieved. The problem stands as a challenge for the future.

Effects of Classroom Environment

Thus far, we have considered the expression of childhood creativity independent of the broader educational context in which it occurs. Children spend a large portion of their time in classrooms, and one would expect the nature of that experience to have a considerable impact on styles of thought. Although it is possible to characterize the climate and organization of classrooms in diverse ways, the distinction that has most clearly captured the imagination of the educational community is that of traditional versus open settings. Although much of the research on this topic treats the traditional versus open contrast as dichotomous, it is more appropriate to think in terms of a continuum. Because a number of different components enter into a classification of a classroom as traditional or open (e.g., the physical environment, the role of the teacher, scheduling of time), a particular classroom might have virtually all, some, or virtually none of the attributes of open education. Certainly, it would be quite legitimate to characterize some classrooms as mixed, and a few researchers in the field have done so.

The issue of creativity is highly relevant to the traditional versus the open-education contrast because one of the justifications of the open-education movement is the presumed inhibitory effect on creativity of the highly structured authoritarian mode considered prototypical of traditional classroom contexts. Over the last 15 years, a number of empirical studies have been carried out to test the foregoing idea as well as other hypotheses respecting differences between traditional and open settings. Initial studies strongly supported the open-education/creativity hypothesis. Haddon and Lytton (1968), for example, gave the Torrance (1966) test battery to 11- to 12-year-old children drawn from traditional and open classrooms and found that the children in the latter scored significantly higher on virtually all of the divergent-thinking indices. Further, a follow-up four years later demonstrated the continued superiority of the open-education students, despite the diversity of educational environments to which they were currently exposed (Haddon & Lytton, 1971). These effects were obtained despite the comparability of verbal-reasoning ability in the two groups. Such matching, of course, does not guarantee that the traditional and open subsamples were of equal divergent-thinking ability prior to their exposure to these different modes of instruction. This is a problem that plagues much of the research on the present topic.

Although matching on diverse ability and SES measures has become more sophisticated in the recent work, the impossibility of random assignment in real-world educational settings necessarily implies that children drawn from different classrooms might be initially unequal on the dependent variables of interest. The solution to the problem, of course, lies in longitudinal research in which pretests are obtained prior to, or at the very beginning of, explicit classroom instruction—whether traditional, open, or mixed. Because there is also some indication (Wilson, Stuckey, & Langevin, 1972) that children exposed to open education for a long (six years) as opposed to a short period of time (one year) demonstrate differential effects (a longer time associated with higher divergent-thinking scores), longitudinal studies would have to be pursued for a considerable time period. Research on the effects of open versus traditional modes of instruction within such a long-term longitudinal perspective has not yet appeared in the published literature (at least in relation to the creativity construct).

Beginning in the mid 1970s, a series of studies were published that offered highly equivocal support or no support whatever for the view that traditional instruction inhibits and open education fosters creativity. In one of the first of these investigations, Ramey and Piper (1974) selected children from the first, fourth, and eighth grades of purportedly traditional and open schools. They observed that children in open classrooms generated higher scores on figural tasks, whereas children in traditional classrooms performed at a higher level on verbal tasks taken from the Torrance (1966) battery. Ramey and Piper (1974) interpreted their unexpected findings along the lines of the kinds of activities stressed in traditional versus open classrooms—children in the latter setting spending more time manipulating concrete objects and children in the former exercising linguistic skills. If the foregoing argument is valid, one might also expect classroom differences in verbal versus performance IQ, and here it is regrettable that such control measures were not obtained.

In subsequent research, methodological improvements can be noted along lines of explicit IQ and SES matching of children in traditional versus open settings and the use of measuring instruments for quantifying the extent of openness manifested in the classroom. The first of these studies (Ward & Barcher, 1975) employed second, third, and fourth graders and reported an IQ moderator effect. For low-IQ pupils, the traditional versus open contrast did not yield any outcome difference on verbal and figural tests from Torrance (1966) and Wallach and Kogan (1965). In the case of the high-IQ pupils, on the other hand, children in the traditional classrooms relative to their peers in the open setting generated significantly higher creativity (i.e., divergent-thinking) scores. For the first time, then, we have a set of results in which no advantage whatever accrued to open instruction in respect to the facilitation of creativity. Indeed, the effect was reversed in the high-IQ subgroup. In a similar study based on fifth graders, R. J. Wright (1975) also failed to confirm a linkage between open education and creative performance. Comparable findings were reported by Forman and McKinney (1978) in a sample of second-grade children selected from open and traditional classes and matched for age, IQ, race, and SES. An exceptionally complex pattern of findings was obtained in which higher fluency and uniqueness scores were obtained for some of the Wallach and Kogan (1965) tasks in the traditional setting and for other tasks in the open setting. The tasks failed to divide along a simple verbal-figurative contrast as in the Ramey and Piper (1974) research discussed earlier. In sum, for all of the studies conducted during the decade of the 1970s, neither traditional nor open instruction emerged as a clear-cut facilitator of divergent-thinking performance.

In virtually all of the research described thus far, classrooms were dichotomized as predominantly traditional or open, and longitudinal designs were *not* used. In a marked departure from earlier research, Thomas and Berk (1981) designed a study that (1) added an intermediate category to the traditional versus open distinction (labeled formal vs. informal by those authors) and that (2) included a pretest and a posttest administered in the fall and spring of the school year respectively. Thomas and Berk (1981) offer the hypothesis that it may be the intermediate classroom that is most facilitative of creativity, and they further suggest that the lesser statistical power of designs lacking a pretest might have contributed to the conflicting results obtained in the past.

Working with the foregoing three-way categorization of first- and second-grade classrooms and using the Torrance (1966) tests as a criterion, Thomas and Berk (1981) obtained clear-cut evidence for classroom effects on divergent-thinking performance. However, the curvilinear hypothesis—that intermediate classrooms would prove more facilitative than formal or informal classrooms—was not consistently confirmed. Depending on the child's sex or the particular divergent-thinking component at issue, the largest fall-to-spring improvement sometimes was found in intermediate classrooms, sometimes in informal classrooms and sometimes, in fact, in formal classrooms. This last outcome was quite rare, however, and it would be reasonable to assert that the Thomas and Berk (1981) study represents one of the very few successful efforts to show that formal or traditional schooling suppresses the development of divergent-thinking skills. In no sense does this imply, of course, that such suppression will be maintained on a long-term basis.

In some of the classroom-climate studies treated thus far, children have been divided by IQ and sex in search of possible moderator effects. Of course, IQ and sex do not exhaust the ways in which children can be classified. Solomon and Kendall (1976) have used a variety of children's motivational and cognitive measures to construct a typology by means of cluster analysis. Only one of the child-type clusters—"compliant, conforming orientation"—had any impact on creativity, with more compliant children yielding higher divergent-thinking scores in the open-classroom setting. Results such as these reinforce Wallach's (1971) thesis that a portion of the variance in ideational-fluency scores can be attributed to the child's need to please an examiner by generating a large quantity of responses. It is not at all obvious, however, why the foregoing effect occurs in the open rather than the traditional context.

In all of the research discussed here, creativity has been treated as an outcome variable. When operationalized as performance on divergent-thinking tasks, there is an implicit assumption of the validity of such tasks as creativity criteria. As we have previously noted, however, divergent thinking is likely to be a highly imperfect predictor of real-world creativity. To equate divergent-thinking scores with creativity as an outcome variable is to give the former much more credit than it deserves. Because divergent thinking represents a predictor rather than a criterion of creativity, it is puzzling that so little attention has been paid to the possibility that divergent thinking should be joined with classroom climate on the predictor or independent-variable side of the equation, with the dependent-variable side reserved for a diversity of cognitive and socioemotional *behaviors*.

Research by Trickett (1983) represents an initial effort to conceptualize the problem in the manner indicated above. Working with first-grade children selected from traditional, open, and intermediate or mixed classrooms, Trickett administered selected Wallach and Kogan (1965) divergent-thinking tasks and the Otis-Lennon Mental Ability Test (where IQ information was not available in school records). The dependent variables of the study consisted of teacher ratings of children's classroom behaviors, teacher ratings of preference (likability) and overall academic standing, children's responses to a self-concept scale, and children's school attendance record. These became the dependent measures in a multiple-regression analysis. IQ, divergent thinking, classroom climate, and their respective interactions constituted the predictors or independent variables. Whereas divergent thinking had no impact on any of the dependent variables for boys, girls high in divergent thinking received higher ratings for school involvement, self-reliant learning, achievement anxiety, and likability. It should be further noted that no significant interactions were observed between divergent thinking and classroom climate in respect to behavioral outcomes. In other words for the first-grade girls of the present sample, divergent thinking on the whole was associated with positive behavioral outcomes *regardless of classroom climate*. Comparable effects were reported by Thomas and Berk (1981). The link to higher achievement anxiety observed by Trickett (1983) points to a possible negative connotation for a divergent-thinking style.

There is reason to believe, however, that the anxiety of high-divergent thinkers may reflect a greater introspective awareness of inner states—in other words, lesser defensiveness (see Singer, 1973; Wallach, 1970).

It is evident that the Trickett (1983) research, although based on a different paradigm than the other studies discussed here, fails to provide any support for the view that divergent thinking and open education represent a winning combination. Before we dispose of an attractive hypothesis completely, however, one can fairly ask whether the problem possibly lies in the use of divergent-thinking indices as creativity assessors. Perhaps a more positive picture would have ensued if the creativity assessments were more closely tied to classroom achievements. In this regard, note should be taken of Bennett's (1976) research in British primary schools. Children in open, mixed, and traditional classrooms were asked to engage in a creative-writing exercise. An introductory paragraph was provided in which children were to imagine themselves invisible for a day. Although analysis revealed a striking sex difference (girls received higher imaginativeness ratings), there was no indication whatever that any one teaching style facilitated creative writing more than another.

Although the weight of the evidence points to the rejection of the straightforward hypothesis that open instruction is advantageous for pupils whose style of thinking is strongly divergent, this discussion must necessarily end on an ambivalent note. In the one study (Thomas & Berk, 1981) in which pretests controlled for individual differences in initial divergent-thinking levels, open and intermediate classrooms were observed to have a facilitative effect in comparison with the more formal classroom setting. Of course, variables other than the presence or absence of a pretest cannot be ignored. The Thomas and Berk (1981) research employed first- and second-graders, an age where facilitative effects can conceivably be demonstrated most readily. To quote Forman and McKinney (1978, p. 106), "it is possible that an open environment has different effects on creativity at different periods of development."

As indicated earlier, there are good grounds for objecting to the use of divergent-thinking tests as outcome variables. Given the far-from-perfect association between divergent-thinking and creativity criteria in the real world, it makes much more sense to view the former as predictors of pedagogically relevant outcomes. If the combination of divergent thinking and open education is particularly conducive to positive intellective and socioemotional behavior in the classroom, significant interactions can be anticipated. As the Trickett (1983) research demonstrated, however, no such interactions were found in first-grade samples. The overall thrust of the findings suggest, then, that a child's divergent-thinking status does not imply any special advantage or disadvantage in one type of classroom as opposed to another.

Long-term Stability of Divergent-Thinking Performance

Given the enormous interest in the creativity topic over the past three decades, it is rather astonishing to note how little effort has been devoted to the issue of long-term stability. Relative to his or her peers, does the child who performs well (or poorly) on divergent-thinking tasks in the preschool years continue to perform well (or poorly) in primary school, secondary school, college, and so on? Only a few data sets are addressed to this issue and all appear to span the period from later childhood or early adolescence to middle or later adolescence. Because divergent-thinking tasks can be administered reliably to children of preschool age, it is apparent that there are crucial gaps in our knowledge about long-term stability.

In one of the earlier studies, Cropley and Clapson (1971) examined the five-year stability of divergent nonverbal and verbal tests taken from the batteries of Torrance (1966) and French, Ekstrom, and Price (1963) respectively. Of a sample of 320 pupils tested at approximately 12 years of age, 110 were available for retesting five years later. Regrettably, those participating in the retesting represented a somewhat biased sample as reflected by higher mean IQs relative to the initial total sample of pupils. The five-year stability coefficients were significant for both sexes, although of somewhat greater magnitude in the male sample.

Possibly, the most definitive investigation of the long-term stability of divergent thinking has been carried out by Magnusson and Backteman (1978). Those authors were able to test the entire school population in a small Swedish town (approximately 1,000 pupils) when the pupils were 13 and 16 years of age. Swedish versions of Guilford-type divergent-thinking tests were employed, with different tests administered at the two age levels. On each testing occasion, both verbal and figural tasks were used and were scored exclusively for fluency. Intelligence test data were also obtained. Stability coefficients were fairly comparable for both verbal and figural tests and averaged .46 for boys and .42 for girls. Worthy of note is the evidence that these co-efficients were lower than those observed for intelligence data. In the case of verbal intelligence, coefficients ranged from the mid-.60s to the low .70s. Magnusson and Backteman (1978) attribute the difference to the greater variation in the content of the divergent-thinking measures on the two testing occasions relative to the intelligence assessments where a higher level of similarity prevailed. Of further interest in the Magnusson and Backteman investigation is the use of a multivariable-multioccasion matrix for the intelligence and creativity data. Thus, it was possible to demonstrate that the stability coefficients for divergent-thinking measures were consistently higher than those between divergent thinking and intelligence for both simultaneous and cross-time assessments.

In the sole study devoted to the longitudinal stability of the Wallach and Kogan (1965) tasks, Kogan and Pankove (1972) examined consistency of divergent-thinking performance over a five-year period extending from the fifth to tenth grade. At the initial fifth-grade assessment, the tasks were administered to all of the children individually. Five years later, individual administration was employed in one of the school systems involved, whereas only group administration was feasible in the other school system. This variation in task context differentially influenced the magnitude of stability coefficients for boys and girls. In the case of boys, highly significant stability coefficients (ranging from the high .30s to the low .50s) were obtained for fluency and uniqueness when the tenth-grade assessments were carried out in the impersonal-group context. Girls, on the other hand, failed to manifest consistency in that context. Instead, stability coefficients for girls reached significant levels only where tenth-grade assessments were individually based (and, hence, similar to fifth-grade assessments). The individual-testing context at tenth grade, by contrast, generated nonsignificant stability coefficients for boys.

In summary, the accumulated evidence is in general support of the long-term longitudinal stability of divergent-thinking performance across the years of middle childhood (approximately age 10) through a substantial portion of adolescence (approximately ages 16 to 17). There is a dearth of information regarding longitudinal stability outside the age range indicated. Despite the general pattern of support for longitudinal stability, the research of Kogan and Pankove (1972) suggests that the magnitude of the coefficients can vary substantially as a function of testing context and sex of subject. Note further that these coefficients rarely exceed .50 (even with cor-rections for attenuation). The longitudinal stability of IQ assessments for a comparable age range is considerably higher (coefficients generally ranging from about .6 to .8). This difference in magnitude cannot be attributed entirely to variation in tests between first and second administrations, as in the Magnusson and Backteman research, for both Cropley and Clapson (1971) and Kogan and Pankove (1972) employed the same instruments on the two testing occasions, yet obtained lower stability coefficients for divergent-thinking than for IQ assessments. Given evidence cited earlier that divergent-thinking performance is more susceptible to test-context effects than are IQ assessments, and given that these effects may not be constant across age, the lesser magnitude of the stability coefficients for divergent thinking relative to IQ becomes comprehensible.

Longitudinal study of creativity has not gone beyond stability coefficients to the examination of developmental functions, that is, changes in mean levels of performance with age. This seems to mirror the state of affairs in respect to other individual-difference dimensions (Wohlwill, 1973, 1980). What little evidence exists is based on no more than two data points, hardly sufficient for investigation of developmental trends over time. The limited data available (e.g., Cropley & Clapson, 1971; Kogan & Pankove, 1972) points to increases in the fluency and uniqueness components of divergent thinking from late childhood into adolescence (although not without exceptions). In the case of the Wallach and Kogan tasks, cross-sectional comparisons (Wallach & Kogan, 1965; Wallach & Wing, 1969) suggest that growth in fluency proceeds at a more accelerated pace in the case of verbal than of figural measures. Conceivably, the differential task strategies evoked by the verbal and figural items (recall the earlier discussion of the Kogan and Morgan, 1969, data) may account for the apparent difference in developmental growth rate. Increases in experiential repertoires with age may be more conducive to use of the category-exhaustion strategies presumed relevant to verbal tasks. It is dubious, however, whether sheer size of repertoires would be of great consequence for figural tasks.

Concurrent Validity of Divergent Thinking

This discussion deals with the issue of the relation between performance on divergent-thinking tests and real-world behaviors purportedly relevant to creativity. Earlier, we examined the relation of the former to make-believe play activity. Such research

is in the construct-validational tradition of theoretically bridging domains distinguished by common psychological processes. Here, we shift emphasis to products or outcomes that most experts in
the field would deem relevant to the manifestation of
real-world creativity for a specified age range. In the
case of young children, for example, drawing and
sculpting (out of clay) represent spontaneous activities that lead to products whose level of creativity
(as well as other characteristics) can presumably be
rated. It should be noted in this regard that the alleged creativity reflected in divergent-thinking tasks
and the creativity judged to be present in a child's art
work do not share any apparent common properties.
In the case of the Wallach and Kogan (1965) tasks,
for example, both the verbal and figural items require verbal responses from the child, whereas
drawing is a patently nonverbal activity. This is not
to imply that some higher order theoretical process
could not account for a relationship if one were to be
found. For the present, however, it would seem advisable to treat the issue within a predictor-criterion
framework, with divergent thinking cast in the former and drawing assigned the latter role. Because
drawing is a typical activity within the child's life
experience in a way that divergent-thinking tests are
not, the foregoing predictor-criterion distinction can
be justified.

Research by Wallbrown and Huelsman (1975)
represents one of the few attempts to study the present issue in children. They administered the Wallach and Kogan (1965) tasks to third and fourth graders and then obtained two crayon drawings and a
clay product from each child. The art products were
rated for originality and effectiveness of expression
(aesthetic quality) by four knowledgeable judges.
Note that the correlation between ratings of originality and aesthetic quality was .89, a value sufficiently high to suggest that even sophisticated judges
are unable to distinguish between those two components of a child's art work. Of primary interest in the
Wallbrown and Huelsman research is the evidence
that the Wallach and Kogan divergent-thinking tasks
(with intelligence controlled) proved to be significant predictors of the rated originality and aesthetic
quality of children's clay products. In sum, the evidence clearly favors the view that, despite the disparate nature of the behaviors represented in the predictor and criterion tasks, divergent-thinking ability
has a direct and substantial impact on a real-life creative activity in children. Unanswered in the Wallbrown and Huelsman research, however, is the
question of why divergent thinking and originality of

art products are significantly related.

One possible direction for an explanation is offered in a study of kindergarten children by Singer
and Whiton (1971). Again, the Wallach and Kogan
(1965) tasks were employed (verbal only). The children were also asked to draw a picture of a person.
These figure drawings were scored for facial expressiveness, movement (tension, directionality, or
action), and spontaneous elaboration (addition of
animals, costumes, scenery, or more than one person). Significant interrater agreement was obtained.
Both the facial expressiveness and movement ratings were significantly related to divergent-thinking
scores but only marginally related to IQ assessments. Singer and Whiton interpret their findings in
terms of a construct of response constriction. Thus,
children constricted in their associations to divergent-thinking items are also presumed to be constricted in expressing affect in the face and body of
their human-figure drawings.

Whether such an explanation can also account for
the Wallbrown and Huelsman (1975) results in older
children, of course, depends on the degree to which
the expressiveness component entered into the
judges' ratings of the originality and aesthetic quality of the children's art products. Clearly needed, in
other words, is further information regarding the
bases for judging an art work to be of low or high
originality and aesthetic quality. Worthy of note in
the present context is other evidence indicating that
openness to affect among children of high divergent-
thinking ability is manifested as greater introspective self-awareness and lesser defensiveness (Wallach, 1970, 1971; Wallach & Kogan, 1965). Hence,
a more constricted inner life, inhibitions of expressiveness in human-figure drawings, and low divergent-thinking performance seem to form a coherent cluster.

As children progress through the school system,
a variety of additional creativity criteria become
available for study. In the Wallach and Wing (1969)
research on graduating high school seniors, for example, seven separate domains of potentially creative nonacademic attainment were delineated—
leadership, art, social service, writing, dramatic
arts, music, and science. Attainment in four of these
domains was significantly predicted by ideational-
fluency indices derived from the Wallach and Kogan
tasks—leadership, art, writing, and science. None
of these were predicted by the verbal and mathematical scores of the College Board's Scholastic Aptitude Test. Note that the domains of social service,
dramatic arts, and music at the high school level are

not likely to involve innovative activities but rather reflect prosocial behaviors (social service) or interpretive skills (dramatic arts and music).

The modest success of Wallach and Wing (1969) in establishing a connection between divergent-thinking indicators and talented nonacademic attainments has encouraged others to seek such relationships in subjects younger than high school age. The most extreme example is represented by a study based on 7-year-olds (Rotter, Langland, & Berger, 1971). Small but significant correlations were found between divergent-thinking performance and several activities—creative writing, dramatics, and life sciences. Because these latter activities seem well beyond the capacity of 7-year-old children, the Rotter et al. (1971) data may represent a confirmation of the Wallach (1971) argument that more fluent children are especially eager to please an examiner and, hence, check off numerous activities to create a favorable impression of themselves.

Although the study of a broad range of creativity criteria in elementary school children seems ill advised, it is quite likely that one can begin to do predictor-criterion research well before the senior year of secondary school. Vernon (1971), for example, worked with junior high school pupils and employed such criteria as "rated creativity of an autobiography," "creativity of a draw-a-man procedure," and "artistic leisure-time interests." All of these proved to be significantly correlated with performance on the Wallach and Kogan (1965) tasks when these were administered under relaxed conditions.

Predictive Validity of Divergent Thinking

Consider next the issue of predictive validity—the extent to which divergent-thinking assessments at a particular point in time can predict creative performance at some later point in time. Such a study was carried out by Cropley (1972), who administered a battery of Guilford-type divergent-thinking tests to junior high school pupils and, five years later, assessed the level of nonacademic attainment in four of the Wallach and Wing (1969) domains—art, drama, literature, and music. Unfortunately, Cropley's claim of significant canonical correlations was proven to be erroneous in a reanalysis reported by Jordan (1975). The actual magnitude of the relation between predictors and criteria did not deviate significantly from chance.

In a study exploring the long-term predictive validity of the Wallach and Kogan (1965) tasks (Kogan & Pankove, 1974), children who had been given those tasks in fifth grade (Pankove & Kogan, 1968) were followed up in their senior year of high school, at which time they filled out the Wallach and Wing (1969) questionnaire of activities and accomplishments. Results clearly indicated that fifth-grade divergent-thinking assessments had no predictive power in respect to overall accomplishments. When separate analyses were carried out for the seven fields of nonacademic attainment, little change in the pattern of findings was observed. Not surprisingly, a tenth-grade index of nonacademic attainments proved to be the best predictor of such attainments upon graduation.

Results such as those reported above raise severe doubts about the value of childhood divergent-thinking assessments as predictors of creativity in the adolescent and adult years. Of course, one can question the relevance of the Wallach and Wing (1969) indices for genuine creativity, but it is difficult to envision a superior device for use with samples of high school age. At the same time, one should keep in mind that the Kogan and Pankove (1974) data in no way detracts from the concurrent and construct validity of children's divergent-thinking abilities. One also must allow for the possibility that children's divergent-thinking performance may have greater import for eventual choice of a field of study than for the extent of creative accomplishment within that field. Thus, Hudson (1966) has offered a strong case for an affinity between choice of the arts and humanities as a field of concentration and the tendency to do well on divergent-thinking tests. Physical science concentrators, by contrast, perform relatively less well on such tests but tend to obtain high scores on tests of the convergent type.

The Kogan and Pankove (1972, 1974) evidence favors the view that extracurricular activities and accomplishments are distinguished by a high degree of consistency during the secondary school years. Very conceivably, the roots of this consistency might be traced back to an earlier period in the pupil's schooling. The necessary evidence is not currently available. We do know, however, that secondary school activities and accomplishments are predictive of comparable behaviors in the college years (e.g., Richards, Holland, & Lutz, 1967). If these latter behaviors, in turn, should prove predictive of adult creativity, the use of divergent-thinking tests as creativity predictors could be seriously questioned. Instead, a good case could be made for what Wallach (1976, p. 189) has called persistence forecasting—"the best way to predict whether someone will manifest particular forms of behavior in the future is to determine whether the person has displayed those or similar behaviors in the past. . . .'' Of course, such persistence forecasting is contingent on the development of satisfactory operational definitions for creativity in mature adults, a goal that is difficult to achieve in the light of the diverse requirements of adult occupational roles (see Kogan, 1973). Further, the base rates for adult creativity are rather low, and, hence, it is hardly surprising that psychologists have preferred to use the retrospective method with adults whose creativity is already acknowledged by peers (e.g., Barron, 1963) rather than engage in painstaking, lifespan research aimed at predicting who among a particular cohort of children or adolescents will manifest real-world creativity at some later stage of life. It is to the credit of Torrance (1972, 1975) that he has attempted the latter kind of long-term research. Students tested in high school have been followed up 12 years later (around 30 years of age). Significant product-moment and canonical correlations have been reported between the Torrance test scores and criteria of creative achievement. At the same time, IQ scores were also significantly correlated with the criteria, but Torrance and his associates appear reluctant to make use of multiple-regression analyses that would yield information about the incremental validity of the Torrance instruments over and beyond the predictive power of the IQ. It would also prove useful to add an index of high school extracurricular accomplishments to the prediction equation. Until such analyses are carried out, evidence for the long-term predictive validity of the Torrance instruments must be considered equivocal at best.

The foregoing review clearly casts doubt on the long-term predictive validity of divergent-thinking indices when these are assessed in the years extending from late childhood (ages 10 to 11) through late adolescence. One cannot, of course, generalize from the research described in the present section to studies of earlier portions of the life span. In this connection, Harrington et al. (1983) have recently reported striking success in validating divergent-thinking performance at ages 4 and 5 against a teacher-rating criterion of creativity in the sixth grade. Given earlier evidence reviewed by Wallach and Kogan (1965) seriously questioning the utility of teacher ratings in the light of massive halo effects, it is very much to the credit of Harrington et al. (1983) that they have been able to overcome this measurement problem. They were able to do so through the use of the *California Child Q-Set* (Block & Block, 1981), an ipsative rating procedure in which 100 descriptive

items are sorted for each child into nine categories to yield a preestablished frequency distribution. It appears that the use of a large number of items of widely varying content in an ipsative measurement framework can reduce halo effects and concomitantly enhance discriminative validity.

Modification and Training of Divergent Thinking

Despite the admonishment of Wallach (1971) regarding the futility of training subjects on a creativity predictor rather than a criterion, modification research has continued to be a major preoccupation of numerous creativity researchers. The nub of Wallach's argument concerns the mistaken belief that enhancement of divergent-thinking scores is tantamount to a genuine creativity increase. Because divergent thinking is but an imperfect predictor of real-world creativity, one obviously cannot generalize from a predictor to a criterion in the interpretation of training effects. In Wallach's view, effort could be more usefully expended in teaching children and adolescents to be better writers, painters, scientific thinkers, and so on. One cannot take issue with Wallach's argument, although it is important to realize that modification and training experiments do not always have the simple goal of creativity enhancement. Instead, such experiments often serve the useful scientific purpose of providing greater insight into the psychological processes underlying divergent-thinking ability.

Incentives

An example of a theoretical approach is offered by Ward et al. (1972). In that study, a monetary incentive (a penny per response) was used with a sample of predominantly black, low SES fifth graders. The general aim of the study was to test a motivational versus cognitive interpretation of divergent-thinking performance. If poor performance reflects a weak incentive to produce associates to the respective test items, it would be expected that monetary incentives should yield a marked rise in the generation of such associates. A pure motivational interpretation could be advanced, in fact, if the incentives were to bring the low divergent thinkers up to the level of their high divergent-thinking peers. Such an outcome would be feasible if the latter subjects were putting forth maximal effort prior to the introduction of monetary incentives. The Ward et al. (1972) results failed to support the pure motivational interpretation because the monetary incentives essentially added a constant increment to the children's performance and did not disrupt the preincentive rank ordering of the children on an ideational-fluency dimension. In sum, incentives provide a motivational boost to ideational output, but the stability of individual differences points to the importance of cognitive factors—variation in the size of ideational repertoires or more versus less effective strategies of ideational production.

Variations on the Ward et al. (1972) experiment have been reported by R. A. Johnson (1974) and by Milgram and Feingold (1977). In the R. A. Johnson study, three grade levels of both disadvantaged and relatively advantaged children were employed. Consistent with the Ward et al. (1972) outcomes, the lower SES children were more fluent under both reward conditions relative to a no-reward control group. For the higher SES children, on the other hand, the reward and control conditions yielded similar levels of fluency. The Milgram and Feingold (1977) investigation used somewhat older children—seventh graders in an Israeli school who were officially designated as disadvantaged. Incentive conditions generated significant increases in fluency (relative to a control group), with a concrete incentive (candy) approximately twice as effective as verbal praise. Base-line and posttreatment fluency scores were significantly and substantially correlated, thus lending support to the Ward et al. (1972) finding that incentives do not disrupt the pretreatment rank ordering of the children.

The three foregoing studies are in fundamental agreement concerning the efficacy of concrete incentives for raising the level of ideational fluency displayed by disadvantaged children in the third through seventh grades. The R. A. Johnson (1974) finding for more advantaged children suggests that the observed effect is distinctive for children of low SES. Indeed, with the use of concrete incentives, the performance of the lower SES children in the R. A. Johnson investigation *exceeded* that of their higher SES peers. The effect was in the opposite direction when incentives were absent.

Models

The use of reinforcers represents but one of several methods that psychologists have employed to enhance children's level of divergent production. Given the general effectiveness of modeling procedures for inducing subjects to perform specific behaviors, it is hardly surprising that this social learning tradition (Bandura, 1969) has been extended to encompass children's divergent thinking. An initial effort along these lines is reported by Zimmerman and Dialessi (1973). Fifth-grade children were randomly assigned to one of four treatment groups formed on the basis of the high or low fluency and flexibility (number of response categories) of an adult model's verbal responses to a divergent-thinking item. Results unequivocally demonstrated that a fluent model enhanced and a flexible model depressed both fluency and flexibility in children's responses to the divergent-thinking tasks. These effects were particularly prominent for the female members of the sample. A highly flexible model had less of an inhibiting effect on boys if the model also exhibited high fluency.

Zimmerman and Dialessi (1973) argue that model flexibility has an evaluative connotation for the child because it implies self-monitoring of responses to insure that they are dissimilar to one another. Given the high correlations of .70 and .84 between fluency and flexibility on the divergent-thinking items employed, the Zimmerman and Dialessi findings strongly suggest that the route to flexibility lies through fluency. Although these authors do not interpret their outcomes along associative lines, they are clearly consistent with the Mednick (1962) and Wallach and Kogan (1965) positions. If the child believes that he or she must search for different categories of response, the nonlogical associative flow is evidently disrupted and both fluency and flexibility are reduced. It is apparent that the response category shifts (indexed by the flexibility score) must emerge from a spontaneous, associative flow of ideas if that score is to represent a valid indicator of the flexibility of a child's divergent-thinking performance.

No attempt was made in the foregoing investigation to explore divergent-thinking components other than fluency and flexibility. A subsequent study by Belcher (1975) in a sample of fourth and fifth graders examined the impact of a videotaped model who offered original or unoriginal ideas. Level of originality was indexed by the norms provided in the Torrance (1966) manual. A comparison of the two modeling conditions pointed to a facilitating effect of an original model for boys and the inhibiting effect of such a model for girls. It will be recalled that a flexible model in the Zimmerman and Dialessi (1973) study also had a more deleterious effect on girls than on boys. It appears, then, that the introduction of flexibility and originality into a model's performance raises the evaluative apprehension of girls, hence disrupting the spontaneous associative flow (fluency) through which flexibility and originality are mediated. The foregoing finding is consistent with other evidence reported by Kogan (1974, 1976b) indicating the greater susceptibility of girls (vs. boys) to context effects in the creativity domain.

Direct Instruction

Another technique for improving divergent-thinking performance can best be described as teaching to the test. Typically, children are exposed to exercises designed to foster a divergent mode of thought. Sometimes these exercises are carried out for an hour or more each day for a period of several days or weeks. Control groups are exposed to other kinds of materials—presumably of equal interest and irrelevant to divergent thinking. In a study of 9- to 10-year-olds by Franklin and Richards (1977), for example, a variety of objects were brought into the classroom (e.g., bricks, apples, coins) and children were taught to develop question-asking techniques about the diversity of possible uses for such objects. Control groups were exposed to art lessons "providing a variety of new and stimulating experiences" (p. 68). After 10 weeks of training, the experimental and control children were found to differ significantly on the Torrance (1966) verbal tasks but not on the figural tasks taken from the same test battery. In a similar study based on kindergarten children, Cliatt, Shaw, and Sherwood (1980) exposed their experimental group to a daily regimen of divergent-thinking questions by appropriately trained teachers over an 8-week period. Teachers in the matched control groups were also instructed to ask questions, but without any specification as to their character. As in the Franklin and Richards (1977) investigation, the enhanced divergent-thinking performance in the experimental group was obtained for the verbal, but not for the figural subtests of the Torrance (1966) battery. The specificity of the effects in the case of both of the foregoing studies is surprising, given the extended length of the training period and given the fact that verbal and figural divergent thinking are at least moderately correlated.

Creativity Games

In the foregoing examples, the intervention efforts were designed to permit children to practice the very skills presumed critical for doing well on divergent-thinking tasks. An alternative approach is to offer the child a wide diversity of creativity-relevant experiences in the hope that the compounding of effects will have an impact on divergent thinking as well as other types of creativity tasks. Such a study was carried out in an experimental summer camp for sixth- and seventh-grade disadvantaged children in Israel (Goor & Rapoport, 1977). The experimental group participated in a variety of creativity games, whereas the control group participated in the usual camp activities. A significant advantage on the Torrance (1966) tests for the experi-

mental group was observed in both an immediate posttest and a four-month follow-up. Goor and Rapoport (1977) attribute the sticking power of the treatment to anecdotal evidence suggesting that the experimental children continued to play the creativity games during breaks in their formal schooling.

An evaluation of the Goor and Rapoport research must acknowledge its practical impact. Disadvantaged children generate higher divergent-thinking scores when exposed to a rich and varied diet of creativity games. The theoretical shortcoming of the research (one that applies to all studies of the present type) lies in the impossibility of pinpointing the source of the significant effects. Conceivably, only those games highly similar in character to the Torrance (1966) test materials were responsible for the improved divergent-thinking scores of the children in the training group. The lack of any experimental treatment for the control group opens up the possibility of motivational Hawthorne-type effects. Finally, to reiterate the Wallach (1971) argument, we do not know whether the enhancement of divergent thinking has any relevance for creative activities in school or out-of-school contexts.

Humor

Another prevalent theme that distinguishes efforts to facilitate divergent-thinking performance is that of humor. Ziv (1976), for example, exposed Israeli tenth graders to a recording of one of their country's best comedians. Relative to a control group, enhanced performance on the verbal subtests of the Torrance (1966) battery was observed. In respect to humor, it is important to note that the more original responses to divergent-thinking items (particularly alternate uses) are likely to have a humorous quality. When Hudson (1968), in research based on adolescent subjects, provided an example item with 10 imaginative responses (many of them quite amusing), he was able to raise levels of fluency and originality to a significant degree. It is thus apparent that humor has a liberating effect on adolescents. A dual function appears to be served by humor—it reduces the anxiety of the testing situation, hence liberating the subject to extend the limits of what are deemed to be acceptable responses, and it offers a model for the production of such responses. It would be of interest to find out whether younger children would respond to humor in a similar manner.

Summary

A broad array of approaches have been pursued in the effort to enhance the level of divergent thinking in children and adolescents. In brief, subjects have been offered incentives, models, exercises of the divergent-thinking-type, a range of creativity-relevant games, and humorous stimuli. Most of these interventions have been successful to varying degrees. The available evidence suggests that these training efforts do not disrupt the ordering of individual differences, implying that those initially high or low on the divergent-thinking dimension remain so at the conclusion of the intervention. Although diverse means have been found to raise divergent-thinking scores, particular approaches have varied in their theoretical value. Thus, the use of incentives to raise performance has suggested that individual differences in divergent thinking are more cognitively than motivationally based. High scorers, in other words, do not appear to earn that status by simply trying harder.

The fact that fluent, but *not* flexible or original, models enhance all three of those divergent-thinking components offers a strong case for an associative view of the creative process. Models that generate original responses spread over diverse categories actually inhibit divergent production. A fluent model, in contrast, is more likely to simulate an associative process (i.e., a nonlogical flow of ideas), hence reinforcing the view that the route to originality and flexibility is through fluency. Humorous models have also been employed, generally to good effect in raising divergent-thinking levels. Humor appears to have a disinhibition function, allowing for the production of divergent-thinking responses that might otherwise undergo self-censoring.

Of lesser theoretical interest are those studies that provide a variety of creativity-relevant experiences (often over an extended period) with the intent of facilitating divergent thinking. Such efforts have generally met with a measure of practical success, but the diversity of the experiences offered has made it difficult to achieve any genuine understanding of the particular elements in the interventions that account for the observed outcomes. Further, where control conditions are of the no-treatment-type, the possibility of Hawthorne-type effects cannot be ruled out.

Sex, Race, and SES Differences

The most thorough survey of sex differences in cognitive abilities and styles can be found in the Maccoby and Jacklin (1974) volume. Contained within that book are brief sections on sex differences in both verbal and nonverbal divergent-thinking measures. For the former, Table 3.13 from Maccoby

and Jacklin indicates virtually no sex differences in the preschool years and a modest trend toward superiority in girls beginning around age 10. For nonverbal measures, on the other hand, Table 3.14 in Maccoby and Jacklin suggests the absence of a systematic sex difference across the age span extending from preschool through young adulthood. If divergent thinking has some predictive validity for creative accomplishment in the real world, the underrepresentation of women among the ranks of the most creative in the arts and sciences cannot, on the basis of the data surveyed above, be attributed to the lack of creativity potential. Instead, factors other than those reflected by divergent-thinking processes would have to be invoked to account for such creativity differences in an occupational or professional context. Discussion of such matters would extend well beyond the scope of the present chapter. The author has written about these matters elsewhere (Kogan, 1976b), with further commentary offered by Sheldon and Jenness (1976) and by Helson (1976).

Although the evidence points strongly to the absence of systematic mean differences between the sexes in divergent-thinking ability, a similar conclusion does not apply to the relation between divergent-thinking indicators, on the one hand, and various personal and environmental measures, on the other hand. In other words, divergent-thinking scores appear to correlate differently with other variables for males and females. For example, high scorers on divergent-thinking tests tend to be non-defensive in the sense of a willingness to admit to negative personal characteristics (see Yando et al., 1979), but the effect appears to be considerably stronger in males than in females (Kogan & Morgan, 1969; Wallach & Kogan, 1965). Possible antecedents of the foregoing correlational difference are discussed by Kogan (1974). That paper also describes other evidence suggesting that males are less susceptible than females to variation in assessment context. It appears that males' performance in the divergent-thinking domain may be more under the control of intrinsic task requirements, whereas females' performance may be more readily influenced by such external task factors as the evaluative or interpersonal context in which an assessment is carried out. Kogan (1974) has further raised the possibility that this more contextually bound performance of females might contribute to the reported sex differences in real-world creative accomplishments.

Consider next the matter of race and SES differences. Approximately a decade ago, Rohwer (1971) offered the provocative hypothesis that SES would make a difference for "formal conceptual activity"—that is, for tasks typically employed to assess intelligence (e.g., Raven Progressive Matrices)—but would have limited effect on tasks requiring "imaginative conceptual activity"—that is, tasks of the divergent-thinking type. The former type of task is presumed to involve the "mastery and application of a well-defined set of rules . . . that . . . permit little deviation from their culturally agreed upon form" (p. 202). The latter type of task, by contrast, obviously depends on self-generated images and ideas.

Rohwer (1971) did not test the foregoing hypothesis in the framework of the distinction between convergent and divergent thinking because that author's concerns were more directly focused on determinants of learning proficiency. Others, however, have pursued the issue in question more directly. Warden and Prawat (1975) tested both black and white, higher and lower status adolescents (eighth graders), on two divergent-thinking and three convergent-thinking tasks taken from Guilford (1967). In the case of the former, no significant race or SES effects were observed. For the convergent-thinking tasks, in contrast, significant race and SES effects were found that favored whites and higher status adolescents. Results virtually identical to these were obtained in a sample of sixth and seventh graders given the Wallach and Kogan (1965) tasks by Rosenbaum (1974). That investigator also varied the race of the experimenter and the task context (test vs. game), but neither of these interacted with the race or SES of the subject in affecting divergent-thinking performance.

One of the most extensive investigations of SES and race effects on children's cognitive performance is that recently reported by Yando et al. (1979) on samples of second and third graders. Included within that study were two divergent-thinking tasks of the Guilford-type scored for fluency, flexibility, and originality. Both a matched-groups and typical-groups design were employed. In the former, children in the four race-by-SES groups (black and white of lower and higher SES) were matched for MA and IQ; in the latter, the groups were equated only for chronological age. In the matched-groups design, no significant race or SES differences in divergent thinking were obtained. Of course, such a design necessarily implies that the children in the demographic subgroups are somewhat atypical, given the linkage in the population between race and SES on the one hand and MA and IQ on the other hand. This problem does not arise in the typical-groups portion of the research. Here, one finds that the disadvantaged (lower SES) children yielded higher fluency and flexibility scores despite the higher MA and IQ of the advantaged children. On the other hand, the latter children produced a larger percentage of original responses than did their disadvantaged peers. It is also important to note that the significant effects described were confined to SES; no significant race effects were found.

Yando et al. (1979) explain the patterning of the three divergent-thinking measures in respect to SES as indicative of lesser concern for quality in the disadvantaged children. It is argued that the more advantaged children engage in self-censoring of responses that do not meet an internalized standard of acceptability. Because the disadvantaged children do produce high-quality as well as low-quality responses, Yando and her associates maintain that the SES difference is of a stylistic rather than of an ability character. The disadvantaged children are presumed to be more adventuresome and spontaneous, the advantaged children more constricted and self-critical.

In conclusion, one can state rather unequivocally that low SES children are not necessarily handicapped relative to their more advantaged peers in responding to tasks of the divergent-thinking type. This appears to represent one of the few areas within the broad cognitive domain where such a state of affairs prevails. There is still some uncertainty, however, as to whether the facts are indicative of no-difference or of a disadvantage for the more advantaged child. In the latter, the effect is clearly mitigated by the evidence for quality differences favoring the more advantaged children. The Yando et al. (1979) argument for an SES-style difference is persuasive, but its post hoc nature clearly calls for a more direct empirical test of that interpretation.

Overview

The intrinsic nature of the creativity construct virtually insures against its disappearance as a topic of scientific inquiry. Creativity in one form or another stands as one of the major values in virtually all literate societies. There are societies, of course, in which the leadership will suppress any manifestation of creativity in the arts and humanities. Even in such societies, however, scientific creativity is likely to be highly valued, if only for its practical consequences in the competition between nations. It is quite likely that there would be a common core of agreement between psychologists and laypersons in respect to the essential meaning of creativity and that this attributed meaning would be different for the construct of intelligence. Indeed, in a study based on judgments of fictitious divergent-thinking protocols (Hammaker, Shafto, & Trabasso, 1975), it was clearly demonstrated that lay judges distinguished semantically between creativity and intelligence in much the same manner as psychologists concerned with that issue.

In the preceding pages, we have tried to highlight those aspects of the creativity construct that would be of special interest to developmental psychologists. Some of these aspects have been pursued for a considerable number of years, and it is unlikely that there is much more to be learned. Thus, the separation of divergent and convergent thinking at the correlational or factorial level has been well established in children (as well as adults). Also well confirmed is the indication that divergent-thinking performance in children can be enhanced by a variety of procedures—for example, direct instruction, incentives, role playing, and modeling. In the realm of educational implications, the general expectation that primary-level open education would facilitate creative performance in comparison to traditional education has not been conclusively demonstrated. There may, of course, be other benefits associated with an open-classroom climate. Concurrent validity for children's divergent-thinking performance has been demonstrated, but the evidence for long-term predictive validity is much more equivocal. Of course, this latter type of longitudinal research involves lengthy time commitments on the part of investigators; hence, it is doubtful whether this issue will be resolved soon. Further, given the strong involvement of motivational, specific-talent, and environmental factors in real-world creativity, it is dubious whether the predictive validity of divergent-thinking tests will ever be more than modest at best.

It is in the research linking creativity to symbolic functioning broadly conceived that the present topic comes closest to articulating with current research concerns in developmental psychology. We have noted the close connection between make-believe play in early childhood and performance on divergent-thinking tasks. Next, we will take up the topic of children's metaphor and figurative language and will demonstrate how these relate to divergent thinking as well. It appears that the study of the symbolic functions in childhood offers a broad-gauged theoretical approach into which divergent-thinking research might fit as a significant subtopic.

No doubt, some will perceive such a trend as a form of downgrading, insisting that the creativity topic must continue to occupy the center of the stage. There is the constant danger, given the dramatic connotations of the creativity construct, that the field can become encapsulated and pursued in cultlike fashion in highly specialized journals devoted to its promotion. Such a trend is regrettable because it is unlikely that much progress will take place if creativity research is cut off from a theoretical base in developmental as well as other branches of psychology.

As a final note, I should like to reiterate that the present treatment of the creativity issue cannot be considered exhaustive and has been slanted toward the concerns of developmental psychologists. Those wishing to supplement the present review with a broader and more exhaustive perspective on the topic would be well advised to consult the recent contribution by Barron and Harrington (1981).

METAPHOR AND FIGURATIVE LANGUAGE

General Background

Beginning in the mid-1970s, a lengthy series of articles, monographs, book chapters, and books have been published that deal with the general topic of metaphor and figurative language. Given the relative dearth of such work during the preceding decade and a half, the sudden emergence of interest in the area of metaphor generates considerable scientific curiosity. Various explanations have been advanced for this phenomenon, and they are treated in an historically oriented chapter by Honeck (1980). That author points to the "barren 60s" as the period when generative-transformational linguistics dominated the psychological scene. The emphasis on syntax and deep-structure semantics left little room for the agrammatical realm of metaphor. There were also positive forces at work, of course, that led to the resurgence in the mid-1970s. Honeck (1980) offers brief biographical accounts of the influences on contemporary researchers that produced the veritable explosion of current metaphor research.

It is clearly beyond the scope of the present chapter to review all of the recent theoretical and empirical developments in the field of metaphor. Only a portion of the work relates to developmental issues and, within this perspective, only a relatively small fraction is concerned with individual variation among children. A review of the developmental literature on metaphor is available in Gardner, Winner, Bechhofer, and Wolf (1978) and in Pollio, Barlow, Fine, and Pollio (1977). We will refrain from covering the same ground here. Most of the research oriented around individual differences has appeared since the publication of the foregoing contributions and, hence, will represent the major focus of the present portion of the chapter.

One might reasonably inquire about the rationale for a section on metaphor in a chapter devoted to stylistic variation. Viewed from an individual-differences perspective, the study of metaphor is quite young in comparison to research on divergent thinking and cognitive styles. Of course, the relative youth of a construct does not necessarily represent an accurate guide to its importance. In this author's view, the domain of metaphor fills what could be considered a conspicuous gap in the literature on stylistic variation in childhood and adolescence.

The issue of perceived similarity provides a bridge between metaphor on the one hand and divergent thinking and cognitive styles on the other hand. Within the cognitive-style domain, styles of conceptualization concern grouping of stimuli on the basis of complementarity or similarity. The kinds of similarity that have been typically examined include the perceptual analytic (sharing of parts), locational (objects found in the same place), and nominal categorical (each object as an exemplar of a category). The shift in children's conceptualizations from complementarity to similarity and, within the latter, from perceptual to nominal bases of grouping has been a major concern of cognitive developmentalists (e.g., Bruner, Olver, & Greenfield, 1966; Denney, 1975; Denney & Moulton, 1976; Inhelder & Piaget, 1964). Much of this work has taken place within the framework of the growth of logical thought. There is a type of similarity that is not encompassed by the forms considered above however. Metaphoric similarity is typically a cross-category phenomenon in which objects and events ordinarily unrelated are brought together by virtue of some shared feature. Children can be expected to differ in their sensitivity to such cross-categorical similarities, and it is the purpose of the present section to examine the source of such differences within a developmental framework.

The similarity issue links metaphor to creativity as well because, in process terms, a divergent-thinking task taps the breadth of a child's similarity class. As tolerance for less clearly appropriate instances increases, it is quite conceivable that the child forges an association to the task stimulus on largely metaphoric grounds. If so, one might expect such responses to earn high quality ratings and resultant scores to correlate with performance on a more ex-

plicitly metaphorical task. This hypothesis is, in fact, tested in research reported later in this discussion.

Measures of Metaphor

Virtually all of the research devoted to the role of metaphor in children's cognitive and language functioning began with an emphasis on developmental change or growth. Multiple measures have been generated for the foregoing purpose, and it should not come as too great a surprise to learn that developmental curves vary as a function of the particular measures employed. In due course, one would like to know whether these diverse measures are assessing the same constructs in children and whether these assessments tap the same construct in children of different ages. At this point, of course, one is working solidly within an individual-differences framework.

The remainder of this section describes the variety of metaphor tasks that have entered into individual-differences research with children and adolescents. For this purpose, I will draw heavily on the work of M. R. Pollio and her associates (Pollio & Pickens, 1980; Pollio & Pollio, 1974, 1979) and that of the author (Kogan, 1980a; Kogan, Connor, Gross, & Fava, 1980). In the case of the Pollio investigations, emphasis has been placed on two polarities—frozen versus novel metaphor and production versus comprehension of metaphor. Frozen figures are those that have been part of the lexicon for a long time, although the nonliteral roots of the figure can be discerned (e.g., the foot of a mountain). Novel figures are those that elicit surprise in the scorer; they are unique or occur quite rarely. In its purest form, production of metaphor carries the implication of spontaneous generation, that is, the eliciting conditions largely derive from the child rather than from materials provided by the experimenter in any specific sense. Thus, a request for a composition on a particular topic represents a prototypical metaphor-production task for older children and adolescents. A task of that sort clearly carries no explicit or implicit demand for the production of figurative language. In a comprehension task on the other hand, a metaphor is inherent within the materials provided, and the child's task is to recognize or explain it.

Examination of the number of frozen and novel figures indicates that the production of these two kinds of figures in a composition task is uncorrelated in elementary school samples (Pollio & Pollio, 1974). This finding evokes little surprise because frozen figures are probably no different from standard lexical entries and, hence, should have little bearing on the child's disposition to produce genuinely novel metaphors. The corpus of metaphors produced in the foregoing production task were used as stimuli in the construction of a metaphoric comprehension task for children in grades four through eight (Pollio & Pollio, 1979). An equal number of frozen and novel figures were selected—17 of each type—and four alternative response choices were offered for each item—the correct metaphoric interpretation, an incorrect metaphoric interpretation, and two incorrect literal interpretations. In striking contrast to the production data where, it will be recalled, frozen and novel figures were unrelated, the comprehension data indicated a consistently significant correlation between frozen and novel items (r's across grades ranging from .50 to .80). Again, it does seem reasonable that a child who understands the more difficult novel figures should be able to handle the easier frozen figures as well. Although no vocabulary data were collected, we would be not at all surprised to find such scores correlating substantially with metaphoric comprehension as assessed in the Pollios' task.

The lack of any frozen versus novel consistency in the case of production is attributed by Pollio and Pollio (1974, 1979) to the hesitancy on the part of elementary school children to risk novel metaphoric usage in school compositions for fear that it would result in a lowered grade. There is no evidence, however, to indicate that children deliberately suppress figurative in favor of literal usage in the writing of a composition. Further, if a risk-avoidant process is involved, one can understand how it might reduce the *incidence* of novel figures, but it is far from evident why it should affect the *correlation* between frozen and novel usage (unless, of course, the incidence is low enough to bring about a highly restricted range of scores).

The development of the Metaphoric Triads Task (MTT) has been fully explicated in a recent monograph by Kogan et al. (1980). A briefer description with emphasis on educational implications is also available (Kogan, 1980a). Whereas the research of Pollio and her associates is firmly anchored in a psycholinguistic context, the work of the present author grew out of his long-standing interest in the domain of cognitive styles. The dominant measurement tradition in the cognitive-style area has emphasized nonverbal procedures, and this tradition was followed in the construction of the MTT. Of course, metaphors are most typically expressed as figurative language; hence, one might reasonably ask why a nonverbal approach was chosen. Our rationale was that metaphor is primarily a cognitive process involving cross-categorical similarity. Although such similarities are frequently expressed in linguistic forms, we are in full agreement with Verbrugge's (1979) argument to the effect that the roots of a metaphor lie in the prelinguistic motor and iconic functioning of early childhood. Indeed, although the evidence is far from definitive, it has even been claimed that primitive metaphoric operations can be detected in infants under 1 year of age (Wagner, Winner, Cicchetti, & Gardner, 1981; Winner, Wagner, Cicone, & Gardner, 1979).

The MTT contains 29 triads of chromatic pictures (reproduced in achromatic form in the appendix to Kogan et al., 1980). Each triad offers three pairing possibilities, one of which is metaphoric in character. Item No. 15, for example, offers pictures of a toddler on the grass, a brightly colored watering can, and a rosebud. The toddler can play with the colorful watering can, or one can sprinkle water on the rosebud with the watering can—both thematic-functional pairings. Finally, linking the toddler and the rosebud because of their stage of development or growth potential is clearly metaphoric in character. The foregoing item is conceptual in nature because there is no physical resemblance between a toddler and a rosebud. Other items contained within the MTT are of a configurational character. One of these is comprised of a flying flock of geese, soldiers marching in formation, and a rifle. Instructions to the child emphasized that he or she form and explain as many pairs as possible. These instructions reflected our interest in the capacity rather than the preferential aspect of the child's performance.

Cross-sectional age differences on the MTT exhibited a progressive increase in comprehension across an age span extending from kindergarten to young adulthood. Considerable variation in item-difficulty levels was observed, with some metaphors recognized considerably more easily than others. Item difficulty, however, did not relate directly to the conceptual-configurational contrast, despite the expectation from Piaget's (1970) theory that perceptually based metaphors might prove easier at younger ages. Instead, the salience of the configural cues and the presence or absence of conflicting conceptual cues were prime determinants of metaphor difficulty. Mean-item differences across age also suggest a more rapid growth rate for the conceptual as opposed to the more difficult configurational items.

It should be noted that the measures described do not exhaust the instruments that have been used to study individual variation in children's production and comprehension of metaphor. Most of these remaining instruments, however, represent item collections for which no information exists regarding item analyses or overall reliability. Malgady (1977) constructed 11 similes from comparisons reported in Koch (1970)—for example, ''The thunder is like bowling.'' Pollio and Pickens (1980) adapted a preference task developed by Gardner, Kircher, Winner, and Perkins (1975) for use in an exploratory study of individual differences. A simile stem was offered along with four alternative endings (e.g., His voice was as quiet as _____: [a] the quietest sound we've heard: [b] a mouse sitting in a room: [c] dawn in a ghost town: [d] a family going on a trip.). The four alternatives for the item above were coded as literal, conventional, appropriate, and inappropriate respectively, although interest focused solely on the middle two, given their alleged similarity to the frozen versus novel distinction discussed earlier. In both the Malgady (1977) and Pollio and Pickens (1980) studies, significant performance increases with age were observed. In the latter investigation, the conventional exceeded the appropriate (novel) choice at each grade level (3 to 11).

The Kogan et al. (1980) study reported the development of a metaphoric-triads task in a verbal format. Some of the items were directly adapted from the pictorial MTT, and new items were derived from diverse published and unpublished sources. These, along with original MTT items, were administered to children in the second and fifth grades. Consistent with the age differences observed on the standard MTT, the older children obtained higher metaphoric-comprehension scores on the verbal triads as well (Chadrow, Parlow, & Kogan, 1981).

Convergent Validation of Metaphor Measures

Possibly the most ambitious effort to demonstrate the convergent validity of metaphor measures in children and adolescents can be credited to Pollio and Pickens (1980). Four tasks were administered to children and adolescents in grades, 3, 5, 6, 7, 9, and 11. Three of the four tasks were described earlier—a composition task (production), the Pollio and Pollio (1979) multiple-choice instrument (comprehension), and the Gardner et al. (1975) similes task (preference). The fourth task involved oral explication of the child's choices in the Pollio and Pollio (1979) comprehension measure. Because each of the four tasks contained a novel and frozen component, correlational analyses at each age level were based on eight measures. Given the instability of correlations based on an N of 30, Pollio and Pickens (1980) combined the children in grades 3, 5, and 6 and the

adolescents in grades 7, 9, and 11 and carried out a separate factor analysis for each.

It is of interest to compare the within-task (frozen vs. novel) consistency across the two age groups. For comprehension and explication, frozen and novel figures exhibited individual covariation at both age levels. Conceivably, these particular operations are linked to general verbal skills. Regrettably, Pollio and Pickens (1980) did not include a verbal IQ or MA index among their variables. In striking contrast to the comprehension and explication data, the incidence of frozen and novel figures was inversely related in the production data for both age groups. The dynamic here is less clear. Perhaps, those children and adolescents who generated novel figures found frozen figures rather trite. A developmental shift is most apparent in the preference area. The orthogonality of preference for novel and conventional figures in childhood turned into a strong inverse relationship in adolescence. Conceivably, at the latter age level, the more intellectually able subjects were attuned to the higher imaginativeness of the novel relative to the conventional similes.

Consider next the nature of the intertask associations. Here, we can examine the overall factor structures for the child and the adolescent groups. In the case of the latter, production, comprehension, preference, and explication were found to be completely independent of one another. The factor-analytic results for the children on the other hand pointed to a general factor shared by the comprehension, explication, and novel-preference measures. Production and conventional preferences loaded on separate and weaker factors. Pollio and Pickens (1980) argue that the foregoing results are strongly indicative of an age-linked increase in differentiation (i.e., multidimensionality) in the metaphor domain. The general factor yielded by the children's data broke down into specific task factors in the adolescent data. Full acceptance of a differentiation interpretation would appear to be premature, however, in the light of ceiling effects on two of the tasks employed. This would necessarily reduce the intertask correlations on which the factor analyses were based, hence facilitating the emergence of task-specific factors in the adolescent sample. For the general factor obtained in the analysis of the children's data, one is again forced to speculate (in the absence of IQ or MA information) whether verbal competence was actually being measured. Because the factor analysis combined data from children across three grades—three, five, and six—such an alternative interpretation has considerable credibility.

Consider next the convergent validity of the pictorial MTT and its verbal analogue (Connor &

Kogan, 1980; Kogan et al., 1980). In a sample of high school seniors, correlation coefficients between comprehension of pictorial and verbal items were of moderate magnitude and highly significant. Comparable levels of convergence were observed in samples of second-grade and fifth-grade children in a recent study by Chadrow et al. (1981). It should be noted that these significant correlations were *not* based on identical metaphoric content across the pictorial and verbal modalities.

Contrary to a hypothesis advanced in Kogan et al. (1980) based on findings in other cognitive domains (e.g., Reznick, 1977), there does not appear to be any special advantage to pictorial over verbal representations of metaphoric content for younger as opposed to older children (second graders vs. fifth graders). Indeed, there is some indication in the outcomes of the Chadrow et al. (1981) study that both younger and older children find the verbal form of configurational items somewhat easier. Because a number of these items have multiple encodings in their original pictorial form, the lesser difficulty of the verbal equivalent can be attributed to the provision of an appropriate encoding. This is a necessary condition, if not a sufficient one, for comprehension of the metaphoric similarity. Whether such a verbal advantage would hold for children younger than 7 years of age is moot in the absence of relevant data. In respect to the issue of pictorial-verbal consistency, the evidence strongly supports its developmental generality across the broad age span extending from about 7 to 18 years of age. In line with dual-coding views (Paivio, 1979), subjects might verbally encode pictorial stimuli when making metaphoric connections, or they might bring imagery to bear upon the verbal stimuli. At the present time, there is more evidence for the role of verbal encoding (Kogan et al., 1980). The foregoing evidence has not directly addressed developmental issues in metaphor however. Hence, the application of the dual-coding theory to such issues represents a challenging research topic for the future.

In sum, the evidence for the convergent validation of metaphor measures is mixed. When such measures cut across media (pictures vs. words), considerable convergence is found for tasks with the same structural format (triads). Such cross-media generality proved to be developmentally invariant from age 7 on. Where tasks reflect different kinds of metaphoric operations (preference, comprehension, explication), generality in childhood is gradually transformed into specificity in adolescence. Metaphoric production (as in the writing of compositions) seems to stand apart from other kinds of metaphoric assessments at all ages studied. A note of caution must be sounded in connection with the convergent-validation issue in children because the research conducted thus far has been quite limited in scope. There is a range of functions, conceivably closely linked to metaphor, that have not yet been combined with more typical metaphor instruments in correlational studies based on children. The crossmodal sensory linkages (e.g., color and music) of synesthesia (e.g., Gardner, 1974; Marks, 1978) and the physiognomic sensitivities (e.g., emotions reflected in expressive line patterns) described by Werner and Kaplan (1963) and Wallach and Kogan (1965) are both strong candidates for membership in a cluster of metaphoric operations. Kogan et al. (1980) report highly significant correlations between MTT performance and physiognomic sensitivity in college students. To date, however, the interrelations among synesthetic, physiognomic, and other types of metaphor have not been systematically examined in samples of children.

Correlates of Metaphoric Processes

As a cognitive process tapping sensitivity to cross-categorical similarity, metaphoric operations are unlikely to be totally independent of a variety of other cognitive functions. In regard to comprehension and preference, a metaphoric response often connotes a performance of higher quality than is reflected by alternative options. Accordingly, one might expect metaphoric sensitivity to correlate with indices of intellective ability or cognitive developmental stage. Another important feature of metaphor (excluding the frozen variety discussed earlier) is the surprise occasioned by the juxtaposition of elements that had not previously been experienced in a particular combination. As we have seen, children vary in their preference for, and comprehension of, such metaphoric figures. It would be of interest to observe whether such variation has anything in common with the domain of divergent thinking. The latter, it will be recalled, frequently entails a search for alternative categories of response appropriate to a particular stimulus. Indeed, a case could be made for the view that high-quality divergent-thinking responses earn that status by virtue of their metaphoric originality.

Intellective Abilities

In connection with their research on the MTT, the author and his associates (Kogan, 1980a; Kogan et al., 1980) examined its relation to scores on various standardized tests of aptitude and achievement that were available in the school records of the children participating in the research. Although virtually all of the many ensuing correlations were positive, a substantial number were not significant. A comparable pattern was found by Malgady (1977). It is, thus, apparent that metaphoric comprehension does not share with divergent thinking the property of independence from assessments of intelligence or convergent thinking. Because metaphoric comprehension is assessed in a convergent-thinking format in which the metaphoric connection is keyed correct, the link to intelligence is not unreasonable. One might further note—consistent with Ortony, Reynolds, and Arter (1978)—that successful performance on a metaphor task generally depends on some real-world knowledge on the part of the child, and such knowledge is often a prerequisite to success on intelligence tests (or portions thereof) as well.

High-scoring MTT children were also found to do significantly better than their low-scoring counterparts on the difficult foil analogies contained within the Achenbach (1969) instrument. It must be acknowledged that the conceptual items of the MTT represent implicit analogies—the baby-rosebud comparison could be converted into the explicit analogy of baby is to adult as rosebud is to a fully blossoming rose. Although we do not know whether children engage in this analogical reasoning process on the MTT, it is of interest that 8 of the 10 MTT items significantly associated with analogies performance were conceptual and, hence, implicitly analogical. Configurational items, by contrast, require that children recognize a perceptual resemblance to gain credit. There is no analogical basis for recognition of a configural similarity between a winding river and coiled snake for example.

The full complexity of the metaphor-analogy relationship has been highlighted by the work of Sternberg and his associates (Sternberg, Tourangeau, & Nigro, 1979; Tourangeau & Sternberg, 1981). Although that work is not based on child samples, its relevance for an individual-differences perspective on metaphor is considerable; hence, some discussion of the approach is warranted here. In the case of their representational model, the critical components are the within-domain and between-domain distances of the topic and vehicle terms in the metaphor. Eight domains were selected for study (birds, land mammals, sea creatures, ships, aircraft, land vehicles, U.S. historical figures, and modern world leaders). Exemplars from each of these domains can be located on prestige and power-aggression dimensions, and these provide the within-domain assessments. Thus, the within-domain similarity of an eagle to a tiger is greater than that of an eagle to a squirrel on the prestige and power-aggression dimensions. The former type of metaphoric comparison was judged of higher quality than

the latter. It is also possible, of course, to scale the eight domains themselves for similarity, and these between-domain distances yielded a marginal positive association with quality (greater between-domain distances associated with higher quality).

Individual differences impinge on the model, in the sense of possible relations between the distance parameters and relevant external variables. In this regard, Tourangeau and Sternberg (1981) included an analogies test and a test of poetry appreciation in their study, in the expectation that these would reduce the distance between remote domains. This expectation was not confirmed nor did the ability dimensions relate to perceived quality or comprehensibility of metaphor. These outcomes for college students are not consistent with those obtained for children by Kogan et al. (1980).

The negative outcome reported above by Tourangeau and Sternberg (1981) contrasts with the Sternberg et al. (1979) statement that an information processing model developed for analogical reasoning is equally applicable to the domain of metaphor. The latter can be cast in analogical form. Hence, the component processes presumed to comprise analogical reasoning should prove equally relevant for metaphors. Of course, metaphors are often implicit analogies, in the sense that terms are missing. Such deletions can be accommodated within an information processing framework because one would anticipate increased response times by virtue of the greater cognitive work required in interpretation. The critical question, of course, is whether the similarity in information processing between nonmetaphoric and metaphoric analogies necessarily implies that the latter can be reduced to, or are merely a special case of, the former.

In a relevant theoretical paper, Ortony (1979a) has argued that the explanation of metaphor in analogical terms is insufficient. According to that author, it is the phenomenon of nonliteral similarity y that is in need of explanation and that phenomenon can be as much a characteristic of analogies as of metaphors. From an individual-differences standpoint, there is good reason to believe that metaphoric comprehension and analogical reasoning are correlated variables, but there is clearly no basis for asserting that the ability to reason by analogy is a precursor of metaphoric understanding.

Divergent Thinking

One of the 10-year-old samples employed in the Kogan et al. (1980) research responded to two of the Wallach and Kogan (1965) tasks—alternate uses and pattern meanings. Both were scored for fluency and idea quality, and these scores were examined in relation to MTT performance. For fluency, 3 of 12 possible correlations were significant. For quality, the proportion rose to 10 of 12. These outcomes are clearly consistent with the view that it is the quality rather than fluency of ideas generated in tasks of divergent thinking that bears some relation to metaphoric processing. Despite the fact that divergent thinking is a production task, its quality component shared considerable variance with the MTT—a task of comprehension. Comparable findings were reported by Malgady (1977), who observed significant associations in a sample of 5- to 12-year-olds between interpretation of similes and performance on the Torrance (1966) divergent-thinking tests.

The Kogan et al. (1980) data open up the possibility that the failure to find any associations between production and comprehension in the metaphoric domain (recall the research of the Pollios) may simply reflect the choice of composition writing as a production task. Such tasks make no explicit mention to subjects of generating metaphors, with the result that their incidence is quite low. A divergent-thinking task, by contrast, offers an opportunity for much metaphorlike output as the child searches for remote matches between the stimulus (word or picture) provided and other objects and events in her real or imaginative worlds. It would be premature, then, to conclude that production and comprehension of metaphor are unrelated in school-age children until further research with other task formats is undertaken.

Modification of Metaphoric Processing

Although metaphoric processing represents a relatively new dimension of individual differences in childhood and adolescence, it has already become a target for training efforts. There are diverse theoretical and practical reasons for such a step apart from the customary American penchant in the cognitive developmental field of attempting to demonstrate that any cognitive structure or process worthy of a label can be advanced through one or another experimental intervention. A fundamental issue concerns the extent to which metaphoric processing in childhood represents a stylistic preference or an ability-like dimension. If metaphoric comprehension has much in common with analogical reasoning, it should prove more difficult to modify than would be the case if metaphor is simply another style of conceptualization—a domain in which children have been shown to change with alacrity (e.g., Denney, 1972). Of course, one must bear in mind that metaphor has been examined in its preferential, comprehension, and production aspects, and these might

well show differential susceptibility to change. Further, these different aspects of metaphor have been examined with a variety of tasks, and, hence, it would be of interest to know to what extent task factors are interfering with the display of metaphoric competence.

In a more global and practical vein, various writers have discussed the importance of metaphor in the sciences, education, and social policy (see Ortony, 1979b), whereas still other scholars have emphasized metaphor's relevance to the visual arts (Gombrich, 1963) and literature (Wheelwright, 1962). Indeed, in the light of the multidisciplinary ramifications of the metaphor construct, one can only express surprise at its relative neglect until quite recently as a topic for intensive empirical inquiry. There is no pretense, of course, that the facilitation of metaphoric skills in children and adolescents will necessarily prepare them for the later utilization of metaphor in real-world professional contexts. Nevertheless, it is this author's belief that sufficient justification exists to proceed.

Two types of training studies have been reported in the published literature on metaphor. The first type comprises experimentation in the naturalistic context and has assumed the form of comparing children in control and experimental classrooms. Children in the latter have been exposed to programmed materials intended to enhance figurative-language production, and the effect of such exposure is then examined through appropriate pretest versus posttest comparisons.

The overall contribution of this work has proved disappointing owing to defects in research design (admitted by Pollio and his associates, 1977), but it would be unfortunate if the outcomes were to discourage further experimentation in the classroom context. Kogan (1980a) has, in fact, offered suggestions for classroom experiments in metaphor within an aptitude-treatment interaction (ATI) framework (Cronbach & Snow, 1977).

The second type of research is more in the tradition of the laboratory, in the sense of examining pretest versus posttest differences in individual experimental and control children as a function of particular interventions (Kogan et al., 1980). The first two studies were based on 7- and 9-year-olds randomly divided into experimental and control groups. Training consisted of a review of pretest items with each child. The control children played a 20-questions game with the experimenter. Children in both age groups who received feedback from the experimenter on pretest items exhibited a posttest increment significantly greater than that observed in control children.

Several factors could be operating to produce the improvements in MTT performance described. Conceivably, some children consider the categorical and functional pairings to be more desirable and, hence, fail to report the metaphoric pairing when all three choices are not required. Further, the metaphoric connections may increase in desirability by virtue of their endorsement by the examiner in the feedback-training period. One must also allow for the possibility that the metaphoric pairs may be more difficult to detect. The examiner's demonstration of metaphoric possibilities makes the metaphoric linkage more accessible.

In a third experiment, based on 10-year-olds, we focused attention on the picture-encoding process in the MTT. If the child does not encode the critical pictures appropriately, there is little likelihood that he or she will succeed in making the necessary metaphoric connections. To insure appropriate encoding, one group of children was provided with verbal labels for all of the pictures within the triads. One of the control groups provided their own labels for the pictures; the other group was a standard control. The outcome was quite clearcut. Provision of appropriate verbal labels raised MTT performance significantly beyond that obtained in the two control conditions. It is thus evident that competence on the MTT involves more than skill at making metaphoric connections. Attention to, and selection of, relevant stimulus dimensions in the pictures is a critical prerequisite.

The three training studies taken as a whole have pointed to diverse task factors that interfere with metaphoric comprehension in the pictorial MTT. It is evident that children's metaphoric competence is somewhat underestimated by the standard MTT because brief interventions can significantly raise performance. It is important to keep in mind, however, that the homogeneity-of-regression assumption of the analysis of covariance was met in all three training studies, implying that the rank ordering of children did not change much from pretest to posttest. Although a child's metaphoric comprehension on the MTT can be significantly raised, his or her standing relative to other children in the sample appears to be maintained. Metaphoric comprehension, in other words, continues to function as a stable individual-differences variable.

Overview

The period extending from the mid-1970s to the present day has been an active and productive one for metaphor theory and research. A simple count yields three major psychologically oriented books

(Honeck & Hoffman, 1980; Ortony, 1979b; Pollio et al., 1977), three journal or chapter reviews (Billow, 1977; Gardner et al., 1978; Ortony et al., 1978), a research monograph (Kogan et al., 1980), and a steady stream of theoretical and empirical contributions published in journals or as book chapters. As noted earlier, only portions of these published works concern developmental and individual-differences issues.

Although much progress has been made, one cannot read the present discussion on metaphor with the sense that the major issues in the field have been resolved. From an individual-differences perspective, convergent and discriminant validation are of critical importance—in both of these respects, much remains to be learned. Those with a psycholinguistic orientation have paid inadequate attention to the role of verbal-intellective processes. Metaphor measures deriving from a cognitive-style perspective have shown modest convergent and discriminant validity, but little effort has thus far been devoted to exploring linkages between such measures (e.g., the MTT) and psycholinguistic indices of figurative language use and comprehension.

This discussion of metaphor has made little reference to the evidence for metaphoric comprehension and production in preschool children (e.g., Gentner, 1977; Winner, McCarthy, & Gardner, 1980) because such research has essentially ignored the issue of individual variation in early childhood. Yet, much early metaphor occurs in the context of symbolic make-believe play, and as we noted (see *Creativity*), children vary in their inclination toward such play. Further, such variation was shown to relate significantly to the child's divergent-thinking capacity. Given the previously reported evidence linking divergent thinking and metaphoric comprehension in older children, it might prove fruitful to examine such relationships in preschoolers in a symbolic-play context. This would go a long way toward strengthening the link between an older tradition of creativity research and the more recent work on the developmental psychology of metaphor.

FIELD DEPENDENCE-INDEPENDENCE (FDI)

General Background

No chapter on stylistic variation in children would be complete without a discussion of FDI. Indeed, a major portion of the Kagan and Kogan (1970) chapter was devoted to that construct. When the latter was written, eight years had passed since the publication of *Psychological Differentiation* (Witkin et al., 1962) and no critical summary of research published subsequently was available in the literature. Given the enormous popularity of the FDI construct, a substantial body of work had appeared during the foregoing eight-year period, much of it representing a departure from the theory outlined in Witkin et al. (1962). Hence, the FDI domain was ripe for the evaluative review that appeared in the 3rd edition of *Carmichael's Manual of Child Psychology* (1970).

A very different set of conditions prevails currently. Beginning in the mid-1970s and continuing into the present, Witkin and his associates have published a series of reviews encompassing virtually every aspect of FDI theory and research. There are FDI reviews presently available in the domains of learning and memory (Goodenough, 1976), cross-cultural differences (Witkin & Berry, 1975), interpersonal behavior (Witkin & Goodenough, 1977), educational applications (Witkin, Moore, Goodenough, & Cox, 1977), and developmental origins (Witkin & Goodenough, 1981). In addition, several recent publications report on the current theoretical status of the FDI construct and the theory of psychological differentiation considered as a whole (Witkin, 1978; Witkin & Goodenough, 1981; Witkin, Goodenough, & Oltman, 1979). Readers seeking detailed research summaries of the FDI literature and interpretations of that literature by the founders of the theory would be well advised to consult the references cited here.

The construct of FDI evolved from laboratory research on basic perceptual processes (Witkin et al., 1954). In field-dependent (FD) perception, there is considerable difficulty in perceiving parts of a field as separable from the whole; in other words, the FD person is relatively handicapped in disembedding parts from their context. In contrast, field-independent (FI) perception is characterized by analysis of the field into discrete parts, that is, the FI person demonstrates disembedding skill. Although the FDI dimension is conceived to be bipolar, the distribution of persons along the FDI continuum does not exhibit bimodality but rather is consistent with a normal curve.

The step from strictly perceptual processes to the more comprehensive theory of psychological differentiation (Witkin et al., 1962) led to an emphasis upon the component of "self-nonself segregation," that is, the degree to which the person relies primarily on internal or external referents in processing information from the self and the surrounding field. As the theory evolved (e.g., Witkin, 1978), the referents were given an interpersonal focus—FI individuals described as autonomous in their relations with others in contrast to FD persons who are described as prone to rely on others (particularly in situations where information is ambiguous). In a further extension, the FI and FD poles of the dimension are viewed as reflecting an impersonal and interpersonal orientation respectively. Thus, FI individuals, by virtue of their impersonal orientation and reliance on internal referents, do well at tasks requiring restructuring (e.g., spatial perspective taking, sequential hypothesis testing in concept-attainment problems). FD individuals, by contrast, perform poorly on restructuring tasks.

The focus on the interpersonal domain marked a major change from the formulation favored in the Witkin et al. (1962) volume. That earlier version of the theory was strongly value laden—FI associated with a cluster of psychological virtues, FD distinguished by a syndrome of deficits. In the current formulation, the bipolarity of the dimension is conceived to be value free, with FI, at one extreme, tied to restructuring skills, and FD, at the opposite extreme, indicative of interpersonal competencies. Later, in this discussion, the adequacy of the current formulation will be examined in the context of relevant recent research.

The problem of coping with the sheer quantity of FDI research is rendered somewhat less formidable by the fact that much of that research is based on adult samples (exclusive of parent/child interaction). It is important to remember that FDI is essentially rooted in a theory of cognition and personality and has been examined within an individual-differences perspective across the entire lifespan (Kogan, 1973, 1982). Although the theory in its most current form subsumes the FDI construct within a more abstract and higher level construct of psychological differentiation, the fact remains that the theory did not originally derive from a concern about developmental issues. Instead, as is the case with numerous personality constructs, FDI was first established as a viable construct in adults with the applicability of the construct to children following later.

One may well inquire as to why developmentalists should be at all concerned with FDI. The answer must lie in the broad ramifications that one's FDI status has for diverse areas of functioning. FDI impinges on many of the cognitive processes that have been examined in children and adolescence—learning, memory, problem solving, spatial cognition, social versus task orientations and competencies. Indeed, there are probably few psychological domains where one would be at a loss to offer a prediction derived from FDI theory. Because most of the domains cited have been foci of developmental investigation, one cannot ignore the possibility that at a particular age or stage, FDI may represent a moderator of performance. If, indeed, FDI serves this kind of moderator function, one should examine it rather closely in its own right. What are its measurement properties, its causal origins, and its plasticity?

Conceptual and Methodological Issues and Controversies

Although a diversity of tasks have been advanced as legitimate assessors of FDI, two particular procedures—the Embedded Figures Test (EFT) and the Rod-and-Frame Test (RFT)—have emerged as the overwhelmingly dominant choices of investigators engaged in FDI research. Many studies rely on only one of the foregoing measures, although the cumulation of genuine FDI variance by means of an EFT/RFT composite has been considered a methodologically advisable course. Both tasks have been presumed to tap the ability to overcome an embedding context—the complex figure and the frame in the EFT and RFT respectively—and, hence, the magnitude of the relation between the tasks has been used as the primary indicator of the coherence of the FDI construct.

One Construct or Two

In their most recent publication, Witkin and Goodenough (1981) outline the possibility that EFT and RFT may, in fact, be tapping distinctive, although *related,* psychological processes. In this reconceptualization, EFT is treated as an index of restructuring ability in the spatial/configurational domain, whereas RFT is presumed relevant to a dimension of visual versus vestibular sensitivity in perception of the upright.

Given a battery of spatial tasks, do EFT and RFT load on distinct factors? Vernon (1972) was one of the first investigators to raise the issue of the relative distinctiveness of EFT and RFT in a study of Canadian eighth-grade students. Factor analysis of a battery of spatial tests pointed to a space factor with considerably higher loadings for EFT than for RFT. Further, EFT and RFT did not correlate in the same fashion with an array of other cognitive and social-personality variables. The Vernon research also demonstrated that EFT could not be teased apart from either *g* (general intelligence) or spatial ability. Those familiar with the FDI literature will recognize the foregoing lack of discriminant validity as a persistent controversial issue in the area, one that has generated evidence on both sides. In striking contrast to Vernon (1972), Satterly (1976), working with a sample of British 10- to 11-year-old boys, obtained distinct FDI and spatial-ability factors. Regrettably, however, the RFT was not included in the

Satterly battery of tests and, hence, the possibility of an EFT/RFT separation could not be examined.

A careful and thorough examination of the relative distinctiveness of EFT and RFT has been recently offered by Linn and Kyllonen (1981) in a study based on a sample of high school seniors given a battery of 34 tests (including 12 measures presumed relevant to FDI). Three independent analyses of the data clearly indicated that an EFT-like test and the RFT loaded on different factors and were members of different clusters. Hence, the Linn and Kyllonen (1981) results strongly support both Vernon's (1972) earlier suggestion and Witkin and Goodenough's (1981) recent speculation regarding the distinctiveness of the restructuring and perception-of-the-upright components of FDI. There is, however, the unresolved issue of whether RFT belongs on a visuokinesthetic factor (as suggested by both Vernon, 1972, and Witkin & Goodenough, 1981) or can be more appropriately assigned to a familiar field factor (as proposed by Linn & Kyllonen, 1981). The latter factor involves the matching of visual material to a familiar template (such as the true vertical). Finally, there is the puzzling contradiction in connection with the water-level bottles' task, wherein prior research assimilated judgments of horizontality into a restructuring cluster (e.g., Liben, 1978; Signorella & Jamison, 1978) in contrast with Linn and Kyllonen's (1981) findings linking the water-level task to the RFT and the familiar-field factor.

Some discussion of the developmental implications of the foregoing issues is clearly called for. As indicated earlier, Kogan (1976a) based his case for the coherence of FDI in preschool children largely on the EFT/RFT correlation. This would now appear to be the wrong question to be asking. If, in fact, there are two distinct components to FDI (as has been suggested by research on adolescent samples), the question then becomes one of the degree of structural continuity across the years of later and earlier childhood. Conceivably, the splitting of FDI into two components is a postchildhood phenomenon. Only further research directed to this issue can provide the necessary clarification.

The Error Pattern on the RFT

At the outset, it is important to note that several versions of the RFT have become available and that there is no guarantee that a child's status on FDI would remain perfectly constant across different versions. The original RFT (Witkin et al., 1954) placed a luminous rod and frame in a completely dark room. The portable RFT (Oltman, 1968) has the subject peering into a barrel. Where younger children are concerned, the task is sometimes made more interesting by superimposing a human figure over the rod (S. Coates cited in Kogan, 1976a; H. Gerard cited in Kagan & Zahn, 1975). Finally, the manipulation of the rod can be strictly under the experimenter's control (e.g., Kojima, 1978) or under the subject's control (Morell, 1976). The impact of these various RFT contrasts on performance in different age groups is virtually unknown.

Consider next the matter of scoring. Only deviations from the true vertical in the direction of the tilted frame are consistent with FDI theoretical expectations. The evidence clearly indicates that the majority of errors are in the direction of the tilted frame for subjects ranging in age from 5 to 18 (Kagan & Zahn, 1975; Keogh & Ryan, 1971; Kojima, 1978; Morell, 1976). Such findings clearly support FDI theory but, nevertheless, raise the question of the basis for errors in a direction opposite to that of the tilted frame (ranging from 12% to 37% in the various studies cited).

The major question at issue, of course, is the extent to which these opposite-to-frame deviations represent systematic as opposed to random variance. The weight of the evidence favors the former. Morell (1976) approached the problem by developing two separate deviation scores—an absolute score that ignores direction and an algebraic score that takes direction into account. Significant moderate correlations with EFT performance were obtained for absolute, but not algebraic, RFT scores. Because the latter are presumed to be a more adequate reflection of genuine FDI variance than the former, Morell (1976) contends that the RFT, as customarily assessed, is more a measure of a general ability or inability to perceive the true upright than an index of the influence of an embedding field.

An alternative approach to the problem is offered by Kojima (1978). If errors in the direction of the frame reflect FDI variance, those children who exhibit such deviations in their judgments of the true vertical should have lower EFT scores than do children whose judgments deviate from the vertical in a direction opposite to that of the frame. Results consistent with the foregoing prediction were particularly striking for boys—the frame-dependent group averaging half as many EFT items correct as the counter-frame-error group. In the case of the girls on the other hand, the two error groups had essentially similar EFT scores that were considerably below that of the frame-independent group. Such sex differences seem to be quite common in the FDI area in particular as well as in the cognitive-style domain more generally (Kogan, 1976b; Maccoby & Jacklin, 1974).

The outcomes reported above strongly suggest that counterframe errors in young children contribute genuine FDI variance. Further support for such an inference comes from data collected by Kagan and Zahn (1975) indicating that both kinds of errors contributed to the predictive capacity of the RFT with respect to academic achievement (reading and mathematics). On this basis, those authors proposed that the RFT "may measure something independent of errors toward the frame, perhaps ability to perceive the true upright, carefulness, or motivation to be exactly correct" (p. 647).

Implications

On the basis of the foregoing review of a selected portion of the FDI literature, one would have to conclude that the present construct is at a conceptual crisis point. For many years, EFT and RFT have been employed as virtually interchangeable indices on the assumption that both reflect the ability to separate elements from embedding contexts. We now observe that such a basis for the oft-observed significant correlations between EFT and RFT is difficult to defend in light of factor-analytic outcomes and evidence regarding RFT error patterns. Indeed, even Witkin and Goodenough (1981) now acknowledge the distinctiveness of RFT (relative to EFT) by virtue of its vestibular component. It is clearly unwarranted to maintain that the presence of significant correlations between EFT and RFT are a mere reflection of motivation to be correct, because that would imply a lack of differentiation among cognitive tasks that is belied by accumulated empirical evidence. Instead, it appears that either or both EFT and RFT are factorially multidimensional but share some variance in common. It is the precise nature of this shared variance that requires explanation. We have no choice, then, but to end the present discussion on a tentative note. At the same time, a sense of despair is clearly not warranted. There is now an enormous body of evidence relating both the EFT and RFT to a host of other variables. Sorting out the variance distinctive for each and shared by both has already begun. Further work along such lines is deserving of strong encouragement.

FDI in Preschool Children

In the chapter devoted to FDI in Kogan (1976a), the Preschool Embedded Figures Test (PEFT) (Coates, 1972) was carefully evaluated for its appropriateness as a measure of FDI in early childhood (ages 3 to 5). This test seemed to meet the necessary reliability and validity criteria. One of the findings that the test generated evoked some surprise however. Contrary to results obtained with older children, girls performed at a significantly higher level than boys did. Coates (1974a, 1974b) attempted to explain this sex difference in terms of the Maccoby (1966) model wherein optimal intellectual functioning is associated with the midpoint of a passivity-activity continuum. In the preschool years, girls are presumed closer to the hypothetical midpoint than boys are. Beyond the preschool years, however, girls' passivity is presumed to increase and boys' activity to decrease, hence producing the shifts away from female toward male superiority in disembedding skill. Kogan (1976a) offered as an alternative, more parsimonious hypothesis the possibility that girls' biologically based developmental maturity may be more advanced than that of boys during the preschool years. Other evidence scattered through the Kogan (1976a) volume supported the latter hypothesis.

Overlooked in the above line of reasoning is the radical change in the character of the PEFT items (relative to the standard EFT) introduced to increase the interest value of the task for young children. Whereas the standard EFT uses geometric shapes, the PEFT employs meaningful pictures of persons and objects in which a simple geometric form is embedded. Kojima (1978) has raised the possibility that the social content of Coates's (1972) PEFT is responsible for the early sex difference favoring girls. Waber (1979) presses the argument somewhat further, maintaining that child and adult versions of the EFT may, in fact, be tapping different psychological processes by virtue of the more complex task demands inherent in the adult EFT.

In response to such arguments, Kojima (1978) has developed a simplified, strictly geometric EFT appropriate for 5- to 6-year-olds in Japan. This instrument demonstrated satisfactory validity, at least in respect to expected correlations with WPPSI scales and the RFT. Further, the sex difference was found significantly to favor the boys. Kojima (1978) also cites a personal communicaton from investigators who administered the Coates (1972) PEFT to Japanese children and, consistent with results for American children, found that girls outperformed boys. A logical next step, of course, would be to administer the Kojima EFT to American children. Conceivably, investigators in the present area have been unduly pessimistic about American preschoolers' ability to disembed simple forms in a strictly geometric mode. On the other hand, it must be noted that Japanese children appeared to be two years ahead of their American and Israeli peers in patterns of performance in the R-I domain (Salkind, Kojima, & Zelniker, 1978).

A further consideration in respect to Kojima's (1978) EFT is his use of 5- and 6-year-olds. We have no evidence of that test's appropriateness for children as young as 3, an age at which the Coates (1972) PEFT can be comfortably administered. This implies that Kojima's (1978) research is not at all informative regarding the issue of sex differences before the age of 5. Further, it must be noted that 5-year-old girls outperformed their male-age peers on the RFT (Vaught, Pittman, & Roodin, 1975) and on another often-used FDI indicator, the draw-a-person task scored for articulation of body concept (Ford, Stern, & Dillon, 1974). Results such as these detract from Kojima's (1978) argument that preschool FDI sex differences favoring females necessarily reflect the social content of the PEFT. At the current stage of knowledge, the evidence favors the view advanced by Kogan (1976a) of the greater cognitive maturity of girls than boys during the preschool years. The indication that such sex differences generalize across several cognitive domains suggests that maturational factors are predominant, although the contribution of psychosocial determinants cannot be ruled out. The question of the basis for these early sex differences is but one aspect of the broader issue of the origins and antecedents of FDI, a matter that will now concern us.

Socialization Influences

Any inquiry into the origins of FDI leads inevitably to the purported crucial role of child-rearing practices in the development of an FD or FI cognitive style. This theme was stressed in the Witkin et al. (1962) volume and was further emphasized in subsequent articles by Dyk and Witkin (1965) and Dyk (1969). The impact of child-rearing practices on FDI has been most succinctly summarized by Witkin and Goodenough (1981):

Child-rearing practices that encourage separate autonomous functioning foster the development of differentiation, in general and, more particularly, of a field-independent cognitive style. In contrast, child-rearing practices that encourage continued reliance on parental authority are likely to make for less differentiation and a more field-dependent cognitive style. (pp. 81–82)

The early work by Witkin and his associates relied heavily on interviews with mothers and children's TAT productions scored for perception of parental figures. Subsequent research in a variety of cultures (reviewed by Witkin & Berry, 1975) reinforced the earlier exploratory studies in showing that cultures with strict parental socialization practices fostered FD, whereas those with socialization practices of a looser nature appeared to produce more FI individuals.

Despite the extensiveness and apparent consistency of these socialization effects, the relevant research has not been free of methodological artifacts (see Kagan & Kogan, 1970). For example, interviewers in the Witkin et al. (1962) study employed global ratings of mothers' level of differentiation. These are particularly susceptible to bias when the mothers' extensive interview protocols permit the interviewer to infer the FDI status of the child. Accordingly, investigation of these issues has continued to the present day with particular emphasis on the observed dyadic interaction between mother and child. The underlying assumption of this work is that socialization processes should be reflected in short-term laboratory-based mother/child interaction.

Before proceeding to these laboratory-based studies, however, an investigation in the questionnaire-interview tradition is worthy of some discussion. Claeys and DeBoeck (1976) were able to obtain a sample in the Netherlands of adopted children and their adoptive parents, where two thirds of the children were adopted prior to 3 months of age. Such a sample makes it possible to examine the influence of parental characteristics on FDI without concern for the hereditary link between the parents' and children's mental capacities. No significant relations appeared between parental child-rearing inventory responses and the Children's Embedded Figures Test (CEFT) (Witkin, Oltman, Raskin, & Karp, 1971) performance. However, in the interview data, adoptive mothers who were rated highly on reinforcement of competition and independence had adopted sons and daughters who performed more successfully on the CEFT than did the adopted children of mothers rated highly on reinforcement of obedience and docility. This latter finding supports the original hypothesis of Witkin et al. (1962) and is noteworthy in the light of the high interrater reliability of the interview dimensions and the control over the hereditary parent/child linkage by virtue of the nature of the sample employed. Claeys and DeBoeck (1976) are appropriately cautious, however, in noting that no causal inferences can be drawn because ''a mother's behavior might be induced by that particular child's characteristics'' (pp. 843–844).

Consider next the laboratory-based studies that have sought to test the hypothesis that variation among children in FDI will be associated with differences in patterns of mother/child interaction. In a well-designed study, Hoppe, Kagan, and Zahn (1977) examined conflict resolution among RFT-assessed FI and FD third- and fourth-grade children and their mothers (drawn from Anglo-American and Mexican-American cultural backgrounds). Three role-play scenes were created containing content likely to produce mother/child disagreement (e.g., mother and child wanting to watch different TV programs scheduled at the same time). There was no indication that mothers of FD children insisted on obedience or inhibited their children's assertiveness. For boys, consistent with expectations, FI was associated with greater assertiveness; for girls, in striking contrast, FDs were more assertive than their FI peers. No such sex reversal has ever been posited in the socialization hypotheses advanced by Witkin and his colleagues. On the basis of the Hoppe et al. (1977) data, it would not be possible to assert that variation among children in FDI is traceable to maternal child-directed behaviors.

In a second relevant study, Laosa (1980), working with Chicano families, examined maternal teaching strategies associated with both maternal and child (average age of 5½) FDI levels. Correlations between the maternal-behavior categories and children's FDI levels were relatively low and failed to show a consistent pattern across sex of child and FDI index (CEFT, block design, figure drawing). On the other hand, the mother's own FDI level was significantly related to three of the behavioral categories: FI was associated with mother's inquiry (asking questions of child) and praise of the child, whereas FD was related to modeling behavior (child observing mother working on the model). Laosa (1980) argues that the causal direction proceeds from maternal cognitive style to maternal teaching behaviors and that these findings are consistent with FDI theory, assertions that are highly debatable.

It is important to bear in mind that the task employed (Tinkertoy construction) relies on spatial visualization; hence, FI children should learn it more readily. If there is a correlation between mothers' and children's FDI levels, the use of inquiry and praise by FI mothers would indicate their children's greater sense of security with, and success at, solving the Tinkertoy task. Correspondingly, FD mothers may have to resort to modeling to facilitate their children's performance on what may be an uncongenial task. Consistent with this conjecture is evidence indicating that mothers using negative physical control (punishment or manual restraints) were more likely to have FD children. It is unfortunate that data relevant to these alternative interpretations were not presented. In the absence of such information, the interpretation of Laosa's (1980) results is equivocal, and in no sense can one consider them to be supportive of the Witkin et al. (1962) socialization hypotheses.

The final study considered here (Moskowitz, Dreyer, & Kronsberg, 1981) is based on longitudinal data extending over a two-and-one-half-year period. The social and exploratory behaviors and maternal interactions of 1-year-old infants were assessed. At age 3½, these same behaviors were examined and the PEFT was administered. For both ages (1 and 3½), maternal behaviors possessed no predictive power whatever in respect to FDI assessed with the PEFT. Conceivably, Moskowitz et al. (1981) may not have sampled the appropriate maternal behaviors or, if such behavior does in fact exert an influence on FDI, its effects may simply not be felt until later in childhood. Arguing against the latter alternative is the evidence cited in Kogan (1976a) pointing to the significant stability of PEFT assessments over the preschool years from 3 to 5.

The outcomes of the three studies examining the characteristics of short-term mother/child interactions in relation to FDI can only be described as disappointing to proponents of the view that FI and FD children have been exposed to differential maternal-socializing influences. Although the investigators in all three studies have made every effort to engage their subjects in involving and naturalistic-type situations, one can readily maintain that the mother/child interactions were of too brief a duration, or were unrepresentative relative to the typical interaction between mother and child, or that the critical interaction variables were overlooked, or that the research was doomed from the start merely by virtue of participation in an experiment (putting mothers and children on their best behavior, so to speak). The Claeys and DeBoeck (1976) outcomes support the original Witkin et al. (1962) socialization hypotheses but, despite the control for hereditary linkage, are based on a Dutch sample (in contrast to the American and Chicano samples employed in the interactional studies). Thus, ethnicity represents still another variant. The controversy surrounding socialization influences on FDI clearly cannot be resolved here. Future research might profitably consider the examination within the same sample of general child-rearing beliefs, self-reported and child-reported child-rearing practices, and ongoing parent/child interactional behaviors. Replication across at least two age levels would also be desirable, and FDI should be assessed to include both the restructuring and perception-of-the-upright components. An exhaustive study of the foregoing type would not offer any final resolution of the issue, but it could not help advancing our knowledge of the specific processes that mediate between parental socialization influences and a child's standing on the FDI dimension.

Interpersonal Behavior

As outlined in Witkin et al. (1962), FDI theory has changed considerably over the years, with possibly the most dramatic change reflected in the positive attributes assigned to FD individuals in the interpersonal domain. Witkin and Goodenough (1977) offer an extensive review of the literature relating FDI to interpersonal behavior. A very small portion of that literature is based on children or adolescents however. Early relevant research has already been critically evaluated by Kagan and Kogan (1970), and work based on preschool samples has been thoroughly discussed by Kogan (1976a). In general, the reviewed research has tended to support the view that FD children are person oriented, whereas FI children are object or task oriented. The present section will focus on the researches of Nakamura and his colleagues (Ruble & Nakamura, 1972; Nakamura & Finck, 1980), for these represent the only major child-based investigations that have not yet received critical attention.

In the Ruble and Nakamura (1972) study, second- and third-grade children were classified as FI or FD on a modified RFT procedure. They also responded to two types of tasks—an object-assembly puzzle and a squares game. The critical aspect of these tasks was the provision of distinctive cues by the experimenter. In the case of the object-assembly puzzles, children in the experimental group were informed that the examiner (E) would simultaneously work on the same puzzle. The results showed that FI children were generally more successful. Ruble and Nakamura (1972) explain these outcomes on the basis of the focus of the children's glances. The FI children apparently glanced at E's hands as she worked on the puzzle, whereas FD children glanced at E's face. It is evident that the former type of glancing would have instrumental value for problem solution, whereas the latter type would not. At the same time, it should be noted that the spatial object-assembly task is likely to be more congenial to FI children; hence, FD children may have been disadvantaged from the start.

In contrast to the object-assembly puzzle, the squares task provided the type of social cue that FD children could utilize in the service of problem solution, and their performance improved accordingly. There does not appear to be much doubt, then, that the FDI dimension is highly relevant to task versus social orientation in children. These authors take special pains to disclaim any value bias in the latter distinction by noting that there are situational contexts in which sensitivity to social cues can enhance effective functioning.

The foregoing point is heavily emphasized in Nakamura and Finck (1980). It should be noted that FDI is not the focus of their research. Instead, these authors have attempted to delineate relatively effective and ineffective task-oriented and socially oriented children by means of a self-report questionnaire, and they have related this classification to FDI for purposes of construct validation. Despite this shift from the customary central role occupied by the FDI construct in most of the research devoted to that topic, Nakamura and Finck (1980) shed useful light on the interpersonal component of FDI.

The foregoing authors devised the Hypothetical Situation Questionnaire (HSQ) for use with a sample of 9- to 12-year-olds in a school setting. Each item described a classroom-related activity, with the child selecting one of four alternatives to express what he or she would do in the situation described. Some items contain situations relevant to a social orientation; other items are intended to tap a task orientation. Further, some items were designed to assess self-assurance, thereby permitting a subclassification of task-oriented and socially oriented children into those, within each orientation, who are relatively effective and ineffective. Children were given both the RFT and a short form of the EFT.

The most prominent result was the uniformly higher FI scores (on both the RFT and EFT) for low-social task-effective children. On the other hand, a social orientation, whether or not a task orientation was also present and whether the orientation was effective or ineffective, was associated with higher levels of FD. There appears to be little doubt, then, that social sensitivity is more closely linked to FD than FI. Such sensitivity, however, does not necessarily imply social competence or effectiveness.

The major obstacle at present to the further specification of the interpersonal aspect of FD is the one-dimensional constraint in the FDI construct. Indexing a strength in the interpersonal area by means of a deficit in perception-of-the-upright or restructuring ability poses both conceptual and methodological difficulties (Kogan, 1980c). There may well be distinctive social sensitivities and competencies associated with both FI and FD. The further delineation of these remains a task for the future.

Training Effects

In their most recent review, Witkin and Goodenough (1981) devote several pages to the issue of training FDI. Given that the founders of the theory have long maintained that FDI represents a highly stable and pervasive construct with deep roots in personality and possibly even in biology, one would expect efforts to improve performance on the EFT and RFT to be doomed to failure. Hence, the impact of direct training on those critical measures of FDI assumes considerable importance in respect to the very origins of that construct. In the light of that importance, the exceedingly small number of such training studies in children is surprising.

Morell (1976) is one of a very small group of investigators who have attempted to modify performance on a measure of FDI—RFT in this case. Three age groups (11-, 14-, and 18-year-olds) were randomly divided into control and experimental groups with the latter given feedback training designed to improve RFT performance on the Oltman (1968) apparatus. This consisted of the opportunity to examine the deviation from the vertical on each trial and to correct and recorrect it if necessary. Subjects were also pretested and posttested on the EFT as a check on generalization effects. No significant training effects were obtained for either the RFT or the EFT. One must tentatively conclude, then, that FDI (at least its RFT component) is not readily trainable in children or adolescents.

In regard to the training of EFT performance in children, it should be noted that the issue has been pursued within a sex-differences context. Given the massive amount of evidence reported in Maccoby and Jacklin (1974) that is suggestive of greater FI in males than in females during the childhood and adolescent years, investigators have begun to ask the question of whether the female disadvantage could be erased by means of appropriate training on EFT items. The underlying rationale was first advanced by Sherman (1967), and asserts that young girls have had lesser opportunity than young boys to practice on spatial visualization and restructuring tasks. Hence, training might serve a catch-up function because boys are presumed to have already attained their maximal FI level.

Two similar studies by the same team of investigators have focused on the foregoing training issue. In the first (Connor, Serbin, & Schackman, 1977), 6- to 10-year-old children were randomly assigned to a training condition or to a control group. The principal training condition employed an overlay technique in which a complex geometric figure was made progressively more simple through removal of a series of three overlays to facilitate recognition of the simple embedded figure (a diamond shape). Consistent with the predictions, no significant differences across groups were obtained for boys, whereas the overlay training boosted the CEFT of girls relative to the other conditions. Connor et al. (1977) maintained that their results are congruent with the Sherman (1967) hypothesis. Also advanced as a possible explanation is a motivational hypothesis—attributed to Goldstein and Chance (1965)—that accounts for girls' improvement on the basis of the increased confidence in the spatial domain occasioned by the insights gained from the overlay procedure.

The second study (Connor, Schackman, & Serbin, 1978) differed from the first in the use of CEFT pretests and a generalization task of a spatial character. The findings pointed to significant practice effects from pretest to posttest on the CEFT as well as a significant training effect over and beyond the influence of practice. Girls appeared to benefit more than boys from practice, but training effects were comparable across sex. Performance on the generalization task was stronger for girls than for boys (in the sense of training vs. control differences within sex). In general, practice appeared to vitiate initial sex differences on the CEFT, an outcome similar to that obtained by Goldstein and Chance (1965) with adults.

The most provocative results reported by Connor et al. (1978) concern the CEFT pretest versus posttest correlations. These were significant in the control groups and diminished to nonsignificance, although remaining positive, in the training groups. In contrast to most training studies that show increments in performance with little disruption in the ranking of individuals, the present data suggest that children may, in fact, reorder themselves along the FDI dimension following a relatively brief training experience. Results such as these are quite damaging to the view that FDI represents an individual-difference dimension that is highly stable (in the interindividual sense) across most of the lifespan. Hence, the Connor et al. (1978) findings deserve careful scrutiny. Note first that the correlation differences between training and control groups were not significant (at least for the CEFT pretest and posttest measures). One must also take account of the absence of any delayed posttests. Conceivably, the disruption in the initial rank ordering of the children represents a temporary, short-term phenomenon. Only further research incorporating such delayed posttesting (perhaps carried out within a longitudinal framework) can answer the major question of whether the FDI dimension is truly stable or susceptible to disruption by transient experimental interventions.

In their most current theoretical statement, Witkin and Goodenough (1981) appear sanguine in their views about training of FDI. This stance is quite puzzling in the light of the conceptual incongruities that such training effects bring in their wake. One such problem (the possible disruption of presumably stable individual differences) has already been discussed. Another glaring incongruity comes about by virtue of the intended direction of training, namely, toward greater FI. If FDI theory has become truly value neutral, as Witkin and Goodenough (1981) have recently asserted, the basis for training for FI rather than FD is difficult to defend.

Witkin and Goodenough (1981) defend their optimistic view of FI training on the ground that it promotes mobility of functions. In other words, the ideal state is one in which a particular child could express FI or FD dispositions dependent on the requirements of the situation. Once again, however, a theoretical ideal is undercut by assessment constraints. As Kogan (1980c) has previously observed:

> It is simply not possible for an individual to fluctuate between FI and FD when these are opposite poles of a single dimension. One cannot be both superior and inferior on the FI-FD indexes, for these are very much in the nature of abilities. (p. 597)

It is difficult at the present juncture to offer any definitive judgment regarding the impact of training research on FDI theory. As we have noted, such research has been quite limited thus far, and much of it has become tied to the sex-differences issue. The latter is important in its own right, but the overlap with training concerns is only partial. The conceptual implications of various training outcomes can be readily spelled out. In the absence of an adequate data base, however, such speculation represents little more than an interesting theoretical exercise.

The Question of Origins

Two separate but related questions have been asked about the origins of FDI. The more general question concerns the source of individual differences in FDI in the population as a whole. The second more specific question inquires into the basis for the frequently observed sex differences in FDI. In regard to the first more general question, an earlier discussion briefly reviewed some recent empirical studies of parental child-rearing practices and mother/child interaction. Such research bears on the issue of socialization and, hence, is relevant to the question of origins. That body of work, however, represents but a small portion of the socialization research brought to bear upon the FDI dimension.

The primary approach has involved cross-cultural study of subsistence-level peoples (see Witkin & Berry, 1975), with socialization representing a major component within an ecocultural model (Berry, 1976).

In broad outline, that model distinguishes between migratory hunter-and-gatherer cultures on the one hand and sedentary agricultural cultures on the other hand. The former yield higher FI scores than the latter. Such an outcome is consistent with the idea that cognitive-restructuring skills are adaptive for the nomadic existence of hunter-gatherers but have little real-world applicability for sedentary agricultural groups. In corresponding fashion, social competencies (representing high FD) are considered to be of minor relevance to hunter-gatherers but of great importance in the stratified societies typical of agricultural groups. Berry (1976) offers a wide range of evidence suggesting that these contrasting modes of existence are related to socialization practices that foster a cognitive style appropriate to the ecocultural context. The ecocultural model is also relevant to the second question posed earlier—the source of sex differences in FDI. Males exhibit higher FI than do females in agricultural groups, whereas sex differences in FDI appear to be negligible in groups of hunter-gatherers. This cross-cultural difference is attributed to socialization for conformity in agricultural socieites and for autonomy in hunter-gatherers.

Although Berry (1976) limited his research to subsistence-level cultures, it should be noted that the socialization aspects of the ecocultural model have been examined on a broad global scale. A typical approach has involved the selection of contrasting subcultures or villages within a particular country that differ in their emphasis on socialization for conformity. Where such an emphasis is strong, children are expected to be FD; where the emphasis is weak, FI is anticipated. Witkin and Goodenough (1981) review research of the foregoing type carried out across a large number of countries and conclude that the outcomes favor "the starting hypothesis relating field dependence-independence and restructuring ability to extent of stress on social conformity in the society" (p. 91).

With so broad-gauged a starting hypothesis, it is inevitable that reports of exceptions would eventually be forthcoming. Thus, Nedd and Gruenfeld (1976) did not find anticipated differences in FDI among 14- to 15-year-old adolescents drawn from six separate subcultures on the island of Trinidad. A further exception is noted by Dinges and Hollenbeck (1978), who compared 9½-year-old Navajo children

with Anglo norms on the CEFT provided by Witkin et al. (1971). Contrary to what might have been expected on the basis of Navajo socialization practices, Navajo children obtained CEFT scores that significantly exceeded the Anglo norms. Consider next a study based on 3- to 7-year-olds in rural Guatemala (Irwin, Engle, Klein, & Yarbrough, 1976). In contrast to most of the research that relied on communitywide assessments of traditionalism, the foregoing authors obtained individual family data on the Inkeles and Smith (1974) modernity scale. Correlations between children's EFT scores and mothers' modernity scores were negligible. Finally a study of Moroccan children by Wagner (1978) strongly indicated that extent of formal schooling was a rather powerful predictor of CEFT performance. In contrast, the rural/urban distinction (presumed reflective of socialization differences) had little impact on CEFT scores. It is, thus, apparent that the Witkin and Berry (1975) proposals regarding FDI and cross-cultural socialization practices cannot be given an unqualified endorsement. A detailed analysis of the supporting and contradictory data, however, is well beyond the scope of the present chapter.

Simultaneous with the extensive research on socialization practices and FDI, other investigators have pursued the origins of FDI in the biological realm. Witkin and Goodenough (1981) describe hormonal and genetic factors, and Waber (1976, 1977b) and Zoccolotti and Oltman (1978) have implicated central nervous system (CNS) factors such as hemispheric lateralization. A thorough analysis of this vast literature cannot be undertaken here. Much of the biologically oriented research has been carried out within a sex-differences perspective and has been extensively reviewed in the L. J. Harris (1978) chapter and the Wittig and Petersen (1979) volume. Also available is a book by Sherman (1978) written from a sex-role, antibiological perspective. A large portion of the reviewed research is concerned with spatial ability rather than FDI as such.

In general, FDI investigators have pursued either social-environmental or biological determinants with little attempt made to pose competing hypotheses within a comprehensive explanatory perspective. Waber (1977a) is one of the few to give the matter theoretical attention, and she has come down rather firmly on the biological side. One must recognize, however, that the social-environmental approach, as reflected, for example, in the examination of sex role as a mediator of cognitive performance, has also become more sophisticated. Nash (1979) makes a persuasive case for sex-role influences, and there are several observations reported in her chapter where a test of competing neuropsychological and sex-role hypotheses would be feasible (see Kogan & Marcuse, 1981). In short, despite the enormous progress that has been made in our knowledge of sex-related differences in FDI and related processes, we still have much to learn about the relative contribution of, and interaction between, biological and social processes.

Overview

In the preceding pages, this author has tried to highlight some of the current controversial issues in FDI theory and research. To undertake such a review under conditions of space limitation is to guarantee a measure of disappointment because FDI has sprawled over the psychological landscape, defying any reviewer to achieve an adequate grasp of its breadth and depth. One simply cannot do justice to the full scope of FDI in anything less than a book-length contribution. There is need for such a work because virtually all of the available published reviews have been prepared by the original proponents of the theory and their disciples. A genuine appraisal of FDI theory and research would require the painstaking effort of a neutral sophisticated outsider willing to sift through the vast corpus of published and unpublished work with a critical eye.

Given the selectivity of the present review, there will no doubt be readers who object to the neglect of particular portions of FDI research. Especially conspicuous in this regard is the absence of the large body of research devoted to educational applications. The latter includes some interesting work on associations with reading performance (e.g., Kogan, 1980b) and other forms of school achievement (e.g., Satterly, 1976) as well as on implications for mental retardation (e.g., Massari & Mansfield, 1973) and learning disabilities (e.g., Guyer & Friedman, 1975). Such applications of FDI theory to educationally relevant problems will surely continue, and may, in fact, represent that domain where future expansion of FDI research will be most pronounced.

With the untimely death of Herman A. Witkin in 1979, however, the future course of research and theoretical development in the FDI domain becomes clouded. Although FDI has attracted researchers in virtually every branch of psychology, the activities of Witkin and his immediate associates have represented the basic core of the overall enterprise. The series of bibliographic listings, the periodic symposia and conferences, the preparation of detailed reviews of the various portions of the FDI entity—all of these activities will undoubtedly undergo some retrenchment. It is highly dubious, however, that FDI will disappear because the fertility of the construct has led to periodic renewal and constant articulation with other popular areas and issues that capture the attention of psychologists at the time. Some good examples are:

1. The impact of sex roles on cognitive functioning.
2. Hemispheric lateralization and cognition.
3. The cross-cultural analysis of cognitive functioning.
4. The relevance of individual differences for instruction.
5. The development of spatial cognition.

In a subsequent discussion, efforts to integrate FDI with Piagetian constructs are examined. There is good reason to believe, then, that the Witkin legacy will be with us for some time to come.

REFLECTION-IMPULSIVITY (R-I)

General Background

The cognitive style of reflection-impulsivity (R-I), also referred to as conceptual or cognitive tempo, indexes the extent to which a child delays a response in the course of searching for the correct alternative in a context of response uncertainty. Latency to first response and the accuracy of that response constitute the joint measures of the style. The most common instrument for assessing R-I is the Matching Familiar Figures Test (MFFT), developed by Kagan, Rosman, Day, Albert, and Phillips (1964). The MFFT requires the child to match a standard figure with one of six variants, one of which is, in fact, identical to the standard. Latency of response and error incidence are obtained for all test items. These two variables have correlated negatively with each other in the range of $-.3$ to $-.6$ (Messer, 1976). The comparison of the fast-responding/high-error (impulsive) child with the slow-responding/low-error (reflective) child on various other tasks or in observed behaviors represents the focus of much R-I research. The fast-responding/low-error child and the slow-responding/high-error child were frequently omitted from consideration during the early years of R-I research, but more recent work has acknowledged their presence.

Since the publication of Messer's (1976) comprehensive review of the R-I literature, the study of this cognitive style has been pursued in several directions. First, the validity of the basic R-I construct itself has been questioned, a controversy initiated by the exchange between Block, Block, and Harrington (1974, 1975) and Kagan and Messer (1975). This controversy as well as other more strictly psychometric concerns have led to a searching examination of the MFFT as the primary index of conceptual tempo. Second, there has been increased attention directed at the strategies used by reflective and impulsive children to solve problems under varying stimulus and task conditions. A final trend in the R-I literature over the past 10 years is the increasing interest in the applicability of the MFFT to the field of education in general and, more specifically, to the assessment and understanding of children distinguished by various handicapping conditions.

Measurement Issues

Psychometric Credibility of the MFFT

Since Messer's (1976) review, there has been an increasing amount of criticism of the MFFT as the primary measure of R-I. The first formal critique of this kind was offered by Ault, Mitchell, and Hartmann (1976). Their concerns centered around the inherently low reliability of the MFFT error component as well as the measurement implications of a negative correlation between error and latency scores. In regard to the former, low reliability of error scores may have four unfortunate consequences:

1. The likelihood of subject misclassification is enhanced when the traditional double-median-split procedure is used.
2. The threat of regression toward the mean is exacerbated for error scores in any repeated measures design.
3. It is more difficult to find significant differences in error-change scores with smaller samples owing to the relative lack of statistical power.
4. Correlations between MFFT errors and other variables will be underestimated unless a correction for attenuation is applied.

The second concern focuses on methods of analyzing MFFT data. More frequently than not, the method used to test for differences in performance between reflective and impulsive children on some external criterion has been to create a 2×2 median-split classification based on errors and latency. Such a procedure results in the sacrifice of valuable information because scores that are continuous in nature are dichotomized. The use of regression models with errors and latency as separate variables is the recommended alternative.

Egeland and Weinberg (1976) have extended the work of Ault et al. (1976) by exploring the short-term stability of three different versions of the MFFT (Forms F, S, and K) for children in kindergarten, second grade, and fifth grade respectively. The evidence points to relatively low short-term stability for all three forms, with one form (F) not recommended for use with kindergarten children. Although this recommendation has been questioned by others (Margolis, Leonard, Brannigan, & Heverly, 1980), serious doubts about the psychometric adequacy of the original MFFT continue to plague research in the R-I area.

Item Analysis of the MFFT

Research by Kojima (1976) suggests that the location of the correct variant on an MFFT item may exert considerable influence on how children respond to that item. That author tested a large sample of Japanese children on the elementary form of the MFFT and found that they generally preferred variant two (located immediately below the standard) over the other five as their first choice. In addition, some alternatives that are more dissimilar than others from the standard tend to occupy the same position across items. As might be expected, incorrect responses are less likely to occur for such alternatives. Much of the data reviewed in Kojima's paper needs additional analysis, but one tentative conclusion seems clear: an important source of variability in MFFT performance is item difficulty as reflected by the location of the correct variant.

A potentially effective method for controlling proximity would be to have the six variants surrounding the standard in a circular fashion so that each of the variants is equidistant from the standard. In such a way, variance in performance resulting from the differential distance between the standard and each variant is eliminated. Of course, if it is the order in which variants are examined rather than proximity that influences item difficulty, the circular arrangement would not necessarily represent a methodological advance. Only further research can settle the issue.

Alternative Measures of R-I

In light of the foregoing criticisms of the MFFT, the development of a more psychometrically adequate instrument would clearly represent a constructive step. By far the most successful attempt at introducing a new instrument to assess R-I has been the development of the MFFT 20 by Cairns and Cammock (1978). The primary goal of those authors was "to improve the reliability of MFFT error scores by increasing the number of items and selecting, through item-total error performance, only those items providing an efficient discrimination index" (p. 556).

From earlier versions of the MFFT, 30 items were selected and were administered to a sample of 11- to 12-year-old boys. Of these items, significant error differences were found between reflectives and impulsives on 25, with item-total correlations ranging from .18 through .60. Interestingly, the correlations were lowest for those items where the correct variant occupied positions directly below the standard. These latter findings lend support to Kojima's (1976) conclusion that target position of the correct variant influences the assessment of R-I in young children. As a next step, Cairns and Cammock (1978) examined the reliability of their new instrument—20 items selected from the original set of 30 to satisfy diverse psychometric criteria. Split-half reliability coefficients approximated .90 for both errors and latencies. In addition, a test-retest coefficient (across a five-week interval) for errors of .77 far exceeded the previous levels reported by Egeland and Weinberg (1976). A test-retest coefficient for latency of .85 was also much higher than earlier estimates cited by Ault et al. (1976).

The lack of attention paid to sound psychometric principles in the initial development of the MFFT has undoubtedly contributed to some of the inconsistent findings that have characterized the R-I literature over the past 15 years. Of course, if the MFFT had been designed to meet the highest psychometric standards, conflicting data from similar studies might still have resulted. Nevertheless, the source of explanation for such disagreement could not have been the questionable psychometric properties of the instrument itself. Clearly, the enormous attractiveness of the R-I construct and the intuitive appeal of the MFFT encouraged investigators to ignore some of the questionable properties of this major instrument.

Construct Validity

The Meaning of Error and Latency Scores

Beginning with the early work of Kagan et al. (1964), errors and latency have been used simultaneously to define R-I, although the original definition stressed the speed of response rather than accuracy. Kagan and Messer (1975) contend that the stress on speed or tempo was intended as a departure from traditional considerations of competence. At the same time, however, the quality of response was retained as a component of the R-I style. The conceptual emphasis on the latency, as opposed to the error component, was attacked by Block et al. (1974, 1975) on the basis of evidence indicating that errors relate substantially to children's personal characteristics, whereas latencies (at least as main effects) account for little personality variance. In support of the foregoing view, both Haskins and McKinney (1976) and Mitchell and Ault (1979) have observed that MFFT errors relate much more strongly than do MFFT latencies to problem-solving performance. At the base of the significant interchange between Block et al. (1974, 1975) and Kagan and Messer (1975) is the issue of whether R-I is best represented by a combined latency-error index or exclusively by an accuracy or error dimension. If the latter, the very use of such value-laden terms as reflective and impulsive (or conceptual tempo) is open to question.

More recently, another group of investigators entered the fray, maintaining that latency represents the critical component of the R-I construct (Zelniker, Bentler, & Renan, 1977; Zelniker & Jeffrey, 1976, 1979). In the view of Zelniker, Bentler, and Renan (1977), "consistent individual differences in cognitive style stemming from differences in modes of perceptual analysis are reflected in latency while accuracy varies depending on the task employed" (p. 301). Reflective children are presumed to engage in detail analysis of stimuli, which requires more time than the global analysis presumably preferred by impulsive children. Accuracy, then, would be a by-product of the particular task employed, that is, whether more readily solved by a detail or by a global strategy of analysis.

In support of their argument, Zelniker, Bentler, and Renan (1977) carried out a factor analysis of item data gathered on a fourth-grade sample by Zelniker and Jeffrey (1976). Latency and error scores were available for two sets of items—those demanding detail analysis as opposed to global analysis for efficient solution. The factor-analytic outcomes pointed to a single latency factor cutting across the detail versus global contrast, as opposed to two distinct accuracy factors—one for detail and the other for global items. Further, none of the error scores loaded substantially on the latency factor, suggesting that response latencies to different kinds of stimuli are relatively independent of the quality of performance. In short, strategies of information processing tied to latencies are given causal priority and major significance in respect to performance on tasks like those of the MFFT.

None of the foregoing is intended to imply a fundamental contradiction between the views put forth by the Block and Zelniker research groups. The former were concerned with the socioemotional correlates of MFFT performance in preschool children. Many more such correlates were observed for the error than for the latency score. Zelniker and her associates on the other hand focused on the information processing aspects of the MFFT itself in middle childhood. Clearly, the two approaches at issue have posed distinctly different questions in children widely discrepant in age. Hence, to ask the question in the general form of which is more important—latency or errors—is to court confusion. It is evidently essential that the question be posed in a specific context. Also important, of course, is consideration of possible developmental changes in the meaning of latency and errors. Kogan (1976a) offers some discussion of this issue for the preschool period, but the task of integrating preschool data with that of later childhood and adolescence has not yet been accomplished.

R-I and Cognitive Efficiency

A model of R-I that conceptually and methodologically integrates speed and accuracy was proposed by Salkind and Wright (1977). Those authors contend that error and latency scores on such tasks as the MFFT are products of an interaction between children's basic information processing efficiency and choices between strategies that emphasize speed versus accuracy. The model acknowledges the joint determination of cognitive tempo by synthesizing raw latency and error scores and by converting them into the constructs of impulsivity (I) and efficiency (E). Impulsivity is defined as the difference between standardized scores for speed and accuracy (hence, reflecting the child's position on the speed-accuracy tradeoff). Efficiency is defined as the sum of standardized scores for speed and accuracy, given that both of these tap the dimension at issue. Thus, it can be seen that the speed component contributes in the same direction to both efficiency and impulsivity, whereas the accuracy component affects efficiency and impulsivity in opposite directions. Hence, the Salkind and Wright (1977) measures were designed to insure that efficiency and impulsivity would be uncorrelated.

It is unlikely, however, that the foregoing ideal can be realized because such orthogonality assumes that the latency and error measures are equally reliable. A review of the relevant evidence (Kogan, 1976a; Messer, 1976) clearly indicates differential reliability—errors more reliable than latencies in the preschool years and latencies more reliable than errors in school-age children. Indeed, preschool latency reliabilities are often close to chance level, suggesting that the error component in such data is predominant. The application of the Salkind and Wright formulas to preschoolers, then, would produce exceptionally high correlations between I and E scores. In other words, the separation of stylistic and ability variance—the original intent of the Salkind and Wright model—cannot be accomplished for such children. Although this represents a psychometric shortcoming of the model, the substantive aspect is of greater importance because impulsivity in preschoolers may, in fact, have more to do with a capacity deficit than with a style of functioning.

In later childhood, reliabilities are substantially above chance for both errors and latencies, although higher in the latter case. Hence, we would expect I and E scores to exhibit a modest positive correlation—that is, greater impulsiveness associated with higher levels of efficiency. In the present case, however, we are more likely to be dealing with a psychometric artifact than with a genuine substantive finding.

It is apparent that the attempt to separate stylistic from ability variance within the context of performance on a single test—the psychometrically flawed MFFT—does pose serious problems. Even if error and latency reliabilities were both high and equally reliable (an objective that has apparently been achieved by the MFFT 20 described earlier), the resultant independence of the stylistic and ability component is a psychometric necessity rather than a substantive outcome. Accordingly, it is imperative that I and E scores be validated against external variables. Despite the conceptual and methodological promise of the Salkind and Wright (1977) approach, their proposed model has not been distinguished by widespread adoption. Conceivably, investigators hesitate to make use of it for fear that their studies would lack continuity with prior relevant research. One particular paper, that of Miyakawa (1981), is worthy of mention because it bears directly on the validity of the Salkind and Wright (1977) model. If the purpose of the separate impulsivity and efficiency scores is to distinguish stylistic from ability variance respectively, then, one might expect the latter to relate to other ability measures (such as performance on IQ-type tests), whereas the former (the stylistic index) should be relatively independent of ability measures. Miyakawa (1981) tested this hypothesis in samples of Japanese first and fourth graders. A puzzling developmental trend was observed in the data. The expected effect was found in the older children, but a reversed outcome—impulsivity rather than efficiency relating to IQ performance (inversely)—was obtained in the younger children. It, thus, appears that a strategic preference—toward speed or accuracy—has implications for intellective performance in younger but not in older children. On the other hand, the efficiency with which a particular strategy is employed begins to relate to intellective test performance as the child ages. Although findings such as these may reflect a substantive developmental trend, the mediating processes responsible for the observed effects remain unclear. Regrettably, Miyakawa (1981) nowhere provides information regarding the reliabilities of the error and latency measures used to derive the I and E scores. Such information is essential to achieve an understanding of the basis for the striking age differences reported.

Although the use of I and E scores represents a conceptual advance over the implicitly accepted view that fast-inaccurate (impulsive) performance implies inefficiency and that slow-accurate (reflective) performance implies efficiency, the evidence is not yet available to accept or reject the Salkind and Wright (1977) model. On the one hand, the use of a single index to reflect impulsivity is an attractive methodological advance over classifying children discretely, and the relationship of intelligence indicators to E scores provides some evidence for the validity of the measure (if only in older children). On the other hand, the overall validational evidence is quite limited, and the difficulties posed by the differential reliabilities of error and latency scores have not been effectively addressed.

Convergent and Discriminant Validity

At least two studies have examined the convergent and discriminant validity of R-I through the use of the multitrait-multimethod analysis outlined by Campbell and Fiske (1959). Despite the general methodological elegance of the Campbell and Fiske model, its application to the R-I domain raises some complex conceptual issues. Because R-I does, in fact, possess convergent validity, that is, generalizes across tasks with response uncertainty (Messer, 1976), an appropriate task for purposes of discriminant validity would have to offer comparable content to a task, such as the MFFT, without the response-uncertainty feature. This is difficult to accomplish, of course, and, regrettably, neither of the relevant

studies (Bentler & McClain, 1976; Hall & Russell, 1974), in fact, concerned themselves with this crucial problem. In the case of the Hall and Russell (1974) work, an attempt was made to distinguish conceptual tempo from intelligence in a sample of third-grade boys. Unfortunately, all of the instruments contained a salient response-uncertainty feature, hence clouding the distinction between convergent and discriminant validation.

Bentler and McClain (1976) selected four personality and motivational constructs—extraversion, test anxiety, impulsivity, and academic-achievement motivation—for which some theoretical argument could be made for a linkage to R-I. In a sample of fifth-grade children, the foregoing four constructs were assessed by means of three methods—self-, peer-, and teacher-ratings. A high degree of convergent and discriminant validity was observed for the four contructs, something of a surprise, given the purported linkage of each to the R-I domain. Scores generated by the four personality-motivational measures for each of the three methods were then correlated with the MFFT indices and two motor-inhibition tasks. The significant r's were few enough in number to suggest that they could be attributed to chance. It must be noted that Bentler and McClain have not applied a multitrait-multimethod analysis to the R-I construct itself but rather to possible correlates of R-I. Hence, their study does not directly address the matter of convergent and discriminant validation of the MFFT and related response-uncertainty indices.

Relation to Self-regulatory Behaviors

Does MFFT performance relate to behaviors that have a self-regulatory but not a response-uncertainty character? In a review of relevant research based on preschool samples, Kogan (1976a) pointed to both positive and negative evidence on the issue in respect to motor-inhibition tasks where children had to perform as slowly as possible. The general hypothesis of the foregoing research is that reflectives should do better on such tasks because reflection implies a delay in venturing a response on the MFFT (i.e., higher latencies in the service of greater accuracy). It appears, however, that inhibition within perceptual-matching and motor-performance contexts may represent different psychological processes.

Despite the equivocality of previous findings in the area, a study by Toner, Holstein, and Hetherington (1977) offers a further exploration of the issue in a preschool sample. In addition to motor-inhibition tasks, these authors employed measures of delay of gratification and of resistance to temptation. The correlational outcomes involving the three types of tasks indicated that a coherent or consistent construct of self-regulatory behavior is not present at the preschool level. Where significant correlations were found, age and IQ also sometimes were implicated in the relationship, yet no partial correlations are reported. One is forced to conclude, therefore, that the equivocality surrounding the issue of the self-regulatory implications of R-I has not been abated by the outcomes of the Toner et al. (1977) investigation.

Concurrent Behavioral Validity

A most striking feature of the evidence on this topic is the sharp discrepancy in the outcomes reported in the preschool and elementary school years. In the earlier period, R-I is associated with a broad band of behaviors. In contrast, when school age is reached, R-I appears to stand apart from indices of behavioral impulsivity. Indeed, little evidence exists for any real-world behavioral correlates of R-I, a fact that led Kagan and Messer (1975) to proclaim that R-I should not be generalized beyond cognitive tasks distinguished by response uncertainty.

Let us first consider data based on older children. The negative outcomes of the Bentler and McClain (1976) study have been reported earlier. McKinney (1975) examined teacher ratings of task orientation, distractibility, and extroversion-introversion in relation to R-I in second-grade classes. Reflective boys were rated as more task oriented than impulsive boys, but no such difference was found in the case of the girls. When 7- to 10-year-old children were actually observed in the school setting and rated on a set of behavioral categories (e.g., working independently, attending, distracted, aggressive), no evidence for behavioral differences between reflective and impulsive children was found (Moore, Haskins, & McKinney, 1980).

Where preschool children are concerned, behavioral correlates are indeed found, but the behaviors do not relate to MFFT performance in ways consistent with R-I labeling. Block et al. (1974) offer the classic study in the area. They essentially report that children assigned to the impulsive category on the basis of their MFFT performance do not manifest behavioral impulsivity as indexed by teachers' Q-sort ratings. Instead, such children appear to be anxious, vulnerable, cautious, and self-doubting. Hence, fast-inaccurate responding is presumed to reflect the child's urge to escape a task quickly, particularly where that task is perceived by the child to be beyond his competence to deal with it. Impulsive

behavior turned out to be most characteristic of the slow-inaccurate children. On the basis of such outcomes, Block et al. (1974, 1975) and Kagan and Messer (1975) have disagreed regarding the appropriate conceptualization of R-I. The arguments on both sides of the issue are discussed by Kogan (1976a).

A more recent study of R-I in preschoolers (Susman, Huston-Stein, & Friedrich-Cofer, 1980) employed the Salkind and Wright (1977) analytic model for scoring the error and latency data. A variety of social behaviors were rated in classrooms designated as of high (adult-imposed) or low structure. Impulsivity was found to relate to a variety of behaviors but only in the less-structured classrooms. Impulsive children (relative to their reflective peers) were rated as less aggressive and demanding, more responsible, and waiting patiently during delays. Again, we have a syndrome that is not indicative of behavioral impulsivity; indeed, some similarity to the Block et al. (1974) characterization is present. That significant effects were found only in the less structured setting is attributed by Susman et al. (1980) to the greater opportunity in such a setting for free-play and independent activity, factors that might contribute to the enhancement of individual-differences variance. Of further interest is the indication that E scores were not associated with social behaviors. One could view this as a partial validation of the Salkind and Wright (1977) model on the grounds that style should be more likely than capacity to have noncognitive social consequences. This is a debatable point, however, and clearly one that is not consistent with the Block et al. (1974) argument concerning the greater importance of error than latency scores in respect to behavioral correlates. On one point, however, there is no disagreement: impulsivity assessed on response-uncertainty tasks is not equivalent to impulsivity as a behavioral syndrome or personality trait.

The research described here has sought behavioral and personality correlates of R-I in the child's natural settings of school and home. A more narrow-gauged approach is represented in the work of Brodzinsky (1975, 1977), who has examined links between R-I and responsivity to humor in elementary school children. The rationale for the research derives from the information processing requirements that distinguish varieties of humor—from salient affective and cognitive properties on the one hand to subtle incongruities on the other hand. These were expected to map onto the strategies of information processing favored by impulsives and reflectives respectively.

In the initial study (Brodzinsky, 1975), 6- and 8-year-old reflective children revealed better humor comprehension than impulsives, an effect that vanished in the 10-year-olds. The R-I differences were particularly pronounced for cartoons with high affective salience, suggesting that impulsives are quite poor at suppressing such cues with adverse consequences for comprehension. At the same time, impulsive children laughed more at these high-affective cartoons (and to a lesser extent at cartoons in general), pointing to the greater emotional lability of that subgroup.

In a second study, Brodzinsky (1977) confirmed the foregoing findings in a sample of fourth-grade children, suggesting (contrary to the findings reported above) that the effects do not vanish by 10 years of age. This study, however, was based on verbal jokes, in contrast to the pictorial cartoons previously employed. These varied in type of linguistic ambiguity—phonological, lexical, surface structural, and deep structural. The relation between comprehension and mirth (affective responsivity) is further developed, the evidence indicating that reflective children modulate their affective expression consistent with the extent of joke comprehension, whereas impulsives' mirth levels appear to be independent of degree of comprehension. This linkage of cognition and affect in reflective children has also been demonstrated on the MFFT itself by Brodzinsky and Rightmyer (1976). Incorrect MFFT choices bring about a reduction in positive facial affect for reflective third graders and fourth graders, in contrast to impulsives who display little affect discrepancy between correct and incorrect choices.

One further outcome of the Brodzinsky (1977) investigation is worthy of notice. In addition to spontaneous comprehension, that author also employed several prompts whenever the explanation of the humor fell short. Use of this prompted-comprehension score essentially wiped out conceptual-tempo (R-I) differences, suggesting the presence of a production deficiency rather than a lack of capacity in the impulsive (and slow-inaccurate) children. Probing questions apparently focused the attention of these children on critical features of the humor stimulus. Comparable effects were obtained in a related study in which fourth graders and seventh graders were required to paraphrase the meaning of sentences containing nonhumorous linguistic ambiguities (Brodzinsky, Feuer, & Owens, 1977).

In sum, although the R-I dimension may not relate to elementary school children's behaviors in a natural setting (as rated by teachers, peers, and parents), the work of Brodzinsky and his colleagues strongly suggests that R-I implicates socioemotional processes in children beyond the preschool years. These relationships have been demonstrated in respect to humor comprehension and responsivity in a testlike context. Humor, particularly appropriate for the study of elicited affect, eventually led the investigators to the discovery that impulsive children are more emotionally labile than their reflective peers. If this is indeed the case, one might well expect R-I differences to generalize beyond the confines of the humor response. At present, however, very little is known about the extent of this generalization.

Developmental Change/Continuity

In norming the MFFT, Salkind (1978) assembled developmental data on over 2,800 children (52.6% male, with an age range of 5 to 12 years). A brief report based on these data has been published by Salkind and Nelson (1980). Children appear to become more reflective through 10 years of age by virtue of a progressive decrease in errors coupled with longer latencies. After this age, there is a decrease in latency as well as a stabilization in errors or, in the terms of Salkind and Wright (1977), an increase in efficiency of performance. What is especially interesting about the shapes of the curves for both males and females is that they challenge the popularly accepted notion that reflection continues to increase with age during the childhood years. Salkind and Nelson (1980) offer a possible reason for the observed outcomes. They suggest that children at around 10 years of age become maximally aware of the speed-accuracy tradeoff. No independent evidence is offered to support such an inference however.

In addition to cross-sectional mean differences, Salkind and Nelson (1980) report latency-error correlations across the 5- to 12-year age span. These achieved their highest levels for 9- and 10-year-olds ($r = -.57$ and $-.58$ respectively). Correlational magnitudes dropped to the .40s at younger and older levels. As Kogan (1976a) has reported, these correlations drop into the $-.30$s for 3- to 4-year-olds. Such low correlations, in fact, prompted Kagan and Messer (1975) to raise the question of whether comparable psychological processes distinguish younger and older children on the MFFT. Conceivably, these lower correlations can be attributed to a combination of match-to-sample demands that are too difficult for a preschooler, and the likelihood that the same/different distinction is not firmly established in children below 5 years of age. Fein and Eshleman (1974) have found that young children understand the concept of ''different'' better than that of the ''same.'' Vurpillot (1976) has observed that an identity relationship is not firmly established in preschoolers, implying that ''same'' responses are often based on partial equivalences in early childhood. In light of the instructions on the MFFT (''Find the one that is exactly the same . . .''), the question arises as to how developmental processes interact with the expression of stylistic variance in the assessment of R-I in the preschool years. Research devoted to this issue is scant (but see Achenbach & Weisz, 1975, and relevant discussions by Kogan, 1976a, and Zelniker & Jeffrey, 1979).

In addition to the matter of comparability between preschoolers and older children, there is the issue of developmental transitions within the preschool period itself. For the most part, investigators have found that errors tend to decrease and latencies tend to increase between the ages of 3 and 6 years (Kogan, 1976a). This trend toward increased reflection was manifested on the original preschool form of the MFFT. J. C. Wright (1971) has constructed a match-to-sample task intended exclusively for use with preschoolers—the Kansas Reflection-Impulsivity Scale for Preschoolers (KRISP)—and, hence, it would be of interest to determine whether the two instruments yield comparable outcomes. In this connection, Salkind and Schlecter (1982) investigated the feasibility of using the KRISP and the MFFT as analogous measures of cognitive tempo in kindergarten children. The extent of congruity in a child's classification on the two instruments was well in excess of chance, although only 53% of the children were classified identically. Of course, use of a multiple-regression rather than a classification paradigm would very likely bring the two instruments into closer correspondence.

In due course, the comparability of R-I processes in early and later childhood will be better understood as longitudinal-data sets extending across that period become available. A longitudinal study of R-I across a later period of the life span (fifth to eighth grade) has recently been reported by Messer and Brodzinsky (1981). The major significant outcome of that work is the indication that the construct of R-I seems to have integrity as an individual-differences variable up through the age of at least 14 years. The transition from the late preadolescent to the early adolescent period apparently does not severely disrupt the rank ordering of individuals on the R-I dimension. Match-to-sample tasks have also been used with younger and older adults (see Kogan, 1982), but it is not yet clear whether such tasks tap identical psychological processes across the entire lifespan.

Strategies and Task Demands

If one can speak of a new look in R-I research, that label must deservedly be applied to the work of Zelniker and Jeffrey and their associates. A 1976 Society for Research in Child Development Monograph represents the major empirical contribution. A subsequent chapter (Zelniker & Jeffrey (1979) places the empirical work in a broader theoretical context. Unlike the exhaustive, but largely descriptive, Messer (1976) survey, the Zelniker and Jeffrey (1979) essay offers a review deriving from a coherent conceptual position regarding the basis for the distinction between reflective and impulsive functioning. That position stresses information processing differences associated with R-I, reflective children analyzing stimuli into components and consequently excelling on tasks requiring attention to details, impulsive children focusing more on the stimulus as a whole, hence, performing better on tasks requiring a more global analysis.

Zelniker and Jeffrey (1976) offer several illustrations of the foregoing information processing differences. The principal experiment involved the construction of two alternative forms of the MFFT—one containing items demanding detail analysis for efficient solution, the other comprising items emphasizing contour variations that could more readily be solved through global analysis. Children designated reflective or impulsive on the standard MFFT responded to both kinds of items. As expected, reflective children performed better than their impulsive peers on the detail items; a slight nonsignificant difference favoring impulsive children emerged on global items.

Of interest is the basis for the asymmetry in the magnitude of the R-I difference across detail items (a large R advantage) and global items (a small I advantage). Zelniker and Jeffrey (1979) argue that global items do not readily lend themselves to detail analysis, hence forcing reflective children to employ a less favored global strategy. In contrast, detail items can be processed with either a detail or global strategy. The impulsive children inappropriately use the latter, thereby enhancing their error rates relative to that of their reflective peers. In short, superior or inferior performance is not attributed to intrinsic characteristics of reflective or impulsive children, but rather to the degree of match between the information processing strategy favored by the child and the nature of the stimulus materials. Given earlier reviews of evidence on R-I (Kogan, 1976a; Messer, 1976) suggestive of the general cognitive superiority of the reflective child, the Zelniker and Jeffrey approach represents a striking departure from earlier formulations.

A logical next question concerns the generalizability of the foregoing effects. Are they confined to MFFT-type items or can R-I differences in strategy use be found in other task contexts? The latter seems to be true. Thus, in a concept-attainment framework (Zelniker & Jeffrey, 1976), reflective children isolated the components of a stimulus and considered one dimension at a time. The impulsive child on the other hand preferred to handle two or more dimensions of the stimulus simultaneously. These have been labeled part-scanning and whole-scanning strategies respectively by Bruner, Goodnow, and Austin (1956). In spite of the strategy difference, however, no R-I effects were found for number of problems actually solved.

Along similar lines (Zelniker, Renan, Sorer, & Shavit, 1977), the strategies employed by reflective and impulsive children in a 20-question game (Mosher & Hornsby, 1966) were examined. The former asked more constraint-seeking (CS) questions than did the latter, who were more likely to ask hypothesis-seeking questions about single stimulus items (HS questions). Of course, CS questions permit the child to eliminate a class of possible answers from further consideration. Much of the literature on the 20-questions procedure has supported the view that the use of CS and HS questions reflect higher and lower levels of cognitive maturity respectively. Zelniker, Renan, Sorer, and Shavit (1977) observed that the proportion of CS questions was significantly greater for the reflectives than for the impulsives drawn from a sample of Israeli second graders. Despite the foregoing difference, however, the mean number of questions to solution in the 20-questions task proved generally unrelated to R-I. If CS questions imply greater efficiency in problem solving, how can one account for the paradoxical findings reported? Zelniker, Renan, Sorer, and Shavit (1977) note that certain kinds of questions may appear to be CS when, in fact, they are not. The child asking "Is it red?" may be focusing on the detail of a specific picture rather than attempting to eliminate or establish a color class. Given the reflective child's penchant for detail, in other words, their CS questions may, in fact, be of a pseudoconstraint character.

Consistent with the Zelniker and Jeffrey (1979)

approaches to R-I is a study by Weiner and Berzonsky (1975). The latter authors compared the performance of reflective and impulsive children in an incidental-learning paradigm. The former children were better than the latter with intentional learning as the criterion of competent performance. The reverse proved to be the case with an incidental-learning criterion. Although Weiner and Berzonsky (1975) attributed the R-I difference to a developmental lag in the impulsives' attention-deployment pattern, one must note that the findings are consistent with R-I differences in detail versus global processing.

Although the evidence in favor of the Zelniker and Jeffrey (1976, 1979) hypothesis is now considerable, a recent study (Loper, Hallahan, & McKinney, 1982) has generated results that are not consistent with it. In that study, children averaging 7½ and 11 years of age (classified as reflective and impulsive) were given the Conceptual Styles Test (Kagan et al., 1963) under spontaneous conditions and under conditions in which either analytic or global hypotheses were reinforced (with candy). Both younger and older children, regardless of their status as reflective or impulsive, generated hypotheses consistent with the nature of the reinforcement. There was no indication of the predicted interaction effect—that is, reflective children profiting more from analytic and impulsive children from global reinforcement. These results are compatible, however, with Kagan's (1976) assertion that the disposition toward analytic or global strategies can be substantially modified under strong incentive conditions. Despite the lack of congruence between the Zelniker and Jeffrey (1976) expectations and the Loper et al. (1982) findings, however, it would be quite premature to abandon the former point of view. Denney (1972) demonstrated the ease with which strategies on the Conceptual Styles Test can be dramatically modified. Conceivably, that instrument does not offer a sufficiently sensitive measure for a test of competing theories in the present domain.

There is now evidence to suggest that the detail processing of reflective children places them at an advantage in Western educational systems. Thus, reflection is associated with concurrent academic achievement (Haskins & McKinney, 1976), although the evidence for the MFFT as a predictor of future achievement is somewhat more mixed (Barrett, 1977). More puzzling, however, are results reported by Bush and Dweck (1975) indicating that reflective children do better than their impulsive peers on response-uncertainty tasks even when these are presented in a format emphasizing speed of response. Under such conditions, one could expect the detail-processing strategies of reflective children to be disrupted, thereby eliminating whatever advantage such children possess when time per item is not limited. Instead, the reflective children were actually faster (completed more items) than their impulsive peers and committed fewer errors. In other words, the reflectives appeared to be converted into fast accurates, suggesting a marked increase in efficiency in Salkind and Wright's (1977) terms.

The Bush and Dweck (1975) outcomes strongly suggest that reflective children exhibit tempo flexibility, whereas impulsive children are locked into a less adaptive style. These conclusions are directly challenged by Barstis and Ford (1977) who examined (in kindergarten and second-grade children) the changes produced on the MFFT itself. When instructions emphasized accuracy (''Find the *right* picture on the *very first guess*'') versus speed (''Choose the right picture *just as fast as you can*''), impulsives were more likely than reflectives to alter their performance in a direction consistent with the instructional sets provided. Second graders as a whole also showed greater adaptive flexibility than did kindergarten children.

Because appropriateness of shifts in the Barstis and Ford (1977) work combined what happens under both accuracy and speed sets, it is difficult to translate their findings into a form that would be relevant for understanding the ease with which reflectives and impulsives can shift to global and detail processing respectively. Further, although the outcomes reported appear to contradict the Bush and Dweck (1975) results, the procedural differences between the two studies render explicit comparisons difficult and force the tentative conclusion that the relation between style and flexibility in the R-I domain is uncertain at the present time.

Whatever the eventual resolution of the foregoing issue, it appears dubious that the distinction between detail and global processing constitutes an exhaustive explanation of R-I phenomena. Other factors clearly contribute to R-I differences, and Zelniker and Jeffrey (1979) have alluded to some of these. Thus, Broadbent (1977) proposes a relation between processing systems and degree of expenditure of effort. Global processing can be accomplished with considerably less effort than can detail processing. In the case of the Bush and Dweck (1975) study, where the tasks—digit-symbol substitution and Raven Progressive Matrices—presumably required detail processing, the reflective children seemed able to mobilize much effort in successfully carrying out the task under speeded

conditions. Indeed, Zelniker and Jeffrey (1979) even offer the possibility that the commitment of effort ''may influence the strategy that the individual would be likely to employ'' (p. 292). Kagan (1976) argues along similar lines in pointing to the ''motivation of reflectives to perform well on intellectual tasks, a disposition which leads them to adopt an analytic strategy on difficult problems'' (p. 51). Reflective children may share in the culturally accepted view that an analytic strategy is more effective and elegant. As yet, however, we lack evidence concerning the causal direction of the association between motivation and type of processing.

A further source of R-I differences are metacognitive processes, particularly those concerned with the estimation of task difficulty (e.g., Brown, 1977). Zelniker and Jeffrey (1979) suggest two alternative possibilities. First, impulsives may underestimate task difficulty and, hence, fail to mobilize sufficient effort to perform the task adequately. Second, by virtue of a history of failure, impulsive children may perceive tasks of easy-to-moderate difficulty to be beyond their capacity and, hence, may fail to make the modest expenditure of effort required to solve such tasks. Zelniker and Jeffrey (1979) make no choice between these alternatives, although the weight of the evidence would appear to favor the latter. As indicated earlier, impulsivity is associated with lower levels of academic achievement, suggesting that such children are more likely to experience school failure. Further, personality data described by Block et al. (1974) suggest that impulsive children are fearful and self-doubting in unfamiliar situations and, hence, respond rapidly to escape a setting where feelings of incompetence are prominent.

Let us next consider the training implications of the Zelniker and Jeffrey (1979) position. If one begins with the premise that the strategies—detail versus global—favored by reflective versus impulsive children do not entail differential value, the pedagogical ideal would be one in which optimal instructional environments are created for the two types of children in question. Within the perspective of the ATI model (Cronbach & Snow, 1977) described earlier, reflective children should flourish in educational environments that encourage detail processing, whereas impulsive children should prosper with instructional methods that favor more global types of analysis. This utopian ideal is unfortunately difficult to implement in the absence of guidelines for translating from the microprocess level of task strategies to the macroprocess level of matching instructional styles and curricular materials. One can also question the desirability of such a step if, in fact, global strategies have the kinds of motivational and metacognitive implications discussed earlier. From a pragmatic standpoint, it would appear to make sense to enhance the flexibility of the impulsive child by fostering greater competence in the use of detail-processing strategies. As Zelniker and Jeffrey (1976) noted, reflective children seem able to switch over to global processing when the task clearly calls for it, even though such a strategy is not generally favored.

It is not feasible in the present chapter to offer a review of all of the modification studies, the large majority of which have been discussed by Messer (1976). Instead, such research studies will be cited here as they bear on issues raised in the present discussion. The accumulated evidence indicates that conceptual tempo can be modified through delay, feedback, verbal instruction, visual-scanning training, and modeling (e.g., Debus, 1970; Egeland, 1974; Meichenbaum & Goodman, 1971; Ridberg, Parke, & Hetherington, 1971; Zelniker, Cochavi, & Yered, 1974). In the earlier studies, latencies were increased but error rates remained unchanged. Where the stress in the training procedure focuses on accuracy, however, whether through scanning techniques (Egeland, 1974), detailed verbal-analytic explanation (Zelniker et al., 1974), or training children to talk to themselves as a means of control (Meichenbaum & Goodman, 1971), error rates have been successfully modified. It has proven exceedingly difficult, however, to reduce impulsive children's error rate to the level manifested by reflective children in the standard MFFT administration. Further, we have little information on the long-term staying power of such modification efforts.

If the detail processing of reflectives implies attentional focusing on the distinctive features of stimuli, an observation reported by Odom, McIntyre, and Neale (1971) a number of years ago and confirmed more recently by Hartley (1976) and Cairns (1978), training efforts that increase the salience of distinctive features should reduce the MFFT error rate of impulsive children. To facilitate such a goal, Zelniker, Jeffrey, Ault, and Parsons (1972) devised a differentiation training procedure. This required that the child find the variant in an array that is *different* from the standard. All other variants were identical to the standard. Such a display obviously forces the child to continue scanning until a nonmatching feature is detected. In the standard MFFT, a child can readily declare an incorrect variant to be the "same" as the standard because of failure to scan all relevant features. Differentiation training proved more effective than direct training on the

MFFT in facilitating a reduction in the error rates of impulsive children on a subsequent posttest MFFT. The effectiveness of differentiation training can be traced to its dual properties. Such training not only induces impulsive children to pay particular attention to distinctive features but it also forces such children into expending greater effort in attentional scanning. The relative contribution of each of these factors to the subsequent improved MFFT performance cannot be readily gauged.

There appears to be little doubt, then, that impulsive children can be trained to adopt a processing strategy resembling that of the reflective child. There is still much doubt, however, as to whether impulsive children can be trained to the point where they are indistinguishable from reflective children. Little effort has been made to promote a more global processing strategy in reflectives. As discussed earlier, the fact that reflective children do not appear to be disadvantaged on global-type problems would appear to render such training superfluous. Conceivably, if some advantage to global processing could be demonstrated outside of the immediate match-to-sample context, more active training efforts along such lines would commence.

Overview

It should be apparent from the foregoing review that R-I research has proceeded on a number of different fronts, often with little effort at seeking connections. Psychometrically oriented investigators have focused their energies on the primary assessment instrument—the MFFT. We have been made acutely aware of that test's deficiencies, and diverse improvements have been proposed, ranging from alternative methods for analysis of MFFT-type data to the construction of a new MFFT with highly desirable psychometric properties. Such methodological improvements in the assessment and design of research in the area of conceptual tempo deserve our close attention. Regrettably, however, methodological advances often come too late for their full force to be felt. Methodological critiques did not begin to appear in print until more than 10 years had passed since the initial publication on conceptual tempo (Kagan et al., 1964). With a lag of that nature (no doubt found in other areas of psychology as well), the direction of research in a field has been set and recommendations for methodological change meet with nods of approval but with little effort toward implementation. There is good reason to believe that the apex of basic research on conceptual tempo was reached some time ago, if incidence of publication is a reliable guide. This suggests that the various methodological advances of the past few years will have their most pronounced effect on applied R-I research. Such work continues to appear regularly in a diversity of educational and learning-disability journals.

As in the case of FDI, no attempt has been made to encompass all of the current R-I research in the present review. Applied research on various kinds of handicapped children is clearly beyond the scope of the present discussion. For those readers interested in such special populations, R-I studies have been carried out with mentally retarded and learning-disabled children (e.g., Cullinan, Epstein, Lloyd, & Noel, 1980; Rotatori, Cullinan, Epstein, & Lloyd, 1978; Tarver & Maggiore, 1979), with deaf children (e.g., R. I. Harris, 1978), and with emotionally disturbed children (e.g., Finch & Montgomery, 1973; Montgomery & Finch, 1975). Research on the link between R-I and reading achievement has been reviewed by Kogan (1980b). In contrast to the abundant cross-cultural research on FDI, there is but a single published study (Salkind et al., 1978) based on cross-cultural data. Japanese children exhibit a high degree of precocity, manifesting patterns of R-I performance two years earlier than they emerge in American and Israeli children. Salkind et al. (1978) suggest that the iconic nature of the Japanese language renders it similar to an MFFT-like task, in contrast to the dissimilarity between the latter and the phonetic English and Hebrew languages.

The present review of R-I research has emphasized the Zelniker and Jeffrey (1979) approach to the topic, given its theoretical coherence and empirical support. These authors strongly favor a value-neutral stance in which impulsive children do not necessarily employ a *deficient* information processing strategy but one that is merely *different* from the strategy favored by reflective children. This view is an appealing one, but it would be premature to claim complete validity for it in the light of some of the data described earlier. There is little doubt that the issue of whether R-I is value free or value laden will serve as a focus of controversy for quite some time to come. It will be recalled that Block et al. (1974) offered a strong case for the maladaptive value of particular R-I strategies in preschoolers. Given the longitudinal commitment intrinsic to the work of those authors, future data sets might serve to keep the R-I area in ferment for some time to come.

A PIAGETIAN PERSPECTIVE

To this point, the present chapter has succeeded in discussing developmentally relevant research on creativity, metaphor, and cognitive styles without touching on the theoretical tradition that has dominated the cognitive developmental area for more than three decades. The work of Jean Piaget essentially ignored the issue of individual differences and impinged on the topics of creativity, metaphor, and cognitive styles in a relatively tangential way. This has not stopped developmentalists concerned with these topics from employing the Piagetian system as a point of departure for new theoretical formulations and related research. These extrapolations from Piaget have taken diverse forms that have varied with the topic at issue. In the creativity domain, as we will presently see, there has been much theoretical speculation as to how one might reconcile the universal stages postulated by Piaget with the atypicality or uniqueness implied by the creativity construct. In addition, research has been carried out in search of a creative stage beyond formal operations. In the metaphor domain, relevant research has been limited in extent and has focused on the Piagetian operations that constitute prerequisites for particular metaphoric competencies. It is within the cognitive-style domain that the linkage to Piagetian thought structures have been pursued most vigorously and diversely. Given the presence of individual difference in the rate at which Piagetian stages emerge and in the fact that numerous individuals apparently do not attain formal operations, the question of the basis for such variation has been posed; one of the answers has focused on the role of cognitive styles. Much of this work has been directed toward the competence/performance issue (Flavell & Wohlwill, 1969), particularly the individual-difference factors that might account for decrements in performance relative to the child's expected level of competence. These issues and related illustrative research receive extended treatment later.

Creativity

One of the criticisms that has been leveled against Piagetian stage theory is its unilinear character. This theme has been taken up by dialectical psychologists, especially Riegel (e.g., 1973), who view the unilinear approach as one that stifles individuality and creativity. Dialectical operations are proposed as an antidote to account for both inter-variability and intravariability among children, adolescents, and adults. Riegel's (1973) proposals bear some similarity to those earlier put forth by Werner (1957), which are discussed at length in Kagan and Kogan (1970). The Wernerian stance is multilinear, allowing for both movement across stages and for greater differentiation within stages across the developmental spectrum. In Riegel's (1973) view, the process goes a step further, with dialectic operations representing a final period of cognitive development. There is a lack of explicitness regarding the meaning of dialectical operations in a developmental context. The general thrust of the argument seems to be that the availability of more than one developmental period can create dialectical conflicts and contradictions, and these represent a fundamental property of thought. In fact, "the individual accepts these contradictions as a basic property of thought and creativity" (Riegel, 1973, p. 366).

The dialectical approach is consistent with empirical data in some of its aspects, but other parts of the theory have not yet been put to the test. In its stress on the availability of multiple stage operations in children and adults, there is an abundance of evidence to support a dialectical approach, although none of the relevant research was explicitly guided by such an approach. For example, a review of the work on styles of categorization and conceptualization clearly indicated that "early styles do not drop out of the child's repertoire but continuously re-emerge in more complex and sophisticated forms over the life span" (Kogan, 1976a, p. 125). The more complex aspect—asserting that multilinear or dialectical operations allow for the expression of creativity—may conceivably bear some relation to empirical reality, but no evidence to support such a view has yet been put forth. Indeed, the vagueness surrounding this issue in the theory as stated hinders the possibility of conducting relevant empirical tests.

A second speculative effort to link Piagetian theory and creativity has recently been advanced in a volume by Feldman (1980). The general thrust of the approach is that analogous processes account for the child's transition to higher Piagetian stages and for the reorganization of a thought structure in creative problem solving. Although the processes are presumed to be similar and related to Piaget's (1977) ideas about disequilibration during developmental transitions, the products are, of course, quite different in the two cases. Concrete operations represent an almost universal achievement, whereas creativity obviously entails the generation of ideas or products that are original from the observer's perspective. The attainment of concrete operations by a specific child represents a unique and profound achievement relative to a prior mode of thought for that child, but creativity in scientific usage has not employed such an intraindividual criterion.

In an "Afterword" to the Feldman (1980) book, H. Gruber has noted other distinctions between Piagetian stage transitions and genuine creativity. The latter has a purposeful quality that the former lacks. Further, in Gruber's view, developmental changes in the Piagetian framework bring about greater cognitive similarities between children, whereas creativity involves notions of rarity and distinctiveness. Despite these differences, one must credit Feldman (1980) for providing a stimulating metaphor to bridge the gap between the universal and the unique in development. Regrettably, it is likely to remain no more than a metaphor because no guidelines whatever are offered for subjecting the process analogy to empirical research. A more detailed critique has been outlined by Brainerd (1981); Feldman (1981) has offered a rejoinder to this critique.

A third and final approach to linking Piagetian stages and creativity has been advanced by Arlin (1975). Unlike the purely speculative arguments described above, the proposal offered by Arlin is subjected to an empirical test. In brief, Arlin argues that formal operations with their hypothetic-deductive mode of thought do not necessarily represent a final equilibrium or stage of development. Instead, formal operations are alleged to constitute a problem-solving stage that is then followed in some individuals by a problem-finding stage. The latter is presumed to tap the kind of problem or hypothesis generation that frequently is dubbed creative. To qualify as a fifth stage, in Arlin's (1975) view, all problem finders should have mastered formal operations but not all problem solvers should be problem finders—the stage criterion of sequencing.

Problem finding was assessed by asking respondents (college seniors) to generate questions about an array of 12 common objects placed before them. These were scored according to the intellectual-products category of Guilford's (1967) structure-of-intellect model from lowest order (units) to highest order (implications). The expected sequencing of problem solving and problem finding was obtained. Regrettably, a replication (Cropper, Meck, & Ash, 1977) found no evidence whatever for the sequencing required to contemplate a fifth stage. Apart from the lack of empirical consistency, however, one can criticize the Arlin (1975) work on a number of grounds. From a Piagetian perspective, Fakouri (1976) argues that problem solving and problem finding vary in content, not structure, hence implying a quantitative rather than a qualitative distinction. A more trenchant criticism is that processes akin to problem finding in the form of play behavior and divergent thinking are found in children as young as nursery school age. It is quite likely, then, that formal operations and creativity (as conceptualized in the present chapter) represent independent processes.

Metaphor

The area of metaphor has been brought into correspondence with Piagetian operations in a speculative essay by Gallagher (1978). Thus, the transfer of meaning from a better known vehicle to a lesser known topic that is characteristic of most good metaphors is considered analogous in many respects to the assimilation concept (Piaget, 1971)—that is, "The stress on qualitative restructuring of the known through the incorporation of the unknown to arrive at a new level of understanding" (Gallagher, 1978, p. 88). Elsewhere in the essay, it is proposed that the interaction between the topic and vehicle of a metaphor "is analogous to the coordination of likenesses and differences" described in Piaget's (1977) treatment of the equilibration concept (Gallagher, 1978, p. 89). These alleged correspondences represent a metaphor in their own right, but (as in the case of the Feldman, 1980, treatise on creativity discussed earlier) there is no apparent way to establish the empirical truth or falsity of the alleged similarities. Unlike the case of creativity, however, the metaphor area has witnessed at least two attempts to explore the linkage between *specific* Piagetian operations (Inhelder & Piaget, 1958, 1964) and comprehension of metaphor. In the studies described below, Piagetian operations have been examined as possible cognitive prerequisites for metaphoric thinking.

Consider first the research of Billow (1975). That author distinguishes between simpler similarity metaphors (e.g., "hair is spaghetti") and more complex metaphors that have the character of analogies with missing terms (e.g., "spring is a lady in a new coat"). It was expected that the possession of concrete operations (as reflected in competence at class inclusion) would insure understanding of similarity metaphors, whereas formal operations (as assessed by a combinatorial reasoning task) would be required to grasp the meaning of analogical metaphors. For children in the age range of 5 to 7, comprehension of similarity metaphors and the class-inclusion index were significantly correlated (with age and IQ statistically controlled). On the other hand, there was no indication whatever that success at class inclusion (concrete operations) was necessary to interpret the similarity metaphors. In regard to formal operations and analogical metaphors, a significant correlation (IQ and age held constant)

was obtained in 9- to 13-year-olds. However, the evidence is far from clear that formal operations, as indexed by combinatorial reasoning, constitute a logical prerequisite for the comprehension of analogical metaphors. The data were not analyzed so as to offer a direct resolution of the issue. It can be argued, of course, that class inclusion and combinatorial reasoning represented a poor choice of concrete and formal operational tasks respectively in the context of research on metaphor. Regrettably, Billow (1975) does not offer a strong case for process comparability across the metaphor and Piagetian tasks employed in his research.

A second attempt to link metaphoric comprehension and Piagetian operations is reported by Cometa and Eson (1978). Those authors fault Billow (1975) for choosing inappropriate Piagetian tasks as possible precursors of metaphoric comprehension and for employing a verbal criterion as an index of concrete operations. They maintain that metaphoric understanding depends less upon class-inclusion operations than upon what Inhelder and Piaget (1964) have called intersectional classification, that is, constructing an element representing the overlap or co-occurrence of two classes on the basis of a common, shared property. The capacity to solve the Inhelder and Piaget intersection-matrix tasks occurs toward the latter part of the concrete-operational stage. Cometa and Eson (1978) argue that children would have to achieve the foregoing skill before they are able to *explicate* metaphoric meaning. In the earlier phase of concrete operations, the child's skill at intersectional classification would not be fully operational, and as a consequence, children at that level, according to the foregoing authors, would be able to *paraphrase*, but not explicate, metaphors.

Middle-class children from grades K, 1, 3, 4, and 8 were classified as preoperational, concrete operational, intersectional, or formal operational on the basis of their performance on tasks of conservation of amount, intersection matrices, and the Inhelder and Piaget (1958) combination-of-chemicals task. Results were quite consistent with the Cometa and Eson hypotheses. Preoperational children could not paraphrase; concrete-operational children could not explicate, but some of these children could paraphrase; intersectional children could paraphrase, and the majority could explicate; formal operational children could explicate, but the performance increment relative to the intersectional children was small. The findings as a whole lend support to the view that paraphrase and explication represent separate stages of metaphoric comprehension (see also Winner, Rosenstiel, & Gardner, 1976). It would also appear that formal operations are not a prerequisite for metaphoric explication. Instead, metaphoric explication seems almost fully operational by the time the child has mastered intersectional class structures.

The Cometa and Eson (1978) research represents a sophisticated blending of a Piagetian stage approach and metaphoric operations in the linguistic domain. In response to the argument that exposure to adult language might account for differences in metaphoric comprehension, the foregoing authors note that the preoperational and concrete-operational children were virtually identical in age, IQ, and SES background. At the same time, there seems to be little question that explication requires a more elaborated linguistic statement than does paraphrase; hence, it is difficult to discount the possibility that the child's developing linguistic skills facilitate the leap from paraphrase to explication. That intersectional classification represents a logical precondition rather than a correlate of metaphoric explication has not been conclusively established. On the other hand, the evidence is quite strong that formal operations are not a prerequisite for metaphoric comprehension.

Cognitive Styles

It is in the cognitive-style domain that the interface between Piagetian operations and individual differences has been pursued most vigorously. As indicated earlier, much of the relevant research has sought to account for performance deficiencies under conditions where competence is expected. Although much attention has focused on interfering task factors, there has also been a growing interest in cognitive-style differences as a possible contributor to the nonuniversal incidence or delay in emergence of formal operations. Other research has focused on spatial egocentrism and concepts of horizontality and verticality. The two cognitive-style dimensions that have played a dominant role are those reviewed earlier—FDI and R-I.

Formal Operations

The first relevant study on this topic (Saarni, 1973) proved quite unpromising. No relation between Piagetian level (concrete operational, transitional, and formal operational) and FDI (RFT) was found for 11- to 15-year-old boys, whereas formal operational girls of that age performed significantly more poorly on the RFT than did their concrete operational and transitional same-sex peers.

Subsequent work has yielded a consistent effect indicating that FI adolescents are at a distinct advantage on formal-operational tasks. Lawson (1976) administered the bending-rods and balance-beam tasks (Inhelder & Piaget, 1958) and the RFT to a sample of sixth-grade boys and girls averaging about 11½ years of age. Correlations between the two formal-operational procedures and the RFT were sufficiently high—.81 and .77 respectively—for Lawson to conclude "that a degree of field independence is required for the development of formal stage reasoning" (1976, p. 982). Such an inference is not warranted, of course, on the basis of correlation evidence alone. In possibly the most exhaustive study of the topic, Neimark (1975) found relationships between both FDI (EFT) and R-I (MFFT) on the one hand and a variety of indices derived from formal-operational and related tasks on the other hand in samples of children in the third through sixth grades. Further, EFT and MFFT appear to tap somewhat different aspects of performance in the formal-operational domain, suggesting that the cognitive-style effects are additive. Expanding upon these outcomes, Neimark (1975) argues for common task elements across the cognitive-style and formal-operational procedures. Thus, the withholding of a response until information is properly evaluated (a reflective approach) should contribute to problem solving on Piagetian tasks. Similarly, the analytic attitude of the FI subject—the separation of critical from irrelevant salient information—should also function to enhance performance in the formal-operational area.

More recent work described by Stone and Day (1980) lends further weight to the role of FDI in formal-operational thought. Children and adolescents (9 to 14 years of age) were given two successive presentations of the Inhelder and Piaget (1958) bending-rods task. Between these presentations, a "minimally directive means of eliciting the control-of-variables strategy was presented" (Stone & Day, 1980, p. 342). Children were divided into three groups—spontaneous deployers (successful on the initial presentation), latent deployers (successful on the second presentation), and nonusers who were unable to deploy an appropriate strategy. Of three individual-difference variables employed—measures of short-term memory, selective attention, and FDI (assessed with the Wechsler Intelligence Scale for Children [WISC] block-design test)—only FDI effectively discriminated between the spontaneous and latent deployers. The latter were more FD and, hence, apparently required the additional bit of structuring provided by the experimental prompt before the control-of-variables strategy could become accessible. Such an outcome points, of course, to possible interactions between cognitive-style and instructional or other task factors as an influence on performance in the formal-operations domain.

In support of such an interactional position consider a study by Linn (1978). That author required her subjects (seventh and ninth graders) to use the separation-of-variables schema described by Inhelder and Piaget (1958). Two tasks were employed (both involving spheres rolling down a ramp), but in one case conflicting information was introduced and in the other case not. In the latter instance, no performance differences were found between FD and FI adolescents. Where conflicting information was present, however, the performance of FDs dropped to near-zero levels, whereas the performance of FIs remained fairly stable. It is apparent from these results that a cognitive style can influence some aspects of formal thinking more than others. This conclusion is further reinforced in the work of Huteau and Rajchenbach (1978), who observed that FDI differentiates performance only for those Piagetian tasks that require the overcoming of an embedded figurative context. Hence, FDI was related to volume conservation but not to permutations in 14-year-old boys. At an earlier age (7 years), FDI related to liquid conservation but not to seriation. Neimark's (1975) views regarding common elements or features across Piagetian and cognitive-style tasks are, thus, further reinforced.

An alternative approach to the examination of formal operations/cognitive-style relationships derives from the psychometric study of abilities and is best illustrated by the research of Linn and Swiney (1981). Those authors raise the question of how much of the variance in performance on formal-reasoning tasks can be assimilated to factors of ability and cognitive style. The research was based on high school seniors of relatively high ability. A formal reasoning composite (combining controlling, analyzing, naming, and proportional reasoning) yielded a reliability coefficient of .63. Of this reliable variance, 49% was accounted for by the combination of Gc (crystalized ability), Gfv (fluid visualization ability, which loaded FDI restructuring tasks) and Ff (familiar field, which loaded the RFT). An additional 12% of reliable variance was attributed to physics knowledge. Given the selective nature of the sample employed, it is not surprising that Gc was the most powerful predictor of formal reasoning because, as Horn and Cattell (1966) have shown, Gc involves the retrieval of well-learned information from memory. The lesser predictive power of the FDI-relevant factors in the present context suggests that inferring new relationships in the formal-reasoning tasks was of lesser importance than the application of available strategies. Of the two FDI-relevant factors, Gfv and Ff, the former was the stronger predictor, suggesting that the restructuring component of FDI has more to do with formal reasoning than do the processes tapped by the RFT. On the whole, it is evident that formal reasoning is not a unique cognitive dimension but rather overlaps substantially with specific abilities and cognitive styles. Although the Linn and Swiney (1981) work is not developmental in emphasis, its replication in younger and less selective samples could conceivably yield highly informative data regarding the stable or changing import of abilities and styles in formal reasoning across the adolescent years.

Perception of Horizontality and Verticality

The development of a euclidean spatial system was examined by Piaget and Inhelder (1956) who administered various tasks to assess the child's concepts of horizontality and verticality. The former was examined by asking children to anticipate the position of liquid in tipped bottles; the latter was studied, for example, by asking children to place straight objects on the sides of hills. Although Piaget and Inhelder (1956) asserted that a euclidean system of spatial coordinates is typically established by early childhood, later research has shown that college students are often unsuccessful at water-level tasks (e.g., Thomas & Jamison, 1975; Willemsen & Reynolds, 1973). These studies as well as others conducted with children (Liben, 1974, 1975) have also pointed to strong sex differences favoring males.

Of particular interest in the present context is research by Liben (1978) with high school seniors relating concepts of horizontality and verticality to FDI assessed with the EFT. The relevant correlations were statistically significant for both concepts in both boys and girls. Further, these correlations remained significant when spatial ability (assessed with the Guilford-Zimmerman Test of Spatial Orientation) was held constant. Hence, it is clearly disembedding skill rather than spatial aptitude as such that relates to performance on Piagetian spatial tasks. The latter would seem to require the ability to disembed the water line or a plumb line from the surrounding field, hence contributing to the observed relations with FDI. Sex differences on the Piagetian tasks were again found, including a difference in the magnitude of the correlation between the horizontality and verticality tasks—highly significant in males, low and nonsignificant in females. Liben

(1978) speculates about the sex difference in both performance and competence terms and leans toward the latter on the grounds that training the horizontality concept had little effect on performance. Hence, she concludes that females' difficulties may well reflect the lack of an integrated system of spatial reference.

Spatial Perspective Taking

With the present topic, we leave the domain of adolescent thinking and return to the thought of the child. According to Piaget and Inhelder (1956), young children exhibit spatial egocentrism in the sense of a failure to distinguish between the perspective of self and other. With growth, the coordination of perspectives improves and is presumed to be firmly established by 9 to 10 years of age. In a recent paper, Brodzinsky (1980) has raised the possibility that distinctive styles of information processing may influence the rate at which various operational competencies are attained. Such styles would presumably have little influence before these competencies have begun to develop and after they have been fully consolidated. In other words, cognitive styles, in Brodzinsky's (1980) view, are most influential during transitional phases of development. To test this hypothesis, that author employed the MFFT as an index of R-I and two multiple-object farm scenes as spatial-perspective tasks. In the latter, children had to represent the perspectives of another observer (a small doll) placed at 45° increments around the scene. Children who were 4, 6, 8, and 10 were divided into reflectives and impulsives on the basis of median splits for errors and latencies. Consistent with expectations, cognitive-style effects were observed only in 6- and 8-year-olds, reflective children exceeding their impulsive peers in perspective-taking performance. Further, the kinds of errors varied, impulsives more likely to make egocentric errors and reflectives more inclined toward adjacent errors. Some ambiguity of interpretation remains, for as Brodzinsky (1980) notes, reflectives may be more developmentally advanced than impulsives (the competence view) or reflectives may be better able to deploy their operational skills (the performance view). Similar ambiguity surrounds the research of Finley, Solla, and Cowan (1977), who reported that the perspective-taking performance of second-grade FI children significantly exceeded that of their FD age peers.

In an effort to explore possible causal linkages between cognitive style and perspective taking, the children employed in the Brodzinsky (1980) study were reexamined after a two-year interval on both the MFFT and perspective-taking measures (Brodzinsky, 1982). Through the use of structural equation models (Jöreskog & Sörbom, 1976), it is possible to make *tentative* inferences as to whether cognitive-style or operational-thought variables have cause or effect status in respect to one another. Promising results were obtained over the 6- to 8-year-old age range. Application of the causal model indicated that the direction of effects seemed to flow from R-I level at age 6 to perspective-taking performance at age 8—as opposed to the contrary direction. One is, thus, tempted to conclude that style of information processing affects the rate of emergence of operativity—spatial perspective taking in the present case.

Despite the provocative quality of the foregoing findings, Brodzinsky (1982) has judiciously offered several cautions. The inference of unidirectional causation is undermined by the possibility that other unobserved variables are ultimately responsible for the observed outcomes. A proposed alternative to causal modeling of longitudinal data would involve a training paradigm in which children's reflectivity or operativity are experimentally enhanced and the effects on the nontrained variable noted. One would obviously have to take special care in such studies to insure that any immediate experimental effects have some degree of staying power. Brodzinsky (1982) has also acknowledged that longitudinal data do not provide an answer to the competence-performance issue, namely, "are reflective children more intelligent or developmentally precocious, or does their information processing style simply allow for easier access to existing knowledge" (p. 625). This points to a limitation in the sense that cognitive-style information may sometimes account for considerable variance in operativity levels during transitional periods of development but may nevertheless be unable to explain the actual cognitive processes responsible for the individual differences in operativity.

Conservation

In one of the very few studies devoted to the topic, Barstis and Ford (1977) have raised the possibility that R-I might be relevant to perceptual centration effects (see also Grant, 1976). If impulsive children, for example, are dominated by immediate perceptions and, hence, are unable to decenter, one might well expect such children to have difficulty in suppressing the salient perceptual stimuli present in tasks of conservation. In second-grade children, R-I had no impact on conservation performance (number and amount), largely reflecting the fact that the large majority of those children were classified as fully conserving. In the case of the kindergarten children on the other hand, 80% of the reflectives were conserving or in a transition phase, whereas 75% of the impulsives were classified as nonconserving. Further, mean latencies on the conservation tasks were significantly longer for reflective kindergartners. Despite this strong association between R-I and conservation, however, it is not possible, as Barstis and Ford (1977) note, to consider reflection as a prerequisite for conservation in the presence of a minority of impulsive children who were classified as conserving. Nevertheless, there is little doubt that reflective children are at an advantage on conservation tasks because a slow and deliberate information processing style appears to be consistent with the strategy required to do well in the conservation domain.

In a similar vein, Brodzinsky (1982) observed that impulsivity was negatively related to both mass and weight conservation. Further, impulsivity at age 6 was negatively related to weight conservation at age 8, pointing to *possible* causal directionality. Of further significance is the indication that the latency component of MFFT performance proved more prognostic of conservation ability than did the error component. This finding tends to support the Zelniker and Jeffrey (1976, 1979) argument concerning the strategic significance of latencies in response-uncertainty tasks. It would appear that the conservation task is one that rewards a slow and deliberate perceptual-analytic strategy, precisely the type of strategy that reflective children favor. Because FI children would also be expected to favor such a strategy, one is not surprised by evidence indicating that these children (relative to their FD peers) are more likely to conserve liquid and weight (Finley et al., 1977) and length and volume (Hill, 1980). The latter study also found that the FDI-conservation association was stronger in younger (6½- to 7½-year-olds) than in older children (8- to 11-year olds). Of further interest is evidence indicating that the foregoing association disappears for 5- to 8-year-olds after their exposure to conservation training (Case, 1977). Apparently, in the view of that author, FD children are taught the inadequacy of perceptually global strategies during the course of training, thereby disrupting the "natural" FDI-conservation relationship.

Theoretical Contributions

As we have just seen, a small band of investigators has been making a concerted effort to articulate cognitive-style variables with Piagetian thought structures. In addition to the empirical work reviewed, theoretical essays have begun to appear that echo this integrative theme (e.g., Neimark, 1979, 1981; Overton & Newman, 1982; Sigel & Brodzinsky, 1977; Stone & Day, 1980). It should be noted that some of these essays extend well beyond the topic of cognitive styles to deal with the broader issue of competence vis-à-vis activation/utilization. It is important to note that cognitive styles represent but a single class of variables impinging upon the general theme of the competence/performance contrast. Lack of exclusivity, of course, does not necessarily imply lack of importance.

The role of cognitive styles (in particular FDI) in cognitive development receives considerable emphasis in what may well be the most comprehensive (and possibly the most inaccessible) of the theories designed to articulate the Piagetian structural approach with individual and task variation in performance. This theory has been advanced by Pascual-Leone (e.g., Pascual-Leone, 1976, 1980) in prose that can best be described as formidable. The interested reader approaching the theory for the first time might find it helpful to consult such secondary sources as Case (1974) and Chapman (1981). I have leaned quite heavily on those sources in the following exceedingly brief description.

Note first that there are two broad distinctions within the theory—that part that describes all directed thinking and that part that deals with developmental and individual variation. The first part describes the three kinds of schemes that constitute the basic units of thought—the figurative and operative schemes described by Piaget (e.g., 1970) and the executive schemes reminiscent of the construct of plans in Miller, Galanter, and Pribram (1960). The executive scheme is presumed to determine the particular figurative and operative schemes activated in problem situations. In this first part of the Pascual-Leone theory, consideration is also given to the manner in which new schemes are acquired and to the specific processes by which these schemes are engaged in goal-directed activity.

The second part of the theory—the part of most immediate interest for our purposes—concerns both cross-age and within-age differences in scheme repertoires, activation, and utilization. A crucial concept is the notion of M-power (also sometimes labeled M-capacity or M-space)—the maximum number of schemes that the individual is able to activate at any single time. The currently favored instrument for the assessment of M-power is a test of backward digit span (Case, 1972). This M-power is presumed to increase linearly with age from the early preoperational to the late formal-operational period (approximately ages 3–4 to 15–16). Hence, problem-solving performance will depend on the match between the child's M-power and the M-demand of the task. Within age, variation in performance is attributed to the extent to which subjects utilize the full M-power at their disposal, and the relative weight assigned cues from the perceptual field as opposed to task instructions or other sources. The individual differences for the foregoing two components are presumed to be highly correlated and explanatory of the FDI cognitive style. In other words, FD individuals are presumed to expend less mental effort and, hence, are unlikely to break down gestalts into their elements. Further, they are more likely to give disproportionate weight to perceptually salient but misleading cues. By contrast, FI individuals are expected to utilize most of their M-power and to give minimal weight to misleading salient cues.

Although the Pascual-Leone theory was formulated more than a decade ago, the number of direct empirical tests of the FDI component of the theory (in the published literature) is quite small. Case and Globerson (1974) examined correlations between FDI indices and independent measures of M-power in 7- to 8-year-old children. Moderate but significant correlations were obtained. In a related study, Case (1974) offered highly specific predictions as to how FI and FD children would perform on Piagetian formal-operational tasks. These predictions (deriving from Pascual-Leone's M-power construct) were quite discrepant from those flowing from a strictly Piagetian perspective. Thus, the majority of FI 7- to 8-year-olds were able to solve formal-operational problems (bending rods and spinning wheels), a minority of FD 7- to 8-year-olds were capable of such solutions, and virtually no FI 5- to 6-year-olds were capable of solving the problems. Case (1974) demonstrates how the control-of-variables scheme can be acquired by means of concrete operations and shows how M-power (relative to M-demand of the task) can explain age and FI-FD differences. In a subsequent study, Case (1975) examined the M-power and FDI dimensions in children varying in social class and essentially found no relationships of consequence.

Although other empirical tests of the Pascual-Leone theory are available in the published literature, none have specifically incorporated the FDI dimension in the designs employed. Where FDI has been used, its function has been that of a control variable. A study of combinatorial reasoning in children 9 to 15 years of age (Scardamalia, 1977) deliberately used subjects one standard deviation above the mean on the WISC block-design index of FDI to guarantee that only those children and adolescents making full use of their M-power would participate in the research. Highly impulsive subjects on the MFFT were also excluded, although the theoretical basis for doing so is less clear. Hence, although FDI is acknowledged as a source of variance in performance on Piagetian tasks, recent research in the Pascual-Leone tradition has not directly examined its effects. Instead, emphasis has been placed on the M-power construct as such, as opposed to factors that affect the utilization of M-power.

Overview

This discussion demonstrates that creativity, metaphor, and cognitive style do not represent an esoteric set of constructs far removed from the mainstream of cognitive developmental research. To the degree that the Piagetian tradition and its derivatives represent a current dominant force in the field, one must acknowledge that the topics treated in this chapter represent a rivulet feeding into the mainstream. As we have seen, each of the major topics articulates with the Piagetian corpus in distinctive ways. In the case of creativity, the linkage has not advanced much beyond the kind of theoretical speculation that resists empirical attack, although one must acknowledge the abortive effort to establish a fifth problem-finding stage beyond formal operations. It is possible that the Piagetian neglect of the creativity issue reflects a failure to consider a stage of dialectic operations. It is also possible that there are analogies between Piagetian stage transitions and a creative breakthrough for the child experiencing these changes. In neither of the above cases, however, does one know how to graft an empirical handle onto the speculative propositions offered.

In the metaphor area, the bridge to Piagetian theory has taken the form of searching for cognitive prerequisites for the comprehension of metaphor. There have been but two such efforts, one relatively less and the other relatively more successful. The shortcoming of this Piagetian-flavored metaphor research lies in the neglect of possible psycholinguistic influences on the decoding of metaphoric sentences. One possible reason for the dearth of Piagetian-inspired metaphor research is the development of a stagelike model for metaphoric operations in their own right (Winner et al., 1976). In this latter respect, the Piagetian tradition has had an impact, both direct and indirect, on the developmental study of metaphor.

It is in the domain of cognitive styles that the integration of individual differences and Piagetian operativity constructs has flowered. The distinction between competence and performance is clearly one of the most important (as well as controversial) issues in the cognitive-developmental area, and a small group of investigators has tried to show that research on cognitive styles can make a contribution to a better understanding of the distinction. Departing from the dominant approach of seeking task factors accounting for the competence/performance distinction, the foregoing investigators focused their efforts on possible organismic determinants and opted for cognitive styles as potentially most likely to account for individual variation on diverse measures of operational thought. On the basis of the research reviewed earlier, one would have to conclude that the effort has been a striking success. Whether employing a developmental or psychometric approach or whether guided by intuitive hunches or a highly formalized model with quantitative parameters, the overall pattern of results clearly demonstrates that cognitive styles (FDI and R-I) have a major effect on performance in both the concrete-operational and formal-operational domains. These effects are not always across the board, so to speak, but are often moderated by task factors. As might be expected, the effects are strongest when the operational-thought and cognitive-style indices share task features in common. It has also been demonstrated that cognitive style-operational thought linkages are most evident during transitional periods before operational thought structures are fully consolidated. One of the more provocative suggestions is that cognitive styles may have a causal influence on the developmental rate for operative thought structures, but there are presently too many methodological unknowns to draw any firm conclusions about causal directionality. In sum, there is good reason to believe that cognitive styles remain alive, well, and actively engaged in the search for moderators of competence.

CONCLUSIONS

Three broad topic areas, each with its own distinctive history, have been brought together in the present chapter. As Vernon (1973) has shown, intellectual precursors of cognitive styles flourished in German typological theories of the 1920s and early 1930s. One of the intellectual roots of metaphor and figurative-language research also is of German origin—Gestalt psychology in the present instance—but as Honeck (1980) has indicated, other influences deriving from philosophy, rhetoric, linguistics, and neobehavioristic psychology were also at work. Finally, the creativity domain is distinctively American in derivation, particularly that aspect emerging from Guilford's (1950) initial formulation of the divergent-thinking abilities.

The Role of IQ and Mental Age (MA)

The confluence of the three domains in the present chapter, despite their divergent historical roots, reflects more than an idiosyncratic selection on the part of this author. Possibly the most striking feature linking the three domains is their emphasis on the examination of cognitive achievements and processes that have not typically been included under the rubric of intelligence or intellectual development. This is not to imply, of course, that the forms of thinking comprising what we commonly consider intelligence are independent of the core constructs under review in this chapter. One can choose to define intelligence so broadly that all cognitive processes must fall within its net. Guilford (1967) would clearly opt for such inclusiveness. The fact remains, however, that the study of cognitive styles, metaphor, and creativity has maintained a reasonable independence from the intelligence domain, although articulating with it empirically and conceptually. On the one extreme, the FDI dimension has been conceived, even by its founder, as equivalent to a form of analytic intelligence. In this regard, one often finds a particular subtest of a major intelligence scale—block design from the WISC—used as an appropriate index of FDI. At the opposite extreme, as we have seen, much of the energy of researchers in the divergent-thinking area has been devoted to efforts to separate that mode of thinking from the convergent abilities that typically are assessed by intelligence tests.

Within the two extremes outlined above, one finds intelligence data employed in a variety of contexts. Often, one would like to determine the relative contribution of stylistic and ability variance to a particular behavioral outcome. Partial- and multiple-correlation techniques are customarily employed to address such questions. In another context, intelligence information can shed light on the meaning of different stylistic components, for example, latency and error scores from the MFFT measure of R-I. Although no published evidence is available as yet, the development of causal models for longitudinal data should eventually lead investigators to raise the issue of the casual priority of stylistic and ability indicators. It is entirely feasible that a child's style may affect his or her performance on an IQ test rather than the other way around. We are accustomed to think of intelligence as more basic and central (possibly as a result of its longer history), but its causal role vis-à-vis stylistic disposition remains an open question.

It is important to recognize that IQ as such is not a developmental construct, although its MA component is of immediate developmental significance. Focus upon this component has led to the formulation of the developmental-lag hypothesis, namely, variation on alleged cognitive-style indicators reflects developmental-level rather than trait variance. Because children become more FI and reflective over time, the notion of lag implies that FD and impulsive children are developmentally less advanced and, therefore, of lower MA (e.g., Achenbach & Weisz, 1975; Weisz, O'Neill, & O'Neill, 1975). Zelniker and Jeffrey (1979) have delivered an effective response to the advocates of the developmental-lag idea. One inference that flows from it is an expected decline in score variability as subjects become older, with the virtual elimination of such variance in a normal-adult sample. Such an inference does not conform to the facts. Further, there is no justification for posing the issue in either/or developmental versus trait terms. For example, FDI declines with age, yet persists as a trait (Witkin, Goodenough, & Karp, 1967). In the case of R-I (examined over the age range from 11 to 14), the evidence tentatively points to trait persistence in the absence of developmental change (Messer & Brodzinsky, 1981). Conceivably, the latter finding reflects the age range studied because evidence at earlier ages reported in Kogan (1976a) is suggestive of both developmental change and trait persistence.

Domain Interrelationships

Ample evidence is now available to suggest that the creativity, metaphor, and cognitive-style domains are not completely independent of each other. Linkages between divergent thinking and metaphor have been described in this chapter and Messer (1976) reported significant associations between FDI and R-I. Kogan (1976a) devoted a chapter to style interrelationships in preschool children.

Despite the foregoing research on connections between stylistic dimensions during childhood and adolescence, little effort has been devoted to combining stylistic variables to achieve better predictions of behavior in given situations. Thus, FI in combination with high divergent thinking may have

quite different behavioral consequences than FI in combination with low divergent thinking. It will be recalled that Neimark (1975) used both FDI and R-I measures in trying to account for individual variation in formal-operational thought and found that these two styles combined additively in the prediction equation. On the whole, however, researchers have barely begun to study the complexities of stylistic combinations and their effects on behavior and experience across the lifespan.

An approach that offers some promise for a better integration of stylistic dimensions has been advanced by Block and Block (1980). A major goal of those authors is to integrate a broad array of cognitive, personality, and behavioral data within a two-dimensional theory of ego control and ego resiliency. The ego-control dimension extends from the polar extremes of undercontrol to overcontrol and has implications for the extent of impulse containment, delay of gratification, vulnerability to distraction, and inhibition of actions and affects. Ego resiliency refers to the degree to which the ego structures are effective in modulating ego-control levels to meet environmental demands. For each of these broad dimensions, an array of experimental tasks, observer Q-sort descriptors, and self-report assessments have been employed in a longitudinal study beginning with children at age 3. The Block and Block (1980) report carries these children through ages 4, 5, and 7, but the work is ongoing, with the subjects now in their midadolescent years.

It is important to note that the research of the Blocks extends well beyond the stylistic dimensions considered in this chapter because their aim is the very broad one of demonstrating concurrent and predictive as well as convergent and discriminant validity for diverse indices of the ego-control and ego-resiliency constructs. The interest in stylistic variables—R-I (Block et al., 1974, 1975), intolerance of ambiguity (Harrington, Block, & Block, 1978), breadth of categorization (Block et al., 1981), and creativity (Harrington et al., 1983)—is to a considerable extent governed by the goal of locating these variables within the two-dimensional space of ego control and ego resiliency. This is a perfectly reasonable goal, of course, that can often help to illuminate the cognitive and affective dynamics underlying stylistic dispositions and strategic choices. At the same time, the Block and Block (1980) approach necessarily implies that any integration of the stylistic dimensions discussed in this chapter would necessarily take place within their particular personality-based framework. Although it is a framework of proven conceptual value, it is important to recognize that other integrative modes may well be possible.

Style Similarities and Contrasts

The four stylistic dimensions reviewed in this chapter share some characteristics and differ on others. Each has spawned a set of assessment devices that meet reasonable reliability criteria, although the R-I domain has been marked by intensive efforts to enhance the reliability of the traditional MFFT instrument. In regard to convergent validity, all four constructs have shown some cross-task generality, particularly where task formats are structurally similar. Thus, divergent-thinking and metaphor tasks exhibit picture versus word generality when response formats remain constant. Also, FDI tasks have yielded a substantial degree of response consistency, although recent theorizing and research have raised the possibility that the EFT and RFT may tap somewhat different facets of the FDI construct.

The issue of discriminant validity in respect to intelligence has been discussed in an earlier subsection. In respect to longitudinal stability, the empirical evidence is supportive of the view that individual rank orders remain relatively constant across the primary through secondary school years for FDI, RI, and, to a lesser extent, for divergent thinking. Longitudinal research has been virtually nonexistent in the metaphor area, except for the observation of six-month stability on the MTT in elementary school children (Kogan et al., 1980).

Evidence for modifiability is present for all four constructs under review. These are not across-the-board effects however. Success rates vary markedly with the particular training procedures employed, and some constructs are fundamentally less difficult to modify than others. In no case has evidence been adduced to support the long-term sticking power of experimental-training outcomes. This latter consideration is of particular importance for a construct, such as FDI, for which genetic and other biological causal explanations have been advanced.

This chapter has not focused on data gathered on infants and preschoolers. Some of the generalizations reported here would cease to hold for children not yet of primary school age. As Kogan (1976a) has shown, different kinds of questions arise in the study of such young populations. Sex differences were found to be widespread during that early period; except for FDI (where much controversy continues), these sex differences appear to be markedly reduced

if not vitiated during the school-age years. The foregoing observation refers exclusively to mean differences, not to correlational pattern differences across the sexes. There is much evidence for the latter in regard to personality-cognition relationships but, despite an interesting speculative model offered by Maccoby (1966) quite some time ago, little empirical follow-through or systematization has taken place.

Possibly, the most striking contrast among the four stylistic constructs under review concerns their theoretical breadth or sweep. At the one extreme, FDI has been viewed as a master construct with implications for virtually all aspects of human functioning. Personality processes, social behaviors, educational choices and outcomes, child-rearing patterns—these are but a few of the areas on which FDI is expected to have a major impact. It is of interest to contrast the foregoing expansive view with the Kagan and Messer (1975) assertion that R-I should not be generalized beyond performance on response-uncertainty tasks. This stricture has not been heeded in practice because numerous investigators continue to explore the relevance of R-I for educational outcomes and child psychopathology. Divergent thinking has also been the target of numerous extrinsic validity studies, particularly in respect to the search for school-relevant talents and behaviors. Most limited in its generality at the present time is the metaphor construct. Given the recency of the individual-differences research in that domain, the foregoing limitation can be readily understood.

The clear developmental relevance of the four constructs has been amply described. All have been examined for cross-age differences, both cross-sectionally and longitudinally. All have been studied from the perspective of longitudinal stability, and in at least one case (R-I), causal models have been applied to establish the priority of a stylistic dimension relative to other cognitive outcomes in childhood. Finally, at both the theoretical and empirical level, all four constructs have been linked to the cognitive-developmental achievements that have flowed from the tradition of research inspired by Piaget, Inhelder, and their associates.

Changing Conceptions of Styles

Because some styles have now been with us for more than 30 years, it is reasonable to ask whether there has been any apparent shift in emphasis over that period of time. On balance, the answer is yes. In general, there has been a shift away from styles as strictly traitlike to a position in which styles are viewed as highly susceptible to task and situational influences. In this respect, one can note parallels to the trait-situation controversy in the personality domain (Magnusson & Endler, 1977).

Although an interactional framework has taken hold in the present area, it is important to note that the manifestations assume somewhat different forms across the diverse constructs. In the case of FDI, the shift has been away from the claim of the generalized superiority of FI functioning to the recognition of the numerous social contexts in which FD individuals excel. A somewhat analogous development has distinguished the R-I construct. Whereas the early research suggested that impulsiveness is handicapping across a wide range of cognitive tasks, more recent work has at least raised the possibility that impulsiveness may prove beneficial for particular kinds of tasks.

The foregoing developments point to the adaptive possibilities of previously undervalued modes of cognitive functioning vis-à-vis a specified class of situations. Note that these shifts have not really endangered the constructs as such; instead, the theories from which they derive have had to become more elaborated and articulated to accommodate extrinsic task factors. Such factors, however, can operate to affect the measurement of the construct itself. Thus, verbal and figural tasks yield different outcomes in the domains of categorization and conceptualizational styles (see Kogan, 1976a; Saarni & Kogan, 1978). As one might expect, such task variation will affect the kinds of inferences one can draw in regard to developmental change.

The shift from a strictly traitlike view of styles to one moderated by task factors is analogous in some respects to a shift away from a strictly defined view of stages in the cognitive-developmental literature. In a summary of evidence pro and con in respect to the existence of Piaget's concrete-operational and formal-operational stages, Flavell (1977) comes down strongly on the antistage side. Although acknowledging that stages continue to have their advocates (e.g., Wohlwill, 1973), Flavell (1977) suggests that the coherence of cognitive operations required by a stage conception falls far short of the ideal. Similarly, styles are not monolithic dispositions; their impact on performance is frequently modulated by task and situational contingencies.

General Reflections on Past, Present, and Future

In a review of cognitive styles published more than 10 years ago, this author (Kogan, 1971b) delin-

eated nine cognitive styles (plus risk-taking cautiousness). The present review has included two (excluding divergent thinking and metaphor), and one is tempted to speculate about the reason for this. Although it is often the case that a domain of psychological inquiry can sustain itself after the demise of its principal initiator or founder, there are times when the premature withdrawal of an investigator can break the momentum of the development of a field and initiate a process of decline. Five of the nine styles outlined in Kogan (1971b) derived from the ego-psychoanalytic tradition, and all of these withered in the absence of successors to George Klein and Riley W. Gardner. A similar case can be made in respect to James Bieri's withdrawal from the study of cognitive complexity. One might argue, of course, that the foregoing intellectual traditions had run their course, hence leaving few leads for further study. There is no obvious right or wrong answer to these opposing arguments, and it would probably make sense to turn over such issues to the historians and sociologists of science.

It is, nevertheless, of interest to speculate about the forces that have kept FDI and R-I from following in the path of the other, relatively dormant styles. In the case of FDI, the dominant influence of Herman A. Witkin must be acknowledged, and his recent death should shed some light on the issue of the relative importance of major investigator and the merit of his ideas on the further development of those ideas. Although Jerome Kagan ceased doing R-I research some time ago, one must keep in mind that the construct is the youngest of the nine styles and Kagan generated enough momentum to keep investigators working on it through the 1970s. Both FDI and R-I have now captured the attention of applied researchers in developmental, clinical, and educational psychology; hence, both constructs appear to be assured of quite a few more years on the psychological scene. Further, a small but dedicated group of investigators have seized on FDI and R-I as important to the understanding of the competence/performance distinction. Hence, there is no imminent danger that FDI and R-I will fade out of basic developmental research. As other writers have noted, the surplus meaning associated with particular constructs—the value connotations that adhere to such terms as FDI and R-I—attracts investigators by their implied sense of psychological significance. The accessibility of the major research instruments and a plausible, but not completely delineated, conceptual framework also contribute to the desire to pursue further research on these topics.

Do the creativity and metaphor domains fit the pattern described herein? In the case of the former, the most persistent advocate of children's creativity research—Paul Torrance—has been too applied and mission oriented to attract many basic researchers in developmental psychology. It is the Wallach and Kogan (1965) research that probably provided the major impetus for much of the theoretically based divergent-thinking work carried out with children from the late 1960s through the 1970s. As indicated earlier, the divergent-thinking tradition is likely to be assimilated into the current work on the development of symbolic processes. The area of metaphor belongs to the latter tradition; hence, one would expect metaphor research to flourish for some time to come. It is simply too early to know, however, whether interest will develop in the individual-differences aspect of metaphoric production and comprehension in children. Several instruments for such study described earlier are now available, but it is obviously premature to attempt to guess how widely any of them will be adopted for future research in the metaphor area.

It is difficult to envision what a review of the present areas would look like a decade or more from now. Of one thing, we can be fairly sure: it will bear little resemblance to the present chapter. In the case of all of the constructs reviewed, the creative high point may have been reached and passed. This implies that some of the material discussed here will become a matter of largely historical interest. Other parts will hopefully become integrated with other constructs or systems and, hence, continue to lead a useful scientific life. The ultimate question, of course, the one whose answer is so difficult to predict, concerns the specific constructs that will survive and the possible transformations they will undergo.

REFERENCES

Achenbach, T. M. Cue learning, associative responding, and school performance in children. *Developmental Psychology*, 1969, *1*, 717–725.

Achenbach, T. M., & Weisz, J. R. Impulsivity-reflectivity and cognitive development in preschoolers: A longitudinal analysis of developmental and trait variance. *Developmental Psychology*, 1975, *11*, 413–414.

Arlin, P. K. Cognitive development in adulthood: A fifth stage? *Developmental Psychology*, 1975, *11*, 602–606.

Ault, R. L., Mitchell, C., & Hartmann, D. P. Some methodological problems in reflection-impulsivity research. *Child Development*, 1976, *47*, 227–231.

Baltes, P. B., & Nesselroade, J. R. The developmental analysis of individual differences on multiple measures. In J. R. Nesselroade & H. W. Reese (Eds.), *Life-span developmental psychology: Methodological issues*. New York: Academic Press, 1973.

Bandura, A. *Principles of behavior modification*. New York: Holt, Rinehart & Winston, 1969.

Barrett, D. E. Reflection-impulsivity as a predictor of children's academic achievement. *Child Development*, 1977, *48*, 1443–1447.

Barron, F. *Creativity and psychological health*. Princeton, N.J.: Van Nostrand, 1963.

Barron, F., & Harrington, D. M. Creativity, intelligence, and personality. *Annual Review of Psychology*, 1981, *32*, 439–476.

Barstis, S. W., & Ford, L. H., Jr. Reflection-impulsivity, conservation, and the development of ability to control cognitive tempo. *Child Development*, 1977, *48*, 953–959.

Belcher, T. L. Modeling original divergent responses: An initial investigation. *Journal of Educational Psychology*, 1975, *67*, 351–358.

Bennett, N. *Teaching style and pupil progress*. Cambridge, Mass.: Harvard University Press, 1976.

Bentler, P. M., & McClain, J. A. Multitrait-multimethod analysis of reflection-impulsivity. *Child Development*, 1976, *47*, 218–226.

Berry, J. W. *Human ecology and cognitive style*. New York: Halsted Press, 1976.

Bieri, J. Cognitive complexity and personality development. In O. J. Harvey (Ed.), *Experience, structure, and adaptability*. New York: Springer Publishing, 1966.

Billow, R. M. A cognitive developmental study of metaphor comprehension. *Developmental Psychology*, 1975, *11*, 415–423.

Billow, R. M. Metaphor: A review of the psychological literature. *Psychological Bulletin*, 1977, *84*, 81–92.

Block, J., & Block, J. H. *The California child Q-set*. Palo Alto, Calif.: Consulting Psychologists Press, 1981.

Block, J., Block, J. H., & Harrington, D. M. Some misgivings about the Matching Familiar Figures Test as a measure of reflection-impulsivity. *Developmental Psychology*, 1974, *10*, 611–632.

Block, J., Block, J. H., & Harrington, D. M. Comment on the Kagan-Messer reply. *Developmental Psychology*, 1975, *11*, 249–252.

Block, J., Buss, D. M., Block, J. H., & Gjerde, P. F. The cognitive style of breadth of categorization: Longitudinal consistency of personality correlates. *Journal of Personality and Social Psychology*, 1981, *40*, 770–779.

Block, J. H., & Block, J. The role of ego-control and ego-resiliency in the organization of behavior. In W. A. Collins (Ed.), *Minnesota Symposia on Child Psychology* (Vol. 13). Hillsdale, N.J.: Erlbaum, 1980.

Brainerd, C. J. Stages II: A review of *Beyond universals in cognitive development* by D. H. Feldman. *Developmental Review*, 1981, *1*, 63–81.

Broadbent, D. E. The hidden preattentive processes. *American Psychologist*, 1977, *32*, 109–119.

Brodzinsky, D. M. The role of conceptual tempo and stimulus characteristics in children's humor development. *Developmental Psychology*, 1975, *11*, 843–850.

Brodzinsky, D. M. Children's comprehension and appreciation of verbal jokes in relation to conceptual tempo. *Child Development*, 1977, *48*, 960–967.

Brodzinsky, D. M. Cognitive style differences in children's spatial perspective taking. *Developmental Psychology*, 1980, *16*, 151–152.

Brodzinsky, D. M. The relationship between cognitive style and cognitive development: A two-year longitudinal study. *Developmental Psychology*, 1982, *18*, 617–626.

Brodzinsky, D. M., Feuer, V., & Owens, J. Detection of linguistic ambiguity by reflective, impulsive, fast/accurate, and slow/inaccurate children. *Journal of Educational Psychology*, 1977, *69*, 237–243.

Brodzinsky, D. M., & Rightmyer, J. Pleasure associated with cognitive mastery as related to children's conceptual tempo. *Child Development*, 1976, *47*, 881–884.

Brown, A. L. Development, schooling, and the acquisition of knowledge about knowledge. In R. C. Anderson, R. J. Spiro, & W. E. Montague (Eds.), *Schooling and the acquisition of knowledge*. Hillsdale, N.J.: Erlbaum, 1977.

Bruner, J. S. Nature and uses of immaturity. *American Psychologist*, 1972, *27*, 687–708.

Bruner, J. S., Goodnow, J. J., & Austin, G. A. *A study of thinking*. New York: Wiley, 1956.

Bruner, J. S., Olver, R. R., & Greenfield, P. M. (Eds.), *Studies in cognitive growth*. New York: Wiley, 1966.

Bush, E. S., & Dweck, C. S. Reflections on conceptual tempo: Relationship between cognitive style and performance as a function of task characteristics. *Developmental Psychology*, 1975, *11*, 567–574.

Cairns, E. Role of task strategy and stimulus processing in reflective and impulsive tactual matching performance. *Perceptual and Motor Skills*, 1978, *47*, 523–529.

Cairns, E., & Cammock, T. Development of a more reliable version of the Matching Familiar Figures Test. *Developmental Psychology*, 1978, *14*, 555–560.

Campbell, D. T., & Fiske, D. W. Convergent and discriminant validation by the multitrait-multimethod matrix. *Psychological Bulletin*, 1959, *56*, 81–105.

Case, R. Validation of a neo-Piagetian capacity construct. *Journal of Experimental Child Psychology*, 1972, *14*, 287–302.

Case, R. Structures and strictures: Some functional limitations on the course of cognitive growth. *Cognitive Psychology*, 1974, *6*, 544–573.

Case, R. Social class differences in intellectual development: A neo-Piagetian investigation. *Canadian Journal of Behavioral Science*, 1975, *7*, 244–261.

Case, R. Responsiveness to conservation training as a function of induced subjective uncertainty, *M*-space, and cognitive style. *Canadian Journal of Behavioral Science*, 1977, *9*, 12–25.

Case, R., & Globerson, T. Field independence and central computing space. *Child Development*, 1974, *45*, 772–778.

Caudle, F. M. Instructional effects of divergent thinking: Attention deployment or experimenter demand? (Doctoral dissertation, New School for Social Research, 1975). *Dissertation Abstracts International*, 1976, *36*, 4222B. (University Microfilms No. 75–25,445)

Chadrow, M., Parlow, S., & Kogan, N. Age and modality effects in metaphoric comprehension. Paper presented at the meeting of the Eastern Psychological Association, New York, April 1981.

Chapman, M. Pascual-Leone's theory of constructive operators: An introduction. *Human Development*, 1981, *24*, 145–155.

Claeys, W., & DeBoeck, P. The influence of some parental characteristics on children's primary abilities and field independence: A study of adopted children. *Child Development*, 1976, *47*, 842–845.

Cliatt, M. J. P., Shaw, J. M., & Sherwood, J. M. Effects of training on the divergent-thinking abilities of kindergarten children. *Child Development*, 1980, *51*, 1061–1064.

Coates, S. *Preschool embedded figures test*. Palo Alto, Calif.: Consulting Psychologists Press, 1972.

Coates, S. Sex differences in field dependence-independence between the ages of 3 and 6. *Percep-*

tual Motor Skills, 1974, *39*, 1307–1310. (a)

Coates, S. Sex differences in field independence among preschool children. In R. C. Friedman, R. M. Richart, & R. L. Vande Wiele (Eds.), *Sex differences in behavior*. New York: Wiley, 1974. (b)

Cometa, M. S., & Eson, M. E. Logical operations and metaphor interpretation: A Piagetian interpretation. *Developmental Psychology*, 1978, *49*, 649–659.

Connor, J. M., Schackman, M., & Serbin, L. A. Sex-related differences in response to practice on a visual-spatial test and generalization to a related test. *Child Development*, 1978, *49*, 24–29.

Connor, J. M., Serbin, L. A., & Schackman, M. Sex differences in children's response to training on a visual-spatial test. *Developmental Psychology*, 1977, *13*, 293–294.

Connor, K., & Kogan, N. Topic-vehicle relations in metaphor: The issue of asymmetry. In R. P. Honeck & R. R. Hoffman (Eds.), *Cognition and figurative language*. Hillsdale, N.J.: Erlbaum, 1980.

Cronbach, L. J. The two disciplines of scientific psychology. *American Psychologist*, 1957, *12*, 671–684.

Cronbach, L. J., & Snow, R. E. *Aptitudes and instructional methods*. New York: Irvington, 1977.

Cropley, A. J. A five-year longitudinal study of the validity of creativity tests. *Developmental Psychology*, 1972, *6*, 119–124.

Cropley, A. J., & Clapson, L. G. Long-term test-retest reliability of creativity tests. *British Journal of Educational Psychology*, 1971, *41*, 206–208.

Cropper, D. A., Meck, D. S., & Ash, M. J. The relation between formal operations and a possible fifth stage of cognitive development. *Developmental Psychology*, 1977, *13*, 517–518.

Cullinan, D., Epstein, M. H., Lloyd, J., & Noel, M. Development of cognitive tempo in learning disabled children. *Learning Disability Quarterly*, 1980, *3*, 46–53.

Dansky, J. L. Make-believe: A mediator of the relationship between play and associative fluency. *Child Development*, 1980, *51*, 576–579. (a)

Dansky, J. L. Cognitive consequences of sociodramatic play and exploration training for economically disadvantaged preschoolers. *Journal of Child Psychology and Psychiatry*, 1980, *20*, 47–58. (b)

Dansky, J. L., & Silverman, I. W. Effects of play on associative fluency in preschool-aged children. *Developmental Psychology*, 1973, *9*, 38–43.

Dansky, J. L., & Silverman, I. W. Play: A general facilitator of associative fluency. *Developmental Psychology*, 1975, *11*, 104.

Debus, R. L. Effects of brief observation of model behavior on conceptual tempo of impulsive children. *Developmental Psychology*, 1970, *2*, 22–32.

Denney, D. R. Modeling effects upon conceptual style and cognitive tempo. *Child Development*, 1972, *43*, 105–119.

Denney, D. R. Developmental changes in concept utilization among normal and retarded children. *Developmental Psychology*, 1975, *11*, 359–368.

Denney, D. R., & Moulton, P. A. Conceptual preferences among preschool children. *Developmental Psychology*, 1976, *12*, 509–513.

Dinges, N. G., & Hollenbeck, A. R. Field dependence-independence in Navajo children. *International Journal of Psychology*, 1978, *13*, 215–220.

Dyk, R. B. An exploratory study of mother-child interaction in infancy as related to the development of differentiation. *Journal of the American Academy of Child Psychiatry*, 1969, *8*, 657–691.

Dyk, R. B., & Witkin, H. A. Family experiences related to the development of differentiation in children. *Child Development*, 1965, *30*, 21–55.

Egeland, B. Training impulsive children in the use of more efficient scanning techniques. *Child Development*, 1974, *45*, 165–171.

Egeland, B., & Weinberg, R. A. The Matching Familiar Figures Test: A look at its psychometric credibility. *Child Development*, 1976, *47*, 483–491.

Fakouri, M. E. Cognitive development in adulthood: A fifth stage? A critique. *Developmental Psychology*, 1976, *12*, 472.

Fein, G. G., & Eshleman, S. Individuals and dimensions in children's judgment of same and different. *Developmental Psychology*, 1974, *10*, 793–796.

Feitelson, D., & Ross, G. The neglected factor— play. *Human Development*, 1973, *16*, 202–223.

Feldman, D. H. *Beyond universals in cognitive development*. Norwood, N.J.: Ablex, 1980.

Feldman, D. H. The role of theory in cognitive developmental research: A reply to Brainerd. *Developmental Review*, 1981, *1*, 82–89.

Finch, A. J., Jr., & Montgomery, L. E. Reflection-impulsivity and information seeking in emotionally disturbed children. *Journal of Abnormal Child Psychology*, 1973, *1*, 358–362.

Finley, G. E., Solla, J., & Cowan, P. A. Field dependence-independence, egocentrism and conservation in young children. *Journal of Genetic Psychology*, 1977, *131*, 155–156.

Flavell, J. H. *Cognitive development*. Englewood Cliffs, N.J.: Prentice-Hall, 1977.

Flavell, J. H., & Wohlwill, J. F. Formal and functional aspects of cognitive development. In D. Elkind & J. H. Flavell (Eds.), *Studies in cognitive development*. New York: Oxford University Press, 1969.

Ford, M. A., Stern, D. N., & Dillon, D. J. Performance of children ages 3 to 5 on the draw-a-person task: Sex differences. *Perceptual and Motor Skills*, 1974, *38*, 1188.

Forman, S. G., & McKinney, J. D. Creativity and achievement of second graders in open and traditional classrooms. *Journal of Educational Psychology*, 1978, *70*, 101–107.

Franklin, B. S., & Richards, P. N. Effects on children's divergent thinking abilities of a period of direct teaching for divergent production. *British Journal of Educational Psychology*, 1977, *47*, 66–70.

French, J. W., Ekstrom, R. B., & Price, L. A. *Manual for kit of reference tests for cognitive factors*. Princeton: Educational Testing Service, 1963.

Gallagher, J. M. The future of formal thought research: The study of analogy and metaphor. In B. Z. Presseisen, D. Goldstein, & M. H. Appel (Eds.), *Topics in cognitive development* (Vol. 2). New York: Plenum, 1978.

Gardner, H. Metaphors and modalities: How children project polar adjectives onto diverse domains. *Child Development*, 1974, *45*, 84–91.

Gardner, H., Kircher, M., Winner, E., & Perkins, D. Children's metaphoric productions and preferences. *Journal of Child Language*, 1975, *2*, 125–141.

Gardner, H., Winner, E., Bechhofer, R., & Wolf, D. The development of figurative language. In K. E. Nelson (Ed.), *Children's language* (Vol. 1). New York: Gardner Press, 1978.

Gardner, R. W., & Moriarty, A. *Personality development at preadolescence: Exploration of structure formation*. Seattle: University of Washington Press, 1968.

Gentner, D. Children's performance on a spatial analogies task. *Child Development*, 1977, *48*, 1034–1039.

Goldstein, A. G., & Chance, J. E. Effects of practice on sex-related differences in performance on embedded figures. *Psychonomic Science*, 1965, *3*, 361–362.

Gombrich, E. H. *Meditations on a hobby horse.*

London: Phaidon Press, 1963.

Goodenough, D. R. The role of individual differences in field dependence as a factor in learning and memory. *Psychological Bulletin*, 1976, *83*, 675–694.

Goor, A., & Rapoport, T. Enhancing creativity in an informal educational framework. *Journal of Educational Psychology*, 1977, *69*, 636–643.

Grant, R. A. The relation of perceptual activity to Matching Familiar Figures Test accuracy. *Developmental Psychology*, 1976, *12*, 534–539.

Gray, J. L. Stability and generalizability of conceptual style. *Psychology in the Schools*, 1974, *11*, 466–475.

Guilford, J. P. Creativity. *American Psychologist*, 1950, *14*, 469–479.

Guilford, J. P. *The nature of human intelligence*. New York: McGraw-Hill, 1967.

Guyer, B. L., & Friedman, M. P. Hemispheric processing and cognitive styles in learning-disabled and normal children. *Child Development*, 1975, *46*, 658–668.

Haddon, F. A., & Lytton, H. Teaching approach and the development of divergent thinking abilities in primary school. *British Journal of Educational Psychology*, 1968, *38*, 171–180.

Haddon, F. A., & Lytton, H. Primary education and divergent-thinking abilities: Four years on. *British Journal of Educational Psychology*, 1971, *41*, 136–147.

Hall, V. C., & Russell, W. J. C. Multitrait-multimethod analysis of conceptual tempo. *Journal of Educational Psychology*, 1974, *66*, 932–939.

Hammaker, M. K., Shafto, M., & Trabasso, T. Judging creativity: A method for assessing how and by which criteria it is done. *Journal of Educational Psychology*, 1975, *67*, 478–483.

Hargreaves, D. J., & Bolton, N. Selecting creativity tests for use in research. *British Journal of Psychology*, 1972, *63*, 451–462.

Harrington, D. M., Block, J. H., & Block, J. Intolerance of ambiguity in preschool children: Psychometric considerations, behavioral manifestations, and parental correlates. *Developmental Psychology*, 1978, *14*, 242–256.

Harrington, D. M., Block, J. H., & Block, J. Predicting creativity in preadolescence from divergent thinking in early childhood. *Journal of Personality and Social Psychology*, 1983, in press.

Harris, L. J. Sex differences in spatial ability: Possible environmental, genetic and neurological factors. In M. Kinsbourne (Ed.), *Asymmetrical function of the brain*. New York: Cambridge University Press, 1978.

Harris, R. I. The relationship of impulse control to

parent hearing status, manual communication, and academic achievement in deaf children. *American Annals of the Deaf*, 1978, *123*, 52–67.

Hartley, D. G. The effect of perceptual salience on reflective-impulsive performance differences. *Developmental Psychology*, 1976, *12*, 218–225.

Harvey, O. J. System structure, flexibility, and creativity. In O. J. Harvey (Ed.), *Experience, structure, and adaptability*. New York: Springer Publishing, 1966.

Haskins, R., & McKinney, J. D. Relative effects of response tempo and accuracy on problem solving and academic achievement. *Child Development*, 1976, *47*, 690–696.

Hattie, J. Conditions for administering creativity tests. *Psychological Bulletin*, 1977, *84*, 1249–1260.

Hattie, J. Should creativity tests be administered under testlike conditions? An empirical study of three alternative conditions. *Journal of Educational Psychology*, 1980, *72*, 87–98.

Helson, R. Commentary: Reality of masculine and feminine trends in personality and behavior. In S. Messick & associates (Eds.), *Individuality in learning*. San Francisco: Jossey-Bass, 1976.

Hill, D. Relation of field independence to development of conservation. *Perceptual and Motor Skills*, 1980, *50*, 1247–1250.

Hocevar, D. Ideational fluency as a confounding factor in the measurement of originality. *Journal of Educational Psychology*, 1979, *71*, 191–196.

Honeck, R. P. Historical notes on figurative language. In R. P. Honeck & R. R. Hoffman (Eds.), *Cognition and figurative language*. Hillsdale, N.J.: Erlbaum, 1980.

Honeck, R. P., & Hoffman, R. R. (Eds.), *Cognition and figurative language*. Hillsdale, N.J.: Erlbaum, 1980.

Hoppe, C. M., Kagan, S. M., & Zahn, G. L. Conflict resolution among field-independent and field-dependent Anglo-American and Mexican-American children and their mothers. *Developmental Psychology*, 1977, *13*, 591–598.

Horn, J. L., & Cattell, R. B. Refinement and test of the theory of fluid and crystallized general intelligence. *Journal of Educational Psychology*, 1966, *57*, 253–270.

Houtz, J. C., & Speedie, S. M. Processes underlying divergent thinking and problem solving. *Journal of Educational Psychology*, 1978, *70*, 848–854.

Hudson, L. *Contrary imaginations*. London: Methuen, 1966.

Hudson, L. *Frames of mind*. New York: W. W. Norton, 1968.

Huteau, M., & Rajchenbach, F. Hétérogènéité du niveau de développment opératoire et dépendance-indépendance à l'égard du champ. *Enfance*, 1978, *4–5*, 181–196.

Hutt, C. Exploration and play in children. In T. A. Jewell & C. Loizos (Eds.), *Play, exploration, and territory in mammals*. New York: Academic Press, 1966.

Hutt, C., & Bhavnani, R. Predictions from play. In J. S. Bruner, A. Jolly, & K. Sylva (Eds.), *Play: Its role in development and evolution*. New York: Basic Books, 1976.

Inhelder, B., & Piaget, J. *The growth of logical thinking from childhood to adolescence: An essay on the construction of formal operational structures*. New York: Basic Books, 1958.

Inhelder, B., & Piaget, J. *The early growth of logic in the child*. New York: Harper & Row, 1964.

Inkeles, A., & Smith, D. H. *Becoming modern*. Cambridge, Mass.: Harvard University Press, 1974.

Irwin, M., Engle, P. L., Klein, R. E., & Yarbrough, C. Traditionalism and field dependence. *Journal of Cross-Cultural Psychology*, 1976, *4*, 463–472.

Johnson, J. E. Relations of divergent thinking and intelligence test scores with social and non-social make-believe play of preschool children. *Child Development*, 1976, *47*, 1200–1203.

Johnson, R. A. Differential effects of reward versus no-reward instructions on the creative thinking of two economic levels of elementary school children. *Journal of Educational Psychology*, 1974, *66*, 530–533.

Jordan, L. Use of canonical analysis in Cropley's "A five-year longitudinal study of the validity of creativity tests." *Developmental Psychology*, 1975, *11*, 1–3.

Jöreskog, K. G., & Sörbom, D. *LISREL III: Estimation of linear structural equation systems by maximum-likelihood methods*. Chicago: National Educational Resources, 1976.

Kagan, J. Commentary on "Reflective and impulsive children: Strategies of information processing underlying differences in problem solving." *Monographs of the Society for Research in Child Development*, 1976, *41*(5, Serial No. 168).

Kagan, J., & Kogan, N. Individual variation in cognitive processes. In P. H. Mussen (Ed.), *Carmichael's manual of child psychology* (Vol. 1) (3rd ed.). New York: Wiley, 1970.

Kagan, J., & Messer, S. B. A reply to "Some misgivings about the Matching Familiar Figures Test as a measure of reflection-impulsivity." *Developmental Psychology*, 1975, *11*, 244–248.

Kagan, J., Moss, H. A., & Sigel, I. E. Psychological significance of styles of conceptualization. In J. C. Wright & J. Kagan (Eds.), Basic cognitive processes in children. *Monographs of the Society for Research in Child Development*, 1963, *28*(2, Serial No. 86).

Kagan, J., Rosman, B. L., Day, D., Albert, J., & Phillips, W. Information processing in the child: Significance of analytic and reflective attitudes. *Psychological Monographs*, 1964, *78*(1, Whole No. 578).

Kagan, S., & Zahn, G. L. Field dependence and the school achievement gap between Anglo-American and Mexican-American children. *Journal of Educational Psychology*, 1975, *67*, 643–650.

Kenny, D. A. *Correlation and causality*. New York: Wiley, 1979.

Keogh, B. K., & Ryan, S. R. Use of three measures of field organization with young children. *Perceptual and Motor Skills*, 1971, *33*, 466.

Koch, K. *Wishes, lies, and dreams*. New York: Chelsea House, 1970.

Kogan, N. A clarification of Cropley and Maslany's analysis of the Wallach-Kogan creativity tests. *British Journal of Psychology*, 1971, *62*, 113–117. (a)

Kogan, N. Educational implications of cognitive styles. In G. S. Lesser (Ed.), *Psychology and educational practice*. Glenview, Ill.: Scott, Foresman, 1971. (b)

Kogan, N. Creativity and cognitive style: A life-span perspective. In P. B. Baltes & K. W. Schaie (Eds.), *Life-span developmental psychology: Personality and socialization*. New York: Academic Press, 1973.

Kogan, N. Creativity and sex differences. *Journal of Creative Behavior*, 1974, *8*, 1–14.

Kogan, N. *Cognitive styles in infancy and early childhood*. Hillsdale, N.J.: Erlbaum, 1976. (a)

Kogan, N. Sex differences in creativity and cognitive styles. In S. Messick & associates (Eds.), *Individuality in learning*. San Francisco: Jossey-Bass, 1976. (b)

Kogan, N. A cognitive style approach to metaphoric thinking. In R. E. Snow, P. A. Federico, & W. E. Montague (Eds.), *Aptitude, learning, and instruction: Cognitive process analyses* (Vol. 1). Hillsdale, N.J.: Erlbaum, 1980. (a)

Kogan, N. Cognitive styles and reading performance. *Bulletin of the Orton Society*, 1980, *30*, 63–78. (b)

Kogan, N. A style of life, a life of style. (Review of *Cognitive styles in personal and cultural adaptation* by H. A. Witkin.) *Contemporary Psychology*, 1980, *25*, 595–598. (c)

Kogan, N. Cognitive styles in older adults. In T. Field, A. Houston, H. Quay, L. Troll, & G. Finley (Eds.), *Review of human development*. New York: Wiley, 1982.

Kogan, N., Connor, K., Gross, A., & Fava, D. Understanding visual metaphor: Developmental and individual differences. *Monographs of the Society for Research in Child Development*, 1980, *45*(1, Serial No. 183).

Kogan, N., & Marcuse, Y. Review of *Sex-related differences in cognitive functioning: Developmental issues* (M. A. Wittig & A. C. Petersen, Eds.). *Sex Roles*, 1981, *7*, 463–469.

Kogan, N., & Morgan, F. T. Task and motivational influences on the assessment of creative and intellective ability in children. *Genetic Psychology Monographs*, 1969, *80*, 91–127.

Kogan, N., & Pankove, E. Creative ability over a five-year span. *Child Development*, 1972, *43*, 427–442.

Kogan, N., & Pankove, E. Long-term predictive validity of divergent-thinking tests. *Journal of Educational Psychology*, 1974, *66*, 802–810.

Kojima, H. Some psychometric problems of the Matching Familiar Figures Test. *Perceptual and Motor Skills*, 1976, *43*, 731–742.

Kojima, H. Assessment of field dependence in young children. *Perceptual and Motor Skills*, 1978, *46*, 479–492.

La Greca, A. M. Can children remember to be creative? An interview study of children's thinking processes. *Child Development*, 1980, *51*, 572–575.

Laosa, L. M. Maternal teaching strategies and cognitive styles in Chicano families. *Journal of Educational Psychology*, 1980, *72*, 45–54.

Lawson, A. E. Formal operations and field independence in a heterogeneous sample. *Perceptual and Motor Skills*, 1976, *42*, 981–982.

Liben, L. Operative understanding of horizontality and its relation to long-term memory. *Child Development*, 1974, *45*, 416–424.

Liben, L. Long-term memory for pictures related to seriation, horizontality, and verticality concepts. *Developmental Psychology*, 1975, *11*, 795–806.

Liben, L. Performance on Piagetian spatial tasks as a function of sex, field dependence, and training. *Merrill-Palmer Quarterly*, 1978, *24*, 97–110.

Lieberman, J. N. *Playfulness: Its relationship to imagination and creativity*. New York: Academic Press, 1977.

Linn, M. C. Influence of cognitive style and training on tasks requiring the separation of variables schema. *Child Development*, 1978, *49*, 874–877.

Linn, M. C., & Kyllonen, P. The field dependence-independence construct: Some, one, or none. *Journal of Educational Psychology*, 1981, *73*, 261–273.

Linn, M. C., & Swiney, J. F., Jr. Individual differences in formal thought: Role of expectations and aptitudes. *Journal of Educational Psychology*, 1981, *73*, 274–286.

Loper, A. B., Hallahan, D. P., & McKinney, J. D. The effect of reinforcement for global or analytic strategies on the performance of reflective and impulsive children. *Journal of Experimental Child Psychology*, 1982, *33*, 55–62.

Maccoby, E. E. Sex differences in intellectual functioning. In E. E. Maccoby (Ed.), *The development of sex differences*. Stanford, Calif.: Stanford University Press, 1966.

Maccoby, E. E., & Jacklin, C. N. *The psychology of sex differences*. Stanford, Calif.: Stanford University Press, 1974.

Maddi, S. R. Motivational aspects of creativity. *Journal of Personality*, 1965, *33*, 330–347.

Magnusson, D., & Backteman, G. Longitudinal stability of person characteristics: Intelligence and creativity. *Applied Psychological Measurement*, 1978, *2*, 481–490.

Magnusson, D., & Endler, N. S. (Eds.), *Personality at the crossroads: Current issues in interactional psychology*. Hillsdale, N.J.: Erlbaum, 1977.

Malgady, R. G. Children's interpretation and appreciation of similes. *Child Development*, 1977, *48*, 1734–1738.

Margolis, H., Leonard, H. S., Brannigan, G. G., & Heverly, M. A. The validity of Form F of the Matching Familiar Figures Test with kindergarten children. *Journal of Experimental Child Psychology*, 1980, *29*, 12–22.

Marks, L. E. *The unity of the senses: Interrelations among the modalities*. New York: Academic Press, 1978.

Massari, D. J., & Mansfield, R. S. Field dependence and outer-directedness in the problem solving of retardates and normal children. *Child Development*, 1973, *44*, 346–350.

McKinney, J. D. Problem-solving strategies in reflective and impulsive children. *Journal of Educational Psychology*, 1975, *67*, 807–820.

McKinney, J. D., & Forman, S. G. Factor structure of the Wallach-Kogan tests of creativity and measures of intelligence and achievement. *Psychology in the Schools*, 1977, *14*, 41–44.

Mednick, S. A. The associative basis of the creative process. *Psychological Review*, 1962, *69*, 220–232.

Meichenbaum, D. H., & Goodman, J. Training impulsive children to talk to themselves: A means of developing self-control. *Journal of Abnormal Psychology*, 1971, *77*, 115–126.

Messer, S. B. Reflection-impulsivity: A review. *Psychological Bulletin*, 1976, *83*, 1026–1053.

Messer, S. B., & Brodzinsky, D. M. Three-year stability of reflection-impulsivity in young adolescents. *Developmental Psychology*, 1981, *17*, 848–850.

Milgram, R. M., & Feingold, S. Concrete and verbal reinforcement in creative thinking of disadvantaged children. *Perceptual and Motor Skills*, 1977, *45*, 675–678.

Milgram, R. M., & Milgram, N. A. Group versus individual administration in the measurement of creative thinking in gifted and non-gifted children. *Child Development*, 1976, *47*, 563–565.

Milgram, R. M., Milgram, N. A., Rosenbloom, G., & Rabkin, L. Quantity and quality of creative thinking in children and adolescents. *Child Development*, 1978, *49*, 385–388.

Milgram, R. M., & Rabkin, L. Developmental test of Mednick's associative hierarchies of original thinking. *Developmental Psychology*, 1980, *16*, 157–158.

Miller, G. A., Galanter, E., & Pribram, K. H. *Plans and the structure of behavior*. New York: Holt, Rinehart & Winston, 1960.

Mitchell, C., & Ault, R. L. Reflection-impulsivity and the evaluation process. *Child Development*, 1979, *50*, 1043–1049.

Miyakawa, J. Some comments on Salkind and Wright's model for reflection-impulsivity. *Perceptual and Motor Skills*, 1981, *52*, 947–954.

Montgomery, L. E., & Finch, A. J., Jr. Reflection-impulsivity and locus of conflict in emotionally disturbed children. *Journal of Genetic Psychology*, 1975, *126*, 89–91.

Moore, M. G., Haskins, R., & McKinney, J. D. Classroom behavior of reflective and impulsive children. *Journal of Applied Developmental Psychology*, 1980, *1*, 59–75.

Morell, J. A. Age, sex, training, and the measurement of field dependence. *Journal of Experimental Child Psychology*, 1976, *22*, 100–112.

Mosher, F. A., & Hornsby, J. R. On asking questions. In J. S. Bruner, R. R. Olver, & P. M. Greenfield (Eds.), *Studies in cognitive growth*. New York: Wiley, 1966.

Moskowitz, D. S., Dreyer, A. S., & Kronsberg, S. Preschool children's field independence: Prediction from antecedent and concurrent maternal and child behavior. *Perceptual and Motor Skills*, 1981, *52*, 607–616.

Mussen, P. H. (Ed.), *Carmichael's manual of child*

psychology (Vol. 1) (3rd ed.). New York: Wiley, 1970.

Nakamura, C. Y., & Finck, D. N. Relative effectiveness of socially oriented and task-oriented children and predictability of their behaviors. *Monographs of the Society for Research in Child Development*, 1980, *45*(3–4, Serial No. 185).

Nash, S. C. Sex role as a mediator of intellectual functioning. In M. A. Wittig & A. C. Petersen (Eds.), *Sex-related differences in cognitive functioning: Developmental issues*. New York: Academic Press, 1979.

Nedd, A. N. B., & Gruenfeld, L. W. Field dependence-independence and social traditionalism. *International Journal of Psychology*, 1976, *11*, 23–41.

Neimark, E. D. Individual differences and the role of cognitive style in cognitive development. *Genetic Psychology Monographs*, 1975, *91*, 171–225.

Neimark, E. D. Current status of formal operations research. *Human Development*, 1979, *22*, 60–67.

Neimark, E. D. Confounding with cognitive style factors: An artifact explanation for the apparent nonuniversal incidence of formal operations. In I. E. Sigel, D. M. Brodzinsky, & R. Golinkoff (Eds.), *Piagetian theory and research: New directions and applications*. Hillsdale, N.J.: Erlbaum, 1981.

Nelson, K. Individual differences in language development: Implications for development and language. *Developmental Psychology*, 1981, *17*, 170–187.

Nelson, K. E., & Bonvillian, J. D. Concepts and words in the two-year-old: Acquisition of concept names under controlled conditions. *Cognition*, 1973, *2*, 435–450.

Nelson, K. E., & Bonvillian, J. D. Early language development: Conceptual growth and related processes between 2 and 4½ years of age. In K. E. Nelson (Ed.), *Children's language* (Vol. 1). New York: Gardner Press, 1978.

Nesselroade, J. R., & Baltes, P. B. (Eds.) *Longitudinal research in the study of behavior and development*. New York: Academic Press, 1979.

Nicholls, J. G. Some effects of testing procedure on divergent thinking. *Child Development*, 1971, *42*, 1647–1651.

Odom, R. D., McIntyre, C. W., & Neale, G. The influence of cognitive style on perceptual learning. *Child Development*, 1971, *42*, 883–891.

Oltman, P. K. A portable rod-and-frame apparatus. *Perceptual and Motor Skills*, 1968, *26*, 503–506.

Ortony, A. Beyond literal similarity. *Psychological Review*, 1979, *86*, 161–180. (a)

Ortony, A. (Ed.) *Metaphor and thought*. New York: Cambridge University Press, 1979. (b)

Ortony, A., Reynolds, R. E., & Arter, J. A. Metaphor: Theoretical and empirical research. *Psychological Bulletin*, 1978, *85*, 919–943.

Overton, W. F., & Newman, J. L. Cognitive development: A competence-activation/utilization approach. In T. Field, A. Houston, H. Quay, L. Troll, & G. Finley (Eds.), *Review of human development*. New York: Wiley, 1982.

Paivio, A. Psychological processes in the comprehension of metaphor. In A. Ortony (Ed.), *Metaphor and thought*. New York: Cambridge University Press, 1979.

Pankove, E., & Kogan, N. Creative ability and risk taking in elementary school children. *Journal of Personality*, 1968, *36*, 420–439.

Pascual-Leone, J. On learning and development, Piagetian style, II: A critical historical analysis of Geneva's research programme. *Canadian Psychological Review*, 1976, *17*, 289–297.

Pascual-Leone, J. Constructive problems for constructive theories: The current relevance of Piaget's work and a critique of information-processing simulation psychology. In R. Kluwe & H. Spada (Eds.), *Developmental models of thinking*. New York: Academic Press, 1980.

Pepler, D. J., & Ross, H. S. The effects of play on convergent and divergent problem solving. *Child Development*, 1981, *52*, 1202–1210.

Pettigrew, T. F. The measurement and correlates of category width as a cognitive variable. *Journal of Personality*, 1958, *26*, 532–544.

Piaget, J. Piaget's theory. In P. H. Mussen (Ed.), *Carmichael's manual of child psychology* (Vol. 1) (3rd ed.). New York: Wiley, 1970.

Piaget, J. *Biology and knowledge*. Chicago: University of Chicago Press, 1971.

Piaget, J. *The development of thought: Equilibration of cognitive structures*. New York: Viking, 1977.

Piaget, J., & Inhelder, B. *The child's conception of space*. New York: W. W. Norton, 1956.

Pollio, H. R., Barlow, J. M., Fine, H. J., & Pollio, M. R. *Psychology and the poetics of growth*. Hillsdale, N.J.: Erlbaum, 1977.

Pollio, M. R., & Pickens, J. D. The developmental structure of figurative competence. In R. P. Honeck & R. R. Hoffman (Eds.), *Cognition and fig-*

urative language. Hillsdale, N.J.: Erlbaum, 1980.

Pollio, M. R., & Pollio, H. R. Development of figurative language in school children. *Journal of Psycholinguistic Research*, 1974, *3*, 185–201.

Pollio, M. R., & Pollio, H. R. A test of metaphoric comprehension and some preliminary developmental data. *Journal of Child Language*, 1979, *6*, 111–120.

Ramey, C. T., & Piper, V. Creativity in open and traditional classrooms. *Child Development*, 1974, *45*, 557–560.

Reznick, H. M. Developmental changes in children's strategies for processing pictorial information. *Merrill-Palmer Quarterly*, 1977, *23*, 143–162.

Richards, J. M., Jr., Holland, J. L., & Lutz, S. W. Prediction of student accomplishment in college. *Journal of Educational Psychology*, 1967, *58*, 343–355.

Ridberg, E. H., Parke, R. D., & Hetherington, E. M. Modification of impulsive and reflective cognitive styles through observation of film mediated models. *Developmental Psychology*, 1971, *5*, 369–377.

Riegel, K. F. Dialectic operations: The final period of cognitive development. *Human Development*, 1973, *16*, 346–370.

Rohwer, W. D., Jr. Learning, race, and school success. *Review of Educational Research*, 1971, *41*, 191–210.

Rosenbaum, D. Assessment of divergent thinking in children; effects of task context, race and socioeconomic status (doctoral dissertation, New School for Social Research, 1973). *Dissertation Abstracts International*, 1974, 34, 3507B–3508B. (University Microfilms No. 74-158)

Rotatori, A., Cullinan, D., Epstein, M. H., & Lloyd, J. Cognitive tempo in educable mentally retarded children. *Journal of Psychology*, 1978, *99*, 135–137.

Rotter, D. M., Langland, L., & Berger, D. The validity of tests of creative thinking in seven-year-old children. *Gifted Child Quarterly*, 1971, *15*, 273–278.

Ruble, D. N., & Nakamura, C. Y. Task orientation versus social orientation in young children and their attention to relevant social cues. *Child Development*, 1972, *43*, 471–480.

Saarni, C. I. Piagetian operations and field independence as factors in children's problem-solving performance. *Child Development*, 1973, *44*, 338–345.

Saarni, C. I., & Kogan, N. Kognitive stile. In G. Steiner (Ed.), *Die Psychologie des 20 Jahrhunderts*. (Vol. 7) Zurich: Kindler, 1978.

Salkind, N. J. The development of norms for the Matching Familiar Figures Test. *Journal Supplement Abstract Service*, 1978, *8*(Ms. No. 1718).

Salkind, N. J., Kojima, H., & Zelniker, T. Cognitive tempo in American, Japanese, and Israeli children. *Child Development*, 1978, *49*, 1024–1027.

Salkind, N. J., & Nelson, C. F. A note on the developmental nature of reflection-impulsivity. *Developmental Psychology*, 1980, *3*, 237–238.

Salkind, N. J., & Schlecter, T. Comparability of the KRISP and the MFF in kindergarten children. *Child Study Journal*, 1982, *12*, 1–5.

Salkind, N. J., & Wright, J. C. The development of reflection-impulsivity and cognitive efficiency. *Human Development*, 1977, *20*, 377–387.

Saltz, E., Dixon, D., & Johnson, J. E. Training disadvantaged preschoolers on various fantasy activities: Effects on cognitive functioning and impulsive control. *Child Development*, 1977, *48*, 367–380.

Saltz, E., & Johnson, J. E. Training for thematic-fantasy play in culturally disadvantaged children: Preliminary results. *Journal of Educational Psychology*, 1974, *66*, 623–630.

Santostefano, S. *A biodevelopmental approach to clinical child psychology: Cognitive controls and cognitive control therapy*. New York: Wiley, 1978.

Satterly, D. J. Cognitive styles, spatial ability, and school achievement. *Journal of Educational Psychology*, 1976, *68*, 36–42.

Scardamalia, M. Information processing capacity and the problem of horizontal décalage: A demonstration using combinatorial reasoning tasks. *Child Development*, 1977, *48*, 28–37.

Sheldon, E. B., & Jenness, D. Commentary: Complexity of sex comparisons. In S. Messick & associates (Eds.), *Individuality in learning*. San Francisco: Jossey-Bass, 1976.

Sherman, J. A. Problem of sex differences in space perception and aspects of intellectual functioning. *Psychological Review*, 1967, *74*, 290–299.

Sherman, J. A. *Sex-related cognitive differences*. Springfield, Ill.: Charles C. Thomas, 1978.

Sigel, I. E. *SCST manual: Instructions and scoring guide*. Detroit: Merrill-Palmer Institute, 1967.

Sigel, I. E. The development of classificatory skills in young children: A training program. In W. W. Hartup (Ed.), *The young child: Review of re-*

search (Vol. 2). Washington, D.C.: National Association for the Education of Young Children, 1972.

Sigel, I. E., & Brodzinsky, D. M. Individual differences: A perspective for understanding intellectual development. In H. L. Hom, Jr., & P. A. Robinson (Eds.), *Psychological processes in early education*. New York: Academic Press, 1977.

Signorella, M. L., & Jamison, W. Sex differences in the correlations among field dependence, spatial ability, sex role orientation, and performance on Piaget's water-level task. *Developmental Psychology*, 1978, *14*, 689–690.

Singer, D. L., & Rummo, J. Ideational creativity and behavioral style in kindergarten-age children. *Developmental Psychology*, 1973, *8*, 154–161.

Singer, D. L., & Whiton, M. B. Ideational creativity and expressive aspects of human figure drawing in kindergarten age children. *Developmental Psychology*, 1971, *4*, 366–369.

Singer, J. L. *The child's world of make-believe*. New York: Academic Press, 1973.

Smilansky, S. *The effects of sociodramatic play on disadvantaged children*. New York: Wiley, 1968.

Smith, P. K., and Dutton, S. Play and training in direct and innovative problem solving. *Child Development*, 1979, *50*, 830–836.

Smith, P. K., & Syddall, S. Play and non-play tutoring in preschool children: Is it play or tutoring which matters? *British Journal of Educational Psychology*, 1978, *48*, 315–325.

Solomon, D., & Kendall, A. J. Individual characteristics and children's performance in "open" and "traditional" classroom settings. *Journal of Educational Psychology*, 1976, *68*, 613–625.

Sternberg, R. J., Tourangeau, R., & Nigro, G. Metaphor, induction, and social policy: The convergence of macroscopic and microscopic views. In A. Ortony (Ed.), *Metaphor and thought*. New York: Cambridge University Press, 1979.

Stone, C. A., & Day, M. C. Competence and performance models and the characterization of formal operational skills. *Human Development*, 1980, *23*, 323–353.

Susman, E. J., Huston-Stein, A., & Friedrich-Cofer, L. Relation of conceptual tempo to social behaviors of Head Start children. *Journal of Genetic Psychology*, 1980, *137*, 17–20.

Sylva, K., Bruner, J. S., & Genova, P. The role of play in the problem-solving of children 3–5 years old. In J. S. Bruner, A. Jolly, & K. Sylva (Eds.),

Play: Its role in development and evolution. New York: Basic Books, 1976.

Tarver, S., & Maggiore, R. P. Cognitive development in learning disabled boys. *Learning Disability Quarterly*, 1979, *2*, 78–84.

Thomas, H., & Jamison, W. On the acquisition of understanding that still water is horizontal. *Merrill-Palmer Quarterly*, 1975, *21*, 31–44.

Thomas, N. G., & Berk, L. E. Effects of school environments on the development of young children's creativity. *Child Development*, 1981, *52*, 1153–1162.

Toner, I. J., Holstein, R. B., & Hetherington, E. M. Reflection-impulsivity and self-control in preschool children. *Child Development*, 1977, *48*, 239–245.

Torrance, E. P. *Torrance tests of creative thinking*. Princeton, N.J.: Personnel Press, 1966.

Torrance, E. P. Predictive validity of the Torrance tests of creative thinking. *Journal of Creative Behavior*, 1972, *6*, 236–252.

Torrance, E. P. Creativity research in education: Still alive. In I. A. Taylor & J. W. Getzels (Eds.), *Perspectives in creativity*. Chicago: Aldine, 1975.

Tourangeau, R., & Sternberg, R. J. Aptness in metaphor. *Cognitive Psychology*, 1981, *13*, 27–55.

Trickett, P. K. The interaction of cognitive styles and classroom environment in determining first-graders' behavior. *Journal of Applied Developmental Psychology*, 1983, *4*, in press.

Vandenberg, B. Play, problem-solving and creativity. In K. H. Rubin (Ed.), *New directions for child development: Children's play* (No. 9). San Francisco: Jossey-Bass, 1980.

Vaught, G. M., Pittman, M. D., & Roodin, P. A. Developmental curves for the portable rod-and-frame test. *Bulletin of the Psychonomic Society*, 1975, *5*, 151–152.

Verbrugge, R. R. The primacy of metaphor in development. In E. Winner & H. Gardner (Eds.), *New directions for child development: Fact, fiction, and fantasy in childhood* (No. 6). San Francisco: Jossey-Bass, 1979.

Vernon, P. E. Effects of administration and scoring on divergent thinking tests. *British Journal of Educational Psychology*, 1971, *41*, 245–257.

Vernon, P. E. The distinctiveness of field independence. *Journal of Personality*, 1972, *40*, 366–391.

Vernon, P. E. Multivariate approaches to the study of cognitive styles. In J. R. Royce (Ed.), *Multivariate analysis and psychological theory*. New York: Academic Press, 1973.

Vurpillot, E. *The visual world of the child*. New York: International Universities Press, 1976.

Waber, D. P. Sex differences in mental abilities: A function of maturation rate? *Science*, 1976, *192*, 572–574.

Waber, D. P. Biological substrates of field dependence: Implications of the sex difference. *Psychological Bulletin*, 1977, *84*, 1076–1087. (a)

Waber, D. P. Sex differences in mental abilities, hemispheric lateralization, and rate of physical growth at adolescence. *Developmental Psychology*, 1977, *13*, 29–38. (b)

Waber, D. P. Cognitive abilities and sex-related variation in the maturation of cerebral cortical functions. In M. A. Wittig & A. C. Petersen (Eds.), *Sex-related differences in cognitive functioning: Developmental issues*. New York: Academic Press, 1979.

Wagner, D. A. The effects of formal schooling on cognitive style. *Journal of Social Psychology*, 1978, *106*, 145–151.

Wagner, S., Winner, E., Cicchetti, D., & Gardner, H. "Metaphorical" mapping in human infants. *Child Development*, 1981, *52*, 728–731.

Wallach, M. A. Creativity. In P. H. Mussen (Ed.), *Carmichael's manual of child psychology* (Vol. 1) (3rd ed.). New York: Wiley, 1970.

Wallach, M. A. *The intelligence/creativity distinction*. Morristown, N.J.: General Learning Press, 1971.

Wallach, M. A. Psychology of talent and graduate education. *In* S. Messick & associates (Eds.), *Individuality in learning*, San Francisco: Jossey-Bass, 1976.

Wallach, M. A., & Kogan, N. *Modes of thinking in young children*. New York: Holt, Rinehart & Winston, 1965.

Wallach, M. A., & Wing, C. W., Jr. *The talented student: A validation of the creativity-intelligence distinction*. New York: Holt, Rinehart & Winston, 1969.

Wallbrown, F. H., & Heulsman, C. B., Jr. The validity of the Wallach-Kogan creativity operations for inner-city children in two areas of visual art. *Journal of Personality*, 1975, *43*, 109–126.

Ward, W. C. Creativity in young children. *Child Development*, 1968, *39*, 737–754.

Ward, W. C. Creativity and environmental cues in nursery school children. *Developmental Psychology*, 1969, *1*, 543–547. (a)

Ward, W. C. Rate and uniqueness in children's creative responding. *Child Development*, 1969, *40*, 869–878. (b)

Ward, W. C., Kogan, N., & Pankove, E. Incentive effects in children's creativity. *Child Development*, 1972, *43*, 669–676.

Ward, W. D., & Barcher, P. R. Reading achievement and creativity as related to open classroom experience. *Journal of Educational Psychology*, 1975, *67*, 683–691.

Warden, P. G., & Prawat, R. S. Convergent and divergent thinking in black and white children of high and low socioeconomic status. *Psychological Reports*, 1975, *36*, 715–718.

Weiner, A. S., & Berzonsky, M. D. Development of selective attention in reflective and impulsive children. *Child Development*, 1975, *46*, 545–549.

Weisz, J. R., O'Neill, P., & O'Neill, P. C. Field dependence-independence on the Children's Embedded Figures Test: Cognitive style or cognitive level? *Developmental Psychology*, 1975, *11*, 539–540.

Werner, H. The concept of development from a comparative and organismic point of view. In D. B. Harris (Ed.), *The concept of development: An issue in the study of human behavior*. Minneapolis: University of Minnesota Press, 1957.

Werner, H., & Kaplan, B. *Symbol formation: An organismic-developmental approach to language and the expression of thought*. New York: Wiley, 1963.

Wheelwright, P. *Metaphor and reality*. Bloomington: Indiana University Press, 1962.

Willemsen, E., & Reynolds, B. Sex differences in adults' judgment of the horizontal. *Developmental Psychology*, 1973, *8*, 309.

Williams, T. M., & Fleming, J. W. Methodological study of the relationship between associative fluency and intelligence. *Developmental Psychology*, 1969, *1*, 155–162.

Wilson, F. S., Stuckey, T., & Langevin, R. Are pupils in the open plan school different? *Journal of Educational Research*, 1972, *66*, 115–118.

Winner, E., McCarthy, M., & Gardner, H. The ontogenesis of metaphor. In R. P. Honeck & R. R. Hoffman (Eds.). *Cognition and figurative language*. Hillsdale, N.J.: Erlbaum, 1980.

Winner, E., Rosenstiel, A. K., & Gardner, H. The development of metaphoric understanding. *Developmental Psychology*, 1976, *12*, 289–297.

Winner, E., Wapner, W., Cicone, M., & Gardner, H. Measures of metaphor. In E. Winner & H. Gardner (Eds.), *New directions for child development: Fact, fiction, and fantasy in childhood* (No. 6). San Francisco: Jossey-Bass, 1979.

Witkin, H. A. *Cognitive styles in personal and cultural adaptation: The 1977 Heinz Werner lec-*

tures. Worcester, Mass.: Clark University Press, 1978.

Witkin, H. A., & Berry, J. W. Psychological differentiation in cross-cultural perspective. *Journal of Cross-Cultural Psychology,* 1975, *6,* 4–87.

Witkin, H. A., Dyk, R. B., Faterson, H. F., Goodenough, D. R., & Karp, S. A. *Psychological differentiation*. New York: Wiley, 1962.

Witkin, H. A., & Goodenough, D. R. Field dependence and interpersonal behavior. *Psychological Bulletin,* 1977, *84,* 661–689.

Witkin, H. A., & Goodenough, D. R. *Cognitive styles: Essence and origins*. New York: International Universities Press, 1981.

Witkin, H. A., Goodenough, D. R., & Karp, S. A. Stability of cognitive style from childhood to young adulthood. *Journal of Personality and Social Psychology,* 1967, *7,* 291–300.

Witkin, H. A., Goodenough, D. R., & Oltman, P. K. Psychological differentiation: Current status. *Journal of Personality and Social Psychology,* 1979, *37,* 1127–1145.

Witkin, H. A., Lewis, H. B., Hertzman, M., Machover, K., Meissner, P. B., & Wapner, S. *Personality through perception*. New York: Harper, 1954.

Witkin, H. A., Moore, C. A., Goodenough, D. R., & Cox, P. W. Field-dependent and field-independent cognitive styles and their educational implications. *Review of Educational Research,* 1977, *47,* 1–64.

Witkin, H. A., Oltman, P. K., Raskin, E., & Karp, S. A. *A manual for the children's embedded figures test*. Palo Alto, Calif.: Consulting Psychologists Press, 1971.

Wittig, M. A., & Petersen, A. C. (Eds.), *Sex-related differences in cognitive functioning: Developmental issues*. New York: Academic Press, 1979.

Wohlwill, J. F. *The study of behavioral development*. New York: Academic Press, 1973.

Wohlwill, J. F. Cognitive development in childhood. In O. G. Brim, Jr., & J. Kagan (Eds.), *Constancy and change in human development*. Cambridge, Mass.: Harvard University Press, 1980.

Wright, J. C. *The Kansas reflection-impulsivity scale for preschoolers (KRISP)*. St. Louis: CEMREL, 1971.

Wright, R. J. The affective and cognitive consequences of an open education elementary school. *American Educational Research Journal,* 1975, *12,* 449–468.

Yando, R., Seitz, V., & Zigler, E. *Intellectual and personality characteristics of children: Social class and ethnic-group differences*. Hillsdale, N.J.: Erlbaum, 1979.

Zelniker, T., Bentler, P. M., & Renan, A. Speed versus accuracy as a measure of cognitive style: Internal consistency and factor analyses. *Child Development,* 1977, *48,* 301–304.

Zelniker, T., Cochavi, D., & Yered, J. The relationship between speed of performance and conceptual style: The effect of imposed modification of response latency. *Child Development,* 1974, *45,* 779–784.

Zelniker, T., & Jeffrey, W. E. Reflective and impulsive children: Strategies of information processing underlying differences in problem solving. *Monographs of the Society for Research in Child Development,* 1976, *41*(5, Serial No. 168).

Zelniker, T., & Jeffrey, W. E. Attention and cognitive style in children. In G. A. Hale & M. Lewis (Eds.), *Attention and cognitive development*. New York: Plenum, 1979.

Zelniker, T., Jeffrey, W. E., Ault, R. L., & Parsons, J. Analysis and modification of search strategies of impulsive and reflective children on the Matching Familiar Figures Test. *Child Development,* 1972, *43,* 321–335.

Zelniker, T., Renan, A., Sorer, I., & Shavit, Y. Effect of perceptual processing strategies on problem solving of reflective and impulsive children. *Child Development,* 1977, *48,* 1436–1442.

Zimmerman, B. J., & Dialessi, F. Modeling influences on children's creative behavior. *Journal of Educational Psychology,* 1973, *65,* 127–134.

Ziv, A. Facilitating effects of humor on creativity. *Journal of Educational Psychology,* 1976, *68,* 318–322.

Zoccolotti, P., & Oltman, P. K. Field dependence and lateralization of verbal and configurational processing. *Cortex,* 1978, *14,* 155–163.

SOME CURRENT ISSUES IN THE STUDY OF THE ACQUISITION OF GRAMMAR* | 11

MICHAEL MARATSOS, *Institute of Child Development, University of Minnesota*

CHAPTER CONTENTS

*The major draft of this chapter was written while the author was a fellow at the Center for Advanced Study in the Behavioral Sciences at Stanford, California. I wish to express my gratitude for the working conditions available at the Center and to the following sources for funding during that period: National Institute of Mental Health Grant No. 5–T32–MH14851–05 and the Andrew W. Mellon Foundation; I also wish to thank the University of Minnesota, which gave me sabbatical support during this period.

On the basis of the best information now available, it seems reasonable to suppose that a child cannot help constructing a particular sort of transformational grammar to account for the data presented to him, any more than he can control his perception of solid objects or his attention to line and angle.

N. Chomsky, *Aspects of the theory of syntax* (1965)

Grammar, with its mixture of general rule and arbitrary exception, proposes to the young mind a foretaste of what will be offered to him by law, ethics, and all those other systems by which man seeks to codify his instinctive experience.

M. Yourcenar, *The memoirs of Hadrian* (1963)

A great many things keep happening, some of them good, some of them bad.

Gregory of Tours, *The history of the Franks* (597)

A review written at this point in time about the state of grammatical acquisition as a field cannot objectively present a certain and unified picture. Things are unsettled.

The recent origins of interest in the field lay in Noam Chomsky's work in transformational grammar. Pretransformational structural linguistics had already analyzed how a language system is a system of rules that exceeds the data (Brown, 1957; Gleason, 1961; Harris, 1951). Berko's (1958) famous demonstration that a speaker exposed to one use of a novel term, never heard before, could predict a new grammatical use for the term appropriately, grew out of this tradition. One tells the subject something like "Today John glizzes. Yesterday he did the same thing. Yesterday he _____," and the subject knows to fill in *glizzed*, although never having heard *glizzed* before. Such demonstrations showed that speakers, indeed, assimilate a system of rules exceeding memorized uses. Russian investigators were almost simultaneously giving similar demonstrations with Russian noun-gender systems (Bogoyavlenskiy, 1957/1973). But Chomsky's work in transformational grammar indicated that the acquisition of grammar was an even more formidable problem. His claims were that first, grammatical competence itself—the rules for producing and comprehending sequences of morphemes or for judging them for acceptability—has a purely *formal* component represented without respect to meaning. Abstract rules of transformational rearrangements, deletion, and substitution operate on underlying and intermediate syntactic strings to produce surface structures (the

structures actually heard), which thus comprise only a kind of tip of the derivational iceberg. Furthermore, Chomsky held that language acquisition is essentially best considered as instantaneous, that grammar is learned without tutoring or feedback about correctness or uncorrectness of utterances, and that the input to the child (judging from what was known about adult speech to adults) was likely to be a degenerate, error-filled sample because of memory problems or other performance problems. Under such conditions, Chomsky believed, it was impossible to hold that the child learned grammar in any normal sense. Instead, to devise such complex structures so quickly and under such unfavorable conditions, the child must begin the task already equipped with highly developed and abstract ideas about the general possible forms of grammar.

In a sense, the present chapter is a review of the state of Chomsky's claims, although much current work has taken on impetus and interest of its own. Because of space limitations, the chapter is devoted to those problems of acquisition studied empirically in the grammatical acquisition of normal children under normal conditions. In particular, the following problems have been emphasized:

1. Can abstract grammatical relations and categories, such as subject and object or noun, verb, and adjective, be justified in the description of early grammar? What kinds of categories and rules do characterize early grammar?

2. How do such categories evolve? What is the relative role of cognitive, semantic, and formal analyses in their evolution?

3. What is the evidence that transformational grammars as they have been conceived give a psychologically real account of what the child acquires?

4. What is the nature of linguistic input to the child? Is it degenerate, error filled, and misleading or not? Does parental input give the child feedback on the correctness or comprehensibility of the child's utterances?

5. What are some general characteristics of children's acquisition of linguistic rules? Is rule acquisition and change virtually instantaneous or is it gradual? Does the child begin with the most general formulation suggested by the data or work up from lower level analyses? Do all children go through similar acquisitional sequences in acquiring grammar? What can explain those similarities that are found?

In the past few years, many of these issues have been raised most sharply in the study of children's early simple-sentence constructions (Bloom, 1970; Bloom, Miller, & Hood, 1975; Bowerman, 1973, 1975, 1976; Braine, 1963, 1976; Brown, 1973; de Villiers & de Villiers, 1978; Ingram, 1979; Maratsos & Chalkley, 1980; Schieffelin, in press; Schlesinger, 1971, 1974, 1981; Slobin, 1981). A significant characteristic of recent research is the increased interest in the early acquisition of languages that differ importantly from English in their major structural characteristics (MacWhinney, 1975; Schieffelin, in press; Slobin, 1981). These results will be treated after those that are centered on issues arising in English acquisition and related findings.

THE STUDY OF EARLY GRAMMATICAL ACQUISITION: THE PROBLEM OF EARLY CATEGORIES

The chief stimulus to the greatly accelerated interest in children's acquisition of grammatical structure almost certainly lay in the implications of complex transformational grammatical descriptions. Paradoxically, recent years have seen a primary interest in children's early combinations, such as *mommy eat, get ball,* or *his table*—utterances for the explication of which transformational grammars would likely never have been formulated. Why should this have happened? There are a number of evident reasons. There is always a feeling that the organism's first approaches to a problem show its basic analytic tendencies. There were also important particular questions. Nativists, such as McNeill (1966), for example, claimed that children's early grammatical constructions make use of purely grammatical relations, such as subject, verb, and object. As these have been described for adult grammar, they cannot be tied directly to nonlinguistic categories such as actor and action, or to simple linear positions in sentences such as first word or last word. Children's immediate use of such abstract grammatical categories would, thus, imply innate linguistic predispositions to impose them actively on the incoming data. An early purpose of investigation was to see if children's early combinatorial rules required use of such categories or could be otherwise explained.

In general, investigators have agreed that there is truly some kind of systematic patterning in children's earliest utterances. Where there is such patterning, it must be that the child has indeed induced or analyzed *categories* for the purpose of describing regularities of word combinations. The principal task of the study of early grammatical acquisition has, thus, been to try to analyze what kinds of categories the child uses and what kinds of properties these involve. These categories and their constituent properties have fallen into a number of types. But their basic properties may be profitably analyzed as arising from relatively pure forms of structural analysis that have recurred throughout the history of the analysis of grammar. Before proceeding to an examination of the empirical data and theoretical arguments, it will, thus, be useful to outline these kinds of analysis in relatively clear form.

Semantic Versus Distributional Analyses

Lyons (1968) discusses two major kinds of sentential structural analysis that have recurred in the history of grammatical analysis. The first of these is *distributional* analysis: an analysis of linguistic units purely in terms of the manner in which classes of units combine with each other grammatically, largely without reference to meaning. The second will here generally be called *semantic-based* analysis: meanings conveyed by the terms contain the basis for stating the generalizations about how they may be sequenced.

These two kinds of analysis can be illustrated briefly by a consideration of a very small corpus of utterances: *hit ball, get spoon, I hit, you get, find shoe, mommy find, mommy get.* In a distributional analysis, terms that combine similarly with other terms are formed into classes for the statements of general rules summarizing the grammatical structure of the corpus. In the present corpus, we might describe the terms as falling into three major classes of grammatical behavior that will be called neutrally X_1, X_2, and X_3—X_3 consists of terms that occur only at the ends of utterances: *spoon, dog,* and *shoe;* X_1 terms occur only at the beginning: *I, you, mommy;* X_2 terms, *hit, get,* and *find,* occur either at the end or the beginning. Furthermore, members of X_2 can combine with either members of X_1 or X_3, whereas members of the last two classes cannot combine with each other. All these criteria justify the initial positing of three classes and a simple pair of rules to describe the general structure of the corpus:

$$\text{Utterance} = \begin{Bmatrix} x_1 + x_2 \\ x_2 + x_3 \end{Bmatrix}$$

An important characteristic of these rules is that they are productive: they predict new, unheard combinations. For example, because *hit* is an X_2 term and *shoe* an X_3 term, the rules predict that an acceptable utterance might be *hit shoe.* The rules also predict the unacceptability of other, unheard utterances.

For example, the rules say utterances must have an X_2 term; *you spoon* or *mommy ball* are, thus, ruled out.

In a semantic-structural analysis, the terms are classified in terms of their general semantic properties to see if these properties can be used to describe the general combinatorial structure. One possible classification scheme of the sample corpus is that the utterances employ three semantic categories to order the terms: agent, one who initiates an action; action; and patient, a traditional grammatical description for the recipient of the force of an action. In such a scheme, *mommy, I,* and *you* may all be classified as agents (assuming Englishlike interpretations of the meanings of the utterances); *hit, get,* and *find* as action terms; and *ball, spoon,* and *shoe* as patients. Two rules, then, account for the above corpus as well as predict other possible utterances:

$$\text{Utterance} = \left\{ \begin{array}{l} \text{Agent + Action} \\ \text{Action + Patient} \end{array} \right\}$$

Either of the above descriptions is an adequate possible analysis of this small corpus. In psychological terms, of course, these descriptions imply very different kinds of understanding. A speaker who actually used a distributional analysis might well be making semantic analyses of the meanings of the terms. But these would be irrelevant to his analysis of the possibilities of combinations of terms. Suppose the speaker saw his mother hit a shoe for example. Wishing to say something happened concerning the hitting and the shoe, he would find that *hit* was classified as an X_2 word and *shoe* as an X_3 word. Thus, the utterance *hit shoe* would be possible. Notice that if we take the above analysis literally, the speaker could see a shoe hit his mother and say *mother hit* because mother is an X_1 word and *hit* an X_2 word.

The semantic analysis claims that just certain aspects of the semantic analysis are relevant to the construction of sentences: the relations of agency, patienthood, and actionality. In talking about hitting a ball, because hitting is an action and the ball is a recipient of the action, the rules dictate the placement of *ball* after *hit*. It is only these very general semantic analyses that are relevant. Although the fact that *hit* refers to a contact between two objects is relevant to the choice of the word *hit* to describe the action, it is not relevant to the ordering of the terms because whether or not there is contact does not indicate whether a term denotes an action.

Even for this limited corpus, however, other possible rules for sentence formulation may easily be devised. The concepts of agent, action, and patient, for example, are very general ones. To classify hitters, getters, and finders all alike as agents is to abstract from each kind of activity a small part of the conceptual structures of the respective situational roles. Perhaps our speaker, even though using a semantic basis to guide his productions, instead learned specific formulas revolving around the more particular roles and meanings involved in finding, getting, and bitting (e.g., placing the term denoting the finder before the term denoting the action of finding). The speaker's knowledge would, thus, consist of six binary combinatorial rules: finder+*find, find*+found, getter+*get, get*+gotten object, hitter+*hit, hit*+hit object. Or the speaker's understanding might be in terms of general semantic concepts, but not the ones we thought. Another adequate description of the corpus above, for example, would be:

$$\text{Utterance} = \left\{ \begin{array}{l} \text{Animate Being + Action} \\ \text{Action + Inanimate Object} \end{array} \right\}$$

In these rules, the situational role of the referent of the word is irrelevant. All that matters for sequencing the words is whether the word denotes an animate being or an inanimate being.

As a last example, we could imagine that the speaker's knowledge encompasses a combination of distributional and semantic formulas, such as the following kind. He knows that each utterance must contain an X_2 word. For each of these X_2 terms, there is also a specific semantic-structural correspondence, such as *get*+word = getting+gotten object, word+*get* = getter+getting, that gives the meaning of the combination. As will be seen, much of adult grammar turns out to have such a mixed analytic character (Maratsos, 1979).

The difficulty of making a convincing single choice of an analysis is well illustrated by the plethora of analyses available for the small corpus above. The speaker of this hypothetical corpus could be given various learning, production, and judgment tasks to see how he has actually encoded these rules. But it is now more to the point instead to deal with what has been proposed and found out about young children. Students of children's language deal with larger but often less orderly corpora. The ingenuity of investigators in determining as much as they have has been considerable.

Distributional Accounts of Early Grammar

Before going on, it will be useful to define early grammar. The basic measure of linguistic advancement that has been used in the analysis of English and in the analysis of the early periods of other languages is MLU: the mean length of the child's utterances in morphemes (Brown, 1973; Brown, Cazden, & Bellugi, 1969; de Villiers & de Villiers, 1974). An utterance like *see dog* is just two morphemes long. *See dogs* is three morphemes long because *dogs* is comprised of two morphemes, the stem *dog* and plural marking *-s*.

Brown (1973) divided acquisition through an MLU of 4.0 (after which average length often fails to rise much) into five major MLU points that he called stages: 1.75, 2.25, 2.75, 3.50, 4.00. Investigators often refer to early speech as Stage I speech, meaning speech in an MLU range of about 1.00+ through about 1.75, although some have extended it to higher MLUs (Bloom, Miller, & Hood, 1975).

The earliest descriptions of children's speech were purely distributional descriptions. Such descriptions had been the prevalent mode in American structural linguistics of past decades (Gleason, 1961; Harris, 1951). Investigators recorded children's utterances spoken in the home and analyzed their speech distributionally (Braine, 1963; Brown & Bellugi, 1964; Miller & Ervin, 1964).

The first description of this kind to attract widespread interest was Braine's (1963). Braine collected corpora of the earliest two-word combinations of three children learning English. The basic facts that struck Braine are obvious from a selection of some of the utterances from his subject Andrew:

> *more car, more cereal, more cookie, more fish, more high, more hot, more juice, more read, more sing, outside more;* (*more*+X); *no bed, no down, no fix, no home, no name, no more, no pee, no plug, no water, no wet;* (*no*+X); *boot off, light off, pants off, shirt off, shoe off, water off;* (X+*off*).

The major feature of the data was the frequent use by each of the three children of a few words in mostly fixed position and in combination with a larger set of words that were each used less frequently and not necessarily in fixed position. Distributional criteria converged on a division into two main distributional classes. There were the fixed-position words that could not generally occur together, and there were the nonfixed, infrequent words that sometimes did occur together. The fixed-position words Braine called *pivots* because sentences seemed to pivot around them. The nonfixed-position words were called *open* words because they seemed to accept new members easily. Pivot words were further divided into two subclasses: P_1 (words that always occurred initially) and P_2 (words that always occurred finally).

As Braine noted, at least some of the pivot-open

combinations were definitely productive; novel utterances were produced according to the rules, such as *more hot, more read,* and *no wet.* As in normal distributional analysis, Braine's description made no use of semantic analyses. Indeed, Braine held that the bizarreness of some of the combinations indicated the unimportance of semantic analysis in the children's combinations.

Semantic-Based Descriptions of Early Speech

Braine's analysis was proclaimed a universal of early speech (McNeill, 1966), but it also attracted both reinterpretation (McNeill, 1966, 1970) and criticism (Bloom, 1970; Bowerman, 1973; Brown, 1973). Some of these criticisms concerned the distributional adequacy of Braine's original analyses (Bowerman, 1973); others centered on children whose utterances did not have a "pivot-look" (Bowerman, 1973; Brown, 1973). The most important criticism, however, arose from the possibility that purely distributional analyses underestimate the degree to which children might be encoding semantic-structural correspondences in their speech rather than simply encoding generalizations about the positional possibilities of words *per se* (Bloom, 1970; Schlesinger, 1971). For example, consider the formula *more*+X. Braine (1963) said that *more* was simply a word analyzed as appearing initially in utterances and that X was any term that had no analyzed fixed position. Suppose, however, that the speech contexts in which children's utterances are heard are interpreted by the adult to give a probable semantic interpretation of what the child meant to communicate with the utterance (Bloom, 1970; Schlesinger, 1971). Then, utterances, such as *more hot* or *more cereal*, seem to encode either a recurrence or a desire for recurrence of the referent of the word following *more*, much as in normal adult usage. Thus, the condition for being X in the formula *more*+X is a semantic one, that is, the word must denote a recurrent (or desired-to-be recurrent) entity.

Similar kinds of analyses were quickly applied to other commonly occurring formulas in children's early speech: *no*+X = *no*+disappeared entity, *that*+X = *that*+named or categorized entity, *want*+X = *want*+desired entity, and so on (Bloom, 1970; Braine, 1976; Brown, 1970, 1973). Such formulas are quite constrained in certain ways. They still seem to pivot around a key term—in this case, a term denoting a relation; the other position is defined by a semantic category determined by the relation, that is, something recurrent (*more*+X), disappeared, rejected, wanted, named, noticed, and so on. Bloom (1970) and Schlesinger (1971), however, noted that in children's early utterances, one could also find orderly combinations in which both positional locations seemed to be defined by semantic categories that could freely accept new members. Consider a child like Kendall, studied by Bowerman (1973), who produced among her utterances the following sequences:

> *Kendall sit, Kendall read, Mommy read, Melissa walk, Daddy hide, Daddy write, Daddy walk, Kimmy bite, Bill talk, spider move, horse walk, horse run, ant away* (means, roughly, "ant went away"), *Melissa away.*

It is possible that what Kendall knew was a large variety of individual word formulas, such as X+*walk*, X+*bite*, and X+*away*. But the variety of terms in both positions points instead to the formulation of a pattern not tied to individual terms. Instead, the pattern might be described as something like actor+action. That is, a word denoting an action may be preceded by a word denoting the being that carried out the action.

Investigators (Bloom, 1970; Bowerman, 1973; Brown, 1973) found that English-speaking children produced utterances that could be analyzed according to the following patterns: agent-action (already discussed); action-patient, that is, a word denoting an action may be placed before a word denoting the recipient of the force of the action (e.g., *put book, hit ball*); agent-patient, that is, a word denoting the initiator of an activity may be placed before a word denoting the recipient of the force (e.g., *mommy sock*, said as mommy is putting on the child's sock; *mommy lunch*, said as mommy is having lunch); possessor-possessed object (e.g., *Adam checker, mommy sock*, said of mother's sock); action-location, that is, a word denoting an action may be placed before a word denoting the place or endpoint of the action (e.g., *walk street, come here*); located object-location, that is, a word denoting an object may be placed before a word denoting the location of the object (e.g., *sweater chair*, said of a sweater resting on a chair; *book table*, said of a book on a table; *doggy here*); attribute-object, that is, a word denoting an attribute of an object may be placed before the word denoting the object (e.g., *big train, red book*). Brown (1973) also noted the common use of what he called referential operations, including nomination+named object (*that book, it cat*); notice+noticed object (*hi mommy, hi belt, hi chair*); recurrence (*more milk, more cereal, other nut*); and nonexistence+nonexistent or disappeared object (*no rattle, no more juice*). Other languages, of course, might have different word orders from those of English, such as possessed object+possessor in Dutch. But the semantic relations relevant to the ordering of words appeared to be highly similar across transcripts of children speaking many different languages (Brown, 1973).

A set of semantic-structural relations commonly proposed for the early grammars of children learning English is reprinted here, adapted slightly, from Brown (1970, p. 220):

I. **Relations**

	Examples (from various children)
agent-action	*Adam put, Eve read*
action-patient	*put book, hit ball*
agent-patient	*mommy sock, mommy lunch*
possessor-possessed object	*Adam checker, mommy sock*
action-location or goal of action	*walk street, come here*
located object-location	*sweater chair, book table*
attribute-modified object	*big train, red book*

II. **Referential operations**

nomination	*that book, it cat*
notice	*hi mommy, hit belt, hi chair*
recurrence	*more milk, more cereal, other nut*
nonexistence	*no rattle, no more juice*

The most important result of the study of early speech is the now common agreement that semantic-cognitive categories, such as actionality, actorhood, location, recurrence, possession, and nomination, play central roles in the child's grammatical analyses; that is, the child analyzes aspects of the situational meanings of words to account for how they may be ordered with respect to each other. Furthermore, many of these meanings, Sinclair (1971, 1973) and Brown (1973) note, seem like ones that would be paramount in the child's general cognitive development at the time. Because of the child's changing notions of the permanence of objects, for example, the child could be expected to have interest in the recurrence of objects, of object types, or of their disappearance. That children would be interested in actions upon objects is clear as well as that they would be interested in possession. Such general cognitive analyses, then, seem to suggest themselves as hypotheses to the child to account for how words that express them are ordered as well. Chomsky's original suggestion of the possible irrelevance of situational meaning is clearly invalidated.

The use of semantic-cognitive categories—such as possessor, recurrer, location, and actor—thus represents perhaps the most important analytic outcome of the study of early grammar. Beyond this generally adopted use, however, remain a large number of questions. Preliminary to discussing these, it will be useful to discuss another of the major developments of recent years, that is, a gradually growing awareness of methodological problems of interpretation in attributing a construction to a child. Such methodological preliminaries form a necessary backdrop to all our further discussions.

Methodological Problems, Cautions, and Techniques of Inference

In the end, of course, methodology shades inexorably into interpretation. Individual problems require individual analyses. The purpose here is to bring up some general problems that form a useful background in dealing with any corpus.

1. Number and consistency. A problem raised by Braine (1976) is that investigators may propose analyses unjustified by simple criteria for simple numerical frequency and consistency of grammatical marking. He notes cases in which previous investigators had credited a child with a general construction, when only a few examples of the possible construction occurred or the examples were inconsistent in word order when contrasted with a stable adult ordering. As a beginning requirement, Braine suggests, a child should use the appropriate grammatical marking, such as word order, at an above-chance level. For example, to attribute a child with a stable observance of any pattern X + Y, there should be at least 6 examples out of 6 that actually have the order X + Y, 9 of 10 examples in consistent order, and so forth.

(Of course, the investigator should also be sensitive to cases where the adult language potentially employs both orders or makes special exceptions. For example, in English, the usual order for locational expressions is located object + location [e.g., *sweater (on) chair, dog (to) house*]. There are a few locative terms, however, that can appear either initially or finally, for example, *dog (is) here, here('s) dog*. If a child has some instances of location + located object but they are mostly of the form *here* + X or *there* + X, this is not a reason to conclude the child does not have knowledge of the order located object + location.)

2. Variety of instantiation. Another difficulty, and a very important one, is that even though a good number of instances are consistent with a potential general semantic-structural pattern, the child's corpus on closer inspection may make it plausible that more specific semantic-structural patterns are being used (Braine, 1976; Brown, Cazden, & Bellugi, 1969). For example, Jonathan (Braine, 1976) produced the following possible action-patient sequences in his second corpus: *eat dessert, eat fork, bite top, bite block, bounce ball, drink water, have-it egg, have-it milk, have-it fork*. This group consists of nine potential action-patient utterances in the appropriate order. Strikingly, however, most of the combinations have to do with oral ingestion. Jonathan might know a broader action-patient pattern and simply be reflecting motivational restrictions. But it is clear that the data do not justify attributing more to Jonathan than perhaps something like ingestion + ingested substance as a possible formula.

It cannot be too strongly emphasized how frequently close internal inspection of a corpus may show potential general patterns to be comprised of smaller ones. Even when a child's corpus seems to exemplify a wider variety within a potential semantic-structural relation, careful analysis may still show limitations that reduce the plausibility of this attribution. For example, David (Braine, 1976), a child with an MLU of 1.7, produced a number of utterances that at a very broad level could be analyzed as including actor-action, action-patient, or actor-action-patient sequences. They were: *want break it, want fix it, can I fix it, I can't open door, I can't get open door, can I have put in, can I have break it, I can't get it, I can't come in, gimme ball, gimme that, gimme that . . . blow* ("give me that to blow out"), *I get, get ball, I get ball, get car, I get car, get hat, I get book, I get mike, open door, look (at) light, look (at) chicken, help it, break it, fix it, hold it, roll it, hit me.*

But clear limitations in the utterances and their

contexts of use make it difficult to attribute such broad semantic-structural knowledge to David (Braine, 1976). The possible patient terms are frequently *it*, for example, *break it, fix it, get it, hold it, roll it, help it*. When action terms are used just with *it*, this suggests that the child may in fact be analyzing sequences like *break-it, fix-it*, and so forth, as single units (Brown et al., 1969), a conclusion for which Braine (1976) also finds additional evidence in David's speech. *Open door* apparently simply meant "to open" because it was used to request the opening of boxes and other objects besides doors. This leaves, as possible action-patient utterances, two combinations with *look*, the combinations centering on *get* (*get ball, I get ball, get car, I get car, get hat, I get book, I get mike*) as well as a few more combinations. The combinations with *get* seem clearly to be special learning about *get*, something like $(I) + get + (X)$. Possible actor-action sequences are also clearly limited. The sequences beginning with *can-I+* . . . or *can-I-have* . . . were apparently rather fixed-form requests for an action or object. David was not necessarily to be the doer of a requested action; he said *can-I fix it* in a context that made clear someone else was supposed to fix it. Sequences beginning with *I-can't* . . . were usually requests for something to be done that David could not do. All of these seem more nearly allied to the common request sentences of the form *want+X*, of which there were 47 in David's corpus. This again leaves just the very limited combinations with *get* as potential actor-action sequences, clearly too limited a group to justify a broad formula instead of a highly restricted *I+get+* . . . rule. Thus, despite many utterances that show consistent order, David's corpus shows no good evidence for attribution of broad actor-action or action-patient sequential regularities. In general, Braine's (1976) close analyses of such instances make it clear that each child's corpus may require close internal inspection. Simply counting the number of sequences consistent with a possible general formula is not enough.

3. Developmental sequences. Brown (1973) and Schlesinger (1974) pointed out that even if a possible general construction is well and variegatedly instantiated in a corpus, it is possible that the child's competence might consist of a list of more specific rules. For example, even if we find a child using a wide variety of action-patient sequences, the child might actually have encoded a large number of word-bound or specific-category formulas, such as *bite+X, get+X,* movement+moved object, *find+X*, and so forth. Over a period of time, the accumulation of such a list of more specific rules would come to look like a more general rule, even if this was not yet the case for the child.

Schlesinger (1974) suggested one possible analytic procedure, that of analyzing what structural-semantic formulas were exemplified in grammatical combinations that emerged nearly simultaneously in a child's speech. If the child rather quickly began using many combinations of various kinds that were exemplifications of the formula action-patient, this would give good evidence of the child's having actually analyzed something like this structural-semantic formula. Conversely, if the child only formulated more specific combinations that were possible examples of the action-patient rule, this would support his having analyzed the data in terms of smaller semantic-structural patterns.

The method of seeing what combinations come relatively simultaneously, or fail to do so, has since been used in a number of works, whether inspired by Schlesinger's suggestion or not (e.g., Bloom, Miller, & Hood, 1975; Bowerman, 1976; Braine, 1976). For example, Jonathan, a child studied by Braine (1976), produced no examples of actor-action patterns in his initial corpus. In his second corpus, a few weeks later, he produced the following: *mommy sit, daddy sit, Andrew walk, daddy walk, man walk, boy walk, daddy sleep, Elliot sleep, Andrew sleep, daddy work* (when daddy was going to work), *daddy work* (when daddy was at his desk). Braine remarks that nearly all of these were associated with movement to some place of the actor (outside for walking, bed for sleeping). Thus, they seem narrower than a broad actor-action pattern, involving only movement of the actor by the actor. On the other hand, the fact that the different combinations emerged relatively simultaneously, whereas no other possible actor-action sequences did so, makes it unlikely that Jonathan had simply learned a list of individual word formulas X+*sit*, X+*walk*, X+*sleep*, X+*work*. The developmental evidence, thus, indicates a pattern something like mover (of self)+movement.

Bowerman (1976) has suggested an interesting methodological addition to the method of studying what developmental sequences do occur. In studying her two children, she recorded not only two-word utterances but also one-word utterances. She thus could see not only what combinations did occur but also what combinations did not occur that might have. One of her children, Eva, used the semantically similar terms *more, nomore, allgone*, and *again* as single words, and then began using only *more+X* without employing combinations with the other potential modifier terms. In general, Eva also learned other modifier word combinations individually rather than entering a large number simultaneously into modifier-modified combinations. Bowerman's other child, Christy, contrastively tended to enter semantically similar terms into similar semantic-structural formulas with some simultaneity.

It is always possible (and often likely), of course, that a child initially analyzes as a set of more specific rules what will eventually be analyzed as a more general construction. Thus, piece-by-piece initial learning does not indicate that some general construction is not eventually captured. This is likely to be characteristically true of much in cognitive development (Flavell, 1981).

4. Presence or absence of novel combinations. Sometimes a child will produce utterances that are clearly not imitated from adult speech, yet they seem to show some orderly generalization at work. The most famous instance of this comes from a later period of development, that is, in children's past tense overregularizations such as in *goed* and *knowed*. Examples exist in the study of early speech as well however. Andrew, for example, produced such combinations as *more hot* and *more read*. These clearly do not observe adult restrictions on the use of *more* but do observe the rule *more*+X = "recurrence of 'X'." These combinations, thus, provided strong evidence for the productivity of the *more*+X rule because they were novel, yet orderly. On the other hand, expectable errors may sometimes fail to occur. Braine (1976) notes that Andrew also used a combinatorial formula *all*+X, producing such sequences as *all messy, all done, all buttoned, all dressed, all through,* and *all clean*. As Braine notes, however, the group of terms that can go with *all* is somewhat arbitrary, and they are probably memorized for the adult. If Andrew had had a truly productive formula, he could have been expected to produce erroneous uses, such as *all big,* which he did not. Thus, he probably memorized all of the combinations, showing that he was interested in the use of *all* but that he did not derive a productive rule for its use. (Braine calls such frequent memorized-looking patterns associative patterns).

Again, however, such errors may be ambiguous in interpretation. For example, a child Braine studied produced the reasonable error of *eat water*. This could arise from an overgeneralization of the action-patient rule, but could equally (and more plausibly) arise from an overgeneralization about the use of *eat* per se.

These are some of the major general methodological concerns and analytic means that have become prominent in the last few years. Bowerman (1975) and Brown et al. (1969) note others having to do with sample size, especially relevant in judging sequence of acquisition of constructions. But by and large, most interpretive methods amount to careful inspection of the corpus or the sequence of corpora for internal consistencies or inconsistencies. The gradual accumulation of such methodological awareness has comprised, nevertheless, one of the major outcomes of the study of early speech. In the following discussions, some of the central problems of early speech are treated with these ideas in mind.

Specificity and Generality in Early Grammars

Braine (1976), applying the methodological criteria and cautions outlined above, analyzed corpora from 11 children in early and middle Stage I. These included corpora from Bowerman (1973) of 2 children, 1 learning English and 1 Finnish; corpora from Kernan (1970) of 2 children learning Samoan; corpora from Lange and Larsson (1973) of a child acquiring Swedish; as well as the corpora of the 6 other children available to Braine, all except 1 of whom were learning English (the exception was a child named Odi who was learning Hebrew). The corpora were collected at various points in Stage I. Kendall, for example, had corpora from MLU points 1.10 and 1.42; Tofi, a child learning Samoan, had corpora from MLU 1.6.

Of the 11 children, 6 did not show convincing evidence for a pattern in which both grammatical positions were occupied by a category, for example, such rules as actor-action or possessor-possessed object. Their grammars consisted of patterns such as *want*+X = 'request for 'X,'' or possible associative patterns such as X+*it* (David's *roll-it, hold-it* [Braine, 1976]); or groups of individual word patterns perhaps concentrated on a type of speech act, for example, Odi's (Braine, 1976) *give-me*+X and *where*+X, both of which seemed to function as request patterns. Such predominant use of specific patterns could last late into childhood. David, for example, who had no convincing general patterns, had an MLU of 1.7.

Furthermore, what could look like highly general formulas would often turn out to be more specific ones. Jonathan (Braine, 1976), for example, had a number of utterances that could be analyzed as action-patient but that concentrated on ingestion-ingested sequences (*eat*+X, *bite*+X, *drink*+X). His initial actor-action patterns concentrated on self-mover+movement patterns (e.g., X+*walk*, X+*sit*).

As far as can be told, evidence from other investigators often accords with this picture of more specific formula usage being common, although not universal. Bowerman's (1976) subject Eva is reported to have initially used mostly individual word formulas as she progressed into later grammar, as judged from such evidence as when various individual word patterns came into productive use. Bowerman's other child, Christy, concentrated on general or semigeneral patterns, such as mover-movement or object+class identification. Bloom (1970), Bloom, Miller, and Hood (1975), and Bloom, Lightbown, and Hood (1975) studied four subjects. While they do not print corpora, extensive quantitative summaries and examples are given. Two subjects, Kathryn and Gia, seem to have encoded a good number of fairly general semantic-structural patterns early on. Eric and Peter, however, showed persistent concentration on many highly specific formulas concerning such relations as recurrence and disappearance. Furthermore, as sometimes occurred with Braine's (1976) subjects, Eric and Peter frequently centered what could be analyzed as general semantic-structural relations around one or two words, such as *I* for agency, *my* for possession, *here* and *there* for locative place relations, and *it* for possible patient relations. Bloom, Miller, and Hood (1975) and Bloom, Lightbown, and Hood (1975) although noting the tendency to concentrate on pronominal references in Eric and Peter, judged the relevant utterances nevertheless to comprise exemplars of the potential general semantic-structural patterns. As was seen above, however, this is frequently not justified. The child may be using a far more specific pattern, such as *my* + X = possession of self; uses of *it* in expressions, such as *roll it* or *fix it,* may be associative patterns or segmentation errors (Braine, 1976; Brown et al., 1969). If we are conservative and judge such uses to be highly limited patterns until there is greater variety of instantiation, then we would conclude that more general patterns for location, possession, and agency had not emerged in the speech of these children by the end of Stage I. The fact that children concentrate in varying degrees initially on individual word formulas or on pronominal uses has been much commented on in the literature. Correlations have been made to aspects of the children's speech, such as its usual social use or some other variable (e.g., Horgan, 1978a, 1979; Nelson, 1973, 1975). But there is as yet little clear explanation for the phenomenon, which in any case is not necessarily an all-or-none one within individual children.

Thus, the use of highly general semantic-structural patterns, such as actor-action, actor-action-patient, property+object, located object+location, and so on, do not necessarily form a universal or even common entry into grammatical productivity. Among the general patterns that occur, the kinds of general patterns discussed earlier, such as agent + action or located object+location, do seem to predominate (Bloom, Miller, & Hood, 1975; Braine, 1976). But individual children seem to differ greatly in when and (possibly) how they achieve their use. Furthermore, despite efforts by such investigators as Bloom (1970), Bloom, Lightbown, and Hood (1975), and Wells (1974) to find them, it does not appear easy to discern among the early-acquired patterns any universal pattern of sequence of acquisition. Some children acquire individual word patterns having to do with recurrence or negation early on and actor-action patterns later, but others may reverse this sequence (Braine, 1976). Some may acquire possessor-possessed patterns before actor-action patterns, but others afterward.

Why should children not immediately and quickly evolve such general patterns as actor-action? Given the central importance of actor-action and actor-action-patient patterns in adult grammars as well as the central nature of activity in the picture of cognitive development provided us by investigators (e.g., Piaget), such general patterns seem like a natural beginning point.

No answer to this question is readily apparent. Some of the answer may have to do with the difficulties of certain kinds of grammatical analysis. As will be seen, the proper analysis of actional grammar is not as straightforward as it seems to the adult mind. Other factors beyond grammatical analysis per se could also be important however. A child most interested in requesting or naming things, for example, might simply not begin on the analysis of other kinds of patterns for some time. A child mostly interested in conveying relations about the self will automatically have a more restricted grammar as well. Or more general perceptual analytic tendencies might be involved.

In any case, these findings of great individual variation and great specificity in many children's early grammars constitute one of the major changes in orientations toward early grammar in the 1970s, just as the use of semantic-structural descriptions, such as actor-action, constituted a major change from the early distributional descriptions of the last decade. As can be seen, Stage I cannot be considered a neatly packaged, universal, and clear period for children's development. Instead, there seems to be a family of types of descriptions that children master. As will be seen, all of the kinds of descriptions they make actually have some role in adult grammars. But it is increasingly clear that far more is to be told about grammatical development than can be found in Stage I speech.

Beyond these major findings, there is still a last major result of the study of early grammar to be described. It is a more difficult result because it is a negative one, consisting of failure to find strong evidence for a set of possible analyses. The question is that of whether children's early grammars employ formal categories and relations, such as noun and verb or subject and object. Although the question is not closed (Bloom, Lightbown, & Hood, 1975; Bloom, Miller, & Hood, 1975), there seems to be a growing consensus that such formal categories are not found in early speech (Bowerman, 1973, 1975; Braine, 1976; Ingram, 1979; Maratsos & Chalkley, 1980). Analysis of how and why investigators reach such a conclusion is the focus of the next discussion.

Formal Categories in Early Speech?

In the present discussion, categories, such as noun and verb, will be differentiated from relations, such as subject and object. The differentiation lies in how a term (or phrase) takes on a grammatical classification. For example, for an adult, the word *boy* is a noun as part of its inherent marking. In both *the boy ate a fish* or *a fish ate the boy*, *boy* is a noun. On the other hand, whether or not *boy* is a subject or object depends upon its *role* in the sentence structure. In *the boy ate a fish*, *boy* is head of the subject noun phrase *the boy*. In *a fish ate the boy*, *the boy* is the grammatical object. Grammatical categories, such as noun and verb, are thus separable in principle from grammatical relations such as subject and object. Grammars such as Fillmore's case grammar (1968, 1971) in fact employ noun and verb categories without employing subject and object relations. Conversely, although present subject-object grammars all employ noun and verb categories, it is possible to envisage a grammar with a subject-object distinction that does not. Thus, the problems of lexical formal categories and grammatical relational formal categories will be analytically treated as separate here.

Formal Lexical Categories

What do we mean when we ask if a child's speech has nouns and verbs? They certainly use terms that are nouns and verbs and adjectives in the adult vocabulary, such as *boy*, *walk*, or *big*. Thus, in a certain sense, they do use nouns and verbs.

In a deeper sense, however, what we want to know is whether they group terms into grammatical categories in a way that captures important aspects of the reasons adult grammarians group terms into such categories. They might use the terms but not analyze them in the relevant ways at all.

It is generally agreed that the reason we do not simply use such categories as object-word, action-word, and property-word instead of noun, verb, and adjective is that groups of terms may behave similarly in grammar that do not all share a clear common semantic denotation. For example, consider the nouns *boy*, *dog*, *idea*, *trip*, and *action*. *Boy* and *dog*, like many nouns, denote concrete object classes. But it is hard to say that *idea*, *trip*, and *action* also do. All these terms do, however, share in common certain properties of grammatical combination. For example, they can all appear after various words that denote their definiteness or indefiniteness, such as *the boy*, *the idea*, *an action*, *a dog*, *that boy*, *this idea*, *those actions*, *these trips*. They also can take -*s* to mark plural number, for example, *dogs*, *ideas*, *trips*, *actions*, *ideas*. We could symbolize each of these as small semantic-structural patterns, for example, $X + s = $ 'plural of X,' $the + X = $ 'definite reference to X,' $those + X = $ 'definite plural reference to X,' and so forth. Then, such terms as *idea* and *dog*, despite their highly dissimilar semantic nature, share in common their participation in a group of grammatical patterns. To symbolize this commonality, linguists describe such terms as *nouns*.

Similarly, verbs tend to denote actions. But they also include nonactional terms, such as *like*, *know*, *see*, *hear*, *belong*, *consist*, *want*, and *need*. Despite the semantic differences among *want*, *kick*, *die*, *need*, *belong*, and *push*, however, they too share various characteristic grammatical combinations. For example, they can take -*s* to denote present tense after a third-person-singular noun phrase: *the boy likes it, it dies, she kicks them, it belongs here;* they can take -*ed* to denote past tense (with some irregular exceptions): *wanted, needed, died, kicked, pushed, belonged, consisted;* or they can take forms of *do*, such as *doesn't, didn't, don't, did, does, do,* to denote tense or negation: *doesn't know, didn't die, did hear, does belong, don't push.* Among the terms denoting relations, verbs also have another grammatical privilege in common. They can occur directly after a noun or noun phrase at the beginning of a sentence, for example, *boys like dogs, action inspires people,* and so on.

The unification of classes such as adjectives or prepositions is similar. Although not necessarily unified by common semantic denotation, these classes share in common certain properties of grammatical behavior. Thus, adjectives as semantically diverse as *dead, noisy, loud, big, nice,* and *red* (often highly actional in meaning—*noisy, loud, quick*) share such properties as being able to be used in front of nouns as part of the initial noun phrase of a sentence, for example, *the noisy boy sang, the loud girl ate, the quick beetle died.* (Verbs can be used as prenominal modifiers only when a participial ending, such as *-ing* or *-ed,* is used, e.g., *the singing boy died, the shocked beetle ran.*) Adjectives cannot be marked for tense and negation in the same way as verbs, as shown by the ungrammaticality of **he niced to her,*[1] or **the quick beetle didn't noisy;* adjectives must take preceding forms of *be,* for example, *he wasn't nice to her, the quick beetle was noisy.*

Thus, in adult grammar, grammatical categories such as noun, verb, and adjective are justified because a semantically heterogeneous group of terms shares in a common group of grammatical operations. Such systems are potentially quite productive once the system is known. For example, suppose we hear that *glix* is a word denoting an emotional feeling. By itself, this does not tell us how to use it because it could be a noun (sadness, joy), an adjective (happy, sad), or a verb (enjoy, like). But if we hear it in a grammatical context, such as *John glixes dogs,* we know its grammatical category and, from this, can predict the other uses likely for such a term, for example, *John glixed dogs, Mary doesn't glix dogs, the glixing of dogs by John was surprising, to glix dogs is nice, dogs aren't glixed by most people, glixing dogs is common, my father won't glix this idea,* and so forth.

Do children in Stage I grammar use nouns, verbs, and adjectives in their early speech in the sense outlined above? Do they represent semantically heterogeneous terms as being unified by common grammatical uses? Do such unifications share properties of the adult grammar?

Very briefly, at present, the most reasonable answer appears to be that such categories are lacking in children's early speech (Braine, 1976; Maratsos & Chalkley, 1980). When children's grammatical rules mention general categories, such categories seem to be best analyzed according to the semantic properties or situational-role properties of the word. Thus, a rule, such as actor-action, does include sequences that include adult verbs, for example, *mommy walk, daddy sing.* But action-word is a semantically based description. *Walk, sing,* and *push,* used in such a rule, can be united by their semantic similarity per se. Similarly, 'actor' describes a term according to its situational-semantic role, as the doer or the initiator of the action. It is true that all the terms that denote actors will be adult nouns. But this

is because actors are denoted by concrete animate terms, which have noun status for the adult. For the child, however, it is their semantic denotations that unite them. They are not a semantically heterogeneous group of terms united by participation in common grammatical structures.

In fact, the child will treat differently terms that are united by grammatical category in the adult grammar. For example, in the adult grammar, *want, see, walk,* and *tickle* are all verbs, united by operations that verbs have in common. Various children, however, may treat *want* or *see* quite differently from such terms as *walk* or *tickle.* For example, Bowerman (1976) reports that her daughter Eva began combinations of the form *want*+X at a time when terms that would be verbs in the adult vocabulary were entering into no combinations at all, although appearing as single words; or in David's (Braine, 1976) speech (described earlier), *want*+X was a highly productive combination including both object words and action words as things that could denote wanted entities (e.g., *want cup, want go*), whereas such terms as *hold* or *roll* appeared only with *-it,* for example, *hold-it, roll-it.* Even within what are action verbs for the adult, treatment may be different. Jonathan (Braine, 1976), for example, used *eat, bite,* and *drink* only at the beginnings of sentences (*eat*+X, *bite*+X) without mentioning any actor; he used *sleep, sit, walk,* and *work* as terms that took initial actor arguments (*daddy work, Elliot walk*). Or the child may group together terms that do not fall into the same grammatical category for the adult. For many children, for example, such terms as *off, up, away,* and *back* seem to denote locative actions for some period of time (Bloom, Miller, & Hood, 1975; Bowerman, 1976; Braine, 1976). *Spider away* means something like 'spider going away.' In such cases, the child may treat *walk, away,* and *go* as similar, that is, as part of some kind of actor-action pattern, but treat *want* as part of a different pattern.

Thus, in early speech, the unification of terms into grammatical categories appears to follow from their sharing some semantic property or situational-role property necessary for the particular combination. At present, it does not appear appropriate to describe young children as employing categories such as adultlike noun or verb or adjective. Such unification appears to be a product of later development.

Formal Grammatical Relations

A lexical formal category, such as noun or verb, refers to a group of semantically heterogeneous words drawn together by commonalities of grammatical use. A formal grammatical *relation*, such as subject, object, or modifier of a head, refers to a semantically heterogeneous group of roles or relations drawn together by some aspect of grammatical structure. The discussion here will be limited to the central cases of subject and object (for discussion of grammatical predicate of a sentence, see Bowerman, 1973; Brown, 1973; McNeill, 1966, 1970).

What properties of adult grammar justify role categories, such as subject and object? It will be useful in such a discussion to have available some more general relational terminology from logic and semantic studies (e.g., Reichenbach, 1948). In particular, analysts speak of a basic division of terms into *predicate terms* and their *arguments*. A predicate term is one that denotes some relation among entities, a property of an entity, an activity or state, and so on; an argument is a term or phrase that denotes the entity that is described, related, modified, and so on. Thus, in the sentence *they see dogs,* the major predicate term is the verb *see; see* describes generally a relation between one who sees (a seer) and a seen entity and is, thus, a two-argument predicate term. In *they see dogs, they* denotes the seers, whereas *dogs* denotes the seen entities. The basic predicate-argument rule for *see* is seer+*see*+seen. Similarly, *big* is a one-argument predicate, denoting relatively large size of its single argument. In *that dog is big, that dog* denotes the described entity and thus comprises the single argument of *big*. Similarly, in *big dogs eat bones, big* takes a single argument *dogs;* together, *big*+*dogs* also comprise the initial argument of the predicate *eat,* which takes the general form eater-*eat*-eaten.

Most predicate terms of languages are one- or two-argument predicates, although a few, such as *give (John gave a dog to Mary)*, are often described as three-argument predicates. The basic idea of grammatical subject in English is the following: Under various grammatical and pragmatic circumstances, an English sentence must have a central predicate term from one of the classes of main verb, adjective, preposition, or simply *be* (as in *he is a dog,* where *is* comprises the main predicate term). This central predicate term must take at least one argument placed before the main predicate. This prepredicate argument is the subject. The semantic role of the subject argument is not homogeneous across predicates. If a predicate takes an agentive argument, that argument is virtually always the initial argument. But many predicates do not take agentive arguments. Then, the semantic role of the argument often depends upon a semantic-structural rule

for the individual predicate. For *own,* for example, the initial argument role is that of possessor (*John owns this dog*); for *belong,* the initial argument role is instead that of the possessed object (*this dog belongs to John*). Similarly, one can say either *John likes tables* or *tables please John; John can see the table* or *the table is visible to John; this machine has 40 parts* or *40 parts make up this machine*. Thus, part of what is meant by grammatical subject is an argument of the main predicate that fulfills a general structural requirement. Thus, a semantically heterogeneous group of semantic roles is unified into a larger category by the group's role in fulfilling a general structural requirement. In English, there are other characteristics of subject arguments as well. If the verb or auxiliary verb is modulated according to number (e.g., *he like+s it, they like it*), it agrees in number with this argument role. In English, furthermore, grammatical subjects are referred to pronominally by *they, he, she,* and *I* for the appropriate person-number definite references.

What about grammatical object? Not all predicate terms take grammatical objects. *See* does, for example (*he sees the dog*), but *fall* does not (*he fell*). What is meant by grammatical object is somewhat looser. For English, it seems to mean that if a verb takes a second central argument, the argument follows rather than precedes the main predicate. Thus, we say *John saw the dog,* not **John the dog saw*. Again, it follows from the considerations above that grammatical objects are also semantically heterogeneous. For example, they can be the experienced stimulus (*John likes tables*) or the experiencer (*tables please John*). A problem that comes up with respect to grammatical objects is what the status is of postprepositional objects, such as *John* in *Sam relies on John* or *Sam* in *John talks to Sam*. In some sense, it often feels as though combinations, such as *rely on* or *talk to,* are single semantic units, but their parts also seem to have some grammatical and semantic separateness. Arguments that form the object of a preposition that is semantically (and often grammatically) unified with a main verb are often called oblique objects. Their grammatical status and semantic status are often problematic (see Bresnan, in press, for further discussion).

If we were to look for a more general cross-cultural definition of grammatical subject and object, we could not refer exclusively to English-characteristic properties, such as word order. In many languages, for example, inflections on the noun make clear its grammatical role so that subjects are not always in one position. Or, in fact, the verb may be consistently marked to agree in number and person with what we call the subject, but the subject role need not be represented by a separate noun-phrase argument at all. Languages that have both of the above properties include Latin, Turkish, and Spanish. What can be said for such languages is that the subject is a role of the verb, which still consistently fills some grammatical role, such as being the role that the verb agrees with in number and person or the role that is marked with some inflection that characteristically appears on such a noun-phrase argument.

Typically, as well, the grammatical subject is the natural *topic* of the sentence, the argument that the main predicate is generally "about." This is only, however, a statistical generalization. For example, in *we ate it*—said as an answer to "What happened to the roast?"—*it* refers to the roast, which is the topic. Or in *Harry got fired*—said as an answer to "What happened today at the office?"—the topic is really what had happened—*Harry got fired* is, thus, a comment on a topic in another sentence.

In many languages, there is an important construction that is responsible for the common differentiation between *grammatical* or *surface* subject and object from what are often called *underlying* or *logical* subject and object. This construction is the passive. In passives, for example, *John was liked (by Mary),* there is still an argument fulfilling the grammatical requirement of a prepredicate argument with which a verbal element agrees in number, for example. But for a given two-argument verb, the semantic-argument role which usually characterizes the structural role of the grammatical object instead fills the grammatical subject. For *like*, for example, it is usually the liker that fills the grammatical subject role in most sentence structures. In a passive form such as *John was liked (by Mary)*, however, the role of the liked being now fills the grammatical role of the grammatical subject. In English, this general reversal of the usual grammatical- and semantic-role correspondences is marked by use of a past participal form of the verb and a form of preceding *be* as well as the *by*-marking. Rather than simply describing passive verbs as completely separate from the active forms, linguists analyze the passive verb as being the same verb, but in a different grammatical-semantic configuration. The argument role that fills the structural role of the grammatical subject in active-form sentences is called the logical or underlying subject; the argument role that fills the grammatical-object position in actives but the grammatical-subject role in passives is called the underlying object. Participation in the passive is much of what is responsible for justifying the category of grammatical objects in English (Bowerman, 1973).

Do children's Stage I grammars show clear evidence of underlying (or even surface) formal grammatical relations comprising part of their analysis of the language? It is clear that the entire ensemble of adult knowledge is not present. For example, part of adult knowledge consists of knowledge of what lexical categories can appear as the main predicate of a sentence to begin with, such categories as verb (*he ate*), adjective (*he is nice*), preposition (*he (is) in the house*), or adverb (*he (is) here*). Children have not formulated such grammatical categories (as far as can be told) nor do they observe adult limitations in other ways. In rules such as *more*+X, for example, *more* is a single-argument predicate denoting recurrence or desired recurrence. Thus, *more*+X can be viewed as a single-argument predicate rule. But it is not a member of the predicate classes that can be a main, subject- or object-taking predicate in English.

Nor do children's early grammars show evidence of knowledge or rules such as the passive-active relation. Such knowledge is responsible for giving grammatical relations much of their "abstract" character (Bowerman, 1973).

We can still ask, however, if children have captured other major properties of the language that are in some broad sense highly analogous to the kinds of properties referred to by structural analyses such as grammatical subject and object, that is, the unification of semantically diverse argument roles of predicates because of their perceived structural similarities of use. Analysts such as McNeill (1966, 1970) and Bloom (1970) noted the occurrence of utterances in children's language that seemed to exemplify these relations—utterances such as *mommy walk* (subject-verb), *eat orange* (verb-object), or *mommy eat orange*—by the end of Stage I (subject-verb-object). Thus, it seemed to them that children's speech did employ grammatical relations.

The problem, however, is the familiar one. Children may produce combinations that would be described with certain categories in an adult grammar, but the children may not analyze them as belonging to similar underlying categorical patterns. Bowerman (1973) argued that properties of children's grammars throughout Stage I made it difficult to credit them with having achieved relational categories such as object and subject. For grammatical subjects, the major problem Bowerman pointed out was a lack of semantic diversity of initial-argument roles. Suppose, she proposed, we look at those predicates in children's speech that in the adult language are ones that can be main predicates and can take obligatory initial arguments. In the reports available to her, nearly all such early predicates in Stage I grammars were actional predicates that took initial agentive arguments, for example, X+*go*, X+*eat*, X+*kick*, and so on. There were few instances of nonagentive predicates, such as *like, need, afraid, belong, own, big*, and so on. In fact, even among actional predicates, most took initial-animate agents. Few were like *break* or *fall* (*cup break, glass fall*), in which the initial argument is in some sense an actor but not an animate instigator. She concluded the most parsimonious description of such combinations of initial argument+predicate is thus a semantic-structural formula such as agent+action. Even when some children, usually toward the end of Stage I, begin to produce utterances, such as *cup fall*, these might best be described as additions to the more general agent+action rule of a few individual lexical rules, such as X+*fall*.

Bloom, Miller, and Hood (1975), however, note that if one does not require an actual predicate term to be present, then some children's early grammars do show semantic-structural formulas in which initial-argument roles have semantic diversity. For example, children who produce agent-action sequences often also produce possessor-possessed sequences, for example, *mommy hat, daddy chair;* in possessor-possessed sequences, the initial term can be considered the possessor-argument role, and the second term can be considered the possessed-object role of an underlying, although unexpressed, relation of possession. Similarly, some children early on produce located object-location utterances, such as *sweater chair*, in which the first term can be analyzed as denoting a located-object role and the second argument as denoting a location role of an underlying (although unexpressed) locative relation. Thus, some children during Stage I, such as Gia and Kathryn in Bloom's records or Kendall in Bowerman's (1973) records, have rules such as agent-action, located object-location, and possessor-possessed object; there is semantic diversity among initial-argument roles of these formulas.

But such diversity of semantic roles for initial arguments is not by itself sufficient to demonstrate the existence of the second aspect of grammatical subject structure: the unification of such diverse semantic-structural roles because of their commonly analyzed role in the grammar of the language (Bowerman, 1975; Braine, 1976; Maratsos & Chalkley, 1980). The child might simply consider these to be separate semantic-structural formulas, actor-action, located object-location, and possessor-possessed object. What evidence suggests that although the child analyzes the semantic diversity of these structures, the child also analyzes them as part of

some larger grammatical pattern? For example, in adult speech (as we saw), such semantically diverse initial arguments are unified by their role in fulfilling a general structural requirement of the language: that a sentence have an overall argument-predicate- . . . form. In Stage I grammar, the same child that says *Elliott walk* or *daddy coffee* is also likely to be producing combinations such as *little hat, big balloon*, or *more glass* as complete utterances. In these, the argument is placed after the predicate, not before. Strikingly, in fact, such terms as *big, little*, or *red* actually can take initial arguments in adult grammar (e.g., *book is big, hat is little*); but children frequently do not use or impose these orders, using predicate+argument orders, such as *big book* or *little hat* instead. Thus, children who use argument+predicate orders such as agent-action, also use orders such as predicate+argument. They seem to show no particular awareness of an overall argument+predicate . . . or even argument+ . . . configuration for English; this overall configurational pattern is much of what unifies the diverse argument roles we call subject roles into a grammatical category.

It is possible, however, that children might somehow psychologically group together some diverse set of semantic-structural rules as a beginning on this system. The difficulty is in finding psychological evidence that they do so. Bloom, Lightbown, and Hood (1975) and Bloom, Miller, and Hood (1975), for example, note that Kathryn and Gia in particular, acquired a number of the argument-initial patterns in a relatively brief period of time. This might suggest their relatively sudden seeing of some kind of overall pattern. As far as can be judged from tables in Bloom et al. (1975) and Braine (1976), however, such children seem to be learning a number of grammatical patterns quickly within the same period. Some of these may be argument-initial patterns but others seem to be predicate-initial patterns. Thus, the developmental evidence does not strongly suggest such early unification either.

What about grammatical objects? Bowerman (1973) noted that the interpretable semantic diversity of what could be object-of-verb arguments in adult grammar is indeed greater than the semantic diversity of roles of initial arguments of actually occurring predicates. Some second arguments are desired or demanded objects (*want*+X), some are brought-into-being references (e.g., *make house*), some are acted-on objects (*eat orange*). Again, however, the problem is finding evidence that these are psychologically unified by the child. As will be recalled, Braine (1976) found that often, such patterns were really likely to be more specific ones, such as ingestion + ingested object, or really, only some narrower patterns such as *want* + X were truly convincingly productive. A piece of interesting evidence that a semantically diverse set may not be unified is provided by remarks of Gvozdev (1949 cited in Slobin, 1981) on the grammatical development of Zhenya. Zhenya was learning Russian, which marks grammatical-object roles (at least usually) with an accusative inflection marker on the noun. Zhenya used predicates that take a variety of what would be object roles for the adult, such as *read, draw, give,* and *carry.* When he began to use the accusative inflectional marker, however, he attached the marker consistently at first only to arguments denoting something moved or carried, such as arguments denoting carried or given objects. If he had formulated a grammatical-object category, it might be expected that he would have analyzed the broader range of application of the accusative marker correctly with more alacrity. His use suggests the analysis of a transferred-object category combined with a variety of other individual lexical predicate-argument rules.

Thus at present, there is little strong evidence that Stage I children have formed analyses corresponding to adult grammatical subject and object. It is likely that children eventually draw together diverse predicate-argument patterns in some way into the broader patterns described by grammatical relations. They must do so in a way so that they retain semantic-structural patterns, such as agent-action-patient, which remains a structurally valid generalization within subject-object systems. In connection with this, a danger must be noted in the conscientious use of skeptical arguments that characterize the preceding discussions. Strong skepticism could prevent the analysis of the beginnings of such grammatical unification in subsets of the system, or even prevent analysis of the complete system. A problem for future research is thus how to find such beginnings as they occur. In any case, the best present summaries of what children seem to learn in Stage I grammar include rules such as *want* + X, which are centered on particular words, or rules of varying breadth such as possessor-possessed, mover-movement, agent-action, and so forth. Positive evidence for formal grammatical relations is presently lacking.

Three Further Facets of Early Grammatical Development

The foregoing results comprise the major findings of study of early grammatical development (at least in English and languages similar to English early on). There remain, however, other points and problems that reflect importantly on our understanding of the process of grammatical analysis in children. All of these concern (as will be seen) the directness (or lack of it) of relations between cognition per se and grammar, even for rules such as agent-action.

The Word-Bound Nature of General Semantic-Structural Rules

The first point concerns the child's analyses of rules such as agent-action or agent-action-patient. Such rules seem to apply to individual word meanings to produce grammatical combinations in a freely productive fashion. For example, a plausible interpretation of the rule agent-action-patient is: If an animate agent causes an action by exertion of force upon some recipient of the force, a word denoting the agent can be placed before a word denoting the action, which in turn precedes a word denoting the patient. Thus, in *John hit Sam,* John causes hitting to come about, with the result of exerting force on Sam.

This very broad interpretation, however, is incorrect. For example, suppose a girl brings about the falling of a vase by letting it go from her hands. By the above interpretation of the rule agent-action-patient, we could say *the girl fell the vase* because the girl was the causer of the falling and the vase was the recipient of the force. Or if someone made an animal eat, we could say *she* (causer of eating) *ate* (caused action) *the animal* (recipient of force), which is a sentence of English, but it means something else.

The problem is that rules such as agent-action-patient are not freely productive in the fashion above. Instead, they must operate with detailed predicate-argument configurations learned individually for each predicate. Each predicate specifies very detailedly the specific situational role(s) and number of its arguments. The predicate *fall,* for example, only takes one argument, one denoting an object that changes downward in location. Because there is only one argument, the agent-action-patient rule does not apply to it. *Eat* takes two arguments. But these are very specifically analyzed. One argument denotes a being that ingests food; the other, an object that is ingested. At a general level, one argument role denotes what is plausibly interpreted as an agent; the other, what is interpretable as a patient. Thus, the agent-action-patient rule properly orders the eater argument first and the eaten argument second. It does not, however, give license to place initially a term or phrase denoting someone who caused the eating in some vague fashion. Thus, a rule like agent-action or agent-action-patient actually works in the following fashion. First, each predicate must be individually analyzed for the number and specific semantic nature of its arguments. Then, if a general rule is applicable, it can be applied to order the arguments.

In early speech, children usually seem to form their analyses of such general rules appropriately. They do not produce such utterances as *mommy fall toy* or *I go car here* in early combinations (Bloom et al., 1975; Bowerman, 1974, 1982). Nor are they reported to produce combinations such as *mommy eat* to mean 'mommy causes eating to occur' in the erroneous senses above. These findings imply that children seem to form general semantic-structural rules in a way that coordinates with the specific nature of individual predicate-argument configurations. Instead of writing sentence → agent + action + patient, a more exact rewriting might be: predicate (argument [+ agentive], argument [+ patient]) → agent-action-patient; that is, such rules order already given unordered predicate-argument sets.

It is clear that the savings from such rules are not as great as they might seem. They do not obviate the necessity to make detailed analyses of individual predicate-argument analyses. The economy involved is in ordering those predicate-argument sets to which some general rule is applicable. For such predicate-argument sets, ordering can be referred to the general rule (once it is formed) rather than being stored individually with each predicate.

Thus it is not accurate to speak of general rules such as agent-action-patient being opposed to, or completely supplanting, individual grammatical analyses of individual predicates. Rather than opposition, there is complex coordination between individual predicate grammar and the grammar of general rules.

The Relation of Semantic-Structural Categories to Cognitive Categories

A second problem that has recently begun to attract attention (Bloom, Miller, & Hood, 1975; Bowerman, 1976; Braine & Wells, 1978; Schlesinger, 1977) is how grammatical use and cognitive categories are related. A fairly straightforward theory that suggests itself from study of Stage I speech is that certain general cognitive categories such as agency and patienthood are mirrored fairly directly in grammatical use. Lately, however, both empirical and analytic study have made this relationship more problematic even for apparently straightforward semantic-structural categories. In the discussion above, it was seen how such general categories

might have to be fit to coordinate with individual predicate grammars. A second type of problem is how grammatical use selects or shapes boundaries among semantic-cognitive categories, and the child's observation of this.

One form of this argument concerns fuzzy boundaries among semantic categories relevant to grammar. A very eloquent statement of the problem can be found in Schlesinger (1977):

> Consider first that a concept has been acquired only to the extent that one knows what belongs to it and what does not. Now what are the boundaries of the agent concept: Mummy handing the bottle to the child is no doubt an event where an agent is performing some action, but what about mummy just holding the bottle? To take one further step, can the bottle be said to be an agent "containing" the milk in the same way that mother is an agent holding the bottle? Clearly there are gradations here of "agentiveness." In our adult judgment of what does and does not fall under the agent concept, we are very much influenced by what our languages express as an agent. (pp. 6–7)

In fact, there may well be differences in how languages fix such boundaries. Inanimate causal agents may indeed be causal subjects in English (e.g., *the key opened the door*), but are excluded from doing so in Dutch (Bates & MacWhinney, 1982). Thus, how far this boundary extends may be fixed by how elements are treated grammatically in the language. Developmentally, it seems likely that such somewhat fuzzily defined semantic-grammatical categories might spread out around clearer bundles of grammatical-semantic properties. Early actor arguments very much tend to be clear animate doers of the action (Bloom, 1970; Bowerman, 1973; Braine, 1976). Sentences in which the agent-actors are inanimate, such as *ball fall* or *pencil write,* occur later (Bloom, Lightbown, & Hood, 1975; Bowerman, 1973; Braine, 1976). Among patients, clearly acted upon inanimate arguments are earliest. Less common are patients that have some independent movement of their own. A dropped object, for example, has some independent movement after it is dropped and is, thus, less clearly simply passive (Braine, 1976). Animate patients, as in *kiss mommy* or *push daddy,* are also rare early on (Bloom, 1970; Bowerman, 1973; Brown, 1973), In fact, in some cases where children attempt these less clear semantic-grammatical uses early on, there may be numbers of erroneous uses. Kendall (Bowerman, 1973; Braine, 1976) for some time consistently placed animate patients of activities in sentence-initial position; she produced such sentences as *Kimmy kick* = 'kick Kimmy,' even as she consistently placed inanimate patients in correct postpredicate position (e.g., *read book, bite finger*). De Villiers and de Villiers (1973b) found that early Stage I subjects were random when they acted out actional sentences in which both agent and patient were animates (e.g., *make the boy kiss the girl*). Given the available naturalistic data, this might reflect general underlying problems with animate patients. Braine (1976) also found that two of his subjects had difficulty with achieving stable word orders for arguments denoting inanimate moving objects such as pulled or falling objects. Bowerman (1981) noted errors such as *cup put* (an object that is put somewhere also moves) in her children's very early combinations. Such errors are not universal among subjects (Bloom et al., 1975). But in conjunction with data from developmental lateness of such mixed cases, these errors indicate that the less clear cases may indeed develop later than the clearer semantic-structural cores of such categories.

The problem of somewhat unclear semantic-structural boundaries may be distinguished from the related case in which grammar functions to make a choice among possible semantic properties as definers of use. For English, this point has been illustrated in work by Braine and Wells (1978) on the problem of transitive versus intransitive predicates. The problem in which these researchers were interested was that of perceived semantic similarity among argument roles. For example, consider the subjects and object of the following sentences: *the boy dropped the cup; the boy ran; the cup fell*. We might hold that *the boy* in *the boy dropped the cup* and *the boy ran* are the two most similar arguments, being animate agents. Similarly, we might hold that *the cup* in *the boy dropped the cup* and *the cup fell* are similar because in both, the cup is a basically passive sufferer of some action. Braine and Wells had children group together sentence arguments on the basis of semantic similarity (see Braine & Wells, 1978, for a description of methods) and found something different from this. According to their results, *the boy* of *the boy ran* and *the cup* of *the cup fell* were perceived as similar to each other. Contrastively, *the boy* and *the cup* of *the boy dropped the cup* were each members of two semantic-structural categories separate from the first category. They suggest (see also Atkinson, Hardy, & Braine, 1981) that over time, the child learns that in one-argument sentences, the single argument is placed initially. This leads to the

formation of a semantic-structural category, 'object of attribution' (Braine & Wells, 1978) that applies to all single arguments of intransitive predicates. It is just in transitive sentences, in which there are two grammatically relevant argument roles, that distinctions such as agent and patient are relevant for governing correct placement. This thus leads to the formation of the corresponding categories. Therefore, grammatical use leads to the formation of a rather semantically undistinguished intransitive-argument category, as opposed to agent and patient categories for transitives, despite the clear cognitive similarities, for example, between intransitive and transitive agents. Braine and Wells's results concern 4- and 5-year-olds. But the result is in fact mirrored rather exactly in a naturalistic study of early acquisition in a New Guinean language called Kaluli (Schieffelin, in press). The relevant aspect of Kaluli grammar is an inflection -ɛ (pronounced eh). This inflection is applied to transitive agents that are in focus (see *Exceptions from Other Languages*), but not to intransitive ones. That is, the marker might be applied to *mommy* in *mommy drank water* but not to *mommy* in *mommy walked* or *mommy sat*. Schieffelin found that her subjects sometimes incorrectly applied the -ɛ marker to nonfocused transitive agents, but they never generalized it to intransitive agents. In other words, Kaluli maintains a general distinction between agents of transitive versus intransitive predicates rather than treating all agents like, and Schieffelin's three Kaluli subjects easily observed this distinction early on rather than generalizing the marker to all agents.

Thus, such analyses all indicate that even more cognitive-based categories such as agent and patient, are not the simple result of a direct imposition onto language of general cognitive categories. Instead the language may fix boundaries among possible cognitive-semantic categories or properties according to different use. The evolution of semantic-structural grammatical categories is a product of semantic-cognitive and structural similarity rather than of cognitively analyzed similarity per se. It will be seen later how structural similarity comes to exert even stronger influence upon the evolution of grammatical categories in the period after early speech.

Pragmatics, Inflection, and 'Natural' Word Order

Finally, recent work in other languages reflects on another kind of indirectness of relation between natural cognitive structure and linguistic structure: the problem of 'natural' category order and natural grammatical order. One of the marked characteristics of English simple sentences is their observation of a relatively fixed word order for expressing basic semantic-cognitive relations. The general English order is subject-verb-(object)—for example, *Harvey drank milk; Mary ran*—corresponding in actional sentences to the order agent-action-(patient). More complex constructions provide ample opportunity for the use of other orders. The order may be reversed (*milk was drunk by Harvey*), as in passives, or otherwise changed (*it's milk that Harvey drinks* = O . . . S V). But so strong is the basic SV(O) (agent-action-[patient]) order in simple sentences that deviations from it are often intuitively felt to be some kind of reordering of this basic order; they are in fact also later occurring constructions (Bever, 1970).

Furthermore, this particular general order, especially to speakers of English, seems a cognitively 'natural' order. One can easily imagine that the order of actional events in the world is that an action begins with (is initiated by) an agent and, taking shape there, passes to the recipient or patient of the force. Thus, the natural order is agent-action-patient, exactly the basic order of English.

English does not, however, provide a universal pattern. Perhaps a good place to see this is to inspect briefly an almost diametrically opposite language, Turkish (Slobin, 1982). In Turkish, any of the six possible orders of subject, object, and verb is actually found in simple sentences: SOV, SVO, OSV, OVS, VSO, VOS. To an English speaker, this looks like entirely free-word order, and such languages are often described this way. They are free, however, only in respect to major predicate-argument relations. In Turkish, as in many other languages of the world, major constituent order is controlled in large part by another variable of a kind not yet considered here: pragmatic analysis (Bates, 1976), in particular the pragmatic variable called *focus*. Pragmatic variables in general concern aspects of the meanings of sentences controlled by, or expressive of, the perspective or informational states of the speaker and listener. Topic, previously mentioned, is one such variable. Focus is yet another, and is found pervasively in grammatical analysis. In general, the constituent with the most salient or important pragmatic information is in the focus variable. It denotes what is at issue, what is in contrast to previous declarations, or it presents new information. In English simple sentences, it is generally conveyed by stress. If a child wants herself to be the one who eats some cake, for example, it would be natural for her to say "*I'll* eat the cake." If she wants it to be the cake that

she eats, the stress pattern would be "I'll eat the *cake*." The stressed element is the focused one in each sentence. These examples are only a subtype of the broad range covered by focus (see Jackendoff, 1972, for further discussion).

In many languages, focus affects word order itself, even in simple sentences. In Turkish, for example, if there is a focused upon element, it must be placed in front of the verb. A child who wishes to say that she should be the eater (not someone else), might say either *cake I eat* or *I eat cake*, placing *I* before *eat*. (For various reasons, *cake eat I* would be best for focusing on what is to be eaten.)

Thus, in Turkish, word order itself cannot distinctly clarify who is doing what to whom. Often this is not necessary anyway. Any combination of *I, eat,* and *cake* is likely to mean that *I* denotes the eater, and *cake,* the eaten. But suppose the verb is something like *kiss* so that either of two mentioned persons might be kisser or kissed? In Turkish, such relations are generally clear because the grammatical object, if it refers to some definite instance (akin to the meaning given in English by prefixing *the*), receives a distinctive inflectional marker on the noun. The shape of this marker is regulated by the phonology of the stem. If the stem of the noun object contains a front vowel, such as /i/ (pronounced "ee") or /e/ for example, the accusative object marker is /i/ or /ï/ (pronounced "ee" with rounded lips). If the stem contains a back vowel, such as /a/ (pronounced "ah") or /u/, the marker is /u/ or /ü/ (rounded lips pronunciation of /u/). Thus, to transliterate, any of the orders *cat dog-u chased, dog-u cat chased, dog-u chased cat, cat chased dog-u, chased dog-u cat,* or *chased cat dog-u* would signal that the dog was the chased creature, and the cat, thus, the chaser.

It is extremely common in the world's languages for the use of pragmatic variables to control major constituent order in some degree and in combination with the use of inflectional markers to denote predicate-argument role relations; Indo-European and non-Indo-European languages, such as Russian, Latin, Italian, German, Hungarian, and Kaluli, also allow such reflection of pragmatic expression in ordering. In some cases, inflectional markings for grammatical role relations are not always clear (e.g., Serbo-Croation, German); then, word order may be used to make them unambiguous.

Languages in which the usual order is not a fixed 'natural' SVO order clearly offer interesting investigative opportunities. Suppose there is a cognitively natural order and children naturally tend to impose it upon grammar. Then children might tend to have difficulties with languages that do not have this as their basic order (in some languages the most common order may be SOV or VSO for example). Children might have difficulties learning such languages or even impose the fixed SVO order initially (a prediction made by Osgood & Bock, 1977). Beyond this, other queries suggest themselves. For example, inflections occur commonly only after Stage I in such languages as English (Brown, 1973). Are grammatical systems intrinsically more difficult or confusing in which inflections are used to express basic predicate-argument relations instead of word order?

Not all languages nor all children are alike, so perhaps a uniform answer to the question should not be expected. But overall it does not seem that the SVO, agent-action-patient order is absolutely basic. Bowerman (1973) found that in learning Finnish, her subject Seppo adopted the probability distribution of his mother, mostly SVO, but he used other orders as well—about as often as this was true of his mother's speech. In Samoan, the verb is generally first, an order analyzed readily by Tofi (Kernan, 1970). MacWhinney (1976) notes that either agents or patients are recorded as occurring initially for children learning Hungarian. Slobin (Aksu & Slobin, in press; Slobin, 1982) found that his Turkish subjects used the same variety of orders used by adults and in roughly the same proportions; OVS was a little more frequent than in adult use. Schieffelin found appropriate observation of pragmatic-grammatical regularities in her three Kaluli-learning subjects, although SVO sequences appeared earlier than SOV orders for two of them. Park (1970) notes that his daughter, exposed to Korean, seemed to fix on SVO consistently, even though Korean has as much constituent order freedom as any language. But his German subjects used all six possible orders of S, O, and V. Zhenya, studied by Gvozdev (1949) fixed upon an SOV order for Russian at first, although the most common Russian order is SVO. Overall, the evidence certainly does not favor a strong hypothesis that children will initially fix on an SVO order even if this is not present or dominant in their language. Nor is difficulty indicated in languages in which SVO order is not dominant or available.

How well do children perform in learning an inflectional system to convey grammatical and semantic relationships? This seems to depend on the clarity with which such relationships are expressed in the language (Slobin, 1982). Turkish seems to provide particularly clear inflectional morphology (whatever an English speaker might think of its vowel harmony

system) compared to such languages as German, Russian, or Serbo-Croatian. Preliminary analyses indicate that Turkish children use appropriate inflectional morphology to express basic relations such as patienthood or possession or location, even in two-word or single-word utterances (Aksu & Slobin, in press). Perhaps even more interesting are results of comprehension studies performed with sentences equivalent to the English *the dog chases the cat*. Slobin (1982) reports on results for such sentences administered in four interestingly contrasted languages: English, Italian, Serbo-Croatian, and Turkish. For English-speaking children, of course, the only available simple sentence order is SVO: *the dog chases the cat*. For Turkish (as noted above), any of the SVO, SOV, OSV, OVS, VSO, and VOS orders should be comprehensible as long as the grammatical object is appropriately marked. In fact, Turkish-speaking 2-year-olds who received all six possible orders comprehended these better than English-speaking children of the same general age and level comprehended the single-order SVO. Furthermore, Turkish-speaking children did not automatically adopt a strategy of using the most common word order (SOV) to analyze semantic-structural relations if the inflectional marker for the grammatical object was absent. Instead, younger children interpreted all such unmarked sentences randomly; only at a much later age did they tend to analyze the first noun phrase as the agent if marking were absent. (See Slobin, 1982, for further results; see also Hakuta, 1977, for an interesting comprehension study of Japanese.)

The available results thus do not indicate that there is a natural order for grammar fixed by some natural order of thoughts. Instead, children readily observe the order (or orders) of the language they hear, even if it is not such a natural order. They readily analyze the use of constituent order to mark pragmatic rather than predicate-argument role relations if this characterizes the language of their community. Finally, they may find inflectional systems such as those of Turkish clear systems to analyze for the marking of basic semantic-structural role relations. Such findings expand our notions of what is 'natural' in a language and the relations between grammar and thought. These findings will also prove important for our understanding of what is thought of as underlying or deep-sentence structure in later analyses discussed in this chapter.

Early Speech: Discussion of Findings

In summary, what are some of the chief findings of early grammar? What kinds of analytic abilities and biases does the child show in the first attempts at the analyses of sequences?

The major result of early grammatical study is surely the finding that semantic properties such as actionality, agency, location, or possession, seem to provide defining properties for many early grammatical categories. Added to this are pragmatic factors such as focus, which is prominent in basic word order in many inflectional languages. Sometimes the relevant categories are narrower than first inspection suggests (Braine, 1976), but overall the relevance of meaning and pragmatic use for early grammar are clearly established. Second, grammatical rules may revolve around individual words, in such rules as *want*+desired object. Thus, the basic analytic elements of early grammar include semantic analysis, pragmatic analysis, phonological analysis (for a word is a combination of a particular sound sequence and a meaning), and sequential analysis.

Early speech does not, however, seem to involve the complex coordinations of these kinds of analysis that are required for formal categories, such as noun and verb or subject and object. Part of the nativist argument has been the great speed of acquisition. Given the complexity of the analyses to be made, nonnativist arguments and explanations require more time for the child to achieve such analyses. As will be seen, such findings are not decisive with respect to the nativist argument. But they are certainly relevant to the general questions, and fail to provide the nativist viewpoint strong support.

Finally, early speech shows only limited uniformity among children. A reasonably small set of structural meanings and combination types appears sufficient to characterize the body of findings. But within this set, individual children differ in how specific or general their early analyses are and in the sequence of attaining analyses. It is not likely, however, that such differences signal different basic linguistic capacities or ways of analyzing grammar because all of the types of analyses children employ in early grammar are also required to command various parts of adult grammar (Maratsos & Chalkley, 1980). Such differences may thus arise because of such factors as what the child prefers to talk about or the differences in cognitive style that result in different emphases in how such capacities are applied.

No review of a topic as extended as early speech can prove exhaustive. In particular, the review of problems such as whether there is some kind of grammatical knowledge in one-word speech has been foregone here. The interested reader can find discussions of such problems in such studies as Antinucci and Parisi (1973), Bloom (1973), Bowerman (1978), Braine (1974, 1976), Branigan (1979), Brown (1973), Dore (1975), McNeill (1970) and Rodgon (1976).

LATER GRAMMATICAL ACQUISITION

The problems of later grammatical development do not hang together around as closely unified a set of problems as those of Stage I grammar. Instead, analyses of a large number of major problems characterizes this work. Before beginning such analyses of particular problems, however, it may be useful to have a broader overview of the chronology of post Stage I grammatical development. In particular, such an overview has been provided for English by Brown's (1973) summary of the major structural developments as they are correlated with his periods as marked off by MLU. We have already discussed the major development of Stage I grammar, that is, the beginning of the use of major predicate-argument combinations. Some of the major developments Brown notes for the remaining periods can be briefly summarized:

Stage II. In the development of English, Stage II sees the beginning appearances of many small morphemes and inflections, such as *a, the, in, on,* noun plural *-s,* possessive inflection *'s* (e.g., *'s* in *John's dog*), and verb morphology marking tense and aspect (e.g., *-s* of *it goes here* and progressive *-ing* of *he's singing*). Just as major constituent structure that begins in Stage I does not achieve stable command by the child until much later, such small morphemes are not used consistently when required for months or even years after they begin to appear (Brown, 1973). But enough small morphemes begin to appear around Stage II to make their beginning appearance a characteristic marker of this period.

Stage III. In English, there are a number of verbs called auxiliary verbs, such as *do, can, will, have,* or forms of *be,* that play central roles in the English systems of negation and interrogation. For example, these verbs typically carry the negative marker *n't* (*he isn't coming, I don't need it*), and their sentence-initial appearances are important grammatical markers of interrogation (*can he come?, does he know?*). Such forms begin to appear numerously in declarative sentences in Stage III; then they spread to uses in questions. One of the best known developmental phenomena of English is the error some children commonly make in misplacing such verbs in *wh*-questions, for example, *why he will come?* (Brown, 1970; Klima & Bellugi, 1966; Knapp, 1979).

Stage IV. Even as previous developments continue, one of the essential mechanisms of language, sentence embedding, begins to appear in common use (Brown, 1973; Hafitz, Gartner, & Bloom, 1980; Limber, 1973). In sentence embedding, a whole sentence may comprise a single argument of a predicate (e.g., *I think he will come,* in which *he will come* denotes what is thought); or a whole sentence may be grammatically modified to act as a modifier or specifier of a noun-phrase argument of the main clause, for example, *you saw,* in *here's the onion (that) you saw.*

Stage V. The major characteristic frequent development of this period is the use of conjunctions. This may include conjunctions of whole sentences (*the wind blew and my coat came off*), verb phrases (*he sang a song and ate dinner*), or noun phrases (*I ate some cereal and some eggs*). Conjunctions with *and* appear earliest; these are followed by conjunctions expressing a variety of other relations among clauses (Bloom, Lahey, Hood, Lifter, & Fiess, 1980; Brown, 1973).

The highest point of development for which MLU is a good marker seems to be Stage V, or an MLU of 4.0. After this point complexity increases do not bring stable increases in sentence length and MLU remains largely stable (Brown, 1973). There are, nevertheless, many important systems that appear to develop after the child has reached an MLU of 4.0. Simple actional passives, such as *the boy was kissed by the girl* appear to be comprehended just around Stage V or so (de Villiers & de Villiers, 1974). But children who comprehend such passives may fail to comprehend nonactional passives, such as *John was liked by Mary,* well into the school years (Becker & Maratsos, 1979; Maratsos, Kuczaj, Fox, & Chalkley, 1979). The use of the passive in the full range of underlying subject and object sentences thus appears to be a long development (see also Horgan, 1978b). Another important construction that apparently requires more time is the analysis of adjective+infinitive phrase constructions such as *John is eager to please* (*John* = subject of *please*) versus *John is easy to please* (*John* = object of *please*). C. Chomsky (1969) found that children have difficulty with such constructions until about the age of 9. Other investigators have found, however, that reliable competence may be found by a mental age of about 6½ if easier testing methods are used (Cromer, 1970; Fabian-Krauss & Ammon, 1980; Kessel, 1970). Finally, no developmental norms are known for many constructions central in adult linguistic theoretical treatments. Perhaps not surprisingly, for example, little is known about when chil-

dren have mastered the set of rules responsible for such sentences as *John was thought by Mary to have been scratched by Sam,* or when their use of *wh*-questions allows questioning of a constituent in a highly embedded sentence, as in *who do you think Mary could ask Sam to talk to about that?* (Rosenbaum, 1967; Ross, 1967). What is important about such findings is that for whatever reason, many central constructions of adult grammar are apparently not mastered in the early preschool years.

The provision of a chronological outline of development comprises an important general task of the study of language development. But the discussion of many problems often cuts across different chronological developments, structural developments, and developmental periods. Such issues include the nature and importance of mothers' speech to children, the determinants of sequences of acquisition or of acquisition itself, the nature of children's formal categories and their manner of constructing them, the reality or lack of reality of transformational grammars as descriptions of speakers' psychological analysis of language, and other problems connected to the problem of whether language acquisition requires recruitment of some innate linguistic faculty as an explanatory factor. In Brown's study of the acquisition of 14 morphemes (Brown, 1973), many of these issues are woven together in a study that cannot be conveniently sliced into small pieces for topical discussions. Our discussion will, thus, begin with a review of Brown's study, after which we will then look at the individual problems.

THE 14 MORPHEMES: DESCRIPTION AND DEVELOPMENT

For the second part of his monumental research and review monograph, *A First Language: The Early Stages* (1973), Brown chose to study a set of 14 morphemes that begin to appear in Stage II and give that period its characteristic developmental appearance. The morphemes do not belong to any coherent structural group. Instead, the morphemes appear to have been chosen because of their methodological amenability for the study of the sequence of acquisition. In particular, Cazden (1968) and Brown (1973) chose forms that had a number of convenient scoring properties. First, the forms are frequent in adult use. Thus, child failure to use the form could not be attributed to the child's following a general low frequency of use. Nor could it arise from the not-particularly-interesting reason that the form is rarely heard. Second, one could score with reasonable confidence that the form should have been used in a particular semantic-grammatical environment. This allows one to calculate a quantifiable measure of the *proportion* of use of the morpheme when it should have been used, making a quantitative measure of acquisition possible. Thus, for example, suppose a child in a transcript fails to use past tense *-ed* five times when it should have been used (e.g., the child says *I push it* after pushing something) and does use it five times when it should have been used (e.g., the child says *he kicked it* after someone has kicked something). The child can be assigned a score of .50 for use of *-ed* past tense in the transcript. If the form is frequent in its occasions for use, such scores may have some usefulness as a measure of the child's command of use.

Brown (1973) used the same criterion for scoring acquisition of all 14 morphemes. Stable acquisition corresponded to use in obligatory contexts of use over 90% of the time in three consecutive 2-hr. samples; in each relevant sample, opportunities for use of the morpheme had to be at least five in number. This requirement asks that the child not only understand the general range of occurrence of a morpheme but also that the child have analyzed that the morpheme must be used whenever possible; it is thus a fairly conservative criterion. It could reasonably be applied to all of the 14 morphemes uniformly however.

What are the 14 morphemes? They are not, as already mentioned, members of a single structural set; they are not all word inflections nor are they all aspects of the verb system or noun system. They are simply 14 commonly occurring, relatively easy-to-score morphemes or morpheme sets. These morphemes are:

1. The progressive *-ing* affix on verbs, denoting an activity in progress, for example, *-ing* of *he's kicking it* or *we're singing.*

2–3. Auxiliary forms of *be* required for preceding a verb with *-ing* affix, for example, *'re* of *we're singing, is* of *he is coming,* or *was* of *was he running?* This set of uses of *be* was called the auxiliary *be* by Brown because it is auxiliary to the *-ing* affixed verb. The *be*-forms are further subdivided into two sets:

(a) Contractible *be: be* in an environment where the *be*-form can appear contracted or not. Such an environment, for example, is *he +_____+ singing,* where either *is* or its contracted form *-s* is possible: *he is singing—*

he's singing. It should be noted that even though *is* is not contracted in *he is singing,* it could be and, thus, is scored as an example of contractible *be.*

(b) Uncontractible *be:* a required *be* in an environment where the *be*-form cannot be contracted. For example, in questions one can say *are you coming?* but not *'reyou coming?* Or in answer to a question, one might be able to say *yes, he is,* but not **yes, he's.*

4. Verb present tense, third-person-singular *-s.* This morpheme denotes a habitual tendency to occur for the relation denoted by the verb. It occurs only with a third-person-singular subject. Examples include *-s* in *he likes it* or *-s* in *the boy knows it.*

5. Irregular third-person-singular present tense. Every main verb of English takes *-s* after third-person-singular subjects to denote the present tense. With the verbs *have* and *do,* however, there is also a stem change so that the result is *has* instead of **haves* and *does* instead of **doos.* Opportunities for use of *has* and *does* occur frequently, and Brown (1973) counted these two uses together as instances of the irregular third-person-singular present.

6. Verb past tense *-ed.* For example, *-ed* in *he kicked it.*

7. Verb irregular past tense. Many verbs of English do not take *-ed* to mark simple past, for example, *run/ran, know/knew, think/thought, break/broke, see/saw.* Perhaps misleadingly, Brown counted all the past forms as instances of the past irregular morpheme. This is really a *list* of verb forms that appear in the grammatical-semantic context characteristic of *-ed* past.

8–9. Contractible and uncontractible copula *be.* Grammarians have generally distinguished between two major classes of the verb *to be.* One is auxiliary *be,* that is, *be* used in conjunction with a main verb. The other occurs when a form of *be* occurs with an adjective, preposition, prepositional phrase, or noun phrase to form the sentence predicate. Examples include *'s* in *he's big, are* in *they are inside, was* in *was he by the house?,* and *be* in *he will be a sorry plumber.* Again, Brown scored for two categories: forms of *be* that should occur in an environment where contraction is possible (e.g., *is* or *'s* of *he is big, he's big; are* or *'re* of *they are inside, they're inside*) and forms that should occur in an environment where contraction is not possible, for example, *are* of *are you tired?* or *is* of *yes, he is.*

10. The preposition *in.*

11. The preposition *on.*

12. The articles *a* and *the.* These were scored as

though a single morpheme because one could not always tell whether one or the other should have been used.

13. The noun plural -s. For example, -s of *I see cats*.

14. The noun possessive inflection -s. For example, -s of *I want John's cat* or *I want John's*.

Crystal (1973) and Kuczaj (1977a) point out that it may not always be as easy as it seems to score whether some morpheme should be present or not or to score an utterance as counting as an error or not. For example, if someone points to a cup someone else has and says *give me cup*, should it be *give me the cup*, *give me that cup*, or *give me your cup?* Kuczaj (1977a) found more specific problems in scoring the irregular past tense. Often children would say *breaked* or *broked*, for example, where *broke* alone should have been used. He found that if he scored the irregular past tense as correct only when the irregular form alone (such as *broke*) was used, then after overregularizations set in, .90 use of the irregular past tense did not occur for months to years after the other morphemes. This is contrary to the relatively early mastery of the irregular past tense reported by Brown (1973). In the following exposition, Brown's original results will be retained, but these possible problems should not be forgotten.

The first of Brown's major findings was that full use of a morpheme or set of morphemes is not a single, sudden step in the child's development. Instead, the frequency of the child's use of a morpheme in an obligatory context rises gradually, often over a period of months or years. Thus, such learning curves may be gradual rather than resembling sudden extension of a rule-guided insight.

Second, the overall sequence of acquisition of the 14 morphemes was remarkably stable across Brown's three subjects. A morpheme or morpheme set acquired early by one child was very likely to be acquired early by another child; a morpheme acquired late by one child was likely to be acquired late by another child. The average correlation of acquisitional order between any two of the three subjects (Adam, Eve, and Sarah) was .85, a correlation significant even with such a small sample. The average order of acquisition found by Brown was:

1. present progressive affix -*ing*.
2. *on*.
3. *in*.
4. noun plural -*s*.
5. irregular past morphemes, for example, *broke, ran, made*.

6. noun possessive -'*s*.
7. uncontractible copula *be*-forms.
8. articles *a* and *the*.
9. past regular -*ed*.
10. third-person regular -*s*.
11. third-person-singular irregular -*s* (i.e., *has, does*).
12. uncontractible auxiliary *be*-forms.
13. contractible copula *be*-forms.
14. contractible auxiliary *be*-forms.

These orders have been subsequently validated with one or two exceptions by cross-sectional studies (de Villiers & de Villiers, 1973a; Kuczaj, 1977a). Across a wide range of children, stable use of the various morphemes thus appears in relatively consistent order.

After this finding, the major question is why such stability of order is found. Something interesting is that at a major level, simple phonological factors do not seem important. For example, -*s* is the form of noun plural -*s*, possessive -'*s*, third-person-singular regular -*s*, third-person-singular irregular -*s*, and third-person-singular contracted *be* (*he's singing, he's big*). But these were acquired at different times. Another major factor considered by Brown (1973) was frequency of parental use. He found that among the three children's parents, there was a relatively stable frequency profile: forms used more frequently by one parent were used more frequently by another parent. But the frequency of use by parents in Stage I samples (before the morphemes began to appear commonly) was a poor predictor of the children's order of acquisition. The overall correlation between frequency of parental input and order of acquisition in the child was just .26, a nonsignificant correlation in this sample and certainly incapable of explaining the .85 correlation among acquisitional orders of the three children. Frequency of use might, of course, be important when comparing constructions that are rarely heard at all to frequently heard ones (Limber, 1973). But among these 14 frequently heard morphemes, frequency of use played little determining role.[2]

The problem then remains of finding explanations for the obtained stability of acquisitional order. The basic answer given by Brown (1973) is that it is the complexity of the analytic puzzle offered by the morpheme or morpheme set that must determine order. Some meanings are probably more difficult than others, making analysis of the morpheme with the harder meaning more difficult as well. Or a morpheme may require many grammatical steps for its realization, or many grammatical choices. As a particularly clear example, consider the progressive construction, which has two parts: use of *-ing* and choice of an appropriate form of *be* preceding the main verb, for example, *he is singing, they're going, I was writing, were you eating?*, and so on. The rule for adding the *-ing* is relatively straightforward: If the verb denotes an activity ongoing at the time of the referred to event, add *-ing*. It does not matter whether the sentence is a question or not, what the number and person of the subject are, or what the general tense is; the use of *-ing* is controlled directly by the progressive meaning and the verb-category membership of the major relational term. Consider, in contrast, the complexities of choosing the appropriate form and position of *be*. Use of *be* is also dictated by the progressive meaning of the verb. But to choose properly among the forms *is, are, am, was, were, 's, 're,* and *be,* one must take into account the number and person of the subject (e.g., within present tense: *am* for first-person singular; *are* for second-person, first-person plural, and third-person plural; *is* for third-person singular); one must also take into account general sentence tense (*I am singing, I was singing; they are singing; they were singing*); choice of contractible forms requires registration of the appropriate grammatical context (*they're coming,* but not *'rethey coming?*); appropriate placement of the *be* morpheme requires analysis of interrogative-declarative relations (*is he coming?—he is coming*); and so on. It is clear that choice and placement of the appropriate *be*-form is a much more complex puzzle on virtually any grounds than choice of the *-ing* form.

Often, however, ideas about relative semantic or structural complexity are at best intuitive. For example, *in* and *on* are relatively early, and the articles *a* and *the* appear later. The meanings of *in* and *on* might seem intuitively more straightforward, but no general theory of semantic complexity can easily determine this. On the other hand, there are conditions under which predictions of complexity can be made more straightforwardly. Suppose for a particular type of property, either semantic or grammatical, that morpheme A has properties x and y and that morpheme B has properties x and y as well as other properties. Then, morpheme B is more *cumulatively complex* than A. In general, Brown proposes that if a construction B is cumulatively more complex than another construction A, it will be acquired later.

This proposition is not itself tautologically true. For example, the child might use a construction without having analyzed all its properties, so that it is relatively less complex for him than for the adult. If the proposition were generally true, however, it might give a way of studying the relative psychological complexity of constructions through the study of acquisition, a conclusion generally clearly hoped for in Brown and Hanlon (1970) and Brown (1973).

In his analysis, Brown focused on two types of cumulative complexity: (1) semantic cumulative complexity and (2) grammatical cumulative complexity, as measured by the number of transformational operations required to produce the construction. For this later analysis, Brown used a transformational grammar of the kind summarized by Jacobs and Rosenbaum (1968). How successful were these as predictors? Brown (1973) found them to be reasonably successful. For example, noun plural *-s* can be viewed as involving just one semantic distinction, singular versus plural; distinguishing among forms of *be* can be viewed as involving singular versus plural, first versus second versus third person, and past tense versus present tense. Thus, noun plural *-s* might be predicted to be acquired earlier, which it is. On the whole, such semantic-based predictions worked well when they were possible. There are two caveats, however. First (as Brown notes), irregular and regular forms of past and present tense share the same semantics but are acquired at different development points. This shows that semantic complexity alone cannot predict all of the different acquisitional orders. Second (as Brown notes), most relative ordering predictions could not be made by cumulative complexity. For example, definite and indefinite articles could not be compared to any other forms on the list. It should also be noted that if Kuczaj's (1977a) analysis that past irregular is late is accepted (as seems reasonable), a few of the 27 predictions made for the three children are then not confirmed by the data, but most still remain.

What about predictions made by transformational complexity? Brown finds that 18 such predictions can be made, all of which are confirmed. This point, however, will be discussed in the section *Transformational Grammars and the Study of Developmental Sequence;* there it will turn out that success in general—and in Brown's (1973) study in particular—is in fact not very good.

Thus, the general results of Brown's study are the following:

1. For many constructions, the course of acquisition is gradual rather than sudden and general.

2. There is a relatively stable order of acquisition of small morphemes among different children.

3. The order of acquisition cannot be accounted for by simple frequency of parental use.

4. The order of acquisition may sometimes be predicted by a measure of cumulative complexity, such as semantic complexity of the morphemes, although morphemes of the same semantic complexity may also be acquired at different times; transformational complexity (as will be seen) actually fares less well.

Brown's study touches, often deeply, upon some of the central problems of grammatical acquisition: What are the psychologically real operations of grammatical construction for the child? What are the determinants of acquisition and acquisitional order? How uniform are acquisitional sequences? Are rules acquired in all-or-none fashion? (Why not?) How can we judge whether a construction has been acquired at all? These problems will be taken up in the following discussions, with the addition of one other problem, that is, the evolution of formal categories after Stage I—a problem that has recently attracted much attention (Bates & MacWhinney, 1982; Grimshaw, in press; Karmiloff-Smith, 1979; Kiss, 1973; Maratsos, 1979, 1982; Maratsos & Chalkley, 1980; Pinker, in press; Schlesinger, 1974; Slobin, 1966, 1982). The first set of questions taken up will center on the nature and effects of parental input to children.

INPUT AND ACQUISITION

Brown's (1973) study of the effects of parental frequency of use is one of many recent studies concerning the general problem of the nature and effects of linguistic input to the child. Research on the problem drew much of its impetus from the claims that Chomsky (1965) made about the child's linguistic environment. He claimed that children formulate with remarkable quickness an abstract transformational grammar to account for the utterances they hear. Furthermore, it seemed to him that children's data for inducing grammar would be extremely unhelpful in various ways. Parents, he claimed, do not train children for grammar by carefully molding their children's utterances through reinforcement for grammatical utterances and some kind of punishment for ungrammatical utterances (a process commonly held at that time to be central in learning theory, e.g., Miller & Dollard, 1941). Furthermore, studies of adult speech have indicated that adult speech is highly ungrammatical and full of errors, false starts, and misleading pauses. Under these conditions, Chomsky (1965) held that the child's nearly instantaneous achievement of an abstract grammar could only be accounted for by the child's having

innate principles that suggest and limit hypotheses about the possible underlying form and operations of grammars. It also seemed to him that there was no basis for the claim that situationally determined meaning might be helpful in the formation of grammar. These claims led soon to a large body of research on these problems. What were some of the results?

Do Parental Reactions Mold Grammar?

One primary question is actually twofold. Do parental reactions to children's utterances motivate grammatical development by positive reactions to more grammatical utterances and negative reactions to less grammatical utterances? Do parental reactions thus give children feedback about the adequacy or lack of adequacy of their usage?

The bulk of available evidence indicates that there is no such molding or feedback. The focal evidence is found in Brown and Hanlon's (1970) study of parental reaction to grammatical and ungrammatical forms in the speech of Adam, Eve, and Sarah. The findings fall into two main parts: the study of parental reinforcement practices and the study of the communication effectiveness of more grammatical and less grammatical utterances. In the study of parental reinforcement practices, Brown and Hanlon classified parental reactions as either signs of approval, such as *that's right, correct, very good,* or *yes,* or as signs of disapproval in reactions, such as *that's not right, that's wrong,* or *no.* The question was whether signs of approval would be more common after grammatically correct utterances, such as *there's the animal farmhouse,* and whether disapproval would occur more frequently after such utterances as *her curl my hair.*

The results were clear, and negative. Parental approval was about twice as frequent as disapproval following grammatical and ungrammatical utterances alike. For parents gave approval or disapproval not on the basis of the grammaticality of the utterance, but on its truth value. *Her curl my hair,* for example, met with an approving *uh-huh* because the child's mother was curling her hair. *There's the animal farmhouse,* conversely, led to *no, that's a lighthouse.* Contrary to their own frequent report, parents do not seem to respond much to grammaticality per se at all; they are listening and judging for content.

Perhaps, however, there is another kind of environmental contingency: perhaps grammatical utterances are better understood. Brown and Hanlon (1970) concretized this problem by seeing whether grammatical constructions uttered in both mature and immature forms at the same developmental point communicated equally well. For example, in learning *wh*-questions, a child might oscillate among forms, such as *where we going?* (missing auxiliary), *where we should go?* (misplaced auxiliary), or *what will we eat?* (correct). Do the more grammatical forms communicate more effectively? Brown and Hanlon asked this question for three forms in such transition: yes/no questions, negatives, and *wh*-questions. To do so, they classified parental responses into two major classes: sequiturs and non sequiturs. A sequitur was a natural continuation of the conversation, such as a reasonable response to a question or a further comment. A nonsequitur was a lack of response to a question, a query for clarification, a clear misunderstanding, or some other response of this kind. A repeat of the child's utterance was thought to be ambiguous and not scored. (Because repeats were the residual category, it appears from tables in Brown & Hanlon, 1970, that they were, in fact, roughly equal in frequency after grammatical and ungrammatical utterances.) It turns out that more primitive and correct utterances elicited virtually the same proportion of sequiturs. It may be true that early on the primitiveness of the child's grammar may impair understanding, although even most early utterances appear to be clear in context (Slobin, 1982). But clearly, grammatical advance can and does take place without either discernible differential approval or comprehension distinguishing among ungrammatical and grammatical utterances.

Brown and Hanlon's studies thus indicate little role for environmental contingencies either in motivating the child to avance in grammar or in molding the child's grammar by selecting out incorrect utterances. Preschool children thus receive little direct guidance in formulating grammar. What parents and others do is to supply examples from which the child must draw the general patterns. Are the examples as poor as Chomsky (1965) and others have believed? What are the characteristics of the speech the child hears? How might these characteristics affect language learning? Are there characteristics of the speech that might be helpful to children?

The Nature of Parental Speech (as well as Others' Speech)

Chomsky's guesses about the degeneracy and irrelevance of adult speech seem to have been largely incorrect. First, it turns out that adult speech to adults is itself overwhelmingly grammatical, especially once clearly marked false starts are edited out (Newport, 1976). Furthermore, although major clause boundaries may not always be clearly auditorily marked (Broen, 1972), there are subtle and consistent phonological characteristics that mark off boundaries between hierarchical units such as noun phrases (Sorenson, Cooper, & Paccia, 1978). Speakers attempting to deal with more complex problems probably may make more errors. But in ordinary adult speech, grammaticality is dominant.

What about speech to children? Virtually all sentences are complete well-formed sentences or well-formed fragments (e.g., *the red ball* in *get the red ball . . . the red ball*). There are fewer disfluencies or broken sentences than in adult speech and fewer sentences with subordinate, coordinated, or embedded sentential clauses. Small morphemes and inflections are fewer. Imperatives and questions are proportionally more common in early speech to children than in adult-to-adult speech. There is more repetition of all or of parts of previous children's utterances as well as more adult self-repetition. (Blount, 1972; Broen, 1972; Brown et al., 1969; Drach, 1969; Newport, 1976; Phillips, 1973; Shatz & Gelman, 1973; Snow, 1972, 1974). Phonologically, adult speech to children is characterized by higher pitch, exaggerated intonation, clear enunciation, slower tempo, and distinct pauses between utterances and between major clause boundaries (Brown, 1977; Brown et al., 1969; DePaulo & Bonvillian, 1975; Drach, 1969; Ferguson, 1964, 1977; Newport et al, 1975; Phillips, 1973; Sachs & Devlin, 1976). The major semantic relations expressed by grammatical combinations are more limited. The topic of speech is far more likely to be restricted to the here and now, the vocabulary to be more restricted, and the major content words more likely to denote concrete objects, activities, and properties (Blount, 1972; Cross, 1977; Drach, 1969; Ferguson, 1977; Phillips, 1973; Shatz & Gelman, 1973; Snow, 1972, 1974). There are various changes as the child gets older: MLU rises and declaratives are used more frequently (Brown & Hanlon, 1970; Lord, 1976; Newport et al, 1975). Much of the increase in MLU comes from less use of imperatives (e.g., *pick this up*), which are short utterances (Newport et al, 1977). Interestingly, increases in a mother's MLU can apparently be accounted for by changes in the child's age per se because parental MLU goes up with the child's age, even if the child's MLU does not go up (Lord, 1976).

These speech characteristics are not necessarily universal. There are cross-cultural differences among adult speakers in their attitudes toward children's learning to talk, toward children, and toward conversations with them (Schieffelin, in press;

Snow, in press). These special speech characteristics are nevertheless common and also characterize much of older children's speech to younger children (Sachs & Devlin, 1976; Shatz & Gelman, 1973). This is important because in many cultures other children are likely to form the major source of speech samples for younger ones (Schieffelin, in press; Slobin, 1973).

Are mothers in some sense attempting to aid their children in learning to talk through such practices—as they often report they are (Brown, 1977)? The best guess is that they probably are not speaking in these ways to aid language learning (Brown, 1977; Snow, in press). Brown (1977) notes that many of these speech characteristics are common to utterances made to foreigners or to speech between lovers, where presumably the goal is not to teach the listeners to talk. The fact that parental MLU rises with the child's age per se rather than with the increasing child's MLU also indicates something else is going on. The most likely guess is that parents are attempting to keep the children interested and make sure they understand rather than attempting to tutor them in grammar.

But whether or not the speech characteristics are intended to be particularly useful in the child's language acquisition, the question arises of whether they are helpful anyway. By and large, the special characteristics of such speech are probably generally useful (Brown, 1977; de Villiers & de Villiers, 1978; Snow, 1974). First, with an exception to be noted later, the input is generally grammatical, contrary to Chomsky's original claim. Even if only examples of underlying patterns are provided, the examples are at least accurate ones. Utterances are furthermore generally short and about immediate, clear situations. There is some evidence from comprehension studies (Shipley, Smith, & Gleitman, 1969) that children may not respond to a sentence if it is too complex or contains too much they do not understand. As MacNamara (1972) notes, despite Chomsky's disclaimers about the necessity of semantic or situational information, theories of grammar in fact incorporate semantic information heavily as part of the description of the speaker's knowledge of grammar. A speaker who said *the dog bit the cat* when, in fact, the cat bit the dog (and said it not as a joke) would utter an acceptable English sequence, but we would not credit him with knowledge of English grammar. As is already clear in Stage I speech, many rules of grammar that children analyze involve general semantic notions such as agency, location, recurrence, or possession, that refer to real-world relations. Analyzing relations such as underlying

grammatical subject and object must also involve semantic and situational analysis. How could one analyze the notion of *John* as the underlying subject of *like* in both *John likes Mary* and *Mary is liked by John* in contrast to *Mary is liked despite John* if not for the fact that the situational context of use and the meaning of *like* indicate that *John* stands in the same relation to *like* in *John likes Mary* and *Mary is liked by John*, but not in *Mary is liked despite John?* This property of standing in the same role relation despite differences of structural use is part of what constitutes the analysis of notions such as underlying subject or underlying object. As MacNamara remarks, to break into the code of how combinations encode meaning, the meaning and code must initially both be given some description.

Investigators have also been interested in various particular parental practices that might enrich or make particularly useful the speech children hear. Brown et al. (1969) note one that they call *occasional questions*. Part of the grammar of *wh*-questions is that the initial *wh*-word (e.g., *what* in *what do you want?*) may stand in the same relation to other parts of the sentence as a constituent in another part of the sentence. Thus, *what* in *what do you want?* denotes the object of *want*, similar to *you want something* or *you want what?* The last example, in which the *wh*-form is in declarativelike position, is called an occasional question. A mother receiving no answer to a *wh*-question such as *what do you want?* may repeat it in occasional-question form, and this form may be more likely to receive an answer than the first (Brown et al., 1969; Moerk, 1972). (Of course, it is not clear what would happen if the mother simply repeated the initial *wh*-question.) Investigators have also discussed various forms of elaboration parents may do in repeating their children's utterances. One such practice discussed by Brown et al. (1969) was called expansion by them. The parent, hearing an utterance such as *having lunch*, may repeat it in full form: *yes, mommy's having lunch;* the full form contains necessary missing constituents omitted in the child's utterance, and in particular, it supplies omitted inflections and small morphemes; Brown et al. (1969) thought expansion might be especially useful for learning such inflections and small morphemes. In an initial naturalistic investigation of this hypothesis with Brown's et al. (1969) three subjects, however, it was found that Sarah's mother used fewer expansions than Adam's and Eve's mothers, but if anything, Sarah used more inflections at the same MLU level than Adam and Eve did. Cazden (1968) and Feldman (1971) attempted more rigorous experimental tests. An experimenter expanded every utterance of the child, offered a new utterance about the situation, or did nothing. The group hearing *new* utterances improved on various tests over time, whereas the expansion groups did not. It has been noted (Nelson, 1973) that the experimental populations were black populations in which the missing inflections were often not obligatory, but Gonzales (1973) found similar results in a population in which this difficulty did not apply. Brown et al. (1969) wonder whether the adults in the pure-expansion condition might not have become very uninteresting to listen to. Other investigators have, in fact, achieved some favorable results with a related training technique sometimes called expatiation. Nelson, Carskaddon, and Bonvillian (1973) found that if experimenters followed a child's utterance with a sentence that both filled in incomplete parts *and* added new changes—such as a change from declarative to question (which they called a recast sentence group)—the result was that the children used more complex predicate forms compared to a control group. In a later study, Nelson (1975) gave 28- and 29-month-old children experience with recast sentences involving either complex questions or more complex verb constructions in the recast forms. The groups showed more increase in sentence complexity over time than a control group; furthermore, they showed improvement discriminately, depending on the type of construction to which they were exposed. Cross (1977, 1978) performed a correlational study. She found groups of children who actually were progressing more rapidly linguistically, and she investigated characteristics of the speech they heard. In general, she found that mothers whose speech more frequently incorporated semantic material from the preceding children's utterances had more quickly progressing children. In Cross's study, naturally, the causal direction is difficult to discern. The mothers' speech practices might have been important or perhaps rapidly progressing children are also more likely to say things that make it more interesting for adults to continue what they are saying. The collected group of results, however, indicates that coherent new sentences by themselves can make development faster as can sentences that also continue parts of one spoken by the child. These studies are not of expansions in the old sense, however, because they are not simply repetitions with missing material filled in.

The Nelson et al. and Cross studies bring up some points about parental utterances as possible signs to the child about the correctness of her utterances. One might hold that expansions, in which a following parental utterance added material (which an adult knows to be missing material), might signal the child that something was incorrect in her own utterance. Or if a child says *what we should do?* and the parent says *what should we do?*, the change might signal something is wrong to the child. But the child, in fact, may also hear continuations in which changes do *not* necessarily sign something wrong with the old sentence. Is it likely, for example, that a child who says *the boy's swimming* and hears *is the boy swimming hard?* will decide that she should have had a form of *be* at the beginning of the sentence in her utterance instead of after the subject? Thus, it is still up to the child to decide somehow whether lack of match signals a problem or not.

The fact that maternal speech may have special characteristics that appear to aid learning seems sometimes to give the impression, as Cromer (1981) notes, that somehow the problem of language acquisition is solved or enormously eased for the child by the nature of the input. But there are fundamental problems with such a position. First, it is clear that various helpful practices are not necessary for linguistic development to occur. Lieven (1978a,b) found a mother-child pair in which the mother virtually never linked her utterances to previous ones of the child for example, yet the child learned to speak. There is very great variety of circumstances and care under which children must learn language. In fact, in some cultures parental attitudes are even hostile to the child's learning to speak (Schieffelin & Eisenberg, in press). It would be surprising if very delicate, fine-grained interactions were required for the learning of language. Second, it is clear that not all parental patterns are helpful because some children receive more beneficial patterns; this shows that other children also learn to speak when practices are less helpful. Newport, Gleitman, and Gleitman (1975, 1977) studied both a variety of measures of acquisition over time and measures of parental speech uses. They found that particular grammatical systems were sometimes aided by particular parental practices. For example, acquisition of auxiliary verbs seemed more rapid in children whose mothers used more sentence-initial auxiliaries in questions (*would you like some?, is he coming?*), and noun plurals were acquired more rapidly in children whose parents used more deictic utterances, such as *this is X*. But other major kinds of developments, such as the number of main verbs per utterance, did not seem much affected by differential parental practices. Newport et al. (1975) suggest an interesting hypothesis that more universal aspects of languages such as complementation and coordination might not be so affected in rate by differential practices, whereas aspects more specific to a particular language (such as its inflectional systems or auxiliary systems) might be. (Since inflectional and auxiliary systems tend to be very common, however, and to inflect for similar kinds of meanings quite commonly across languages (Pinker, in press; Slobin, 1982); this last suggestion might be somewhat qualified). Wells (1980) notes that in his studies, not all children whose parents showed various helpful practices progressed rapidly; nor did all rapid progressors have parents who displayed these practices very often. Third, it is not really clear that parental speech is absolutely ideal for grammatical acquisition, as sometimes seems to be implied. For example, speech to children contains many fragments that are repetitions of previous utterances as well as many imperatives (*get the ball*) that, relative to declaratives, have omitted parts. One of the often-noted characteristics of children's early speech is that children produce many sentences with missing or omitted parts, at least compared to the adult grammar. But they also hear many fragments. If they do not, for example, properly interpret that initial arguments are missing from imperatives because of the difference in pragmatic force, they are simply hearing many examples of sentences without initial arguments, as Brown (1973) points out. Newport (1976) also notes another possible difficulty. If one holds that the end product of grammatical acquisition is a transformational grammar with underlying structure differing from surface structure, declaratives tend to be closer to this underlying structure than imperatives or questions. Yet, speech to children in the earliest stages of grammars has proportionately fewer declaratives than adult-to-adult speech or than adult speech to older preschool children. As noted later, it is no longer clear that transformational grammars are the end point of acquisition. But Newport's argument at least points out that early input cannot be considered ideal under all assumptions, as does the problem of fragments.

The most important point, however, is that input cannot *solve* the problem of acquisition for the child. The problem is to induce general patterns from specific examples. Most of the advantages that have been discussed have to do with making individual examples more analyzable because they are comprehensible in context. As Cromer (1981) remarks, children change their grammars over time against what is essentially little change in input. The fact that much is left out early or not even attempted shows that it is up to the child to arrive at interpretations of what is needed. Furthermore, it is very clear in various ways that it is *how* the child interprets the

data that is important. For example, children could interpret various examples grossly incorrectly, although reasonably. When children hear markers such as *a* and *the* and *-s* used on terms such as *dog* and *cat,* they are hearing them used with object words. Words such as *you* or *Elliott* are also object words, but they do not generalize these privileges to such words (de Villiers & de Villiers, 1973a). One can only say that children analyze such factors as 'denotes a class' versus 'denotes an individual' appropriately as is relevant to the uses; no one can tell them to do so. On the other hand, children also make errors that do not correspond straightforwardly to individually heard utterances (such as *knowed* and *breaked* or *where we should put it?*). All of these are simply illustrations of the basic point, that is, the task of ferreting out the appropriate patterns is the child's.

In summary, parental speech to children does not (at least according to present evidence), carefully shape their grammatical acquisition by feedback such as noncomprehension or disapproval of incorrect utterances. Incorrect utterances are generally comprehended and usually approved, much like correct utterances. On the other hand, input to children is not as misleading and degenerate as Chomsky (1965) implied. Parental input marks major boundaries with pauses, uses brief utterances that are largely about surrounding context, and appears generally comprehensible. Furthermore, it is likely that speech of other children to young children is adjusted in similar ways (Sachs & Devlin, 1976; Shatz & Gelman, 1973). On the whole, however, the basic problem of analyzing the underlying patterns in the welter of examples is the child's; it cannot be solved for the child by the input.

Because this is so, the chief problem of acquisition is what the child analyzes from the multiply interpretable data. In the next discussions, these problems are taken up, beginning with a problem that has begun to attract attention in the study of later development, much as it did in the study of Stage I speech, that is, the relative role of structural factors and semantic factors in explaining the course and content of development.

SEMANTIC FACTORS, FORMAL FACTORS, AND THE DEVELOPMENT OF FORMAL CATEGORIES

In the past years, no doubt encouraged partly by the negative findings for formal categories in early speech and an increasing recognition of the role of semantic factors in adult grammar (e.g., Fillmore, 1968; Lakoff, 1971), a new kind of approach to grammatical acquisition has become common (Bates, 1976). In this approach, the eminence of semantic and pragmatic factors as explanations of overall grammatical development is foremost. This kind of approach implies that conceptual development per se and the fairly straightforward use of major semantic factors organized around cognitively central notions such as 'object,' 'agent,' 'topic,' 'action,' and 'patient' are capable of accounting for development in two major senses: first, in the sense of explaining sequence of acquisition; second, in the sense of providing the required analytic framework for grammatical analysis in most or all of grammar (Bates & MacWhinney, 1982; Schlesinger, 1974, 1981). At the same time, however, a number of voices are being raised in qualification of many such claims (e.g., Bowerman, 1981; Cromer, 1981; Karmiloff-Smith, 1979; Maratsos & Chalkley, 1980; Schlesinger, 1977; Slobin, 1982). Two such qualifications have already been discussed. First, there is the pervasive evidence that children do not have extraordinary difficulty learning a grammar in which major constituent orders do not generally follow the cognitively "natural" order of agent-action-patient (Slobin, 1982). Second, there is the fact that structural uses in a language may be essential in fixing boundaries among grammatical concepts and may differ across languages (Braine & Wells, 1978; Schlesinger, 1977). However, what about other claims? Can semantic complexity and, underlying it, cognitive complexity explain the sequence of acquisition satisfactorily? Can semantic properties per se, properly bundled, provide sufficient analytic material for the construction of even what look like more formal categories, such as subject, verb, and object? These questions comprise the foci of the next discussions.

Semantic and Conceptual Development and Acquisition Order

One type of prediction between semantic complexity and acquisition has been discussed already, that is, Brown's (1973) findings that for the 14 morphemes, cumulative semantic complexity would provide good predictions of the acquisitional order of a subgroup of the morphemes. Recent years have evidenced an interest in the extent to which semantic development as it rests more broadly upon general conceptual development could provide predictions concerning the sequence of children's grammatical acquisition. Regarding early speech, for example, Brown (1973), Bloom (1970), and Sinclair (1971) have all noted that the meanings encoded early in

grammatical acquisition, such as agency, location, recurrence, and disappearance of objects, correspond to underlying cognitions portrayed as undergoing important developments at the end of the sensorimotor period in Piaget's work. Complementarily, cognitive complexity has been used to explain the late acquisition of some constructions. Gvozdev (1949) found that in Russian, inflections for noun plurality, diminutiveness imperative, and past tense appeared relatively early, whereas the conditional marker, although formally very much like the early past tense marker, appears rather late. Gvozdev (1949) held that the early-appearing meanings are distinguished by their especially concrete and graphic meanings or their important social functions. Cromer (1974) similarly noted that the *have*-perfective (e.g., *I've eaten* or *have you seen this?*) is formally similar to other auxiliary verb constructions, such as the progressive, and that it is heard relatively frequently in parental speech. Yet, Brown's (1973) subjects did not produce examples of the *have* = perfective for months to years after they productively used other auxiliary verb constructions. It seemed to Cromer (1974) that the semantic complexity of the *have* - perfective and, underlying that, its conceptual complexity (it is usually analyzed as denoting pastness extending into the present or as denoting past relations having present relevance) might account for its late occurrence. Cromer (1974) found experimental evidence in a nonlinguistic cognitive task for children's relative late appreciation of such subtle temporal notions.

Conceptual development probably affects children's grammatical acquisition in a number of ways. First, it supplies requisite analyses for semantic factors relevant to analyzing individual morphemes or regularities of grammatical structure (MacNamara, 1972). Second, it may affect what the child is interested in talking about. As conceptual development makes various concepts available, the child may search for ways of talking about them. Or the child may use utterances in which these concepts are part of the child's underlying communicative intent, even if unexpressed grammatically (Slobin, 1973). Third, if a concept is less concrete or otherwise more complex, even if the child has the concept cognitively available, it may be more difficult for the child to associate a particular word or morpheme with the concept.

Analysts such as Cromer (1981), however, have seen an hypothesis emerging that is far too strong—this is the hypothesis that cognitive development per se is not only a necessary but also a sufficient explanation of when a grammatical construction can appear. That is, development of the corresponding nonlinguistic concept will make it possible by itself for a corresponding grammatical expression to be mastered and expressed.

If this hypothesis were true, constructions encoding similar meanings should appear at the same time. This prediction is falsified by a large body of findings (Brown, 1973; Brown & Hanlon, 1970; Hakuta, 1976; Kuczaj, 1979; Slobin, 1973, 1982). Within the same language, constructions expressing the same meaning may appear at different times. For example, Brown (1973) and Kuczaj (1978a) note the different acquisitional points for the irregular and regular past, which express the same meanings. Kuczaj (1979) has shown that within the English system of auxiliary verbs (e.g., *can, should, could, will, would, gonna,* and others) stable expression of a particular meaning (e.g., possibility or permission) with one verb does not entail simultaneous or even temporally close acquisition of another verb expressing the same meaning. Across languages, the times of acquisition of constructions having similar meanings may be very different because of the differing structural complexity of expression (Slobin, 1973, 1982). Slobin (1973) cites one dramatic case study (Mikés, 1967) of two children who simultaneously learned Hungarian and Serbo-Croatian. In Hungarian, locative meanings are marked as suffixes on the located noun. In Serbo-Croatian, there is a complex formal system involving prepositional markings and noun gender. As Slobin notes, presumably the children's cognitive development was similar when acquiring both languages; but the locative meanings were marked much earlier on Hungarian nouns than on the Serbo-Croatian ones.[3] Other cross-linguistic findings demonstrate the same general point equally well. For example, English yes/no question meaning can be conveyed by intonation alone (*he go?*); in Finnish such questions require a special particle and initial placement for the verb. Utterances interpretable as questions appear much later in Finnish than in English (Bowerman, 1973). Multiplying examples to be found in such sources as Slobin (1973, 1982), Hakuta (1976), Schieffelin (in press), and others, would only serve as further illustration.

Overall, the variety of formal means within and across languages for expressing the same meanings is so great that children's acquiring relevant constructions simultaneously could be accounted for only by supposing that the formal problems of analyzing grammar are so simple for children that it is only conceptual development that prevents instantaneous grammatical analysis. This is an hypothesis that might warm the heart of the most ardent nativist. Instead, semantic-conceptual complexity can provide partial prediction of the sequence of acquisition of constructions; but complete prediction must depend upon the incorporation of such factors as structural complexity and phonological clarity (Brown, 1973; Slobin, 1973), as well as other factors (MacWhinney, 1978).

The Evolution of Formal Categories

There is another aspect of language learning where it seems doubtful that acquisition can simply consist of an expression of underlying major semantic properties, that is, the evolution of formal categories, such as subject and object or verb and adjective and noun. As will be seen, however, there is considerable disagreement about the relative importance of central semantic properties of the classes in both the ontogenetic processes leading to the adult state and in the characterization of the adult state itself.

Formal grammatical categories, such as subject and object or verb and adjective, are categories that group terms or roles into classes relevant for grammar; but unlike earlier categories, such as agent or possessor, they cannot be defined according to the semantic properties of their members alone. The formation of formal categories does not signal the end of utility for more semantically based distinctions (such as agency) or other semantic distinctions. They are, however, apparently categories that require different principles of organization, at least in part.

The last years have seen growing agreement (Bates & MacWhinney, 1982; Bowerman, 1973; Braine, 1976; Grimshaw, in press; MacNamara, 1977; Maratsos & Chalkley, 1980; Pinker, in press; Schlesinger, 1974, 1981; Slobin, 1981) that such formal categories are not present in Stage I grammar (see Bloom et al., 1975, for disagreement on this point). The central questions regarding such categories have come to be the degree to which they can nevertheless be described as involving semantic properties, such as agency or concrete objecthood, in development or final form. Some theorists (Bates & MacWhinney, 1982; Schlesinger, 1974, 1981) hold that the modal semantic tendencies of such classes play a primary role in both the development and the final form in defining the category. Other theorists hold that at some point, categories may come to be formed or shaped essentially by the shared combinatorial properties that they hold in common so that the core semantic modality of the category is partially or completely transcended.

These latter theorists divide roughly into two major groups. A first group are those who believe that the central semantic tendencies, such as agency for subjecthood or actionality for verbs, play important ontogenetic roles in the early development of the categories. A second group holds that it is possible that formal categories arise solely on the basis of the shared combinatorial properties that characterize the category (probably Bowerman, 1973, for subjects; Maratsos & Chalkley, 1980, for verbs, adjectives, and subjects; and Kiss, 1973, for form classes).

The major formal categories of languages are categories such as subject and object or verb, noun, and adjective. Interestingly, however, some of the major findings regarding formal categories in recent years have come from investigations of such subclasses as arbitrary noun gender in such languages as Russian, German, Polish, Spanish, French, and Hebrew. As anyone knows who has learned any of these or similar languages, such categories seem only peripherally tied to meaning. Evidence summarized in Slobin (1973) concerning Slavic gender systems, furthermore, indicated long-drawn-out, error-filled acquisitional processes for such clearly nonsemantically based categories. This picture contrasted strongly with the apparently near error-free, more rapid formation of categories such as noun and verb. Such evidence thus suggested that formal categories of the latter kind must have at least some kind of ontogenetic semantic core that accounts for their early and effortless learning.

In recent years, however, the empirical data concerning the acquisition of such systems have begun to look different. These data indicate that children can organize formal gender systems by the age of 3 or so, with often surprising skill and accuracy. We will thus first discuss noun gender acquisition before turning to the more problematic case of other formal category learning.

Arbitrary Noun-Gender Categories

In various languages, nouns of the language are divided into two, three, or more sets on the basis of their subset differences in how they take (depending on the language) noun inflections in different case contexts, determiner endings, adjectival endings, pluralization markers, verb agreement markers, or different sets of coreferential pronouns. Typically, except for a few nouns that cluster together semantically, meaning offers no good cue. In German, for example, it is true that the words for 'boy,' 'man,' and other truly masculine entities are all in one noun declension (leading to its being called the masculine noun gender). However, the word for 'knife' is

neuter, the word for 'spoon' is masculine, and the word for 'fork' is feminine, as an example of the general arbitrariness of such systems—another example, in Spanish the word for 'pants' is feminine.

It is confusing, however, simply to lump together all such systems because of the negative characteristic that meaning generally provides little cue as to class. It turns out that for some, the phonological shape of the noun stem itself can nearly always (as in Hebrew) or usually (as in French or Spanish) provide some cue for gender. In such languages as German, Polish, and Russian, in contrast, the phonological shape of the stem is usually irrelevant. Thus, in the following discussion, findings from these kinds of categories will be examined separately.

Stem-Based Systems. In Hebrew and in much of French and Spanish, the phonological form of the stem itself predicts which of various subsets of inflectional or other morphemes are associated with the noun. In Hebrew, for example, nouns that end in stressed *-a* or (less common) unstressed *-at* or *-et* take *-ot* as noun plural and various other sets of verb agreement and adjective agreement markers; this set is called the feminine gender because, for animate nouns, true gender is also a predictor of the set. Nouns that end in other sounds take the masculine plural marker *-im* and a separate set of verb agreement and adjective agreement markers. Thus, the phonological shape of the stem itself, once analyzed, can be correlated to sets of grammatical markers that combine with the nouns. Similarly, in French, elements such as the set of determiners or the relevant set of pronouns to refer to a noun can usually (although not always) be predicted from the phonological shape of the noun, as is true for Spanish.

Such systems cause errors in acquisition (Karmiloff-Smith, 1979; Levy, in press, a,b; Tolbert, 1978). Central aspects of such systems seem, however, to be acquired by the age of 3, as measured variously by naturalistic observations or experimental tasks with nonsense words. There are even overregularizations on the basis of phonological shape. For example, Levy, in press, b; reports that errors are common when a noun (e.g., *beitza*, ['egg']) happens to end in the phonological shape characteristic of one gender (feminine for *beitza*) but takes markers characteristic of the other gender.

In such systems, however, one might wonder whether children first construct the grammatical categories on the basis of the small set of truly sexed masculine and feminine nouns and then somehow form the other classes by perhaps interpreting nonsexed nouns as somehow truly sexed or by somehow expanding the original semantically based class. There are various kinds of evidence that they do not do this. Levy (in press, a,b), for example, discusses longitudinal and experimental studies of Hebrew. As she notes, the children's errors seem all to be determined by phonological characteristics; there is no evidence of the errors stemming from some kind of judgment of natural masculinity or femininity. Karmiloff-Smith (1979) provides relevant evidence from French. Her subjects were 3-year-old through school-age children. She showed them, for example, nonsense pictures of novel inanimate and animate objects and beings. The animates were novel but could be clearly identified as male or female from various characteristics. She found that children could actually use phonological shape as a predictor for appropriately chosen inanimate-object words before they could use inherent gender for animate-sexed beings, the words for which gave no phonological cues to gender use. Thus, her evidence makes it implausible that children had analyzed the gender sets on the basis of inherent gender first and then constructed appropriate interpretations or categories on that basis for nonsexed terms. A very interesting facet of Karmiloff-Smith's study is that she also asked children their reasons for answering as they did. They could give no reasons at all, and this for years after their answers showed they knew something about the system. When they could do so, their answers centered on natural gender. None of their answers concerned the phonological characteristics of the nouns, except in a very few instances by older children. Thus, her interview data show both how systematically applied linguistic knowledge may be completely unavailable to conscious introspection and also how speakers' conscious intuitions almost always overestimate or center upon semantic variables, even when nonsemantic ones are actually analyzed and applied earlier.

Thus, there is considerable available evidence that children can form productive systems of rules relating the phonological shape of the noun to various sets of determiners, pronouns, adjective endings, plural markers, and other grammatical markers by the age of 3. Such learning must first involve considerable analysis of how nouns individually take individual grammatical uses. Over time, the unconscious analytic system of long-term storage must sift out the appropriate phonological predictors from all the possible predictive systems available. Such a process implies both a considerable capacity for detailed analyses in long-term memory as well as capacity to produce the resultant constructed grammatical categories.

Systems Based on Shared Combinations. In languages such as German, Polish, and Russian, however, even the phonological shape of the stem itself is rarely a good predictor. Instead, the various sets of determiners, or noun inflections, must instead be analyzed for how they predict each other. Nouns that overlap in the set of grammatical markers they take per se must be organized into classes. How do children fare with such systems?

Russian is one of the earlier reported languages so studied (Gvozdev, 1949 [summarized or drawn upon in Slobin, 1973]; Popova, 1958/1973; Zakharova, 1958/1973). Like Turkish, Russian employs inflections on the nouns themselves to mark various grammatical cases. Russian has six such grammatical cases: nominative, accusative, instrumental, dative, genitive, and what is called the prepositional. There is some, but not thoroughgoing, correspondence to major grammatical or semantic relational categories. What would be the grammatical subject in English is marked with the nominative, the indirect object with the dative, and what would be the grammatical object, the accusative (usually). But like most such systems, the full system includes a number of idiosyncracies. The instrumental case, for example, can mark not only instruments but also under some circumstances predicate nominals (such as *soldier* in the equivalent of 'he will be a soldier') (Slobin, 1973).

Further complicating the systems is the fact that nouns fall into three different gender sets of noun inflections to mark these cases. For example, in the singular, what are called feminine nouns (the most common) take -*a* to mark the nominative, -*u* to mark the accusative, and -*oy* to mark the instrumental (an ending also used for many other gender-case markings). Masculine nouns take no endings in the nominative and accusative but -*om* in the instrumental. Neuter nouns take stressed -*o* on the nominative and -*om* in the instrumental.

Truly masculine nouns tend to be assigned to the masculine set and truly feminine ones to the feminine set; aside from these, assignments are apparently made with no particular semantic basis. Nor does the phonological shape of the noun itself generally give much of a cue. Thus, the child sometimes hears -*a*, sometimes -*o*, and sometimes nothing on nominative forms; sometimes -*u*, sometimes nothing on accusative forms; sometimes -*oy*, sometimes -*om* on instrumental forms (all in the singular)— with none of these being correlated to noun meaning or sound. How can the child form a predictive, productive system? What the child must analyze, apparently, is the following: nouns that take -*a* in the nominative, take -*u* in the accusative and -*oy* in the instrumental; nouns that take no ending in the nominative, take nothing in the accusative and -*om* in the instrumental; nouns that take -*o* in the nominative, take nothing in the accusative and -*om* in the instrumental; and so forth. That is, for each noun, first the child must memorize which case marker the noun takes in the various case environments. Then, the child's internal analytic system must notice that nouns tend to share markings (i.e., nouns that take nominative -*a*, take accusative -*u*, and so forth). From this information, at some point, the child must construct categories that summarize this information about the related uses of nouns.

As if this were not enough, it turns out that there are confusing subclasses and irregularities in the system. Many masculine nouns, for example, end in -*a*, such as *Papa* ('papa'). Thus, in the nominative, they look like nouns that take -*a* as an inflection. A number of nouns take the unstressed vowel -*ə* (pronounced like "uh") as the nominative ending. Such nouns may be either feminine or neuter in the rest of their uses, something that must be memorized for each noun. If a noun stem ends with what is called a palatalized consonant, it takes no ending in the nominative and otherwise is arbitrarily assigned to the masculine or feminine set of uses. (These examples do not exhaust the irregularities.) Thus, the system is both semantically arbitrary and, in various ways, confusing or irregular as well.

Slobin (1973) summarizes reports in Gvozdev (1949) and Zakharova (1958) that indicate that children analyze case distinctions accurately and early. That is, from an early age, they do not use an accusative ending where a nominative is appropriate for example. This is attributed to the semantic basis of case categories by Slobin (1973), although he elsewhere notes the often-arbitrary nature of case categories. In contrast to the skill with case categories, however, errors in gender use may persist into the school years, which begin at 7 or 8 in Russia. Early on, for example, children may mark all accusatives with feminine -*u*. Or they may pass through different favored markings, briefly favoring masculine and neuter -*om* for the instrumental case, then overusing feminine -*oy*. Such inflectional imperialisms, as Slobin describes them, end reasonably early, but other gender errors are made for years. Slobin analyzed this and evidence from other Slavic systems as indicating that semantic-based categorical distinctions are learned easily but that semantically arbitrary systems, such as noun gender, are extremely difficult for children to construct.

In recent years, however, the picture has begun to shift. Maratsos and Chalkley (1980) note that Zakharova (1958/1973), whose evidence was both observational and experimental, did find gender errors through the preschool years. Such errors that occurred late were, however, confined to those nouns in which the nominative form ends in unstressed -*o* or palatalized consonants. As will be recalled, these are the cases where even knowledge of the general system cannot give correct prediction of other forms from the nominative. For nouns ending in nominative inflection -*a*, stressed -*o*, or most consonants (i.e., no nominative inflection), Zakharova's reports along with Gvozdev's (1949) indicate that productive control is present by about the age of 3. Considering both the complexity of the analysis and the confusing nature of some of it, such productive control is remarkably early.

Even more striking are results reported for Polish by Smoczynska (in press). Polish is essentially similar to Russian in the singular; nominative -*a* predicts one set of other noun endings, nominative -*o* predicts another set, and so forth. But in Polish, various problems, such as masculine nouns for which the stem ends in -*a*, or other confusing uses, are not present. According to the available cross-sectional and longitudinal evidence, Polish children also begin to use case-gender inflections around the age of 2 or before. But there is only a brief period of errors and no evidence of inflectional imperialism. Thus, the learning of the arbitrary, but comparatively regular, Polish system is both relatively early and accurate. Therefore, the Polish results indicate that it is apparently the exceptions, confusions, and irregularities of Russian that lead to the persistent and common errors of Russian acquisition, not the semantic arbitrariness of the system.

A third language that has received study is German (MacWhinney, 1978; Mills, in press; Walter, 1975). German has four cases—nominative, accusative, genitive, and dative—and three noun-gender subdivisions that are variously marked for definite and indefinite determiners, pronouns, and adjectives. Again, there is usually little semantic cue from the noun, nor is there usually a phonological cue (except for a small set). Perhaps because the inflections are not marked directly on the nouns themselves, the relevant uses appear a little later in German, beginning with determiners around the age of 2½. According to various diary studies and experimental studies, case errors (e.g., using nominative forms in accusative contexts or genitives in dative contexts) are more common than gender errors (MacWhinney, 1978; Mills, in press; Walter, 1975). Gender errors are variously reported as being virtually absent (as in sources summarized in Mac-Whinney, 1978) or tend to occur rarely, with feminine *die* being overused a little. Productive knowledge of the system can be shown in various degrees at the age of 3 (MacWhinney, 1978; Mills, in press). Thus, again, children turn out to be surprisingly skillful and accurate in constructing a complex, semantically arbitrary system. And experimental evidence with nonsense words (Böhm & Levelt, 1979) indicates that conflicting evidence from natural gender and formally assigned gender leads to assignment of gender use on the basis of the formal cues.

Thus, in all of these languages, available evidence indicates that children can skillfully construct formal categories in which phonological properties or shared combinatorial uses of terms are the determining properties. Nor is there any evidence indicating that children begin by analyzing the small set of truly sexed nouns and then generalize this knowledge to the nonsexed nouns. Available evidence indicates the earlier or stronger defining role of the formal correspondences per se. Levy (in press, a) notes as well that various kinds of evidence indicate, if anything, that children under 3 are rather poor in making cognitive gender distinctions. She also cites evidence from Ervin-Tripp and Kluwin (in preparation) that indicates that English-speaking children during this period (i.e., under 3 years of age) have not analyzed correctly such uses as *he* versus *she*, despite the actual semantic gender basis for this distinction. Thus, evidence overall suggests that both phonological stem-based systems and systems based on shared grammatical uses are learned without such a basis. In addition, the available evidence shows how children can construct such formal categories from analysis of patterns that must be initially analyzed for terms individually. These are drawn out when various properties, whether phonological or shared uses, become good enough predictive systems. Children's skill in constructing such systems comprises one of the major empirical findings of the past years.

Major Lexical Categories: Verb, Adjective, Noun

Major lexical categories such as verb, adjective, and noun, or relational categories such as subject and object, have certain analytic properties in common with noun-gender classes (Kiss, 1973; Maratsos & Chalkley, 1980). Like gender categories, they seem to contain semantically heterogeneous members unified by shared grammatical uses. Contrastively, however, they also seem to center more upon semantic qualities, such as actionality, objecthood, stable qualities, agency, and patienthood. Thus, theories of three major kinds concerning lexical categories have grown up: (1) theories that they are like noun-gender categories in being essentially constructed from shared grammatical operations per se (e.g., Kiss, 1973; Maratsos & Chalkley, 1980); (2) theories that major semantic-structural categories such as objecthood or agency play some important ontogenetic role in forming the basis for lexical categories, such that combinatorial processes are somehow added to, shape, or suggest the abstraction of a more formal category from such early semantic-based beginnings (Bowerman, 1973; Brown, 1958; Gentner, 1982; Grimshaw, in press; MacNamara, 1977; Maratsos, 1981; Slobin, 1966, 1981); or (3) theories in which the central semantic properties remain in some form the defining core of one or more of such categories, at least through childhood (Bates & MacWhinney, 1982; Schlesinger, 1974, 1981). Each of these three major types of theorization contains within it many different types of approaches, but they seem to correspond to major overall developmental theories. Ideas and findings centered around these approaches will be considered in this review only for lexical classes, such as noun, verb, and adjective, for which more post Stage I findings are available. (For speculations—but only a few data—about subject and object, see Bates & MacWhinney, 1982; Bowerman, 1973; Grimshaw, in press; Maratsos & Chalkley, 1980; Pinker, in press; Schlesinger, 1974, 1981).

At this point in the study of language acquisition, perhaps the major question is the degree to which semantic properties are capable of supplying the defining properties for major formal categories throughout development as a whole. Thus, for example, Bates and MacWhinney (1982) claim that for lexical categories, even the end state of development comprises a semantically based system of organization. Verbs, despite the apparent diversity of meaning shown by terms such as *hit, kick, run, sleep, read, like, want, need, belong, consist,* and *have,* are generally distinguishable on the basis of their semantic properties from adjectives (including a semantic range from *big* and *tall* through *nice* and *careful* to *noisy, loud, quick, busy,* and *fast*) and from nouns (ranging from *Mary, John, Paris, dog, table, chair* through *idea, action, game, trip, relation and sadness*). Just as early on, children control grammatical uses through such analyses as the semantic properties of terms, grammatical categories remain semantically defined, although possibly structural forms might suggest which meanings are to be grouped together.

What Bates and MacWhinney (1982) suggest (and as Schlesinger, 1981, also implies for verbs), is that although not all verbs, for example, are clear examples of the best actions, they draw off a pool of properties centering on the cluster found in the prototypically best examples. Such a pool of properties might include instantaneousness, intentionality, change, and specified physical movement among others. Thus, *throw* would be a better verb than *imagine,* which nevertheless contains enough of the relevant pool of qualities (intentional control, internally active quality) to be distinguished from adjectives or nouns. Nouns similarly center around object qualities of stable existence, shape, and solidity, whereas adjectives center around qualities such as stability and nonobjecthood. There might be a few bad members of classes that have to be arbitrarily assigned and marked as such, but these should be few in number. Bates and MacWhinney (1982) and Schlesinger (1974, 1981) also use another mechanism for aiding in this. Terms less near the focal meanings of their category are hypothesized to be interpreted as being more consistent with these focal meanings because they are used in grammatical environments characteristic of such good members. Thus, *idea* and *action* acquire more 'objectlike' interpretation and analysis because they are heard in uses that are like those of clear object terms; *want* and *need* and *belong* and *like* presumably acquire more dynamic encodings because they are used in grammatical environments characteristic of good examples of dynamic terms. These accounts suggest that grammatical privileges might be organized first around the semantically better members. Terms that resemble these better members more in meaning and that appear in similar structural context are assimilated into the earlier categories, resulting in the grouping together of semantically heterogeneous terms.

In a sense, such a theory is developmentally conservative. The best supported categories of early speech consist of semantically defined ones. What is being suggested is a continuation of such grouping principles into later grammar. Grammatical structure and sequence may suggest which properties might be grouped together or how terms should be interpreted (Schlesinger, 1977); but they nevertheless do not form a basis for the analytic defining properties of the classes.

Aside from the fact that the theory is in some ways parsimonious (because it employs developmental processes that seem well supported in early speech), what other kinds of support are evident for it? Bates and MacWhinney (1982) argue that, in general, children's (and adults') processing capacity is limited and language is itself a limited channel, with only various ordering and inflectional devices as its main resources. Thus, such resources would be preferably devoted by the child to marking major functional qualities, such as agency, topicality, actionality, and so on, rather than being used for the intricate and difficult analyses required by more formal analyses of structures. Schlesinger (1974, 1981) argues that children actively prefer to use meaning to explain grammar. Other types of arguments concern adult intuitions, such as those that nouns have a certain "object" quality about them.

First, however, as regards the adult state, it is generally counterintuitive that the general lack of overlap among semantic categories is as great as Bates and MacWhinney (1982) and Schlesinger (1974, 1981) propose. It is very difficult to think of nonactional verbs such as *consist, belong, have, know, think* (in the sense of 'to have an opinion'), *feel* (good), and others, being more actional than adjectives such as *noisy, loud, quick, fast, active, busy,* or even *nasty, nice, obnoxious, careful,* and *clever,* which generally denote ways of acting. It is true that objecthood in particular has coherent relations to grammar, in that terms denoting objects are typically treated similarly in languages, which category is thus called nouns; but otherwise semantic properties seem to overlap highly across classes.

The second problem lies in the developmental phenomena. For example, the theory proposes that children "actionalize" the meanings of verbs to make them fit into the action-term category. Among English verbs, there are certain constructions that are applied most readily to actional or intentional actional verbs. These include the progressive (e.g., *he's singing*), which denotes ongoing activity, or the imperative (*leave the house!*), which denotes a controlable activity (Fillmore, 1968; Lakoff, 1966). If children attributed more dynamic qualities to verbs such as *want, need, see, hear, know, think* (in the sense of 'to have an opinion') and *belong,* one might at least expect such errors as **I'm knowing it* or **need some dinner!* Such errors are generally absent (Brown, 1973; Cazden, 1968), a fact best explained by children's having analyzed the nonactional nature of such terms (Kuczaj, 1978b; Slobin, 1973). Yet, children treat such less actional verbs like more actional ones where appropriate. For example, children apply to them such operations as *-ed* past tensing productively, as shown by overregularizations such as *knowed, thinked, thoughted, seed, sawed, heared,* and *feeled.* Maratsos et al. (1979) show that children overregularize such terms as soon as they show evidence of being able to make past reference to the relevant situations; Maratsos and Kuczaj

(1979) further provide evidence that overregularization occurs about as frequently for these as for more actional verbs. These findings all argue that such terms are treated productively as members of the verb class, despite their properly analyzed nonactionlike semantics. The second kind of evidence concerns nonoccurring errors. Terms, such as *noisy, busy, careful*, and others, clearly have various actional qualities. They might be expected to be terms that would have to be assigned to the adjective class as arbitrary exceptions. Or at least, there should be some difficulties getting right the boundary categories between them and nonactional verbs, which have so many qualities characteristic of nonverbs. Yet, such errors as *noisied, *it noises, *I didn't loud, *he happied (*happy* is similar to many emotion verbs in meaning), and others, are extremely rare, as are most errors of treating members of one form class grammatically like members of other form classes (Cazden, 1968, Maratsos, 1981). Cazden (1968), for example, found not one error in the samples of Adam, Eve, and Sarah in Stages I through V of treating adjectives like verbs in inflectional markings; in fact, verb markings were applied to a nonverb just once, in the use of *stand ups*, which could well have resulted from a temporary segmentation problem with *stand-up* (temporarily treating it as a single word). Maratsos (1981) similarly investigated 55 hr. of longitudinal samples from one child in Stage V and after as well as 19 hr. from 20 other children in Stage V and above, and he found no errors of treating adjectives as verbs (or vice versa). Such accuracy of use, of course, might be attributed to very great use of memorization by children. But the problem with this is that errors such as applying *-ed* past to irregular verbs are quite frequent so that we know that such operations are productive; thus, accuracy cannot be attributed to memorization per se.

Third, general developmental phenomena as well as characteristics of adult languages argue that Bates and MacWhinney's (1982) general assumptions about the nature of the child's processing capacity and expressive inclinations are not overpoweringly supported. Children in Stage I, for example, turn out to spend much of their grammatical resources on various word-based formulas or narrow-scope formulas rather than concentrating them initially or reliably on major semantic relations, such as agency (Bowerman, 1976; Braine, 1976; Ingram, 1979). It turns out that 2-year-olds are able to analyze complex formal systems such as arbitrary noun gender in Russian, German, Polish, French, Spanish, and Hebrew with surprising skill

and accuracy; irregularity and confusing evidence seems to give more problems than necessity for complex tabulation of data or nonsemantic-based category distinctions per se.

If formal categories such as noun and verb are not defined through development by the semantic properties of their members per se however, how are they constructed? Although they fall into many different particular ideas, with different presuppositions, the remaining ideas seem to converge on shared structural properties being some kind of eventual shaper of major formal categories. Thus, terms such as *know* and *see,* for example, are not semantically very similar to many terms that take *-ed* past tensing. But terms such as *know* and *see* do resemble terms that take *-ed* past tensing in many combinatorial properties, such as taking *-s* tensing (*he kicks, he knows*); similar auxiliaries (*he will kick, he will know, he didn't kick, he didn't know, did you kick?, do you know?*); and appearance with similar arguments in similar ways (*I kick, I know, they kick, they know*). Thus, this similarity somehow leads to their inclusion in the same grammatical class, leading to the susceptibility of such nonactional terms to take the *-ed* past-tensing characteristic of the class (*he knowed, he thoughted, he seed*), although their nonactional analysis prevents them from taking verb operations reserved for actional verbs. Conversely, because actional adjectives such as *noisy* and *loud* do not share enough similar combinations with most verbs, this prevents them from being categorized similarly to *make* or *kick* in the way *know* and *think* are. Structural properties must thus somehow end in being partial- or complete-defining properties to regulate the relevant grammatical uses.

There seem to be two major kinds of hypotheses to explain how formal categories can acquire such structural organization. In one, major semantic properties, such as objecthood and actionality, form an ontogenetic beginning point (at least) for the formal categories for which they are modal meanings. Thus, children analyze object words as taking determiners, such as *a* and *the,* to form arguments of predicates, as taking property word modifiers, and so on; action words are analyzed as taking auxiliary forms such as preceding *don't* and *can't,* or tense markers such as *-ed* past and present tense *-s.* Suppose, as they are acquired, such combinatorial properties are also encoded as characteristic defining properties of the class. Later in development, words that do not exactly fit the semantic analyses of the major categories are nevertheless heard in similar structural contexts (e.g., *I heard a noise, let's take a trip, I don't want that, he likes me*) for such nonobject and nonaction words as *noise, trip, want,* and *like*. Such terms are assimilated into the earlier originally semantically bounded classes. Over time, the structural properties thus become more reliable in defining properties of the category than the original semantic properties, although the latter may still be available to introspection as characteristic of the class or even provide best guesses about the category meaning (Brown, 1957). Such a position seems to be espoused (or at least suggested as plausible) implicitly or explicitly in such works as Brown (1958), Gentner (1982), MacNamara (1977), Maratsos (1981), and Slobin (1981). Recent nativist proposals have sought to make a link from major categorial semantic properties to more structural categories in another fashion. Grimshaw (in press) has recently proposed that the child may have a predisposition to expect good object terms to provide examples of noun usage and good action terms to provide good examples of verb usage; the child may particularly attend to particular kinds of markers, such as tense inflections on action terms, as indicators of the general category (Pinker, in press). From this beginning, the child's innate knowledge would be able to begin describing the language in terms of formal categories not necessarily linked to the cuing semantic categories. (Also see de Villiers, 1980, for an interesting discussion of the roles of central semantic properties in the adult representation of verbs and nouns.)

A second type of theory attempts to obtain formal classes from the reliable combinations that characterize them per se. For example, Kiss (1973) has shown that if frequent words are given greater weight, form-class categories can be made to arise in a computer simulation by a distributional process; that is, words that frequently precede or follow the same words are unified into categories. Oliver (1968) has shown similar results. Maratsos and Chalkley (1980) have proposed that, for verbs, the most likely organizers are the grammatical operations most reliably characteristic of the class, such as use of preceding *do*-forms, use of *-s* tense markers, and so forth.

For nouns, in fact, most analysts have found it intuitively compelling (Gentner, 1982; MacNamara, 1977; Maratsos, 1981; Slobin, 1966) that objecthood would provide some kind of early organizer for class privileges. The account is intuitively appealing on many grounds. Objecthood is a clear basic cognitive category, one that would be expected to be analyzed as a relevant aspect of the reference of a word and as a possible determinant of many grammatical regularities (Gentner, 1982). Across the world's languages (including English), although not all nouns denote objects, objects are virtually always contained within a single grammatical category, the noun category (actually, it is called the noun category in other languages because it contains the object words) (Gleason, 1961). Thus, there is good reason to think that objecthood is a powerful grammatical organizer. Developmentally, children's terms in early grammar that are nouns for adults are almost universally object words (MacNamara, 1977); nonobject words appear later.

What about verbs? The modal semantic quality for verbs is actionality, itself a better or worse compound of qualities such as movement, intentionality, brevity, cause, change, and other semantic properties (depending on the action term). As Gentner (1982) notes, there is something more slippery about relational qualities than about object qualities in many ways. It is often harder to say whether something is actional or not, and the semantic slippage among grammatical categories seems to be larger for actional qualities than for object qualities. The developmental picture is really not as straightforward for actional and verb properties either. Various less actional future verbs are present early on, such as *sleep, want, need,* nonmotional *sit,* nonmotional *fit* (e.g., *it fits here*), nonmotional *go* (it goes here to refer to a habitual location), and others. Furthermore (as discussed previously), many adult nonverbs seem to function as the action predicates of sentences for many children—such terms as *away, up, down, back,* and *bye-bye* (Bloom, Lightbown, & Hood, 1975; Bloom, Miller, & Hood, 1975; Bowerman, 1976). Some of the latter may last as action predicates of sentences as late as MLU 3.30 (as far as can be told from tabulations in Bloom, Lightbown, & Hood, 1975, and Bloom, Miller, & Hood, 1975). Nor is it the case that characteristic verb operations distribute neatly on all actional terms, and just on actional terms. Morphemes such as *don't* and *can't* are used with largely nonoverlapping sets of terms around Stage II (Bellugi, 1967), including uses with many less actional terms, such as *need, want, know, like,* and *sleep* (examples in Bellugi, 1967; Braine, 1976). The first uses of present tense *-s* tend to be on static locative uses of terms such as *fit* (*it fits here*) *go* (*it goes here*, in the sense of belonging at a location) or *sit*. Progressive *-ing* appears on many terms relatively rapidly. These tend to denote actions that go on for a while, such as walking or singing. Past tense *-ed* and irregular past uses tend to appear earliest on a few frequently used terms and on terms denoting changes of state or achievement, which tend not to overlap with those that take progressive *-ing*

(Bloom, Hafitz, & Lifter, 1980). Furthermore, perhaps strikingly, actional predicate nonverbs, such as *away, back,* and *bye-bye,* do not take such verb markers as they are being acquired, even though these terms are still frequently used as major action predicates around Stages II or III according to analyses in Bloom, Miller, and Hood (1975). Various kinds of semantic subclasses of action predicates also seem to differ in the proportion with which they take, for example, their initial arguments (Bloom, Miller, & Hood, 1975).

It is fairly clear that whatever is going on, there is little striking impression of a major actional class that is organizing grammatical properties characteristic of verbs in a focused way during this period. Maratsos and Chalkley (1980), particularly struck by the absence of *-ing* errors on actional nonverbs, such as *away* or *bye-bye,* give another analysis. They assume that actionality is an early organizer for major predicate-argument rules, such as agent-action, although some results, in fact, such as those in Bloom et al. (1975), make it less clear if all actional predicates are analyzed alike early on (also see Braine & Wells, 1978). But actionality is analyzed as not being an accurate predictor for various more specific combinations, as judged from the data above. When strong evidence emerges for the organization of a general class coordinating verb operation—such as the pattern of overregularization of *-ed* past on actional and nonactional verbs, but continuing lack of error with nonverbs—the verb class appears to have achieved its more adultlike form without preceding evidence for an earlier action category organizing verb privileges. Thus, Maratsos and Chalkley (1980) hold that eventually, after a period of initial nonoverlap, the terms that take various distinctive verb operations finally overlap sufficiently to justify the formation of a category on much the same kind of basis that is used to form such categories as noun gender. That is, terms that participate in overlapping combinations, even if not organized clearly by meaning per se, are organized into a category constructed for this purpose. This does not preclude properties such as actionality from being available for discrimination of operations that apply to actional versus nonactional verbs (or more vs. less actional adjectives for that matter); but it is not the category used to regulate distinctive verb operations.

Maratsos and Chalkley's argument that actionality is not a strong organizer early on because of the failure of verb operations to be used on actional nonverbs (e.g., **awaying*) is not, however, a strong

one. They make use themselves of a mechanism in which initial uses of a construction are memorized specifically upon words that take it, even if the terms already fall into a general category. Empirically, their account implies that significant overlap among verbs in the relevant kinds of operations should be attained around Stages IV and V, when *-ed* overregularizations show the patterns they hold to be symptomatically important. It would thus be positive supporting evidence if other kinds of generalizations potentially organized around the nonsemantically defined verb class, such as reliable supplying of initial noun-phrase arguments, seemed to occur around that time. In Stages II and III, in fact, such overlap seems not to be common, according to the analyses of Bloom et al. (1980). But no evidence is presently available for the kinds of developments Maratsos and Chalkley seem to imply (although it is interesting that Brown, 1973, remarks that by Stage V, terms that take progressive *-ing* also take present tense *-s*). Thus, for the verb category, more evidence is available than for other categories; but a clear overall resolution does not yet emerge, although it seems clear that some kind of more formal organization is in place by Stage V or so.[4]

Summary and Afterword

To summarize, presently available findings indicate that semantic properties of terms per se cannot provide the sole sources of lexical categories or subcategories throughout childhood. The earliest general categories, such as located object or agent appear to be of this semantically defined kind. But by the ages of 3 or 4, such categories as verb, adjective, and noun gender have achieved organizations in which shared grammatical combinations provide bases for category organization.

A discussion of children's abilities to construct structurally defined categories must not, however, imply a kind of systematic replacement of semantic and pragmatic analysis by formal analyses in grammar nor does it imply that the different kinds of analyses are used for different rules. Far more common in languages is that particular rules and categories involve complex admixtures of formal, semantic, and pragmatic analyses. For example, consider the English rule of adding present tense *-s* to the verb after a third-person-singular subject. The rule applies to a formally defined category verb that cannot be adequately characterized in terms of semantic denotation alone. But the rule itself expresses a certain meaning, a complex general tendency for the relation denoted by the verb to be true of the subject (*he* *eats cereal* means it is a general characteristic of his to eat cereal, unlike *he's eating cereal*). The rule only applies when the subject denotes a third-person-singular noun phrase. The notion of 'singular' is semantic, with underlying roots in cognition, whereas the notion 'third person' means someone or something that is not the speaker or the listener, a pragmatic analysis. Finally, the marker *-s* itself is pronounced either /s/ (e.g., he *eats*), /z/ (e.g., *he knows*), or /iz/ (e.g., *he seizes it*), depending on the phonology of the verb stem (Berko, 1958). Thus, the rule freely mixes formal, semantic, pragmatic, and phonological analyses of specific and general kinds rather than being one of these exclusively.

Grammar may also exhibit systematic relations between more formal and more semantically defined categories. For example, not all subjects are agents, certainly. But if a verb takes an agentive argument, that argument is virtually always the subject. Furthermore, there are rules for various treatments of subjects that require the subject to be an agent, such as the English progressive (when used of animate subjects) or imperative. 'Subject' thus does not replace 'agent'; there are instead regular relations between the two constructs. Finally, mixtures of formal and semantic analysis often enter into the definitional basis of categories, such as underlying subject and object. For example, an important aspect of the analysis of underlying subject and object is the relation between active and passive sentences. This relation is certainly partly formal. It obtains only for verbs, for example; even though a statement such as **Mary was nastied to by John* is semantically comprehensible, it is formally deviant. At the same time, however, the key to the analysis is the fact that for a given verb, the semantic role of the noun phrase following the *by* is the same as the semantic role of the noun phrase in surface subject position in the active. That is, the underlying subject of *John was liked by Mary* is *Mary* because *Mary* bears the same relation to *like* in both sentences, that of liker. It is not simply a formal correspondence among structural forms per se that is central. For example, for every sentence of the form $NP_1 + \ldots + Verb + NP_2$, there is a corresponding sentence form $NP_2 + \ldots BE + Verb + Past Participle + despite + NP_2$ (e.g., *Mary likes John; John is liked despite Mary*). But because the object of *despite* does not bear the same relation to the verb semantically as does the subject of the active, no one is tempted to make an underlying grammatical relation out of this.

Thus, some kind of complex admixture of formal and meaningful properties seems to be the rule rather than the exception in the analysis of grammar. It seems to me that in the past years, semantic, pragmatic, and formal analyses have been treated as being some kind of opposition. But I do not think the way in which development displays the child's ability to formulate categories upon more structurally defined bases after Stage I should imply that the child's language acquisition therefore becomes 'formal' rather than 'semantic.' An adequate analysis of language acquisition will instead require attempts to understand how the child coordinates these different kinds of analyses appropriately.

TRANSFORMATIONAL OPERATIONS AND LANGUAGE ACQUISITION

Much of the apparatus for describing formal categories arose in pre-Chomskyan linguistics. However, it was the complexity of grammar as described by transformational analyses that comprised one of the major initial motivations for the study of grammatical acquisition. At one time, it was generally presupposed, for example, McNeill (1966, 1970) that the child formulated a set of transformational rules—rules that operated on what may be distantly related underlying syntactic structures—to give the surface forms of sentences. Some analysts argued that given the nature of the child's evidence and the remoteness of the required underlying structures, innate acquisitional ideas must be inferred to explain the child's acquisition (Chomsky, 1965; McNeill, 1966, 1970). Others, however, held that even if we presuppose a transformational grammar to be part of what the child acquires, the available evidence in combination with more general analytic procedures might make transformations derivable without appeal to innate linguistic knowledge (e.g., Bowerman, 1973; Braine, 1971; Ervin-Tripp, 1971; Maratsos, 1979).

In recent years, however, it has come increasingly under question whether transformations comprise a psychologically real part of sentence processing (Fodor, Bever, & Garrett, 1974; Fodor & Garrett, 1966) or part of the speaker's knowledge at any level (Bresnan, 1978, in press-a, in press-b; Gazdar, in press; Maratsos, 1978; Pinker, in press; Prideaux, 1976; Woods, 1970). However, transformational rules have still found supporters and defenders as well (Bever, Katz, & Langendoen, 1976; Erreich, Valian, & Winzemer, 1980; Fay, 1978; Hurford, 1975). This problem of whether transformations are psychologically real has thus become a dominant one in the literature on the transformational acquisition.

Justifying Transformational Rules

To begin with, what are transformations? Transformations are rules that rearrange, delete, add, or substitute new elements for old in an already ordered sequence of grammatical elements. Transformations typically account for structurally related constructions, such as questions versus declaratives, passives versus actives, subjectless versus full sentential complements, tags versus full questions, affirmatives versus negatives, or different particle placements. They have also been claimed, however, to be part of the production of even the simplest declarative sentences of English (Bever, Fodor, & Weksel, 1965; Chomsky, 1957; McNeill, 1966). For most linguists, the essential justification for transformations was the manner in which they led to a more elegant description of the underlying regularities of grammatical patterns (Akmajian & Heny, 1976; Chomsky, 1957). Let us see how this works.

Some of the best known transformational rules are *movement* rules, rules that rearrange the order of grammatical elements. Well-known rules include the rule of auxiliary verb movement, which derives interrogatives from underlying declarativelike sequences (e.g., Q *you are coming* aux mov't *are you coming?*); the passive, which derives passives from an underlying activelike structure (e.g., *John Past like Mary* passive *Mary Past BE+ed like by John*); and *wh*-movement, which derives *wh*-questions from an underlying declarativelike form (e.g., *John will eat what* wh-mov't *what John will eat,* followed by auxiliary movement to give *what will John eat?*).

One might ask why such sentences are not simply described as having their surface ordering immediately rather than receiving an initial ordering that is then rearranged. To see this, we can look at one of the best justified transformational derivations, that deriving *wh*-questions from underlying declarativelike forms by two major steps: (1) *wh*-movement: for example, *he is eating what* aux-mov't *what he is eating* and (2) auxiliary movement: *what he is eating* aux-mov't *what is he eating?* We will be concerned here with only the justification for the first operation, that of *wh*-movement.

One basic kind of justification comes from what are called co-occurrence restrictions, that is, restrictions on how various grammatical elements may require the presence of some other element. Some of these restrictions may be very general, for example, a tensed main verb generally requires a noun-phrase subject before it in English. Other restrictions may be specific, for example, the verb *blame* generally requires a succeeding noun-phrase direct object. We

may say *he blamed someone* or *he blamed something,* but not the semantically similar **he blamed.* Because some transitive verbs can omit their objects (e.g., we may say *he ate something* or *he ate*), whether a verb that can take such an object *must* take one has to be marked individually for each transitive verb. Thus, a grammatical description of English requires a statement for *blame* something like +[_____+NP], where the _____ denotes a place for the verb *blame.*

But *wh*-questions such as *who(m) did he blame?* or *what will he blame?* seem to violate the usual co-occurrence restriction that *blame* take such a directly succeeding noun-phrase object. The presence of a *wh*-NP in front seems to correspond to the absence of the usual NP after *blame.* One way of simplifying this problem is to generate the sentence by the following sequence of operations: (1) generate the *wh*-phrases in post-*blame* position. The initial syntactic structure for *who(m) did he blame?* would, thus, be *he blamed who(m);* therefore, *blame* acts as usual. The relevant co-occurrence restriction can be stated just once at this initial level of description. Then (2) move the *wh*-phrases to the front, to give the actual surface string—thus, *he blamed who* becomes *who he blamed.* If *blame* were the only case of this sort, of course, this procedure would not be worthwhile. But the case of *blame* is only one of a potentially infinite number of such instances. For the presence of a *wh*-morpheme at the beginning of a sentence seems to correspond to the exception in a usually reliable co-occurrence restriction for various verbs and prepositions; for example, in **he talked to, to* requires an object, but apparently no object is required in *who did he talk to?,* or again, **he liked,* but *who did he like?* All of these can be simplified in the same way, that is, state the usual co-occurrence restriction at some initial level of description. At this initial level of description, the *wh*-phrase is generated in declarativelike position. Then, move the *wh*-phrase to the front of the sentence to account for the actual surface form. Thus, the introduction of an underlying level of description (deep structure) and a single transformation results in a considerable overall simplification of co-occurrence restriction statements in the grammar.

It is important that at its core, this kind of justification has nothing to do with explicating meaningful semantic relations among declaratives and questions. Its justification lies in the overall simplification introduced in the grammar, although its superiority in clarifying more semantic kinds of relations might be pointed to afterward as further support for the superiority of the description (Chomsky, 1957).

In 1963, however, Katz and Fodor suggested that semantic interpretation of underlying syntactic structures might also be made a systematic part of grammar. This led to another kind of argument for transformational rules. Consider again the case of *blame*. Part of the knowledge of an English speaker is that the direct-object argument of *blame* denotes someone or something held responsible for an odious occurrence. To capture this, we might write a general rule something like this: NP_1 + *blame* + NP_2: NP_2 = 'party held responsible for odious occurrence by NP.' (Actually the description would probably not be as close to ordinary language, but that is another matter.) But now suppose we look at a sentence, such as *who did John blame?* The usual rule does not apply. For even though *who* is a noun phrase asking for the identity of the party held responsible, it does not directly follow *blame*. Suppose, however, the semantic interpretive rule, *blame* + NP_2: NP_2 = 'responsible party' is applied to the underlying structure *John blamed who*. Then, the usual semantic interpretive rule can apply to interpret *who* as the party held responsible (the use of *who* adds the information that there is a request for the identity of the party). Afterward, the transformational rule again accounts for the surface form. Again, the transformational rule supplies a considerable simplification, especially when one considers that there is a large set of semantic interpretive rules that have in common the same kind of structurally correlated exception.

Similar kinds of justifications can be given for rules of syntactic deletion of underlying elements. One example to consider is the English imperative, consisting of subjectless verb phrases such as *go away, tell Mary I'm coming,* and *wash yourself up*. These are commonly derived (Klima, 1964) from underlying forms *you will* + VP in which *you* and *will* are then deleted. But why not simply generate verb phrases directly, with a note that such sentences are to be understood semantically as being commands to someone? Why actually generate the morphemes *you* and *will,* only to delete them?

We will only consider here one of the arguments for underlying *you*. This argument arises from the pattern of reflexive use in imperatives. Reflexives are such words as *yourself, himself, herself*. In general, they must occur after a noun phrase (which has the same reference within the same clause). Thus, we can say *you hurt yourself,* but not **you hurt himself;* or *Mary liked herself,* but not **Mary liked himself*. In imperatives, the second person reflexives *yourself* or *yourselves* can be used (*wash yourself!; give yourself a break!*) but no other reflexives

(**wash himself!; *give myself a break!*). A way of avoiding the use of special co-occurrence restrictions on reflexives—but just for imperatives—is to describe them as having underlying *you* in initial position, for example, *you wash you*. The rule for reflexives can then operate on this structure to give *yourself* because of the initial *you*. To give the surface form, the *you* must then be deleted.

At the same time, placing underlying *you* would also simplify rules for interpreting the semantic effects of grammatical combinations. The fact that *you* is understood as the subject of any imperative follows if the usual semantic interpretive rules are applied to the pretransformed structure in which *you* is still present.

Transformations are thus a kind of descriptive device; they employ certain kinds of methodological presuppositions about how co-occurrence restrictions or semantic interpretive rules may be stated initially and what kinds of simplicity are to be preferred. A psychologist might wonder (e.g., Watt, 1970) whether similar kinds of simplicity are important for speakers. A linguist may question whether there are not other kinds of ways of capturing such generalizations (Bresnan, in press-b; Lakeoff & Thompson, 1975).

But such doubts took some time to grow for most psychologists and linguists. Initially, for example, psycholinguistic investigations with adults found that the more transformations a sentence contained, the more time subjects might take to respond to them or that sentences with more transformations seemed to take up more memory space (Miller, 1962; Savin & Perchonok, 1965). Negatives, passives, and questions, for example, seemed to be responded to more slowly than simple declaratives and to take up more memory space. Combinations of these (e.g., negative questions, negative passives, passive questions, negative passive questions) showed even sharper effects.

With time, however, various kinds of contrary evidence began to appear. Various constructions that were more complex by transformational description did not always cause slower response. For example, sentences such as *John runs faster than Bill* are transformationally more complex than ones such as *John runs faster than Bill runs,* but not psychometrically so. Adjective-noun combinations such as *red ducks,* are transformationally derived from embedded modifiers, such as *ducks that are red,* in many transformational derivations (Smith, 1964), but they are easier to understand than the complex embedded modifier forms. Fodor, Bever, and Garrett (1974) and Fodor and Garrett (1966) offer useful summaries of the failure of the hypothesis that transformational complexity necessarily predicts complexity of processing for adults. Fodor et al. (1974) nevertheless hold that transformational grammar may give a correct psychological characterization of how speakers represent grammar. But they hypothesize speakers also construct various strategies and heuristics for analyzing underlying structure from surface structure by various shortcuts so that psychometric studies do not reflect this transformational structure accurately. But others hold that transformations might not describe psychologically real structure at all (Bresnan, 1978, in press a,b; Kaplan, 1972; Kaplan & Bresnan, in press; Wanner & Maratsos, 1978; Woods, 1970). Under these circumstances, it might be hoped (especially by those supporting transformational analyses) that somehow language acquisition itself would offer more striking clues and evidence concerning the reality of transformational grammars. The adult has had time to derive processing strategies and shortcuts. The child, however, may show the underlying structural ensemble more clearly because she is learning it; it might display itself more clearly in aspects of the sequence of learning (Brown & Hanlon, 1970) or in the kinds of errors children make while formulating the relevant grammatical structures (Bellugi, 1971; Brown et al., 1969; Erreich et al., 1980; Fay, 1978; Hurford, 1975). Thus, the study of acquisition might help analyze adult competence better than the direct study of adult competence itself. The study of sequence and the study of errors comprise the two major methodological tools psycholinguists have employed in studying this question. What have been the results?

Transformational Grammars and the Study of Developmental Sequence

The first hypothesis to be considered is that the derivational complexity of a sentence as predicted by the number of transformations required to produce it in a grammar can serve to predict its relative order of acquisition. In particular, Brown and Hanlon (1970) and Brown (1973) have employed the idea of cumulative complexity, that is, if construction$_x$ requires all the transformations required by construction$_y$ and still more, then construction$_x$ is said to be cumulatively more complex than construction$_y$. As these researchers note, this seems like the best comparison. For example, if a first construction requires two transformations and a second construction requires just one transformation but the transformations are completely different transformations, it might be that differences in acquisition are caused by a greater difficulty of a particular one of the transfor-

mations rather than by overall transformational complexity.

What kinds of constructions are cumulatively more complex than one another? Brown and Hanlon (1970) and Brown (1973) drew cases from various transformational grammars available in the mid-1960s (Chomsky, 1965; Jacobs & Rosenbaum, 1968; Klima, 1964). Most of their examples came from operations in the English auxiliary verb system, including negation, interrogation, truncation, and various affixing functions. For example, in most transformational grammars of the period, questions were derived from declarativelike orders by a transformation moving the auxiliary verb to the front, for example, Q he is coming aux mov't is he coming? Thus, using the notation A < B to denote that A is transformationally less complex than B, we can write Declarative < Question. Similarly, at that time, negatives were more complex in adult grammar because they were held to begin with a deep structure in which the negative particle was initial (Klima, 1964), such as Neg he is coming, and were produced by movement of this particle inward, thus, Neg he is coming neg mov't he is + Neg coming—therefore, Declarative < Negative. Another such operation was truncation of the sentence after the first auxiliary verb to account for such sentences as yes, he is or I can (e.g., is he here? Ans.: yes, he is). Thus, yes, he is is derived by truncation if the part of the sentence after the initial auxiliary is identical with the postauxiliary part of a preceding sentence—therefore, Declarative < Truncate. Truncation, auxiliary movement, and negation may also be variously combined into truncated questions (e.g., is he?), truncated negatives (e.g., no, he isn't), negative questions (e.g., isn't he coming?), or truncated negative questions (e.g., isn't he coming?). As can be seen, there are a number of predictions about sequence of acquisition possible from these analyses. Simple declaratives should be acquired before negatives, questions, and truncates, which should in turn be acquired before negative questions, negative truncates, truncated questions, which should in turn be acquired before truncated negative questions. As Brown and Hanlon (1970) note, some of the transformationally complex forms, such as isn't he? are in fact even shorter than the corresponding full forms so that simple morpheme length would not make all of the same predictions.

In analyzing their three subjects' transcripts, Brown and Hanlon set as a criterion of acquisition six examples of use that were not routinelike because in a 700-utterance sample, six examples was the lower boundary of use in adult speech. They also felt that this generally was associated with sufficient variety of use within the construction to have some confidence that the child's uses did not arise from a much more specific construction. (There was one case where the six-example criterion was not used because of this problem. Adam, for a while, frequently produced apparent questions of the form *d' you want* + VP without any other questions that contained sentence-initial auxiliaries.) Most of the predictions made by cumulative complexity were successful in the sample.

Brown (1973) also used transformational formulations to make predictions of cumulative complexity for his 14 morphemes. In his book, he used a Jacobs and Rosenbaum (1968) featural grammar, one in which grammatical features on the verb lead to realizing segments in the string. For example, the deep structure of *he kicked* would represent *kick* as a verb marked [+past], thus: $he + kick \atop [+past]$. The presence of [+past] would lead to placing *-ed* on the end of the stem, thus: ${kick \atop [+past]} \rightarrow kicked$. Similarly, Jacobs and Rosenbaum derive progressives, such as *he is singing,* from a structure in which the verb is marked +[progressive]. This leads to placement of a form of *be* before the verb; $he \,{sing \atop [+prog]} \rightarrow he \; be \,{sing \atop [+prog]}$. If a +[prog] verb has a form of be in front of it, the affix -ing is added, thus: $he \; Be \,{sing \atop [+prog]} \rightarrow he \; Be \,{sing \atop [+prog]} + ing$. Other transformations then attach relevant tense and subject number features to the form of Be, marking it as third-person singular present to give *he is singing.* Brown believed the above descriptions warranted the following predictions. First, irregular past forms, such as *broke,* do not have the featural transformation adding *-ed* and thus are transformationally less complex than regular *-ed* forms. Irregular past forms are, in fact, acquired earlier in Brown's analysis. Second, by similar reasoning, irregular present forms (*has, does*) are less complex than regular present tense and should be acquired earlier, as they were. Third, the affix *-ing* involves just a transformation of adding an *-ing* segment to the verb; use of progressive *be* involves a transformation realizing *be* in front as well as operations marking number, person, and tense besides. Thus forms of *be* should arise later, which they do. (Brown notes that because irregular forms might require a specification blocking application of the regular tense operations, however, some of the above derivations are somewhat tentative.)

On the whole, then, findings within the auxiliary system do support the prediction that transformational complexity, as measured by transformational grammars of the mid-1960s, might predict acquisitional order. Before accepting these findings as strongly supporting the hypothesis, however, a number of difficulties must be brought up. First, in

Brown (1973) there are problems with his predictions. They partly depend, for example, on the particular grammar chosen. It is true that in Jacobs and Rosenbaum (1968), regular tensed verbs are derived by a transformation, whereas irregulars are not. On the other hand, in older (and, throughout the 1960 decade, more common) derivations, such as that of Chomsky (1957), both regular and irregular are derived from an underlying structure of the form NP + Tense + Verb . . . (e.g., *he Past kick . . . he Past break . . .*). In these, for various reasons, the tense marker then hops to the end of the verb, thus: *he Past kick* affixhop *he kick + past; he Past sing* affixhop *he sing + Past*. In this derivation, clearly, there are no transformational differences between regular and irregular. Furthermore, if Jacobs and Rosenbaum's (1968) derivations are retained, there is still the problem raised by Kuczaj (1977a), that is, if later overregularizations such as *breaked* are counted against showing early learning of the irregular past, then the irregular past is late, not early, and Brown's derivational predictions do not work. Use of the Jacobs and Rosenbaum (1968) grammar for the progressive can also be viewed as not leading to an accurate prediction. Technically, the Jacobs and Rosenbaum derivation adds the *-ing* affix to the verb only if it follows a form of previously added *be*. Thus, in the derivation, presence of *be* is the precondition for use of *-ing*. In acquisition, of course, *-ing* appears reliably far earlier. Or if one wants to put it in terms of number of operations per se in its derivation, *-ing* requires transformational production of *be* beforehand as well as production of *-ing*. Production of *be* requires both production of *be* as well as number-person-tense marking. Thus, the constructions cannot be placed in cumulatively complex relations, because they each involve an operation or operations not common to the other.

The predictions in Brown and Hanlon (1970) fare better. Often, however, other forms of complexity can also predict the same results (Bever, 1970; Maratsos, 1979; Tolbert, 1978). First, the transformationally derived forms are often more semantically complex than the exactly corresponding less complex form. For example, *he isn't coming* has both an extra morpheme and an extra negative meaning compared to *he is coming*. Similarly, questions are usually held to be more semantically complex than declaratives. Aside from these differences of cumulative semantic complexity, the later acquired forms often also require analysis of semantically and syntactically related forms across greater syntactic distances. For example, analyzing how truncates are used always requires analyses of correspondences between a preceding utterance and the truncate. One does not say *yes, you are* or *yes, he is* out of the blue. What can be omitted depends on analysis of the preceding utterance; thus, there are semantic and formal dependencies across speakers' utterances that must be analyzed to analyze both the individual examples of truncates and the general pattern. Such analytic problems might make many of the later acquired forms more difficult to analyze, even if transformational operations were not involved in their description.

It cannot be denied, however, that it would be quite compelling if transformational complexity according to an adult grammar designed on independent grounds consistently turned out to be a good predictor of acquisitional order. In fact, however, it cannot be expected that transformational grammars of the mid-1960s will prove to be such generally accurate predictors. Investigators have begun to note a number of exceptions to the predicted acquisitional sequences, and some more will be noted here as well (Hecht & Morse cited in de Villiers & de Villiers, 1978; Ingram & Tyack, 1979; Knapp, 1979; Maratsos, 1978; Tager-Flusberg, de Villiers, & Hakuta, 1982).

Exceptions from English

1. Conjunction. In Chomsky (1957), full sentential conjunctions such as *John sang and John danced* or *John sang and Mary sang* provided the underlying sources for phrasal conjunctions such as *John sang and danced* or *John and Mary sang*. The shorter forms were derived from the fuller sentential forms by deletion of identical elements and conjunction of the nonidentical ones, if these were constituents of the same kind. Some experimental evidence from children's imitations seemed to indicate that sentential conjunctions might be simpler (Lust, 1977). But Tager-Flusberg, de Villiers, and Hakuta (1982) found in naturalistic analyses of Brown's samples for Adam, Eve, and Sarah that sentential and phrasal conjunctions appeared together. If anything, sentential conjunctions were less common initially than they became later. Gartner, Hood, and Bloom (1980) have found similar results in the records of their four subjects. (See Lust, 1977, for some contrary results.)

2. Possessives. Brown (1973) notes that the possessive marker '*s* appears stably earlier on truncated possessives, such as *John's* in *that's John's*, than on full possessives, as in *that's John's dog*, although the full possessive is the underlying form in transformational derivations.

3. Subjectless complements. In transformational descriptions (Rosenbaum, 1967), verb-phrase complements, such as *to sing a song* in *I want (to sing a song)*, are derived from an underlying fuller complement form by deletion of the complement subject if it is identical to a noun-phrase argument of the main clause. Thus, *I want to sing a song* derives from *I want (I sing a song)* by complement-subject deletion. Subjectless complement forms such as *I wanna sing*, however, appear to arise earlier in children's grammars than forms with specified complement subjects, such as *I want mommy sing* (Maratsos, 1978).

4. Truncated passives. In transformational derivations, truncated passives, such as *he was kicked* or *it got broken*, derive from full passives, such as *he was kicked by someone* or *it got broken by something*, by deletion of the *by*-phrase. Truncated passives, however, both appear and are comprehended as early as, or earlier than, full passives (Baldie, 1976; Horgan, 1978b; Maratsos & Abramovitch, 1975; Maratsos, Fox, Becker, & Chalkley, in preparation).

5. Possessives. In many transformational descriptions, simple possessives, such as *John's dog*, are derived from complex embedded sentence structures such as *the dog that John has*, which are converted into an intermediate form *the dog of John's* (compare to *that dog of John's, a dog of John's, the dog of John's you mentioned*) and, finally, to the simple possessive, for example, *John's dog*. However, it is clear that simple possessives generally appear earlier in children's acquisition than embedded sentences (Maratsos, 1978).

6. Adjectives. In common transformational derivations (e.g., Smith, 1964), adjective constructions such as *the big dog* derive from underlying relative clauses (*dogs that are big*) which in turn are sometimes described as deriving from underlying conjunctions (Thompson, 1968). This initial embedded-sentence form is transformed by *be*-deletion into an intermediate form that is ungrammatical for simple adjectives, for example, **the dog big*, which is in turn converted obligatorily by a last transformation into the final order, *the big dog*. But in children's speech, the simple prenominal adjective appears (Maratsos, 1978) before sentence embedding generally. For some children, in fact, orders such as *big dog* appear before ones such as *dog big* in early speech.

7. Imperatives. In most transformational derivations, imperatives, such as *go away!*, are derived from underlying full sentences with underlying *you will*, for example, *you will go away*. Imperatives appear earlier than sentences with *will*, however, (see Brown, 1973, for early use of imperatives; Klima & Bellugi, 1966, for later use of *will*).

8. Various uses of *that*. *That* is often used to mark an embedded complement sentence (as in *I know that he will come*) or a relative clause (as in *I see the onion that you picked*). Most of these forms, however, can also appear without *that* under various circumstances (*I know you will come; I see the onion you picked*). Children seem to use the forms without *that* before the forms that contain *that,* although the former are derived from the latter by deletion of *that* in transformational derivations (Bloom, Lahey, Hood, Lifter, & Fiess, 1980; Maratsos, 1979).

9. *Wh*-questions. As Brown and Hanlon (1970) note, *wh*-questions are derivationally more complex than yes/no questions. There seem to be children who master correct auxiliary verb placement in yes/no questions before *wh*-questions, often producing persistent misplaced auxiliaries in the latter form, for example, *why we can't do that?* (Brown, 1970; Labov & Labov, 1978). In various cross-sectional and longitudinal studies, however, it appears likely that such a difference is not at all universal (Hecht & Morse cited in de Villiers & de Villiers, 1978; Ingram & Tyack, 1979; Knapp, 1979, who produces detailed longitudinal evidence for her subjects) and may be uncommon.

Many foreign languages also seem likely to supply instances in which derivational complexity, using mid-1960s transformational grammar, does not provide good predictions of acquisitional order. Such grammars always gave a fixed underlying order to subject, object, and verb in a given language, deriving other orders by transformation or other rearrangements (Chomsky, 1965). Thus, in the acquisition of freer order languages children might be predicted to fix upon this underlying order initially, before deriving the transformed orders. Second, such transformational grammars represented the subject and object as consistently present in underlying structure, even if these were absent in surface structure. But in many languages, one or both subject and object may be omitted if pragmatically redundant. Thus, children might be predicted to supply these, even redundantly, before omitting them in languages in which omission is common. Such implicit predictions presently seem to meet with contradictions.

Exceptions from Other Languages

1. Contradictions of fixed underlying order. As already reported, children learning Turkish, German, Hungarian, Italian, and Finnish do not seem to fix initially upon a single order of subject, object, and verb before using other orders. Instead, children acquiring these languages may use a variety of orders very quickly or immediately (Bowerman, 1973; MacWhinney, 1976; Mills, in press; Park, 1970; Slobin, 1982). There do seem to be cases in which a child seizes upon a fixed order in a freer word-order language. Zhenya (Gvozdev, 1949), for example, initially used fixed order SOV in learning Russian (in which the most common order is actually SVO). There are also individual cases noted, however, in which children learning a more fixed-order language seem to use more flexible order (e.g., Burling, 1959), reports that his child used flexible order in learning English at first. Thus, the overall picture does not indicate a uniform tendency to seize upon the fixed underlying order and then use other orders later.

2. Kaluli and the use of the agentive (or subject) transitive -ɛ focus marker. In Kaluli, an agent or subject is marked with -ɛ, only if it denotes a focused element and is agent or subject of a transitive sentence. Thus, if *Mary* denotes a focused element, the usage would be roughly *paper-ɔ Mary-ɛ cut* because *cut* is a transitive verb; but the proper form for *Mary* with *walk* or *die* would be *Mary-ɔ die* or *Mary-ɔ walk,* because *die* and *walk* are intransitives. Suppose, however, the object argument of a transitive verb is omitted because of pragmatic redundancy so that the major constituents are simply *Mary* and *cut* (e.g., someone might have said, "John cut the bread," and the speaker might be saying on contradiction "No, *Mary* cut"). The marker is still -ɛ because *cut* is what could be called an underlying transitive verb, even though only one argument is realized in the surface string. A normal transformational derivation would perhaps give as the deep structure of *Mary cut* something like *bread +Mary+cut* so that the -ɛ marker could be correctly assigned because the sentence is transitive. Then, the object argument could be omitted. The very clear derivational prediction is that children should first produce the -ɛ marker in sentences in which the object argument is present because these sentences are closer to underlying form. In fact, however, Schieffelin (in press) reports that Kaluli children produce the -ɛ marker initially in sentences in which the redundant argument is omitted, contrary to the prediction. (This finding is very interesting in itself because it indicates that underlying transitivity can control grammatical marking, even if there is little evidence that surface-structure transitivity is responsible.)

3. Spanish. In Spanish, the verb may be marked for number and person, with the subject either present (e.g., 'I' + verb+first-person singular) or not (verb+first-person singular). There are indications, however, that the child does not first use only forms with pronominal subjects and then forms with the

subject deleted (Tolbert, 1978), even though the full form would be derivationally less complex. Again, more investigation of Spanish and similar languages is needed to follow up these tentative indications; but such patterns, if confirmed, run counter to usual derivational predictions.

Thus, on the whole, there seem to be plentiful exceptions to a general principle of cumulative transformational complexity predicting acquisitional order.[5] Although there may be various reasons for the exceptions, there might also be reasons other than hypothesized transformational complexity for the consonances, as has already been described. On the whole, it no longer appears likely that such cumulative complexity will predict acquisitional order.

There are good reasons, however, to wonder if sequence of acquisition can be expected to model faithfully the step-by-step processes of even a psychologically real adult grammar. Maratsos (1978) and Bowerman (1978) note that the child's initial analysis of a construction may not reflect the eventual adult analysis for a variety of reasons. The formulas of Stage I speech, for example, are only later drawn into various more general or abstract systems of determiner classes, formal grammatical relations, or other formal classes. It could be argued that only under highly constrained and ideal conditions might the child actually give immediate transformational analyses to constructions related transformationally in adult grammar. Instead, initial analysis of many eventually related forms might have to be made more specifically or individually before the growing pattern in the data made a transformational analysis compelling. For example, as noted before, it is partly the presence of reflexives, such as *wash yourself* and *he cut himself*, that justify derivation of imperatives from forms with underlying *you will*. The child might well give an initially less complex analysis to imperatives and only gradually revise the imperative rule in the light of later acquired constructions. A transformationalist might prefer to see transformational analyses predict order of acquisition unambiguously and successfully. But the failure of acquisition order to do so cannot be considered a decisive blow against transformational analyses.

Transformational Grammar and Errors

Is there any other kind of evidence that can be mustered from development itself that might bear upon the questions? Perhaps, when transformations are actually being formulated, there might be perturbations in the child's productions that display this learning process. One such perturbation that has been proposed (Bellugi, 1971; Brown et al., 1969; Erreich, et al., 1980; Fay, 1978) concerns errors children make as they acquire constructions such as yes/no questions, *wh*-questions, particle placement, negation, and other constructions in which transformations are involved. Analysts such as Kuczaj (1976,a), Maratsos (1978), Maratsos and Kuczaj (1978,a,b), and Prideaux (1976), on the other hand, hold that many errors that might be expected by the same logic are not found and, furthermore, that the occurring errors might profitably receive other explanations.

The basic proposal of those who believe the relevant errors occur while the child is mastering a transformational rule is that the child's command of the rule may be unstable while the rule is being mastered. Thus, under various conditions, the rule is not carried out or is carried out only partly. There are a few transformational rules that are especially relevant to this discussion. It is also necessary to specify some of the details of how a movement is analyzed into more basic operations (Erreich et al., 1980; Fay, 1978). There are five transformational rules and operations that are relevant to the present discussion: *wh*-movement, auxiliary verb movement, negative placement, affix-hopping, and *do*-support.

1. *Wh*-movement. The *wh*-movement transformational rule (already discussed) moves a *wh*-constituent from a declarative position to a position at the front of the sentence, thus: *John saw what wh-mov't what John saw*.

2. Auxiliary verb movement. The rule of auxiliary verb movement (also already mentioned) moves an auxiliary verb from postsubject to presubject position in yes/no questions and *wh*-questions, thus: *he will come aux mov't will he come?; what he will do aux mov't what will he do?*

3. Negative placement. For various rather complex reasons in adult speech, English negatives are described (Klima, 1964) as having a negative particle in sentence-initial position in deep structure. The particle then moves into a position after the first auxiliary, thus: *Neg he can come neg mov't he can + Neg come; Neg he is happy neg mov't he is+Neg happy*. It is eventually realized as *not* and optionally contracted to *n't* on most auxiliary verbs.

4. Affix-hopping. Giving the overall motivation for the affix-hopping rule requires more space than is available here (see Chomsky, 1957, for the original exposition or Akmajian & Heny, 1976, for a clear

exposition). The basic idea is that in underlying structure, tense or aspect markers (e.g., progressive -*ing*, past tense -*ed*, present tense -*s*, past participle -*ed* or -*en*) are described as being positioned in deep structure in front of the verbal elements they eventually end up affixed to. For example, the surface structure of *he is coming* is generally analyzed as *he BE+Present come+ing*. Its underlying structure is analyzed as *he Present BE+ing come*. The present and -*ing* markers hop over the succeeding verb forms, giving *he BE+Present come + ing*. Similarly, the surface structure of *he pushed* is *he push+Past*. The underlying structure is analyzed as *he Past push;* hopping of past over *push* gives *he push+Past*. Syntactically, for various complex reasons, *would* is considered the syntactic past of *will*, *should* the syntactic past of *shall*, *could* the syntactic past of *can*, and *might* the syntactic past of *may*. Thus, the underlying structure for *he could come* is *he Past can come*, converted by affix-hopping to *he could+Past come*.

5. *Do*-support. If the simple active affirmative declarative form of a sentence has an auxiliary verb, this auxiliary verb is in presubject position for questions, carries the negative marker, or is the sentence terminal point in truncations, for example, *he will like it, will he like it?, he won't like it (won't = will+Neg), oh yes, he will*. If, however, the simple affirmative form has only a main verb, sometimes tensed (*pushed*), sometimes not (*they push too hard*), then in the related question, negative, and truncated forms, a form of *do* acts like other auxiliary verbs, for example, *did he push?, why did he push?, he didn't push, oh yes, he did*. There have been various proposals for how to handle the exceptional behavior of such sentences. Klima (1964), for example, proposed that *do* is always present in underlying structure and sometimes deleted. The best known proposal, however, is Chomsky's (1957) proposal for a rule called *do*-support. Essentially, the proposal works this way. One of the alternatives for expansion of the auxiliary component in underlying structure is to realize it as a simple tense marker, either past or present, with no other auxiliary element present. Thus, the underlying structure of *he pushed* is *he Past push*. This lone tense marker is treated like a normal auxiliary verb in negation, interrogation, and truncation operations. Thus, the underlying question-form Q *he Past push* is converted by auxiliary movement into *Past he push?* Negation in *Neg he Past push* gives *he Past+Neg push*. Truncation of a structure such as *yes, he Past push* gives *yes, he Past*. Chomsky's second proposal was the following: if at the end of a sentence derivation, the

element, a form of *do* should be prefixed to the tense marker. Thus, *Past he push? do*-support *do + Past he push?* (did he push?); *he Past + Neg push do*-support *he do + Past + Neg push (he didn't push); yes, he Past do*-support *Yes, he do + Past (yes, he did)*. Thus, underlying structure, transformations, and rule of *do*-support are all set up so that *do*-support can work in this fashion, which in the end generates the related forms in a strikingly economical fashion. It is a very ingenious jigsaw puzzle.

Having briefly seen the relevant five transformations, we need the point about the formal analysis of movement rules. The point is that basic transformational analysis divides a movement of a constituent into two steps: first, copying of the constituent in its new position; second, deletion in the old position. That is, generally speaking, movement of A in a rule such as b A C *A mov't* A b c occurs in the following way. First, copying of A in new position: b A c A *copy* A b A c; second, deletion in the old position: A b A c *A deletion* A b c . Thus, for example, the rule hopping the past affix in the transformation *he Past push* affix-hop *he push+Past* actually occurs in two steps: (1) *he Past push copy he Past push+Past* and (2) *he Past push+Past delete he push+Past*.

How would failure or partial failure of such rules look? If the rule completely fails, then the moved constituent would be left in its original position. If the rule is only partly carried out, then the result is that the moved constituent is copied in its new position, but not deleted in its old position; thus, it is left appearing in two places in the string. Supporters of what Erreich et al. (1980) call the basic operations hypothesis claim that a number of children's errors are best accounted for by these kinds of explanations; opponents claim other explanations are more revealing.

First let us look at the kinds of errors that are found and the corresponding basic-operations explanations:

1. A well-known error is discussed in Brown et al. (1969), Brown (1970), and Bellugi (1971). Some children produce *wh*-questions with misplaced auxiliary verbs, such as *where we can go?, why he can't come?*, and *what we should do now?* One explanation of this error is that the children carry out the *wh*-placement rule successfully, but then fail to carry out the auxiliary movement operation because of information processing overload. Thus, they carry out the step *we can go where wh*-mov't *where we can go*, but they do not carry out the step moving the auxil-

iary in front of the subject. This leaves the erroneous *where we can go?* Bellugi (1971) notes that this error seems to persist even longer for negative *wh*-questions, and she attributes this error persistence to the still extra information load contributed by negation. Labov and Labov (1978), however, note that nearly all *wh*-negative questions are *why* questions and that misplacements, in general, persist longer for *why* questions than other *wh*-questions in both negative and affirmative forms (also see Maratsos et al., 1979, for similar evidence). Thus, the negation does not seem to contribute extra load. But the error could still be seen as resulting from problems carrying out the second auxiliary verb movement transformation.

2. Reduplications of the auxiliary element in questions. Klima and Bellugi (1966) list examples of errors such as *did he made it?*, *does it rolls?*, and *where should we should go?* Hurford (1975) also lists such examples from his daughter, and Kuczaj (1976a,b) notes them in both a cross-sectional sample and in a sample of his own son. These might all result from copying without deletion. An error, such as *did he made it*, for example, might result from incomplete auxiliary movement in the following way:

(a) Copying of tense in initial position: Q *he Past make it* aux copy *Past he Past make it?* Failure to delete the original past marker leaves *Past he Past make it?*

(b) *Affix-hopping for original Past element: Past he Past make it* affix hop *Past he make+Past it?*

(c) Do-support for first past: *Past he make+Past it* do-support *do+Past he make+Past it?*, this is spelled out eventually as *did he made it?*

Thus, failure of tense deletion in the movement rule plus carrying out of the other rules as usual gives a sentence redundantly marked for tense in the question. Similar failure of deletion in original position plus carrying out of the other rules can give question errors, such as *is he is making it?*, *what's he is doing?*, and so forth—errors of the kind that Hurford (1975) notes as occurring.

3. Reduplication of past tense in declaratives. Erreich et al. (1980) note the occurrence in one subject of a few errors of the form *I did broke it*. This could occur as follows:

(a) Affix-hopping, first step: *I Past break it* aux copy *I Past break+Past it.*

(b) Failure to delete original tense marker.

(c) *Do*-support for initial tense marker: *I Past break+Past it* Do-support *I do+Past break+Past it,* which is spelled out as *I did broke it.*

(d) Reduplication of particles. Fay (1978) notes

that his son went through a period of reduplicating verb particles, such as *up,* in *I phoned up my friend up.* Menyuk (1969) also notes such errors occurring in a cross-sectional sample. The proposed explanation is that there is a movement transformation converting verb+particle combinations into the verb+NP+particle form, for example, *I called up my friend* prt copy *I called up my friend up.* Failure to delete the original particle gives *I called up my friend up.*

Most of the errors, it should be noted, concern copying without deletion. Just the well-known *wh*-errors (*where we should go?*) might result from complete failure of an operation.

The transformationalist explanation of these errors is interesting and follows from combining some reasonable assumptions about sentence production with the formal analysis of adult transformational descriptions. The problems with the explanation that critics have brought up are: (1) There are other explanations of the errors; these explanations might also explain errors of similar kinds that are not well handled by the transformationalist explanation. (2) Far fewer errors occur than might be expected because there are far more possibilities for failure than in these few examples (Kuczaj, 1976a,b; Maratsos, 1978; Maratsos & Kuczaj, 1978; Prideaux, 1976).

Let us take the point about nonoccurring errors first. The problem is that there are many other rules that should be able to fail in similar ways; but the expectable errors seem rarely or never to occur. Various failures of affix-hopping, for example, would result in such sentences as: *he does be going, he did can go, he ising go, did can he go?, he had be singing, he does will like it,* and so on. Incomplete affix-hopping would give such errors as: *he ising going, he did could go, did would he like it, he does is going,* and so on. But such errors are not recorded (*he does be going* is of a type that might occur in dialects where the general type is grammatical; but it does not occur in dialects where it is not) (Maratsos, 1978; Maratsos & Kuczaj, 1978). Similarly, in *wh*-questions, there seem to be no errors resulting from copying without deletion of the *wh*-word (e.g., *what did he see what?*) nor errors such as *will he go where?*, resulting from failure to move the *wh*-word to the front (nor do there seem to be pragmatically inappropriate uses of sentences such as *he will go where?*). Finally, outside the range of auxiliary-related operations there are many rules that might be expected to show similarly caused errors, such as *he is trying him(self) to go* (failure to delete complement subject), *it got broken it* (copying without deletion in passive), *not he won't go* (copying without deletion in negative placement), and errors following from commonly accepted transformational derivations of adjectives, such as *I see the house big* (failure to prepose adjective) (Maratsos, 1978). Thus, within the constructions on which interest has centered, many errors do not seem to occur that might; and many typologically similar errors do not seem to occur at all in other ranges of constructions.

Second (as mentioned before), there are other explanations of the various errors. Some of these may also better expain similar-looking errors that cannot be elucidated very well by the basic operations hypothesis (Brown & Hanlon, 1970; Kuczaj, 1976a,b; Maratsos & Kuczaj, 1978). Brown and Hanlon (1970) note that errors such as *what he is doing?*, do have a possible source in something besides a failed transformation. There are what are called embedded questions, such as *tell me what he is doing* or *I want to know what he is doing*. In these, a *wh*-word heads a clause that serves as an embedded sentence object of a main verb. For example, in *tell me (what he is doing), (what he is doing)* denotes what is to be told. These forms often have the pragmatic function of questions (one could say *I want to know what he is doing, tell me what he is doing,* or simply *what is he doing?*); these forms have the auxiliary verb in postsubject position (note the position of *is* in *tell me what he is doing*). Thus, errors in auxiliary verb placement in the nonembedded forms might come from confusion with the embedded forms, which are in fact being heard and produced at the time the *wh*-errors occur (Brown & Hanlon, 1970). A number of further assumptions must be made to explain why the confusion seems to affect the main clause form and only rarely the embedded form (Maratsos et al., 1979). One reason might be that the embedded form does have the more usual postsubject order.

What about the reduplication or overtensing errors (e.g., *is he is going?* or *did he made it?*)? Maratsos and Kuczaj (1978) note that in their data (4 longitudinal subjects, 6 hr. apiece for 13 cross-sectional subjects) only the redundant *do*-form errors occur with anything but the barest frequency. For example, they find just one possible transformational redundant *be*-use in 1 longitudinal subject and 13 cross-sectional subjects—*what's that is?* As they note, one also finds in these records the error *I thought so 'cept they're weren't t*, in which there is a redundant *be*-marking that has no known possible transformational error source. It is likely that children produce a certain very low amount of redundant

marking because a child becomes momentarily confused by the possibility of marking the same element in different places where it can in fact be marked. The exception in the auxiliary system to this very usual low error rate of redundant marking is in the use of *do*-forms. Children do produce forms such as *did he made it? does it rolls?, it didn't disappeared, did I didn't mean to?,* or *I did broke it* (Erreich et al., 1980; Fay, 1978; Hurford, 1975; Klima & Bellugi, 1966; Kuczaj, 1976,a,b; Maratsos & Kuczaj, 1978). As noted above, the errors seem confined to the cases where only a main verb otherwise appears in the clause. There are no errors such as *he did can go, he did could go, does will he come?,* and so on, although these are all expectable by the transformationalist hypothesis.

But such redundant markings of tense on the main verb with accompanying *do*-forms require some explanation. The most likely explanation might be that the *do*-system does have a kind of exceptional character. As noted before, for the other auxiliary verbs, the relations among interrogatives, negatives, truncates, and declaratives are quite regular. *Do* is more of a special case, and this may introduce performance errors so that children mark with *do,* but they also lose track of this and also mark the main verb. This would result in a redundant main verb tensing. Kuczaj (1976,a,b) and Maratsos and Kuczaj (1978,a,b) note that overtensed negatives such as *it didn't broke* or *it didn't disappeared* would also follow from difficulties with controlling such relations between *do*-form use and the main verb form, but this cannot be readily explained by the basic operations hypothesis. The problem is reasonably technical (see Maratsos & Kuczaj, 1978), but perhaps it can be briefly summarized. Suppose the presupposition is made that in evaluating the transformational hypothesis, adult-form rules should be used. This presupposition is made, it should be noted, by Fay (1978) and Erreich et al. (1980), who support the basic operations hypothesis. The underlying structure for tensed negatives is something like this: *Neg it Past disappear* (for *it didn't disappear*). Negative placement gives *it Past+Neg disappear*. At this point, however, there is no evident opportunity for occurrence of an error of copying with deletion because tense markers only hop over immediately succeeding verbs. In forms such as *it Past+ Neg disappear,* the negative intervenes, preventing hopping of the past marker over onto the main verb. Thus, only *do*-support is possible, giving the correct *it didn't disappear*. The basic operations hypothesis thus cannot explain such observed errors as *it didn't disappeared*. Another point noted by Maratsos and Kuczaj (1978) is that within the obtained *do*-errors in the overtensed past tense questions there is a notable peculiarity. The errors, such as *did I made it?*, *did he came?*, or *did it broke?* are all with irregular past verb forms (Hurford, 1975; Maratsos & Kuczaj, 1978). There seem to be no errors reported of the form *did he pushed it?* or *did I maked it?* These researchers believe the problem is that if the child mistakenly tenses the irregular form, it still looks more like the acceptable untensed stem and thus less easily monitored. The basic operations explanation of overtensed errors does not lead easily to a similar explanation.

To summarize briefly, it has been suggested that errors in carrying out transformational rules might account for various kinds of obtained children's errors, such as *where we should go?* or *did I made it?* (Erreich et al., 1980; Fay, 1978). Critics have noted that there are other possible explanations of such errors (Brown & Hanlon, 1970; Kuczaj, 1976,a,b; Maratsos & Kuczaj, 1978; Prideaux, 1976). Furthermore, some similar violations occur that the other explanations seem to handle more easily. In addition, a very great range of errors that might be expected by the basic operations hypothesis seem not to be observed. Many of those that are observed appear to be very rare, only as frequent as similar but more random-seeming errors that also occur. At the present time, it thus seems to me that the transformationalist position fails to find strong support in the data from children's errors.

Transformational Analysis and Sentence Judgment

Valian, Caplan, and de Sciora (1976) have wondered if another kind of evidence, however, might not indicate the reality of transformational analyses. They thought that perhaps children (grade-school children, 6- to 10-year-olds in this study) might consistently choose derivationally less complex sentences as clearer communications, where "derivationally less complex" .is again given by a mid-1960s transformational grammar. In the game modeled for the child, the child is given a sentence to say, such as "Bobby put his shirt on." The experimenter would say "what?" asking for a clarification. The child was then told that she was to do something to clarify what she had said, by repeating the original sentence or modifying it. The hypothesis was that derivationally simpler forms would be more often simply repeated by the child, whereas the more complex forms would be more often modified. Thus, for example, most transformational derivations would make *Bobby put on his shirt* less com-

plex than *Bobby put his shirt on;* according to the hypothesis, the child should repeat the first form more often but modify the second form to the first more often when attempting to clarify.

Valian et al. (1976) experimented with 12-pair types relatable by transformational derivation. For these, in 8 of the 12 pairs, results were consonant with the prediction, although they were contrary to prediction or nonindicative for the other 4 pairs.

De Villiers and de Villiers (1978) point out, however, that it seems likely that the particular pairs chosen were ones intuitively more likely to work. They list pair types where it seems to them the derivationally less complex form would be likely to come out as more complex, for example, *the horse that was brown won the race* versus *the brown horse won the race* (the second sentence is derivationally more complex); *the boy ate an apple and the boy ate an orange* versus (derivationally more complex) *the boy ate an apple and an orange; that he smoked bothered me* versus (derivationally more complex) *it bothered me that he smoked*. Although the experiment has not been tried, de Villiers and de Villiers's proposed experiment seems quite reasonable to me, as does their prediction about the results. Sentences more complex by transformational derivation are often less complex in other ways.

Nontransformational Approaches

At the present time, transformational accounts of sentential structure have thus failed to find consistent support in adult psycholinguistic studies, in studies of acquisitional order among children, in children's error patterns or (probably) in their patterns of judgment. To many developmentalists, such an accumulation of negative findings might argue that transformational grammar is not an interesting tool for the study of development per se and furthermore, that it is not likely to be a psychologically real model of the grammatical knowledge the child acquires.

If transformational derivations remained the only available adequate description of human grammatical knowledge, such conclusions would probably be unwarranted. Reasons have already been mentioned as to why transformational descriptions might be psychologically adequate descriptions of the *product* of development without providing useful predictors of the *sequence* of development. Similarly, reasons can easily be devised as to why transformational accounts of linguistic competence might be correct but might not result in errors in sentence production. Hamburger and Wexler (1975) argue that they find that transformational formulations at least are adequate for an account of acquisition which in theory can lead to determination of an adequate adult grammar, and they challenge other accounts to do the same.

It is, however, no longer the case that only transformational formulations are available to describe the underlying regularities of grammar. Over the past years, proposals have increasingly appeared for the treatment of various constructions, such as the passive, conjunction, prenominal adjectives, nominalizations, possessives, and omissions, by nontransformational rule mechanisms (e.g., Brame, 1978; Bresnan, 1978, in press-b; Chomsky, 1970, 1980; Dougherty, 1970; Gazdar, in press; Jackendoff, 1972, 1975; Lakoff & Thompson, 1975; Monahan, in press; Perlmutter & Postal, 1977), with a culmination in some systematic proposals for the complete elimination of transformations from grammatical description (e.g., Bresnan, in press-b; Kaplan & Bresnan, in press; Lakoff & Thompson, 1975). Psycholinguists have also made proposals for treating many processes of grammatical use and knowledge by nontransformational processes (Ford, Bresnan, & Kaplan, in press; Kaplan, 1972, 1975; Maratsos, 1978; Pinker, in press; Prideaux, 1976; Schlesinger, 1971; Wanner & Maratsos, 1978; Woods, 1970).

How do such derivations work and what implicit or explicit presuppositions do they involve about how the child analyzes and relates constructions? Such treatments generally involve, as apparently any adequate grammatical treatment must, distinctions between simple aspects of surface form and the underlying grammatical and semantic relatedness of constituents. For example, it is a fact that the initial arguments of sentences with the active verb form (e.g., *John* in *John likes Mary*) bear the same semantic role relation with respect to the verb, as do post *by*-arguments of the same verbs in passive forms (e.g., *John* in *Mary liked by John*). This is true whether or not one captures this relation by converting an activelike form into a passive one or by some other means. Similarly, it is a fact in Kaluli that the transitive agentive focus marker -ɛ may be used even if there is only a subject argument present, as long as the verb in some sense is understood to be transitive—an analysis that arises from the fact that in other sentences the verb takes both subject and object arguments. That is, the properties of human language per se require the child to analyze the systematic relations between various underlying functions and different surface forms. The major difference is that transformational descriptions require uniform underlying grammatical strings to represent underlying similar functions; the necessary rearrangement or deletion of these underlying elements to account for surface form explains much of the abstractness of transformational descriptions. In nontransformational descriptions, underlying functions are mapped onto different surface forms or affect surface forms directly without operations of rearrangement, substitution, deletion, or addition on the underlying sequences of grammatical elements.

A few examples may make the operation of such analyses clearer. Such formulations have been particularly well worked out in various accounts (e.g., Brame, 1978; Bresnan, 1978, in press-a; Perlmutter & Postal, 1977) of the passive construction. We will not follow any of the accounts in detail, but simply employ some of their general characteristics. Such accounts generally distinguish between what can be called grammatical subject and object and underlying or logical subject and object. Grammatical subject and object are grammatical functions determined by regularities in surface form/function relations in the language. In English, for example, many sentence operations or constraints converge to justify the construct of grammatical subject, such as the requirement in main-clause sentences that there be a preverbal argument, number and person agreement with this argument, various pronominalization phenomena, choice of arguments that can be omitted in infinitival complements, and other rule regularities. In both *John likes dogs dogs are liked by John*, the initial argument plays this role of grammatical subject, *John* in the first sentence, *dogs* in the second. In general, for each major predicate term, there is a particular semantic role that fills the role of grammatical subject. Because of the passive, however, it is not always the same semantic role for transitive verbs. Under the structural conditions corresponding to the passive (use of past participial verb, preceding form of BE, optional use of a *by*-phrase after the verb), the semantic role which usually provides the grammatical object, fills instead the grammatical subject structural role. The semantic role which usually fills the grammatical subject role, may appear in the postverbal *by*-phrase as a type of oblique object, as in *John was liked by Mary* or it may simply be understood, as in *John was liked*. (There are languages, such as Arabic, in which only short passives, such as *John was kissed,* are allowed; this suggests that the major function of the passive is to allow reference only to the usual object argument and to topicalize it.)

Acquisitionally, both a transformational account and a nontransformational account claim that when the child is faced with sentences such as *the ball got hit* or *it got broken,* he does not analyze these as forms of *hit* and *break* that are completely separate from the active uses (which the child might be expected to do because these uses do not observe the usual semantic-structural configurations of active *hit* and *break*). Instead, by hypothesis, the child analyzes these as being uses of the same verbs as the active form but with the grammatical subject role being held by the semantic role that usually is indicated by the grammatical object. In both accounts, analysis of this relation leads to an hypothesized distinction between the underlying predicate-argument relations and the grammatical functional relations in the following form. In the passive structure, the semantic role characteristic of the object plays the grammatical subject role; if as a result this semantic role is given a separate categorical description from the grammatical object, it can be said that in passives, the underlying or logical object is the grammatical subject. Similarly, the underlying or logical subject role plays the grammatical role of oblique object with preceding *by* when it is realized at all in passives. Where the accounts differ is in how the child is viewed as instantiating this analysis in sequential analysis. In the transformational analysis, there is an assumption that various methodological and analytic preferences will lead the child to state co-occurrence restrictions and semantic-interpretive rules on ordered strings. Thus, underlying grammatical relations will be read into a uniformly ordered sequence for both passives and actives to capture such relations economically and the underlying structure will be logical subject-verb-logical object. Passives are then necessarily derived from this underlying order by a rearrangement transformation. In a nontransformational analysis, the assumption is that co-occurrence and semantic-interpretive rules can be stated upon unordered underlying functional descriptions. For example, the underlying functional representation of both *John liked Mary* and *Mary was liked by John* would be something such as this *like* (subject = *John;* object = *Mary*). The fact that John is the feeler of positive emotions toward Mary can be read directly off this underlying unordered functional description for both passive and active forms. The active form, then, results from making the logical subject the grammatical subject and making the logical object the grammatical object; these decisions result in the order *John-like-Mary*. The passive form results not from a rearrangement of this activelike order, but instead from a decision to make the underlying object the grammatical subject, and the underlying subject, the object of an oblique postverbal *by*-phrase; the result is a direct realization of the surface order *John-like-by Mary*. Other aspects of the analysis account for the differences in the forms of the verb. That is, the two derivations work approximately as follows:

Transformational: Co-occurrence, semantic interpretation on *John like Mary;* transformation gives *Mary is liked by John*.

Nontransformational: Co-occurrence, semantic interpretation on unordered set *like* (subject = *John;* object = *Mary*): realization of logical subject as grammatical oblique object, logical object as grammatical subject, gives *Mary is liked by John*.

What about short passives, such as *Mary was kissed?* In a transformational account, this is derived from an underlying activelike form by two steps: *Someone* (past) *kiss Mary* $\xrightarrow{passive}$ *Mary* (Past *be+ed*) *kiss by someone* $\xrightarrow{by+someone\ deletion}$ *Mary* (Past *be+ed*) *kiss*. (I am ignoring details of affix-hopping.) In a nontransformational account, a possibility in English is simple nonrealization of the underlying subject role in passives. Thus, roughly, *like* (subject = unspecified; object = Mary) can lead to a direct realization of *Mary* as grammatical subject in a passive-form sentence.

Both accounts thus require the child to analyze many of the same underlying and surface grammatical functions and to analyze similar function/form relationships. The difference is that nontransforma-tional accounts do not require the presupposition that the child analyzes a uniformly ordered and realized underlying grammatical string for all thus functionally related sentences. Acquisitionally (as we have seen with respect to the passive and underlying fixed order in general) (1) there is little evidence that children assume or impose upon their analysis the assumption that languages have single underlying fixed orders for the realization of similar grammatical relations (evidence from Turkish, Hungarian, German, and so on) and (2) short passives, which are derivationally more complex in the transformational derivation, do not appear later in acquisition; if anything, they may appear earlier.

Similarly, nontransformational derivations would treat the similar underlying functional relations of *wh*-words and declarative-position constituents as not arising from similar underlying positions but from alternative realizations of underlying functional structures; the similar underlying functional relations of prenominal adjectives to nouns (e.g., *red hat*) and predicate nominative adjectives to subjects (*hat [is] big*) are also not analyzed as arising from identical underlying ordered representations. Both of these are consistent with various developmental facts, such as the earlier occurrence of prenominal adjective orderings, often earlier than the full sentential forms that are supposed to give rise to them in full transformational derivations.

Finally, at the most general level, Pinker (in press) has demonstrated that one particular nontransformational formulation (Bresnan, in press-b) can be demonstrated to be learnable in the same sense as transformational formulations, for example, those employed by Hamburger and Wexler (1975). Thus, nontransformational accounts have a number of promising explanatory and descriptive properties (also see de Villiers et al., 1978; Maratsos, 1978; Prideaux, 1976; Schlesinger, 1971; Tager-Flusberg et al., 1982, for applications of nontransformational descriptions to acquisitional problems).

The past failures of various transformational descriptions, however, should not be taken as automatic positive support for nontransformational formulations. Perhaps the most compelling aspect of various nontransformational accounts lies in an intuitive kind of parsimony. Both transformational and nontransformational accounts must frequently presuppose analysis by the child of similar kinds of form/function relations; but nontransformational accounts claim that the perceived set and ordering of elements is the full set for a sentence. This gives such accounts the intuitive appeal of claiming that what is heard is roughly what it appears to be. This property plus gradually growing advantages to be found for nontransformational accounts in linguistic description per se (Bresnan, 1978, in press-a,b; Perlmutter & Postal, 1977), in descriptions of adult psycholinguistic processing (Ford et al., in press), and in descriptions of acquisitional phenomena make these descriptions promising candidates for the provision of analytic frameworks in the analysis of acquisition. The possibility that language is nontransformational in the outlined sense thus serves to remove some of the great distance between underlying and realized surface structure that made the child's task of formulation seem so immensely formidable. But it does not make the child's task elementary. As only too briefly outlined above, both transformational and nontransformational accounts must frequently presuppose similar analyses on the child's part of complex analyses of form/function relations; these apparently are properties of human languages under any reasonable linguistic description.

SOME GENERAL ASPECTS OF RULE ACQUISITION

The preceding discussions have centered upon a few relatively focused questions. Embedded in these treatments, a number of other general facets of development have also been brought up, but not necessarily systematically. At the cost of some redundancy, some of these emerging facets of development will be briefly reviewed here, with the addition of new material where it is relevant. The more general causes of development are treated in the final discussions.

Specificity, Irregularity, and Subclasses

A commonly held theory of the past concerning language acquisition was that children seem to analyze and apply rules in highly general fashion (McNeill, 1966, 1970; Slobin, 1973; and perhaps Chomsky, 1965). Results from recent investigations, however, temper this picture.

Lexical Specificity and Acquisition

A recurring finding of recent years is that children often make highly specific analyses of combinations and apply possible generalizations cautiously rather than make highly rapid general analyses that are productively extended immediately. Stage I speech findings (already summarized) indicate how word-bound or narrow-category patterns may be common early on (Bowerman, 1976; Braine, 1976; Ingram, 1979). In later learning, there also seems to be much individual lexical learning of new constructions, even when the emerging constructions could be construed in terms of more general categories. In the acquisition of the verb system (already discussed), there seems to be individual lexical learning of which individual predicates take progressive *-ing*, past tense *-ed*, and use of *don't* and *can't* as negators among other aspects of inflectional learning (Bellugi, 1967; Brown, 1973; Cazden, 1968; Kuczaj, 1978b; Maratsos & Chalkley 1980). Bowerman (1978, 1981); Brown in his unpublished grammars; R. Clark (1977); Hafitz, Gartner, and Bloom (1980); MacWhinney (1978); Maratsos (1979); and Park (1978) all give extensive evidence of how initial lexical memorization may characterize children's entry into systems such as noun pluralization, English auxiliary verb use in interrogatives, complements of individual verbs, small-scale regularities of English, and inflectional learning across many languages (for an important review of the latter in particular, see MacWhinney, 1978).

In fact, if enough members of a general category fail to take a construction characteristic of the category, the rule may fail to be reliably productive in adult use (Baker, 1979; Bowerman, 1974, 1978, 1981; Maratsos & Chalkley, 1980). For example, many verbs denoting changes of state show the following alternation pattern between transitive and intransitive forms: *it melted, John melted it; the cup broke, Mary broke the cup*. The subject of the transitive denotes the causer of the change; the object of the transitive or the subject of the intransitive denotes the changed entity. Many verbs show this alternation; but if it were freely productive, the pattern would also result in errors such as **John fell the cup* (from *the cup fell*), or **Mary died the bug*. To take another such case, many adjectives take the prefix *un-* to denote an opposite quality (*happy; unhappy*). But the exceptions so far outnumber the instances (**unsad, *unnice, *untall*) that the rule is generally described as unproductive, although quite likely in some sense known. Nouns may sometimes be used as verbs (*a hammer; he hammered it*) but not reliably (*a broom; *he broomed it*).

Adults often seem to know that there is a generalization. But they also implicitly know that one can only be certain a particular term of the relevant type takes the construction if it is known to do so, a peculiar mixture of general rule and memorized instance (which Maratsos & Chalkley, 1980, however, hypothesize characterizes the initial stages of acquisition of all productive constructions). Some investigators have emphasized that children do seem to produce novel examples that follow from productive use of such constructions. Bowerman (1974) discusses causative errors, such as **I fell it* in her children's speech, which she analyzes as having become common after an initial period of accurate use of the relevant verbs. In Bowerman (1978, 1981), a number of such productive uses of other patterns that are unproductive for the adult are discussed. E. V. Clark (1981) similarly cites errors such as *I broomed it* as demonstrating children's productive use of the possibility of using nouns as verbs and vice versa.

But there is also evidence that such errors may be very rare at least in many children. Cazden (1968) noted no cases of nouns being used as verbs and just one causative transitive error (*I falled it*) in all of Adam, Eve, and Sarah's transcripts through MLU Stage V (MLU = 4.0). Maratsos (1982) analyzed 55 hr. of speech from 1 child and 19 hr. from 20 other children, all in Stage V and beyond. He found just two cases of nouns used as verbs (e.g., *you were catching, not balling* [pitching]) and just one or two cases of possible causative-related errors, neither of them very clear examples. Here, the estimated sample size was 15,000 to 25,000 utterances. These results stand in contrast to claims (e.g., in Bowerman, 1974, or E. V. Clark, 1981) that naturalistically recorded errors such as causatives or noun-verb uses are frequent.

It is likely that children differ greatly in how frequently they make such errors. There is also a possibility, however, that differences in sampling are important. Examples such as those that are cited by Bowerman (1974) and E. V. Clark (1981) come from parents taking down individual interesting utterances they hear from children, usually their own children. The effective sample size in this procedure can be very large. A reasonably talkative child can easily produce 350 utterances an hour or more (Brown, 1973; Maratsos, 1982). An adult who was listening just 2 hr. a day would, thus, hear around 250,000 utterances a year. An error rate of 1 in 10,000 utterances for a given error possibility would thus produce 25 examples in a year, which over a few years would come to look like a large corpus. When the possible systematic errors are this rare, it may be necessary to worry about how often less systematic errors also occur.

For some of these processes, however, occasional clear overgeneralizations occur, such as *unsad* (Bowerman, 1981; Maratsos, 1982), that must result from productive use of an adult pattern. Aspects of developmental patterning also make it plausible that some kind of general learning has gone on for more problematic cases such as the causative (Bowerman, 1974, 1982). But the apparent rareness of such errors simultaneously shows that even in the preschool years, children, like adults, may do some lexical monitoring of how infrequently some grammatical processes are applied. The adult state of competence may comprise more a continuation, with a little honing up, of natural analytic tendencies in the child rather than a clearly different imposition of strong lexical inhibitory processes.

But certainly some rules with exceptions nevertheless become very productive. The *-ed* past-tensing rule, which eventually results in frequent errors such as *runned* and *knowed,* provides a prime example of this. It has been commonly believed that once such a general rule becomes available and productive, the child actively avoids or banishes exceptions for at least some time (McNeill, 1966, 1970; Slobin, 1973). Early observations for *-ed* overregularizations indicated that when *-ed* overregularizations finally begin to occur, children replace earlier correct memorized uses, such as *broke* and *ran,* with overregularizations like *breaked* which follow from the productive general rule. It appeared that only after such a stage of banishing exceptions do children gradually relearn the exceptions (*broke*) (McNeill, 1966, 1970; Slobin, 1973).

More recent evidence, however, indicates that conflicting general rules and specific lexical exceptions are not incompatible for the child. Cazden (1968) found that when Eve began to use *goed,* she did not stop using *went.* Instead, the two forms were both used for the five-month period Cazden investigated. Kuczaj (1977b) examined longitudinal samples for 1 subject, and 6-hr. cross-sectional samples for 13 children of different levels of competence. Again, no evidence indicates that *-ed* overregularizations drove out irregular past forms. Instead, even within individual verbs, overregularized and irregular forms alternated, often for periods of months to years. Overregularization, in general, ranged in frequency from .20 to .60 of the children's uses. Kuczaj (1978a) also elicited judgments from 3- through 9-year-old children of various regular, irregular, and overregular forms. He found, for example, that irregular past forms, such as *broke,* were always judged acceptable (Experiment 2, 1978, p. 324), whereas acceptability for overregularized forms ranged from .20 through .80, depending upon age and form.

These results thus indicate that the child is neither an ideological generalist (as proposed by McNeill, 1966) nor so limited by long-term-memory capacity that she actively banishes exceptions because they take up such storage capacity (Slobin, 1973). Instead, a conflict between individual lexical exceptions and productive general rule leads to retention of both. It would be interesting to see in other cases in which children have been reported to banish one form in favor of a competitor (e.g., inflectional imperialism) if there is in fact some alternation among uses. The *-ed* results indicate this would be likely.

All these data indicate children may retain individual lexical specifications, even as general constructions are being formed. Does this mean individual lexical specifications are never lost? This seems unlikely. One suspects that if a general rule proves to be productive and accurate for members of a specifiable general category, individual specifications are eventually given up and the general rule

applies with complete freedom when appropriate. The nature and course of this highly likely process, however, has never been studied in detail.

Subcategories and General Categories

When we are dealing with problems of a general rule versus individual lexical items that do not follow the rule, it is fairly clear what is meant by irregularity or lexical exception. But suppose a generalization is characteristic of a large number of terms that belong to major class C, but does not apply to a specifiable subclass C_1 of C. Are members of C_1 an exception to the rule? Will the members of C_1 be highly susceptible to being treated like other members of C? Are rules first formulated for C in general, then special analyses made for C_1?

Some results indicate that children may initially form rules for a general category C before they establish subclass differences in treatment. Thus, children may treat mass nouns like common nouns, producing forms such as **sugars* or **a sugar.* Children commonly make errors of treating members of one gender class or subclass like those of another. Slobin (1973) held that in general, children preferred to treat terms as though they were members of the general category initially, formulating subcategory specifications later if necessary.

But there are other cases where the evidence is good that the natural analytic direction may be the other way. That is, if the examples the child hears of a construction are within a definable or available major subclass C_1, the child will confine the application of the construction to C_1 rather than extending it to all members of the general category C. For example, English-speaking children apparently confine class-denoting common noun privileges such as uses of articles (*a, the*) or pluralization (*-s*) to common nouns rather than overgeneralizing their use to the category of nouns in general (which would lead to uses such as **the Fido*) (Katz, Baker,& MacNamara, 1974). Turkish children, conversely apparently use the definiteness marker on all nouns, as is appropriate, but confine its use to nouns used in the accusative case, as is also appropriate. In neither English nor Turkish do children appear simply to extend the use of the definiteness markers to all nouns before confining the use to appropriate subcategories. Similarly, English-speaking children appear appropriately to confine the use of present tense *-s* to a context after third-person-singular subjects (*he likes it, the boy eats*) rather than extending it initially to all present tense uses (**they eats*) after all subjects before they confine it to the relevant subcategory of subjects. In general, if children consistently applied operations in terms of the most general category to which the data show they might apply, acquisition would show far more errors of use than it actually does (Maratsos, 1979; Pinker, in press). For the use of some kind of subcategory specification in linguistic rules is common, not exceptional.

The observation of relevant subcategory boundaries requires analyses in which specific analyses of incoming constructions are made and retained so that initially many properties of the domain and context of use are stored. Only if future uses indicate that some of these properties are not relevant are they dropped from the analysis. In this way, analysis that proceeds up through relevant subcategories to more general categories (if this is appropriate) follows naturally. Judging from children's often accurate observation of subcategory boundaries, this kind of procedure appears to be common or even dominant.

But if working up through subcategories is a dominant procedure, how can errors that cross subcategory boundaries be explained? It is probably impossible to account for all of these systematically, but there are possibilities to cover some. First, even if the subcategory specification is in place, there may be problematic individual cases for judging whether it is relevant. For example, the common mass-noun distinction is based upon that of formless stuff versus articulated individuals (Jackendoff, 1976). But sugar, for example, could easily be considered either as stufflike because it is in masses or as being articulated individuals because it has such characteristics, that is, it is in grains. The language chooses to consider it stuff, but it is clear how this might not be easy to retain consistently and how it might lead to errors such as *sugars. Similarly, some gender-category boundaries are unclear, even once formed, as in Russian (see *Arbitrary Noun Gender Categories*) for some nouns. Second, it may be that the relevant subcategory is simply not formed yet and requires some time for analysis. This is very likely in the case of many noun-gender systems. As the noun operations become common enough to be productive, there is no subcategory boundary to prevent uses across what are adult subcategories. In the end, however, it is unlikely all subcategory/general category errors can be explained systematically. Sometimes children observe a distinction in one domain of grammatical functioning and simultaneously ignore the same distinction in another. For example, Schieffelin (in press) notes that her Kaluli subjects observed the focus/nonfocus in their use of word order, but not in marking transitive agents. On the whole, however, it presently seems reasonable to say that children are relatively skillful in observing subcategory/general category distinctions as they learn. This indicates that they usually work up through levels of specification rather than beginning with the most general analysis and working down.

Alternation Between Old and New

Another characteristic developmental finding of the last few years is the frequently nonstagelike nature of rule acquisition. For example, even after children have begun to produce complete argument-predicate combinations such as *mommy read book,* fragments such as *mommy read, read book,* or *mommy book* may continue to occur (Bloom, 1970; Brown, 1973). Such omission may continue well past Stage I, into Brown's MLU Stage III and beyond, judging from tabulations in Bloom, Miller, and Hood (1975). Brown (1973) and Cazden (1968) have shown that children consistently supply small morphemes, such as *-ed* past or definite *the* or forms of *be,* only sometime after they have begun to be used; use does not shift quickly from consistent omission to consistent production. In learning to use auxiliary verbs in questions, children may go back and forth between use and nonuse (e.g., *he coming, is he coming?; why he coming?, why is he coming?*) for some period of time (Knapp, 1979; Labov & Labov, 1978).

Alternations may also occur among different forms or ordering of the same terms. Children's oscillation among irregular and overregular past forms has already been discussed. Some children also alternate between correct placement and misplacement of *wh*-auxiliaries (e.g., *where should we go?, where we should go?*) (Bellugi, 1971; Knapp, 1979; Labov & Labov, 1978).

Why should such gradual transitions or alternations among omission and production be so common, especially given that the child seems to have some knowledge of how and when to produce the correct forms? One possibility many investigators have suggested is that failures of production or incorrect production might frequently occur because of information processing limitations upon the child's memory or programming capacity during sentence production. Antinucci and Parisi (1973) and Bloom (1970) held that children who sometimes omit basic predicate or argument constituents probably do so because of information processing constraints. Bloom (1970) and Bloom, Miller, and Hood (1975) furthermore produce some evidence that the presence of negation (e.g., *not, no*), two-part verbs (*call up, give away*), or newer verbs, among other properties, are associated with a lower probability of use of other constituents; this suggests that such conditions result in less of the child's limited information processing capacity being available for the production of other basic constituents.[6] Knapp (1979) produces similar evidence in analyzing children's probability of producing correctly placed auxiliary verbs in questions. Bellugi (1971) finds that the use of negation makes misplacement of auxiliary verbs more likely in *wh*-questions (e.g., *where should we go?* versus *why we can't go?*). (Also see Tolbert, 1978, for possible relations of information processing constraints and sequence of acquisition.)

Such suggestions have great plausibility and probably some truth. But it is unlikely that information processing capacity limitations during sentence production can account for all such alternations among omission and production or between correct and incorrect forms because there are so many other plausible causes of such alternation. Let us consider some of these arguments briefly for the case of alternating omission and commission (e.g., a child who sometimes puts something in and sometimes leaves it out). To begin with, there is no general reason a child should operate under the assumption that because something is known to be expressed, it always should be expressed whenever possible. Grammatical subjects are obligatorily encoded in English declaratives; but in many of the world's languages, they may be left unencoded if pragmatically or contextually redundant. Verb tensing is obligatory where possible in standard English. But it is optional in many dialects of black English; in Chinese, it is possible but only rarely bothered about. To analyze that something is always supplied when possible, the child must apparently analyze that for every occasion that something could have been supplied, it actually was.

It is clear that such a tabulation process is potentially complex. Furthermore, it may depend upon complex differences in kind of tabulation for different constructions. For example, if the child has the construct of grammatical subject available, obligatory use can be gauged by noting that a subject was employed wherever possible. At the same general level, however, grammatical object arguments of verbs may be omitted or not (e.g., *he ate* or *he ate something*). But this general level of control is inappropriate for grammatical objects; instead, the necessary tabulation is at the level of the individual verb. Some individual verbs can take their objects optionally or not (such as *eat*), whereas others must

take an object if the verb takes one at all (e.g., one cannot say *he liked* or *he blamed*). Brown (unpublished grammars) notes that by Stage V, his subjects had become very accurate in observing such individual verb requirements. [In fact interestingly, and for whatever reasons, children seem to supply obligatory objects more reliably through Stage III than obligatory subject arguments according to tabulations for four subjects in Bloom, Miller, and Hood (1975); this may reflect greater pragmatic interest in the content of object arguments or some other cause.] Children are probably capable of tabulation at different levels at once. As Slobin (1971) notes, for example, irregular verbs make up more than half of the past tense uses children hear. This means that tabulation of -*ed* past at the general level alone would give a ratio of less than 50% use of -*ed* past where possible. The actual level of -*ed* use with irregular verbs seems to range between 20% and 60% (Kuczaj, 1977a). But children at this point supply -*ed* past 1.00 of the time with regular verbs, as they should. Thus, children somehow capture the fact that the individual verbs that should take -*ed* past always do so, even if the generally tabulated level of use of -*ed* past is less than .50.

Beyond this clear complexity, conditions of obligatory versus nonobligatory use may present other kinds of complications for analysis. Brown (1973) notes that English subject arguments are commonly omitted in imperatives (*eat your dinner*) and other constructions. Until the child appreciates such conditions appropriately, the only possible tabulation is that initial arguments can be left unencoded optionally. Finally, information processing constraints might well apply in children's comprehension as well as during production (Shipley et al., 1969). A child hearing *the boys are eating oranges* might only hear or process *eat . . . orange* or *boy . . . orange* sometimes, automatically providing analytic models for fragments or omissions. The presence of negation or new verbs or other kinds of factors cited in sources such as Bloom, Miller, and Hood (1975) might reduce information processing capacity available for analysis of surrounding sentence parts during comprehension so that the child analyzes other aspects of sentence structure unreliably for a longer period when hearing such constructions.

Similarly, analysts have sometimes suggested other reasons besides information processing constraints during production in accounting for oscillation among correct and incorrect orderings or markings. For example, Brown and Hanlon (1970) note that *wh*-questions with an auxiliary after the subject (e.g., *where we should go now*) actually do appear with similar semantic intention in sentences such as *I want to know where we should go now,* in which the *wh*-question is an argument of a verb. A child who did not always hear the first part of the sentence, analyze it correctly, or appreciate the subtle distinction between *wh*-questions in isolation versus those that are embedded would be hearing many *wh*-questions in which the auxiliary followed the subject, which is otherwise the most common order.

Thus, gradual transitions and alternations among forms have proven to be common in children's language acquisition. There are many plausible explanations of this at present, each with something to recommend them. In the end, investigation of the problem perhaps serves to make it all the more remarkable that children can sort out the relevant conditions of use at all.

Individual Differences and Similarities

One of the major goals of developmental studies is to plot the course of development and from this to infer the underlying causes of development. Clearly, such a goal is more easily attained when the course of development is consistently across different children. Such consistency does seem to be obtained within various limits. As mentioned earlier, Stage I children seem to draw from a common pool of major semantic-structural or pragmatic analyses in regulating early grammar. Brown (1973) plotted out a fairly general developmental progression for children learning English that seems to have some cross-cultural application (for highly general constructions, such as conjunction or embedding) and has documented surprising similarities of order of acquisition across children for the 14 morphemes (or morpheme sets) discussed earlier. Errors such as *-ed* overregularizations seem to be universally found.

There have always been, however, reports of individual differences among children. Some children may differ from others in amount of overall error (Brown et al., 1969; Ramer, 1976, Smoczynska, in press) so that they make generally far more errors. Children may differ in detailed sequence of when various early formulas are acquired or in appearing variously specific or general in their analyses early on (Bloom, 1970; Bowerman, 1976; Brown, 1973; and especially Braine, 1976). It also turns out that children may differ seriously in to what degree they make various particular errors in acquiring certain grammatical constructions. For example, it is well documented that some children commonly misplace auxiliary verbs in *wh*-questions (e.g., *where we should go?*) far more frequently and longer than for yes/no questions (see reports in Bellugi, 1971; Brown, 1970; Knapp, 1979; Labov & Labov, 1978). But other children seem to make such errors rarely or no more commonly than for yes/no questions (Hecht & Morse cited in de Villiers & de Villiers, 1978; Ingram & Tyack, 1979; Knapp, 1979). Similar differences are found in the production of errors, such as tense overmarking (*did he made it?; it didn't disappeared*) (Maratsos & Kuczaj, 1978), early forms of negation (the de Villiers & de Villiers, 1978 discussion of Bellugi, 1967, Bloom, 1970, and data of their own), later forms of negation (e.g., compare remarks about multiple negation in Bellugi, 1967, with Menyuk, 1969), and other forms of English. Individual differences in children's making errors are reported or implicit in studies of acquisition in Finnish (Bowerman, 1973), German (MacWhinney, 1978; Mills, in press), Polish (Smoczynska, in press), and Kaluli (Schieffelin, in press) among others.

Individual variation should not be allowed to overshadow the important general uniformities that are found and the important general uniformities in basic acquisitional processes that necessarily underlay all children's acquisition. First, however, it requires substantive explanation in its own right where it occurs; it may be linked to differences in how long children wait to accumulate data before using a construction (Knapp, 1979; Kuczaj & Maratsos, 1975) or to other kinds of individual differences in interests, self-monitoring, or cognitive style (Brown et al., 1969; Horgan, 1978a, 1979; Nelson, 1973; Ramer, 1976). Second, at times it presents considerable interpretive and methodological problems. The production of misplaced auxiliary verbs in *wh*-questions (e.g., *where we should put this?*) seemed at one time to be a universal stage in acquisition and has attracted much theorization concerning its causes (Bellugi, 1971; Brown et al., 1969; Brown & Hanlon, 1970; Erreich et al., 1980; Fay, 1978). But it now appears to be frequently characteristic of only some children, perhaps a minority. Should its appearance in some be taken, nevertheless, to provide evidence about underlying analytic processes in all children learning the construction? Or does it represent more idiosyncratic problems of some children? More broadly, the fact of individual variation makes it more difficult to verify the broad course of acquisition in a given language through investigation of one or two subjects. This is unfortunate, because naturalistic transcription performed longitudinally is a time-consuming process. In any case, individual variation embedded within more general trends of acquisition now appears to be a well-documented finding of developmental studies.

THEORIES OF ACQUISITION

This is the point in review chapters at which review of available theories is undertaken, to be compared to the obtained findings. There is some point to this; for throughout the history of science, the most important work has usually been done in attempts to gather evidence for the proof or disproof of major theories (Crombie & Hoskin, 1970). However, what are clearly important findings are often not easily accommodated within various major theories or are not particularly relevant to their proof or disproof; a discussion of the theories per se can have an important masking effect on the retention of such findings. I think there is a good chance that this is presently so within the field of grammatical acquisition, which shows distinct signs of being in various kinds of transitional states. Thus, I do not think the present discussion should be thought of as a kind of culmination toward which all the previous data were gathered, even if the theories or positions exposited here were often important motivations for such investigations. With this caution in mind let us proceed to a discussion of available major ideas and findings.

Behaviorist Learning Theories and Grammatical Acquisition

For quite a long time, Chomsky (1959, 1965) was able to take behaviorist learning theories as the major opponents to a nativist theory. If the disproof of such theories were sufficient to prove linguistic nativism, theoretical formulations would no longer be necessary. Behaviorism, as Chomsky (1959) showed, can only deal with the many problems presented by language acquisition through a careful ad hoc relabeling of various phenomena, such as the stimulus that the child seizes upon for generalization, the discrimination made among stimuli, and so on. Thus, in the case of noun-gender systems, the stimulus gradient for generalization turns out to be other case-gender combinations in which the noun is used; in the case of various tensing rules, the stimulus is one of pastness, and so on.

Most important, present findings (Brown & Hanlon, 1970) do not indicate environmental contingencies that act directly on the child to shape the appropriate stimulus and response generalization and discrimination gradients. As Brown and Hanlon show for their sample, ungrammatical sentences are comprehended as well as grammatical, as far as can be told. Furthermore, like grammatical sentences, two thirds of the parental reactions children receive for ungrammatical utterances are ones of approval (e.g., *her curl my hair; uh huh*); thus, there is good reason for such ungrammatical uses to persist according to behavioral theory. Because no one claims (as far as we know) that human behavior is unsusceptible to shaping or, at least, to encouragement or discouragement on the basis of environmental contingencies, we probably have to save this generalization by proposing that children (correctly) do not think such parental reactions to be relevant to grammaticality versus ungrammaticality.

In connection with behaviorist formulations, a side issue has arisen about whether imitation might in some way contribute to linguistic development (Bloom, Hood, & Lightbown, 1974; R. Clark, 1977; Ervin, 1964; Leonard & Kaplan, 1976; Snow, in press). Grammatical acquisition in behaviorist theory, however, seems to require environmental shaping of the appropriate generalization gradients of such imitations; without such shaping, the possible importance of imitation is greatly reduced in a theory of acquisition. Thus, the question has shifted to whether imitation might have *some* role. Ervin (1964) reported that children's imitations were nonprogressive, that is, their imitations were not more advanced than their spontaneous utterances. Bloom et al. (1974) reopened the issue by showing that for two children who imitated frequently in early language acquisition, imitations tended to be of relatively new words or constructions just being learned. What is the possible significance of such findings? First, various children never imitate very much at all (Bloom et al., 1974), thus, overt imitation cannot be extremely important. Second, what is the function of overt imitation in those who do? The major function might be to help fix the example for storage by overt repetition (Bloom et al., 1974). It is not clear whether or not imitation even has this function (Leonard & Kaplan, 1976). Present evidence is that its function for the child is actually to allow continuation of the conversation; of course, it might have the other function anyway. If it does, this might be simply a low-level processing aid for some children, but it has little to do with the major problem of analyzing generalizations from individual examples. Without environmental contingencies to shape such responses into the general patterns, the findings on overt imitation in naturalistic speech situations cannot achieve very great general theoretical importance, whatever the interest is that the phenomenon occurs in some children.

Nativist Theories

Nativism, in general, is simply the belief that the child is not an unbiased observer and processor of stimuli. This is almost certainly true. Even in the realm of classical conditioning, investigators such as Garcia (e.g., Garcia & Revusky, 1970) have shown that the classical conditioning laws of association, contiguity, and so on, do not apply to all stimuli and responses (Nisbett & Ross, 1980). Garcia has shown, for example, that a novel taste experienced hours before an upset stomach is induced is associated to the upset stomach; the same novel taste experienced just before the upset stomach is not so associated. The evolutionary reasons for such asymmetries are clear enough, but such facts violate all the classical laws of conditioning. In virtually all physiological, perceptual, or other domains carefully investigated, some kind of nonequipotentiality of stimuli is common, not exceptional (Nisbett & Ross, 1980). Thus, why should the same not be true of language (Chomsky, 1959, 1975)?

Chomsky is probably correct in holding that much of the aversion held toward nativism in general is more ideological than empirically founded. In the case of language, however, there are other factors at work. First, no one really knows how long an evolutionary history language might have. In the case of other systems, such as perception, digestion, or even social organization, the evolutionary history of various aspects is likely to go back a long time, often millions of years. In the case of language, contrastively, it has even been recently suggested that Neanderthal man might not have had language as we know it because of the articulatory limitations inferable from Neanderthal jaw structure (Lieberman, 1975). For all we know, language has an evolutionary history of only some thousands of years. Second, a demonstration of general plausibility of some kinds of innate tendencies or biases does not indicate where such tendencies or biases take their origin. Humans might have exceptionally good systems of intermodal transfer among visual, auditory, sequential, and other kinds of analysis; these would be required for anyone's theory of grammar. Various biases might be caused by more general cognitive biases (McNeill, 1970, calls universals of language caused by such cognitive biases weak linguistic universals, to distinguish them from universals peculiar to language itself). Thus, the plausibility of some kinds of innate constraints or biases in the human cognitive processing that is relevant to language does not indicate how or at what level such special analytic propensities may operate. This being said,

let us look briefly at some of the present empirical evidence and theoretical proposals.

First, there is the status of the particular empirical and theoretical claims made initially by Chomsky (1959, 1965). Briefly these claims were:

1. Language has a complex transformational structure so that surface structures are radically different from underlying syntactic structures.
2. Syntactic structure cannot be shown to have a straightforward relation to semantic analyses, thus, the role of situational analyses of occasions of linguistic use in acquisition is at best uncertain.
3. Children learn language very quickly—for all practical purposes, instantaneously.
4. The input is degenerate, full of errors, and provides little feedback about the correctness of utterances.

Of these claims, the last is partly substantiated by available evidence; the child apparently does not receive feedback in the form of noncomprehension or disapproval of ungrammatical utterances, as far as can be presently determined (Brown & Hanlon, 1970). This is possibly the central finding concerning grammatical acquisition to have been obtained in the last 20 years. The other claims, however, have been generally falsified or weakened. Transformational grammar itself has come under increasing attack as a predictor of behavioral indices, such as sequence of acquisition, errors, or adult psycholinguistic processing (de Villiers & de Villiers, 1978; Fodor et al., 1974; Maratsos, 1978), and as an adequate model of human grammatical competence per se (Bresnan, 1978, in press-a,b; Lakoff & Thompson, 1975; Perlmutter & Postal, 1977). There is no longer reason to presuppose that surface structure differs radically from underlying structure. Furthermore, semantic analysis is clearly part of grammatical acquisition, even if not sufficient in itself to account for all developments. Similarly, it is also a major aspect of grammatical description of adult language in the relation of surface structures to underlying functional relations in nontransformational grammars (Bresnan, in press a,b; Kaplan & Bresnan, in press; Lakoff, 1966), however explicitly or implicitly this is done (also see Chomsky, 1980). Children's language acquisition is no longer seen as being performed as quickly as it was once believed. Various constructions traditionally viewed as important to showing the abstractness of the relation of surface form to underlying form (or relations), such as the passive, *easy to please* versus *eager to please* constructions, or *wh*-questions in which highly embedded constituents are questioned, seem not to be learned before the end of the preschool years, if that early (C. Chomsky, 1969; Cromer, 1970; de Villiers & de Villiers, 1978; Kessell, 1970; Maratsos et al., in preparation). Finally, the input may not carefully shape children's advancement, but it nevertheless seems to provide reasonably good examples of use in interpretable contexts; it is not degenerate, error filled, and misleading or irrelevant. All these considerations are important. Given the provable complexity of language under any conceivable description, more general inductionist accounts would require time in which to operate upon the data and would require at least respectable examples of the system. Such findings, of course, cannot falsify the nativist hypothesis. A nativist might claim, for example, that part of the evolutionary knowledge children implicitly have is that languages can differ in various ways; thus, the child might be maturationally set not to make final analyses of many types until preliminary data collection and description at a lower level have been completed. This being the case, let us look very briefly at some present nativist ideas and claims.

A common type of nativist argument is to point to regularities of grammatical phenomena that are common among the world's languages. Such regularities provide likely candidates for innate knowledge or constraints on the child's acquisition. The child's acquisition of language, it is usually claimed, would be impossible without such constraints, given the potentially confusing nature of the data.

One well-known type of argument of this kind has to do with the child's construction of formal classes, such as noun, verb, and adjective. These are, in theory, constructible on the basis of shared combinations of the terms, whether these are described purely distributionally (Kiss, 1973) or with the incorporation of some meaning (Maratsos & Chalkley, 1980). The nativist asks, however, why there should tend to be a common number of such categories across the world (usually nouns, verbs, and adjectives as the major lexical categories; sometimes just nouns and a major predicate class, usually called verbs, as in Chinese or Chinook). Second, there is potentially much confusion in the evidence for children. For example, what look like similar stems often appear in both noun and verb uses (e.g., *here's a hammer; he hammered it*). Or dissimilar word clases may appear in similar sequential-combinatorial environments, for example, the common appearance of *go* and *dog* in *watch that dog!* and *watch that go!* Finally, across the world's languages, various formal categories are associated

with a limited set of marked meanings. For example, across the world's languages, nouns may be marked for number, sex, shape, animacy, grammatical case (related to predicate role), intentionality, definiteness and indefiniteness, nearness versus farness, status, and other meanings. But markings for color, or usefulness, or degree of civilization are uncommon. Similarly, among verbs, markings for tense, aspect, number and person of arguments, transitivity of verb, animacy or definiteness of some argument, causitivity, knowledge of event by hearsay or direct witness, shape and size of handled objects (for verbs of handling), passivity, and a few other meanings are reasonably common. But other meanings, such as time of day, emotive value, and so on, are not marked (Pinker, in press). Grimshaw (in press) has suggested that what the child might innately know is that there is a limited number of possible general categories in a language, with a limited number of possible general meaning-structure correlates (e.g., agents will always be subjects in languages; "good" action terms will be members of the verb category, "good" object terms will be members of the noun category). Pinker (in press) has further suggested that the detailed semantic analyses children are often capable of carrying out with such terms (e.g., early analyses of tense and aspect inflections on verbs) might be best accounted for by some kinds of innate expectations limiting the possibilities.

What is the status of such arguments? They are interesting, but not presently certain. For example, let us consider the common claim that purely distributional analyses (analyses of terms into classes purely on the basis of their sequential behavior, without respect to meaning) are incapable of giving appropriate class groupings because of overlapping privileges of occurrence, such as *watch that dog* and *watch that go*. It is true that there are examples of such overlap. But Oliver (1968) and Kiss (1973) have each shown that if various stochastic biases or criteria are built in, such as taking into account how common various combinations are, which words appear more frequently, and so on, that in fact such procedures converge on appropriate form class distributions. The nativist argument that distributional analyses could not work is simply not true. Similarly, as has been seen, there is considerable possible complexity and confusion in the analysis of arbitrary noun-gender classes in various languages. It is not yet clear that nativists wish to incorporate such classes into the child's innate expectations. But analyses appropriate for such classes can give analyses of other kinds of formal classes as well, even with meaningful analyses incorporated. The point is reasonable that the child must analyze a great many meanings very specifically to construct systems such as case systems, or to analyze accurately whether determiners are used only with class-denoting nouns versus any nouns. Thus, some kind of limitation on meanings or greater access to certain types of meanings might be useful. But at present, a nonlinguistic nativist might argue that these are what McNeill (1970) called weak universals. Such meanings might be more naturally associated with nouns and verbs for various more general cognitive reasons. For example, it might be natural for humans to think of actions in temporal frameworks or for them implicitly to have recorded on the predicate terms describing situations, various situational factors such as animacy of actors, number of actors, and so forth. A nativist would need, first, proof that children actually do have more difficulty learning markings that encode other kinds of meanings and, second, evidence that these associations or possible biases cannot be accounted for by more general cognitive or semantic-expressive biases.

Chomsky (1975) has recently tended to argue that constraints on transformational operations provide the strongest evidence for innate constraints. The basic argument is that across the world's languages there are constraints on the free generalization of various transformational or interpretive devices that are not easy to predict on general grounds, yet speakers may observe these constraints without direct evidence. For example, no language has operations requiring counting, as in "put X marker on the third word"; or languages do not have such rules as "to make a question, invert the complete sentence (i.e., make a mirror image)." Or to refer to a common constraint on wh-questions, no language recorded when Chomsky (1975) wrote allows a wh-term to question a constituent within a relative clause. That is, for example, the question corresponding to *John knows the girl who ate what?* would be *what does John know the girl who ate?* Chomsky argues that speakers know these to be ungrammatical without ever having heard examples uttered and disapproved and despite the fact that wh-words can question constituents inside other kinds of embeddings (e.g., *what does John think Mary saw?*). This suggests that speakers have such a constraint as an innate part of their grammatical knowledge.

Chomsky is correct that these facts are interesting and require accounting for, but they do not necessarily lead to postulation of innate constraints. For example, the fact that languages do not require counting or have mirror-image rules might easily

follow from the fact that preschool children (the ones who are to learn language) are not guaranteed to be very good at either. So it is not surprising that human languages do not generally involve these. What about the argument that speakers can recognize something as ungrammatical that they have never heard disapproved? This is an interesting phenomenon, but by itself does not prove innate constraints against the type of operation. First, there are types of operations allowable in some languages that are not allowable in others. In many languages, for example, wh-questioning of embedded constituents is not allowed in general (Ross, 1967). Something like *what does John think Mary saw?* is unacceptable and probably incomprehensible to such speakers. Because such structures are acceptable in other languages, their unacceptability in some cannot be attributed to some innate prohibition against them. In fact, recent evidence indicates that although questioning out of relative clauses is not allowed in some languages, it is allowed in the Scandinavian languages (Maling & Zahnen, in press). Thus, an English speaker's rejection of these cannot similarly be laid to a universal innate constraint. In fact, within English, speakers find unacceptable and sometimes incomprehensible (I have found) a sentence like *John is possible to come.* It is unlikely that anyone has heard this kind of sentence disapproved, but it is also a type that appears generally within the language. *Possible* is semantically and structurally similar to other adjectives, such as *likely* (e.g., *that he'll come is [possible, likely]*). *John is likely to come* is in fact acceptable and comprehensible. It is, thus, hard to make a case that *John is possible to come* is unacceptable on general grounds. Thus, speakers are quite capable of holding constructions to be unacceptable and indeed hard to comprehend even without there being some kind of universal or general constraint. How they keep track of what is in effect not done, is not easy to tell, but they do.

But if there is a tendency for questioning out of embedded clauses in general to be unacceptable—and a gradient of unacceptability so that embedded relative clauses are highest in unacceptability, does this not argue some kind of general tendency or bias at work? It does. But again this does not mean that the bias is necessarily specific to linguistic knowledge or that it is something known ahead of time as a specific fact. It might be that there are cognitive reasons that have to do with the processing of such structures that make them difficult and that make relative-clause operations of this kind the most difficult; if this is so, such a gradient is otherwise explicable (Bever, 1970; Schlesinger, 1974). Thus again, although there may be some provable general tendency for some restriction or universal, there remains the problem of showing that it cannot be accounted for in terms of some processing factor or some more general cognitive bias or tendency. There is something else that might be added. I think one of the problems with some of the proposals is that they claim to be part of a general evolutionary way of thinking; but in fact, it is often hard to see the adaptive value, either positive or negative, of having the constraint or not having it. Of course, where it is possible to find such adaptive value, then it is reasonable to posit such value as the reason languages tend to evolve historically in the appropriate direction without giving this tendency a genetic explanation.

At present, it seems to me that the question of innate constraints or knowledge is open and that it would not be at all surprising if various biases, abilities, or processing heuristics specific to language acquisition are found. (Also see work in the learnability of languages, e.g., Anderson, 1976; Gold, 1967; Pinker, 1979, in press.)[7] But the question of which aspects of acquisition are best accounted for by positing biases and ideas or procedures specific to linguistic capacities seems problematic at the present time.

Apes and Nativism

A major line of work so far not considered here is recent work that attempts to teach apes language (Gardner & Gardner, 1980; Patterson, 1980; Premack, 1971; Savage-Rumbaugh & Rumbaugh, 1980; Terrace, Petitto, Sanders, & Bever, 1980). Few problems have generated as much interest and controversy. Although there is controversy even here (Terrace et al., 1980), it seems likely from the present evidence that apes can probably learn to use signs to communicate meanings. As this used to be the old boundary for language, it seems unfair to raise the ante and say that this is not really language. But the problem of whether apes can use ordered grammars with significant characteristics of human grammars is far more problematic. It is simply not clear whether various procedures might not be eliciting complex game behaviors rather than real communication behavior from some apes (Terrace et al., 1980). The cases where it is safest at present to say there is real communicative use of signs is in the apes learning American sign language (Gardner & Gardner, 1980; Terrace et al., 1980). Terrace et al. have pointed out serious problems in interpretations that give the apes very much credit for achievements so far. For example, evidence is unclear that sen-

tence length really increases systematically over time, as original records indicated (Brown, 1973), or that word order is really regulated systematically by general relations, such as agency. In opposition, Gardner and Gardner (1980) have defended much of their data that support such claims. No one can say what the limits of ape acquisition might be. For example, chimpanzees, such as Nim Chimpsky, have been raised in unusual caretaking situations that seem to have caused emotional stress (Terrace et al., 1980). But at present, the safest estimates of ape competence do not place competence very high.

It is thus hard to tell what future experimental results might be. It would not be surprising, however, if apes, for example, could not achieve such a system as underlying grammatical relations controlling different surface forms in provably systematic ways. If apes could do so, however, it would not demonstrate that the linguistic nativist position was correct. Such relations even in nonnativist formulations require quite complex coordinations of tabulation and sifting of lexical, semantic, and structural analyses. Apes might fail to achieve such analyses because of failures to have similarly complex systems of cross-modal analysis of sequence, visual input, motor movement, and so on. In the end, it seems to me, that it is likely that the answer as to whether the most complex forms of language displayed by humans require specifically linguistic innate constraints and ideas will rest upon analyses and studies of normal human children learning language. However, see important studies of children devising their own languages (e.g., Goldin-Meadow, 1979, and Goldin-Meadow & Feldman, 1975, 1977); also see studies of children learning American sign language for related problems; (Bellugi & Klima, 1979; Newport, 1980); and finally see Curtiss's report on Genie (Curtiss, 1977), a child not exposed to language until after puberty. Such work is not reviewed here because of space limitations.

Cognitivist Theories of Grammatical Acquisition

What can be called cognitivist theories are simply ones that emphasize the possibility that language grows out of some kind of general cognitive analytic abilities (e.g., Anderson, 1976, 1980; Bates & MacWhinney, 1982; Bloom, 1970; Karmiloff-Smith, 1979; Kiss, 1973; MacWhinney, 1978; Maratsos, 1979; Maratsos & Chalkley, 1980; Schlesinger, 1971, 1974, 1981; Slobin, 1973). This does not prevent fairly radical disagreements from being found within this group. In particular, some theorists hold that major developmental trends or outcomes stem largely or solely from semantic-conceptual properties; they emphasize that part of language development that has to do with the concepts language encodes, even if these can be modified or grouped by grammatical use (e.g., Bates & MacWhinney, 1982; Schlesinger, 1971, 1974, 1981). Others assume that aspects of the linguistic medium itself, such as sequence and phonological analysis per se can form important defining properties of grammatical analyses as a matter of fairly natural course (e.g., Anderson, 1980; Karmiloff-Smith, 1979; Kiss, 1973; Maratsos & Chalkley, 1980). Many theorists take various kinds of intermediate positions on these issues (e.g., Slobin, 1981,1982).

Perhaps unfairly, a kind of prototypical cognition-major semantics-grammar position can be constructed from a number of positions that claim that major semantic factors in grammatical acquisition are able to account both for central phenomena of acquisition and for the fact of acquisition itself. Bowerman (1981), Cromer (1981), Maratsos and Chalkley (1980), and Pinker (in press) among others have noted the growth of this position as a kind of consensus among present workers in the field of language acquisition:

1. Children are active agents in language learning, taking their motivation for learning and grammatical advancement from their active desire to express meanings that conceptual development makes available to them.

2. The major aspects of the analysis of grammar can be accounted for by the child's active application of major cognitive-based semantic categories, such as agent, action, location, focus, topic, and so forth.

3. Factors of the above type remain the major defining properties for categories throughout linguistic development.

4. Following directly from (2) and (3), the acquisition of grammar is essentially fairly straightforward, requiring little information processing capacity, which is a good thing because the child has very little.

5. What (1), (2), and (3) in combination cannot account for, the structure of parental linguistic input can.

6. Analyses that cannot be carried out through the above mechanisms are unnatural, difficult for the child, and acquired very late.

Like most general accounts, the strong cognitivist account seizes appropriately on various positive aspects of the available data. In particular, in the early 1970s, a consensus had grown that major semantic categories such as agent and action and patient, located object and location, or other cognition-derived meanings (e.g., recurrence and negation) provide the major core of Stage I grammatical competence (Brown, 1973). Children do not simply combine words that can go together for formal distributional reasons without respect to the meaning conveyed by the combinations, which had been implied or stated in earlier descriptions, such as those of Braine (1963), Miller and Ervin (1964), or Brown and Fraser (1964). Available evidence (Slobin, 1973) further indicated clearly that purely formally defined systems, such as arbitrary noun gender, were not mastered until the end of the preschool years, if not later; much error and inappropriate overgeneralization attended the construction of these systems. Parental input, although not shaping responses (Brown & Hanlon, 1970), was turning out to be far better input than Chomsky (1965) had believed. Although findings from acquisition had not yet indicated the problems of transformational grammar as a predictor of acquisition, it was clear from linguistics itself that purely formally based transformational grammar was no longer a commonly held linguistic description. Fillmore's case grammar (1968) seemed highly semantic-based. Another group of linguists had been working on a mode of description called generative semantics (Lakoff, 1971; Lakoff & Ross, 1968; McCawley, 1970, 1971; Postal, 1970), which depicted transformational operations as beginning directly on fully realized semantic descriptions of sentences. Actually, the "deep structures" of generative semantics were far further removed from the surface than those of Chomskyan transformational grammars, but many psycholinguists simply saw the importantly indicated role of meaning and assumed this made matters simpler somehow. Theorists such as Slobin (1973) proposed various strategies and heuristics that seemed to give fairly simple ways of operating upon grammatical descriptions to give at least initial analyses (also see Bever, 1970). Bates's (1976) book introduced pragmatic analyses as important in grammar (which they are) and further proposed the central relation of Piagetian cognition to language development in strong terms. MacNamara (1972) demonstrated that meaning must play a role in syntactic acquisition.

All of these points are important. They require incorporation into any theory of acquisition. Without losing some of the major achievements of the last few years which form the basis for such a view, however, we can also now point out the incompleteness or incorrectness of this strong cognitivist position in dealing with grammatical acquisition. In doing so, I will by and large simply restate points or findings discussed more fully in earlier sections of this chapter.

First, it is true that input to the child appears potentially more helpful and certainly more accurate than Chomsky's original portrayal. It does not, however, shape acquisition or motivate grammatical advancement (already discussed). At best, it seems to provide good examples of use in meaningful contexts and perhaps offers hints to an organism intelligent enough to figure them out. The major task of drawing out generalizations from the ambiguous individual examples remains that of the child.

Second, even when semantic factors are central to defining grammatical rules, their connections with grammar are not completely direct. Children do not seem to be constrained to cognitively 'natural' orders (Slobin, 1982). Whether or not a major pragmatic or semantic variable operates in a language depends upon the language itself. Within semantic categories relevant to grammar, subdivisions or organizations of the relevant properties—for example, common versus proper- and pronominal-noun operations—are governed by the structure of the language (Schlesinger, 1977) rather than simply following from completely 'natural' organizations of these. Nor are all the relevant factors for grammar that are semantic always general semantic properties. Children's early rules include many rules such as $no + X =$ 'negation of X' or narrow category rules such as mover + movement. Adult rules require analyses at the same level to capture many regularities of grammar, such as the fact that *own* takes a possessor argument initially, whereas *belong* takes possessed objects in subject position.

Finally, it is true that the earliest general grammatical categories seem to have semantic properties as defining properties. But children's achievement of formal organizations for vowel harmony systems, noun gender systems, or form class systems appears early in the preschool years, with less error and difficulty than earlier accounts have implied. Such analyses would by their nature require some time to pass in a general inductionist account. They require the tabulation of many detailed lexical analyses in long-term storage until internal analytic procedures draw out the relevant generalizations about how phonological characteristics of words predict grammatical combinations the words may take part in, or how a set of semantically heterogeneous terms or phrases may participate in a common set of operations. Children's considerable ability to carry out these operations belies the description of them as having highly limited long-term storage capacity (e.g., Bates & MacWhinney, 1982; Slobin, 1973). Limitations are far more likely in the domain of short-term processing (Bloom, Lightbown, & Hood, 1975; Bloom, Miller, & Hood, 1975; Knapp, 1979; Tolbert, 1978); this problem becomes gradually alleviated by automatization and the formation of appropriate general categories (Knapp, 1979).

In short, aspects of the strong cognitivist position seem strongest in dealing with early grammar (and not all of that, as has been noted previously). Non-nativist positions that can account for development beyond this point must be able to account naturally for the child's great ability to interweave general and specific semantic factors, formal factors, lexical analyses, and general categorical construction. Chomsky's picture of a richly equipped organism in a generic sense must be correct. The problem is yet whether or not this richness is in some degree uniquely fitted for linguistic analyses or stems from a complex coordination of cognitive analyses and biases of more general kinds.

APPENDIX: SOME NOTES ON METHODOLOGY

Because of the centrality of naturalistic observation in the empirical study of language acquisition, most of the methodological remarks in this chapter have been concerned with such methods. In the past few years, however, important methodological findings have been obtained concerning experimental methods such as judgment, comprehension, and imitation. It appears, for example, that what have been often treated as substantive findings are in fact simply methodological problems with one type of task (comprehension) (Bowerman, 1979; Cromer, 1981). In other cases, critical findings regarding the use of these methods are clearly relevant not only to basic research but also to applied uses. For these reasons, some justification can be given for a brief and admittedly selective review of some of the findings regarding these methods.

Judgment Methods

The chief methodological tool of the linguist is judgment—judgment of sentence grammaticality, meaning, or relatedness to other sentence forms (Chomsky, 1957; Lees, 1959). Linguists have naturally suggested eliciting judgments from children as a way of enriching the empirical base of developmental studies (Lees, 1964; Chomsky, 1964).

Unfortunately, tacit knowledge of underlying

grammatical structure versus the ability to think about grammar and give judgments of sentences appear to be different things. We have already seen in the work of Karmiloff-Smith (1979) how children could not give reasons for their correct answers about French noun gender for years. Furthermore, when they could, they could only talk about semantic-based factors and tended to overestimate the importance of these. They could virtually never talk about phonological bases for their answers, although they had developed such competence earlier.

Nor does simple judgment of whether a sentence is grammatical or not seem to correspond to the knowledge shown in actual spontaneous production. Children who observe correct word order from Stage I on are apparently unable to recognize consistently the syntactic unacceptability of such sentences as *teeth your brush* until Stage V, nor are they able to give corrections of such sentences consistently until that stage (de Villiers & de Villiers, 1974). Hakes, Evans, and Turner (1981) similarly found that judgment of grammaticality is a skill that falls behind actual use, and they connect this skill to general cognitive development.

It is probably not the case that judgment tasks are systematically unusable. Kuczaj's experimental results with judgments of past tense sentences reasonably complement and supplement available naturalistic observations (Kuczaj, 1978a). Gleitman, Gleitman, and Shipley (1972) found interesting results in their subjects' remarks and judgments about sentences, although they also note considerable methodological problems. On the whole, however, it appears that judgment methods can at best be used with great caution to supplement other results. Children's ability to judge and explain what they unconsciously know may lag behind unconscious knowledge for years or never catch up. Indeed, adults understand very little about how the grammar that was internalized years before actually works, although they are capable of making various kinds of judgments about sentences.

Comprehension Tasks and Comprehension Strategies

In comprehension methods, it is hoped the child will show something of his knowledge of a construction by his nonlinguistic response to a sentence that contains it. Children hearing *the boy was kissed by the girl* might be shown a picture of a boy kissing a girl and one of a girl kissing a boy and then asked to point to the picture that goes with the sentence (Fraser, Bellugi, & Brown, 1963). Or the child might be given a boy doll and a girl doll and asked to act out the sentence (Bever, 1970). Comprehension tests may be profitably used to investigate children's knowledge of constructions that appear rarely in their speech or for which naturalistic collection would be arduous and time consuming.

The most straightforward problem with comprehension studies that has emerged over the last decade or so is that these studies seem easily to underestimate children's knowledge when comparisons with rigorously analyzed naturalistic findings can be made (Brown, 1973). Brown suggests that the presence of carefully matched pictures that are different only in the crucial response may be confusing in picture-comprehension tasks. Dale (1976) notes that there may well be attentional and motivational problems. After all, the child spontaneously speaks only if interested but may give some kind of comprehension response to a construction because of experimenter pressure, not from interest. The task may also require an inference beyond the linguistic knowledge tested (Kessel, 1970, discussing C. Chomsky, 1969). The literature now indicates that the age estimates for the same competence may be lowered by years through a change in procedure (Cromer, 1970; Fabian-Krauss & Ammon, 1980; Kessel, 1970).

Perhaps more central is the problem of comprehension strategies, a concept centrally introduced in developmental studies by Bever (1970). The basic problem is that a child who does not understand a construction, instead of responding randomly or simply saying "I don't know" may instead adopt some kind of consistent guess to get through the task in some way. Or the child may use some strategy to choose a response even when the child's knowledge would allow a more accurate response.

Bever (1970) discusses many types of such strategies. The first major type is the strategy of interpreting the referents of the individual words as standing in their most likely real-world relations. For example, a sentence that includes the words *mommy, dog,* and *pat* is more likely to mean that mommy pats the dog whatever the arrangement of words. A sentence with the words *drink, milk,* and *mommy* is even more certain to have a real-world interpretation. Children may sometimes only pay attention to probable or almost-certain real-world relations instead of analyzing the grammar of the sentence (Bever, 1970; Slobin, 1966). Children may even perform badly on constructions they actually understand if enticed by such relations, although pretraining can alleviate such problems (Strohner & Nelson, 1974).

In another type of strategy, the child may transfer some kind of knowledge of another construction actively to the task at hand. A well-known case of this in English comprehension studies is children's incorrect comprehension of passives such as *the dog was bitten by the cat* as though they were actives (*the dog . . . bit . . . the cat*) (Bever, 1970; Fraser et al., 1963). Children apparently begin by randomly interpreting such sentences earlier in their linguistic development. They then become more likely to treat passives like actives later in development before they finally attain accurate interpretations (Bever, 1970; de Villiers & de Villiers, 1973b). Such results look as though children are getting worse at the passive. Of course, they are not. Instead, what they are doing is more actively generalizing the active structure to the uncomprehended passive sentence. Thus these results are in a sense studies of the generalization of the active to the uncomprehended, unanalyzed passive more than they are studies of children's developing analyses of the passive. It is not that children have an analysis of the passive that is incorrect. It is that they have no analysis of it and use something derived from the active to get through the task.

Bever (1970) also discusses other strategies, such as the order-of-mention strategy (e.g., interpreting *the boy left after the girl sang* in the order *the boy left . . . the girl sang*). Other experimenters have sometimes found similar results (e.g., Clark, 1972; see Bowerman, 1979, for a summary).

The methodological problem with such results is clear. The subject's responses to a construction may not show anything of the subject's actual developing analyses of the construction per se. The responses may have more to do with particular task strategies the child adopts to get through the task. This clearly can make it difficult to study what might be hoped to be actual stages in the child's developing knowledge because such strategies may be what one is actually studying.

The second major problem is whether such strategies may have something important to do with how the child makes such analyses in the real world and arrives at grammatical analyses rather than simply being studies of children's strategies in experimental tasks. It is presently not very easy to be optimistic regarding this possibility. For example, how would use of a strategy that noun-verb-noun = actor-action-patient (Bever, 1970) help the child learn the passive? If anything, it seems as though it would hinder learning but not have much to do with the actual process of correct analysis that must begin at some time (Cromer, 1981). Or consider the strategy of comprehending sentences according to the likely or present real-world relations among actors, without regard to actual word order or other syntactic markings. How would this aid the child in actually analyzing the appropriate correlations among real world relations, word order, and syntactic markings? It is extremely interesting that in fact most utterances are interpretable in context without understanding how grammar also expresses the relations among words (Slobin, 1973), especially in early grammar. But referring to the child's lack of need to correlate grammatical devices to utterance meaning does not explain very much about how the child, nevertheless, does this anyway. Finally, it is becoming evident that slight task variations or even attempts to reproduce the same task can produce different apparent strategies in children's comprehension of the same constructions (Bowerman, 1979, gives an excellent review of this problem; Carey, 1978, reviews the same problem in the area of word-meaning studies). Given how easily variability may be induced by slight experimental variations, it is difficult to see how one can generalize from the task situations to naturalistic situations.

Thus, comprehension methods may underestimate the child's knowledge by introducing unforeseen difficulties, or they may be unrepresentative of underlying knowledge (or the lack of it) because of children's use of task strategies. For the first problem, it seems that little can be done except two things: (1) the experimenter must attempt to simplify the task and make sure the child understands those aspects of it that are not relevant to the particular linguistic competence being tested and (2) the experimenter might attempt to show that different methods or variations of method converge upon the same results. Correlation of some of the results to well-established naturalistic findings might also be useful. The same basic methods may be useful in attempting to eliminate the effects of task strategies in the interpretation. Or the experimenter may be able to come up with more particular controls, such as using nonsense morphemes in key positions to give a baseline of how the child understands the construction without its key markers (e.g., one might give children passives such as *the boy gom pushed po the bear* to see how the child interprets uncharacteristic activelike sentences).

Imitation Tasks

Imitation tasks consist of the child attempting to repeat a sentence said by the experimenter. If the sentence is short enough, the child may simply imitate correctly through the use of general motoric-perceptual skills, without processing the sentence through the linguistic system (Fraser et al., 1963). But if the sentence is too long for the child to do this, the child may instead process the sentence through underlying semantic-structural competence in interesting ways (Knapp, 1979; Kuczaj & Maratsos, 1975; Menyuk, 1969; Slobin & Welch, 1973; Smith, 1970). The child may rearrange the sentence greatly but give a semantically sensible imitation anyway, showing some comprehension of the underlying meaning (Slobin & Welch, 1973). Or the child may supply missing morphemes left out in the experimenter's model or correct incorrect orders (Knapp, 1979; Kuczaj & Maratsos, 1975; Smith, 1970); in a few cases, the child may even do so prior to actually using the relevant construction spontaneously (Knapp, 1979; Kuczaj & Maratsos, 1975; Smith, 1970), although such cases appear not to be usual (Knapp, 1979; Kuczaj, 1976,a,b).

Such results indicate imitation may be a very powerful method of investigation under ideal circumstances. But it now appears that there is considerable individual variation in how children respond to the task. A few children appear actually to enjoy the task. Slobin & Welch's (1973) subject Echo imitated about 1,000 sentences a month for nearly a year (Slobin, 1975; Slobin & Welch, 1973, report only on the first month's data). Such a subject can be compared to the 3-year-old in Maratsos (1976) who, asked to imitate "I like to drive cars," "So what?" More systematically, Bloom (1974) found that Peter, a subject she studied longitudinally, could not successfully imitate sentences he had uttered himself the day before. Hood (1977) found great individual variation of response. Compared to naturalistic records of their competence, some subjects imitated well, whereas other subjects at the same linguistic level imitated poorly.

Such results clearly have more applied implications. It is clear that clinicians would like to be able to achieve a relatively quick and general analysis of a child's linguistic ability through the use of test batteries. Lee (1969) has in fact devised such batteries that employ the comprehension and imitation methods reviewed earlier. Given the apparently task-dependent and individually variable nature of the relation between children's underlying competence and experimental measures, such tests clearly cannot be relied on as the sole or even central index of the child's actual linguistic ability.

These remarks on methodological findings of the last few years do not comprise a complete analysis or summary of important emerging methods. In particular, the use of computer simulations (e.g., Anderson, 1976; Kiss, 1973) or mathematical proofs of the learnability of a system and its developmental assumptions (Anderson, 1976; Hamburger & Wexler, 1975; Pinker, 1979, in press) are likely to emerge as increasingly important methods with their own advantages and interpretive problems in the upcoming years. (See Pinker, 1979, or Wexler, 1982, for an introduction to the goals and methods of such investigations). Only constraints of space and subject matter make inappropriate the discussion of these methods, which may be especially prominent in future years in dealing with the problems of advanced development.

NOTES

1. In linguistic description, unacceptable sentences are prefixed with an * to denote their unacceptability. This practice will be followed in the present chapter as well.

2. In a recent article, Moerk (1980) has questioned whether input frequency made as little difference as Brown (1973) concluded. He notes that Brown took his sample from a period before Stage II and correlated these parental frequencies to acquisitional order often far beyond this stage (reasons for this are given in Brown, 1973). Moerk (1980) makes the reasonable suggestion that one might look at those morphemes acquired soon after the parental sample was taken to see if sampling made any difference. For Adam (Brown, 1973), for example, *-ing, in, on,* and noun plural *-s* were acquired in that order in Stages II and III and had been used 65, 37, 20, and 57 times respectively by his parents. The correlation between parental use and earliness of acquisition is .56. Similar correlations for morphemes acquired in Stage II and parental frequency were .66 for Sarah and .76 for Eve (Brown, 1973). These figures were not statistically significant because of the small numbers but are, as Moerk (1980) notes, much more impressive than Brown's (1973) overall figure of .26.

Moerk's (1980) analysis rests on a peculiar analytic artifact however. It correlates order of acquisition and parental frequency of use just for those morphemes that actually reached acquisition criterion in Stages II and III. A look at Brown's (1973) tables shows that the most frequently used morphemes before Stage II were the articles *a* and *the* (used 233 times by Adam's parents) and copula *be* in uncontracted form (used 154 times by Adam's parents). These were not acquired at all during Stages II and III, even though they were the highest in parental frequency of use before this time. This is the sort of finding that led to parental frequency failing to predict aquisitional order very well. Moerk's (1980) analysis seems plausible when one simply looks at the tables he presents, but it appears to be incorrect in essential ways.

3. Slobin (1973) uses this finding and others to support a generalization that children more easily analyze affixes attached to the ends of words than morphemes that appear before them. Although Mac-Whinney (1978) has brought up considerations that weaken Slobin's claim, Kuczaj (1979) has produced experimental evidence in a training task that strongly supports Slobin's claim.

4. Maratsos and Chalkley (1980) actually seriously consider the idea that categories such as ''verb'' might not be formed internally at all. Instead, children might simply store the information that terms taking one type of operation reliably (or nearly reliably) take still others, with operations encoded with more primitive representational means. This idea is quite problematic for reasons partially discussed in Maratsos (1981) and will not be discussed in any further detail here.

5. Many of the examples cited also contradict a number of processing principles proposed by investigators such as Bever (1970) and Slobin (1973), Behavioral Strategies (Bever, 1970) or Operating Principles (Slobin, 1973). For example, both investigators hypothesize that omission of underlying material or omission of markers that clarify semantic-structural relationships leads to later acquisition. But the examples just cited above contain many cases in which the earlier acquired form has what can be interpreted as omitted material compared to the later appearing form. (Also see Cromer, 1981, and Maratsos, 1979, for further counterexamples to this proposal.) Second, Slobin (1973) proposes that structures involving rearrangement of underlying order are more difficult. Again, findings concerning freer word-order languages are not consistent with this if the notion of underlying order is traced to usual transformational formulations as it generally has been.

6. There is, however, a change in the underlying theoretical apparatus between Bloom (1970) and Bloom et al., (1975a). In particular, in Bloom (1970) it is clearly implied that if all information processing constraints were lifted, the child would reliably fill in obligatory basic sentence constituents. This is not the intended position in Bloom et al (1975) (Bloom, 1980). What seems to be the intended position is that the arguments understood as obligatory for the adult are always understood to be part of the underlying grammatical structure for the child, but information processing constraints supply only part of the reason they are not reliably pro-

duced. This position is difficult to evaluate through the use of behavioral data, although it is quite reasonable for dealing with various acquisitional phenomena. I am in this chapter thus only discussing the simpler proposition that informational processing constraints per se account for omissions of structures that are sometimes produced. (Also see Braine, 1974, 1976, for important alternative analyses of these problems.)

7. In learnability work, the problem is to evaluate whether a model employing various assumptions and constraints can be shown to be capable of inducing an adult grammar from incoming linguistic and situational data. In the end, the basic questions for such work revolve around which assumptions are the appropriate ones and whether the necessary constraints are linguistic or not, much as in the section on *Nativist Theories*. For this reason, a more extended discussion of this important work would overlap considerably in the end with our previous discussion. Given space constraints, these considerations have led to a decision not to review the work here.

REFERENCES

Akmajian, A., & Heny, F. *An introduction to the principles of transformational syntax*. Cambridge: MIT Press, 1976.

Aksu, A., & Slobin, D. I. The acquisition of Turkish. In D. I. Slobin (Ed.), *Cross-linguistic studies in language acquisition*. Hillsdale, N.J.: Erlbaum, in press.

Anderson, J. *Language, memory, and thought*. Hillsdale, N.J.: Erlbaum, 1976.

Anderson, J. A theory of language acquisition based on general learning principles. Unpublished manuscript, Carnegie-Mellon University, 1980.

Antinucci, F., & Parisi, D. Early language acquisition: A model and some data. In C. A. Ferguson & D. I. Slobin (Eds.), *Studies of child language development*. New York: Holt, Rinehart & Winston, 1973.

Atkinson Hardy, J., & Braine, M. Categories that bridge between meaning and syntax in five-year-olds. In W. Deutsch (Ed.), *The child's construction of language*. New York: Academic Press, 1981.

Baker, C. L. Syntactic theory and the projection problem. *Linguistic Inquiry*, 1979, *10*, 533–583.

Baldie, B. The acquisition of the passive voice. *Journal of Child Language*, 1976, *3*, 331–348.

Bates, E. *Language and context: The acquisition of*

pragmatics. New York: Academic Press, 1976.

Bates, E., & MacWhinney, B. A functionalist approach to grammatical development. In L. Gleitman & H. E. Wanner (Eds.), *Language acquisition: The state of the art*. Cambridge: At the University Press, 1982.

Becker, J., & Maratsos, M. P. *Development of comprehension of the passive*. Paper presented at the meeting of the Society for Research in Child Development, San Francisco, March 1979.

Bellugi, U. *The acquisition of negation*. Unpublished doctoral dissertation, Harvard University, 1967.

Bellugi, U. Simplification in children's language. In R. Huxley & E. Ingram (Eds.), *Language acquisition: Models and methods*. New York: Academic Press, 1971.

Bellugi, U., & Klima, E. S. *The signs of language*. Cambridge, Mass.: Harvard University Press, 1979.

Berko, J. The child's learning of English morphology. *Word*, 1958, *14*, 150–177.

Bever, T. G. The cognitive basis for linguistic structures. In J. R. Hayes (Ed.), *Cognition and the development of language*. New York: Wiley, 1970.

Bever, T. G., Fodor, J. A., & Weksel, W. On the acquisition of syntax. *Psychological Review*, 1965, *72*, 467–482.

Bever, T., Katz, J., & Langendoen, D. *An integrated theory of linguistic ability*. New York: Thomas Crowell, 1976.

Bloom, L. *Language development: Form and function in emerging grammars*. Cambridge: MIT Press, 1970.

Bloom, L. Talking, understanding, and thinking. In R. L. Schiefelbusch & L. L. Lloyd (Eds.), *Language perspectives—Acquisition, retardation, and intervention*. Baltimore: University Park Press, 1974.

Bloom, L. Personal communication, 1980.

Bloom, L., Hafitz, E., & Lifter, K. Schematic organization of verbs in child language and the acquisition of grammatical morphemes. *Language*, 1980, *56*, 386–412.

Bloom, L., Hood, L., & Lightbown, P. Imitation in language development: If, when, and why? *Cognitive Psychology*, 1974, *6*, 380–420.

Bloom, L., Lahey, M., Hood, L., Lifter, K., & Fiess, K. Complex sentences: Acquisition of syntactic connections and the semantic relations they encode. *Journal of Child Language*, 1980, *7*, 235–256.

Bloom, L., Lightbown, P., & Hood, L. Structure and variation in child language. *Monographs of the Society for Research in Child Development*, 1975, *40*(2, Serial No. 160).

Bloom, L., Miller, P., & Hood, L. Variation and reduction as aspects of competence in language development. In A. D. Pick (Ed.), *Minnesota Symposia on Child Psychology* (Vol. 9). Minneapolis: University of Minnesota Press, 1975.

Blount, B. G. Parental speech and language acquisition: Some Luo and Samoan examples. *Anthropological Linguist*, 1972, *14*, 119–130.

Bogoyavlenskiy, D. N. *Psikhologiya usvoyeniya orfografi*. Moscow: Akad. Pedag. Nauk RSFSR, 1957. English translation of pp. 261–271: The acquisition of Russian inflections, reprinted in C. A. Ferguson & D. I. Slobin, *Studies of child language acquisition*. New York: Holt, Rhinehart & Winston, 1973.

Böhm, K., & Levelt, W. J. M. *Children's use and awareness of natural and syntactic gender*. Paper presented at the Conference on Linguistic Awareness and Learning to Read, Victoria, B.C., June 1979.

Bowerman, M. *Early syntactic development: A cross-linguistic study with special reference to Finnish*. Cambridge: At the University Press, 1973.

Bowerman, M. Learning the structure of causative verbs. A study in the relationship of cognitive, semantic, and syntactic development. *Papers and Reports on Child Language Development*. Stanford: Stanford University Committee on Linguistics, 1974, *8*, 142–178.

Bowerman, M. Commentary on Structure and variation in children's language. *Monographs of the Society for Research in Child Development*, 1975, *41*(Serial No. 160).

Bowerman, M. Semantic factors in the acquisition of rules for word use and sentence construction. In D. M. Morehead & A. E. Morehead (Eds.), *Normal and deficient child language*. Baltimore: University Park Press, 1976.

Bowerman, M. Semantic and syntactic development. In R. L. Schiefelbusch (Ed.), *The bases of language intervention*. Baltimore, Md.: University Park Press, 1978.

Bowerman, M. The acquisition of complex sentences. In P. Fletcher & M. Gorman (Eds.), *Language acquisition*. Cambridge: At the University Press, 1979.

Bowerman, M. Keynote address, Child Language Research Forum, Stanford University, Stanford, Calif., April 1981.

Bowerman, M. Personal communication, 1981.

Bowerman, M. Evaluating competing linguistic models with language acquisition data: Implications of developmental errors with causative verbs. *Semantica*, 1982, *3*, 1–73.

Braine, M. D. S. The ontogeny of English phrase structure: The first phase. *Language*, 1963, *39*, 3–13.

Braine, M. D. S. The acquisition of language in infant and child. In C. Reed (Ed.), *The learning of language*. New York: Appleton-Century-Crofts, 1971.

Braine, M. D. S. Length constraints, reduction rules, and holophrastic processes in children's word combinations. *Journal of Verbal Learning and Verbal Behavior*, 1974, *13*, 448–456.

Braine, M. D. S. Children's first word combinations. *Monographs of the Society for Research in Child Development*, 1976, *41*(1, Serial No. 164).

Braine, M. D. S., & Wells, R. S. Case-like categories in children: The actor and some related categories. *Cognitive Psychology*, 1978, *10*, 100–122.

Brame, M. *Base generated syntax*. Seattle: Noit Amrofer, 1978.

Branigan, G. Some reasons why successive single word utterances are not. *Journal of Child Language*, 1979, *6*, 411–421.

Bresnan, J. A realistic transformational grammar. In M. Halle, J. Bresnan, & G. A. Miller (Eds.), *Linguistic theory and psychological reality*. Cambridge: MIT Press, 1978.

Bresnan, J. The passive in lexical-functional grammar. In J. Bresnan (Ed.), *The mental representation of grammatical relations*. Cambridge: MIT Press, in press. (a)

Bresnan, J. A theory of grammatical representation. In J. Bresnan (Ed.), *The mental representation of grammatical relations*. Cambridge: MIT Press, in press. (b)

Broen, P. A. The verbal environment of the language learning child. *Monographs of the American Speech and Hearing Association*, 1972, *17*.

Brown, R. *Unpublished grammars for Adam, Eve, and Sarah*. Harvard University, no date.

Brown, R. Linguistic determinism and the part of speech. *Journal of Abnormal and Social Psychology*, 55, 1957, 1–5.

Brown, R. *Words and things*. New York: Free Press, 1958.

Brown, R. *Psycholinguistics. Selected Papers*. New York: Free Press, 1970.

Brown, R. *A first language: The early stages*. Cambridge: Harvard University Press, 1973.

Brown, R. Preface. In C. E. Snow & C. A. Ferguson (Eds.), *Talking to children: Language input and acquisition*. Cambridge: At the University Press, 1977.

Brown, R., & Bellugi, U. Three processes in the child's acquisition of syntax. *Harvard Educational Review*, 1964, *34*, 133–151.

Brown, R., Cazden, C. B., & Bellugi, U. The child's grammar from I to III. In J. P. Hill (Ed.), *Minnesota Symposia on Child Psychology* (Vol. 2). Minneapolis: University of Minnesota Press, 1969.

Brown, R., & Fraser, C. The acquisition of syntax. In U. Bellugi & R. Brown (Eds.), *The acquisition of language*. Chicago: University of Chicago Press, 1964.

Brown, R., & Hanlon, C. Derivational complexity and order of acquisition. In J. R. Hayes (Ed.), *Cognition and the development of language*. New York: Wiley, 1970.

Burling, R. Language development of a Garo and English-speaking child. *Word*, 1959, *15*, 45–68.

Carey, S. The child as a word learner. In M. Halle, J. Bresnan, & G. A. Miller (Eds.), *Linguistic theory and psychological reality*. Cambridge: MIT Press, 1978.

Cazden, C. B. The acquisition of noun and verb inflections. *Child Development*, 1968, *39*, 433–438.

Chomsky, C. *The acquisition of syntax in children from 5 to 10*. Cambridge: MIT Press, 1969.

Chomsky, N. *Syntactic structures*. The Hague: Mouton, 1957.

Chomsky, N. Review of *Verbal behavior* by B. F. Skinner. *Language*, 1959, *35*, 26–58.

Chomsky, N. Formal discussion: The development of grammar in child language. In U. Bellugi & R. Brown (Eds.), *The acquisition of language*. *Monographs of the Society for Research in Child Development: # 92*, 1964, *29*(1), 35–39.

Chomsky, N. *Aspects of the theory of syntax*. Cambridge: MIT Press, 1965.

Chomsky, N. Remarks on nominalization. In R. A. Jacobs & P. S. Rosenbaum (Eds.), *Readings in English transformational grammar*. Waltham, Mass.: Ginn, 1970.

Chomsky, N. *Reflections on language*. New York: Pantheon, 1975.

Chomsky, N. On binding. *Linguistic Inquiry*, 1980, *11*, 1–80.

Clark, E. V. On the acquisition of the meaning of *before* and *after*. *Journal of Verbal Learning and Verbal Behavior*, 1972, *11*, 750–758.

Clark, E. V. How children learn to create new

words. In W. Deutsch (Ed.), *The child's construction of language*. London: Academic Press, 1981.

Clark, R. What's the use of imitation? *Journal of Child Language*, 1977, *4*, 341–358.

Crombie, A. C., & Hoskin, M. The scientific movement and the diffusion of scientific ideas, 1688–1751. In J. S. Bromley (Ed.), *The new Cambridge modern history*, vol. 6, *The rise of Great Britain and Russia, 1688–1725*. Cambridge: At the University Press, 1971.

Cromer, R. F. Children are nice to understand: Surface structure clues for the recovery of deep structure. *British Journal of Psychology*, 1970, *61*, 397–408.

Cromer, R. F. The development of language and cognition: The cognition hypothesis. In B. Foss (Ed.), *New perspectives in child development*. Harmondsworth, Middlesex, England: Penguin Books, 1974.

Cromer, R. F. Reconceptualizing language acquisition and cognitive development. In R. Schieffelbusch & D. Bricker (Eds.), *Early language: Acquisition and intervention*. Baltimore: University Park Press, 1981.

Cross, T. G. Mother's speech adjustments: The contribution of selected child listener variables. In C. E. Snow & C. A. Ferguson (Eds.), *Talking to children: Input and acquisition*. New York: Cambridge University Press, 1977.

Cross, T. G. Mother's speech and its association with rate of linguistic development in young children. In N. Waterson & C. E. Snow (Eds.), *The development of communication*. New York: Wiley, 1978.

Crystal, D. Non-segmental phonology in language acquisition: A review of the issues. *Lingua*, 1973, *32*, 1–45.

Curtiss, S. *Genie: A study of a modern-day "wild child."* New York: Academic Press, 1977.

Dale, P. S. *Language development* (2nd ed.). New York: Holt, Rinehart & Winston, 1976.

DePaulo, B., & Bonvillian, J. D. The effect on language development of the special characteristics of speech addressed to children. *Unpublished paper, Harvard University, 1975*.

de Villiers, J. G. The process of rule learning in children: A new look. In K. E. Nelson (Ed.), *Children's language* (Vol. 2). New York: Gardner Press, 1980.

de Villiers, J. G., & de Villiers, P. A. A cross-sectional study of the acquisition of grammatical morphemes in child speech. *Journal of Psycholinguistic Research*, 1973, *2*, 267–278. (a)

de Villiers, J. G., & de Villiers, P. A. Development of the use of word order in comprehension. *Journal of Psycholinguistic Research*, 1973, *2*, 331–341. (b)

de Villiers, J. G., & de Villiers, P. A. Competence and performance in child language: Are children really competent to judge? *Journal of Child Language*, 1974, *1*, 1–10.

de Villiers, J. G., & de Villiers, P. A. *Language acquisition*. Cambridge: Harvard University Press, 1978.

de Villiers, P. A., & de Villiers, J. G. Form and function in the development of sentence negation. *Papers and reports in child language*, 1979, *17*, 57–64. Stanford, California.

Dore, J. Holophrases, speech acts and language universals. *Journal of Child Language*, 1975, *2*, 21–40.

Dougherty, R. A grammar of coordinate conjoined structures. *Language*, 1970, *46*, 2–70.

Drach, K. M. *The language of the parent: A pilot study*. Working paper No. 14. Berkeley: University of California, 1969.

Erreich, A., Valian, V., & Winzemer, J. Aspects of a theory of language acquisition. *Journal of Child Language*, 1980, *7*, 157–187.

Ervin, S. M. Imitation and structural change in children's language. In E. H. Lenneberg (Ed.), *New directions in the study of language*. Cambridge: MIT Press, 1964.

Ervin-Tripp, S. An overview of theories of grammatical development. In D. Slobin (Ed.), *The ontogenesis of grammar*. New York: Academic Press, 1971.

Ervin-Tripp, S., & Kluwin, T. *The development of the pronoun system in English-speaking children*. Article in preparation.

Fabian-Krauss, V., & Ammon, P. Assessing linguistic competence: When are children hard to understand? *Journal of Child Language*, 1980, *7*, 401–415.

Fay, D. Reply to Kuczaj (1976). *Journal of Child Language*, 1978, *5*, 143–149.

Feldman, C. *The effects of various types of adult responses in the syntactic acquisition of two to three-year olds*. Unpublished paper, University of Chicago, 1971.

Ferguson, C. A. Baby talk in six languages. *American Anthropologist*, 1964, *66*, 103–114.

Ferguson, C. A. Baby talk as a simplified register. In C. E. Snow & C. A. Ferguson (Eds.), *Talking to children: Language input and acquisition*. Cambridge: At the University Press, 1977.

Ferguson, C. A., & Slobin, D. I. (Eds.). *Studies of*

child language development. New York: Holt, Rinehart & Winston, 1973.

Fillmore, C. J. The case for case. In E. Bach & R. T. Harms (Eds.), *Universals in linguistic theory*. New York: Holt, Rinehart & Winston, 1968.

Fillmore, C. J. Types of lexical information. In D. D. Steinberg & L. A. Jakobovits (Eds.), *Semantics: An interdisciplinary reader in philosophy, linguistics and psychology*. Cambridge: At the University Press, 1971.

Flavell, J. H. Personal communication, 1981.

Fodor, J. A., Bever, T. G., & Garrett, M. F. *The psychology of language*. New York: McGraw-Hill, 1974.

Fodor, J. A., & Garrett, M. F. Some reflections on competence and performance. In J. Lyons & R. J. Wales (Eds.), *Psycholinguistic papers: The proceedings of the 1966 Edinburgh Conference*. Edinburgh: Edinburgh University Press, 1966.

Ford, M., Bresnan, J., & Kaplan, R. A competence-based theory of syntactic closure. In J. Bresnan (Ed.), *The mental representation of grammatical relations*. Cambridge: MIT Press, in press.

Fraser, C., Bellugi, U., Brown, R. Control of grammar in imitation, comprehension, and production. *Journal of Verbal Learning and Verbal Behavior*, 1963, *2*, 121–135.

Garcia, J., & Revusky, S. Learned associations over long delays. In G. Bower (Ed.), *The psychology of learning and motivation: Advances in research and theory*. New York: Academic Press, 1970.

Gardner, B. T., & Gardner, R. A. Two comparative psychologists look at language acquisition. In K. E. Nelson (Ed.), *Children's language* (Vol. 2). New York: Gardner Press, 1980.

Gazdar, G. Phrase structure grammar. In P. Jacobson & G. K. Pullum (Eds.), *The nature of syntactic representation*. Cambridge: At the University Press, in press.

Gentner, D. Why nouns are learned before verbs: Linguistic relativity vs. natural partitioning. In S. A. Kuczaj II (Ed.), *Language development: Syntax and semantics*. Hillsdale, N.J.: Erlbaum, 1982.

Gleason, H. A. *An introduction to descriptive linguistics* (Rev. ed.). New York: Holt, Rinehart & Winston, 1961.

Gleitman, L. R., Gleitman, H., & Shipley, E. F. The emergence of the child as a grammarian. *Cognition*, 1972, *1*: 137–164.

Gold, E. Language identification in the limit. *Information and Control*, 1967, *16*, 447–474.

Goldin-Meadow, S. Structure in a manual commu-nication system developed without a language model: Language without a helping hand. In A. Whittaker & H. A. Whittaker (Eds.), *Studies in neurolinguistics* (Vol. 4). New York: Academic Press, 1979.

Goldin-Meadow, S., & Feldman, H. The creation of a communication system: A study of deaf children of hearing parents. Paper presented at the meeting of the Society for Research in Child Development, Denver, April 1975.

Goldin-Meadow, S., & Feldman, H. The development of language-like communication without a language model. *Science*, 1977, *197*, 401–403.

Gonzales, J. L. The effects of maternal stimulation on early language development of Mexican-American children. *Diss. Abstr.*, 1973, 33(7-A): 3436.

Gregory, Bishop of Tours. History of the Franks. Original date, 597. New York: Penguin books, 1975. Translated by E. Brehaut.

Grimshaw, J. Form, function, and the language acquisition device. In C. L. Baker & J. McCarthy (Eds.), *The logical problem of language acquisition*. Cambridge: MIT Press, in press.

Gvozdev, A. N. *Formirovaniye u rebenka grammaticheskogo stroya*. Moscow: Akad. Pedag. Navk RSFSR, 1949.

Hafitz, J., Gartner, B., & Bloom, L. Giving complements when you're two: The acquisition of complement structures in child language. Paper presented at the Boston University Conference on Language Development, Boston, July 1980.

Hakes, D., Evans, J., & Turner, W. *The development of psycholinguistic abilities in children*. New York: Springer-Verlag, 1981.

Hakuta, K. A case study of a Japanese child learning English. *Language Learning*, 1976, *26*, 321–351.

Hakuta, K. Word order and particles in the acquisition of Japanese. In *Papers and Reports on Child Language Development; No. 13*. Stanford: Department of Linguistics, 1977, 110–117.

Hamburger, H., & Wexler, K. A mathematical theory of learning transformation grammar. *Journal of Mathematical Psychology*, 1975, *12*, 137–177.

Harris, Z. S. *Methods in structural linguistics*. Chicago: University of Chicago Press, 1951.

Hood, L. Experimental competence in imitation compared to naturalistic production. Unpublished paper, 1977.

Horgan, D. How to answer questions when you've got nothing to say. *Journal of Child Language*, 1978, *5*, 159–166. (a)

Horgan, D. The development of the full passive. *Journal of Child Language*, 1978, *5*, 65–80 (b).

Horgan, D. *Nouns: Love 'em or leave 'em*. Unpublished manuscript, Illinois State University, 1979.

Hurford, J. R. A child and the English question formation rule. *Journal of Child Language*, 1975, *2*, 299–301.

Ingram, D. *Early patterns of grammatical development*. Paper presented at the conference "Language Behavior in Infancy and Early Childhood," October 13–19, 1979, Santa Barbara, California.

Ingram, D., & Tyack, C. Inversion of subject NP and aux in children's questions. *Journal of Psycholinguistic Research*, 1979, *8*, 333–341.

Jackendoff, R. S. *Semantic interpretation in generative grammar*. Cambridge: MIT Press, 1972.

Jackendoff, R. S. Morphological and semantic regularities in the lexicon. *Language*, 1975, *51*, 639–671.

Jackendoff, R. S. Toward an explanatory semantic representation. *Linguistic Inquiry*, 1976, 89–150.

Jacobs, R. A., & Rosenbaum, P. S. *English transformational grammar*. Waltham, Mass: Ginn, 1968.

Kaplan, R. Augmented transition networks as psychological models of sentence comprehension. *Artificial Intelligence*, 1972, *3*, 77–100.

Kaplan, R. On process models for sentence analysis. In D. A. Norman & D. E. Rumelhart (Eds.), *Explorations in cognition*. San Francisco: W. H. Freeman, 1975.

Kaplan, R., & Bresnan, J. A formal system for grammatical representation. In J. Bresnan (Ed.), *The mental representation of grammatical relations*. Cambridge: MIT Press, in press.

Karmiloff-Smith, A. *A functional approach to child language*. Cambridge: At the University Press, 1979.

Katz, J. J., & Fodor, J. A. The structure of a semantic theory. *Language*, 1963, *39*, 170–210.

Katz, N., Baker, E., MacNamara, J. What's in a name: A study of how children learn common and proper names. *Child Development*, 1974, *45*, 469–473.

Kernan, K. T. Semantic relationships and the child's acquisition of language. *Anthropological Linguist*, 1970, *12*, 171–187.

Kessel, F. S. The role of syntax in children's comprehension from ages six to twelve. *Monographs of the Society for Research in Child Development*, 1970, *35*(Serial No. 139).

Kiss, G. Grammatical word classes: A learning model and its simulation. In G. H. Bower (Ed.), *The psychology of learning and motivation: Advances in research and theory* (Vol. 7). New York: Academic Press, 1973.

Klima, E. S., & Bellugi, U. Syntactic regularities in the speech of children. In J. Lyons & R. J. Wales (Eds.), *Psycholinguistic papers: The proceedings of the 1966 Edinburgh conference*. Edinburgh: Edinburgh University Press, 1966.

Klima, E. S. Negation in English. In J. A. Fodor & J. J. Katz (Eds.), *The structure of language*. Englewood Cliffs, N.J.: Prentice-Hall, 1964.

Knapp, D. *Information-processing constraints and children's acquisition of auxiliary verbs in interrogatives*. Unpublished doctoral dissertation, University of California at San Diego, 1979.

Kuczaj, S. A., II. Arguments against Hurford's 'aux copying rule.' *Journal of Child Language*, 1976, *3*, 423–427. (a)

Kuczaj, S. A., II. *The development of the auxiliary system in children*. Unpublished manuscript, 1976. (b)

Kuczaj, S. A., II. The acquisition of regular and irregular past tense forms. *Journal of Verbal Learning and Verbal Behavior*, 1977, *16*, 589–600. (a)

Kuczaj, S. A., II. *Old and new forms, old and new meanings: The form-function hypothesis revisited*. Paper presented at the meeting of the Society for Research in Child Development, New Orleans, March, 1977. (b)

Kuczaj, S. A., II. Children's judgments of grammatical and ungrammatical irregular past tense verbs. *Child Development*, 1978, *49*, 319–326. (a)

Kuczaj, S. A., II. Why do children fail to overgeneralize the progressive inflection? *Journal of Child Language*, 1978, *5*, 167–171. (b)

Kuczaj, S. A., II. Evidence for a language learning strategy. On the relative ease of acquisition of prefixes and suffixes. *Child Development*, 1979, *50*, 1–13.

Kuczaj, S. A., II, & Maratsos, M. P. What children can say before they will. *Merrill-Palmer Quarterly*, 1975, *21*, 89–111.

Labov, W., & Labov, T. Learning the syntax of questions. In R. Campbell & P. T. Smith (Eds.), *Recent advances in the psychology of language*. New York: Plenum, 1978.

Lakoff, G. Stative adjectives and verbs in English. In *Harvard Computational Laboratory Report NSF 17*, 1966.

Lakoff, G. On generative semantics. In D. D. Steinberg & L. A. Jakobovits (Eds.), *Semantics: An interdisciplinary reader in philosophy, linguistics and psychology*. London: Cambridge University Press, 1971.

Lakoff, G., & Thompson, H. Introducing cognitive grammar. In C. Cogen, H. Thompson, G. Thurgood, K. Whistler, & J. Wright (Eds.), *Proceedings of the 2nd annual meeting of the Berkeley Linguistic Society*. Berkeley, Calif., 1975.

Lakoff, G., & Ross, J. R. Is deep structure necessary? Indiana University Linguistics Club, 1968.

Lange, S., & Larsson, K. Syntactical development of a Swedish girl Embla, between 20 and 42 months of age, I: Age 20–25 months. *Report no. 1, Project child language syntax, Institutionem for nordiska sprak*, Stockholm Universitet, 1973.

Lee, L. *Northwestern Syntax Screening Test*. Evanston, Ill.: Northwestern University Press, 1969.

Lees, R. Formal discussion: The acquisition of syntax. In U. Bellugi & R. Brown (Eds.), The acquisition of language. Monographs of the Society for Research in Child Development: #92, 1964, 29(1), 92–98.

Leonard, L. B., & Kaplan, L. A note on imitation and lexical acquisition. *Journal of Child Language*, 1976, *3*, 449–455.

Levy, Y. It's frogs all the way down. *Cognition*, in press, a.

Levy, Y. The acquisition of Hebrew plurals—the case of the missing gender category. *Journal of Child Language*, in press, b.

Lieberman, P. *On the origins of language*. New York: Macmillan, 1975.

Lieven, E. V. M. Different registers in speech to children. *Proceedings of the 1978 Child Language Research Forum* at Stanford University. Stanford Committee on Linguistics, 1978. (a)

Lieven, E. V. M. Turn-taking and pragmatics: Two issues in early child language. In R. N. Campbell & P. T. Smith (Eds.), *Recent advances in the psychology of language*. New York: Plenum, 1978. (b)

Limber, J. The genesis of complex sentences. In T. E. Moore (Ed.), *Cognition and the acquisition of language*. New York: Academic Press, 1973.

Lord, C. *Language acquisition and the linguistic environment*. Unpublished doctoral dissertation, Harvard University, 1976.

Lust, B. Conjunction reduction in child language. *Journal of Child Language*, 1977, *4*, 257–288.

Lyons, J. *Introduction to theoretical linguistics*. London: Cambridge University Press, 1968.

MacNamara, J. Cognitive basis of language learning in infants. *Psychological Review*, 1972, *79*, 1–13.

MacNamara, J. From sign to language. In J. MacNamara (Ed.), *Language learning and thought*. New York: Academic Press, 1977.

MacWhinney, B. Rules, rote and analogy in morphological formations by Hungarian children. *Journal of Child Language*, 1975, *2*, 65–77.

MacWhinney, B. Hungarian research on the acquisition of morphology and syntax. *Journal of Child Language*, 1976, *3*, 377–410.

MacWhinney, B. The acquisition of morphophonology. *Monographs of the Society for Research in Child Development*, 1978, *43*(1–2, Serial No. 174).

Maling, J., & Zahnen, A. A base-generated account of "extraction phenomena" in Scandinavian languages. In P. Jacobson & G. K. Pullum (Eds.), *The nature of syntactic representation*. Cambridge: At the University Press, in press.

Maratsos, M. P. *The use of definite and indefinite reference in young children*. London: Cambridge University Press, 1976.

Maratsos, M. P. New models in linguistics and language acquisition. In M. Halle, J. Bresnan, & G. A. Miller (Eds.), *Linguistic theory and psychological reality*. Cambridge: MIT Press, 1978.

Maratsos, M. P. How to get from words to sentences. In D. Aaronson & R. J. Rieber (Eds.), *Psycholinguistic research: Implications and applications*. Hillsdale, N.J.: Erlbaum, 1979.

Maratsos, M. P. Problems in categorical evolution: Can formal categories arise from semantic ones? In W. Deutsch (Ed.), *The child's construction of language*. London: Academic Press, 1981.

Maratsos, M. P. The child's construction of grammatical categories. In L. Gleitman & H. E. Wanner (Eds.), *Language acquisition: The state of the art*. Cambridge: At the University Press, 1982.

Maratsos, M. P. & Abramovitch, R. How children understand full, truncated, and anomalous passives. *Journal of Verbal Learning and Verbal Behavior*, 1975, *14*, 145–157.

Maratsos, M. P., & Chalkley, M. A. The internal language of children's syntax: The ontogenesis and representation of syntactic categories. In K. E. Nelson (Ed.), *Children's language* (Vol. 2). New York: Gardner Press, 1980.

Maratsos, M. P., Fox, D. E. C., Becker, J., & Chalkley, M. A. *Semantic restrictions on children's early passives*. Article in preparation.

Maratsos, M. P., & Kuczaj, S. A., II. Against the transformationalist hypothesis: A simpler account of redundant tense markings. *Journal of Child Language,* 1978, *5,* 337–346.

Maratsos, M. P., & Kuczaj, S. A., II. Patterns of overregularizations in children's speech. Paper presented at the Meeting of the Society for Research in Child Development, San Francisco, March 1979.

Maratsos, M. P., Kuczaj, S. A., II, Fox, D. E. C., & Chalkley, M. A. Some empirical studies in the acquisition of transformational relations. In W. A. Collins (Ed.), *Minnesota Symposia on Child Psychology* (Vol. 12). Hillsdale, N.J.: Erlbaum, 1979.

McCawley, J. D. Semantic representation. In P. L. Garvin (Ed.), *Cognition: A multiple view.* New York: Spartan Books, 1970.

McCawley, J. D. Where do noun phrases come from? In D. D. Steinberg & L. A. Jakobovits (Eds.), *Semantics: An interdisciplinary reader in philosophy, linguistics and psychology.* Cambridge: At the University Press, 1971.

McNeill, D. Developmental psycholinguistics. In F. Smith & G. A. Miller (Eds.), *The genesis of language: A psycholinguistic approach.* Cambridge: MIT Press, 1966.

McNeill, D. *The acquisition of language: The study of developmental psycholinguistics.* New York: Harper & Row, 1970.

Menyuk, P. *Sentences children use.* Cambridge: MIT Press, 1969.

Mikés, M. Acquisition des categories grammaticales dans le langage de l'enfant. *Enfance,* 1967, *20,* 289–298.

Miller, G. A. Some psychological studies of grammar. *American Psychologist,* 1962, *17,* 748–762.

Miller, N., & Dollard, J. *Social learning and imitation.* New Haven, Conn.: Yale University Press, 1941.

Miller, W., & Ervin, S. M. The development of grammar in child language. In U. Bellugi & R. Brown (Eds.), *The acquisition of language. Monographs of the Society for Research in Child Development,* 1964, *29,* Serial No. 92.

Mills, A. The acquisition of German. D. I. Slobin (Ed.), *Cross-linguistic studies in language acquisition.* Hillsdale, N.J.: Erlbaum, in press.

Moerk, E. Principles of interaction in language learning. *Merrill-Palmer Quarterly,* 1972, *18,* 229–257.

Moerk, E. L. Relationship between parental input frequencies and children's language acquisition: A reanalysis of Brown's data. *Journal of Child Language,* 1980, *7,* 105–118.

Monahan, K. P. Grammatical relations and clause structure in Malayalam. In J. Bresnan (Ed.), *The mental representation of grammatical relations.* Cambridge: MIT Press, in press.

Nelson, K. Structure and strategy in learning to talk. *Monographs of the Society for Research in Child Development,* 1973, *38* (1–2, Serial No. 149).

Nelson, K. Individual differences in early semantic and syntax development. In D. Aaronson & R. J. Rieber (Eds.), *Developmental psycholinguistics and communication disorders. Annals of the New York Academy of Sciences,* 1975. (Special Issue)

Nelson, K. E., Carskaddon, G., & Bonvillian, J. D. Syntax acquisition: Impact of experimental variation in adult verbal interaction with the child. *Child Development,* 1973, *44,* 497–504.

Newport, E. L. Motherese: The speech of mothers to young children. In J. J. Castellan, D. B. Pisoni, & G. R. Potts (Eds.), *Cognitive theory* (Vol. 3). Hillsdale, N.J.: Erlbaum, 1976.

Newport, E. L. Constraints on structure: Evidence from American sign language and language learning. W. A. Collins (Ed.), *Minnesota Symposia on Child Psychology* (Vol. 14). Hillsdale, N.J.: Erlbaum, 1980.

Newport, E. H., Gleitman, H., & Gleitman, L. R. Mother, I'd rather do it myself: Some effects and non-effects of maternal speech style. In C. E. Snow & C. A. Ferguson (Eds.), *Talking to children: Language input and acquisition.* Cambridge: At the University Press, 1977.

Newport, E. L., Gleitman, L. R., & Gleitman, H. *A study of mothers' speech and child language acquisition.* Paper presented at the 7th Child Language Research Forum, Stanford University, Stanford, Calif., September 1975.

Nisbett, R., & Ross, L. *Human inference: Strategies and shortcomings of social judgment.* Englewood Cliffs, N.J.: Prentice-Hall, 1980.

Oliver, D. A stochastic mechanism for inducing form classes. Unpublished manuscript, Harvard University, 1968.

Osgood, C., & Bock, K. Salience and sentencing: Some production principles. In S. Rosenberg (Ed.), *Sentence production: Developments in research and theory.* Hillsdale, N.J.: Erlbaum, 1977.

Park, T. A. The acquisition of German syntax. Unpublished paper. University of Berne, Psychological Institute, 1970.

Park, T. A. Plurals in child speech. *Journal of Child Language,* 1978, *5,* 237–250.

Patterson, F. G. Innovative uses of language by a gorilla: A case study. In K. E. Nelson (Ed.), *Children's language* (Vol. 2). New York: Gardner Press, 1980.

Perlmutter, D., & Postal, P. Toward a universal characterization of passivization. In *Proceedings of the 3rd annual meeting of the Berkeley Linguistics Society*. Berkeley, Calif.: Department of linguistics, 1977.

Phillips, J. R. Syntax and vocabulary of mothers' speech to young children: Age and sex comparisons. *Child Development*, 1973, *44*, 182–185.

Pinker, S. Formal models of language learning. *Cognition*, 1979, *7*, 112–173.

Pinker, S. A theory of the acquisition of lexical-interpretive grammars. In J. Bresnan (Ed.), *The mental representation of grammatical relations*. Cambridge: MIT Press, in press.

Popova, M. I. Grammatichiskiye elementy yazyka v rechi detey preddoshkol'nogo voz rasta Voprosy psiklaologii. [Grammatical elements of language in the speech of pre-school children.] In C. A. Ferguson & D. I. Slobin (Eds.), *Studies of child language development*. New York: Holt, Rinehart & Winston, 1973. (Originally published, 1958.)

Postal, P. M. The surface verb 'remind.' *Linguistic Inquiry*, 1970, *1*, 37–120.

Premack, D. Language in chimpanzee? *Science*, 1971, *172*, 802–822.

Prideaux, G. D. A functional analysis of English question acquisition: A response to Hurford. *Journal of Child Language*, 1976, *3*, 417–422.

Ramer, A. L. H. Styles in emerging syntax. *Journal of Child Language*, 1976, *3*, 49–62.

Reichenbach, H. *Elements of symbolic logic*. New York: The Free Press, 1948.

Rogdon, M. *Single-word usage, cognitive development, and the beginnings of combinatorial speech: A study of ten English-speaking children*. Cambridge: At the University Press, 1976.

Rosenbaum, P. *The grammar of English predicate complement constructions*. Cambridge: MIT Press, 1967.

Ross, J. R. Class lectures, 1969.

Ross, J. R. *Constraints on variables in syntax*. Unpublished doctoral dissertation, MIT, 1967.

Sachs, J., & Devlin, J. Young children's use of age-appropriate speech styles in social interaction and role-playing. *Journal of Child Language*, 1976, *3*, 81–98.

Savage-Rumbaugh, E. S., & Rumbaugh, D. Language analogue project I phase II: Theory and tactics. In K. E. Nelson (Ed.), *Children's language* (Vol. 2). New York: Gardner Press, 1980.

Savin, H., & Perchonok, E. Grammatical structure and the immediate recall of English sentences. *Journal of Verbal Learning and Verbal Behavior*, 1965, *4*, 348–353.

Schieffelin, B. *How Kaluli children learn what to say, what to do, and how to feel*. Cambridge: At the University Press, in press.

Schieffelin, B., & Eisenberg, A. Cultural variation in dialogue. In R. L. Schiefelbusch (Ed.), *Communicative competence: Acquisition and intervention*. Baltimore: University Park Press, in press.

Schlesinger, I. M. Production of utterances and language acquisition. In D. I. Slobin (Ed.), *The ontogenesis of grammar*. New York: Academic Press, 1971.

Schlesinger, I. M. Relational concepts underlying language. In R. L. Schiefelbusch & L. L. Lloyd (Eds.), *Language perspectives—Acquisition, retardation, and intervention*. Baltimore: University Park Press, 1974.

Schlesinger, I. M. The role of cognitive development and linguistic input in linguistic development. *Journal of Child Language*, 1977, *4*, 1–35.

Schlesinger, I. M. Semantic assimilation in the development of relational categories. In W. Deutsch (Ed.), *The child's construction of language*. London: Academic Press, 1981.

Shatz, M., & Gelman, R. The development of communication skills: Modifications in the speech of young children as a function of listener. *Monographs of the Society for Research in Child Development*, 1973, *38*(5, Serial No. 152).

Shipley, E. F., Smith, C. S., & Gleitman, L. R. A study in the acquisition of language: Free responses to commands. *Language*, 1969, *45*, 322–342.

Sinclair, H. Sensorimotor action patterns as a condition for the acquisition of syntax. In R. Huxley & E. Ingram (Eds.), *Language acquisition: Models and methods*. New York: Academic Press, 1971.

Sinclair, H. Language acquisition and cognitive development. In T. E. Moore (Ed.), *Cognitive development and the acquisition of language*. New York: Academic Press, 1973.

Slobin, D. I. Comments on "developmental psycholinguistics," by D. McNeill. In G. A. Miller & F. Smith (Eds.), *The genesis of language*. Cambridge: MIT Press, 1966.

Slobin, D. I. On the learning of morphological rules: A reply to Palermo and Eberhart. In D. I. Slobin (Ed.), *The ontogenesis of grammar*. New York: Academic Press, 1971.

Slobin, D. I. Cognitive prerequisites for the development of grammar. In C. A. Ferguson & D. I. Slobin (Eds.), *Studies of child language development*. New York: Holt, Rinehart & Winston, 1973.

Slobin, D. I. Personal communication, 1975.

Slobin, D. I. The origin of grammatical encoding of events. In W. Deutsch (Ed.), *The child's construction of language*. New York: Academic Press, 1981.

Slobin, D. I. Universal and particular in the acquisition of language. In L. R. Gleitman & H. E. Wanner (Eds.), *Language acquisition: The state of the art*. Cambridge: At the University Press, 1982.

Slobin, D. I., & Welch, C. A. Elicited imitation as a research tool in developmental psycholinguistics. In C. A. Ferguson & D. I. Slobin (Eds.), *Studies of child language development*. New York: Holt, Rinehart & Winston, 1973.

Smith, C. S. Determiners and relative clauses in generative grammar of English. *Language*, 1964, *40*, 37–52.

Smith, C. S. An experimental approach to children's linguistic competence. In J. R. Hayes (Ed.), *Cognition and the development of language*. New York: Wiley, 1970.

Smoczynska, M. The acquisition of Polish. In D. I. Slobin (Ed.), *Cross-linguistic studies in language acquisition*. Hillsdale, N.J.: Erlbaum, in press.

Snow, C. E. Mother's speech to children learning language. *Child Development*, 1972, *43*, 549–565.

Snow, C. E. *Mother's speech research: An overview*. Paper presented at the S.S.R.C. Conference on Language Input and Acquisition, Boston, July 1974.

Snow, C. E. Parent-child interaction and the development of communicative ability. In R. L. Schiefelbusch (Ed.), *Communicative competence: Acquisition and intervention*. Baltimore: University Park Press, in press.

Sorensen, J., Cooper, W., & Paccia, J. Speech timing of grammatical categories. *Cognition*, 1978, 135–153.

Strohner, J., & Nelson, K. E. The young child's development of sentence comprehension: Influence of event probability, nonverbal context, syntactic form, and strategies. *Child Development*, 1974, *45*, 564–576.

Tager-Flusberg, H., de Villiers, J. G., & Hakuta, K. The development of sentence coordination. In S. A. Kuczaj II (Ed.), *Language development*, vol. I: *Syntax and semantics*. Hillsdale, N.J.: Erlbaum, 1982.

Terrace, H. S., Petitto, L. A., Sanders, R. J., & Bever, T. G. On the grammatical capacity of apes. In K. E. Nelson (Ed.), *Children's language* (Vol. 2). New York: Gardner Press, 1980.

Thompson, J. Relative clauses and conjunctions. *The Ohio State University Working Papers in Linguistics*, 1968, *1*, 80–99.

Tolbert, K. *A study of the acquisition of grammatical morphemes in Spanish and Mayan Cachiquel*. Unpublished doctoral dissertation, Harvard University, 1978.

Valian, V., Caplan, J., & de Sciora, A. M. M. *Children's use of abstract linguistic knowledge in an everyday speech situation*. Paper presented at the First Annual Boston University Conference on Language Development, July 1976.

Walter, S. *Zur Entwicklung Morphologischer Strukturen bei Kinder*. Heidelberg: Diplomarbeit, 1975.

Wanner, H. E., & Maratsos, M. P. An ATN approach to comprehension. In M. Halle, J. Bresnan, & G. Miller (Eds.), *Linguistic theory and psychological reality*. Cambridge: MIT Press, 1978.

Watt, W. C. On two hypotheses concerning psycholinguistics. In J. R. Hayes (Ed.), *Cognition and the development of language*. New York: Wiley, 1970.

Wells, G. Learning to code experience through language. *Journal of Child Language*, 1974, *1*, 243–249.

Wells, G. Apprenticeship in meaning. In K. Nelson (Ed.), *Children's Language* (Vol. 2). New York: Gardner Press, 1980.

Wexler, K. A principle theory for language acquisition. In L. Gleitman & H. E. Wanner (Eds.), *Language acquisition: The state of the art*. Cambridge: At the University Press, 1982.

Woods, W. Transition network grammars for natural language analysis. *Communications of the ACM*, 1970, *3*, 591–606.

Yourcenar, M. *Memoirs of Hadrian*. Translated from the French by G. Frick. New York: Farrar, Strauss, and Giroux, 1963.

Zakharova, A. V. Acquisition of forms of grammatical case by preschool children. In C. A. Ferguson & D. I. Slobin (Eds.), *Studies of child language development*. New York: Holt, Rinehart & Winston, 1973.

Zakharova, A. V., Usvoyeniye doshKol 'niKami padeshnykh form. [Acquisition of forms of grammatical case by preschool children.] In C. A. Ferguson & D. I. Slobin (Eds.), *Studies of child language development*. New York: Holt, Rinehart & Winston, 1973. (Originally published, 1958.)

MEANINGS AND CONCEPTS* | 12

EVE V. CLARK, *Stanford University*

CHAPTER CONTENTS

Meanings—that is, word, phrase, and sentence meanings—and concepts are as different as apples and oranges. Although they are often discussed as if

*This chapter was begun while I was a Fellow at the Center for Advanced Study in the Behavioral Sciences, Stanford, 1979–1980. Its preparation was supported in part by CASBS, the Spencer Foundation, and the National Science Foundation (BNS80–07349). I am grateful to the many students and colleagues who have influenced my thinking about meanings and concepts over the last few years: their discussions, comments, and criticisms have caused me to rethink my position on many occasions on many issues. Some of these changes will be apparent in this chapter. I am particularly indebted to Herbert H. Clark, John H. Flavell, and Ellen M. Markman for their invaluable contributions to the content and form of many of the arguments put forward here.

they were equivalents, the distinctions between them are crucial—not only in talking about development but also in considering the relation between language and thought. Let me begin with two commonplace illustrations of their differences, and then present by way of a metaphor the approach I will take in discussing them.

Meanings and concepts can best be distinguished when we compare the single words available for describing objects, situations, and states in different languages. My first illustration of this is verbs for putting on clothes in English and Japanese. English speakers essentially content themselves with one verb, *to put on*, and use it for talking about a whole range of different actions of putting on: for hats, scarves, shirts, dresses, pants, socks, rings, glasses, and other less clothinglike accessories. Despite the paucity of linguistic devices, we all know the different actions required for different pieces of clothing. For example, we can easily interpret mimed actions for dressing. Our conceptual knowledge about this domain, then, is much more diverse and elaborate than the terms we have for talking about it. Japanese speakers, in contrast, have a much more elaborated vocabulary for talking about putting things on and commonly use at least four contrasting verbs: *kaburu* for actions of covering the head (e.g., with a scarf or even nongarments), *kiru* for garments on the upper body (shirts, coats, dresses, etc.), *haku* for garments on the lower body (pants, shorts, socks), and *hameru* (the most general verb) for accessories and various small items (e.g., rings, gloves). One can also use additional verbs for some specific items: *kakeru* (to hang) for putting on glasses, *tsukeru* (to attach) for putting on a badge, *maku* (put around) for putting on a (neck) scarf, or *noseru* for putting one thing on top of another, and so on (Backhouse, 1981). Japanese goes further in the direction of supplying separate word meanings for concepts, but the conceptual categories are still more diverse than the terms available. For instance, we are all aware of the differences of action in putting on a shirt compared to putting on a sweater, yet Japanese speakers use *kiru* for both.

For my second illustration, let's take basic color terms in English and Dani, a language spoken in Papua New Guinea. English has some 11 basic color terms: *black, white, red, blue, green, brown, yellow, orange, purple, pink,* and *grey.* Dani, in contrast, has only two: *mili* (black) and *mola* (white), which divide up the spectrum by grouping dark, warm colors versus light, cold ones. However, Dani speakers appear to organize colors in memory and use colors in matching tasks in just the same way as English speakers: the concepts appear to be much the same, even though the terms available for talking about them differ in the two languages (Berlin & Kay, 1969; Heider & Olivier, 1972).

The meanings of single words in a language, then, make reference to only part of our conceptual knowledge. And the word meanings available are always fewer than the concepts they are used to talk about. As speakers, we have to make do with the words we have and those depend largely on which language we speak.[1]

The speaker of a language is something like a marine biologist. The trained biologist knows an enormous amount about the different species living in the oceans—what they look like, what their life cycles are, what they feed on, how they reproduce, where their preferred habitats are, and so on. The marine biologist is also skilled at devising ways to find particular species on demand, constructing devices of all kinds to fish with: nets of different sizes and shapes that are trawled or drawn over the bottom, lines with different bait, hooks, flies in profusion—each device designed to fish up a particular species. The contents of the seas and oceans are analogous to the conceptual contents of our minds. And the array of nets, hooks, and other devices for catching specific species is analogous to the repertoire of word meanings available in a language. As children, we learn which devices—which words—pick out, catch, hook which concepts and can thus be used to convey the concepts we are thinking about.[2]

But the ocean with all its inhabitants is vast, and the set of fishing devices available to the marine biologist does not begin to cover the whole domain. In some areas, the biologist may have devised more ways of capturing sea life than in others and can therefore be more certain of bringing up a certain kind of fish. In other parts of the ocean where currents make fishing harder, the biologist may have to be content with a net that pulls in several kinds at once, thus not distinguishing directly among them. And marine biologists specializing in corals versus dolphins versus sole versus herring may also differ in how specific their fishing devices are for each domain. Analogously, words in some domains are finely graded to pick out closely related conceptual categories and keep them distinct. In other domains, there are fewer words available and so fewer distinctions made within the language. Languages vary considerably in which lexical domains are elaborated and which are not (Clark & Clark, 1978) and so do speakers: experts on a domain have more words for the categories in it than the person on the street, even though both are speakers of the same language.

Three questions fundamental to the development of concepts and meanings provide the foci of this chapter: What concepts do children acquire first? How do they relate their concepts to words? How do they find out which concepts there are words for? I will look first at the concepts children acquire during their first 2 years or so, with emphasis on the kinds of concepts they *must* acquire, given that all languages offer ways of talking about objects, situations, and states. Then I will take up the nature of the conventional relations between concept and word meaning, the relations among different word meanings, and whether word meanings themselves can be decomposed into smaller elements that pick out parts of conceptual categories or are better considered simply as ''names'' for the categories they pick out. These issues, together with the question of how children decide which concepts there are likely to be words for and which not, pervade the second half of the chapter.

There are other questions of universality in the acquisition of word meaning. What is the significance of universal versus individual patterns of development? Do all children go through the same stages in acquiring a word? Is the sequence of such stages an invariant one? Do children all follow the same route—a universal course of acquisition? Or are there alternative routes to the goal of acquiring adult meanings? Can one chart what is universal or highly general across children both within a particular language group and across different language groups in the ways they acquire early meanings? Are universals of language acquisition a reflection of cognitive constraints on how children relate their conceptual categories to the word meanings available? Some universals in acquisition patterns presumably reflect processing constraints imposed by such factors as memory, attention, and the ability to retrieve pertinent information (Clark & Clark, 1977, 1978). They may also reflect cognitive pacesetters, such that children will initially only look for words to convey familiar concepts. Concept acquisition would then set the pace for children acquiring particular word meanings (e.g., Johnston & Slobin, 1978; Slobin, in press).[3] The amount of individual variation in the acquisition of concepts and of meanings has been given much less attention. There could be many different entry points for acquiring vocabulary once children start to relate concepts to words. Where they start could provide an index of possible individual variations. However, there is surprising uniformity in early vocabularies (E. V. Clark, 1977a, 1979; Nelson, 1973b). Many of these questions, though, will only be touched on tangentially in this chapter.

This chapter is planned as follows. In the first section, I shall consider what concepts are and take up concepts young children must acquire, given the words available in a particular language. In doing this, I will draw on whatever evidence I have been able to find about the kinds of concepts acquired in the first two years. In the second section, I shall present a general account of the characteristics of early word meanings, noting the parallels between concepts and meanings. I shall then consider what happens to those early meanings as children acquire more vocabulary and show that the available data render current theories of meaning acquisition inadequate.

In the next part of the chapter, I shall propose a new view of children's acquisition of word meanings—lexical contrast theory—and show how it an-

swers a number of questions left by other theories and also fills in for many of their shortcomings. Then I shall show how the theory of lexical contrast can be extended—unlike previous theories—to account for two other ways in which children (and adults) commonly expand their vocabulary, through word coinages and figurative uses. I will end with a brief summary of what is now known about meanings and concepts and what may be some important gaps to fill in the next decade.

EARLY CONCEPTUAL DEVELOPMENT

What kinds of concepts do young children need? Which do they acquire during their first 2 or 3 years? One approach to these questions is to consider the kinds of concepts needed to use any language appropriately. In fact, becoming a member of the language community represents a major goal of conceptual development—the goal of attaining the concepts conventionally conveyed by the linguistic means available in a particular language. But first we need to agree on what a concept is.

Concepts and Categories

I shall use the term *concept* to designate a set of properties that are associated with each other in memory and thus form a unit. The properties can be of any type, transitory or permanent, concrete or abstract, perceptual or functional, combined in all sorts of ways. Concepts can be concepts of *individuals*—sets of properties associated with a particular person (Uncle Ian), object (the Speedwell), or event (the Boston tea party)—or concepts of *kinds*—a group of individuals of similar nature, sharing certain properties in common. Some examples of kinds are tigers, marathons, lemons, and oaks (see S. P. Schwartz, 1977) or chairs, bicycles, and books. In considering early conceptual development, I will be concerned with children's concepts of kinds rather than with their concepts of individuals. Concepts, then, are units of representation. They provide reference points for categorizing the world around us.

The instantiation of a concept is a category. Whether an object belongs to a particular category or not is determined, I will assume, by testing that item against the relevant concept with some rule for deciding whether or not it meets the criteria for membership. The decision rule may take any of several forms, depending in part on the nature of the concept (Smith & Medin, 1981). For example, a spoonbill might be adjudged a member of the category bird based on the degree of family resemblance holding between spoonbills and other birds (Rosch & Mervis, 1975). Or a black-edged square might be assigned to the category of black-edged objects because it meets the necessary condition for such membership.[4] Much recent research has been concerned with the nature of such rules and how people decide on category membership (e.g., Bourne, Dominowski, & Loftus, 1979).

Categorization can take place at several levels. A spaniel, for instance, is a member of the category spaniel, of the category dog, and of the category animal (among others). The level of categorization may play an important role developmentally because one level, the so-called basic level, appears privileged: categories at that level are better remembered, better recognized, and more easily named than categories at other levels (Rosch, Mervis, Gray, Johnson, & Boyes-Braem, 1976). The basic level is generally defined as the level at which the members of a category are most like each other and least like the members of neighboring categories. Take the category table as an example. Tables have a number of properties in common with each other—a family resemblance—and share relatively few properties with such neighboring categories as cupboards, sofas, or rugs. At one level lower, however, a kitchen table shares many properties in common with a dining room table or with a coffee table, both of which are members of neighboring categories. And at one level above, tables share almost no properties with such fellow members of the category furniture as cupboards, beds, bookcases, or armchairs. Are basic-level categories the first to be acquired? Perhaps, but that assumes that basic-level categories for adults are basic level ones for children, an assumption that may not always be warranted (E. V. Clark, 1978a; Mervis & Mervis, 1982).

The members of a category all share varying degrees of family resemblance with each other. Some members, though, may have more of the properties that identify them as members of that category than others. The greater the number of such properties, the more that member of the category is considered prototypical. For example, robins are regarded as much more typical birds than penguins. Robins have feathers, fly, sing, perch on branches, build nests in trees. Such properties considered all together bring robins much closer to being prototypical birds than penguins. The members of a category, then, exhibit the internal structure of the category in their relative prototypicality. So membership in a category is not delimited along a strict boundary, with objects clearly in or out. Membership is a matter of degree (Rosch & Mervis, 1975).

Categorization can also take place across differ-

ent domains, with one object being simultaneously a member of several different categories. To return to our spaniel: besides being a member of the spaniel-dog-animal hierarchy, it is also a member of the category pet, of the category hunting dog, and of the category droopy-eared, and so on. Some categories may be more accessible than others, in that they have specific linguistic expressions as labels and, hence, appear to represent a conventional classification. Other categories, such as things one can carry on one's head, may have a more ad hoc character that makes them harder to remember and name (see Barsalou, 1981).

Objects, Situations, and States

Since many categories have linguistic labels that pick them out, such categories provide a convenient starting point for any inquiry into children's concepts. Children must eventually acquire the different linguistic means for talking about these categories and so they must at some point acquire the necessary concepts. I will focus here on three major domains of categories—objects, situations, and states—and then consider the evidence for young children's developing concepts for kinds within those domains during their first 2 years.

Children must construct categories of *objects*. The domain of objects, though, is far from uniform. Consider the kinds of objects exemplified by the categories dog, piano, and tree. Each contains many members with different properties, but the members are sufficiently alike to be identified as dogs (e.g., Labradors, boxers, Chihuahuas, dachshunds); pianos (e.g., Steinways, Bechsteins, Baldwins); and trees (e.g., oaks, ashes, birches) respectively. Category members may have properties that are discrete in place and time—as do dogs, trees, or pianos—or continuous—as do members of the categories sand, flour, and water. But within both types of object category, there is much the same diversity of membership.

Children must also construct categories of *situations* (Comrie, 1976; Vendler, 1967). Situations, like objects, do not comprise a homogeneous conceptual domain. They have to be divided into at least two subtypes, *processes* (i.e., ongoing activities of limited duration) and *events* (activities that result in a change of state). And within these subparts of the domain, there are many different kinds, just as with objects.

And children must also construct categories of *states*. States include many kinds of properties, ranging from form, size, and color to function and even movement. (Many states provide the bases for membership decisions for object and situation categories.)

Given these three broad domains, can we look, for each one, at which concepts very young children develop first? Ideally, we should be able to go from each of these domains to studies of the acquisition of concepts in that domain. But because few developmentalists have put the question about what has to be acquired in quite this way, there are many gaps in the studies that have been done. Researchers have pursued the development of particular concepts regardless of their relation to later linguistic development. In taking an alternative perspective, I will necessarily be selective. My emphasis will be on the domains of objects, situations, and states and on what we can infer about children's early development of concepts within these domains.

The focus will therefore be on the outcomes of different studies, on the evidence that children do possess certain concepts that allow them to contrast some categories of objects, situations, and states early on. I will not be directly concerned with the particular mechanisms by which children form such concepts, for example, storage of single exemplars versus feature extraction, or template matching versus the construction of prototypes (Brooks, 1978; Kossan, 1981; Palmer, 1978; Smith & Medin, 1981). Some kinds of concepts, of course, may be more salient than others on just those dimensions that make concepts more accessible to acquisition. Thus the nature of the mechanism may play a basic role in what is mastered early and what is not. This issue, though, falls outside the scope of the present chapter.

Objects

Infants have access to visual information about objects from birth. Several studies suggest that they form concepts of objects by processing the available visual information. Cohen and Caputo (1978) contrasted 6-month-old infants' ability to generalize to new instances when habituated to either a single exemplar of a category (a particular face) or several exemplars (several different faces). To habituate the infants, they showed them a stimulus over and over again until their attention began to wane, and then they showed them a novel instance. The infants' renewed interest in looking, measured by an increase in sucking or in heart rate, is taken as a measure of recognition of novelty or of difference from the original stimulus. Cohen and Caputo found that only those infants habituated to several exemplars generalized (by showing continued habituation) to

novel faces. At 7½ months, infants could learn to respond to specific female faces, regardless of orientation, and to female faces in general (Cohen & Strauss, 1979). At 10 months, infants could abstract featural information that differed for different faces, for example, nose length or separation between the eyes, and form a concept of the category by averaging feature values. This was inferred from their ability to treat novel faces as either members (showing habituation) or nonmembers of the category, depending on whether the feature values of the novel faces fitted the concept (Strauss, 1979).

These studies suggest that infants may be extracting prototypes or the best characteristic instances—objects that share most properties in common with other distinct but allied category members. To generalize, they must be able to deal with degrees of similarity among potential category members. Bornstein (1981) argued more generally that the infant must rely on *equivalence*—degree of similarity—to organize perceptual input combined with the prototypicality of the percepts received as input in order to form concepts. It is the equivalence classification of perceptual input that allows the infant to make sense of his world. Because each stimulus is *not* new, objects and situations are not unique. But neither are memories exact. If they were, they would be disruptive to conceptual development, for each stimulus would be treated as different. Bornstein suggested, therefore, that judgments of approximate similarity are the forerunners to concept formation.

However, notice that in these experiments, all the stimuli shown to the infants are relevant. They are all members of the same conceptual category and simply vary in how much they have in common with the other members shown. This is somewhat different from the situation that confronts infants in the real world. There they are not exposed to an array of instances selected as belonging to the same category. Rather they may see one instance and then not see another for some time. Or they may see several instances that are fairly disparate in their properties, although they happen to be members of the same category. Moreover, a single object can be a member of many different categories and so is pertinent to the formation of a variety of different concepts. All this suggests that infants must have considerable memory capacity to store all kinds of information pertinent to potential categories. Otherwise, they would find it impossible to construct representations or concepts of every instance to which they are exposed and somehow later sift them to find possible categories.

Until recently, most research on children's acquisition of concepts studied artificial concepts, after the elegant paradigm initiated by Bruner, Goodnow, and Austin (1956). For example, children might be shown various geometric shapes with different kinds of borders and have to form the concept of a triangle with a wavy line inside its edges. Although this paradigm was very productive for examining the kinds of hypotheses and the strategies used in forming such concepts (Bourne et al., 1979), there has been little research on the natural acquisition of everyday concepts. The research by Cohen and his colleagues on faces, therefore, represents one of the first attempts to get at when infants are able to group different objects as members of a category.

The natural acquisition of categories has been studied by Mervis with somewhat older children, aged 4 to 5 (Mervis & Pani, 1980). The categories she used were sets of toys designed to have the kinds of properties and distribution of properties characteristic of many natural categories. She contrasted the acquisition of a conceptual category through exposure to prototypical instances—good exemplars of the category—with acquisition through exposure to poor exemplars. The objects Mervis constructed fitted a gradient of membership from highly prototypical (the best instance characteristic of that category) to fairly marginal. Those children who had learned the category from the better exemplars generalized more easily to new instances than children who had learned from poor exemplars. Mervis argued that prototypical exemplars must play a critical role in the acquisition of concepts for natural kinds just as they evidently did in her studies of the acquisition of an artificial kind.

Although the children Mervis worked with were already 5 and thus considerably older than the 1- to 2-year-old who is setting up all sorts of conceptual categories based on experience of the world so far, her results may indeed be typical of what younger children do. In a study by Saltz, Dixon, Klein, and Becker (1977), 2- and 4-year-olds were asked to choose pictures when asked for a cat, say. The 2-year-olds showed a stronger preference for pictures of prototypical instances (here, of cats) than the 4-year-olds. In another study by Kuczaj (1979), young children, aged 1 year 9 months to 2 years 4 months, showed a strong preference for prototypical instances in a word-comprehension task. Hearing the word *dog*, for example, they would pick prototypical examples over less prototypical ones, but as they got older, they extended their choices of possible referents of the word to include less prototypical members of the category as well. Their choices were invariably of appropriate referents. These observa-

tions extend those made by Thomson and Chapman (1977). However, both Kuczaj (1979) and Thomson and Chapman were concerned more with the children's comprehension of the words used than with the prototypical character of the referents.

The studies by Cohen and his colleagues and by Mervis suggest that children can form concepts for object categories early and that such concepts may well have a prototypical structure. There is other evidence that young children know about the category membership of various kinds of objects very early. I will first take up evidence from some studies of sorting and then turn to some studies of matching or equivalence judgments.

Sorting is one way to show that children have certain concepts. Nelson (1973a) found that children between 1 year 7 months and 1 year 10 months would spontaneously group objects like small toy cars mixed in with small toy planes into two separate groups—cars and planes. They would also sort out plastic eating utensils from plastic animals, again placing them into two distinct groups. A more complete study was carried out by Ross (1980) who used the sorting and the looking preferences of 1-, 1½-, and 2-year-olds to argue that they had certain conceptual categories before they had acquired any linguistic labels for those same categories.

Ross (1980) combined habituation tests with preference ones in her study of categorization. The preference technique is to look at which toy a child prefers to play with, a familiar one or a novel one. In general, children pay more attention to a novel object, just as they show greater interest in novel objects after habituation. Ross showed 150 children (50 at each age) toys from six categories: M-shaped forms, O-shaped forms, men, four-legged animals, food, and furniture. The children then saw another object from the same category together with one from a new category as well to see whether they showed greater interest in a new stimulus from a different category. They showed strong habituation for M's, O's, and men, but not for animals, food, or furniture. (Note that the members of the latter categories are more disparate in their properties than members of the first three.) On the preference measures, the children showed a preference for the novel item in all six categories. Lastly, Ross found that comprehension of words for members of these categories was unrelated to the habituation and preference shown by these 1- to 2-year-olds.

In another study of early concepts, Starkey (1981) looked at infants' ability to sort objects and at their preferences. He presented 6-, 9-, and 12-month-olds with eight sets of four small manipulable objects and then looked at the order in which infants touched the different objects in the set and the groupings they made. The sequential touching of like objects increased with age. For instance, no infant touched four like objects sequentially at 6 months, compared to 50% of the 9-month-olds and 69% of the 12-month-olds who did. The 6-month-olds did little grouping of like objects, but 81% of the 9-month-olds formed object pairs. And 12-month-olds did this even more often.

Starkey's results suggest that children begin to categorize objects as early as 6 months: some at this age could pair like objects. By 9 months, some infants could sort out one complete group of like objects from the set of two groups, and by 12 months, they regularly sorted both groups in a set. This study, even more than Ross's (1980), shows that even very young infants can distinguish members of one category from another and can demonstrate this in their sequential touching and their primitive sorting.

One final point that should be made about sorting studies: in a recent paper, Markman, Cox, and Machida (1981) have argued that the standard sorting task itself may both misrepresent and underestimate children's ability to categorize. They asked 3- and 4-year-olds to sort objects *into* plastic bags versus *onto* separate sheets of paper and showed that with the plastic bags, these children sorted objects from the categories of furniture, people, vehicles, and trees in a more adultlike way. When sorting onto pieces of paper, they were much more likely to construct designs or scenes in which the categories remained intermingled and thus gave rise to what investigators like Vygotsky (1962) talked of as the ''chaining'' characteristic of younger children's conceptual organization. Younger children may indeed be more easily diverted in how they organize particular objects, so sorting tasks probably underestimate their ability to categorize. Sorting, then, even with Markman's improvements, should probably be regarded as a minimal rather than as a maximal measure of what young children know about particular categories. This view would fit more compatibly with the wealth of observations in diaries that have been kept of overall development from birth to 2 or 3. Even very young infants, for example, know how to treat a new bottle—which way up to hold it, which end to suck, and so on. And from 7 or 8 months, they frequently show that they know what to do with certain toys, which way to stand them or how to manipulate them, even when they are new instances of particular categories (e.g., Perez, 1892; Piaget, 1962; Preyer, 1882).

Another approach to finding out about children's knowledge of category membership has been to ask them to make matching and equivalence judgments. For example, Daehler, Lonardo, and Bukatko (1979) asked children between 1 year 8 months and 2 years 8 months to select one of four pictures to match a label, another picture, or both. They also asked them to pair objects with objects versus pictures with pictures. In a third study, they asked them to match objects that were related but not perceptually identical to compare the ease with which the children could match pictures of identical objects, basic-level objects or different-level objects from the same superordinate category, and associated objects (e.g., a nail and a hammer) at 1 year 9 months, 2 years 3 months, and 2 years 8 months. The order of ease in making these matches was: identical objects, then members of basic-level categories, then members of the same superordinate category, and hardest of all, associated objects (e.g., bucket and spade). Daehler and his colleagues argued that both perceptual information and linguistic labels make important contributions to children's performance in matching and identification. Their ability to match and judge objects as equivalent is based on their recognition of identity or of some degree of similarity for category members.

Similar assumptions have governed some research on infants' object concepts in studies of object permanence. LeCompte and Gratch (1972) looked at the effect on children 9, 12, and 18 months old of substituting another toy for one they had watched being hidden in a trick box. Even the youngest infants reacted to the trick trials as if they expected the same toy to appear in the box where it had been hidden. However, the 9-month-olds simply looked puzzled when a different toy appeared upon the box being opened; the older infants were more likely to search actively in the box for the original toy. This technique of surprising children might be used with advantage to look at their notions of identity versus category membership, for instance, by substituting a toy spaniel for a toy Labrador. So far it has been used to look only at identity.

There is, then, some evidence that children acquire conceptual categories for objects at a fairly early age. Although few studies have looked at infants under 9 months, what evidence there is shows that 9-month-olds can put objects from two different categories into appropriate groups: they will touch like objects in sequence and will even on occasion sort them into groups. Habituation and preference measures give the same results. These experimental findings are strongly backed by the large observational literature in the diary studies from earlier this century: infants clearly construct some conceptual categories of objects during their very first year.

One final note—all the sorting and judgment studies considered here have been concerned with the children's concepts of kinds of objects that are countable. I have been unable to find any research on children's concepts of objects that consist of substances like water or sand. Presumably infants attend to substances just as they do to discrete objects and must form some preliminary concepts of these kinds too in their first year. Their exposure to substances may be somewhat more limited: water, milk, other liquids, earth (dirt), sand, and gravel. Whether they view noodles, rice, and other foods of that type as substances could be debatable; individual pieces may be the entities they categorize first.

Situations

There has been little attempt in studies of early perceptual and conceptual development to look at concepts of situations. Concepts of kinds of objects, yes, but not concepts of kinds of situations. What I will do in this discussion is simply look at what little evidence there is that young children are attentive to activities pertinent to the categorization of situations. First, there is a great deal of observational and anecdotal information about infants' propensity to attend to motion as opposed to stasis. This is documented repeatedly in the diary studies (see Kagan, 1970). In general, if infants have a choice between looking at something that is moving versus something that is still, they attend to the movement. Repetitive activities in particular seem to attract the attention of very young infants. They will attend to rattles and bells—both of which also make a noise when moving. They will watch hands moving—finger play—with no accompanying noise. They will watch dogs or birds moving—indeed, any moving object—with greater attentiveness than something that is still (e.g., Piaget, 1962; Stern, 1924). And infants presumably start to categorize the many routine activities they see every day—walking, sitting, feeding, and so on.

Earlier I distinguished *processes* and *events*. Processes are activities that last for a specifiable stretch of time and have no particular outcome or result. That is, the activity itself does not change the state of the person or object doing the activity. The act of running, for instance, exemplifies a process. In contrast, a race, with specified starting and finishing points and the selection at the end of a winner is an event, even though the same activity appears in both the process of running and the event of a race. Events, then, involve an activity with an outcome or distinct result. Indeed, the activity in an event often

produces a change of state in the person or object affected by the activity. Because there has apparently been no research on what infants and 1- or 2-year-olds know about kinds of processes, there is little that can be said at the moment about infants' categories of processes.

Is there any evidence that processes are distinguished from events? Do infants distinguish motion that produces a result from motion that produces no change? Do they categorize them differently? Several studies suggest young children do indeed attend to changes of state, that is, to the results that are the outcome of some motion. Borton (1979) looked at 3-month-olds' attention to three different settings. In the first, X moves toward Y, touches Y, and Y moves on. In the second, X moves but stops short of Y, and Y then moves on; and in the third, X simply moves all the way across a screen. Borton videotaped infants attending to the displays and examined their looking patterns for the collision versus noncollision settings. He found they spent more time looking at noncontact (setting 2) than they did at either the contact settings (where X hit Y) or the motion alone (where X moved across the screen). Borton argued that this attention to the noncontact setting, given the infants also looked away more often here, suggests they were searching for "magical events," and he inferred from this that 3-month-olds are sensitive to the necessity for spatial contact in the triggering of Y's movement by X. This might be preliminary evidence that processes are distinguished from events, provided the children attend both to activities categorizable as processes and activities categorizable as events. What is the evidence?

In a similar study with 4- and 8-month-olds, Leslie (1979) presented events with a temporal rather than a spatial gap. Like Borton, Leslie argued from his results that the infants distinguished the causal sequences, with contact between two objects in both space and time, from contingent sequences where there was no temporal or spatial contact. Although these two studies are clearly aimed toward another goal, they do suggest that infants are able to distinguish some processes from events at an early age. The evidence here is necessarily indirect, however, and not in itself evidence for categorization.

A somewhat different source of evidence about children's concepts of everyday events comes from studies of agency and of the results of a change of state. The studies of agency have largely concerned infants' and young children's attention to the agent of an action, for example, a film strip showing first one person, A, standing at one side of a table and another, B, at the other side, then A leans on the table and pushes it over to touch B, and then B pushes it back. Golinkoff and Kerr (1978) looked at whether children aged 1 year 3 months to 1 year 6 months attended to changes in role, whether A or B was the pusher. Using habituation, they showed that the children were aware of changes in role regardless of the direction of the action (pushing). Moreover, they showed more recovery of attention to situations where both agents were people than to those where the switch was from a man to a chair as agent. Golinkoff and Kerr had expected greater recovery to the man/chair switch in roles because chairs are anomalous agents. The finding that children this age attend to roles suggests that the categories of agent and of object affected must begin to develop before language does. However, this study provides no evidence for the identification of agency with animate rather than inanimate beings.

In a similar study, Robertson and Suci (1980) studied the attention children aged 1 year 5 months to 1 year 6 months paid to short films of events to see whether they looked more at the agents, at the activities, or at the recipients of the activities. Because the children attended much more to the agent than to either the activity or the recipient, Robertson and Suci concluded that agency played an important role in children's attention to events. Finally, Leslie's (1979) and Borton's (1979) studies provide evidence that infants as young as 3 months realize there has to be spatial and temporal contiguity for there to be a causal sequence, that is, an event rather than a process.

The other property of events that has been studied is their results, the outcomes of actions. Keil (1979), for example, examined the surprise reactions of 1½- and 2½-year-olds in a setting where they could predict the outcome of a particular action producing a change of state. For instance, to gauge their intuitions about cause, he looked at their surprise when a construction made of blocks failed to collapse with the removal of certain crucial blocks that supported the construction. (Surprise was measured as in LeCompte & Gratch, 1972.) When the action that should produce the change of state was carried out in full view of children, both age groups were surprised at the outcome—at the failure of the structure to collapse. When the action was screened from view, neither age showed surprise; with even simpler events, only the 2½-year-olds showed surprise. Essentially, what Keil did was check up on these young children's predictions of what the result should be for certain events by measuring their surprise when the expected outcomes did not occur. The results led Keil to conclude that children this age need knowledge of each component in an event to understand the event fully. Simpler events, where the law of support alone was involved, were easier for the children to understand than more complex ones, where both support and balance were used in the block constructions.

In a study of slightly older children, Gelman, Bullock, and Meck (1980) looked at their knowledge of events by examining the sequences involved in changes of state, both in going from a canonical to a noncanonical state and in going back from an end state to the original one. The task was to complete picture sequences by adding a third one in the appropriate slot. For example, given a picture of a glass on the left and of a hammer to its right, children had to place a third picture, of a broken glass, to the right of the hammer. Children had to place the picture of the initial state, the instrument, or the resultant state, for both familiar and bizarre sequences. Both 3- and 4-year-olds were able (1) to predict what the transformed state would be, (2) to retrieve what the initial state had been, and (3) to give evidence of understanding the kinds of actions that could link state 1 and state 2. This study, in combination with Keil's, suggests that fairly young children must know a good deal about changes of state and causality, and hence about *events*. But, one caveat: although Keil's study was of children under 2½, that of Gelman et al. was of 3- and 4-year-olds. There is, therefore, considerable need to look at children's concepts of kinds of processes and events in a much younger population.

What is known about the earliest emergence of notions of causality comes largely from Piaget's observational studies of his own children (e.g., 1952, 1954, 1962). He documented their growing awareness, from infancy, that their own actions were effective in producing such outcomes as shaking a rattle, moving a frill by pulling a string, or making a doll's feet move. He noted that between 8 and 11 months, they progressed from a general (and usually fortuitous) sense of efficacy in repeating whatever action they happened to be doing when the interesting result occurred to the realization that spatial contiguity plays an important role in one event causing another. The younger infant may pull on a string—any string—and expect the toy hung above him to move. The older infant looks for the string attached to that toy and pulls that string. Observations like these together with the findings of such researchers as Leslie (1979) and Borton (1979) strongly suggest that infants become aware fairly early that there are connections between activities and results, but the nature of these connections emerges rather slowly (see *Gelman & Baillargeon, vol. III, chap. 3*). Moreover, how soon infants categorize the distinctions they perceive as processes versus events among different kinds of situations has yet to be determined.

States

Little is known about very young children's categorization of states, that is, the temporary or permanent properties of objects and situations, but some research in perception has focused on which properties infants as young as 5 months can discriminate (see *Gibson & Spelke, vol. III, chap. 1*). For example, Gibson and her colleagues have used the habituation paradigm to find out if infants that age treat shape as an invariant property of objects. The infants were first habituated to a sponge undergoing a rigid motion and showed no dishabituation when the sponge was shown with a different rigid motion. They did dishabituate though to that rigid motion when they had initially been habituated to a deforming motion (the sponge being squeezed and released). They also dishabituated when the shape of the sponge was changed, even though the rigid motions remained the same (Gibson, Owsley, & Johnston, 1978; Gibson, Owsley, Walker, & Megaw-Nyce, 1979). Although these studies show that infants can discriminate such properties as shape and motion, they cannot tell us directly about the kinds of states children might categorize early on as properties or states.

One suggestive source of information about the kinds of properties 1-year-olds attend to and may use in categorizing is the large body of diary observations collected at the beginning of the century. From them, as well as from more recent diaries like Piaget's (1962), it is clear that children rely on properties like shape, size, movement, sound, and taste when deciding whether a word can be applied to an object for which they lack a label (see E. V. Clark, 1973b). Most 1- to 2-year-olds also normally know all the conventionalized versions of different animal noises and can match animal noises to the appropriate pictures with ease. They generally know about characteristic movements for different animals as well, and they can inventory body parts and common appendages like collars, saddles, and reins. They also show apparent distress upon detecting imperfections. For instance, if they find a crack in a plate, a broken edge, a button missing, or some spilt food, they will point at it or pick at it as if to indicate there is something different about this particular object (Church, 1966; Kagan, 1981). Although these observations are all clues to which states or properties may be the most salient and most used for categorizing by children aged 1 or so, there has been little attempt to study which conceptual categories of states are established earliest.

However, the general priority of shape as a property noted in the diary studies is backed up by studies of free sorting where 2-year-olds consistently used shape in preference to size and color in categorizing cardboard figures. Denney (1972) found this preference both in free classification tasks ("Put together the things that are alike") and in tasks where the children were asked to put together things with the same name. Similar attention to shape and to details of shape was noted for 1- and 2-year-olds by Ricciuti (Ricciuti, 1963, 1965; Ricciuti & Johnson, 1965) as well as for 3-year-olds by Donaldson and Wales (1970).

Finally, what 3- and 4-year-olds consider characteristic properties of things that are *alive* has been studied in some detail by Carey (1978b). She asked children about a person, a dog, a bug, and a plant, for example, whether each thing breathed, moved, ate, had young, and so on. Her main finding was that young children this age were very sure about those properties expected to go with some kinds of living things but that their knowledge of other categories was still limited. How to ask similar questions of much younger children to find out what they know about kinds of states and properties poses another problem altogether.

Summary

This brief account of the concepts of kinds—objects, situations, and states—known in the first year or so of life is clearly limited by the data available. It is clear, because they go on to learn the appropriate language, that children develop concepts of kinds of objects, kinds of situations, and kinds of states. But very little is known still about the nature of children's earliest conceptual categories, and still less about which concepts of kinds emerge first or the relation between adult and child conceptual categories during the first 2 years.

Evidence for infants' and young children's concepts of objects comes from several sources—categorization studies of faces and other kinds as well as free- and constrained-sorting studies, among others—although there has been little observational research on the early *emergence* of concepts of objects. Again, diary studies provide numerous provocative observations, but these are not always reported in enough detail to answer all the questions one would like to ask. But by age 2 or so, it is clear that young children have already acquired a large fund of knowledge about objects in the world around them.

Direct evidence for their concepts of situations—processes and events—is much sketchier. It is known that infants are attentive to movement and to the results of an event where there is a change of state. This in itself tells us little about the kinds of situations children might acquire concepts of early on. Here, then, is a large gap in our knowledge about what infants know.

Information about children's concepts of states is just as limited. Young children use certain properties in sorting tasks; they can also identify characteristic properties of some objects. Infants are probably aware of some of the usual or normal attributes of shape, size, position, and so on, for familiar objects around them: they show this in part by their attention to nonnormal properties or orientations. However, relatively little is known still about which properties are salient for infants, whether there are any hierarchies among properties and states, or how infants come to set up categories of states in contrast to categories of objects or situations.

What I have outlined here is sufficient to show that there are many gaps in what is known about the conceptual categories possessed by infants and young children. These gaps are in part the result of questions about early concept attainment *not* being formulated in terms of the concepts children will eventually come to talk about. If one looks back from the vantage point of what one *can* talk about with a particular language, it may be possible to ask more direct questions about children's emerging concepts of objects, situations, and states. Language provides an elaborate symbolic system for talking about kinds, so it seems only reasonable to treat it as a guide in asking about the whys, whens, and hows of early conceptual development.

I shall turn next to the meanings children acquire early and show that these do indeed fall into several domains: words that pick out objects, situations, and states. However, children's early concepts are not all equally represented in early language. Whether this is because children's conceptual categories are developed to different degrees by age 1 or so or whether other factors affect the earlier stages of language development is a question I will raise again later.

THE ACQUISITION OF WORDS

In trying to study the contents of the oceans, the marine biologist must decide which species to focus on and then find an appropriate device for drawing it to the surface. Similarly, children have to find the right words for pointing to conceptual categories and particular members of categories. But children in this situation are more akin to the student biologist than to the one who is fully qualified. They have to work out which device—which word or expression—maps onto which concept before they can use particular devices to draw up an instance of a particular concept for others. And because many conceptual categories lack words to encode them in one language or another, children have to work out, for their language, which concepts are encoded linguistically and which are not. In the same way, the student biologist has to learn which species can be captured with the devices available and which cannot.

Working out the relations between a rich and elaborate set of conceptual categories and a system of conventional linguistic devices for talking about concepts is a complex process. As Slobin (1979) has pointed out, this is mainly because the relation between concepts and word meanings is itself an indirect one:

> Language *evokes* ideas; it does not represent them. Linguistic expression is thus not a straightforward map of consciousness or thought. It is a highly selective and conventionally schematic map. (p. 6)

Words, I shall argue, simply *flag* concepts—they serve to evoke them—and learning the meanings of words is a matter of learning which concept or concepts each word conventionally picks out within a specific language community.

The first concepts children focus on when they begin to map words onto concepts, I have suggested, should be those concepts children start to acquire early, namely concepts of certain objects, situations, and states. Each language encodes these or selections of them, but languages also vary in many of the other concepts that could be encoded. Some, through various grammatical devices, such as word endings, code explicitly such notions as number (singular versus plural), person (first person *I* versus third person *he*), gender (masculine versus feminine), animacy (words for people and animals versus words for inanimate objects), time of the event relative to the time of the utterance, contour of the event (completed, in progress, repetitive, etc.), and so on. In essence, a large number of grammatical distinctions can be used to modulate the meanings of terms that evoke objects, situations, and states. In this chapter I am concerned primarily with word meanings rather than utterance meanings so I will not go into any detail about grammaticalized modulations (but see Bowerman, 1976, 1978b; Slobin, 1979, in press). Instead, because all languages have terms for objects, situations, and states, I shall focus on how children map such terms onto their conceptual categories of these kinds.

How can one follow the route children take in acquiring their first word meanings? It has been done mainly by observing children's usage, whether congruent or not with the adult's, and from that, inferring what concepts children have mapped onto particular words and hence the meanings of those words. However, children have not only to learn what the conventional meaning is for each word they acquire; they must also realize that each word contrasts with its fellow words and that the contrasts among words reflect contrasts among concepts.

What are the primary components in the process of acquiring meanings? First, children must look for, and establish, consistencies in adult uses of words to pick out particular conceptual categories— the *conventions* that govern different words. Second, they must observe the *contrasts* adults observe. Convention and contrast together rule the whole vocabulary. Of course, children's initial hypotheses about adult consistencies may be erroneous or incomplete. In either case, children's consequent misuses of words in production or misinterpretations in comprehension are likely to be revealing about the course of acquisition itself.

Early Lexical Development

What are the first vocabulary domains to emerge in children's speech? Children 1- to 1½- years old talk about people: *Dada* or *Papa, Mama* or *Mummie,* and *baby* (the latter often in self-reference). They talk about animals—*dog, cat* or *kitty, bird, duck* or *hen, cow, horse,* and *sheep*—by the age of 1½ or 2 (Nice, 1915). They talk about vehicles, the commonest ones being *car, truck, boat,* and *train.* They talk about toys, with *ball, block, book,* and *doll* usually the ones they label earliest. They talk about food: *juice, milk, cookie, bread,* and *drink,* to list the commonest terms used. They talk about body parts: starting with such terms as *eye, nose, mouth,* and *ear,* and only later going beyond the face to upper and lower limbs and other body parts (Andersen, 1978). They talk about some articles of clothing and household implements: *hat, shoe, spoon, clock,* and *key.* They will often have a greeting term, like *hi, bye,* or *night-night;* and they may have a few terms for actions or states: *up, away* or *no more, off.* In addition to these domains, children use a deictic or pointing spatial term, like *that* or *here.* And they may also have a few game-routine terms, like *peekaboo* and *pattycake.* These early vocabulary domains have been extensively documented in recent studies by Benedict (1978, 1979), Nelson (1973b), and Rescorla (1980). Some of the older work on children's early vocabularies has been summarized in E. V. Clark (1977a, 1979). Interestingly, recent studies like Nelson's of the first 50 or so words that children acquire show exactly the same patterns and to a large extent the same vocabulary as studies from 50 years or more ago (E. V. Clark, 1979).[5]

To what extent does this early vocabulary contain labels for conceptual categories in the three major domains of objects, situations, and states?

Object Words

Which categories of objects do children pick out with their first object words? First, there is growing evidence that the first referents for children's early words tend to be prototypical instances of the category denoted. For example, a child is more likely to learn the word *bird* first for such exemplars as robins or blackbirds and only later for spoonbills or ostriches. This is probably in large part because adults choose good exemplars as instances to point out and name for their children (Anglin, 1977). Second, many of the first words children acquire for contrasting one category with another tend to be basic-level terms for adults. For example, in naming pictures for children, adults typically use terms like *dog* or *tree* rather than the more specific *collie* or *oak* or than the more general superordinate *animal* or *plant* (Brown, 1958). As Rosch and her colleagues (1976) have shown, basic-level terms are those that pick out categories at the level where members of the same category are most likely to be judged both more like each other and less like the members of any neighboring category. Another way to put this is that what, for adults, are basic-level terms are the ones that contrasting conceptual categories map onto most easily. However, one must be careful not to assume that basic-level categories for adults are all necessarily basic-level ones for children (see E. V. Clark, 1978a; Mervis & Mervis, 1982), although basic-level terms are probably more frequent in speech to children than in speech to other adults (Anglin, 1977).

But do young children assume that words pick

out categories rather than individuals or do they act at first as if each word, each category label, is simply a proper name? Observations of young children's usage suggests they quickly use terms for kinds, not just for individuals. There are, of course, some domains where children may first discriminate individuals (e.g., parents and pets) and learn names for them and only later learn to treat them as kinds, as members of categories, too. In other domains (e.g., blocks, beads, bottles), children may be encouraged to treat objects as kinds, as members of categories, from the start. This premise led Katz, Baker, and Macnamara (1974) to study children's acquisition of nonsense words introduced with or without an article (i.e., used as a common noun with *a* or *the* for the category or as a proper noun without any article for an individual). With dolls, girls as young as 1 year 5 months made a distinction between words presented with articles (picking out an instance of the category) versus words without articles (picking out a particular individual). With blocks, however, Katz et al. found no differences.[6] The differentiation between dolls and blocks suggests that the emerging linguistic distinction between category label and proper name was grounded on prior knowledge that people, or dolls representing people, were more likely to have names (be treated as individuals) than blocks. Had the distinction been grounded on the presence or absence of an article with each "new" word, the results for objects from both categories should have been identical.

Although children appear first to acquire basic-level terms—terms of the greatest utility in the child's world, according to Brown (1958)—they have at some point to begin acquiring labels for both more general (superordinate) and more specific (subordinate) categories. The mapping that is required for this is rather harder than for basic-level terms. At the superordinate level, category membership is much more diverse than at the basic level: various kinds of furniture are more unlike each other than are various kinds of chairs. And at the subordinate level, category members are harder to keep apart: various kinds of chairs, armchairs and deck chairs, for instance, are more like each other than are chairs and tables or chairs and cupboards. These conceptual factors are reflected in languages to the degree that most languages tend to have a more elaborated basic-level vocabulary than either a superordinate or subordinate one (e.g., Berlin, Breedlove, & Raven, 1973; Brown, Kolar, Torrey, Trùong-Quang, & Volkman, 1976), and many languages lack terms at the subordinate and superordinate levels. One caveat: basic levels are not necessarily the same from language to language and will not always coincide with the basic level identified by Rosch et al. (1976).

When do children begin to acquire superordinate- and subordinate-level terms for hierarchically structured categories? And do they acquire such terms in any particular order? Various early vocabulary studies show no evidence of ordering. In the domain of animal terms, for instance, young children begin to use both superordinate (e.g., *animal, insect*) and subordinate (e.g., *spaniel, monarch*) once they have acquired certain basic-level terms (e.g., *dog, butterfly*). The question here, and it may be a crucial one, is whether these superordinate and subordinate terms have that status for 3- and 4-year-olds (E. V. Clark, 1978a). There has been little attempt to establish exactly what terms like *animal* or *spaniel* mean to young children in contrast to *dog*. And observations like that of François (1978) that before about 3½ her daughter rejected such predications as "a dog is an animal" with anger (see also Ervin-Tripp, 1974), suggest that children that age have not yet realized that the terms for some categories include more than others.

To attain this realization, children must learn that the members of some categories can be grouped together and treated alike at some higher level of classification: the lower level categories are *included* in the higher level one—both daisies and roses are flowers. Learning about class inclusion is a problem that was extensively studied by Piaget (1928). But class inclusion is not the only such relation children must acquire. Some categories can be grouped together as *parts* of another category—one's hand is part of one's body, a tree is part of a forest. Such part-whole relations seem to be mastered earlier and to take precedence over inclusion when children have to analyze unfamiliar domains (see Markman, Horton, & McLanahan, 1980). Nonetheless, when given utterances like "A robin is a bird" and "A mib is a bird," 6- and 7-year-olds seem able to make appropriate inferences about the attributes a mib should have as a member of the category bird (Harris, 1975). This suggests that 6-year-olds have learned some basic level to superordinate-level relations. Smith (1979), following up this issue, found that such relations were harder to learn in some domains than others. This suggests that inclusion relations have to be acquired separately for each domain and that Smith may have been tapping some domains known to the children and some that were simply unfamiliar and therefore more difficult (see Horton, 1982). She also suggested that part of the difficulty might be due to how children attended to the forms of the questions asked (see also Shipley, 1975). This point was examined explicitly by Markman et al.

(1980) by teaching new class-inclusion hierarchies to children between 6 and 17, either by pointing and saying, for instance, "These are trees," "These are oaks" or by pointing and saying "Oaks and pines are two kinds of trees." With the latter information, even 6-year-olds correctly took the relation to be one of class inclusion and not one of part-whole.

The form in which children acquire category labels for superordinate- and subordinate-level categories, then, appears critical for their organization of linguistic—and perhaps even conceptual—hierarchies in different domains. The nature of the categories themselves leads children to first seek labels for those categories most easily distinguished from each other and for which membership is most clearly assignable through family resemblances: basic-level categories. The fact that linguistic labels for superordinate- and subordinate-level categories are acquired quite a bit later suggests labels for such categories may be less useful or even that they may be harder to map onto conceptual categories. In any case, this finding is compatible with the lesser prominence of both superordinate- and subordinate-level categorization abilities in adults (Rosch et al., 1976).

Things Versus Material. Most of the object categories mentioned so far have as their members objects with discrete boundaries, things like dogs, chairs, or leaves. But some categories consist of material that forms a mass, such as sand, milk, or water. The distinction between these two types of object category is captured in English by the distinction between count nouns (used with articles, pluralizable) and mass nouns (no articles, no plural form). Brown (1957) noted that young children seemed sensitive to this linguistic contrast, even though the majority of their words for object categories were words for countable things. They always gave correct grammatical treatment to words for materials like milk, orange juice, and dirt; none said things like *a milk* or *some dirts*. To check these observations, Brown devised a small experiment to look at 3- and 4-year-olds' ability to identify the appropriate grammatical devices for distinguishing count versus mass nouns in English. He showed children a picture, for instance a pair of hands kneading a mass of red stuff in a container. He then asked such things as, "Do you know what a sib is? In this picture you can see a sib. Now show me another sib"—as he showed them three more pictures: one of hands kneading another colored mass in another container, one of a mass of red material, and one of the original container. In asking about the material, he introduced it by saying, "Have you ever seen any

sib? In this picture you see some sib. Now show me some more sib"—again pointing to the three other pictures. Of the 16 children who took part, 11 picked out countable things in response to count nouns and 12 picked out material in response to mass nouns. Use of *a* versus *any*, it seems, provides 3- and 4-year-olds with certain clues to meanings for new words. The fact that they take such clues into account suggests they have already acquired part of the linguistic distinction. That, in turn, suggests that they must already distinguish things from materials as conceptual categories of objects.

Objects Versus Situations. Brown's study also indicated that children took account of the linguistic distinction between nouns (for objects) and verbs (for situations). With instructions like, "Do you know what it means to sib? In this picture you can see sibbing. Now show me another picture of sibbing," children consistently chose the picture of hands kneading another mass of material in contrast to pictures of the material or of the container alone. Brown also compared the verbs used spontaneously by the children with the first 1,000 words in the Thorndike-Lorge (adult-based) and the Rinsland (child-based) word lists. In the nonoverlapping portions of these lists, Brown noted that only 33% of the verbs on the adult list named human or animal movement. But of the child verbs not on the adult list, 67% named human or animal activities. The everyday view that verbs pick out actions is far truer for young children than for adults.

Indirect evidence that objects and situations are treated differently during language acquisition comes from various asymmetries in how young children treat terms for the two kinds of categories. For example, there are three to four times as many nouns as verbs in children's early vocabularies (E. V. Clark, 1978a; Gentner, 1978a, 1982; Goldin-Meadow, Seligman, & Gelman, 1976). These numbers are not, of course, simply based on adult part-of-speech assignments but on the object or situation that seems to be being picked out by the child's words. For instance, some children choose the term *door* for talking about opening or separating one object from another, whereas other children in the same settings choose the term *open* (e.g., Griffiths & Atkinson, 1978): both *door* and *open* would be counted here as verbs.

This preference for terms for objects over situations also shows up in sorting tasks where 2- and 3-year-olds are given novel objects and asked to sort them. They tend to do so according to properties of form rather than according to their activities (e.g., Tomikawa & Dodd, 1980), R. G. Schwartz (1978) also found that 1-year-olds were much more likely to produce new words spontaneously (ones they had just been taught) for referent objects than for referent activities. He observed the same asymmetry when he deliberately elicited the words just taught. This suggests that children's conceptual categories for objects may be better established than their categories for situations, at least during the earlier stages of acquiring words.

Asymmetries of this type are not necessarily evidence for a distinction between the two kinds of categories. However, research by Huttenlocher and Lui (1979) suggests that these early asymmetries could be reflecting a fundamental difference in how categories of objects and situations are organized conceptually. They looked at children's organization in memory of concepts picked out by either nouns or verbs by giving 3-, 4-, and 5-year-olds short lists of nouns or verbs to recall. They found few changes with age, but a large difference in recall of nouns versus verbs, with nouns being much better. Huttenlocher and Lui attributed this to differences in memory organization: Nouns were more likely to be related to other nouns that picked out related categories at the same level or at superordinate or subordinate levels, for example, *cat-dog-horse* or *cat-animal-Siamese,* and so on, whereas verbs were more likely to be related to the nouns for the object categories that might perform the particular activities named by the verb rather than to other verbs, for example, *dig-spade-garden, play-toy-baby,* and so on, and were, therefore, harder to retrieve.

Situation Words

When children start to talk about situations, they do not necessarily use the words an adult might expect. They may use *open,* for example, for talking about a door being opened or shut, for an orange being peeled, for a coat being undone, for a shoe being taken off as well as for a tap or a radio being turned on (Guillaume, 1927). Or they use *door* for a similar range of situations. From an adult perspective, the forms children pick up first for talking about situations may be verbs, nouns, or particles, like *off* or *up* (e.g., *take off, pick up*). But once they have started to talk about situations, they gradually add more and more forms that for adults are verbs. However, children's earliest verb uses, even then, make it difficult to tell whether they distinguish processes from events. The problem is that their verbs lack all the clues that might be provided by various endings, such as tense (the time of the utterance relative to the action), aspect (completion or noncompletion of the action), person (action of the speaker, of the addressee, or of a third person), or number (action of one or more than one instigator). But children soon begin to use a few verb endings and their selective uses of ones like *-ed* and *-ing* for instance, suggest they use them initially to distinguish processes from events.

Children appear to do this by focusing on some of the aspectual properties of situations. Aspect, roughly speaking, encompasses the "contour" of an activity—whether it lasts for a limited amount of time or not; whether it results in a change of state or not (see Bull, 1960; Comrie, 1976). Processes are activities that last for some amount of time without any discernible change of state, whereas events are activities that produce a change of state as their result or outcome. When they begin to use verb endings, children acquiring English tend to use *-ing* only with verbs used to talk about ongoing activities (processes)—for example, *play, write, eat*—and *-ed* with verbs for activities that result in a change of state (events)—for example, *find, break, spill* (Antinucci & Miller, 1976; Bloom, Lifter, & Hafitz, 1980). The differences in contour—whether the activity continues for some limited period or whether it produces a change of state—are the first to be marked explicitly when children begin to talk about situations in a variety of other languages as well (Slobin, in press).

Events par excellence are situations where there is a clear cause or instigator of the change of state and a distinct result that follows from the instigator's activity (Slobin, 1981). Several recent studies have looked at how children talk about cause and result. Early on, they appear to focus on results alone: they talk about the outcomes of actions—*up* (for a toy just placed out of reach), *broken* (for a puzzle piece thrown down the stairs), *stuck* (of a finger poked into a small hole), *off* (for the lid pulled off a box), and so on. In these events, children comment only on the outcome—the states that result. But by age 2 or so, they begin to use verbs like *make* in talking about causation itself, as in "He made it come" alongside *"He comed it"[7] (Bowerman, 1974, 1982). And they often talk about both the causing activity and the result, as in "Make it be up" or "Make it be on."

Such explicit expressions of cause provide further evidence that events are conceptually distinct from processes. Moreover, expressions of causation with verbs like *make* or *get* (e.g., English, "He made the boy sit down") appear at about the same time in children acquiring languages as different as English, Serbo-Croatian, Italian, and Turkish (Ammon & Slobin, 1979), even though crosslinguistic differences in the encoding of space, time, agency, and causation make for differences in how easy various expressions of causation are to understand (Ammon, 1981a, 1981b).

Children's linguistic expressions for talking about situations, then, lend support to the view that they already distinguish process categories from event categories. Their earliest uses of the verb endings -ing and -ed are on process and event verbs respectively. (Later, of course, they learn that both endings can occur on both types of verbs.) They also talk about some events initially by focusing on the state that results from the activity (the change of state) and then add verbs like make so as to encode both activity and result in a single utterance.

Situations Versus States.   Although most verbs pick out situations, some are more akin to adjectives, in that they pick out states, for example, *want, hear,* or *be*. Two kinds of linguistic evidence suggest that children distinguish situations from states at the same time that they distinguish between types of situations. First, children rely heavily on general purpose verbs, like *do, make,* and *go,* from age 2 or earlier, for talking about a wide variety of different situations, thus differentiating situations from states (Berman, 1978; E. V. Clark, 1978a), although not events from processes. Second, as Brown (1973) has amply documented, children acquiring the verb ending -ing rarely add this ending to stative verbs like *be* or *want*. It can be used only on process and event verbs in adult speech, and it generally appears only on those types of verbs in young children's speech too.

State Words

Finally, I want to turn to the evidence that children rely on their concepts of states or properties in acquiring their first linguistic terms for states. Nelson (1976) looked at children's earliest uses of terms to pick out states of objects, for example, in utterances like ''Big dog'' or ''Plate hot.'' She found a steady increase with age in the use of attributive adjectives (those in a position preceding the noun in English). However, the first states children talked about all tended to be what Nelson called transient states of objects, for example, *dirty, broken,* or *wet* predicated of objects temporarily in those states. Note that such states all appear to be the result or outcome of prior actions. Next, at around age 2 or so, children began to talk about less transient properties as well, in such a way as to subcategorize certain kinds of objects, for example, *car-smoke* versus *house-smoke* (E. V. Clark, 1981a). By 2- to 2½-

years Nelson found that children talked about a variety of transient states, using such terms as *broken, dirty, cold, hot, missing, allgone, fixed, open, on, off,* and *stuck;* they also distinguished some objects according to size or color, with terms like *big, bigger, little, baby,* or *red* used to modify the noun that picked out the object in question; and they commonly distinguished instances of an object category according to possession or use (e.g., *my chair, Daddy shoe*).

In summary, young children's first 50 to 200 words include terms for objects, for situations, and for states. The linguistic contrasts children make suggest that they have either already established the pertinent conceptual categories or do so simultaneously with the acquisition of the pertinent linguistic expressions. So far, however, I have simply considered which words children commonly use for categories of objects, situations, and states. I now wish to turn to the meanings children attribute to those words and the process of working out those meanings—finding out which conceptual category each word conventionally picks out in the language being acquired.

MEANING ACQUISITION

In discussing children's early vocabularies, I have up to now ignored the relation of the child's meanings to the adult's meanings. Adults know the language whereas children are only just getting a foothold on it. Thus, if animal terms are taken as an example, for adults, the word *dog* contrasts with the words for other animal categories at the same level of abstraction, for example, *cow, horse,* and *sheep*. It also contrasts with both superordinate and subordinate terms, like *animal, canine, terrier,* or *Pekingese*. To go further, the term *dog* for adults, at some level or another, contrasts with every other term known to them. These contrasts are smaller in number, of course, for children who have only a minute vocabulary by comparison. At the same time, there is no way that, simply by pointing to an instance of a category and naming it, adults can convey to children exactly what it is that a particular word picks out. Is it the object as a whole, the shape, the color, the texture, the motion, the object in that setting, the orientation, or what?

What children have to do is look for *consistencies* from one occasion to the next in order to form an initial hypothesis about what a word might be picking out. They can then test the hypothesis by trying out the word on potentially appropriate occasions and making the necessary adjustments in light of still further evidence from subsequent adult uses as well as their own uses where they are understood, misunderstood, or corrected.[8]

The relations between a child's first hypotheses and the actual adult meanings could vary widely. I will sketch some of the logically possible relations first and then consider how characteristics of children's early word production fit those possibilities.

Child Meanings Versus Adult Meanings

The first general principle children might assume in trying to work out word meanings is that they have stability: they do not change from one time to another or from one speaker to another. It is only under this assumption that it would make sense to look for consistency and try out different hypotheses. If consistency and stability are assumed, there appear to be five logically possible relations that a child's first meanings could bear to the adult's:

1. The child's meanings might be *overextensions* of the adult ones. For example, a word like *dog* might be overextended from dogs to pick out sheep, cows, cats, and other four-legged mammals as well.

2. The child's meanings might be *underextensions*. For example, *dog* might be used for one particular dog or only for dogs lying down.

3. The child's meanings might *overlap* with the adult's, such that the child uses the word *dog* to refer to large dogs, and not to small ones, but also to pick out sheep, calves, and other four-legged mammals of about the same size. The child's use of the word *dog* here both overlaps in part with the adult's use and extends beyond it. (This is really a combination of underextension and overextension.)

4. The child's meanings might *coincide* with the adult's meanings. Although this would appear easy to observe, it may be harder to establish in fact.

5. The child's meanings might *mismatch* the adult's meanings entirely.

Suppose, instead, that children assumed instability of meaning from one occasion to the next. For example, a child might assume that a word served to pick out whatever was of most interest to him at that moment. The word, then, might be a general purpose pointer to direct someone's attention, and little more. In one sense, this would not be unlike the case of deictic or pointing words like *here* or *that*, which pick out, for the person addressed, a place or an object identifiable only by reference to where the speaker is on the occasion of the particular utterance. Unstable meaning-concept relations

should be much harder for both child and observer to pin down. But if words are taken to be unstable in this way, one might expect to find a child using a word like *dog*, for instance, as if it were deictic, just like *here* or *that*.

What is known about each of these logically possible relations? And are there other options, less obvious a priori, that children take as they work out the relations of words to conceptual categories as well as of words to other words? The abundant data from both old and new diary studies as well as from more detailed studies of the emergence of particular word meanings allow one to assess these possibilities in some detail. Most of the data, however, pertain to production only, not to comprehension. (Some of the problems this raises will be discussed later.)

Overextension

Overextensions (e.g., the use of *ball* for balls as well as for oranges, apples, the moon, and doorknobs; or *fly* for flies, specks of dirt, dust, toes, and crumbs of bread) are widely reported in the classical diary studies (see Anglin, 1977; E. V. Clark, 1973b). They usually appear in children's speech between 1 and 2½, and may last anywhere up to several months. From these studies, however, it is hard to assess how prevalent overextensions are in each child's vocabulary or whether they are equally probable in all domains.

More recent observations suggest that over a third of children's very early vocabulary may be overextended (e.g., Rescorla, 1976, 1980). Moreover, across six children, Rescorla (1976) noted that words for object categories, such as *cat, shoe,* or *ball,* were much more likely to be overextended than words for other, nonobject categories, for example, *up, stop.* And words for objects in some domains were more often overextended than others. For example, a small group of words for alphabetic letters (*A, B, C,* etc.) were all overextended, as were many of the words for vehicles (*car, truck*) and clothing (*shoe, hat*). Words for animals were somewhat less likely to be overextended, although *car* or *kitty* and *dog* were overextended by most of the children studied. Many of the words overextended by most or all of the children were also very high-frequency words in the children's speech.

Finally, the proportion of words overextended by Rescorla's six children decreased as they acquired more vocabulary. For example, Daniel overextended 15 of his first 25 words, but only 10 of the next 25, and only 5 of the next 25 after that. This pattern, as the data in Table 1 show, is typical.

Table 1. Percentage of Words Overextended with Increasing Vocabulary Size

Words	1–25	26–50	51–75
Andrea	36	20	17
Daniel	60	40	20
Donald	40	40	32
Erica	44	20	12
Evan	48	40	0
Rachel	44	52	36
Means	45	35	20

(Based on Rescorla, 1976)

What is the basis for the overextensions children use? The diary data, summarized originally in E. V. Clark (1973b) and reported on subsequently by Anglin (1977), are backed by more recent observations by Bowerman (1976, 1978a) and Braunwald (1978) as well as by studies like Rescorla's. Overextensions are most likely to be based on the *appearance* of the referent objects, their resemblance in shape, size, texture, taste, or movement to members of the original "correct" (i.e., adult) referent category. Those based on shape predominate and in many of the accounts constitute between 80% and 90% of the documented overextensions. Movement, size, taste, and texture make up a much smaller group. And a still smaller set involves terms that appear to pick out activities rather than objects: these are words that appear to be precursers to verbs. Typical examples of each class of overextension are shown in Tables 2, 3, and 4.

The typical age range in which overextensions are usually observed is between 1 and 2½ (E. V. Clark, 1973b; Rescorla, 1976). The same age range has been documented in diaries of children acquiring quite different languages. The duration of individual instances of overextension is highly variable. Some children overextend a word for only a couple of days; others may persist in overextending one for several months. The critical factor appears to be the point of acquisition of a more appropriate word for the category in question. Leopold (1949) observed a recurring pattern of change where the domains of overextended words were "narrowed down" by the addition of new and better words for the pertinent categories. Essentially, once a child who has been overextending *dog* to cows, say, acquires the word *cow* and adds it to his repertoire, he no longer uses *dog* to pick out instances of the category cow. Several examples from Leopold's bilingual daughter, documenting the points of acquisition of her new words, are given in Table 5.

The process of overextending a word is strikingly similar regardless of the language being acquired. For instance, one animal term is often overextended to pick out other four-legged mammals; a term for a ball or a round piece of fruit is frequently overextended to pick out other small round objects, and so on (see Table 2). This suggests that overextensions themselves may also offer indirect clues to the conceptual representations children have of certain categories (E. V. Clark, 1977b). Children seem to judge on the basis of similarities with neighboring categories whether a word can be extended to pick out that further kind of referent as well. The ability to make similarity judgments, then, appears crucial not only for the formation of conceptual categories and other cognitive representations (Tversky, 1977) but also for decisions about word use.

Table 2. Overextensions Based on Shape

Word	First Referent	Domain of Application
buti	ball	toy, radish, stone spheres on park gates
nénin	breast	button on garment, point of bare elbow, eye in portrait, face in portrait, face in photo
gumene	coat button	collar stud, door handle, light switch, anything small and round
ticktock	watch	clocks, all clocks and watches, gas meter, firehose wound on spool, bath scale with round dial
baw	ball	apples, grapes, eggs, squash, bell clapper, anything round
kotibaiz	bars of cot (crib side)	large toy abacus, toast rack, picture of building with columned facade
tee	stick	cane, umbrella, ruler, (old-fashioned) razor, board of wood, all sticklike objects
mum	horse	cow, calf, pig, moose, all four-legged animals

(Based on E. V. Clark, 1973b)

Table 3. Overextensions Based on Movement, Size, Sound, Taste, and Texture

Word	First Referent	Domain of Application
sch	sound of train	all moving machines
ass	toy goat on wheels, with rough hide	sister, wagon (things that move), all things that move, all things with a rough surface
fly	fly	specks of dirt, dust, all small insects, child's own toes, crumbs of bread, a toad
em	worm	flies, ants, all small insects, heads of timothy grass
fafer	sound of train	steaming coffeepot, anything that hissed or made noises
cola	chocolate	sugar, tarts, grapes, figs, and peaches
sizo	scissors	all metal objects
wau-wau	dog	all animals, toy dog, soft house slippers, picture of old man in furs

(Based on E. V. Clark, 1973b)

Table 4. Overextensions Based on Activity

Word	First Referent	Domain of Application
our (= open)	opening or closing father's door	peeling fruit, opening/closing a box shelling peas, undoing shoe laces
atta (= allgone)	departures	opening or closing doors, raising a box lid, any disappearance of an object from sight

(Based on E. V. Clark, 1973b)

Table 5. Narrowing Down Overextensions by Adding New Words

Word	Initial and Subsequent Domain of Application	More Appropriate Words for Part of Initial Domain
Papa	father, grandfather, mother 1;0, any man 1;2	mama 1;3 Mann 1;5
Mann	pictures of adults 1;5, any adult 1;6	Frau 1;7
baby	self and other children 1;2, pictures of children 1;4, any child 1;8	boy 1;8
ball	balls (including crocheted) 1;0, balloon and ball of yarn 1;4, observatory dome 1;8, balls of tinfoil and paper (called paper ball), marbles, ovoid ball (called egg ball), spherical bead (once ball bead) 1;11	balloon 1;10 bead 1;9
wauwau	dogs 1;1, stone lion 1;1, horses (bronze bookends), toy dog, soft slippers with face 1;3, fur-clad man in poster 1;4, porcelain elephant 1;6, picture of a sloth 1;8, lamb made of cake 1;9	Mann 1;5 shoe 1;6 cake 1;9 hottey (horse) 1;10 dog 1;11
cake	candy 1;6, real cakes and sand cakes 1;9	candy 1;10

(Data from Leopold, 1949; based on Barrett, 1978)

Underextension

Underextensions, where a child uses a word like *car* only for one particular car or only for cars ridden in, have not been observed to the same degree. There are two problems in detecting underextensions: first, any uses that are made of the word *car,* for example, are appropriate, and second, it is difficult if not impossible to interpret children's *nonuses* of words. If a child fails to use the word *car* on occasions where it would have been appropriate, the child could be underextending the word *car,* could simply lack interest on that occasion, or could even be attending to something else. So our ability to detect underextensions is more limited than our ability to notice overextensions.

A few careful observers, however, have documented instances of underextension and followed children's uses of such words over time. Reich (1976), for instance, observed his son's early comprehension of the word *shoes,* starting at 8 months. Asked ''Where're the shoes?,'' at first he would crawl only to those on a shoe rack in his mother's closet. No other shoes would do. He then began to include the shoes in both his father's and mother's closets, but not shoes outside the closets. Next included were shoes outside on the floor as well as shoes in the closets. And finally, some two months later, the baby would also turn to, and play with, shoes that were being worn. This child, then, progressively enlarged the category of objects picked out by *shoes,* even though he himself did not yet produce the word.

In production, there are many fewer observed underextensions well documented. Bloch (1924) noted that one child first produced *papa* only in connection with one person, but later extended it to everyone in the household. Greenfield (1973) provided a similar account of the acquisition of *dada.* Bloom (1973) observed that her daughter initially used *car* only for a car moving by on the street below, as seen from the living room window. She did not apply *car* to either still or moving cars seen when she was down on the street.[9] This highly restricted use of *car* then vanished from the child's vocabulary for some six months. When it reappeared, it had a much more adultlike extension. Huttenlocher (1974) reported that one of the children she observed at 10 months used *hi* as someone came into the room when she was in her crib, but not elsewhere. Very soon, however, this baby extended *hi* to other settings regardless of her own location.

Some of the underextensions reported concern address terms, such as *mama* or *papa* or the name of a family pet. And there, one could argue, the child is treating the term as a proper name. But even in these domains, the diary data contain conflicting observations: some children do underextend a term like *dada,* others do not. Whether underextensions might constitute a first stage in the use of any word (E. V. Clark, 1973b), the first step in mapping a word onto a conceptual category, remains an open question.

Overlap and Coincidence

Overlap occurs when the child's use of a word overlaps partially with two (or more) adult words. For example, a child who thinks *dog* picks out large dogs and calves, but not small dogs or cows, has a meaning for *dog* that overlaps with the adult's *dog* and *cow.* In essence, such overlaps involve simultaneous underextension and overextension and may be hard to distinguish from underextensions on the one hand, and overextensions on the other. Overlaps are also hard to distinguish from coincident uses where the child's use of a word appears to coincide with the adult's use on the occasions observed. But without checking further, it may be impossible to tell whether the child's coincident uses really coincide fully with the adult conventions for the word or not. Both overlap and coincidence may be difficult to detect and hard to establish. With overlaps, though, there should be some evidence of error in the child's uses, error compatible with both underextension and overextension.

Researchers studying the acquisition of meanings (as well as of syntactic and morphological structure) have generally focused first on onset of usage and second on evidence of erroneous use; they then made inferences from the patterns of erroneous use, up to the point when errors disappear. Apparently correct uses, like those that coincide with adult uses, appear at first glance to be less informative than errors about the process of acquiring meanings. But coincident word meanings (which, according to Rescorla, 1976, 1980, make up about two thirds of the vocabulary of a child aged 1½ to 2) do provide an important source of information nonetheless. The fact of coincidence suggests that the boundaries between the object categories denoted by such words are clearer so that it is easier to map words onto conceptual categories. An alternative explanation is that children are exposed to better exemplars or a small range of exemplars for those categories so that their mapping of word to category is made simpler.

There is one final point about coincident usage. Children acquire some words as parts of routines or formulaic expressions. As long as they use these only in the contexts in which they first acquired them, their language appears adultlike. But, as

Bowerman (1978a, 1979) and Karmiloff-Smith (1977, 1981) have noted, initially correct but limited uses of words or constructions may be followed some time later by errors. Bowerman suggested that once children realize that various meanings acquired independently of each other are related, they begin to organize them differently and for a time may become confused by newly observed similarities of meaning among them. For example, *put* and *make* share some meaning in common, in that *put* expresses the meaning of "make be/go in some place." Children who recognize the shared elements of meaning may then retrieve the wrong word on occasion, using *put* for *make* (e.g., *"You put a place for Eva to be in" [3 years 1 month]) or *make* for *put* (e.g., *"I make some butter my sandwich" [2 years 2 months]) (Bowerman, 1978a). Karmiloff-Smith (1977) put forward a slightly different explanation for the late-occurring errors she observed, suggesting that children start out learning only one of the conventional meanings of a word, such as French *même* [same one, same kind]. Later, when children learn the other meaning, they may create a new form to distinguish the meaning of *same (one)* from *same (kind)*, for example, by using *la même vache* versus *la même de vache* respectively. Once they realize that certain contrasting meanings happen to be carried by the same form nonetheless, they revert to adult usage.

Mismatch

Mismatches are those instances where the child starts out with a wrong hypothesis about the adult convention governing the meaning of a word, a hypothesis so wrong that the child's meaning is quite different from that of the adult. Take the instance noted by Maccoby (cited in Clark & Clark, 1977, p. 486) of a child who frequently forgot to wipe his boots when he came in. On one occasion, his mother reacted with, "Young man, you did that on purpose!" When asked later what *on purpose* meant, the child replied, "It means you're looking at me." This child made a quite reasonable guess about what *on purpose* meant, it is just that his hypothesis was wrong.

Another clear mismatch comes from Bowerman (1976). She reported that Christy, aged 1½, began to use *hi* as she balanced her tiny toys on the end of a finger, as she slid her hands under a blanket, as she stuck her hand into a mitten-shaped potholder, and when a shirt fell over her foot in her crib. Bowerman suggested that the child's hypothesis was that *hi* had to do with something resting on or covering her hands or feet and that this hypothesis was derived

from those occasions when she saw finger-puppets on her mother's fingers that nodded and said "hi" to her. Christy, instead of taking *hi* in its greeting sense, focused on the relationship between finger and finger-puppet and from that constructed her first hypothesis about the meaning—the adult convention—for *hi*.

What happens when children come up with a wrong hypothesis of this kind? If the child receives no evidence of understanding on the adult's part, he presumably desists from using a word and probably drops it from his repertoire. This makes mismatches hard to detect in the early stages of language acquisition. Children sometimes use a word on a few occasions and then drop it for as long as six months (Bloch, 1924; Bloom, 1973; Huttenlocher, 1974). Mismatches of this type have not been noted very often, but they could be relatively common in the early stages. Many initial mismatches may never become evident. Consider a child trying out a hypothesis about the meaning of a new word. He forms a hypothesis and then looks for consistency the next time he hears the word. And he can detect none. He has selected inappropriate information about the object or the situation, information that simply does not "repeat" on the next occasion; he therefore has to start all over again with a new hypothesis.

Do these five possible relations of child to adult meaning tell the full story of what goes on as children try to work out what word meanings are? At best, accounts based on overextension or underextension, overlap, and coincidence alone can provide only a static account of what happens as children try out their hypotheses. The other part of the account must deal with the fact that children *need* words for certain uses and that may force them to call on their "old," or already established, vocabulary at certain times, in certain ways. But one can see this only by following individual words over time.

Meanings in Context

When one follows the developmental history of individual words, it becomes clearer that children are struggling with two major factors as they acquire meanings. They are working out what category each word picks out (the reference) and how adjacent word meanings contrast with each other (the sense), *and* they are trying to communicate with others with the aid of a limited linguistic repertoire. Consider one example from Stephen who numbered the word *hat* among his first 10 words at 1 year 2 months. At first, he produced *hat* for his own winter hat and various toy hats (a cowboy hat, a fireman's hat, a matador's hat). But he also used *hat* for a winter boot, various boxes, a Frisbee, a page from a newspaper, a coloring book, and a set of keys. At first, according to Gruendel (1977), each object was called *hat* as soon as Stephen had placed it on his head. Then he narrowed *hat* to objects that were containerlike—he stopped overextending *hat* for paper and keys, for example, but added boxes to the domain of *hat*. Finally, he dropped all nonhats as referents and used the word only for hats. (Although Gruendel did not indicate when during this progression Stephen acquired productive use of the words *paper, key,* and *box,* all three words entered during the period just described.)

This general pattern of development has been observed for other words too. Braunwald (1978) noted that her daughter Laura, aged 1, used *down* first as a request to get down from her high chair, then for requesting other positional changes where *up, out,* or *in* were needed. But by 1 year 4 months, Laura had narrowed her uses to settings where *down* was appropriate. *Up* entered Laura's repertoire a month after *down* and was first used when she was holding onto her mother's legs begging to be picked up. She then extended *up* to being picked up and also used it as a request to be put into her high chair or her stroller. *Down* meanwhile became more restricted so that it contrasted with *up: down* did not overlap with *up*. The commonest use of *up* four months later continued to be as a request to be picked up. By 1 year 3 months, Laura began to use *out* as well, first as a request to be helped out of a wading pool; it was then extended to getting out of the pool or the bathtub and out of her high chair or crib. By 1 year 4 months, Laura contrasted *down* with both *up* and *out*.

A still more complex sequence can be seen in Laura's acquisition of the meaning of *cookie*. This word first entered her vocabulary in comprehension at 9 months 8 days, and was imitated by 1 year 22 days. She first produced the word at 1 year 2 months for cookies and crackers, then extended it on the basis of perceptual and perhaps functional similarity to other round edible objects, including a bagel (1 year 3 months), cheerios—a doughnut shaped cereal Laura had never seen or eaten before (1 year 3 months 17 days), and a round slice of cucumber (1 year 3 months 30 days). Each extension allowed Laura to ask for foods new to her, foods not regularly served in her parents' household. Concurrent with these extensions of *cookie* was a second subjective or affective extension of the word, apparently on the basis of some dimension of pleasure, that is, to request music on the hi-fi or the car radio and to identify the sound of music (1 year 3 months 13 days); to

request that someone rock her, to pick out the motion of rocking or the rocking chair (1 year 3 months 19 days); and to talk about ice cream (1 year 3 months 21 days). In each instance, there was also an element of roundness in the settings: records are round, the seat of the rocking chair was round, an ice-cream bowl or cone is round. However, Braunwald suggested that the basis for these overextensions was actually the child's affective state. This interpretation is supported by Laura's use of another word later on, which became used for both ice cream (1 year 6 months 1 day) and for rocking (1 year 6 months 22 days).

The complexity of children's initial word uses, shown so clearly in studies as detailed as Braunwald's (1978), suggests that children are strongly influenced by their desire to communicate when they extend and overextend a limited vocabulary. Working out adult meanings does not occur in vacuo: children are also producing words to try to make themselves understood while talking about a much wider range of objects, situations, and states than they have words for. Patterns of use in production reflect both children's ongoing attempts to identify the conceptual category or categories conventionally picked out by particular words and their attempts to make themselves understood. The study of individual words and their neighbors in early vocabularies, especially during the narrowing-down process, reveals that children are continually adjusting the domain of each word as they acquire productive mastery of others (see Table 5). This sometimes makes it appear as if children are using words in a complexive fashion, moving from one criterial feature of meaning applied on one occasion to another criterial feature of meaning applied on another occasion (Bowerman, 1977). Children's early word uses shift, then, with the communicative requirements they are trying to meet as well as with their discovery of what the conventional relations are between words and conceptual categories.

Children are faced with apparent instability in one small group of words that shift their reference from one occasion of use to the next. These are deictic or pointing words like locative *here,* demonstrative *that,* or even a verb like *see* or *look*. Children use these deictics to pick out salient objects or situations in a variety of settings. So there is normally no relation whatever from one time to the next between the properties of the referents thus picked out. This apparent instability of reference, though, is not really instability but simply a reflection of the shifting nature of deictic reference, something that is observed by adults too.

Summary

There are a limited number of relations holding between children's early word meanings and their adult equivalents. The data available show that over-extensions are common and may involve a third or more of early vocabularies. As children's repertoires reach 100 words or so, the overextensions dwindle. Underextensions are harder to catch, at least in pro-duction, but may be typical of the very first stage of comprehension as the child begins to map words onto conceptual categories. Overlaps are hard to dis-tinguish from underextensions and overextensions. They are poorly documented because, as with under-extensions, one is hard put to interpret nonuses of words. Coincidences, although common (up to two thirds of early vocabularies), are also hard to estab-lish for sure, again because of nonuses; but they also offer a different kind of information about the word-to-concept mappings, perhaps identifying categories that are easier for children to pick out with words. Mismatches have been little studied and may be hard to detect. These relations, though, provide only one facet of the acquisition process: the other stems from children's communicative needs. The same child can successively underextend, overextend, and overlap the same word with the adult's uses or over-extend it in different ways on different occasions, depending on what he needs words for. The crucial dimension here is provided by the relation between the vocabulary the child has at his disposal and the range of objects, situations, and states he tries to talk about. The early meanings of words, therefore, have to be assessed against the other words (and their meanings) that are available to the child.

Comprehension and Production

Virtually all the facts and characteristics of early language acquisition and the inferences about chil-dren's early meanings have been based on what chil-dren say, not on what they understand. Yet in-ferences based on what they say may give a distorted picture of what the child's meanings for particular words are. Recent research reveals an asymmetry between comprehension and production in early lan-guage, an asymmetry akin to that found in adult speakers as well. As adults, we understand many different varieties of English—different dialects, different social-class ranges, and different varieties of English (Australian English, American English, Indian English, etc.)—that we are quite incapable of producing. We also have a huge passive vocabulary, words that we recognize when we hear them but that we never ourselves produce. Very young children

show something of the same tendency: they appear to understand more than they produce.

What is the evidence for this asymmetry during acquisition? Diarists like Grégoire (1937), Leopold (1949), and Lewis (1951) noted that the children they were following appeared to understand words long before they produced them. This observation is common to virtually all the diaries (see also Bene-dict, 1978; Huttenlocher, 1974; Rescorla, 1976). Goldin-Meadow et al. (1976) used a comprehension and production test for a variety of nouns and verbs representative of the vocabularies of 2-year-olds to look more closely at the content of the comprehen-sion-production asymmetry. They found that all 12 of the children they studied (aged 1 year 2 months to 2 years 2 months) were more likely to understand a word than to produce it.

The asymmetry, though, turned out not to be as simple as understanding words before producing them. Goldin-Meadow and her colleagues found ev-idence for more specific asymmetries signaled by the proportions of nouns and verbs understood and produced. The younger children whose language was less mature (they produced few or no multiword utterances) understood more nouns than verbs and produced only nouns. The children with greater lin-guistic sophistication at this age (a larger vocabulary and more multiword utterances) differed from the younger children on three counts: they understood more verbs, they produced more nouns, and they also produced some verbs.

Verb meanings, then, appear to be more difficult for young children in both comprehension and pro-duction. Why? The categories of actions that verbs pick out—the situations—typically differ from cate-gories of objects (see E. V. Clark, 1978a).

1. Situations are typically transitory in nature: compare objects that remain available for inspec-tion, even though their orientation, lighting, or color may change over time.

2. The range covered by a particular action is vague. Take the activity of opening, a common ac-tivity that often preoccupies small children. At what point does an action count as opening? If we pause to visualize the precise action normally used in opening doors, windows, boxes, bottles, cans, and curtains, say, we can glimpse the difficulty posed by the range included as instances of opening. The category of "open" situations appears to be much more diverse than any object category. In fact, situations often look as though they are as diverse at the basic level as object categories are at a superordinate level: the diversity of kinds picked out by *animal* seems more

comparable to the diversity of actions picked out by *open* than the diversity of objects picked out by *horse* or *sheep*.

3. There is also a boundary problem. Where does one draw the boundary for an action's beginning and ending? Consider the actions of opening just listed: as one opens a door, one steps closer to it, grasps the handle, and turns or pulls the handle to effect the action of opening itself; once the door is open, one lets go and then goes on to some other action. At what point does the act of opening itself begin and end? Take other kinds of opening: opening a briefcase, opening a box, opening a jar. What counts as being part of the situation and what does not? Identifying boundaries for an action in situation categories, then, is a difficult business (see also Gentner, 1978a, 1978b, 1982).

Huttenlocher and Lui (1979) attributed the difficulty with verbs in part to children's representations in memory—situations, they suggested, are linked in memory to object categories as if in a matrix. In contrast, object categories (picked out by nouns) are linked hierarchically to other object categories via their hierarchical or basic-level relations. These differences in memory representations make for differences in how easily verbs or nouns are retrieved and may ultimately be connected to the intrinsic differences between situations and objects I just noted.

In an effort to get at early comprehension more systematically, Oviatt (1980) trained infants between 9 and 17 months on the name of a salient object in one setting and the name of a simple action in another. She then probed the infants for comprehension of the newly trained words, taking account of gestures and gaze as well as any vocalizations. Few of the infants, even those aged 15 to 17 months, made any effort to pronounce the words taught. Instead, they might produce another word already known to them. For instance, 7 of the 14 infants who appeared to understand the object word when asked, ''Where's the *X?*'' produced either a semantically related object word (overextended for the occasion) or a demonstrative, like *there,* while pointing at the referent. Oviatt found that words for objects and situations seemed to be learned equally well, but only 4 of the 17 infants who had understood the situation word produced any intelligible vocalization. This was in marked contrast to the numbers who overextended words for objects from neighboring categories. The apparent disinclination to name actions, though, appears quite consistent with the observations of production made by Goldin-Meadow et al. (1976) as well as by Benedict (1978).

The lag of production behind comprehension has shown up in overextensions too. In a study by Thomson and Chapman (1977), some children overextended words in both comprehension and production, whereas others overextended them only in production. Thomson and Chapman looked at five children between 1 year 9 months and 2 years 3 months, identifying four words that each child had overextended in spontaneous speech. They then tested the children's comprehension by showing them pairs of pictures and asking them, for example, ''Show me the doggie.'' The pictures were of appropriate referents (dogs) paired with inappropriate ones (e.g., cows or horses) to which the word had been overextended previously by the child. Of the five children, four preferred the appropriate referent for at least half the words they had overextended in production. Thus one child, aged 1 year 11 months, overextended the word *apple* in production to a variety of other spherical and round objects—balls, tomatoes, cherries, onions, and so on—yet, in comprehension, consistently identified the appropriate referent, apples. In contrast, another child overextended all four of her words studied (*cow, doggie, fish,* and *catsup*) in comprehension as well as in production. She showed no preference for the appropriate referent when asked for a *cow* and shown pictures of a cow and a horse. The other children also overextended one or two words each in comprehension as well as in production.

These findings suggest that children may go through several stages as they try to work out word meanings. First they form some hypothesis about the meaning of a word—that *doggie,* for example, picks out mammal-shaped objects. They then rely on that hypothesis both when trying to understand which object is being picked out by another speaker and when producing a word to pick out an instance of such a category. Next, as children gather more information about the adult referents of *doggie,* they add to the information already accumulated about use of the word. And as a result, they become able to pick out more, and more appropriate, referents in the category dog when they hear the word. But because these children still lack words for nearby categories (horses, cows, sheep, etc.), they may continue to produce *doggie* for both appropriate and inappropriate instances. This account is compatible with observations from diaries like Moore's (1896) as well as studies like Thomson and Chapman's (1977). Overextension in production (but not in comprehension) at this point appears to be more a consequence of having only a small vocabulary than of having incomplete meanings (E. V. Clark, 1975, 1978a, 1978c; Fremgen & Fay, 1980).

In summary, language acquisition should be considered from both perspectives, production *and* comprehension. In production, the child has in mind the conceptual category he intends to talk about, and searches through a memory store for the appropriate word that will pick out that concept for his addressee. Production, then, is dependent on the retrieval from memory of known words appropriate to express the desired meaning. In comprehension, the child is trying to recognize the words he hears and then identify the conceptual categories they pick out. Production is not simply the inverse of comprehension; the two processes are quite distinct. Production requires an active search for available words and expressions combined with an evaluation of whether these are appropriate to label the concepts to be conveyed and to call up those concepts in the addressee. Comprehension requires recognition of a word as known, followed by a search for the conceptual category usually picked out by that term to arrive at the speaker's intended meaning.

To credit children with having acquired a particular word, one must therefore consider both comprehension and production. Mastery in comprehension does not guarantee mastery in production, and failure in production may not be good evidence that children do not yet understand a particular word. Consideration of only one of these processes may distort our view of the process of acquisition and the stages children go through in mastering the relations of words to concepts.

Later Lexical Development

So far, I have focused on the words children acquire very early for objects, situations, and states and some of the relations those bear to the adult terms and their meanings. By age 6, though, the average child is estimated to have a vocabulary of around 14,000 words (Templin, 1957). To achieve this, a child beginning at 18 months would have to add new words to his vocabulary at the rate of nine a day. Not surprisingly, then, studies of later vocabulary development have tended to focus on the words for a particular domain rather than on the vocabulary as a whole.

These studies fall into two groups: (1) those relying on comprehension tasks, usually experimental, often cross-sectional and (2) those observing spontaneous production, often longitudinal in design. The results from the two types of study sometimes conflict, with the observational studies of production attributing more to children than comprehension studies do. This is because of a tendency to assume that anything said by a child has the adult value for

the words used. But production alone, however adultlike it *sounds*, is not necessarily a good guide to what children know about the meanings in question.

Order of Acquisition

What determines the order in which children acquire new words and their meanings? One factor is the relative complexity of each meaning within a particular domain, with more complex terms being acquired later. Complexity, of course, has to be evaluated independently and is usually characterized by the number of conditions that have to be met before a word is used appropriately. The more complicated the conditions of application, the later a word meaning seems to be acquired.

A second factor affecting order of acquisition is children's reliance on nonlinguistic strategies, strategies based on their a priori conceptual organization of object and situation categories. These appear to play a critical role in children's first hypotheses about the meanings of new words.

Both factors play a role in children's acquisition of word meanings from the start. However, the role of relative complexity can only be assessed once children have begun to acquire sets of words related in meaning. Complexity (conditions of application) and nonlinguistic strategies interact with each other. Here, I will consider some studies that trace the effects of both in children's gradual working out of new meanings.

Relative Complexity of Meaning

One finding common to many different lexical domains is that where a set of words is related in meaning, the more complex among them are acquired later. Let me illustrate this finding with studies of three different domains: dimensionality, kinship, and time.

Dimensional terms, such as *big, small, high, low, wide,* and *narrow* were some of the first to be studied. Donaldson and Wales (1970) found that *big* and *small* (in Scots, *wee*) were mastered first, followed by "vertical" terms like *high,* whereas *deep* did not appear at all before age 5. However, they did not systematically examine the whole domain or look at children's comprehension of each member of a pair. I used a word game in which the child supplied opposites, either in response to a single word or in response to a phrase, to examine the sequence of acquisition suggested by Donaldson and Wales more closely (E. V. Clark, 1972). Children acquired the pair *big-small* first, then *tall-short, high-low,* and *long-short*. Terms that picked out a specific dimension (e.g., *high-low* or *long-short*) were the first mastered after the general three-dimensional terms *big* and *small*. Only after these did children start to grasp pairs like *wide-narrow* and *deep-shallow*.

The order in which children mastered the different adjective pairs largely matched the relative complexity computed by the conditions of application that each term required for appropriate use (Bierwisch, 1967)—the simpler the adjectives, the earlier they were acquired. This ordering of dimensional adjectives appears to be a very stable one (e.g., Bartlett, 1976; Brewer & Stone, 1975).

A second domain in which semantic complexity has been examined is that of kinship terms. Anthropologists have generally isolated three dimensions along which different kin terms may contrast: generation, sex, and lineality. Haviland and Clark (1974) took some 14 English kin terms and looked at children's ability to give adultlike definitions that reflected knowledge of these three factors in specifying the relationship of each kin type to a particular reference point. The kin terms fell into four groups, based on the complexity of their conditions of application. And children's definitions showed that the simpler the kin term, the earlier a child was likely to give an adultlike account of it (see also Deutsch, 1979).

A third domain where complexity has been shown to play an important role is that of temporal terms. Children between 3 and 5 were given descriptions containing *before* and *after,* which they had to use in acting out two events (E. V. Clark, 1971). On the basis of the errors made, I suggested that the conditions of application for *before* were simpler than those for *after,* and this was one reason why children appeared to master the conjunction *before* earlier than *after* (see also Ferreiro, 1971). This study provoked a number of follow-up studies that looked at such factors as the role of main versus subordinate clauses (e.g., Amidon & Carey, 1971; Coker, 1978; Johnson, 1975) and of logically constrained versus arbitrary sequences of events (French & Brown, 1977; Kavanaugh, 1979). Neither clause order nor logically constrained sequences by themselves account for the greater ease of *before* over *after;* both, though, probably play a role in getting children to attend to the differences between the two conjunctions (see Ehri & Galanis, 1980).

Complexity of meaning also appears to be a factor for other temporal terms. Both experimental and observational studies suggest that the first temporal contrast children master is *now* versus *then* (e.g., Decroly & Degand, 1913; Lewis, 1951; Stern & Stern, 1928), followed a little later by *today* versus *yesterday* or *tomorrow* (e.g., Decroly & Degand, 1913; Harner, 1975; Snyder, 1914). Harner (1975)

also established that children tend to acquire the meaning of *yesterday* before *tomorrow*. They also understand and produce the terms *first* and *last* before *before* and *after* (E. V. Clark, 1970, 1971; Coker, 1978). This is corroborated by data from an opposites task where 4- and 5-year-olds mastered the pair *first-last* before *before-after* and sometimes substituted *first* for *before* and *last* for *after* (E. V. Clark, 1972).

In summary, there is widespread evidence that semantic complexity is one factor governing the order in which children acquire sets of words related in meaning. The order of acquisition follows the complexity of the conditions of application for different words in the same domain.

Nonlinguistic Strategies

But complexity of meaning is not the only factor at work. Children also rely on nonlinguistic knowledge not only for constructing their hypotheses about the meanings of words but also as a source of strategies for dealing with settings in which they do not yet know the meanings of some words. Semantic complexity makes predictions about order of acquisition, but it does not account for where children start from nor does it account for the strategies they use while working out a meaning. I suggest that what children know conceptually is an important ingredient in their initial hypotheses about meanings as well as in their gradual acquisition of the adult conventions.

How might hypotheses based on a priori conceptual organization affect lexical development? One argument is that the child's nonlinguistic knowledge provides another way of measuring what should be easy and what should be hard for the child to acquire as he works out various meanings. If the adult meaning of a word coincides in its conditions of application with some conceptual organization that the child can readily impose on particular settings, that meaning ought thereby to be easier for the child to master. The word meaning fits his strategy for dealing with such settings from the start. Where there is a poor fit, or no fit at all, between an adult meaning and the child's conceptual organization, word meanings should be harder to acquire.

This approach assumes that children rely on a limited number of organizational principles derived from their conceptual structures. One of the first studies that took this approach explicitly was a study of the earliest locative terms children acquire: *in, on,* and *under* (E. V. Clark, 1973a, 1977a). Children were given a simple imitation task, where the experimenter simply said "Do what I do" and then, say, put a small cube into an upright glass. Each child was provided with an identical cube and glass. Below age 2, children would copy the placing of objects in containers but seemed incapable of placing objects outside and next to containers. Equally, they could place objects on supports, such as blocks, but seemed incapable of placing them beside potential supports. The same nonlinguistic preferences appeared when children aged 1½ and up were asked to carry out instructions using the words *in, on,* and *under:* they showed systematic preferences in the kinds of actions they were willing to carry out. These preferences could be predicted from the properties of the objects that were to be acted upon. If one object was a container, the child would always place a smaller object inside it. If the reference object was instead a support, the child would place other objects on it. The children therefore appeared always to get instructions with *in* right. They got *on* right only with supports and never got *under* right at all for containers or supports.

Nonlinguistic constraints like these appear to operate across a variety of different objects, both realistic and contrived (e.g., Cook, 1978). And the order of acquisition—*in* and *on* before *under*—holds for other languages too (e.g., Dromi, 1979), even for American Sign Language, where one might expect the iconic nature of the locative signs for *in, on,* and *under* to dispel all doubt in the child's mind as to what the locative relation was intended to be (Bernstein, 1981).

Nonlinguistic strategies, then, provide one factor in predicting which meanings will be the easiest to acquire. But there is a real problem in such studies. The data make it appear that children understand the word *in* from the very start; they never make errors with it. But children can only be said to have acquired the meaning of *in* when they systematically contrast it with *on* or with some other meaning from the same domain. Nonetheless, it may still be easier for children to acquire the meaning of *in* because the adult meaning coincides from the start with the primary strategy that children rely on—the placement of smaller objects inside a container. *On* should be rather harder to acquire because children should only get it right when they are dealing with reference objects that provide support but have no containerlike properties. And *under* should be the hardest of the three because it does not coincide with either of these two early nonlinguistic strategies that children display for organizing objects in relation to each other in space.

The extent to which these nonlinguistic strategies are applied and their consistency across children in different settings has been shown in further studies of locative words. In the acquisition of vertical terms—*up-down, on top of-at the bottom, over-under,* and *above-below*—children seemed to master the positive or "upper" term first (E. V. Clark, 1977a). They made relatively few mistakes with instructions that contained *up, at the top of, over,* and *above,* and their errors on other instructions consisted mainly of "top" placements. In other words, they seemed to be relying on the same support strategy found in earlier studies of locatives. The same strategy also appears to account for the earlier comprehension of "up" terms in pairs like *higher-lower, above-below,* and *rising-falling* studied by Friedenberg and Olson (1977). They also found that placement errors, for the most part, consisted of choices of the top surface.

The ordering of these terms and the terms studied by E. V. Clark (1977a) also fit a scenario where the more complex the conditions of application, the later the pair is acquired. But the simpler terms linguistically are also the ones congruent with the child's nonlinguistic strategies (E. V. Clark, 1973a; H. H. Clark, 1973). Nonlinguistic factors, then, appear to govern which meanings children try to work out first. Another illustration of this comes from the progressive acquisition of contrasts among the orientational terms *top, bottom, front,* and *back* (E. V. Clark, 1980b). Initially, children appeared to understand *top* in designating one side of a cube but on the other three instructions also chose the top side—yet another application of the support or top-surface strategy. Next children contrasted *top* with *bottom,* but they continued to make errors on *front* and *back.* Most of the errors were choices of the top surface, but some children contrasted *front* and *back* by choosing the top and bottom surfaces respectively. Next the children contrasted *front* and *back* as a pair with *top* and *bottom,* but they assigned them, more or less at random, to a nonvertical dimension: children picked the left or right, the near or far, or the far or near sides of the cube. It was only much later that children made the contrast between them a consistent one. Orientation, then, is another domain where the contrasts among word meanings are worked out gradually and predictably in terms of children's nonlinguistic strategies—the source of their hypotheses about the meanings of these words.

One final point about *in, on,* and *under:* some observational studies of these three terms have suggested that when children begin to produce them (around 2 to 2½), they tend to do so without any noticeable errors (e.g., Brown, 1973). However, my own records of spontaneous speech from 2-year-olds show numerous errors of application. One child used *on* and *in* erroneously a large number of times over a period of some six months before sorting them out. The confusions may have been due in part to their phonetic similarity, particularly in contexts where the vowel is unstressed. Thus, one child talked about a band-aid being *in* rather than *on* his knee and a book being *in* instead of *on* the table. This kind of confusion has been observed in a variety of other studies (e.g., E. V. Clark, 1978c; Museyibova, 1974; Stern, 1924). I also found numerous misuses in production from the same children whose comprehension was reported in E. V. Clark (1973a, 1977a).

Another domain where nonlinguistic strategies have been studied in some detail is that of deixis. Studies of *here, there, this,* and *that* have shown that different initial hypotheses about what these words mean make for different routes in working out the adult meanings. The order of acquisition across different children, though, appears to be remarkably similar.

For adults, the words *here* and *there* contrast in that *here* denotes a space relatively near and including the speaker; it may encompass just the particular spot where the speaker is standing or the whole universe. *There,* in contrast, denotes a space where the speaker is not. When children start acquiring deictic terms, they may contrast *here* and *there,* but not do so on the dimension of spatial proximity. *Here* is often deictic, but *there* tends to mean completion or result, as in "There you go" or "There it is!" (e.g., Carter, 1978). But the hypothesis about what *here* picks out seems to vary from child to child. Some children decide that it always picks out some object relatively near the child himself (a child-centered view of things), whereas others decide that *here* always picks out something near the speaker (a speaker-centered view). These two starting points make for different nonlinguistic strategies in the initial stages of acquiring the meanings of *here* and *there.* Child-centered children always pick objects near themselves regardless of where the speaker is. Speaker-centered ones do the reverse, in the sense that they always pick out something near the speaker: an object nearby when the speaker is next to them, an object opposite when the speaker is seated opposite.

These nonlinguistic strategies, then, lead to different strategies being applied at the same stage of acquisition (Charney, 1979; Clark & Sengul, 1978; Webb & Abrahamson, 1976). The more complex the deictic term and the less congruent with the child's nonlinguistic strategy, the later it appears to be acquired. The contrast between *here* and *there* is mastered before that between *this* and *that,* and both of these contrasts are acquired before those between *come* and *go* and *bring* and *take* (E. V. Clark, 1978b; Clark & Garnica, 1974). But the picture is complicated yet again when we compare children's acquisition of some of these terms in comprehension versus production. In production, the data collected by Richards (1976) appear at first to show that children can contrast *come* and *go* somewhat earlier than they can in comprehension. But should one take children at face value, or rather sound value, here? Many of the settings studied by Richards were ones in which the children might use collocations—words readily associated in set phrases like *go to school* or *come home*—and this might account for their performance (but see also Tanz, 1980). Observations of misuses in spontaneous speech are rare, mainly because it is always possible to construct an appropriate interpretation. It is only when children combine two deictic words that are normally incompatible that one may realize children have not yet mastered the adult meanings—for instance when *come* is combined with *there* instead of *here* (Bowerman, 1974) or *I* with *there,* as in the response to, "Where are you?": *I am there* (van der Geest, 1975).

Summary
Semantic complexity and nonlinguistic strategies interact with the setting of acquisition, the context in which children are exposed to new words. This is clear from observational studies of the emergence of comprehension and production of individual words (e.g., Braunwald, 1978; Carter, 1978). The context of acquisition provides the setting in which children form their first hypotheses about word meanings, about which categories words pick out from one occasion to the next. Children may have to refine their initial hypotheses considerably as they establish what is consistent from one occasion to the next and work out how new words contrast with others already in their repertoires. It would be unrealistic to expect all children to form the same initial hypotheses about meanings or to follow the same steps in working out the adult meanings, hence some of the diversity in words for objects, situations, and states in very young children. Nonetheless, their strategies for dealing with certain kinds of settings appear quite consistent, at least in domains like that of locative prepositions or deictic terms, where children apply a limited number of strategies during acquisition.

The limited range of strategies suggest that there are conceptual limits on the kinds of hypotheses children will come up with initially for such relational words as locative prepositions. What these findings do is lead us back to a generalization, one made when the study of language universals was first moved in the early 1960's, that is, the complexity of ideas is mirrored in the complexity of language. In terms of word meanings—where the conditions of application are complex, meanings should be acquired later. This is often mirrored in the actual forms of words as well: a more complicated word form, for example, *grandfather* versus *father*, in general expresses a more complicated idea. This argument of Greenberg's (1966) has been readvocated more recently in language processing (e.g., Clark & Clark, 1977, 1978). And in acquisition, Slobin (1973) has argued for the same position, that conceptual complexity is reflected in linguistic complexity. The relation between concepts and meanings in acquisition, then, is such that simpler concepts should be easier to map onto words than more complex ones.

THEORIES OF MEANING ACQUISITION

So far, I have given little indication of what theories might accommodate the facts that have been presented. Most theories that have been put forward have been proposed to account for specific observations, so it is hard to generalize from them to the acquisition of meanings elsewhere in the lexicon, much less to utterance meanings in general, for either single words or larger expressions. Accounts of meaning acquisition have generally been too limited in scope for one to draw clear conclusions about the process of acquiring meaning as a whole. Most researchers have focused on one issue or on one domain of the vocabulary and followed development by observing children's production of the relevant words. Few theories, though, have tried to make reference to the whole body of data available to provide a more general account of meaning acquisition.

Nelson (1974), for instance, focused on the basis for children's earliest word uses. She argued that children aged 1 to 2 relied on their knowledge of object functions, how objects moved or could be manipulated, when first attaching a label to a category. This would suggest that children should overextend their uses of a word to other objects with like functions, for example, the word *ball* overextended to any object that was thrown. However, most overextensions of words appeared to be based on shape rather than function (Bowerman, 1977).[10] Nelson, then, appeared to be concerned with the initial basis for word use by very young children, but her approach made no predictions about what differences might be expected in the acquisition of different domains in the lexicon nor about what might make words easy or difficult to acquire. Her concern appeared to be more with the information children might use in building up conceptual categories than with the process of acquiring the pertinent word meanings.

Other researchers have focused on the idea that children acquire parts of meanings before they master the whole. For example, Bowerman (1974) made a detailed analysis of the acquisition of forms to express causation in the verb itself. Before children could be credited with knowledge of a component like CAUSE in event verbs, they had to give evidence that they were aware of CAUSE as a component of their meanings. The evidence that they have acquired CAUSE seems to appear simultaneously on two fronts: children begin to use verbs like *make* and *get* with causative meaning (e.g., "I made it fall"), and they also begin to treat other verbs and even adjectives as if they could be used for talking about events. For example, Bowerman noted uses like "I come it closer so it won't fall" (2 years 3 months) said as the child pulled a bowl closer to her; "Mommy, can you stay this open?" (2½), said as the child tried to hold the refrigerator door open; "I'm singing him" (3 years 1 month) as she pulled the string on a musical toy; "How would you flat it?" (2 years 11 months), asked of paper on a magic slate; or "I wanta . . . wanta . . . round it" (3 years 1 month), as the child reached for the handle of the eggbeater. Overregularization errors of this type provide strong evidence that the verbs in question were being treated as event verbs and, hence, that the children had acquired the component CAUSE as part of the meanings.

Although the general view that parts of meanings are acquired before the whole is given strong support by this and other studies of verb meaning by Bowerman (1982, in press) as well as by investigators like Gentner (1978a), what follows for the acquisition of meaning in general is less clear. This approach makes no direct predictions about how children might acquire different domains of terms, for instance animal terms or kin terms, as opposed to certain types of verbs. Nor does it make direct predictions about order of acquisition within particular domains of the vocabulary. The merit of Bowerman's approach is the careful attention to the different factors that might account for the patterns of errors children produce as they work out how to encode such components as CAUSE in a particular language.

Both Bowerman (1978a, 1981) and Carey

(1978a) have argued that children initially pick up words in highly specific contexts and may therefore use them apparently correctly for some time. The initial relating of a word to a category has been characterized by Carey as a "fast mapping"; this process is then followed by a much longer period in which the child works out the details of the adult meaning. Bowerman (1978a) has argued further that once children begin to analyze word meanings and realize some are related or overlap in meaning, they begin to make "late" errors. Bowerman's data were again drawn from verb uses rather than uses of nouns. However accurate this account of meaning acquisition is, it provides no theory about what meanings children focus on first or why, nor does it provide predictions about the acquisition of particular domains of words.

Few investigators have looked very closely at the acquisition of words for taxonomies of objects, for example, the acquisition of words for furniture or vehicles (but see Rescorla, 1981). But Rosch et al. (1976) have argued that because category structure is much clearer at the basic-level of organization, children should find it easier to learn basic-level terms (e.g., *dog, tree*) before superordinate (*animal, plant*) or subordinate ones (*spaniel, apple tree*). And Anglin (1977) showed that adults were more likely to use basic-level terms when talking to young children than when talking to other adults. This prediction is clearly pertinent for the many domains of nouns that are used for talking about various kinds of taxonomies. Again, though, this prediction is an extremely general one and provides little insight into how children work out the meanings, whether of basic-level, superordinate, or subordinate terms. Moreover, the prediction assumes that what are basic-level terms for the adult will also be basic-level ones for the child. This assumption may not always be warranted (Brown, 1958; Mervis & Mervis, 1982).

In summary, most of the proposals about meaning acquisition are partial theories. Few have tackled more than one domain of the lexicon, and different researchers have focused on different aspects of the acquisition process—the initial mapping of words onto conceptual categories; the setting of that initial mapping; the discovery, documented by errors, of a particular component as part of a meaning; and so on. Generalizations become difficult, though, because of the diversity of lexical relations represented (Fillmore, 1978) and because few of the results appear to overlap. One attempt at providing a more general framework in which to consider meaning acquisition is the semantic feature hypothesis (E. V. Clark, 1973b), but it too fails.

The Semantic Feature Hypothesis

Linguistics has a long tradition of analyzing word meanings into smaller elements—semantic markers, components, or features. For instance, the meaning of *father* can be broken down into such elements as male (in contrast to *mother*), adult (in contrast to *child*), parent of (in contrast to *son*), animate (in contrast to *lamp*), and so on. Such analyses can be used to capture both the relatedness of neighboring word meanings and the differences where meanings contrast (e.g., Bierwisch, 1967). Under this view, word meanings can be represented as lists of those features that, on the analogue of a dictionary, make up their lexical entries (e.g., Bierwisch, 1970; Katz & Fodor, 1963).

The features in a lexical entry can be represented in several ways. For example, the element male in *father* can simply be listed as (Male), in contrast to the (Female) in *mother*. But this notation does not indicate these two features are mutually exclusive. This is expressed by a rule specifying that words with (Male) in their entries cannot have (Female) as well. Alternatively, this information can be incorporated into the notation itself by using a single term for the feature and adding plus or minus values to it. *Father* can be specified as +Male and *mother* as −Male, *father* as +Adult and *child* as −Adult, *father* as +Animate and *lamp* as −Animate, and so on. Lexical entries, then, are lists or features with values attached that specify the details of a word meaning.

The semantic feature hypothesis began from the assumption that meanings break down into combinations of units—components or features—smaller than those represented by words and that those smaller units, in turn, are based (ultimately) on perceptual and conceptual units common to all human beings (E. V. Clark, 1973b). This hypothesis was put forward originally to answer two questions: (1) Where do children start in the acquisition of meanings—what are the first semantic components or features they identify? (2) What determines the order in which children acquire particular meanings? I began from the assumption that children have to learn word meanings. When they first begin to use words, therefore, they do not know the full meanings, but have only parts of the adult meanings available. The acquisition of semantic knowledge consists of adding further components or features of meaning until the child meanings match adult meanings. One prediction, then, is that children's production and comprehension of words may differ considerably from the adult's in the early stages of acquisition, but over time will come to correspond to the adult models.

As soon as children have some meaning attached to a word, they can use that information in trying to understand the word and in deciding when to produce it. But in production, their partial meanings should often make children's uses diverge from adult ones. This prediction is strongly supported. As we have seen, some children overextend 40% or more of their earliest acquired words (see Table 1). The overextension data also suggested that the first semantic components or features children pick up are features of appearance—with shape predominating but other factors, like size, movement, taste, and sound, also playing a role. Initially (E. V. Clark, 1973b), I proposed that one could infer from the overextensions in the domain of any one word what the child considered its meaning to be. For instance, a child who uses *ball* for balls, doorknobs, snaps, oranges, and beads could be said to have something like "small round object" as his meaning for *ball*. However, if the same child picks out a picture of a ball rather than one of a doorknob when asked for a *ball,* it is clear that "small round object" is not the only meaning attached to *ball*. But it must have *at least* that as its meaning to account for overextensions in production (E. V. Clark, 1975) alongside the lack of overextension in comprehension.

Another set of predictions made by this theory concerned the acquisition of words related in meaning and their relative order of acquisition. If two words shared meaning components or features in common, then children who had not acquired their full meanings might well confuse the words in production and comprehension. For instance, if all children knew about the meanings of *more* and *less* was that they both picked out "amount," they might easily use one word instead of the other or they might misunderstand what the adult intended. Not until they learn that *more* picks out a positive amount and *less* a negative one will they get the two words straight. Similarly, for words that pick out categories where one is included within the other, for example, *boy* and *brother,* children should get the meaning of the more general term right first (*boy*) because there are fewer semantic features to acquire than for *brother*. Moreover, the meaning of *brother* could at one stage be treated as equivalent to that of *boy* if children had only mastered those features held in common by the two words.

The theory also predicted that when children were learning semantic components or features, they should learn the more general ones first, where these were the features held in common by several words. Moreover, if word meanings consisted of features related to each other hierarchically, then the order of acquisition for features should be top-down, from the most general feature first, with the others acquired in order of hierarchical dependence. For instance, children initially learn that words like *first* and *last* have to do with time, then that they contrast with other time words, like *now,* in having to do with sequence rather than simultaneity. This reflects the analysis of the feature +Time being hierarchically superordinate to the features +Simultaneous and −Simultaneous.

Finally, because children have to discover what meaning or meanings each word has, the acquisition of a feature or some combination of features as the meaning of one word does not imply that children will recognize automatically that other words related in meaning are indeed so related. First, they have to work out which features make up the meaning of a new word. For example, they may have learned that *first* has the features +Time, −Simultaneous, and +Prior, but they still have to learn for *before* that it also contains that combination of features.

The semantic feature hypothesis was put forward to account for two major sets of data: the large literature on overextensions in early language production and a growing body of experimental data on particular domains of the lexicon. These data showed that, for sets of words related in meaning, such as dimensional terms, children tended to produce and understand some words before others. This suggested that there was a consistent order of acquisition within domains such as dimensionality and kinship, an order predicted by the relative semantic complexity of the meanings of different terms.

However, as investigators tested the predictions of the semantic feature hypothesis over a wider domain, its shortcomings become more and more apparent. I will now take up four of its major problems: the status of semantic features, the addition of features during acquisition, the general-to-specific direction of acquisition for features, and the differences between production and comprehension.

Semantic Features

What elements constitute semantic features? The features identified (e.g., "furry," "moves," "round") clearly do not represent the universal primitives posited by Bierwisch (1970) or Postal (1966). Instead they appear to represent the basis on which children set up some contrast between neighboring categories. For instance, a child who previously called cows and dogs *dog,* upon acquiring the word *cow* might use "has horns" as a criterion in deciding whether to call a particular animal *cow* or *dog*. But "has horns" is only one of the candidate differences the child might seize on as pertinent. Potential semantic features of that type appear to vary considerably in complexity: one like "round" seems simpler than "array of parallel vertical bars" (see Tables 2 and 3). There is no way, however, within the framework of the semantic feature hypothesis to justify all the choices of features as features.

In accounts of the adult lexicon, features are identified and justified on the basis of their use to mark contrasts between meanings. For instance, a feature like +Animate is justified because of the contrasts in meaning between nouns that denote animate objects and those that denote inanimate ones. The number and nature of the features to be postulated are a function of the contrasts to be described within the vocabulary and grammar as a whole. Children's semantic features, derived from their erroneous word uses, rarely map onto adult ones. What is the relation, for instance, between a feature like "moves" and +Animate? Does "moves" get refined into some abstract criterion for living things that is eventually best captured as +Animate? The status of such semantic features attributed to children is unclear, both as regards the criteria for identifying a semantic feature and as regards the relation of such features to features postulated for adult meanings.

Another more general problem rears its head when we probe further into the source of semantic features. To what extent is one talking about semantic features and to what extent about conceptual knowledge of the category? Some linguists, in proposing semantic features as components of the meaning of a word, have tried to draw a line between semantic knowledge (the word meaning) and knowledge about the conceptual category a word picks out (e.g., Katz & Fodor, 1963). Others have argued that such a line is in principle impossible to draw when one componentializes word meanings (Bolinger, 1965). But the aim is to account for the child's knowledge about meanings as distinct from his knowledge about the pertinent conceptual categories.

The difficulty of distinguishing one's mental "dictionary" from one's "encyclopedia" remains a problem for anyone who assumes that the lexicon as a whole can be componentialized. Although some words appear to yield up certain semantic features quite readily, others do not. For instance, the adjective *tall* can be analyzed as containing the features +1Dimension, +Vertical, +Extent, +Polar, so that its meaning contrasts with the meanings of other dimensional adjectives on each of the various features (e.g., Bierwisch, 1967). But a componential analysis of a word like *chair,* in the domain of furniture words, appears to defy all the attempts that have

been made (Miller & Johnson-Laird, 1976). In fact, most taxonomies appear hard, if not impossible, to characterize in terms of semantic features. This suggests that only some words or sets of words are amenable to this form of semantic analysis; the analysis cannot be applied to the vocabulary as a whole. But if it cannot, the semantic feature hypothesis is then very restricted in the domains about which it can make predictions.

In summary, the reification of semantic features as they were originally proposed and incorporated into the semantic feature hypothesis makes it difficult, if not impossible, to relate acquisitional *facts* to any descriptions of the adult system. Although part of the fault probably lies in the kinds of accounts given of the adult system, the identification of semantic features per se for child or adult remains an unsolved problem.

Adding Semantic Features to Lexical Entries

The only process of change proposed in the semantic feature hypothesis was the adding of further semantic features to the lexical entries for particular words as children learned more about their meanings. But what about underextensions and overlaps? Both require the dropping of semantic features as well. The focus on addition alone as children learn more about adult meanings is in part an artifact of the focus on overextension data. There, one would have to add features in order to narrow down an overextension. But this is not the only case. Children might have to add, subtract, and organize or reorganize features during the course of acquisition (e.g., Bowerman, 1978a, 1982).

General-to-Specific Features Acquisition

Originally, I proposed that lexical entries that contained hierarchically structured features would be acquired from the most general to the most specific feature. This proposal was based on evidence from the acquisition of the meanings of the words *before* and *after* in which children appeared to acquire the component features top-down. They first mastered +Time, then +Simultaneous (in such words as *now* or *then*), then −Simultaneous, and finally ±Prior.

There are two problems with the proposal. First, it is often hard to determine whether features are hierarchically structured or not within lexical entries (see Bierwisch, 1969); second, there is considerable evidence against this view in data collected on the acquisition of opposites (E. V. Clark, 1972). When children acquire the meanings of adjective pairs like *tall* and *short* or *deep* and *shallow,* they learn first that such terms refer to dimensionality. And

+Dimension is the superordinate feature in their lexical entries. However, the next feature they master is ±Polar, where the word picks out the positive end of the dimension (*tall, deep*) with +Polar or the negative one (*short, shallow*) with −Polar (e.g., Bartlett, 1976; Brewer & Stone, 1975). Only after this do they acquire the features that differentiate the vertical dimension, +Vertical, in *tall* and *short* from the nonvertical one, −Vertical, in *deep* and *shallow*. Thus, for at least one set of terms where the hierarchical structure of the features appears well established, children do not acquire the features top-down. The prediction, then, does not hold as a general case.

Comprehension Versus Production

The semantic feature hypothesis relied on the overextensions made to infer what meaning a child had for a particular word. But the overextensions documented in the diary literature were all overextensions in production. Since then, several researchers have found that overextension in comprehension is rarer than in production (see *Meaning Acquisition*). These findings, combined with evidence that children rely on nonlinguistic strategies prior to understanding a word, led to modifications in the semantic feature hypothesis (E. V. Clark, 1975, 1977a).

Originally, it was assumed that the child's meaning for a word could be inferred from the patterns of errors made. But if children do not overextend in comprehension while doing so in production, this approach clearly underestimates their knowledge of word meanings. I therefore proposed that the errors noted with overextensions in production provided evidence that children had *at least* that meaning attached to the word in question instead of *just* that meaning.

At the same time, evidence that children relied on nonlinguistic strategies prior to comprehension suggested that much of the comprehension data might also require reinterpretation (e.g., E. V. Clark, 1973a, 1980b). Rather than taking correct responses to a single word like *more* or *in* at face value, I argued that children should only be credited with adultlike comprehension once they contrasted the pertinent meaning with the meanings of other, neighboring words in the same domain.

Both major sources of support for the semantic feature hypothesis, then, have had to be qualified in light of alternative interpretations. Overextensions in production appear to depend more on communicative strategies and the need to stretch one's vocabulary than on having grasped only a few of the components making up the adult meanings. And the comprehension data that appeared to favor the acquisition of some word meanings before others appear to be the result of combining partial meanings with certain nonlinguistic strategies. These reassessments resulted from closer scrutiny of some of the differences between producing language and understanding it. The original version of the semantic feature hypothesis was derived from a mixture of the two, with no discussion of the differences.

Summary

There is considerable evidence against the semantic feature hypothesis. The most critical concerns semantic features themselves: the criteria for their identification are vague, their status vis-à-vis features postulated in accounts of adult meanings is unclear, and only certain domains of the lexicon allow word meanings to be decomposed into features or components of meaning. In addition to this, there is evidence against the addition of features to lexical entries being the only developmental process and against there being a particular order for the acquisition of features that are hierarchically structured. (This is partly a problem of finding criteria for identifying features in a lexical entry as hierarchical.) Finally, data based on production and on comprehension yield different assessments of what children know about meanings. The semantic feature hypothesis failed to take account of these differences.

Where the semantic feature hypothesis remains useful is in its predictions about order of acquisition for domains containing words that differ in the complexity of their meanings. In such domains, the prediction is that the relatively less complex word meanings will be acquired before the more complex ones, where complexity is measured cumulatively by the number of conditions for application shared in common by the different words. But semantic complexity is only one of several factors that affect order of acquisition. Patterns of usage in the language, experience with the objects or situations denoted, and compatibility with a priori organizational principles at the conceptual level, to name but a few, may also contribute to order of acquisition.

Overall, the force of the semantic feature hypothesis has been considerably eroded. As it stands now, it makes predictions about the relative order of acquisition of words related in meaning, whose meanings can be decomposed into features or components. It is just as limited in its scope, then, as other accounts that have been put forward over the last decade. It is clearly time to take a fresh look at what is involved in the acquisition of meaning, especially the acquisition of word meanings.

LEXICAL CONTRAST THEORY

In acquiring meanings, I shall propose, children work off two basic principles of language and lexical organization, namely *contrast* and *conventionality*. These principles combined with the conceptual salience of certain categories and relations that give rise to nonlinguistic strategies account for the data available as well as for data not usually considered in discussions of the acquisition of meaning, data on word coinage and metaphor.

Let me begin by describing the two principles. The first is that of lexical *contrast* (de Saussure, 1968; Lyons, 1968). Consider a brief analogy to dictionary writing. In making a dictionary for some hitherto unknown language, one would elicit words, write them down in the left-hand column, and then elicit definitions for them, to be written opposite in the right-hand column of the page. Word 1, then, has its definition beside it—definition 1; below is word 2 aligned with definition 2, and so on down the pages throughout the dictionary. Word 1 contrasts in meaning with word 2; word 2, in turn, contrasts with word 3. In fact, any two elements in the dictionary may be said to contrast: they have different meanings and therefore flag different conceptual categories when used by speakers of that language. Sometimes one word may have several meanings: those will contrast both with each other and with the meanings of other words. This notion of lexical contrast can be expressed as follows:

> *Principle of Contrast*. The conventional meanings of every pair of words (or word-formation devices) contrast.

This principle, like the next, is linguistic, in that it applies to words, not to categories.

Contrasts among word meanings depend, in turn, on the conventional meanings assigned by speakers of each language. Words only maintain their contrasts over time, from one occasion of use to the next, if speakers agree on what meanings the words conventionally carry. This can be represented in a second principle:

> *Principle of Conventionality*. For certain meanings, there is a conventional word or word-formation device that should be used in the language community.

These two principles play a crucial role in language use. In acquisition, these two principles of lexical contrast theory combine with certain adjunct theories to account for the course children follow as they acquire word meanings. These adjuncts will include, for instance, an account of children's hypotheses about what words can be used for; an account of the hypotheses children entertain about word meanings (why initial hypotheses are based on nonlinguistic knowledge, whereas later ones may also draw on linguistic information); an account of how order of acquisition among related meanings is linked to the complexity of the hypotheses children are able to start from; and an account of the strategies children follow in acquiring word-formation devices. These, with lexical contrast theory, will make for both a more heterogeneous and a more complete theory of meaning acquisition.

When a speaker wishes to convey a particular meaning to his addressee, he must choose terms and expressions that he judges appropriate for the addressee to be able to select and identify his intended meaning (Grice, 1957). Thus, the system used for communication—the language—must be such that it allows for coordination between speaker and addressee (see Clark & Marshall, 1981). One property of language that contributes to coordination on an everyday basis is the common possession of a large stock of conventional lexical items known or partly known to both speaker and addressee as native speakers of the language. The communicative utility of such a conventional vocabulary lies in the fact that each meaning contrasts with every other one.

In the acquisition of such a system, children should be looking for two things. First, they should seek the conventional word for an object, situation, or state and, in doing so, assume consistency from one occasion to the next. This assumption seems amply borne out by children's earliest steps in language. They attempt adult forms and themselves treat them as consistent from one occasion to the next; they ask for the names of things unfamiliar to them; and they repair their own word choices, for example, switching *shoe* to *sandal,* from an early age. Second, children should assume that word meanings contrast and that any new word therefore contrasts with those already known to them. This assumption too is strongly supported. For example, when children narrow down the domains of previously overextended words, they do so by contrasting newly acquired words with old ones (see Table 5); they are consistent in their own uses of words, which automatically requires that they contrast them with each other; and, presented with a new word, children act as if it must contrast with words they already know in the same domain (e.g., Carey, 1978a; Dockrell, 1981). In summary, there is strong evidence that children attend to both conventionality and contrast from the earliest stages of language on (E. V. Clark, 1980a).

Under this view of lexical acquisition, the word learner's goal is to *fill lexical gaps* in finding words for whatever conceptual categories he wants to talk about. The theory I want to present here, then, makes the following assumptions:

1. Children will look for new words as they become aware of a gap. By this, I mean becoming aware of wanting to talk about a particular category to someone else and finding no word readily available for it.

2. When children hear new words, they assume that those words contrast with ones they already know and that they must therefore map onto hitherto unlabeled conceptual categories.

In the earliest stages, I have suggested that children look for words to label members of categories that are salient to them (see *The Acquisition of Words*). Thus a child interested in cars, for instance, may attend much more to words for cars initially than to words for other object categories (e.g., Rescorla, 1981). But as soon as children have acquired some language, the relating of words to categories must become more of a two-way street, so that contrasting conceptual categories can trigger a search for contrasting words and exposure to new words can trigger a search for pertinent conceptual contrasts. For example, a child who has set up several categories of animals may then listen for words for those categories, whereas another child may notice new words in the animal domain and then start "looking for" the categories they flag.

What predictions does this view of word meanings make about the process of acquisition? If children are to fill lexical gaps, they must find some means for doing so. I will argue that there are three major options young children rely on. Two of them have been considered under previous views of meaning acquisition: children's overextensions and their reliance on general-purpose words like *that*. These two sets of data, though, have not been linked to each other theoretically. The third option I will discuss is children's coinage of new words with meanings that contrast with those of words they already know. For children, these three options provide ways of filling gaps in their current vocabulary. And each of these communicative strategies provides evidence for children's observance of both conventionality and contrast.

Overextensions Revisited. The first option available to the child with a limited repertoire who wishes to express a new meaning is that of stretching current (known) vocabulary in production to pick out categories for which the child has no words. This process is essentially described by Slobin's (1973) precept, "Use old forms to express new functions" (i.e., new meanings). This is best illustrated by the large body of data on children's overextensions (*Meaning Acquisition*). Children who wish to talk about categories for which they lack words (gaps in their vocabulary) often stretch well-known words in production—words for kinds of objects (e.g., *dog* extended to pick out all sorts of four-legged mammals), situations (e.g., *open* for opening things and removing any sort of obstacle to access), and states (e.g., *hot* applied to all temperatures alike). Since children demonstrate good comprehension of their overextended words, it seems clear that they must be overextending for communicative purposes, in order to be able to talk about categories for which they still lack separate words.

This remedy, of course, must be a temporary one: overextensions operate for the occasion on which the child wanted to talk about some other category, but in the next breath, those words are re-relegated to picking out the particular categories the child assumes they really denote. A particular word, under this view, might be overextended to pick out nearby categories on different occasions over a period of months or only once. It depends on when the child acquires the conventional word or words for those nearby categories. Moreover, the same word may be used on different occasions to pick out nearby categories that each resemble the original category in quite different ways (e.g., Bowerman, 1977). For example, *dog* might be extended on separate occasions to cats because they are four-legged, to bedroom slippers because they are furry, and to a fur wrap because of the animal face with eyes at one end of it. The determining factors, then, are what the child wants to talk about and what he actually has words for. There is nothing in principle to constrain the kinds of overextension made except the child's ability to see some dimension of similarity sufficient to justify stretching one word rather than another.

The child's aim, as speaker, is to fill a particular gap on a particular occasion. Stretching known words to pick out neighboring categories appears to be an option particularly favored in the earliest stages of acquisition. Lexical contrast theory predicts that, under these circumstances, children may overextend words in production. It also predicts that children will not overextend a word from one category to pick out another when they already have a word for the latter in their repertoire. Both predictions appear to be well supported by the data. Children overextend many but not all the words in their early vocabularies (see Tables 1 to 4), and they cease to overextend words to those parts of a domain for which a new (conventional) word has been acquired (see Table 5).

General-Purpose Words. The second option children may take in filling lexical gaps is to rely on general-purpose terms, words whose intended meanings are construable only in the context in which they are uttered. Children rely on such terms for talking about objects and situations. The classic general-purpose term for picking out objects is the demonstrative *that*. The referent of *that*, though, can only be identified in the context of each utterance. Children rely on demonstratives from a very early stage; indeed, a demonstrative word often appears among the first 10 and certainly among the first 50 words of a child's vocabulary (Clark & Sengul, 1978). Another general-purpose term for objects is *thing*: reliance on this word seems to appear at a slightly later stage, but some children use it heavily (e.g., Bühler, 1930; Geodakian & Kurghinian, 1976). These terms pick out kinds of objects: the addressee has to be present to understand which one on each occasion. These words are also frequently, if not invariably, accompanied by pointing gestures that make the referent quite clear in context (see Pechmann & Deutsch, 1980).

Children also use general-purpose words for situations, especially for kinds of events. The terms they rely on most heavily are general-purpose verbs like *do, make,* and *go* (Berman, 1978; E. V. Clark, 1978a, 1978c). Again, as for demonstratives, the intended meanings of these general-purpose verbs can only be understood in context on the occasion of their utterance. Hearing a child's speech out of context (e.g., on a tape-recording), merely gives one the illusion of understanding everything. For instance, consider the following utterances transcribed from a child aged 2 years 2 months:

1. "I do it again."
2. "You . . . do . . . doing that."
3. "You do do it, okay?"
4. "The clown do!"

Without their contexts, it is impossible to know what situations were actually being talked about. In fact, (1) was a comment as the child knocked over some blocks; (2) a comment as he watched an adult build blocks up into a tower; (3) a request to the adult to unroll some computer tape the child had been trying unsuccessfully to unroll himself; and (4) a request to have a toy clown perform as a clown should (E. V. Clark, 1978c).

At first glance, neither overextensions nor general-purpose words fit the principle of contrast: the same form is used from one occasion to the next to pick out different conceptual categories. Use of general-purpose terms clearly violates the preference for one meaning to one form (Slobin, 1973), an ideal version of the principle of contrast. But there is, of course, a contrast in the speaker's *intended* meaning on each occasion on which he uses an overextension or a general-purpose term. This is why it is critical that analysis of overextensions and especially of general-purpose terms take into account the intended meaning on each occasion. For general-purpose terms, and for demonstratives and deictics generally, the focus has been on their general purpose nature rather than on intended meanings. The difficulty lies in keeping track of the exact settings of use and making sure that one has identified the object or situation the child as speaker was trying to pick out on each occasion.

Coinages. A third option children could take is to construct new word forms to carry new meanings. Again, the principle of contrast predicts that they should do this only to fill gaps—to convey meanings for which they have no readily available words. This third option *is* an option for children, although it is not perhaps exploited as early as overextensions or general-purpose terms. Children's coinages include terms for both objects and situations. The kinds of words they coin include terms for agents and objects affected by different activities (e.g., E. V. Clark, 1981a; Clark & Hecht, 1982). They also coin terms for situations, and as is the case for general purpose verbs, these are mainly events (e.g., E. V. Clark, 1982; Clark & Clark, 1979). I will take up this option—coining new words—in greater detail later.

The three options just described all follow from a theory in which the need to fill lexical gaps, and hence follow the principle of contrast, is primary. All three options represent temporary solutions for speakers with limited means at their disposal. They allow children to fill gaps; but eventually children must acquire the stock of conventional lexical items available to any adult speaker of that language. (Of course, adults too have to expand that stock on occasion and then they take up at least some of the same options, using general-purpose terms or newly coined words to convey their meanings.)

The next step is to acquire more terms to carry further contrasts. To do this, children have in many cases to find "new forms for old functions" (old meanings previously expressed some other way). To make further contrasts explicit, they need to add lexical items so they can be sure their listeners pick out the right conceptual category when they talk about such categories out of context. And they must be able to do this with displaced speech as well as in talking about the here and now. This is particularly critical for uses of general-purpose terms and over-extensions of conventional terms.

The process of adding words to keep categories in the same domain distinct through linguistic contrasts is clearly seen when children narrow down previously overextended terms. As they acquire a new word, they drop the overextension previously relied on. For instance, with the acquisition of the word *cow,* a child who previously overextended *dog* to pick out cows stops doing so. This is precisely what is predicted by the principle of contrast. The pervasiveness of this process is well documented in Leopold's (1949) data where one can chart the take-over points where conventional terms entered his daughter's vocabulary and immediately replaced her earlier overextensions (Barrett, 1978; see also Table 5). The addition of new terms to pick out existing conceptual contrasts in a domain makes those contrasts linguistically explicit. And the addition of new terms helps children communicatively: because they have more words at their disposal, they do better as speakers in picking out the objects they wish to talk about. Adding to their vocabulary helps children communicate more effectively.

Children not only acquire more terms to pick out more kinds of objects but also more kinds of situations and states. For example, in talking about events, they begin to contrast an original term like *open* with *shut, turn on, turn off, pull off, put on,* and so on, thus dividing up the domain formerly grouped together by overextensions of words like *open, shut,* or *door.* They do this by acquiring the appropriate—conventional—adult terms for the different kinds of events. They also acquire more terms for processes and begin to contrast *kick,* say, with terms like *wave, shake,* and *move.* In talking about states, children make themselves better understood as they add further locative terms and use not only *in* and *on* in production but also contrast *in* and *on* with *to, from, out, off,* and *up* (e.g., Braunwald, 1978; Gruendel, 1977). The addition of each new word in a domain makes explicit in children's speech the further contrasts they can now mark in talking, contrasts mapped onto already existing contrasts among conceptual categories of objects, situations, and states.

Children also replace general-purpose terms with words that make the contrasts among different situations, for instance, quite explicit. In the contexts of the verb *do,* for example, 2-year-olds use more and more specific verbs to pick out particular events and processes as time goes by (say from age 2 to 3). In building blocks and then knocking them down, earlier use of *do* alone yields to *knock down* or *hit;* in playing with paper or playdough where the child was cutting out different shapes, *do* yields to *cut* or *cut out;* in drawing pictures, *do* yields to *draw* or *write;* and so on. In each case, the general-purpose verb *do,* used to pick out a particular kind of event in context, gives way to more specific verbs that can pick out the event both in and out of context.[11] One advantage of the more specific verb is precisely that it is less tied to the context of the actual utterance than is general-purpose *do* (e.g., E. V. Clark, 1978a, 1978c).

The same goes for general-purpose verbs used to pick out processes rather than events. For instance, *go* as well as *do* is used for several kinds of activities. But the contexts in which *go* is used early on gradually give way to uses of more specific verbs such as *ride, walk, drive, bicycle, run,* and *fly.* Where general-purpose *go* is used for the activity of making a noise, it yields to more specific verbs like *shout, whisper, yell,* and *cry.* In summary, children gradually give up using general-purpose verbs as broadly in favor of more precise labels for many of the conceptual categories they want to talk about. The essence of both narrowing down overextensions and replacing general-purpose terms (for objects as well as situations) is an explicit linguistic marking of conceptual contrasts through words with meanings that contrast.

Hierarchy in Taxonomies

So far I have talked about contrasts within particular domains—contrasts among animal terms, among locative terms, among activity terms, and so on. But linguistic and conceptual contrasts need not all be made at the same level. Concepts and meanings can be organized hierarchically, with varying degrees of elaboration in a taxonomy. How do children acquire words for categories at different levels within a hierarchy? And when do they do this? As yet, we know little about this aspect of conceptual and linguistic development, and lexical contrast theory makes no direct predictions here. The few analyses that have been done suggest that in domains like those of animals, children first acquire several words that contrast with each other at the same level. (These words may or may not be words adults would use for basic-level categories.) Then children begin to add both superordinate and subordinate terms to the domain in no particular order (e.g., E. V. Clark, 1978a).

But even quite simple hierarchies seem to take quite a long time to set up at the linguistic level: this presumably reflects the difficulty of doing so at the conceptual level too. Rosch and her colleagues (1976) have shown that contrasts between categories are less clear both above and below the basic level. Above the basic level, there may be little or even no family resemblance between the categories grouped together in the superordinate category. For example, bookshelves, beds, chairs, rugs, sofas, and lamps are all members of the superordinate category of furniture, but rugs have very little in common with bookshelves, and so on. Equally, with subordinate categories, below the basic level, contrasts are based on much finer details and are, therefore, harder to maintain. Consider the small differences that distinguish dining tables from kitchen tables, bedside tables, coffee tables, occasional tables, and sofa tables.

The difficulty even adults have in keeping categories apart at the lower level and realizing where the lines should be drawn for categories at the upper level seems to be reflected in the greater length of time it takes children to learn terms for superordinate and subordinate categories. And learning the relevant words is only part of the task: they have to be learned together with their hierarchical status. For instance, it is possible to make inferences about unknown objects provided one knows which superordinate category they belong to. Told that a *mib* is a bird, one can assume that a mib has wings, flies, lays eggs, and so on. While 5- to 7-year-olds are able to make a number of inferences from such information, younger children do not appear able to make use of it (Harris, 1975; Smith, 1979). In part, of course, this also reflects the fact that making such inferences requires extensive general knowledge about the domain (see Horton, 1982).

Order of Acquisition

Some domains of the lexicon contain word meanings that overlap or share parts of their meanings with neighboring terms rather than labeling distinct categories. Such terms are typically terms for relations and thus more likely to be words for situations and states than for objects. Domains like those of dimensional adjectives (e.g., *tall, long, wide*), verbs of possession (e.g., *have, give, buy*), and kinship terms (e.g., *son, grandfather, aunt*) exhibit a stable order of acquisition for the different word meanings included in each "field." This stability has been attributed to the relative semantic complexity of the

words involved, with the simpler terms (those with fewer semantic components) being acquired before their relatively more complex neighbors (e.g., E. V. Clark, 1972). Under the present view, the relative complexity of different meanings still resides in the degree of overlap of the meanings and in working out the different conditions of application. But the focus is on the motivation for working out how each of the related meanings is used, that is, on the discovery of how each dimensional adjective, for instance, *contrasts* with its neighbors and hence what the *conventional* uses are to which each adjective can be put.

The point at which a child starts trying to work out the conditions of application for *big* and *small*, for instance, probably varies from child to child. And the nonlinguistic basis for a child's initial hypotheses about the meanings of *big* and *small*, or other dimensional terms, will also vary because children's initial exposure to each dimensional term and the number of terms already being worked on varies (see Keil & Carroll, 1980). If the child is trying to establish the basis for contrasts in meaning within a domain, each new word added to the domain may upset some contrasts already worked out. Thus, the child may go through several stages of incorrect uses before getting the adultlike set of contrasts fully established (e.g., Gathercole, 1982; Maratsos, 1973, 1974). Under the present view, these fluctuations reflect the patterns of contrasts children are gradually working out as they discover the conditions of application for each word—its conventional meaning—and how each contrasts with the other words in the domain. The addition of any new term to the domain will require adjustments by the child in both the conventional meanings and the contrasts he has already set up.

For terms like *more* and *less,* the present theory initially makes the same interpretation as that in E. V. Clark (1973a), namely, that the child knows the meaning of neither term and is relying on a nonlinguistic strategy of choosing the object with greater extension or mass. This will make it appear that the child (1) understands *more* and (2) treats *less* as if it means *more*. Under the present theory, there is no reason to assume the meaning of *more* is simpler than that of *less*. What the child has to do, though, is work out how they contrast. And acquisition of their meanings can only be assumed once children do contrast them consistently (see also E. V. Clark, 1980b).

A similar analysis applies to temporal terms like *before* and *after*. The initial pattern of errors has always been attributed to a nonlinguistic strategy of assuming that the order of mention mirrors the order of occurrence (E. V. Clark, 1971). This initial strategy appears to be replaced by another that assumes the second event—taken to be described in the second clause (as in the order of mention strategy)—is introduced by a conjunction to mark its place in sequence. This strategy coincides with the meaning of *before* and makes it appear to be acquired before that of *after*. However, under the present view, children cannot be said to know fully the meanings of either *before* or *after* until they have mastered the contrast between them as well as how they contrast with other neighboring temporal terms. And, just as in the domain of dimensional adjectives, temporal terms differ in their conditions of application. These are what make *first* and *last* easier to master than *before* or *tomorrow*. The addition of each new term to the domain likewise can produce fluctuations and even errors in how children interpret and produce the different terms.

In summary, lexical contrast theory, combined with certain adjuncts such as a theory about children's initial hypotheses about meanings, can account for the data that have been considered previously in both supporting and disconfirming the semantic feature hypothesis. Children's acquisition of word meanings depends on the numbers of contrasts involved and the conditions of application. Where these are more complex, the series of contrasts involved are also more complicated to analyze and then acquire. Other word meanings may take a long time to acquire because one word has several meanings, making it more difficult for children to come up with hypotheses compatible with the conditions of application for each meaning. Complexity of word meanings, then, is assumed to reside in the conditions on their use. And those, in turn, spring from the contrasts each conventional word meaning bears to its neighbors.

Some Advantages of Lexical Contrast Theory

What are the advantages of taking an approach that focuses on lexical contrasts rather than on semantic features? First, a theory based on contrasts of meaning motivates word acquisition itself: to pick out contrasting conceptual categories, one needs contrasting word meanings. The notion of contrast, in effect, is basic to both conceptual and linguistic organization.

Lexical contrast theory also gets away from the reification of semantic features implicit in the various componential approaches (see *Theories of Meaning Acquisition*). The present view of word meanings is not one where words have lexical entries with listable features or components that can be added or deleted as children work out what else belongs with the meaning of word *X*. Instead, it is one where children learn that a particular label or flag simply picks out a particular conceptual category. This view of meaning solves the problem of how a word is related to the mass of information that can be linked to a single conceptual category. Speakers depend on the particular linguistic or nonlinguistic context and on mutual knowledge for their listeners to be able, on different occasions, to pick out different pieces from all the information potentially pertinent to a category. For example, the word *dog*, uttered following an earlier discussion about sport, should lead the addressee to focus on what he knows about dogs in various kinds of sport, whereas *dog* uttered in the context of talking about highly trained animals should lead the addressee to retrieve any knowledge pertinent to dogs in circuses, sheep dog trials, guide dogs for the blind, and so on. Under this view, speakers can use the same word on different occasions to evoke different segments of their addressees' conceptual category. There is no need to posit any complex set of disjunctions as lists of properties within the lexical entry for the word *dog*. *Dog* is simply the linguistic device—the word—that flags the conceptual category bearing the label (see further Kripke, 1972; Putnam, 1970).

A third advantage is that lexical contrast theory retains an important distinction, that between conceptual categories and word meanings. As I argued in the introduction, the two are not equivalent, although the terms cognitive and semantic have often been used interchangeably in discussions of early meanings (e.g., Nelson, 1974; Nelson, Rescorla, Gruendel, & Benedict, 1978). The problem is that this leaves no way for one to talk about the conceptual categories for which we lack words; it does not allow one to compare different languages and the means of expression conventionalized within each nor to compare the kinds of expressions speakers can create to fill gaps. Keeping concepts and meanings distinct is an important consideration not only for the discussion of concepts and meanings but also for the analysis of how speakers make the language serve their purpose to convey which conceptual categories they want to talk about.

Fourth, lexical contrast theory makes communication primary. It views the acquisition of word meanings as based on two fundamental principles governing the lexicon as a whole—the principles of conventionality and contrast. And by focusing on speakers' reasons for wishing to enlarge the lexicon, namely the need to fill lexical gaps, the theory can readily account for the data on early word uses—children's reliance on overextensions, general-purpose terms, and word coinages. It can also account for the gradual restriction of some of these options as children add more words to their repertoires, words whose meanings contrast with those acquired earlier. Underextensions and overlaps are also both possible in this theory. But they are not explicitly predicted because they will depend on the specific set of contrasts each child has worked out and the hypotheses he has about new words subsequently acquired. But the addition of a new word with a meaning that contrasts with other words already known does not necessarily result in appropriate usage. Because the conventions that govern each word have to be learned, children may take a long time to work out the precise dimensions of contrast among sets of meanings. Despite this, studies in a variety of lexical domains have shown considerable uniformity in the stages children go through as they map the meanings of dimensional adjectives, spatial prepositions, temporal adverbs and conjunctions, and deictic terms among others.

Finally, as I have already indicated, lexical contrast theory does not work alone. It applies together with certain adjunct theories in order to account for the acquisition of meanings. One such adjunct consists of the principles and strategies children rely on as they acquire a repertoire of word-formation devices. In the next section, I will show how lexical contrast theory, together with this adjunct theory, accounts for children's word coinages.

Extending Lexical Contrast Theory

This theory of meaning acquisition makes further predictions about both children's and adults' word use. First, where children lack a word for some conceptual category, they can draw on yet another resource for communicating: they can coin a new word with the requisite meaning just for the occasion. This resource, of course, becomes more available to children as they learn more about their language. And it is a resource constantly exploited by adults. Second, both children and adults can stretch known words, not by overextending them (as in the earlier stages of acquisition) but by relying on comparison—overtly as in similes (e.g., *x is like y*) or covertly as in metaphors (*x is a y*). In this final section, I will briefly review what is known about children's uses of these two options and argue that both lend further support to lexical contrast theory.

Coining New Words

When children add to their vocabulary, they look for words that conventionally flag further categories they wish to talk about. But if they fail to find a conventional label when they look, they still need a way to fill this gap in the lexicon, a way to convey this meaning not yet attached to a word form. And so they may construct a word for that particular purpose on that particular occasion (e.g., E. V. Clark, 1981a, 1982). Taking up this option, of course, depends on their knowing how to construct the necessary new word forms.

What kinds of forms do children construct to carry new meanings? They are presumably guided by the word-formation patterns available in their language. English, for example, relies on three major word-formation processes: affixation, conversion, and compounding.

Affixation. Affixes in English come in two types, prefixes added to the beginnings of words and suffixes added to the ends. The former are fewer in number and, unlike the latter, rarely change the word class of the base, e.g., making a noun into a verb or vice versa. Among the most productive prefixes are *un-,* used to express reversal, and *re-,* used to express repetition.

Suffixes typically alter the word class of the base form. They can be grouped according to their end product, for example, whether they result in a noun or verb, and by the bases they apply to. For instance, the noun-forming *-er* can be added to both noun and verb bases to form agentive or instrumental nouns (*jumper, forker*). Other noun-forming suffixes, like *-ness* or *-ing,* form nouns from adjectives (*darkness*) and verbs (*washing*) respectively. The verb-forming suffixes *-ize* and *-ify* can be added to either noun or adjective bases, as in *beautify, finalize.* Adjective-forming *-y, -ly,* and *-ful* are added to noun bases (*rocky, friendly*), while *-able* is added to verbs (*jumpable*). This list, of course, contains only some of the affixes used in English, mostly ones that seem to be fairly productive for contemporary speakers (Adams, 1973; Marchand, 1969). Affixation is often referred to as the process of derivation.

Conversion. Conversion, or zero derivation, which changes word class without the addition of any affix, is a very productive word formation process of English. It operates to make nouns into verbs, verbs into nouns, adjectives into verbs, and nouns into adjectives, to name but a few of the possible changes in word class. For instance, many nouns can be used as verbs, for example, *to launderette, to trumpet* (Clark & Clark, 1979), and certain verbs can be used as nouns, for example, *an attempt, a wrench.* Adjectives can become nouns, for example, *some bitter, a final,* and verbs, for example, *to calm, to soundproof.* The process of conversion has been in use for centuries and remains very productive.

Some types, though, are much commoner than others.

Compounding. Compounding is also a common process in English. Compounds are made up of combinations of noun bases or noun and verb bases, and may have various suffixes added as well. They are usually identified by their stress pattern: most compounds have heavier stress on the first element and lighter stress on the last one, as in *post-man* or *fire-engine*. Compounds are usually distinguished from simple nouns or verbs in having meanings that are related to, but not inferrable from, their parts. For instance, a *dark-room* is dark and is a room, but there is nothing in this combination to give the meaning of a room used for photographic processing that can be made dark as needed. Equally, although a compound like *dog-sled* may seem transparent because it does denote a kind of *sled,* the relation between *sled* and *dog* is not in any sense "given." There is no a priori reason why this word should not denote a sled for carrying dogs or food for dogs, a sled decorated with pictures of dogs, a sled that once ran over a dog, and so on. It just happens that, conventionally, it denotes a sled drawn by dogs, a meaning that has to be learned for this compound (Downing, 1977).

The many types of compounds in English have been classified in various ways. Those in which the two (or more) bases are nouns have often been characterized by a short list of paraphrases for the relation between Noun–1 and Noun–2. For example, three very productive types are: (1) the type *door-knob,* Noun–1 *has* Noun–2; (2) the type *frog-man,* Noun–2 *is like* Noun–1; and (3) the type *tea-room,* Noun–2 *is for* Noun–1 (e.g., Adams, 1973). These paraphrases are often convenient, but they do not adequately account for all the relations expressed in compounds.

Compounds containing a verb base, in contrast, have usually been classified by the grammatical relations the bases would have had in a full sentence. For instance, a compound like *sun-rise* falls into the group Subject + Verb, while *sight-seeing* is Object + Verb (with the verb made into a noun with the suffix *-ing*) as is *tax-payer* (with the verb made into an agentive noun with the suffix *-er*). These types together with compounds patterned like *swimming-pool, day-dreaming, baby-sitter,* and *home-work* are among the most productive in modern English (Adams, 1973; Marchand, 1969).

These three options all appear in young children's speech when they coin new words, but the patterns children rely on are initially limited compared to the range available to adults. As in the rest of the lexicon, children's acquisition of word-forma-

tion patterns is governed by the principles of conventionality and contrast. In addition, several other principles appear to affect how easy different word-formation patterns or devices are to acquire. Among them, for example, is the *simplicity* of the word form used. The simplest word forms appear to be those where there is no change at all, beyond the change of word class. Making nouns into verbs using conversion, therefore, ought to be a very simple affair. And children's innovative verbs support this view: as young as age 2, they use verbs like *needle* for *mend, bell* for *ring, stick* for *hit with a stick, cracker* for *drop crackers into,* and so on. New words that require the addition of suffixes, like *-er* or *-ly,* appear only later.

Simplicity of form interacts with *transparency* of meaning, another factor in children's coinages. For example, for 2- and 3-year-olds, the earliest coinages of agent nouns (for the instigators of actions) tend to be compounds formed from a base noun to which they add the noun *-man,* for example, *rat-man* (for a psychologist who worked with rats), *plant-man* (for a gardener), and *fire-man* (for someone who burns things) (E. V. Clark, 1981a). Because children already know the meaning of *man,* the use of that noun in their compounds makes the meaning of the compounds more transparent for the expression of new kinds of agency.

A third factor that affects the word formation patterns children use is the *productivity* of different devices—whether a particular pattern is regularly available in the language for constructing new forms or whether it occurs in only a few well-established words. Productive patterns provide the models for innovative words, models that adults and children alike rely on when they coin new words. Young children pick productive devices over unproductive ones when all other things are equal (e.g., E. V. Clark, 1981b). For example, English relies on *-er* much more than on *-ist* to form new agent nouns and young children's spontaneous coinages of agent nouns with suffixes make exclusive use of *-er* (E. V. Clark, 1981a).

A fourth factor that governs new word formation is one I have called *regularization*. If children can organize new word forms into existing paradigms, something that is helped by reliance on productive patterns of word formation, the coining process appears to be easier. Paradigms essentially act as an aide-mémoire, both for producing and for understanding new forms (E. V. Clark, 1980a; MacWhinney, 1978).

Ideally, in coining a new word, one should be able to draw on a paradigm with a large number of model exemplars (regularization and productivity), with simple mappings of meanings to forms (transparency), and simple rather than complex word forms (simplicity). The four factors just described (and possibly others) interact with each other to result in a particular order of acquisition for word-formation devices. What that order actually is depends on the resources available in each particular language. The same principles for the acquisition of new word forms may have different outcomes in English, Hungarian, Russian, and Hebrew. The places where there are one-to-one mappings between meaning and form vary from one language to another, and the productivity of the devices carrying particular meanings also varies from language to language. Nonetheless, each factor affects the new forms children construct to carry their new meanings.

What is common to all such innovations is that the new meanings are always meanings that *contrast* with the meanings of words already known to the child coiners. Furthermore, these new meanings yield priority to *conventional* ones. When children learn a conventional lexical item for picking out a particular category, they give up the innovative form used for that meaning previously. Conventionality, then, takes priority over innovation, and innovations always conform to the principle of contrast: new meanings contrast with meanings already known to the child.

Data from a variety of languages show that children construct innovative word forms from as early as (and sometimes earlier than) age 2. These new words, often nonce words (used on only one occasion) fill in for words the children lack. The gaps in their vocabularies can have two sources: they have not acquired the conventional word adults would use to convey a particular meaning or there simply isn't one (E. V. Clark, 1981a, 1982). For adults, the latter—real gaps—are the ones to be filled, when need be, with innovative words (e.g., Clark & Clark, 1979).

Where are children most likely to construct innovative words—for which conceptual categories? Any answer to this question has to take into account the word-formation options available in particular languages and the principles governing their acquisition. Although the data are not yet in, there do appear to be certain domains in which children are more likely to feel a need for new lexical items. For example, children quite often coin new words for actions. In doing so, they rely on labels for objects involved in the actions, particularly for instruments, for example, after his mother had nursed his baby sister: "*Mommy nippled Anna*" (2 years 11

months); watching a man open a door with a key: "*He's keying the door*" (3 years 21 days) pretending to shoot his mother with a stick: "*I'm going to gun you*"(3 years 2 months); asking if the pants his mother was mending were ready: "*Is it all needled?*" (3 years 2 months); or after getting into the car: "*I seat-belted myself*" (4½) (E. V. Clark, 1978a, 1982). Children also coin a large number of agent and instrument nouns, both spontaneously and on demand, for example, for agents: *a plant-man* (gardener), *a present-man* (someone who gives presents), *a smile-person* (someone who smiles at people), *a hitter-man* (someone who hits things), *an opener* (someone who opens doors); and for instruments: *a chop* (an axe), *a knock-thing* (something for knocking with), *a rock-machine* (a machine for throwing things), *a hugging-machine* (a thing for hugging people) (see E. V. Clark, 1981a; Clark & Hecht, 1982).

The largest category of coinages, perhaps, is simply words for categories of objects, and, in particular, words for subcategories of objects. It is here that the principle of contrast can be seen at work most clearly. Having acquired a word for an object category, children later divide that category into different subkinds, related by their membership in the larger category but distinct from one another. In English, children usually rely on compounds in constructing innovative nouns for talking about subkinds. For example, one 2-year-old, who distinguished different kinds of smoke, talked about *house-smoke* for smoke from a chimney, *car-smoke* for exhaust, and *pipe-smoke* for the tobacco smoke from someone's pipe. One also finds contrasts like that between *bottle* as a word to pick out the category and *baby-bottle* for a bottle the child had used as a baby. (Notice that the latter meaning contrasts with that commonly found in children's speech with *baby-* used as a size modifier in compounds.)

In summary, children as young as 2 have already acquired some word-formation patterns or devices that allow them to construct new words. This in turn allows children to extend their vocabularies when they need to find a way of talking about a particular category, a category for which they lack a word. In general, their spontaneous coinages conform to the word-formation patterns of their language, and children acquiring different languages appear to apply much the same principles in their acquisition of word-formation options. Moreover, a cursory inspection of the available data suggests that children's coinages fall into similar conceptual groupings across different languages: new words for objects, agents, and instruments, for example, predominate among their innovative nouns. But the order of acquisition of the various devices and the effects of different acquisition principles on that order have still to be established in detail.

Using Figurative Language

Another way of extending the lexicon predicted by lexical contrast theory is the extension of old forms to carry new meanings, in this case figurative meanings. The use of conventional terms with figurative senses may be hard at times to distinguish from the earlier overextensions produced by very young children. However, there is strong evidence that children do not understand figurative extensions or make much use of them until they have mastered the primary or nonfigurative uses to which a word is put. Asch and Nerlove (1960), for example, found that children aged between 3 and 11 would apply adjectives to physical objects first and only later apply them to attitudes as well. The adjectives Asch and Nerlove studied were *sweet, hard, soft, cold, warm, bright, deep,* and *crooked.* Figurative senses, even when conventional (as are many uses of these adjectives), take a long time to acquire. The younger children simply appeared not to know the nonliteral or figurative meanings of these adjectives.

But there are some extended uses children find relatively easy to understand and produce. Gentner (1977) found that 4-year-olds were easily able to assign six body parts (head, shoulders, arms, stomach, knees, and feet) to drawings of trees and mountains presented in various orientations in response to questions like, ''If the mountain had a stomach, where would it be?'' Gentner found this analogical ability well developed even in the youngest children she looked at. Children, then, can make appropriate inferences about how to map a set of properties from one object onto another not normally thought of as having those properties. They were extending their body-part terms, words from a domain established very early and therefore very well known to children of 4 or 5 (Andersen, 1978).

Other studies of early metaphoric development have concentrated on children's ability to interpret figurative uses, either by explaining a word use presented in a sentence or by selecting an appropriate paraphrase. Winner, Rosenstiel, and Gardner (1976) found that children under 10 had a harder time than older children in interpreting metaphors appropriately. On the other hand, 6-year-olds often seemed to interpret metaphors as descriptions of magical situations, thereby taking figurative word uses to be literal uses. Winner (1978) looked at very early metaphoric language, distinguishing it from

overextensions where the child has not yet acquired words for some conceptual categories; she found a number of instances in the speech of one child followed longitudinally from age 2: the child would rename a familiar object that he transformed through his actions, for example, putting his foot in a wastebasket, he called it a *boot* (2 years 4 months); holding a horn like an eggbeater and making the appropriate turning motions, he called it a *mixer* (2 years 5 months); or he called a piece of string his *tail,* but immediately afterwards explained that it was *string* (2 years 11 months). Similes like these appear to be the earliest figurative extensions children make. Winner's findings, then, appear to present the natural precursor to the results Gentner reported for the extension of body-part terms to trees and mountains.

The acquisition of figurative usage is complicated by there being all sorts of conventional metaphors and similes in the language. The meanings of these have to be acquired just like those of conventional lexical items. For instance, the meanings of *to spill the beans, to be left high and dry, to hit the sack,* or *by and large* cannot be computed by knowing the meanings of the words contained in the whole expression; they have to be learned just like the meanings of *horse, river,* and *climb.* Conventional metaphors like these are used for talking about objects, situations, and states, so the child has to learn that a particular word may pick out several quite different categories, for example, the uses of *sweet* in *sweet cherry, sweet tooth,* and *sweet nature.*

The preference for concrete or literal meanings noted by these researchers suggests that the concrete or basic meaning has priority in acquisition. Presumably this could vary, though, for some words, depending on children's initial exposure and subsequent hypotheses about the meaning. Just as children have to learn that the meaning of *dogsled* is in fact a sled that is pulled by dogs (rather than one decorated with dogs, for instance), they also have to learn the relations between basic and figuratively extended uses of conventional words in the language. This may be difficult, because there is nothing about a word a priori that tells one whether it has a conventional figurative meaning in addition to its basic meaning or not. And, of course, figurative extensions can be created, just as new word forms can, to carry new meanings.

The presence of conventional figurative expressions may contribute to the difficulty children have in working out word meanings. They are just beginning to work out what the basic uses of such words as *hard* and *soft* are; for example, they have identified the dimension involved and how the terms apply to different objects. At this point, to hear the same words extended to feelings, colors, and voices is probably a source of considerable confusion. The dimensions identified with uses of *hard* and *soft* have suddenly vanished, and although the extensions of *hard* and *soft* to these other domains is conventional, it is not necessarily transparent. The lack of transparency is easily seen when one considers how sounds, colors, feelings, and voices are described in other languages. Sometimes the same dimensional adjectives get extended to these other domains, but often the adjectives extended may be taken from quite a different part of the vocabulary (e.g., Rosaldo, 1975).

So lexical contrast theory predicts here that, provided children construct meanings that contrast with those conventional meanings they have already acquired, they may extend their vocabulary through figurative extensions as well as by coining new words. Overall, children appear to make less use of the figurative option to extend their vocabulary during their first 5 or 6 years than they do of word coinages and, even earlier, of various types of overextension and general-purpose words for the categories they are trying to talk about. The greater difficulty of figurative language can probably be attributed in large part to the absence of transparent connections between the basic or literal meanings of words and their figurative extensions, especially for conventional figurative language.

Summary

Acquiring a vocabulary is a complex process that depends critically on two factors: (1) *conventionality,* the observation of conventions governing language use within a speech community and (2) *contrast,* the requirement that new meanings contrast with those already known. In the acquisition of new words, whether part of the well-established lexicon or not, children look first for contrasts in meaning. Lexical contrast theory, founded on these two principles, provides motivation for the acquisition of vocabulary and for the patterns of acquisition found. Children initially overextend words to fill lexical gaps; they rely heavily on general-purpose words; they coin new words; and, later, they extend known words figuratively to new domains. But lexical contrast theory itself still needs further elaboration. What it can do is account for the roles played by conventionality and contrast. Children observe these two principles very early, and this accounts for how they go about exploiting the options available in each language for expressing the meanings they want to convey to others.

Lexical contrast theory requires further ingredients: one is an account of the hypotheses about meanings children start out with, and how they elaborate these hypotheses as they work out word meanings, both the relations conventional meanings bear to the conceptual categories they pick out and the relations they bear to each other. It will also require further examination of the contribution made by various conceptual capacities. Some of the information children use in judging similarity and in identifying category members is revealed in the nonlinguistic strategies they rely on. These strategies are strategies for organizing objects, situations, and states, but they have been relatively little studied, despite their prominence as a source of hypotheses about new word meanings (e.g., E. V. Clark, 1973a, 1977a, 1980a).

Another ingredient is the social setting of language use. I have focused on contrasts of meaning that parallel contrasts among the categories being talked about. But there are other "layers" of contrasts that also come into play in language use. Different words for the same category—apparent synonyms—may still contrast, but they do so in the register or social attitude conveyed. Compare uses of *cop* versus *policeman, tea* versus *marijuana, guy* versus *man,* and so on (Nunberg, 1978). The word chosen to pick out a particular category not only contrasts that category with others in the same domain but also can serve to identify the speaker as a member of a particular group, as holding a particular attitude, or as being formal or informal. Thus, even apparent synonyms normally contrast, but the dimension of contrast may be one of social or emotional rather than semantic significance. These aspects of contrast have received little or no attention in the acquisition of word meanings (but see Andersen, 1977; Bates, 1976).

Finally, children can only take proper account of convention and contrast once they begin to relate conceptual categories to words. But this process poses a difficult selection problem: children have to decide which categories are likely to have a linguistic representation—a single word to flag just that category—and which are not (see Slobin, 1979). Practically nothing is known about how children decide that a category is a likely candidate for linguistic encoding or about how they actually link categories with words. It seems reasonable to suggest, though, that children rely on what they already know conceptually when they start to form hypotheses about what kind of object, situation, or state a word might serve to pick out.

CONCLUSION

The focus in the present chapter has been on young children's concepts and meanings, the emergence of certain types of conceptual categories and the subsequent acquisition of words for talking about those categories. But to study concepts and meanings, it is essential to keep them distinct. Words serve to flag or pick out particular categories or, depending on the context, particular facets of a category. The relation between concepts and meanings, therefore, is necessarily an indirect one. Words (and their meanings) simply evoke concepts; they do not represent them. Thus information pertinent to forming a conceptual category may have no role in the meaning of the word used to pick out that category.

This view poses a problem when it comes to investigating young children's conceptual categories. The language—the words—they use may not be the best guide to the conceptual categories they have established nor to the contents of those categories. To investigate young children's conceptual categories, therefore, one has two major choices: one can construct an epistemology to encompass the kinds of concepts children acquire first, when they acquire them, and how they acquire them. But there have been few attempts to take on such a difficult task. Or one can start from language by looking at which kinds of categories are invariably talked about, whatever the language, and asking when and how those develop in young children, even prior to any use of language. Using the latter perspective, I examined the evidence for children having categories of objects, situations, and states, from early infancy onwards. The data available are such, though, that there are many gaps in our knowledge about how and when different kinds of conceptual categories are established.

Nonetheless, it is clear that between birth and age 2, children set up conceptual categories of objects, situations, and states. The evidence for this comes from studies of memory, recognition, and sorting behaviors from children during the first two years of life. However, the range of categories established during this period and the processes by which this is done in the natural setting have received relatively little attention so far. All one can conclude is that children aged 1 to 2 do already have certain categories of objects, situations, and states available to

which they can attach words when they come to acquire language. Their earliest words, in fact, pick out mainly objects and situations, but by 2 they usually flag some states as well. This in turn suggests that when children try to work out what words mean, they look first to the conceptual categories they already know.

Using a word and knowing what an adult would mean by that word are two different things. Children's hypotheses about what categories words pick out do not necessarily coincide with adult meanings. Children may pick out too large a category (overextension), too small a category (underextension), or set the boundaries wrongly (overlap). They may also pick roughly the right category so that their word use and the adult's coincide. Whether the categories for which children's word meanings tend to coincide with those of adults are more easily distinguished from each other than other categories has yet to be investigated. There is evidence in young children's word uses of all four kinds of relations between child and adult meanings: overextension, underextension, overlap, and coincidence.

Studies of later meaning acquisition have concentrated on particular semantic domains, such as locative words, possession verbs, dimensional adjectives, or kinship terms. In many such domains, children appear to acquire the different words in an orderly way, with some meanings being consistently earlier or easier to master than others. However, data based on production of words have often led investigators to different conclusions from data based on comprehension. This is true also of studies of very early meaning acquisition. The process in language use—production or comprehension—appears, then, to play an important role in limiting the kinds of inferences that can be made about children's knowledge of word meanings.

The theories of meaning acquisition developed in the last decade or so are probably best characterized as partial theories. Most were presented to account for data from particular domains rather than from the vocabulary as a whole. Some were based on production data alone, others on comprehension data, and still others on an undifferentiated mixture of the two. The most extensive theory, the semantic feature hypothesis, has been widely tested. Proposed originally to account for overextensions data (production) and data from the comprehension of dimensional and temporal terms, it has since been found lacking on several grounds. The most critical concerns the notion of semantic feature. The theory itself placed no constraints on what might be considered a feature and lacked principled criteria for identifying features or accounting for changes in features from child to adult meanings. Consideration of such weaknesses and of further data have led to the rejection of this theory as an adequate account of meaning acquisition.

It was clearly time for a new approach. The proposal presented here, in a preliminary form, is for a theory based on principles that govern the lexicon as a whole, for adults and children alike. In a system based on convention and contrast, the acquisition of new lexical items is governed by the need to make further distinctions and convey meanings not conveyed by words already known. In the earlier stages of acquisition, such an approach predicts that children may overextend known words to talk about neighboring categories and rely on general-purpose words like *do* or *that* for situations and objects respectively. But the patterns of use for each child will depend on the system already acquired and the contrasts already set up. This approach also predicts that children will coin new words to convey their new meanings—and this as soon as they start to master some word-formation devices. And, somewhat later perhaps, they will even extend their available vocabulary by using it figuratively.

Essentially, all these options represent ways of filling lexical gaps—places where the speaker lacks a word for the category he wants to talk about. Some of the options are ones that will only really be exploited during language acquisition. For instance, overextensions yield to the available conventional words for each part of a domain like that of animals. And the extensive use of general-purpose terms becomes modulated by the need to be more specific, especially when talking about things displaced in space and time. But general-purpose terms continue to be used, when needed, by adult speakers. Word formation, the coining of innovative lexical items to carry new meanings that contrast with those already available, is a highly productive option for adults as well as for children. It is an option that allows for continual renewal and expansion of the conventional lexicon: innovations that are generally accepted become in their turn well-established words in the vocabulary of the language.

Although still in the process of being developed, lexical contrast theory shows promise of providing a more extensive and communicatively motivated framework in which to study children's acquisition of meanings. It can account for the data originally covered by the semantic feature hypothesis and for the data disconfirming that hypothesis. And it extends to two other domains not previously considered in connection with meaning acquisition: coining new words and using figurative language. It also adheres in a motivated way to the distinction between concepts and meanings. Lexical gaps can only be defined in terms of categories children want to talk about but lack words for. But such gaps can only be defined if meanings and concepts are distinct.

I have ended this chapter by introducing a theory that is motivated by the need to fill gaps, lexical gaps, in the child's or adult's vocabulary. I hope that the approach adopted in the chapter as a whole may also lead to the filling of some of the gaps in what is known about the nature of children's earliest conceptual categories and how they come to relate such categories to the words and expressions in their first language. After all, it is only once they have words that they can freely call up those conceptual categories they wish to talk about.

NOTES

1. These illustrations have focused on single words but of course phrases or even whole utterances can be used to convey an equivalent meaning where there is not just one word available.

2. There has been a long tradition in psychology (and elsewhere) of equating thinking (and hence concepts) with language, with the corollary assumption that one needs a word before one can form the relevant concept. In the present chapter, I shall assume the reverse—that initially at least, children begin to form concepts before they look for words for them. Concepts indeed make up the foundation on which children begin to build the structure of their language (e.g., Slobin, 1973, 1979). Once children have acquired a certain amount of language, of course, the developmental process goes both ways: the emergence of new concepts prompts children to look for new words and hearing new words prompts them to form further concepts.

3. The complexity of a concept, though, merely sets a lower bound on when children might be ready to acquire a particular word meaning. The form of the pertinent word, its complexity as part of the language to be acquired, could delay children's acquisition till long after they had mastered the requisite concept (Slobin, 1973).

4. The relation between concept and category, then, is equivalent to that between *intension* and *extension* (Allwood, Andersson, & Dahl, 1977). The intension specifies the qualities or properties needed for membership, and the extension comprises those entities that have the required properties.

5. Although most of the vocabulary lists sampled were from children acquiring English, the diaries available from other languages (French, German, Hungarian, Polish, Russian) show a very similar set of terms being among the first 50 or so acquired.

6. The small boys tested by Katz et al. (1974) treated dolls just like blocks, and for both dolls and blocks treated the nonsense word as a kind term (for the category), whether it occurred with or without an article.

7. Utterances or examples preceded by an asterisk are unacceptable or ungrammatical for adult speakers of the language with the meanings or forms specified.

8. Children's earliest tests of any such hypotheses may be constrained by their phonological development. Making oneself understood is no mean feat when one only pronounces the first consonant and vowel, say, of most words attempted. Lexical development is intricately bound up with other facets of the language, especially its sound system (e.g., Vihman, 1981).

9. It is of course possible that the child did not recognize that the same kind of object was involved in both settings. Yet another problem in the detection of underextensions is what for the child constitutes "similar enough."

10. It is not clear quite how Nelson's (1974) proposal about the initial mapping could really be tested, since she herself suggested that children then go on to extend their words on the basis of similarity of shape, size, and so on. What is clear is that conceptual categories must contain all kinds of information about their members; such information is clearly not restricted to properties of appearance alone.

11. The greater specificity that comes with the replacement of general-purpose terms as well of overextensions also makes for greater informativeness, following the conversational maxims laid out by Grice (1975).

REFERENCES

Adams, V. *An introduction to modern English word formation*. London: Longman, 1973.

Allwood, J., Andersson, L. G., & Dahl, O. *Logic in linguistics*. Cambridge: At the University Press, 1977.

Amidon, A., & Carey, P. Why five-year-olds cannot understand before and after. *Journal of Verbal Learning and Verbal Behavior*, 1972, *11*, 417–423.

Ammon, M. S. Development in the comprehension of lexical causatives. Paper presented at the meeting of the Society for Research in Child Development, Boston, April 1981. (a)

Ammon, M. S. Development in the interpretation of innovative causative expressions. Paper presented at the meeting of the Society for Research in Child Development, Boston, April 1981. (b)

Ammon, M. S., & Slobin, D. I. A cross-linguistic study of the processing of causative sentences. *Cognition*, 1979, *7*, 3–17.

Andersen, E. S. Learning to speak with style: A study of the sociolinguistic skills of children. Unpublished doctoral dissertation, Stanford University, 1977.

Andersen, E. S. Lexical universals of body-part terminology. In J. H. Greenberg (Ed.), *Universals of human language, vol. 3, Word structure*. Stanford, Calif.: Stanford University Press, 1978.

Anglin, J. M. *Word, object, and conceptual development*. New York: W. W. Norton, 1977.

Antinucci, F., & Miller, R. How children talk about what happened. *Journal of Child Language*, 1976, *3*, 167–189.

Asch, S. E., & Nerlove, H. The development of double function terms in children. In B. Kaplan & S. Wapner (Eds.), *Perspectives in psychological theory*. New York: International Universities Press, 1960.

Backhouse, A. E. Japanese verbs of dress. *Journal of Linguistics*, 1981, *17*, 17–29.

Barrett, M. D. Lexical development and overextension in child language. *Journal of Child Language*, 1978, *5*, 205–219.

Barsalou, L. W. The determinants of graded structure in categories. Unpublished doctoral dissertation, Stanford University, 1981.

Bartlett, E. J. Sizing things up: The acquisition of the meaning of dimensional adjectives. *Journal of Child Language*, 1976, *3*, 205–219.

Bates, E. *Language and context: The acquisition of pragmatics*. New York: Academic Press, 1976.

Benedict, H. Language comprehension in 9–15 month old children. In R. N. Campbell & P. T. Smith (Eds.), *Recent advances in the psychology of language: Language development and mother-child interaction*. New York: Plenum, 1978.

Benedict, H. Early lexical development: Comprehension and production. *Journal of Child Language*, 1979, *6*, 183–200.

Berlin, B., Breedlove, D. E., & Raven, P. H. General principles of classification and nomenclature in folk biology. *American Anthropologist*, 1973, *75*, 214–242.

Berlin, B., & Kay, P. *Basic color terms: Their universality and evolution*. Berkeley and Los Angeles: University of California Press, 1969.

Berman, R. A. Early verbs: Comments on how and why a child uses his first words. *International Journal of Psycholinguistics*, 1978, *5*, 21–39.

Bernstein, M. E. Acquisition of locative expressions by deaf children learning American Sign Language. Unpublished doctoral dissertation, Boston University, 1981.

Bierwisch, M. Some semantic universals of German adjectivals. *Foundations of Language*, 1967, *3*, 1–36.

Bierwisch, M. On certain problems of semantic representations. *Foundations of Language*, 1969, *5*, 153–184.

Bierwisch, M. On semantics. In J. Lyons (Ed.), *New horizons in linguistics*. London: Penguin, 1970.

Bloch, O. La phrase dans le langage de l'enfant. *Journal de Psychologie*, 1924, *21*, 18–43.

Bloom, L. M. *One word at a time: The use of single word utterances before syntax*. The Hague: Mouton, 1973.

Bloom, L. M., Lifter, K., & Hafitz, J. Semantics of verbs and the development of verb inflection in child language. *Language*, 1980, *56*, 386–412.

Bolinger, D. L. The atomization of meaning. *Language*, 1965, *41*, 555–573.

Bornstein, M. H. Two kinds of perceptual organization near the beginning of life. In W. A. Collins (Ed.), *Minnesota symposia on child psychology, vol. 14: Aspects of the development of competence*. Hillsdale N.J.: Erlbaum, 1981.

Borton, R. W. The perception of causality in infants. Paper presented at the meeting of the Society for Research in Child Development, San Francisco, March 1979.

Bourne, L. E., Dominowski, R. L., & Loftus, E. F. *Cognitive processes*. Englewood Cliffs, N.J.: Prentice-Hall, 1979.

Bowerman, M. Learning the structure of causative verbs: A study in the relationship of cognitive, semantic, and syntactic development. *Papers and Reports on Child Language Development* (Stanford University), 1974, *8*, 142–179.

Bowerman, M. Semantic factors in the acquisition of rules for word use and sentence construction. In D. M. Morehead & A. E. Morehead (Eds.), *Normal and deficient child language*. Baltimore: University Park Press, 1976.

Bowerman, M. The acquisition of word meaning: An investigation of some current concepts. In P. N. Johnson-Laird & P. C. Wason (Eds.), *Thinking*. Cambridge: At the University Press, 1977.

Bowerman, M. Systematizing semantic knowledge: Changes over time in the child's organization of word meaning. *Child Development*, 1978, *49*, 977–987. (a)

Bowerman, M. Words and sentences: Uniformity, individual variation, and shifts over time in patterns of acquisition. In F. D. Minifie & L. L. Lloyd (Eds.), *Communicative and cognitive abilities—Early behavioral assessment*. Baltimore: University Park Press, 1978. (b)

Bowerman, M. Explorations in recombinant semantics: The child's acquisition of patterns for lexicalizing the notion of motion. Paper presented at the Workshop on Words and Concepts, Stanford University, March 31, 1979.

Bowerman, M. Beyond communicative adequacy: From piecemeal knowledge to an integrated system in the child's acquisition of language. In *Papers and Reports on Child Language Development* (Stanford University), 1981, *20*, 1–24.

Bowerman, M. Reorganizational processes in lexical and syntactic development. In E. Wanner & L. R. Gleitman (Eds.), *Language acquisition: The state of the art*. Cambridge: At the University Press, 1982.

Bowerman, M. Evaluating competing linguistic models with language acquisition data: Implications of developmental errors with causative verbs. *Quaderni di Semantici*, in press.

Braunwald, S. R. Context, word, and meaning: Toward a communicative analysis of lexical acquisition. In A. Lock (Ed.), *Action, gesture and symbol*. N.Y.: Academic Press, 1978.

Brewer, W. F., & Stone, J. B. Acquisition of spatial antonym pairs. *Journal of Experimental Child Psychology*, 1975, *19*, 299–307.

Brooks, L. Nonanalytic concept formation and memory for instances. In E. Rosch & B. B. Lloyd (Eds.), *Cognition and categorization*. Hillsdale, N.J.: Erlbaum, 1978.

Brown, C. H., Kolar, J., Torrey, B. J., Trùòng-Quang, T., & Volkman, P. Some general principles of biological and non-biological folk classification. *American Ethnologist*, 1976, *3*, 73–85.

Brown, R. W. Linguistic determinism and the part of speech. *Journal of Abnormal and Social Psychology*, 1957, *55*, 1–5.

Brown, R. W. How shall a thing be called? *Psychological Review*, 1958, *65*, 14–21.

Brown, R. W. *A first language: The early stages*. Cambridge, Mass.: Harvard University Press, 1973.

Bruner, J. S., Goodnow, J. J., & Austin, G. A. *A study of thinking*. New York: Wiley, 1956.

Bühler, K. *The mental development of the child*.

New York: Harcourt, Brace, 1930.

Bull, W. E. *Time, tense, and the verb*. Berkeley and Los Angeles: University of California Press, 1960. (University of California publications in linguistics, Vol. 19.)

Carey, S. The child as word learner. In M. Halle, J. Bresnan, & G. A. Miller (Eds.), *Linguistic theory and psychological reality*. Cambridge, Mass.: MIT Press, 1978. (a)

Carey, S. The child's concept of *animal*. Paper presented at the Psychonomics Society Meeting, San Antonio, Tex., November 1978. (b)

Carter, A. L. From sensori-motor vocalizations to words: A case study of the evolution of attention-directing communication in the second year. In A. Lock (Ed.), *Action, gesture, and symbol*. N.Y.: Academic Press, 1978.

Charney, R. The comprehension of ''here'' and ''there.'' *Journal of Child Language*, 1979, *6*, 69–80.

Church, J. (Ed.) *Three babies: Biographies of cognitive development*. New York: Random House, 1966. (Vintage Books)

Clark, E. V. How young children describe events in time. In G. B. Flores d'Arcais & W. J. M. Levelt (Eds.), *Advances in psycholinguistics*. Amsterdam: North-Holland, 1970.

Clark, E. V. On the acquisition of the meaning of *before* and *after*. *Journal of Verbal Learning and Verbal Behavior*, 1971, *10*, 266–275.

Clark, E. V. On the child's acquisition of antonyms in two semantic fields. *Journal of Verbal Learning and Verbal Behavior*, 1972, *11*, 750–758.

Clark, E. V. Non-linguistic strategies and the acquisition of word meanings. *Cognition*, 1973, *2*, 161–182. (a)

Clark, E. V. What's in a word? On the child's acquisition of semantics in his first language. In T. E. Moore (Ed.), *Cognitive development and the acquisition of language*. New York: Academic Press, 1973. (b)

Clark, E. V. Knowledge, context, and strategy in the acquisition of meaning. In D. P. Dato (Ed.), *Georgetown University round table on languages and linguistics 1975: Developmental psycholinguistics*. Washington, D.C.: Georgetown University Press, 1975.

Clark, E. V. Strategies and the mapping problem in first language acquisition. In J. Macnamara (Ed.), *Language learning and thought*. New York: Academic Press, 1977. (a)

Clark, E. V. Universal categories: On the semantics of classifiers and children's early word meanings. In A. Juilland (Ed.), *Linguistic studies offered to Joseph Greenberg, on the occasion of his sixtieth birthday*. Saratoga, Calif.: Anma Libri, 1977. (b)

Clark, E. V. Discovering what words can do. In D. Farkas, W. M. Jacobsen, & K. W. Todrys (Eds.), *Papers from the parasession on the lexicon*. Chicago: Chicago Linguistic Society, 1978. (a)

Clark, E. V. From gesture to word: On the natural history of deixis in language acquisition. In J. S. Bruner & A. Garton (Eds.), *Human growth and development: Wolfson College Lectures 1976*. Oxford: Oxford University Press, 1978. (b)

Clark, E. V. Strategies for communicating. *Child Development*, 1978, *49*, 953–959. (c)

Clark, E. V. Building a vocabulary: Words for objects, actions, and relations. In P. Fletcher & M. Garman (Eds.), *Language acquisition*. Cambridge: At the University Press, 1979.

Clark, E. V. Convention and innovation in acquiring the lexicon. In *Papers and Reports on Child Language Development* (Stanford University), 1980, *19*, 1–20. (a)

Clark, E. V. Here's the *top:* Nonlinguistic strategies in the acquisition of orientational terms. *Child Development*, 1980, *51*, 329–338. (b)

Clark, E. V. Lexical innovations: How children learn to create new words. In W. Deutsch (Ed.), *The child's construction of language*. London: Academic Press, 1981. (a)

Clark, E. V. Negative verbs in children's speech. In W. Klein & W. J. M. Levelt (Eds.), *Crossing the boundaries in linguistics*. Dordrecht: Reidel, 1981. (b)

Clark, E. V. The young word-maker: A case study of innovation in the child's lexicon. In E. Wanner & L. R. Gleitman (Eds.), *Language acquisition: The state of the art*. Cambridge: At the University Press, 1982.

Clark, E. V., & Clark, H. H. When nouns surface as verbs. *Language*, 1979, *55*, 767–811.

Clark, E. V., & Garnica, O. K. Is he coming or going? On the acquisition of deictic verbs. *Journal of Verbal Learning and Verbal Behavior*, 1974, *13*, 556–572.

Clark, E. V., & Hecht, B. F. Learning how to coin agent and instrument nouns. *Cognition*, 1982, *12*, 1–24.

Clark, E. V., & Sengul, C. J. Strategies in the acquisition of deixis. *Journal of Child Language*, 1978, *5*, 457–475.

Clark, H. H. Space, time, semantics, and the child. In T. E. Moore (Ed.), *Cognitive development and the acquisition of language*. New York: Academic Press, 1973.

Clark, H. H., & Clark, E. V. *Psychology and lan-*

guage: An introduction to psycholinguistics. New York: Harcourt Brace Jovanovich, 1977.

Clark, H. H., & Clark, E. V. Universals, relativity, and language processing. In J. H. Greenberg (Ed.), *Universals of human language,* vol. 1, *Method and theory.* Stanford, Calif.: Stanford University Press, 1978.

Clark, H. H., & Marshall, C. R. Definite reference and mutual knowledge. In A. Joshi, B. Webber, & I. Sag (Eds.), *Elements of discourse structure.* Cambridge: At the University Press, 1981.

Cohen, L. B. Concept acquisition in the human infant. Paper presented at the meeting of the Society for Research in Child Development, New Orleans, March 1977.

Cohen, L. B., & Caputo, N. F. Instructing infants to respond to perceptual categories. Paper presented at the meeting of the Midwestern Psychological Association, Chicago, May 1978.

Cohen, L. B., & Strauss, M. S. Concept acquisition in the human infant. *Child Development,* 1979, *50,* 419–424.

Coker, P. L. Syntactic and semantic factors in the acquisition of *before* and *after. Journal of Child Language,* 1978, *5,* 261–277.

Comrie, B. *Aspect.* Cambridge: At the University Press, 1976.

Cook, N. In, on and under revisited again. *Papers and Reports on Child Language Development* (Stanford University), 1978, *15,* 38–45.

Daehler, M. W., Lonardo, R., & Bukatko, D. Matching and equivalence judgments in very young children. *Child Development,* 1979, *50,* 170–179.

Decroly, O., & Degand, J. Observations relatives au développement de la notion du temps chez une petite fille. *Archives de Psychologie,* 1913, *13,* 113–161.

Denney, N. W. A developmental study of free classification in children. *Child Development,* 1972, *43,* 221–232.

de Saussure, F. *Cours de linguistique générale.* (Publié par C. Bally et A. Sechehaye, avec la collaboration de A. Riedlinger.) Paris: Payot, 1968.

Deutsch, W. The conceptual impact of linguistic input: A comparison of German family-children's and orphans' acquisition of kinship terms. *Journal of Child Language,* 1979, *6,* 313–327.

Dockrell, J. E. The child's acquisition of unfamiliar words: An experimental study. Unpublished doctoral dissertation, University of Stirling, 1981.

Donaldson, M., & Wales, R. J. On the acquisition

of some relational terms. In J. R. Hayes (Ed.), *Cognition and the development of language.* New York: Wiley, 1970.

Downing, P. On the creation and use of English compounds. *Language,* 1977, *53,* 810–842.

Dromi, E. More on the acquisition of locative prepositions: An analysis of Hebrew data. *Journal of Child Language,* 1979, *6,* 547–562.

Ehri, L. D., & Galanis, H. Teaching children to comprehend propositions conjoined by *before* and *after. Journal of Experimental Child Psychology,* 1980, *30,* 308–324.

Ervin-Tripp, S. Is second language learning like the first? *TESOL Quarterly,* 1974, *8,* 111–127.

Ferreiro, E. *Les relations temporelles dans le langage de l'enfant.* Geneva and Paris: Librairie Droz, 1971.

Fillmore, C. J. On the organization of semantic information in the lexicon. In D. Farkas, W. M. Jacobsen, & K. Todrys (Eds.), *Papers from the parasession on the lexicon.* Chicago: Chicago Linguistic Society, 1978.

François, D. Du pré-signe au signe. In F. François, D. François, E. Sabau-Jouannet, & M. Sourdot, *La syntaxe de l'enfant avant 5 ans.* Paris: Larousse, 1978.

Fremgen, A., & Fay, D. Over-extensions in production and comprehension: A methodological clarification. *Journal of Child Language,* 1980, *7,* 205–211.

French, L. A., & Brown, A. L. Comprehension of *before* and *after* in logical and arbitrary sequences. *Journal of Child Language,* 1977, *4,* 247–256.

Friedenberg, L., & Olson, G. M. Children's comprehension of simple descriptions of vertical arrays. *Child Development,* 1977, *48,* 265–269.

Gathercole, V. C. M. Decrements in children's responses to *big* and *tall:* A reconsideration of the potential cognitive and semantic causes. *Journal of Experimental Child Psychology,* 1982, *34.*

Gelman, R., Bullock, M., & Meck, E. Preschoolers' understanding of simple object transformations. *Child Development,* 1980, *51,* 691–699.

Gentner, D. Children's performance on a spatial analogies task. *Child Development,* 1977, *48,* 1034–1039.

Gentner, D. On relational meaning: The acquisition of verb meaning. *Child Development,* 1978, *49,* 988–998. (a)

Gentner, D. What looks like a jiggy but acts like a zimbo? A study of early word meaning using artificial objects. *Papers and Reports on Child*

Language Development (Stanford University), 1978, *15*, 1–6. (b)

Gentner, D. Why nouns are learned before verbs: Linguistic relativity versus natural partitioning. In S. A. Kuczaj II (Ed.), *Language development*, vol. 2: *Language, thought, and culture*. Hillsdale, N.J.: Erlbaum, 1982.

Geodakian, I., & Kurghinian, V. An attempt to group psycholinguistically the early utterances of a child. *Neurolinguistics*, 1976, *5*, 105–407.

Gibson, E. J., Owsley, C. J., & Johnston, J. Perception of invariants by five-month-old infants: Differentiation of two types of motion. *Developmental Psychology*, 1978, *14*, 407–415.

Gibson, E. J., Owsley, C. J., Walker, A., & Megaw-Nyce, J. Development of the perception of invariants: Substance and shape. *Perception*, 1979, *8*, 609–619.

Goldin-Meadow, S., Seligman, M. E. P., & Gelman, R. Language in the two-year-old. *Cognition*, 1976, *4*, 189–202.

Golinkoff, R. M., & Kerr, J. L. Infants' perception of semantically defined action role changes in filmed events. *Merrill-Palmer Quarterly*, 1978, *24*, 53–61.

Greenberg, J. H. *Language universals*. The Hague: Mouton, 1966.

Greenfield, P. M. Who is "Dada"? Some aspects of the semantic and phonological development of a child's first words. *Language and Speech*, 1973, *16*, 34–43.

Grégoire, A. *L'apprentissage du langage*, vol. 1, *Les deux premières années*. Liège and Paris: Librairie Droz, 1937.

Grice, H. P. Meaning. *Philosophical Review*, 1957, *66*, 377–388.

Grice, H. P. Logic and conversation. In P. Cole & J. L. Morgan (Eds.), *Syntax and semantics*, vol. 3, *Speech acts*. New York: Academic Press, 1975.

Griffiths, P., & Atkinson, M. A *door* to verbs. In N. Waterson & C. E. Snow (Eds.), *The development of communication: Social and pragmatic factors*. New York: Wiley, 1978.

Gruendel, J. M. Referential extension in early language development. *Child Development*, 1977, *48*, 1567–1576.

Guillaume, P. Les débuts de la phrase dans le langage de l'enfant. *Journal de Psychologie*, 1927, *24*, 1–25.

Harner, L. *Yesterday* and *tomorrow:* Development of early understanding of the terms. *Developmental Psychology*, 1975, *11*, 864–865.

Harris, P. Inferences and semantic development. *Journal of Child Language*, 1975, *2*, 143–152.

Haviland, S. E., & Clark, E. V. "This man's father is my father's son": A study of the acquisition of English kin terms. *Journal of Child Language*, 1974, *1*, 23–47.

Heider, E. R., & Olivier, D. C. The structure of the color space in naming and memory for two languages. *Cognitive Psychology*, 1972, *3*, 337–354.

Horton, M. S. Category familiarity and taxonomic organization in young children. Unpublished doctoral dissertation, Stanford University, 1982.

Huttenlocher, J. The origins of language comprehension. In R. L. Solso (Ed.), *Theories in cognitive psychology*. New York: Wiley, 1974.

Huttenlocher, J., & Lui, F. The semantic organization of some simple nouns and verbs. *Journal of Verbal Learning and Verbal Behavior*, 1979, *18*, 141–162.

Johnson, H. L. The meaning of *before* and *after* for preschool children. *Journal of Experimental Child Psychology*, 1975, *19*, 88–99.

Johnston, J. R., & Slobin, D. I. The development of locative expressions in English, Italian, Serbo-Croatian, and Turkish. *Journal of Child Language*, 1979, *6*, 531–547.

Kagan, J. The determinants of attention in the infant. *American Scientist*, 1970, *58*, 298–306.

Kagan, J. *The second year: The emergence of self-awareness*. Cambridge, Mass.: Harvard University Press, 1981.

Karmiloff-Smith, A. More about the same: Children's understanding of post-articles. *Journal of Child Language*, 1977, *4*, 377–394.

Karmiloff-Smith, A. The grammatical marking of thematic structure in the development of language production. In W. Deutsch (Ed.), *The child's construction of language*. London: Academic Press, 1981.

Katz, J. J., & Fodor, J. A. The structure of a semantic theory. *Language*, 1963, *39*, 170–210.

Katz, N., Baker, E., & Macnamara, J. What's in a name? A study of how children learn common and proper names. *Child Development*, 1974, *45*, 469–473.

Kavanaugh, R. D. Observations on the role of logically constrained sentences in the comprehension of "before" and "after." *Journal of Child Language*, 1979, *6*, 353–357.

Keil, F. The development of the young child's ability to anticipate the outcomes of simple causal events. *Child Development*, 1979, *50*, 455–462.

Keil, F., & Carroll, J. J. The child's acquisition of "tall": Implications for an alternative view of semantic development. *Papers and Reports on*

Child Language Development (Stanford University), 1980, *19*, 21–28.

Kossan, N. E. Developmental differences in concept acquisition strategies. *Child Development*, 1981, *52*, 290–298.

Kripke, S. Naming and necessity. In D. Davidson & G. Harman (Eds.), *Semantics of natural language*. Dordrecht: Reidel, 1972.

Kuczaj, S. A. Young children's over-extensions of object words in comprehension and/or production: Support for a prototype theory of early object word meaning. Paper presented at the meeting of the Society for Research in Child Development, San Francisco, March 1979.

LeCompte, G. K., & Gratch, G. Violation of a rule as a method of diagnosing infants' levels of object concept. *Child Development*, 1972, *43*, 385–396.

Leopold, W. F. *Speech development of a bilingual child: A linguist's record* (Vol. 3). Evanston, Ill.: Northwestern University Press, 1949.

Leslie, A. M. The discursive representation of perceived causal connection in infancy. Paper presented at the Conference on Knowledge and Representation, The Netherlands Institute of Advanced Studies, Wassenaar, March 1979.

Lewis, M. M. *Infant speech: A study of the beginnings of language*. London: Kegan Paul, 1951.

Lyons, J. *Introduction to theoretical linguistics*. Cambridge: At the University Press, 1968.

MacWhinney, B. The acquisition of morphophonology. *Monographs of the Society for Research in Child Development*, 1978, *43*(Serial No. 174).

Maratsos, M. P. Decrease in the understanding of the word "big" in preschool children. *Child Development*, 1973, *44*, 747–752.

Maratsos, M. P. When is a high thing a big one? *Developmental Psychology*, 1974, *10*, 367–375.

Marchand, H. *The categories and types of present-day English word formation* (2nd ed.). Munich: Verlag C. H. Beck, 1969.

Markman, E. M., Cox, B., & Machida, S. The standard sorting task as a measure of conceptual organization. *Developmental Psychology*, 1981, *17*, 115–117.

Markman, E. M., Horton, M. S., & McLanahan, A. G. Classes and collections: Principles of organization in the learning of hierarchical relations. *Cognition*, 1980, *8*, 227–241.

Mervis, C. B., & Mervis, C. A. Leopards are kitty-cats: Object labeling by mothers for their thirteen-month-olds. *Child Development*, 1982, *53*, 267–273.

Mervis, C. B., & Pani, J. R. Acquisition of object

categories. *Cognitive Psychology*, 1980, *12*, 496–522.

Miller, G. A., & Johnson-Laird, P. N. *Language and perception*. Cambridge, Mass.: Harvard University Press, 1976.

Moore, K. C. The mental development of a child. *Psychological Review, Monograph Supplement*, 1896, *1* (3).

Museyibova, T. A. [The development of an understanding of spatial relations and their reflection in the language of children of pre-school age.] In B. G. Anan'yev & B. F. Lomov (Eds.), *Problemy vospriyatiya prostranstva i prostranstvennykh predstavleniy*. Moscow, 1961. (Trans., Problems of spatial perception and spatial concepts, NASA, June 1964.)

Nelson, K. Some evidence for the cognitive primacy of categorization and its functional basis. *Merrill-Palmer Quarterly*, 1973, *19*, 21–39. (a)

Nelson, K. Structure and strategy in learning to talk. *Monographs of the Society for Research in Child Development*, 1973, *38*(Serial No. 149). (b)

Nelson, K. Concept, word, and sentence: Interrelations in acquisition and development. *Psychological Review*, 1974, *81*, 267–285.

Nelson, K. Some attributes of adjectives used by young children. *Cognition*, 1976, *4*, 13–30.

Nelson, K., Rescorla, L., Gruendel, J. M., & Benedict, H. Early lexicons: What do they mean? *Child Development*, 1978, *49*, 960–968.

Nice, M. M. The development of a child's vocabulary in relation to environment. *Pedagogical Seminary*, 1915, *22*, 35–64.

Nunberg, G. Slang, usage conditions, and l'arbitraire du signe. In D. Farkas, W. M. Jacobsen, & K. Todrys (Eds.), *Papers from the parasession on the lexicon*. Chicago: Chicago Linguistic Society, 1978.

Oviatt, S. L. The emerging ability to comprehend language: An experimental approach. *Child Development*, 1980, *51*, 97–106.

Palmer, S. E. Fundamental aspects of cognitive representation. In E. Rosch & B. B. Lloyd (Eds.), *Cognition and categorization*. Hillsdale, N.J.: Erlbaum, 1978.

Pechmann, T., & Deutsch, W. From gesture to word and gesture. *Papers and Reports on Child Language Development* (Stanford University), 1980, *19*, 113–120.

Pérez, B. *Les trois premières années de l'enfant*. Paris: Alcan, 1892.

Piaget, J. *Judgment and reasoning in the child*. London: Kegan Paul, 1928.

Piaget, J. *The origins of intelligence in children*.

New York: International Universities Press, 1952.

Piaget, J. *The construction of reality in the child* (M. Cook, trans.). New York: Basic Books, 1954.

Piaget, J. *Play, dreams, and imitation in childhood* (C. Gattegno & F. M. Hodgson, trans.). New York: W. W. Norton, 1962.

Postal, P. M. Review article: André Martinet, *Elements of general linguistics. Foundations of Language*, 1966, *2*, 151–186.

Preyer, W. *Die Seele des Kindes: Beobachtungen über die geistige Entwicklung des Menschen in den ersten Lebensjahren*. Leipzig: Schaefer, 1882.

Putnam, H. Is semantics possible? In H. E. Kiefer & M. K. Munitz (Eds.), *Language, belief, and metaphysics*. Albany, N.Y.: State University of New York Press, 1970.

Reich, P. A. The early acquisition of word meaning. *Journal of Child Language*, 1976, *3*, 117–123.

Rescorla, L. Concept formation in word learning. Unpublished doctoral dissertation, Yale University, 1976.

Rescorla, L. Overextension in early language development. *Journal of Child Language*, 1980, *7*, 321–335.

Rescorla, L. Category development in early language. *Journal of Child Language*, 1981, *8*, 225–238.

Ricciuti, H. N. Geometric form and detail as determinants of similarity judgments in young children. In U.S. Office of Education, *A basic research program on reading, final report* (Cooperative Research Project No. 539), 1963.

Ricciuti, H. N. Object grouping and selective ordering behavior in infants 12 to 24 months old. *Merrill-Palmer Quarterly*, 1965, *11*, 129–148.

Ricciuti, H. N., & Johnson, L. J. Developmental changes in categorizing behavior from infancy to the early pre-school years. Paper presented at the meeting of the Society for Research in Child Development, Minneapolis, March 1965.

Richards, M. M. *Come* and *go* revisited: Children's use of deictic verbs in contrived situations. *Journal of Verbal Learning and Verbal Behavior*, 1976, *15*, 655–665.

Robertson, S. S., & Suci, G. J. Event perception by children in the early stages of language production. *Child Development*, 1980, *51*, 89–96.

Rosaldo, M. It's all uphill: The creative metaphors of Ilongot magical spells. In M. Sanches & B. Blount (Eds.), *Sociocultural dimensions of language use*. New York: Seminar Press, 1975.

Rosch, E., & Mervis, C. B. Family resemblances:

Studies in the internal structure of categories. *Cognitive Psychology*, 1975, *7*, 573–605.

Rosch, E., Mervis, C. B., Gray, W., Johnson D., & Boyes-Braem, P. Basic objects in natural categories. *Cognitive Psychology*, 1976, *8*, 382–439.

Ross, G. Concept categorization in 1 to 2 year olds. *Developmental Psychology*, 1980, *16*, 391–396.

Saltz, E., Dixon, D., Klein, S., & Becker, G. Studies of natural language concepts: III. Concept overdiscrimination in comprehension between two and four years of age. *Child Development*, 1977, *48*, 1682–1685.

Schwartz, R. G. Words, objects, and actions in early lexical acquisition. Unpublished doctoral dissertation, Memphis State University, 1978.

Schwartz, S. P. Introduction. In S. P. Schwartz (Ed.), *Naming, necessity, and natural kinds*. Ithaca, N.Y.: Cornell University Press, 1977.

Shipley, E. F. Comparisons and class-inclusion. In D. P. Dato (Ed.), *Georgetown University round table on languages and linguistics 1975: Developmental psycholinguistics*. Washington, D.C.: Georgetown University Press, 1975.

Slobin, D. I. Cognitive prerequisites for the acquisition of grammar. In C. A. Ferguson & D. I. Slobin (Eds.), *Studies of child language development*. New York: Holt, Rinehart & Winston, 1973.

Slobin, D. I. The role of language in language acquisition. Address to the meeting of the Eastern Psychological Association, Philadelphia, April 1979.

Slobin, D. I. The origins of grammatical encoding of events. In W. Deutsch (Ed.), *The child's construction of language*. London: Academic Press, 1981.

Slobin, D. I. (Ed.). *The crosslinguistic study of language acquisition*. Hillsdale, N.J.: Erlbaum, in press.

Smith, C. L. Children's understanding of natural language hierarchies. *Journal of Experimental Child Psychology*, 1979, *27*, 437–458.

Smith, E. E., & Medin, D. L. *Three views of concepts*. Cambridge, Mass.: Harvard University Press, 1981.

Snyder, A. D. Notes on the talk of a two-and-a-half year old boy. *Pedagogical Seminary*, 1914, *21*, 412–424.

Starkey, D. The origins of concept formation: Object sorting and object preference in early infancy. *Child Development*, 1981, *52*, 489–497.

Stern, C., & Stern, W. *Die Kindersprache*. Leipzig: Barth, 1928.

Stern, W. *Psychology of early childhood up to the*

sixth year of age. New York: Holt, 1924.

Strauss, M. S. Abstraction of prototypical information by adults and 10-month-old infants. *Journal of Experimental Psychology,* 1979, *5,* 618–632.

Tanz, D. *Studies in the acquisition of deictic terms.* Cambridge: At the University Press, 1980.

Templin, M. C. Certain language skills in children: Their development and interrelationships. *University of Minnesota Institute of Child Welfare Monograph,* 1957, *26.*

Thomson, J. R., & Chapman, R. S. Who is "Daddy"? The status of two-year-olds' over-extended words in use and comprehension. *Journal of Child Language,* 1977, *4,* 359–375.

Tomikawa, S. A., & Dodd, D. H. Early word meanings: Perceptually or functionally based? *Child Development,* 1980, *51,* 1103–1109.

Tversky, A. Features of similarity. *Psychological Review,* 1977, *84,* 327–352.

van der Geest, T. *Some aspects of communicative competence and their implications for language acquisition.* Amsterdam: Van Gorcum, 1975.

Vendler, Z. *Linguistics in philosophy.* Ithaca, N.Y.: Cornell University Press, 1967.

Vihman, M. M. Phonology and the development of the lexicon: Evidence from children's errors. *Journal of Child Language,* 1981, *8,* 239–264.

Vygotsky, L. S. *Thought and language.* Cambridge, Mass.: MIT Press, 1962.

Webb, P. A., & Abrahamson, A. A. Stages of egocentrism in children's use of *this* and *that:* A different point of view. *Journal of Child Language,* 1976, *3,* 349–367.

Winner, E. New names for old things: The emergence of metaphoric language. *Papers and Reports on Child Language Development* (Stanford University), 1978, *15,* 7–16.

Winner, E., Rosenstiel, A. K., & Gardner, H. The development of metaphoric understanding. *Developmental Psychology,* 1976, *12,* 289–297.

COMMUNICATION* | 13

MARILYN SHATZ, *University of Michigan*

CHAPTER CONTENTS

*Both institutions and individuals provided invaluable assistance to me as I prepared this chapter. The Rackham Graduate School of the University of Michigan, the John R. Simon Guggenheim Foundation, and the Wisconsin Center for Education Research (through a grant from the National Institute of Education, NIE–G–81–0009) provided financial support. Bolt Beranek and Newman and the Wisconsin Center provided space and secretarial help. Dorrit Billman, Philip R. Cohen, Jacquelynne Eccles, and Louise Cherry Wilkinson made many useful comments on sections of earlier drafts. I am especially grateful to Dorrit Billman for her help in researching the vast literature bearing on communication skills. My thanks also to Ellen M. Markman and John H. Flavell, for both their comments and their patience. Of course, the end product does not necessarily reflect the views of any of the above.

We casually take as instances of communication a variety of activities involving the sharing of information between entities, from the sentences of a researcher presenting her work at a professional meeting to the interactional games parents play with their children to the glances of lovers across a room. As Colin Cherry (1957) said, "communication is essentially a social affair."

Differences among various instances of communication can be characterized by their content, by the channels used to convey messages, by the naturalness or conventionality of the signal, and by the intentionality of the sender. Because this chapter deals with the development of the child's ability to communicate, I focus on those aspects that are most likely to show change in the individual over time, namely those related to the acquisition of a conventional system primarily utilizing linguistic symbols. This kind of communication system contributes to the production of social behavior, but is itself based on a broad range of cognitive skills. Hence, a review of the development of communicative competence is inevitably a discussion of such traditional cognitive concerns as the nature of knowledge representations, processing capacity, and the content of knowledge. To expand on Cherry, communication may be essentially a social affair, but it is fundamentally a cognitive activity as well.

There are, of course, other interesting issues in communication apart from those focusing on language, for example, the possibly universal production and comprehension of facial expressions (Ekman, 1971; Hiatt, Campos, & Emde, 1979; Izard, 1971) and the relationship of human to animal behavior (R. Brown, 1970; Seidenberg & Petitto, 1979; Thorpe, 1972). These will be addressed only insofar as they bear on theoretical issues in the acquisition of conventional systems.

Over the years a large literature on the acquisition of conventional communicative systems has accrued, much of it motivated by an interest in evaluating particular theories of grammar acquisition (Bruner, 1975; McNeill, 1970; Shatz, 1982) or cognitive development (Piaget, 1926; Shatz & Gelman, 1973). Recently researchers have begun to define the domain of communication skills per se and to investigate the mechanisms of development within that domain (Ammon, 1981; Flavell, 1976; Flavell, Botkin, Fry, Wright, & Jarvis, 1968; Higgins, Fondacaro, & McMann, 1981; Shatz, 1978c). There now exists a considerable body of facts about behaviors—ranging from infant-parent interactions to sophisticated perspective taking—that are all loosely termed communicative but for which there is still little in the way of a unifying theoretical framework. In light of this deficit, this review chapter has several goals: first, to report the descriptions of developing communicative behaviors that have been collected and to relate them to the various theoretical issues, whether cognitive, linguistic or social, that motivated them; and second, to begin to explore the possible relations the various lines of work in communication development have to one another. The purpose of the latter goal is to suggest questions of theoretical interest that can guide future research in the area.

The chapter is divided into five major sections. In the first section I consider in more detail the domain of communication research, particularly with regard to the defining characteristics of conventional communication systems. In the second section I take up the theoretical questions that have motivated much of the research on the development of communication skills. For both expository and historical reasons, this section is comprised of three segments with either a linguistic, cognitive, or social focus. The section titled *The Knowledge Bases of Communication* is the major review section, organizing the literature according to the knowledge bases necessary for conventional communicative behavior. The next section considers both the methodological and explanatory implications of children's variable performance in communication tasks. The final section returns to theoretical concerns, addressing the implications of the literature to date for a theory of communication skills and future work in the area.

CHARACTERISTICS OF CONVENTIONAL COMMUNICATION SYSTEMS

Natural and Conventional Signs

Signs are the units of information carrying meaning within a communication system. Some signs are natural, in that they are virtually universally expressed by members of a given species and each member of the species understands them in essentially the same way. Certain facial expressions would appear to be natural signs (Ekman, 1971). Conventional signs, on the other hand, are those whose meaning depends on a culturally agreed-on set of rules or standards, however tacit these may be. Although most conventional signs do not iconically represent their meaning, the lack of iconicity is not a necessary feature of such signs nor is iconicity necessary to natural signs. Moreover, natural signs or certain aspects of them can be recruited for conventional use by overlaying a secondary sign-meaning relation above and beyond the original one, although not all conventional signs are created this way.

Conventional signs imply some degree of learning on the part of the user. Whereas the role maturation and experience play in the expression and understanding of natural signs is a question of current debate (Campos & Stenberg, 1980), there is no argument that experience is crucial for the acquisition of a conventional sign system (Curtiss, 1977), although the nature of the requisite experience is at issue (see Snow & Ferguson, 1977).

Because experience is likely to play a greater role in the acquisition of conventional signs than natural ones, there is more opportunity for misunderstanding in a communication system characterized by conventional signs. Presumably all sufficiently mature individuals will be able to produce and comprehend the natural signs of their species. Conventional signs, on the other hand, can foster different interpretations in receivers who have acquired partial or slightly divergent knowledge of the rules governing their use. The following examples illustrate how gaps in children's knowledge (semantic, idiomatic, and illocutionary) can lead to misunderstanding a more knowledgeable speaker.

Mother: He's three and three-quarters. (Child looks puzzled.)
Mother: How old are you?
Child: Four and two dollars.

6-year-old (after being badgered by her brother): Hold your horses!
4-year-old: But I don't have any horses in my hands!

Experimenter (inquiring about a 3-year-old's ability): Can you tie your shoes?
Child: They are tied.

These sorts of misunderstandings suggest that sender/receiver differences in knowledge about, and interpretation of, conventional signs must be taken account of in a theory of human communication. The concepts of intentionality and internal representation help do so.

Intentions and Internal Representations

Communicative behavior must be characterized in terms that recognize its essentially active and social nature, as distinct from instances of passive signaling or knee-jerk responsiveness to signals. Hence, it is necessary to distinguish between the sorts of behaviors that are directed toward a receiver and those that, like the crying of a newborn, may have social or informational consequences but would have occurred even in the absence of a receiver. True communication, then, depends on the sender taking the receiver's capacity to understand into account. Similarly, an important construct in speech act theory is based on the notion of speaker intentions: illocutionary force is the way in which a speaker intends his utterance to be taken by a listener (Searle, 1969). Thus, the banging of a radiator would not be communicative, even if it directly caused a hearer to know that the heat was on, because the radiator cannot be said to have intended its behavior to influence the hearer's knowledge state.

We are certain of the radiator's inability to communicate because we assume a radiator has no means to represent an intention and an intended receiver internally. We ascribe communicative intentionality only to entities that have systems for representing both their goal states and knowledge of their receivers and that can produce appropriate actions on the basis of those representations. Likewise, receivers can be described as having knowledge and goal states involving a sender. *Understanding* a message, then, presumes some compatibility between the internal representations of sender and receiver; *misunderstanding,* some degree of incompatibility (Rommetveit, 1974; Shatz, 1978b). As illustrated by our dialogues above, misunderstandings occur when interpretive knowledge is not shared by participants. Because conventional signs are by definition based on interpretive information, they are more subject to misunderstanding than are natural ones.

Note that the capacity for communication is not limited to humans but to entities capable of the internal representation of knowledge and goal states of interactive partners. Thus, when equipped with representational systems that encode the relationships subsumed by beliefs, plans, and goals, computers do a passable job (in limited circumstances at least) of modeling human understanding (see Cohen & Perrault, 1979; Perrault & Allen, 1980; Schank & Abelson, 1977). The work of computer scientists on natural language processing is of interest to cognitive psychologists because it provides a method for modeling very specifically the understanding process. The computer scientist's job is to find a representational system and a set of operations ranging over that system that will succeed in producing appropriate behavior. The cognitive psychologist can then consider whether such a scheme fits adult experimental data as an appropriate model of human understanding.

Finding adequate models of behavior is an even more difficult task for the developmental psychologist than for the computer scientist or cognitive psychologist because developmental theory observes an additional empirical constraint, namely, that changes in behavior over time as well as behavior at particular points in time must be accounted for. The representational system that is handy and effective for talking about particular points may be unwieldy or unenlightening for talking about change. For the developmentalist, successful systems are those that are compatible both with accounts of behavior at anchor points in time and with accounts of change between those points. However, investigating the causes of change directly is a difficult business, and the best strategy for narrowing the set of candidate mechanisms for change is to describe with some certainty the anchor states. Hence, although their ultimate concerns may be somewhat different from those of the typical computer scientist, developmentalists may, nonetheless, find the computer scientist's successful accounts of anchor states informative and useful, at least as heuristic guides to their own study of whether and when children's behavior can be called intentional and whether and how they represent information about their coparticipants in communicative interactions.

Channels of Information and the Complexity of Communicative Behavior

Recent research has confirmed that participants in communicative interactions construe interpretations of messages from a variety of information sources (Bransford & McCarrell, 1974; Gunter, 1974; Rommetveit, 1974). If the message involves a linguistic component, then there is, of course, syntactic and semantic information available. There may also be various paralinguistic sources, such as intonation and prosody, as well as accompanying nonlinguistic features, such as hand gestures and facial expressions. The location of a message in the flow of discourse also affects its interpretation. Moreover, conventional signs are not limited to the linguistic channel but can be developed for other channels as well, for example, the gestural one. Even patterns of signs co-occurring across channels often take on conventional meanings, with different speech styles or registers having specific discourse and paralinguistic characteristics as well as particular lexical and syntactic features. (The most pertinent example of speech style for us would be the baby-talk registers described by Ferguson, 1977, which include not only syntactic and lexical simplifications, e.g., bye-bye for goodbye, but also paralinguistic clarifying procedures, such as the exaggeration of intonational contours.)

The implications of the above for a description of communicative competence are awesome. Indeed, the complexity of the communicative process has led some theorists to argue that a characterization of it goes beyond any purely linguistic enterprise and must be formulated within a theory of complex human social interaction (see, e.g., Bierwisch, 1980). As for the developmental implications, it is clear that children must acquire not only the language they hear but also an understanding of all the other channels of information their culture recruits for communicative tasks, and they must integrate these sources of information into a coherent functioning system (Cook-Gumperz & Gumperz, 1978).

Summary

We seek to explain the growth of children's ability to use a communication system consisting largely of conventional signs embedded in information-rich contexts. To be successful with such a system, children must acquire the ability to represent various kinds of knowledge, to integrate them, and to evaluate their relevance in context. A theory of the acquisition of communicative competence, then, must make reference to children's representational and processing capabilities as well as to the content of their social and linguistic knowledge.

More traditionally, communicative abilities have been considered primarily from either a linguistic, cognitive, or social perspective. To understand better the motivation for the research done to date, we turn now to a discussion of how communication has been related to theoretical questions in the areas of language, cognition, social behavior, and development.

THEORETICAL ISSUES RELATED TO COMMUNICATION

The theoretical issues in other domains that bear on questions concerning the development of communication often have their grounding in nondevelopmental questions. Although it is beyond the scope of this chapter to give a detailed report on the history or even the current state of these issues, it is useful to have a framework in which to situate the developmental issues. Therefore, each of the following sections on language, cognition, and social behavior includes a short overview of the broader issues.

Language and Communication

Obviously, language and communication have a close and complex relationship, which philosophers and linguists have puzzled over for centuries. Many of their efforts have centered on two issues: the descriptive question of how to characterize language formally and the ontogenetic question concerning the origins of language. Both of these issues and the theories they have motivated have implications for research on the development of communication.

The Descriptive Question

On the surface, what should or should not be included in a description of language does not appear to be a difficult question. Languages are strings of symbols that represent meaning in some perceptible medium, usually sound. Descriptions of languages would presumably include the rules for representing the sound characteristics of symbols, the rules for combining those symbols, and the rules for interpreting them, that is, the phonological, syntactic, and semantic properties of languages. Unfortunately, the reality of language use makes this story less neat. Although lexical items and syntactic strings can be said to have formally specifiable meanings, the sense in which particular utterances of such strings are to be taken is often not completely specified by those traditional syntactic and semantic accounts. Hence, some theorists have argued that if descriptions of languages are to be complete descriptions of sound-meaning relations, then they should include in some way those aspects of an utterance's meaning not traditionally accounted for, namely, those accruing to it by virtue of its being uttered in a certain context (Searle, 1969, 1972).

The problem with attempting an expansion of the traditional domain of linguistic description is that it quite definitely opens Pandora's box. A given utterance of a linguistic string in a particular context involving two particular participants can stand for something quite different from the meaning derivable from an analysis of its syntactic and semantic properties. In some cases, utterance meaning can be derived from traditional grammatical principles in combination with rather simple and general rules of contextual interpretation. For example, competent speakers of English know that requests for action can be expressed by questioning the ability of the hearer to do the desired act in a context where hearer ability is not truly an issue, as in the utterance, "Can you get me a cup of coffee?" (see Searle, 1975). In other cases, however, utterance meaning may depend to a great extent on the unique experiences of the participants. The utterance, "It's that time of night again," may also be a request for a cup of coffee, but it is likely to be interpreted as such only by a roommate familiar with the evening-snack ritual and not by every speaker of the language. Such cases have suggested to some the hopelessness of producing linguistic formalisms that would completely account for utterance meaning (Katz, 1977; Katz & Langendoen, 1976; Morgan & Sellner, 1980).

A solution proposed by Bierwisch (1980) is to keep language and communication separate. He cites three reasons for doing so: there are uses of language that are not communicative (see also Rees, 1973); there are certainly cases of communication that are nonlinguistic; and finally, the rules underlying the linguistic and communicative facets of verbal communication differ. There is, of course, a close relation between language and communication, and it is speech acts that form the bridge between them. Bierwisch says, "A speech act makes a linguistic utterance, mainly by virtue of its meaning, the bearer of what would best be called a communicative sense. Notice that a communicative sense belongs to the domain of social interaction" (1980, p. 3). Speech act theory, then, belongs to the theoretical realm of social interaction, although it is the part that relates social theory to linguistic theory.

Bierwisch's solution seems on balance to be a reasonable way of continuing to make progress in linguistic description without ignoring or obscuring the equally important issues of communication and their relation to language. The advantage of his approach is that it takes account of the fact that the behavioral domains of language and communication are not completely overlapping ones. Moreover, it recognizes that the knowledge bases for the two kinds of behavior also are to some extent distinct. It is not without disadvantages however. One is that, although the claim that language and social interaction have different rule systems seems true, it may also obscure similarities between them. The form of any human complex rule system may be constrained in similar ways by principles of learnability or accessibility. Certainly, more is known about the rules of language than about the rules of social interaction. Until more is known about both, it may be a disservice to suggest that there are no interesting parallels between them (Shatz, 1981). Second, the strong form of Bierwisch's argument implies that language description can proceed without reference to communicative factors and that no communicative phenomena can be captured by the tools of traditional linguistic analysis. With regard to the latter implication, several researchers have argued that some pragmatic and discourse phenomena, such as deictic pronouns—which make reference to speaker-listener relations but are defined similarly across a range of contexts—remain within the realm of linguistic analysis (Reichman, 1981; Shatz, 1980). For example, the rules of interpretation for *here* and *there* specify the relative spatial relations between speaker, hearer, and referent, regardless of whether speaker and hearer are, say, casual acquaintances or good friends. The rules are pragmatic in that they describe a relation between language users that is necessary to a complete characterization of the terms in question; yet the rules can be learned by any speaker of the language and applied without further reference to the background social conditions obtaining in given contexts. Because such phenomena remain relatively independent of the vagaries of social context, they should not be eliminated as candidates for linguistic description on the grounds of their pragmatic character alone.

As for the implication that language description

can proceed without any reference to communicative factors, even Bierwisch's (1980) own linguistic description makes reference to seemingly intentional phenomena (e.g., attitudes) in its account of linguistic devices such as grammatical mood that directly express communicative sense. Although Bierwisch smoothly differentiates the notions of a linguistic attitude expressed in a string and the intended attitude of an utterance, he does not address whether the distinction is psychologically appropriate (but see Bach & Harnish, 1979). The existence of grammatical devices with the potential for explicitly marking communicative sense is evidence for a close tie between language form and communicative function, although it is insufficient support for the argument that the form of the language is the direct outcome of communicative pressures. That argument has recently been stated in the context of questions about the phylogeny and ontogeny of language.

The Phylogenetic Question

Why languages have the form they do is a question that has long intrigued students of language. As with the descriptive question discussed earlier, the question of the historical development of languages again involves the issue of the relative autonomy of language as a system apart from communicative considerations. Obviously, languages must be of a form that allows them to be useful tools in communicative tasks, but whether this constraint fully or primarily determines the form they can take is unclear. Theories that argue for an important degree of constraint are called functionalist theories. Bates and MacWhinney (1979) note that there is a strong and a weak version of the functionalist view. In the weak one, the existence of grammatical devices is correlated with communicative functions and the processing constraints of the communicators; in the strong one, grammatical forms are determined and maintained by those factors. The strong form is subject to the criticism that it has not been put forth in a complete or explicit enough way that would allow a reasonable test of it. Moreover, several aspects of syntax (e.g., gender marking) come to mind as ones that may be especially hard to account for on communicative grounds. The weaker form also suffers from expository vagueness, but even if explicit correlations were proposed and confirmed empirically, it is unclear what they would signify other than a restatement of the obvious fact noted above that languages must function as successful modes of communication. In contrast, nonfunctionalist theories put less weight on communicative factors per se as

determinants of particular forms within the language. In the next section, we see that the issue of the relationship between linguistic form and communicative factors also must be confronted when considering development of the child.

Ontogenetic Considerations

It seems reasonable, having spent some time on nondevelopmental issues as background, to begin with some caveats. It is easy to make inappropriate inferences from theoretical arguments to developmental issues. For example, just because neat linguistic theories can be developed by keeping linguistic and communicative issues relatively separate, it does not follow that those are the linguistic descriptions that are learned by a child acquiring language or that the child learns them independently of communicative considerations. Similarly, even if a strong functional position regarding the etiology of the forms of languages were true, it would not necessarily follow that the development of a child's grammar was likewise completely determined by the communicative pressures on the child. It may be painfully obvious that it is dangerous to conflate formal and developmental issues on the one hand and the questions of the origins of language generally with the origin of an individual's language on the other hand. Nevertheless, the literature on early language and communicative development is littered with examples of such conflations. It is important to keep in mind that how separate language and communication are in the child's representations or how much communicative pressures account for the child's acquisition of language are empirical questions.

The data relevant to these issues are relatively sparse, but there are some pieces of evidence that argue for some separation of language and communication on developmental grounds. First, ability in one area does not seem to be a necessary and sufficient condition for the other: there are certainly children who can communicate but who have a variety of linguistically based difficulties, and recently a child has been reported to have achieved some measure of grammatical skill in the absence of normal communicative development (Blank, Gessner, & Esposito, 1979). Second, attempts to account for language acquisition on the basis of developmentally prior communication systems have generally been vague, and efforts to specify them better have not been particularly successful (Shatz, 1982). Finally, there are reports of stages of organization and reorganization in children's grammars that appear to be the results not of communicative pressure but of the children's internal notions of orderliness within what Karmiloff-Smith (1981) has called "a formal problem-space" (also see Bowerman, 1982). This is not to argue that there are no facilitative effects of communicative experience on language acquisition (see Hoff-Ginsberg & Shatz, 1982, for a review). Instead, the point is that the questions of one area do not appear reducible to, or equatable with, the questions in the other. Just what relation they do bear to one another is an important area of research. As a heuristic, it seems most reasonable to adopt the view that the areas are disparate, albeit related.

Cognition and Communication

As might be expected, given our earlier discussion, the primary foci of work relating cognition and communication are issues involving representation—its nature, its development, and the processes by which representations are recruited for communicative tasks.

Adult Work

As already noted, communication involves mental representations. It is no surprise, then, that communication research has a close tie to cognitive studies as well as to language studies. Relevant cognitive research can be divided into that which investigates the nature of representations and that focusing more on the process by which those representations are utilized in the production of behavior. Work on representational systems has been carried out largely by philosophers and computer scientists. It has its roots in arguments by Grice (1957) that the understanding of speaker meaning essentially involves the speaker's construction of a plan for listener understanding and the listener's recognition of that plan. Drawing both on Grice (1957) and Austin (1962), Searle (1969) has proposed that plan recognition is effected by reference to a set of appropriateness conditions on speech acts that can be used as an evaluation metric to determine the intentions behind utterances in specific contexts. Taking a different route, Schiffer (1972) has argued that the representation of mutual beliefs as such is crucial to a characterization of plan recognition. Formalisms based on the work of both Searle (1969) and Schiffer (1972) are currently being devised by computer scientists (see Cohen & Levesque, 1980; Perrault & Allen, 1980; Perrault, Allen, & Cohen, 1978).

Little data on adults exist to evaluate the psychological reality of the representational systems thus far proposed. For example, models based on Searle's (1969, 1975) view presume two separate representations of a sentence, such as "Can you shut the door?": a literal reading as a question about listener ability and an alternative reading (in appropriate contexts) as a request for listener action. However, results of comprehension-time studies provide equivocal evidence in support of such models (Clark & Lucy, 1975; Gibbs, 1979). As for processing considerations, the major effort here has again been with regard to comprehension issues (Bransford & McCarrell, 1974; Clark & Haviland, 1974). Basically, comprehension models all call for some parsing of incoming linguistic information and integration of that information with prior knowledge (although not necessarily in a simple two-step order, see H. H. Clark, 1979). The empirical work on these models lends credence to the view that language interpretation involves more than the analysis of linguistic strings based on linguistic information alone, although the specific principles governing how information is accessed, integrated, and utilized are far from established.

Two other concepts primarily from adult cognitive research have a bearing on communication work as well. The first is the notion of a limited capacity processor. Because communication tasks involve an integration of information from a variety of sources in real time, their accomplishment is presumably subject to the constraints of the capacity limitations of the processing system. There have been some proposals for how such constraints operate, but there is no single, well-accepted position on them. The second concept involves an executive function. If communicative behavior is goal directed, then the question arises of an executor that sets goals and selects means of achieving them. The idea of an executive faculty that organizes cognitive activity has received mixed reviews from cognitive psychologists, but it seems to survive in spite of the lack of clear formulations of it. A related notion in the developmental literature is found in discussions of metacognition and its value for accessing and organizing appropriate behaviors (see A. L. Brown, 1978; Flavell, 1978b).

Developmental research involving cognition and communication is related to the above issues, although it was motivated less by the adult literature than by the work of Piaget. (However, see Shatz, 1978b, for a discussion of the implications of developmental research for Searle's, 1969, 1975, theory.) Regardless of the source of the motivation, the issues already mentioned, namely, the nature of representations and the process of using those representations in real time, are central questions in developmental work on communication.

The Ontogenesis of Representation

It is generally agreed that there is some form of representation that is nonanalogue and symbolic that underlies much of cognitive activity, including the sorts of communicative systems under discussion (see *Mandler, vol. III, chap. 7*). One question that has occupied developmentalists is where this representational ability comes from. Piaget (1952, 1962) has proposed that it is the result of the child's sensorimotor interactions with the world of objects during his first months of life. From such interactions comes the ability to represent absent objects and potential states as well as means-end relations, in other words, the ability to have intentional states. These achievements are considered to be prerequisites for higher order acquisitions such as language. Indeed, the view that early language depends on sensorimotor development has attained some popularity (see Bloom, 1973; R. Brown, 1973). However, in a recent review of the pertinent literature, Corrigan (1979) has argued that evaluating the evidence for a strong Piagetian position is difficult because there are neither agreed-on measures of representational capacity nor specific enough characterizations of the language behavior for which they should account. Nor has the nature of the sought-for relationships between cognition and language been clearly enough specified. The same can be said of early cognition-communication relationships (see Bates, Benigni, Bretherton, Camaioni, & Volterra, 1979, for a discussion in this area).

Others have argued that the representational ability demonstrated by intentional states is essentially innate (Fodor, 1975). Trevarthen and Hubley (1978) have claimed that the change observed in infants' interactive behavior at about 9 months of age is due to maturational factors that allow for the integration of multiple social and physical objects into single representations. The behavioral change Trevarthen and Hubley reported has been noted by other researchers (e.g., Bates et al., 1979), although few go so far as to argue that such behaviors are innately programmed. Schaffer (1979) grants the child some innate capacity but as a basically interactive organism seeking out social stimulation. He argues that development is an outcome of the early interactive patterns between parent and child.

In support of this more social perspective, a review of the literature on infant interactions with people and objects suggests that there may be important differences between early representations of the social world and those of the physical world (Gelman & Spelke, 1980). If that is the case, one would expect Piagetian theory not to be particularly successful at predicting the course of communicative development. In any event, the mechanisms accounting for the development of what Bretherton and Bates (1979) have called the child's "theory of interfacing minds" are presently unclear. Sometime within the period of 9 to 18 months, infants evidence the ability to have intentional states and to base interactive behavior on such states. We will review the work to date investigating the biological, cognitive, and social precursors of those states, but as Gelman and Spelke (1980) point out, further research on this question is needed.

The issue of the causes of growth does not disappear with the advent of representational skills and early childhood. A basic division between a more socially oriented view and a Piagetian position that sees development as primarily a result of the child's actions on her world of physical objects continues to surface in theoretical discussions of later developments as well.

The Basis for Later Developments in Representation

As Bretherton and Bates (1979) point out, theories of interfacing minds are not constructed in a day. The ability to understand conventional signals, to plan selectively and appropriately for their use, and to execute those plans are abilities that are only gradually acquired. Such abilities depend on complex representations of one's own abilities, a view of others in one's social world, and a knowledge of the conventions governing the behavior of participants in that world. In Piaget's terms, the child must be able to decenter, to take multiple perspectives of a situation, and to integrate them into a nonegocentric picture of reality. Decentering occurs only when the child has acted on the world enough to have developed schemes that may on occasion come into conflict with one another. The resolution of the conflict requires reorganization and coordination, the consequences of which are the integrated schemes that underlie decentered behavior (see Inhelder, Sinclair, & Bovet, 1974).

In contrast to such internally controlled development, Wertsch (1977, 1979) has presented a view of development based on the writings of Soviet psychologists, primarily Vygotsky (1978, in preparation), in which the chief source of developmental progress is external.[1] In this view, the parent supplies the perspective and planning functions for a child in any given cognitive task, thus providing examples for him that gradually become internalized as his competence with lower level aspects of the task grows and that eventually allow him to take over more of the higher functions. Hence, cognitive work is seen initially as a joint or social effort that is only gradually taken over by the child exclusively. The importance of this sort of view for communication should be obvious. The social agent of change, usually the mother, essentially communicates a cognitive organization to her child. Communication, then, is no longer a by-product of cognition but is a determinant of it.

One concern the Vygotskyan view raises is how the child has the cognitive apparatus to understand and incorporate the parental communications if it is the communications that seem to be the basis for the development of cognitive structure. Wertsch (1977) has addressed this apparent circularity by outlining a hierarchy of communicative acts that require more linguistic and conventional knowledge on the part of the child to understand or use the acts as he moves up the hierarchy. Thus, a ''pure intended effect act'' requires little from the child other than that he notice the result of the parent's act. The successful utilization of more sophisticated acts would presumably depend on the progress fostered in the child by prior acts. There is some evidence suggesting that mothers do produce for very young children the sorts of low-level acts Wertsch describes (Schnur & Shatz, in press; Wood, Bruner, & Ross, 1976). As for cross-cultural data, Cole[2] has informally reported that parental structuring of everyday tasks to accommodate a child's participation occurs in other cultures besides Western ones. However, Ochs (1980) reports that, at least in the language domain, Samoan caregivers do not support children's early communicative efforts the way American middle-class mothers do. Hence, there is as yet little firm evidence for the claim that such acts are necessary or sufficient for cognitive development or even that they are facilitative of it. Although Wertsch's (1977, 1979) account makes Vygotsky's position tenable, it is unproven.

The Uses of Representations

Currently, much developmental research focuses on the processes by which knowledge is recruited to the production of communicative behavior. Interestingly, the work culminating in this focus on process has its origins in the tradition of Piagetian structuralism. Initially, when children were found to be inadequate communicators, they were typically labeled egocentric, incapable of taking another's perspective. As Asher (1979) notes, this conflation of communicative failure with egocentrism appears in the writings of Piaget himself. That is, Piaget (e.g., 1926) used differences in behavior between

children of different ages or between children and adults to argue for a particular sort of structural difference, and this line of reasoning was adopted by others. However, as the results of studies using a variety of research methods began to accumulate, they stimulated questions about the necessity of linking communicative inadequacy to one kind of structural deficit.[3] For one, some studies looking for evidence of perspective taking in children were successful in finding such evidence (e.g., Maratsos, 1973; Shatz & Gelman, 1973). For another, studies of referential communication showed that young children often produced messages that were inadequate even for themselves (Asher & Oden, 1976). It was difficult to see how such messages could be termed egocentric if they could not adequately convey even private meaning to their originator. One conclusion derived from these lines of work was that communicative inadequacy was not necessarily evidence for egocentrism.

The view that has gained popularity with the demise of the egocentrism construct characterizes communicative competence as a confluence of subskills, each of which has to be acquired before adequate performance is achieved (see Flavell et al., 1968; Glucksberg, Krauss, & Higgins, 1975). On this account, children's inadequate performance is attributable to the absence of one subskill or another in their knowledge base. Although the component-skills view has merit, proofs that children completely lack a particular subskill or kind of knowledge have been exceedingly hard to come by. Instead, as we will see, children are more likely sometimes to display and sometimes not to display a particular subskill. This intraindividual variation in the quality of performances seems to depend on the information processing demands of the tasks used to measure them. Such variation is precisely what is difficult for structurally based stage models to explain. As an alternative, a developmental process model that distributes the explanatory burden between structural change and processing constraints accounts for both between- and within-subject behavioral variation (Shatz, 1978c). Such a model has much in common with other recent attempts to build information processing concerns into developmental theories (e.g., Case, 1978; Fischer, 1980; Wilkinson, 1981). Moreover, accounts such as Fischer (1980) and Shatz's (1978c) have an affinity with recent work in other areas of psychology that have questioned the wisdom of trying to characterize human cognition in very general and abstract terms (e.g., Nisbett & Ross, 1980).

In sum, this brief review of cognitive issues suggests that the framework Piaget's monumental theory provided for research in communication development is no longer sufficient or fully appropriate. Piaget's search for structural principles at the most general level resulted in the neglect of several phenomena, such as the differences between social and nonsocial objects, the processing constraints on the organism, and the organizing social influences on the organism, all of which subsequent research has shown to be important for any characterization of the cognitive apparatus recruited for communicative tasks. Still, it should be noted that, as a good scientific theory should, Piaget's work promoted its own demise by stimulating the research from which a new framework is evolving. In later sections, we will examine more closely the kinds of data on children's knowledge and performance for which a new framework will have to account.

Social Issues and Communication

The discussions of language and cognition have demonstrated the importance of social considerations for explanations of communicative behavior. I have already alluded to two issues of relevance to communication that are addressed in the social literature, namely the genesis of meaningful social behavior and the use of social information in interpreting messages. These issues are considered in more detail here.

The Origins of Social Understanding

The ethological view on the beginnings of meaningful social behavior places them in the context of the phylogenetic heritage of the species. In this view, the human comes prepared with devices that control his social relationships. As in the animal world, these "natural" social behaviors presumably communicate threat, submission, and dominance (Hinde, 1970). Recent research confirms that children do produce some facial expressions that are morphologically and functionally analogous to those observed in nonhuman primates (Camras, 1977). Camras is currently attempting to determine whether more sophisticated social behaviors involving language can be related to these early "natural" behaviors.[4] Even if some can, it is unclear how much sophisticated social behavior will ultimately be accounted for in this way.

Other theorists concerned with the beginnings of social awareness have labeled experience in the social world as the source of meanings individuals attach to actions (Cooley, 1908; Mead, 1934; Shotter, 1978; Vygotsky, 1962, 1978). Such writers argue

that social development involves learning to see oneself as others do (Mead) or to interpret one's actions as well as others' actions in culturally determined ways (Shotter). This process is carried out by observing how others respond to one's actions (Cooley) or by having others comment on and set one's actions in a larger meaningful framework (Vygotsky).

Although the above sorts of explanations account well for both differences across cultures and commonalities across individuals within cultures in the way individual actions generally are viewed, it is unclear whether they account for self-perception and its development. If people's views of themselves depend solely on the way they have been viewed by others, then, ceteris paribus, they should view themselves as others do. Shrauger and Schoeneman (1979) point out that the results of correlational studies relating self-perception to the actual perceptions by others are ambiguous: half of the studies show no significant correlations, whereas the others report significant but low relationships. Moreover, although people modify their self-description in response to feedback from others, the nature of their modifications depends on a variety of factors that suggest the demand characteristics of test situations may have influenced the findings. No long-range studies of the indirect effect of feedback on developing self-concept have been carried out. Thus, there is no clear evidence for the view that self-concept is derived wholly or mainly from others' perceptions of the self.

Studies from the attribution literature suggest that evidence for the view may be long in coming. The same objective task performance (success or failure) is likely to be assigned a different cause (ability or luck), depending on whether the subject is assessing his own or another's performance (Jones & Nisbett, 1972; Kelley & Michela, 1980). That is, people view the causes of their own successes and failures differently from the way they view those of others. Hence, the assessment of their own performance by others would not conform to their own. How then, if the attribution studies are tapping into genuine or natural patterns of behavior assessment, could self-perceptions possibly derive wholly or primarily from the perceptions of others?

Monson & Snyder (1977) have suggested that people judge themselves differently from others because they have more and better information about their own performances than they do about those of others. Because children, like adults, show differences in self/other judgments (Stipek & Hoffman, 1980), it appears that they too have special access to information about their actions. Only when confronted with a novel task on which they have no prior information about their own success, do children judge their own performance in the same way they judge another's (Parsons, 1980). As noted earlier, the lack of clear correlations between self-perception and perception by others suggests that the source of additional information about the self need not be social. How this information is acquired, represented, and integrated with social sources of information to arrive at self-reflexive understanding remains an unanswered question. To the extent that there are internal sources, however, the positions of Mead (1934) and Vygotsky (1962, 1978) are weakened.

The above discussion is relevant to an important problem in communication, that of misunderstanding. We have all felt at times that what we want to communicate is misunderstood by our listener. That is, the listener sees our actions in a way different from the way we ourselves see them. At such times, we often try to justify our actions by providing our listener with more information about ourselves or our motives. It is unknown how such communicative behavior would alter judgments on attribution tasks. Nor is it known what the relation is between self-awareness and the ability to recognize and repair misunderstandings. As we will see, only recently have researchers begun to be concerned with the development of monitoring ability.

The Use of Social Information

Regardless of how children come to assign meaning to social actions, one can ask how they use what they know and whether they use it appropriately. The issue of appropriateness has received much attention in both the psychological and sociolinguistic literature, with the result that children have been shown to be remarkably adept at producing socially adapted behavior. Yet, it may be a mistake to presume that communicators learn a set of general social-interpretation rules that are applied uniformly across situations. Higgins et al. (1981) argue that whatever information either adult or child participants recruit for a communication task depends on the roles and goals of the participants in the particular situation. For example, 4-year-olds talk differently to 2-year-olds when they see themselves in a teaching role from when they are trying to engage a younger child in informal play (Shatz & Gelman, 1977). Hence, in assessing what subjects know and how they use their knowledge, researchers must take account of the goals the subjects themselves may have for any given task. This caveat is especially important in research with children, who are less likely than adult subjects to share the goals a researcher intuitively assumes are represented in her task setting.

In addition, the selection of social information depends on the cognitive resources available to utilize it. For example, Higgins (1980) has argued that there are several processes of social judgment that involve different kinds of inferences on the part of the judge. Which inference process is utilized will depend not only on the demands and goals of a given task but also on the ease with which the judge can execute the various processes as well as how facile she is with the information each process requires. In other words, the selection of a particular process as well as the information requisite to it depend in a particular situation on the most efficient distribution of the processor's limited resources (Shatz, 1978c).

The issue is not whether social interactions involve systematic knowledge. Much literature confirms the existence of stereotypes, speech registers, and ritual interactions, all of which suggest that there is social knowledge stored at a relatively general level. It is possible that one function of such knowledge is to ease the process of producing appropriate, meaningful behavior in complex social situations. The alternative to general knowledge would be continual negotiation about meaning and acceptability. Although recent work has shown that negotiation does indeed occur (e.g., Garfinkel, 1967; Newman, 1978), it seems most reasonable that interactions vary in the degree to which participants utilize prior knowledge to assign meaning or negotiate meaning in dealing with one another. The point is that when they rely on stored knowledge, its use is subject to factors like the cognitive resources available for the task and the goals they wish to accomplish. Likewise, whether they use stored knowledge is subject to the same factors. It appears, then, that separating the factors of social competence from cognitive performance in accounting for developing communicative behavior will be an extremely difficult task.

Toward a Theory of Communication

The discussion of theoretical issues bearing on communication research has included issues that regularly occur in the developmental literature. There are questions of ontogeny and phylogenetic relationships, issues of the continuity of behaviors over time, and questions about the role of heredity and environment as determinants of behavior and changes in behavior. Other issues have been raised that are less classically or uniquely developmental, for example: What knowledge systems are required for communicative behavior? How are they represented? How are they integrated with other systems in the process of producing behavior? Answers to such questions will be good answers insofar as they can account for developmental data as well as adult data. Obviously, a comprehensive theory of communication behavior and its development should provide accounts for all the issues raised. Given the recalcitrance of the issues it must address, such a theory is not likely to appear on the horizon in the very near future. For the intrepid, however, we turn now to a review of the data it would explain.

THE KNOWLEDGE BASES OF COMMUNICATION

We have alluded to the kinds of knowledge required to be a successful linguistic communicator. In this section, we examine evidence for the kinds of skills children possess and address the question of how they come to acquire them. Obviously, one kind of knowledge requisite to linguistic communication is grammatical: participants are presumed to possess the semantic and syntactic systems of their linguistic community. A full discussion of how children acquire such knowledge is not included in this chapter (see *Clark, vol. III, chap. 12; Maratsos, vol. III, chap. 11*), although we do consider the relationship of grammar to other skills necessary for communicative competence. Instead, we focus on what makes a grammatical system usable for communication: the existence of an intentional system, the understanding of discourse relations, the ability to apply relevant background knowledge to communicative situations, and the ability to make social inferences. In addition, we examine the acquisition of the knowledge of such conversational mechanics as turn taking and topic maintenance.

In considering what kinds of knowledge children have and how they come to acquire them, one confronts the problem of continuity in development. For example, can a child who points at a mitten be said to be carrying out an act of reference in the same sense as the 4-year-old who says, "This is a mitten"? Early behaviors that have some similarity in form or function to later, more complex behaviors are often taken to be precursors of later ones. When precursor is taken in the strong sense as the source from which later behavior emerges, the resulting view of development is one of continuity. An apparent virtue of continuous models of development is that they avoid the burden of explicating mechanisms to account for discontinuous change (see Flavell, 1971, and Shatz,

1978c, for a discussion of the difficulties of discontinuous models). Yet, precursor models often seem equally mysterious insofar as the claims for the emergence of later behaviors from earlier ones are not founded on principled grounds (for attempts at establishing operational criteria for continuity, see Bates et al., 1979; Bower, 1974; & Bruner, 1978). Research on early communication skills has often been motivated by a belief in continuity. Consequently, much work has focused on the description of prelinguistic behaviors that might function as precursors. However, little has been done to justify empirically or theoretically the assumption of continuity (for an extended discussion, see Shatz, in press). Therefore, in reviewing the literature on the development of communication skills, I consider the prelinguistic period separately, taking a conservative position on the question of whether early skills are necessary or sufficient to account for later behaviors.

The Prelinguistic Period

Preparedness for Communication

One claim that exists in the literature is that the infant comes equipped to participate in social interactions (see Schaffer, 1974, 1979). There is little doubt that certain neonatal behaviors are responded to as if they were informative. Not only do Western parents use crying, smiling, attentiveness, and body posture as cues to assess the state of their infants and respond appropriately to them, but on the basis of such behaviors, they often attribute to their infants the ability to communicate intentionally. As a member of a hospital nursery staff commented when asked why she talked to her young charges, "It's never too early to start relating to infants as people" (Rheingold & Adams, 1980). Yet, clearly the preparedness claim can be separated from the claim that the very young infant cries to get his wants attended to. Initially at least, it is more reasonable to assume that such behaviors are simply natural expressions of physical states.

Although they may not be intentional, these explicit behavioral expressions of internal states may still be preparatory to the establishment of later intentional communication systems. Adults recognize the internal states for which these behavioral expressions stand; they can, then, infer a commonality between themselves and the creature producing these expressions. This feeling of alikeness gives them reason to believe that they will eventually be able to get such a creature to understand what they themselves are thinking and feeling. Thus, insofar as infants come equipped with expressive behaviors that allow appropriate inferences to their internal states, they are prepared to be admitted into the company of participants in interpersonal communication. Indeed, when disordered infants do not produce the normal range of these behaviors, it seems to have a deleterious effect on their parents' behavior toward them. It is, of course, unlikely that the development of such children would ultimately result in normal outcomes, regardless of parental behaviors. Still, the argument that it is to the advantage of the normal child to be equipped with behaviors immediately certifying him as like-kind seems reasonable.

Westerners go a step further and attribute intentionality to infants on the basis of this attribution of alikeness. That is a possible, but not necessary, inference from the attribution of alikeness. Not every culture rushes to grant intentionality to the infant solely on the basis of early expressive behaviors. Ochs reports that in Samoa "the actions and vocalizations of infants are treated more as natural reflexes of physiological states . . . than as intentional, spontaneous acts" (1980, p. 23). Because Samoan children do learn to communicate, the very early attribution of intentionality to infants must not be essential to the development of their communicative skill. Whether it has any effect on the rate and nature of development is a question that has not yet been answered.

The question of whether the infant has particular preprogrammed patterns of interaction that will ultimately structure communication is also unresolved. Some researchers have suggested the neonate shows patterns of responding to social stimuli that are well timed and reciprocal in nature (see Bullowa, 1976; Fafouti-Milenkovic & Uzgiris, 1979; Freedle & Lewis, 1977). But just what patterns can justifiably be taken as precursors of which more sophisticated behaviors is unclear. For example, Condon and Sander (1974) reported on the co-occurring action patterns neonates produce in connection with adult speech sounds. They suggested a direct relation between such patterns and later conversational behavior. In apparent compatibility with this view, turn overlaps and co-occurrence were found to be the predominant vocalization patterns between mothers and their 3- and 4-month-old infants (Anderson, Vietze, & Dokecki, 1977; Stern, Jaffe, Beebe, & Bennett, 1975). However, rather than being important as precursors to later conversational patterns, overlapping turns may be fully appropriate to early infant-adult interaction as an end in themselves, in that they serve the function of establishing and maintaining contact. Indeed, Stern et al. suggest that both co-occurring vocalizations and the Condon and Sander (1974) phenomenon serve an essentially separate function from the ones expressed by the alternating patterns more common to conversations, in that the former mark the fact of interaction. Further, these investigators argue that analogous co-occurring forms, like chorusing and oath taking, are the true issue of these early patterns, preserved as solidarity markers in adult interactions. In the above view, conversational turn taking does not differentiate out of patterns of co-occurrence but has a separate origin. The view seems reasonable. To the extent that neither the forms nor the functions of early turn taking are transferred from the realm of early infant-caretaker interactions to the conversational setting, the argument that there is continuity between them is weakened.

Bateson (1975) has argued that the alternating patterns she observed in a mother's interactions with her 2- to 4-month-old infant were instances of early protoconversations from which later behaviors would emerge. However, even the occurrence of alternating turns does not necessarily index any preparedness for, or competence at, turn control on the part of the infant. Nonoverlapping turns may occur primarily for two reasons. For one, as Schaffer, Collis, and Parsons (1977) suggest, it is just hard to attend and behave at the same time. Second, the early occurrence of nonoverlapping turns seems to depend to a large extent on the degree to which the mother accommodates her behavior to her child's performances (Hayes & Elliott, 1979; Stern, 1977; Trevarthen, 1977). Just when children attempt to avoid overlapping turns on communicative grounds is unclear. It would be of interest to examine the interactional behavior of children in the 1st year of life for any evidence indicating awareness that overlaps can be a problematic interaction pattern, for example, cases where children start over or relinquish a turn to repair overlaps. At present, then, there is no clear evidence that some infant behaviors index explicit preparation for later conversational participation.

The Influence of Parental Behavior

The rhythm and structure of children's early interactive patterns cannot be taken as indicating that infants are directly prepared for conversational turn taking. Yet, when woven by parents into elaborated exchanges, the early behaviors described above possibly still do facilitate growth. As noted, several researchers have observed that mothers work their infants' repertoires into joint-action patterns by accommodating their behavior to that of their children.

Wood et al. (1976) have argued that this kind of scaffolding creates for the child a structured interaction more elaborate than one she herself could create but one in which she is still a central element. Unfortunately, no studies have been done to determine whether the degree to which, or time at which, a child is engaged in structured protoconversations influences the onset or degree of skill at later conversational tasks. Freedle and Lewis (1977) did find positive correlations between the degree to which mothers were responsible for initiating vocalization sequences with their 3-month-olds and the children's later language development as measured by their mean length of utterance (MLU) at 2 years of age. However, Freedle and Lewis measured MLU and not conversational skill per se. They point out that in any case such correlations are best taken as indicating a motivational factor: an attentive, interested mother of a 3-month-old is likely to be the same sort of mother when her child is old enough to utilize the kind of information she has been providing, perhaps unnecessarily, for some period of time.

There are, of course, some aspects of turn allocation that must be learned from experience. Various languages and cultures have different devices for managing turn allocation. Snow (1977a) showed that Western maternal speech to children as young as 3 months includes many examples of interrogative devices, such as subject-verb-inversion, tag questions, and question intonation, all of which function in adult conversations as turn allocators. Thus, parents often behave as though their children can take turns, and in so doing, they provide data for them on the kinds of devices that their language and culture recognize as conversationally appropriate. Again, it is unclear just when children begin to take advantage of such information. (We consider later what they do know by the time they are preschoolers.) Nor do we know how much early experience the child needs to learn the system. It is possible that parents' conventional conversational overtures to their very young children are unnecessary in the sense that such young infants do not learn from them at that time. However, such efforts may still be compatible with an evolutionary perspective. It may be more efficient to create a device that continually emits as its output an input that is ultimately relevant for the learner than to create one so sensitive to the child's progress that it turns on only when the child is ready. Indeed, there is some evidence, at least with regard to linguistic levels, that parents are not especially well tuned to their children's progress (Gleason, 1976). In short, Western parents treat their prelinguistic infants as potentially competent social par-

ticipants. It is unclear whether they do so because it directly helps the child gradually learn about conversations or whether it assures appropriate parental behavior when the infant is ready to benefit, in which case it has only an indirect relation to the child's later development.

The above discussion suggests that parental structuring of infant behaviors needs to be evaluated in light of such other factors as cultural differences before it can be accepted as a cause for growth. Recent research suggests that maturation is another factor that must be considered as well. Whereas early on, infants focus on either persons or objects, by 8 to 10 months, they seem to be able to integrate them into one behavioral sequence. For example, Sugarman-Bell describes as "co-ordinated person-object orientation" a sequence where the child looks up, touches the adult's arm and, after being acknowledged by the adult, reaches for an object in the adult's possession. These sorts of sequences occur at about the same time or shortly after infants show the ability to use one object as an instrument to gain or manipulate a second object. Thus, object-object instrumentality and person-object instrumentality are closely related in time (Sugarman-Bell, 1978). The fact that these sorts of results are consistent across studies and with fairly large samples of children in more than one culture (Bates et al., 1979) suggests that there may be a maturational factor involved in the child's ability to perform such coordinations. Indeed, Trevarthen and Hubley (1978) argue this position. To the extent that this is so, parental scaffolding of early child behaviors would not appear to be sufficient to induce the more sophisticated behaviors, although it still may be necessary to the achievement of coordination. Sugarman-Bell also reports that institutionalized children exhibited the same pattern and timing of development in their progress toward coordination as home-reared children; yet, their speech was delayed relative to the home-reared group. Thus, it is possible that the achievement of coordinated instrumentality is relatively independent of early interactive experience, but both coordination and interactive experience are requisite to language onset. If this is so, then one would expect to find effects of early experience only after adequate maturational progress.

Demonstrating Intentional Communication

As Sugarman-Bell (1978) points out, coordinated person-object orientation is not in itself evidence for intentional communication (in the sense discussed earlier). Nor are the sequences of eye contact and vocalization that Harding and Golinkoff

(1979) describe as intentional vocalizations. Children who exhibit these behaviors may have intentions, in that they have goals they seek to have accomplished. Moreover, they may have expectations about the value of objects, including social objects, as instruments for the attainment of their goals. Yet, it seems important to distinguish between expectations about the efficacy of an instrument and a genuine understanding of the workings of that instrument.[5] Intentional communication (as opposed to intentions) involves a representation of the social object as an individual capable of understanding one's intentions. Obviously, it is difficult to garner direct evidence that 10-month-olds have such representations.

Golinkoff (1981) argues the child's use of vocalizations accompanied by eye contact to achieve goals is evidence for intentional communication because vocalization and eye contact are distal rather than proximal modes of interaction for influencing an agent and depend not only on the achievement of a means-ends analysis but also (apparently) on an understanding of the agent as a self-propelled actor as well. However, the use of distal means need not index that the child has a view of the other as a being capable of understanding one's communicative intentions. Presumably, a belief in one's magical power over another's behavior could as readily underlie the instigating distal behavior that results in a listener accomplishing a desired activity. Similarly, the regular but idiosyncratic vocalizations reportedly used consistently to signal common functions (Carter, 1978a; Dore, 1974; Halliday, 1975) are not obviously instances of intentional communication in the strict sense outlined above. In fact, if the child had a belief in the magical ability of his own (distal) actions to influence others, one might well expect to see these sorts of unconventional but fixed behaviors used to effect particular results.

In a recent article, Greenfield (1980) presents some examples of children persisting in attempts to achieve their goals despite misunderstandings on the part of their interlocutors. Often, these attempts take the form of alternative forms of expression, with the children adjusting their behavior in view of the adult's responses until they can confirm the appropriateness of the adult's interpretation. Greenfield's examples are taken from children with some linguistic ability, considerably older than the children in studies cited earlier that focus on consistent vocalizations. Wilcox and Webster (1980) report similar results with children who use primarily one- or two-word utterances. These children reformulate their messages in response to evidence of misunderstand-

ing more than they do to the request for clarification, "*What?*". In the latter case, children are as likely to repeat as to reformulate. Of course, the clearest proof of intentional communication rather than simple perseverance toward a goal would be the cessation of varied attempts as a function of the listener indicating mutual understanding despite the lack of compliance. It is possible that examining the data of prelinguistic children with regard to repair behaviors would indicate that they do adjust their behavior until they are assured of genuine understanding, if not compliance. Golinkoff (in press) is conducting such work. Depending on her findings, one might be more willing to grant that prelinguistic children view their interlocutors as capable of understanding rather than merely as controllable instruments. In the absence of such evidence, however, one cannot dismiss the possibility that such sophistication on the part of the child waits, at least in part, on the advent of a linguistic system in which the "negotiated interpretation of intention," as Greenfield (1980) calls it, can be carried out.[6]

Summary

Recent investigations have described the child's growth in interactive abilities during the prelinguistic period. Clearly, infants are social creatures who are often treated early on as communicative partners. However, it is unclear whether prelinguistic developments form a continuous and direct line to the communicative patterns of the linguistic period. It does appear, on the basis of cross-cultural evidence, that early parental molding of the child's expressive behaviors into communicative sequences is not a prerequisite for later development to occur. Finally, I have argued that the observations of children using idiosyncratic but consistent signals for specific interactive functions are insufficient evidence of true communication in the strict sense defined herein. Whether truly intentional communication can be said to occur in the prelinguistic period is still an open question.

A review of the prelinguistic period makes obvious how useful a tool language is for the experimenter if not for the neophyte communicator. Without language as a tool of measurement, it is often extremely difficult, if not impossible, to investigate the existence or extent of a particular communicative ability. I have suggested several topics that may be amenable to further investigation with such young children, namely, their attempts to repair misunderstandings and misfires in communicative patterns of turn taking. Surely, creative researchers will find others. For the moment, it is with some relief that we turn to a discussion of one kind of knowledge displayed by the child's use of her new-found linguistic skills in conversation, the understanding of discourse relations.

Discourse Knowledge

An investigation of the development of communicative skill necessarily involves a consideration not just of isolated utterances but of the relationship between the child's communicative behaviors and those of his or her partner. There are, of course, a multiplicity of ways in which communicators can take account of their partners in their own behavior (see Ferguson, 1977). For example, they can speak louder to a person who is hard of hearing or limit the topics under discussion to those understandable by their listeners, as older children and mothers do when talking to young children (Shatz & Gelman, 1977; Snow, 1977a). However, some of the most fundamental adjustments one can make have to do with producing behaviors responsive to prior discourse. A mother who continually responded to her child's questions with a complete change of topic would fail by any reasonable measure of communicative skill, no matter how appropriate the topics introduced were to her child's age or stage. Hence, learning to make one's utterances contingent upon prior discourse is a crucial development. Such knowledge depends not only on assessing a particular partner's abilities and intentions but also on recognizing and using the ways in which the language provides opportunities for creating and marking shared knowledge. Indeed, recent efforts to describe adult language have demonstrated that adequate characterizations of the rules governing aspects of the language, such as reference, anaphora, and ellipsis, require analysis at the level of discourse rather than the sentence (Clark & Marshall, 1980; Holzman, 1971; Reichman, 1981). Presumably, these aspects of language are acquired in the context of discourse.

The early discourse environments that young children experience apparently differ across cultures. In Western culture, the dyadic discourse context is taken to be the primary natural environment in which children are exposed to language and in which they acquire communicative skill. Schieffelin (in press) reports that prelinguistic Kaluli children in Papua New Guinea are talked about rather than talked to, often in the presence of siblings who do much of the talking about them. Clearly, Kaluli children develop into culturally adequate communicators despite this difference. Whether their developmental route to achieving mature status varies significantly from Western children is as yet unclear. Future cross-cultural research on this issue would be most useful; for the present, the following discussion is necessarily based on Western children only.

By the time they are 19 months of age, children are sensitive to discourse contexts and make efforts to maintain discourse (Bloom, Rocissano, & Hood, 1976; Shatz, 1978b). Yet, children's early abilities to participate in sustained discourse are limited, and some of the devices they use to create cohesion are rare in adult discourse. For example, the full repetition of a partner's utterance is a common device found primarily in children's speech (Billman & Shatz, 1981; Keenan, 1977; McTear, 1978). Thus, one kind of knowledge a child must acquire includes the means by which the adult speech community achieves conversational coherence. In this section, I review the work that has described the child's developing knowledge of discourse phenomena by considering first children's ability to carry on extended, contingent discourse. I then examine their knowledge of devices for carrying on particular discourse-related activities, such as the use of ellipsis and making reference.

Discourse Coherence

In a fundamental study, Bloom et al. (1976) investigated the extent to which child utterances were dependent on, and related to, preceding adult utterances. They examined four children over a period of development that corresponded to the three language-acquisition stages described by R. Brown (1973): Stage 1 (mean length of utterance < 2), Stage 2 (MLU 2.0–2.75), and Stage 5 (MLU 3.5–4.0). They found that at Stage 1, the children were more likely to talk in response to an adult utterance than to initiate a conversation. Much of the speech produced following adult utterances, however, was not contingent in either form or topic on the prior utterance. Bloom et al. (1976) suggested that Stage 1 children know a simple rule of interaction, such as: take a conversational turn immediately following a partner's turn. They also report that their subjects knew even more than this. At all stages of development, the children produced more linguistically (semantically and structurally) contingent utterances in response to adult questions than to nonquestions. Imitations, noncontingent responses, and no response were more likely to follow nonquestions. Two possible reasons for this result are (1) that children see questions as requiring a relevant verbal response or (2) that questions are simply easier to respond to (possibly because they make response requirements more obvious) and, hence, they are more likely to elicit relevant responses. In either case, the children appear to know more than just to take a turn following a turn.

Several studies provide evidence for the view that early on children discriminate questions from nonquestions and that they do so primarily on the basis of form. By their 2nd year, children often respond to yes/no questions with formally canonical replies of "yes" and "no," even when those replies are semantically inappropriate (Ervin-Tripp, 1970; Horgan, 1978; Steffensen, 1978). That their behavior is based on an analysis of form is further supported by the fact that even when they recognize the force of a yes/no question (e.g., Can you shut the door?) as a request for action and not information, they are more likely to accompany their action response to such questions with yes replies than when the request is an imperative (Shatz, 1978a). Moreover, even a question/nonquestion distinction does not fully capture the extent of their knowledge of form. Not only do children seem sensitive to the answerhood condition on questions (Katz, 1972), but some give evidence in their responses of differentiating yes/no questions from wh questions at remarkably early stages. Crosby (1976) reports on a child, who, at the age of 1 year 5 months, had two virtually mutually exclusive response categories for questions: "no" for yes/no questions and intelligible words other than "no" for wh questions. Another child at 1 year 3 months is reported to have produced affirmative replies regularly to yes/no and tag questions but not to wh questions (Horgan, 1978). Rodgon (1979) reports similar data from three other children.

One might be tempted to conclude on the basis of the above data that a child learns the constraints of discourse agreement by means of a syntactic route—by first taking note of the sequence of forms canonically prescribed by the language. Further support for this view comes from Ervin-Tripp's observation (1970) that children know *because* is a canonical response to *why* questions, although their use of the word is often the only proper relation their replies have to propositions of causality. However, there is some evidence that criteria of form are not applied as generally as they might be. For example, *why don't* sentences do not elicit *because* replies. Children regularly see these sorts of utterances as requests for action without assigning a verbal answerhood condition to them (Ervin-Tripp, 1970; Shatz, 1978b). It is possible that the supremacy of functional over formal concerns as a determinant of response form comes about in this instance because children have

few occasions to witness *why don't* utterances receiving verbal replies.

Moreover, although children seem to recognize some of the formal constraints on sequences of discourse, it is clear that they do not have adultlike rules of discourse contingency. Simple response procedures characterizing children's behavior in both natural and experimental contexts can sometimes account for young children's apparently sophisticated responding. For example, I have proposed such a procedure to account for the patterns of responses children produce to utterances such as Can you shut the door? that can function as requests for information or action (Shatz, 1978a, 1978b). Rather than being granted a wide range of formal rules governing the interpretation of indirect speech acts, the child is assumed to respond according to the following response procedure:

> Respond with action a or with action on an object o *unless* l or c is present, where a and o are members of the set S, the elements of which consist of actions or objects identifiable from the speech stream; l is a member of the set L and c is a member of the set C, the elements of which are stop-action markers identifiable from a reading of the linguistic input and from the physical, interpersonal, or social context respectively.

In less formal terms, the child's strategy is to act on identifiable items unless there is some salient cue for doing otherwise. As an example of such a cue from the realm of linguistic context, I suggested that the kinds of test-question routines mothers often engage their children in should function as stop-action markers for young children. That is, wh questions might serve solely to inhibit action responding and promote the response patterns associated with the routines. Using both experimental and naturalistic data, Allen & Shatz (in press) found some confirming evidence for this suggestion. The responses of 16-month-old infants to what questions were closely related to the wh routines in which their mothers had engaged them. Such demonstrations suggest that children's early attempts to participate in conversations are based on a blend of incomplete formal and functional knowledge. It is likely that one aspect of communicative development is the gradual differentiation and reintegration of these kinds of information into separate but related rule-governed knowledge bases.

Further evidence that children's functional and formal knowledge of discourse contingencies are at first somewhat conflated comes from an examination of children's imitations of adult utterances occurring in conversations. Very immature language learners have often been reported to produce imitations in response to utterances that are either anomalous or beyond their linguistic or cognitive abilities (Boskey & Nelson, 1980; Shipley, Smith, & Gleitman, 1969). It has been argued that such imitations are a strategic response to the obligation to take a turn when the requisite skills to make an appropriate response are lacking. For example, Boskey and Nelson (1980) asked young children to respond to wh questions, half of which were unanswerable either because they were anomalous or because the children did not have the knowledge to answer. Children classed as imitators on the basis of previous conversations produced more imitations than nonimitators, with most of their imitations occurring in response to unanswerable questions. Boskey & Nelson did not include nonquestions in their protocols; hence, they report no base-line measures of tendency to imitate nonquestions. Because other studies have reported imitation following nonquestions (Bloom et al., 1976) and commands (Shipley et al., 1969), it is unclear how to describe the knowledge Boskey and Nelson's (1980) subjects had: Were they aware of discourse constraints on wh questions per se, on questions versus nonquestions, on turn taking generally or were their imitations merely a response to lack of understanding, regardless of their knowledge of conversational obligations (cf. Rees, 1975)?

A study of spontaneous imitations by five children in the second half of their 2nd year of age suggests that the occurrence of imitations depends not only on lack of knowledge but also on the relative appropriateness of applying other response strategies as well. Folger and Chapman (1978) found that their subjects produced more imitations in response to parental imitations, descriptions, and requests for information than to requests for action. As noted earlier, I have suggested that young children are turned away from action responses toward other modes of responding by linguistic or contextual cues. Folger and Chapman argue that their subjects were led to imitate in nonaction contexts by such cues. It is possible that verbal imitation is one mode of discursive response a child tries out in nonaction contexts at this early stage of expanding response modes. It would be useful to have additional controlled studies that examine the kinds of pragmatic and linguistic cues children first use to distinguish situations calling for action versus those that elicit other strategies for responding, such as imitation.

There is some evidence that parental conversational styles influence the kinds of response devices children adopt. Children who produce imitative responses are likely to have parents who amply demonstrate imitation in their responses to their children's utterances (Folger & Chapman, 1978; Seitz & Stewart, 1975), although the imitations parents produce have different conversational purposes, such as requesting confirmation. There is also a report of a child who used *hmm* in much the same way as the Folger and Chapman (1978) subjects used imitation (Shatz, 1981). Her mother frequently used *hmm* either to acknowledge utterances or with rising intonation to prompt an answer from her child. In both the *hmm* case and the imitation cases, the children seem to have borrowed conversational response types from their parents without observing the contingent discourse constraints on them found in parental speech. These cases are reminiscent of early semantic development when children use conventional words in unconventional ways. The cases are also reminiscent of an aspect of Piaget's collective monologues, namely, the use of a discourse device without apparent recognition of its interactive function (Piaget, 1926). The language is full of such devices (e.g., *by the way, as you know, even so,* etc.), each of which serves to orient the listener to the way what is coming in the discourse relates to what went before. Apparently children tend to pick up devices like these quite readily from parental speech. Using them with functional appropriateness seems to be another matter. It would be interesting to know whether the ability to pair a discourse device appropriately with a conversational function is eventually influenced by conversational experiences or whether it is primarily dependent on the child's own cognitive and social development.

The studies cited above all indicate that, by the age of 2, children have a sense of their conversational responsibilities, at least to the extent that they make attempts to respond in situations calling for a response. They also recognize that the same response is not always acceptable but that responses must somehow fit the particular discourse context. Moreover, they often manage a fit on formal grounds without achieving either a semantic or pragmatic match. This fact suggests that syntactic markings of differing discourse contingencies may be early guides for children's growing awareness of varying intentions. A second source of information about partner intention may be in the language games in which parents engage their children (Ratner & Bruner, 1978). The consistent pairings of form and function typical of such games may do for the younger learner what R. Brown (1980) suggests they do for the researcher: allow a more confident assessment of the relevance and irrelevance of particular responses. Ordinary discourse, even that directed to young children, is considerably less regular than games with regard to the pairing of form and function (Shatz, 1979). It is not surprising, then, that children have a difficult time achieving discourse coherence on the multiple bases of syntax, semantics, and pragmatics. Given the widespread belief that children understand on nonlinguistic grounds the intent of utterances addressed to them, it is surprising, however, that many of their first attempts at discourse coherence are based at least as much on form as on function.

Learning to respond appropriately is, however, only a partial solution to the discourse problem because conversations are typically more than two-turn affairs. In a recent study, Kaye and Charney (1980) showed that it is mothers who take the responsibility of maintaining conversations with 2-year-olds beyond the two-turn level. They do so by a variety of devices, including what Kaye and Charney call turnabouts, that is, turns in which a speaker both responds to the listener's prior utterance and makes another request of the listener to respond again. (Also see Wells, MacLure, & Montgomery, 1979, for a discussion of devices for extending conversation.) Because children are reasonably compliant about responding, such maternal strategies assure some success at keeping the interaction going beyond two turns. Interestingly, there was no connection between the degree of maternal maintenance tactics and a child's later language development as measured by scores on the Peabody Picture Vocabulary Test (PPVT) six months later. As these authors themselves point out, the PPVT is not necessarily an appropriate measure of parental influence on language development let alone of influence on conversational skills. It is also possible that no correlation was found because the high incidence of turnabouts the authors observed was due to the unique testing situation in which mothers knew their children's language was being observed and were trying to get them to perform. In any event, it appears that producing a response that is related to the prior turn at least formally is often within the ken of 1- to 2-year-olds; simultaneously managing aspects of dialogue, such as turnabout turns, that require both a response to prior utterances and an attempt to expand or extend the interaction, may not be.

Children are surprisingly inventive however. Several reports of early communicative behavior suggest that very young children devise means of carrying on contingent discourse before they have all the conventional tools to do so. For example, Scollon (1976) found that a 1-year-old produced in multiple one-word utterances the same content that would later occur in multiword utterances. At times, it appeared that the child was waiting for confirmation of understanding or attention to her first word (the topic) before proceeding to the second (the comment). The effect of these vertical constructions was to make the sequences of dialogue this child participated in longer than two turns. Extended sequences of dialogue have also been reported by Keenan (1974, 1977). Her twins during the 3rd year used repetition for a variety of pragmatic functions, sometimes producing long strings of repetitive dialogue. Keenan argues that repetition is a way for an immature speaker who lacks the syntactic means to mark shared knowledge to make presumed shared knowledge explicit. Another way Keenan's twins maintained dialogue was to produce turns consisting of phonological substitutions made on prior turn constituents (Keenan & Klein, 1975). An example of this would be a child responding "zoom-zoom" to the prior utterance, "boom-boom." Keenan suggests that early discourse devices, such as repetition and phonological substitution, are utilized generally by young children and not just by twins.

However, although another twin pair was observed to rely heavily on repetition during extended dialogue sequences, a pair of unrelated but familiar 2-year-olds at the same syntactic level did not; nor did they exhibit any other special means of extending dialogue (Billman & Shatz, in press). Similarly, Hiebert and Cherry (1978) found no evidence among familiar but unrelated peer dyads of the device of phonological substitution. The question of just how common the development of idiosyncratic patterns of contingent dialogue is in young children requires further research, as does the question of whether the exhibition of such patterns truly indexes the marking of sophisticated conversational knowledge that Keenan (1974, 1977) argues it does. Garvey and Berninger (1981) provide the kinds of analyses that may prove useful in determining whether repetitive behavior at least is truly conversational. They used the timing and length of utterances to reveal differences between ritual verbal play and adapted conversation, with ritual being less variable internally than conversation. Claims such as Keenan's could be buoyed with analyses showing that repetition sequences conform to the timing of conversation rather than ritual play.

Recent work examining contingent queries in children's conversations confirms that the integration of the cognitive procedures underlying successful discourse is a process extending over a number of years. Garvey (1977, 1979) has distinguished contingent queries on the basis of the specificity and type of answer they require. For example, the following queries are some that can be made in response to the utterance, "I want a ball":

1. Nonspecific: "What?"
2. Request for confirmation: "A ball?"
3. Specific request for repetition: "A what?"
4. Request for specification: "Which one?"

Gallagher (1981) reports that even children under 2 respond to requests for confirmation (although occasionally not appropriately) and also to nonspecific requests. Children's responses to "What?" are often repetitions of their earlier utterances, but children sometimes revise their prior utterances as well (also see Wilcox & Webster, 1980). The occurrence of such revisions suggests that even very young children may have a theory of the listener as being one who is helped by reformulation and not just by repetition (see Valian & Caplan, 1979). In this regard, it would be interesting to explore more specifically than has been done to date just what kinds of revisions very young children make and how appropriate they are to the context of their occurrence.[7]

One difference between nonspecific and specific requests is that nonspecific requests make no demand on children to tailor their reformulations to the specifically stated needs of the listener, whereas specific requests do. Thus, specific requests would appear to be more difficult for speakers, in that their prior utterance must be examined in light of the listener's specific query and the next speaker utterance adjusted accordingly. Indeed, Gallagher's (1981) data give no evidence that Stage 1 children are capable of doing this. By age 3, however, children can give appropriate specific answers to specific requests, although they themselves do not often generate such requests in playroom conversation with one another (Garvey, 1977).

Other situations do elicit more querying from young children. A recent study examining children's behavior in an experimental setting found that even 3-year-olds regularly produced requests for clarification or more information in response to ambiguous requests from adults (Revelle, Karabenick, & Wellman, 1981). However, 4-year-olds were better at asking for clarification only when it was actually required and at tailoring the form of their request to the particular type of ambiguity experienced. Hence, the making of requests would seem to be more difficult than responding to them because 3-year-olds appear to be better at the latter than the former task. Making requests may be more difficult because they require monitoring of one's understanding in addition to the other operations described earlier for responding. Perhaps in the Revelle et al. study, the younger children realized that understanding might be a problem, but finding it difficult to monitor along with everything else, they adopted a strategy of regularly making a contingent query, even though one might not actually be necessary in a particular instance.

Sometime in their 2nd year, children can respond to nonspecific requests; in their 3rd year, they can make them. By age 3, they can respond to specific requests; by age 4 they can make specific requests as well. The earliest accomplishment would seem at bottom to require only some discourse rule such as "What?" → repetition. The second accomplishment requires, in addition, an ability to recognize one's own need for more information. The third requires an ability to compare utterances to one another and adjust one's reply accordingly. The fourth requires self-monitoring, comparing of utterances, and linguistic adjustment. It should not be surprising, then, that the integration of these cognitive operations into appropriate communicative behavior is a relatively late and fragile accomplishment of the preschool period (also see Flavell, Speer, Green, & August, 1981).

Ellipsis

Ellipsis involves omitting from utterances elements of grammatical sentences that can be taken as understood in context. The appropriate use of ellipsis by children might, thus, be a reasonable measure of their understanding of what is and what is not shared knowledge in a conversational context. A child who responds "Shovel" to the question "What do you want?" may be demonstrating an understanding that a concern for his desires is shared and that only the object of them is new information requiring mention. On the other hand, it seems equally possible that, given his limited productive power, he is simply expressing the most salient thing to him, without regard to the information he shares with the listener. When a child is at the one-word stage, it is extremely difficult to confirm whether his communicative representation is rich. Indeed, Greenfield argues that informativeness is first defined by the child from his own perspective (Greenfield, 1978; Greenfield & Zukow, 1978). Evidence from children who have begun to string two words together suggests that children at this stage at least try to mark new information for their listeners. Wieman (1976) found that, despite the fact that stress in two-word utterances was regularly used to mark semantic relations, the marking of new information being added to the discourse overrode semantic marking rules. Thus, a child who regularly used stress on the locative to mark the semantic relations in noun + locative constructions (e.g., sweater chàir) used stress instead on the following two occasions to mark new information.

1. M: What is on the side of the milk truck?
   C: Milk-truck B̀.
2. M: What's in the street?
   C: Firètruck street.

Again one can raise the question (although perhaps less forcefully) of whether the marked word simply encodes the concept that is in some way, apart from discourse requirements, salient for the child. The child could also have used a fully elliptical utterance and responded with only "firetruck." However, the fact that he did not do so should not be taken as evidence for the salience argument and against an awareness of what is new and what is shared knowledge. Even adults do not universally observe a minimal redundancy rule by producing only essential information in their messages. Redundancies of the "firetruck street" sort may serve all sorts of purposes from explicitly marking understanding of the prior utterance to the use of repetition as a social-cohesion device. One sort of data that might address the question more directly would be to examine the child's behavior when his perspective is pitted against dialogue constraints to see just how much the child's early use of ellipsis and stress is indeed founded on beliefs in mutual knowledge.

By the age of 3, children also produce elliptical utterances in response to nonquestions as well as questions. "I do too" or "Me too" are all-too familiar responses of children when one of their peers or siblings has voiced a desire for a cookie, a turn, or whatever (see Holzman, 1971). Here too, such responses may reflect something other than a clear understanding of the discourse constraints on ellipsis. Instead, they may be fairly stereotypic messages in contexts where rights or privileges are at issue. It should be relatively easy to determine whether children inappropriately persist in the use of such utterances when it is unclear whether the preceding utterance has been adequately understood by its intended recipient.

Appropriate ellipsis is also constrained by syntactic considerations. Suppose, for example, a listener must select a particular ball from a set of different colored balls. She asks the speaker, "Which ball do I pick?" The speaker can reply, "The green one" or "The green" but not just "Green," although that could be considered equally informative in this context. Somewhat surprisingly, there appear to be few studies examining the use of ellipsis in children on this level; it would seem to be a profitable place in which to examine the relative effects of syntactic and communicative constraints on language productions.

Reference

It has been suggested that linguistic reference evolves out of prelinguistic capacities for sharing attention (Bruner, 1975, 1977). The sort of referential activity that would be most compatible with this hypothesis is exophoric, that is, it is an indication toward something existing in the physical environment. Carter (1978b) reports on one child whose preverbal attention-directing behavior apparently evolved into verbal labeling. Dore (1978) argues that such development depends on corequisites: prelinguistic skills at attention sharing plus an ability to see that sound sequences arbitrarily (and eventually conventionally) represent concepts. Children have ample opportunity to observe a close relation between nonverbal indicating and verbalizations. Mothers of 9- to 34-month-olds have rarely been observed pointing without verbalizing simultaneously (Murphy & Messer, 1977; Shatz, 1982). By the second half of their 2nd year, children also regularly accompany their indicating gestures with vocalizations (Murphy, 1978). However, some children apparently make the mistake of assuming that any language accompanying attention-directing gestures also serves an attentional function. Having observed his parents pointing and saying, "What's that?", a child began to use the phrase to draw attention to objects, for example, "What's that birdie?" (Atkinson, 1979). Once again, the child seems to have adopted a parental conversational behavior without understanding its conventional meaning or implications for discourse. Thus, it appears that another thing about communication that the child has to learn is the relations gesture and co-occurrent language can have to one another. It is hard to see how this knowledge would be derivable solely or even primarily from the preverbal roots of referential skill.

E. V. Clark (1977) makes a similar point when she argues that there are linguistic components to deictic terms that have no analogue in the gestural sphere. For example, the appropriate use of the pronouns *I* and *you* implies an understanding that such terms are mapped to the roles of speaker and listener, not of self and other. The same is true of locational terms, such as *here, there, this,* and *that.* The distinction between speaker perspective and self-perspective is not an issue in the gestural domain. Work by Charney (1979) and de Villiers and de Villiers (1974) has shown that by the age of 3½, children are quite consistent in mapping deictic terms to speaker roles. Charney's (1979) data on still younger children are particularly interesting with regard to the questions of when children show an awareness of the relevance of speaker roles or whether there is a stage in the acquisition of such terms during which they are consistently interpreted from the perspective of the self. In Charney's study, children aged 2½ to 3½ were seated on the floor with the experimenter and two toys. Three different spatial arrangements of toys (T_1 and T_2), experimenter (E), and child (C) determined the three different conditions under which the same questions were asked. In the *same-perspective* condition, both E and C sat together, with T_1 near them and T_2 in a straight line farther away. Thus, for both E and C, T_1 was near and T_2 far. In the *neutral-perspective* condition, C, T_2, and E, with T_1 placed directly in front of her, formed three angles of an equilateral triangle. Thus, C was equidistant from the toys (in a neutral position), whereas E was near T_1 and far from T_2. In the *opposite-perspective* condition, E and C were directly across from each other, with one toy in front of each of them. Thus, C was near T_1 and far from T_2; the opposite was true for E. In each condition, the child was asked:

> "See the airplane?"
> "See the train?"
> "Which one is here/there?"

The crucial data are responses in the neutral-perspective condition. If children can operate only from their own perspectives, then given no information from that perspective, they should choose randomly or show confusion. If they do see the relevance of speaker roles, then they should answer according to E's perspective, even if in the opposite-perspective condition information from their own perspective gets in the way, makes the task more difficult, and derogates their performance. What Charney found was that even the younger children in the sample performed about as well in the neutral-perspective as in the same-perspective condition, with the opposite-perspective condition being the worst (although more than 72% of the responses in this condition were correct). Thus, she found no evidence for a stage in which the self is used exclusively as the

reference point. Error analyses confirmed this and exposed a range of reasons why children erred. For example, some children behaved as though *here* made reference to a speaker relation but *there* was appropriate to use only when it made reference to the relation between the object and both participants, not just the speaker (as in *over there*). Charney argues that other studies (e.g., Clark & Sengul, 1978; Webb & Abrahamson, 1976) that found evidence for the self-perspective stage used more difficult tasks and that subjects older than hers may have adopted the self-perspective strategy when faced with cognitive overload induced by the demands of those tasks. (Her argument is a specific case of Shatz's (1978c) general explanation of intraindividual variation in performance on communication tasks and suggests that difficulties with her opposite-perspective condition may have stemmed in part from its added complexity. That is, active inhibition of one's own perspective is an extra component of that condition not present in the neutral condition.) Thus, Charney's data suggest that children at a remarkably early age acquire some truly pragmatic ability (in the linguistic sense) that has no direct analogue in the preverbal world.

If linguistic reference developed largely from gesture, then one might expect gestural behavior to wither away with the advent of language. However, that does not generally appear to be so. Pechmann and Deutsch (in press) found that even adults used pointing and a partial verbalization rather than a complete verbal description in referential situations in which gesturing could be unambiguously designative. The difference between younger and older children was not how much they used gesture or language in such situations, but whether they could adjust their behavior to be more linguistic when gesturing was inadequate. 3-year-olds did not spontaneously produce full verbal descriptions; older children and adults did so more readily when the situation called for them. Similarly, Van Hekken, Vergeer, and Harris (1980) found that in preschoolers' spontaneous conversations with one another, pronominal references that could be disambiguated either by verbal or nonverbal means were unambiguous more than 82% of the time, with almost 90% of these disambiguated by nonverbal means. On the other hand, in cases where only verbalizations were appropriate to disambiguation, almost two thirds of those cases remained ambiguous. Interestingly, peer listeners gave little indication of problems with the ambiguities. Virtually none of them were noted explicitly, and ambiguous reference was responded to with social speech about as often as unambiguous reference. (Unfortunately, no adult comparison group was included in this study.)

In an attempt to extract more complete verbal referential descriptions from children, Deutsch and Pechmann (1982) used a gift-selection task with feedback. Children were asked to select the gift they liked best from an array of eight so that the experimenter could take it to a birthday party. If the children's responses were inadequate, a request for more information, such as "Which ball?", was made. Deutsch and Pechmann argue that the 3-year-olds' deficits in initial descriptions are not attributable to linguistic constraints on length or complexity because at other times they spontaneously produced utterances equal in complexity to those required for adequate messages in their task. They point out that their young subjects responded very well when asked for more information, and they contend this result follows from the fact that such requests for more information (in conjunction with the child's prior utterance) narrow the field of potential targets (e.g., from all the objects in the field to only those that are balls) on which the child must perform perceptual-comparative analyses in his search for critical descriptive features. There is other evidence as well that preschoolers' performance on communicative tasks is adversely affected when they are confronted with a complex or large array of items to analyze (see Ackerman, 1981a, 1981b; Shatz, 1978c).

The sorts of stimuli used in the Deutsch and Pechmann (1982) task leave open another possibility, namely, that the children did not at first fully recognize that the situation called for attributive reference, where the description exactly identifies the referent (see Donellan, 1966). The stimulus sets in their task always included items from more than one class. Hence, a question such as "Which ball?" always both narrowed the class of objects to be considered and clarified the need for attributive reference. Other studies have shown that instructions that clarify the attributive nature of a referential task can facilitate the quality of preschoolers' descriptions (Harris, Macrae, & Bassett, 1978; Higgins & Akst, 1975). It is possible that asking "Which ball?", even when a large array is comprised only of tokens of a single class of objects would have a positive effect on the quality of the description. In this case, no simplification of the perceptual array is possible and facilitation would be evidence that children have difficulty spontaneously recognizing their conversational obligations in a task rather than just having difficulty carrying them out. There is some reason to doubt such an outcome however. Only 30% of the

almost 700 potentially ambiguous references in the Van Hekken et al. (1980) study actually were ambiguous. It is hard to believe that children fortuitously achieve disambiguity in 70% of their utterances without striving to do so.

In any case, these data suggest that when the attributive nature of the task is made clear to them, children's difficulties stem less from a lack of knowledge about what such tasks require than from deficits in the means to fulfill these requirements. Ackerman (1979) has shown that children as young as 6 understand the communicative obligations behind attributive reference, despite the fact that they sometimes fail on more traditional tests of referential communication (Glucksberg et al., 1975). The Deutsch and Pechmann (1982) data (as well as those of Harris et al., 1978, and Higgins & Akst, 1975) suggest that 3-year-olds have similar understandings. The most they appear to be guilty of is either being a bit slow to identify situations requiring attributive reference or finding it difficult to carry out their obligations because of overload.

The early referential successes of young children are impressive, yet the high susceptibility to failure in complex referential tasks suggests that those skills still need to be consolidated in as-yet unspecifiable ways. Furthermore, there are other sorts of referential abilities for which even 5-year-olds show quite limited ability. Endophoric reference, in which reference is made to propositions occurring earlier in the discourse and not to objects in the environment, is one example. *That* in the sequence below would be an example of endophoric reference.

1. "Please tell me what time I should be home."
   "That depends on whether you want to eat dinner here."

Little is known about children's ability to understand and use referents of this sort. Baumgardner and Lasky (1978) report that about half the time 5-year-olds can correctly identify the sentential referent of *that* upon hearing sentence pairs such as:

2. Jim was spanked, but Nancy was never spanked.
   Jim was spanked but that never happened to Nancy.

Second graders are almost perfect on the task. Pratt (1978) suggests that endophoric reference is more difficult because it places more memory load on the child than does exophoric reference, for which perceptual information is usually available.

He supports his claim with data from a task in which children hear a short story such as: "Bill got a white kitten for Christmas and Nancy got a black one." Such stories are either presented alone or along with a picture depicting the appropriate scene. The children are then asked, "Which one got the kitten?" Whether one wants to argue that this is a task in the detection of discourse anomaly rather than referential ambiguity, the facts are that children are much more likely to detect a problem in the picture condition than in the language-alone condition.

Differences in memory requirements may not be the only kind of difference accounting for a likely advantage of exophoric over endophoric reference. In both cases the child has the problem of delineating what is mutual knowledge and what she must communicate. In the exophoric case, however, she has information not only about the object of reference but also about the listener. For example, one can check whether the listener's eyes are open or whether the object is in his line of sight. Quite young children do seem to take account of such information (Flavell, 1978a). In the endophoric case, such information is lacking. Instead, one must rely not only on one's own memory for prior discourse but one must also make judgments about the listener's ability to make appropriate inferences from discourse. For instance, in the Baumgardner and Lasky (1978) example, the propositional referent, "Nancy was spanked," is never explicitly stated and must be inferred by both speaker and listener. Thus, although children may be able to take account of listener characteristics that are readily observable, taking account of more covert characteristics may prove too difficult.

What do children do in cases where overt information about listeners is not available? Languages typically establish conventions of discourse to account for instances in which the listener's knowledge state is indeterminant. For example, the first mention of a new character in a discourse or text is conventionally accomplished by the use of the indefinite article, with the definite article marking second and later mentions. The following anecdotes suggest that the learning of such conventions and their conditions of application is not completed in the preschool years. (Also see Maratsos, 1974; Warden, 1976.) A 5-year-old wrote a story beginning, "One morning the little old woman. . . ." Her brother, aged 7, criticized her:

> Bro: You should have said "a little old woman."

Sis: Why? What's wrong with *the?*
Bro: You don't know who the woman is yet. You have to use *a* when you don't know her.

However, a little learning is a dangerous thing. Bro overapplied the *first mention takes the indefinite* rule to produce the following error, which Sis, a year older and wiser by this time, gleefully corrected:

> Bro: Where's a woffel? (Woffel was a nickname for the family dog.)
> Sis: *A* woffel? *The* woffel. There's only one woffel in the whole world.

We have seen that appropriate referential performance requires in all but the simplest cases coordination among a variety of subskills: the ability to assess the listener's knowledge state, knowledge of the referential conventions of the language, inferential ability, and memory for discourse. There is no evidence that any one of these subskills is completely out of preschoolers' range of competence, although clearly the content and richness of any of these areas grows with experience. It does appear that children's deficient performance on complex referential tasks is well explained by the difficulty they have in maximally utilizing their partial and still-fragile subskills in tasks requiring their confluence.

Illocutionary Knowledge

The Representation Question

Closely related to some of the issues involved in discourse coherence is the question of the child's ability to understand the illocutionary force of the utterances she hears when understanding utterances involves taking them as their speakers meant them to be taken. In other words, the listener is able to recognize when particular speech acts, such as offering, promising, requesting, and so on, have been performed. There are various linguistic and psycholinguistic proposals about the processes involved in determining illocutionary force. As noted in the theoretical discussion of language and communication, speech act theory can be considered as the bridge between theories of language and social theories. At the moment, however, there is considerable controversy about the proper formulation of speech act theory.[8]

Most important for our purposes is that there are few specific psychological proposals about the nature of illocutionary information, that is, how it is represented mentally and accessed procedurally. Knowledge of how to relate utterances to social information to derive interpretations can be considered speech act knowledge. However, it is unclear whether that knowledge is indeed something with independent status related to, but distinct from, either linguistic or social knowledge. Cohen and Levesque (1980) suggest that, at least for artificial intelligence systems, discourse comprehension does not necessarily depend on a separate level of speech act knowledge. On the other hand, there is some reason to believe, on the basis of arguments about both mature processes and the development of them, that humans may indeed have illocutionary knowledge. For example, adults can make consistent judgments about the conventionality and politeness of a list of forms expressing such requests as: "Can you tell me your name?" / "Won't you tell me your name?" / "Have I already asked you your name?" (Clark & Schunk, 1980). It is hard to explain how subjects would be able to rate such expressions for their conventionality if they did not have some general knowledge about the likelihood a form would be used for a particular function. I have argued that the kind of form/function data to which children are exposed early in the language-learning process is the sort that would allow for the acquisition of illocutionary knowledge (Shatz, 1980). In the next section, I will describe the input data that would give the child information about the likelihood that a particular form fulfills a particular function as well as the range of forms by which particular functions are likely to be expressed. Thus, attributing illocutionary knowledge to humans helps explain not only how it is that adults can perform judgment tasks of language use but also why parents talk the way they do to their children (information necessary to the construction of that knowledge should be extractable from the input data).

Of course, having evidence that illocutionary knowledge exists is quite different from describing its nature. Becker (1982) suggests that speech act understanding depends on "an interlocking, co-predictive system of rules or conventions . . . similar in nature to that Maratsos (1982) describes for grammatical categories and Rosch (Rosch & Mervis, 1975) describes for natural categories." However, as Gleitman (1981) has recently pointed out, much of the research on natural concepts tells us about the ability of people to judge good exemplars of concepts and not really about the structure of the concepts themselves. Before proposals about the nature of illocutionary knowledge representations can be

evaluated, further work on both theoretical and empirical levels is necessary. Keeping that in mind, we turn to children's abilities to discriminate and respond to illocutionary forces of different kinds.

Contextual Adjustments

Regardless of their differences, all speech act theorists recognize in one way or another that the definite determination of the illocutionary force of a specific utterance is intimately tied to the situation of that utterance in a particular conversational context. That is, isolated utterances are often ambiguous with regard to the force a speaker can intend in using them. For example, the sentence, "Would you like to drive the car?" can be a request for information, an offer, a directive, or even a challenge, depending on the context in which it is uttered. Clearly, knowledge about the way utterances can fulfill various illocutionary functions in appropriate contexts is important information for children to have if they are to carry on natural discourse. Recent studies have addressed the question of when and how children use both linguistic information and context in determining the force of an utterance. In particular, is their ability to determine force confined primarily to those forms in the language most highly conventionalized and associated with a unique function (e.g., "Pick up your toys" or "Can you pass the salt?") or can children discern utterance meanings even when the sentences expressing them do so less directly or conventionally?

Both naturalistic and experimental studies have been conducted on children's ability to discern illocutionary force. The naturalistic studies have focused on preschoolers in playschool settings (e.g., Dore, 1977; Garvey, 1975), whereas the experimental studies have investigated a broader age range of subjects in a variety of tasks (Ackerman, 1978; Reeder, 1980; Shatz, 1978b). All studies are surprisingly consonant, however, in demonstrating at least some ability in children to adjust their response behaviors on the basis of differences in context. The more difficult question remains of how to characterize the knowledge on which they base their adaptive behaviors.

It is often tempting to argue on the basis of their spontaneous behavior that children have sophisticated knowledge of how speech acts are performed. By age 4 or 5, children produce requests that vary appropriately in form to take account of differing aspects of the interactive situation. (Some of the specific adjustments child speakers make will be discussed later. For a complete review of children's requestive behavior, see Becker, 1982.) Moreover, these children comprehend a variety of utterances as requests, even when those utterances are not explicitly expressed as such. For example, Garvey (1975) found that preschoolers responded to indirect requests for action, such as "I need a wheel now," with justifications of noncompliance that made reference to their inability to do the requested act, the lack of necessity that they comply, and so on. That is, they not only recognized the intended act that was indirectly expressed, but in making their replies, they seemed to be responding to the sorts of appropriateness conditions on such acts proposed by Searle (1969). Garvey (1975) argues that such behavior is evidence children have knowledge similar to that of adults. However, even though children's behavior may be similar to that of adults, the bases for their behavior may be different. For example, adults' theories often stress, as a basis for such behavior, the dependence of indirect interpretations on representations of direct readings of propositional content (although, as noted earlier, the evidence for such theories is equivocal). On the other hand, children seem biased to focus first on the implications of a message for their own response performance rather than on the specifics of the propositional content (Ackerman, 1981a). Hence, children might produce the sort of behavior Garvey (1975) reports as a consequence of their performative bias and not as a function of fully analyzing the propositional content and relating it to a list of contextual appropriateness conditions to derive an indirect interpretation. It would be useful to examine children's responses to a different kind of speech act for which the appropriateness conditions did not relate so directly to the listener's action responses.

The above argument is consonant with an experimental investigation of still younger children's responses to illocutionary ambiguity. As noted earlier, the findings of Shatz (1978b) suggest that 2-year-olds' performance may be based more on primitive response strategies than on inferential analysis and propositional content. The 2-year-olds were exposed to such test sentences as "Can you talk on the telephone?", which can be interpreted as either requests for action or for information. Each subject heard such utterances embedded in two different linguistic contexts that fostered one or the other interpretation. Even the young 2-year-olds showed some ability to adjust their behavior according to linguistic context. However, all the children, especially the younger ones, showed a bias to act in response to such utterances, regardless of context. Recall that I argued that this action bias is a default response strategy that diminishes as the child learns more about contextual or linguistic markers that indicate what sort of response is appropriate. Again, it appears that young children's seemingly appropriate response behavior should not necessarily be taken as evidence that they share with adults the rather sophisticated speech act knowledge or inferential processes that have been associated with adults' indirect language use.

Using a different paradigm, Reeder (1980) found that children as young as 2½ chose different paraphrases of the utterance, "Would you like to play on the train?", depending on whether the nonlinguistic context supported a request interpretation (and the paraphrase, "I want you to play on the train") or an offer interpretation ("I'll let you play on the train"). However, from these data one cannot argue that children have an understanding that would-you sentences can be paraphrased in at least two ways. As Reeder notes, crucial control trials were missing from his experiment, namely, ones in which the initial stimulus sentence was not a would-you form but something unrelated. Without this control, it is impossible to determine whether the children were actually selecting what they considered an acceptable functional paraphrase of the would-you sentence or whether they were simply selecting the utterance most appropriate to their interactional understanding without actual reference to the earlier stated utterance. Hence, it is unclear whether they demonstrated sophisticated knowledge of form/function relationships or just the understanding of two different situations on primarily nonlinguistic grounds. Nevertheless, because Shatz's (1978b) subjects of the same age did show the ability to process across sentences, it is at least plausible, if not proven, that Reeder's (1980) subjects were in fact relating the earlier utterance to the later ones.

The question of whether children of such a young age recognize the possibility of multiple functional paraphrases for a single form is important because it is at the heart of understanding the flexibility of human language. On the other hand, the existence of multiple form/function relationships would seem to complicate the process of language acquisition because unique mappings presumably make the problem of relating form to meaning easier (Shatz, 1979). Indeed, Grimshaw (1981) has argued that the child must start out hypothesizing unique mappings if he is to acquire the grammar at all. As she points out, this is not because the grammar favors such mappings, quite the contrary. Instead, without the assumption of one-to-one mappings, there are too many candidate hypotheses consistent with the initial data and no way to select among them. Hence, the child assumes such mappings as an evaluation metric and waits on additional data to suggest otherwise. Applying this notion to the problem of how children assign potential forces to particular utterance forms, one might expect that children would first show some tendency to assume a given form could express only one force. There is some evidence that younger children do use a smaller variety of forms to express requests than do older children (Bates, 1976; Ervin-Tripp, 1974, 1977), but only for the youngest children who are essentially still presyntactic is there some evidence of one-to-one form/function mappings (Halliday, 1975).

One possible reason why children create multiple mappings fairly early on is that they are exposed to them early on. For example, mothers of beginning language learners generally produced as many forms per function and functions per form for questions addressed to their children as did mothers of more adept speakers, although the former were more likely to use particular mappings (characteristic pairs) with greater frequency relative to other mappings (Shatz, 1979). Similarly, Schneiderman (1980) found that although mothers of younger children (1½ to 2) were more likely to express their action directives as imperatives than were mothers of older children, even the mothers of the youngest children used forms other than the imperative more than 40% of the time. Likewise, children as young as 3 have been observed making requests using a variety of forms (Dore, 1977; Read & Cherry, 1978). It is also possible that requests for action are an especially easy class of illocutionary concepts for a child to learn. If children are biased to interpret language as taking action responses, then requests for action would be a function or "meaning" that would be readily assignable to forms, particularly in default cases when no other intention was apparent.

There are surprisingly little data about the variety of forms children use to express other functions (although see Dore, 1977, for a taxonomy of the functions children spontaneously produce). Nor is much known about their understanding of the conditions of appropriate use on particular performatives, like *promise, warn,* and so on. We do know that children as young as 2 can take linguistic context into account when deciding how to respond to an utterance. However, they also exhibit a general tendency to focus on, and respond to, potential action-response obligations. Although children from 2 to 5 can be turned from this performative bias by manipulations of context (Ackerman, 1981a; Shatz, 1978b), it is only around the age of 6 that children show explicit

awareness of the potential illocutionary ambiguity of some utterances. At this age, they enjoy riddles and jokes about illocutionary ambiguity (Hirsh-Pasek, Gleitman, & Gleitman, 1978) and even make such jokes themselves (Shatz, 1978c). Metalinguistic appreciation of this sort may require an awareness of messages as objects in themselves, things extractable from and applicable to a multiplicity of contexts, rather than as integral and inseparable parts of a larger interaction space. (Flavell and his colleagues have suggested something similar. See Flavell et al., 1981; Singer & Flavell, 1981.) Potter (1979) suggests one reason why children may have so much trouble treating symbols objectively, that is, to develop symbolic thinking in the first place, children must create a tight relation between the arbitrary symbol and external reality. To some extent, that step is too well learned and must be partially unlearned before the relations among symbols themselves can become objects of contemplation for children. Hence, one should expect to find little metacommunicative awareness until children have acquired a solid system of mapping symbols to reality.

Knowledge of Conversational Rules

In addition to knowledge of form/function relationships, there is another kind of knowledge that is implicated in the appropriate use of language. Grice (1975) has argued that implicit principles of conversation guide conversational participants in both their choice of messages and their interpretations of them. For example, cooperative partners are expected to avoid ambiguity, say what is believed to be true, and be direct and concise. The violations of such principles are taken to be evidence that the speaker wants to imply something other than what he is actually saying but that he is unwilling to make that implication explicit. For example, if in response to the query, "How do you like your new secretary?", the boss responds, "Well, she dresses nicely," one might infer that he is less than pleased with her typing. What do children know about such rules? Do they follow them? Can they detect violations? Do they know how to interpret violations?

Elsewhere, I have reported evidence that children as young as 2 expect cooperation from their listeners, and they complain about lack of it (Shatz, 1978c). Moreover, the messages of children aged 3 to 5 suggest that they take account of conversational principles in deciding what to say. Children as young as 4 mark the degree of certainty with which they make statements, especially when talking to listeners likely to challenge them (Shatz & Gelman,

1977). They also have been shown to take more care introducing new elements into the discourse for listeners who they know have had no prior experience with those elements (Menig-Peterson, 1975). The work on referential behavior already discussed shows that children try to be unambiguous when the need to do so is made clear to them. Likewise, Ackerman (1981a) has shown that children as young as 5 reveal an ability to detect referential ambiguity when the task is structured so that they are led to focus on that issue alone and not on the production of action responses.

Ackerman's data may seem surprising in light of the research of Flavell, Markman, and others reporting young children's difficulty in detecting ambiguity. His findings are evidence that an understanding of message ambiguity itself is not beyond the capacity of a preschooler. Yet, as Singer and Flavell (1981) remark, an important question coming to the fore is why such an ability is so fragile and evidence for it so hard to capture. One possibility is that the integration of various kinds of knowledge, some of which are not firmly acquired, is a costly cognitive process, one that children do not always have the resources to carry out completely. Another possibility is that some of their understandings about communication may be different from those of educated adults. For example, children seem to expect listeners to carry a considerable amount of the burden of figuring out what is being said. They are more likely to blame the listener for communicative failures than the speaker, even in the face of ambiguous or inadequate messages (see Robinson, 1981), and they say they believe a listener who claims to be able to identify a target referent, even when they know the message the listener received was inadequate (Beal & Flavell, 1981). Adults, sadly enough, seem to have less faith in the omniscience of their listeners as a means to save them from communicative disaster. Children have some reason to believe as they do. Throughout their preschool years they are given little feedback about the inadequacy of their messages. They are more often than not paired with not only cooperative but also relatively solicitous listeners who value their attempts at communication and do indeed try to understand them. As Brown and Hanlon (1970) noted some years ago, parents respond as well to the badly expressed messages of their children as to the well-expressed ones.

The question of whether children have adultlike conversational principles has been examined in another study by Ackerman (1981c). He used an experimental context to study children's ability, both to detect violations of other conversational princi-

ples and to interpret such violations appropriately. The principles investigated concern the requirements that responses to prior discourse be contingent or relevant to the earlier discourse and that the responses be informative and not completely redundant to what went before. Kindergarten-, first-, and second-grade subjects were asked to assign responses to a short discourse to one of two puppets, depending on whether the response was straightforward or not. The puppets had been described as "smart alecky" or "truthful." First- and second-grade children could appropriately assign violations and nonviolations, although they were less likely to do so for redundancy violations than for topic-relevance ones. However, when in a second experiment, first and third graders were asked to explain why speakers might have produced such violations, first graders were able to make reasonable inferences only 37% of the time; third graders did so 73% of the time. Ackerman suggests that the ability to interpret violations may require more experience with such indirect speech (and with subtly devious speakers) than first graders have had. He also points out, quite rightly, that his situation may have resulted in an underestimation of these sorts of skills because they were not measured in familiar contexts. That argument would also seem pertinent to the kindergartners' failure even to discriminate violations. Ackerman contends that the kindergartners did understand the task because in the same task format they could make discriminations of utterances with more severe violations in them. But, if, indeed, the task was difficult and the discrimination of the subtler conversational violations was difficult, then the two sources of difficulty may have combined to obscure the kindergartners' knowledge of the principles under investigation. In any case, there is some evidence that by the age of 6, children expect conversation to adhere to certain principles of cooperation and they evidence those expectations in both their speaking and listening behavior. More research is needed to determine whether younger children's principles actually differ from those of adults or whether the same principles are more fragile and harder to apply.

Sociolinguistic Knowledge

Utterances can express not only the intentions of the speaker but also a whole range of social information. A speaker's choice of an utterance form can reflect the status of the listener relative to the society at large as well as the relationship of the listener to the speaker. Of course, languages differ with regard to how much and which societal distinctions in status are marked in the language. Some cultures make quite marked distinctions, for example, between women's language and that of men (Lakoff, 1973), and virtually all cultures have some special devices reserved for talking to children (Ferguson, 1977). The appropriate use of these general registers is based on such characteristics as age, sex, and occupation of the listener. Language choice can also mark the relative relationship between a particular speaker and listener on a variety of dimensions from relative status (e.g., expert to novice) to familiarity (formal versus informal styles of address). To use language appropriately, children have to learn when and how to mark both general distinctions and relative ones. It is not obvious which sort of distinction would be easier for a child to make. On the one hand, general distinctions require learning only the characteristics of the listener and whether and how these are taken note of by the language, whereas relative distinctions require the inclusion of a comparison between the relative status of self and listener as part of the language-selection process. On the other hand, the relationship of self to others may be particularly salient for the child and, hence, possibly easier to learn than more general status variables that the society at large marks. The literature reviewed here is examined with an eye to addressing the question of the kinds of status relationships children are able to discriminate and express in their language.

Age- and Status-Related Adjustments

In 1973, Shatz and Gelman showed that 4-year-olds produce shorter and generally less complex sentences to 2-year-olds than they do to either peers or adults. Since then, the finding that children adjust their communicative behavior depending on listener age has become one of the best documented facts in the communication literature. Children as young as 3 show adjustments for younger listeners and even role play such behavior to a doll (Sachs & Devin, 1976). Even 2-year-olds in a nursery school setting are sensitive to listener differences. They talk more to adults and adjust their adult-directed messages more to take account of listener needs than they do for peers (Wellman & Lempers, 1977). This may be because they expect adults in the school context to be more challenging about inadequate messages. Other researchers have found that preschoolers do more question answering (Martlew, Connolly, & Mc-Cleod, 1978) and more informing (Cooper, 1979) with adults than they do with peers.

Despite the number of studies showing differences in children's speech as a function of adult versus child listeners, it is often difficult to discern just what representation of listener characteristics the child has or whether adjustments are a function more of the situation than of differences in representations. For example, did the 5-year-old reported in the Martlew et al. (1978) study answer more of his mother's questions than his friend's because he saw her as a communicative partner of high status who could command responses or did the mother simply ask questions more central to the maintenance of the interaction? In the latter case, it would be the behavior of the mother that would account more for the apparent adjustment of the child rather than some internal representation of listener characteristics that determines differential response obligations. Martlew et al. report that the mother and child did spend more time establishing explicit rules of interaction, whereas the peers tactily assumed the rules and concentrated on mutual fantasy play. For example, the mother explicitly expressed her dissatisfaction with the way the interaction was proceeding by saying, "Come on. I'm getting fed up with doing this. I want to do something different." Her child responded with "All right" and a specific attempt to reengage in fantasy play.

Gearhart (1979) confirms that preschoolers are good at role playing in fantasy situations but not particularly adept at negotiating the conditions of play. Gearhart asked pairs of same-aged girls (3, 5, or 6 years old) to play grocery store with each other. She found that there were virtually no initiations, such as "What do you wanna do?" and only the oldest children actually negotiated about the roles each was to play and the behaviors appropriate to those roles. The 3-year-olds clearly had two-person scripts for the store setting, but they told partners what they wanted them to do rather than trying to negotiate a mutually acceptable plan. These observations suggest that adults and older children may organize their interactions with younger children to make the conditions of interaction themselves a topic of conversation, and young children's responses to such initiations may account, at least in part, for differences in speech directed to adult versus peer listeners.

This is not to suggest that preschoolers are simply pawns in the hands of more sophisticated conversational partners and that they have no internalized knowledge of listener characteristics. As noted earlier, Sachs and Devin (1976) found that children as young as 3 did not need feedback from a live listener to produce appropriately adjustive speech behavior. (They did, however, find that the quantity and quality of role playing increased with age.) This suggests that children have some internal representations of listener characteristics to which they adjust. Children aged 2½ to 5 have shown in their role-playing performances that they select directive forms on the basis of age and status characteristics of their listeners. In one study on directives, they produced more imperatives when acting as a superior addressing a subordinate than vice versa (Corsaro, 1979b). In fact, one child explicitly stated that he expected his partner, the ''boss,'' to order him around. In another study, subjects aged 4 to 7 showed knowledge not only of status relationships within the family but also of other culturally defined roles, such as doctors, teachers, and nurses. Andersen (1978) asked children to use puppets to role play several different characters. She found that ''parents'' gave more directives to children than vice versa, but fathers used relatively more imperatives and mothers more hints to do so. Doctors used more imperatives to nurses than nurses did to doctors, with nurses using more hints to doctors. However, women were not always prohibited from frequent use of imperatives. As (women) teachers, the children regularly produced imperatives addressed to students. Thus, the use of hints by both nurses and mothers does not appear to be due to the possibility that children see hinting as a necessary feature of female speech. The use of hints addressed to children by mothers and not fathers may be a reflection of the children's view of either the relative status of the two parents with regard to each other or the relative power each parent exercises over the child. In the former case, the child may be conflating the societal view of male/female status relations with the specific status relations between parent and child. In any event, role-playing tasks appear to be a fruitful paradigm for confirming that children have some conventional knowledge of the kinds of participant relationships that bear on choice of directive forms.

It is not surprising that by the age of 4 or 5 children are reasonably good at adjusting to familial-status relations. They have considerable experience with them after all. What is worth noting is that children also seem aware of less common status relations, such as doctor/nurse relationships, with which they would have had considerably less experience. It is possible that status, in terms of who has control over whom, is a very salient issue in the young child's life, and, hence, the knowledge of appropriate directive forms even for less familiar relationships is a relatively early acquisition. There is some evidence that other kinds of distinctions that adults commonly make in the language are less available to the young child. For example, Edelsky (1977) found

that first graders were inconsistent in judging expressions like ''Oh dear'' or ''I'll be damned'' as primarily either male or female speech. By sixth grade, children's judgments were much like adults'. Similarly, in an examination of Hungarian children's understanding of the personal pronoun system that differentiates familiarity and politeness, Hollos (1977) found that children did not correctly role play the more complex adult system until about the age of 9 (although they had mastered the system for children at a far earlier age).

Not only are children still acquiring sociolinguistic knowledge in their school years but they are also apparently learning the culture's system of evaluating different modes of talking. Cremona and Bates (1977) examined the attitudes of first- to fifth-grade Italian children who began school speaking the Valmontonese dialect of Italian. Their school encouraged the use of standard Italian. In a task requiring the children to judge who spoke ''better,'' a standard speaker or a dialect speaker, first graders' preferences for standard Italian were no better than chance. Third graders chose the standard speaker 100% of the time, although they themselves still showed stable vestiges of the dialect in their speech.

Conventional wisdom has it that first impressions are often founded in large measure on the way one speaks. Apparently, even though they have not yet learned all the characteristics of conventionally acceptable speech in their culture, preschoolers too use language as a way to take the measure of their interactive partners. In a study to uncover the cues 4-year-olds use in determining how to adjust their speech, Masur (1978) had 4-year-olds talk to 2-year-olds with either high or low syntactic abilities. She found that at first the 4-year-olds were sensitive to the listeners' syntactic capacities, but that as the interaction progressed, they adjusted more to the 2-year-olds' abilities to hold up their end of the conversation. (Apparently conversational skill is not perfectly correlated with syntactic knowledge even in 2-year-olds!) Interestingly, as interaction time lengthened, the 4-year-olds were able to respond to a broader analysis of their listeners' abilities.

Scripts, Routines, and Rituals

Not only does society dictate how language should be spoken but also it often dictates what should be said. It is common for a society to have prescribed ways of performing greetings, leave-takings, the giving and receiving of goods and favors, and so on. In a study of children aged 2 to 5, Grief and Gleason (1980) examined children's productions of hi, *thanks,* and *goodbye* in situations calling for them. The children produced verbal greetings and leave-takings only about one fourth of the times they were required and *thanks* only 7% of the time. Parental rates of production were considerably higher than these, as were the children's rates after they were prompted by their parents. Parental urgings were quite explicit, often taking the form "Say *X*." This kind of parental tuition bears strong similarity to the teaching frames Schieffelin (1979) describes in the speech of Kaluli mothers talking to their children in Papua New Guinea. Schieffelin reports, "When a Kaluli wants someone else to 'say what I say' he says the message plus the word ɛlɛma. The Kaluli word ɛlɛma is a contraction of two words, ɛlɛ (like this/that) and *sama* (present tense singular imperative speak/say) and means *say like this/that*" (1979, p. 86). For example, a mother said to her child, "Mother, I want pandanus (a tropical vegetable), ɛlɛma." Schieffelin's transcripts are full of such examples of mothers explicitly instructing their children on how to conduct an appropriate social interaction by telling them just what to say, most often to a third party. It is of some interest that interaction rituals and social scripts prompt direct parental tuition, whereas most other aspects of language acquisition and language use do not.

In addition to direct teaching, parents do engage their children, especially when they are very young, in a variety of caretaker-infant games involving limited and repetitious uses of language (see Bruner & Sherwood, 1976). Parent/child pairs differ as to which games they play, and those differences do seem to influence the way the young child uses language in other contexts. In an experimental study of 16-month-olds' responses to questions beginning with *what* (e.g., "What does a doggie say?"), Allen and Shatz (in press) found that one of the best predictors of the kind of response a given subject would make was the type of routines in which her mother commonly engaged her. Of course, such a finding says nothing about how the child eventually learns the rules of the language. Instead, it is interesting because it suggests that the child makes use of her prior discourse history when confronted with a new conversational situation requiring her participation.

The notion that children make use of conversational routines to structure their interactions is related to a suggestion by Nelson and Gruendel (1979). They argue that when children have a script for an activity that is being talked about, they do a better job of creating a cohesive, coherent dialogue. The authors define a script as a "conceptual structure that describes appropriate sequences of events in a particular context" (p. 78). Scripts, or knowledge

structures, for common events within a child's world are likely to be shared with other children of the same culture. Like games, they provide the child with mutually known contexts where the behavior of dialogic partners is at least somewhat predictable. For a child who still has to put considerable effort into accomplishing all of the subtasks involved in creating a verbal turn in a conversation, having a shared context that greatly constrains the situation would seem to be a genuine help. It should not be surprising then that when children engage in dialogue over topics on which they share considerable knowledge and experience, their conversations are more extended and look somewhat more cohesive.

How to Do Things by Talking

In any society, language does social work: it is used to gain access to groups, give permission, establish agreements, and resolve arguments. Part of what children must learn are the often tacit but, nonetheless, culturally accepted ways of carrying out such work with language. Recently, several studies have examined how children accomplish social work with language. Corsaro (1979a) studied groups of 2- and 3-year-olds in a playschool to determine how they gained access to playgroups. He found that nonverbal strategies were most common (and most likely to be met with rejection!). When they did manage to produce verbal behavior, their speech was often appropriate and met with success. Slightly older preschoolers are considerably more adept at negotiating rights of access as well as ownership on a regular basis (Newman, 1978). In a study of spontaneous conflict resolutions, Eisenberg and Garvey (1981) found that preschoolers were quite aware of the need to give a reason for a negative response. They also made compromise attempts, suggesting they took their antagonist's position into account.

The rather sophisticated skills observed in preschoolers' natural interactions are not observed in less natural tasks however. The use of a role-playing task to examine conflict resolution (Brenneis & Lein, 1977) resulted in the occurrence of simpler response behaviors involving more redundancy and less negotiation than Eisenberg and Garvey (1981) observed. Similarly, Howie-Day (1979) found that first graders were no different from older children in the kinds of appeals they chose as potentially effective for children to use in persuading listeners to give up a toy; but older children were considerably more adept at providing reasons for why those arguments would be effective. Thus, children learn to do at least some things by talking fairly early on, but talking about doing those things appears more difficult for the preschooler.

Where Does All the Knowledge Come from?

Our review of the kinds of knowledge children bring to communicative settings has focused on the years between 1 and 7 because it is clear that a great deal of development takes place during that time (although 7-year-olds are far from ideal communicative partners). Where does all the knowledge come from? I have taken a rather skeptical stand on the view that infancy will provide us many of the answers. Instead, it seems that the kinds of knowledge feeding into mature communicative behavior are so diverse that one must look at development within each domain for answers to questions of etiology. In a few cases, it appears that direct tuition is implicated; in others, conventional structures built up by experience in a culture seem relevant. In still others, the child's analysis of formal properties of linguistic structure appears to provide entrée into the world of coherent discourse. In short, there may be as many kinds of learning involved in the development of communication skills as there are ways of asking someone to pass the salt.

This is not to say that there are no general principles that can be uncovered in studying the development of communication. For one thing, the question of how children put these diverse bits of knowledge together to produce coherent behavior is an important issue. Communication is an elegant example of complex human behavior, recruiting information processing capacities to their fullest. Hence, it is an excellent area for studying the processing capacities of young children under varying task conditions. Indeed, it is possible that looking at the varying levels of performance in children under different task conditions will provide clues to how complex tasks are accomplished. We turn now to a discussion of issues bearing on the problem of variation in performance across tasks.

VARIABILITY IN COMMUNICATIVE PERFORMANCE

How and when do children use the kinds of knowledge I have been describing? Research over the last decade suggests that, although children may have considerable knowledge that is relevant to communication tasks, they do not always make use of it. Reviews of the literature on children's communicative performance reveal that the context in which communicative skills are assessed can have

considerable effect on performance (see Dickson, 1981; Shatz, 1978c). Thus, many of the explanations proposed over the years to account for children's lack of ability have had to be revised as the employment of different tasks often revealed the presence of knowledge or a skill thought to be lacking. For example, children have been shown to be able to take account of their listeners (e.g., Maratsos, 1973; Menig-Peterson, 1975; Shatz & Gelman, 1973, 1977), to do comparison processes (Whitehurst & Sonnenschein, 1981), and to detect ambiguity (Ackerman, 1981b) and inconsistency (Wimmer, 1979). All these factors were previously assumed to be outside the ken of the average 5- or 6-year-old. What then are the conditions that facilitate or inhibit children's performance on communicative tasks?

Do Child and Experimenter Agree on the Task?

Developmentalists are perenially plagued by the problem of assuring that their young subjects understand the task they are required to do. What makes that problem especially difficult in the communication domain is that children are accustomed to doing communicative work in the everyday world that may look very similar to the tasks the experimenter assigns them. Thus, the child may be fooled into behaving as he would in the everyday world, despite subtle differences in task conditions between those two worlds. For example, I argued earlier that by the age of 5, children are in the habit of communicating in a discourse context with cooperative interlocutors, who use context to help understand the child's messages and who are unlikely to be intentionally ambiguous, inconsistent, or tricky. It is reasonable for a child placed in an experimental context and given vague instructions about the task to believe those conversational conditions still pertain. Often, however, they do not. Many referential communication tasks dispense with a listener altogether or at least provide no interpretive context to aid a listener. Thus, the child is immediately faced with a situation quite different from the one in which his everyday messages occur. We have seen that using instructions that make clear to the child his listener has no other information on which to rely but that which the child himself must provide increases the young child's performance on referential tasks. Similarly, using a response mode that leads the child away from performative responses allows the child to show that he can determine what is an adequate or inadequate communication. In other words, the job of the experimenter in testing the child's skill is to be certain that the child can overcome his bias to respond the way he typically would in an everyday world, a world in which he must show his cooperativeness through his responses and in which the likelihood of communicative success is facilitated by interlocutors who infer, repair, and give feedback. This can be accomplished by giving the subject explicit instructions with regard to what is required and also by structuring the task so that everyday responses are clearly insufficient or inappropriate to the task at hand.

Why is it that these kinds of precautions seem less necessary with older children? One obvious answer is that older children's everyday experience is different from that of younger children, at least in Western societies in which schooling is common. The kinds of tasks that so often assess referential skill are ones that focus on analytic abilities. For example, the type of "password" tasks in which children are required to communicate information about word pairs (see Asher, 1979) and the tasks in which fixed features of stimulus sets are varied from trial to trial (e.g., Whitehurst & Sonnenschein, 1978) both focus on the child's ability to give contrastive, nonredundant messages. Children who have had some experience in school settings, where analysis in terms of critical features is stressed in a variety of domains, may be more inclined spontaneously to see these communication tasks as requiring the application of analytic skills. In other words, by virtue of their experience, they may see the goals of these tasks differently from younger children. Higgins et al. (1981) have commented on the likelihood that younger children see the goals of communication differently from older children and adults, and Dickson (1982) has suggested that this sort of argument can be made not only for older versus younger children but also for any groups (e.g., middle class vs. lower class or educated vs. uneducated) for whom the levels of experience with analytic tasks differ. Thus, in selecting a task in which to examine group differences, the researcher needs to consider how the task structure relates to the communicative experience of the subjects to be tested.

It is worth stressing here that the issue is not whether children have sufficient experience to have acquired a given capacity. (I address that issue later.) Instead, the present concern is that the child and the experimenter must share assumptions about the need to display a given skill in a given context. Young children may not have sufficient experience with similar tasks to see the function of the task in the same light as the experimenter. Indeed, it is apparently quite easy to teach a child that a given skill she already possesses is conventionally appropriate in

particular contexts (Whitehurst & Sonnenschein, 1981). It is also worth noting that the behaviors children exhibit inappropriately by an experimenter's standards in a given task may be quite functional in other contexts. For example, Deutsch (1976) found that subjects were able to identify objects like small red triangles faster when given messages that included noncriterial, redundant information than when they were given contrastive, nonredundant messages. At least for Deutsch's task, redundancy—a common feature in young children's referential descriptions (Whitehurst, 1976)—facilitates listener response performance and, hence, can be considered a positive attribute. Similarly, children may at times recruit more context than they should for the rather restrictive laboratory tasks they are often asked to do, but recruiting context to create an interpretation is a very basic aspect of language comprehension and one that adults do with regularity (see Brown, Smiley, Day, Townsend, & Lawton, 1977). The point is that what children do when they do not perform as experimenters expect them to is not necessarily ignorant or inappropriate from their perspective. To put it simply, experimenters could be less egocentric[9] when trying to determine why children do not perform as expected.

The above points are not to be taken as a claim that careful and sensitive experimentation will result in the disappearance of all developmental differences on communication tasks. What such work has been doing, and hopefully will continue to do, is make simplistic explanations of those differences hard to accept. In the next section, we will consider some consistent deficits in children's performance and ways to investigate the nature of their causes.

A Growing Knowledge Base: Some Things Children Do Not (or May Not) Know

I have already commented on several areas of knowledge that are still incomplete in the preschooler. Obviously, semantic, syntactic, and pragmatic knowledge continue to expand beyond kindergarten. For example, although children as young as 4 show some understanding of the logical presuppositions of certain words, such as *think* and *know* (Johnson & Maratsos, 1977), the understanding of other words supporting logical inference, such as *even* and *only,* is still incomplete at that age. Thus, children told, "Even the rabbit is in the cage" inappropriately answer the question, "Which animals are in the cage?" by indicating that the rabbit is alone (Kail, 1981).[10] As noted earlier, children may lack the social experience necessary to interpret violations of conversational rules that form the basis of sarcasm and other forms of language use requiring subtle inferences of intent.

One of the most far-reaching deficits that children appear to have is in the organizational quality of their knowledge. On a variety of tasks, younger children appear to have their knowledge less well or less complexly organized than older children and adults. For example, Pratt, Scribner, and Cole (1977) found that preschoolers adjusted as much as first graders the information that they gave to a listener concerning the rules of a board game, depending on whether or not the listener had the game materials. The preschool children, however, produced the information in a much more disorganized fashion. Similarly, Menig-Peterson and McCabe (1978) found that although both preschoolers and school-age children produced phrases that oriented their listeners to the time, location, and character aspects of their narratives, school-age children were better at giving orienting information at the beginning of their narratives. It seems plausible to assume that increased structural organization develops with experience and increased knowledge in a domain (see Chi, 1978). One consequence of more systematized knowledge is a saving of cognitive resources. The more organized one's knowledge, the less work required to retrieve the essential pieces of information and order them in appropriate ways for the task at hand. Hence, differences in the organization of knowledge structures would have serious consequences for the way children perform on communicative tasks, virtually all of which make some demands for the retrieval of stored knowledge. Older children with more organized knowledge presumably could accomplish a given task better with the same amount of resources as a younger child with less organized knowledge. That is, a greater degree of organization in knowledge stores is a way of stretching cognitive resources (see Shatz, 1978c).

There are several suggestions for research derivable from this view. First, giving children an external means of stretching resources, by providing an organization or by reducing the overall cognitive work load of the task in some other way, should result in better performance. There is some evidence that providing prosthetics of one sort or another are indeed beneficial to children's performance. Pratt, Bates, and Wickens (1980) compared children's performances on a message-evaluation task under conditions that either required the child to work strictly from memory or allowed him a picture as a memory aid. Children did better in the memory-aid condition. The work of Patterson and her colleagues showing improvement in listeners' performance when they are given plans for asking questions also seems relevant here (Patterson & Kister, 1981).

The technique of providing prosthetics could be brought to bear on the hypothesis of difference in structural organization in an interesting way. It is possible that younger children's organization does not always differ from adults or older children in any important way but that the burdens of doing complex tasks are generally heavier on them and, hence, there are no resources remaining to display their knowledge in appropriately organized ways. If this is the case, then relieving cognitive work load in other portions of a task that has in the past shown younger children to be less organized than older children should result in improving their performance on precisely the organizational components of the message. If the child actually lacks organizational structure, however, work-load prosthetics may improve other aspects of task performance but should have little effect on organizational components. Whitehurst and Sonnenschein (1981) have suggested that training studies are a means to determining whether a child has a skill and just does not know when to apply it or whether the skill is lacking completely. If, after short and relatively explicit training, a child's performance improves on the trained factor and stays improved over time, then, they argue, it is likely the child has not learned a new skill but only when to apply an accustomed one. The use of prosthetics is another method for determining whether a skill, however fragile, actually exists, but in this case, its absence from performance is not due to the child's lack of knowledge about when to apply it. Instead, it is attributed to the drain on resources required elsewhere that its display would entail.

That the question of whether and how children's knowledge is structured is an important one gains support from Markman (1981). She notes that it is only structured, meaningful information that we can say is understood. Thus, we do not say we understand our telephone numbers. She points out that children may have a different view of understanding from adults because their principles of organization are incomplete. (Knowledge of logical inference and conventional rules, such as those discussed earlier, count as principles of organization.) In essence, recognition that something is relevant to understanding is prior to monitoring whether one does indeed understand that something. One implication of Markman's argument is that one's ability to detect that one does not understand (by adult standards) should improve as a by-product of increasing the organizational structure of knowledge.

There are, of course, other considerations as well. For example, children may have different strategies from adults for flagging difficulties. Markman suggests that in a comprehension task, children may pick a favored interpretation and then wait for disconfirming evidence, whereas adults evaluate incoming information for ambiguities of interpretation. This difference in strategies may be related in part to style differences and not just age differences. Both Pratt et al. (1980) and Asher and Wigfield (1981) report that reflective children (as assessed by the Matching Familiar Figures Test [MFFT]) do better on communicative tasks that involve evaluating ambiguities and comparison activities than do impulsive children. It is also the case that the ability to monitor one's understanding in any given situation depends on having the resources to do that (Markman, 1981; Shatz, 1978c). It may be that certain children who do a task more slowly have no more resources per unit time than do children who do it quickly but over the full time they allot for doing the task, they will accrue a larger resource pool. Hence, children with longer latencies on tasks like the MFFT may generally take longer to do communicative tasks as well and, hence, have more cognitive resources to allot to monitoring and comparison activities. It would be interesting to apply time measurements to children's performances in communication tasks to explore this possibility further.

The issues raised about monitoring ability are appropriate to questions of metacommunicative skill generally. Flavell (1981) suggests that "being able to talk about communications reflects (imperfectly to be sure) the ability to *think* about them, and that is probably an important development. . . ." The question I raise here is whether *thinking* about messages, in the sense stated earlier of taking the message as an object of thought, is truly beyond the capacity of the preschooler or whether that too would be more readily displayed given the appropriate prosthetics. Thinking about messages in the abstract no doubt becomes more common with age; why that is the case remains to be explained.

The moral in all of this is that one must proceed with caution in deciding what children do and do not know. It is undoubtedly the case that children's knowledge increases with time in important ways. However, it will take clever and sensitive research to determine how the display of competence in performance relates both to the structure of knowledge and the process of using that knowledge.

The Generality of Knowledge: Communication Skills or Skills for Communication?

I began this chapter by noting that a variety of activities are typically labeled communicative. The fact that acts having quite different characteristics and contexts of occurrence can all be given the same label is both useful and potentially misleading. It is useful because it forces us to ask what is common across these occurrences that we intuitively feel have some relation. It may be misleading because a child successful on one communicative task is often expected to be successful on other communication tasks. It is an easy but unjustified inference that acts that are given the same name necessarily draw on the same set of skills to accomplish them. The question of the generality of a child's knowledge is an important issue for any developmental theory. Indeed, Piaget's theory, which made broad claims for general knowledge, has been found wanting to the extent that the evidence for that claim has been considered weak (see Shatz, 1978c; *Gelman & Baillargeon, vol. III, chap. 3*).

There are two aspects to the question of the generality of knowledge or skill. One is whether the knowledge displayed in one set of tasks (e.g., conservation) will evidence itself in a related set of tasks (e.g., classification). Another is whether even within a set of tasks (e.g., number vs. mass conservation), a capacity will generally be displayed. Examining the evidence for knowledge components of the sort discussed earlier both within a variety of communication tasks as well as across tasks from other domains will begin to address the question of what knowledge or subskill, if any, is unique to communicative competence (cf. Ammon, 1981).

The paradigm used to investigate the generality-of-knowledge question has been a correlational one. Children are tested on a variety of tasks and their performances across them are correlated. Early studies examining the influence of particular factors (like role taking) in performances across domains were disappointing with regard to their success at finding support for a single general factor largely responsible for performance across domains (e.g., K. Rubin, 1974). Looking at a range of tasks all within the referential communication domain, Wigfield and Asher (1978) correlated third and fifth graders' performances on a task requiring picture descriptions, a word-clue task, and a task requiring the child to communicate about locations around the school to another child. Third graders' performances did not correlate across tasks. For the fifth graders, performances on the first two tasks were positively correlated. The authors propose that the relative lack of correlations suggests that different tasks draw on different sets of skills. Of course, at one level that must be true. Two tasks that are not identical will involve elements of knowledge or skill in each that the other does not share. However, it is still of interest to determine whether a child showing competence with a subcomponent of one task will also show it on another. One cannot discover how generally a child's knowledge is represented unless one examines performance across tasks. What one needs to be sure of in looking for correlations across tasks is that the elements that differ across tasks do not take differential amounts of resources for their execution. If they do, overall task performances are likely to differ as well. One common reason why a subcomponent draws large amounts of resources is that it is incompletely acquired. It may be that fifth graders and not third graders produced correlated performances across tasks in the Wigfield and Asher (1978) study because the unrelated components in both tasks were likely to be learned better by the fifth graders than by the younger children. Hence, similar performance across tasks was less likely to be masked by incomplete acquisition of some unrelated exponent of one task or the other for any given older subject.

A note of caution seems appropriate here. It is usual to conclude on the basis of correlated performances across tasks that children producing such behavior have acquired general knowledge structures that apply to those tasks. Our earlier discussion of the correlations between performance on the MFFT and various communication tasks should make us cautious about such claims. It is possible that the way children process certain kinds of information and recruit possible related, but not isomorphic, knowledge structures to various tasks is what determines whether their performances across tasks will be correlated. Again, it would seem impossible to learn much about the structure or representation of knowledge without considering as well how that knowledge is used.

Variable Criteria for Success

It may by now be tiresomely obvious that whether a child is considered successful or not as a communicator will depend as much on the criteria the experimenter sets for success as on the objective characteristics of the child's behavior. An experimenter who is looking for evidence that a particular subskill is to some extent available seems more likely than not to find that evidence, provided she takes the sorts of precautions discussed throughout this chapter. The generality and organization of those subskills into spontaneous, unprompted performance without feedback is another matter. How much we should hold children to that sort of performance is an issue worth considering. Adults, too, often show inadequate performance by these and some of the other standards that researchers in the field have applied to children (see Shatz, 1978c, for some examples). Again, this is not to argue against the view that communication skill develops with age. Instead, the point is only that the researcher often makes a tacit evaluation of what is important in communicative performance without an explicit theoretical justification for that judgment. The consequences of not examining one's criteria may be wasteful indeed. For example, much has been made in the literature of the young child's inability to produce referential communications that are contrastive and nonredundant. Given that nonredundancy has yet to be shown to be an especially useful or important aspect of normal mature, successful referential communication, it hardly seems worthwhile to invest time and effort in perfecting training procedures to induce children to produce such messages.

On the other hand, certain kinds of analytic skills are important to adequate communication performance, at least in a technological society. It is important to be able to apply logical principles to the comprehension of discourse and to be able to assess both messages and one's understanding of them for gaps, ambiguities, and contradictions. Imagine the success-to-failure ratio of the efforts of a computer programmer lacking such skills. Still, the question of how people should operate in a technological environment can be separated from the question of how ordinary interactions are conducted, just as the question of what children can do is separable from the question of what they usually do.

CONCLUSIONS
What Is Missing and Why

My apologies to the reader who took the *what* in the above subtitle to stand for the abilities children lack. The ambiguity was intentional. My *what* refers to the topics that have not been addressed in this chapter, not because they were outside of the scope of the domain I delineated but because in some cases the topics are well covered by recent review papers or books and in other cases very little is known at present about the areas. Finally, I, too, am a limited-capacity processor and found the range of literature bearing on even the narrowed domain I outlined quite staggering. Hence, selectivity was a necessity.

I chose to focus the bulk of this review on the

preschool years because that is the time period of development that has received the most attention in recent years (see Dickson, 1982). That fact is not surprising in light of the review of the theoretical issues which underlie much of the research (see *Theoretical Issues Related to Communication*). The questions of the relationship between early communicative behaviors and language acquisition, the role of egocentrism in preschool cognitive and communicative behavior, and the induction of the child into a social world have quite naturally led to a focus on early experience and development. I suspect that emphasis is likely to change as concerns with communication performance itself and what governs it throughout the life span begin to play a larger role in developmental researchers' thinking about communication skill. Although sociolinguists have been concerned with these sorts of questions for some time (see Gumperz & Hymes, 1972), psychologists are likely to bring a different perspective to them.

I have attended relatively little to demographic variables other than age, in part because reviews organized around such concerns exist elsewhere. Higgins (1976) deals extensively with the influence of social class on communicative performance, as does Dickson (1982) in his review of referential communication research, which also covers the influences of IQ, verbal ability, and age. Most of these variables are particularly relevant to the problem of successful communication in the classroom, another topic not addressed here. The display of many of the kinds of knowledge discussed earlier (*The Knowledge Bases of Communication*) have been observed in classroom contexts (e.g., illocutionary and sociolinguistic knowledge). Wilkinson (1982) includes discussions of such observations as well as studies of the language of teaching. A related topic is, of course, communication in the written mode. Only recently has writing begun to receive concerted attention among researchers. Rubin (1980) has explored the differences between oral and written communication, as have Higgins (1978) and Olson (1977). Several volumes concerned with the cognitive and developmental processes involved in writing have recently appeared (Frederiksen, 1981; Gregg & Steinberg, 1980). This recent emphasis on modes of communication other than the oral has prompted some preliminary but promising investigations into children's preparedness for literacy (Cole, Anderson, & Teal, 1981; Scollon & Scollon, 1979). It would not be surprising to find in the next edition of the Handbook a chapter devoted to the development of literacy.

Finally, I have rarely included a consideration of the communicative behavior of abnormal popula-

tions. If communicative performance depends in large measure on the confluence of social, linguistic, and cognitive skills, it would indeed be interesting to examine how deviant development in each of these domains redounds on communicative performance. I know of no work that attempts to do this kind of factor analysis, although the communicative performance of children with cognitive and linguistic deficits has received considerable attention (e.g., Guralnick & Paul-Brown, 1977; Hoy & McKnight, 1977; Johnston, in press; Paccia-Cooper & Curcio, 1982). Clearly, any theoretical arguments based on the performance of normal children must also be consonant with what is learned about disordered populations. Thus far, the information processing approach dominating the organization of this chapter seems to hold promise for integrating some of the findings on language-disordered children with those of normal populations (see Johnston, 1981; Shatz, Bernstein, & Shulman, 1980). Further efforts along these lines would be informative.

Past and Future Research

Research in children's communicative performance has produced a variety of findings bearing on the issues raised in the earlier discussion (*Theoretical Issues Related to Communication*). With regard to the question of the relation between language and communication development, we have seen an explosion of work that has carefully described early interactive patterns between infants and their caretakers. Yet, any real evidence that patterns of interaction developed in the early months or even the 1st year have any direct bearing on the speed or order of language-acquisition skill is lacking. Nor is it easy to uncover clear influences of early behavior on later communicative skills. Moreover, the few studies on cross-cultural patterns of mother-child interaction suggest that children can flourish in cultural contexts that do not necessarily attribute intentionality to their every behavior. It is also the case that children seem to acquire some formal aspects of language that they produce even in the absence of pragmatic or functional knowledge. At other times, children fall back on pragmatic strategies when formal acquisition is incomplete. In sum, there is evidence that language and communicative development have somewhat independent courses early in childhood. It will be of interest in future years to investigate how those systems grow to be more integrated, particularly as children learn those formal aspects of language that more explicitly encode pragmatic considerations.

Perhaps the area that has seen the most dramatic

advances in recent years is the cognitive one. Whereas 10 or 15 years ago egocentrism explanations dominated the research that sought to describe and account for children's communicative failures, there is now considerably more respect for the abilities children show in appropriate contexts as well as more sophisticated attempts at theoretical explanations for their variable performance. There has also been a new emphasis on the organizational aspects of performance, especially with regard to the question of how much conscious monitoring, inference, and decision making account for differences between mature and immature performance. If these factors should prove to be crucial, the question of how those abilities themselves are acquired would warrant further attention. At the moment, there seem to be no direct comparisons between the two divergent views on the etiology of these sorts of abilities, one being that parental behavior demonstrates the executive function and guides the child to it; the other being that these abilities will spontaneously develop as the child acquires experience with both logical and cultural principles and has sufficient resources for explicit executive activities.

Finally, we have seen that clarifying the goals of a communicative task positively influences children's performance. This finding suggests that children do indeed often see different purposes in an interaction from those adults see. Much of this may have to do with their different views of role rights and obligations. Future work on children's understanding of participant obligations in conventional interactions would be useful in clarifying the role social knowledge plays both in communicative behavior and in children's understandings of communicative tasks.

Knots in Theoretical Lines

The view that seems most naturally derived from the research reviewed is that communicative skills develop as a function of growing knowledge in a variety of cognitive, social, and linguistic domains and as the child becomes better able to organize and utilize his knowledge. One of the most striking deficits in this view as stated is its lack of attention to a question that has received much attention elsewhere in developmental psychology, at least in the areas of linguistic and cognitive development: What aspects of communicative knowledge are universal and what are culture bound? For example, much has been made of perspective taking or role taking as an important element in mature communicative performance. Even non-Piagetian frameworks, such as

those found in philosophy or artificial intelligence, use terminology that implies a concern with the relation of one individual belief system to another as a central issue in communication. Yet, many societies do not have the view of the individual as an independent agent that Western society does, and this difference is often reflected in language structure (e.g., the absence of well-differentiated personal-pronoun systems[11]). What would be requisite knowledge for successful communication in such cultures? Would the perspective-taking factor play an equal role or any role at all? Another aspect of communicative performance that seems especially likely to be affected by cultural differences has to do with communicative goals. We have already seen that many of the tasks used to assess communicative competence are defined according to a Western value system extolling the virtues of analytic thinking. It is unclear how general this model of adult performance is. In sum, it is likely that a general theory of communicative development will need an account of what is universal and what is culture specific in communicative performance.

A related issue concerns the ecological validity of our conclusions about children's communicative ability versus their knowledge of skills feeding that ability. As Dickson (1982) has noted, it may be nice to know that in simple, controlled contexts, children can do this or that subtask successfully. But will the same child be able to function adequately in the more complex world of the classroom, the grocery store, or even the playground? Saying that we are interested in competence and are satisfied to find that a child can indeed do *x* or *y* when it is taken out of a complex context may make us inordinately complacent about genuine communicative difficulties the child may face. In language research, an interest in competence involved an abstraction away from the vagaries of everyday performance. In communication, the phrase *communicative competence*, taken in that light, almost seems like a contradiction in terms. Examining the child's performance in a variety of ways and a variety of contexts is indeed a useful method for uncovering the child's knowledge, but all too often researchers who select one method or another work within a single paradigm and fail to reconstruct the whole child when creating explanations, training programs, or therapy programs.

Finally, process concerns seem to have crept into even the most structurally based approaches to communicative development. Although that is to be applauded as an obvious attempt to create more reasonable theories, much theoretical work still needs to be done. If such theories are to become truly predictive, then we must develop ways to compare the workload levels of task components. That is, one needs a metric in which to examine the quantity and distribution of resources. Such a metric still eludes cognitive psychologists who use the limited-capacity model to investigate other cognitive behaviors. Yet, the difficulty of the task does not diminish its importance.

One Last Message

Work in communicative development has been the focus of a research explosion in recent years. In part, this is due to an expansion of the sorts of communicative behaviors considered worthy of investigation. Another aspect of the explosion seems to be a paradigm shift away from Piagetian structural concerns to a focus on component skills and processing questions. The promise of the new paradigm is in its ability to accommodate data of various sorts and its comfort with complex models of performance.

In summary, the story on communication is much more complex than one might have expected reading Piaget (1926) or even that classic empirical study of Krauss and Glucksberg (1969). In some regard, our increased knowledge about children's abilities has opened Pandora's box, creating more questions and issues to be addressed. Yet, the progress in discovering children's abilities and the rapidity with which a new framework has been developing for doing further research in the area are startling and laudable. Hopefully, for the researcher in communication development, what has been learned so far will be an impetus to progress in the future.

NOTES

1. Admittedly, for Piaget, social interchanges may motivate development but, as Inhelder et al. (1974) emphasize, always via the mediation of internal schemes and resolutions of conflicts among them.

2. M. Cole in a colloquium, Department of Psychology, Harvard University, in February 1981.

3. These lines of work have been discussed ably and extensively elsewhere (see Asher, 1979; Glucksberg, Krauss, & Higgins, 1975; Shatz, 1978c; and the recent volume edited by Dickson, 1981); hence, only a few are reported here as examples.

4. L. Camras in a research proposal, "Dominance and display in children's social interaction," at DePaul University in 1980.

5. See Bretherton and Bates (1979) for a view of intentionality that relies heavily on expectation.

6. In this view, communication involves more than "the coordination of separate activities of two or more individuals into a single social activity"— the definition provided by R. A. Clark (1978). In my opinion, Clark's definition is more appropriately taken as a definition of interaction than of communication.

7. See Gallagher and Darnton (1978) for a comparison of the responses to "What?" by language-disordered and normal children.

8. The interested reader should see Bach and Harnish (1979), H. H. Clark (1979), Katz (1977), and Searle (1969, 1975) for examples of theoretical and experimental work on speech acts.

9. Ethnocentric might be a better term here because I am trying to convey the notion that task expectations are to some extent dependent on culturally determined experiences.

10. Also see Markman (1976, 1978) for further evidence that children have difficulty dealing with the logical implications of language.

11. R. Harré in a colloquium, Graduate School of Education, Harvard University, in December 1980.

REFERENCES

Ackerman, B. P. Children's understanding of speech acts in unconventional directive frames. *Child Development*, 1978, *49*, 311–318.

Ackerman, B. P. Children's understanding of definite descriptions: Pragmatic influences to the speaker's intent. *Journal of Experimental Child Psychology*, 1979, *28*, 1–15.

Ackerman, B. P. Performative bias in children's interpretations of ambiguous referenial communications. *Child Development*, 1981, *52*, 1224–1230. (a)

Ackerman, B. P. The understanding of young children and adults of the deictic adequacy of communications. *Journal of Experimental Child Psychology*, 1981, *31*, 256–270. (b)

Ackerman, B. P. When is a question not answered? The understanding of young children of utterances violating or conforming to the rules of conversational sequencing. *Journal of Experimental Child Psychology*, 1981, *31*, 487–507. (c)

Allen, R., & Shatz, M. "What says meow?" The role of context and linguistic experience in very young children's responses to "what" questions. *Journal of Child Language*, in press.

Ammon, P. Communication skills and communicative competence: A neo-Piagetian process—structural view. In W. P. Dickson (Ed.), *Children's oral communication skills*. New York: Academic Press, 1981.

Andersen, E. Will you don't snore please? Directives in young children's role-play speech. *Papers and Reports on Child Language Development*, 1978, *15*, 140–150.

Anderson, B. J., Vietze, P., & Dokecki, P. R. Reciprocity in vocal interactions of mothers and infants. *Child Development,* 1977, *48,* 1676–1681.

Asher, S. R. Referential communication. In G. J. Whitehurst & B. J. Zimmerman (Eds.), *The functions of language and cognition*. New York: Academic Press, 1979.

Asher, S. R., & Oden, S. Children's failure to communicate: An assessment of comparison and egocentrism explanations. *Developmental Psychology,* 1976, *12,* 132–139.

Asher, S. R., & Wigfield, A. Training referential communication skills. In W. P. Dickson (Ed.), *Children's oral communication skills*. New York: Academic Press, 1981.

Atkinson, M. Prerequisites for reference. In E. Ochs & B. Schieffelin (Eds.), *Developmental pragmatics*. New York: Academic Press, 1979.

Austin, J. *How to do things with words*. Cambridge: Harvard University Press, 1962.

Bach, K., & Harnish, R. M. *Linguistic communication and speech acts*. Cambridge, Mass.: MIT Press, 1979.

Bates, E. *Language and context: The acquisition of pragmatics*. New York: Academic Press, 1976.

Bates, E., Benigni, L., Bretherton, I., Camaioni, L., & Volterra, V. *The emergence of symbols*. New York: Academic Press, 1979.

Bates, E., & MacWhinney, B. A functionalist approach to the acquisition of grammar. In E. Ochs & B. Schieffelin (Eds.), *Developmental pragmatics*. New York: Academic Press, 1979.

Bateson, M. C. Mother-infant exchanges: The epigenesis of conversational interaction. In D. Aaronson & R. W. Rieber (Eds.), *Developmental psycholinguistics and communication disorders*. New York: New York Academy of Sciences, 1975. (Annals of the New York Academy of Sciences [Vol. 263])

Baumgardner, M. J., & Lasky, E. Z. Acquisition of comprehension of the verb phrase anaphora construction. *Journal of Speech and Hearing Research*, 1978, *21*, 166–173.

Beal, C. R., & Flavell, J. H. Young speakers' eval-uations of their listener's comprehension in a referential communication task. Unpublished manuscript, Stanford University, 1981.

Becker, J. Children's strategic use of requests to mark and manipulate social status. in S. Kuczaj (Ed.), *Language development: Language, thought, and culture*. Hillsdale, N.J.: Erlbaum, 1982.

Bierwisch, M. Semantic structure and illocutionary force. In J. R. Searle, F. Kiefer, & M. Bierwisch (Eds.), *Speech act theory and pragmatics*. Dordrecht, the Netherlands: D. Reidel, 1980.

Billman, D., & Shatz, M. Interactive devices of two-year-old dyads: A twin and nontwin comparison. *Discourse Processes,* in press.

Blank, M., Gessner, M., & Esposito, A. Language without communication: A case study. *Journal of Child Language,* 1979, *6*, 329–352.

Bloom, L. *One word at a time*. The Hague: Mouton, 1973.

Bloom, L., Rocissano, L., & Hood, L. Adult-child discourse: Developmental interaction between information processing and linguistic knowledge. *Cognitive Psychology,* 1976, *8*, 521–552.

Boskey, M., & Nelson, K. *Answering unanswerable questions: The role of imitation*. Paper presented at the Boston University Conference on Language Development, October 1980.

Bower, T. G. R. Repetition in human development. *Merrill-Palmer Quarterly,* 1974, *20*, 303–318.

Bowerman, M. Reorganizational processes in language development. In E. Wanner & L. R. Gleitman (Eds.), *Language acquisition: The state of the art*. Cambridge: At the University Press, 1982.

Bransford, J., & McCarrell, N. A sketch of a cognitive approach to comprehension: Some thoughts about understanding what it means to comprehend. In W. Weimer & D. Palermo (Eds.), *Cognition and the symbolic processes*. Hillsdale, N.J.: Erlbaum, 1974.

Brenneis, D., & Lein, L. "You fruithead": A sociolinguistic approach to children's dispute settlement. In S. Ervin-Tripp & C. Mitchell-Kernan (Eds.), *Child discourse*. New York: Academic Press, 1977.

Bretherton, I., & Bates, E. The emergence of intentional communication. *New Directions for Child Development,* 1979, *4,* 81–100.

Brown, A. L. Knowing when, where and how to remember: A problem of metacognition. In R. Glaser (Ed.), *Advances in instructional psychology*. New York: Halsted Press, 1978.

Brown, A. L., Smiley, S. S., Day, J. D., Townsend, M. A., & Lawton, S. C. Intrusion of a thematic idea in children's comprehension and retention of stories. *Child Development,* 1977, *48,* 1454–1466.

Brown, R. The first sentences of child and chimpanzee. In R. Brown (Ed.), *Psycholinguistic papers.* New York: Free Press, 1970.

Brown, R. *A first language.* Cambridge, Mass.: Harvard University Press, 1973.

Brown, R. The maintenance of conversation. In D. Olson (Ed.), *The social foundations of language and thought.* New York: W. W. Norton, 1980.

Brown, R., & Hanlon, C. Derivational complexity and order of acquisition in child speech. In J. R. Hayes (Ed.), *Cognition and the development of language.* New York: Wiley, 1970.

Bruner, J. S. The ontogenesis of speech acts. *Journal of Child Language,* 1975, *2,* 1–20.

Bruner, J. S. Early social interaction and language acquisition. In H. R. Schaffer (Ed.), *Studies in mother-infant interaction.* London: Academic Press, 1977.

Bruner, J. S. From communication to language: A psychological perspective. In I. Markova (Ed.), *The social context of language.* New York: Wiley, 1978.

Bruner, J. S., & Sherwood, V. Early rule structure: The case of peekaboo. In J. S. Bruner, A. Jolly, & K. Sylva (Eds.), *Play: Its role in evolution and development.* New York: Basic Books, 1976.

Bullowa, M. From non-verbal communication to language. *International Journal of Psycholinguistics,* 1976, *3.*

Campos, J., & Stenberg, C. R. Perception, appraisal, and emotion: The onset of social referencing. In M. Lamb & L. Sherrod (Eds.), *Infant social cognition.* Hillsdale, N.J.: Erlbaum, 1980.

Camras, L. Facial expressions used by children in a conflict situation. *Child Development,* 1977, *48,* 1431–1435.

Carter, A. L. The development of systematic vocalizations prior to words: A case study. In N. Waterson & C. E. Snow (Eds.), *The development of communication.* New York: Wiley, 1978. (a)

Carter, A. L. From sensori-motor vocalizations to words: A case study of the evolution of attention-directing communication in the second year. In A. Lock (Ed.), *Action, gesture, and symbol.* London: Academic Press, 1978. (b)

Case, R. Intellectual development from birth to adulthood: A neo-Piagetian interpretation. In R.

Siegler (Ed.), *Children's thinking: What develops?* Hillsdale, N.J.: Erlbaum, 1978.

Charney, R. The comprehension of "here" and "there." *Journal of Child Language,* 1979, *6,* 69–80.

Cherry, C. *On human communication.* Cambridge, Mass.: MIT Press, 1957.

Chi, M. T. H. Knowledge structures and memory development. In R. Siegler (Ed.), *Children's thinking: What develops?* Hillsdale, N.J.: Erlbaum, 1978.

Clark, E. V. From gesture to word: On the natural history of deixis in language acquisition. In J. S. Bruner & A. Garton (Eds.), *Human growth and development: Wolfson College lectures 1976.* Oxford: Oxford University Press, 1977.

Clark, E. V., & Sengul, C. J. Strategies in the acquisition of deixis. *Journal of Child Language,* 1978, *5,* 457–475.

Clark, H. H. Responding to indirect speech acts. *Cognitive Psychology,* 1979, *11,* 430–477.

Clark, H. H., & Haviland, S. E. Psychological processes as linguistic explanation. In D. Cohen (Ed.), *Explaining linguistic phenomena.* Washington, D.C.: Hemisphere, 1974.

Clark, H. H., & Lucy, P. Understanding what is meant from what is said: A study in conversationally conveyed requests. *Journal of Verbal Learning and Verbal Behavior,* 1975, *14,* 56–72.

Clark, H. H., & Marshall, C. R. Definite reference and mutual knowledge. In A. K. Joshi, I. A. Sag, & B. L. Webber (Eds.), *Proceedings of the workshop on computational aspects of linguistic structure and discourse setting.* New York: Cambridge University Press, 1980.

Clark, H. H., & Schunk, D. H. Polite responses to polite requests. *Cognition,* 1980, *8,* 111–143.

Clark, R. A. The transition from action to gesture. In A. Lock (Ed.), *Action, gesture, and symbol.* London: Academic Press, 1978.

Cohen, P. R., & Levesque, H. J. *Speech acts and the recognition of shared plans.* Proceedings of the Third Conference of the Canadian Society for Computational Studies of Intelligence, Victoria, B.C., Can., 1980.

Cohen, P. R., & Perrault, C. R. Elements of a plan-based theory of speech acts. *Cognitive Science,* 1979, *3,* 177–212.

Cole, M., Anderson, L., & Teal, W. *Literacy experiences of low-income children at home, preschool, and kindergarten.* Paper presented at the Conference on Home Influences on School

Achievement, University of Wisconsin, Madison, October 1981.

Condon, W., & Sander, L. Synchrony demonstrated between movements of the neonate and adult speech. *Child Development*, 1974, *45*, 456–462.

Cook-Gumperz, J., & Gumperz, J. J. Context in children's speech. In N. Waterson & C. E. Snow (Eds.), *The development of communication*. New York: Wiley, 1978.

Cooley, C. A study of the early use of self words by a child. *Psychological Review*, 1908, *15*, 6.

Cooper, M. G. Verbal interaction in nursery schools. *British Journal of Educational Psychology*, 1979, *49*, 214–225.

Corrigan, R. Cognitive correlates of language: Differential criteria yield differential results. *Child Development*, 1979, *50*, 617–631.

Corsaro, W. A. "We're friends, right?": Children's use of access rituals in a nursery school. *Language in Society*, 1979, *8*, 315–336. (a)

Corsaro, W. A. Young children's conception of status and role. *Sociology of Education*, 1979, *52*, 46–59. (b)

Cremona, C., & Bates, E. The development of attitudes toward dialect in Italian children. *Journal of Psycholinguistic Research*, 1977, *6*, 223–232.

Crosby, F. Early discourse agreement. *Journal of Child Language*, 1976, *3*, 125–126.

Curtiss, S. *GENIE: A psycholinguistic study of a modern day "wild child."* New York: Academic Press, 1977.

Deutsch, W. *Sprachliche Redundanz und Objcktidentifikation*. Unpublished doctoral dissertation, University of Marburg/Lahn, W. Germany, 1976.

Deutsch, W., & Pechmann, T. Social interaction and the development of definite descriptions. *Cognition*, 1982, *11*, 159–184.

de Villiers, P. A., & de Villiers, J. G. On this, that, and the other: Non-egocentrism in very young children. *Journal of Experimental Child Psychology*, 1974, *18*, 438–447.

Dickson, W. P. (Ed.) *Children's oral communication skills*. New York: Academic Press, 1981.

Dickson, W. P. Two decades of referential communication research: A review and meta-analysis. In C. J. Brainerd & M. Pressley (Eds.), *Progress in cognitive development research*, vol. 2, *Verbal processes in children*. New York: Springer-Verlag, 1982.

Donellen, K. Reference and definite descriptions. *Philosophical Review*, 1966, *75*, 281–304.

Dore, J. A pragmatic description of early language development. *Journal of Psycholinguistic Research*, 1974, *4*, 423–430.

Dore, J. "Oh them sheriff": A pragmatic analysis of children's responses to questions. In S. Ervin-Tripp & C. Mitchell-Kernan (Eds.), *Child discourse*. New York: Academic Press, 1977.

Dore, J. Conditions for the acquisition of speech acts. In I. Markova (Ed.), *The social context of language*. New York: Wiley, 1978.

Edelsky, C. Acquisition of an aspect of communicative competence: Learning what it means to talk like a lady. In S. Ervin-Tripp & C. Mitchell-Kernan (Eds.), *Child discourse*. New York: Academic Press, 1977.

Eisenberg, A. R., & Garvey, C. Children's use of verbal strategies in resolving conflict. *Discourse Processes*, 1981, *4*, 149–170.

Ekman, P. Universals and cultural differences in facial expressions of emotion. In J. Cole (Ed.), *Nebraska Symposium on Motivation* (Vol. 18). Lincoln: University of Nebraska Press, 1971.

Ervin-Tripp, S. Discourse agreement: How children answer questions. In J. R. Hayes (Ed.), *Cognition and the development of language*. New York: Wiley, 1970.

Ervin-Tripp, S. The comprehension and production of requests by children. *Papers and Reports of Child Language Development*, 1974, *8*, 188–196.

Ervin-Tripp, S. Wait for me, roller-skate! In S. Ervin-Tripp & C. Mitchell-Kernan (Eds.), *Child discourse*. New York: Academic Press, 1977.

Fafouti-Milenkovic, M., & Uzgiris, I. C. The mother-infant communication system. *New Directions for Child Development*, 1979, *4*, 41–56.

Ferguson, C. A. Baby talk as a simplified register. In C. E. Snow & C. A. Ferguson (Eds.), *Talking to children*. Cambridge: At the University Press, 1977.

Fischer, K. W. A theory of cognitive development: Control and construction of a hierarchy of skills. *Psychological Review*, 1980, *87*, 477–531.

Flavell, J. H. Stage-related properties of cognitive development. *Cognitive Psychology*, 1971, *2*, 421–453.

Flavell, J. H. *The development of metacommunication*. Paper presented at the Symposium on Language and Cognition, 21st International Congress of Psychology, Paris, July 1976.

Flavell, J. H. The development of knowledge about visual perception. In C. B. Keasey (Ed.), *Nebraska Symposium on Motivation 1977*. Lincoln: University of Nebraska Press, 1978. (a)

Flavell, J. H. Metacognitive development. In J. M.

Scandura & C. J. Brainerd (Eds.), *Structural/process theories of complex human behavior*. Alpen a.d. Rijn, the Netherlands: Sijthoff & Noordhoff, 1978. (b)

Flavell, J. H. Personal communication, November 1981.

Flavell, J. H., Botkin, P. I., Fry, C. L., Jr., Wright, J. W., & Jarvis, P. E. *The development of role-taking and communication skills in children*. New York: Wiley, 1968.

Flavell, J. H., Speer, J. R., Green, F. L., & August, D. L. The development of comprehension monitoring and knowledge about communication. *Monographs of the Society for Research in Child Development*, 1981, *46*(5, Serial No. 192).

Fodor, J. A. *The language of thought*. New York: T. Y. Crowell, 1975.

Folger, J. P., & Chapman, R. S. A pragmatic analysis of spontaneous imitation. *Journal of Child Language*, 1978, *5*, 25–38.

Frederiksen, C. H. *Writing: The nature, development, and teaching of written communication*. Hillsdale, N.J.: Erlbaum, 1981.

Freedle, R., & Lewis, M. Prelinguistic conversations. In M. Lewis & L. A. Rosenblum (Eds.), *Interaction, conversation, and the development of language*. New York: Wiley, 1977.

Gallagher, T. M. Contingent query sequences within adult-child discourse. *Journal of Child Language*, 1981, *8*, 51–62.

Gallagher, T. M., & Darnton, B. A. Conversational aspects of the speech of language-disordered children: Revision behaviors. *Journal of Speech and Hearing Research*, 1978, *21*, 118–135.

Garfinkel, H. *Studies in ethnomethodology*. Englewood Cliffs, N.J.: Prentice-Hall, 1967.

Garvey, C. Requests and responses in children's speech. *Journal of Child Language*, 1975, *2*, 41–60.

Garvey, C. The contingent query: A dependent act in conversation. In M. Lewis & L. A. Rosenblum (Eds.), *Interaction, conversation, and the development of language*. New York: Wiley, 1977.

Garvey, C. Contingent queries and their relations in discourse. In E. Ochs & B. Schieffelin (Eds.), *Developmental pragmatics*. New York: Academic Press, 1979.

Garvey, C., & Berninger, G. Timing and turn-taking in children's conversation. *Discourse Processes*, 1981, *4*, 27–58.

Gearhart, M. *Social planning: Role play in a novel situation*. Paper presented at the meeting of the Society for Research in Child Development, San Francisco, March 1979.

Gelman, R., & Spelke, E. The development of thoughts about animates and inanimates: Implications for research on social cognition. In J. H. Flavell & L. Ross (Eds.), *New directions in the study of social-cognitive development*. Cambridge: At the University Press, 1980.

Gibbs, R. W. Contextual effects in understanding indirect requests. *Discourse Processes*, 1979, *2*, 1–10.

Gleason, J. B. *Parental judgment of children's language abilities*. Paper presented at the meeting of the Linguistic Society of America, Philadelphia, December 1976.

Gleitman, L. R. *What some concepts might not be*. Paper presented at the Symposium of the Jean Piaget Society, Philadelphia, May 1981.

Glucksberg, S., Krauss, R. M., & Higgins, E. J. The development of referential communication skills. In F. D. Horowitz (Ed.), *Review of child development research* (Vol. 4). Chicago: University of Chicago, 1975.

Golinkoff, R. M. The influence of Piagetian theory on the study of development of communication. In I. E. Sigel, D. Brodzinsky, & R. M. Golinkoff (Eds.), *New directions in Piagetian theory and practice*. Hillsdale, N.J.: Erlbaum, 1981.

Golinkoff, R. M. The preverbal negotiation of failed messages: Insights into the transition period. In R. M. Golinkoff (Ed.), *The transition from prelinguistic to linguistic communication*. Hillsdale, N.J.: Erlbaum, in press.

Greenfield, P. M. Informativeness, presupposition, and semantic choice in single-word utterances. In N. Waterson & C. Snow (Eds.), *The development of communication*. New York: Wiley, 1978.

Greenfield, P. M. Towards an operational and logical analysis of intentionality: The use of discourse in early child language. In D. Olson (Ed.), *The social foundations of language and thought*. New York: W. W. Norton, 1980.

Greenfield, P. M., & Zukow, P. G. Why do children say what they say when they say it?: An experimental approach to the psychogenesis of presupposition. In K. Nelson (Ed.), *Children's language* (Vol. 1). New York: Gardner Press, 1978.

Gregg, L. W., & Steinberg, E. *Cognitive processes in writing*. Hillsdale, N.J.: Erlbaum, 1980.

Grice, H. P. Meaning. *Philosophical Review*, 1957, *66*, 377–388.

Grice, H. P. Logic and conversation. In P. Cole & J. L. Morgan (Eds.), *Speech acts: Syntax and se-*

mantics (Vol. 3). New York: Academic Press, 1975.

Grief, E. B., & Gleason, J. B. Hi, thanks, and goodbye: More routine information. *Language in Society*, 1980, *9*, 159–166.

Grimshaw, J. Form, function, and the language acquisition device. In C. L. Baker & J. J. McCarthy (Eds.), *The logical problem of language acquisition*. Cambridge, Mass.: MIT Press, 1981.

Gumperz, J. J., & Hymes, D. (Eds.) *Directions in sociolinguistics*. New York: Holt, Rinehart & Winston, 1972.

Gunter, R. *Sentences in dialog*. Columbia, S.C.: Hornbeam Press, 1974.

Guralnick, M. J., & Paul-Brown, D. The nature of verbal interactions among handicapped and non-handicapped preschool children. *Child Development*, 1977, *48*, 254–260.

Halliday, M. A. K. *Learning how to mean: Explorations in the development of language*. London: Edward Arnold, 1975.

Harding, C. G., & Golinkoff, R. M. The origins of intentional vocalizations in prelinguistic infants. *Child Development*, 1979, *50*, 33–40.

Harris, P. L., Macrae, A., & Bassett, E. Disambiguation by young children. In R. N. Campbell & P. T. Smith (Eds.), *Recent advances in the psychology of language: Language development and mother-child interaction*. New York: Plenum, 1978.

Hayes, A., & Elliott, J. *Gaze and vocalization in mother-infant dyads: Conversation or coincidence*. Paper presented at the meeting of the Society for Research in Child Development, San Francisco, March 1979.

Hiatt, S., Campos, J., & Emde, R. Facial patterning and infant emotional expression: Happiness, surprise, and fear. *Child Development*, 1979, *50*, 1020–1035.

Hiebert, E. H., & Cherry, L. J. Language play in young children's interactions with three co-participants. In D. Farkas, W. M. Jacobsen, & K. B. Todrys (Eds.), *Papers from the 14th regional meeting of the Chicago Linguistic Society*. Chicago: Chicago Linguistic Society, 1978.

Higgins, E. T. Social class differences in verbal communicative accuracy: A question of "Which question?" *Psychological Bulletin*, 1976, *83*, 695–714.

Higgins, E. T. Written communication as functional literacy: A developmental comparison of oral and written communication. In R. Beach & P. D. Pearson (Eds.), *Perspectives on literacy*. Minneapolis: College of Education, University of Minnesota, 1978.

Higgins, E. T. Role-taking and social judgment: Alternative developmental perspectives and processes. In J. H. Flavell & L. Ross (Eds.), *New directions in the study of social-cognitive development*. Cambridge: At the University Press, 1980.

Higgins, E. T., & Akst, L. *Comparison processes in the communication of kindergartners*. Paper presented at the meeting of the Society for Research in Child Development, Denver, April 1975.

Higgins, E. T., Fondacaro, R., & McCann, D. Rules and roles: The "communication game" and speaker-listener processes. In W. P. Dickson (Ed.), *Children's oral communication skills*. New York: Academic Press, 1981.

Hinde, R. A. *Animal behavior: A synthesis of ethology and comparative psychology* (2nd ed.) New York: McGraw-Hill, 1970.

Hirsh-Pasek, K., Gleitman, L. R., & Gleitman, H. What did the brain say to the mind? A study of the detection and report of ambiguity by young children. In A. Sinclair, R. J. Jarvella, & W. J. M. Levelt (Eds.), *The child's conception of language*. New York: Springer-Verlag, 1978.

Hoff-Ginsberg, E., & Shatz, M. Linguistic input and the child's acquisition of language. *Psychological Bulletin*, 1982, *92*, 3–26.

Hollos, M. Comprehension and use of social rules in pronoun selection by Hungarian children. In S. Ervin-Tripp & C. Mitchell-Kernan (Eds.), *Child discourse*. New York: Academic Press, 1977.

Holzman, M. Ellipsis in discourse: Implications for linguistic analysis by computer, the child's acquisition of language, and semantic theory. *Language and Speech*, 1971, *14*, 86–98.

Horgan, D. How to answer questions when you've got nothing to say. *Journal of Child Language*, 1978, *5*, 159–165.

Howie-Day, A. M. *Metapersuasion: The development of reasoning about persuasive strategies*. Paper presented at the meeting of the Society for Research in Child Development, San Francisco, March 1979.

Hoy, E. A., & McKnight, J. R. Communication style and effectiveness in homogeneous and heterogeneous dyads of retarded children. *American Journal of Mental Deficiency*, 1977, *81*, 587–598.

Inhelder, B., Sinclair, H., & Bovet, M. *Learning and the development of cognition* (S. Wedgwood, trans.). Cambridge, Mass.: Harvard University Press, 1974.

Izard, D. *The face of emotion*. New York: Appleton-Century-Crofts, 1971.

Johnson, C. N., & Maratsos, M. P. Early comprehension of mental verbs: Think and know. *Child Development*, 1977, *48*, 1743–1747.

Johnston, J. Paper presented at the Conference on the Transition from Prelinguistic to Linguistic Communication, University of Delaware, September 1981.

Johnston, J. The language disordered child. In N. Lass, J. Northern, D. Yoder, & L. McReynolds (Eds.), *Speech, language, and hearing*. Philadelphia: W. B. Saunders, in press.

Jones, E. E., & Nisbett, R. E. The actor and the observer: Divergent perceptions of the causes of behavior. In E. E. Jones, D. E. Kanouse, H. H. Kelley, R. E. Nisbett, S. Valins, & B. Weiner (Eds.), *Attribution: Perceiving the causes of behavior*. Morristown, N.J.: General Learning Press, 1972.

Kail, M. Personal communication, June 1981.

Karmiloff-Smith, A. The grammatical marking of thematic structure in the development of language production. In W. Deutsch (Ed.), *The child's construction of language*. London: Academic Press, 1981.

Katz, J. J. *Semantic theory*. New York: Harper & Row, 1972.

Katz, J. J. *Propositional structure and illocutionary force*. New York: T. Y. Crowell, 1977.

Katz, J. J., & Langendoen, D. T. Pragmatics and presupposition. In T. G. Bever, J. J. Katz, & D. T. Langendoen (Eds.), *An integrated theory of linguistic abilities,* New York: T. Y. Crowell, 1976.

Kaye, K., & Charney, R. How mothers maintain "dialogue" with two-year-olds. In D. Olson (Ed.), *The social foundations of language and thought*. New York: W. W. Norton, 1980.

Keenan, E. O. Conversational competence in children. *Journal of Child Language*, 1974, *1*, 163–185.

Keenan, E. O. Making it last: Uses of repetition in children's discourse. In S. Ervin-Tripp & C. Mitchell-Kernan (Eds.), *Child discourse*. New York: Academic Press, 1977.

Keenan, E. O., & Klein, E. Coherency in children's discourse. *Journal of Psycholinguistic Research*, 1975, *4*, 365–378.

Kelley, H. H., & Michela, J. L. Attribution theory. In M. R. Rosenzweig & L. W. Porter (Eds.), *Annual review of psychology*, 1980, *31*.

Krauss, R. M., & Glucksberg, S. The development of communication: Competence as a function of age. *Child Development*, 1969, *40*, 255–266.

Lakoff, R. Language and woman's place. *Language in Society*, 1973, *2*, 45–80.

Maratsos, M. P. Nonegocentric communication abilities in preschool children. *Child Development*, 1973, *44*, 697–700.

Maratsos, M. P. Preschool children's use of definite and indefinite articles. *Child Development*, 1974, *45*, 446–455.

Maratsos, M. P. Grammatical categories: Establishment and evaluation. In E. Wanner & L. R. Gleitman (Eds.), *Language acquisition: The state of the art*. Cambridge: At the University Press, 1982.

Markman, E. M. Children's difficulty with word-referent differentiation. *Child Development*, 1976, *47*, 742–749.

Markman, E. M. Empirical versus logical solutions to part-whole comparison problems concerning classes and collections. *Child Development*, 1978, *49*, 168–177.

Markman, E. M. Comprehension monitoring. In W. P. Dickson (Ed.), *Children's oral communication skills*. New York: Academic Press, 1981.

Martlew, M., Connolly, K., & McCleod, C. Language use, role, and context in a five-year-old. *Journal of Child Language*, 1978, *5*, 81–99.

Masur, E. F. Preschool boys' speech modifications: The effect of listeners' linguistic levels and conversational responsiveness. *Child Development*, 1978, *49*, 924–928.

McNeill, D. The development of language. In P. Mussen (Ed.), *Carmichael's manual of child psychology* (3rd ed.) (Vol. 1) New York: Wiley, 1970.

McTear, M. *Towards a model for analyzing conversations involving children*. Paper presented at the Seminar on Linguistic Interaction Between Children and Adults at Home and at School, University of Bristol, Eng., September 1978.

Mead, G. H. *Mind, self, and society*. Chicago: University of Chicago Press, 1934.

Menig-Peterson, C. L. The modification of communicative behavior in preschool-aged children as a function of the listener's perspective. *Child Development*, 1975, *46*, 1015–1018.

Menig-Peterson, C. L., & McCabe, A. Children's orientation of a listener to the context of their narratives. *Developmental Psychology*, 1978, *14*, 582–592.

Monson, T. C., & Snyder, M. Actors, observers, and the attribution process. *Journal of Experimental Social Psychology*. 1977, *13*, 89–111.

Morgan, J. L., & Sellner, M. B. Discourse and linguistic theory. In R. J. Spiro, B. C. Bruce, & W. F. Brewer (Eds.), *Theoretical issues in reading comprehension*. Hillsdale, N.J.: Erlbaum, 1980.

Murphy, C. M. Pointing in the context of a shared

activity. *Child Development,* 1978, *49,* 371–380.

Murphy, C. M., & Messer, D. Mothers, infants and pointing: A study of a gesture. In H. R. Schaffer (Ed.), *Studies in mother-infant interaction.* London: Academic Press, 1977.

Nelson, K., & Gruendel, J. M. At morning it's lunchtime: A scriptal view of children's dialogues. *Discourse Processes,* 1979, *2,* 73–94.

Newman, D. Ownership and permission among nursery-school children. In J. Glick & K. A. Clarke-Stewart (Eds.), *The development of social understanding.* New York: Gardner Press, 1978.

Nisbett, R. E., & Ross, L. *Human inference: Strategies and shortcomings of social judgment.* Englewood Cliffs, N.J.: Prentice-Hall, 1980.

Ochs, E. *Talking to children in Western Samoa.* Unpublished manuscript, University of Southern California, 1980.

Olson, D. R. From utterance to text: The bias of language in speech and writing. *Harvard Educational Review,* 1977, *47,* 257–281.

Paccia-Cooper, J., & Curcio, F. Language processing and forms of immediate echolalia in autistic children. *Journal of Speech and Hearing Research,* 1982, *25,* 42–47.

Parsons, J. *The development of attributions, expectancies, and persistence.* Unpublished manuscript, University of Michigan, 1980.

Patterson, C. J., & Kister, M. C. The development of listener skills for referential communication. In W. P. Dickson (Ed.), *Children's oral communication skills.* New York: Academic Press, 1981.

Pechmann, T., & Deutsch, W. The development of verbal and nonverbal devices for reference. *Journal of Experimental Child Psychology,* in press.

Perrault, C. R., & Allen, J. F. A plan-based analysis of indirect speech acts. *American Journal of Computational Linguistics,* 1980, *6,* 167–182.

Perrault, C. R., Allen, J. F., & Cohen, P. R. *Speech acts as a basis for understanding dialogue coherence.* Proceedings of Second Conference on Theoretical Issues in Natural Language Processing: Champaign-Urbana, Ill.: 1978.

Piaget, J. *The language and thought of the child.* New York: Harcourt, Brace, 1926.

Piaget, J. *The origins of intelligence in children.* New York: International Universities Press, 1952.

Piaget, J. *Play, dreams, and imitation.* New York: W. W. Norton, 1962.

Potter, M. C. Mundane symbolism: The relation among objects, names, and ideas. In N. R. Smith & M. B. Franklin (Eds.), *Symbolic functioning in childhood.* Hillsdale, N.J.: Erlbaum, 1979.

Pratt, M. W. *Deixis, detection, and development.* Paper presented at the Atlantic Provinces Linguistic Association Meetings, Halifax, N.S., Can., December 1978.

Pratt, M. W., Bates, K., & Wickens, G. *Checking it out: Cognitive style and perceptual support as factors influencing message evaluation by young listeners and speakers.* Unpublished manuscript, Mount St. Vincent University, Halifax, N.S., Can., 1980.

Pratt, M. W., Scribner, S., & Cole, M. Children as teachers: Developmental studies of instructional communication. *Child Development,* 1977, *48,* 1475–1481.

Ratner, N., & Bruner, J. S. Games, social exchange and the acquisition of language. *Journal of Child Language,* 1978, *5,* 391–402.

Read, B. K., & Cherry, L. J. Preschool children's production of directive forms. *Discourse Processes,* 1978, *1,* 233–245.

Reeder, K. The emergence of illocutionary skills. *Journal of Child Language,* 1980, *7,* 13–28.

Rees, N. S. Noncommunicative functions of language in children. *Journal of Speech and Hearing Disorders,* 1973, *38,* 98–110.

Rees, N. S. Imitation and language development: Issues and clinical implications. *Journal of Speech and Hearing Disorders,* 1975, *40,* 339–350.

Reichman, R. *Plain speaking: A theory and grammar of spontaneous discourse.* Unpublished doctoral dissertation, Harvard University, 1981.

Revelle, G. L., Karabenick, J. D., & Wellman, H. M. *Comprehension monitoring in preschool children.* Paper presented at the meeting of the Society for Research in Child Development, Boston, April 1981.

Rheingold, H. L., & Adams, J. L. The significance of speech to newborns. *Developmental Psychology,* 1980, *16,* 397–403.

Robinson, E. J. The child's understanding of inadequate messages and communication failure: A problem of ignorance or egocentrism? In W. P. Dickson, (Ed.), *Children's oral communication skills.* New York: Academic Press, 1981.

Rodgon, M. M. Knowing what to say and wanting to say it: Some communicative and structural aspects of single-word responses to questions. *Journal of Child Language,* 1979, *6,* 81–90.

Rommetveit, R. *On message structure.* New York: Wiley, 1974.

Rosch, E., & Mervis, C. Family resemblances:

Studies in the internal structure of categories. *Cognitive Psychology,* 1975, *7,* 573–605.

Rubin, A. D. A theoretical taxonomy of the differences between oral and written language. In R. J. Spiro, B. C. Bruce, & W. F. Brewer (Eds.), *Theoretical issues in reading comprehension.* Hillsdale, N.J.: Erlbaum, 1980.

Rubin, K. The relationship between spatial and communicative egocentrism in children and young and old adults. *Journal of Genetic Psychology,* 1974, *125,* 295–301.

Sachs, J., & Devin, J. Young children's use of age-appropriate speech styles in social interaction and role-playing. *Journal of Child Language,* 1976, *3,* 81–98.

Schaffer, H. R. Early social behavior and the study of reciprocity. *Bulletin of the British Psychological Society,* 1974, *27,* 209–216.

Schaffer, H. R. Acquiring the concept of the dialogue. In M. H. Bornstein & W. Kessen (Eds.), *Psychological development from infancy: Image to intention.* Hillsdale, N.J.: Erlbaum, 1979.

Schaffer, H. R., Collis, G. M., & Parsons, G. Vocal interchange and visual regard in verbal and preverbal children. In H. R. Schaffer (Ed.), *Studies in mother-infant interaction.* London: Academic Press, 1977.

Schank, R. C., & Abelson, R. *Scripts, plans, goals, and understanding.* Hillsdale, N.J.: Erlbaum, 1977.

Schieffelin, B. Getting it together: An ethnographic approach to the study of the development of communicative competence. In E. Ochs & B. Schieffelin (Eds.), *Developmental pragmatics.* New York: Academic Press, 1979.

Schieffelin, B. Cross-cultural perspectives on the transition: What difference do differences make? In R. M. Golinkoff (Ed.), *The transition from prelinguistic to linguistic communication.* Hillsdale, N.J.: Erlbaum, in press.

Schiffer, S. R. *Meaning.* London: Oxford University Press, 1972.

Schneiderman, M. H. *"Do what I mean, not what I say": Mothers' action-directives to their young children.* Unpublished doctoral dissertation, University of Pennsylvania, 1980.

Schnur, E., & Shatz, M. The role of maternal gesturing in conversations with one-year-olds. *Journal of Child Language,* in press.

Scollon, R. *Conversations with a one year old: A case study of the developmental foundation of syntax.* Honolulu: University Press of Hawaii, 1976.

Scollon, R., & Scollon, S. *The literate two-year-old: The fictionalization of self.* Unpublished manuscript, University of Alaska, 1979.

Searle, J. R. *Speech acts.* Cambridge: At the University Press, 1969.

Searle, J. R. Chomsky's revolution in linguistics. *New York Review of Books,* June 29, 1972.

Searle, J. R. Indirect speech acts. In P. Cole & J. L. Morgan (Eds.), *Speech acts: Syntax and semantics,* vol. 3. New York: Academic Press, 1975.

Seidenberg, M. S., & Petitto, L. A. Signing behavior in apes: A critical review. *Cognition,* 1979, *7,* 177–215.

Seitz, S., & Stewart, C. Expanding on expansions and related aspects of mother-child communication. *Developmental Psychology,* 1975, *11,* 763–769.

Shatz, M. Children's comprehension of question-directives. *Journal of Child Language,* 1978, *5,* 39–46. (a)

Shatz, M. On the development of communicative understandings: An early strategy for interpreting and responding to messages. *Cognitive Psychology,* 1978, *10,* 271–301. (b)

Shatz, M. The relationship between cognitive processes and the development of communication skills. In C. B. Keasey (Ed.), *Nebraska Symposium on Motivation* (Vol. 25). Lincoln: University of Nebraska Press, 1978. (c)

Shatz, M. How to do things by asking: Form-function pairings in mothers' questions and their relation to children's responses. *Child Development,* 1979, *50,* 1093–1099.

Shatz, M. *Pragmatics from a psychologist's point of view.* Address presented at the Conference on Developmental Pragmatics, SUNY at Buffalo, October 1980.

Shatz, M. Learning the rules of the game: Four views of the relation between social interaction and syntax acquisition. In W. Deutsch (Ed.), *The child's construction of language.* London: Academic Press, 1981.

Shatz, M. On mechanisms of language acquisition: Can features of the communicative environment account for development? In E. Wanner & L. R. Gleitman (Eds.), *Language acquisition: The state of the art.* Cambridge: At the University Press, 1982.

Shatz, M. On transition, continuity, and coupling: An alternative approach to communicative development. In R. M. Golinkoff (Ed.), *The transition from prelinguistic to linguistic communication.* Hillsdale, N.J.: Erlbaum, in press.

Shatz, M., Bernstein, D., & Shulman, M. The responses of language disordered children to indirect directives in varying contexts. *Applied Psycholinguistics*, 1980, *1*, 295–306.

Shatz, M., & Gelman, R. The development of communication skills: Modifications in the speech of young children as a function of listener. *Monographs of the Society for Research in Child Development*, 1973, *38*(5, Serial No. 152).

Shatz, M., & Gelman, R. Beyond syntax: The influence of conversational constraints on speech modifications. In C. E. Snow & C. A. Ferguson (Eds.), *Talking to children*. Cambridge: At the University Press, 1977.

Shipley, E. F., Smith, C. S., & Gleitman, L. R. A study in the acquisition of language: Free responses to commands. *Language*, 1969, *45*, 322–342.

Shotter, J. The cultural context of communication studies: Theoretical and methodological issues. In A. Lock (Ed.), *Action, gesture, and symbol*. London: Academic Press, 1978.

Shrauger, J. S., & Schoeneman, T. J. Symbolic interactionist view of self-concept: Through the looking glass darkly. *Psychological Bulletin*, 1979, *86*, 549–573.

Singer, J. B., & Flavell, J. H. Development of knowledge about communication: Children's evaluations of explicitly ambiguous messages. *Child Development*, 1981, *52*, 1211–1215.

Snow, C. E. The development of conversation between mothers and babies. *Journal of Child Language*, 1977, *4*, 1–22. (a)

Snow, C. E. Mothers' speech research: From input to interaction. In C. E. Snow & C. A. Ferguson (Eds.), *Talking to Children*. Cambridge: At the University Press, 1977. (b)

Snow, C. E., & Ferguson, C. A. (Eds.) *Talking to children*. Cambridge: At the University Press, 1977.

Steffensen, M. Satisfying inquisitive adults: Some simple methods of answering yes/no questions. *Journal of Child Language*, 1978, *5*, 221–236.

Stern, D. Mother and infant at play: The dyadic interaction involving facial, vocal, and gaze behaviors. In M. Lewis & L. A. Rosenblum (Eds.), *Interaction, conversation, and the development of language*. New York: Wiley, 1977.

Stern, D., Jaffe, J., Beebe, B., and Bennett, S. Vocalizing in unison and in alternation: Two modes of communication within the mother-infant dyad. In D. Aaronson & R. W. Rieber (Eds.), *Developmental psycholinguistics and communication disorders*. New York: New York Academy of Sciences, 1975. (*Annals of the New York Academy of Sciences* [Vol. 263])

Stipek, D. J., & Hoffman, J. M. Development of children's performance-related judgments. *Child Development*, 1980, *51*, 912–914.

Sugarman-Bell, S. Some organizational aspects of pre-verbal communication. In I. Markova (Ed.), *The social context of language*. New York: Wiley, 1978.

Thorpe, W. H. The comparison of vocal communication in animals and man. In R. A. Hinde (Ed.), *Non-verbal communication*. Cambridge: At the University Press, 1972.

Trevarthen, C. Descriptive analyses of infant communicative behavior. In H. R. Schaffer (Ed.), *Studies in mother-infant interaction*. London: Academic Press, 1977.

Trevarthen, C., & Hubley, P. Secondary intersubjectivity: Confidence, confiding, and acts of meaning in the first year. In A. Lock (Ed.), *Action, gesture, and symbol*, London: Academic Press, 1978.

Valian, V., & Caplan, J. S. What children say when asked "What?". A study of the use of syntactic knowledge. *Journal of Experimental Child Psychology*, 1979, *28*, 424–444.

Van Hekken, S. M. J., Vergeer, M. M., & Harris, P. L. Ambiguity of reference and listeners' reaction in a naturalistic setting. *Journal of Child Language*, 1980, *7*, 555–563.

Vygotsky, L. S. *Thought and language*. Cambridge, Mass.: MIT Press, 1962.

Vygotsky, L. S. *Mind in society*. Cambridge, Mass.: Harvard University Press, 1978.

Vygotsky, L. S. The genesis of higher mental functions. In J. V. Wertsch (Ed.), *The concept of activity in Soviet psychology*. Book in preparation, 1982.

Warden, D. A. The influence of context on children's use of identifying expressions and references. *British Journal of Psychology*, 1976, *67*, 101–112.

Webb, P. A., & Abrahamson, A. A. Stages of egocentrism in children's use of "this" and "that": A different point of view. *Journal of Child Language*, 1976, *3*, 349–367.

Wellman, H. M., & Lempers, J. D. The naturalistic communicative abilities of two-year-olds. *Child Development*, 1977, *48*, 1052–1057.

Wells, G., MacLure, M., & Montgomery, M. Some strategies for sustaining conversation *Sixth Lacus Forum 1979*. Columbia, S.C.: Hornbeam Press, 1979.

Wertsch, J. V. *Metacognition and adult-child interaction*. Paper presented at the Northwestern University Annual Conference on Learning Disabilities, Evanston, Ill., May 1977.

Wertsch, J. V. From social interaction to higher psychological processes. A clarification and application of Vygotsky's theory. *Human Development*, 1979, *22*, 1–22.

Whitehurst, G. J. The development of communication: Changes with age and modeling. *Child Development*, 1976, *47*, 473–482.

Whitehurst, G. J., & Sonnenschein, S. The development of communication: Attribute variation leads to contrast failure. *Journal of Experimental Child Psychology*, 1978, *25*, 454–490.

Whitehurst, G. J., & Sonnenschein, S. The development of informative messages in referential communication: Knowing when vs. knowing how. In W. P. Dickson (Ed.), *Children's oral communication skills*. New York: Academic Press, 1981.

Wieman, L. Stress patterns of early child language. *Journal of Child Language*, 1976, *3*, 283–286.

Wigfield, A., & Asher, S. R. *Age differences in children's referential communication performance: An investigation of task effects*. Center for the Study of Reading (Tech. Rep. No. 96). Urbana-Champaign: University of Illinois, July 1978.

Wilcox, M. J., & Webster, E. J. Early discourse behavior: An analysis of children's responses to listener feedback. *Child Development*, 1980, *51*, 1120–1125.

Wilkinson, A. C. *Children's partial knowledge of counting*. Unpublished manuscript, University of Wisconsin, Madison, 1981.

Wilkinson, L. C. (Ed.), *Communicating in the classroom*. New York: Academic Press, 1982.

Wimmer, H. Processing of script deviations by young children. *Discourse Processes*, 1979, *2*, 301–310.

Wood, D., Bruner, J. S., & Ross, G. The role of tutoring in problem solving. *Journal of Child Psychology and Psychiatry*, 1976, *17*, 89–100.

AUTHOR INDEX

Note: "n" following name indicates name is to be found in "notes."

SUBJECT INDEX

Make-believe play:
  divergent thinking and, 641–642
  metaphor with, 662
Manipulation of objects, in infancy,
  9
Manual exploration, 6
Mappings:
  one-to-one, 866–867
  reality, 867
  of words, 816
Maps:
  medium-sized spatial
    representations assessed by,
    450–451, 452
  understanding of, 41
Mass nouns, count nouns distinct
  from, 800
Matching:
  category membership and, 793
  tasks, 207
Matching Familiar Figures Test
    (MFFT), 672, 673–674,
    675, 676, 677, 678, 679,
    680, 681, 682, 875
Matching Familiar Figures Test 20
    (MFFT20), 674, 675
Materials, nature of for learning,
  85, 102–104
Mathematics, 81
  didactics of Genevan school,
    253–254
  see also Numerical ability
Meanings, see Word meanings
Meaning systems, in problem
  solving, 236, 240–241
Mean length of utterance (MLU),
  710–711
  later grammatical acquisition and,
    727–728
  in parental speech to children,
    733, 734
Mechanical events, causality and,
  22
Mechanism, as causal principle,
  211–213
Mechanistic-process approach, to
  verbal comprehension, 393
Mediation theory, of learning,
  346
Mediators, for learning, 147–149
Medium-scale spaces, representation
  of, 448–449, 451
Memory, 78
  early development of, 86, 87–90
  infant concept development of,
    837
  in information processing theory
    of intelligence, 398–399
  metamemory, 83, 96, 108–110,
    133, 396, 397–398

recall:
  of behavior perception from
    films, 500, 501
  of categorical information, 471
  in infancy, 428–429
  knowledge and, 96–98
  rote, 105
  of stories, 462–464
  recognition, 103–104
  rote, 105, 116–117
  scene perception and, 454
  strategies and, 82
  verbal reports and, 108
  verb comprehension and, 810
  see also Rehearsal; Retention
Memory organization packets
  (MOPs), 457
Mental age (MA):
  cognitive style and, 692
  intelligence and, 352
  perspective taking and, 522
Mental capacity, see M-power
Mental energy:
  intelligence and, 354–355
  as quantitative principle of
    cognition, 369
Mental illnesses, Genevan school
  on, 252–253
Mental retardation:
  field dependence-independence
    and, 672
  reflection-impulsivity and, 683
  spatial perspective taking and,
    516–518
Mental rotation, spatial visualization
  and, 395–396
Mental space, of learner, 100–101
Mental verbs, 324–325
Metacognition, 60, 95, 133, 396–
  398, 466
  accessibility and, 433
  Binet and Simon and, 349
  communication and, 847
  declarative knowledge and, 83
  definition, 106–107
  experience, 397
  knowledge and, 397, 398
  reflection-impulsivity and
    processes of, 681
  research in, 81, 82–83
  roots of, 107–108
    executive control, 83, 110–117
    other-regulation, 122–124
    self-regulation, 117–122
    verbal reports, 108–110
  status of as concept, 124–126
Metacommunication, 867, 875
Metacomponents:
  as cognitive-monitoring skills,
    397

information processing theory
    and, 371, 372, 373
  in intelligence, 400–402
Metalinguistic awareness,
    children's, 244–247
Metalinguistic knowledge, 185
Metamemory, 83, 96, 108–110,
    133, 396, 397–398
Metaphor, 655–656, 693
  analogies linked with, 660
  breadth of, 693
  coinages by, 826–829
  correlates of processes of, 659–
    661
  current status of research in,
    695
  divergent thinking and, 660–661,
    692
  explication and, 685–686
  frozen, 656–657, 658
  information processing model for,
    660
  intellectual abilities and, 659–
    660
  intelligence and, 691–692
  lexical contrast theory and, 829–
    830
  measures of, 656–658, 693
    convergent validation of, 658–
      659, 662
    Metaphoric Triads Task, 657,
      658–659, 660, 662
  multidisciplinary ramifications of
    the, 661
  novel, 656–657, 658
  paraphrase and, 685–686
  Piagetian theory and, 683, 685–
    686, 690
  in preschool children, 662
  training efforts in, 661–662
Metaphoric Triads Task (MTT),
    657, 658–659, 660, 662
Metaprocedural reorganization,
    119–120
Metric accuracy, of spatial
    representation, 453
Microgenetic approach, 84, 93
Miller Analogies Test, 406
Mismatch, child meanings versus
    adult meanings and, 807,
    809
Misunderstanding, in
    communication, 843, 851,
    855
Mixed model, of linear syllogistic
    reasoning, 384
Mnemonic elaboration, 82, 88,
    104–105
Modal logic, 264–265, 274, 319–
    324

Models:
  divergent thinking enhanced by,
    651
  morality and, 566
Modified counting task, 185
Modus Ponens, 272, 283, 285, 288,
    292, 293, 296, 303, 304,
    305
Modus Tollens, 283–284, 285, 290,
    293, 303, 304, 305
Monitoring:
  cognitive, 396–397
  developmental studies of, 114–
    117
    comprehension monitoring,
      114–116
    effort allocation while
      studying, 116–117
Monitor process, 401
Mood, moral decision making and,
    565. *See also* Emotions
Moral course of action:
  determining ideal, 611–613
  valued outcomes for, 563–569
Moral dilemmas, *see* Morality
Moral education, 566, 568, 569,
    597–598, 600
Moral evaluation, 612–614, 615
Moral ideal, deformation of, 561–
    563
Moral internalization, moral
    motivation and, 566–568
Morality, 616–617
  aptitude and, 595
  authority conceptions and, 530
  behavior related to, 600–602
  change in, 595–600, 616–617
    disequilibrium and, 596–597
  cognitive development and:
    cognitive psychology with,
      614–615, 616
    moral course of action and,
      562–563
  cognitive nature of, 591–595
  components, 569–575
    I (interpreting situation), 559–
      561, 591, 594, 600
    II (ideal moral course of
      action), 561–563, 591, 594,
      600, 616
    III (valued outcomes for moral
      course of action), 563–569,
      591, 600
    IV (implementing intentions),
      569, 591, 600
  comprehension studies in, 592
  consequences and, 612–614
  of constraint, 571
  cooperation and, 568, 571, 616
  course of action, 561–569

cross-cultural studies of, 595,
    598–599
decision making and, 564–565
Defining Issues Test research,
    583–589. *See also* six-stage
    model of, *below*
definition, 556–558, 569–570
economics and, 608
educational programs fostering,
    566, 568, 569, 597–598,
    600
ego strength in, 569
emotions involved in, 570
empathy and, 557, 560–561
ideal deformation and, 561–563
ideology and, 592–593
information processing accounts
    and, 614, 615–616, 617
intentionality and, 612–614, 615
internalization, 566–568
interpersonal relationships and,
    608
justice and, 574
Kohlberg on, 574, 575–580
  conventional level, 576, 578,
    580, 582
  Damon compared with, 603–
    604
  Heinz dilemma, 561–562, 563,
    579, 580, 581, 582, 584,
    600, 601
  justice and, 574, 577
  Piaget compared with, 574–
    575, 578, 579, 580
  postconventional (principled)
    level, 577, 578–579, 582
  preconventional level, 575,
    576, 578, 582
  scoring system of, 575, 577,
    579, 580–583
  stage theories of, 574, 575–
    580
  see also six-stage model of,
    below
law and, 608
moral dilemma, 561–563, 597
  Heinz dilemma, 561–562, 563,
    579, 580, 581, 582, 584,
    600, 601
  prosocial moral reasoning and,
    606–608
  young children and, 602–606
moral evaluation, 612–614, 615
moral philosophy for evaluating,
    581–582
motivation of, 565–569
parents and, 567, 595
peer interaction and, 575, 594–
    595, 596
perspective taking and, 593, 598

politics and, 608
post-Piagetian research on, 612–
    616
prosocial behavior and, 517–518,
    527–529, 557–558. *See also*
    Empathy
qualitative/quantitative
    distinction, 580
religion and, 608
responsibility and, 614
role-taking and, 593–595
six-stage model of, 589–590
  behavior relating to moral
    judgment and, 600–602
  change in moral judgment and,
    595–600
  developmental sequence of
    morality in, 590–591
  sexist nature of, 599
  see also Morality, Kohlberg on
social cognition and, 567
social convention and, 608–610
social-historical contexts and, 561
social norms and, 539, 562, 563,
    572–573, 610–612
social psychology and, 610–612,
    617
socioeconomic status and, 595
stage theories of, 563, 586–587,
    616
  Defining Issues Test research,
    583–589
  Piaget, 570–573, 574, 577,
    579, 580, 586, 593, 596
  prerequisites to, 593–594
  see also Morality, Kohlberg
    on; Morality, six-stage
    model of
values and, 558, 564, 601
verbal ability and, 595
of young children, 602–606
see also Altruism
Moral Judgment of the Child, 570–
    571
Moral philosophy, 558, 581–582
Moral reasoning, 502. *See also*
    Morality
Moral sensitivity, moral behavior
    and, 559
Morphemes:
  cumulative complexity and, 751
  expansion for, 734–735
  grammatical acquisition and, 727,
    728–732
  grammatical role acquisition and,
    764
  mean length of utterance and,
    710–711
Morphosyntactic markers, functional
    aspects of, 243